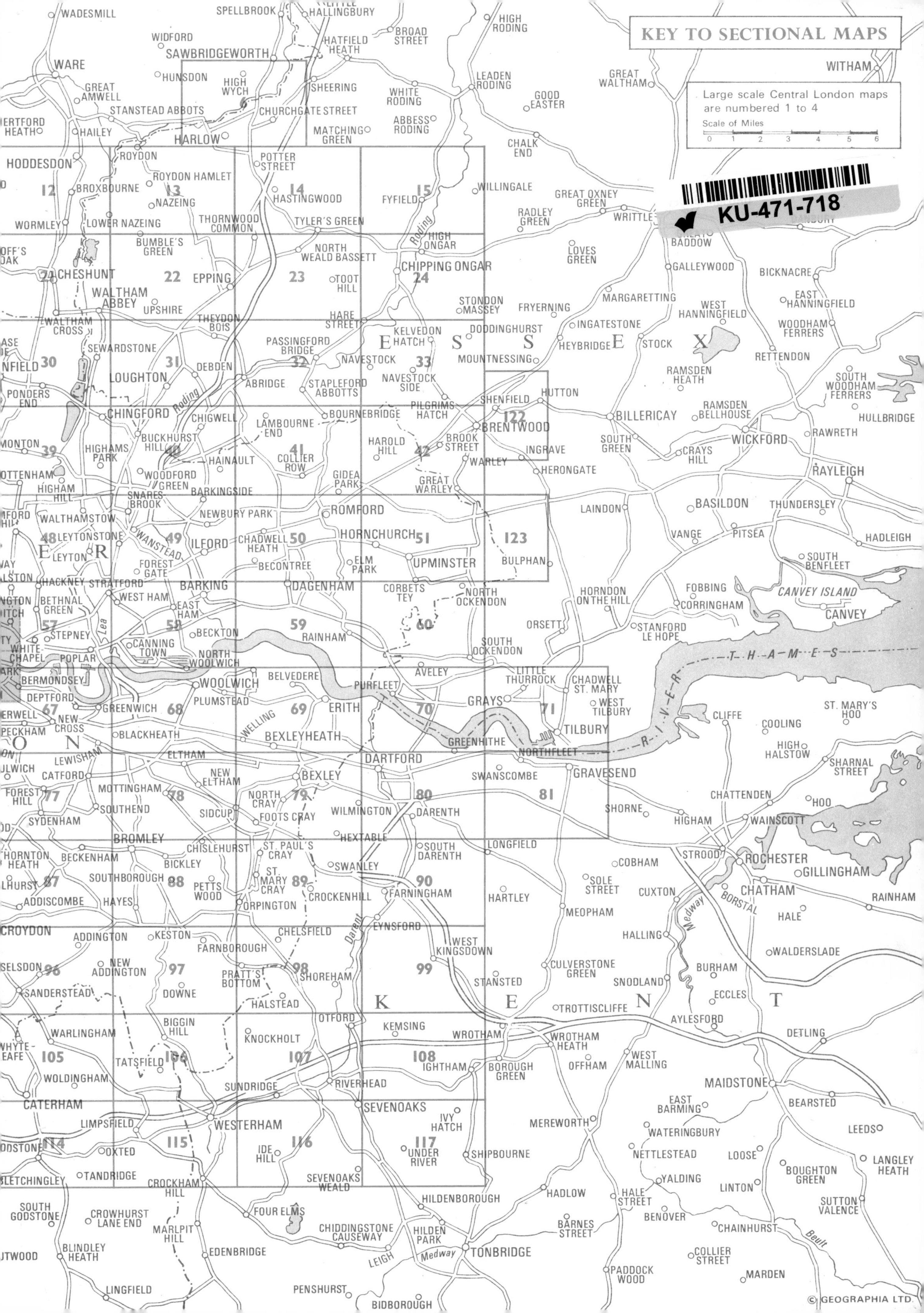

KEY TO SECTIONAL MAPS

Large scale Central London maps are numbered 1 to 4

Scale of Miles

KU-471-718

© GEOGRAPHIA LTD.

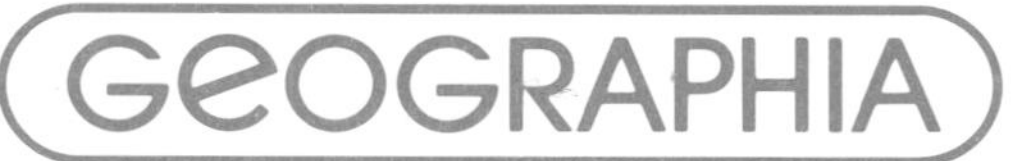

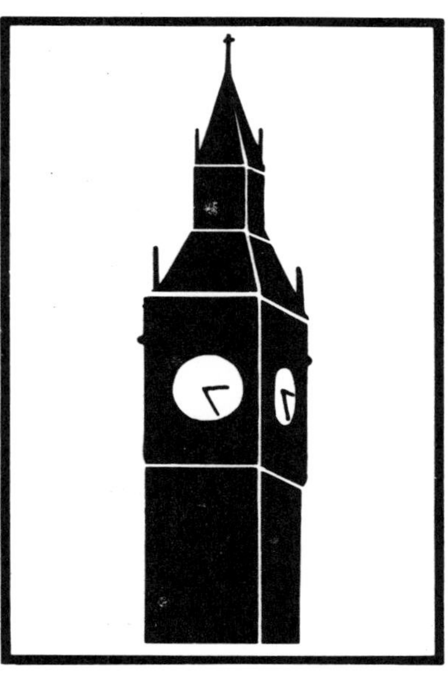

GREATER LONDON
STREET ATLAS

Scale: Outer Area .... 3·17 inches to 1 mile

Central Area .... 5·5 inches to 1 mile

Published by Geographia Ltd.
63,Fleet Street.London.EC4
Tel.01-353 2701/2

Based upon the Ordnance Survey Maps with the Sanction of the Controller of H.M.Stationery Office.

The Ordnance Survey is not responsible for the accuracy of the National Grid on this production.

We wish to acknowledge the co-operation of the Post Office in the preparation of the postal information used in this atlas.

First Published 1977
Second Revised Edition 1978
Third Revised Edition 1981

Index Photoset by The Halesworth Press,Halesworth,Suffolk

Atlas printed offset litho jointly by Harrier Offset,Belvedere,Kent,and The Anchor Press Ltd.Tiptree,Essex.

Preliminary pages designed by M A Preedy MSIAD and J.T.Wright for Geographia Ltd.

Paper supplied by G.R.Macmillan Paper Ltd.London,SE13.

Bound by William Brendon of Tiptree,Essex.

ISBN 0 09 202790 3

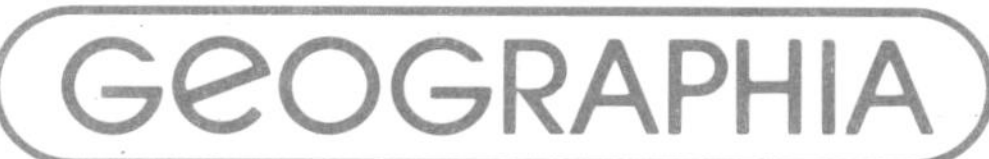

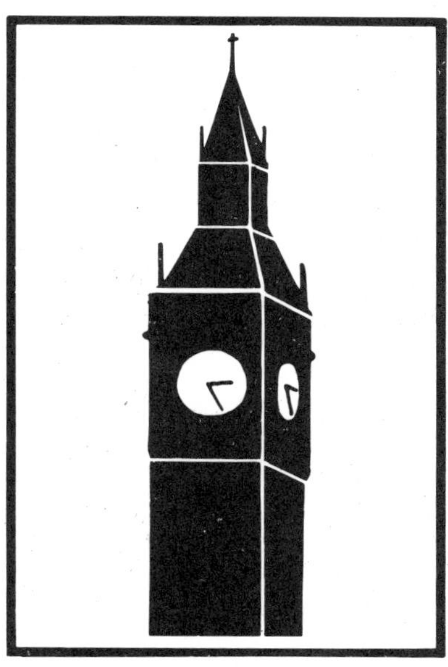

GREATER LONDON STREET ATLAS

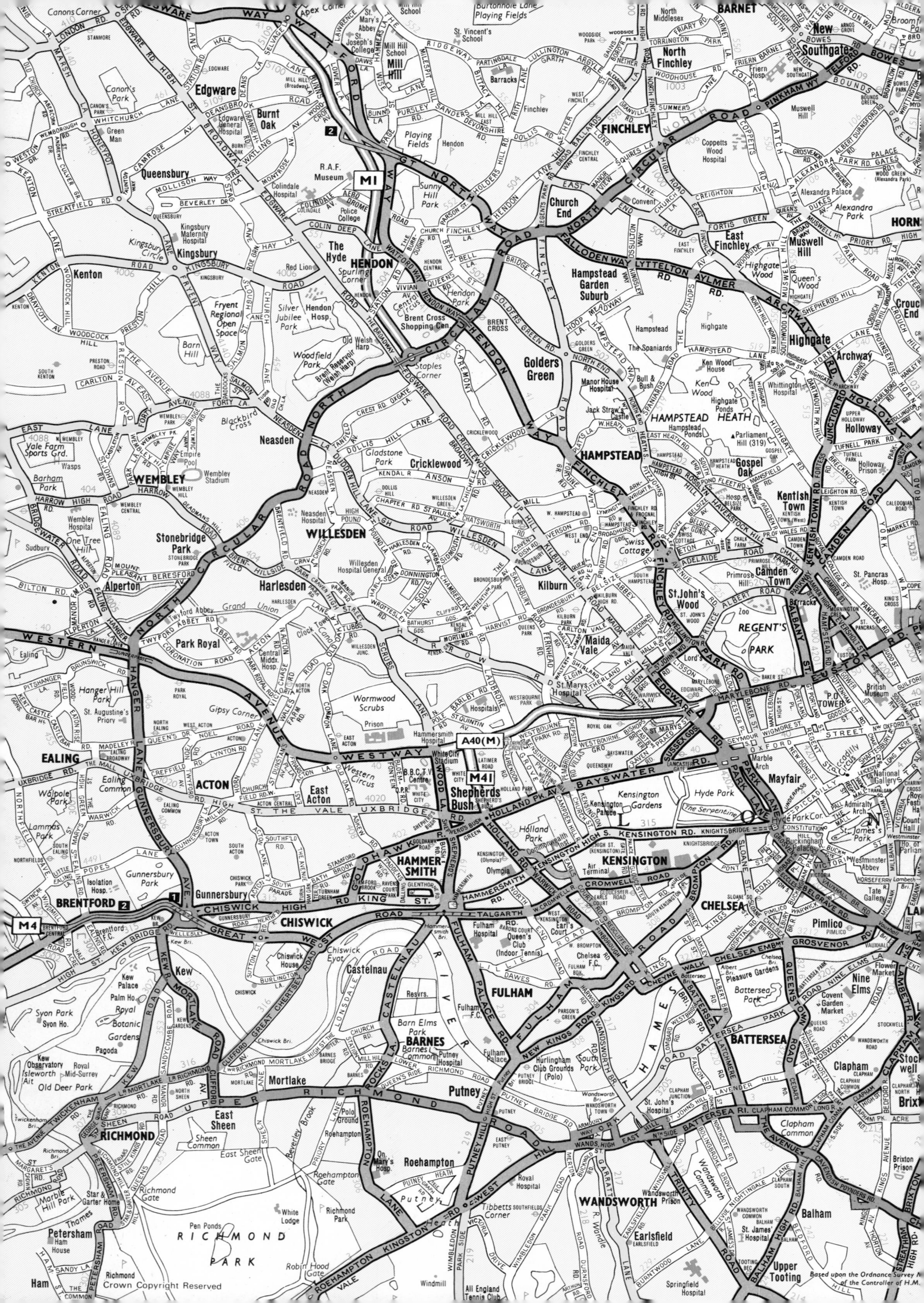

Edgware
Burnt Oak
Mill Hill
North Finchley
Finchley
New Southgate
Queensbury
Kingsbury
Kenton
The Hyde
Hendon
Church End
East Finchley
Muswell Hill
Hampstead Garden Suburb
Highgate
Golders Green
Archway
Hampstead Heath
Hampstead
Holloway
Neasden
Wembley
Cricklewood
Gospel Oak
Kentish Town
Willesden
Stonebridge Park
Harlesden
Kilburn
Camden Town
Alperton
St. John's Wood
Regent's Park
Park Royal
Maida Vale
Ealing
Acton
East Acton
Shepherds Bush
Mayfair
Hyde Park
Kensington Gardens
Hammersmith
Kensington
Chiswick
Brentford
Gunnersbury
Chelsea
Pimlico
Fulham
Kew
Castelnau
Barnes
Battersea
Nine Elms
Mortlake
Putney
Clapham
East Sheen
Richmond
Roehampton
Wandsworth
Balham
Richmond Park
Petersham
Earlsfield
Upper Tooting
Ham
M1
M4
A40(M)
M41
River Thames
London
Crown Copyright Reserved
Based upon the Ordnance Survey Map with the sanction of the Controller of H.M.

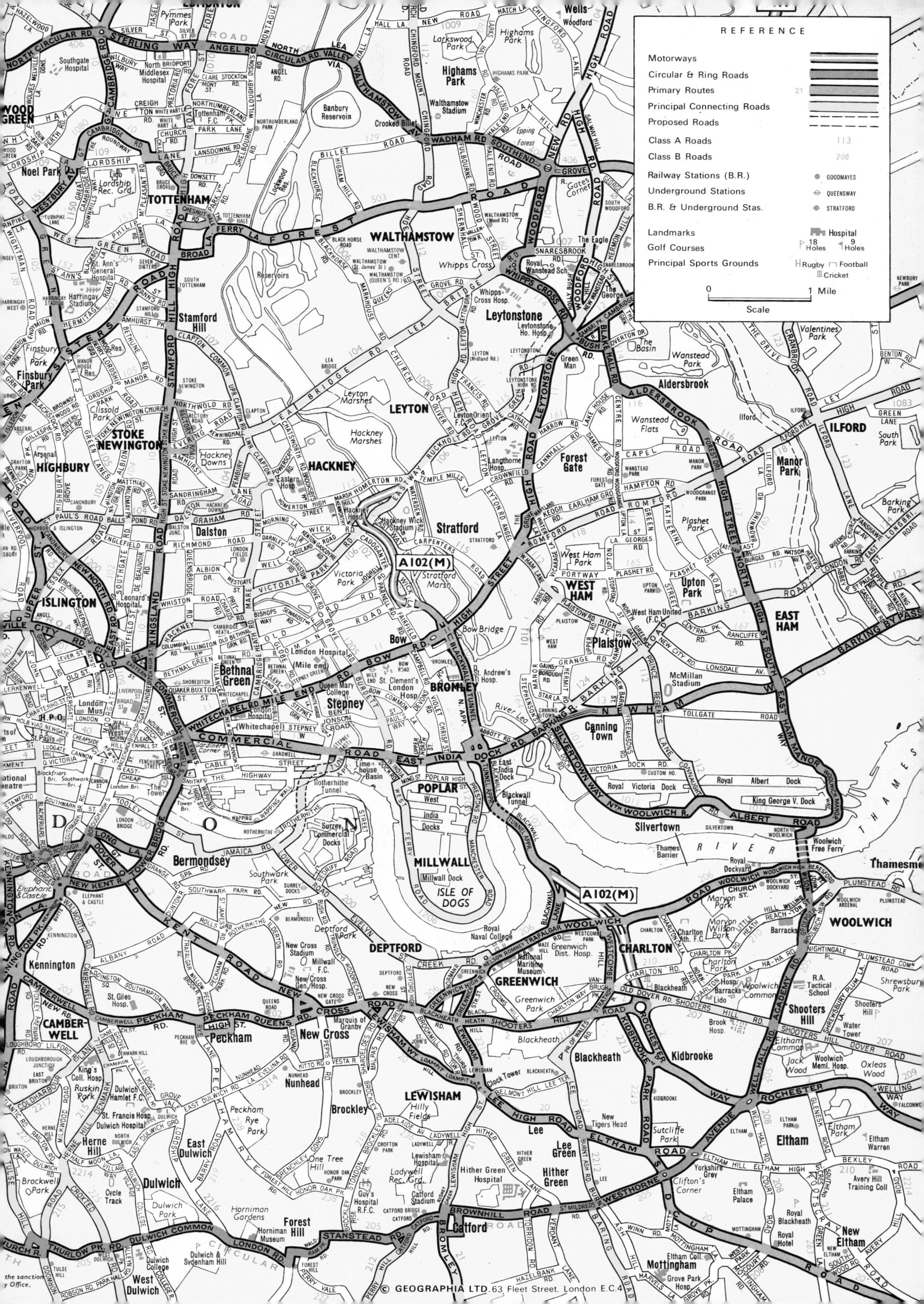
REFERENCE
Motorways
Circular & Ring Roads
Primary Routes
Principal Connecting Roads
Proposed Roads
Class A Roads
Class B Roads
Railway Stations (B.R.)
Underground Stations
B.R. & Underground Stas.
GOODMAYES
QUEENSWAY
STRATFORD
Landmarks
Hospital
Golf Courses
18 Holes
9 Holes
Principal Sports Grounds
Rugby
Football
Cricket
0
1 Mile
Scale
TOTTENHAM
WALTHAMSTOW
Leytonstone
Stamford Hill
STOKE NEWINGTON
HIGHBURY
HACKNEY
LEYTON
Forest Gate
Stratford
Dalston
ISLINGTON
WEST HAM
Upton Park
EAST HAM
ILFORD
Bethnal Green
Stepney
BROMLEY
Bow
Plaistow
Canning Town
POPLAR
Silvertown
MILLWALL
ISLE OF DOGS
Bermondsey
DEPTFORD
GREENWICH
CHARLTON
WOOLWICH
Kennington
CAMBER WELL
Peckham
New Cross
LEWISHAM
Blackheath
Kidbrooke
Eltham
Lee
Brockley
Nunhead
East Dulwich
Dulwich
Forest Hill
Catford
Hither Green
Mottingham
Shooters Hill
A102(M)
RIVER THAMES
© GEOGRAPHIA LTD. 63 Fleet Street, London E.C.4

Central Booking Offices

British Transport Hotels Limited,
PO Box 179, St. Pancras Chambers, London NW1 2TU
Tel 01–278 4211
Telex 27863

Centre Supranational Hotel Reservations,
20–26 Cursitor Street, London, EC4A 1PB.
Tel: *Individual Reservations* 01–404 0404; *Group Reservations* 01–404 0511; *Sales & Administration* 01–404 0611.
Telex 263561

Crest Hotel Reservations,
PO Box 38, Empire Way, Wembley, HA9 8UN.
Tel 01–903 6422
Telex 923842

De Vere Hotels and Restaurants Limited,
Sales Division, The Connaught Rooms, Great Queen Street, London, WC2B 5DA
Tel 01–404 0991 and 01–405 7811
Telex 8953644

Embassy Hotels Limited,
34 Queen's Gate, London, SW7 5JA
Tel 01–584 8222
Telex 8813387

EMI Hotels,
170 Tottenham Court Road, London W1P 0HA
Tel 01–388 5055
Telex 24616

Grand Metropolitan Hotels Limited,
Grand Metropolitan House, Stratford Place, London, W1A 4YU
Tel 01–629 6618
Telex 25971

Holiday Inn International,
10–12 New College Parade, Finchley Road, London, NW3
Tel 01–722 7755
Telex 27574

Hotel Representative Incorporated,
15 New Bridge Street, London, EC4V 6AU
Tel 01–583 3050
Telex 265497
For: Berkeley, Claridges, Connaught, Savoy, Hyde Park

Imperial London Hotels Limited,
Imperial Hotel, Russell Square, London, WC1B 5BB
Tel 01–278 7871
Telex 263951

Inter Hotels,
29 Harrington Gardens, London, SW7 4JT
Tel 01–373 3241
Telex 8951994

Ladbroke Hotels,
PO Box 137, Millbuck House, Clarendon Road, Watford, Herts, WD1 1DN
Tel 01–734 6000
Telex 897618

M F North Limited (North Hotels),
58 Cromwell Road, London, SW7 5BZ
Tel 01–589 1212
Telex 262180

Norfolk Capital Hotels Limited,
8 Cromwell Place, London, SW7 2JN
Tel 01–589 7000
Telex 23241

Prestige Hotels,
Central Office, Strand House, Great West Road, Brentford, Middlesex
Reservations: 01–568 6841
Administration/Brochures: 01–568 1009
Telex 8811951

Rank Hotels Limited,
Central Reservations, 16 Young Street, London, W8
Tel 01–262 2893
Telex 267270

Reo Stakis Hotels,
210–211 Grand Buildings, London, WC2N 5HN
Tel 01–930 0342

Select Hotels,
Central Booking Office, Strand House, Great West Road, Brentford, Middlesex
Tel 01–568 1361
Telex 8811951

Swallow Hotels Limited,
Sales and Reservations, The Brewery, Sunderland, Co Durham, SR1 3AN
Tyne and Wear Tel 77324
Telex 53168
Bookings also for Anchor Hotels and Taverns Ltd, GW Hotels and Lorimer Inns

Trust Houses Forte Hotels Limited,
71–75 Uxbridge Road, London, W5 5SL
Tel 01–567 3444
Telex 934946

Booking Agencies

Exp-O-Tel *(Hotel Reservations)* Ltd
Strand House, Great West Road, Brentford, Middlesex, TW8 9EX
Tel 01–568 8765
Telex 8811951
Hours: Mon–Fri 9am–5.30pm Sat 9.30am–12noon. No Charges.
London Bookings: 01–568 8855
Provincial: 01–568 1991
Overseas: 01–568 5151
Room Space Ltd: Private bookings, 01–568 4143
Telex 8967788
(Mon–Fri 9.15–5.30. Sat 9.30–12 noon)

Prospectus *(conference reservations)* Ltd:
01–741 4041
Exhibitex *(fairs and travel)* Ltd:

01–741 4494
Supersports *(Travel)* Ltd, Banda House, Cambridge Grove, Hammersmith, London, W6 0LE
Tel 01–741 4575

Hotel & Personal Accommodation Ltd,
10 Lower Belgrave Street, London, SW1
Tel 01–730 6181
Telex 918837
Hours: Mon–Fri 9.30am–5.30pm. Closed Sat, Sun & Bank Holidays. No charges.
We also make group bookings.

HBI – Hotac Hotel Accommodation Service Ltd,
Globegate House, Pound Lane, London, NW10 2LB
Tel 01–451 2311

and 01–459 1212
Telex 8814032
Hours: 9.30am–5.30pm. Mon–Fri. No charges.
Also branches at London (Heathrow) Airport
Terminal 1: 01–759 2710 8am–11pm
Terminal 2: 01–897 0821 7am–11pm
Terminal 3: 01–897 0507 7am–11pm
(Gatwick 0293 30266 8am–11pm)
Specialising in airport traffic

Hotel Booking Service Ltd,
137 Regent Street, London, W1R 8EB
Tel 01–437 5052
Telex 262892
Hours: Mon–Fri 9am–6pm *(1pm Sat, May–Sep)*. Closed Sun. £1 booking fee. Free service to business house clients.

Hotelguide,
Faraday House, 8–10 Charing Cross Road, London, WC2H PHG
Tel 01–836 5561
Telex 22650
Hours: Mon–Fri 9am–5.30pm (1pm Sat) Closed Sun. No charges.

In listing the above mentioned organisations the Association is only recording their existence. The Association cannot accept liability for any circumstances arising from their use by members.

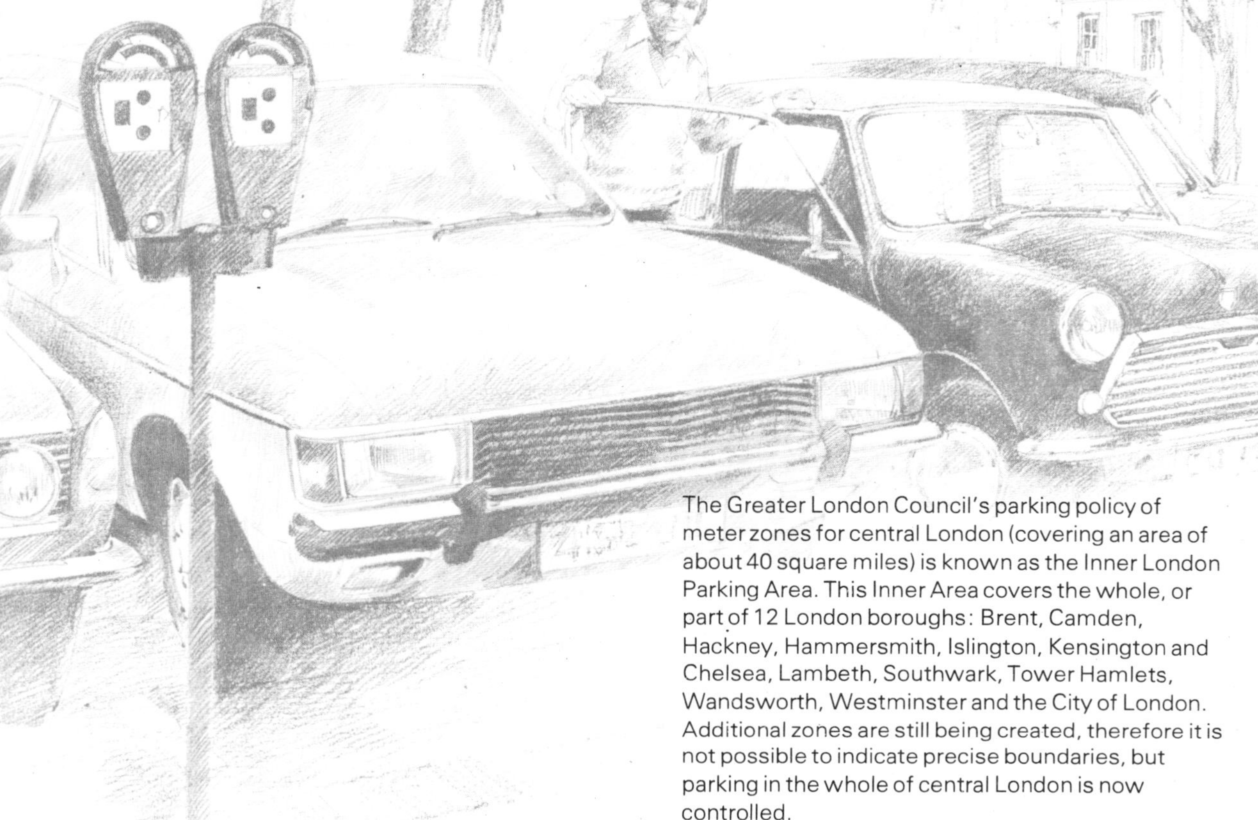

The Greater London Council's parking policy of meter zones for central London (covering an area of about 40 square miles) is known as the Inner London Parking Area. This Inner Area covers the whole, or part of 12 London boroughs: Brent, Camden, Hackney, Hammersmith, Islington, Kensington and Chelsea, Lambeth, Southwark, Tower Hamlets, Wandsworth, Westminster and the City of London. Additional zones are still being created, therefore it is not possible to indicate precise boundaries, but parking in the whole of central London is now controlled.

There are also parking zones in outer London, most of which include meters.

Brief details of how meters operate are given in the Street Parking section which follows.

Street Parking Parking Zones

Controlled zones are indicated by signs at their boundary points, giving the hours of operation. Special regulations may also apply in areas near to the wholesale markets and where Sunday street markets are held. Street parking other than at officially designated places is prohibited during the specified hours. In many zones, some parking places may be found reserved exclusively for residents, or other classes of users specified on nearby plates.

Meter Regulations

There are some differences in the charges, and variations in the length of time for which parking is allowed.

The car must be parked within the limits of the parking bay, indicated by the white lines on the road. Also it must be facing the same direction as the traffic flow, unless angle parking is indicated by road marking.

Payment must be made immediately, although unexpired meter time, paid for by a previous occupant of the space, may be used. After the initial payment has been made, additional parking time may not be bought by making any further payments. A vehicle should be removed before the permitted time has elapsed and no vehicle may be returned to any bay in the same parking place within one hour.

If a vehicle is left at a meter beyond the time paid for, a ticket may be placed on it, to show a high rate excess charge which is payable to the local authority. This allows a further short period of parking before an offence is committed.

Waiting Restrictions

The usual system of yellow lines should indicate these, but their omission does not necessarily mean there is no effective restriction. In addition, any vehicle waiting on a road may be judged to be causing 'unnecessary obstruction', without proof that other vehicles or persons may have actually been obstructed, and a prosecution could ensue.

Vehicle Removal

A car left on the road causing actual obstruction, or not left in a parking place and judged to be creating an 'unnecessary obstruction' on the highway, may be removed by the Police and held in a Pound. If a vehicle has been removed a driver should contact the nearest Police Station, who will have the details of any official removal. On collection, a substantial fee is payable for the removal, in addition to any other parking or penalty charges.

Disabled People – Orange Badge Scheme

Certain disabled drivers, passengers and institutions caring for the disabled who operate specially adapted mini-buses or similar vehicles, may apply to become members of the Orange Badge Scheme run by local authorities. The badges are for identification only and do not entitle the holder to parking concessions. Concessions derive from exceptions written into traffic regulation orders by individual local authorities, and the badges are valid throughout the country except for the following areas of central London. The cities of London and Westminster, the Borough of Kensington and Chelsea, and the Borough of Camden who operate their own concessionary schemes. Extensions to the existing regulations came into effect on 1 June 1975. They extend the eligibility for an orange badge to a blind person (as a passenger) who is registered under the National Assistance Act 1948. They allow badge holders to park for up to two hours on yellow lines except where there is a ban on loading or unloading in force at the time, or in a bus lane. They must set an orange disc at the time of arrival. The badge holder is entitled to park free of charge and without time restriction, at parking meters and where parking is limited.

Special Restrictions

No stopping Regulations apply at many dangerous junctions, at a number of school entrances, in cab parking places and on bus stop clearways. In a few areas spaces are reserved for diplomatic cars, doctors, invalid carriages and pedal cycles.

Parking at Night

Cars, motor cycles, invalid carriages, pedal cycles and goods vehicles under 30cwt unladen weight not being a vehicle, in any case, to which a trailer is attached, can park without lights provided that:

a The road is subject to a speed limit of 30mph or less.

b No part of the vehicle is within 15 yards of a road junction.

c The vehicle is parked close to the kerb and parallel to it, and except in one way streets, with its nearside to the kerb.

Vehicles 30cwt or more unladen weight, or carrying eight or more passengers, must show two white lights to the front and two red lights with an illuminated number plate to the rear, in any night parking situation.

Similarly, if the road is not subject to a 30mph speed limit, a vehicle left standing on the highway at night must conform to the lighting regulations as above.

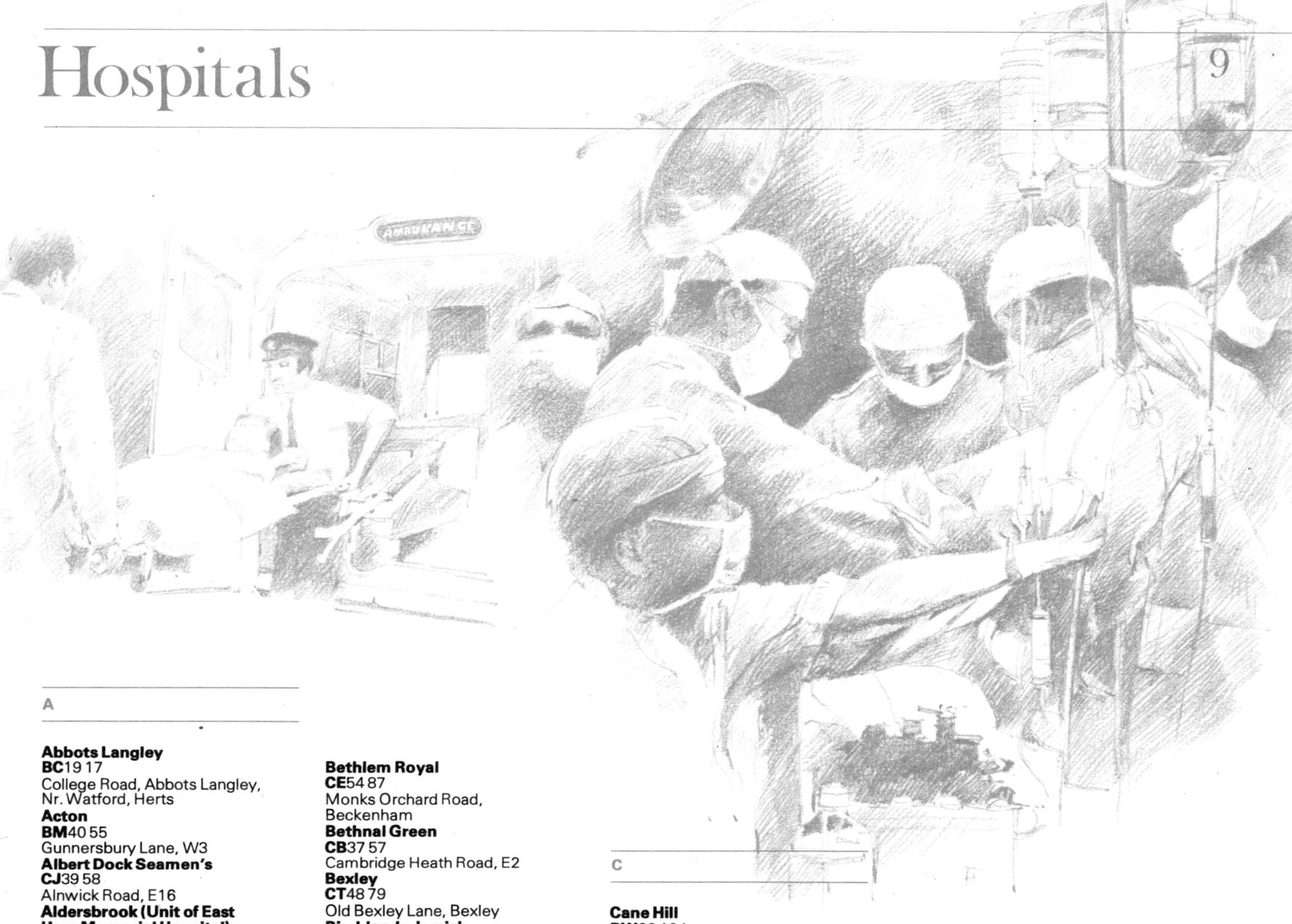

A

Abbots Langley
BC19 17
College Road, Abbots Langley,
Nr. Watford, Herts
Acton
BM40 55
Gunnersbury Lane, W3
Albert Dock Seamen's
CJ39 58
Alnwick Road, E16
**Aldersbrook (Unit of East
Ham Memorial Hospital)**
CH34 49
Aldersbrook Road, E11
All Saints
BY42 4
Austral Street, SE11
Ashford
AY48 73
London Road, Ashford
Atkinson Morley's
BP50 75
Copse Hill, Wimbledon, SW20

B

Banstead
BT59 95
Downs Road, Sutton
Barking
CN36 58
Upney Lane, Barking
Barnes
BO45 65
South Worple Way, SW14
Barnet General
BQ24 28
Wellhouse Lane, Barnet
Beckenham
CD51 87
379 Croydon Road, Beckenham
Beckenham Maternity
CE52 87
Stone Park Avenue, Beckenham
Beechcroft
AS62 100
Heathside Road, Woking, Surrey
Belgrave Children's
BY43 66
Clapham Road, SW9
Belmont
BS58 95
Brighton Road, Sutton

Bethlem Royal
CE54 87
Monks Orchard Road,
Beckenham
Bethnal Green
CB37 57
Cambridge Heath Road, E2
Bexley
CT48 79
Old Bexley Lane, Bexley
Birchlands Jewish
BU47 76
Birchlands Avenue,
Wandsworth Common, SW12
Bolingbroke
BU46 76
Bolingbroke Grove,
Wandsworth Common, SW11
Botleys Park
AU56 91
Guildford Road, Chertsey, Surrey
Bow Arrow
CX46 80
Dartford, Kent
Brentford
BK43 64
Boston Manor Road, Brentford
Brentwood District
DC26 122
Crescent Drive, Brentwood, Essex
**British Home and Hospital
for Incurables**
BY49 76
Crown Lane, SW16
**British Hospital for Mothers
and Babies**
CK42 68
Samuel Street, SE18
Bromley
CH52 88
Cromwell Avenue, Bromley
Brompton
BT42 3
Fulham Road, SW3
Brook General
CK44 68
Shooters Hill Road, SE18
Brookwood
AO63 100
Knaphill, Woking, Surrey
Bushey District
BH26 36
Windmill Street, Bushey Heath,
Herts

C

Cane Hill
BW62 104
Coulsdon
**Carshalton, Beddington &
Wallington District**
BU56 95
The Park, Carshalton
Cassel
BK49 74
Ham Common, Richmond
Caterham & District
CB64 105
Croydon Road, Caterham Valley
Cell Barnes
BK14 9
Highfield Lane, St. Albans, Herts
Central Middlesex
BN38 55
Acton Lane, NW10
Chadwell Heath
CO32 50
Grove Road, Chadwell Heath,
Romford, Essex
Charing Cross
BQ42 65
Fulham Palace Road, W6
Chase Farm
BY23 29
The Ridgeway, Enfield
Cheam
BQ55 85
London Road, North Cheam
Chelsea Hospital for Women
BT42 3
Dovehouse Street, SW3
Cheshunt Cottage
CC18 21
Church Lane, Cheshunt, Herts
Cheyne
CF55 87
Woodland Way, West Wickham
Children's
CD49 77
Sydenham Road, Sydenham,
SE26

Chingford
CF27 39
Larkshall Road, Chingford, E4
City of London Maternity
BX33 47
65 Hanley Road, N4
Claremont
BK53 84
St. James's Road, Surbiton
Claybury
CL29 40
Woodford Bridge, Woodford
Green, Essex
Clayponds
BL42 65
Occupation Lane,
South Ealing, W5.
Clerks Croft (Netherne)
BZ70 114
Bletchingley, Surrey
**Cobham & District
Cottage Hospital**
BC60 92
Portsmouth Road, Cobham,
Surrey
Colindale
BN30 37
Colindale Avenue, NW9
Coppetts Wood
BU30 38
Coppetts Road, Muswell Hill, N10
Cray Valley
CP51 89
St. Paul's Cray
Croydon General
BZ54 87
London Road, Croydon
Cuddington
BR60 94
Banstead, Surrey
Cumberland House
BU52 86
Whitford Gardens, Mitcham

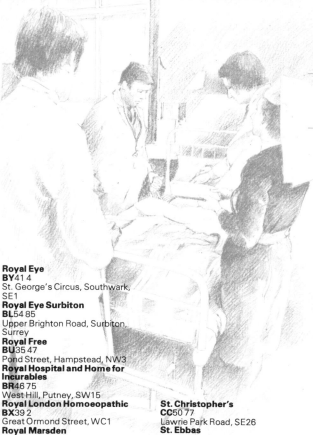

Moorfields Eye
BX39 2
High Holborn, WC1
Mothers (S.A.)
CB35 48
143–153 Lower Clapton Road, E5
Mount Pleasant
BF39 54
North Road, Southall
Mount Vernon
AZ29 35
Northwood
Murray House
AU57 91
Ottershaw, Surrey

N

Napsbury
BJ17 18
Napsbury, Nr. St. Albans, Herts
National Heart
BV39 1
Westmorland Street, W1
National Hospital for Nervous Diseases
BX38 2
Queens Square, WC1
National Temperance
BW38 1
Hampstead Road, NW1
Neasden
BN36 55
Brentfield Road, NW10
Nelson
BR51 85
Kingston Road, Merton, SW20
Netherne
BW64 104
Coulsdon
Newham Maternity
CG35 49
Forest Lane, E7
New Cross
CC43 67
Avonley Road, New Cross, SE14
New End
BT35 47
Hampstead, NW3
New Victoria
BO51 85
184 Coombe Lane West, Kingston upon Thames
Normansfield
BK50 74
Kingston Road, Teddington
North Middlesex
CA28 39
Silver Street, Edmonton, N18
Northwick Park
BJ33 45
Watford Road, Harrow
Northwood, Pinner & District
BC30 35
Pinner Road, Northwood
Norwood & District
BZ50 77
Hermitage Road, SE19

O

Oldchurch
CT32 50
Oldchurch Road, Romford
Ongar War Memorial
CX16 24
Shelley, Ongar, Essex
Orme Lodge
BJ29 36
Gordon Avenue, Stanmore
Orpington
CN56 97
Orpington
Ottershaw
AU57 91
Ottershaw, Surrey
Oxted & Limpsfield
CF67 114
Eastlands Way, Oxted, Surrey

P

Paddington Green Children's
BT39 1
Paddington Green, W2

Perivale Maternity
BH38 54
Greenford
Plaistow
CJ37 58
Samson Street, Plaistow, E13
Poplar
CF39 57
East India Dock Road, E14
Port of London Isolation
DJ46 81
Denton, Nr. Gravesend, Kent
Potters Bar & District
BS20 20
Mutton Lane, Potters Bar, Herts
Prince of Wales General
CA31 48
Tottenham Green East, N15
Princess Alexandra
CM10 6
Hamstel Road, Harlow, Essex
Princess Louise
BQ39 55
St. Quinton Avenue, W10
Purley & District War Memorial
BY59 95
Brighton Road, Purley
Putney
BQ45 65
Commondale, Putney, SW15

Q

Queen Charlotte's Maternity
BP41 65
Goldhawk Road, W6
Queen Elizabeth
BT62 104
Holly Lane, Banstead Wood, Surrey
Queen Elizabeth House
BU47 76
Nightingale Lane, SW12
Queen Elizabeth II
BS10 5
Howlands, Welwyn Garden Herts
Queen Elizabeth Hospital for Children
CB37 57
Hackney Road, E2
Queen Mary's Hospital for Children
BV58 95
Carshalton, Surrey
Queen Mary's
CO50 79
Frognal Avenue, Sidcup
Queen Mary's
BP46 75
Roehampton Lane, SW15
Queen Mary's Maternity
BT34 47
124 Heath Street, NW3
Queen Mary's for the East End
CF36 57
West Ham Lane, Stratford, E15
Queens
BZ53 87
Queens Road, Croydon

R

Redhill General
BU71 121
Earlswood Common, Redhill, Surrey
Rowley Bristow Orthopaedic
AW61 101
Pyrford, Nr. Woking, Surrey
Roxbourne
BF34 45
Rayners Lane, South Harrow
Royal
BL45 65
Kew Foot Road, Richmond
Royal Dental
BW40 3
32 Leicester Square, WC2
Royal Ear
BW38 1
Huntley Street, WC1
Royal Earlswood
BV72 121
Princess Road, Redhill, Surrey

Royal Eye
BY41 4
St. George's Circus, Southwark, SE1
Royal Eye Surbiton
BL54 85
Upper Brighton Road, Surbiton, Surrey
Royal Free
BU35 47
Pond Street, Hampstead, NW3
Royal Hospital and Home for Incurables
BR46 75
West Hill, Putney, SW15
Royal London Homoeopathic
BX39 2
Great Ormond Street, WC1
Royal Marsden
BT42 3
Fulham Road, SW3
Royal Marsden (Surrey Branch)
BT58 95
Downs Road, Sutton
Royal Masonic
BP41 65
Ravenscourt Park, W6
Royal National Ear, Nose & Throat
BX38 2
Grays Inn Road, WC1
Royal National Ear, Nose & Throat
BW40 3
Golden Square, W1
Royal National Orthopaedic
BV39 1
234 Great Portland Street, W1
Royal National Orthopaedic
BK27 36
Brockley Hill, Stanmore
Royal Northern
BX34 47
Holloway Road, N7
Royal Surrey County
AQ71 118
Farnham Road, Guildford, Surrey
Rush Green
CT34 50
Dagenham Road, Romford

S

St. Albans City
BG12 9
Normandy Road, St. Albans, Herts
St. Andrew's
CE38 57
Devons Road, E3
St. Ann's General
BZ32 48
St. Ann's Road, South Tottenham, N15
St. Anthony's
BQ54 85
London Road, North Cheam
St. Bartholomew's
BY39 2
West Smithfield, EC1
St. Bernard's
BG41 64
Uxbridge Road, Southall
St. Charles'
BQ39 55
Exmoor Street, W10

St. Christopher's
CC50 77
Lawrie Park Road, SE26
St. Ebbas
BN58 94
Hook Road, Epsom, Surrey
St. Faith's
DA27 42
London Road, Brentwood, Essex
St. Francis
CA45 67
St. Francis Road, SE22
St. George's
CV35 51
117 Suttons Lane, Hornchurch
St. George's
BT49 76
Blackshaw Road, SW17
St. Giles'
CA44 67
St. Giles' Road, Camberwell, SE5
St. Helier
BT54 86
Wrythe Lane, Carshalton, Surrey
St. James's
BU47 76
Sarsfeld Road, SW12
St. James's
DG47 81
Trafalgar Road, Gravesend, Kent
St. John's
CF44 67
Morden Hill, SE13
St. John's
BT45 66
St. John's Hill, Battersea, SW11
St. John's for Diseases of the Skin
BW1 3
Lisle Street WC2
St. John's
AY38 53
Kingston Lane, Uxbridge
St. John's
BJ47 74
Amyand Park Road, Twickenham
St. Lawrence's
BZ65 105
Caterham, Surrey
St. Leonard's
CA37 2
Nuttall Street, Kingsland Road, N1
St. Luke's
AS71 118
Warren Road, Guildford, Surrey
St. Luke's Woodside
BV31 47
Woodside Avenue, N10
St. Margaret's
CO18 23
Ongar Road, Epping, Essex

11

St. Mark's
BY38 2
City Road, EC1
St. Mary's
CH37 58
Upper Road, Plaistow, E13
St. Mary's Maternity
BY54 86
St. James's Road, Croydon
St. Mary's Cottage
BE51 84
Upper Sunbury Road, Hampton
St. Mary's
BT39 1
Praed Street, W2
St. Mary's
BS39 56
Harrow Road, W9
St. Mary Abbots
BS41 66
Marloes Road, W8
St. Matthew's
BZ38 2
Shepherdess Walk, N1
St. Michael's
BZ23 30
19 Chase Side Crescent, Enfield
St. Nicholas
CN42 68
Tewson Road, Plumstead, SE18
St. Olave's
CC41 67
Lower Road, Rotherhithe, SE16
St. Pancras & Tropical
Disease
BW37 1
4 St. Pancras Way, NW1
St. Paul's
BX39 2
Endell Street, WC2
St. Peter's
AU55 82
Guildford Road, Chertsey, Surrey
St. Peter's
BX40 4
Henrietta Street, WC2
St. Peter's Hospitals
BX39 2
Sheffield Street, Kingsway, WC2
St. Stephen's
BQ25 28
Mays Lane, Barnet
St. Stephen's
BT43 66
Fulham Road, SW10
St. Teresa's
BQ50 75
12 The Downs, SW20
St. Thomas'
BX41 4
Lambeth Palace Road, SE1
Samaritan for Women
BU39 1
Marylebone Road, NW1
Schiff
BE61 102
Knowle Hill Park, Cobham, Surrey
Seamen's see under
    Dreadnought Seamen's
Sevenoaks
CV64 108
St. John's Hill, Sevenoaks, Kent
Shabden Park
BU64 104
High Road, Chipstead, Surrey
Shaftesbury
BX39 2
172 Shaftesbury Avenue, WC2
Shenley
BL20 19
Black Lion Hill, Shenley,
St. Albans, Herts
Sidcup Cottage
CO48 79
Birkbeck Road, Sidcup
Southall-Norwood
BE41 64
The Green, Southall
South London, for Women &
Children
BV46 76
Clapham Common, SW4
South Middlesex
BH46 74
Mogden Lane, Isleworth
South Ockendon
DB38 60
South Road, South Ockendon,
Essex

South Western
BX45 66
Landor Road, SW9
Southwood
BV33 47
Southwood Lane, Highgate, N6
Springfield
BU48 76
61, Glenburnie Road, SW17
Staines
AW50 73
Kingston Road, Staines
Stone House
CY46 80
London Road, Dartford, Kent
Sundridge
CQ67 116
Sevenoaks, Kent
Surbiton General
BL53 85
Ewell Road, Surbiton
Sutton & Cheam General
BS58 95
Cotswold Road, Sutton

T

Teddington Memorial
BH50 74
Hampton Road, Teddington
Temple Hill House
BS34 47
5 West Heath Road, NW3
Thames Ditton
BH54 84
Weston Green Road,
Thames Ditton, Surrey
The Manor
BM59 94
Christchurch Road, Epsom,
Surrey
Thomas Barlow House
BW32 47
80 Shepherds Hill, Highgate, N6
Thorpe Coombe
CF31 48
714 Forest Road,
Walthamstow, E17
Thurrock
DE40 71
Long Lane, Grays, Essex
Tolworth
BM55 85
Red Lion Road, Tolworth
Tooting Bec
BV49 76
Tooting Bec Road, Tooting, SW17
Tropical Diseases
    see under St. Pancras
    & Tropical Diseases

U

University College
BW38 1
Gower Street, WC1
    Royal Ear
    BW38 1
    Huntley Street, WC1
    Dental
    BW38 1
    Mortimer Market, WC1
    Obstetric
    BW38 1
    Huntley Street, WC1
    Private Wing
    BW38 1
    Grafton Way, WC1
Upton
AP41 62
Slough, Berks
Uxbridge & District
AX35 44
Harefield Road, Uxbridge

V

Victoria Maternity
BR24 28
Wood Street, Barnet
Victoria
CT31 50
Pettits Lane, Romford

W

Waddon
BX54 86
Purley Way, Croydon
Waltham Abbey
War Memorial
CF20 21
Farm Hill Road, Waltham Abbey,
Essex
Walton General
BC55 83
Sidney Road, Walton on Thames,
Surrey
Wandle Valley
BU54 86
Mitcham Junction
Wanstead
CH31 49
Hermon Hill, Wanstead, E11
Warley
DA28 42
Warley Hill, Brentwood, Essex
Warlingham Park
CE61 105
Warlingham, Surrey
Watford General
(Peace Memorial Wing)
BC24 26
Rickmansworth Road, Watford,
Herts
Watford General
(Shrodells Wing)
BC25 26
Vicarage Road, Watford, Herts
Watford General
(Holywell Wing)
BB26 35
Tolpits Lane, Watford, Herts
Weir Maternity
BW47 76
Weir Road, SW12
Welwyn Garden City Cottage
BQ8 5
Church Road,
Welwyn Garden City, Herts
Wembley
BK36 54
Fairview Avenue, Wembley
Western Opthalmic
BU39 1
Marylebone Road, NW1
West Hendon
BO32 46
Goldsmith Avenue, NW9
West Hill
CV46 80
Dartford, Kent
West London
BQ42 65
Hammersmith Road, W6
West Middlesex
BJ44 64
Twickenham Road, Isleworth
Westminster
BX42 4
Dean Ryle Street, SW1
Westminster Children's
BW42 3
Vincent Square, SW1
West Park
BL59 94
Epsom, Surrey
Wexham Park
AR38 52
Wexham, Slough, Berks
Weybridge
AZ56 92
Church Street, Weybridge, Surrey
Whipps Cross
CF32 48
Whipps Cross Road, Leytonstone,
E11
Whittington
BV34 47
Highgate Hill, N19
    Highgate Wing
    BV34 47
    Dartmouth Park Hill
    Archway Wing
    BW33 47
    Archway Road
    St. Mary's Wing
    BW33 47
    Highgate Hill
Willesden General
BP36 55
Harlesden Road, NW10

Wilson
BU52 86
Cranmer Road, Mitcham, Surrey
Wimbledon
BP50 75
Thurstan Road, Copse Hill, SW20
Woking Victoria
AS61 100
Chobham Road, Woking, Surrey
Woodford Jubilee
CH29 40
Woodford Green, Essex
Wood Green & Southgate
BW29 38
Bounds Green Road, N11

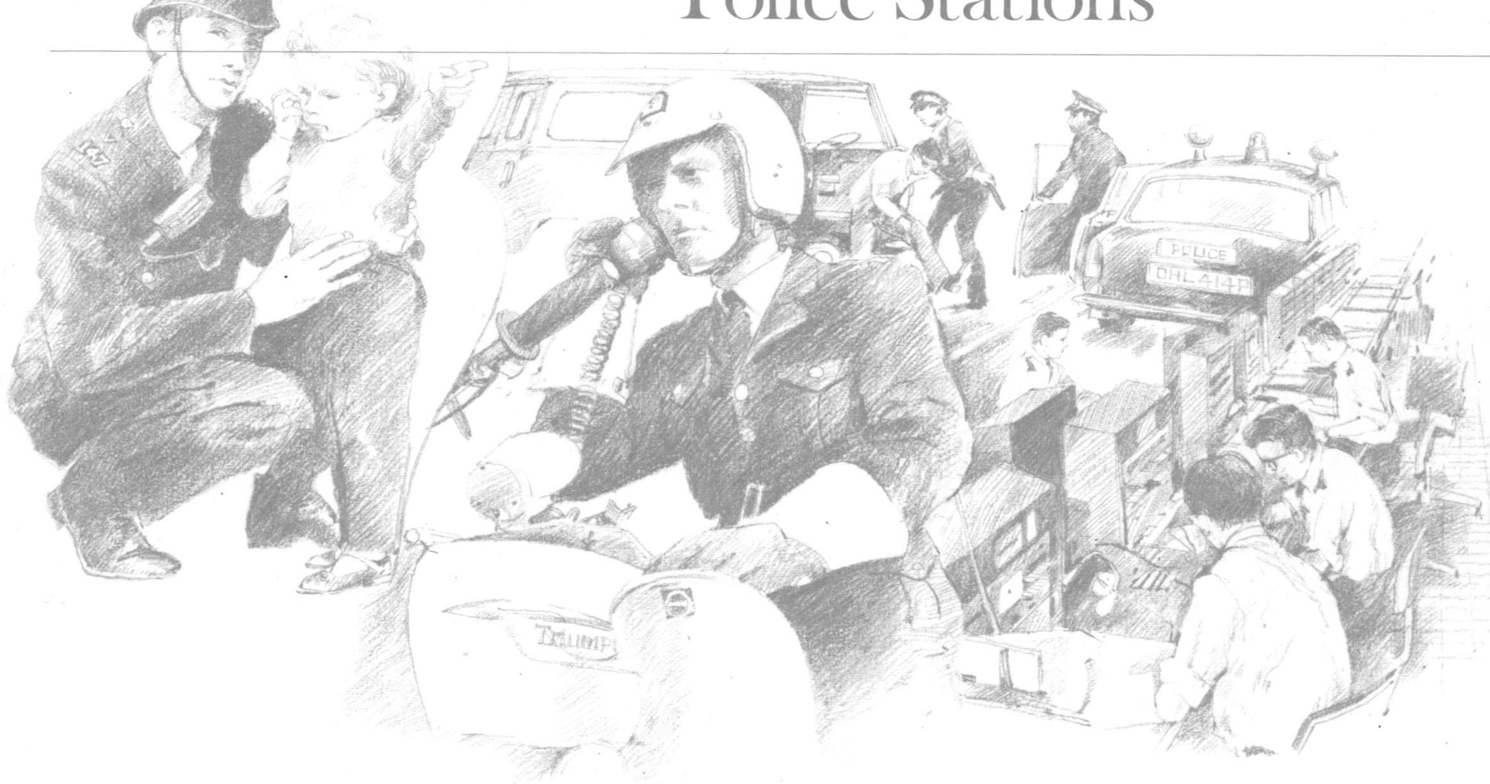

Acton BM40 55
250 High Street, W3
Addington CE56 96
Addington Village Road
Albany Street BV38 1
60 Albany Street, NW1
Arbour Square CC39 57
East Arbour Street, E1

Banstead BS61 104
High Street
Barking CM36 58
6 Ripple Road
Barkingside CM31 49
1 High Street
Barnes BO44 65
92–102 Station Road, SW13
Barnet BR24 28
26 High Street
Battersea BU44 66
112 Battersea Bridge Road, SW11
Belvedere CR42 69
2 Nuxley Road
Bethnal Green CB38 57
458 Bethnal Green Road, E2
Bexleyheath CR45 69
49 Broadway
Biggin Hill CJ62 106
195 Main Road
Bishopsgate CA39 2
182 Bishopsgate, EC2
Blackwall CF40 57
19 Coldharbour, E14
Boreham Wood BN23 28
Elstree Way
Bow CE38 57
111 Bow Road, E3
Bow Street BX39 2
28 Bow Street, WC2
Brentford BK43 64
The Half Acre
Brentwood DA27 42
London Road
Brixton BY45 66
367 Brixton Road, SW9
Brockley CD45 67
4 Howson Road, SE4
Bromley CH51 88
Widmore Road

Bushey BF26 36
43 Clay Hill

Camberwell BZ44 67
22a Camberwell Church Street,
SE5
Cannon Row BX41 4
1 Cannon Row, SW1
Carter Street BZ42 4
292 Walworth Road, SE17
Catford CF48 77
333 Bromley Road, SE6
Chadwell Heath CP33 50
14 Wangey Road
Chelsea BU42 3
2 Lucan Place, SW3
Cheshunt CC18 21
101 Turners Hill
Chigwell CM29 40
24 Brook Parade, High Street
Chingford CF26 39
Kings Head Hill, E4
Chislehurst CL50 78
47 High Street
Chiswick BO42 65
205 Chiswick High Road, W4
City Road BZ38 2
4 Shepherdess Walk, N1
Clapham BW44 66
51 Union Grove, SW8
Claybury CK29 40
Manor Road, Woodford Bridge
Cobham BC60 92
Portsmouth Road
Collier Row CS30 41
22 Collier Row Lane
Croydon BZ55 87
71 Park Lane

Dagenham CS35 50
561 Rainham Road South
Dalston CA36 57
39 Dalston Lane, E8

Dartford CV47 80
Instone Road
Deptford CD43 67
116 Amersham Vale, SE14
Dorking BJ71 119
Moores Road

Ealing BK40 54
67 Uxbridge Road, W5
Earlsfield BT48 76
522 Garratt Lane, SW17
East Dulwich CB46 77
173–183 Lordship Lane, SE22
East Ham CK37 58
4 High Street South, E6
East Molesey BG53 84
1 Walton Road
Edgware BM29 37
Whitchurch Lane
Edmonton CB28 39
320 Fore Street, N9
Egham AT49 72
High Street
Eltham CK44 68
20 Well Hall Road, SE9
Enfield BZ24 30
Baker Street
Epsom BO60 94
Church Street
Erith CT42 69
22 High Street
Esher BF56 93
113 High Street

Farnborough CL55 88
Farnborough Common
Feltham BD47 74
34 Hanworth Road
Finchley BS29 38
193 Ballards Lane, N3

Forest Gate CH35 49
370 Romford Road, E7
Fulham BS43 66
Heckfield Place, SW6

Gerald Road BV42 3
5 Gerald Road, SW1
Gipsy Hill CA50 77
16 Central Hill, SE19
Golders Green BR32 46
1069 Finchley Road, NW11
Gravesend DG47 81
Windmill Street
Grays DD42 71
Orsett Road
Greenford BG38 54
21 Oldfield Lane
Greenwich CF43 67
31 Royal Hill, SE10
Guildford AR71 118
Margaret Road

Hackney CC35 48
2 Lower Clapton Road, E5
Ham BK48 74
Ashburnham Road
Hammersmith BQ42 65
226 Shepherds Bush Road, W6
Hampstead BT35 47
26½ Rosslyn Hill, NW3
Hampton BF51 84
68 Station Road
Harefield AX30 35
24 Rickmansworth Road
Harlesden BO36 55
76 Craven Park, NW10
Harlow CM11 13
Crown Gate, The High
Harold Hill CW28 42
Gooshays Drive

Harrow BG34 45
74 Northolt Road
Harrow Road BS38 56
325 Harrow Road, W9
Hatfield BP11 10
St. Alban's Road East
Hayes BA39 53
755 Uxbridge Road
Heathrow AZ45 63
Heathrow Airport, Hounslow
Hemel Hempstead AX13 8
Combe Street
Hendon BQ31 46
133 Brent Street North, NW4
Highbury Vale BY34 47
211 Blackstock Road, N5
Highgate BV32 47
407 Archway Road, N6
Hoddesdon CE12 12
High Street
Holborn BX39 2
70 Theobalds Road, WC1
Holloway BX34 47
284 Hornsey Road, N7
Hornchurch CV34 51
74 Station Lane
Hornsey BX31 47
98 Tottenham Lane, N8
Hounslow BF45 64
5 Montague Road
Hyde Park BU40 3
North of Serpentine, W2

Ilford CL34 49
40 High Road
Isle of Dogs CE42 67
West Ferry Road, E14
Islington BY36 56
277 Upper Street, N1

Kenley BZ60 96
94 Godstone Road
Kennington Road BY41 4
49 Kennington Road, SE1
Kensington BS41 66
72 Earl's Court Road, W8
Kentish Town BV35 47
12a Holmes Road, NW5
Kilburn BR37 55
2–4 Harvist Road, NW6
Kingsbury BM32 46
3 The Mall, Kenton
Kingston upon Thames
BK51 84
5 High Street
Kings Cross Road BX38 2
76 Kings Cross Road, WC1

Lavender Hill BV45 66
176 Lavender Hill, SW11
Leatherhead BJ64 102
44 Kingston Road
Lee Road CG46 68
418 Lee High Road, SE12
Leman Street CA39 2
74 Leman Street, E1
Lewisham CE46 77
2 Ladywell Road, SE13
Leyton CF33 48
215 Francis Road, E10
Leytonstone CG34 49
470 High Road, E11
Limehouse CE40 57
29 West India Dock Road, E14

Loughton CK24 31
158 High Road

Marylebone BV39 1
1–9 Seymour Street, W1
Mill Hill BN28 37
11 Deans Drive
Mitcham BU52 86
58 Cricket Green
Muswell Hill BU31 47
Fortis Green, N2

New Malden BO52 85
184 High Street
New Southgate BV28 38
High Road, N11
Nine Elms BV43 66
147 Battersea Park Road, SW8
Norbury BX51 86
1516 London Road, SW16
Northwood BB29 35
2 Murray Road
North Woolwich CL41 68
Pier Road, E16
Norwood Green BE42 64
190 Norwood Road, Southall
Notting Hill BR40 55
101 Ladbroke Road, W11

Ockenden DA39 60
Darenth Lane, Daiglen Drive
Oxted CG68 115
Church Lane

Paddington Green BS38 56
4 Harrow Road, W2
Peckham CB44 67
177 Peckham High Street, SE15
Penge CC50 77
175 High Street, SE20
Pinner BE31 45
Bridge Street
Plaistow CH38 58
444 Barking Road, E13
Plumstead CN42 68
216 Plumstead High Street, SE18
Ponders End CC24 30
204 High Street
Potters Bar BT19 20
The Causeway
Putney BQ45 65
215 Upper Richmond Road, SW15

Radlett BJ20 18
193 Watling Street
Rainham CV38 60
3 New Road
Redhill BT70 121
79 Reigate Road
Richmond BK46 74
8 Red Lion Street
Rickmansworth AX26 35
High Street

Rochester Row BW42 3
63 Rochester Row, SW1
Roehampton BP47 75
117 Danebury Avenue, SW15
Romford CT31 50
19 Main Road
Rotherhithe CC41 67
99 Lower Road, SE16
Ruislip BB33 44
The Oaks

St. Albans BG13 9
Victoria Street
St. Anns Road BZ32 48
289 St. Anns Road, N15
St. John's Wood BU37 1
20½ New Court Street, NW8
St. Mary Cray CP53 89
79 High Street
Sevenoaks CT65 107
Morewood Close
Shenley BM20 19
The Terrace, Harris Lane
Shepherds Bush BP40 55
252 Uxbridge Road, W12
Shooters Hill CK44 68
Shooters Hill, SE18
Sidcup CO49 79
87 Main Road
Slough AP41 62
Windsor Road
Snow Hill BY39 2
5 Snow Hill, EC1
Southall BF40 54
67 High Street
Southgate BW26 38
25 Chase Side, N14
South Norwood CA52 87
83 High Street, SE25
Southwark BZ41 4
323 Borough High Street, SE1
Staines AW49 73
2 London Road
Stoke Newington CA35 48
33 Stoke Newington High Street, N16
Stoneleigh BO56 94
358 Kingston Road, Ewell
Streatham BX49 76
101 Streatham High Road, SW16
Sunbury BC50 73
69 Staines Road East
Surbiton BL54 85
299 Ewell Road, Tolworth
Sutton BS56 95
6 Carshalton Road West
Swanley CT52 89
London Road
Sydenham CC48 77
179 Dartmouth Road, SE26

Teddington BH50 74
18 Park Road
Thamesmead CP41 69
1 Tavy Bridge, SE2
Tilbury DF44 71
Dock Road
Tooting BU50 76
Mitcham Road, SW17
Tottenham CA31 48
398 High Road, N17
Tottenham Court Road
BW39 1
56 Tottenham Court Road, W1
Tower Bridge CA41 4
209 Tooley Street, SE1
Twickenham BJ47 74
41 London Road

Upminster CY34 51
223 St. Mary's Lane
Uxbridge AX36 53
49 Windsor Street

Vine Street BW40 3
10 Vine Street, W1

Wallington BW57 95
84 Stafford Road
Waltham Abbey CF20 21
35 Sun Street
Walthamstow CD31 48
360 Forest Road, E17
Walton on Thames BC54 83
New Zealand Avenue
Wandsworth BS46 76
146 High Street, SW18
Wanstead CH32 49
Spratt Hall Road, E11
Wapping CB40 57
98 Wapping High Street, E1
Waterloo Pier BX40 4
Victoria Embankment, WC2
Wealdstone BH31 45
78 High Street
Watford Central BC23 26
Shady Lane, Clarendon Road
Watford North BC20 17
Kingsway, Garston
Welling CO45 69
60–62 High Street
Welwyn Garden City BQ7 5
The Campus
Wembley BK36 54
603 Harrow Road
Westcombe Park CH42 68
11 Combedale Road, SE10
West Drayton AY41 63
Station Road
West End Central BW40 3
27 Savile Row, W1
West Ham CG37 58
18 West Ham Lane, E15
West Hampstead BS35 47
21 Fortune Green Road, NW6
West Hendon BP33 46
West Hendon, Broadway, Edgware Road, NW9
West Wickham CF55 87
9 High Street
Whetstone BT27 38
1170 High Road, N20
Willesden Green BP36 55
96 High Road, NW10
Wimbledon BS50 76
15 Queens Road, SW19
Winchmore Hill BY26 38
687 Green Lanes, N21
Windsor AO44 61
Alma Road
Woking AS62 100
Heath Side Road
Woodford Green CH28 40
509 High Road
Wood Green BX29 38
347 High Road, N22
Wood Street BZ39 2
37 Wood Street, EC2
Woolwich CL42 68
29 Market Street, SE18
Worcester Park BP55 85
154 Central Road

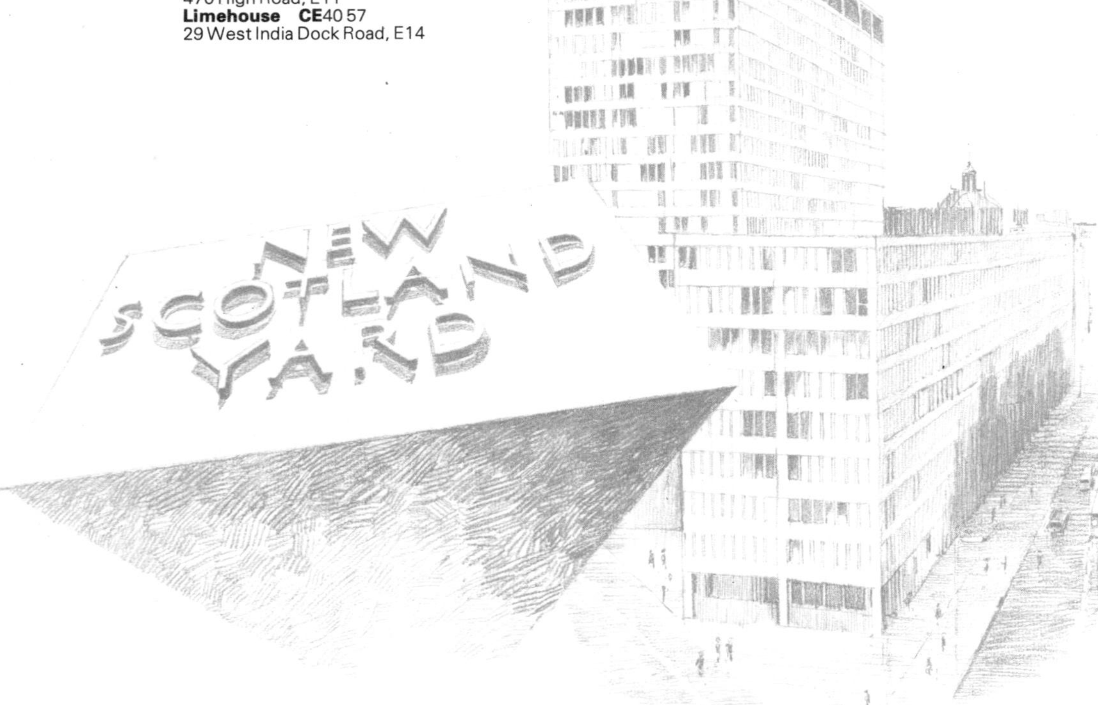

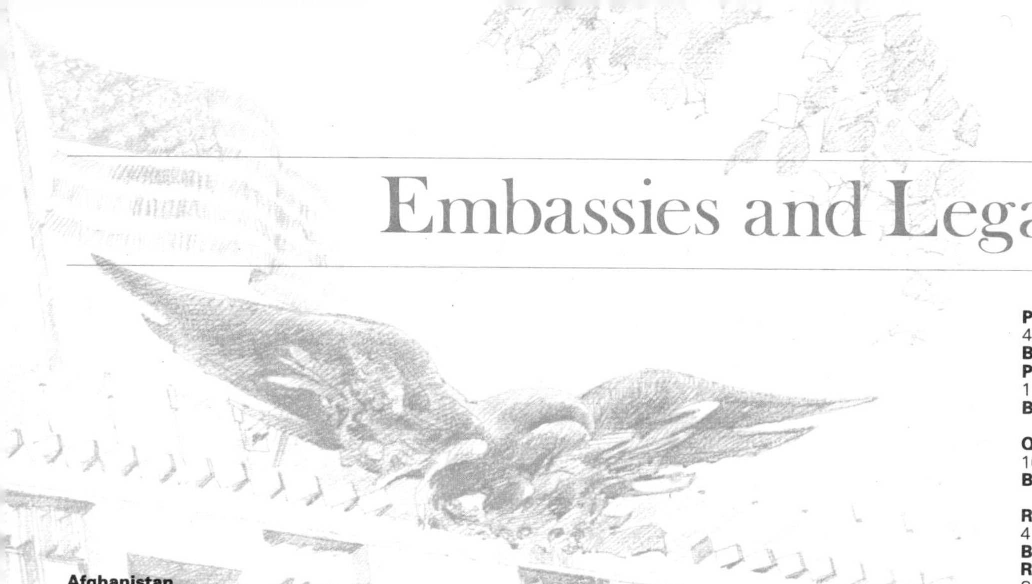

Afghanistan
31 Prince's Gate, SW7
BT41 3
Algeria
54 Holland Park, W11
BR40 55
America
See United States of America
Argentine Republic
9 Wilton Crescent, SW1
BV41 3
Austria
18 Belgrave Mews West, SW1
BV41 3

Bahrain
98 Gloucester Road, SW7
BT41 3
Belgium
105 Eaton Square, SW1
BV41 3
Bolivia
106 Eaton Square, SW1
BV41 3
Brazil
32 Green Street, W1
BV40 3
Bulgaria
186 Queen's Gate, SW7
BT41 3
Burma
19A Charles Street, W1
BV40 3

Cameroon
84 Holland Park, W11
BR40 55
Chile
12 Devonshire Street, W1
BV39 1
China, People's Republic
110 Westcombe Park Road, SE3
CG43 68
Colombia
3 Hans Crescent, SW1
BU41 3
Costa Rica
225 Cromwell Road, SW5
BS42 66
Cuba
57 Kensington Court, W8
BS41 66
Czechoslovakia
25 Kensington Palace Gardens, W8
BS40 56

Denmark
55 Sloane Street, SW1
BU41 3
Dominican Republic
4 Braemar Mansions,
Cornwall Gardens, SW7
BS41 66

Ecuador
3 Hans Crescent, SW1
BU41 3
Egypt, Arab Republic of
75 South Audley Street, W1
BV40 3
Eire
See Ireland, Republic of
El Salvador
16 Edinburgh House,
9B Portland Place, W1
BV39 1

Ethiopia
17 Prince's Gate, SW7
BU41 3

Federal Republic of Germany
23 Belgrave Square, SW1
BV41 3
Finland
38 Chesham Place, SW1
BV41 3
France
58 Knightsbridge, SW1
BU41 3

Gabon
48 Kensington Court, W8
BS41 66
German Democratic Republic
34 Belgrave Square, SW1
BV41 3
Germany
West Germany: see
Federal Republic of Germany
East Germany: see
German Democratic Republic
Greece
1A Holland Park, W11
BR40 55

Haiti
17 Queen's Gate, SW7
BT41 3
Honduras
48 George Street, W1
BU39 1
Hungary
35 Eaton Place, SW1
BV41 3

Iceland
1 Eaton Terrace, SW1
BV42 3
Indonesia
38 Grosvenor Square, W1
BV40 3
Iran
16 Prince's Gate, SW7
BT41 3
Iraq
21/22 Queen's Gate, SW7
BT41 3
Ireland, Republic of
17 Grosvenor Place, SW1
BV41 3
Israel
2 Palace Green, Kensington, W8
BS40 56
Italy
14 Three King's Yard,
Davies Street, W1
BV40 3
Ivory Coast
2 Upper Belgrave Street, SW1
BV41 3

Japan
43–46 Grosvenor Street, W1
BV40 3
Jordan
6 Upper Phillimore Gardens, W8
BS41 66

Korea
4 Palace Gate, W8
BT41 3
Kuwait
40 Devonshire Street, W1
BV39 1

Laos
5 Palace Green, W8
BS40 56
Lebanon
21 Kensington Palace Gardens,
W8
BS40 56
Liberia
21 Prince's Gate, SW7
BT41 3
Libya, Arab Republic
58 Prince's Gate, SW7
BT41 3
Luxembourg
27 Wilton Crescent, SW1
BV41 3

Mexico
8 Halkin Street, SW1
BV41 3
Mongolia
7 Kensington Court, W8
BS41 66
Morocco
49 Queen's Gate Gardens, SW7
BT41 3

Nepal
12A Kensington Palace Gardens,
W8
BS40 56
Netherlands
38 Hyde Park Gate, SW7
BT41 3
Nicaragua
8 Gloucester Road, SW7
BT41 3
Norway
25 Belgrave Square, SW1
BV41 3

Oman
64 Ennismore Gardens, SW7
BU41 3

Pakistan
35 Lowndes Square, SW1
BU41 3
Panama
109 Jermyn Street, SW1
BW40 3
Paraguay
Braemar Lodge,
Cornwall Gardens, SW7
BS41 66
Peru
52 Sloane Street, SW1
BU41 3
Philippines
9A Palace Green, W8
BS40 56

Poland
47 Portland Place, W1
BV39 1
Portugal
11 Belgrave Square, SW1
BV41 3

Qatar
10 Reeves Mews, W1
BV40 3

Romania
4 Palace Green, W8
BS40 56
Russia (U.S.S.R.)
See under Soviet Union

Saudi Arabia
30 Belgrave Square, SW1
BV41 3
Senegal
11 Phillimore Gardens, W8
BS41 66
Somali
60 Portland Place, W1
BV39 1
South Africa
South Africa House,
Trafalgar Square, WC2
BW40 3
Soviet Union
13 Kensington Palace Gardens,
W8
BS40 56
Spain
24 Belgrave Square, SW1
BV41 3
Sudan
3 Cleveland Row, SW1
BW40 3
Sweden
23 North Row, W1
BV40 3
Switzerland
16–18 Montagu Place, W1
BU39 1
Syria, Arab Republic
8 Belgrave Square, SW1
BV41 3

Thailand
29/30 Queen's Gate, SW7
BT41 3
Tunisia
29 Prince's Gate, SW7
BT41 3
Turkey
43 Belgrave Square, SW1
BV41 3

United Arab Emirates
30 Prince's Gate, SW7
BT41 3
United States of America
24 Grosvenor Square, W1
BV40 3
Uruguay
48 Lennox Gardens, SW1
BU41 3

Venezuela
1 Cromwell Road, SW1
BS42 66
Vietnam
12 Victoria Road, W8
BT41 6

Yemen, Arab Republic
41 South Street, W1
BV40 3
**Yemen, People's Democratic
Republic**
57 Cromwell Road, SW7
BT42 3
Yugoslavia
5 Lexham Gardens, W8
BS42 66

Zaire
26 Chesham Place, SW1
BV41 3

Australia

Australia House
Strand, WC2
BX39 2

States

New South Wales
66 Strand, WC2
BX40 4

Queensland
392 Strand, WC2
BX40 4

South Australia
50 Strand, WC2
BX40 4

Tasmania
458 Strand, WC2
BX40 4

Western Australia
115–116 Strand, WC2
BX40 4

Victoria
Victoria House, Melbourne
Place, WC2
BX39 2

Canada

Canada House
Trafalgar Square, SW1
BW40 3

Provinces

Alberta
Alberta House
37 Hill Street, W1
BV40 3

British Columbia
1 Regent Street, SW1
BW40 3

Nova Scotia
14 Pall Mall, SW1
BW40 3

Ontario
Ontario House
13 Charles II Street, SW1
BW40 3

Quebec
12 Upper Grosvenor Street, W1
BV40 3

Saskatchewan
14–16 Cockspur Street, SW1
BW40 3

New Zealand

New Zealand House
Haymarket, SW1
BW40 3

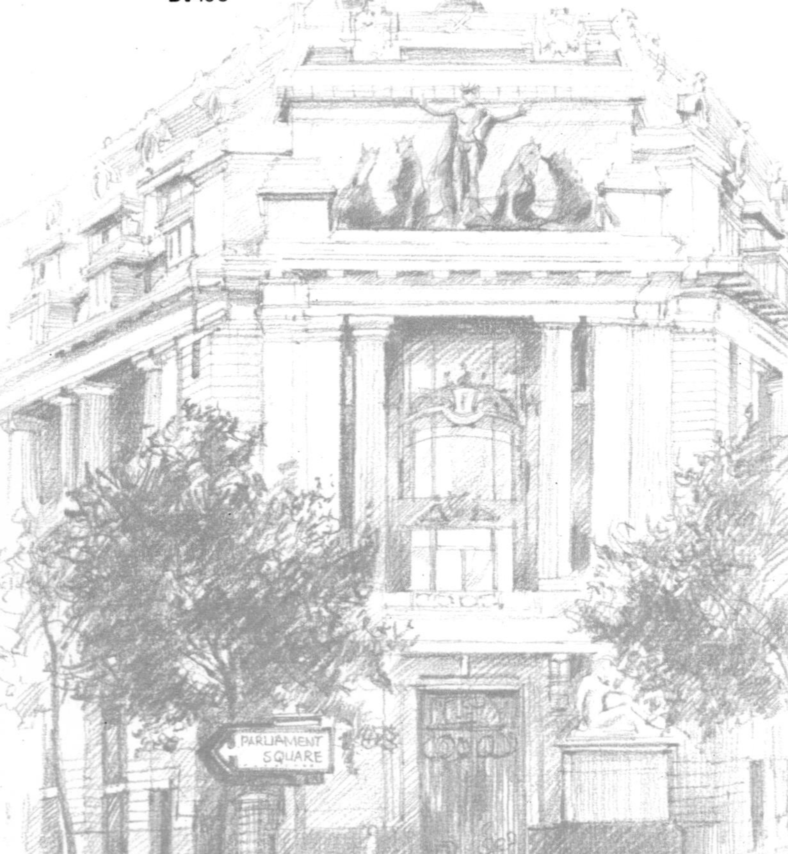

Bahamas

39 Pall Mall, SW1
BW40 3

Bangladesh

28 Queens Gate, SW7
BT41 3

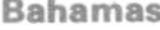

Barbados

6 Upper Belgrave Street, SW1
BV41 3

Botswana

162 Buckingham Palace Road, SW1
BW42 3

Cyprus

93 Park Street, W1
BV40 3

Fiji

34 Hyde Park Gate, SW7
BT41 3

Gambia

60 Ennismore Gardens, SW7
BU41 3

Ghana

13 Belgrave Square, SW1
BV41 3

Grenada *West Indies*

102 Grand Buildings,
Trafalgar Square, SW1
BX40 4

Guyana

3 Palace Court, Bayswater Road,
W2
BS40 56

Hong Kong

6 Grafton Street, W1
BV40 3

India

India House
Aldwych, WC2
BX40 4

Jamaica

50 St. James's Street, SW1
BW40 3

Kenya

45 Portland Place, W1
BV39 1

Lesotho

16A St. James's Street, SW1
BW40 3

Malawi

33 Grosvenor Square, W1
BV40 3

Malaysia

45 Belgrave Square, SW1
BV41 3

Malta GC

24 Haymarket, SW1
BW40 3

Mauritius

32 Elvaston Place, SW7
BT41 66

Nauru

11 Carturet Street, SW1
BW41 3

Nigeria

Nigeria House
9 Northumberland Avenue, WC2
BX40 4

Papua New Guinea

14 Waterloo Place, W1
BW40 3

Sierra Leone

33 Portland Place, W1
BV39 1

Singapore

2 Wilton Crescent, SW1
BV41 3

Sri Lanka

13 Hyde Park Gardens, W2
BT40 3

Swaziland

58 Pont Street, SW1
BU41 3

Tanzania

43 Hertford Street, W1
BV40 3

Tonga

17th Floor
New Zealand House,
Haymarket, SW1
BW40 3

Trinidad & Tobago

42 Belgrave Square, SW1
BV41 3

Uganda

Uganda House
Trafalgar Square, WC2
BW40 3

Zambia

Zambia House
7–11 Cavendish Place, W1
BV39 1

Agricultural Research Council
BV38 1
160 Great Portland Street, W1
Arts Council of Great Britain
BV40 3
105 Piccadilly, W1

British Airports Authority
BW41 3
2 Buckingham Gate, SW1
British Airways AZ45 63
Speedbird House, London Airport
**British Broadcasting
Corporation BV**39 1
Broadcasting House, Portland
Place, W1
British Gas Corporation
BU39 1
59 Bryanston Street, W1
British Library BW39 1
14 Store Street, WC1
British Railways Board
BN38 1
Euston Square, PO Box 100, NW1
British Standards Institution
BV40 3
2 Park Street, W1
British Steel Corporation
BV41 3
33 Grosvenor Place, SW1
British Tourist Authority
BW40 3
64 St. James's Street, SW1
**British Transport Docks
Board BU**38 1
Melbury House, Melbury Terrace,
NW1
British Waterways Board
BU38 1
Melbury House, Melbury Terrace,
NW1
Board of Customs and Excise
CA40 4
Kings Beam House, Mark Lane,
EC3
Board of Inland Revenue
BX40 4
Somerset House, WC2

**Central Electricity Generating
Board BY**39 2
15 Newgate Street, EC1
Central Office of Information
BY41 4
Hercules Road, SE1
Charity Commission
BW40 3
14 Ryder Street, St. James's, SW1
Church Commissioners
BX41 4
1 Millbank, Westminster, SW1
Civil Aviation Authority
BX39 2
43/45 Kingsway, WC2
Civil Service Department
BX40 4
Whitehall, SW1
**College of Arms or Heralds
College BY**40 4
Queen Victoria Street, EC4
**Commonwealth Development
Corporation BV**40 3
33 Hill Street, W1
**Corporation of London Records
Office BZ**39 2
Guildhall, EC2
Corporation of Trinity House
CA40 4
Trinity House, Tower Hill, EC3
Council on Tribunals
BW40 3
6 Spring Gardens, SW1
**Criminal Injuries Compensation
Board BX**38 2
10–12 Russell Square, WC1
Crown Estate Commissioners
BW40 3
13 Carlton House Terrace, SW1

**Department for National
Savings BR**41 65
375 Kensington High Street, W14

**Department of Education and
Science BX**41 4
Elizabeth House, York Road, SE1
Department of Employment
BW41 3
Caxton House, Tothill Street, SW1
**Department of Health and Social
Security BY**42 4
Alexander Fleming House,
Elephant & Castle, SE1
Department of Industry
BW41 3
1 Victoria Street, SW1
**Department of the
Environment BW**41 3
2 Marsham Street, SW1
Design Council BW40 3
28 Haymarket, SW1
Development Commission
BX41 4
11 Cowley Street, SW1
Duchy of Cornwall BW41 3
10 Buckingham Gate, SW1
Duchy of Lancaster BX40 4
Lancaster Place, Strand, WC2

Electricity Council
BX42 4
30 Millbank, SW1
**Exchequer and Audit
Department BY**40 4
Audit House, Victoria
Embankment, EC4
**Export Credits Guarantee
Department BZ**39 2
PO Box 272, Aldermanbury House,
Aldermanbury, EC2

**Foreign and Commonwealth
Office BX**41 4
King Charles Street, SW1
Forestry Commission
BW40 3
London Office
25 Savile Row, W1

**Gaming Board for Great
Britain BX**39 2
Berkshire House,
168–173 High Holborn, WC1
Government Actuary
BX39 2
22 Kingsway, WC2
Government Hospitality Fund
BW40 3
2 Carlton Gardens, SW1

HM Land Registry BX39 2
Lincoln's Inn Fields, WC2
HM Stationery Office
BY39 2
Atlantic House,
Holborn Viaduct, EC1
Historic Buildings Councils
BW40 3
25 Savile Row, W1
Home Office BW41 3
150 Queen Anne's Gate, SW1
Horserace Totalisator Board
BY39 2
Tote House,
8–12 New Bridge Street, EC4
Housing Corporation
BW38 1
149 Tottenham Court Road, W1

**Independent Broadcasting
Authority BU**42 3
70 Brompton Road, SW3
**Institute of Geological
Sciences BT**41 3
Exhibition Road, SW7

Law Officer's Department
BX39 2
Attorney-General's Chambers,
Royal Courts of Justice, WC1

London Transport Executive
BW41 3
55 Broadway, SW1
Lord Advocate's Department
BX41 4
Fielden House,
Great College Street, SW1

Medical Research Council
BV38 1
20 Park Crescent, W1
**Ministry of Agriculture Fisheries
and Food**
BX40 4
Whitehall Place, SW1
Ministry of Defence BX40 4
Main Building, Whitehall, SW1
**Monopolies and Mergers
Commission BX**39 2
New Court, 48 Carey Street, WC2

National Bus Company
BY39 2
55 New Street Square, EC4
National Debt Office BZ39 2
Royex House,
Aldermanbury Square, EC2
**National Economic
Development Office BX**42 4
Millbank Tower, Millbank, SW1
National Freight Corporation
BV38 1
Argosy House,
215 Great Portland Street, W1
National Ports Council
BX39 2
Commonwealth House,
1 New Oxford Street, WC1
**National Research Development
Council BW**41 3
Kingsgate House,
66 Victoria Street, SW1
National Theatre Board
BY40 4
Upper Ground, South Bank, SE1
National Water Council
BW41 3
1 Queen Anne's Gate, SW1
Northern Ireland Office
BW41 3
Great George Street, SW1

**Office of Manpower
Economics BX**39 2
22 Kingsway, WC2
**Office of Population Censuses
and Surveys BX**39 2
St. Catherine's House,
10 Kingsway, WC2

Patent Office BY39 2
25 Southampton Buildings,
Chancery Lane, WC2
**Political Honours Scrutiny
Committee BX**40 4
Standard House, Northumberland
Avenue, WC2
Port of London Authority
CB40 4
1 Thomas More Street, E1
Post Office Board BW39 1
23 Howland Street, W1
**Prices and Consumer Protection
Department BW**41 3
1 Victoria Street, SW1
**Public Health Laboratory
Service BO**30 37
Colindale Avenue, NW9

Public Record Office BY39 2
Chancery Lane, WC2
Public Trustee Office
BX39 2
24 Kingsway, WC2
Pilgrim Trust BX41 4
Fielden House,
Little College Street, SW1

Registry of Friendly Societies
BV40 3
17 North Audley Street, W1
**Royal Commission on
Environmental Pollution**
BW41 3
Church House,
Great Smith Street, SW1
**Royal Commission on Historic
Monuments**
BW40 3
23 Savile Row, W1
Royal Fine Art Commission
BW40 3
2 Carlton Gardens, SW1
Royal Mint CA40 4
Tower Hill, EC3

**Social Science Research
Council BY**40 4
Hamilton House, 1 Temple Avenue,
EC4
Sports Council BU42 3
70 Brompton Road, SW3

Thames Water Authority
BY38 2
New River Head, Rosebery
Avenue, EC1
The British Council BW40 3
10 Spring Gardens, SW1
**The House of Lords Record
Office BX**41 4
House of Lords, SW1
The National Trust BW41 3
42 Queen Anne's Gate, SW1
The Press Council BY39 2
1 Salisbury Square, EC4
The Treasury BX41 3
18 Parliament Street, SW1

**United Kingdom Atomic Energy
Authority BW**40 3
11 Charles II Street, SW1

Value Added Tax Tribunals
BV40 3
17 North Audley Street, W1

Wine Standards Board
BZ40 4
68½ Upper Thames Street, EC4

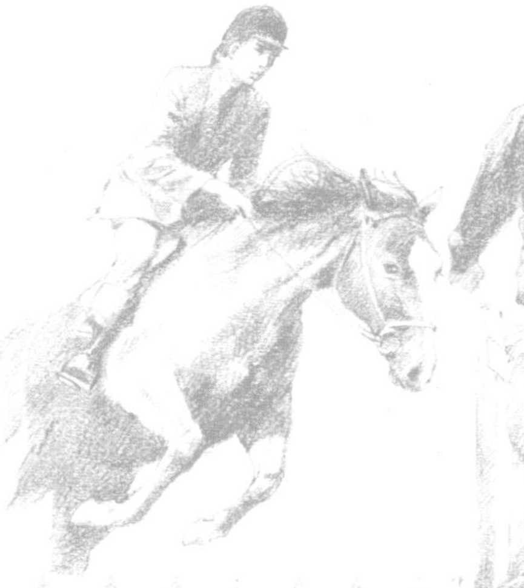

Association Football

Arsenal BY34 47
Avenell Road, N5
Brentford BK43 64
Griffin Park, Brentford, Middx
Charlton Athletic CJ42 68
The Valley, SE7
Chelsea BS43 66
Stamford Bridge, Fulham Road,
SW6
Crystal Palace CA52 87
Selhurst Park, SE25
Fulham BQ44 65
Craven Cottage,
Stevenage Road, SW6
Millwall CC43 67
The Den, New Cross, SE14
Orient CE34 48
Leyton Stadium,
Brisbane Road, E10
**Queen's Park Rangers
BP**40 55
Loftus Road, W12
**Tottenham Hotspur
CB**29 39
White Hart Lane, N17
Watford BC25 26
Vicarage Road, Watford, Herts
West Ham United CJ37 58
Boleyn Ground, Upton Park, E13
Wimbledon BT49 76
Plough Lane, SW19

Rugby Union

Blackheath CH43 68
Rectory Field, SE3
Harlequins BH46 74
Twickenham & Stoop Memorial
Ground, Twickenham
London Irish BC51 83
The Avenue, Sunbury on Thames
London Scottish BK45 64
Richmond Athletic Ground
London Welsh BL45 65
Old Deer Park, Kew Road,
Richmond
**Metropolitan Police
BG**54 84
Ember Court, East Molesey,
Surrey
Richmond BK45 64
Richmond Athletic Ground
Rosslyn Park BO45 65
Upper Richmond Road, SW15
St. Mary's Hospital BJ50 74
Udney Park Road, Teddington
Saracens BV25 29
Green Road, Southgate, N14

**Streatham and Croydon
BY**53 86
Brigstock Road, Thornton Heath
Wasps BK35 45
Repton Avenue, Sudbury
Woodford CG29 40
High Road, Woodford Green

Cricket Grounds

Blackheath CH43 68
Rectory Field, SE3
Brentwood DC27 122
Old Cricket Ground
Ilford CL33 49
Valentine's Park, Cranbrook
Road, Ilford
Leyton CE33 48
Youth Sports Grounds,
Crawley Road, E10
Lord's BT38 1
St. John's Wood, NW8
Kennington BX43 66
The Oval, SE11
Romford CU30 41
Gallows Corner Sports Ground,
Gidea Park

Athletics Centres

**Ashton Playing Fields
CJ**29 40
Woodford Green
**Crystal Palace National
Sports CB**50 77
Crystal Palace Park, SE19
**New River Sports Centre
BY**29 38
White Hart Lane, N22
**Parliament Hill Fields
BU**35 47
Gospel Oak, NW3
Victoria Park CD37 57
Victoria Park, E9
**West London Stadium
BP**39 55
Wormwood Scrubs, W12

Tennis Clubs

All England BR49 75
Church Road, SW19
**Bank of England
BO**46 75
Priory Lane, Roehampton

**Coolhurst Lawn Tennis and
Squash Club BW**32 47
Coolhurst Road, N8
Hazelwood BZ26 39
Ridge Avenue, N21
Holland Park BR41 65
1 Addison Road, W14
Hurlingham BR45 65
Fulham, SW6
Paddington BS38 56
Castellain Road, W9
Queen's BR42 65
Palliser Road, W14
Roehampton BP45 65
Roehampton Lane, SW15

Greyhound Racing

Catford CE46 77
Greyhound Stadium, SE6
Crayford, Kent CT46 79
Crayford Road
Hackney Wick CE36 57
Waterden Road, E15
Harringay BZ32 48
Green Lanes, N4
Romford CS32 50
London Road
Slough, Berks AQ41 62
Uxbridge Road
Walthamstow CE29 39
Chingford Road, E17
Wembley BM35 46
Stadium Way
White City BQ40 55
Wood Lane, W12
Wimbledon BT49 76
Plough Lane, SW19

Boxing

**Newington Sports Hall
BY**42 4
Manor Place, SE17
Royal Albert Hall BT41 3
Kensington Gore, SW7
**Wembley Stadium
and Arena BM**35 46
Empire Way, Wembley
York Hall CC37 57
Old Ford Road, E2

Horse Racing

Epsom BO63 103
On B290, Epsom, Surrey
Kempton Park BD51 84
On A308, near Sunbury
Sandown Park BG55 84
On A3, near Esher
Windsor AM43 61
On A308, near Windsor

Sports Centres

Crystal Palace CB50 77
National Sports Centre,
Norwood, SE19
**Hampstead Swimming Baths
BT**36 56
Avenue Road, NW3
**Michael Sobell Sports Centre
BX**34 47
Hornsey Road, N7
**Picketts Lock Centre
CC**26 39
Picketts Lock Lane, N9
**Rainham Sports Centre
CV**39 60
Lambs Lane, Rainham, Essex
**Walnut Sports Centre
CO**54 89
Orpington, Kent

Motor Racing

Brands Hatch CZ56 99
London Road

Town Halls

Greater London Council
BX41 4
The County Hall, SE1 7PB
Barking CR34 50
Civic Centre,
Dagenham, RM10 7DR
Barnet BP31 46
Town Hall, The Burroughs,
Hendon, NW4 4BG
Bexley CQ45 69
Civic Offices, Broadway,
Bexleyheath, DA7
Brent BM34 46
Town Hall, Forty Lane, Wembley
Bromley CH51 88
Town Hall, Widmore Road,
Bromley, BR1 1SB
Camden BX38 2
Town Hall,
Euston Road, NW1 2RU
City of London Corporation
BZ39 2
P.O. Box 270 Guildhall, EC2P 2EJ
Croydon BZ55 87
Town Hall, Taberner House,
Park Lane, Croydon CR9 3JS
Ealing BK40 54
Town Hall, New Broadway, W5
Enfield BZ24 30
Civic Centre, Silver Street, Enfield
Greenwich CL42 68
Town Hall, Wellington Street,
Woolwich, SE18
Hackney CB36 57
Town Hall, Mare Street, E8 1EA
Hammersmith BP42 65
Town Hall, King Street, W6 9JU
Haringey BX30 38
Civic Centre, P.O. Box
264, High Road, N22 4LE
Harrow BH31 45
Civic Centre, Harrow, Middlesex
Havering CT31 50
Town Hall, Main Road, Romford
Hillingdon AX37 53
Civic Centre,
Uxbridge, UB8 1UW

Hounslow BF44 64
Civic Centre, Lampton Road,
Hounslow
Islington BY36 56
Town Hall, Upper Street, N1 2UD
Kensington & Chelsea
BS41 66
Town Hall,
Hornton Street, W8 4SQ
Kingston upon Thames
BK51 84
Guildhall, 19 High Street
Lambeth BX45 66
Town Hall, Brixton Hill, SW2 1RW
Lewisham CE47 77
Town Hall, Catford, SE6 4RU
Merton BR50 75
Town Hall, P.O. Box
364, The Broadway, SW19 7NR
Newham CK37 58
Town Hall, East Ham, E6 2RP
Redbridge CL34 49
Town Hall, High Road,
Ilford, IG1 1DD
Richmond upon Thames
BK46 74
Town Hall, York House,
Twickenham, TW1 3AA
Southwark CA44 67
Town Hall,
Peckham Road, SE5 8UB
Sutton BS56 95
Town Hall, 3 Throwley Way,
Sutton, SM1 4AB
Tower Hamlets CB37 57
Town Hall, Patriot Square, E2 9LN
Waltham Forest CE31 48
Town Hall, Forest Road,
Walthamstow, E17 4JA
Wandsworth BS46 76
Town Hall,
High Street, SW18 2PU
Westminster, City of
BW41 3
City Hall,
Victoria Street, SW1E 6QW

District Council Offices

Beaconsfield District
AP41 62
Windsor Road, Slough, SL1 2HN
Brentwood District DB27 42
Ingrave Road,
Brentwood, CM15 8AY
Broxbourne District
CB18 21
Manor House, Turners Hill,
Cheshunt, EN8 8LE
Dacorum District AX13 8
Civic Centre, Marlowes,
Hemel Hempstead, HP1 1HH
Dartford District CW47 80
High Street, Dartford, DA1 1DR
Elmbridge District BB54 83
Town Hall, New Zealand
Avenue, Walton on Thames,
Surrey, KT12 1PS
Epping Forest District
CN19 22
323 High Street, Epping, Essex
Epsom and Ewell District
BN60 94
P.O. Box 5, Town Hall,
The Parade, Epsom, KT18 5BY
Gravesham District DG47 81
Civic Centre,
Gravesend, DA12 1AU
Guildford District AS71 118
Millmead House, Guildford,
Surrey, GU2 5BB
Harlow District CM11 13
Town Hall, Harlow,
Essex, CM20 1HJ
Hertsmere District BN23 28
Elstree Way, Borehamwood,
Hertfordshire

Mole Valley District
BK71 119
Pippbrook, Dorking, RH4 1SJ
Reigate and Banstead District
BS70 121
Town Hall, Castlefield Road,
Reigate, RH2 0SH
Runnymede District
AX56 92
Station Road, Addlestone,
Weybridge, Surrey, KT15 2AH
St. Albans District BG139
16 St. Peter's Street,
St. Albans, AL1 3ND
Sevenoaks District
CU66 116
Argyle Road, Sevenoaks,
Kent, TN13 1HG
Slough District AO40 61
Town Hall, Bath Road, Slough
Spelthorne District
AW49 73
Knowle Green,
Staines, TW18 1XB
Tandridge District CB65 105
Harestone Valley Road,
Caterham, Surrey, CR3 6YN
Three Rivers District
AY26 35
17–23 & 46 High Street,
Rickmansworth, WD3 1JE
Thurrock District DE42 71
Whitehall Lane, Grays,
Essex, RM17 6SL
Watford District BC24 26
Town Hall, Watford, WD1 3EX
Welwyn Hatfield District
BQ7 5
The Campus,
Welwyn Garden City,
Hertfordshire, AL8 6AE

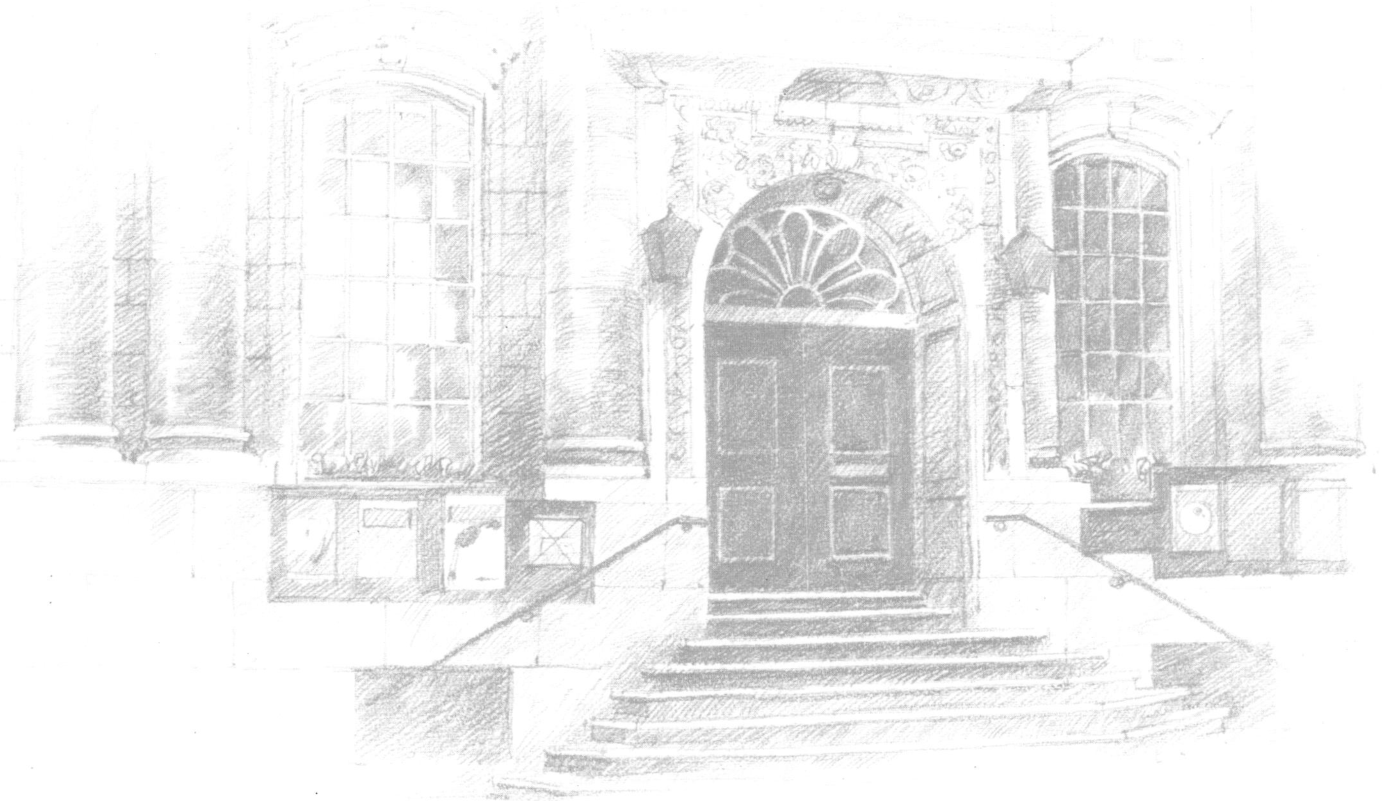

ER Eastern Region
LMR London Midland Region
SR Southern Region
WR Western Region

Abbey Wood *SR*
Acton Central *LMR*
Acton Main Line *WR*
Addiscombe *SR*
Addlestone *SR*
Albany Park *SR*
Anerley *SR*
Angel Road *ER*
Apsley *LMR*
Ashford *SR*
Ashtead *SR*

Balham and Upper Tooting *SR*
Bank *Waterloo & City*
Banstead *SR*
Barbican *LMR*
Barking *ER*
Barnehurst *SR*
Barnes *SR*
Barnes Bridge *SR*
Bat and Ball *SR*
Battersea Park *SR*
Beckenham Hill *SR*
Beckenham Junction *SR*
Beddington Lane Halt *SR*

Bush Hill Park *ER*
Byfleet and New Haw *SR*

Caledonian Road and Barnsbury *LMR*
Cambridge Heath *ER*
Camden Road *LMR*
Canning Town *ER*
Cannon Street *SR*
Canonbury *LMR*
Carpenders Park *LMR*
Carshalton *SR*
Carshalton Beeches *SR*
Castle Bar Park *WR*
Caterham *SR*
Catford *SR*
Catford Bridge *SR*
Chadwell Heath *ER*
Charing Cross *SR*
Charlton *SR*
Cheam *SR*
Chelsfield *SR*

Erith *SR*
Esher *SR*
Essex Road *ER*
Euston *LMR*
Ewell East *SR*
Ewell West *SR*
Eynsford *SR*

Bellingham *SR*
Belmont *SR*
Belvedere *SR*
Berkhamsted *LMR*
Berrylands *SR*
Bethnal Green *ER*
Bexley *SR*
Bexleyheath *SR*
Bickley *SR*
Bingham Road *SR*
Birkbeck *SR*
Blackfriars *SR*
Blackheath *SR*
Black Horse Road *ER*
Bookham *SR*
Bowes Park *ER*
Boxhill and Westhumble *SR*
Brentford Central *SR*
Brentwood and Warley *ER*
Bricket Wood *LMR*
Brimsdown *ER*
Brixton *SR*
Broad Street *LMR*
Brockley *SR*
Bromley North *SR*
Bromley South *SR*
Brondesbury *LMR*
Brondesbury Park *LMR*
Brookman's Park *ER*
Bruce Grove *ER*
Burnham (Bucks) *WR*
Bushey *LMR*

Chertsey *SR*
Cheshunt *ER*
Chessington North *SR*
Chessington South *SR*
Chingford *ER*
Chipstead *SR*
Chislehurst *SR*
Chiswick *SR*
Chorley Wood and Chenies *LMR*
Clandon *SR*
Clapham *SR*
Clapham Junction *SR*
Clapton *ER*
Claygate *SR*
Clock House *SR*
Cobham and Stoke D'Abernon *SR*
Coombe Road *SR*
Coulsdon North *SR*
Coulsdon South *SR*
Crayford *SR*
Crews Hill *ER*
Cricklewood *LMR*
Crofton Park *SR*
Crouch Hill *LMR*
Croxley Green *LMR*
Crystal Palace *SR*
Cuffley and Goff's Oak *ER*
Custom House (Victoria Dock) *ER*

Dagenham Dock *ER*
Dalston Junction *LMR*

Dartford *SR*
Datchet *SR*
Deepdene *SR*
Denham *WR*
Denham Golf Club *WR*
Denmark Hill *SR*
Deptford *SR*
Dorking *SR*
Dorking Town *SR*
Drayton Green *WR*
Drayton Park *ER*
Dunton Green *SR*

Ealing Broadway *WR*
Earlsfield *SR*
Earlswood *SR*
East Croydon *SR*
East Dulwich *SR*
East Tilbury *ER*
Eden Park *SR*
Effingham Junction *SR*
Egham *SR*
Elephant and Castle *SR*
Elmers End *SR*
Elmstead Woods *SR*
Elstree and Borehamwood *LMR*
Eltham Park *SR*
Eltham (Well Hall) *SR*
Emerson Park Halt *ER*
Enfield Chase *ER*
Enfield Lock *ER*
Enfield Town *ER*
Epsom *SR*
Epsom Downs *SR*

Falconwood *SR*
Farningham Road and Sutton-at-Hone *SR*
Farringdon *LMR*
Feltham *SR*
Fenchurch Street *ER*
Finchley Road and Frognall *LMR*
Finsbury Park *ER*
Forest Gate *ER*
Forest Hill *SR*
Fulwell *SR*

Gidea Park and Squirrels Heath *ER*
Gipsy Hill *SR*
Goodmayes *ER*
Gordon Hill *ER*
Gospel Oak for Highgate *LMR*
Grange Park *ER*
Gravesend Central *SR*
Grays *ER*
Greenford (Central Line) *WR*
Greenhithe *SR*
Greenwich *SR*
Grove Park *SR*
Guildford *SR*
Gunnersbury *LMR*

Hackbridge *SR*
Hackney Downs *ER*
Hadley Wood *ER*
Hampstead Heath *LMR*
Hampton *SR*
Hampton Court *SR*

Hampton Wick *SR*
Hanwell *WR*
Harlesden *LMR*
Harlow Mill *ER*
Harlow Town *ER*
Harold Wood *ER*
Harringay Stadium *ER*
Harringay West *ER*
Harrow and Wealdstone *LMR*
Harrow-on-the-Hill *LMR*
Hatch End *LMR*
Hatfield *ER*
Haydons Road *SR*
Hayes *SR*
Hayes and Harlington *WR*
Headstone Lane *LMR*
Hemel Hempstead and Boxmoor *LMR*
Hendon *LMR*
Herne Hill *SR*
Hersham *SR*
Highams Park and Hale End *ER*
Highbury and Islington *LMR*
Hinchley Wood *SR*
Hither Green *SR*
Holborn Viaduct *SR*
Honor Oak Park *SR*
Hornsey *ER*
Horsley *SR*
Hounslow *SR*

Ilford *ER*
Isleworth *SR*
Iver *WR*

Kempton Park *SR*
Kemsing *SR*
Kenley *SR*
Kensal Green *LMR*
Kensal Rise *LMR*
Kent House *SR*
Kentish Town *LMR*
Kenton *LMR*
Kew Bridge *SR*
Kew Gardens *LMR*
Kidbrooke *SR*
Kilburn High Road *LMR*
Kings Cross *ER*
King's Langley and Abbot's Langley *LMR*
Kingston *SR*
Kingswood and Burgh Heath *SR*
Knockholt *SR*

Ladywell *SR*
Langley (Bucks.) *WR*
Lea Bridge *ER*
Leatherhead *SR*
Lee *SR*
Lewisham *SR*
Leyton Midland Road *ER*
Leytonstone High Road *ER*
Liverpool Street *ER*
London Bridge *SR*
London Fields *ER*
London Road (Guildford) *SR*
Loughborough Junction *SR*
Lower Edmonton *ER*
Lower Sydenham *SR*

Malden Manor *SR*
Manor Park *ER*
Maryland *ER*
Marylebone *LMR*
Maze Hill *SR*
Merstham *SR*
Merton Park *SR*
Mill Hill Broadway *LMR*
Mitcham *SR*
Mitcham Junction *SR*
Moorgate *LMR*
Morden Road Halt *SR*
Morden South *SR*
Mortlake *SR*
Motspur Park *SR*
Mottingham *SR*

New Barnet *ER*
New Beckenham *SR*
New Cross *SR*
New Cross Gate *SR*
New Eltham *SR*
New Malden *SR*
New Southgate and Friern Barnet *ER*
Norbiton *SR*
Norbury *SR*
North Dulwich *SR*
Northfleet *SR*
Northolt Park *LMR*
North Sheen *SR*
Northumberland Park *ER*
North Wembley *LMR*
North Woolwich *ER*
Norwood Junction *SR*
Nunhead *SR*

Oakleigh Park *ER*
Ockendon *ER*
Orpington *SR*
Otford *SR*
Oxshott *SR*
Oxted *SR*

Paddington *WR*
Palmers Green and Southgate *ER*
Park Street and Frogmore *LMR*
Peckham Rye *SR*
Penge East *SR*
Penge West *SR*
Petts Wood *SR*
Plumstead *SR*
Ponders End *ER*
Potters Bar and South Mimms *ER*
Primrose Hill *LMR*
Purfleet *ER*
Purley *SR*
Purley Oaks *SR*
Putney *SR*

Queen's Park *LMR*
Queen's Road (Battersea) *SR*
Queen's Road Peckham *SR*

Radlett *LMR*
Rainham *ER*
Ravensbourne *SR*
Raynes Park *SR*
Rectory Road *ER*
Redhill *SR*
Reedham *SR*
Reigate *SR*
Richmond *LMR and SR*
Riddlesdown *SR*
Romford *ER*

St. Albans Abbey *LMR*
St. Albans City *LMR*
St. Helier *SR*
St. John's *SR*
St. Margaret's *SR*
St. Mary Cray *SR*
St. Pancras *LMR*
Sanderstead *SR*
Selhurst *SR*
Selsdon *SR*
Seven Kings *ER*
Sevenoaks *SR*
Seven Sisters *ER*
Shenfield and Hutton *ER*
Shepperton *SR*
Shoreham *SR*
Shortlands *SR*
Sidcup *SR*

Silver Street *ER*
Silvertown *ER*
Slade Green *SR*
Slough *WR*
Smitham *SR*
South Acton *LMR*
Southall *WR*
South Bermondsey *SR*
Southbury *ER*
South Croydon *SR*
South Greenford Halt *WR*
South Hampstead *LMR*
South Kenton *LMR*
South Merton *SR*
South Ruislip *WR*
South Tottenham *ER*
Staines Central *SR*
Stamford Hill *ER*
Stanford-le-Hope *ER*
Stepney (East) *ER*
Stoke Newington *ER*
Stonebridge Park *LMR*
Stoneleigh *SR*
Stratford *ER*
Stratford (Low Level) *ER*
Strawberry Hill *SR*
Streatham *SR*
Streatham Common *SR*
Streatham Hill *SR*
Sudbury and Harrow Road *LMR*
Sudbury Hill Harrow *LMR*
Sunbury *SR*
Sundridge Park *SR*
Sunnymeads *SR*
Surbiton *SR*
Sutton *SR*
Sutton Common *SR*
Swanley *SR*
Swanscombe Halt *SR*
Sydenham *SR*
Sydenham Hill *SR*
Syon Lane *SR*

Tadworth and Walton on the Hill *SR*
Tattenham Corner *SR*
Teddington *SR*
Thames Ditton *SR*
Theobalds Grove *ER*
Thornton Heath *SR*
Tilbury (Riverside) *ER*
Tilbury Town *ER*
Tolworth *SR*
Tooting *SR*
Tottenham Hale *ER*
Tulse Hill *SR*
Turkey Street *ER*
Twickenham *SR*

Upminster *ER*
Upper Halliford Halt *SR*
Upper Holloway *LMR*
Upper Warlingham *SR*

Vauxhall *SR*
Victoria *SR*

Waddon *SR*
Waddon Marsh Halt *SR*
Wallington *SR*
Waltham Cross and Abbey *ER*
Walthamstow *ER*
Walthamstow Queen's Road *ER*
Walthamstow St. James Street *ER*
Walthamstow Wood Street *ER*
Walton on Thames *SR*

Wandsworth Common *SR*
Wandsworth Road *SR*
Wandsworth Town *SR*
Wanstead Park *ER*
Waterloo *SR*
Watford High Street *LMR*
Watford Junction *LMR*
Watford North *LMR*
Watford West *LMR*
Welling *SR*
Welwyn Garden City *ER*
Wembley Central *LMR*
Wembley Complex *LMR*
Westbourne Park *WR*
West Byfleet *SR*
Westcombe Park *SR*
West Croydon *SR*
West Drayton and Yiewsley *WR*
West Dulwich *SR*
West Ealing *WR*
West Hampstead Midland *LMR*
West Horndon *ER*
West Norwood *SR*
West Ruislip *WR*
West Sutton *SR*
West Wickham *SR*
Weybridge *SR*
White Hart Lane *ER*
Whitton *SR*
Whyteleafe *SR*
Whyteleafe South *SR*
Willesden Junction *LMR*
Wimbledon *SR*
Wimbledon Chase *SR*
Winchmore Hill *ER*
Windsor and Eton Central *WR*
Windsor and Eton Riverside *SR*
Woking *SR*
Woldingham *SR*
Woodgrange Park *ER*
Wood Green (Alexandra Park) *ER*
Woodmansterne *SR*
Woodside *SR*
Woolwich Arsenal *SR*
Woolwich Dockyard *SR*
Worcester Park *SR*
Worplesdon *SR*
Wraysbury *SR*

York Road *ER*

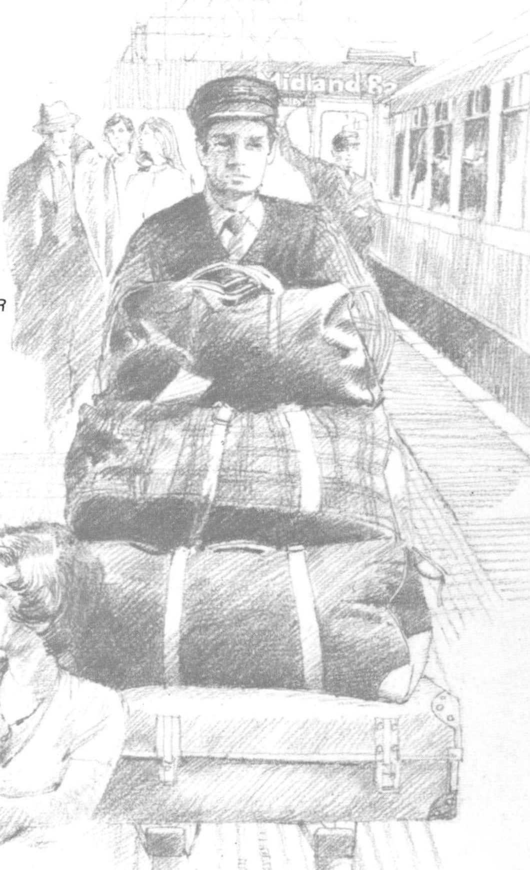

B'loo   Bakerloo
Cent   Central
Circle   Circle
Dist   District
J'lee   Jubilee
Met   Metropolitan
N'thn   Northern
Picc   Piccadilly
Vic   Victoria

Acton Town   Dist and Picc
Aldgate   Met and Circle
Aldgate East   Dist and Met
Aldwych   Picc
Alperton   Picc
Angel   N'thn
Archway   N'thn
Arnos Grove   Picc
Arsenal   Picc

Baker Street   B'loo, Met,
    Circle and J'lee
Balham   N'thn
Bank   N'thn and Cent
Barbican   Met and Circle
Barking   Dist and Met
Barkingside   Cent
Barons Court   Dist and Picc
Bayswater   Dist and Circle
Becontree   Dist
Belsize Park   N'thn
Bethnal Green   Cent
Blackfriars   Dist and Circle
Blackhorse Road   Vic
Blake Hall   Cent
Bond Street   Cent and J'lee
Borough   N'thn
Boston Manor   Picc

Bounds Green   Picc
Bow Road   Met and Dist
Brent Cross   N'thn
Brixton   Vic
Bromley by Bow   Met and Dist
Buckhurst Hill   Cent
Burnt Oak   N'thn
Bushey   B'loo

Caledonian Road   Picc
Camden Town   N'thn
Cannon Street   Dist and Circle
Canons Park   J'lee
Carpenders Park   B'loo
Chalk Farm   N'thn
Chancery Lane   Cent
Charing Cross   B'loo, N'thn and
    J'lee
Chigwell   Cent
Chiswick Park   Dist
Chorley Wood   Met
Clapham Common   N'thn
Clapham North   N'thn
Clapham South   N'thn
Cockfosters   Picc
Colindale   N'thn
Collier's Wood   N'thn
Covent Garden   Picc
Croxley   Met

Dagenham East   Dist

Dagenham Heathway   Dist
Debden   Cent
Dollis Hill   J'lee

Ealing Broadway   Dist and Cent
Ealing Common   Dist and Picc
Earl's Court   Dist and Picc
East Acton   Cent
Eastcote   Met and Picc
East Finchley   N'thn
East Ham   Dist and Met
East Putney   Dist
Edgware   N'thn
Edgware Road   Met, Dist, B'loo
    and Circle
Elephant and Castle   N'thn and
    B'loo
Elm Park   Dist
Embankment   B'loo, N'thn,
    Dist and Circle
Epping   Cent
Euston   N'thn
Euston Square   Circle and Met

Fairlop   Cent
Farringdon   Met and Circle
Finchley Central   N'thn
Finchley Road   B'loo and J'lee
Finsbury Park   Picc and Vic
Fulham Broadway   Dist

Gants Hill   Cent
Gloucester Road   Picc, Dist
    and Circle
Golders Green   N'thn
Goldhawk Road   Met
Goodge Street   N'thn

Grange Hill   Cent
Great Portland Street   Met and
    Circle
Greenford   Cent
Green Park   Picc, Vic and J'lee
Gunnersbury   Dist

Hainault   Cent
Hammersmith   Met, Picc and
    Dist
Hampstead   N'thn
Hanger Lane   Cent
Harlesden   B'loo
Harrow and Wealdstone   B'loo
Harrow-on-the-Hill   Met
Hatch End   B'loo
Hatton Cross   Picc
Headstone Lane   B'loo
Heathrow Central   Picc
Hendon Central   N'thn
High Barnet   N'thn
Highbury and Islington   Vic
Highgate   N'thn
High Street Kensington   Dist and
    Circle
Hillingdon   Met and Picc
Holborn   Cent and Picc
Holland Park   Cent
Holloway Road   Picc
Hornchurch   Dist
Hounslow Central   Picc
Hounslow East   Picc
Hounslow West   Picc
Hyde Park Corner   Picc

Ickenham   Met and Picc

Kennington   N'thn
Kensal Green   B'loo

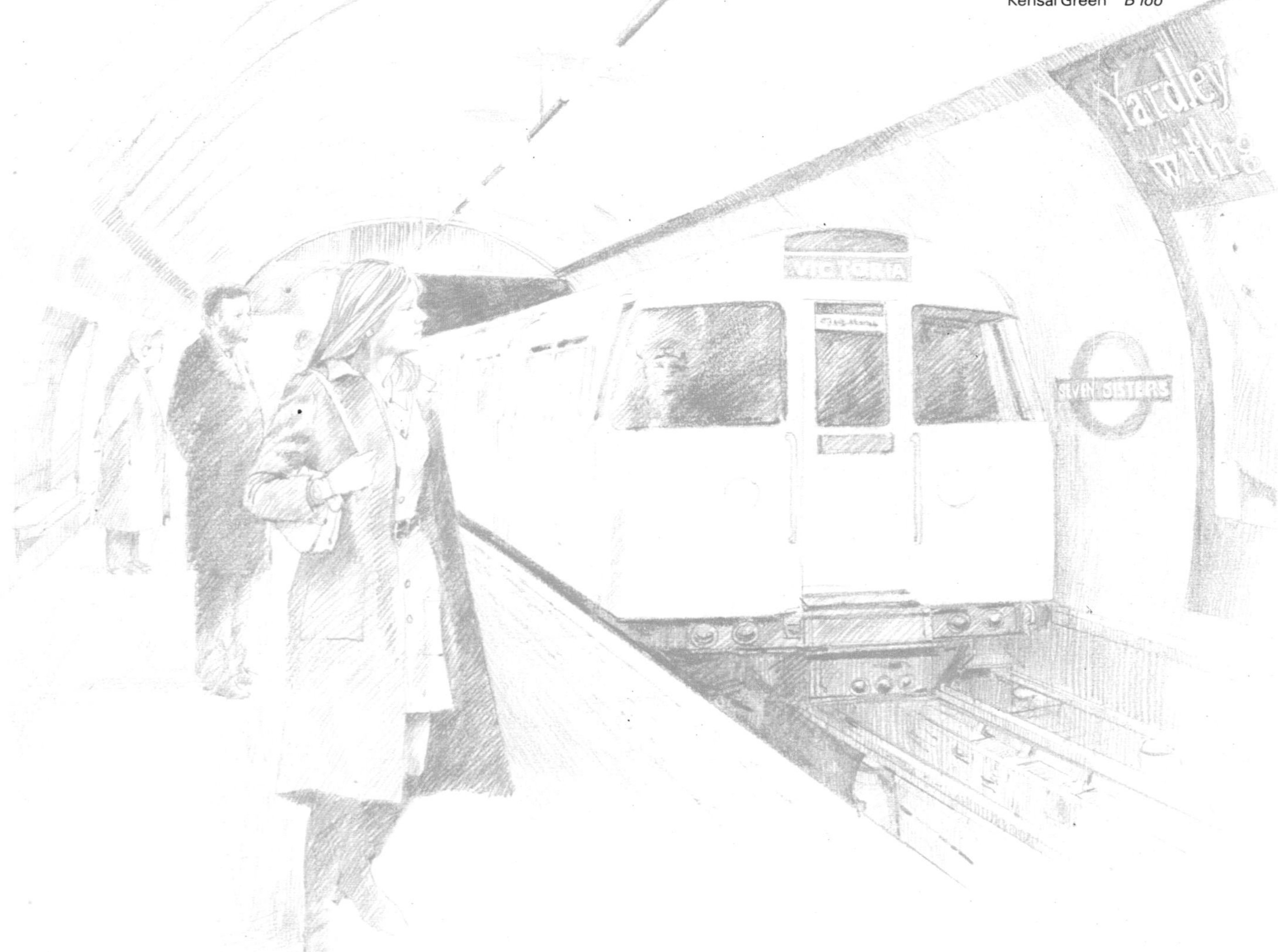

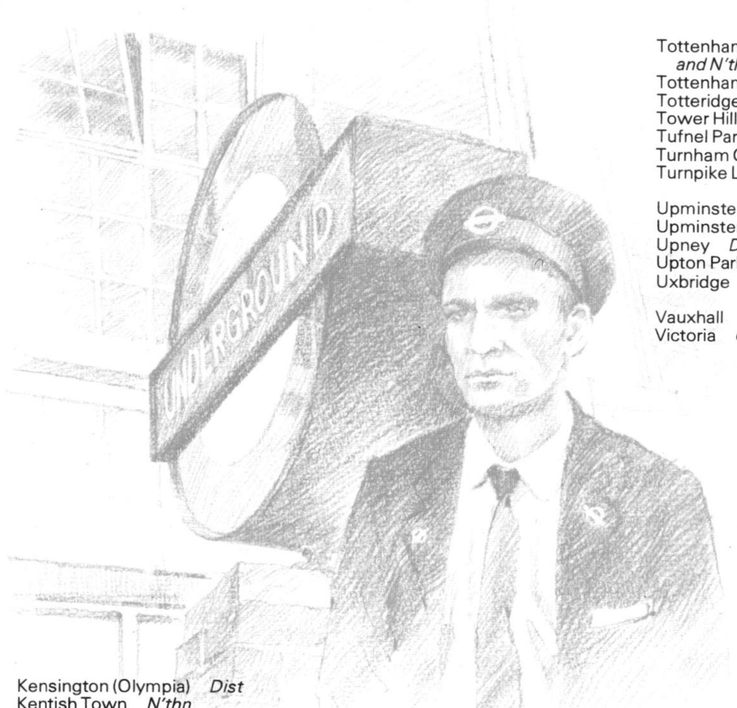

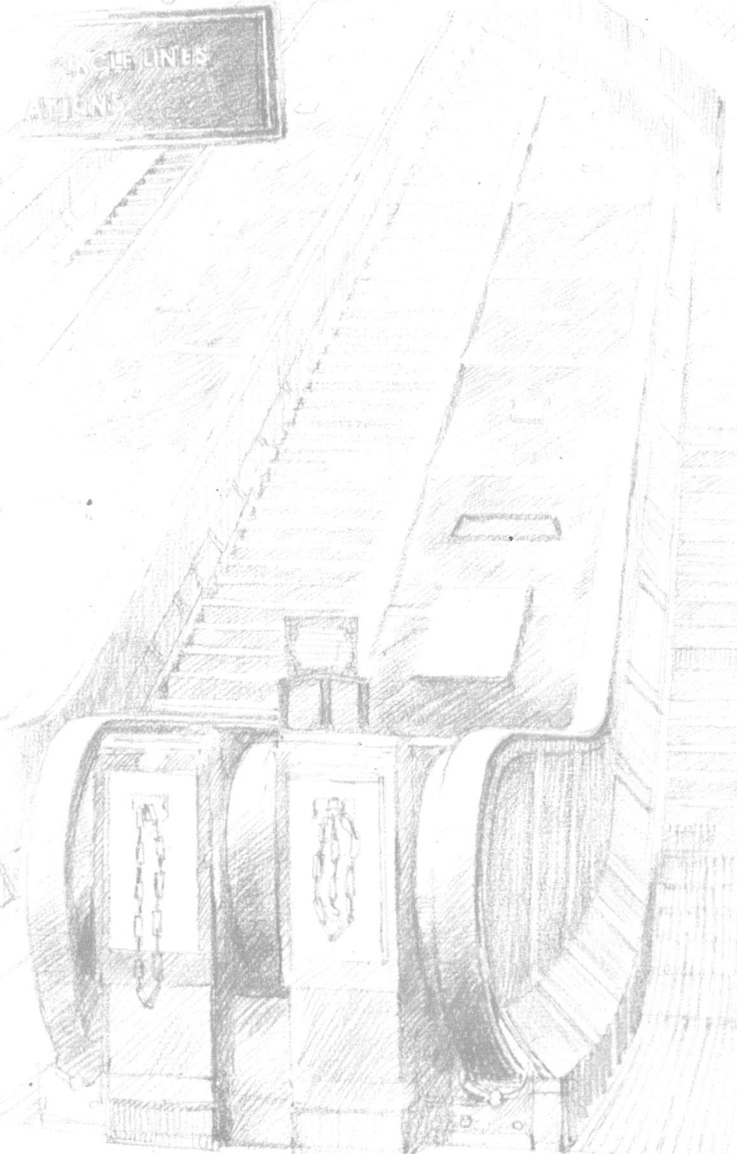

Tottenham Court Road   *Cent and N'thn*
Tottenham Hale   *Vic*
Totteridge and Whetstone   *N'thn*
Tower Hill   *Circle and Dist*
Tufnel Park   *N'thn*
Turnham Green   *Dist*
Turnpike Lane   *Picc*

Upminster   *Dist*
Upminster Bridge   *Dist*
Upney   *Dist*
Upton Park   *Dist and Met*
Uxbridge   *Met and Picc*

Vauxhall   *Vic*
Victoria   *Circle, Dist and Vic*

Walthamstow Central   *Vic*
Wanstead   *Cent*
Wapping   *Met*
Warren Street   *N'thn and Vic*
Warwick Avenue   *B'loo*
Waterloo   *N'thn and B'loo*
Watford   *Met*
Watford High Street   *B'loo*
Watford Junction   *B'loo*
Wembley Central   *B'loo*
Wembley Park   *B'loo and J'lee*
West Acton   *Cent*
Westbourne Park   *Met*
West Brompton   *Dist*
West Finchley   *N'thn*
West Ham   *Met and Dist*
West Hampstead   *J'lee*
West Harrow   *Met*
West Kensington   *Dist*
Westminster   *Circle and Dist*
West Ruislip   *Cent*
Whitechapel   *Met and Dist*
White City   *Cent*
Willesden Green   *J'lee*
Willesden Junction   *B'loo*
Wimbledon   *Dist*
Wimbledon Park   *Dist*
Woodford   *Cent*
Wood Green   *Picc*
Woodside Park   *N'thn*

Kensington (Olympia)   *Dist*
Kentish Town   *N'thn*
Kenton   *B'loo*
Kew Gardens   *Dist*
Kilburn   *J'lee*
Kilburn Park   *B'loo*
Kingsbury   *J'lee*
King's Cross, St. Pancras   *N'thn, Picc, Met, Circle and Vic*
Knightsbridge   *Picc*

Ladbroke Grove   *Met*
Lambeth North   *B'loo*
Lancaster Gate   *Cent*
Latimer Road   *Met*
Leicester Square   *N'thn and Picc*
Leyton   *Cent*
Leytonstone   *Cent*
Liverpool Street   *Met, Circle and Cent*
London Bridge   *N'thn*
Loughton   *Cent*

Maida Vale   *B'loo*
Manor House   *Picc*
Mansion House   *Dist and Circle*
Marble Arch   *Cent*
Marylebone   *B'loo*
Mile End   *Cent, Met and Dist*
Mill Hill East   *N'thn*
Monument   *Dist and Circle*
Moorgate   *N'thn, Met and Circle*
Moor Park   *Met*
Morden   *N'thn*
Mornington Crescent   *N'thn*

Neasden   *J'lee*
Newbury Park   *Cent*
New Cross   *Met*
New Cross Gate   *Met*
North Acton   *Cent*
North Ealing   *Picc*
Northfields   *Picc*
North Harrow   *Met*
Northolt   *Cent*
North Weald   *Cent*
North Wembley   *B'loo*
Northwick Park   *Met*
Northwood   *Met*
Northwood Hills   *Met*
Notting Hill Gate   *Cent, Dist and Circle*

Oakwood   *Picc*
Old Street   *N'thn*
Ongar   *Cent*
Osterley   *Picc*
Oval   *N'thn*
Oxford Circus   *B'loo, Cent and Vic*

Paddington   *B'loo, Met, Dist and Circle*
Park Royal   *Picc*
Parsons Green   *Dist*

Perivale   *Cent*
Piccadilly Circus   *Picc and B'loo*
Pimlico   *Vic*
Pinner   *Met*
Plaistow   *Met and Dist*
Preston Road   *Met*
Putney Bridge   *Dist*

Queensbury   *J'lee*
Queen's Park   *B'loo*
Queensway   *Cent*

Ravenscourt Park   *Dist*
Rayners Lane   *Met and Picc*
Redbridge   *Cent*
Regent's Park   *B'loo*
Richmond   *Dist*
Rickmansworth   *Met*
Roding Valley   *Cent*
Rotherhithe   *Met*
Royal Oak   *Met*
Ruislip   *Met and Picc*
Ruislip Gardens   *Cent*
Ruislip Manor   *Met and Picc*
Russell Square   *Picc*

St. James's Park   *Dist and Circle*
St. John's Wood   *J'lee*
St. Paul's   *Cent*
Seven Sisters   *Vic*
Shadwell   *Met*
Shepherd's Bush   *Cent and Met*
Shoreditch   *Met*
Sloane Square   *Dist and Circle*
Snaresbrook   *Cent*
South Ealing   *Picc*
Southfields   *Dist*
Southgate   *Picc*
South Harrow   *Picc*
South Kensington   *Picc, Dist and Circle*
South Kenton   *B'loo*
South Ruislip   *Cent*
South Wimbledon   *N'thn*
South Woodford   *Cent*
Stamford Brook   *Dist*
Stanmore   *J'lee*
Stepney Green   *Dist and Met*
Stockwell   *N'thn and Vic*
Stonebridge Park   *B'loo*
Stratford   *Cent*
Sudbury Hill   *Picc*
Sudbury Town   *Picc*
Surrey Docks   *Met*
Swiss Cottage   *J'lee*

Temple   *Circle and Dist*
Theydon Bois   *Cent*
Tooting Bec   *N'thn*
Tooting Broadway   *N'thn*

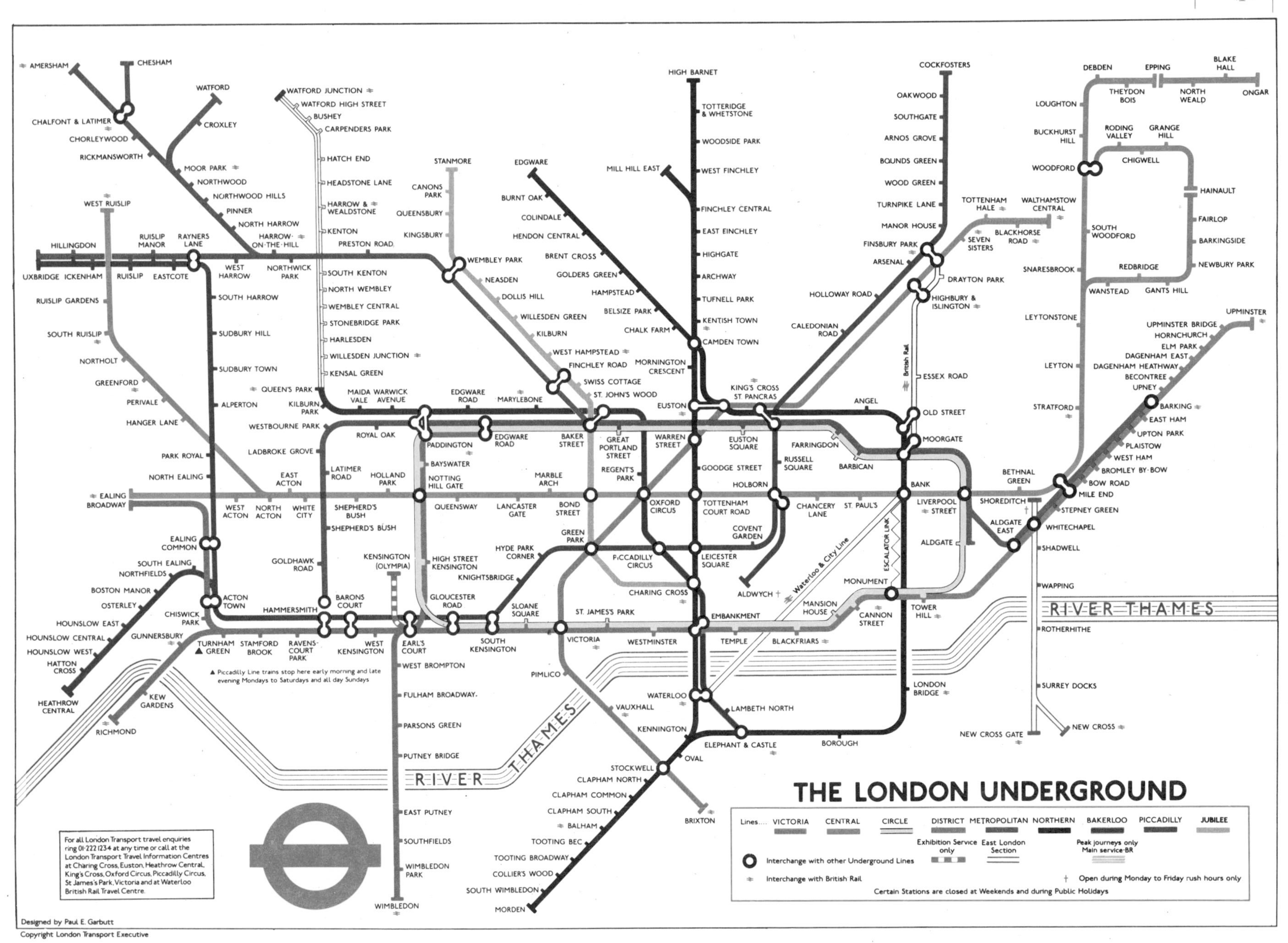

THE LONDON UNDERGROUND

Lines . . . . . . VICTORIA   CENTRAL   CIRCLE   DISTRICT   METROPOLITAN   NORTHERN   BAKERLOO   PICCADILLY   JUBILEE

Exhibition Service only   East London Section

○ Interchange with other Underground Lines

⊕ Interchange with British Rail

Peak journeys only
Main service BR

+ Open during Monday to Friday rush hours only

Certain Stations are closed at Weekends and during Public Holidays

For all London Transport travel enquiries
ring ℡ 222 1234 at any time or call at the
London Transport Travel Information Centres
at Charing Cross, Euston, Heathrow Central,
King's Cross, Oxford Circus, Piccadilly Circus,
St James's Park, Victoria and at Waterloo
British Rail Travel Centre

Designed by Paul E. Garbutt

Copyright London Transport Executive

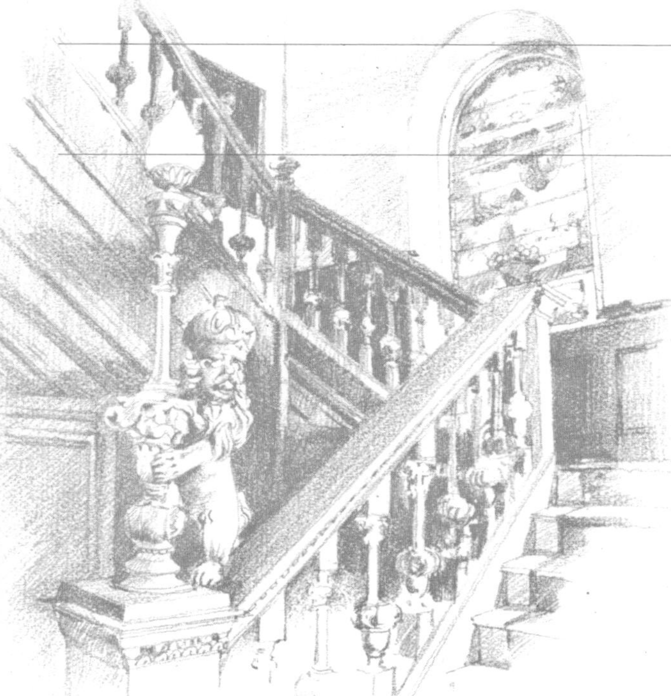

Apothecaries
Black Friars Lane, EC4
This charming seventeenth century building has a most attractive courtyard. The poet, John Keats here became a Licentiate. The portrait gallery contains his picture and there are portraits of James I and Charles I.

Armourers & Brasiers
81 Coleman Street, EC2
Historic edifice first erected about 1450 and reconstructed in 1840 by J. H. Good.

Bakers
Harp Lane, EC3
This is a modern building standing on an historic site—the fourth building of this Livery Company. The first was built in 1506, the last building fell to enemy action in 1940. The present one dates from 1960 and is the work of Trehearne, Preston and Partners.

Barber-Surgeons
Monkwell Square, EC2
Modern building adjoining the famous Barbican site. It replaces the ancient Hall destroyed in the Blitz.

Brewers
Aldermanbury Square, EC2
On its historic site, first occupied in 1420, but rebuilt in 1960 by Sir Hubert Worthington and T. W. Sutcliffe. It had been damaged by enemy action in the Second World War.

Butchers
Bartholomew Close, EC1
The traditional Hall in Bartholomew Close is augmented by an additional building in adjoining Little Britain. It is all conveniently close to the great traditional meat market of Smithfield.

Carpenters
Throgmorton Avenue, EC2
Although there was a Hall on this site for at least 500 years, the Victorian replacement was bombed in 1941. The present Hall dates from 1956. A commemorative stone was unveiled at the time the new foundation stone was laid.

Clothworkers
Dunster Court, EC3
The first Hall on this site was built in 1456. A second was erected in 1482, and was burned down in the Great Fire. There have been three others including a Victorian one which was destroyed by bombing

in 1941. The present neo-Georgian Hall was built in 1958. The ancient archives survived; also among the treasures is a loving-cup, the gift of Samuel Pepys, Master of the Company in 1677.

Coopers
13 Devonshire Square, EC2
Historic Company dating from time of Edward II. New address (above) in addition to Coopers Corner in the Guildhall.

Cutlers
4 Warwick Lane, EC4
This building, is distinguished by fine terracotta reliefs executed by Benjamin Creswick in 1867.

Drapers
Throgmorton Street, EC2
Part seventeenth century building but with considerable Victorian restoration work. It was again the subject of careful restoration after the Blitz, this work being carried out in 1949. Inside there are some fine portraits and valuables, including the Elizabethan Lambard Cup. The famous mulberry tree still flourishes in the garden.

Dyers
10 Dowgate Hill, EC4
This is a mainly Victorian building though with some later alterations. The Company is privileged to keep swans on the Thames.

Fanmakers' Hall
This quaint building in the churchyard of St. Botolph's, Bishopsgate, was originally built as a church school in 1861. The entrance is still flanked by Coade stone figures of two charity children.

Fishmongers
London Bridge, EC4
This Victorian classical Hall was the work of Henry Roberts and Sir Gilbert Scott. It was the first of the Halls to suffer fire damage during the Second World War. A previous Hall on that site was destroyed in the Great Fire of 1666. This is one of the very ancient Companies, its foundation dating from before the reign of Henry II.

Founders
13 St. Swithin's Lane, EC4
The original Hall had to be rebuilt in 1877 but following damage in the Second World War was again restored in 1967.

Girdlers
Basinghall Avenue, EC2
This Company met originally in

Westcheap. The medieval Hall did not survive the Great Fire. Its replacement was destroyed in the Second World War, and the present building is modern.

Goldsmiths
Foster Lane, EC2
This building has an extremely handsome exterior which is late-Georgian Renaissance. It stands on the site of both the medieval and seventeenth century forerunners.

Grocers
Princes Street, EC2
This, the fourth Hall on the site is mainly Victorian with some modern restoration made necessary by bomb damage. It was unlucky enough to be damaged by fire in 1965 and was again restored, and re-opened in 1967.

Haberdashers
Staining Lane, EC2
A modern block called Garrard House contains the entrance to the new Haberdashers Hall. The first medieval one perished in the Great Fire, and its replacement was destroyed in the Second World War.

Innholders
College Street, EC4
Built in 1670 this handsome Hall escaped the damage that afflicted so many of the Livery Halls of the City of London.

Ironmongers
Barbican, EC2
This building dates from 1925, the historic original having been destroyed in the daylight bombing raid of 1917. This Company is the smallest among the 'Great' companies of the City Livery.

Leathersellers
15 St. Helen's Place, EC3
This Victorian edifice, built in 1878 was extended by the addition of a courtroom and other offices in 1926. Damaged by air-raids in 1941, the place was again restored and retains its handsome and imposing entrance. This Company is one of the oldest in the City, dating from the fourteenth century.

Master Mariners
The sloop *Wellington* was purchased by the Master Mariners from the Admiralty to be their Company Hall in 1947. It has been berthed permanently since 1948 in the Thames at Temple Stairs.

Mercers
Ironmonger Lane, EC2
In Becket House after original Hall was destroyed in 1941 bombing. Richest of the City Livery Companies, and first in precedence.

Merchant Taylors
30 Threadneedle Street, EC2
Home of the largest of the City Livery Companies. The medieval Hall was replaced after the Great Fire. The building was burned out after a raid in 1940, but restored in 1959 by Sir Albert Richardson.

Painter Stainers
9 Little Trinity Lane, EC4
The original building was rebuilt in 1668 and a new wing added in 1880, and again in 1915.

Pewterers
Oat Lane, EC2
The present building is neo-Georgian, rebuilt in 1960. The original Hall dated from 1496, and was in Lime Street, but the new Court Room contains much panelling and some fittings rescued from the old place after it was bombed.

Plaisterers
This modern building at No. 1, London Wall makes a vivid contrast with the neighbouring portions of the Roman wall. The decor throughout is a faithful reproduction of the eighteenth century Robert Adam style. The Great Hall, with its minstrel gallery at one end is the largest Livery Hall in the City.

Saddlers
Gutter Lane, EC2
One of the oldest of all City Companies, this new Hall built by Sylvester Sullivan was opened in 1958. The former Hall, destroyed in the bombing, stood in Wood Street. This Company claims to have been formed in Saxon times.

Salters
Fore Street, EC2
The present Hall was opened in 1976 and has been built in a truly modern style, comprising an ash-panelled Banqueting Hall, Committee and Court Rooms. It also commands a very fine view over London Wall and St. Paul's Cathedral.

Skinners
6 Dowgate Hill, EC4
The Hall has an eighteenth century facade to a seventeenth century building which was rebuilt following the Great Fire of 1666. It has some large panel paintings, the work of Sir Frank Brangwyn in 1902.

Stationers & Newspaper Makers
Stationers Hall, EC4
This Hall built soon after the Great Fire was given a stone facade in 1800 with a Victorian wing added around 1887. The interior suffered damage in the Second World War but has been carefully restored. The ancient records, dating from 1402 also include the registration of the First Folio of Shakespeare's Works.

Tallowchandlers
4 Downgate Hill, EC4
This building is mainly Victorian reconstruction dating circa 1871.

Vintners
Upper Thames Street, EC4
The medieval court room survives from the first building which was otherwise destroyed in the Great Fire. The rest of the Hall dates from 1671. Remodelling of the exterior occurred between 1908–1910. This is the Hall of one of the twelve 'Great' Livery Companies and it has rich sixteenth century tapestries and paintings.

Wax Chandlers
Gresham Street, EC2
Postwar reconstruction upon ancient foundations. The Company itself has a history of some 500 years of prominence in the City.

NB
Livery Halls may be visited only by appointment. The City Information Centre in St. Paul's Churchyard supply information in this connection, and about special days on which the Halls may be open to the public.

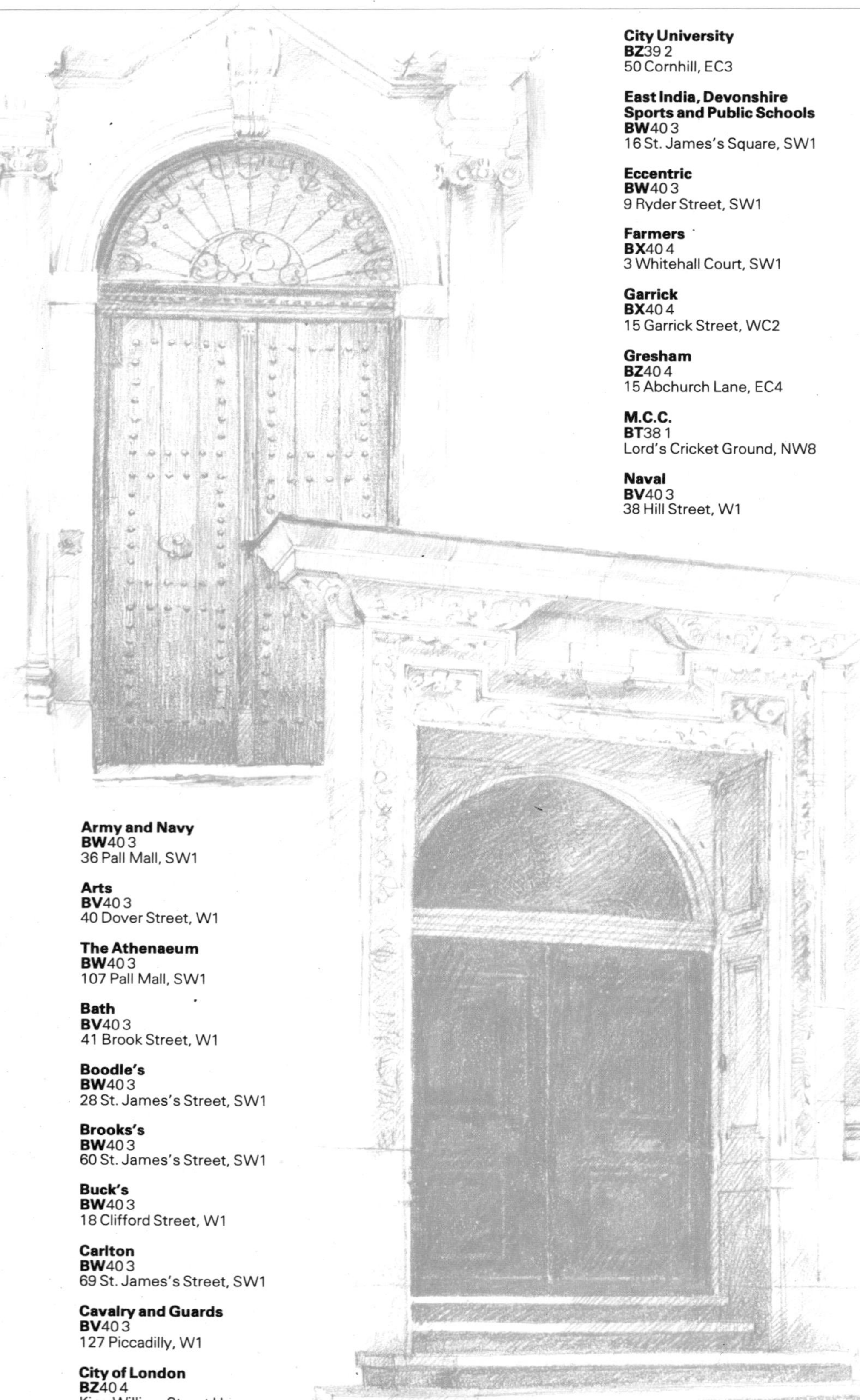

City University
BZ39 2
50 Cornhill, EC3

East India, Devonshire Sports and Public Schools
BW40 3
16 St. James's Square, SW1

Eccentric
BW40 3
9 Ryder Street, SW1

Farmers
BX40 4
3 Whitehall Court, SW1

Garrick
BX40 4
15 Garrick Street, WC2

Gresham
BZ40 4
15 Abchurch Lane, EC4

M.C.C.
BT38 1
Lord's Cricket Ground, NW8

Naval
BV40 3
38 Hill Street, W1

Naval and Military
BV40 3
94 Piccadilly, W1

Pratt's
BW40 3
14 Park Place, SW1

Press
BY39 2
International Press Centre,
76 Shoe Lane, EC4

Reform
BW40 3
104 Pall Mall, SW1

Royal Air Force
BV40 3
128 Piccadilly, W1

Royal Automobile
BW40 3
89 Pall Mall, SW1

Royal Thames Yacht
BU41 3
60 Knightsbridge, SW1

Savage
BY40 3
9 Fitzmaurice Place, W1

Travellers
BW40 3
108 Pall Mall, SW1

Turf
BW40 3
5 Carlton House Terrace, SW1

United Oxford and Cambridge
BW40 3
71 Pall Mall, SW1

University Women's
BV40 3
2 Audley Square, W1

Whites
BW40 3
37 St. James's Street, SW1

Wig and Pen
BY39 2
229 Strand, WC2

Army and Navy
BW40 3
36 Pall Mall, SW1

Arts
BV40 3
40 Dover Street, W1

The Athenaeum
BW40 3
107 Pall Mall, SW1

Bath
BV40 3
41 Brook Street, W1

Boodle's
BW40 3
28 St. James's Street, SW1

Brooks's
BW40 3
60 St. James's Street, SW1

Buck's
BW40 3
18 Clifford Street, W1

Carlton
BW40 3
69 St. James's Street, SW1

Cavalry and Guards
BV40 3
127 Piccadilly, W1

City of London
BZ40 4
King William Street House
Arthur Street, EC4

Museums and Art Galleries

Battle of Britain Museum
BP30 37
Hendon, NW9

Bear Gardens Museum
BY40 4
Bankside, Southwark, SE1

Bethnal Green Museum
CB39 57
Cambridge Heath Road, E2

Borough Museum
CW47 80
Market Street, Dartford

British Museum
BW39 1
Great Russell Str. WC1

Chartered Insurance Institute Museum
BZ39 2
20 Aldermanbury, EC2

Church Farmhouse Museum
BP31 46
Church End, Hendon, NW4

City Museum
BH13 9
Hatfield Road, St. Albans

Clock Museum
Guildhall Library
BZ39 2
Aldermanbury, EC2

Commonwealth Institute
BS41 66
Kensington High Street, W8

Courtauld Institute Galleries
BW38 1
Woburn Square, W1

Cuming Museum
BZ42 4
155 Walworth Road, SE17

Dulwich College Picture Gallery
CA47 77
College Road, SE21

Fenton House
BT34 47
Hampstead Grove, NW3

Forty Hall Museum
CA22 30
Forty Hill, Enfield

Geffrye Museum
CA37 2
Kingsland Road, E2

Geological Museum
BT41 3
Exhibition Road, SW7

Guards Museum Wellington Barracks
BW41 3
Birdcage Walk, SW1

Guildhall Art Gallery
BZ39 2
King Street, EC2

Gunnersbury Park Museum
BM41 65
Gunnersbury Park, W3

Ham House
BK47 74
Richmond

Haringey Borough Museum
CA30 39
Bruce Castle, Lordship Lane, N17

Hayward Gallery
BX40 4
South Bank, SE1

Historic Ship Collection
CA40 4
St. Katharine's Dock, E1

Horniman Museum
CB47 77
London Road, Forest Hill, SE23

Imperial War Museum
BY41 4
Lambeth Road, SE1

Institute of Contemporary Arts
BW40 3
Nash House, The Mall, SW1

Iveagh Bequest
BU33 47
Kenwood, Hampstead, NW3

Jewish Museum
BW38 1
Upper Woburn Place, WC1

Keats House & Museum
BU35 47
Keats Grove, Hampstead, NW3

Leighton House Art Gallery & Museum
BR41 65
Holland Park Road, W14

London Transport Collection
BX40 4
Covent Garden, WC2

Museum of Mankind
BW40 3
6 Burlington Gardens, W1

Musical Museum
BK43 64
368 High Street, Brentford

National Army Museum
BU42 3
Royal Hospital Road, SW3

National Gallery
BW40 3
Trafalgar Square, WC2

National Maritime Museum
CF43 67
Romney Road, Greenwich, SE10

National Portrait Gallery
BX40 4
St. Martin's Place, WC2

National Postal Museum
BZ39 2
King Edward Street, EC1

Natural History Museum
BT41 3
Cromwell Road, SW7

Passmore Edwards Museum
CG36 58
Romford Road, E15

Percival David Foundation of Chinese Art
BW38 1
53 Gordon Square, WC1

Pollocks' Toy Museum
BW39 1
1 Scala Street, W1

Public Record Office Museum
BY39 2
Chancery Lane, WC2

Rotunda Museum
CK42 68
Woolwich Common, SE18

Royal Academy of Arts
BW40 3
Burlington House, Piccadilly, W1

Royal Air Force Museum
BP30 37
Hendon, NW9

Royal Society of Painters in Watercolours
BV40 3
26 Conduit Street, W1

Science Museum
BT41 3
Exhibition Road, SW7

Serpentine Gallery
BT41 3
Kensington Gardens, W2

Sir John Soane's Museum
BX39 2
Lincoln's Inn Fields, WC2

South London Art Gallery
CA44 67
Peckham Road, SE5

Syon Park
BK44 64
Brentford

Tate Gallery
BX42 4
Millbank, SW1

The Mall Art Galleries
BW40 3
The Mall, SW1

The Museum of London
BZ39 2
London Wall, EC2

The Queen's Gallery
BV41 3
Buckingham Palace Road, SW1

Thomas Coram Foundation
BX35 2
40 Brunswick Square, WC1

Verulamium Museum
BF13 9
St. Michael's Str, St. Albans

Victoria & Albert Museum
BT41 3
Cromwell Road, SW7

Wallace Collection
BV39 1
Manchester Square, W1

Wellington Museum
BV41 3
Apsley House, Hyde Park Corner W1

Wesley's House and Chapel
BY37 2
City Road, EC1

Whitechapel Art Gallery
CA39 2
Whitechapel High Street, E1

William Morris Gallery & Brangwyn Gift
CE31 48
Lloyd Park, Forest Road, Walthamstow, E17

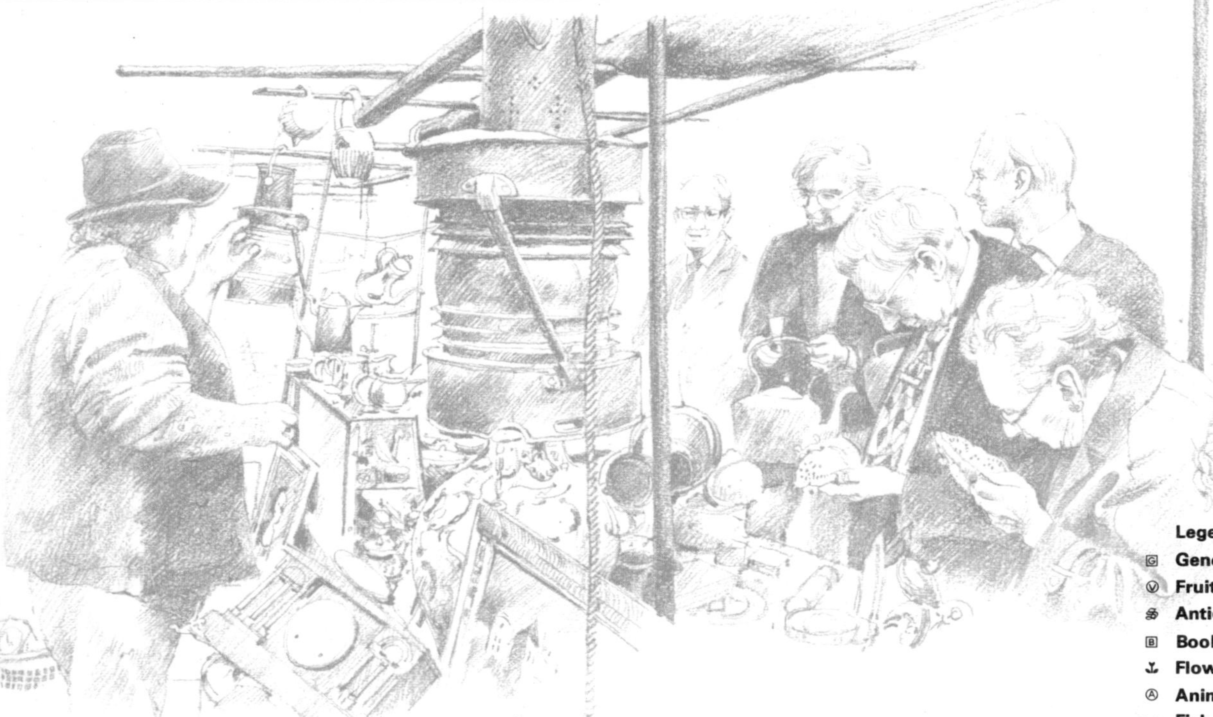

Legend
🄖 General market
🅥 Fruit & Vegetables
🖎 Antiques
🄑 Books
⚘ Flowers
🄐 Animals & Birds
🠦 Fish

B

Bacon Street CA38 2
London E1
Sun am only 🅥
Battersea High Street
BT44 66
London SW11
Mon–Sat (Wed am only) 🄖
Bell Lane CA39 2
London E1
Sun am only 🄖
Bell Street BU39 1
London NW1
Mon–Sat 🄖
Beresford Square CL42 68
London SE18
Mon–Sat (Thu am only) 🄖
Bermondsey Street CA41 4
London SE1
Fri only 🄖
Bermondsey Square CA41 4
London SE1
Fri only 🖎
Berwick Street BW39 1
London W1
Mon–Sat 🄖
Bethnal Green Road CA38 2
London E2
Mon–Sat 🄖
Brick Lane CA38 2
London E1
Sun am only 🄖
Brixton Station Road
BY45 66
London SW9
Mon–Sat (Wed am only) 🄖
Broadway CB37 57
London E8
Mon–Sat 🄖
Burdett Road CD38 57
London E3
Mon–Sat 🄖

C

Camden Passage BY37 2
London N1
Mon–Sat (Wed until 8pm) 🖎

Chalton Street BW38 1
London NW1
Mon–Sat 🄖
Chapel Market BY37 2
London N1
Mon–Sat am (Thu am only) 🄖
Chatsworth Road CC35 48
London E5
Mon–Sat 🄖
Cheshire Street CA38 2
London E2
Sun am only 🄖
Choumert Road CB44 67
London SE15
Mon–Sat (Thu am only) 🄖
Church Street BT39 1
London NW8
Mon–Sat 🄖
Cobb Street CA39 2
London E1
Sun am only 🄖
Colomb Street CG42 68
London SE10
Mon–Sat 🄖
Columbia Road CA38 2
London E2
Sun am only ⚘
Crown Street BM40 55
Acton, London W3
Thu only 🄖
Cygnet Street CA38 2
London E1
Sun am only 🄖

D

Dawes Street BZ42 4
London SE17
Sun only 🄖
Deptford High Street
CE43 67
London SE8
Sat only 🄖
Devons Road CE38 57
London E3
Mon–Sat 🄖
Douglas Way CD43 67
Deptford, London SE8
Fri and Sat 🄖

E

Earlham Street BW39 1
Holborn, London WC2
Mon–Sat 🄖 🖎
Earlswood Street CG42 68
London SE10
Mon–Sat 🄖
East Street BZ42 4
London SE17
Tues–Sun am (Thu am only) 🄖
Exmouth Street BY38 2
London EC1
Mon–Sat (Thu am only) 🄖

F

Fairfield West BL51 85
Kingston, Surrey
Mon am only 🄖
Farringdon Road BY39 56
London EC4
Mon–Sat (Thu am only) 🄑

G

Golborne Road BR39 55
London W10
Mon–Sat (Thu am only) 🄖
Goodge Place BW39 1
London W1
Mon–Sat 🅥
Goulston Street CA39 2
London E1
Mon–Fri and Sun am 🄖
Greenman Street BZ36 57
Essex Road, London N1
Mon–Sat (Thu am only) 🅥

H

High Street BN60 94
Epsom
Sat only 🄖

High Street CD32 48
Walthamstow, London E17
Mon–Sat 🄖
Hildreth Street BV47 76
Balham, London SW12
Mon–Sat (Wed am only) 🄖
Holloway Road BX34 47
London N7
Mon–Sat (Thu am only) 🄖
Hoxton Street CA37 2
London N1
Mon–Sat 🄖

I

Inverness Street BV37 1
London NW1
Mon–Sat 🄖

J

Jubilee Market BX40 4
Covent Garden, London WC2
Mon–Fri 🄖

K

Kingsland Road CA36 57
London E8
Sat only 🄖

L

Leather Lane BY39 2
London EC1
Mon–Sat lunchtimes 🄖
Leeds Street CB28 39
London N18
Mon–Sat 🄖
Leyden Street CA39 2
London E1
Sun am only 🄖
Lower Marsh BY41 4
London SE1
Mon–Sat (Thu am only) 🄖

M

Maple Road　**CC**50 77
Penge, London SE20
Tue–Sat (Wed am only) Ⓥ
Market Place　**BK**51 84
Kingston, Surrey
Mon–Sat Ⓖ
Market Place　**CT**32 50
Romford, Essex
Wed, Fri & Sat Ⓖ
Market Square　**AS**62 100
Woking, Surrey
Tue, Fri & Sat Ⓖ
Middlesex Street　**CA**39 2
(Petticoat Lane)
London E1
Sun am only Ⓖ
Mile End Road　**CC**39 57
London E1
Mon–Sat Ⓖ

N

New Goulston Street
CA39 2
London E1
Sun am only Ⓖ
Northcote Road　**BU**46 76
Battersea, London SW11
Mon–Sat (Wed am only) Ⓖ
North End Road　**BR**42 65
London W14
Mon–Sat Ⓖ
North Street　**AR**71 118
Guildford, Surrey
Fri & Sat Ⓖ

O

Old Castle Street　**CA**39 2
London E1
Sun am only Ⓖ

P

Petticoat Lane　**CA**39 2
see under Middlesex Street
Plender Street　**BW**37 1
London NW1
Mon–Sat Ⓥ ⌣
Portobello Road　**BR**39 55
London W10
Mon–Fri (Thu am only) Ⓖ
Sat mainly ⬧

Q

Queen's Crescent　**BV**35 47
London NW5
Mon–Sat Ⓖ

R

Ridley Road　**CA**35 48
London E8
Mon–Sat Ⓖ
Roman Road　**CD**38 57
London E3
Mon–Sat Ⓖ
Rupert Street　**BW**40 3
London W1
Mon–Sat Ⓥ

S

Salmon Lane　**CD**39 57
London E14
Mon–Sat Ⓖ
Sclater Street　**CA**38 2
London E1
Sun am only Ⓖ Ⓐ
Slyfield Green　**AS**68 109
Guildford, Surrey
Wed & Bank Hols Ⓖ
Stamford Road　**CO**37 59
Dagenham, Essex
Mon–Sat Ⓖ

Strutton Ground　**BW**41 3
London SW1
Mon–Fri & Sat am Ⓖ
Strype Street　**CA**39 2
London E1
Sun am only Ⓖ
Surrey Street　**BZ**55 87
Croydon, Surrey
Mon–Sat Ⓖ

T

Tachbrook Street　**BW**42 3
London SW1
Mon–Sat Ⓖ
Tower Bridge Road　**CA**41 4
London SE1
Mon–Sat (Thu am only) Ⓖ
Toynbee Street　**CA**39 2
London E1
Mon–Fri & Sun am only Ⓖ
Tyler Street　**CG**42 68
London SE10
Mon–Sat Ⓖ

W

Watney Street　**CB**39 57
London E1
Mon–Sat Ⓖ
Well Street　**CC**36 57
London E9
Mon–Sat Ⓖ
Wentworth Street　**CA**39 2
London E1
Mon–Fri & Sun am only Ⓖ
Westmoreland Road
BZ43 67
London SE17
Daily (Thu and Sun am only) Ⓖ
Whitechapel Road　**CB**39 57
London E1
Mon–Sat Ⓖ
Whitecross Street　**BZ**38 2
London EC1
Mon–Sat (Thu am only) Ⓖ
Wilcox Road　**BX**43 66
London SW8
Mon–Sat (Thu am only) Ⓖ

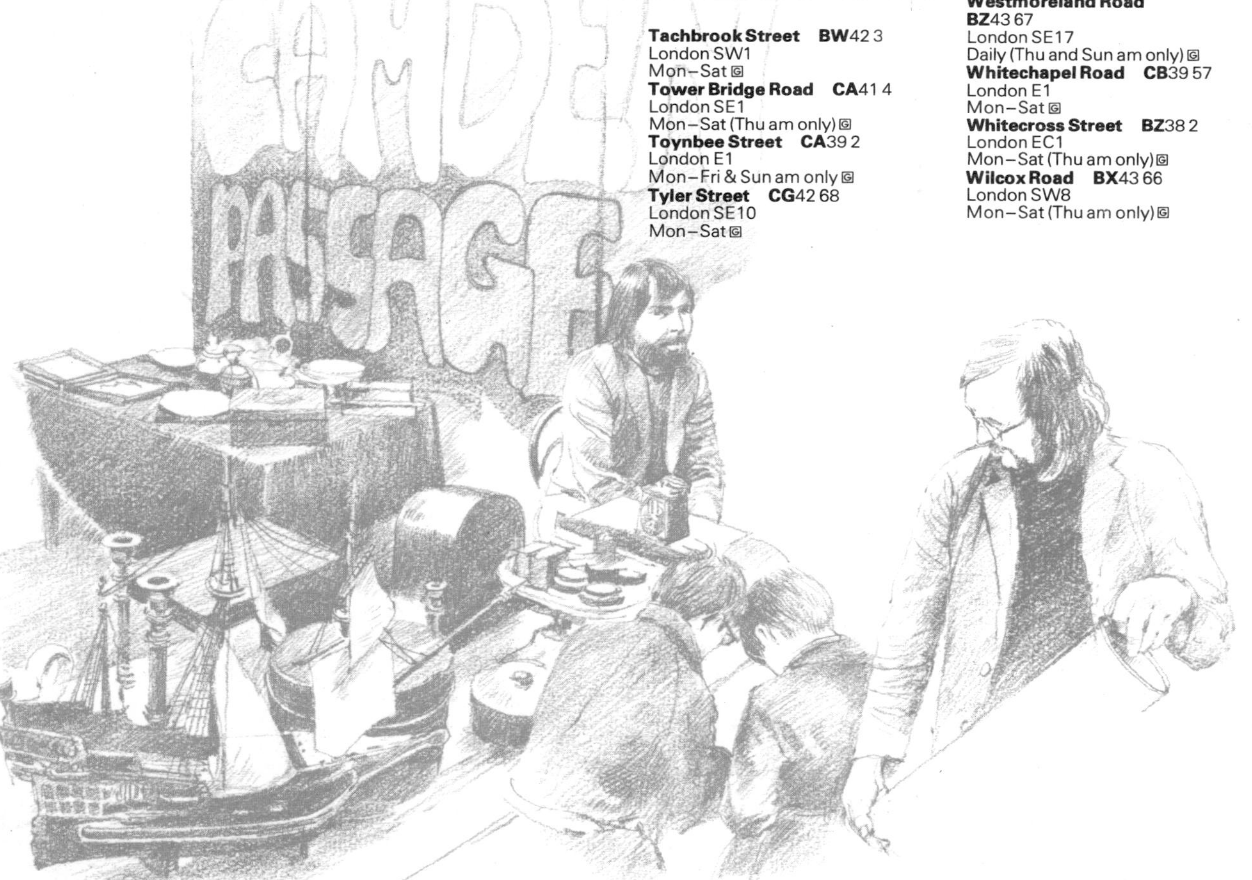

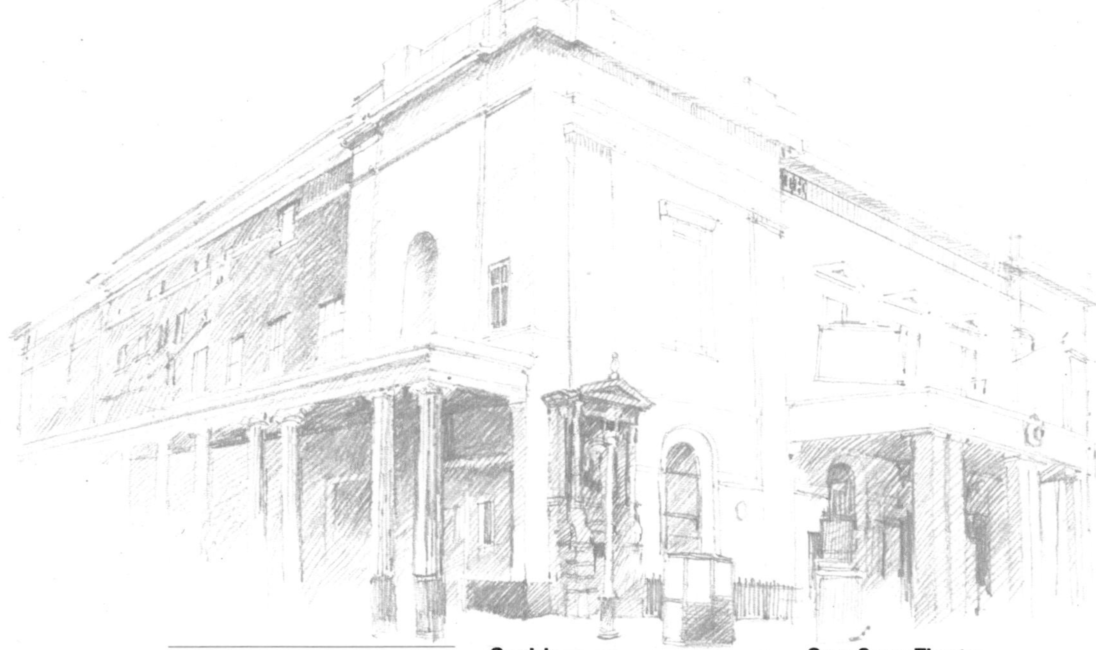

Theatres in Central London

Adelphi
BX40 4
The Strand
Albery
BX40 4
St. Martin's Lane
Aldwych
BX39 2
Aldwych
Ambassadors
BW39 1
West Street
Apollo
BW40 3
Shaftesbury Avenue
Arts
BX40 4
(Theatre Club) Gt. Newport Street
Astoria
BW39 1
Charing Cross Road

Cambridge
BX39 2
Earlham Street
Cockpit
BU38 1
Gateforth Street, NW8
Coliseum
BX40 4
St. Martin's Lane
Comedy
BW40 3
Panton Street
Cottesloe
BX40 4
National Theatre, South Bank
Criterion
BW40 3
Piccadilly

Drury Lane
BX39 2
Theatre Royal, Catherine Street
Duchess
BX40 4
Catherine Street
Duke of York's
BX40 4
St. Martin's Lane

Fortune
BX39 2
Russell Street

Garrick
BX40 4
Charing Cross Road
Globe
BW40 3
Shaftesbury Avenue
Greenwood
BZ41 4
Weston Street

Haymarket
BW40 3
Theatre Royal, Haymarket
Her Majesty's
BW40 3
Haymarket

Jeannetta Cochrane
BX39 2
Theobalds Road

Kings Road Theatre
BT42 3
Kings Road

Lyric
BW40 3
Shaftesbury Avenue
Lyric
BO42 65
King Street, W6
Lyttleton
BX40 4
National Theatre, South Bank

Mayfair
BV40 3
Stratton Street
Mermaid
BY40 4
Puddle Dock, Blackfriars

National Theatre
BX40 4
(Cottesloe Lyttleton & Olivier Theatres) South Bank
New London
BX39 2
Parker Street

Old Vic
BY41 4
Waterloo Road
Olivier
BX40 4
National Theatre, South Bank
Open Air Theatre
BV38 1
Inner Circle, Regents Park

Open Space Theatre
BW38 1
303/307 Euston Road

Palace
BW39 1
Shaftesbury Avenue
Palladium
BW39 1
Argyll Street
Phoenix
BW39 1
Charing Cross Road
Piccadilly
BW40 3
Denman Street
Prince Edward
BW39 1
Old Compton Street
Prince of Wales
BW40 3
Coventry Street

Queen's
BW40 3
Shaftesbury Avenue

Royal Court
BV42 3
Sloane Square
Royal Opera House
BX39 2
Covent Garden
Royalty
BX39 2
Portugal Street

Sadler's Wells
BY38 2
Rosebery Avenue
St. Martin's
BX40 4
West Street
Savoy
BX40 4
Strand
Shaftesbury
BX39 2
Shaftesbury Avenue
Shaw
BW38 1
Euston Road
Strand
BX40 4
Aldwych

Vanbrugh
BW38 1
Malet Street

Vaudeville
BX40 4
Strand
Victoria Palace
BW41 3
Victoria Street

Warehouse
BX39 2
Earlham Street
Westminster
BW41 3
Palace Street
Whitehall
BX40 4
Whitehall
Windmill
BW40 3
Gt. Windmill Street
Wyndham's
BW40 3
Charing Cross Road

Young Vic
BY41 4
The Cut

Cinemas in Central London

ABC
BT42 3
Fulham Road
ABC 1 & 2
BW39 1
Shaftesbury Avenue
Academy 1, 2 & 3
BW39 1
Oxford Street
Astral
BW40 3
Rupert Street, W1

Biograph
BW42 3
Wilton Road

Centa
BW40 3
Piccadilly
Cinecenta, 1, 2, 3 & 4
BW40 3
Panton Street
Classic 1, 2, 3, 4 & 5
BV39 1
Oxford Street
Classic 1, 2 & 3
BW40 3
Haymarket
Classic
BW40 3
Charing Cross Road
Classic Victoria
BW41 3
Victoria Street
Columbia
BW40 3
Shaftesbury Avenue
Curzon
BV40 3
Curzon Street

Dominion
BW39 1
Tottenham Court Road

Empire
BW40 3
Leicester Square
Eros
BW40 3
Piccadilly Circus

Film Centa 1, 2 & 3
BW40 3
Charing Cross Road

Gala Royal
BU39 1
Marble Arch
Gate Two
BX38 2
Brunswick Square, WC1

Institute of Contemporary Arts
BW40 3
Carlton House Terrace

Jacey
BX40 4
Trafalgar Square

Leicester Square Theatre
BW40 3
Leicester Square

London Pavilion
BW40 3
Piccadilly Circus

Moulin Complex
BW40 3
Great Windmill Street, W1

Minema
BU41 3
Knightsbridge

National Film Theatre 1 & 2
BX40 4
South Bank

Odeon
BT39 1
Edgware Road

Odeon
BW40 3
Haymarket

Odeon
BU42 3
Kings Road

Odeon
BW40 3
Leicester Square

Odeon
BU40 3
Marble Arch

Odeon
BX40 4
St. Martin's Lane

Paris Pullman
BT42 3
Drayton Gardens

Plaza 1, 2, 3 & 4
BW40 3
Regent Street

Prince Charles
BW40 3
Leicester Place

Rialto
BW40 3
Coventry Street

Ritz
BW40 3
Leicester Square

Scene 1, 2, 3 & 4
BW40 3
Swiss Centre, Leicester Square

Sherlock Holmes Centre
BU39 1
182 Baker Street, NW1

Starlight Cinema
BV40 3
Mayfair Hotel, Stratton Street

Studio 1 & 2
BW39 1
Oxford Street

Times Centa 1 & 2
BU38 1
Chiltern Court, Baker Street

Warner West End 1, 2, 3 & 4
BW40 3
Cranbourn Street

Concert and Exhibition Halls in Central London

Bishopsgate Institute
CA39 2
Bishopsgate

Caxton Hall
BW41 3
Caxton Street

Central Hall
BW41 3
Storeys Gate

Conway Hall
BX39 2
Red Lion Square

Earls Court Ltd
BS42 66
Warwick Road

Holland Park
BR41 65
Kensington

Kingsway Hall
BX39 2
Kingsway

Olympia Ltd
BR41 65
Hammersmith Road

Purcell Room
BX40 4
South Bank

Queen Elizabeth Hall
BX40 4
South Bank

Royal Albert Hall
BT41 3
Kensington Gore

Royal College of Music
BT41 3
Prince Consort Road

Royal Festival Hall
BX40 4
South Bank

Royal Horticultural Society New Hall
BW41 3
Greycoat Street

Rudolf Steiner Hall
BU38 1
Park Road

Seymour Hall
BU39 1
Seymour Place

St. Pancras Town Hall
BX38 2
Euston Road

Wigmore Hall
BV39 1
Wigmore Street

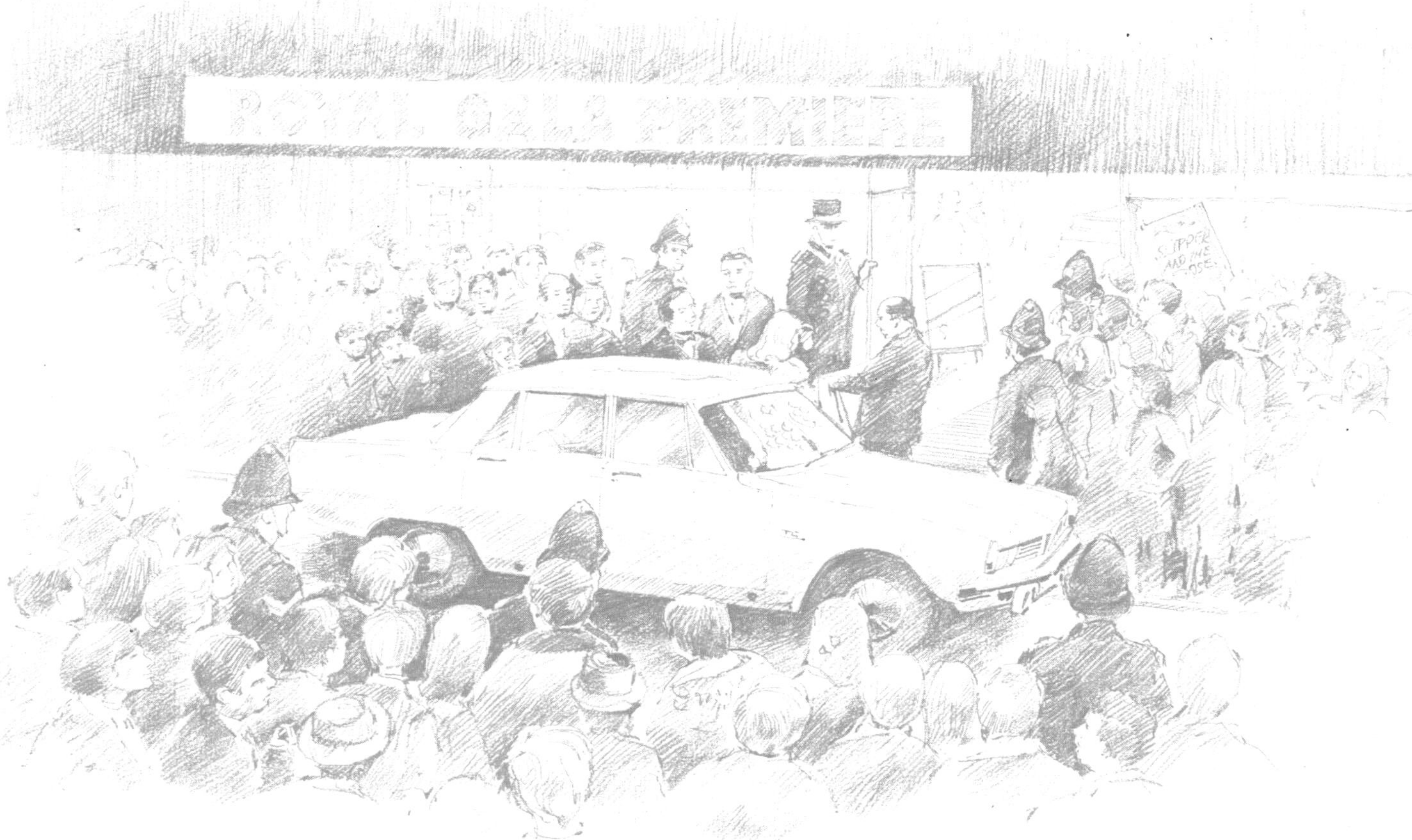

Index

The street name and postal district or locality of an entry is followed by a grid reference and number of the map on which the name will be found e.g. Abbey Rd, SW19 will be found in square **BT50** on map **76** and Norfolk Crescent, Sidcup in square **CN47** on map **78** (you will see from the map the latter location is in postcode boundary DA15).

The index contains some names for which there is insufficient space on the map. The adjoining thoroughfare to such roads is shown in italics e.g. Agar Place, NW1 is off *Agar Grove* the latter being found in square **BW36** on map **56**.

A strict alphabetical order is followed in which Avenue, Close, Gardens etc, although abbreviated, are read as part of the preceeding name.
For example Andrews Rd comes before Andrew St, and Abbey Orchard St before Abbey Rd.

Legend

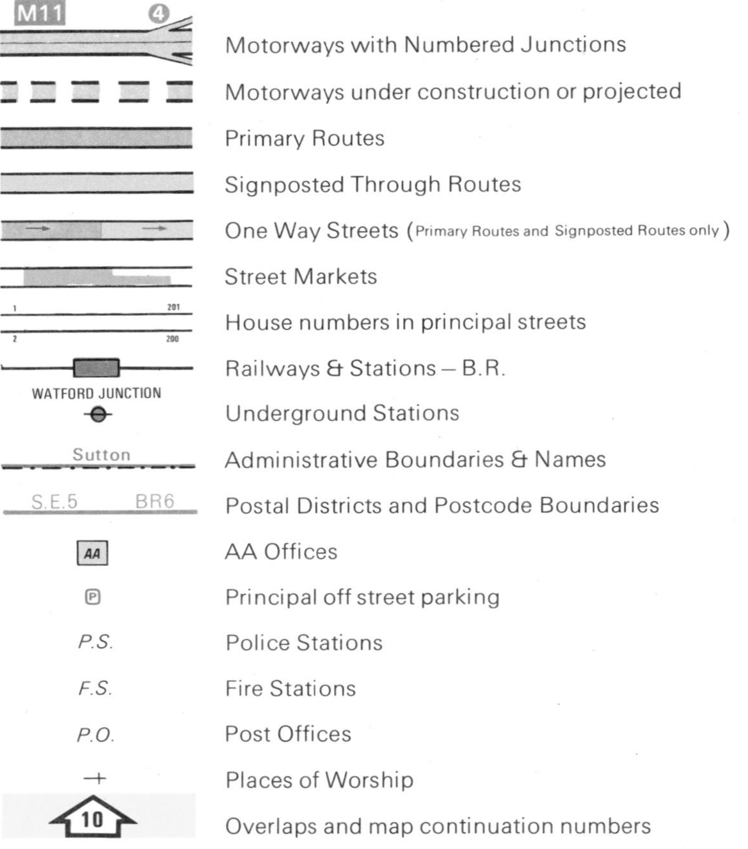

Motorways with Numbered Junctions

Motorways under construction or projected

Primary Routes

Signposted Through Routes

One Way Streets (Primary Routes and Signposted Routes only)

Street Markets

House numbers in principal streets

Railways & Stations – B.R.

Underground Stations

Administrative Boundaries & Names

Postal Districts and Postcode Boundaries

AA Offices

Principal off street parking

P.S. Police Stations

F.S. Fire Stations

P.O. Post Offices

Places of Worship

Overlaps and map continuation numbers

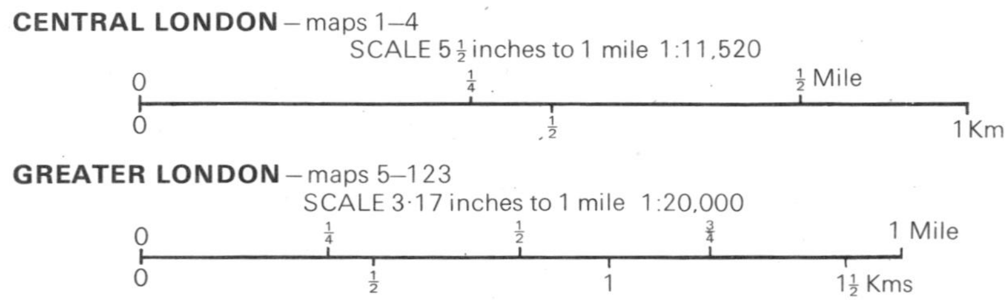

CENTRAL LONDON – maps 1–4
SCALE 5½ inches to 1 mile 1:11,520

GREATER LONDON – maps 5–123
SCALE 3·17 inches to 1 mile 1:20,000

Greater London Street Atlas

Maps on pages 1 to 4 are of Central London and are indicated in
red shading on 'Key to Sectional Maps' on the inside front cover.
These maps are at the enlarged scale of 5½ inches to one mile.
Maps 5 to 123 cover the entire area of Greater London at the
general scale of 3.17 inches to the mile.
Street names,where they appear at both scales are printed in
bold type to indicate the enlarged pages.

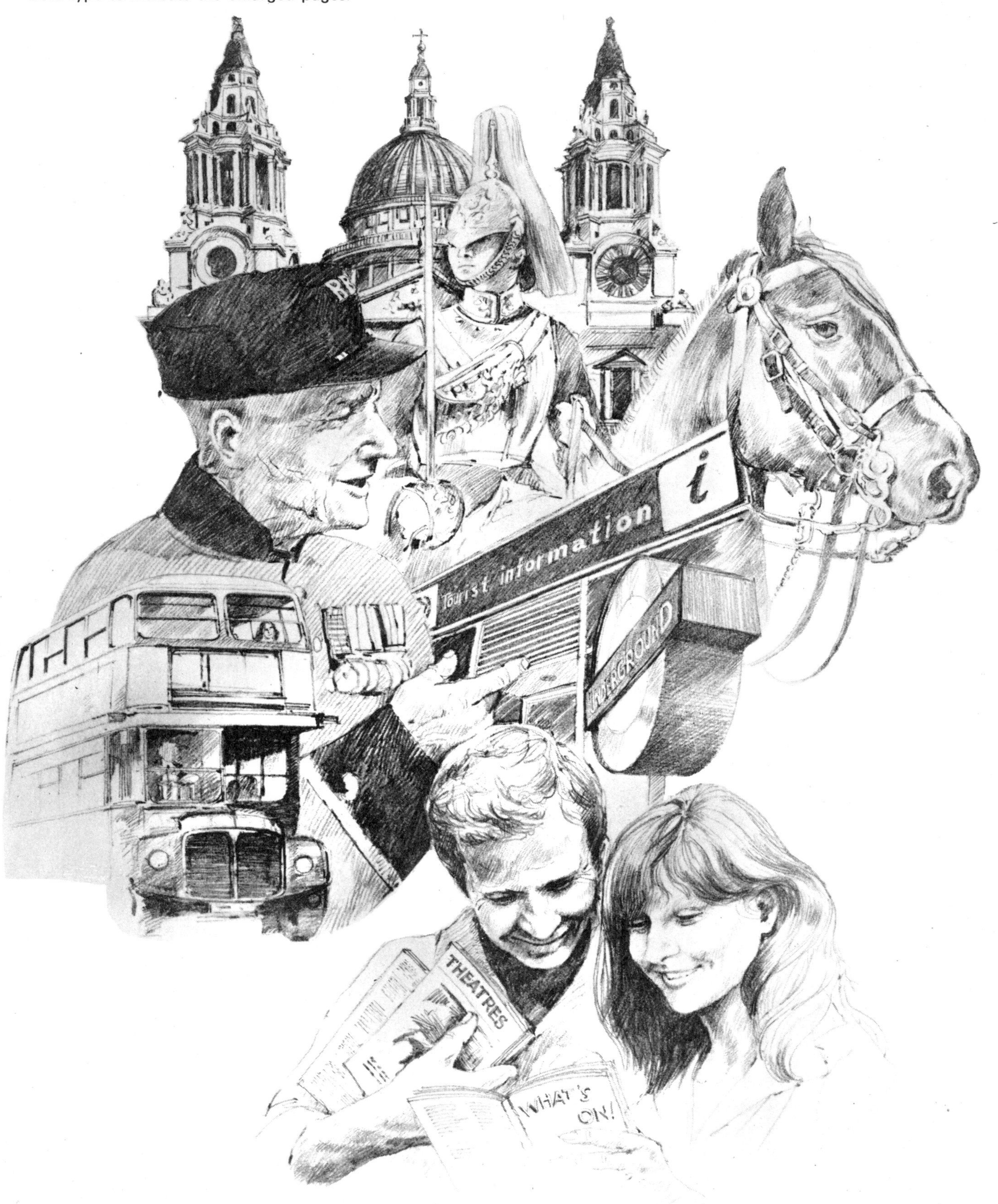

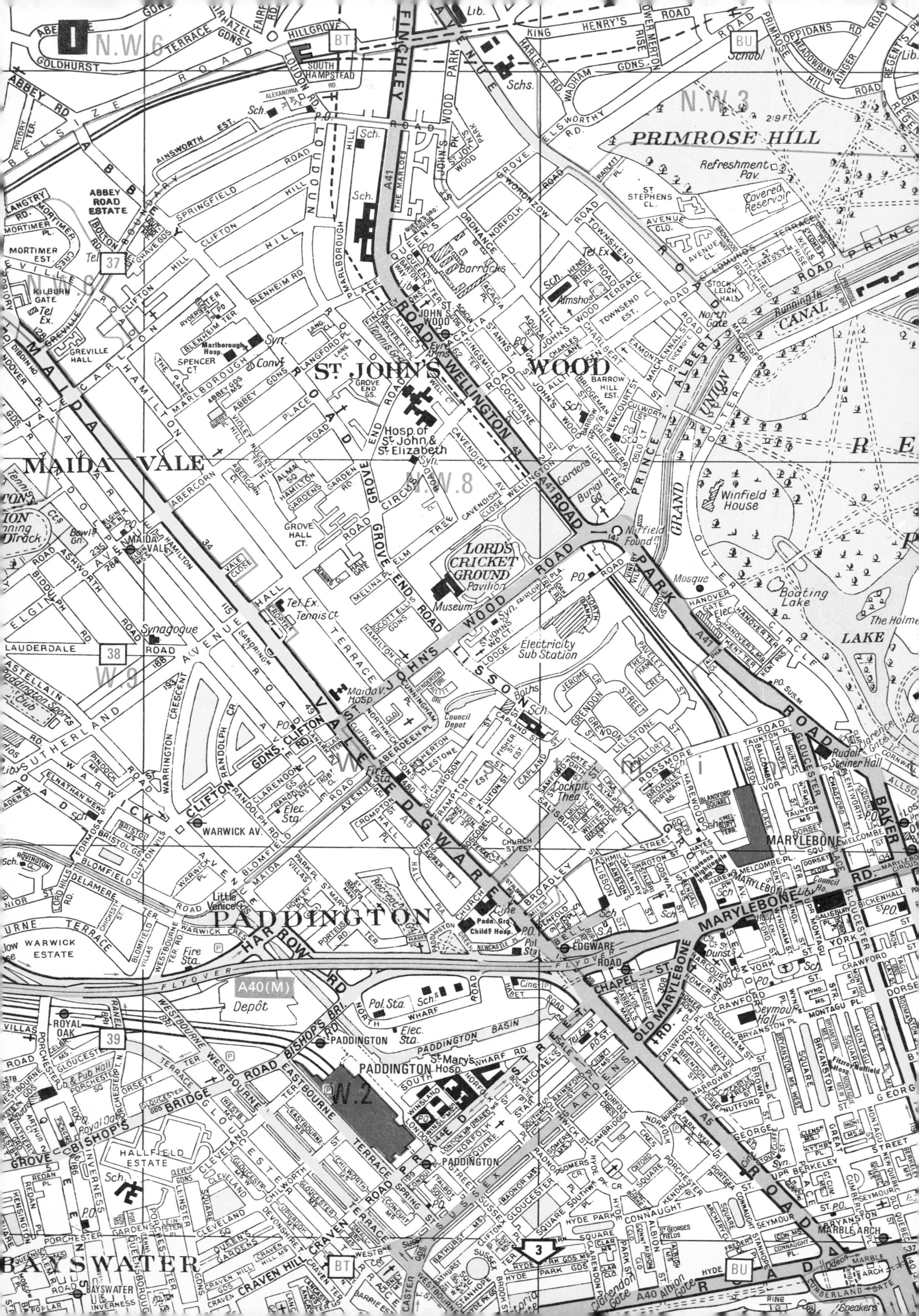

N.W.6
N.W.3
N.W.8
W.9
W.2
ST. JOHN'S WOOD
MAIDA VALE
PADDINGTON
BAYSWATER
PRIMROSE HILL
LORD'S CRICKET GROUND
Pavilion
Museum
Hosp. of St John & St Elizabeth
Barracks
Electricity Sub Station
Winfield House
Boating Lake
LAKE
The Holme
Mosque
Nuffield Found.
Refreshment Pav.
Covered Reservoir
Rudolf Steiner Hall
Cockpit Thea.
Council Depot
MARYLEBONE
MARBLE ARCH
PADDINGTON
ROYAL OAK
WARWICK AV.
EDGWARE ROAD
MAIDA VALE
SOUTH HAMPSTEAD
Little Venice
ABBEY ROAD ESTATE
MORTIMER EST.
WARWICK ESTATE
HALLFIELD ESTATE
Synagogue
Tel. Ex.
Sch.
P.O.
Pol. Sta.
Fire Sta.
Depôt
A40(M)
FLYOVER
GRAND UNION CANAL
Running Tk.
PADDINGTON BASIN
PADDINGTON Hosp.
St Mary's Hosp.
Seymour Hall
Marylebone Hosp.
Maida V. Hosp.
Fitzroy Nuffield Hosp.
Padn. Grn. Childr. Hosp.
FINCHLEY ROAD
WELLINGTON ROAD
PARK ROAD
PRINCE ALBERT ROAD
OUTER CIRCLE
MAIDA VALE
EDGWARE ROAD
ST. JOHN'S WOOD ROAD
GROVE END ROAD
HAMILTON TERRACE
CLIFTON HILL
ABBEY ROAD
BELSIZE ROAD
GOLDHURST TERRACE
KING HENRY'S ROAD
ELSWORTHY RD.
AVENUE ROAD
BLENHEIM RD.
SPRINGFIELD ROAD
CARLTON HILL
MARLBOROUGH PLACE
ABERCORN PL.
LISSON GROVE
HARROW ROAD
BISHOP'S BRIDGE ROAD
WESTBOURNE TERRACE
EASTBOURNE TERRACE
PRAED ST.
SUSSEX GARDENS
MARYLEBONE RD.
BAKER ST.
GLOUCESTER PLACE
OLD MARYLEBONE RD.
BRYANSTON SQUARE
MONTAGU SQUARE
HYDE PARK GDS
BAYSWATER ROAD
CRAVEN HILL
PORCHESTER TERRACE
WARWICK AVENUE
RANDOLPH AVENUE
SUTHERLAND AVENUE
BLOMFIELD ROAD
DELAMERE TER.
CLIFTON GDNS.
Albion Gate
Speakers
A41
A5
A40
BT
BU
37
38
39
3

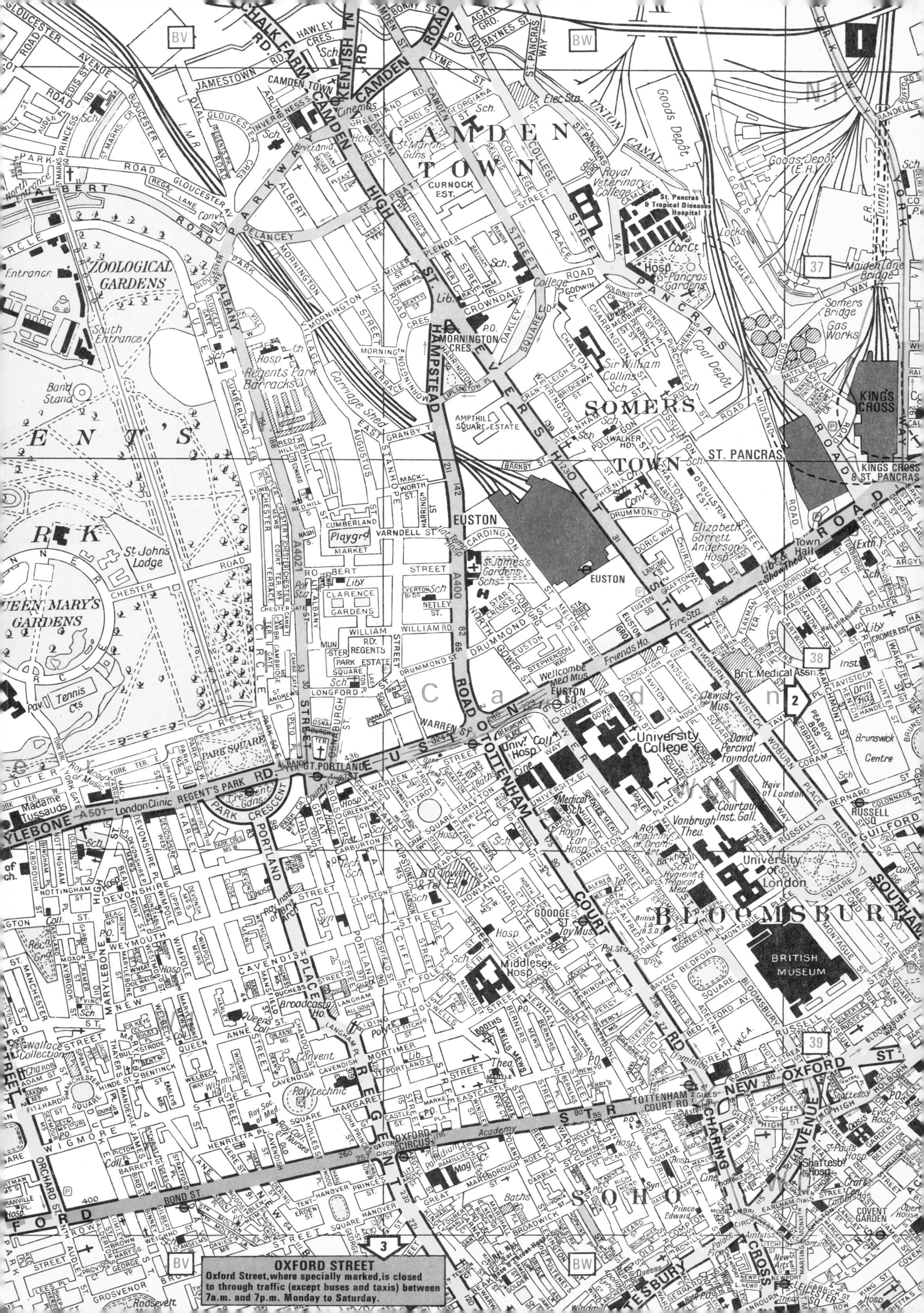

OXFORD STREET
Oxford Street, where specially marked, is closed to through traffic (except buses and taxis) between 7a.m. and 7p.m. Monday to Saturday.

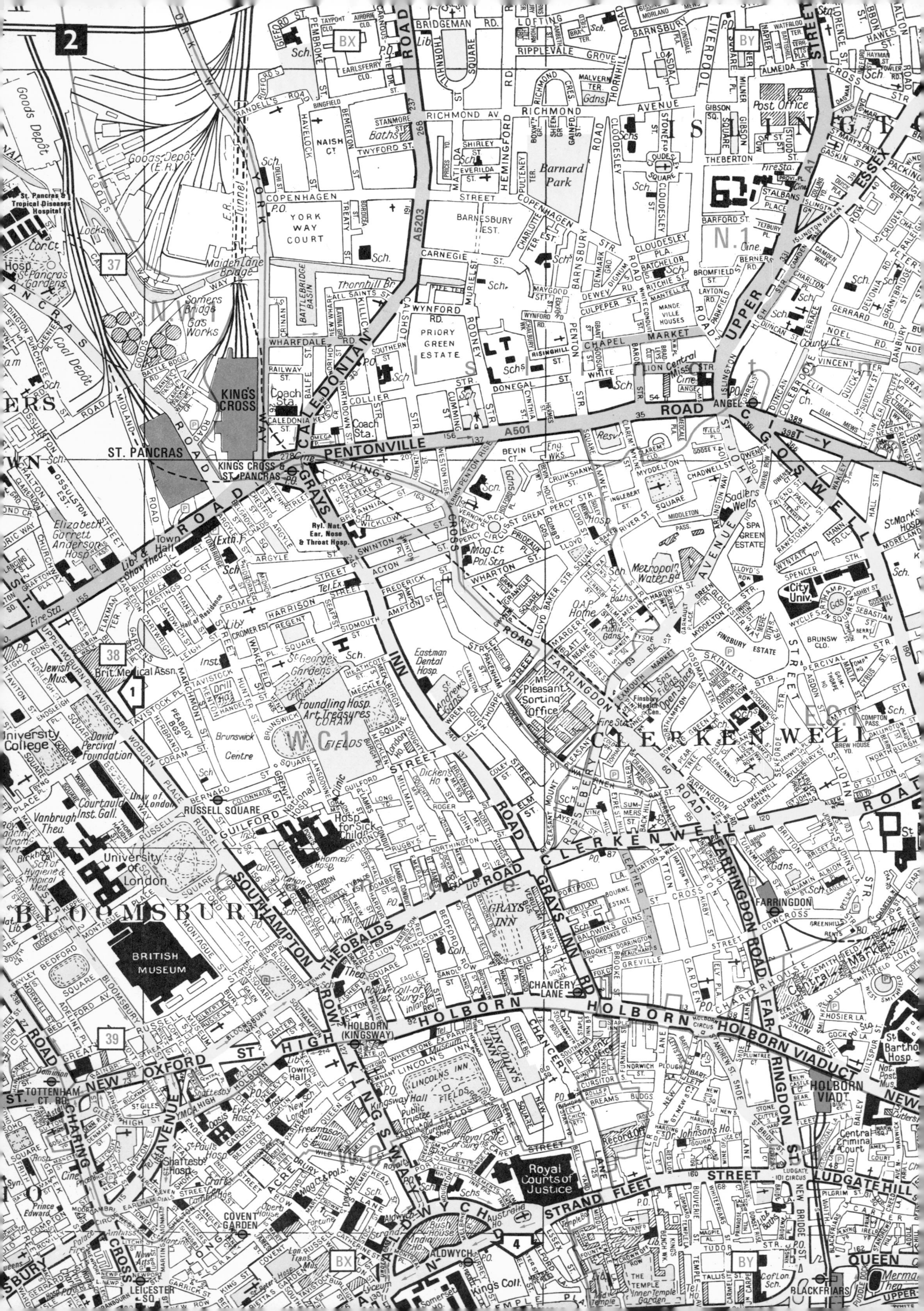
2
BX
BY
ISLINGTON
N.1
Barnard Park
Post Office
YORK WAY COURT
BARNESBURY EST.
PRIORY GREEN ESTATE
KING'S CROSS
ST. PANCRAS
KINGS CROSS & ST. PANCRAS
Somers Bridge Gas Works
Goods Depot
Coal Depot
St. Pancras & Tropical Diseases Hospital
PENTONVILLE ROAD
A501
A5203
CALEDONIAN ROAD
YORK WAY
GRAYS INN ROAD
KING'S CROSS ROAD
EUSTON ROAD
UPPER STREET
GOSWELL ROAD
ST. JOHN STREET
ANGEL
Metropoln Water Bd
Sadlers Wells
City Univ.
FINSBURY ESTATE
SPA GREEN ESTATE
Mt. Pleasant Sorting Office
Ryl. Nat. Ear, Nose & Throat Hosp.
Eastman Dental Hosp.
CLERKENWELL
EC1
WC1
Foundling Hosp. Art Treasures
CORAM FIELDS
Brunswick Centre
Elizabeth Garrett Anderson Hosp.
Town Hall
Brit. Medical Assn.
University College
David Percival Foundation
Univ. of London
RUSSELL SQUARE
Courtauld Inst. Gall.
Vanbrugh Thea.
University of London
BLOOMSBURY
BRITISH MUSEUM
SOUTHAMPTON ROW
THEOBALDS ROAD
CLERKENWELL ROAD
FARRINGDON ROAD
FARRINGDON
GRAYS INN
CHANCERY LANE
HOLBORN
HOLBORN (KINGSWAY)
HOLBORN VIADUCT
NEW OXFORD ST.
TOTTENHAM CT. RD.
CHARING CROSS ROAD
SHAFTESBURY AVENUE
KINGSWAY
LINCOLN'S INN FIELDS
Royal Courts of Justice
STRAND
FLEET STREET
ALDWYCH
Bush House
King's Coll.
COVENT GARDEN
LEICESTER SQ.
LUDGATE HILL
Central Criminal Court
Central Markets
BLACKFRIARS
THE TEMPLE
37
38
39
1
4

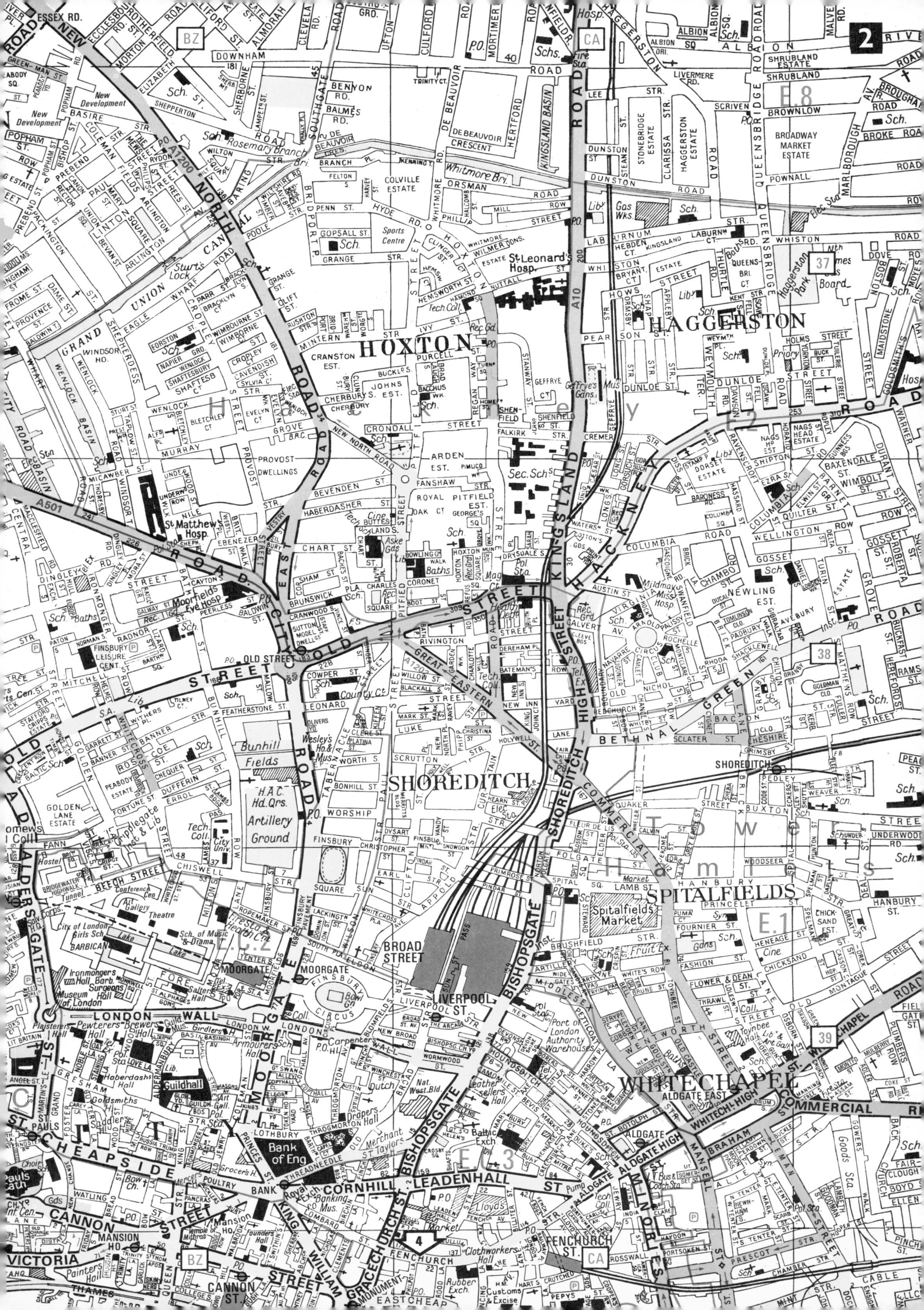
2
HOXTON
HAGGERSTON
SHOREDITCH
SPITALFIELDS
WHITECHAPEL
CITY
E.8
E.2
E.1
E.C.2
E.C.3
BZ
CA
37
38
39
4
NEW NORTH ROAD
KINGSLAND ROAD
HACKNEY ROAD
OLD STREET
CITY ROAD
EAST ROAD
GRAND UNION CANAL
REGENT'S CANAL
QUEENSBRIDGE ROAD
GREAT EASTERN STREET
COMMERCIAL STREET
SHOREDITCH HIGH STREET
BISHOPSGATE
MOORGATE
BETHNAL GREEN ROAD
WHITECHAPEL HIGH STREET
COMMERCIAL ROAD
ALDGATE HIGH STREET
LEADENHALL STREET
CORNHILL
CHEAPSIDE
CANNON STREET
QUEEN VICTORIA STREET
KING WILLIAM STREET
GRACECHURCH STREET
FENCHURCH STREET
LONDON WALL
ALDERSGATE
MINORIES
Bunhill Fields
H.A.C. Hd. Qrs. Artillery Ground
BROAD STREET
LIVERPOOL ST.
Spitalfields Market
Bank of Eng
Guildhall
Lloyds
FENCHURCH ST.
ALDGATE
ALDGATE EAST
MOORGATE
OLD STREET
SHOREDITCH
St Leonard's Hosp.
St Matthew's Hosp.
Moorfields Eye Hosp
Geffrye Mus.
Finsbury Leisure Cent.
Haggerston Park
Broadway Market Estate
Port of London Authority Warehouses
Tower Hamlets
Hackney

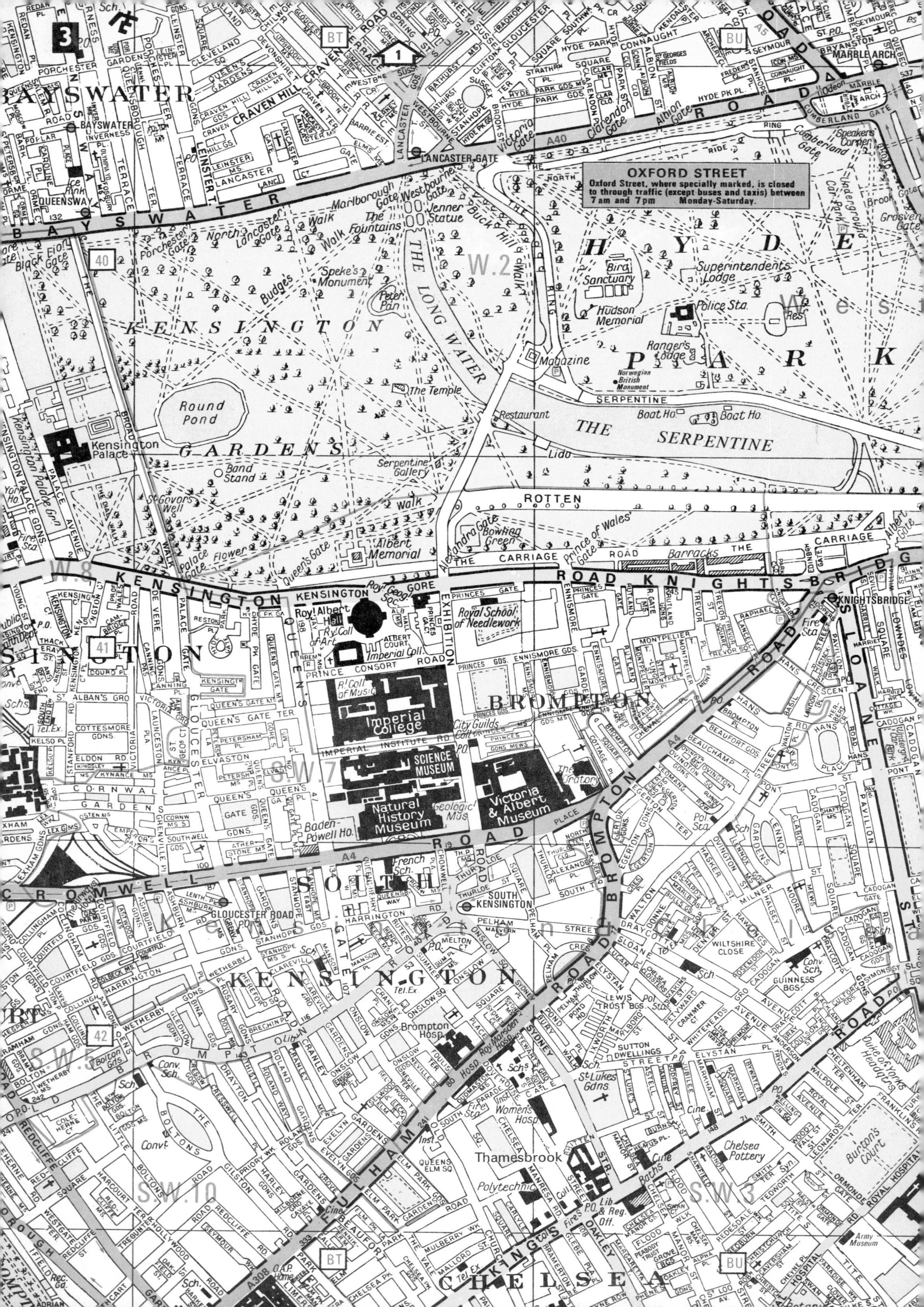

3
BT
1
BU
BAYSWATER
BAYSWATER ROAD
LANCASTER GATE
QUEENSWAY
MARBLE ARCH
OXFORD STREET
Oxford Street, where specially marked, is closed to through traffic (except buses and taxis) between 7am and 7pm Monday-Saturday.
HYDE PARK
KENSINGTON GARDENS
W.2
40
The Long Water
Round Pond
Kensington Palace
Speke's Monument
Peter Pan
The Temple
Magazine
Bird Sanctuary
Hudson Memorial
Police Sta.
Superintendents Lodge
Ranger's Lodge
Norwegian British Monument
THE SERPENTINE
Restaurant
Boat Ho.
Lido
Serpentine Gallery
Band Stand
ROTTEN ROW
Albert Memorial
Alexandra Gate
Bowling Green
Prince of Wales' Gate
Barracks
Speakers' Corner
W.8
KENSINGTON ROAD
KNIGHTSBRIDGE
Roy! Albert Hall
Imperial Coll.
Royal School of Needlework
Imperial College
PRINCE CONSORT ROAD
EXHIBITION ROAD
41
BROMPTON
SCIENCE MUSEUM
Natural History Museum
Victoria & Albert Museum
The Oratory
S.W.7
CROMWELL ROAD
SOUTH KENSINGTON
GLOUCESTER ROAD
KENSINGTON
42
S.W.5
Brompton Hosp.
Roy! Marsden Hosp.
FULHAM ROAD
SLOANE STREET
Guinness BGS.
Chelsea Pottery
Burton's Court
Duke of York's Head Qrs
S.W.10
THE BOLTONS
Thamesbrook
Polytechnic
S.W.3
KINGS ROAD
CHELSEA
Army Museum
ROYAL HOSPITAL ROAD

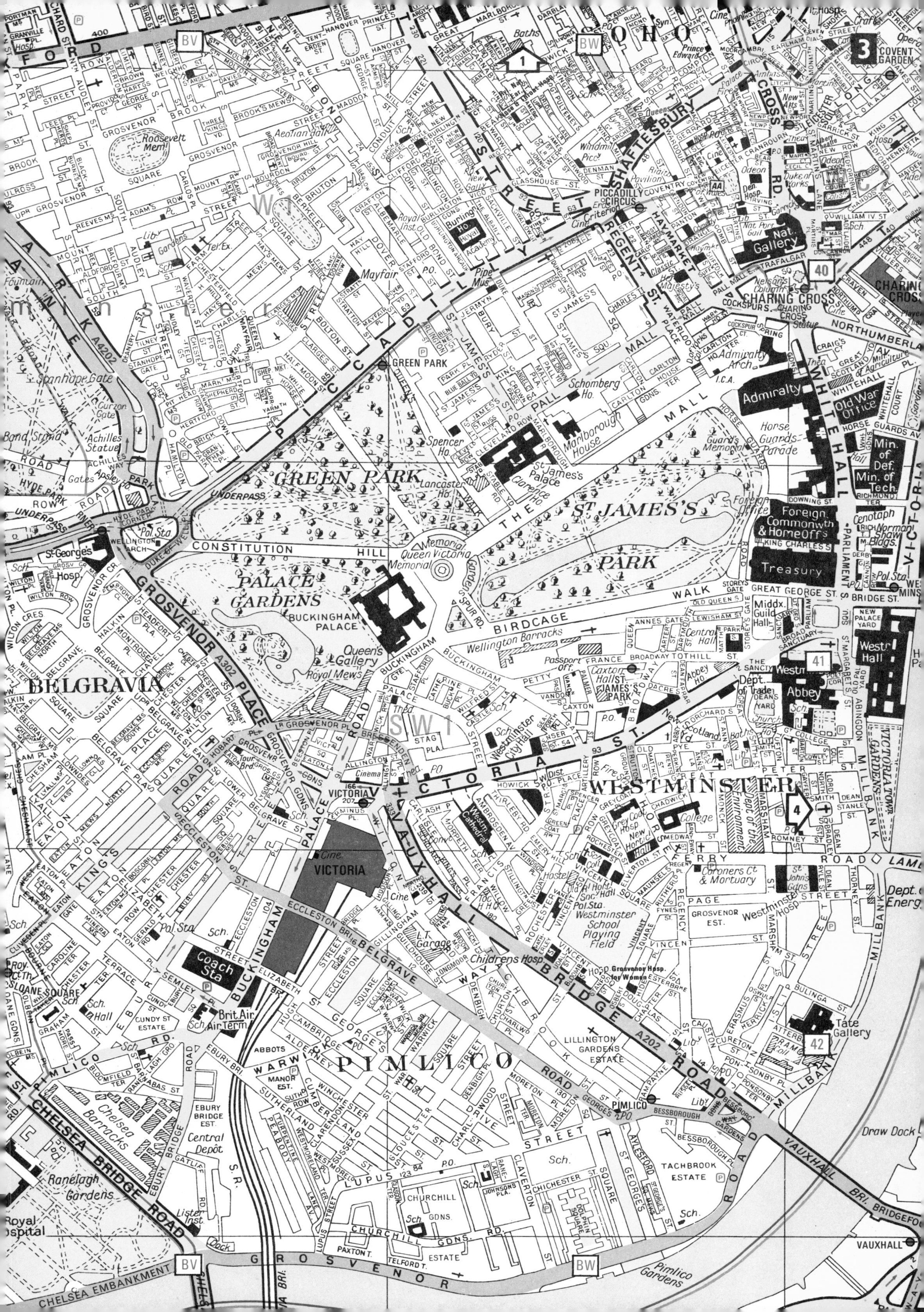

SOHO
3
COVENT GARDEN
MAYFAIR
W1
Roosevelt Mem!
GROSVENOR SQUARE
PICCADILLY
PICCADILLY CIRCUS
SHAFTESBURY AV
REGENT ST
HAYMARKET
Nat. Gallery
TRAFALGAR SQ
CHARING CROSS
Admiralty Arch
Admiralty
WHITEHALL
Old War Office
Horse Guards Parade
Min. of Def.
Min. of Tech.
Foreign, Commonwlth & HomeOffs
Treasury
ST JAMES'S PARK
St James's Palace
Marlborough House
Clarence Ho
Lancaster Ho
Spencer Ho.
GREEN PARK
CONSTITUTION HILL
Queen Victoria Memorial
BUCKINGHAM PALACE
PALACE GARDENS
Queen's Gallery
Royal Mews
BIRDCAGE WALK
Wellington Barracks
Hyde Park Corner
Wellington Arch
Apsley Ho
Achilles Statue
St George's Hosp
GROSVENOR PLACE
BELGRAVIA
SW1
VICTORIA
VICTORIA ST
Westminster City Hall
Westr. Cathedral
New Scotland Yard
Caxton Hall
Central Hall
Westr. Abbey
Westr. Hall
WESTMINSTER
VICTORIA TOWER GARDENS
MILLBANK
Tate Gallery
Coach Sta
Brit.Air Air Term
VAUXHALL BRIDGE ROAD
PIMLICO
Chelsea Barracks
Ranelagh Gardens
Royal Hospital
CHELSEA BRIDGE ROAD
CHELSEA EMBANKMENT
GROSVENOR ROAD
Pimlico Gardens
CHURCHILL GDNS. ESTATE
LILLINGTON GARDENS ESTATE
TACHBROOK ESTATE
Westminster School Playing Field
Westminster Hosp
Grosvenor Hosp. for Women
Draw Dock
VAUXHALL
BV
BW
40
41
42
1
4

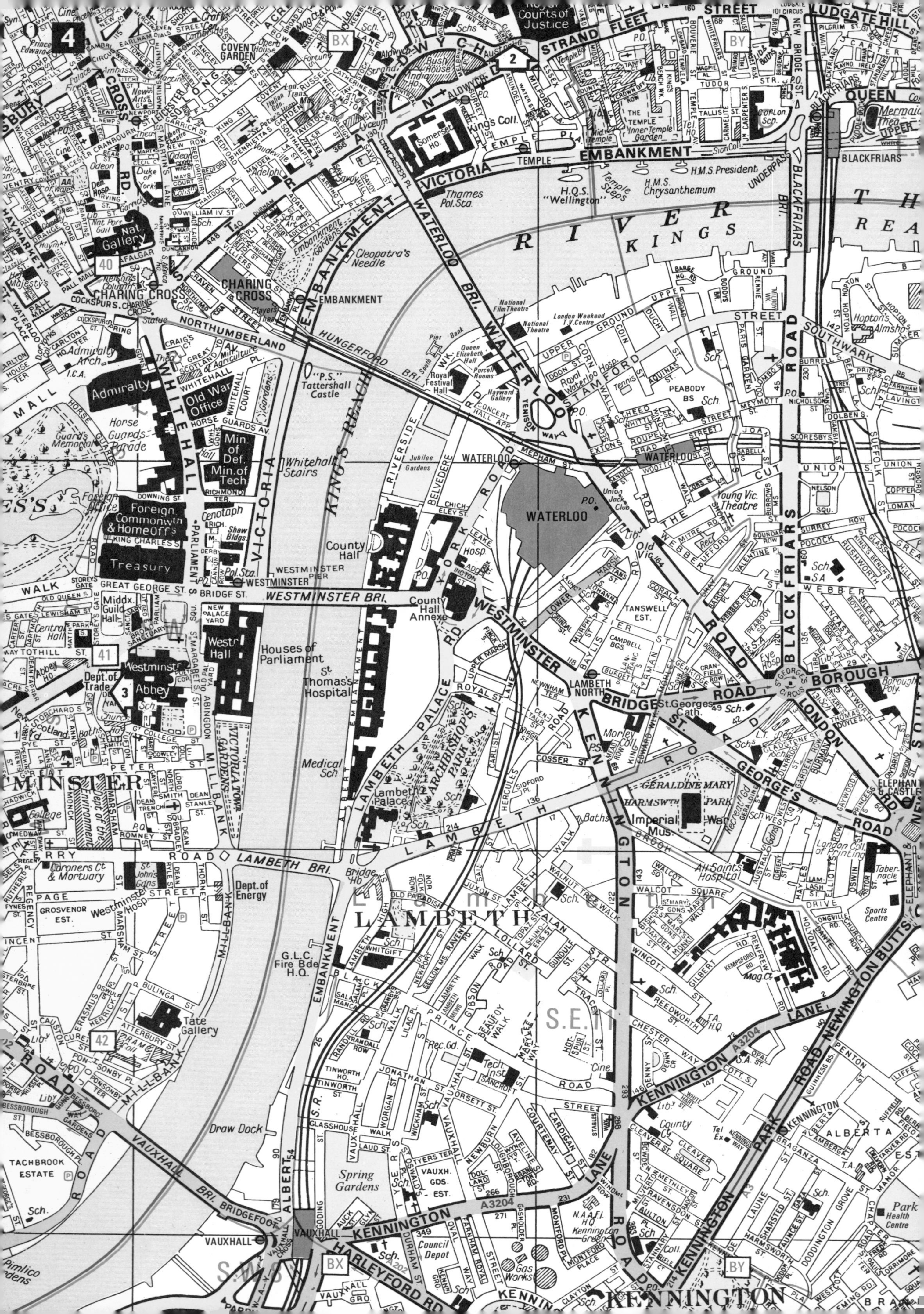
4
BX
BY
Courts of Justice
FLEET STREET
LUDGATE HILL
STRAND
ALDWYCH
Bush House
COVENT GARDEN
Somerset Ho.
King's Coll.
TEMPLE
VICTORIA EMBANKMENT
H.M.S. President
H.M.S. Chrysanthemum
H.Q.S. "Wellington"
Temple Steps
Thames Pol. Sta.
BLACKFRIARS
BLACKFRIARS BRI.
UNDERPASS
QUEEN
Mermaid Theatre
RIVER
KINGS
REACH
Nat. Gallery
TRAFALGAR SQ
40
CHARING CROSS
EMBANKMENT
Cleopatra's Needle
WATERLOO BRI.
National Film Theatre
National Theatre
London Weekend T.V. Centre
UPPER GROUND
STAMFORD ST.
SOUTHWARK ST.
BLACKFRIARS ROAD
Hopton's Almshouses
NORTHUMBERLAND AV.
HUNGERFORD BRI.
Admiralty Arch
Admiralty
Old War Office
Min. of Agriculture
WHITEHALL
Horse Guards Parade
Guards Memorial
"P.S." Tattershall Castle
Royal Festival Hall
Queen Elizabeth Hall
Purcell Rooms
Hayward Gallery
Royal Waterloo Hosp.
PEABODY BS
WATERLOO
Min. of Def.
Min. of Tech
Whitehall Stairs
Jubilee Gardens
THE CUT
Young Vic. Theatre
Union Jack Club
Foreign Office
Foreign Commonwealth & Home Offs
Cenotaph
DOWNING ST.
Treasury
VICTORIA EMBANKMENT
KING'S REACH
County Hall
WESTMINSTER PIER
WESTMINSTER
WESTMINSTER BRI.
GREAT GEORGE ST.
BRIDGE ST.
County Hall Annexe
Old Vic
WESTMINSTER BRIDGE RD.
TANSWELL EST.
Middx. Guild Hall
Westr. Hall
Houses of Parliament
St. Thomas's Hospital
41
Westminster Abbey
Dept. of Trade
3
New Scotland Yd.
LAMBETH NORTH
ST. GEORGE'S ROAD
St. George's Cath.
BOROUGH
LONDON ROAD
ST. GEORGE'S CIRCUS
Morley Coll.
KENNINGTON ROAD
ARCHBISHOP'S PARK
LAMBETH PALACE RD.
Medical Sch
Lambeth Palace
VICTORIA TOWER GARDENS
MILLBANK
WESTMINSTER
Dept. of the Environment
GERALDINE MARY HARMSWORTH PARK
Imperial War Mus.
ELEPHANT & CASTLE
LAMBETH RD.
LAMBETH BRI.
Coroners Ct & Mortuary
St. John's Gdns
Dept. of Energy
All Saints Hospital
London Coll. of Printing
Tabernacle
Sports Centre
LAMBETH
G.L.C. Fire Bde H.Q.
ALBERT EMBANKMENT
GROSVENOR EST.
Westminster Hosp.
S.E.11
NEWINGTON BUTTS
Tate Gallery
42
KENNINGTON LANE
KENNINGTON PARK ROAD
Tech. Inst.
Cine
County Ct.
Draw Dock
VAUXHALL BRI. ROAD
TACHBROOK ESTATE
BESSBOROUGH GARDENS
Spring Gardens
VAUXH. GDS. EST.
A3204
VAUXHALL
HARLEYFORD RD.
Council Depot
Gas Works
N.A.A.F.I. HQ
Kennington Green
Park Health Centre
KENNINGTON
Pimlico Gardens
S.W.8

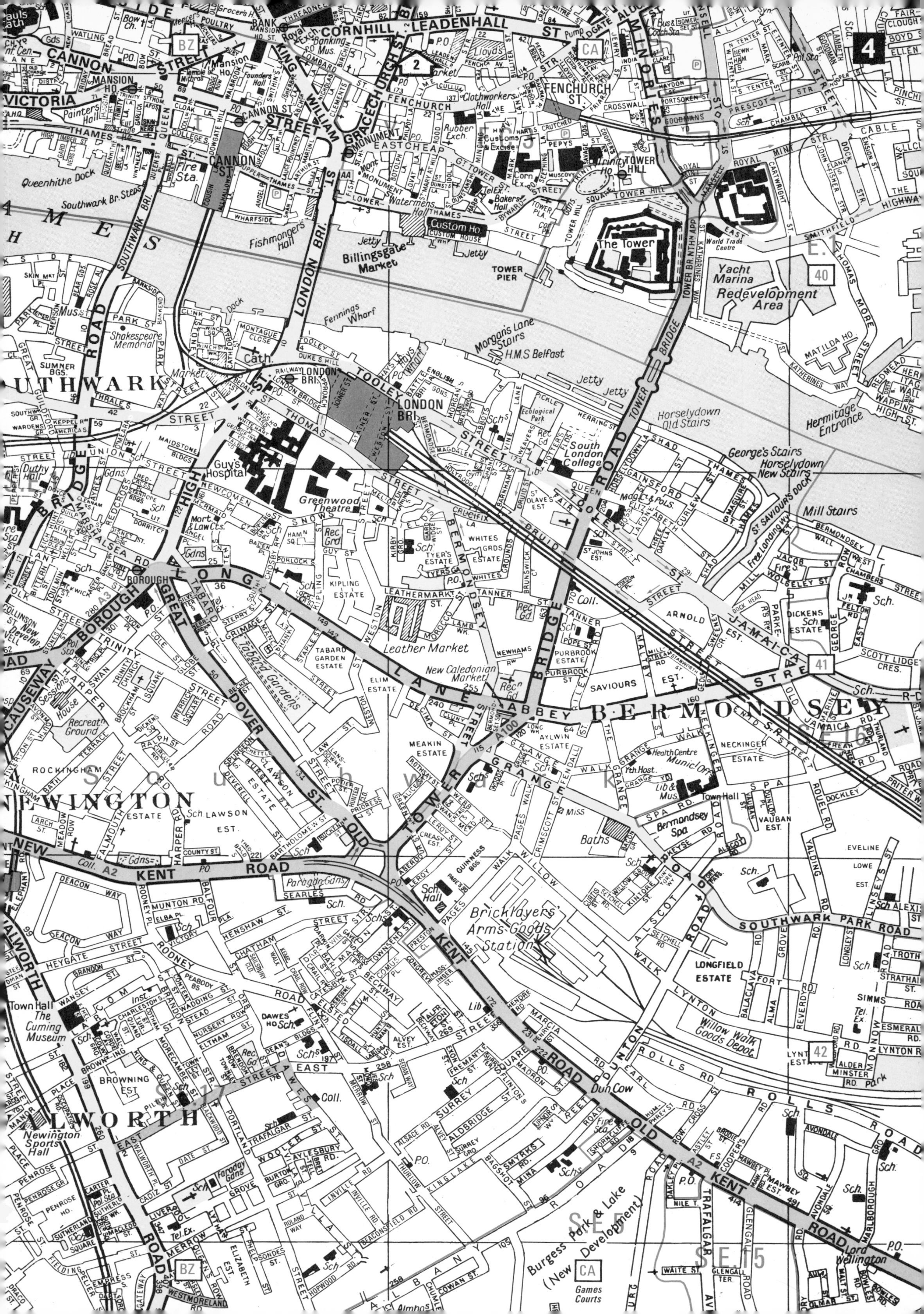

4
CANNON STREET
CORNHILL
LEADENHALL ST
MINORIES
VICTORIA
MANSION HO.
KING WILLIAM STREET
GRACECHURCH ST.
FENCHURCH ST.
EASTCHEAP
MONUMENT
TOWER HILL
Trinity Ho
Lloyds
Custom Ho.
Billingsgate Market
Fishmongers Hall
Watermens Hall
Queenhithe Dock
The Tower
World Trade Centre
Yacht Marina Redevelopment Area
TOWER PIER
TOWER BRIDGE
LONDON BRI.
SOUTHWARK BRI.
THAMES
Fennings Wharf
Morgans Lane Stairs
H.M.S Belfast
SOUTHWARK
Shakespeare Memorial
Cath.
TOOLEY STREET
LONDON BRI.
Guy's Hospital
Greenwood Theatre
South London College
Horselydown Old Stairs
George's Stairs
Horselydown New Stairs
St Saviour's Dock
Mill Stairs
Hermitage Entrance
WAPPING HIGH ST.
JAMAICA ROAD
BOROUGH HIGH STREET
LONG LANE
GREAT DOVER ST.
TOWER BRIDGE ROAD
ABBEY STREET
BERMONDSEY
Leather Market
New Caledonian Market
Tabard Gardens
Recreat'n Ground
NEWINGTON
Southwark
Town Hall
Bermondsey Spa
Baths
Bricklayers' Arms Goods Station
Willow Walk Goods Depot
NEW KENT ROAD
OLD KENT ROAD
SOUTHWARK PARK ROAD
ROLLS ROAD
WALWORTH
WALWORTH ROAD
Town Hall
The Cuming Museum
Newington Sports Hall
Burgess Park & Lake (New Development)
Games Courts
ALBANY ROAD
Duh Cow
Lord Wellington
S.E.1
S.E.17
S.E.5
S.E.15
S.E.16
40
41
42
BZ
CA

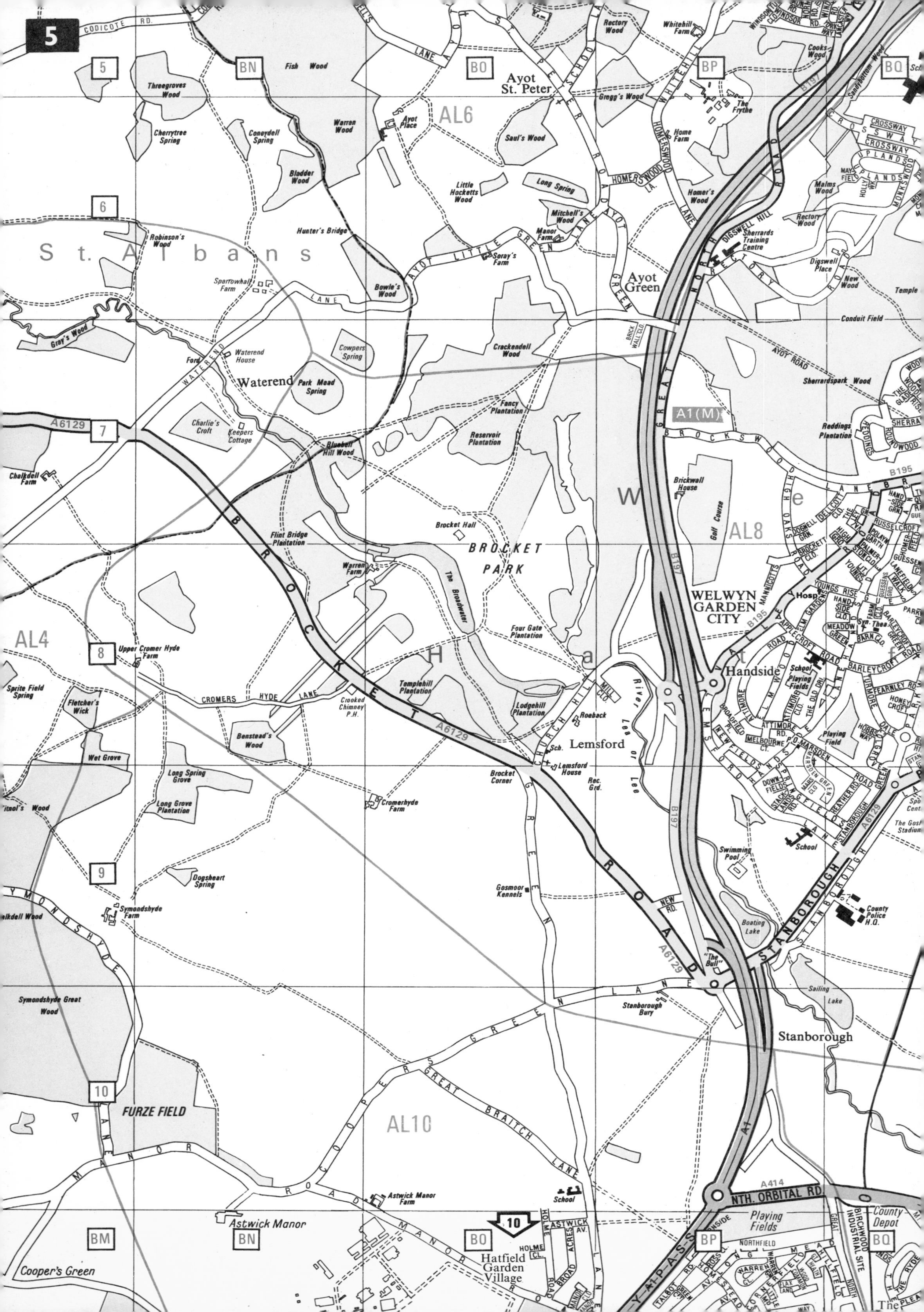
CODICOTE RD.
BN
BO
BP
BQ
Fish Wood
Ayot St. Peter
Rectory Wood
Whitehill Farm
Cooks Wood
Threegroves Wood
Cherrytree Spring
Coneydell Spring
Warren Wood
Ayot Place
AL6
Gregg's Wood
Saul's Wood
The Frythe
Home Farm
CROSSWAY
UPLANDS
Bladder Wood
Little Hocketts Wood
Long Spring
HOMERSWOOD LA.
Homer's Wood
Malms Wood
Rectory Wood
Robinson's Wood
Hunter's Bridge
Mitchell's Wood
Manor Farm
DIGSWELL HILL
Sherrards Training Centre
St. Albans
Soray's Farm
AYOT LITTLE GREEN LANE
Ayot Green
RECTORY ROAD
Digswell Place
New Wood
Temple
Sparrowhall Farm
Bowle's Wood
Conduit Field
Gray's Wood
Cowpers Spring
Crackendell Wood
BRICK WALL CLO.
AYOT ROAD
Ford
Waterend House
WATEREND
Waterend
Park Mead Spring
Sherrardspark Wood
Fancy Plantation
A1(M)
Reddings Plantation
A6129
7
Charlie's Croft
Keepers Cottage
Reservoir Plantation
BROCKSWOOD LANE
Bluebell Hill Wood
Chalkdell Farm
Brickwall House
B195
Golf Course
AL8
Brocket Hall
Flint Bridge Plantation
BROCKET PARK
Warren Farm
The Broadwater
WELWYN GARDEN CITY
Hosp.
AL4
Four Gate Plantation
8
Upper Cromer Hyde Farm
Handside
School
Playing Fields
Sprite Field Spring
Fletcher's Wick
CROMERS HYDE LANE
Crooked Chimney P.H.
Templehill Plantation
Lodgehill Plantation
MILL CLO.
River Lea
Roeback
Lemsford
Sch.
Lemsford House
Rec. Grd.
Benstead's Wood
Wet Grove
Long Spring Grove
Long Grove Plantation
Brocket Corner
Cromerhyde Farm
Playing Field
B197
School
Swimming Pool
9
Dogsheart Spring
Gosmoor Kennels
Symondshyde Farm
SYMONDSHYDE
NEW RD.
County Police H.Q.
Boating Lake
STANBOROUGH ROAD
"The Bull"
Symondshyde Great Wood
LANE
Stanborough Bury
Sailing Lake
Stanborough
10
FURZE FIELD
AL10
GREAT BRAITCH LANE
COOPERS GREEN
A1
MANOR ROAD
Astwick Manor Farm
School
A414
NTH. ORBITAL RD.
Playing Fields
Astwick Manor
10
BM
Hatfield Garden Village
Cooper's Green
County Depot
BIRCHWOOD INDUSTRIAL SITE

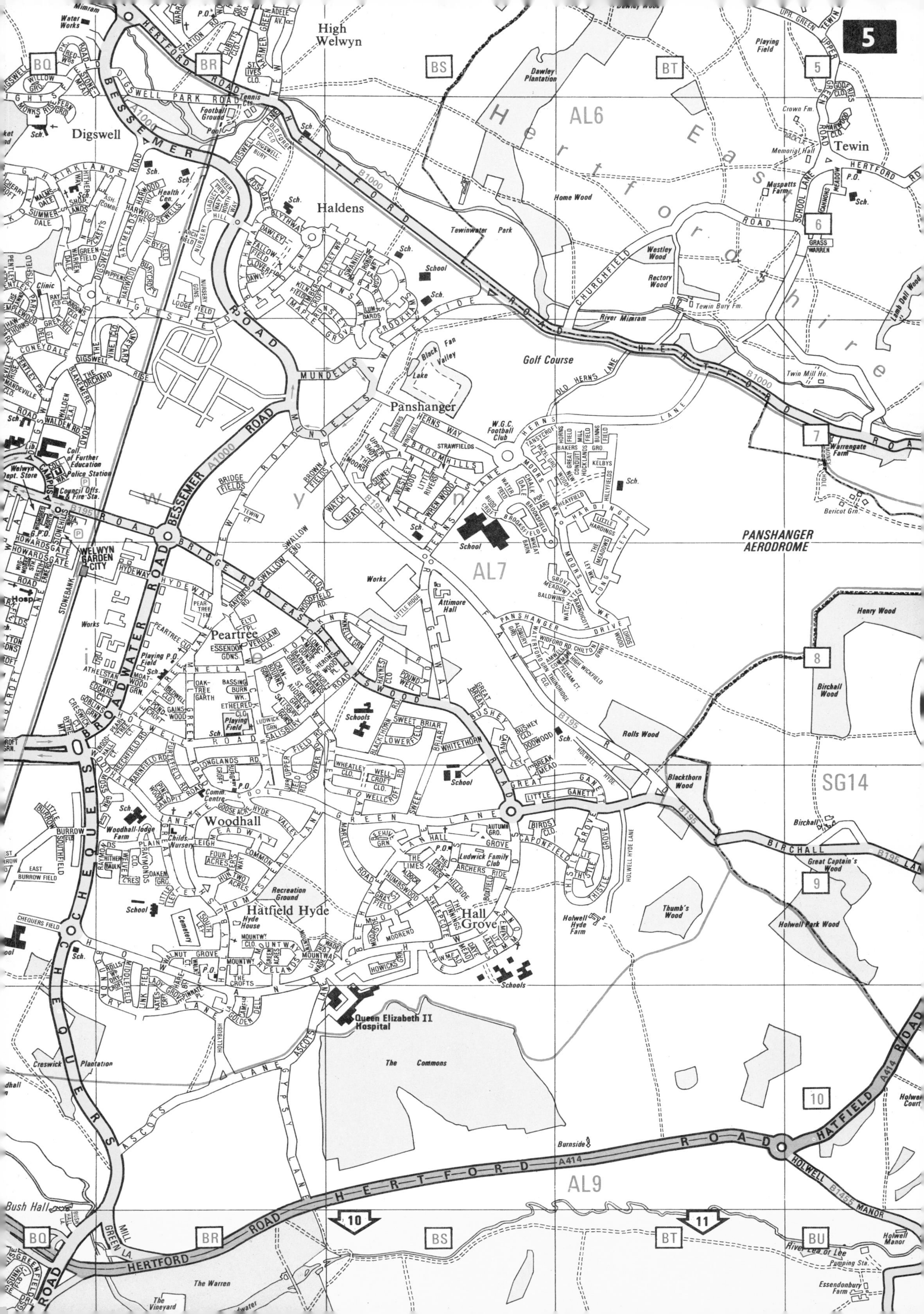
High Welwyn
Digswell
Haldens
Tewin
Panshanger
Peartree
Woodhall
Hatfield Hyde
Hall Grove
WELWYN GARDEN CITY
PANSHANGER AERODROME
Queen Elizabeth II Hospital
The Commons
Golf Course
Dawley Plantation
Home Wood
Tewinwater Park
Westley Wood
Rectory Wood
River Mimram
Black Fan Valley
Rolls Wood
Blackthorn Wood
Thumb's Wood
Henry Wood
Birchall Wood
Holwell Park Wood
Great Captain's Wood
Creswick Plantation
Bush Hall
The Warren
The Vineyard
Holwell Manor
Essendonbury Farm
Attimore Hall
Holwell Hyde Farm
Warrengate Farm
Muspatts Farm
Crown Fm.
Tewin Bury Fm.
Twin Mill Ho.
Bericot Grn.
Burnside
Pumping Sta.
River Lea or Lee
W.G.C. Football Club
Coll. of Further Education
Police Station
Council Offs. & Fire Sta.
Welwyn Dept. Store
Woodhall-lodge Farm
Recreation Ground
Cemetery
Hyde House
Ludwick Family Club
Works
Schools
AL6
AL7
AL9
SG14
Hertfordshire
Welwyn
BQ
BR
BS
BT
BU
5
6
7
8
9
10
11
BESSEMER ROAD
HERTFORD ROAD
BROADWATER ROAD
BRIDGE ROAD EAST
HERNS LANE
CHEQUERS
HATFIELD ROAD
HOLWELL MANOR
BIRCHALL LANE
DIGSWELL PARK ROAD
MUNDELLS
WATERSIDE
CHURCHFIELD ROAD
GREEN LANE
HOWLANDS
ASCOTS LANE
GYPSY LANE
PANSHANGER DRIVE
A1000
A414
B1000
B195
B1455

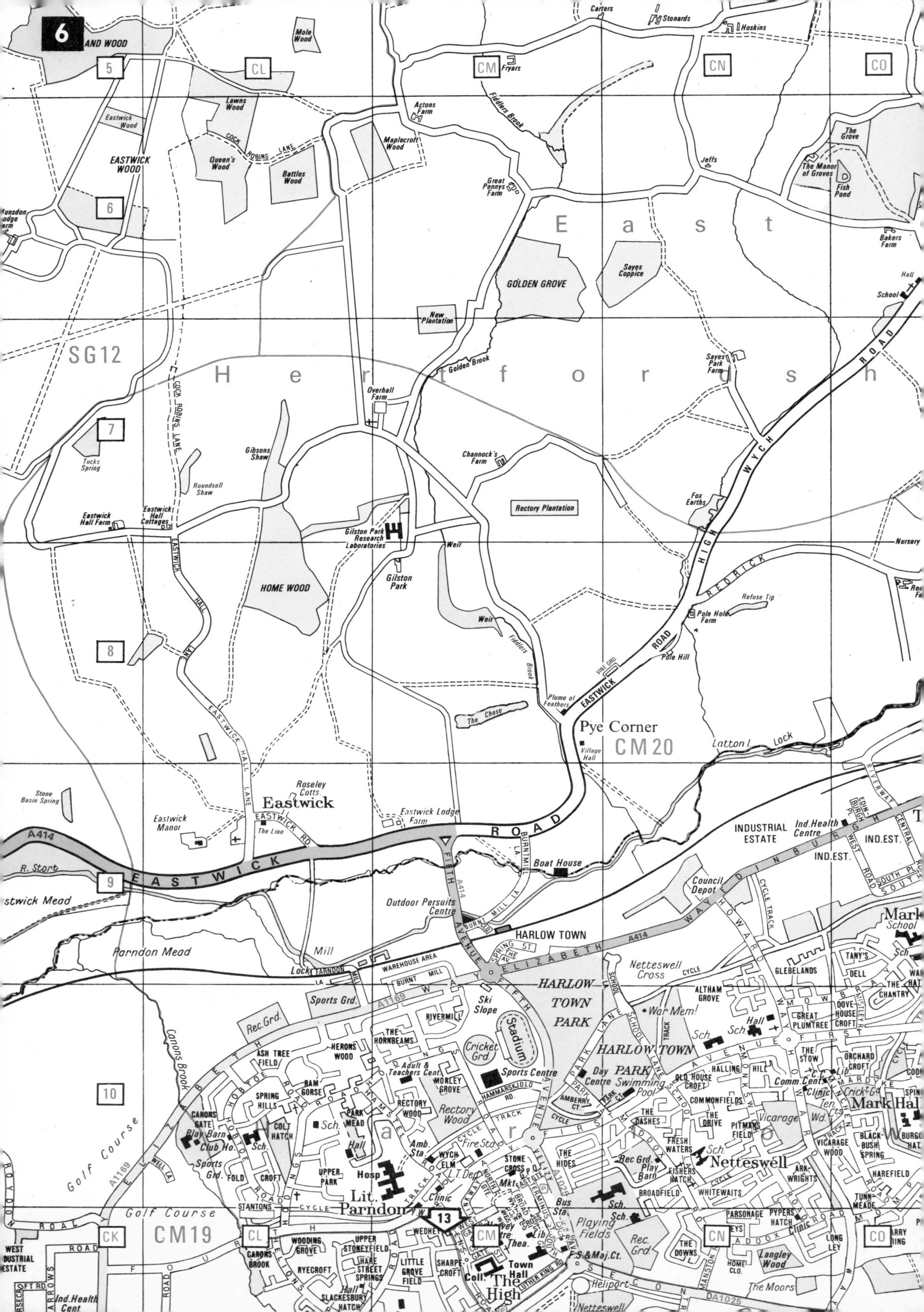

6
EASTWICK WOOD
Queen's Wood
Battles Wood
Maplecroft Wood
Actons Farm
Fiddlers Brook
Great Pennys Farm
East
GOLDEN GROVE
Sayes Coppice
New Plantation
SG12
Hertfordshire
Overhall Farm
Golden Brook
Gibsons Shaw
Roundsell Shaw
Tucks Spring
Eastwick Hall Farm
Eastwick Hall Cottages
Channock's Farm
Rectory Plantation
Gilston Park Research Laboratories
Gilston Park
HOME WOOD
Weir
Fox Earths
HIGH WYCH ROAD
REDRICK
Refuse Tip
Pole Hole Farm
Pole Hill
EASTWICK ROAD
Plume of Feathers
The Chase
Pye Corner
Village Hall
CM20
Latton Lock
Eastwick
Roseley Cotts.
Eastwick Manor
The Lion
Eastwick Lodge Farm
Stone Basin Spring
A414
EASTWICK ROAD
R. Stort
Eastwick Mead
Boat House
Outdoor Persuits Centre
FIFTH AVENUE
HARLOW TOWN
INDUSTRIAL ESTATE
Ind.Health Centre
IND.EST.
Council Depot
EDINBURGH WAY
Parndon Mead
Mill
Lock
WAREHOUSE AREA
ELIZABETH WAY
Netteswell Cross
HARLOW TOWN PARK
Sports Grd.
Rec.Grd.
Ski Slope
Stadium
Cricket Grd.
Sports Centre
War Mem.
HARLOW TOWN PARK
Swimming Pool
Canons Brook
Golf Course
Rectory Wood
Fire Sta.
Hosp
Lit. Parndon
Netteswell
Mark Hall
Playing Fields
Rec. Grd.
Town Hall
Coll.
The High
Heliport
The Moors
Langley Wood
CM19
CK
CL
CM
CN
CO
5
6
7
8
9
10
13

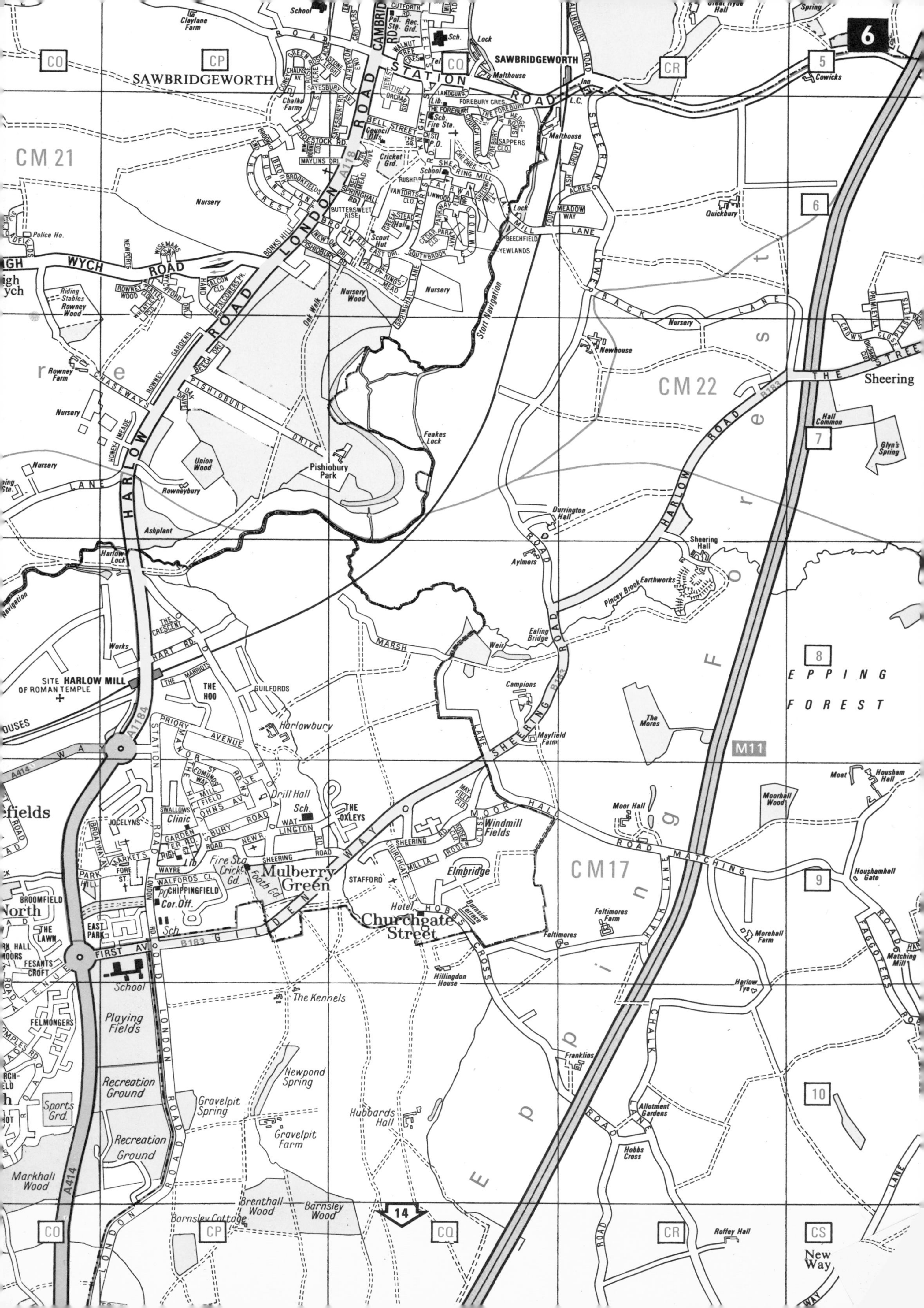

6
SAWBRIDGEWORTH
SAWBRIDGEWORTH
STATION ROAD
Claylane Farm
School
Sch.
Lock
Malthouse
Malthouse
Inn
L.C.
ALLINGBURY ROAD
SHEERING LOWER ROAD
Spring
Cowicks
CM 21
CM 22
CM 17
CO
CP
CQ
CR
CS
5
6
7
8
9
10
14
LONDON ROAD
HARLOW ROAD
A1184
A1184
A414
M11
B183
BELL STREET
Lib.
Sch.
Fire Sta.
Council Offs.
P.O.
Cricket Grd.
School
SHEERING MILL LANE
Nursery
Police Ho.
HIGH WYCH ROAD
High Wych
Riding Stables
Rowney Wood
Rowney Farm
Nursery
Nursery
Nursery Wood
Oak Walk
Stort Navigation
Feakes Lock
PISHIOBURY DRIVE
Pishiobury Park
Union Wood
Rowneybury
Ashplant
Harlow Lock
Navigation
Lock
BEECHFIELD
YEWLANDS
MEADOW WAY
ACRES
BACK LANE
Nursery
Newhouse
Quickbury
THE STREET
Sheering
Hall Common
Glyn's Spring
Durrington Hall
SHEERING ROAD
Aylmers
Sheering Hall
Earthworks
Pincey Brook
Ealing Bridge
Weir
MARSH LANE
Campions
Mayfield Farm
EPPING FOREST
Epping Forest
The Mores
Moat
Housham Hall
Moorhall Wood
Moor Hall
Windmill Fields
MOOR HALL ROAD
MATCHING ROAD
Houshamhall Gate
Feltimores Farm
Feltimores
Morehall Farm
Harlow Tye
FAGGOTERS LANE
Matching Mill
THE CRESCENT
HART RD.
Works
SITE OF ROMAN TEMPLE
HARLOW MILL
THE MARRIOTS
THE HOO
GUILFORDS
Harlowbury
PRIORY AVENUE
STATION ROAD
OLD ROAD
Drill Hall
Sch.
THE OXLEYS
WATLINGTON RD.
Clinic
Lib.
Fire Sta.
Cricket Gd.
Mulberry Green
Footb. Gd.
SHEERING ROAD
GILDEN WAY
STAFFORD
Hotel
Churchgate Street
CHURCHGATE STREET
HOBBS CROSS
Elmbridge
Hillingdon House
CHALK LANE
Franklins
Allotment Gardens
Hobbs Cross
Burnside Terrace
Roffey Hall
New Way
CHIPPINGFIELD
Cor.Off.
Sch.
FIRST AV.
School
Playing Fields
Recreation Ground
Recreation Ground
Sports Grd.
Markhall Wood
The Kennels
Newpond Spring
Gravelpit Spring
Hubbards Hall
Gravelpit Farm
Brenthall Wood
Barnsley Wood
Barnsley Cottage
LONDON ROAD
North
BROOMFIELD
FELMONGERS
FESANTS CROFT
EAST PARK
THE LAWN

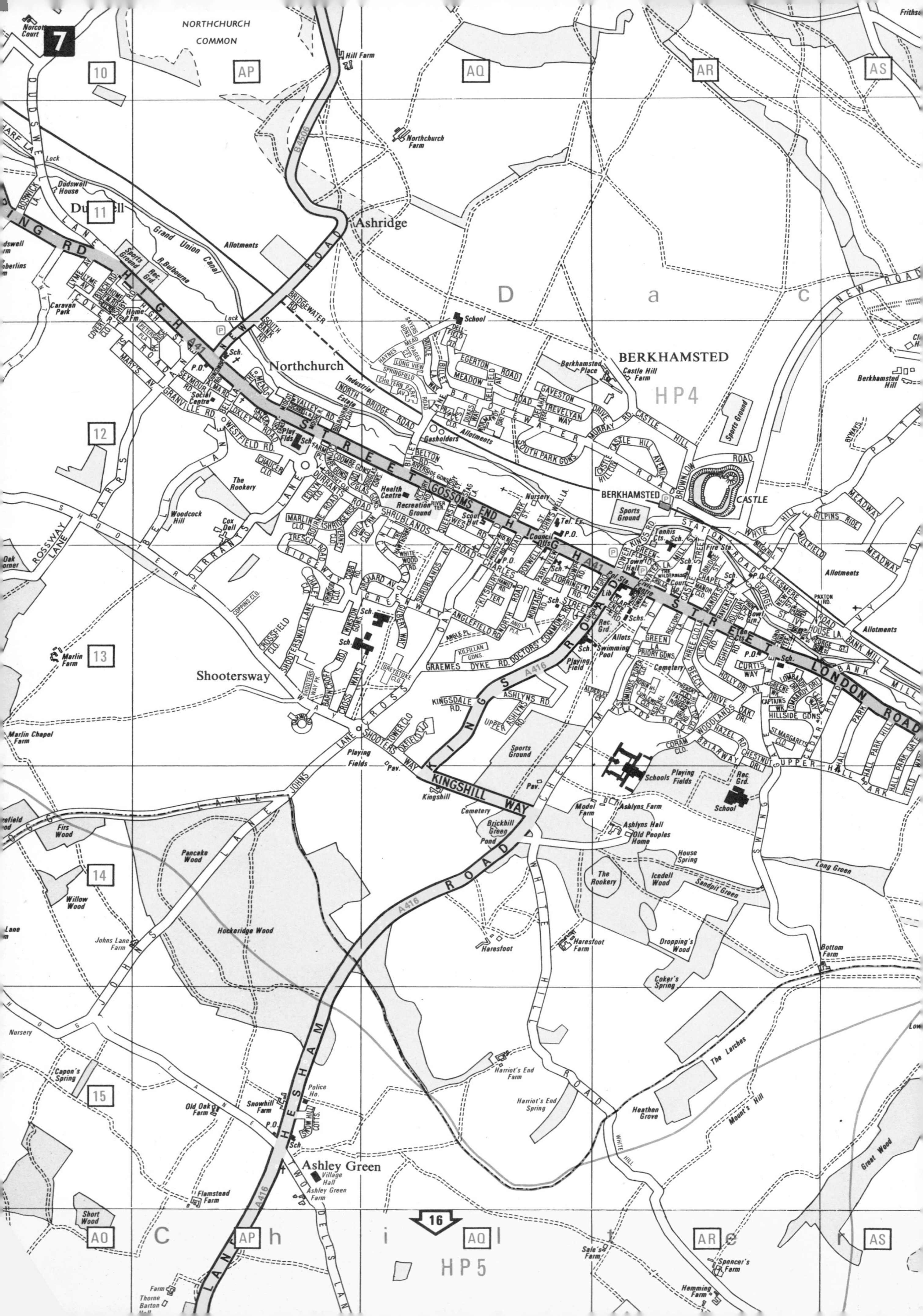
7
NORTHCHURCH
COMMON
Norcott Court
Hill Farm
Northchurch Farm
10
AP
AQ
AR
AS
Frithsden
Lock
Dudswell House
Dudswell
11
Grand Union Canal
R. Bulbourne
Allotments
Ashridge
Sports Ground
Rec. Grd.
Caravan Park
Home Fm.
BRIDGEWATER RD.
SOUTH BANK RD.
D
a
c
School
NEW ROAD
Northchurch
BERKHAMSTED
Berkhamsted Place
Castle Hill Farm
HP4
Berkhamsted Hill
Industrial Estate
NORTH BRIDGE ROAD
EGERTON ROAD
MEADOW ROAD
GAVESTON DRIVE
TREVELYAN WAY
Allotments
Gasholders
SOUTH PARK GDNS.
CASTLE HILL
CASTLE HILL AVENUE
Sports Ground
BROWNLOW ROAD
CASTLE
12
HIGH STREET
A41
GOSSOMS END
Health Centre
Recreation Ground
SHRUBLANDS
Nursery
BERKHAMSTED
Sports Ground
STATION ROAD
GILPINS RIDE
MEADWAY
MILLFIELD
Allotments
The Rookery
Woodcock Hill
Cox Dell
SHOOTERSWAY
ROSSWAY LANE
Oak Corner
COPPINS CLO.
CROSSFIELD CLO.
SHOOTERSWAY LANE
GREENWAY
ANGLEFIELD RD.
Tel. Ex.
P.O.
Council Offs.
Town Hall
Tennis Cts.
Fire Sta.
Allotments
PAXTON RD.
Allotments
BANK MILL
LONDON ROAD
13
Marlin Farm
Shootersway
KILFILLAN GDNS.
GRAEMES DYKE RD.
DOCTORS COMMONS RD.
Rec. Grd.
Allots.
Swimming Pool
Playing Field
GREEN LA.
PRIORY GDNS.
Cemetery
CURTIS WAY
HOLLY DRI.
HILLSIDE GDNS.
KINGSDALE RD.
ASHLYNS RD.
UPPER ASHLYNS RD.
A416
KINGS ROAD
Marlin Chapel Farm
Playing Fields
Pav.
KINGSHILL WAY
Kingshill
Sports Ground
Pav.
CHESHAM ROAD
Schools
Playing Fields
Rec. Grd.
School
CORAM CLO.
BRIARWAY
CHESTNUT DRI.
UPPER HALL PARK
Cemetery
Brickhill Green Pond
Model Farm
Ashlyns Farm
Ashlyns Hall
Old Peoples Home
House Spring
Firs Wood
Pancake Wood
14
Willow Wood
The Rookery
Icedell Wood
Sandpit Green
Long Green
Hockeridge Wood
Johns Lane Farm
Haresfoot
Haresfoot Farm
Dropping's Wood
Coker's Spring
Bottom Farm
ROAD
Nursery
Capon's Spring
15
Old Oak Farm
Snowhill Farm
Police Ho.
Harriot's End Farm
Harriot's End Spring
The Larches
Heathen Grove
Mount's Hill
WHITE HILL
Great Wood
P.O.
Sch.
Ashley Green
Village Hall
Ashley Green Farm
Flamstead Farm
Short Wood
16
AO
AP
AQ
AR
AS
C
h
i
t
e
r
HP5
Sale's Farm
Spencer's Farm
Hemming Farm
Thorne Barton Hall
CHESHAM LANE
DELLS LANE

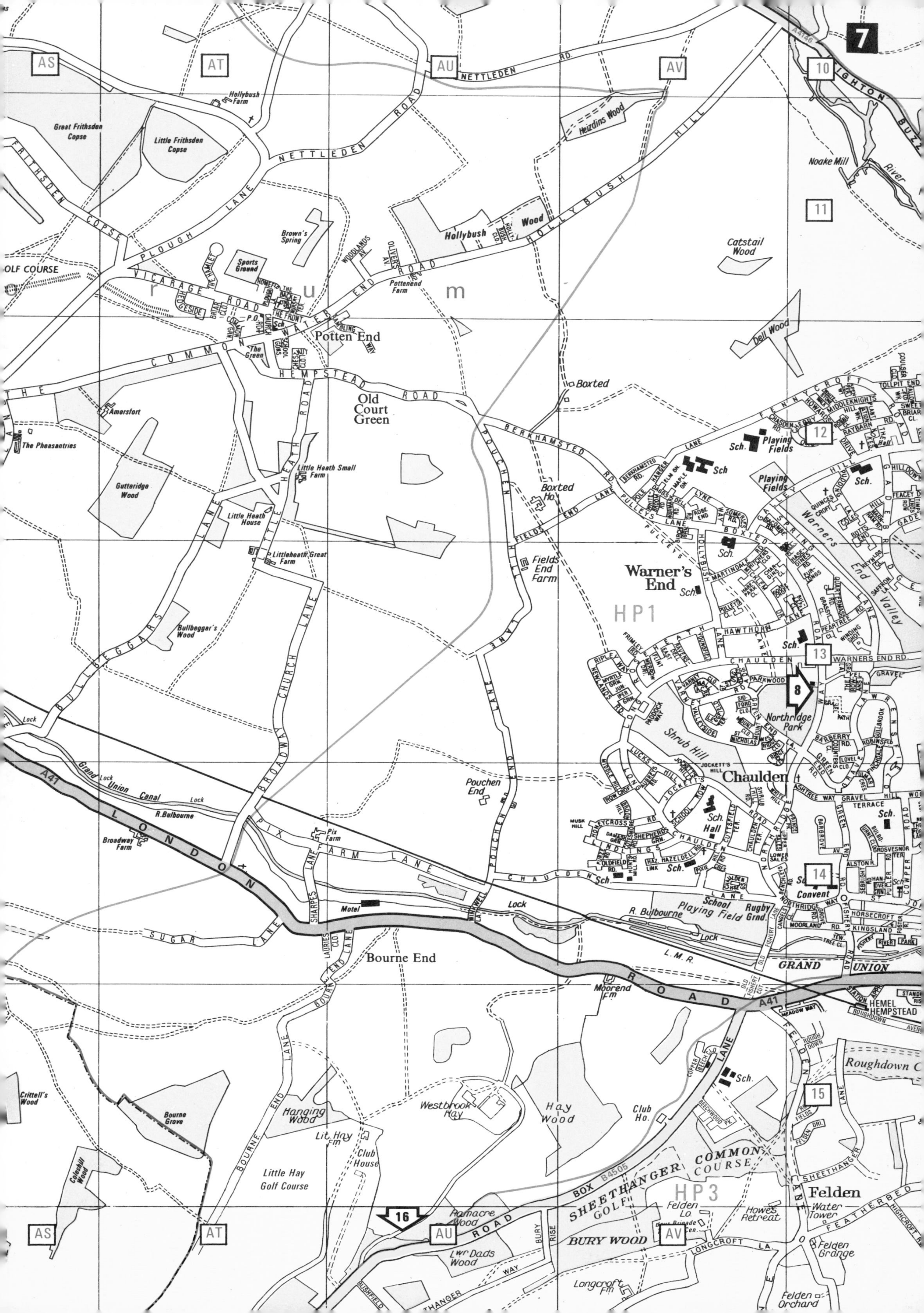

7
AS
AT
AU
AV
10
11
12
13
14
15
8
16
NETTLEDEN RD.
NETTLEDEN ROAD
Hollybush Farm
Great Frithsden Copse
Little Frithsden Copse
FRITHSDEN COPSE
PLOUGH LANE
Heizdins Wood
HOLLYBUSH HILL
Noake Mill
River
Catstail Wood
Brown's Spring
Hollybush Wood
OLF COURSE
Sports Ground
VICARAGE ROAD
Pottenend Farm
Potten End
Dell Wood
THE COMMON
HEMPSTEAD ROAD
Boxted
Old Court Green
Amersfort
The Pheasantries
BERKHAMSTED RD.
FENNYCROFT RD.
Playing Fields
Sch.
Little Heath Small Farm
Gutteridge Wood
Little Heath House
Boxted Ho.
FIELDS END LANE
PULLEYS LANE
Warners End Valley
Littleheath Great Farm
Fields End Farm
Warner's End
HP1
Bullbeggar's Wood
BULLBEGGARS LANE
CHURCH LANE
POUCHEN END LANE
HAWTHORN LANE
CHAULDEN LANE
WARNERS END RD.
Northridge Park
Shrub Hill
Chaulden
Lock
Grand Union Canal
R. Bulbourne
A41
LONDON ROAD
Pouchen End
Pix Farm
PIX FARM LANE
Broadway Farm
Sch. Hall
Convent
Motel
SUGAR LANE
School Playing Field
Rugby Grnd.
GRAND UNION
L.M.R.
Bourne End
Moorend Fm
HEMEL HEMPSTEAD
Roughdown Common
Crittell's Wood
Bourne Grove
Hanging Wood
Westbrook Hay
Hay Wood
Club Ho.
Lit Hay Fm
Club House
Little Hay Golf Course
BOURNE END LANE
Coleshill Wood
SHEETHANGER COMMON GOLF COURSE
BOX LANE
B4505
HP3
Felden
Felden Lo.
Howes Retreat
Water Tower
Ramacre Wood
BURY WOOD
Lwr Dads Wood
LONGCROFT LA.
Felden Grange
Longcroft Fm
Felden Orchard
FEATHERBED LANE

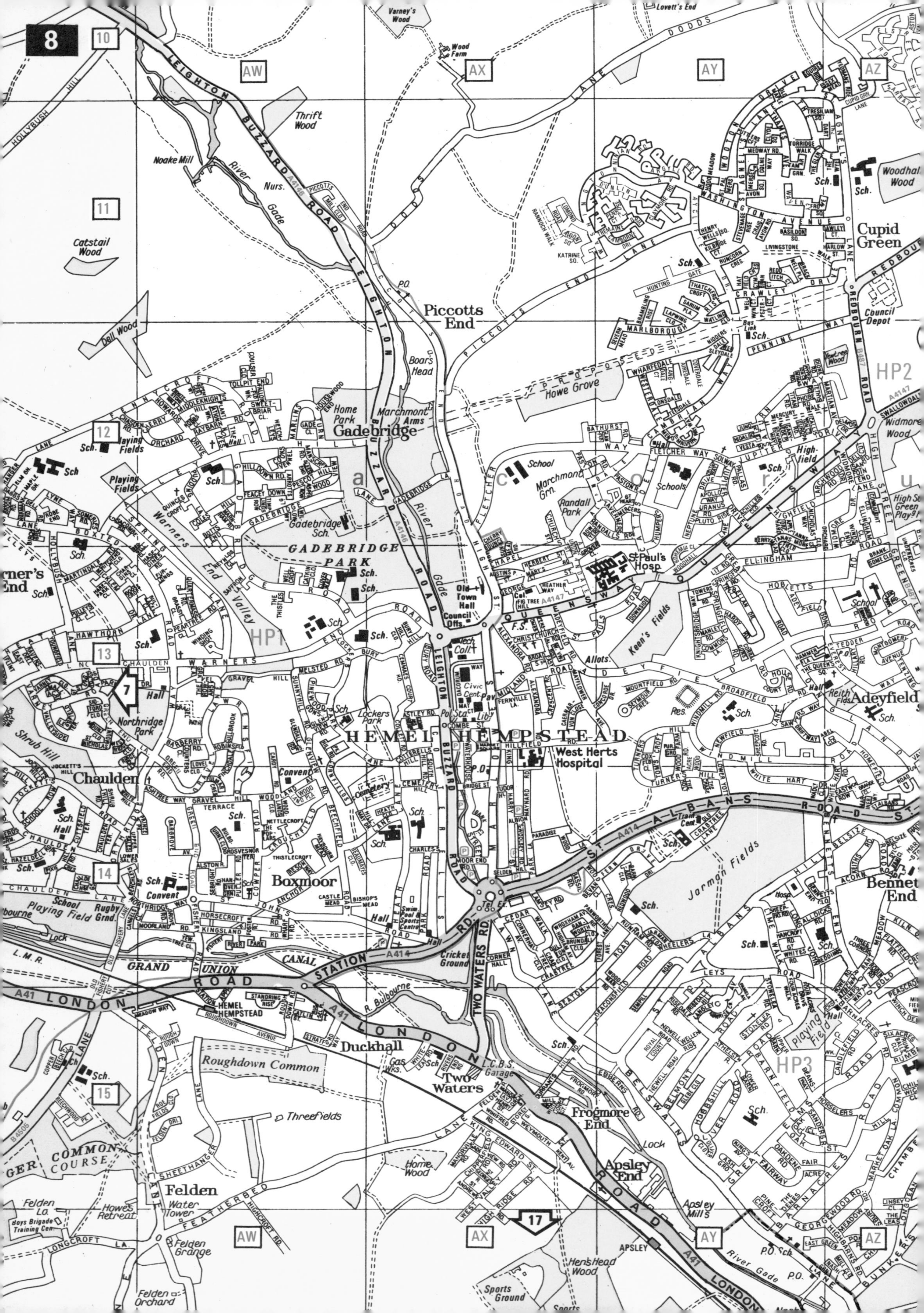

8
10
11
12
13
14
15
7
17
AW
AX
AY
AZ
HP1
HP2
HP3
Varney's Wood
Lovett's End
Wood Farm
DODDS LANE
Thrift Wood
Noake Mill
River Gade
Nurs.
LEIGHTON BUZZARD ROAD
Catstail Wood
Dell Wood
Piccotts End
PICCOTTS END LANE
Boar's Head
Howe Grove
PROPOSED
Cupid Green
WASHINGTON AVENUE
Woodhall Wood
REDBOURN ROAD
Council Depot
Ventree Wood
Widmore Wood
Home Park
Marchmont Arms
Gadebridge
Playing Fields
GADEBRIDGE PARK
Gadebridge Sch.
Warners End Valley
School
Marchmond Grn.
Randall Park
Schools
High-field
St Paul's Hosp.
QUEENSWAY
Keen's Fields
Old Town Hall
Council Offs.
Tech. Coll.
Civic Cent.
Lib.
HEMEL HEMPSTEAD
West Herts Hospital
Adeyfield
ADEYFIELD ROAD
Res.
Northridge Park
Shrub Hill
Chaulden
CHAULDEN LANE
Lockers Park
Cemetery
Convent
Boxmoor
ST. ALBANS ROAD
Jarman Fields
Bennetts End
School Playing Field
Rugby Grnd.
GRAND UNION CANAL
L.M.R.
STATION ROAD
LONDON ROAD
A41
A414
A4146
A4147
Cricket Ground
TWO WATERS RD.
HEMEL HEMPSTEAD
R. Bulbourne
Duckhall
Roughdown Common
Gas Wks.
L.C.B.S. Garage
Two Waters
Frogmore End
Threefields
Home Wood
Apsley End
Lock
Apsley Mills
APSLEY
River Gade
Felden
Felden La.
Howes Retreat
Boys Brigade Training Cen.
Water Tower
FEATHERBED
Felden Grange
LONGCROFT LA.
Hen's Head Wood
Sports Ground
Felden Orchard
GER COMMON COURSE
Playing Field

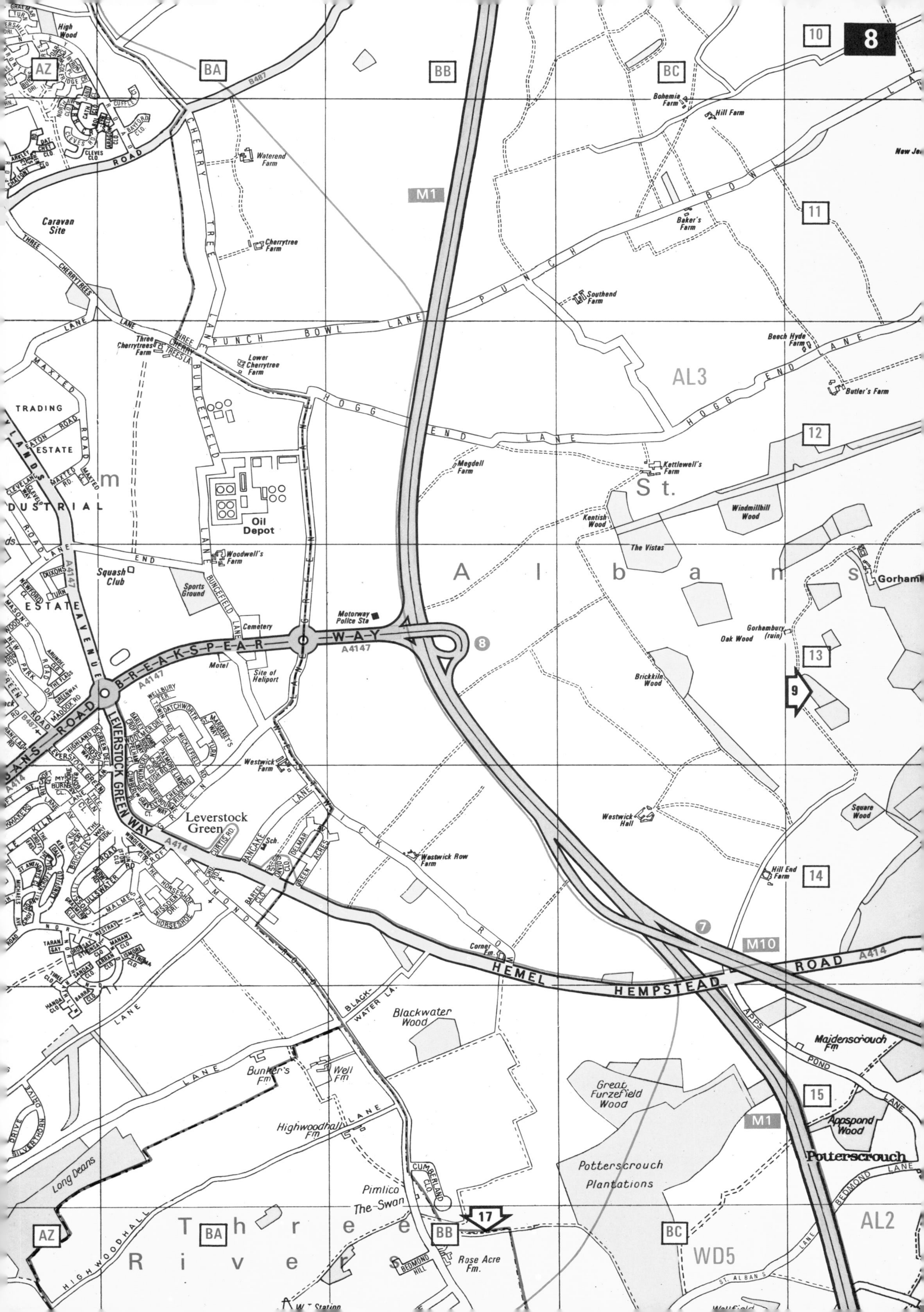
AZ
BA
BB
BC
10
11
12
13
14
15
9
17
High Wood
B487
Bohemia Farm
Hill Farm
New Jersey
Waterend Farm
M1
Caravan Site
THREE CHERRYTREES LANE
Cherrytree Farm
CHERRY TREE LANE
PUNCH BOWL LANE
Baker's Farm
Southend Farm
Three Cherrytrees Farm
Lower Cherrytree Farm
Beech Hyde Farm
HOGG END LANE
AL3
Butler's Farm
TRADING ESTATE
MAXTED ROAD
BUNCEFIELD LANE
Megdell Farm
Kettlewell's Farm
St. Albans
Windmillhill Wood
Kentish Wood
INDUSTRIAL
Oil Depot
The Vistas
Woodwell's Farm
Squash Club
Sports Ground
ESTATE
Gorhambury
Motorway Police Sta.
Cemetery
BREAKSPEAR WAY
A4147
Gorhambury (ruin)
Oak Wood
Motel
Site of Heliport
Brickkiln Wood
LEVERSTOCK GREEN WAY
Westwick Farm
Leverstock Green
A414
Westwick Hall
Square Wood
Westwick Row Farm
Hill End Farm
M10
Corner Fm.
HEMEL HEMPSTEAD ROAD
BEDMOND ROAD
BLACKWATER LANE
Blackwater Wood
APPS POND LANE
Maidenscrouch Fm
Bunker's Fm
Well Fm
Great Furzefield Wood
Appspond Wood
Highwoodhall Fm
Potterscrouch
Potterscrouch Plantations
Long Deans
Pimlico
The Swan
AL2
Three Rivers
WD5
Rose Acre Fm.
BEDMOND HILL
HIGHWOODHALL LANE
ST. ALBANS LANE

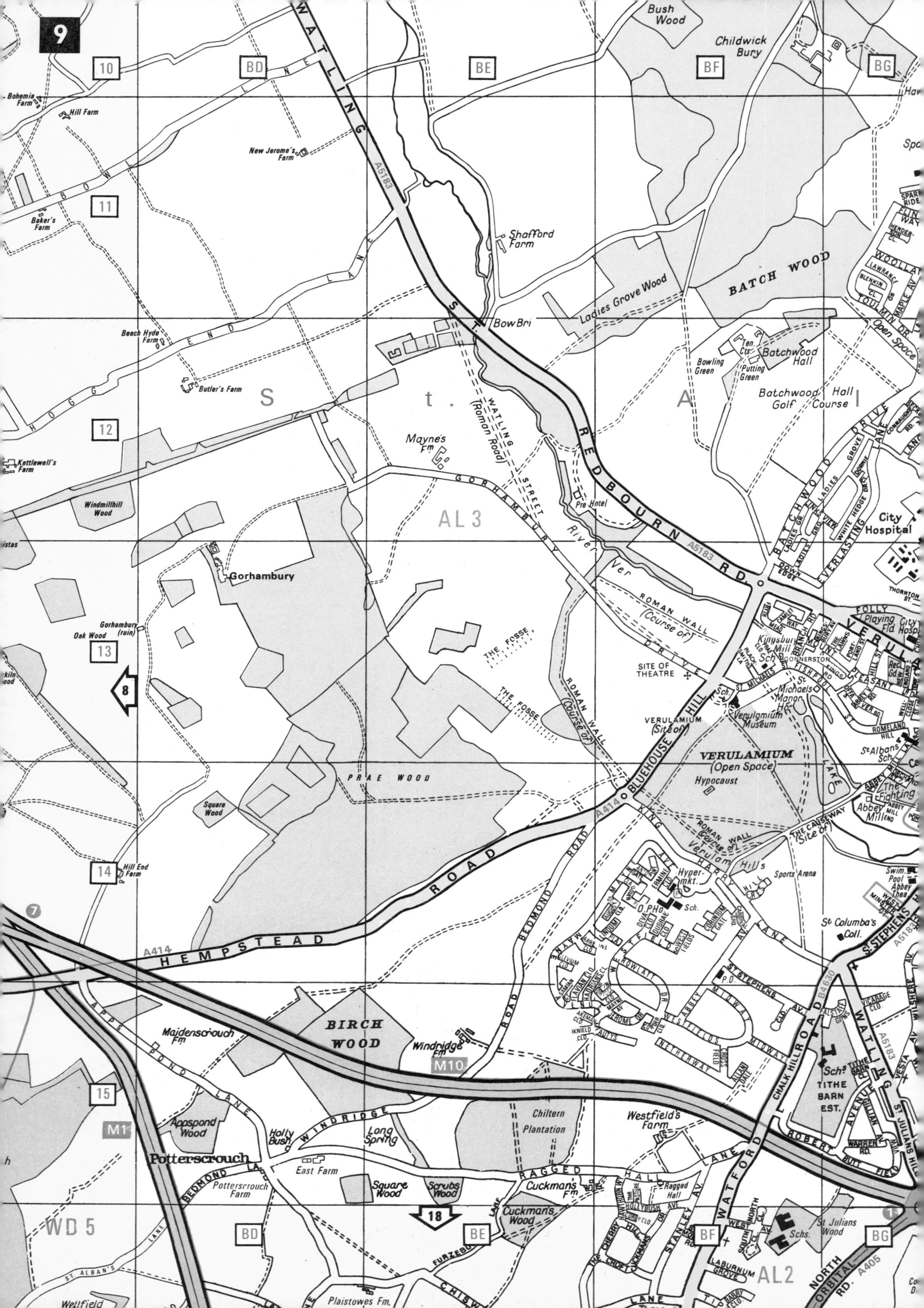

9
10
11
12
13
14
15
BD
BE
BF
BG
Bush Wood
Childwick Bury
Bohemia Farm
Hill Farm
New Jerome's Farm
Baker's Farm
BOW LANE
WATLING ST.
A5183
Shafford Farm
Ladies Grove Wood
BATCH WOOD
Bow Bri
Beech Hyde Farm
HOGG END LANE
Butler's Farm
S t . A l
Bowling Green
Ten. Cts.
Putting Green
Batchwood Hall
Batchwood Hall Golf Course
WATLING STREET (Roman Road)
Mayne's Fm
REDBOURN RD.
Kettlewell's Farm
Windmillhill Wood
GORHAMBURY DRIVE
AL3
Pre Hotel
River Ver
City Hospital
Gorhambury
ROMAN WALL (Course of)
Gorhambury (ruin)
Oak Wood
THE FOSSE
SITE OF THEATRE
8
ROMAN WALL (Course of)
VERULAMIUM (Site of)
Verulamium Museum
VERULAMIUM (Open Space)
Hypocaust
BLUEHOUSE HILL
PRAE WOOD
Square Wood
A414
KING HARRY LANE
ROMAN WALL (Course of)
Verulam Hills
THE CAUSEWAY (Site of)
Sports Arena
Hill End Farm
HEMPSTEAD ROAD
BEDMOND ROAD
Hyper-mkt.
Sch.
St Columba's Coll.
ST STEPHENS AV
A414
APPS POND LANE
Maidenscrouch Fm
BIRCH WOOD
Windridge Fm
M10
WESTFIELDS
NETHERWAY
MIDWAY
CHALK HILL ROAD
WATLING ST.
TITHE BARN EST.
Chiltern Plantation
Westfield's Farm
ROBERT BUTT FIELD
Appspond Wood
M1
Holly Bush
WINDRIDGE
Long Spring
Potterscrouch
East Farm
BEDMOND LANE
Potterscrouch Farm
Square Wood
Scrubs Wood
RAGGED HALL LANE
Cuckman's Fm
Ragged Hall
Cuckman's Wood
18
WD5
WATFORD RD.
St Julians Wood
Schs.
LABURNUM GROVE
AL2
NORTH ORBITAL RD.
A405
ST. ALBAN'S LANE
Wellfield
Plaistowes Fm.

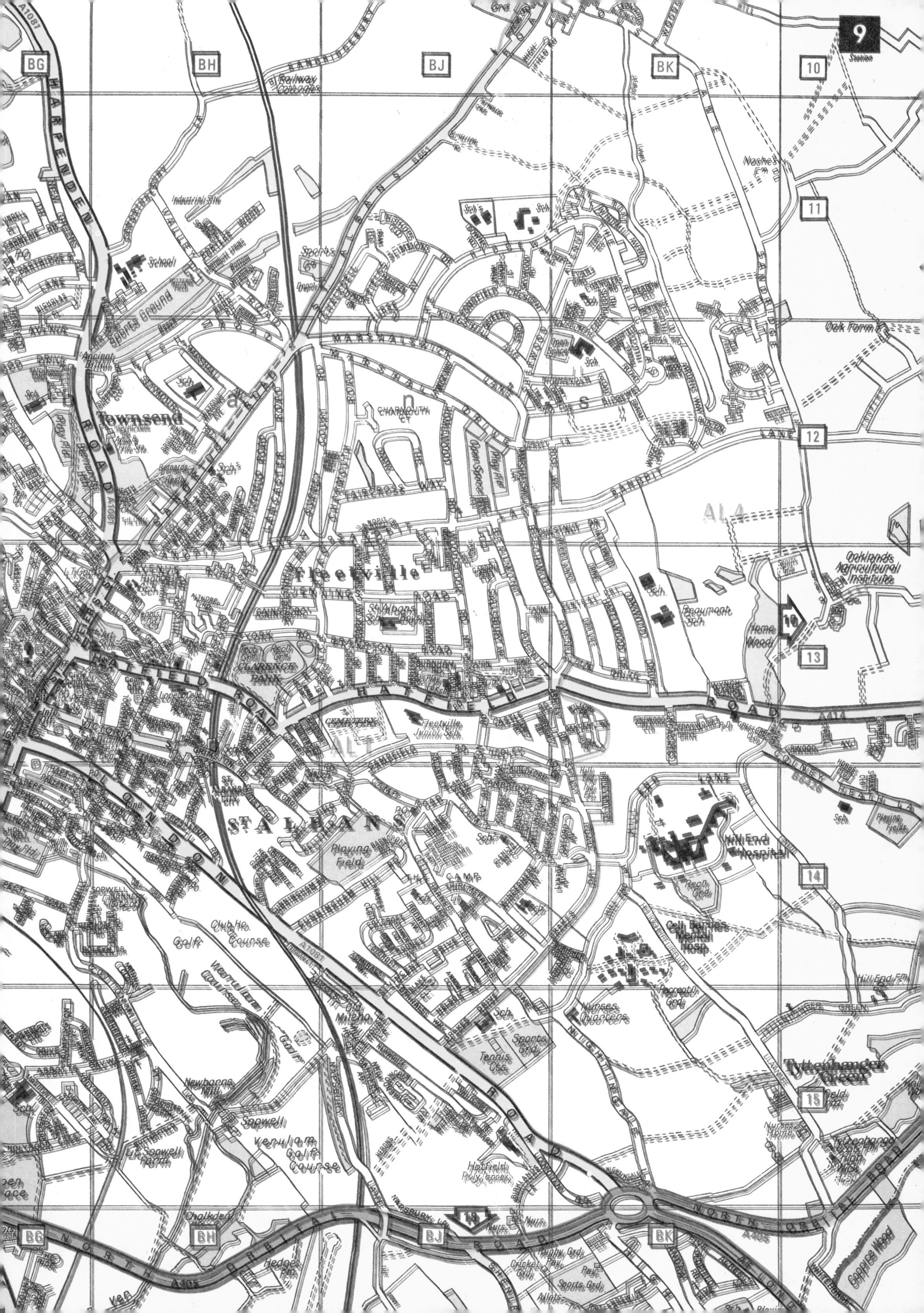
BG
BH
BJ
BK
10
11
12
13
14
15
Station
Railway Cottages
HARPENDEN ROAD
A1081
Industrial Site
School
Sports Ground
Townsend
Play Fld.
Sports Gd.
MARSHALSWICK LANE
Sch.
Open Space
Play Fld.
Nashe's Fm.
Oak Farm
SANDRIDGE
SANDPIT LANE
CHARMOUTH CT
FAIRCROSS WAY
AL4
Fleetville
JENNINGS ROAD
Oaklands Agricultural Institute
Beaumont Sch.
Home Wood
HATFIELD ROAD
A414
CLARENCE PARK
Cemetery
Fleetville Junior Sch.
AL1
ST. ALBANS
VICTORIA
LONDON ROAD
Playing Field
CAMP
Hill End Hospital
Recn. Grd.
Cell Barnes Mental Hosp.
Playing Fields
Club Ho.
Golf Course
A1081
Verulam Course
Hill End Fm.
Nurses Quarters
NIGHTINGALE
Sch.
Sports Grd.
Tennis Ccs.
Tyttenhanger Green
Newbarns Mill
Sopwell Mill
Verulam Golf Course
Sopwell
Hatfield Polytechnic
Chalkdell
Hedges
NORTH ORBITAL ROAD
A405
Rugby Grd.
Cricket Grd.
Sports Grd.
Allots.
Coppice Wood

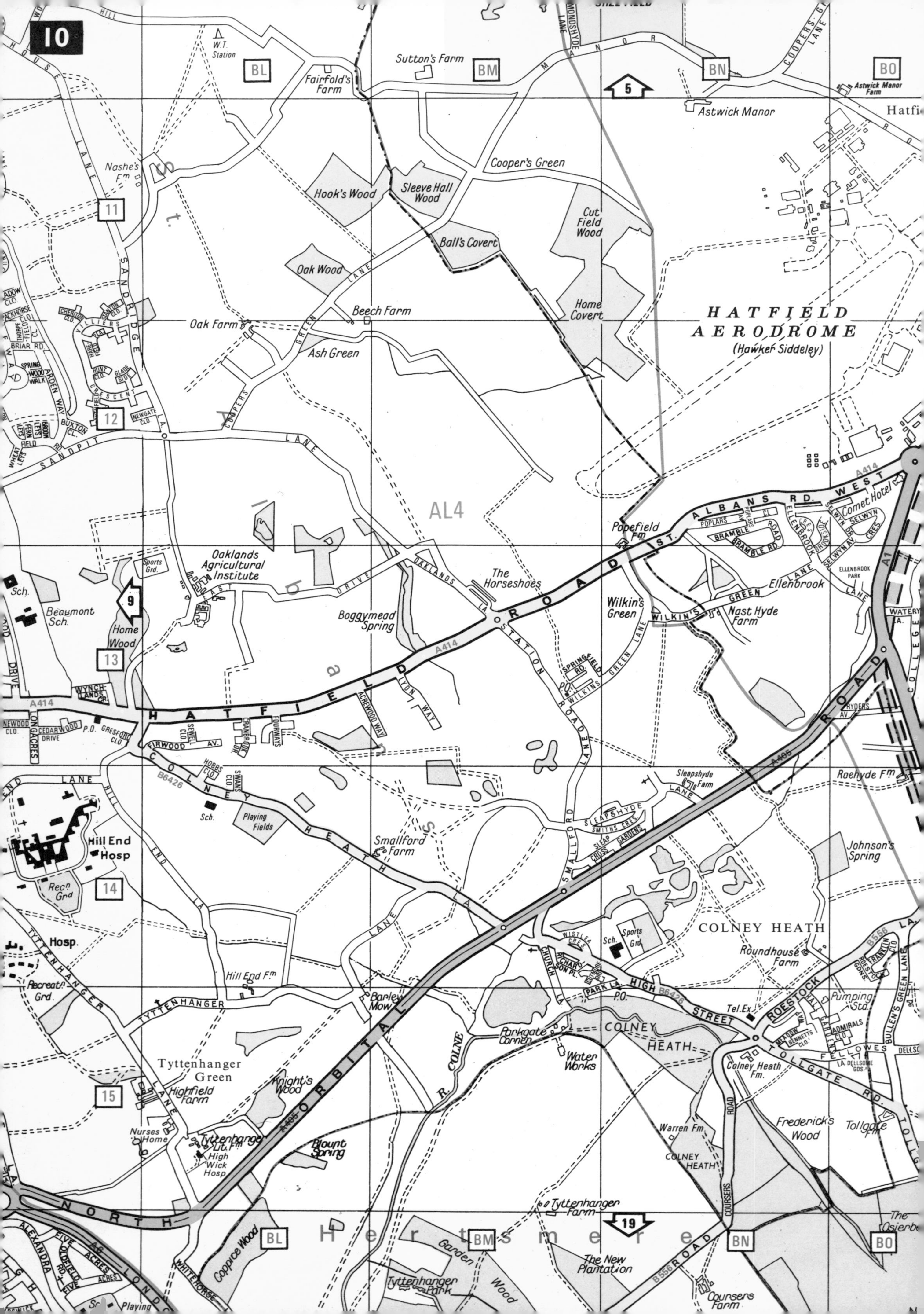

Hatfield Aerodrome (Hawker Siddeley)
AL4
St. Albans
Hertsmere
Colney Heath
Sutton's Farm
Fairfold's Farm
Astwick Manor
Astwick Manor Farm
W.T. Station
Manor Rd
Coopers Green Lane
Cooper's Green
Hook's Wood
Sleeve Hall Wood
Ball's Covert
Cut Field Wood
Home Covert
Oak Wood
Beech Farm
Oak Farm
Ash Green
Green Lane
Coopers Lane
Sandpit Lane
Sandridge La.
Nashe's Fm
House Lane
Oaklands Agricultural Institute
Oaklands Drive
Oaklands La.
The Horseshoes
Popefield Fm
St. Albans Rd. West
Hatfield Road
A414
Comet Hotel
Ellenbrook
Ellenbrook Lane
Ellenbrook Park
Nast Hyde Farm
Wilkin's Green
Wilkin's Green Lane
Boggymead Spring
Station Road
Smallford Lane
Sleapshyde
Sleapshyde Farm
Sleapshyde Lane
Smiths Cres.
Sleap Cross Gardens
Roehyde Fm
Ryders Av.
Watery La.
Johnson's Spring
Road
A405
A1
Beaumont Sch.
Home Wood
Sports Grd.
Sch.
Hill End Hosp
Hosp.
Recn Grd
Recreatn Grd.
Hill End Lane
Colney Heath La.
B6426
Playing Fields
Smallford Farm
Hill End Fm
Barley Mow
Tyttenhanger
Tyttenhanger Green
Highfield Farm
Highfield Lane
Nurses Home
Tyttenhanger Lt. Fm
High Wick Hosp
Knight's Wood
Blount Spring
North Orbital Road
R. Colne
Parkgate Corner
Water Works
Church La.
Park La.
High Street
P.O.
Tel. Ex.
Roestock
Roundhouse Farm
Pumping Sta.
Tollgate Rd.
Tollgate Fm
Fredericks Wood
Colney Heath Fm.
Warren Fm
Coursers Road
Coursers Farm
Tyttenhanger Farm
The New Plantation
Garden Wood
Tyttenhanger Park
Coppice Wood
B556 Road
Bullen's Green Lane
Fellowes
Dellsome
The Osierbed
Alexandra
Five Acres
Whitehorse
London
A6
Playing
Firwood Av.
Lyon Way
Acrewood Way
Fourways
Cranbrook Dr.
Gresford Clo.
Cedarwood Drive
Longacres
Wynchlands Cr.
Buxton Cl.
Newgate Clo.
Villiers Crescent
Arden Way
Briar Rd
Springfield Rd.
Wilkins Green
Poplars
Bramble Rd
Selwyn Av
Selwyn Cres.
Wistlea Cres.
Richardson Pl.
Bennetts Clo.
Admirals Clo.
Franklin Clo.
Hatfi
BL
BM
BN
BO
5
9
11
12
13
14
15
19

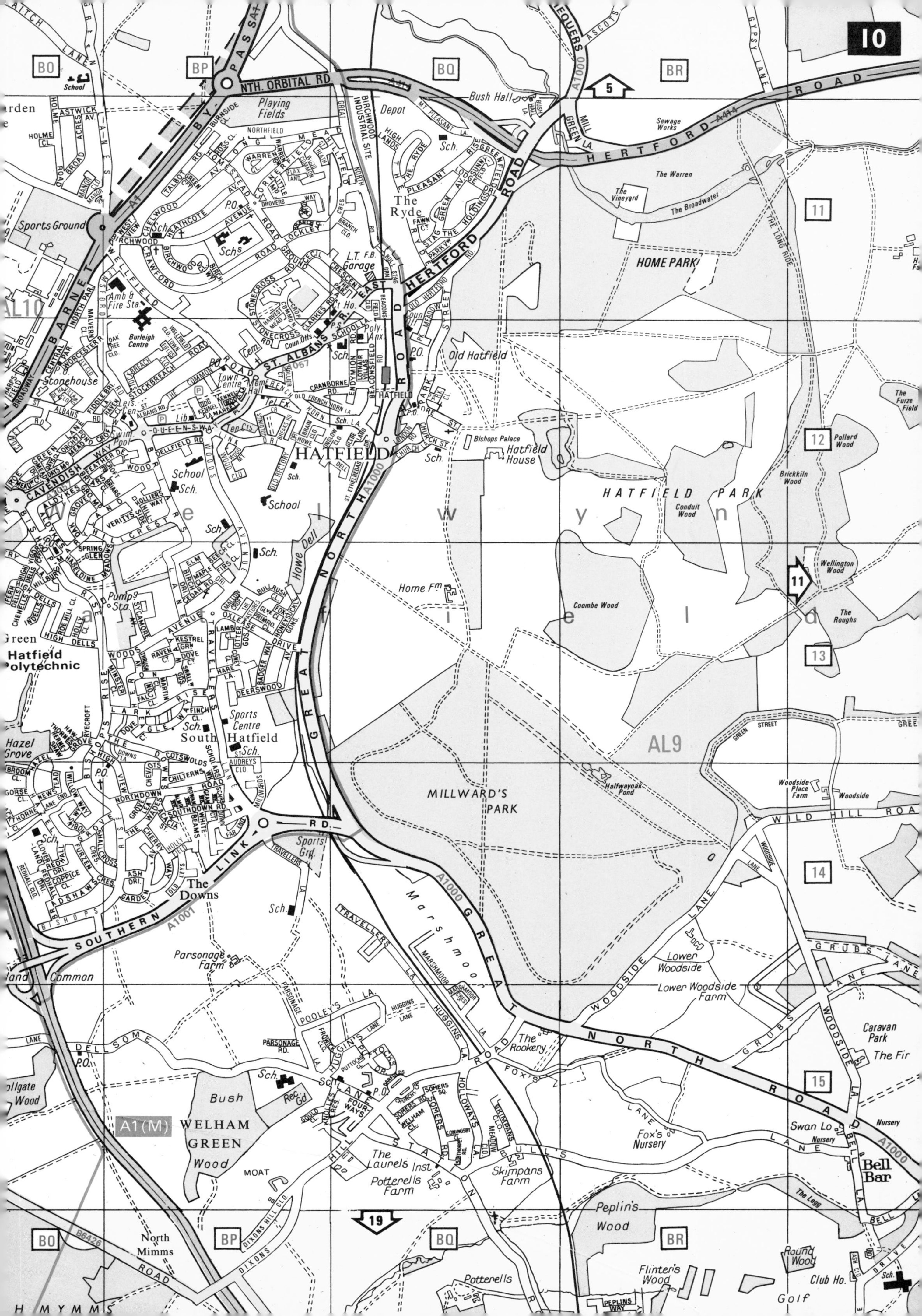
10
BO
BP
BQ
BR
5
11
12
13
14
15
19
NTH. ORBITAL RD.
HERTFORD ROAD
BARNET BY-PASS
A1
A414
A1000
A1001
A1(M)
B6426
Playing Fields
Birchwood Industrial Site
Depot
Bush Hall
Sewage Works
The Warren
The Vineyard
The Broadwater
The Long Ride
HOME PARK
The Ryde
Sports Ground
Amb & Fire Sta.
Burleigh Centre
Stonehouse
Town Centre
Old Hatfield
HATFIELD
Bishops Palace
Hatfield House
HATFIELD PARK
Conduit Wood
Brickkiln Wood
Pollard Wood
The Furze Field
Wellington Wood
Coombe Wood
The Roughs
Home Fm
Howe Dell
Welwyn Hatfield
Hatfield Polytechnic
Hazel Grove
South Hatfield
Sports Centre
AL9
AL10
Halfwayoak Pond
MILLWARD'S PARK
GREAT NORTH ROAD
SOUTHERN LINK RD.
The Downs
Marshmoor
Woodside Place Farm
Woodside
WILD HILL ROAD
Lower Woodside
Lower Woodside Farm
Caravan Park
The Fir
Swan Lo
Nursery
Bell Bar
Parsonage Farm
Common
The Rookery
Fox's Nursery
Bush Wood
WELHAM GREEN
Wood
MOAT
The Laurels Inst.
Potterells Farm
Skimpans Farm
Peplin's Wood
The Legg
Round Wood
Flinter's Wood
Club Ho.
Golf
Potterells
North Mimms
H MYMMS
Tollgate Wood

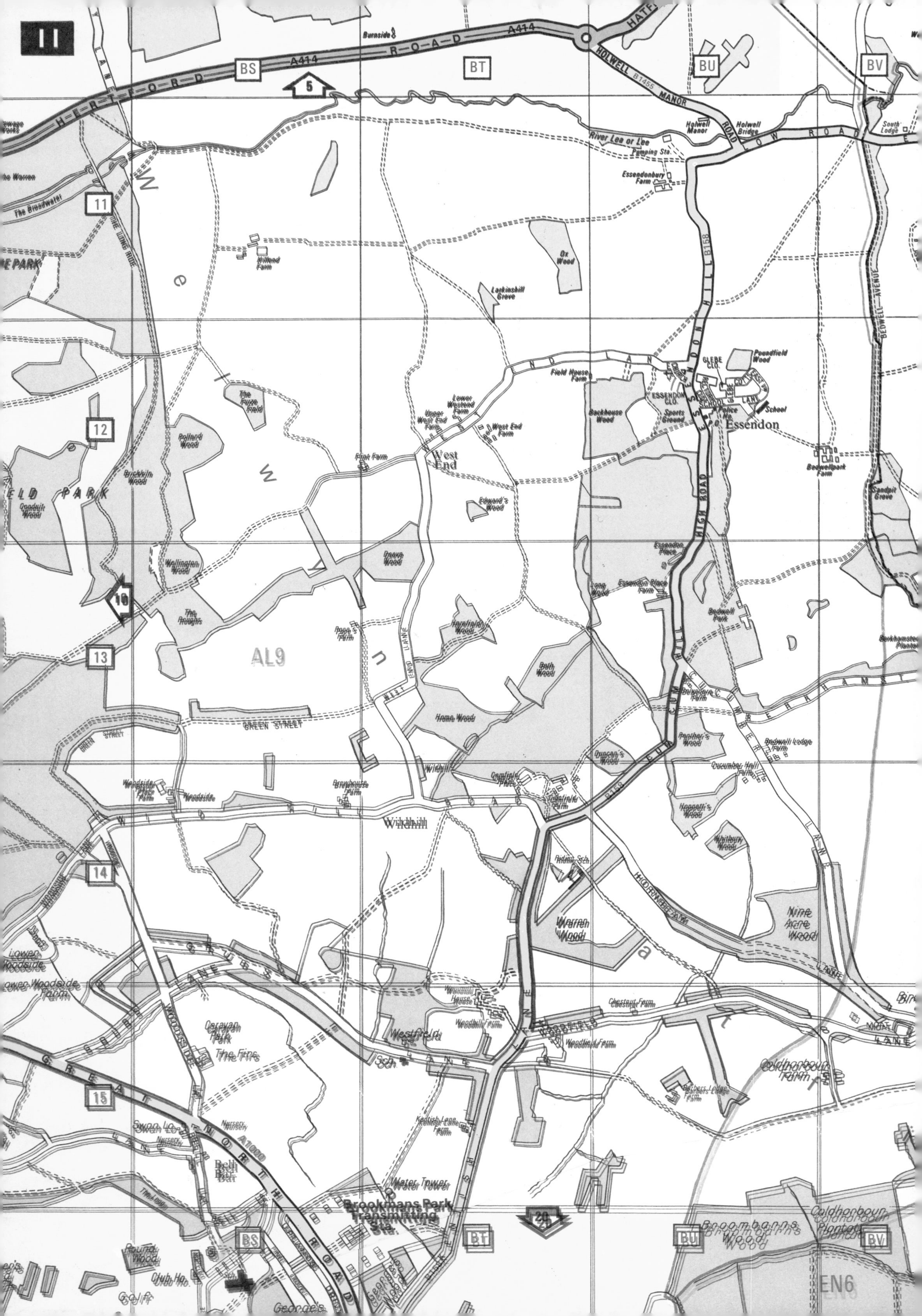
11
HERTFORD ROAD A414
HOLWELL MANOR B1455
BS
BT
BU
BV
5
Burnside
River Lea or Lee
Holwell Manor
Holwell Bridge
LOW ROAD
South Lodge
Pumping Sta.
Essendonbury Farm
The Warren
The Broadwater
THE LONG RIDE
11
12
13
14
15
10
Ox Wood
Larkinshill Grove
ESSENDON HILL B158
BEDWELL AVENUE
Poundfield Wood
GLEBE CLO.
Field House Farm
ESSENDON CLO.
SCHOOL LANE
Sports Ground
Police Ho.
School
Essendon
Backhouse Wood
Lower Westend Farm
Upper West End Farm
West End Farm
West End
Flint Farm
Bedwellpark Farm
Sandpit Grove
Pollard Wood
Brickkiln Wood
The Furze Field
Conduit Wood
Edward's Wood
Drove Wood
Wellington Wood
The Roughs
HIGH ROAD
Essendon Place
Long Wood
Essendon Place Farm
Bedwell Park
Harefield Wood
Bath Wood
AL9
WEST END LANE
Home Wood
GREEN STREET
Woodside Place Farm
Woodside
Brewhouse Farm
Wildhill
WILDHILL ROAD
Camfield Place
Camfield Farm
Duncan's Wood
Panther's Wood
Bedwell Lodge Farm
Cucumber Hill Farm
Hornbeam Lane
Hoppett's Wood
Whitbury Wood
Riding Sch.
Warren Wood
Nine Acre Wood
Lower Woodside
Lower Woodside Farm
Woodhill House
Woodhill Farm
Westfield
Chestnut Farm
Woodfield Farm
WOODFIELD LANE
MOTT LANE
Caravan Park
The Firs
Coldharbour Farm
Barbers Lodge Farm
Kentish Lane Farm
Swan Lo.
Nursery
GREAT NORTH ROAD A1000
Bell Bar
Water Tower
Brookmans Park Transmitting Stn.
Round Wood
Club Ho.
Golf
George's
20
Broombanks Wood
Coldharbour Plantation
EN6
KENTISH LANE

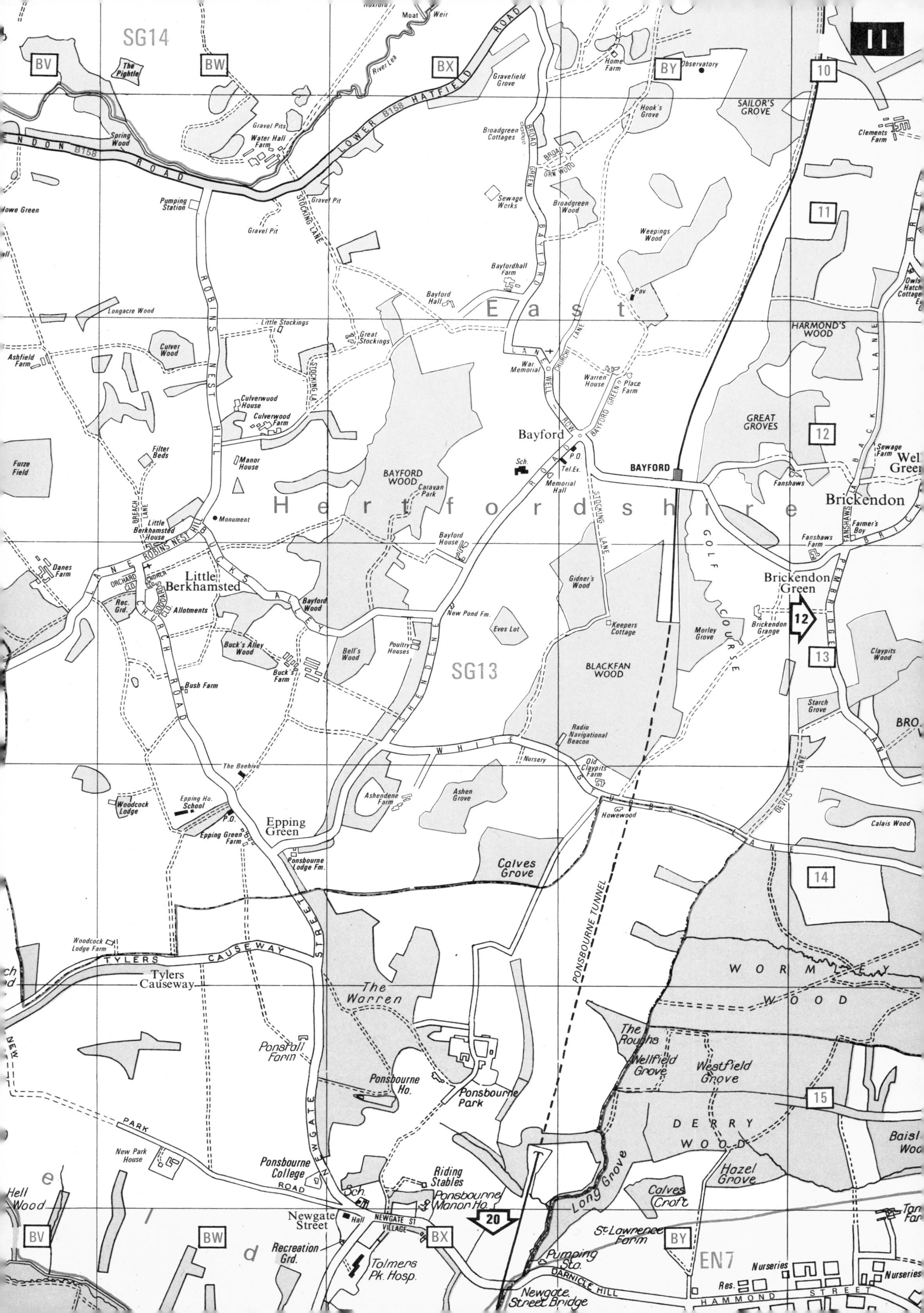

11
SG14
BV
BW
BX
BY
10
Moat
Weir
River Lea
The Pightle
Spring Wood
LOWER B158 HATFIELD ROAD
Gravefield Grove
Home Farm
Observatory
SAILOR'S GROVE
Clements Farm
Gravel Pits
Water Hall Farm
Hook's Grove
Broadgreen Cottages
BROAD GREEN
BROAD GRN WOOD
Pumping Station
Gravel Pit
STOCKING LANE
Sewage Works
Broadgreen Wood
Weepings Wood
11
Bayfordhall Farm
BAYFORD
Bayford Hall
Pav
East
Longacre Wood
Little Stockings
Great Stockings
Culver Wood
Ashfield Farm
HARMOND'S WOOD
War Memorial
CHURCH LANE
WELL ROW
Warren House
Place Farm
BAYFORD GREEN
Culverwood House
Culverwood Farm
GREAT GROVES
BACK LANE
Bayford
12
Sewage Farm
Filter Beds
Manor House
Sch.
P.O.
Tel.Ex.
Memorial Hall
BAYFORD
Furze Field
BAYFORD WOOD
Caravan Park
Fanshaws
Brickendon
Monument
Hertfordshire
BREACH LANE
Little Berkhamsted House
ROBINS NEST HILL
Bayford House
GOLF COURSE
Fanshaws Farm
Farmer's Boy
FANSHAWS LANE
Danes Farm
Little Berkhamsted
ORCHARD CLO.
CHURCH CLO.
GODDARDS CLO.
BUCKS ALLEY
Gidner's Wood
STOCKING LANE
Brickendon Green
PEMBRIDGE
Rec. Grd.
Allotments
Bayford Wood
New Pond Fm.
Eves Lot
Keepers Cottage
Morley Grove
Brickendon Grange
12
13
Buck's Alley Wood
Bell's Wood
Poultry Houses
Claypits Wood
Buck's Farm
SG13
BLACKFAN WOOD
CHURCH ROAD
Bush Farm
ASHENDENE
Starch Grove
Radio Navigational Beacon
WHITE
Nursery
DEVILS LANE
The Beehive
Old Claypits Farm
STUDDS
Ashendene Farm
Ashen Grove
Howewood
Epping Ho. School
Woodcock Lodge
P.O.
Epping Green
Epping Green Farm
Calais Wood
LANE
Ponsbourne Lodge Fm.
Calves Grove
14
Woodcock Lodge Farm
TYLERS CAUSEWAY
Tylers Causeway
STREET
PONSBOURNE TUNNEL
WORMLEY WOOD
The Warren
The Roughs
NEW
Ponsfall Farm
Wellfield Grove
Westfield Grove
Ponsbourne Ho.
Ponsbourne Park
15
PARK
DERRY WOOD
New Park House
Ponsbourne College
NEWGATE
Riding Stables
Long Grove
Hazel Grove
Calves Croft
Hell Wood
ROAD
Sch.
Ponsbourne Manor Ho.
Newgate Street
Hall
NEWGATE ST VILLAGE
20
St Lawrence Farm
BV
BW
BX
BY
Recreation Grd.
Tolmers Pk. Hosp.
Pumping Sta.
EN7
Nurseries
Nurseries
Res.
DARNICLE HILL
HAMMOND STREET
Newgate Street Bridge

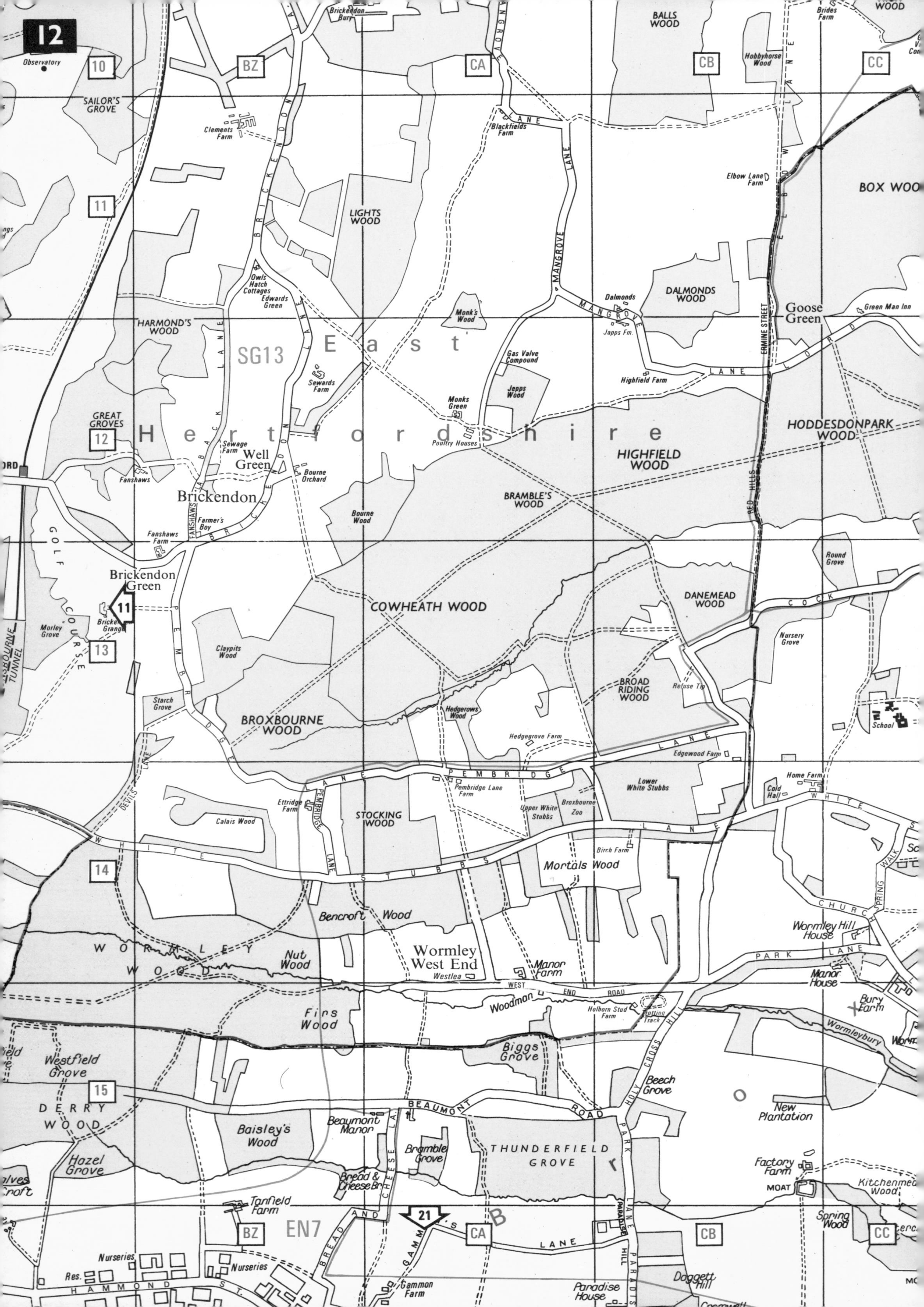
Observatory
SAILOR'S GROVE
Brickendon Bury
BALLS WOOD
Brides Farm
Hobbyhorse Wood
BZ
CA
CB
CC
10
11
12
13
14
15
Clements Farm
Blackfields Farm
LIGHTS WOOD
Elbow Lane Farm
BOX WOOD
Owls Hatch Cottages
Edwards Green
HARMOND'S WOOD
Monk's Wood
Dalmonds
DALMONDS WOOD
Goose Green
Green Man Inn
Japps Fm
SG13
East
Hertfordshire
Gas Valve Compound
Sewards Farm
Jepps Wood
Highfield Farm
Monks Green
GREAT GROVES
Poultry Houses
HODDESDONPARK WOOD
Sewage Farm
Well Green
Bourne Orchard
HIGHFIELD WOOD
Fanshaws
Brickendon
BRAMBLE'S WOOD
Bourne Wood
Farmer's Boy
Fanshaws Farm
GOLF COURSE
Brickendon Green
Round Grove
DANEMEAD WOOD
COWHEATH WOOD
Morley Grove
Brickendon Grange
Nursery Grove
BROXBOURNE TUNNEL
Claypits Wood
BROAD RIDING WOOD
Refuse Tip
Starch Grove
Hedgerows Wood
School
BROXBOURNE WOOD
Hedgegrove Farm
Edgewood Farm
Pembridge Lane Farm
Lower White Stubbs
Home Farm
Cold Hall
Ettridge Farm
STOCKING WOOD
Upper White Stubbs
Broxbourne Zoo
Calais Wood
Birch Farm
Mortals Wood
Bencroft Wood
Wormley Hill House
WORMLEY WOOD
Nut Wood
Wormley West End
Manor Farm
Westlea
Manor House
Woodman
Holborn Stud Farm
Trotting Track
Bury Farm
Firs Wood
Wormleybury
Biggs Grove
Westfield Grove
Beech Grove
DERRY WOOD
New Plantation
Beaumont Manor
Baisley's Wood
Bramble Grove
THUNDERFIELD GROVE
Hazel Grove
Factory Farm
Bread & Cheese Br
MOAT
Kitchenmead Wood
Tanfield Farm
Spring Wood
21
EN7
Nurseries
Res.
Doggett Hill
Gammon Farm
Paradise House
Fanshaws Lane
White Stubbs Lane
Pembridge Lane
Brickendon Lane
Back Lane
Mangrove Lane
Lord Lane
Ermine Street
Red Hills
Cock Lane
Church Lane
Spring Walk
Park Lane
West End Road
Holy Cross Hill
Beaumont Road
Paradise Hill
Park Lane
Bread and Cheese La.
Gammon's Lane
Hammond St.
Devils Lane

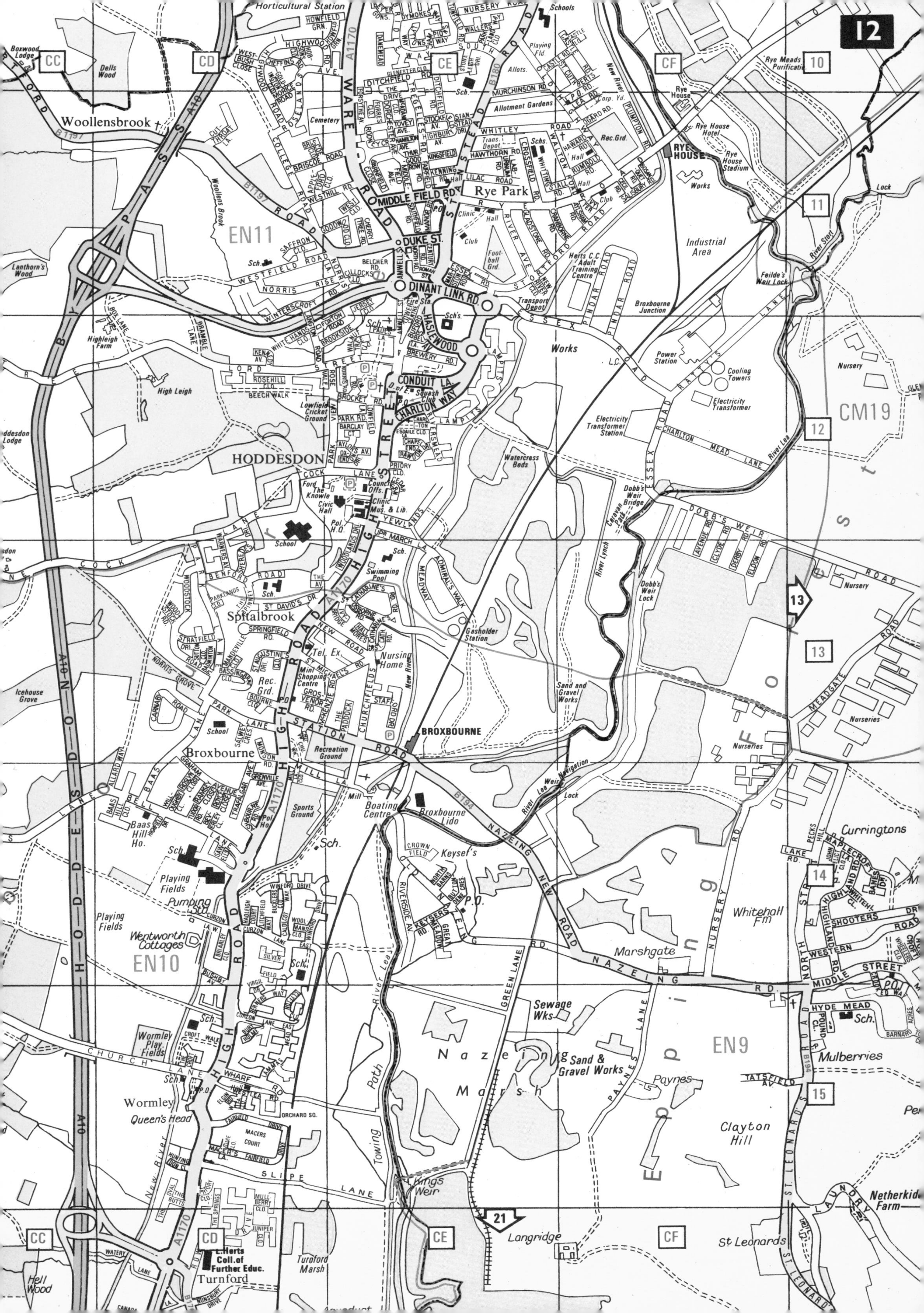

Horticultural Station
Woollensbrook
HODDESDON
Rye Park
Spitalbrook
Broxbourne
BROXBOURNE
Wormley
Turnford
EN11
EN10
EN9
CM19
Nazeing Marsh
Epping Forest
Industrial Area
Rye House
Broxbourne Lido
Marshgate
Whitehall Fm
Clayton Hill
St Leonards
Netherkidd Farm
Curringtons
Mulberries
Paynes
Langridge
Turnford Marsh
Hell Wood
Kings Weir
E. Herts Coll. of Further Educ.
CC
CD
CE
CF
10
11
12
13
14
15
21

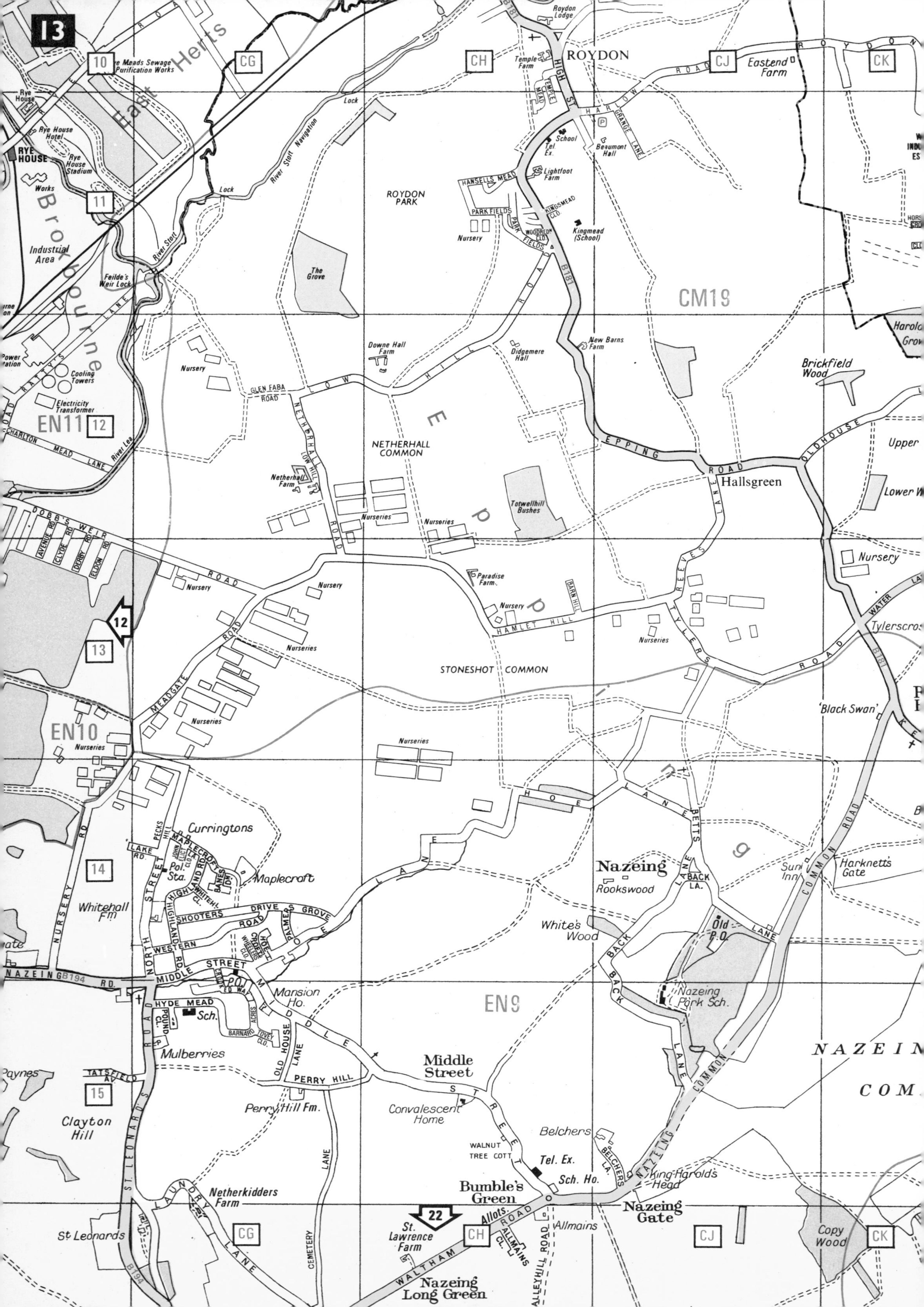
13
Roydon
Roydon Lodge
Temple Farm
High St.
Harlow Road
Grange Lane
School
Beaumont Hall
Lightfoot Farm
Hansells Mead
Park Fields
Kingsmead Cl.
Woodred Clo.
Kingmead (School)
Roydon Park
Nursery
Eastend Farm
Rye House
Rye House Hotel
Rye House Stadium
Rye Meads Sewage Purification Works
East Herts
River Stort Navigation
Lock
River Stort
Feilde's Weir Lock
Broxbourne
Industrial Area
Works
Power Station
Cooling Towers
Electricity Transformer
Ratty's Lane
Charlton Mead Lane
River Lea
EN11
EN10
EN9
CM19
The Grove
Downe Hall Farm
Didgemere Hall
New Barns Farm
Low Hill Road
Glen Faba Road
Netherhall Road
Netherhall Common
Netherhall Farm
Nurseries
Totwellhill Bushes
Epping Road
Hallsgreen
Oldhouse
Brickfield Wood
Harold's Grove
Upper
Lower
Reeves Lane
Dobb's Weir Road
Avenue Rd.
Clyde Rd.
Derby Rd.
Eldon Rd.
Paradise Farm
Hamlet Hill
Barn Hill
Tylers Road
Water Lane
Tylerscross
Stoneshot Common
Meadgate Road
'Black Swan'
Hoe Lane
Betts Lane
Back La.
Nazeing
Rookswood
White's Wood
Old P.O.
Nazeing Park Sch.
Back Lane
Common Road
Sun Inn
Harknetts Gate
Nazeing Common
Curringtons
Maplecroft
Pecks Hill
Lake Rd.
North Street
Pol. Sta.
Highland Rd.
Shooters Drive
Palmers Grove
Western Rd.
Middle Street
Nazeing B194 Rd.
Hyde Mead
Pound Cl.
Sch.
Mansion Ho.
Old House Lane
Perry Hill
Perry Hill Fm.
Mulberries
Tatsfield Av.
Paynes
Clayton Hill
Nursery Rd.
Whitehall Fm.
Middle Street
Convalescent Home
Belchers
Belchers La.
Walnut Tree Cott
Tel. Ex.
Sch. Ho.
King Harolds Head
Bumble's Green
Nazeing Gate
Allmains
Alleyhill Road
Waltham Road
St. Lawrence Farm
Nazeing Long Green
Cemetery Lane
Laundry Lane
Netherkidders Farm
St Leonards
St. Leonard's Road
Copy Wood
CG
CH
CJ
CK
10
11
12
13
14
15
22

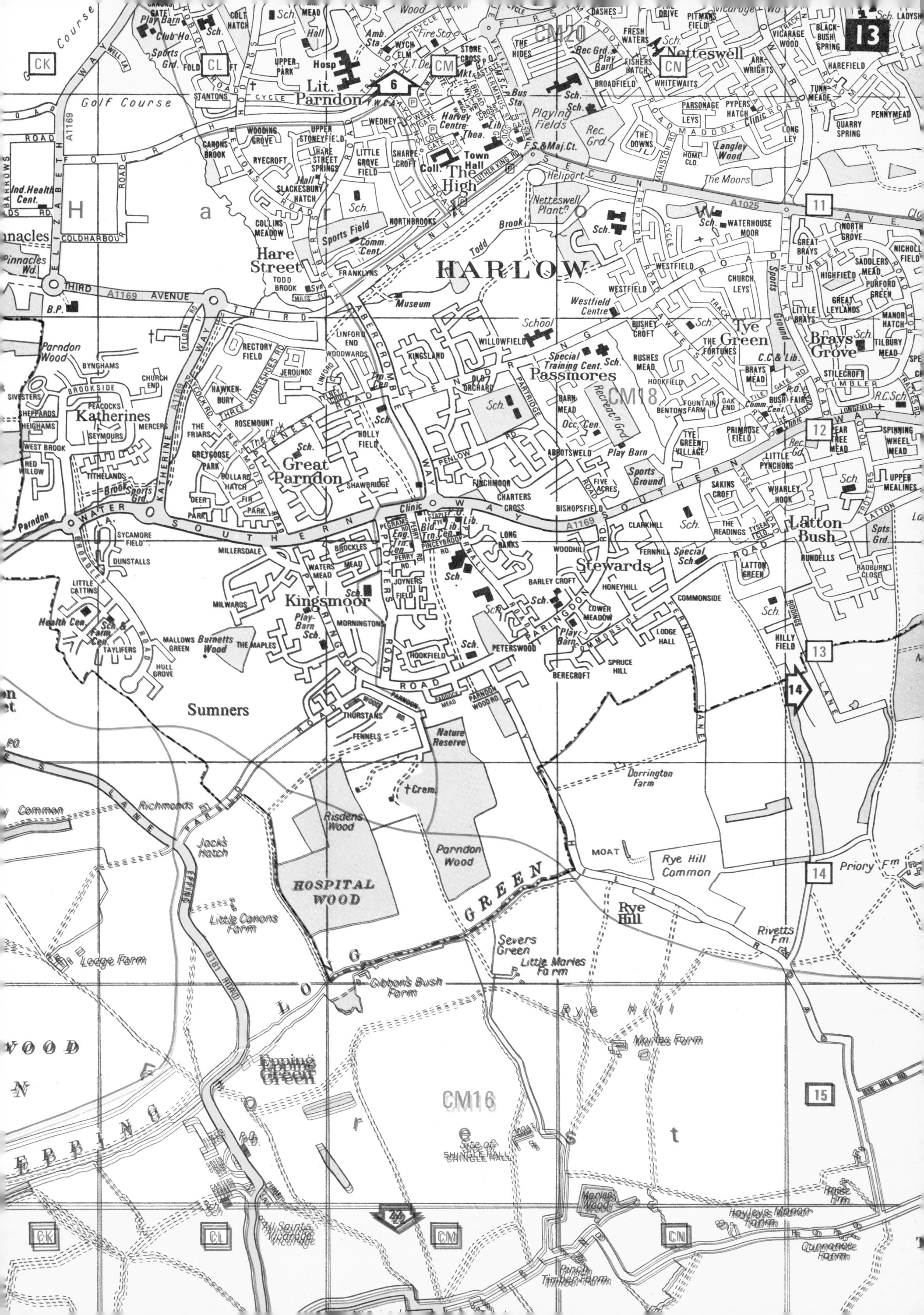
CK
CL
CM
CN
Golf Course
Play Barn
Club Ho.
Sports Grd.
Sch.
COLT HATCH
STANTONS
UPPER PARK
Hosp
Amb. Sta.
Fire Sta.
WYCH ELM
STONE CROSS
Lit. Parndon
6
CM20
DASHES
THE DRIVE
PITMANS FIELD
THE HIDES
FRESH WATERS
Netteswell
Rec Grd.
Play Barn
FISHERS HATCH
BROADFIELD
WHITEWAITS
ARKWRIGHTS
VICARAGE WOOD
BLACKBUSH SPRING
HAREFIELD
TUNNMEADE
PENNYMEAD
QUARRY SPRING
LONG LEY
PARSONAGE LEYS
PYPERS HATCH
THE DOWNS
HOME CLO.
Langley Wood
The Moors
Golf Course
ROAD
A1169
Ind. Health Cent.
H
a
r
l
o
w
COLDHARBOUR
Pinnacles Wd.
Playing Fields
Rec. Grd.
Bus Sta.
F.S.& Maj.Ct.
Harvey Centre
Thea.
Lib.
Town Hall
Coll.
The High
Heliport
SECOND AVENUE
A1025
11
WOODING GROVE
CANONS BROOK
UPPER STONEYFIELD
RYECROFT
HARE STREET SPRINGS
LITTLE GROVE FIELD
SHARPECROFT
WEDNEY
SLACKESBURY HATCH
COLLINS MEADOW
Sports Field
Comm. Cent.
NORTHBROOKS
Hare Street
TODD BROOK
FRANKLYNS
Museum
Todd Brook
Netteswell Plantn
WATERHOUSE MOOR
WESTFIELD
Westfield Centre
HARLOW
CHURCH LEYS
GREAT BRAYS
NORTH GROVE
NICHOLLS FIELD
SADDLERS MEAD
HIGHFIELD
PURFORD GREEN
GREAT LEYLANDS
LITTLE BRAYS
MANOR HATCH
Brays Grove
TILBURY MEAD
THIRD AVENUE
A1169
B.P.
Parndon Wood
BYNGHAMS
SIVESTERS
SHEPPARDS
HEIGHAMS
PEACOCKS
BROOKSIDE
CHURCH END
Katherines
MERCERS
SEYMOURS
WEST BROOK
RED WILLOW
TITHELANDS
Sports Grd.
RECTORY FIELD
HAWKENBURY
JEROUNDS
LINFORD END
WOODWARDS
KINGSLAND
WILLOWFIELD
School
BUSHEY CROFT
Special Training Cent.
Passmores
RUSHES MEAD
THE FORTUNES
Tye Green
C.C.& Lib.
BRAYS MEAD
STILECROFT
ROSEMOUNT
THE FRIARS
GREYGOOSE PARK
POLLARD HATCH
DEER PARK
FIR PARK
Great Parndon
HOLLY FIELD
SHAWBRIDGE
OLD ORCHARD
Recreat'n Grd
CM18
BARN MEAD
Occ. Cen.
HOOKFIELD
FOUNTAIN FARM
OAK END
BENTONS
Comm. Cent.
BUSH FAIR
R.C.Sch.
12
SPINNING WHEEL MEAD
ABBOTSWELD
Play Barn
TYE GREEN VILLAGE
PRIMROSE FIELD
LITTLE PYNCHONS
PENLOW
FINCHMOOR
CHARTERS CROSS
Sports Ground
FIVE ACRES
UPPER MEALINES
WHARLEY HOOK
SAKINS CROFT
Clinic
SOUTHERN WAY
A1169
BISHOPSFIELD
Parndon
WATER LA.
SYCAMORE FIELD
DUNSTALLS
MILLERSDALE
BROCKLES MEAD
WATERS MEAD
Lib.
Sch.
LONG BANKS
WOODHILL
CLARKHILL
FERNHILL
Special Sch.
THE READINGS
Latton Bush
Spts. Grd.
RUNDELLS
RADBURN CLOSE
LATTON GREEN
LITTLE CATTINS
Stewards
BARLEY CROFT
HONEYHILL
COMMONSIDE
MILWARDS
Kingsmoor
Health Cen.
Play-Barn
MORNINGTONS
LOWER MEADOW
LODGE HALL
HILLY FIELD
13
MALLOWS GREEN
Burnetts Wood
THE MAPLES
TAYLIFERS
HULL GROVE
HOOKFIELD
PETERSWOOD
SPRUCE HILL
BERECROFT
Sumners
THURSTANS
FENNELS
Nature Reserve
14
Crem.
Dorrington Farm
Common
Richmonds
Risdens Wood
Jack's Hatch
Parndon Wood
MOAT
Rye Hill Common
Priory Fm
HOSPITAL WOOD
14
Little Canons Farm
GREEN
Rye Hill
Severs Green
Rivetts Fm.
Lodge Farm
Little Maries Farm
Gibbon's Bush Farm
LONG
Rye Hill
Maries Farm
WOOD
EPPING
Epping Green
CM16
15
Forest
Site of Shingle Hall
P.O.
Sch.
Marles Wood
Rose Fm.
Hayleys Manor Farm
42
All Saints Vicarage
Cunnnnce Farm
Punch Timber Farm
CK
CL
CM
CN

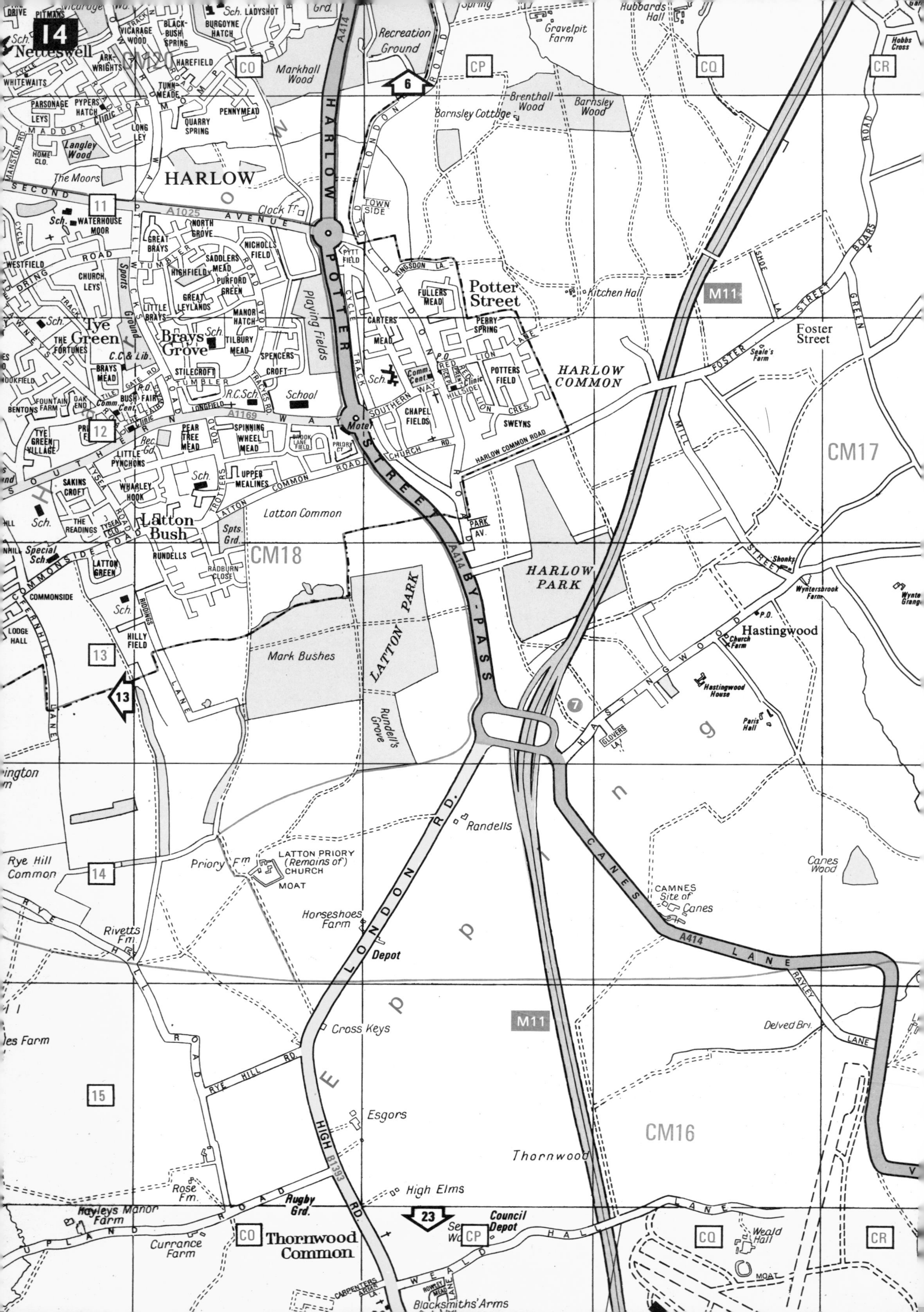
HARLOW
Netteswell
Potter Street
HARLOW COMMON
Tye Green
Brays Grove
Latton Bush
LATTON PARK
HARLOW PARK
Hastingwood
Foster Street
Thornwood Common
Thornwood
Latton Common
Mark Bushes
Recreation Ground
Markhall Wood
Brenthall Wood
Barnsley Wood
Barnsley Cottage
Gravelpit Farm
Hubbards Hall
Kitchen Hall
Playing Fields
LATTON PRIORY (Remains of) CHURCH
MOAT
Priory Fm
Randells
Horseshoes Farm
Depot
Cross Keys
Esgors
High Elms
Rose Fm.
Hayleys Manor Farm
Currance Farm
Rugby Grd.
Council Depot
Weald Hall
Blacksmiths' Arms
Rivetts Fm.
Rye Hill Common
Canes Wood
CAMNES Site of Canes
Delved Bri.
Rundell's Grove
Hastingwood House
Paris Hall
Church Farm
Wyntersbrook Farm
Seale's Farm
Shonks
Langley Wood
The Moors
CM17
CM18
CM16
CM20
M11
A414
A1025
A1169
B1393
HARLOW ROAD
POTTER STREET BY-PASS
LONDON RD.
HIGH RD.
CANES LANE
SECOND AVENUE
SOUTHERN WAY
HARLOW COMMON ROAD
HASTINGWOOD ROAD
FOSTER STREET
RYE HILL RD.
UPLAND ROAD
HALL LANE
WEALD
RAYLEY LANE
CO
CP
CQ
CR
6
7
11
12
13
14
15
23
Epping

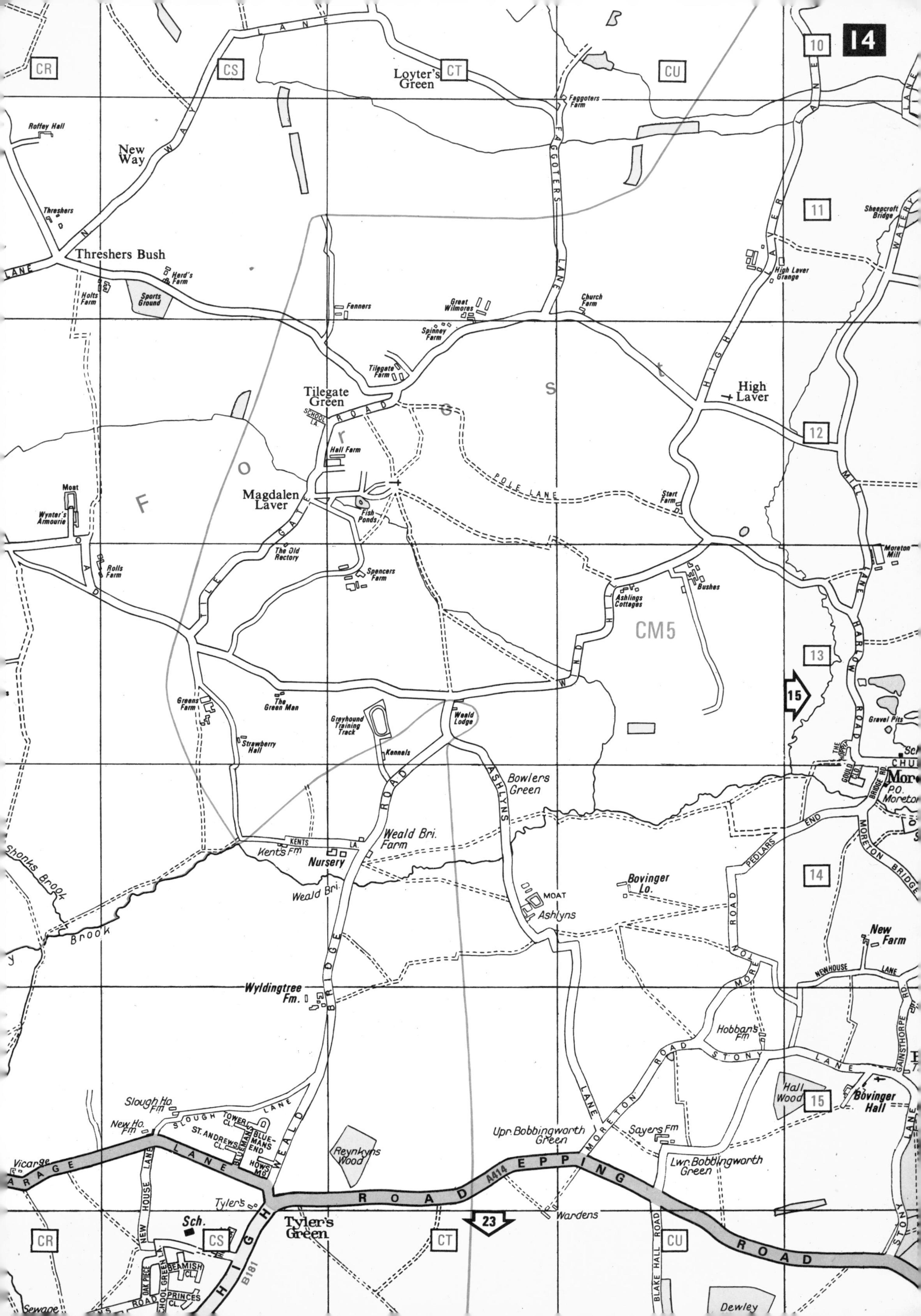
CR
CS
CT
CU
10
11
12
13
14
15
Loyter's Green
Faggoters Farm
Roffey Hall
New Way
Threshers
Threshers Bush
Herd's Farm
Holts Farm
Sports Ground
Fenners
Great Wilmores
Spinney Farm
Church Farm
Tilegate Farm
Tilegate Green
High Laver
High Laver Grange
Sheepcroft Bridge
School La.
Hall Farm
Magdalen Laver
Moat
Wynter's Armourie
Fish Ponds
Pole Lane
Start Farm
Moreton Mill
The Old Rectory
Rolls Farm
Spencers Farm
Ashlings Cottages
Bushes
CM5
Greens Farm
The Green Man
Greyhound Training Track
Weald Lodge
Kennels
Strawberry Hall
Gravel Pits
Bowlers Green
Kents La.
Kents Fm
Nursery
Weald Bri. Farm
Weald Bri.
Shonks Brook
Brook
Bovinger Lo.
Moat
Ashlyns
Pedlars End
Moreton Bridge
P.O.
New Farm
Newhouse Lane
Wyldingtree Fm.
Hobbans Fm
Stony Lane
Hall Wood
Bovinger Hall
Gainsthorpe Rd.
Slough Ho. Fm
New Ho. Fm
Slough Lane
Tower Cl.
St. Andrews Cl.
Bluemans End
Hows Md
Weald Bridge Road
Reynkyns Wood
Upr. Bobbingworth Green
Sayers Fm
Lwr. Bobbingworth Green
Moreton Road
Vicarage Lane
A414 Epping Road
Tyler's
Tyler's Green
Wardens
23
Sch.
New House Lane
High Road
B181
Beamish Cl.
Oak Piece
School Green
Princes Cl.
Sewage
Blake Hall Road
Dewley
Faggoters Lane
High Laver
Mill Lane
Harlow Road
Watery Lane
Ashlyns
Forest

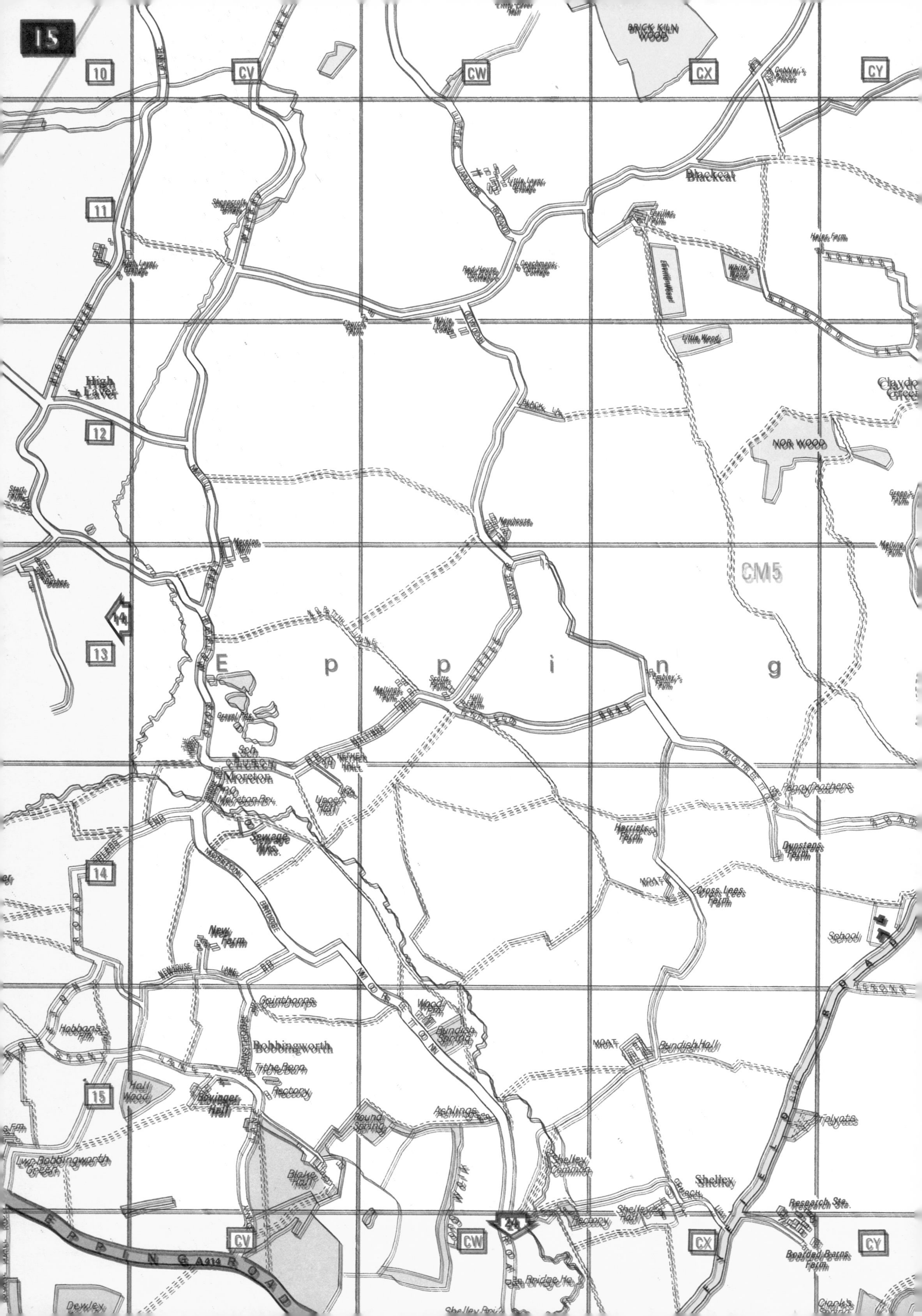
10
CV
CW
CX
CY
BRICK KILN WOOD
LANE
Cobbler's Pieces
Blackcat
Little Laver Grange
Sheepcroft Grange
Sevilles Farm
High Laver Cottage
Red House Cottages
Coachmans Cottage
Hales Farm
White's Wood
Little Wood
Church Farm
White Lodge
11
12
13
14
15
HIGH LAVER
High Laver
Claydon Green
BLACK LA
NOR WOOD
Start Farm
Newhouse
Green's Farm
Moreton Hall
Melting Farm
CM5
14
E p p i n g
Maltings Farm
Scotts Farm
Hill Farm
Embley's Farm
Gravel Pits
Sch
Moreton
Moreton Br.
CHURCH
NETHER HALL
Upper Hall
Poorfeathers
Sewage Wks.
Harriets Farm
Dunstans Farm
MOAT
Cross Lees Farm
School
New Farm
NEWHOUSE LANE
Gainthorps
Wood Farm
Bundish Spring
Hobbans Fm
Bobbingworth
MOAT
Bundish Hall
Tithe Barn
Hall Wood
Rectory
Bovinger Hall
Round Spring
Achlings
Takelys
Shelley Common
Blake Hall
Lwr Bobbingworth Green
Shelley
Shelley Hall
Rectory
Research Sta.
Boarded Barns Farm
24
EPPING ROAD
A414
Dewley
Bridge Ho
Shelley Bri.
Clark's

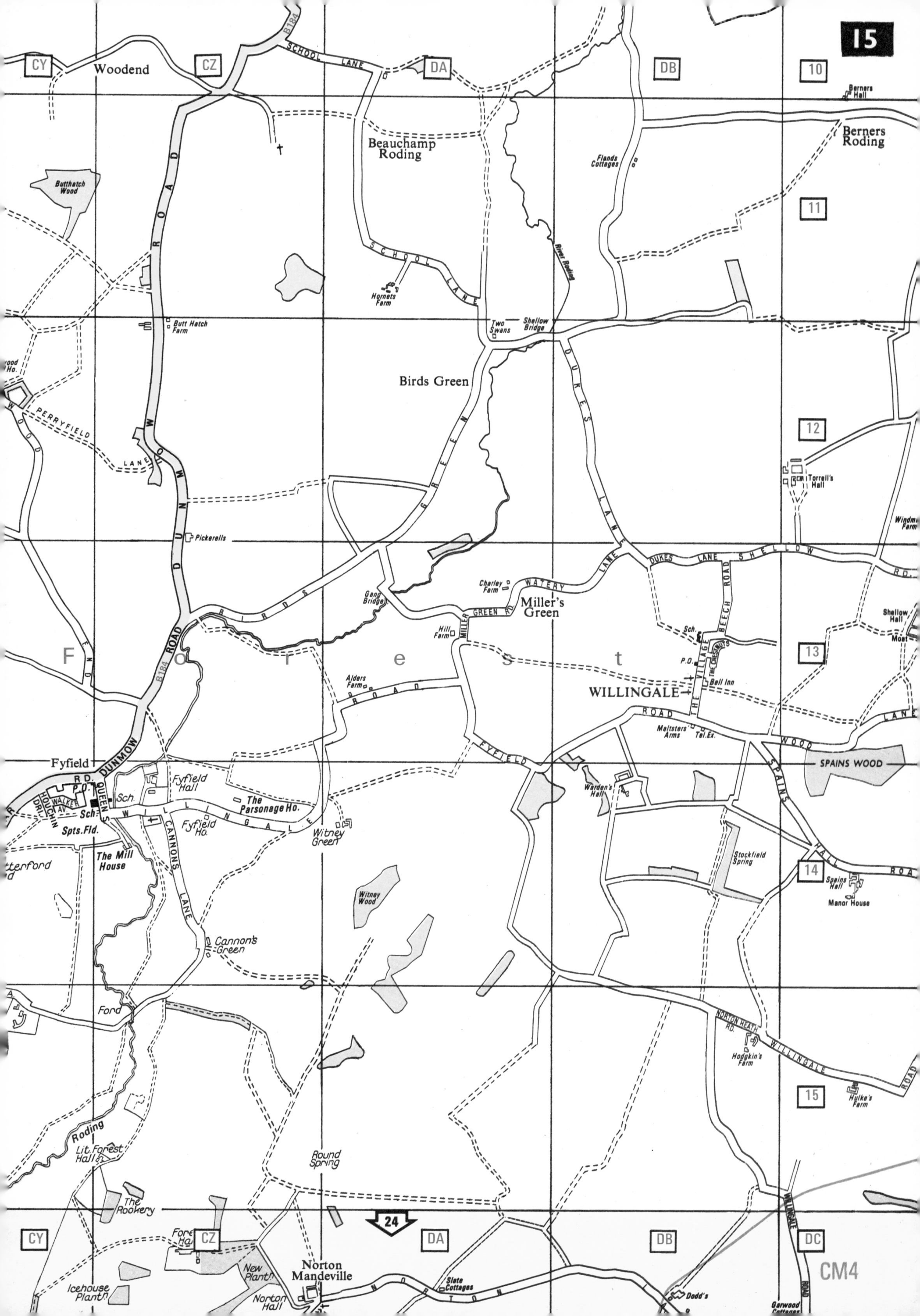

CY
CZ
DA
DB
10
Woodend
B184
SCHOOL LANE
Beauchamp Roding
Berners Hall
Berners Roding
Flands Cottages
Butthatch Wood
11
DUNMOW ROAD
SCHOOL LANE
Hornets Farm
River Roding
Butt Hatch Farm
Two Swans
Shellow Bridge
Birds Green
DUKES LANE
12
Torrell's Hall
PERRYFIELD LANE
WOOD END
GREEN
Pickerells
DUKES LANE SHELLOW RD.
BEECH ROAD
Charley Farm
WATERY LANE
Gang Bridge
BIRDS
Miller's Green
MILLER GREEN RD.
Hill Farm
Shellow Hall
Moat
Sch.
13
P.O.
THE CHESTNUTS
Bell Inn
Forest
WILLINGALE
THE VILLAGE
Alders Farm
ROAD
Meltsters Arms
Tel.Ex.
WOOD LANE
FYFIELD ROAD
Fyfield
RD. DUNMOW
SPAINS WOOD
QUEENS
Sch.
Fyfield Hall
The Parsonage Ho.
Warden's Hall
SPAINS HALL ROAD
HOUCHIN DR.
WALKER AV.
Sch
Spts. Fld.
WILLINGALE
CANNONS LANE
Fyfield Ho.
Witney Green
The Mill House
Stockfield Spring
14
Spains Hall
Manor House
Witney Wood
Cannon's Green
Ford
NORTON HEATH RD.
WILLINGALE ROAD
Hodgkin's Farm
15
Hylke's Farm
Roding
Lit. Forest Hall
Round Spring
The Rookery
24
CY
CZ
DA
DB
DC
Forest Hall
Norton Mandeville
New Plantn
Icehouse Plantn
Norton Hall
Slate Cottages
NORTON
Dodd's
WILLINGALE ROAD
Garwood Cottages
CM4

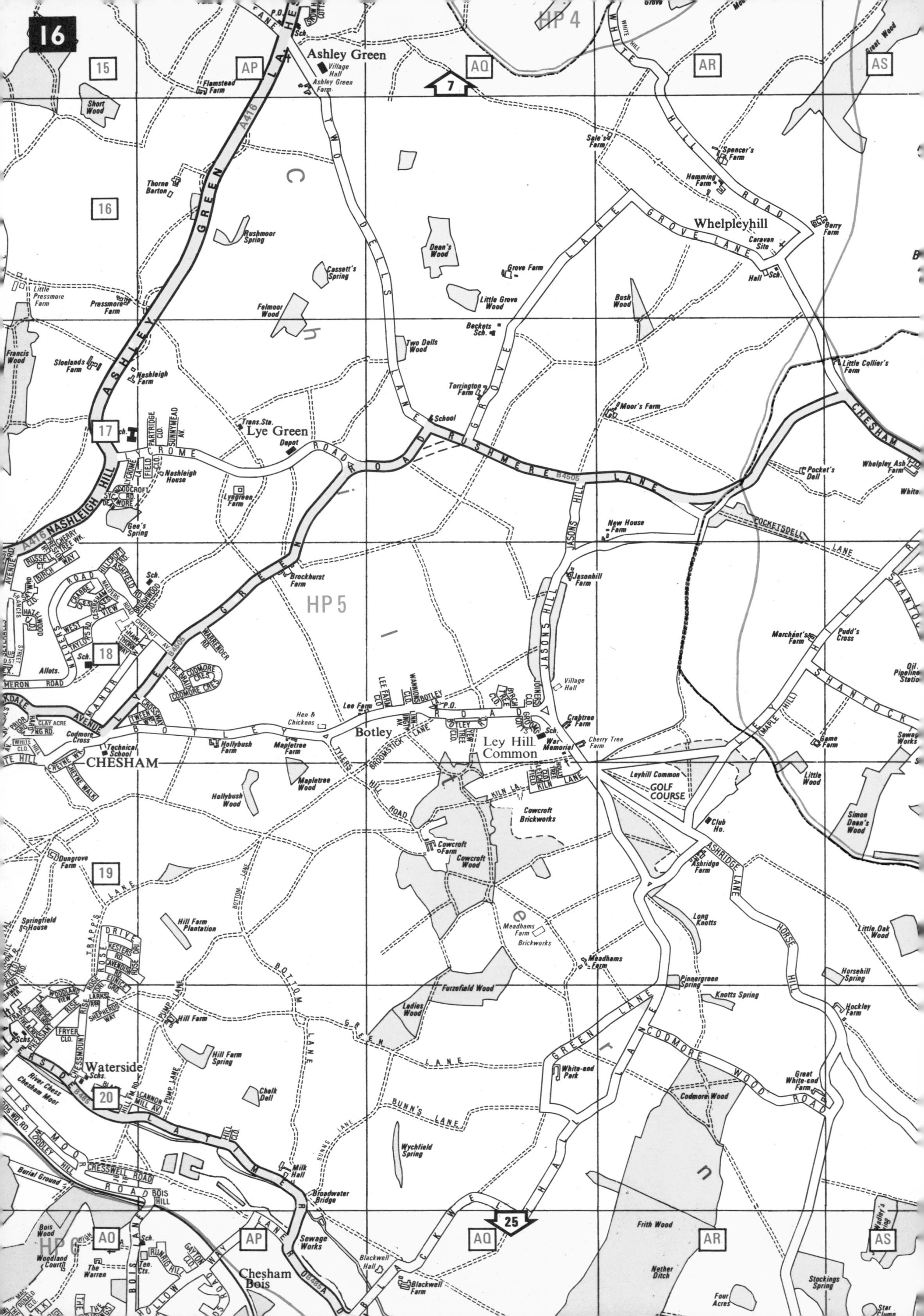
16
HP 4
HP 5
HP 6
15
16
17
18
19
20
AP
AQ
AR
AS
AO
7
25
Ashley Green
Village Hall
Ashley Green Farm
Flamstead Farm
Short Wood
Thorne Barton
Rushmoor Spring
Little Pressmore Farm
Pressmore Farm
Felmoor Wood
Cassett's Spring
Francis Wood
Sloelands Farm
Nashleigh Farm
ASHLEY GREEN
A416
TWO DELLS LANE
Dean's Wood
Grove Farm
Little Grove Wood
Beckets Sch.
Two Dells Wood
Torrington Farm
School
Sale's Farm
Spencer's Farm
Hemming Farm
Berry Farm
Whelpleyhill
Caravan Site
Hall
Sch.
GROVE LANE
WHITE HILL ROAD
Bush Wood
Little Collier's Farm
Moor's Farm
CHESHAM
Whelpley Ash Farm
Pocket's Dell
POCKETSDELL LANE
Great Wood
Trans. Sta.
Lye Green
Depot
LYCROME ROAD
PARTRIDGE CLO.
SUNNYMEAD AV.
Nashleigh House
Lyegreen Farm
Gee's Spring
NASHLEIGH HILL
RUSHMERE LANE
B4505
New House Farm
JASONS HILL
Jasonhill Farm
Brockhurst Farm
WARRENDER RD.
CODMORE CRES.
Village Hall
Merchant's Farm
Pudd's Cross
Oil Pipeline Station
SHANTOCK
Lee Farm
LEE FARM CLO.
WARNERS CLO.
BOTLEY RD.
P.O.
Hen & Chickens
Botley
Ley Hill Common
War Memorial
Crabtree Farm
Cherry Tree Farm
Codmore Cross
Technical School
CHESHAM
Hollybush Farm
Mapletree Farm
Mapletree Wood
Hollybush Wood
BROOMSTICK LANE
TYLERS HILL ROAD
KILN LANE
Leyhill Common
GOLF COURSE
Club Ho.
Game Farm
Sewage Works
Little Wood
Simon Dean's Wood
Cowcroft Brickworks
Cowcroft Farm
Cowcroft Wood
Ashridge Farm
ASHRIDGE LANE
Dungrove Farm
BOTTOM LANE
Springfield House
Hill Farm Plantation
Meadhams Farm
Brickworks
Long Knotts
Little Oak Wood
HORSE HILL
Horsehill Spring
Hockley Farm
Furzefield Wood
Ladies Wood
Pinnergreen Spring
Knotts Spring
Hill Farm
PUMP LANE
GREEN LANE
Hill Farm Spring
Waterside
Schs.
River Chess
Chesham Moor
Chalk Dell
White-end Park
CODMORE WOOD ROAD
Great White-end Farm
Codmore Wood
BUNN'S LANE
Wychfield Spring
LATIMER ROAD
CRESSWELL ROAD
Burial Ground
BOIS MOOR ROAD
BOIS HILL
Milk Hall
Broadwater Bridge
Sewage Works
Frith Wood
Nether Ditch
Four Acres
Stockings Spring
Bois Wood
Woodland Court
The Warren
Ten. Cts.
Chesham Bois
Blackwell Hall
Blackwell Farm
BLACKWELL HALL LANE
B485

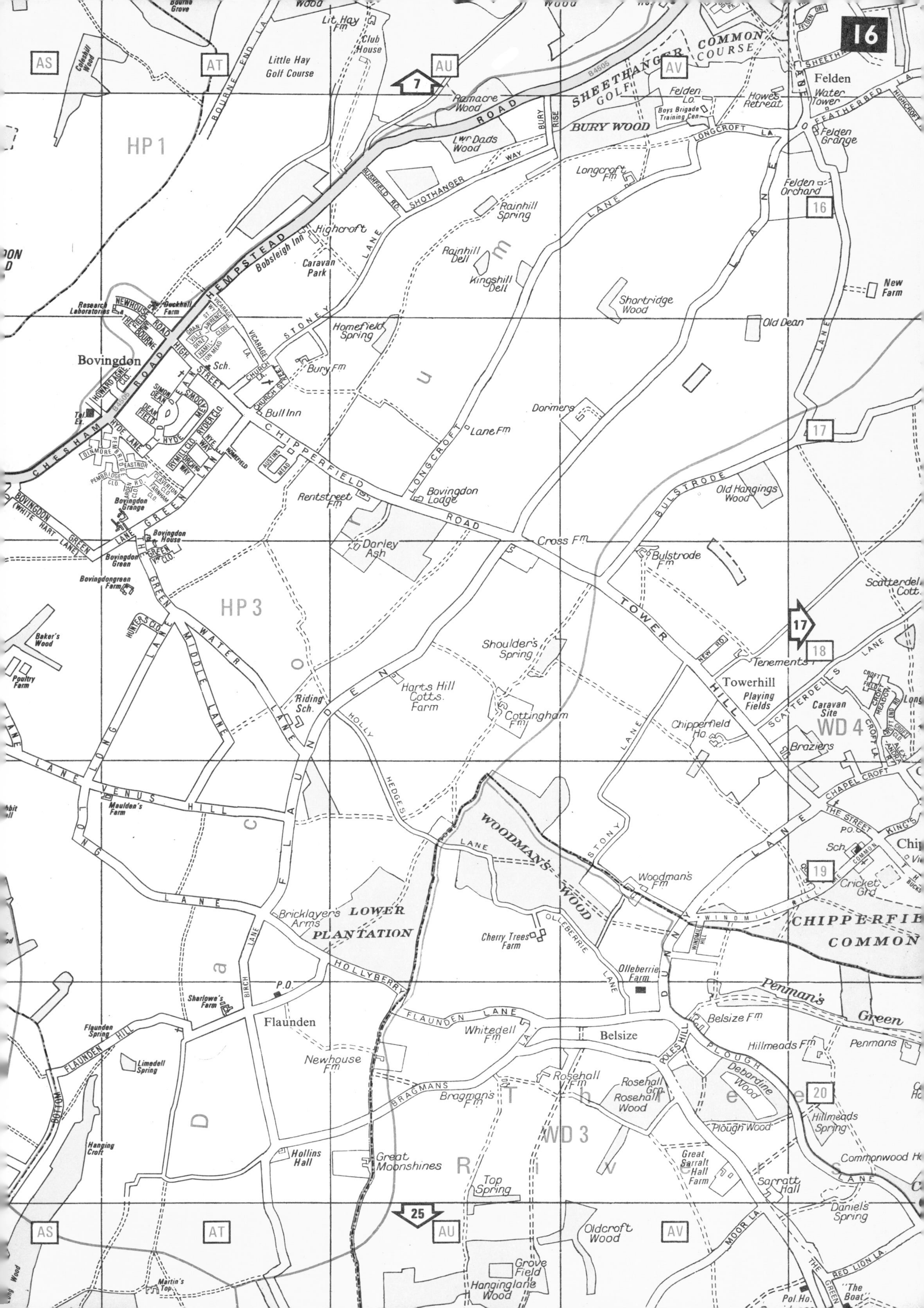
16
AS
AT
AU
AV
7
25
17
18
19
20
HP 1
HP 3
WD 3
WD 4
Little Hay
Golf Course
Lit Hay Fm
Club House
Coleshill Wood
Bourne Grove
BOURNE END LA
SHEETHANGER
GOLF
COMMON
COURSE
Felden
Water Tower
Felden Lo.
Boys Brigade Training Cen.
Howes Retreat
Ramacre Wood
Lwr Dads Wood
BURY WOOD
BURY RISE
BOXSHANGER WAY
LONGCROFT LA.
Felden Grange
FEATHERBED LA
HIGHCROFT
Felden Orchard
Longcroft Fm
Rainhill Spring
Rainhill Dell
Kingshill Dell
Shortridge Wood
Old Dean
New Farm
BUSHFIELD RD.
SHOTHANGER
HEMPSTEAD
ROAD
B4505
Highcroft
Bobsleigh Inn
Caravan Park
Duckhall Farm
Research Laboratories
NEWHOUSE ROAD
THE BOURNE
Bovingdon
HIGH STREET
CHESHAM ROAD
VICARAGE LA.
STONEY LANE
Homefield Spring
Bury Fm
CHURCH ST.
Bull Inn
Sch.
Tel. Ex.
HOWARD AGNE CLO.
SIMON DEAN
DEAN FIELD
HYDE LANE
HYDE MEAD
RYDER CLO.
DINMORE
PEMBRIDGE CLO.
EASTNOR
RYMILL CLO.
ORCHARD WAY
HOMEFIELD
AUSTINS MEAD
Dormers
Lane Fm
LONGCROFT
CHIPPERFIELD ROAD
Bovingdon Lodge
Rentstreet Fm
Darley Ash
Cross Fm
BULSTRODE
Old Hangings Wood
Bovingdon Grange
BOVINGDON (WHITE HART LANE)
GREEN LANE
Bovingdon House
Bovingdon Green
Bovingdongreen Farm
Bulstrode Fm
Scatterdells Cott.
TOWER HILL
NEW RD.
Tenements
Towerhill
Playing Fields
HUNTERS CLO.
Baker's Wood
Poultry Farm
WATER LANE
MIDDLE LANE
Shoulder's Spring
Harts Hill Cotts. Farm
Cottingham Fm
Riding Sch.
FLAUNDEN
HOLLY HEDGES
Chipperfield Ho.
Caravan Site
Braziers
SCATTERDELLS LANE
CROFT LA.
CHAPEL CROFT
THE STREET
P.O.
Sch.
Cricket Grd
LONG LANE
VENUS HILL
Meulden's Farm
WOODMAN'S WOOD
STONY LANE
Woodman's Fm
WINDMILL HILL
CHIPPERFIELD
COMMON
LOWER PLANTATION
Bricklayers Arms
BIRCH LANE
Cherry Trees Farm
OLLEBERRIE LANE
Olleberrie Farm
DUNNY LANE
Penman's Green
HOLLYBERRY
P.O.
Sharlowe's Farm
Flaunden
FLAUNDEN LANE
Whitedell Fm
Belsize
POLES HILL
Belsize Fm
Hillmeads Fm
Penmans
PLOUGH LANE
Flaunden Spring
FLAUNDEN HILL
Limedell Spring
BOTTOM
Newhouse Fm
BRAGMANS LANE
Bragman's Fm
Rosehall Fm
Rosehall Grn.
Rosehall Wood
Debardine Wood
Plough Wood
Hillmeads Spring
Hanging Croft
Hollins Hall
Great Moonshines
Top Spring
Great Sarratt Hall Farm
Sarratt Hall
Commonwood Ho
Daniels Spring
Oldcroft Wood
MOOR LA.
RED LION LA.
Grove Field
Hanginglane Wood
Martin's Top
Pol. Ho.
"The Boat"
THE GREEN
Long Wood

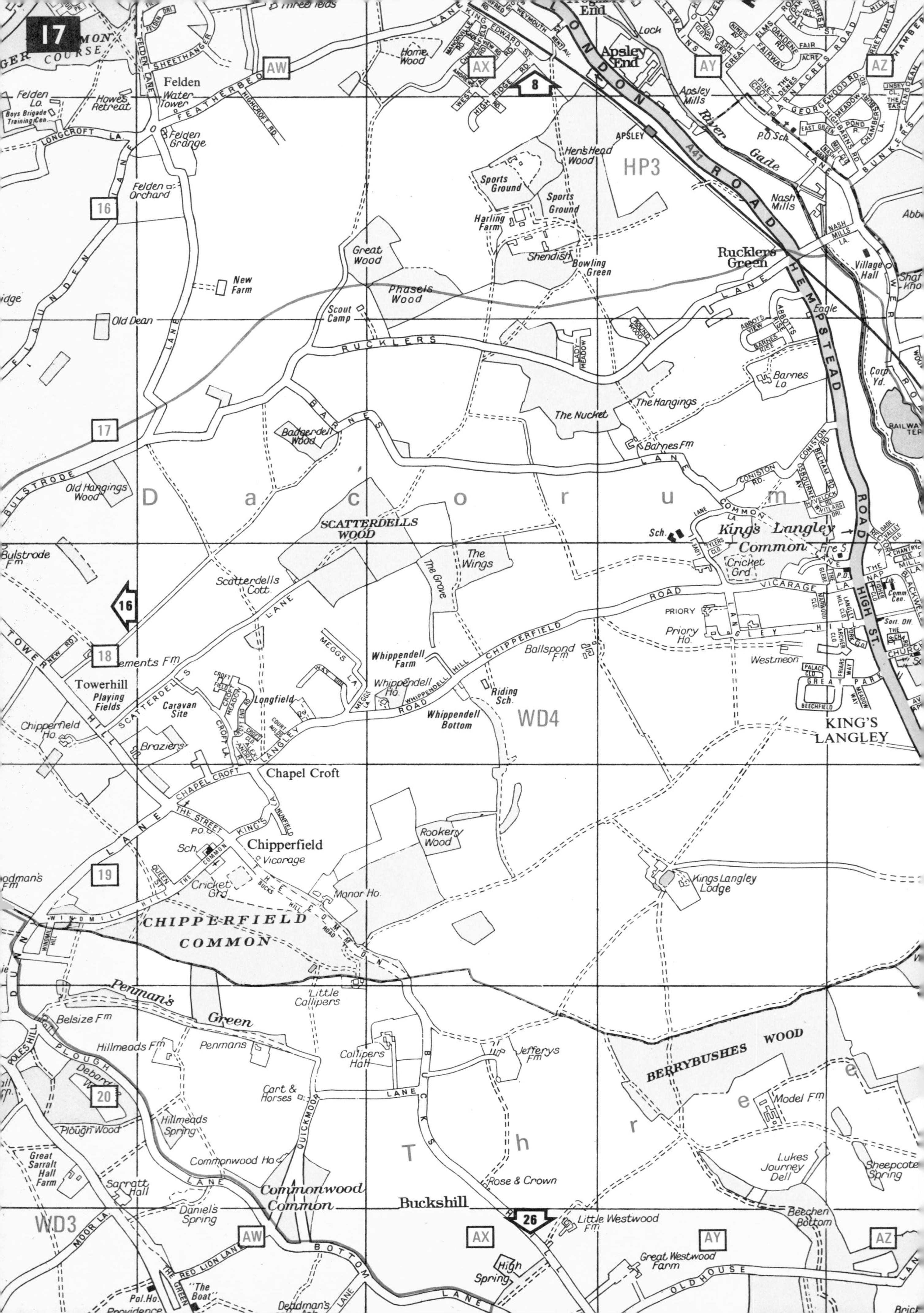
Felden
Felden Water Tower
Felden Lo.
Howes Retreat
Boys Brigade Training Cen.
Felden Grange
Felden Orchard
Home Wood
Apsley End
Lock
Apsley Mills
APSLEY
Hens Head Wood
HP3
River Gade
Nash Mills
Sports Ground
Harling Farm
Shendish
Bowling Green
Great Wood
New Farm
Phasels Wood
Scout Camp
Old Dean
Rucklers Green
Village Hall
RUCKLERS LANE
The Nuckett
The Hangings
Barnes Lo
Barnes Fm
Badgerdell Wood
Old Hangings Wood
Dacorum
SCATTERDELLS WOOD
The Wings
The Grove
King's Langley Common
Cricket Grd.
Sch.
Fire S.
Bulstrode Fm
Scatterdells Cott.
PRIORY
Priory Ho.
Westmeon
Ballspond Fm
Whippendell Farm
Whippendell Ho.
Riding Sch.
Whippendell Bottom
WD4
KING'S LANGLEY
Towerhill Playing Fields
Clements Fm
Caravan Site
Longfield
Chipperfield Ho.
Braziers
Chapel Croft
Chipperfield
Vicarage
Rookery Wood
Kings Langley Lodge
Cricket Grd
Manor Ho.
CHIPPERFIELD COMMON
Little Callipers
Penman's Green
Belsize Fm
Hillmeads Fm
Penmans
Callipers Hall
Jefferys Fm
BERRYBUSHES WOOD
Model Fm
Cart & Horses
Plough Wood
Hillmeads Spring
Commonwood Ho
Great Sarratt Hall Farm
Sarratt Hall
Three Rivers
Lukes Journey Dell
Sheepcote Spring
Rose & Crown
Commonwood Common
Buckshill
Daniels Spring
Little Westwood Fm
Beechen Bottom
WD3
Great Westwood Farm
High Spring
"The Boat"
Pol. Ho.
AW
AX
AY
AZ
8
16
17
18
19
20
26
LONDON ROAD
HEMPSTEAD ROAD
HIGH ST.
BULSTRODE
FLAUNDEN LANE
LONGCROFT LA.
FEATHERBED LA.
BARNES LANE
VICARAGE ROAD
CHIPPERFIELD ROAD
WHIPPENDELL HILL
TOWER HILL
SCATTERDELLS LANE
WINDMILL HILL
PLOUGH LANE
QUICKMOOR LANE
BUCKS HILL
BOTTOM LANE
OLDHOUSE LANE
RED LION LANE
MOOR LA.
THE STREET
CHAPEL CROFT

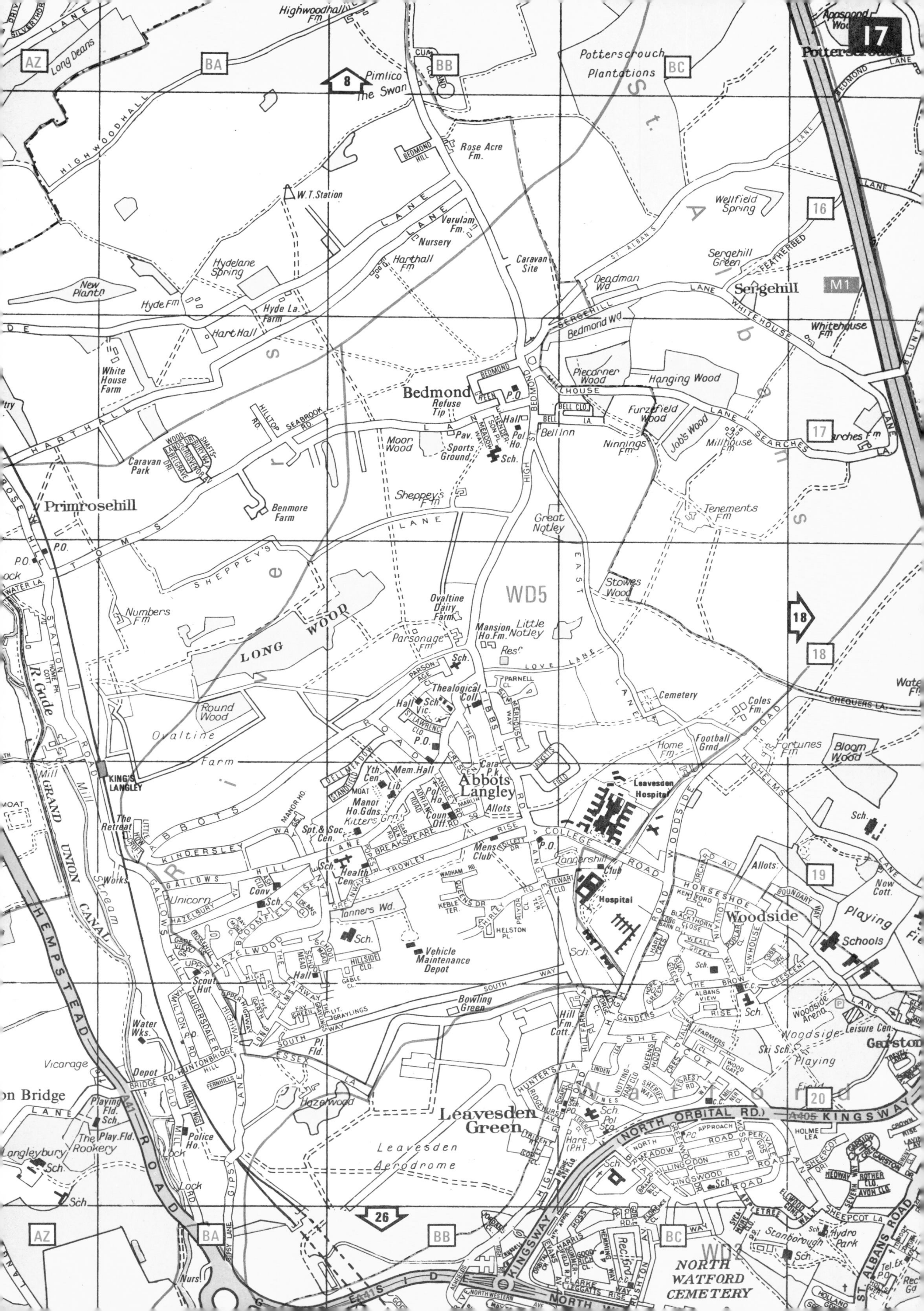
17
8
18
26
AZ
BA
BB
BC
16
17
18
19
20
Pimlico
The Swan
Potterscrouch Plantations
Highwoodhall Fm
Long Deans
HIGHWOODHALL
Rose Acre Fm.
BEDMOND HILL
W.T. Station
Verulam Fm.
Nursery
Harthall Fm
Hydelane Spring
New Plantn
Hyde Fm
Hyde La. Farm
Hart Hall
White House Farm
Caravan Site
Wellfield Spring
Sergehill Green
Deadman Wd
Sergehill
M1
Bedmond Wd
Whitehouse Fm
Piecorner Wood
Hanging Wood
Furzefield Wood
Job's Wood
Ninnings Fm
Millhouse Fm
Bedmond
Refuse Tip
Bell Inn
Moor Wood
Sports Ground
Caravan Park
Primrosehill
Benmore Farm
Sheppey's Fm
Great Notley
Tenements Fm
Stowes Wood
WD5
Numbers Fm
LONG WOOD
Ovaltine Dairy Farm
Mansion Ho.Fm.
Little Notley
Parsonage Fm
LOVE LANE
Round Wood
Ovaltine Farm
Theological Coll
Cemetery
Coles Fm.
Football Grnd
Home Fm
Fortunes Fm
Bloom Wood
CHEQUERS LA.
R. Gade
KING'S LANGLEY
GRAND UNION CANAL
The Retreat
Abbots Langley
Leavesden Hospital
Mem. Hall
Manor Ho.Gdns.
Kitters Grn
Allots
Mens Club
Tannershill Club
Hospital
Health Cen
Tanners Wd.
Vehicle Maintenance Depot
Woodside
Playing Fields
Schools
Bowling Green
Hill Fm. Cott.
Woodside Arena
Leisure Cen.
Garston
Water Wks.
Vicarage
Depot
Police Ho.
Hazelwood
Leavesden Green
Leavesden Aerodrome
NORTH ORBITAL RD.
A405 KINGSWAY
Langleybury Sch.
The Rookery
WD2
NORTH WATFORD CEMETERY
Stanborough Park
Hydro Park
HEMPSTEAD ROAD
A41
St Albans
Watford

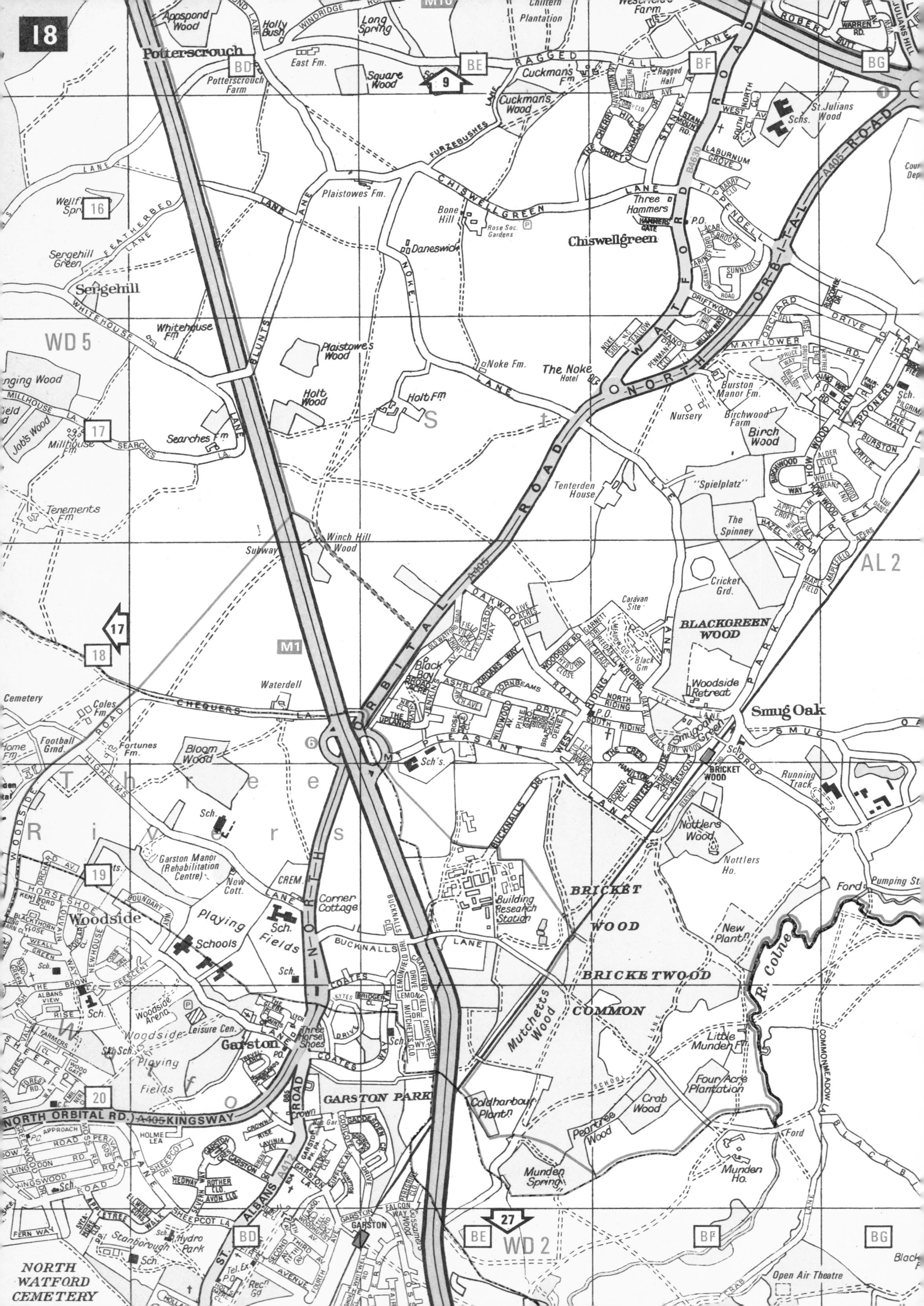
Potterscrouch
Potterscrouch Farm
Appspond Wood
Holly Bush
Windridge
Long Spring
East Fm.
Square Wood
Chiltern Plantation
Westfield Farm
Ragged Hall Lane
Ragged Hall
Cuckmans Fm.
Cuckmans Wood
Furzebushes Lane
Robert
Warren Rd.
Butt
St. Julians Wood
Schs.
North Orbital Road A405
Watford Road B4630
Chiswellgreen
Chiswellgreen Lane
Three Hammers
Hammers Gate
P.O.
Tippendell
Laburnum Grove
Stanley Av.
Stanmount Rd.
Cherry Hill
Cuckmans Dr.
The Croft
Sunnydell
Driftwood Av.
Plaistowes Fm.
Bone Hill
Rose Soc. Gardens
Daneswick
Noke Lane
Noke Fm.
The Noke Hotel
Plaistowes Wood
Holt Wood
Holt Fm.
Blunts Lane
Searches Fm
Searches La.
Millhouse La.
Millhouse Fm
Job's Wood
Hanging Wood
Sergehill
Sergehill Green
Sergehill Lane
Featherbed Lane
Whitehouse Lane
Whitehouse Fm
Wellfield Spr.
WD 5
Tenements Fm
Winch Hill Wood
Subway
Tenterden House
Lye Lane
"Spielplatz"
Nursery
Burston Manor Fm.
Birchwood Farm
Birch Wood
Mayflower Rd.
Orchard Drive
Burston Drive
Spooners Dr.
The Mall
How Wood
Birchwood Way
The Spinney
Hazel Rd.
Maple Field
AL 2
Cricket Grd.
Caravan Site
Blackgreen Wood
Black Boy Wood
Woodside Retreat
Smug Oak
Smug Oak Lane
Smugoak Green
Park Street
Bricket Wood
Drop Lane
Running Track
Oakwood
Five Acres Av.
Old Watford Road
Jordans Way
Ashridge
Hornbeams
Woodside Road
North Riding
South Riding
West Riding
Mount Pleasant
Sch's.
The Uplands
Black Boy
Broad Acre
Jenkins Av.
Black Grn
Hunters Ride
The Cres.
Station
Bucknalls Dr.
Bucknalls Lane
Building Research Station
Bricket Wood
Bricketwood Common
Mutchetts Wood
Nottlers Wood
Nottlers Ho.
New Plantn
R. Colne
Ford
Pumping St.
Little Munden Fm.
Four Acre Plantation
Crab Wood
Peartree Wood
Coldharbour Plantn
Munden Spring
Munden Ho.
Commonmeadow Lane
Blackbirds
Open Air Theatre
WD 2
Waterdell
Chequers La.
Coles Fm.
Cemetery
Football Grnd.
Home Fm.
Fortunes Fm.
Bloom Wood
Three Rivers
Highelms
Garston Manor (Rehabilitation Centre)
New Cott.
Crem.
Corner Cottage
Sch. Fields
Playing Fields
Schools
Woodside
Horseshoe
Boundary Way
Newhouse
Crescent
The Brow
Albans View
Woodside Arena
Leisure Cen.
Garston
Three Horse Shoes
Coates Way
Garston Park
North Orbital Rd. A405 Kingsway
St. Albans Road A412
Sheepcot Lane
Appletree Walk
Stanborough
Hydro Park
Garston
Tel. Ex.
North Watford Cemetery
M1
M10
BD
BE
BF
BG
16
17
18
19
20
9
17
27
6

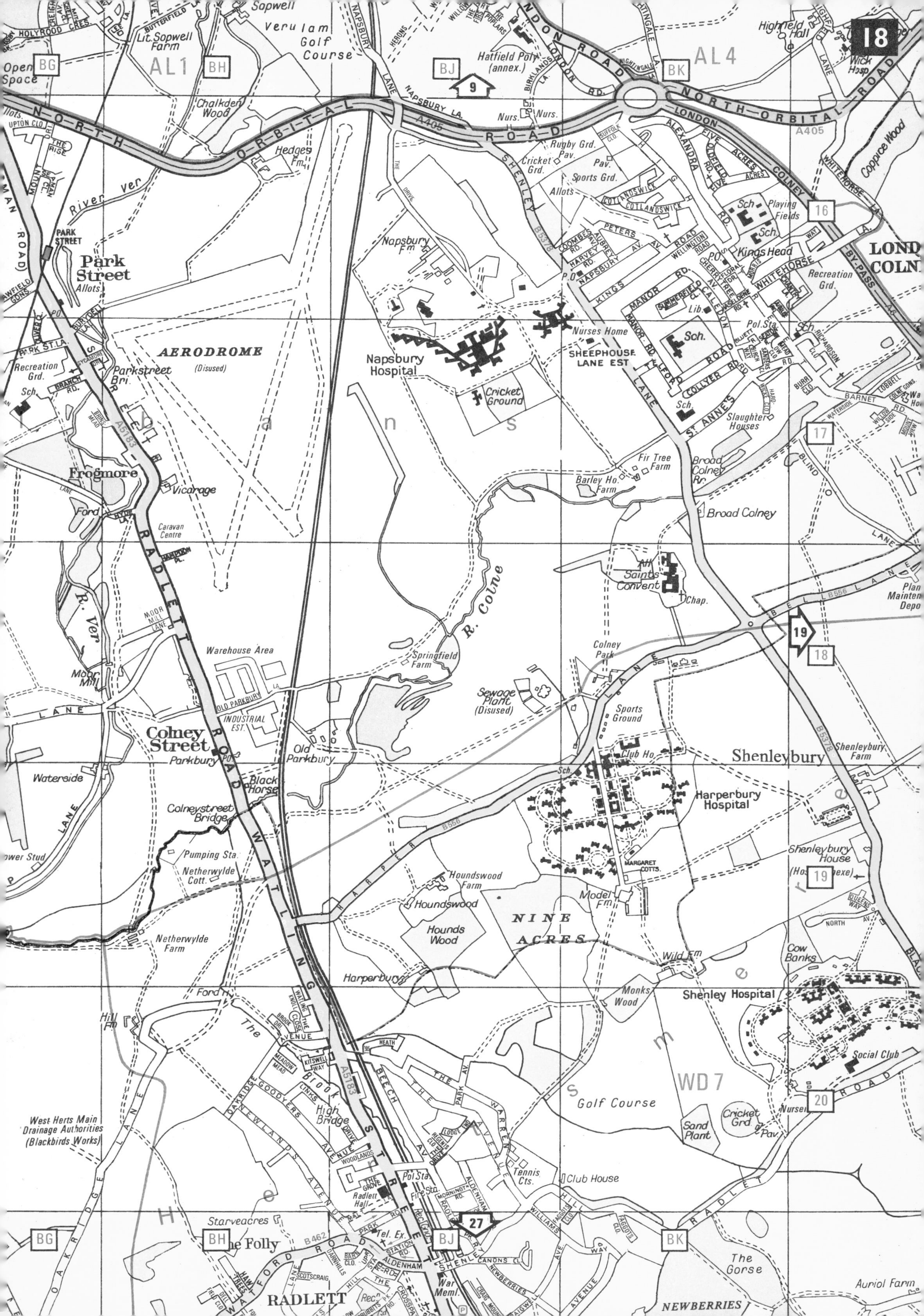
Sopwell
Verulam Golf Course
Lit. Sopwell Farm
Hatfield Poly (annex.)
Highfield Hall
Wick Hosp
AL1
AL4
Open Space
Chalkden Wood
Hedges Fm.
NORTH ORBITAL ROAD
LONDON ROAD
NAPSBURY LA.
Nurs.
Rugby Grd. Pav.
Cricket Grd.
Sports Grd.
Allots
Playing Fields
Coppice Wood
River Ver
Park Street
Allots.
Napsbury Fm.
Kings Head
LONDON COLNEY
Recreation Grd.
AERODROME (Disused)
Parkstreet Bri.
Napsbury Hospital
Nurses Home
SHEEPHOUSE LANE EST
Cricket Ground
Slaughter Houses
Frogmore
Vicarage
Fir Tree Farm
Barley Ho. Farm
Broad Colney
Caravan Centre
All Saints Convent
Chap.
R. Ver
R. Colne
Moor Mill
Warehouse Area
Springfield Farm
Colney Park
Sewage Plant (Disused)
Colney Street
Parkbury
Old Parkbury
Black Horse
Sports Ground
Club Ho.
Shenleybury
Shenleybury Farm
Waterside
Colneystreet Bridge
Harperbury Hospital
Pumping Sta.
Netherwylde Cott.
Houndswood Farm
Houndswood
Hounds Wood
NINE ACRES
Model Fm.
MARGARET COTTS.
Shenleybury House (Hosp. Annexe)
Netherwylde Farm
Harperbury
Wild Fm
Monks Wood
Cow Banks
Shenley Hospital
Social Club
Hill Fm
WD7
Golf Course
West Herts Main Drainage Authorities (Blackbirds Works)
High Bridge
Sand Plant
Cricket Grd.
Pav.
Tennis Cts.
Club House
Radlett Hall
Starveacres
The Folly
RADLETT
The Gorse
Auriol Farm
NEWBERRIES
WATLING STREET
RADLETT ROAD
HARPER LANE
BELL LANE
A405
A5183
B5378
B556
B462
9
16
17
18
19
20
27

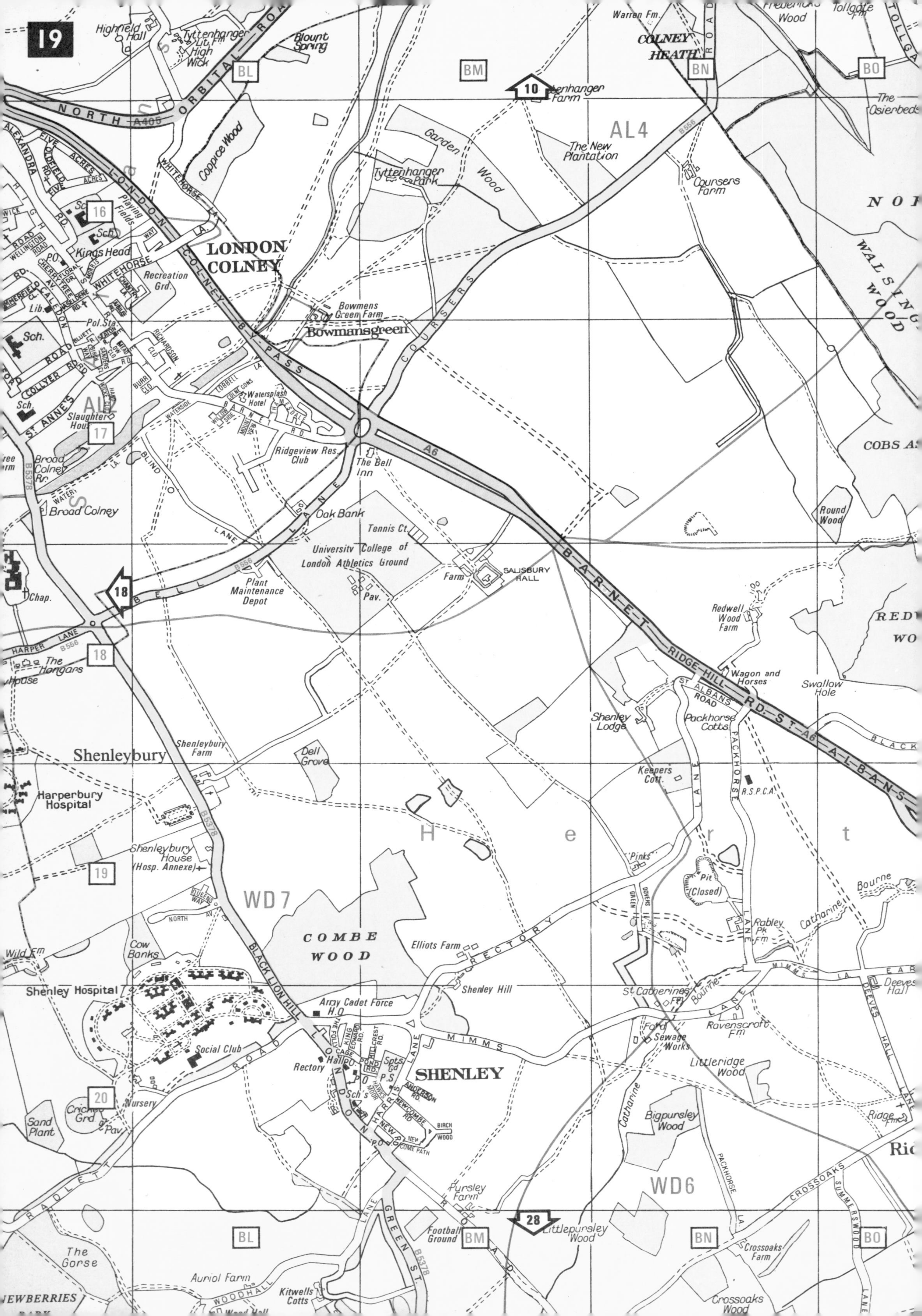

Highfield Hall
Tyttenhanger Lit. Fm
High Wick
Blount Spring
Warren Fm.
Colney Heath
Tollgate Fm
BL
BM
BN
BO
10
Tyttenhanger Farm
The Osierbeds
North Orbital Road A405
Coppice Wood
Garden Wood
AL4
The New Plantation
Tyttenhanger Park
Coursers Farm
B556
Alexandra
Five Acres
Oldfield Rd.
Whitehorse La.
Playing Fields
16
Sch.
Kings Head
P.O.
Wellington Road
Cherry Tree
Whitehorse
Recreation Grd.
London Colney
London Colney By-Pass
Coursers
Bowmens Green Farm
Bowmansgreen
Lib.
Pol. Sta.
Richardson Clo.
Collyer Rd.
St. Anne's
AL2
Slaughter House
17
Waterside
Watersplash Hotel
Barnet Rd
Ridgeview Res. Club
The Bell Inn
A6
Broad Colney Fr.
Blind La.
Watery La.
Broad Colney
B5378
Oak Bank
Tennis Ct.
University College of London Athletics Ground
Farm
Salisbury Hall
Bell Lane
Plant Maintenance Depot
Pav.
18
Chap.
Harper Lane
The Hangars
Barnet
Ridge Hill
St. Albans Road
Redwell Wood Farm
Wagon and Horses
Swallow Hole
Round Wood
Cobs Ash
Redwell Wood
Walsingham Wood
Shenley Lodge
Packhorse Cotts.
Packhorse Lane
Keepers Cott.
R.S.P.C.A.
Shenleybury
Shenleybury Farm
Dell Grove
Harperbury Hospital
Herts
Shenleybury House (Hosp. Annexe)
19
Queens Way
North Av.
WD7
Pinks
Pit (Closed)
Bourne
Catharine
Rabley Pk Fm
Combe Wood
Elliots Farm
Rectory
Wild Fm
Cow Banks
Black Lion Hill
Shenley Hospital
Shenley Hill
St Catherines Fm
Mimms La
Deeves Hall
Army Cadet Force H.Q.
The Folly
King Edward Rd.
Hill Crest Rd.
Mimms Lane
Ravenscroft Fm
Ford
Sewage Works
Social Club
Road
Rectory
Hall
Cage Pond Rd.
Spts. Gd
P.S.
P.O.
Sch's
Shenley
Anderson Rd.
Littleridge Wood
20
Nursery
Cricket Grd
Pav.
Sand Plant
London Road
Harris Lane
Newcombe Rd.
New Rd.
Birch Wood
New Come Path
Bigpursley Wood
Ridge Fm
Radlett Road
Pursley Farm
Packhorse La.
WD6
Crossoaks Lane
Summerswood Lane
28
Littlepursley Wood
Football Ground
Green St.
B5378
The Gorse
Auriol Farm
Woodhall
Kitwells Cotts
Newberries
Crossoaks Farm
Crossoaks Wood

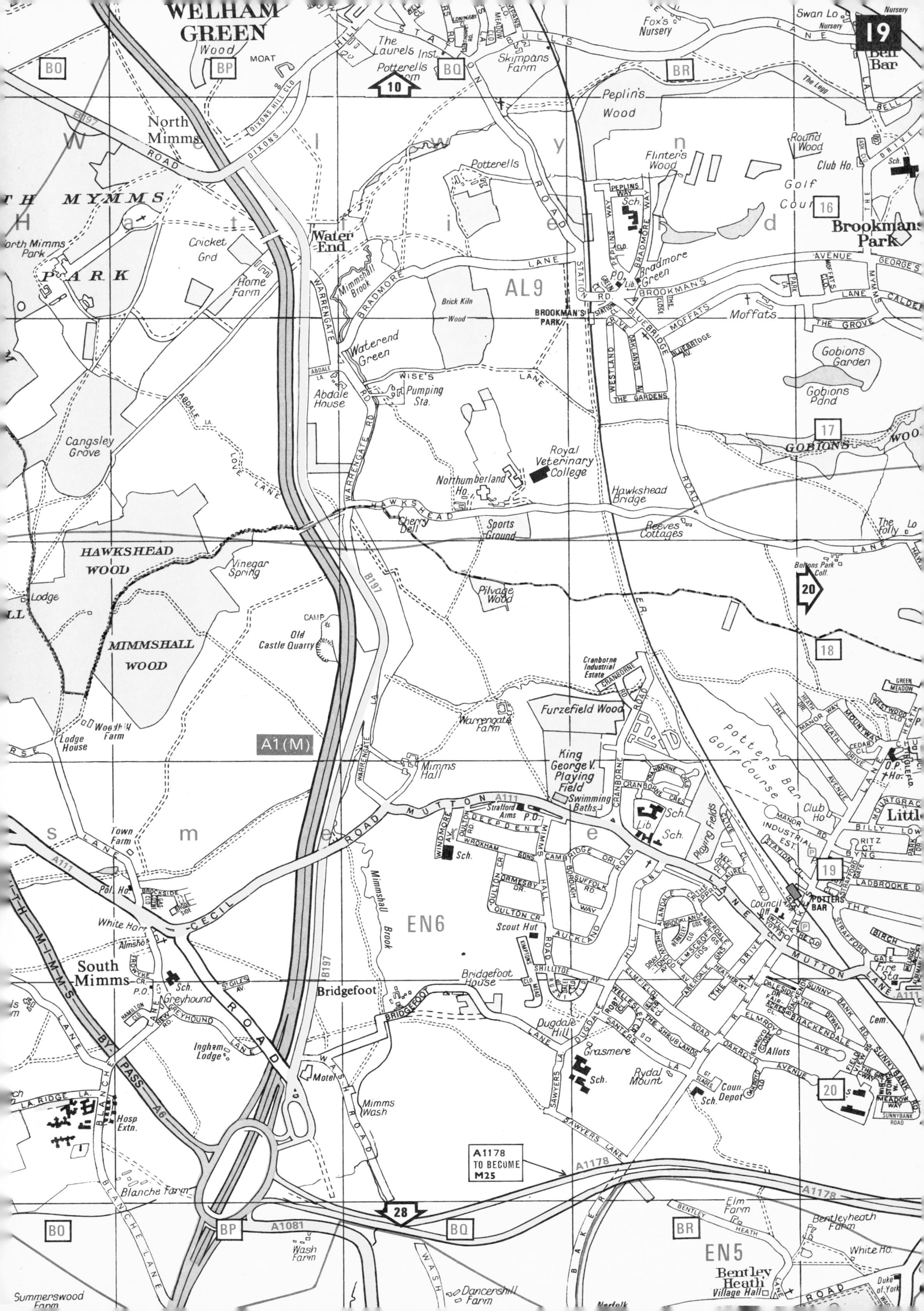
WELHAM GREEN
Wood
MOAT
BO
BP
BQ
BR
10
The Laurels Inst.
Potterells Farm
Skimpans Farm
Fox's Nursery
Swan Lo
Nursery
Bell Bar
Peplin's Wood
The Legg
North Mimms
Round Wood
Flinter's Wood
Potterells
Club Ho.
Golf Course
16
Brookmans Park
Water End
Cricket Gnd
Home Farm
North Mimms Park
PARK
Mimmshall Brook
Brick Kiln Wood
AL9
BROOKMAN'S PARK
Bradmore Green
Moffats
THE GROVE
Gobions Garden
Gobions Pond
Waterend Green
Abdale House
Pumping Sta.
Cangsley Grove
17
GOBIONS
Royal Veterinary College
Northumberland Ho.
Hawkshead Bridge
Cherry Dell
Sports Ground
Reeves Cottages
The Folly
HAWKSHEAD WOOD
Vinegar Spring
Lodge
Pilvage Wood
Gobions Park Coll.
20
CAMP
Old Castle Quarry
MIMMSHALL WOOD
18
Cranborne Industrial Estate
Furzefield Wood
Warrengate Farm
Woodhill Farm
Lodge House
Potters Bar Golf Course
A1(M)
King George V. Playing Field
Swimming Baths
Mimms Hall
Strafford Arms
P.O.
Sch.
Lib.
Playing Fields
Club Ho.
Little
Town Farm
19
POTTERS BAR
Council Off.
EN6
Mimmshall Brook
White Hart
Almshos
South Mimms
Greyhound
Scout Hut
Bridgefoot
Bridgefoot House
Fire Sta.
Cem.
Ingham Lodge
Dugdale Hill
Grasmere
Rydal Mount
Allots
Coun. Depot
20
Motel
Mimms Wash
Hosp Extn.
A1178 TO BECOME M25
A1178
Blanche Farm
Elm Farm
Bentleyheath Farm
BO
BP
A1081
28
BQ
BR
Wash Farm
EN5
White Ho.
Bentley Heath
Village Hall
Duke of York
Summerswood Farm
Dancershill Farm

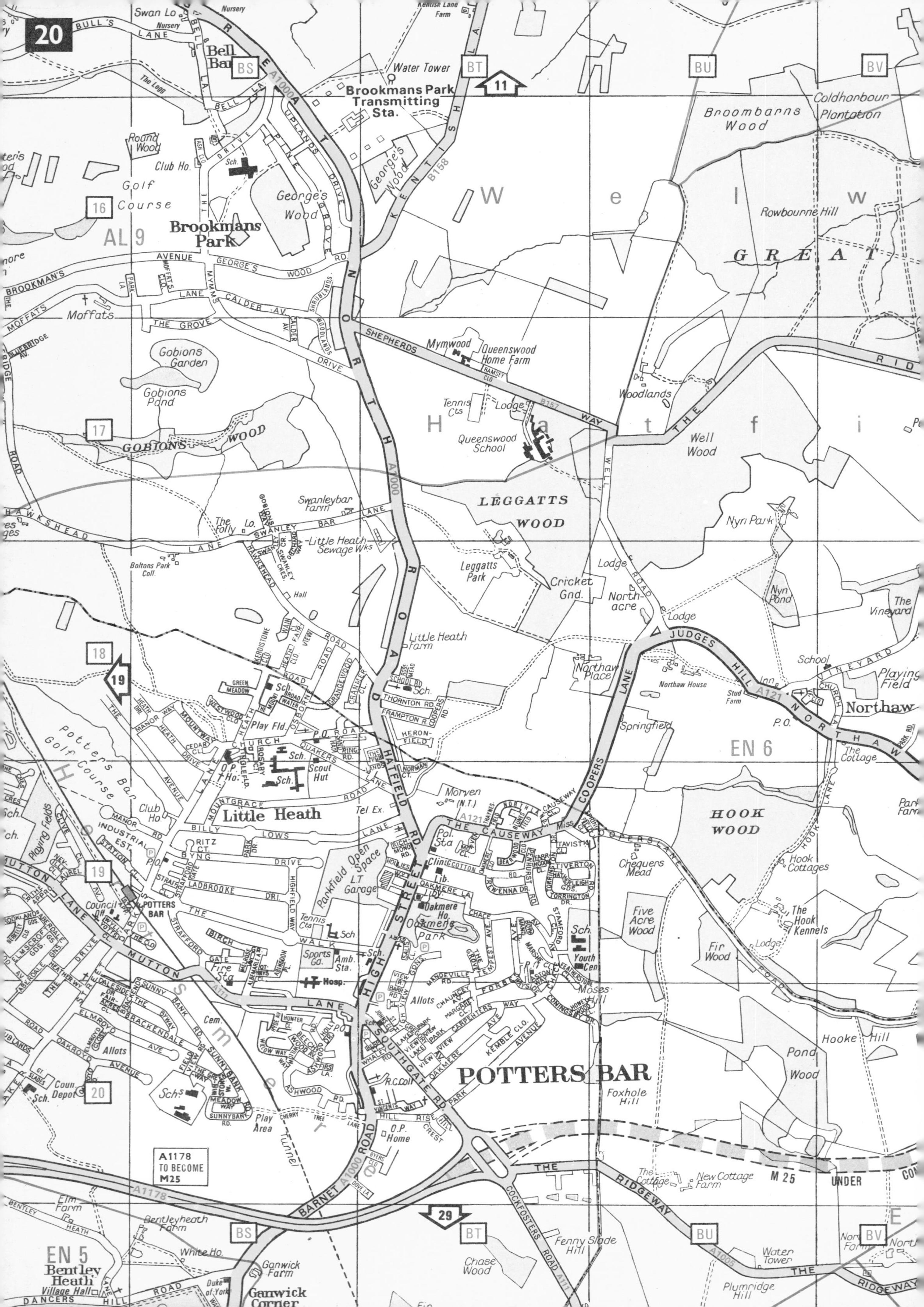

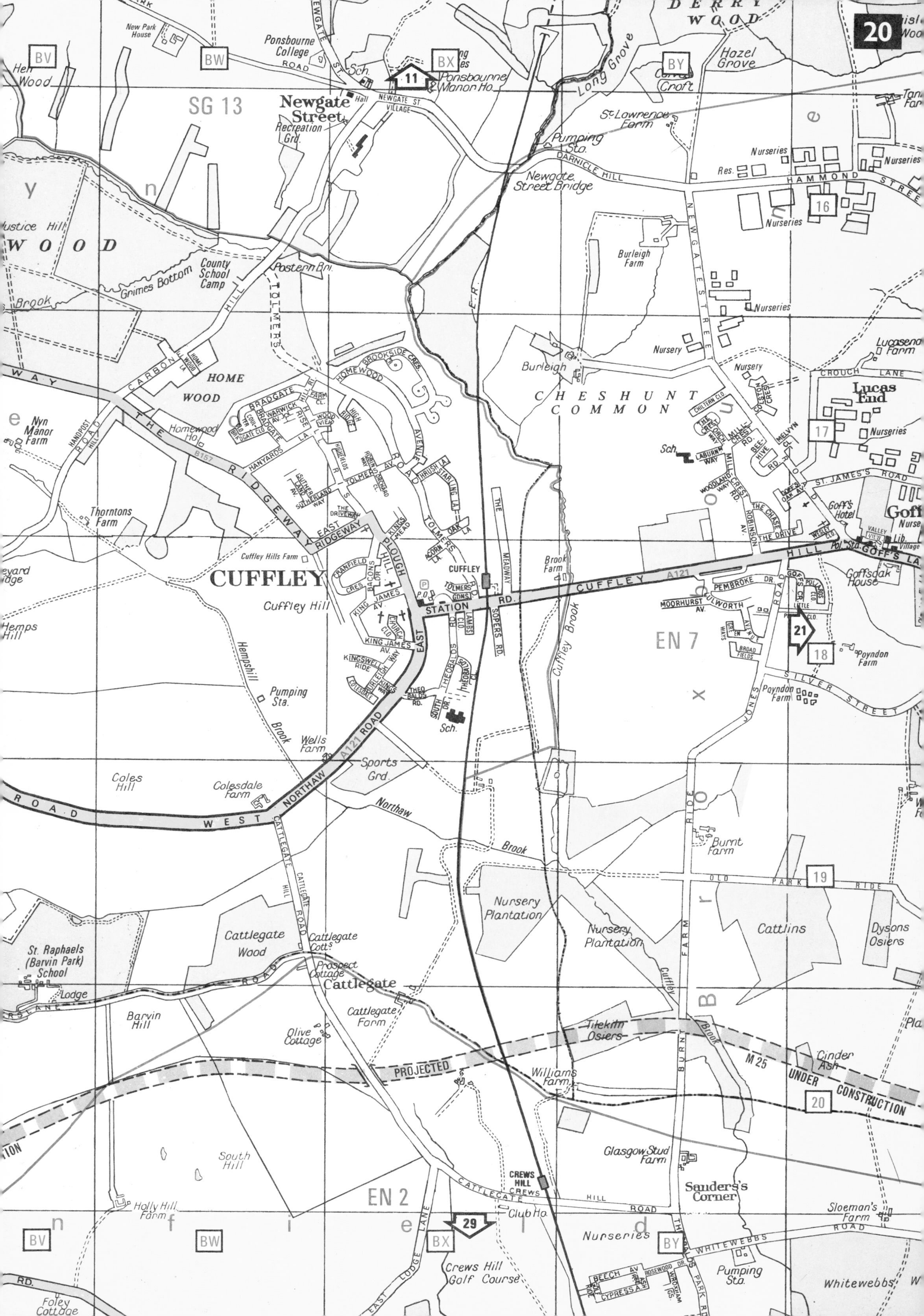
New Park House
Ponsbourne College
Ponsbourne Manor Ho.
DERRY WOOD
Hazel Grove
Long Grove
Hen Wood
SG 13
Newgate Street
Recreation Grd.
St. Lawrence Farm
Pumping Sta.
DARNICLE HILL
Newgate Street Bridge
HAMMOND STREET
Nurseries
Justice Hill
WOOD
Postern Bri.
County School Camp
Grimes Bottom
Brook
Burleigh Farm
TOLMERS
Burleigh
CHESHUNT COMMON
Lucasend Farm
CROUCH LANE
Lucas End
HOME WOOD
Homewood Ho.
Nyn Manor Farm
THE RIDGEWAY
ST. JAMES'S ROAD
Goffs Hotel
Thorntons Farm
Cuffley Hills Farm
CUFFLEY
Cuffley Hill
STATION RD.
CUFFLEY HILL
Brook Farm
Goffsoak House
Hemps Hill
Hempshill
Pumping Sta.
EN 7
Poyndon Farm
SILVER STREET
Wells Farm
Sports Grd.
Coles Hill
Colesdale Farm
NORTHAW ROAD WEST
Northaw Brook
Burnt Farm
OLD PARK RIDE
Nursery Plantation
Cattlins
Dysons Osiers
St. Raphaels (Barvin Park) School
Lodge
Cattlegate Wood
Cattlegate Cotts
Prospect Cottage
Cattlegate
Cattlegate Farm
Barvin Hill
Olive Cottage
Titekiln Osiers
PROJECTED
M 25 UNDER CONSTRUCTION
Cinder Ash
Williams Farm
Glasgow Stud Farm
South Hill
CREWS HILL
CATTLEGATE ROAD
Sauders's Corner
EN 2
Holly Hill Farm
Club Ho.
Sloeman's Farm
WHITEWEBBS ROAD
Nurseries
Crews Hill Golf Course
EAST LODGE LANE
Pumping Sta.
THEOBALDS PARK RD
Whitewebbs
Foley Cottage

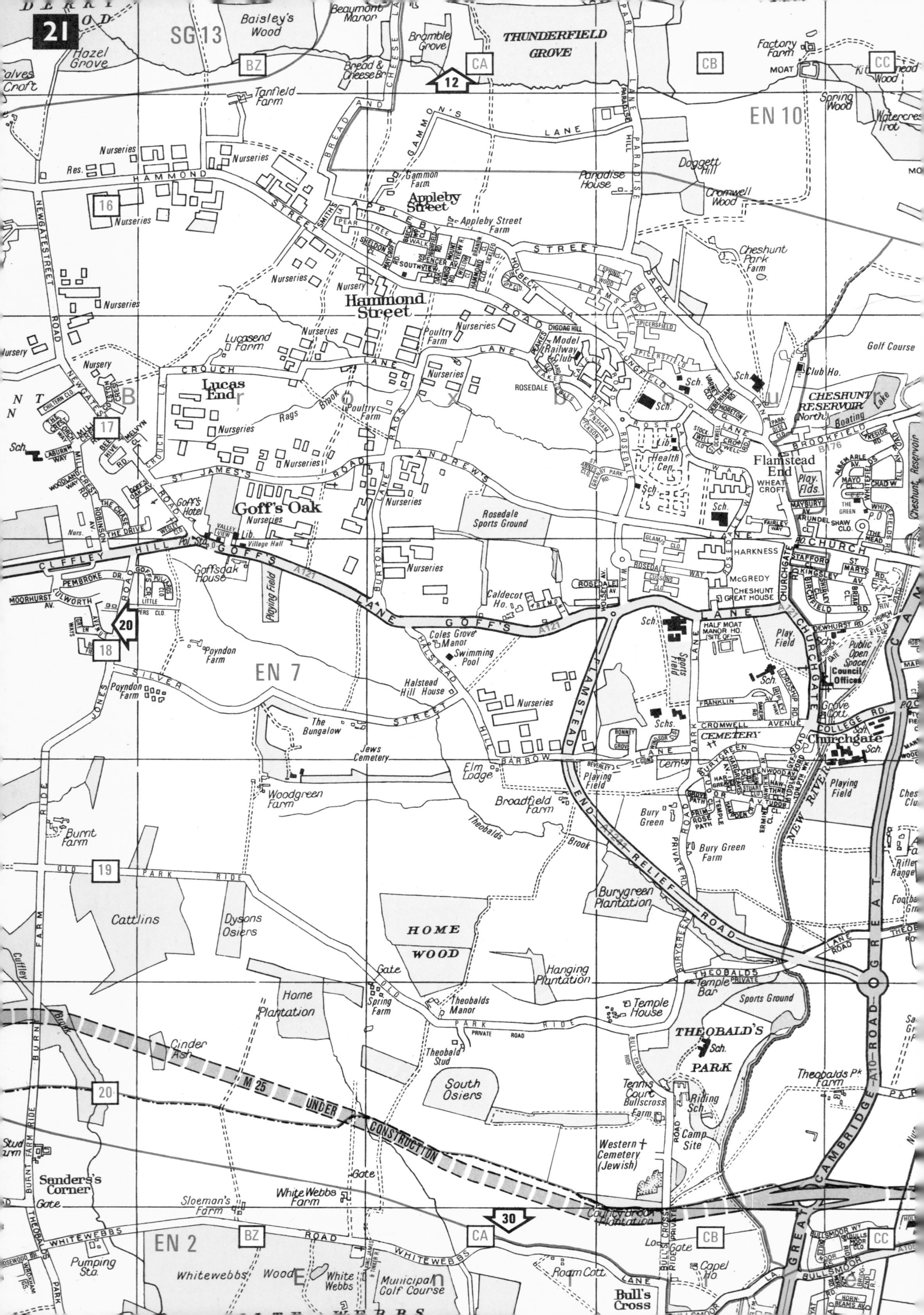

SG 13
EN 10
EN 7
EN 2
BZ
CA
CB
CC
12
30
16
17
18
19
20
Hazel Grove
Baisley's Wood
Beaumont Manor
Bramble Grove
Bread & Cheese Br
THUNDERFIELD GROVE
Factory Farm
MOAT
Spring Wood
Tanfield Farm
Nurseries
Res.
HAMMOND STREET
BREAD AND CHEESE LANE
GAMMON'S LANE
PARADISE HILL
Doggett Hill
Paradise House
Cromwell Wood
Gammon Farm
Appleby Street
Appleby Street Farm
NEWGATESTREET ROAD
Hammond Street
Cheshunt Park Farm
Lucasend Farm
Lucas End
CROUCH LANE
Poultry Farm
Model Railway Club
ROSEDALE
Golf Course
Club Ho.
CHESHUNT RESERVOIR (North)
Boating Lake
Flamstead End
Rags
Brook
Poultry Farm
ST JAMES'S ROAD
ST ANDREW'S ROAD
Goff's Oak
Goff's Hotel
Lib.
Village Hall
Rosedale Sports Ground
Goffsoak House
Playing Field
GOFF'S LANE
A121
CUFFLEY HILL
Caldecot Ho.
Coles Grove Manor
Swimming Pool
Poyndon Farm
SILVER STREET
Halstead Hill House
The Bungalow
Jews Cemetery
BARROW LANE
Elm Lodge
Woodgreen Farm
Broadfield Farm
Theobalds Brook
Burnt Farm
OLD PARK RIDE
Cattlins
Dysons Osiers
HOME WOOD
Hanging Plantation
Burygreen Plantation
FLAMSTEAD END RELIEF ROAD
Bury Green
Bury Green Farm
CEMETERY
Churchgate
Council Offices
Playing Field
NEW RIVER
Gate
Spring Farm
Theobalds Manor
Home Plantation
PARK RIDE
PRIVATE ROAD
Temple Bar
Temple House
Sports Ground
THEOBALD'S PARK
Cinder Ash
M 25 UNDER CONSTRUCTION
Theobald Stud
South Osiers
Tennis Court
Bullscross Farm
Riding Sch.
Camp Site
Western Cemetery (Jewish)
Theobalds Pk Farm
GREAT CAMBRIDGE ROAD A10
Sanders's Corner
Gate
Sloeman's Farm
White Webbs Farm
County Brook Plantation
WHITEWEBBS ROAD
Pumping Sta.
Whitewebbs Wood
White Webbs
Municipal Golf Course
Roam Cott.
Bull's Cross
Capel Ho.
BULLSMOOR LANE
BURNT FARM RIDE
THEOBALDS PARK ROAD

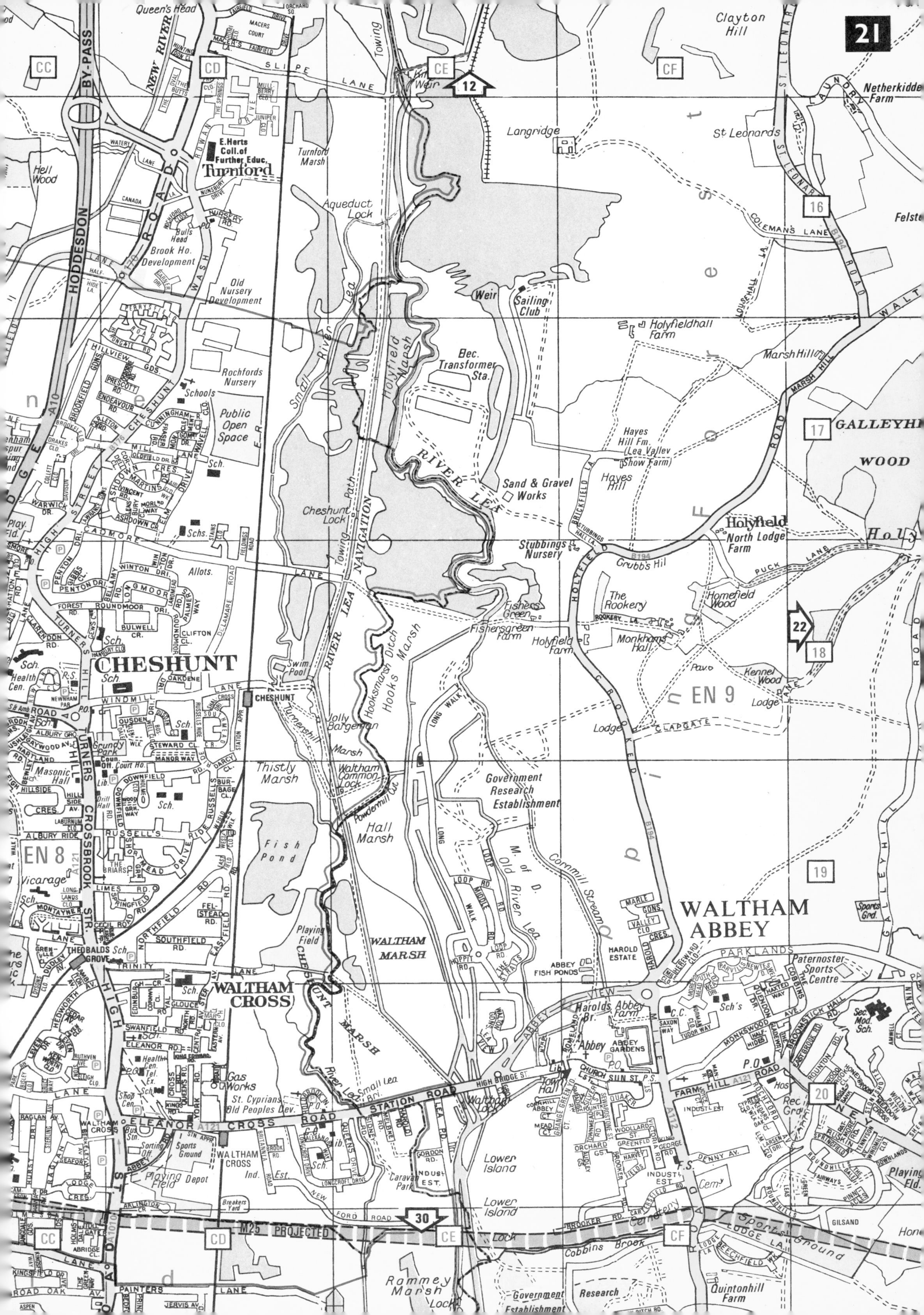

CHESHUNT
WALTHAM CROSS
WALTHAM ABBEY
Turnford
Holyfield
EN 8
EN 9
HODDESDON BY-PASS
A10
RIVER LEA NAVIGATION
RIVER LEA
Small River Lea
Old River Lea
Cornmill Stream
Turnford Marsh
Holyfield Marsh
Hooks Marsh
Hall Marsh
Thistly Marsh
WALTHAM MARSH
Aqueduct Lock
Cheshunt Lock
Waltham Common Lock
Waltham Lock
Rammey Marsh Lock
Fish Pond
Sand & Gravel Works
Elec. Transformer Sta.
Sailing Club
Weir
Government Research Establishment
Rochfords Nursery
Public Open Space
E.Herts Coll.of Further Educ.
Hell Wood
Clayton Hill
Langridge
St Leonards
Netherkidders Farm
Holyfieldhall Farm
Hayes Hill Fm. (Lea Valley Show Farm)
Holyfield North Lodge Farm
The Rookery
Monkhams Hall
Kennel Wood
Homefield Wood
GALLEYHILL WOOD
Stubbings Nursery
Fishers Green
Fishersgreen Farm
Holyfield Farm
Harolds Abbey Farm
ABBEY GARDENS
Abbey
Paternoster Sports Centre
Lower Island
Gas Works
Playing Field
Sports Ground
M25 PROJECTED
SLIPE LANE
STATION ROAD
ELEANOR CROSS ROAD
HIGH BRIDGE ST.
FARM HILL ROAD
CROOKED MILE
B194
A121
A112
CC
CD
CE
CF
12
16
17
18
19
20
22
30

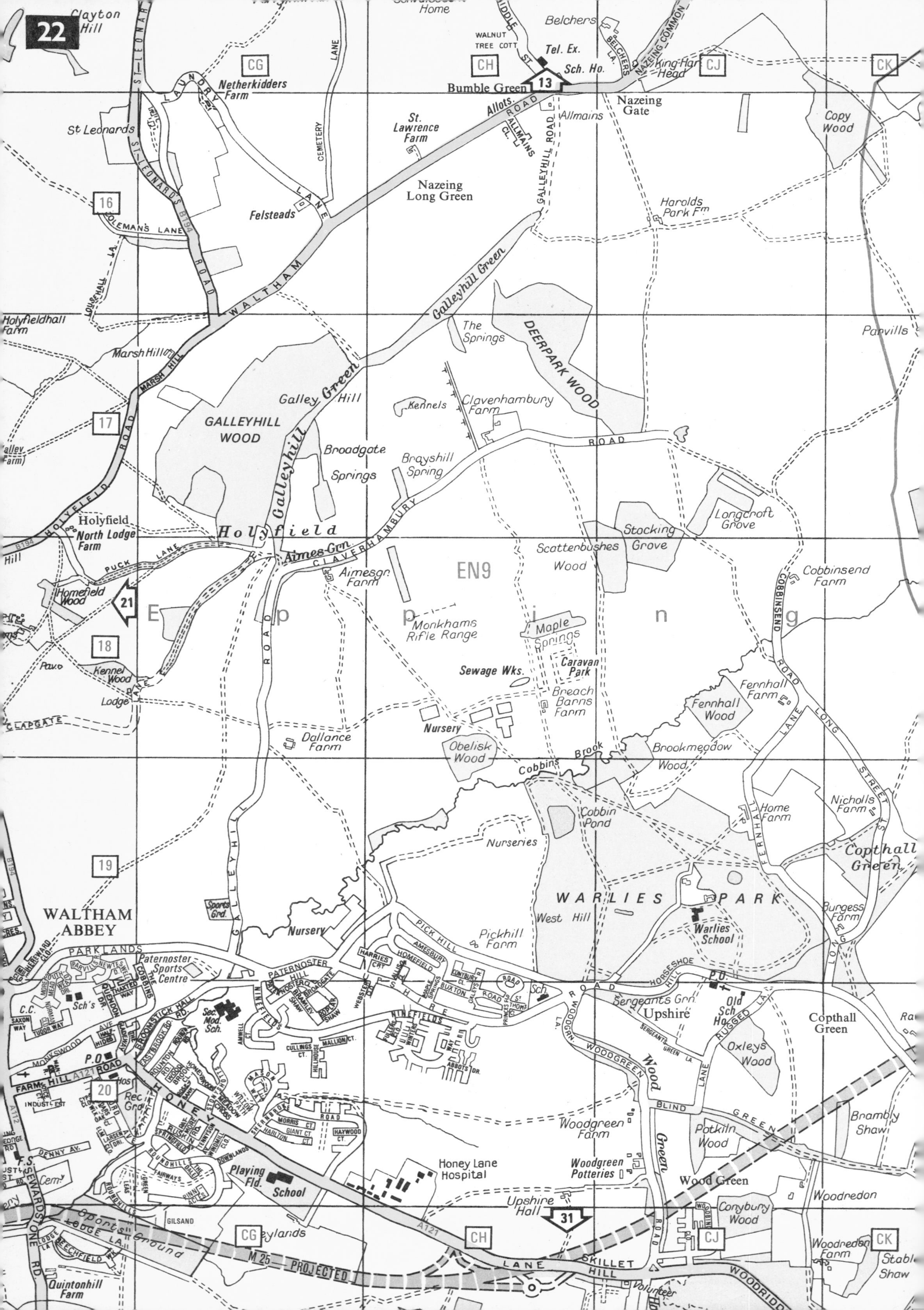
Clayton Hill
CG
CH
CJ
CK
Netherkidders Farm
Bumble Green
13
Tel. Ex.
Sch. Ho.
Belchers
King Harold's Head
Nazeing Gate
St Leonards
St. Lawrence Farm
Allmains
Copy Wood
Nazeing Long Green
Felsteads
Harolds Park Fm
16
WALTHAM ROAD
Galleyhill Green
The Springs
DEERPARK WOOD
Holyfieldhall Farm
Marsh Hill
Parvills
Galley Green Hill
Kennels
Clavenhambury Farm
GALLEYHILL WOOD
17
Broadgate Springs
Brayshill Spring
Holyfield
North Lodge Farm
Holyfield
Stocking Grove
Longcroft Grove
Aimes Grn
Scatterbushes Wood
Aimesgn Farm
EN9
Cobbinsend Farm
Homefield Wood
21
Epping
Monkhams Rifle Range
Maple Springs
Caravan Park
18
Kennel Wood
Lodge
Sewage Wks.
Breach Barns Farm
Fernhall Farm
Fernhall Wood
CLAPGATE
Dallance Farm
Nursery
Obelisk Wood
Cobbins Brook
Brookmeadow Wood
Cobbin Pond
Home Farm
Nicholls Farm
Nurseries
19
Copthall Green
WALTHAM ABBEY
Sports Grd.
WARLIES PARK
West Hill
Warlies School
Burgess Farm
Nursery
Pickhill Farm
PARKLANDS
Paternoster Sports Centre
Sch's
Sec. Mod. Sch.
Sch
Sergeants Grn.
Upshire
Old Sch Ho.
P.O.
Copthall Green
P.O.
20
Rec Grd.
Woodgreen Wood
Oxleys Wood
Woodgreen Farm
Potkiln Wood
Brambly Shaw
Honey Lane Hospital
Playing Fld.
School
Woodgreen Potteries
Wood Green
Woodredon
Cem.
Upshire Hall
31
Conybury Wood
Sports Ground
CG
Heylands
CH
CJ
CK
Woodredon Farm
M 25 PROJECTED
SKILLET HILL
Stable Shaw
Quintonhill Farm
Volunteer

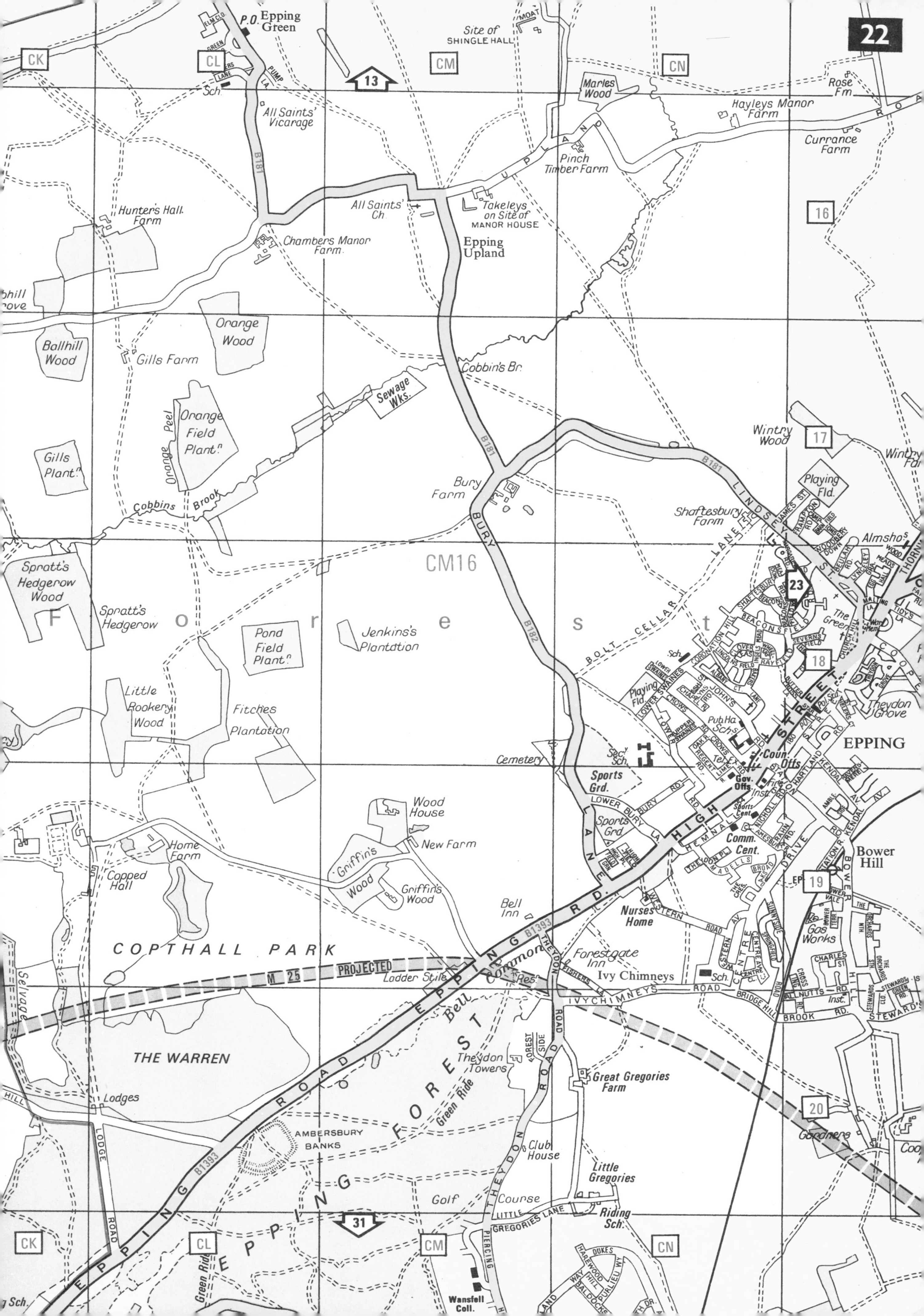
Epping Green
P.O.
Site of SHINGLE HALL
CK
CL
CM
CN
13
Marles Wood
Rose Fm.
Hayleys Manor Farm
All Saints' Vicarage
Currance Farm
UPLAND
Pinch Timber Farm
B181
16
Hunter's Hall Farm
All Saints' Ch.
Takeleys on Site of MANOR HOUSE
Chambers Manor Farm
Epping Upland
Orange Wood
Ballhill Wood
Gills Farm
Cobbin's Br.
Sewage Wks.
Orange Field Plant.n
Orange Peel
Gills Plant.n
Wintry Wood
17
Playing Fld.
Bury Farm
Cobbins Brook
Shaftesbury Farm
BURY
LINDSEY
LANE
CM16
Spratt's Hedgerow Wood
Spratt's Hedgerow
Almshos
23
F o r e s t
Pond Field Plant.n
Jenkins's Plantation
B182
BOLT CELLAR
BEACONSFIELD
The Green
18
Little Rookery Wood
Fitches Plantation
Playing Fld
Sch.
Theydon Grove
EPPING
Cemetery
Sports Grd.
Coun. Offs
Gov. Offs
Wood House
LOWER BURY
Sports Grd.
HIGH
STREET
Home Farm
New Farm
Comm. Cent.
Bower Hill
Copped Hall
Griffin's Wood
Griffin's Wood
Bell Inn
19
Nurses Home
Gas Works
COPTHALL PARK
EPPING RD.
B1393
Forestgate Inn
M 25 PROJECTED
Ladder Stile
Bell Common
Ivy Chimneys
Sch.
IVYCHIMNEYS ROAD
BROOK RD.
Selvage
THE WARREN
THEYDON ROAD
Theydon Towers
FOREST SIDE
Great Gregories Farm
Lodges
Green Ride
20
Goodnere
AMBERSBURY BANKS
EPPING FOREST
Club House
LODGE ROAD
Little Gregories
Golf Course
EPPING ROAD
B1393
31
LITTLE GREGORIES LANE
Riding Sch.
CK
CL
CM
CN
Green Ride
PIERCING HILL
Wansfell Coll.

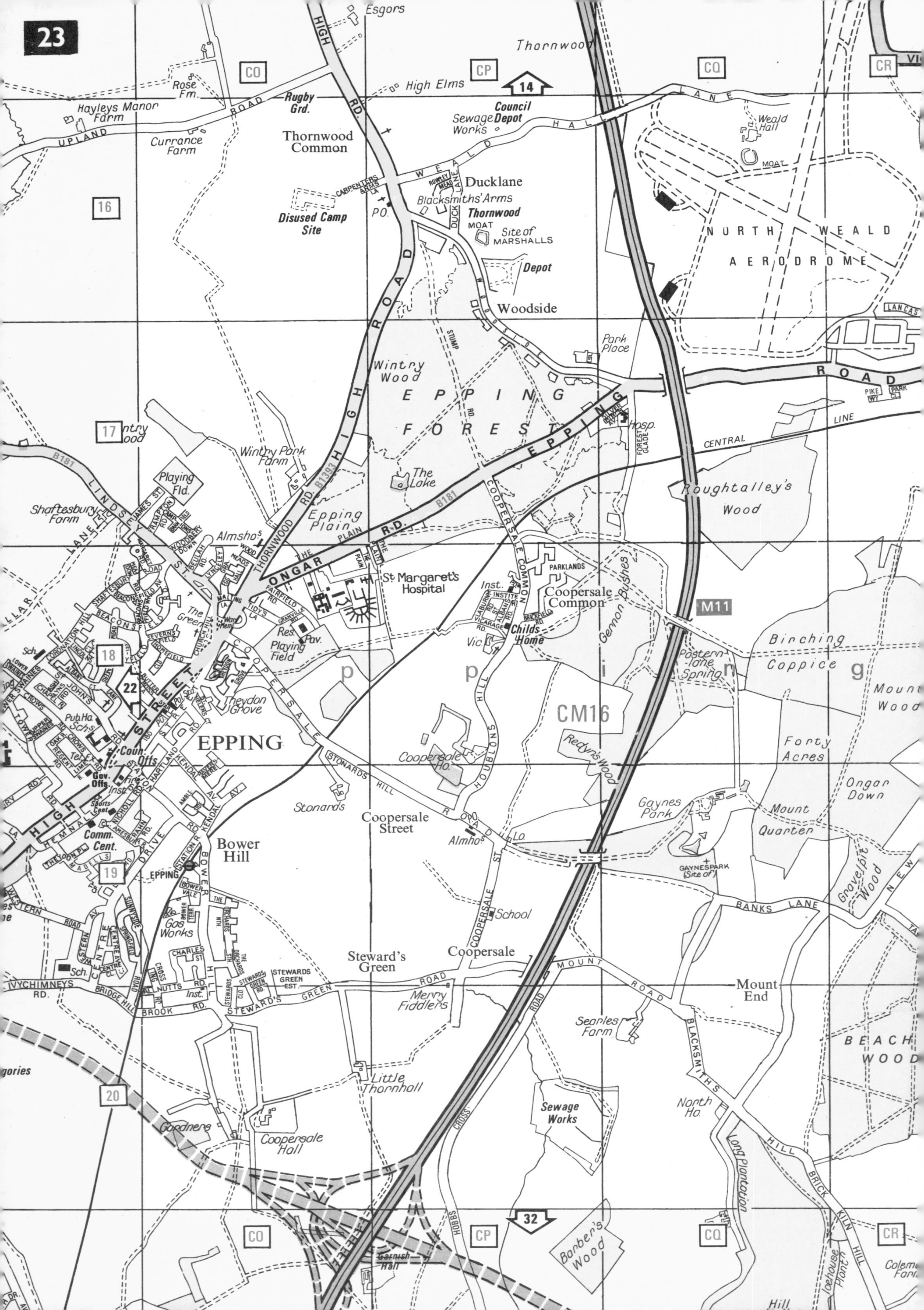

Esgors
Thornwood
CO
CP
CQ
CR
14
Rose Fm.
High Elms
Hayleys Manor Farm
UPLAND ROAD
Rugby Grd.
Council Depot
Sewage Works
WEALD HALL LANE
Weald Hall
MOAT
Currance Farm
Thornwood Common
16
CARPENTERS ARMS
Ducklane
Blacksmiths' Arms
P.O.
Disused Camp Site
Thornwood
MOAT
Site of MARSHALLS
NORTH WEALD AERODROME
Depot
HIGH ROAD
WOODSIDE
Woodside
Park Place
Wintry Wood
EPPING FOREST
ROAD
PIKE WY
PARK CL
17
Wintry Park Farm
Hosp.
CENTRAL LINE
Playing Fld.
B181
B1393
LINDSEY ST
The Lake
Roughtalley's Wood
Shaftesbury Farm
Epping Plain
PLAIN RD.
EPPING
Almsho's
THORNWOOD RD.
COOPERSALE COMMON
ONGAR
St Margaret's Hospital
PARKLANDS
Inst.
Coopersale Common
Gernon Bushes
M11
FAIRFIELD RD.
The Green
Childs Home
Vic.
Res. Pav.
Playing Field
Birching Coppice
Postern lane Spring
18
22
Sch.
HIGH STREET
Theydon Grove
COOPERSALE
Epping
CM16
Mount Wood
EPPING
Coun. Offs
Gov. Offs.
Redyn's Wood
Forty Acres
STONARDS HILL
Coopersale Ho.
HOUBLONS HILL
Ongar Down
Stonards
Gaynes Park
Mount Quarter
Coopersale Street
Almho's
Lo.
Comm. Cent.
Bower Hill
Sports Cent
GAYNESPARK (Site of)
19
EPPING
BANKS LANE
Gravelpit Wood
Gas Works
School
Steward's Green
Coopersale
MOUNT ROAD
Mount End
IVYCHIMNEYS RD.
BRIDGE HILL
BROOK RD.
STEWARD'S GREEN ROAD
STEWARDS GREEN EST.
Merry Fiddlers
Searles Farm
BEACH WOOD
BLACKSMITHS HILL
20
Little Thornhall
Sewage Works
North Ho.
Gardners
Coopersale Hall
Long Plantation
BRICK KILN HILL
32
Barber's Wood
Garnish Hall
HOBBS CROSS ROAD
Icehouse Plant
Hill

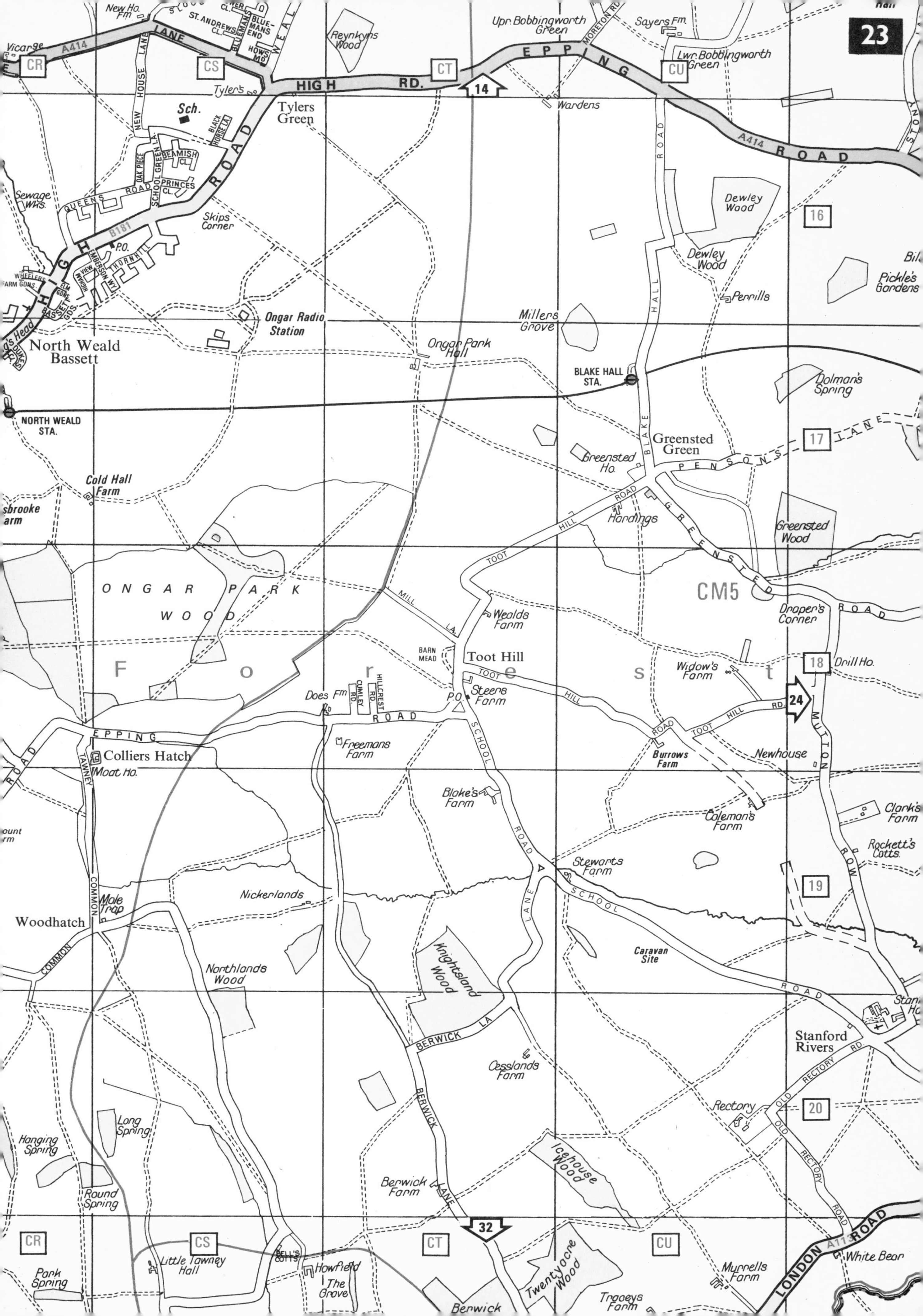
North Weald Bassett
Tylers Green
Ongar Radio Station
Ongar Park Hall
Millers Grove
BLAKE HALL STA.
NORTH WEALD STA.
Greensted Green
Greensted Ho.
Hardings
Greensted Wood
Dewley Wood
Perrills
Pickle's Gardens
Dolman's Spring
Upr. Bobbingworth Green
Lwr. Bobbingworth Green
Sayers Fm.
Wardens
Reynkyns Wood
HIGH RD.
EPPING ROAD
A414
B181
Skips Corner
Sewage Wks.
Cold Hall Farm
ONGAR PARK WOOD
Forest
CM5
Toot Hill
TOOT HILL ROAD
Wealds Farm
MILL LA.
BARN MEAD
Steens Farm
P.O.
Does Fm.
Freemans Farm
Colliers Hatch
Moat Ho.
Burrows Farm
Newhouse
Draper's Corner
Drill Ho.
Widow's Farm
Coleman's Farm
Clark's Farm
Rockett's Cotts.
MUTTON ROW
Blake's Farm
SCHOOL ROAD
Stewarts Farm
Caravan Site
Nickerlands
Mole Trap
Woodhatch
TAWNEY COMMON
Northlands Wood
Knightsland Wood
BERWICK LA.
Cesslands Farm
Stanford Rivers
RECTORY RD.
Rectory
OLD RECTORY ROAD
Long Spring
Hanging Spring
Round Spring
Icehouse Wood
Berwick Farm
BERWICK LANE
Little Tawney Hall
BELL'S COTTS.
Howfield
The Grove
Twentyacre Wood
Traceys Farm
Murrells Farm
White Bear
LONDON ROAD A113
Park Spring
Berwick
14
16
17
18
19
20
24
32
CR
CS
CT
CU

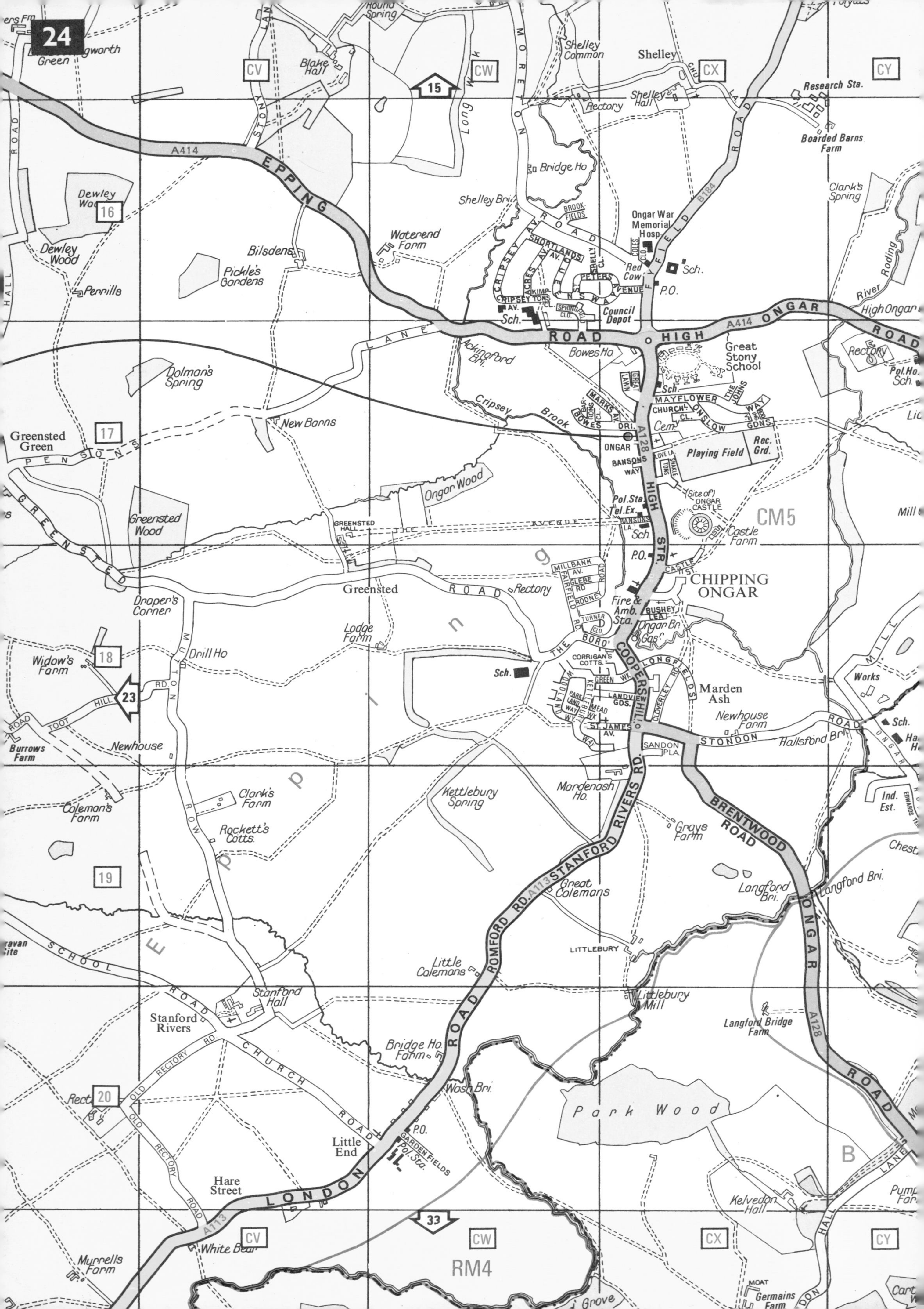
CV
CW
CX
CY
15
33
23
16
17
18
19
20
Blake Hall
Round Spring
Shelley Common
Shelley
Shelley Hall
Rectory
Research Sta.
Boarded Barns Farm
Long Walk
MORETON
STONY LANE
EPPING
A414
ROAD
Bridge Ho
Shelley Bri.
Clark's Spring
Dewley Wood
Waterend Farm
Bilsdens
Pickle's Gardens
Pennills
Ongar War Memorial Hosp.
Red Cow
Sch.
P.O.
FYFIELD
B184
Council Depot
CRIPSEY AV.
SHORTLANDS AV.
BROOKFIELDS
PETERS
AVENUE
ROAD
HIGH
ONGAR
High Ongar
River Roding
Rectory
Pol.Ho.
Sch.
Bowes Ho.
Great Stony School
Ackingford Bri.
LANE
Dolman's Spring
Cripsey Brook
New Barns
MAYFLOWER
CHURCH CL.
ONSLOW GDNS.
Cem.
ONGAR
A128
BANSONS WAY
Playing Field
Rec. Grd.
Greensted Green
PENSONS
GREENSTED
Ongar Wood
Greensted Wood
GREENSTED HALL
HIGH STR.
Pol.Sta.
Tel.Ex.
(Site of) ONGAR CASTLE
Castle Farm
CM5
Mill
Greensted
ROAD
Rectory
Draper's Corner
MILLBANK AV.
GLEBE RD
RODNEY
CHIPPING ONGAR
Fire & Amb. Sta.
BUSHEY LEA
Ongar Br.
Gas
Lodge Farm
THE BORO'
TURNER CL.
COOPERSHILL
LONGFIELDS
Drill Ho
Widow's Farm
MUTTON ROW
TOOT HILL RD.
Sch.
Marden Ash
Works
Sch.
Newhouse Farm
STONDON ROAD
Hallsford Bri.
ST JAMES AV.
SANDON PLA.
Burrows Farm
Newhouse
Clark's Farm
Kettlebury Spring
Mardenash Ho.
Ind. Est.
Coleman's Farm
Rockett's Cotts.
Grays Farm
BRENTWOOD ROAD
STANFORD RIVERS RD.
Great Colemans
Langford Bri.
Langford Bri.
ONGAR
Epping
Caravan Site
SCHOOL ROAD
LITTLEBURY
Little Colemans
ROMFORD RD.
A113
Stanford Hall
Stanford Rivers
Littlebury Mill
Langford Bridge Farm
A128
RECTORY RD.
CHURCH ROAD
Bridge Ho. Farm
Wash Bri.
ROAD
Rect.
OLD RECTORY ROAD
P.O.
Little End
GARDEN FIELDS
Pol.Sta.
Park Wood
B
Hare Street
LONDON
Kelvedon Hall
HALL LANE
White Bear
RM4
Murrells Farm
Grove
MOAT
Germains Farm

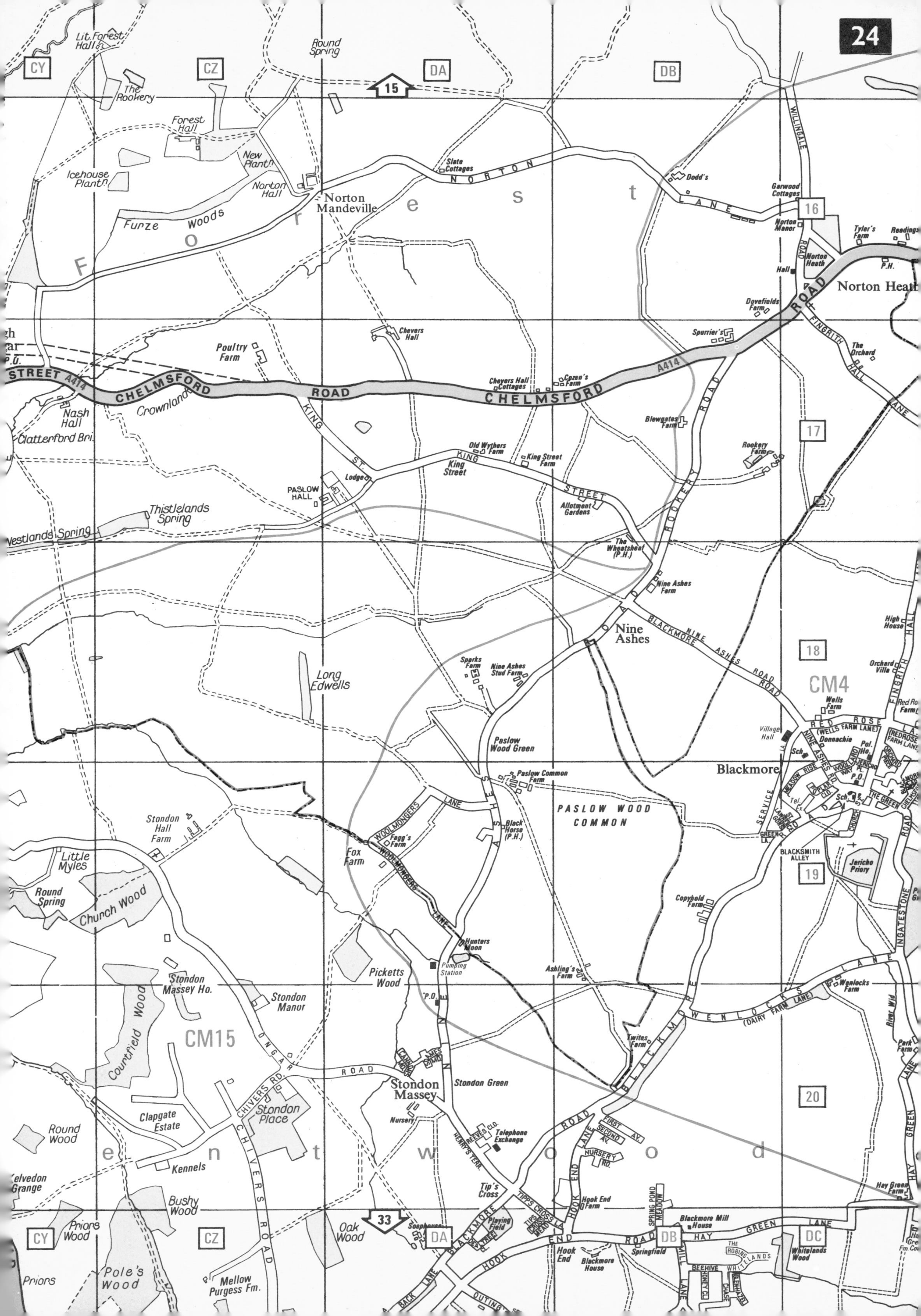
CY
CZ
DA
DB
DC
15
33
16
17
18
19
20
Lit. Forest Hall
Round Spring
The Rookery
Forest Hall
New Plantn
Icehouse Plantn
Norton Hall
Norton Mandeville
Furze Woods
Forest
Slate Cottages
NORTON LANE
Dodd's
WILLINGALE
Garwood Cottages
Norton Manor
Tyler's Farm
Readings
Norton Heath
Hall
P.H.
Dovefields Farm
Spurrier's
FINGRITH HALL LANE
The Orchard
Chevers Hall
Poultry Farm
STREET A414
CHELMSFORD ROAD
A414
Chevers Hall Cottages
Cozen's Farm
Crownland
Nash Hall
Clatterford Bri.
KING ST.
Old Wythers Farm
King Street Farm
King Street
KING STREET
Blewgates Farm
Rookery Farm
ROOKERY ROAD
PASLOW HALL
Lodge
Allotment Gardens
Thistlelands Spring
Westlands Spring
The Wheatsheaf (P.H.)
Nine Ashes Farm
Nine Ashes
BLACKMORE NINE ASHES ROAD
High House
Orchard Villa
CM4
Long Edwells
Sparks Farm
Nine Ashes Stud Farm
Wells Farm
RED ROSE LANE
(WELLS FARM LANE)
Red Rose Farm
(REDROSE FARM LANE)
Donnachie
Village Hall
Sch.
Pol. Ho.
Paslow Wood Green
Paslow Common Farm
Blackmore
PASLOW WOOD COMMON
P.O.
THE GREEN
Tel. Ex.
SERVICE
Black Horse (P.H.)
WOOLMONGERS LANE
Fagg's Farm
Fox Farm
Stondon Hall Farm
Little Myles
Round Spring
Church Wood
BLACKSMITH ALLEY
Jericho Priory
CHURCH
Copyhold Farm
Hunters Moon
Pumping Station
Picketts Wood
Ashling's Farm
INGATESTONE
Wenlocks Farm
WENLOCKS LANE
(DAIRY FARM LANE)
Stondon Massey Ho.
Stondon Manor
Countfield Wood
CM15
River Wid
Park Farm
Twites Farm
ONGAR ROAD
BLACKMORE ROAD
Stondon Massey
Stondon Green
CHIVERS RD.
Stondon Place
Clapgate Estate
Round Wood
Nursery
REEVES CLO.
HENRY'S TERR.
Telephone Exchange
FIRST AV.
SECOND AV.
NURSERY RD.
HOOK END LANE
Kennels
Kelvedon Grange
CHIVERS ROAD
Tip's Cross
Hook End Farm
Bushy Wood
TIPPS CROSS LA.
Playing Field
Hay Green Farm
SPRING POND MEADOW
Blackmore Mill House
HAY GREEN LANE
Priors Wood
Oak Wood
Soaphouse
HOOK END ROAD
MILL LANE
Springfield
Hook End
Blackmore House
THE ROBINS
WHITELANDS
Whitelands Wood
BEEHIVE
Pole's Wood
Priors
Mellow Purgess Fm.
BACK LANE
OUTING

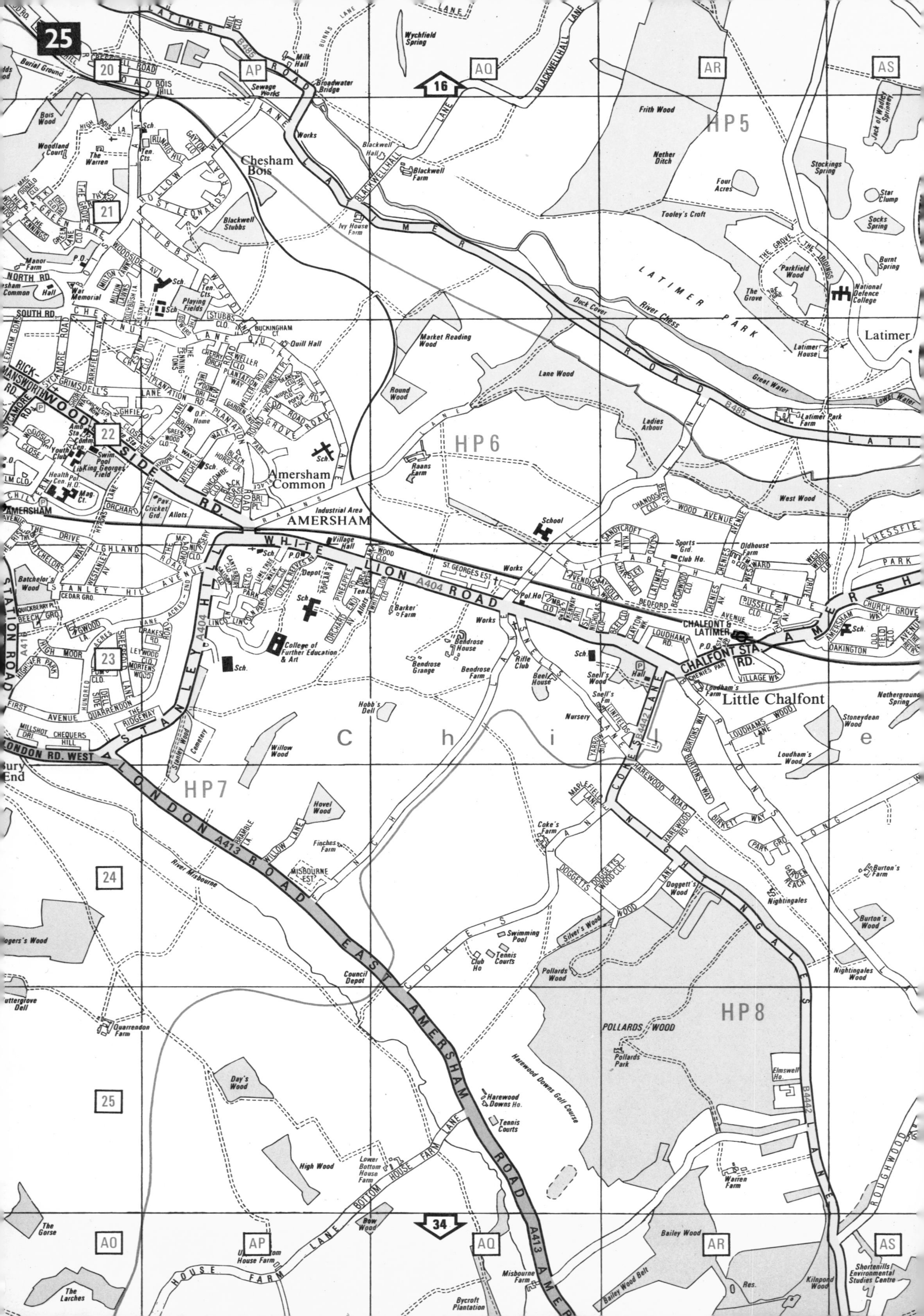

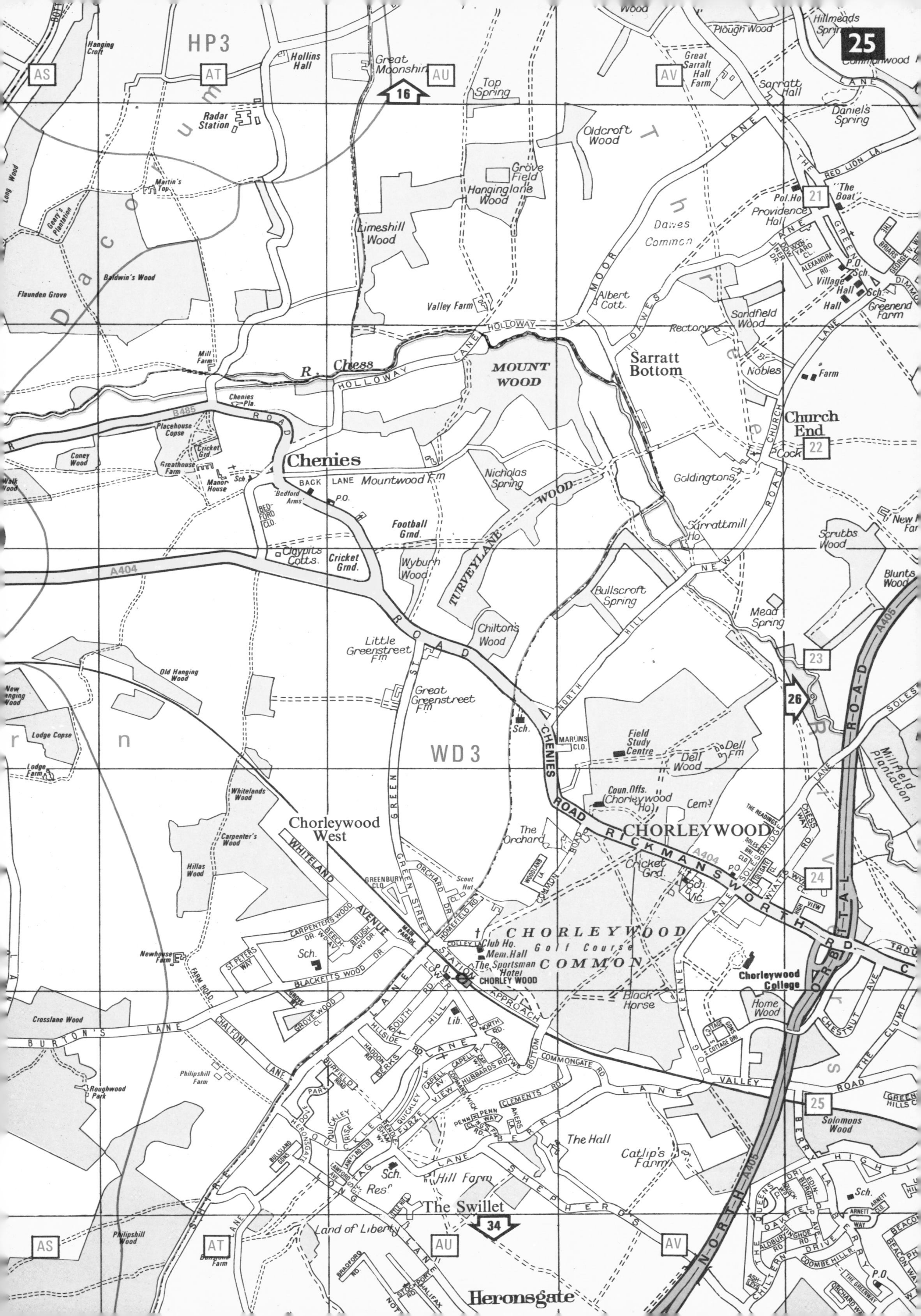

25
HP3
WD3
AS
AT
AU
AV
16
26
34
21
22
23
24
25
Hanging Croft
Hollins Hall
Great Moonshine
Top Spring
Plough Wood
Hillmeads Spring
Great Sarratt Hall Farm
Sarratt Hall
Commonwood
Daniels Spring
Radar Station
Oldcroft Wood
Grove Field
Hanginglane Wood
Long Wood
Martin's Top
Geary's Plantation
Limeshill Wood
Dawes Common
Moor Lane
Red Lion La.
"The Boat"
Pol. Ho.
Providence Hall
Baldwin's Wood
Flaunden Grove
Valley Farm
Albert Cott.
Village Hall
Sch.
P.O.
Greenend Farm
Sandfield Wood
Rectory
Holloway La.
Mill Farm
R. Chess
Holloway Lane
Mount Wood
Sarratt Bottom
Nobles
Farm
Chenies Pla.
B485
Road
Placehouse Copse
Cricket Grd.
Coney Wood
Greathouse Farm
Manor House
Chenies
Back Lane
Mountwood Fm
Nicholas Spring
Church End
Cock
Goldingtons
Church Road
'Bedford Arms'
Bedford Clo.
Football Grnd.
Wood
Sarrattmill Ho
New
Scrubbs Wood
Claypits Cotts.
Cricket Grnd.
A404
Wyburn Wood
Turveylane
Bullscroft Spring
Blunts Wood
Hill
Mead Spring
A405
Chiltons Wood
Little Greenstreet Fm
Old Hanging Wood
Great Greenstreet Fm
North
Sch.
Marlins Clo.
Field Study Centre
Dell Fm
Dell Wood
Millfield Plantation
Lodge Copse
Lodge Farm
Whitelands Wood
Coun. Offs. (Chorleywood Ho)
Cemy
Chorleywood West
Carpenter's Wood
Hillas Wood
Whiteland Avenue
Green
The Orchard
Chorleywood
Rickmansworth
Cricket Grd.
Chess Way
Orbital Road
Greenbury Clo.
Orchard Dr.
Scout Hut
Woodland La
Common Road
Sch.
Vic.
Wyatt's Rd
High View
Carpenters Wood Dr.
Beechwood Dr.
Brushwood Dr.
Main Parade
Station
Chorleywood Golf Course
Chorleywood Common
Club Ho.
Mem. Hall
The Sportsman Hotel
Newhouse Farm
St Peters Way
Blacketts Wood Dr.
Chorley Wood
Approach
Farm Road
Chorleywood College
Black Horse
Home Wood
Kennel Lane
Chestnut Ave
The Clump
Crosslane Wood
Burton's Lane
Chalfont Lane
Grove Wood Cl.
Lib.
Hillside Rd
South Rd
North Rd
Haddon Rd
Berks
Lower Rd
Cottage Dri
Commongate Rd
Valley Road
Philipshill Farm
Roughwood Park
Burfield Road
Park
Quickley Rise
Quickley La.
Capell Av.
View
Hubbards Rd
Clements Rd
Lane
Green Hills Cl.
Solomons Wood
Heronsgate Rd
Penn Way
Berry Lane
Akers
The Hall
Catlip's Farm
Bullsland Gdns
Hill Farm
Sch.
Res.
Shepherds Lane
High Field
Berry La.
Queens Dri.
Edinburgh Dr.
Oakfield Av.
Sch.
Arnett Way
Beacon Way
Long Lane
The Swillet
Land of Liberty
Philipshill Wood
Bullsland Farm
Shire Lane
North Orbital Road
Aldbury Rd
Coombe Hill Rd
Chiltern Drive
The Greenway
Orchard Way
P.O.
Bradford Rd
Stockport Rd
Halifax
Heronsgate

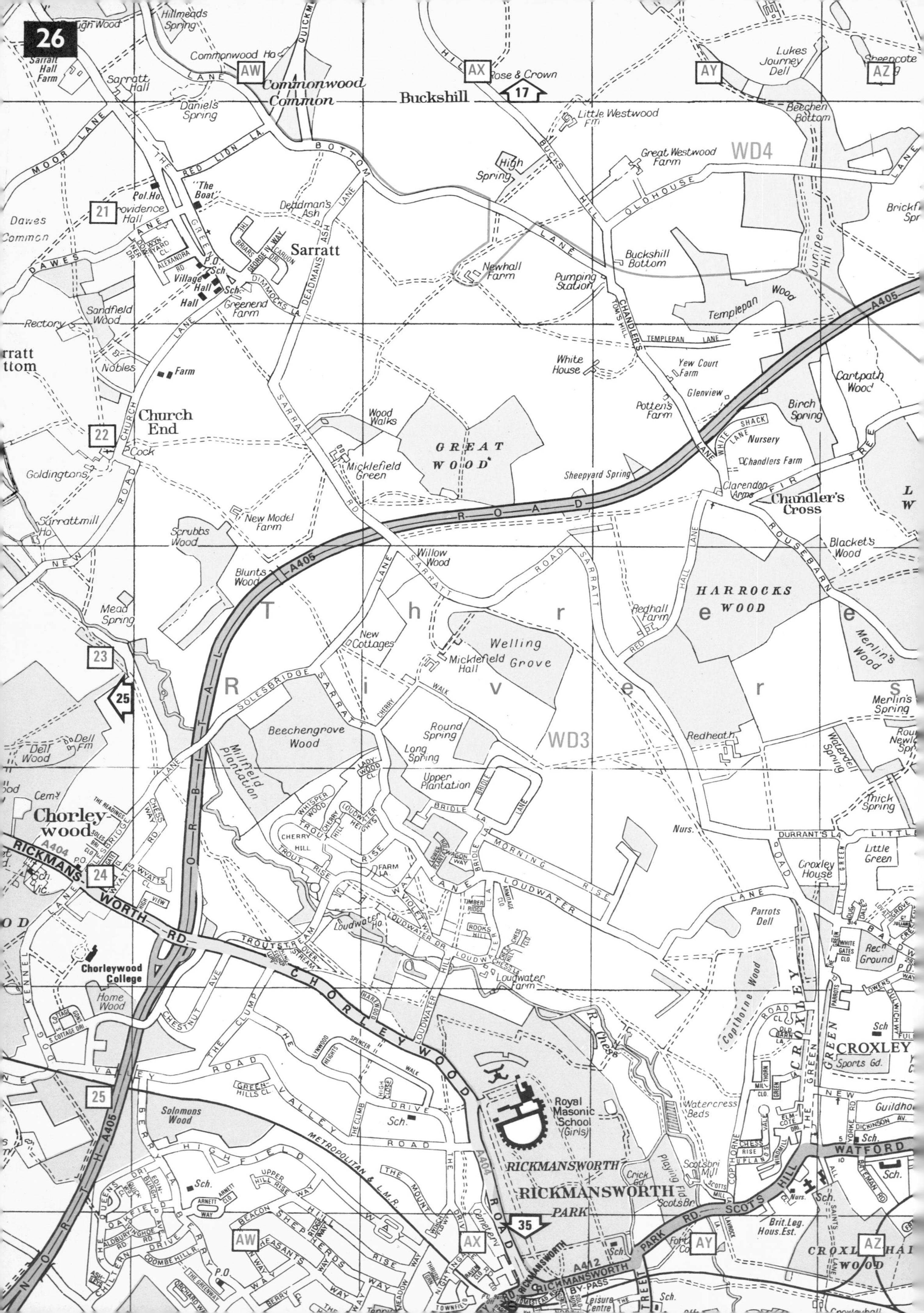
26
Hillmeads Spring
Commonwood Ho
AW
Commonwood Common
AX
Rose & Crown
17
Buckshill
AY
Lukes Journey Dell
AZ
Sheepcote
Sarratt Hall Farm
Sarratt Hall
Daniel's Spring
Little Westwood Fm
Beechen Bottom
Great Westwood Farm
WD4
MOOR LANE
RED LION LA.
BOTTOM
"The Boat"
Pol.Ho
High Spring
Deadman's Ash
OLDHOUSE
21
Providence Hall
Dawes Common
Sarratt
Buckshill Bottom
Newhall Farm
Pumping Station
Juniper Hill
Village Hall
P.O.
Sch.
Greenend Farm
Templepan Wood
Sandfield Wood
Rectory
TEMPLEPAN LANE
Sarratt Bottom
Nobles
Farm
White House
Yew Court Farm
Cartpath Wood
Church End
Glenview
Potten's Farm
Birch Spring
Wood Walks
22
Cock
GREAT WOOD
WHITE SHACK LANE
Nursery
Chandlers Farm
Goldingtons
Micklefield Green
Sheepyard Spring
Clarendon Arms
Chandler's Cross
FIR TREE
New Model Farm
ROAD
Sarrattmill Ho
Scrubbs Wood
A405
Willow Wood
Blacket's Wood
ROUSEBARN
Blunts Wood
Mead Spring
HARROCKS WOOD
Redhall Farm
Three Rivers
Welling Grove
New Cottages
Micklefield Hall
Merlin's Wood
23
25
SOLESBRIDGE
Merlin's Spring
Beechengrove Wood
Round Spring
WD3
Dell Fm
Dell Wood
Redheath
Waterdell Spring
Long Spring
Millfield Plantation
Upper Plantation
Cemy
Chorleywood
Thick Spring
BRIDLE LA
Nurs.
DURRANT'S LA
LITTLE
Little Green
A404
RICKMANSWORTH RD.
MORNING
Croxley House
24
LOUDWATER
RISE
Parrots Dell
Loudwater Ho
TROUTSTREAM
CHORLEYWOOD
Rec Ground
Chorleywood College
Loudwater Farm
Home Wood
Copthorne Wood
Sch
CHESTNUT AVE
R. Chess
CROXLEY
Sports Gd.
VALLEY ROAD
25
Solomons Wood
Royal Masonic School (Girls)
Watercress Beds
Guildho
Sch.
METROPOLITAN & L.M.R.
HIGHFIELD
RICKMANSWORTH
Scotsbri Mill
WATFORD
RICKMANSWORTH PARK
SCOTS HILL
Playing Fld
Scots Br
35
Cemetery
Brit.Leg. Hous.Est.
AW
AX
AY
AZ
CROXLEY HALL WOOD
A412
RICKMANSWORTH BY-PASS
Leisure Centre
NORTH ORBITAL RD.
P.O.

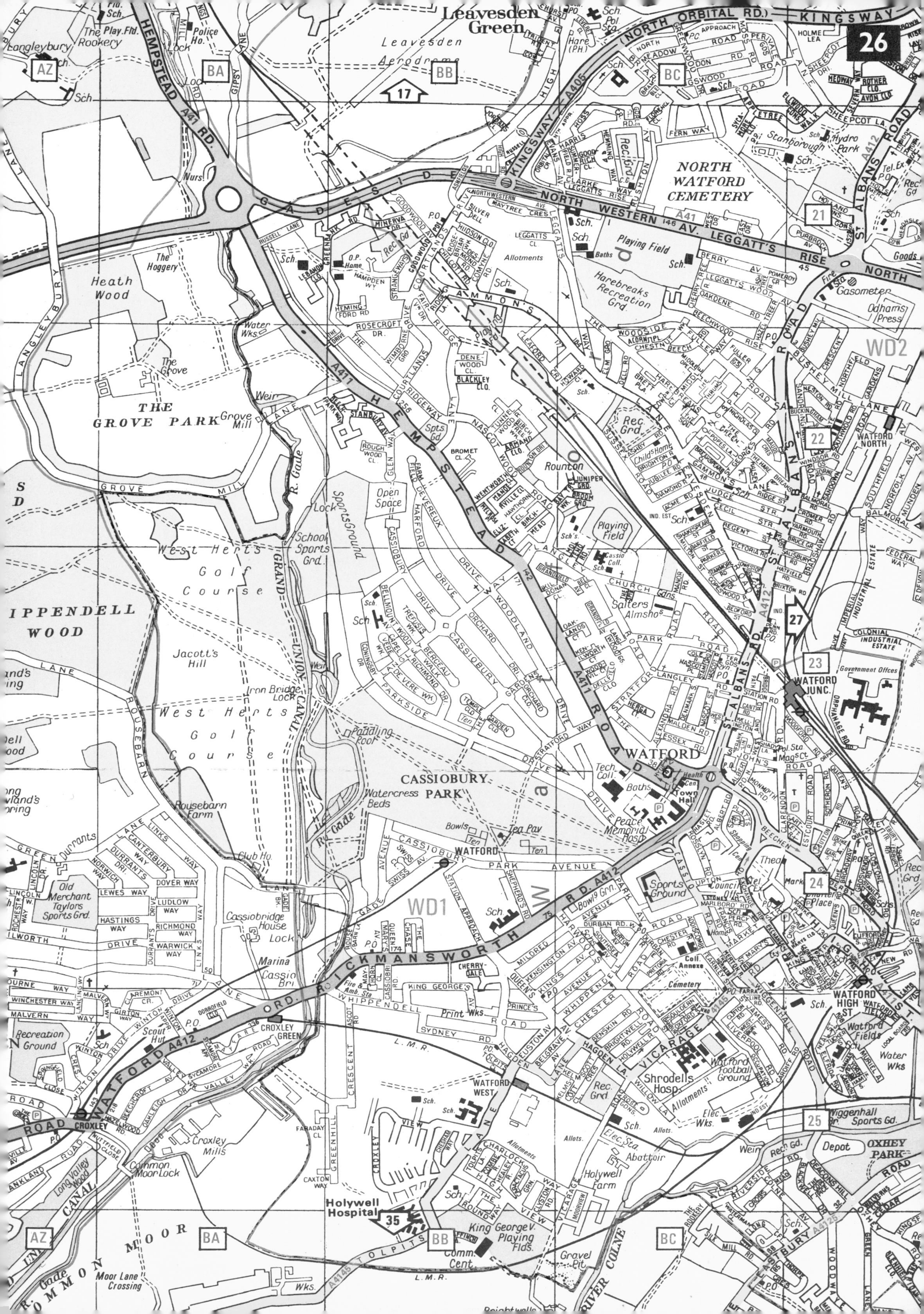
Leavesden Green
Leavesden Aerodrome
17
AZ
BA
BB
BC
NORTH ORBITAL RD.
KINGSWAY
A405
HEMPSTEAD RD.
A41
GADESIDE
NORTH WESTERN AV.
LEGGATT'S RISE
NORTH WATFORD CEMETERY
Playing Field
Harebreaks Recreation Grd.
Heath Wood
The Hoggery
The Grove
THE GROVE PARK
Grove Mill
Water Wks.
Weir
R. Gade
GROVE MILL LANE
West Herts Golf Course
WHIPPENDELL WOOD
Jacott's Hill
ROUSEBARN LANE
Rousebarn Farm
GRAND UNION CANAL
School Sports Grd.
Sports Ground
Iron Bridge Lock
HEMPSTEAD ROAD
A411
CASSIOBURY PARK
Watercress Beds
Paddling Pool
Bowls
Tea Pav
CASSIOBURY PARK AVENUE
WATFORD
Cassiobridge House Lock
Marina
RICKMANSWORTH RD.
A412
WATFORD ROAD
CROXLEY
CROXLEY GREEN
WD1
WD2
North Merchant Taylors Sports Grd.
Recreation Ground
Croxley Mills
Common Moor Lock
COMMON MOOR
Moor Lane Crossing
Holywell Hospital
35
King George V. Playing Flds.
Comm. Cent.
Gravel Pit
RIVER COLNE
TOLPITS
A4145
WATFORD WEST
L.M.R.
Shrodells Hosp.
Watford Football Ground
VICARAGE RD.
Cemetery
Holywell Farm
Abattoir
Elec. Wks.
WATFORD JUNC.
23
Government Offices
ST. ALBANS RD.
A412
27
21
22
24
25
WATFORD NORTH
Gasometer
Odhams Press
IMPERIAL INDUSTRIAL ESTATE
COLONIAL INDUSTRIAL ESTATE
Tech. Coll.
Town Hall
Peace Memorial Hosp.
Salters Almshs.
Cassio Coll.
Playing Field
Rounton
Open Space
Stanborough
Hydro Park
WATFORD HIGH ST
Watford Fields
Water Wks.
Wiggenhall Sports Gd.
Depot
OXHEY PARK
Charter Place
Market
Council Offs.
Coll. Annexe
Print Wks.
CASSIO

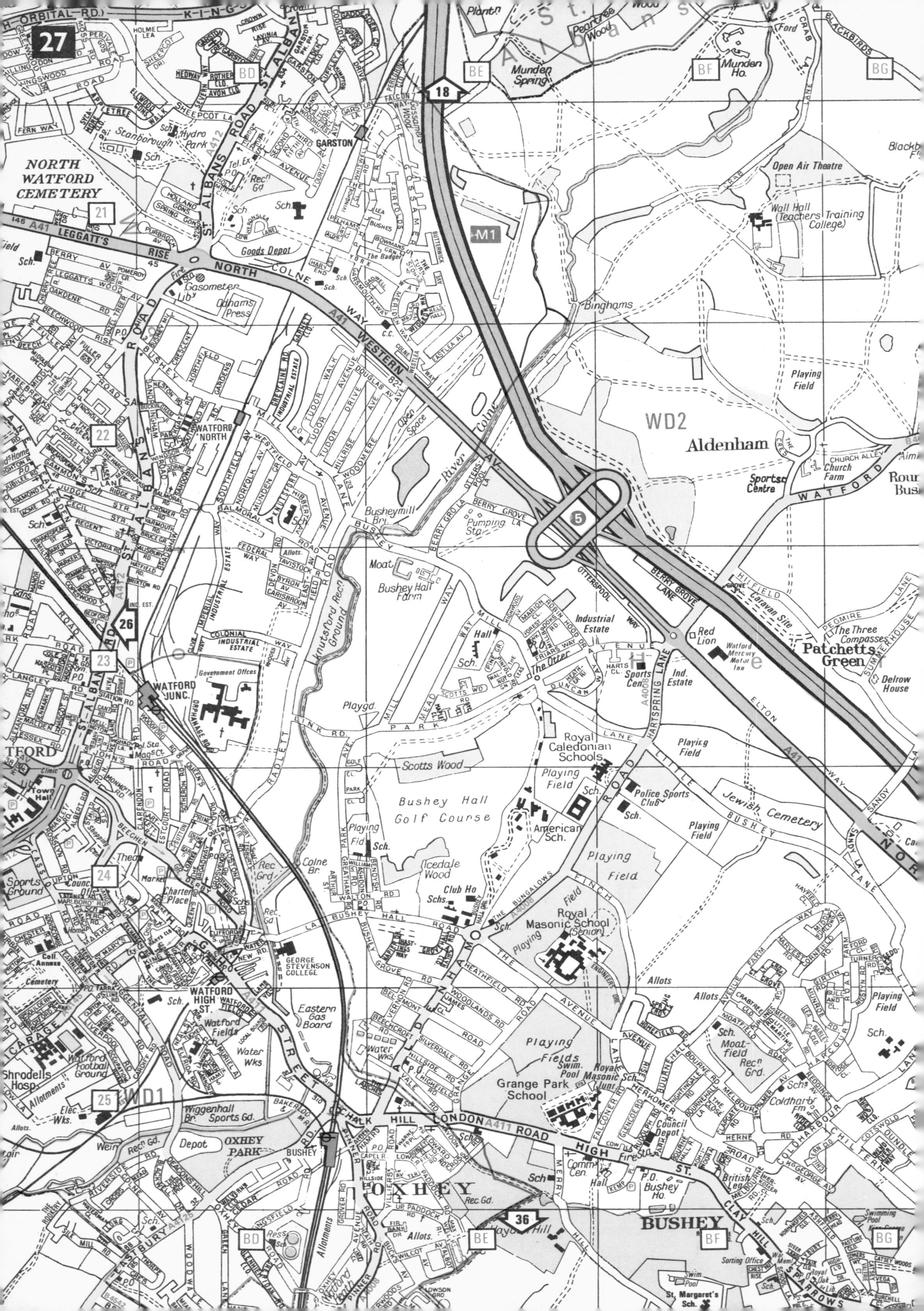

27
NORTH
WATFORD
CEMETERY
Stanborough
Hydro
Park
GARSTON
ST. ALBANS ROAD
A412
LEGGATT'S RISE
A41
NORTH
WESTERN
AV.
Gasometer
Odhams
Press
Goods Depot
The Badger
WATFORD
NORTH
BUSHEY MILL LANE
Open
Space
River
Colne
Busheymill
Bri.
Pumping
Sta.
M1
18
21
22
23
24
25
26
36
BD
BE
BF
BG
Munden
Spring
Munden
Ho.
Peartree
Wood
Open Air Theatre
Wall Hall
(Teachers Training
College)
Binghams
Playing
Field
WD2
Aldenham
Church
Farm
Sports
Centre
WATFORD
5
BERRY GROVE
LANE
Caravan Site
The Three
Compasses
Patchetts
Green
Delrow
House
Red
Lion
Watford
Mercury
Motor
Inn
Industrial
Estate
The Otter
Ind.
Estate
HARTSPRING LANE
A4008
ELTON
WAY
Moat
Bushey Hall
Farm
Knutsford Rec'n
Ground
IMPERIAL
INDUSTRIAL ESTATE
COLONIAL
INDUSTRIAL
ESTATE
Government Offices
WATFORD
JUNC.
Playgd.
Scotts Wood
Bushey Hall
Golf Course
Icedale
Wood
Club Ho
Royal
Caledonian
Schools
American
Sch.
Police Sports
Club
Jewish Cemetery
Playing
Field
Royal
Masonic School
(Senior)
Colne
Br.
GEORGE
STEVENSON
COLLEGE
Eastern
Gas
Board
WATFORD
HIGH
ST.
Watford
Fields
Water
Wks
Watford
Football
Ground
Shrodells
Hosp.
WD1
Wiggenhall
Sports Gd.
Depot
OXHEY
PARK
BUSHEY
OXHEY
Playing
Fields
Grange Park
School
Royal
Masonic
Junr
Council
Depot
HIGH
ST.
Comm'y
Cen.
Bushey
Ho.
BUSHEY
CLAY
HILL
Coldharb'r
Fm
Moat-
field
Rec'n
Grd.
Allots
LONDON
ROAD
A411
CHALK
HILL
Hayden Hill
Rec. Gd.
St. Margaret's
Sch.
Sorting Office
Allotments
Charter
Place
Market
Sports
Ground

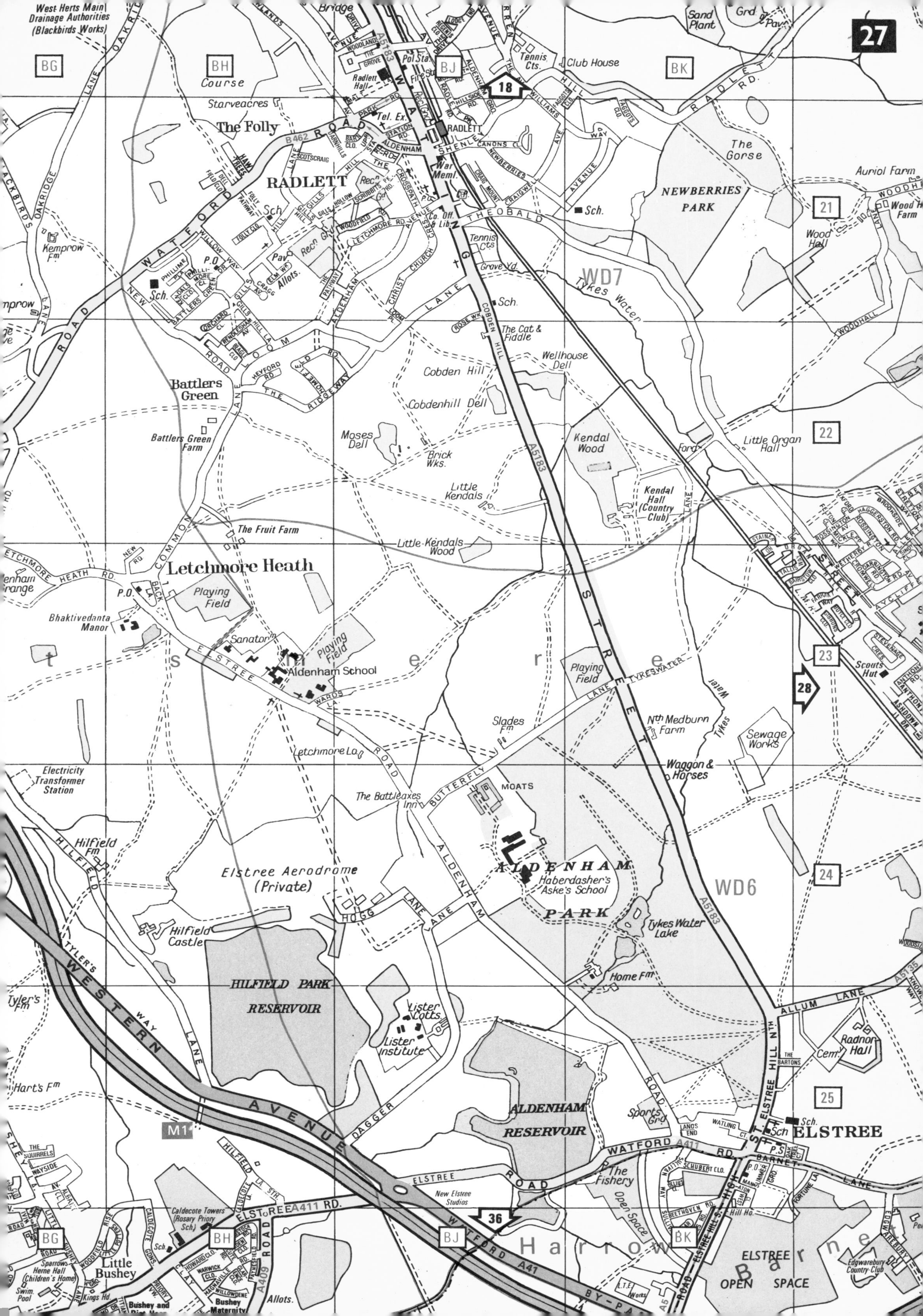
RADLETT
The Folly
Battlers Green
Letchmore Heath
Aldenham School
NEWBERRIES PARK
The Gorse
Kendal Wood
Kendal Hall (Country Club)
Cobden Hill
Cobdenhill Dell
Moses Dell
Little Kendals
The Fruit Farm
Little-Kendals Wood
Bhaktivedanta Manor
Elstree Aerodrome (Private)
Hilfield Castle
HILFIELD PARK RESERVOIR
ALDENHAM RESERVOIR
ALDENHAM PARK
Haberdasher's Aske's School
Tykes Water Lake
Home Fm
Lister Institute
Lister Cotts
The Battleaxes Inn
Slades Fm
Nth Medburn Farm
Waggon & Horses
Sewage Works
ELSTREE
ELSTREE OPEN SPACE
Little Bushey
WATLING STREET
WATFORD ROAD
ALDENHAM ROAD
WESTERN AVENUE
Radnor Hall
Wood Hall
Auriol Farm
Little Organ Hall
Kemprow Fm
Electricity Transformer Station
Hilfield Fm
Tyler's Fm
Hart's Fm
Sports Grd
The Fishery
New Elstree Studios
Edgwarebury Country Club
WD7
WD6
Hertsmere
Harrow
Barnet
M1
A5183
A411
18
28
36
21
22
23
24
25
BG
BH
BJ
BK

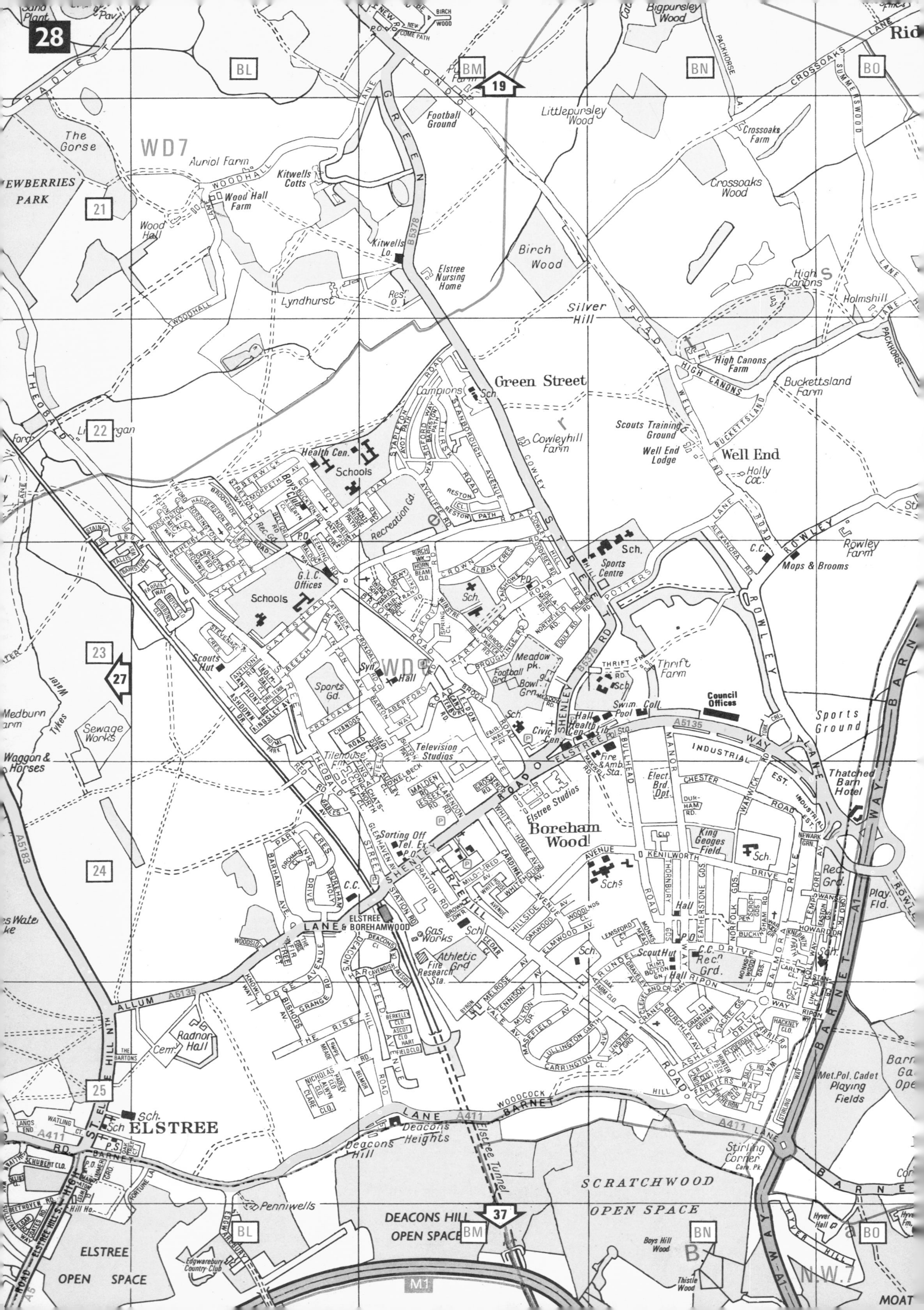
BL
BM
BN
BO
19
WD7
The Gorse
Auriol Farm
Kitwells Cotts
Football Ground
Littlepursley Wood
Bigpursley Wood
Crossoaks Farm
Crossoaks Wood
Crossoaks Lane
Ridge
Packhorse Lane
Summerswood Lane
Newberries Park
21
Wood Hall Farm
Wood Hall
Woodhall Lane
Kitwells Lo.
Elstree Nursing Home
Birch Wood
Lyndhurst
Silver Hill
High Canons
Holmshill Lane
High Canons Farm
Buckettsland Farm
Buckettsland Lane
Green Street
Campions
Cowleyhill Farm
Scouts Training Ground
Well End Lodge
Well End
Holly Cot.
Well End Road
Theobald Street
22
Ford
Health Cen.
Schools
Recreation Gd.
Rec. Gd.
G.L.C. Offices
Sports Centre
Potters Lane
Alexandra Road
C.C.
Rowley Farm
Mops & Brooms
Rowley Lane
23
27
Scouts Hut
Sports Gd.
Syn.
Hall
Meadow pk.
Football Grd.
Bowl. Grn.
Thrift Farm
Swim. Pool
Coll.
Council Offices
Medburn Farm
Water Tykes
Sewage Works
Waggon & Horses
Tilehouse Fm.
Television Studios
Civic Cen.
Fire & Amb. Sta.
Elstree Studios
Elect. Brd. Dpt.
Industrial Est.
Sports Ground
Thatched Barn Hotel
A5135
Elstree Way
Shenley Road
Boreham Wood
King Georges Field
A5183
24
Sorting Off
Tel. Ex.
Elstree & Borehamwood
Gas Works
Athletic Grd.
Fire Research Sta.
Rec. Grd.
Play. Fld.
Allum Lane
Radnor Hall
Cem.
25
Elstree
Deacons Heights
Deacons Hill
Stirling Corner
Scratchwood Open Space
Met. Pol. Cadet Playing Fields
A411
Barnet Lane
Woodcock Hill
Elstree Tunnel
Barnet Way A1
Penniwells
37
Deacons Hill Open Space
Elstree Open Space
Edgwarebury Country Club
Boys Hill Wood
Thistle Wood
Hyver Hall
Hyver Hill
M1
N.W.7
Moat

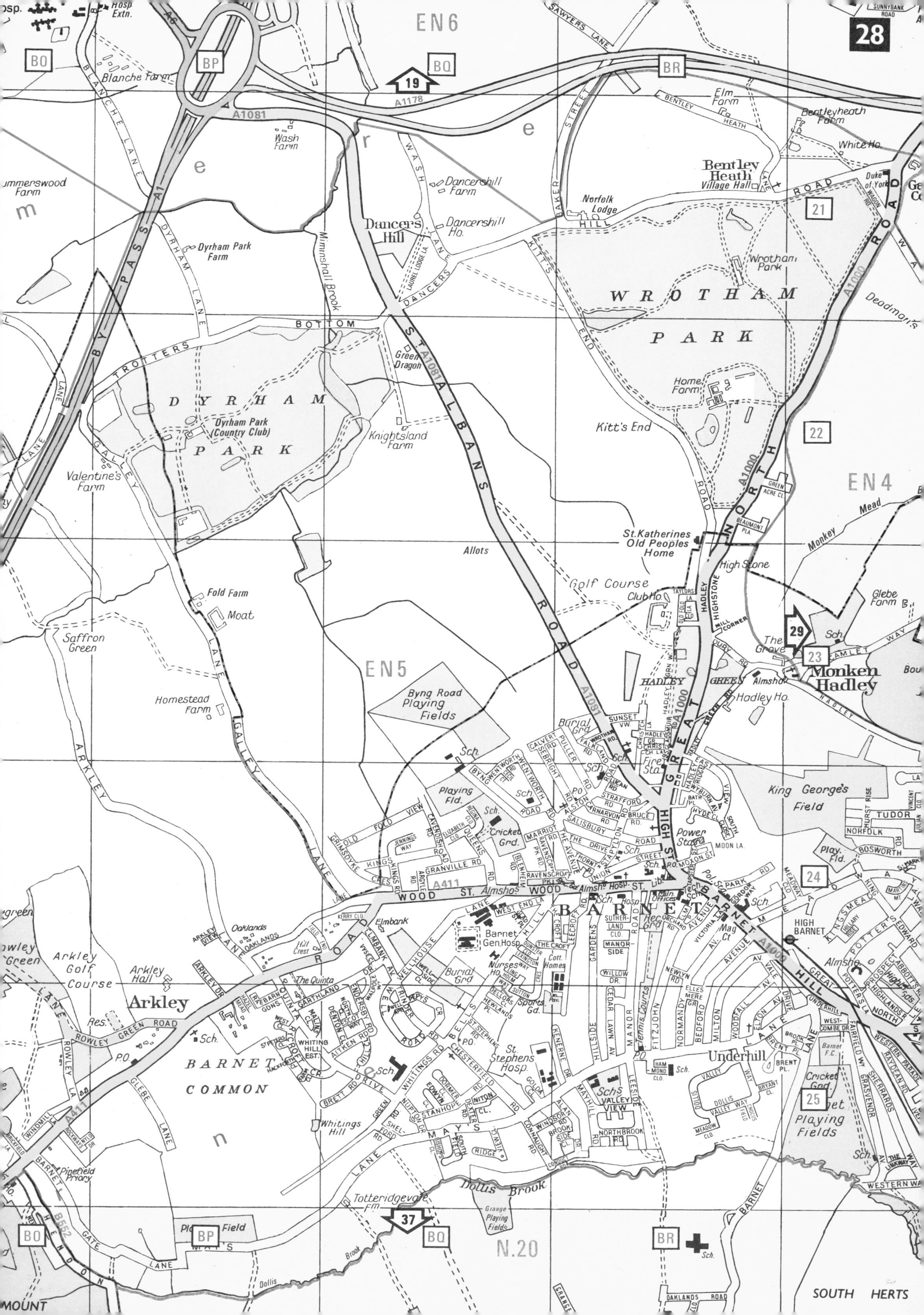
EN6
BO
BP
BQ
BR
19
A1178
A1081
Blanche Farm
Blanche Lane
Wash Farm
Sawyers Lane
Elm Farm
Bentley Heath
Bentleyheath Farm
White Ho.
Bentley Heath Village Hall
Dancershill Farm
Dancers Hill
Dancershill Ho.
Wash Lane
Laurel Lodge La.
Mimmshall Brook
Norfolk Lodge
Baker Street
Hill Road
Duke of York
21
Dyrham Park Farm
Dyrham Lane
By Pass
A1
Dancers
Bottom
Trotters
Kitts End
W R O T H A M
P A R K
Wrotham Park
Deadman's
Green Dragon
St. Albans Road
A1081
D Y R H A M
P A R K
Dyrham Park (Country Club)
Knightsland Farm
Home Farm
Kitt's End
22
Valentine's Farm
Galley
Great North Road
A1000
EN4
Green Acre Cl.
Beaumont Pla.
Monkey Mead
St.Katherines Old Peoples Home
Allots
High Stone
Golf Course
Club Ho.
Fold Farm
Moat
Glebe Farm
Saffron Green
29
The Grove
Sch.
23
Monken Hadley
Hadley Green
Almsho.
Hadley Ho.
EN5
Byng Road Playing Fields
Homestead Farm
Arkley Lane
Galley Lane
Burial Grd.
Fire Sta.
King George's Field
Playing Fld.
Cricket Grd.
Tudor
Norfolk
Bosworth
Power Sta.
Moon La.
Play. Fld.
Old Fold View
Wood St.
A411
Almsho.
Hosp.
Lib.
Mun. Offices
24
B A R N E T
High Barnet
Oaklands
Elmbank
Barnet Gen.Hosp.
Hill Crest
Arkley Golf Course
Arkley Hall
The Quinta
Burial Grd.
Nurses Homes
Sports Gd.
Arkley
Res.
Rowley Green Road
Sch.
P.O.
B A R N E T
C O M M O N
St. Stephens Hosp.
Underhill
Barnet F.C.
Cricket Gnd.
Western Parade
25
Playing Fields
Valley View
Dollis Valley Way
Whitings Hill
Mays Lane
Northbrook Rd.
Pinefield Priory
Dollis Brook
Totteridgevale Fm.
Grange Playing Fields
37
N.20
Hendon Lane
B552
Mays Lane
Dollis Brook
Oaklands Road
Mount
South Herts

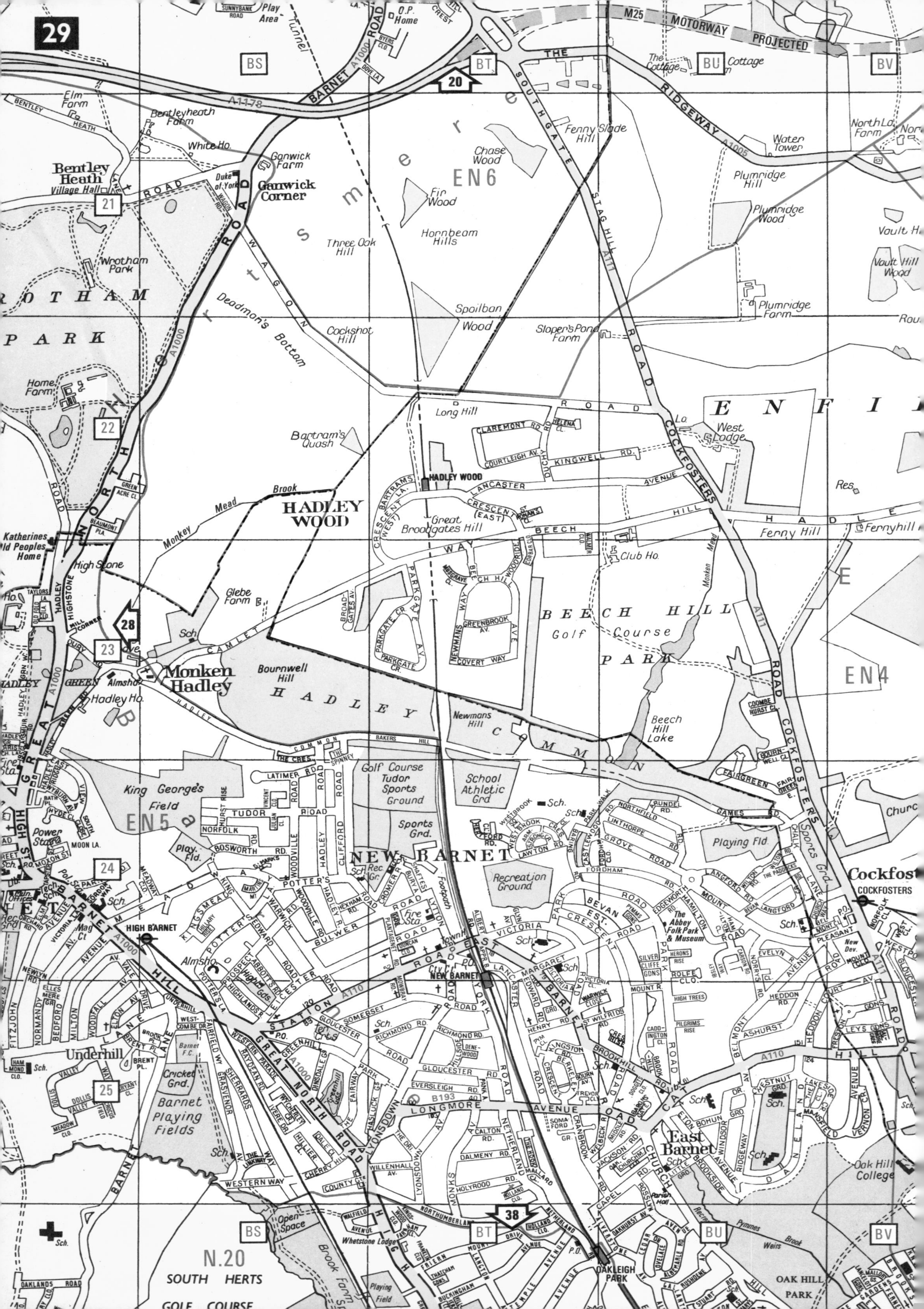

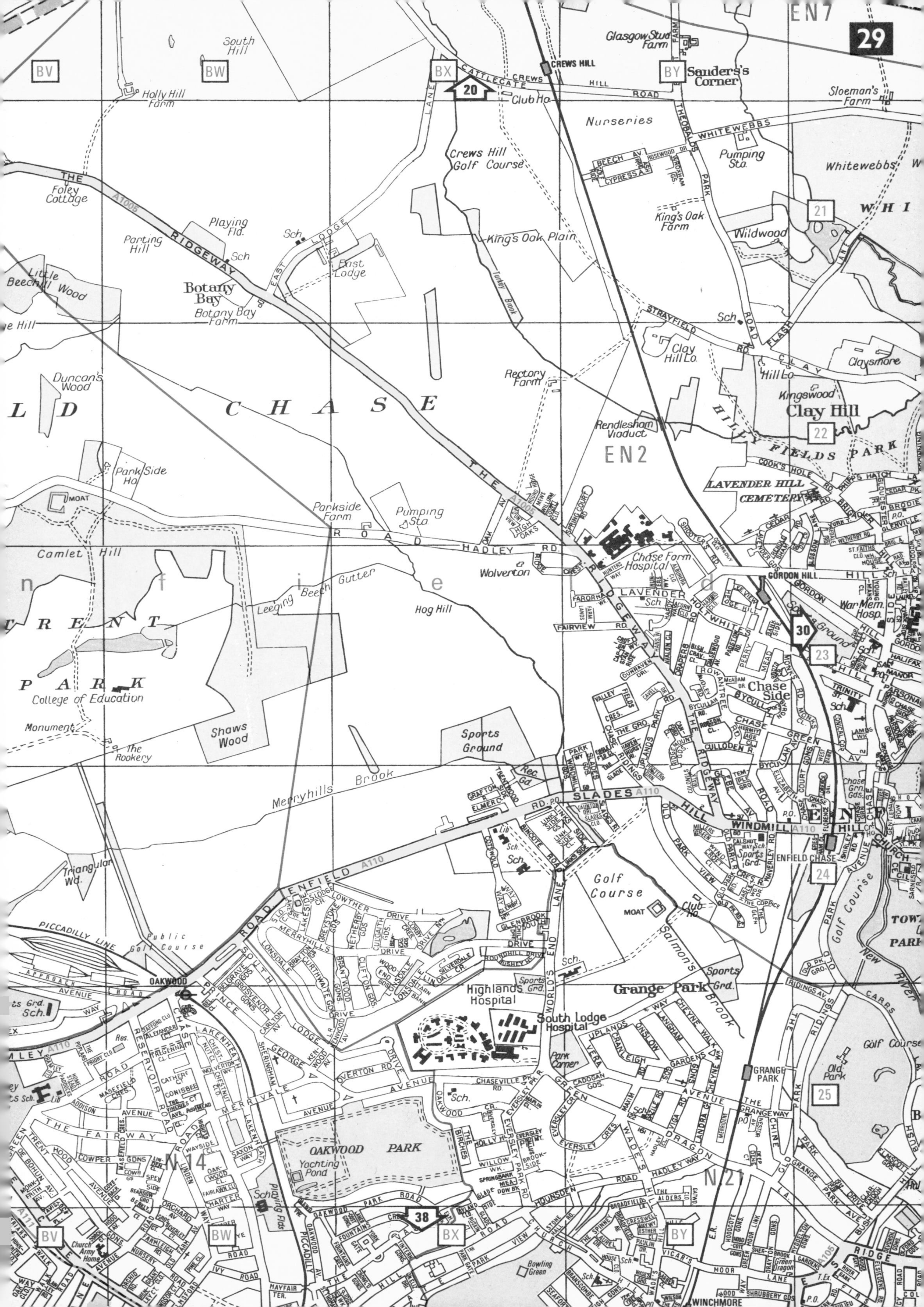
EN7
BV
BW
BX
BY
20
South Hill
Holly Hill Farm
Glasgow Stud Farm
CREWS HILL
Sanders's Corner
CATTLEGATE
CREWS HILL ROAD
Club Ho.
Sloeman's Farm
Nurseries
WHITEWEBBS
Pumping Sta.
Whitewebbs
Crews Hill Golf Course
THE RIDGEWAY
A1005
Foley Cottage
Playing Fld.
Parting Hill
Sch
EAST LODGE
East Lodge
King's Oak Plain
King's Oak Farm
Wildwood
21
Little Beechill Wood
Botany Bay
Botany Bay Farm
Turkey Brook
STRAYFIELD RD.
Clay Hill Lo.
Hill Lo.
Claysmore
Kingswood
Clay Hill
22
Duncan's Wood
Rectory Farm
C H A S E
Rendlesham Viaduct
EN2
HILLY FIELDS PARK
Park Side Ho.
MOAT
LAVENDER HILL CEMETERY
Parkside Farm
Pumping Sta.
HADLEY RD.
Camlet Hill
Wolverton
Chase Farm Hospital
GORDON HILL
War Mem. Hosp.
Leeging Beech Gutter
Hog Hill
30
23
Chase Side
P A R K
College of Education
Monument
Shaws Wood
The Rookery
Sports Ground
Rec. Gd.
Merryhills Brook
SLADES HILL
A110
WINDMILL HILL
ENFIELD CHASE
24
Triangular Wd.
ENFIELD ROAD
Golf Course
MOAT
Club Ho.
PICCADILLY LINE
Public Golf Course
OAKWOOD
Salmon's Brook
Sports Grd.
Grange Park
Highlands Hospital
South Lodge Hospital
WORLD'S END LANE
Park Corner
GRANGE PARK
Old Park
Golf Course
25
OAKWOOD PARK
Yachting Pond
N14
N21
Playing Flds
38
BV
BW
BX
BY
Bowling Green
WINCHMORE

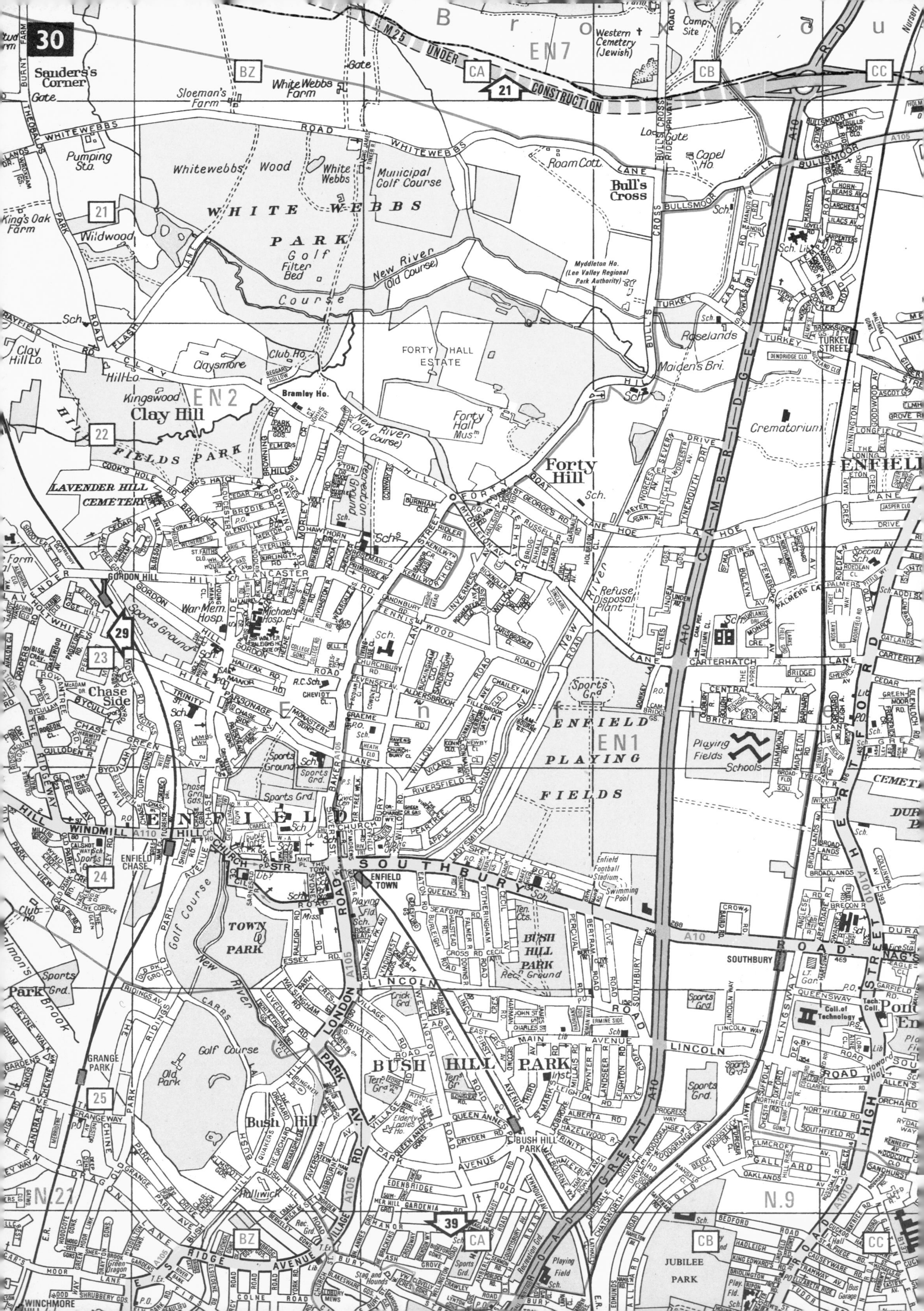
Broxbourne
EN7
EN2
EN1
N.21
N.9
BZ
CA
CB
CC
21
22
23
24
25
29
39
M25 UNDER CONSTRUCTION
Sanders's Corner
Western Cemetery (Jewish)
Camp Site
Sloeman's Farm
White Webbs Farm
WHITEWEBBS ROAD
Pumping Sta.
Whitewebbs Wood
White Webbs
Municipal Golf Course
WHITE WEBBS PARK
Golf
Filter Bed
New River (Old Course)
Roam Cott.
Bull's Cross
Capel Ho.
Myddleton Ho. (Lee Valley Regional Park Authority)
King's Oak Farm
Wildwood
Clay Hill Lo.
Claysmore
Club Ho.
FORTY HALL ESTATE
Forty Hall Mus.
Bramley Ho.
Kingswood
Clay Hill
Raselands
Maiden's Bri.
Crematorium
FIELDS PARK
LAVENDER HILL CEMETERY
Forty Hill
Recreation Ground
War Mem. Hosp.
St. Michael's Hosp.
Sports Ground
Refuse Disposal Plant
Chase Side
Sports Grd.
ENFIELD
ENFIELD PLAYING FIELDS
Playing Fields
Schools
ENFIELD CHASE
ENFIELD TOWN
SOUTHBURY ROAD
A10
A105
A110
A1010
Enfield Football Stadium
Swimming Pool
Golf Course
TOWN PARK
BUSH HILL PARK
Rec. Ground
SOUTHBURY
Coll. of Technology
GREAT CAMBRIDGE ROAD
LONDON ROAD
LINCOLN ROAD
Golf Course
Old Park
GRANGE PARK
BUSH HILL PARK
Bush Hill
Halliwick
Elderly Ladies Ho.
Playing Field
JUBILEE PARK
Stag and Hounds
WINCHMORE
RIDGE AVENUE
HERTFORD ROAD
HIGH STREET
Sports Grd.

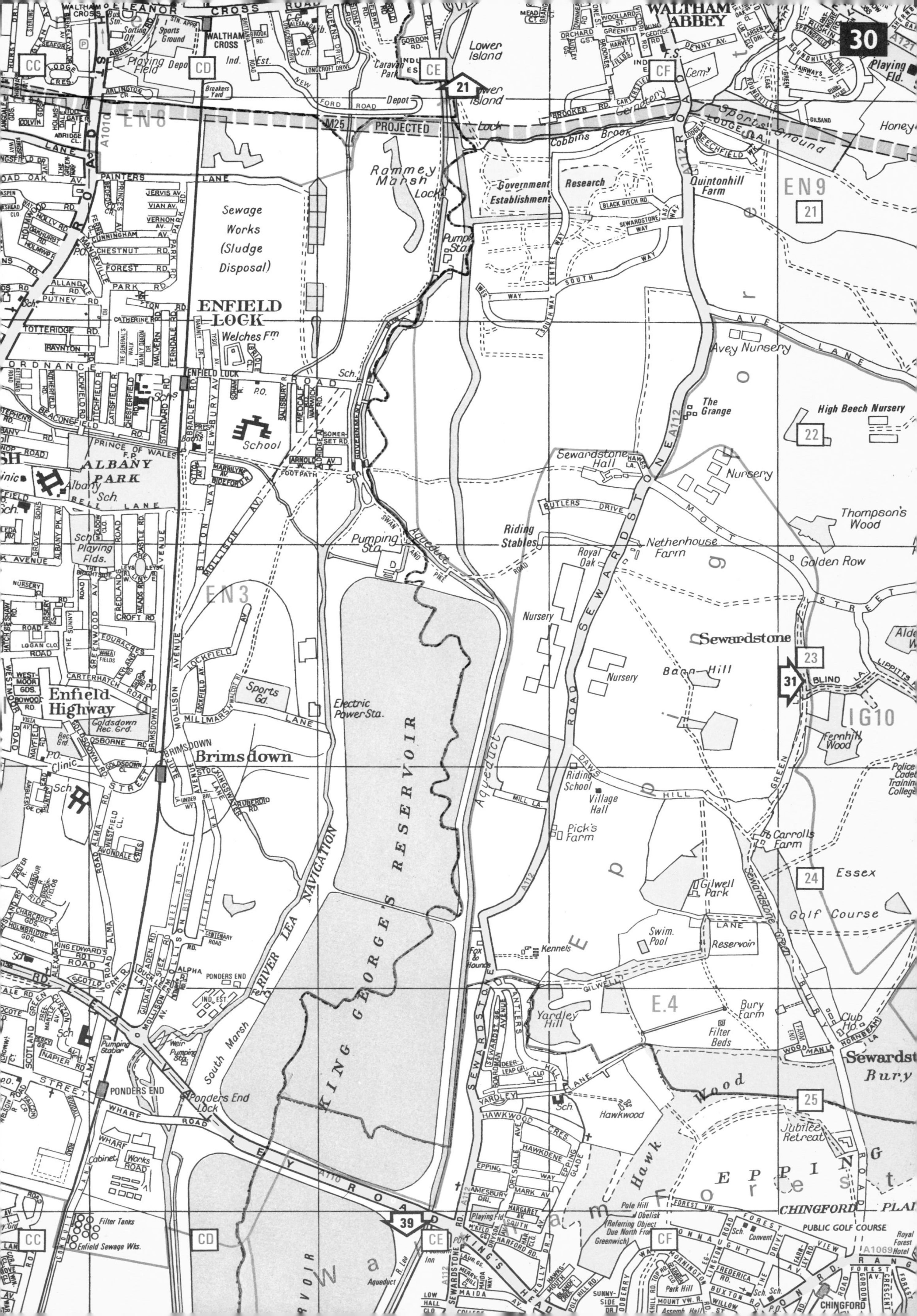

WALTHAM ABBEY
WALTHAM CROSS
ELEANOR CROSS
Lower Island
Lower Island
Lock
M25 PROJECTED
EN8
EN9
EN3
IG10
E.4
Rammey Marsh
Lock
Sewage Works (Sludge Disposal)
Government Establishment
Research
Quintonhill Farm
Cobbins Brook
Sports Ground
Cemy
ENFIELD LOCK
Welches Fm.
Avey Nursery
AVEY LANE
High Beech Nursery
The Grange
Sewardstone Hall
Nursery
Thompson's Wood
Riding Stables
Netherhouse Farm
Golden Row
Royal Oak
Nursery
Sewardstone
Bury Farm
ALBANY PARK
School
Pumping Sta.
Pumping Sta.
Electric Power Sta.
Sports Gd.
KING GEORGE'S RESERVOIR
RIVER LEA NAVIGATION
Aqueduct
Enfield Highway
Goldsdown Rec. Grd.
Brimsdown
Riding School
Village Hall
Pick's Farm
Carrolls Farm
Essex
Golf Course
Gilwell Park
Swim. Pool
Reservoir
Kennels
Fox & Hounds
Yardley Hill
Filter Beds
Sewardstone Bury
Hawkwood
Hawk Wood
Jubilee Retreat
EPPING FOREST
Waltham Forest
CHINGFORD
PUBLIC GOLF COURSE
Royal Forest Hotel
Pole Hill Obelisk (Referring Object Due North From Greenwich)
South Marsh
Ponders End Lock
Weir
PONDERS END
Filter Tanks
Enfield Sewage Wks.
SEWARDSTONE ROAD
LEA VALLEY ROAD
KING'S HEAD HILL
Fernhill Wood
Police Cadet Training College
21
22
23
24
25
31
39
CC
CD
CE
CF

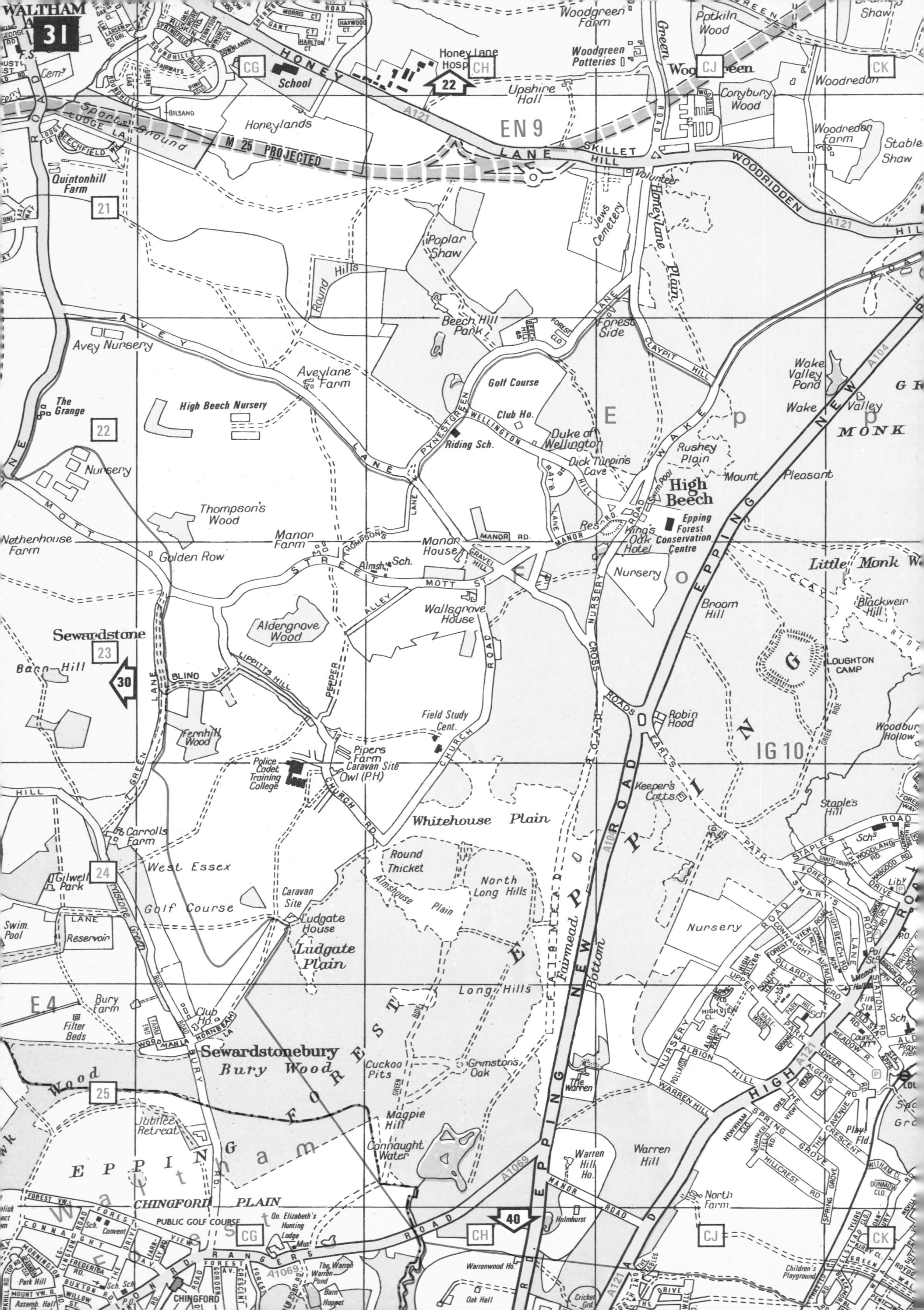

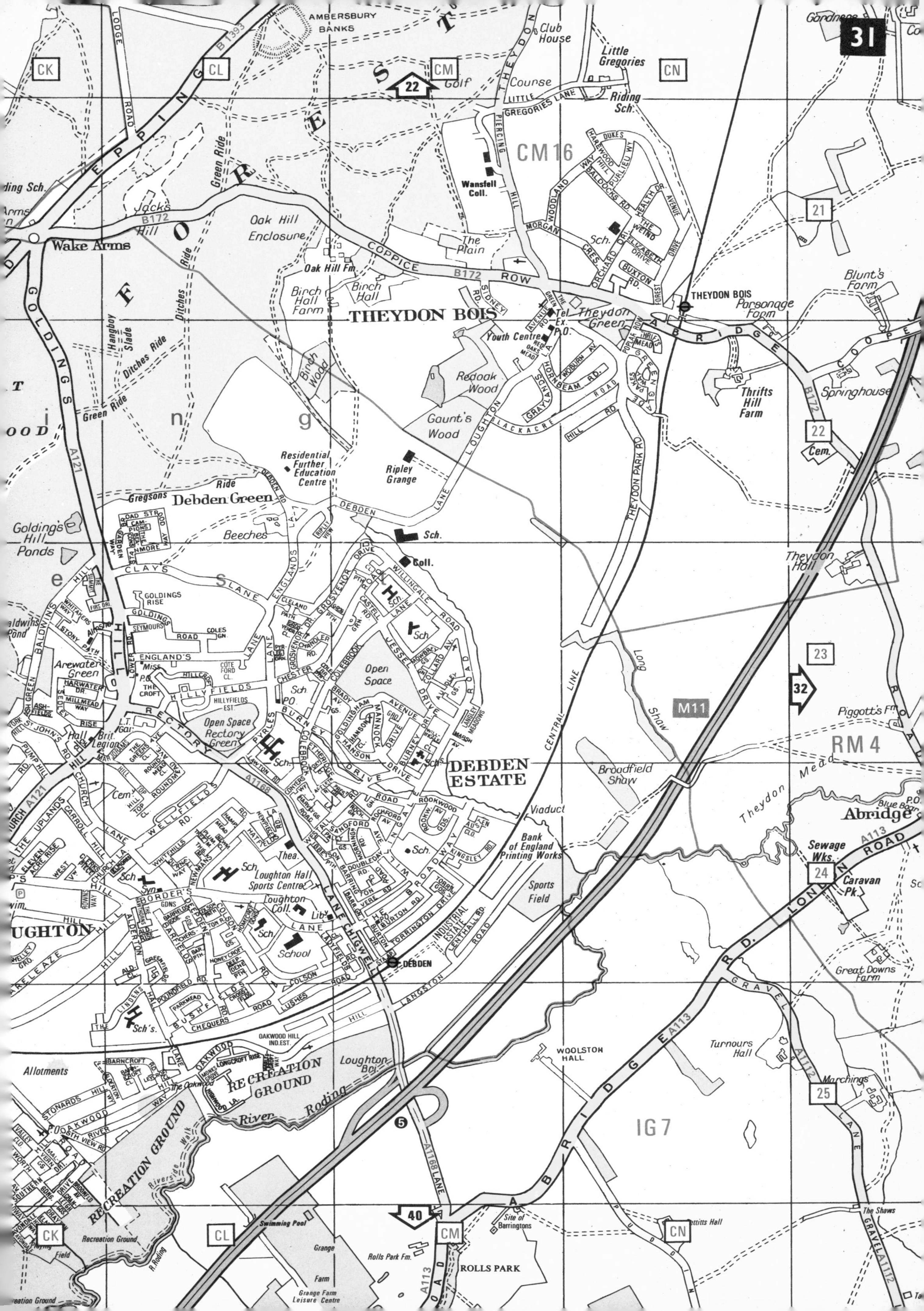

AMBERSBURY BANKS
CK
CL
CM
CN
22
Golf Course
Club House
Little Gregories
LITTLE GREGORIES LANE
Riding Sch.
CM16
Wansfell Coll.
EPPING FOREST
Wake Arms
Jacks Hill
B172
Oak Hill Enclosure
Oak Hill Fm.
COPPICE ROW
The Plain
Birch Hall Farm
Birch Hall
THEYDON BOIS
Theydon Green
Youth Centre
Redoak Wood
Gaunt's Wood
Birch Wood
Hangboy Slade
Ditches Ride
Green Ride
GOLDINGS
A121
Residential Further Education Centre
Ripley Grange
Debden Green
Gregsons Ride
Golding's Hill Ponds
Beeches
CLAYS LANE
21
Blunt's Farm
Parsonage Farm
ABRIDGE
Thrifts Hill Farm
Springhouse
22
Cem.
Theydon Hall
23
32
M11
Piggott's Fm
RM4
Long Shaw
Broadfield Shaw
Theydon Mead
Abridge
Sewage Wks.
24
Caravan Pk.
LONDON ROAD
A113
Great Downs Farm
DEBDEN ESTATE
Open Space
CENTRAL LINE
Viaduct
Bank of England Printing Works
Sports Field
INDUSTRIAL ESTATE
Loughton Hall Sports Centre
Loughton Coll.
LOUGHTON
DEBDEN
Arewater Green
Open Space Rectory Green
RECTORY
CHURCH HILL
OAKWOOD HILL IND. EST.
RECREATION GROUND
Allotments
River Roding
Loughton Brk
WOOLSTON HALL
Turnours Hall
Marchings
25
A1112
IG7
ABRIDGE RD.
GRAVEL LANE
A1168
40
Swimming Pool
Recreation Ground
Grange Farm
Grange Farm Leisure Centre
Rolls Park Fm.
ROLLS PARK
Site of Barringtons
Pettits Hall
The Shaws

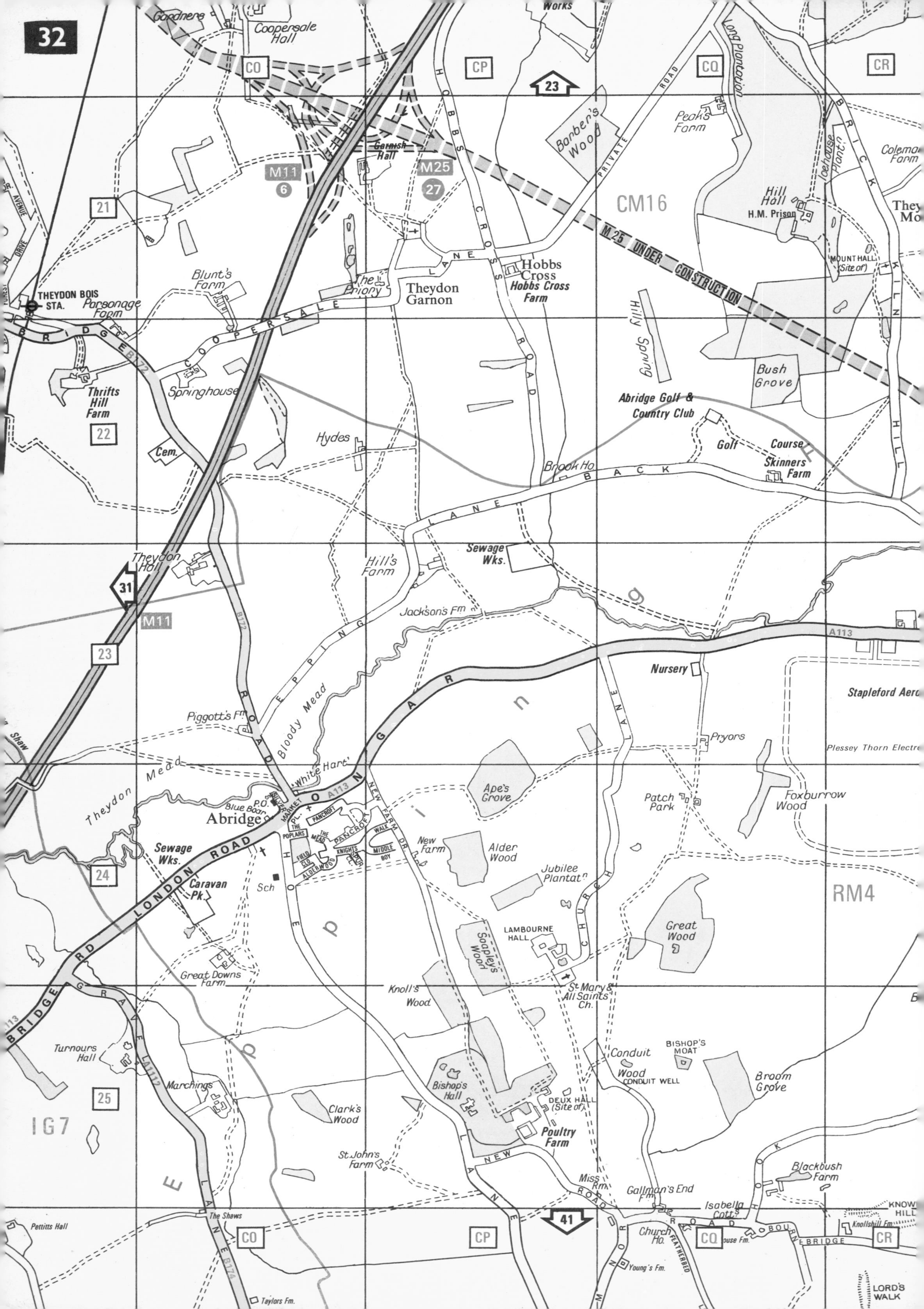
Gardners
Works
Coopersale Hall
CO
CP
CQ
CR
23
Long Plantation
Peaks Farm
Barber's Wood
PRIVATE ROAD
HOBBS CROSS ROAD
Garnish Hall
M11
6
M25
27
Coleman Farm
Icehouse Plantn
BRICK KILN HILL
Hill Hall
H.M. Prison
CM16
M25 UNDER CONSTRUCTION
21
AVENUE
FOREST DRIVE
Blunt's Farm
The Priory
LANE
Hobbs Cross
Hobbs Cross Farm
Theydon Garnon
MOUNT HALL (Site of)
THEYDON BOIS STA.
Parsonage Farm
BRIDGE
COOPERSALE
B172
Hilly Spring
Thrifts Hill Farm
Springhouse
Bush Grove
Abridge Golf & Country Club
22
Hydes
Golf Course
Skinners Farm
Cem.
Brook Ho.
BACK LANE
Sewage Wks.
Theydon Hall
Hill's Farm
31
M11
Jackson's Fm
A113
23
EPPING
Nursery
Stapleford Aero
Bloody Mead
Piggott's Fm
ROAD
Pryors
Shaw
Plessey Thorn Electr
Theydon Mead
White Hart
ONGAR
Ape's Grove
LANE
Patch Park
Foxburrow Wood
Blue Boar
P.O.
MARKET PL.
Abridge
THE POPLARS
PANCROFT
THE MEAD
NEW FARM DR.
WALK
FIELD CLO.
KNIGHTS
MIDDLE BOY
ALDERWOOD
New Farm
Alder Wood
Sewage Wks.
LONDON ROAD
24
Caravan Pk.
Sch
Jubilee Plantatn
RM4
LAMBOURNE HALL
Soapley's Wood
CHURCH
Great Wood
Great Downs Farm
Knoll's Wood
St Mary & All Saints Ch.
BRIDGE RD
GRAVEL LA.
A113
Turnours Hall
Conduit Wood
CONDUIT WELL
BISHOP'S MOAT
Broom Grove
Marchings
Bishop's Hall
25
IG7
Clark's Wood
DEUX HALL (Site of)
Poultry Farm
St John's Farm
NEW ROAD
Miss Rm
Gallman's End Fm
Blackbush Farm
KNOW HILL
The Shaws
Pettitts Hall
CO
CP
41
Isabella Cotts
Knollshill Fm
Church Ho.
FEATHERBED
CQ
ouse Fm.
BOURNEBRIDGE
CR
LANE B174
Young's Fm.
Taylors Fm.
LORD'S WALK

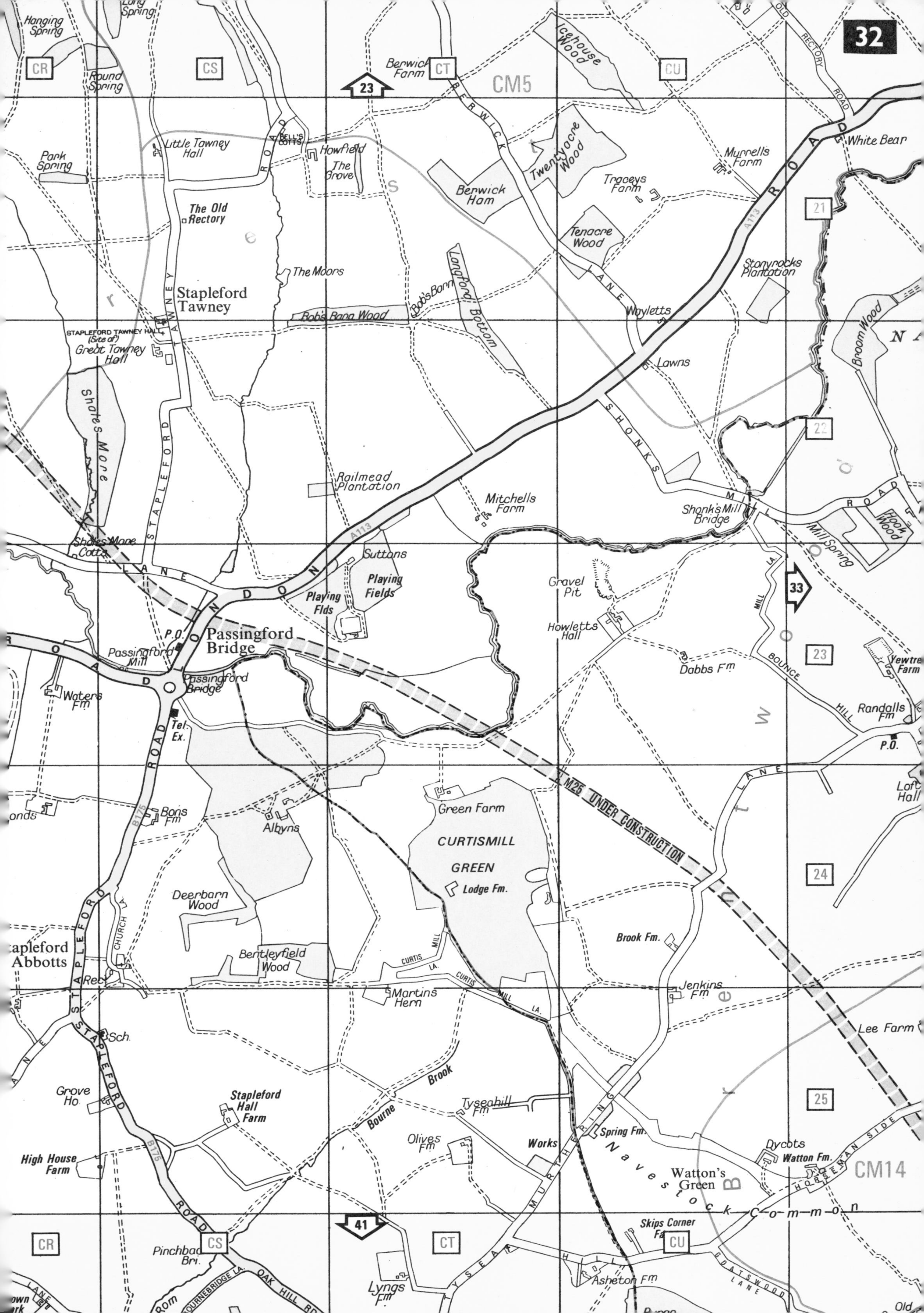

Hanging Spring
Long Spring
Round Spring
Berwick Farm
CM5
Icehouse Wood
23
Little Tawney Hall
Park Spring
Howfield
The Grove
Berwick Ham
Twentyacre Wood
Murrells Farm
White Bear
Traceys Farm
The Old Rectory
Tenacre Wood
The Moors
Stapleford Tawney
Bob's Barn Wood
Bob's Barn
Langford Bottom
Stonyrocks Plantation
Wayletts
Broom Wood
STAPLEFORD TAWNEY HALL (Site of)
Great Tawney Hall
Lawns
Shales More
Railmead Plantation
Mitchells Farm
Shonk's Mill Bridge
Hook Wood
Mill Spring
Shales More Cotts
Suttons
Playing Fields
Playing Flds
Gravel Pit
Howletts Hall
33
Passingford Bridge
Passingford Mill
Waters Fm
Tel. Ex.
Dabbs Fm
Yewtree Farm
Randalls Fm
P.O.
M25 UNDER CONSTRUCTION
Green Farm
Bons Fm
Albyns
CURTISMILL GREEN
Lodge Fm.
Loft Hall
Deerbarn Wood
Brook Fm.
Stapleford Abbotts
Bentleyfield Wood
Rec
Martins Hern
Jenkins Fm
Lee Farm
Sch.
Grove Ho.
Stapleford Hall Farm
Bourne Brook
Tyseahill Fm
Spring Fm.
Olives Fm
Works
Navestock Common
Dycots
Watton Fm.
Watton's Green
CM14
High House Farm
41
Skips Corner Fa
Pinchback Bri.
Asheton Fm
Lyngs Fm
OAK HILL RD
OLD RECTORY ROAD
BERWICK LANE
SHONKS MILL ROAD
LONDON ROAD
STAPLEFORD ROAD
TAWNEY ROAD
BOUNCE HILL
CURTIS MILL LA.
CHURCH LA.
TYSEA HILL
MURTHERING LANE
GOATSWOOD LANE
HORSEMAN SIDE
LANE

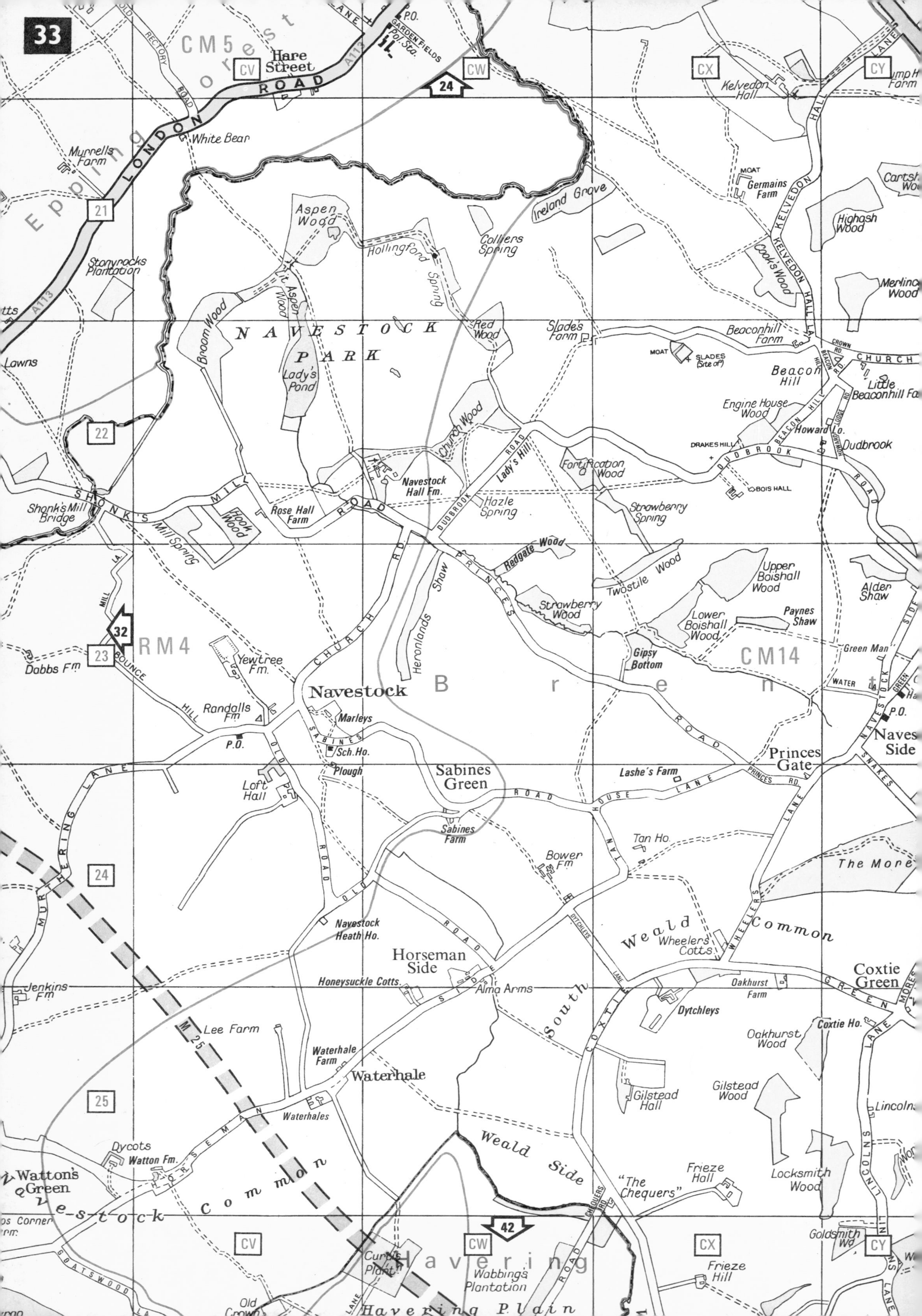

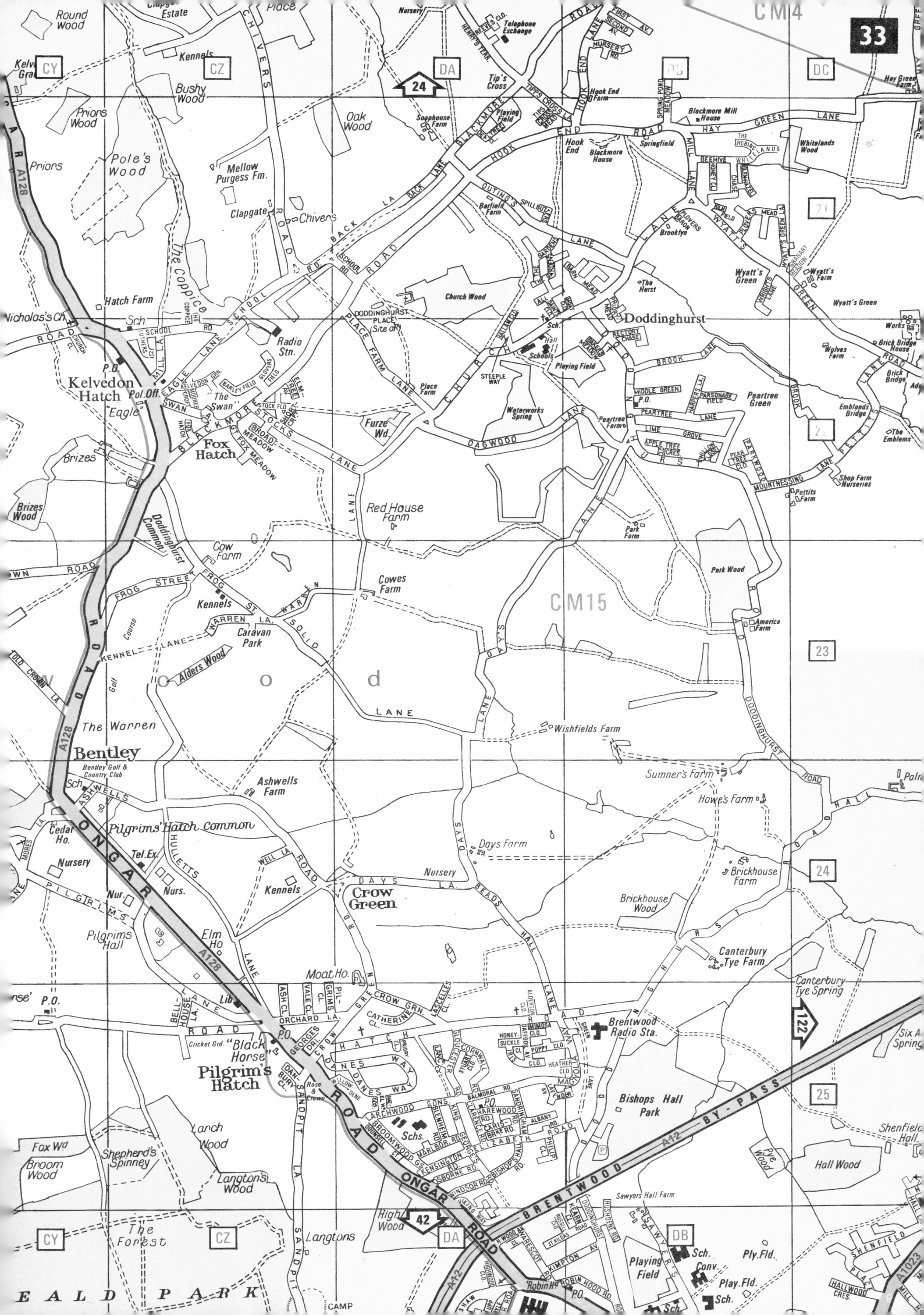

33
CM4
CM15
CY
CZ
DA
DB
DC
24
42
122
23
24
25
Round Wood
Kennels
Bushy Wood
Priors Wood
Pole's Wood
Priors
A128
Mellow Purgess Fm.
Clapgate
Chivers
The Coppice
Oak Wood
Soaphouse Farm
Tip's Cross
Telephone Exchange
Playing Field
Hook End Farm
Hook End
Blackmore House
Springfield
Blackmore Mill House
HAY GREEN LANE
Whitelands Wood
Hay Green Farm
Barfield Farm
Brooklyn
Wyatt's Green
Wyatt's Farm
Church Wood
The Hurst
Doddinghurst
Hatch Farm
Sch.
SCHOOL RD
BACK LA
SCHOOL ROAD
DODDINGHURST PLACE (Site of)
Radio Stn.
Kelvedon Hatch
P.O.
Pol.Off.
"Eagle"
"The Swan"
Fox Hatch
Furze Wd.
Place Farm
Steeple Way
Waterworks Spring
Schools
Playing Field
BROOK LANE
Peartree Green
Peartree Farm
DAGWOOD LANE
MOUNTNESSING LANE
Works
Brick Bridge House
Wolves Farm
Brick Bridge
Emblands Bridge
The Emblems
Shop Farm Nurseries
Pettits Farm
Brizes
Brizes Wood
Doddinghurst Common
Red House Farm
Cow Farm
Park Farm
Park Wood
FROG STREET
Kennels
Cowes Farm
Caravan Park
WARREN LA.
KENNEL LANE
Alders Wood
OLD CROWN LA.
America Farm
Wood
Golf Course
The Warren
Bentley
Bentley Golf & Country Club
Wishfields Farm
Sumner's Farm
Howe's Farm
Ashwells Farm
Pilgrims' Hatch Common
Cedar Ho.
Nursery
Tel.Ex.
Nurs.
Days Farm
Kennels
Nursery
DAYS LA.
Crow Green
Brickhouse Farm
Brickhouse Wood
Canterbury Tye Farm
Canterbury Tye Spring
Pilgrims Hall
Elm Ho.
Moat Ho.
Lib.
P.O.
ORCHARD LA.
CROW GRN.
Brentwood Radio Sta.
Six Acre Spring
Cricket Grd.
"Black Horse"
Pilgrim's Hatch
Rose & Crown
Bishops Hall Park
Shenfield Hall
Larch Wood
Fox Wd
Broom Wood
Shepherd's Spinney
Langton's Wood
Schs.
Pye Wood
Hall Wood
Sawyers Hall Farm
BRENTWOOD A12 BY-PASS
ONGAR ROAD
High Wood
The Forest
Langtons
Playing Field
Sch.
Conv.
Ply.Fld.
Play.Fld.
Sch.
ROBIN HOOD RD
"Robin Hd"
KIMPTON AV.
SHENFIELD PLACE
HALLWOOD CRES.
A1023
WEALD PARK
CAMP

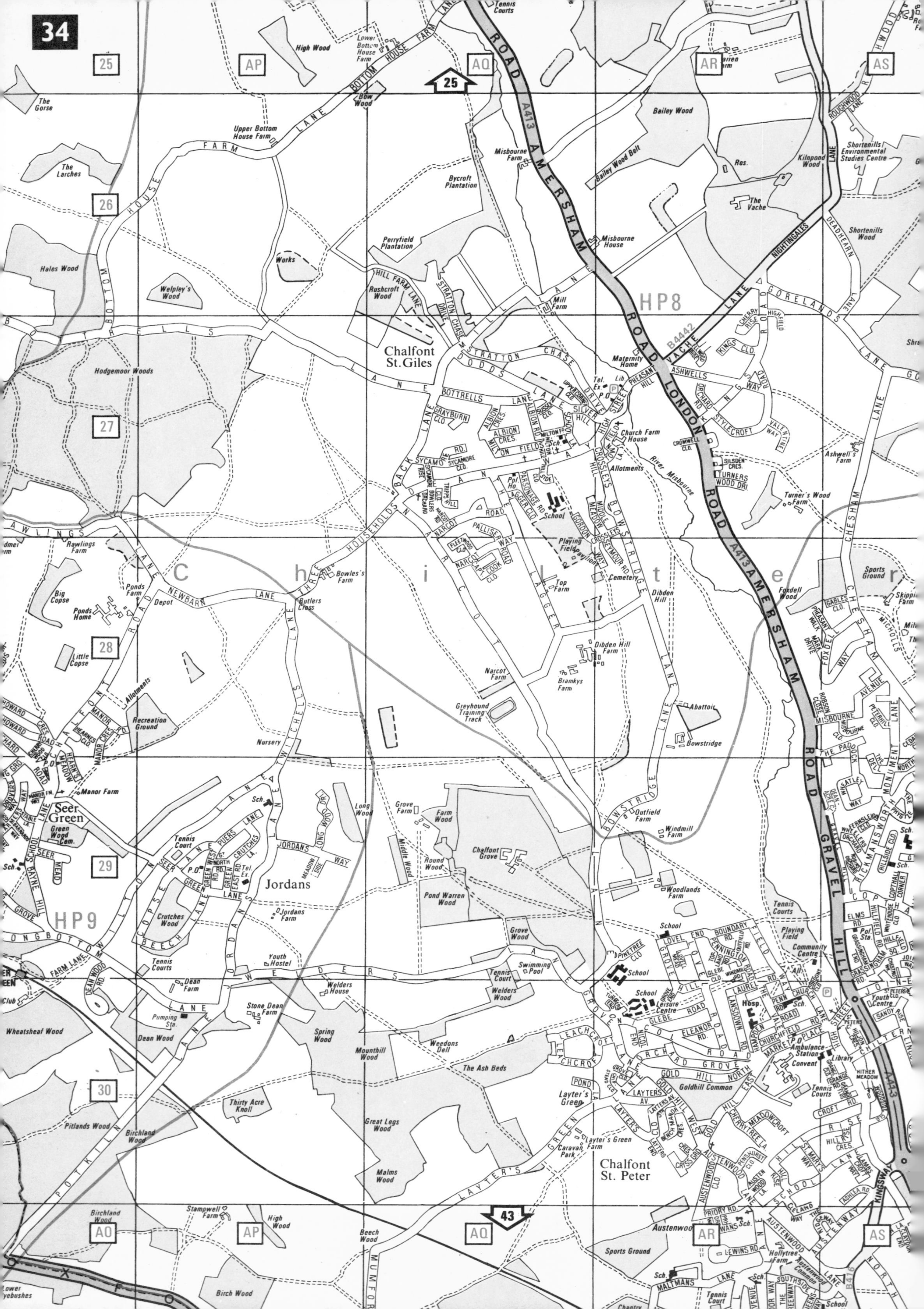

Chalfont St. Giles
Seer Green
Jordans
Chalfont St. Peter
HP8
HP9
Chiltern
AMERSHAM ROAD
LONDON ROAD
GRAVEL HILL
A413
B4442
Hodgemoor Woods
Hales Wood
High Wood
Bailey Wood
Bycroft Plantation
Perryfield Plantation
Rushcroft Wood
Welpley's Wood
Little Copse
Big Copse
Long Wood
Middle Wood
Round Wood
Farm Wood
Chalfont Grove
Pond Warren Wood
Grove Wood
Spring Wood
Mounthill Wood
Great Legs Wood
Malms Wood
Beech Wood
Thirty Acre Knoll
Birchland Wood
Pitlands Wood
Wheatsheaf Wood
Dean Wood
Birch Wood
Stampwell Farm
Austenwood
Sports Ground
Goldhill Common
Layter's Green
Greyhound Training Track
Dibden Hill
Bowstridge
Misbourne Farm
Misbourne House
The Vache
Shortenills Environmental Studies Centre
Shortenills Wood
Kilnpond Wood
Foxdell Wood
Turner's Wood Farm
Ashwell's Farm

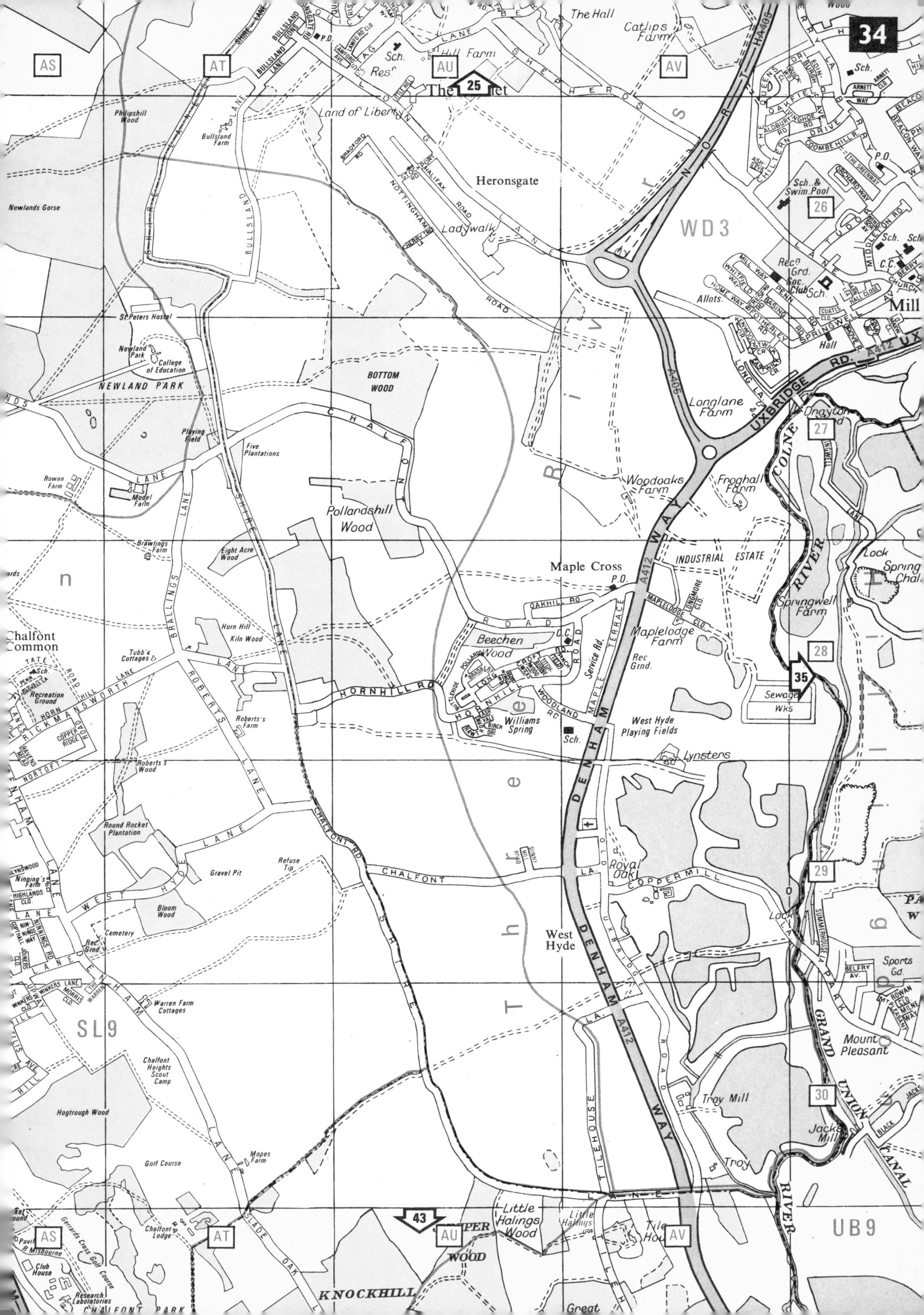
34
AS
AT
AU
AV
25
43
35
26
27
28
29
30
The Hall
Catlips Farm
Hill Farm
Sch.
Land of Liberty
Philipshill Wood
Bullsland Farm
Heronsgate
Newlands Gorse
WD3
Ladywalk
St Peters Hostel
Newland Park
College of Education
NEWLAND PARK
BOTTOM WOOD
Playing Field
Five Plantations
Rowan Farm
Model Farm
Pollardshill Wood
Brawlings Farm
Eight Acre Wood
Maple Cross
P.O.
INDUSTRIAL ESTATE
Horn Hill Kiln Wood
Chalfont Common
Beechen Wood
Maplelodge Farm
Springwell Farm
Tubb's Cottages
Recreation Ground
Roberts's Farm
Williams Spring
Sch.
West Hyde Playing Fields
Sewage Wks
Lynsters
Roberts's Wood
Round Rocket Plantation
Refuse Tip
Gravel Pit
Royal Oak
Bloom Wood
Cemetery
West Hyde
Warren Farm Cottages
SL9
Chalfont Heights Scout Camp
Hogtrough Wood
Troy Mill
Mount Pleasant
Sports Gd.
Golf Course
Mopes Farm
Troy
Little Halings Wood
Chalfont Lodge
Club House
Research Laboratories
KNOCKHILL
UB9
Longlane Farm
Woodoaks Farm
Froghall Farm
Lock
Jacks Mill
Allots.
Hall
Mill
UXBRIDGE RD.
DENHAM WAY A412
A405
RIVER COLNE
GRAND UNION CANAL
CHALFONT LANE
HORNHILL RD
SHIRE LANE
ROBERTS LANE
BRAWLINGS LANE
WEST HYDE LANE
COPPERMILL LA.
TILEHOUSE LANE
DENHAM LANE
Service Rd.
MAPLE TERRACE

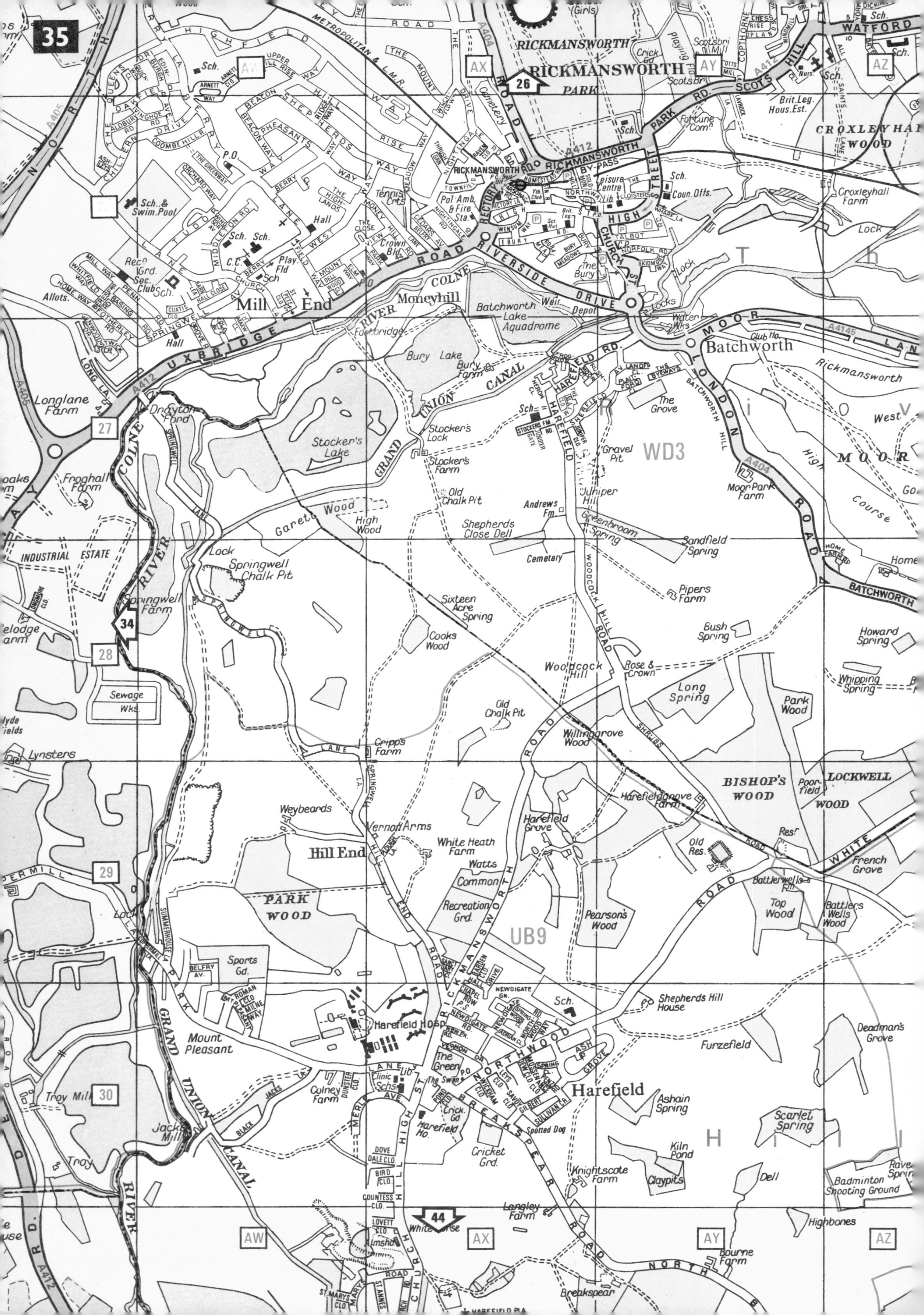

35
RICKMANSWORTH
RICKMANSWORTH PARK
26
AW
AX
AY
AZ
WATFORD
SCOTS HILL
CROXLEY HALL WOOD
Croxleyhall Farm
Brit. Leg. Hous. Est.
Fortune Com.
Scotsbridge Mill
METROPOLITAN & L.M.R.
HIGHFIELD
UPPER HILL RISE
SHEPHERDS WAY
PHEASANTS WAY
BEACON WAY
Cemetery
NIGHTINGALE RD
RICKMANSWORTH BY-PASS
Leisure Centre
Coun. Offs.
HIGH STREET
CHURCH ST
Pol. Amb. & Fire Sta.
Tennis Crts
Crown Bld.
Mill End
Moneyhill
RIVER COLNE
RIVERSIDE DRIVE
Batchworth Lake Aquadrome
Bury Lake
Bury Farm
Weir
Depot
Locks
Water Wks
Batchworth
MOOR LANE
A4145
LONDON ROAD
BATCHWORTH HILL
Rickmansworth
The Grove
UXBRIDGE ROAD
A412
A405
Longlane Farm
Drayton Ford
27
Stocker's Lake
GRAND UNION CANAL
Stocker's Lock
Stocker's Farm
HAREFIELD RD
WD3
Gravel Pit
Juniper Hill
Moor Park Farm
MOOR
West
High
Course
Froghall Farm
INDUSTRIAL ESTATE
Gareth Wood
High Wood
Old Chalk Pit
Andrews Fm
Shepherds Close Dell
Greenbroom Spring
Sandfield Spring
Cemetary
Lock
Springwell Chalk Pit
Springwell Farm
34
28
Sewage Wks.
Sixteen Acre Spring
Cooks Wood
Pipers Farm
WOODCOCK HILL ROAD
Bush Spring
Howard Spring
BATCHWORTH
Home Farm
Woodcock Hill
Rose & Crown
Long Spring
Whipping Spring
Park Wood
Old Chalk Pit
Willingrove Wood
Lynsters
Cripps Farm
LANE
SPRINGWELL LA.
BISHOP'S WOOD
Poorfield
LOCKWELL WOOD
Harefieldgrove Farm
Harefield Grove
Res.
Old Res.
WHITE HILL ROAD
French Grove
Battlerwells Fm.
Top Wood
Battlers Wells Wood
Weybeards
Vernon Arms
Hill End
White Heath Farm
Watts Common
Recreation Grd.
29
PARK WOOD
HILL END ROAD
RICKMANSWORTH ROAD
UB9
Pearson's Wood
Sports Gd.
Harefield Hosp.
Shepherds Hill House
Mount Pleasant
Deadman's Grove
Furzefield
Harefield
The Green
NORTHWOOD ROAD
Colney Farm
Ashain Spring
30
Troy Mill
Jacks Mill
Troy
Harefield Ho.
Crick. Gd
Spotted Dog
Cricket Grd.
BREAKSPEAR ROAD
Scarlet Spring
Kiln Pond
Claypits
Knightscote Farm
Dell
Badminton Shooting Ground
Highbones
Langley Farm
44
White Horse
Almshouses
Bourne Farm
Breakspear
NORTH
RIVER COLNE
HIGH ST
CHURCH HILL

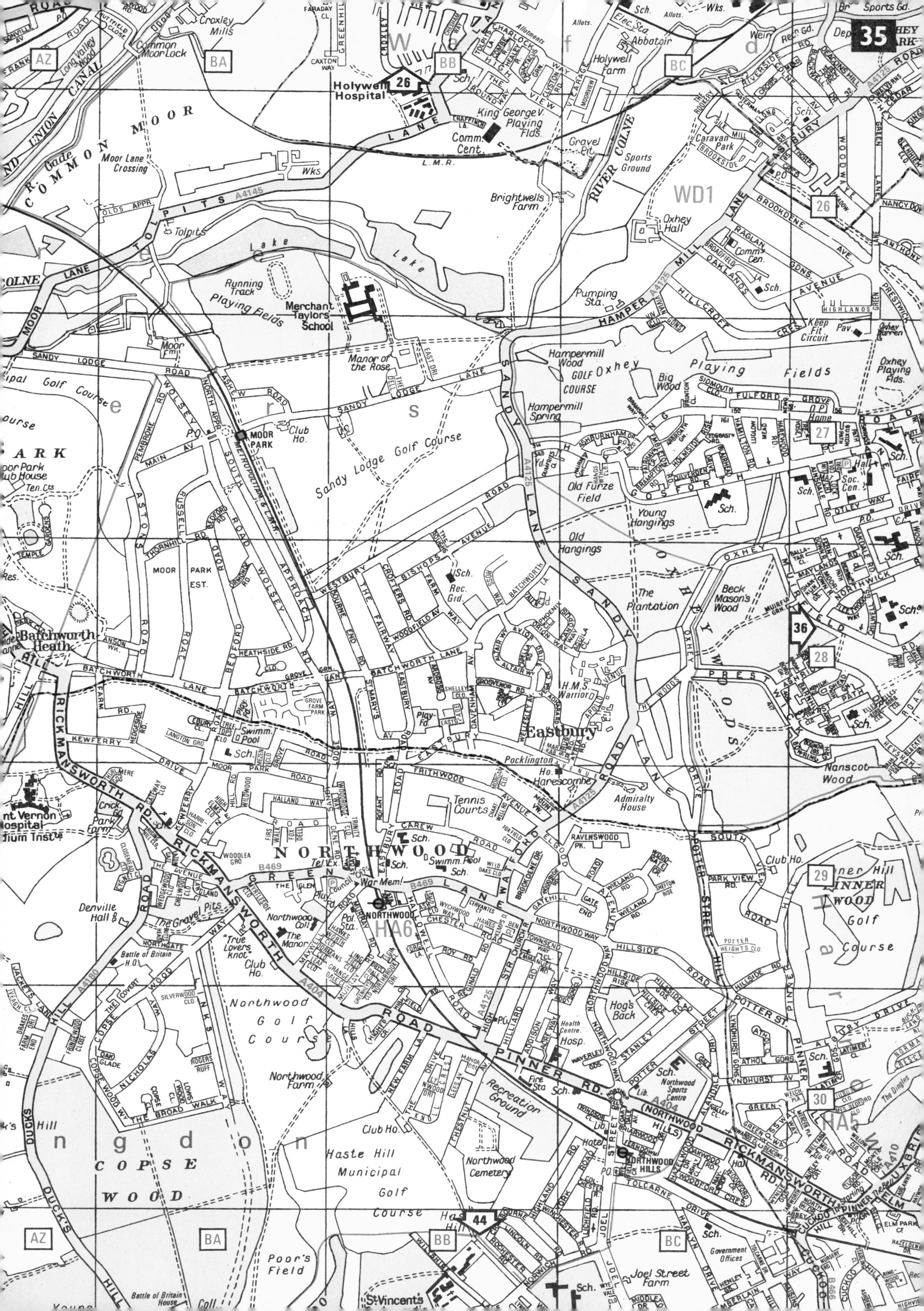
AZ
BA
BB
BC
26
Holywell Hospital
Croxley Mills
Common Moor Lock
Long Valley Wood
GRAND UNION CANAL
R. Gade
COMMON MOOR
Moor Lane Crossing
TOLPITS LANE
A4145
Tolpits
COLNE
MOOR LANE
Lake
Running Track
Playing Fields
Merchant Taylors' School
King George V. Playing Flds.
Comm. Cent.
L.M.R.
Gravel Pit
Sports Ground
RIVER COLNE
Brightwells Farm
Abbatoir
Holywell Farm
Elec. Sta.
Caravan Park
WD1
Oxhey Hall
HAMPER MILL LANE
A4125
Pumping Sta.
Keep Fit Circuit
Oxhey Warren
Oxhey Playing Flds.
Playing Fields
Hampermill Wood
OXHEY GOLF COURSE
Big Wood
Hampermill Spring
SANDY LODGE ROAD
Moor Fm.
Manor of the Rose
SANDY LODGE LANE
MOOR PARK
Club Ho.
Sandy Lodge Golf Course
Moor Park Club House
Ten. Cts.
MOOR PARK EST.
Batchworth Heath
BATCHWORTH LANE
Old Furze Field
Young Hangings
Old Hangings
The Plantation
Beck Mason's Wood
OXHEY WOODS
PRESTWICK
H.M.S. Warrior
Eastbury
Swimm. Pool
Pocklington Ho.
Harescombe
Admiralty House
Nanscot Wood
Tennis Courts
NORTHWOOD
Swimm. Pool
War Mem.
Council Offs.
NORTHWOOD
HA6
Northwood Coll.
The Manor
Denville Hall
The Gravel Pits
"True Lovers' Knot"
Club Ho.
Battle of Britain H.Q.
Mount Vernon Hospital
Crick. Gd.
Park Farm
RICKMANSWORTH RD.
A404
Northwood Golf Course
Northwood Farm
PINNER RD.
Recreation Ground
Fire Sta.
Health Centre
Hosp.
Hog's Back
Northwood Sports Centre
Lib.
(NORTHWOOD HILLS)
NORTHWOOD HILLS
Northwood Cemetery
Club Ho.
Haste Hill Municipal Golf Course
44
Poor's Field
St. Vincent's
Joel Street Farm
Government Offices
COPSE WOOD
Hillingdon
Duck's Hill
DUCK'S HILL
Battle of Britain House
Pinner Hill
PINNER WOOD
Golf Course
Harrow
HA5
The Dingles
27
28
29
30
36
Sch.
TOLCARNE DRIVE
POTTER STREET
HILLSIDE ROAD
NORTHWOOD WAY
GREEN LANE
HALLOWELL RD.
CHESTER ROAD
FRITHWOOD AVENUE
CAREW ROAD
GOSFORTH LANE
OXHEY LANE
SOUTH VIEW ROAD
NORTHWICK RD.
HIGH ST.
REGINALD RD.
HILLIARD RD.
EMMANUEL RD.
STANLEY RD.
POTTER ST.
LYNDHURST AV.
ATHOL GDNS.
PINNER HILL RD.
ALBURY DRIVE
ELM PARK
CUCKOO HILL
BATCHWORTH HILL
EASTBURY ROAD
EASTBURY AVENUE
WESTBURY
BISHOPS AVENUE
WOODFIELD AV.
SOUTH APPROACH
WOLSEY ROAD
ASTONS ROAD
BEDFORD ROAD
RUSSELL RD.
THORNHILL RD.
KEWFERRY DRIVE
KEWFERRY RD.
HALLAND WAY
MOOR PARK ROAD
DENE ROAD
COPSE WOOD WAY
THE BROAD WALK
NICHOLAS WAY
JACKETS LANE
A4180

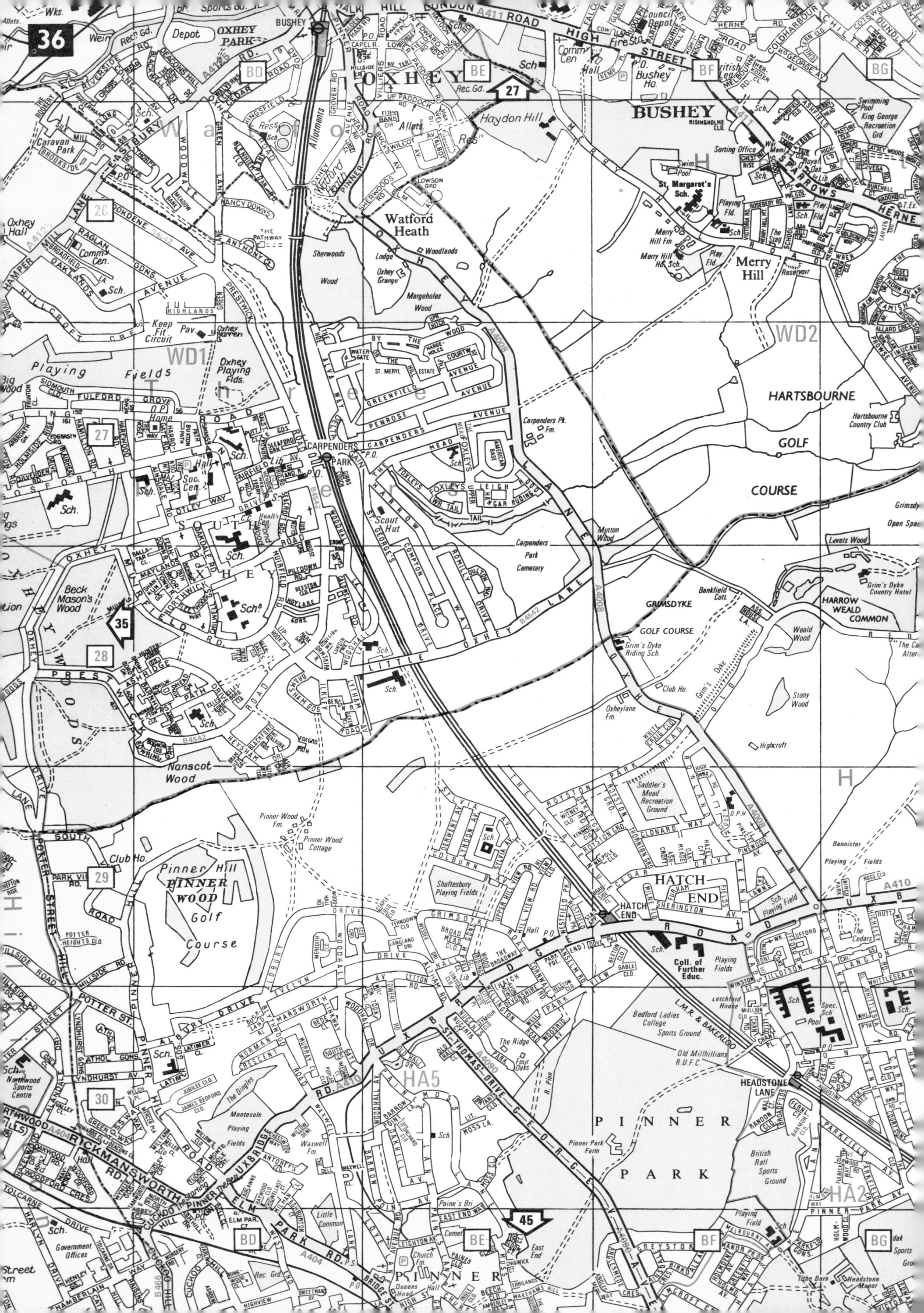
OXHEY
OXHEY PARK
BUSHEY
HIGH STREET
Haydon Hill
Watford Heath
Sherwoods Wood
Oxhey Grange
Margeholes Wood
St. Margaret's Sch.
Merry Hill
Merry Hill Fm
WD1
WD2
HARTSBOURNE
Hartsbourne Country Club
GOLF
COURSE
Oxhey Playing Flds.
Playing Fields
CARPENDERS PARK
SOUTH OXHEY
Carpenders Park Cemetery
Mutton Wood
Carpenders Pk. Fm.
GRIMSDYKE GOLF COURSE
Grim's Dyke Riding Sch.
Grim's Dyke Country Hotel
HARROW WEALD COMMON
Weald Wood
Stony Wood
Levels Wood
Bankfield Cott.
Oxheylane Fm.
Highcroft
Beck Mason's Wood
Nanscot Wood
Pinner Wood Fm.
Pinner Wood Cottage
Pinner Hill
PINNER WOOD
Golf Course
Shaftesbury Playing Fields
Saddler's Mead Recreation Ground
HATCH END
Coll. of Further Educ.
Bedford Ladies College Sports Ground
Old Millhillians R.U.F.C.
Montesole Playing Fields
The Dingles
Waxwell Fm.
HA5
HA2
PINNER PARK
Pinner Park Farm
British Rail Sports Ground
HEADSTONE LANE
Headstone Manor
Tithe Barn
Little Common
PINNER
Northwood Sports Centre
Government Offices
RICKMANSWORTH RD.
UXBRIDGE RD.
ELM PARK RD.
UXBRIDGE RD.
ST. THOMAS' DRIVE
GEORGE V AVENUE
OXHEY LANE
OXHEY DRIVE
PRESTWICK RD.
BD
BE
BF
BG
26
27
28
29
30
35
45

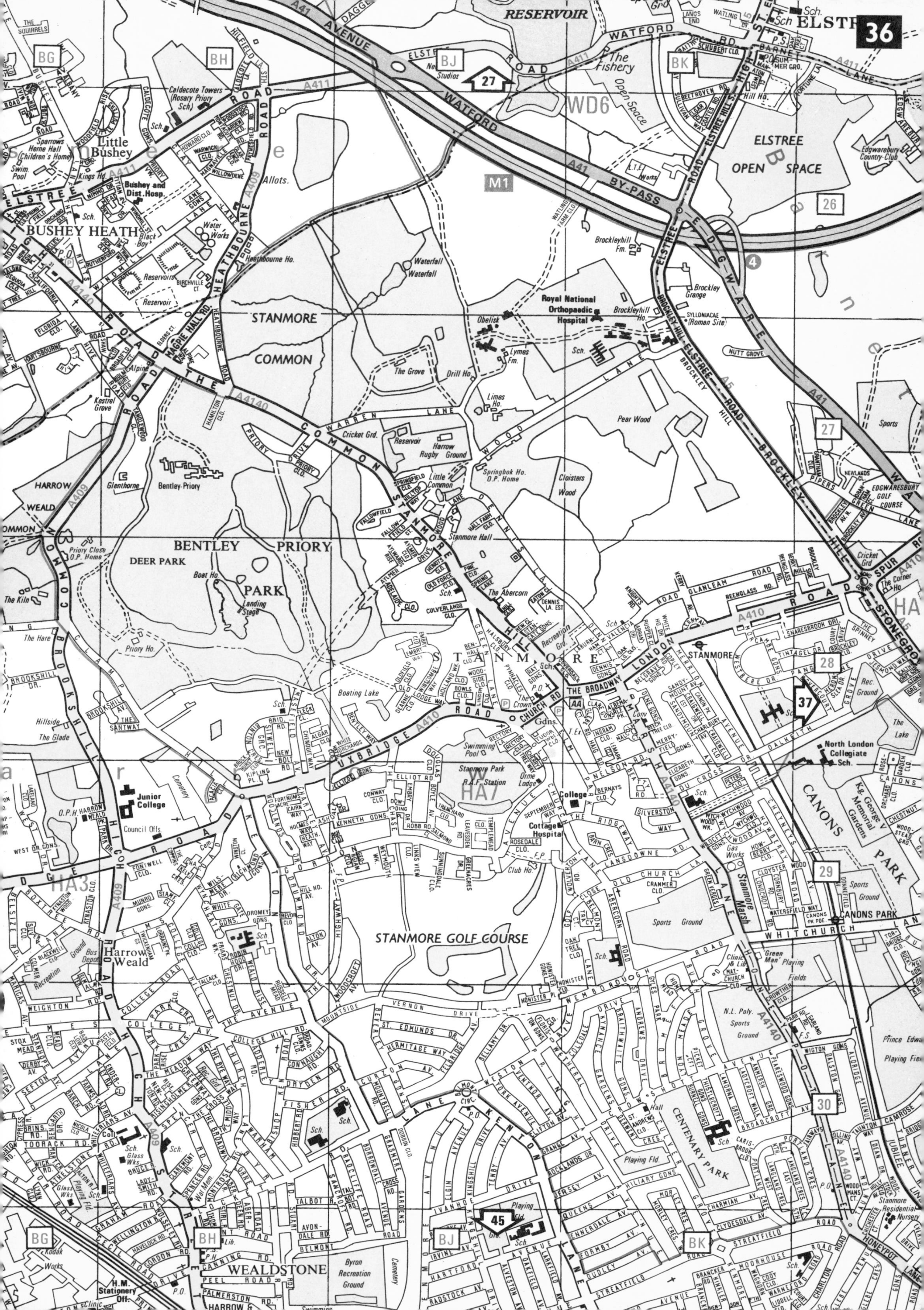
RESERVOIR
ELSTREE
WATFORD ROAD
The Fishery
Open Space
WD6
27
BG
BH
BJ
BK
Caldecote Towers (Rosary Priory Sch)
Little Bushey
Sparrows Herne Hall (Children's Home)
Bushey and Dist. Hosp.
BUSHEY HEATH
Allots.
Water Works
Reservoirs
Reservoir
Heathbourne Ho.
HEATHBOURNE ROAD
M1
A41 BY-PASS
ELSTREE OPEN SPACE
26
Edgwarebury Country Club
Brockleyhill Fm.
Waterfall
Royal National Orthopaedic Hospital
Obelisk
Brockleyhill Ho.
Brockley Grange
SYLLONIACAE (Roman Site)
NUTT GROVE
STANMORE COMMON
The Grove
Drill Ho.
Lymes Fm.
Limes Ho.
Pear Wood
WARREN LANE
Cricket Grd.
Reservoir
Harrow Rugby Ground
Little Common
Springbok Ho. O.P. Home
Cloisters Wood
27
Sports
EDGWARESBURY GOLF COURSE
Cricket Grd
Kestrel Grove
Glenthorne
Bentley Priory
HARROW WEALD COMMON
Priory Close O.P. Home
DEER PARK
BENTLEY PRIORY PARK
Boat Ho
Landing Stage
Stanmore Hall
The Abercorn
The Kiln
The Hare
Priory Ho.
STANMORE
Recreation Grd.
THE BROADWAY
STANMORE
28
37
Rec. Ground
The Lake
North London Collegiate Sch.
Hillside
The Glade
Boating Lake
UXBRIDGE ROAD
The Crown
Swimming Pool
Stanmore Park R.A.F. Station
Orme Lodge
Cemetery
Junior College
Council Offs.
O.P.H.
HA7
College
Cottage Hospital
CANONS PARK
Kg. George V Memorial Gardens
HA3
Club Ho.
Sports Ground
Gas Works
Stanmore Marsh
29
Sports Ground
CANONS PARK
STANMORE GOLF COURSE
Harrow Weald
Bus Depot
Recreation Ground
Green Man Playing Fields
N.L. Poly. Sports Ground
Prince Edward Playing Fields
Hall
CENTENARY PARK
30
Playing Fld.
Glass Wks
Playing Fld.
Playing Fld.
45
Stanmore Residential Nursery
Kodak Works
WEALDSTONE
Byron Recreation Ground
Cemetery
H.M. Stationery Off.
HONEYPOT LANE

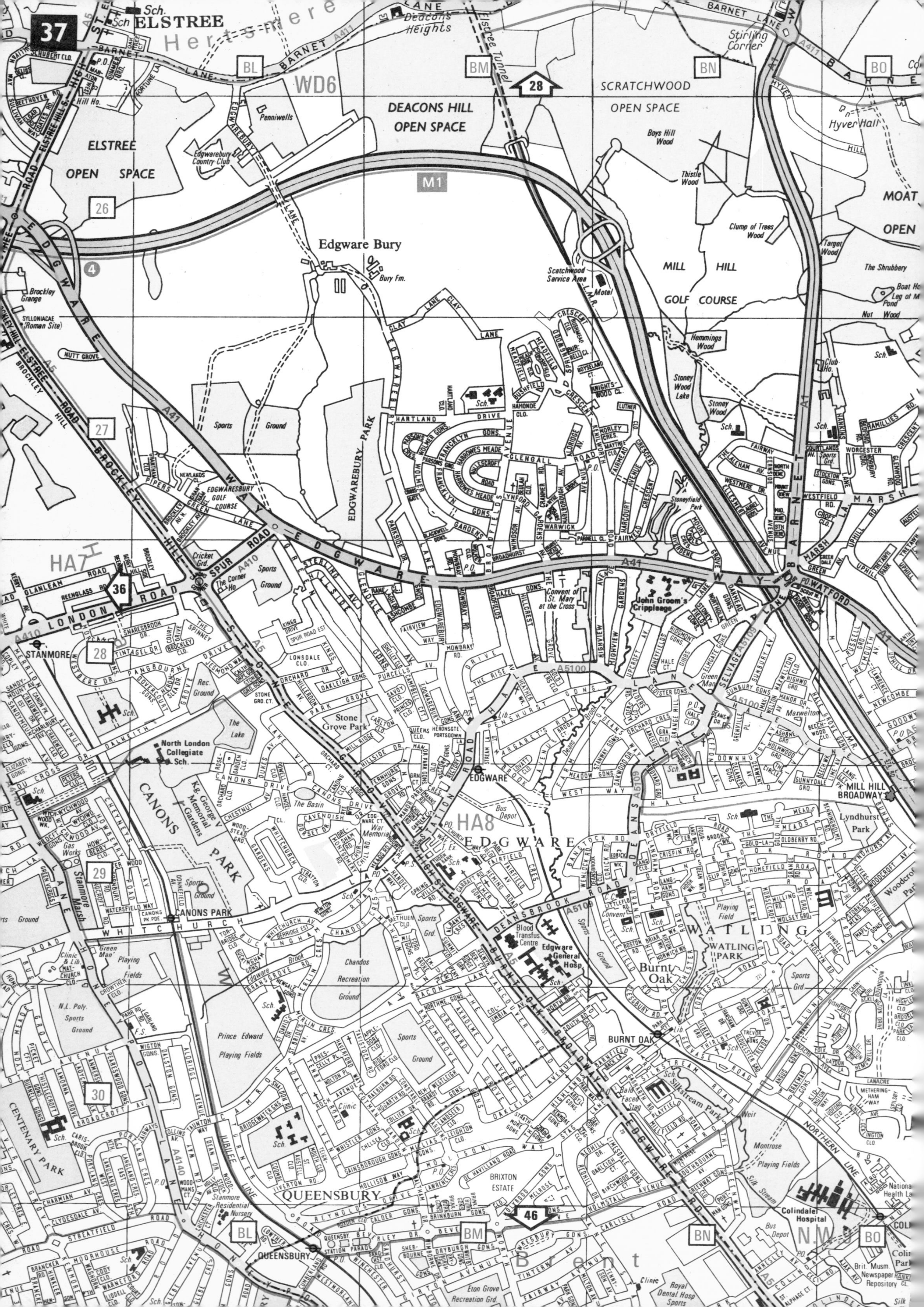
ELSTREE
Hertsmere
WD6
DEACONS HILL
OPEN SPACE
Deacons Heights
SCRATCHWOOD
OPEN SPACE
Stirling Corner
Hyver Hall
ELSTREE
OPEN SPACE
Edgwarebury Country Club
Penniwells
Boys Hill Wood
Thistle Wood
M1
Clump of Trees Wood
MOAT
OPEN
Elstree Tunnel
Edgware Bury
Bury Fm.
Brockley Grange
SYLLONIACAE (Roman Site)
Scratchwood Service Area
Motel
MILL HILL
GOLF COURSE
Target Wood
The Shrubbery
Boat Ho
Leg of Mutton Pond
Nut Wood
Hemmings Wood
Stoney Wood Lake
Stoney Wood
EDGWAREBURY PARK
Sports Ground
EDGWARESBURY GOLF COURSE
HA7
Cricket Grd.
Sports Ground
The Corner Ho
EDGWARE
WAY
John Groom's Crippleage
Convent of St. Mary at the Cross
Stoneyfield Park
WATFORD
STANMORE
Rec. Ground
The Lake
North London Collegiate Sch.
Stone Grove Park
CANONS PARK
Kg. George V Memorial Gardens
The Basin
War Memorial
HA8
EDGWARE
Bus Depot
MILL HILL BROADWAY
Lyndhurst Park
Maxwelton
Woodcroft Park
CANONS PARK
Stanmore Marsh
Gas Works
Chandos Recreation Ground
Blood Transfus Centre
Edgware General Hosp.
Burnt Oak
WATLING
WATLING PARK
Playing Field
Sports Grd
N.L. Poly. Sports Ground
Prince Edward Playing Fields
Sports Ground
BURNT OAK
Silkstream Park
Montrose Playing Fields
CENTENARY PARK
QUEENSBURY
BRIXTON ESTATE
Stanmore Residential Nursery
Colindale Hospital
National Health La
N.W.9
Brit. Musm. Newspaper Repository
Brent
Eton Grove Recreation Grd
Royal Dental Hosp Sports
A5
A41
A410
A411
A1
A5100
A5109
A4140
BL
BM
BN
BO
26
27
28
29
30
28
36
46
4

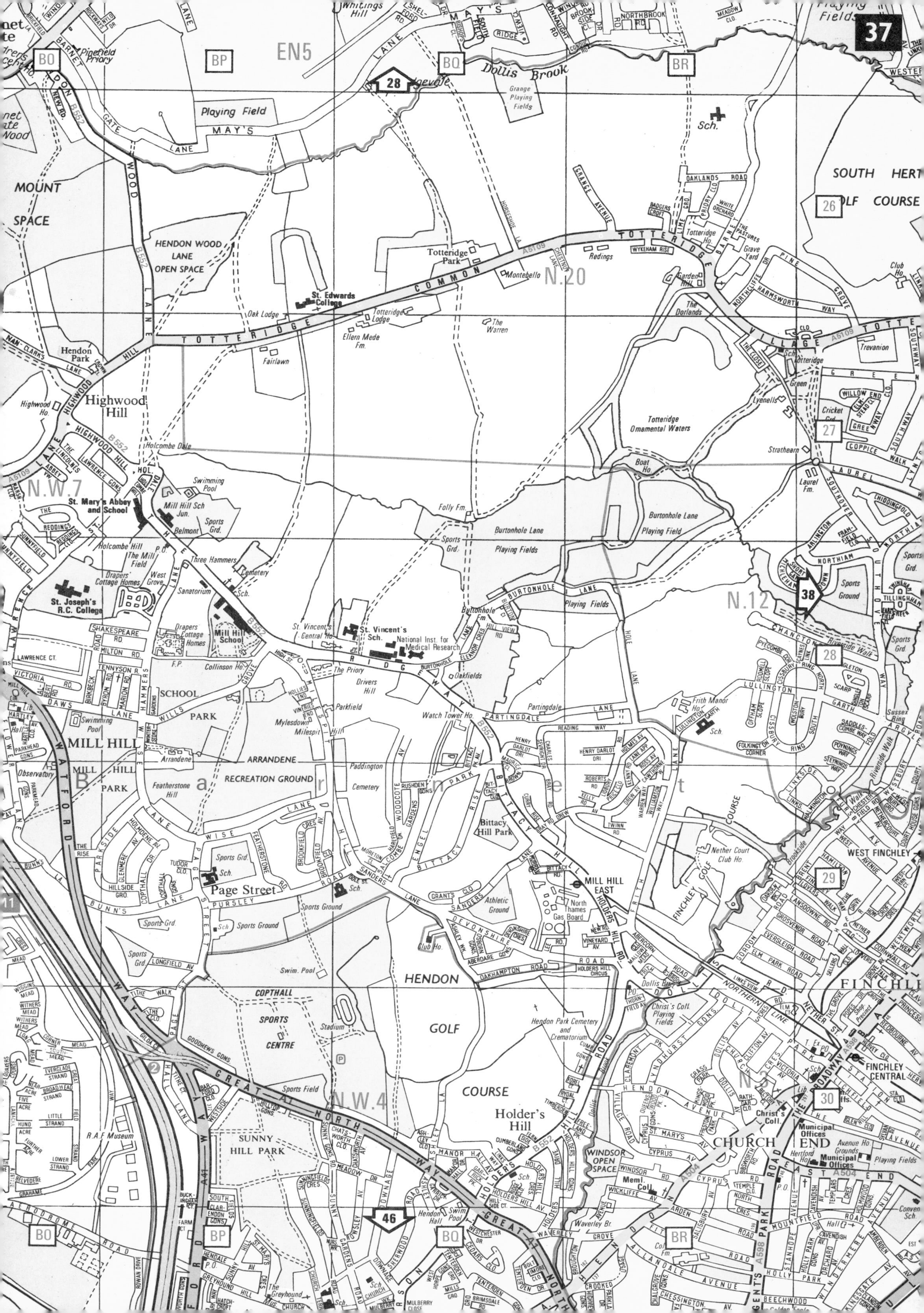
EN5
BO
BP
BQ
BR
28
Dollis Brook
Playing Field
MAY'S LANE
Grange Playing Fields
Sch.
MOUNT SPACE
HENDON WOOD LANE OPEN SPACE
SOUTH HERTS GOLF COURSE
26
OAKLANDS ROAD
BADGERS CROFT
WHITE ORCHARD
THE PASTURES
Totteridge Ho.
Grave Yard
TOTTERIDGE COMMON
A5109
Totteridge Park
Redings
WYKEHAM RISE
Montebello
N.20
Garden Hill
St. Edwards College
Oak Lodge
Totteridge Lodge
Ellern Mede Fm.
The Warren
The Dorlands
NORTHCLIFFE DR
HARMSWORTH WAY
PINE GROVE
Club Ho.
TOTTERIDGE VILLAGE
Trevanion
SOUTHWAY
Hendon Park
Fairlawn
Totteridge Green
Lyenells
WILLOW END
Cricket Gd.
GREENWAY
27
COPPICE WALK
Highwood Hill
Highwood Ho.
HIGHWOOD HILL
B552
Holcombe Dale
Totteridge Ornamental Waters
Strathearn
Boat Ho.
LAUREL
Laurel Fm.
N.W.7
St. Mary's Abbey and School
Swimming Pool
Mill Hill Sch Jun.
Belmont
Sports Grd.
Folly Fm.
Burtonhole Lane Playing Field
Burtonhole Lane Playing Fields
Holcombe Hill
The Mill Field
Drapers' Cottage Homes
West Grove
Three Hammers
Cemetery
Sports Grd.
NORTHIAM
St. Joseph's R.C. College
Sanatorium
Sch.
BURTONHOLE LANE
Playing Fields
N.12
38
Sports Ground
Buttonhole Fm
Drapers Cottage Homes
Mill Hill School
St. Vincent's Central Ho.
St. Vincent's Sch.
National Inst. for Medical Research
SHAKESPEARE RD
MILTON RD
LAWRENCE CT.
TENNYSON R.
VICTORIA RD
Collinson Ho.
RIDGEWAY
Oakfields
Riverside Walk
Sports Grd
28
HIGH ST.
The Priory
Drivers Hill
DAWS LANE
SCHOOL
HAMMERS
PARK
WILLS GROVE
Parkfield
Frith Manor Ho.
Sch.
Watch Tower Ho.
PARTINGDALE LANE
Partingdale
HOLE LANE
Swimming Pool
MILL HILL
Mylesdown Milespit Hill
READING WAY
HENRY DARLOT DRI
ARRANDENE
Arrandene
Paddington Cemetery
CHARLES SEVRIGHT DR
FOLKINGTON CORNER
MILL HILL PARK
Observatory
RECREATION GROUND
Featherstone Hill
RUSHDEN GDNS
BITTACY
Barnet
COURSE
Riverside Walk
WATFORD
WISE LANE
WOODCOTE AV
Bittacy Hill Park
Nether Court Club Ho
WEST FINCHLEY
29
THE RISE
PARKSIDE
HOLMDENE AV
TUDOR CLO.
Sports Grd.
Sch.
Page Street
BROOKFIELD CRES
MORETON
SANDERS LANE
ENGEL PARK
BITTACY HILL
MILL HILL EAST
FINCHLEY GOLF
BUNN'S LANE
PURSLEY RD
Sch.
Sports Ground
GRANT'S CLO
Athletic Ground
North Thames Gas Board
HOLDERS HILL RD.
FRITH LANE
LANSDOWNE RD
GROSVENOR ROAD
EVERSLEIGH ROAD
ELM PARK ROAD
Sports Grd.
Sch
Sports Ground
DEVONSHIRE ROAD
Club Ho.
VINEYARD AV.
LONGFIELD AV
Swim. Pool
ABERDARE GDNS
OAKHAMPTON ROAD
HOLDERS HILL CIRCUS
HENDON
Dollis
NORTHERN LINE
FINCHLEY
TITHE WALK
COPTHALL SPORTS CENTRE
Stadium
GOLF
Hendon Park Cemetery and Crematorium
Christ's Coll. Playing Fields
DOLLIS AV
LYNDHURST GDNS
CLIFTON AV
FINCHLEY CENTRAL
GOODWIN'S GDNS
Sports Field
COURSE
Holder's Hill
N.W.4
HENDON AVENUE
N.3
30
CHURCH END
Christ's Coll.
Municipal Offices
Avenue Ho Grounds
Playing Fields
R.A.F. Museum
GREAT NORTH WAY
SUNNY HILL PARK
WINDSOR OPEN SPACE
Meml. Coll.
CYPRUS AV
ST MARY'S AV
EAST END ROAD
A504
A41
46
MANOR HALL AV
HOLDERS HILL AV
Hendon Hall
Swim Pool
WICKLIFFE AV
ARDEN
REGENT'S PARK ROAD
A598
MOUNTFIELD ROAD
Convent Sch.
AERODROME ROAD
BO
BP
BQ
BR
Waverley Br.
ALLANDALE AVENUE
HOLLY PARK
WINDERMERE AV
The Greyhound
CHURCH
BEECHWOOD
CHESSINGTON AV.
GREYHOUND HILL

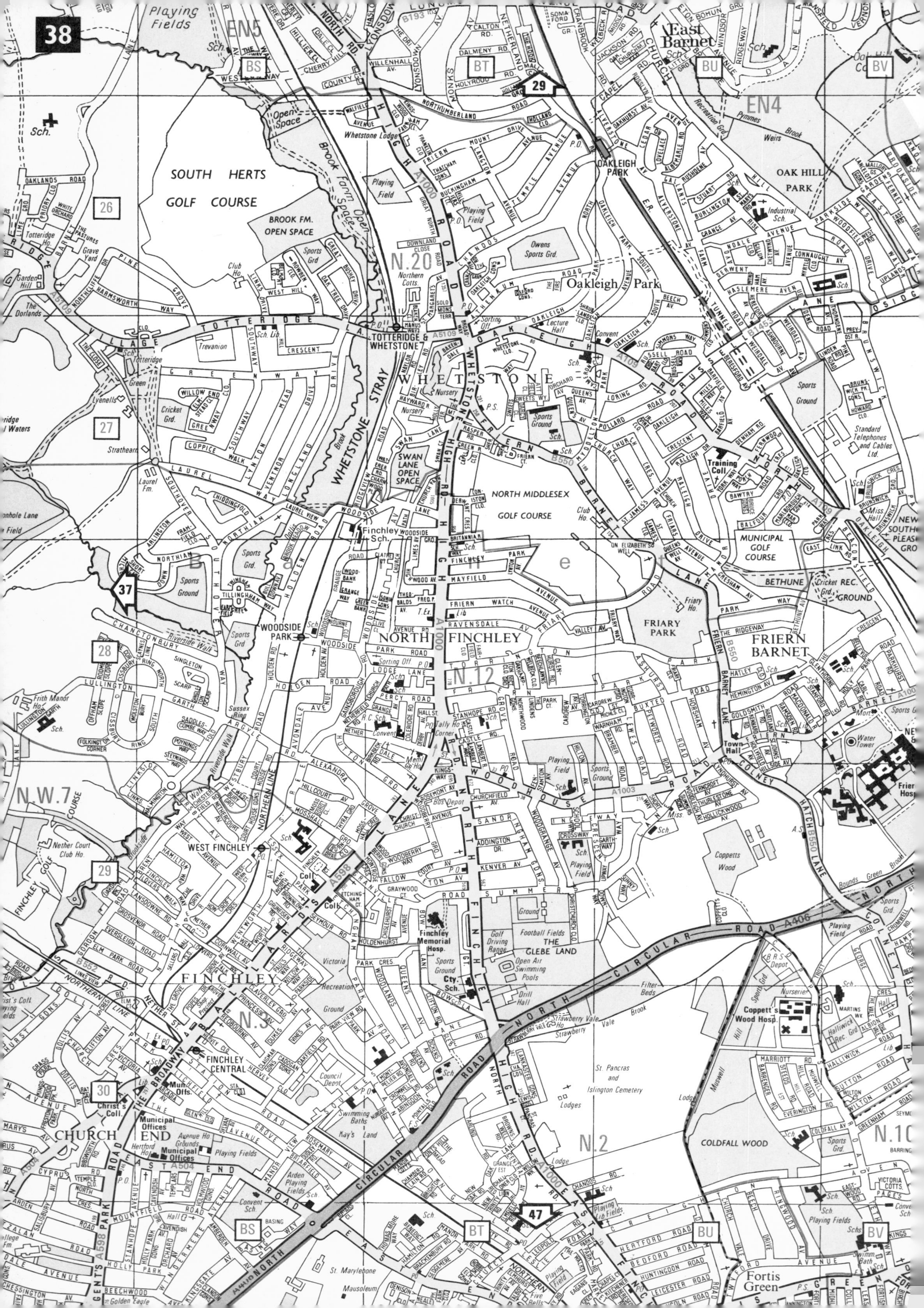
38
Playing Fields
EN5
BS
BT
BU
BV
29
East Barnet
EN4
Oak Hill Park
SOUTH HERTS GOLF COURSE
BROOK FM. OPEN SPACE
26
27
28
29
30
37
47
N.20
Oakleigh Park
OAKLEIGH PARK
TOTTERIDGE & WHETSTONE
TOTTERIDGE LA.
WHETSTONE
WHETSTONE STRAY
SWAN LANE OPEN SPACE
NORTH MIDDLESEX GOLF COURSE
MUNICIPAL GOLF COURSE
Standard Telephones and Cables Ltd.
WOODSIDE PARK
NORTH FINCHLEY
FRIARY PARK
FRIERN BARNET
N.12
Coppetts Wood
N.W.7
WEST FINCHLEY
FINCHLEY
Finchley Memorial Hosp.
THE GLEBE LAND
NORTH CIRCULAR ROAD
N.3
FINCHLEY CENTRAL
CHURCH END
St. Pancras and Islington Cemetery
N.2
COLDFALL WOOD
Coppett's Wood Hosp.
N.10
St. Marylebone Mausoleum
Fortis Green

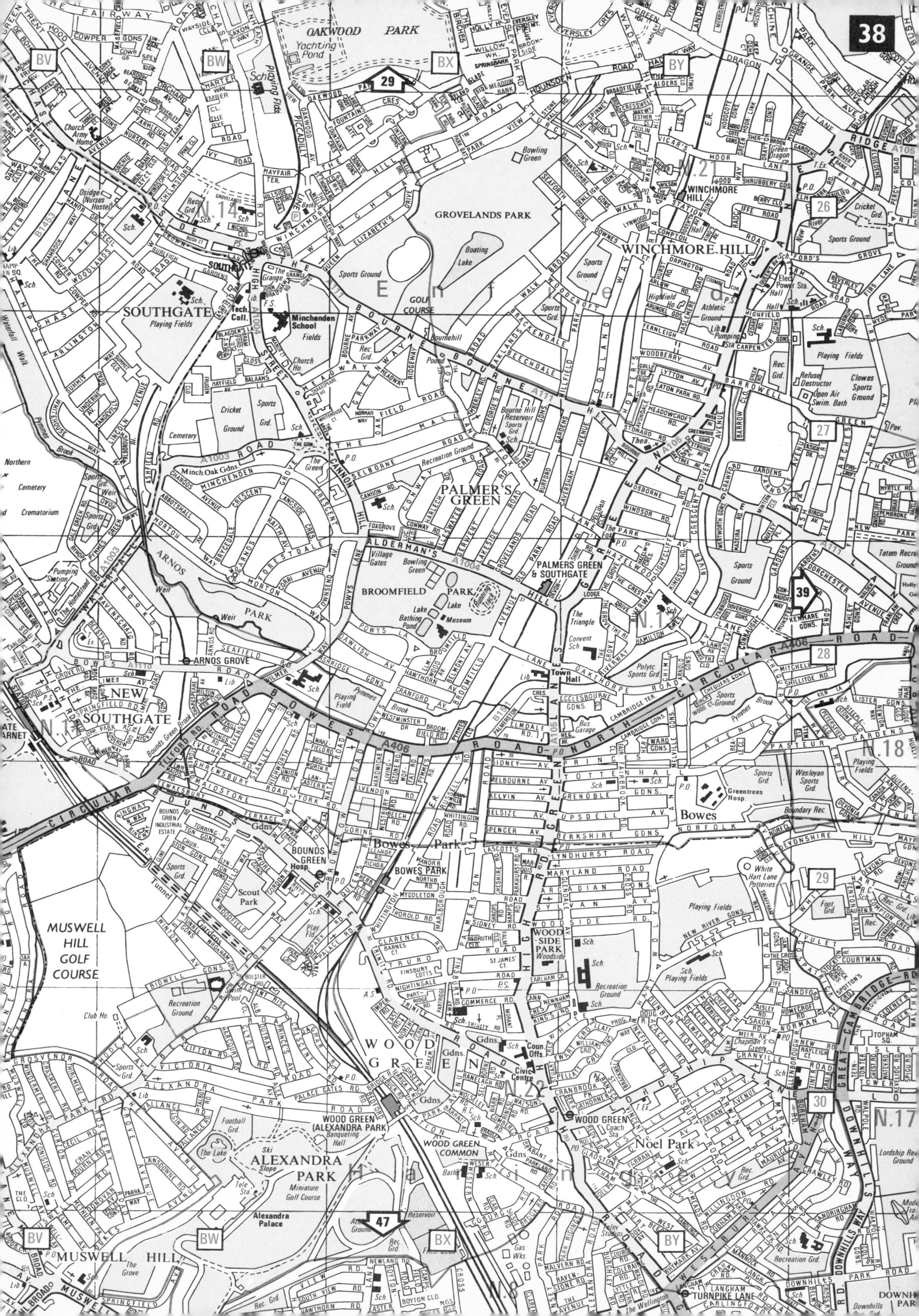
OAKWOOD PARK
Yachting Pond
29
BV
BW
BX
BY
SOUTHGATE
Playing Fields
Minchenden School
GROVELANDS PARK
Boating Lake
Sports Ground
GOLF COURSE
Enfield
WINCHMORE HILL
WINCHMORE HILL
N.21
N.14
26
27
PALMER'S GREEN
PALMERS GREEN & SOUTHGATE
BROOMFIELD PARK
Museum
ARNOS PARK
ARNOS GROVE
NEW SOUTHGATE
Northern Cemetery
Crematorium
39
28
NORTH CIRCULAR ROAD
A406
N.18
N.11
Bowes
Town Hall
BOWES PARK
BOUNDS GREEN
MUSWELL HILL GOLF COURSE
29
WOOD GREEN
N.22
WOOD GREEN (ALEXANDRA PARK)
WOOD GREEN COMMON
ALEXANDRA PARK
Alexandra Palace
Noel Park
Haringey
30
N.17
47
MUSWELL HILL
TURNPIKE LANE
N.8
Lordship Rec. Ground
Recreation Grd.
Clowes Sports Ground
Tatem Recreation Ground
Greentrees Hosp.
Wesleyan Sports Grd.
White Hart Lane Potteries
Playing Fields
Recreation Ground
Scout Park
Cricket Ground
Cemetery
WOODSIDE PARK
Civic Centre
Coun. Offs.

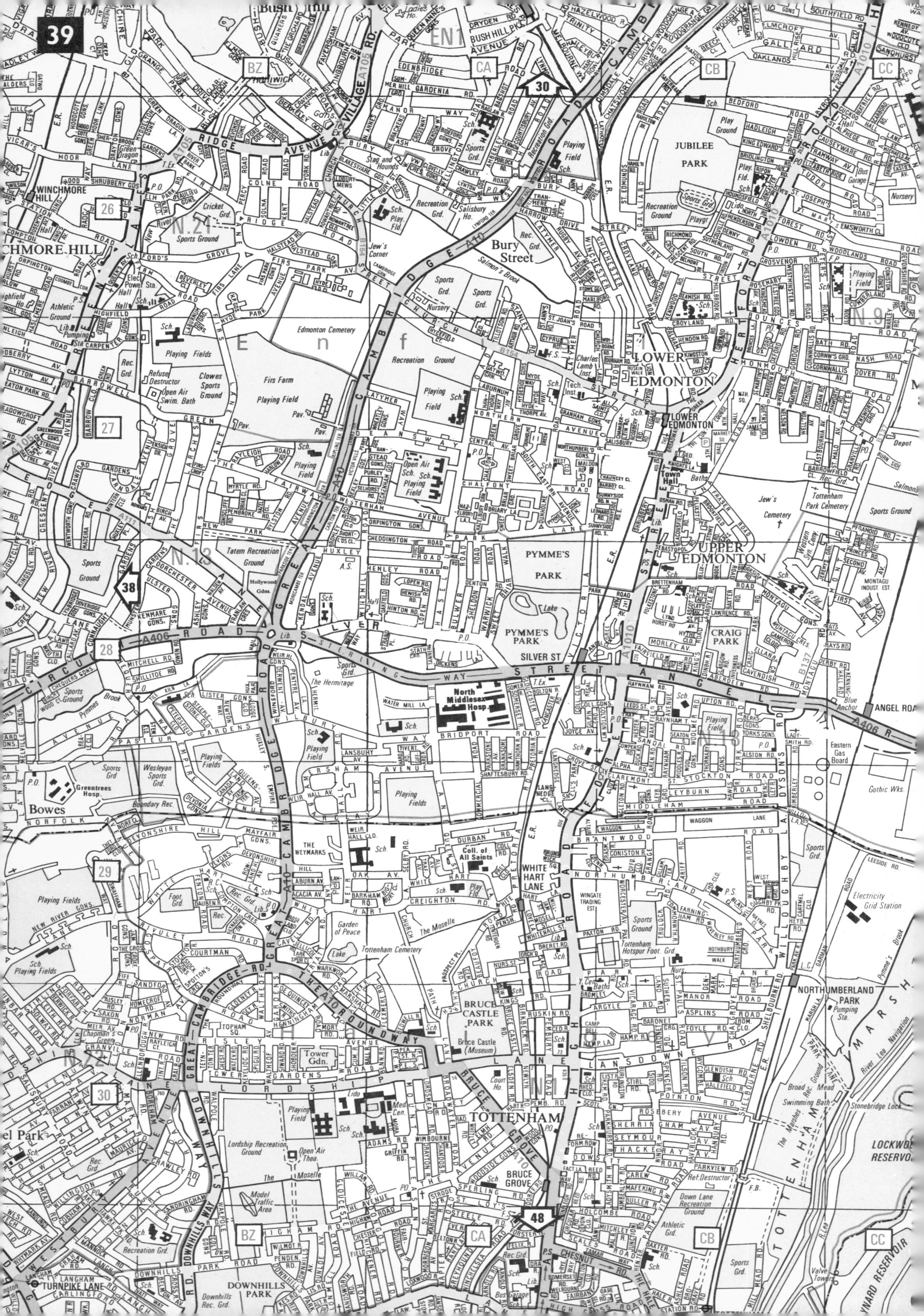
Bush Hill
EN1
BZ
CA
CB
CC
30
WINCHMORE HILL
26
N.21
27
28
29
30
N.13
38
N.9
N.18
N.17
48
WINCHMORE HILL
Ridge Avenue
Bury Street
Jubilee Park
Edmonton Cemetery
Firs Farm Playing Field
Recreation Ground
LOWER EDMONTON
UPPER EDMONTON
Jew's Cemetery
Tottenham Park Cemetery
Pymme's Park
Silver St
Craig Park
Angel Road
North Middlesex Hosp.
Tatem Recreation Ground
Sports Ground
Greentrees Hosp.
Bowes
The Weymarks
Coll. of All Saints
White Hart Lane
Tottenham Hotspur Foot. Grd.
Tottenham Cemetery
Bruce Castle Park
Bruce Castle (Museum)
Northumberland Park
TOTTENHAM
Bruce Grove
Lordship Recreation Ground
Downhills Park
Turnpike Lane
Lockwood Reservoir
Great Cambridge Road
Sterling Way
North Circular Road
Angel Road
Hertford Road
High Road
Lordship Lane
Downhills Way
Tottenham Marshes
River Lee Navigation
Electricity Grid Station
Eastern Gas Board
Gothic Wks.
Montagu Indust. Est
Wingate Trading Est
Pymme's Brook
Salmon's Brook
The Moselle

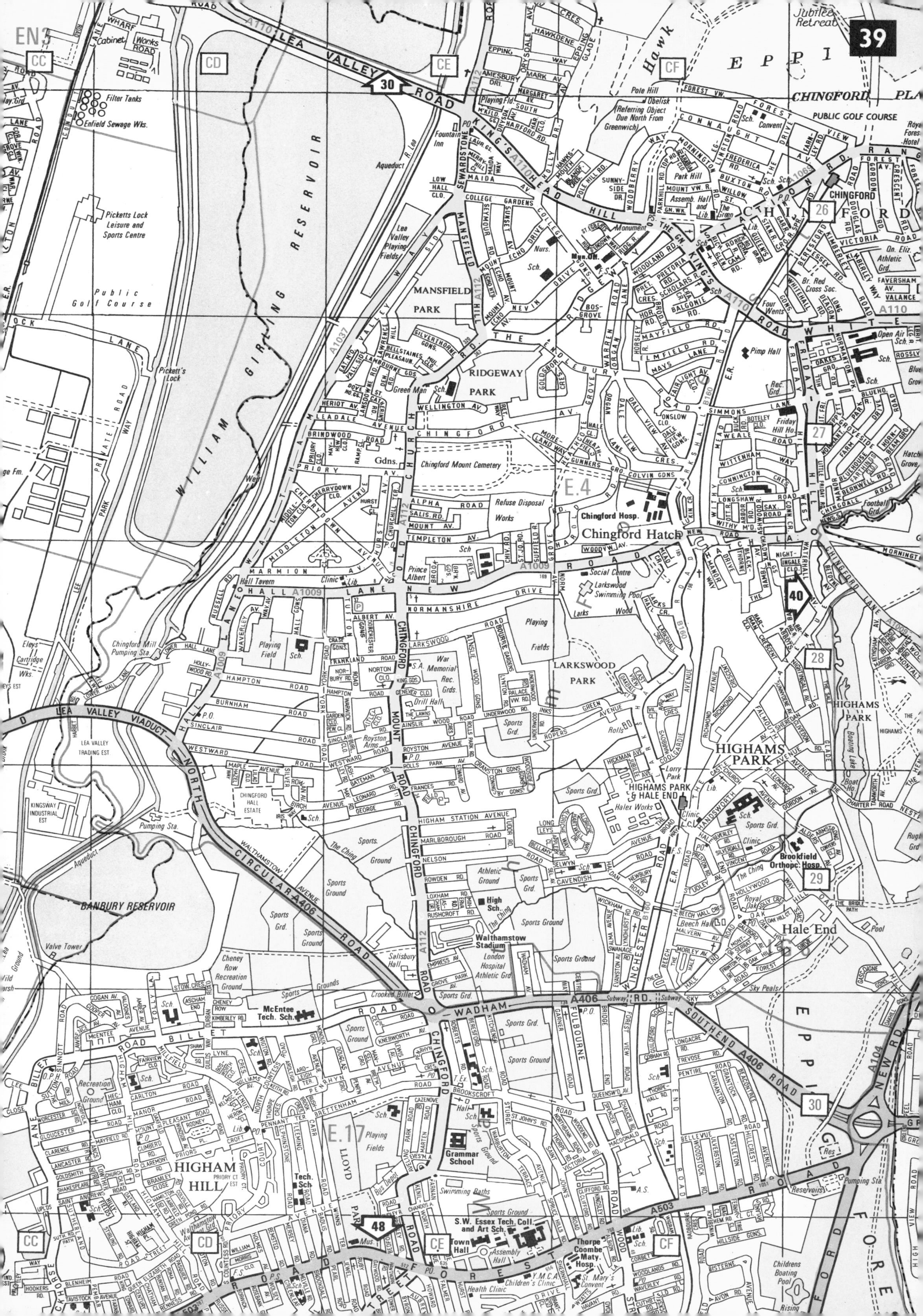

EN3
CC
CD
CE
CF
LEA VALLEY ROAD
A110
30
Filter Tanks
Enfield Sewage Wks.
Picketts Lock Leisure and Sports Centre
Public Golf Course
WILLIAM GIRLING RESERVOIR
Aqueduct
R. Lea
Fountain Inn
Lea Valley Playing Fields
MANSFIELD PARK
RIDGEWAY PARK
Pickett's Lock
PRIVATE ROAD
LEE PARK WAY
Chingford Mount Cemetery
Refuse Disposal Works
E.4
Chingford Hosp.
Chingford Hatch
Social Centre
Larkswood Swimming Pool
Larks Wood
Playing Fields
LARKSWOOD PARK
Chingford Mill Pumping Sta.
Eleys Cartridge Wks.
LEA VALLEY VIADUCT
LEA VALLEY TRADING EST
KINGSWAY INDUSTRIAL EST
CHINGFORD HALL ESTATE
NORTH CIRCULAR ROAD
A406
Pumping Sta.
BANBURY RESERVOIR
Valve Tower
WALTHAMSTOW AVENUE
The Ching
Sports Ground
Walthamstow Stadium
London Hospital Athletic Grd
Salisbury Hall
Crooked Billet
Cheney Row Recreation Ground
McEntee Tech. Sch.
WADHAM RD.
SOUTHEND ROAD
A406
HIGHAMS PARK
HIGHAMS PARK & HALE END
Halex Works
Brookfield Orthopc. Hosp.
Hale End
Sky Peals
EPPING FOREST
A104
NEW RD.
Pumping Sta.
Reservoirs
Res
A503
FOREST ROAD
E.17
HIGHAM HILL
Grammar School
Swimming Baths
S.W. Essex Tech. Coll. and Art Sch.
Town Hall
Assembly Hall
Thorpe Coombe Maty. Hosp.
St. Mary's Convent
Y.M.C.A.
Children's Clinic
Health Clinic
Childrens Boating Pool
Lloyd Park
Bus Depot
Mus.
48
Jubilee Retreat
Hawk Wood
CHINGFORD PLAIN
PUBLIC GOLF COURSE
Royal Forest Hotel
Pole Hill
Obelisk (Referring Object Due North From Greenwich)
Convent
CHINGFORD
26
Qn. Eliz. Athletic Grd.
Br. Red Cross Soc.
Four Wents
Open Air Sch.
Pimp Hall
Friday Hill Ho.
27
Football Grd.
40
28
29
HIGHAMS PARK
Boating Lake
Boat Ho.
The Charter Road
Royal Oak
Beech Hall
KINGS HEAD HILL
THE RIDGEWAY
CHINGFORD MOUNT ROAD
OLD CHURCH ROAD
NEW ROAD
HALL LANE
CHINGFORD ROAD
A112
A1009
A1037
B160
Monument
Green Man
Prince Albert
Hall Tavern
War Memorial Rec. Grds.
Drill Hall
Royston Arms
Sports Grd.

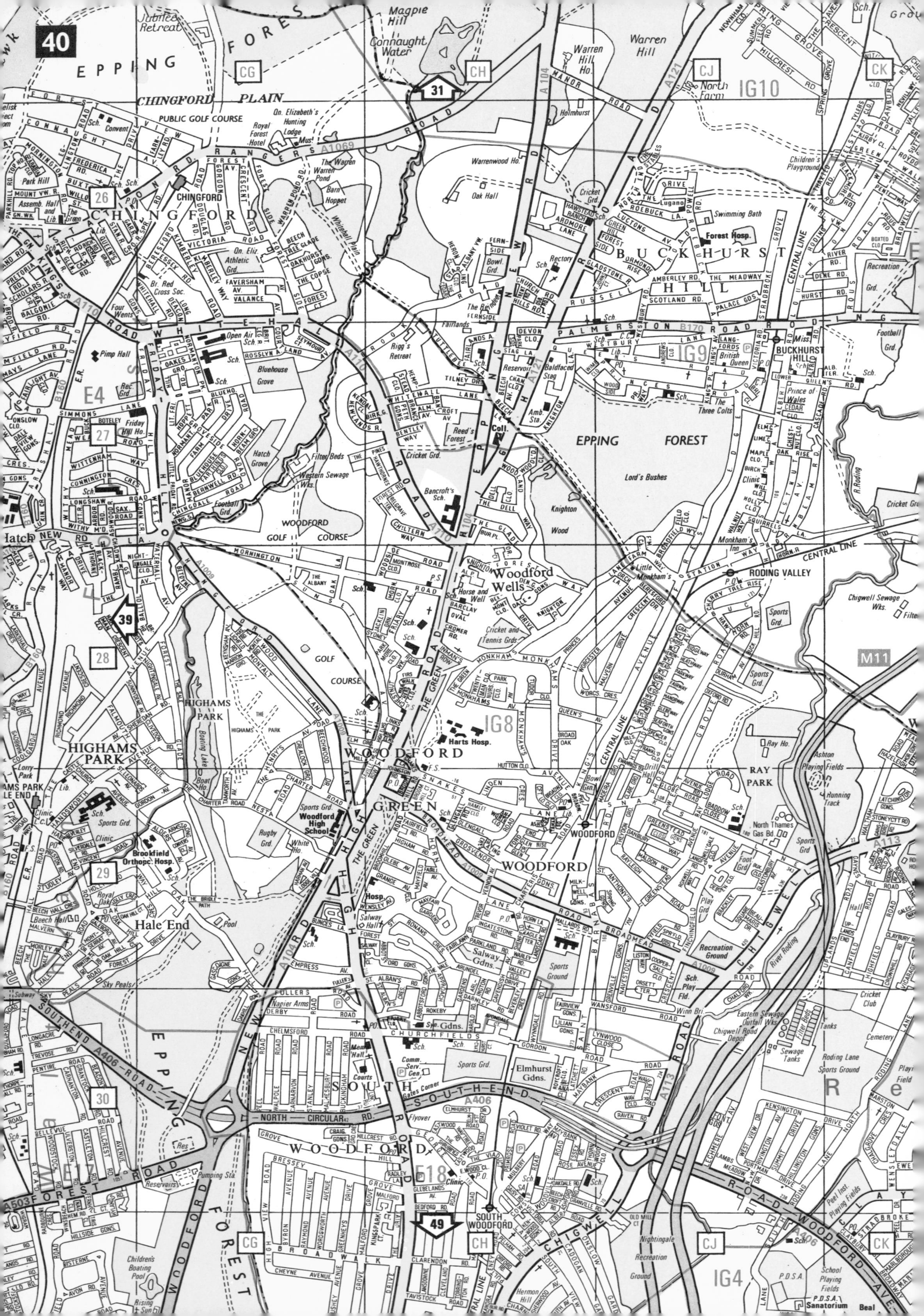
EPPING FOREST
CHINGFORD PLAIN
PUBLIC GOLF COURSE
Connaught Water
Magpie Hill
Warren Hill
IG10
CHINGFORD
BUCKHURST HILL
IG9
EPPING FOREST
Lord's Bushes
Knighton Wood
E4
WOODFORD GOLF COURSE
Woodford Wells
RODING VALLEY
HIGHAMS PARK
WOODFORD
IG8
Harts Hosp.
RAY PARK
WOODFORD GREEN
Woodford High School
Brookfield Orthopc. Hosp.
Hale End
WOODFORD
Salway Gdns.
Elmhurst Gdns.
SOUTH WOODFORD
NORTH CIRCULAR RD.
SOUTHEND ROAD
E17
E18
IG4
WOODFORD NEW ROAD
FOREST ROAD
M11
CENTRAL LINE
A406
A104
A110
A121
A113
A1009
A1069
A503
B170
B160
CG
CH
CJ
CK
31
39
49
26
27
28
29
30

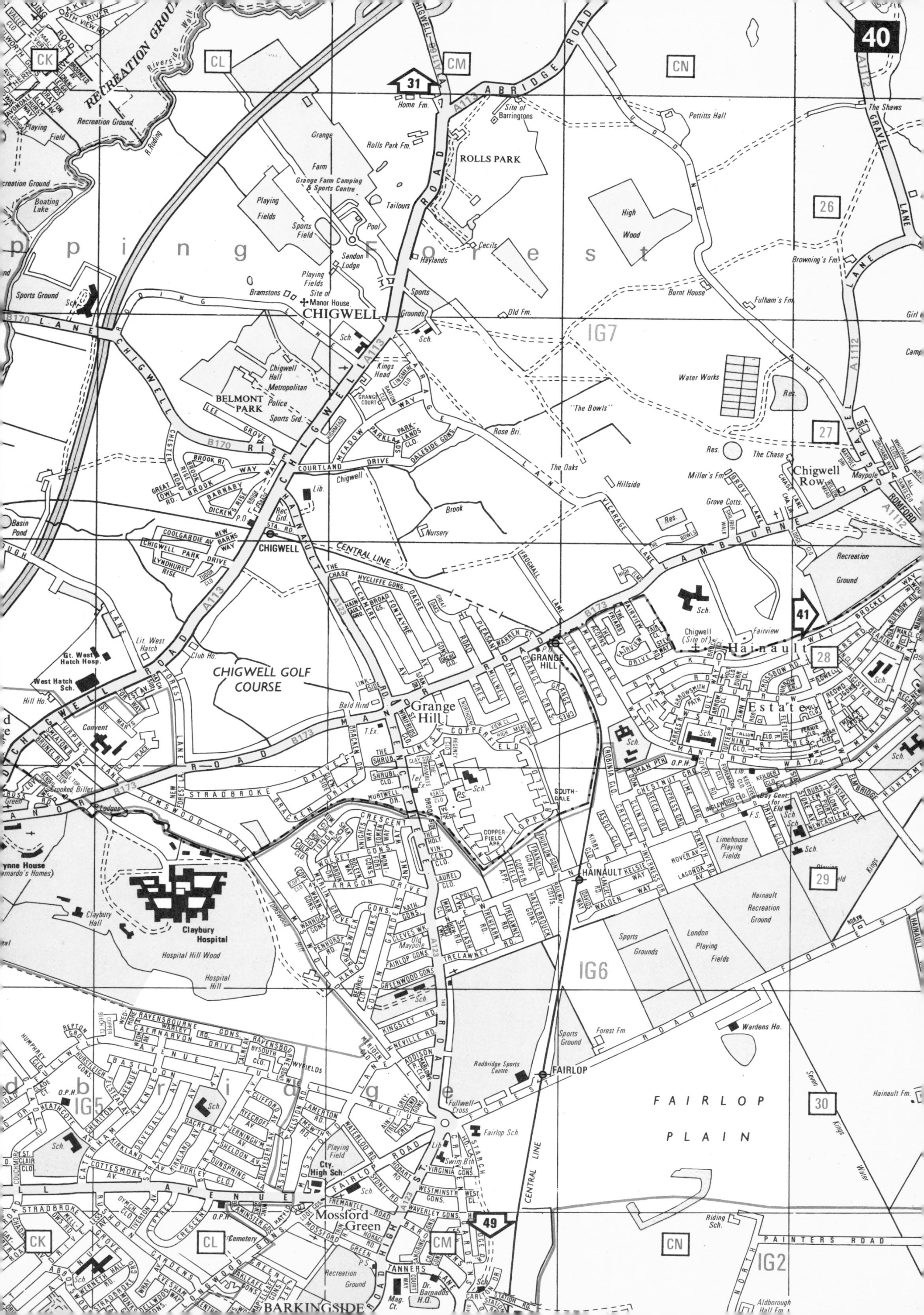
CK
CL
CM
CN
31
41
49
26
27
28
29
30
CHIGWELL
ROLLS PARK
High Wood
Grange Farm Camping & Sports Centre
Playing Fields
Chigwell Hall Metropolitan Police Sports Grd.
BELMONT PARK
Chigwell Row
IG7
IG6
IG5
IG2
CHIGWELL GOLF COURSE
Grange Hill
Hainault Estate
HAINAULT
FAIRLOP
FAIRLOP PLAIN
Claybury Hospital
Hospital Hill Wood
Hainault Recreation Ground
London Playing Fields
Redbridge Sports Centre
Mossford Green
BARKINGSIDE
CENTRAL LINE
Water Works
Recreation Ground
Sports Ground
West Hatch Sch.
Gt. West Hatch Hosp.
Epping Forest
Redbridge

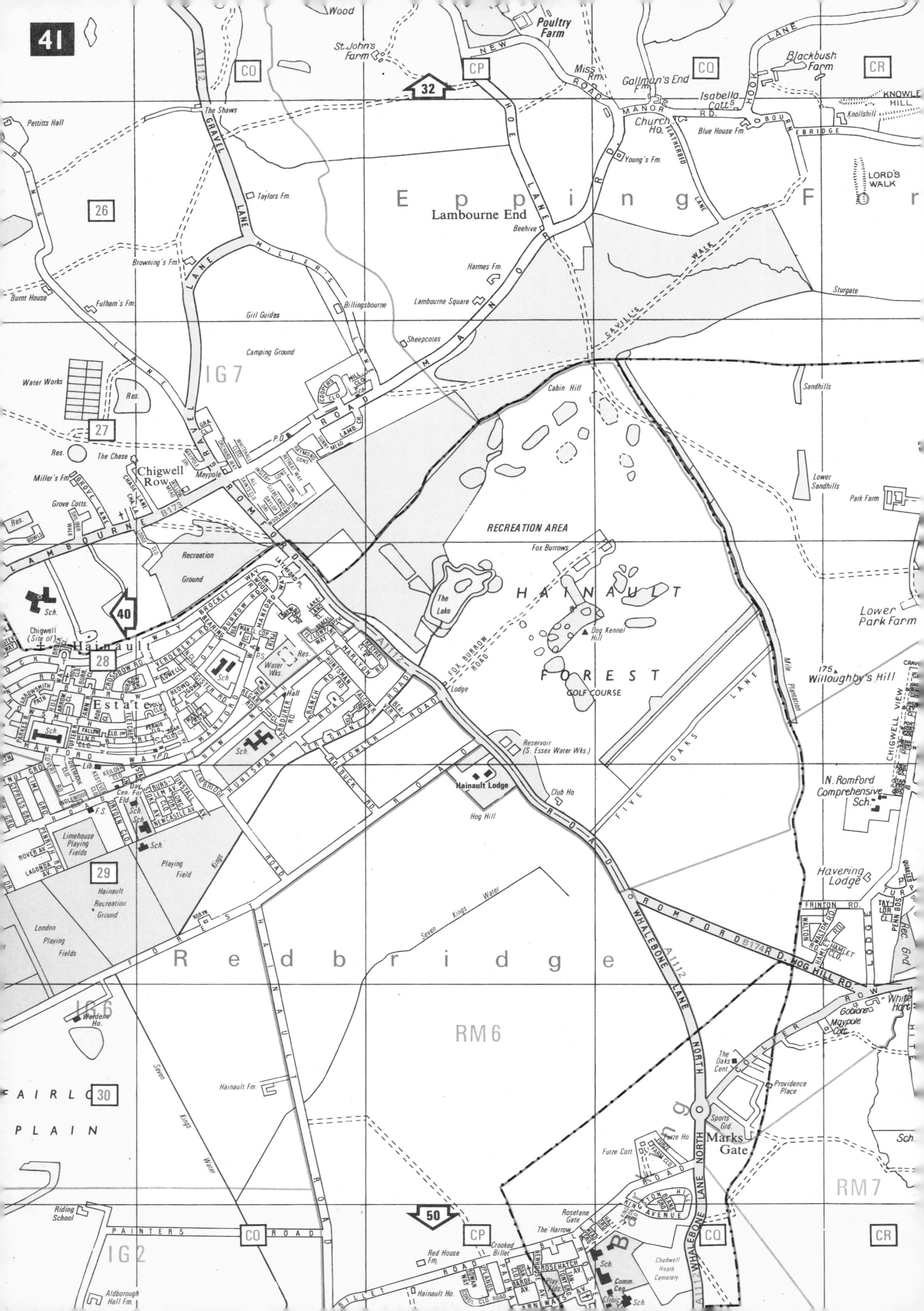

Poultry Farm
St. John's Farm
Blackbush Farm
Gallman's End Fm.
Isabella Cotts.
Church Ho.
Blue House Fm.
Knollshill
Pettitts Hall
The Shaws
Taylors Fm.
Young's Fm.
Epping For
Lambourne End
Beehive
Browning's Fm.
Harmes Fm.
Burnt House
Fulham's Fm.
Billingsbourne
Lambourne Square
Sturgate
Girl Guides
Camping Ground
Sheepcotes
IG7
Water Works
Res.
Cabin Hill
Sandhills
The Chase
Miller's Fm.
Chigwell Row
Maypole
Grove Cotts.
Lower Sandhills
Park Farm
RECREATION AREA
Fox Burrows
Recreation Ground
HAINAULT FOREST
The Lake
Dog Kennel Hill
GOLF COURSE
Lower Park Farm
Chigwell (Site of)
Hainault Estate
Willoughby's Hill
Reservoir (S. Essex Water Wks.)
Hainault Lodge
Club Ho
Hog Hill
N. Romford Comprehensive Sch.
Limehouse Playing Fields
Playing Field
Havering Lodge
Hainault Recreation Ground
London Playing Fields
Seven Kings Water
Redbridge
IG6
Wardens Ho.
RM6
Gobions
Maypole Cott.
White Hart
The Oaks Cent.
Providence Place
Hainault Fm.
FAIRLOP PLAIN
Sports Grd.
Furze Ho.
Marks Gate
Furze Cott.
RM7
Riding School
Roselane Gate
The Harrow
IG2
Red House Fm.
Crooked Billet
Chadwell Heath Cemetery
Hainault Ho.
Aldborough Hall Fm.

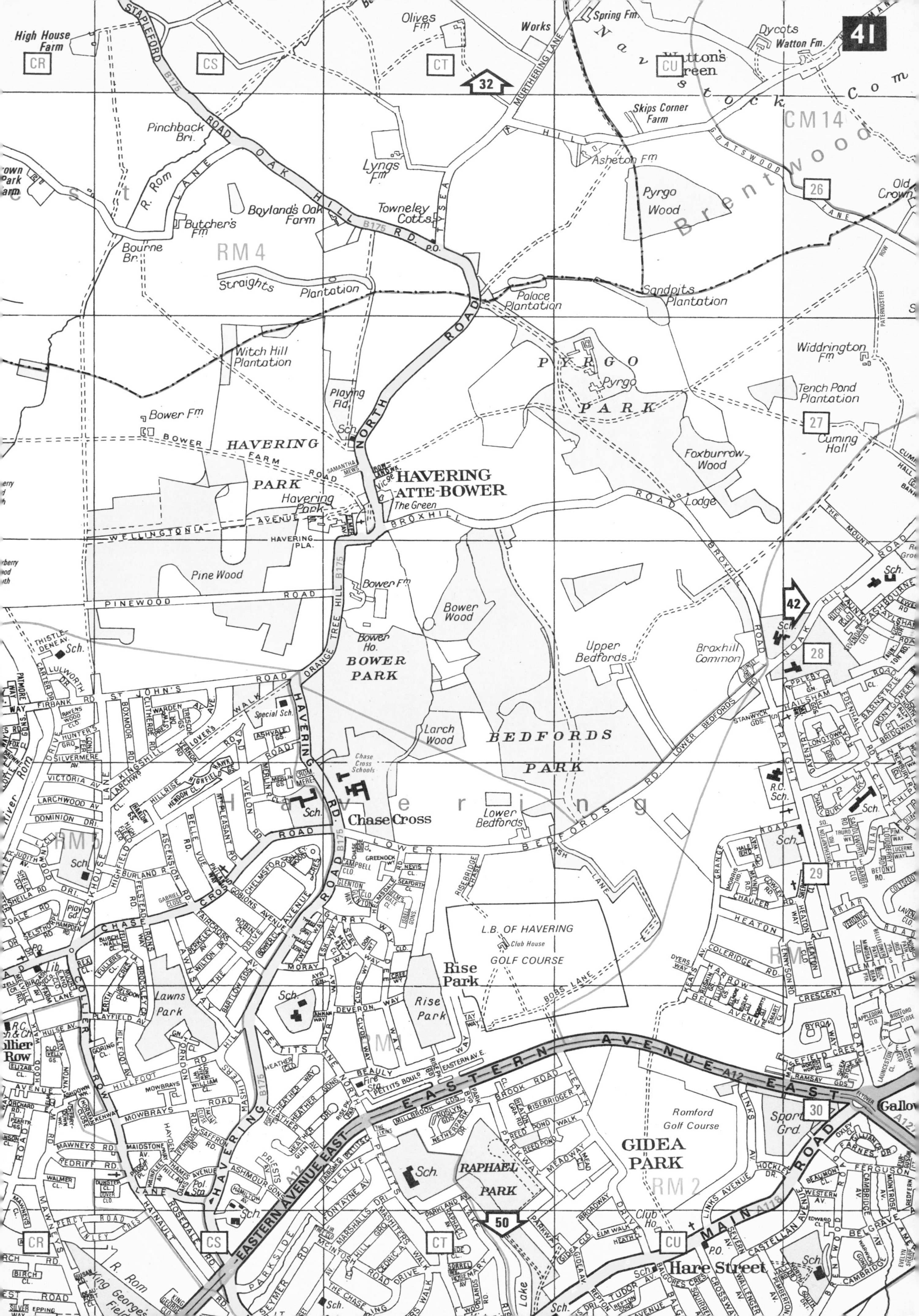

High House Farm
Olives Fm
Works
Spring Fm
Dycots
Watton Fm.
Wattons Green
Skips Corner Farm
Navestock Common
CM14
Brentwood
Pinchback Bri.
Stapleford Road
Oak Hill Rd.
Asheton Fm
Pyrgo Wood
Lyngs Fm
Towneley Cotts
Boyland's Oak Farm
Butcher's Fm
Bourne Br.
RM4
Straights Plantation
Palace Plantation
Sandpits Plantation
Witch Hill Plantation
Pyrgo Park
Widdrington Fm
Tench Pond Plantation
Cuming Hall
Foxburrow Wood
Bower Fm
Havering Park
Havering-atte-Bower
The Green
Broxhill Road
Lodge
North Road
Wellingtonia Avenue
Pine Wood
Pinewood Road
Bower Wood
Bower Ho.
Bower Park
Upper Bedfords
Broxhill Common
Larch Wood
Bedfords Park
Chase Cross
Lower Bedfords
Lower Bedfords Road
Havering
L.B. of Havering Golf Course
Club House
Rise Park
Lawns Park
Collier Row
Eastern Avenue East
Romford Golf Course
Gidea Park
RM2
Raphael Park
Hare Street
Main Road
Sport Grd.
Gallows Corner
King Georges Field
R. Rom
32
26
27
28
29
30
42
50
CR
CS
CT
CU

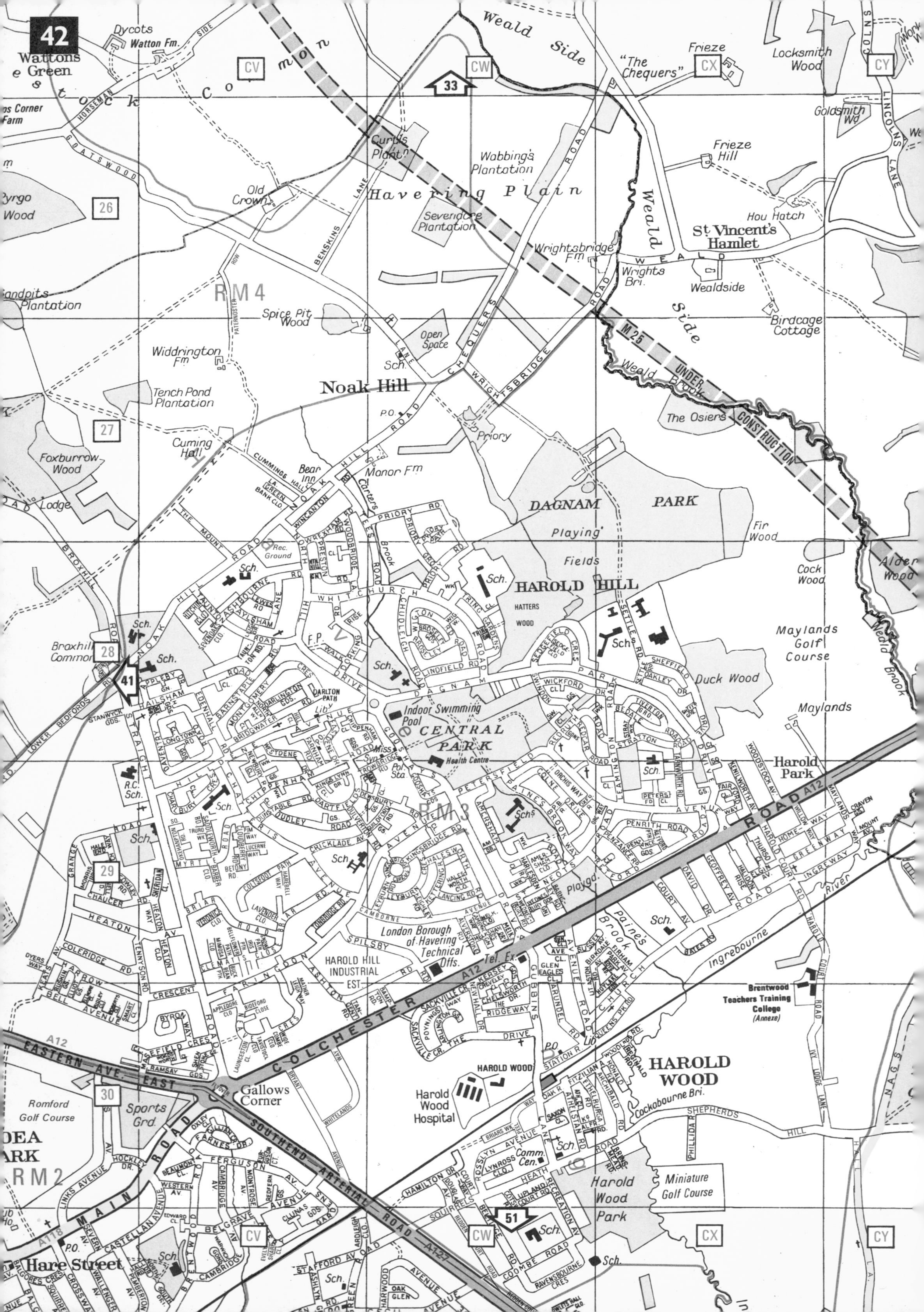

Havering Plain
Noak Hill
HAROLD HILL
DAGNAM PARK
CENTRAL PARK
HAROLD WOOD
Harold Park
St Vincent's Hamlet
Gallows Corner
Harold Wood Hospital
Harold Wood Park
Hare Street
Romford Golf Course
Maylands Golf Course
Brentwood Teachers Training College (Annexe)
London Borough of Havering Technical Offs.
HAROLD HILL INDUSTRIAL EST
Indoor Swimming Pool
Health Centre
Duck Wood
Cock Wood
Fir Wood
Alder Wood
The Osiers
Priory
Manor Fm
Wrightsbridge Fm
Wealdside
Birdcage Cottage
Frieze Hill
Frieze
Locksmith Wood
Goldsmith Wd
"The Chequers"
Weald Side
Weald Brook
M25 UNDER CONSTRUCTION
Severidore Plantation
Wobbing's Plantation
Curtis's Plantn
Old Crown
Spice Pit Wood
Widdrington Fm
Tench Pond Plantation
Cuming Hall
Foxburrow Wood
Broxhill Common
Sandpits Plantation
Pyrgo Wood
Dycots
Watton Fm.
Open Space
Miniature Golf Course
Sports Grd.
COLCHESTER ROAD A12
EASTERN AVE. EAST
SOUTHEND ARTERIAL ROAD A127
MAIN ROAD A118
RM4
RM3
RM2
CV
CW
CX
CY
26
27
28
29
30
33
41
51

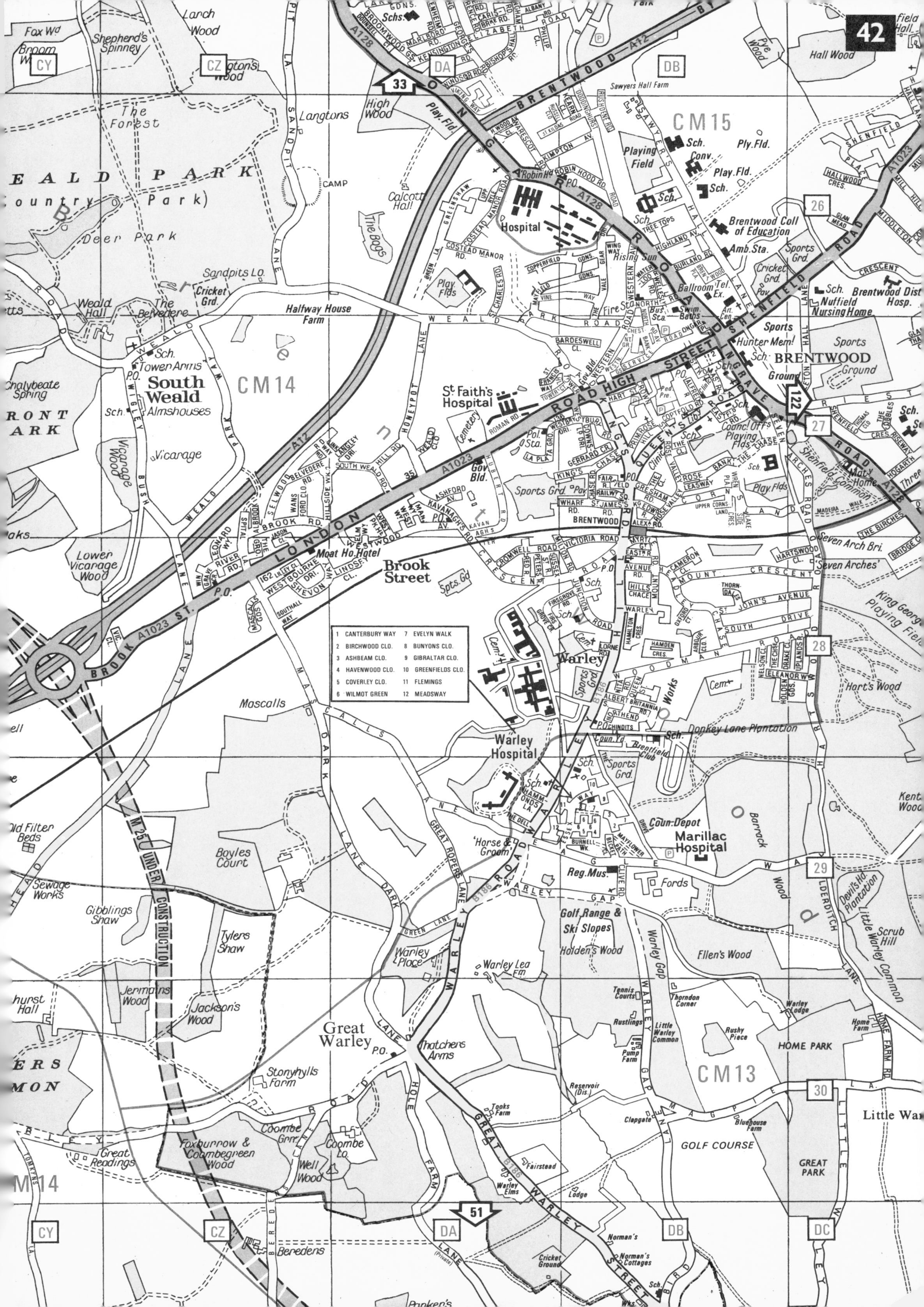

1 CANTERBURY WAY
2 BIRCHWOOD CLO.
3 ASHBEAM CLO.
4 HAVENWOOD CLO.
5 COVERLEY CLO.
6 WILMOT GREEN
7 EVELYN WALK
8 BUNYONS CLO.
9 GIBRALTAR CLO.
10 GREENFIELDS CLO.
11 FLEMINGS
12 MEADSWAY
CY
CZ
DA
DB
DC
33
51
26
27
28
29
30
122
CM15
CM14
CM13
BRENTWOOD
South Weald
Brook Street
Warley
Great Warley
Little Warley
WEALD PARK
(Country Park)
Deer Park
Fox Wd
Larch Wood
Shepherd's Spinney
Langtons Wood
The Forest
Langtons
High Wood
CAMP
Calcott Hall
The Bogs
Sandpits Lo.
Cricket Grd.
Weald Hall
The Belvedere
Halfway House Farm
Towen Arms
Chalybeate Spring
Almshouses
Vicarage
Vicarage Wood
Lower Vicarage Wood
Moat Ho. Hotel
Hospital
St. Faith's Hospital
Warley Hospital
Marillac Hospital
Brentwood Coll of Education
Sawyers Hall Farm
Pre Wood
Hall Wood
Nuffield Nursing Home
Brentwood Dist Hosp.
Hunter Mem!
Seven Arch Bri.
'Seven Arches'
King George's Playing Fields
Hart's Wood
Donkey Lane Plantation
Mascalls
Boyles Court
Old Filter Beds
Sewage Works
Gibblings Shaw
Tylers Shaw
Jermains Wood
Jackson's Wood
'Horse & Groom'
Reg.Mus.
Fords
Golf Range & Ski Slopes
Holden's Wood
Warley Gap
Fllen's Wood
Barrack Wood
Devil's Hd. Plantation
Little Warley Common
Scrub Hill
Warley Place
Warley Lea Fm
Tennis Courts
Thorndon Corner
Rustlings
Little Warley Common
Rushy Piece
Pump Farm
Warley Lodge
Home Farm
HOME PARK
Thatchens Arms
Stonyhylls Farm
Reservoir (Dis.)
Tooks Farm
Clapgate
Bluehouse Farm
GOLF COURSE
GREAT PARK
Coombe Grn.
Coombe Lo.
Foxburrow & Coombegreen Wood
Great Readings
Well Wood
Fairstead
Warley Elms
Lodge
Norman's
Norman's Cottages
Cricket Ground
Beredens
M25 UNDER CONSTRUCTION
A12
A128
A1023
B186
BRENTWOOD
LONDON ROAD
BROOK ST.
HIGH STREET
SHENFIELD ROAD
INGRAVE ROAD
KINGS ROAD
WEALD ROAD
WARLEY HILL
GREAT WARLEY STREET
MAGPIE LANE
CM14

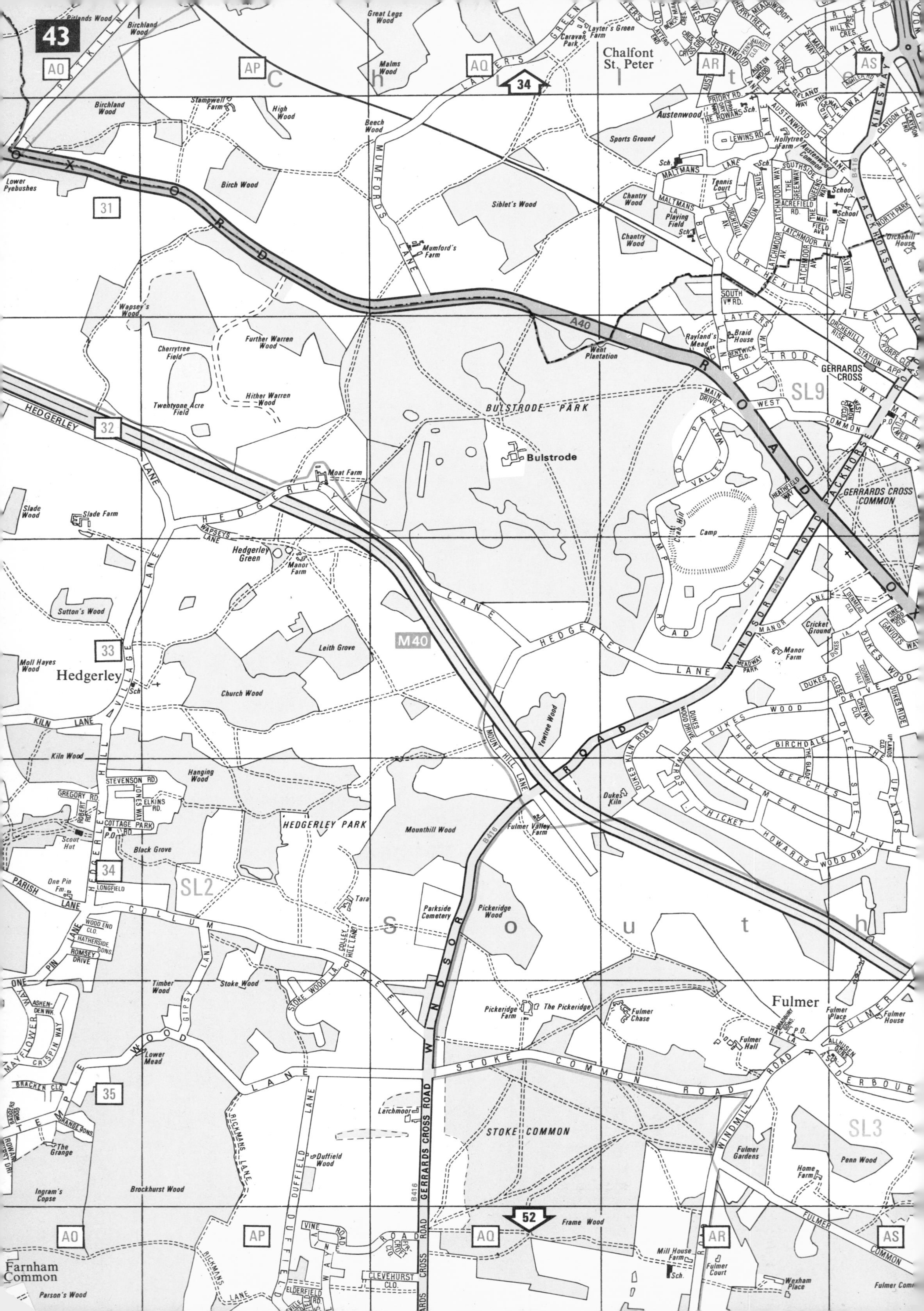

Chalfont St. Peter
Austenwood
Gerrards Cross
Bulstrode Park
Bulstrode
Gerrards Cross Common
Hedgerley
Hedgerley Green
Hedgerley Park
Fulmer
Stoke Common
Farnham Common
Oxford Road
A40
M40
Windsor Road
Gerrards Cross Road
Hedgerley Lane
Collum Lane
Stoke Common Road
Windmill Road
Fulmer Road
Mumfords Lane
Packhorse Road
Camp Road
Wood Lane
Kiln Lane
Parish Lane
Church Wood
Mounthill Wood
Pickeridge Wood
Stoke Wood
Brockhurst Wood
Siblet's Wood
Birch Wood
Leith Grove
Black Grove
Hanging Wood
Sutton's Wood
Slade Farm
Moat Farm
Fulmer Valley Farm
Manor Farm
Mumford's Farm
Stampwell Farm
Fulmer Chase
The Pickeridge
Pickeridge Farm
Fulmer Hall
Fulmer Gardens
Penn Wood
Home Farm
Duffield Wood
Lerchmoor
Parkside Cemetery
Sports Ground
SL2
SL3
SL9

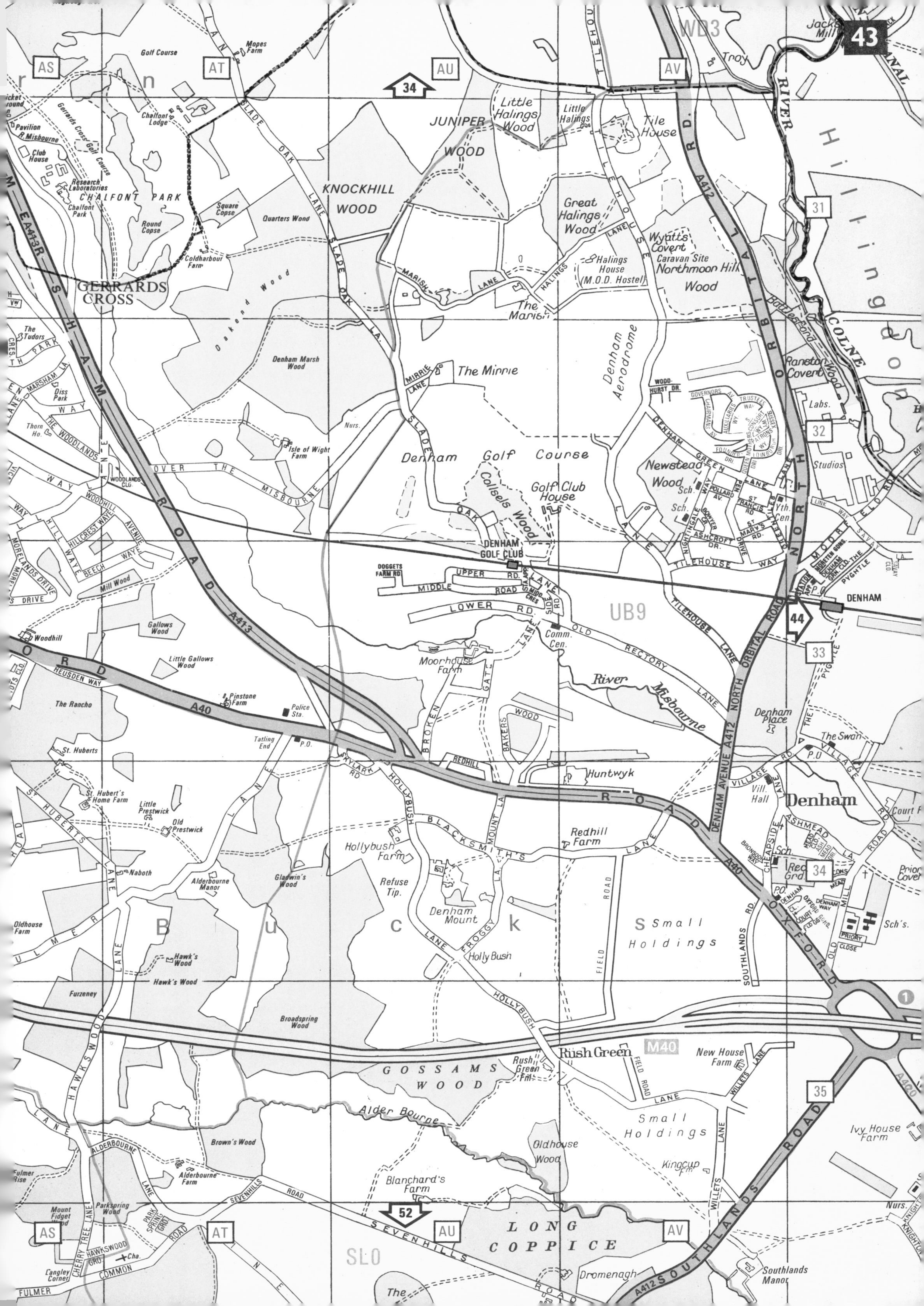
AS
AT
AU
AV
34
52
44
31
32
33
34
35
WD3
UB9
SL0
Golf Course
Mopes Farm
Chalfont Lodge
Gerrards Cross Golf Course
Pavilion
R. Misbourne
Club House
Research Laboratories
CHALFONT PARK
Chalfont Park
Square Copse
Round Copse
Quarters Wood
Coldharbour Farm
GERRARDS CROSS
Oakend Wood
Denham Marsh Wood
JUNIPER WOOD
KNOCKHILL WOOD
Little Halings Wood
Little Halings
Tile House
Great Halings Wood
Wyatt's Covert
Caravan Site
Halings House (M.O.D. Hostel)
Northmoon Hill Wood
The Marish
MARISH LANE
HALINGS LANE
SLADE OAK LANE
TILEHOUSE LANE
The Tudors
Diss Park
MARSHAM LA.
THE WOODLANDS
Thorn Ho.
The Mirrie
MIRRIE LANE
Denham Aerodrome
WOODHURST DR.
Isle of Wight Farm
OVER THE MISBOURNE
Nurs.
Denham Golf Course
Collsels Wood
Golf Club House
DENHAM GOLF CLUB
DOGGETS FARM RD
UPPER RD.
MIDDLE ROAD
LOWER RD.
Newstead Wood
Sch.
Yth. Cen.
POLLARD AV.
ST FRANCIS RD.
ST MARY'S RD.
ASHCROFT DR.
NIGHTINGALE WAY
TILEHOUSE WAY
DENHAM GREEN LANE
Labs.
Studios
Ranston Covert
Bottleford Wood
RIVER COLNE
Hillingdon
NORTH ORBITAL RD.
A412
DENHAM
STATION APP.
PYGHTLE
MOORFIELD RD
SAVAY LA.
WOODLANDS CL.
HILLCREST WAYE
BEECH WAYE
MORELANDS DRIVE
Mill Wood
Woodhill
Gallows Wood
Little Gallows Wood
A413
AMERSHAM ROAD
OXFORD ROAD
A40
HEUSDEN WAY
The Rancho
Pinstone Farm
Police Sta.
Tatling End
P.O.
St. Huberts
St. Hubert's Home Farm
Little Prestwick
Old Prestwick
ST HUBERTS LANE
Naboth
Alderbourne Manor
Gladwin's Wood
Oldhouse Farm
FULMER LANE
Hawk's Wood
Furzeney
Broadspring Wood
HAWKSWOOD LANE
Moorhouse Farm
Comm. Cen.
OLD RECTORY LANE
River Misbourne
BROKEN GATE
BAKERS WOOD
REDHILL
Huntwyk
SKYLARK RD
HOLLYBUSH
BLACKSMITH'S LANE
MOUNT LA.
Hollybush Farm
Refuse Tip.
Redhill Farm
Denham Mount
FROGGY LANE
Holly Bush
FIELD ROAD
Small Holdings
Bucks
SOUTHLANDS RD.
Denham Place
The Swan
VILLAGE RD.
Vill. Hall
Denham
Court Fm.
ASHMEAD
CHEAPSIDE
Rec. Grd.
Sch's.
PRIORY CLOSE
OLD MILL RD.
Prior Covert
M40
Rush Green
Rush Green Fm.
GOSSAMS WOOD
New House Farm
WILLETS LANE
Alder Bourne
Brown's Wood
Oldhouse Wood
Kingcup Fm.
Ivy House Farm
A4007
Alderbourne Farm
ALDERBOURNE LANE
Fulmer Rise
Mount Fidget Wood
Parkspring Wood
PARK SPRING GRO.
SEVENHILLS ROAD
Blanchard's Farm
LONG COPPICE
SOUTHLANDS ROAD
Nurs.
Southlands Manor
Dromenagh
The
CHERRY TREE LANE
HAWKSWOOD GRO.
Cha.
Cangley Corner
COMMON ROAD
FULMER

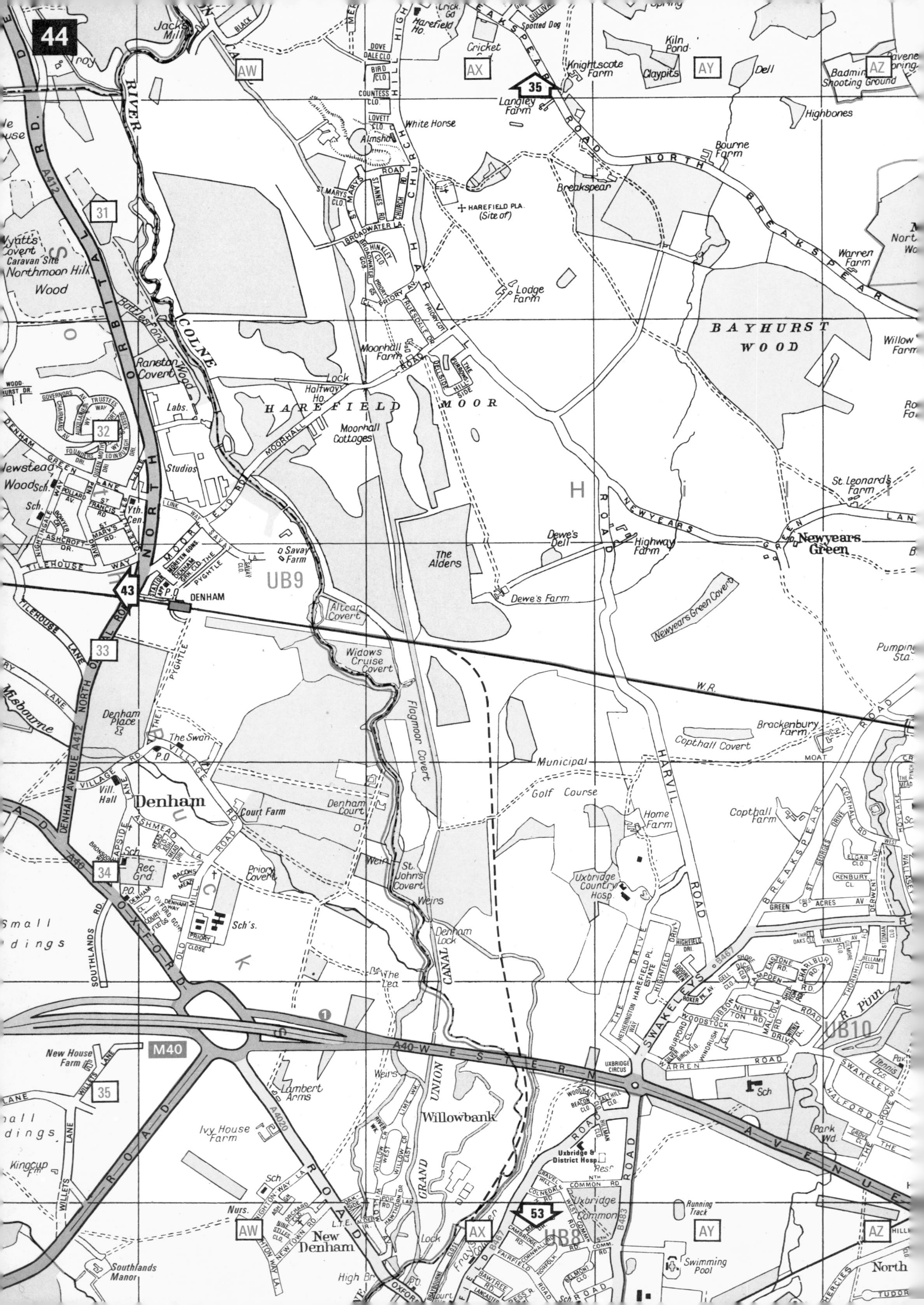
AW
AX
AY
AZ
35
31
32
33
34
43
53
UB9
UB10
UB8
M40
A40 WESTERN AVENUE
NORTH ORBITAL RD.
A412
DENHAM AVENUE A412
RIVER COLNE
HAREFIELD MOOR
BAYHURST WOOD
Knightscote Farm
Claypits
Kiln Pond
Dell
Badminton Shooting Ground
Highbones
Langley Farm
Bourne Farm
Breakspear
NORTH BREAKSPEAR ROAD
BREAKSPEAR ROAD
Warren Farm
Spotted Dog
Cricket Gd
Harefield Ho.
White Horse
Almshouses
HAREFIELD PLA. (Site of)
Lodge Farm
HARVIL ROAD
CHURCH HILL
BROADWATER LA.
Moorhall Farm
MOORHALL ROAD
Halfway Ho.
Lock
Moorhall Cottages
Ranston Covert
Battlesford Wood
Labs.
Studios
Northmoon Hill Wood
Wyatts Covert
Caravan Site
Newstead Wood
Sch.
Yth. Cen.
TILEHOUSE WAY
TILEHOUSE LANE
Savay Farm
DENHAM
P.O.
Altcar Covert
Widows Cruise Covert
Flagmoor Covert
The Alders
Dewe's Dell
Dewe's Farm
Highway Farm
NEWYEARS GREEN LANE
Newyears Green
Newyears Green Covert
St. Leonard's Farm
Pumping Sta.
W.R.
Brackenbury Farm
Copthall Covert
MOAT
Copthall Farm
Municipal Golf Course
Home Farm
Uxbridge Country Hosp.
Misbourne
Denham Place
The Swan
VILLAGE RD
Vill. Hall
Denham
Court Farm
Denham Court
Rec. Grd.
Priory Covert
Sch's.
Weir
Weirs
St. John's Covert
Denham Lock
The Lea
Small Holdings
SOUTHLANDS RD.
OXFORD ROAD
New House Farm
WILLETS LANE
Kingcup Fm
Ivy House Farm
Lambert Arms
A4020
Willowbank
GRAND UNION CANAL
UXBRIDGE CIRCUS
SWAKELEYS ROAD
B467
HAREFIELD PL. ESTATE
WARREN ROAD
R. Pinn
Sch
Park Wd.
Uxbridge & District Hosp.
Uxbridge Common
COMMON RD
B483
Running Track
Swimming Pool
Nurs.
New Denham
L.T.E.
Southlands Manor
High Br.
North

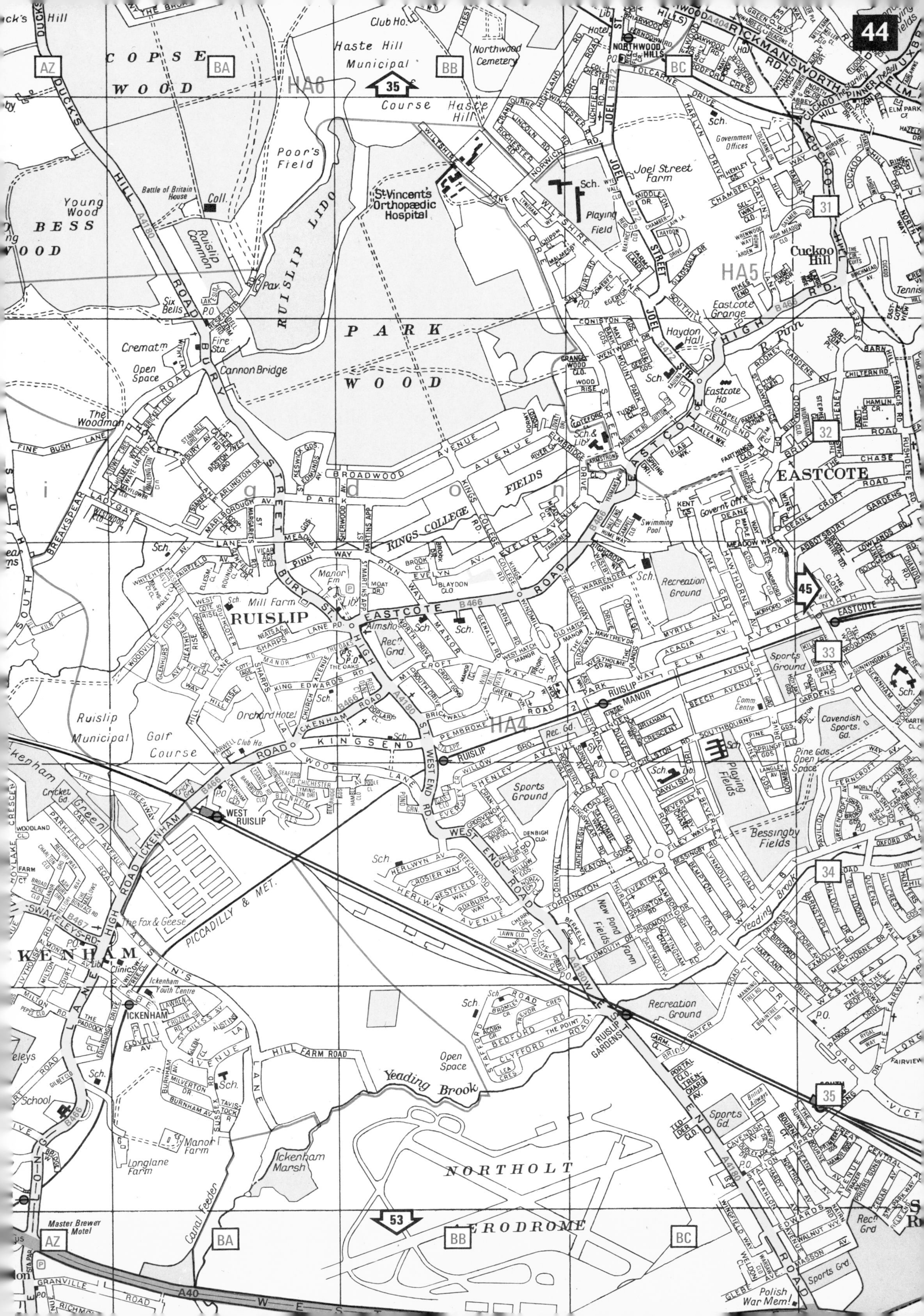
AZ
BA
BB
BC
35
53
45
31
32
33
34
35
HA6
HA5
HA4
COPSE WOOD
BESS WOOD
Young Wood
Battle of Britain House
Coll.
Ruislip Common
DUCK'S HILL
HILL ROAD
BURY ROAD
Haste Hill Municipal Course
Haste Hill
Club Ho.
Northwood Cemetery
NORTHWOOD HILLS
Poor's Field
RUISLIP LIDO
St. Vincent's Orthopaedic Hospital
PARK WOOD
Six Bells
Pav.
Cremat'm
Fire Sta.
Open Space
Cannon Bridge
The Woodman
FINE BUSH LANE
BREAKSPEAR
BROADWOOD AV.
PARK AVENUE
KINGS COLLEGE FIELDS
Joel Street Farm
JOEL STREET
Playing Field
Sch.
Eastcote Grange
Haydon Hall
Cuckoo Hill
RICKMANSWORTH RD.
Government Offices
Eastcote Ho
EASTCOTE
HIGH RD.
R. Pinn
Swimming Pool
Recreation Ground
Govern't Off's
RUISLIP
Mill Farm
Manor Fm
Lib.
Almshouses
Rec. Grd.
EASTCOTE ROAD
HIGH ST.
BURY ST.
MANOR
PARK WAY
ELM AVENUE
Ruislip Municipal Golf Course
Orchard Hotel
Club Ho.
KINGSEND
ICKENHAM ROAD
WEST END RD.
RUISLIP
Rec. Gd.
Comm. Centre
Sports Ground
Cavendish Sports Gd.
Playing Fields
Pine Gds. Open Space
Bessingby Fields
Cricket Gd.
WEST RUISLIP
PICCADILLY & MET.
The Fox & Geese
SWAKELEYS RD.
ICKENHAM
Clinic
Ickenham Youth Centre
Herlwyn Av.
New Pond Fields Farm
Recreation Ground
RUISLIP GARDENS
Open Space
Yeading Brook
HILL FARM ROAD
Manor Farm
Longlane Farm
Ickenham Marsh
Canal Feeder
NORTHOLT AERODROME
Sports Gd.
British Airways
Master Brewer Motel
Polish War Mem!
Sports Grd
Rec'n Grd
A40
A4180
B466
B467
B472
A404

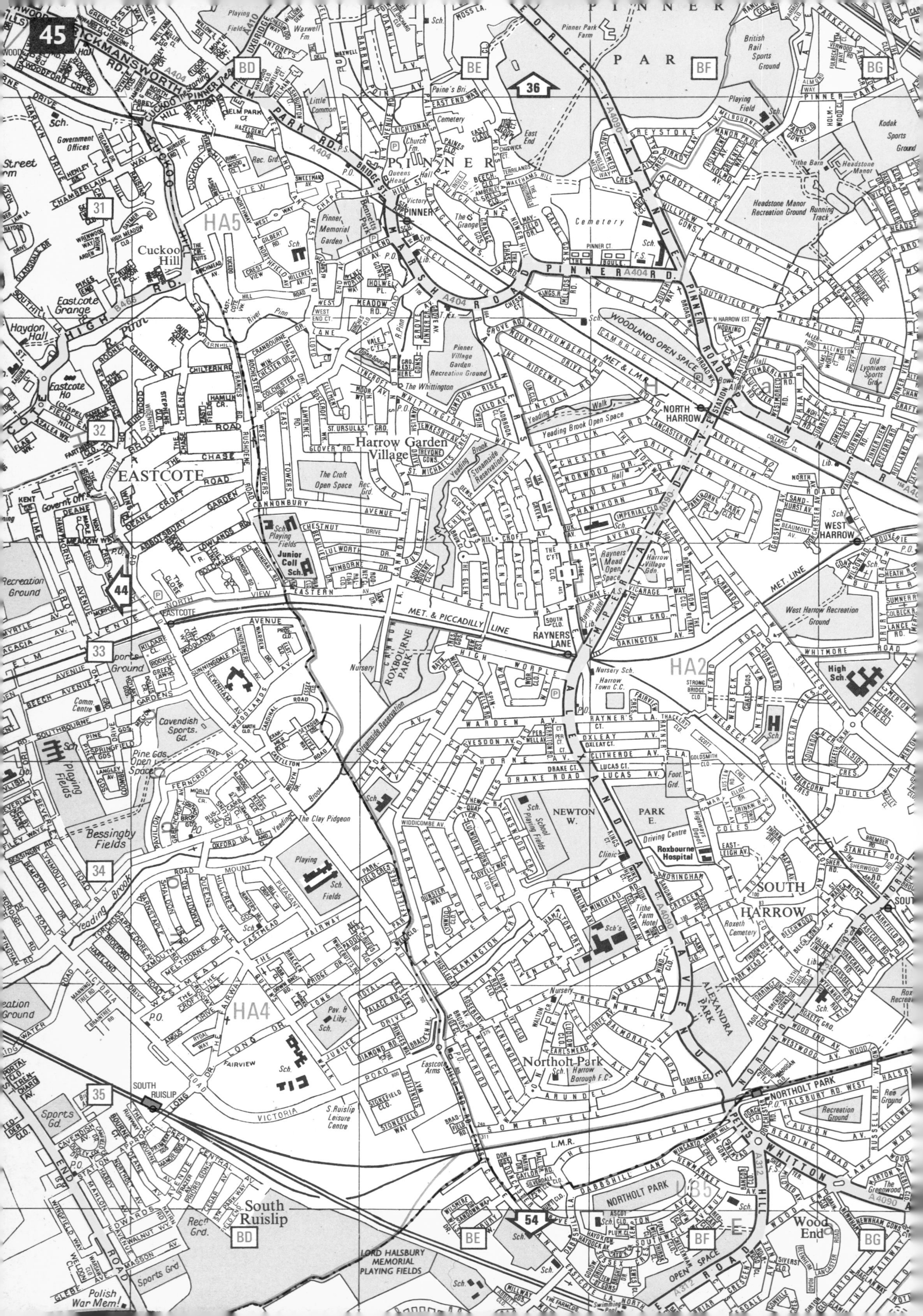

45
PINNER PARK
Pinner Park Farm
36
BD
BE
BF
BG
British Rail Sports Ground
Playing Field
Kodak Sports Ground
Headstone Manor
Headstone Manor Recreation Ground
Running Track
PINNER
Little Common
Cemetery
Church Fm.
Queens Head
Pinner Memorial Garden
East End
The Grange
Cemetery
HA5
Cuckoo Hill
Government Offices
Eastcote Grange
Haydon Hall
Eastcote Ho
31
32
33
34
35
44
54
Pinner Village Garden Recreation Ground
The Whittington
Harrow Garden Village
The Croft Open Space
Woodlands Open Space
Yeading Brook Open Space
NORTH HARROW
Old Lyonians Sports Grd.
WEST HARROW
West Harrow Recreation Ground
EASTCOTE
Junior Coll Sch.
Recreation Ground
Sports Ground
MET. & PICCADILLY LINE
RAYNERS LANE
ROXBOURNE PARK
Streamside Reservation
HA2
High Sch.
Harrow Town C.C.
Rayners Mead Open Space
Cavendish Sports Gd.
Pine Gds. Open Space
Playing Fields
Bessingby Fields
The Clay Pidgeon
Playing Sch. Fields
NEWTON W.
PARK E.
Roxbourne Hospital
Driving Centre
SOUTH HARROW
Roxeth Cemetery
Tithe Farm Hotel
ALEXANDRA PARK
HA4
Pav. & Liby. Sch.
Eastcote Arms
Northolt Park
Harrow Borough F.C.
SOUTH RUISLIP
S. Ruislip Leisure Centre
Sports Gd.
South Ruislip
Recn Grd.
L.M.R.
NORTHOLT PARK
UB5
Recreation Ground
Rec Ground
Wood End
LORD HALSBURY MEMORIAL PLAYING FIELDS
Polish War Mem.
Sports Grd

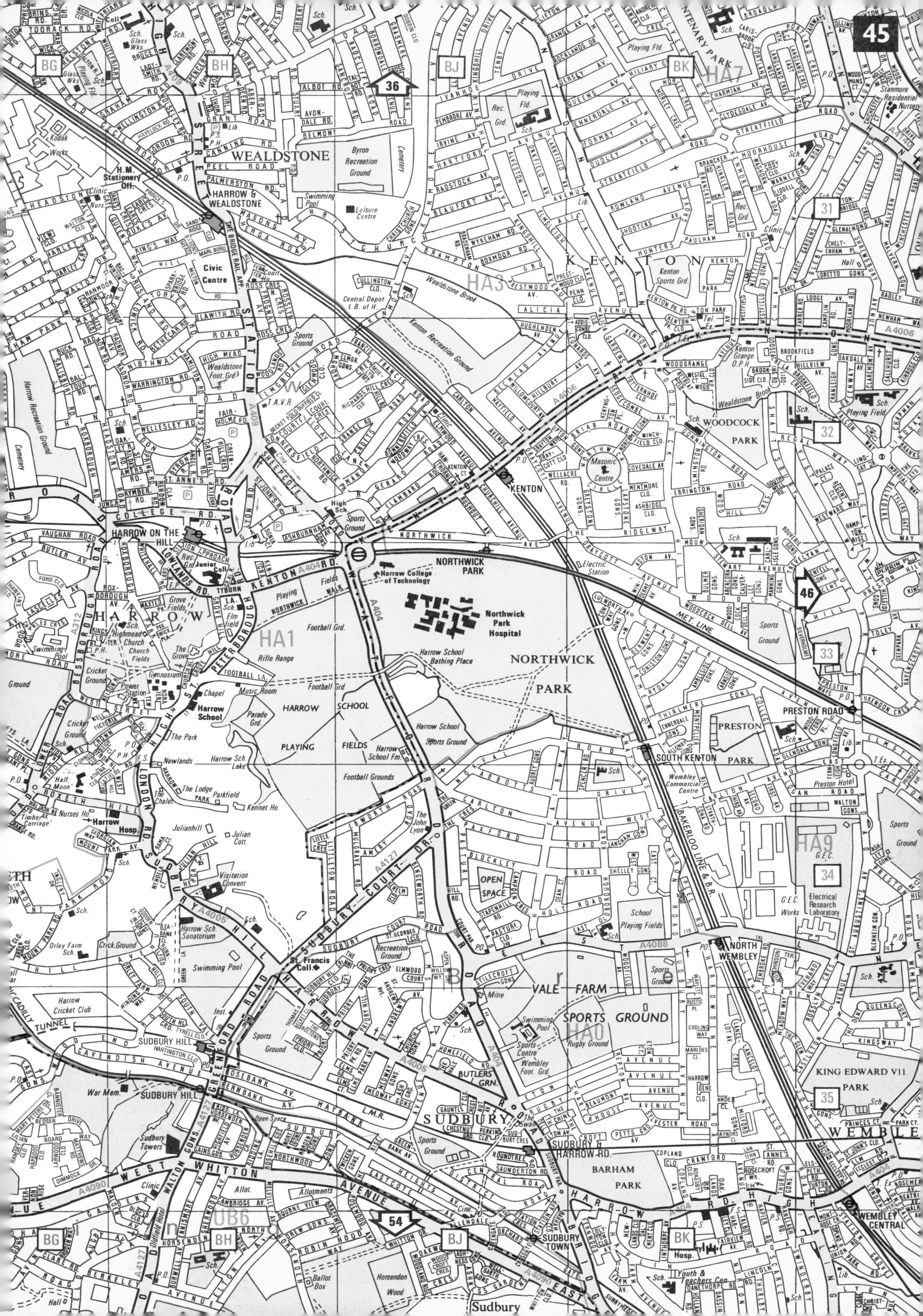

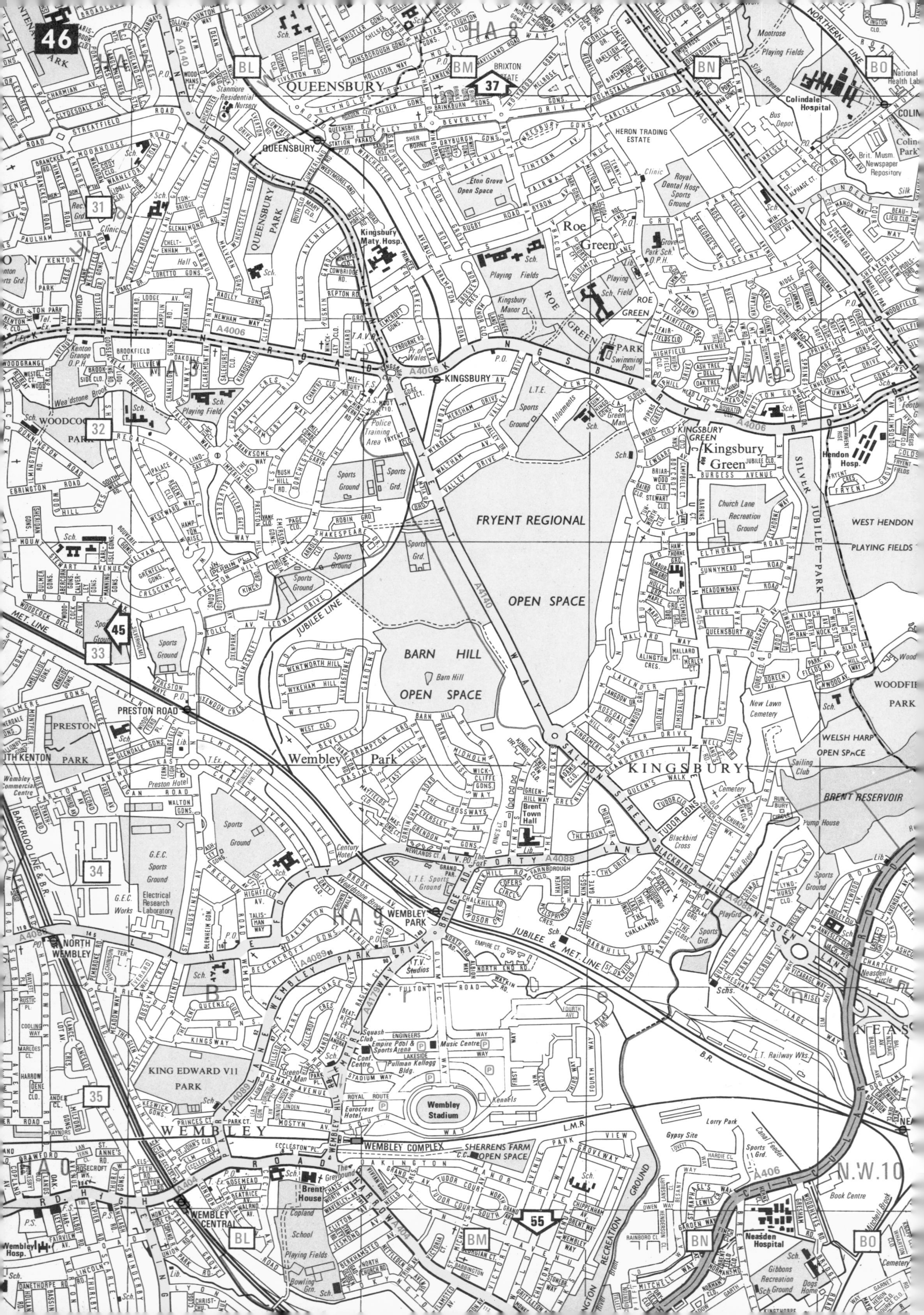

46
HA 8
BL
BM
BN
BO
37
QUEENSBURY
Stanmore Residential Nursery
Montrose Playing Fields
National Health Lab
Colindale Hospital
Bus Depot
HERON TRADING ESTATE
Brit. Musm. Newspaper Repository
Royal Dental Hosp Sports Ground
Eton Grove Open Space
Roe Green
Kingsbury Maty. Hosp.
QUEENSBURY PARK
Playing Fields
Kingsbury Manor
ROE GREEN PARK
Swimming Pool
KENTON ROAD
A4006
KINGSBURY ROAD
KINGSBURY
Kenton Grange O.P.H.
Pr. of Wales
T.A.V.R.
L.T.E. Sports Ground
Allotments
NW9
Kingsbury Green
Hendon Hosp.
WOODCOCK PARK
Playing Field
Police Training Area
Sports Ground
FRYENT REGIONAL
OPEN SPACE
FRYENT WAY
A4140
Church Lane Recreation Ground
WEST HENDON
PLAYING FIELDS
SILVER JUBILEE PARK
JUBILEE LINE
MET. LINE
45
33
31
32
BARN HILL
Barn Hill
OPEN SPACE
PRESTON ROAD
PRESTON PARK
SOUTH KENTON
Preston Hotel
Wembley Commercial Centre
Wembley Park
KINGSBURY
New Lawn Cemetery
WOODFIELD PARK
WELSH HARP OPEN SPACE
Sailing Club
BRENT RESERVOIR
Pump House
Brent Town Hall
Blackbird Cross
Cemetery
34
G.E.C. Sports Ground
G.E.C. Works
Electrical Research Laboratory
Century Hotel
FORTY AVENUE
A4088
FORTY LANE
BLACKBIRD HILL
L.T.E. Sports Ground
WEMBLEY PARK
HA 9
NORTH WEMBLEY
JUBILEE & MET. LINE
T.V. Studios
OLYMPIC WAY
Neasden Circle
NEASDEN
Sports Grd.
PlayGrd.
KING EDWARD VII PARK
35
Squash Club
Empire Pool & Sports Arena
Music Centre
Conf. Centre
Pullman Kellogg Bldg.
Wembley Stadium
Kennels
Eurocrest Hotel
L.T. Railway Wks.
B.R.
L.M.R.
Lorry Park
Gypsy Site
Canal Feeder
WEMBLEY
WEMBLEY COMPLEX
SHERRENS FARM OPEN SPACE
A406
N.W.10
HA 0
HIGH ROAD
WEMBLEY CENTRAL
Brent House
Copland School Playing Fields
Bowling Grn.
Wembley Hosp.
55
RECREATION GROUND
Neasden Hospital
Book Centre
Gibbons Recreation Ground
Dogs Home
Cemetery

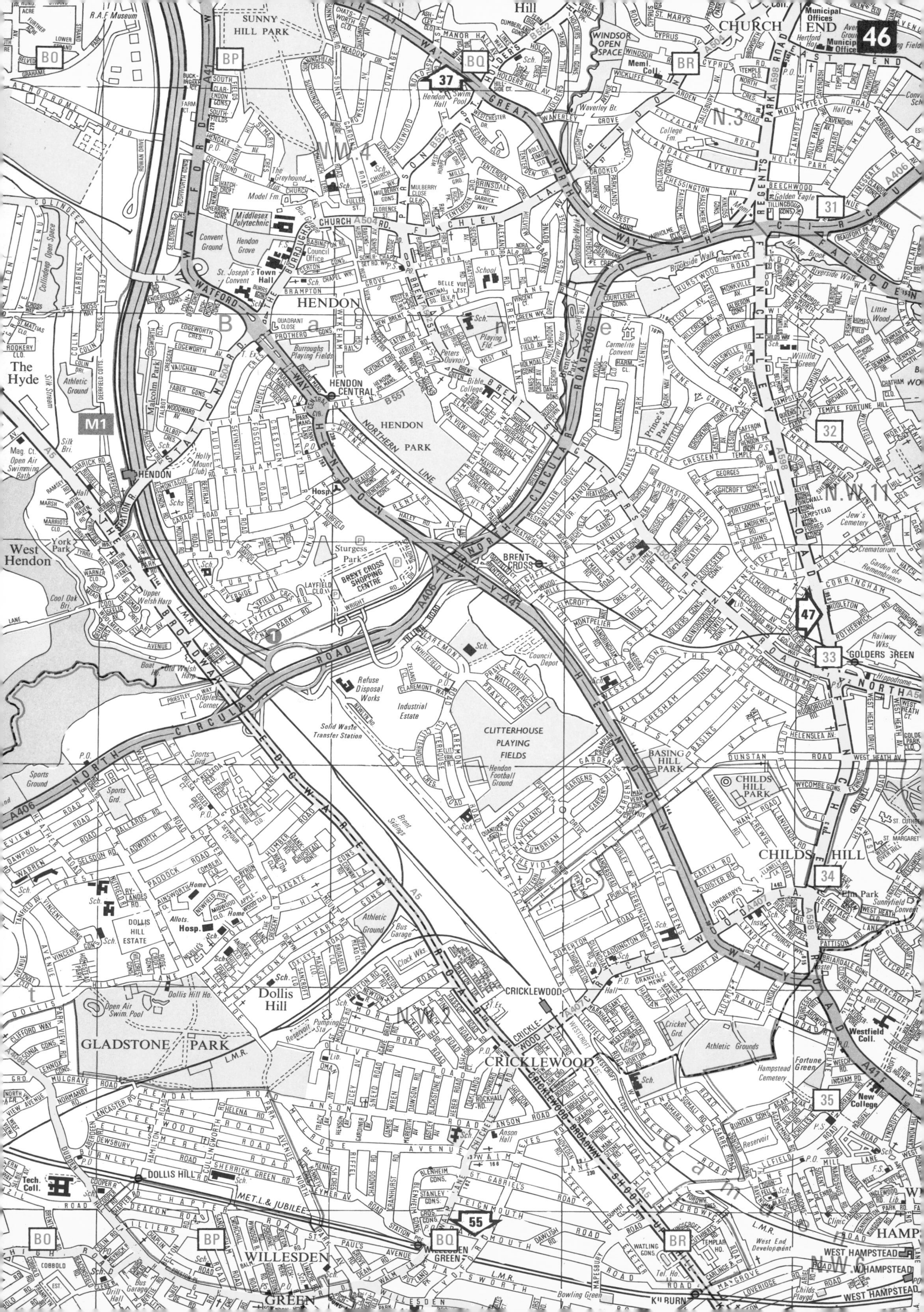

R.A.F. Museum
SUNNY HILL PARK
Hill
WINDSOR OPEN SPACE
CHURCH END
Municipal Offices
37
BO
BP
BQ
BR
N.3
N.W.4
The Greyhound
Model Fm.
Middlesex Polytechnic
Hendon Grove
Convent Ground
St. Joseph's Convent
Town Hall
HENDON
Burroughs Playing Fields
HENDON CENTRAL
HENDON NORTHERN PARK
The Hyde
Colindeep Open Space
Athletic Ground
Malcolm Park
M1
Holly Mount (Club)
HENDON
West Hendon
York Park
Upper Welsh Harp
Cool Oak Bri.
Old Welsh Harp
Mag. Ct.
Open Air Swimming Bath
Sturgess Park
BRENT CROSS SHOPPING CENTRE
BRENT CROSS
Carmelite Convent
Prince's Park
Little Wood
Willifield Green
31
32
N.W.11
Jew's Cemetery
Crematorium
Garden of Remembrance
47
Railway Wks.
33
GOLDERS GREEN
Hippodrome
Refuse Disposal Works
Industrial Estate
Solid Waste Transfer Station
Council Depot
CLITTERHOUSE PLAYING FIELDS
Hendon Football Ground
Brent Sidings
BASING HILL PARK
CHILDS HILL PARK
CHILDS HILL
34
Elm Park
Westfield Coll.
Athletic Grounds
Cricket Grd.
Hampstead Cemetery
Fortune Green
35
New College
Reservoir
Sports Ground
Sports Grd.
DOLLIS HILL ESTATE
Athletic Ground
Bus Garage
Clock Wks.
Dollis Hill
Dollis Hill Ho.
Open Air Swim. Pool
GLADSTONE PARK
CRICKLEWOOD
N.W.2
Pumping Sta.
Reservoir
Anson Hall
Tech. Coll.
DOLLIS HILL
MET.L.& JUBILEE
55
WILLESDEN GREEN
WILLESDEN
GREEN
KILBURN
West End Development
N.W.6
WEST HAMPSTEAD
HAMP
Bowling Green
NORTH CIRCULAR ROAD
WATFORD WAY
EDGWARE ROAD
HENDON WAY
FINCHLEY ROAD
CRICKLEWOOD BROADWAY
GREAT NORTH WAY

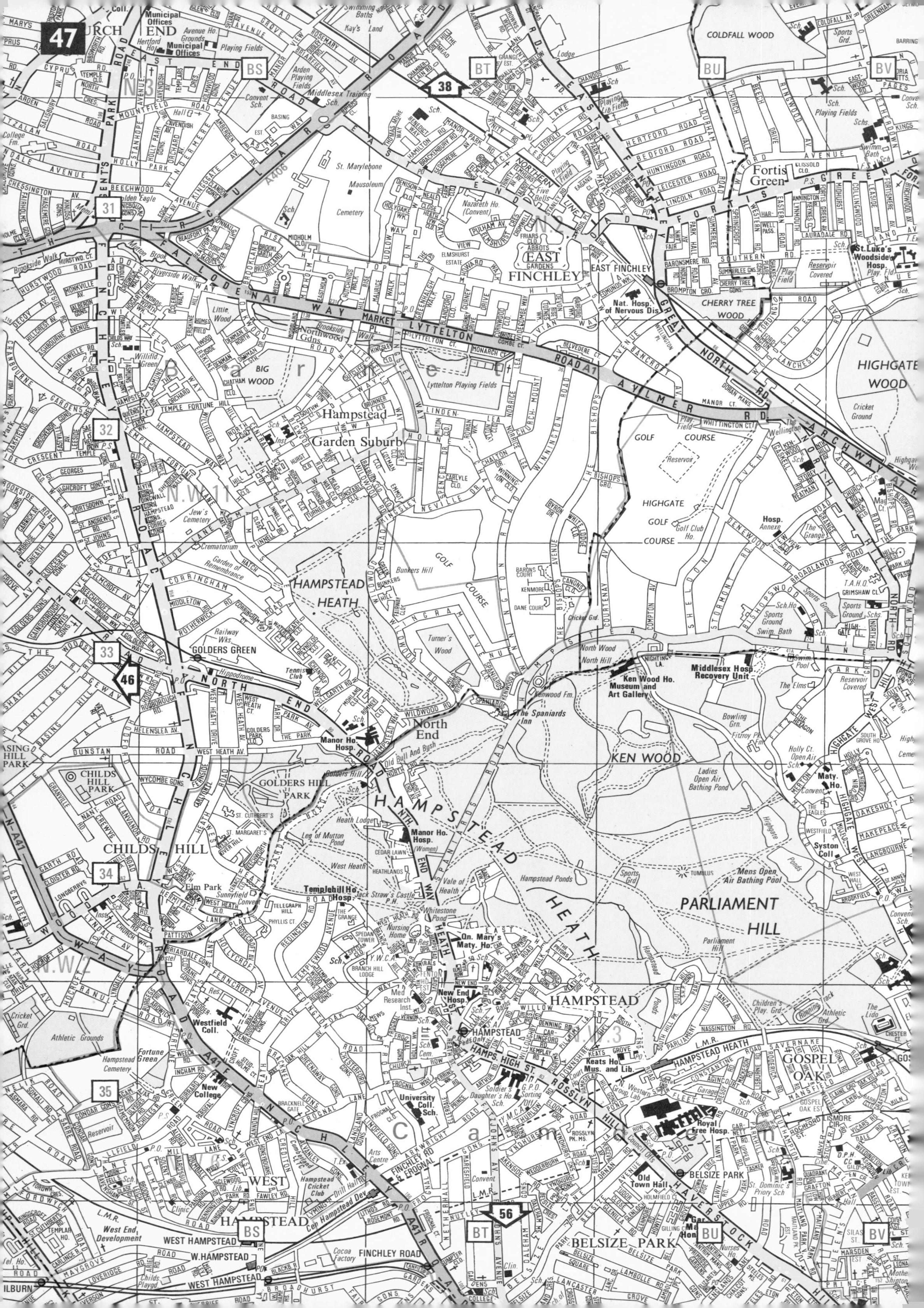
BS
BT
BU
BV
38
31
32
33
34
35
46
56
N3
N.2
N.W.11
N.W.2
N.W.3
COLDFALL WOOD
Fortis Green
EAST FINCHLEY
EAST GARDENS
St. Marylebone Cemetery
Mausoleum
Nazareth Ho. (Convent)
Middlesex Training Sch.
CHERRY TREE WOOD
Nat. Hosp. of Nervous Dis.
HIGHGATE WOOD
Cricket Ground
St. Luke's Woodside Hosp.
Reservoir Covered
LYTTELTON ROAD A1
AYLMER RD
ARCHWAY RD
GREAT NORTH RD
FALLODEN WAY A1
MARKET PL.
Northwood Gdns.
BIG WOOD
Little Wood
Lyttelton Playing Fields
Hampstead Garden Suburb
Jew's Cemetery
Crematorium
Garden of Remembrance
HAMPSTEAD HEATH
Bunkers Hill
GOLF COURSE
Turner's Wood
HIGHGATE GOLF COURSE
Golf Club Ho.
Hosp. Annexe
The Grange
Sports Ground
GOLDERS GREEN
Railway Wks.
Hippodrome
Tennis Club
NORTH END ROAD
Manor Ho. Hosp.
North End
Old Bull And Bush
The Spaniards Inn
Kenwood Fm.
North Wood
North Hill
Ken Wood Ho. Museum and Art Gallery
Middlesex Hosp. Recovery Unit
The Elms
Bowling Grn.
KEN WOOD
Ladies Open Air Bathing Pond
Holly Ct. Open Air Sch.
Maty. Ho.
Convent
Syston Coll
CHILDS HILL PARK
GOLDERS HILL PARK
CHILDS HILL
Heath Lodge
Leg of Mutton Pond
Manor Ho. Hosp. (Women)
West Heath
Templehill Ho. Hosp.
Jack Straw's Castle P.H.
Whitestone Pond
Vale of Health
Hampstead Ponds
TUMULUS
Mens Open Air Bathing Pool
PARLIAMENT HILL
HAMPSTEAD HEATH
Parliament Hill
Elm Park
Sunnyfield Convent
Nursing Home
Qn. Mary's Maty. Ho.
Branch Hill Lodge
Med Research Inst.
New End Hosp.
HAMPSTEAD
Children's Play Grd.
Running Track
Athletic Grd.
The Lido
Westfield Coll.
Athletic Grounds
Cricket Grd.
Hampstead Cemetery
Fortune Green
New College
Reservoir
HAMPS. HIGH ST.
Soldier's Daughter's Ho. Sch.
Keats Ho. Mus. and Lib.
ROSSLYN HILL
HAMPSTEAD HEATH
GOSPEL OAK
Royal Free Hosp.
University Coll. Sch.
Arts Centre
Hampstead Cricket Club
WEST HAMPSTEAD
West End Development
W.HAMPSTEAD
WEST HAMPSTEAD
Cocoa Factory
FINCHLEY ROAD
Old Town Hall
BELSIZE PARK
HAVERSTOCK HILL
St. Dominic's Priory Sch
FINCHLEY RD
A41
A406
A1
KILBURN

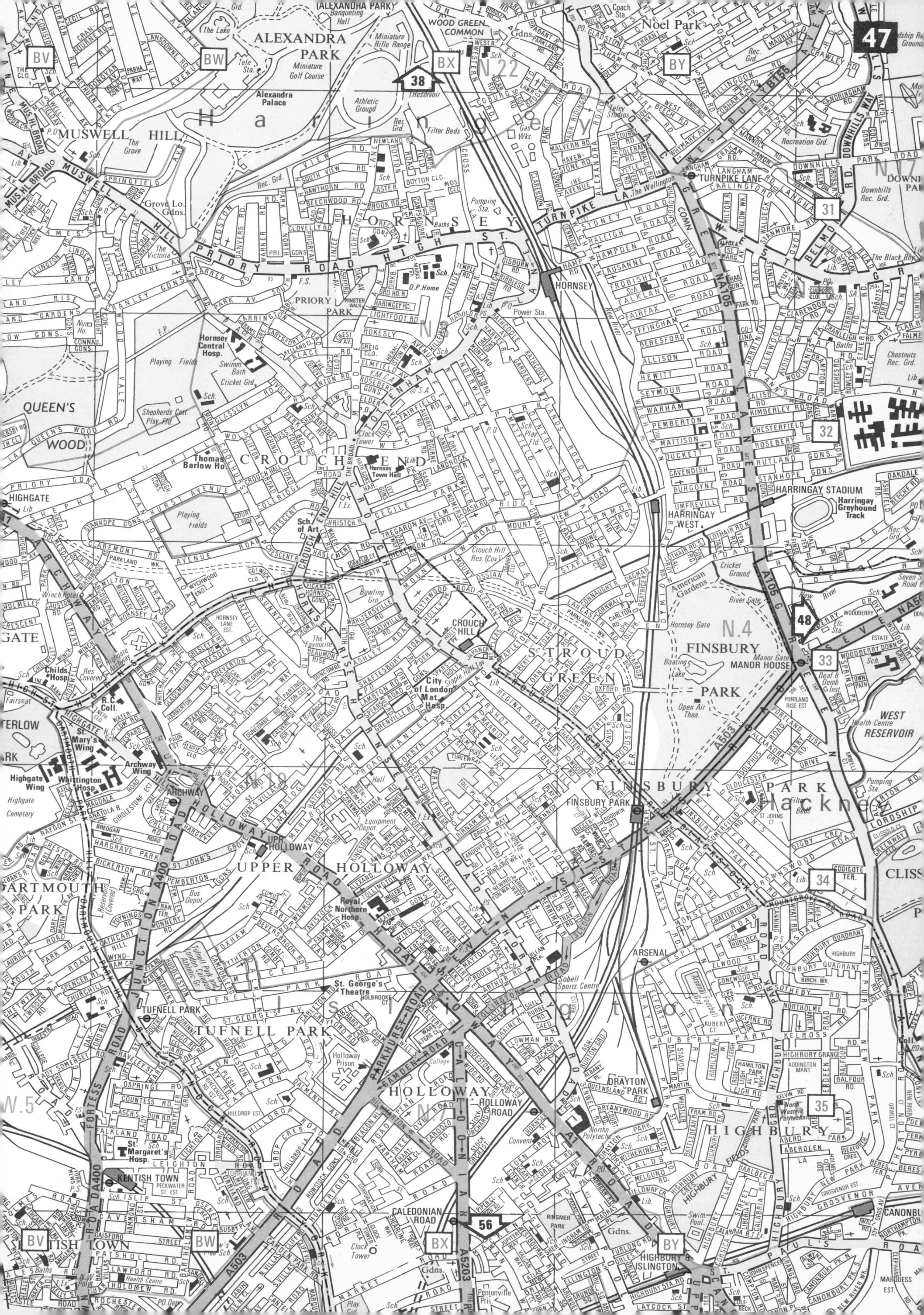
ALEXANDRA PARK
Alexandra Palace
MUSWELL HILL
WOOD GREEN COMMON
Noel Park
N.22
Haringey
TURNPIKE LANE
HORNSEY
PRIORY PARK
Hornsey Central Hosp.
QUEEN'S WOOD
CROUCH END
Hornsey Town Hall
HIGHGATE
HARRINGAY WEST
HARRINGAY STADIUM
Harringay Greyhound Track
CROUCH HILL
STROUD GREEN
FINSBURY PARK
MANOR HOUSE
WEST RESERVOIR
N.4
N.19
ARCHWAY
Whittington Hosp.
Highgate Cemetery
UPPER HOLLOWAY
Royal Northern Hosp.
DARTMOUTH PARK
TUFNELL PARK
St. George's Theatre
Islington
Hackney
ARSENAL
DRAYTON PARK
Holloway Prison
HOLLOWAY
HOLLOWAY ROAD
HIGHBURY
N.7
KENTISH TOWN
St. Margaret's Hosp.
CALEDONIAN ROAD
HIGHBURY & ISLINGTON
CANONBURY
Pentonville Pris.
38
31
32
33
34
35
48
56
BV
BW
BX
BY

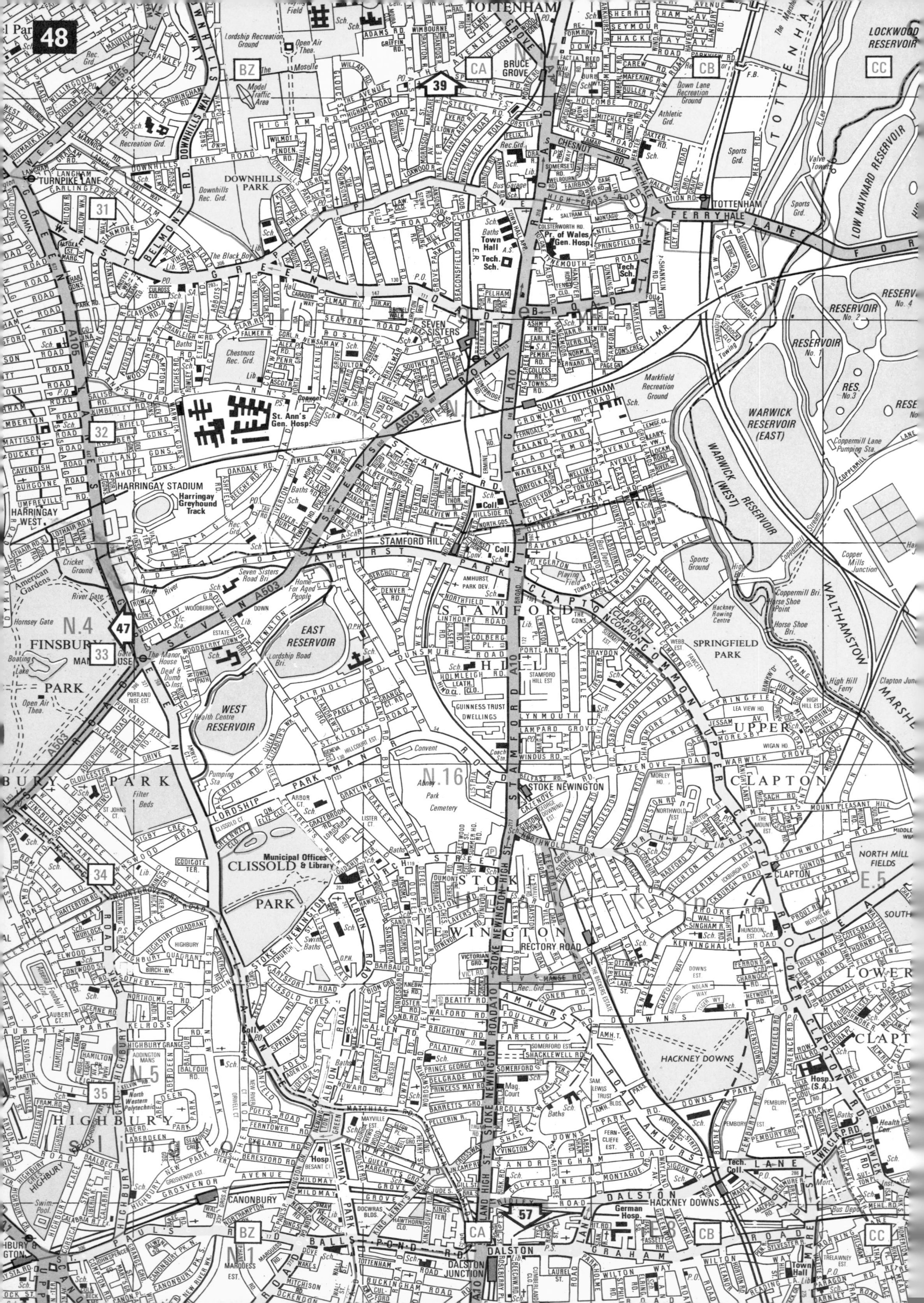
TOTTENHAM
BRUCE GROVE
SEVEN SISTERS
SOUTH TOTTENHAM
STAMFORD HILL
STAMFORD HILL
STOKE NEWINGTON
UPPER CLAPTON
LOWER CLAPTON
HIGHBURY
CANONBURY
DALSTON
DALSTON JUNCTION
HACKNEY DOWNS
CLAPTON
HARRINGAY STADIUM
HARRINGAY WEST
TURNPIKE LANE
DOWNHILLS PARK
FINSBURY PARK
CLISSOLD PARK
SPRINGFIELD PARK
EAST RESERVOIR
WEST RESERVOIR
WARWICK RESERVOIR (EAST)
WARWICK (WEST) RESERVOIR
LOW MAYNARD RESERVOIR
LOCKWOOD RESERVOIR
WALTHAMSTOW MARSHES
Abney Park Cemetery
St. Ann's Gen. Hosp.
Pr. of Wales Gen. Hosp.
German Hosp.
NORTH MILL FIELDS
N.4
N.5
N.15
N.16
N.17
E.5
N.1
BZ
CA
CB
CC
31
32
33
34
35
39
47
57

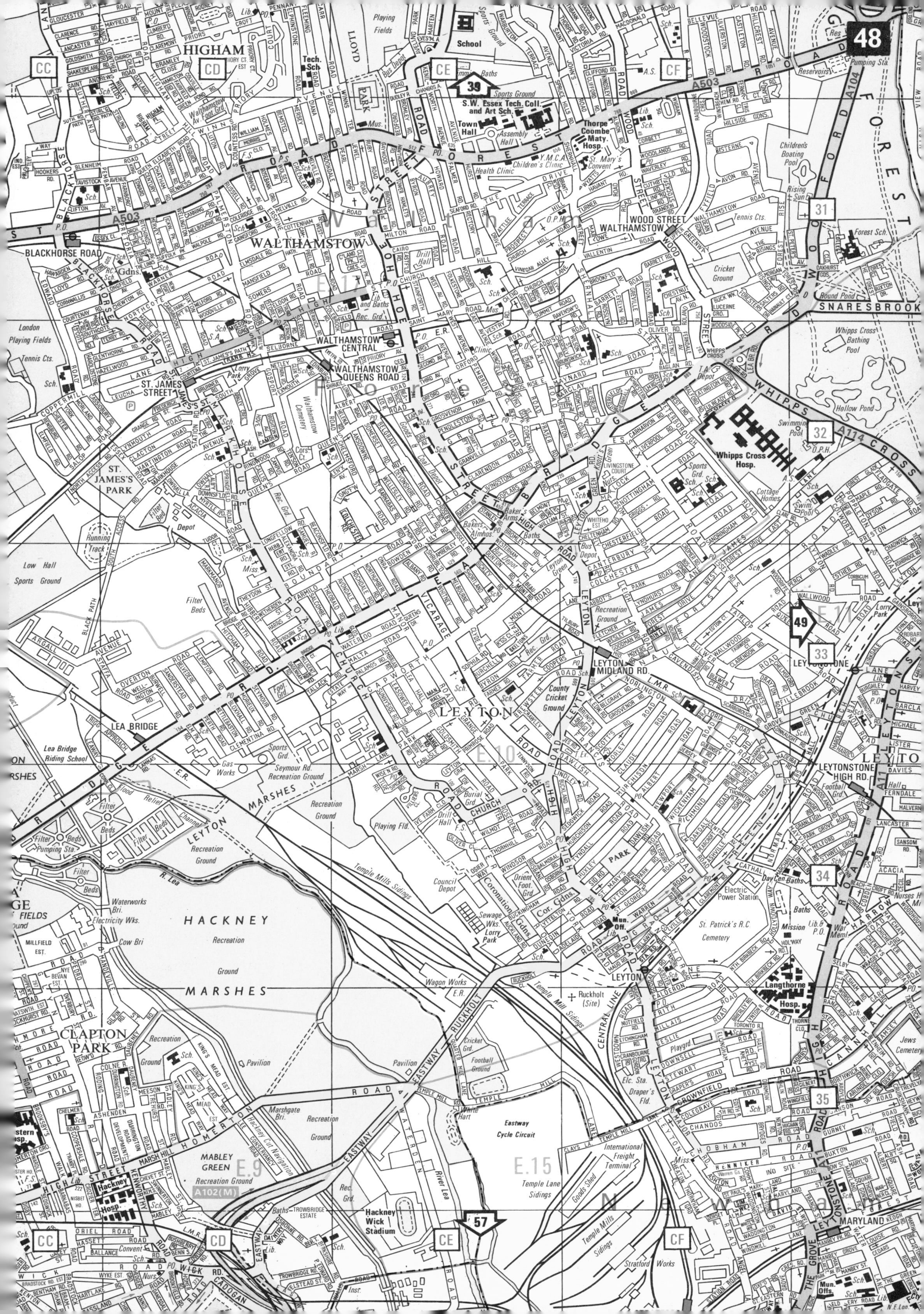
48
HIGHAM
WALTHAMSTOW
BLACKHORSE ROAD
WALTHAMSTOW CENTRAL
WALTHAMSTOW QUEENS ROAD
ST. JAMES STREET
WOOD STREET WALTHAMSTOW
SNARESBROOK
Whipps Cross Hosp.
Whipps Cross Bathing Pool
Hollow Pond
S.W. Essex Tech. Coll. and Art Sch.
Town Hall
Thorpe Coombe Maty. Hosp.
ST. JAMES'S PARK
Low Hall Sports Ground
London Playing Fields
Filter Beds
LEA BRIDGE
Lea Bridge Riding School
LEYTON
LEYTON MIDLAND RD.
LEYTONSTONE
LEYTONSTONE HIGH RD.
County Cricket Ground
Leyton Green
HACKNEY Recreation Ground
MARSHES
LEYTON MARSHES
Temple Mills Sidings
Coronation Gdns.
Orient Foot. Grd.
Langthorne Hosp.
St. Patrick's R.C. Cemetery
Electric Power Station
CLAPTON PARK
MABLEY GREEN Recreation Ground
Hackney Hosp.
Hackney Wick Stadium
Eastway Cycle Circuit
International Freight Terminal
MARYLAND
E.9
E.10
E.15
E.17
E.11
CC
CD
CE
CF
31
32
33
34
35
39
49
57
A503
A104
A114
A11
A102(M)

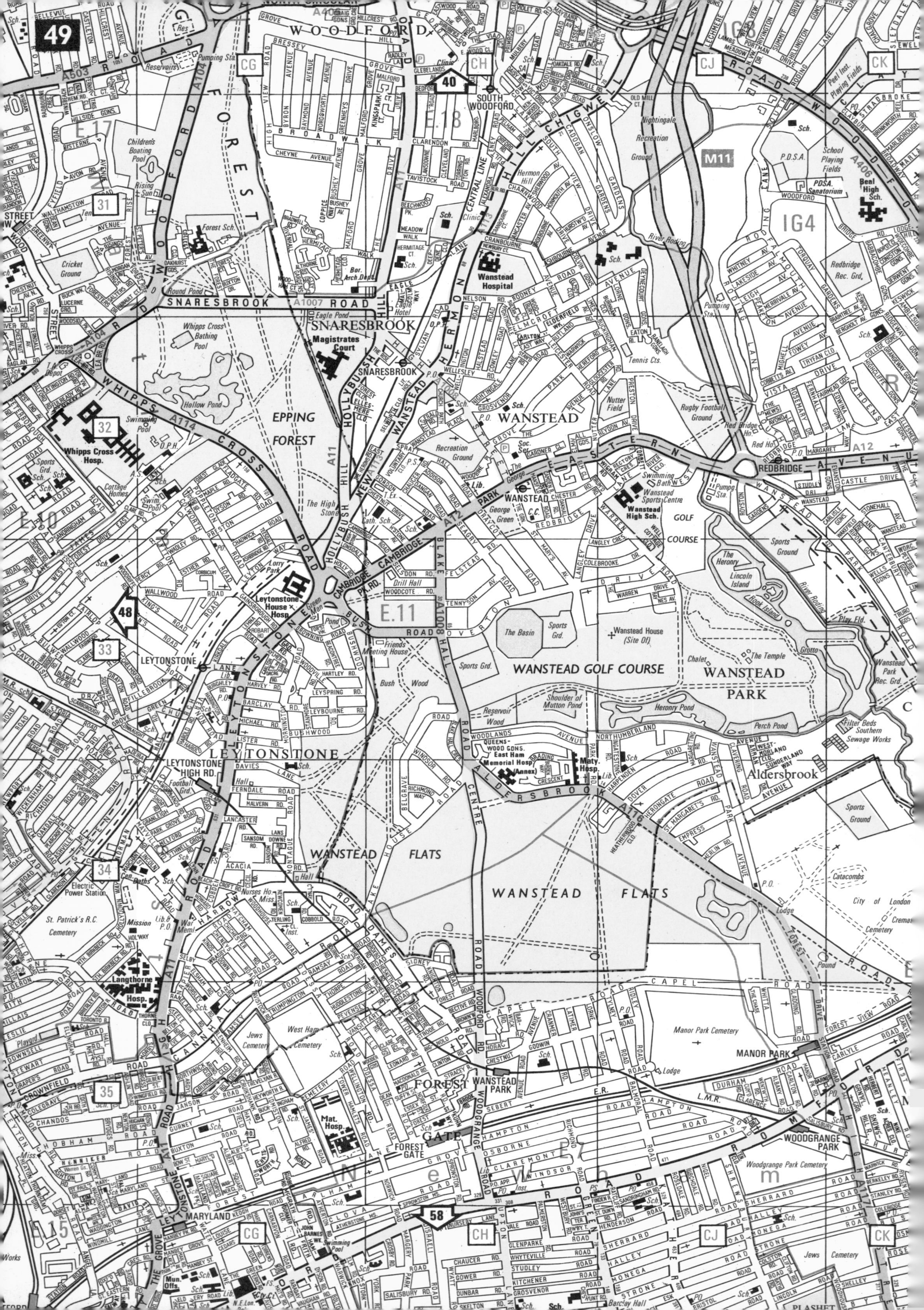

WOODFORD
SOUTH WOODFORD
E.18
E.17
E.11
E.10
E.15
E.7
IG4
IG8
CG
CH
CJ
CK
40
31
32
33
34
35
48
58
M11
A104
A503
A1007
A114
A11
A12
A113
A116
A406
A117
FOREST
WOODFORD NEW ROAD
SNARESBROOK ROAD
SNARESBROOK
Magistrates Court
Eagle Pond
Whipps Cross Bathing Pool
Hollow Pond
Round Pond
Children's Boating Pool
Cricket Ground
Forest Sch.
Whipps Cross Hosp.
WHIPPS CROSS ROAD
EPPING FOREST
HOLLYBUSH HILL
HERMON HILL
CHIGWELL
CENTRAL LINE
Wanstead Hospital
WANSTEAD
EASTERN AVENUE
REDBRIDGE
Recreation Ground
Nightingale Recreation Ground
River Roding
Rugby Football Ground
Redbridge Rec. Grd.
Beal High Sch.
School Playing Fields
Wanstead High Sch.
GOLF COURSE
Sports Ground
The Heronry
Lincoln Island
Rook Island
The Basin
Wanstead House (Site Of)
The Temple
WANSTEAD GOLF COURSE
WANSTEAD PARK
Shoulder of Mutton Pond
Heronry Pond
Perch Pond
Reservoir Wood
Bush Wood
Filter Beds Southern Sewage Works
Aldersbrook
East Ham Memorial Hosp (Annex)
Maty. Hosp.
ALDERSBROOK ROAD
LEYTONSTONE
LEYTONSTONE HIGH RD.
Leytonstone House Hosp.
CAMBRIDGE PARK
Green Man
Friends Meeting House
WANSTEAD FLATS
City of London Cemetery
Catacombs
St. Patrick's R.C. Cemetery
Electric Power Station
Langthorne Hosp.
Jews Cemetery
West Ham Cemetery
Manor Park Cemetery
MANOR PARK
CAPEL ROAD
WOODFORD ROAD
FOREST GATE
WANSTEAD PARK
Mat. Hosp.
WOODGRANGE PARK
Woodgrange Park Cemetery
ROMFORD ROAD
MARYLAND
THE GROVE
PLASHET

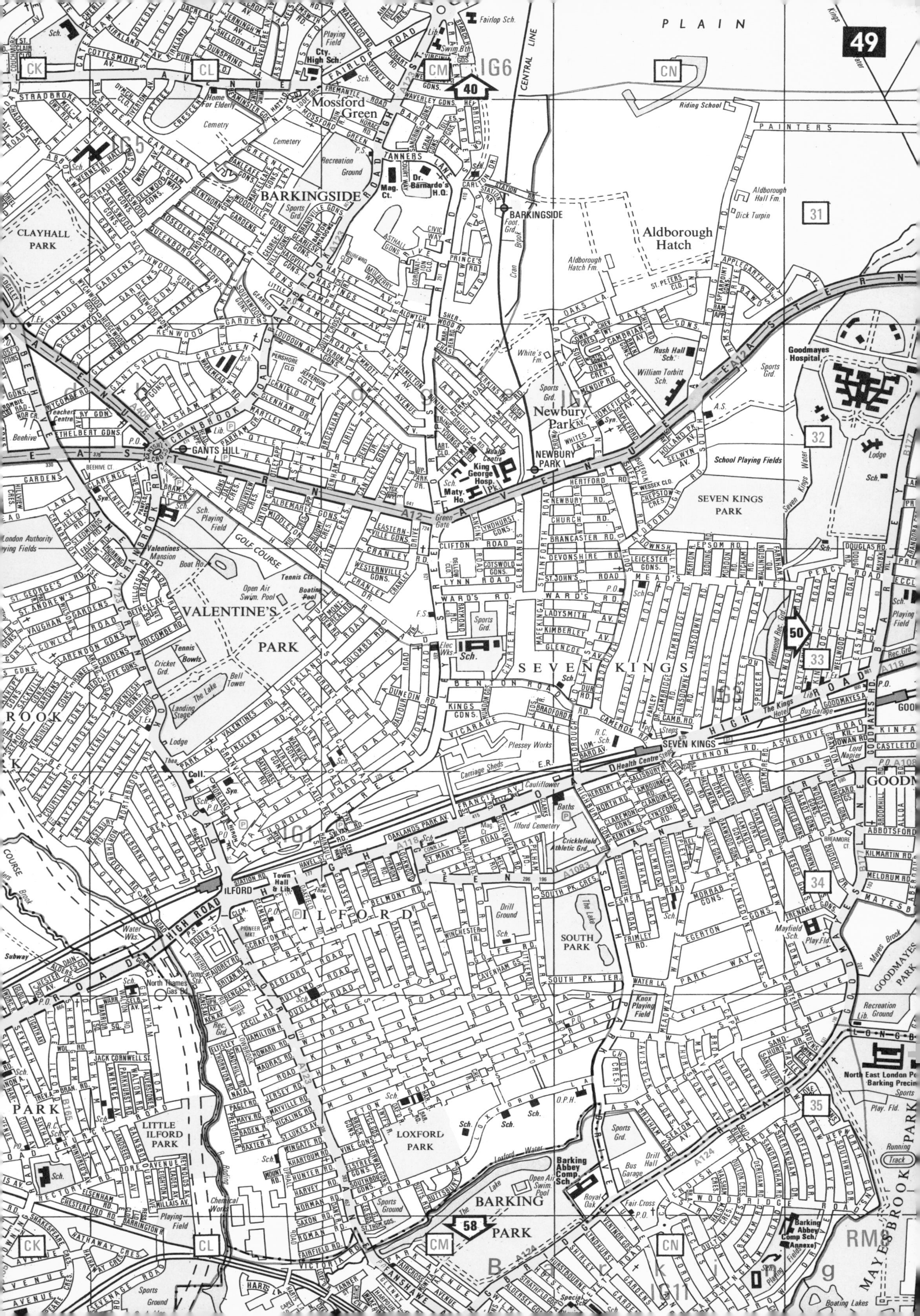
PLAIN
CK
CL
CM
CN
IG6
40
Mossford Green
CENTRAL LINE
Riding School
PAINTERS
IG5
Cemetery
Recreation Ground
BARKINGSIDE
Dr. Barnardo's H.Q.
CLAYHALL PARK
Aldborough Hatch
31
Goodmayes Hospital
GANTS HILL
IG2
Newbury Park
NEWBURY PARK
King George Hosp.
32
School Playing Fields
SEVEN KINGS PARK
EASTERN AVENUE
A12
GOLF COURSE
Valentines Mansion
VALENTINE'S PARK
SEVEN KINGS
50
33
IG3
Plessey Works
SEVEN KINGS
IG1
Ilford Cemetery
Town Hall & Lib.
ILFORD
HIGH ROAD
SOUTH PARK
34
Drill Ground
GOODMAYES PARK
Knox Playing Field
LITTLE ILFORD PARK
LOXFORD PARK
North East London Polytechnic Barking Precinct
35
Barking Abbey Comp. Sch.
BARKING
58
PARK
Barking Abbey Comp Sch. (Annexe)
RM8
MAYESBROOK PARK
IG11
Barking
Boating Lakes

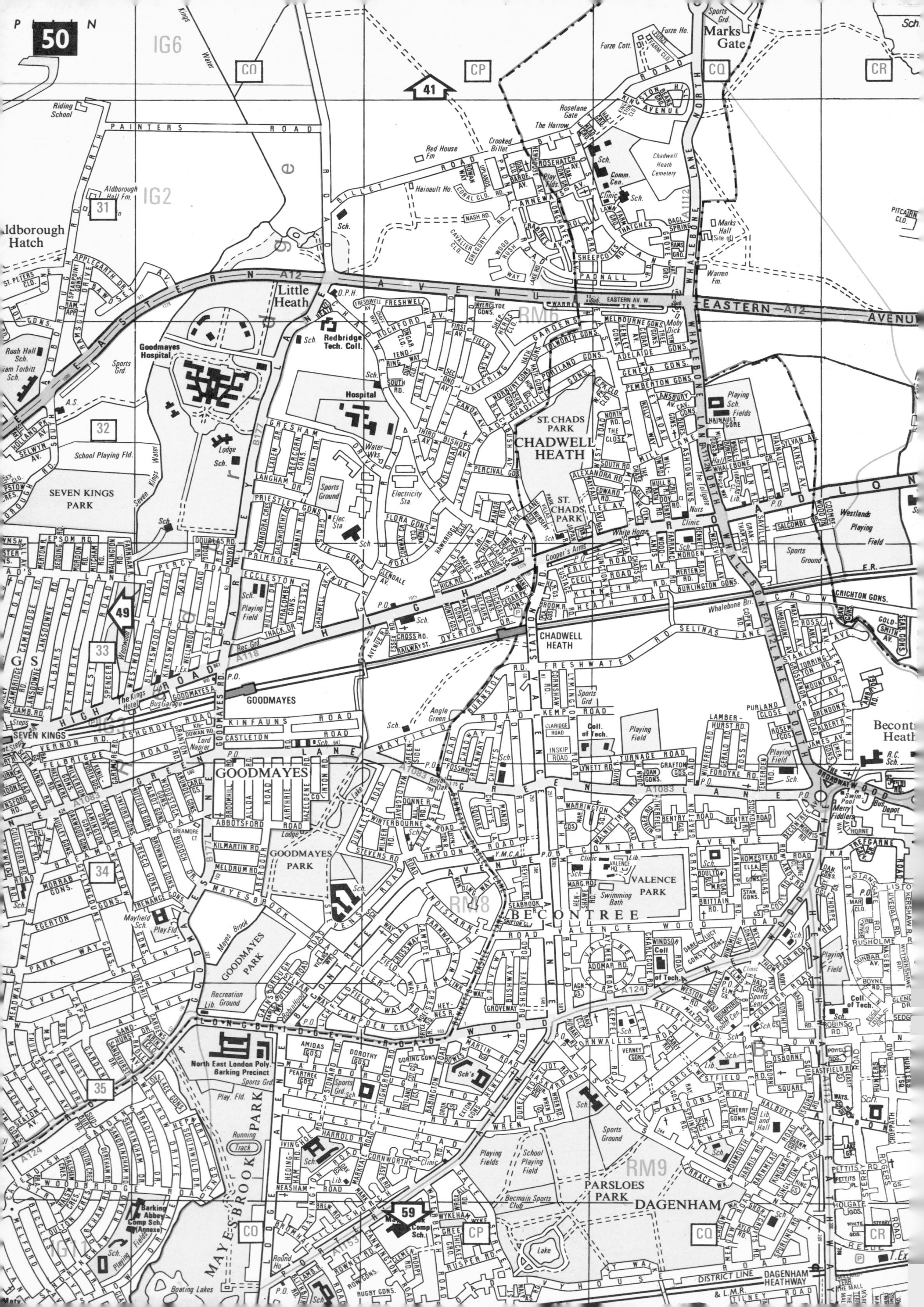
IG6
CO
CP
41
CQ
CR
Marks Gate
Furze Ho.
Furze Cott.
Riding School
PAINTERS ROAD
Roselane Gate
The Harrow
Crooked Billet
Red House Fm
Hainault Ho.
BILLET ROAD
Chadwell Heath Cemetery
Comm. Cen.
Clinic
Sch.
WHALEBONE LANE NORTH
Aldborough Hall Fm.
IG2
31
Aldborough Hatch
Marks Hall (Site of)
Warren Fm.
EASTERN AVENUE A12
Little Heath
RM6
Goodmayes Hospital
Redbridge Tech. Coll.
Hospital
Rush Hall Sch.
Sports Grd.
32
School Playing Fld.
Seven Kings Water
SEVEN KINGS PARK
Lodge
Water Wks
Electricity Sta.
Sports Ground
ST. CHADS PARK
CHADWELL HEATH
Playing Fields
Westlands Playing Field
Sports Ground
White Horse
Cooper's Arms
Clinic
Lib.
49
33
HIGH ROAD
A118
Playing Field
GOODMAYES
Rec. Grd.
Bus Garage
The Kings Hotel
CHADWELL HEATH
Whalebone Bri.
SELINAS LANE
FRESHWATER RD.
SEVEN KINGS
Coll. of Tech.
Playing Field
Sports Grd.
Becontree Heath
Angle Green
GOODMAYES
GREEN LANE A1083
Royal Oak
Bus Depot
Merry Fiddlers
34
GOODMAYES PARK
Mayfield Sch.
Play Fld.
BECONTREE AVENUE
VALENCE PARK
Swimming Bath
RM8
BECONTREE
Mayes Brook
GOODMAYES PARK
Recreation Ground
LONGBRIDGE ROAD
A124
Coll of Tech.
Coll. of Tech.
North East London Poly. Barking Precinct
35
Play. Fld.
Running Track
Sports Grd.
Sports Ground
Playing Fields
School Playing Field
RM9
PARSLOES PARK
DAGENHAM
Becmain Sports Club
Barking Abbey Comp Sch. (Annexe)
59
IG11
MAYES BROOK PARK
Boating Lakes
Lake
DISTRICT LINE
& L.M.R.
DAGENHAM HEATHWAY
VALENCE AVENUE
Sch.

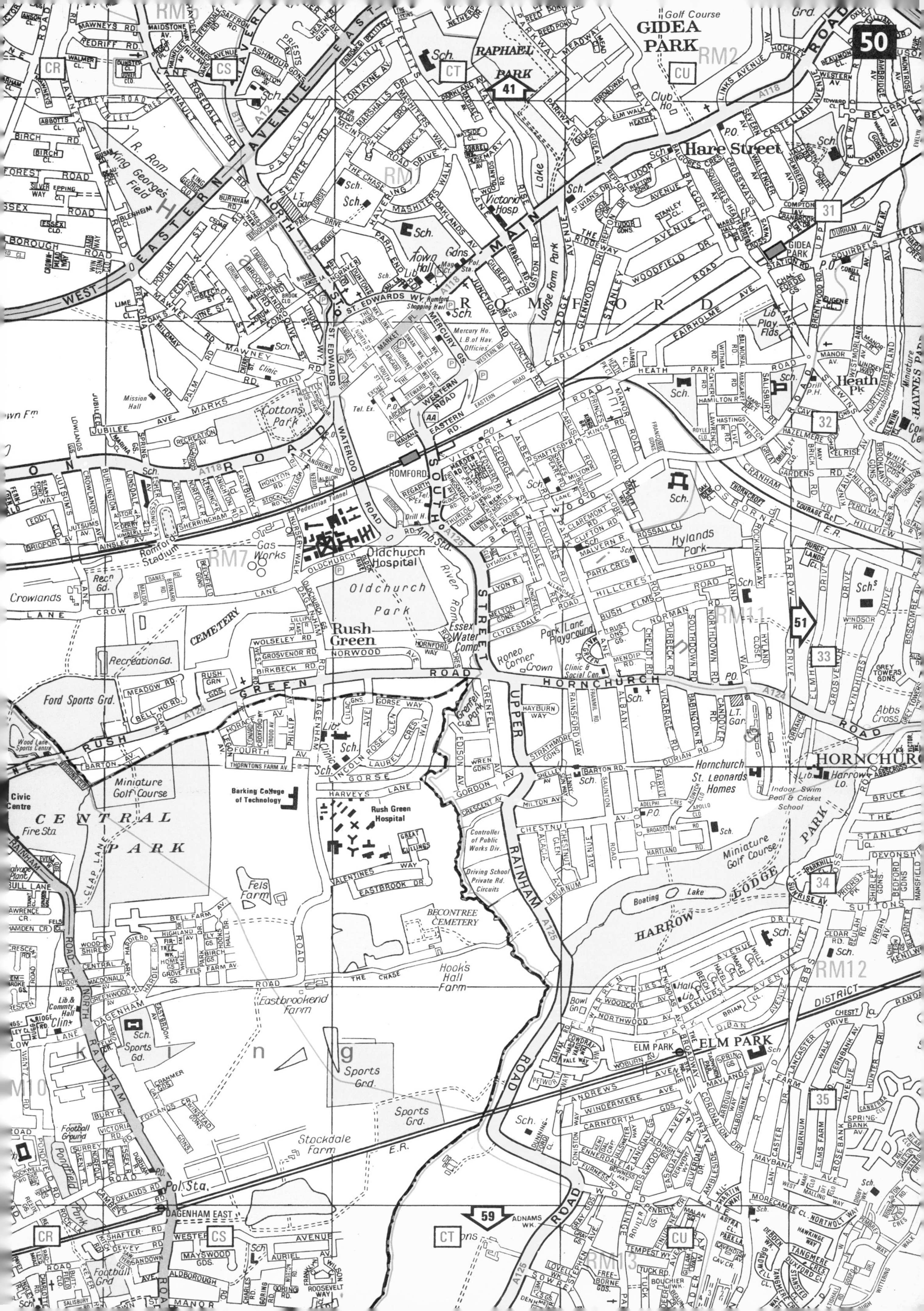

GIDEA PARK
RM2
Golf Course
RAPHAEL PARK
41
Club Ho.
Hare Street
Sch.
P.O.
CR
CS
CT
CU
RM5
RM1
RM7
RM11
RM12
RM13
RM10
EASTERN AVENUE
WEST
NORTH ST.
King George's Field
R. Rom
A12
A118
A125
A124
B175
Victoria Hosp.
Town Hall
Lib.
Pol. Sta.
Romford Shopping Hall
MAIN ROAD
ROMFORD
Lodge Farm Park
Lake
Mercury Ho. L.B. of Hav. Offices
HEATH PARK ROAD
Heath Pk
GIDEA PARK
STATION RD.
31
32
33
34
35
51
59
Lib. Play. Flds
Cottons Park
Mission Hall
Clinic
Tel. Ex.
AA
ROMFORD
Pedestrian Tunnel
Romford Stadium
Gas Works
Oldchurch Hospital
Oldchurch Park
River Rom
Amb. Sta.
Drill H.
Crowlands
CROW LANE
CEMETERY
Rush Green
Recreation Gd.
Recn Gd.
Essex Water Comp.
Roneo Corner
Crown
Park Lane Playground
Clinic & Social Cen.
Hylands Park
HORNCHURCH ROAD
RUSH GREEN ROAD
UPPER RAINHAM ROAD
SOUTH STREET
Ford Sports Grd.
Wood Lane Sports Centre
Miniature Golf Course
Civic Centre
CENTRAL PARK
Fire Sta.
Barking College of Technology
Rush Green Hospital
Grenfell Park
Controller of Public Works Div.
Driving School Private Rd. Circuits
Hornchurch St. Leonards Homes
L.T. Gar.
HORNCHURCH
Harrow Lo.
Indoor Swim Pool & Cricket School
Miniature Golf Course
Boating Lake
HARROW LODGE PARK
Fels Farm
BECONTREE CEMETERY
Hook's Hall Farm
Eastbrookend Farm
THE CHASE
Sports Grd.
Sports Gd.
Stockdale Farm
E.R.
Lib. & Commty. Hall
Clin.
Football Ground
Pondfield Park
Pol. Sta.
DAGENHAM EAST
Football Grd
Bowl Gn.
Hall
ELM PARK
DISTRICT
ABBS CROSS
Abbs Cross
Grey Towers Gdns
Miniature Golf
RAINHAM ROAD
ADNAMS WK.

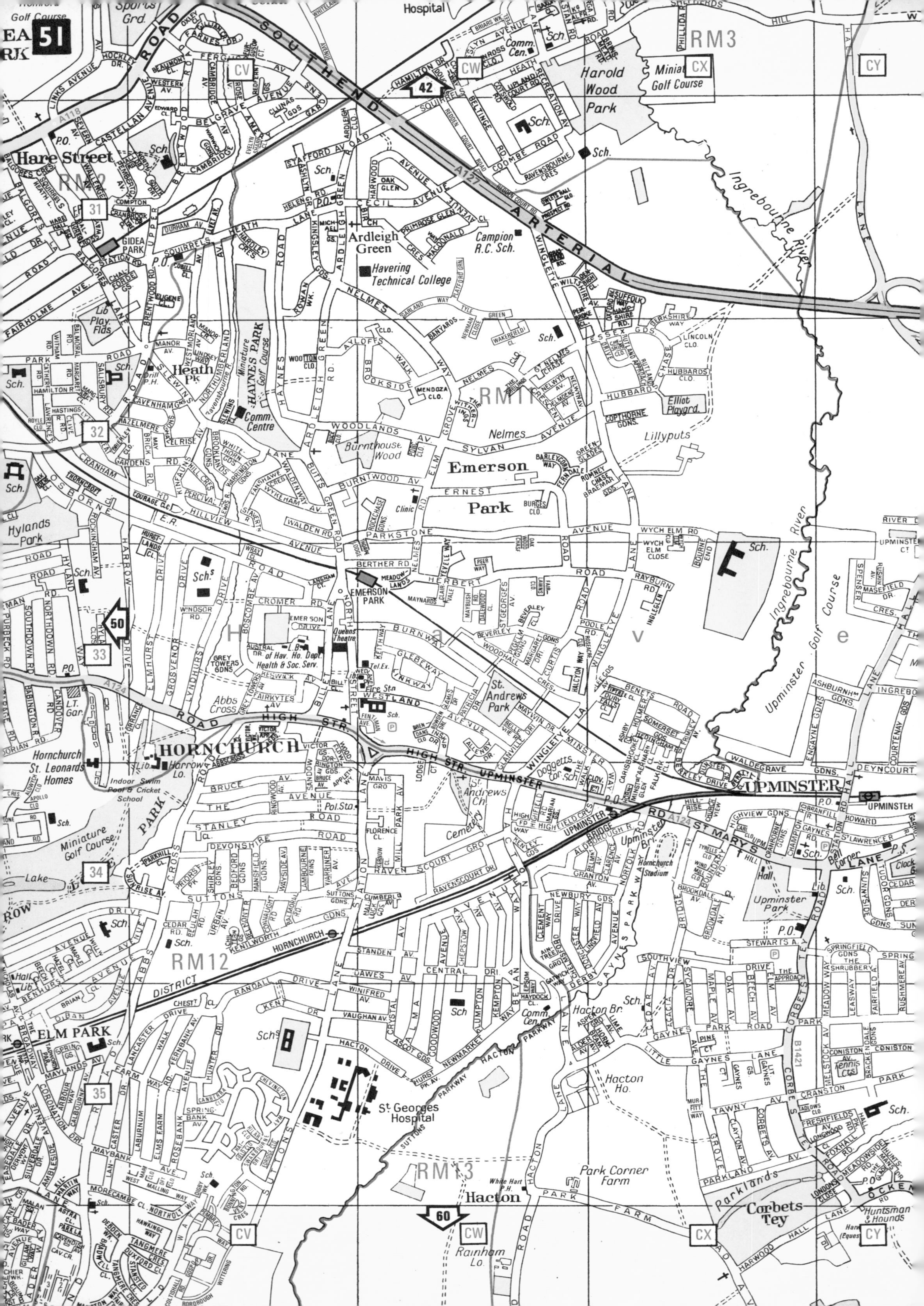
51
Hare Street
RM2
Gidea Park
Station Rd.
Southend Arterial
A127
A118
42
CV
CW
CX
CY
RM3
Harold Wood Park
Miniature Golf Course
Ingrebourne River
Ardleigh Green
Havering Technical College
Campion R.C. Sch.
Nelmes
RM11
Emerson Park
Burnthouse Wood
Heath Pk.
Haynes Park Golf Course
Comm. Centre
Lillyputs
Elliot Playgrd.
Hylands Park
50
31
32
33
34
35
Emerson Park
Queens Theatre
L.B. of Hav. Ho. Dept. Health & Soc. Serv.
Grey Towers Gdns
Abbs Cross
St. Andrews Park
A124
High Str.
Hornchurch
Harrow Lo.
Hornchurch St. Leonards Homes
Indoor Swim Pool & Cricket School
Miniature Golf Course
Lake
St. Andrews Ch.
Cemetery
Doggetts Cor. Sch.
Upminster
Upminster Rd.
Upminster Bri.
Hornchurch Stadium
Upminster Golf Course
Ingrebourne River
St Marys Lane
Hall
Upminster Park
Corbets Tey Road
B1421
Hornchurch
District
RM12
Elm Park
Hacton Br.
Hacton Ho.
St Georges Hospital
Park Corner Farm
RM13
White Hart P.H.
Hacton
60
Rainham Lo.
Parklands
Corbets Tey
Huntsman & Hounds
Harwood Hall Lane
Tennis Cts

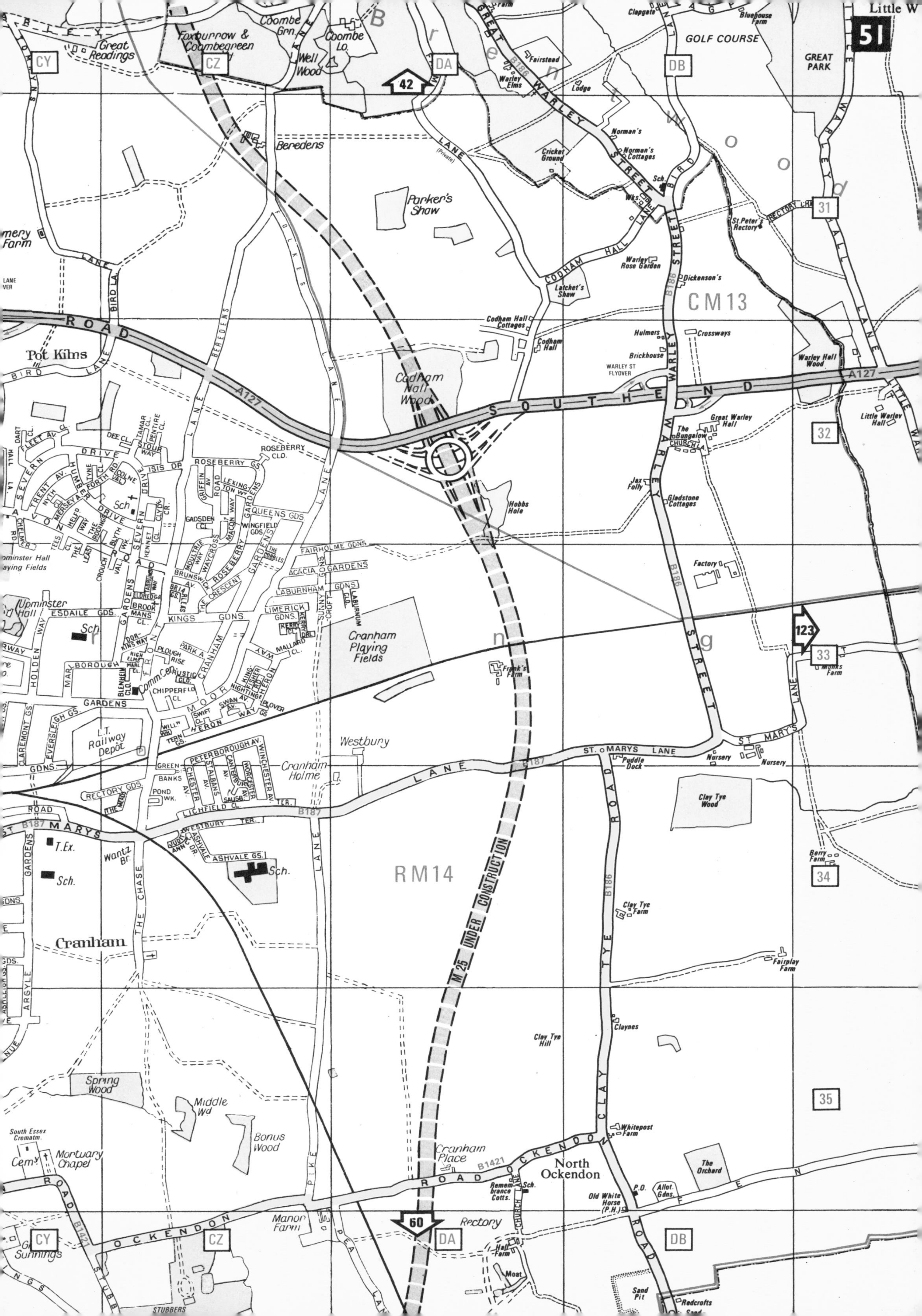

42
60
123
CY
CZ
DA
DB
31
32
33
34
35
Foxburrow & Coombegreen
Coombe Grn.
Coombe Lo.
Well Wood
Great Readings
Beredens
Parker's Shaw
GOLF COURSE
GREAT PARK
Fairstead
Warley Elms
Lodge
Norman's
Norman's Cottages
Cricket Ground
St.Peter's Rectory
Warley Rose Garden
Dickenson's
Latchet's Shaw
CM13
Codham Hall Cottages
Codham Hall
Hulmers
Crossways
Brickhouse
Warley Hall Wood
WARLEY ST FLYOVER
Codham Hall Wood
SOUTHEND ROAD
A127
Little Warley Hall
Great Warley Hall
The Bungalow
Jax Folly
Gladstone Cottages
Hobbs Hole
Pot Kilns
Factory
Cranham Playing Fields
Frank's Farm
Westbury
Cranham Holme
Puddle Dock
Nursery
Monks Farm
Clay Tye Wood
L.T. Railway Depôt
ST. MARYS LANE
B187
RM14
M 25 UNDER CONSTRUCTION
Berry Farm
Clay Tye Farm
Fairplay Farm
Claynes
Clay Tye Hill
Cranham
Spring Wood
Middle Wd
Bonus Wood
South Essex Crematm.
Cemy.
Mortuary Chapel
Cranham Place
North Ockendon
Whitepost Farm
The Orchard
Rememberance Cotts.
P.O.
Allot. Gdns.
Old White Horse (P.H.)
OCKENDON ROAD
B1421
Manor Farm
Rectory
Hall Farm
Moat
Sand Pit
Redcrofts
Sunnings
STUBBERS
CLAY TYE ROAD
WARLEY STREET
B186
GREAT WARLEY STREET
CODHAM HALL LANE
BIRD LANE
FOLKES LANE
PIKE LANE
THE CHASE
Upminster Hall
Sch.
T.Ex.
Comm.Cen.

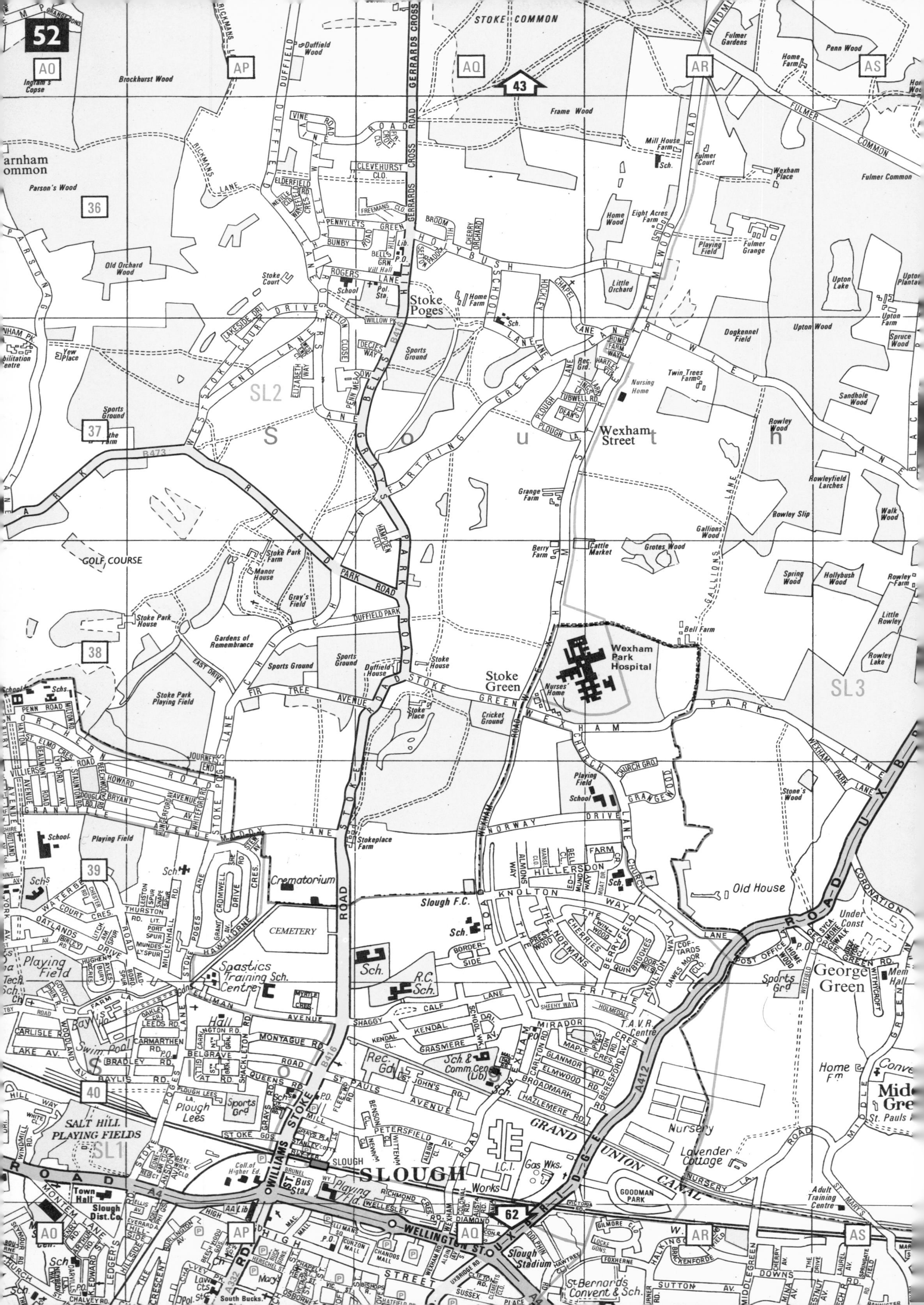
52
AO
AP
AQ
AR
AS
43
62
36
37
38
39
40
STOKE COMMON
Duffield Wood
Brockhurst Wood
Ingram's Copse
Farnham Common
Parson's Wood
Old Orchard Wood
Frame Wood
Fulmer Gardens
Penn Wood
Home Farm
FULMER COMMON
Fulmer Common
Mill House Farm
Fulmer Court
Wexham Place
Home Wood
Eight Acres Farm
Playing Field
Fulmer Grange
Little Orchard
Upton Lake
Upton Wood
Upton Farm
Spruce Wood
Dogkennel Field
Twin Trees Farm
Sandhole Wood
Nursing Home
Rowley Wood
Wexham Street
Rowleyfield Larches
Rowley Slip
Walk Wood
Grange Farm
Gallions Wood
Grotes Wood
Berry Farm
Cattle Market
Spring Wood
Hollybush Wood
Rowley Farm
Little Rowley
Rowley Lake
Bell Farm
Wexham Park Hospital
Nurses' Home
Stoke Green
Cricket Ground
SL3
SL2
SL1
Stoke Poges
Stoke Court
School
Pol. Sta.
Vill Hall
Home Farm
Sch.
Sports Ground
Yew Place
Sports Ground
GOLF COURSE
Stoke Park Farm
Manor House
Gray's Field
Stoke Park House
Gardens of Remembrance
Sports Ground
Duffield House
Stoke House
Stoke Place
Stoke Park Playing Field
Stone's Wood
Old House
Crematorium
Stokeplace Farm
CEMETERY
Slough F.C.
Spastics Training Sch. Centre
R.C. Sch.
George Green
Sports Grd
Under Const
T.A.V.R. Centre
Home Fm
Middle Green
St. Pauls
Nursery
Lavender Cottage
GOODMAN PARK
Adult Training Centre
GRAND UNION CANAL
Gas Wks.
Works
SLOUGH
Coll. of Higher Ed.
Bus Sta.
Playing Fld
Town Hall
Slough Dist. Co.
SALT HILL PLAYING FIELDS
Plough Lees
Sports Grd
Swim Pool
Hall
Slough Stadium
St. Bernard's Convent & Sch.
South Bucks.
Law Cts.
Rec. Gd.
Sch. & Comm. Cen. (Lib)
GERRARDS CROSS ROAD
STOKE ROAD
PARK ROAD
WEXHAM ROAD
FRAMEWOOD ROAD
ROWLEY LANE
WEXHAM PARK LANE
UXBRIDGE ROAD
A412
A4
B416
B473
A332
WELLINGTON ST.
HIGH STREET
KNOLTON WAY
NORWAY DRIVE
GALLIONS LANE
CHURCH LANE
FARTHING GREEN
HOLLYBUSH HILL
STOKE GREEN
FIR TREE AVENUE
DUFFIELD PARK
NORTHERN ROAD
BAYLIS RD.
MONTAGUE RD.
ST. PAULS AVENUE
PETERSFIELD AV.
BROADMARK RD.
HAZLEMERE RD.
GRASMERE AV.
KENDAL DR.
CALF LANE
FRITHE
HOLMEDALE
MIRADOR CRES.
BERESFORD AV.
GLANMOR RD.
ELMWOOD RD.
MAPLE CRES.
CARLTON RD.
NURSERY LA.
VICTORIA RD.
GILMORE CL.
HALKINGCROFT
FOXHERNE
SUTTON AV.
DOWNS

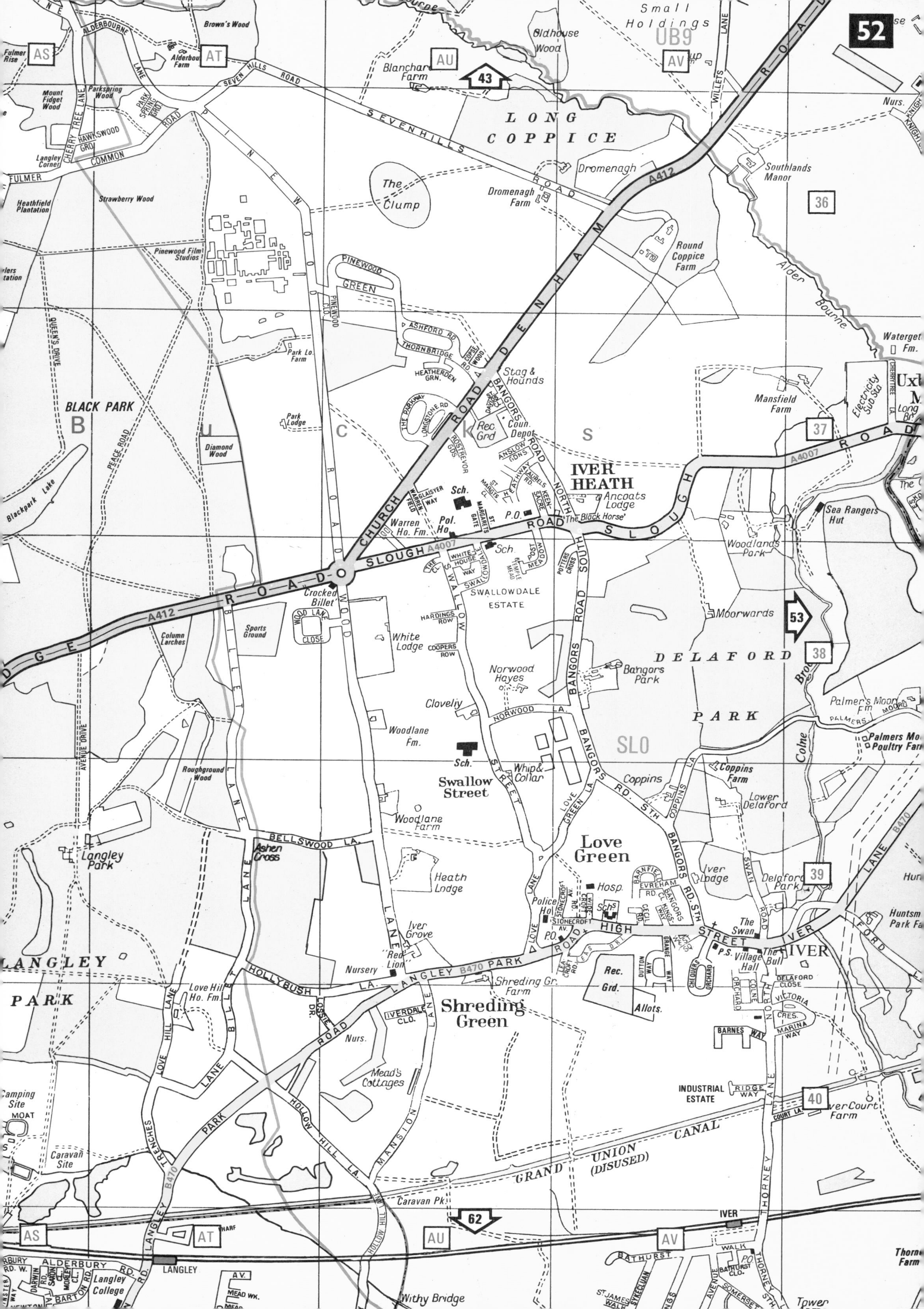
Small Holdings
UB9
Oldhouse Wood
Brown's Wood
Alderbourne Farm
Blanchard Farm
43
LONG COPPICE
SEVEN HILLS ROAD
SEVENHILLS ROAD
Fulmer Rise
Mount Fidget Wood
Parkspring Wood
CHERRY TREE LANE
HAWKSWOOD GRO.
Langley Corner
COMMON ROAD
FULMER
Heathfield Plantation
Strawberry Wood
PINEWOOD ROAD
The Clump
Dromenagh
Dromenagh Farm
A412
DENHAM ROAD
Southlands Manor
Nurs.
36
Pinewood Film Studios
PINEWOOD GREEN
PINEWOOD CLO.
Round Coppice Farm
Alder Bourne
Waterget Fm.
ASHFORD RD.
THORNBRIDGE RD.
HEATHERDEN GRN.
Park Lo. Farm
QUEEN'S DRIVE
Stag & Hounds
Mansfield Farm
Electricity Sub.Sta.
Long Br.
37
BLACK PARK
BUCKS
Park Lodge
Diamond Wood
PEACE ROAD
Blackpark Lake
Rec. Grd.
Coun. Depot
ANSLOW GDNS.
IVER HEATH
Ancoats Lodge
'The Black Horse'
A4007
SLOUGH ROAD
Sea Rangers Hut
CHURCH ROAD
Sch.
Pol. Ho.
P.O.
Warren Ho. Fm.
Woodlands Park
SLOUGH A4007
WHITE HOUSE WAY
SWALLOWDALE
SWALLOWDALE ESTATE
Sch.
POST MEADOW
TEMPLE MEAD
POTTERS CROSS
SOUTH ROAD
Crocked Billet
WOOD LANE CLOSE
Moorwards
53
A412
ROAD
EDGE
Sports Ground
Column Larches
HARDINGS ROW
White Lodge
COOPERS ROW
DELAFORD PARK
38
Norwood Hayes
Bangors Park
BANGORS ROAD
Cloveliy
NORWOOD LA.
Palmer's Moor Fm
PALMERS MOOR
Palmers Moor Poultry Farm
AVENUE DRIVE
Woodlane Fm.
SL0
Colne
BILLET LANE
Roughground Wood
Sch.
Swallow Street
SWALLOW STREET
Whip & Collar
Coppins
Coppins Farm
Lower Delaford
Woodlane Farm
LOVE GREEN LA.
BANGORS RD. STH.
BELLSWOOD LA.
Ashen Cross
Langley Park
Love Green
Hosp.
Iver Lodge
Delaford Park
39
Heath Lodge
LANE
Police Ho.
STONECROFT AV.
Sch.
The Swan
Iver Grove
HIGH STREET
P.O.
P.S.
Village Hall
The Bull
IVER
Huntsmoor Park Farm
LANGLEY
Red Lion
Nursery
LANGLEY B470 PARK ROAD
Rec. Grd.
DUTTON WAY
GRANGE WAY
CHEQUERS
ORCHARD
DELAFORD CLOSE
VICTORIA CRES.
PARK
Love Hill Ho. Fm.
HOLLYBUSH LA.
COSTE DR.
Shreding Gr. Farm
Shreding Green
Allots.
BARNES WAY
MARINA WAY
IVERDALE CLO.
Nurs.
LOVE HILL LANE
Mead's Cottages
INDUSTRIAL ESTATE
RIDGE WAY
40
COURT LA.
Iver Court Farm
Camping Site
MOAT
TRENCHES
HOLLOW HILL LA.
MANSION LANE
GRAND UNION CANAL (DISUSED)
Caravan Site
B470
Caravan Pk.
62
THORNEY LANE
IVER
AS
AT
AU
AV
HOLLOW HILL LA.
ALDERBURY RD.
ALDERBURY RD. W.
DARWIN RD.
SAXON CL.
MORLEY CL.
Langley College
BARTON RD.
LANGLEY RD.
LANGLEY
MEAD WK.
Withy Bridge
BATHURST WALK
ST JAMES WALK
AVENUE
BATHURST CLO.
P.O.
SOMERSET
THORNEY STH.
Tower
Thorney Farm

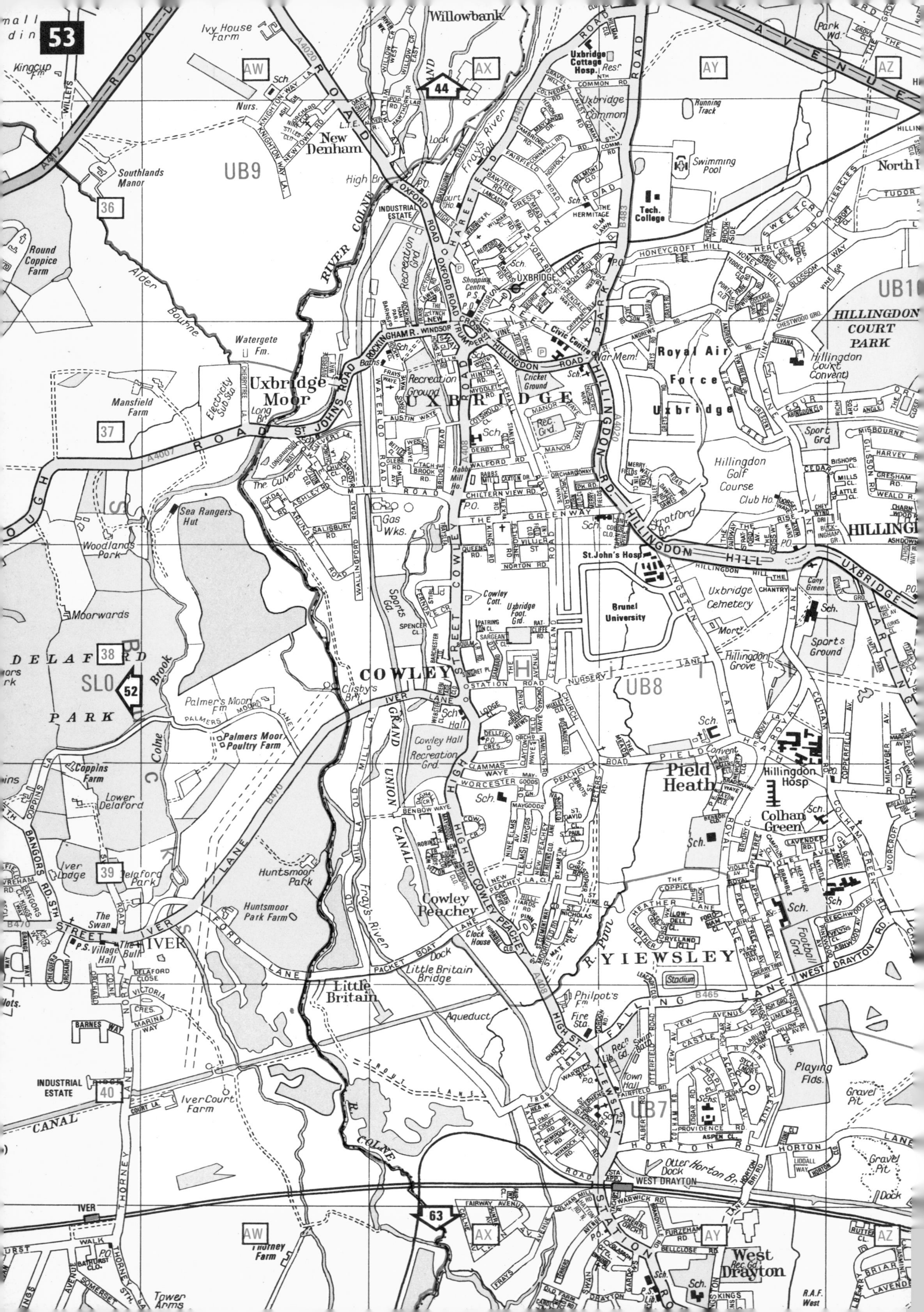
Willowbank
Ivy House Farm
Kingcup Fm.
New Denham
UB9
Southlands Manor
Round Coppice Farm
Alden Bourne
Watergete Fm.
Uxbridge Moor
Mansfield Farm
Sea Rangers Hut
Woodlands Park
Moorwards
DELAFORD PARK
SL0
Palmers Moor Fm
Palmers Moor Poultry Farm
Coppins Farm
Lower Delaford
Iver Lodge
Delaford Park
Huntsmoor Park
Huntsmoor Park Farm
The Swan
IVER
Village Hall
Little Britain
Iver Court Farm
INDUSTRIAL ESTATE
CANAL
IVER
Thorney Farm
Tower Arms
RIVER COLNE
OXFORD ROAD
INDUSTRIAL ESTATE
Uxbridge Cottage Hosp.
Uxbridge Common
Running Track
Swimming Pool
Tech. College
UXBRIDGE
Civic Centre
Royal Air Force Uxbridge
Hillingdon Golf Course
HILLINGDON COURT PARK
Hillingdon Court Convent
UB10
North
HILLINGDON HILL
UXBRIDGE ROAD
St.John's Hosp.
Brunel University
Uxbridge Cemetery
Hillingdon Grove
Sports Ground
UB8
COWLEY
Cowley Hall Recreation Grd.
GRAND UNION CANAL
Pield Heath
Hillingdon Hosp
Colham Green
Cowley Peachey
YIEWSLEY
Little Britain Bridge
Aqueduct
Playing Flds.
Gravel Pit
UB7
WEST DRAYTON
West Drayton
R.A.F. West
AW
AX
AY
AZ
44
36
37
38
39
40
52
63

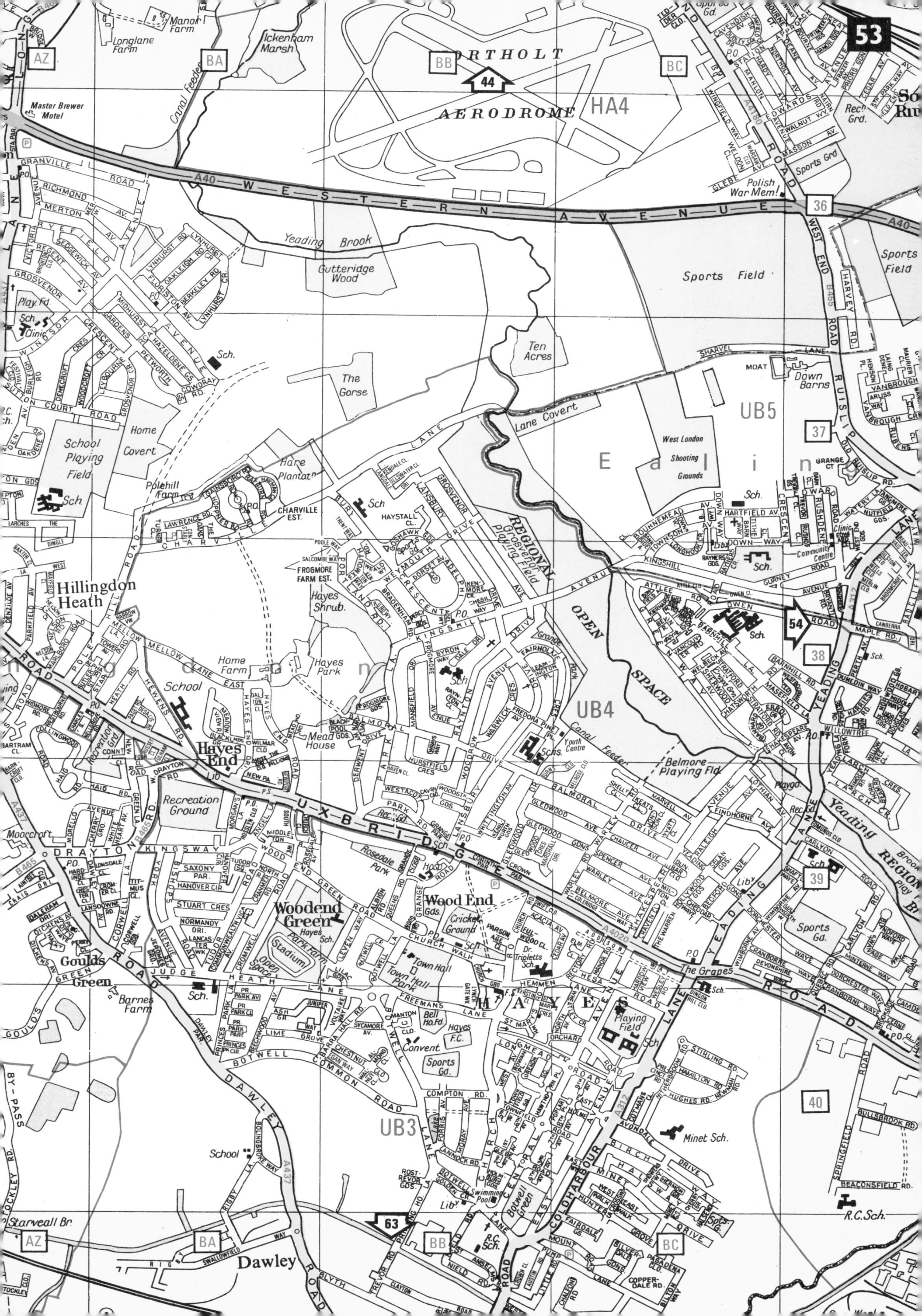
53
Manor Farm
Longlane Farm
Ickenham Marsh
NORTHOLT AERODROME
44
HA4
Master Brewer Motel
Canal Feeder
WESTERN AVENUE
A40
36
Polish War Meml.
Yeading Brook
Gutteridge Wood
Sports Field
Sports Field
Ten Acres
The Gorse
Sharvel Lane
Moat
Down Barns
UB5
Lane Covert
37
West London Shooting Grounds
Ealing
Home Covert
School Playing Field
Hare Plantatn
Polehill Farm
Charville Est.
Haystall Cl.
Frogmore Farm Est.
Hayes Shrub.
Regional Grosvenor Playing Field
Open Space
Kingshill Avenue
Owen Road
54
38
Hillingdon Heath
Hillingdon
Home Farm
Hayes Park
School
Mead House
Hayes End
Uxbridge Road
UB4
Youth Centre
Belmore Playing Fld.
Recreation Ground
Rosedale Park
Wood End
Woodend Green
Hayes Sch.
Park Farm
Stadium
Open Space
Cricket Ground
Town Hall
Town Hall Park
Dr. Tripletts Sch.
The Grapes
39
Sports Gd.
Yeading
Goulds Green
Barnes Farm
Bell Ho. Fd.
Hayes F.C.
Convent
Sports Gd.
HAYES
Playing Field
UB3
School
Dawley Road
A437
Minet Sch.
40
Lib.
Swimming Pool
Botwell Green
Coldharbour Lane
A312
R.C. Sch.
Starveall Br.
63
Dawley
AZ
BA
BB
BC

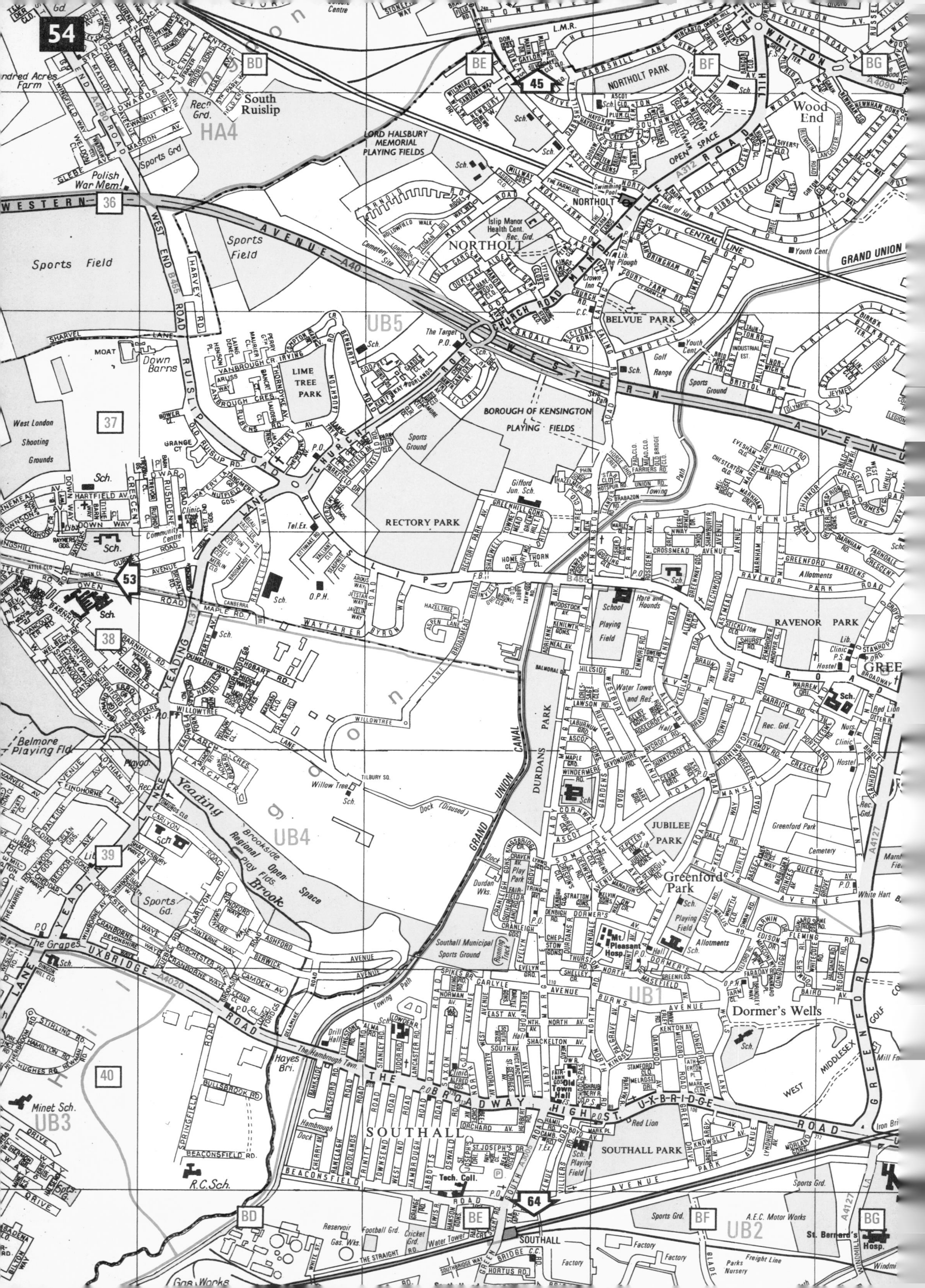
BD
BE
BF
BG
45
36
37
38
39
40
53
64
South Ruislip
HA4
LORD HALSBURY MEMORIAL PLAYING FIELDS
NORTHOLT PARK
Wood End
OPEN SPACE
Northolt
NORTHOLT
Islip Manor Health Cent.
WESTERN AVENUE
A40
Sports Field
UB5
LIME TREE PARK
BELVUE PARK
BOROUGH OF KENSINGTON PLAYING FIELDS
GRAND UNION
West London Shooting Grounds
RECTORY PARK
Gifford Jun. Sch.
RAVENOR PARK
DURDANS PARK
GRAND UNION CANAL
Belmore Playing Fld.
Yeading Brook
Brookside Regional Open Space Play Flds.
UB4
JUBILEE PARK
Greenford Park
Mt. Pleasant Hosp.
Southall Municipal Sports Ground
UB1
Dormer's Wells
WEST MIDDLESEX GOLF COURSE
UXBRIDGE ROAD
The Grapes
The Hambrough Tavn.
Hayes Bri.
THE BROADWAY
SOUTHALL
Old Town Hall
Red Lion
SOUTHALL PARK
Tech. Coll.
Minet Sch.
UB3
R.C.Sch.
Reservoir
Gas Wks.
Football Grd.
Cricket Grd.
Water Tower
A.E.C. Motor Works
St. Bernard's Hosp.
UB2
Gas Works
Factory
Parks Nursery
Freight Line

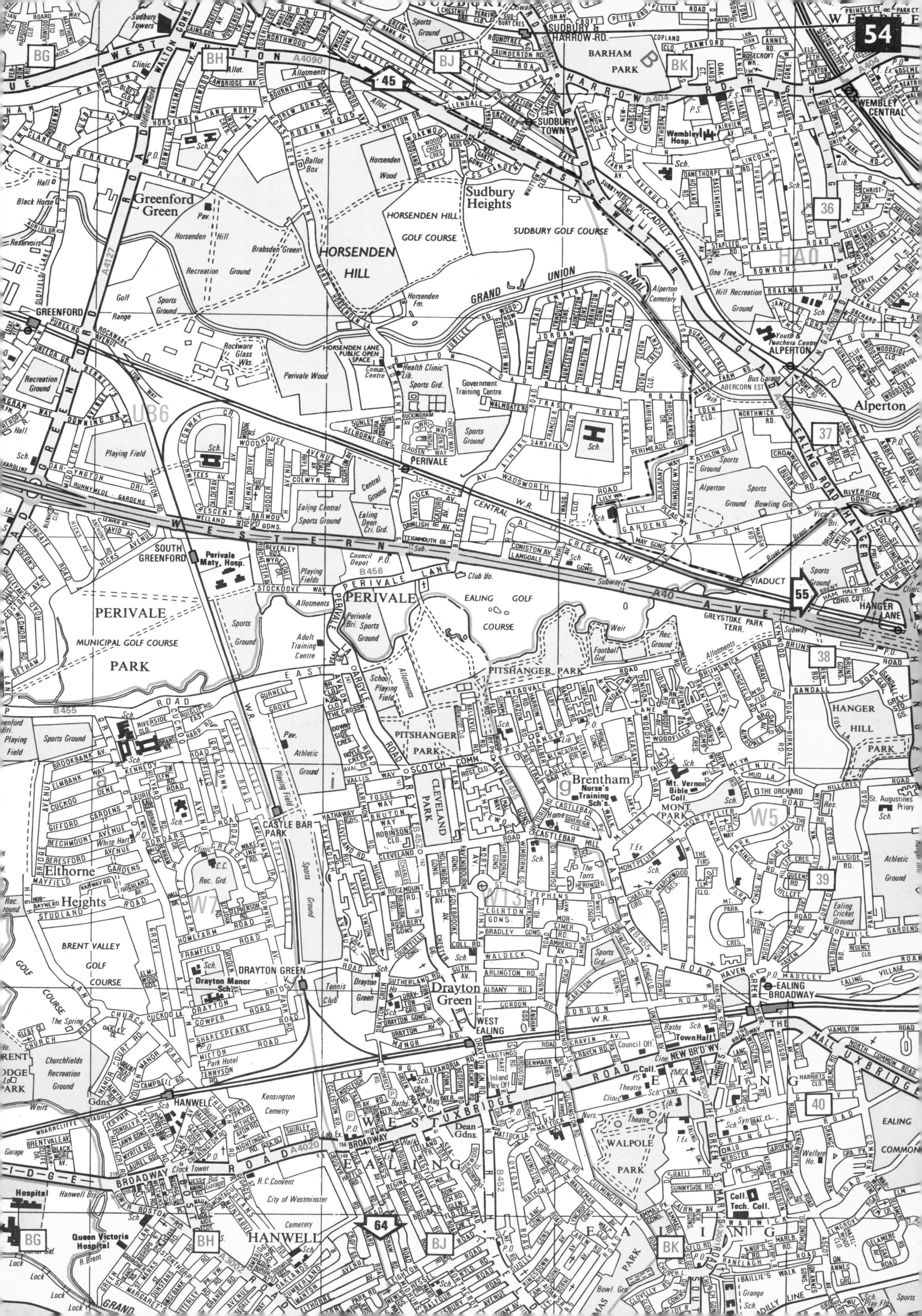

Sudbury Towers
Barham Park
Wembley Hosp.
Wembley Central
Sudbury & Harrow Rd.
Sudbury Town
Greenford Green
Horsenden Hill Golf Course
Horsenden Hill
Sudbury Heights
Sudbury Golf Course
Grand Union Canal
Alperton Cemetery
Alperton
Horsenden Wood
Greenford
Perivale Wood
Government Training Centre
Perivale
Rockware Glass Wks.
Recreation Ground
Playing Field
Ealing Central Sports Ground
Alperton Sports Ground
South Greenford
Perivale Maty. Hosp.
Western Avenue
Ealing Golf Course
Hanger Lane
Perivale Park
Municipal Golf Course
Pitshanger Park
Hanger Hill Park
Brentham
Mt. Vernon Bible Coll.
Castle Bar Park
Cleveland Park
Elthorne Heights
Brent Valley Golf Course
Drayton Green
Drayton Manor Sch.
West Ealing
Ealing Broadway
Town Hall
Ealing Common
Walpole Park
Hanwell
Kensington Cemetery
West Ealing
Broadway
Uxbridge Road
City of Westminster Cemetery
Queen Victoria Hospital
Churchfields Recreation Ground
Coll. Tech. Coll.
45
55
64
36
37
38
39
40
BG
BH
BJ
BK

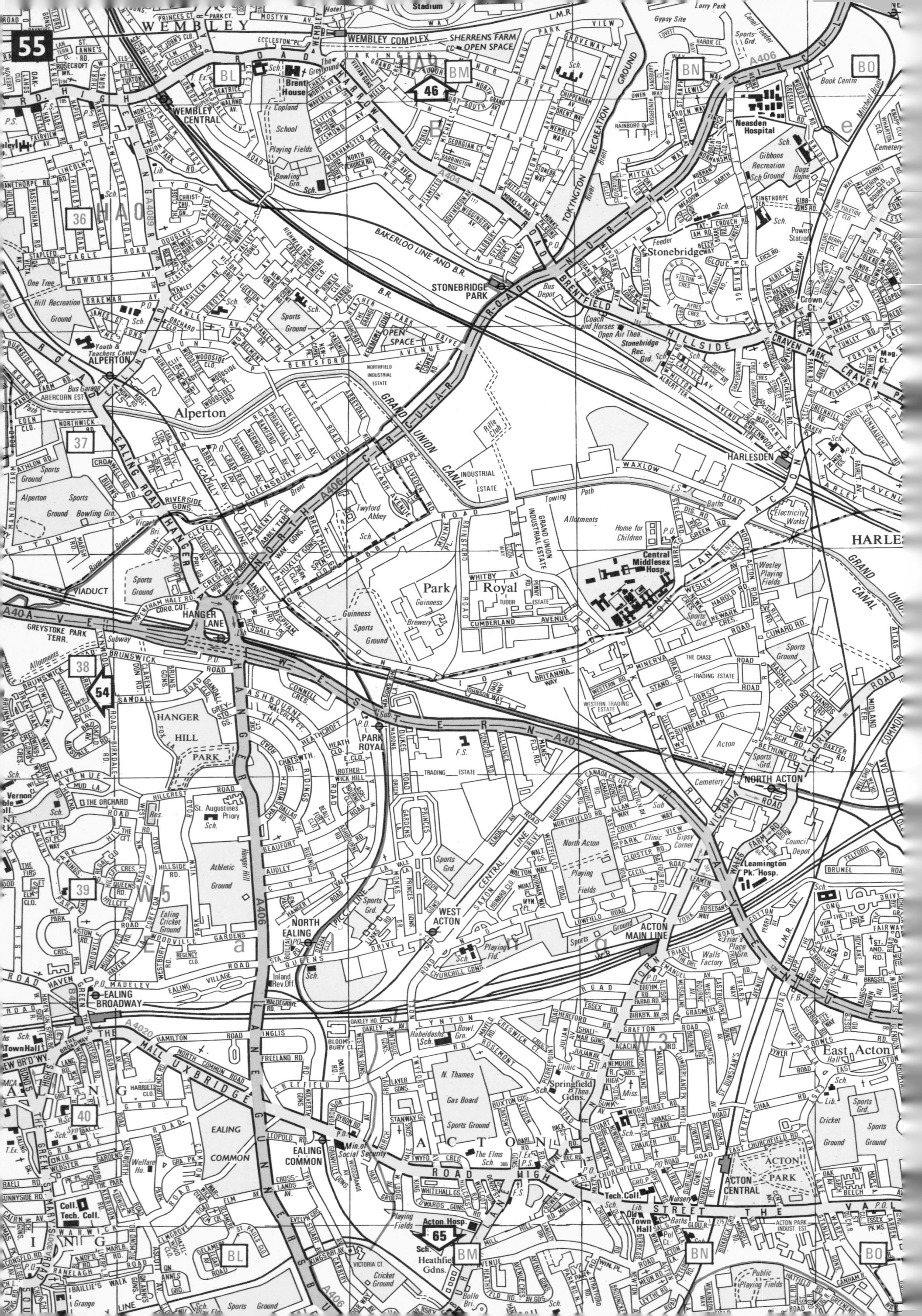
WEMBLEY
WEMBLEY COMPLEX
SHERRENS FARM OPEN SPACE
WEMBLEY CENTRAL
Brent House
Copland School Playing Fields
46
BL
BM
BN
BO
Neasden Hospital
Gibbons Recreation Ground
Dogs Home
Power Station
Book Centre
HA0
HA9
36
37
38
39
40
54
65
BAKERLOO LINE AND B.R.
STONEBRIDGE PARK
Stonebridge
Coach and Horses Open Air Thea.
Stonebridge Rec. Grd.
HILLSIDE
CRAVEN PARK
HARLESDEN
HARLES
GRAND UNION CANAL
NORTH CIRCULAR ROAD
A406
A404
A40
A4020
Alperton
ALPERTON
Youth & Teachers Centre
One Tree Hill Recreation Ground
Alperton Sports Ground
Bowling Grn.
OPEN SPACE
NORTHFIELD INDUSTRIAL ESTATE
Rifle Club
INDUSTRIAL ESTATE
GRAND UNION INDUSTRIAL ESTATE
WAXLOW ROAD
Allotments
Home for Children
Central Middlesex Hosp.
Electricity Works
Wesley Playing Fields
Twyford Abbey
Park Royal
Guinness Brewery
Guinness Sports Ground
HANGER LANE
VIADUCT
GREYSTOKE PARK TERR.
HANGER HILL PARK
WESTERN AVENUE
PARK ROYAL
TRADING ESTATE
THE CHASE TRADING ESTATE
WESTERN TRADING ESTATE
Acton Cemetery
NORTH ACTON
Council Depot
Leamington Pk. Hosp.
St. Augustines Priory
Athletic Ground
Ealing Cricket Ground
W5
NORTH EALING
WEST ACTON
North Acton Playing Fields
ACTON MAIN LINE
Walls Factory
Friar's Place Grn.
EALING BROADWAY
Inland Rev. Off.
Town Hall
EALING
EALING COMMON
UXBRIDGE ROAD
N. Thames Gas Board Sports Ground
Min. of Social Security
Springfield Gdns.
W3
ACTON
HIGH STREET
The Elms Sch.
Tech. Coll.
ACTON CENTRAL
ACTON PARK
East Acton
Cricket Ground
Sports Ground
Acton Hosp.
Heathfield Gdns.
Public Playing Fields
Bollo Bri.
THE VALE
ACTON PARK INDUST. EST.

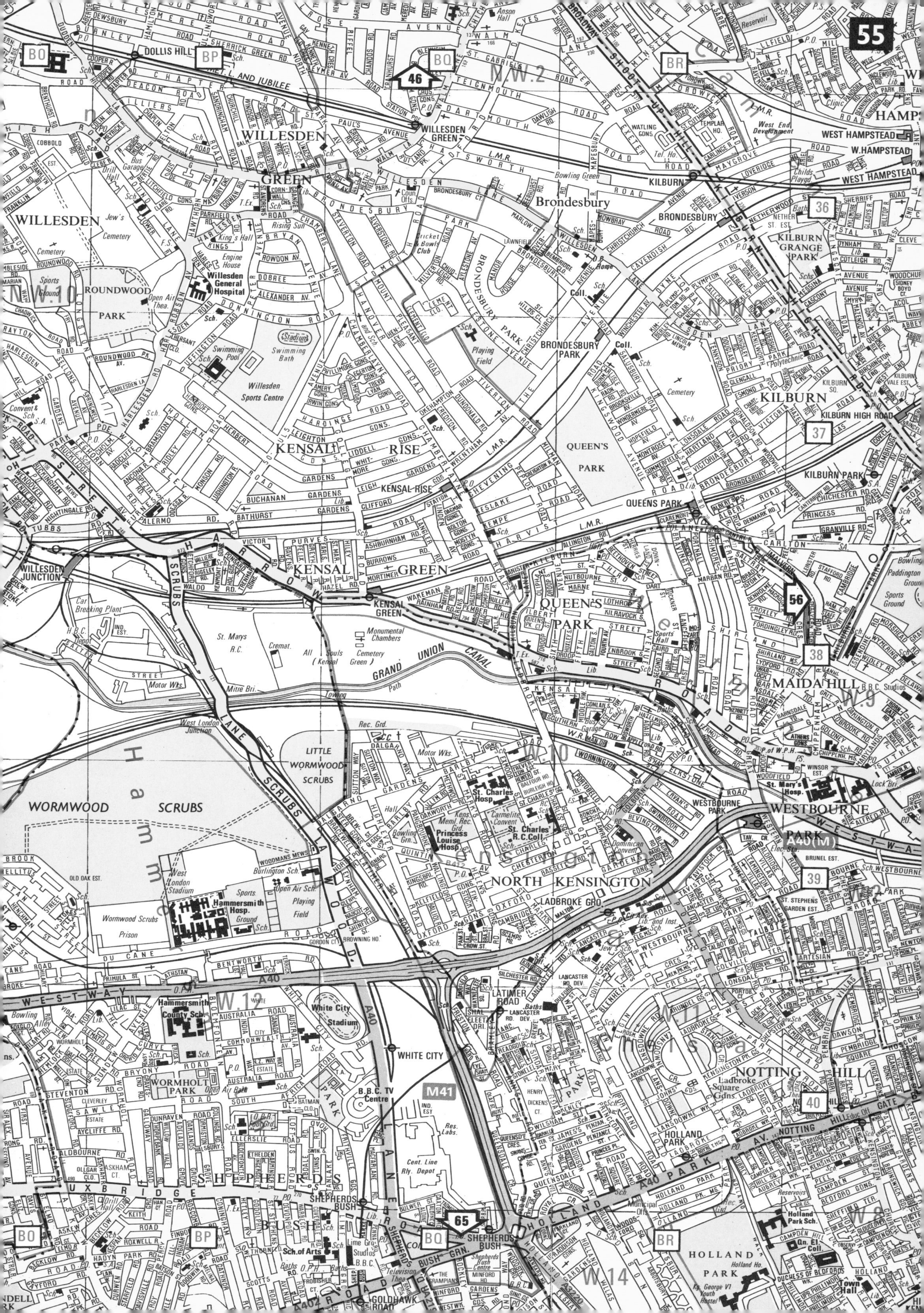
DOLLIS HILL
N.W.2
46
WILLESDEN GREEN
WILLESDEN
GREEN
KILBURN
WEST HAMPSTEAD
W.HAMPSTEAD
WEST HAMPSTEAD
Brondesbury
BRONDESBURY
36
KILBURN GRANGE PARK
WILLESDEN
Jew's Cemetery
Willesden General Hospital
ROUNDWOOD PARK
Sports Ground
N.W.10
N.W.6
BRONDESBURY PARK
Playing Field
Cemetery
KILBURN
KILBURN HIGH ROAD
Willesden Sports Centre
Swimming Pool
Swimming Bath
Stadium
QUEEN'S PARK
37
KENSAL RISE
KENSAL RISE
KILBURN PARK
QUEENS PARK
WILLESDEN JUNCTION
KENSAL GREEN
KENSAL GREEN
QUEEN'S PARK
56
Car Breaking Plant
St. Marys R.C.
Cremat.
All Souls (Kensal Green) Cemetery
Monumental Chambers
GRAND UNION CANAL
38
MAIDA HILL
W.9
W.10
LITTLE WORMWOOD SCRUBS
WORMWOOD SCRUBS
St. Charles Hosp.
Princess Louise Hosp.
St. Charles' R.C. Coll.
Dominican Convent
WESTBOURNE PARK
WESTBOURNE PARK
St. Mary's Hosp.
A40(M)
39
W.2
NORTH KENSINGTON
LADBROKE GRO.
West London Stadium
Hammersmith Hosp.
Wormwood Scrubs Prison
Playing Field
WESTWAY
A40
W.12
Hammersmith County Sch.
White City Stadium
WHITE CITY
LATIMER ROAD
W.11
NOTTING HILL
40
M41
B.B.C. TV Centre
Cent. Line Rly. Depot
WORMHOLT PARK
HOLLAND PARK
SHEPHERDS BUSH
SHEPHERDS BUSH
65
HOLLAND PARK
Holland Park Sch.
W.8
W.14
A40 HOLLAND PARK AV.
NOTTING HILL GATE
UXBRIDGE ROAD
GOLDHAWK ROAD
BO
BP
BQ
BR
BO
BP
BQ
BR

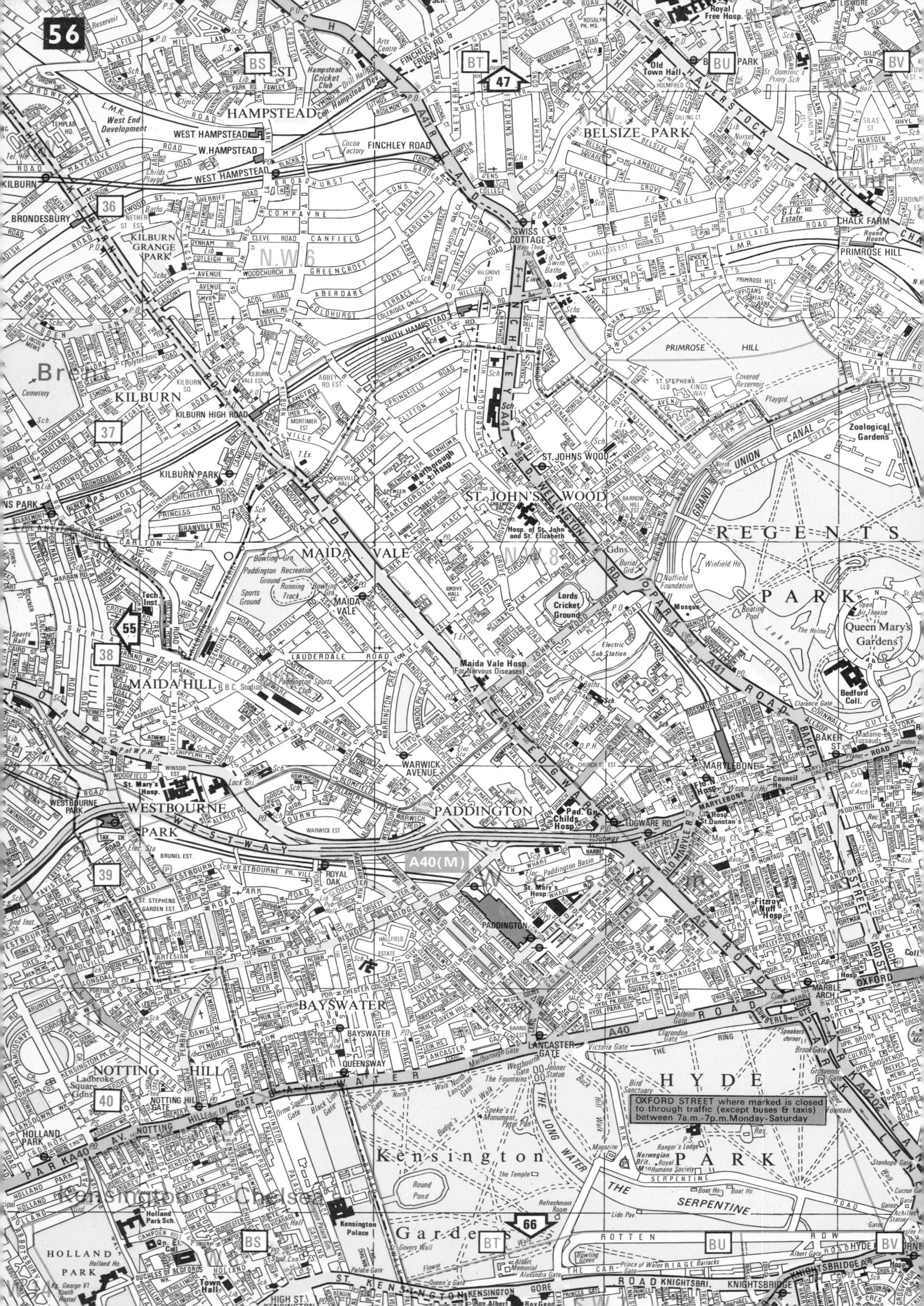
BS
BT
BU
BV
47
HAMPSTEAD
WEST HAMPSTEAD
W. HAMPSTEAD
Hampstead Cricket Club
West End Development
FINCHLEY ROAD
Cocoa Factory
BELSIZE PARK
Old Town Hall
Royal Free Hosp.
CHALK FARM
PRIMROSE HILL
SWISS COTTAGE
KILBURN
BRONDESBURY
KILBURN GRANGE PARK
N.W.6
36
37
38
39
40
55
KILBURN PARK
KILBURN HIGH ROAD
SOUTH HAMPSTEAD
PRIMROSE HILL
Zoological Gardens
REGENTS PARK
Queen Mary's Gardens
Open Air Theatre
Bedford Coll.
ST. JOHN'S WOOD
ST.JOHNS WOOD
Hosp. of St. John and St. Elizabeth
Marlborough Hosp.
N.W.8
Lords Cricket Ground
Winfield Ho.
Nuffield Foundation
Mosque
Boating Pool
MAIDA VALE
Paddington Recreation Ground
Running Track
Sports Ground
Maida Vale Hosp. (For Nervous Diseases)
MAIDA HILL
B.B.C. Studios
Paddington Sports Club
Electric Sub Station
BAKER ST
Madame Tussauds
MARYLEBONE
Council Ho.
WARWICK AVENUE
St. Mary's Hosp.
WESTBOURNE PARK
PADDINGTON
Pad. Gn. Childs Hosp.
EDGWARE RD.
WESTWAY
A40(M)
ROYAL OAK
Paddington Basin
PADDINGTON
Fitzroy Nuff Hosp.
BAYSWATER
QUEENSWAY
LANCASTER GATE
MARBLE ARCH
OXFORD
NOTTING HILL
Ladbroke Square Gdns
NOTTING HILL GATE
HOLLAND PARK
HYDE PARK
OXFORD STREET where marked is closed to through traffic (except buses & taxis) between 7a.m.-7p.m. Monday-Saturday
Kensington Gardens
THE LONG WATER
THE SERPENTINE
Round Pond
Kensington Palace
Speke's Monument
Peter Pan
The Fountains
Bird Sanctuary
Speakers Corner
Holland Park Sch.
Town Hall
HOLLAND PARK
Holland Ho.
66
ROTTEN ROW
Albert Memorial
KENSINGTON GORE
KNIGHTSBRIDGE
Kensington & Chelsea

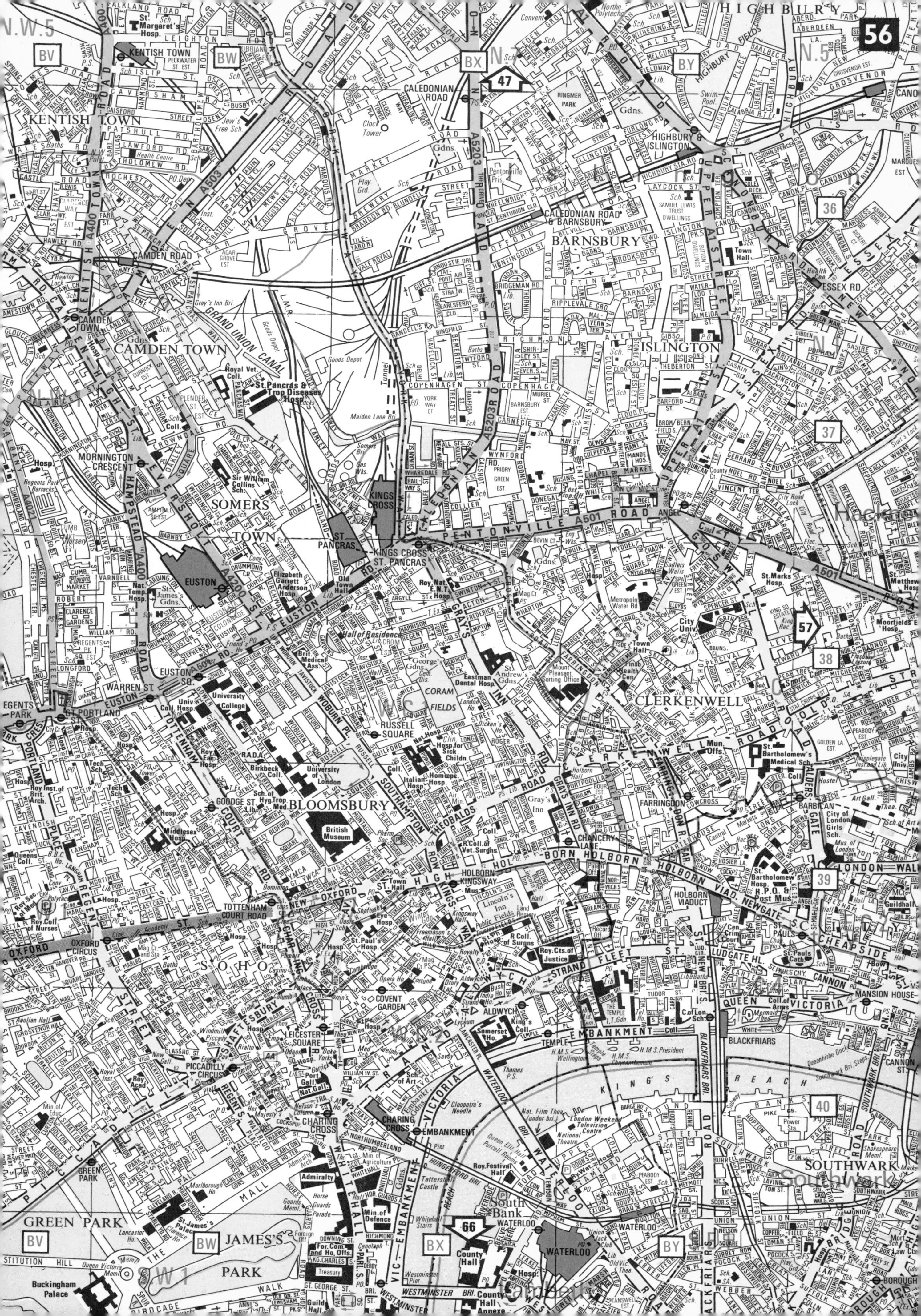

56
HIGHBURY
N.W.5
N.5
N.7
BV
BW
BX
BY
47
36
37
38
39
40
57
66
KENTISH TOWN
CAMDEN TOWN
CAMDEN ROAD
SOMERS TOWN
EUSTON
ST PANCRAS
KINGS CROSS
KINGS CROSS ST. PANCRAS
CALEDONIAN ROAD
CALEDONIAN ROAD & BARNSBURY
BARNSBURY
ISLINGTON
HIGHBURY & ISLINGTON
ANGEL
CLERKENWELL
MORNINGTON CRESCENT
EUSTON SQ.
WARREN ST.
GT PORTLAND
RUSSELL SQUARE
BLOOMSBURY
British Museum
University of London
University College
GOODGE ST.
TOTTENHAM COURT ROAD
OXFORD CIRCUS
HOLBORN KINGSWAY
CHANCERY LANE
FARRINGDON
BARBICAN
ST. PAULS
MANSION HOUSE
BLACKFRIARS
SOHO
LEICESTER SQUARE
COVENT GARDEN
PICCADILLY CIRCUS
CHARING CROSS
EMBANKMENT
TEMPLE
ALDWYCH
GREEN PARK
ST. JAMES'S PARK
Buckingham Palace
WATERLOO
SOUTHWARK
BOROUGH
GRAND UNION CANAL
PENTONVILLE ROAD
EUSTON ROAD
A501
A503
A400
A4200
A5203
A5203 ROAD
KING'S REACH
WATERLOO BRI.
BLACKFRIARS BRI.
WESTMINSTER BRI.
HUNGERFORD BRI.
VICTORIA EMBANKMENT
STRAND
FLEET ST.
HOLBORN VIADUCT
NEWGATE ST.
CHEAPSIDE
LONDON WALL
QUEEN VICTORIA ST.
CANNON ST.
LUDGATE HL.
CORAM FIELDS
Gray's Inn
Lincoln's Inn Fields
Roy. Cts. of Justice
Somerset Ho.
National Theatre
Roy. Festival Hall
County Hall
Admiralty
Min. of Defence
Nat. Gall.
Middlesex Hosp.
St. Bartholomew's Hosp.
Mount Pleasant Sorting Office
City Univ.
Sadlers Wells
Pentonville Pris.
Highbury Fields
Regents Park Barracks
S.W.1
W.C.1

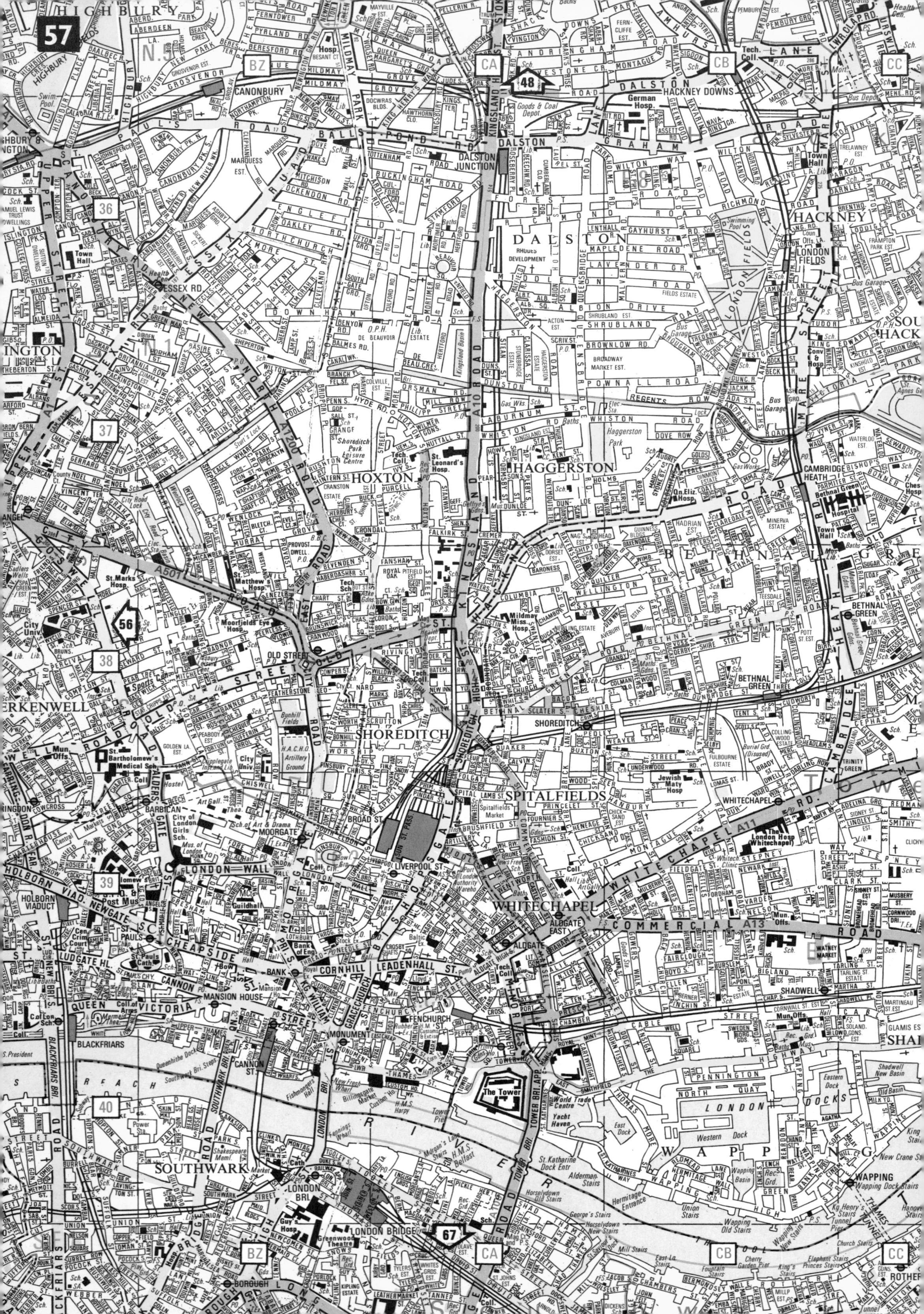

57
HIGHBURY
BZ
CA
CB
CC
48
36
37
38
39
40
56
67
CANONBURY
DALSTON
HACKNEY DOWNS
DALSTON JUNCTION
HACKNEY
LONDON FIELDS
HAGGERSTON
HOXTON
SHOREDITCH
BETHNAL GREEN
CAMBRIDGE HEATH
SPITALFIELDS
WHITECHAPEL
ALDGATE EAST
ALDGATE
SHADWELL
WAPPING
LONDON DOCKS
SOUTHWARK
LONDON BRIDGE
BLACKFRIARS
MANSION HOUSE
MONUMENT
BANK
MOORGATE
LIVERPOOL ST.
OLD STREET
BARBICAN
ANGEL
HOLBORN VIADUCT
ST. PAULS
CANNON ST.
FENCHURCH
BOROUGH
CLERKENWELL
ISLINGTON
The Tower
RIVER THAMES
KINGSLAND ROAD A10
NEW NORTH ROAD A1200
CITY ROAD
COMMERCIAL ROAD A13
WHITECHAPEL ROAD A11
CHEAPSIDE
CORNHILL
LEADENHALL ST.
LONDON WALL
BISHOPSGATE
TOWER BRIDGE
ESSEX RD.
UPPER STREET
HACKNEY ROAD
MARE STREET
CAMBRIDGE HEATH ROAD
REGENTS CANAL
BALLS POND RD.
GRAHAM ROAD
QUEEN VICTORIA ST.

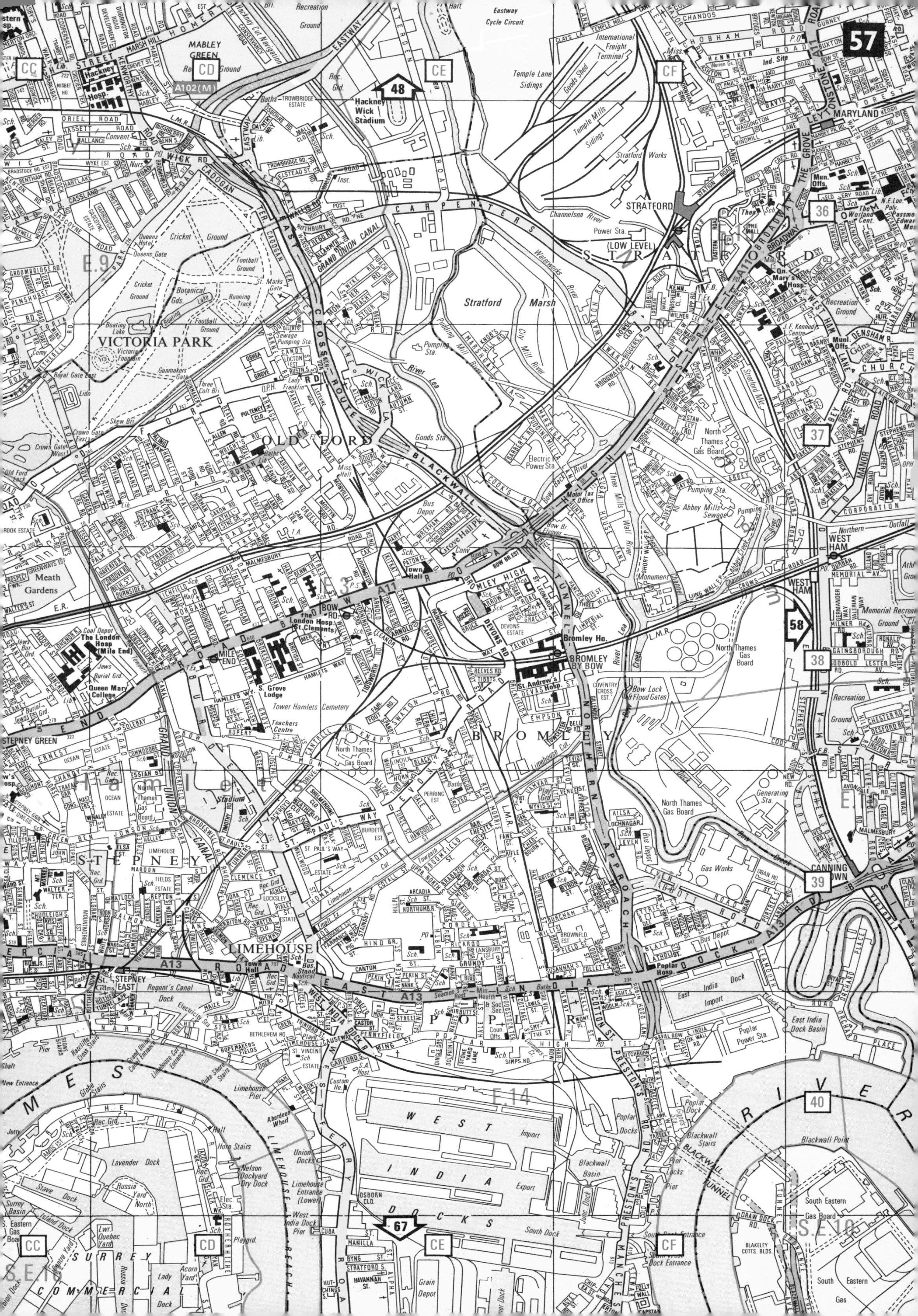

57
CC
CD
CE
CF
48
36
37
58
38
39
40
67
MABLEY GREEN
Hackney Wick Stadium
Eastway Cycle Circuit
International Freight Terminal
Temple Lane Sidings
Temple Mills Sidings
Stratford Works
STRATFORD
(LOW LEVEL)
STRATFORD
MARYLAND
E.9
VICTORIA PARK
Stratford Marsh
Channelsea River
Waterworks River
River Lea
Pudding Mill River
City Mill River
OLD FORD
BLACKWALL
Bus Depot
Grove Hall Pk.
E.3
BOW
Bow Road
The London Hosp (Mile End)
Queen Mary College
MILE END
Tower Hamlets Cemetery
Bromley Ho.
BROMLEY BY BOW
St. Andrew's Hosp.
BROMLEY
North Thames Gas Board
Abbey Mills Sewage
Pumping Sta.
WEST HAM
Memorial Recreation Ground
Bow Lock & Flood Gates
Limehouse Cut
Generating Sta.
Gas Works
CANNING TOWN
STEPNEY GREEN
Meath Gardens
Hamlets
STEPNEY
LIMEHOUSE
Regent's Canal Dock
STEPNEY EAST
POPLAR
East India Dock
East India Dock Basin
Poplar Power Sta.
A13
A11
A102(M)
E.14
WEST INDIA DOCKS
Limehouse Pier
Poplar Docks
Blackwall Basin
Blackwall Point
RIVER
Lavender Dock
Surrey Basin
SURREY COMMERCIAL
S.E.16
S.E.10
South Eastern Gas Board
Grain Depot
South Dock

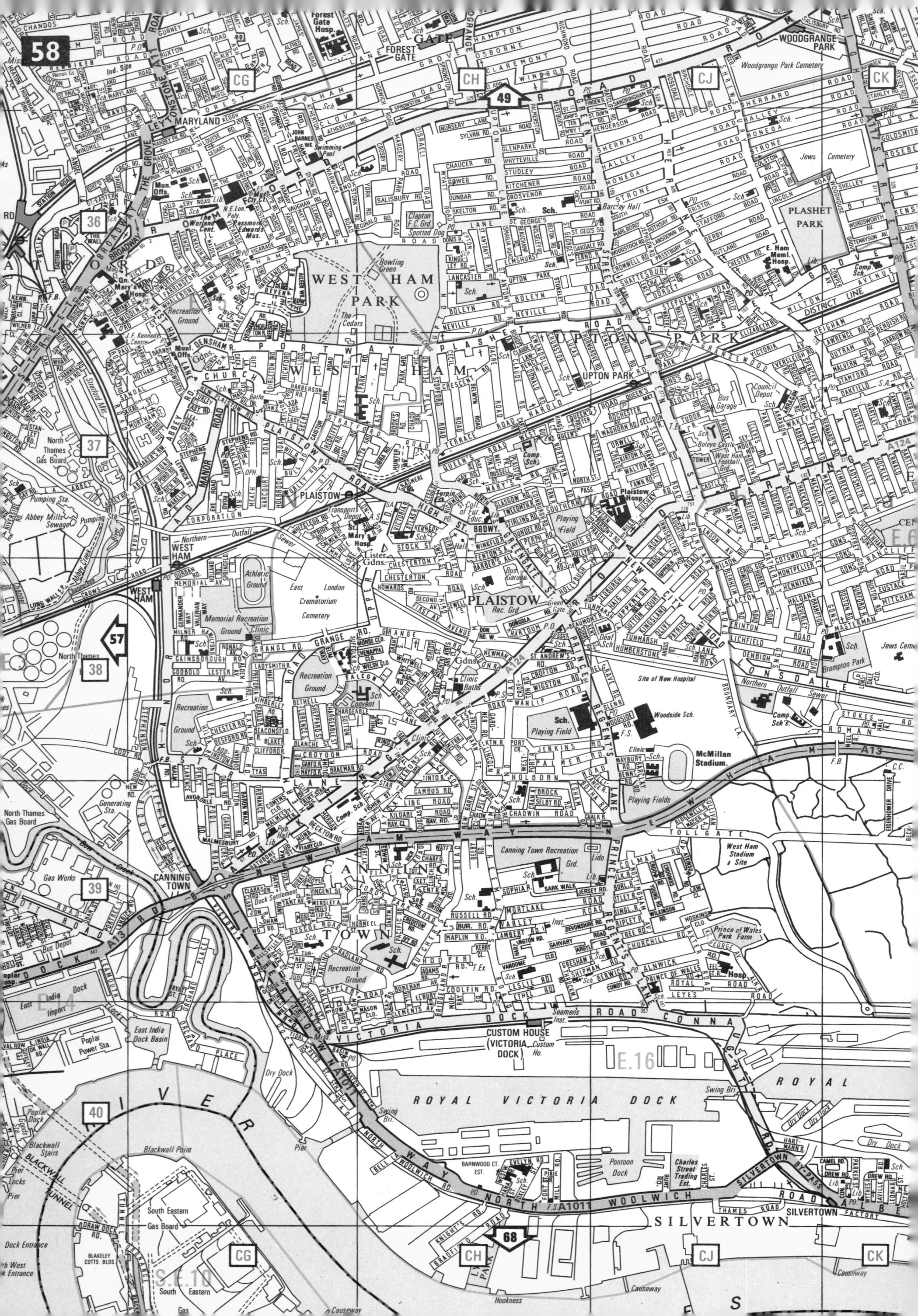
FOREST GATE
WOODGRANGE PARK
Woodgrange Park Cemetery
MARYLAND
WEST HAM PARK
Jews Cemetery
PLASHET PARK
UPTON PARK
WEST HAM
PLAISTOW
East London Crematorium Cemetery
Memorial Recreation Ground
North Thames Gas Board
Abbey Mills Sewage Pumping Sta.
Northern Outfall Sewer
DISTRICT LINE
Site of New Hospital
McMillan Stadium
Woodside Sch.
Canning Town Recreation Grd.
CANNING TOWN
West Ham Stadium Site
Prince of Wales Park Farm
CUSTOM HOUSE (VICTORIA DOCK)
ROYAL VICTORIA DOCK
ROYAL
East India Dock Basin
Poplar Power Sta.
Blackwall Point
BLACKWALL TUNNEL
RIVER
South Eastern Gas Board
Pontoon Dock
Charles Street Trading Est.
SILVERTOWN
E.16
S.E.10
CG
CH
CJ
CK
49
57
68
36
37
38
39
40

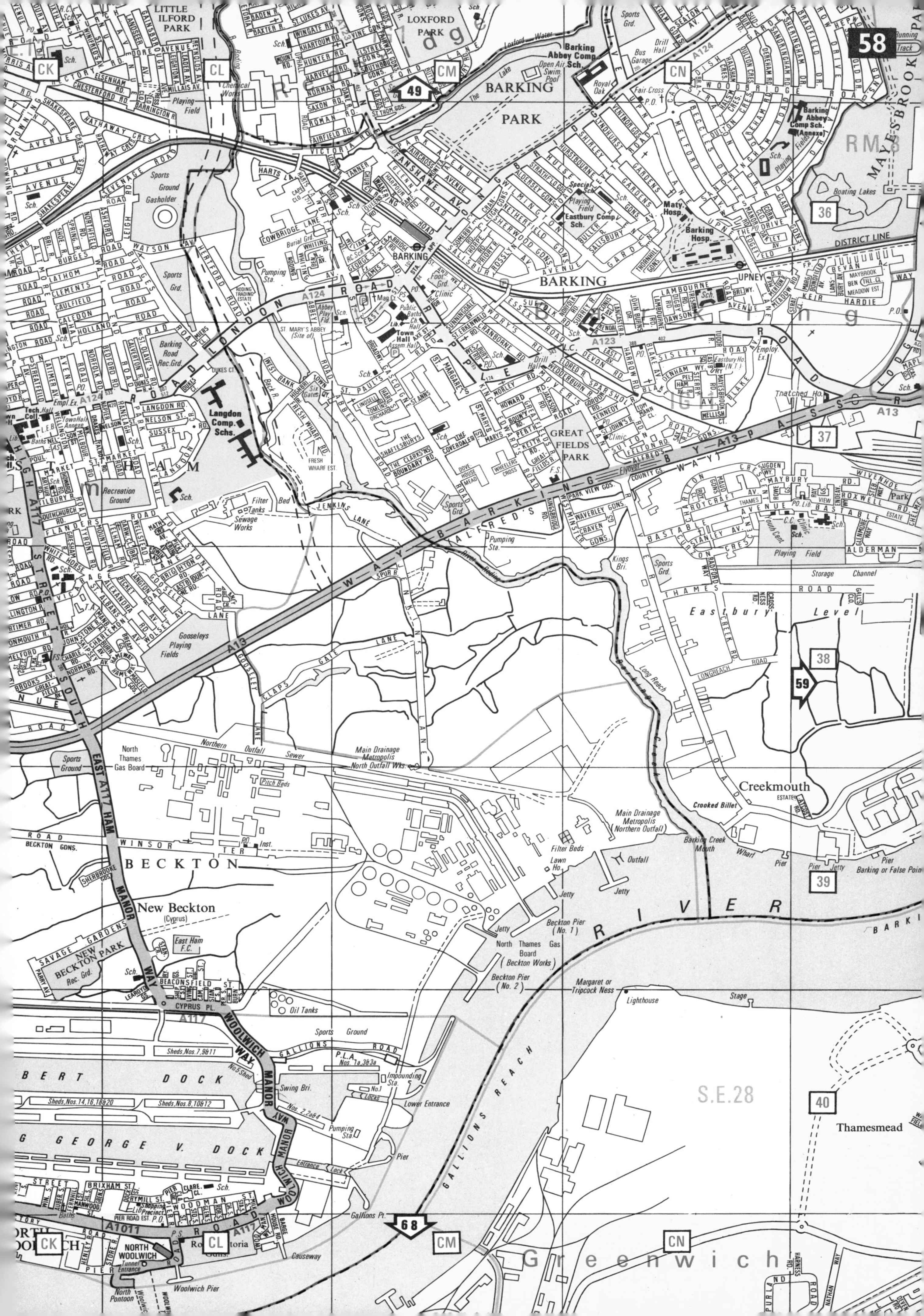
LITTLE ILFORD PARK
LOXFORD PARK
CK
CL
CM
CN
49
BARKING PARK
Barking Abbey Comp. Sch.
Barking Abbey Comp Sch. (Annexe)
RM8
MAYESBROOK
Boating Lakes
36
DISTRICT LINE
BARKING
UPNEY
Town Hall
ST. MARY'S ABBEY (Site of)
Langdon Comp. Schs.
Eastbury Comp Sch.
Maty. Hosp.
Barking Hosp.
GREAT FIELDS PARK
BARKING BY-PASS
A13
A124
A123
A117
A1011
37
Thatched Ho.
Recreation Ground
Sewage Works
Filter Tanks
Gooseleys Playing Fields
Eastbury Level
Storage Channel
THAMES ROAD
LONGREACH ROAD
Long Reach
Barking Creek
38
59
Creekmouth
Crooked Billet
Barking Creek Mouth
Barking or False Point
39
North Thames Gas Board
Main Drainage Metropolis North Outfall Wks.
Northern Outfall Sewer
Main Drainage Metropolis (Northern Outfall)
Filter Beds
Outfall
Jetty
BECKTON
New Beckton (Cyprus)
East Ham F.C.
NEW BECKTON PARK
CYPRUS PL.
Beckton Pier (No. 1)
North Thames Gas Board (Beckton Works)
Beckton Pier (No. 2)
Margaret or Tripcock Ness
Lighthouse
RIVER
Oil Tanks
Sports Ground
ALBERT DOCK
KING GEORGE V. DOCK
GALLIONS REACH
Gallions Pt.
S.E.28
40
Thamesmead
68
NORTH WOOLWICH
Woolwich Pier
Greenwich

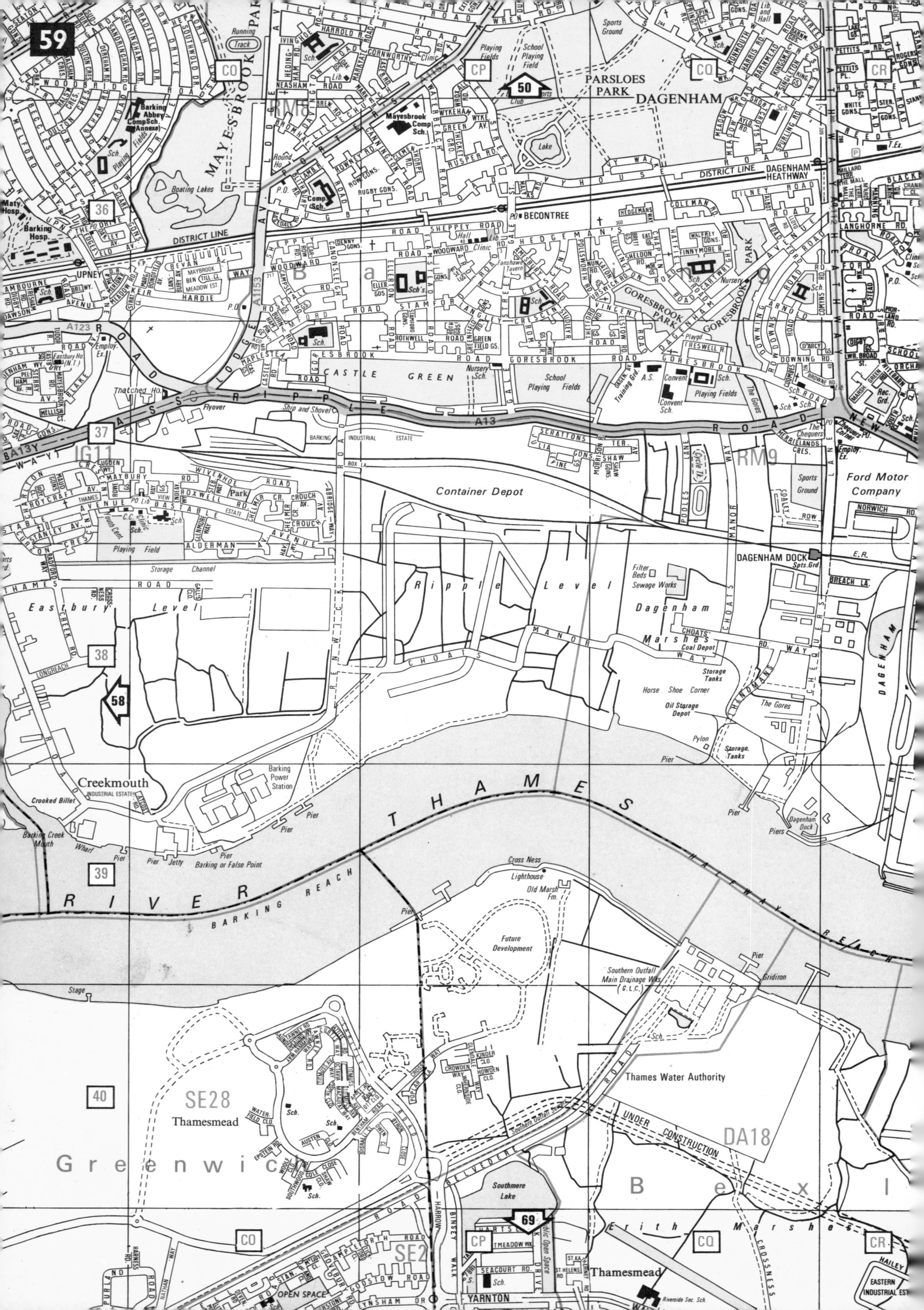
MAYESBROOK PARK
PARSLOES PARK
DAGENHAM
Sports Ground
Playing Fields
School Playing Field
Lake
Boating Lakes
Running Track
Barking Abbey Comp.Sch. (Annexe)
Mayesbrook Comp Sch.
Barking Hosp.
Maty. Hosp.
DISTRICT LINE
UPNEY
BECONTREE
DAGENHAM HEATHWAY
Fanshawe Tavern
GORESBROOK PARK
CASTLE GREEN
School Playing Fields
Playing Fields
The Gores
Convent Sch.
Training Grd.
Thatched Ho.
Flyover
Ship and Shovel
BARKING INDUSTRIAL ESTATE
RIPPLE ROAD
A13
The Chequers
Chequers Corner
Ford Motor Company
Container Depot
Sports Ground
DAGENHAM DOCK
Playing Field
Storage Channel
THAMES ROAD
Eastbury Level
Ripple Level
Dagenham Marshes
Filter Beds
Sewage Works
Coal Depot
Storage Tanks
Horse Shoe Corner
Oil Storage Depot
Pylon
Pier
Creekmouth INDUSTRIAL ESTATE
Crooked Billet
Barking Power Station
Barking Creek Mouth
Wharf
Jetty
Barking or False Point
Dagenham Dock
Piers
RIVER THAMES
BARKING REACH
HALFWAY REACH
Cross Ness Lighthouse
Old Marsh Fm.
Future Development
Southern Outfall Main Drainage Wks (G.L.C.)
Gridiron
Stage
Thames Water Authority
UNDER CONSTRUCTION
SE28
Thamesmead
Greenwich
Southmere Lake
Bexley
Erith Marshes
BELVEDERE ROAD
HARROW
BINSEY WALK
Public Open Space
OPEN SPACE
YARNTON
Riverside Sec. Sch.
EASTERN INDUSTRIAL EST
SE2
DA18
IG11
RM9
RM8
CO
CP
CQ
CR
36
37
38
39
40
50
58
69

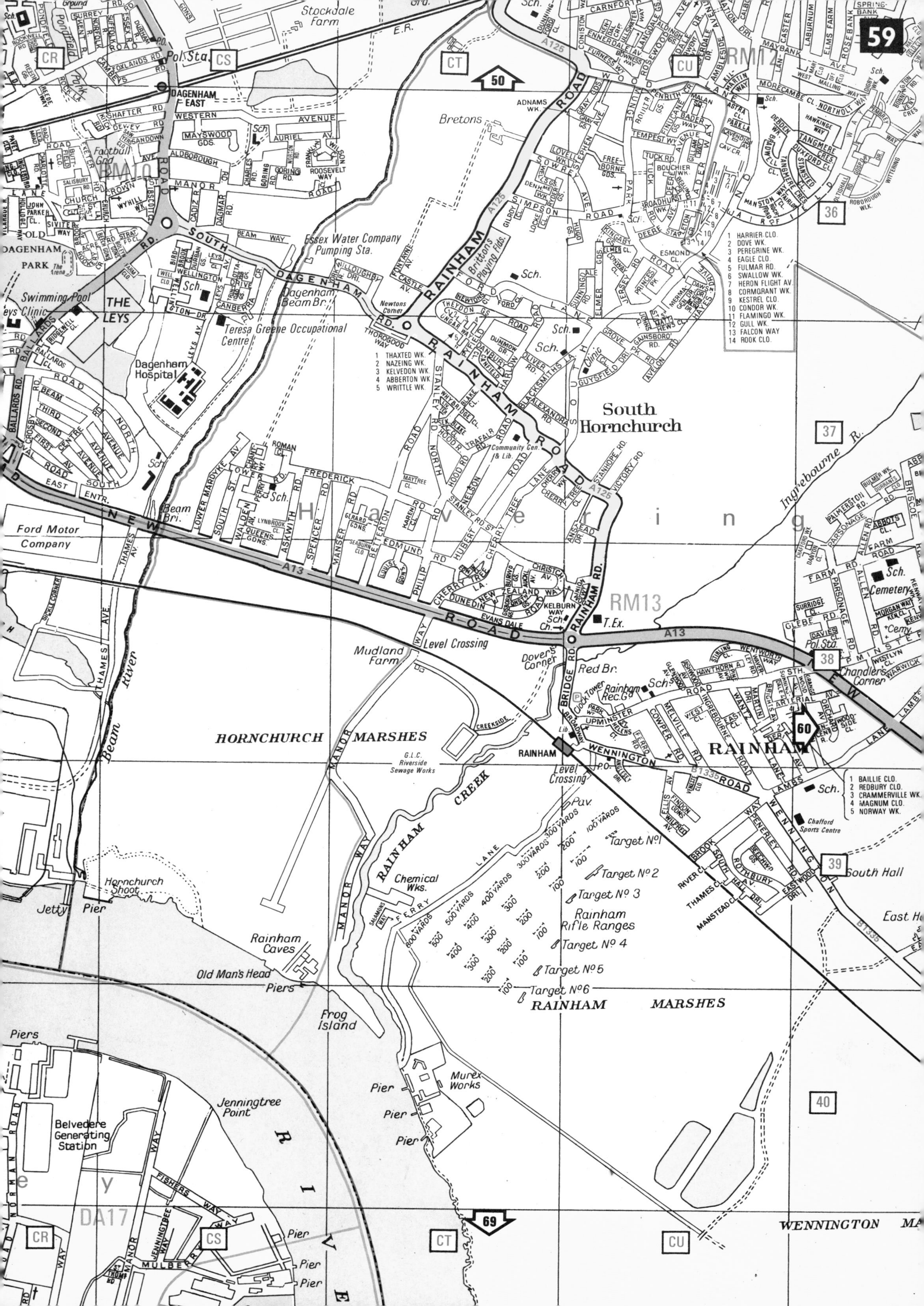

Stockdale Farm
CR
CS
CT
CU
50
RM12
Pol.Sta.
DAGENHAM EAST
SHAFTER RD.
WESTERN AVENUE
MAYSWOOD GDS.
AURIEL AV.
ALDBOROUGH RD.
GORING RD.
ROOSEVELT WAY
MANOR ROAD
CADIZ RD.
DAGMAR RD.
Football Gnd
RM10
CHURCH
CROWN
WYHILL WK.
OLD DAGENHAM PARK
The Arena
SOUTH RD.
BEAM WAY
Essex Water Company Pumping Sta.
Bretons
ADNAMS WK.
WOOD LANE
Swimming Pool
THE LEYS
WELLINGTON
Sch.
CANBERRA CR.
DAGENHAM RD.
Dagenham Beam Br.
Newtons Corner
RAINHAM RD.
Brittons Playing Flds.
THOROGOOD WAY
Teresa Greene Occupational Centre
Dagenham Hospital
1 THAXTED WK.
2 NAZEING WK.
3 KELVEDON WK.
4 ABBERTON WK.
5 WRITTLE WK.
1 HARRIER CLO.
2 DOVE WK.
3 PEREGRINE WK.
4 EAGLE CLO.
5 FULMAR RD.
6 SWALLOW WK.
7 HERON FLIGHT AV.
8 CORMORANT WK.
9 KESTREL CLO.
10 CONDOR WK.
11 FLAMINGO WK.
12 GULL WK.
13 FALCON WAY
14 ROOK CLO.
36
BALLARDS RD.
BEAM AVENUE
NORTH AVENUE
SOUTH AVENUE
EAST ENTR.
ROMAN CL.
FREDERICK RD.
LOWER MARDYKE AV.
ASKWITH RD.
SPENCER RD.
MANSER RD.
EDMUND RD.
PHILIP RD.
CHERRY TREE LA.
SOUTH END RD.
South Hornchurch
Community Cen. & Lib.
Clinic
37
Ingrebourne R.
Beam Bri.
Ford Motor Company
NEW ROAD
A13
Havering
THAMES AV.
RM13
T.Ex.
RAINHAM RD.
Mudland Farm
Level Crossing
Dovers Corner
Red Br.
BRIDGE RD.
Rainham Rec.Gd
Clock Tower
UPMINSTER RD.
WENNINGTON RD.
B1335
RAINHAM
Lib.
Level Crossing
38
Pol.Sta.
Chandlers Corner
Cemetery
60
HORNCHURCH MARSHES
MANOR WAY
G.L.C. Riverside Sewage Works
RAINHAM CREEK
CREEKSIDE
1 BAILLIE CLO.
2 REDBURY CLO.
3 CRAMMERVILLE WK.
4 MAGNUM CLO.
5 NORWAY WK.
Chafford Sports Centre
39
South Hall
East Ha
Beam River
Hornchurch Shoot
Jetty
Pier
Chemical Wks.
FERRY LANE
Target No 1
Target No 2
Target No 3
Rainham Rifle Ranges
Target No 4
Target No 5
Target No 6
RAINHAM MARSHES
Rainham Caves
Old Man's Head
Piers
Frog Island
Piers
Murex Works
Jenningtree Point
Belvedere Generating Station
Pier
40
RIVER
DA17
FISHERS WAY
NORMAN ROAD
MANOR WAY
JENNINGTREE WAY
69
WENNINGTON MA

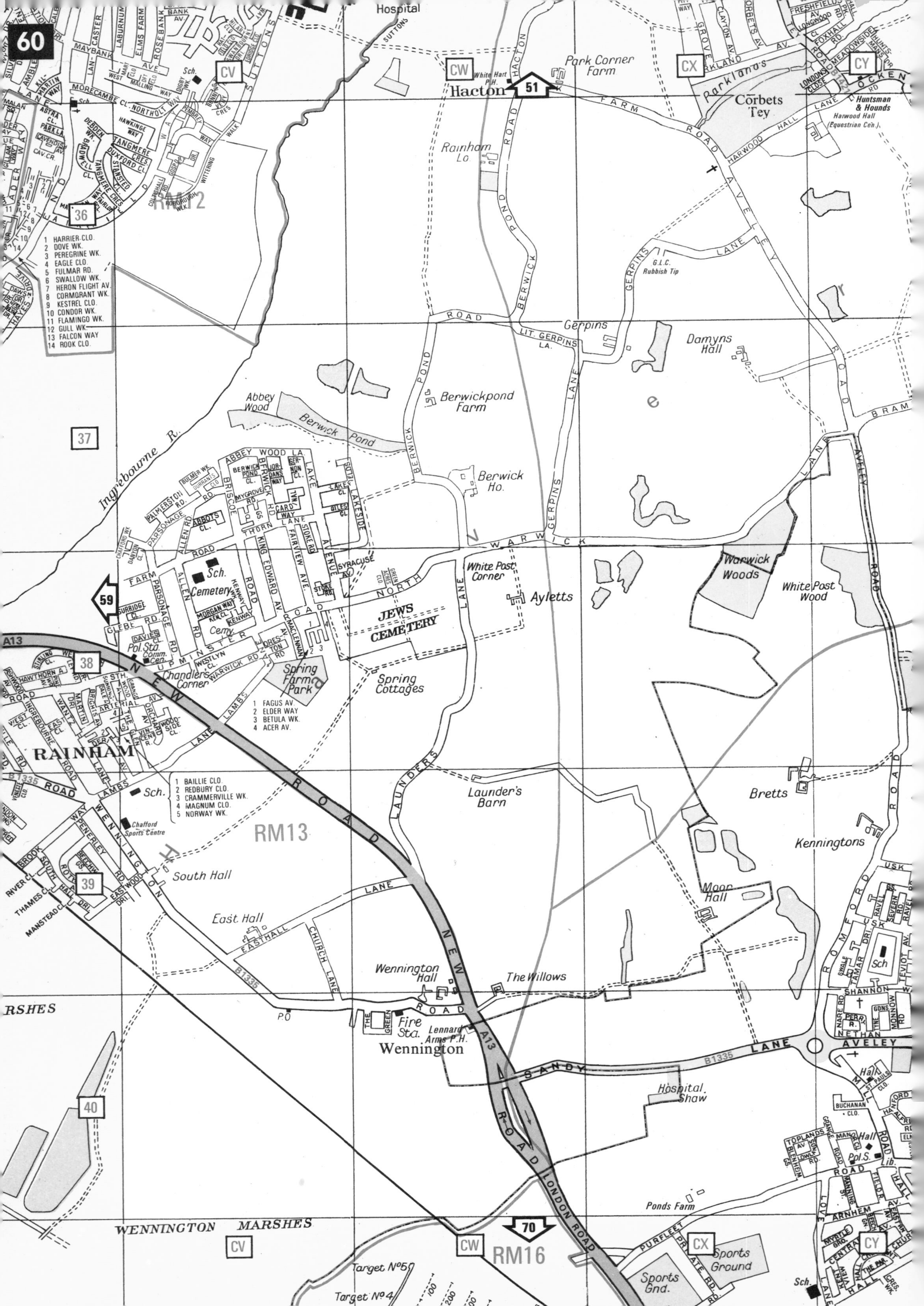
Hospital
Hacton
51
Park Corner Farm
Corbets Tey
Huntsman & Hounds
Harwood Hall (Equestrian Cen.)
Rainham Lo
RM12
1 HARRIER CLO.
2 DOVE WK.
3 PEREGRINE WK.
4 EAGLE CLO.
5 FULMAR RD.
6 SWALLOW WK.
7 HERON FLIGHT AV.
8 CORMORANT WK.
9 KESTREL CLO.
10 CONDOR WK.
11 FLAMINGO WK.
12 GULL WK.
13 FALCON WAY
14 ROOK CLO.
G.L.C. Rubbish Tip
Gerpins
Damyns Hall
Abbey Wood
Berwick Pond
Berwickpond Farm
Berwick Ho.
Ingrebourne R.
59
White Post Corner
Ayletts
JEWS CEMETERY
Warwick Woods
White Post Wood
Spring Farm Park
Spring Cottages
Chandlers Corner
1 FAGUS AV.
2 ELDER WAY
3 BETULA WK.
4 ACER AV.
RAINHAM
1 BAILLIE CLO.
2 REDBURY CLO.
3 CRAMMERVILLE WK.
4 MAGNUM CLO.
5 NORWAY WK.
Chafford Sports Centre
RM13
Launder's Barn
Bretts
Kenningtons
South Hall
Moor Hall
East Hall
Wennington Hall
The Willows
Fire Sta.
Lennard Arms P.H.
Wennington
Hospital Shaw
WENNINGTON MARSHES
70
RM16
Ponds Farm
Sports Ground
Sports Gnd.
Target No5
Target No4
CV
CW
CX
CY
36
37
38
39
40
A13
B1335
NEW ROAD
LONDON ROAD
SANDY LANE
AVELEY ROAD

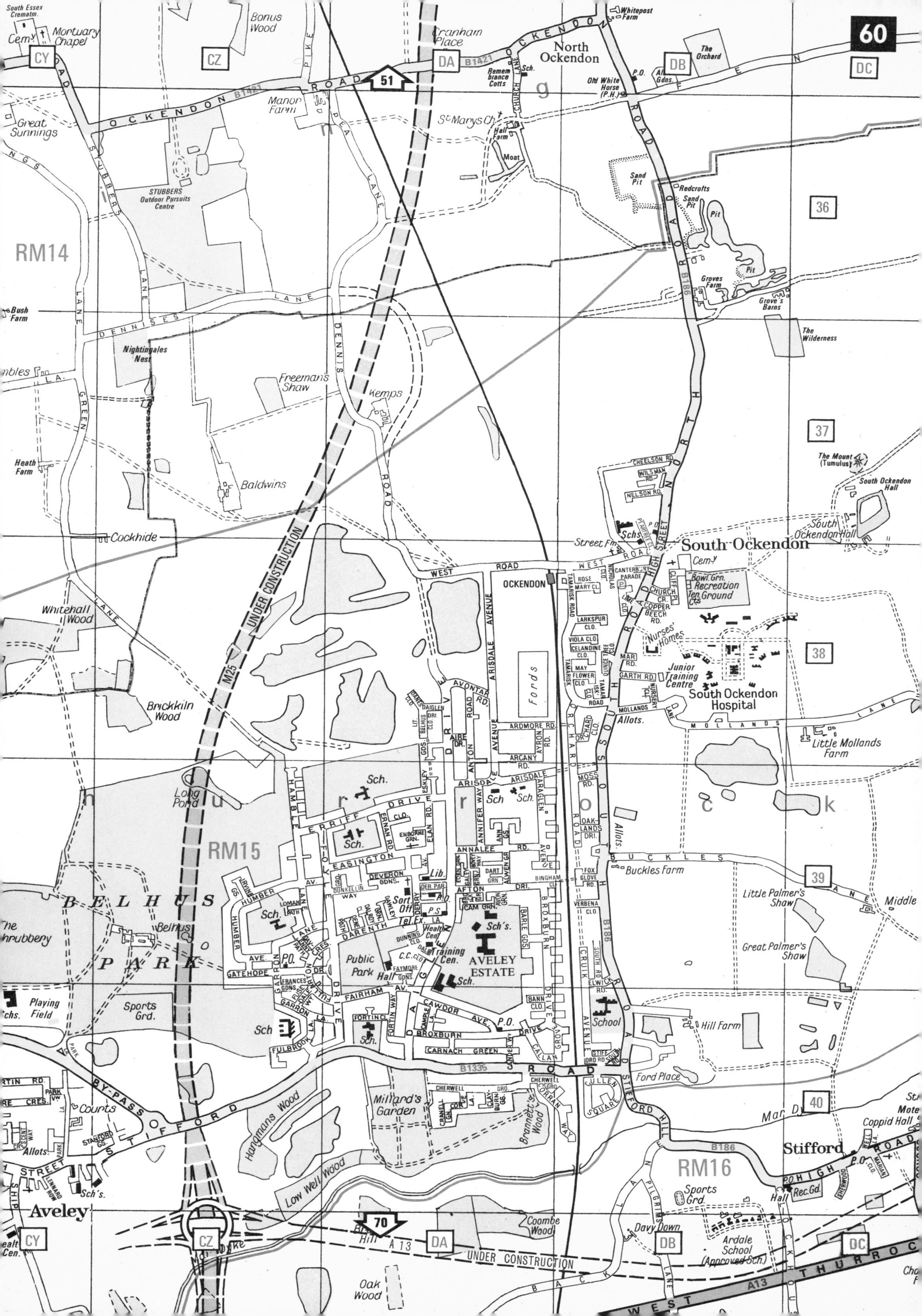

South Essex Cremat.
Cemy
Mortuary Chapel
CY
CZ
DA
DB
DC
Bonus Wood
Cranham Place
51
B1421
OCKENDON ROAD
North Ockendon
Whitepost Farm
The Orchard
Remembrance Cotts
Sch.
CHURCH LANE
P.O.
Old White Horse (P.H.)
Great Sunnings
Manor Farm
St Marys Ch.
Hall Farm
Moat
STUBBERS LANE
STUBBERS Outdoor Pursuits Centre
PEA LANE
Sand Pit
Redcrofts
Pit
36
RM14
Groves Farm
Grove's Barns
B186
Bush Farm
DENNISES LANE
Nightingales Nest
DENNIS ROAD
The Wilderness
GREEN LANE
Freeman's Shaw
Kemps
NORTH ROAD
37
Heath Farm
The Mount (Tumulus)
Baldwins
CHEELSON RD.
WILSMAN RD.
NELSON RD.
South Ockendon Hall
Cockhide
M25 UNDER CONSTRUCTION
Street Fm.
Schs
South Ockendon
WEST ROAD
OCKENDON
Cemy
Bowl. Grn.
Recreation Ground
Ten. Cts
Whitehall Wood
ARISDALE AVENUE
Fords
LARKSPUR CLO.
Nurses' Homes
38
Junior Training Centre
South Ockendon Hospital
Brickkiln Wood
AVONTAR RD.
ARDMORE RD.
Allots.
MOLLANDS LANE
Little Mollands Farm
Sch.
Long Pond
RM15
ERRIFF DRIVE
ORCHARD ROAD
SOUTH ROAD
Allots.
BUCKLES LANE
Buckles Farm
39
Little Palmer's Shaw
Middle
BELHUS PARK
Belhus
The Shrubbery
EASINGTON
Lib.
Sort. Off.
Sch's.
AVELEY ESTATE
Public Park
Training Cen.
Great Palmer's Shaw
Playing Field
Sports Grd.
Sch.
FAIRHAM AV.
CAWDOR AVE.
BROXBURN DRIVE
School
Hill Farm
B1335
STIFFORD BY-PASS
STIFFORD ROAD
CARNACH GREEN
Ford Place
Courts
Millard's Garden
Hangmans Wood
Brannett's Wood
CULLEN SQUARE
STIFFORD HILL
40
Mar Dyke
Coppid Hall
Allots.
B186
Stifford
RM16
HIGH ROAD
HIGH STREET
Sch's.
Low Well Wood
Sports Grd.
Rec. Gd.
Hall
Aveley
70
Coombe Wood
Davy Down
Ardale School (Approved Sch.)
A13
UNDER CONSTRUCTION
Mar Dyke
Oak Wood
BACK LANE
WEST THURROCK

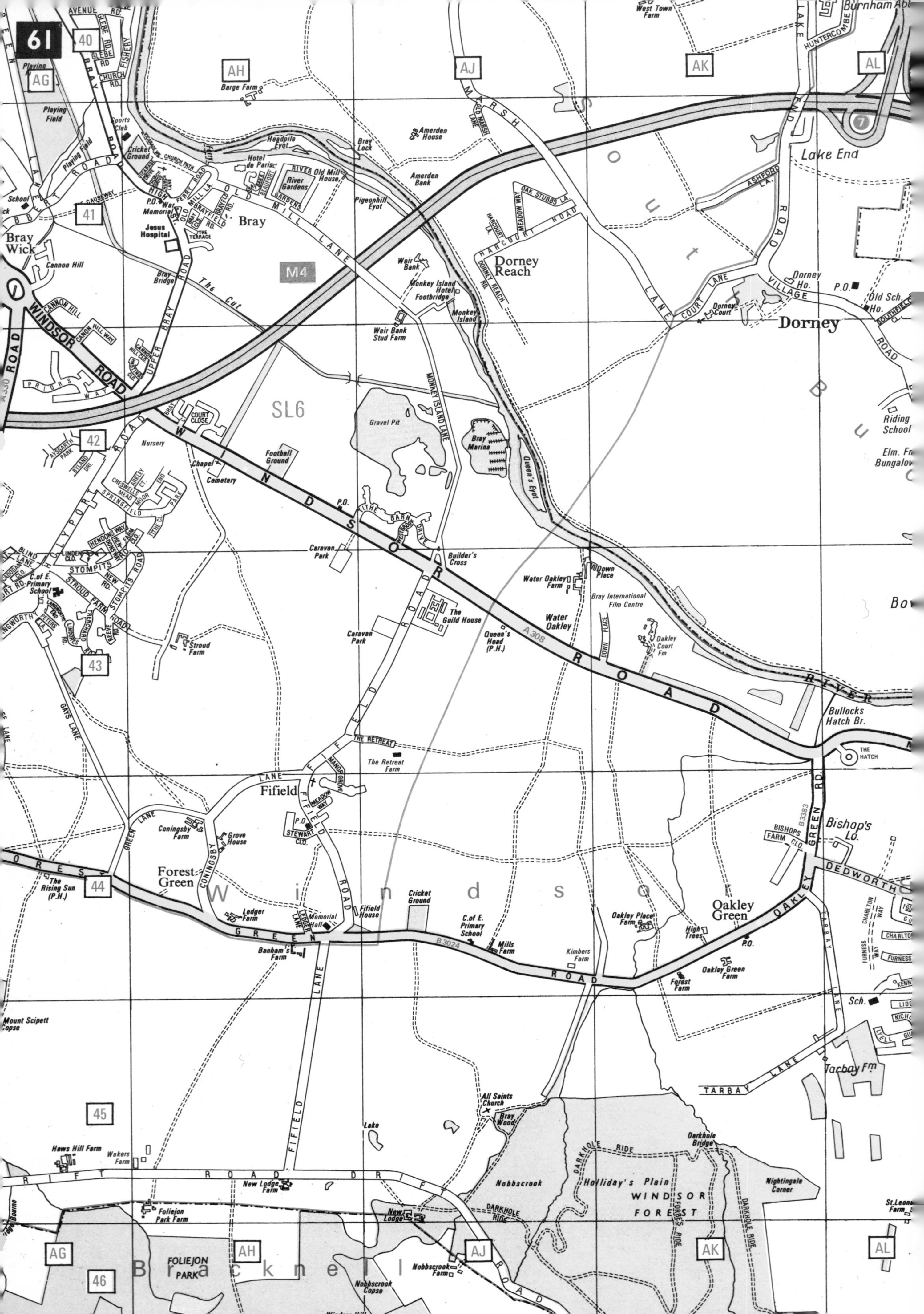
Bray
Bray Wick
Dorney Reach
Dorney
Lake End
Burnham Abbey
Fifield
Forest Green
Oakley Green
Water Oakley
Windsor
Bracknell
South Bucks
SL6
M4
WINDSOR ROAD
A308
B3024
B3383
River Thames
Monkey Island
Queen's Eyot
Bray Marina
Gravel Pit
Bray Lock
Headpile Eyot
Pigeonhill Eyot
Weir Bank Stud Farm
Monkey Island Hotel
Hotel de Paris
Jesus Hospital
Cannon Hill
Amerden House
Amerden Bank
Barge Farm
West Town Farm
Dorney Court
Dorney Ho.
Old Sch. Ho.
Riding School
Builder's Cross
The Guild House
Queen's Head (P.H.)
Down Place
Bray International Film Centre
Water Oakley Farm
Oakley Court Fm
Bullocks Hatch Br.
The Hatch
Bishop's Lo.
The Retreat Farm
Coningsby Farm
Grove House
Stroud Farm
Ledger Farm
Memorial Hall
Fifield House
Cricket Ground
C.of E. Primary School
Mills Farm
Kimbers Farm
Banham's Farm
Oakley Place Farm
High Trees
Forest Farm
Oakley Green Farm
Tarbay Fm
The Rising Sun (P.H.)
Mount Scipett Copse
Haws Hill Farm
Wakers Farm
New Lodge Farm
Foliejon Park Farm
FOLIEJON PARK
New Lodge
Nobbscrook
Nobbscrook Farm
Nobbscrook Copse
All Saints Church
Bray Wood
Lake
Holliday's Plain
WINDSOR FOREST
Oarkhole Bridge
Nightingale Corner
DRIFT ROAD
FIFIELD ROAD
DARKHOLE RIDE
FORBES RIDE
TARBAY LANE
OAKLEY GREEN ROAD
DEDWORTH
GREEN LANE
MONKEY ISLAND LANE
OLD MILL LANE
MARSH LANE
COURT LANE
ROAD LANE
HOLYPORT ROAD
STOMPITS ROAD
GAYS LANE
AG
AH
AJ
AK
AL
40
41
42
43
44
45
46
7

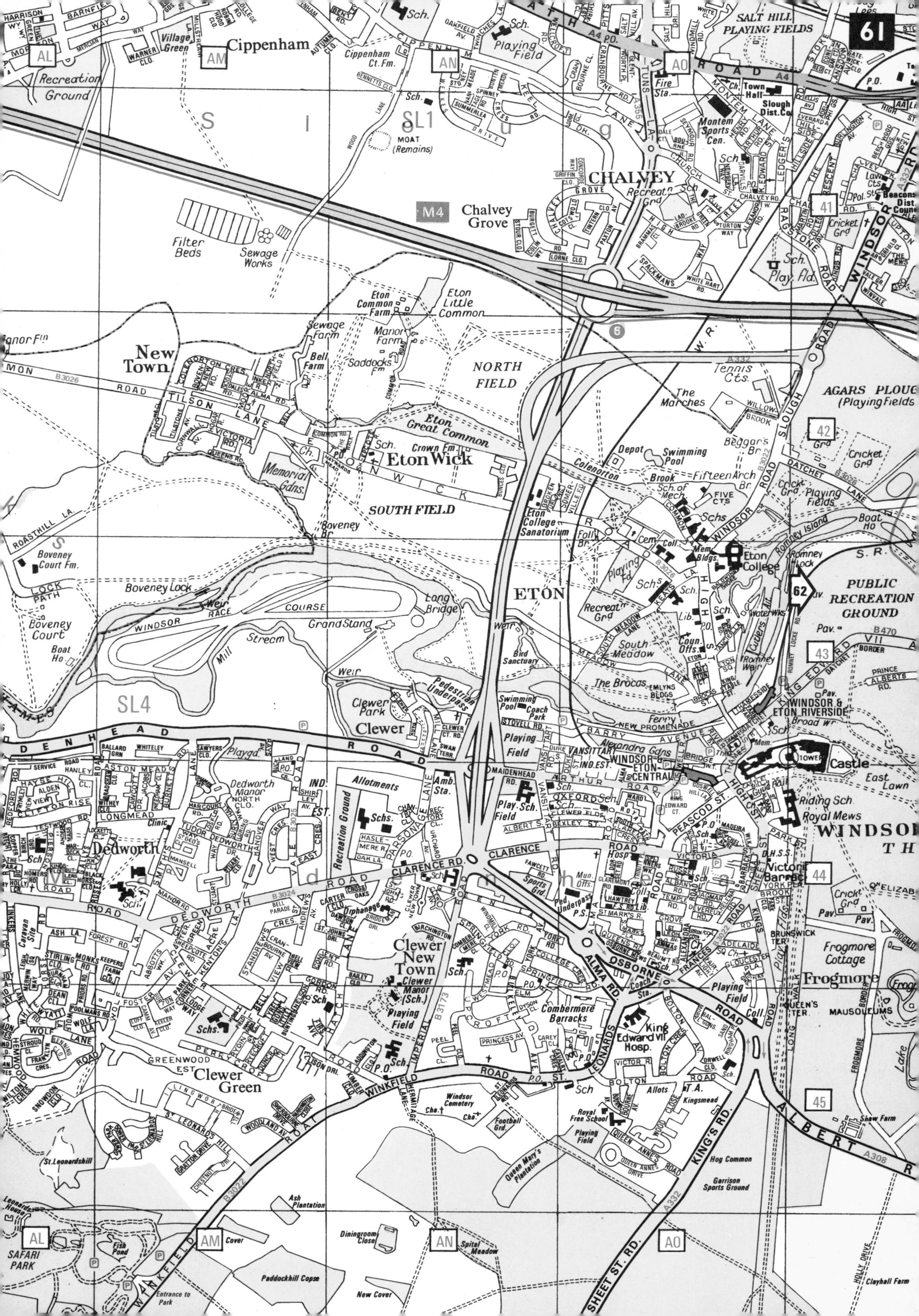

61
Cippenham
Village Green
Recreation Ground
Cippenham Ct. Fm.
SALT HILL PLAYING FIELDS
Playing Field
MOAT (Remains)
SL1
Slough
Town Hall
Slough Dist. Co
Montem Sports Cen.
Fire Sta.
CHALVEY
Chalvey Grove
Recreatn Grd
M4
Filter Beds
Sewage Works
Cricket Grd
Play. Fld.
Eton Common Farm
Eton Little Common
Sewage Farm
Manor Farm
Bell Farm
Saddocks Fm
NORTH FIELD
Tennis Cts.
The Marches
AGARS PLOUG (Playing Fields
New Town
Eton Great Common
Crown Fm.
Eton Wick
Memorial Gdns.
SOUTH FIELD
Depot
Swimming Pool
Beggars Br.
Cricket Grd
Colenorton Brook
Fifteen Arch Br.
Playing Fields
Eton College Sanatorium
Boveney Br.
Boveney Court Fm.
Boveney Lock
Weir
RACE COURSE
WINDSOR
Grand Stand
Long Bridge
ETON
Eton College
Romney Island
Romney Lock
PUBLIC RECREATION GROUND
Boveney Court
Boat Ho.
Mill Stream
Bird Sanctuary
South Meadow
Romney Weir
The Brocas
SL4
Clewer Park
Clewer
Pedestrian Underpass
Swimming Pool
Coach Park
Playing Field
WINDSOR & ETON RIVERSIDE
WINDSOR & ETON CENTRAL
Castle
East Lawn
DENHEAD ROAD
Dedworth Manor
Allotments
Recreation Ground
Amb. Sta.
Riding Sch.
Royal Mews
WINDSOR
Dedworth
Victoria Barracks
Frogmore Cottage
Frogmore
MAUSOLEUMS
Clewer New Town
Clewer Manor (Sch.)
Playing Field
Combermere Barracks
King Edward VII Hosp.
Clewer Green
Windsor Cemetery
Football Grd.
Royal Free School
Playing Field
St. Leonardshill
Queen Mary's Plantation
Hog Common
Garrison Sports Ground
Shaw Farm
Ash Plantation
Diningroom Close
Spital Meadow
SAFARI PARK
Fish Pond
Cover
Paddockhill Copse
New Cover
Entrance to Park
Clayhall Farm

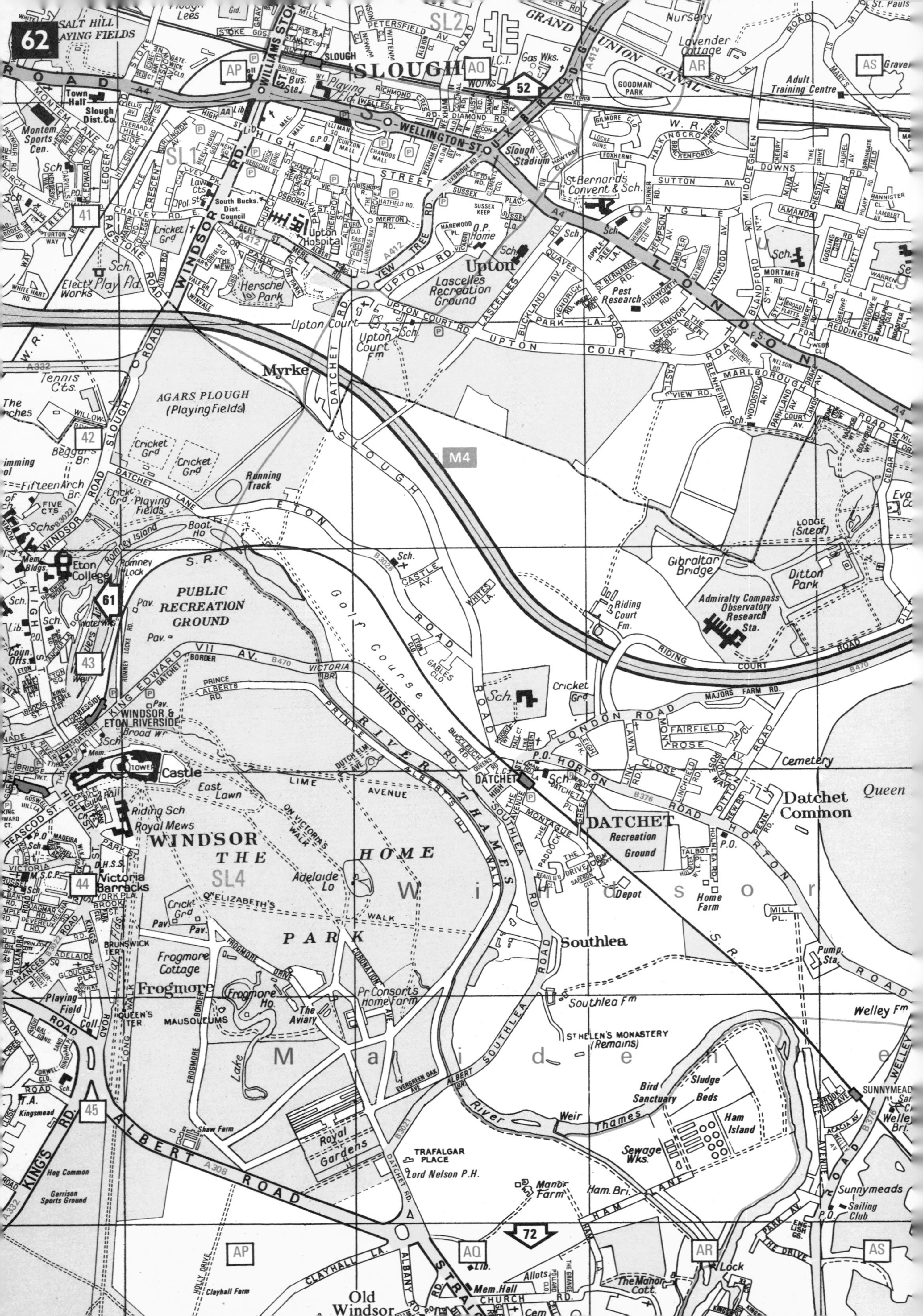
SLOUGH
SL2
SL1
SL4
AP
AQ
AR
AS
52
41
42
43
44
45
61
72
GRAND UNION CANAL
Town Hall
Slough Dist. Co.
Montem Sports Cen.
Bus Sta.
Playing Fld.
Gas Wks.
GOODMAN PARK
Adult Training Centre
Lavender Cottage
Nursery
WELLINGTON ST.
HIGH STREET
Slough Stadium
St Bernard's Convent & Sch.
South Bucks. Dist. Council
Upton Hospital
Upton
Lascelles Recreation Ground
O.P. Home
Herschel Park
Electy Works
Pest Research
Upton Court
Upton Court Fm
Myrke
M4
AGARS PLOUGH (Playing Fields)
Running Track
Tennis Cts.
Beggars Br.
Fifteen Arch Br.
Eton College
Romney Island
Romney Lock
Boat Ho
PUBLIC RECREATION GROUND
Golf Course
Riding Court Fm.
Gibraltar Bridge
Ditton Park
LODGE (Site of)
Admiralty Compass Observatory Research Sta.
RIDING COURT ROAD
KING EDWARD VII AV.
VICTORIA BR.
WINDSOR & ETON RIVERSIDE
Castle
East Lawn
LIME AVENUE
Riding Sch.
Royal Mews
WINDSOR
THE HOME PARK
Victoria Barracks
Adelaide Lo
RIVER THAMES
DATCHET
DATCHET Recreation Ground
Datchet Common
Queen
Cemetery
Home Farm
Depot
Southlea
Southlea Fm
ST HELEN'S MONASTERY (Remains)
Welley Fm
Windsor
Maidenhead
Frogmore Cottage
Frogmore
Frogmore Ho.
MAUSOLEUMS
Lake
The Aviary
Pr Consort's Home Farm
Royal Gardens
TRAFALGAR PLACE
Lord Nelson P.H.
Manor Farm
Bird Sanctuary
Sludge Beds
Ham Island
Sewage Wks.
Ham Bri.
Weir
SUNNYMEAD
Sunnymeads
Sailing Club
Playing Field
Kingsmead
Hog Common
Garrison Sports Ground
ALBERT ROAD
KING'S RD.
Shaw Farm
Clayhall Farm
CLAYHALL LA.
Old Windsor
Mem. Hall
Lock
The Manor Cott.
Allots

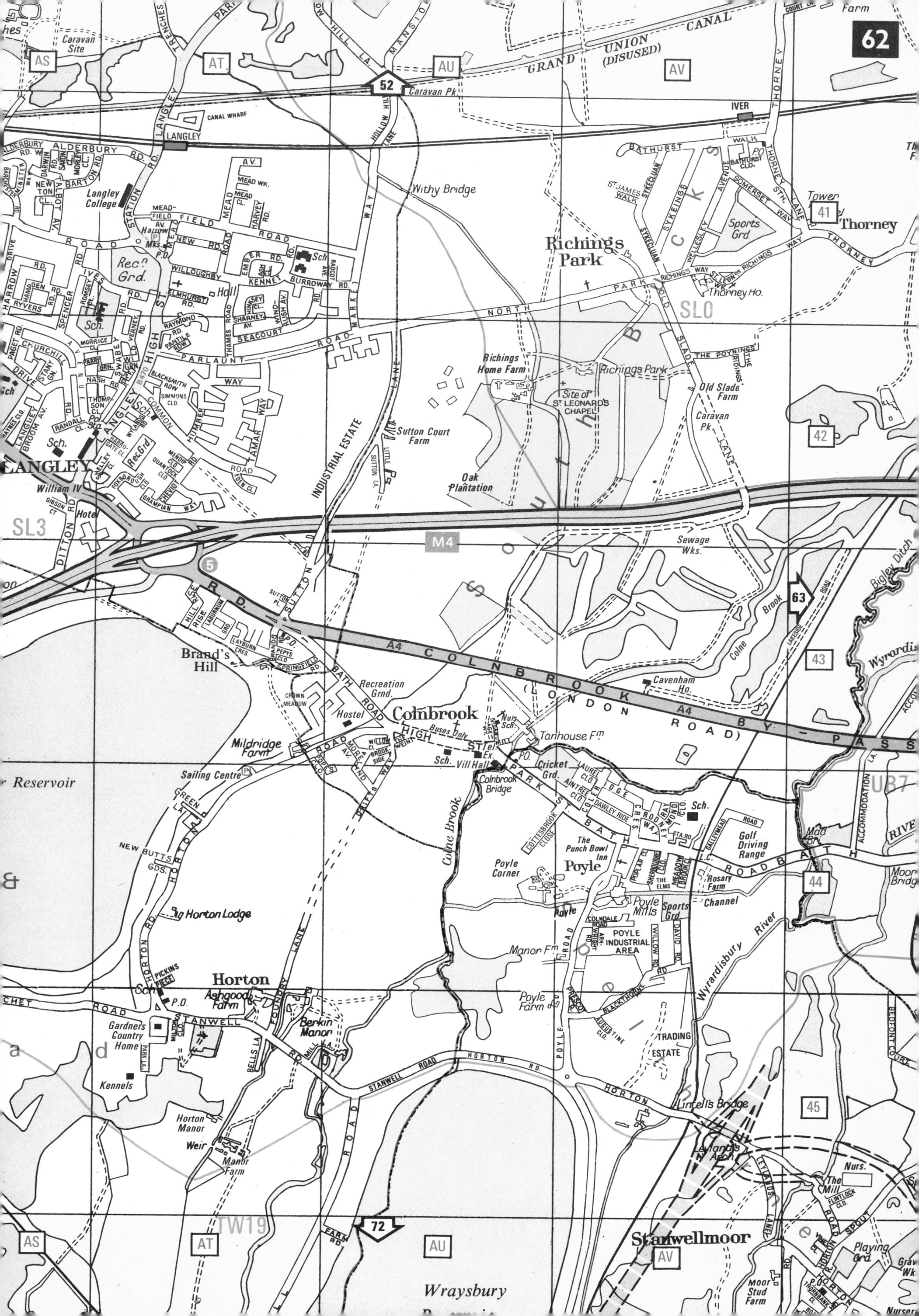
Caravan Site
GRAND UNION CANAL (DISUSED)
Caravan Pk
CANAL WHARF
LANGLEY
IVER
Withy Bridge
Langley College
Richings Park
Thorney
Tower
Sports Grd.
Thorney Ho.
SL0
Rec.n Grd.
Hall
INDUSTRIAL ESTATE
Richings Home Farm
Site of ST LEONARD'S CHAPEL
Old Slade Farm
Caravan Pk.
Sutton Court Farm
Oak Plantation
LANGLEY
William IV
Hotel
SL3
M4
Sewage Wks.
Colne Brook
Bigley Ditch
A4 COLNBROOK BY-PASS (LONDON ROAD)
Brand's Hill
Recreation Grnd.
Colnbrook
Hostel
Cavenham Ho.
Wyrardisbury
Tanhouse Fm
Mildridge Farm
Sailing Centre
Reservoir
Colnbrook Bridge
Cricket Grd.
Golf Driving Range
Poyle Corner
The Punch Bowl Inn
Poyle
Rosary Farm
Channel
Poyle Mills
POYLE INDUSTRIAL AREA
Manor Fm
Horton Lodge
Horton
Ashgood Farm
Poyle Farm
Wyrardisbury River
Gardners Country Home
Berkin Manor
TRADING ESTATE
Kennels
Horton Manor
Weir
Manor Farm
Lintell's Bridge
Leyland's Arch
The Mill
Nurs.
TW19
Stanwellmoor
Playing Grd.
Moor Stud Farm
Wraysbury

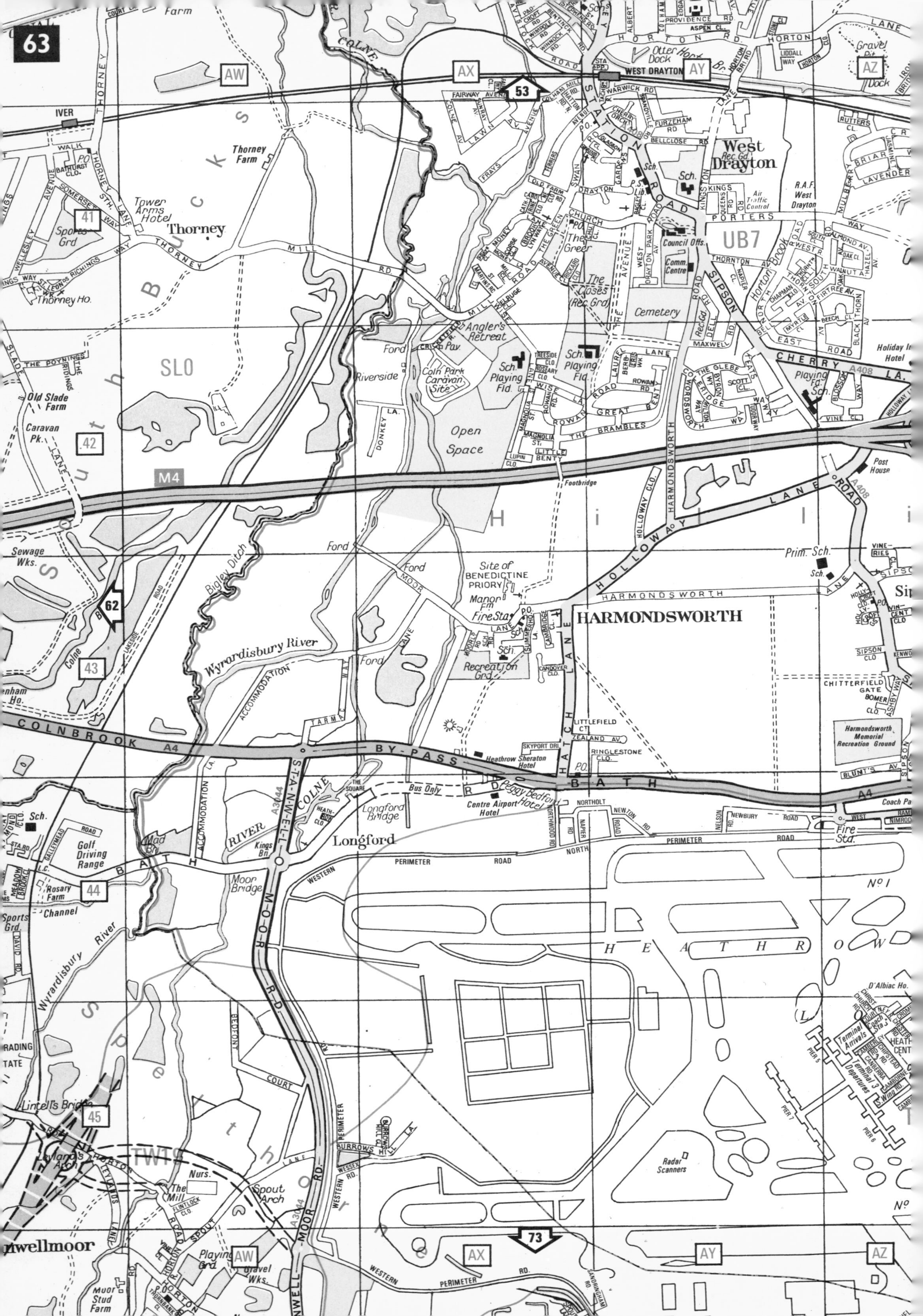
AW
AX
AY
AZ
53
IVER
WEST DRAYTON
Thorney Farm
Tower Arms Hotel
Thorney
Thorney Ho.
Bucks
SL0
Old Slade Farm
Caravan Pk.
41
42
43
44
45
M4
Sewage Wks.
62
Colne
Bigley Ditch
Wyrardisbury River
COLNBROOK BY-PASS
A4
West Drayton
UB7
R.A.F. West Drayton
Air Traffic Control
Council Offs.
Comm. Centre
The Green
The Closes (Rec. Grd)
Cemetery
Angler's Retreat
Colne Park Caravan Site
Riverside
Open Space
Sch. Playing Fld.
Footbridge
Holiday Inn Hotel
Post House
CHERRY LA.
HOLLOWAY LANE
HARMONDSWORTH
Site of BENEDICTINE PRIORY
Manor Fm
Fire Sta.
Recreation Grd
Prim. Sch.
Harmondsworth Memorial Recreation Ground
Heathrow Sheraton Hotel
Centre Airport Hotel
Peggy Bedford Hotel
BATH RD.
Bus Only
Longford
Longford Bridge
Moor Bridge
Kings Br.
Mad Br.
Golf Driving Range
Rosary Farm
Channel
Sports Grd.
STANWELL MOOR RD.
A3044
PERIMETER ROAD
NORTHERN PERIMETER ROAD
WESTERN PERIMETER RD.
Fire Sta.
H E A T H R O W
No 1
Terminal 3
Radar Scanners
Lintell's Bridge
Leyland's Arch
TW19
The Mill
Spout Arch
Nurs.
Playing Grd.
Gravel Wks.
Moor Stud Farm
Stanwellmoor
Spelthorne
73

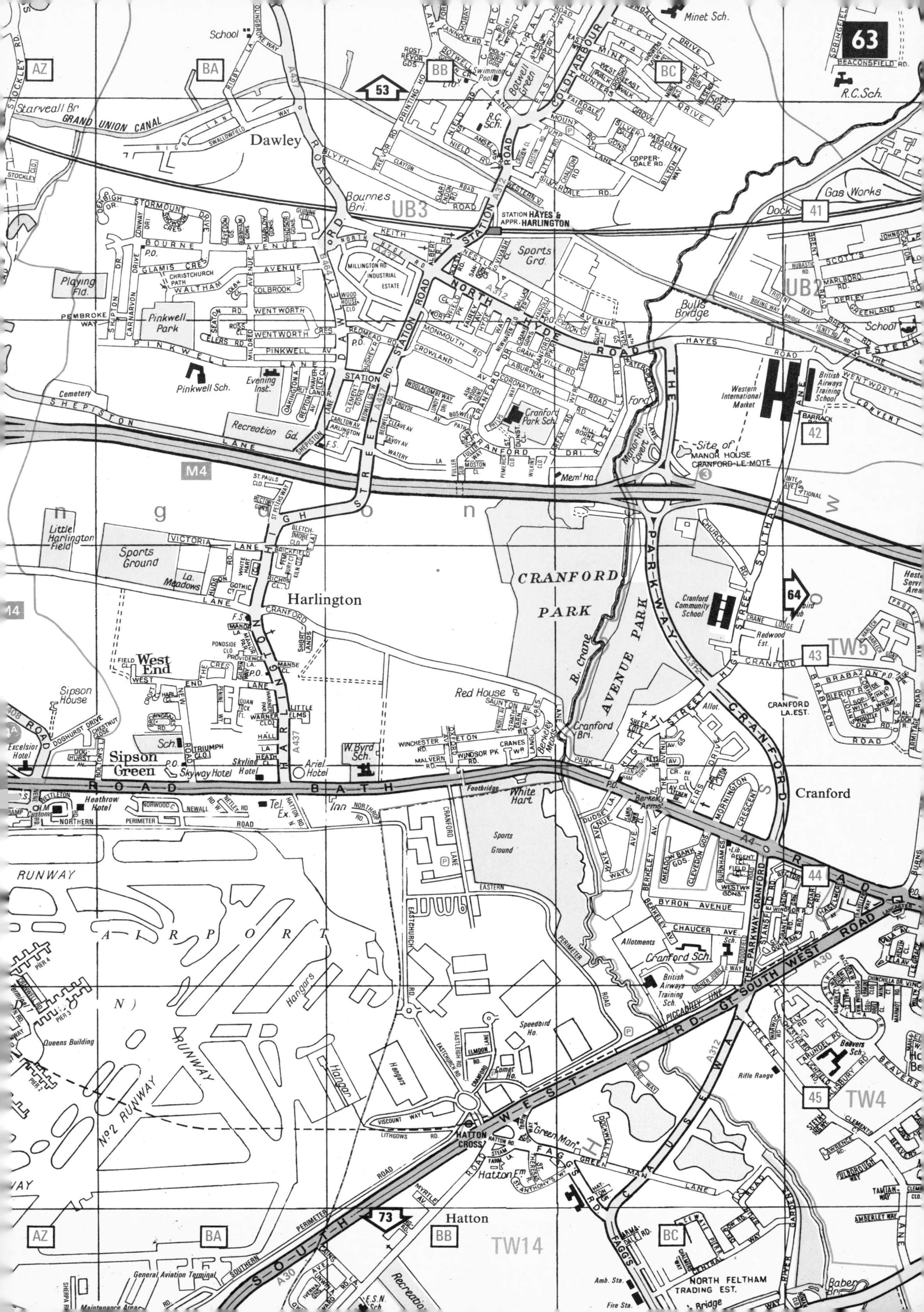
AZ
BA
BB
BC
53
Starveall Br
GRAND UNION CANAL
Dawley
School
Minet Sch.
R.C.Sch.
Swimming Pool
Botwell Green
COLDHARBOUR
Bournes Bri.
UB3
STATION HAYES & HARLINGTON
Gas Works
Dock
41
UB2
Bulls Bridge
Playing Fld.
Pinkwell Park
Pinkwell Sch.
Evening Inst.
Cemetery
Recreation Gd.
SHEPISTON LANE
M4
Sports Grd.
Cranford Park Sch.
HAYES ROAD
NORTH HYDE ROAD
Western International Market
British Airways Training School
42
Site of MANOR HOUSE CRANFORD-LE-MOTE
Mem! Ha.
Little Harlington Field
Sports Ground
La. Meadows
Harlington
CRANFORD PARK
AVENUE PARK
R. Crane
THE PARKWAY
Cranford Community School
64
Redwood Est.
43
TW5
West End
Sipson House
Sipson Green
Excelsior Hotel
Skyway Hotel
Skyline Hotel
Ariel Hotel
W. Byrd Sch.
Red House
Cranford Bri.
CRANFORD LA. EST.
Cranford
BATH ROAD
Heathrow Hotel
H.M. Customs
Tel. Ex.
Inn
Footbridge
White Hart
'Berkeley Arms'
Sports Ground
44
RUNWAY
AIRPORT
Hangars
Hangar
Queens Building
RUNWAY
No 2 RUNWAY
Allotments
Cranford Sch.
British Airways Training Sch.
PICCADILLY LINE
GT. SOUTH WEST ROAD
A30
A312
Speedbird Ho.
Comet Ho.
Rifle Range
Beavers Sch.
45
TW4
HATTON CROSS
Green Man
Hatton Fm.
73
Hatton
TW14
General Aviation Terminal
NORTH FELTHAM TRADING EST.
Amb. Sta.
Fire Sta.
Baber Bri.

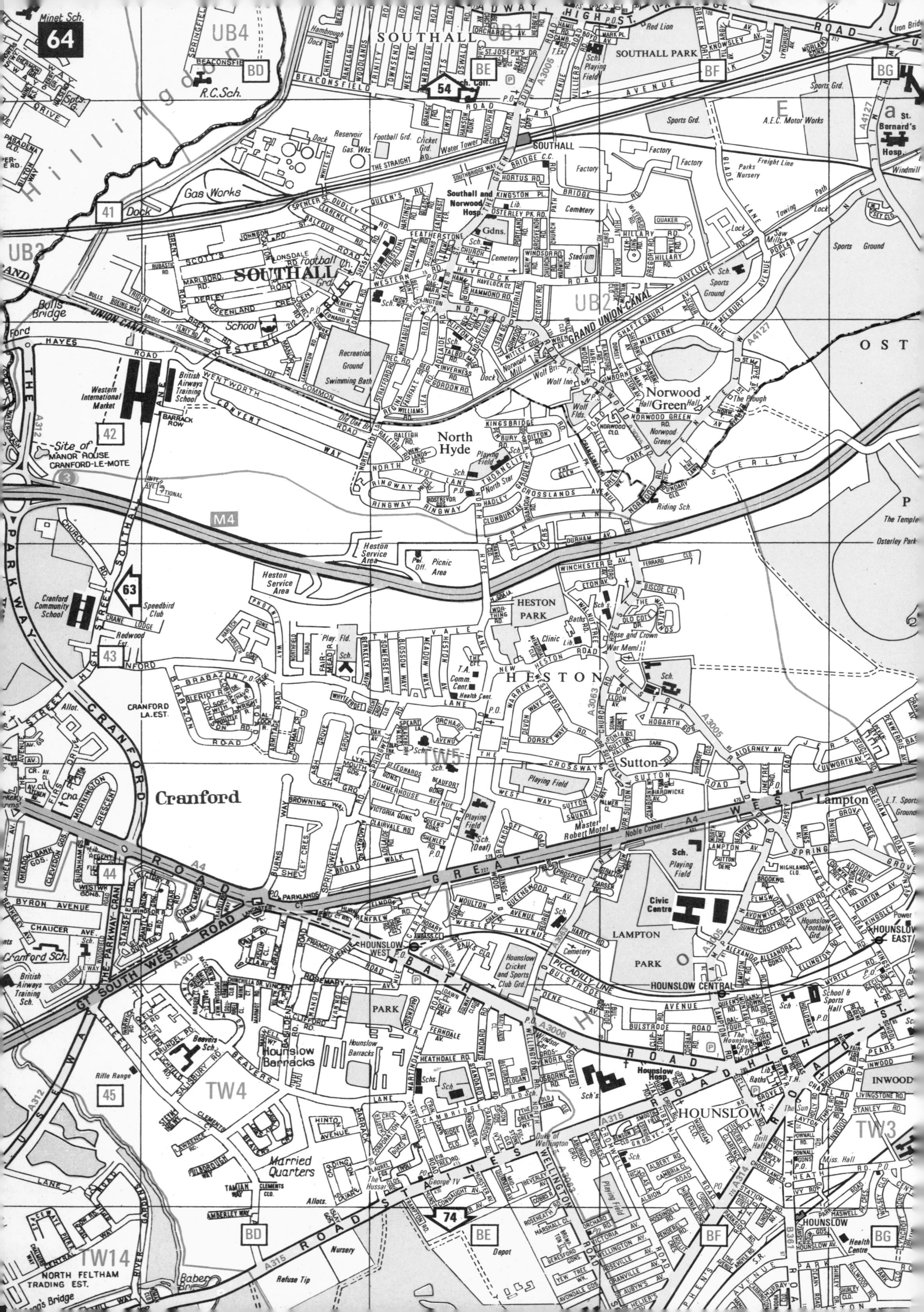
SOUTHALL
Southall Park
Southall and Norwood Hosp.
Gas Works
Hillingdon
Balls Bridge
Union Canal
Grand Union Canal
Western International Market
British Airways Training School
Site of Manor House Cranford-le-Mote
North Hyde
Norwood Green
The Plough
Wolf Inn
Osterley Park
The Temple
M4
Heston Service Area
Picnic Area
Cranford Community School
Speedbird Club
Heston Park
HESTON
Sutton
Cranford
Lampton
Great West Road
Civic Centre
Lampton Park
Hounslow West
Hounslow Central
Hounslow East
Hounslow Barracks
Hounslow Hosp.
HOUNSLOW
Married Quarters
Staines Road
North Feltham Trading Est.
Rifle Range
Refuse Tip
Nursery
Depot
A.E.C. Motor Works
St. Bernard's Hosp.
Sports Ground
UB4
UB1
UB2
UB3
TW5
TW4
TW3
TW14
41
42
43
44
45
54
63
74
BD
BE
BF
BG

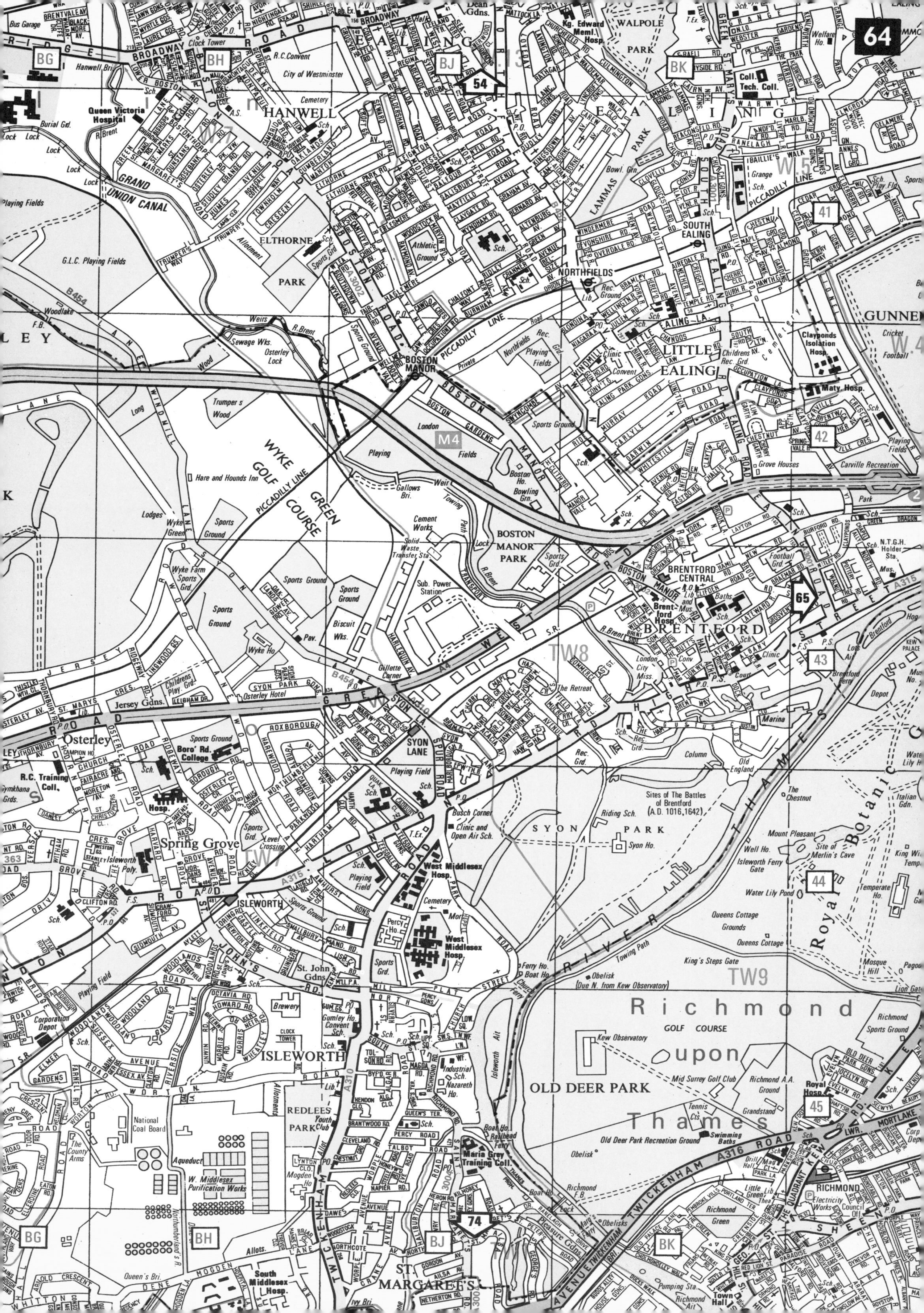

BG
BH
BJ
BK
54
HANWELL
EALING
W.13
W.5
W.7
W.4
Queen Victoria Hospital
Kg. Edward Meml. Hosp.
WALPOLE PARK
LAMMAS PARK
Coll. Tech. Coll.
GRAND UNION CANAL
Playing Fields
G.L.C. Playing Fields
ELTHORNE PARK
Athletic Ground
SOUTH EALING
NORTHFIELDS
PICCADILLY LINE
LITTLE EALING
GUNNERSBURY
Clayponds Isolation Hosp.
Maty Hosp.
BOSTON MANOR
41
42
43
44
45
65
74
M4
A4
A315
A310
A316
B454
WYKE GREEN GOLF COURSE
Trumper's Wood
Hare and Hounds Inn
BOSTON MANOR PARK
Sewage Wks.
Osterley Lock
Cement Works
Sub. Power Station
Biscuit Wks.
Gillette Corner
BRENTFORD CENTRAL
BRENTFORD
TW8
TW7
TW9
GREAT WEST ROAD
Osterley
Boro' Rd. College
R.C. Training Coll.
Spring Grove
Isleworth Poly.
SYON LANE
SYON PARK
Syon Ho.
Sites of The Battles of Brentford (A.D. 1016,1642)
West Middlesex Hosp.
ISLEWORTH
RIVER THAMES
Royal Botanic Gardens
Richmond upon Thames
Kew Observatory
OLD DEER PARK
Mid Surrey Golf Club
Old Deer Park Recreation Ground
RICHMOND
Royal Hosp.
National Coal Board
W. Middlesex Purification Works
REDLEES PARK
Maria Grey Training Coll.
South Middlesex Hosp.
ST. MARGARET'S
TWICKENHAM ROAD
MOGDEN LANE
Pleasure Gdns.

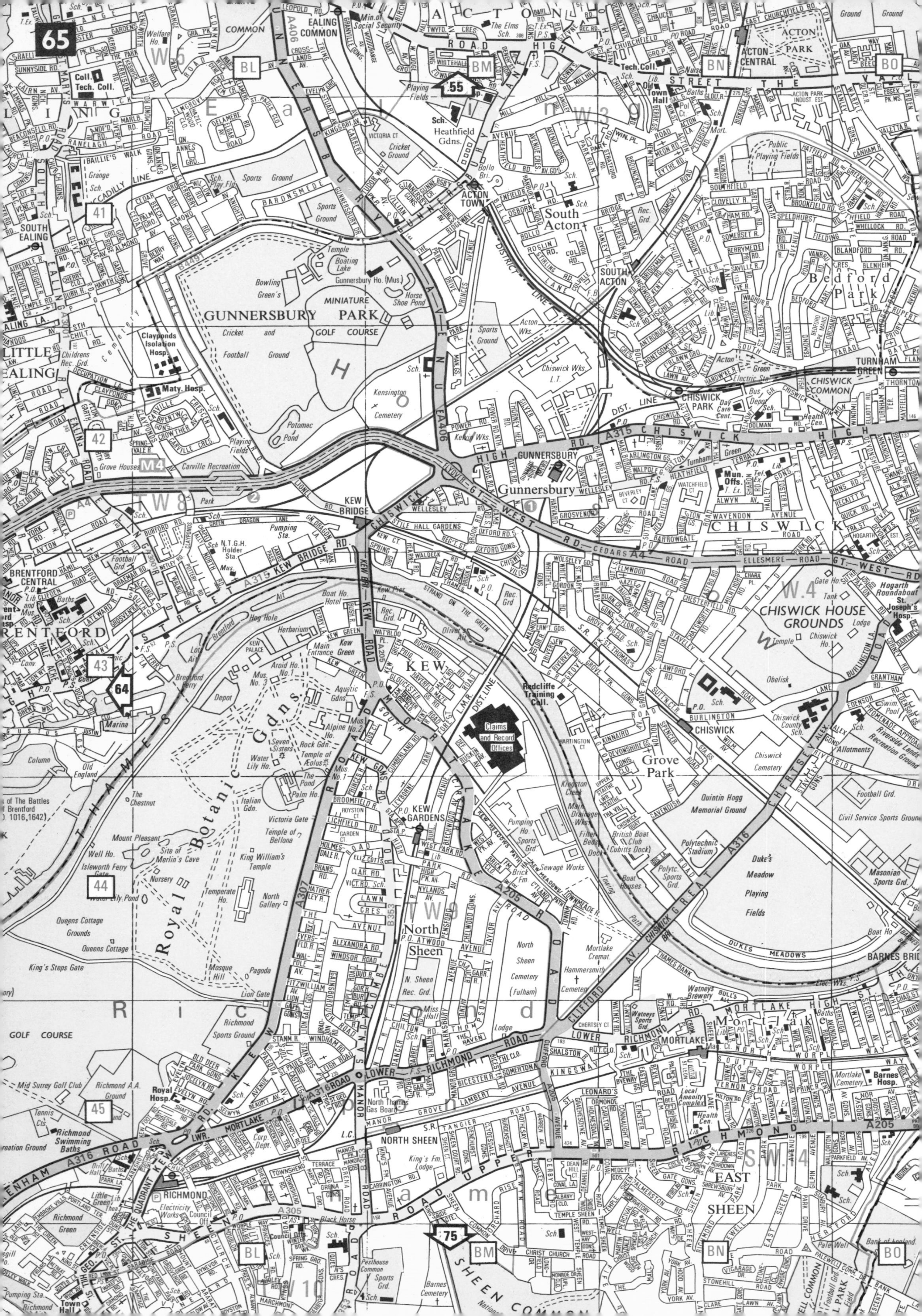

EALING COMMON
ACTON
ACTON CENTRAL
ACTON PARK
Heathfield Gdns.
Cricket Ground
ACTON TOWN
South Acton
SOUTH ACTON
Bedford Park
TURNHAM GREEN
CHISWICK COMMON
CHISWICK PARK
SOUTH EALING
LITTLE EALING
Claypond Isolation Hosp.
Maty. Hosp.
GUNNERSBURY PARK
Gunnersbury Ho. (Mus.)
MINIATURE GOLF COURSE
Temple
Boating Lake
Horse Shoe Pond
Potomac Pond
Kensington Cemetery
Acton Wks.
Chiswick Wks. L.T.
Sports Ground
Gunnersbury
GUNNERSBURY
KEW BRIDGE
BRENTFORD CENTRAL
BRENTFORD
Pumping Sta.
CHISWICK
CHISWICK HOUSE GROUNDS
Hogarth Roundabout
Chiswick Ho.
Obelisk
Grove Park
Quintin Hogg Memorial Ground
Polytechnic Stadium
Duke's Meadow Playing Fields
DUKES MEADOWS
BARNES BRIDGE
Chiswick Cemetery
Redcliffe Training Coll.
Claims and Record Offices
KEW
Kew Green
Herbarium
KEW PALACE
Royal Botanic Gdns.
Temple of Æolus
Palm Ho.
The Pond
Temperate Ho.
North Gallery
Pagoda
Queens Cottage Grounds
Lion Gate
Victoria Gate
KEW GARDENS
North Sheen
N. Sheen Rec. Grd.
North Sheen Cemetery (Fulham)
Mortlake Cremat.
Hammersmith Cemetery
Sewage Works
Mortlake
MORTLAKE
EAST SHEEN
NORTH SHEEN
King's Fm. Lodge
RICHMOND
Richmond Green
Royal Hosp.
Richmond Sports Ground
Old Deer Park
GOLF COURSE
Mid Surrey Golf Club
Richmond Swimming Baths
Barnes Cemetery
Pesthouse Common
SHEEN COMMON
LOWER RICHMOND ROAD
UPPER RICHMOND ROAD
MORTLAKE ROAD
GREAT WEST RD.
CHISWICK HIGH RD.
KEW ROAD
GUNNERSBURY AVENUE
THAMES
W.4
TW9
TW8
SW.14
W.3
W.5
55
64
75

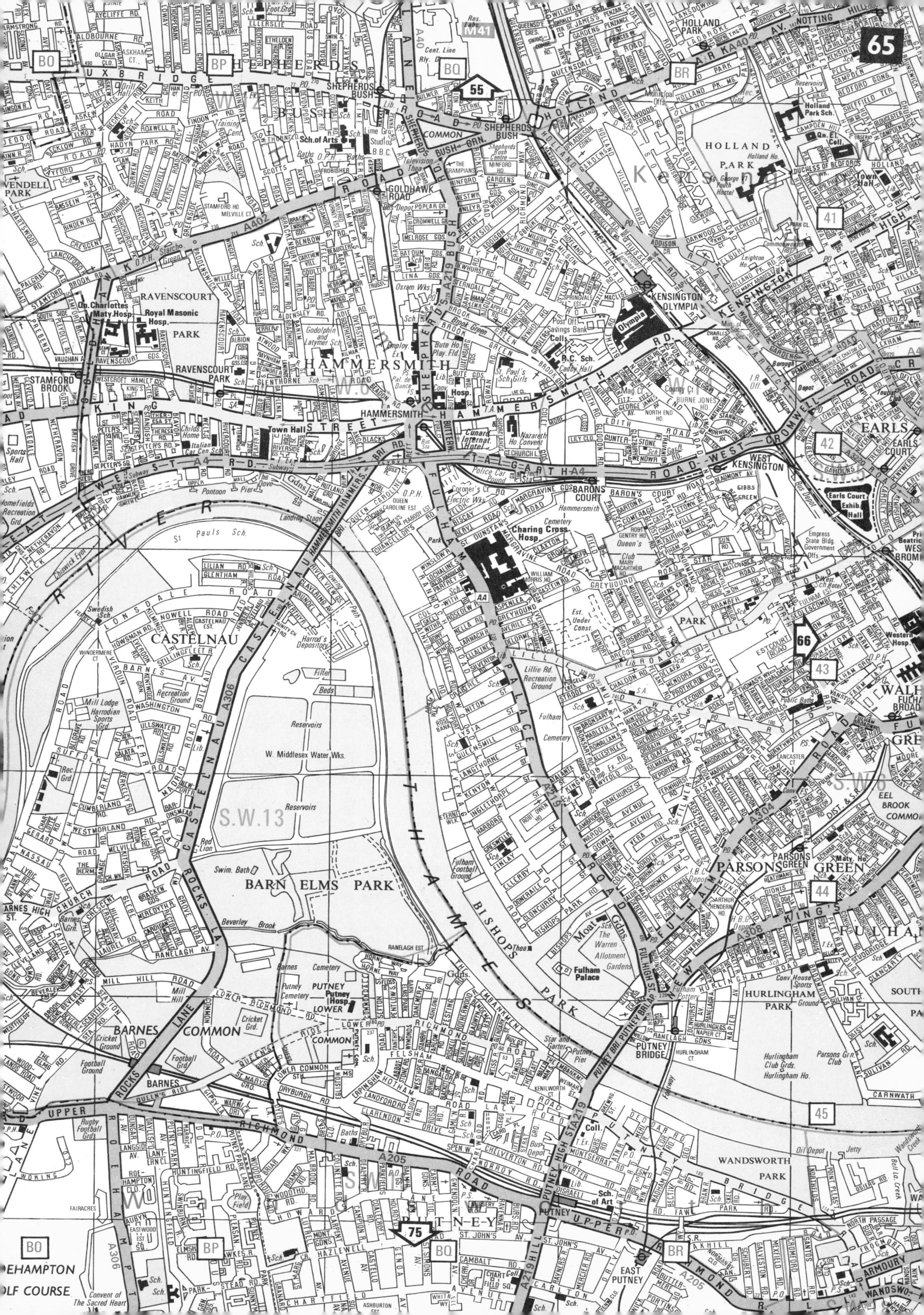
65
SHEPHERDS BUSH
HOLLAND PARK
NOTTING HILL
KENSINGTON OLYMPIA
Kensington
HAMMERSMITH
RAVENSCOURT PARK
STAMFORD BROOK
BARONS COURT
WEST KENSINGTON
EARLS COURT
CASTELNAU
BARN ELMS PARK
Reservoirs
W. Middlesex Water Wks.
S.W.13
RIVER THAMES
BARNES COMMON
BARNES
PUTNEY
EAST PUTNEY
PUTNEY BRIDGE
PARSONS GREEN
HURLINGHAM PARK
WANDSWORTH PARK
FULHAM
Fulham Palace
BISHOPS PARK
Fulham Cemetery
Charing Cross Hosp.
Royal Masonic Hosp.
Qn. Charlottes Maty. Hosp.
Earls Court Exhib. Hall
ROEHAMPTON GOLF COURSE
UXBRIDGE ROAD
KING STREET
GREAT WEST RD.
HAMMERSMITH ROAD
TALGARTH ROAD
WEST CROMWELL ROAD
FULHAM PALACE ROAD
FULHAM ROAD
NEW KING'S ROAD
UPPER RICHMOND ROAD
PUTNEY HIGH ST.
LOWER RICHMOND ROAD
ROCKS LA.
CASTELNAU
BO
BP
BQ
BR
55
41
42
43
44
45
66
75
A40
A402
A4
A306
A219
A3220
A304
A308
A205
M41
S.W.6
W.6
W.14
S.W.15

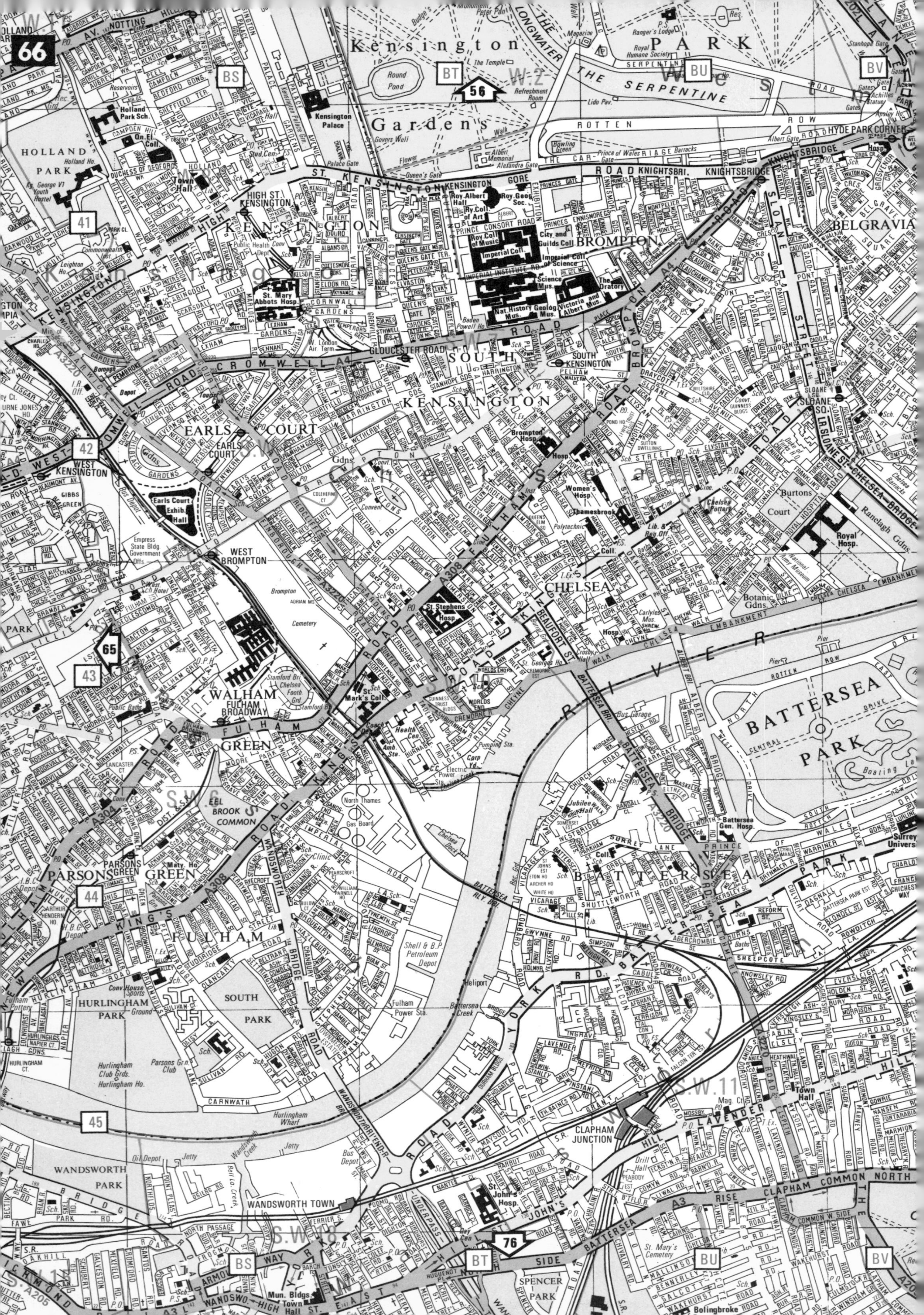

66
Kensington Gardens
PARK
THE SERPENTINE
ROTTEN ROW
HYDE PARK CORNER
KNIGHTSBRIDGE
HOLLAND PARK
Kensington Palace
Round Pond
Albert Memorial
Roy. Albert Hall
Imperial Coll.
Science Mus.
Nat. History Geolog. Mus.
Victoria and Albert Mus.
The Oratory
KENSINGTON
HIGH ST KENSINGTON
BROMPTON
BELGRAVIA
SOUTH KENSINGTON
CROMWELL ROAD
GLOUCESTER ROAD
EARLS COURT
Earls Court Exhib. Hall
WEST KENSINGTON
WEST BROMPTON
Brompton Cemetery
St. Stephens Hosp.
CHELSEA
SLOANE SQ.
Royal Hosp.
Burtons Court
Chelsea Barracks
Botanic Gdns.
CHELSEA EMBANKMENT
RIVER
BATTERSEA PARK
BATTERSEA
BATTERSEA BRIDGE
ALBERT BRIDGE
WALHAM GREEN
FULHAM BROADWAY
Stamford Bri. Chelsea Footb. Grd.
KINGS ROAD
FULHAM ROAD
EEL BROOK COMMON
PARSONS GREEN
FULHAM
HURLINGHAM PARK
SOUTH PARK
Hurlingham Club Grds.
WANDSWORTH BRIDGE
Fulham Power Sta.
Shell & B.P. Petroleum Depot
CLAPHAM JUNCTION
LAVENDER HILL
YORK ROAD
WANDSWORTH PARK
WANDSWORTH TOWN
St. John's Hosp.
CLAPHAM COMMON NORTH SIDE
St. Mary's Cemetery
SPENCER PARK
Mun. Bldgs.
BATTERSEA RISE
41
42
43
44
45
56
65
76
BS
BT
BU
BV

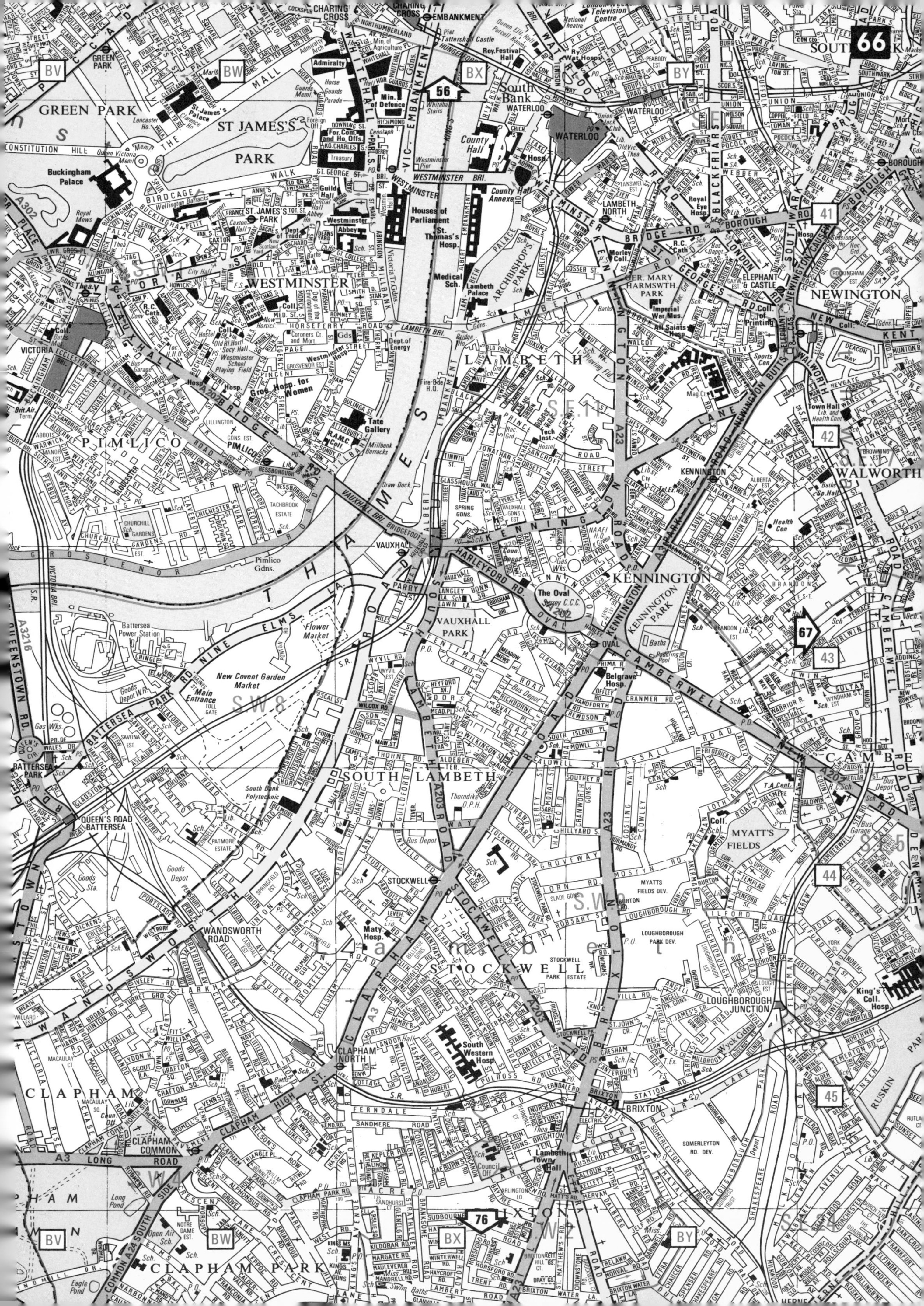
GREEN PARK
ST JAMES'S PARK
Buckingham Palace
WESTMINSTER
Houses of Parliament
Westminster Abbey
County Hall
WATERLOO
South Bank
LAMBETH
Lambeth Palace
ELEPHANT & CASTLE
NEWINGTON
WALWORTH
PIMLICO
VICTORIA
THAMES
VAUXHALL
KENNINGTON
The Oval
Surrey C.C.C.
VAUXHALL PARK
KENNINGTON PARK
Battersea Power Station
New Covent Garden Market
SOUTH LAMBETH
STOCKWELL
MYATT'S FIELDS
LOUGHBOROUGH JUNCTION
King's Coll. Hosp.
QUEEN'S ROAD BATTERSEA
WANDSWORTH ROAD
CLAPHAM
CLAPHAM NORTH
CLAPHAM COMMON
CLAPHAM PARK
BRIXTON
Lambeth Town Hall
BV
BW
BX
BY
56
67
76
41
42
43
44
45

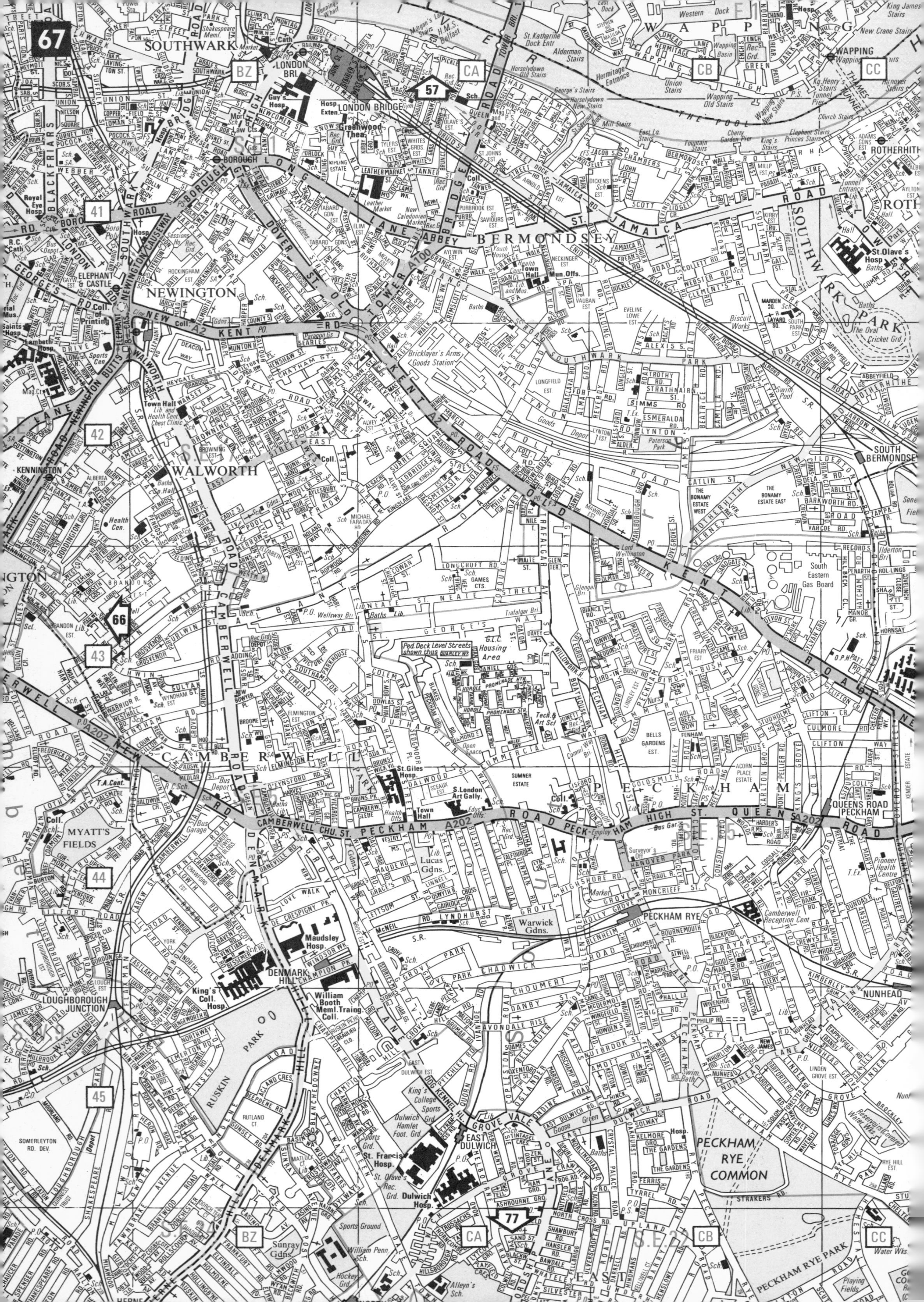
67
SOUTHWARK
LONDON BRI
LONDON BRIDGE
57
BZ
CA
CB
CC
WAPPING
WAPPING
THE POOL
ROTHERHITHE
BOROUGH
NEWINGTON
ELEPHANT & CASTLE
BERMONDSEY
JAMAICA ROAD
TOWER BRIDGE ROAD
LONG LANE
KENT ROAD
NEW KENT ROAD
OLD KENT ROAD
SOUTHWARK PARK
Bricklayer's Arms Goods Station
WALWORTH
41
42
43
44
45
66
KENNINGTON
CAMBERWELL
CAMBERWELL ROAD
CAMBERWELL NEW ROAD
PECKHAM
PECKHAM HIGH ST.
QUEENS ROAD
QUEENS ROAD PECKHAM
SOUTH BERMONDSEY
South Eastern Gas Board
MYATT'S FIELDS
PECKHAM RYE
PECKHAM RYE COMMON
PECKHAM RYE PARK
NUNHEAD
DENMARK HILL
Maudsley Hosp.
King's Coll. Hosp.
LOUGHBOROUGH JUNCTION
RUSKIN PARK
EAST DULWICH
Dulwich Hosp.
St. Francis Hosp.
GROVE VALE
77
Sunray Gdns.
Sports Ground

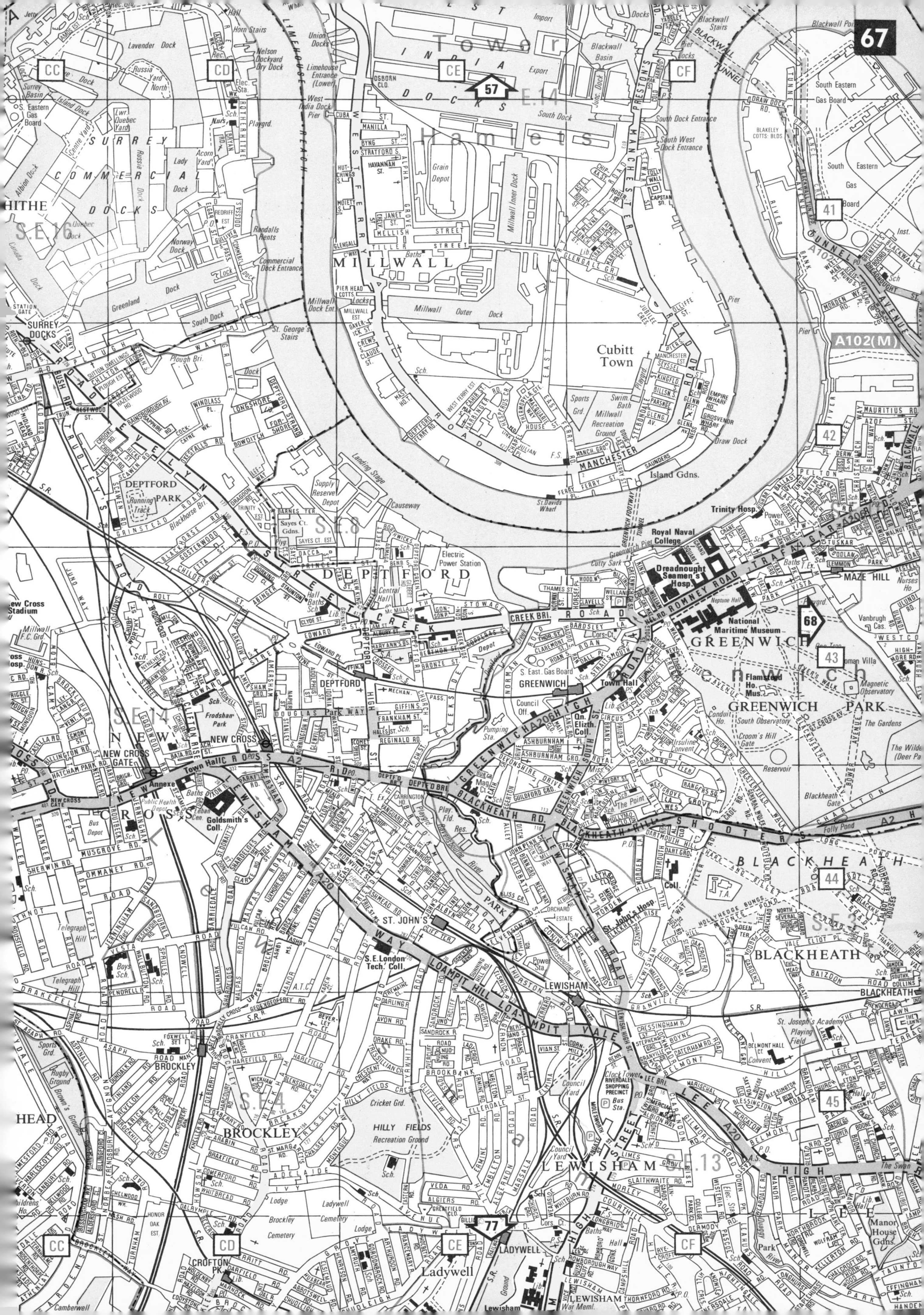

CC
CD
CE
CF
57
Tower
INDIA
DOCKS
E.14
Hamlets
SURREY
COMMERCIAL
DOCKS
HITHE
S.E.16
Lavender Dock
Russia Dock
Island Dock
Greenland Dock
South Dock
Norway Dock
Commercial Dock Entrance
SURREY DOCKS
LIMEHOUSE REACH
Limehouse Entrance (Lower)
West India Dock Pier
Union Docks
Import
Export
South Dock
Blackwall Basin
Blackwall Stairs
BLACKWALL TUNNEL
South Dock Entrance
South West Dock Entrance
South Eastern Gas Board
Grain Depot
Millwall Inner Dock
Millwall Outer Dock
MILLWALL
Millwall Dock Ent.
Cubitt Town
Millwall Recreation Ground
Island Gdns.
Draw Dock
Pier
41
42
43
44
45
A102(M)
BLACKWALL TUNNEL AVENUE
DEPTFORD PARK
Running Track
Plough Bri.
Landing Stage
Supply Reserve Depot
Causeway
S.E.8
DEPTFORD
Electric Power Station
GREENWICH FOOTWAY TUNNEL
Greenwich Pier
Cutty Sark
Royal Naval College
Dreadnought Seamen's Hosp.
Trinity Hosp.
National Maritime Museum
GREENWICH
68
ROMNEY ROAD
TRAFALGAR RD.
MAZE HILL
Vanbrugh Cas.
Flamsteed Ho. Mus.
GREENWICH PARK
Magnetic Observatory
The Gardens
Reservoir
Blackheath Gate
CHARLTON
Folly Pond
A2
SHOOTERS HILL
BLACKHEATH
S.E.3
New Cross Stadium
Millwall F.C. Grd.
S.E.14
NEW CROSS
NEW CROSS GATE
Goldsmith's Coll.
Telegraph Hill
BROCKLEY
HILLY FIELDS Recreation Ground
Cricket Grd.
Brockley Cemetery
Ladywell Cemetery
S.E.London Tech. Coll.
ST. JOHN'S
LOAMPIT HILL
LOAMPIT VALE
LEWISHAM
Lewisham High St.
Riverdale Shopping Precinct
S.E.13
A20
LEE
Manor House Gdns.
77
Ladywell
LADYWELL
CROFTON PK.
HONOR OAK EST.
Camberwell
Lewisham War Meml.
St. Joseph's Academy Playing Field
Ravensbourne River
St. John's Hosp.
Town Hall
Greenwich A206
A2
A21
A2 NEW CROSS RD.
Bus Depot
Deptford Creek
CREEK RD.
EVELYN STREET

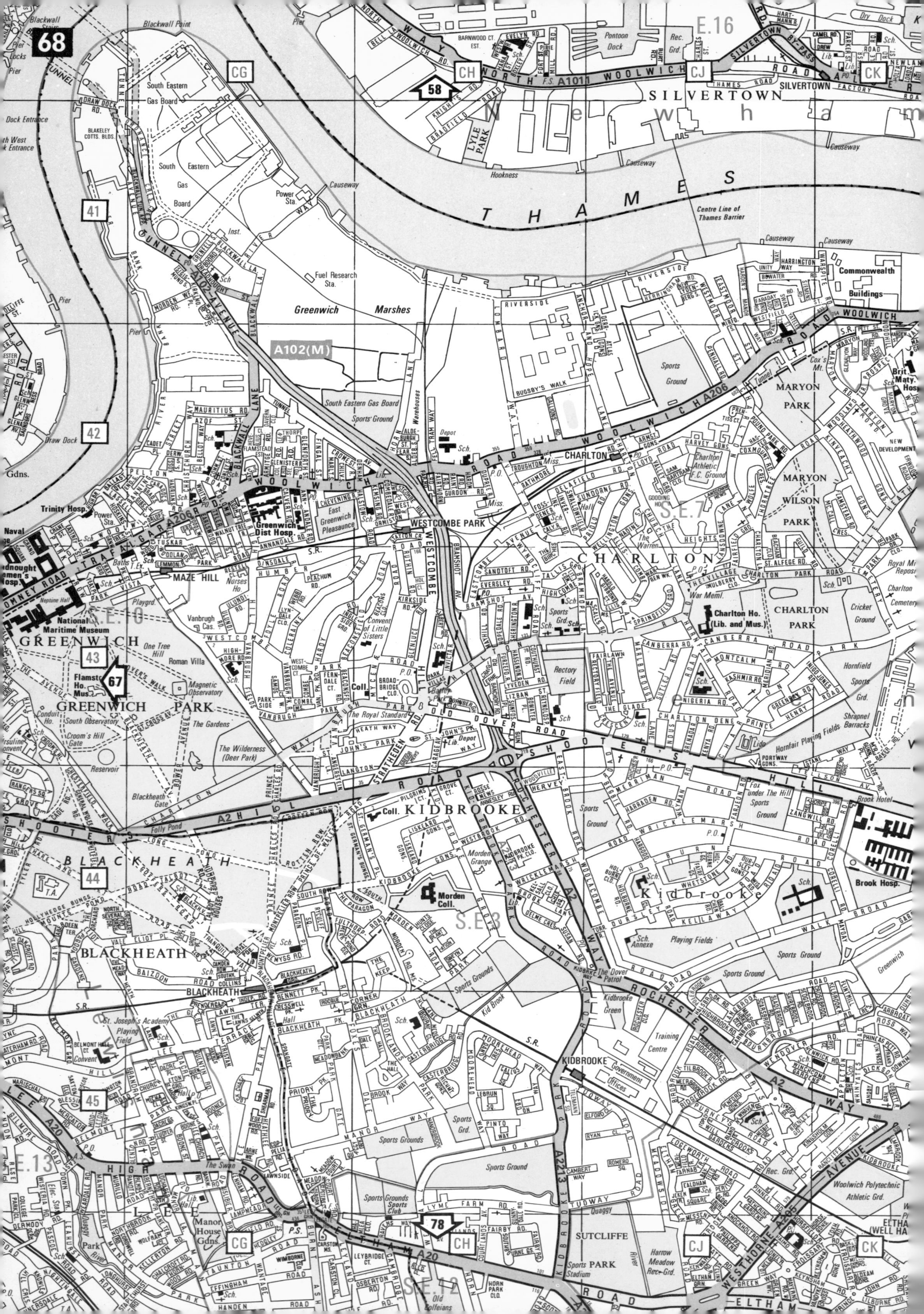
SILVERTOWN
E.16
NORTH WOOLWICH ROAD A1011
SILVERTOWN BY-PASS
Pontoon Dock
Lyle Park
Hookness
Causeway
THAMES
Centre Line of Thames Barrier
Blackwall Point
South Eastern Gas Board
Power Sta.
Fuel Research Sta.
Greenwich Marshes
A102(M)
BLACKWALL TUNNEL
A102 AVENUE
South Eastern Gas Board Sports Ground
Commonwealth Buildings
Sports Ground
WOOLWICH ROAD A206
CHARLTON
Charlton Athletic F.C. Ground
MARYON PARK
MARYON WILSON PARK
WESTCOMBE PARK
Greenwich Dist Hosp.
East Greenwich Pleasaunce
Trinity Hosp.
MAZE HILL
TRAFALGAR ROAD A206
ROMNEY ROAD
National Maritime Museum
GREENWICH
S.E.10
S.E.7
CHARLTON
Charlton Ho. (Lib. and Mus.)
CHARLTON PARK
Cricket Ground
Hornfield Sports Grd.
Shrapnel Barracks
Hornfair Playing Fields
Vanbrugh Cas.
One Tree Hill
Roman Villa
Magnetic Observatory
Flamsteed Ho. Mus.
GREENWICH PARK
South Observatory
The Gardens
The Wilderness (Deer Park)
Reservoir
Blackheath Gate
Convent of Little Sisters
The Royal Standard
DOVER ROAD
SHOOTER'S HILL
A2 HILL ROAD
KIDBROOKE
Morden Grange
Morden Coll.
Kidbrooke
Brook Hosp.
Playing Fields
Sports Ground
BLACKHEATH
S.E.3
Sports Grounds
Kid Brook
The Dover Patrol
Kidbrooke Green
ROCHESTER WAY
Training Centre
KIDBROOKE
Government Offices
A2 WAY
St. Joseph's Academy Playing Field
LEE
E.13
A20 HIGH ROAD
The Swan
Manor House Gdns.
ELTHAM ROAD A20
S.E.12
A2213
KIDBROOKE PARK ROAD
Sports Ground
SUTCLIFFE PARK
Sports Stadium
Harrow Meadow Rec. Grd.
Quaggy
Woolwich Polytechnic Athletic Grd.
WESTHORNE AVENUE A205
Rec. Grd.
Old Colfeians
CG
CH
CJ
CK
41
42
43
44
45
58
67
78

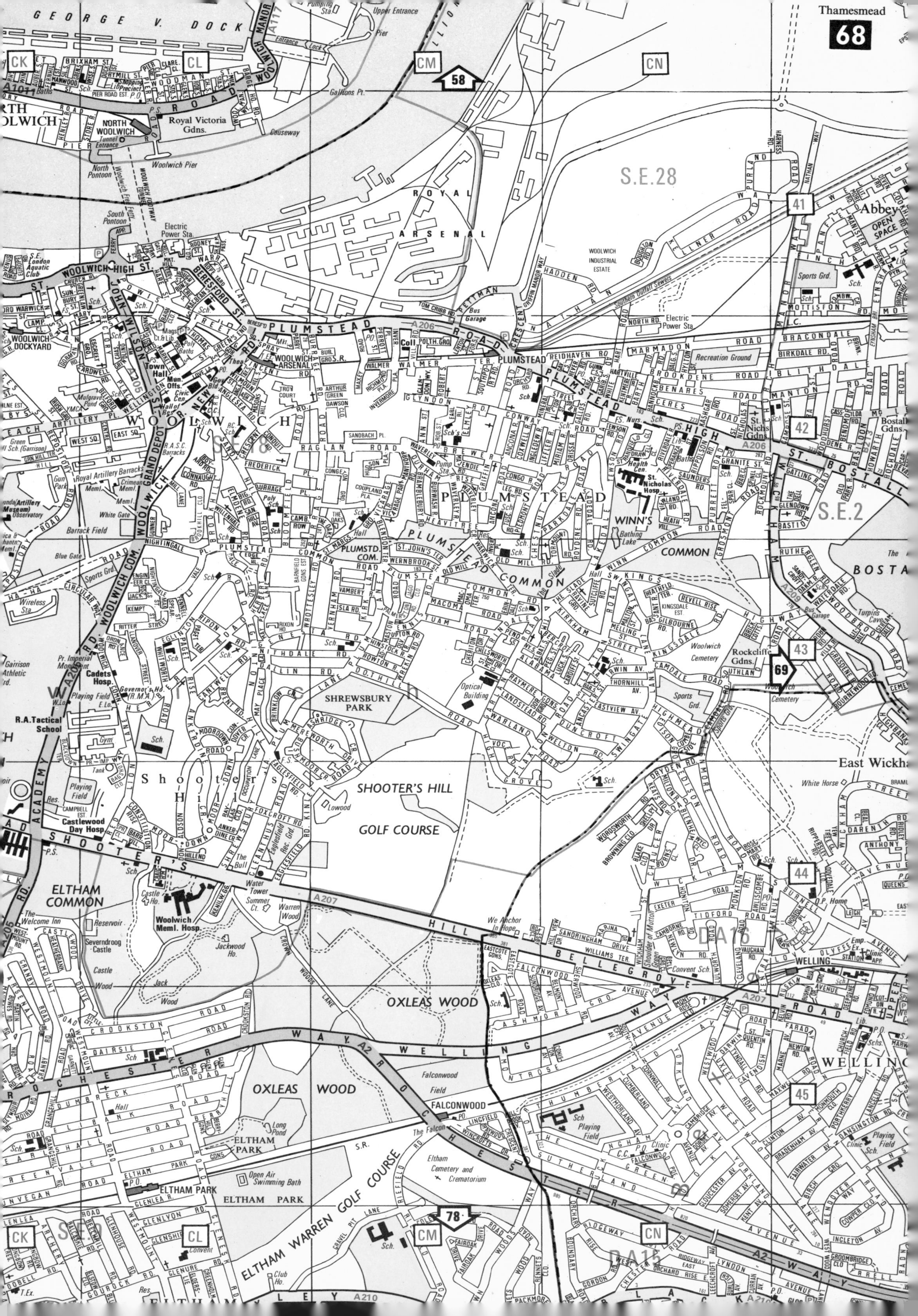
GEORGE V. DOCK
CK
CL
CM
CN
58
78
41
42
43
44
45
69
NORTH WOOLWICH
Royal Victoria Gdns.
Woolwich Pier
North Pontoon
South Pontoon
Electric Power Sta.
Galleons Pt.
Causeway
Upper Entrance
ROYAL ARSENAL
S.E.28
WOOLWICH INDUSTRIAL ESTATE
Abbey
OPEN SPACE
Sports Grd.
WOOLWICH HIGH ST.
WOOLWICH DOCKYARD
PLUMSTEAD ROAD
WOOLWICH ARSENAL
Town Hall
WOOLWICH
S.E.18
Royal Artillery Barracks
Barrack Field
GRAND DEPOT RD.
PLUMSTEAD HIGH ST.
Recreation Ground
PLUMSTEAD
St. Nicholas Hosp.
WINN'S COMMON
PLUMSTEAD COMMON
S.E.2
BOSTALL
Woolwich Cemetery
Rockcliffe Gdns.
Wireless Sta.
Garrison Athletic Grd.
Cadets Hosp.
R.A.Tactical School
SHREWSBURY PARK
Optical Building
Shooters Hill
SHOOTER'S HILL GOLF COURSE
East Wickham
White Horse
Castlewood Day Hosp
SHOOTER'S HILL
ELTHAM COMMON
Woolwich Meml. Hosp.
Severndroog Castle
Castle Wood
Jack Wood
Water Tower
Warren Wood
We Anchor In Hope
BELLEGROVE ROAD
WELLING
DA16
OXLEAS WOOD
ROCHESTER WAY
WELLING WAY
Falconwood Field
FALCONWOOD
The Falcon
ELTHAM PARK
Open Air Swimming Bath
Eltham Cemetery and Crematorium
ELTHAM WARREN GOLF COURSE
DA15
A2
A205
A206
A207
A209
A210

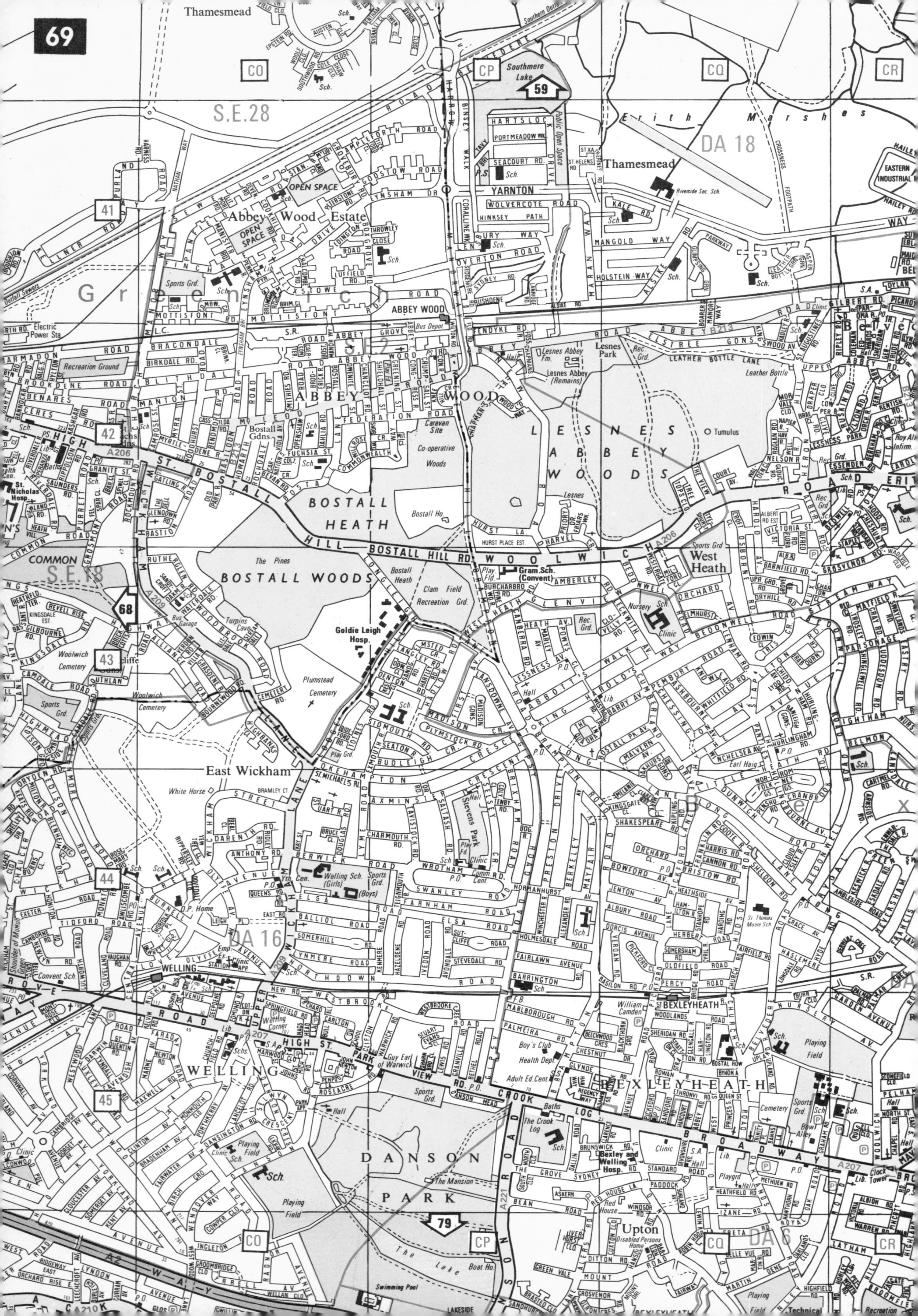
Thamesmead
CO
CP
CQ
CR
Southmere Lake
59
S.E.28
Erith Marshes
DA 18
Thamesmead
HARTSLOCK
PORTMEADOW WK.
SEACOURT RD.
YARNTON
WOLVERCOTE ROAD
HINKSEY PATH
Public Open Space
Riverside Sec. Sch.
MANGOLD WAY
HOLSTEIN WAY
EASTERN INDUSTRIAL
OPEN SPACE
Abbey Wood Estate
41
Greenwich
Sports Grd.
ABBEY WOOD
Bus Depot
Electric Power Sta.
S.E.2
Recreation Ground
Lesnes Abbey Fm.
Lesnes Abbey (Remains)
Lesnes Park
LEATHER BOTTLE LANE
Leather Bottle
ABBEY WOOD
LESNES ABBEY WOODS
Tumulus
42
Bostall Gdns.
Caravan Site
Co-operative Woods
St. Nicholas Hosp.
BOSTALL HEATH
Bostall Ho.
BOSTALL HILL RD.
WOOLWICH
HURST PLACE EST.
West Heath
COMMON
S.E.18
The Pines
BOSTALL WOODS
Bostall Heath
Clam Field Recreation Grd.
Gram. Sch. (Convent)
68
Goldie Leigh Hosp.
Turpins Cave
Bus Garage
Nursery Sch.
Clinic
43
Woolwich Cemetery
Plumstead Cemetery
East Wickham
White Horse
Stevens Park
Earl Haig
Bexley
44
Welling Sch. (Girls)
(Boys)
O.P. Home
DA 16
WELLING
Shoulder of Mutton
Convent Sch.
BEXLEYHEATH
William Camden
St Thomas Moore Sch.
Playing Field
WELLING
Guy Earl of Warwick
Welling Corner
Boy's Club
Health Dept.
Adult Ed. Cent.
BEXLEYHEATH
45
Sports Grd.
DANSON PARK
The Mansion
The Crook Log
Baths
Bexley and Welling Hosp.
Red House
Upton
Disabled Persons Home
79
The Lake
Boat Ho.
Swimming Pool
DA 6
Playing Field
Technical
Recreation
Clock Tower
A206
A207
A209
A221
A210
A2
B213

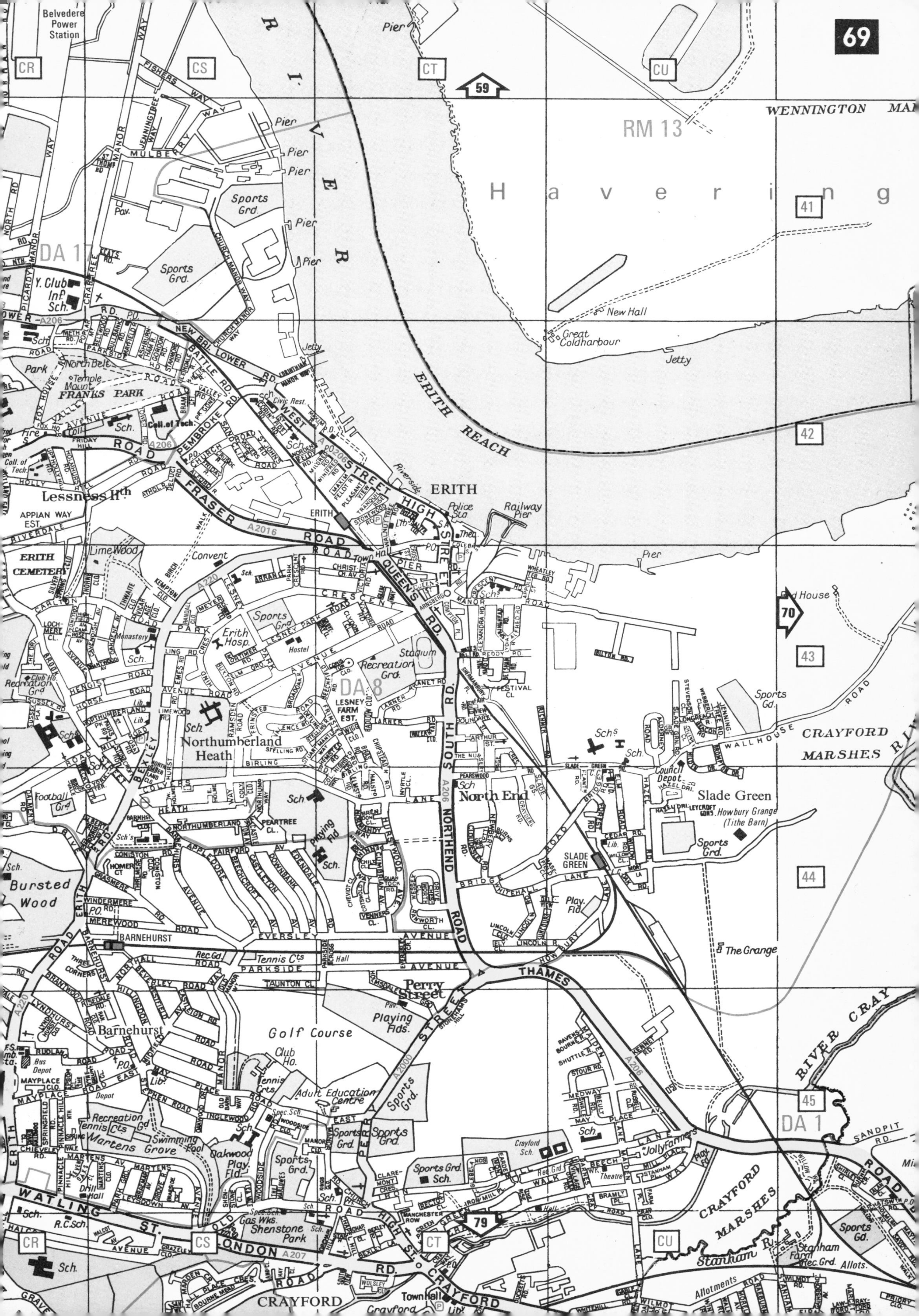

RIVER
Belvedere Power Station
CR
CS
CT
CU
59
WENNINGTON MARSHES
RM 13
Havering
41
42
43
44
45
70
79
DA 17
DA 8
DA 1
ERITH REACH
ERITH
New Hall
Great Coldharbour
Jetty
Pier
Sports Grd.
Railway Pier
Police Sta.
Lesness Hth
APPIAN WAY EST.
ERITH CEMETERY
FRANKS PARK
Northumberland Heath
Erith Hosp.
Stadium
Recreation Grd.
LESNEY FARM EST.
North End
Slade Green
Howbury Grange (Tithe Barn)
CRAYFORD MARSHES
The Grange
Perry Street
Golf Course
Club Ho.
Playing Flds.
Adult Education Centre
Barnehurst
BARNEHURST
Bursted Wood
Martens Grove
Swimming Pool
Oakwood Play. Fld.
Shenstone Park
Gas Wks.
WATLING ST.
LONDON RD.
CRAYFORD
Crayford
Town Hall
RIVER CRAY
Stanham Farm
Jolly Farmers
Theatre
THAMES ROAD
NORTHEND ROAD
FRASER ROAD
HIGH STREET
QUEENS RD.
WALLHOUSE ROAD
SANDPIT ROAD

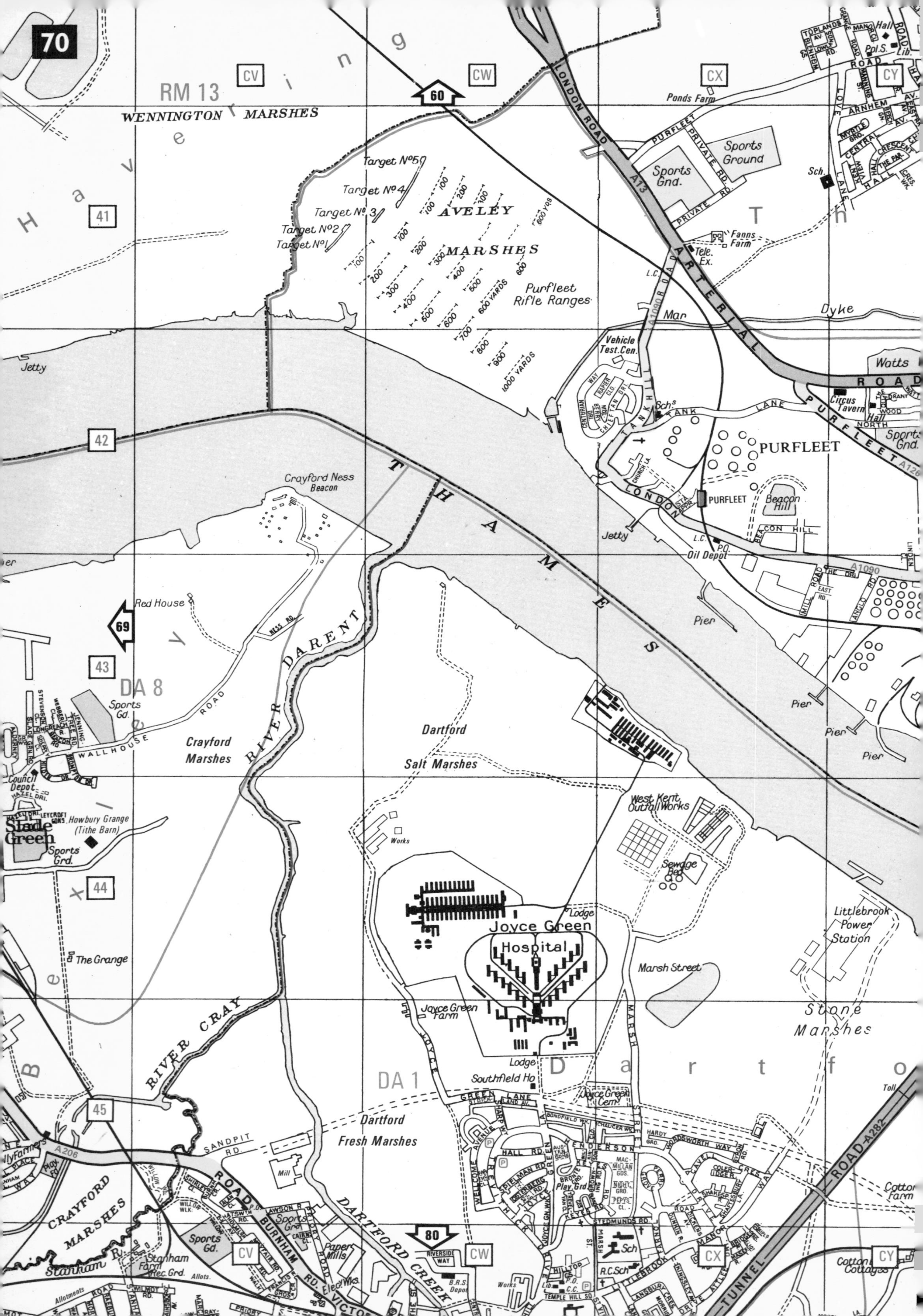
RM 13
WENNINGTON MARSHES
AVELEY MARSHES
Purfleet Rifle Ranges
Target No1
Target No2
Target No3
Target No4
Target No5
LONDON ROAD
A13
ARTERIAL ROAD
Ponds Farm
Sports Ground
Sports Gnd.
Fanns Farm
Tele. Ex.
Mar Dyke
Vehicle Test.Cen.
TANK LANE
PURFLEET
Beacon Hill
Oil Depot
Jetty
Pier
Circus Tavern
Watts
THAMES
Crayford Ness Beacon
Red House
NESS RD.
RIVER DARENT
DA 8
WALLHOUSE ROAD
Crayford Marshes
Dartford Salt Marshes
West Kent Outfall Works
Sewage Bed
Slade Green
Howbury Grange (Tithe Barn)
Council Depot
The Grange
Joyce Green Hospital
Lodge
Joyce Green Farm
Marsh Street
Littlebrook Power Station
Stone Marshes
Southfield Ho
DA 1
Dartford
RIVER CRAY
Dartford Fresh Marshes
SANDPIT RD.
A206
CRAYFORD MARSHES
Stanham Farm
Paper Mills
DARTFORD CREEK
RIVERSIDE WAY
TUNNEL ROAD A282
Cotton Farm
Cotton Cottages
CV
CW
CX
CY
41
42
43
44
45
60
69
80

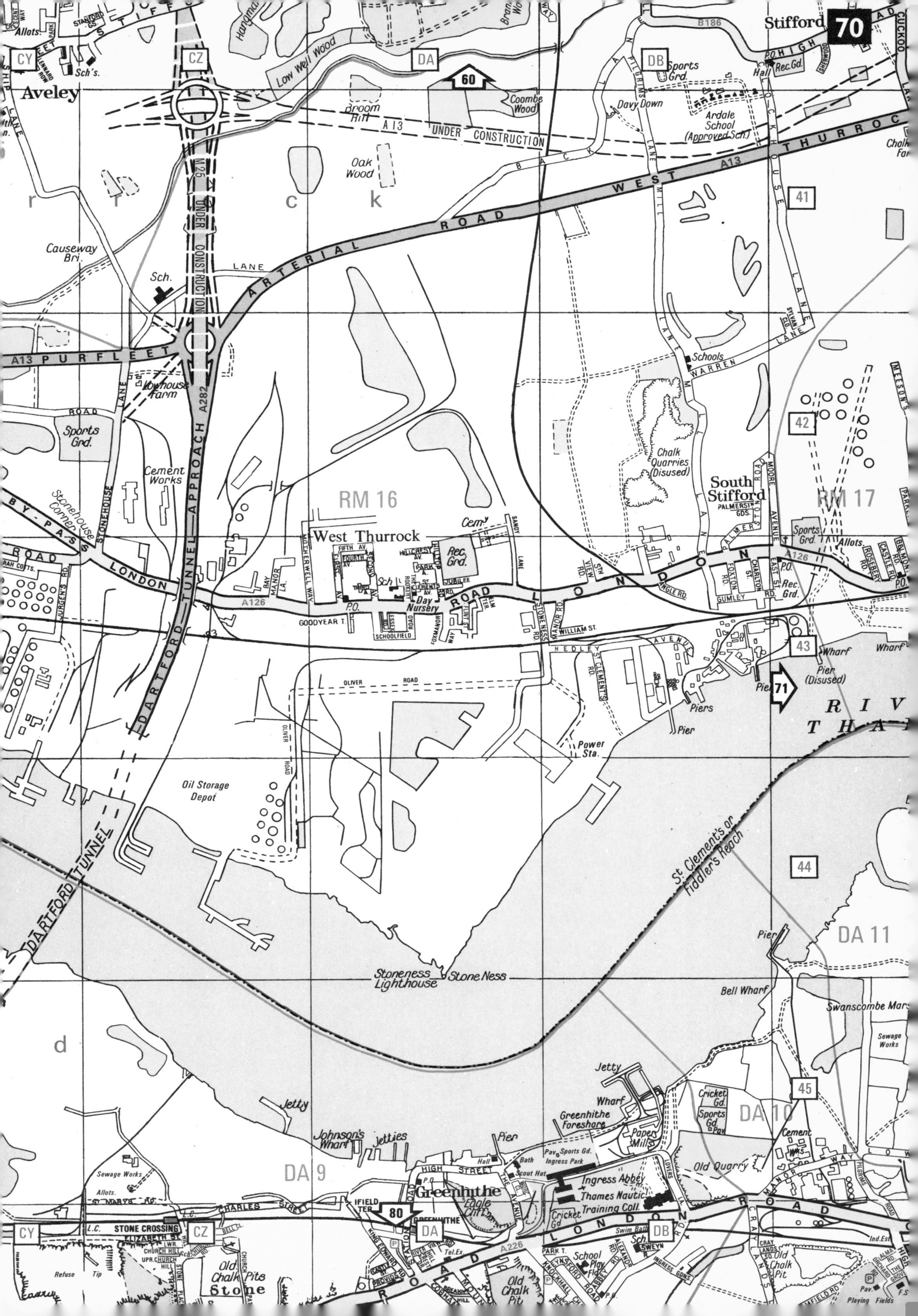

70
Stifford
Aveley
Low Well Wood
Coombe Wood
Broom Hill
A13 UNDER CONSTRUCTION
Davy Down
Ardale School (Approved Sch.)
WEST THURROCK
Oak Wood
ARTERIAL ROAD
Causeway Bri.
M25 UNDER CONSTRUCTION
PURFLEET
A282
Sports Grd.
Cement Works
Stonehouse Corner
DARTFORD TUNNEL APPROACH
RM 16
RM 17
West Thurrock
South Stifford
Chalk Quarries (Disused)
LONDON ROAD
A126
Oliver Road
Oil Storage Depot
Power Sta.
Piers
Pier (Disused)
St Clement's or Fiddler's Reach
Stoneness Lighthouse
Stone Ness
DARTFORD TUNNEL
DA 11
DA 10
DA 9
Bell Wharf
Swanscombe Marsh
Jetty
Wharf
Greenhithe Foreshore
Paper Mills
Johnson's Wharf
Jetties
HIGH STREET
Greenhithe
Ingress Abbey
Thames Nautical Training Coll.
Old Quarry
STONE CROSSING
LONDON ROAD
A226
Old Chalk Pits
Stone
Old Chalk Pit
Sewage Works
Refuse Tip

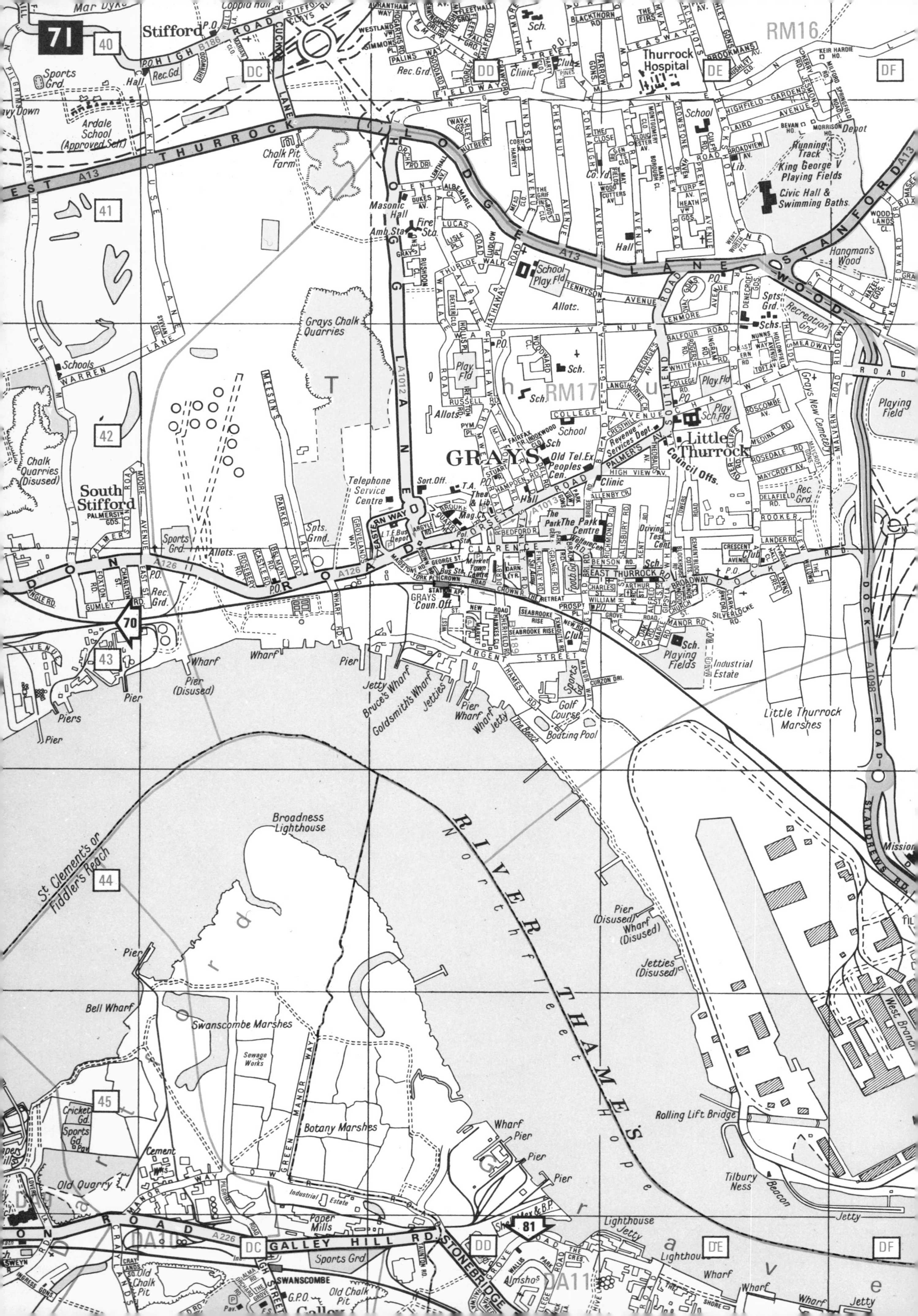
71
Stifford
RM16
Thurrock Hospital
Sports Grd.
Ardale School (Approved Sch.)
WEST THURROCK A13
Chalk Pit Farm
Masonic Hall
Fire Sta.
Amb. Sta.
LODGE LANE
A13
STANFORD
Civic Hall & Swimming Baths
King George V Playing Fields
Running Track
Hangman's Wood
Grays Chalk Quarries
Schools
WARREN LANE
Chalk Quarries (Disused)
South Stifford
RM17
GRAYS
Little Thurrock
Council Offs.
Old Tel. Ex.
Peoples Cen.
Telephone Service Centre
Revenue Services Dept.
Clinic
The Park Centre
Grays New Cemetery
Playing Field
A1012
A126
A1013
DOCK ROAD
A1089
LONDON ROAD
Grays Coun. Off.
Industrial Estate
Little Thurrock Marshes
Wharf
Pier
Pier (Disused)
Piers
Jetty
Bruce's Wharf
Goldsmith's Wharf
Jetties
Golf Course
Boating Pool
The Beach
St. Clement's or Fiddler's Reach
Broadness Lighthouse
RIVER THAMES
Northfleet Hope
Pier (Disused)
Wharf (Disused)
Jetties (Disused)
Bell Wharf
Swanscombe Marshes
Sewage Works
Botany Marshes
Rolling Lift Bridge
Tilbury Ness
Beacon
Cricket Gd.
Sports Gd.
Cement Wks.
Old Quarry
Industrial Estate
Paper Mills
GALLEY HILL RD.
A226
STONEBRIDGE
Lighthouse Jetty
Sports Grd.
Swanscombe
Old Chalk Pit
DA10
DA11
81
70
40
41
42
43
44
45
DC
DD
DE
DF
Mission
West Branch

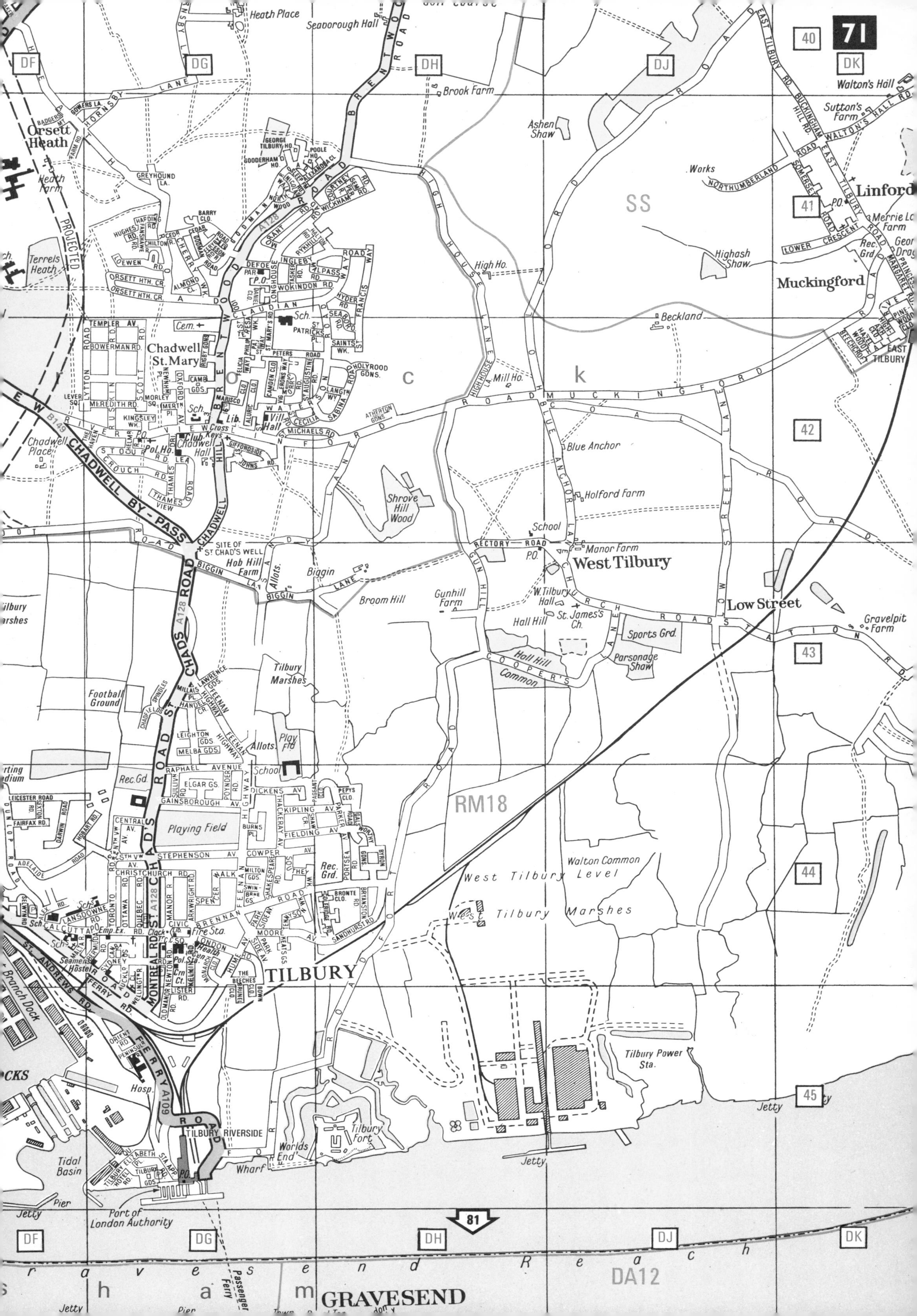

71
40
41
42
43
44
45
DF
DG
DH
DJ
DK
Heath Place
Seaborough Hall
Brook Farm
Walton's Hall
Sutton's Farm
Linford
Works
NORTHUMBERLAND
Ashen Shaw
SS
Orsett Heath
Heath Farm
Terrels Heath
HORNSBY LANE
GOWERS LA.
GREYHOUND LA.
BRENTWOOD ROAD
HIGH HOUSE LANE
High Ho.
Highash Shaw
LOWER CRESCENT
Rec. Grd.
Muckingford
Beckland
EAST TILBURY
Chadwell St. Mary
Cem.
Sch.
Lib.
Vill. Hall
Cross Keys
Club
Pol. Ho.
Chadwell Hall
Chadwell Place
Mill Ho.
MUCKINGFORD ROAD
Blue Anchor
BLUE ANCHOR LANE
Holford Farm
Shrove Hill Wood
School
Manor Farm
RECTORY ROAD
P.O.
West Tilbury
W. Tilbury Hall
St. James's Ch.
Hall Hill
Gunhill Farm
Broom Hill
Biggin
BIGGIN LANE
Hob Hill Farm
SITE OF ST. CHAD'S WELL
CHADWELL BY-PASS
CHADWELL HILL
ST. CHADS ROAD
A128
Low Street
LOW STREET LANE
Gravelpit Farm
STATION ROAD
Sports Grd.
Parsonage Shaw
Hall Hill Common
COOPER'S
Tilbury Marshes
Football Ground
Allots.
Play Fld
School
Rec. Gd.
Playing Field
Rec. Grd.
RM18
Walton Common Level
West Tilbury Level
West Tilbury Marshes
FORT ROAD
TILBURY
Fire Sta.
Pol. Sta.
Health Cen.
Emp. Ex.
Seamens Hostel
Branch Dock
ST. ANDREWS RD.
FERRY ROAD
A109
Hosp.
TILBURY RIVERSIDE
Tidal Basin
Pier
Jetty
Port of London Authority
Wharf
Worlds End
Tilbury Fort
Tilbury Power Sta.
Jetty
81
Gravesend Reach
DA12
GRAVESEND
Passenger Ferry
Jetty
Pier

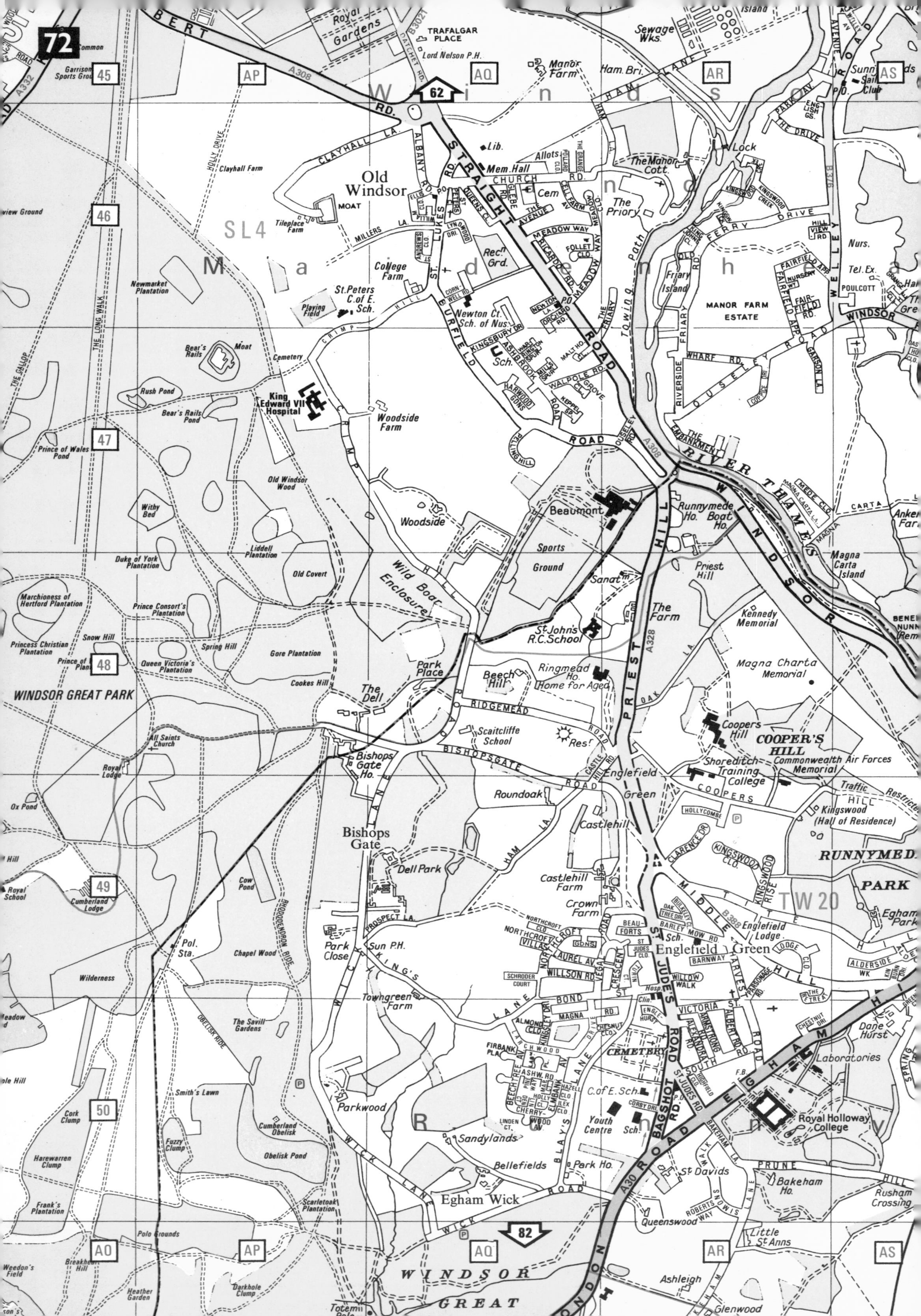

62
82
45
46
47
48
49
50
AO
AP
AQ
AR
AS
Royal Gardens
TRAFALGAR PLACE
Lord Nelson P.H.
DATCHET RD.
B3021
A308
A332
Garrison Sports Grd.
Common
Sewage Wks.
Manor Farm
Ham Bri.
HAM LANE
Island
Sunnymeads
Sailing Club
P.O.
ENGLISH GS.
THE DRIVE
PARK AV.
WELLEY AVENUE
WELLEY RD.
Lock
CLAYHALL LA.
Clayhall Farm
HOLLY DRIVE
ALBANY RD.
STRAIGHT ROAD
Lib.
Mem. Hall
Allots.
THE GRANGE
POLLARD CLO.
The Manor Cott.
CHURCH RD.
Old Windsor
MOAT
Tileplace Farm
MILLERS LA.
ST. LUKES RD.
PETERS CL.
QUEENS CL.
GLEBE RD.
THE AVENUE
CELL FARM AV.
MEADOW CLO.
Cem
The Priory
KINGSWOOD CREEK
FERRY DRIVE
HILL VIEW RD.
B376
Nurs.
Tel. Ex.
SL4
Windsor and Maidenhead
MEADOW WAY
RICARDO RD.
FOLLET CLO.
Rec.n Grd.
College Farm
ST. ANDREWS CLO.
LYNWOOD DRI.
CORNWELL RD.
Towing Path
Friary Island
FRIARY RD.
MANOR FARM ESTATE
FAIRFIELD APP.
NURSERY WY.
FAIRFIELD RD.
POULCOTT
WINDSOR RD.
THE FRIARY
Newmarket Plantation
THE LONG WALK
St. Peters C. of E. Sch.
Playing Field
CRIMP HILL
BURFIELD RD.
Newton Ct. Sch. of Nus.
NEWTON LA.
ORCHARD RD.
KINGSBURY DR.
ASHBROOK RD.
Sch.
MALT HO. CL.
WALPOLE RD.
GROVE CL.
HARWOOD GDNS.
KEPPEL SP.
WHARF RD.
RIVERSIDE
OUSELEY RD.
COPPICE DRI.
GARSON LA.
THE GALLOP
Bear's Rails
Moat
Cemetery
Rush Pond
Bear's Rails Pond
King Edward VII Hospital
Woodside Farm
PELLING HILL
ROAD
THE EMBANKMENT
RIVER THAMES
Prince of Wales Pond
Old Windsor Wood
Withy Bed
Woodside
Beaumont
Runnymede Ho.
Boat Ho.
MEDE CLO.
MAGNA CARTA LA.
CARTA
MAGNA
WINDSOR RD.
Magna Carta Island
Liddell Plantation
Duke of York Plantation
Old Covert
Wild Boar Enclosure
Sports Ground
Sanat.m
Priest Hill
Marchioness of Hertford Plantation
Prince Consort's Plantation
Snow Hill
Spring Hill
Gore Plantation
St. John's R.C. School
The Farm
Kennedy Memorial
Princess Christian Plantation
Prince of Wales Plantation
Queen Victoria's Plantation
WINDSOR GREAT PARK
Cookes Hill
Park Place
Beech Hill
Ringmead Ho.
Home for Aged
Magna Charta Memorial
PRIEST HILL
A328
The Dell
RIDGEMEAD ROAD
OAK LA.
All Saints Church
Scaitcliffe School
Res.r
Coopers Hill
COOPER'S HILL
Royal Lodge
Bishops Gate Ho.
BISHOPSGATE ROAD
CASTLE HILL RD.
Englefield Green
Shoreditch Training College
Commonwealth Air Forces Memorial
Traffic Restricted
COOPERS HILL
Ox Pond
Roundoak
HOLLYCOMBE
Kingswood (Hall of Residence)
Castlehill
Bishops Gate
HAM LA.
CLARENCE DR.
KINGSWOOD CLO.
RUNNYMEDE
Dell Park
Cow Pond
Castlehill Farm
KINGSWOOD RISE
PARK
Royal School
Cumberland Lodge
RHODODENDRON RIDE
Crown Farm
MIDDLE HILL
TW20
B388
BILKELEY CL.
TREE DRI.
BARLEY MOW RD.
Sch.
Englefield Lodge
Egham Park
PROSPECT LA.
Pol. Sta.
Park Close
Sun P.H.
NORTHCROFT CLO.
NORTHCROFT VILLAS
GDNS.
BEAUFORTS
ST. JUDES CLO.
Englefield Green
LODGE CLO.
BARNWAY
HARVEST RD.
ALDERSIDE WK.
Chapel Wood
KING'S LANE
WICK LANE
AUREL AV.
WILLSON RD.
VEGA CRES.
ST. JUDE'S ROAD
WILLOW WALK
PARSONAGE RD.
THE TREK
Wilderness
Towngreen Farm
SCHRODER COURT
BOND ST.
Hosp.
Clin.
VICTORIA ST.
ALBERT RD.
OBELISK RIDE
The Savill Gardens
ALMOND CLO.
KINGSBURY DR.
MAGNA RD.
CHESNUT CLO.
ENGLEHURST
ARMSTRONG RD.
ALEXANDRA RD.
CHESTNUT DRI.
Dane Hurst
FIRBANK PLA.
LARCHWOOD
CEMETERY
SOUTH RD.
Laboratories
EGHAM HILL
BEECHTREE AV.
ASHW. RD.
HOLLY
ELMBANK AV.
HAZELL CLO.
ILEX CLO.
CHERRYWOOD AV.
LINDEN CT.
C. of E. Sch.
CORBY DRI.
ST. JUDES RD.
F.B.
Royal Holloway College
Smith's Lawn
Cork Clump
Parkwood
Cumberland Obelisk
Youth Centre
Sch.
BAGSHOT RD.
Sandylands
Runnymede
Fuzzy Clump
Obelisk Pond
Harewarren Clump
BLAY'S LANE
Bellefields
Park Ho.
BAKEHAM LA.
St. Davids
PRUNE HILL
Bakeham Ho.
Rusham Crossing
Frank's Plantation
Scarletoak Plantation
Egham Wick
ROAD
ROBERTS WAY
SNOWS LANE
Queenswood
A30 LONDON ROAD
Polo Grounds
WICK LANE
Little St. Anns
Weedon's Field
Breakheart Hill
WINDSOR GREAT
Ashleigh
Heather Garden
Darkhole Clump
Totem Pole
Glenwood

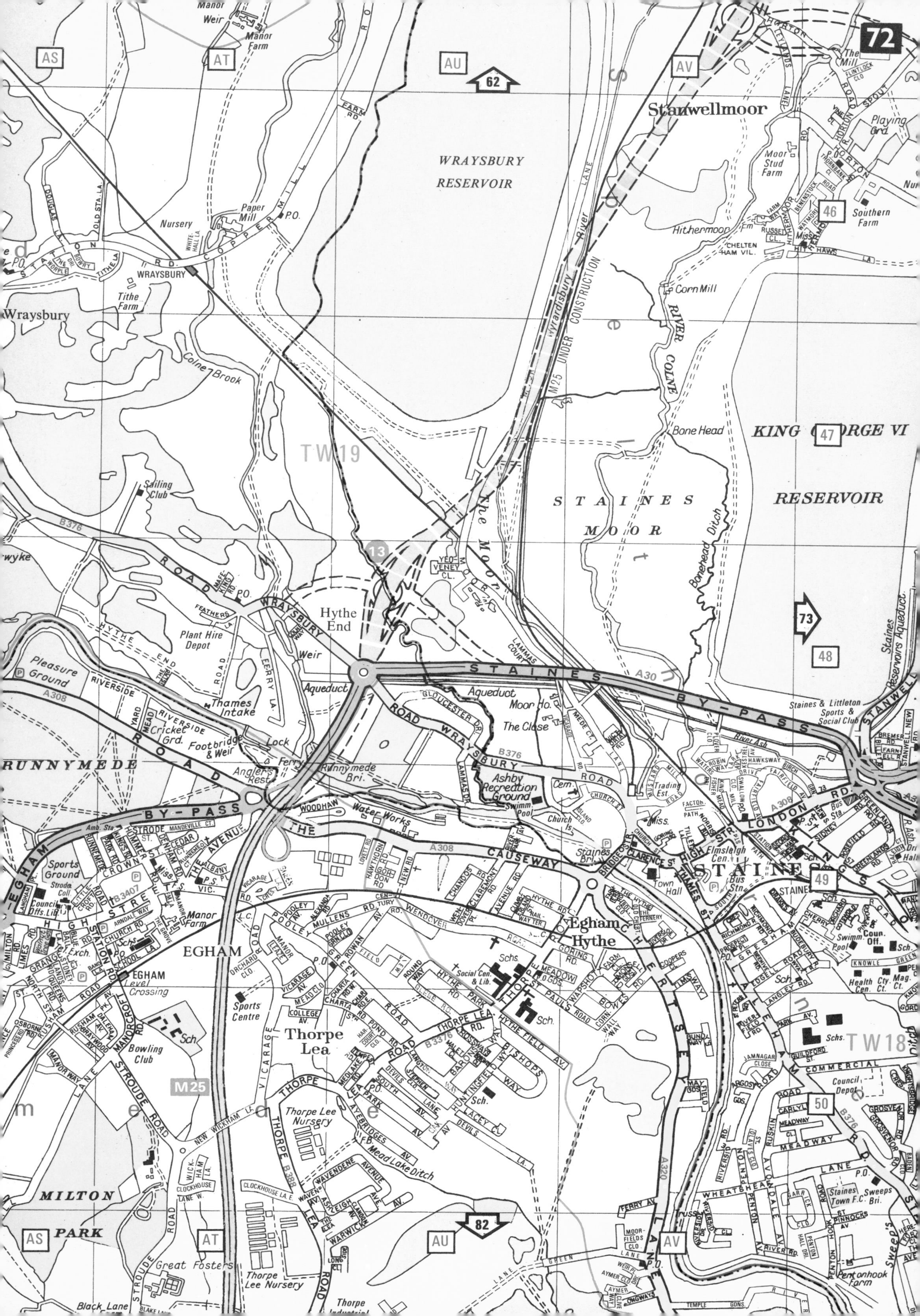

AS
AT
AU
AV
62
Stanwellmoor
WRAYSBURY
RESERVOIR
Wraysbury
WRAYSBURY
Colne Brook
Paper Mill
Nursery
Tithe Farm
Manor Farm
The Mill
Moor Stud Farm
Playing Grd.
Southern Farm
46
Hithermoon Fm
Corn Mill
RIVER COLNE
M25 UNDER CONSTRUCTION
Wyrardisbury River
Bone Head
KING GEORGE VI
47
RESERVOIR
STAINES
MOOR
Bonehead Ditch
73
48
TW19
Sailing Club
B376
13
Hythe End
Plant Hire Depot
Pleasure Ground
Weir
Aqueduct
Thames Intake
Cricket Grd.
Footbridge & Weir
Lock
Ferry
Angler's Rest
Runnymede Bri.
RUNNYMEDE
STAINES BY-PASS
A30
Moor Ho.
The Close
Ashby Recreation Ground
Swimm. Pool
Trading Est.
Staines & Littleton Sports & Social Club
River Ash
STANWELL
Water Works
THE CAUSEWAY
A308
LONDON RD.
Staines Bri.
STAINES
49
Town Hall
Elmsleigh Cen.
Bus Stn.
Sports Ground
EGHAM
HIGH STREET
Manor Farm
Egham Hythe
Coun. Off.
Swimm. Pool
Health Cen.
Mag. Ct.
EGHAM
Level Crossing
Sports Centre
Thorpe Lea
Social Cen. & Lib.
Schs.
Sch.
Bowling Club
M25
TW18
Council Depot
50
Thorpe Lee Nursery
Mead Lake Ditch
MILTON
PARK
82
A320
Staines Town F.C.
Sweeps Bri.
Great Fosters
Thorpe Lee Nursery
Pentonhook Farm
Black Lane
Thorpe Industrial

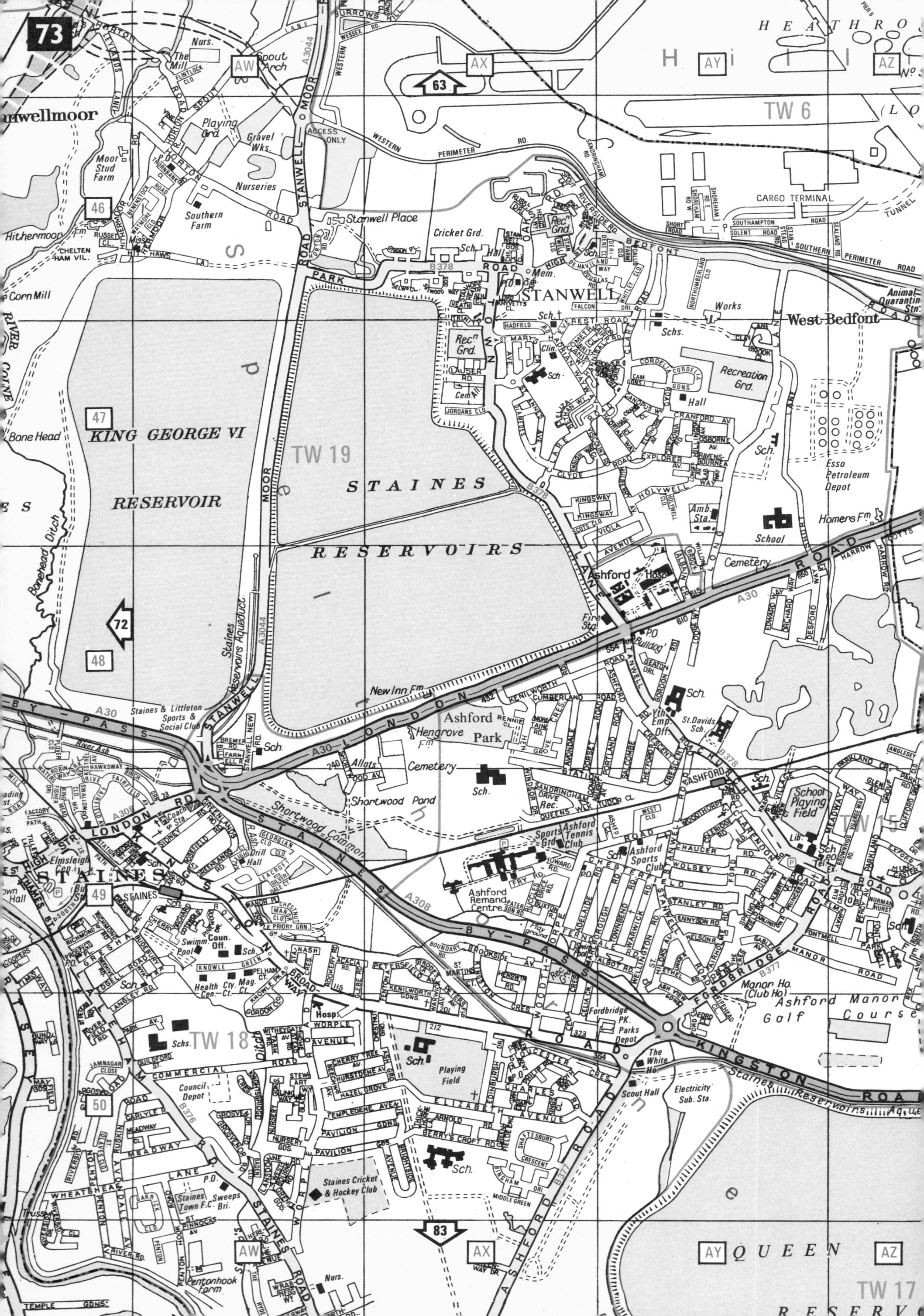
Stanwellmoor
King George VI Reservoir
Staines Reservoirs
Stanwell
West Bedfont
Ashford
Staines
Heathrow
TW 6
TW 19
TW 15
TW 18
TW 17
Cargo Terminal
Southern Perimeter Road
Western Perimeter Rd.
London Road
Staines By-Pass
Kingston Road
Stanwell Moor Road
Esso Petroleum Depot
Ashford Hosp.
Ashford Park
Ashford Manor Golf Course
Ashford Remand Centre
Shortwood Common
Shortwood Pond
Staines Reservoirs Aqueduct
Queen
Staines Cricket & Hockey Club
Staines Town F.C.
Pentonhook Farm
Hithermoor Fm.
Moor Stud Farm
Southern Farm
Stanwell Place
Bone Head
Bonehead Ditch
River Colne
River Ash
Recreation Grd.
Homers Fm.
New Inn Fm.
Hengrove Fm.
Fordbridge Pk.
The White Ho.
Electricity Sub. Sta.
63
72
83

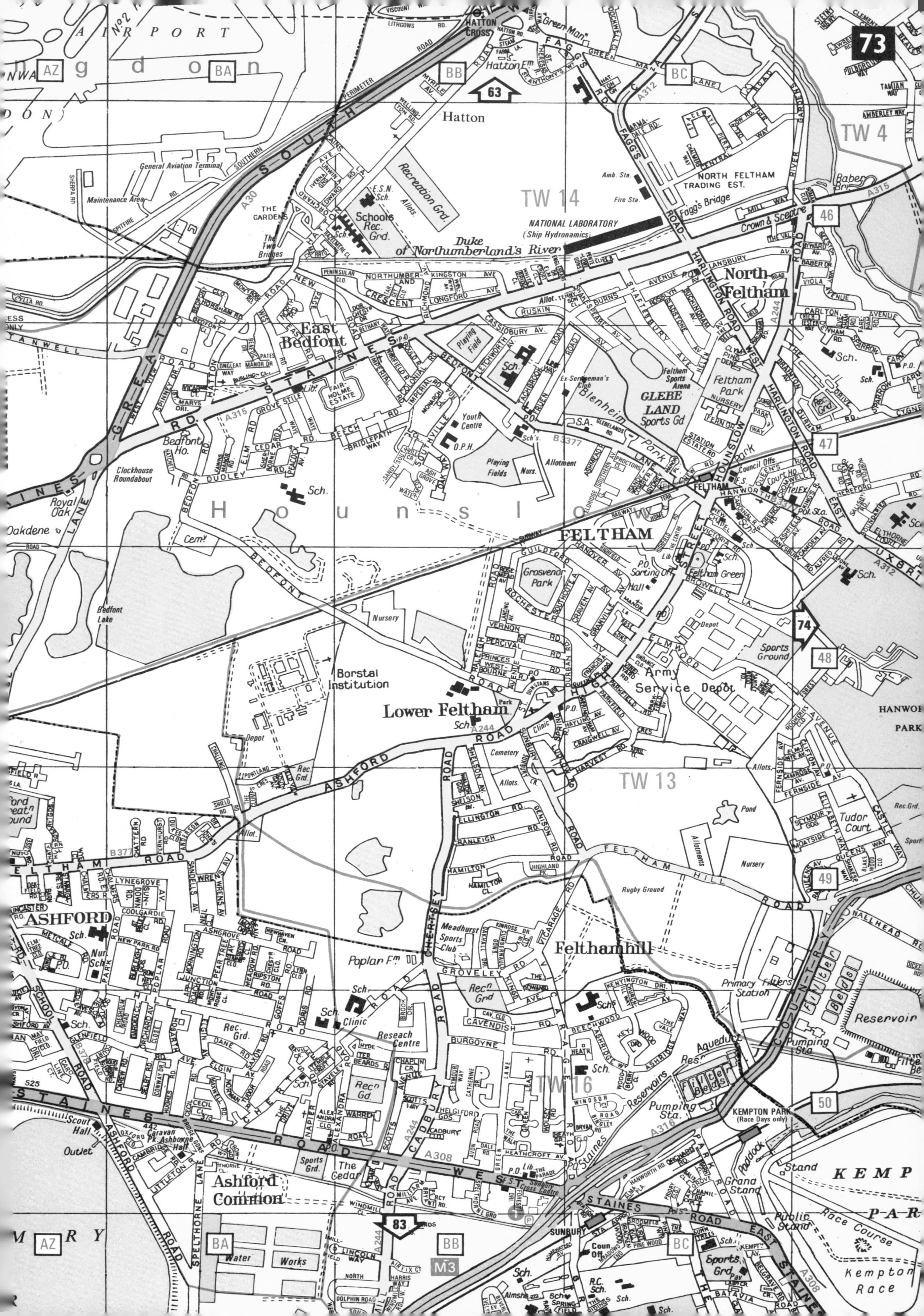

AIRPORT
AZ
BA
BB
BC
63
Hatton Cross
Hatton
TW 4
TW 14
NORTH FELTHAM TRADING EST.
General Aviation Terminal
Maintenance Area
Recreation Grd.
Schools Rec. Grd.
NATIONAL LABORATORY (Ship Hydronamics)
Duke of Northumberland's River
Fagg's Bridge
Crown & Sceptre
46
North Feltham
East Bedfont
FAIR-HOLME ESTATE
Playing Field
Youth Centre
O.P.H.
Playing Fields
GLEBE LAND Sports Gd
Feltham Park
Blenheim Park
47
Clockhouse Roundabout
Bedfont Ho.
Royal Oak
Oakdene
Hounslow
FELTHAM
Grosvenor Park
Feltham Green
Bedfont Lake
Nursery
Borstal Institution
74
Sports Ground
48
Army Service Depot
Lower Feltham
TW 13
Cemetery
Allots.
Tudor Court
Pond
Allotments
Nursery
49
Rugby Ground
ASHFORD
Meadhurst Sports Club
Poplar Fm.
Felthamhill
Primary Filters Station
Reservoir
Reseach Centre
TW 16
Aqueduct
Reservoirs
Pumping Sta.
KEMPTON PARK (Race Days only)
50
Ashford Common
The Cedars
Sunbury Cross Centre
83
M3
Water Works
SUNBURY STA.
Kempton Race Course
Public Stand
Grand Stand
Paddock
A30
A315
A312
A244
A308
A316
B3377

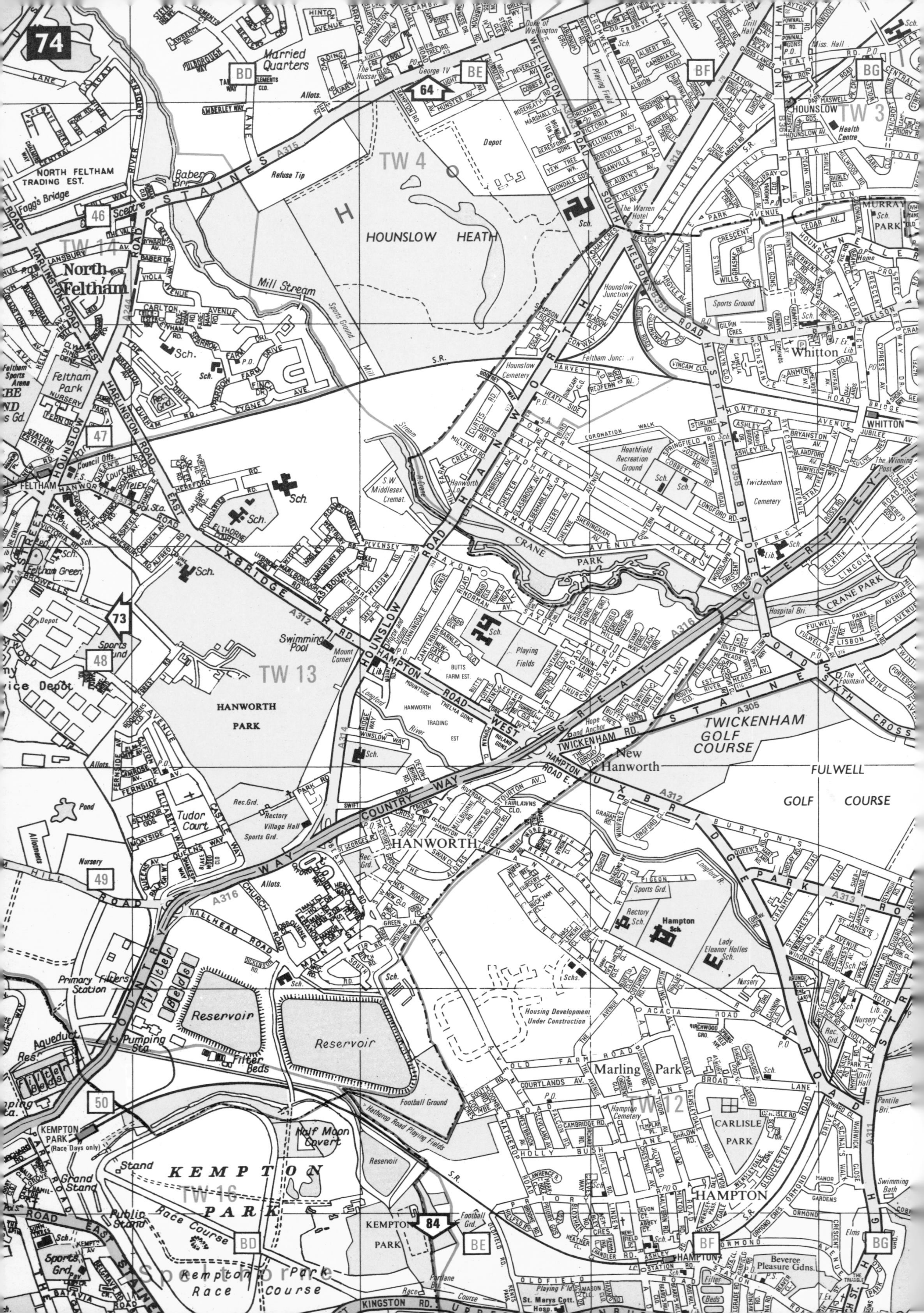
Married Quarters
BD
BE
BF
BG
64
George IV
The Hussar
Duke of Wellington
Allots.
AMBERLEY WAY
Depot
TW 4
TW 3
Refuse Tip
HOUNSLOW
Health Centre
NORTH FELTHAM TRADING EST.
Fogg's Bridge
Baber Bri.
STAINES ROAD
A315
46
Sceptre
HOUNSLOW HEATH
Mill Stream
The Warren Hotel
Hounslow Junction
Sports Ground
TW 14
North Feltham
Feltham Sports Arena
Feltham Park
Sch.
P.O.
Rec. Grd.
S.R.
Feltham Junction
Hounslow Cemetery
Whitton
WHITTON
47
CYGNET AVE.
Council Offs.
FELTHAM
Heathfield Recreation Ground
CORONATION WALK
S.W. Middlesex Cremat.
Twickenham Cemetery
The Winning Post
Feltham Green
73
CRANE PARK
Crane Park
Hospital Bri.
UXBRIDGE ROAD
A312
Swimming Pool
Mount Corner
Depot
48
Sports Ground
Service Depot
TW 13
HANWORTH PARK
HOUNSLOW ROAD
HAMPTON ROAD WEST
BUTTS FARM EST.
HANWORTH TRADING EST.
Playing Fields
A316
The Fountain
Hope and Anchor
TWICKENHAM ROAD
New Hanworth
TWICKENHAM GOLF COURSE
FULWELL GOLF COURSE
A305
STAINES ROAD
GREAT CHERTSEY ROAD
Pond
Allots.
Allotments
Nursery
Tudor Court
Rec. Grd.
Rectory Village Hall
Sports Grd.
COUNTRY WAY
HANWORTH
49
HILL ROAD
A316
Allots.
Sports Grd.
Rectory Sch.
Hampton Sch.
Lady Eleanor Holles Sch.
A313
Primary Filters Station
Filter Beds
Reservoir
Reservoir
Housing Development Under Construction
Marling Park
Aqueduct
Res.
Filter Beds
Pumping Sta.
Football Ground
50
KEMPTON PARK (Race Days only)
Hatherop Road Playing Fields
Half Moon Covert
Reservoir
TW 12
CARLISLE PARK
Hampton Cemetery
Pantile Bri.
Swimming Bath
Grand Stand
Stand
KEMPTON PARK
TW 16
Public Stand
Race Course
84
KEMPTON PARK
Football Grd.
HAMPTON
BD
BE
BF
BG
Beveree Pleasure Gdns.
Sports Grd.
Kempton Park Race Course
Portlane Bri.
St. Marys Cott. Hosp.
KINGSTON RD.
A311

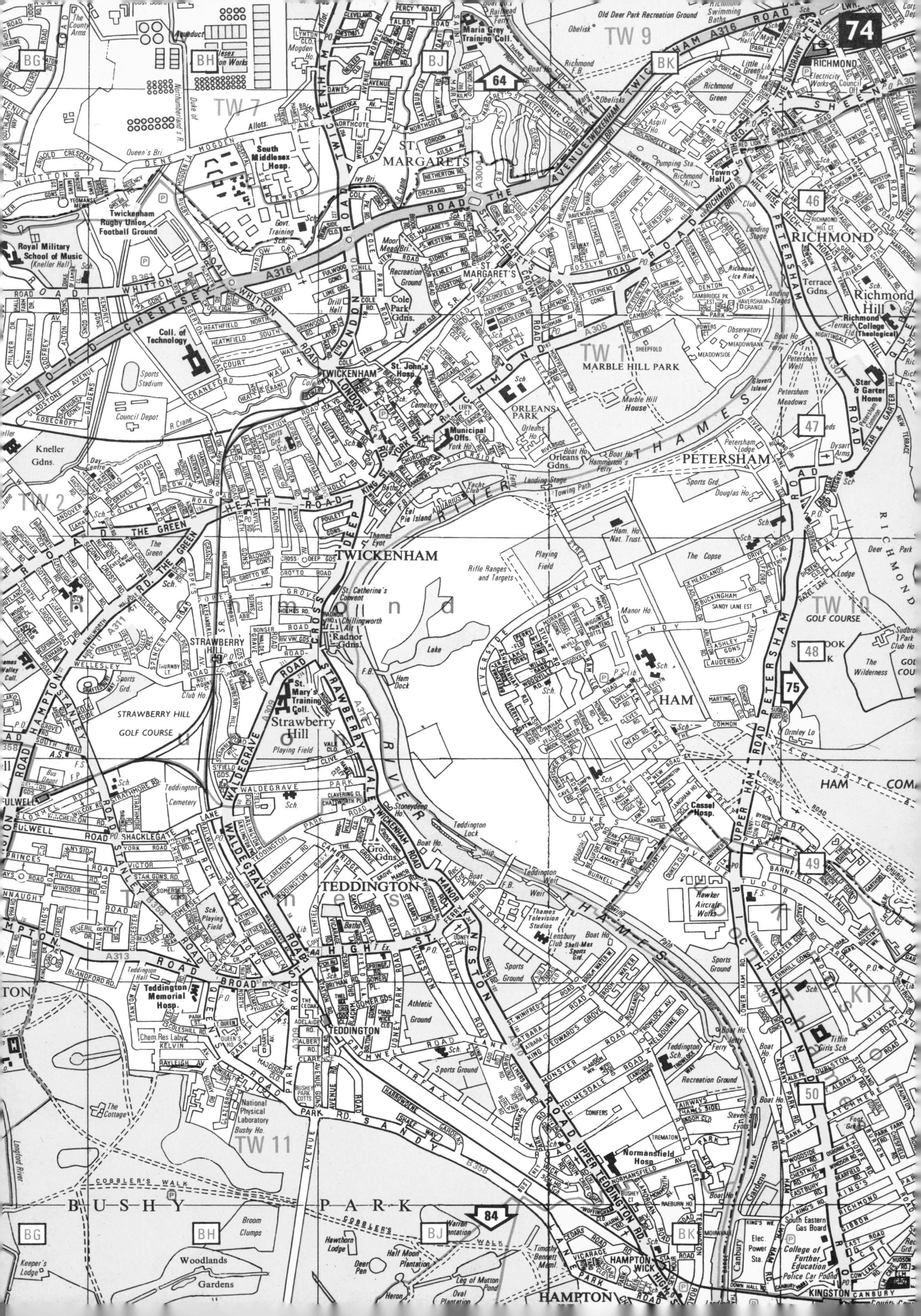
TW 9
TW 7
TW 1
TW 2
TW 10
TW 11
KT 2
BG
BH
BJ
BK
64
46
47
48
49
50
75
84
RICHMOND
Richmond Green
Richmond Hill
Richmond College Theological
Star & Garter Home
Old Deer Park Recreation Ground
Richmond Swimming Baths
ST. MARGARETS
South Middlesex Hosp.
Twickenham Rugby Union Football Ground
Royal Military School of Music (Kneller Hall)
Coll. of Technology
Kneller Gdns.
Council Depot
Sports Stadium
TWICKENHAM
St. John's Hosp.
Municipal Offs.
Cole Park Gdns.
Recreation Ground
MARBLE HILL PARK
Marble Hill House
ORLEANS PARK
Orleans Gdns.
Hammerton's Ferry
PETERSHAM
Petersham Meadows
Glovers Island
Eel Pie Island
Thames Eyot
Rifle Ranges and Targets
Playing Field
Lake
Ham Dock
The Copse
Ham Ho. Nat. Trust
Manor Ho.
HAM
Cassel Hosp.
HAM COMMON
Hawker Aircraft Works
GOLF COURSE
The Wilderness
Ormley Lo
St. Catherine's Convent
Chillingworth Alt
Radnor Gdns.
STRAWBERRY HILL
St. Mary's Training Coll.
Strawberry Hill
STRAWBERRY HILL GOLF COURSE
Teddington Cemetery
Teddington Lock
Teddington Weir
Thames Television Studios
Lensbury Club
TEDDINGTON
Athletic Ground
Teddington Memorial Hosp.
National Physical Laboratory Bushy Ho.
Normansfield Hosp.
Tiffin Girls Sch.
South Eastern Gas Board
College of Further Education
Elec. Power Sta.
HAMPTON WICK
KINGSTON
BUSHY PARK
COBBLER'S WALK
Woodlands Gardens
Broom Clumps
Warren Plantation
Half Moon Plantation
Leg of Mutton Pond
Oval Plantation
Hawthorn Lodge
Deer Pen
Keeper's Lodge
The Cottage
Longford River
RIVER THAMES
CHERTSEY ROAD
WHITTON ROAD
TWICKENHAM ROAD
RICHMOND ROAD
PETERSHAM ROAD
UPPER HAM ROAD
HEATH ROAD
WALDEGRAVE ROAD
STRAWBERRY VALE
KINGSTON ROAD
UPPER TEDDINGTON RD.
BROAD ST.
HIGH ST.
HAMPTON ROAD
STANLEY ROAD
SANDY LANE
FULWELL

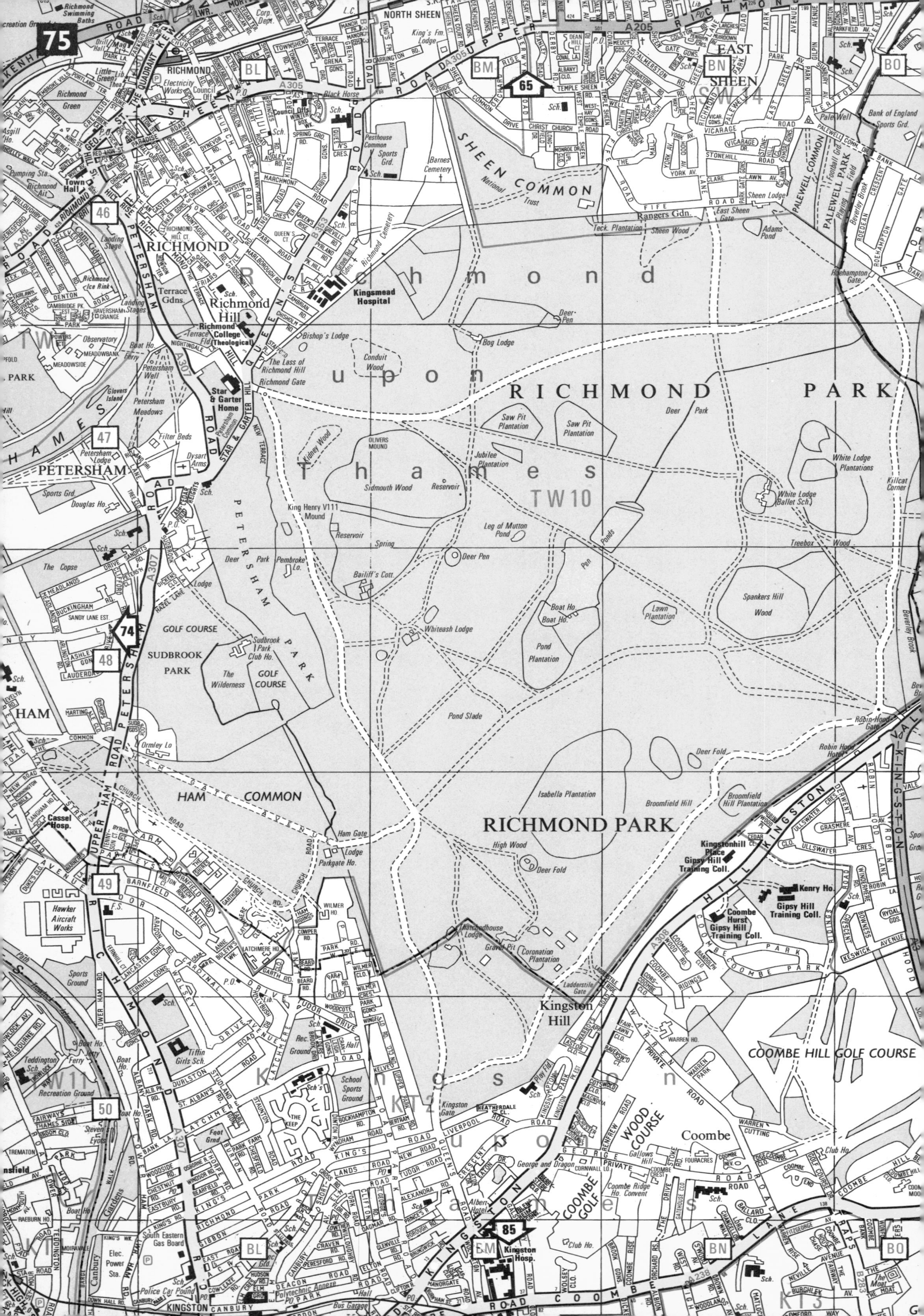
75
NORTH SHEEN
RICHMOND
EAST SHEEN
SW14
Sheen Common
National Trust
Temple Sheen
Richmond Green
Town Hall
Richmond Ait
Pumping Sta.
Landing Stage
Richmond Ice Rink
Terrace Gdns.
Richmond Hill
Richmond College (Theological)
Kingsmead Hospital
Richmond Cemetery
East Sheen Cemetery
Barnes Cemetery
Pesthouse Common Sports Grd.
Observatory
Petersham Well
Petersham Meadows
Glovers Island
Star & Garter Home
Richmond Gate
Bishop's Lodge
Conduit Wood
Bog Lodge
Deer Pen
Rangers Gdn.
East Sheen Gate
Sheen Lodge
Adams Pond
Sheen Wood
Teck. Plantation
Palewell Common
Bank of England Sports Grd.
Roehampton Gate
Richmond upon Thames
RICHMOND PARK
Saw Pit Plantation
Jubilee Plantation
Kidney Wood
Olivers Mound
Sidmouth Wood
Reservoir
King Henry VIII Mound
White Lodge Plantations
White Lodge (Ballet Sch.)
Killcat Corner
TW10
Leg of Mutton Pond
Pen Ponds
Deer Pen
Treebox Wood
Spring
Bailiff's Cott.
Pembroke Lo.
Deer Park
Petersham Park
PETERSHAM
Dysart Arms
Filter Beds
Sports Grd.
Douglas Ho.
The Copse
Whiteash Lodge
Boat Ho.
Pond Plantation
Lawn Plantation
Spankers Hill Wood
Beverley Brook
Golf Course
Sudbrook Park
Sudbrook Park Club Ho.
The Wilderness
Pond Slade
Robin Hood Gate
Robin Hood Hotel
Deer Fold
Isabella Plantation
Broomfield Hill
Broomfield Hill Plantation
HAM COMMON
Ham Gate
Ham Gate Avenue
Ormley Lo
HAM
Cassel Hosp.
RICHMOND PARK
High Wood
Deer Fold
Kingstonhill Place
Gipsy Hill Training Coll.
Kenry Ho.
Coombe Hurst
Parkgate Ho.
Wilmer Ho.
Hawker Aircraft Works
Sports Ground
Thatched House Lodge
Gravel Pit
Coronation Plantation
Ladderstile Gate
Kingston Hill
Tiffin Girls Sch.
Rec. Ground
School Sports Ground
Coombe Hill Golf Course
Warren Ho.
Teddington Lock
Recreation Ground
TW11
Kingston upon Thames
KT2
Kingston Gate
Coombe
Coombe Wood Golf Course
George and Dragon
Gallows Hill
Coombe Ridge Ho. Convent
Club Ho.
Albert Hotel
Kingston Hosp.
South Eastern Gas Board
Elec. Power Sta.
Canbury Gardens
Police Car Pound
Polytechnic Annexe
Bus Garage
KT1
KT3
46
47
48
49
50
65
74
85
BL
BM
BN
BO
EM

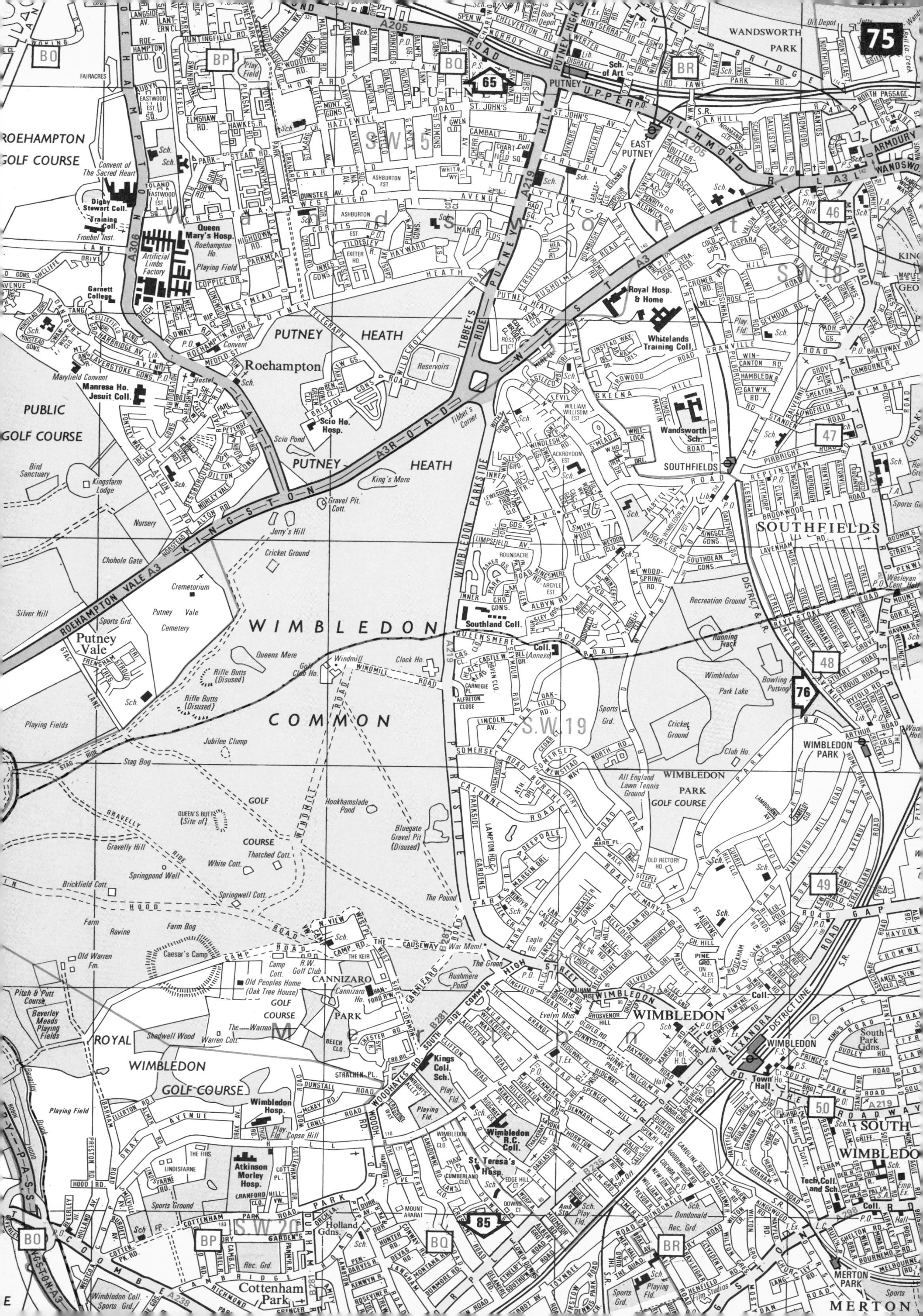

ROEHAMPTON GOLF COURSE
PUTNEY
WANDSWORTH PARK
S.W.15
S.W.18
S.W.19
S.W.20
EAST PUTNEY
PUTNEY HEATH
Roehampton
PUBLIC GOLF COURSE
Queen Mary's Hosp.
Convent of The Sacred Heart
Digby Stewart Coll.
Training Coll.
Froebel Inst.
Garnett College
Manresa Ho. Jesuit Coll.
Maryfield Convent
Royal Hosp. & Home
Whitelands Training Coll.
Wandsworth Sch.
SOUTHFIELDS
Southland Coll.
WIMBLEDON COMMON
Putney Vale
Putney Vale Cemetery
Crematorium
Queens Mere
Windmill
Rifle Butts (Disused)
Playing Fields
GOLF COURSE
Caesar's Camp
CANNIZARO PARK
ROYAL WIMBLEDON GOLF COURSE
Wimbledon Hosp.
Atkinson Morley Hosp.
Cottenham Park
Kings Coll. Sch.
Wimbledon R.C. Coll.
St. Teresa's Hosp.
WIMBLEDON
WIMBLEDON PARK
WIMBLEDON PARK GOLF COURSE
All England Lawn Tennis Ground
Wimbledon Park Lake
Town Hall
SOUTH WIMBLEDON
MERTON PARK
KINGSTON ROAD
ROEHAMPTON VALE
PUTNEY HILL
WEST HILL
RICHMOND ROAD
UPPER RICHMOND ROAD
PARKSIDE
WIMBLEDON PARKSIDE
A3
A205
A219
A306
A218
A238
B281
A298

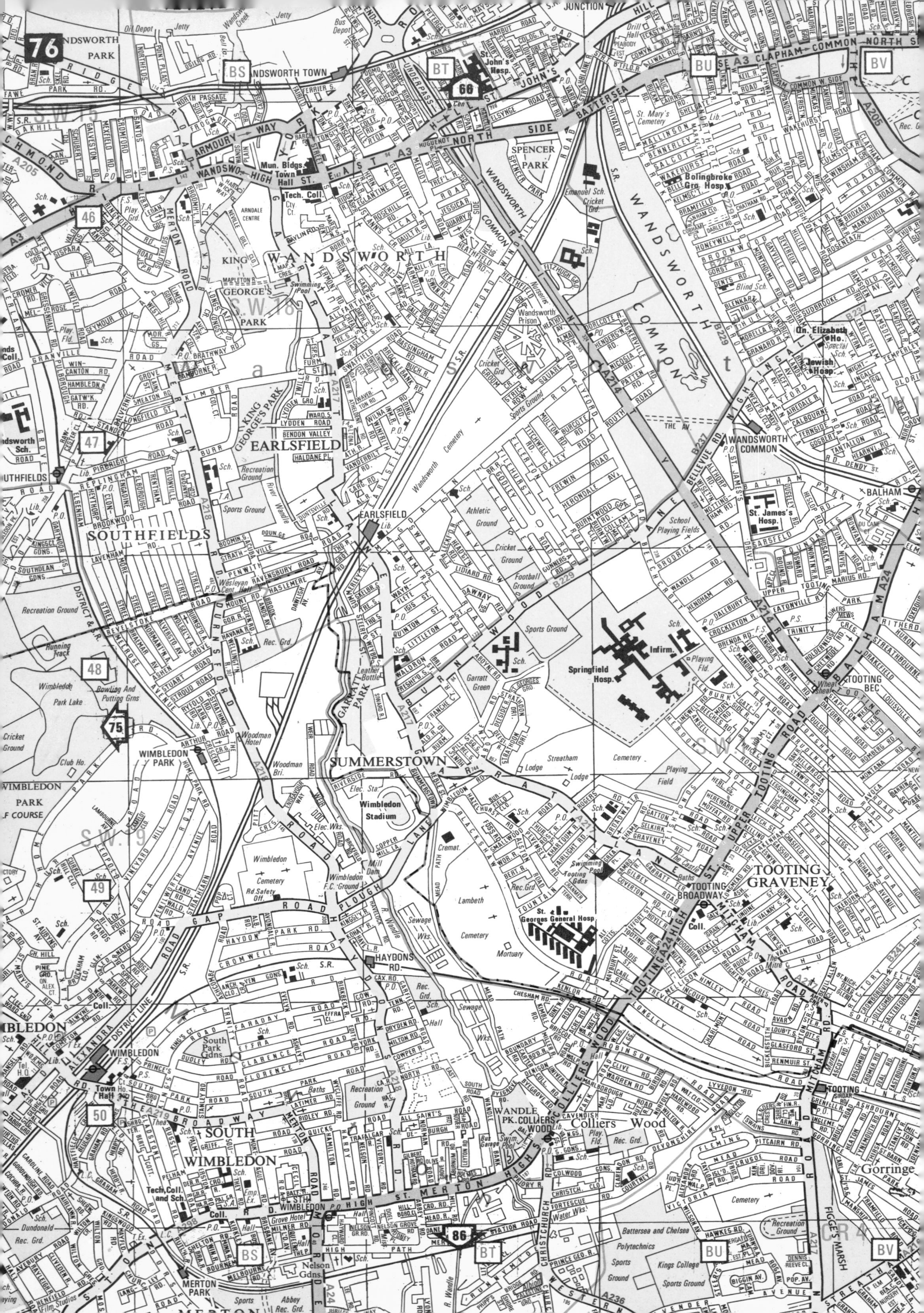

76
BS
BT
BU
BV
66
46
47
48
49
50
75
86
WANDSWORTH
EARLSFIELD
SOUTHFIELDS
SUMMERSTOWN
WIMBLEDON PARK
SOUTH WIMBLEDON
TOOTING GRAVENEY
TOOTING BEC
TOOTING BROADWAY
WANDSWORTH COMMON
BALHAM
Colliers Wood
Gorringe
SPENCER PARK
KING GEORGE'S PARK
Wandsworth Prison
Springfield Hosp.
St. Georges General Hosp.
Wimbledon Stadium
Wimbledon Cemetery
Lambeth Cemetery
Streatham Cemetery
Wandsworth Cemetery
Wimbledon Park Lake
Garratt Green
GARRATT PARK
Bolingbroke Gro. Hosp.
St. James's Hosp.
Qn. Elizabeth Ho.
S.W.18
S.W.19
S.W.15

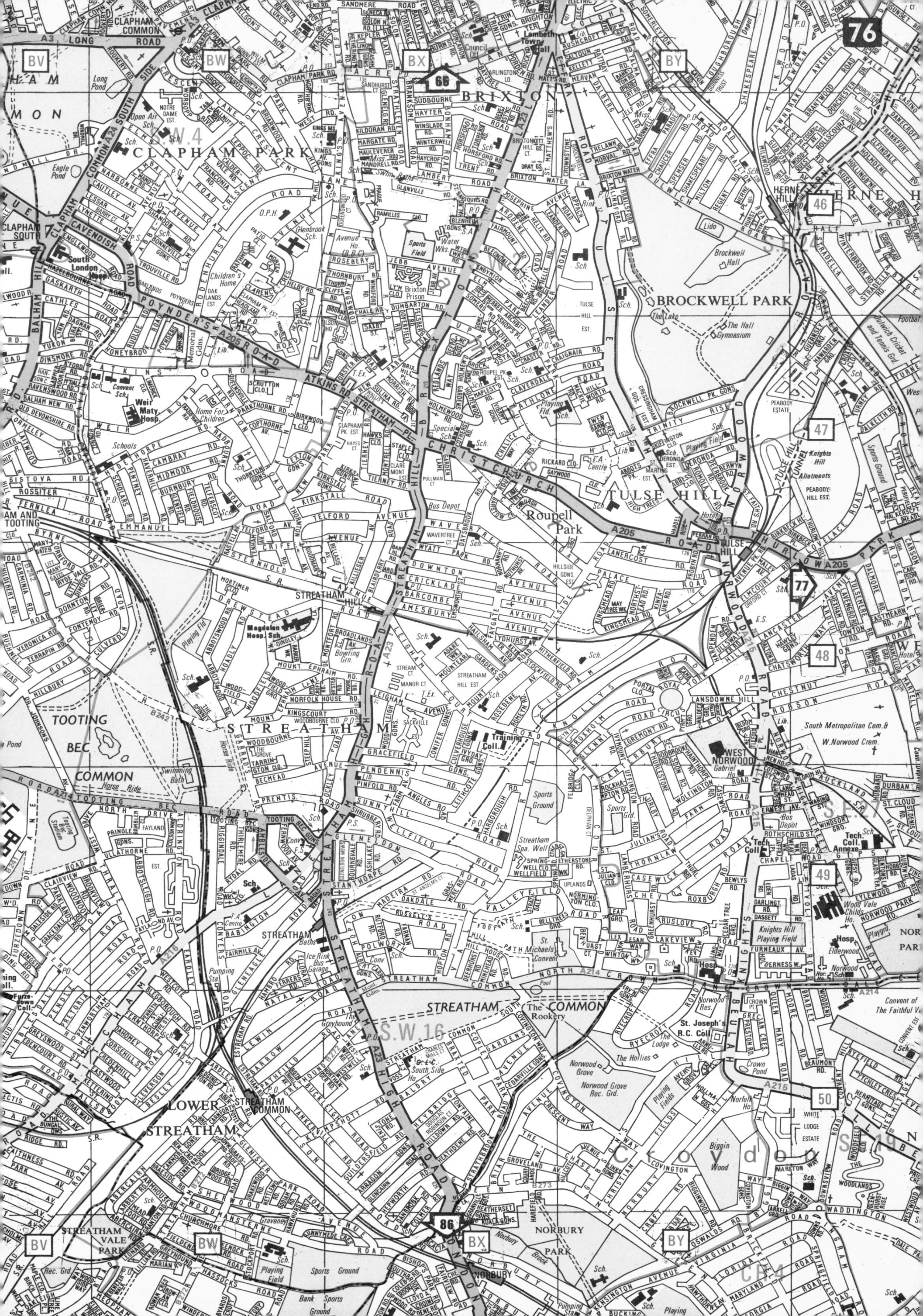
BV
BW
BX
BY
66
CLAPHAM COMMON
LONG ROAD
BRIXTON
S.W.4
CLAPHAM PARK
CLAPHAM SOUTH
South London Hosp.
Eagle Pond
Long Pond
46
HERNE HILL
Brockwell Hall
BROCKWELL PARK
The Lake
The Hall Gymnasium
Brixton Prison
Sports Field
Water Wks.
Lido
POYNDER'S ROAD
ATKINS RD.
STREATHAM PL.
CHRISTCHURCH
47
Knights Hill
Allotments
PEABODY HILL EST.
TULSE HILL
Roupell Park
A205
THURLOW PARK
77
STREATHAM HILL
Bus Depot
Magdalen Hosp. Sch.
Bowling Grn.
48
STREATHAM HILL EST.
Training Coll.
South Metropolitan Cem. & W. Norwood Cem.
WEST NORWOOD
TOOTING BEC COMMON
STREATHAM
Swimming Bath
Horse Ride
Sports Ground
Streatham Spa. Well
SE.27
Tech. Coll.
Tech. Coll. Annexe
49
Wood Vale Childs Ho.
Knights Hill Playing Field
St. Michaels Convent
Ice Rink
Baths
STREATHAM COMMON
The Rookery
S.W.16
St. Joseph's R.C. Coll.
The Hollies
Norwood Grove
Norwood Grove Rec. Grd.
Playing Fields
Crown Pond
50
WHITE LODGE ESTATE
LOWER STREATHAM
STREATHAM COMMON
Croydon
Biggin Wood
SE.19
86
BX
BY
BV
BW
STREATHAM VALE PARK
NORBURY
NORBURY PARK
Playing Field
Sports Ground
Bank Sports Ground
CR4
Convent of The Faithful V.
A23
A214
A215
A216
B242
B273

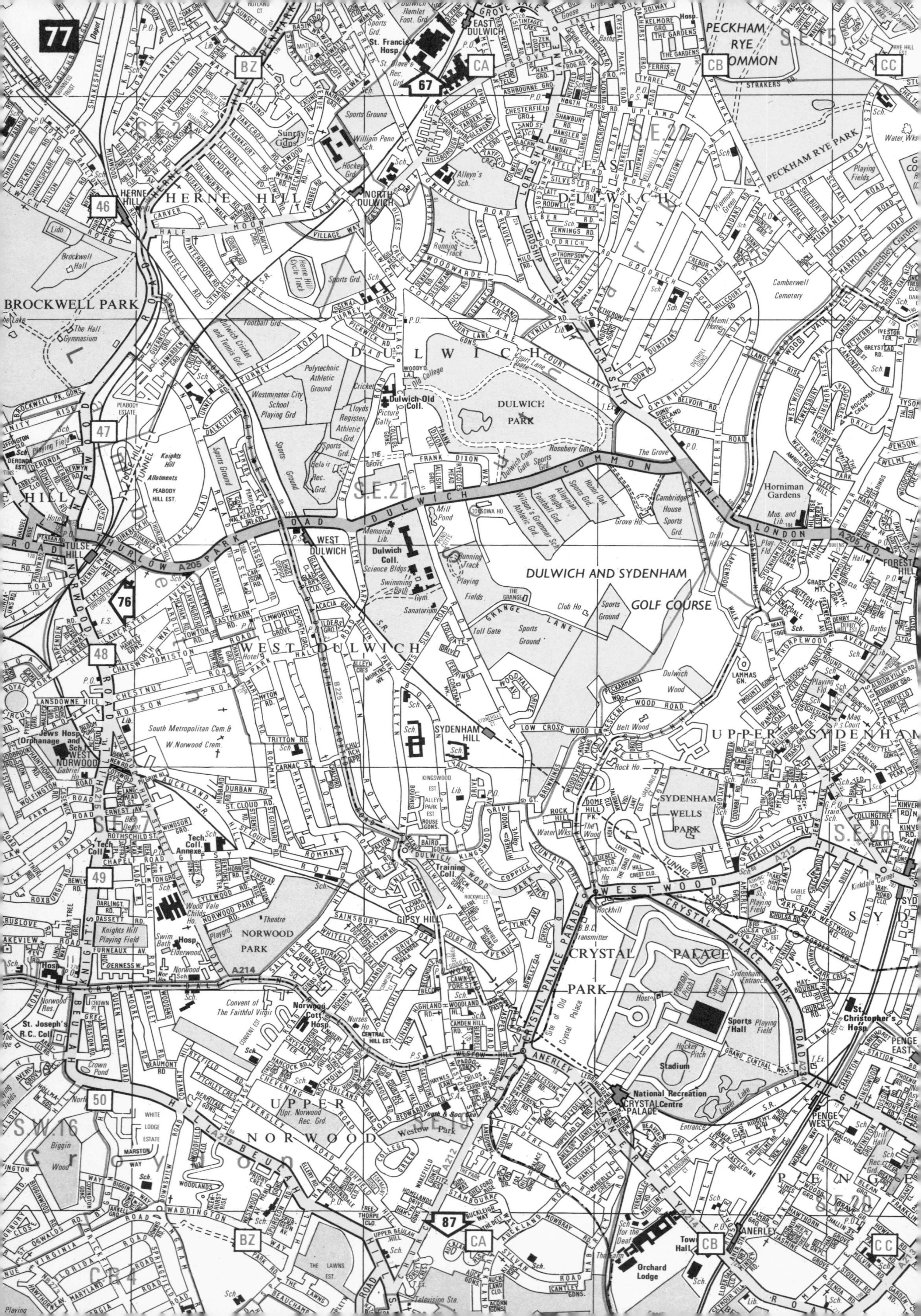

77
BZ
CA
CB
CC
67
46
47
48
49
50
76
87
PECKHAM RYE COMMON
PECKHAM RYE PARK
S.E.15
S.E.24
S.E.22
S.E.21
S.E.27
S.E.26
S.E.20
S.E.19
S.W.16
HERNE HILL
EAST DULWICH
NORTH DULWICH
DULWICH
WEST DULWICH
BROCKWELL PARK
Brockwell Hall
Lido
DULWICH PARK
DULWICH AND SYDENHAM GOLF COURSE
Dulwich Old Coll.
Picture Gally.
Dulwich Coll.
Science Bldgs.
Swimming Bath
Gym.
Sanatorium
Mill Pond
Running Track
Playing Fields
Dulwich Wood
Belt Wood
SYDENHAM HILL
UPPER SYDENHAM
SYDENHAM WELLS PARK
Horniman Gardens
Mus. and Lib.
Camberwell Cemetery
TULSE HILL
WEST NORWOOD
Jews Hosp (Orphanage) and Sch.
South Metropolitan Cem.& W.Norwood Crem.
Knights Hill Allotments
PEABODY HILL EST.
Westminster City School Playing Grd
Polytechnic Athletic Ground
Dulwich Cricket and Tennis Grd
Herne Hill Cycle Track
St. Francis Hosp.
Sunray Gdns
William Penn Sch.
Alleyn's Sch.
NORWOOD PARK
Knights Hill Playing Field
Tech. Coll.
Tech. Coll. Annexe
Training Coll.
GIPSY HILL
CRYSTAL PALACE PARK
Site of Old Crystal Palace
B.B.C. Transmitter
Sports Hall
Stadium
Hockey Pitch
National Recreation Centre
CRYSTAL PALACE
Lower Lake
UPPER NORWOOD
Westow Park
Norwood Cott. Hosp.
Convent of The Faithful Virgin
St. Joseph's R.C. Coll.
Crown Pond
Biggin Wood
WHITE LODGE ESTATE
THE LAWNS EST.
Television Sta.
Town Hall
Orchard Lodge
Sch. for the Deaf
ANERLEY
PENGE
PENGE WEST
PENGE EAST
St. Christopher's Hosp.
LONDON RD. A205
DULWICH COMMON
THURLOW PARK ROAD A205
CRYSTAL PALACE PARADE
WESTWOOD HILL
CRYSTAL PALACE PARK ROAD
BEULAH HILL A215
CROWN DALE
KNIGHT'S HILL A215
A214
A212
A234
SYD
FOREST HILL

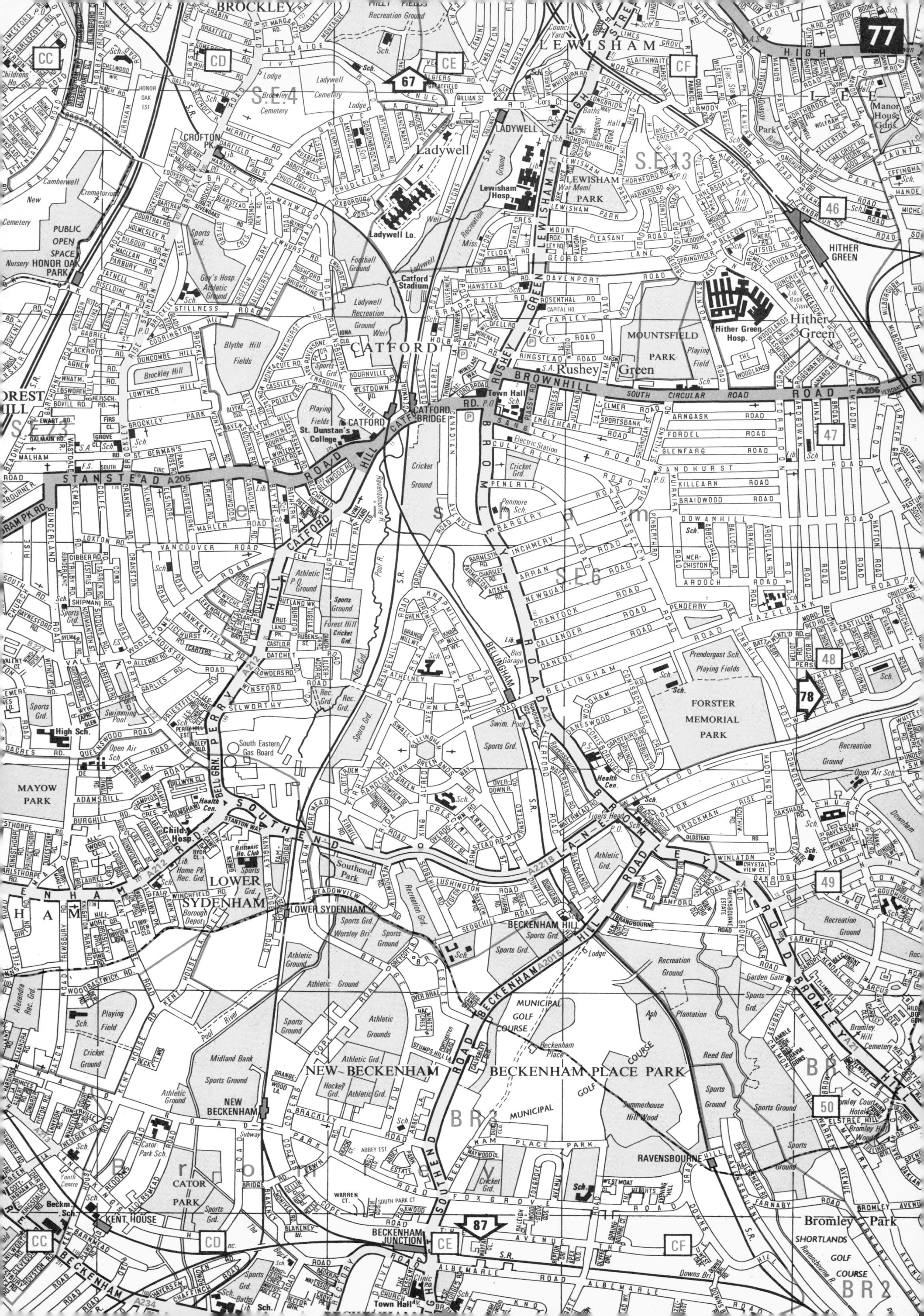
77
BROCKLEY
LEWISHAM
LEE
S.E.4
S.E.13
S.E.6
S.E.23
Ladywell
Ladywell Cemetery
LADYWELL
Lewisham Hosp.
LEWISHAM PARK
Ladywell Lo.
CROFTON PK.
Camberwell New Cemetery
Crematorium
PUBLIC OPEN SPACE
HONOR OAK PARK
HITHER GREEN
Hither Green
Hither Green Hosp.
MOUNTSFIELD PARK
Catford Stadium
Ladywell Recreation Ground
CATFORD
Blythe Hill Fields
Rushey Green
Town Hall
CATFORD BRIDGE
CATFORD
St. Dunstan's College
FOREST HILL
SOUTH CIRCULAR ROAD
BROWNHILL RD.
STANSTEAD ROAD A205
Cricket Ground
Lewisham
BROMLEY ROAD
BELLINGHAM
Forest Hill Cricket Grd.
Prendergast Sch. Playing Fields
FORSTER MEMORIAL PARK
South Eastern Gas Board
PERRY HILL
BELL GRN.
SOUTHEND LANE
MAYOW PARK
High Sch.
Swimming Pool
LOWER SYDENHAM
Southend Park
BECKENHAM HILL
BECKENHAM HILL RD. A2015
MUNICIPAL GOLF COURSE
BECKENHAM PLACE PARK
NEW BECKENHAM
Midland Bank Sports Ground
CATOR PARK
KENT HOUSE
BECKENHAM JUNCTION
RAVENSBOURNE
Bromley Park
SHORTLANDS GOLF COURSE
BR3
BR2
BR1
Bromley
Downham
Recreation Ground
Summerhouse Hill Wood
Beckenham Place
Reed Bed
Plantation
Town Hall
CC
CD
CE
CF
67
87
78
46
47
48
49
50

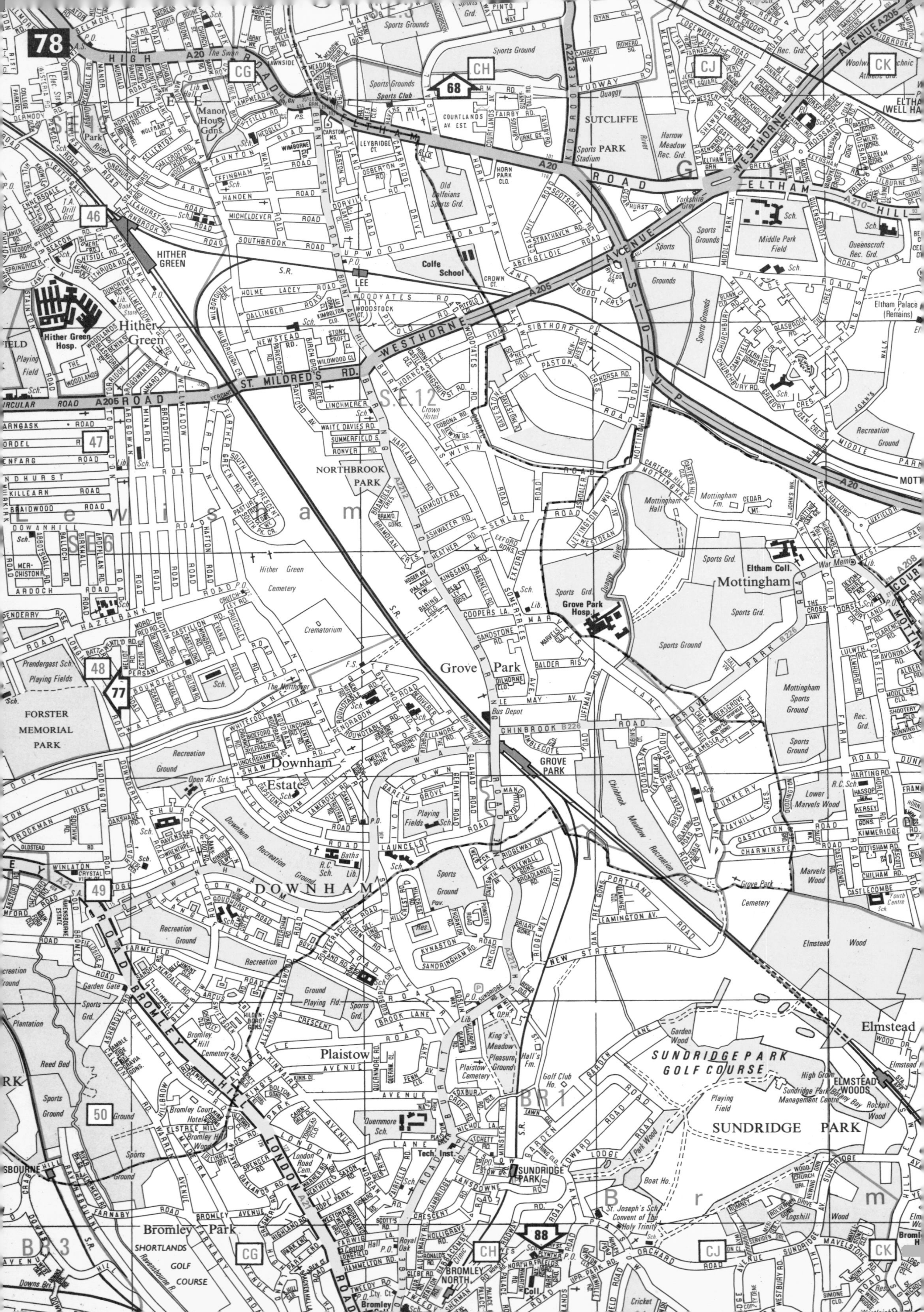
78
CG
CH
CJ
CK
68
46
47
48
77
49
50
88
HIGH ROAD
LEE
Manor House Gdns.
ELTHAM ROAD
A20
SUTCLIFFE PARK
Sports Ground
Kidbrooke
Harrow Meadow Rec. Grd.
WESTHORNE AVENUE
A205
A210
Middle Park Field
Queenscroft Rec. Grd.
Eltham Palace (Remains)
HITHER GREEN
Hither Green
Hither Green Hosp.
Playing Field
S.R.
Colfe School
SIDCUP ROAD
ST. MILDRED'S RD.
S.E.12
SOUTH CIRCULAR ROAD
Lewisham
SE6
NORTHBROOK PARK
A2212
Recreation Ground
MOTTINGHAM LANE
Mottingham Hall
Mottingham Fm.
Mottingham
Eltham Coll.
Hither Green Cemetery
Crematorium
Grove Park Hosp.
Sports Ground
Grove Park
Prendergast Sch. Playing Fields
FORSTER MEMORIAL PARK
Downham Estate
GROVE PARK
Chinbrook Meadow Recreation Grd.
Mottingham Sports Ground
Lower Marvels Wood
Marvels Wood
Grove Park Cemetery
Elmstead Wood
DOWNHAM
Downham Recreation Ground
Bus Depot
Elmstead
SUNDRIDGE PARK GOLF COURSE
ELMSTEAD WOODS
SUNDRIDGE PARK
Plaistow
King's Meadow Pleasure Ground
Plaistow Cemetery
Golf Club Ho.
BR1
Bromley Hill Cemetery
BROMLEY HILL
LONDON ROAD
A21
Quernmore Sch.
Tech. Inst.
SUNDRIDGE PARK
Boat Ho.
Bromley
St. Joseph's Sch. Convent of the Holy Trinity
Bromley Park
SHORTLANDS GOLF COURSE
BR3
BROMLEY NORTH
Reed Bed
Plantation

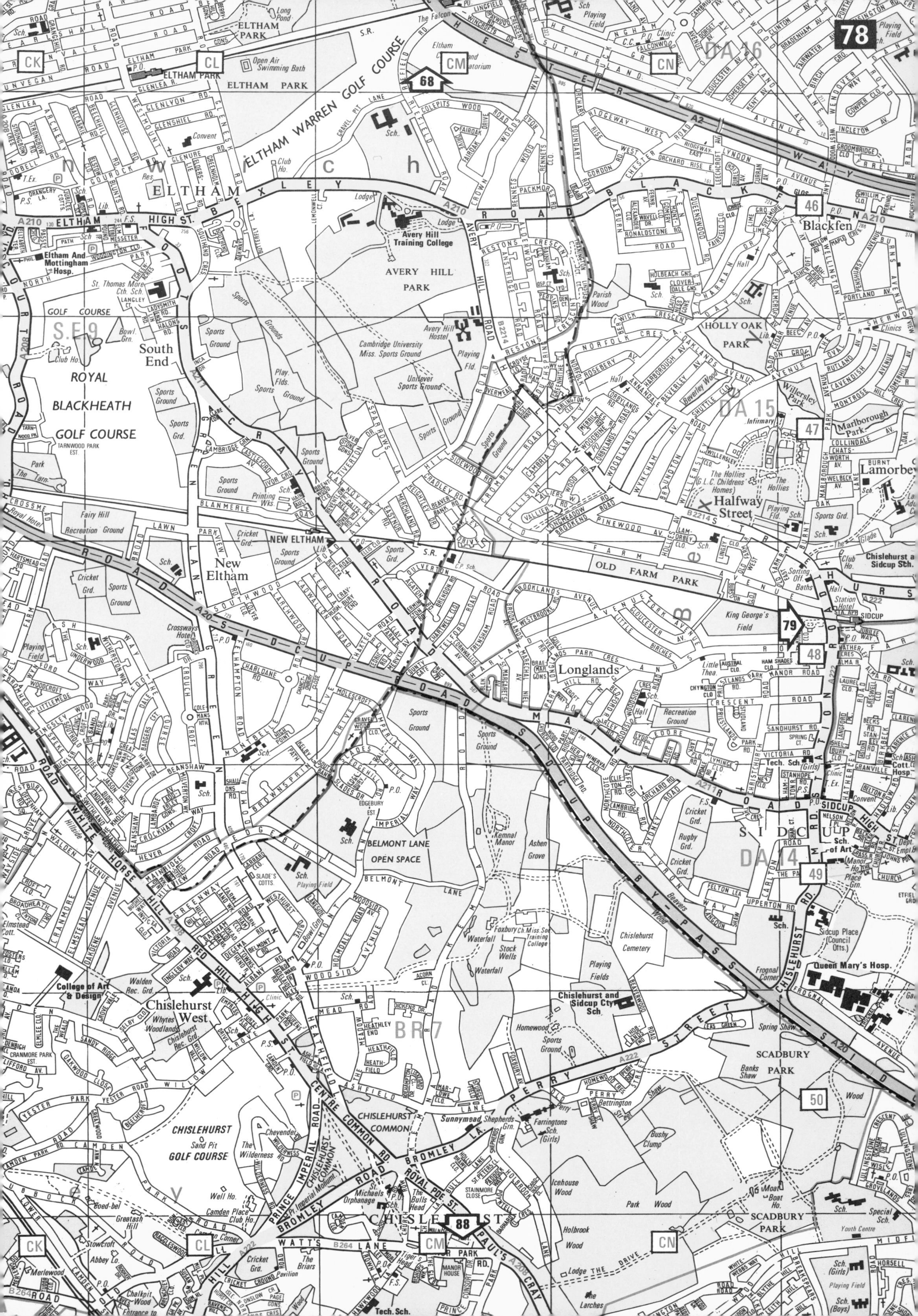
78
CK
CL
CM
CN
68
79
88
46
47
48
49
50
ELTHAM
ELTHAM PARK
ELTHAM WARREN GOLF COURSE
Open Air Swimming Bath
Convent
BEXLEY ROAD
ELTHAM HIGH ST.
Eltham And Mottingham Hosp.
St. Thomas More Cth. Sch.
GOLF COURSE
S.E.9
South End
ROYAL BLACKHEATH GOLF COURSE
TARNWOOD PARK EST.
The Tarn
Avery Hill Training College
AVERY HILL PARK
Avery Hill Hostel
Cambridge University Miss. Sports Ground
Unilever Sports Ground
Sports Ground
Playing Fld.
Parish Wood
Blackfen
HOLLY OAK PARK
Willersley Park
Marlborough Park
DA 15
DA 16
Infirmary
The Hollies (G.L.C. Childrens' Homes)
Halfway Street
Lamorbey
Chislehurst and Sidcup Sch.
Fairy Hill Recreation Ground
NEW ELTHAM
New Eltham
Royal Hotel
Crossways Hotel
OLD FARM PARK
King George's Field
SIDCUP
Longlands
Little Thea.
Recreation Ground
SIDCUP HIGH ST.
Sch. of Art
DA 14
SIDCUP BY-PASS
Sidcup Place (Council Offs.)
Queen Mary's Hosp.
Frognal Corner
SIDCUP ROAD
MAIN ROAD
BELMONT LANE OPEN SPACE
Kemnal Manor
Ashen Grove
Foxbury
Ch. Miss. Soc. Training College
Stock Wells
Waterfall
Chislehurst Cemetery
Playing Fields
Chislehurst and Sidcup Cty. Sch.
Homewood
BR 7
SCADBURY PARK
Banks Shaw
Spring Shaw
Bushy Clump
Park Wood
Icehouse Wood
Holbrook Wood
Moat
College of Art & Design
Chislehurst West
Whytes Woodlands
Chislehurst Rec. Grd.
Walden Rec. Grd.
CHISLEHURST GOLF COURSE
Sand Pit
The Wilderness
CHISLEHURST COMMON
Prince Imperial Monument
St. Michaels Orphanage
The Bulls Head
CHISLEHURST
Camden Place Club Ho.
Camden Corner
Coed-bel
Greatash Hill
Stowcroft
Abbey Lo.
Merlewood
Chalkpit Wood
Cricket Grd.
The Briars
Tiger's Head
Manor House
Tech. Sch.
Youth Centre
Special Sch.
Sch. (Girls)
Sch. (Boys)
RED HILL
WHITE HORSE HILL
PERRY STREET
WATTS LANE
BROMLEY ROAD
BROMLEY LA.
ROYAL PDE.
ST. PAUL'S CRAY RD.
The Larches
Lodge THE DRIVE
Farringtons Sch. (Girls)
Shepherds Grn.
Sunnymead
Edgebury Est.
Slade's Cotts.

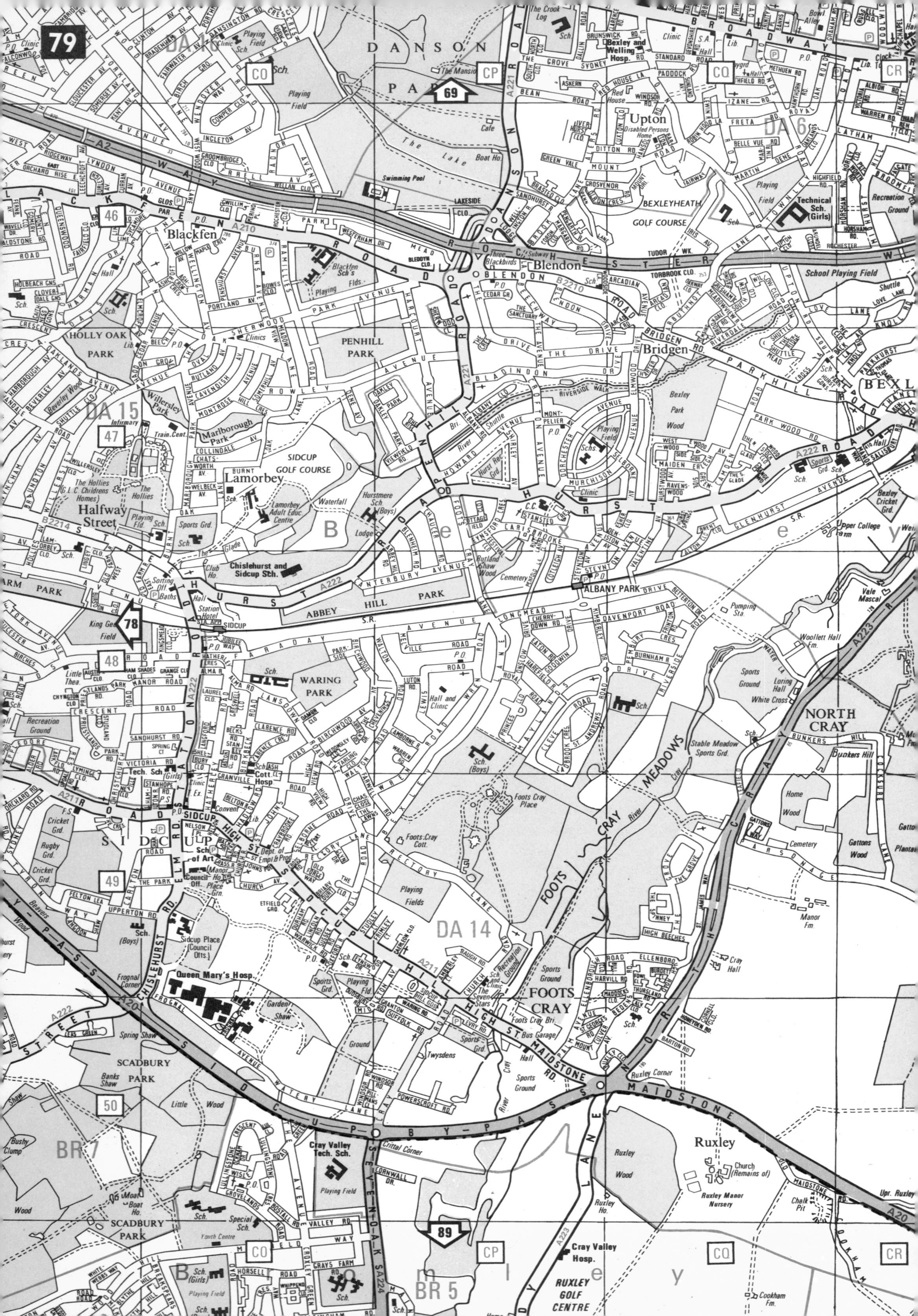
DANSON PARK
69
The Mansion
The Lake
Boat Ho.
Swimming Pool
Lakeside
Playing Field
Upton
Bexley and Welling Hosp.
BROADWAY
DA 6
DA 16
BEXLEYHEATH GOLF COURSE
Technical Sch. (Girls)
Recreation Ground
School Playing Field
Blendon
Three Blackbirds
Blackfen
Blackfen Sch's Flds.
PENHILL PARK
Bridgen
Bexley Park Wood
HOLLY OAK PARK
Willersley Park
Marlborough Park
DA 15
Lamorbey
SIDCUP GOLF COURSE
Lamorbey Adult Educ. Centre
Hurstmere Sch. (Boys)
The Hollies (G.L.C. Childrens Homes)
Halfway Street
Chislehurst and Sidcup Sch.
Bexley
ABBEY HILL PARK
Rutland Shaw Wood
Cemetery
ALBANY PARK
SIDCUP
78
King George Field
WARING PARK
Hall and Clinic
Woollett Hall Fm.
Sports Ground
NORTH CRAY
Bunkers Hill
Stable Meadow Sports Grd.
FOOTS CRAY MEADOWS
Foots Cray Place
Home Wood
Gattons Wood
Cemetery
SIDCUP
Recreation Ground
Tech. Sch.
Cott. Hosp.
Sch. of Art
Council Off.
Manor Ho.
Place Grn.
Playing Fields
DA 14
Sidcup Place (Council Offs.)
Queen Mary's Hosp.
Frognal Corner
Garden Shaw
FOOTS CRAY
Sports Ground
Recreation Ground
The Seven Stars
Foots Cray Bri.
Bus Garage
Twysdens
Manor Fm.
Cray Hall
Ruxley Corner
SCADBURY PARK
Little Wood
Spring Shaw
Banks Shaw
SIDCUP BY-PASS
MAIDSTONE ROAD
Crittal Corner
Cray Valley Tech. Sch.
BR 7
BR 5
Ruxley Wood
Ruxley
Church (Remains of)
Ruxley Manor Nursery
Chalk Pit
89
Cray Valley Hosp.
RUXLEY GOLF CENTRE
Bushy Clump
Moat
SCADBURY PARK
Special Sch.
Youth Centre
Bromley
Cookham Fm.
46
47
48
49
50
CO
CP
CQ
CR
A2
A20
A210
A211
A221
A222
A223
A224
B2210
B2214

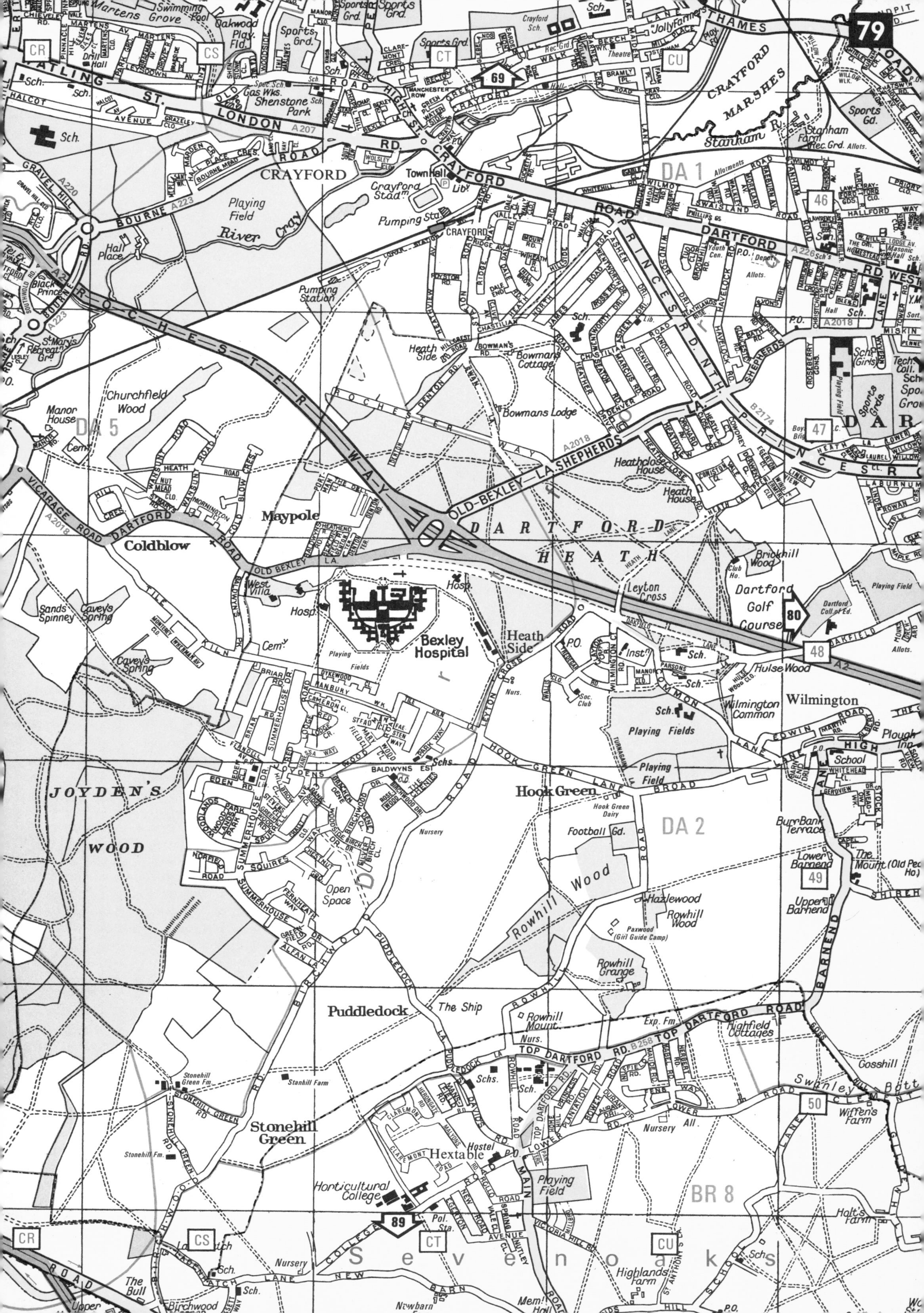
CRAYFORD
Crayford Stadm
Town Hall
Lib'y
Pumping Stan
Playing Field
River Cray
Hall Place
Black Prince
Shenstone Park
Gas Wks.
Swimming Pool
Oakwood Play. Fld.
Sports Grd.
Crayford Sch.
Jolly Farmers
THAMES
CRAYFORD MARSHES
Stankham R.
Stankham Farm
Rec. Grd.
Allotments
Sports Gd.
WATLING ST.
LONDON RD.
CRAYFORD RD.
DARTFORD RD.
BOURNE RD.
GRAVEL HILL
HALCOT AVENUE
DA 1
DA 2
DA 5
BR 8
Pumping Station
Heath Side
Bowmans Cottage
Bowmans Lodge
Heathclose House
Heath House
ROCHESTER WAY
OLD BEXLEY LA.
SHEPHERDS LA.
PRINCES RD.
Churchfield Wood
Manor House
Cemy
Maypole
Coldblow
DARTFORD HEATH
Brickhill Wood
Dartford Golf Course
Dartford Coll. of Ed.
Playing Field
Leyton Cross
Hulse Wood
West Villa
Hosp.
Bexley Hospital
Playing Fields
Heath Side
Sands Spinney
Caveys Spring
JOYDEN'S WOOD
Wilmington Common
Wilmington
Playing Fields
Playing Field
Hook Green
Hook Green Dairy
Football Gd.
School
Burr Bank Terrace
Lower Barnend
Upper Barnend
The Mount (Old Peo. Ho.)
Rowhill Wood
Hazlewood
Rowhill Wood
Paxwood (Girl Guide Camp)
Rowhill Grange
Open Space
Puddledock
The Ship
Rowhill Mount
Exp. Fm.
Highfield Cottages
TOP DARTFORD RD.
Gosshill
Swanley Bott.
Wiffen's Farm
Holt's Farm
Stonehill Green Fm.
Stanhill Farm
Stonehill Green
Stonehill Fm.
Hextable
Hostel
Horticultural College
Playing Field
Nursery
Pol. Sta.
Sevenoaks
Highlands Farm
The Bull
Upper
Birchwood
Newbarn
Mem. Hall
69
80
89
46
47
48
49
50
CR
CS
CT
CU

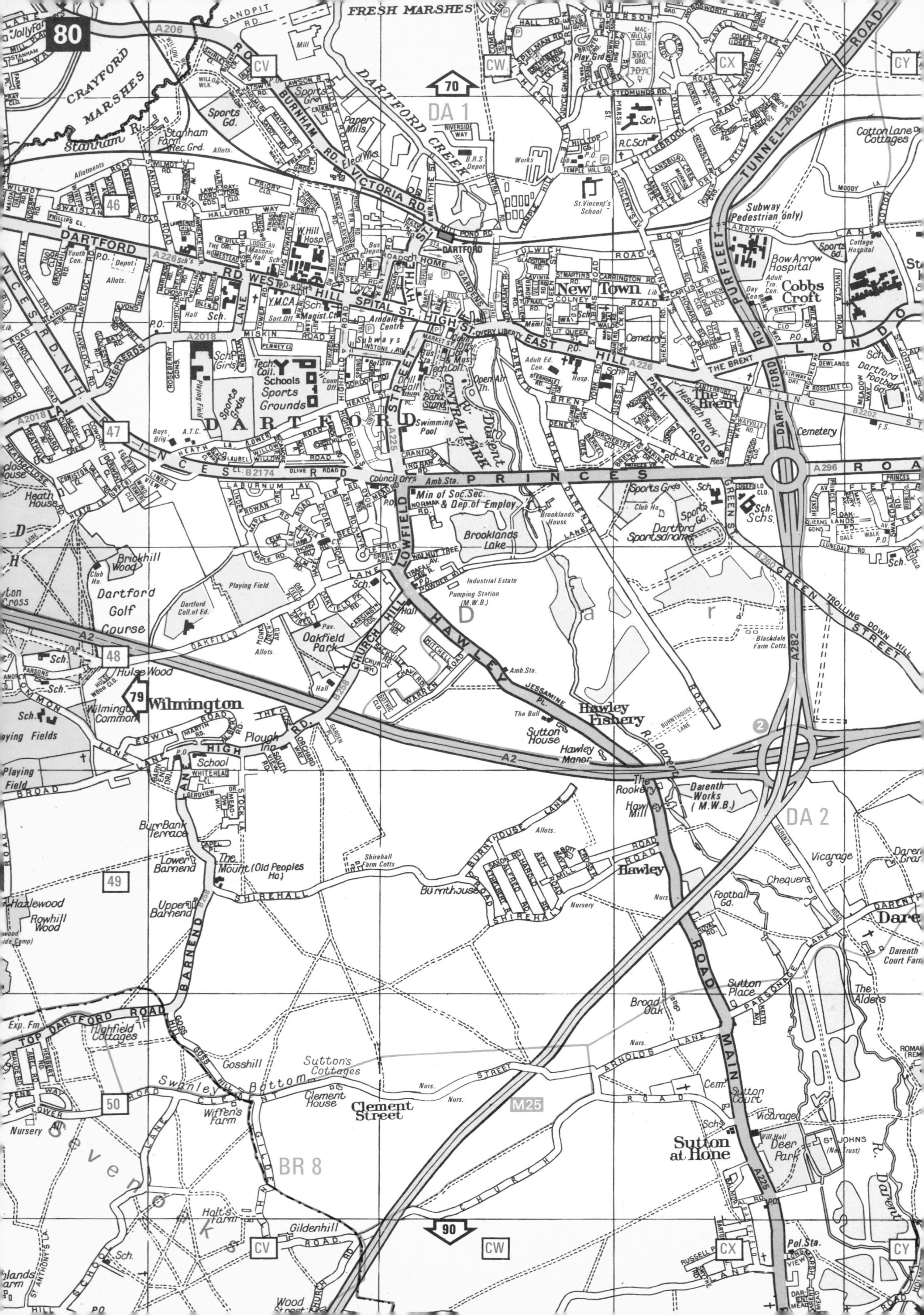
FRESH MARSHES
CRAYFORD MARSHES
DARTFORD CREEK
70
DA 1
CV
CW
CX
CY
Paper Mills
BURNHAM RD.
VICTORIA RD.
Stanham Farm
Sports Gd.
St. Vincent's School
Temple Hill Sq.
DARTFORD
New Town
Cobbs Croft
Bow Arrow Hospital
Subway Pedestrian only
Cotton Lane Cottages
TUNNEL ROAD
PURFLEET RD.
A282
46
47
48
49
50
DARTFORD RD. WEST HILL
SPITAL ST.
HIGH ST.
EAST HILL
Arndale Centre
Central Park
Swimming Pool
Sports Grounds
Tech. Coll.
Schools
PRINCES RD.
The Brent
Hesketh Park
Cemetery
Heath House
Brooklands Lake
Dartford Sportsdrome
Dartford Golf Course
Brickhill Wood
Dartford Coll. of Ed.
Oakfield Park
LOWFIELD ST.
HAWLEY RD.
CHURCH HILL
Industrial Estate
Pumping Station (M.W.B.)
Wilmington
Wilmington Common
79
Hulse Wood
Plough Inn
HIGH RD.
School
Hawley Fishery
Sutton House
Hawley Manor
The Bull
The Rookery
Hawley Mill
Darenth Works (M.W.B.)
DA 2
A2
2
Hawley
Burnthouse
Chequers
Vicarage
Football Gd.
Lower Barnend
Upper Barnend
BARNEND LA.
The Mount (Old Peoples Ho.)
Burr Bank Terrace
Hazlewood
Rowhill Wood
TOP DARTFORD ROAD
Highfield Cottages
Gosshill
Sutton's Cottages
Swanley Bottom
Clement House
Clement Street
Wiffen's Farm
Nursery
M25
BR 8
Broad Oak
Sutton Place
PARSONAGE LANE
MAIN ROAD
ARNOLDS LANE
Sutton Court
Sutton at Hone
Deer Park
ST JOHNS (Nat Trust)
The Alders
Darenth Court Farm
R. Darent
Holt's Farm
Gildenhill
90
Sevenoaks
Wood Street
Pol. Sta.
A225
A226
A296
A2018
B2174
B258
B260
GREEN ST.
TROLLING DOWN HILL
DARTFORD FOOTBALL GD.
WATLING ST.

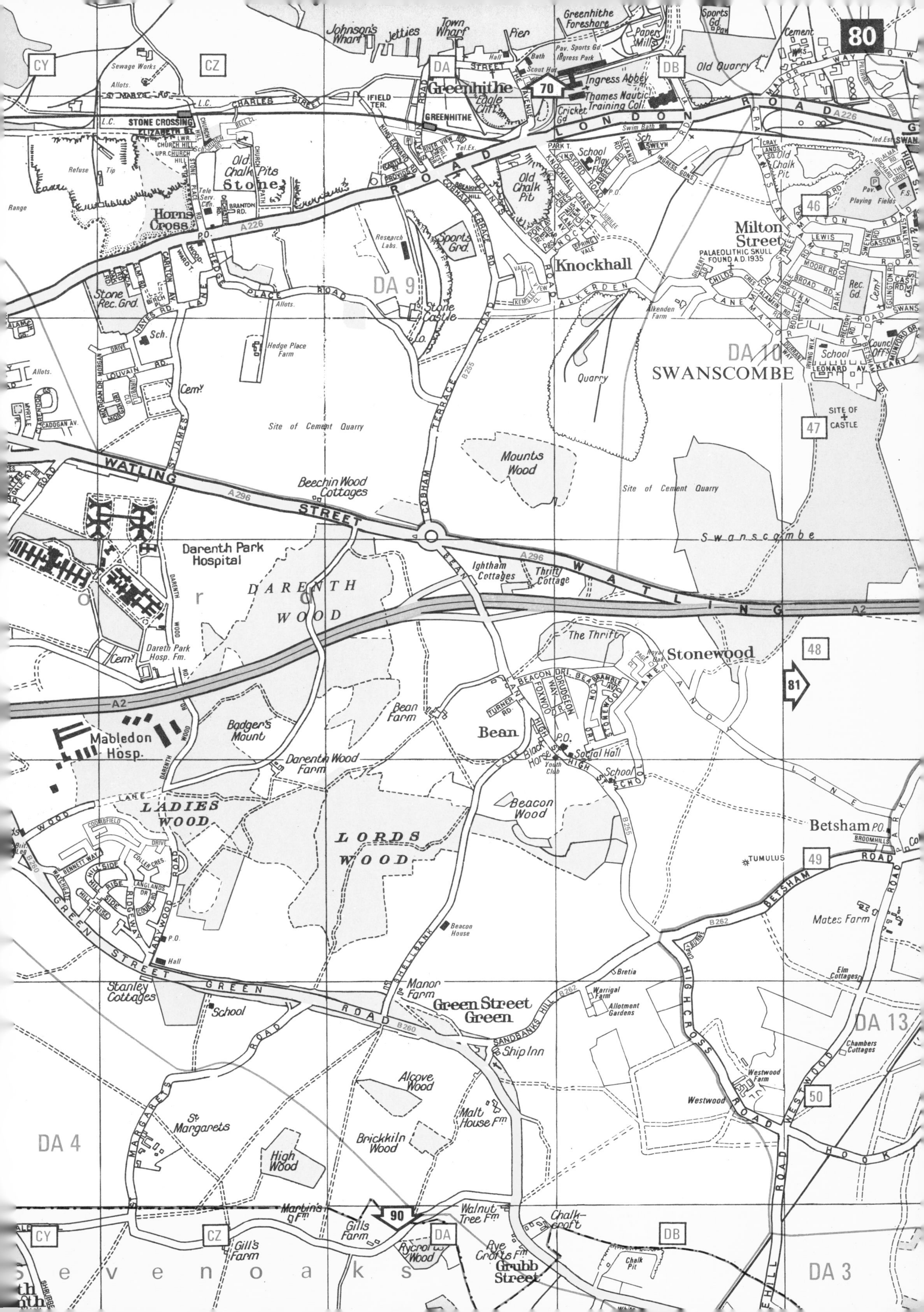

Greenhithe
Stone
Horns Cross
Knockhall
Milton Street
SWANSCOMBE
Darenth Park Hospital
DARENTH WOOD
Stonewood
Bean
Mabledon Hosp.
LADIES WOOD
LORDS WOOD
Betsham
Green Street Green
St Margarets
Grubb Street
Westwood
WATLING STREET
LONDON ROAD
A2
A226
A296
B255
B260
B262
DA 9
DA 10
DA 4
DA 13
DA 3
70
81
90

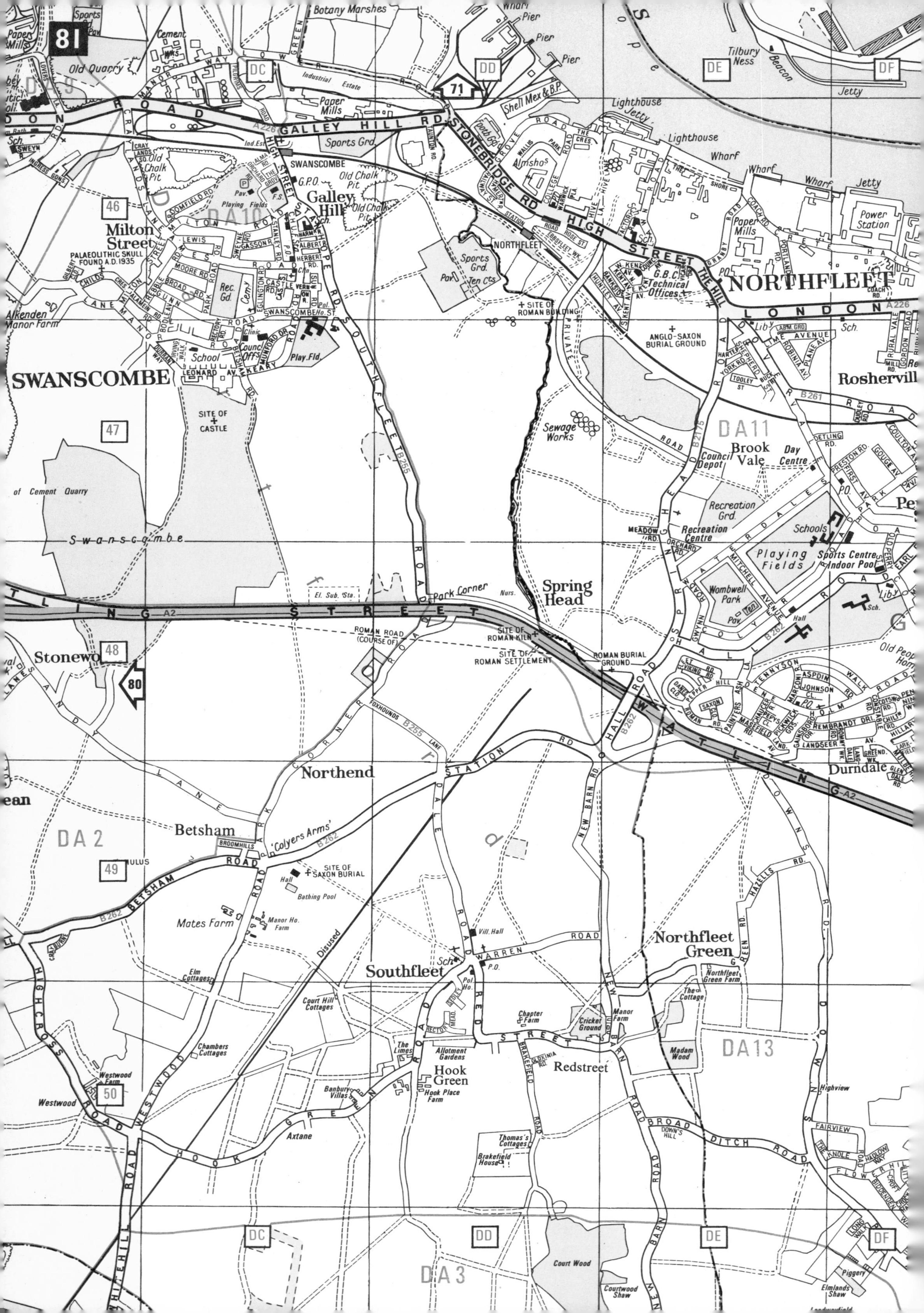
81
71
80
SWANSCOMBE
NORTHFLEET
Galley Hill
Milton Street
Northend
Betsham
Southfleet
Hook Green
Redstreet
Northfleet Green
Spring Head
Brook Vale
Durndale
DA10
DA11
DA2
DA13
DA3
DC
DD
DE
DF

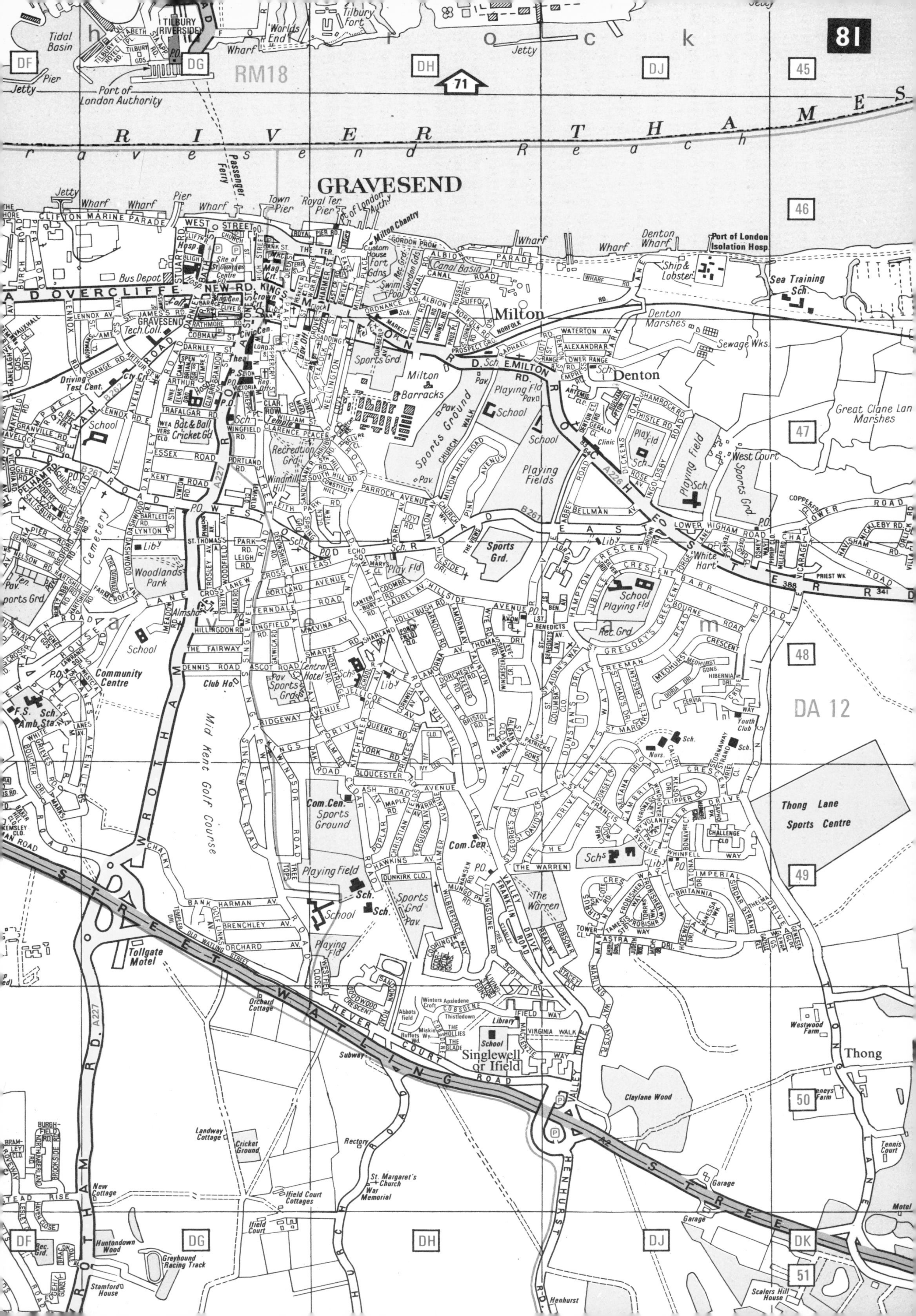
GRAVESEND
RIVER THAMES
Gravesend Reach
TILBURY (RIVERSIDE)
Tidal Basin
Tilbury Fort
Worlds End
Port of London Authority
RM18
DA 12
71
DF
DG
DH
DJ
DK
45
46
47
48
49
50
51
Milton
Denton
Thong
Singlewell or Ifield
Denton Marshes
Great Clane Lane Marshes
Sewage Wks.
Port of London Isolation Hosp.
Sea Training Sch.
Ship & Lobster
Milton Barracks
Sports Ground
Playing Fields
Recreation Grd.
Windmill Hill
Woodlands Park
Cemetery
Mid Kent Golf Course
Thong Lane Sports Centre
Tollgate Motel
Claylane Wood
Huntondown Wood
Greyhound Racing Track
Cricket Ground
The Warren
Westwood Farm
Tennis Court
Scalers Hill House
Stamford House
Henhurst
St. Margaret's Church
War Memorial
Ifield Court Cottages
Ifield Court
Landway Cottage
Rectory
Orchard Cottage
New Cottage
Community Centre
Com. Cen. Sports Ground
Bat & Ball Cricket Gd.
Bus Depot
Canal Basin
Clifton Marine Parade
Overcliffe
Wrotham Road
Watling Street
Pelham Road
Old Road
Parrock Avenue
Valley Drive
Hever Court Road
Church Road
Henhurst Rd.
Thong Lane
Lower Higham Road
A226
A227
A2
B261
B262

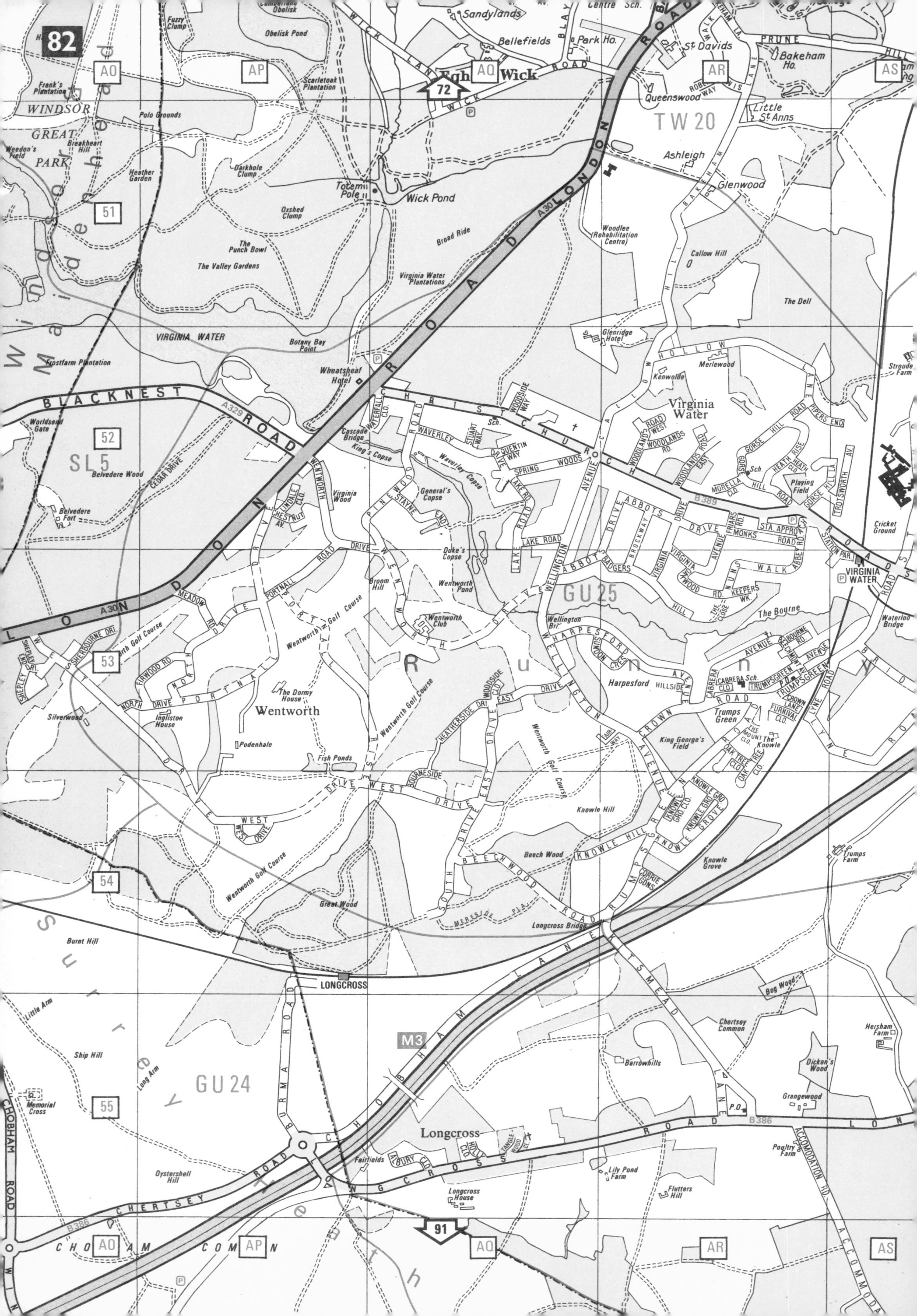

AO
AP
AQ
AR
AS
51
52
53
54
55
72
91
WINDSOR GREAT PARK
Frank's Plantation
Polo Grounds
Breakheart Hill
Weedon's Field
Heather Garden
Fuzzy Clump
Obelisk Pond
Scarletoak Plantation
Darkhole Clump
Totem Pole
Wick Pond
Oxshed Clump
The Punch Bowl
The Valley Gardens
Broad Ride
Virginia Water Plantations
VIRGINIA WATER
Botany Bay Point
Frostfarm Plantation
Wheatsheaf Hotel
Sandylands
Bellefields
Park Ho.
St Davids
Bakeham Ho.
Queenswood
Little St Anns
TW 20
Ashleigh
Glenwood
Woodlee (Rehabilitation Centre)
Callow Hill
The Dell
Glenridge Hotel
Merlewood
Kenwolde
Virginia Water
Stroude Farm
Egham Wick
WICK ROAD
WICK LANE
LONDON ROAD
A30
BLACKNEST ROAD
A329
Worldsend Gate
SL5
Belvedere Wood
CEDAR DRIVE
Belvedere Fort
Cascade Bridge
King's Copse
Waverley Copse
Virginia Wood
General's Copse
Duke's Copse
Broom Hill
Wentworth Pond
Wentworth Club
Wentworth Golf Course
CHRISTCHURCH ROAD
B389
WOODSIDE WAY
WAVERLEY
STUART WAY
QUENTIN WAY
SPRING WOODS
LAKE ROAD
WOODLANDS ROAD WEST
WOODLANDS RD.
WOODLANDS ROAD EAST
GORSE HILL ROAD
PIPERS END
HEATH RISE
Playing Field
TROTSWORTH AV.
Cricket Ground
ABBOTS DRIVE
BROCKWAY
VIRGINIA DRIVE
FRIARS RD.
MONKS ROAD
STA. APPROACH
STATION PAR.
VIRGINIA WATER
NUNS WALK
KEEPERS WK.
THE CLOSE
GU 25
The Bourne
Waterloo Bridge
Wellington Bri.
WELLINGTON AVENUE
HARPESFORD AVENUE
Harpesford
HILLSIDE
CABRERA AVENUE
TRUMPSGREEN AVENUE
CROWN ROAD
Trumps Green
King George's Field
The Knowle
LYNE ROAD
SL5
PORTNALL DRIVE
PORTNALL ROAD
MEADOW
NORTH DRIVE
FIRWOOD RD.
SHERBOURNE DRI.
SHEPLEY END
Silverwood
Ingliston House
The Dormy House
Wentworth
Podenhale
Fish Ponds
WEST DRIVE
BOURNESIDE
HEATHERSIDE DRI.
WOODSIDE CLO.
EAST DRIVE
SOUTH DRIVE
Knowle Hill
Beech Wood
KNOWLE HILL
KNOWLE GROVE
TRUMPSGREEN ROAD
CORRIE GDNS.
BEECHWOOD ROAD
Knowle Grove
Trumps Farm
Great Wood
Longcross Bridge
Burnt Hill
LONGCROSS
Surrey Heath
Little Arm
Ship Hill
Long Arm
GU 24
Memorial Cross
CHOBHAM ROAD
M3
BURMA ROAD
CHOBHAM LANE
KITSMEAD LANE
Bog Wood
Chertsey Common
Hersham Farm
Barrowhills
Dicken's Wood
Grangewood
P.O.
B386
Longcross
LONGCROSS ROAD
ABURY CLO.
Fairfields
Lily Pond Farm
Flutters Hill
Longcross House
Poultry Farm
ACCOMMODATION RD.
Oystershell Hill
CHERTSEY ROAD
CHOBHAM COMMON

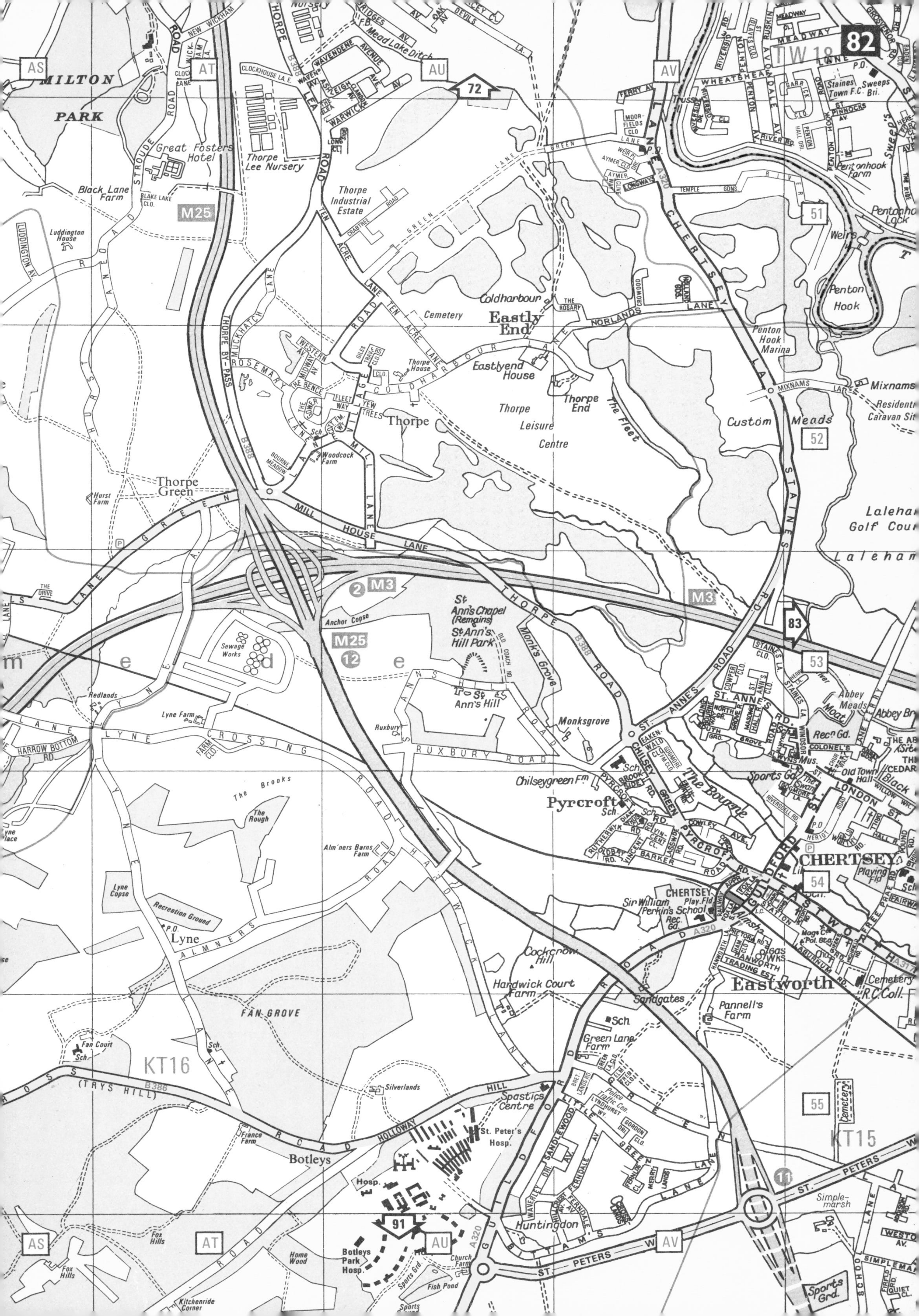
82
72
83
91
MILTON PARK
Great Fosters Hotel
Thorpe Lee Nursery
Thorpe Industrial Estate
Black Lane Farm
Luddington House
M25
M3
Coldharbour
Eastly End
Cemetery
Eastlyend House
Thorpe House
Thorpe
Thorpe End
Thorpe Leisure Centre
The Fleet
Custom Meads
Penton Hook
Penton Hook Marina
Pentonhook Farm
Penton Hook Lock
Weirs
Mixnams
Staines Town F.C.
Sweeps Bri.
Laleham Golf Course
Thorpe Green
Hurst Farm
Woodcock Farm
Anchor Copse
St Ann's Chapel (Remains)
St Ann's Hill Park
St Ann's Hill
Monk's Grove
Monksgrove
Sewage Works
Redlands
Lyne Farm
Ruxbury
Chilseygreen Fm
Pyrcroft
The Bourne
CHERTSEY
Sir William Perkin's School
The Brooks
The Rough
Alm'ners Barns Farm
Lyne Copse
Recreation Ground
Lyne
Cockcrow Hill
Hardwick Court Farm
Eastworth
Sandgates
Pannell's Farm
Green Lane Farm
FAN GROVE
Fan Court
KT16
KT15
Silverlands
Spastics Centre
St. Peter's Hosp.
France Farm
Botleys
Botleys Park Hosp.
Huntingdon
Home Wood
Fox Hills
Kitchenride Corner
Church Farm
Fish Pond
Sports Grd.
Simplemarsh
Cemetery
R.C. Coll.
Old Town Hall
TW18
AS
AT
AU
AV
51
52
53
54
55

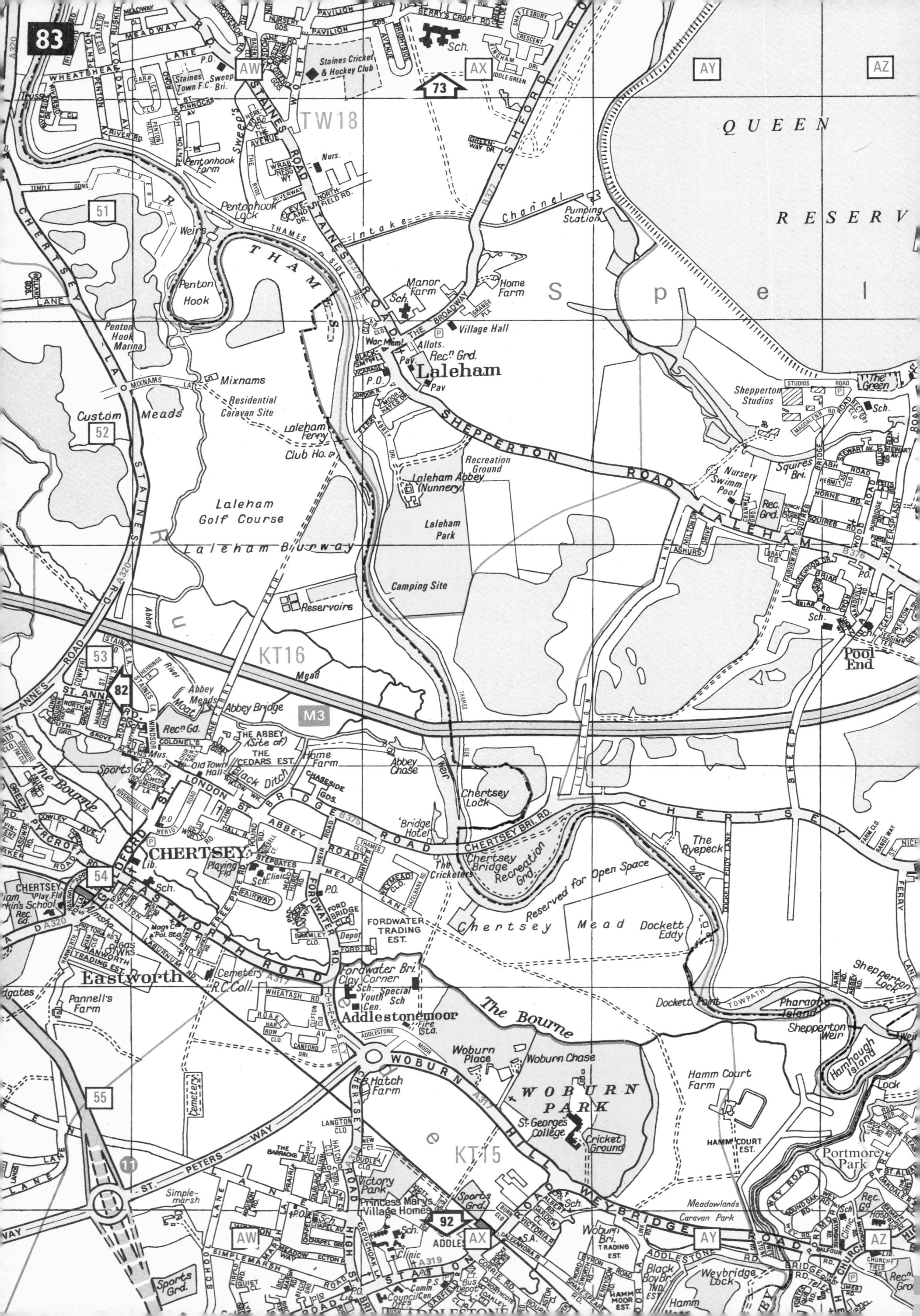

AW
AX
AY
AZ
73
TW18
QUEEN
RESERV
S p e l
Staines Cricket & Hockey Club
Staines Town F.C.
Sweep's Bri.
Pentonhook Farm
Pentonhook Lock
Weirs
Penton Hook
Penton Hook Marina
THAMES
Intake Channel
Pumping Station
Manor Farm
Home Farm
Village Hall
Laleham
Rec^n Grd.
Mixnams
Residential Caravan Site
Custom Meads
Laleham Ferry Club Ho.
Laleham Golf Course
Laleham Burway
Laleham Abbey (Nunnery)
Recreation Ground
Laleham Park
Camping Site
Reservoirs
SHEPPERTON ROAD
Shepperton Studios
Nursery
Swimm. Pool
Squires Bri.
Pool End
KT16
M3
Mead
Abbey Meads
Abbey Bridge
THE ABBEY (Site of)
THE CEDARS EST.
Home Farm
Abbey Chase
Chertsey Lock
Black Ditch
Old Town Hall
CHERTSEY
Playing Fld
Sports Gd.
The Bourne
'Bridge Hotel'
CHERTSEY BRI. RD.
Chertsey Bridge Recreation Grd.
The Cricketers
Reserved for Open Space
Chertsey Mead
Dockett Eddy
The Ryepeck
FORDWATER TRADING EST.
Fordwater Bri.
Clay Corner
Addlestonemoor
Eastworth
Pannell's Farm
The Bourne
Woburn Place
Woburn Chase
WOBURN PARK
St.George's College
Cricket Ground
Hatch Farm
Dockett Point
Pharaoh's Island
Shepperton Lock
Shepperton Weir
Hamhaugh Island
Hamm Court Farm
HAMM COURT EST.
Portmore Park
KT15
Cemetery
Simplemarsh
Victory Park
Princess Mary's Village Homes
Sports Grd.
92
Meadowlands Caravan Park
Woburn Bri.
Black Boy Br.
Weybridge Lock
Hamm
51
52
53
54
55
82
11

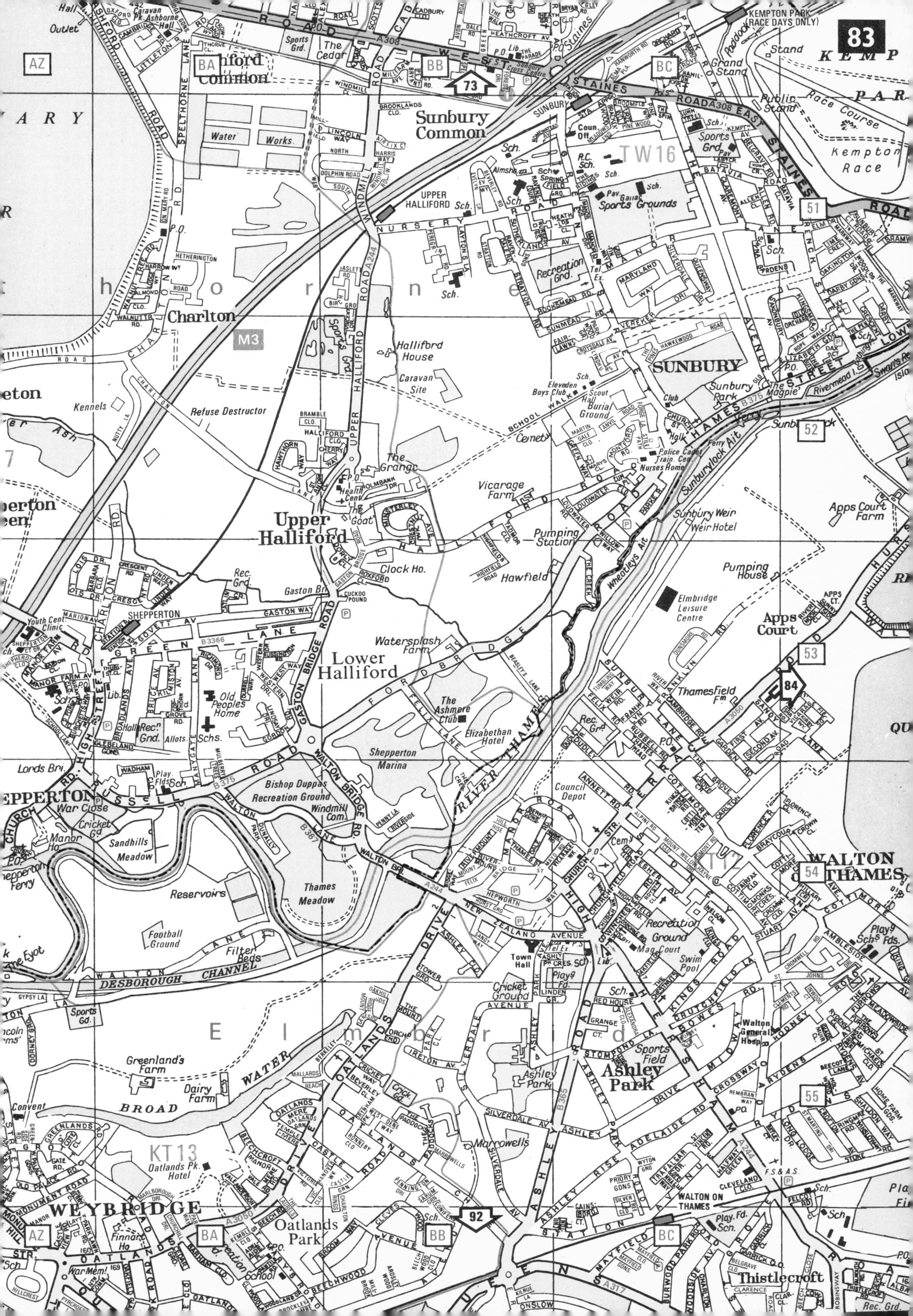

AZ
BA
BB
BC
73
92
51
52
53
54
55
84
Ashford Common
Sunbury Common
Sunbury
TW16
Kempton Park (Race Days Only)
Kempton Race Course
Grand Stand
Public Stand
Paddock
Stand
Water Works
Upper Halliford
Charlton
M3
Halliford House
Caravan Site
Kennels
Refuse Destructor
The Grange
Upper Halliford
Clock Ho.
Rec. Grd.
Gaston Bri.
Cuckoo Pound
Shepperton
Watersplash Farm
Lower Halliford
Vicarage Farm
Pumping Station
Hawfield
Cemetery
Sports Grounds
Recreation Grd.
Sunbury Park
Sunbury Lock
Sunbury Weir
Weir Hotel
Wheatleys Ait
Sunburylock Ait
Apps Court Farm
Apps Court
Pumping House
Elmbridge Leisure Centre
Thamesfield Fm.
River Thames
The Ashmere Club
Elizabethan Hotel
Shepperton Marina
Old Peoples Home
Bishop Duppas Recreation Ground
Windmill Com.
Council Depot
Walton on Thames
KT12
Shepperton
War Close
Cricket Gd.
Manor Ho.
Sandhills Meadow
Lords Bri.
Shepperton Ferry
Reservoirs
Thames Meadow
Football Ground
Filter Beds
Walton Bri.
Desborough Channel
Town Hall
Recreation Ground
Swim Pool
Mag. Court
Cricket Ground
Walton General Hosp.
Ashley Park
Sports Field
Sports Gd.
Greenland's Farm
Dairy Farm
Broad Water
Convent
KT13
Oatlands Pk. Hotel
Weybridge
Oatlands Park
Marrowells
Walton on Thames
Thistlecroft
Elmbridge
Staines Road
Windmill Road
Upper Halliford Road
Gaston Bridge Road
Walton Bridge Rd.
Fordbridge Road
Russell Road
Green Lane
High Street
Charlton Road
Nursery Road
Thames Street
Hersham Road
Ashley Road
Oatlands Drive
Oatlands Avenue
Queens Road
Station Avenue
New Zealand Avenue
Walton Lane
A308
A244
A3050
A317
B375
B3366
B365
B367

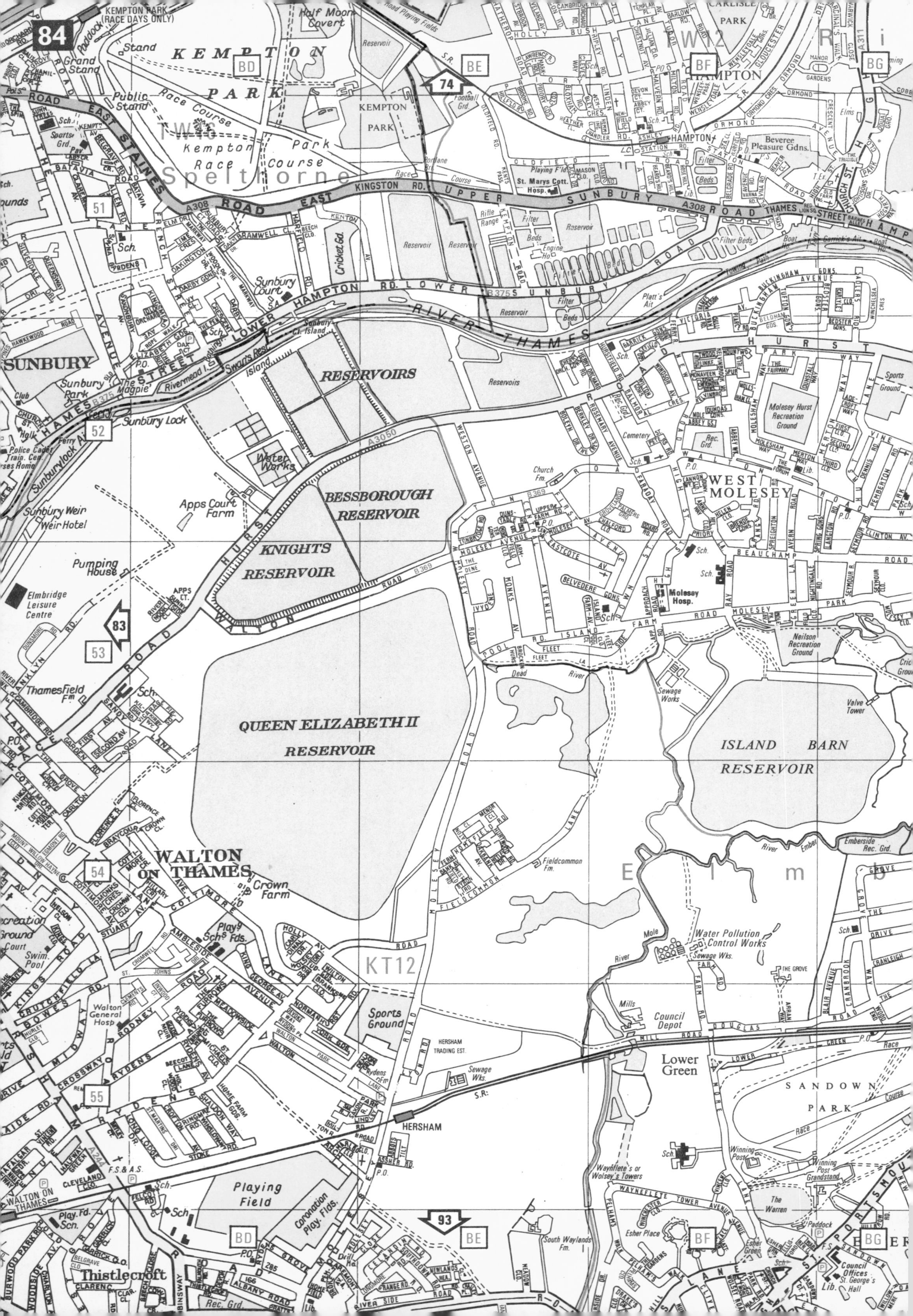
KEMPTON PARK (RACE DAYS ONLY)
Half Moon Covert
KEMPTON PARK
Kempton Race Course
Spelthorne
HAMPTON
TW12
TW16
Beveree Pleasure Gdns.
St. Marys Cott. Hosp.
UPPER SUNBURY ROAD
A308
KINGSTON RD.
THAMES STREET
LOWER SUNBURY RD.
B375
RIVER THAMES
SUNBURY
Sunbury Court
Sunbury Lock
Sunbury Weir
Weir Hotel
Platt's Ait
Garrick's Ait
RESERVOIRS
Reservoirs
BESSBOROUGH RESERVOIR
KNIGHTS RESERVOIR
QUEEN ELIZABETH II RESERVOIR
ISLAND BARN RESERVOIR
Water Works
Apps Court Farm
Pumping House
Elmbridge Leisure Centre
HURST ROAD
A3050
WALTON ROAD
B369
WEST MOLESEY
Molesey Hosp.
Molesey Hurst Recreation Ground
Neilson Recreation Ground
Sports Ground
Cemetery
Church Fm.
Dead River
Sewage Works
Valve Tower
River Ember
Embereside Rec. Grd.
Elmb
Thamesfield Fm.
WALTON ON THAMES
Crown Farm
Fieldcommon Fm.
KT12
River Mole
Water Pollution Control Works
Sewage Wks.
THE GROVE
Mills
Council Depot
Walton General Hosp.
Sports Ground
HERSHAM TRADING EST.
Sewage Wks.
Rydens Fm
HERSHAM
S.R.
Lower Green
SANDOWN PARK
Race Course
Winning Post
Winning Post Grandstand
The Warren
Wayneflete's or Wolsey's Towers
WAYNEFLETE TOWER AVENUE
Esher Place
South Waylands Fm.
Playing Field
Coronation Play. Flds.
Thistlecroft
WALTON ON THAMES
Council Offices
St. George's Hall
Lib.
Esher Green
BD
BE
BF
BG
51
52
53
54
55
74
83
93

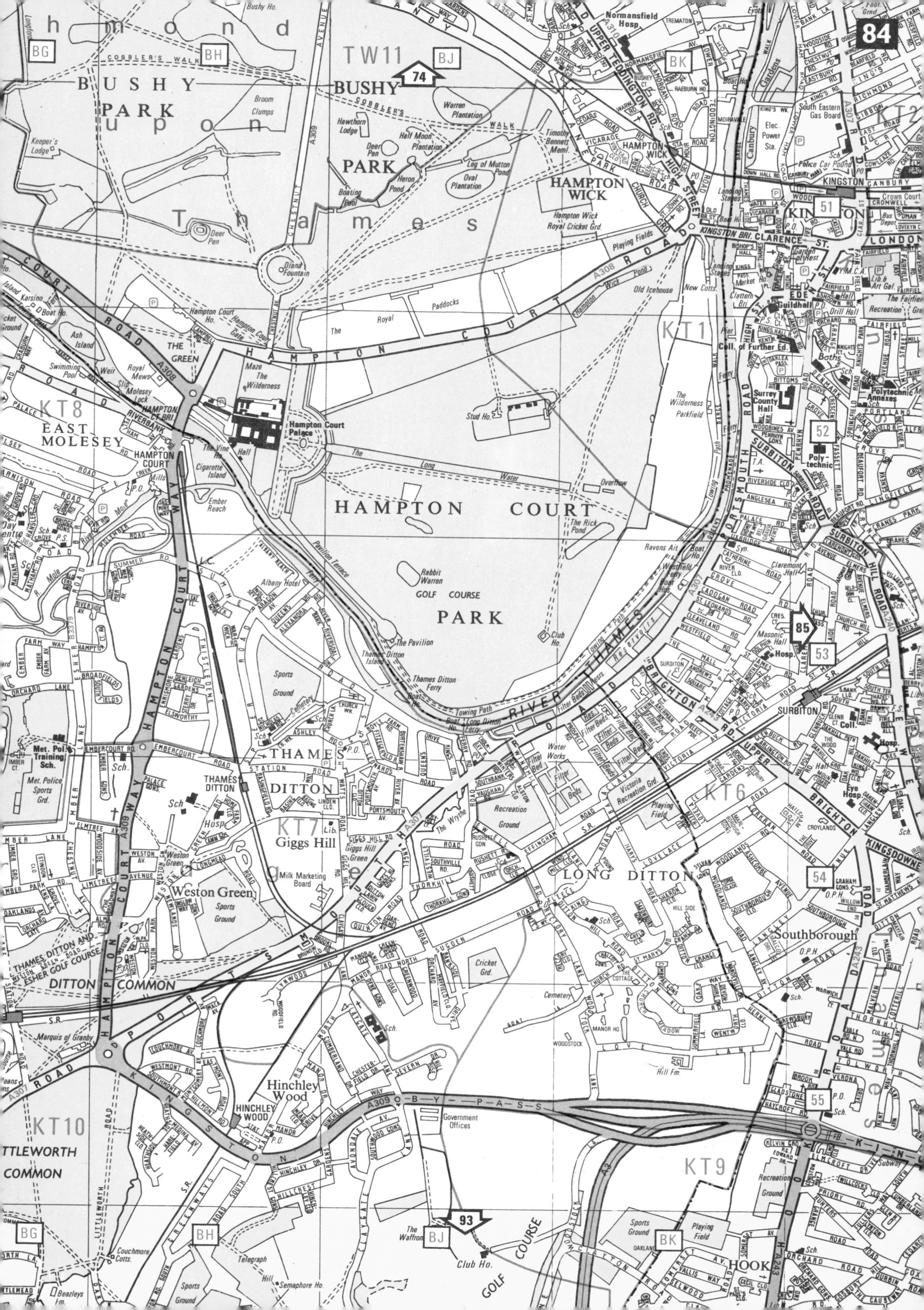

BG
BH
BJ
BK
TW11
74
BUSHY PARK
Richmond upon Thames
COBBLER'S WALK
Keeper's Lodge
Broom Clumps
Warren Plantation
Hawthorn Lodge
Deer Pen
Half Moon Plantation
Leg of Mutton Pond
Oval Plantation
Heron Pond
Boating Pool
Timothy Bennett Meml.
Diana Fountain
CHESTNUT AVENUE
A309
Normansfield Hosp.
TREMATON
UPPER TEDDINGTON RD.
HAMPTON WICK
HIGH STREET
Hampton Wick Royal Cricket Grd.
Playing Fields
KINGSTON BRI.
CLARENCE ST.
KINGSTON
51
Canbury Gardens
Elec. Power Sta.
South Eastern Gas Board
Police Car Pound
Crown Court
Bus Depot
Guildhall
Coll. of Further Ed.
Surrey County Hall
Polytechnic Annexes
52
Polytechnic
HAMPTON COURT ROAD
A308
Hampton Court Ho.
Hampton Court Gate
THE GREEN
Ash Island
Karsino
Swimming Pool
Weir
Royal Mews
Molesey Lock
Maze
The Wilderness
Hampton Court Palace
The Royal Paddocks
Old Icehouse
New Cotts.
Hampton Wick Pond
KT1
KT8
EAST MOLESEY
HAMPTON CT. BRI.
HAMPTON COURT
The Vine Ho.
Cigarette Island
Ember Reach
Stud Ho.
The Long Water
Overflow
HAMPTON COURT PARK
The Rick Pond
Rabbit Warren
GOLF COURSE
The Wilderness Parkfield
Towing Path
PORTSMOUTH ROAD
A307
Ravens Ait
Boat Ho.
Claremont Hall
85
53
Masonic Hall
Hosp.
SURBITON
SURBITON HILL ROAD
A240
Pavilion Terrace
Albany Hotel
The Pavilion
Thames Ditton Island
Thames Ditton Ferry
Boat Ho.
RIVER THAMES
Reservoirs
Filter Beds
Water Works
Victoria Recreation Grd.
KT6
BRIGHTON RD.
A243
Met. Pol. Training Sch.
Met. Police Sports Grd.
EMBERCOURT RD.
HAMPTON COURT WAY
A309
THAMES DITTON
KT7
Giggs Hill
Giggs Hill Green
Milk Marketing Board
Weston Green
Sports Ground
Recreation Ground
The Wythe
Playing Field
LONG DITTON
Southborough
54
KINGSDOWNE
THAMES DITTON AND ESHER GOLF COURSE
DITTON COMMON
Marquis of Granby
S.R.
Cricket Grd.
Cemetery
The Cottage
Manor Ho
Woodstock
Hill Fm.
Hinchley Wood
HINCHLEY WOOD
KINGSTON ROAD
A309 BY-PASS
Government Offices
55
KT10
LITTLEWORTH COMMON
KT9
A3
Recreation Ground
Sports Ground
Playing Field
GOLF COURSE
Club Ho.
93
The Waffron
Telegraph Hill
Semaphore Ho.
Couchmore Cotts.
Beazleys Fm.
HOOK
A243

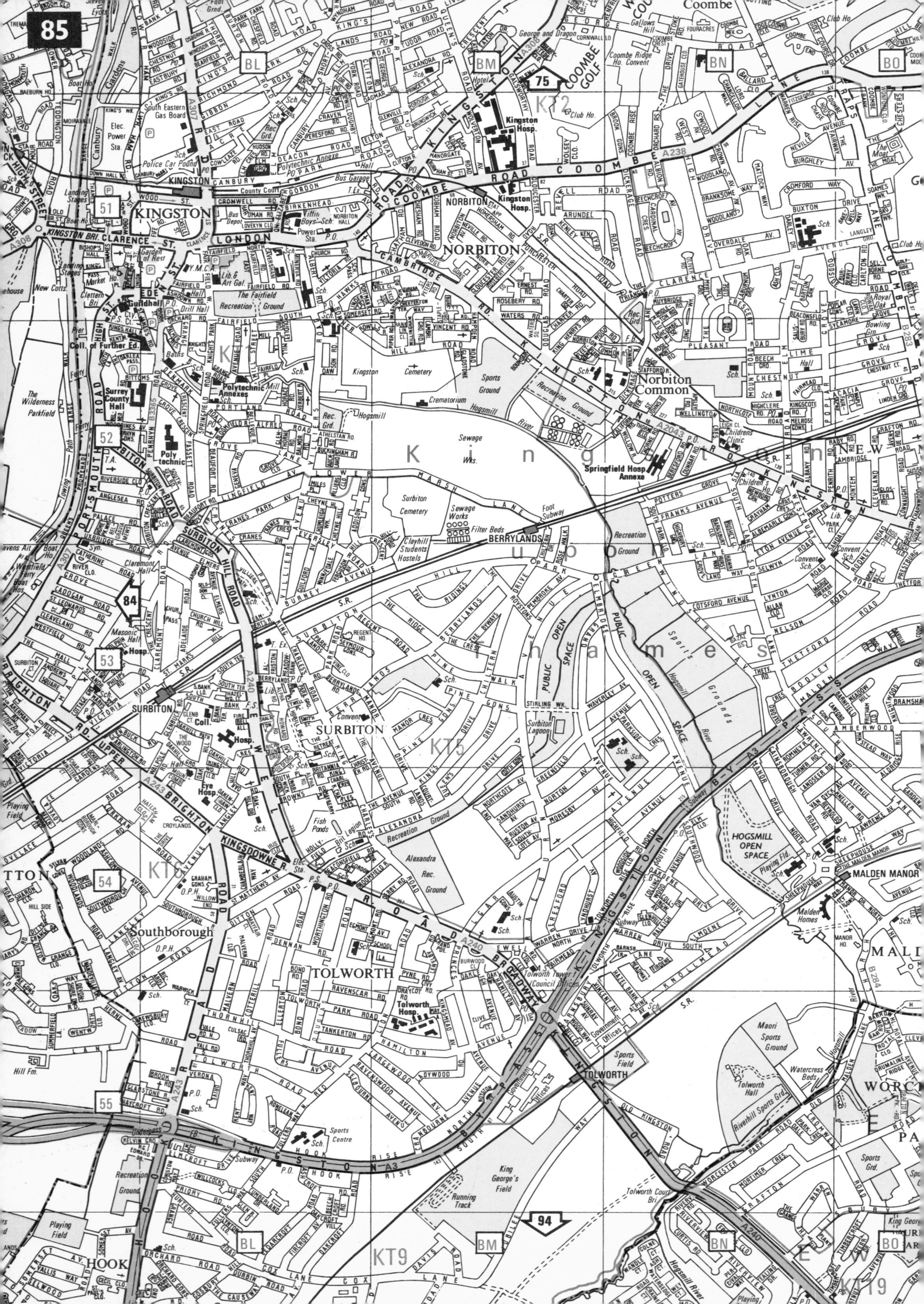

85
BL
BM
BN
BO
75
51
52
53
54
55
84
94
Coombe
KINGSTON
NORBITON
Norbiton Common
SURBITON
TOLWORTH
Southborough
HOOK
MALDEN MANOR
KT2
KT5
KT6
KT9
KT19
Kingston upon Thames
COOMBE GOLF
Kingston Hosp.
Kingston Cemetery
Crematorium
Sewage Wks.
Surbiton Cemetery
BERRYLANDS
Recreation Ground
Sports Ground
PUBLIC OPEN SPACE
HOGSMILL OPEN SPACE
Alexandra Rec. Ground
Surbiton Lagoon
King George's Field
Running Track
Maori Sports Ground
Watercress Beds
Tolworth Hall
Riverhill Sports Grd.
Tolworth Hosp.
Tolworth Tower / Council Offices
Sports Field
Springfield Hosp. Annexe
Surrey County Hall
Coll. of Further Ed.
Guildhall
Polytechnic Annexes
Poly technic
Kingston Bri.
The Wilderness Parkfield
Raven's Ait
South Eastern Gas Board
Elec. Power Sta.
Police Car Pound
Clayhill Students Hostels
Filter Beds
Malden Homes
Playing Field
Hill Fm.
A3
A238
A240
A243
A307
A308
A2043
B284
B3365
KINGSTON BY-PASS
KINGSTON ROAD
COOMBE ROAD
COOMBE LANE
EWELL ROAD
HOOK ROAD
BRIGHTON ROAD
PORTSMOUTH ROAD
LONDON ROAD
KINGSDOWNE R.
CAMBRIDGE RD.
SURBITON HILL ROAD
HIGH STREET

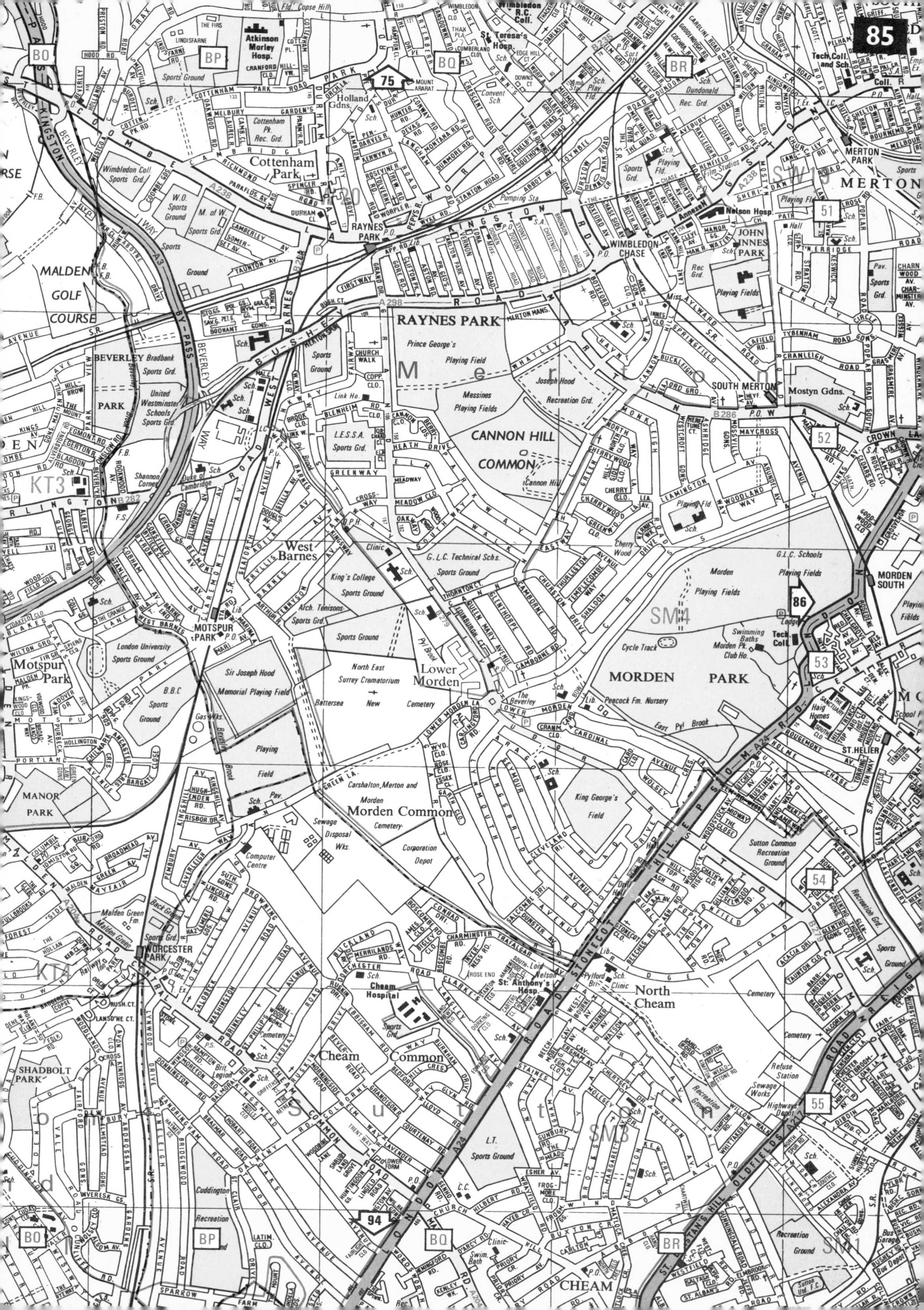

BO
BP
BQ
BR
75
Atkinson Morley Hosp.
Wimbledon R.C. Coll.
St. Teresa's Hosp.
Cottenham Park
Cottenham Pk. Rec. Grd.
Wimbledon Coll. Sports Grd.
W.O. Sports Ground
M. of W. Sports Grd.
Holland Gdns.
Convent Sch.
Dundonald Rec. Grd.
Nelson Hosp.
John Innes Park
Merton Park
MERTON
SW19
51
52
53
54
55
86
94
MALDEN GOLF COURSE
KINGSTON BY-PASS
A3
A238
A298
B282
B286
B279
A24
A217
RAYNES PARK
Raynes Park
Wimbledon Chase
Prince George's Playing Field
Messines Playing Fields
Joseph Hood Recreation Grd.
CANNON HILL COMMON
Cannon Hill
South Merton
Mostyn Gdns.
BEVERLEY
PARK
Bradbank Sports Grd.
United Westminster Schools Sports Grd.
L.E.S.S.A. Sports Grd.
KT3
Shannon Corner
Duke of Cambridge
West Barnes
King's College Sports Ground
G.L.C. Technical Schs. Sports Ground
Arch. Tenisons Sports Grd.
Sports Ground
G.L.C. Schools Playing Fields
Morden Playing Fields
MORDEN SOUTH
SM4
Cycle Track
Swimming Baths
Morden Pk. Club Ho.
Tech. Coll.
MORDEN PARK
Peacock Fm. Nursery
East Pyl Brook
Pyl Brook
Motspur Park
MOTSPUR PARK
London University Sports Ground
Sir Joseph Hood Memorial Playing Field
B.B.C. Sports Ground
North East Surrey Crematorium
Battersea New Cemetery
Lower Morden
Playing Field
MANOR PARK
Carshalton, Merton and Morden Cemetery
Morden Common
Sewage Disposal Wks.
Corporation Depot
King George's Field
St. Helier
Haig Homes
Sutton Common Recreation Ground
Computer Centre
Malden Green Fm.
WORCESTER PARK
KT4
Cheam Hospital
Cheam Common
St. Anthony's Hosp.
North Cheam
Cemetery
Refuse Station
Sewage Works
Highways Depot
Recreation Grd.
SHADBOLT PARK
SM3
L.T. Sports Ground
Cuddington Recreation Ground
Sutton
CHEAM
Recreation Ground
SM1
Bus Garage
Sutton Utd. F.C.

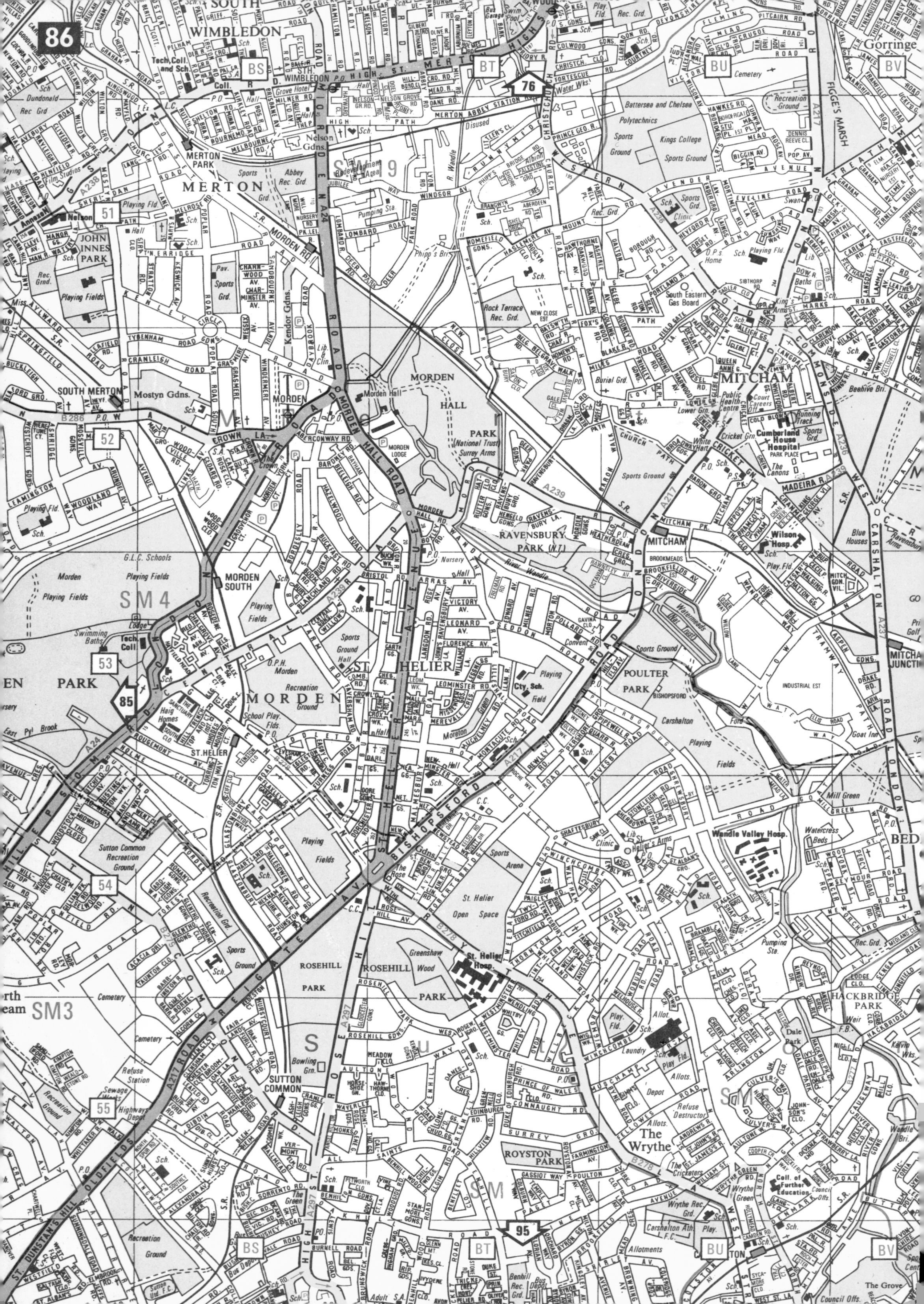
SOUTH WIMBLEDON
WIMBLEDON
BS
BT
BU
BV
Gorringe
76
MERTON
MERTON PARK
JOHN INNES PARK
Nelson
51
SM19
Abbey Rec. Grd.
Battersea and Chelsea Polytechnics Sports Ground
Kings College Sports Ground
Cemetery
FIGGE'S MARSH
SOUTH MERTON
Mostyn Gdns.
MORDEN
MORDEN HALL PARK (National Trust)
Morden Hall
MORDEN HALL ROAD
Rock Terrace Rec. Grd.
South Eastern Gas Board
MITCHAM
Public Health Centre
Cumberland House Hospital
52
G.L.C. Schools
Morden Playing Fields
SM4
MORDEN SOUTH
RAVENSBURY PARK (N.T.)
River Wandle
Wilson Hosp.
Blue Houses
53
85
PARK
MORDEN
ST. HELIER
POULTER PARK
Carshalton Playing Fields
INDUSTRIAL EST
Haig Homes
Mill Green
Wandle Valley Hosp.
Sutton Common Recreation Ground
54
Sports Arena
St. Helier Open Space
St. Helier Hosp.
Greenshaw Wood
ROSEHILL PARK
ROSEHILL PARK
HACKBRIDGE PARK
SM3
Cemetery
Refuse Station
55
SUTTON COMMON
Bowling Grn.
The Wrythe
SM5
ROYSTON PARK
Wythe Rec. Grd.
Coll. of Further Education
Recreation Ground
95
Allotments
Carshalton Ath. F.C.
BS
BT
BU
BV
ST. DUNSTAN'S HILL
A217 REIGATE AVENUE
A24
A297
A239
A217
A236
B278
B286
The Grove

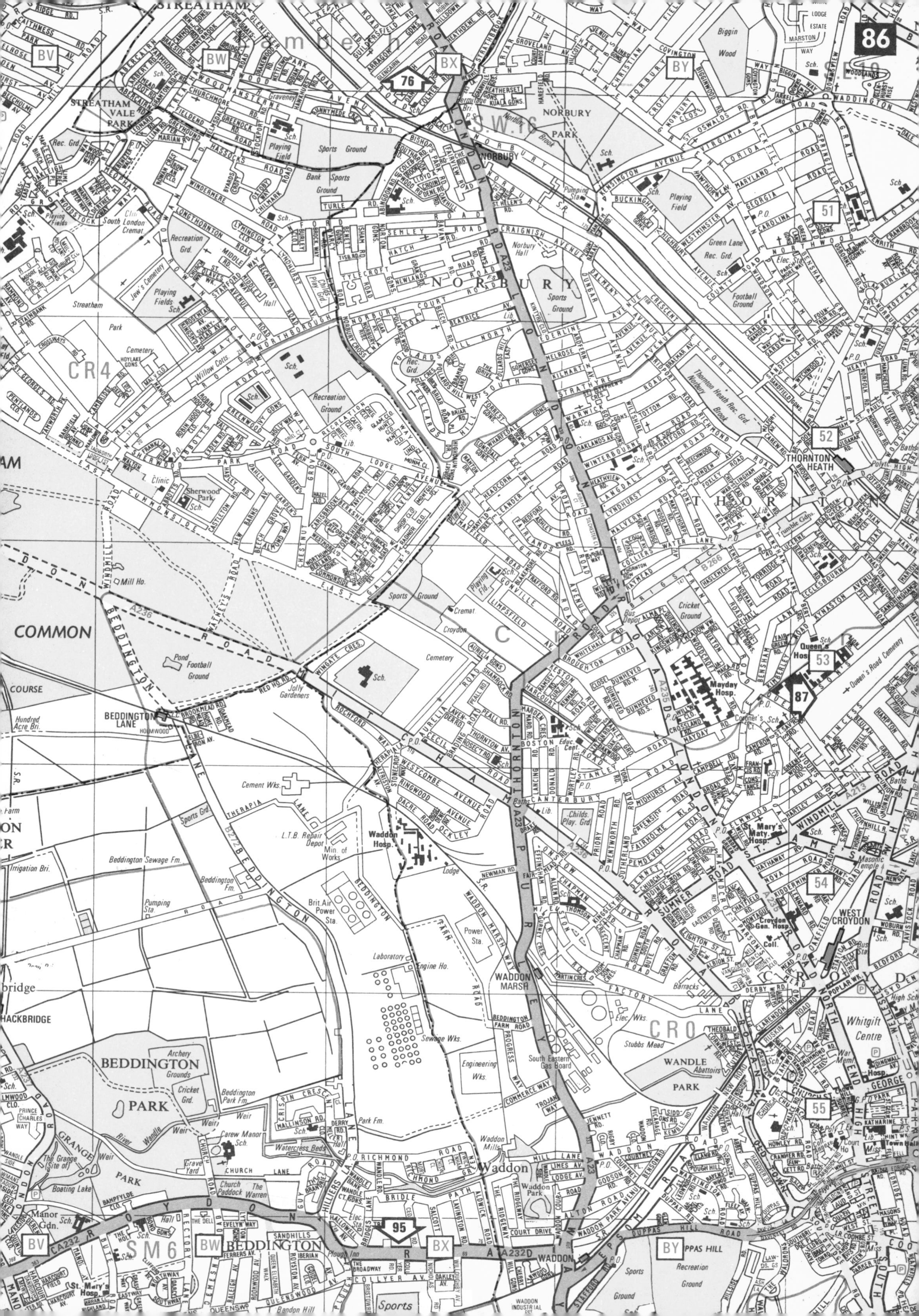
STREATHAM
BV
BW
BX
BY
76
STREATHAM VALE PARK
NORBURY
NORBURY PARK
S.W.16
CR4
N O R B U R Y
51
52
53
54
55
87
95
THORNTON HEATH
T H O R N T O N
COMMON
Mayday Hosp.
Queen's Road Cemetery
Croydon Cemetery
BEDDINGTON LANE
BEDDINGTON PARK
WADDON MARSH
Waddon
WADDON
CR0
WANDLE PARK
WEST CROYDON
Whitgift Centre
C R O Y D
SM6
BEDDINGTON
HACKBRIDGE
Sports Ground
Recreation Ground
Sewage Wks.
Beddington Sewage Fm.
Waddon Hosp.
Power Sta.
Cement Wks.
Playing Field
Croydon Gen. Hosp.
St. Mary's Maty. Hosp.
Stubbs Mead
Town Hall
Recreation Ground

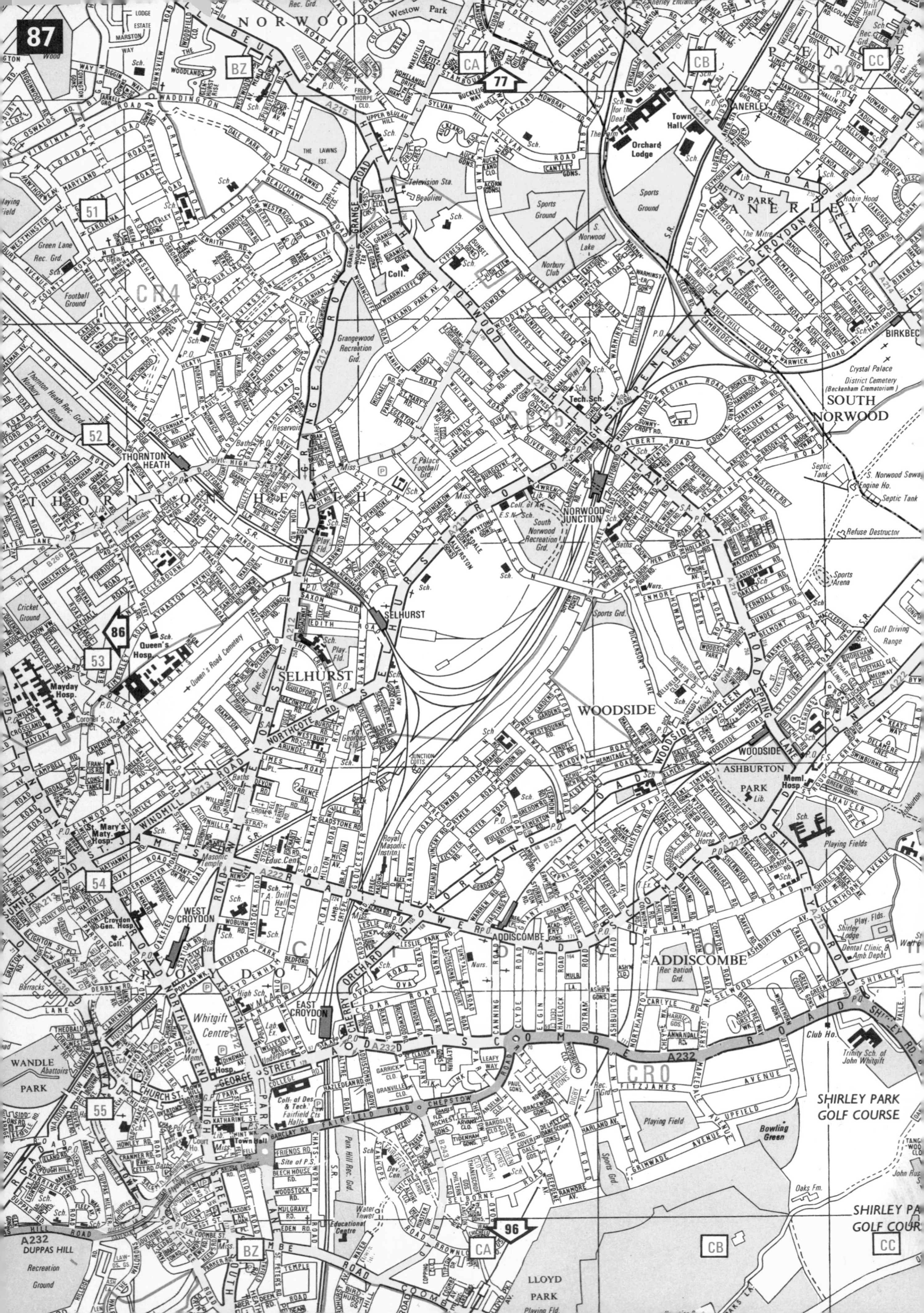
NORWOOD
Westow Park
BZ
CA
CB
CC
77
P E N G E
ANERLEY
Town Hall
Orchard Lodge
Sch. for the Deaf
Sports Ground
Television Sta.
Beaulieu
The Lawns Est.
Green Lane Rec. Grd.
Football Ground
CR4
51
52
53
54
55
86
96
Thornton Heath Rec. Grd.
Norbury Brook
THORNTON HEATH
T H O R N T O N   H E A T H
Grangewood Recreation Grd.
C. Palace Football Grd.
S. Norwood Lake
Norbury Club
Betts Park
A N E R L E Y
The Mitre
Robin Hood
BIRKBECK
Crystal Palace District Cemetery (Beckenham Crematorium)
SOUTH NORWOOD
Tech. Sch.
NORWOOD JUNCTION
South Norwood Recreation Grd.
S. Norwood Sewage Engine Ho.
Septic Tank
Refuse Destructor
Sports Arena
Golf Driving Range
SELHURST
Queen's Hosp.
Mayday Hosp.
Queen's Road Cemetery
Cricket Ground
WOODSIDE
ASHBURTON PARK
Meml. Hosp.
Playing Fields
Royal Masonic Instit.
St. Mary's Maty. Hosp.
Croydon Gen. Hosp.
WEST CROYDON
Educ. Cent.
Masonic Temple
C R O Y D O N
EAST CROYDON
ADDISCOMBE
Rec'eation Grd.
Whitgift Centre
Coll. of Des & Tech. Fairfield Cts Halls
Town Hall
WANDLE PARK
Abattoirs
Barracks
CR0
Trinity Sch. of John Whitgift
Club Ho.
SHIRLEY PARK GOLF COURSE
Shirley Lodge
Dental Clinic & Amb Depot
Playing Field
Bowling Green
Park Hill Rec. Grd.
Water Tower
Educational Centre
Oaks Fm.
DUPPAS HILL Recreation Ground
LLOYD PARK
A212
A213
A214
A215
A222
A232
A236
B243
B266

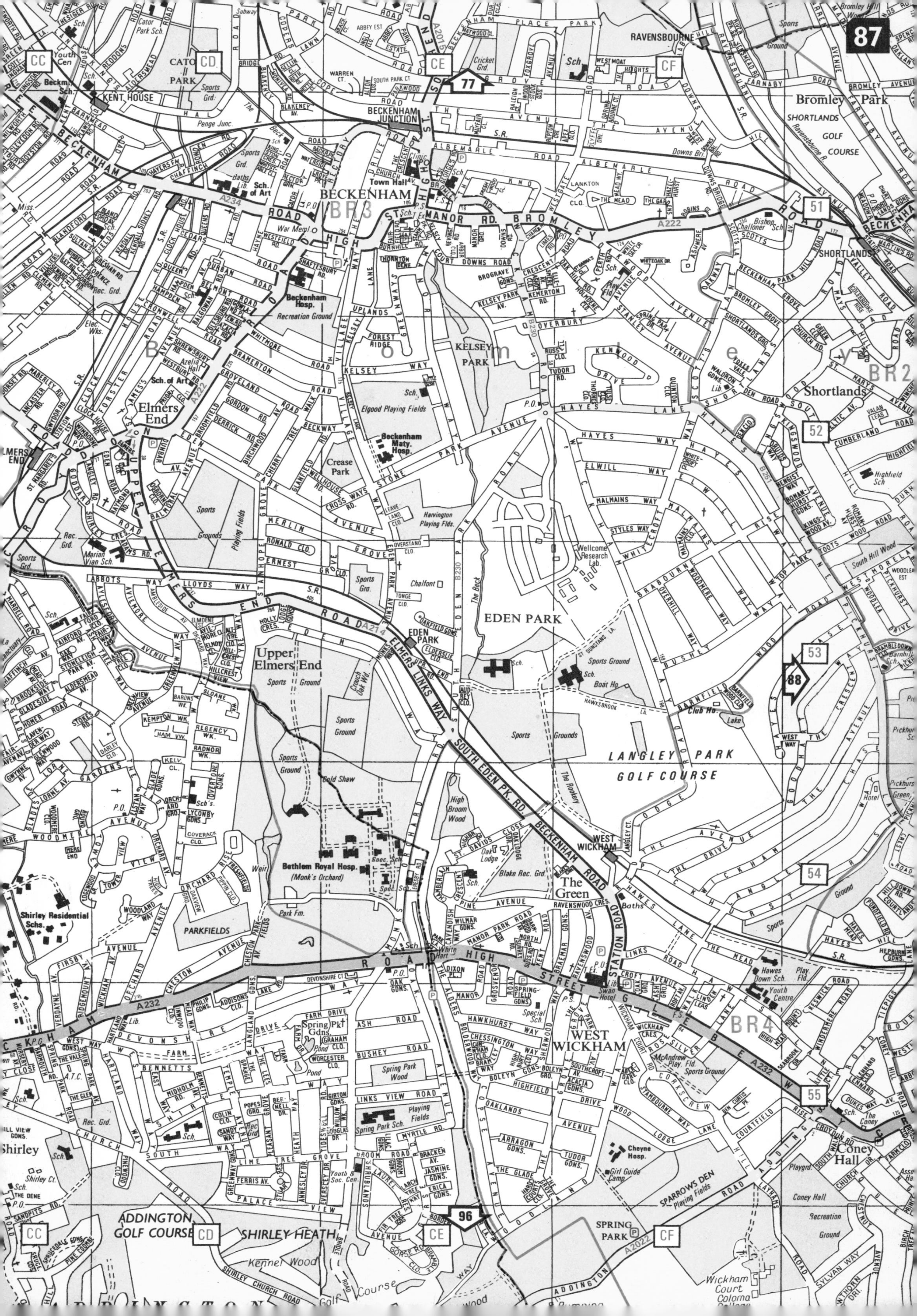

87
CC
CD
CE
CF
77
RAVENSBOURNE
Bromley Park
SHORTLANDS GOLF COURSE
Ravensbourne R.
Downs Bri.
KENT HOUSE
CATOR PARK
Cator Park Sch.
Penge Junc.
BECKENHAM JUNCTION
BECKENHAM
BR3
Town Hall
Beckenham Hosp.
Recreation Ground
Sch. of Art
War Meml.
KELSEY PARK
Elgood Playing Fields
Beckenham Maty. Hosp.
Crease Park
Harvington Playing Flds.
Elmers End
ELMERS END
Marian Vian Sch.
Sports Grounds
Playing Fields
Chalfont
EDEN PARK
Wellcome Research Lab.
Upper Elmers End
Sports Ground
Cold Shaw
Bethlem Royal Hosp. (Monk's Orchard)
Park Fm.
PARKFIELDS
High Broom Wood
Blake Rec. Grd.
The Green
WEST WICKHAM
LANGLEY PARK GOLF COURSE
Club Ho.
Lake
The Rookery
88
Shortlands
SHORTLANDS
BR2
51
52
53
54
55
Highfield Sch.
South Hill Wood
Shirley Residential Schs.
Shirley
ADDINGTON GOLF COURSE
SHIRLEY HEATH
Kennel Wood
Spring Park Wood
Spring Park Sch.
Playing Fields
Youth & Soc. Cen.
96
WEST WICKHAM
BR4
Swan Hotel
Hawes Down Sch.
Youth Centre
McAndrew Play. Fld.
Sports Ground
Cheyne Hosp.
Girl Guide Camp
SPARROWS DEN Playing Fields
SPRING PARK
Coney Hall
Coney Hall Recreation Ground
Wickham Court
A234
A222
A214
A232
A2022
B230
B251
BECKENHAM ROAD
HIGH STREET
ELMERS END ROAD
SOUTH EDEN PK. RD.
WICKHAM ROAD
HAYES LANE
STATION ROAD

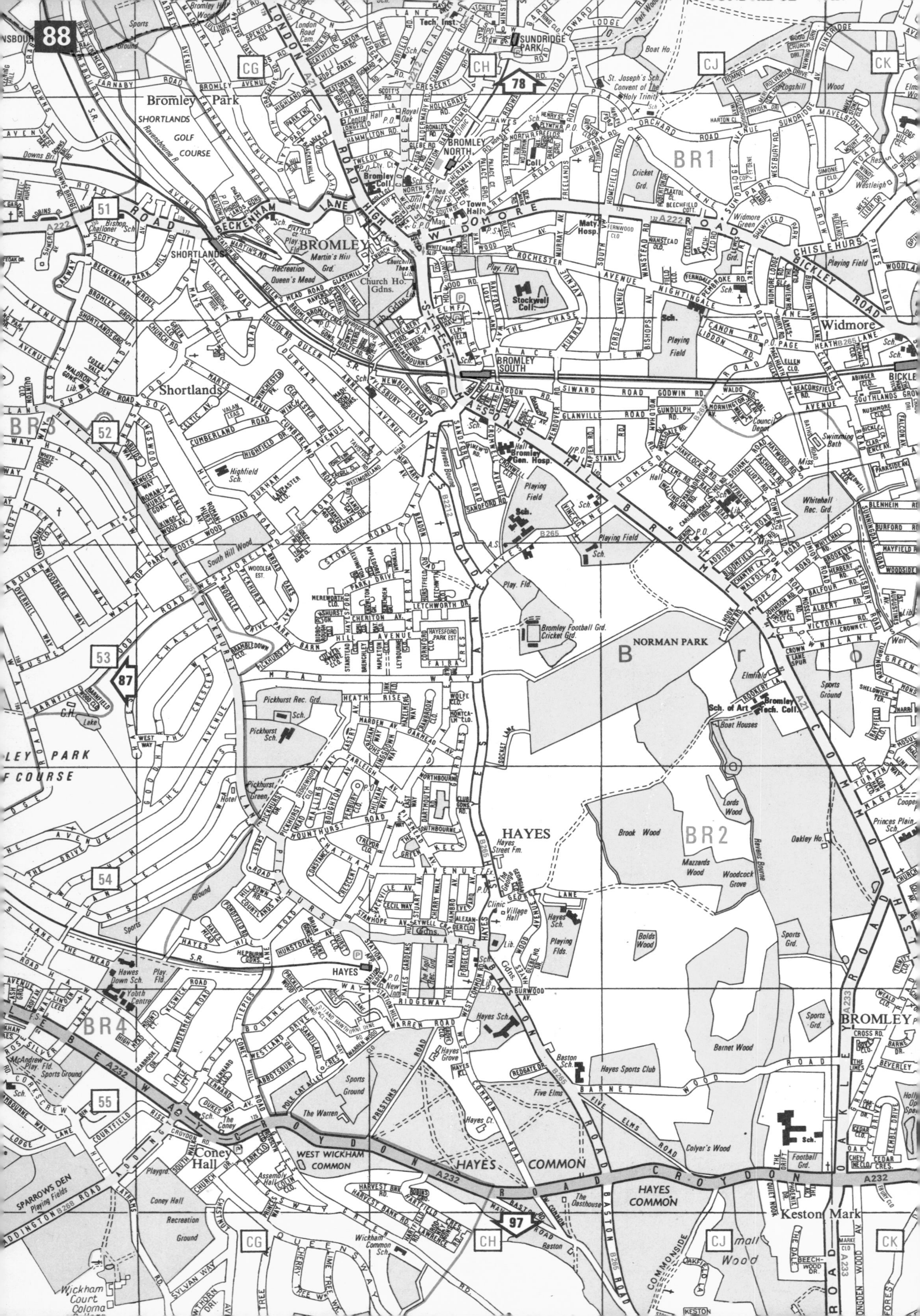
CG
CH
CJ
CK
78
87
97
51
52
53
54
55
BR1
BR2
BR3
BR4
Bromley Park
SHORTLANDS GOLF COURSE
Shortlands
SHORTLANDS
BROMLEY
BROMLEY NORTH
BROMLEY SOUTH
SUNDRIDGE PARK
Widmore
BICKLEY
NORMAN PARK
HAYES
HAYES COMMON
WEST WICKHAM COMMON
Coney Hall
Keston Mark
BROMLEY COMMON
Bromley Gen. Hosp.
Stockwell Coll.
Bromley Coll.
Town Hall
Martin's Hill Grd.
Queen's Mead Recreation
Church Ho. Gdns.
Bromley Football Grd. Cricket Grd.
Bromley Tech. Coll.
Sch. of Art
Pickhurst Rec. Grd.
Pickhurst Sch.
Highfield Sch.
South Hill Wood
Brook Wood
Lords Wood
Mazzards Wood
Woodcock Grove
Bolds Wood
Barnet Wood
Colyer's Wood
Five Elms
Hayes Sports Club
Hayes Sch.
Baston Sch.
Hayes Street Fm.
Hawes Down Sch.
Youth Centre
Coney Hall Recreation Ground
Sparrows Den Playing Fields
Wickham Court
Wickham Common Sch.
The Warren
Hayes Ct.
Hayes Grove
The Oasthouse
Oakley Ho.
Princes Plain Sch.
Whitehall Rec. Grd.
Cricket Grd.
Sports Ground
Playing Field
Elmfield
Boat Houses
Ravens Bourne
LONDON ROAD
HIGH STREET
WIDMORE ROAD
BECKENHAM LANE
MASONS HILL
BICKLEY ROAD
CHISLEHURST ROAD
HAYES ROAD
HAYES LANE
HAYES STREET
BASTON ROAD
CROYDON ROAD
WEST WICKHAM
FIVE ELMS ROAD
BARNET WOOD ROAD
OAKLEY ROAD
A21
A222
A232
A233
B265
B228
B2212
B268
Keston

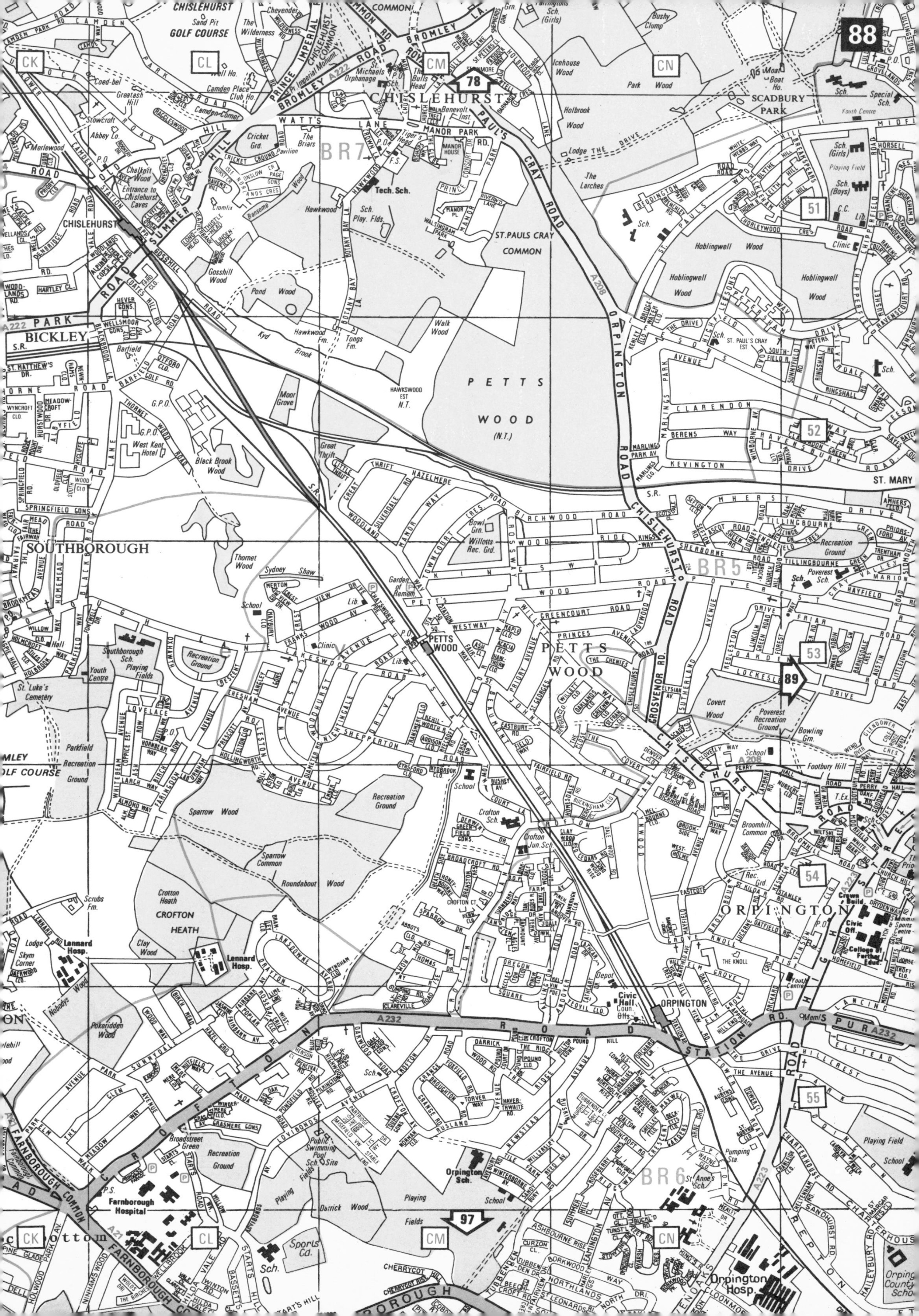
CK
CL
CM
CN
78
CHISLEHURST
Sand Pit
GOLF COURSE
The Wilderness
PRINCE IMPERIAL
BROMLEY ROAD
BROMLEY LA.
Camden Place Club Ho.
Icehouse Wood
Park Wood
Moat
Boat Ho.
SCADBURY PARK
Holbrook Wood
MANOR PARK
WATT'S LANE
PAUL'S CRAY ROAD
BR7
Cricket Grd.
The Briars
Chalkpit Wood
Entrance to Chislehurst Caves
CHISLEHURST
Tech. Sch.
Hawkwood
Sch. Play. Flds.
ST.PAULS CRAY COMMON
The Larches
Hoblingwell Wood
51
Gosshill Wood
Pond Wood
Walk Wood
Hawkwood Fm.
Tongs Fm.
Kyd Brook
BICKLEY
PARK ROAD
HAWKSWOOD EST N.T.
PETTS WOOD (N.T.)
Moor Grove
ORPINGTON ROAD
CLARENDON
BERENS WAY
KEVINGTON DRIVE
52
West Kent Hotel
Black Brook Wood
Great Thrift
ST. MARY
SOUTHBOROUGH
Thornet Wood
Sydney Shaw
Willetts Rec. Grd.
KINGSWAY
BR5
Recreation Ground
POVEREST
CHISLEHURST ROAD
PETTS WOOD
53
89
Covert Wood
Poverest Recreation Ground
Southborough Sch. Playing Fields
Recreation Ground
Youth Centre
St. Luke's Cemetery
Parkfield Recreation Ground
GOLF COURSE
Sparrow Wood
Recreation Ground
Crofton Sch.
Footbury Hill
Broomhill Common
54
ORPINGTON
Civic Off.
Sparrow Common
Roundabout Wood
Crotton Heath
CROFTON HEATH
Clay Wood
Lennard Hosp.
THE KNOLL
Civic Hall
ORPINGTON
Pokeridden Wood
A232
CROFTON ROAD
STATION RD.
55
Playing Field
School
Broadstreet Green
Recreation Ground
Farnborough Hospital
Public Swimming Pool
Darrick Wood
Playing Fields
Orpington Sch.
BR6
97
Sports Cd.
Orpington Hosp.
FARNBOROUGH COMMON

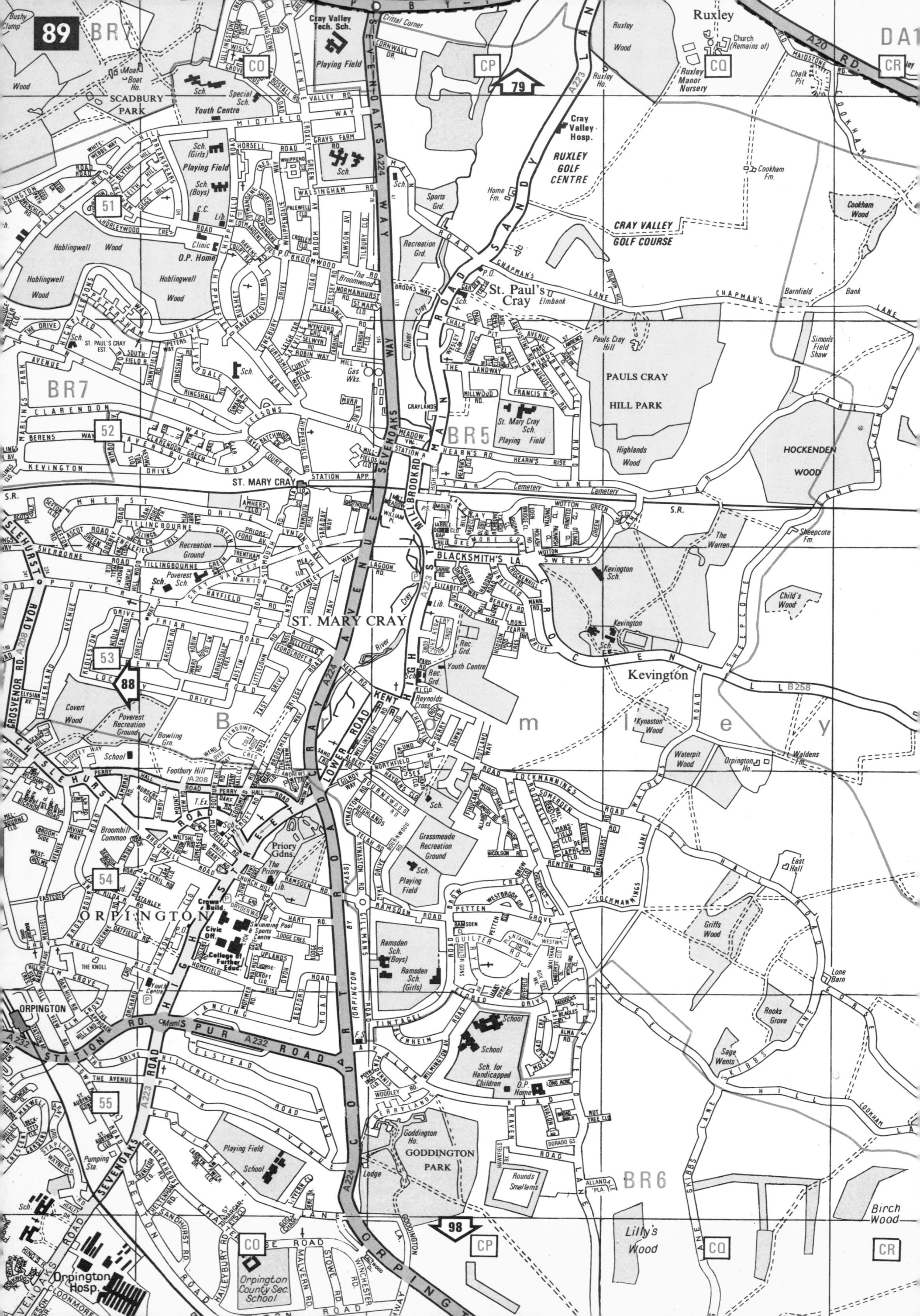
BR7
DA1
BR5
BR6
CO
CP
CQ
CR
79
88
98
51
52
53
54
55
Ruxley
Ruxley Wood
Church (Remains of)
Ruxley Manor Nursery
Ruxley Ho.
Chalk Pit
Cray Valley Tech. Sch.
Playing Field
Crittal Corner
Cornwall Dr.
Cray Valley Hosp.
RUXLEY GOLF CENTRE
CRAY VALLEY GOLF COURSE
Cookham Fm.
Cookham Wood
Home Fm.
Sports Grd.
Recreation Grd.
Moat Boat Ho.
SCADBURY PARK
Bushy Clump
Wood
Special Sch.
Youth Centre
Sch. (Girls)
Sch. (Boys)
Hoblingwell Wood
O.P. Home
Clinic
St. Paul's Cray
Elmbank
Chapman's Lane
Barnfield
Bank
Simon's Field Shaw
Pauls Cray Hill
PAULS CRAY HILL PARK
Highlands Wood
HOCKENDEN WOOD
St. Mary Cray Sch. Playing Field
Gas Wks.
Graylands
ST. MARY CRAY
St. Mary Cray Station
Station App.
Cemetery
Star Lane
S.R.
The Warren
Sheepcote Fm.
Kevington Sch.
Kevington
Child's Wood
Recreation Ground
Poverest Sch.
Blacksmith's La.
Sweeps
Youth Centre
Rec. Grd.
Reynolds Cross
Kynaston Wood
Waterpit Wood
Orpington Ho.
Waldens Fm.
Bromley
Covert Wood
Poverest Recreation Ground
Bowling Grn.
Footbury Hill
Cockmannings
East Hall
Broomhill Common
Priory Gdns.
The Priory
Grassmeade Recreation Ground
Playing Field
ORPINGTON
Crown Build.
Civic Off.
Swimming Pool Sports Centre
College of Further Educ.
The Knoll
Youth Centre
Griffs Wood
Ramsden Sch. (Boys)
Ramsden Sch. (Girls)
Lone Barn
Rooks Grove
Sage Wents
School
Sch. for Handicapped Children
O.P. Home
Goddington Ho.
GODDINGTON PARK
Lodge
Rounds Smallams
Pumping Sta.
Playing Field
School
Lilly's Wood
Birch Wood
Orpington Hosp.
Orpington County Sec. School
SEVENOAKS WAY
SEVENOAKS ROAD
COURT ROAD
SPUR ROAD
STATION RD.
HIGH STREET
CHISLEHURST ROAD
SANDY LANE
MAIN ROAD
HIGH ST.
LOWER ROAD
KENT ROAD
CRAY AVENUE
SKIBBS LANE
CHESTERFIELD
HOCKENDEN LANE
SHEEPCOTE LANE
ORPINGTON BY PASS
A20
A223
A224
A232
A208
B258

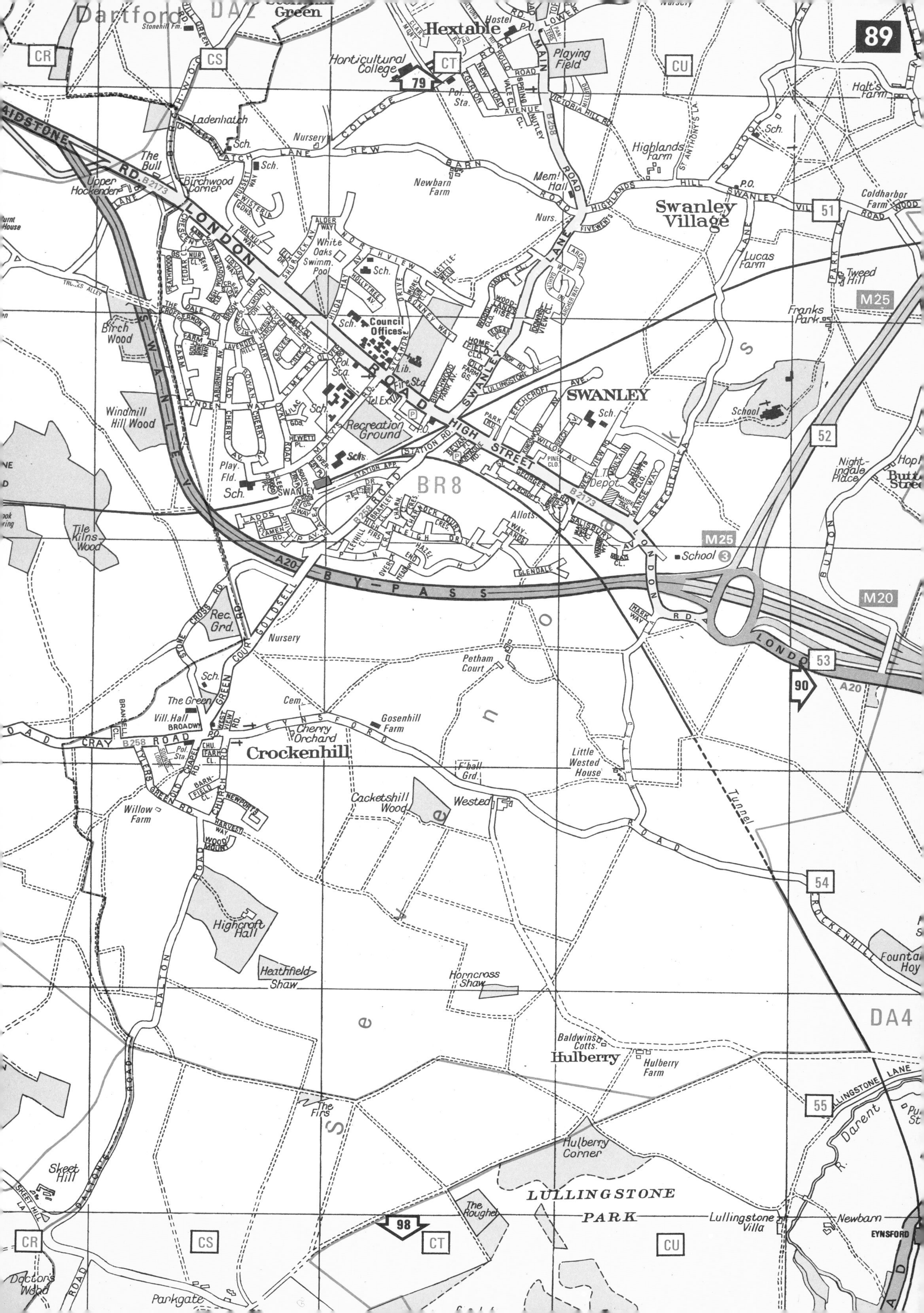

Hextable
Horticultural College
Playing Field
Ladenhatch
The Bull
Upper Hockenden
Birchwood Corner
Newbarn Farm
Highlands Farm
Swanley Village
Lucas Farm
Coldharbor Farm
Holt's Farm
Tweed Hill
Franks Park
White Oaks Swimm. Pool
Council Offices
Birch Wood
Windmill Hill Wood
Recreation Ground
SWANLEY
BR8
Tile Kilns Wood
School
Night-ingale Place
A20
BY-PASS
M25
M20
Rec. Grd.
Nursery
Petham Court
The Green
Vill. Hall
Cherry Orchard
Gosenhill Farm
Crockenhill
Little Wested House
F'ball Grd.
Cacketshill Wood
Wested
Willow Farm
Tunnel
Highcroft Hall
Heathfield Shaw
Horncross Shaw
DA4
Baldwins Cotts.
Hulberry
Hulberry Farm
The Firs
Hulberry Corner
Skeet Hill
LULLINGSTONE PARK
Lullingstone Villa
Newbarn
EYNSFORD
The Rougher
Doctor's Wood
Parkgate
R. Darent
Dartford
DA2
CR
CS
CT
CU
79
90
98
51
52
53
54
55

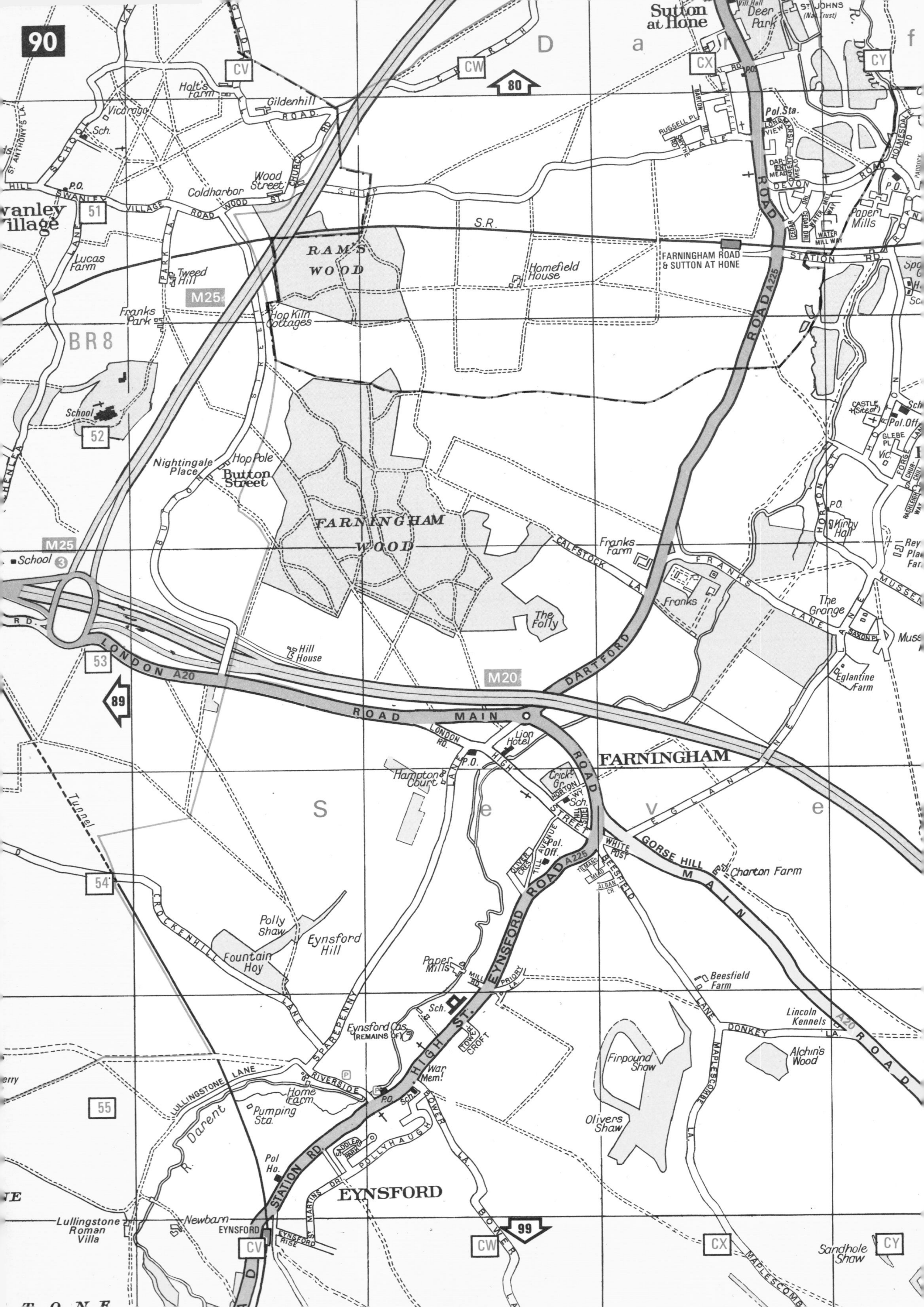
Sutton at Hone
Deer Park
ST JOHNS (Nat Trust)
Vill.Hall
CV
CW
CX
CY
80
Holt's Farm
Gildenhill
Vicarage
Sch.
SCHOOL
ST ANTHONY'S LA.
HILL
P.O.
Swanley Village
51
Coldharbor
Wood Street
CHURCH RD
GILDENHILL ROAD
SWANLEY VILLAGE ROAD
WOOD ST.
Lucas Farm
Tweed Hill
PARK LA.
M25
RAM'S WOOD
S.R.
Homefield House
FARNINGHAM ROAD & SUTTON AT HONE
STATION RD
Hop Kiln Cottages
Franks Park
BR8
School
52
RUSSELL PL.
BARTON RD
BLYTHE RD
LANE
Pol.Sta.
LONGMARSH VIEW
DEVON RD
Paper Mills
HOLMESDALE RD
ROAD A225
Nightingale Place
Hop Pole
Button Street
FARNINGHAM WOOD
Franks Farm
CALFSTOCK LA.
Franks
FRANKS LANE
The Folly
The Grange
CASTLE (Site of)
Sch.
Pol.Off.
GLEBE PL.
Vic.
HORTON ST.
P.O.
Kirby Hall
MUSSENDEN
SAXON PL.
Eglantine Farm
School
M25
3
53
LONDON A20
Hill House
M20
89
DARTFORD
ROAD MAIN
LONDON RD.
P.O.
Lion Hotel
HIGH
FARNINGHAM
Crick. Gr.
HORTON WY.
Sch.
STREET
ROAD
Hampton Court
LANE
EGLANTINE
S
e
v
e
Tunnel
GORSE HILL
WHITE POST
BEESFIELD
Charton Farm
MAIN
TILL AVENUE
OLIVER CRES.
Pol. Off.
A225
TILMANS MEAD
ALBAN CR.
54
CROCKENHILL
Polly Shaw
Eynsford Hill
Fountain Hoy
EYNSFORD ROAD
Paper Mills
MILL RD
PRIORY LA.
Beesfield Farm
LANE
Sch.
HIGH ST.
TOWN CROFT
Eynsford Cas. (REMAINS OF)
SPAREPENNY
Lincoln Kennels
DONKEY LA.
A20
ROAD
Alchin's Wood
Firpound Shaw
MAPLESCOMBE
War Mem.
LULLINGSTONE LANE
RIVERSIDE
Home Farm
P.O.
Sch.
BOWER
Pumping Sta.
55
Darent
R.
POLLYHAUGH
SADDLERS PARK
Olivers Shaw
Pol Ho.
STATION RD.
ST MARTINS DR.
EYNSFORD
LA.
BOWER
Lullingstone Roman Villa
Newbarn
EYNSFORD
EYNSFORD RISE
99
CW
CX
CY
MAPLESCOMBE
Sandhole Shaw

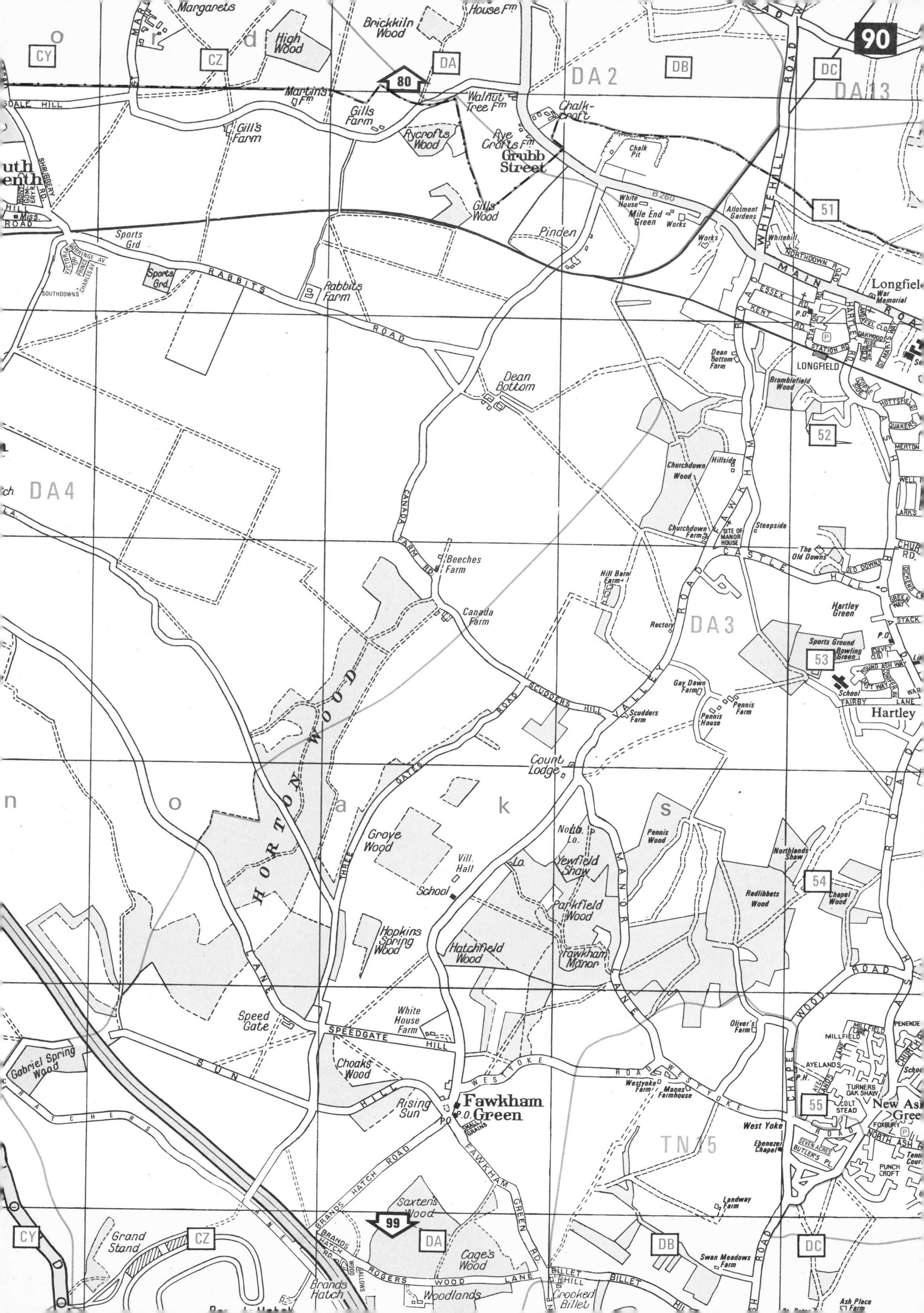

90
80
99
DA2
DA13
DA4
DA3
TN15
CY
CZ
DA
DB
DC
51
52
53
54
55
Margarets
Brickkiln Wood
High Wood
House Fm
Martin's Fm
Gills Farm
Walnut Tree Fm
Chalk-croft
Gill's Farm
Rycrofts Wood
Rye Crofts Fm
Grubb Street
Chalk Pit
Gills Wood
White House
Mile End Green
Works
Allotment Gardens
B260
Pinden
Whitehill
Sports Grd
Sports Grd.
RABBITS ROAD
Rabbits Farm
SOUTHDOWNS
Longfield
War Memorial
LONGFIELD
MAIN ROAD
WHITEHILL ROAD
NORTHDOWN ROAD
ESSEX RD.
KENT RD.
STATION RD
P.O.
Dean Bottom Farm
Dean Bottom
Bramblefield Wood
Churchdown Wood
Hillside
Churchdown Farm
SITE OF MANOR HOUSE
Steepside
FAWKHAM ROAD
CANADA FARM RD.
Beeches Farm
Canada Farm
CASTLE HILL
The Old Downs
OLD DOWNS
Hill Barn Farm
Rectory
Hartley Green
Sports Ground
Bowling Green
School
Hartley
FAIRBY LANE
VALLEY ROAD
SCUDDERS HILL ROAD
Scudders Farm
Gay Dawn Farm
Pennis Farm
Pennis House
Count Lodge
HORTON WOOD
THREE GATES
Grove Wood
Vill. Hall
School
Pennis Wood
Northlands Shaw
Redlibbets Wood
Chapel Wood
Yewfield Shaw
Parkfield Wood
Hopkins Spring Wood
Hatchfield Wood
Fawkham Manor
MANOR LANE
ASH ROAD
CHAPEL WOOD ROAD
Speed Gate
White House Farm
SPEEDGATE HILL
SUN LANE
Gabriel Spring Wood
Choaks Wood
WESTYOKE ROAD
Westyoke Farm
Manns Farmhouse
Oliver's Farm
MILLFIELD
AYELANDS
TURNERS OAK SHAW
New Ash Green
Rising Sun
Fawkham Green
P.O.
BRANDS HATCH ROAD
FAWKHAM GREEN RD.
West Yoke
Ebenezer Chapel
NORTH ASH RD
PUNCH CROFT
Saxten's Wood
Cage's Wood
Grand Stand
Landway Farm
Swan Meadows Farm
ROGERS WOOD LANE
BILLET HILL
Crooked Billet
Brands Hatch
Woodlands
Ash Place Farm

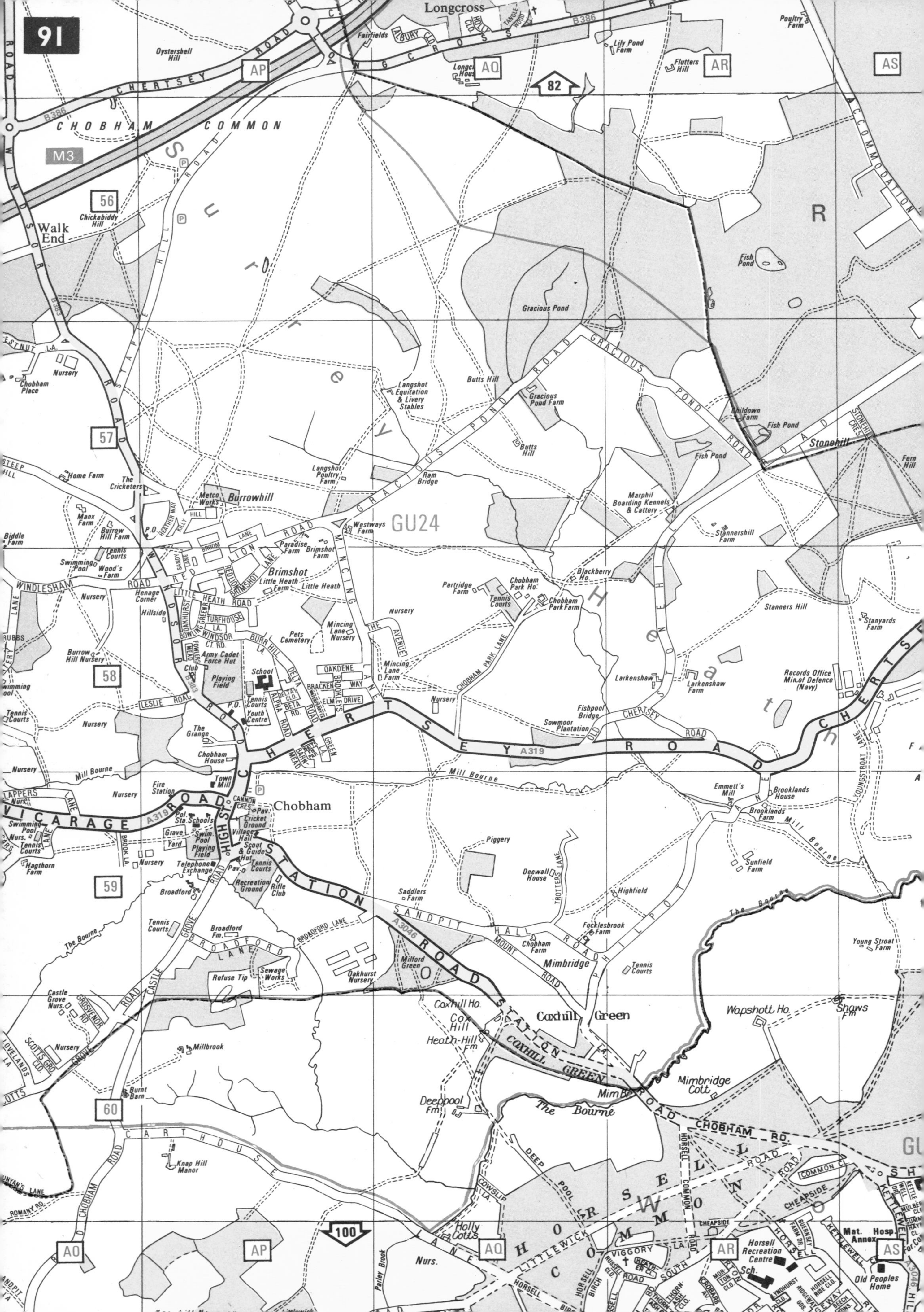
Longcross
Poultry Farm
Oystershell Hill
CHERTSEY ROAD
AP
AQ
AR
AS
82
Fairfields
Lily Pond Farm
Flutters Hill
B386
CHOBHAM COMMON
M3
56
Chickabiddy Hill
Walk End
WINDSOR ROAD
STAPLE HILL ROAD
Surrey
R
Fish Pond
Gracious Pond
Chobham Place
Nursery
Langshot Equitation & Livery Stables
Butts Hill
Gracious Pond Farm
GRACIOUS POND ROAD
Childown Farm
Fish Pond
Stonehill
STONEHILL ROAD
Fern Hill
57
Home Farm
The Cricketers
Langshot Poultry Farm
Ram Bridge
Metco Works
Burrowhill
Marphil Boarding Kennels & Cattery
Stannershill Farm
Manx Farm
Burrow Hill Farm
Biddle Farm
P.O.
Westways Farm
GU24
Paradise Farm
Brimshot Farm
Tennis Courts
Swimming Pool
Wood's Farm
Brimshot
Little Heath Farm
Little Heath
MINCING LANE
Blackberry Ho.
WINDLESHAM ROAD
Henage Corner
Nursery
LITTLE HEATH ROAD
Partridge Farm
Chobham Park Ho.
Tennis Courts
Chobham Park Farm
Heath
Stanners Hill
Stanyards Farm
Hillside
Nursery
THE AVENUE
Pets Cemetery
Mincing Lane Nursery
Burrow Hill Nursery
Army Cadet Force Hut
Club
School
OAKDENE
Mincing Lane Farm
CHOBHAM PARK LANE
Larkenshaw
Larkenshaw Farm
Records Office Min. of Defence (Navy)
58
Playing Field
LESLIE ROAD
Tennis Courts
Youth Centre
Nursery
Fishpool Bridge
Sowmoor Plantation
CHERTSEY ROAD
A319
Nursery
The Grange
Chobham House
Mill Bourne
Fire Station
Town Mill
Chobham
Emmett's Mill
Brooklands House
Brooklands Farm
VICARAGE ROAD
Swimming Pool
Pol. Sta.
Schools
Cricket Ground
Village Hall
Scout & Guide Hut
Tennis Courts
Playing Field
Grave Yard
Hagthorn Farm
Nursery
Telephone Exchange
Piggery
Deewall House
Sunfield Farm
59
Broadford
Recreation Ground
Rifle Club
STATION ROAD
A3046
Saddlers Farm
SANDPIT HALL ROAD
Highfield
Tennis Courts
The Bourne
Broadford Fm.
BROADFORD LANE
Chobham Farm
Focklesbrook Farm
Milford Green
Mimbridge
Young Stroat Farm
Refuse Tip
Sewage Works
Oakhurst Nursery
Castle Grove Nurs.
Coxhill Ho.
Coxhill Green
Wapshott Ho.
Shaws Fm.
Heath-Hill Fm
Nursery
Millbrook
COXHILL GREEN
Mimbridge Cott
Burnt Barn
Deeppool Fm.
The Bourne
60
CARTHOUSE LANE
CHOBHAM RD.
Knap Hill Manor
CHOBHAM ROAD
DEEP POOL
HORSELL COMMON
COWSLIP LA.
Holly Cotts
100
AO
AP
AQ
AR
AS
Nurs.
LITTLEWICK
VIGGORY LA.
Horsell Recreation Centre
Sch.
Mat. Hosp. Annex
Old Peoples Home
Parley Brook

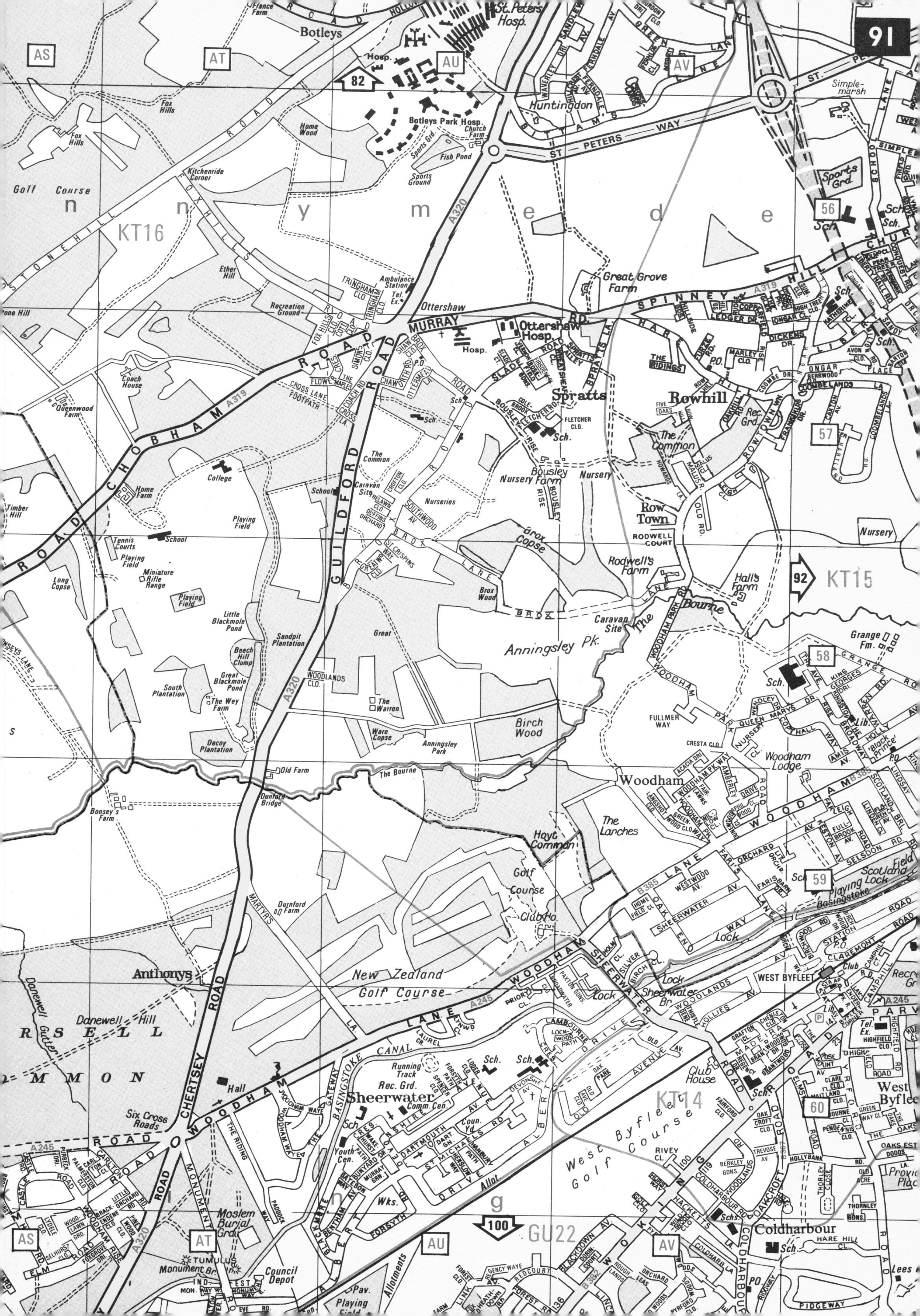

Botleys
St. Peters Hosp.
82
Botleys Park Hosp.
Huntingdon
ST. PETERS WAY
Fox Hills
Golf Course
KT16
Kitchenride Corner
Home Wood
Fish Pond
Sports Ground
A320
Ether Hill
Recreation Ground
Ambulance Station
Ottershaw
MURRAY RD.
Ottershaw Hosp.
Great Grove Farm
SPINNEY HILL
A319
Simplemarsh
Sports Grd.
56
CHOBHAM ROAD
Queenwood Farm
Coach House
College
Home Farm
GUILDFORD ROAD
The Common
Caravan Site
Nurseries
Spratts
Rowhill
The Common
Bousley Nursery Farm
Row Town
57
Timber Hill
Playing Field
School
Tennis Courts
Miniature Rifle Range
Long Copse
Little Blackmole Pond
Beech Hill Clump
Great Blackmole Pond
South Plantation
The Wey Farm
Decoy Plantation
Sandpit Plantation
The Warren
Ware Copse
Anningsley Park
Brox Copse
Brox Wood
BROX LANE
Rodwell's Farm
Anningsley Pk.
Birch Wood
The Bourne
Caravan Site
Hall's Farm
92
KT15
Grange Fm.
58
Woodham Lodge
Woodham
Old Farm
Dunford Bridge
Bonsey's Farm
Hoyt Common
The Larches
Golf Course
Club Ho.
59
Playing Field
Scotland Lock
Basingstoke
Durnford Farm
Anthonys
New Zealand Golf Course
Danewell Hill
Danewell Gutter
WOODHAM LANE
A245
CHERTSEY ROAD
Hall
Six Cross Roads
Sheerwater
Running Track
Rec. Grd.
Comm. Cen.
Youth Cen.
BASINGSTOKE CANAL
Club House
KT14
West Byfleet Golf Course
WEST BYFLEET
60
West Byfleet
Coldharbour
Moslem Burial Grd.
TUMULUS
Monument Br.
Council Depot
Wks.
Allotments
100
GU22
AS
AT
AU
AV
Lees

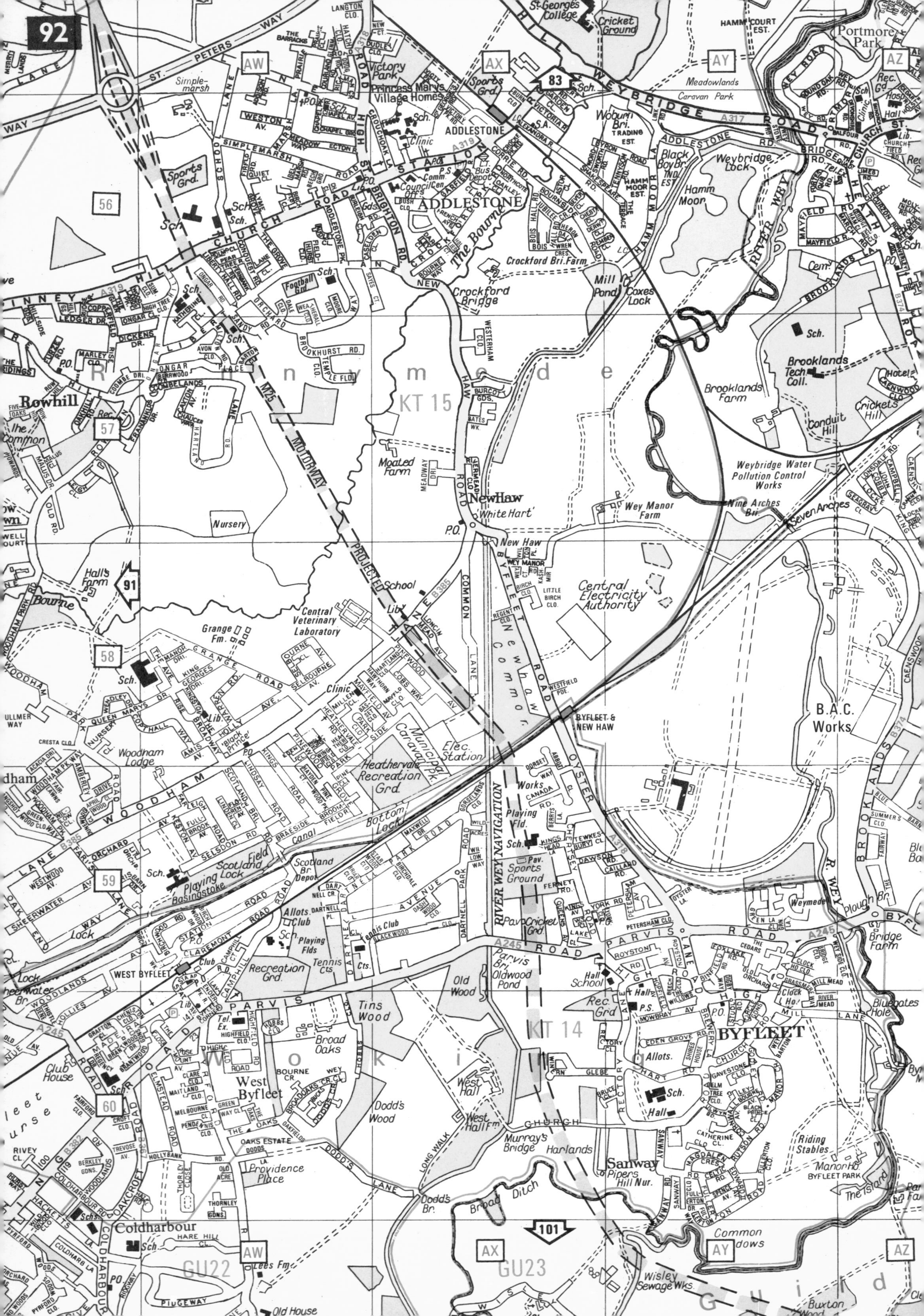
AW
AX
AY
AZ
83
56
57
58
59
60
91
101
St. Georges College
Cricket Ground
HAMM COURT EST.
Portmore Park
Meadowlands
Caravan Park
WEYBRIDGE ROAD
A317
Victory Park
Princess Marys Village Homes
Simplemarsh
ST. PETERS WAY
Sports Grd.
ADDLESTONE
ADDLESTONE
STATION RD.
CHURCH ROAD
A319
Woburn Bri. TRADING EST.
Black Boy Br. IND. EST.
HAMM MOOR EST.
Weybridge Lock
Hamm Moor
RIVER WEY
The Bourne
Crockford Bri. Farm
Crockford Bridge
Mill Pond
Coxes Lock
Football Grd.
Rowhill
Runnymede
KT 15
Brooklands Farm
Brooklands Tech. Coll.
Conduit Hill
Crickets Hill
Weybridge Water Pollution Control Works
Nine Arches Br.
Seven Arches
Moated Farm
New Haw
'White Hart'
Wey Manor Farm
Nursery
M25 MOTORWAY PROJECTED
Hall's Farm
Bourne
Central Electricity Authority
Central Veterinary Laboratory
Grange Fm.
B.A.C. Works
BYFLEET & NEW HAW
Woodham Lodge
Heathervale Recreation Grd.
Municipal Caravan Pk.
Elec. Station
WOODHAM LANE
B385
Bottom Lock
Scotland Lock
Playing Field
Basingstoke Canal
Scotland Br. Depot
RIVER WEY NAVIGATION
Playing Fld.
Sports Ground
Cricket Grd.
Plough Br.
Bridge Farm
Weymede
Allots. Club
Playing Flds
Tennis Club
Tennis Cts.
Recreation Grd.
WEST BYFLEET
Old Wood
Parvis Bri.
Oldwood Pond
A245
PARVIS ROAD
Tins Wood
Broad Oaks
West Byfleet
Woking
KT 14
BYFLEET
Bluegates Hole
Club House
Dodd's Wood
West Hall
West Hall Fm.
Murray's Bridge
Harlands
Sanway
Pipers Hill Nur.
Riding Stables
Manor Ho.
BYFLEET PARK
The Island
Providence Place
Dodd's Br.
Broad Ditch
Common Meadows
Coldharbour
Lees Fm.
GU22
GU23
Wisley Sewage Wks.
Old House
PLOUGEWAY

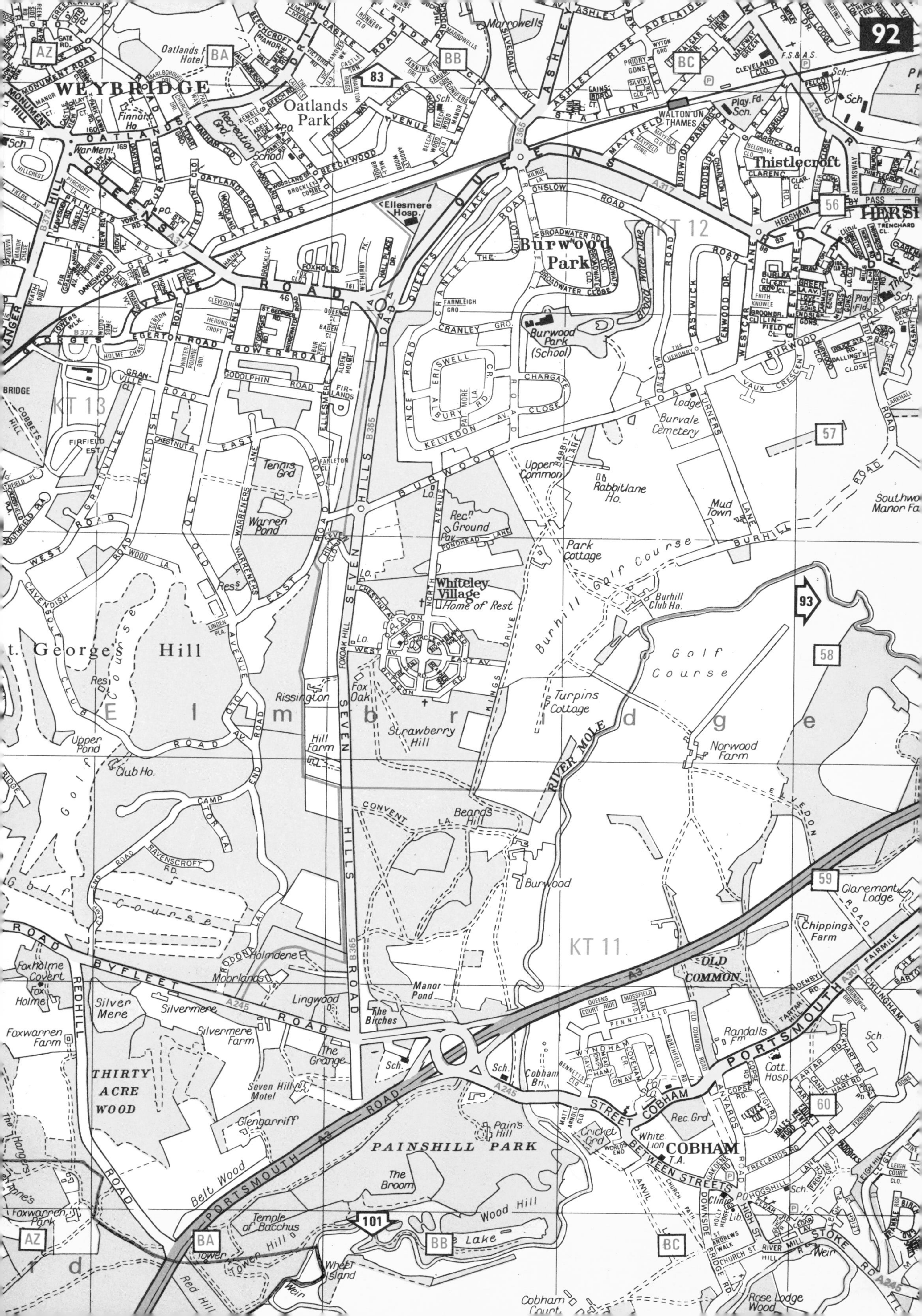

92
WEYBRIDGE
Oatlands Park
Oatlands Park Hotel
83
AZ
BA
BB
BC
WALTON ON THAMES
Thistlecroft
HERSHAM
56
57
58
59
60
93
101
KT 12
KT 13
KT 11
Burwood Park
Burwood Park (School)
Broad Water Lake
Ellesmere Hosp.
QUEENS ROAD
OATLANDS DRIVE
ST. GEORGES AVENUE
GOWER ROAD
GODOLPHIN ROAD
EGERTON ROAD
ONSLOW ROAD
BURWOOD ROAD
HERSHAM ROAD
SEVEN HILLS ROAD
Burvale Cemetery
Upper Common
Rabbitlane Ho.
Mud Town
Park Cottage
Southwood Manor Fa
Burhill Golf Course
Burhill Club Ho.
Whiteley Village
Home of Rest
St. George's Hill
Tennis Grd
Warren Pond
Rissington
Fox Oak
Strawberry Hill
Hill Farm
Upper Pond
Club Ho.
Golf Course
Turpins Cottage
Norwood Farm
RIVER MOLE
Elmbridge
CONVENT LA.
Beards Hill
Burwood
Claremont Lodge
Chippings Farm
OLD COMMON
Manor Pond
Holmdene
Moorlands
Lingwood
The Birches
The Grange
Foxholme Covert
Fox Holme
Silver Mere
Silvermere
Silvermere Farm
Foxwarren Farm
BYFLEET ROAD
REDHILL ROAD
THIRTY ACRE WOOD
Seven Hills Motel
Glengarriff
Belt Wood
PORTSMOUTH ROAD
A3
PAINSHILL PARK
Pain's Hill
The Broom
Temple of Bacchus
Wood Hill
Tower Hill
Wheel Island
Red Hill
Foxwarren Park
Cobham Court
Cobham Bri.
Cricket Grd
White Lion
COBHAM
Rec. Grd
Cott. Hosp.
Randalls Fm
STREET COBHAM
BETWEEN STREETS
HIGH ST.
Rose Lodge Wood
Weir

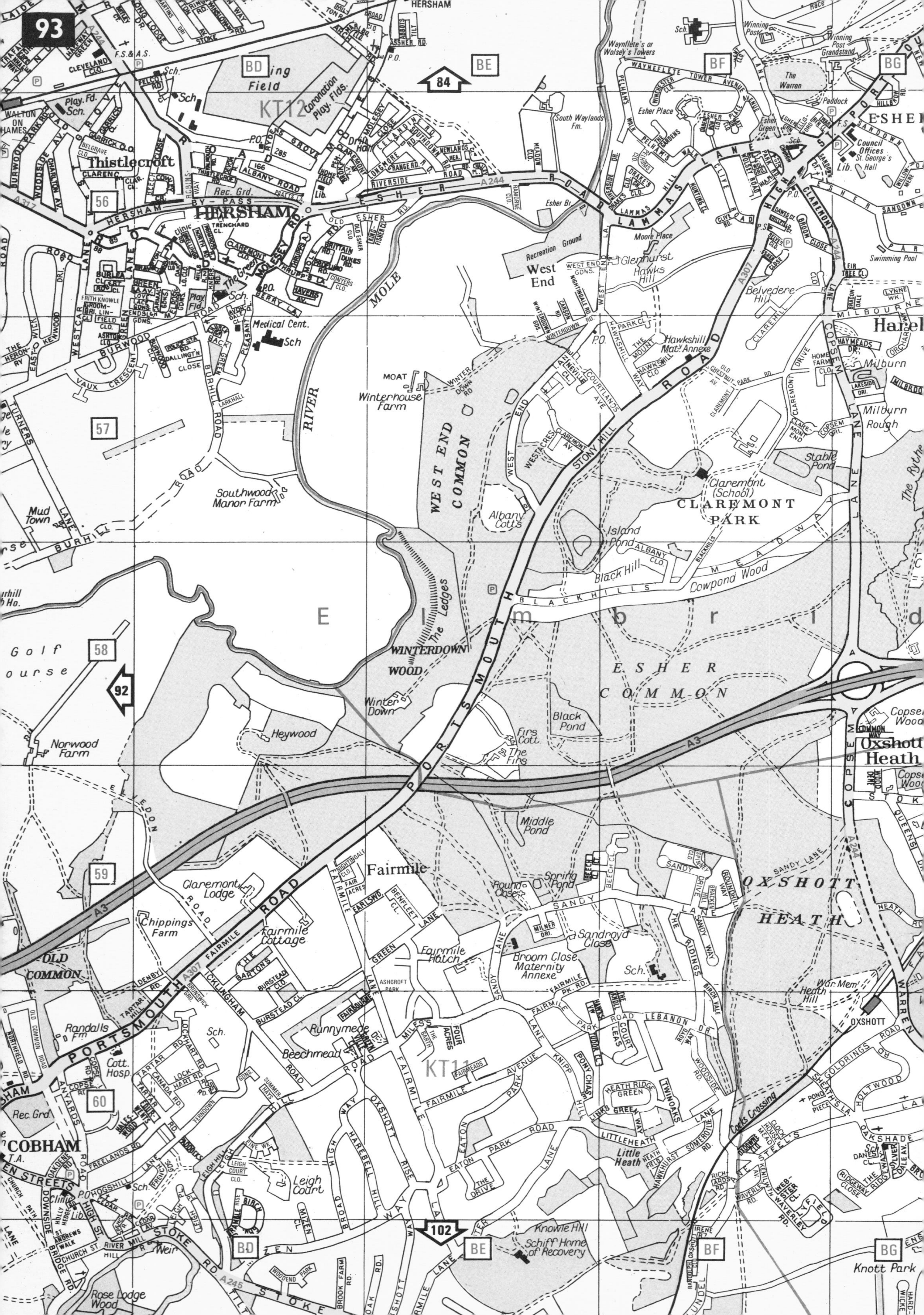
HERSHAM
BD
BE
BF
BG
84
KT12
Coronation Play. Flds.
Field
Play. Fd.
Sch.
Walton on Thames
Thistlecroft
Cleveland Clo.
Felcot Rd.
F.S.&A.S.
Burwood Park Rd.
Woodside
Charlton Av.
Rydens Grove
Albany Road
Rec. Grd.
56
Hersham By-Pass
HERSHAM
Esher Road
A244
A317
Riverside
Old Esher
Molesey Rd.
Mole Rd.
Burwood
Vaux Crescent
Medical Cent.
Burhill Road
Pleasant Pl.
Westcar Lane
Turners Lane
57
River Mole
Moat
Winterhouse Farm
Southwood Manor Farm
Mud Town
Burhill
West End Common
Winter Down Rd.
Albany Cotts
Esher Br.
Recreation Ground
West End
South Waylands Fm.
Waynflete's or Wolsey's Towers
Wayneflete Tower Avenue
Esher Place
Pelhams Walk
Esher Green
Lammas Lane
Moore Place
Glenhurst
Hawks Hill
Hawkshill Mat. Annexe
Stony Hill
Portsmouth Road
A307
High St.
Claremont Lane
Council Offices
St. George's Hall
ESHER
Lib.
Sandown
The Warren
Winning Post
Winning Post Grandstand
Paddock
Race
Swimming Pool
Belvedere Hill
Milbourne
Harel
Milburn
Milburn Rough
Copsem Lane
Stable Pond
Claremont (School)
CLAREMONT PARK
Island Pond
Black Hill
Blackhills
Cowpond Wood
Elmbridge
Golf Course
58
92
The Ledges
Winterdown Wood
Winter Down
ESHER COMMON
Black Pond
Firs Cott.
The Firs
Heywood
Norwood Farm
A3
Middle Pond
Oxshott Heath
Copse Wood
Fairmile
Claremont Lodge
59
Chippings Farm
Fairmile Cottage
Round Close
Spring Pond
Sandy Lane
Sandroyd Close
Broom Close Maternity Annexe
Fairmile Hatch
Old Common
Fairmile Lane
Ashcroft Park
Runnymede
Beechmead
Randalls Fm
Cott. Hosp.
Tartar Rd.
KT11
OXSHOTT HEATH
Heath Hill
War Mem.
OXSHOTT
Warren
Goldrings Road
Holtwood
Cocks Crossing
Littleheath
Little Heath
Lebanon Dr.
Woodside Rd.
Eaton Park Road
Fairmile Park Road
Oxshott Rise
Harebell Hill
60
Rec. Grd.
COBHAM
Clinic
Lib.
Church St.
River Hill
Stoke Rd.
A245
Weir
Rose Lodge Wood
Leigh Court
Knowle Hill
Schiff Home of Recovery
102
Knott Park
Steel's La.
Waverley Rd.

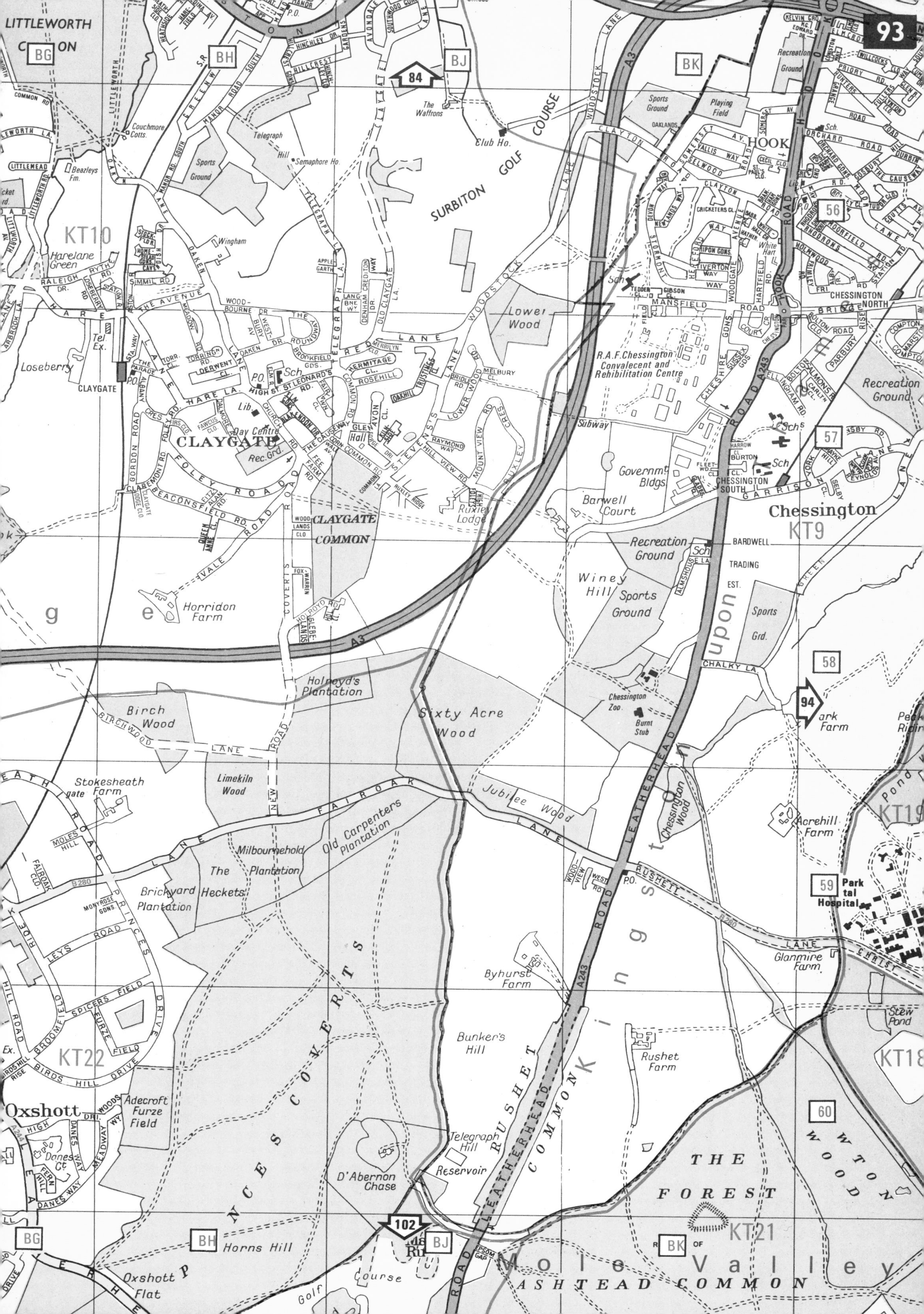
LITTLEWORTH COMMON
CLAYGATE
Claygate Common
SURBITON GOLF COURSE
HOOK
R.A.F. Chessington Convalescent and Rehibilitation Centre
Chessington
KT9
KT10
KT22
KT21
Chessington Zoo
Sixty Acre Wood
Birch Wood
Limekiln Wood
Jubilee Wood
Horridon Farm
Holroyd's Plantation
Old Carpenters Plantation
Milbournehold Plantation
The Heckets
Brickyard Plantation
Stokesheath Farm
Oxshott
Adecroft Furze Field
D'Abernon Chase
Telegraph Hill
Reservoir
Bunker's Hill
Byhurst Farm
Rushet Farm
Glanmire Farm
Acrehill Farm
Recreation Ground
Winey Hill
Sports Ground
Barwell Court
Ruxley Lodge
Lower Wood
Loseberry
Harelane Green
THE FOREST
ASHTEAD COMMON
Mole Valley
Kingston upon Thames
Horns Hill
Oxshott Flat
PRINCES COVERTS
RUSHET COMMON
LEATHERHEAD ROAD
A3
A243
84
94
102

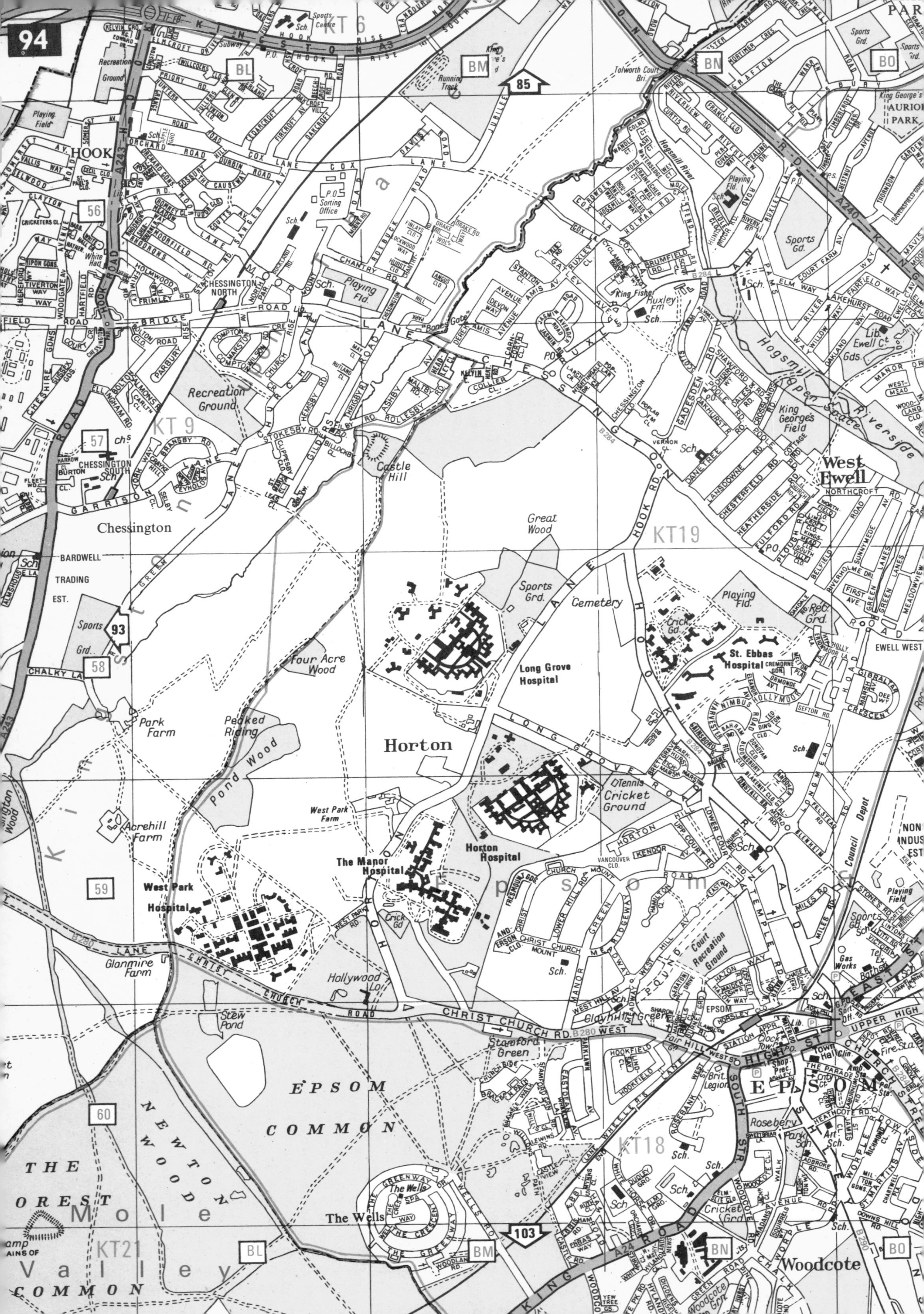
HOOK
CHESSINGTON NORTH
CHESSINGTON SOUTH
Chessington
BARDWELL TRADING EST.
Recreation Ground
Castle Hill
Great Wood
Four Acre Wood
Park Farm
Peaked Riding
Pond Wood
Horton
Long Grove Hospital
St. Ebbas Hospital
West Park Hospital
The Manor Hospital
Horton Hospital
Acrehill Farm
West Park Farm
Glanmire Farm
Hollywood Lo.
Stew Pond
Stamford Green
EPSOM COMMON
NEWTON WOOD
THE FOREST
Mole Valley
COMMON
The Wells
West Ewell
King George's Field
Hogsmill Open Space
Riverside
Cricket Ground
Court Recreation Ground
EPSOM
Rosebery Park
Woodcote
Cemetery
Sports Grd.
Playing Fld.
Running Track
Tolworth Court Bri.
Hogsmill River
King George's AURIOL PARK
KT6
KT9
KT19
KT18
KT21
BL
BM
BN
BO
56
57
58
59
60
85
93
103
A243
A240
A24
B284
B280
HOOK ROAD
CHRIST CHURCH ROAD
CHESSINGTON ROAD
HORTON LANE
LONG GROVE ROAD
HOOK ROAD
KINGSTON ROAD
HIGH ST
EAST ST
UPPER HIGH ST
SOUTH ST
COX LANE
GARRISON LANE
CHALKY LA
HOLLYMOOR LA
TEMPLE RD
DOWNS HILL
Council Depot
Gas Works

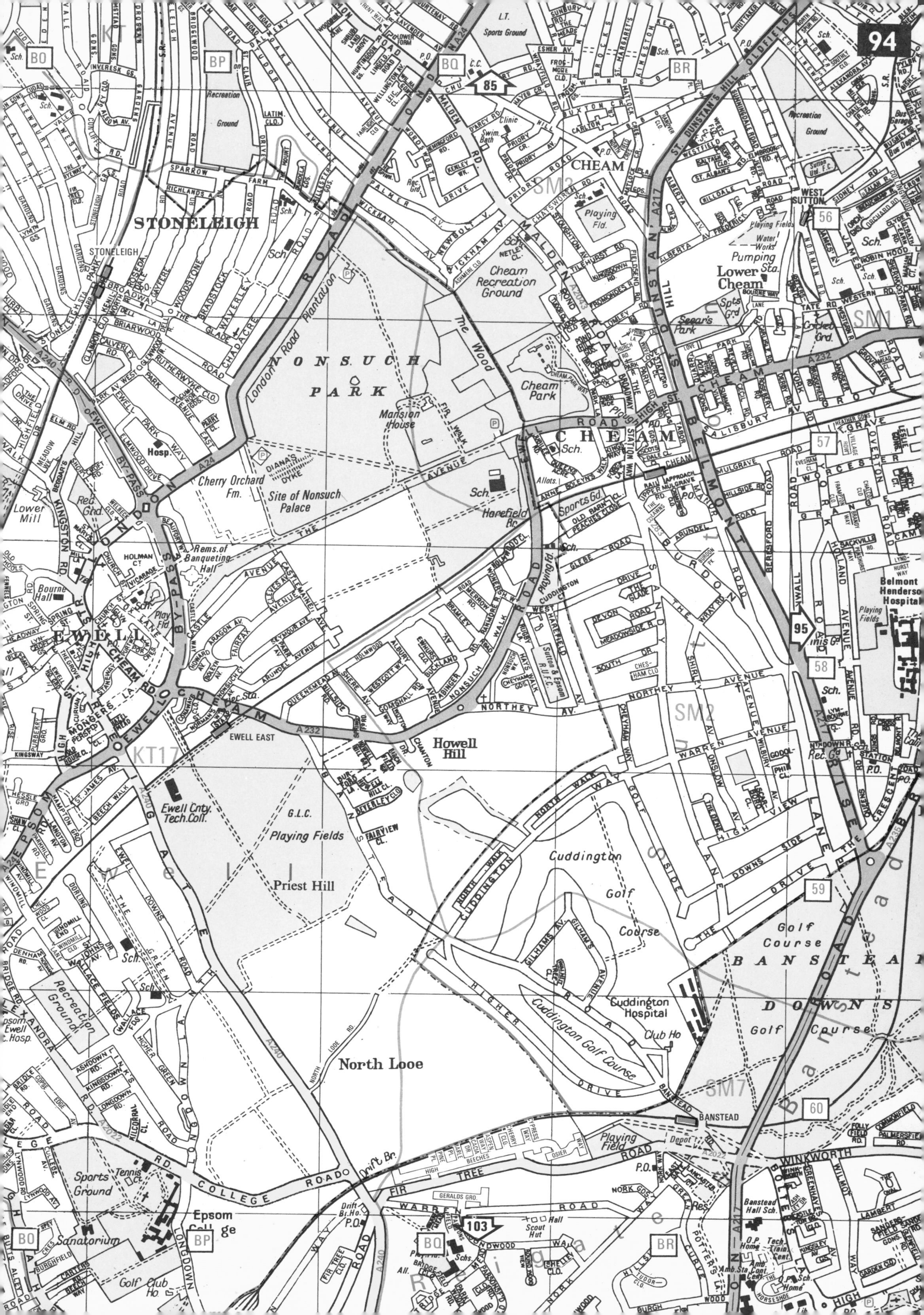
BO
BP
BQ
BR
85
STONELEIGH
Stoneleigh
Recreation Ground
CHEAM
SM3
Playing Fld.
Lower Cheam
Pumping Sta.
Water Works
Playing Fields
WEST SUTTON
56
Recreation Ground
Sutton Utd. F.C.
Bus Garage
Bus Depot
SM1
Cricket Grd.
Spts Grd
Seear's Park
NONSUCH PARK
London Road Plantation
The Wood
Cheam Recreation Ground
Cheam Park
Mansion House
Diana's Dyke
Cherry Orchard Fm.
Site of Nonsuch Palace
Hosp.
Lower Mill
Rec. Grd.
Bourne Hall
Rems. of Banqueting Hall
Play Fld.
EWELL
EWELL BY-PASS
EWELL EAST
KT17
CHEAM
57
Sports Gd.
Harefield Br.
Sutton & Epsom R.U.F.C.
Belmont Henderson Hospital
Playing Fields
95
58
SM2
Howell Hill
Ewell Cnty. Tech.Coll.
G.L.C. Playing Fields
Priest Hill
Cuddington Golf Course
Golf Course
BANSTEAD DOWNS
59
Cuddington Hospital
Club Ho
Cuddington Golf Course
North Looe
SM7
60
BANSTEAD
Playing Field
Depot
Recreation Ground
Epsom Ewell Hosp.
Sports Ground
Tennis Ct.
Epsom College
Sanatorium
Golf Club Ho.
Drift Br.
Drift Br.Ho.
103
Scout Hut
Hall
Schs.
Banstead Hall Sch.
O.P. Home
Tech. Train. Cent.
Amb. Sta.
LONDON ROAD
A24
A232
A217
A240
A2022
A2043
CHEAM ROAD
EWELL ROAD
BELMONT RISE
BRIGHTON ROAD
COLLEGE ROAD
REIGATE ROAD
HIGHER DRIVE
NORTHEY AV.
WARREN AV.
ST. DUNSTAN'S HILL
MALDEN RD.
HIGH ST.
THE AVENUE
THE DRIVE
DOWNS SIDE
WINKWORTH
GREEN LANE
NONSUCH WALK

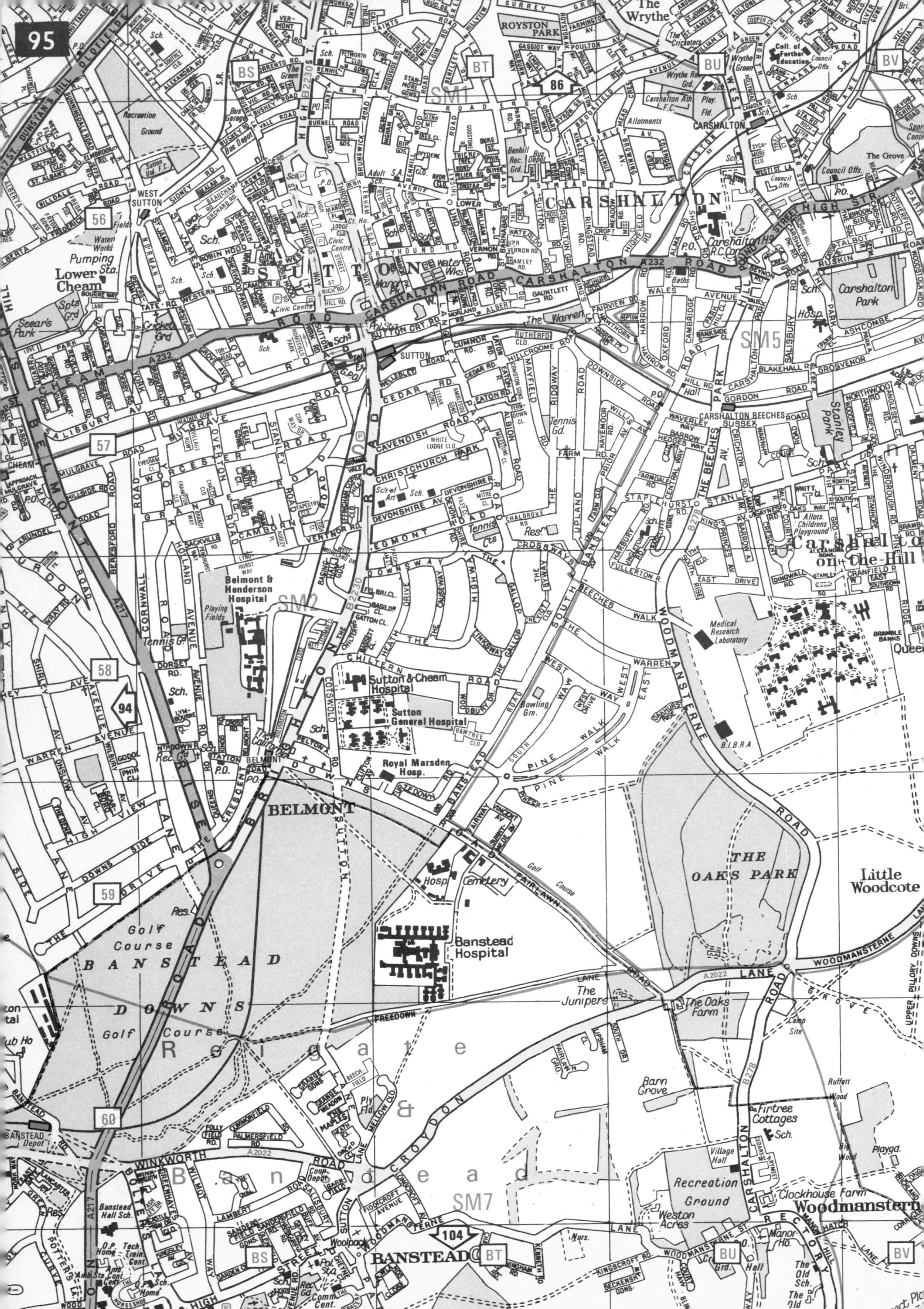

The Wrythe
ROYSTON PARK
SM1
86
BS
BT
BU
BV
Recreation Ground
Carshalton Ath. F.C.
CARSHALTON
Coll. of Further Education
The Grove
Council Offs.
CARSHALTON
SUTTON
Lower Cheam
Pumping Sta.
WEST SUTTON
Sutton Utd. F.C.
Civic Centre
Carshalton Park
SM5
Seears Park
Cricket Grd
56
57
58
59
60
94
CARSHALTON BEECHES
Stanley Park
Carshalton on-the-Hill
Belmont & Henderson Hospital
SM2
Playing Fields
Tennis Gd.
Medical Research Laboratory
Sutton & Cheam Hospital
Sutton General Hospital
Royal Marsden Hosp.
B.I.B.R.A.
BELMONT
THE OAKS PARK
Little Woodcote
Golf Course
BANSTEAD DOWNS
Banstead Hospital
The Junipers
The Oaks Farm
Reigate & Banstead
Barn Grove
Firtree Cottages
Village Hall
Recreation Ground
Clockhouse Farm
Woodmansterne
Weston Acres
SM7
104
BANSTEAD
Banstead Hall Sch.

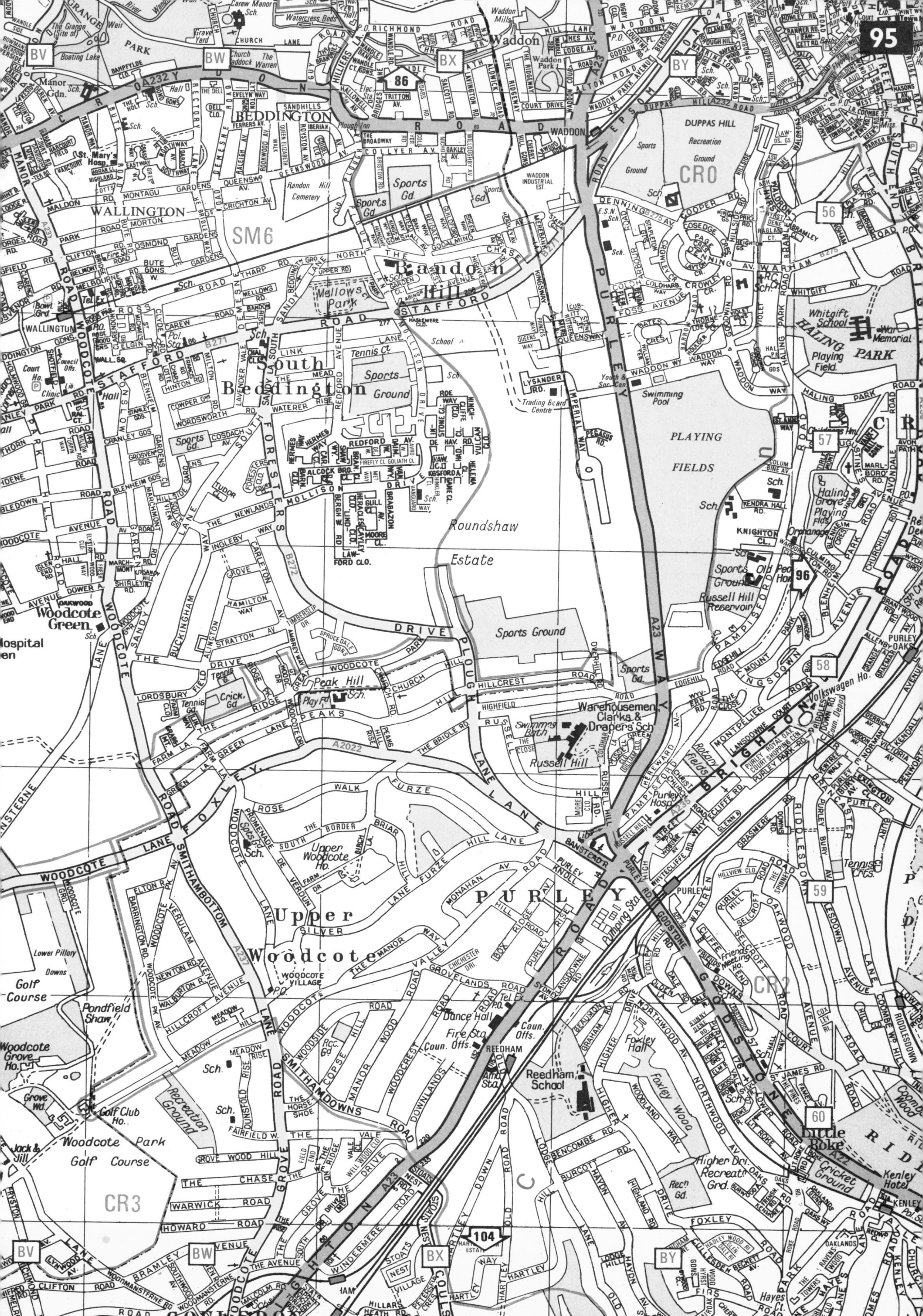

BV
BW
BX
BY
86
Waddon
BEDDINGTON
WALLINGTON
SM6
CR0
Duppas Hill Recreation Ground
Sports Ground
Randon Hill Cemetery
Waddon Industrial Est.
Roundshaw Estate
Sports Ground
Playing Fields
Whitgift School
Haling Park
War Memorial
Playing Field
South Beddington
Mellows Park
Trading Board Centre
Swimming Pool
Russell Hill Reservoir
Warehousemen Clarks & Drapers Sch
Russell Hill
Rotary Fields
Purley Hosp.
Peak Hill
Woodcote Green
Hospital
Upper Woodcote Ho.
Upper Woodcote
PURLEY
Purley
Woodcote Village
Lower Pillory Downs
Golf Course
Pondfield Shaw
Woodcote Grove Ho.
Grove Wd.
Golf Club Ho.
Woodcote Park Golf Course
Jack & Jill
Recreation Ground
Reedham
Reedham School
Foxley Hall
Foxley Wood
Higher Dnl. Recreat'n Grd.
Recn Gd.
Little Roke
Cricket Ground
Kenley Hotel
Kenley
Haling Grove Playing Flds
Orphanage
Sports Ground
Volkswagen Ho.
CR2
CR3
56
57
58
59
60
96
104
A232
A23
A237
A2022
A235
A22
B271
B272
B275
PURLEY WAY
BRIGHTON ROAD
STAFFORD ROAD
WOODCOTE ROAD
FOXLEY LANE
PLOUGH LANE
WOODCOTE LANE
SMITHAMBOTTOM LANE
GODSTONE ROAD

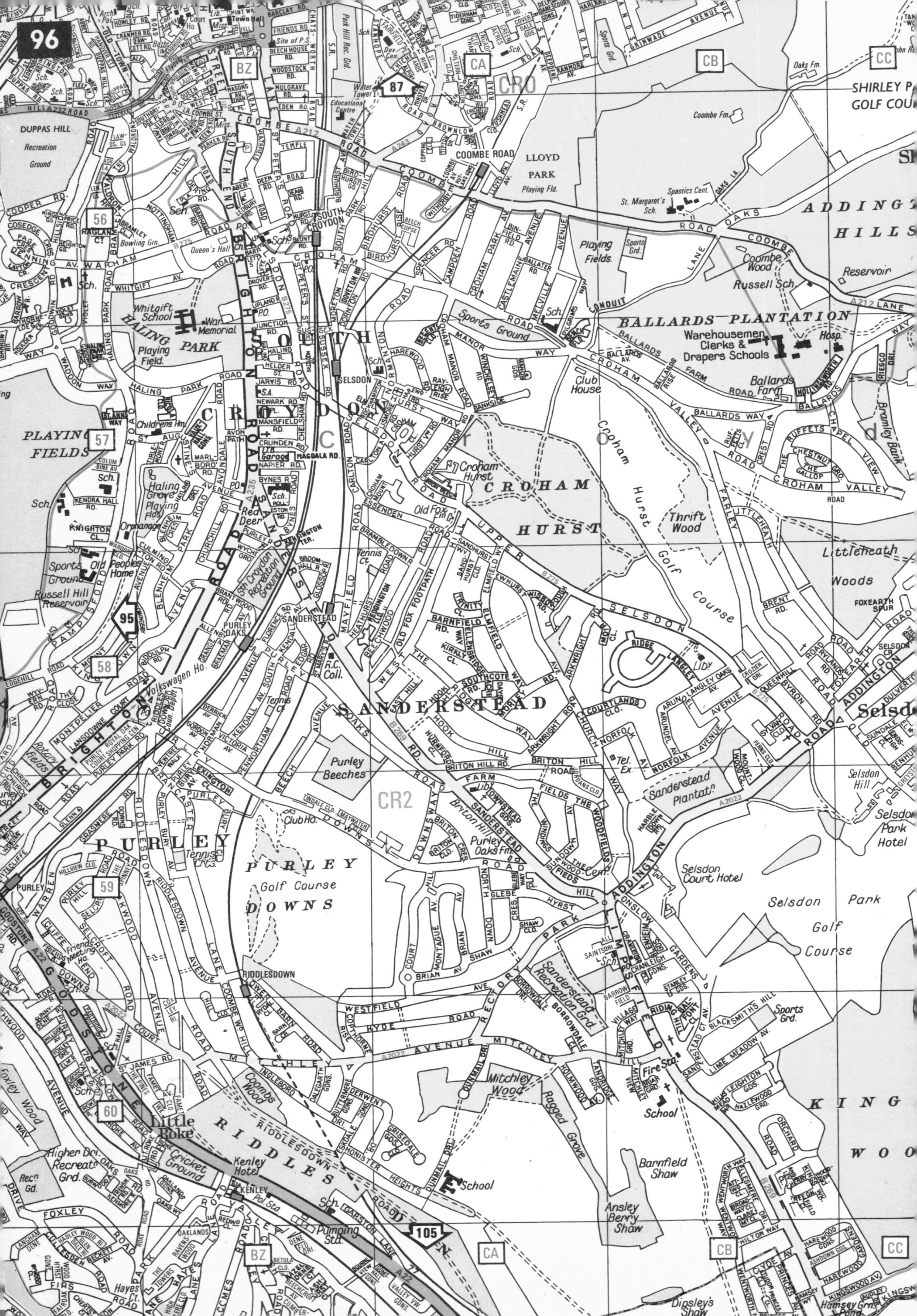

BZ
CA
CB
CC
CR0
CR2
87
56
57
58
59
60
95
105
SHIRLEY PARK GOLF COURSE
Oaks Fm.
Coombe Fm.
DUPPAS HILL Recreation Ground
Town Hall
COOMBE ROAD
LLOYD PARK Playing Fld.
Spastics Cent.
St. Margaret's Sch.
ADDINGTON HILLS
Coombe Wood
Russell Sch.
Reservoir
Playing Fields
Sports Grd.
Water Tower
Educational Centre
SOUTH CROYDON
Queen's Hall
Bowling Grn.
Whitgift School
War Memorial
HALING PARK
Playing Field
SOUTH CROYDON
CROYDON
BALLARDS PLANTATION
Warehousemen Clerks & Drapers Schools
Hosp.
Ballards Farm
Club House
Sports Ground
SELSDON
PLAYING FIELDS
Childrens Hm.
Garage
Croham Hurst
CROHAM HURST
Croham Hurst Golf Course
Thrift Wood
Littleheath Woods
FOXEARTH SPUR
Haling Grove Playing Flds.
Orphanage
Red Deer
Old Fox
Tennis Ct.
Sports Ground
Russell Hill Reservoir
Old Peoples Home
South Croydon Recreation Ground
PURLEY OAKS
SANDERSTEAD
R.C. Coll.
Volkswagen Ho.
SANDERSTEAD
Selsdon
Purley Beeches
Tel. Ex.
Sanderstead Plantatn
Selsdon Hill
Selsdon Park Hotel
Rotary Fields
PURLEY
PURLEY DOWNS Golf Course
Club Ho.
Purley Oaks Fm.
Selsdon Court Hotel
Selsdon Park Golf Course
Tennis Cts.
Friends Meeting Ho.
RIDDLESDOWN
Sanderstead Recreation Grd
Sports Grd.
Mitchley Wood
Ragged Grove
Fire Sta.
School
Coombs Wood
Little Roke
Cricket Ground
Kenley Hotel
RIDDLESDOWN
KENLEY
Pol. Sta.
Pumping Sta.
Higher Dr. Recreatn Grd.
Recn Gd.
Foxley Wood
School
Barnfield Shaw
Ansley Berry Shaw
KING'S WOOD
Dipsley's Shaw
Hayes Ct.
BRIGHTON ROAD
GODSTONE ROAD
ADDINGTON ROAD
LIMPSFIELD ROAD
MITCHLEY AVENUE
SANDERSTEAD ROAD
SELSDON ROAD
CROHAM ROAD
COOMBE ROAD

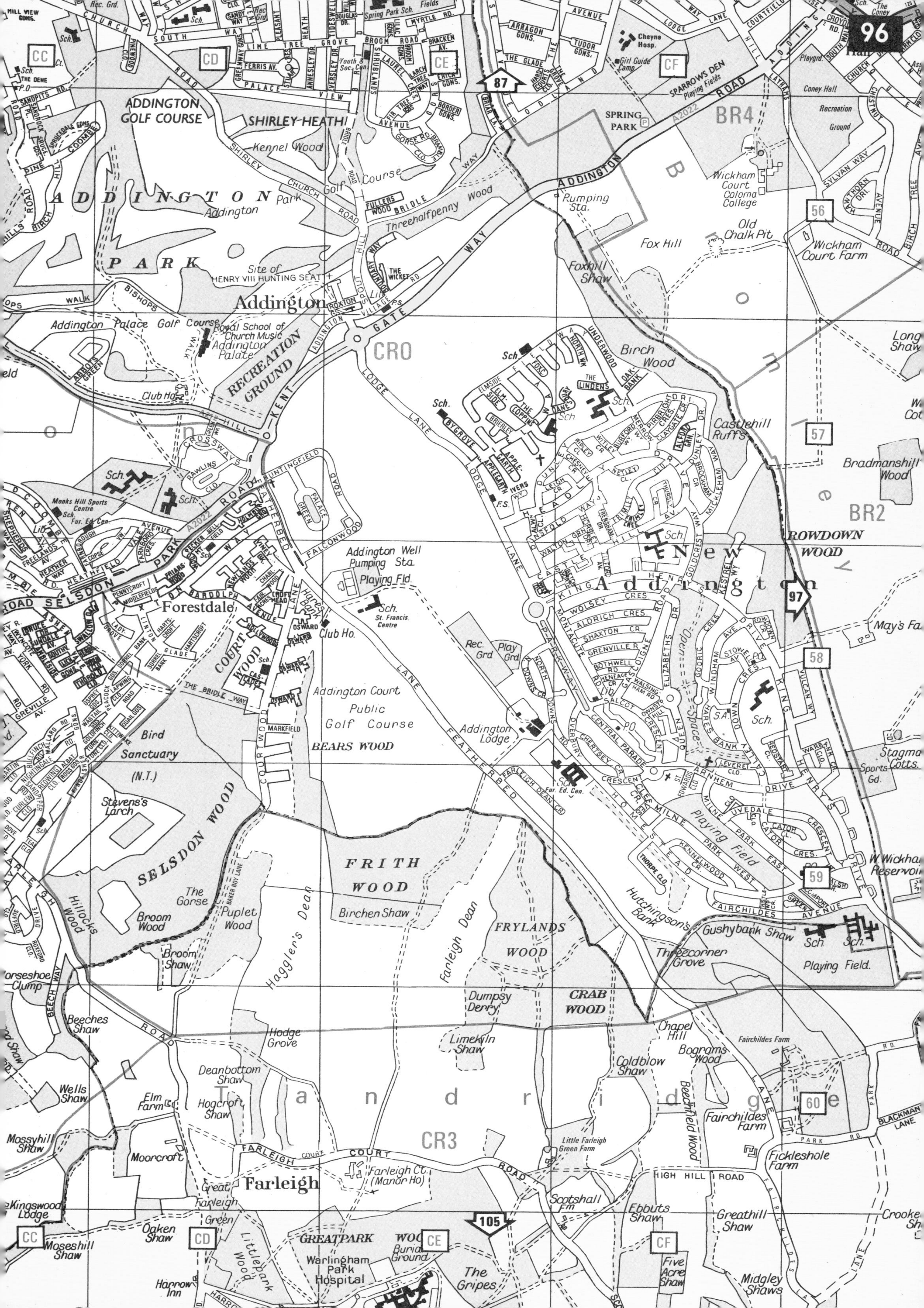
ADDINGTON GOLF COURSE
SHIRLEY HEATH
ADDINGTON PARK
Addington
Addington Palace Golf Course
RECREATION GROUND
Forestdale
New Addington
Addington Court Public Golf Course
BEARS WOOD
FRITH WOOD
SELSDON WOOD
Bird Sanctuary (N.T.)
FRYLANDS WOOD
CRAB WOOD
Farleigh
Tandridge
CR3
CR0
BR4
BR2
ROWDOWN WOOD
GREATPARK WOOD
Warlingham Park Hospital
Fox Hill
Birch Wood
Castlehill Ruffs
Bradmanshill Wood
Wickham Court Colonia College
Wickham Court Farm
Fairchildes Farm
Fickleshole Farm
87
97
105
56
57
58
59
60
CC
CD
CE
CF

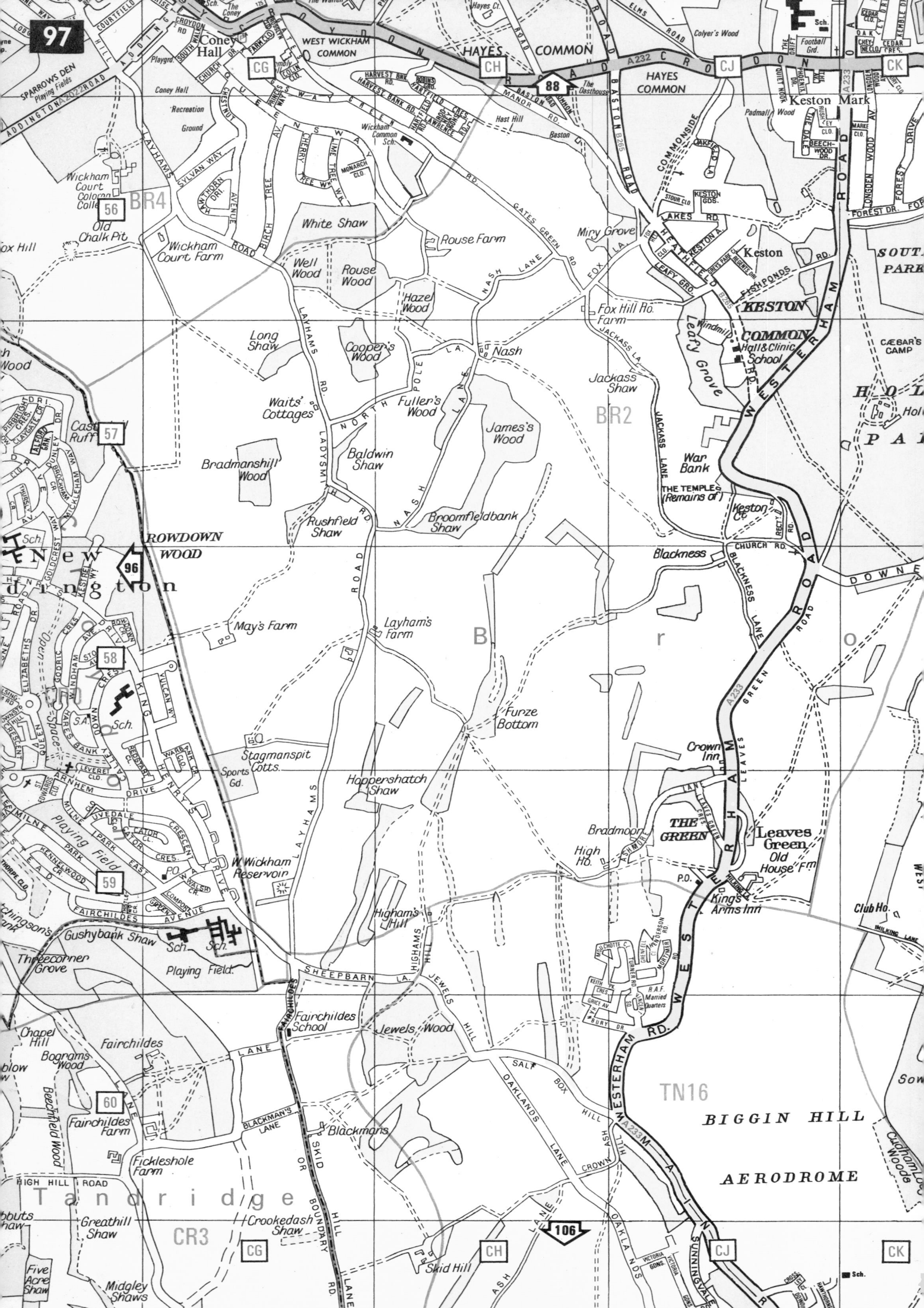

Coney Hall
WEST WICKHAM COMMON
HAYES COMMON
HAYES COMMON
CROYDON ROAD
A232
88
Keston Mark
Sparrows Den Playing Fields
ADDINGTON ROAD A2022
Coney Hall Recreation Ground
Wickham Court Colonial College
BR4
56
Old Chalk Pit
Fox Hill
White Shaw
Rouse Farm
Wickham Court Farm
Well Wood
Rouse Wood
Hazel Wood
Miry Grove
Keston
KESTON COMMON
Fox Hill Rd. Farm
Long Shaw
Cooper's Wood
Nash
Windmill
Leafy Grove
Hall & Clinic
School
CÆSAR'S CAMP
Jackass Shaw
Waits' Cottages
Fuller's Wood
BR2
Castle Ruff
57
James's Wood
Baldwin Shaw
War Bank
Bradmanshill Wood
THE TEMPLE (Remains of)
Keston Ct.
Rushfield Shaw
Broomfieldbank Shaw
ROWDOWN WOOD
96
New Addington
Blackness
May's Farm
Layham's Farm
58
Bromley
Furze Bottom
Crown Inn
Stagmanspit Cotts.
Sports Gd.
Hoppershatch Shaw
Bradmoor
THE GREEN
Leaves Green
High Ho.
Old House Fm.
W. Wickham Reservoir
P.O.
King's Arms Inn
59
Club Ho.
Higham's Hill
Gushybank Shaw
Threecorner Grove
Playing Field
SHEEPBARN LA.
R.A.F. Married Quarters
Chapel Hill
Fairchildes School
Jewels Wood
Fairchildes
Bograms Wood
TN16
60
BIGGIN HILL
Fairchildes Farm
Beechfield Wood
Blackmans
AERODROME
Fickleshole Farm
HIGH HILL ROAD
Tandridge
Greathill Shaw
Crookedash Shaw
CR3
106
Skid Hill
Five Acre Shaw
Midgley Shaws
CG
CH
CJ
CK

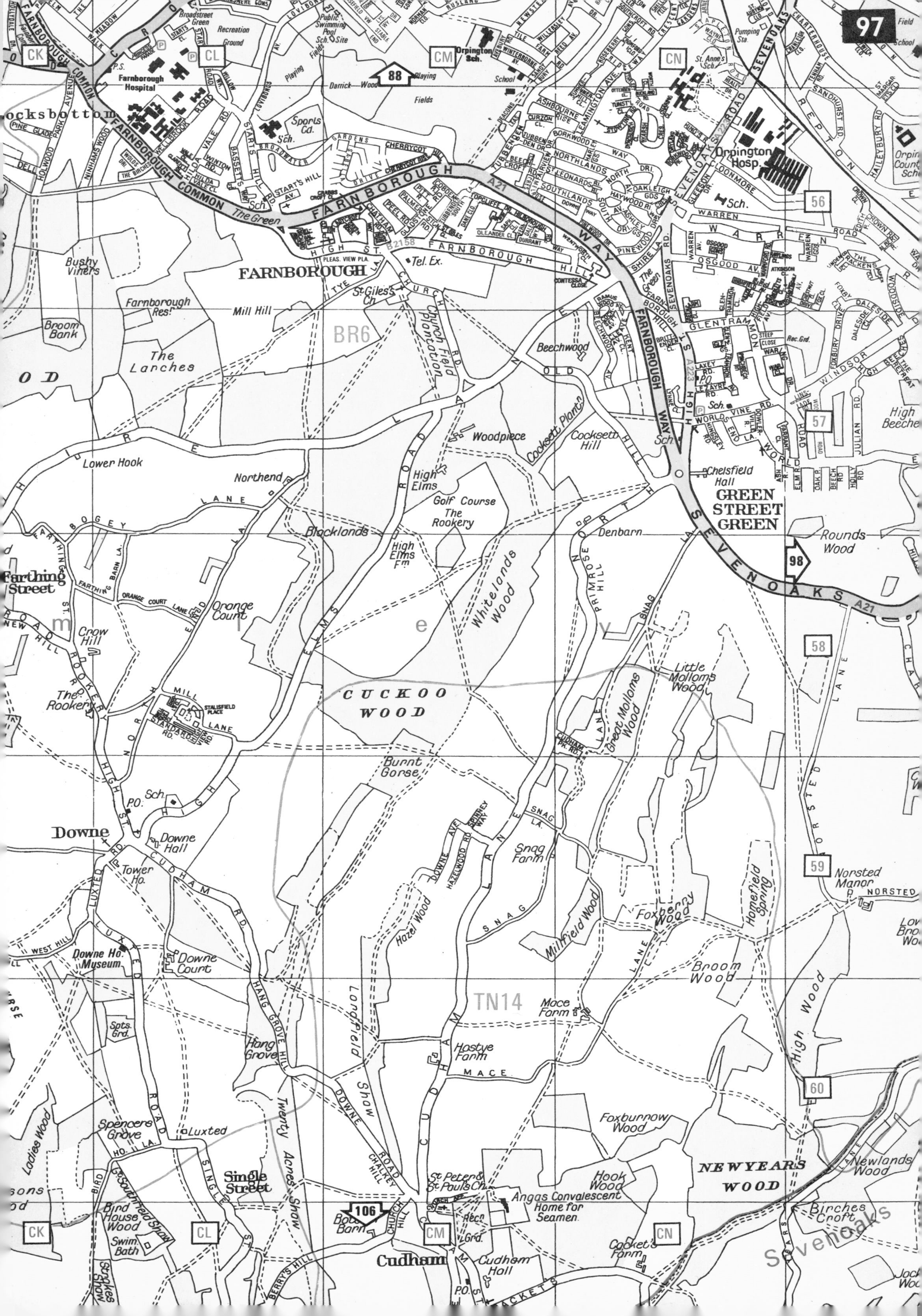

Farnborough Hospital
Farnborough Common
Locksbottom
FARNBOROUGH
Farnborough Resr.
Mill Hill
Bushy Viners
Broom Bank
The Larches
BR6
Church Field Plantation
St Giles's Ch.
Tel. Ex.
High St.
Farnborough Way
Farnborough Hill
Beechwood
Old Lane
Woodpiece
Cocksett Plantn.
Cocksett Hill
Lower Hook
Northend
Bogey Lane
High Elms
Golf Course
The Rookery
Blacklands
High Elms Fm.
Whitelands Wood
Denbarn
North Rd.
Primrose Hill
Snag Lane
Farthing Street
Farthing Barn La.
Orange Court Lane
Orange Court
Crow Hill
The Rookery
Rookery Rd.
Cuckoo Wood
Little Malloms Wood
Great Malloms Wood
Burnt Gorse
Downe
Downe Hall
Tower Ho.
Cudham Rd.
Snag Farm
Hazel Wood
Millfield Wood
Foxberry Wood
Homefield Spring
Broom Wood
Downe Ho. Museum
Downe Court
West Hill
Luxted Rd.
Hang Grove Hill
Hang Grove
Longfield Show
TN14
Mace Farm
Hostye Farm
Mace Lane
Cudham Lane
Spencers Grove
Luxted
Ladies Wood
Single Street
Twenty Acres Show
Downe Road
Foxburrow Wood
Hook Wood
Newyears Wood
St Peter & St Paul's Ch.
Angas Convalescent Home for Seamen
Bird House Wood
Southfield Shaw
Swim. Bath
Berry's Hill
Cudham
Cudham Hall
Church Hill
Cackets Farm
Birches Croft
Newlands Wood
Sevenoaks
Green Street Green
Chelsfield Hall
Orpington Hosp.
Sevenoaks Road
A21
A223
B2158
Rounds Wood
Norsted Manor
Norsted Lane
High Wood
High Beeches
Glentrammon
Worlds End La.
Warren Road
Orpington Sch.
Playing Fields
Darrick Wood
Sports Gd.
CK
CL
CM
CN
56
57
58
59
60
88
98
106

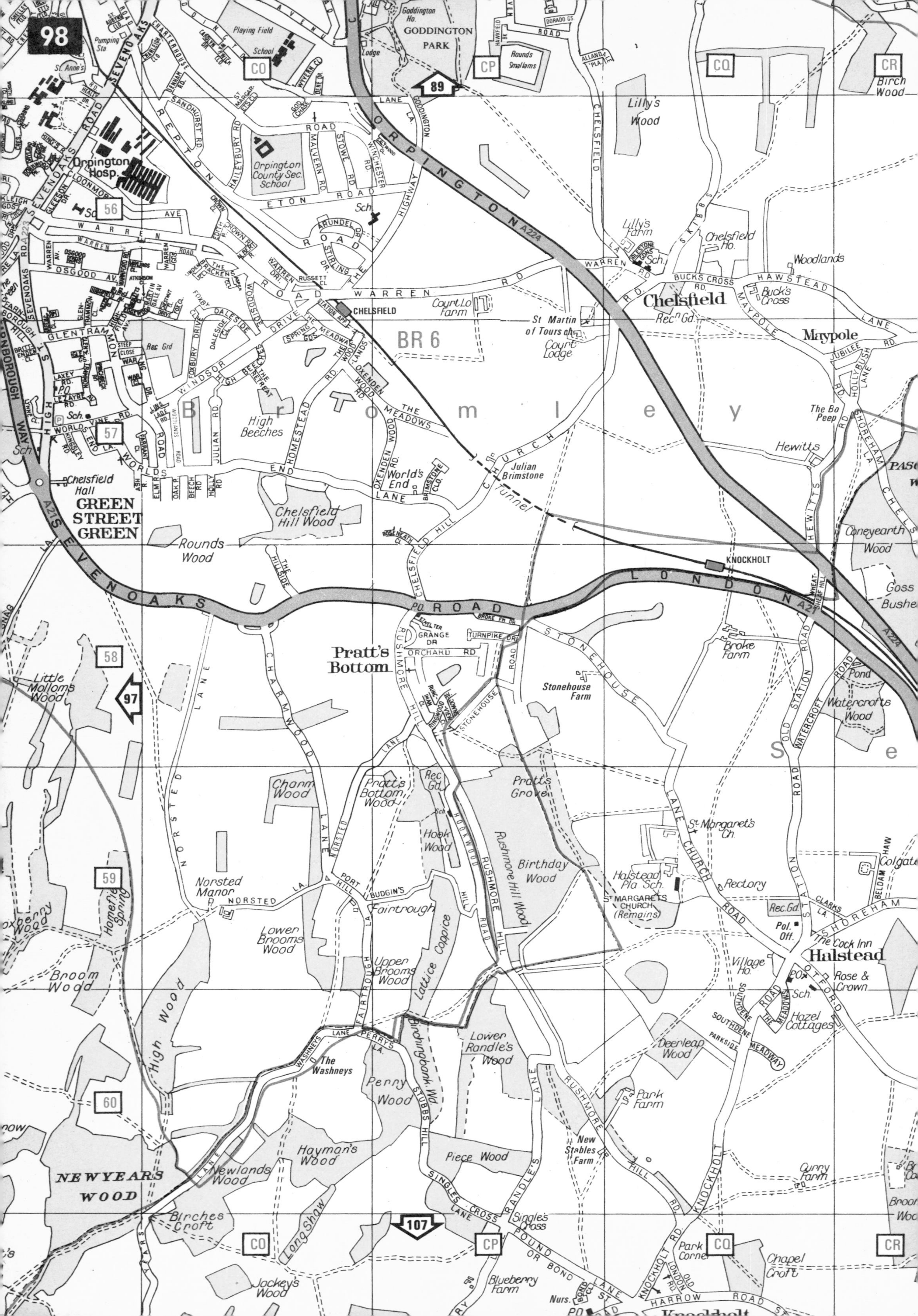

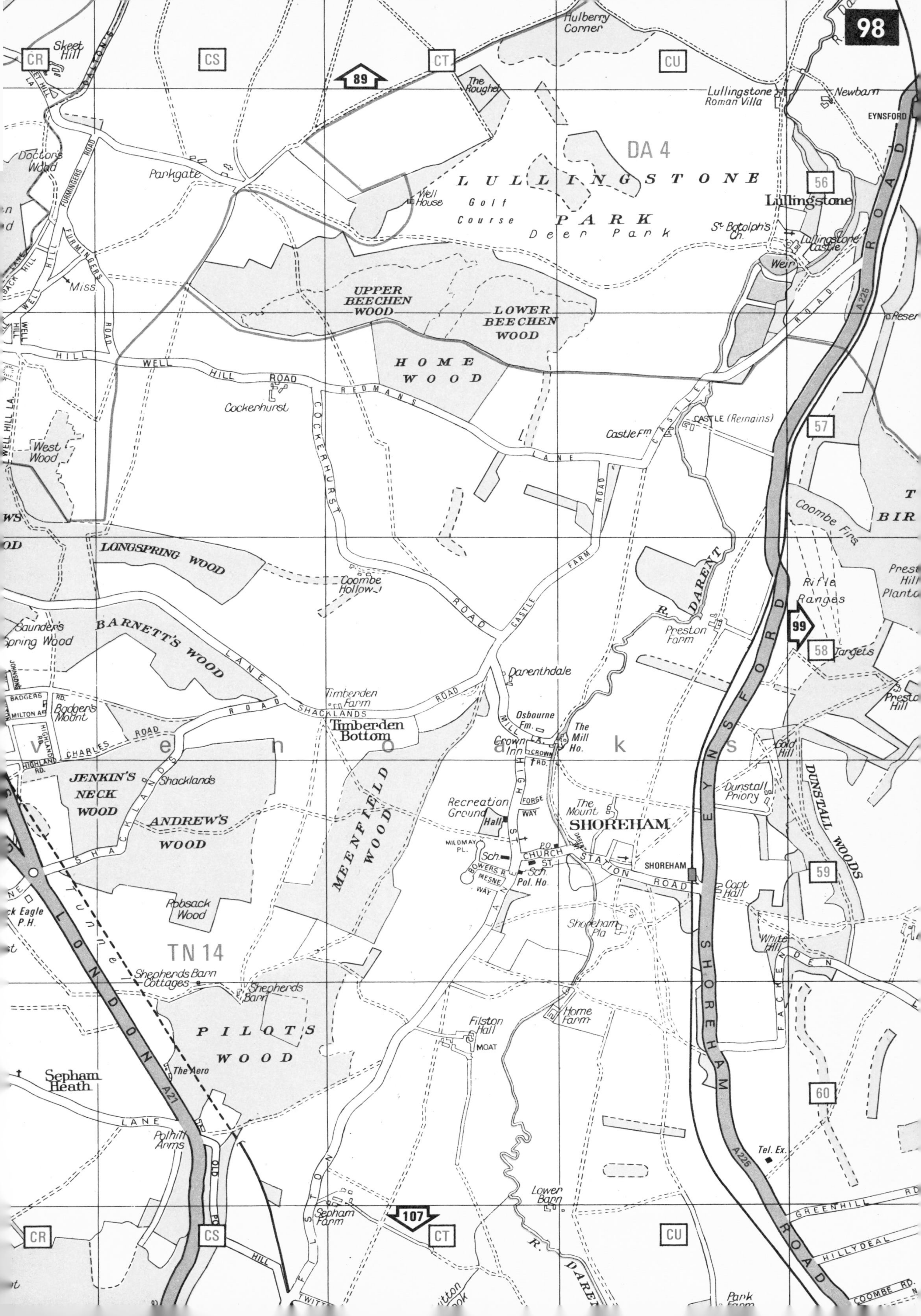

89
99
107
DA 4
TN 14
LULLINGSTONE PARK
Golf Course
Deer Park
Lullingstone
Lullingstone Roman Villa
Lullingstone Castle
St. Botolph's Ch.
Hulberry Corner
The Roughet
Newbarn
EYNSFORD
Skeet Hill
Doctors Wood
Parkgate
Well House
UPPER BEECHEN WOOD
LOWER BEECHEN WOOD
HOME WOOD
Cockerhurst
West Wood
LONGSPRING WOOD
Coombe Hollow
BARNETT'S WOOD
Saunder's Spring Wood
Timberden Farm
Timberden Bottom
Darenthdale
Osbourne Fm.
The Mill Ho.
Crown Inn
JENKIN'S NECK WOOD
ANDREW'S WOOD
Shacklands
MEENFIELD WOOD
Recreation Ground
Hall
SHOREHAM
The Mount
Sch.
Pol. Ho.
Robsack Wood
Shepherds Barn Cottages
Shepherds Barn
PILOTS WOOD
The Aero
Sepham Heath
Polhill Arms
Filston Hall
MOAT
Home Farm
Shoreham Pla
Lower Barn
Sepham Farm
Castle Fm.
CASTLE (Remains)
Preston Farm
R. DARENT
Coombe Fms.
Rifle Ranges
Targets
Gold Hill
Dunstall Priory
DUNSTALL WOODS
Copt Hall
White Hill
Tel. Ex.
SHOREHAM
EYNSFORD ROAD
SHOREHAM ROAD
A225
A21
LONDON ROAD
Tunnel
Sevenoaks
WELL HILL ROAD
REDMANS LANE
COCKERHURST ROAD
CASTLE FARM ROAD
SHACKLANDS ROAD
CHARLES ROAD
STATION ROAD
CHURCH ST
HIGH ST
FORGE WAY
CROWN RD.
MILL LA.
FURMINGERS ROAD
DALTONS ROAD
BADGERS RD.
HIGHLAND RD.
Badger's Mount
GREENHILL RD
HILLYDEAL
COOMBE RD.
FACKENDEN LA.
56
57
58
59
60
CR
CS
CT
CU

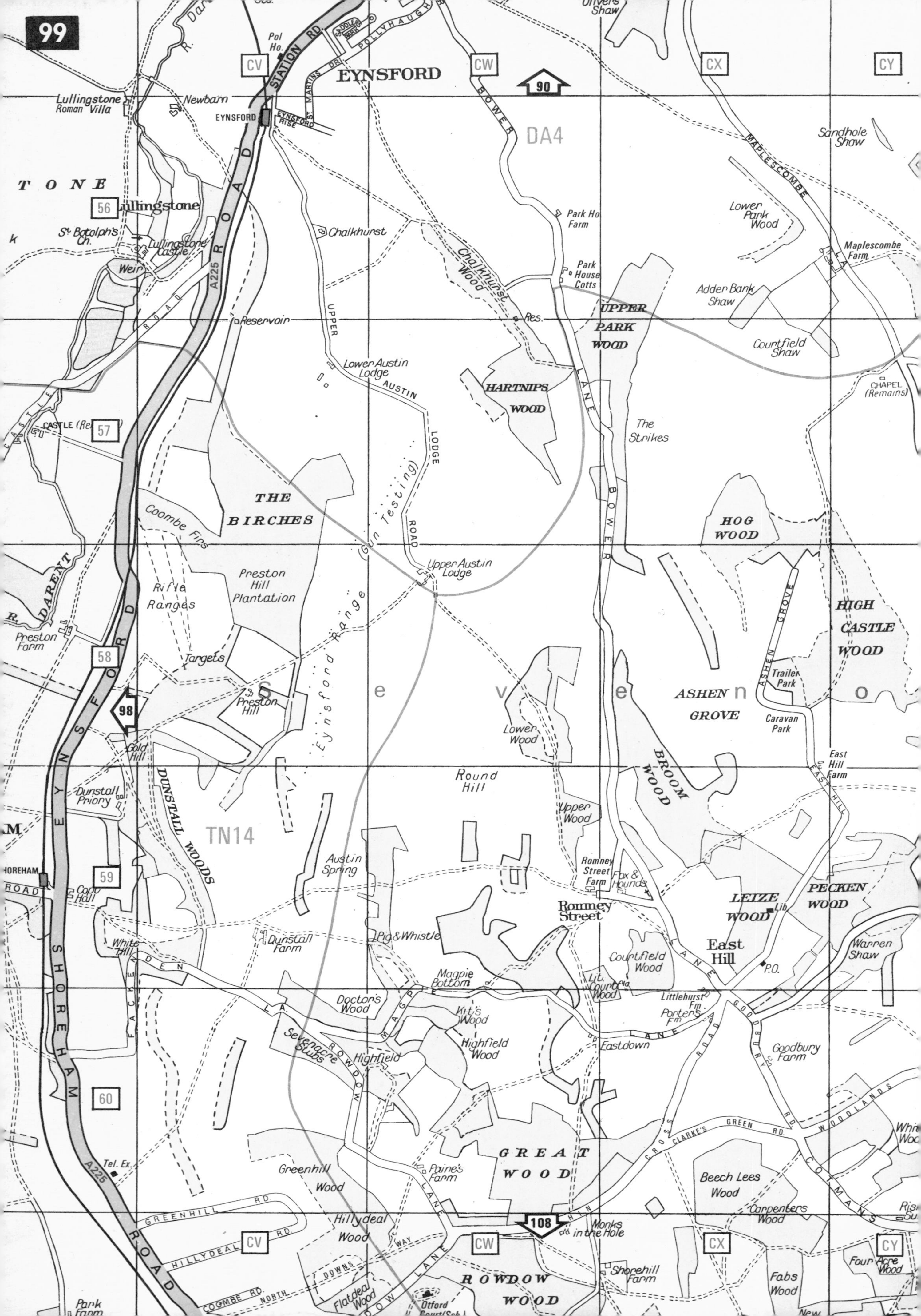

EYNSFORD
STATION RD.
POLLYHAUGH
ST. MARTINS DR.
EYNSFORD RISE
Pol Ho.
Lullingstone Roman Villa
Newbarn
Lullingstone
St. Botolph's Ch.
Lullingstone Castle
Weir
Reservoir
CASTLE RD
CASTLE (Remains)
Chalkhurst
Chalkhurst Wood
Res.
UPPER AUSTIN LODGE ROAD
Lower Austin Lodge
HARTNIPS WOOD
BOWER LANE
Park Ho Farm
Park House Cotts
UPPER PARK WOOD
The Strikes
DA4
MAPLESCOMBE LA
Sandhole Shaw
Lower Park Wood
Maplescombe Farm
Adder Bank Shaw
Courtfield Shaw
CHAPEL (Remains)
THE BIRCHES
Coombe Fins
Preston Hill Plantation
Rifle Ranges
Targets
Preston Hill
Preston Farm
R. DARENT
Eynsford Range (Gun Testing)
Upper Austin Lodge
HOG WOOD
HIGH CASTLE WOOD
ASHEN GROVE
Trailer Park
Caravan Park
Lower Wood
BROOM WOOD
East Hill Farm
EAST HILL
Round Hill
Upper Wood
Gold Hill
Dunstall Priory
DUNSTALL WOODS
TN14
Austin Spring
Romney Street Farm
Fox & Hounds
Romney Street
LEIZE WOOD
PECKEN WOOD
Lib
East Hill
P.O.
Warren Shaw
SHOREHAM
SHOREHAM ROAD
EYNSFORD ROAD
A225
Copt Hall
White Hill
FACKENDEN LA
Dunstall Farm
Pig & Whistle
Magpie Bottom
Courtfield Wood
Lit. Courtfield Wood
Doctor's Wood
MAGPIE BOTTOM
Kit's Wood
Littlehurst Fm.
Porter's Fm.
GOODBURY RD
Goodbury Farm
Sevenacre Stubs
ROWDOW
Highfield
Highfield Wood
Eastdown
LANE
CROSS ROAD
CLARKE'S GREEN RD.
WOODLANDS
COTMANS
Tel. Ex.
Greenhill Wood
Paine's Farm
GREAT WOOD
Beech Lees Wood
Carpenters Wood
GREENHILL RD
HILLYDEAL RD.
Hillydeal Wood
Monks in the Hole
DOWNS WAY
ROWDOW LANE
Shorehill Farm
Fabs Wood
Four Acre Wood
COOMBE RD. NORTH
Park Farm
Flatdeal Wood
Otford Court (Sch.)
ROWDOW WOOD
TONE
Sevenoaks
CV
CW
CX
CY
56
57
58
59
60

90
98
108

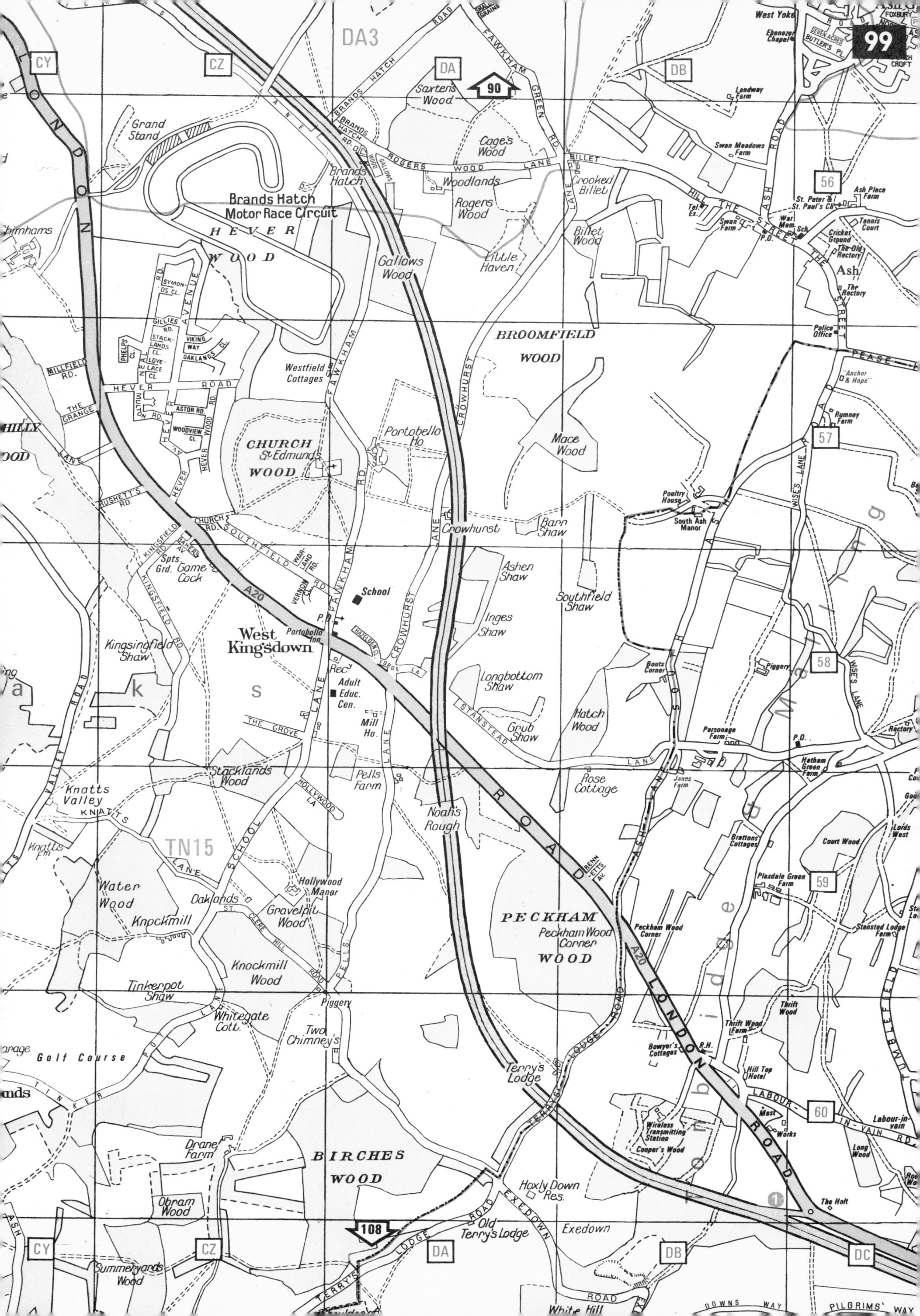
99
DA3
CY
CZ
DA
DB
DC
90
108
56
57
58
59
60
TN15
LONDON ROAD
A20
Grand Stand
Brands Hatch Motor Race Circuit
HEVER WOOD
Brands Hatch
BRANDS HATCH ROAD
BRANDS HATCH RD.
FAWKHAM GREEN RD.
Saxten's Wood
Cage's Wood
ROGERS WOOD LANE
Woodlands
Rogers Wood
Gallows Wood
Little Haven
Crooked Billet
BILLET HILL
Billet Wood
West Yoke
Ebenezer Chapel
SEVEN ACRES
BUTLER'S PL.
FOXBURY
Landway Farm
Swan Meadows Farm
ASH ROAD
THE STREET
Swan Farm
Tel. Ex.
P.O.
War Mem.
Sch.
St. Peter & St. Paul's Ch.
Ash Place Farm
Tennis Court
Cricket Ground
The Old Rectory
Ash
The Rectory
Police Office
PEASE
"Anchor & Hope"
Rumney Farm
Chimhams
SYMONDS CL.
GILLIES RD.
STACKLANDS CL.
LOVELACE CL.
PHELPS CL.
VIKING WAY
OAKLANDS CL.
NEAL RD.
AVENUE
MILLFIELD RD.
HEVER ROAD
THE GRANGE
MULTON RD.
ASTOR RD.
WOODVIEW CL.
HEVER WOOD RD.
HEVER AV.
HILLY
LANE
Westfield Cottages
FAWKHAM RD.
CHURCH WOOD
St. Edmund's
Portobello Ho.
CROWHURST LANE
BROOMFIELD WOOD
Mace Wood
Poultry House
South Ash Manor
WISE'S LANE
RUSHETT'S RD.
CHURCH RD.
SOUTHFIELD RD.
KINGSFIELD RD.
BAKERS AV.
Spts. Grd.
Game Cock
WARLAND RD.
VERNON CL.
School
P.O.
Portobello Inn
West Kingsdown
Crowhurst
Barn Shaw
Ashen Shaw
Southfield Shaw
Inges Shaw
Kingsingfield Shaw
VALLEY ROAD
HAZELDEN CL.
FORGE LA.
Rec.
Adult Educ. Cen.
Longbottom Shaw
Bouts Corner
Piggery
WISE'S LANE
Rectory
THE GROVE
Mill Ho.
STANSTEAD LANE
Grub Shaw
Hatch Wood
Parsonage Farm
P.O.
Hatham Green Farm
Stacklands Wood
Pells Farm
HOLLYWOOD LA.
Rose Cottage
Janes Farm
Knatts Valley
KNATTS LANE
Knatts Fm.
Noah's Rough
Brettons Cottages
Court Wood
Lords West
SCHOOL LANE
Hollywood Manor
BENNETTS AV.
Plaxdale Green Farm
Water Wood
Oaklands
Knockmill
ST. CLERE HILL ROAD
Gravelpit Wood
PECKHAM WOOD
Peckham Wood Corner
Stansted Lodge Farm
Knockmill Wood
PELLS LANE
Tinkerpot Shaw
Piggery
Whitegate Cott.
Two Chimney's
TERRY'S LODGE ROAD
Thrift Wood
Thrift Wood Farm
Bowyer's Cottages
P.H.
TUMBLEFIELD
Golf Course
TINKER POT LANE
Terry's Lodge
Hill Top Hotel
LABOUR-IN-VAIN RD.
Labour-in-vain
Mast
Works
Wireless Transmitting Station
Cooper's Wood
Long Wood
Drane Farm
BIRCHES WOOD
Haxly Down Res.
EXEDOWN ROAD
The Holt
Obram Wood
Old Terry's Lodge
Exedown
TERRY'S LODGE ROAD
Summeryards Wood
White Hill
DOWNS WAY
PILGRIMS' WAY

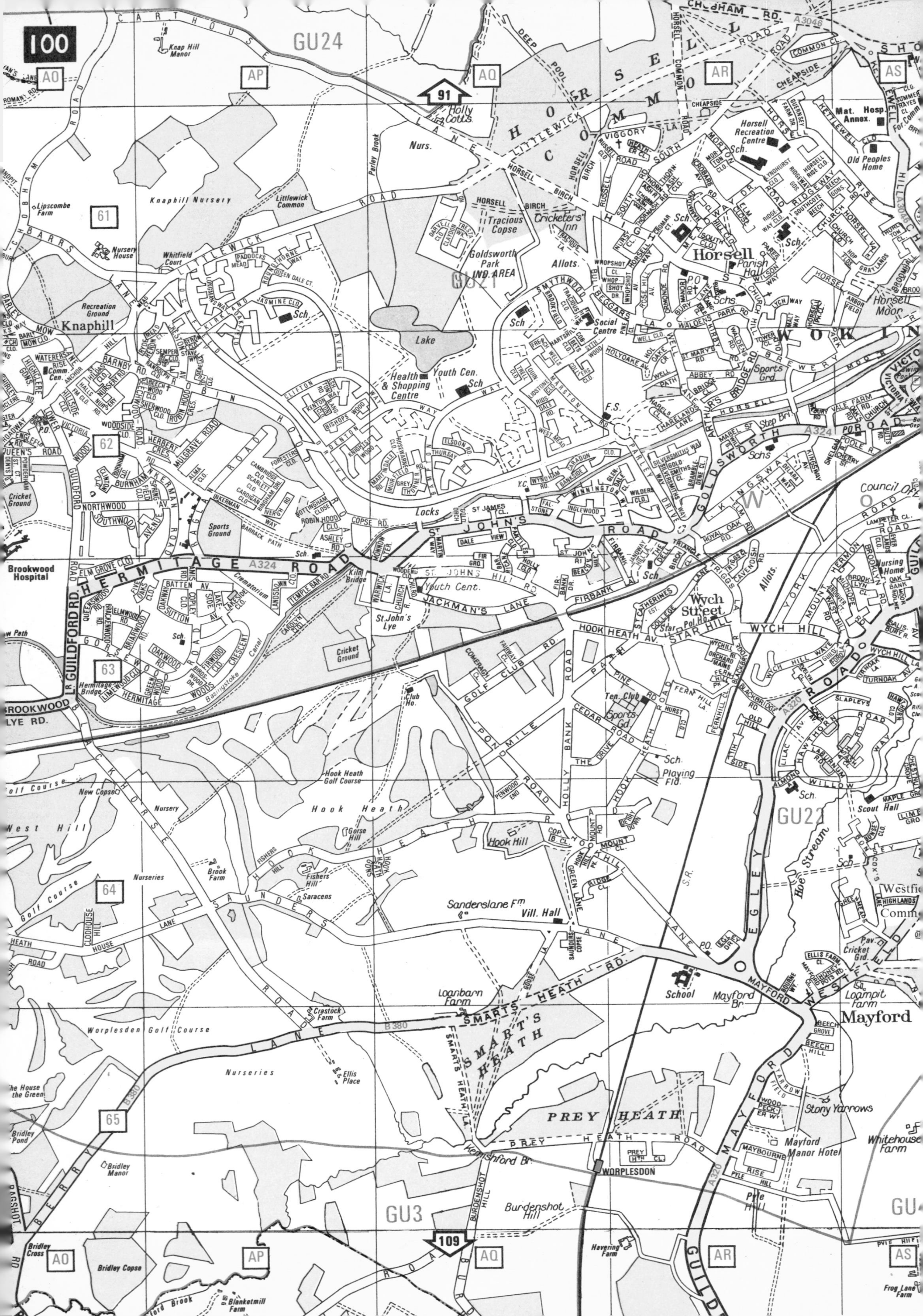

GU24
AO
AP
AQ
AR
AS
91
CARTHOUSE
Knap Hill Manor
Holly Cotts.
HORSELL COMMON
CHOBHAM RD.
A3046
COMMON CL.
CHEAPSIDE
Mat. Hosp. Annex.
Horsell Recreation Centre
Old Peoples Home
Nurs.
Parley Brook
Knaphill Nursery
Lipscombe Farm
61
Littlewick Common
LITTLEWICK ROAD
HORSELL BIRCH
Tracious Copse
Cricketers' Inn
Goldsworth Park IND. AREA
GU21
Allots.
Horsell
Parish Hall
Sch.
Nursery House
Whitfield Court
Recreation Ground
Knaphill
Lake
Health & Shopping Centre
Youth Cen.
Social Centre
WOKING
Sports Grd.
BREWERY
Horsell Moor
HORSELL MOOR
ARTHUR'S BRIDGE RD.
GOLDSWORTH ROAD
A324
F.S.
Step Bri.
ROBIN HOOD ROAD
62
INKERMAN ROAD
RAGLAN ROAD
Cricket Ground
GUILDFORD ROAD
NORTHWOOD AV.
Sports Ground
Locks
ST. JOHN'S ROAD
ST. JOHNS HILL RD.
JACKMAN'S LANE
Kiln Bridge
Youth Cent.
St. John's Lye
Brookwood Hospital
HERMITAGE ROAD
Crematorium
Basingstoke Canal
63
Hermitage Bridge
BROOKWOOD LYE RD.
Council Offs.
Nursing Home
Wych Street
Star Pol. Ho.
HOOK HEATH AV.
STAR HILL
WYCH HILL
WYCH HILL LA.
Cricket Ground
Club Ho.
GOLF CLUB RD.
PONTMILE ROAD
Ten. Club
Sports Gd.
CEDAR ROAD
Playing Fld.
HOLLYBANK ROAD
HOOK HEATH ROAD
Hook Heath Golf Course
Hook Heath
Golf Course
New Copse
Nursery
West Hill
Gorse Hill
Hook Hill
GU22
Hoe Stream
Scout Hall
Nurseries
Brook Farm
Fishers Hill
Saracens
64
CLODHOUSE HILL
HEATH HOUSE ROAD
SAUNDERS LANE
Sanderslane Fm
Vill. Hall
GREEN LANE
EGLEY RD.
Westfield Common
Pav. Cricket Grd.
School
Mayford Br.
MAYFORD
Loampit Farm
Mayford
Loanbarn Farm
Crastock Farm
SMARTS HEATH RD.
Smart's Heath
B380
Worplesden Golf Course
Nurseries
Ellis Place
The House in the Green
65
Bridley Pond
Bridley Manor
PREY HEATH
PREY HEATH ROAD
Kemishford Br.
WORPLESDON
Stony Yarrows
Mayford Manor Hotel
Whitehouse Farm
A320
Pyle Hill
GU3
Burdenshot Hill
BURDENSHOT HILL
109
Havering Farm
Bridley Cross
Bridley Copse
Blanketmill Farm
Frog Lane Farm

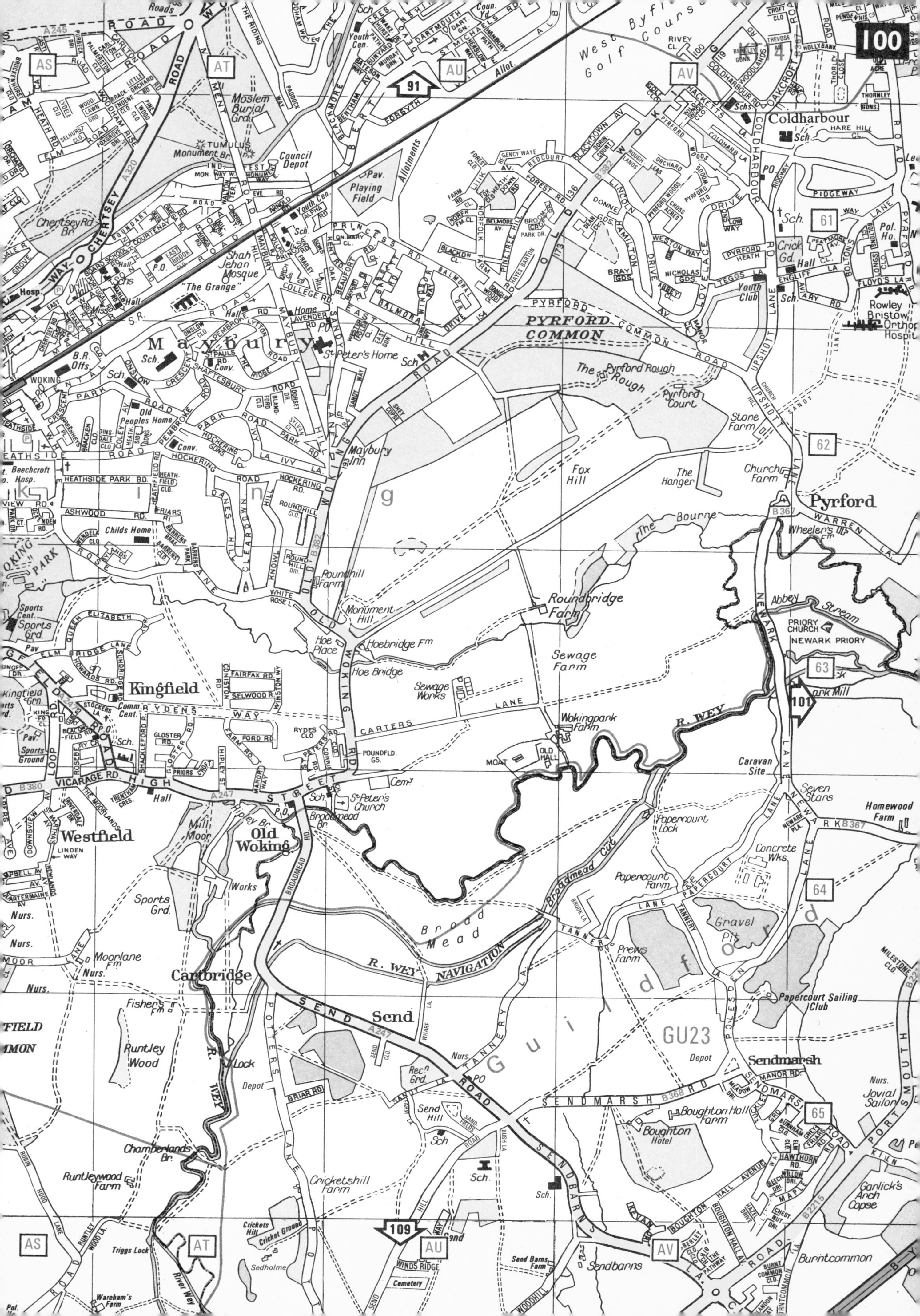
AS
AT
AU
AV
91
West Byfleet Golf Course
KT14
Coldharbour
Moslem Burial Grd.
Tumulus
Monument Br.
Council Depot
Pav. Playing Field
Allotments
Chertsey Rd Br.
Chertsey Road
Shah Jehan Mosque
"The Grange"
Maybury
St Peter's Home
B.R. Offs.
Woking
Old Peoples Home
Beechcroft Hosp.
Heathside Park Rd.
Childs Home
Hockering Rd.
Pyrford Common
The Pyrford Rough
Pyrford Court
Stone Farm
Maybury Inn
Fox Hill
The Hanger
Church Farm
Pyrford
The Bourne
Wheeler's Fm
61
62
63
64
65
101
Roundhill Farm
Monument Hill
Roundbridge Farm
Abbey Stream
Priory Church
Newark Priory
Hoe Place
Hoebridge Fm
Hoe Bridge
Sewage Farm
Sewage Works
Carters Lane
Wokingpark Farm
Old Hall
Moat
R. Wey
Kingfield
Sports Cent.
Sports Grd.
Westfield
Old Woking
St Peter's Church
Broadmead Br.
Papercourt Lock
Caravan Site
Seven Stars
Homewood Farm
Concrete Wks
Papercourt Farm
Broadmead Cut
Broad Mead
R. Wey Navigation
Gravel Pit
Prews Farm
Papercourt Sailing Club
Guildford
GU23
Sendmarsh
Depot
Moorlane Fm
Cartbridge
Send
Send Road
Fishers Fm
Runtley Wood
Lock
Chamberlands Br.
Runtleywood Farm
Rec.n Grd.
Send Hill
Sch.
Cricketshill Farm
Boughton Hall Farm
Boughton Hotel
Sendmarsh Rd
Jovial Sailor
Garlick's Arch Copse
Burntcommon
Sendbarns
Send Barns Farm
Triggs Lock
River Wey
Wareham's Farm
Sedholme
Cricket Ground
Winds Ridge
Cemetery
109
Portsmouth Road

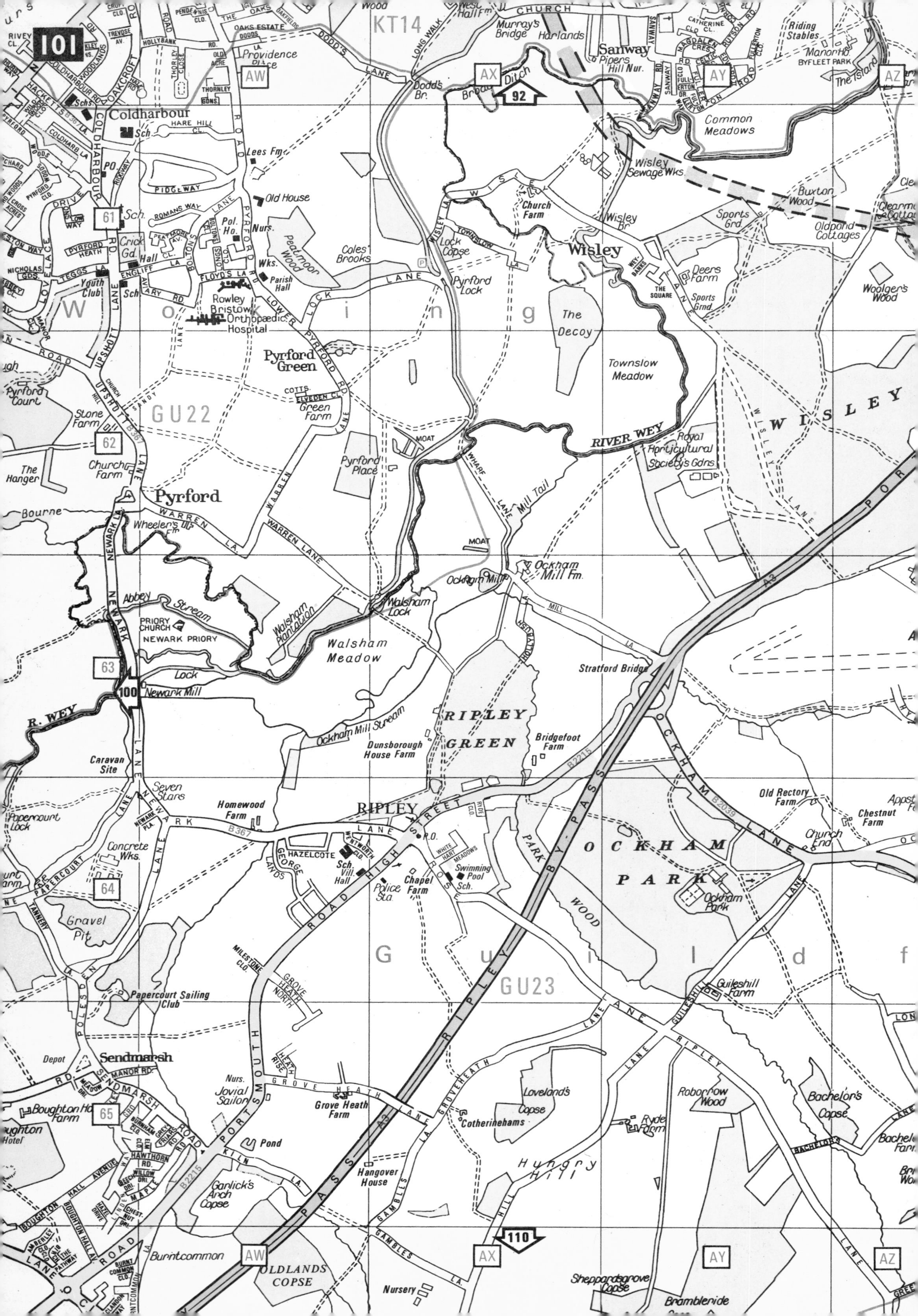
KT14
GU22
GU23
AW
AX
AY
AZ
92
110
100
61
62
63
64
65
Coldharbour
Providence Place
Oaks Estate
Murray's Bridge
Harlands
Sanway
Pipers Hill Nur.
Byfleet Park
The Island
Broad Ditch
Dodd's Br.
Common Meadows
Lees Fm.
Old House
Wisley Sewage Wks.
Buxton Wood
Oldpond Cottages
Church Farm
Wisley Br.
Sports Grd.
Peatmoor Wood
Coles' Brooks
Lock Copse
Wisley
Deers Farm
Woolger's Wood
Parish Hall
Pyrford Lock
The Square
Rowley Bristow Orthopaedic Hospital
Woking
The Decoy
Pyrford Green
Townslow Meadow
Green Farm
Pyrford Court
Stone Farm
River Wey
Royal Horticultural Society's Gdns.
Pyrford Place
The Hanger
Church Farm
Pyrford
Bourne
Wheeler's Fm.
Mill Tail
Moat
Ockham Mill
Ockham Mill Fm.
Abbey Stream
Priory Church
Newark Priory
Walsham Lock
Walsham Plantation
Walsham Meadow
Lock
Newark Mill
Stratford Bridge
R. Wey
Ripley Green
Ockham Mill Stream
Dunsborough House Farm
Bridgefoot Farm
Caravan Site
Seven Stars
Papercourt Lock
Homewood Farm
Ripley
Old Rectory Farm
Chestnut Farm
Church End
Ockham Park
Concrete Wks.
Hazelcote
Sch.
Vill. Hall
Police Sta.
Chapel Farm
Swimming Pool
Park Wood
Gravel Pit
Guildford
Papercourt Sailing Club
Guileshill Farm
Ripley By Pass
Depot
Sendmarsh
Jovial Sailor
Grove Heath Farm
Loveland's Copse
Roborrow Wood
Bachelor's Copse
Boughton Hall Farm
Cotherinehams
Ryde Farm
Pond
Hungry Hill
Garlick's Arch Copse
Hangover House
Burntcommon
Oldlands Copse
Nursery
Sheppardsgrove Copse
Portsmouth Road
A3
B2215
B367
B2039
Ockham Lane
Wisley Lane
Newark Lane
Warren Lane
Pyrford Road
High Street
Ripley Lane
Guileshill Lane
Send Marsh Road
Boughton Hall Avenue

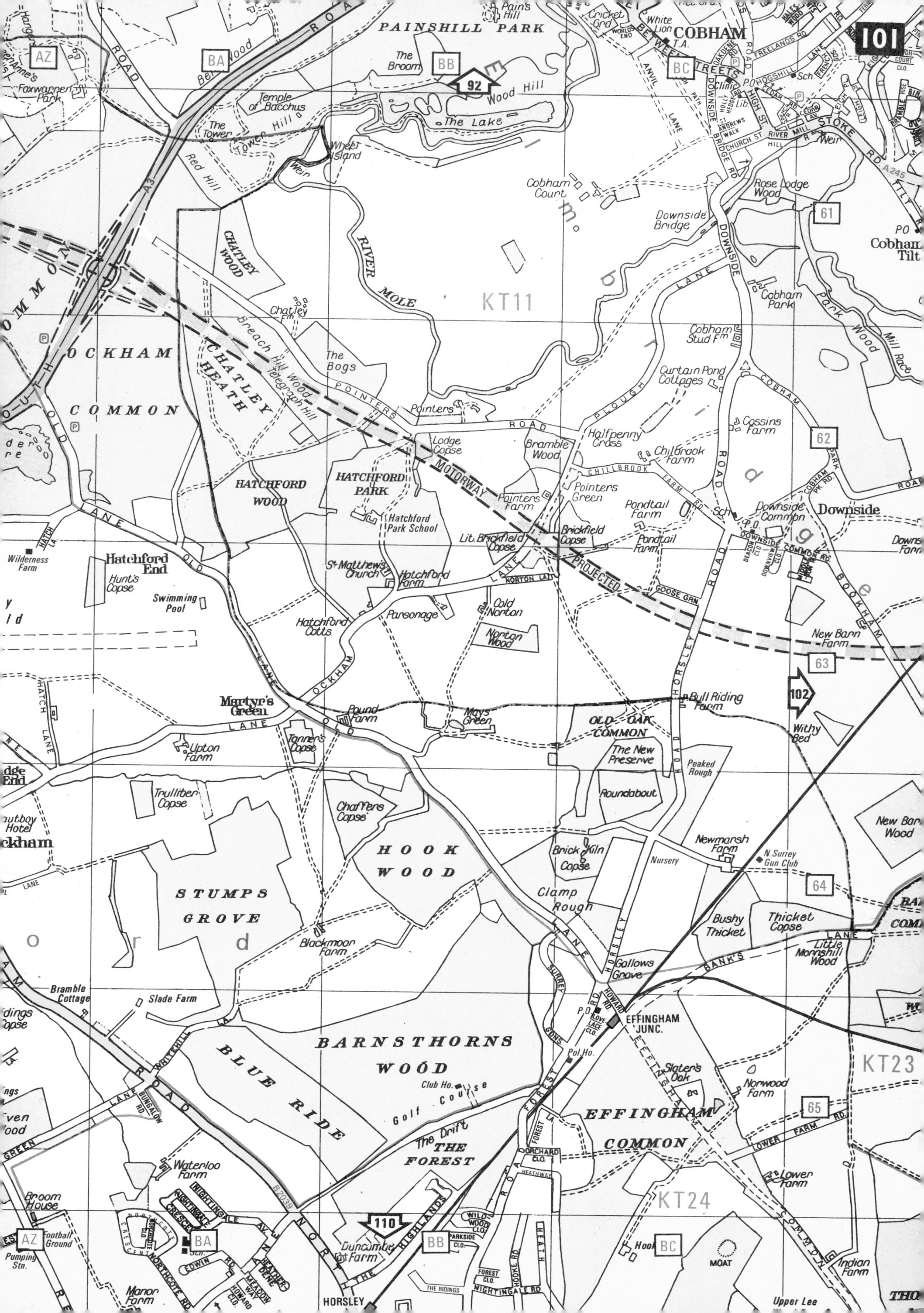

PAINSHILL PARK
COBHAM
Temple of Bacchus
The Lake
RIVER MOLE
Cobham Court
Downside Bridge
KT11
OCKHAM COMMON
CHATLEY HEATH
CHATLEY WOOD
HATCHFORD WOOD
HATCHFORD PARK
Hatchford Park School
Hatchford End
Martyr's Green
OLD OAK COMMON
HOOK WOOD
STUMPS GROVE
BARNSTHORNS WOOD
BLUE RIDE
EFFINGHAM COMMON
EFFINGHAM JUNC.
THE FOREST
Downside
KT23
KT24
HORSLEY

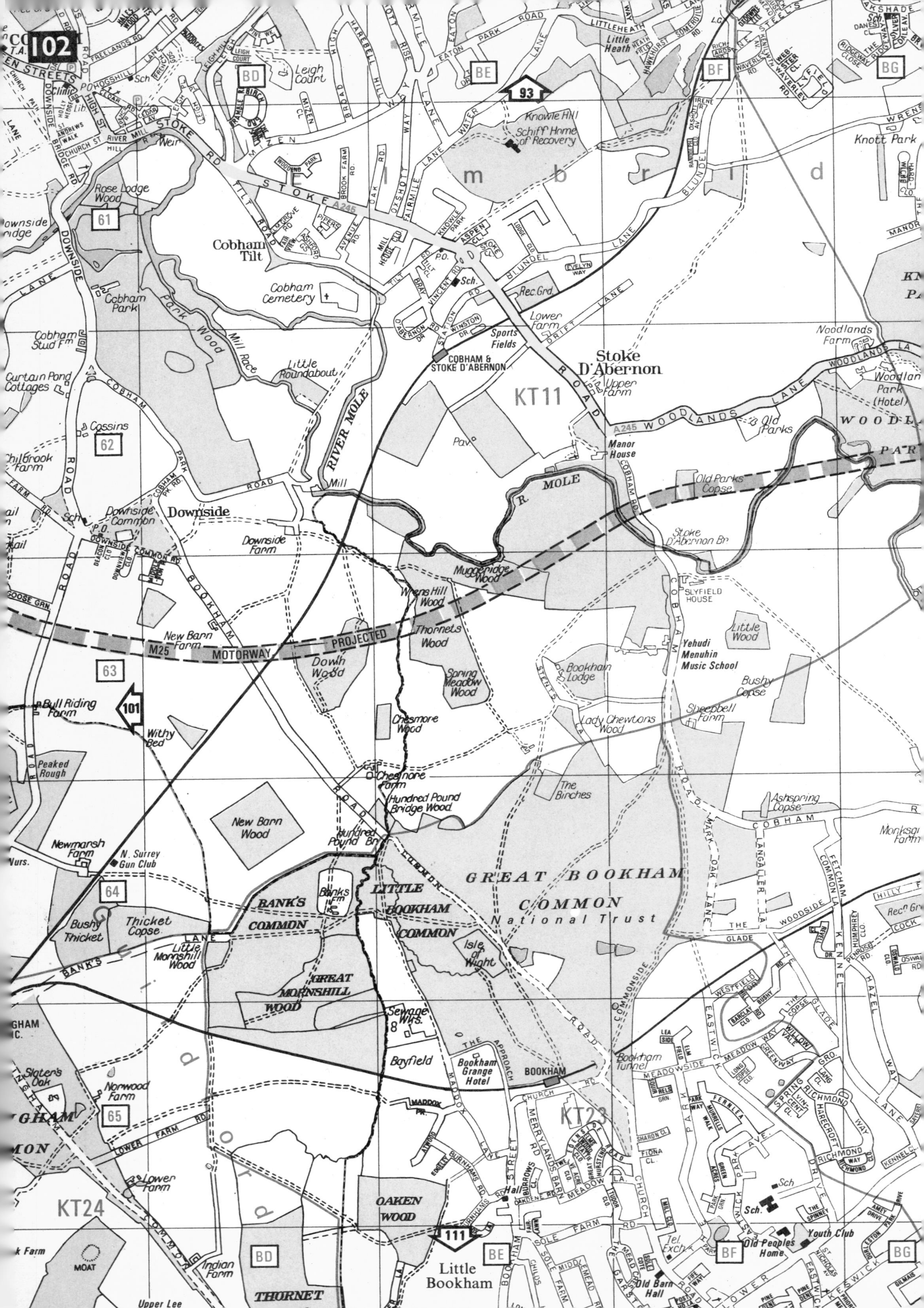

Leigh Court
Little Heath
93
Knowle Hill
Schiff Home of Recovery
Knott Park
Rose Lodge Wood
Cobham Tilt
Cobham Cemetery
Cobham Park
Park Wood
Mill Race
Cobham Stud Fm
Curtain Pond Cottages
Little Roundabout
River Mole
Cobham & Stoke D'Abernon
Sports Fields
Lower Farm
Stoke D'Abernon
Upper Farm
KT11
Woodlands Farm
Woodlands Park (Hotel)
Old Parks
Manor House
Cossins
Chilbrook Farm
Downside
Downside Common
Downside Farm
Mill
R. Mole
Old Parks Copse
Stoke D'Abernon Br
Muggeridge Wood
Wrens Hill Wood
Slyfield House
New Barn Farm
M25 Motorway Projected
Thornets Wood
Little Wood
Yehudi Menuhin Music School
Bookham Lodge
Down Wood
Spring Meadow Wood
Bushy Copse
Bull Riding Farm
101
Withy Bed
Chesmore Wood
Sheepbell Farm
Lady Chewtons Wood
Peaked Rough
Chesmore Farm
The Birches
Hundred Pound Bridge Wood
Hundred Pound Br
Ashspring Copse
New Barn Wood
Monksgrove Farm
Newmarsh Farm
N. Surrey Gun Club
Banks Fm
Little Bookham Common
Great Bookham Common
National Trust
Bank's Common
Bushy Thicket
Thicket Copse
Little Mornshill Wood
Isle of Wight
Great Mornshill Wood
Sewage Wks.
Slater's Oak
Bayfield
Bookham Grange Hotel
Bookham
Bookham Tunnel
Norwood Farm
KT23
Lower Farm
Oaken Wood
KT24
111
Moat
Indian Farm
Little Bookham
Old Barn Hall
Old Peoples Home
Youth Club
Thornet
Upper Lee
Great Bookham

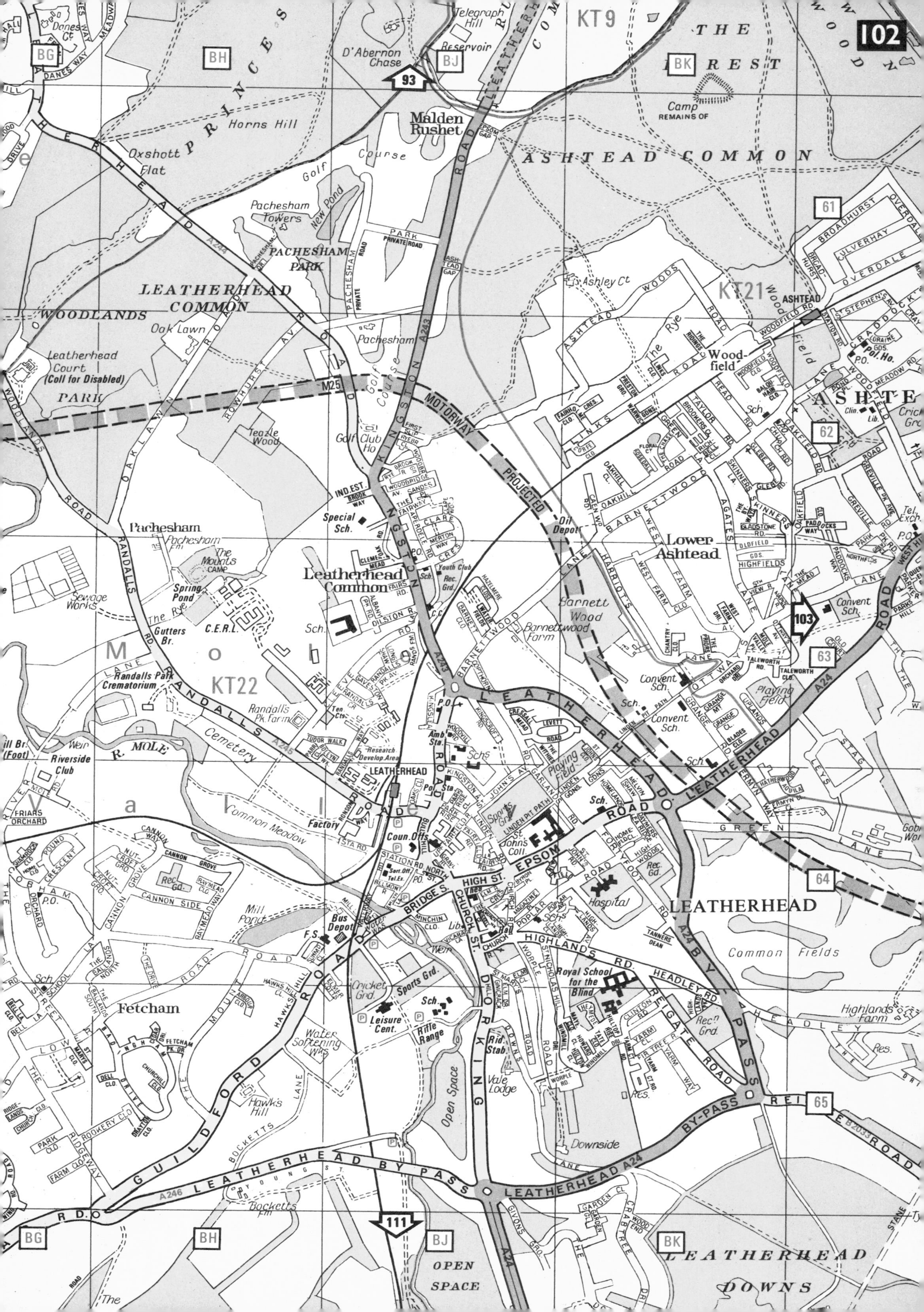

93
Malden Rushet
ASHTEAD COMMON
THE FOREST
PRINCES COVERT
Horns Hill
Oxshott Flat
Pachesham Towers
PACHESHAM PARK
LEATHERHEAD COMMON
WOODLANDS
Oak Lawn
Leatherhead Court (Coll for Disabled)
M25 MOTORWAY PROJECTED
KT9
KT21
KT22
ASHTEAD
Woodfield
Lower Ashtead
Barnett Wood
Leatherhead Common
Pachesham
Sewage Works
C.E.R.L.
Randalls Park Crematorium
R. MOLE
Cemetery
Riverside Club
Mole Valley
Fetcham
LEATHERHEAD
Hospital
Royal School for the Blind
Common Fields
Highlands Farm
Leisure Cent.
Rifle Range
Open Space
Vale Lodge
Downside
Hawk's Hill
Bocketts Fm
LEATHERHEAD BY PASS
GUILDFORD ROAD
KINGSTON ROAD
EPSOM ROAD
DORKING ROAD
REIGATE ROAD
HEADLEY ROAD
RANDALLS ROAD
OPEN SPACE
LEATHERHEAD DOWNS
61
62
63
64
65
103
111

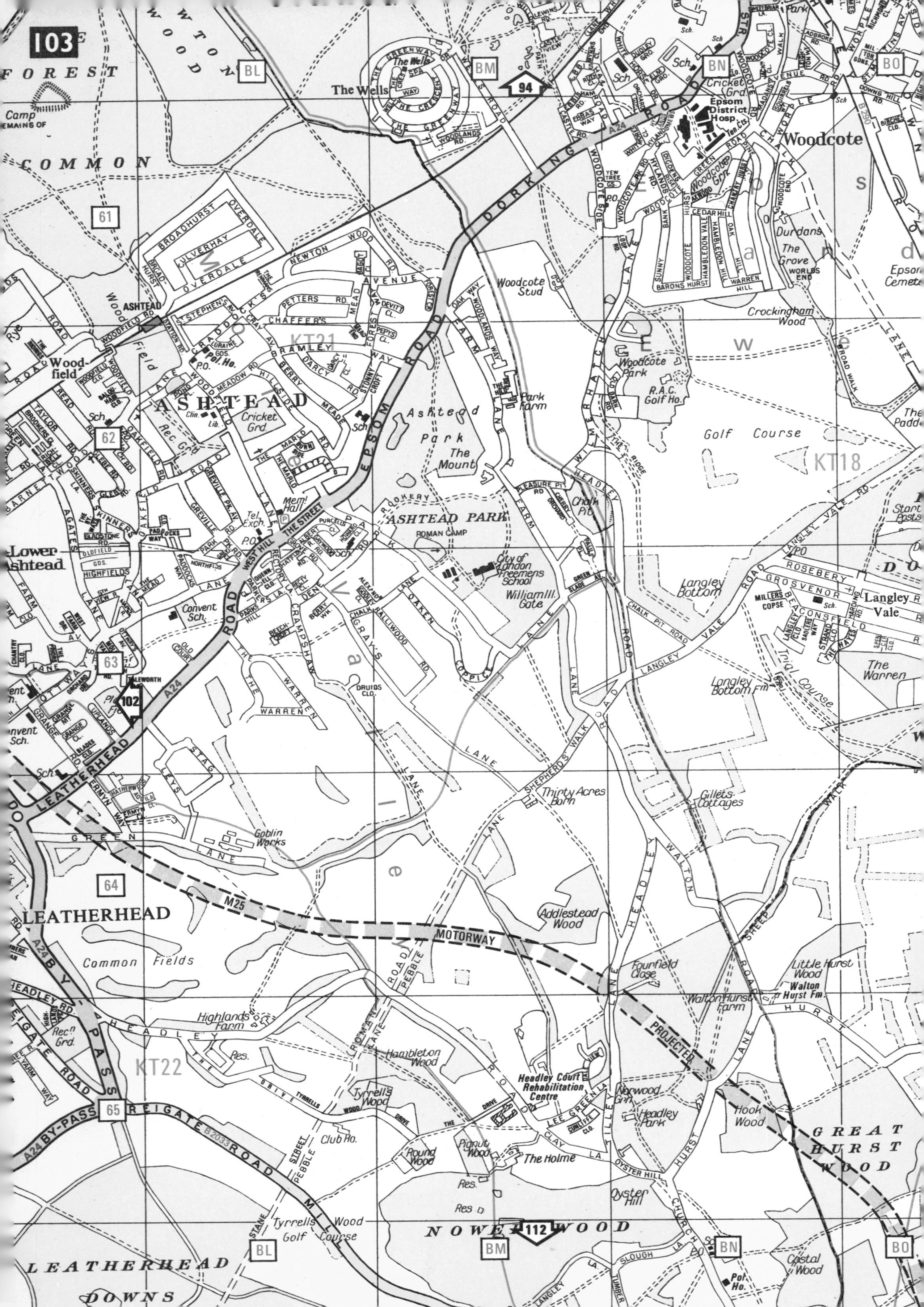
ASHTEAD
LEATHERHEAD
Woodcote
Langley Vale
Lower Ashtead
Woodfield
The Wells
Epsom District Hosp
Ashtead Park
ASHTEAD PARK
City of London Freemens School
Headley Court Rehabilitation Centre
Golf Course
R.A.C. Golf Ho.
Woodcote Park
Woodcote Stud
Park Farm
Crockingham Wood
Durdans
The Grove
Langley Bottom
Langley Bottom Fm
Thirty Acres Barn
Gillets Cottages
Goblin Works
Addlestead Wood
Fourfield Close
Walton Hurst Farm
Little Hurst Wood
Hook Wood
GREAT HURST WOOD
Highlands Farm
Hambleton Wood
Tyrrells Wood
Tyrrells Wood Golf Course
Round Wood
Pignut Wood
The Holme
Norwood Grn
Headley Park
Oyster Hill
NOWER WOOD
LEATHERHEAD DOWNS
Common Fields
Costal Wood
The Warren
DORKING ROAD
EPSOM ROAD
LEATHERHEAD ROAD
REIGATE ROAD
A24 BY-PASS
M25 MOTORWAY
PROJECTED
KT18
KT21
KT22
BL
BM
BN
BO
61
62
63
64
65
94
102
112

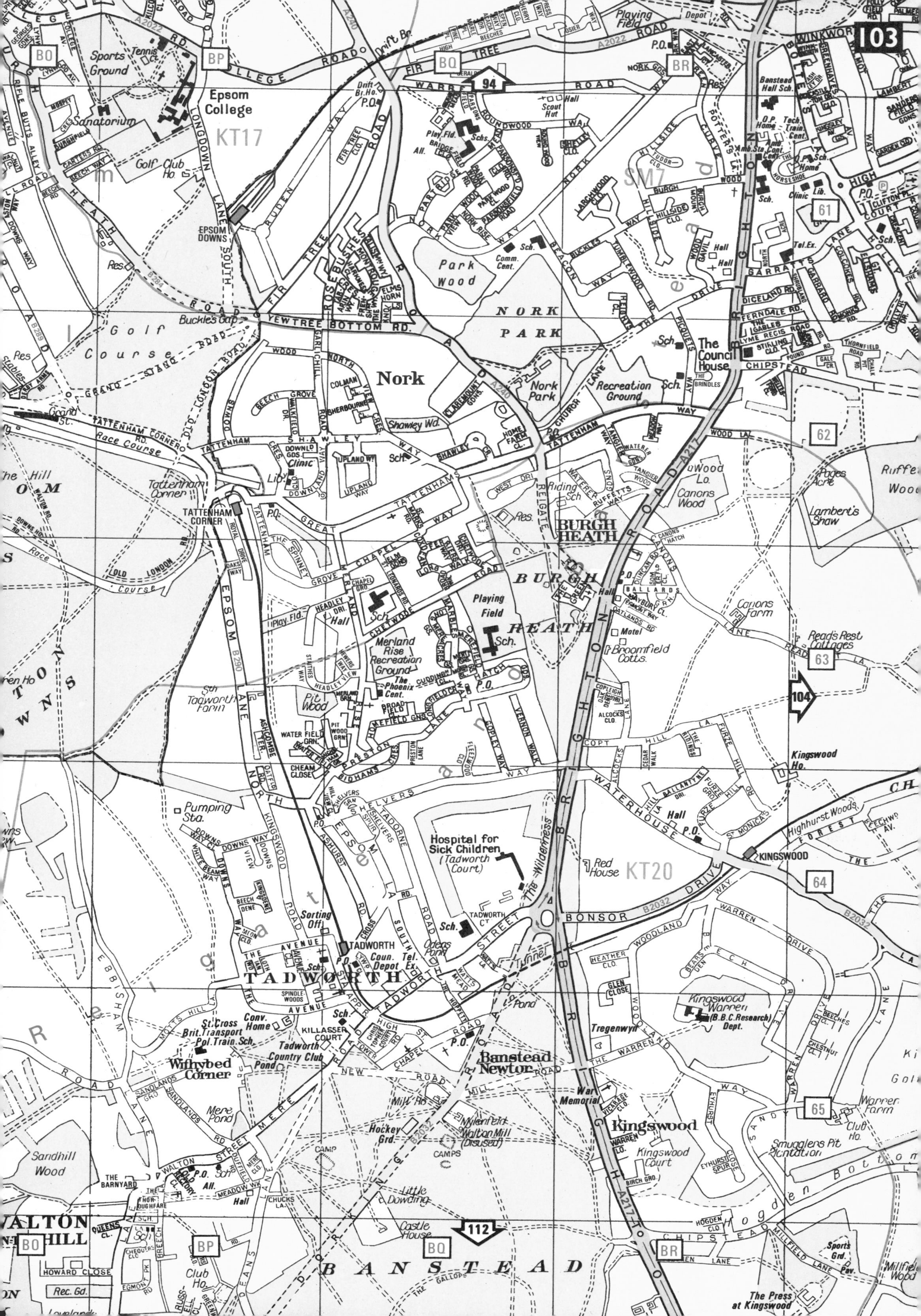
Epsom College
Sports Ground
Sanatorium
Golf Club Ho.
KT17
EPSOM DOWNS
Nork
NORK PARK
Park Wood
The Council House
Recreation Ground
SM7
Golf Course
Race Course
Tattenham Corner
TATTENHAM CORNER
BURGH HEATH
Canons Wood
Lambert's Shaw
Canons Farm
Read's Rest Cottages
Merland Rise Recreation Ground
Playing Field
Hospital for Sick Children (Tadworth Court)
KT20
Kingswood Ho.
KINGSWOOD
TADWORTH
Banstead Newton
Kingswood Warren (B.B.C. Research) Dept.
Kingswood
Kingswood Court
Sandhill Wood
WALTON ON THE HILL
Smugglers Pit Plantation
Little Dowding
Castle House
BANSTEAD
The Press at Kingswood
BRIGHTON ROAD A217
REIGATE ROAD
94
104
112
62
63
64
65

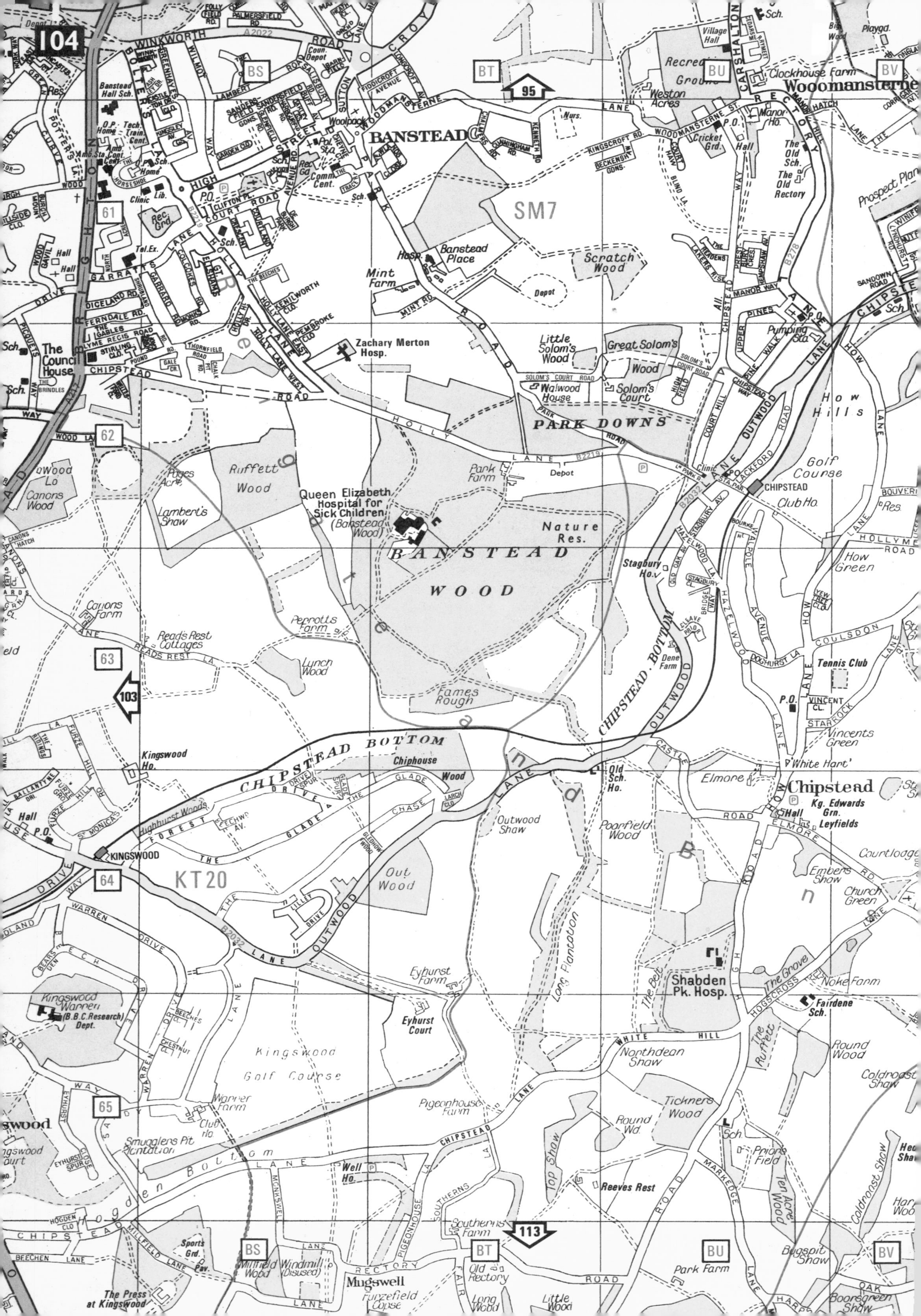

104
BS
BT
BU
BV
95
103
113
61
62
63
64
65
SM7
KT20
BANSTEAD
Woodmansterne
WINKWORTH ROAD
FOLLY FIELD RD.
PALMERSFIELD RD.
A2022
Coun. Depot
Banstead Hall Sch.
O.P. Tech. Home
Train. Cent.
Amb. Sta.
Clinic
Lib.
Rec. Grd.
Tel. Ex.
Hall
HIGH STREET
LAMBERT RD.
SALISBURY RD.
SUTTON LANE
CROYDON LANE
FIDDICROFT AVENUE
LONGCROFT AV.
WOODMANSTERNE LANE
Woolpack
Pol. Sta.
Comm. Cent.
P.O.
CLIFTON PL.
COURT ROAD
B2219
GARRATTS LANE
HOLLY LANE
HOLLY LANE EAST
HOLLY LANE WEST
KENILWORTH CLO.
PEMBROKE CLO.
DICELAND RD.
FERNDALE RD.
THE GABLES
LYME REGIS ROAD
STIRLING CLO.
POUND RD.
THORNFIELD ROAD
CHALK PIT RD.
CHIPSTEAD ROAD
The Council House
Sch.
THE BRINDLES
POTTERS WAY
BURGH HEATH
BRIGHTON ROAD
A217
Mint Farm
MINT RD.
Hosp.
Banstead Place
Zachary Merton Hosp.
Scratch Wood
Depot
Little Solom's Wood
Great Solom's Wood
SOLOM'S COURT ROAD
Walwood House
Solom's Court
PARK DOWNS
PARK ROAD
HOLLY LANE
Park Farm
Ruffett Wood
Pages Acre
Lambert's Shaw
Wood Lo.
Canons Wood
Queen Elizabeth Hospital for Sick Children (Banstead Wood)
BANSTEAD WOOD
Nature Res.
Canons Farm
Read's Rest Cottages
READS REST LA.
Perrotts Farm
Lunch Wood
Fames Rough
Stagbury Ho.
Dene Farm
CHIPSTEAD BOTTOM
OUTWOOD LANE
B2032
Chiphouse Wood
FOREST DRIVE
THE GLADE
THE CHASE
Kingswood Ho.
KINGSWOOD
Hall
P.O.
Hughhurst Woods
WARREN DRIVE
Out Wood
Outwood Shaw
Old Sch. Ho.
Poorfield Wood
Long Plantation
Eyhurst Farm
Eyhurst Court
Kingswood Warren (B.B.C. Research) Dept.
Kingswood Golf Course
Warren Farm
Club Ho.
Smugglers Pit Plantation
Hogden Bottom
HOGDEN LANE
Pigeonhouse Farm
Well Ho.
CHIPSTEAD LANE
Sports Grd.
Pav.
Millfield Wood
Windmill (Disused)
Mugswell
RECTORY LANE
The Press at Kingswood
Furzefield Copse
Southerns Farm
Old Rectory
Long Wood
Little Wood
Top Shaw
Reeves Rest
Round Wd.
Tickners Wood
Northdean Shaw
WHITE HILL
Shabden Pk. Hosp.
The Belt
HIGH ROAD
Priors Field
Ten Acre Wood
Park Farm
Bugspit Shaw
Coldroast Shaw
Round Wood
Fairdene Sch.
Noke Farm
The Grove
HOGSCROSS LANE
Church Green
Embers Shaw
Countlodge
Chipstead
Kg. Edwards Grn.
Leyfields
Elmore
ELMORE ROAD
'White Hart'
Vincents Green
STARROCK LANE
Tennis Club
P.O.
VINCENT CL.
DOGHURST LA.
COULSDON LANE
How Green
HOLLYMEAD ROAD
Golf Course
CHIPSTEAD
Club Ho.
How Hills
Pumping Sta.
MANOR WAY
RECTORY LANE
B2278
The Old Sch.
The Old Rectory
Manor Ho.
Cricket Grd.
Hall
KINGSCROFT RD.
BECKENSHAW GDNS.
Weston Acres
Recreation Ground
Village Hall
Clockhouse Farm
CARSHALTON ROAD
Nurs.
Prospect Place
SANDOWN ROAD
Stagbury

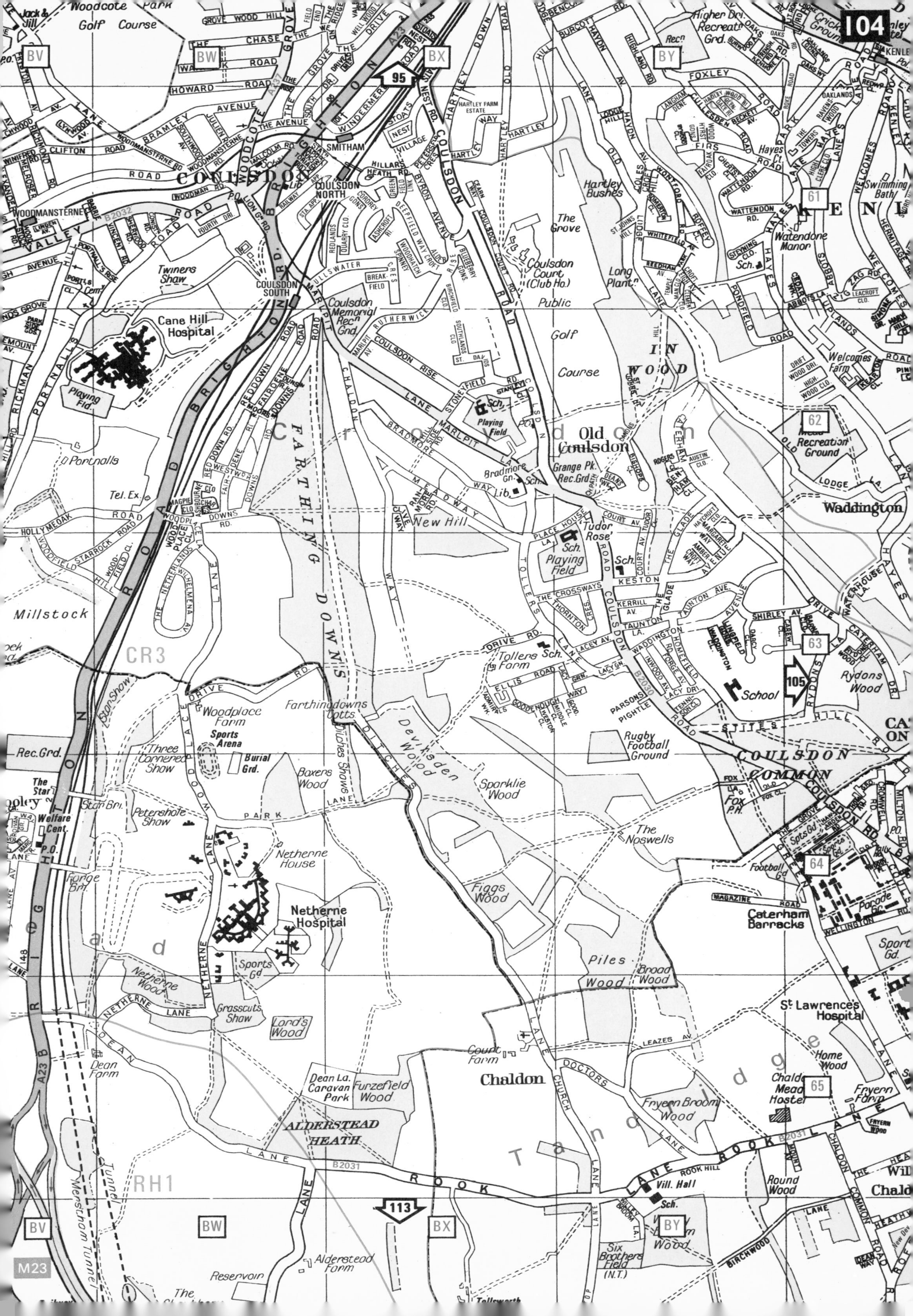
104
BV
BW
BX
BY
95
113
105
61
62
63
64
65
CR3
RH1
M23
Woodcote Park Golf Course
COULSDON
SMITHAM
COULSDON NORTH
COULSDON SOUTH
Cane Hill Hospital
Playing Fld.
Twiners Shaw
Portnalls
Tel. Ex.
Millstock
Coulsdon Memorial Recn Gnd.
FARTHING DOWNS
Hartley Bushes
The Grove
Coulsdon Court (Club Ho.)
Public Golf Course
Long Plantn
HAPPY VALLEY
Old Coulsdon
Grange Pk. Rec.Grd
Bradmore Gn.
New Hill
'Tudor Rose'
Sch. Playing Field
Tollers Farm
Farthingdowns Cotts
Woodplace Farm
Sports Arena
Burial Grd.
Three Cornered Shaw
Boxers Wood
Devilsden Wood
Sparklie Wood
Rugby Football Ground
COULSDON COMMON
Fox P.H.
The Noswells
Petershole Shaw
Netherne House
Netherne Hospital
Figgs Wood
Piles Wood
Broad Wood
Netherne Wood
Grasscuts Shaw
Lord's Wood
Court Farm
Chaldon
Dean Farm
Dean La. Caravan Park
Furzefield Wood
ALDERSTEAD HEATH
Fryern Broom Wood
Vill. Hall
Six Brothers Field (N.T.)
Alderstead Farm
Reservoir
Merstham Tunnel
Round Wood
Caterham Barracks
St Lawrence's Hospital
Home Wood
Fryern Farm
Rydons Wood
School
Waddington
Mead Recreation Ground
Watendone Manor
Welcomes Farm
Higher Dri. Recreatn Grd.
Hayes Ct.
Swimming Bath
The Star
Welfare Cent.
Forge Bri.
Rec.Grd.
Football Gd
Sports Gd
BRIGHTON ROAD
A23
B2032
B2030
B2031
ROOK LANE
CHALDON COMMON ROAD
COULSDON ROAD
Tandridge

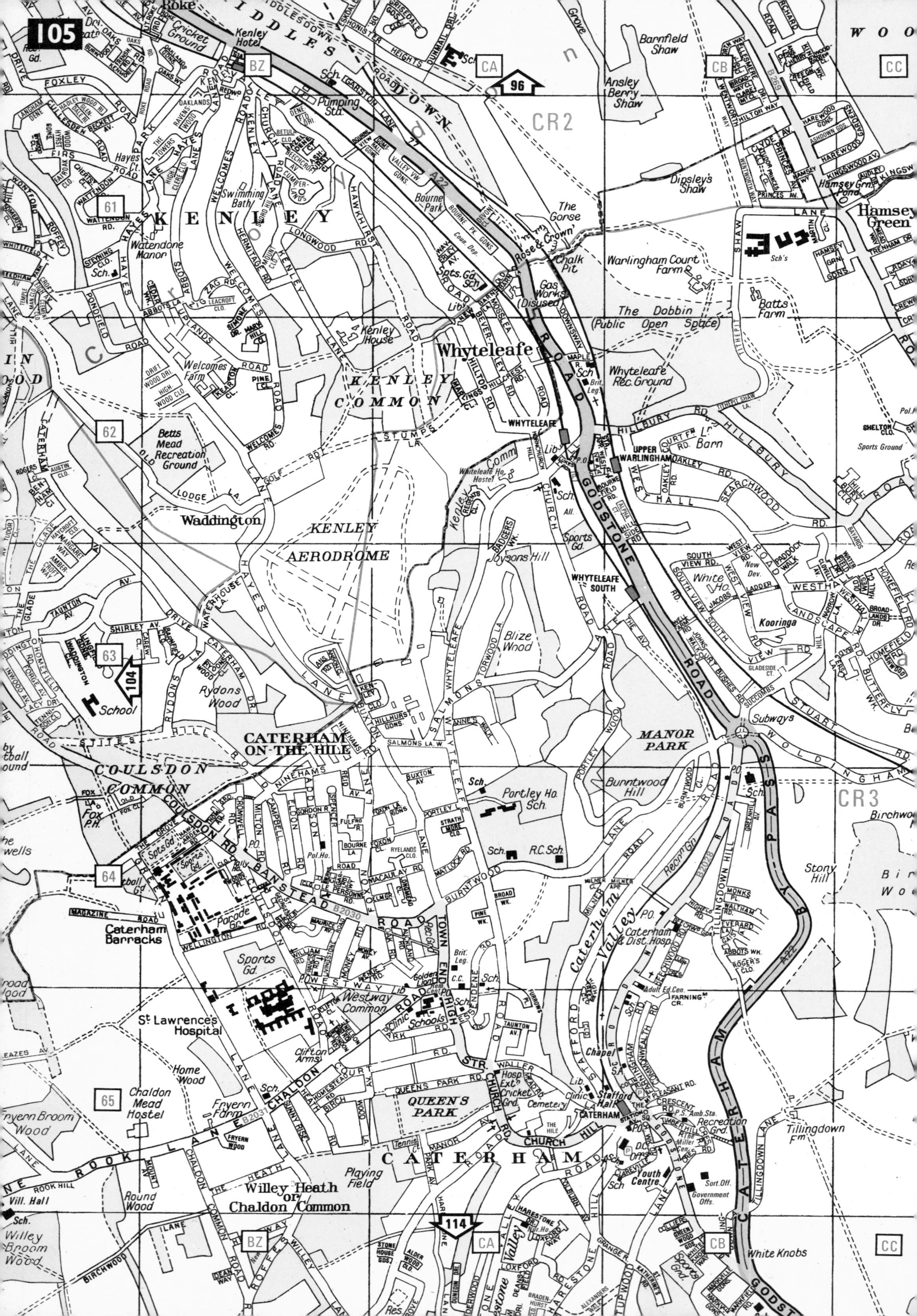

Roke
Kenley Hotel
Cricket Ground
FOXLEY
BZ
CA
CB
CC
96
Pumping Sta.
GARSTON LANE
HONISTER HEIGHTS
Barnfield Shaw
Ansley Berry Shaw
CR2
Dipsley's Shaw
The Gorse
Hamsey Green
Hamsey Grn. Pond
KINGSWOOD AV.
HILTON WAY
B269
A22
Hayes Ct.
61
K E N L E Y
Swimming Bath
Bourne Park
Watendone Manor
LONGWOOD RD.
Rose & Crown
Chalk Pit
Warlingham Court Farm
Sch's
Batts Farm
Gas Works (Disused)
The Dobbin (Public Open Space)
Kenley House
Welcomes Farm
Whyteleafe
K E N L E Y COMMON
Whyteleafe Rec. Ground
62
Betts Mead Recreation Ground
WHYTELEAFE
UPPER WARLINGHAM
HILLBURY RD.
Waddington
KENLEY AERODROME
Joysons Hill
Sports Gd.
WHYTELEAFE SOUTH
GODSTONE ROAD
White Ho.
Kooringa
Blize Wood
63
104
School
Rydons Wood
CATERHAM ON-THE-HILL
MANOR PARK
Subways
COULSDON COMMON
Portley Ho. Sch.
Burntwood Hill
CR3
Fox P.H.
Stony Hill
64
R.C. Sch.
Parade Gd.
BANSTEAD ROAD
B2030
Caterham Barracks
Caterham Valley
Caterham & Dist. Hosp.
Sports Gd.
Westway Common
Schools
St Lawrence's Hospital
Clifton Arms
Home Wood
65
Chaldon Mead Hostel
Fryern Farm
Fryern Broom Wood
QUEENS PARK
Cemetery
CHURCH HILL
CATERHAM
Recreation Grd.
Tillingdown Fm
CATERHAM BY-PASS
C A T E R H A M
ROOK LANE
Playing Field
Willey Heath or Chaldon Common
Round Wood
Vill. Hall
Youth Centre
Government Offs.
Sort. Off.
114
Willey Broom Wood
White Knobs

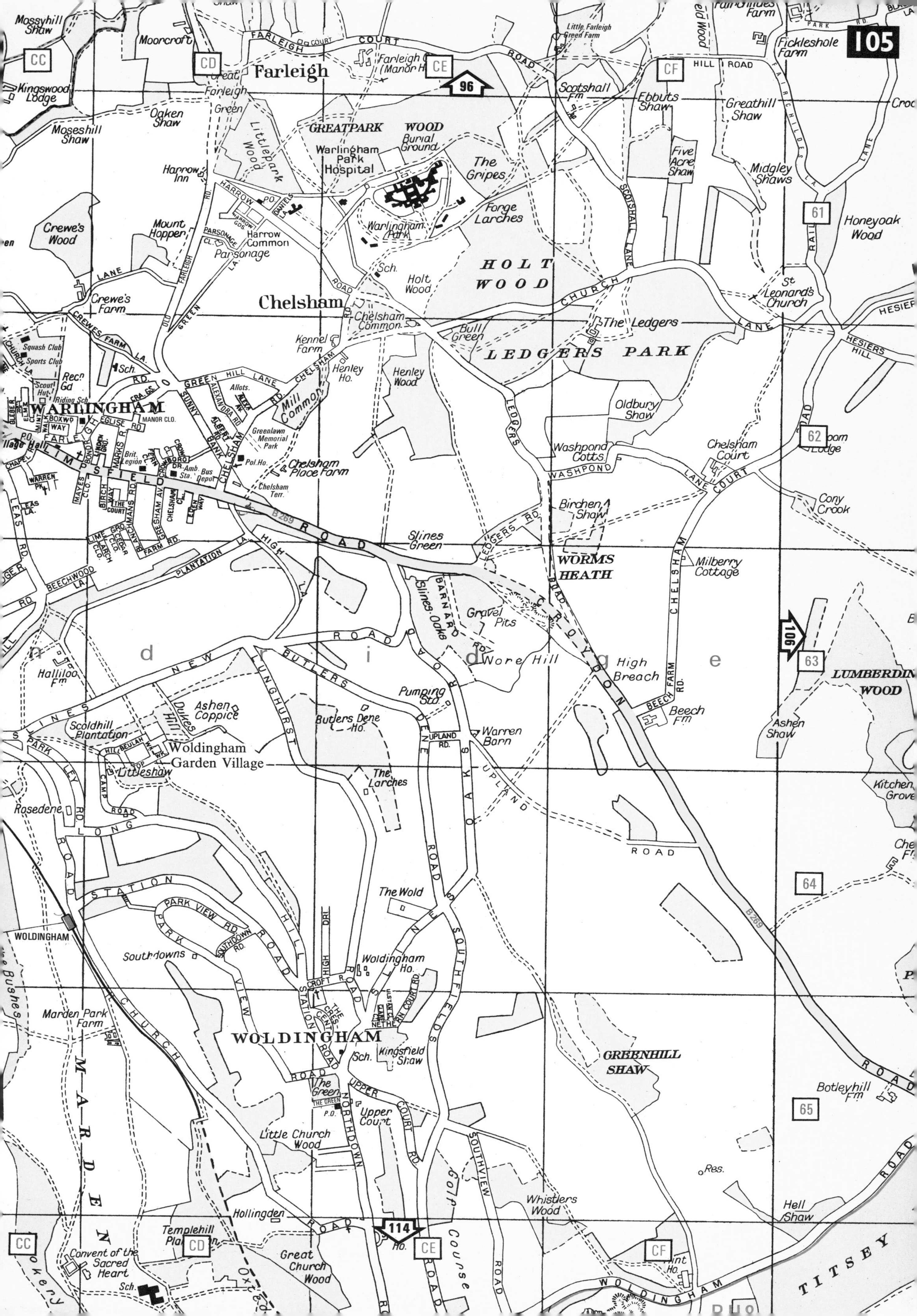

Mossyhill Shaw
Moorcroft
CC
CD
CE
CF
Farleigh
FARLEIGH COURT ROAD
Little Farleigh Green Farm
Farleigh Ct (Manor H)
Fickleshole Farm
HILL ROAD
Kingswood Lodge
Great Farleigh Green
96
Scotshall Fm
Ebbuts Shaw
Greathill Shaw
Oaken Shaw
Moseshill Shaw
GREATPARK WOOD
Burial Ground
Littlepark Wood
Warlingham Park Hospital
The Gripes
Five Acre Shaw
Midgley Shaws
FAIRCHILDES LANE
Harrow Inn
HARROW RD
Forge Larches
61
Honeyoak Wood
Crewe's Wood
Mount Hopper
Warlingham Park
SCOTSHALL LANE
Harrow Common
Parsonage
Sch.
HOLT WOOD
Holt Wood
St Leonard's Church
Crewe's Farm
Chelsham
CHURCH LANE
The Ledgers
HESIERS HILL
Chelsham Common
Bull Green
CREWES FARM LA.
Squash Club
Sports Club
Kennel Farm
LEDGERS PARK
Henley Ho.
Henley Wood
GREEN HILL LANE
Recn Gd
Scout Hut
Riding Sch.
Allots.
Mill Common
WARLINGHAM
MANOR CLO.
Oldbury Shaw
Greenlawn Memorial Park
LEDGERS RD
Washpond Cotts
Chelsham Court
62
Village Hall
Brit. Legion
Pol. Ho.
Chelsham Place Farm
WASHPOND LANE
COURT LANE
Amb. Sta.
Bus Depot
Chelsham Terr.
LIMPSFIELD ROAD
Cony Crook
Birchen Shaw
B269
Slines Green
WORMS HEATH
Milberry Cottage
PLANTATION LA.
BEECHWOOD LA.
HIGH LA.
BARNARD RD.
Slines Oaks
Gravel Pits
CROYDON ROAD
CHELSHAM RD.
106
NEW ROAD
BUTLERS ROAD
Nore Hill
High Breach
63
LUMBERDINE WOOD
Halliloo Fm
Pumping Sta.
BEECH FARM RD.
Beech Fm
Ashen Coppice
Dukes Hill
Butlers Dene Ho.
UPLAND RD.
Warren Barn
Ashen Shaw
Scoldhill Plantation
Woldingham Garden Village
Littleshaw
The Larches
Kitchen Grove
Rosedene
LONG HILL
ROAD
STATION ROAD
PARK VIEW RD.
The Wold
64
WOLDINGHAM
SOUTHDOWN RD.
Southdowns
Woldingham Ho.
SOUTHFIELDS
Marden Park Farm
WOLDINGHAM
Kingsfield Shaw
GREENHILL SHAW
Sch.
The Green
P.O.
UPPER COURT RD
Botleyhill Fm
65
Little Church Wood
NORTHDOWN
SOUTHVIEW ROAD
Res.
Golf Course
Whistlers Wood
Hell Shaw
Hollingden
114
Templehill Plantn.
Convent of the Sacred Heart
Great Church Wood
MARDEN
TITSEY ROAD
WOLDINGHAM ROAD

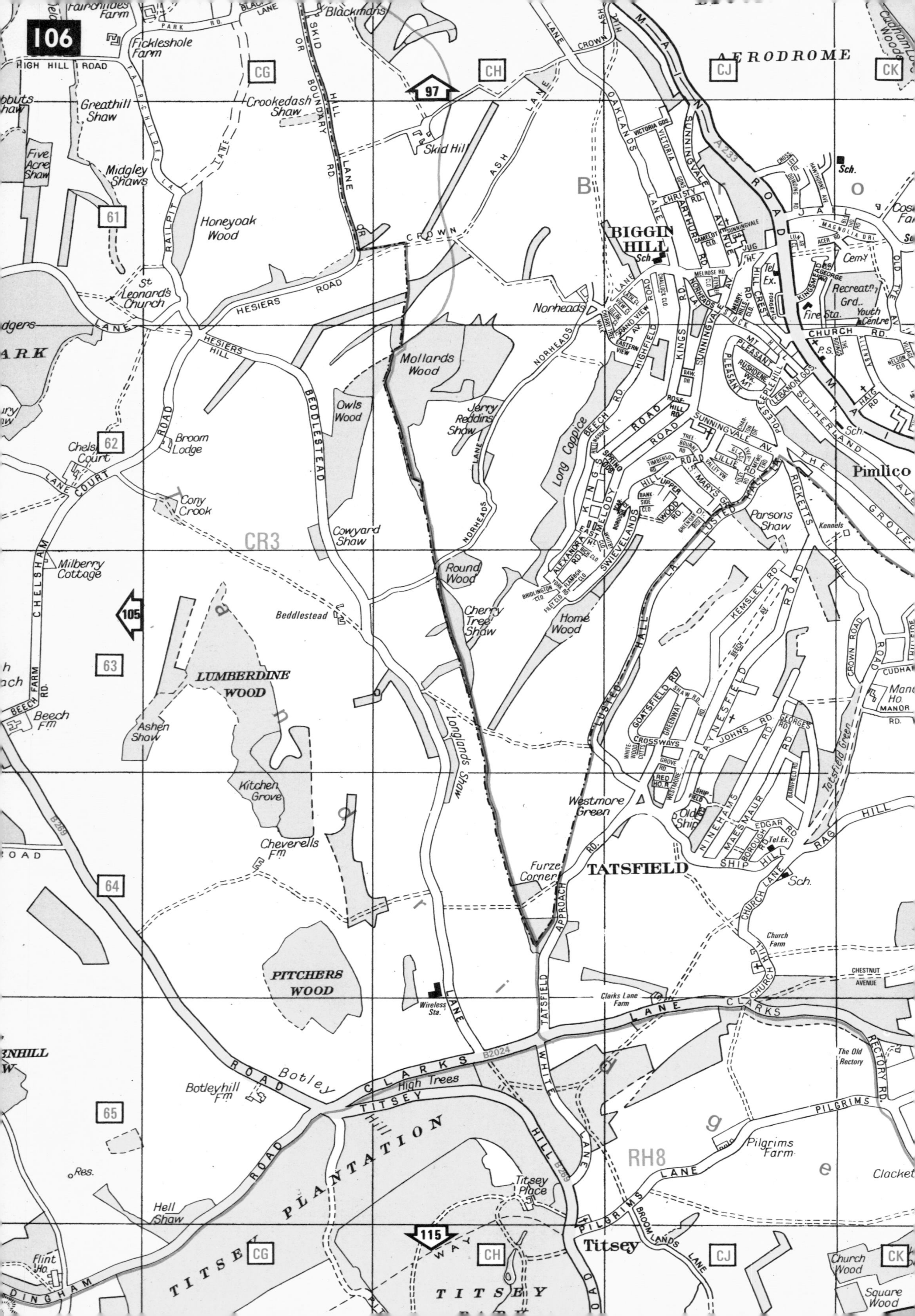

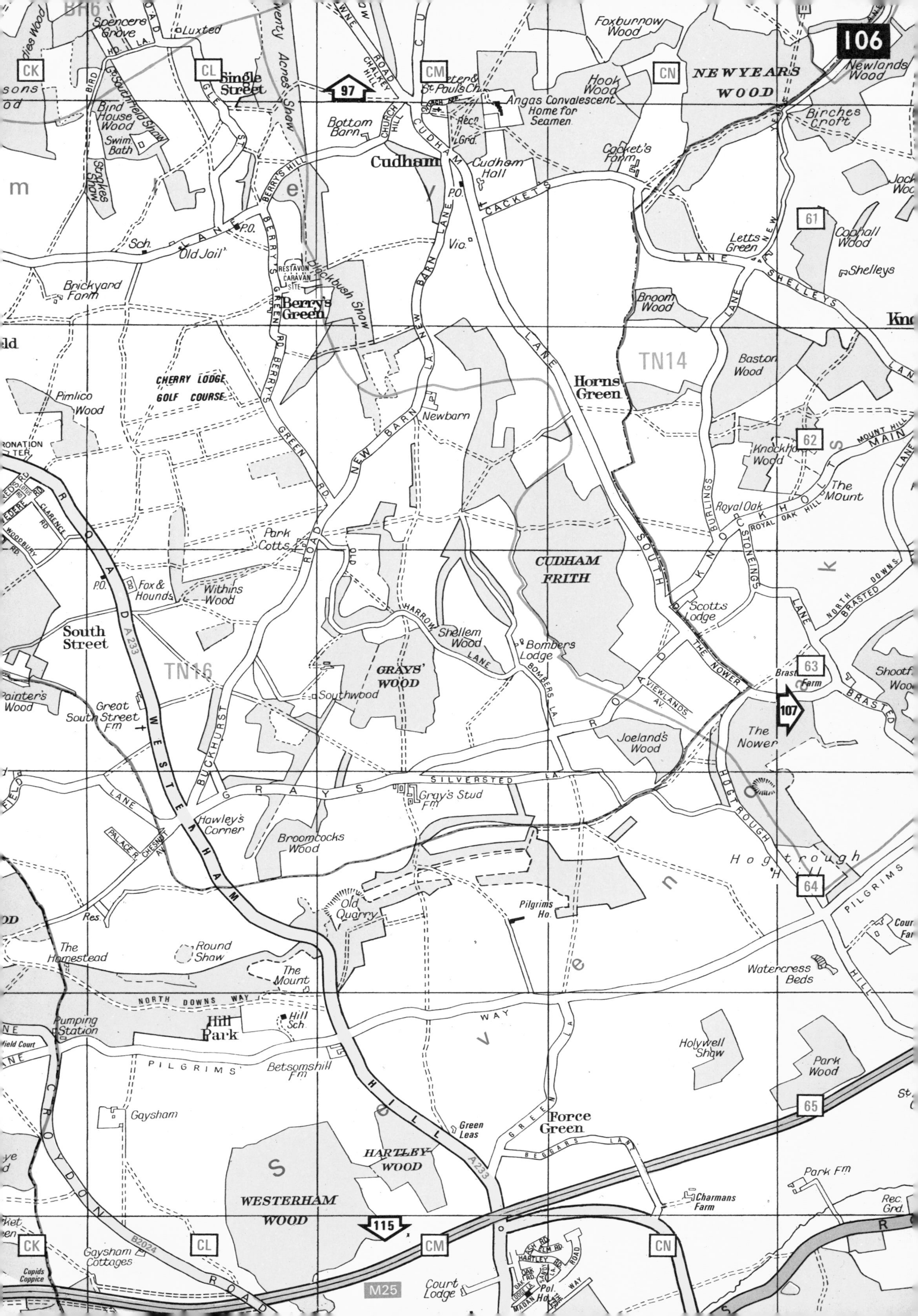
Spencers Grove
Luxted
Foxburrow Wood
Newlands Wood
CK
CL
Single Street
97
CM
St Peter & St Paul's Ch.
CN
NEWYEARS WOOD
Hook Wood
Angas Convalescent Home for Seamen
Birches Croft
Bird House Wood
Swim. Bath
Bottom Barn
Recn. Grd.
Cudham
Cudham Hall
Cacket's Farm
Strakes Shaw
CACKETS
P.O.
Vic.
61
Copthall Wood
Letts Green
Sch.
Old Jail
Brickyard Farm
RESTAVON CARAVAN SITE
Blackbush Show
Berry's Green
Broom Wood
Shelleys
SHELLEYS
TN14
Baston Wood
CHERRY LODGE GOLF COURSE
Pimlico Wood
Horns Green
Newbarn
NEW BARN LANE
BERRY'S GREEN RD.
62
Knockholt Wood
The Mount
Royal Oak
ROYAL OAK HILL
BURLINGS
STONEINGS
KNOCKHOLT
CLARENCE RD
WOODBURY RD.
Park Cotts
CUDHAM FRITH
P.O.
Fox & Hounds
Withins Wood
NORTH DOWNS
BRASTED
South Street
HARROW
Shellem Wood
Bombers Lodge
Scotts Lodge
TN16
GRAYS' WOOD
Southwood
THE NOWER
63
Painter's Wood
Great South Street Fm
VIEWLANDS AV.
BOMBERS LA.
107
The Nower
Joeland's Wood
BUCKHURST
WESTERHAM
A233
SILVERSTED LA.
GRAYS
Gray's Stud Fm
HOGTROUGH
Hawley's Corner
Broomcocks Wood
PALACE RD
CHESNUT AV.
Hogtrough Hill
64
Old Quarry
Pilgrims Ho.
PILGRIMS
Res.
The Homestead
Round Shaw
The Mount
Watercress Beds
NORTH DOWNS WAY
WAY
Pumping Station
Hill Park
Hill Sch.
PILGRIMS'
Betsomshill Fm
Holywell Shaw
Park Wood
65
Gaysham
Green Leas
Force Green
HARTLEY WOOD
GREEN
BEGGARS LANE
Park Fm
WESTERHAM WOOD
Charmans Farm
Rec. Grd.
CROYDON ROAD
B2024
115
CK
CL
CM
CN
Gaysham Cottages
Cupids Coppice
Court Lodge
Pol. Ho.
M25
HILL
A233

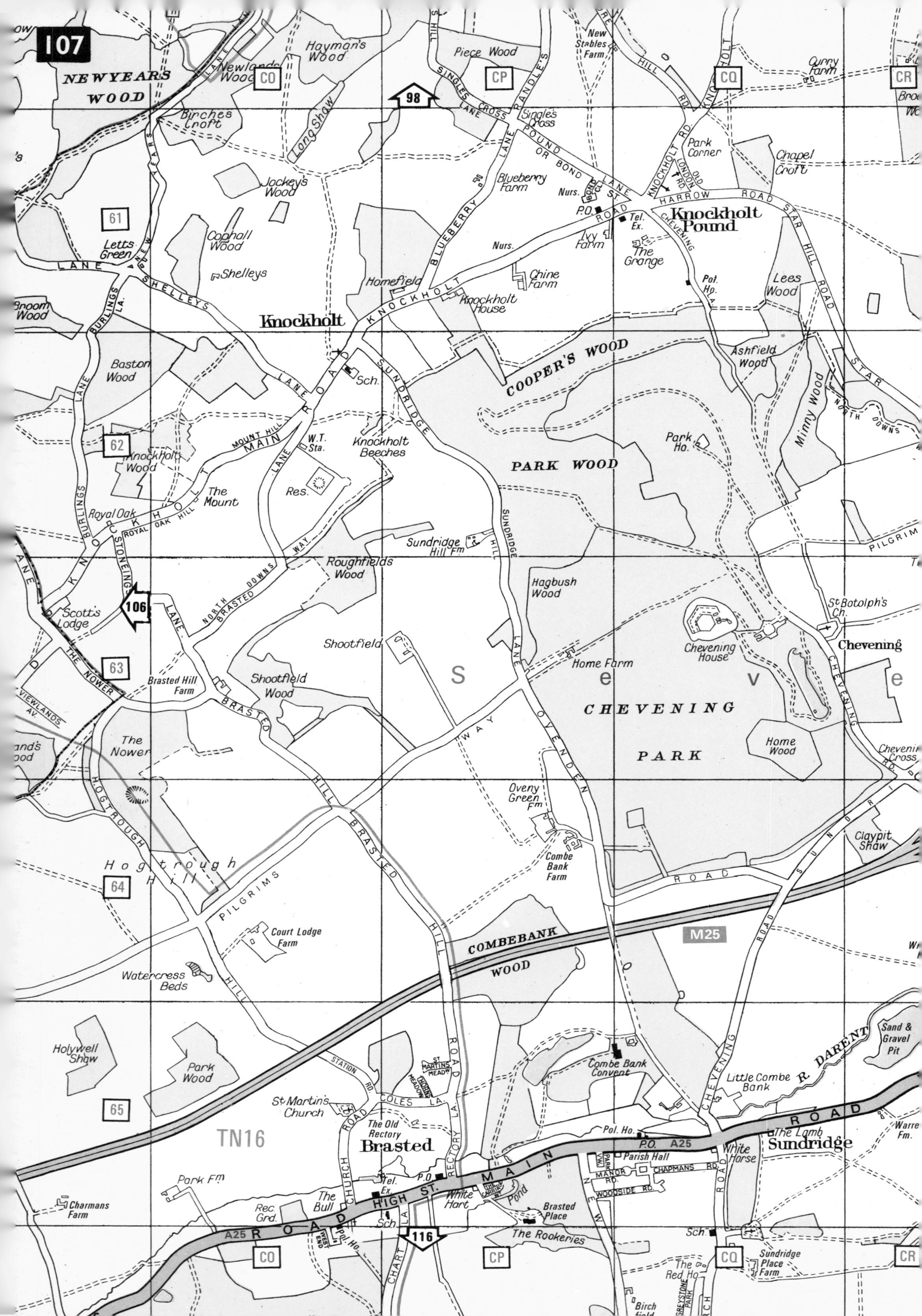
NEWYEARS WOOD
Newlands Wood
Hayman's Wood
Piece Wood
New Stables Farm
Curry Farm
CO
CP
CQ
CR
98
Birches Croft
Long Shaw
Singles Cross
Park Corner
Chapel Croft
Jockey's Wood
Blueberry Farm
Knockholt Pound
61
Letts Green
Cophall Wood
Shelleys
Ivy Farm
The Grange
Chine Farm
Lees Wood
Homefield
Knockholt House
Broom Wood
Knockholt
COOPER'S WOOD
Ashfield Wood
Baston Wood
Sch.
Minny Wood
62
Knockholt Wood
Knockholt Beeches
Park Ho.
PARK WOOD
The Mount
Res.
Royal Oak
Sundridge Hill Fm
Roughfields Wood
Hagbush Wood
106
Scott's Lodge
St Botolph's Ch.
Chevening
Shootfield
Chevening House
63
Brasted Hill Farm
Shootfield Wood
Home Farm
CHEVENING
PARK
The Nower
Home Wood
Chevening Cross
Oveny Green Fm
Claypit Shaw
Combe Bank Farm
Hogtrough Hill
64
M25
Court Lodge Farm
COMBEBANK WOOD
Watercress Beds
Holywell Shaw
Park Wood
Combe Bank Convent
Sand & Gravel Pit
R. DARENT
Little Combe Bank
65
St Martin's Church
The Old Rectory
TN16
Brasted
The Lamb
Sundridge
White Horse
Park Fm
Charmans Farm
The Bull
White Hart
Pond
Brasted Place
Rec. Grd.
The Rookeries
116
Sundridge Place Farm
The Red Ho.
Birch field
KNOCKHOLT ROAD
SUNDRIDGE ROAD
OVENDEN LANE
BRASTED HILL
PILGRIMS WAY
NORTH DOWNS WAY
HIGH ST.
MAIN ROAD
A25
CHEVENING ROAD
STAR HILL ROAD
HARROW ROAD
POUND OR BOND LANE
CHURCH ROAD
RECTORY LA.
CHART LA.
STATION RD
COLES LA.
THE NOWER
HOGTROUGH HILL
BURLINGS LANE
SHELLEYS LANE
STONEINGS LANE
ROYAL OAK HILL
MOUNT HILL

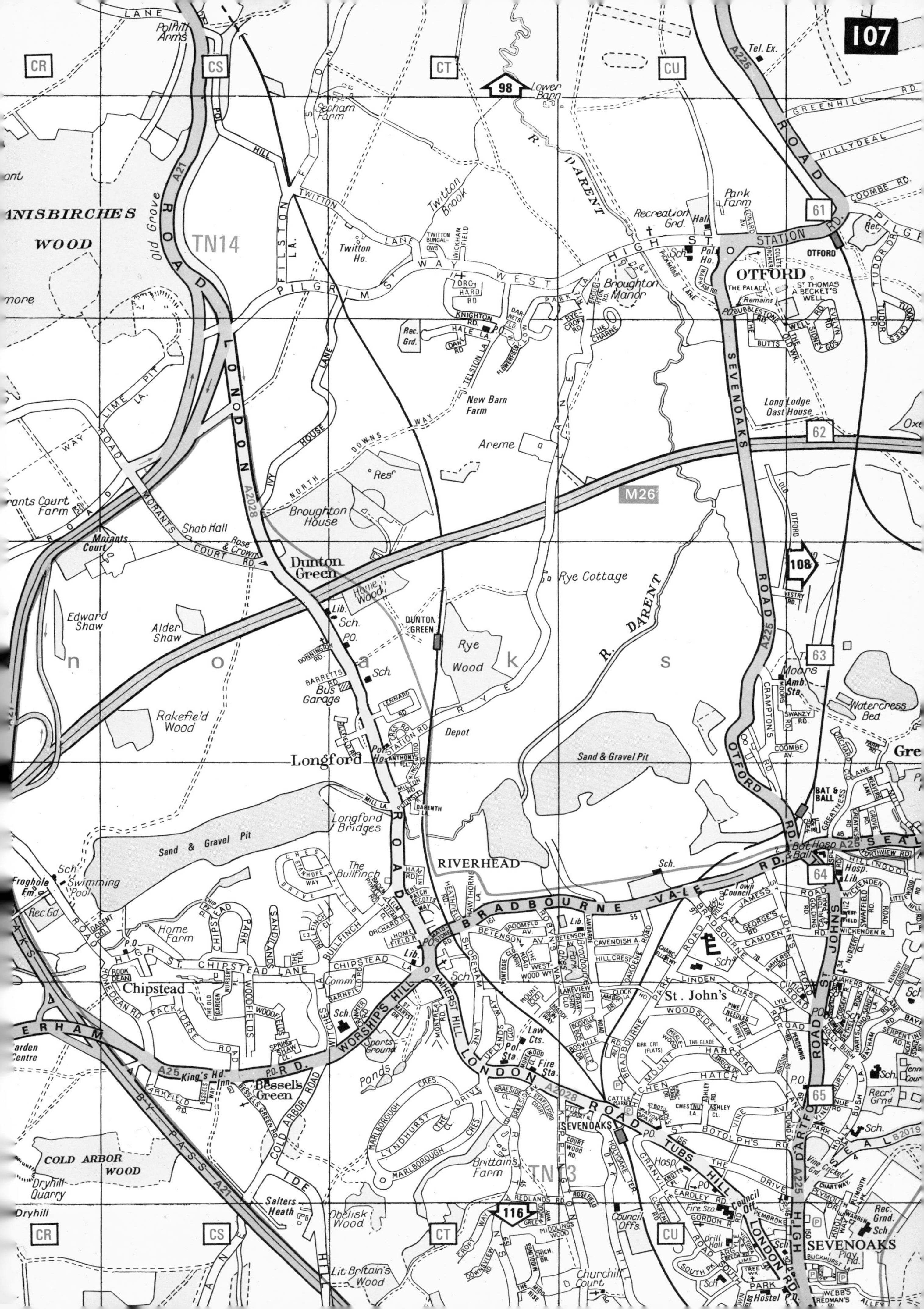
CR
CS
CT
CU
98
108
116
TN14
TN13
M26
A21
A25
A225
A2028
B2019
61
62
63
64
65
Polhill Arms
Sepham Farm
Lower Barn
Tel. Ex.
GREENHILL RD.
HILLYDEAL
COOMBE RD.
Park Farm
Recreation Grd.
Hall
OTFORD
THE PALACE (Remains)
ST THOMAS A BECKET'S WELL
STATION RD.
HIGH ST.
PILGRIMS' WAY WEST
Twitton Brook
Twitton Ho.
TWITTON LANE
FILSTON LA.
Broughton Manor
R. DARENT
Rec. Grd.
KNIGHTON RD.
HALE LA.
TELSTON LA.
New Barn Farm
Long Lodge Oast House
Areme
NORTH DOWNS WAY
IVY HOUSE LANE
LONDON ROAD
SEVENOAKS ROAD
Broughton House
Res
Morants Court Farm
MORANTS COURT RD.
Morants Court
Shab Hall
Rose & Crown
Dunton Green
Home Wood
DUNTON GREEN
Edward Shaw
Alder Shaw
Rye Wood
Rye Cottage
LIME PIT LA.
Old Grove
ANISBIRCHES WOOD
VESTRY RD.
Moors
Amb. Sta.
CRAMPTONS RD.
SWANZY RD.
COOMBE AV.
Watercress Bed
Rakefield Wood
Bus Garage
Depot
Longford
Sand & Gravel Pit
OTFORD RD.
BAT & BALL
Longford Bridges
MILL LA.
RIVERHEAD
Sch.
Lib.
P.O.
Froghole Fm.
Swimming Pool
Rec. Gd.
The Bullfinch
BRADBOURNE VALE RD.
Town Council
ST JOHN'S HILL
ST JOHNS RD.
SEAL RD.
Home Farm
CHIPSTEAD LANE
HIGH ST.
Chipstead
St. John's
WORSHIPS HILL
AMHERST HILL
Sports Ground
Law Cts.
Pol. Sta.
Fire Sta.
LONDON ROAD
King's Hd. Inn
Bessel's Green
ERHAM
Garden Centre
Ponds
Brittains Farm
SEVENOAKS
TUBS HILL
Hosp.
Council Offs.
COLD ARBOR WOOD
Dryhill Quarry
Dryhill
Salters Heath
Obelisk Wood
Lit Britain's Wood
Churchill Court
Hostel
Vine Cricket Grd.
Rec. Grnd.
Play Fld.
BY-PASS

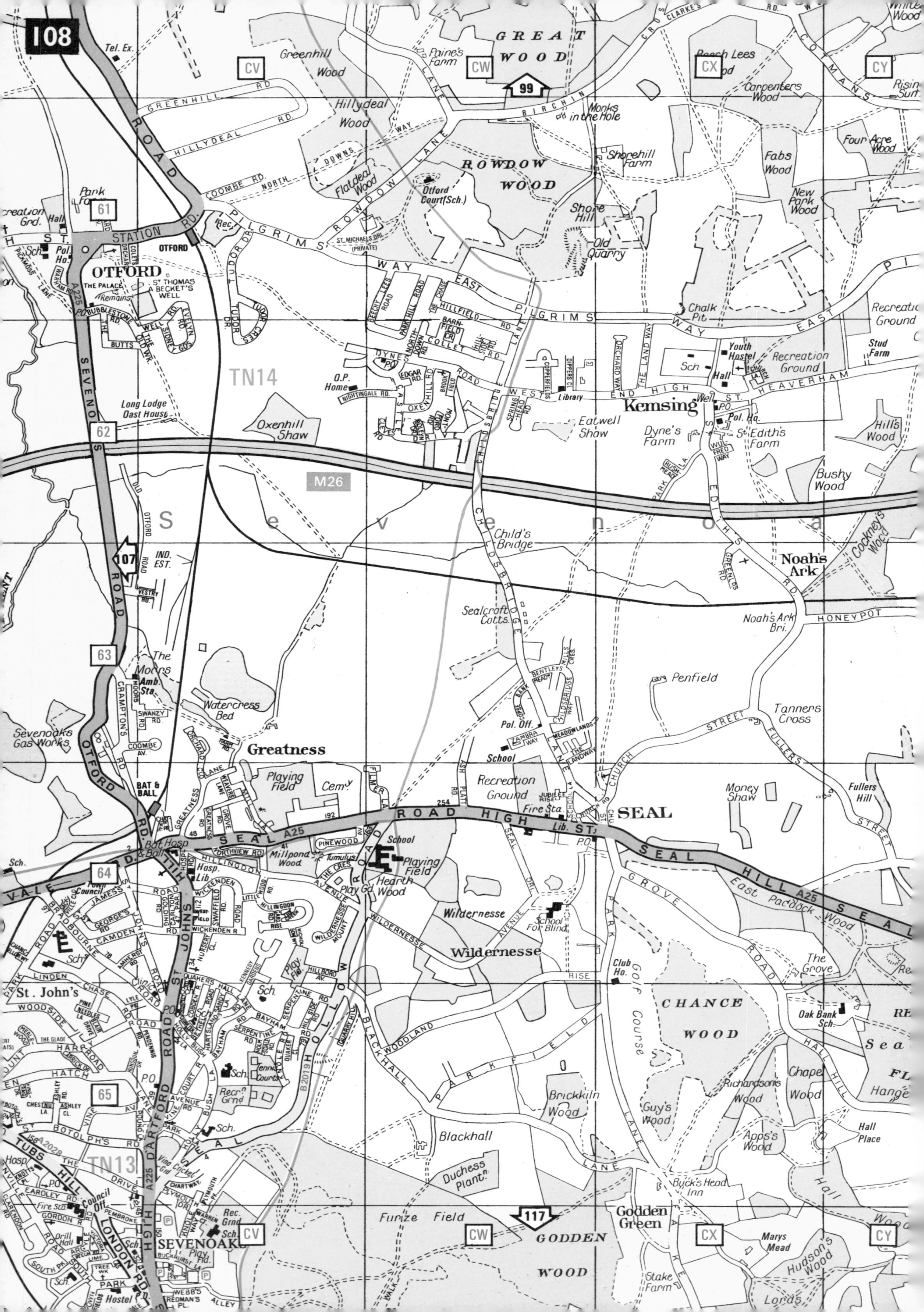
Tel. Ex.
Greenhill Wood
Paine's Farm
GREAT WOOD
Beech Lees Wood
Carpenters Wood
CV
CW
CX
CY
99
GREENHILL RD.
HILLYDEAL RD.
Hillydeal Wood
BIRCHIN
Monks in the Hole
Shorehill Farm
Fabs Wood
Four Acre Wood
DOWNS
COOMBE RD.
NORTH
Flatdeal Wood
ROWDOW LANE
Otford Court (Sch.)
ROWDOW WOOD
New Park Wood
Shore Hill
Old Quarry
Park Farm
Hall
61
STATION RD.
OTFORD
ROAD
PILGRIMS WAY EAST
TUDOR DR.
ST. MICHAELS DR.
OTFORD
THE PALACE
ST. THOMAS A BECKET'S WELL
Remains
P.O.
BUBBLESTONE RD.
THE BUTTS
EVELYN RD.
TUDOR CRES.
BEECHY LEES ROAD
PARK HILL ROAD
THE CHASE
HILLFIELD RD.
Chalk Pit
Recreation Ground
Youth Hostel
Sch.
Hall
Recreation Ground
Stud Farm
HEAVERHAM
CHURCH
Pol. Ho.
COLLET RD.
DYNES ROAD
P.O.
O.P. Home
NIGHTINGALE RD.
EDGAR RD.
OXENHILL RD.
WEST END
HIGH ST.
COPPERFIELDS
DIPPERS CL.
ORCHARD WAY
THE LAND WAY
Library
Kemsing
Well
TN14
Long Lodge Oast House
62
Oxenhill Shaw
SPRING HEAD RD.
Eatwell Shaw
Dyne's Farm
St. Edith's Farm
WULFRED WAY
Hill's Wood
Bushy Wood
M26
CHILDSBRIDGE LANE
OTFORD ROAD
SEVENOAKS ROAD
Sevenoaks
107
IND. EST.
VESTRY RD.
Child's Bridge
GREEN LDS RD.
Noah's Ark
Cockney's Wood
Sealcroft Cotts.
Noah's Ark Bri.
HONEYPOT
63
The Moors
Amb. Sta.
CRAMPTONS
SWANZY RD.
Watercress Bed
Penfield
BENTLEYS MEAD
CHILDSBRIDGE WAY
Tanners Cross
Sevenoaks Gas Works
COOMBE AV.
Greatness
Pol. Off.
ZAMBRA WAY
MEADOWLANDS
THE LANDWAY
STREET
FULLERS
BAT & BALL
Playing Field
Cem.
School
Recreation Ground
Money Shaw
Fullers Hill
Fire Sta.
JUBILEE RISE
SEAL
GREATNESS LANE
254
192
48
ROAD HIGH ST.
SEAL A25
P.O.
Lib.
Bat & Ball
Hosp.
PINEWOOD
School
Playing Field
Millpond Wood
Tumulus
HILLINGDON
THE CRES.
Hearth Wood
Play Gd.
SEAL HILL A25
GROVE ROAD
East Paddock Wood
64
VALE
Council
JAMES'S
Hosp. Lib.
WICKENDEN RD.
HILLINGDON AV.
WILDERNESSE AV.
WILDERNESSE MOUNT
Wildernesse
School For Blind
Wildernesse
The Grove
Sch.
LINDEN CHASE
St. John's
Clinic
QUAKERS HALL LANE
Sch.
Golf Course
Club Ho.
RISE
CHANCE WOOD
Oak Bank Sch.
WOODSIDE
HARRY ROAD
BAYHAM RD.
SERPENTINE RD.
HOLLOW LANE
QUARRY HILL
WOODLAND
PARKFIELD
HALL HILL
HATCH
P.O.
Sch.
Tennis Courts
Brickkiln Wood
Guy's Wood
Richardson's Wood
Chapel Wood
65
AVENUE
Recn. Grnd
B2019
BLACKHALL
Blackhall
Apps's Wood
Hall Place
Sch.
BOTOLPH'S RD.
TUBS HILL
A2028
TN13
THE DRIVE
Vine Cricket Gd.
Duchess Plantn.
LANE
Buck's Head Inn
DARTFORD ROAD
ST. JOHNS ROAD
A225
Hosp.
P.O.
EARDLEY RD.
Fire Sta.
Council Off.
GORDON RD.
Drill Hall
CHARTWAY
PLYMOUTH
Rec. Grnd
Furze Field
117
Godden Green
GODDEN WOOD
Marys Mead
Hudson's Wood
HIGH ST.
LONDON RD.
SEVENOAKS
Sch.
Sch.
SOUTH PK.
PARK
Hostel
Play Fld.
BUCKHURST LA.
WEBB'S ALLEY
REDMAN'S PL.
Stake Farm
Lords
WALK

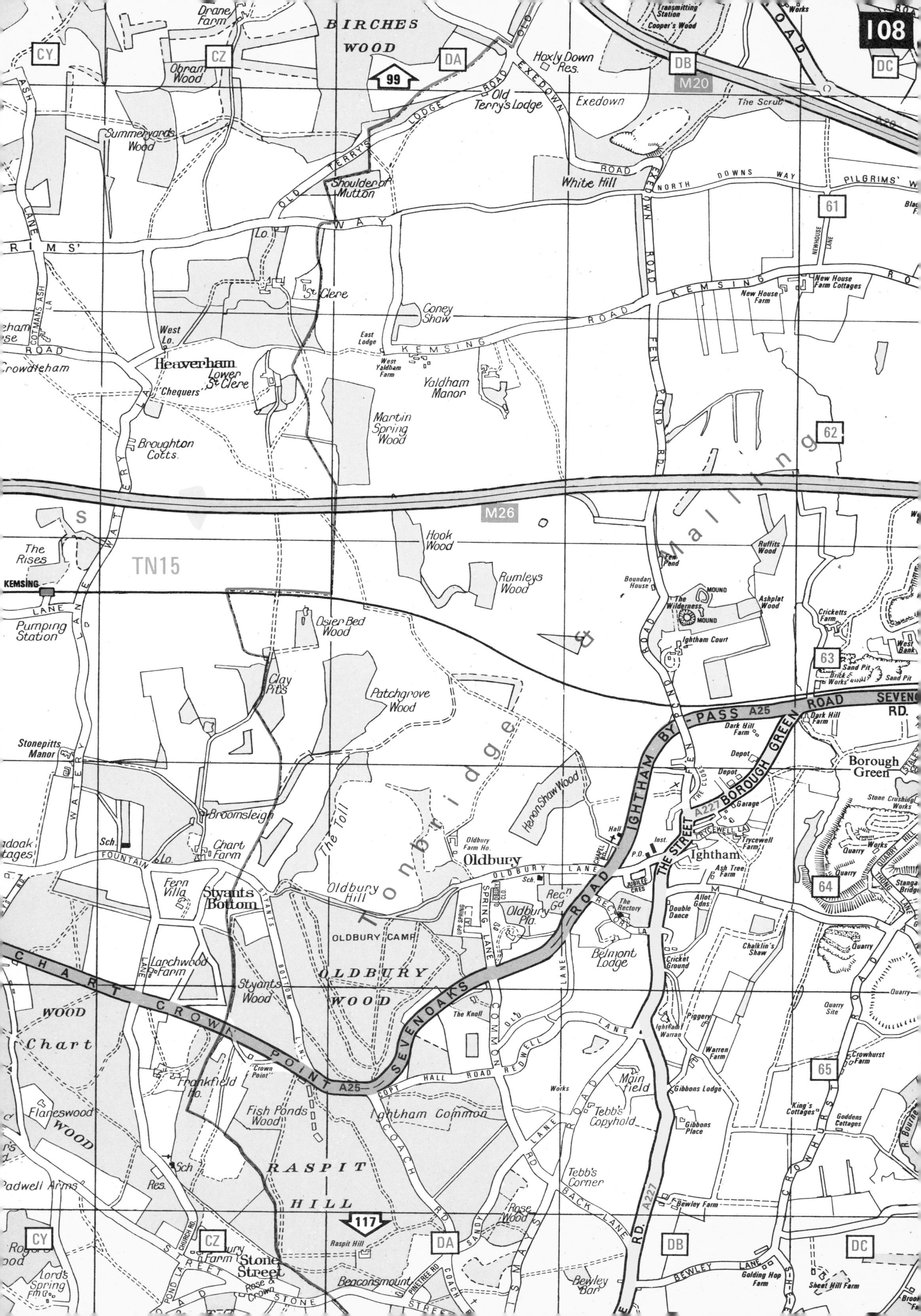
CY
CZ
DA
DB
DC
99
117
61
62
63
64
65
M20
M26
A25
A227
TN15
BIRCHES WOOD
Drane Farm
Obram Wood
Hoxly Down Res.
Transmitting Station
Cooper's Wood
Works
Exedown
The Scrub
Old Terry's Lodge
OLD TERRY'S LODGE ROAD
EXEDOWN ROAD
Summeryards Wood
Shoulder of Mutton
White Hill
WHITE HILL ROAD
NORTH DOWNS WAY
PILGRIMS' WAY
ASH LANE
Lo.
St Clere
Coney Shaw
COTMANS ASH LA
New House Farm Cottages
New House Farm
NEWHOUSE LANE
KEMSING ROAD
FEN POND RD.
West Lo.
East Lodge
West Yaldham Farm
Heaverham
Lower St Clere
Chequers
Crowdleham
Yaldham Manor
Martin Spring Wood
Broughton Cotts.
WATERY LANE
Hook Wood
Rumleys Wood
Ruffits Wood
Fen Pond
Boundary House
The Wilderness
MOUND
Ashplat Wood
Ightham Court
Cricketts Farm
West Bank
Sand Pit
Brick Works
The Rises
KEMSING
LANE
Pumping Station
Osier Bed Wood
Clay Pits
Patchgrove Wood
Tonbridge & Malling
IGHTHAM BY-PASS
BOROUGH GREEN ROAD
SEVENOAKS RD.
Dark Hill Farm
Depot
Borough Green
Stone Crushing Works
Stonepitts Manor
Broomsleigh
The Toll
Heron Shaw Wood
THE CLOSE
Garage
TRYCEWELL LA
Trycewell Farm
Hall
Inst.
P.O.
THE STREET
Ightham
Quarry
QUARRY HILL
Sch.
Chart Farm
Oldbury Farm Ho.
Oldbury
OLDBURY LANE
CHAPEL RD.
JUBILEE CRES
Ash Tree Farm
Stangate Bridge
FOUNTAIN
Fern Villa
Styants Bottom
STYANTS BOTTOM
Oldbury Hill
UPP SPRING
SPRING LANE
OLDBURY CLO.
Rec'n Gd
Oldbury Pla.
The Rectory
RECTORY LA
Double Dance
Allot. Gdns.
Chalklin's Shaw
OLDBURY CAMP
CHART CROWN POINT
SEVENOAKS ROAD
Larchwood Farm
OLDBURY WOOD
Styants Wood
Belmont Lodge
Cricket Ground
Quarry Site
WOOD
Chart
The Knoll
OLD COMMON
REDWELL LANE
Ightham Warren
Piggery
Warren Farm
Crowhurst Farm
Crown Point
Frankfield Ho.
COPT HALL ROAD
Works
Main field
Gibbons Lodge
Fish Ponds Wood
Ightham Common
COACH RD.
Tebb's Copyhold
Gibbons Place
King's Cottages
Goddens Cottages
Flaneswood
Sch
Res.
RASPIT HILL
Padwell Arms
Tebb's Corner
BACK LANE
CROWHURST
Rose Wood
Bewley Farm
Raspit Hill
SANDY
CHURCH RD.
Stone Street
Rose & Crown
STONE STREET
POND LANE
Beaconsmount
PINETREE RD
ST MARY'S RD
Bewley Bar
BEWLEY LANE
Golding Hop Farm
Sheet Hill Farm
Lord's Spring Fm

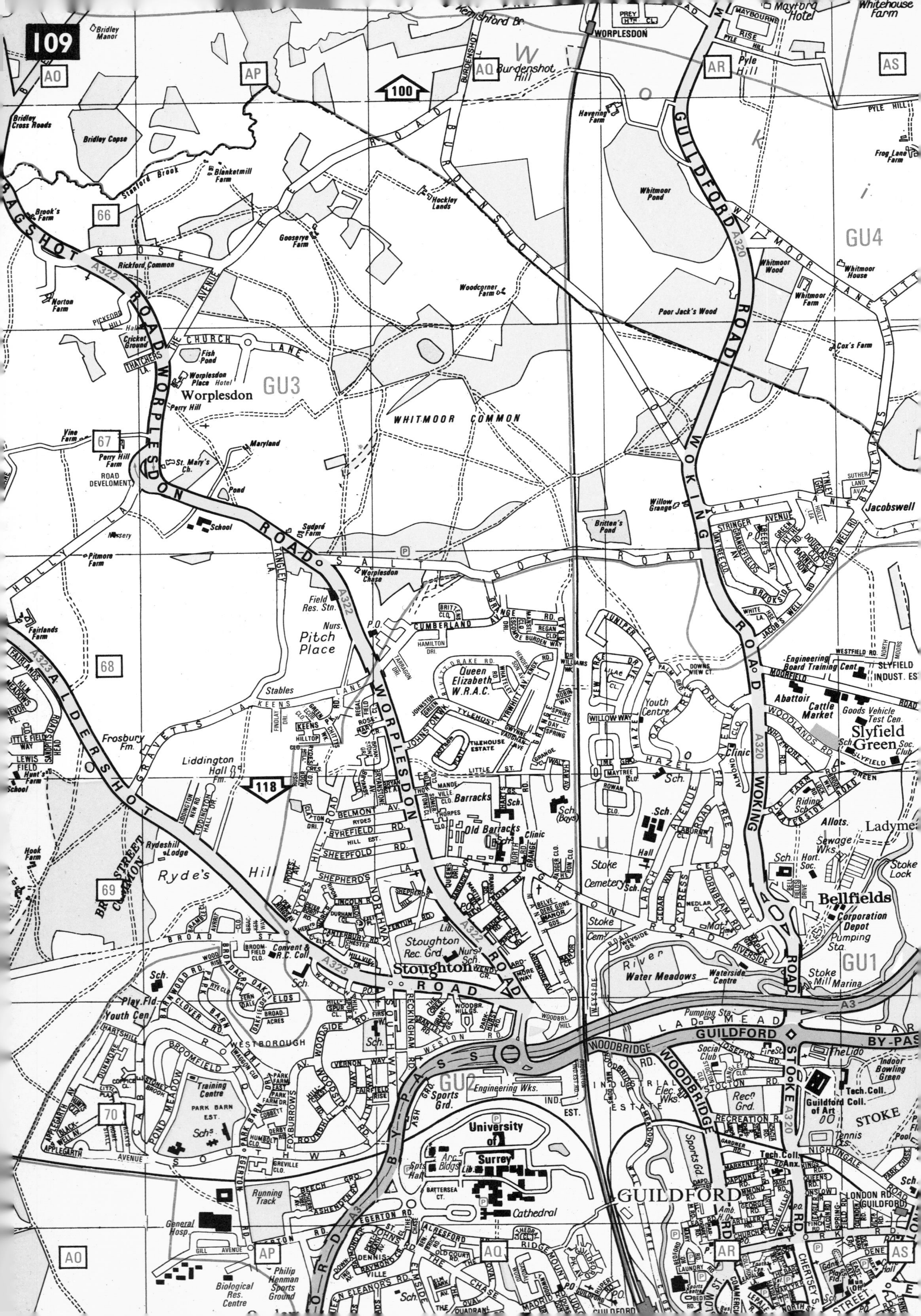
Bridley Manor
Kemishford Br.
Worplesdon
Mayford Hotel
Whitehouse Farm
AO
AP
AQ
AR
AS
100
Burdenshot Hill
Pyle Hill
Bridley Cross Roads
Bridley Copse
Stanford Brook
Blanketmill Farm
Havering Farm
Frog Lane Farm
Whitmoor Pond
Brook's Farm
66
Hockley Lands
Gooserye Farm
GU4
Goose
Rickford Common
A322
Norton Farm
Woodcorner Farm
Whitmoor Wood
Whitmoor House
Whitmoor Farm
Poor Jack's Wood
Pickford Hill
Cricket Ground
The Church Lane
Fish Pond
Cox's Farm
Thatchers La.
Worplesdon Place Hotel
Worplesdon
GU3
Perry Hill
Whitmoor Common
Vine Farm
67
Perry Hill Farm
Maryland
St. Mary's Ch.
Road Develoment
Pond
Willow Grange
Clay Lane
Jacobswell
School
Sudpré Farm
Nursery
Britten's Pond
Pitmore Farm
Holly La.
Salt Box Road
Worplesdon Chase
Field Res. Stn.
Fairlands Farm
Nurs.
P.O.
Cumberland Av.
Pitch Place
68
Queen Elizabeth W.R.A.C.
Engineering Board Training Cent.
Slyfield Indust. Est.
Stables
Keens La.
Abattoir
Cattle Market
Goods Vehicle Test Cen.
Youth Centre
Slyfield Green
Frosbury Fm.
Gravetts La.
Liddington Hall Fm.
118
Clinic
Hazel
Barracks
Old Barracks
Sch.
Riding Sch.
Allots.
Ladymead
Hook Farm
Rydeshill Lodge
Sewage Wks.
Hort. Soc.
Stoke Lock
Ryde's Hill
Stoke Cemetery
Hall
69
Broad Street Common
Bellfields
Corporation Depot
Pumping Sta.
Aldershot Road
A323
Worplesdon Road
Woking Road
A320
Guildford Road
Broad St.
Convent & R.C. Coll.
Stoughton Rec. Grd.
Nurs. Sch.
Stoughton Road
River Water Meadows
Waterside Centre
GU1
Stoke Mill
Marina
Play. Fld.
Youth Cen.
Westborough
Weston Rd.
Ladymead
Guildford By-Pass
A3
Woodbridge Rd.
Stoke Rd.
The Lido
Indoor Bowling Green
Training Centre
Park Barn Est.
GU2
Sports Grd.
Engineering Wks.
Industrial Estate
Elec. Wks.
Rec. Grd.
Tech. Coll.
Guildford Coll. of Art
Stoke
70
University of Surrey
Sports Gd.
Tennis Cts.
Pool
Applegarth Av.
Southway
Nightingale Rd.
Running Track
Libr.
Cathedral
Guildford
London Rd.
General Hosp.
Egerton Rd.
Gill Avenue
Philip Henman Sports Ground
Biological Res. Centre
Ridgemount
Chertsey St.
Dene Rd.
York Rd.

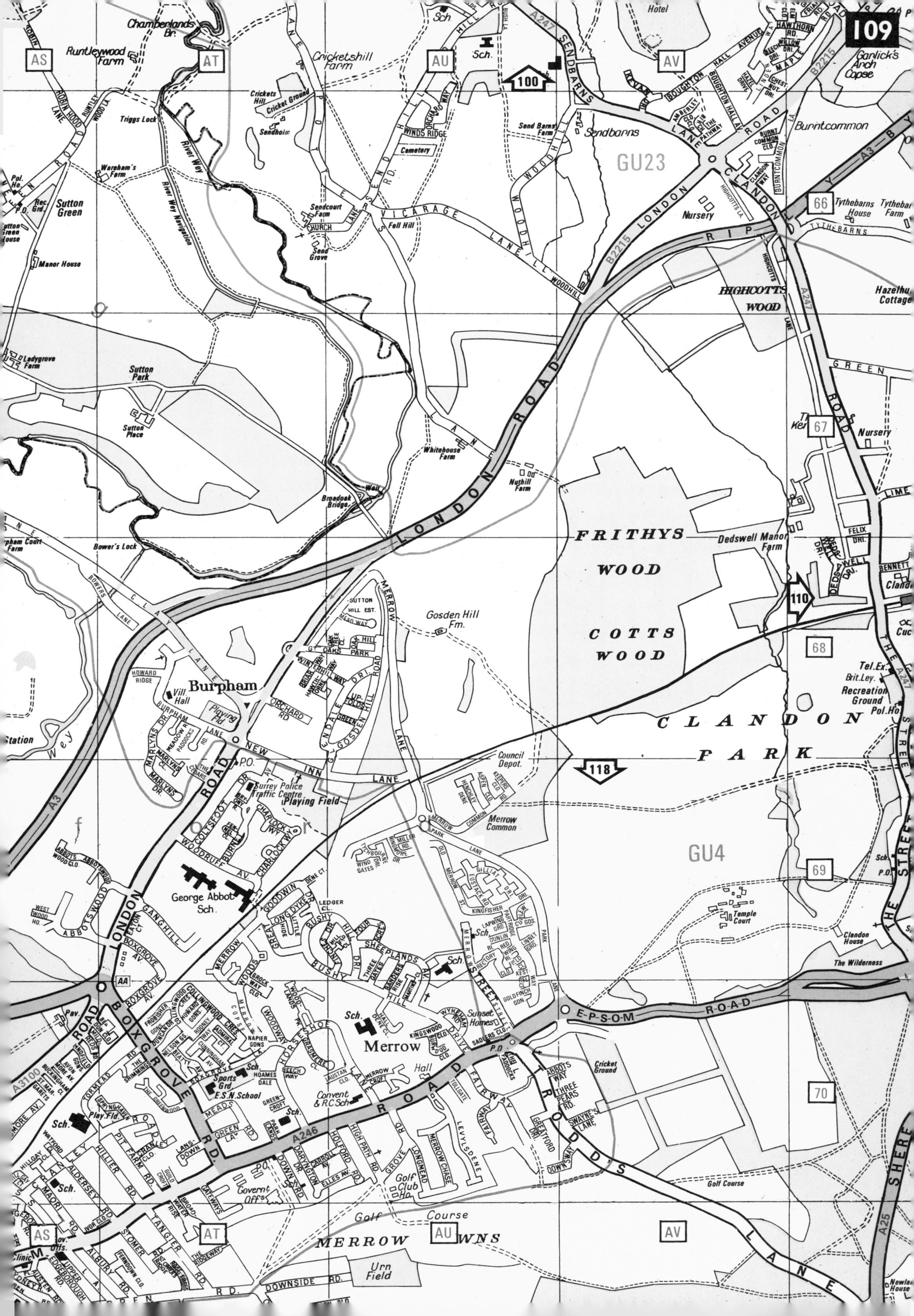
Chamberlands Br.
AS
AT
AU
AV
Runtleywood Farm
Cricketshill Farm
Sch.
Hotel
100
SENDBARNS
HAWTHORN RD.
BOUGHTON HALL AVENUE
Garlick's Arch Copse
Crickets Hill
Cricket Ground
Triggs Lock
ROBIN HOOD LANE
RUNTLEY WOOD LA.
ROAD
Sendholm
ORCHARD WAY
WINDS RIDGE
Cemetery
Send Barns Farm
Sendbarns
GU23
Burntcommon
BURNT COMMON CLO.
Wareham's Farm
River Wey
River Wey Navigation
SEND HILL
SEND RD.
VICARAGE LANE
WOODHILL
LONDON
CLANDON
Nursery
HIGHCOTTS LA.
66
Tythebarns House
TYTHEBARNS
Pol. Ho.
Rec. Grd.
Sutton Green
Manor House
Sendcourt Farm
CHURCH LANE
Fell Hill
Send Grove
B2215
RIPLEY
HIGHCOTTS WOOD
A247
Ladygrove Farm
Sutton Park
Sutton Place
Whitehouse Farm
Nuthill Farm
GREEN
ROAD
67
Nursery
LIME
Broadoak Bridge
Weir
FRITHYS WOOD
Dedswell Manor Farm
FELIX DRI.
BENNETT
Bower's Lock
BOWERS LANE
CLAY LANE
MERROW
SUTTON HILL EST.
MEAD WAY
Gosden Hill Fm.
110
COTTS WOOD
68
Tel. Ex.
Brit. Ley.
Recreation Ground
Pol. Ho.
HOWARD RIDGE
Burpham
Vill. Hall
Playing Fld.
ORCHARD RD.
GOSDEN HILL ROAD
CLANDON
PARK
Station
Wey
BURPHAM LANE
MARLYNS DR.
MEADOW RD.
NEW INN LANE
P.O.
Surrey Police Traffic Centre
Playing Field
Council Depot.
118
A3
ROAD
COLTSFOOT DR.
CHARLOCK WY.
WOODRUFF AV.
Merrow Common
GU4
ABBOTSWOOD
George Abbot Sch.
GANGHILL
LONDON
69
THE STREET
A247
Temple Court
Clandon House
The Wilderness
BOXGROVE AV.
MERROW WOODS
BUSHY HILL DRI.
SHEEPLANDS AV.
MERROW STREET
Sch.
AA
A3100
BOXGROVE ROAD
EPSOM ROAD
Sunset Homes
Merrow
KINGSWOOD
Sports Grd.
E.S.N. School
Play. Fld.
Hall
Convent & R.C. Sch.
Cricket Ground
70
A246
ROAD
Sch.
PIT FARM RD.
CRANLEY RD.
HIGH PATH RD.
GROVE RD.
LONGMEAD
MERROW CHASE
LEVYLSDENE
FAIRWAY
TRODD'S LANE
Golf Club Ho.
Govern't Offs.
Golf Course
SHERE
A25
MERROW DOWNS
Golf Course
Urn Field
DOWNSIDE RD.
EPSOM ROAD
Newlands House

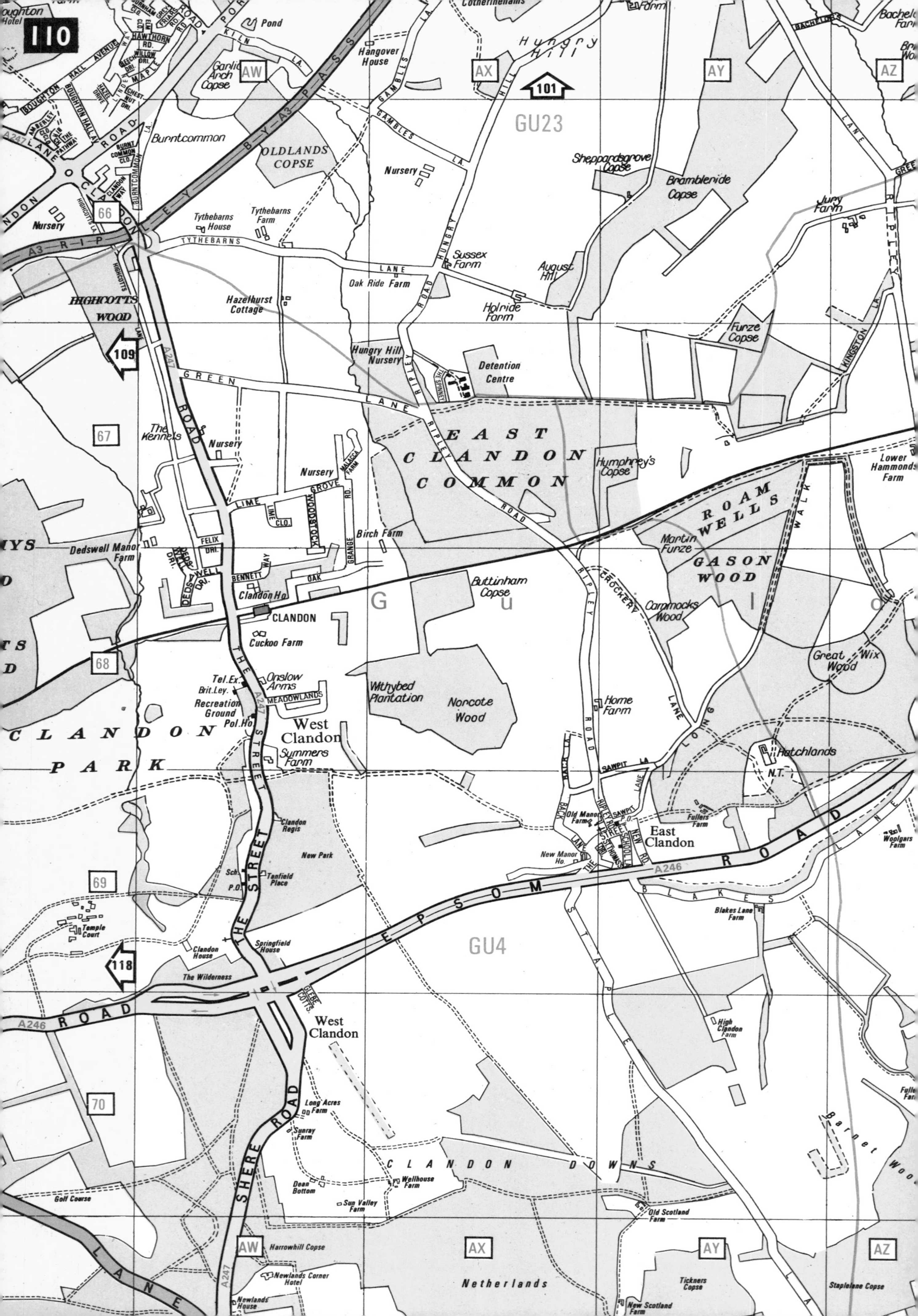

Pond
Hangover House
Hungry Hill
101
GU23
Garlic Arch Copse
Burntcommon
OLDLANDS COPSE
Nursery
Sheppardsgrove Copse
Brambleride Copse
Jury Farm
Tythebarns House
Tythebarns Farm
TYTHEBARNS LANE
Sussex Farm
August Hill
Oak Ride Farm
Holride Farm
HIGHCOTTS WOOD
Hazelhurst Cottage
Furze Copse
109
Hungry Hill Nursery
Detention Centre
GREEN LANE
RIPLEY ROAD
EAST CLANDON COMMON
The Kennels
Nursery
Lower Hammonds Farm
Humphrey's Copse
ROAM WELLS
GASON WOOD
Martin Furze
Birch Farm
Dedswell Manor Farm
Buttinham Copse
Cammocks Wood
Clandon Ho
CLANDON
Cuckoo Farm
Great Wix Wood
Tel. Ex.
Brit. Ley.
Onslow Arms
Recreation Ground
Withybed Plantation
Norcote Wood
Home Farm
Pol. Ho.
West Clandon
CLANDON PARK
Summers Farm
Hatchlands
N.T.
Clandon Regis
New Park
Old Manor Farm
Fullers Farm
East Clandon
New Manor Ho.
Woolgars Farm
Tanfield Place
EPSOM ROAD
A246
Blakes Lane Farm
Temple Court
Springfield House
Clandon House
GU4
118
The Wilderness
West Clandon
High Clandon Farm
Long Acres Farm
Sunray Farm
CLANDON DOWNS
Barnet Wood
Wellhouse Farm
Dean Bottom
Sun Valley Farm
Golf Course
Old Scotland Farm
Harrowhill Copse
Newlands Corner Hotel
Netherlands
Tickners Copse
Staplelane Copse
Newlands House
New Scotland Farm
SHERE ROAD
THE STREET

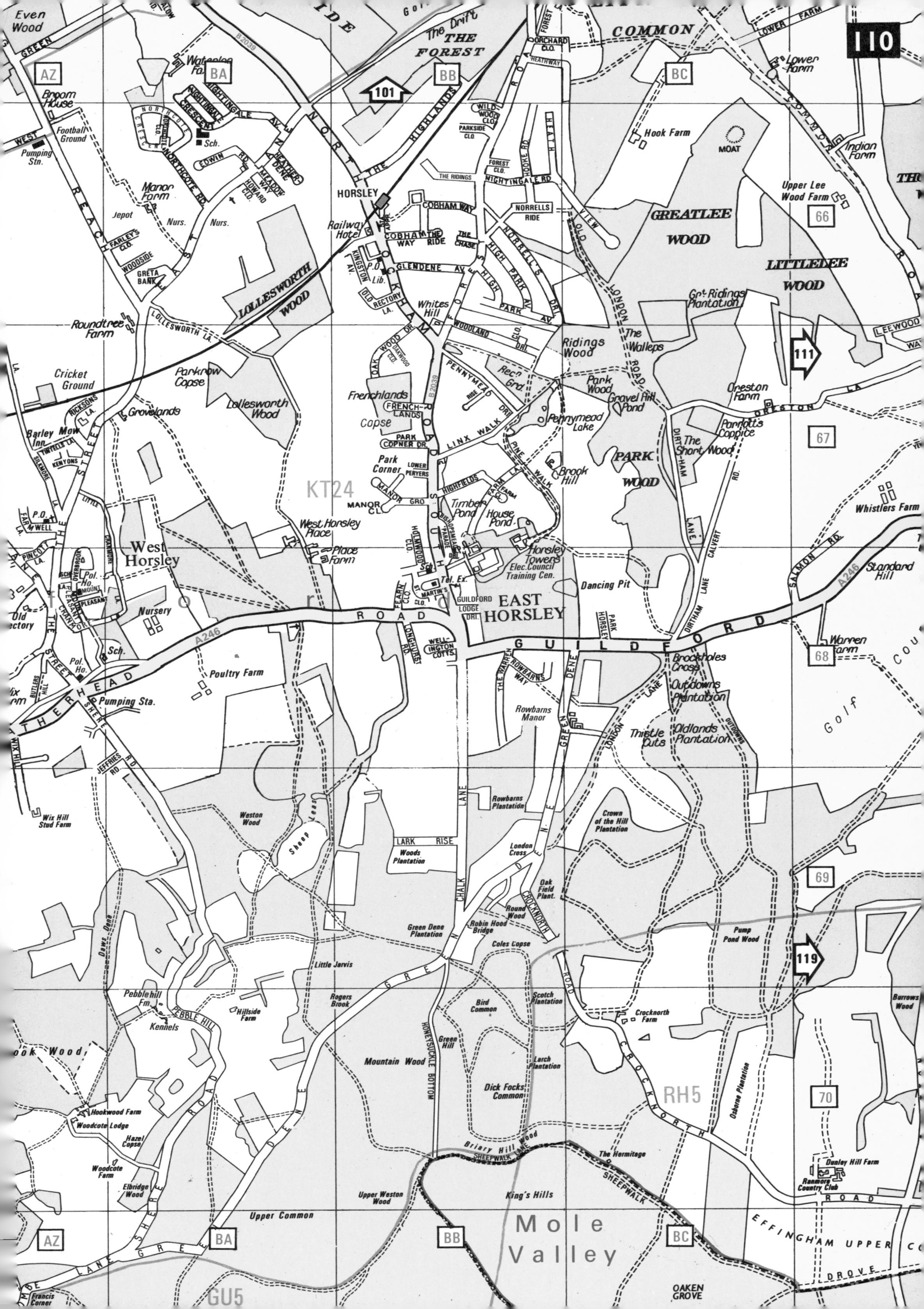
110
Even Wood
COMMON
The Drift
THE FOREST
101
AZ
BA
BB
BC
Broom House
Waterloo Farm
NIGHTINGALE AV.
NIGHTINGALE CRESCENT
NORTHCOTE CRES.
NORTHCOTE RD.
Sch.
EDWIN RD.
HEATHER DENE
MEADOW WAY
HOWARD CL.
WEST
Pumping Stn.
Football Ground
Manor Farm
Jepot
Nurs.
FARLEYS CL.
WOODSIDE
GRETA BANK
THE HIGHLANDS
HORSLEY
Railway Hotel
KINGSTON AV.
P.O.
Lib.
OLD RECTORY LA.
GLENDENE AV.
COBHAM WAY
THE RIDE
THE CHASE
THE RIDINGS
WILD WOOD CL.
PARKSIDE CL.
FOREST CL.
ORCHARD CL.
HEATHWAY
NIGHTINGALE RD.
HOOKE RD.
HEATH
NORRELLS RIDE
NORRELLS DRI.
HIGH PARK AV.
PARK AV.
Whites Hill
Hook Farm
MOAT
Lower Farm
LOWER FARM
Indian Farm
Upper Lee Wood Farm
66
GREATLEE WOOD
LITTLELEE WOOD
Grt. Ridings Plantation
LEEWOOD
LOLLESWORTH WOOD
Roundtree Farm
LOLLESWORTH LA.
Cricket Ground
Parkrow Copse
Lollesworth Wood
RICKSONS LA.
Grovelands
Barley Mow Inn
TINTELLS LA.
KENYONS
OAK WOOD DR.
OAKWOOD CL.
WOODLAND DRI.
PENNYMEAD DRI.
RISE
Recn. Grd.
Ridings Wood
The Walleps
111
Park Wood
Gravel Hill Pond
Pennymead Lake
Oreston Farm
ORESTON LA.
Parrotts Coppice
The Short Wood
DIRTHAM LANE
CALVERT RD.
67
Frenchlands Copse
FRENCHLANDS
PARK CORNER DR.
LINX WALK
PINE WALK
Brook Hill
PARK WOOD
Park Corner
LOWER PERYERS
MANOR GRO.
MANOR CL.
HIGHFIELDS
FARM CL.
Timber Pond
House Pond
KT24
Whistlers Farm
West Horsley Place
Place Farm
West Horsley
PINCOTT LA.
FARM WELL
P.O.
Pol. Ho.
Sch.
OVERBROOK
CHARMORE
LITTLE
SILKMORE
HOLMWOOD CL.
BISHOPSMEAD
PARADE
Tel. Ex.
ST. MARTIN'S CL.
FEARN CL.
GUILDFORD LODGE DRI.
Horsley Towers
Elec. Council Training Cen.
Dancing Pit
SALMON RD.
Standard Hill
A246
EAST HORSLEY
Nursery
PLEASANT
Old Rectory
ROAD
A246
PARK HORSLEY
GUILDFORD
Warren Farm
68
LONGHURST RD.
WELLINGTON COTTS.
THE WARREN
ROWBARNS WAY
Brockholes Cross
Outdowns Plantation
Poultry Farm
Pumping Sta.
THE STREET
BUTLERS HILL
OCKHAM RD.
Pol. Ho.
Sch.
SHERE
HEAD
Rowbarns Manor
GREEN DENE
LONDON LANE
Thistle Cuts
Oldlands Plantation
OUTDOWNS
Golf
WIX HILL
JEFFRIES RD.
Wix Hill Stud Farm
Weston Wood
Sheep Leas
Rowbarns Plantation
Crown of the Hill Plantation
LARK RISE
Woods Plantation
London Cross
Oak Field Plant.
69
CHALK LANE
CROCKNORTH
Round Wood
Robin Hood Bridge
Green Dene Plantation
Coles Copse
Pump Pond Wood
119
Daws Dene
Little Jarvis
Pebblehill Fm.
PEBBLE HILL
Kennels
Hillside Farm
Rogers Brook
Bird Common
Scotch Plantation
Crocknorth Farm
Burrows Wood
Mountain Wood
Green Hill
HONEYSUCKLE BOTTOM
Larch Plantation
Dick Focks Common
RH5
Osborne Plantation
70
Hookwood Farm
Woodcote Lodge
Hazel Copse
Woodcote Farm
Elbridge Wood
Briary Hill Wood
SHEEPWALK LANE
The Hermitage
Dunley Hill Farm
Ranmore Country Club
King's Hills
Upper Weston Wood
Upper Common
Mole Valley
EFFINGHAM UPPER
DROVE
GU5
OAKEN GROVE
Francis Corner

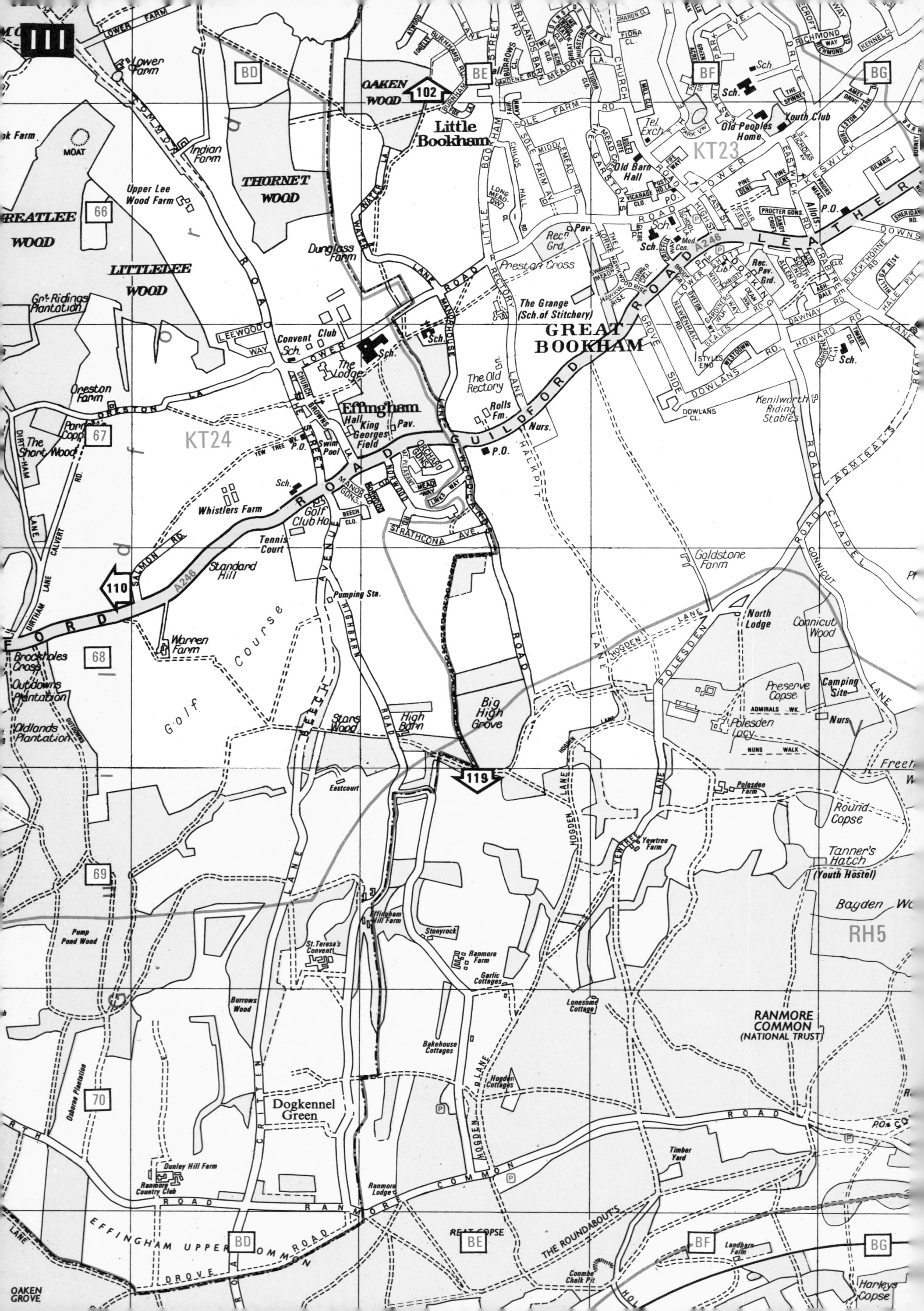

Lower Farm
Indian Farm
Upper Lee Wood Farm
THORNET WOOD
OAKEN WOOD
102
Little Bookham
GREATLEE WOOD
LITTLELEE WOOD
Gt. Ridings Plantation
Dunglass Farm
Convent Sch.
Club
The Lodge
Effingham
Hall
King Georges Field
Oreston Farm
KT24
KT23
The Short Wood
Whistlers Farm
Golf Club Ho.
Tennis Court
Standard Hill
110
Warren Farm
Brockholes Cross
Outdowns Plantation
Oldlands Plantation
Golf Course
Pumping Sta.
Stars Wood
High Barn
Big High Grove
119
Eastcourt
Old Barn Hall
Youth Club
Old Peoples Home
Preston Cross
The Grange (Sch. of Stitchery)
GREAT BOOKHAM
The Old Rectory
Rolls Fm.
Kenilworth Riding Stables
Goldstone Farm
North Lodge
Connicut Wood
Preserve Copse
Camping Site
Polesden Lacy
Polesden Farm
Round Copse
Tanner's Hatch (Youth Hostel)
Bayden Wood
RH5
Yewtree Farm
Effingham Hill Farm
Stonyrock
St. Teresa's Convent
Ranmore Farm
Garlic Cottages
Lonesome Cottage
RANMORE COMMON (NATIONAL TRUST)
Pump Pond Wood
Burrows Wood
Bakehouse Cottages
Hogden Cottages
Osborne Plantation
Dogkennel Green
Timber Yard
Dunley Hill Farm
Ranmore Country Club
Ranmore Lodge
RANMORE COMMON ROAD
EFFINGHAM UPPER COMMON ROAD
DROVE
THE ROUNDABOUTS
REAT COPSE
Coombe Chalk Pit
Landbarn Farm
Harleys Copse
OAKEN GROVE
GUILDFORD ROAD
A246

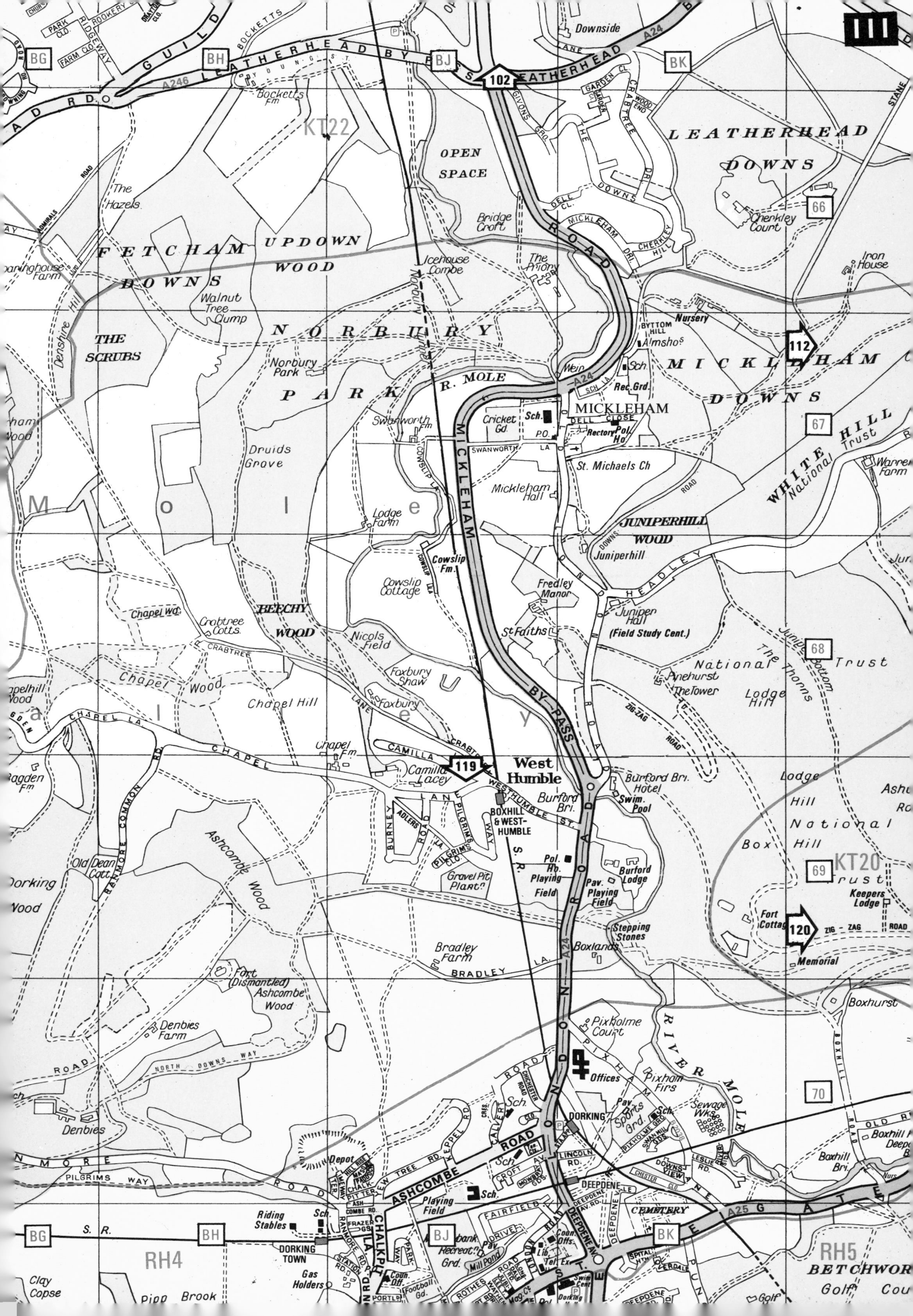
LEATHERHEAD BY PASS
GUILDFORD RD.
A246
A24
102
Downside
Bocketts Fm
KT22
OPEN SPACE
LEATHERHEAD DOWNS
Cherkley Court
66
The Hazels
Bridge Croft
FETCHAM DOWNS
UPDOWN WOOD
Icehouse Combe
The Priory
MICKLEHAM ROAD
Iron House
Walnut Tree Clump
THE SCRUBS
NORBURY PARK
Norbury Park
R. MOLE
Nursery
Almshos
112
MICKLEHAM DOWNS
MICKLEHAM
Swanworth Fm
Cricket Gd.
Rec. Grd.
Rectory
67
Druids Grave
St. Michaels Ch
Mickleham Hall
WHITE HILL
National Trust
Warren Farm
Mole Valley
Lodge Farm
JUNIPERHILL WOOD
Juniperhill
Cowslip Fm.
Cowslip Cottage
Fredley Manor
HEADLEY ROAD
Chapel Wd.
Crabtree Cotts.
BEECHY WOOD
Nicols Field
St Faiths
Juniper Hall (Field Study Cent.)
68
Chapel Wood
Chapel Hill
Foxbury Shaw
Foxbury
National Trust
Pinehurst
The Tower
Lodge Hill
ZIG-ZAG ROAD
MICKLEHAM BY-PASS
Chapel Fm.
CAMILLA
119
West Humble
Camilla Lacey
Burford Bri. Hotel
Swim. Pool
Bagden Fm
Burford Bri.
BOXHILL & WEST-HUMBLE
Box Hill National Trust
RANMORE COMMON RD.
Ashcombe Wood
Old Dean Cott.
Dorking Wood
Gravel Pit Plant.
Playing Field
Burford Lodge
69
KT20
Keepers Lodge
Fort Cottage
120
Stepping Stones
Bradley Farm
BRADLEY LA.
Boxlands
Memorial
Fort (Dismantled)
Ashcombe Wood
Boxhurst
Denbies Farm
Pixholme Court
RIVER MOLE
NORTH DOWNS WAY
Offices
Pixham Firs
70
Denbies
DORKING
Sports Grd.
Sewage Wks.
Boxhill Bri.
RANMORE ROAD
PILGRIMS WAY
Depot
ASHCOMBE ROAD
DEEPDENE
CEMETERY
A25
Riding Stables
Playing Field
BG
BH
BJ
BK
S. R.
DORKING TOWN
RH4
RH5
Clay Copse
Pipp Brook
Gas Holders
Football Gd.
Mill Pond
BETCHWORTH
Golf Course

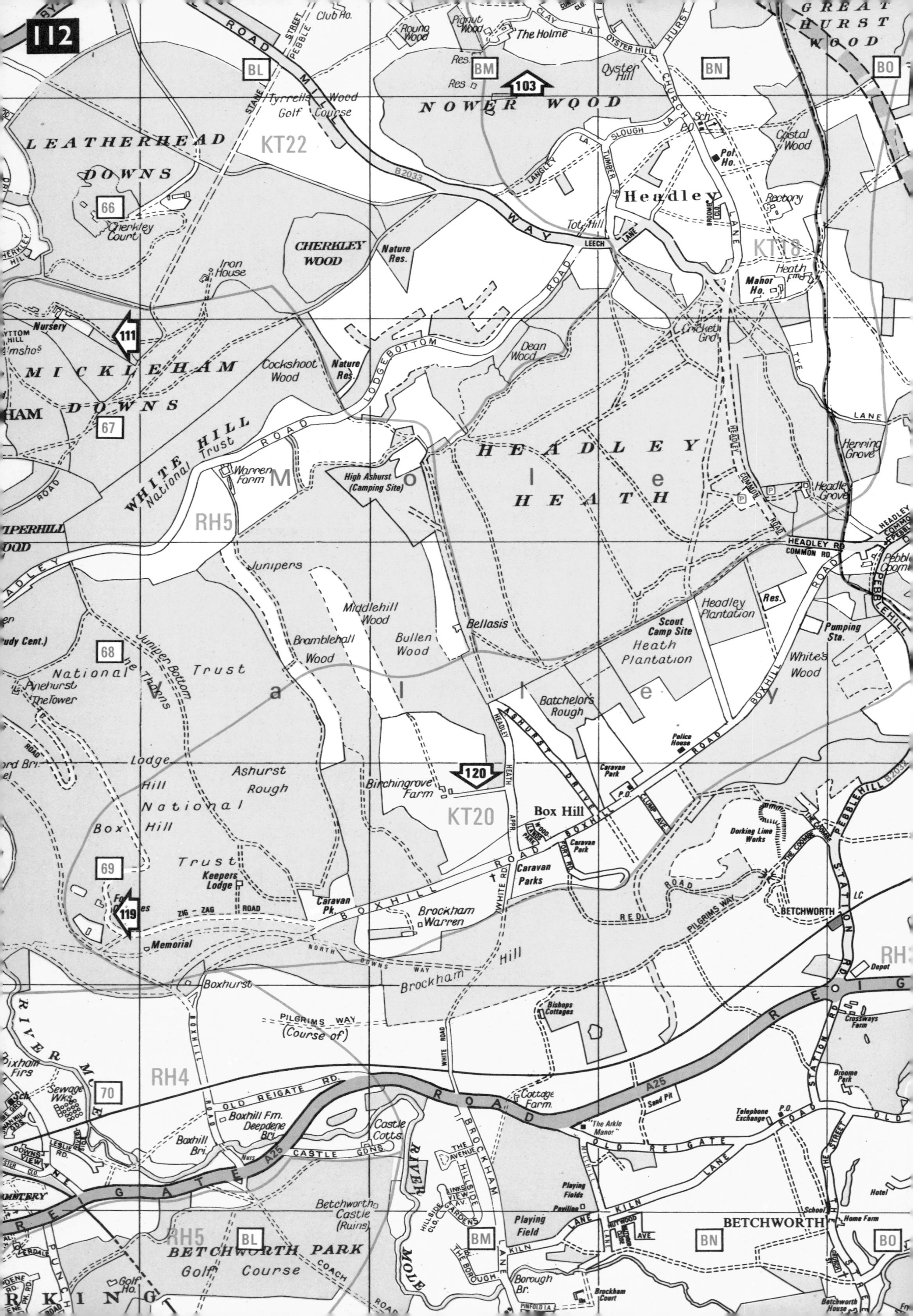
BL
BM
BN
BO
103
111
119
120
66
67
68
69
70
KT22
KT18
KT20
RH5
RH4
LEATHERHEAD DOWNS
Cherkley Court
CHERKLEY WOOD
Nature Res.
Iron House
Tyrrells Wood Golf Course
NOWER WOOD
GREAT HURST WOOD
Round Wood
Pignut Wood
The Holme
Club Ho.
Oyster Hill
Res
Castal Wood
Headley
Pol. Ho.
Rectory
Tot Hill
Manor Ho.
Heath Fm.
Cricket Grd.
B2033
MILL WAY ROAD
LEECH LANE
SLOUGH LA.
TIMBER ST.
LANGLEY LA.
CHURCH LA.
HURST LA.
OYSTER HILL
CLAY LA.
PEBBLE STREET
STANE ST.
Nursery
MICKLEHAM DOWNS
Cockshoot Wood
Nature Res.
LODGEBOTTOM
Dean Wood
WHITE HILL
National Trust
Warren Farm
High Ashurst (Camping Site)
HEADLEY HEATH
Mole Valley
HEADLEY COMMON ROAD
HEADLEY RD.
COMMON RD.
Headley Grove
Herring Grove
TYE LANE
Junipers
Middlehill Wood
Bramblehall Wood
Bullen Wood
Bellasis
Juniper Bottom
The Thatons
Headley Plantation
Scout Camp Site
Heath Plantation
Res.
Pumping Sta.
White's Wood
National Trust
Pinehurst
The Tower
Batchelor's Rough
Police House
BOXHILL ROAD
Lodge Hill
Ashurst Rough
Box Hill National Trust
Birchingrove Farm
Box Hill
Caravan Park
P.O.
ASHURST DRIVE
HEADLEY HEATH APPR.
CLUMP AVE.
Caravan Park
Caravan Parks
FORT RD.
Dorking Lime Works
THE COOMBE
PEBBLEHILL
Keepers Lodge
ZIG - ZAG ROAD
Caravan Pk.
Brockham Warren
WHITE RD.
RED ROAD
PILGRIMS WAY
BETCHWORTH
Memorial
NORTH DOWNS WAY
Brockham Hill
Boxhurst
STATION RD.
Depot
REIGATE ROAD
A25
PILGRIMS WAY (Course of)
Bishops Cottages
Crossways Farm
RIVER MOLE
Pixham Firs
Sewage Wks.
Sch.
OLD REIGATE RD.
Boxhill Fm.
Deepdene Bri.
Boxhill Bri.
Castle Cotts
Cottage Farm
Sand Pit
"The Arkle Manor"
Telephone Exchange
P.O.
Broome Park
BOXHILL RD.
LESLIE RD.
DOWNS VIEW
CASTLE GDNS.
THE AVENUE
BROCKHAM
HILLSIDE
LINKS VIEW AV.
HILLSIDE GARDENS
HILLSIDE CLO.
OLD REIGATE RD.
KILN LANE
Playing Fields
Pavilion
Playing Field
Betchworth Castle (Ruins)
BETCHWORTH PARK Golf Course
COACH ROAD
Golf Ho.
DORKING
PUNCHBOWL
THE BOROUGH
KILN LANE
Borough Br.
Brockham Court
PINFOLD LA.
HUTWOOD RD.
SCHOOL
School
Home Farm
BETCHWORTH
Hotel
THE STREET
CHURCH ST.
Betchworth House
Depot
LC

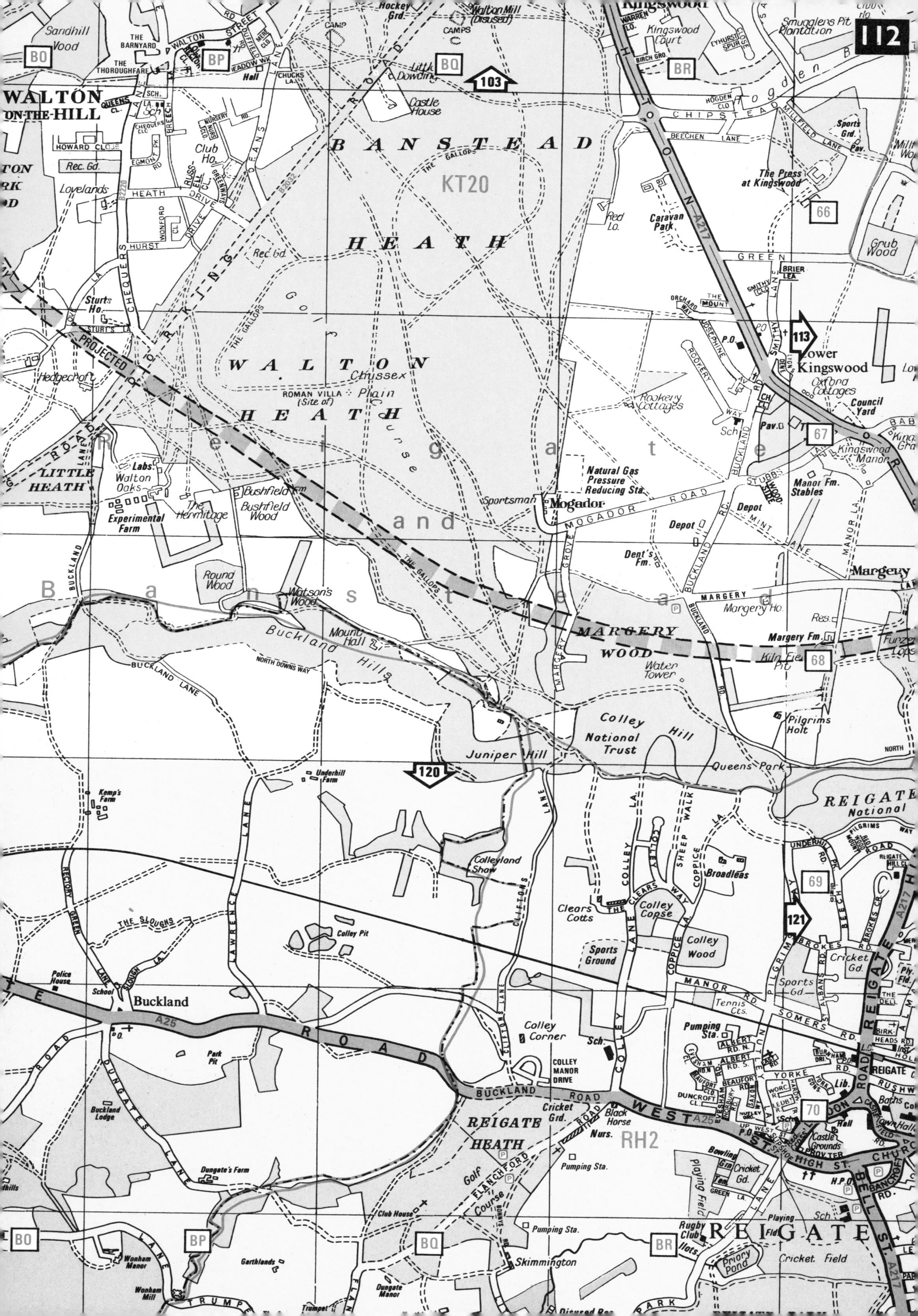
WALTON ON-THE-HILL
BANSTEAD HEATH
WALTON HEATH
KT20
Lower Kingswood
Mogador
Margery
MARGERY WOOD
Colley Hill
REIGATE HEATH
RH2
REIGATE
Buckland
103
113
120
121

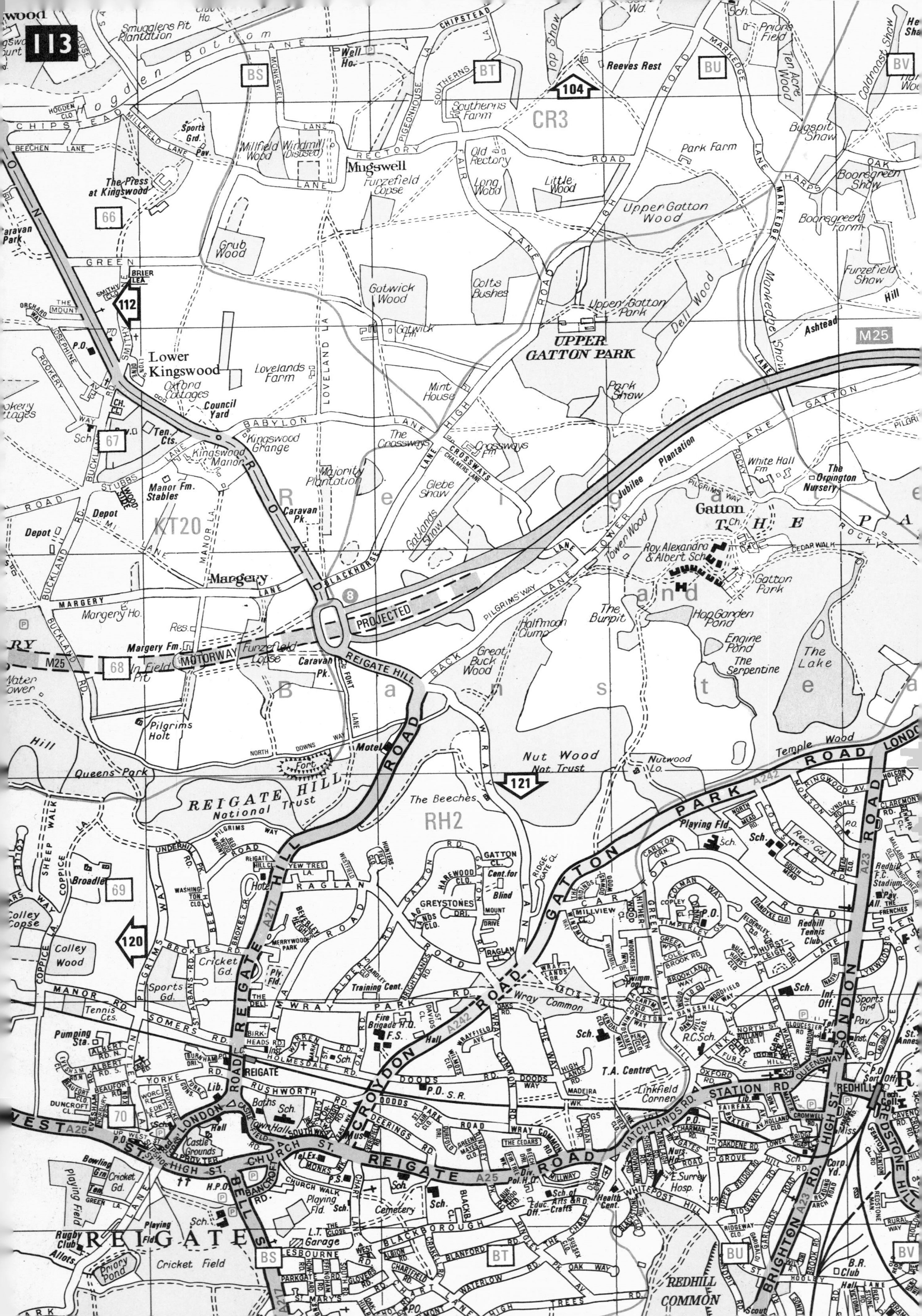
Smugglers Pit Plantation
Ogden Bottom
Chipstead Lane
Well Ho.
BS
BT
BU
BV
104
Southerns La
Top Shaw
Reeves Rest
Markedge
Priors Field
Ten Acre Wood
Coldharbour Shaw
Monkswell
Pigeonhouse La
Southerns Farm
CR3
Hogden Clo
Chipstead
Millfield Lane
Sports Grd.
Pav.
Beechen Lane
Millfield Wood
Windmill (Disused)
Rectory
Mugswell
Old Rectory
Road
Park Farm
Bugspit Shaw
Lane
Funzefield Copse
Long Wood
Little Wood
Fair Lane
The Press at Kingswood
Boorsgreen Shaw
Boorsgreen Farm
Harps Oak
66
Upper Gatton Wood
Caravan Park
Grub Wood
Green
Brier Lea
Smithy Clo
112
The Mount
Orchard Way
Gatwick Wood
Colts Bushes
Upper Gatton Park
Dell Wood
Furzefield Shaw
Hill
Monkedge Shaw
Ashtead
Gatwick Fm
Josephine
P.O.
Rookery Way
Lower Kingswood
Oxford Cottages
Lovelands Farm
Loveland La
UPPER GATTON PARK
M25
Mint House
Park Shaw
Council Yard
Babylon Lane
High Lane
Gatton
Ten. Cts.
67
Sch.
Kingswood Grange
The Crossways
Crossways Fm
Crossways
Chalmers Lane
Kingswood Manor
Stubbs
Woodside
Manor Fm. Stables
Majority Plantation
Glebe Shaw
Jubilee Plantation
White Hall Fm
The Orpington Nursery
Pilgrims Way
Road
Depot
KT20
Caravan Pk.
Gatlands Shaw
Gatton
T. Ch.
Tower Wood
Roy. Alexandra & Albert Sch
Cedar Walk
Rocky Lane
Reigate and Banstead
Buckland Rd.
Manor La.
Margery
Margery Lane
Blackhorse
Lane
Tower Lane
Gatton Park
Margery Ho.
8
Pilgrims' Way
Projected
The Burpit
Hop Garden Pond
Halfmoon Clump
Engine Pond
Res.
Margery Fm.
Motorway
Funzefield Copse
Reigate Hill
The Lake
Great Buck Wood
The Serpentine
68
In Field Pit
Caravan Pk.
Fort Lane
Back Lane
Water Tower
Pilgrims Holt
Hill
North Downs Way
Motel
Wray Lane
Temple Wood
Nut Wood
Nat. Trust
Nutwood Lo.
Road
London
Queens Park
Fort
121
Park Road
A242
Reigate Hill
REIGATE HILL National Trust
The Beeches
Ringwood Av.
Lyndale
RH2
Monson
Colesmead
Rec. Gd.
Holcon Ct.
Claremont Rd.
Playing Fld.
Sch.
Pilgrims Way
Underhill Rd.
Hunters
Gatton Cl.
Cent. for Blind
Ridgegate Cl.
Gatton Park Road
Carlton Grn.
Colman Way
South Mead
Redhill F.C. Stadium
Coppice La.
Sheep Walk
Colley Way
Broadlea
69
Yew Tree La.
Reigate Hill Cl.
Raglan
Road
Westfield
Harewood Clo.
Greystones Dri.
Mount Drive
Millview Cl.
Hotel
Washington Clo.
Beech Rd.
Brokes Cr.
Timperley Gs.
P.O.
Redhill Tennis Club
Colley Copse
Beverley Heights
Raglan
Road
120
Colley Wood
Brokes Rd.
Merrywood Park
Cricket Gd.
Woodcrest
Green Lane
Brook Rd.
Brooklands Way
Nash
Lynwood
Coppice La.
Pilgrims Way
Sports Gd.
St Albans Rd.
Ply. Fld.
Training Cent.
Brightlands Rd.
Alders
Swimm. Pool
Sch.
Inf. Off.
Sports Grd
Manor Rd.
Tennis Cts.
The Dell
Wray Park
Wray Common
Pav.
Pumping Sta.
Albert Rd. N.
Somers Rd.
Reigate Road
Birkheads Rd.
Fire Brigade H.Q.
F.S.
Hall
Wrayfield Ave
Common
The Way
Sch.
Daneshill
R.C.Sch.
North St.
Gloucester Rd.
Evesham
Albert Rd. S.
Yorke
Holmesdale
Sch.
Croydon Road
A242
Doods
P.O.
S.R.
Doods Way
Madeira
High Lands Rd.
T.A. Centre
Linkfield Corner
Oxford Rd.
Queensway
Redhill
Beaufort
Duncroft Cl.
70
Reigate
Rushworth
Lib.
Baths
Sch.
Doods Park
Deerings Rd.
Road
Station Rd.
Fairfax
Baxter
Cromwell
Tech. Coll.
West
A25
Sch.
Hall
Town Hall
South Wk.
Mus.
Wray Common
The Cedars
Hatchlands Rd.
P.O.
Charman
High St.
Castle Grounds
Church St.
Reigate Road
A25
Lower Bridge Rd.
London
Bowling Grn
Cricket Gd.
Tel. Ex.
Monks
Div. Pol. H.Q.
Millway
Nuts. Ho.
E. Surrey Hosp.
Grove
Brighton Rd.
A23
Playing Field
Green La.
H.P.O.
Bell St.
Church Walk
Chart Lane
Sch.
Health Cent.
Whitepost Hill
Ridgeway
Corp. Yd.
Sch.
Playing Fld.
Sch.
Cemetery
Blackborough
Educ. Off.
Sch. of Arts & Crafts
Reading Arch
Rugby Club
Allots.
REIGATE
Playing Fld.
L.T. Garage
Blackborough Rd.
The Chase
Ridgeway Clo.
BS
BT
BU
BV
Priory Pond
Cricket Field
Lesbourne Rd.
Blanford Rd.
Oak Way
Hooley Lane
B.R. Club
Parkgate Rd.
St. Mary's
Waterlow
Redhill Common
Scout
Chartfield Rd.

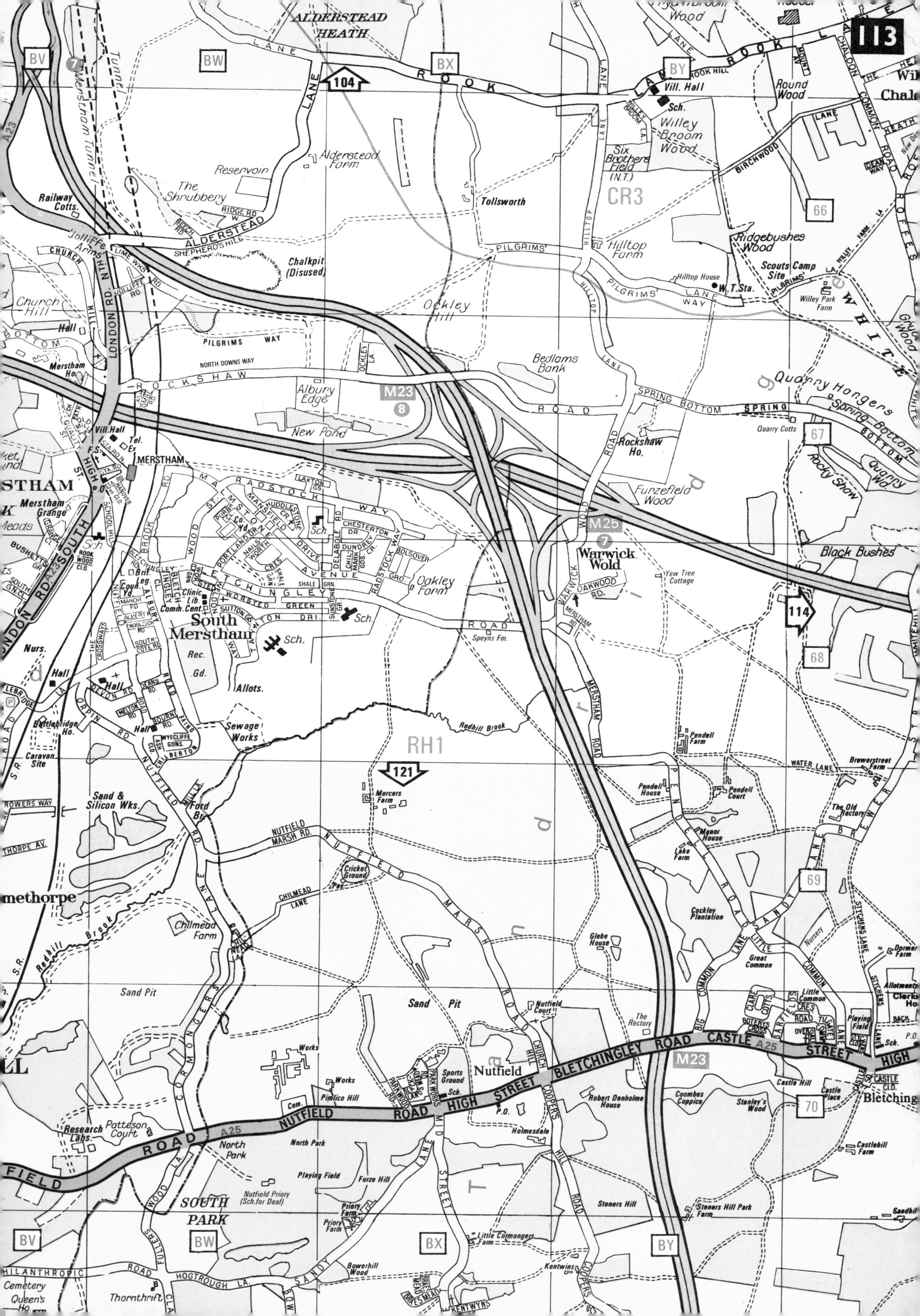
ALDERSTEAD HEATH
ROOK LANE
104
Alderstead Farm
Reservoir
The Shrubbery
Railway Cotts.
Jolliffe Arms
ALDERSTEAD
Chalkpit (Disused)
Tollsworth
Willey Broom Wood
Six Brothers Field (N.T.)
CR3
Vill. Hall
Sch.
Round Wood
Ridgebushes Wood
Hilltop Farm
PILGRIMS' WAY
Scouts Camp Site
W. T. Sta.
Ockley Hill
Church Hill
PILGRIMS WAY
NORTH DOWNS WAY
ROCKSHAW ROAD
Albury Edge
M23
New Pond
Bedlams Bank
SPRING BOTTOM ROAD
Quarry Hangers
Rockshaw Ho.
Quarry Cotts
Rocky Shaw
Funzefield Wood
MERSTHAM
Merstham Grange
M25
Warwick Wold
Yew Tree Cottage
Black Bushes
114
South Merstham
Oakley Farm
Speyns Fm.
Rec. Gd.
Allots.
Sewage Works
Redhill Brook
RH1
121
Mercers Farm
Pendell Farm
Pendell House
Pendell Court
Brewerstreet Farm
WATER LANE
The Old Rectory
Manor House
Lake Farm
Battlebridge Ho.
Caravan Site
Sand & Silicon Wks.
Ford Br.
NUTFIELD MARSH RD.
Cricket Ground
Chilmead Farm
Cockley Plantation
Glebe House
Great Common
Little Common
Nursery
Sand Pit
Nutfield Court
The Rectory
Nutfield
BLETCHINGLEY ROAD
CASTLE STREET
A25
Works
Pimlico Hill
Sports Ground
Research Labs.
Patteson Court
North Park
Robert Denholme House
Coombes Coppice
Stanley's Wood
Castle Hill
Castle Place
Bletching
Castlehill Farm
Holmesdale
Playing Field
Furze Hill
Nutfield Priory (Sch.for Deaf)
SOUTH PARK
Priory Farm
Steners Hill
Steners Hill Park Farm
Little Cormongers Farm
Kentwins
Bowerhill Wood
PHILANTHROPIC ROAD
HOGTROUGH LA.
Thornthrift
Cemetery
Queen's Ho.
BV
BW
BX
BY
66
67
68
69
70

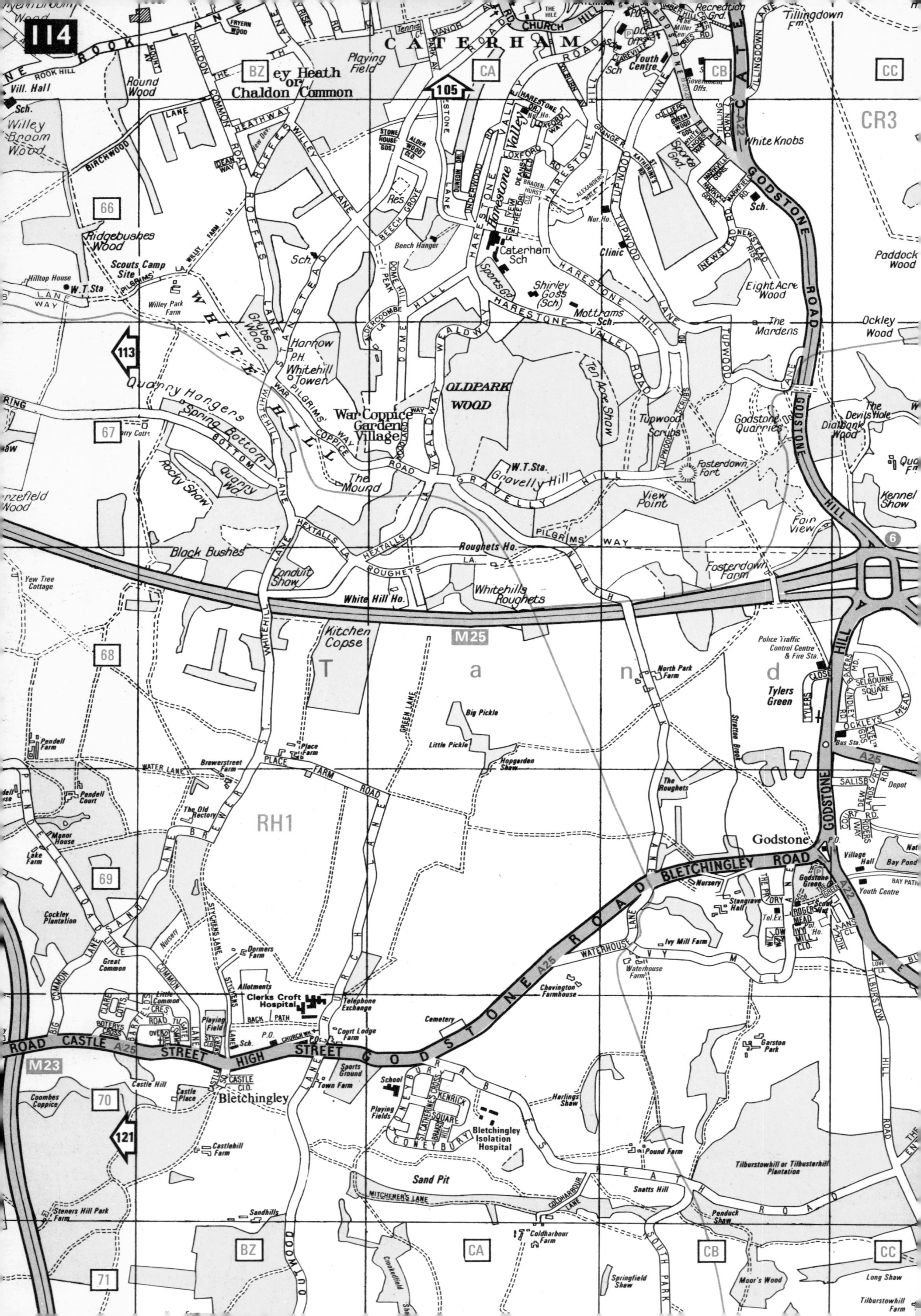
CATERHAM
ROOK LANE
ROOK HILL
Vill. Hall
Sch.
Willey Broom Wood
Round Wood
ey Heath or Chaldon Common
CHALDON COMMON ROAD
HEATHWAY
BIRCHWOOD LANE
DEAN WAY
Playing Field
Tennis Ct.
MANOR
CHURCH HILL
105
BZ
CA
CB
CC
CR3
Youth Centre
Government Offs.
Tillingdown Fm.
TILLINGDOWN LANE
White Knobs
GODSTONE ROAD
A22
66
Ridgebushes Wood
Scouts Camp Site
Hilltop House
W.T.Sta.
PILGRIMS' LA.
WILLEY FARM LA.
Willey Park Farm
WHITE HILL
Grubs Wood
ROFFES LANE
STANSTEAD ROAD
WILLEY LANE
BEECH GROVE
Res.
Beech Hanger
Sch.
HARESTONE VALLEY ROAD
Harestone Valley
LOXFORD
DEANS
BRADENHURST CLO.
ALEXANDERS
TUPWOOD LANE
GRANGER
KATHERINES
Sports Grd.
Nur. Ho.
Clinic
Caterham Sch
Sports Gd.
Shirley Goss (Sch)
Mottrams Sch.
HARESTONE HILL
NEWSTEAD RISE
Sch.
Paddock Wood
Eight Acre Wood
The Mardens
Ockley Wood
113
Quarry Hangers
Harrow P.H.
Whitehill Tower
ALDERCOMBE LA.
DOME HILL
PEAK
WEALDWAY
OLDPARK WOOD
Ten Acre Shaw
Tupwood Scrubs
TUPWOOD SCRUBS
Godstone Quarries
The Devils Hole
Dialbank Wood
67
Spring Bottom
BOTTOM
Rocky Shaw
Quarry Wd.
War Coppice Garden Village
WAR COPPICE ROAD
WOODLANDS WAY
The Mound
W.T.Sta.
Gravelly Hill
View Point
Fosterdown Fort
Kennel Shaw
Fair View
6
Black Bushes
Yew Tree Cottage
HEXTALLS LA.
Roughets Ho.
ROUGHETS LA.
PILGRIMS' WAY
NORTH PARK LANE
Conduit Shaw
White Hill Ho.
Whitehills Roughets
Fosterdown Farm
M25
Kitchen Copse
68
T a n d
North Park Farm
Police Traffic Control Centre & Fire Sta.
Tylers Green
TYLERS CLOSE
SELBOURNE SQUARE
OCKLEYS MEAD
Bus Sta.
Big Pickle
Little Pickle
Hopgarden Shaw
GREEN LANE
Place Farm
PLACE FARM ROAD
Brewerstreet Farm
WATER LANE
Pendell Farm
Pendell Court
The Old Rectory
BREWER ST.
RH1
The Roughets
Stratton Brook
A25
SALISBURY RD.
Depot
COURT
DEW LANDS
RIDERS
Godstone
P.O.
Village Hall
Bay Pond
BAY PATH
Youth Centre
Manor House
Lake Farm
69
BLETCHINGLEY ROAD
Nursery
THE PRIORY
Stangrave Hall
Tel.Ex.
Godstone Green
Scout Hut
Pol. Ho.
HICKMANS CL.
IVY MILL CLO.
Cockley Plantation
SANDY LANE
STYCHENS LANE
Nursery
Ivy Mill Farm
WATERHOUSE LANE
Waterhouse Farm
Great Common
LITTLE COMMON LANE
Dormers Farm
Allotments
Clerks Croft Hospital
Telephone Exchange
Chevington Farmhouse
LOVE LA.
TILBURSTOW HILL ROAD
BIG COMMON LANE
Little Common
CRES.
ROAD
Playing Field
BACK PATH
Cemetery
Court Lodge Farm
Garston Park
ROAD CASTLE STREET
HIGH STREET
GODSTONE ROAD
CHURCH WK.
P.O.
Sch.
M23
Castle Hill
Castle Place
CASTLE CLO.
Bletchingley
Sports Ground
Town Farm
School
CONEYBURY
KENRICK SQUARE
ST. CATHERINES CROSS
Playing Fields
Bletchingley Isolation Hospital
Harlings Shaw
70
Coombes Coppice
121
Castlehill Farm
Sand Pit
Pound Farm
Tilburstowhill or Tilbusterhill Plantation
MITCHENER'S LANE
COLDHARBOUR LANE
Snatts Hill
HEATH ROAD
Steners Hill Park Farm
Sandhills
Penduck Shaw
OUTWOOD
Coldharbour Farm
SOUTH PARK
71
Crookedfield
Springfield Shaw
Moor's Wood
Long Shaw
Tilburstowhill Farm

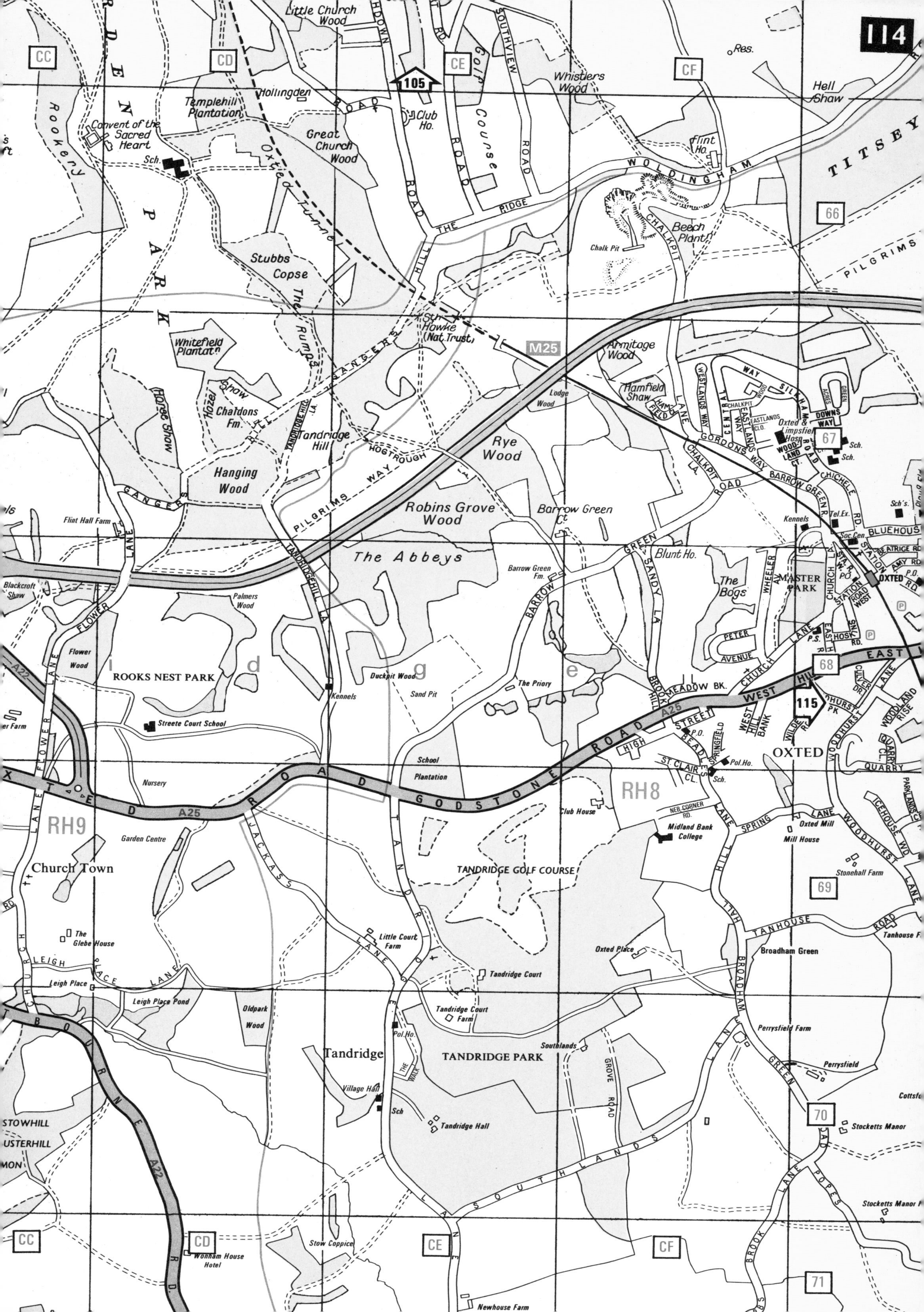

Little Church Wood
Templehill Plantation
Hollingden
Convent of the Sacred Heart
Great Church Wood
Oxted Tunnel
Club Ho.
Golf Course
Whistlers Wood
Hell Shaw
Flint Ho.
WOLDINGHAM
TITSEY
THE RIDGE
Beech Plant.
Chalk Pit
Stubbs Copse
The Rumps
St. Hawke (Nat. Trust)
M25
Armitage Wood
Hamfield Shaw
Whitefield Plantat.n
Chaldons Fm.
Hanging Wood
Tandridge Hill
Rye Wood
Robins Grove Wood
Barrow Green Ct.
PILGRIMS WAY
The Abbeys
Blunt Ho.
The Bogs
MASTER PARK
OXTED
Barrow Green Fm.
Palmers Wood
ROOKS NEST PARK
Duckpit Wood
Sand Pit
The Priory
Kennels
Streete Court School
School Plantation
Nursery
GODSTONE ROAD
A25
RH8
RH9
Garden Centre
Church Town
Club House
Midland Bank College
TANDRIDGE GOLF COURSE
Oxted Mill
Mill House
Stonehall Farm
The Glebe House
Little Court Farm
Oxted Place
Broadham Green
Tandridge Court
Leigh Place
Leigh Place Pond
Oldpark Wood
Tandridge Court Farm
Tandridge
TANDRIDGE PARK
Southlands
Perrysfield Farm
Perrysfield
Village Hall
Tandridge Hall
Stocketts Manor
STOWHILL
Stow Coppice
Wonham House Hotel
Newhouse Farm
A22
105
115
CC
CD
CE
CF
66
67
68
69
70
71

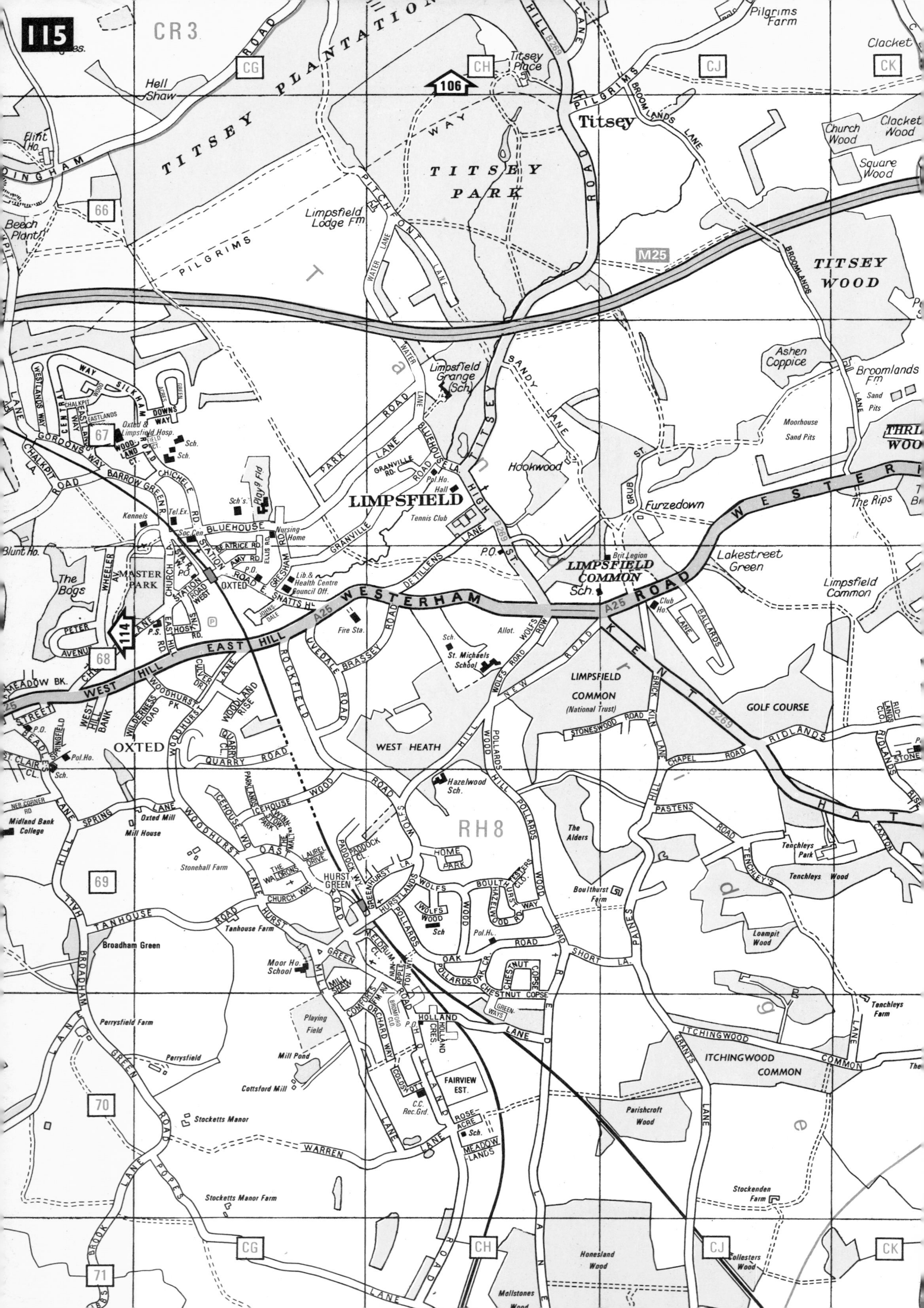
CR3
CG
CH
CJ
CK
106
114
66
67
68
69
70
71
Hell Shaw
TITSEY PLANTATION
Flint Ho.
Beech Plantn
Titsey Place
Pilgrims Farm
Clacket
Titsey
PILGRIMS
BROOMLANDS LANE
Church Wood
Clacket Wood
Square Wood
TITSEY PARK
PILGRIMS WAY
Limpsfield Lodge Fm
PITCHFONT LANE
WATER LANE
M25
TITSEY WOOD
BROOMLANDS
Ashen Coppice
Broomlands Fm
Sand Pits
Moorhouse Sand Pits
Limpsfield Grange (Sch)
SANDY LANE
Hookwood
Furzedown
GRUB ST.
The Rips
WESTERHAM ROAD
Lakestreet Green
Limpsfield Common
LIMPSFIELD
Tennis Club
Pol.Ho.
Hall
GRANVILLE RD.
PARK LANE
PARK ROAD
BLUEHOUSE LA.
HIGH ST.
TITSEY HILL
Brit Legion
LIMPSFIELD COMMON
Sch.
P.O.
Club Ho.
BALLARDS LANE
A25
B269
WESTLANDS WAY
CENTRAL WAY
CHALKPIT WOOD
EASTLANDS
SILKHAM WAY
DOWNS WAY
Oxted & Limpsfield Hosp.
GORDONS WAY
CHALKPIT LA.
BARROW GREEN RD.
CHICHELE RD.
Play'g Fld
Sch's.
Kennels
Tel.Ex.
Soc.Cen.
BLUEHOUSE
Nursing Home
BEATRICE RD.
AMY RD.
ELLIS RD.
GRESHAM RD.
GRANVILLE
DETILLENS LANE
Blunt Ho.
The Bogs
WHEELER AV.
MASTER PARK
CHURCH LA.
STATION ROAD WEST
STATION ROAD EAST
OXTED
Lib. & Health Centre
Council Off.
SNATTS HL.
JOHNS DALE
Fire Sta.
Allot.
WOLFS ROW
NEW ROAD
PETER AVENUE
P.S.
EAST HILL
HOSKINS RD.
EAST HILL
WEST HILL
MEADOW BK.
CULVER DR.
WOODLAND RISE
UVEDALE ROAD
BRASSEY ROAD
ROCKFIELD ROAD
Sch.
St. Michaels School
WOLFS ROAD
LIMPSFIELD COMMON (National Trust)
STONESWOOD ROAD
BRICK KILN LANE
KENT HATCH
GOLF COURSE
RIDLANDS
RIDLANDS LANE
CHAPEL ROAD
STREET
BEADLES
SPRINGFIELD
WEST HILL BANK
WILDERNESS ROAD
WOODHURST PK
WOODHURST
QUARRY CL.
QUARRY ROAD
OXTED
Pol.Ho.
ST. CLAIRS CL.
Sch.
WEST HEATH
Hazelwood Sch.
WOLFS HILL
POLLARDS WOOD HILL
POLLARDS HILL
PASTENS ROAD
The Alders
RH8
Tenchleys Park
TENCHLEY'S LANE
Tenchleys Wood
CAXTON
NEB CORNER RD
Midland Bank College
SPRING LANE
Oxted Mill
Mill House
ICEHOUSE WD.
ICEHOUSE WOOD
PARKLANDS
WOODHURST LANE
Stonehall Farm
OAST
THE MALTINGS
LAUREL DRIVE
PADDOCK CL.
PADDOCK WY.
HURST GREEN
HOME PARK
THE WALDRONS
CHURCH WAY
GREENHURST LA.
HURSTLANDS
WOLFS WOOD
Sch
BOULTHURST WAY
HAZELWOOD RD.
HESTERS CLO.
Boulthurst Farm
PAINES HILL
Loampit Wood
HILL
TANHOUSE ROAD
Tanhouse Farm
HURST ROAD
Broadham Green
Moor Ho. School
MILL LANE
GREEN
MELDRUM CL.
POLLARDS
OAK ROAD
POLLARDS OAK CR.
CHESTNUT COPSE
SHORT LA.
RED LANE
MILL SHAW
COMFORTS FM AV.
ORCHARD WAY
BROMFORD CLO.
HOLLAND ROAD
HOLLAND CRES.
GREEN WAYS
LANE
Tenchleys Farm
Playing Field
BROADHAM GREEN ROAD
Perrysfield Farm
Perrysfield
Mill Pond
P.O.
COLDSHOTT
FAIRVIEW EST.
ITCHINGWOOD COMMON
ITCHINGWOOD COMMON LANE
GRANTS LANE
Cottsford Mill
C.C. Rec.Grd.
Parishcroft Wood
ROSE ACRE
Sch.
MEADOW LANDS
Stocketts Manor
WARREN LANE
POPES LANE
BROOK LANE
Stocketts Manor Farm
Stockenden Farm
Honesland Wood
Collesters Wood
Mollstones Wood
THRL WOO

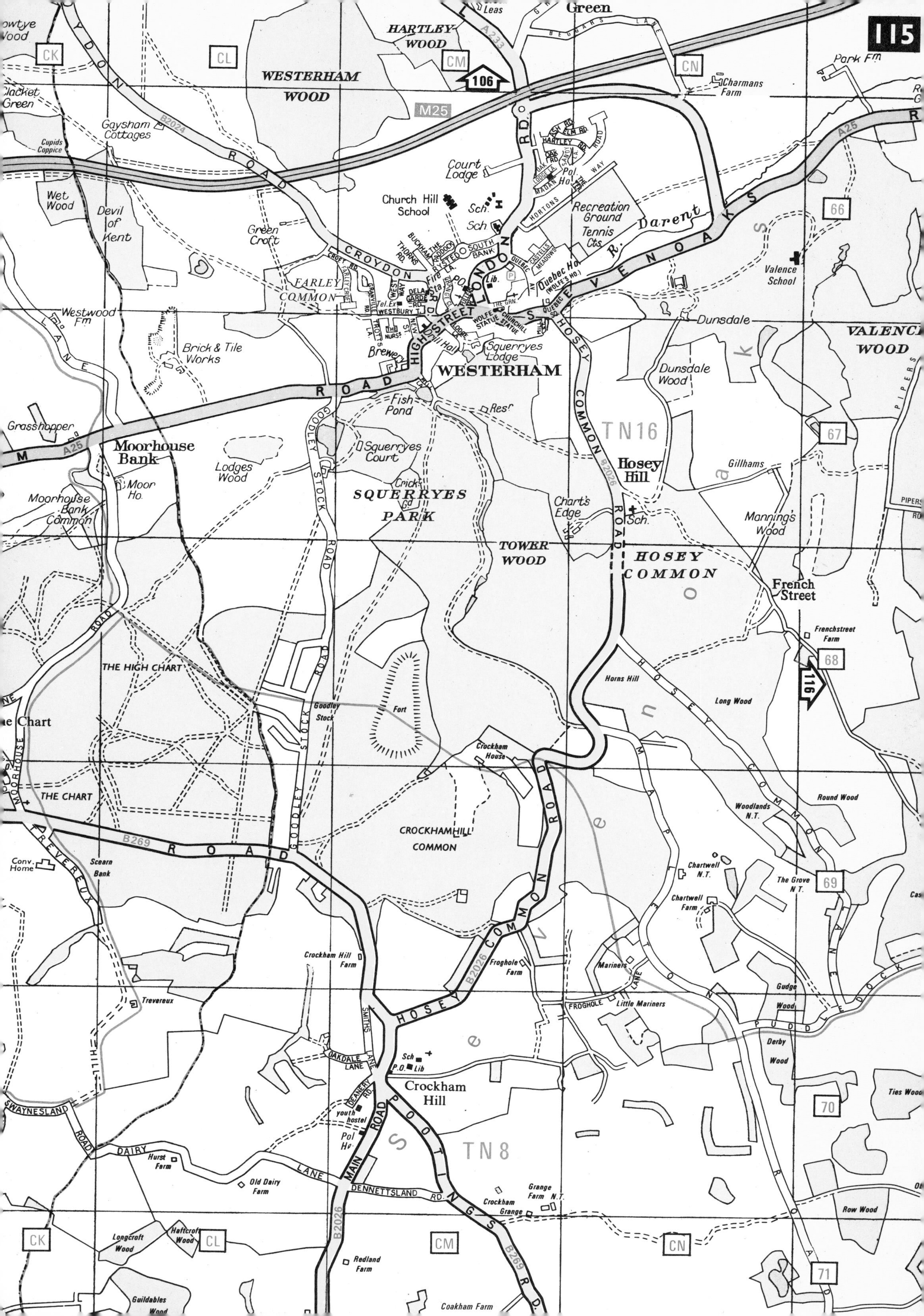
WESTERHAM
WESTERHAM WOOD
HARTLEY WOOD
M25
A25
106
116
TN16
TN8
SQUERRYES PARK
TOWER WOOD
HOSEY COMMON
CROCKHAM HILL COMMON
THE HIGH CHART
THE CHART
Moorhouse Bank
Moorhouse Bank Common
Hosey Hill
French Street
Crockham Hill
VALENCE WOOD
Valence School
Church Hill School
Court Lodge
Recreation Ground
Squerryes Court
Squerryes Lodge
Lodges Wood
Brick & Tile Works
Westwood Fm
Gaysham Cottages
Wet Wood
Devil of Kent
Green Croft
FARLEY COMMON
Dunsdale
Dunsdale Wood
Chart's Edge
Manning's Wood
Gillhams
Frenchstreet Farm
Horns Hill
Long Wood
Crockham House
Fort
Goodley Stock
Woodlands N.T.
Round Wood
Chartwell N.T.
Chartwell Farm
The Grove N.T.
Mariners
Little Mariners
Froghole Farm
Crockham Hill Farm
Gudge Wood
Derby Wood
Ties Wood
Row Wood
Grange Farm N.T.
Crockham Grange
Old Dairy Farm
Hurst Farm
Longcroft Wood
Haftcroft Wood
Guildables Wood
Redland Farm
Coakham Farm
Trevereux
Scearn Bank
Conv. Home
Grasshopper
Charmans Farm
Park Fm
Clacket Green
Cupids Coppice
Fish Pond
CROYDON ROAD
LONDON RD.
HIGH STREET
SEVENOAKS RD.
HOSEY COMMON ROAD
GOODLEY STOCK ROAD
MAIN ROAD
POOTINGS RD.
DAIRY LANE
DENNETTSLAND RD.
SWAYNESLAND ROAD
FREVEREUX HILL
MOORHOUSE RD.
PUDDEDOCK LANE
MAPLETON RD.
SMITHS LANE
OAKDALE LANE
DEANERY RD.
FROGHOLE LANE
B2024
B2026
B269
A233
66
67
68
69
70
71
CK
CL
CM
CN

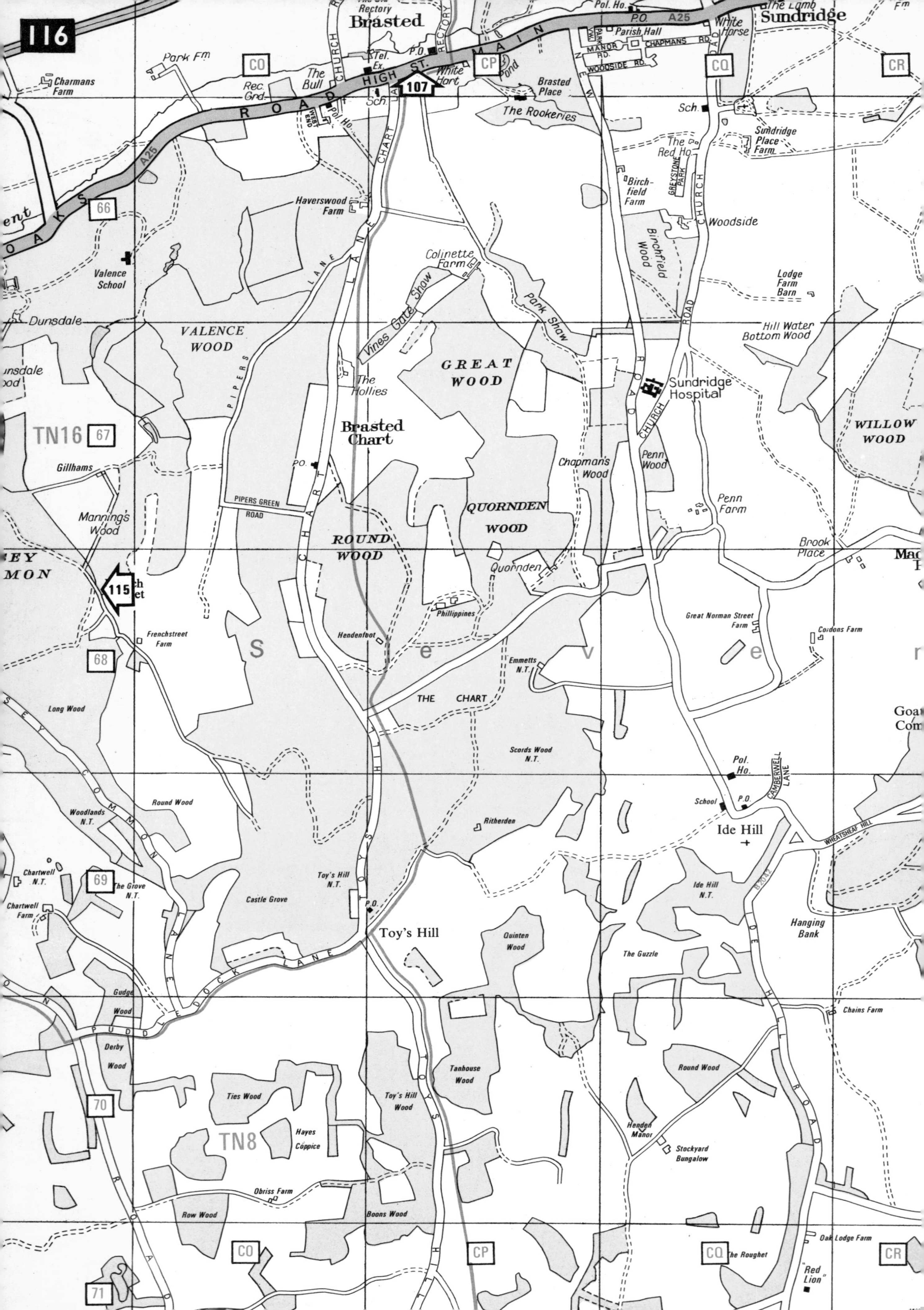

116
Brasted
Rectory
Pol. Ho.
The Lamb
Sundridge
Fm
P.O.
A25
White Horse
Parish Hall
CHAPMANS RD.
MANOR RD.
WOODSIDE RD.
Park Fm
Charmans Farm
CO
CP
CQ
CR
Tel. Ex.
The Bull
Rec. Grd.
CHURCH
RECTORY
MAIN
HIGH ST.
ROAD
White Hart
107
Pond
Brasted Place
The Rookeries
Sch.
Pol. Ho.
WEST END
CHART
Sundridge Place Farm
The Red Ho.
GREYSTONE PARK
Birch-field Farm
Birchfield Wood
Woodside
OAKS
66
Haverswood Farm
LANE
Colinette Farm
Valence School
Dunsdale
Vines Gate Shaw
Park Shaw
Lodge Farm Barn
VALENCE WOOD
Hill Water Bottom Wood
GREAT WOOD
PIPERS
The Hollies
Sundridge Hospital
WILLOW WOOD
TN16
67
Brasted Chart
Chapman's Wood
Penn Wood
Gillhams
P.O.
PIPERS GREEN ROAD
QUORNDEN WOOD
Penn Farm
Manning's Wood
ROUND WOOD
Brook Place
Quornden
115
Phillippines
Frenchstreet Farm
Hendenfoot
Great Norman Street Farm
Cordons Farm
68
Emmetts N.T.
THE CHART
Long Wood
Scords Wood N.T.
Pol. Ho.
CAMBERWELL LANE
Round Wood
School
P.O.
Woodlands N.T.
Ritherden
Ide Hill
WHEATSHEAF HILL
Chartwell N.T.
69
The Grove N.T.
Toy's Hill N.T.
Ide Hill N.T.
B2042
Chartwell Farm
Castle Grove
TOYS HILL
Hanging Bank
Toy's Hill
Quinten Wood
The Guzzle
DOCK LANE
Gudge Wood
Chains Farm
PUDDLEDOCK
Derby Wood
Tanhouse Wood
Round Wood
Ties Wood
Toy's Hill Wood
70
Hayes Coppice
TN8
Henden Manor
Stockyard Bungalow
Obriss Farm
Row Wood
Boons Wood
IDE HILL ROAD
Oak Lodge Farm
The Roughet
"Red Lion"
71

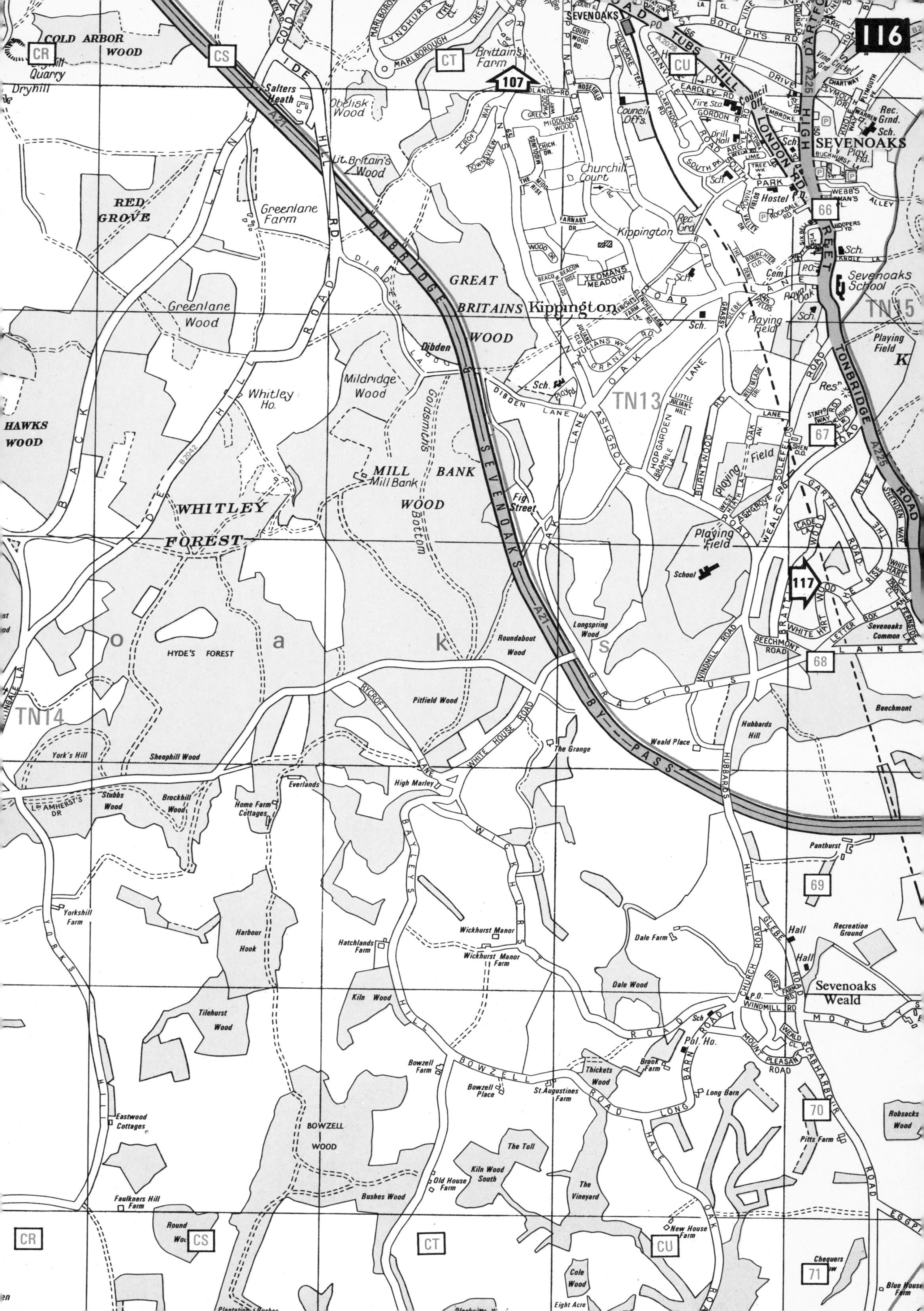
116
SEVENOAKS
Kippington
TN13
TN14
TN15
GREAT BRITAINS WOOD
MILL BANK WOOD
WHITLEY FOREST
HYDE'S FOREST
RED GROVE
HAWKS WOOD
COLD ARBOR WOOD
Greenlane Wood
Greenlane Farm
Mildridge Wood
Whitley Ho.
Dibden
Fig Street
Sevenoaks School
Sevenoaks Weald
Sevenoaks Common
BOWZELL WOOD
Dale Wood
Dale Farm
Wickhurst Manor
Hubbards Hill
Beechmont
Panthurst
Pitfield Wood
Roundabout Wood
Longspring Wood
Weald Place
The Grange
High Marley
Everlands
Sheephill Wood
York's Hill
Stubbs Wood
Brockhill Wood
Harbour Hook
Tilehurst Wood
Kiln Wood
Kiln Wood South
Hatchlands Farm
Bowzell Farm
Bowzell Place
St.Augustines Farm
Thickets Wood
Brook Farm
Long Barn
Pitts Farm
Robsacks Wood
The Toll
The Vineyard
Old House Farm
Bushes Wood
Faulkners Hill Farm
Eastwood Cottages
Yorkshill Farm
New House Farm
Cole Wood
Eight Acre
TONBRIDGE ROAD
SEVENOAKS BY PASS
A21
A225
B2042
CR
CS
CT
CU
107
117
66
67
68
69
70
71

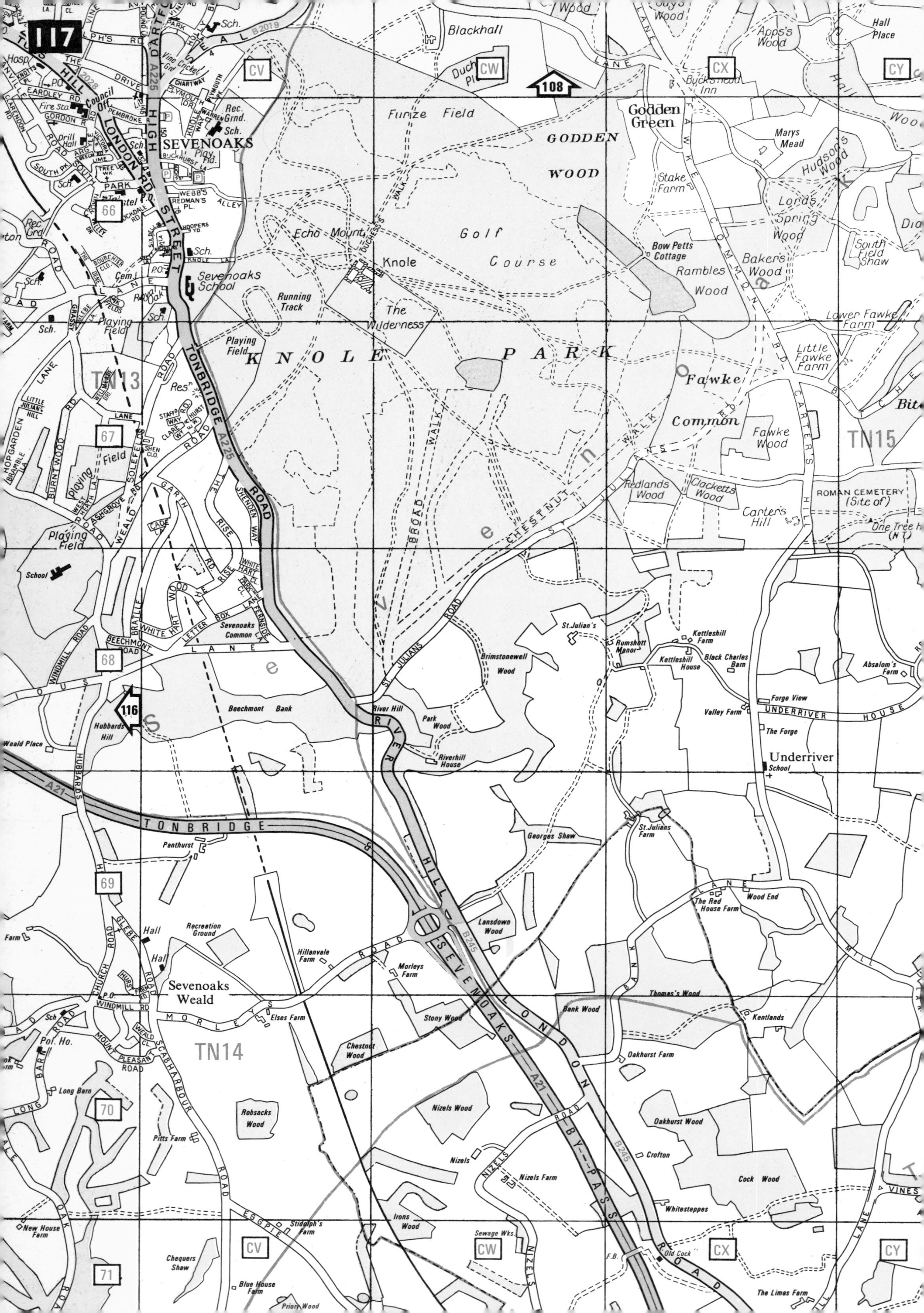

117
108
116
CV
CW
CX
CY
Blackhall
Apps's Wood
Hall Place
Bucks Head Inn
Furze Field
Godden Green
GODDEN WOOD
Marys Mead
Hudson's Wood
Stake Farm
Lords Spring Wood
SEVENOAKS
Echo Mount
Golf Course
Knole
Bow Petts Cottage
Rambles Wood
Baker's Wood
South Field Shaw
Running Track
The Wilderness
Lower Fawke Farm
Little Fawke Farm
Playing Field
KNOLE PARK
Fawke Common
Fawke Wood
TN13
TN15
TN14
Sevenoaks School
Redlands Wood
Clacketts Wood
ROMAN CEMETERY (Site of)
Carter's Hill
One Tree Hill (NT)
TONBRIDGE ROAD
A225
A21
B245
HIGH STREET
LONDON RD
BROAD WALK
CHESTNUT WALK
ST. JULIANS ROAD
WHITE HART WOOD RD
Sevenoaks Common
LETTER BOX LANE
BEECHMONT ROAD
WINDMILL ROAD
Beechmont Bank
Hubbards Hill
Weald Place
St. Julian's
Rumshott Manor
Kettleshill Farm
Kettleshill House
Black Charles Barn
Absalom's Farm
Brimstonewell Wood
River Hill
Park Wood
Riverhill House
Forge View
Valley Farm
UNDERRIVER HOUSE
The Forge
Underriver
School
St.Julians Farm
Georges Shaw
RIVER HILL
TONBRIDGE
Panthurst
Recreation Ground
Hall
Lansdown Wood
Hillanvale Farm
Morleys Farm
Sevenoaks Weald
MORLEYS ROAD
Elses Farm
Stony Wood
Bank Wood
Thomas's Wood
Kentlands
The Red House Farm
Wood End
SEVENOAKS
LONDON
BY-PASS
Chestnut Wood
Oakhurst Farm
Oakhurst Wood
Long Barn
Nizels Wood
Robsacks Wood
Pitts Farm
Crofton
Nizels
Nizels Farm
Cock Wood
Whitesteppes
Irons Wood
Sewage Wks.
Stidolph's Farm
EGGPIE LANE
New House Farm
Chequers Shaw
Blue House Farm
Priory Wood
Old Cock
F.B.
The Limes Farm
SCABHARBOUR ROAD
MOUNT PLEASANT ROAD
CHURCH ROAD
66
67
68
69
70
71

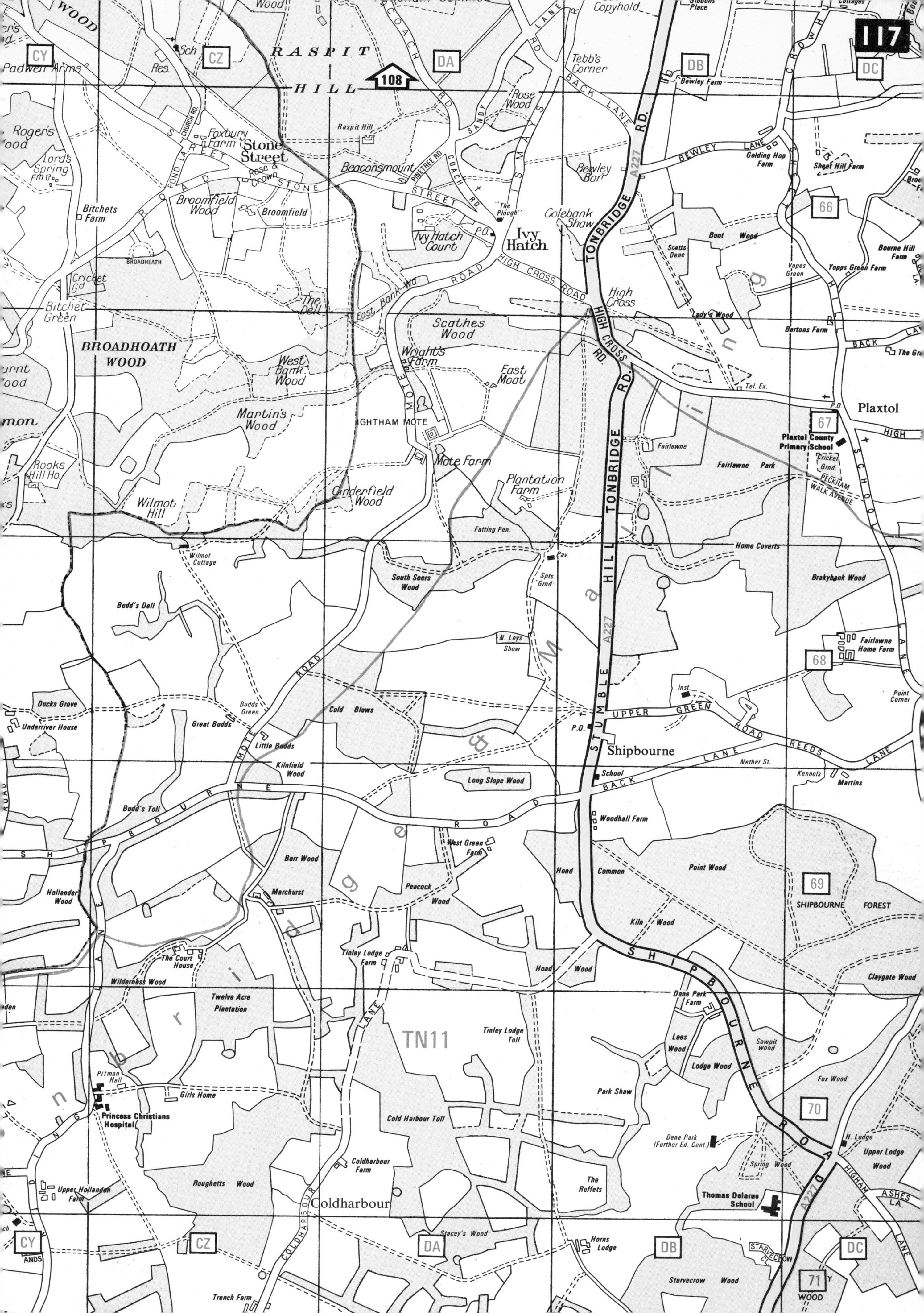

117
CY
CZ
DA
DB
DC
108
RASPIT
HILL
Copyhold
Tebb's Corner
Bewley Farm
Rose Wood
Raspit Hill
Stone Street
Foxbury Farm
Rose & Crown
Roger's Wood
Lord's Spring Fm
Padwell Arms
Beaconsmount
Bitchets Farm
Broomfield Wood
Broomfield
BROADHEATH
Cricket Gd
Bitchet Green
BROADHOATH WOOD
Ivy Hatch
Ivy Hatch Court
"The Plough"
Colebank Shaw
Bewley Bar
Golding Hop Farm
Sheet Hill Farm
Boot Wood
Scatts Dene
Bourne Hill Farm
Vopes Green
Yopps Green Farm
High Cross
Lady's Wood
Bartons Farm
The Dell
East Bank Wd
Scathes Wood
Wright's Farm
West Bank Wood
East Moat
Martin's Wood
IGHTHAM MOTE
Mote Farm
Plantation Farm
Tel. Ex.
Plaxtol
Plaxtol County Primary School
Cricket Grnd.
Fairlawne
Fairlawne Park
PECKHAM WALK AVENUE
Rooks Hill Ho.
Wilmot Hill
Cinderfield Wood
Fatting Pen.
Home Coverts
Wilmot Cottage
South Seers Wood
Pav.
Spts Grnd.
Brakybank Wood
Budd's Dell
N. Leys Show
Fairlawne Home Farm
Ducks Grove
Underriver House
Budds Green
Great Budds
Cold Blows
Inst
UPPER GREEN ROAD
Point Corner
P.O.
Shipbourne
REEDS LANE
Little Budds
Kilnfield Wood
Long Slope Wood
School
Nether St.
Kennels
Martins
Budd's Toll
BACK LANE
SHIPBOURNE ROAD
Woodhall Farm
West Green Farm
Barr Wood
Hoad Common
Point Wood
Hollanden Wood
Marchurst
Peacock Wood
SHIPBOURNE FOREST
Kiln Wood
The Court House
Tinley Lodge Farm
Hoad Wood
Claygate Wood
Wilderness Wood
Twelve Acre Plantation
Dene Park Farm
TN11
Tinley Lodge Toll
Lees Wood
Sawpit wood
Lodge Wood
Pitman Hall
Girls Home
Park Shaw
Fox Wood
Princess Christians Hospital
Cold Harbour Toll
Dene Park (Further Ed. Cent.)
N. Lodge
Upper Lodge Wood
Coldharbour Farm
Spring Wood
Upper Hollanden Farm
Roughetts Wood
The Ruffets
Thomas Delarue School
ASHES LA.
Coldharbour
Stacey's Wood
Horns Lodge
STARVECROW CL.
Starvecrow Wood
Trench Farm
WOOD
TONBRIDGE RD.
HIGH CROSS RD.
STUMBLE HILL
A227
66
67
68
69
70
71

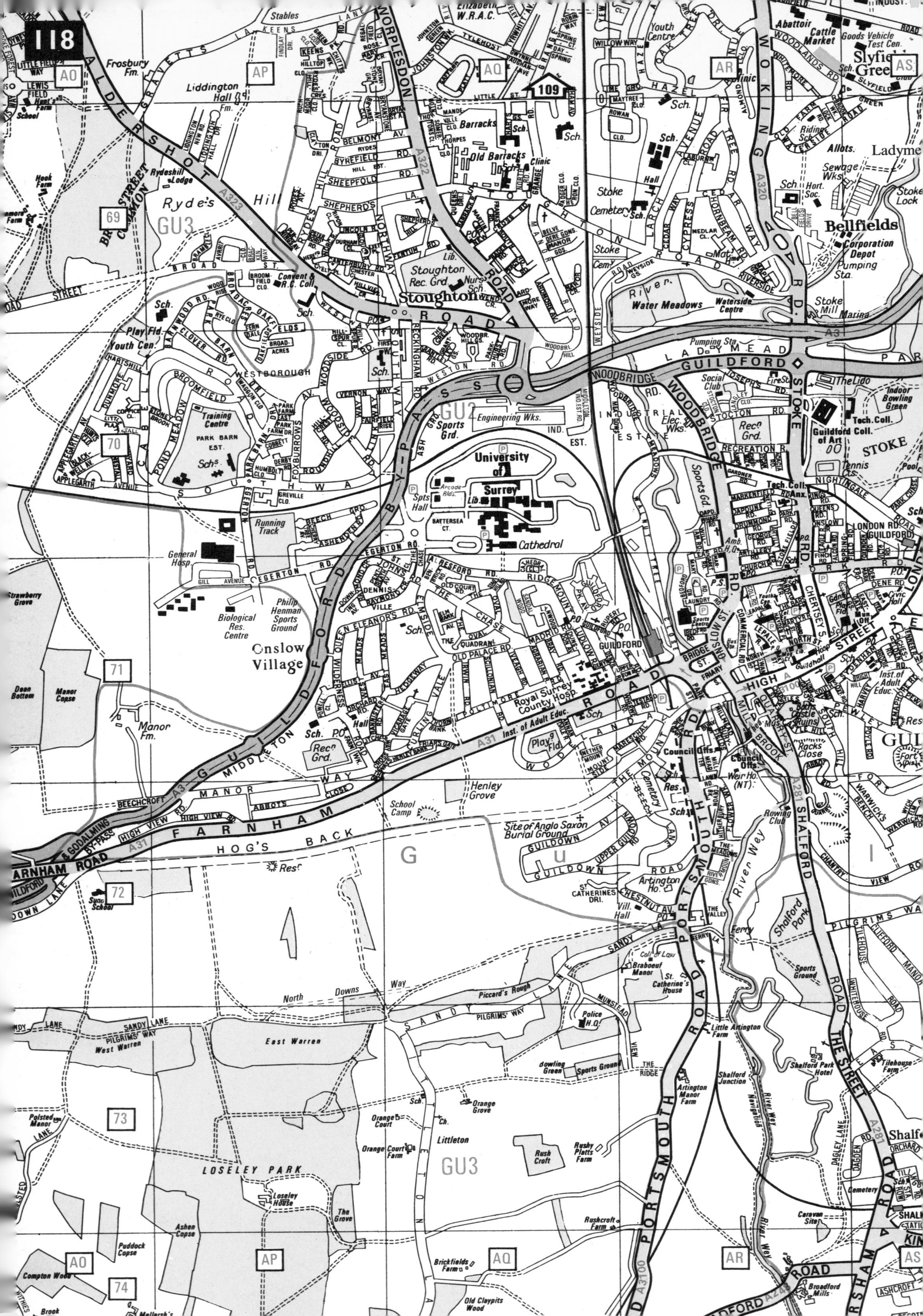

AO
AP
AQ
AR
AS
109
Frosbury Fm.
Liddington Hall Fm.
Stables
Keens
Norpledson Road
A322
Elizabeth W.R.A.C.
Barracks
Old Barracks
Clinic
Youth Centre
Abattoir
Cattle Market
Goods Vehicle Test Cen.
Slyfield Green
Ladymead
Aldershot Road
A323
Rydeshill Lodge
Ryde's Hill
GU3
69
Broad Street Common
Hook Farm
Stoughton Rec. Grd.
Stoughton
Stoughton Road
Convent & R.C. Coll.
Sch.
Play Fld.
Youth Cen.
Westborough
Broomfield
Training Centre
Park Barn Est.
70
Applegarth Avenue
Southway
Stoke Cemetery
River Wey
Water Meadows
Waterside Centre
Bellfields
Corporation Depot
Pumping Sta.
Stoke Mill
Marina
Sewage Wks.
Stoke Lock
A320
Woking Road
A3
Guildford By-Pass
GU2
Ladymead
Guildford
Woodbridge Road
Stoke Road
The Lido
Indoor Bowling Green
Tech. Coll.
Guildford Coll. of Art
Stoke
Industrial Estate
Engineering Wks.
Sports Grd.
University of Surrey
Cathedral
Spts Hall
Running Track
General Hosp.
Biological Res. Centre
Philip Henman Sports Ground
Strawberry Grove
Onslow Village
71
Manor Fm.
Dean Bottom
Manor Copse
Egerton Rd.
Ridgemount
Guildford
Royal Surrey County Hosp.
Inst. of Adult Educ.
Farnham Road
A31
Hog's Back
72
Guildford & Godalming By-Pass
Middleton Road
Manor Way
Henley Grove
School Camp
Site of Anglo Saxon Burial Ground
Guildown
Council Offs.
Weir Ho. (NT)
Rowing Club
Portsmouth Road
A3100
Shalford Road
A281
High Street
Guildhall
Castle Ruins
Racks Close
Chertsey St.
London Rd.
Artington Ho.
Catherines Dri.
Vill. Hall
Ferry
Shalford Park
Sports Ground
Coll. of Law
Braboeuf Manor
St. Catherine's House
North Downs Way
Piccard's Rough
Pilgrims' Way
Sandy Lane
West Warren
East Warren
Police H.Q.
Little Artington Farm
Shalford Junction
Bowling Green
Sports Ground
Artington Manor Farm
Shalford Park Hotel
Tilehouse Farm
The Street
73
Polsted Manor
Orange Grove
Orange Court
Orange Court Farm
Littleton
Rush Croft
Rushy Platts Farm
GU3
Loseley Park
Loseley House
The Grove
Ashen Copse
Rushcroft Farm
Caravan Site
Cemetery
Puddock Copse
Compton Wood
74
Brickfields Farm
Old Claypits Wood
Broadford Mills
Ashcroft
Brook

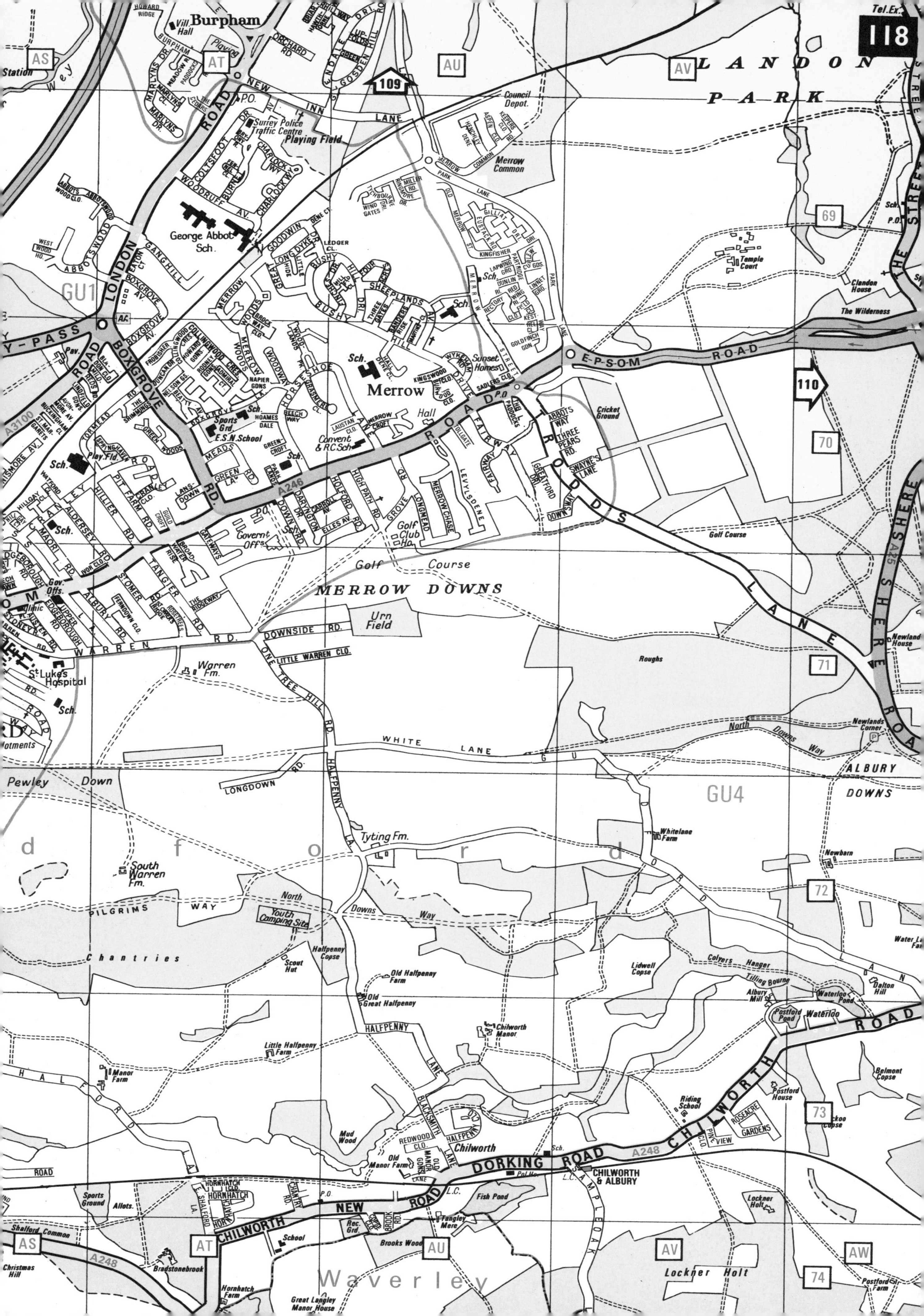
Burpham
Merrow
MERROW DOWNS
CLANDON PARK
EPSOM ROAD
LONDON ROAD
BOXGROVE RD.
TRODDS LANE
WARREN RD.
WHITE LANE
DORKING ROAD
CHILWORTH ROAD
NEW ROAD
George Abbot Sch.
Surrey Police Traffic Centre
Merrow Common
Golf Course
Urn Field
St. Luke's Hospital
Warren Fm.
Tyting Fm.
South Warren Fm.
Pewley Down
PILGRIMS WAY
North Downs Way
Youth Camping Site
Chantries
Chilworth
Chilworth Manor
CHILWORTH & ALBURY
ALBURY DOWNS
Newlands Corner
Lockner Holt
Waverley
Guildford
GU1
GU4
109
110

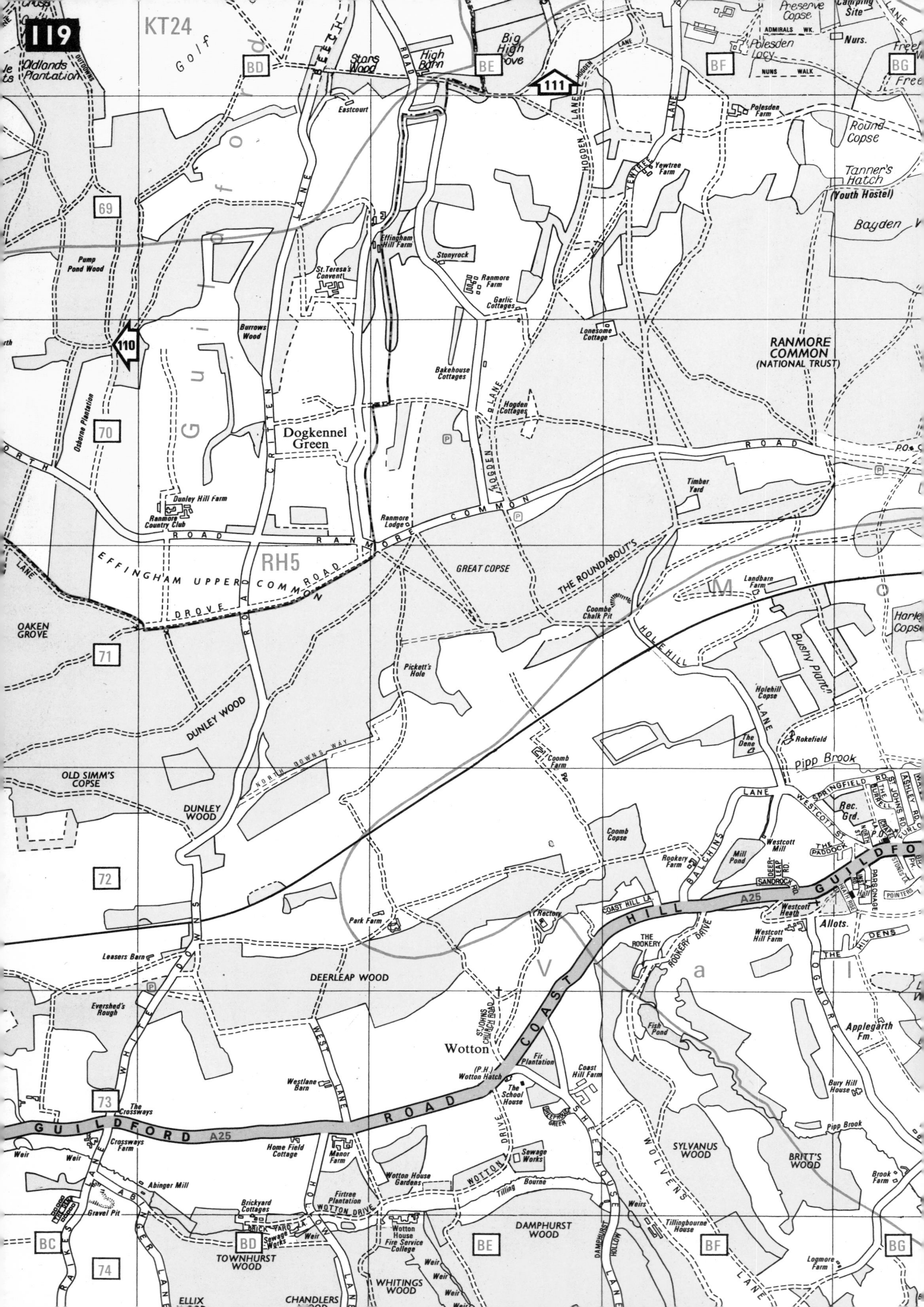
KT24
Oldlands Plantation
Golf
BD
BEECH
Stars Wood
High Barn
ROAD
BE
Big High Grove
111
HOGDEN LANE
BF
Preserve Copse
ADMIRALS WK.
Polesden Lacey
NUNS WALK
Nurs.
Camping Site
BG
Eastcourt
Guildford
Polesden Farm
Round Copse
Yewtree Farm
YEWTREE LANE
Tanner's Hatch (Youth Hostel)
Bayden
69
Pump Pond Wood
Effingham Hill Farm
Stonyrock
St. Teresa's Convent
Ranmore Farm
Garlic Cottages
110
Burrows Wood
Lonesome Cottage
RANMORE COMMON (NATIONAL TRUST)
Bakehouse Cottages
Osborne Plantation
70
CRITTEN LANE
Hogden Cottages
Dogkennel Green
NORTH
ROAD
Timber Yard
Dunley Hill Farm
Ranmore Country Club
Ranmore Lodge
COMMON
RANMORE
RH5
EFFINGHAM UPPER COMMON
DROVE ROAD
GREAT COPSE
THE ROUNDABOUTS
Landbarn Farm
OAKEN GROVE
Coombe Chalk Pit
HOLEHILL
Bushy Plantn
71
Pickett's Hole
Holehill Copse
DUNLEY WOOD
The Dene
Rokefield
NORTH DOWNS WAY
Coomb Farm
Pipp Brook
OLD SIMM'S COPSE
DUNLEY WOOD
SPRINGFIELD RD.
ST JOHNS RD.
ASHLEY RD.
Rec. Grd.
WESTCOTT ST.
Coomb Copse
Westcott Mill
THE PADDOCK
72
Rookery Farm
Mill Pond
BALCHINS LANE
DEER LEAP RD.
SANDROCK RD.
PARSONAGE
POINTERS
A25
GUILDFORD
Park Farm
Rectory
COAST HILL LA.
Westcott Heath
Allots.
Westcott Hill Farm
THE HILDENS
Leasers Barn
THE ROOKERY
ROOKERY DRIVE
DEERLEAP WOOD
Vale
LOGMORE
Applegarth Fm.
Evershed's Rough
WHITE DOWNS
WEST LANE
ST JOHNS CHURCH ROAD
Fish Pond
Wotton
COAST HILL
Fir Plantation
Coast Hill Farm
(P.H.) Wotton Hatch
The School House
Bury Hill House
73
The Crossways
Westlane Barn
SHEEPHOUSE GREEN
SHEEPHOUSE LANE
GUILDFORD ROAD
A25
Pipp Brook
Weir
Crossways Farm
Home Field Cottage
Manor Farm
Sewage Works
SYLVANUS WOOD
BRITT'S WOOD
WOTTON DRIVE
Wotton House Gardens
WOLVENS LANE
Brook Farm
Abinger Mill
ABINGER LANE
Firtree Plantation
Tilling Bourne
Gravel Pit
Brickyard Cottages
WOTTON DRIVE
Weirs
BRICKYARD LA.
Wotton House Fire Service College
DAMPHURST WOOD
Tillingbourne House
BC
BD
Sewage Works
Weir
BE
BF
BG
RAIKES LANE
74
TOWNHURST WOOD
DAMPHURST HOLLOW
Logmore Farm
WHITINGS WOOD
ELLIX
CHANDLERS

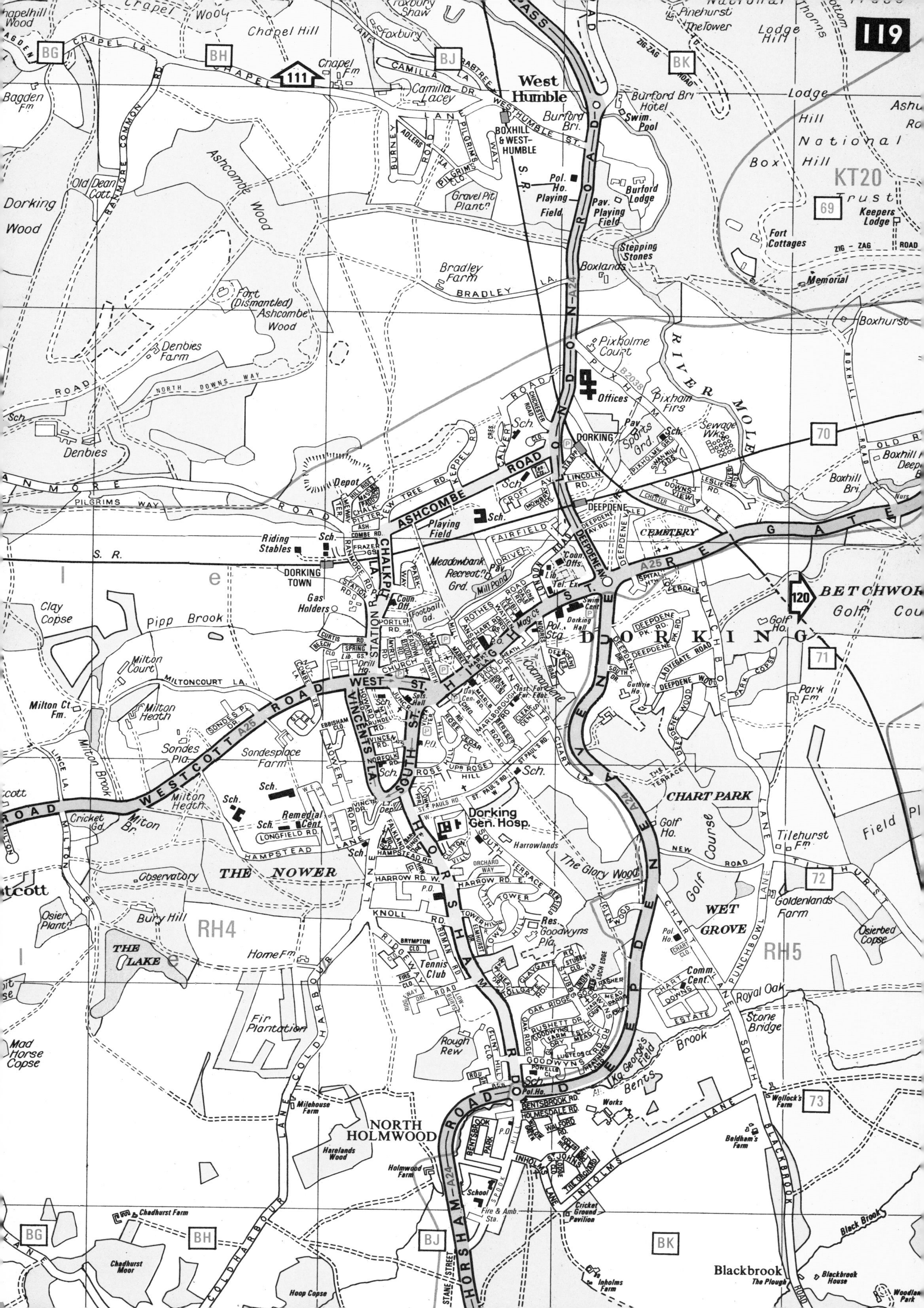
Chapel Hill
Chapel La.
111
Camilla La.
Camilla Dr.
Lacey
West Humble
Westhumble St.
Boxhill & Westhumble
Burford Bri Hotel
Burford Bri.
Swim. Pool
Pinehurst
The Tower
Lodge Hill
Box Hill National Trust
KT20
69
Keepers Lodge
Fort Cottages
Zig-Zag Road
Memorial
Bagden Fm
Ranmore Common Rd.
Old Dean Cott
Dorking Wood
Ashcombe Wood
Gravel Pit Plant
Pol. Ho.
Playing Field
Pav.
Burford Lodge
Stepping Stones
Boxlands
Bradley Farm
Bradley La.
Fort (Dismantled)
Denbies Farm
North Downs Way
Denbies
Pilgrims Way
Pixholme Court
Pixham Firs
River Mole
Sewage Wks.
Offices
Dorking
Sports Grd.
Boxhurst
70
Boxhill Rd.
Boxhill Bri.
Ashcombe Road
Playing Field
Deepdene
Cemetery
Reigate Road
A25
Riding Stables
S. R.
Dorking Town
Meadowbank Recreat. Grd.
Mill Pond
Gas Holders
Station Rd.
Chalkpit La.
Football Gd.
Betchworth Golf Course
120
Golf Ho.
71
Clay Copse
Pipp Brook
Milton Court
Miltoncourt La.
Milton Ct. Fm.
Milton Heath
West St.
High St.
Dorking Hall
Swim. Cent.
Dorking
Deepdene Wood
Ladygate Road
Punchbowl La.
Park Fm
Sondes Pla.
Sondesplace Farm
Westcott Road
Milton Brook
Lince La.
Sch.
Remedial Cent.
Longfield Rd.
Hampstead La.
Dorking Gen. Hosp.
Harrowlands
South St.
Chart Park
Golf Ho.
New Road
Tilehurst Fm
Field Place
72
The Nower
Observatory
Bury Hill
RH4
The Lake
Home Fm
Osier Plant.
Harrow Rd. W.
Harrow Rd. E.
Knoll Rd.
The Glory Wood
Golf Course
Wet Grove
Goldenlands Farm
Osierbed Copse
RH5
Tennis Club
Res.
Goodwyns Pla.
Chart Downs Estate
Comm. Cent.
Royal Oak
Stone Bridge
Fir Plantation
Coldharbour Lane
Rough Rew
Mad Horse Copse
Kg. George's Field
Bents
Brook
Milehouse Farm
North Holmwood
Harelands Wood
Holmwood Farm
Inholms La.
Wollock's Farm
73
Beldham's Farm
Blackbrook Road
Chadhurst Farm
Chadhurst Moor
School
Fire & Amb. Sta.
Cricket Ground Pavilion
Horsham Road A24
Stane Street
Hoop Copse
Inholms Farm
Black Brook
Blackbrook
The Plough
Blackbrook House
Woodlands Park
BG
BH
BJ
BK

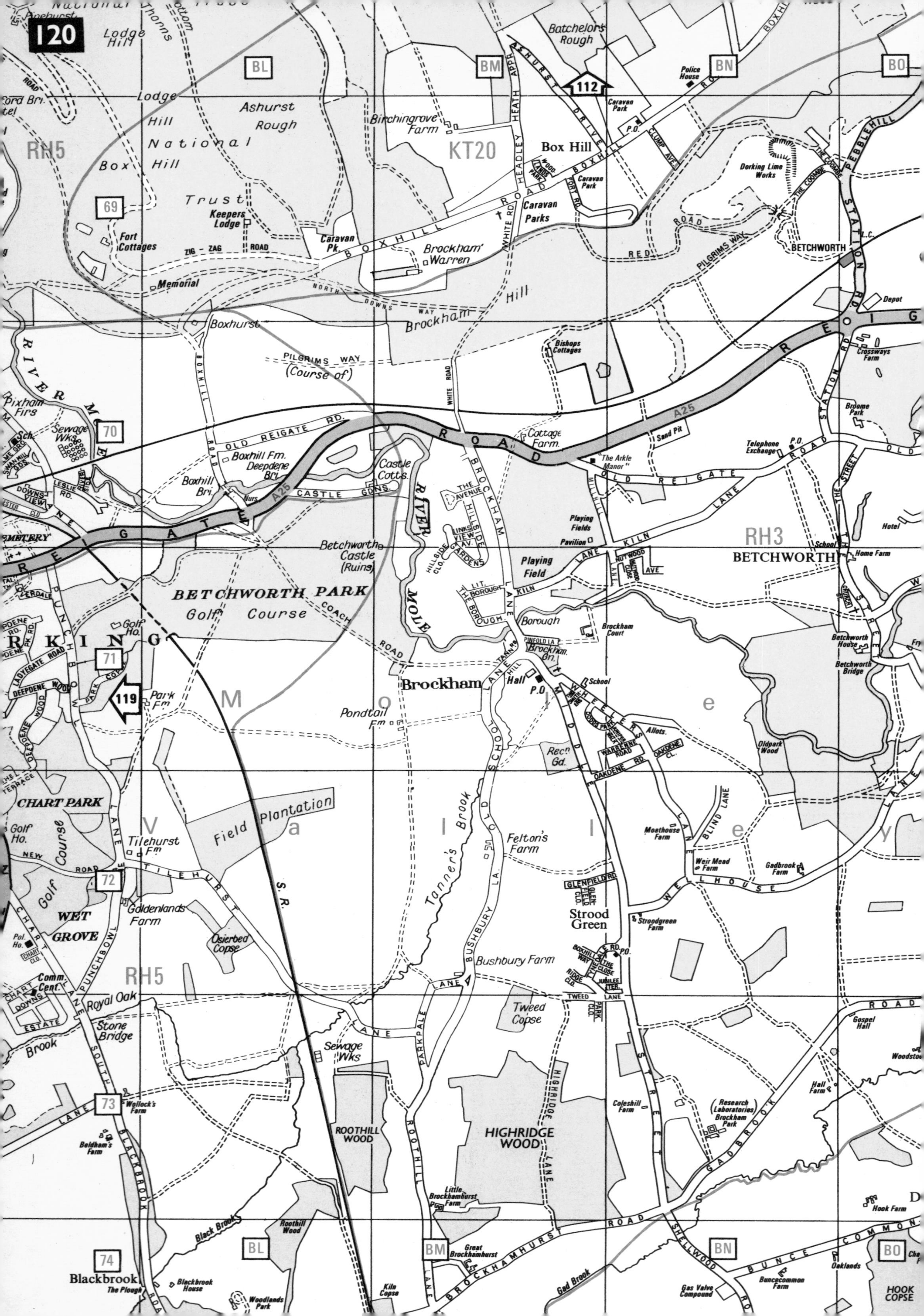
BL
BM
BN
BO
112
Batchelors Rough
Lodge Hill
Ashurst Rough
Birchingrove Farm
KT20
Box Hill
Lodge Hill National Trust
Box Hill
RH5
69
Keepers Lodge
Fort Cottages
ZIG - ZAG ROAD
Caravan Pk.
BOXHILL ROAD
Brockham Warren
Caravan Parks
Caravan Park
Police House
P.O.
HEADLEY HEATH APPR.
ASHURST DRIVE
WHITE ROAD
CLUMP AVE.
Dorking Lime Works
PEBBLEHILL
THE COOMBE
RED ROAD
PILGRIMS WAY
BETCHWORTH
L.C.
Memorial
NORTH DOWNS WAY
Brockham Hill
Depot
Boxhurst
RIVER MOLE
PILGRIMS WAY
(Course of)
Bishops Cottages
STATION RD
Crossways Farm
Pixham Firs
Sewage Wks.
70
OLD REIGATE RD.
Boxhill Fm.
Deepdene Bri.
Boxhill Bri.
Castle Cotts.
Cottage Farm
REIGATE ROAD
A25
Sand Pit
"The Arkle Manor"
Broome Park
Telephone Exchange
P.O.
OLD REIGATE ROAD
KILN LANE
LESLIE RD.
DOWNS VIEW
CASTLE GDNS.
THE AVENUE
HILLSIDE
LINKS VIEW AV.
BROCKHAM LANE
Playing Fields
Pavilion
RH3
BETCHWORTH
Hotel
School
Home Farm
CEMETERY
Betchworth Castle (Ruins)
HILLSIDE CL.
GARDENS
Playing Field
NUTWOOD AVE
BETCHWORTH PARK
Golf Course
COACH ROAD
LIT. BOROUGH
THE BOROUGH
Borough
Brockham Court
Betchworth House
Betchworth Bridge
DORKING
PUNCHBOWL LANE
LADYGATE ROAD
DEEPDENE WOOD
71
Golf Ho.
119
Park Fm.
Mole
Brockham
PINFOLD LA.
Brockham Grn.
Hall
P.O.
School
WHEELERS LA.
Pondtail Fm.
Allots.
Oldpark Wood
Rec. Gd.
WARRENNE ROAD
OAKDENE RD.
OAKDENE CL.
MIDDLE STREET
CHART PARK
Golf Ho.
Golf Course
Field Plantation
Tanner's Brook
OLD SCHOOL LA.
Felton's Farm
Vale
BLIND LANE
Moathouse Farm
Tilehurst Fm.
NEW ROAD
72
TILEHURST LANE
S.R.
Weir Mead Farm
Gadbrook Farm
WELLHOUSE LANE
Goldenlands Farm
GLENFIELD RD.
Strood Green
Stroodgreen Farm
WET GROVE
Golf
CHART LANE
Pol. Ho.
Osierbed Copse
BUSHBURY LA.
Bushbury Farm
P.O.
RH5
Comm. Cent.
Royal Oak
Stone Bridge
Brook
TWEED LANE
PARK CL.
Tweed Copse
Gospel Hall
ROAD
Sewage Wks
PARKPALE LANE
Woodstock
HIGHRIDGE LANE
Hall Farm
73
Wellock's Farm
Beldham's Farm
ROOTHILL WOOD
ROOTHILL LANE
HIGHRIDGE WOOD
Coleshill Farm
(Research Laboratories) Brockham Park
GADBROOK ROAD
Little Brockhamhurst Farm
Hook Farm
Black Brook
Roothill Wood
BROCKHAMHURST ROAD
SHELLWOOD ROAD
BUNCE COMMON
74
BL
BM
Great Brockhamhurst
BN
BO
Blackbrook
The Plough
Blackbrook House
Woodlands Park
Kiln Copse
Gad Brook
Gas Valve Compound
Buncecommon Farm
Oaklands
HOOK COPSE
BLACKBROOK ROAD

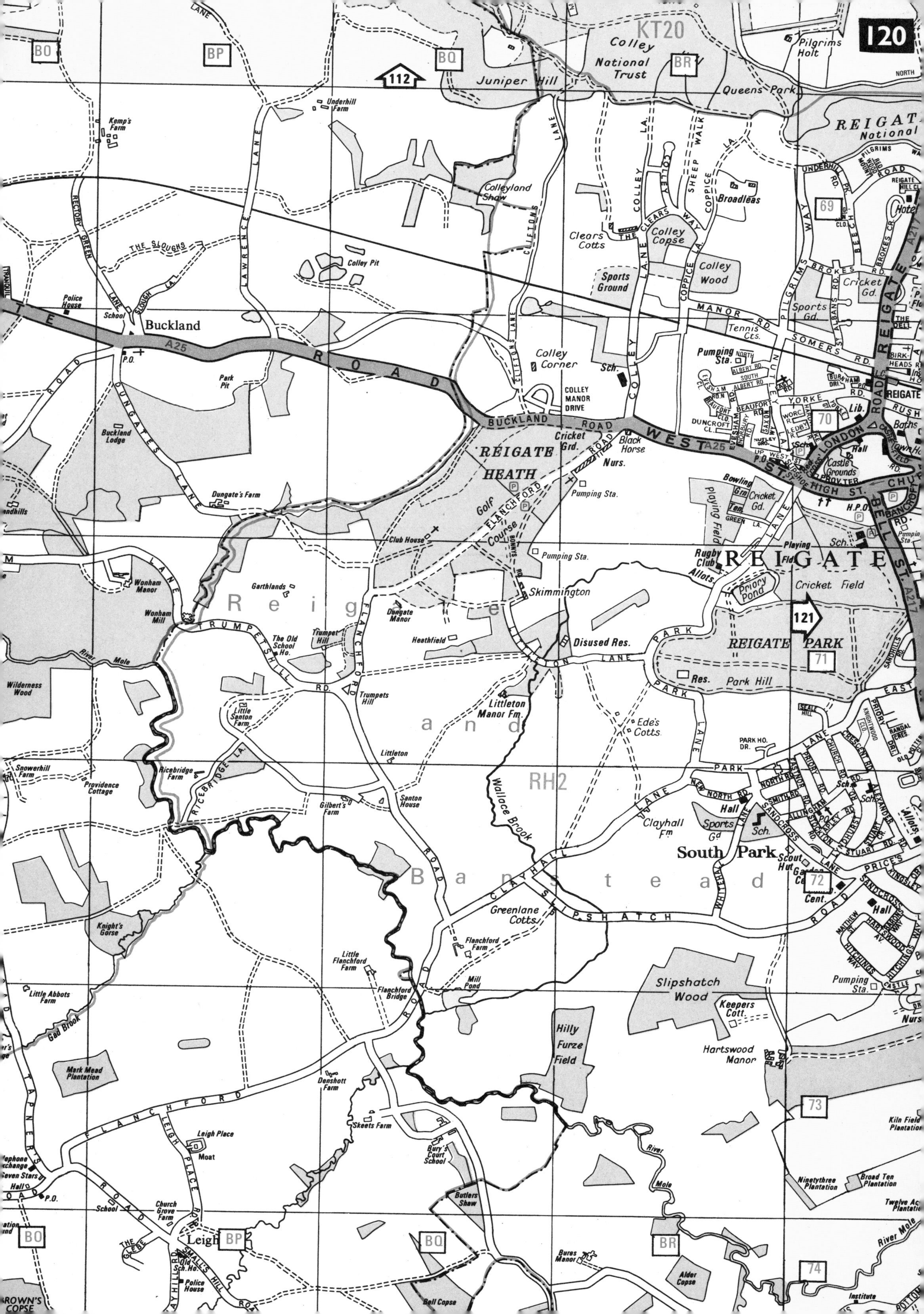

KT20
Colley
National Trust
Juniper Hill
Queens Park
Pilgrims Holt
112
REIGATE
National
Underhill Farm
Kemp's Farm
Colleyland Shaw
Colley Pit
Clears Cotts
Colley Copse
Broadleas
Colley Wood
Sports Ground
Buckland
Police House
School
P.O.
A25
ROAD
Park Pit
Buckland Lodge
Dungate's Farm
Colley Corner
COLLEY MANOR DRIVE
Sch.
BUCKLAND ROAD
WEST ST.
REIGATE HEATH
Cricket Grd.
Black Horse
Nurs.
Pumping Sta.
Golf Course
Club House
FLANCHFORD
Wonham Manor
Wonham Mill
Garthlands
Skimmington
Reigate
and
Banstead
Dungate Manor
Heathfield
Trumpet Hill
The Old School Ho.
TRUMPETSHILL RD.
River Mole
Wilderness Wood
Trumpets Hill
Littleton Manor Fm.
Disused Res.
Little Santon Farm
Ricebridge Farm
RICEBRIDGE LA.
Snowerhill Farm
Providence Cottage
Littleton
Santon House
Gilbert's Farm
Wallace Brook
RH2
Ede's Cotts
Knight's Gorse
Little Abbots Farm
Gad Brook
Mark Mead Plantation
Greenlane Cotts
Flanchford Farm
Little Flanchford Farm
Flanchford Bridge
Mill Pond
CLAYHALL
SLIPSHATCH
Slipshatch Wood
Keepers Cott.
Hilly Furze Field
Hartswood Manor
Denshott Farm
Skeets Farm
Leigh Place
Moat
Bury's Court School
Butlers Shaw
Church Grove Farm
School
Leigh
THE GLEBE
SMALL'S HILL
Old Sch. Ho.
Police House
Bures Manor
Alder Copse
Bell Copse
River Mole
Ninetythree Plantation
Broad Ten Plantation
Twelve Acre Plantation
Kiln Field Plantation
Institute
Seven Stars
Hall
P.O.
Telephone Exchange
BROWN'S COPSE
BO
BP
BQ
BR
69
70
71
72
73
74
121
REIGATE
Rugby Club
Allots.
Priory Pond
Cricket Field
REIGATE PARK
Park Hill
Res.
PARK LANE
Playing Field
Bowling Grn
Cricket Gd.
Tennis Cts.
Pumping Sta.
Sports Gd.
MANOR RD.
SOMERS RD.
Castle Grounds
HIGH ST.
BELL ST.
A217
Lib.
Baths
Hall
Sch.
H.P.O.
South Park
Clayhall Fm
Sports Gd
Hall
Scout Hut
Cent.
Pumping Sta.
Hotel
Cricket Gd.
LONDON ROAD
PARK
NORTH RD.
SANDCROSS LANE
PRICE'S
HITCHINGS WAY
HARTSWOOD AV

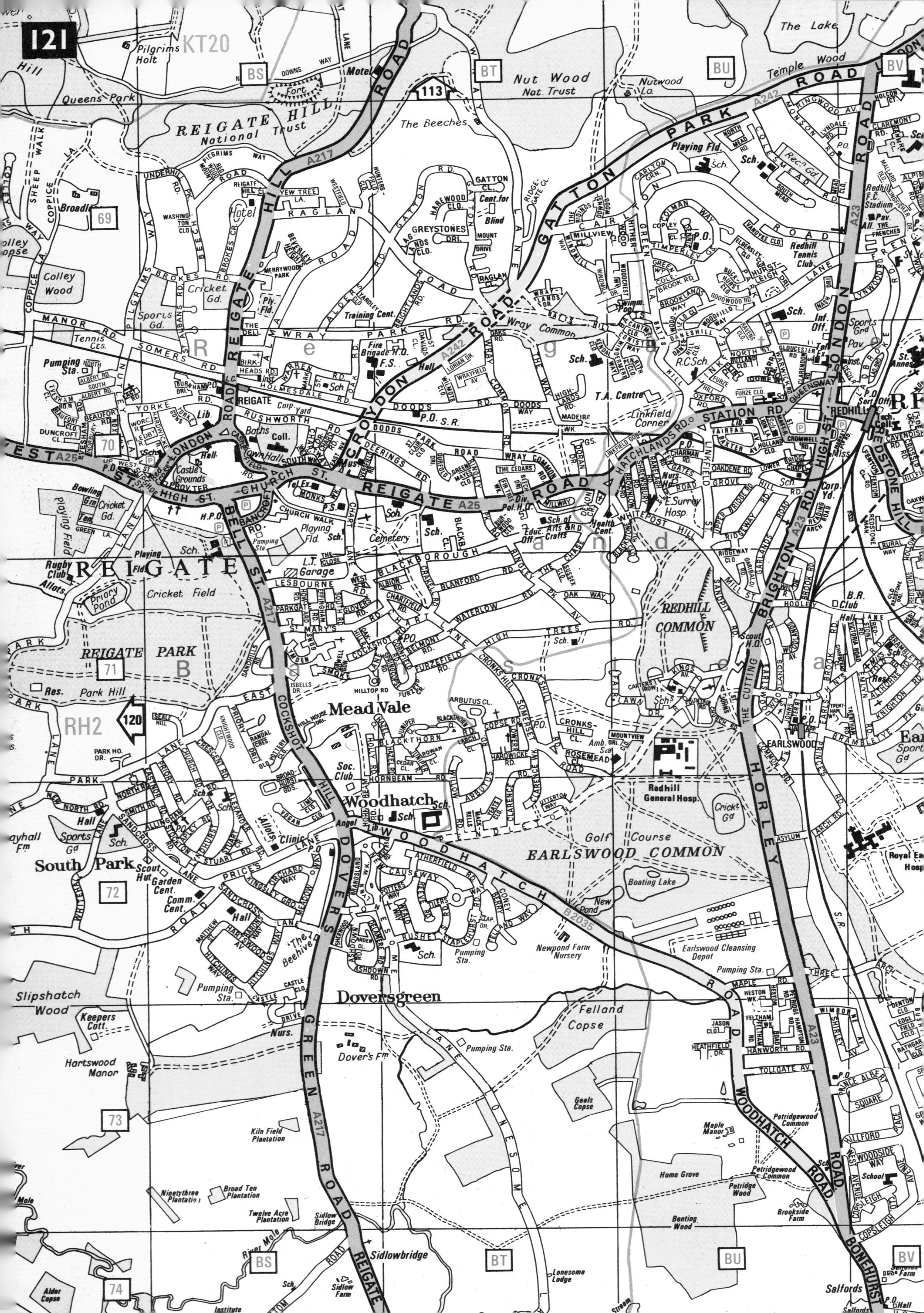

Pilgrims Holt
KT20
BS
BT
BU
BV
113
Queens Park
Fort
Motel
Nut Wood
Nat. Trust
Nutwood Lo.
The Lake
Temple Wood
GATTON PARK ROAD
REIGATE HILL
National Trust
The Beeches
Broadlands
69
Colley Copse
Colley Wood
Cricket Gd.
Sports Gd.
Hotel
Cent. for Blind
GREYSTONES DRI.
Playing Fld.
Redhill F.C. Stadium
Redhill Tennis Club
MANOR RD.
Tennis Cts.
SOMERS RD.
Pumping Sta.
Training Cent.
Fire Brigade H.Q.
Wray Common
T.A. Centre
Linkfield Corner
STATION RD
REDHILL
REIGATE
Corp. Yard
Baths
Coll.
Lib.
70
WEST ST.
HIGH ST.
CHURCH ST.
REIGATE ROAD
Castle Grounds
Town Halls
Bowling Grn
Cricket Gd.
Playing Field
E. Surrey Hosp.
Cemetery
Sch. of Arts & Crafts
L.T. Garage
REIGATE
Rugby Club
Allots.
Priory Pond
Cricket Field
REDHILL COMMON
REIGATE PARK
71
Res.
Park Hill
120
RH2
Mead Vale
Woodhatch
Soc. Club
Redhill General Hosp.
B.R. Club
EARLSWOOD
Golf Course
EARLSWOOD COMMON
Boating Lake
New Pond
South Park
72
Garden Cent.
Comm. Cent.
Hall
The Beehive
Newpond Farm Nursery
Earlswood Cleansing Depot
Pumping Sta.
Slipshatch Wood
Keepers Cott.
Doversgreen
Felland Copse
Dover's Fm
Hartswood Manor
Geals Copse
73
Kiln Field Plantation
Petridgewood Common
Maple Manor
Home Grove
Petridge Wood
Brookside Farm
Ninetythree Plantation
Broad Ten Plantation
Twelve Acre Plantation
Sidlow Bridge
River Mole
Benting Wood
Sidlowbridge
Lonesome Lodge
74
Alder Copse
Sidlow Farm
Salfords
DOVERS GREEN ROAD
REIGATE ROAD
WOODHATCH ROAD
BRIGHTON RD.
HORLEY
LONDON ROAD
CROYDON ROAD
COCKSHOT HILL
BELL ST.
A217
A25
A242
A23
B2035

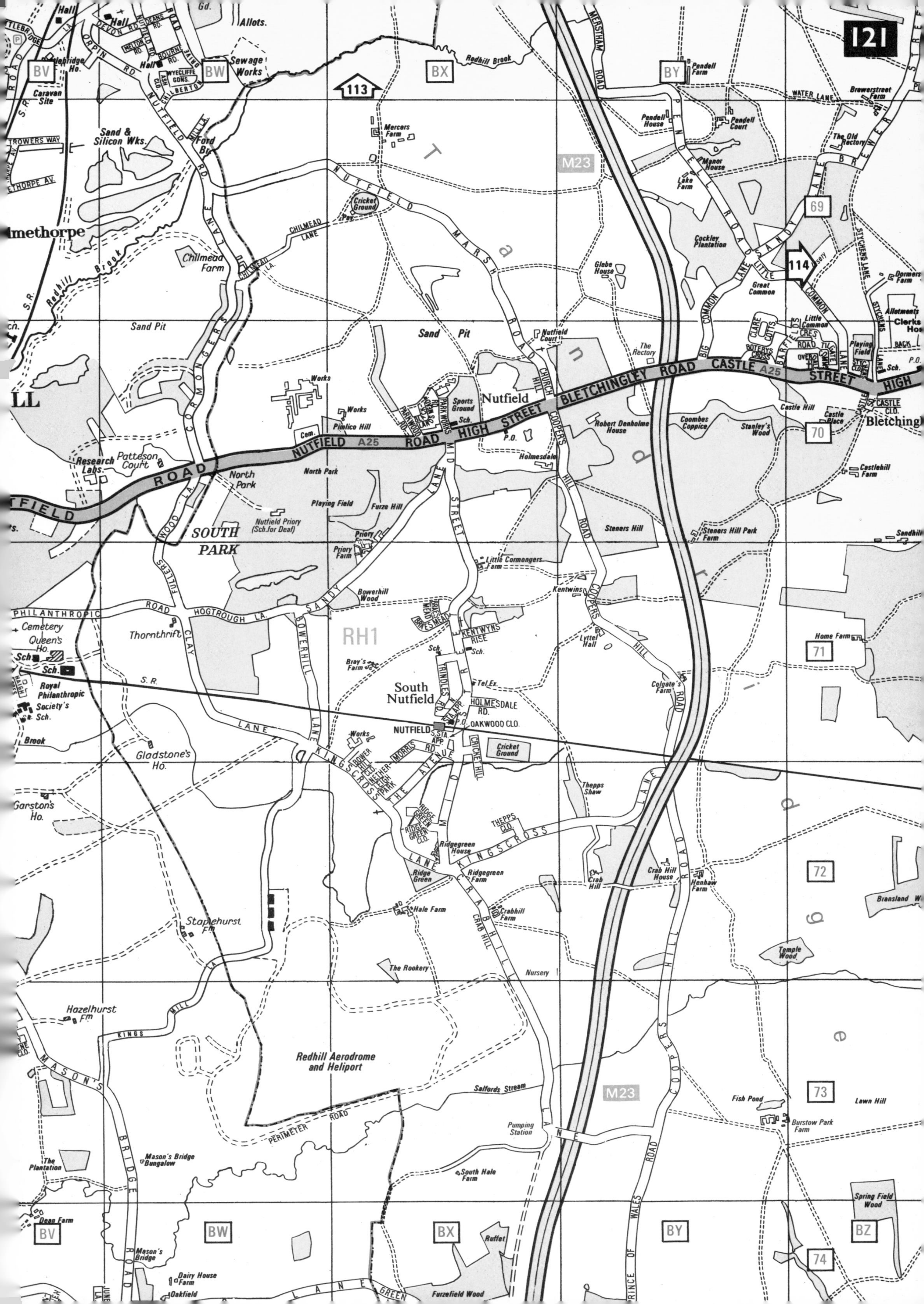
BV
BW
BX
BY
113
114
69
70
71
72
73
74
M23
A25
RH1
Sewage Works
Allots.
Redhill Brook
Pendell Farm
Water Lane
Brewerstreet Farm
Caravan Site
Sand & Silicon Wks.
Ford Br.
Mercers Farm
Pendell House
Pendell Court
Manor House
Lake Farm
The Old Rectory
Cockley Plantation
Cricket Ground
Chilmead Lane
Chilmead Farm
Nutfield Marsh Road
Glebe House
Great Common
Little Common
Sand Pit
Nutfield Court
The Rectory
Cormongers Lane
Works
Pimlico Hill
Sports Ground
Nutfield
Bletchingley Road
Castle Street
High Street
Castle Hill
Castle Place
Bletchingley
Robert Denholme House
Coombes Coppice
Stanley's Wood
Holmesdale
Research Labs.
Patteson Court
Nutfield Road
North Park
Playing Field
Furze Hill
Castlehill Farm
Nutfield Priory (Sch. for Deaf)
South Park
Priory Farm
Steners Hill
Steners Hill Park Farm
Sandhill
Little Cormongers Farm
Kentwins
Bowerhill Wood
Philanthropic Road
Hogtrough La.
Cemetery
Queen's Ho.
Thornthrift
Home Farm
Lyttel Hall
Bray's Farm
Royal Philanthropic Society's Sch.
South Nutfield
Colgate's Farm
Nutfield Sta.
Holmesdale Rd.
Oakwood Clo.
Cricket Ground
Gladstone's Ho.
Kingscross Lane
Thepps Shaw
Garston's Ho.
Ridgegreen House
Ridge Green
Ridgegreen Farm
Crab Hill
Crab Hill House
Henhaw Farm
Bransland Wood
Hale Farm
Crabhill Farm
Staplehurst Fm.
The Rookery
Nursery
Temple Wood
Coopers Hill Road
Hazelhurst Fm.
Kings Mill Lane
Redhill Aerodrome and Heliport
Salfords Stream
Mason's Bridge Road
Perimeter Road
Pumping Station
Fish Pond
Burstow Park Farm
Lawn Hill
The Plantation
Mason's Bridge Bungalow
South Hale Farm
Spring Field Wood
Prince of Wales Road
Dean Farm
Mason's Bridge
Ruffet
Dairy House Farm
Oakfield
Green Lane
Furzefield Wood

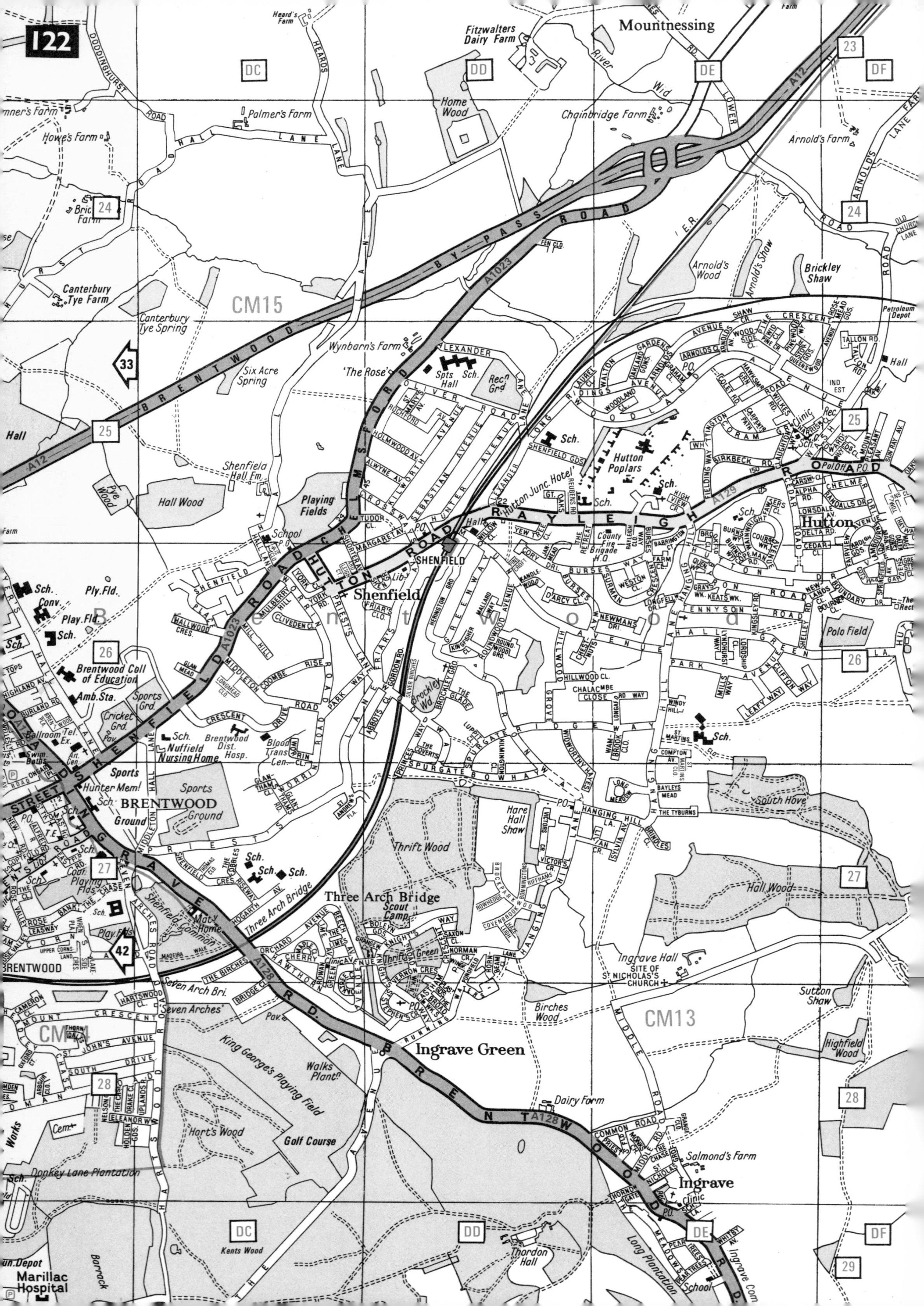
Mountnessing
Fitzwalters Dairy Farm
Heard's Farm
Palmer's Farm
Howe's Farm
Home Wood
Chainbridge Farm
River Wid
Arnold's Farm
Canterbury Tye Farm
Canterbury Tye Spring
BRENTWOOD BY-PASS ROAD
A12
A1023
CM15
Six Acre Spring
Wynbarn's Farm
'The Rose'
Spts Hall
Sch.
Recn Grd
Arnold's Wood
Arnold's Shaw
Brickley Shaw
Hall
Shenfield Hall Fm.
Hall Wood
Pye Wood
Playing Fields
Hutton Poplars
Hutton Junc. Hotel
RAYLEIGH ROAD
A129
HUTTON ROAD
SHENFIELD
Shenfield
Hutton
County Fire Brigade H.Q.
Polo Field
Brentwood
Brentwood Coll of Education
Amb. Sta.
Sports Grd.
Cricket Grd.
Nuffield Nursing Home
Brentwood Dist. Hosp.
Blood Trans. Cen.
Brockley Wd
BRENTWOOD
Sports Ground
Hunter Mem!
Hare Hall Shaw
Thrift Wood
South Hove
Hall Wood
Three Arch Bridge
Scout Camp
Thrift Green
Shenfield Common
Seven Arch Bri.
'Seven Arches'
A128
Ingrave Hall
SITE OF ST NICHOLAS'S CHURCH
Birches Wood
CM13
Sutton Shaw
Highfield Wood
CM14
Ingrave Green
King George's Playing Field
Walks Plantn
Hart's Wood
Golf Course
Dairy Farm
BRENTWOOD ROAD
Salmond's Farm
Ingrave
Donkey Lane Plantation
Kents Wood
Thordon Hall
Long Plantation
Marillac Hospital
Barrack
33
42
DC
DD
DE
DF
23
24
25
26
27
28
29

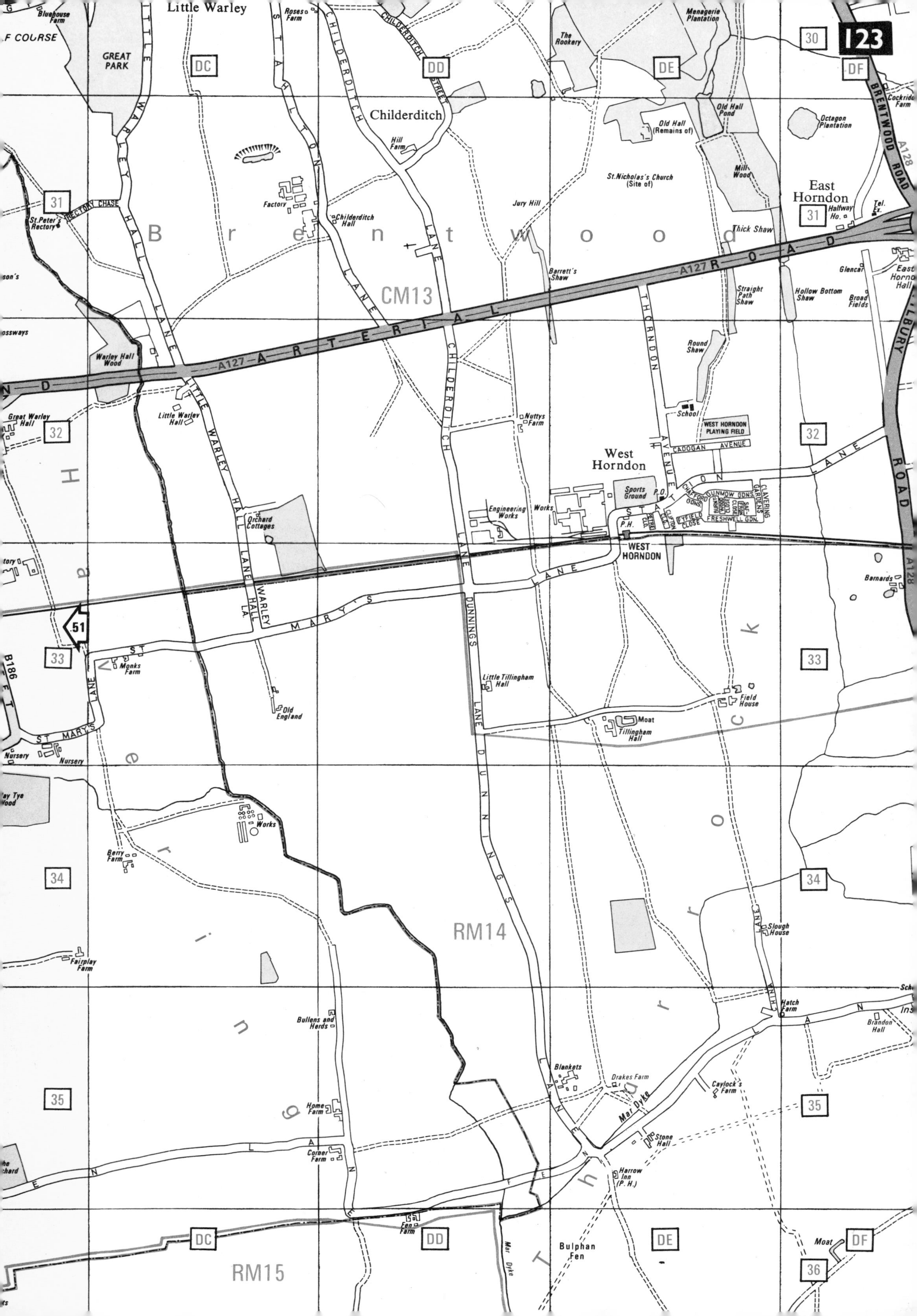

123
Little Warley
Bluehouse Farm
GREAT PARK
Roses Farm
DC
DD
DE
DF
30
31
32
33
34
35
36
Childerditch
Hill Farm
Menagerie Plantation
The Rookery
Old Hall Pond
Old Hall (Remains of)
Octagon Plantation
Cockridden Farm
BRENTWOOD ROAD
A128
Mill Wood
St.Nicholas's Church (Site of)
Jury Hill
East Horndon
Halfway Ho.
Tel. Ex.
Thick Shaw
Factory
Childerditch Hall
RECTORY CHASE
St.Peter's Rectory
Brentwood
Barrett's Shaw
CM13
A127
ARTERIAL ROAD
Straight Path Shaw
Hollow Bottom Shaw
Broad Fields
Glencar
East Horndon Hall
TILBURY ROAD
Round Shaw
Warley Hall Wood
Great Warley Hall
Little Warley Hall
LITTLE WARLEY HALL LANE
CHILDERDITCH LANE
THORNDON AVENUE
Nuttys Farm
School
WEST HORNDON PLAYING FIELD
CADOGAN AVENUE
West Horndon
Sports Ground
P.O.
STATION LANE
CHAPFORD GDNS
DUNMOW GDNS
CLAVERING GARDENS
EYFIELD CLOSE
FRESHWELL GDNS
P.H.
Engineering Works
Works
Orchard Cottages
WEST HORNDON
Bernards
MARY'S LANE
WARLEY HALL LA.
51
B186
ST MARY'S LANE
Monks Farm
Nursery
DUNNINGS LANE
Little Tillingham Hall
Old England
Field House
Moat
Tillingham Hall
Havering
Thurrock
Works
Berry Farm
RM14
Slough House
Fairplay Farm
Bullens and Herds
Hatch Farm
Brandon Hall
Blankets
Drakes Farm
Caylock's Farm
Home Farm
Mar Dyke
Stone Hall
Corner Farm
FEN LANE
Harrow Inn (P.H.)
Fen Farm
Mar Dyke
Bulphan Fen
Moat
RM15

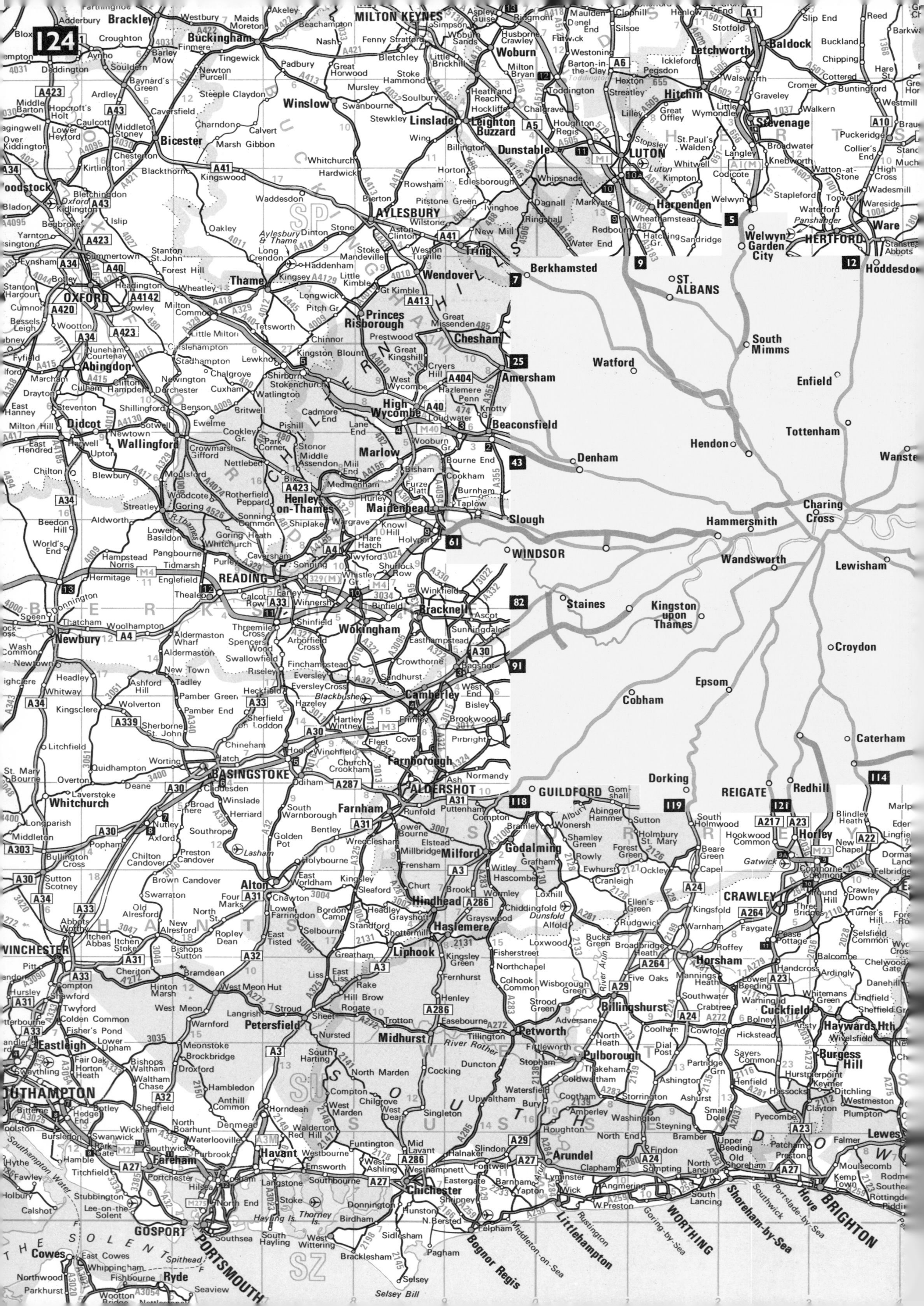
124
MILTON KEYNES
Brackley
Buckingham
Woburn
Letchworth
Baldock
Winslow
Linslade
Leighton Buzzard
Hitchin
Stevenage
Bicester
Dunstable
LUTON
Harpenden
Woodstock
AYLESBURY
Welwyn Garden City
HERTFORD
Ware
Hoddesdon
Tring
Berkhamsted
ST. ALBANS
OXFORD
Thame
Wendover
Princes Risborough
Chesham
South Mimms
Abingdon
Amersham
Watford
Enfield
Didcot
Wallingford
High Wycombe
Beaconsfield
Tottenham
Hendon
Marlow
Denham
Henley-on-Thames
Maidenhead
Slough
Charing Cross
Hammersmith
WINDSOR
Wandsworth
Lewisham
READING
Newbury
Staines
Kingston upon Thames
Bracknell
Wokingham
Croydon
Epsom
Cobham
Camberley
Farnborough
Caterham
BASINGSTOKE
ALDERSHOT
Whitchurch
Dorking
GUILDFORD
REIGATE
Redhill
Farnham
Godalming
Milford
Horley
Alton
Hindhead
CRAWLEY
Haslemere
WINCHESTER
Liphook
Horsham
Petersfield
Billingshurst
Cuckfield
Haywards Hth
Eastleigh
Midhurst
Petworth
Pulborough
Burgess Hill
SOUTHAMPTON
Havant
Fareham
Arundel
Lewes
Chichester
Littlehampton
WORTHING
Shoreham-by-Sea
Hove
BRIGHTON
GOSPORT
PORTSMOUTH
Bognor Regis
Cowes
Ryde
Selsey Bill
THE SOLENT
SP
SU
SZ

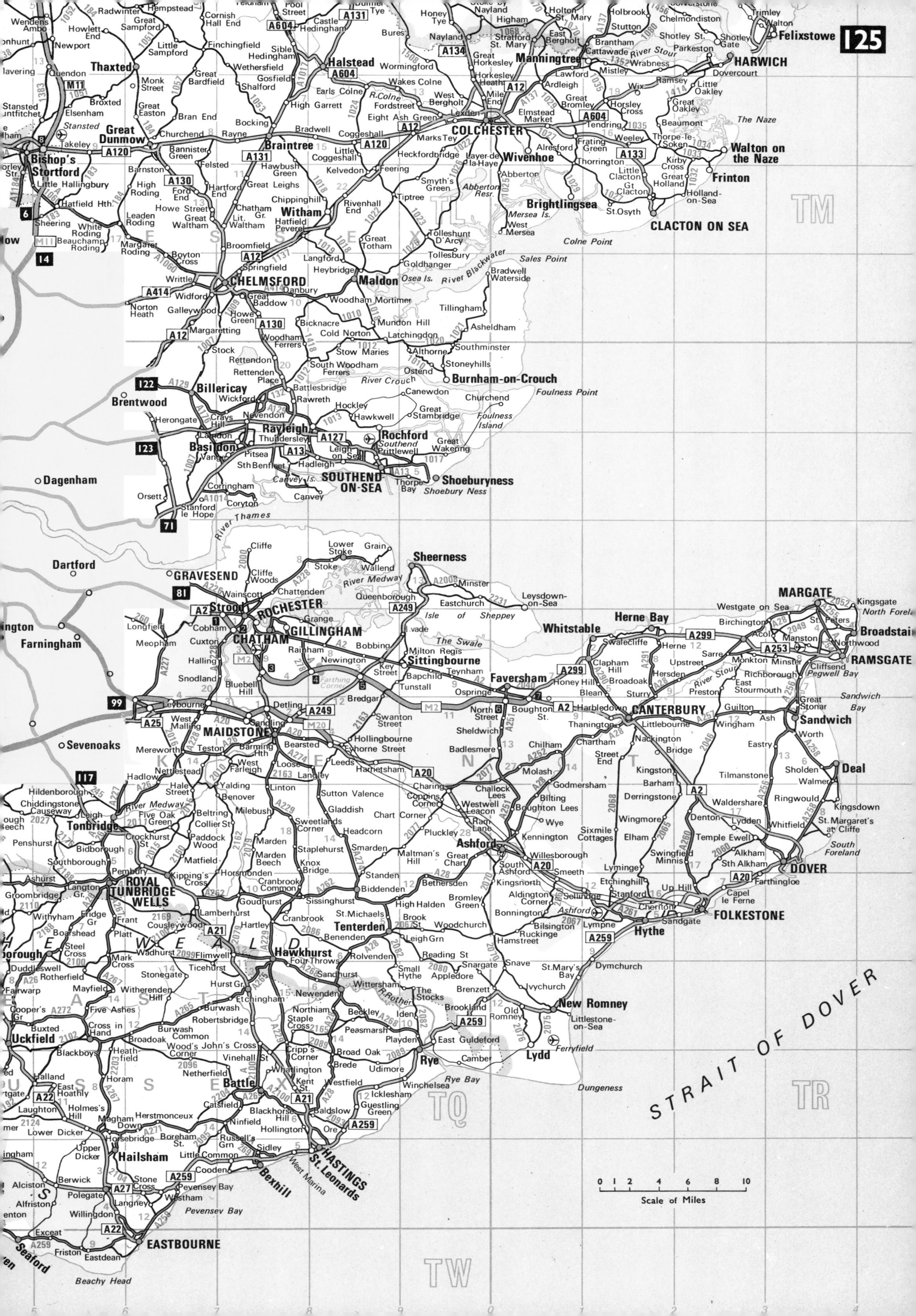
Felixstowe
HARWICH
Dovercourt
Manningtree
Mistley
Halstead
Thaxted
Great Dunmow
Bishop's Stortford
Braintree
Coggeshall
COLCHESTER
Wivenhoe
Walton on the Naze
Frinton
Brightlingsea
CLACTON ON SEA
St.Osyth
Mersea Is.
West Mersea
Colne Point
Witham
Maldon
Osea Is.
River Blackwater
Sales Point
Bradwell Waterside
Tillingham
Asheldham
Southminster
Burnham-on-Crouch
Foulness Point
Foulness Island
River Crouch
CHELMSFORD
Brentwood
Billericay
Wickford
Rayleigh
Basildon
Rochford
Southend
SOUTHEND-ON-SEA
Shoeburyness
Shoebury Ness
Canvey Is.
Dagenham
Orsett
Corringham
Coryton
Stanford le Hope
River Thames
Dartford
GRAVESEND
Cliffe
Grain
Sheerness
Minster
Leysdown-on-Sea
Eastchurch
Isle of Sheppey
The Swale
Queenborough
River Medway
Strood
ROCHESTER
CHATHAM
GILLINGHAM
Sittingbourne
Faversham
Whitstable
Herne Bay
MARGATE
Westgate on Sea
Birchington
Broadstairs
RAMSGATE
Pegwell Bay
Sandwich Bay
Sandwich
Deal
Walmer
Kingsdown
St. Margaret's at Cliffe
South Foreland
DOVER
FOLKESTONE
Hythe
CANTERBURY
Farningham
Sevenoaks
MAIDSTONE
Tonbridge
ROYAL TUNBRIDGE WELLS
Crowborough
Ashford
Tenterden
Hawkhurst
Cranbrook
New Romney
Lydd
Ferryfield
Dungeness
Rye
Rye Bay
Winchelsea
Camber
Uckfield
Battle
HASTINGS
St. Leonards
Bexhill
Hailsham
Pevensey Bay
EASTBOURNE
Beachy Head
Seaford
STRAIT OF DOVER
TL
TM
TQ
TR
TW
0 1 2 4 6 8 10
Scale of Miles

Index to Greater London Streets

For details of indexing system see page 32 of preliminary section. Certain streets named in the Index are to be found both in the Central London enlarged-scale section, maps 1 to 4, as well as in parts of maps on pages 56,57,66 and 67. In order to distinguish between the two the name of the street which is duplicated is given first in **bold type** (indicating the Central London Section), followed immediately by the same name in ordinary type.

Abbreviations of District Names

Amer.	Amersham	Grav.	Gravesend	Ruis.	Ruislip
Ashf.	Ashford	Grnf.	Greenford	St.Alb.	St.Albans
Ash.	Ashtead	Green.	Greenhithe	Saw.	Sawbridgeworth
Bans.	Banstead	Guil.	Guildford	Sev.	Sevenoaks
Bark.	Barking	Hmptn.	Hampton	Shep.	Shepperton
Barn.	Barnet	Harl.	Harlow	Sid.	Sidcup
Beac.	Beaconsfield	Har.	Harrow	Slou.	Slough
Beck.	Beckenham	Hart.	Hartley	Sthl.	Southall
Belv.	Belvedere	Hat.	Hatfield	Sth.Croy.	South Croydon
Berk.	Berkhamsted	Hav.	Havering-atte-Bower	S.Dnth.	South Darenth
Bet.	Betchworth	Hem.H.	Hemel Hempstead	S.Ock.	South Ockendon
Bex.	Bexley	Hert.	Hertford	Stai.	Staines
Bexh.	Bexleyheath	Hodd.	Hoddesdon	S.le H.	Stanford le Hope
Bish.	Bishops Stortford	Horn.	Hornchurch	Stan.	Stanmore
Borwd.	Boreham Wood	Hort.K.	Horton Kirby	Sun.	Sunbury-on-Thames
Brent.	Brentford	Houns.	Hounslow	Surb.	Surbiton
Brom.	Bromley	Ilf.	Ilford	Sutt.	Sutton
Brwd.	Brentwood	Ing.	Ingatestone	S.at H.	Sutton at Hone
Brox.	Broxbourne	Islw.	Isleworth	Swan.	Swanley
Buck.H.	Buckhurst Hill	Ken.	Kenley	Swans.	Swanscombe
Bush.	Bushey	Kes.	Keston	Tad.	Tadworth
Cars.	Carshalton	Kings.on T.	Kingston on Thames	Tedd.	Teddington
Cat.	Caterham	Kings.L.	Kings Langley	Th.Hth.	Thornton Heath
Ch.St.G.	Chalfont St.Giles	Leath	Leatherhead	Til.	Tilbury
Cher.	Chertsey	Long.	Longfield	Ton.	Tonbridge
Chesh.	Chesham	Loug.	Loughton	Twick.	Twickenham
Chess.	Chessington	Lthd.	Leatherhead	Upmin.	Upminster
Chig.	Chigwell	Maid.	Maidenhead	Uxb.	Uxbridge
Chis.	Chislehurst	Mitch.	Mitcham	Vir.W.	Virginia Water
Cob.	Cobham	Mord.	Morden	Wall.	Wallington
Couls.	Coulsdon	New A.G.	New Ash Green	Wal.Abb.	Waltham Abbey
Croy.	Croydon	N.Mal.	New Malden	Wal.Cr.	Waltham Cross
Dag.	Dagenham	Nthlt.	Northolt	Walt.	Walton-on-Thames
Dart.	Dartford	Nthwd.	Northwood	Warl.	Warlingham
Dor.	Dorking	Ong.	Ongar	Wat.	Watford
E.Mol.	East Molesey	Orp.	Orpington	Well.	Welling
Eden.	Edenbridge	Oxt.	Oxted	Welw.	Welwyn
Edg.	Edgware	Pnr.	Pinner	Welw.G.C.	Welwyn Garden City
Egh.	Egham	Pot.B.	Potters Bar	Wem.	Wembley
Enf.	Enfield	Pur.	Purley	West.	Westerham
Epp.	Epping	Rad.	Radlett	West Dr.	West Drayton
Eyns.	Eynsford	Rain.	Rainham	Wey.	Weybridge
Farn.	Farningham	Red.	Redhill	Whyt.	Whyteleafe
Fawk.	Fawkham	Reig.	Reigate	Wdf.Grn.	Woodford Green
Felt.	Feltham	Rich.	Richmond	W.Wick.	West Wickham
Ger.Cr.	Gerrards Cross	Rick.	Rickmansworth	Wind.	Windsor
Gdse.	Godstone	Rom.	Romford	Wok.	Woking
				Wor.Pk.	Worcester Park

General Abbreviations

All.	Alley	Fld.	Field	Pk.	Park
App.	Approach	Gdns.	Gardens	Pass.	Passage
Arc.	Arcade	Gth.	Garth	Peritr.	Perimiter
Av.	Avenue	Gte.	Gate	Pl.	Place
Bk.	Back	Gra.	Grange	Pr.	Prince,Princess
Bnk.	Bank	Gt.	Great	Prom.	Promenade
Boul.	Boulevard	Grn.	Green	Qn.	Queen
Br.	Bridge	Gro.	Grove	Ri.	Rise
Bldgs.	Buildings	Hth.	Heath	Rd.	Road
Chyd.	Churchyard	Hr.	Higher	S. Sth.	South
Circ.	Circle	Hl.	Hill	Sq.	Square
Cir.	Circus	Ho.	House	Sta.	Station
Clo.	Close	Kg.	King	St.	Street
Cor.	Corner	La.	Lane	Ter.	Terrace
Cotts.	Cottages	Lit.	Little	Trd.	Trading
Ct.	Court	Lo.	Lodge	Upr.	Upper
Cres.	Crescent	Lwr.	Lower	Vall.	Valley
Cft.	Croft	Mans.	Mansion	Vw.	View
Dr.	Drive	Mkt.	Market	Vill.	Villas
Dws.	Dwellings	Ms.	Mews	Wk.	Walk
E.	East	Mt.	Mount	W.	West
Embk.	Embankment	N. Nth.	North	Wf.	Wharf
Esp.	Esplanade	Orch.	Orchard	Wd.	Wood
Est.	Estate	Pde.	Parade	Yd.	Yard

Alan Rd. SW19 BR49 75
Alanthus Clo. SE12 CG46 78
Alaska St. SE1 BY40 56
Cornwall Rd.
Albacore Cres. SE13 CE46 77
Alba Gdns. NW11 BR32 46
Albain Cres. Ashf. AY48 73
Alban Av. St. Alb. BG12 9
Alban Cres. Borwd. BM23 28
Alban Cres. Farn. CX54 90
Albans La. NW11 BS33 47
West Hth. Dr
Albans Vw. Wat. BC20 17
Albany Clo. SW14 BM45 65
Albany Clo. Bex. CP47 79
Albany Clo. Bush. BG25 27
Albany Clo. Esher BF58 93
Albany Clo. N15 BY36 47
Albany Clo. Uxb. AZ35 44
Albany Cotts. Esher BE57 93
Albany Ct. NW9 BN30 37
Albany Cres. Edg. BM29 37
Albany Cres. Esher BH57 93
Albany Mans. SW11 BU43 66
Albany Ms. SE17 BZ43 67
Albany Rd.
Albany Pde. Brent BL43 65
Albany Rd.
Albany Pk. Av. Enf. CC23 30
Albany Pk. Rd. Kings. on T. BK50 74
Albany Pk. Rd. Lthd. BJ63 102
Albany Pass Rich. BL46 75
Albany Pl. N7 BY35 47
Albany Pl. Brent. BK43 64
Albany Rd.
Albany Pl. Egh. AT49 72
Albany Pl. Epp. CN18 22
Albany Reach Surb. BH53 84
Albany Rd. E10 CE33 48
Albany Rd. E12 CJ35 49
Albany Rd. E17 CD32 48
Albany Rd. N4 BY32 47
Albany Rd. N18 CC28 39
Albany Rd. SE5 BZ43 67
Albany Rd. SE5 CA43 4
Albany Rd. SW19 BS49 76
Albany Rd. W13 BJ39 54
Albany Rd. Belv. CQ43 69
Albany Rd. Bex. CP47 79
Albany Rd. Brent. BK43 64
Albany Rd. Brwd. DA25 33
Albany Rd. Chis CL49 78
Albany Rd. Enf. CC22 30
Albany Rd. Horn. CU33 50
Albany Rd. N. Mal. BN52 85
Albany Rd. Rich. BL46 75
Albert Rd.
Albany Rd. Rom. CQ32 50
Albany Rd. Walt. BD56 93
Albany Rd. Wind. AO44 61
Albany Rd. Wind. AQ46 72
Albany St. NW1 BV37 1
Albany St. NW1 BV37 56
Albany Ter. NW1 BV38 1
Albany Ter. NW1 BV38 56
Euston Rd.
Albany, The W1 BW40 3
Albany, The W1 BW40 56
Vigo St.
Albany, The Wdf. Grn. CG28 40
Albany Vw. Buck. H. CH26 40
Alba Pl. W11 BR39 55
Portobello Rd.
Albatross Gds. Sth. Croy. CC59 96
Albatross St. SE18 CM43 68
Albemarle App. Ilf. CL32 49
Albemarle Av. Pot. B. BS19 20
Abermarle Av. Wal. Cr. CC17 21
Albemarle Clo. Grays. DD41 71
Albemarle Gdns. Ilf. CL32 49
Albemarle Gdns. N. Mal. BN52 85
Albemarle Pk. Stan. BK28 36
Albemarle Rd. Barn. BU26 38
Albemarle Rd. Beck. CE51 87
Albemarle St. W1 BV40 3
Albemarle St. W1 BV40 56
Albemarle Way, EC1 BY38 2
Albemarle Way EC1 BY38 56
Clerkenwell Rd.
Albermarle Av. Twick. BE47 74
Alberon Gdns. NW11 BR31 46
Alberta Av. Sutt. BR56 94
Alberta Est. SE17 BY42 66
Alberta Rd. Enf. CA25 30
Alberta Rd. Erith CR44 69
Alberta St. SE17 BY42 4
Alberta St. SE17 BY42 66
Albert Av. E4 CE28 39
Albert Av. SW8 BX43 66
Albert Av. Ilf. CM34 49
High Rd.
Albert Br. SW3 BU43 66
Albert Br. SW11 BU43 66
Albert Br. Rd. SW11 BU43 66
Albert Carr Gdns. SW16 BX49 76
Albert Clo. N22 BW30 38
Albert Ct. SW7 BT41 3
Albert Ct. SW7 BT41 66
Albert Ct. SW19 BR47 75
Albert Cres. E4 CE28 39
Albert Dr. SW19 OR48 75
Albert Dr. Wok. AU60 91
Albert Dr. Wok. AU61 100
Albert Embankment, SE1 BX42 4
Albert Embankment, SE1 BX42 66
Albert Gdns. E1 CC39 57
Albert Gdns. NW6 BR37 55
Albert Gate SW1 BU41 66
Rotten Row
Albert Gro. SW20 BQ51 85
Albert Hall Ms SW7 BT41 3
Albert Hall Ms SW7 BT41 66
Prince Consort Rd.
Albert Mans. SW11 BU44 66
Albert Ms. W8 BT41 3
Albert Pl. N3 BS30 38
Popes Dr.
Albert Pl. W8 BS41 3
Albert Pl. W8 BS41 66
Albert Rd. E10 CF34 48
Albert Rd. E17 CE32 48
Albert Rd. E18 CH31 49
Albert Rd. N4 BX33 47
Albert Rd. N15 CA32 48
Albert Rd. N22 BW30 38
Albert Rd. NW4 BQ31 46
Albert Rd. NW6 BR37 55
Albert Rd. NW7 BO28 37
Albert Rd. SE9 CK48 78
Albert Rd. SE20 CC50 77
Albert Rd. SE25 CB52 87
Albert Rd. W5 BJ38 54
Albert Rd. Ash. BL62 103
Albert Rd. Ashf. AY49 73
Albert Rd. Barn. BT24 29
Albert Rd. Belv. CQ42 69
Albert Rd. Bex. CR47 79
Albert Rd. Brom. CJ53 88
Albert Rd. Buck H. CJ27 40
Albert Rd. Dag. CQ33 50
Albert Rd. Dart. CV48 80
Albert Rd. Egh. AR50 72
Albert Rd. Epsom. BO60 94
Albert Rd. Har. BG31 45
Albert Rd. Hayes. BB41 63
Albert Rd. Hmptn. BG49 74
Albert Rd. Houns. BF45 64
Albert Rd. Ilf. CL34 49
Albert Rd. Kings. on T. BL51 85
Albert Rd. Mitch. BU52 86
Albert Rd. N. Mal. BO52 85
Albert Rd. Orp. CO53 89
Albert Rd. Orp. CO56 98
Albert Rd. Red. BW68 113
Albert Rd. Rich. BL46 75
Albert Rd. Rom. CT32 50
Albert Rd. Sthl. BD41 64
Albert Rd. Sutt. BT56 95
Albert Rd. Swans. DC46 81
Albert Rd. Tedd. BH50 74
Albert Rd. Twick. BH47 74
Albert Rd. Warl. CD62 105
Albert Rd. West Dr. AY40 53
Albert Rd. Wey. AX55 83
Albert Rd. Wind. AO45 61
Albert Rd. Est. Belv. CQ42 69
Albert Rd. N. Wat. BC24 26
Albert Rd. S. Wat. BC24 26
Albert Sq. E15 CG35 49
Albert Sq. SW8 BX43 66
Albert St. N12 BT28 38
Lodge La.
Albert St. NW1 BV37 1
Albert St. NW1 BV37 56
Albert St. Brwd. DB28 42
Albert Stg. St. Alb. BG14 9
Albert St. Slou. AP41 62
Albert St. Wat. BD24 27
Queen's Rd.
Albert St. Wind. AN44 61
Albert Ter. NW1 BV37 1
Albert Ter. Ms. NW1 BV37 1
Albert Ter. NW1 BV37 56
Albert Ter. NW10 BO37 55
Albion Av. N10 BV30 38
Albion Av. SW8 BW44 66
Albion Bldgs EC1 BZ39 57
Bartholomews Clo.
Albion Cl. W2 BU40 3
Albion Clo. W2 BU40 56
Albion St.
Albion Clo. Rom. CS32 50
Albion Clo. Slou. AQ40 52
Albion Cres. Ch. St. G. AQ27 34
Albion Dr. E8 CA36 2
Albion Dr. E8 CA36 57
Albion Est. SE16 CC41 67
Albion Gdns. W6 BP42 65
Albion Gdns. Dag. CR35 50
Albion Gte. W2 BT40 56
Albion Gro. N16 BZ35 48
Albion Hill SE13 CE44 67
Albion Hill, Hem. H. AX14 8
Albion Hill Loug. CJ25 31
Albion Ms. W2 BU40 3
Albion Ms. W2 BU40 56
Albion Par. Grav. DH46 81
Albion Pk. Loug. CJ25 31
Albion Pl. EC1 BY39 2
Albion Pl. EC1 BY39 56
Albion Pl. SE25 CB52 87
High St.
Albion Rd. E17 CF31 48
Albion Rd. N16 BZ34 48
Albion Rd. N17 CA30 39
Reform Row
Albion Rd. Bexh. CR45 69
Albion Rd. Ch. St. G. AQ27 34
Albion Rd. Grav. DH47 81
Albion Rd. Hayes BB39 53
Albion Rd. Houns. BF45 64
Albion Rd. Kings. On T. BN51 85
Albion Rd. Reig. BT71 121
Albion Rd. St. Alb. BH13 9
Albion Rd. Sutt. BT57 95
Albion Rd. Twick. BH47 74
Albion Sq. E8 CA36 2
Albion Sq. E8 CA36 57
Albion St. E15 CF37 57
Albion St. SE16 CC41 67
Albion St. W2 BU39 1
Albion St. W2 BU39 56
Albion St. Croy. BY54 86
Albion Ter. E8 CA36 57
Albion Ter. Grav. DH46 81
Albion Villas Rd. SE26 CC48 77
Albion Way, SE13 CF45 67
Albion Way, Wem. BM34 46
Aldbridge St. SE17 CA42 4
Albrighton Rd, SE22 CA45 67
Albrook, Brwd. CZ27 42
Albuhera Clo. Enf. BY23 29
Albury Av. Islw. BH43 64
Albury Av. Sutt. BQ58 94
Albury Clo. Cher. AQ55 82
Albury Clo. Hamptn. BF50 74
Albury Dr. Pnr. BD29 36
Albury Dr. Pnr. BD30 36
Albury Gro. Wal. Cr. CC18 21
Albury Ride, Wal. Cr. CC19 21
Albury Rd. Bexh. CQ44 69
Albury Rd. Chess. BL56 94
Albury Rd. Guil. AS71 118
Albury Rd. Watt. BB57 92
Albury St. SE8 CE43 67
Albury Wk. Wal. Cr. CC19 21
Albyfield Brom. CK52 88
Albyn Rd. SE8 CE44 67
Albyns Cl. Rain CU36 59
South End Rd.
Alcester Cres. E5 CB34 48
Alcester Rd. Wall. BV56 95
Alcock Clo. Wall. BW57 95
Alcock Rd. Houns. BD43 64
Alcocks Clo. Tad BR63 103
Alcocks La. Tad. BR64 103
Alconbury Rd. E5 CB34 48
Alcorn Clo. Sutt. BS55 86
Aldam Pl. N16 CA34 48
High St.
Aldborough Rd. Dag. CS36 59
Aldborough Rd. Ilf. CN33 49
Aldborough Rd. Upmin. CW34 51
Aldborough Rd. N. Ilf. CN32 49
Aldborough Rd. S. Ilf. CN33 49
Aldborough Spur. Slou. AP39 52
Aldbourne Rd. W12 BO40 55
Aldbridge St. SE17 CA42 67
Aldbury Av. Wem BM36 55
Aldbury Clo. Wat. BD21 27
Aldbury Gro. Welw. G. C. B58 5
Aldbury Mews N9 CZ26 39
Aldbury Rd. Rick. AV26 34
Aldbury St. SE8 CE43 67
Aldebert Ter. SW8 BX43 66
Aldeburgh Clo. E5 CB34 48
Southwold Rd.
Aldeburgh Pl. Wdf. Grn. CH28 40
Aldeburgh St. SE10 CH42 68
Alden Av. E15 CG38 58
Aldenham Av. Rad. BJ21 27
Aldenham Gro. Rad. BJ20 18
Aldenham Rd. Borwd. BJ24 27
Aldenham Rd. Rad. BJ21 27
Aldenham Rd. Wat. BD25 27
Aldenham St. NW1 BW37 1
Aldenham St. NW1 BW37 56
Aldenholme, Wey. BB57 92
Aldensley Rd. W6 BP41 65
Alden Vw. Wind. AL44 61
Alder Av. Upmin. CW35 51
Alderbourne La. Iver AT35 43
Alderbourne La. Slou. AR35 43
Aldebrook Rd. SW12 BV46 76
Alderbury Rd. SW13 BP43 65
Alderbury Rd. Slou. AS41 62
Aldebury Rd. W. Slou. AS41 62
Alder Clo. SE15 CA43 67
Alder Clo. St. Alb. BG17 18
Aldercoome La. Cat. CA67 114
Alder Croft Couls. BX57 95
Aldercroft Couls. BX61 104
Alder Gro. NW2 BP34 46
Aldergrove Wk. Horn. CV36 60
Airfield Way
Alderholt Way, SE15 CA43 67
Bedenham Way
Alderley Ct. Berk. AQ13 7
Alderman Av. N. Slou. AQ41 62
Alderman Av. Bark. CO38 59
Aldermanbury, EC2 BZ39 2
Aldermanbury, EC2 BZ39 57
Aldermanbury Sq. EC2 BZ39 2
Aldermanbury Sq. EC2 BZ39 57
Alderman Clo. Hat. BQ15 10
Dixon's Hill Rd.
Alderman Judge Mall.
Kings on T. BL51 85
Eden St.
Alderman's Hill N13 BX28 38
Aldermans Wk. EC2 CA39 57
Bishopsgate
Aldermary Rd. Brom. CH51 88
Aldermas St. W10 BQ39 55
Alderminster Rd. SE1 CB42 4
Alderminster Rd. SE1 CB42 67
Aldermoor Rd. SE6 CD48 77
Alderney Av. Houns. BF43 64
Alderney Gdns. Nthlt. BE36 54
Alderney Rd. E1 CC38 57
Alderney Rd. Erith CU43 69
Alderney St. SW1 BV42 3
Alderney St. SW1 BV42 66
Alder Rd. SW14 BN45 65
Alder Rd. Sid. CN48 78
Alder Rd. Uxb. AX36 53
Alders Av. Wdf. Grn. CG29 40
Aldersbrook Av. Enf. CA23 30
Aldersbrook Dri.
Kings. on T. BL50 75
Aldersbrook La. E12 CK34 49
Aldersbrook Rd. E11 CH34 49
Aldersbrook Rd. E12 CH34 49
Alders Clo. Edg. BN28 37
Aldersey Gdns. Bark. CM36 58
Aldersey Rd. Guil. AS70 118
Aldersford Clo. SE4 CC45 67
Aldersford Clo. SE4 CD45 67
Frendsbury Rd.
Aldersgate St. EC1 BZ39 2
Aldersgate St. EC1 BZ39 57
Alders Gro. E. Mol. BG53 84
Aldersgrove Wal. Abb. CG20 22
Roundhills
Aldersgrove Av. SE9 CJ48 78
Aldershot Rd. NW6 BR37 55
Aldershot Rd. Guil. AO68 109
Aldershot Rd. Guil. AO69 118
Aldershot Ter. SE18 CK43 68
Imperial Way
Alderside Clo. Egh. AS49 72
Alderside Wk. Egh. AS49 72
Aldersmead Av. Croy. CC53 87
Aldersmead Rd. Beck. CD50 77
Alderson St. W10 BR38 55
Kensal Rd.
Alders Rd. Edg. BO28 37
Alders Rd. Reig. BS69 121
Alderstead La. Red. BW66 113
Alders, The, N21 BY25 29
Alders, The, Felt. BE49 74
Alders, The, Houns. BE42 64
Alders, The, W. Wick. CE54 87
Alderton Clo. SE5 BZ45 67
Alderton Clo. Brwd. DA25 42
Alderton Clo. Loug. CL24 31
Alderton Cres. NW4 BP32 46
Alderton Hall La. Loug. CL24 31
Alderton Hill Loug. CK25 31
Alderton Rise. Loug. CL24 31
Alderton Rd. SE24 BZ45 67
Alderton Rd. Croy. CA54 87
Alderton Way NW4 BP32 46
Alderton Cres.
Alderton Way Loug. CK25 31
Alderville Rd. SW6 BR44 65
Alder Way Swan. CS51 89
Alderwick Dr. Houns. BG45 64
Alderwood Clo. Cat. CA66 114
Alderwood Rd. SE9 CM46 78
Alderwood Rom. CO24 32
Aldford St. W1 BV40 3
Aldford St. W1 BV40 56
Aldgate, EC3 CA39 2
Aldgate Av. E1 CA39 57
Aldgate High St. EC3 CA39 2
Aldgate High St. EC3 CA39 57
Aldham Hall, E11 CH32 49
Aldin Av. Slou. AQ41 62
Aldine Ct. W12 BQ41 65
Aldine Cres. W12 BQ41 65
Aldine St. W12 BQ41 65
Aldingham Gdns. Horn. CU35 50
Aldington Rd. SE7 CJ41 68
Aldis Ms. SW17 BU49 76
Aldis St.
Aldis St. SW17 BU49 76
Aldock, Welw. G. C. BS9 5
Aldred Rd. NW6 BS35 47
Aldren Rd. SW17 BT48 76
Aldrich Cres. Croy. CF58 96
Aldriche Way, E4 CF29 39
Aldridge Av. Edg. BM27 37
Aldridge Av. Enf. CE22 30
Aldridge Av. Ruis. BD34 45
Aldridge Av. Stan. BL30 37
Aldridge Rise N. Mal. BO54 85
Aldridge Rd. Vill. W11 BR39 55
Aldridge Walk N14 BX26 38
Aldrington Rd. SW16 BW49 76
Aldsworth Clo. W9 BS38 56
Amberley Est.
Aldwick Clo. SE9 CM48 78
Aldwick Ct. St. Alb. BJ14 9
Aldwick Rd. Croy. BX55 86
Aldworth Gr. SE13 CF46 77
Aldworth Rd. E15 CG36 58
Aldwych WC2 BX39 2
Aldwych, WC2 BX40 4
Aldwych, WC2 BX40 56
Aldwych Av. Ilf. CM31 49
Aldwych Clo. Horn. CU34 50
Aldykes Hat. BO12 10
Alers Rd. Bexh. CP46 79
Alexander Av. NW10 BP36 55
Alexander Clo. Brom. CH54 88
Alexander Clo. Sid. CN46 78
Alexander Clo. Twick. BH48 74
Alexander Ct. N14 BW25 29
Alexander Godley Clo.
Ash. BL63 103
Alexander La. Brwd. DD25 122
Alexander Ms. W2 BS39 56
Alexander St.
Alexander Pl. SW7 BU42 3
Alexander Pl. SW7 BU42 66
Alexander Rd. N19 BX34 47
Alexander Rd. W13 BJ40 54
Alexander Rd. Bexh. CP44 69
Alexander Rd. Chis. CL49 78
Alexander Rd. Couls. BV61 104
Alexander Rd. Green. DB46 80
Alexander Rd. Reig. BS72 121
Alexander Sq. SW3 BU41 66
Alexander Sq. SW3 BU42 3
Alexander St. W2 BS39 56
Alexanders Wk. Cat. CA66 114
Alexandra Av. Warl. CD62 105
Alexandra Av. N22 BW30 38
Alexandra Av. SW11 BV44 66
Alexandra Av. W4 BN43 65
Alexandra Av. Har. BE33 45
Alexandra Av. Sthl. BE40 54
Alexandra Av. Sutt. BS55 86
Alexandra Clo. Ashf. BA50 73
Alexandra Clo. Grays. DG41 71
Alexandra Clo. Har. BF34 45
Alexandra Clo. Stai. AX50 73
Alexandra Clo. Walt. BC55 83
Alexandra Cotts. SE14 CD44 67
Alexandra Ct. W9 BT38 1
Alexandra Ct. Wem. BL35 46
Alexandra Cres. Brom. CG50 78
Alexandra Dr. SE19 CA49 77
Alexandra Dr. Surb. BM54 85
Alexandra Gdns. N10 BV31 47
Alexandra Gdns. W4 BO43 65
Alexandra Gdns. Cars. BU58 95
Alexandra Gdns. Houns. BF44 64
Alexandra Gro. N4 BY33 47
Alexandra Gro. N12 BS29 38
Alexandra Ms. NW8 BS37 56
Alexandra Pk. Rd. N10 BV30 38
Alexandra Pk. Rd. N22 BV30 38
Alexandra Pl. NW8 BT37 1
Alexandra Pl. NW8 BT37 56
Alexandra Pl. SE25 BZ53 87
Alexandra Pl. Croy. CA54 87
Alexandra Rd. E6 CL38 58
Alexandra Rd. E10 CF34 48
Alexandra Rd. E17 CD32 48
Alexandra Rd. E18 CH31 49
Alexandra Rd. N8 BY31 47
Alexandra Rd. N9 CB26 39
King Edwards Rd.
Alexandra Rd. N10 BV30 38
Alexandra Rd. N15 BZ32 48
Alexandra Rd. NW4 BQ31 46
Alexandra Rd. NW8 BS37 56
Alexandra Rd. NW8 BT37 56
Alexandra Rd. SE26 CC50 77
Alexandra Rd. SW14 BN45 65
Alexandra Rd. SW19 BR50 75
Alexandra Rd. W4 BN41 65
Alexandra Rd. Ashf. BA50 73
Alexandra Rd. Borwd. BN22 28
Alexandra Rd. Borwd. BN23 28
Alexandra Rd. Brent. BK43 64
Alexandra Rd. Brwd. DB27 42
Alexandra Rd. Croy. CA54 87
Alexandra Rd. Egh. AR50 72
Alexandra Rd. Egh. AT49 72
Alexandra Rd. Enf. CC24 30
Alexandra Rd. Epsom BO60 94
Alexandra Rd. Erith CT43 69
Alexandra Rd. Grav. DJ47 81
Alexandra Rd. Hem. H. AX13 8
Alexandra Rd. Houns. BF44 64
Alexandra Rd. Kings. L. AW18 17
Alexandra Rd. Kings. L. AZ18 17
Alexandra Rd. Kings. on T. BM50 75
Alexandra Rd. Mitch. BU50 76
Alexandra Rd. Rain. CT37 59
Alexandra Rd. Rich. BL44 65
Alexandra Rd. Rick. AW21 26
Alexandra Rd. Rom. CP32 50
Alexandra Rd. Rom. CQ32 50
Alexandra Rd. Rom. CT32 50
Alexandra Rd. St. Alb. BH13 9
Alexandra Rd. St. Alb. BK16 18
Alexandra Rd. Slou. AO41 61
Alexandra Rd. Surb. BH53 84
Alexandra Rd. Til. DF44 71
Alexandra Rd. Twick. BK46 74
Alexandra Rd. Uxb. AX37 53
Alexandra Rd. Warl. CD62 105
Alexandra Rd. Wat. BC23 26
Alexandra Rd. West. CH63 106
Alexandra Rd. Wey. AX56 92
Alexandra Sq. Mord. BS53 86
Alexandra St. E16 CH39 58
Alexandra St. SE14 CD43 67
Bowerman Av.
Alexandra Ter. Guil. AS71 118
Alexandra Wk. SE19 CA49 77
Alexandra Way, Wal. Cr. CD20 21
Alexandra Rd. W13 BJ40 54
Alexis St. SE16 CB42 4
Alexis St. SE16 CB42 67
Alex St. Chesh. AO18 16
Alfan La. Dart. CS49 79
Alford Grn. Croy. CF57 96
Alford Pl. N1 BZ37 57
Shepherders Wk.
Alford Rd. SW8 BW44 66
Union Gro.
Alford Rd. Erith CS42 69
Alfoxton Av. N15 BY31 47
Alfreda St. SW11 BV44 66
Alfred Cotts. SW17 BU49 76
Alfred Gdns. Sthl. BE40 54
Alfred Ms. W1 BW39 1
Alfred Ms. W1 BW39 56
Alfred Ms. W3 BN40 55
Alfred Pl. N1 BZ37 2
Alfred Pl. WC1 BW39 1
Alfred Pl. WC1 BW39 56
Alfred Pl. Grav. DF47 81
Doves Rd. East
Alfred Rd. E15 CG35 49
Alfred Rd. SE25 CB53 87
Alfred Rd. W2 BS39 56
Alfred Rd. W3 BN40 55
Alfred Rd. W13 BJ40 54
Alfred Rd. Belv. CQ42 69
Alfred Rd. Brwd. DB27 42
Alfred Rd. Buck. H. CJ27 40
Alfred Rd. Dart. CW49 80
Alfred Rd. Felt. BD48 74
Alfred Rd. Grav. DG48 81
Alfred Rd. Kings. on T. BL52 85
Alfred Rd. S. Ock. CW40 60
Alfred Rd. Sutt. BT56 95
Alfred's Gdns. Bark. CN37 58
Alfred St. E3 CD38 57
Alfred St. E16 CG40 58
Alfred St. Grays. DE43 71
Alfred's Way Bark. CM37 58
Alfreton Clo. SW19 BQ48 75
Alfreton St. SE17 CA42 4
Alfreton St. SE17 CA42 67
Alfriston Surb. BL53 85
Alfriston Av. Croy. BX54 86
Alfriston Av. Har. BF32 45
Alfriston Rd. SW11 BU45 66
Algar Clo. Islw. BJ45 64
Algar Clo. Stan. BH28 36
Algar Rd. Islw. BJ45 64
Algarve Rd. SW18 BS47 76
Algernon Rd. NW4 BP32 46
Algernon Rd. NW6 BS37 56
Algernon Rd. SE13 CE45 67
Algers Clo. Loug. CJ25 31
Algers Mead. Loug. CJ25 31
Algers Rd. Loug. CJ25 31
Algiers Rd. SE13 CE45 67
Alibon Gdns. Dag. CR35 50
Alibon Rd. Dag. CR35 50
Alice Gilliat Ct. W14 BR43 65
Alice St. SE1 CA41 4
Alice St. SE1 CA41 67
Alicia Av. Har. BJ31 45
Alicia Clo. Har. BK31 45
Alicia Gdns. Har. BJ31 45
Alie St. E1 CA39 2
Alie St. E1 CA39 57
Alington Cres. NW9 BN33 46
Alington Gro. Wall. BW58 95
Alison Clo. Wok. AS60 100
Grange Rd.
Aliwal Rd. SW11 BU45 66

Street	Grid	Page
Alkerden La. Green.	DB46	80
Alkerden Rd. W4	BO42	65
Alkham Rd. N16	CA33	48
Allan Clo. Dart.	CY47	80
Allan Clo. N. Mal.	BN53	85
Allandale Av. N3	BR31	46
Allandale Pla. Orp.	CP55	89
Allandale Rd. Enf.	CC21	30
Allandale Rd. Horn.	CT33	50
Allanmouth Rd. E3	CD36	57
Allan Way W3	BN39	55
Allard Clo. Orp.	CP54	89
Allard Clo. Wal. Cr.	CA17	21
Allard Cres. Bush.	BG27	36
Allard Way, Brox.	CD14	12
Allardyce St. SW9	BX45	66
Allas Rd. E2	CC38	57
Allbrook Clo. Tedd.	BH49	74
Alldicks Rd. Hem. H.	AY14	8
Allenby Av. Sth. Croy.	BZ58	96
Allenby Clo. Grnf.	BF38	54
Allenby Cres. Grays.	DD42	71
Allenby Dr. Horn.	CW33	51
Allenby Rd. SE23	CD48	77
Allenby Rd. Sthl.	BF38	54
Allenby Rd. West	CK62	106
Allen Clo. Sun.	BC51	83
Allendale St. Alb.	BF15	9
Allendale Av. Sthl.	BF39	54
Allendale Rd. SE5	BZ44	67
Allendale Rd. Grnf.	BJ36	54
Allendale Rd. Hem. H.	AX12	8
Allendale Rd. Hem. H.	AX13	8
Allen Edwards Dr. SW8	BX44	66
Allen Rd. E3	CD37	57
Allen Rd. N16	CA35	48
Allen Rd. Beck.	CC51	87
Allen Rd. Croy.	BX54	86
Allen Rd. Lthd.	BF66	111
Allen Rd. Rain.	CV38	60
Allen Rd. Sun.	BC51	83
Allen's Rd. Enf.	CC25	30
Allen St. W8	BS41	66
Allenswood Rd. SE9	CK45	68
Allerford Ct. Har.	BF32	45
Allerford Rd. SE6	CE48	77
Allerton Clo. Borwd.	BL22	28
Allerton Rd. N16	BZ34	48
Allerton Rd. Borwd.	BL22	28
Allerton Wk. N7	BX34	47
Andover Est.		
Allerton Wk. N7	BX34	47
Durham Rd.		
Allestree Rd. SW6	BR43	65
All Hallows Rd. N17	CA30	39
Roundway, The		
Alleyn Cres. SE21	BZ48	77
Alleyndale Rd. Dag.	CP34	50
Alleyn Pk. SE21	BZ47	77
Alleyn Pk. Sthl.	BE42	64
Alleyn Pk. Est. SE21	CA49	77
Alleyn Rd. SE21	BZ48	77
All Saints Clo. N9	CB27	39
All Saints Clo. Brwd.	DA21	33
All Saints Clo. Chig.	CO27	41
Romford Rd.		
All Saints Dr. SE3	CG44	68
All Saints Dr. SE3	CG44	68
All Saints Dr. Sth. Croy.	CA59	96
All Saints La. Rick.	AZ25	26
All Saints Pass SW18	BS46	76
Wandsworth High St.		
All Saint's Rd. SW19	BT50	76
All Saints Rd. W3	BN41	65
All Saints Rd. W11	BR39	55
All Saints Rd. Grav.	DF47	81
All Saints Rd. Sutt.	BS55	86
All Saints St. N1	**BX37**	**2**
All Saints St. N1	BX37	56
All Souls Av. NW10	BP37	55
All Souls Pl. W1	**BV39**	**1**
All Souls Pl. W1	BV39	56
Langham Pl.		
Allfarthing La. SW18	BS46	76
Allgood Clo. Mord.	BQ53	85
Allhallows La. EC4	**BZ40**	**4**
Allhallows La. EC4	BZ40	57
Allhusen Gdns. Slou.	AS35	43
Alliance Rd. E13	CJ38	58
Alliance Rd. SE18	CO43	69
Alliance Rd. W3	BM38	55
Allingham Ct. NW3	BU35	47
Haverstock Hill		
Allingham Rd. Reig.	BS72	121
Allingham St. N1	**BZ37**	**2**
Allingham St. N1	BZ37	57
Allington Av. N17	CA29	39
Allington Clo. SW19	BQ49	75
Allington Rd. NW4	BP32	46
Allington Rd. SW2	BX46	76
Allington Rd. W10	BR37	55
Allington Rd. Har.	BG32	45
Allington Rd. Orp.	CM55	88
Allington St. SW1	**BV41**	**3**
Allington St. SW1	BV41	66
Allison Clo. SE3	CF44	67
Allison Clo. SE10	CF44	67
Shooters Hill Rd.		
Allison Clo. Wal. Abb.	CH19	22
Allison Gro. SE21	CA47	77
Allison Rd. N8	BY32	47
Allison Rd. W3	BN39	55
Allitsen Rd. NW8	**BU37**	**1**
Allitsen Rd. NW8	BU37	56
Allmains Clo. Wal. Abb.	CH16	22
Allnutts Rd. Epp.	CO20	23
Allnutt Way SW4	BW46	76
Alloa Rd. SE8	CC42	67
Alloa Rd. Ilf.	CO34	50
Allonby Gdns. Wem.	BK33	45
Windermere Av.		
Alloway Clo. Wok.	AQ62	100
Alloway Rd. E3	CD38	57
All Saints Clo. Swans.	DC46	81
High St.		
All Saints Dri. Sth. Croy.	CA59	96
Allsop Pl. NW1	**BU38**	**1**
Allsop Pl. NW1	BU38	56
Allum La. Borwd.	BK25	27
Allum Way N20	BT27	38
Manus Way		
Allyn Clo. Stai.	AV50	72
Penton Rd.		
Alma Av. E4	CF29	39
Alma Av. Horn.	CW35	51
Almack Rd. E5	CC35	48
Alma Clo. Wok.	AP62	100
Alma Cres. Sutt.	BR56	94
Alma Cut. St. Alb.	BH14	9
Alma Gro. SE1	**CA42**	**4**
Alma Gro. SE1	CA42	67
Alma Pl. Sun.	BC50	73
Alma Pl. Th. Hth.	BY53	86
Alma Pl. N10	BV29	38
Alma Rd. SW18	BT45	66
Alma Rd. Berk.	AP12	7
Alma Rd. Cars.	BU56	95
Alma Rd. Enf.	CC25	30
Alma Rd. Esher	BH54	84
Alma Rd. Har.	BG29	36
Alma Rd. Orp.	CP55	89
Alma Rd. Reig.	BS70	121
Alma Rd. St. Alb.	BH14	9
Alma Rd. Sid.	CO48	79
Alma Rd. Sthl.	BE40	54
Alma Rd. Swans.	DC46	81
Alma Rd. Wind.	AM42	61
Alma Rd. Wind.	AO44	61
Alma Sq. NW8	**BT38**	**1**
Alma Sq. NW8	BT38	56
Alma St. E15	CF36	57
Alma St. NW5	BV36	56
Alma Ter. SW18	BT47	76
Almeida St. N1	**BY36**	**2**
Almeida St. N1	BY36	56
Almeric Rd. SW11	BU45	66
Almer Rd. SW20	BP50	75
Almington St. N4	BX33	47
Almners Rd. Cher.	AT54	82
Almond Av. West Dr.	AZ41	63
Almond Av. W5	BK41	64
Almond Av. Cars.	BU55	86
Almond Av. Uxb.	AZ34	44
Almond Av. Wok.	AR63	100
Almond Cl. Egh.	AQ50	72
Almond Clo. Grays.	DG41	71
Almond Clo. SE15	CB44	67
Almond Clo. Brom.	CL54	88
Almond Clo. Guil.	AR68	109
Almond Clo. Guil.	AR69	118
Almond Clo. Hayes	BB40	53
Almond Clo. Ruis.	BB34	44
Almond Clo. Ruis.	BC34	44
Almond Clo. Shep.	BA51	83
Almond Dr. Swan.	CS51	89
Almond Gro. Brent.	BJ43	64
Almond Rd. N17	CB29	39
Trulock Rd.		
Almond Rd. SE16	CB42	67
Almond Rd. Epsom	BN59	94
Almond Rd. Dart.	CY47	80
Almond Av. Buck. H.	CH27	40
Almond Wk. Hat.	BP14	10
Almond Way Borwd.	BM24	28
Whitehouse Av.		
Almond Way Brom.	CL54	88
Almond Way Har.	BF30	36
Almond Way Mitch.	BW53	86
Almons Way Slou.	AQ39	52
Almorah Rd. N1	BZ36	57
Almorah Rd. Houns.	BD44	64
Almorah St. N1	**BZ36**	**2**
Alms Heath Wok.	AZ64	101
Almshouse La. Chess.	BK58	93
Almshouse La. Enf.	CB22	30
Alnwick Gro. Mord.	BS52	86
Abbotsbury Rd.		
Alnwick Rd. E16	CJ39	58
Alnwick Rd. SE12	CH46	78
Alperton La. Alp.	BK38	54
Alpha Clo. NW1	**BU38**	**1**
Alpha Clo. NW1	BU38	56
Alpha Ct. Whyt.	CB62	105
Alpha Gro. E14	CE41	67
Alpha Pl. NW6	BS37	56
Alpha Pl. SW3	**BU43**	**3**
Alpha Pl. SW3	BU43	66
Alpha Rd. E4	CE27	39
Alpha Rd. N18	CB29	39
Alpha Rd. SE14	CD44	67
Alpha Rd. Brwd.	DE25	122
Alpha Rd. Croy.	CA54	87
Alpha Rd. Enf.	CD24	30
Alpha Rd. Surb.	BL53	85
Alpha Rd. Surb.	BL54	85
Alpha Rd. Tedd.	BG49	74
Alpha Rd. Uxb.	AZ38	53
Alpha Rd. Wok.	AP58	91
Alpha Rd. Wok.	AT61	100
Alpha St. SE15	CB44	67
Alpha St. Slou.	AP41	62
Alpine Av. Surb.	BN55	85
Alpine Clo. Croy.	CA55	87
Alpine Copse Brom.	CL51	88
Alpine Rd. SE16	CC42	67
Alpine Rd. Red.	BV69	121
Alpine Rd. Walt.	BC54	83
Alpine St. W10	BR39	55
Alpine Wk. Bush.	BH27	36
Alp St. W10	BR38	55
Alresford Rd. Guil.	AQ71	118
Alric Av. NW10	BN36	55
Alric Av. N. Mal.	BO52	85
Alroy Rd. N4	BY33	47
Alsacre Rd. SE17	CA42	4
Alsacre Rd. SE17	CA42	67
Alscot Rd. SE1	**CA42**	**4**
Alscot Rd. SE1	CA42	67
Alsike Rd. SE2	CP41	69
Alsike Rd. Belv.	CP41	69
Alsom Av. Wor. Pk.	BP56	94
Alston Clo. Surb.	BJ54	84
Alston Rd. N18	CB28	39
Alston Rd. SW17	BT49	76
Alston Rd. Barn.	BR24	28
Alston Rd. Hem. H.	AW14	8
Altair Clo. N17	CA29	39
Altair Clo. N18	CB29	39
Brantwood Rd.		
Altair Way Nthwd.	BB28	35
Altash Way SE9	CK48	78
Altenburg Av. W13	BJ41	64
Altenburg Gdns. SW11	BU45	66
Alt Gro. SW19	BR50	75
Altham Grove Harl.	CN10	6
Altham Rd. Pnr.	BE29	36
Althea St. SW6	BS44	66
Althorne Gdns. E18	CG31	49
Althorne Rd. Red.	BV71	121
Althrone Way Dag.	CR34	50
Althorpe Gro. SW11	BT44	66
Westbridge Rd.		
Althorpe Rd. Har.	BG32	45
Althorpe Rd. St. Alb.	BH13	9
Althorpe Rd. SW17	BU47	76
Altmore Av. E6	CK36	58
Alton Av. Stan.	BH29	36
Alton Clo. Bex.	CQ47	79
Alton Clo. Islw.	BH44	64
Alton Gdns. Beck.	CE50	77
Alton Gdns. Twick.	BG47	74
Alton Rd. N17	BZ31	48
Alton Rd. SW15	BP47	75
Alton Rd. Croy.	BY55	86
Alton Rd. Rich.	BL45	65
Alton St. E14	CE39	57
Altyre Clo. Beck.	CD53	87
Altyre Rd. Croy.	BZ55	87
Altyre Way Beck.	CD53	87
Alvanley Gdns. NW6	BS35	47
Alva Way Wat.	BD27	36
Alverstoke Rd. Rom.	CW29	42
Alverstone Av. SW19	BS48	76
Alverstone Av. Barn.	BU26	38
Alverstone Gdns. SE9	CM47	78
Alverstone Rd. E12	CL35	49
Alverstone Rd. NW2	BQ36	55
Alverstone Rd. N. Mal.	BO52	85
Alverstone Rd. Wem.	BL33	46
Alverston Gdns. SE25	CA52	87
Alverston St. SE8	CD42	67
Alveston Av. Har.	BJ31	45
Alvey Est. SE17	**CA42**	**4**
Alvey Est. SE17	CA42	67
Alvey St. SE17	**CA42**	**4**
Alvey St. SE17	CA42	67
Alvington Cres. E8	CA35	48
Alway Av. Epsom	BN56	94
Alwen Grn. S. Ock.	DA39	60
Alwood Cres. SE12	CH46	78
Alwyn Av. W4	BN42	65
Alwyn Clo. Borwd.	BL25	28
Alwyn Clo. Croy.	CE57	96
Alwyne Av. Brwd.	DD25	122
Alwyne La. N1	BY36	56
Alwyne Pl. N1	BZ36	57
Alwyne Rd. N1	BZ36	57
Alwyne Rd. SW19	BR50	75
Alwyne Rd. W7	BH40	54
Alwyne Sq. N1	BZ36	57
Alwyne Vill. N1	BY36	56
Alwyn Gdns. W3	BM39	55
Noel Rd.		
Alwyns Clo. Cher.	AW53	83
Alwyns St. Cher.	AV53	82
Alyth Gdns. NW11	BS32	47
Amanda Ct. Slou.	AR41	62
Amazon St. E1	CB39	57
Ambassador Clo. Houns.	BE44	64
Amber Av. E17	CD30	39
Amber Croft Way, Couls.	BY59	95
Ambercroft Way, Couls.	BY62	104
Ambercroft Way, Couls.	BY63	104
Ambergeen Av. N3	BS31	47
Ambergate St. SE17	**BY42**	**4**
Ambergate St. SE17	BY42	66
Amberley Clo. Pnr.	BE31	45
Amberley Clo. Wok.	AV66	109
Amberley Ct. Sid.	CP49	79
Amberley Dri. Wey.	AV59	91
Amberley Gdns. Enf.	CA26	39
Amberley Gdns. Epsom	BO56	94
Amberley Gro. SE26	CB49	77
Amberley Gro. Croy.	CA54	87
Amberley Ms. W9	BS38	56
Amberley Rd. E10	CE33	48
Amberley Rd. N13	BX27	38
Amberley Rd. SE2	CP43	69
Amberley Rd. W9	BS38	56
Amberley Rd. Buck. H.	CJ26	40
Amberley Rd. Enf.	CA26	39
Amberley Way Houns.	BD46	74
Amberley Way Mord.	BR54	85
Amberley Way Rom.	CR31	50
Amberry Ct. Harl.	CM10	6
Amber St. E15	CF36	57
Salway Rd.		
Amberwood Rise N. Mal.	BN53	85
Amblecote Clo. SE12	CH48	78
Amblecote Rd. SE12	CH48	78
Ambler Rd. N4	BY34	47
Ambleside Brom.	CF50	77
Ambleside Av. SW16	BW49	76
Ambleside Av. Beck.	CD53	87
Ambleside Av. Horn.	CU35	50
Ambleside Av. Walt.	BD54	84
Ambleside Clo. E9	CC35	48
Churchill Wk.		
Ambleside Cres. Enf.	CC24	30
Ambleside Epp.	CO19	23
Ambleside Gdns. Ilf.	CK31	49
Ambleside Gdns. Sth. Croy.	CC58	96
Ambleside Gdns. Sutt.	BT57	95
Ambleside Gdns. Wem.	BK33	45
Ambleside Rd. NW10	BO36	55
Ambleside Rd. Bexh.	CR44	69
Ambrey Way Pur.	BW58	95
Ambridge Rd. Dag.	CR33	50
Ambrooke Rd. Belv.	CR41	69
Sheridan Rd.		
Ambrooke Rd. Belv.	CR42	69
Gertrude Rd.		
Ambrosden Av. SW1	**BW41**	**3**
Ambrosden Av. SW1	BW41	66
Ambrose Av. NW11	BR33	46
Ambrose St. SE16	CB42	67
Southwark Pk. Rd.		
Ambrose Wk. E3	CE37	58
Malmesbury Rd.		
Ambroth Clo. SE23	CB47	77
Horniman Dr.		
Amelia St. SE17	**BY42**	**4**
Amelia St. SE17	BY42	66
Amen Ct. EC4	**BY39**	**2**
Amen Ct. EC4	BY39	56
America Sq. EC3	**CA40**	**4**
America St. SE1	**BZ40**	**4**
America St. SE1	BZ40	57
Great Guildford St.		
Amerland Rd. SW18	BR46	75
Amersham Av. N18	BZ29	39
Amersham Clo. Rom.	CW29	42
Amersham Dr. Rom.	CW29	42
Amersham Gro. SE14	CD43	67
Amersham Rd. SE14	CD43	67
Amersham Rd. Amer.	AR23	25
Amersham Rd. Ch. St. G.	AQ25	25
Amersham Rd. Ch. St. G.	AQ26	34
Amersham Rd. Ch. St. G.	AR28	34
Amersham Rd. Croy.	BZ53	87
Amersham Rd. Ger. Cr.	AS31	43
Amersham Rd. Har.	BH32	45
Amersham Rd. Rom.	CW29	42
Amersham Val. SE14	CD43	67
Amersham Wk. Rom.	CW29	42
Amersham Way, Amer.	AS23	25
Amerton Ct. Wind.	AO43	61
Amery Gdns. NW10	BP37	55
Amery Gdns. Rom.	CV31	51
Amery Rd. Har.	BJ34	45
Amesbury Wal. Abb.	CH19	22
Amesbury Av. SW2	BX48	76
Amesbury Clo. Epp.	CN19	22
Amesbury Clo. Wor. Pk.	BQ54	85
Amesbury Dr. E4	CE25	30
Amesbury Rd. Brom.	CJ52	88
Amesbury Rd. Dag.	CP36	59
Amesbury Rd. Epp.	CN19	22
Amesbury Rd. Felt.	BD48	74
Ames Rd. Swans.	DC46	81
Amethyst Rd. E15	CF35	48
Amey Dr. Lthd.	BG65	102
Amherst Av. W13	BJ39	54
Amherst Clo. Orp.	CO52	89
Amherst Dr. Orp.	CN52	88
Amherst Gdns. W13	BK39	54
Amherst Rd.		
Amherst Hill Sev.	CT64	107
Amherst Rd. W13	BK39	54
Amherst Rd. Sev.	CU64	107
Amhurst Gdns. Islw.	BH44	64
Amhurst Park N16	BZ33	48
Amhurst Park Dev. N16	CA33	48
Amhurst Pass E8	CB35	48
Amhurst Rd. E8	CA35	48
Amhurst Rd. N16	CA35	48
Amhurst Ter. E8	CB35	48
Amidas Gdns. Dag.	CO35	50
Amiel St. E1	CC38	57
Colebert Av.		
Amies St. SW11	BU45	66
Amis Av. Epsom	BM57	94
Amis Av. Wey.	AW58	92
Amis Rd. Wok.	AP63	100
Amity Gro. SW20	BQ51	85
Amity Rd. E15	CG37	58
Ammiel Ter. E3	CE37	57
Amner Rd. SW11	BV46	76
Amor Pl. W6	BQ42	65
Amor Rd. W6	BQ41	65
Amos Est. SE16	CC40	57
Amott Rd. SE15	CB45	67
Amour Clo. N7	BX36	56
Roman Way		
Amoy Pl. E14	CE40	57
Birchfield St.		
Ampleforth Rd. SE2	CO41	69
Ampthil Sq. Est. NW1	**BW37**	**1**
Ampthill Sq. Est.	BW37	56
Ampton Pl. WC1	**BX38**	**2**
Ampton Pl. WC1	BX38	56
Ampton St.		
Ampton St. WC1	**BX38**	**2**
Ampton St. WC1	BX38	56
Amroth Clo. SE23	CB47	77
Amton Cres. Sutt.	BS55	86
Amwell Clo. Enf.	BZ25	30
Amwell Common Welw. G. C.	BS8	5
Amwell Ct. N4	BZ33	48
Amwell Ct. Wal. Abb.	CG20	22
Amwell St. EC1	**BY38**	**2**
Amwell St. EC1	BY38	56
Amwell St. Hodd.	CE11	12
Amyand Cotts. Twick.	BJ46	74
Amyand Park Rd.		
Amyand La. Twick.	BJ46	74
Beaconsfield Rd.		
Amyand La. Twick.	BJ47	74
Marble Hill Gdns.		
Amyand Pk. Gdns. Twick.	BJ46	74
Amyand Pk. Rd.		
Amyard Pk. Rd. Twick.	BJ47	74
Amy Rd. Oxt	CG68	115
Amyruth Rd. SE4	CE46	77
Anatola Rd. N19	BV34	47
Ancaster Cres. N. Mal.	BP53	85
Ancaster Rd. Beck.	CC52	87
Ancaster St. SE18	CN43	68
Anchorage Clo. SW19	BS49	76
Anchor Cres. Wok.	AO62	100
Anchor & Hope La. SE7	CH41	68
Anchor La. Hem. H.	AW14	8
Anchor St. SE16	CB42	67
Anchor Yd. EC1	BZ38	57
Old St.		
Ancona Rd. NW10	BP37	55
Ancona Rd. SE18	CM42	68
Andalus Rd. SW9	BX45	66
Ander Clo. Wem.	BK35	45
Andermass Wind.	AL44	61
Anderson Clo. Epsom	BM59	94
Anderson Dr. Ashf.	BA49	73
Anderson Rd. E9	CC36	57
Digby Rd.		
Anderson Rd. Rad.	BM20	19
Anderson Rd. Wey.	BA55	83
Anderson's Pl. Houns.	BF45	64
Anderson St. SW3	**BU42**	**3**
Anderson St. SW3	BU42	66
Anderson St. W10	BR38	55
Kensal Rd.		
Andoe Rd. SW11	BU45	66
Andover Clo. Epsom	BN58	94
Andover Clo. Grnf.	BF38	54
Andover Clo. Uxb.	AW37	53
Andover Ct. Wok.	AR63	100
Andover Pl. NW6	BS37	56
Andover Rd. N7	BX34	47
Andover Rd. Orp.	CN54	88
Andover Rd. Twick.	BG47	74
Andre St. E8	CB35	48
Andrew Borde St. WC2	BW39	56
Charing Cross Rd.		
Andrew Clo. Bex.	CS46	79
Bourne Rd.		
Andrew Pl. SW8	BW44	66
Andrews Clo. Buck. H.	CJ27	40
Andrews Clo. Epsom	BO60	94
Andrews Clo. Orp.	CP51	89
Andrew's Crosse WC2	CM39	58
Bell Yd.		
Andrew's La. Wal. Cr.	CA17	21
Andrew's Rd. E8	CB37	57
Andrew St. E14	CF39	57
Andrews Wk. SE17	BY43	66
Ruskin St.		
Andwell Clo. SE2	CO41	69
Anerley Gro. SE19	CA50	77
Anerley Hill SE19	CA50	77
Anerley Pk. SE20	CB50	77
Anerley Pk. Rd. SE20	CB50	77
Anerley Rd. SE19	CB50	77
Anerley Rd. SE20	CB50	77
Anerley Sta. Rd. SE20	CB51	87
Anerley Val. SE19	CA50	77
Anerly St. SW11	BU44	66
Dagnall St.		
Angas Ct. Wey.	BA56	92
Angel Clo. N18	CA28	39
Angel Ct. EC2	**BZ39**	**2**
Angel Ct. EC2	BZ39	57
Throgmorton St.		
Angel Ct. SW1	**BW40**	**3**
Angel Ct. SW1	BW40	56
King St.		
Angel Ct. SW17	BU49	76
Angelfield Houns.	BF45	64
Angel Hill Sutt.	BS55	86
Angel Hill Dr. Sutt.	BS55	86
Angel La. E15	CF36	57
Angel La. Hayes	BA39	53
Angell Pk. Gdns. SW9	BY45	66
Angell Rd. SW9	BY44	66
Angel Ms. N1	**BY37**	**2**
Angel Ms. N1	BY37	56
Angel Pass EC3	BZ40	57
Wharfside		
Angel Pl. EC4	**BZ40**	**4**
Angel Pl. EC4	BZ40	57
Angel Pl. SE1	**BZ41**	**4**
Angel Pl. SE1	BZ41	67
Borough High St.		
Angel Rd. N18	CB28	39
Angel Rd. Har.	BH32	45
Angel Rd. Surb.	BJ54	84
Angel St. EC1	**BZ39**	**2**
Angel St. EC1	BZ39	57
Angel Wk. W6	BQ42	65
Angel Way Rom.	CT31	50
Angerstein La. SE3	CG43	68
Angle Clo. Uxb.	AZ37	53
Anglefield Rd. Berk.	AQ13	7
Angle Pl. Berk.	AQ13	7
Angle Rd. Grays	DB43	70
Anglers La. NW5	BV36	56
Anglesea Av. SE18	CL42	68
Anglesea Cent. Grav.	DG46	81
New Rd.		
Anglesea Pl. Grav.	DG46	81
Clive Rd.		
Anglesea Rd. SE18	CL42	68
Anglesea Rd. Kings. on T.	BK52	84
Anglesea Rd. Orp.	CO53	89
Anglesea St. E1	CB38	57
Anglesey Clo. Ashf.	AZ48	73
Anglesey Ct. Rd. Cars.	BV57	95
Anglesey Dr. Rain.	CU38	59
Anglesey Gdns. Cars.	BV57	95
Anglesey Rd. Enf.	CB24	30
Anglesey Rd. Wat.	BD28	36
Anglesmede Cres. Pnr.	BF31	45
Anglesmede Wk. Pnr.	BF31	45
Anglesmede Way Pnr.	BF31	45
Angles Rd. SW16	BX49	76
Anglia Wk. E6	CK37	58
Napier Rd.		
Anglo Rd. E3	CD37	57
Anglo Rd. Grays.	CY43	70
Angus Clo. Chess.	BM56	94
Angus Dr. Ruis.	BD35	45
Angus Gdns. NW9	BN30	37
Angus Rd. E13	CJ38	58
Angus St. SE14	CD43	67
Clifton Rise		
Anhalt Rd. SW11	BU43	66
Ankerdine Cres. SE18	CL44	68
Anlaby Rd. Tedd.	BH49	74
Anley Rd. W14	BQ41	65
Anmersh Gro. Stan.	BK30	36
Annabel Clo. E14	CE39	57
Anna Clo. E8	CA37	57
Broadway Mkt. Est.		
Annalee Rd. S. Ock.	DA39	60
Annandale Rd. SE10	CG42	68
Annandale Rd. W4	BO42	65
Annandale Rd. Croy.	CB55	87
Annandale Rd. Guil.	AQ71	118
Annandale Rd. Sid.	CN47	78

Annan Way Rom. CS30 41
Anne Boleyn's Wk. Kings. On T. BL49 75
Anne Bolen's Wk. Sutt. BQ57 94
Anne Of Cleves Rd. Dart. CV46 80
Annersley Walk N19 BW34 47
Girdlestone Est.
Annesley Av. NW9 BN31 46
Annesley Clo. NW10 BO34 46
Annesley Dr. Croy. CD55 87
Annesley Rd. N19 BW34 47
Annesley Rd. SE3 CH44 68
Anne St. E13 CH38 58
Anne's Wk. Cat. CA63 105
Annett Clo. Shep. BB52 83
Up. Halliford Rd.
Annette Clo. Har. BH30 36
Spencer Rd.
Annette Rd. N7 BX34 47
Annett Rd. Walt. BC54 83
Annetts Gro. N1 BZ36 57
Essex Rd.
Anne Way E. Mol. BF52 84
Anne Way Ilf. CM29 40
Ann Gdns. S. Ock. DA39 60
Annifer Way, S. Ock. DA39 60
Anning St. EC2 CA38 57
New Inn Yd.
Annington Rd. N2 BU31 47
Annis Rd. E9 CD36 57
Ann La. SW10 BT43 66
Anns Clo. SW1 Bu41 3
Ann's Clo. SW1 BV41 66
Kinnerton St.
Ann St. SE18 CM42 68
Ann's Vill. W11 BQ41 65
Annsworthy Av. Th. Hth. BZ52 87
Annsworthy Cres. SE25 BZ52 87
Ansdell Rd. SE15 CC44 67
Ansdell St. W8 BS41 3
Ansdell St. W8 BS41 66
St. Alban's Gro.
Ansdell Ter. W8 BS41 3
Ansdell Ter. W8 BS41 66
St. Alban's Gro.
Ansell Gro. Cars. BU54 86
Ansell Rd. SW17 BU48 76
Ansell Rd. Dor. BJ71 119
Anselm Clo. Croy. CB55 87
Anselm Rd. SW6 BS43 66
Anselm Rd. Pnr. BE29 36
Ansford Rd. Brom. CF49 77
Ansleigh Pl. W11 BQ40 55
Ansley Clo. Sth. Croy. CB60 96
Anslow Gdns. Iver AU37 52
Anson Clo. Cat. BZ63 105
Anson Clo. Rom. CR30 41
Anson Clo. St. Alb. BJ14 9
Anson Clo. St. Alb. BK10 9
Anson Rd. N7 BW35 47
Anson Rd. NW2 BQ35 46
Anson Rd. Cat. BZ63 105
Anson Wk. Nthwd. BA28 35
Anstead Dr. Rain. CU37 59
Anstey Rd. SE15 CB45 67
Anstey Wk. N8 BY31 47
Anstridge Rd. SE9 CM46 78
Antelope Rd. SE18 CK41 68
Anthony Clo. NW7 BO28 37
Anthony Clo. Sev. CT63 107
Anthony Clo. Wat. BD26 36
Anthony Rd. SE25 CB53 87
Anthony Rd. Borwd. BL23 28
Anthony Rd. Grnf. BH37 54
Anthony Rd. Well. CO44 69
Anthony St. E1 CB39 57
Antill Rd. E3 CD38 57
Antill Rd. N15 CB31 48
Antill Ter. E1 CC39 57
Antlers Hill E4 CE24 30
Antoney's Clo. Pnr. BD30 36
Antonine Gte. St. Alb. BF14 9
Anton Rd. S. Ock. DA38 60
Anton St. E8 CB35 48
Antrim Gro. NW3 BU36 56
Antrim Mans. NW3 BU36 56
Antrim Rd. NW3 BU36 56
Antrobus Clo. Sutt. BR56 94
Antrobus Rd. W4 BN42 65
Anvil Al. Cob. BC60 92
Anvil Rd. Sun. BC52 83
Anworth Clo. Wdf. Grn. CH29 40
Anyards Rd. Cob. BC60 92
Aperdele Rd. Lthd. BJ62 102
Aperfield Rd. Erith CT43 69
Aperfield Rd. West. CK62 106
Apers Av. Wok. AS64 100
Apex Clo. Beck. CF51 87
Apley Rd. Reig. BS72 121
Aplin Way Islw. BH44 64
Osterley Road
Apollo Av. Brom. CH51 88
Hawes Rd.
Apollo Av. Nthwd. BC28 35
Apollo Clo. Horn. CU34 50
Apollo Pl. SW10 BT43 66
Riley St.
Apollo Pl. SW10 BT44 66
Riley St.
Apollo Way Hem. H. AY12 8
Apothecary St. EC4 BY39 56
New Bridge St.
Appach Rd. SW2 BY46 76
Apper St. WC1 BW38 56
Appian Way Est. Erith. CR42 69
Appleby Clo. E4 CF29 39
Appleby Clo. N15 BZ32 48
Cornwall Rd.
Appleby Clo. Twick. BG48 74
Appleby Dr. Rom. CV28 42
Appleby Grn. Rom. CV28 42
Appleby Rd. E8 CB36 57
Appleby Rd. E16 CG39 58
Appleby St. E2 CA37 2
Appleby St. E2 CA37 57
Appleby St. Wal. Cr. BZ16 21
Applecroft, St. Alb. BF17 18
Applecroft Rd. Welw. G. C. BP8 5
Appledore Slou. AP36 52
Duffield La.
Appledore Av. Bexh. CS44 69
Appledore Av. Ruis. BC34 44
Appledore Clo. SW17 BU48 76
Appledore Clo. Brom. CG53 88
Appledore Clo. Edg. BM30 37
Appledore Clo. Rom. CV30 42
Appledore Cres. Sid. CN48 78
Appleford Clo. Hodd. CD11 12
Appleford Rd. W10 BR38 55
Apple Garth. Brent. BK42 64
Applegarth, Croy. CE57 96
Applegarth Av. Guil. AO70 118
Applegarth Dr. Ilf. CN31 49
Applegarth, Esher BJ56 93
Applegarth Rd. SE28 CO40 59
Applegarth Rd. W14 BQ41 65
Apple Gate Brwd. CZ25 33
Coxtie Grn. Rd.
Apple Gro. Chess. BL56 94
Apple Gro. Enf. CA24 30
Apple Mkt. Kings. on T. BK51 84
Apple Orchard, Hem. H. AY12 8
Apple Rd. SE28 CO40 59
Appleshaw Clo. Grav. DG49 81
Chalky Bank
Appleton Gdns. N. Mal. BP53 85
Appleton Rd. SE9 CK45 68
Appleton Rd. Loug. CL24 31
Appleton Way, Horn. CV34 51
Apple Tree Av. Uxb. & West Dr. AY39 53
Apple Tree Cres. Brwd. DB22 33
Appletree Court. Guil. AV69 118
Old Merrow St.
Appletree La. Slou. AR41 62
Appletree Wk. Chesh. AO20 16
Cresswell Rd.
Appletree Wk. Wat. BC20 17
Apple Tree Yd. SW1 BW40 3
Apple Tree Yd. SW1 BW40 56
Duke Of York St.
Appold St. EC2 CA39 2
Applewood Clo. NW2 BP34 46
April Wood Clo. Wey. AV59 91
Appold St. EC2 CA39 57
Appold St. Erith CT43 69
Approach Clo. N16 CA35 48
Cowper Rd.
Approach Rd. E2 CC37 57
Approach Rd. SW20 BQ51 85
Approach Rd. Ashf. BA49 73
Approach Rd. Barn. BT24 29
Approach Rd. Barn. BV24 29
Approach Rd. E. Mol. BF53 84
Approach Rd. St. Alb. BH14 9
Approach, The, W3 BN39 55
Approach, The, Enf. CB23 30
Approach, The Lthd. BE65 102
Approach, The, Orp. CN55 88
Approach, The, Pot B. BR19 19
Approach, The, Upmin. CX34 51
Apps Ct. Walt. BD53 84
Apps Pond La. St. Alb. BC15 8
Apps Pond La. St. Alb. BD15 9
Aprey Gdns. NW4 BQ31 46
April Clo. Felt. BC48 73
April Glen SE23 CC48 77
Mayow Rd.
Apsley Clo. Har. BG32 45
Apsley Rd. E17 CD32 48
Apsley Rd. SE25 CB52 87
Apsley Rd. N. Mal. BN52 85
Apsley Sq. W1 BV40 56
Sth. Audley St.
Aquarius Way. Nthwd. BC28 35
Apollo Av.
Aquila Clo. Ash. BK64 102
Aquila Clo. Nthwd. BC28 35
Aquila St. NW8 BT37 1
Aquila St. NW8 BT37 56
Aquinas St. SE1 BY40 4
Aquinas St. SE1 BY40 56
Arabella Dr. SW15 BO45 65
Arabia Clo. E4 CF26 39
Mornington Rd.
Arabin Rd. SE4 CD45 67
Araglen Av. S. Ock. DA39 60
Aragon Av. Epsom BP58 94
Aragon Av. Surb. BH53 84
Aragon Clo. Hem. H. BA11 8
Aragon Dr. Ilf. CM29 40
Aragon Dr. Ruis. BD33 45
Aragon Rd. Kings. On T. BL49 75
Aragon Rd. Mord. BQ53 85
Arandora Cres. Rom. CO33 50
Arand St. W11 BQ40 55
Arbor Clo. Beck. CE51 87
Arbor Ct. N16 BZ34 48
Arborfield Clo. Slou. AP41 62
Arbor Rd. E4 CF27 39
Arbour Clo. Brwd. DB28 42
Arbour Clo. Lthd. BH65 102
Arbour Field, Wok. AS61 100
Arbour Rd. Enf. CC24 30
Arbour Sq. E1 CC39 57
Arbour View, Amer. AQ23 25
Bell La.
Arbour Way, Horn. CU35 50
Arbroath Grn. Wat. BC27 35
Arbroath Rd. SE9 CK45 68
Arbrook La. Esher BG57 93
Arbury Rd. E3 CD38 57
Arbury Ter. SE26 CB48 77
Arbuthnot La. Bex. CQ47 79
Arbuthnot Rd. SE14 CC44 67
Arbutus Clo. Red. BT71 121
Arbutus Rd. Red. BT72 121
Arbutus St. E8 CA37 57
Arcade Pl. Rom. CT32 50
Arcade The, E17 CE31 48
Hoe St.
Arcade, The EC2 CA39 2
Arcade, The EC2 CA39 2
Blomfield St.
Arcade, The EC2 CA39 57
Liverpool St.
Arcade, The SE9 CK46 78
Eltham High St.
Arcadia Av. N3 BS30 38
Arcadian Av. Bex. CQ46 79
Arcadin Clo. Bex. CQ46 79
Arcadian Gdns. N22 BX29 38
Arcadian Rd. Bex. CQ46 79
Arcadia Rd. Grav. DF51 81
Arcadia St. E14 CE39 57
Arcany Rd. S. Ock. DA38 60
Archbishop's Pl. SW2 BX47 76
Archdale Rd. SE22 CA46 77
Archel Rd. W14 BR43 65
Archer Clo. Kings L. AZ18 17
Archer Ho. SW11 BT44 66
Archer Rd. SE25 CB52 87
Archer Rd. Orp. CO53 89
Archers Ride. Welw. G. C. BS9 5
Archer St. W1 BW40 3
Archer St. W1 BW40 56
Rupert St.
Archers Walk SE15 CA44 67
Sumner Estate
Archer Way Swan. CV51 89
Archery Clo. W2 BU39 56
Archery Rd. SE9 CK46 78
Arches, The, Har. BG34 45
Arch Field Welw. G.C. BR6 5
Archibald Rd. E3 CE38 57
Archibald Rd. N7 BW35 47
Archibald Rd. Rom. CW30 42
Archibald St. E3 CE38 57
Arch Rd. Walt. BD55 84
Arch St. SE1 BZ41 4
Arch St. SE1 BZ41 67
Archway Clo. SW19 BS49 76
Endeavour Rd.
Archway, Dor. BJ71 119
Arch Way Rom. CU29 41
Archway Mall N19 BW34 47
Archway Rd. N6 BU32 47
Archway Rd. N19 BV33 47
Archway St. SW13 BO45 65
Arcola St. E8 CA35 48
Arctic St. NW5 BV35 47
Arcus Rd. Brom. CG49 78
Ardbeg Rd. SE24 BZ46 77
Arden Clo. Bush. BH26 36
Arden Clo. Har. BG34 45
Arden Clo. Hem. H. AT17 16
Arden Clo. Reig. BS72 121
Arden Cres. Dag. CP36 59
Arden Est. N1 CA38 57
Arden Rd. N3 BR31 46
Arden Rd. W13 BJ40 54
Arden Way, St. Alb. BK12 9
Adern BC31 44
Ardfern Av. SW16 BY52 86
Ardfillan Rd. SE6 CF47 77
Ardgowan Rd. SE6 CG47 78
Ardilaun Rd. N5 BZ35 48
Ardintinny St. Alb. BH14 9
London Rd.
Ardleigh Clo. Horn. CV31 51
Ardleigh Ct. Brwd. DC26 122
Ardleigh Gdns. Brwd. DF26 122
Ardleigh Gdns. Sutt. BS54 86
Ardleigh Grn. Rd. Horn. CV32 51
Ardleigh Mews, Ilf. CL34 49
Bengal Rd.
Ardleigh Rd. E17 CD30 39
Ardleigh Rd. N1 CA36 57
Ardley Clo. NW10 BO34 46
Ardley Clo. SE23 CD48 77
Ardley Clo. Ruis. BA33 44
Ardliegh Ct. Brwd. DC26 122
Hutton Rd.
Ardlui Rd. SE27 BZ48 77
Ardmay Gdns. Surb. BL53 85
Ardmere Rd. SE13 CF46 77
Ardmore Av. Guil. AQ69 118
Ardmore La. Buck. H. CH26 40
Ardmore Rd. S. Ock. DA38 60
Ardmore Way, Guil. AQ69 118
Ardoch Rd. SE6 CF48 77
Ardrossan Gdns. Wor. Pk. BP55 85
Ardross Av. Nthwd. BB28 35
Ardshiel Clo. SW15 BQ45 65
Bemish Rd.
Ardshiel Dr. Red. BU71 121
Fairlawn Dr.
Ardsley Wood, Wey. BB56 92
Ardwell Av. Ilf. CM32 49
Ardwell Rd. SW2 BX48 76
Ardwick Rd. NW2 BS35 47
Argall Av. E10 CC33 48
Argent St. SE1 BY41 4
Argent St. Grays. DD43 71
Argon Ms. SW6 BS43 66
Argosy Gdns. Stai. AV50 72
Argosy La. Stai. AX47 73
Clare Rd.
Argus Way, W3 BM41 65
Argus Way Nthlt. BE38 54
Argyle Av. Houns. BF46 74
Argyle Clo. W13 BJ38 54
Argyle Est. SW19 BQ48 75
Argyle Gdns. Upmin. CY35 51
Argyle Mans. Rich. BK48 74
Argyle Pass. N17 CB30 39
Argyle Rd.
Argyle Pl. W6 BP42 65
Argyle Rd. E1 CC38 57
Argyle Rd. E15 CG35 49
Argyle Rd. E16 CH39 58
Argyle Rd. N12 BS28 38
Argyle Rd. N17 CB30 39
Argyle Rd. N18 BC28 39
Argyle Rd. W13 BJ38 54
Argyle Rd. W13 BJ39 54
Argyle Rd. Barn. BQ24 28
Argyle Rd. Grays. DD42 71
Argyle Rd. Har. BF32 45
Argyll Rd. Hem. H. AY11 8
Argyle Rd. Houns. BF46 74
Argyle Rd. Ilf. C34 49
Argyle Rd. Sev. CU66 116
Argyle Rd. Tedd. BH49 74
Argyle Sq. WC1 BX38 2
Argyle Sq. WC1 BX38 56
Argyle St. W1 BW39 1
Argyle St. WC1 BX38 2
Argyle St. WC1 BX38 56
Argyle Wk. WC1 BX38 2
Argyle Wk. WC1 BX38 56
Argyll Av. Sthl. BF40 54
Argyll Gdns. Edg. BM30 37
Argyll Rd. W8 BS41 66
Argyll St. W1 BW39 56
Arica Rd. SE4 CD45 67
Arie Dr. S. Ock. DA38 60
Ariel Clo. Grav. DJ49 81
Ariel Rd. NW6 BS36 56
Arisdale Ave. S. Ock. DA38 60
Aristotle Rd. SW4 BW45 66
Arkell Gro. SE19 BY50 76
Arkindale Rd. SE6 CF48 77
Arkley Ct. Maid AH42 61
Arkley Cres. E17 CD32 48
Arkley Dr. Barn. BP24 28
Arkley La. Barn. BO23 28
Arkley Rd. E17 CD32 45
Arkley Rd. Barn. BP24 28
Arkley Rd. Hem. H. AZ11 8
Arkley Vw. Barn. BP24 28
Arklow Rd. SE14 CD43 67
Arkwright, Harl. CN10 6
Arkwright Rd. NW3 BT35 47
Arkwright Rd. Slou. AV44 62
Arkwright Rd. Sth. Croy. CA58 96
Arkwright Rd. Til. DG44 71
Arkwright St. E16 CG39 58
Arlesford Rd. SW9 BX45 66
Arlesley Clo. SW15 BR46 75
Arlingford Rd. SW2 BY46 76
Arlington N12 BS28 38
Arlington Ave. N1 BZ37 2
Arlington Av. N1 BZ37 57
Arlington Clo. Sid. CN47 78
Arlington Clo. Sutt. BS55 86
Arlington Clo. Twick. BK46 74
Arlington Ct. Hayes. BB42 63
Arlington Cres. Wal. Cr. CD20 21
Arlington Dr. Cars. BU55 86
Arlington Dr. Ruis. BA32 44
Arlington Gdns. W4 BN42 65
Arlington Gdns. Ilf. CL33 49
Arlington Gdns. Rom. CW30 42
Arlington Lo. SW2 BX45 66
Arlington Pass Tedd. BH49 74
Arlington Rd. N14 BV27 38
Arlington Rd. NW1 BV37 1
Arlington Rd. NW1 BV37 56
Arlington Rd. W13 BJ39 54
Arlington Rd. Ashf. AY49 73
Arlington Rd. Rich. BK48 74
Arlington Rd. Surb. BK53 84
Arlington Rd. Tedd. BH49 74
Arlington Rd. Wdf. Grn. CH30 40
Arlington Sq. N1 BZ37 2
Arlington Sq. N1 BZ37 57
Arlington St. SW1 BW40 3
Arlington St. SW1 BW40 56
Arlington Way, EC1 BY38 2
Arlington Way, EC1 BY38 56
Arliss Way Nthlt. BD37 54
Arlow Rd. N21 BY26 38
Armadale Cl. N15 CB31 48
Armadale Rd. SW6 BS43 66
Armadale Rd. Felt. BC46 73
Armada St. SE8 CE43 67
Armfield Av. Mitch. BU51 86
Armfield Clo. E. Mol. BE53 84
Armfield Rd. Enf. BZ23 30
Arminger Rd. W12 BP40 55
Armitage Clo. Rick. AX24 26
Armitage Rd. NW11 BR33 46
Armitage Rd. SE10 CG42 68
Armitage Rd. Houns. BD43 64
Armond Clo. Wat. BB22 26
Armoury Way, SW18 BS46 76
Armstead Wk. Dag. CR36 59
Armstrong Av. Wdf. Grn. CG29 40
Armstrong Clo. Ruis. BC32 44
Armstrong Cres. Bdrn. BT24 29
Armstrong Gdns. SE7 CJ42 68
Armstrong Pl. Hem. H. AX13 8
High St.
Armstrong Rd. W3 BO40 55
Armstrong Rd. Egh. AR50 72
Armstrong Rd. Felt. BE49 74
Arnal Cres. SW18 BR47 75
Arndale Est. SW18 BS46 76
Arndale Way Egh. AT49 72
Arne Gro. Orp. CN55 88
Arne St. WC2 BX39 2
Arnett Clo. Rick. AW25 26
Arnett Way, Rick. AW25 26
Arne Wk. SE3 CG45 68
Arneways Av. Rom. CP31 50
Arneway St. SW1 BW41 3
Arneway St. SW1 BW41 66
Horseferry Rd.
Arnewood Cl. SW15 BP47 75
Alton Rd.
Arneys La. Mitch. BV53 86
Arngask Rd. SE6 CF47 77
Arnhem Av. S. Ock. CW40 60
Arnhem Av. S. Ock CY41 70
Arnhem Dr. Croy. CF58 96
Arnhem Dr. Croy. CF59 96
Arnhem Way, SE22 CA46 77
Dulwich Gro.
Arnison Rd. E. Mol. BG52 84
Arnold Av. E. Enf. CD22 30
Arnold Av. W. Enf. CD22 30
Arnold Cir. E2 CA38 2
Arnold Circus, E2 CA38 57
Arnold Clo. Har. BL32 46
Arnold Cres. Islw. BG46 74
Arnold Est. SE1 CA41 4
Arnold Est. SE1 CA41 67
Arnold Gdns. N13 BY28 38
Arnold Rd. E3 CE38 57
Arnold Rd. N15 CA31 48
Arnold Rd. SW17 BU50 76
Arnold Rd. Dag. CQ36 59
Arnold Rd. Grav. DH48 81
Arnold Rd. Nthlt. BE36 54
Arnold Rd. Stai AX50 73
Arnold Rd. Wok. AT61 100
Arnolds Av. Brwd. DE25 122
Arnolds Clo. Brwd. DE25 122
Arnold's La. S. At H. CW50 80
Arnolds La. S. At H. CX50 80
Arnold, S Farm La. Brwd. DF24 122
Arnos Gro. N14 BW28 38
Arnos Rd. N11 BW28 38
Arnott Clo. SE28 CP40 59
Arnott Clo. W4 BN42 65
Fish La.
Arnott Rd. SE28 CP40 59
Arnould Av. SE5 BZ45 67
Arnsberg Rd. Erith CT43 69
Arnside Gdns. Wem. BK33 45
Arnside Rd. Bexh. CR44 69
Arnside St. SE17 BZ43 4
Arnside St. SE17 BZ43 67
Arnulf St. SE6 CE49 77
Arnulls Rd. SW16 BY50 76
Arodene Rd. SW2 BX46 76
Arondel Gr. N16 CA35 48
Arpley Rd. SE20 CC50 77
Arragon Gdns. SW16 BX50 76
Arragon Gdns. W. Wick. CE55 87
Arragon Rd. E6 CJ37 58
Arragon Rd. Twick. BJ47 74
Arran Clo. Erith CS43 69
Arran Clo. Hem. H. BA14 8
Arran Clo. Wall. BW56 95
Arran Dr. E12 CJ33 49
Arran Dr. Stan. BJ28 36
Arran Rd. SE6 CE48 77
Arran Wk. N1 BZ36 57
Marquess Est.
Arran Way Esher BF55 84
Arras Av. Mord. BT53 86
Arrentine Clo. St. Alb. BE14 9
Arrol Rd. Beck. CC52 87
Arrow Rd. E3 CE38 57
Arrowscout Wk. Nthlt. BD38 54
Arrowscout Wk. Nthlt. BE38 54
Wayfarer Rd.
Arrowsmith Clo. Chig. CN28 40
Arrowsmith Path, Chig. CN28 40
Arrowsmith Rd. Chig. CN28 40
Arrowsmith Rd. Loug. CK24 31
Arsenal Rd. SE9 CK44 68
Artemis Clo. Grav. DJ47 81
Arterberry Rd. SW20 BQ50 75
Arterial Av. Rain CU38 59
Artesian Clo. Horn. CT33 50
Artesian Rd. W2 BS39 56
Arthingworth St. E15 CG37 58
Arthur Ct. W2 BS39 1
Arthur Ct. W2 BS39 56
Queensway
Arthurdon Rd. SE4 CE46 77
Arthur Grn. SE18 CM42 68
Arthur Gro. SE18 CM42 68
Arthur Henderson Ho. SW6 BR44 65
Arthur Ms. N7 BX36 56
Arthur Rd. E6 CK37 58
Arthur Rd. N7 BX34 47
Arthur Rd. N9 CA27 39
Arthur Rd. SW19 BS48 76
Arthur Rd. Kings. On T. BM50 75
Arthur Rd. N. Mal. BP53 85
Arthur Rd. Rom. CP33 50
Arthur Rd. St. Alb. BJ13 9
Arthur Rd. Slou. AO41 61
Arthur Rd. West. CJ61 106
Arthur Rd. Wind. AN44 61
Arthur's Bridge Rd. Wok. AR62 100
Arthur St. EC4 BZ40 4
Arthur St. EC4 BZ40 57
Arthur St. Bush. BD24 27
Arthur St. Erith. CT43 69
Arthur St. Grav. DG47 81
Arthur St. Grays. DE43 71
Arthur St. W. Grav. DG47 81
Arthur Toft Ho. Grays DD43 71
New Rd.
Artichoke Hl. E1 CB40 57
Pennington St.
Artillery Clo. Ilf. CM32 49
Artillery La. E1 CA39 2
Artillery La. E1 CA39 57
Artillery Pass. E1 CA39 2
Artillery Pl. SE18 CK42 68
Artillery Rd. Guil. AR70 118
Artillery Row SW1 BW41 3
Artillery Row SW1 BW41 66
Artillery Ter. Guil. AR70 118
Artillery Yd. EC2 CA38 57
Worship St.
Artington Clo. Opr. CM56 97
Isabella Dri.
Artizan St. E1 CA39 2
Artizan St. E1 CA39 57
Harrow Pl.
Arty Pass. E1 CA39 57
Sandy's Row
Arundel Av. Epsom. BP58 94
Arundel Av. Mord. BR52 85
Arundel Av. Sth. Croy. CB58 96
Arundel Clo. E15 CG35 49
Arundel Clo. Bex. CQ46 79
Arundel Clo. Croy. BY55 86
Arundel Clo. Hamptn. BF49 74
Aruindel Clo. Hem. H. AZ13 8
Arundel Clo. Wal. Cr. CB17 21
Arundel Ct. Slou. AR42 62
Arundel Dr. Borwd. BN24 28
Arundel Dr. Har. BE35 45
Arundel Dr. Orp. CO56 98
Arundel Dr. Wdf. Grn. CH29 40
Arundel Gdns. N21 BY26 38

Arundel Gdns. W11 BR40 55
Arundel Gdns. Ilf. CO34 50
Arundell Gdns. Edg. BN29 37
Cressingham Rd.
Arundel Pl. N1 BY36 56
Arundel Rd. Barn. BU24 29
Arundel Rd. Croy. BZ53 87
Arundel Rd. Dor. BJ71 119
Arundel Rd. Houns. BD45 64
Arundel Rd. Kings. on T. BM51 85
Arundel Rd. Rom. CW30 42
Arundel Rd. Sutt. BR57 94
Arundel Rd. Uxb. AW37 53
Arundel Sq. N7 BY36 56
Arundel St. WC2 BX40 4
Arundel St. WC2 BX40 56
Arundel Ter. SW13 BP43 65
Arvon Rd. N5 BY35 47
Ascalon St. SW8 BW43 66
Ascension Rd. Rom. CS29 41
Ascham Dr. E4 CE29 39
Ascham End E17 CD30 39
Ascham St. NW5 BW35 47
Aschurch Rd. Croy. CA54 87
Ascot Av. W5 BL41 65
Ascot Clo. Borwd. BM25 28
Ascot Clo. Ilf. CN29 40
Ascot Clo. Nthlt. BF36 54
Ascot Gdns. Enf. CC22 30
Ascot Gdns. Sthl. BE39 54
Ascot Rd. E6 CK38 58
Ascot Rd. N15 BZ32 48
Ascot Rd. N18 CB28 39
Ascot Rd. SW17 BV50 76
Ascot Rd. Felt. AZ48 73
Ascot Rd. Grav. DG48 81
Ascot Rd. Orp. CN52 88
Ascot Rd. Wat. BB25 26
Ascots La. Hat. BR10 5
Ashbourne Av. E18 CH31 49
Ashbourne Av. N20 BU27 38
Ashbourne Av. NW11 BR32 46
Ashbourne Av. Bexh. CQ43 69
Ashbourne Av. Har. BG34 45
Ashbourne Clo. N12 BS28 38
Ashbourne Clo. W5 BM39 55
Ashbourne Clo. Couls. BW58 95
Ashbourne Clo. Couls. BW62 104
Ashbourne Gro. NW7 BN28 37
Ashbourne Gro. SE22 CA45 67
Ashbourne Gro. W4 BO42 65
Ashbourne Rise Orp. CM56 97
Ashbourne Rd. W5 BL38 55
Ashbourne Rd. Brox. CD14 12
Ashbourne Rd. Mitch. BV50 76
Ashbourne Rd. Rom. CV28 42
Ashbourne Ter. SW19 BR50 75
Ashbridge Rd. E11 CG33 49
Ashbridge St. NW8 BU38 56
Ashbrook Rd. N19 BW33 47
Ashbrook Rd. Dag. CR34 50
Ashbrook Rd. Wind. AQ47 72
Ashburn Gdns. SW7 BT42 3
Ashburn Gdns. SW7 BT42 66
Ashburnham Av. Har. BH32 45
Ashburnham Clo. N2 BT31 47
Stanley Rd.
Ashburnham Clo. Wat. BC27 35
Ashburnham Dr.
Ashburnham Dr. Wat. BC27 35
Ashburnham Gdns. Har. BH32 45
Ashburnham Gdns. Upmin. CY33 51
Ashburnham Gro. SE10 CE43 67
Ashburnham Pl. SE10 CE43 67
Ashburnmham Retreat SE10 CE43 67
Ashburnham Rd. NW10 BQ38 55
Ashburnham Rd. SW10 BT43 66
Ashburnham Rd. Belv. CS42 69
Ashburnham Rd. Rich. BJ48 74
Ashburn Ms. SW7 BT42 3
Ashburn Ms. SW7 BT42 66
Ashburn Pl. SW7 BT42 3
Ashburn Pl. SW7 BT42 66
Ashburton Av. Croy. CB54 87
Ashburton Av. Ilf. CN35 49
Ashburton Clo. Croy. CB54 87
Ashburton Ct. Pnr. BD30 36
Ashburton Est. SW15 BQ46 75
Ashburton Gdns. Croy. CB55 87
Ashburton Gro. N7 BY35 47
Ashburton Rd. E16 CH39 58
Ashburton Rd. Croy. CB55 87
Ashburton Rd. Ruis. BC34 44
Ashburton Ter. E13 CH37 58
Grasmere Rd.
Ashbury Clo. Hat. BO12 10
St. Albans Rd. West.
Ashbury Dr. Uxb. AZ34 44
Ashbury Gdns. Rom. CP32 50
Ashbury Rd. SW11 BU45 66
Ashby Av. Chess. BM57 94
Ashby Clo. Horn. CW33 51
Ashby Clo. Horn. CX33 51
Ashby Gro. N1 BZ36 48
Ashby Gro. N1 BZ36 57
Ashby Ms SE4 CD44 67
Ashby Rd. N15 CB32 48
Ashby Rd. SE4 CD44 67
Ashby Rd. Berk. AO11 7
Ashby Rd. Wat. BC22 26
Ashby St. EC1 BY38 2
Ashby St. EC1 BY38 56
Ashby Wk. Croy. BZ53 87
Beulah Gro.
Ashby Way, West Dr. AZ43 63
Ashchurch Ct. W12 BP41 65
Ashchurch Gro. W12 BP41 65
Ashchurch Pk. Vill. W12 BP41 65
Ashchurch Rd. W12 BP41 65
Ashchurch Ter. W12 BP41 65
Ash Clo. SE20 CC51 87
Ash Clo. Brwd. CZ25 33
Ash Clo. Cars. BU55 86
Ash Clo. Hat. BS16 20
Ash Clo. N. Mal. BN51 85
Ash Clo. Orp. CM53 88
Ash Clo. Red. BW68 113
Ash Clo. Rom. CR29 41
Ash Clo. Sid. CO48 79
Ash Clo. Slou. AT41 62
Ash Clo. Stan. BJ29 36
Ash Clo. Swan. CS51 89
Ash Clo. Wat. BA19 17
Ash Clo. Wok. AS63 100
Ashcombe Av. Surb. BK54 84
Ashcombe Gdns. Edg. BM28 37
Ashcombe Pk. NW2 BO34 46
Ashcombe Rd. SW19 BS49 76
Ashcombe Rd. Cars. BV57 95
Ashcombe Rd. Dor. BJ70 119
Ashcombe Sq. N. Mal. BN52 85
Ashcombe St. SW6 BS44 66
Ashcombe Ter. Tad. BP63 103
Ashcombe Welw. G.C. BR6 5
Ash Ct. Epsom BN56 94
Ashcroft Pnr. BF29 36
Ashcroft Av. Sid. CO46 79
Ashcroft Clo. Guil. AS74 118
Ashcroft Cres. Sid. CO46 79
Ashcroft Dr. Uxb. AV32 43
Ashcroft Gdns. SW2 BY47 76
Trinity Rise
Ashcroft Park Cob. BE59 93
Ashcroft Rise Couls. BX57 95
Ashcroft Rise Couls. BX61 104
Ashcroft Rd. E3 CD38 57
Ashcroft Rd. Chess. BL55 85
Ashdale. Lthd. BF66 111
Ashdale Clo. Twick. BF47 74
Ashdale Gro. Stan. BH29 36
Ashdale Rd. SE12 CH47 78
Ashdale Way Twick. BF47 74
Ashdale Clo.
Ashdene, Pnr. BD31 45
Ashdene Clo. Ashf. BA50 73
Cambridge Rd.
Ashdon Clo. Wdf. Grn. CH29 40
Ashdon Rd. NW10 BO37 55
Ashdon Rd. Bush. BD24 27
Ashdown Cr. NW5 BV35 47
Ashdown Cres. Wal. Cr. CD17 21
Ashdown Dr. Borwd. BL23 28
Ashdowne Clo. Beck. CE51 87
Ashdown Gdns. Sth. Croy. CB61 105
Ashdown Rd. Enf. CC24 30
Ashdown Rd. Epsom BO60 94
Ashdown Rd. Kings. on T. BL51 85
Ashdown Rd. Reig. BS72 121
Ashdown Rd. Uxb. AZ37 53
Ashdown Rd. Wat. BD28 36
Woodhall La.
Ashdown Wk. Rom. CR30 41
Ash Dr. Hat. BP14 10
Ashendene Rd. Hert. BX13 11
Ashenden Rd. E5 CC35 48
Ashenden Rd. Guil. AP70 118
Ashenden Wk. Slou AO35 43
Ashen Dr. Dart. CU46 79
Ashen Gro. SW19 BS48 76
Ashen Gro. Farn. CX58 99
Ashentree Ct. EC4 BY39 56
Whitefriars St.
Ashen Vale Sth. Croy. CC58 96
Ashes La. Ton. DC70 117
Ashfield Av. Bush. BF26 36
Ashfield Av. Felt. BC47 73
Ashfield Clo. Rich. BL47 75
Ashfield La. Chis. CL50 78
Ashfield Pde. N14 BW26 38
Ashfield Rd. N4 BZ32 48
Ashfield Rd. N14 BW27 38
Ashfield Rd. W3 BO40 55
Ashfield Rd. Chesh. AO18 16
Ashfields Loug. CK23 31
Ashfields Wat. BB21 26
Ashfield St. E1 CB39 57
Ashford Av. N8 BX31 47
Ashford Av. Ashf. AZ50 73
Ashford Av. Brwd. DA27 42
Ashford Av. Hayes BD39 54
Ashford Clo. E17 CD32 48
Ashford Clo. Ashf. AY49 73
Ashford Cres. Ashf. AY48 73
Ashford Cres. Enf. CC23 30
Ashford Gdns. Cob. BD61 102
Ashford Grn. Wat. BD28 36
Ashford La. Wind. AK41 61
Ashford Rd. E6 CL36 58
Ashford Rd. E18 CH30 40
Ashford Rd. N17 CD29 39
Tenterden Rd.
Ashford Rd. NW2 BQ35 46
Ashford Rd. Ashf. BA50 73
Ashford Rd. Felt BA49 73
Ashford Rd. Iver AU37 52
Ashford Rd. Stai. AX51 83
Ashford St. N1 CA38 57
Ash Grn. Loughton CK23 31
Ash Grn. Uxb. AW36 53
Ash Gro. E8 CB37 57
Ash Gro. N13 BZ27 39
Ash Gro. NW2 BQ35 46
Ash Gro. SE20 CC51 87
Ash Gro. W5 BL41 65
Ash Gro. Enf. CA26 39
Ash Gro. Felt. BB47 73
Ash Gro. Guil. AQ70 118
Ash Gro. Hayes BA40 53
Ash Gro. Hem. H. AY15 8
Ash Gro. Houns. BD44 64
Ash Gro. Saw. CR6 6
Ash Gro. Stai. AX50 73
Ash Gro. Sthl. BF39 54
Ash Gro. Uxb. AX30 35
Ash Gro. Wem. BJ35 45
Ash Gro. West Dr. AY40 53
Ash Gro. W. Wick. CF55 87
Ashgrove Rd. Ashf. BA49 73
Ashgrove Rd. Brom. CF50 77
Ashgrove Rd. Ilf. CN33 49
Ashgrove Rd. Sev. CU67 116
Ash Hill Clo. Bush. BF26 36
Ash Hill Dr. Pnr. BD31 45
Ashington Ct. SE26 CB49 77
Ashington Rd. SW6 BR44 65
Ashlake Rd. SW16 BX49 76
Ashland Pl. W1 BV39 1
Ashland Pl. W1 BV39 56
Ash La. Rom. CU29 41
Ash La. Sev. CY61 108
Ash La. Sev. DB59 99
Ash la. Wind. AL44 61
Ashlar Pl. SE18 CL42 68
Ash Latt Rd. Sev. CW63 108
Ashlea Rd. Ger. Cr. AS30 43
Ashleigh Av. Egh. AT50 72
Ashleigh Gdns. Sutt. BS55 86
Ashleigh Gdns. Upmin. CY35 51
Ashleigh Rd. SE20 CB52 87
Ashleigh Rd. SW14 BO45 65
Ashley Av. Epsom BN60 94
Ashley Av. Ilf. CL30 40
Ashley Av. Mord. BS53 86
Ashley Clo. NW4 BQ30 37
Ashley Clo. Pnr. BC30 35
Ashley Clo. Sev. CU65 107
Ashley Clo. Walt. BB54 83
Ashley Cres. N22 BY30 38
Ashley Cres. SW11 BV45 66
Ashley Dr. Bans. BS60 95
Ashley Dr. Borwd. BN25 28
Ashley Dr. Twick. BF47 74
Ashley Dr. Walt. BC55 83
Ashley Gdns. N13 BZ28 39
Ashley Gdns. Grays. DE40 71
Ashley Gdns. Orp. CN56 97
Ashley Gdns. Rich. BK48 74
Ashley Gdns. Wem. BL34 46
Ashley Green La. Chesh. AO17 16
Ashley Green Rd. Chesh. AP15 7
Ashley La. NW4 BO30 37
Ashley La. Croy. BY56 95
Ashley Park Cres. Walt. BB55 83
Ashley Park Cres. Walt. BB54 83
Ashley Park Rd. Walt. BC55 83
Ashley Pl. SW1 BW41 66
Ashley Rise, Watt. BB56 92
Ashley Rd. E4 CE29 39
Ashley Rd. E7 CJ36 58
Ashley Rd. N17 CB31 48
Ashley Rd. N19 BX33 47
Ashley Rd. SW19 BS50 76
Ashley Rd. Dor. BG72 119
Ashley Rd. Enf. CC23 30
Ashley Rd. Epsom BN60 94
Ashley Rd. Hamptn. BF51 84
Ashley Rd. Rich. BL45 65
Jocelyn Rd.
Ashley Rd. St. Alb. BK13 9
Ashley Rd. Surb. BH53 84
Ashley Rd. Th. Hth. BX52 86
Ashley Rd. Uxb. AW37 53
Ashley Rd. Watt. BB56 92
Ashley Rd. Wok. AP62 100
Ashleys. Rick. AV26 34
Ashley Wk. NW7 BQ29 37
Ashling Rd. Croy. CB54 87
Ashlin Rd. E15 CF35 48
Ashlone Rd. SW15 BQ45 65
Ashlyn Clo. Bush. BE24 27
Ashlyn Gro. Horn. CV31 51
Ashlyns La. Epp. CT13 14
Ashlyns Rd. Berk. AQ13 7
Ashlyns Rd. Epp. CN18 22
Ashmead N14 BW25 29
Ashmead Dri. Uxb. AW34 44
Ashmead La. Uxb. AW34 44
Ashmead Rd. SE8 CE44 67
Ashmead Rd. Felt. BC47 73
Ashmere Av. Beck. CF51 87
Ashmere Clo. Sutt. BQ56 94
Ashmere Gdns. SW2 BX45 66
Ashmill St. NW1 BU39 1
Ashmill St. NW1 BU39 56
Ashmole Pl. SW8 BX43 66
Ashmole St. SW8 BX43 66
Ashmore Gdns. Hem. H. AZ14 8
Ashmore Gro. Well. CM45 68
Ashmore La. Kes. GJ59 97
Ashmore Rd. W9 BR38 55
Ashmount Rd. N15 CA32 48
Ashmount Rd. N19 BW33 47
Ashmour Gdns. Rom. CS30 41
Ashness Gdns. Grnf. BJ36 54
Ashness Rd. SW11 BU46 76
Ash Pl. SW1 BW41 3
Ash Ride Enf. BY21 29
Ashridge Clo. Har. BK32 45
Ashridge Clo. Hem. H. AS17 16
Pembridge Rd.
Ashridge Cres. SE18 CL43 68
Ashridge Dr. St. Alb. BE18 18
Ashridge Dr. Wat. BC28 35
Ashridge Gdns. N13 BW28 38
Ashridge Gdns. Pnr. BE31 45
Ashridge La. Chesh. AR19 16
Ashridge Rise, Berk. AP12 7
Ashridge Way Mord. BR52 85
Ashridge Way Sun. BC50 73
Ash Rd. E15 CG35 49
Ash Rd. Croy. CE55 87
Ash Rd. Dart. CV47 80
Ash Rd. Dart. CW49 80
Ash Rd. Grav. DH49 81
Ash Rd. Hart. DC52 90
Ash Rd. Orp. CN57 97
Ash Rd. Sev. DB56 99
Ash Rd. Shep. AZ52 83
Ash Rd. Sutt. BR54 85
Ash Rd. West. CM66 115
Ash Rd. Wok. AS63 100
Ash Row Brom. CL54 88
Ashtead Gap Lthd. BJ61 102
Ashtead Rd. E5 CB33 48
Ashtead Woods Rd. Ash. BK62 102
Ashton Clo. Sutt. BR56 94
Gandergreen La.
Ashton Clo. Walt. BC57 92
Ashton Clo. Wey. BC57 92
Green La.
Ashton Gdns. Houns. BE45 64
Ashton Gdns. Rom. CQ32 50
Ashton Rd. E15 CF35 48
Ashton Rd. Enf. CD21 30
Ashton Rd. Rom. CV29 42
Ashton Rd. Wok. AP62 100
Ashton St. E14 CF40 57
Ashtree Av. Mitch. BT51 86
Ash Tree Clo. Croy. CD53 87
Ash Tree Dell, NW9 BN32 46
Ash Tree Field, Harl. CL10 6
Ashtree Rd. Wat. BC21 26
Ash Tree Way, Croy. CD53 87
Ashtree Way, Hem. H. AW14 8
Ashurst Clo. Ken. BZ61 105
Ashurst Clo. Nthwd. BB29 35
Ashurst Dr. Ilf. CL32 49
Ashurst Dr. Shep. AY52 83
Ashurst Dr. Tad. BM68 112
Ashurst Rd. N12 BU28 38
Ashurst Rd. Barn. BU25 29
Ashurst Wk. Croy. CB55 87
Ash Vale, Rick. AU28 34
Ashvale Dr. Upmin. CZ34 51
Ashvale Gdns. Rom. CS28 41
Ashvale Gdns. Upmin. CZ34 51
Ashvale Rd. SW17 BU49 76
Ash View Gdns. Ashf. AY49 73
Ashville Rd. E11 CF34 48
Ashwater Rd. SE12 CH47 78
Ashwell Rd. E3 CC37 57
Ashwells Rd. Brwd. CY24 33
Ashwell St. St. Alb. BG13 9
Ashwells Way, Ch. St. G. AR27 34
Ashwin St. E8 CA36 57
Ashwood Warl. CC63 105
Ashwood Av. Rain. CU38 59
Ashwood Av. Uxb. AZ39 53
Ashwood Gdns., Hayes BB42 63
Ashwood Rd. E4 CF27 39
Ashwood Rd. Egh. AQ50 72
Ashwood Rd. Pot. B. BS20 20
Ashwood Rd. Wok. AS62 100
Ashworth Rd. W9 BS38 1
Ashworth Rd. W9 BS38 56
Askern Clo. Bexh. CP45 69
Aske St. N1 CA38 57
Pitfield St.
Askew Bldgs. W12 BP41 65
Askew Rd.
Askew Cres. W12 BO41 65
Askew Rd. W12 BO40 55
Askew Rd. Nthwd. BA27 35
Askham Ct. W12 BP40 55
Askham Rd. W12 BP40 55
Askill Dr. SW15 BR46 75
Askwith Rd. Rain. CS38 59
Aslett St. SW18 BT47 76
Asley Rd. Sev. CU65 107
Asmara Rd. NW2 BR35 46
Asmuns Hl. NW11 BS32 47
Asmuns Pl. BR32 46
Asmuns Rd. NW11 BR32 46
Aspdin Rd. Grav. DE48 81
Aspect Row, Hem. H. AW12 8
Aspen Clo. Cob. BE61 102
Aspen Clo. Guil. AU69 118
Aspen Clo. Orp. CO56 98
Aspen Clo. S. Ock. DB38 60
Aspen Clo. West Dr. AY40 53
Aspen Clo. West Dr. AY40 53
Aspen Copse Brom. CK51 88
Aspen Dr. Wem. BJ34 45
Aspen Gdns. W6 BP42 65
Bridge Av.
Aspen Gdns. Mitch. BV53 86
Aspen Grn. Belv. CQ41 69
Aspen Gro. Upmin. CW35 51
Aspen La. Nthlt. BE38 54
Aspenlea Rd. W6 BQ43 65
Aspen Way Bans. BQ60 94
Aspen Way, Enf. CC21 30
Aspinall Rd. SE4 CC45 67
Aspinden Rd. SE16 CB42 67
Aspley Rd. SW18 BS46 76
Asplins Rd. N17 CB30 39
Assam St. E1 CB39 2
Assam St. E1 CB39 57
Assembly Ms. E1 CC39 57
Assembly Pass E1 CC39 57
Assembly Wk. Cars. BU54 86
Assher Rd. Walt. BE55 84
Ass House La. Har. BF28 36
Astall Clo. Har. BH30 36
Astbury Rd. SE15 CC44 67
Astell St. SW3 BU42 3
Astell St. SW3 BU42 66
Aster Pl. SE1 BZ41 4
Aster Pl. SE1 BZ41 67
Aste St. E14 CF41 67
Astey's Row N1 BY36 56
Asthall Gdns. Ilf. CM31 49
Astle Dr. Sev. CW62 108
Astle St. SW11 BV44 66
Astley Av. NW2 BQ35 46
Astley Rd. Hem. H. AX13 8
Astley St. SE1 CA42 4
Astley St. SE1 CA42 67
Aston Av. Har. BK33 45
Aston Clo. Sid. CO48 79
Aston Grn. Houns. BC44 63
Aston Mead. Wind. AM44 61
Aston Mews. Rom. CP33 50
Reynolds Av.
Aston Rd. SW20 BQ51 85
Approach Rd.
Aston Rd. W5 BK39 54
Aston Rd. Esher BH57 93
Astons Rd. Nthwd. BA27 35
Aston St. E14 CD39 57
Aston View Hem. H. AZ10 8
Astonville St. SW18 BS47 76
Aston Way Epsom BO61 103
Aston Way Pot. B. BT19 20
Astor Av. Rom. CS32 50
Astor Clo. Kings. On T. BM50 75
Astor Clo. Wey. AX56 92
Astoria Wk. SW9 BY45 66
Astor Rd. Sev. CZ57 99
Astra Clo. Horn. CU36 59
Astra Dr. Grav. DJ49 81
Astrop Ms. W6 BQ41 65
Astrop Ter. W6 BQ41 65
Astwick Av. Hat. BO11 10
Astwood Ms. SW7 BS42 3
Astwood Ms. SW7 BS42 66
Asylum Arch Rd. Red. BU72 121
Asylum Rd. SE15 CB43 67
Atalanta St. SW6 BQ44 65
Atbara Ct. Tedd. BJ50 74
Atbara Rd. Tedd. BJ50 74
Atcham Rd. Houns. BG45 64
Atcost Rd. Bark. CO39 59
Atheldene Rd. SW18 BS47 76
Athelney St. SE6 CE48 77
Athelstan Clo. Rom. CW30 42
Athelstane Gro. E3 CD37 57
Athelstane Mews N4 BY33 47
Stroud Green Rd.
Athelstane Rd. N4 BY34 47
Athelstan Rd. Kings. on T. BL52 85
Villiers Rd.
Athelstan Rd. Rom. CW30 42
Athelstan Wk. Welw. G. C. BR8 5
Athelstone Rd. Har. BG30 36
Athelstone Rd. Hem. H. AY15 8
Athena Clo. Har. BG34 45
Athenaeum Rd. N20 BT26 38
Athenlay Rd. SE15 CC46 77
Athens Gdns. W9 BS38 56
Atherden Rd. E5 CC35 48
Atherfield Rd. Reig. BT72 121
Atherfold Rd. SW9 BX45 66
Atherstone Ms. E7 CG36 58
Atherstone Ms. SW7 BT42 3
Atherston Ms. SW7 BT42 66
Atherton Dr. SW19 BQ49 75
Atherton End Saw. CQ5 6
Atherton Gdns. Grays. DH42 71
Atherton Heights Wem. BK36 54
Bridgewater Rd.
Atherton Pl. Har. BG31 45
Atherton Pl. Sthl. BF40 54
Atherton Rd. E7 CG35 49
Atherton Rd. SW13 BP43 65
Atherton Rd. Ilf. CK30 40
Atherton St. SW11 BU44 66
Athlone Clo. E5 CB35 48
Goulton Rd.
Athlone Rd. SW2 BX47 76
Athlone Sq. Wind. AO44 61
Ward Royal
Athlone St. NW5 BV36 56
Athlone Rd. Wem. BK37 54
Athol Clo. Pnr. BC30 35
Athole Gdns. Enf. CA25 30
Athol Gdns. Pnr. BC30 35
Atholl Rd. Ilf. CO33 50
Athol Rd. Erith. CS42 69
Athol St. E14 CF39 57
Athol Way Uxb. AZ38 53
Atkinson Clo. Orp. CN56 97
Atkinson Rd. E16 CJ39 58
Atkins Clo. Wok. AQ62 100
Greythorne Rd.
Atkins Rd. E10 CE32 48
Atkins Rd. SW12 BW47 76
Atlantic Rd. SW9 BY45 66
Atlas Gdns. SE7 CJ42 68
Atlas Mews N7 BX36 47
Atlas Rd. E13 CH37 58
Atlas Rd. NW10 BO38 55
Atlas Rd. Wem. BN35 46
Atley Rd. E3 CE37 57
Atney Rd. SW15 BR45 65
Atria Rd. Nthwd. BC28 35
Atterbury Rd. N4 BY32 47
Wightman Rd.
Atterbury St. SW1 BW42 3
Atterbury St. SW1 BX42 66
Attewood Av. NW10 BO34 46
Attewood Rd. Nthlt. BE36 54
Arnold Rd.
Attfield Clo. N20 BT27 38
Attimore Clo. Welw. G. C. BP8 5
Attimore Rd. Welw. G. C. BP8 5
Attle Clo. Hayes BC38 53
Attle Clo. Uxb. AZ37 53
Attlee Dr. Dart. CW46 80
Attlee Dr. Dart. CX46 80
Attlee Rd. SE28 CO40 59
Attlee Rd. Hayes BC38 53
Attlee Ter. E17 CE31 48
Attneave St. WC1 BY38 2
Attneave St. WC1 BY38 56
Attwood Clo. Sth. Croy. CB60 96
Atwater Clo. SW2 BY47 76
Atwell Rd. SE15 CB44 67
Atwood Lthd. BE65 102
Atwood Av. Rich. BM44 65
Atwood Rd. W6 BP42 65
Atwood's Alley Rich. BM44 65
Kew Gardens Rd.
Atworth St. E14 CF41 67
Auberon St. E16 CK40 58
Aubert Ct. N5 BY35 47
Aubert Pk. N5 BY35 47
Aubrey Av. St. Alb. BK16 18
Aubrey Pl. NW8 BT37 1
Aubrey Rd. E17 CE31 48
Aubrey Rd. N8 BX32 47
Aubrey Rd. W8 BR40 55
Aubreys Rd. Hem. H. AV14 7
Aubrey Wk. W8 BR40 55
Aubyn Hl. SE27 BZ49 77
Aubyn Sq. SW15 BP46 75
Auckland Av. Rain. CT38 59
Auckland Clo. SE19 CA51 87
Auckland Clo. Enf. CB22 30
Auckland Clo. Til. DG44 71
Auckland Gdns. SE19 CA51 87
Auckland Hl. SE27 BZ49 77
Auckland Ri. SE19 CA51 87
Auckland Rd. SE19 CA51 87
Auckland Rd. SW11 BU45 66
Auckland Rd. Cat. CA64 105
Auckland Rd. Ilf. CL33 49
Auckland Rd. Kings. on T. BL52 85
Auckland Rd. Pot. B. BR19 19

Auckland St. SE11 BX42 66
Kennington Lane
Auden Pl. NW1 BV37 1
Auden Pl. NW1 BV37 56
Audley Clo. Borwd. BM24 28
Audley Clo. Wey. AW56 92
Audley Ct. E18 CG31 49
Audley Ct. Pnr. BD30 36
Audley Ct. Twick. BG48 74
Audley Dr. Warl. CC61 105
Audley Gdns. Ilf. CN34 49
Audley Gdns. Loug. CM23 31
Audley Gdns. Wal. Abb. CF20 21
Audley Pl. Sutt. BS57 95
Audley Rd. NW4 BP32 46
Audley Rd. W5 BL39 55
Audley Rd. Enf. BY23 29
Audley Rd. Rich. BL46 75
Audley Sq. W1 BV40 3
Audrey Clo. Beck. CE53 87
Audrey Gdns. Wem. BJ34 45
Audrey Rd. Ilf. CL34 49
Audrey St. E2 CB37 57
Audreys Clo. S. Hat. BP13 10
Audwick Clo. Wal. Cr. CD17 21
Ashdown Cr.
Augurs La. E13 CH38 58
Augusta Rd. Twick. BG48 74
Augustas Clo. St. Alb. BF14 9
Augusta St. E14 CE39 57
Augustine Clo. Slou. AV45 62
Augustine Rd. W14 BQ41 65
Augustine Rd. Har. BG30 36
Augustine Rd. Orp. CP52 89
Augustine Clo. Brent. BK43 64
Augustus Rd. SW19 BQ47 75
Augustus St. NW1 BV37 1
Augustus St. NW1 BV37 56
Aukingford Gdns. Ong. CW17 24
Epping Rd.
Aulay St. SE1 CB43 4
Aulay St. SE1 CB43 67
Aultone Way, Cars. BU55 86
Aulton Way Sutt. BS55 86
Aulton Pl. SE11 BY42 4
Aulton St. SE11 BY42 66
Aurelia Gdns. Croy. BX53 86
Aurelia Rd. Croy. BX53 86
Auric Clo. Grays. DG42 71
Auriel Av. Dag. CS36 59
Auriga Mews N1 BZ35 48
Auriol Dr. Grnf. BG36 54
Auriol Rd. W14 BR42 65
Austell Gdns. NW7 BO27 37
Austen Clo. SE28 CO40 59
Austen Clo. Green. DB46 80
Austen Clo. Loug. CM24 31
Austen Clo. Til. DH44 71
Coleridge Rd.
Austen Gdns. Dart. CW45 70
Austen Pl. Guil. AS71 118
Austen Rd. Guil. AS71 118
Austen Rd. Har. BF34 45
Austenway, Ger. Cr. AR31 43
Austenwood Clo. Ger. Cr. AR30 34
Austenwood La. Ger. Cr. AR30 34
Austenwood La. Ger. Cr. AR31 43
Austin Av. Brom. CK53 88
Austin Clo. SE6 CD47 77
Brockley View
Austin Clo. Ken. BY62 104
Austin Friars EC2 BZ39 2
Austin Friars EC2 BZ39 57
Austin Friars Pass EC2 BZ39 57
Austin Friars
Austin Rd. SW11 BV44 66
Austin Rd. Grav. DF47 81
Austin Rd. Hayes. BB41 63
Austin Rd. Orp. CO53 89
Austins La. Uxb. BA35 44
Austins Mead, Hem. H. AT17 16
Austins S. La. Uxb. BA34 44
Austins Pl. Hem. H. AX13 8
Austin St. E2 CA38 2
Austin St. E2 CA38 57
Austin Waye, Uxb. AX37 53
Austral Clo. Sid. CN48 78
Longlands Rd.
Austral Dr. Horn. CV33 51
Australia Rd. W12 BP40 55
Australia Rd. Slou. AQ41 62
Australia St. SE11 BY42 4
Austria St. SE11 BY42 66
Aust Rd. Grav. DH47 81
Austyn Gdns. Surb. BM54 85
Autumn Clo. Enf. CB23 30
Autumn Clo. Slou. AM40 61
Autumn Gro. Welw. G. C. BS9 5
Autumn St. E3 CE37 57
Auxiliaries Wy. Uxb. AV32 43
Avalon Clo. Enf. BY23 29
Avalon Clo. Orp. CP55 89
Avalon Cres. W13 BJ39 54
Avalon Rd. SW6 BS44 66
Avalon Rd. W13 BJ38 54
Avalon Rd. Orp. CO55 89
Avalon Ter. Rich. BL45 65
Avard Gdns. Orp. CM56 97
Isabella Dri.
Avarn Rd. SW17 BU50 76
Avcliffe Clo. Kings. on T. BM51 85
Avebury Est. E2 CB38 57
Avebury Pk. Surb. BK54 84
Avebury Rd. E11 CF33 48
Avebury Rd. SW19 BR51 85
Avebury Rd. Orp. CM55 88
Avebury St. N1 BZ37 2
Aveley Clo. S. Ock. CW40 60
Aveley Clo. S. Ock. CY40 60
High St.
Aveley Rd. Rom. CS31 60
Aveley Rd. Upmin. CX36 60
Aveline St. SE11 BX42 4
Aveline St. SE11 BX42 66
Aveling Park Rd. E17 CE30 39
Avelon Rd. Rain. CU37 59
Avelon Rd. Rom. CS29 41
Ave Maria La. EC4 BY39 2
Ave Maria La. EC4 BY39 56
Ludgate Hill
Avenell Rd. N5 BY34 47
Avening Ter. SW18 BS46 76
Avenons Rd. E13 CH38 58
Avenue App. Kings L. AZ18 17
Avenue Clo. N14 BW25 29
Avenue Clo. NW8 BU37 1
Avenue Clo. NW8 BU37 56
Avenue Clo. Houns. BC44 63
Avenue Clo. Rom. CW29 42
Avenue Clo. Tad. BP64 103
Avenue Clo. West Dr. AX41 63
Avenue Cres. W3 BM41 65
Avenue Cres. Houns. BC43 63
Avenue Dr. Slou. AS39 52
Avenue Elmers Surb. BL53 85
Avenue Gdns. SE25 CA51 87
Avenue Gdns. SW14 BO45 65
Avenue Gdns. W3 BM41 65
Avenue Gdns. Houns. BC43 63
Avenue Gdns. Tedd. BH50 74
Avenue Gte. SE21 CA49 77
Avenue Mews N10 BV31 47
Queen's Av.
Avenue Ms. NW6 BS35 47
Finchley Rd.
Avenue Pk. Rd. SE27 BY48 76
Avenue Rise Bush. BF25 27
Avenue Rd. E7 CH35 49
Avenue Rd. N6 BW33 47
Avenue Rd. N12 BT28 38
Avenue Rd. N14 BV26 38
Avenue Rd. N15 BZ32 48
Avenue Rd. NW3 BT36 1
Avenue Rd. NW3 BT36 56
Avenue Rd. NWU0 BO37 55
Avenue Rd. SE20 CC51 87
Avenue Rd. SE25 CA51 87
Avenue Rd. SW16 BW51 86
Avenue Rd. SW20 BP51 85
Avenue Rd. W3 BM41 65
Avenue Rd. W13 BJ40 54
Avenue Rd. Bans. BS61 104
Avenue Rd. Beck. CC51 87
Avenue Rd. Belv. CR42 69
Avenue Rd. Bexh. CQ45 69
Avenue Rd. Brent. BK42 64
Avenue Rd. Brwd. DB28 42
Avenue Rd. Cat. BZ64 105
Avenue Rd. Cob. BD61 102
Avenue Rd. Epp. CM21 31
Avenue Rd. Epsom BN60 94
Avenue Rd. Erith. CS43 69
Avenue Rd. Felt. BB48 73
Avenue Rd. Hmptn. BF51 84
Avenue Rd. Hodd. CF13 12
Avenue Rd. Islw. BH44 64
Avenue Rd. Kings. on T. BL52 85
Avenue Rd. Maid. AG40 61
Avenue Rd. N. Mal. BO52 85
Avenue Rd. Pnr. BE31 45
Avenue Rd. Rom. CP33 50
Avenue Rd. Rom. CW29 42
Avenue Rd. St. Alb. BH13 9
Avenue Rd. Sev. CV65 108
Avenue Rd. Stai. AU49 72
Avenue Rd. Sthl. BE40 54
Avenue Rd. Sutt. BS58 95
Avenue Rd. Tedd. BJ50 74
Avenue Rd. Wall. BW57 95
Avenue Rd. Wdf. Grn. CJ29 40
Avenue Rd. West. CK63 106
Avenue S. The Surb. BL54 85
Avenue Ter. N. Mal. BN52 85
Avenue Ter. Wat. BE25 27
Avenue, The E4 CF29 39
Avenue, The E11 CH32 49
Avenue, The EC3 CA40 4
Avenue, The EC3 CA40 57
Avenue, The N1 BV28 38
Avenue, The N3 BS30 38
Avenue, The N8 BY31 47
Avenue, The N10 BW30 38
Avenue, The N11 BV28 38
Avenue, The N17 BZ31 48
Avenue, The NW6 BR36 55
Avenue, The SE7 CJ43 68
Avenue, The SE9 CK46 78
Eltham High St.
Avenue, The SE10 CF43 67
Avenue, The SE19 CA49 77
Avenue, The SW4 BV46 76
Avenue, The SW17 BV48 76
Avenue, The SW18 BU47 76
Avenue, The W4 BO41 65
Avenue, The W13 BJ40 54
Avenue, The Amer. AO22 25
Avenue, The Barn. BR24 28
Avenue, The Beck. CE51 87
Avenue, The Bet. BM70 120
Avenue, The Bex. CP47 79
Avenue, The Brom. CJ52 88
Avenue, The Brwd. DC29 122
Avenue, The Bush. BE24 27
Avenue, The Cars. BV57 95
Avenue, The Couls. BW61 104
Avenue, The Croy. CA55 87
Avenue, The Egh. AT49 72
Avenue, The Epsom BP57 94
Avenue, The Esher BH57 93
Avenue, The Grav. DG47 81
Avenue, The Green DA45 70
Avenue, The Guil. AO74 118
Avenue, The Hamptn. BE50 74
Avenue, The Har. BH30 36
Avenue, The Har. BH31 45
Marlborough Rd.
Avenue, The Harl. CM9 6
Avenue, The Hodd. CD13 12
Avenue, The Horn. CV34 51
Avenue, The Houns. BC44 63
Avenue, The Houns. BF46 74
Avenue, The Kes. CJ55 88
Avenue, The Loug. CJ25 31
Avenue, The Nthwd. BA29 35
Avenue, The Orp. CN55 88
Avenue, The Orp. CO50 79
Avenue, The Pnr. BE29 36
Avenue, The Pnr. BE32 45
Avenue, The Pot. B. BS19 20
Avenue, The Rad. BJ20 18
Avenue, The Red. BX72 121
Avenue, The Rich. BL44 65
Avenue, The Rom. CS31 50
Avenue, The Stai. AR45 62
Avenue, The Stai. AW51 83
Avenue, The Sun. BC51 83
Avenue, The Surb. BL53 85
Avenue, The Sutt. BR58 94
Avenue, The Tad. BP64 103
Avenue, The Twick. BJ46 74
Avenue, The Uxb. AX38 53
Avenue, The Uxb. AZ35 44
Avenue, The Wat. BC23 26
Avenue, The Wem. BL33 46
Avenue, The W. Wick. CF54 87
Avenue, The Wey. AW58 92
Avenue, The Whyt. CB63 105
Avenue, The Wind. AQ46 72
Avenue, The Wok. AP58 91
Avenue, The Wor. Pk. BO55 85
Avenue, The Tad. BP65 103
Averil Gro. SW16 BY50 76
Averil St. W6 BQ43 65
Avern Rd. E. Mol. BF53 84
Avery Farm Row SW1 BV42 66
Cundy St.
Avery Gdns. Ilf. CK32 49
Avery Hl. Rd. SE9 CM46 78
Avery Row W1 BV40 3
Avery Row W1 BV40 56
Avey La. Wal. Abb. CG22 31
Aviary Clo. E16 CG39 58
Aviary Rd. Wok. AW61 101
Aviary St. E16 CG39 58
Lawrence St.
Aviemore Clo. Beck. CD53 87
Aviemore Way Beck. CD53 87
Avignon Rd. SE4 CC45 67
Avington Clo. Guil. AS70 118
Avington Gro. SE20 CC50 77
Avington Way SE15 CA43 67
Avior Dr. Nthwd. BB28 35
Avior Dr. Nthwd. BC28 35
Avis Sq. E1 CC39 57
Avoca Rd. SW17 BV49 76
Avon Clo. Grav. DH48 81
Avon Clo. Hayes BC38 53
Avon Clo. Sutt. BT56 95
Avon Clo. Wat. BD20 18
Avon Clo. Wey. AW57 92
Avon Clo. Wor. Pk. BP55 85
Avondale Av. N12 BS28 38
Avondale Av. NW2 BO34 46
Avondale Av. Barn. BU26 38
Avondale Av. Esher BJ55 84
Avondale Av. Stai. AV50 72
Avondale Av. Wor. Pk. BO54 85
Avondale Clo. Loug. CK26 40
Avondale Dr.
Avondale Clo. Walt. BD56 93
Avondale Ct. E16 CG39 58
Off Avondale Rd.
Avondale Ct. E18 CH30 40
Avondale Cres. Enf. CD24 30
Avondale Cres. Ilf. CJ32 49
Avondale Dr. Hayes BC40 53
Avondale Dr. Loug. CK26 40
Avondale Gdns. Houns. BE46 74
Avondale Pk. Rd. W11 BR40 55
Avondale Pk. Gdns. W11 BQ40 55
Avondale Rise SE15 CA45 67
Avondale Rd. E16 CG39 58
Avondale Rd. E17 CE33 48
Avondale Rd. N3 BT30 38
Avondale Rd. N13 BY27 38
Avondale Rd. N15 BY32 47
Avondale Rd. SE9 CK48 78
Avondale Rd. SW14 BN45 65
Avondale Rd. SW19 BS49 76
Avondale Rd. Ashf. AX48 73
Avondale Rd. Brom. CG50 78
Avondale Rd. Har. BH31 45
Avondale Rd. Hayes BC40 53
Avondale Rd. Sth Croy. BZ57 96
Avondale Rd. Wall. CP44 69
Avondale Sq. SE1 CB42 4
Avondale Sq. SE1 CB42 67
Avon Grn. S. Ock. DA39 60
Avonley Rd. SE14 CC43 67
Avonmead Wok. AR62 100
Silversmiths Way
Avon Ms. Pnr. BE29 36
Avonmore Pl. W14 BR42 65
Avonmore Rd.
Avonmouth Rd. W14 BR42 65
Avonmouth St. SE1 BZ41 4
Avon Path Sth. Croy. BZ57 96
Avon Pl. SE1 BZ41 4
Avon Pl. SE1 BZ41 67
Avon Rd. E17 CF31 48
Avon Rd. SE4 CE45 67
Avon Rd. Grnf. BF38 54
Avon Rd. Sun. BB50 73
Avon Rd. Upmin. CY32 51
Avon Sq. Hem. H. AY11 8
Avon St. SE1 BZ41 67
Avontar Rd. S. Ock. DA38 60
Avon Way E18 CH31 49
Tavistock Rd.
Avonwick Rd. Houns. BF44 64
Avril Way E4 CF28 39
Avro Way Wall. BX57 95
Avrrit Clo. Guil. AP69 118
Awlfield Av. N17 BZ30 39
Awliscombe Rd. Well. CN44 68
Axes La. Red. BW74 121
Axe St. Bark. CM37 58
Axholme Av. Edg. BM30 37
Axminster Cres. Well. CP44 69
Axminster Rd. N7 BX34 47
Axtaine Rd. Orp. CP54 89
Axwood Epsom BN61 103
Aybrook St. W1 BV39 1
Aybrook St. W1 BV39 56
Aycliff Clo. Brom. CK52 88
Aycliff Dr. Hem. H. AY11 8
Aycliffe Rd. W12 BP40 55
Aycliffe Rd. Borwd. BL23 28
Ayebridges Av. Egh. AU50 72
Ayelands La. New. A. G. DC55 90
Aylands Rd. Enf. CC21 30
Aylesbury Cres. Slou. AO39 52
Aylesbury Rd. SE17 BZ42 4
Aylesbury Rd. SE17 BZ42 67
Aylesbury Rd. Brom. CH52 88
Aylesbury St. EC1 BY38 2
Aylesbury St. EC1 BY38 56
Aylesbury St. NW10 BN34 46
Aylesford Av. Beck. CD53 87
Aylesford St. SW1 BW42 3
Aylesford St. SW1 BW42 66
Aylesham Rd. Orp. CN54 88
Ayles Rd. Hayes BC38 53
Aylestone Av. NW6 BQ36 55
Aylesworth Spur Wind. AQ47 72
Ashbrook Rd.
Aylett Rd. SE25 CB52 87
Aylett Rd. Islw. BH44 64
Aylett Rd. Upmin. CY34 51
Ayley Croft. Enf. CB25 30
Aylmer Clo. Stan. BJ28 36
Aylmer Dr. Stan. BJ28 36
Aylmer Rd. E11 CG33 49
Aylmer Rd. N2 BU32 47
Aylmer Rd. W12 BO41 65
Aylmer Rd. Dag. CO34 50
Ayloffe Rd. Dag. CQ36 59
Ayloffs Clo. Horn. CW32 51
Ayloffs Wk. Horn. CV32 51
Aylesham La. Rom. CV28 42
Aylsham Rd. Hodd. CF11 12
Aylton Est. SE16 CC41 67
Aylward Rd. SE23 CC48 77
Aylward Rd. SW20 BR51 85
Aylwards Rise Stan. BJ28 36
Aylwards St. E1 CC39 57
Aylwin Est. SE1 CA41 4
Aylwin Est. SE1 CA41 67
Aymer Clo. Stai. AV51 82
Aymer Dr. Stai. AV51 82
Aynhoe Rd. W14 BQ42 65
Aynno St. Wat. BC25 26
Aynscombe Angle Orp. CO54 89
Aynscombe La. SW14 BN45 65
Aynscombe Path SW14 BN44 65
Ayot Grn. Welw. BP6 5
Ayot Little Green La. Welw. BO6 5
Ayot Path Borwd. BM22 28
Ayot Rd. Welw. G. C. BP7 5
Ayot St. Peter Rd. Welw. BO5 5
Ayr Ct. W3 BM39 55
Monks Dr.
Ayres Clo. E13 CH38 58
Ayres Cres. NW10 BN36 55
Ayres St. SE1 BZ41 4
Ayres St. SE1 BZ41 67
Ayr Grn. Rom. CS29 41
Ayron Rd. S. Ock. DA38 60
Ayrsome Rd. N16 CA34 48
Ayr Way Rom. CT30 41
Aysgarth Park Maid. AG42 61
Aysgarth Rd. SE21 BZ46 77
Aytoun Pl. SW9 BX44 66
Aytoun Rd. SW9 BX44 66
Azalea Clo. W7 BH40 54
Azalea Dr. Swan. CS52 89
Azalea Wk. Pnr. BC32 44
Azenby Rd. SE15 CA44 67
Azof St. SE10 CG42 68
Baalbec Rd. N5 BY35 47
Baas Hill Clo. Brox. CD14 12
Baas La. Brox. CD14 12
Babbacombe Clo. Chess. BK56 93
Babbacombe Gdns. Ilf. CK31 49
Babbacombe Rd. Brom. CH51 88
Babbington Ri. Wem. BM36 55
Baber Dr. Felt. BD46 74
Babington Rise Wem. BM36 55
Babington Rd. NW4 BP31 46
Babington Rd. SW16 BW49 76
Babington Rd. Dag. CP35 50
Babington Rd. Horn. CU33 50
Babmaes St. SW1 BW40 3
Babmaes St. SW1 BW40 56
Jermyn St.
Babylon La. Tad. BS67 113
Baccallay St. E3 CD39 57
Bacchus Wk. N1 CA37 2
Bacchus Wk. N1 CA37 57
Bachelors Acre Wind. AO44 61
Bachelor's La. Wok. AY65 101
Baches St. N1 BZ38 2
Baches St. N1 BZ38 57
Back Alley Dor. BJ71 119
Back Church La. E1 CB39 2
Back Churck La. E1 CB39 57
Back Grn. Walt. BD57 93
Back Hill EC1 BY38 2
Back Hill EC1 BY38 56
Back La. N8 BX37 56
New Rd.
Back La. NW3 BT35 47
Flask Wk.
Back La. Bark. CM37 58
Broadway
Back La. Bex. CR47 79
Back La. Brent. BK43 64
St. Paul's Rd.
Back La. Brwd. DA21 33
Back La. Ch. St. G. AQ27 34
Back La. Edg. BN30 37
Back La. Grays. CZ41 70
Back La. Guil. AW69 110
Back La. Hert. BZ12 12
Back La. Reig. BT68 113
Back La. Rich. BK48 74
Back La. Rick. AT22 25
Back La. Rom. CP22 32
Back La. Rom. CP33 50
Station Rd.
Back La. Sev. CR67 116
Back La. Sev. DB65 108
Back La. Sev. DC67 117
Back La. Ton. DB69 117
Back La. Wal. Abb. CJ14 13
Back La. Wat. BH23 27
Back La. Welw. BT6 5
Back Path Red. BZ70 114
Back River Pk. Beck. CD51 87
Back Rd. Sid. CO49 79
Back Row SW17 BU49 76
Totterdown St.
Back St. W3 BM40 55
Back Swan Yd. SE1 CA41 67
Bermondsey St.
Back, The Berk. AT11 7
Bacon Gro. SE1 CA41 4
Bacon Gro. SE1 CA41 67
Bacon La. NW9 BM31 46
Bacon La. Edg. BM30 37
Bacon Link, Rom. CR29 41
Bacons Dr. Pot. B. BX18 20
Bacons La. N6 BV33 47
Bacons Mead Uxb. AW34 44
Bacon St. E1 CA38 2
Bacon St. E1 CA38 57
Bacon St. E2 CA38 2
Bacon St. E2 CA38 57
Bacton St. E2 CC38 57
Digby St.
Badburgham Ct. Wal. Abb. CG20 22
Ninefields
Baddow Clo. Wdf. Grn. CJ29 40
Baddow Wk. N1 BZ37 57
Popham St.
Baden Clo. Stai. AW50 73
Baden Clo. Wey. BB57 92
Baden Pl. SE1 BZ41 4
Baden Pl. SE1 BZ41 67
Baden Powell Rd. Sev. CT64 107
Baden Rd. N8 BW31 47
Baden Rd. Guil. AQ69 118
Baden Rd. Ilf. CL35 49
Bader Wk. Grav. DF48 81
Hillary Av.
Bader Way, Rain. CU36 59
Badger Clo. Guil. AQ69 118
Badger Clo. Houns. BD45 64
Badgers Copse, Wor. Pk. BO55 85
Badgers Cft. N20 BR26 37
Badgers Cft. SE9 CL48 78
Badgers Hill, Vir. W. AR53 82
Badgers Hole, Croy. CC56 96
Badgers La. Warl. CC63 105
Badgers Mt. Grays. DF41 71
Badgers Rd. Sev. CR58 98
Badgers Wk. N. Mal. BO51 85
Badgers Wk. Whyt. CA63 105
Badgers Wood. Slou. AO35 43
Badger Way, Hat. BP13 10
Badingham Dr. Lthd. BH65 102
Badlis Rd. E17 BW31 47
Badmaes St. SW1 BW40 56
Badminton Clo. Borwd. BM23 28
Stratfield Rd.
Badminton Clo. Har. BH31 45
Badminton Clo. Nthlt. BF36 54
Badminton Pl. Brox. CD13 12
Badminton Rd. SW12 BV46 76
Bedshawe Rd. Grays. DD40 71
Badsworth Rd. SE5 BZ44 67
Badwell Clo. Horn. CU36 59
Baftishill St. N1 BY37 2
Bagden Hill, Dor. BG68 111
Bagley Clo. West Dr. AY41 63
Bagley Rd. SW6 BS44 66
Bagley Spring, Rom. CQ31 50
Bagot Clo. Ash. BL61 103
Bagshot Clo. SE18 CL44 68
Bagshot Rd. Egh. AR50 72
Bagshot Rd. Enf. CA26 39
Bagshot Rd. Guil. AO66 109
Bagshot Rd. Wok. AO65 100
Bagshot St. SE17 CA42 4
Bagshot St. SE17 CA42 67
Baildon St. SE8 CD43 67
Bailey Clo. Wind. AN44 61
Bailey Gdns. Rom. CO32 50
Bailey Pl. SE26 CC50 77
Bailey Rd. Dor. BG72 119
Baillie Clo. Rain. CV39 60
Baillie Rd. Guil. AS71 118
Baillie's Wk. W5 BK41 64
Bainbridge Rd. Dag. CQ35 50
Bainbridge St. WC1 BW39 1
Bainbridge St. WC1 BW39 56
Baird Av. Sthl. BF40 54
Baird Clo. NW9 BN32 46
Baird Gdns. SE21 CA49 77
Baird Rd. Enf. CB24 30
Bairstow Clo. Borwd. BK23 27
Baizdon Rd. SE3 CG44 68
Bakeham La. Egh. AR50 72
Baker Boy La. Croy. CD59 96
Baker Ct. Borwd. BM23 28
Brook Rd.
Baker Hill Clo. Grav. DF49 81
Baker La. Mitch. BV51 86
Baker Rd. NW10 BN37 55
Baker Rd. SE18 CK43 68
Bakers Alley SE1 CA40 57
Abbots La.
Bakers Av. Sev. CZ57 99
Baker's Av. E17 CE32 48
Bakers End SW20 BR51 85
Bakers Gro. Welw. G. C. BT7 5
Baker's Hill E5 CB33 48
Bakers Hill Barn. BS23 29
Bakers La. N6 BU32 47
North Hill
Bakers La. W5 BK40 54
Grove, The
Bakers La. Epp. CN18 22
Bakers Md. Gdse. CC68 114
Bakers Meadow Brwd. DB22 33
Bakers Ms. W1 BV39 1
Baker's Ms. W1 BV39 56
Adam St.
Bakers Pas. NW3 BT35 47
Oriel Pl.

Bakers Rd. Uxb. AX36 53
Bakers Rd. Wal. Cr. CB18 21
Baker's Row E15 CG37 58
Baker's Row EC1 BY38 2
Baker's Row EC1 BY38 56
Baker St. NW1 BU38 1
Baker St. NW1 BU38 56
Baker St. W1 BU38 56
Baker St. Enf. BZ24 30
Baker St. Grays. DF40 71
Baker St. Pot. B. BR20 19
Baker St. Pot. B. BR21 28
Baker St. Wey. AZ56 92
Bakers Wood, Uxb. AU33 43
Bakewell Way, N. Mal. BO51 85
Bakley Clo. Bush. BF25 27
Balaams La. N14 BW27 38
Balaam St. E13 CH38 58
Balaclava Rd. SE1 CA42 4
Balaclava Rd. SE1 CA42 67
Balaclava Rd. Surb. BK54 84
Balben Rd. E9 CC36 57
Balcaskie Rd. SE9 CK46 78
Balchen Rd. SE3 CJ44 68
Balchier Rd. SE22 CB46 77
Balchins La. Dor. BF72 119
Balcombe St. NW1 BU38 1
Balcombe St. NW1 BU38 56
Balcorne St. E9 CC36 57
Balder Ri. SE12 CH48 78
Balderton St. W1 BV39 1
Balderton St. W1 BV39 56
Baldocks Rd. Epp. CN21 31
Baldock St. E3 CE37 57
Baldock Way Borwd. BL23 28
Baldry Gdns. SW16 BX50 76
Baldwin Cres. SE5 BZ44 67
Baldwin's Gdns. EC1 BY39 2
Baldwin's Gdns. EC1 BY39 56
Baldwin's Hill, Loug. CK23 31
Baldwin's La. Rick. AZ24 26
Baldwins Pond, Loug. CK23 31
Baldwins Shore, Wind. AO43 61
Baldwin St. EC1 BZ38 2
Baldwin St. EC1 BZ38 57
Baldwin Ter. N1 BZ37 2
Baldwin Ter. N1 BZ37 57
Baldwins, Welw. G. C. BS8 5
Baldwyn Gdns. W3 BN40 55
Baldwyns Est. Dart. CT48 79
Baldwyn's Pk. Bex. CS48 79
Baldwyn's Rd. Bex. CS48 79
Balfern Gro. W4 BO42 65
Balfern St. SW11 BU44 66
Balfe St. N1 BX37 2
Balfe St. N1 BX37 56
Balfont Clo. Sth. Croy. CB60 96
Balfour App. Ilf. CL34 49
Balfour Rd.
Balfour Av. W7 BH40 54
Balfour Av. Wok. AS64 100
Balfour Gro. N20 BU27 38
Balfour Ho. W10 BQ39 55
Balfour Ms. Pl. W1 BV40 3
Balfour Ms. W1 BV40 56
Alford St.
Balfour Pl. W1 BV40 56
Alford St.
Balfour Rd. N5 BZ35 48
Balfour Rd. N9 CB27 39
Victoria Rd.
Balfour Rd. SE25 CB52 87
Balfour Rd. SW19 BS50 76
Balfour Rd. W3 BN39 55
Balfour Rd. W13 BJ41 64
Balfour Rd. Brom. CJ53 88
Balfour Rd. Cars. BU57 95
Balfour Rd. Grays. DE42 71
Balfour Rd. Har. BG32 45
Balfour Rd. Houns. BF45 64
Balfour Rd. Ilf. CL34 49
Balfour Rd. Sthl. BD41 64
Balfour Rd. Wey. AZ56 92
Balfour St. SE17 BZ42 4
Balfour St. SE17 BZ42 67
Balgonie Rd. E4 CF26 39
Balgores Cres. Rom. CU31 50
Balgores La. Rom. CU31 50
Balgores Sq. Rom. CU31 50
Balgowan Clo. N. Mal. BO52 85
Balgowan Rd. Beck. CD52 87
Balgowan St. SE18 CN42 68
Balgrove Rd. W10 BR39 55
Balham Gro. SW12 BV47 76
Balham High Rd. SW12 BV48 76
Balham High Rd. SW17 BV48 76
Balham Hill SW12 BV47 76
Balham New Rd. SW12 BV47 76
Balham Pk. Rd. SW12 BU47 76
Balham Rd. N9 CB27 39
Balham Station Rd. SW12 BV47 76
Ballamore Rd. Brom. CH48 78
Ballance Rd. E9 CC36 57
Ballands S. The Lthd. BH64 102
Ballands S. The Lthd. BH65 102
Ballantine St. SW18 BT45 66
Ballantyne Dr. Tad. BR64 103
Ballard Clo. Kings. on T. BN50 75
Ballard Grn. Wind. AM43 61
Ballards Av. Sth. Croy. CB57 96
Ballards Clo. Dag. CR37 59
Ballards Fm. Rd. Sth. Croy. CB57 96
Ballards Grn. Tad. BR63 103
Ballard's La. N3 BS30 38
Ballard's La. N12 BS30 38
Ballards La. Oxt. CJ68 115
Ballards Rise Sth. Croy. CB57 96
Ballards Rd. NW2 BP34 46
Ballards Rd. Dag. CR37 59
Ballards Way, Croy. CB57 96
Ballards Way, Sth Croy. CB57 96
Ballast Quay SE10 CF42 67
Ballatar Clo. Wat. BD28 36
Ballater Rd. SW2 BX45 66
Ballater Rd. Sth. Croy. CA56 96
Ballina St. SE23 CC47 77
Ballingdon Rd. SW11 BV46 76
Balliol Av. E4 CG28 40
Balliol Rd. N17 BZ30 39
Balliol Rd. W10 BQ39 55
Balliol Rd. Well. CO44 69
Ball La. N14 BW27 38
Balaams La.
Balloch Rd. SE6 CF47 77
Ballogie Av. NW10 BO35 46
Ballow Clo. SE5 BZ43 67
Elmington Estate
Balls Pond Rd. N1 BZ36 57
Balmain Clo. W5 BK40 54
Balmer Rd. E3 CD37 57
Balmes Rd. N1 BZ37 2
Balmes Rd. N1 BZ37 57
Balmoral Av. Beck. CD52 87
Balmoral Clo. SW15 BQ46 75
Westleigh Av.
Balmoral Cres. E. Mol. BF52 84
Balmoral Dr. Borwd. BN25 28
Balmoral Dr. Hayes BB38 53
Balmoral Dr. Hayes. BC39 53
Balmoral Dr. Sthl. BE38 54
Balmoral Dr. Wok. AU61 100
Balmoral Gdns. W13 BJ41 64
Balmoral Gdns. Ilf. CN33 49
Balmoral Gdns. Wind. AO45 61
Balmoral Gro. N7 BX36 56
Brewery Rd.
Balmoral Rd. E7 CJ35 49
Balmoral Rd. E10 CE34 48
Balmoral Rd. Brwd. DA25 33
Balmoral Rd. Enf. CC21 30
Balmoral Rd. Har. BF35 45
Balmoral Rd. Horn. CV34 51
Balmoral Rd. Kings. On. T. BL52 85
Balmoral Rd. Rom. CU32 50
Balmoral Rd. S. at H. CX50 80
Balmoral Rd. Wat. BD22 27
Balmoral Rd. Wor. Pk. BP55 85
Balmore Cres. Barn. BV25 29
Balmuir Gdns. SW15 BQ45 65
Balnacraig Av. NW10 BO35 46
Balouhain Clo. Ash. BK62 102
Baltic Clo. SW19 BT50 76
Baltic St. EC1 BZ38 2
Baltic St. EC1 BZ38 57
Balvernie Gro. SW18 BR47 75
Bamborough Gdns. W12 BQ41 65
Bamford Av. Wem. BL37 55
Bamford Rd. Bark. CA36 57
Bamford Rd. Brom. CF49 77
Bampford Way Rom. CR28 41
Bampfylde Clo. Wall. BW55 86
Bampton Rd. SE23 CC48 77
Bampton Rd. Rom. CW30 42
Bampton Way Wok. AQ62 100
Banbury Clo. Sutt. BS57 95
Banbury Ct. WC2 BX40 56
Long Acre
Banbury Rd. E9 CC36 57
Banbury St. SW11 BU44 66
Banbury St. Wat. BC25 26
Banbury Wk. Nthlt. BF37 54
Leander Rd.
Banchory Rd. SE3 CH43 68
Bancroft Av. N2 BU32 47
Bancroft Av. Buck. H. CH27 40
Bancroft Clo. Ashf. AZ49 73
Bancroft Clo. Reig. BS70 121
Bancroft Rd.
Bancroft Ct. Nthlt. BD37 54
Bancroft Gdns. Har. BG30 36
Bancroft Gdns. Orp. CN54 88
Bancroft Rd. E1 CC38 57
Bancroft Rd. Har. BG30 36
Bancroft Rd. Reig. BS70 121
Banders Rise, Guil. AU70 118
Band La. Egh. AS49 72
Bandon Rise, Wall. BW56 95
Bangalore St. SW15 BQ45 65
Bangor Clo. Nthlt. BF35 45
Bangor Rd. Brent. BL43 65
Bangors Clo. Iver AV39 52
Bangors Rd. N. Iver. AU37 52
Bangors Rd. S. Iver AV38 52
Banim St. W6 BP41 65
Banister Rd. W10 BQ38 55
Bank Av. Mitch. BT51 86
Bank Ct. Dart. CW46 80
Bank Ct. Hem. H. AX14 8
Bankend SE1 BZ40 4
Bankfoot Rd. Brom. CG49 78
Bankhurst Rd. SE6 CD47 77
Bank La. SW15 BO46 75
Bank La. Kings. on T. BL50 75
Bank La. Sev. CX69 117
Bank Mill La. Berk. AS13 7
Bank Pl. Brwd. DB27 42
Bankside SE1 BY40 4
Bankside SE1 BY40 56
Bankside Enf. BY23 29
Bankside, Sth. Croy CA57 96
Bankside, Sthl. BD40 54
Bankside Av. Nthlt. BC37 53
Bankside Clo. Bex. CS49 79
Bankside Clo. Cars. BU57 95
Bankside Clo. West. CJ62 106
Bankside Dr. Surb. BJ54 84
Bankside Way SE19 CA50 77
Central Hill Est.
Bankside Wok. AQ62 100
Banks La. Bexh. CQ45 69
Bank's La. Lthd. BC64 101
Bank St. Grav. DG46 81
Bank, The N6 BV33 47
Bankton Rd. SW2 BY45 66
Bankwell Rd. SE13 CG45 68
Banmore Comm. Rd. Dor. BH69 119
Bann Clo. S. Ock. DA40 60
Banner St. EC1 BZ38 2
Banner St. EC1 BZ38 57
Banning St. SE10 CG42 68
Bannister Clo. SW2 BY47 76
Bannister Clo. Har. BG35 45
Bannister Clo. Slou. AS41 62
Bannister Ho. E9 CC35 48
Bannisters Rd. Guil. AP71 118
Bannock Burn Rd. SE18 CN42 68
Bansons La. Ong. CX17 24
Bansons Way Ong. CX17 24
Banstead Gdns. N9 CA27 39
Banstead Rd. Cars. BT58 95
Banstead Rd. Cat. BZ64 105
Banstead Rd. Epsom BP59 94
Banstead Rd. Pur. BY59 95
Banstead Rd. S. Sutt. BT59 95
Banstead St. SE15 CB45 67
Banstead Way Wall. BX56 95
Banstock Rd. Edg. BM29 37
Banton Clo. Enf. CB23 30
Banyard Rd. SE16 CB41 67
Banyards Horn. CW32 51
Bapchild Pl. Orp. CP52 89
Okemore Gdns.
Baptist Gdns. NW5 BV36 56
Queen's Cres.
Barandon Walk W11 BQ40 55
Lancaster Rd.
Barbara Clo. Shep. AZ53 83
Barbara St. N7 BX36 56
Barbauld Rd. N16 CA34 48
Barber Clo. N21 BY26 38
Barberry Rd. Hem. H. AW13 8
Barber's All. E13 CH38 58
Barber's Rd. E15 CE37 57
Barbican Rd. Grnf. BF39 54
Barbican Site EC2 BZ39 57
Barb Ms. W6 BQ41 65
Shepherds Bush Rd.
Barbon Clo. WC1 BX39 56
Boswell St.
Barbot Clo. N9 CB27 39
Barchard St. SW18 BS46 76
Barchester Clo. Uxb. AX38 53
Barchester Rd. Har. BG30 36
Barchester Rd. Slou. AS41 62
Barchester St. E14 CE39 57
Barclay Clo. SW6 BS43 66
Barclay Clo. Lthd. BF65 102
Barclay Ct. Hodd. CE12 12
Barclay Oval. Wdf. Grn. CH28 40
Barclay Rd. E11 CG33 49
Barclay Rd. E13 CJ38 58
Barclay Rd. E17 CE32 48
Barclay Rd. N18 BZ29 39
Barclay Rd. SW6 BS43 66
Barclay Rd. Croy. BZ55 87
Barcombe Av. SW2 BX48 76
Barden Clo. Uxb. AX29 35
Barden St. SE18 CN43 68
Bardeswell Clo. Brwd. DB27 42
Bardfield Av. Rom. CP31 50
Bardinell Trd. Est. Chess. BK58 93
Bardney Rd. Mord. BS52 86
Bardolph Av. Croy. CD58 96
Bardolph Rd. N7 BX35 47
Bardolph Rd. Rich. BL45 65
St. George's Rd.
Bard Rd. W10 BQ40 55
Bardsey Wk. N1 BZ36 57
Marquess Est.
Bardsley Clo. Croy. CB55 87
Bardsley La. SE10 CF43 67
Bardwell Ct. St. Alb. BG14 9
Bardwell Rd.
Bardwell Rd. St. Alb. BG14 9
Bardwell St. N7 BX35 47
Barfett St. W10 BR38 55
Barfield Av. N20 BU27 38
Barfield Rd. E11 CG33 49
Barfield Rd. Brom. CL52 88
Barfields Loug. CL24 31
Barfields Clo. Loug. CL24 31
Barfields Cres. Red. BY70 121
Barfields Gdns. Loug. CL24 31
Barfields Path Loug. CL24 31
Barfield St. Wat. BC23 26
Barfolds Hat. BQ15 10
Barford Clo. NW4 BP30 37
Barford St. N1 BY37 2
Barford St. N1 BY37 56
Barforth Rd. SE15 CB45 67
Bargate Clo. SE18 CN42 68
Bargate Clo. N. Mal. BP54 85
Barge House Rd. E16 CL41 68
Barge House Rd. SE1 BY40 4
Barge House St. SE1 BY40 56
Barge Rd. E. Mol. BG52 84
Bargery Rd. SE6 CE47 77
Barge Wk. Kings. on T. BK51 84
Barge Wk. Kings. on T. BK52 84
Bargrove Av. Hem. H. AW14 8
Bargrove Clo. SE19 CB50 77
Lullington Rd.
Bargrove Cres. SE6 CD48 77
Barham Av. Borwd. BL24 28
Barham Clo. Brom. CK54 88
Barham Clo. Chis. CL49 78
Barham Clo. Grnf. BJ36 54
Barham Clo. Rom. CR30 41
Barham Clo. Wey. BA56 92
Barham Rd. SW20 BP50 75
Barham Rd. Chis. CL49 78
Barham Rd. Dart. CX47 80
Barham Rd. Epsom BN58 94
Barham Rd. Sth. Croy. BZ56 96
Baring Clo. SE12 CH48 78
Baring Rd. SE12 CH47 78
Baring Rd. Barn. BT24 29
Baring Rd. Croy. CB54 87
Baring St. N1 BZ37 2
Baring St. N1 BZ37 57
Barker Rd. Cher. AV54 82
Barker St. SW10 BT43 66
Barker Wk. SW16 BW48 76
Barkham Rd. N17 BZ29 39
Bark Hart Rd. Orp. CO54 89
Barking By-pass Bark. CM38 58
Barking Ind. Est. Bark. CO37 59
Barking Rd. E6 CJ37 58
Barking Rd. E13 CG39 58
Barking Rd. E16 CG39 58
Barkis Way SE16 CB42 67
Egan Way
Bark Pl. W2 BS40 3
Bark Pl. W2 BS40 56
Barkston Gdns. BS42 66
Barkston Path Borwd. BM22 28
Barkworth Rd. SE16 CB42 67
Barlborough St. SE14 CC43 67
Barlby Gdns. W10 BQ38 55
Barlby Rd. W10 BQ39 55
Barle Gdns. S. Ock. DA39 60
Barley Clo. Bush. BF25 27
Barleycorn Way E14 CD40 57
Narrow St.
Barleycorn Way Horn. CW32 51
Barley Croft Harl. CM13 13
Barley Croft Harl. CN13 13
Barley Cft. Hem. H. BA13 8
Barleycroft Grn. Welw. G. C. BQ8 5
Barleycroft Rd. Welw. G. C. BQ8 5
Barley Field Brwd. CZ22 33
Barley La. Ilf. CO33 50
Barley La. Rom. CO33 50
Barley Mow Clo. Wok. AO62 100
Barley Mow La. Wok. AO61 100
Barley Mow Pass W4 BN42 65
Barley Mow Rd. Egh. AR49 72
Barley Mow Way Shep. AZ52 83
Petts La.
Barlow Clo. Wall. BX57 95
Redford Av.
Barlow Pl. W1 BV40 3
Barlow Pl. W1 BV40 56
Bruton La.
Barlow Rd. NW6 BR36 55
Maygrove Rd.
Barlow Rd. W3 BM40 55
Barlow Rd. Hamptn. BF50 74
Barlow St. SE17 BZ42 4
Barlow St. SE17 BZ42 67
Barmeston Rd. SE6 CE48 77
Barmor Clo. Har. BF30 36
Barmouth Av. Grnf. BH37 54
Barmouth Rd. SW18 BT46 76
Barmouth Rd. Croy. CC55 87
Barnabas Rd. E9 CC35 48
Barnaby Way, Chig. CL27 40
Barnacre Clo. Uxb. AX39 53
Barnacres Cft. Hem. H. AZ15 8
Barnacres Rd. Hem. H. AY16 17
Barnacres Rd. Hem. H. AZ15 8
Barnard Acres Wal. Abb. CG15 13
Barnard Clo. SE18 CL41 68
Powis St.
Barnard Clo. Chis. CM51 88
Barnard Clo. Hem. H. AY14 8
Barnard Clo. Sun. BC50 73
Barnard Clo. Wall. BW57 95
Barnard Gdns. Hayes BC38 53
Barnard Gdns. N. Mal. BP52 85
Barnard Grn. Welw. G. C. BR8 5
Bernard Gro. E15 CC36 58
Barnard Hill N10 BV30 38
Barnard Ms. SW11 BU45 66
Barnard Rd.
Barnardo Dr. Ilf. CM31 49
Ashurst Dr.
Barnardo St. E1 CC39 57
Barnard Rd. SW11 BU45 66
Barnard Rd. Enf. CB23 30
Barnard Rd. Saw. CO5 6
Barnard Rd. Warl. CE63 105
Barnards Inn EC4 BY39 56
Fetter La.
Barnards Way, Beac. AO29 34
Barnby Rd. Wok. AO62 100
Barnby St. E15 CG37 58
Barnby St. NW1 BW37 56
Barnby St. NW1 BW38 1
Barn Clo. Ashf. AZ49 73
Barn Clo. Nthlt. BD37 54
Barn Clo. Rad. BJ21 27
Barn Clo. Welw. G. C. BQ8 5
Barn Cres. Pur. BZ60 96
Barn Cres. Stan. BK29 36
Barncroft Clo. Loug. CL25 31
Barncroft Clo. Uxb. AZ39 53
Barncroft Rd. Berk. AP13 7
Barncroft Rd. Loug. CL25 31
Barncroft Way St. Alb. BJ14 9
Barndicott Welw. G. C. BT8 5
Barnehurst Av. Bexh. CS44 69
Barnehurst Av. Erith CS44 69
Barnehurst Clo. Erith CS44 69
Barnehurst Rd. Bexh. CR44 69
Barn Elms Park SW15 BQ45 65
Barnend Dr. Dart. CV49 80
Barnend La. Dart. CV49 80
Barnes Alley Hmptn. BG51 84
Barnes Av. Chesh. AO18 16
Barnes Av. SW13 BP43 65
Barnes Br. SW13 BO44 65
Barnes Br. W4 BO44 65
Barnesbury Est. N1 BX37 2
Barnes Clo. E12 CJ35 49
Barnes Ct. N22 BX29 38
Barnes Ct. Wdf. Grn. CJ28 40
Durham Av.
Barnes Cray Rd. Dart. CU45 69
Barnesdale Cres. Orp. CO53 89
Barnes End N. Mal. BP53 85
Barnes High St. SW13 BO44 65
Barnes La. Kings. L. AW17 17
Barnes Pikle W5 BK40 54
Mattock La.
Barnes Pikle W5 BK40 54
Mattock La.
Barnes Rise, Kings L. AY17 17
Barnes Rd. N18 CC28 39
Princes Rd.
Barnes Rd. Ilf. CM35 49
Barnes St. E14 CD39 57
Barnes Ter. SE8 CD42 67
Barnes Way, Iver AV40 52
Barnet By-pass N2 BT32 47
Barnet By-pass Barn. BO23 28
Barnet By-pass Hat. BO12 10
Barnet By-pass Hat. BP17 19
Barnet Dr. Brom. CK55 88
Barnet Gate La. Barn. BO25 28
Barnet Gro. E2 CB38 2
Barnet Gro. E2 CB38 57
Barnet Hill Barn. BR24 28
Barnet La. N20 BR26 37
Barnet La. Borwd. BK25 27
Barnet Rd. Barn. BN25 28
Barnet Rd. Barn. BS21 29
Barnet Rd. Pot. B. BM18 19
Barnet Rd. Pot. B. BS20 20
Barnet Rd. St. Alb. BL17 19
Barnet Row Guil. AR68 109
Barnets Fld. Sev. CT61 107
Barnett Clo. Lthd. BJ63 102
Barnetts Shaw, Oxt. CF67 114
Chalkpit Wood
Barnettwood La. Lthd.
& Ash. BJ63 102
Barnet Way NW7 BN27 37
Barnet Way NW7 BN28 37
Barney Clo. SE7 CJ42 68
Charlton Church Rd.
Barnfield Bans. BS60 95
Barn Field, Epp. CO17 23
Barnfield, Hem. H. AY15 8
Barnfield, Iver AV39 52
Barnfield, N. Mal. BN53 85
Barnfield Av. Cray. CC55 87
Barnfield Av. Kings. on T. BK49 74
Barnfield Av. Mitch. BV52 86
Barnfield Clo. Couls. BZ63 105
Barnfield Clo. Hodd. CE11 12
Barnfield Clo. Swan. CS54 89
Barnfield Cres. Sev. CW62 108
Barnfield Gdns. Kings. on T. BL49 75
Barnfield Gdns. Est. SE18 CL43 68
Barnfield Rd. SE18 CL43 68
Barnfield Rd. W5 BK38 54
Barnfield Rd. Belv. CQ43 69
Barnfield Rd. Edg. BN30 37
Barnfield Rd. Orp. CP52 89
Barn Field Rd. St. Alb. BK12 9
Barnfield Rd. Sev. CT65 107
Barnfield Rd. Sth. Croy. CA58 96
Barnfield Rd. Welw. G. C. BR9 5
Barnfield Rd. West. CJ64 106
Barnfield Way Slou. AL40 61
Barnfield Wd. Clo. Beck. CF53 87
Barnfield Wd. Rd. Beck. CF53 87
Barnham Rd. Grnf. BG38 54
Barnham St. SE1 CA41 4
Barnham St. SE1 CA41 67
Barn Hill Harl. CH13 13
Barnhill Pnr. BD32 45
Barn Hill Wem. BM33 46
Barn Hill Av. Brom. CG53 88
Barnhill La. Hayes BC38 53
Barnhill Rd. Hayes BC38 53
Barnhill Rd. Wem. BN34 46
Barnhurst Path Wat. BD28 36
Barnlea Rick AW26 35
Barnlee Clo. Felt. BE48 74
Barn Mead Brwd. DB21 33
Barn Mead Epp. CN21 31
Coppice Row
Barn Mead. Harl. CN12 13
Barnmead Wok. AP58 91
Barnmead Gdns. Dag. CQ35 50
Barn Meadow Clo. Lthd. BE65 102
Barn Meadow La.
Barn Meadow La. Lthd. BE65 102
Barnmead Rd. Beck. CC51 87
Barnmead Rd. Dag. CQ35 50
Barn Rise Wem. BM34 46
Barn Rd. Mitch. BV52 86
Barnsbury Clo. N. Mal. BN52 85
Barnsbury Cres. Surb. BN54 85
Barnsbury Est. N1 BX37 56
Barnsbury Gro. N7 BX36 56
Roman Way
Barnsbury La. Surb. BM55 85
Barnsbury Ms. N1 BY36 56
Brooksby St.
Barnsbury Pk. N1 BY36 56
Barnsbury Rd. N1 BY37 2
Barnsbury Rd. N1 BY37 56
Barnsbury Sq. N1 BY36 56
Barnsbury St. N1 BY36 2
Barnsbury St. N1 BY36 56
Barnsbury Ter. N1 BY36 56
Barnsbury Ter. N1 BX37 2
Barnsdale Rd. W9 BR38 55
Barnsdale Yd. W9 BR38 55
Barnsdale Rd.
Barnsfield Pl. Uxb. AX37 53
Barns La. Wok. AV65 100
Barns La. Wok. AV66 109
Barnsley Rd. Rom. CW29 42
Barnsley St. E1 CB38 57
Barnstaple La. SE13 CF45 67
Lewisham High St.
Barnstaple Path Rom. CV28 42
Barnstaple Rd.
Barnstaple Rd. Rom. CV28 42
Barnstaple Rd. Ruis. BD34 45
Barnston Wk. N1 BZ37 57
Popham St.
Barn St. N16 CA34 48
Church St.
Barnway Egh. AR49 72
Barn Way Wem. BM33 46
Barnwell Rd. SW2 BY46 76
Barnwood Av. W. Wick. CE54 87
Barnwood Clo. W9 BS38 56
Amblerley Est.
Barnwood Clo. Ruis. BA34 44
Barnwood Ct. Est. E16 CH40 58
Barnwood Rd. Guil. AP70 118
Barnyard The Tad. BP65 103
Baroness Rd. E2 CA38 2
Baroness Rd. E2 CA38 57
Baronet Gro. N17 CB30 39
Baronet Rd. N17 CB30 39
Baron Gdns. Ilf. CM31 49
Baron Gro. Mitch. BU52 86
Barons Rd. Dag. CP33 50
Barons Ct. NW9 BN32 46
Baron's Ct. Rd. W14 BR42 65
Baronsfield Rd. Twick. BJ46 74
Barons Gate, Barn. BU25 29
Barons Hurst, Epsom BN61 103

8

»aumont Rd. E13 CH38 58
»aumont Rd. SE19 BZ50 77
»aumont Rd. SW19 BR47 75
»aumont Rd. W4 BN41 65
»aumont Rd. Brox. CA15 12
»aumont Rd. Orp. CM53 88
»aumont Rd. Pur. BY60 95
»aumont Rd. Slou. AO38 52
»aumont Rd. Wind. AO44 61
»aumont Sq. E1 CC39 57
»aumont St. W1 BV39 1
»aumont St. W1 BV39 56
»aumont Vw. Wal. Cr. BZ16 21
Pear Tree Wk.
»aumont Wk. NW3 BU36 56
Adelaide Rd.
»auvais Ter. Nthlt. BD38 54
»auval Rd. SE22 CA46 77
»averbank Rd. SE9 CM47 78
»aver Clo. SE19 CB50 77
»aver Clo. Hamptn. BF51 84
»aver Gro. Nthlt. BD38 54
»aver Gro. Nthlt. BE38 54
Jetstar Way
»aver Rd. Ilf. CP28 41
»avers Cres. Houns. BD45 64
»avers La. Houns. BD45 64
»averwood Rd. Sid. CN49 78
»avor La. W6 BP42 65
»bbington Rd. SE18 CN42 68
»bletts Clo. Orp. CN56 97
»ccles Dr. Bark. CN36 58
»ccles St. E14 CD39 57
»c Clo. Ruis. BD34 45
»ckenham Gdns. N9 CA27 39
»ckenham Gro. Brom. CF51 87
»ckenham Hill Rd. SE6 CE50 77
»ckenham Hill Rd. Beck. CE50 77
»ckenham La. Brom. CG51 88
»ckenham Pl. Pk. Beck. CE50 77
»ckenham Rd. Beck. CC51 87
»ckenham Rd. W. Wick. CE54 87
»ckenshaw Gdns. Bans. BT61 104
»ckers Est. The N16 CB34 48
»cket Av. E6 CL38 58
»cket Clo. SE25 CB53 87
»cket Clo. Brwd. DB29 42
»cket St. SE1 BZ41 4
»cket St. SE1 BZ41 67
»cket Fold, Har. BH32 45
»ckets Sq. Berk. AQ12 7
Bridle Way
»ckett Av. Ken. BY61 104
»cketts Av. St. Alb. BG12 9
»cketts Clo. Houns. BC46 73
Harlington Rd. West.
»cketts Clo. Orp. CN55 88
»ckett Wk. Beck. CD50 77
»ckford Rd. Croy. CA53 87
»ck La. Beck. CC52 87
»cklow Gdns. W12 BP41 65
Becklow Rd.
»cklow Rd. W12 BO41 65
»ck Rd. E8 CB37 57
»cks Rd. Sid. CO48 79
»ckton Gdns. E6 CK39 58
»ckton Pl. Erith. CR44 69
»ckton Rd. E6 CG39 58
»ckton Rd. E16 CG39 58
»ckton St. E16 CG39 58
»ckway, Beck. CD52 87
»ckway Rd. SW16 BW51 86
»ckway St. SE17 BZ42 4
»ckway St. SE17 BZ42 67
»ckwith Rd. SE24 BZ46 77
»clands Rd. SW17 BV50 76
»cmead Av. SW16 BW49 76
»cmead Av. Har. BJ32 45
»condale Rd. SE19 CA49 77
»consfield Rd. W11 BV28 38
»contree Av. Dag. CO35 50
»contree Av. Dag. CQ34 50
»ctive Pl. SW15 BR45 65
»ctive Rd. E7 CH35 49
»ctive Rd. SW15 BR45 65
»dale Rd. Enf. BZ22 30
»dale Rd. Enf. BZ23 30
»dale Rd. Rom. CX28 42
»dale St. SE1 BZ40 4
»dale St. SE1 BZ40 57
»ddington Fm. Rd. Croy. BX54 86
»ddington Gdns. Wall. BV57 95
»ddington Gn. Orp. CN51 88
»ddington Gro. Wall. BW56 95
»ddington La. Croy. BW53 86
»ddington Path, Orp. CN51 88
»ddington Rd. Ilf. CN33 49
»ddington Rd. Orp. CN51 88
»ddlestead La. Warl. CG62 106
»de Clo. Pnr. BD30 36
»denham Way SE15 CA43 67
Hordle Prom. N.
»dens Rd. Sid. CQ50 79
»de Rd. E3 CD39 57
»de Rd. Rom. CP32 50
»dfont Clo. Felt. BA46 73
»dfont Ct. Stai. AW45 63
»dfont La. Felt. BB47 73
»dfont La. Felt. BC47 73
»dfont Rd. Felt. BA47 73
»dfont Rd. Stai. AY46 73
»dford Av. Amer. AR23 25
»dford Av. WC1 BW39 1
»dford Av. WC1 BW39 56
»dford Av. Barn. BR25 28
»dford Av. Hayes BC39 53
»dfordbury WC2 BX40 4
»dfordbury WC2 BX40 56
Chandos Pl.
»edford Clo. N10 BV29 38
»edford Clo. Rick. AT22 25
»edford Ct. WC2 BX40 4
»edford Ct. WC2 BX40 56
Bedford St.
»edford Cres. Enf. CD21 30
»edford Gdns. W8 BS40 56
»edford Gdns. Horn. CV34 51
»edford Hill SW12 BV47 76
Bedford Hill SW16 BV47 76
Bedford Pk. Croy. BZ54 87
Bedford Pk. Mans. W4 BN42 65
Bedford Park Rd. St. Alb. BH13 9
Bedford Pl. WC1 BX39 2
Bedford Pl. WC1 BX39 56
Bedford Pl. Croy. BZ54 87
Bedford Rd. E6 CL37 58
Bedford Rd. E17 CE31 48
Bedford Rd. E18 CH30 40
Bedford Rd. N2 BU31 47
Bedford Rd. N8 BW32 47
Bedford Rd. N9 CB26 39
Bedford Rd. N15 CA31 48
Bedford Rd. N22 BX30 38
Bedford Rd. NW7 BO27 37
Bedford Rd. SW4 BX45 66
Bedford Rd. W4 BN41 65
Bedford Rd. W13 BJ40 54
Bedford Rd. Brent. BL42 65
Claypounds La.
Bedford Rd. Dart. CX47 80
Bedford Rd. Enf. CC23 30
Bedford Rd. Grav. DF48 81
Bedford Rd. Grays. DD42 71
Bedford Rd. Har. BG32 45
Bedford Rd. Ilf. CL34 49
Bedford Rd. Nthwd. BA27 35
Bedford Rd. Orp. CO55 89
Bedford Rd. Ruis. BB35 44
Bedford Rd. St. Alb. BH14 9
Bedford Rd. Sid. CN48 78
Bedford Rd. Twick. BG48 74
Bedford Rd. Wor. Pk. BQ55 85
Bedford Row WC1 BX39 2
Bedford Row WC1 BX39 56
Bedford Sq. WC1 BW39 1
Bedford Sq. WC1 BW39 56
Bedford St. WC2 BX40 4
Bedford St. WC2 BX40 56
Bedford St. Wat. BC23 26
Bedford Way WC1 BW38 1
Bedford Way WC1 BW38 56
Bedgebury Gdns. SW19 BR47 75
Bedgebury Rd. SE9 CJ45 68
Bedivere Rd. Brom. CH48 78
Bedlam Gdns. E. Mol. BF52 84
Bedlow Clo SE2 CP40 59
Glendale Way
Bedlow Way, Croy. BX56 95
Nicholas Rd.
Bedmond Grn. Wat. BB17 17
Bedmond Hill, Hem. H. BB16 17
Bedmond La. St. Alb. BD15 9
Bedmond La. Wat. BC16 17
Bedmond Rd. Hem. H. BA14 8
Bedmond Rd. St. Alb. BE14 9
Bedonwell Rd. Belv. CQ43 69
Bedser Dr. Har. BG35 45
Bedster Gdns. E. Mol. BG51 84
Bedwardine Rd. SE19 CA50 77
Bedwell Av. Hat. BV11 11
Bedwell Clo. Welw. G. C. BR8 5
Bedwell Gdns. E. Hayes BB42 63
Bedwell Gdns. W. Hayes BB42 63
Bedwell Rd. N17 CA30 39
Bedwell Rd. Belv. CQ42 69
Bedwin Way SE16 CB42 67
Catlin St.
Beeby Rd. E16 CH39 58
Beech Av. Lthd. BD68 111
Beech Av. N20 BU26 38
Beech Av. W3 BO40 55
Beech Av. Brent. BJ43 64
Beech Av. Brwd. DC27 122
Beech Av. Buck. H. CH27 40
Beech Av. Enf. BY21 29
Beech Av. Rad. BJ20 18
Beech Av. Ruis. BC33 44
Beech Av. Sid. CO47 79
Beech Av. Sth Croy. BZ59 96
Beech Av. Swan. CT52 89
Beech Av. Upmin. CX35 51
Beech Av. West. CJ63 106
Beech Cl. Hat. BP13 10
Beech Clo. N9 CB25 30
Beech Clo. SW15 BP47 75
Beech Clo. SW19 BQ50 75
Beech Clo. Ashf. BA49 73
Beech Clo. Cars. BU55 86
Beech Clo. Cob. BF59 93
Beech Clo. Dor. BH71 119
Beech Clo. Horn. CU34 50
Beech Clo. Lthd. BD67 111
Beech Clo. Walt. BD56 93
Beech Clo. West Dr. AZ41 63
Beech Clo. Wey. AY59 92
Beech Copse, Brom. CK51 88
Beech Copse, Sth. Croy. CB56 96
Beech Ct. SE9 CK46 78
Beech Ct. Tedd. BK50 74
Broom Water
Beechcroft, Chis. CL50 78
Beechcroft, Guil. AO72 118
Beechcroft, S. le H. DK42 71
Beechcroft, Ash. BL63 103
Beechcroft Av. NW11 BR33 46
Beechcroft Av. Bexh. CS44 69
Beechcroft Av. Har. BF33 45
Beechcroft Av. Ken. BZ61 105
Beechcroft Av. N. Mal. BO51 85
Beechcroft Av. Rick. BA25 26
Beechcroft Av. Sthl. BE40 54
Beechcroft Clo. SW16 BX49 76
Beechcroft Clo. Houns. BE43 64
Beechcroft Clo. Orp. CM56 97
Beechcroft Gdns. Wem. BL34 46
Beechcroft Manor, Wey. BA55 83
Beechcroft Rd. E18 CH30 40
Beechcroft Rd. SW14 BN45 65
Beechcroft Rd. SW17 BU48 76
Beechcroft Rd. Bush. BE25 27
Beechcroft Rd. Chess. BL55 85
Beechcroft Rd. Orp. CM56 97
Beechdale N21 BX27 38
Beechdale Rd. SW2 BX46 76
Beech Dell, Orp. CK56 97
Beechdene, Tad. BP64 103
Beech Dr. Berk. AR13 7
Beech Dr. N2 BU30 38
Beech Dr. Borwd. BL23 28
Beech Dr. Reig. BT70 121
Beech Dr. Saw. CP7 6
Beech Dr. Tad. BR64 103
Beech Dr. Wok. AV65 100
Beechen Clo. Pnr. BE31 45
Beechen Gro. Wat. BC24 26
Beechen La. Tad. BR66 112
Beechenlea La. Swan. CU52 89
Beechen Pl. SE23 CC48 77
Beeches Av. The, Cars. BU57 95
Beeches Clo. Tad. BS65 104
Beeches Rd. SW17 BU48 76
Beeches Rd. Sutt. BR54 85
Beeches, The Bans. BS61 104
Beeches, The St. Alb. BG17 18
Sycamore Dr.
Beeches, The, Til. DG44 71
Beeches Wk. Cars. BT58 95
Beech Farm Rd. Warl. CF63 105
Beech Field, Bans. BS60 95
Beechfield, Kings L. AY18 17
Beechfield, Saw. CQ6 6
Beechfield Cott. Brom. CJ51 88
Beechfield Gdns. Rom. CS33 50
Beechfield Rd. N4 BZ32 48
Beechfield Rd. SE6 CD47 77
Beechfield Rd. Brom. CJ51 88
Beechfield Rd. Erith. CT43 69
Beechfield Rd. Hem. H. AW14 8
Beechfield Wk. Wal. Abb. CF21 30
Beech Gdns. W5 BL41 65
Beech Gdns. Dag. CR36 59
Beech Gdns. Wok. AR61 100
Beech Grn. S. Ock. CY41 70
Beech Grn. Wok. AS61 100
Beech Gro. Amer. AO23 25
Beech Gro. Cat. CA66 114
Beech Gro. Epsom BP62 103
Beech Gro. Guil. AP70 118
Beech Gro. Ilf. CN29 40
Beech Gro. Mitch. BW53 86
Beech Gro. N. Mal. BN52 85
Beech Gro. Wey. AW56 92
Beech Gro. Wok. AR65 100
Beech Hall Cres. E4 CF29 39
Beech Hall Rd. E4 CF29 39
Beech Hill, Barn. BT22 29
Beech Hill Av. Barn. BT23 29
Beech Hill Ct. Berk. AR13 7
Beech Hill Gdns. Wal. Abb. CH22 31
Beechhill Rd. SE9 CL46 78
Beech House Rd. Croy. BZ55 87
Beech La. Beac. AP29 34
Beech La. Buck. H. CH27 40
Beech La. Guil. AR72 118
Beech Lawn, Guil. AS71 118
Beechlawns N2 BT28 38
Beechmont Av. Vir. W. AR53 82
Beechmont Rd. Brom. CG49 78
Beechmont Rd. Sev. CU68 116
Beechmore Gdns. Sutt. BQ55 85
Beechmore Rd. SW11 BU44 66
Beechmount Av. W7 BG39 54
Beecholme Av. Mitch. BV51 86
Beecholme Est. E5 CB34 48
Beechpark Way, Wat. BB22 26
Beech Pl. St. Alb. BG12 9
Beech Rd. N11 BX29 38
Beech Rd. SW16 BX51 86
Beech Rd. Dart. CV47 80
Beech Rd. Epsom BO61 103
Beech Rd. Felt. BB47 73
Beech Rd. Ong. DB13 15
Beech Rd. Orp. CO57 98
Beech Rd. Red. BW66 113
Beech Rd. Reig. BS69 121
Beech Rd. St. Alb. BH12 9
Beech Rd. Sev. CU66 116
Beech Rd. Slou. AS41 62
Beech Rd. Wat. BC22 26
Beech Rd. West. CH62 106
Beech Rd. Wey. BA58 92
Beech Row, Kings. On T. BL49 75
Beech St. E1 BZ39 57
Beech St. EC1 BZ39 57
Beech St. EC2 BZ39 2
Beech St. Rom. CS31 50
Beechtree Av. Egh. AQ50 72
Beech Tree Clo. Stan. BJ28 36
Beech Tree Clo. Stan. BK28 36
Marsh La.
Beech Tree Glade E4 CG26 40
Beech Tree La. Stai. AW51 83
Beech Tree Pl. Sutt. BS56 95
West St.
Beech Wk. NW7 BN29 37
Beech Wk. Dart. CU45 69
Beech Wk. Epsom BP59 94
Beech Wk. Hodd. CD12 12
Beech Way NW10 BN36 55
Beechway, Bex. CP46 79
Beech Way, Croy. CC60 96
Beech Way, Epsom BO61 103
Beech Way, Ger. Cr. AS33 43
Beech Way, Guil. AT70 118
Beech Way, Twick. BF48 74
Beechway Clo. Wal. Cr. CA16 21
Beech Wood Av. Amer. AR22 25
Beechwood Av. Rick. AT24 25
Beechwood Av. Tad. BS64 104
Beechwood Av. N3 BR31 46
Beechwood Av. Couls. BV61 104
Beechwood Av. Grnf. BF38 54
Beechwood Av. Har. BF34 45
Beechwood Av. Hayes BA40 53
Beechwood Av. Orp. CN56 97
Beechwood Av. Pot. B. BS20 20
Beechwood Av. Rich. BM44 65
Beechwood Av. Ruis. BB34 44
Beechwood Av. St. Alb. BJ12 9
Beechwood Av. Stai. AW50 73
Beechwood Av. Sun. BC50 73
Beechwood Av. Th. Hth. BY52 86
Beechwood Av. Uxb. AZ39 53
Beechwood Av. Wey. BA56 92
Beechwood Clo. NW7 BO28 37
Beechwood Clo. Amer. AR23 25
Beechwood Clo. Surb. BK54 84
Beechwood Clo. Wey. BB56 92
Beechwood Clo. Wok. AP62 100
Beechwood Cres. Bexh. CP45 69
Beechwood Dr. Kes. CJ56 97
Beechwood Dr. Wdf. Grn. CG28 40
Beechwood Gdns. W5 BL37 55
St. Anne's Gdns.
Beechwood Gdns. Cat. CB64 105
Beechwood Gdns. Har. BF34 45
Beechwood Gdns. Ilf. CK32 49
Beechwood Gdns. Rain. CU39 59
Beechwood Gdns. Slou. AR41 62
Beechwood La. Warl. CC63 105
Beechwood Manor, Wey. BB56 92
Beechwood Pk. E18 CH31 49
Beechwood Pk. Hem. H. AV15 7
Beechwood Rise, Wat. BC21 26
Beechwood Rd. E8 CA36 57
Beechwood Rd. N8 BW31 47
Beechwood Rd. Cat. CB64 105
Beechwood Rd. Slou. AO39 52
Beechwood Rd. Sth. Croy. BZ58 96
Beechwood Rd. Vir. W. AQ54 82
Beechwood Rd. Wok. AP62 100
Beechwood Ter. E4 CF29 39
Larks Hall Rd.
Beechworth Clo. NW3 BS34 47
Beechy Lees Rd. Sev. CW61 108
Beecot La. Walt. BD55 84
Beecroft Rd. SE4 CD46 77
Beehive Ct. Ilf. CK32 49
Beehive Grn. Welw. G. C. BS9 5
Beehive La. Ilf. CK32 49
Beehive La. Welw. G. C. BS9 5
Beehive Rd. Stai. AV49 72
Beehive Rd. Wal. Cr. BY17 20
Beehive Way, Reig. BS72 121
Sandcross La.
Beehive Whitelands Brwd. DB21 33
Beeken Dene, Orp. CM56 97
Isabella Dr.
Beel Clo. Amer. AR23 25
Beeleigh Rd. Mord. BS52 86
Beesfield La. Farn. CX54 90
Beeston Clo. E8 CB35 48
Ferncliffe Est.
Beeston Clo. Wat. BD28 36
Beeston Pl. SW1 BV41 3
Beeston Pl. SW1 BV41 66
Beeston Rd. Barn. BT25 29
Berkeley Cres.
Beeston Way, Felt. BD46 74
Beethoven Rd. Borwd. BK26 36
Beethoven St. W10 BR38 55
Beeton Clo. Pnr. BF29 36
Begbie Rd. SE3 CJ44 68
Beggar's Hill, Epsom BO57 94
Beggars Hollow, Enf. BZ22 30
Beggars La. West. CM65 106
Beggars La. Wok. AO59 91
Begonia Wk. W12 BO39 55
Du Cane Rd.
Beira St. SW12 BV47 76
Belcher Rd. Hodd. CE11 12
Belchers La. Wal. Abb. CJ15 13
Belcroft Clo. Brom. CG50 78
Hope Park
Belfairs Dr. Rom. CP33 50
Belfairs Grn. Wat. BD28 36
Heysham Dr.
Belfast Av. Slou. AO39 52
Belfast Rd. N16 CA34 48
Belfast Rd. SE25 CB52 87
Belfield Rd. Epsom BN57 94
Belfont Wk. N7 BX35 47
Camden Rd.
Belfont Wk. N7 BX35 47
Warlters Rd.
Belford Gro. SE18 CL42 68
Belford Rd. Borwd. BL22 28
Belfort Rd. SE15 CC44 67
Belfry Av. Uxb. AW29 35
Belfry La. Rick. AX26 35
Belgrade Rd. N16 CA35 48
Belgrade Rd. Hamptn. BF51 84
Belgrave Av. Rom. CV31 51
Belgrave Av. Wat. BB25 26
Belgrave Clo. N14 BW25 29
Belgrave Clo. W3 BM41 65
Avenue Rd.
Belgrave Clo. Walt. BC56 92
Belgrave Cres. Sun. BC51 83
Belgrave Dr. Kings L. BA17 17
Belgrave Gdns. N14 BW24 29
Belgrave Gdns. NW8 BS37 1
Belgrave Gdns. NW8 BS37 56
Belgrave Gdns. Stan. BK28 36
Belgrave Grn. N. Slou. AP40 52
Belgrave Grn. S. Slou. AP40 52
Belgrave Manor, Wok. AS63 100
Brooklyn Rd.
Belgrave Ms. SW1 BV41 3
Belgrave Ms. SW1 BV41 66
Belgrave Ms. Uxb. AX38 53
Belgrave Ms. N. SW1 BV41 3
Belgrave Ms. N. SW1 BV41 66
Belgrave Ms. S. SW1 BV41 3
Belgrave Ms. S. SW1 BV41 66
Belgrave Pl. SW1 BV41 3
Belgrave Pl. SW1 BV41 66
Belgrave Rd. E10 CF33 48
Belgrave Rd. E11 CH34 49
Belgrave Rd. E13 CJ38 58
Belgrave Rd. E17 CE32 48
Belgrave Rd. SE25 CA52 87
Belgrave Rd. SW1 BV42 3
Belgrave Rd. SW1 BV42 66
Belgrave Rd. SW13 BO43 65
Belgrave Rd. Houns. BE45 64
Belgrave Rd. Ilf. CK33 49
Belgrave Rd. Mitch. BT52 86
Belgrave Rd. Slou. AP40 52
Belgrave Rd. Sun. BC51 83
Belgrave Sq. SW1 BV41 3
Belgrave Sq. SW1 BV41 66
Belgrave St. E1 CD39 57
Belgrave St. SW1 BV41 66
Belgrave Ter. Wdf. Green. CH27 40
Belgrave Wk. Mitch. BT52 86
Belgravia Gdns. Brom. CF50 77
Belgravia Mews,
Kings. on T. BK52 84
Belgrove St. WC1 BX38 2
Belgrove St. WC1 BX38 56
Belham Rd. Kings L. AY17 17
Belham St. SE5 BZ44 67
Belham Wk. SE5 BZ44 67
Deynsford Rd.
Belhaven Ct. Borwd. BL23 29
Leeming Rd.
Belhaven St. E3 CD38 57
Belinda Rd. SW9 BY45 66
Belithe Vill. N1 BX36 56
Bell Alley, Houns. BF45 64
Bellamy Clo. SW5 BR42 65
Aisgill Av.
Bellamy Clo. Uxb. AZ34 44
Bellamy Clo. Wat. BC23 26
Bellamy Dr. Stan. BJ30 36
Bellamy Rd. E4 CE29 39
Bellamy Rd. Enf. BZ23 30
Halifax Rd.
Bellamy Rd. Wal. Cr. CD18 21
Bellamy St. SW12 BV47 76
Bellasis Av. SW2 BX48 76
Bell Av. Rom. CU30 41
Bell Av. West Dr. AY42 63
Bell Clo. Green. CZ46 80
Bell Clo. Pnr. BD30 36
Bell Clo. Ruis. BB34 44
Bell Clo. Slou. AQ39 52
Bell Clo. Wat. BC17 17
Bellclose Rd. West Dr. AY41 63
Bell Ct. Surb. BM55 85
Bell Cres. Couls. BV64 104
Bell Dr. SW18 BR47 75
Bellefield Rd. Orp. CO53 89
Bellefields Rd. SW9 BX45 66
Belle Grove Clo. Well. CN44 68
Bellegrove Rd. Well. CN44 68
Bellenden Rd. SE15 CA45 67
Belleville Rd. SW11 BU46 76
Belle Vue, Grnf. BG37 54
Bellevue Gdns. SW9 BX44 66
Bellevue La. Bush. BG26 36
Bellevue Pk. Th. Hth. BZ52 87
Bellevue Rd. E17 CF30 39
Bellevue Rd. N11 BV28 38
Bellevue Rd. NW4 BQ31 46
Bellevue Rd. SW13 BP44 65
Bellevue Rd. SW17 BU47 76
Bellevue Rd. W13 BJ38 54
Belle Vue Rd. Bexh. CQ46 79
Bellevue Rd. Horn. CW33 51
Bellevue Rd. Kings. on T. BL52 85
Belle Vue Rd. Rom. CS29 41
Belle Vue Ter. NW4 BQ31 46
Bellew St. SW17 BT48 76
Bellfield, Croy. CD57 96
Bellfield Av. Har. BG29 36
Bellfields Rd. Guil. AR69 118
Bellflower Path, Rom. CV29 42
Bell Fm. Av. Dag. CS34 50
Bellgale Mews NW5 BV34 47
York Rise
Bell Gdns. Orp. CP53 89
Bell Gate, Hem. H. AV12 8
Bathurst Rd.
Bell Grn. SE26 CD49 77
Bell Grn. La. SE26 CD49 77
Bellhouse La. Brwd. CZ25 33
Bell Ho. Rd. Rom. CS33 50
Bellingham Grn. SE6 CE48 77
Bellingham Rd. SE6 CE48 77
Bell La. E1 CA39 2
Bell La. E1 CA39 57
Bell La. E16 CH40 58
Bell La. NW4 BQ31 46
Bell La. Amer. AQ23 25
Bell La. Berk. AP12 7
Bell La. Brox. CD14 12
Bell La. Enf. CC22 30
Bell La. Hat. BS15 11
Bell La. Hodd. CE12 12
Bell La. Lthd. BG65 102
Bell La. St. Alb. BL18 19
Bell La. Twick. BJ47 74
Bell La. Wat. BB17 17
Bell La. Wind. AM42 61
Bell La. Clo. Lthd. BG65 102
Bellman Av. Grav. DJ47 81
Bell Mead, Saw. CQ6 6
Bell Meadow Gdse. CC69 114
Hickmans Clo.
Bellmount Wood Av. Wat. BB23 26
Bellot Way SE10 CG42 68
Bell Parade, Wind. AM44 61
Bellring Clo. Belv. CR43 69
Bell Rd. E3 CF38 57
Bell Rd. E. Mol. BG53 84
Bell Rd. Enf. BZ23 30
Bell Rd. Houns. BF45 64
Bells All. SW6 BS44 66
Bells Gdns. Est. SE15 CB43 67
Bells Gdns. Rd. SE15 CB43 67
Bells Hill, Barn. BQ25 28
Bells Hill, Slou. AQ37 52
Bells Hill Grn. Slou AQ36 52
Bells La. Slou. AT45 62
Bellsome Gdns. St. Alb. BO15 10
Bellstaines Pleasuance E4 CE27 39
Bell St. NW1 BU39 1
Bell St. NW1 BU39 56
Bell St. Reig. BS70 121
Bell St. Saw. CQ6 6
Bellswood La. Iver AT39 52
Belltrees Gro. SW16 BX49 76
Bell Vw. Wind. AM45 61
Bell Vw. Clo. Wind. AM44 61
Bellvue Clo. Orp. CL58 97
Bell Water Gate SE18 CL41 68
Bellweir Clo. Stai. AT48 72
Wraysbury Rd.

Bell Wharf La. EC4 BZ40 4
Bell Wharf La. EC4 BZ40 57
Upr. Thames St.
Bellwood Rd. SE15 CC45 67
Bell Yard WC2 BY39 2
Bell Yd. WC2 BY39 56
Belmarsh Rd. Wey. AW56 92
Belmont Av. N9 CB26 39
Belmont Av. N13 BX28 38
Belmont Av. N17 BZ31 48
Belmont Av. Barn. BU25 29
Belmont Av. Guil. AP69 118
Belmont Av. N. Mal. BP52 85
Belmont Av. N. Mal. BP53 85
Belmont Av. Sthl. BE41 64
Belmont Av. Upmin. CX34 51
Belmont Av. Well. CN44 68
Belmont Av. Wem. BL37 55
Belmont Circle, Har. BJ30 36
Belmont Clo. N20 BS26 38
Belmont Clo. SW4 BW45 66
Belmont Clo. Barn. BU24 29
Belmont Clo. Uxb. AX36 53
Belmont Clo. Wdf. Grn. CH28 40
Belmont Ct. St. Alb. BG14 9
Belmont Hill
Belmont Gro. SE13 CF45 67
Belmont Gro. W4 BN42 65
Belmont Hall Ct. SE13 CF45 67
Belmont Hill SE13 CF45 67
Belmont Hill, St. Alb. BG14 9
Belmont La. Chis. CL49 78
Belmont La. Stan. BK29 36
Belmont Pk. SE13 CF45 67
Belmont Pk. Clo. SE13 CF45 67
Belmont Pk.
Belmont Park Rd. E10 CE32 48
Belmont Rise, Sutt. BR57 94
Belmont Rd. N15 BZ31 48
Belmont Rd. N17 BZ31 48
Belmont Rd. NW11 BR32 46
Belmont Rd. SW4 BW45 66
Belmont Rd. Beck. CD51 87
Belmont Rd. Bexh. CR43 69
Belmont Rd. Bush. BE24 27
Belmont Rd. Chis. CL49 78
Belmont Rd. Grays. DC43 71
Belmont Rd. Har. BH31 45
Belmont Rd. Hem. H. AY15 8
Belmont Rd. Horn. CV34 51
Belmont Rd. Ilf. CM34 49
Belmont Rd. Lthd. BJ64 102
Belmont Rd. Reig. BT71 121
Belmont Rd. SE25 CB53 87
Belmont Rd. Sutt. BS58 95
Belmont Rd. Twick. BG48 74
Belmont Rd. Uxb. AX36 53
Belmont Rd. Wall. BV56 95
Belmont St. NW1 BV36 56
Belmor, Borwd. BM25 28
Belmore Av. Hayes BC39 53
Belmore Av. Wok. AU61 100
Belmore St. SW8 BW44 66
Belper St. N1 CB36 57
Lofting Rd.
Belsham St. E9 CC36 57
Belsize Av. N13 BX29 38
Belsize Av. NW3 BT36 56
Belsize Av. W13 BJ41 64
Belsize Clo. Hem. H. AZ14 8
Belsize Cres. NW3 BT35 47
Belsize Gdns. Sutt. BS56 95
Belsize Gro. NW3 BU36 56
Belsize La. NW3 BT36 56
Belsize Ms. NW3 BT35 47
Belsize La.
Belsize Pk. NW3 BT36 56
Belsize Pk. Gdns. NW3 BT36 56
Belsize Pk. Ms. NW3 BT35 47
Belsize La.
Belsize Pl. NW3 BT35 47
Belsize La.
Belsize Rd. NW6 BS37 1
Belsize Rd. NW6 BS37 56
Belsize Rd. NW6 BT36 56
Belsize Rd. Har. BG29 36
Belsize Rd. Hem. H. AZ14 8
Belsize Sq. NW3 BT36 56
Belsize Ter. NW3 BT36 56
Belson Rd. SE18 CK42 68
Belswains Grn. Hem. H. AV15 8
Ebberns Rd.
Belswains La. Hem. H. AY15 8
Beltana Dr. Grav. DJ49 81
Beltane Dr. SW19 BQ48 75
Beltinge Rd. Rom. CW31 51
Beltona Gdns. Wal. Cr. CC17 22
Belton Rd. E7 CH36 58
Belton Rd. E11 CG35 49
Belton Rd. N17 CA31 48
Belton Rd. NW2 BP36 55
Belton Rd. Berk. AQ12 7
Belton Rd. Sid. CO49 79
Belton Way E3 CE39 57
Beltran Rd. SW6 BS44 66
Beltwood Rd. Belv. CS42 69
Belvedere NW9 BO30 37
Belvedere Av. SW19 BR49 75
Belvedere Av. Ilf. CL30 40
Belvedere Blds. SE1 BY41 4
Belvedere Bldgs. SE1 BY41 66
Belvedere Clo. Esher BF56 93
Belvedere Clo. Grav. DH47 81
Belvedere Clo. Tedd. BH49 74
Belvedere Ct. N2 BT32 47
Belvedere Ct. SW15 BQ45 65
Upr. Richmond Rd.
Belvedere Dr. SW19 BR49 75
Belvedere Gdns. E. Mol. BE53 84
Belvedere Gdns. Guil. AQ69 118
Belvedere Gro. SW19 BR49 75
Belvedere Pl. SE1 BY41 4
Belvedere Pl. SE1 BY41 66
Borough Rd.
Belvedere Rd. E10 CD33 48
Belvedere Rd. SE1 BX41 4
Belvedere Rd. SE1 BX41 66
Belvedere Rd. SE2 CP40 59
Belvedere Rd. SE19 CA50 77
Belvedere Rd. Bexh. CQ45 69
Belvedere Rd. Brwd. CZ27 42
Belvedere Rd. West. CK62 106
Belvedere Sq. SW19 BR49 75
Belvedere Way, Har. BL32 46
Belvoir Clo. SE9 CK48 78
Nunnington Clo.
Belvoir Rd. SE22 CB47 77
Belvue Clo. Nthlt. BF36 54
Belvue Rd. Nthlt. BF36 54
Bembridge Clo. NW6 BQ36 55
Bembridge Gdns. Ruis. BA34 44
Bemerton St. N1 BX37 2
Bemerton St. N1 BX37 56
Bemish Rd. SW15 BQ45 65
Bempton Dr. Ruis. BC34 44
Bemsted Rd. E17 CD31 48
Benares Rd. SE18 CN42 68
Benbow Clo. St. Alb. BJ14 9
Benbow Rd. W6 BP41 65
Benbow St. SE8 CE43 67
Benbow Waye, Uxb. AX39 53
Benbrick Rd. Guil. AQ71 118
Benbury Clo. Brom. CF49 77
Bence, The Egh. AT52 82
Bench Fld. Sth. Croy. CA57 96
Benchley Gdns. SE23 CC46 77
Bench Manor Cres. Ger. Cr. AR30 34
Bench, The Rich. BK48 74
Back La.
Bencombe Rd. Pur. BX60 95
Bencope St. SE17 CA42 67
Bencroft, Wal. Cr. CB16 21
Bencroft Rd. SW16 BW50 76
Bendall Ms. NW1 BU39 1
Bendall Ms. NW1 BU39 56
Bendemeer Rd. SW15 BQ45 65
Bendish Rd. E6 CK36 58
Bendmore Av. SE2 CO42 69
Bendon Vall. SW18 BS47 76
Bendysh Rd. Bush. BE24 27
Benedict Dr. Felt. BA47 73
Benedict Rd. SW9 BX45 66
Benedict Rd. Mitch. BT52 86
Benedict Way N2 BT31 47
Benenden Grn. Brom. CH53 88
Benenstock Rd. Stai. AW46 73
Benets Rd. Horn. CX33 51
Benett Gdns. SW16 BX51 86
Benfleet Clo. Cob. BE59 93
Benfleet Clo. Sutt. BT55 86
Benford Rd. Hodd. CD13 12
Bengal Rd. Ilf. CL35 49
Bengarth Dr. Har. BG30 36
Bengarth Rd. Nthlt. BD37 54
Bengeworth Rd. SE5 BZ45 67
Bengeworth Rd. Har. BJ34 45
Benhale Clo. Stan. BJ28 36
Benham Clo. SW11 BT45 66
Hope St.
Benham Clo. SW11 BT45 66
Wayland Rd.
Benham Clo. Couls. BY62 104
Benham Rd. W7 BH39 54
Benham St. SW11 BT45 66
Benhill Av. Sutt. BS56 95
Benhill Rd. SE5 BZ43 67
Benhill Rd. Sutt. BT55 86
Benhill Wd. Rd. Sutt. BT55 86
Benhilton Gdns. Sutt. BS55 86
Benhurst Av. Horn. CU35 50
Benhurst Clo. Sth. Croy. CC58 96
Benhurst Ct. SW16 BY49 76
Benhurst Gdns. Sth. Croy. CC58 96
Benhurst La. SW16 BY49 76
Benin St. SE13 CF47 77
Benjamin Clo. Rom. CU32 50
Globe Rd.
Benjamin St. EC1 BY39 2
Benjamin St. EC1 BY39 56
Ben Jonson Rd. E1 CC39 57
Benledi St. E14 CF39 57
Bennerley Rd. SW11 BU46 76
Bennet St. SW1 BW40 3
Bennet St. SW1 BW40 56
Arlington St.
Bennett Clo. Kings. on T. BK51 84
Bennett Clo. Nthwd. BB29 35
Kemps Dr.
Bennett Clo. Well. CO44 69
Bennett Gro. SE13 CE44 67
Bennett Pk. SE3 CG45 68
Bennett Rd. E13 CJ38 58
Bennett Rd. Rom. CQ32 50
Bennetts Av. Croy. CD55 87
Bennett's Av. Grnf. BG37 54
Bennetts Av. Sev. DB59 99
Bennetts Castle La. Dag. CP35 50
Bennetts Clo. N17 CB29 39
Bennetts Clo. Cob. BC60 92
Bennetts Clo. Slou. AN41 61
Bennetts Clo. St. Alb. BN15 10
Bennetts Copse, Chis. CK50 78
Wood Dr.
Bennetts End Clo. Hem. H. AY14 8
Bennetts End Rd. Hem. H. AZ14 8
Bennetts Gate, Hem. H. AZ15 8
Bennetts End Rd.
Bennett St. W4 BO43 65
Bennetts Way, Croy. CD55 87
Bennetts Yd. SW1 BX41 66
Marsham St.
Bennett Way, Dart. CY49 80
Bennett Way, Guil. AW68 110
Benning Clo. Wind. AL45 61
Benningholme Rd. Edg. BO29 37
Bennington Av. Bark. CL36 58
Bennington Rd. N17 CA30 39
Bennington Rd. Wdf. Grn. CG29 40
Forest Dr.
Benns Alley, Hamptn. BF51 84
Thames St.
Benn St. E9 CD36 57
Benrek Clo. Ilf. CM30 40
Bensham Clo. Th. Hth. BZ52 87
Bensham Gro. Th. Hth. BZ51 87
Bensham La. Croy. BY54 86
Bensham Manor Rd. Th. Hth. BZ52 87
Benskin Rd. Wat. BC25 26
Benskins La. Hav. CV26 42
Benson Av. E6 CJ37 58
Benson Clo. Houns. BF45 64
Benson Clo. Slou. AQ40 52
Benson Rd. SE23 CC47 77
Benson Rd. Croy. BY55 86
Benson Rd. Grays. DD43 71
Bensor Clo. Uxb. AY39 53
Bentbrook Pk. Dor. BJ73 119
Bentfield Gdns. SE9 CJ48 78
Benthal Rd. N16 CB34 48
Bentham Av. Wok. AU60 91
Bentham Av. Wok. AU61 100
Bentham Rd. E9 CC36 57
Bentham Rd. SE28 CO40 59
Ben Tillet Clo. Bark. CO36 59
Bentinck Ms. W1 BV39 1
Bentinck Ms. W1 BV39 56
Marylebone La.
Bentinck Rd. West Dr. AX40 53
Bentinck St. W1 BV39 1
Bentinck St. W1 BV39 56
Bentley Dr. Ilf. CM32 49
Bentley Heath La. Barn. BR21 28
Bentley Rd. N1 CA36 57
Tottenham Rd.
Bentley Rd. Slou. AN40 61
Bentleys Meadow, Sev. CW63 108
Bentley St. Grav. DH46 81
Bentley Way, Stan. BJ28 36
Bentley Way, Wdf. Grn. CH27 40
Benston Clo. Houns. BF45 64
Staines Rd.
Benton Rd. E16 CJ40 58
Oriental Rd.
Benton Rd. Wat. BD28 36
Benton Rd. E. Ilf. CM33 49
Benton Rd. W. Ilf. CM33 49
Bentons, Harl. CN12 13
Bentons La. SE27 BZ49 77
Bentons Ri. SE27 BZ49 77
Bentry Clo. Dag. CQ34 50
Bentry Rd. Dag. CQ34 50
Bentsbrook Clo. Dor. BJ73 119
Spook Hill
Bentsbrook Rd. Dor. BJ73 119
Bentsley Clo. St. Alb. BK11 9
Bentwick Clo. Ger. Cr. AR32 43
Benworth Rd. W12 BP39 55
Benwell Rd. N7 BY35 47
Benworth St. E3 CD38 57
Benyon Rd. N1 BZ37 2
Benyon Rd. N1 BZ37 57
Berberis Wk. West. Dr. AY42 63
Berber Rd. SW11 BU46 76
Ashness Rd.
Berceau Wk. Wat. BB23 26
Berecroft, Harl. CN13 13
Beredens La. Upmin. CZ32 51
Berenger Wk. SW10 BT43 66
Worlds End
Berens Rd. NW10 BQ38 55
Berens Rd. Orp. CP53 89
Berens Way, Chis. CN52 88
Beresford Av. N20 BU27 38
Beresford Av. W7 BG39 54
Beresford Av. Slou. AR40 52
Beresford Av. Surb. BM54 85
Beresford Av. Twick. BK46 74
Beresford Av. Wem. BL37 55
Beresford Dr. Brom. CK52 88
St. Michael's Clo.
Beresford Dr. Wdf. Grn. CJ28 40
Beresford Gdns. Enf. CA24 30
Beresford Gdns. Houns. BE46 74
Beresford Gdns. Rom. CQ32 50
Beresford Rd. E4 CG26 40
Beresford Rd. E17 CE30 39
Beresford Rd. N2 BU31 47
Beresford Rd. N5 BZ35 48
Beresford Rd. N8 BY32 47
Beresford Rd. Dor. BJ71 119
Beresford Rd. Grav. DF47 81
Beresford Rd. Har. BG32 45
Beresford Rd. Kings. on T. BL51 85
Beresford Rd. N. Mal. BN52 85
Beresford Rd. Rick. AV26 34
Beresford Rd. St. Alb. BJ14 9
Beresford Rd. Sthl. BD40 54
Beresford Rd. Sutt. BR58 94
Beresford Sq. SE1 CL42 68
Beresford St. SE18 CL41 68
Beresford Ter. N5 BZ35 48
Berestead Rd. W6 BO43 65
Berestead Rd. W6 BO42 65
Berger Clo. Orp. CN53 88
Berger Rd. E9 CC36 57
Bergholt Av. Ilf. CK32 49
Bergholt Cres. N16 CA33 48
Berkeley Av. Grnf. BG36 54
Berkeley Av. Houns. BC44 63
Berkeley Av. Ilf. CL30 40
Berkeley Av. Rom. CS29 41
Berkeley Av. Wal. Cr. CC20 21
Berkeley Clo. Borwd. BM25 28
Berkeley Clo. Guil. AS70 118
Berkeley Clo. Pot. B. BR19 19
Berkeley Clo. Ruis. BC34 44
Berkeley Ct. EC1 BY39 56
Briset St.
Berkeley Ct. N14 BW25 29
Berkeley Ct. Ruis. BB34 44
Berkeley Ct. Stai. AU48 72
Moor La.
Berkeley Ct. Wey. BB55 83
Berkeley Cres. Barn. BT25 29
Berkeley Cres. Dart. CW47 80
Berkeley Gdns. N21 BZ26 39
Berkeley Gdns. W8 BS40 56
Brunswick Gdns.
Berkeley Gdns. Walt. BB54 83
Berkeley Ms. W1 BU39 1
Berkeley Ms. W1 BU39 56
Berkeley Pl. SW19 BQ50 75
Berkeley Rd. E12 CK35 49
Berkeley Rd. N8 BW32 47
Berkeley Rd. N15 BZ32 48
Berkeley Rd. NW9 BM31 46
Berkeley Rd. SW13 BP44 65
Berkeley Rd. Bexh. CP44 69
Berkeley Rd. Uxb. BA36 53
Berkeley Sq. W1 BV40 3
Berkeley Sq. W1 BV40 56
Berkeley St. W1 BV40 3
Berkeley St. W1 BU39 56
Berkeley Wk. N7 BX34 47
Andover Est.
Berkeley Wk. N7 BX34 47
Durham Rd.
Berkeley Waye, Houns. BD43 64
Berkhampstead Rd. Belv. CR42 69
Berkhampstead Rd. Hem. H. AV12 7
Berkhampstead Av. Wem. BL36 55
Berkhampstead Hill, Berk. AS12 7
Berkhampstead La. Hat. BU13 11
Berkhampstead Pl. Berk. AQ12 7
Berkley Ct. Rick. BA25 26
Mayfare
Berkley Clo. Horn. CX34 51
Berkley Dr. E. Mol. BE52 84
Berkley Dr. Horn. CX34 51
Berkley Gdns. Wey. AV60 91
Berkley Gro. NW1 BU36 56
Berkley Rd.
Berkley Rd. NW1 BU36 56
Berkley Rd. SW13 BP44 65
Berks Clo. Cat. BZ64 105
Berks Hill, Rick. AU25 25
Berkshire Clo. Orp. CN54 88
Berkshire Gdns. N13 BX29 38
Berkshire Gdns. N18 CB28 39
Berkshire Rd. E9 CD36 57
Berkshire Sq. Mitch. BX52 86
Berkshire Way, Horn. CX32 51
Berkshire Way, Mitch. BX52 86
Bermans Clo. Brwd. DD27 122
Hanging Hill La.
Berman's Way NW10 BO35 46
Bermondsey Sq. SE1 CA41 4
Bermondsey Sq. SE1 CA41 67
Abbey St.
Bermondsey St. SE1 CA40 4
Bermondsey St. SE1 CA40 57
Bermondsey St. SE1 CA41 4
Bermondsey Wall. E. SE16 CB41 67
Bermondsey Wall. W. SE16 CB41 4
Bermondsey Wall. W. SE16 CB41 67
Mill St.
Bermuda Rd. Til. DG44 71
Bernard Av. W13 BJ41 64
Bernard Cassidy St. E16 CG39 58
Morgan St.
Bernard Gdns. SW19 BR49 75
Bernard Rd. N15 CA32 48
Bernard Rd. Rom. CS33 50
Bernard Rd. Wall. BV56 95
Bernard St. WC1 BX38 2
Bernard St. WC1 BX38 56
Bernard St. St. Alb. BG13 9
Bernays Clo. Stan. BK29 36
Bernays Gro. SW9 BX45 66
Bernell Dr. Croy. CD55 87
Berner Est. E1 CB39 57
Berne Rd. Th. Hth. BZ52 87
Berners Dr. St. Alb. BH16 9
Berners Ms. W1 BW39 1
Berners Ms. W1 BW39 56
Berners Pl. W1 BW39 1
Berners Pl. W1 BW39 56
Berners Rd. N1 BY37 2
Berners Rd. N1 BY37 56
Berners Rd. N22 BY30 38
Berners St. W1 BW39 1
Berners St. W1 BW39 56
Berners Way, Brox. CD15 12
Berney Rd. Croy. BZ54 87
Cromwell Rd.
Bernville Way, Harrow BL32 46
Kenton Rd.
Bernwell Rd. E4 CG27 40
Berota Rd. SE9 CM48 78
Berridge Est. Edg. BL29 37
Berridge Grn. Edg. BM29 37
Berridge Rd. SE19 BZ49 77
Berriman Rd. N7 BX34 47
Berriton Rd. Har. BE33 45
Berrwood Clo. Wey. AW57 92
Berry Av. Wat. BC21 26
Berry Clo. N21 BY26 38
Berry Clo. NW10 BO36 55
Berry Clo. Rick. AW26 35
Berryfield Rd. SE17 BY42 4
Berryfield, Slou. AR39 52
Berry Grn. La. Wat. BE23 27
Berry Gro. La. Wat. BE22 27
Berry Gro. La. Wat. BF23 27
Berryhill SE9 CL45 68
Berry Hill, Stan. BK28 36
Berryhill Gdns. SE9 CL45 68
Berry Ho. Rd. SW11 BU44 66
Dagnall St.
Berrylands SW20 BQ52 85
Berrylands, Orp. CP55 89
Berrylands, Surb. BL53 85
Berrylands Rd. Surb. BL53 85
Berry Ln. Guil. & Wok. AO65 100
Berry La. Rick. AU25 25
Berry La. Rick. AW25 26
Berry La. Rick. AW26 35
Berry La. Walt. BD56 93
Berryman Clo. Dag. CP34 50
Bennetts Castle La.
Berrymans La. SE26 CC49 77
Berrymead, Hem. H. AY12 8
Berry Meade, Ash. BL62 103
Berrymead Gdns. W3 BN41 65
Berrymede Rd. W4 BN41 65
Berry Pl. EC1 BY38 2
Berry Rd. SE17 BY42 66
Berry's Croft Rd. Stai. AX50 73
Berry's Grn. Rd. West. CL61 10
Berry's Hill, West. CL61 10
Berrys La. Wey. AX59 9
Berrystede Clo. Kings. on T. BM50 7
Berry St. EC1 BY38
Berry St. EC1 BY38 5
Dallington St.
Berry Wk. Ash. BL63 10
Berry Way W5 BL41 6
Berry Way, Rick. AW26 3
Bertal Rd. SW17 BT49 7
Berther Rd. Horn. CV33 5
Berthon St. SE8 CE43 6
Bertie Rd. NW10 BP36 5
Bertie Rd. SE26 CC50 7
Bertram Cott. SW19 BS50 7
Bertram Rd. NW4 BP32 4
Bertram Rd. Enf. CA24 3
Bertram Rd. Kings. on T. BM50 7
Bertram St. N19 BV34 4
Bertram Way, Enf. CA24 3
Bertrand St. SE13 CE45 6
Bert Rd. Th. Hth. BZ53 8
Berwick Av. Hayes BD39 5
Berwick Clo. Wal. Cr. CE20 2
Queens Dr.
Berwick Cres. Sid. CN47 7
Berwick La. Ong. CT20 2
Berwick Pond Clo. Rain. CV37 6
Berwick Pond Rd. Rain. CW37 6
Berwick Rd. E16 CJ39 5
Berwick Rd. E17 CD31 4
Berwick Rd. N22 BY30 3
Berwick Rd. Borwd. BL22 2
Berwick Rd. Rain. CV37 6
Berwick Rd. Well. CO44 6
Berwick St. W1 BW39
Berwick St. W1 BW39
Berwyn Av. Houns. BF44 6
Berwyn Rd. SE24 BY47 7
Berwyn Rd. Rich. BM45 6
Beryl Rd. W6 BQ42 6
Besant Ct. N1 BZ35 4
Besant Wk. N7 BX34 4
Andover Est.
Besant Wk. N7 BX34 4
Newington Way
Besant Way NW10 BN35 4
Besley St. SW16 BW50 7
Bessborough Gdns. SW1 BW42
Bessborough Gdns. SW1 BW42 6
Vauxhall Bridge Rd.
Bessborough Pl. SW1 BW42
Bessborough Pl. SW1 BW42 6
Bessborough Rd. SW15 BP47 7
Bessborough Rd. Her. BG33 4
Bessborough St. SW1 BW42
Bessborough St. SW1 BW42 6
Bessborough Way SW1 BW42
Bessborough Way SW1 BW42 6
Besein Pk Rd. W12 BO41 6
Bessels Grn. Rd. Sev. CS65 10
Bessels Way, Sev. CS65 10
Bessemer Rd. SE5 BZ44 6
Bessemer Rd. Welw. G. C. BR7
Bessingby Rd. Ruis. BC34 4
Bessingham Wk. SE4 CC45 6
Bessingham Wk. SE4 CD45 6
Frendsbury Rd.
Besson St. SE14 CC44 6
Bess St. E2 CC38 5
Roman Rd.
Beswick Mews NW6 BS36 5
Lymington Rd.
Bestwood St. SE8 CC42 6
Beta Rd. Wok. AP58 9
Betchworth Rd. Ilf. CN34 4
Betchworth Way, Croy. CF58 9
Betenson Av. Sev. CT64 10
Betham Rd. Grnf. BG38 5
Bethany Waye, Felt. BB47 7
Bethecar Rd. Har. BH32 4
Bethell Av. E16 CG38 5
Bethell Av. Ilf. CL33 4
Bethel Rd. Sev. CV65 10
Bethel Rd. Well. CP45 6
Bethesden Clo. Beck. CD50 7
Bethlehem Ho. E14 CD40 5
Bethnal Grn. Est. E2 CC38 5
Bethnal Grn. Rd. E1 CA38
Bethnal Grn. Rd. E1 CA38 5
Bethnal Grn. Rd. E2 CA38
Bethnal Grn. Rd. E2 CA38 5
Beth Rd. Wok. AT61 10
Princess Rd.
Bethune Av. N11 BU28 3
Bethune Rd. N16 BZ33 4
Bethune Rd. NW10 BN38 5
Bethwin Rd. SE5 BY43 6
Betley Ct. Walt. BC55 8
Betony Rd. Rom. CV29 4
Betoyne Av. E4 CG28 4
Betsham Rd. Erith. CT43 6
Betsham Rd. Grav. DB49 8
Betsham Rd. Grav. DC49 8
Betsham Rd. Swans. DC47 8
Betstyle Rd. N11 BV28 3
Betterton Dr. Sid. CO48 7
Betterton Rd. Rain. CT38 5
Betterton St. WC2 BX39
Betterton St. WC2 BX39 5
Bette St. E1 CB40 5
Bettles Clo. Uxb. AX37 5
Betton Pl. E2 CA37 5
Bettons Pk. E15 CG37 5
Bettons Pk. E15 CG37 5
New Plaistow Rd.
Bettridge Rd. SW6 BR44 6
Betts La. Wal. Abb. CJ14 1
Betts Rd. E16 CH40 5
Victoria Docks Rd.
Betts St. E1 CB40 5
Betts St. E1 CB40 5
Highway, The
Betts Way, Surb. BJ54 8
Betula Clo. Ken. BZ61 10
Betula Wk. Rain. CV38 6

11

12

Borough Rd. West. CJ64 106
Borough Sq. SE1 BZ41 67
Borough, The Bet. BM71 120
Borough Way, Pot. B. BR19 19
Borrodaile Rd. SW18 BS46 76
Borrowdale, Hem. H. AY12 8
Lonsdale
Borrowdale Av. Har. BJ30 36
Borrowdale Clo. Ilf. CK31 49
Borrowdale Clo. Sth. Croy. CA60 96
Borrowdale Dri. Sth. Croy. CA59 96
Borthwick Rd. E15 CG35 49
Borthwick Rd. NW9 BO32 46
Broadway, The
Borthwick St. SE8 CE42 67
Borwick Av. E17 CD31 48
Bosanquet Clo. Uxb. AX38 53
Bosbury Rd. SE6 CF48 77
Boscastle Rd. NW5 BV34 47
Boscobel Pl. SW1 BV42 3
Boscobel Pl. SW1 BV42 66
Boscobel St. NW8 BT38 1
Boscobel St. NW8 BT38 56
Boscombe Av. Grays. DE42 71
Boscombe Av. E10 CF33 48
Boscombe Av. Horn. CV33 51
Boscombe Clo. Egh. AU51 82
Lea Rd.
Boscombe Clo. E5 CD35 48
Durrington Rd.
Boscombe Rd. SW17 BV50 76
Boscombe Rd. SW19 BS51 86
Boscombe Rd. W12 BP40 55
Boscombe Rd. Wor. Pk. BQ54 85
Bosenquet Rd. Hodd. CF11 12
Bosgrove E4 CF26 39
Boss Rd. E3 CE36 57
Rothbury Rd.
Boss St. SE1 CA41 4
Boss St. SE1 CA41 67
Bostal Hill SE2 CO42 69
Bostall Hill Rd. SE2 CP42 69
Bostall La. SE2 CO42 69
Bostall Manor Way SE2 CO42 69
Bostall Pk. Av. Bexh. CO43 69
Bostal Rd. Orp. CO50 79
Bostal Row, Bexh. CO45 69
Boston Gdns. Brent. BJ42 64
Boston Gro. Ruis. BA32 44
Boston Manor Rd. Brent. BJ42 64
Boston Pk. Rd. Brent. BK43 64
Boston Pl. NW1 BU38 1
Boston Pl. NW1 BU38 56
Boston Rd. E6 CK38 58
Boston Rd. E17 CE32 48
Boston Rd. W7 BH40 54
Boston Rd. Croy. BX53 86
Boston Rd. Edg. BN29 37
Boston St. E2 CB37 2
Boston St. E2 CB37 57
Bostonthorpe Rd. W7 BH41 64
Boston Vale W7 BJ42 64
Bosville Dr. Sev. CU65 107
Bosville Rd. Sev. CU65 107
Boswell Clo. Orp. CP54 89
Killewarren Way
Boswell Clo. Wal. Cr. CD18 21
Boswell Ct. WC1 BX39 2
Boswell Ct. WC1 BX39 56
Boswell Pth. Hayes BB42 63
Boswell Rd. Th. Hth. BZ52 87
Boswell St. WC1 BX39 2
Boswell St. WC1 BX39 56
Boswick La. Berk. AO11 7
Bosworth Clo. E17 CD30 39
Bosworth Rd. N11 BW29 38
Bosworth Rd. W10 BR38 55
Bosworth Rd. Barn. BS24 29
Bosworth Rd. Dag. CR34 50
Botany Bay La. Chis. CM51 88
Boteley Clo. E4 CF27 39
Boterys Cross, Red. BY70 121
Botha Rd. E13 CH39 58
Bothwell Clo. E16 CH39 58
Bothwell Rd. Croy. CF58 96
Bothwell St. W6 BQ43 65
Delorme St.
Botley Rd. Chesh. AQ18 16
Botley Rd. Hem. H. AZ11 8
Botolph La. EC3 CA40 4
Botolph La. EC3 BZ40 57
Botolph Pass E3 CE38 57
Botolph Rd.
Botolph Rd. E3 CE38 57
Botsford Rd. SW20 BR51 85
Botsom La. Sev. CY57 99
Bottom House Farm La.
Ch. St. G. AO27 34
Bottom House Farm. La.
Ch. St. G. AQ25 25
Bottom La. Chesh. AP19 16
Bottom La. Rick. AW21 26
Bottrells La. Ch. St. G. AO27 34
Bott Rd. Dart. CW49 80
Botts End, Hem. H. AW12 8
Botts Ms. W2 BS39 56
Chepstow Rd.
Botwell Comm. Rd. Hayes BA40 53
Botwell Cres. Hayes BB39 53
Botwell La. Hayes BB40 53
Boucher Clo. Tedd. BH49 74
Boucher Dr. Grav. DF48 81
Bouchier Wk. Rain. CU36 59
Boughton Av. Brom. CG54 88
Boughton Rd. SE18 CN41 68
Boughton Rd. SE28 CN41 68
Boulcott St. E1 CC39 57
Boulevard, The Pnr. BE31 45
Boulmer Rd. Uxb. AX38 53
Boulogne Rd. Croy. BZ53 87
Boulter Gdns. Horn. CU36 59
Boulthurst Way, Oxt. CH69 115
Boulton Rd. Dag. CQ34 50
Bounce Hill, Rom. CU23 32
Bounces La. N9 CB27 39
Bounces Rd. N9 CB26 39
Boundaries Rd. SW12 BU48 76
Boundaries Rd. Felt. BD47 74
Boundary Clo. CM35 49
Loxford La.
Boundary Clo. Ilf. CN35 49
Loxford La.
Boundary Clo. Kings. on T. BM52 85
Boundary Clo. Sthl. BF42 64
Boundary Ct. Welw. G. C. BR10 5
Hollybush La.
Boundary La. E13 CJ38 58
Boundary La. SE17 BZ43 67
Boundary La. SE17 BZ43 67
Camberwell Rd.
Boundary La. Welw. G. C. BR9 5
Boundary Rd. E13 CJ37 58
Boundary Rd. E17 CD33 48
Boundary Rd. N9 CC25 30
Boundary Rd. N22 BY31 47
Boundary Rd. NW8 BS37 1
Boundary Rd. NW8 BS37 56
Boundary Rd. SW19 BT50 76
Boundary Rd. Ashf. AX49 73
Boundary Rd. Bark. CM37 58
Boundary Rd. Ger. Cr. AR29 34
Boundary Rd. Pnr. BD33 45
Boundary Rd. Rom. CU32 50
Boundary Rd. St. Alb. BH12 9
Boundary Rd. Sid. CN46 78
Boundary Rd. Upmin. CX34 51
Boundary Rd. Wall. BV57 95
Boundary Rd. Wok. AT61 100
Boundary Rd. S. Wall. BV58 95
Boundary Row SE1 BY41 4
Boundary Row SE1 BY41 66
Boundary St. E2 CA38 2
Boundary St. E2 CA38 57
Boundary St. Erith. CT43 69
Boundary Way, Croy. CE56 96
Boundary Way, Wat. BD19 18
Boundary Yd. Wok. AT61 100
Boundary Rd.
Boundfield Rd. SE6 CG48 78
Boundry Dr. Brwd. DF26 122
Bounds Grn. Ind. Est. N11 BW29 38
Bounds Grn. Rd. N11 BW29 38
Bounds Grn. Rd. N22 BW29 38
Bourchier Clo. Sev. CU66 116
Bourchier St. W1 BW40 3
Bourchier St. W1 BW40 56
Wardour St.
Bourdon Pl. W1 BV40 3
Bourdon Pl. W1 BV40 56
Bourdon St.
Bourdon Rd. SE20 CC51 87
Bourdon St. W1 BV40 3
Bourdon St. W1 BV40 56
Bourke Clo. NW10 BO36 55
Bourke Clo. SW2 BX47 76
Bourke Hill, Couls. BU62 104
Bourlet Clo. W1 BW39 1
Bourlet Clo. W1 BW39 56
Riding House St.
Bourlet Clo. W1 BW39 56
Wells St.
Bourn Av. N15 BZ31 48
Bourn Av. Barn. BT25 29
Bournbrook Rd. SE3 CJ45 68
Bourne Av. Hayes BA41 63
Bourne Av. Wind. AO45 61
Bourne Av. N14 BX27 38
Bourne Av. Ruis. BD35 45
Bourne Av. Uxb. AZ38 53
Bournebridge Gdns. Ilf. CO29 41
Bournebridge La. Rom. CQ26 41
Bourne Clo. SW2 BX46 76
Bourne Clo. Brox. CD13 12
Bourne CLo. Brwd. DF26 122
Bourne Ct. Ruis. BC35 44
Bourne Cres. Wey. AW60 92
Bourne End, Horn. CX33 51
Bourne End La. Berk. AT15 7
Bourne End Rd. Nthwd. BB28 35
Bourne Est. EC1 BY39 2
Bourne Est. EC1 BY39 56
Bournefield Rd. Whyt. CA62 105
Bourne Gdns. E4 CE28 39
Bournehall Av. Bush. BF25 27
Bournehall La. Bush. BF25 27
Bournehall Rd. Bush. BF25 27
Bourne Hill N13 BX27 38
Bourne La. Cat. BZ64 105
Bourne La. Sev. DC66 117
Bourne Mead, Bex. CS46 79
Bournemead Av. Nthlt. BC37 53
Bourne Meadow, Cher. AV53 82
Bournemead Way, Nthlt. BC37 53
Bournemouth Rd. SE15 CB44 67
Bournemouth Rd. SW19 BS51 86
Bourne Pk. Gdns. Ken. CA57 96
Bourne Pk. Gdns. Ken. CA61 105
Bourne Pl. W4 BN42 65
Dukes Av.
Bourne Rd. E7 CG34 49
Bourne Rd. N8 BX32 47
Bourne Rd. Berk. AP12 7
Bourne Rd. Bex. CR47 79
Bourne Rd. Brom. CJ52 88
Bourne Rd. Bush. BF25 27
Bourne Rd. Grav. DJ48 81
Bourne Rd. Red. BW68 113
Bourne Rd. Slou. AO41 61
Bourne Rd. Vir. W. AR53 82
Bourneside, Vir. W. AQ54 82
Bourne St. SW1 BV42 3
Bourne St. SW1 BV42 66
Bourne St. Croy. BY55 86
Bourne Ter. W2 BS39 1
Bourne Ter. W2 BS39 56
Bourne, The N14 BW26 38
Bourne, The Hem. H. AT17 16
Bourne Vale, Brom. CG54 88
Bournevale Rd. SW16 BX49 76
Bourne Vw. Grnf. BH36 54
Bourne Vw. Ken. BZ61 105
Bourne Way, Brom. CG55 88
Bourne Way, Epsom BN56 94
Bourne Way, Sutt. BR56 94
Bourne Way, Swan. CS52 89
Bourne Way, Wey. AX56 92
Bourne Way, Wok. AR64 100
Bournewood Rd. SE18 CO43 69
Bournewood Rd. Orp. CO54 89
Bournside Rd. Wey. AX56 92
Bournville Rd. SE6 CE47 77
Bournwell Clo. Barn. BU23 29
Bousfield Rd. SE14 CC44 67
Bousley Rise, Cher. AU57 91
Boutflower Rd. SW11 BU45 66
Bouverie Gdns. Har. BK33 45
Bouverie Pl. W2 BT39 1
Bouverie Pl. W2 BT39 56
Bouverie Rd. N16 CA33 48
Bouverie Rd. Couls. BV62 104
Bouverie Rd. Har. BG32 45
Bouverie St. EC4 BY39 2
Bouverie St. EC4 BY39 56
Bouverie Way, Slou. AS42 62
Bouvier Rd. Enf. CC22 30
Bovay Pl. N7 BX35 47
Holloway Rd.
Bovay St. N7 BX35 47
Boveney New Rd. Wind. AM42 61
Boveney Rd. SE23 CC47 77
Boveney Rd. Wind. AL42 61
Bovey Way, S. Ock. DA39 60
Bovill Rd. SE23 CC47 77
Bovingdon Av. Wem. BM36 55
Bovingdon Cres. Wat. BD20 18
Bovingdon La. NW9 BO29 37
Bovingdon Rd. SW6 BS44 66
Bovingdon Sq. Mitch. BX52 86
Bovington Grn. Hem. H. AS17 16
Bow Arrow La. Dart. CX46 80
Bowater Clo. NW9 BN32 46
Bowater Clo. NW9 BO32 46
Buck La.
Bowater Pl. SE3 CH43 68
Bowater Rd. SE18 CJ41 68
Bow Bridge Est. E3 CE38 57
Bow Common La. E3 CD38 57
Bowden Dr. Horn. CW33 51
Bowden Rd. E17 CE33 48
Bowden St. SE11 BY42 4
Bowden St. SE11 BY42 66
Bowditch SE8 CD42 67
Bowdon Rd. E17 CE33 48
Bowen Dr. SE21 CA48 77
Bowen Rd. Har. BG33 45
Bowen St. E14 CE39 57
Bower Av. SE10 CG44 68
Bower Clo. Nthlt. BD37 54
Bower Clo. Rom. CS29 41
Bowerdeans St. SW6 BS44 66
Bowerdean St. SW8 BS44 66
Bower Fm. Rd. Hav. CS27 41
Bower Hill, Epp. CO19 23
Bower Hill Clo. Red. BX72 121
Bowerhill La. Red. BW71 121
Bower La. Eyns. CX57 99
Bowerman Av. SE14 CD43 67
Bowerman Rd. Grays. DG42 71
Bower Rd. Swan. CU50 79
Bowers Av. Grav. DF49 81
Mulberry Rd.
Bowers La. Guil. AS68 109
Bowers Rd. Sev. CR59 98
Bower St. E1 CC39 57
Bower Ter. Epp. CO19 23
Bower Vale, Epp. CO19 23
Bowes Dr. Ong. CW17 24
Bowes-lyon Clo. Wind. AO44 61
Ward Royal
Bowes Rd. N11 BV28 38
Bowes Rd. N13 BV28 38
Bowes Rd. W3 BO40 55
Bowes Rd. Dag. CP35 50
Bowes Rd. Stai. AV50 72
Bowes Rd. Walt. BC55 83
Bowfell Rd. W6 BQ43 65
Bowford Av. Bexh. CQ44 69
Bowie Clo. SW4 BW47 76
Plummer Rd.
Bow La. EC4 BZ39 2
Bow La. EC4 BZ39 57
Bow La. Mord. BR53 85
Lower Morden La.
Bow La. N12 BT29 38
Bowlers Orchard,
Ch. St. G. AQ27 34
Bowles Gro. Ent. CB21 30
Bowles Rd. SE1 CB43 4
Bowles Rd. SE1 CB43 67
Bowley Clo. SE19 CA49 77
Bowley St. E14 CD40 57
Bowling Grn. Clo. SW15 BP47 75
Bowling Grn. La. EC1 BY38 2
Bowling Grn. La. EC1 BY38 56
Bowling Grn. Pl. SE1 BZ41 4
Bowling Grn. Rd. Wok. AP58 91
Bowling Grn. St. SE11 BY43 66
Bowling Grn. Wk. N1 CA38 2
Bowling Grn. Wk. N1 CA38 57
Bowl La. St. Alb. BD11 9
Bowls Clo. Stan. BJ28 36
Bowls, The Chig. CN27 40
Bowman Av. E16 CG40 58
Bowmans Clo. W13 BJ40 54
Bowmans Clo. Pot. B. BT19 20
Bowmans Grn. Wat. BE21 27
Bowmans Lea SE23 CC47 77
Dunoon Rd.
Bowmans Meadow, Wall. BV55 86
Bowmans Mews N7 BX34 47
Seven Sisters Rd.
Bowman's Pl. N7 BX34 47
Bowmans Pl. N7 BX34 47
Hercules Pl.
Bowman's Rd. Dart. CT47 79
Bowmead SE9 CK48 78
Bowness Clo. E8 CA36 57
Rhodes Dev.
Bowness Cres. SW15 BO49 75
Bowness Dr. Houns. BE45 64
Bowness Rd. SE6 CE47 77
Bowness Rd. Bexh. CR44 69
Bowness Way, Horn. CU35 50
Bowood Rd. SW11 BV45 66
Bowood Rd. Enf. CC23 30
Bowring Grn. Wat. BD28 36
Bow Rd. E3 CD38 57
Bowrons Av. Wem. BK36 54
Bowry Dri. Stai. AS46 72
Bow St. E15 CG35 49
Bow St. WC2 BX39 2
Bow St. WC2 BX39 56
Bowstridge La. Ch. St. G. AR27 34
Bowyer Cres. Uxb. AV32 43
Bowyers, Hem. H. AX12 8
Bowzell Rd. Sev. CT70 116
Boxall Rd. SE21 CA46 77
Boxall Rd. Dag. CQ35 50
Boxfield, Welw. G. C. BS9 5
Boxgrove Av. Guil. AT69 118
Boxgrove La. Guil. AT70 118
Boxgrove Rd. SE2 CO41 69
Boxgrove Rd. Guil. AT70 118
Boxhill Rd. Dor. BL70 120
Boxhill Rd. Tad. BL69 120
Boxhill Rd. Tad. BN68 112
Boxhill Way, Bet. BM72 120
Box La. Bark. CO37 59
Box La. Hem. H. AU16 16
Box La. Hodd. CD12 12
Boxley Rd. Mord. BT52 86
Boxley St. E16 CH40 58
Boxmoor Rd. Har. BJ31 45
Boxmoor Rd. Rom. CS28 41
Box Ridge Av. Pur. BX59 95
Box Rd. Guil. AQ67 109
Boxted Clo. Buck. H. CK26 40
Boxted Rd. Hem. H. AV12 7
Boxtree La. Har. BG30 36
Boxtree Rd. Har. BG29 36
Box Tree Wk. Orp. CP54 89
Boxwell Rd. Berk. AQ13 7
Boxwood Way, Warl. CC62 105
Boxworth Gro. N1 BX37 2
Boyard Rd. SE18 CL42 68
Boyce Clo. Borwd. BL23 28
Boyce Way E13 CH38 58
Boycroft Av. NW9 BN32 46
Boyd Av. Sthl. BE40 54
Boyd Clo. Kings. on T. BM50 75
Crescent Rd.
Boydell Ct. NW8 BT36 56
Boyd Rd. SW19 BT50 76
Boyd St. E1 CB39 2
Boyd St. E1 CB39 57
Boyfield St. SE1 BY41 4
Boyfield St. SE1 BY41 66
Boyland Rd. Brom. CG49 78
Boyle Av. NW4 BQ31 46
Boyle Av. Stan. BJ29 36
Boyle Fm. Rd. Surb. BJ53 84
Boyle St. W1 BW40 56
Savile Row
Boyne Rd. SE13 CF45 67
Boyne Rd. Dag. CR34 50
Boyne Ter. Ms. W11 BR40 55
Boyseland Ct. Edg. BN27 37
Boyson Rd. SE17 BZ43 67
Boyston Rd. SE17 BZ43 67
Camberwell Rd.
Boythorn Way SE16 CB42 67
Bonamy Estate East, The
Boyton Clo. N8 BX31 47
Boyton Rd. N8 BX31 47
Brabant Ct. EC3 BZ40 57
Philpot La.
Brabant Rd. N22 BX30 38
Brabazon Av. Wall. BX57 95
Brabazon Rd. Houns. BD43 64
Brabazon Rd. Nthlt. BF37 54
Brabazon St. E14 CE39 57
Brabourne Cres. Bexh. CQ43 69
Brabourne Rise, Beck. CF53 87
Brabourn Rd. SE15 CC44 67
Bracewell Av. Grnf. BH35 45
Bracewell Rd. W10 BQ39 55
Bracewood Gdns. Croy. CA55 87
Bracey St. N4 BX33 47
Bracken Av. SW12 BV46 76
Bracken Av. Croy. CE55 87
Bracken Bri. Dr. Ruis. BD34 45
Brackenbury Gdns. W6 BP41 65
Brackenbury Rd. N3 BT31 47
Brackenbury Rd. W6 BP41 65
Bracken Clo. Slou. AO35 43
Bracken Clo. Wok. AS62 100
Brackendale N21 BX26 38
Brackendale, Pot. B. BR20 19
Brackendale, Pot. B. BS20 20
Brackendale Ct. Beck. CE50 77
Brackendale Gdns. Upmin. CY35 51
Bracken Dene, Dart. CT49 79
Brackendene, St. Alb. BE18 18
Brackendene Clo. Wok. AT61 100
Bracken Dr. Chig. CL29 40
Brackenford, Slou. AR41 62
Bracken Gdns. SW13 BP44 65
Bracken Hill, Cob. BF59 93
Bracken Hill, Ruis. BE35 45
Bracken Hill Clo. Brom. CG51 88
Bracken Hill La. Brom. CG51 88
Bracken Path, Epsom BM60 94
Brackens, The Enf. CA26 39
Brackens, The Orp. CO56 98
Bracken, The E4 CF26 39
Hortus Rd.
Bracken Way, Guil. AP69 118
Bracken Way, Wok. AP58 91
Brackenwood, Sun. BC51 83
Brackenwood Rd. Wok. AO63 100
Brackley, Wey. BA56 92
Brackley Clo. Wall. BX57 95
Mollison Dr.
Brackley Rd. W4 BO42 65
Brackley Rd. Beck. CD50 77
Brackley Sq. Wdf. Grn. CJ29 40
Brackley St. EC1 BZ39 2
Brackley St. EC1 BZ38 57
Viscount St.
Brackley Ter. W4 BO42 65
Bracklyn Ct. N1 BX37 2
Bracklyn Ct. N1 BZ37 57
Bracklyn St. N1 BZ37 2
Bracknell Gdns. NW3 BS35 47
Bracknell Gate NW6 BS35 47
Bracknell Pl. Hem. H. AY11 8
Brackwell Clo. N22 BY30 38
Bracondale Av. Grav. DF51 81
Bracondale, Esher BG57 93
Bracondale Rd. SE2 CO42 69
Bradbery, Rick. AU28 34
Bradbourne Pk. Rd. Sev. CU65 107
Bradbourne Rd. Bex. CR47 79
Bradbourne St. SW6 BS44 66
Bradbourne Vale Rd. Sev. CT64 107
Bradbourn Rd. Sev. CU64 107
Bradbury Clo. Sthl. BE42 64
Blandford Rd.
Bradbury Gdns. Slou. AR35 43
Bradbury St. N16 CA35 48
Braddon Rd. Rich. BL45 65
Braddon St. SE16 CB41 67
Braddyll St. SE10 CG42 68
Bradenham Av. Well. CO45 69
Bradenham Rd. Har. BJ31 45
Bradenham Rd. Hayes BB38 53
Bradenhurst Clo. Cat. CA66 114
Braden St. W9 BS38 56
Bradfield Clo. Wok. AS62 100
Bradfield Dr. Bark. CO35 50
Bradfield Rd. E16 CH41 68
Bradfield Rd. Ruis. BE35 45
Bradfields Av. Edg. BM28 37
Bradford Cl. SE26 CB49 77
Coombe Rd.
Bradford Clo. Brom. CK54 88
Bradford Dr. Epsom BO57 94
Bradford Rd. SE26 CB49 77
Bradford Rd. W3 BO41 65
Warple Way
Bradford Rd. Ilf. CM33 49
Bradgate, Pot. B. BW17 20
Bradgate Clo. Pot. B. BW17 20
Bradgate Rd. SE6 CE46 77
Brading Cres. E11 CH34 49
Brading Rd. SW2 BX47 76
Brading Rd. Croy. BX53 86
Bradiston Rd. W9 BR38 55
Bradlaugh St. N1 CA37 2
Bradlaugh St. N1 CA37 57
Bradleigh Av. Grays. DD42 71
Bradleigh Rd. Grays. DD42 71
Bradley Clo. N7 BX36 56
Blundell St.
Bradley Clo. N7 BX36 56
Sutterton St.
Bradley Gdns. W13 BJ39 54
Bradley La. Dor. BJ69 119
Bradley Rd. N22 BX30 38
Station Rd.
Bradley Rd. SE19 BZ50 77
Bradley Rd. Enf. CD22 30
Bradley Rd. Slou. AO40 52
Bradleys Clo. N1 BY37 2
Bradleys Clo. N1 BY37 56
White Lion St.
Bradmead SW8 BY43 66
Bradmore La. W6 BQ42 65
Beadon Rd.
Bradmore La. Hat. BQ16 19
Bradmore Pk. Rd. W6 BP41 65
Bradmore Way, Couls. BX62 104
Bradmore Way, Hat. BR16 19
Bradshaw Clo. Wind. AM44 61
Bradshaw Waye, Uxb. AY39 53
Bradshaw Rd. Wat. BD23 27
Bradshaws, Hat. BO14 10
Bradshaw St. SE15 CB43 67
Bradstock Rd. E9 CC36 57
Bradstock Rd. Epsom BP57 94
Bradstock Rd. Est. E9 CC36 57
Brad St. SE1 BY40 4
Brad St. SE1 BY40 56
Bradwell Av. Dag. CR34 50
Bradwell Clo. E18 CG31 49
Bradwell Rd. Buck. H. CK26 40
Brady Av. Loug. CM23 31
Brady St. Dws. E1 CB39 57
Brady St. E1 CB38 57
Brae Clo. Belv. CQ42 69
Brae Ct. Kings. On T. BM51 85
Wolverton Av.
Braefoot Ct. SW15 BQ46 75
Putney Hill
Braemar Av. N22 BX30 38
Braemar Av. NW10 BN34 46
Braemar Av. SW19 BS48 76
Braemar Av. Bexh. CS45 69
Braemar Av. Sth. Croy. BZ58 96
Braemar Av. Th. Hth. BY52 86
Braemar Av. Wem. BK36 54
Braemar Gdns. NW9 BN30 37
Braemar Gdns. Horn. CW32 51
Braemar Gdns. Horn. CX32 51
Braemar Gdns. Sid. CM48 78
Braemar Gdns. W. Wick. CF54 87
Braemar Rd. E13 CG38 58
Braemar Rd. N15 CA32 48
Braemar Rd. Brent. BK43 64
Braemar Rd. Wor. Pk. BP55 85
Braemore Clo. SW15 BP47 75
Alton Rd.
Braeside, Beck. CE49 77
Braeside, Wey. AW59 92
Braeside Av. Sev. CT65 107
Braeside Av. SW19 BR51 85
Braeside Clo. Pnr. BF29 36
Braeside Clo. Sev. CT65 107
Braeside Cres. Bexh. CS45 69
Braeside Rd. SW16 BW50 76
Braemead, Red. BX71 121
Braes St. N1 BY36 56
Brafton Rd. Croy. BZ56 96
Braganza St. SE17 BY42 4
Braganza St. SE17 BY42 66
Bragmans La. Rick. AU20 16
Braham St. E1 CA39 2
Braham St. E1 CA39 57
Braid Av. W3 BN39 55
Braid Clo. Felt. BE48 74

14

Bridge Row, Croy. BZ54 87
Cross Rd.
Bridges Dr. Dart. CX46 80
Bridges La. Croy. BX56 95
Bridges Pl. SW6 BR44 65
Bridges Rd. SW19 BS50 76
Bridges Rd. Stan. BH28 36
Bridge St. SW1 BX41 4
Bridge St. SW1 BX41 66
Bridge St. Berk. AR13 7
Bridge St. Guil. AR71 118
Bridge St. Hem. H. AX14 8
Bridge St. Lthd. BJ64 102
Bridge St. Pnr. BE31 45
Bridge St. Rich. BK46 74
Bridge St. Stai. AV49 72
Bridge St. Walt. BB54 83
Bridge Ter. E15 CF36 57
Bridge, The, Har. BH31 45
Bridge Vw. W6 BQ42 65
Bridgewater Clo. Chis. CN52 88
Bridgewater Gdns. Edg. BL30 37
Bridgewater Rd. Berk. AW12 7
Bridgewater Rd. Wem. BK36 54
Bridgewater Rd. Wey. BA57 92
Bridgewater Sq. EC2 BZ39 2
Bridgewater St. EC2 BZ39 2
Bridgewater St. EC1 BZ39 57
Viscount St.
Bridge Way N11 BW27 38
Bridge Way NW11 BR32 46
Bridge Way Bark. CN36 58
Bridge Way, Couls. BU63 104
Bridge Way, Twick. BG47 74
Bridge Way, Uxb. AZ35 44
Bridgeway, Wem. BL36 55
Bridgeway St. NW1 BW37 1
Bridgeway St. NW1 BW37 56
Bridge Wharf Cher. AX54 83
Bridge Rd.
Bridgewood Clo. SE20 CB50 77
Castledine Rd.
Bridgewood Rd. SW16 BW50 76
Bridgewood Rd. Wor. Pk. BP55 85
Bridgford St. SW18 BT48 76
Bridgman Rd. N1 BX36 56
Bridgman Rd. Tedd. BJ50 74
Bridgwater Clo. Rom. CV28 42
Bridgwater Rd. E15 CF37 57
Bridgwater Rd. Rom. CV28 42
Bridgwater Rd. Ruis. BC35 44
Bridgwater Wk. Rom. CV28 42
Bridle Clo. Enf. CD22 30
Bridle Clo. Epsom BN56 94
Bridle Clo. St. Alb. BH12 9
Bridle End Epsom BO60 94
Bridle La. W1 BW40 3
Bridle La. W1 BW40 56
Bridle La. Rick. AX24 26
Bridle Path, Croy. BX55 86
Bridle Path Rd. Barn. BT23 29
Bridle Path, The Wdf. Grn. CG29 40
Bridlepath Way, Felt. BB47 73
Bridle Rd. Croy. CE55 87
Bridle Rd. Epsom. BO60 94
Bridle Rd. Esher. BJ57 93
Bridle Rd. Pnr. BC32 44
Bridle, The Rd. Pur. BX58 95
Bridle, The Way Croy. CD58 96
Bridle, The Way Wall. BW56 95
Bridle Way, Berk. AQ12 7
Bridle Way Croy. CE56 96
Bridle Way, Hodd. CE10 12
Bridle Way, S. Hodd. CE10 12
Bridlington Clo. West. CH63 106
Bridport Av. Rom. CR32 50
Bridport Pl. N1 BZ37 2
Bridport Pl. N1 BZ37 57
Bridport Rd. N18 CA28 39
Bridport Rd. Grnf. BF37 54
Bridport Rd. Th. Hth. BY52 86
Bridstow Pl. W2 BS39 56
Bridwell Pl. EC4 BY39 56
Tudor St.
Brief St. SE5 BY44 66
Brier Lea. Tad. BR66 112
Brierley Croy. CE57 96
Brierley Av. N9 CC26 39
Brierley Clo. SE25 CB52 87
Brierley Clo. Horn. CU32 50
Brierly Gdns. E2 CC37 57
Cyprus St.
Brierley Rd. E11 CF35 48
Brierley Rd. SW12 BW48 76
Brierly St. E2 CC38 57
Royston St.
Briery Ct. Hem. H. AZ13 8
Briery Rd. Hem. H. AZ12 8
Briery Way, Amer. AP22 25
Brigadier Av. Enf. BZ22 30
Brigadier Av. Enf. BZ23 30
Brigadier Hill, Enf. BZ22 30
Brigadier Hill Enf. BZ23 30
Brightfield Rd. SE12 CG46 78
Bright Hill, Guil. AS71 118
Brightlands Rd. Reig. BT69 121
Brightling Rd. SE4 CD46 77
Brightlingsea Pl. E14 CD40 57
Brightman Rd. SW18 BT47 76
Brighton Av. E17 CD32 48
Brighton Clo. Uxb. AZ36 53
Brighton Clo. Wey. AW56 92
Burleigh Rd.
Brighton Dr. Nthlt. BF36 54
Brighton Gro. SE14 CD44 67
Brighton Rd. E6 CL38 58
Brighton Rd. N2 BT30 38
Brighton Rd. N16 CA35 48
Brighton Rd. Ban. BR60 94
Brighton Rd. Couls. BW62 104
Brighton Rd. Pur. BX60 95
Brighton Rd. Red. BU71 121
Brighton Rd. Red. BV65 104
Brighton Rd. Surb. BK53 84
Brighton Rd. Sutt. BT57 95
Brighton Rd. Tad. BR62 103
Brighton Rd. Tad. BR64 103
Brighton Rd. Wat. BC22 26
Brighton Rd. Wey. AX56 92
Brighton Ter. SW9 BX45 66
Bright Av. Rain. CU38 59
Brightside Av. Stai. AX50 73
Brightside Rd. SE13 CF46 77
Brightside, The Enf. CC23 30
Bright St. E14 CE39 57
Brightwell Cres. SW17 BU49 76
Brightwell Rd. Wat. BC25 26
Brigstock Rd. Belv. CR42 69
Brigstock Rd. Couls. BV61 104
Brigstock Rd. Th. Hth. BY53 86
Brig St. E14 CF42 67
Brim Hill N2 BT31 47
Brimpsfield Clo. SE2 CO41 69
Brimsdown Av. Enf. CD23 30
Brimshot La. Wok. AP58 91
Brimstone Clo. Orp. CP57 98
Brindles, The Bans. BR62 103
Brindles Clo. Brwd. DE27 122
Brindley St. SE14 CD44 67
Brindley Way Sthl. BF40 54
Brindwood Rd. E4 CD27 39
Brinkburn Clo. SE2 CO42 69
Brinkburn Clo. Edg. BM30 37
Brinkburn Gdns. Edg. BM31 46
Brinkley Rd. Wor. Pk. BP55 85
Brinklow Cres. SE18 CL43 68
Brinkworth Rd. Ilf. CK31 49
Brinkworth Way E9 CD36 57
Brinley Clo. Wal. Cr. CC19 21
Brinsdale Rd. NW4 BQ31 46
Brinsley Rd. Har. BG30 36
Brinsme Rd. St. Alb. BG17 18
Brinsmead Rd. Rom. CX30 42
Brinsworth Clo. Twick. BG47 74
Brion Pl. E14 CF39 57
Brisbane Av. SW19 BS50 76
Brisbane Ho. Til. DG44 71
Leicester Rd.
Brisbane Rd. E10 CE34 48
Brisbane Rd. W13 BJ40 54
Brisbane Rd. Ilf. CL33 49
Brisbane St. SE5 BZ43 67
Briscoe Clo. Hodd. CD11 12
Briscoe Rd. SW19 BT50 76
Briscoe Rd. Hodd. CD11 12
Briscoe Rd. Rain. CV37 60
Briset Rd. SE9 CJ45 68
Briset St. EC1 BY39 2
Briset St. EC1 BY38 56
Briset Way N7 BX34 47
Andover Est.
Bristol Clo. Stai. AY46 73
Whitley Clo.
Bristol Gdns. SW15 BP47 75
Bristol Gdns. W9 BS38 1
Bristol Ms. W9 BS38 1
Bristol Gdns. W9 BS38 56
Bristol Park Rd. E17 CD31 48
Hervey Park Rd.
Bristol Rd. E7 CJ36 58
Bristol Rd. E15 CG36 58
Bristol Rd. Grav. DH48 81
Bristol Rd. Grnf. BF37 54
Bristol Rd. Mord. BS53 86
Bristow Rd. SE19 CA49 77
Bristow Rd. Bexh. CQ44 69
Bristow Rd. Croy. BX56 95
Bristow Rd. Houns. BF45 64
Britania Dr. Grav. DJ49 81
Britania W. Y. Stai. AX47 73
Britannia Rd. N12 BT27 38
Britannia Rd. SW6 BS43 66
Britannia Rd. Brwd. DB28 42
Britannia Rd. Ilf. CL34 49
Britannia Rd. Surb. BL54 85
Britannia Rd. Wal. Cr. CD20 21
Britannia Row N1 BY37 2
Britannia Row N1 BY37 56
Britannia St. WC1 BX38 2
Britannia St. WC1 BX38 56
Britannia Wk. N1 BZ38 2
Britannia Wk. N1 BZ38 57
Britannia Way NW10 BM38 55
Britannia Way SW6 BS43 66
Britannia Rd.
British Gro. W4 BO42 65
British Gro. Pass. W6 BO42 65
British Legion Rd. E4 CG27 40
British St. E3 CD38 57
Briton Clo. Sth. Croy. CA59 96
Briton Cres. Sth. Croy. CA59 96
Briton Hill Rd. Sth. Croy. CA58 96
Brittain Rd. Dag. CQ34 50
Brittain Rd. Walt. BD56 93
Brittany St. SE11 BX42 66
Britten Cl. NW11 BS33 47
Chandos Way
Brittenden Clo. Orp. CN57 97
Brittens Clo. Guil. AQ68 109
Britten St. SW3 BU42 3
Britten St. SW3 BU42 66
Britton Av. St. Alb. BG13 9
Britton St. EC1 BY38 56
Britton St. EC1 BY39 2
Brixham Cres. Ruis. BC33 44
Brixham Gdns. Ilf. CN35 49
Brixham Rd. E16 CH39 58
Brixham Rd. Well. CP44 69
Brixham St. E16 CK40 58
Brixton Est. Edg. BM30 37
Brixton Hill SW2 BX47 76
Brixton Hill Ct. SW2 BX46 76
Brixton Hill Pl. SW2 BX47 76
Brixton Oval SW2 BY45 66
Rushcroft Rd.
Brixton Rd. SW9 BY45 66
Brixton Rd. Wat. BC23 26
Brixton Sta. Rd. SW9 BY45 66
Brixton Water La. SW2 BX46 76
Brandon St. Grav. DG47 81
Broad Acre, St. Alb. BE18 18
Broad Acre, Stai. AW49 73
Cherry Orch.
Broadacre Clo. Uxb. AZ34 44
Broadacres, Guil. AP69 118
Broad Acres, Hat. BO11 10
Broadbent St. W1 BV40 3
Broadbent St. W1 BV40 56
Bourdon St.
Broadbridge Clo. SE3 CH43 68
Broad Clo. Walt. BE55 84
Broadcoombe Sth. Croy. CC57 96
Broad Ct. WC2 BX39 2
Broad Ct. WC2 BX39 56
Broadcroft Av. Stan. BK30 36
Broadcroft Rd. Orp. CM54 88
Broad Ditch Rd. Grav. DE50 81
Broadfield, Harl. CN10 6
Broadfield Clo. NW2 BQ34 46
Broadfield Clo. Tad. BQ63 103
Broadfield Ct. Bush. BH27 36
Broadfield La. Wat. BC26 35
Broadfield Rd. SE6 CG47 78
Broadfield Rd. Hem. H. AY13 8
Broadfield Sq. Enf. CB24 30
Broadfields E. Mol. BG53 84
Broadfields Har. BF30 36
Broadfields, Saw. CO6 6
Broadfields, Wal. Cr. BY18 20
Broadfields Av. N21 BY26 38
Broadfields Av. Edg. BM28 37
Broadfield Way Buck. H. CJ28 40
Broadfield Pl. Welw. G. C. BP8 5
Broadford La. Wok. AP59 91
Broadford Rd. Guil. AR74 118
Broadgate, Wal. Abb. CG20 22
Broadgates Av. Barn. BS23 29
Broadgates Rd. SW18 BT47 76
Ellerton Rd.
Broad Grn. Croy. BY54 86
Broad Grn. Hert. BX12 11
Broad Grn. Av. Croy. BY54 86
Broadham Green Rd. Oxt. CF69 114
Broadhead Strand NW9 BO30 37
Broadheath, Sev. CZ66 117
Broadheath Dr. Brom. CK49 78
Broad High Way, Cob. BD61 102
Broadhinton Rd. SW4 BV45 66
Broadhurst, Ash. BL61 103
Broadhurst Av. Edg. BM28 37
Broadhurst Av. Ilf. CN35 49
Broadhurst Gdns. NW6 BS36 56
Broadhurst Gdns. Chig. CM28 40
Broadhurst Gdns. Reig. BS72 121
Broadhurst Gdns. Ruis. BD34 45
Broadhurst Wk. Rain. CU36 59
Broadlands Av. Chesh. AO18 16
Broadlands Av. SW16 BX48 76
Broadlands Av. Enf. CB24 30
Broadlands Av. Shep. BA53 83
Broadlands Clo. N6 BV33 47
Broadlands Clo. Enf. CB24 30
Broadlands Dr. Warl. CC63 105
Broadlands Rd. N6 BU33 47
Broadlands Rd. Brom. CH49 78
Broadlands, The Felt. BE48 74
Broadlands Way N. Nal. BO53 85
Broad La. N15 CA31 48
Broad La. Dart. CU49 79
Broad La. Hamptn. BE50 74
Broad Lawn SE9 CL48 78
Broadlawns Clo. Har. BH30 36
Broadley Rd. Harl. CK13 13
Broadley St. NW8 BT39 1
Broadley St. NW8 BT39 56
Broadley Ter. NW1 BU38 1
Broadley Ter. NW1 BU38 56
Broadmark Rd. Slou. AQ40 52
Broadmead SE6 CE48 77
Broadmead Av. Wor. Pk. BP54 85
Broadmead Clo. Pnr. BE29 36
Broad Meadow, Brwd. CZ22 33
Broadmead Rd. Nthlt. BE38 54
Broadmead Rd. Wdf. Grn. CH29 40
Broad Oak, Wdf. Grn. CH28 40
Broad Oak Av. Enf. CC21 30
Broadoak Rd. Erith CS43 69
Broadoaks, Epp. CN19 22
Broad Oaks, Surb. BM54 85
Broad Oaks, Surb. BM55 85
Kingston by Pass
Broadoaks Cres. Wey. AW60 92
Broad Oaks Way Brom. CG53 88
Broad Platts. Slou. AR41 62
Broad Rd. Swans. DC46 81
Broad St. Av. EC2 CA39 57
Old Broad St.
Broad Sanctuary SW1 BX41 4
Broad Sanctuary SW1 BX41 66
Broadstone Pl. W1 BV39 1
Broadstone Pl. W1 BV39 56
Broadstone Rd. Horn. CU34 50
Broad St. E15 CF36 57
Broad Street Av. EC2 CA39 2
Broad St. Dag. CR36 59
Broad St. Guil. AO69 118
Broad St. Hem. H. AX13 8
Broad St. Tedd. BH49 74
Broad Strood, Loug. CL22 31
Broad Strood, Loug. CL23 31
Broad Walk, The W8 BS40 56
Broad Vw. NW9 BM32 46
Broadview Ave. Grays. DE41 71
Broadview Rd. SW16 BW50 76
Broad Wk. E18 CG31 49
Broad Wk. N21 BX27 38
Broad Wk. NW1 BV37 1
Broad Wk. SE3 CJ44 68
Broad Wk. W1 BU40 3
Broad Walk, The W8 BS40 3
Broad Wk. Cat. CA64 105
Broad Wk. Couls. BV65 104
Broad Wk. Epsom BO62 103
Broad Wk. Epsom BQ63 103
Broad Wk. Har. BF31 45
Broad Walk, Harl. CM10 6
Broad Walk, Harl. CM11 13
Broad Wk. Houns. BD44 64
Broad Wk. Orp. CP55 89
Broad Wk. Sev. CW67 117
Broad Wk. La. NW11 BR33 46
Broad Walk N. Brwd. DD27 122
Broad Walk S. The Brwd. DD28 122
Broad Walk, The. Nthwd. BA30 35
Broadwall, SE1 BY40 4
Broadwall, SE1 BY40 56
Broadwater, Pot. B. BS18 20
Broadwater Clo. Stai. AS47 72
Broadwater Clo. Walt. BC56 92
Broadwater Clo. Walt. BB56 92
Broadwater Clo. Wok. AU59 91
Woodham La.
Broadwater Gdns. Uxb. AW31 44
Broadwater Gdns. Orp. CL56 97
Broadwater La. Uxb. AW31 44
Broadwater Rise, Guil. AT71 118
Broadwater Rd. N17 CA30 39
Broadwater Rd. SW17 BU49 76
Broadwater Rd. Walt. BB56 92
Broadwater Rd. Welw. G. C. BR8 5
Broadwater E13 CH37 58
Broadway E15 CF36 57
Broadway N16 CA33 48
Broad Way N20 BT27 38
Broadway SW1 BW41 3
Broadway SW1 BW41 66
Broadway SW16 BW49 76
Broadway W6 BQ42 65
Hammersmith Rd.
Broadway W7 BH40 54
Broadway W13 BJ40 54
Broadway, Bark. CM37 58
Broadway, Bexh. CQ45 69
Broadway, Edg. BM30 37
Broadway, Epsom BP56 94
Broadway, Grnf. BG38 54
Broadway, Rain. CU38 59
Broadway, Rom. CU30 41
Broad Way, St. Alb. BG13 9
Broadway, Surb. BM54 85
Broadway, Swan. CS53 89
Broadway Anchor Hill, Work. AO62 100
Broadway Av. Croy. BZ53 87
Broadway Av. Harl. CP9 6
Broadway Av. Twick. BJ46 74
Broadway Church La. Berk. AT14 7
Broadway Clo. Sth. Croy. CB60 96
Broadway Clo. Wdf. Grn. CH29 40
Broadway Ct. SW19 BS50 76
Broadway Gdns. Mitch. BU52 86
Broadway, Grays. DE43 71
Broadway, Hat. BO12 10
Broadway Ho. Brom. CF49 77
Broadway Mkt. E8 CB37 57
Broadway Mkt. Est. E8 CA37 57
Broadway Mews N13 BX28 38
Elmdale Rd.
Broadway Mews N21 BY26 38
Compton Rd.
Broadway, Stai. AW49 73
Broadway, Til. DF44 71
Dock Rd.
Broadway, The E4 CF29 39
Broadway, The N3 BS30 38
Broadway, The N8 BX32 47
Broadway, The N9 CB27 39
Fore St.
Broadway, The NW7 BO28 37
Broadway, The NW9 BP33 46
Broadway, The SW14 BO44 65
Terrace, The
Broadway, The SW19 BR50 75
Broadway, The W3 BM41 65
Gunnersbury La.
Broadway, The W5 BK40 54
Broadway, The Croy. BX56 95
Broadway, The Dag. CQ34 50
Broadway, The Har. BH30 36
Broadway, The Horn. CU35 50
Broadway, The Loug. CM24 31
Broadway, The N9 CB27 39
Broadway, The Pnr. BE29 36
Broadway, The Stai. AX52 83
Broadway, The Stan. BK28 36
Broadway, The Sthl. BE40 54
Broadway, The Surb. BH54 84
Broadway, The Sutt. BR57 94
Broadway, The Wat. BD24 27
Broadway, The Wdf. Grn. CH29 40
Snakes La.
Broadway, The Wey. AW58 92
Broadwick St. W1 BW39 1
Broadwick St. W1 BW39 56
Broadwood Av. Ruis. BB32 44
Broad Yd. EC1 BY38 56
Broad Yd. EC1 BY39 2
Brocas Clo. NW3 BT36 56
Chalcotts Est.
Brocas St. Wind. AO43 61
Brockdene Dr. Nthwd. BB29 35
Brockdene Dr. Nthwd. BC29 35
Brockdish Av. Bark. CN35 49
Brockell Hurst E. Mol. BE53 84
Brockenhurst Av. Wor. Pk. BO54 85
Brockenhurst Clo. Wok. AS60 91
Brockenhurst Gdns. NW7 BO28 37
Brockenhurst Gdns. Ilf. CM35 49
Brockenhurst Rd. Croy. CB54 87
Brockenhurst Way SW16 BW51 86
Brocket Clo. Chig. CN28 40
Brocket Rd. Grays. DG41 71
Cherry Wk.
Brocket Rd. Hodd. CE12 12
Brocket Rd. St. Alb. BN7 5
Brockett Clo. Welw. G. C. BP8 5
Brocket Way, Chig. CN28 40
Brock Grn. S. Ock. DA39 60
Brockham Clo. SW19 BR49 75
Brockham Cres. Croy. CF57 96
Brockham Dr. Ilf. CM32 49
Brockhamhurst Rd. Bet. BM74 120
Brockham La. Bet. BM70 120
Brockham St. SE1 BZ41 4
Brockham St. SE1 BZ41 67
Brockhill Cres. SE4 CD45 67
Brockhurst Clo. Stan. BH29 36
Brockhurst Rd. Chesh. AO18 16
Brocklebank Rd. SW18 BT47 76
Brocklehurst St. SE14 CC43 67
Brocklesby Rd. SE25 CB52 87
Brockles Mead, Harl. CM13 13
Brockley Av. Stan. BL27 37
Brockley Av. N. Stan. BL27 37
Brockley Clo. Stan. BL28 37
Brockley Combe, Wey. BA56 92
Brockley Cres. Rom. CS29 41
Brockley Cross SE4 CD45 67
Brockley Footpath SE14 CC45 67
Brockley Gdns. SE4 CD44 67
Brockley Gro. SE4 CD46 77
Brockley Gro. Brwd. DD26 122
Brockley Hall Rd. SE4 CD46 77
Brockley Hill Stan. BK26 36
Brockley Pk. SE23 CD47 77
Brockley Ri. SE23 CD47 77
Brockley Rd. SE4 CD45 67
Brockley Side Stan. BL28 37
Brockley Ter. SE17 CA42 4
Brockley Ter. SE17 CA42 67
Alvey St.
Brockley Vw. SE23 CD47 77
Brockley Way SE4 CC46 77
Brockman Ri. Brom. CF49 77
Brockparkwood, Brwd. DD27 122
Brock Pl. E3 CE38 57
Brock Rd. E13 CH39 58
Brock St. SE15 CC45 67
Evelina Rd.
Brocks Dr. Sutt. BR55 85
Brockside, Pot. B. BP19 19
Brockswood La. Welw. G. C. BP7 5
Brockway, Vir. W. AR53 82
Brockway Clo. Guil. AT70 118
Brockwell Clo. Orp. CN53 88
Brockwell Ct. SW2 BY46 76
Brockwell Pk. Gdns. SE24 BY47 76
Broderick Gro. Lthd. BF66 111
Broderick Rd. SE2 CO42 69
Brodewater Rd. Borwd. BM23 28
Brodia Rd. N16 CA34 48
Brodie Rd. E4 CF26 39
Brodie Rd. Enf. BZ22 30
Brodie Rd. Guil. AS71 118
Brodie St. SE1 CA42 4
Brodie St. SE1 CA42 67
Brodlove La. E1 CC40 57
Brodrick Rd. SW17 BU48 76
Brograve Gdns. Beck. CE51 87
Brograve Rd. N17 CB31 48
Broke Fm. Dr. Orp. CP58 98
Broken Furlong. Wind. AN42 61
Broken Gate La. Uxb. AU33 43
Broken Wf. EC4 BZ40 4
Broken Wharf EC4 BZ40 57
Broken Wharf EC4 BZ40 4
High Timber St.
Broke Rd. E8 CA37 2
Broke Rd. E8 CA37 57
Brokes Cres. Reig. BS69 121
Brokesley St. E3 CD38 57
Brokes Rd. Reig. BS69 121
Broke Walk E8 CA37 57
Broadway Mkt. Est.
Bromar Rd. SE5 CA45 67
Bromboro' Grn. Wat. BD28 36
Bromefield, Stan. BK30 36
Bromehead Rd. E1 CC39 57
Bromehead St. E1 CC39 57
Bromell's Rd. SW4 BW45 66
Brome Rd. SE9 CK45 68
Bromet Clo. Wat. BB22 26
Bromfelde Rd. SW4 BW45 66
Bromfield St. N1 BY37 2
Bromfelde Wk. SW9 BX44 66
Gaskell St.
Bromefield Ct. Wal. Abb. CH20 22
Winters Wy.
Bromfield St. N1 BY37 56
Bromford Clo. Oxt. CH70 115
Bromhall Rd. Dag. CO36 59
Bromhedge SE9 CK48 78
Bromholm Rd. SE2 CO41 69
Bromleigh Clo. Wal. Cr. CD17 21
Ashdown Cres.
Bromley Av. Brom. CG50 78
Bromley Common Brom. CJ52 88
Bromley Cres. Brom. CG51 88
Bromley Cres. Ruis. BB35 44
Bromley Gdns. Brom. CG51 88
Bromley Gro. Brom. CF51 87
Bromley Hall Rd. E14 CF39 57
Lochnager St.
Bromley Hall Rd. E14 CF39 57
Bromley High St. E3 CE38 57
Bromley Hill, Brom. CG49 78
Bromley La. Chis. CM50 78
Bromley Rd. E10 CE32 48
Bromley Rd. E17 CE31 48
Bromley Rd. N17 CA30 39
Bromley Rd. N18 BZ28 39
Bromley Rd. SE6 CE47 77
Bromley Rd. Beck. CE51 87
Bromley Rd. Brom. CE47 77
Bromley Rd. Chis. CL51 88
Bromley St. E1 CC39 57
Brompton Clo. Houns. BE46 74
Brompton Dr. Erith CU43 69
Brompton Gro. N2 BU31 47
Brompton Pk. Rd. N8 BY31 47
High Rd.
Brompton Pl. SW3 BU41 3
Brompton Pl. SW3 BU41 66
Brompton Rd. SW1 BU42 66
Brompton Rd. SW3 BU42 3
Brompton Rd. SW3 BU42 66
Brompton Rd. SW7 BU42 66
Brompton Sq. SW3 BU41 3
Brompton Sq. SW3 BU41 66
Bromwich Av. N6 BV34 47
Bromyard Av. W3 BO40 55
Brondesbury Ct. NW2 BQ36 55
Brondesbury Pk. NW2 BP36 55
Brondesbury Pk. NW6 BP36 55
Brondesbury Rd. NW6 BR37 55
Brondesbury Vill. NW6 BR37 55
Bronhill Ter. N17 CB30 39
Landsdowne Rd.
Bronsart Rd. SW6 BR43 65
Bronson Rd. SW20 BQ51 85

Name	Ref	Pg
Bronsoon Way Uxb.	AV34	43
Bronte Clo. Til.	DH44	71
Bronte Cres. Hem. H.	AZ10	8
Bronte Gro. Dart.	CWS45	70
Bronti Clo. SE17	**BZ42**	**4**
Bronze St. SE8	CE43	67
Brook Av. Dag.	CR36	59
Brook Av. Edg.	BM29	37
Brook Av. Wem.	BL34	46
Brookbank Av. W7	BG39	54
Brookbank Rd. SE13	CE45	67
Brook Clo. SW20	BP52	85
Brook Clo. Rom.	CT30	41
Brook Clo. Ruis.	BB33	44
Brook Clo. Stai.	AY47	73
Brook Ct. Edg.	BM28	37
Brook Ct. Rad.	BJ20	18
Watling Rd.		
Brook Cres. E4	CE28	39
Brook Cres. N9	CB28	39
Brookdale N12	BW28	38
Brookdale Av. Upmin.	CX34	51
Brookdale Clo. Upmin.	CX34	51
Brookdale Rd. E17	CD31	48
Brookdale Rd. SE6	CE46	77
Brookdale Rd. Bex.	CO47	79
Brookdene Av. Wat.	BC26	35
Brookdene Rd. SE18	CN42	68
Brook Dr. SE11	**BY41**	**4**
Brook Dr. SE11	BY41	66
Brook Dr. Har.	BG31	45
Brook Dr. Rad.	BH20	18
Brook Dr. Ruis.	BB33	44
Brook Dr. Sun.	BB50	73
Brooke Av. Har.	BG34	45
Brooke Clo. Bush.	BG26	36
Brookehowse Rd. SE6	CE48	77
Brook End. Saw.	CP6	6
Brookend Rd. Sid.	CN47	78
Brooke Rd. E5	CA34	48
Brooke Rd. E17	CF31	48
Brooke Rd. N16	CA34	48
Brooke Rd. Grays	DD42	71
Brooker Rd. Wal. Abb.	CF20	21
Brooker Rd. Wal. Abb.	CF21	30
Brookers Clo. Ash.	BK62	102
Brooke's Ct. EC1	**BY39**	**2**
Brooke's Ct. EC1	BY39	56
Brookes Ct. EC1	BY39	56
Baldwin's Gdns.		
Brooke St. EC1	**BY39**	**2**
Brooke St. EC1	BY39	56
Brook Farm Rd. Cob.	BD61	102
Brookfield N6	BV34	47
Brookfield Sev.	CW62	108
Brookfield, Wok.	AQ61	100
Brookfield Av. E17	CF31	48
Brookfield Av. NW7	BP29	37
Brookfield Av. W5	BK38	54
Brookfield Av. Sutt.	BT56	95
Brookfield Clo. NW7	BP29	37
Brookfield Clo. Brwd.	DE25	122
Brookfield Ct. Grnf.	BG38	54
Brookfield Ct. Har.	BK32	45
Brookfield Cres. NW7	BP29	37
Brookfield Cres. Har.	BK32	45
Brookfield Gdns. Esher	BH57	93
Brookfield Gdns. Wal. Cr.	CC17	21
Brookfield La. Wal. Cr.	CB17	21
Brookfield Pk. NW5	BV34	47
Brookfield Path Wdf. Grn.	CG29	40
Oak Hill		
Brookfield Rd. E9	CD36	57
Brookfield Rd. N9	CB27	39
Brookfield Rd. W4	BN41	65
Brookfields Enf.	CC24	30
Brookfields, Saw.	CP6	6
Brookfields Av. Mitch.	BU53	86
Brook Flds. Ong.	CW16	24
Brook Gdns. E4	CE28	39
Brook Gdns. SW13	BO45	65
Beverley Rd.		
Brook Gdns. Kings. on T.	BN51	85
Brook Grn. W6	BQ41	65
Brook Hill, Oxt.	CF68	114
Brookhill Close SE18	CL42	68
Brookhill Clo. Barn.	BU25	29
Brookhill Rd. SE18	CL43	68
Brookhill Rd. Barn.	BT25	29
Brook Ho. Gdns. E4	CG28	40
Brookhowse Rd. SE6	CE48	77
Brookhurst Rd. Wey.	AW57	92
Brookland Clo. NW11	BS31	47
Brookland Rise		
Brookland Garth NW11	BS31	47
Brookland Hl. NW11	BS31	47
Brookland Ri. NW11	BS31	47
Brooklands App. Rom.	CS31	50
Brooklands Av. SW19	BS48	76
Brookelands Av. Sid.	CM48	78
Brooklands Clo. Rom.	CS31	50
Brooklands Clo. Sun.	BB51	83
Brooklands Dr. Wem.	BK37	54
Brooklands Gdns. Horn.	CV34	51
Brooklands Gdns. Pot. B.	BR19	19
Brooklands La. Rom.	CS31	50
Brooklands La. Wey.	AZ56	92
Brooklands Pk. SE3	CH45	68
Brooklands Rd. Rom.	CS31	50
Brooklands Rd. Surb.	BH54	84
Brooklands Rd. Wey.	AZ59	92
Brooklands St. SW8	BW44	66
Brooklands Way, Red.	BU69	121
Brook La. SE3	CH44	68
Brook La. Bex.	CP46	79
Brook La. Brom.	CH50	78
Brook La. Brwd.	DB22	33
Brook La. Saw.	CP6	6
Brook La. Wok.	AO59	91
Brooklane Field, Harl.	CO12	14
Brook La. N. Brent.	BK42	64
Brooklea Clo. NW9	BO30	37
Brookleys Wok.	AP58	91
Brooklyn Av. SE25	CB52	87
Brooklyn Av. Loug.	CK24	31
Brooklyn Clo. Wok.	AS63	100
Brooklyn Ct. Loug.	CK24	31
Brooklyn Gro. SE25	CB52	87
Brooklyn Rd. SE25	CB52	87
Brooklyn Rd. Brom.	CJ53	88
Brooklyn Rd. Wok.	AS62	100
Brooklyn Way, West Dr.	AXZ41	63
Brookmans Ave. Grays.	DE40	71
Brookman's Av. Hat.	BR16	19
Brookmans Clo. Upmin.	CZ33	51
Brookmead Epsom	BO57	94
Brookmead Av. Brom.	CK53	88
Brookmead Clo. Orp.	CO54	89
Brook Meadow N12	BS27	38
Brookmead Rd. Croy.	BW53	86
Brookmeads Est. Mitch.	BU53	86
Brookmead Way, Orp.	CO53	89
Brook Ms. NW2	BT40	56
Brook Ms. N. W2	BT40	56
Brookmill Rd. SE8	CE44	67
Brook Parade Chig.	CL27	40
Brook Path Loug.	CK24	31
Brook Pl. Barn.	BS25	29
Brook Rise Chig.	CL27	40
Brook Rd. E7	CH35	49
Brook Rd. N8	BX31	47
Brook Rd. N22	BX31	47
Brook Rd. NW2	BO34	46
Brook Rd. W4	BM43	65
Brook Rd. Borwd.	BM23	28
Brook Rd. Brwd.	CZ27	42
Brook Rd. Buck. H.	CH27	40
Brook Rd. Epp.	CO20	23
Brook Rd. Grav.	DF47	81
Brook Rd. Guil.	AU73	118
Brook Rd. Ilf.	CN32	49
Brook Rd. Loug.	CK24	31
Brook Rd. Red.	BU71	121
Brook Rd. Red.	BW68	113
Brook Rd. Rom.	CT30	41
Brook Rd. Saw.	CQ6	6
Brook Rd. Surb.	BL54	85
Brook Rd. Swan.	CS52	89
Brook Rd. Th. Hth.	BZ52	87
Brook Rd. Twick.	BJ46	74
Brook Rd. Wal. Cr.	CD20	21
Brook Rd. S. Brent.	BK43	64
Brooks Av. E6	CK38	58
Brooksbank St. E9	CC36	57
Brooksby's Ms. N1	CB36	57
Brooksby's St.		
Brooksby St. N1	BY36	56
Brooksby's Wk. E9	CC35	48
Brooks Clo. SE9	CL48	78
Brookscroft Rd. E17	CE30	39
Brooksfield, Welw. G.C.	BS7	5
Brookshill Har.	BG28	36
Brookshill Av. Stan.	BG28	36
Brookshill Dr. Har.	BG28	36
Brookside N21	BX25	29
Brookside Barn.	BU25	29
Brookside Cars.	BV56	95
Brookside, Cher.	AV54	82
Brookside, Guil.	AR68	109
Brookside, Harl.	CK13	13
Brookside, Hodd.	CE12	12
Brookside, Horn.	CW32	51
Brookside, Ilf.	CM29	40
Brookside, Orp.	CN54	88
Brookside, Pot. B.	BP19	19
Brookside, Slou.	AU43	62
Brookside, Uxb.	AY36	53
Brook Side Wal. Abb.	CG19	22
Paternoster Hill		
Brookside, Wat.	BC26	35
Brookside Ave. Stai.	AS45	62
Brookside Av. Ashf.	AX49	73
Brookside Clo. Barn.	BQ25	28
Brookside Clo. Har.	BE35	45
Brookside Clo. Har.	BK32	45
Brookside Cres. Hat.	BN12	10
Brookside Cres. Pot. B.	BX17	20
Brookside Cres. Wor. Pk.	BP54	85
Green La.		
Brookside Gdns. Enf.	CB22	30
Brookside Rd. N9	CB28	39
Brookside Rd. N19	BW34	47
Brookside Rd. NW11	BR32	46
Brookside Rd. Borwd.	BL22	28
Brookside Rd. Borwd.	BL23	28
Brookside Rd. Grav.	DF50	81
Brookside Rd. Hayes	BD40	54
Brookside S. Barn.	BY26	38
Brookside Wk. N3	BR29	37
Brookside Way Croy.	CC53	87
Brook Ms. N. W2	**BT40**	**3**
Brook's Ms. W1	**BV40**	**3**
Brook's Rd. E13	CH37	58
Brook St. N17	CA30	39
High Rd.		
Brook St. W1	**BV40**	**3**
Brook St. W1	BV40	56
Brook St. W2	**BT40**	**3**
Brook St. W2	BT40	56
Brook St. Belv.	CR42	69
Brook St. Brwd.	CY28	42
Brook St. Kings. On T.	BL51	85
Brook St. Wind.	AO44	61
Brooksville Av. NW6	BR37	56
Brooks Way Bush.	BG26	36
Richfield Rd.		
Brooks Way, Orp.	CP51	89
Brookvale, Erith	CR44	69
Brookvale Rd. SW6	BR43	65
Brookview Rd. SW16	BV49	76
Brook Wk. Edg.	BN29	37
Brook Wlk. Guil.	AR69	118
Brook Way SE3	CH45	68
Brook Way, Chig.	CL27	40
Brook Way, Rain.	CU39	59
Brookwood Av. SW13	BO44	65
Brookwood Lye Rd. Wok.	AO63	100
Brookwood Rd. SW18	BR47	75
Brookwood Rd. Houns.	BF44	64
Broom Av. Orp.	CO51	89
Broom Clo. Brom.	CK53	88
Broom Clo. Esher	BF56	93
Broom Clo. Hat.	BO14	10
Broom Clo. Tedd.	BK50	74
Broom Clo. Wal. Cr.	CB17	21
Spicersfield		
Broom Ct. Rich.	BM44	65
Lichfield Rd.		
Broomcroft Av. Nthlt.	BD38	54
Broomcroft Clo. Wok.	AU61	100
Broomcroft Pk. Dr. Wok.	AU61	100
Broome Clo. Epsom	BN66	112
Broome Pla. S. Ock.	CY40	60
Park La.		
Broome Rd. Hampton.	BE50	74
Broome Way SE5	BZ43	67
Broomfield E17	CS33	50
Alexandra Rd.		
Broomfield, Guil.	AP70	118
Broomfield, Harl.	CO9	6
Broomfield, St. Alb.	BG17	18
Broomfield Sun.	BC51	83
Broomfield Ave. Sev.	CT64	107
Broomfield Av. N13	BX28	38
Broomfield Av. Loug.	CK25	31
Broomfield Ct. Wey.	AZ57	92
Broomfield La. N13	BX28	38
Broomfield Pk. Dor.	BG72	119
Broomfield Pl. W13	BJ40	54
Mattock La.		
Broomfield Ride. Lthd.	BG80	93
Broomfield Rd. N13	BX28	38
Broomfield Rd. W13	BJ40	54
Broomfield Rd. Beck.	CD52	87
Broomfield Rd. Bexh.	CR46	79
Broomfield Rd. Guil.	AP69	118
Broomfield Rd. Rich.	BL44	65
Broomfield Rd. Rom.	CP33	50
Broomfield Rd. Surb.	BL54	85
Broomfield Rd. Swans.	DC46	81
Broomfield Rd. Tedd.	BK50	74
Melbourne Rd.		
Broomfield St. E14	CE39	57
Broom Gdns. Croy.	CE55	87
Broom Gro. Wat.	BC22	26
Broomgrove Gdns. Edg.	BM30	37
Broomgrove Rd. SW9	BX44	66
Stockwell Rd.		
Broom Hall, Lthd.	BG60	93
Broom Hall Dr. Lthd.	BG60	93
Broomhall End Wok.	AS61	100
Broomhall La.		
Broomhall La. Wok.	AS61	100
Broomhall Rd. Sth. Croy.	BZ58	96
Broomhall Rd. Wok.	AS61	100
Broom Hill, Hem. H.	AV14	7
Broom Hill, Slou.	AQ36	52
Broom Hill. Wdf. Grn.	CH29	40
Broomhill Rise, Bexh.	CR46	79
Broomhill Rd. SW18	BS46	76
Broomhill Rd. Dart.	CU46	79
Broomhill Rd. Ilf.	CO34	50
Broomhill Rd. Orp.	CO54	89
Broomhill Rd. Wdf. Grn.	CH29	40
Broomhills, Grav.	DC49	81
Broomhills. Welw. G. C.	BS7	5
Broomhouse Gdns. E4	CG28	40
Abbotts Cres.		
Broomhouse La. SW6	BS44	66
Broomhouse Rd. SW6	BS44	66
Broomhurst Ct. Dor.	BJ72	119
Ridgeway Rd.		
Broomlands La. Oxt.	CJ65	106
Broomlands La. Oxt.	CJ66	115
Broom La. Wok.	AP57	91
Broom Leys, St. Alb.	BK12	5
Broomloan La. Sutt.	BS55	86
Broom Lock, Tedd.	BK50	74
Broom Mead Bexh.	CR46	79
Broom Pk. Tedd.	BK50	74
Broom Rd. Croy.	CE55	87
Broom Rd. Tedd.	BJ49	74
Brooms Clo. Welw. G.C.	BQ6	5
Broomsleigh St. NW6	BR35	46
Broomstick Hall Rd. Wal. Abb.	CG20	22
Broomstick La. Chesh.	AQ18	16
Broom Water, Tedd.	BK50	74
Broom Water W. Tedd.	BK49	74
Broom Way, Wey.	BB56	92
Broomwood Gdns. Brwd.	DA25	33
Broomwood Rd. SW11	BU46	76
Broomwood Rd. Orp.	CO51	89
Broseley Gro. SE26	CD49	77
Broseley Rd. Rom.	CW28	42
Brott. St. E1	CC38	57
Mantus Rd.		
Brougham Rd. E8	**CB37**	**2**
Brougham Rd. E8	CB37	57
Brougham Rd. W3	BN39	55
Broughinge Rd. Borwd.	BM23	28
Brough St. SW8	BX43	66
Broughton Av. N3	BR31	46
Broughton Av. Rich.	BK48	74
Broughton Dri. W13	BJ40	54
Broughton Rd.		
Broughton Drive SW9	BY44	66
Loughborough Park Dev.		
Broughton Gdns. N6	BW32	47
Broughton Hall Av. Wok.	AV66	109
Broughton Rd. SW6	BS44	66
Broughton Rd. W13	BJ40	54
Broughton Rd. Orp.	CM55	88
Broughton Rd. Sev.	CU61	107
Broughton Rd. Th. Hth.	BY53	86
Broughton Rd. SW8	BV44	66
Broughton St. SW8	BV44	66
Brouncker Rd. W3	BN41	65
Brow Clo. Orp.	CP54	89
Brow Cres. Orp.	CP54	89
Browells La. Felt.	BC48	73
Brown Clo. Til.	DG45	71
Brown Clo. Wall.	BX57	95
Brown Fields. Welw. G. C.	BR7	5
Brownfield St. E14	CF39	57
Browngraves Rd. Hayes.	BA43	63
Brown Hart Gdns. W1	**BV40**	**3**
Brown Hart Gdns. W1	BV40	56
Brownhill Rd. SE6	CE47	77
Browning Av. W7	BH39	54
Browning Av. Sutt.	BU56	95
Browning Av. Wor. Pk.	BP54	85
Browning Clo. W9	BT38	56
Randolph Av.		
Browning Clo. Hamptn.	BE49	74
Browning Clo. Well.	CN44	68
Browning Est. SE17	**BZ42**	**4**
Browning Est. SE17	BZ42	67
Browning Ho. W12	BQ39	55
Alexandra Rd.		
Browning Ms. W1	**BV39**	**1**
Browning Ms. W1	BV39	56
New Cavendish St.		
Browning Rd. E11	CG33	49
Browning Rd. E12	CK36	58
Browning Rd. Dart.	CX45	70
Browning Rd. Enf.	BZ22	30
Browning Rd. Enf.	BZ23	30
Browning Rd. Lthd.	BG66	111
Browning St. SE17	**BZ42**	**4**
Browning St. SE17	BZ42	67
Browning Wk. Til.	DH44	71
Coleridge Rd.		
Browning Way Houns.	BD44	64
Brownlea Gdns. Ilf.	CO34	50
Brownlow Ms. WC1	**BX38**	**2**
Brownlow Ms. WC1	BX38	56
Brownlow Rd. E7	CH35	49
Brownlow Rd. E8	**CA37**	**2**
Brownlow Rd. E8	CA37	57
Brownlow Rd. N3	BS29	38
Brownlow Rd. N11	BW29	38
Brownlow Rd. NW10	BO36	55
Brownlow Rd. Berk.	AR12	7
Brownlow Rd. Borwd.	BM24	28
Brownlow Rd. Croy.	CA56	96
Brownlow Rd. Red.	BU70	121
Brownlow St. WC1	**BX39**	**2**
Brownlow St. WC1	BX39	56
Brownrigg Rd. Ashf.	AZ49	73
Brown Rd. Grav.	DJ47	81
Browns La. Lthd.	BD67	111
Brownspring Dr. SE9	CL49	78
Browns Rd. E17	CE31	48
Browns Rd. Surb.	BL54	85
Brown St. W1	**BU39**	**1**
Brown St. W1	BU39	56
Brownswell Rd. N2	BT30	38
Brownswood Rd. N2	BT30	38
Oak La.		
Brownswood Rd. N4	BY34	47
Brow, The. Red.	BV73	121
Spencer Way		
Brow, The. Wat.	BC19	17
Broxash Rd. SW11	BV46	76
Broxbourne Av. E18	CH31	49
Broxbourne Rd. E7	CH34	49
Broxbourn Rd. Orp.	CN54	88
Broxburn Dr. S. Ock.	DA39	60
Broxburn Rd. S. Ock.	DA40	60
Broxhill Rd. Hav.	CT27	41
Broxholm Rd. SE27	BY48	76
Brox La. Cher.	AU57	91
Brox Rd. Cher.	AU57	91
Broxted Rd. SE6	CD48	77
Broxwood Way, NW8	**BU37**	**1**
Bruce Av. Horn.	CV34	51
Bruce Av. Shep.	BA53	83
Bruce Castle Rd. N17	CA30	39
Bruce Clo. Well.	CO44	69
Bruce Clo. Wey.	AY60	92
Bruce Dr. Sth. Croy.	CC58	96
Bruce Gro. N17	CA30	39
Bruce Gro. Orp.	CO54	89
Bruce Gro. Wat.	BD22	27
Bruce Rd. E3	CE38	57
Bruce Rd. NW10	BN36	55
Bruce Rd. SE25	BZ52	87
Bruce Rd. Barn.	BR24	28
Bruce Rd. Har.	BH30	36
Bruce Rd. Mitch.	BV50	76
Bruce Wlk. Wind.	AL44	61
Tinkers Rd.		
Bruce Way, Wal. Cr.	CC20	21
Brucket Rd. Welw. G.C.	BN7	5
Brudenell Rd. SW17	BU48	76
Bruffs Meadow Nthlt.	BE36	54
Arnold Rd.		
Brumana Clo. Wey.	AZ57	92
Elgin Rd.		
Brumfield Rd. Epsom	BN56	94
Brummel Clo. Bexh.	CR45	69
Brumwill Rd. W5	BL37	55
Brundall Clo. Hem. H.	AX14	8
Brunel Clo. Nthlt.	BE38	54
Brunel Clo. Til.	DG45	71
Brunel Est. W2	BS39	56
Brunel Pl. Houns.	BF39	54
Brunel Rd. SE16	CC41	67
Brunel Rd. W3	BO39	55
Brunel Rd. Wdf. Grn.	CK28	40
Brunel St. E16	CG39	58
Brune St. E1	**CA39**	**2**
Brunel Wk. N15	CA31	48
Brunel Wy. Slou.	AP40	52
Brune Wy. E1	CA39	2
Brunner Clo. NW11	BS32	47
Brunner Rd. E17	CD32	48
Brunner Rd. W5	BK38	54
Brunswick Av. N11	BW27	38
Brunswick Av. Upmin.	CZ33	51
Brunswick Cent. WC1	BX38	56
Brunswick Clo. EC1	**BY38**	**2**
Brunswick Clo. Bexh.	CP45	69
Brunswick Rd.		
Brunswick Clo. Pnr.	BE32	45
Brunswick Clo. Surb.	BH54	84
Brunswick Ct. SE1	**CA41**	**4**
Brunswick Ct. SE1	CA41	67
Brunswick Ct. Walt.	BD55	84
Brunswick Cres. N11	BV27	38
Brunswick Gdns. W5	BL38	55
Brunswick Gdns. W8	BS40	56
Brunswick Gdns. Ilf.	CM29	40
Brunswick Gro. N11	BV27	38
Brunswick Gro. Cob.	BD60	93
Brunswick Ms. W1	BU39	56
Gt. Cumberland Pl.		
Brunswick Pk. SE5	BZ44	67
Brunswick Pk. Gdns. N11	BV27	38
Brunswick Pk. Rd. N11	BV27	38
Brunswick Pl. N1	**BZ38**	**2**
Brunswick Pl. N1	BZ38	57
Brunswick Pl. SE19	CB50	7
Brunswick Pl. Grav.	DH47	81
Brunswick Rd. E3	CF39	5
Brunswick Rd. E10	CF33	49
Brunswick Rd. E14	CF39	57
Brunswick Rd. N15	CA31	48
West Green Rd.		
Brunswick Rd. W5	BK38	54
Brunswick Rd. Bexh.	CP45	69
Brunswick Rd. Kings. on T.	BM51	85
Brunswick Rd. Sutt.	BS56	95
Brunswick Rd. N17	CA29	39
Brunswick Sq. WC1	**BX38**	**2**
Brunswick Sq. WC1	BX38	56
Brunswick Sq. E17	CF32	48
Brunswick Ter. Wind.	AO44	61
Brunswick Vil. SE5	CA44	67
Brunton Pl. E14	CD39	57
Brushfield St. E1	**CA39**	**2**
Brushfield St. E1	CA39	57
Brushwood Dri. Rick.	AU24	25
Brussels Rd. SW11	BT45	66
Bruton Clo. Brom.	CK50	78
Bullersdown Dr.		
Bruton Clo. Chis.	CK50	78
Bullersdown Dr.		
Bruton La. W1	**BV40**	**3**
Bruton La. W1	BV40	56
Bruton Pl. W1	**BV40**	**3**
Bruton Pl. W1	BV40	56
Bruton Rd. Mord.	BT52	86
Bruton St. W1	**BV40**	**3**
Bruton St. W1	BV40	56
Bruton Way W13	BJ39	54
Bryan Av. NW10	BP36	55
Bryan Clo. Sun.	BC50	73
Bryaneton Ms. E. W1	**BU39**	**1**
Bryan Rd. SE16	CD41	67
Bryanston Av. Twick.	BF47	74
Bryanston Clo. Sthl.	BE42	64
Blandford Rd.		
Bryanston Ms. W. W1	**BU39**	**1**
Bryanston Pl. W1	**BU39**	**1**
Bryanston Sq. W1	**BU39**	**1**
Bryanston St. W1	**BU39**	**1**
Bryanstone Av. Guil.	AQ69	118
Bryanstone Clo. Guil.	AP69	118
Bryanston Ms. W. W1	BU39	56
Bryanston Pl. W1	BU39	56
Bryanstone Rd. N8	BW32	47
Bryan Stone Rd. Guil.	AP68	109
Bryanston Sq. W1	BU39	56
Bryanston St. W1	BU39	56
Bryant Av. Rom.	CV30	42
Bryant Av. Slou.	AO39	52
Bryant Clo. Barn.	BR25	28
Bryant Ct. E2	CA37	57
Bryant Rd. Nthlt.	BD38	54
Bryant St. E15	CF36	57
Bryantwood Rd. N7	BY35	47
Brycedale Cres. N14	BW28	38
Bryce Rd. Dag.	CP35	50
Bryden Clo. SE26	CD49	77
Bryden Gro. SE26	CD49	77
Brydges Pla. WC2	**BX40**	**4**
St. Martin's La.		
Brydges Rd. E15	CF35	49
Bryer Pl. Wind.	AL45	61
Bryett Rd. N7	BX34	47
Tollington Way		
Brymer Rd. SE5	CA43	67
Brympton Clo. Dor.	BJ72	119
Brynford Clo. Wok.	AS61	100
Brynmaer Rd. SW11	BU44	66
Brynmawr Rd. Enf.	CA24	30
Brymer Rd. SE5	**CA45**	**4**
Bryony Rd. Uxb.	AY39	53
Bryony Rd. W12	BP40	55
Bryony Rd. Guil.	AT69	118
Bubblestone Rd. Sev.	CU61	107
Buccleston Cotts. E5	CB33	48
Buccleuch Rd. Slou.	AQ43	62
Buccleuch Ter. E5	CB33	48
Buchanan Clo. S. Ock.	CW40	60
Buchanan Gdns. NW10	BP37	55
Buchan Clo. Uxb.	AY39	53
Buchan Rd. SE15	CC45	67
Bucharest Rd. SW18	BT47	76
Buckbean Pth. Rom.	CV29	42
Buck Clo. Horn.	CV32	51
Buckden Clo. SE12	CG46	78
Upwood Rd.		
Buckenham St. SE1	BZ41	4
Buckenham St. SE1	BZ41	67
Old Kent Rd.		
Buckettsland Borwd.	BN22	19
Buckfast Rd. Mord.	BS52	86
Buckfast St. E2	**CB38**	**2**
Buckfast St. E2	CB38	57
Buck Gdns. Slou.	AP41	52
Buckham Thorns Rd. West.	CM66	115
Buckhold Rd. SW18	BS46	76
Buckhurst Av. Cars.	BU54	86
Buckhurst Av. Sev.	CV66	115
Buckhurst Clo. Red.	BU69	121
Buckhurst La. Sev.	CV66	115
Buckhurst Rd. West.	CL64	106
Buckhurst St. E1	CB38	57
Buckhurst Way Buck. H.	CJ28	40
Buckingham Av. N20	BT26	29
Buckingham Av. E. Mol.	BF52	84

Buckingham Av. Felt. BC46 73
Buckingham Av. Grnf. BJ37 54
Buckingham Av. Th. Hth. BY51 86
Buckingham Av. Well. CN45 68
Buckingham Clo. Enf. CA23 30
Buckingham Clo. Guil. AS70 118
Buckingham Clo. Hamptn. BE49 74
Buckingham Clo. Horn. CV32 51
Woodlands Av.
Buckingham Clo. Orp. CN54 88
Buckingham Ct. NW4 BP30 37
Buckingham Ct. Amer AP22 25
Buckingham Gdns. E. Mol. BF51 84
Buckingham Gdns. Edg. BL29 37
Buckingham Gdns. Th. Hth. BY51 86
Buckingham Gate, SW1 BV41 3
Buckingham Gate, SW1 BW41 66
Buckingham Gro. Uxb. AY37 53
Buckingham Hill Rd. S. Le H. DK41 71
Buckingham Ms. NW6 BS35 47
West End La.
Buckingham Ms. NW10 BO37 55
Buckingham Rd.
Buckingham Palace Rd. SW1 BV42 3
Buckingham Palace Rd. SW1 BV42 66
Buckingham Pl. SW1 BW41 3
Buckingham Pl. SW1 BW41 66
Palace St.
Buckingham Rd. E10 CE34 48
Buckingham Rd. E11 CJ32 49
Buckingham Rd. E15 CG35 49
Buckingham Rd. E18 CG30 40
Buckingham Rd. N1 CA36 57
Buckingham Rd. N22 BX30 38
Buckingham Rd. NW10 BO37 55
Buckingham Rd. Borwd. BN24 28
Buckingham Rd. Edg. BL29 37
Buckingham Rd. Hamptn. BE49 74
Buckingham Rd. Har. BG32 45
Buckingham Rd. Ilf. CM34 49
Buckingham Rd. Kings. on T. BL52 85
Buckingham Rd. Mitch. BX53 86
Buckingham Rd. Rich. BK48 74
Buckingham Rd. Wat. BD22 27
Buckingham St. WC2 BX40 4
Buckingham St. WC2 BX40 56
Watergate Wk.
Buckingham Ter. Sthl. BF41 64
Havelock Rd.
Buckingham Way Wall. BW58 95
Buckland Ave. Slou. AQ42 62
Buckland Cres. NW3 BT36 56
Buckland Cres. Wind. AM44 61
Buckland La. Bet. BP68 112
Buckland La. Tad. BO68 112
Buckland Rise Pnr. BD30 36
Buckland Rd. E10 CF32 48
Buckland Rd. Chess. BL56 94
Buckland Rd. Orp. CN56 97
Buckland Rd. Reig. BQ70 120
Buckland Rd. Sutt. BQ58 94
Buckland Rd. Tad. BR67 112
Bucklands Rd. Tedd. BK50 74
Buckland St. N1 BZ37 2
Buckland St. N1 BZ37 57
Buckland Wk. Mord. BT53 86
Buckland Way Wor. Pk. BQ54 85
Buck La. NW9 BN32 46
Buckleigh Av. SW20 BR52 85
Buckleigh Rd. SW16 BW50 76
Buckleigh Way SE19 CA50 77
Buckler Gdns. SE9 CK49 78
Bucklers All. SW6 BR43 65
Haldane Rd.
Bucklersbury EC4 BZ39 2
Bucklersbury EC4 BZ39 57
Walbrook
Bucklers Clo. Brox. CD14 12
Buckles La. S. Ock. DB39 60
Buckle St. E1 CA39 2
Buckle St. E1 CA39 57
Buckles Way Bans. BR61 103
Buckley Rd. NW6 BR36 55
Buckmaster Rd. SW11 BU45 66
Bucknalls Clo. Wat. BE20 18
Bucknalls Dr. St. Alb. BE19 18
Bucknalls La. Wat. BD19 18
Bucknall St. WC2 BW39 1
Bucknall St. WC2 BW39 56
Buckner Rd. SW2 BX45 66
Buckner St. W10 BR38 55
Bucknills Clo. BN61 103
Bucknills Clo. Epsom BN60 94
Buckrell Rd. E4 CF27 39
Buck Rd. Grav. DE47 81
Bucks Alley, Hert. BW12 11
Bucks Av. Wat. BE26 36
Bucks Clo. Wey. AW60 92
Buckscross Rd. Grav. DF48 81
Bucks Cross Rd. Orp. CQ56 98
Buckshaw Rd. N18 CB29 39
Bucks Hill, Kings L. AX20 17
Bucks Hill, Kings L. AX21 26
Bucks Hill Rd. Kings L. AW19 17
Buckstone Clo. SE23 CC46 77
Buckstone Rd. N18 CB29 39
Buck St. E2 CB37 2
Buck St. NW1 BV36 56
Camden High St.
Buckthorne Rd. SE4 CD46 77
Buckton Rd. Borwd. BL22 28
Buck Wk. E17 CF31 48
Budd Cft. Welw. G. C. BS7 5
Buddings Circ. Wem. BN34 46
Budd's All. Twick. BK46 74
Arlington Clo.
Budebury Rd. Stai. AW49 73
Budge Row EC4 BZ40 4
Budge Row EC4 BZ40 57
Cannon St.
Budgins Hill, Orp. CO59 98
Budleigh Cres. Well. CP43 69
Budoch Dr. Ilf. CO34 50
Buer Rd. SW6 BR44 65
Buff Av. Bans. BS60 95
Buford St. Hodd. CE12 12
Bug Hill, Warl. CC63 105
Bugsby's Way SE7 CH42 68
Bukfield Clo. Hat. BP11 10
Wellfield Rd.
Bulbourne Clo. Berk. AP12 7
Bulbourne Clo. Hem. H. AW14 8
Bulganak Rd. Th. Hth. BZ52 87
Bulinga St. SW1 BX42 4
Bulinga St. SW1 BX42 66
Bulingford Clo. SE4 CD45 67
Frendsbury Rd.
Bulkeley Ave. Wind. AN44 61
Bulkeley Clo. Egh. AR49 72
Bullace Clo. Hem. H. AW13 8
Bullace La. Dart. CW46 80
Bullace Row SE5 BZ44 67
Camberwell Rd.
Bull All. Well. CO45 69
Bullard's Pl. E2 CC38 57
Bullbanks Rd. Belv. CS42 69
Bullbeggars La. Berk. AS13 7
Bullbeggars La. Wok. AQ61 100
Bullbeggars Rd. Gdse. CC69 114
Bullen's Green La. St. Alb. BO15 10
Bullen St. SW11 BU44 66
Buller Clo. SE15 CB43 67
Buller Rd. N17 CB30 39
Buller Rd. NW10 BQ38 55
Buller Rd. Bark. CN36 58
Buller Rd. Th. Hth. BZ51 87
Bullers Clo. Sid. CQ49 79
Bullers Rd. N22 BY30 38
Bullerswood Dr. Chis. CK50 78
Bullescroft Rd. Edg. BM27 37
Bullfields, Saw. CQ5 6
Bullfinch Clo. Sev. CS64 107
Bullfinch Dene Sev. CS64 107
Bullfinch Clo.
Bullfinch La. Sev. CS64 107
Bullfinch Rd. Croy. CC59 96
Bullfinch Rd. Sth. Croy. CC58 96
Bullhead Rd. Borwd. BN23 28
Bull Hill, Lthd. BJ64 102
Bull Inn Ct. WC2 BX40 56
Strand
Bullivant St. E14 CF39 57
Bull La. N18 CA28 39
Bull La. Chis. CM50 78
Bull La. Dag. CR34 50
Bull La. Ger. Cr. AR31 43
Bull Rd. E15 CG37 58
Bullrush Cl. Hat. BP13 10
Bull's Alley SW14 BN44 65
Bullsbrook Rd. Hayes BD40 54
Bull's Cross, Enf. CB22 30
Bulls-Cross Ride, Wal. Cr. CB20 21
Bull's Cross Ride, Wal. Cr. CB21 30
Bulls Gdns. SW3 BU42 3
Bulls Gdns. SW3 BU42 66
Walton St.
Bulls Head Pass, EC3 CA39 57
Gracechurch St.
Bullshead Pl. EC3 CA39 2
Bullsland Gdns. Rick. AT25 25
Bull's La. Hat. BQ15 10
Bullsmoor Clo. Wal. Cr. CC21 30
Bullsmoor Gdns. Wal. Cr. CB21 30
Bullsmoor La. Enf. CB21 30
Bullsmoor Ride, Wal. Cr. CC21 30
Bullsmoor Way, Wal. Cr. CB21 30
Bull Stag Grn. Hat. BQ11 10
Bull Wf. La. EC4 BZ40 4
Bull Wharf La. EC4 BZ40 57
Bull Yd. N15 CA31 48
Stamford Hill High Rd.
Bulmer Gdns. Har. BK33 45
Bulmer Ms. W11 BS40 56
Kensington Pk. Rd.
Bulmer Pl. W11 BS40 56
Bulmer Wk. Rain. CV37 60
Bulow Ct. SW6 BS44 66
Bulstrode Av. Houns. BE44 64
Bulstrode Gdns. Houns. BF45 64
Bulstrode La. Kings L. AV18 16
Bulstrode Pl. W1 BV39 1
Bulstrode Pl. W1 BV39 56
Bulstrode Rd. Houns. BF45 64
Bulstrode St. W1 BV39 1
Bulstrode St. W1 BV40 56
Bulstrode Way, Ger. Cr. AR32 43
Bulwell Cres. Wal. Cr. CD18 21
Bulwer Ct. Rd. E11 CF33 48
Bulwer Gdns. Barn. BT24 29
Bulwer Rd. E11 CF33 48
Bulwer Rd. N18 CA28 39
Bulwer Rd. Barn. BS24 29
Bulwer St. W12 BQ40 55
Bunby Rd. Slou. AP36 52
Bunce Comm. Rd. Reig. BN74 120
Buncefield La. Hem. H. AZ12 8
Bunces Clo. Wind. AN42 61
Bunces La. Wdf. Grn. CG29 40
Bundys Way, Stai. AV50 72
Bungalow Rd. SE25 CA52 87
Bungalow Rd. Wok. AZ65 101
Bungalows, The SW16 BV50 76
Bungalows, The Bush. BE24 27
Bunhill Row EC1 BZ38 2
Bunhill Row EC1 BZ38 57
Bunhouse Pl. SW1 BV42 66
Bourne St.
Bunkers Hill NW11 BT33 47
Bunkers Hill Belv. CR42 69
Bunkers Hill, Sid. CQ48 79
Bunker, S La. Hem. H. AZ16 17
Bunns Field, Welw G.C. BT7 5
Bunns La. NW7 BO29 37
Bunsen St. E3 CD37 57
Kenilworth Rd.
Bunten Meade Slou. AN40 61
Buntingbridge Rd. Ilf. CM32 49
Bunting Clo. Mitch. BU53 86
Bunton St. SE18 CL41 68
Bunyan Rd. E17 BW31 47
Bunyan's La. Wok. AO60 91
Bunyard Dri. Wok. AU60 91
Burbage Clo. Wal. Cr. CD19 21
Burbage Rd. SE21 BZ46 77
Burbage Rd. SE24 BZ46 77
Burberry Clo. N. Mal. BO51 85
Burbridge Rd. Shep. AZ52 83
Burbridge Way N17 CA30 39
Burcham St. E14 CE39 57
Burcharbro Rd. SE2 CP43 69
Burchell Ct. Bush. BG26 36
Burchell Rd. E10 CE33 48
Burchell Rd. SE15 CB44 67
Burchetts Way, Shep. AZ53 83
Burchett Way, Rom. CQ32 50
Burch Rd. Grav. DF46 81
Burchwall Clo. Rom. CS29 41
Burcote Rd. SW18 BT47 76
Burcote, Wey. BA57 92
Burcott Gdns. Wey. AX57 92
Burcott Rd. Pur. BY60 95
Burdenshot Hill, Guil. AQ65 100
Burdenshott Av. Rich. BM45 65
Burden Way E11 CH34 49
Burden Way, Guil. AQ68 109
Burder Clo. N1 CA36 57
Kingsbury Ter.
Burdett Av. SW20 BP51 85
Burdett Clo. Sid. CQ49 79
Burdett Est. E14 CE39 57
Burdett Rd. E3 CD38 57
Burdett Rd. E14 CD38 57
Burdett Rd. Croy. BZ53 87
Burdett Rd. Rich. BL44 65
Burdett St. SE1 BY41 4
Burdett St. SE1 BY41 66
Pearman St.
Burdon La. Sutt. BR57 94
Burdon Pk. Sutt. BR58 94
Burfield Clo. SW17 BT49 76
Burfield Rd. Wind. AQ46 72
Burford Clo. Dag. CP34 50
Bennetts Castle La.
Burford Clo. Ilf. CM31 49
Burford Clo. Uxb. AY35 44
Burford Gdns. N13 BX27 38
Burford La. Epsom BQ59 94
Burford Rd. E6 CK38 58
Burford Rd. E15 CF36 57
Burford Rd. SE6 CD48 77
Burford Rd. Brent. BL42 65
Burford Rd. Brom. CK52 88
Burford Rd. Sutt. BS55 86
Burford Rd. Wor. Pk. BO54 85
Burford Way Croy. CF57 96
Burgandy Croft. Welw. G. C. BR9 5
Burges Clo. Horn. CW32 51
Ernest Rd.
Burges Rd. E6 CK36 58
Burgess Av. NW9 BN32 46
Burgess Cotts. Belv. CR41 69
Burgess Hl. NW2 BS35 47
Burgess Rd. E15 CG35 49
Burgess Rd. Sutt. BS56 95
Burgess St. E14 CE39 57
Burge St. SE1 BZ41 4
Burge St. SE1 BZ41 67
Burgett Rd. Slou. AN41 61
Burghfield Epsom BO61 103
Burghfield Rd. Grav. DF50 81
Burgh Heath Rd. Epsom. BO60 94
Burghill Rd. SE26 CC49 77
Burghley Av. Borwd. BN25 28
Burghley Av. N. Mal. BN51 85
Burghley Gdns. Ilf. CO29 41
Burghley Rd. E11 CG33 49
Burghley Rd. N8 BY31 47
Burghley Rd. NW5 BV35 47
Burghley Rd. SW19 BQ49 75
Burgh Mt. Bans. BR61 103
Burgh St. N1 BY37 2
Burgh St. N1 BY37 56
Burgh Wd. Bans. BR61 103
Burgon St. EC4 BY39 56
Carter La.
Burgos Gro. SE10 CE44 67
Burgoyne Hatch, Harl. CO10 6
Burgoyne Rd. N4 BY32 47
Burgoyne Rd. SE25 CA52 87
Burgoyne Rd. SW9 BX45 66
Burgoyne Rd. Sun. BB50 73
Burgundy St. SE1 CA42 4
Burgundy St. SE1 CA42 67
Burham Clo. SE20 CC50 77
Blenheim Rd.
Burhill Gro. Pnr. BE30 36
Burhill Rd. Walt. BC58 92
Burke Clo. SW15 BO45 65
Burke St. E16 CG39 58
Burland Rd. SW11 BU46 76
Burland Rd. Brwd. DB26 42
Burland Rd. Rom. CS29 41
Burlea Clo. Walt. BC56 92
Burleigh Av. Sid. CN46 78
Burleigh Av. Wall. BV55 86
Burleigh Clo. Wey. AW56 92
Burleigh Gdns. N14 BW26 38
Burleigh Gdns. Ashf. BA49 73
Burleigh Ho. W10 BQ39 55
Burleigh Pl. Mitch. BU53 86
Burleigh Rd. Enf. CA24 30
Burleigh Rd. Hem. H. BA14 8
Burleigh Rd. St. Alb. BJ13 9
Burleigh Rd. Sutt. BR54 85
Burleigh Rd. Uxb. AZ37 53
Burleigh Rd. Wey. AW56 92
Burleigh St. WC2 BX40 4
Burleigh St. WC2 BX40 56
Tavistock St.
Burleigh Way Enf. BZ24 30
Burleigh Way, Pot. B. BX18 20
Burley Clo. E4 CE28 39
Burley Clo. SW16 BW51 86
Burley Rd. E16 CJ39 58
Burleigh Mead Hat. BQ11 10
Gt. Nth. Rd.
Burlingham Clo. Guil. AU69 118
Gilliat Dri.
Burlings La. Sev. CN62 106
Burlington Arc. W1 BW40 3
Burlington Arcade W1 BW40 56
Burlington Gdns.
Burlington Ave. Slou. AR41 62
Burlington Av. Rich. BM44 65
Burlington Av. Rom. CS32 50
Burlington Clo. W9 BR38 55
Elgin Av.
Burlington Clo. Brom. CL55 88
Crofton Rd.
Burlington Clo. Felt. BA47 73
Burlington Gdns. W1 BW40 3
Burlington Gdns. W1 BW40 56
Burlington Gdns. W3 BN40 55
Burlington Gdns. W4 BN42 65
Burlington Gdns. Rom. CQ33 50
Burlington La. W4 BN43 65
Burlington Ms. W3 BO40 55
Burlington Gdns.
Burlington Ms. E. W2 BS39 56
Shrewsbury Rd.
Burlington Ms. W. W2 BS39 56
Ledbury Rd.
Burlington Pl. Wdf. Grn. CH27 40
Burlington Rise Barn. BU26 38
Burlington Rd. N10 BV31 47
Tetherdown
Burlington Rd. N17 CB30 39
Burlington Rd. SW6 BR44 65
Burlington Rd. W4 BN42 65
Burlington Rd. Enf. BZ23 30
Burlington Rd. Islw. BG44 64
Burlington Rd. N. Mal. BO52 85
Burlington Rd. Th. Hth. BZ51 87
Burma Ct. N5 BZ35 48
Green Lanes
Burman St. SE1 BY41 4
Burman St. SE1 BY41 66
Burma Rd. N16 BZ35 48
Burma Rd. Wok. AP53 82
Burmester Rd. SW17 BT48 76
Burnaby Cres. W4 BN43 65
Burnaby Gdns. W4 BM43 65
Burnaby Rd. Grav. DF47 81
Burnaby St. E6 CL40 58
Burnaby St. SW10 BT43 66
Burn Brae Clo. N3 BS29 38
Burnbury Rd. SW12 BW47 76
Burn Clo. Wat. BG24 27
Burn Clo. Wey. AX56 92
Burncroft Av. Enf. CC23 30
Burne Jones Ho. W14 BR42 65
Burne St. NW1 BU39 1
Burnell Av. Twick. BK49 74
Burnell Av. Well. CO44 69
Burnell Gdns. Stan. BK30 36
Burnell Rd. Sutt. BS56 95
Burnell Wk. Brwd. DB29 42
Burnels Av. E6 CL38 58
Burness Clo. N7 BX36 56
Roman Way
Burness Clo. Uxb. AXZ37 53
Burnet Av. Guil. AT69 118
Burnet Gro. Epsom BN60 94
Burnett Clo. E9 CC35 48
Churchill Wk.
Burnetts Rd. Wind. AM44 61
Burney Av. Surb. BL53 85
Burney Clo. Lthd. BG66 111
Burney Dr. Loug. CL23 31
Burney Dr. Loug. CM23 31
Burney Rd. Dor. BJ69 119
Burney St. SE10 CF43 67
Burnfoot Av. SW6 BR44 65
Burnham, Wok. AO62 100
Burnham Av. Uxb. BA35 44
Burnham Clo. E11 CJ31 49
Burnham Clo. Enf. CA22 30
Burnham Clo. Wind. AL44 61
Burnham Clo. Wok. AO62 100
Burnham Ct. NW4 BQ31 46
Burnham Cres. Dart. CV45 70
Burnham Dr. Reig. BS70 121
Burnham Dr. Wok. Pk. BQ55 85
Burnham Gdns. Hayes BA41 63
Burnham Gdns. Houns. BC44 63
Burnham La. Guil. AT68 109
Burnham Rd. E4 CD28 39
Burnham Rd. Dag. CO36 59
Burnham Rd. Dart. CV45 70
Burnham Rd. Mord. BS53 86
Burnham Rd. Rom. CS31 50
Burnham Rd. St. Alb. BJ13 9
Burnham Rd. Sid. CQ48 79
Burnhams Rd. Lthd. BE65 102
Burnhams Rd. Lthd. BE66 111
Burnham St. E2 CC38 57
Burnham St. Kings. on T. BM51 85
Burnham Way W13 BJ41 64
Burnhill Rd. Beck. CE51 87
Burnley Rd. NW10 BO35 46
Burnley Rd. SW9 BX44 66
Burnsall St. SW3 BU42 3
Burnsall St. SW3 BU42 66
Burns Av. Felt. BC46 73
Burns Av. Sid. CO46 79
Burns Av. Sthl. BF40 54
Burns Clo. Cob. BG61 102
Burns Clo. Erith CT44 69
Burns Clo. Hayes BB39 53
Burns Clo. Well. CO44 69
Burns Dri. Hem. H. AZ10 8
Burn Side N9 CC27 39
Burn Side. Ash. BL62 103
Burnside, Saw. CP6 6
Burnside Cl. Hat. BP11 10
Burnside Clo. Barn. BS24 29
Burnside Clo. Twick. BJ46 74
Burnside Cres. Wem. BK37 54
Burnside Rd. E3 CD38 57
Burnside Rd. Dag. CP34 50
Burnside Ter. Harl. CQ9 6
Burns Pl. Til. DG44 71
Burns Rd. NW10 BO37 55
Burns Rd. SW11 BU44 66
Burns Rd. W13 BJ41 64
Burns Rd. Har. BH31 45
Burns Rd. Wem. BL37 55
Burns Way. Brwd. DE25 122
Burns Way Houns. BD44 64
Burnt Ash Hl. SE12 CG46 78
Burns Ash La. Brom. CH50 78
Burns Ash Rd. SE12 CG46 78
Burnt Common Clo. Wok. AV66 109
Burntcommon La. Wok. AV66 109
Burnt Farm Ride, Wal. Cr. BY20 20
Burnt Farm Rd. Enf. BY20 20
Burnthouse La. Dart. CW49 80
Burnthwaite Rd. SW6 BR43 65
Burnt Mill, Harl. CM9 6
Burnt Mill CLo. Harl. CM9 6
Burnt Mill La.
Burntmill La. Harl. CM9 6
Burnt Oak, Edg. BM29 37
Burnt Oak Fields, Edg. BN30 37
East Rd.
Burnt Oak La. Sid. CN46 78
Burntwood Av. Horn. CV32 51
Burntwood, Cat. CA64 105
Burntwood Clo. SW18 BU47 76
Burntwood Clo. Brwd. DE32 123
Burntwood Clo. Cat. CB64 105
Burntwood Gra. Rd. SW18 BT47 76
Burntwood La. SW17 BT48 76
Burntwood Rd. Sev. CU67 116
Burnway Horn. CW33 51
Burrage Gro. SE18 CM42 68
Burrage Pl. SE18 CL42 68
Burrage Rd. SE18 CL43 68
Burrard Rd. E16 CH39 58
Burrard Rd. NW6 BS35 47
Burr Clo. Bexh. CQ45 69
Burr Clo. St. Alb. BL17 19
Burrell Clo. Edg. BM27 37
Burrell Row, Beck. CE51 87
High St.
Burrell St. SE1 BY40 4
Burrell St. SE1 BY40 56
Burrell, The Dor. BG72 119
Burrfield Dr. Orp. CP53 89
Burr Hill La. Wok. AP58 91
Burritt Rd. Kings. on T. BM51 85
Burroughs Gdns. NW4 BP31 46
Burroughs, The NW4 BP31 46
Burroway Rd. Slou. AT41 62
Burrow Clo. Chig. CN28 40
Burrow Fld. Welw. G.C. BQ9 5
Burrow Grn. Chig. CN28 40
Burrow Hill Grn. Wok. AO58 91
Windlesham Rd.
Burrow Rd. Chig. CN28 40
Burrows Clo. Lthd. BE65 102
Burrows Hill Clo. Houns. AW45 63
Burrows Hill La. Houns. AW45 63
Burrows Ms. SE1 BY41 4
Burrows Ms. SE1 BY41 66
Burrows Rd. NW10 BQ38 55
Burrow Walk SE24 BZ47 77
Rosendale Rd.
Burr Rd. SW18 BS47 76
Bursdon Clo. Sid. CN48 78
Burses Way, Brwd. DE25 122
Bursland Rd. Enf. CC24 30
Burslem Av. Ilf. CO29 41
Burslem St. E1 CB39 57
Burstead Clo. Cob. BD59 93
Burstead Gdns. Ilf. CO29 41
Burstock Rd. SW15 BR45 65
Burston Dr. St. Alb. BG17 18
Burston Rd. SW15 BQ45 65
Burstow Rd. SW20 BR51 85
Burtenshaw Rd. Surb. BJ53 84
Burtley Clo. N4 BZ33 48
Burton Av. Wat. BC24 26
Burton Clo. NW7 BQ28 37
Burton Clo. Chess. BK57 93
Burton Ct. SW3 BU42 3
Burton Ct. SW3 BU42 66
Burton Dr. Loug. CM24 31
Burton Gdns. Houns. BE44 64
Burton Gro. SE17 BZ42 4
Burton Gro. SE17 BZ42 67
Burtonhole La. NW7 BQ28 37
Burton Lane SW9 BY44 66
Myatts Fields Dev.
Burton La. Wal. Cr. CA18 21
Burton Pl. WC1 BW38 1
Burton Pl. WC1 BW38 56
Burton St.
Burton Rd. E18 CH31 49
Burton Rd. NW6 BR36 55
Burton Rd. SW9 BY44 66
Burton Rd. Kings. On T. BL50 75
Burton Rd. Loug. CM24 31
Burtons La. Ch. St. G. AR23 25
Burton's La. Ch. St. G. AS25 25
Burton's Rd. Hamptn. BF49 74
Burton St. WC1 BW38 1
Burton St. WC1 BW38 56
Burtons Way. Ch. St. G. AR23 25
Burton Way, Wind. AM45 61
Burtop Rd. SW17 BT48 76
Burt Rd. E16 CJ40 58
Burwash Rd. SE18 CM42 68
Burwell Av. Grnf. BH36 54
Burwell Clo. E1 CB39 57
Burwell Rd. E10 CD33 48
Burwell Wk. E3 CE38 57
Campbell Rd.
Burwood Av. Brom. CH55 88
Burwood Av. Ken. BY60 95
Burwood Av. Pnr. BC32 44
Burwood Clo. Guil. AU70 118
Burwood Clo. Reig. BT70 121
Burwood Clo. Surb. BM54 85
Burwood Clo. Walt. BD57 93
Burwood Gdns. Rain. CT38 59
Burwood Pk. Rd. Walt. BC56 92
Burwood Pl. W2 BU39 1
Burwood Pl. W2 BU39 56
Burwood Rd. Watt. BB57 92
Bury Av. Ruis. BA32 44
Bury Clo. Wok. AR61 100
Bury Ct. EC3 CA39 2
Bury Ct. EC3 CA39 57
Bury Cres. Hayes BB37 53

Street	Grid	Page
Burycroft. Welw. G.C.	BR6	5
Burydell La. St. Alb.	BG17	18
Buryfields, Guil.	AR71	118
Burygreen Rd. Wal. Cr.	CB19	21
Bury Gro. Mord.	BS53	86
Bury Hall Vill. N9	CA26	39
Bury Hill, Hem. H.	AW13	8
Bury Hill Clo. Hem. H.	AX13	8
Bury Holme, Brox.	CD15	12
Bury La. Epp.	CM17	22
Bury La. Rick.	AX26	35
Bury La. Wok.	AR61	100
Bury Meadows, Rick.	AX26	35
Bury Pl. WC1	**BX39**	**2**
Bury Pl. WC1	BX39	56
Bury Rise, Hem. H.	AU16	16
Bury Rd. E4	CG25	31
Bury Rd. N22	BY30	38
Bury Rd. Dag.	CR35	50
Bury Rd. Epp.	CN19	22
Bury Rd. Harl.	CP9	6
Bury Rd. Hem. H.	AX13	8
Bury St. EC3	**CA39**	**2**
Bury St. EC3	CA39	57
Bury St. N9	CA26	39
Bury St. SW1	**BW40**	**3**
Bury St. SW1	BW40	56
Bury St. Guil.	AR71	118
Bury St. Ruis.	BA32	44
Bury St. W. N9	BZ26	39
Bury Wk. SW3	**BU42**	**3**
Bury Wk. SW3	BU42	66
Busby Ms. NW5	BW36	56
Torriano Av.		
Busby Pl. NW5	BW36	56
Busby St. E2	CA38	2
Busby St. E2	CA38	57
Bushberry Rd. E9	CD36	57
Bushbury La. Bet.	BM72	120
Bushby Av. Brox.	CD14	12
Bush Clo. Ilf.	CM32	49
Bush Clo. Wey.	AX56	92
Bush Cotts. SW18	BS46	76
Putney Br. Rd.		
Bush Ct. N14	BW26	38
Bushell Gro. Bush.	BG27	36
Gleed Av.		
Bushell St. E1	**CB40**	**4**
Bushell St. E1	CB40	57
Hermitage Wall		
Bushell Way, Brom.	CL47	78
Bush Elms Rd. Horn.	CU33	50
Bushetts Gro. Red.	BV68	113
Bushey Av. E18	CG31	49
Bushey Av. Orp.	CM54	88
Bushey Clo. Uxb.	AZ34	44
Bushey Clo. Welw. G.C.	BS8	5
Bushey Ct. SW20	BP51	85
Bushey Ct. Kings. On T.	BK50	74
Bushey Crof. Harl.	CN12	13
Bushey Gro. Rd. Bush.	BD24	27
Bushey Hall Dri. Bush.	BE24	27
Bushey Hall Rd. Bush.	BD24	27
Bushey Hill Enf.	BX24	29
Bushey Hill Rd. SE5	CA44	67
Bushey La. Sutt.	BS56	95
Bushey Lea Ong.	CX18	24
Bushey Lees Sid.	CN46	78
Fen Grove		
Bushey Ley. Welw. G.C.	BS8	5
Busheymill Cres. Wat.	BD22	27
Bushey Mill La. Wat.	BD22	27
Bushey Pk. Cotts. Tedd.	BH50	74
Bushey Pk. Rd. Tedd.	BJ50	74
Bushey Rd. E13	CJ37	58
Bushey Rd. N15	CA32	48
Albert Rd.		
Bushey Rd. SW20	BP52	85
Bushey Rd. Croy.	CE55	87
Bushey Rd. Hayes	BB42	63
Bushey Rd. Sutt.	BS56	95
Bushey Rd. Uxb.	AZ34	44
Bushey Way Beck.	CF53	87
Bushey Fair, Harl.	CN12	13
Bushfield Clo. Edg.	BM27	37
Bushfield Cres. Edg.	BM27	37
Bushfield Dr. Red.	BV73	121
Bushfield Rd. Hem. H.	AU16	16
Bushfields Loug.	CL25	31
Bush Gro. NW9	BN33	46
Bush Gro. Stan.	BK29	36
Bushgrove Rd. Dag.	CP35	50
Bush Hall La. Hat.	BQ11	10
Bush Hill N21	BZ26	39
Bush Hill Rd. N21	BZ25	30
Bush Hill Rd. Har.	BL32	46
Bush La. EC4	**BZ40**	**4**
Bush La. EC4	BZ40	57
Bush La. Wok.	AU65	100
Bushmoor Cres. SE18	CL43	68
Bushnell Rd. SW17	BV48	76
Bush Rd. E11	CG33	49
Bush Rd. SE8	CC42	67
Bush Rd. Buck. H.	CJ28	40
Bush Rd. Buck. Hill.	CJ28	40
Bush Rd. Rich.	BL43	65
Bush Rd. Shep.	AY53	83
Bushway, Dag.	CP35	50
Bushwood E11	CG33	49
Bushwood Rd. Rich.	BM43	65
Bushy Cft. Oxt.	CF68	114
High St.		
Bushy Hill Dr. Guil.	AT69	118
Bushy Pk. Gdns. Tedd.	BG49	74
Bushy Rd. E13	CJ37	58
Bushy Rd. Lthd.	BF65	102
Bushy Rd. Tedd.	BH50	74
Busk St. E2	CB37	57
Yorkton St.		
Butcher Row E14	CC40	57
Butcher's Rd. E16	CH39	58
Bute Av. Rich.	BL48	75
Bute Ct. Wall.	BV56	95
Bute Gdns. W6	BQ42	65
Bute Gdns. Wall.	BW56	95
Bute Gdns. W. Wall.	BW56	95
Bute Rd. Croy.	BY54	86
Bute Rd. Ilf.	CL31	49
Bute Rd. Wall.	BW56	95
Bute St. SW7	**BT42**	**3**
Bute St. SW7	BT42	66
Bute Wk. N1	BZ36	57
Marquess Est.		
Buthfield St. W8	BS41	66
Butler Av. Har.	BG33	45
Butler Ho. Grays	DD43	71
Hawkes Clo.		
Butler Rd. NW10	BO36	55
Curzon Cres.		
Butler Rd. Dag.	CO35	50
Butler Rd. Har.	BG33	45
Butlers Clo. Wind.	AL44	61
Butlers Dene Rd. Cat.	CD63	105
Butlers Dr. E4	CF22	30
Butler's Pl. New. A.G.	DC55	90
Butler St. E2	CC38	57
Digby St.		
Butler St. Uxb.	AZ38	53
Butter Cross La. Epp.	CO18	23
Butterfield La. St. Alb.	BH15	9
Butterfields E17	CF32	48
Butterfly La. SE9	CL46	78
Butterfly La. Borwd.	BJ24	27
Butterfly Wk. Warl.	CC63	105
Butter Hill Wall.	BV55	86
Buttermere Clo. N. Mal.	BO53	85
Grand Drive		
Buttermere Gdns. Pur.	BZ60	96
Buttermere Rd. SW15	BR46	75
Buttermere Walk E8	CA36	57
Rhodes Dev.		
Buttersweet Rise, Saw.	CQ6	6
Butterwick W6	BQ42	65
Butterwick Wat.	BE21	27
Buttesland St. N1	BZ38	57
Pitfield St.		
Buttfield Clo. Dag.	CR36	59
Butt Field Vw. St. Alb.	BG15	9
Buttlehide, Rick.	AU28	34
Buttondene Cres. Brox.	CE14	12
Button Meade. Slou.	AN40	61
Button St. Swan.	CV53	90
Butts, The Brox.	CD15	12
Butts, The Sun.	BD52	83
Elizabeth Gdns.		
Buttsbury Rd. Ilf.	CM35	49
Butts Cotts. Felt.	BE48	74
Butts Cres. Felt.	BF48	74
Butts Farm Est. Felt.	BE48	74
Butts Grn. Rd. Horn.	CV32	51
Butts Head, Nthwd.	BA29	35
Butts Rd. Brom.	CG49	78
Butts Rd. Wok.	AS62	100
Butt's, The Brent.	BK43	64
Butts, The Bush.	BG26	36
Butts, The Sev.	CU62	107
Butts, The Sun.	BD52	84
Buxted Clo. E8	CA36	57
Richmond Rd.		
Buxted Rd. N12	BU28	38
Buxton Ave. Cat.	CA64	105
Buxton Clo. St. Alb.	BK12	9
Buxton Clo. Wdf. Grn.	CJ29	40
Buxton Cres. Sutt.	BR56	94
Buxton Dr. E11	CG31	49
Buxton Dr. N. Mal.	BN51	85
Buxton Gdns. W3	BM40	55
Buxton La. Cat.	BZ63	105
Buxton Path Wat.	BD27	36
Buxton Rd. E4	CF26	39
Buxton Rd. E6	CK38	58
Buxton Rd. E15	CG35	49
Buxton Rd. E17	CD31	48
Buxton Rd. NW2	BP36	55
Buxton Rd. SW14	BO45	65
Buxton Rd. Ashf.	AX49	73
Buxton Rd. Epp.	CN21	31
Buxton Rd. Erith	CS43	69
Buxton Rd. Grays.	CF41	71
Buxton Rd. Ilf.	CN32	49
Buxton Rd. Th. Hth.	BY53	86
Buxton Rd. Wal. Abb.	CH20	22
Buxton St. E1	**CA38**	**2**
Buxton St. E1	CA38	57
Byam St. SW6	BT44	66
Byards Cft. SW16	BW51	86
Bycliffe Ter. Grav.	DF47	81
Bycroft Rd. Sthl.	BF38	54
Bycroft St. SE20	CC50	77
Parish La.		
Bycullah Av. Enf.	BY24	29
Bycullah Rd. Enf.	BY23	29
Byegrove Rd. SW19	BT50	76
Byers Clo. Pot. B.	BT20	20
Bye, The W3	BO39	55
Bye Ways Twick.	BF48	74
Byeways, The Rick.	AY27	35
Byeway, The SW14	BN45	65
Byeway, The Epsom	BO56	94
Bye Way, The Har.	BH30	36
Byfield Gdns. SW13	BP44	65
Byfield, Welw. G.C.	BR6	5
Byfield Ct. N. Mal.	BP52	85
Byfield Rd. Islw.	BJ45	64
Byfleet Corner, Wey.	AW60	92
Byfleet Rd. Cob.	AZ59	92
Byfleet Rd. Wey.	AX58	92
Byford Clo. E15	CG36	58
Bygrove Croy.	CE57	96
Bygrove St. E14	CE39	57
Byland Clo. N21	BX26	38
Byland CLo. SE2	CO41	69
Finchale Rd.		
Byland Dri. Maid.	AG42	61
Bylands, Wok.	AT63	100
Byne Rd. SE26	CC50	77
Byne Rd. Cars.	BU55	86
Bynes Rd. Sth. Croy.	BZ57	96
Byng Dr. Pot. B.	BS19	20
Bynghams, Harl.	CK12	13
Byng Pl. WC1	**BW38**	**1**
Byng Pl. WC1	BW38	56
Byng Rd. Barn.	BQ24	28
Byng St. E14	CE41	67
Bynon Av. Bexh.	CQ45	69
Byon Clo. SE26	CD49	77
Byrefield Rd. Guil.	AP69	118
Byrne Rd. SW12	BV47	76
Byron Av. E12	CK36	58
Byron Av. E18	CG31	49
Byron Av. NW9	BM31	46
Byron Av. Borwd.	BM25	28
Byron Av. Couls.	BX61	104
Byron Av. Houns.	BC44	63
Byron Av. N. Mal.	BP52	85
Byron Av. Sutt.	BT56	95
Byron Av. Wat.	BD23	27
Byron Cl. Walt.	BE54	84
Byron Clo. E8	CA37	57
Broadway Mkt. Est.		
Byron Clo. SE28	CP40	59
Byron Clo. Hamptn.	BE49	74
Byron Clo. Wok.	AP62	100
Byron Ct. Enf.	BY23	29
Byron Ct. Rich.	BK49	74
Byron Dr. N2	BT32	47
Byron Gdns. Sutt.	BT56	95
Byron Gdns. Til.	DH44	71
Byron Hill Rd. Har.	BG33	45
Byron Pl. Hem. H.	AZ10	8
Byron Pl. Lthd.	BJ64	102
Byron Rd. E10	CE33	48
Byron Rd. E17	CE31	48
Byron Rd. NW2	BP34	46
Byron Rd. NW7	BP28	37
Byron Rd. W5	BL40	55
Byron Rd. Brwd.	DE26	122
Byron Rd. Har.	BH30	36
Byron Rd. Har.	BH32	45
Byron Rd. Sth. Croy.	CB58	96
Byron Rd. Wem.	BK34	45
Byron Rd. Wey.	AY56	92
Byron St. E14	CE39	57
Byron Way, Hayes	BB38	53
Byron Way Nthlt.	BE38	54
Byron Way, Rom.	CV30	42
Byron Way, West Dr.	AY42	63
Bysouth Clo. Ilf.	CL30	40
By The Wood, Wat.	BE27	36
Bythorn St. SW9	BX45	66
Byton Rd. SW17	BU50	76
Byward Av. Felt.	BD46	74
Byward St. EC3	**CA40**	**4**
Byward St. EC3	CA40	57
Bywater St. SW3	**BU42**	**3**
Bywater St. SW3	BU42	66
By-ways, The Ash.	BK62	102
Byways, The Surb.	BM53	85
Byway, The Pot. B.	BS20	20
Byway, The Sutt.	BT58	95
Bywood Av. Croy.	CC53	87
Bywood Clo. Ken.	BY61	104
Cabbell St. NW1	**BU39**	**1**
Cabbell St. NW1	BU39	56
Cabell Rd. Guil.	AO70	118
Cable St. E1	**CB40**	**4**
Cable St. E1	CB40	57
Cabot Way, E6	CJ37	58
Parr Rd.		
Cabrera Av. Vir. W.	AR53	82
Cabrera Clo. Vir. W.	AR53	82
Cabul Rd. SW11	BU44	66
Cacket's La. Sev.	CM61	106
Cactus Wk. W12	BO39	55
Du Cane Rd.		
Cadbury Cl. Islw.	BJ44	64
Cadbury Clo. Sun.	BB50	73
Cadbury Rd. SE16	CB41	67
Cadbury Rd. Sun.	BB50	73
Caddington Cl. Barn.	BU25	29
Caddington Rd. NW2	BR34	46
Cade La. Sev.	CV67	117
Cade Rd. SE10	CF44	67
Cader Rd. SW18	BT46	76
Cadet Pl. SE10	CG42	68
Cadiz Rd. Dag.	CS36	59
Cadiz St. SE17	**BZ42**	**4**
Cadiz St. SE17	BZ42	67
Cadley Ter. SE23	CC48	77
Cadmore La. Wal. Cr.	CC17	21
Cadogan Ave. Dart.	CY47	80
Cadogan Av. Brwd.	DE32	123
Cadogan Clo. E9	CD36	57
Cadogan Ter.		
Cadogan Clo. Brom.	CF51	87
Albermarle Rd.		
Cadogan Clo. Har.	BF35	45
Cadogan Clo. Maid.	AG43	61
Cadogan Clo. Tedd.	BH49	74
Cadogan Ct. SW3	BU42	66
Draycott Av.		
Cadogan Ct. Sutt.	BS57	95
Cadogan Gdns. E18	CH31	49
Cadogan Gdns. N3	BS30	38
Cadogan Gdns. N21	BY25	29
Cadogan Gdns. SW3	**BU42**	**3**
Cadogan Gdns. SW3	BU42	66
Cadogan Gate SW1	**BU42**	**3**
Cadogan Gte. SW1	BU42	66
Cadogan La. SW1	**BV41**	**3**
Cadogan La. SW1	BV41	66
Cadogan Pl. SW1	**BU41**	**3**
Cadogan Pl. SW1	BU41	66
Cadogan Rd. Surb.	BK53	84
Cadogan Sq. SW1	**BU41**	**3**
Cadogan Sq. SW1	BU41	66
Cadogan St. SW3	**BU42**	**3**
Cadogan St. SW3	BU42	66
Cadogan Ter. E9	CD36	57
Cadoxton Av. N15	CA32	48
Cadwallon Rd. SE9	CL48	78
Caedmon Rd. N7	BX35	47
Caenshill Rd. Wey.	AZ57	92
Caenswood Hill, Wey.	AZ58	92
Caenwood Clo. Wey.	AZ57	92
Caen Wood Rd. Ash.	BK62	102
Caerleon Clo. Sid.	CP49	79
Caerleon Ter. SE2	CO42	69
Caernarvon Clo. Hem. H.	AX13	8
Caernarvon Clo. Horn.	CX33	51
Caernarvon Clo. Mitch.	BX52	86
Caernarvon Dr. Ilf.	CL30	40
Caesar St. E2	**CA38**	**2**
Caesar St. E2	CA38	57
Caesar's Wk. Mitch.	BU53	86
Caesars Way Shep.	BA53	83
Green La.		
Cage Pond Rd. Rad.	BL20	19
Cage St. WC1	**BX39**	**2**
Cahir St. E14	CE42	67
Caillard Rd. Wey.	AY59	92
Cains La. Felt.	BA46	73
Caird St. W10	BR38	55
Cairn Av. W5	BK40	54
Cairndale Clo. Brom.	CG50	78
Cairnfield Av. NW2	BO34	46
Cairns Clo. Dart.	CV46	80
Cairns Rd. SW11	BU46	76
Cairn Way Stan.	BH29	36
Cairo New Rd. Croy.	BY55	86
Cairo Rd. E17	CE31	48
Cairo Rd. Croy.	BY55	86
Caishowe Rd. Borwd.	BM23	28
Caistor Mews SW12	BV47	76
Caistor Rd.		
Caistor Park Rd. E15	CG37	58
Caistor Rd. SW12	BV47	76
Caithness Gdns. Sid.	CN46	78
Caithness Rd. W14	BQ41	65
Caithness Rd. Mitch.	BV50	76
Calabria Rd. N5	BY36	56
Calais St. SE5	BY44	66
Calbourne Av. Horn.	CU35	50
Calbourne Rd. SW12	BU47	76
Calcott Clo. Brwd.	DA26	42
Costead Manor Rd.		
Calcot Wk. SE9	CJ49	78
Calcutta Rd. Til.	DF44	71
Caldbeck Wal. Abb.	CF20	22
Roundhills		
Caldbeck Av. Wor. Pk.	BP55	85
Caldecote Gdns. Bush.	BH26	36
Caldecote La. Bush.	BH26	36
Caldecot Rd. SE5	BZ44	67
Caldecott Way E5	CC34	48
Millfields Rd.		
Caldecot Way, Brox.	CD14	12
Calder Av. Grnf.	BH37	54
Calder Av. Hat.	BS16	20
Calder Clo. Enf.	CA24	30
Calder Gdns. Edg.	BM31	46
Calderon Pl. W10	BQ39	55
St. Quintin Gdns.		
Calderon Rd. E11	CF35	48
Caldervale Rd. SW4	BW46	76
Calderwood St. SE18	CL42	68
Caldew St. SE5	BZ43	67
Caldwell Rd. Wat.	BD28	36
Caldwell St. SW9	BX43	66
Caldwell Yd. EC4	**BZ40**	**4**
Caldwell Yd. EC4	**BZ40**	**4**
High Timber St.		
Caldwell Yd. EC4	BZ40	57
Caldy Rd. Belv.	CR41	69
Caldy Wk. N1	BZ36	57
Marquess Est.		
Caleb St. SE1	**BZ41**	**4**
Caleb St. SE1	BZ41	67
Mint St.		
Caledonian Est. N7	BX36	56
Caledonian Rd. N1	**BX37**	**2**
Caledonian Rd. N1	BX37	56
Caledonian Rd. N7	BX37	56
Caledonian Rd. W10	BQ39	55
Quintin Gdns.		
Caledonia St. N1	**BX37**	**2**
Caledonia St. N1	BX37	56
Caledon Rd. E6	CK37	58
Caledon Rd. St. Alb.	BK16	18
Caledon Rd. Wall.	BV56	95
Cale St. SW3	**BU42**	**3**
Cale St. SW3	BU42	66
Caletock St. SE10	CG42	68
Lenthorp Rd.		
Caletock Way SE10	CG42	68
Glenister Rd.		
Calfstock La. S. Onth.	CW52	90
Calgate Cl. SW19	BR47	75
Calidore Clo. SW2	BX46	76
California La. Bush.	BG26	36
California Rd. N. Mal.	BN52	85
Caliph Clo. Grav.	DJ49	81
Callander Rd. SE6	CE48	77
Callan Gro. S. Ock.	DA40	60
Callard Av. N13	BY28	38
Callcott Rd. NW6	BR36	55
Callcott St. W8	BS40	56
Calley Down Cres. Croy.	CF59	96
Callis Farm Clo. Stai.	AY46	73
Callis Rd. E17	CD32	48
Calliston Ct. Hem. H.	AY12	8
Callow Hill, Egh.	AR51	82
Callow Hill, Vir. W.	AR52	82
Callow St. SW3	**BT43**	**3**
Callow St. SW3	BT43	66
Calmont Rd. Brom.	CF50	77
Calne Av. Ilf.	CL30	40
Calonne Rd. SW19	BQ49	75
Calshot Clo. Enf.	BY24	29
Calshot Rd. Houns.	AZ44	63
Calshot St. N1	**BX37**	**2**
Calshot St. N1	BX37	56
Calshot Way, Houns.	AZ44	63
Calshot Rd.		
Calthorpe Gdns. Stan.	BL28	37
Calthorpe Gdns. Sutt.	BT55	86
Calthorpe St. WC1	**BX38**	**2**
Calthorpe St. WC1	BX38	56
Calton Av. SE21	CA46	77
Calton Rd. Barn.	BT25	29
Calverley Cres. Dag.	CR34	50
Calverley Gdns. Har.	BK33	45
Calverley Gro. N19	BW33	47
Calverley Rd. Epsom.	BP57	94
Calvert Av. E2	**CA38**	**2**
Calvert Av. E2	CA38	57
Calvert Clo. Belv.	CR42	69
Calvert Clo. Sid.	CQ50	79
Calvert Cres. Dor.	BJ70	119
Calverton Rd. E6	CL37	58
Calvert Rd. SE10	CG42	68
Calvert Rd. Barn.	BQ23	28
Calvert Rd. Dor.	BJ70	119
Calvert Rd. Leath.	BC68	110
Calvert St. NW1	BV37	56
Calvin Clo. Orp.	CP52	89
Calvin St. E1	**CA38**	**2**
Calvin St. E1	CA38	57
Calydon Rd. SE7	CH42	68
Camac Rd. Twick.	BG47	74
Cambalt Rd. SW15	BQ46	75
Camberley Av. SW20	BP51	85
Camberley Av. Enf.	CA24	30
Camberley Rd. Houns.	AZ45	63
Cambert Way SE9	CH45	68
Camberwell Church St. SE5	BZ44	67
Camberwell Glebe SE5	BZ44	67
Camberwell Grn. SE5	BZ44	67
Camberwell Gro. SE5	BZ44	67
Camberwell La. Sev.	CQ69	116
Camberell New Rd. SE5	BY43	66
Camberwell Pass. SE5	BZ44	67
Camberwell Rd.		
Camberwell Rd. SE5	BZ43	67
Camberwell Sta. Rd. SE5	BZ44	67
Cambeys Rd. Dag.	CR35	50
Camborne Av. W13	BJ41	64
Camborne Av. Rom.	CV29	42
Camborne Clo. Houns.	AZ45	63
Camborne Rd. S.		
Camborne Mews W11	BR39	55
St. Mark's Rd.		
Camborne Rd. SW18	BS47	76
Camborne Rd. Croy.	CB54	87
Camborne Rd. Houns.	AZ45	63
Camborne Rd. Mord.	BQ53	85
Camborne Rd. N. Houns.	AZ45	63
Camborne Rd.		
Camborne Rd. Sid.	CP48	79
Camborne Rd. Sutt.	BS57	95
Camborne Rd. Well.	CN44	68
Camborne Rd. S. Houns.	AZ45	63
Camborne Rd.		
Camborne Wk. Rich.	BK46	74
Petersham Rd.		
Camborne Way Houns.	BF44	64
Camborne Way, Houns.	AZ45	63
Camborne Rd. S.		
Camborne Way, Rom.	CW29	42
Cambourne Av. N9	CC26	39
Cambourne Dri. Hem. H.	AY11	8
Cambray Rd. SW12	BW47	76
Cambray Rd. Orp.	CN54	88
Cambria Clo. Houns.	BF45	64
Cambria Clo. Sid.	CM47	78
Cambria Ct. Felt.	BC47	73
Cambria Cres. Grav.	DJ49	81
Cambrian Av. Ilf.	CN32	49
Cambrian Clo. SE27	BY48	76
Cambrian Gro. Grav.	DG47	81
Cambrian Rd. E10	CE33	48
Cambrian Rd. Rich.	BL46	75
Cambrian Way, Hem. H.	AY12	8
Cambria Rd. SE5	BZ45	67
Cambria St. SW6	BS43	66
Cambridge Av. NW6	BS37	56
Cambridge Av. Grnf.	BH35	45
Cambridge Av. N. Mal.	BO52	85
Cambridge Av. Rom.	CV30	42
Cambridge Av. Well.	CN45	68
Cambridge Clo. SW20	BP51	85
Cambridge Clo. Houns.	BE45	64
Cambridge Clo. Wal. Cr.	CC18	21
Cambridge Clo. Wok.	AP62	100
Cambridge Clo. West Dr.	AX43	63
Cambridge Cotts. Rich.	BM43	65
Cambridge Cres. E2	CB37	57
Cambridge Cres. Tedd.	BJ49	74
Cambridge Cres. Wat.	BD24	27
Cambridge Dr. SE12	CH46	78
Cambridge Dr. Ilf.	CN33	49
Cambridge Dr. Pot. B.	BQ19	19
Cambridge Dr. Ruis.	BD34	45
Cambridge Gdns. N13	BY28	38
Cambridge Gdns. N17	BZ29	39
Great Cambridge Rd.		
Cambridge Gdns. N21	BZ26	39
Cambridge Gdns. NW6	BS37	56
Cambridge Gdns. W10	BQ39	55
Cambridge Gdns. Enf.	CB23	30
Cambridge Gdns. Grays.	DG42	71
Cambridge Gdns. Kings. on T.	BM51	85
Cambridge Gate NW1	**BV38**	**1**
Cambridge Gate NW1	BV38	56
Cambridge Gate SE17	BZ43	67
Walworth Rd.		
Cambridge Gate Ms. NW1	**BV38**	**1**
Cambridge Gate Ms. NW1	BV38	56
Albany St.		
Cambridge Grn. N9	CA26	39
Cambridge Grn. SE9	CL47	78
Cambridge Gro. SE20	CB51	87
Cambridge Gro. W6	BP42	65
Cambridge Gro. Rd. Kings. on T.	BM52	85
Cambridge Hth Rd. E1	CB39	57
Cambridge Hth Rd. E2	CB39	57
Cambridge Ho. Wind.	AO44	61
Ward Royal		
Cambridge Ms. SW11	BU44	66
Cambridge Pde. Enf.	CB23	30
Cambridge Pk. E11	CH33	49
Cambridge Pk. Twick.	BK46	74
Cambridge Pk. Est. Twick.	BK46	74
Cambridge Pk. Rd. E11	CG33	49
Cambridge Pl. NW6	BS37	56
Cambridge Pl. W8	**BS41**	**3**
Cambridge Pl. W8	BS41	66
Cambridge Pl. W9	BS38	56
Cambridge Rd. E4	CF26	39
Cambridge Rd. E11	CG32	49
Cambridge Rd. NW6	BS38	56
Cambridge Rd. NW11	BF32	45
Cambridge Rd. SE20	CB52	87
Cambridge Rd. SW11	BU44	66
Cambridge Rd. SW13	BO44	65
Cambridge Rd. SW20	BP51	85
Cambridge Rd. W7	BH41	64

Cambridge Rd. Ashf. BA50 73
Cambridge Rd. Bark. CM36 58
Cambridge Rd. Brom. CH50 78
Cambridge Rd. Cars. BU57 95
Cambridge Rd. Hamptn. BE50 74
Cambridge Rd. Houns. BE45 64
Cambridge Rd. Ilf. CN33 49
Cambridge Rd. Kings. on T. BL51 85
Cambridge Rd. Mitch. BV52 86
Cambridge Rd. N. Mal. BN52 85
Cambridge Rd. Pnr. BE31 45
Cambridge Rd. Rich. BM43 65
Cambridge Rd. St. Alb. BJ14 9
Cambridge Rd. Saw. CQ5 6
Cambridge Rd. Sid. CN49 78
Cambridge Rd. Sthl. BE40 54
Cambridge Rd. Tedd. BH49 74
Cambridge Rd. Twick. BK46 74
Cambridge Rd. Uxb. AX36 53
Cambridge Rd. Walt. BC53 83
Cambridge Rd. Wat. BD24 27
Cambridge Rd. N. W4 BM42 65
Cambridge Rd. S. W4 BM42 65
Cambridge Row SE18 CL42 68
Cambridge Sq. W2 BU39 1
Cambridge Sq. W2 BU39 56
Cambridge St. SW1 BV42 3
Cambridge St. SW1 BV42 66
Cambridge Ter. N9 CA26 39
Bury St. W.
Cambridge Ter. N13 BY28 38
Cambridge Ter. NW1 BV38 1
Cambridge Ter. Ms. NW1 BV38 1
Cambridge Ter. NW1 BV38 56
Outer Circle
Cambridge Ter. Berk. AR13 7
Cambridge Ter. Ms. NW1 BV38 56
Albany St.
Cambridge Yd. W7 BH40 54
Cambus Rd. E16 CH39 58
Camdale Rd. SE18 CN43 68
Camden Av. Felt. BD48 74
Camden Av. Hayes. BD40 54
Camden Clo. SW19 BR48 75
Victoria Drive
Camden Clo. Chis. CM51 88
Camden Clo. Grays. DG42 71
Camden Gdns. Sutt. BS56 95
Camden Gdns. Th. Hth. BY52 86
Canden Gro. Chis. CL50 78
Camden High St. NW1 BV36 56
Camden High St. NW1 BV37 1
Camden Hill Rd. SE19 CA50 77
Camdenhurst St. E14 CD39 57
Camden Ms. N7 BW36 56
Murray St.
Camden Pk. Rd. NW1 BW36 56
Camden Pk. Rd. Chis. CK50 78
Camden Pass. N1 BY37 2
Camden Pass. N1 BY37 56
Camden Rd. E11 CH32 49
Camden Rd. E17 CD32 48
Camden Rd. N7 BW36 56
Camden Rd. NW1 BV37 1
Camden Rd. NW1 BW36 56
Camden Rd. Bex. CQ47 79
Camden Rd. Cars. BU56 95
Camden Rd. Sev. CU64 107
Camden Rd. Sutt. BS56 95
Camden Row SE3 CG44 68
Camden Sq. NW1 BW36 56
Camden Square SE15 CA44 67
Sumner Estate
Camden St. NW1 BV36
Camden St. NW1 BW36 56
Camden Ter. NW1 BW36 56
N. Villas
Camden Wk. N1 BY37 2
Camden Wk. N1 BY37 56
Camden Way, Chis. CK50 78
Camden Way Th. Hth. BY52 86
Camelford Wk. W11 BQ40 55
Lancaster Road
Camelia Pl. Twick. BF47 74
Camellia St. SW8 CD43 67
Camelot Clo. SW19 BR49 75
Camelot Clo. West CJ61 106
Camelot St. SE15 CB43 67
Camel Rd. E16 CJ40 58
Drew Rd.
Camera Pl. SW10 BT43 66
Cameron Clo. N20 BT27 38
Cameron Clo. N18 CB28 39
Cameron Clo. Bex. CS48 79
Cameron Clo. Brwd. DB28 42
Cameron Dr. Wal. Cr. CC20 21
Cameron Rd. SE6 CD48 77
Cameron Rd. Brom. CH53 88
Cameron Rd. Chesh. AO18 16
Cameron Rd. Croy. BY53 86
Cameron Rd. Ilf. CN33 49
Cameron St. E6 CL40 58
Camerton Clo. E8 CA36 57
Rhodes Dev.
Camfield, Welw. G.C. BR10 5
Cam Grn. S. Ock. DA39 60
Camilla Clo. Lthd. BF66 111
Pine Dene
Camilla Dr. Dor. BJ68 111
Camilla Rd. SE16 CB42 67
Camlan Rd. Brom. CG49 78
Camlet St. E2 CA38 2
Camlet St. E2 CA38 57
Camlet Way Barn. BS23 29
Camlet Way, St. Alb. BF13 9
Camley St. NW1 BW37 56
Camm Av. Wind. AM45 61
Camley St. NW1 BW37 1
Camm Gdns. Surb. BH54 84
Camomile Av. Mitch. BU51 86
Camomile St. EC3 CA39 2
Camomile St. EC3 CA39 57
Campana Rd. SW6 BS44 66
Campbell Av. Ilf. CL31 49
Campbell Av. Wok. AS64 100
Campbell Blds. SE1 BY41 4
Campbell Cl. Rom. CT29 41
Campbell Clo. Hav. CT29 41
Havering Rd.
Campbell Clo. Ruis. BC32 44
Campbell Clo. Twick. BG47 74
Campbell Ct. NW9 BN32 46
Campbell Croft Edg. BM28 37
Campbell Est. SE18 CK44 68
Campbell Rd. E3 CE38 57
Campbell Rd. E6 CK37 58
Campbell Rd. E17 CD31 48
Campbell Rd. N17 CA30 39
Campbell Rd. W7 BH40 54
Campbell Rd. Cat. BZ64 105
Campbell Rd. Croy. BY54 86
Campbell Rd. E. Mol. BH52 84
Campbell Rd. Grav. DF47 81
Campbell Rd. Twick. BG47 74
Campbell Rd. Wey. AZ57 92
Campdale Rd. N7 BW34 47
Campden Cres. Dag. CO35 50
Campden Cres. Wem. BJ34 45
Campden Gdns. W8 BS40 56
Campden Gro. W8 BS41 66
Campden Hill W8 BS41 66
Campden Hill Gdns. W8 BS40 56
Campden Hill Pl. W8 BR40 55
Campden Hill Rd. W8 BS40 56
Campden Hill Sq. W8 BR40 55
Campden Ho. Clo. W8 BS41 66
Hornton St.
Campden Pl. W8 BR40 55
Campden Rd. Sth. Croy. CA56 96
Campden Rd. Uxb. AY34 44
Campden St. W8 BS40 56
Campen Cl. SW19 BR48 75
Queensmere Rd.
Camp End Rd. Wey. BA59 92
Camperdown St. E1 CA39 2
Camperdown St. E1 CA39 57
Leman St.
Campfield Rd. SE9 CJ47 78
Campfield Rd. St. Alb. BJ13 9
Campfield Walk SW19 BT51 86
Brangwyn Cres.
Camphill Ct. Wey. AW59 92
Camphill Rd. Wey. AW59 92
Campion Clo. Uxb. AY39 53
Campion Ho. Islw. BG43 64
Campion Rd. SW15 BQ44 65
Campion Rd. Islw. BH44 64
Campions, Loug. CL22 31
Campions Epp. CO17 23
Campion Ter. NW2 BQ34 46
Cample Ca. S. Ock. DA40 60
Camplin Rd. Har. BL32 46
Camplin St. SE14 CC43 67
Campon Bldgs. W8 BS40 56
Camp Rd. SW19 BP49 75
Camp Rd. Cat. CD64 105
Camp Rd. Ger. Cr. AR32 43
Camp Rd. St. Alb. BH13 9
Campsbourne Rd. N8 BX31 47
Campsbourne The N8 BX31 47
Rectory Gdns.
Campsey Gdns. Dag. CO36 59
Campsey Rd. Dag. CO36 59
Campsfield Rd. N8 BX31 47
Campshill Pl. SE13 CF46 77
Campshill Pl. SE13 CF46 77
Campshill Rd.
Campshill Rd. SE13 CF46 77
Campus Rd. E17 CD32 48
Campus, The Welw. G. C. BQ7 5
Camp Vw. SW19 BP49 75
Camp View Rd. St. Alb. BJ14 9
Cam Rd. E15 CF37 57
Camrose Av. Edg. BL30 37
Camrose Av. Erith. CR43 69
Camrose Av. Felt. BC49 73
Camrose Clo. Mord. BS52 86
Camrose St. SE2 CO42 69
Cam Ter. Chis. CL50 78
Mill Pl.
Canada Av. N18 BZ29 39
Canada Cres. W3 BN38 55
Canada Farm Rd. S. Dnth. DA52 90
Canada La. Brox. CD16 21
Canada Rd. W3 BN39 55
Canada Rd. Cob. BD60 93
Canada Rd. Slou. AQ41 62
Canada Rd. Wey. AX59 92
Canada Way W12 BP40 55
Canadian Av. SE6 CE47 77
Canal Gro. SE15 CB43 67
Canal Head SE15 CB44 67
Peckham High St.
Canal Rd. E3 CD38 57
Canal Rd. Grav. DH46 81
Canal St. SE5 BZ43 67
Canal Wk. N1 BZ37 57
Canal Wk. SE26 CC49 77
Venner Rd.
Canal Way NW1 BW36 56
Baynes St.
Canberra Clo. Dag. CS36 59
Canberra Clo. Horn. CV35 51
Canberra Clo. St. Alb. BH11 9
Canberra Cres. Dag. CS36 59
Canberra Dr. Hayes. BD38 54
Canberra Rd. E6 CK37 58
Barking Rd.
Canberra Rd. SE7 CJ43 68
Canberra Rd. Bexh. CP43 69
Canberra Rd. Houns. AZ45 63
Canberra Sq. Til. DG44 71
Canbury Av. Kings. on T. BL51 85
Canbury Ms. SE26 CB48 77
Wells Pk. Rd.
Canbury Pk. Rd.
Kings. on T. BL51 85
Canbury Pass, Kings. on T. BK51 84
Canbury Path Orp. CO52 89
Canbury Pl. Kings. on T. BL51 85
Canbury Pass
Cancell Rd. SW9 BY44 66
Candahar Rd. SW11 BU44 66
Cander Way, S. Ock. DA40 60
Candlefield Clo. Hem. H. AZ15 8
Candlefield Rd. Hem. H. AZ15 8
Candlefield Wk. Hem. H. AZ15 8
Candler St. N15 BZ32 48
Candover Clo. West Dr. AX43 63
Candover Rd. Horn. CU33 50
Candover St. W1 BW39 1
Candover St. W1 BW39 56
Foley St.
Candy Croft. Lthd. BF66 111
Candy St. E3 CD37 57
Caneland Ct. Wal. Abb. CG20 22
Shernbroke Rd.
Canes La. Harl. CP13 14
Canfield Clo. Rain. CT37 59
Canfield Dr. Ruis. BC35 44
Canfield Gdns. NW6 BS36 56
Canfield Pl. NW6 BT36 56
Canfield Rd. Wdf. Grn. CK29 40
Canford Av. Nthlt. BE37 54
Canford Clo. Enf. BY23 29
Canford Dr. Wey. AW55 83
Canford Gdns. N. Mal. BN53 85
Canford Rd. SW11 BV45 66
Canham Rd. SE25 CA52 87
Canham Rd. W3 BO41 65
Canmore Gdns. SW16 BW50 76
Cannhall Rd. E11 CG35 49
Cann Hatch Tad. BR62 103
Canning Cres. N22 BX30 38
Canning Cross SE5 CC44 67
Grove La.
Canning Ms. W8 BT41 3
Canning Pass. W8 BT41 3
Canning Pass. W8 BT41 66
Victoria Rd.
Canning Pla. Ms. W8 BT41 66
Canning Pla.
Canning Pl. W8 BT41 3
Canning Pl. W8 BT41 66
Canning Rd. E15 CG37 58
Canning Rd. E17 CD31 48
Canning Rd. N5 BY34 47
Canning Rd. Croy. CA55 87
Canning Rd. Har. BH31 45
Cannington Rd. Dag. CP36 59
Cannizaro Rd. SW19 BQ50 75
Cannonbury Av. Pnr. BD32 45
Cannon Clo. SW20 BQ52 85
Cannon Clo. Hamptn. BF50 74
Cannon Cres. Wok. AP59 91
Cannon Gro. Lthd. BH64 102
Cannon Hill N14 BX27 38
Cannon Hill NW6 BS35 47
Cannon Hill, Maid. AG41 61
Cannon Hill Clo. Maid. AH42 61
Cannon Hill La. SW20 BQ53 85
Cannon Hill La. SW20 BR51 85
Cannon Hill La. SW20 BR52 85
Cannon La. NW3 BT34 47
Cannon La. Pnr. BE32 45
Cannon Mill Ave. Chesh. AP20 16
Cannon Pl. NW3 BT34 47
Cannon Pl. SE7 CK42 68
Maryon Rd.
Cannon Rd. N14 BX27 38
Cannon Rd. Bexh. CQ44 69
Cannon Rd. Wat. BD25 27
Cannon Row SW1 BX41 4
Cannon Row SW1 BX41 66
Bridge St.
Cannon St. EC4 BZ39 2
Cannon St. Rd. E1 CB39 57
Cannons Corner Edg. BL28 37
Cannon Side, Lthd. BH64 102
Cannons Lane, Ong. CZ14 15
Cannons Md. Brwd. DA20 24
Cannons Meadow, Welw. BU6 5
Cannon St. EC4 BZ39 57
Cannon St. St. Alb. BG13 9
Cannon Way E. Mol. BF52 84
Cannon Way, Lthd. BH64 102
Canon Av. Rom. CP32 50
Canon Beck Rd. SE16 CC41 67
Canonbie Rd. SE23 CC47 77
Canonbury Av. N1 BY36 56
Canonbury Rd.
Canonbury Gro. N1 BZ36 57
Canonbury Pk. S. N1 BZ36 57
Canonbury La. N1 BY36 56
Canonbury Pk. N. N1 BZ36 57
Canonbury Pl. N1 BY36 56
Canonbury Rd. N1 BY36 56
Canonbury Rd. Enf. CA23 30
Canonbury Sq. N1 BY36 56
Canonbury St. N1 BZ36 57
Canonbury Vill. N1 BY36 56
Canon Ct. Edg. BL29 37
Canon Murnane Rd. SE1 CA41 67
Canon Pk. Est. Stan. BK28 36
Canon Rd. Brom. CJ52 88
Canons Brook, Harl. CL11 13
Canons Clo. N2 BT33 47
Canons Clo. Edg. BL29 37
Canons Clo. Rad. BJ21 27
Canons Dr. Edg. BL29 37
Canons Gate, Harl. CL10 6
Canons Hatch, Tad. BR62 103
Canons Hill Couls. BY62 104
Canons La. Tad. BR62 103
Canonsleigh Rd. Dag. CO36 59
Canons Pk. Par. Edg. BL29 37
Canon St. N1 BZ37 2
Canon St. N1 BZ37 57
Prebend St.
Canon's Wk. Croy. CC55 87
Canopus Way Nthwd. BC28 35
Canopus Way, Stai. AY47 73
Canrobert St. E2 CB37 57
Canrobert St. E2 CB38 57
Cantelones Rd. BW36 56
Catnerbury Av. Ilf CK33 49
Canterbury Av. Sid. CO48 79
Canterbury Av. Slou. AO38 52
Canterbury Av. Upmin. CZ34 51
Canterbury Clo. Amer. AP23 25
Canterbury Clo. Beck. CE51 87
Tyler Rd.
Canterbury Clo. Brom. CE51 87
The Avenue
Canterbury Clo. Dart. CX47 80
Canterbury Clo. Grnf. BF39 54
Canterbury Cres. SW9 BY45 66
Canterbury Gro. SE27 BY49 76
Canterbury Par. S. Ock. DB38 60
Canterbury Rd. E10 CF33 48
Canterbury Rd. NW6 BR37 55
Canterbury Rd. Borwd. BM23 28
Canterbury Rd. Croy. BX54 86
Canterbury Rd. Felt. BE48 74
Canterbury Rd. Grav. DH48 81
Canterbury Rd. Guil. AP69 118
Canterbury Rd. Har. BF32 45
Canterbury Rd. Mord. BS54 86
Canterbury Rd. Wat. BC23 26
Canterbury Ter. NW6 BS37 56
Canterbury Way, Rick. BA24 26
Cantley Gdns. SE19 CA51 87
Cantley Gdns. Ilf. CM32 49
Cantley Rd. W7 BJ41 64
Canton St. E14 CE39 57
Cantrell Rd. E3 CD38 57
Cantwell Rd. SE18 CL43 68
Canute Gdns. SE16 CC42 67
Canvey St. SE1 BZ40 57
Zoar St.
Cape Clo. Bark. CL36 58
Harts La.
Capel Av. Wall. BX56 95
Capel Clo. N20 BT27 38
Capel Clo. Brom. CK54 88
Capel Ct. EC2 BZ39 2
Capel Ct. EC2 BZ39 57
Bartholomew La.
Capel Gdns. Ilf. CN35 49
Capel Gdns. Pnr. BE31 45
Capella Rd. Nthwd. BB28 35
Capell Ave. Rick. AU25 25
Capell Rd. Rick. AU25 25
Capel Way, Rick. AU25 25
Capel Pl. Dart. CV49 80
Capel Rd. E7 CH35 49
Capel Rd. Barn. BU26 38
Capel Rd. Wat. BD25 27
Capel Vere Wk. Wat. BB23 26
Capener's Clo. SW1 BV41 66
Kinnerton St.
Caperne Rd. SW18 BT47 76
Cargill Rd.
Cape Rd. N17 CB31 48
Cape Rd. Enf. CB21 30
Cape Rd. St. Alb. BJ13 9
Capital Ho. SE6 CE46 77
Capland St. NW8 BT38 1
Capland St. NW8 BT38 56
Caple Rd. NW10 BO37 55
Capon Clo. Brwd. DA26 42
Caponfield. Welw. G. C. BS9 5
Capper St. WC1 BW38 1
Capri Rd. Croy. CA54 87
Capstan Ride Enf. BY23 29
Capstan Sq. E14 CF41 67
Capstone Rd. Brom. CG49 78
Captain Cook Clo.
Ch. St. G. AQ28 34
Captains Wk. Berk. AR13 7
Capthorne Av. Har. BE33 45
Capthorne Ct. Har. BE33 45
Capuchin Clo. Stan. BJ29 36
Templemead Clo.
Capworth St. E10 CE33 48
Caractacus Grn. Wat. BB25 26
Caradoc Clo. W2 BS39 56
Ledbury Rd.
Caradoc St. SE10 CG42 68
Caradon Clo. Wok. AQ62 100
Caradon Way N15 BZ31 48
Caravelle Gdns. Nthlt. BD38 54
Javelin Way
Carberry Rd. SE19 CA50 77
Carbery Av. W3 BL41 65
Carbis Rd. E14 CD39 57
Carbone Hill, Pot. B. BW17 20
Carburton St. W1 BV38 1
Carburton St. W1 BV38 56
Carden Rd. SE15 CB45 67
Cardiff Rd. W7 BJ41 64
Cardiff Rd. Enf. CB24 30
Cardiff Rd. Wat. BC25 26
Cardiff St. SE18 CN43 68
Cardigan Clo. Wok. AP62 100
Cardigan Gdns. Ilf. CO34 50
Cardigan Pl. NW6 BS38 56
Cardigan Rd. E3 CD37 57
Cardigan Rd. SW13 BP44 65
Cardigan Rd. SW19 BT50 76
Cardigan Rd. Rich. BL46 75
Cardigan St. SE11 BY42 4
Cardigan St. SE11 BY42 66
Cardinal Av. Borwd. BM54 85
Cardinal Av. Kings. on T. BL49 75
Cardinal Av. Mord. BR53 85
Cardinal Bourne St. SE1 BZ41 4
Cardinal Bourne St. SE1 BZ41 67
Burge St.
Cardinal Clo. Chis. CM50 78
Cardinal Clo. Mord. BR53 85
Cardinal Cres. N. Mal. BN51 85
Cardinal Dr. Ilf. CM29 40
Cardinal Dr. Walt. BD54 84
Cardinale Way N19 BW33 47
Cardinal Gro. St. Alb. BF14 9
Cardinal Pl. SW15 BQ45 65
Cardinal Rd. Felt. BC47 73
Cardinal Rd. Ruis. BD33 45
Cardinal's Wk. Hmptn. BG50 74
Cardinals Wk. Sun. BB50 73
Seymour Way
Cardinal Way, Rain. CV37 60
Cardington Sq. Houns. BD45 64
Cardington St. NW1 BW38 1
Cardington St. NW1 BW38 56
Cardozo Rd. N7 BX35 47
Cardrew Av. N12 BT28 38
Cardrew Clo. N12 BT28 38
Cardross St. W6 BP41 65
Cardwell Rd. N7 BX35 47
Cardwell Rd. SE18 CL42 68
Cardy Rd. Hem. H. AW13 8
Carew Clo. Couls. BZ63 105
Carew Rd. N17 CB30 39
Carew Rd. W13 BK41 64
Carew Rd. Ashf. BA50 73
Carew Rd. Mitch. BV51 86
Carew Rd. Nthwd. BB29 35
Carew Rd. Th. Hth. BY52 86
Carew Rd. Wall. BW57 95
Carew St. SE5 BZ44 67
Carey Clo. Wind. AN45 61
Carey Gdns. SW8 BW44 66
Stewarts Rd.
Carey Gdns. SW8 BW44 66
Thessaly Rd.
Carey La. EC2 BZ39 2
Carey La. EC2 BZ39 57
Gutter La.
Carey Pl. Wat. BD24 27
Clifford St.
Carey Rd. Dag. CQ35 50
Carey St. WC2 BX39 2
Carey St. WC2 BX39 56
Carfax Rd. Hayes BB42 63
Carfax Rd. Horn. CT35 50
Carfax Sq. SW4 BW45 66
Clapham Pk. Rd.
Cargill Rd. SW18 BS47 76
Cargreen Rd. SE25 CA52 87
Carholme Rd. SE23 CD47 77
Carisbrook Av. Wat. BD23 27
Carisbrook Clo. Stan. BK30 36
Carisbrooke Av. Bex. CP47 79
Carisbrooke Clo. Enf. CA23 30
Carisbrooke Clo. Horn. CX33 51
Carisbrooke Gdns. SE15 CA43 67
Rosemary Rd.
Carisbrooke Rd. E17 CD31 48
Carisbrooke Rd. Brom. CJ52 88
Carisbrooke Rd. Mitch. BW52 86
Carisbrooke Rd. St. Alb. BF16 18
Carl Clo. Upmin. CX34 51
Carleton Av. Wall. BW57 95
Carleton Clo. Esher BG54 84
Carleton Pl. Hort. K. CY52 90
Carleton Rd. N7 BW35 47
Carleton Rd. Wal. Cr. CC17 21
Carlile Clo. E3 CD37 57
Carlingford Gdns. Mitch. BV50 76
Carlingford Rd. N15 BY31 47
Carlingford Rd. NW3 BT35 47
Carlingford Rd. Mord. BQ53 85
Carlisle Av. EC3 CA39 2
Carlisle Av. EC3 CA39 57
Carlisle Av. W3 BO39 55
Carlisle Av. St. Alb. BG12 9
Carlisle Clo. Kings. on T. BM51 85
Carlisle Gdns. Har. BK33 45
Carlisle Gdns. Ilf. CK32 49
Carlisle La. SE1 BX41 4
Carlisle La. SE1 BX41 66
Carlisle Mews, Kings. on T. BM51 85
Carlisle Clo.
Carlisle Pl. N11 BV28 38
Carlisle Pl. N12 BV28 38
Oakleigh Rd.
Carlisle Pl. SW1 BW41 3
Carlisle Pl. SW1 BW41 66
Carlisle Rd. E10 CE33 48
Carlisle Rd. N4 BY33 47
Scarborough Rd.
Carlisle Rd. NW6 BR37 55
Carlisle Rd. NW9 BN31 46
Carlisle Rd. Dart. CX46 80
Carlisle Rd. Hmptn. BF50 74
Carlisle Rd. Rom. CU32 50
Carlisle Rd. Slou. AO40 52
Carlisle Rd. Sutt. BR57 94
Carlisle St. W1 BW39 1
Carlisle St. W1 BW39 56
Soho Sq.
Carlisle Walk, E8 CA36 57
Rhodes Dev.
Carlos Pl. W1 BV40 3
Carlos Pl. W1 BV40 56
Carlow St. NW1 BW37 56
Carlton Ave. Green. CZ46 80
Carlton Ave. Hayes BB42 63
Carlton Av. N14 BW25 29
Carlton Av. Felt. BD46 74
Carlton Av. Har. BJ32 45
Carlton Av. Sth. Croy. BZ57 96
Carlton Av. E. Wem. BK34 45
Carlton Av. W. Wem. BJ34 45
Carlton Clo. Borwd. BN24 28
Carlton Clo. Chess. BL57 94
Carlton Clo. Edg. BM28 37
Carlton Clo. Grays DF41 71
Carlton Clo. Wok. AT60 91
Carlton Ct. NW6 BS37 56
Carlton Cres. Sutt. BR56 94
Carlton Dr. SW15 BQ46 75
Carlton Dr. Ilf. CM31 49
Carlton Gdns. SW1 BW40 3
Carlton Gdns. SW1 BW40 56
Carlton Gdns. W5 BK39 54
Carlton Grn. Red. BU69 121
Carlton Gro. SE15 CB44 67
Carlton Hl. NW8 BS37 1
Carlton Hl. NW8 BS37 56
Carlton House Ter. SW1 BW40 3
Carlton Ho. Ter. SW1 BW40 56
Carlton Ms. SW1 BW40 3
Carlton Pde. Orp. CO54 89
Carlton Pk. Sev. CV64 108
Carlton Pk. Av. SW20 BQ51 85
Carlton Rd. E11 CG33 49
Carlton Rd. E12 CJ35 49
Carlton Rd. E17 CD30 39
Carlton Rd. N4 BY33 47
Carlton Rd. N11 BV28 38
Carlton Rd. N15 CA31 48
Carlton Rd. SW14 BN45 65
Carlton Rd. W4 BN41 65
Carlton Rd. W5 BK40 54
Carlton Rd. Dart. CW47 80

Carlton Rd. Dart. CX47 80
Carlton Rd. Erith. CR43 69
Carlton Rd. Grays DF41 71
Carlton Rd. N. Mal. BO51 85
Carlton Rd. Reig. & Red. BT69 121
Carlton Rd. Rom. CT32 50
Carlton Rd. Sid. CN49 78
Carlton Rd. Slou. AQ40 52
Carlton Rd. Sth. Croy. BZ57 96
Carlton Rd. Sun. BC50 73
Carlton Rd. Walt. BC54 83
Carlton Rd. Well. CO45 69
Carlton Rd. Wok. AT60 91
Carlton Sq. E1 CC38 57
Carlton St. SW1 BW40 3
Carlton St. SW1 BW40 56
Regent St.
Carlton Ter. E7 CJ36 58
Carlton Ter. E11 CH32 49
Carlton Ter. N18 BZ27 39
Carlton Ter. SE26 CC48 77
Carlton Vale NW6 BS38 56
Carlwell St. SW17 BU49 76
Carlyle Av. NW10 BN37 55
Carlyle Av. Brom. CJ52 88
Carlyle Av. Sthl. BE40 54
Carlyle Clo. N2 BT32 47
Carlyle Clo. NW10 BN37 55
Carlyle Clo. E. Mol. BG51 84
Carlyle Gdns. Sthl. BE40 54
Carlyle Rd. E12 CK35 49
Carlyle Rd. SE28 CO40 59
Carlyle Rd. W5 BK42 64
Carlyle Rd. Croy. CB55 87
Carlyle Rd. Stai. AV50 72
Carlyle Rd. Stai. AW50 73
Carlyle Sq. SW3 BT42 3
Carlyle Rd. SW3 BT42 66
Carlyon Av. Har. BE35 45
Carlyon Av. Wok. AS62 100
Carlyon Clo. Wem. BL37 55
Carlyon Clo. Wok. AS62 100
Carlyon Rd. Hayes. BD39 54
Carlyon Rd. Wem. BL37 55
Carmalt Gdns. SW15 BQ45 65
Carmalt Gdns. Walt. BD56 93
Carmarthen Rd. Slou. AP40 52
Carmelite Clo. Har. BG30 36
Carmelite Rd. Har. BG30 36
Carmelite St. EC4 BY40 4
Carmelite St. EC4 BY40 56
Carmelite Wk. Har. BG30 36
Carmelite Way Har. BG30 36
Carmelite Way Hart. DC53 90
Carmen St. E14 CE39 57
Carmichael Rd. SE25 CA53 87
Carminia Rd. SW17 BV48 76
Carnaby Rd. Brox. CD13 12
Carnaby St. W1 BW39 1
Carnaby St. W1 BW39 56
Carnach Grn. S. Ock. DA40 60
Carnac St. SE27 BZ48 77
Carnanton Rd. E17 CF30 39
Carnarvon Av. Enf. CA24 30
Carnarvon Dr. Hayes. BA42 63
Carnarvon Rd. E10 CF32 48
Carnarvon Rd. E15 CG36 58
Carnarvon Rd. E18 CG30 40
Carnarvon Rd. Barn. BR24 28
Carnation St. SE2 CO42 69
Carnbrook Rd. SE3 CJ45 68
Carnecke Gdns. SE9 CK46 78
Carnegie Pl. SW19 BQ48 75
Carnegie Rd. St. Alb. BG11 9
Carnegie St. N1 BX37 2
Carnegie St. N1 BX37 56
Carnfield Dr. NW9 BO29 37
Carnforth Clo. Epsom. BM57 94
Carnforth Gdns. Horn. CU35 50
Carnforth Rd. SW16 BW50 76
Carnoustie Dr. N1 BX36 2
Carnoustie Dr. N1 BX36 56
Carnwath Rd. SW6 BS45 66
Carolina Rd. Th. Hth. BY51 86
Caroline Clo. Croy. CA56 96
Brownlow Rd.
Caroline Clo. West Dr. AX41 63
Caroline Ct. Ashf. AZ50 73
Caroline Ct. Stan. BJ29 36
Chase, The
Caroline Gdns. SE15 CB43 67
Caroline Pl. W2 BS40 3
Caroline Pl. W2 BS40 56
Caroline Pl. Wat. BD25 27
Caroline Pl. Ms. W2 BS40 56
Orme La.
Caroline Rd. SW19 BR50 75
Caroline St. E1 CC39 57
Caroline Ter. SW1 BV42 3
Caroline Ter. SW1 BV42 66
Carol St. NW1 BW37 1
Carol St. NW1 BW37 56
Carolyn Clo. Wok. AP63 100
Carolyn Dr. Orp. CO55 89
Caroon Dr. Rick. AW21 26
Car Pk. Hem. H. AX13 8
Carpenders Av. Wat. BE27 36
Carpenter Gdns. N21 BY27 38
Carpenter Path, Brwd. DE25 122
Carpenters Arms La. Epp. CO16 23
Carpenters Cl. SW1 BU41 3
Carpenters Ct. Twick. BH48 74
Hampton Rd.
Carpenters Pl. SW4 BW45 66
Carpenters Rd. E15 CE36 57
Carpenters Rd. Enf. CC21 30
Carpenter St. W1 BV40 3
Carpenters Way, Pot. B. BT20 20
Carpenters Wood Dr. Rick. AT24 25
Carrara Wk. SW9 BY45 66
Somerleyton Rd. Dev.
Carriage Rd, The SW7 BT41 3
Carriage, The Rd. SW7 BT41 66
Carriageway, The Sev. CP65 107
Carrick Dr. Sev. CU65 107
Carrick Gdns. N17 BZ30 39
Flexmere Rd.
Carrington Av. Borwd. BM25 28
Carrington Av. Houns. BF46 74
Carrington Clo. Borwd. BN25 28
Carrington Ho. SE8 CE44 67
Carrington Rd. Dart. CW46 80
Carrington Rd. Rich. BM45 65
Carrington Rd. Slou. AP40 52
Carrington St. W1 BV40 3
Carrington St. W1 BV40 56
Carrol Clo. NW5 BV35 47
Highgate Rd.
Carroll Av. Guil. AT70 118
Carroll Cld. E15 CG35 49
Carroll Clo. E15 CG35 49
Ash Rd.
Carroll Hill Loug. CK24 31
Carrol Pl. NW5 BV35 47
Carron Clo. E14 CE39 57
Carroun Rd. SW8 BX43 66
Carrow Rd. Dag. CO36 59
Carr Rd. E17 CD30 39
Carr Rd. Nthlt. BF36 54
Carrs La. N21 BZ25 30
Carr St. E14 CD39 57
Carshalton Gro. Sutt. BT56 95
Carshalton Pk. Rd. Cars. BU56 95
Carshalton Pk. Rd. Cars. BU57 95
Carshalton Pl. Cars. BV56 95
Carshalton Rd. Bans. BU60 95
Carshalton Rd. Mitch. BV52 86
Carshalton Rd. Sutt. BT56 95
Carshalton Rd. W. Sutt. BS56 95
Carsington Gdns. Dart. CV48 80
Carslake Rd. SW15 BQ46 75
Carson Rd. E16 CH38 58
Carson Rd. SE21 BZ47 77
Carson Rd. Barn. BU24 29
Carstairs Rd. SE6 CF48 77
Carston Clo. SE12 CG46 78
Carston Ms. SE12 CG46 78
Carswell Clo. Brwd. DE25 122
Carswell Rd. SE6 CF47 77
Carter Clo. Rom. CR29 41
Carter Clo. Wall. BW57 95
Carter Clo. Wind. AN44 61
Carter Ct. EC4 BY39 56
Carter La.
Carter Dr. Rom. CR29 41
Carteret St. SW1 BW41 3
Carteret St. SW1 BW41 66
Carterhatch La. Enf. CA22 30
Carterhatch La. Enf. CA23 30
Caterhatch Rd. Enf. CC23 30
Carter La. EC4 BY39 2
Carter La. EC4 BY39 56
Carter Pl. SE17 BZ42 4
Carter Pl. SE17 BZ42 67
Carter Rd. E13 CH37 58
Carter Rd. SW19 BT50 76
Carters Clo. Loug. CL25 31
Carters Clo. Wor. Pk. BQ55 85
Cartersfield Rd. Wal. Abb. CF21 30
Carter's Hl. Sev. CX67 117
Carter's Hl. SE9 CJ47 78
Carter's Hl. Clo. SE9 CJ47 78
Carters Lane SE23 CD48 77
Carters La. Epp. CL15 13
Carters La. Wok. AU63 100
Carters Mead. Harl. CP12 14
Carters Rd. Epsom. BO61 103
Carter's Row, Grav. DF47 81
Seymour Rd.
Carters Row, Red. BU71 121
Carter St. SE17 BZ43 4
Carter St. SE17 BZ43 67
Carters Yd. SW18 BS46 76
Wandsworth High St.
Carthew Rd. W6 BP41 65
Carthew Vill. W6 BP41 65
Carthouse La. Wok. AP60 91
Carthouse La. Wok. AQ61 100
Carthusian St. EC1 BZ39 2
Carting La. WC2 BX40 4
Carting La. WC2 BX40 56
Cart La. E4 CF26 39
Station Rd.
Cartmel Clo. N18 CB29 39
Cartmel Clo. Red. BU70 121
Cartmell Gdns. Mord. BT53 86
Cartmell Rd. Bexh. CR44 69
Carton St. W1 BU39 1
Carton St. W1 BU39 56
Cartwright Gdns. WC1 BX38 2
Cartwright Gdns. WC1 BX38 56
Cartwright Rd. Dag. CQ36 59
Cartwright St. E1 CA40 4
Cartwright St. E1 CA40 57
Carve Ley, Welw. G.C. BS8 5
Carver Rd. SE24 BZ46 77
Carville Cres. Brent. BL42 65
Carville St. N7 BY34 47
Durham Rd.
Cary Rd. E11 CG35 49
Carysfort Rd. N8 BW32 47
Carysfort Rd. N16 BZ34 48
Cascade Av. N10 BW31 47
Cascade Clo. Orp. CP52 88
Chalk Pit Av.
Cascade Rd. Buck. H. CJ27 40
Cascades Croy. CD58 96
Caselden Clo. Wey. AW56 92
Casella Rd. SE14 CC43 67
Casewick Rd. SE27 BY49 76
Casimir Rd. E5 CC34 48
Casington Way, S. Ock. DA39 60
Casino Av. SE24 BZ46 77
Casket St. E2 CA38 57
Caslon Pl. E1 CB38 57
Cudworth St.
Caslte Rd. Islw. BH44 64
Caspian St. SE5 BZ43 67
Casselden Rd. NW10 BN36 55
Cassidy Rd. SW6 BS43 66
Cassida Rd. SE2 CO42 69
Cassilis Rd. Twick. BJ46 74
Cassiobridge Rd. Wat. BB25 26
Cassiobury Av. Felt. BB46 73
Cassiobury Dr. Wat. BB22 26
Cassiobury Pk. Av. Wat. BB24 26
Cassiobury Rd. E17 CC32 48
Cassio Rd. Wat. BC24 26
Cassland Rd. E9 CC36 57
Cassland Rd. Th. Hth. BZ52 87
Casslee Rd. SE6 CD47 77
Casson St. E1 CB39 2
Casson St. E1 CB39 57
Castalia St. E14 CF41 67
Castellain Rd. W9 BS38 1
Castellain Rd. W9 BS38 56
Castellan Av. Rom. CU31 50
Castello Av. SW15 BQ46 75
Castell Rd. Loug. CM23 31
Castells Meadows, West. CM66 115
Castelnau SW13 BP44 65
Castelnau Est. SW13 BP43 65
Castelnau Pl. SW13 BP43 65
Castelnau Row SW13 BP43 65
Lonsdale Rd.
Casterbridge Rd. SE3 CH45 68
Castile Rd. SE18 CL42 68
Castillon Rd. SE6 CG48 78
Castlands Rd. SE6 CD48 77
Castle Av. Slou. AQ43 62
Castle Av. E4 CF29 39
Castle Av. Epsom. BP58 94
Castle Av. Rain. CT36 59
Castle Av. West Dr. AY40 53
Castlebar Hill W5 BJ39 54
Castlebar Ms. W5 BJ39 54
Castlebar Pk. W5 BK39 54
Castlebar Rd. W5 BK39 54
Castle Baynard St. EC4 BY40 4
Puddle Dock
Castle Clo. E9 CD35 48
Swinnerton St.
Castle Clo. SW19 BQ48 75
Castle Clo. Bush. BF25 27
Castle Clo. Hodd. CF10 12
Castle Clo. Red. BZ70 114
Castle Clo. Reig. BS72 121
Castle Clo. Sun. BB50 73
Millfarm Ave.
Castlecombe Dr. SW19 BQ47 75
Castlecombe Rd. SE9 CK49 78
Castle Ct. EC3 BZ39 57
Birchin Lane
Castledine Rd. SE20 CB50 77
Castle Dr. Ilf. CK32 49
Castle Dr. Reig. BS72 121
Castle Farm Rd. Sev. CT58 98
Castlefield Rd. Reig. BS70 121
Castlefields, Grav. DF51 81
Castleford Av. SE9 CL47 78
Castle Gdns. Dag. CO37 59
Castle Gdns. Dor. BL70 120
Castlegate, Rich. BL45 65
Castle Grn. Wey. BB55 83
Castle Grove Rd. Wok. AP59 91
Castlehaven Rd. NW1 BV36 56
Castle Hill, Berk. AR12 7
Castle Hill, Guil. AR71 118
Castle Hill, Hart. DB53 90
Castle Hill, Wind. AO44 61
Castle Hill Ave. Berk. AR12 7
Castle Hill Av. Croy. CE58 96
Castle Hill Clo. Berk. AR12 7
Castle Hill Rd. Egh. AQ48 72
Castle La. SW1 BW41 3
Castle La. SW1 BW41 66
Castleleigh Ct. Enf. BZ25 30
Castlemaine Av. Epsom BP58 94
Castlemaine Av. Sth. Croy. CA56 96
Castle Mead, Hem. H. AW14 8
Castle Ms. N12 BT28 38
Castlereagh St. W1 BU39 1
Castlereagh St. W1 BU39 56
Castle Rd. N12 BT28 38
Castle Rd. NW1 BV36 56
Castle Rd. Couls. BU63 104
Castle Rd. Dag. CO37 59
Castle Rd. Enf. CD23 30
Castle Rd. Epsom. BM61 103
Castle Rd. Grays DC43 71
Castle Rd. Hodd. CE10 12
Castle Rd. Nthlt. BF36 54
Castle Rd. St. Alb. BJ13 9
Castle Rd. Sev. CU57 98
Castle Rd. Swans. DC46 81
Castle Rd. Wey. BB55 83
Castle Rd. Wok. AS60 91
Castle Sq. Guil. AR71 118
Castle Sq. Red. BZ70 114
Castle St. E6 CJ37 58
Castle St. EC1 BY39 2
Castle St. Berk. AR13 7
Castle St. Green. DA46 80
Castle St. Guil. AR71 118
Castle St. Kings. On T. BL51 85
Castle St. Ong. CX18 24
Castle St. Red. BY70 121
Castle St. Swans. DC46 81
Castleton Av. Bexh. CS44 69
Castleton Av. Erith CS44 69
Castleton Av. Wem. BL35 46
Castleton Clo. Bans. BS61 104
Castleton Dr. Bans. BS60 95
Castleton Rd. E17 CF30 39
Castleton Rd. SE9 CJ49 78
Castleton Rd. Ilf. CO33 50
Castleton Rd. Mitch. BW52 86
Castleton Rd. Ruis. BD33 45
Castletown Rd. W14 BR42 65
Castle Vw. Epsom. BM60 94
Castleview Gdns. Ilf. CK32 49
Castle View Rd. Slou. AR42 62
Castle View Rd. Wey. AZ56 92
Castle Wk. Reig. BS70 121
High St.
Castle Walk, Sun. BD52 83
Elizabeth Gdns.
Castle Way SW19 BQ48 75
Castle Way, Epsom BP58 94
Castle Way, Felt. BD49 74
Castlewood Dr. SE9 CK44 68
Castlewood Rd. N15 CB32 48
Castlewood Rd. N16 CB32 48
Castlewood Rd. Barn. BT24 29
Castle Yd. Rich. BK46 74
Hill St.
Castor St. E14 CE40 57
Caterham Av. Ilf. CK30 40
Caterham By-pass. Cat. CB65 105
Caterham Ct. Wal. Abb. CG20 22
Shernbroke Rd.
Caterham Dr. Couls. BY62 104
Caterham Dr. Couls. BZ63 105
Caterham Rd. SE13 CF45 67
Catesby St. SE17 BZ42 67
Catfield Gro. Felt. BF48 74
Catford Hl. SE6 CD48 77
Catford Rd. SE6 CE47 77
Cathall Rd. E11 CF34 48
Catham Clo. St. Alb. BJ14 9
Cathay St. SE16 CB41 67
Cathay Wk. Nthlt. BF37 54
Leander Rd.
Cathcart Dr. Orp. CN54 88
Cathcart Hl. N19 BW34 47
Cathcart Rd. SW10 BS43 3
Cathcart Rd. SW10 BS43 66
Cathcart St. NW5 BV35 47
Cathedral Clo. Guil. AQ71 118
Cathedral Pl. EC4 BZ39 2
Cathedral Pl. EC4 BY39 56
Newgate St.
Cathedral St. SE1 BZ40 4
Cathedral St. SE1 BZ40 57
Catherall Rd. N5 BZ34 48
Catherine Clo. Brwd. DA25 33
Catherine Clo. Hem. H. AZ11 8
Catherine Clo. Wey. AY60 92
Catherine Ct. N14 BW25 29
Catherine Dr. Sun. BB50 73
Catherine Gdns. Houns. BG45 64
Catherine Gro. SE10 CE44 67
Catherine Pl. SW1 BW41 3
Catherine Pl. SW1 BW41 66
Catherine Rd. Enf. CD21 30
Catherine Rd. Rom. CU32 50
Catherine Rd. Surb. BK53 84
Catherine St. WC2 BX40 4
Catherine St. WC2 BX40 56
Catherine St. St. Alb. BG13 9
Catherine Wheel Yd. Brent BK43 64
High St.
Cat Hill Barn. BU25 29
Cathles Rd. SW12 BV46 76
Cathnor Rd. W12 BP41 65
Catisfield Rd. Enf. CD22 30
Catkin Clo. Hem. H. AW13 8
Catlin Cres. Shep. BA53 83
Catling Clo. SE23 CC48 77
Dacres Rd.
Catlins La. Pnr. BC31 44
Catlin St. SE16 CB42 67
Catlin St. Hem. H. AW15 8
Cator Clo. Croy. CF59 96
Cator Cres. Croy. CF59 96
Cator La. Beck. CD51 87
Cato Rd. SW4 BW45 66
Cator Rd. SE26 CC50 77
Cator Rd. Cars. BU56 95
Cator St. SE15 CA43 67
Cato St. W1 BU39 1
Cato St. W1 BU39 56
Catsey La. Bush. BG26 36
Catsey Wds. Bush. BG26 36
Catterick Way, Borwd. BL23 28
Cattistock Rd. SE9 CK49 78
Cattlegate Hill, Pot. B. BW19 20
Cattlegate Rd. Enf. BX20 20
Cattlegate Rd. Pot. B. BW19 20
Catton St. WC1 BX39 2
Catton St. WC1 BX39 56
Cattsdell, Hem. H. AY13 8
Caulfield Rd. E6 CK37 58
Caulfield Rd. SE15 CB44 67
Causeway Felt. BC45 63
Causeway Clo. Pot. B. BT19 20
Causeway Ct. Wok. AP62 100
Bingham Dr.
Causeway, The N2 BT31 47
Causeway, The SW18 BS46 76
Causeway, The Cars. BV55 86
Causeway, The Chess. BL56 94
Causeway, The Egh & Stai. AT49 72
Causeway, The Esher BH57 93
Causeway, The Pot. B. BT19 20
Causeway, The St. Alb. BF14 9
Causeway, The Sutt. BT58 95
Causeway, The Tedd. BH49 74
Causeyware Rd. N9 CB26 39
Causton Rd. N6 BV33 47
Causton St. SW1 BW42 3
Causton St. SW1 BW42 66
Cautley Av. SW4 BW46 76
Cavalier Clo. Rom. CP31 50
Cavalry Cres. Houns. BD45 64
Cavalry Cres. Wind. AN45 61
Cavan Dr. St. Alb. BG11 9
Cavaye Pl. SW10 BT42 3
Cavaye Pl. SW10 BT42 66
Fulham Rd.
Cavell Cres. Dart. CX45 70
Cavell Dr. Enf. BY23 29
Cavell Rd. N17 BZ29 39
Cavell Rd. Wal. Cr. CA17 21
Cavell St. E1 CB39 57
Cavendish Ave. Sev. CU64 107
Cavendish Av. N3 BS30 38
Cavendish Av. NW8 BT37 1
Cavendish Av. NW8 BT38 56
Cavendish Av. W13 BJ39 54
Cavendish Av. Erith. CR43 69
Cavendish Av. Har. BG35 45
Cavendish Av. Horn. CU36 59
Cavendish Av. N. Mal. BP53 85
Cavendish Av. Ruis. BC35 44
Cavendish Av. Sid. CO47 79
Cavendish Av. Wdf. Grn. CH30 40
Cavendish Av. Well. CN45 68
Cavendish Clo. N18 CB28 39
Cavendish Clo. NW6 BR36 55
Cavendish Clo. NW8 BT38 1
Cavendish Clo. NW8 BT38 56
Cavendish Clo. SW15 BR46 75
St. John's Av.
Cavendish Clo. Amer. AQ23 25
Cavendish Clo. Hayes. BB39 53
Cavendish Clo. Sun. BB50 73
Cavendish Ct. EC3 CA39 57
Houndsditch
Cavendish Ct. Rick. BA25 26
Mayfare
Cavendish Cres. Borwd. BM24 28
Cavendish Cres. Horn. CU36 59
Cavendish Dr. E11 CF33 48
Cavendish Dr. Edg. BL29 37
Cavendish Dr. Esher BH56 93
Cavendish Gdns. Bark. CN35 49
Cavendish Gdns. Ilf. CL33 49
Cavendish Gdns. Red. BV70 121
Cavendish Gdns. Rom. CQ32 50
Cavendish Ms. N. W1 BV39 56
Hallam St.
Cavendish Ms. S. W1 BV39 56
Hallam St.
Cavendish Pl. W1 BV39 1
Cavendish Pl. W1 BV39 56
Cavendish Rd. E4 CF29 39
Cavendish Rd. N4 BY32 47
Cavendish Rd. N18 CB28 39
Cavendish Rd. NW6 BR36 55
Cavendish Rd. SW12 BV46 76
Cavendish Rd. SW19 BT50 76
Cavendish Rd. W4 BN44 65
Cavendish Rd. Barn. BQ24 28
Cavendish Rd. Chesh. AO19 16
Cavendish Rd. Croy. BY54 86
Cavendish Rd. N. Mal. BO53 85
Cavendish Rd. Red. BV70 121
Cavendish Rd. St. Alb. BH13 9
Cavendish Rd. Sun. BB50 73
Cavendish Rd. Sutt. BT57 95
Cavendish Rd. Wey. AZ58 92
Cavendish Rd. Wok. AR63 100
Cavendish Sq. W1 BV39 1
Cavendish Sq. W1 BV39 56
Cavendish St. N1 BZ37 2
Cavendish St. N1 BZ37 57
Cavendish St. W1 BV39 56
Cavendish Way, Hat. BO12 10
Cavendish Way W. Wick. CE54 87
Cavenham Ct. Wok. AS63 100
Brooklyn Rd.
Cavenham Gdns. Horn. CV32 5
Cavenham Gdns. Ilf. CM34 49
Cavenny Path, S. Ock. CZ39 60
Caverleigh Way Wor. Pk. BP54 85
Cave Rd. E13 CH37 58
Cave Rd. Rich. BK49 74
Caversham Av. N13 BY27 38
Caversham Av. Sutt. BR55 85
Caversham Rd. N15 BZ31 4
Caversham Rd. NW5 BW36 56
Caversham Rd. Kings. on T. BL51 85
Fairfield North
Caversham St. SW3 BU43
Caversham St. SW3 BU43 66
Caverswall St. W12 BQ39 6
Eynham Rd.
Caves Clo. Chis. CL51 8
Cave St. N1 BX37 5
Cavil's Wk. Rom. CQ27 4
Cawcott Dr. Wind. AM44 6
Cawdor Ave. S. Ock. DA40 6
Cawdor Cres. W7 BJ41 6
Cawley Rd. E9 CC37 5
Cawnpore St. SE19 CA49 7
Cawsey Way, Wok. AS62 10
Cawthorne Way NW7 BR28 3
Caxton Av. Wey. AW57 9
Caxton Dr. Uxb. AX37 5
Caxton Gro. E3 CE38 5
Caxton La. Oxt. CK69 11
Caxton Rd. N22 BX30 3
Caxton Rd. SW19 BT49 7
Caxton Rd. W12 BQ40 5
Caxton Rd. Sthl. BD41 6
Caxton St. SW1 BW41
Caxton St. SW1 BW41 6
Caxton St. N. E16 CG39 5
Caxton St. S. E16 CG40 5
Caxton Way, Wat. BB25 2
Caygill Clo. Brom. CG52 8
Cayley Clo. Wall. BX57 9
Cayley St. E14 CD39 5
Cayman St. SE16 CB41 6
Cayton Rd. Grnf. BH37 5
Cayton St. EC1 BZ38
Cayton St. EC1 BZ38 5
Cazenove Rd. E17 CE30 3
Cazenove Rd. N16 CA34 4
Cearn Way Couls. BX61 10
Cecil Av. Bark. CM36 5
Cecil Av. Enf. CA24 3
Cecil Av. Horn. CW31 5
Cecil Av. Wem. BL35 4
Cecil Clo. Ashf. BA50 7
Cecil Clo. Chess. BK56 9
Cecil Ct. WC2 BX40 5
St. Martin's La.
Cecil Ct. Barn. BQ24 2
Cecil Ct. Croy. CA55 8
Cecil Cr. Hat. BP11 1
Cecile Park N8 BX32 4
Cecilia Clo. N2 BT31 4
Benedict Way
Cecilia Rd. E8 CA35 4
Cecil Pk. Pnr. BE31 4
Cecil Pl. Mitch. BU53 8
Cecil Rd. E11 CG34 4
Cecil Rd. E13 CH37 5
Cecil Rd. E17 CE30 3
Cecil Rd. N10 BV30 3
Cecil Rd. N14 BW26 3
Cecil Rd. NW9 BN31 4
Cecil Rd. NW10 BN37 5
Cecil Rd. SW19 BS50 7
Cecil Rd. W3 BN39 5
Cecil Rd. Ashf. BA50 7
Cecil Rd. Croy. BX53 8
Cecil Rd. Enf. BZ24 3

21

Charlbury Clo. Rom. CV29 42
Charlbury Cres. Rom. CV29 42
Charlbury Gdns. Ilf. CN34 49
Charlbury Gro. W5 BK39 54
Charlbury Rd. Uxb. AY34 44
Charldane Rd. SE9 CL48 78
Charlecote Gro. SE26 CB48 77
Charlecote Rd. Dag. CQ34 50
Charlemont Rd. E6 CK38 58
Charles Burton Ct. E10 CD35 48
Meeson St.
Charles Clo. Sid. CO49 79
Charles Cres. Har. BG33 45
Charlesfield Way SE9 CJ48 78
Charles Gdns. Slou. AQ39 62
Borderside
Charles Grindling Wk. SE18 CL42 68
Charles Ho. W14 BR42 65
Charles Ho. Wind. AO44 61
Ward Royal
Charles II St. SW1 BW40 56
Charles La. NW8 BU37 1
Charles La. NW8 BU37 56
Charles Mills Ct. SW16 BX50 76
Charles Rd. E7 CJ36 58
Charles Rd. SW19 BS51 86
Shelton Rd.
Charles Rd. W13 BJ39 54
Charles Rd. Dag. CS36 59
Charles Rd. Rom. CP33 50
Charles Rd. Sev. CR58 98
Charles Rd. Sev. CR59 98
Charles Rd. Stai. AX50 73
Charles II St. SW1 BW40 3
Charles Sevright Dr. NW7 BQ28 37
Charles Sq. N1 BZ38 2
Charles Sq. N1 BZ38 57
Charles St. E16 CJ40 58
Charles St. SW13 BO45 65
Charles St. W1 BV40 3
Charles St. W1 BV40 56
Charles St. W5 BK40 54
Lancaster Rd.
Charles St. Berk. AQ13 7
Charles St. Cher. AV54 82
Charles St. Croy. BZ55 87
Charles St. Enf. CA25 30
Charles St. Epp. CO19 23
Charles St. Grays DD43 71
Charles St. Green. CZ46 80
Charles St. Hem. H. AX14 8
Charles St. Houns. BE44 64
Charles St. Uxb. AZ38 53
Charleston St. SE17 BZ42 4
Charleston St. SE17 BZ42 67
Charlesworth St. N7 BX36 56
Charleville Cir. SE26 CB49 77
Charleville Rd. W14 BR42 65
Charlieville Rd. Erith CS43 69
Mill Rd.
Charlmont Rd. SW17 BU50 76
Charlock Way, Guil. AT69 118
Charlock Way, Wat. BB25 26
Charlock Way, Wat. BC25 26
Charlotte Despard Av. SW11 BV44 66
Charlotte Gdns. Rom. CR29 41
Charlotte Ms. W1 BW39 56
Tottenham St.
Charlotte Pl. W1 BW39 1
Charlotte Pl. W1 BW39 56
Goodge St.
Charlotte Rd. EC2 CA38 2
Charlotte Rd. EC2 CA38 57
Charlotte Rd. SW13 BO44 65
Charlotte Rd. Dag. CR36 59
Charlotte Rd. Wall. BW57 95
Charlotte Row SW4 BW45 66
North St.
Charlotte St. W1 BW39 1
Charlotte St. W1 BW39 56
Charlotte Ter. N1 BX37 2
Charlotte Ter. N1 BX37 56
Charlton, Wind. AL44 61
Charlton Av. Walt. BC56 92
Charlton Church La. SE7 CJ42 68
Charlton Clo. Hodd. CE12 12
Charlton Clo. Uxb. AZ34 44
Charlton Cres. Bark. CN37 58
Charlton Dene SE7 CJ43 68
Charlton Dr. West. CJ62 106
Charlton Gdns. Couls. BW62 104
Charlton Gs. Couls. BW58 95
Charlton Kings Rd. NW5 BW35 47
Charlton La. SE7 CJ42 68
Charlton La. Shep. BA52 83
Charlton Mead La. Hodd. CF12 12
Charlton Pk. La. SE7 CJ43 68
Charlton Pk. Rd. SE7 CJ43 68
Charlton Pl. N1 BY37 2
Charlton Pl. N1 BY37 56
Charlton Pl. Wind. AL44 61
Charlton
Charlton Rings, Wey. BB55 83
Charlton Rd. N9 CC26 39
Charlton Rd. NW10 BO37 55
Charlton Rd. SE3 CH43 68
Charlton Rd. SE7 CH43 68
Charlton Rd. Har. BK31 45
Charlton Rd. Shep. BA52 83
Charlton Rd. Shep. BA53 83
Charlton Rd. Wem. BL33 46
Charlton Row, Wind. AL44 61
Charlton
Charlton Sq. Wind. AL44 61
Charlton
Charlton St. Grays DB43 70
Charlton Wk. Wind. AL44 61
Charlton
Charlton Way SE3 CG43 68
Charlton Way SE10 CG44 68
Charlton Way, Hodd. CE12 12
Charlton Way, Wind. AL44 61
Charlwood Clo. Har. BH29 36
Charlwood, Croy. CD58 96
Charlwood Dr. Cob. BG61 102
Charlwood Pl. SW1 BW42 3
Charlwood Pl. SW1 BW42 66
Charlwood Rd. SW15 BQ45 65
Charlwood St. SW1 BW42 3
Charlwood St. SW1 BW42 66
Charlwood Ter. SW15 BQ45 65
Cardinal Pl.
Charman Rd. Red. BU70 121
Charmian Av. Stan. BK30 36
Charminster Av. SW19 BS51 86
Charminster Ct. Surb. BK54 84
Charminster Rd. SE9 CJ49 78
Charminster Rd. Wor. Pk. BQ54 85
Charmouth Ct. St. Alb. BJ12 9
Charmouth Rd. St. Alb. BJ12 9
Charmouth Rd. Well. CP44 69
Charmouth La. Orp. CO58 98
Charne, The Sev. CU62 107
Charnock Ct. Cres. Swan. CT52 89
Charnock Rd. E5 CB34 48
Charnwood Av. SW19 BS51 86
Charnwood Clo. N. Mal. BO52 85
Charnwood Dr. E18 CH31 49
Charnwood Pl. N20 BT27 38
Charnwood Rd. SE25 BZ53 87
Charnwood Rd. Enf. CB21 30
Charnwood Rd. Uxb. AZ37 53
Charnwood St. E5 CB34 48
Charrington Rd. Croy. BY55 86
Charrington St. NW1 BW37 1
Charrington St. NW1 BW37 56
Charriots Pl. Wind. AO44 61
Peascod St.
Charsley Clo. Amer. AR23 25
Charsley Rd. SE6 CE48 77
Chart Clo. Croy. CC53 87
Chart Clo. Brom. CG51 88
Chart Clo. Dor. BK72 119
Chart Downs Est. Dor. BK72 119
Chartecote Gro. SE26 CB48 77
Charter Av. Ilf. CM33 49
Charter Clo. Slou. AP41 62
Hencroft St.
Charter Cres. Houns. BE45 64
Charter Dr. Bex. CQ47 79
Charterhouse Av. Wem. BK35 45
Charterhouse Bldgs. EC1 BY38 56
Goswell Rd.
Charterhouse Ms. EC1 BY39 2
Charterhouse Rd. Orp. CO55 89
Charterhouse Sq. EC1 BY39 2
Charterhouse Sq. EC1 BY39 56
Charterhouse St. EC1 BY39 2
Charterhouse St. EC1 BY39 56
Charteris Rd. N4 BY33 47
Charteris Rd. NW6 BR37 55
Charteris Rd. Wdf. Grn. CH29 40
Charter Rd. Kings. On T. BM52 85
Charter Rd. E. Egh. AU50 72
Charter Rd. Sth. Egh. AU50 72
Charter Rd. W. Egh. AU50 72
Charters Clo. SE19 CA49 77
Charters Cross, Harl. CM12 13
Charter Sq. Kings. On T. BM51 85
Charter, The Rd. Wdf. Grn. CG29 40
Charter Way N3 BR31 46
Regents Pk. Rd.
Charter Way N14 BW25 29
Chartfield Av. SW15 BP46 75
Chartfield Rd. Reig. BT71 121
Chartfield Sq. SW15 BQ46 75
Chartham Gro. SE27 BY48 76
Royal Circus
Chartham Rd. SE25 CB52 87
Chart La. Dor. BK71 119
Chart La. Reig. BS70 121
Chart La. Reig. BT71 121
Chart La. West. CO68 116
Chart La. S. Dor. BK72 119
Chartley Av. NW2 BO34 46
Chartley Av. Stan. BH29 36
Charton Clo. Belv. CQ43 69
Chartridge Way, Hem. H. BA13 8
Chart St. N1 BZ38 2
Chart St. N1 BZ38 57
Chart Way, Reig. BS70 121
Chartway, Sev. CV65 108
Chartwell Clo. SE9 CM48 78
Chartwell Clo. Wal. Abb. CG20 22
Mason Way
Chartwell Pl. Epsom BO60 94
Chartwell Pl. Sutt. BR55 85
Chartwell Rd. Nthwd. BB29 35
Charville Est. Hayes BA37 53
Charville La. Hayes BA38 53
Charville La. W. Uxb. AZ38 53
Charwood SE27 BY49 76
Leigham Ct. Rd.
Chasden Rd. Hem. H. AV12 7
Chase Ct. Gdns. Enf. BZ24 30
Chase Cross Rd. Rom. CS29 41
Chase End, Epsom BN59 94
Chasefield Rd. SW17 BU49 76
Chase Gdns. E4 CE28 39
Chase Gdns. Twick. BG46 74
Chase Grn. Enf. BZ24 30
Chase Grn. Av. Enf. BY23 29
Chase Hill, Enf. BZ24 30
Chase La. Chig. CN27 40
Chase La. Ilf. CM32 49
Chaseley St. E14 CD39 57
Chase Ridings, Enf. BY23 29
Chase Rd. E18 CG30 40
Chase Rd. N14 BW25 29
Chase Rd. NW10 BN38 55
Chase Rd. W3 BN39 55
Chase Rd. Brwd. DB27 42
Chase Rd. Epsom BN59 94
Chase Side N14 BV25 29
Chase Side, Enf. BZ24 30
Chase Side Av. SW20 BR51 85
Chase Side Av. Enf. BZ23 30
Chase Side Clo. Rom. CT29 41
Chase Side Cres. Enf. BZ23 30
Chaseside Gdns. Cher. AW54 83
Chase, The E12 CJ35 49
Chase, The SW4 BV45 66
Chase, The SW16 BX50 76
Chase, The SW20 BR51 85
Chase, The Ash. BK62 102
Chase, The Bexh. CR45 69
Chase, The Brom. CH52 88
Chase, The Brwd. DB27 42
Chase, The Brwd. DB28 42
Chase, The Brwd. DE28 122
Chase, The Chig. CM28 40
Chase, The Couls. BW60 95
Chase, The Edge. BM30 37
Chase, The Guil. AQ71 118
Chase, The Hem. H. AY14 8
Chase, The Leath. BB66 110
Chase, The Lthd. BG61 102
Chase, The Pnr. BD32 45
Chase, The Pnr. BE31 45
Chase, The Reig. BT71 121
Chase, The Rom. CQ32 50
Chase, The Rom. CT31 50
Chase, The Rom. CT34 50
Chase, The Stan. BJ29 36
Chase, The Sun. BC51 83
Staines Rd.
Chase, The Tad. BS64 104
Chase, The Upmin. CZ34 51
Chase, The Uxb. AZ35 44
Chase, The Wal. Cr. BY17 20
Chase, The Wall. BX56 95
Chase, The Wat. BB24 95
Chase, The Wat. BB24 26
Chase, The Sev. CW61 108
Chase, The Trading Est. NW10 BN38 55
Chaseville Pk. Rd. N21 BX25 29
Chase Way N14 BV27 38
Chaseways, Saw. CP7 6
Chasewood Av. Enf. BY23 29
Chastillian Rd. Dart. CT47 79
Chaston St. NW5 BV35 47
Herbert St.
Chatfield Pl. W5 BL39 55
Park Vw. Rd.
Chatfield Rd. SW11 BT45 66
Chatfield Rd. Croy. BY54 86
Chatham Av. N1 BZ38 57
Nile St.
Chatham Av. Brom. CG54 88
Chatham Clo. NW11 BS32 47
Chatham Clo. Sutt. BR54 85
Chatham Hill Rd. Sev. CV64 108
Chatham Pl. E9 CC36 57
Chatham Rd. E17 CD31 48
Chatham Rd. E18 CG30 40
Chatham Rd. SW11 BU46 76
Chatham Rd. Kings. On. T. BM51 85
Chatham Rd. Orp. CM56 97
Chatham St. SE17 BZ42 4
Chatham St. SE17 BZ42 67
Chatsfield, Epsom BP58 94
Chatsworth Av. NW4 BQ30 37
Chatsworth Av. SW20 BR51 85
Chatsworth Av. Brom. CH49 78
Chatsworth Av. Sid. CO47 79
Chatsworth Av. Wem. BL35 46
Chatsworth Clo. NW4 BQ30 37
Chatsworth Clo. Borwd. BM24 28
Chatsworth Ct. W8 BS42 66
Chatsworth Cres. Houns. BG45 64
Chatsworth Dr. Enf. CB26 39
Chatsworth Est. E5 CC35 48
Chatsworth Gdns. W3 BM40 55
Chatsworth Gdns. Har. BF33 45
Chatsworth Gdns. N. Mal. BO53 85
Chatsworth Pde. Orp. CM53 88
Chatsworth Pl. Tedd. BJ49 74
Chatsworth Ri. W5 BL38 55
Chatsworth Rd. E5 CC34 48
Chatsworth Rd. E15 CG35 49
Chatsworth Rd. NW2 BQ36 55
Chatsworth Rd. W4 BN43 65
Chatsworth Rd. W5 BL39 55
Chatsworth Rd. Croy. BZ55 87
Chatsworth Rd. Dart. CV45 70
Chatsworth Rd. Hayes BC38 53
Chatsworth Rd. Sutt. BQ56 94
Chatsworth Way SE27 BY48 76
Chatteris Av. Rom. CV29 42
Chattern Hill, Ashf. AZ49 73
Chattern Rd. Ashf. BA49 73
Chatterton Rd. Brom. CJ52 88
Chatto Rd. SW11 BU46 76
Chaucer Av. Hayes BC39 53
Chaucer Av. Houns. BC44 63
Chaucer Av. Rich. BM44 65
Chaucer Clo. N11 BW28 38
Chaucer Clo. Berk. AP12 7
Chaucer Clo. Til. DH44 71
Coleridge Rd.
Chaucer Gdns. Sutt. BS55 86
Chaucer Grn. Croy. CC54 87
Chaucer Rd. E7 CH36 58
Chaucer Rd. E11 CH32 49
Chaucer Rd. E17 CF30 39
Chaucer Rd. SE24 BY46 76
Chaucer Rd. W3 BN40 55
Chaucer Rd. Ashf. AY49 73
Chaucer Rd. Grav. DE48 81
Chaucer Rd. Rom. CU29 41
Chaucer Rd. Sid. CP47 79
Chaucer Rd. Sutt. BS56 95
Chaucer Rd. Well. CN44 68
Chaucer Wk. Hem. H. AZ10 8
Coleridge Cr.
Chaucer Wk. Dart. CW45 70
Chaucer Way, Dart. CX45 70
Chaucer Way, Wey. AW57 92
Chaulden Ter. Hem. H. AV14 7
Chauncey Av. Pot. B. BT20 20
Chauncey Clo. N9 CB27 39
Chave Rd. Dart. CW48 80
Chaworth Rd. Cher. AU57 91
Cheam Clo. Tad. BP64 103
Cheam Com. Rd. Wor. Pk. BP55 85
Cheam Pk. Way, Sutt. BQ57 94
Cheam Pl. SE5 BZ43 67
Cheam Rd. Epsom BP58 94
Cheam Rd. Sutt. BR57 94
Cheam St. SE15 CB45 67
Nunhead Grn.
Cheapside EC2 BZ39 2
Cheapside EC2 BZ39 57
Cheapside, Wok. AR60 91
Cheapside, Wok. AR61 100
Cheapside La. Uxb. AV34 43
Cheddar Rd. Houns. AZ45 63
Cromer Rd.
Cheddar Waye, Hayes BC39 53
Cheddington Rd. N18 CA27 39
Chedworth Clo. E16 CG39 58
Hallsville Rd.
Cheelson Rd. S. Ock. DA37 60
Cheffins Rd. Hodd. CD10 12
Chequers, Welw. G. C. BQ9 5
Chelford Rd. Brom. CF49 77
Chelmer Cres. Bark. CO37 59
Chelmer Dr. Brwd. DF25 122
Chelmer Rd. E9 CC35 48
Chelmer Rd. Grays DG42 71
Chelmer Rd. Upmin. CY32 51
Chelmsford Av. Rom. CS29 41
Chelmsford Clo. W6 BR43 65
Chelmsford Dr. Upmin. CW34 51
Chelmsford Gnds. Ilf. CK33 49
Chelmsford Rd. E11 CF33 48
Chelmsford Rd. E17 CE32 48
Chelmsford Rd. E18 CG30 40
Chelmsford Rd. N14 BW26 38
Chelmsford Rd. Brwd. DC25 122
Chelmsford Rd. Ing. DC19 24
Chelmsford Rd. Ong. CZ16 24
Chelmsford Rd. Ong. DA17 24
Chelmsford Sq. NW10 BQ37 55
Chelsea Br. BV43 66
Chelsea Br. Rd. SW1 BV42 3
Chelsea Br. Rd. SW1 BV42 66
Chelsea Cloisters SW3 BU42 3
Chelsea Cloisters SW3 BU42 66
Makins St.
Chelsea Clo. NW10 BR37 55
Chelsea Clo. NW10 BN37 55
Winchelsea Rd.
Chelsea Clo. Edg. BM30 37
Chelsea Clo. Hmptn. BG49 74
Chelsea Ct. SW3 BU43 66
Chelsea Embank. SW3 BV43 3
Chelsea Embank. SW3 BU43 66
Chelsea Man. Blds. SW3 BU42 3
Chelsea Manr. Est. SW3 BU43 66
Alpha Pl.
Chelsea Mnr. Gdns. SW3 BU42 3
Chelsea Mnr. Gdns. SW3 BU42 66
Chelsea Mnr. St. SW3 BU42 3
Chelsea Mnr. St. SW3 BU42 66
Chelsea Pk. Gdns. SW3 BT43 3
Chelsea Pk. Gdns. SW3 BT43 66
Chelsea Sq. SW3 BT42 3
Chelsea Sq. SW3 BT42 66
Chelsea Wk. SW3 BU43 66
Chelsfield Av. N9 CC26 39
Mottingham Rd.
Chelsfield Gdns. SE26 CC48 77
Chelsfield Hill, Orp. CP58 98
Chelsfield La. Orp. CP54 89
Chelsfield La. Orp. CR57 98
Chelsfield Rd. Orp. CP53 89
Chelsham Clo. Sutt. BR58 94
Chelsham Clo. Warl. CD62 105
Chelsham Ct. Rd. Warl. CF63 105
Chelsham Rd. SW4 BW45 66
Chelsham Rd. Sth. Croy. BZ57 96
Chelsham Rd. Warl. CD62 105
Chelsing Rise, Hem. H. BA14 8
Chelston Rd. Ruis. BC33 44
Chelsworth Clo. Rom. CW30 42
Chelsworth Dr. SE18 CM43 68
Chelsworth Dr. Rom. CW30 42
Cheltenham Av. Twick. BJ47 74
Cheltenham Clo. Nthlt. BF36 54
Cheltenham Gdns. E6 CK37 58
Cheltenham Gdns. Loug. CK25 31
Cheltenham Pl. W3 BM40 55
Cheltenham Pl. Har. BL31 46
Cheltenham Rd. SE15 CC45 67
Cheltenham Rd. Orp. CO55 89
Cheltenham Ter. SW3 BU42 3
Cheltenham Ter. SW3 BU42 66
Cheltenham Vil. Stai. AV46 72
Chelval St. E14 CE41 67
Chelverton Rd. SW15 BQ45 65
Chelwood Av. Hat. BP11 10
Chelwood Clo. Epsom BO59 94
Chelwood Clo. Nthwd. BA29 35
Chelwood Gdns. Rich. BM44 65
Chelwood Gdns. Pass. Rich. BM44 65
Pensford Av.
Chelwood Wk. SE4 CD45 67
Chenappa Clo. E13 CG38 58
Chenduit Way, Stan. BH28 36
Chenells, Hat. BO13 10
Cheney Rd. NW1 BX37 2
Cheney Rd. NW1 BX37 56
Cheneys Rd. E11 CG34 49
Cheney St. Pnr. BD32 45
Chenies Av. Amer. AR23 25
Chenies Ct. Hem. H. AZ11 8
Chenies Ms. WC1 BW38 1
Chenies Ms. WC1 BW38 56
Chenies Par. Amer. AR23 25
Chenies Pl. NW1 BW37 1
Chenies Pl. NW1 BW37 56
Chenies Rd. Rick. AU23 25
Chenies St. WC1 BW39 1
Chenies St. WC1 BW39 56
Chenies, The Dart. CT49 79
Chenies, The Orp. CN53 88
Cheniston Clo. Wey. AV60 91
Cheniston Gdns. W8 BS41 66
Cheo Rd. Dor. BJ71 119
Chepstow Av. Horn. CW34 51
Chepstow Clo. SW15 BR46 75
Chepstow Cres. W11 BS40 56
Chepstow Cres. Ilf. CN32 49
Chepstow Gdns. Sthl. BE39 54
Chepstow Pl. W2 BS40 56
Chepstow Rise, Croy. CA55 87
Chepstow Rd. W2 BS39 56
Chepstow Rd. W7 BJ41 64
Chepstow Rd. Croy. CA55 87
Chepstow Vill. W11 BR40 55
Chepstow Way SE15 CA44 67
Sumner Estate
Chequers, Welw. G. C. BR8 5
Chequers Clo. Orp. CN52 88
Ravensbury Rd.
Chequers Clo. Tad. BP66 112
Chequers Field, Welw. G. C. BQ9 5
Chequers Gdns. N13 BY28 38
Chequers Hill, Amer. AO23 25
Chequers La. Dag. CQ38 59
Chequers La. Tad. BP66 112
Chequers La. Wat. BD18 18
Chequers Orch. Iver. AV39 52
Chequers Pde. SE9 CK46 78
Chequers Rd. Brwd. CW25 33
Chequers Rd. Loug. CL25 31
Chequers Rd. Rom. CW27 42
Chequers Sq. Uxb. AX36 53
High St.
Chequer St. EC1 BZ38 2
Chequer St. EC1 BZ38 57
Chequer St. St. Alb. BG13 9
Chequers Wk. Wal. Abb. CG20 22
Mason Way
Chequers Way N13 BY28 38
Chequer Tree Clo. Wok. AP61 100
Green Acre
Cherbury Ct. N1 BZ37 2
Cherbury Ct. N1 BZ37 57
Cherbury St. N1 BZ37 2
Cherbury St. N1 BZ37 57
Cherimoya Gdns. E. Mol. BF52 84
Cherington Rd. W7 BH40 54
Cheriton Av. Brom. CG53 88
Cheriton Av. Ilf. CK30 40
Cheriton Clo. W5 BK39 54
Queens Wk.
Cheriton Clo. St. Alb. BK11 9
Cheriton Dr. SE18 CM43 68
Cheriton Sq. SW17 BV48 76
Cherkley Hill, Lthd. BK66 111
Cherries, The Slou. AQ39 52
Cherry Av. Slou. AR41 62
Cherry Av. Brwd. DC27 122
Cherry Av. Sthl. BD40 54
Cherry Av. Swan. CS52 89
Cherry Bounce, Hem. H. AX13 8
Cherry Clo. W5 BK41 64
Cherry Clo. Bans. BQ60 94
Cherry Clo. Cars. BU55 86
Cherry Clo. Mord. BR52 85
Cherry Clo. Ruis. BB34 44
Cherrycot Hill, Orp. CM56 97
Cherrycot Rise, Orp. CM56 97
Cherry Cres. Brent. BJ43 64
Cherry Cft. Welw. G. C. BQ6 5
Cherrydale, Wat. BB24 26
Cherrydown Av. E4 CD27 39
Cherrydown Clo. E4 CD27 39
Cherrydown Rd. Sid. CP48 79
Cherrydown Wk. Rom. CR30 41
Cherry Gdns. Dag. CQ35 50
Cherry Gdn. St. SE16 CB41 67
Cherry Garth, Brent. BK42 64
Cherry Gro. Hayes BC40 53
Cherry Gro. Uxb. AZ39 53
Cherry Hill, Barn. BS25 29
Cherry Hill, Rick. AW24 26
Cherry Hill. St. Alb. BF16 18
Cherry Hill Gdns. Croy. BX56 95
Cherry La. West Dr. AY42 63
Cherry Laurel Wk. SW2 BX46 76
Beechdale Rd.
Cherry Orch. Amer. AP22 25
Cherry Orchard, Ash. BM62 103
Cherry Orchard, Hem. H. AW12 8
Cherry Orchard, Slou. AQ36 52
Cherry Orchard, Stai. AW49 73
Cherry Orchard, West Dr. AY41 63
Cherry Orchard Clo. Orp. CP53 89
Cherry Orchard Gdns. E. Mol. BE52 84
Cherry Orchard La. Brom. CK55 88
Cherry Orchard Rd. Croy. BZ55 87
Cherry Orchard Rd. E. Mol. BE52 84
Cherry Ri. Ch. St. G. AR27 34
Cherry Rd. Enf. CC22 30
Cherry St. Guil. AR71 118
Cherry St. Rom. CS32 50
Cherry St. Wok. AS62 100
Cherry Tree Av. Guil. AP70 118
Cherry Tree Av. St. Alb. BK16 18
Cherry Tree Av. Stai. AW50 73
Cherry Tree Av. West Dr. AY39 53
Cherry Tree Clo. Rain. CT37 59
Cherry Tree Ct. Couls. BX62 104
Coulsdon Rd.
Cherrytree Dr. SW16 BX48 76
Leigham Av.
Cherry Tree Gdns. N2 BU31 47
Cherry Tree Gdns. Croy. BZ54 87
Oval Rd.
Cherry Tree Grn. Sth. Croy. CB60 96
Cherry Tree La. Ger. Cr. AR30 34
Cherry Tree La. Hem. H. BA11 8
Cherrytree La. Iver AW37 53
Cherry Tree La. Pot. B. BS20 20
Cherry Tree La. Rain. CT38 59
Cherry Tree La. Slou. AS36 52
Cherry Tree Rise, Buck. H. CJ28 40
Cherry Tree Rd. Hodd. CE11 12
Cherry Tree Rd. Wat. BC21 26
Cherry Tree Wk. Beck. CD52 87
Cherry Tree Wk. Chesh. AO18 16
Cherry Tree Wk. West. CJ61 106
Cherry Tree Wk. W. Wick. CG56 97
Cherry Tree Way, Stan. BJ28 36
Cherry Wk. Brom. CH54 88
Cherry Wk. Grays. DG41 71
Cherry Wk. Rain. CT37 59
Cherry Wk. Rick. AX23 26
Cherry Way, Epsom BN57 94
Cherry Way, Hat. BP14 10
Cherry Way, Shep. BB52 83
Cherrywood Av. Egh. AQ50 72

23

Street	Grid	Page
Clabon Ms. SW1	BU41	66
Clack St. SE16	CC41	67
Clacton Path SE4	CD45	67
Frendsbury Rd.		
Clacton Rd. E6	CJ38	58
Clacton Rd. E17	CD32	48
Claigmar Gdns. N3	BS30	38
Claire Ct. Clo. N12	BT28	38
Woodside Av.		
Clairvale, Horn.	CW33	51
Clairvale Rd. Houns.	BE44	64
Clairview Rd. SW16	BV49	76
Clairville Ct. Reig.	BT70	121
Wray Com.		
Clairy Gdns. W7	BH40	54
Clammas Waye, Uxb.	AX39	53
Clamp Hill, Stan.	BG28	36
Clancarty Rd. SW6	BS44	66
Clandon Av. N3	BS31	47
Clandon Av. Egh.	AU50	72
Clandon Clo. W3	BM41	65
Avenue Rd.		
Clandon Clo. Epsom	BO57	94
Clandon Rd. Guil.	AS71	118
Clandon Rd. Ilf.	CN34	49
Clandon Rd. Wok.	AV66	109
Clandon St. SE8	CE44	67
Clandon Way, Wok.	AV66	109
Clanfield Way SE15	CA43	67
Hordle Prom. W.		
Clanricarde Gdns. W2	BS40	56
Clapgate La. Wal. Abb.	CF18	21
Clapgate Rd. Bush.	BF25	27
Clapham Com. N. Side SW4	BU45	66
Clapham Com. S. Side SW4	BV46	76
Clapham Com. W. Side SW4	BU45	66
Clapham Cres. SW4	BW45	66
Clapham High St. SW4	BW45	66
Clapham Manor St. SW4	BW45	66
Clapham Pk. Est. SW2	BX47	76
Clapham Pk. Est. SW4	BW46	76
Clapham Pk. Rd. SW4	BW45	66
Clapham Rd. SW9	BX45	66
Clappers La. Wok.	AO59	91
Claps Gate La. Bark.	CL38	58
Clapton Com. E5	CA33	48
Clapton Pass. E5	CC35	48
Lwr. Clapton Rd.		
Clapton Sq. E5	CC35	48
Clapton Ter. N16	CB33	48
Clapton Way E5	CB35	48
Clara Pl. SE18	CL42	68
John Wilson St.		
Clara Pl. SE18	CL42	68
Monk St.		
Clare Clo. Borwd.	BL25	28
Clare Clo. Wey.	AW60	92
Clare Cor. SE9	CL47	78
Clare Cotts. Red.	BY70	121
Clare Cl. N2	BT31	47
Benedict Way		
Clare Ct. Cat.	CE65	105
Clare Cres. Lthd.	BJ62	102
Clarecroft Way W14	BQ41	65
Claredale St. E2	CB37	57
Clare Gdns. E7	CH35	49
Clare Gdns. W11	BR39	55
Westbourne Pk. Rd.		
Clare Gdns. Bark.	CN36	58
Clare Gdns. Stan.	BK28	36
Clare Hall Pl. SE16	CC42	67
Litlington St.		
Clarehill Clo. Esher	BF56	93
Clarehill Rd. Esher	BF57	93
Clare La. N1	BZ36	57
Clare Lawn Av. SW14	BN46	75
Clare Mkt. WC2	**BX39**	**2**
Clare Mkt. WC2	BX39	56
Portugal St.		
Claremont, Wal. Cr.	CA18	21
Claremont Av. Esher	BE57	93
Claremont Av. Har.	BL32	46
Claremont Av. N. Mal.	BP53	85
Claremont Av. Sun.	BC51	83
Claremont Av. Walt.	BD56	93
Claremont Av. Wok.	AS63	100
Claremont Clo. E16	CL40	58
Claremont Clo. N1	**BY37**	**2**
Claremont Clo. N1	BY37	56
Claremont Clo. Orp.	CL56	97
Claremont Clo. Sth. Croy.	CB60	96
Claremont Clo. Walt.	BD56	93
Claremont Ct. Dor.	BJ72	119
Rose Hill		
Claremont Cres. Dart.	CT45	69
Claremont Cres. Rick.	BA25	26
Claremont Dr. Esher	BF58	93
Claremont Dr. Wok.	AS63	100
Claremont End, Esher	BF57	93
Claremont Est. SW2	BX47	76
Claremont Gdns. Dart.	CY47	80
Claremont Gdns. Ilf.	CN34	49
Claremont Gdns. Surb.	BL52	85
Claremont Gdns. Upmin.	CY33	51
Claremont Gro. Wdf. Grn.	CJ29	40
Claremont La. Esher	BF56	93
Claremont Pk. N3	BR30	37
Claremont Pk. Rd. Esher	BF57	93
Claremont Rd. E7	CH35	49
Claremont Rd. E11	CF34	48
Claremont Rd. E17	CD30	39
Claremont Rd. N6	BV33	47
Claremont Rd. NW2	BQ33	46
Claremont Rd. W9	BR37	55
Claremont Rd. W13	BJ39	54
Claremont Rd. Barn.	BT22	29
Claremont Rd. Brom.	CK52	88
Claremont Rd. Croy.	CB54	87
Claremont Rd. Esher	BH57	93
Claremont Rd. Har.	BH30	36
Claremont Rd. Horn.	CU32	50
Claremont Rd. Red.	BV69	121
Claremont Rd. Stai.	AU49	72
Claremont Rd. Surb.	BL53	85
Claremont Rd. Swan.	CT50	79
Claremont Rd. Tedd.	BH49	74
Claremont Rd. Twick.	BJ46	74
Claremont Rd. Wey.	AW59	92
Claremont Rd. Wind.	AO44	61
Claremont Sq. N1	**BY37**	**2**
Claremont Sq. N1	BY37	56
Claremont St. E16	CL40	58
Claremont St. N18	CB29	39
Claremont St. SE10	CE43	67
Claremont Way NW2	BQ33	46
Claremount, St. Alb.	BF19	18
Claremount Gdns. Epsom	BQ62	103
Clarence Av. SW4	BW47	76
Clarence Av. Brom.	CK52	88
Clarence Av. Ilf.	CL32	49
Clarence Av. N. Mal.	BN51	85
Clarence Av. Upmin.	CX34	51
Clarence Clo. Bush.	BH26	36
Clarence Clo. Walt.	BC56	92
Clarence Cres. SW4	BW46	76
Clarence Cres. Sid.	CO48	79
Clarence Cres. Wind.	AO44	61
Clarence Dr. Egh.	AR49	72
Clarence Gdns. NW1	**BV38**	**1**
Clarence Gdns. NW1	BV38	56
Clarence La. SW15	BO46	75
Clarence Ms. E5	CB35	48
Clarence Pl.		
Clarence Pass. NW1	**BX37**	**2**
Clarence Pl. E5	CB35	48
Clarence Pl. Grav.	DG47	81
Clarence Rd. E5	CB35	48
Clarence Rd. E12	CJ35	49
Clarence Rd. E16	CG38	58
Clarence Rd. E17	CC30	39
Clarence Rd. N15	BZ32	48
Clarence Rd. N22	BX29	38
Clarence Rd. NW6	BR36	55
Clarence Rd. SE9	CK48	78
Clarence Rd. SW19	BS50	76
Clarence Rd. W4	BM42	65
Clarence Rd. Berk.	AR13	7
Clarence Rd. Bexh.	CQ45	69
Clarence Rd. Brom.	CJ52	88
Clarence Rd. Brwd.	DA23	33
Clarence Rd. Croy.	BZ54	87
Clarence Rd. Enf.	CB25	30
Clarence Rd. Grav.	DH46	81
Clarence Rd. Grays	DD42	71
Clarence Rd. Red.	BT72	121
Clarence Rd. Rich.	BL44	65
Clarence Rd. St. Alb.	BH13	9
Clarence Rd. Sid.	CO48	79
Clarence Rd. Sutt.	BS56	95
Clarence Rd. Tedd.	BH50	74
Clarence Rd. Wall.	BV56	95
Clarence Rd. Walt.	BC56	92
Clarence Rd. West.	CK62	106
Clarence Rd. Wind.	AN44	61
Clarence Row, Grav.	DG47	81
Clarence St. Egh.	AS50	72
Clarence St. Kings. on T.	BK51	84
Clarence St. Rich.	BL45	65
Clarence St. Stai.	AV49	72
Clarence St. Sthl.	BD41	64
Clarence Ter. NW1	**BU38**	**1**
Clarence Ter. NW1	BU38	56
Cornwall Ter.		
Clarence Ter. Houns.	BF45	64
Clarence Wk. SW4	BX44	66
Jeffrey's Rd.		
Clarence Wk. Red.	BT72	121
Clarence Way NW1	BV36	56
Clarence Way Est. NW1	BV36	56
Clarence Yd. SE17	**BZ42**	**4**
Clarendon Av. SE5	BZ43	67
Councillor St.		
Clarendon Clo. W2	**BU40**	**3**
Clarendon Clo. W2	BU40	56
Clarendon Pl.		
Clarendon Clo. Orp.	CO52	89
Clarendon Ct. NW11	BR31	46
Finchley Rd.		
Clarendon Cres. Twick.	BG48	74
Clarendon Cross W11	BR40	55
Portland Rd.		
Clarendon Dr. SW15	BQ45	65
Clarendon Gdns. NW4	BP31	46
Clarendon Gdns. W9	**BT38**	**1**
Clarendon Gdns. W9	BT38	56
Clarendon Gdns. Ilf.	CK33	49
Clarendon Gdns. Wem.	BK35	45
Clarendon Grn. Orp.	CO52	89
Clarendon Gro. NW1	**BW38**	**1**
Clarendon Gro. NW1	BW38	56
Phoenix Rd.		
Clarendon Gro. Mitch.	BU52	86
Clarendon Gro. Orp.	CO52	89
Clarendon Ms. W2	**BU40**	**3**
Clarendon Ms. W2	BU40	56
Clarendon Pl.		
Clarendon Path, Orp.	CO52	89
Clarendon Pl. W2	**BU40**	**3**
Clarendon Pl. W2	BU40	56
Clarendon Ri. SE13	CF45	67
Clarendon Rd. E11	CF33	48
Clarendon Rd. E17	CE32	48
Clarendon Rd. E18	CH31	49
Clarendon Rd. N8	BX31	47
Clarendon Rd. N15	BY31	47
Clarendon Rd. N18	CB29	39
Clarendon Rd. N22	BX30	38
Clarendon Rd. SW19	BU50	76
Clarendon Rd. W5	BL38	55
Clarendon Rd. W11	BR40	55
Clarendon Rd. Ashf.	AY49	73
Clarendon Rd. Borwd.	BM24	28
Clarendon Rd. Croy.	BY55	86
Clarendon Rd. Har.	BH32	45
Clarendon Rd. Hayes	BB41	63
Clarendon Rd. Red.	BU70	121
Clarendon Rd. Sev.	CU65	107
Clarendon Rd. Sev.	CU66	116
Clarendon Rd. Wal. Cr.	CC18	21
Clarendon Rd. Wall.	BW57	95
Clarendon Rd. Wat.	BC24	26
Clarendon St. SW1	**BV42**	**3**
Clarendon St. SW1	BV42	66
Clarendon Ter. W9	**BT38**	**1**
Clarendon Ter. W9	BT38	56
Maida Vale		
Clarendon Wk. W11	BQ40	55
Lancaster Rd.		
Clarendon Way N21	BZ25	30
Clarendon Way, Chis.	CN52	88
Clarendon Way, Orp.	CN52	88
Clarens St. SE6	CD48	77
Clare Rd. E11	CF32	48
Clare Rd. NW10	BP36	55
Clare Rd. Grnf.	BG36	54
Clare Rd. Houns.	BE45	64
Clare Rd. Stai.	AX47	73
Clare St. E2	CB37	57
Claret Gdns. SE25	CA52	87
Clareville Gro. SW7	**BT42**	**3**
Clareville Gro. SW7	BT42	66
Clareville Rd. Cat.	CB65	105
Clareville Rd. Orp.	CM55	88
Clareville St. SW7	**BT42**	**3**
Clareville St. SW7	BT42	66
Gloucester Rd.		
Clare Way, Bexh.	CQ44	69
Clare Way, Sev.	CV67	117
Clare Wood, Lthd.	BJ62	102
Clarewood Mans. SW9	BY45	66
Coldharbour La.		
Clarewood Wk. SW9	BY45	66
Somerleyton Rd. Dev.		
Clarges Ms. W1	**BV40**	**3**
Clarges Ms. W1	BV40	56
Clarges St. W1	**BV40**	**3**
Clarges St. W1	BV40	56
Claribel Rd. SW9	BY44	66
Claridge Rd. Dag.	CP33	50
Clarina Rd. SE20	CC50	77
Clarissa Rd. Rom.	CP33	50
Clarissa St. E8	**CA37**	**2**
Clarissa St. E8	CA37	57
Clark Clo. Erith	CU44	69
Forest Rd.		
Clarke's Av. Wor. Pk.	BQ54	85
Clarke Path N16	CB33	48
Braydon Rd.		
Clarke Path N16	CB33	48
Oldhill St.		
Clarkes Rd. Hat.	BP12	10
Clarke Way, Wat.	BC21	26
Clarke's Grn. Rd. Sev.	CX60	99
Clarkhill, Harl.	CN12	13
Clarks La. Epp.	CN19	22
Hemnall St.		
Clarks La. Sev.	CQ59	98
Clarks La. West.	CG65	106
Clarks Mead, Bush.	BG26	36
Clarkson Rd. E16	CG39	58
Clarksons, The Bark.	CM37	58
Clarkson St. E2	CB38	57
Clarks Rd. Ilf.	CM34	49
Clark St. E1	CB39	57
Clark Way, Houns.	BE43	64
Springwell Rd.		
Claston Clo. Dart.	CT46	79
Iron Mill La.		
Clatre Ct. N12	BT28	38
Claude Rd. E10	CF34	48
Claude Rd. E13	CH37	58
Claude Rd. SE15	CB44	67
Goodman Rd.		
Claude St. E14	CE42	67
Claudian Pl. St. Alb.	BF14	9
Claudian Way, Grays	DG41	71
Claudia Pl. SW19	BR47	75
Augustus Rd.		
Claughton Rd. E13	CJ37	58
Claughton Way, Brwd.	DE25	122
Clausen Way, Grnf.	BJ37	54
Clauson Av. Nthlt.	BF35	45
Clavell St. SE10	CF43	67
Claverdale Rd. SW2	BX47	76
Claverhambury Rd. Wal. Abb.	CG18	22
Clavering Av. SW13	BP43	65
Clavering Clo. Twick.	BJ49	74
Clavering Gdns. Brwd.	DE32	123
Clavering Rd. E12	CJ33	49
Claverley Gro. N3	BS30	38
Claverley Vill. N3	BS30	38
Claverley Gro.		
Claverton Clo. Hem. H.	AT17	16
Claverton St. SW1	**BW42**	**3**
Claverton St. SW1	BW42	66
Clave St. E1	CC40	57
Claxton Gro. W6	BQ42	65
Clay Acre, Chesh.	AO18	16
Claybridge Rd. SE12	CJ49	78
Clayburn Gdns. S. Ock.	DA40	60
Claybury Bush.	BF26	36
Claybury Broadway, Ilf.	CK31	49
Claybury Rd. Wdf. Grn.	CK29	40
Clay Cft. Welw. G. C.	BS7	5
Hazel Gro.		
Claydon End, Ger. Cr.	AS31	43
Claydon La. Ger. Cr.	AS31	43
Claydon Rd. Wok.	AQ61	100
Clay Fm. Rd. SE9	CM48	78
Claygate Clo. Horn.	CT35	50
Carfax Rd.		
Claygate Cres. Croy.	CF57	96
Claygate La. Esher	BJ54	84
Claygate Lodge Clo. Esher	BH57	93
Claygate Rd. W13	BJ41	64
Claygate Rd. Dor.	BJ72	119
Clayhall Av. Ilf.	CK31	49
Clayhall La. Reig.	BQ72	120
Clayhall La. Wind.	AP46	72
Clay Hill Bush.	BF25	27
Clay Hill, Enf.	BY22	29
Clay Hill, Enf.	BZ22	30
Clayhill Cres. SE9	CJ49	78
Clayhill Pound La. Epsom	BM60	94
Clayhill Rd. Reig.	BP74	120
Claylands Pl. SW8	BY43	66
Claylands Rd. SW8	BX43	66
Clay La. Bush.	BH26	36
Clay La. Edg.	BM27	37
Clay La. Epsom	BM65	103
Clay La. Guil.	AR67	109
Clay La. Red.	BW71	121
Clay La. Stai.	AY47	73
Claymore Rd. Hem. H.	AY11	8
Claypit Hill, Loug.	CJ22	31
Claypole Rd. E15	CF37	57
Claypounds Av. Brent.	BL42	65
Claypounds Gdns. W5	BK42	64
Claypounds La. Brent.	BL42	65
Clay Ride, Loug.	CK25	31
Clay Side, Chig.	CM28	40
Clays La. E15	CF35	48
Clay's La. Loug.	CL23	31
Clay St. W1	**BU39**	**1**
Clay St. W1	BU39	56
Dorset St.		
Clayton Av. Upmin.	CX35	51
Clayton Av. Wem.	BL36	55
Clayton Cres. Brent.	BK42	64
Clayton Cft. Dart.	CU48	79
Clayton Dr. Guil.	AP69	118
Clayton Mead NW9	BO29	37
Clayton Rd. SE15	CB44	67
Clayton Rd. Chess.	BK56	93
Clayton Rd. Epsom	BO60	94
Clayton Rd. Hayes	BB41	63
Clayton Rd. Islw.	BH45	64
Clayton Rd. Rom.	CS33	50
Clayton St. SE11	**BY43**	**4**
Clayton St. SE11	BY43	66
Clayton Wk. Amer.	AR23	25
Clayton Waye, Uxb.	AX38	53
Clay Tye Rd. Upmin.	DB35	51
Claywood Clo. Orp.	CN54	88
Cleanthus Rd. SE18	CL44	68
Clearbrook Way E1	CC39	57
W. Arbour St.		
Cleardene, Dor.	BJ71	119
Cleardown, Wok.	AT63	100
Clears, The Reig.	BR69	120
Clearwell Dr. W9	BS38	56
Amberley Est.		
Cleave Av. Hayes	BB42	63
Cleave Av. Orp.	CN57	97
Cleaveland Rd. Surb.	BK53	84
Cleave Prior, Couls.	BU63	104
Cleaverholme Clo. SE25	CB53	87
Cleaver Sq. SE11	**BY42**	**4**
Cleaver Sq. SE11	BY42	66
Cleaver St. SE11	**BY42**	**4**
Cleeve Hill SE23	CB47	77
Cleeve Rd. Lthd.	BJ63	102
Cleeves Clo. Hem. H.	AZ11	8
Cleeves Cres. Croy.	CF59	96
Clegg Pl. SW15	BQ45	65
Clegg St. E1	CB40	57
Prusom St.		
Clegg St. E13	CH37	58
Cleland Path, Loug.	CL23	31
Cleland Way, Ger. Cr.	AR30	34
Cleland Way, Ger. Cr.	AR31	43
Clematis Clo. Rom.	CV29	42
Clematis St. W12	BP40	55
Clem Av. SW4	BW45	66
Clemence St. E14	CD39	57
Clement Clo. NW6	BQ36	55
Clement Clo. W4	BN41	65
Winston Wk.		
Clement Clo. Pur.	BY57	95
Clement Clo. Pur.	BY61	104
Clement Clo. Wal. Cr.	CD17	21
Clement Gdns. Hayes	BB42	63
Clementhorpe Rd. Dag.	CP36	59
Clementine Rd. E10	CD33	48
Clement Mead, Lthd.	BJ63	102
Clement Rd. SW19	BR49	75
Clement Rd. Beck.	CC51	87
Clements Av. E16	CH40	58
Clements Clo. Slou.	AQ41	62
Clements Ct. Houns.	BD45	64
Clements Inn WC2	**BX39**	**2**
Clements Inn WC2	BX39	56
Strand		
Clements Inn Pass. WC2	**BX39**	**2**
Clements La. EC4	**BZ40**	**4**
Clement's La. EC4	BZ40	57
Clements La. Ilf.	CL34	49
Clement's Pl. Brent.	BK42	64
Challis Rd.		
Clements Rd. E6	CK36	58
Clement's Rd. SE16	CB41	67
Clements Rd. Ilf.	CL34	49
Clements Rd. Rick.	AU25	25
Clements Rd. Walt.	BC55	83
Clement St. Swan.	CV50	80
Clement Way, Upmin.	CW34	51
Clenches Fm. La. Sev.	CU66	116
Clenches Fm. Rd. Sev.	CU66	116
Clendon Way SE18	CM42	68
Polthorne Gro.		
Clennam St. SE1	**BZ41**	**4**
Clennam St. SE1	BZ41	67
Southwark Bridge Rd.		
Clensham Ct. Sutt.	BS55	86
Clensham La. Sutt.	BS55	86
Clenston Ms. W1	**BU39**	**1**
Clenston Ms. W1	BU39	56
Seymour Pl.		
Clephane Rd. N1	BZ36	48
Cleremont Rd. E9	CC37	57
Clere Pl. EC2	**BZ38**	**2**
Clere Pl. EC2	BZ38	57
Clere St.		
Clere St. EC2	**BZ38**	**2**
Clere St. EC2	BZ38	57
Clerkenwell Clo. EC1	**BY38**	**2**
Clerkenwell Clo. EC1	BY38	56
Clerkenwell Grn. EC1	**BY38**	**2**
Clerkenwell Grn. EC1	BY38	56
Clerkenwell Rd. EC1	**BY38**	**2**
Clerkenwell Rd. EC1	BY38	56
Clerks Piece, Loug.	CK24	31
Clevedon, Wey.	BA56	92
Clevedon Clo. N16	CA34	48
Smalley Rd.		
Clevedon Gdns. Hayes	BA41	63
Clevedon Gdns. Houns.	BC44	63
Clevedon Pass N16	CA34	48
High St.		
Clevedon Rd. SE20	CC51	87
Clevedon Rd. Kings. On T.	BM51	85
Clevedon Rd. Twick.	BK46	74
Clevedon St. N16	CA34	48
Sanford La.		
Clevehurst Clo. Slou.	AQ36	52
Cleveland, Hem. H.	AZ12	8
Cleveland Av. SW20	BR51	85
Cleveland Av. W4	BO42	65
Cleveland Av. Hamptn.	BE50	74
Cleveland Clo. Walt.	BC55	83
Cleveland Ct. W13	BJ39	54
Kent Av.		
Cleveland Cres. Brwd.	BN25	28
Cleveland Dr. Stai.	AW51	83
Cleveland Est. E1	CC38	57
Cleveland Gdns. N4	BZ32	48
Cleveland Gdns. NW2	BQ34	46
Cleveland Gdns. SW13	BO44	65
Cleveland Gdns. W2	**BT39**	**1**
Cleveland Gdns. W2	BT39	56
Cleveland Gdns. W13	BJ39	54
Argyle Rd.		
Cleveland Gdns. Wor. Pk.	BO55	85
Cleveland Gro. E1	CC38	57
Cleveland Way		
Cleveland Ms. W1	**BW39**	**1**
Cleveland Ms. WC1	BW39	56
Maple St.		
Cleveland Pk. Av. E17	CD31	48
Cleveland Pk. Cres. E17	CD31	48
Cleveland Pl. SW1	BW40	56
King St.		
Cleveland Rise, Mord.	BQ54	85
Cleveland Rd. E18	CH31	49
Cleveland Rd. N1	**BZ36**	**2**
Cleveland Rd. N1	BZ36	57
Cleveland Rd. N9	CB26	39
Cleveland Rd. SW13	BO44	65
Cleveland Rd. W4	BN41	65
Cleveland Rd. W13	BJ39	54
Cleveland Rd. Ilf.	CL34	49
Cleveland Rd. Islw.	BJ45	64
Cleveland Rd. N. Mal.	BO52	85
Cleveland Rd. Uxb.	AX38	53
Cleveland Rd. Well.	CG44	68
Cleveland Rd. Wor. Pk.	BO55	85
Cleveland Row SW1	**BW40**	**3**
Cleveland Row SW1	BW40	56
Cleveland Sq. W2	**BT39**	**1**
Cleveland Sq. W2	BT39	56
Cleveland St. W1	**BV38**	**1**
Cleveland St. W1	BW38	56
Cleveland Ter. W2	**BT39**	**1**
Cleveland Ter. W2	BT39	56
Cleveland Way E1	CC38	57
Cleveland Way, Hem. H.	AZ12	8
Cleveley Cres. W5	BL37	55
Cleveleys Rd. E5	CB34	48
Cleverley Est. W12	BP40	55
Cleve Rd. NW6	BS36	56
Cleve Rd. Sid.	CP48	79
Cleves Av. Epsom	BP58	94
Cleves Clo. Cob.	BC60	92
Cleves Rd. E6	CJ37	58
Cleves Rd. Hem. H.	AZ11	8
Cleves Rd. Rich.	BK48	74
Cleves Rd. Sev.	CW62	108
Cleves Wk. Ilf.	CM29	40
Cleves Way, Hamptn.	BE50	74
Cleves Way, Ruis.	BD33	45
Cleves Wood, Wey.	BB56	92
Cleve Yd. SW1	**BW40**	**3**
Clew Av. Wind.	AN44	61
Clewer Ct. Rd. Wind.	AN43	61
Clewer Cres. Har.	BG30	36
Clewer Flds. Wind.	AN44	61
Clewer Hill Rd. Wind.	AM44	61
Clewer Pk. Wind.	AN43	61
Clichy Est. E1	CC39	57
Clifden Rd. E5	CC35	48
Clifden Rd. Brent.	BK43	64
Clifden Rd. Twick.	BH47	74
Cliffe End, Pur.	BY59	95
Cliffe Rd. Sth. Croy.	BZ56	96
Cliff Gro. Grav.	DG47	81
Clifford Av. SW14	BM45	65
Clifford Av. Chis.	CK50	78
Clifford Av. Ilf.	CL30	40
Clifford Av. Wall.	BW56	95
Clifford Clo. Nthlt.	BE37	54
Clifford Ct. NW2	BO35	46
Clifford Dr. SW9	BY44	66
Loughborough Pk. Dev.		
Clifford Gdns. NW10	BQ37	55
Clifford Gro. SE20	CC50	77
Clifford Gro. Ashf.	AZ49	73
Clifford Manor Rd. Guil.	AS72	118
Clifford Rd. E16	CG38	58
Clifford Rd. E17	CF30	39
Clifford Rd. N9	CC25	30
Clifford Rd. SE25	CB52	87
Clifford Rd. Barn.	BS24	29
Clifford Rd. Houns.	BD45	64
Clifford Rd. Rich.	BK48	74
Clifford Rd. Wem.	BK36	54
Clifford's Inn EC4	BY39	56
Fleet St.		
Clifford St. W1	**BW40**	**3**
Clifford St. W1	BW40	56
Clifford St. Wat.	BD24	27
Clifford Way NW10	BO35	46
Cliff Pl. S. Ock.	DB38	60
Cliff Rd. NW1	BW36	56
Cliff Ter. SE8	CE44	67
Cliffview Rd. SE13	CE45	67
Cliff Vill. NW1	BW36	56
Cliff Wk. E16	CG39	58
Clifton Av. E17	CC31	48
Clifton Av. N3	BR30	37
Clifton Av. W12	BO41	65
Clifton Av. Felt.	BD48	74
Clifton Av. Stan.	BJ30	36
Clifton Av. Sutt.	BS58	95
Clifton Av. Wem.	BL36	55
Clifton Clo. Brwd.	DE32	123

Clifton Clo. Cat. BZ65 105
Clifton Clo. Orp. CL56 97
Clifton Clo. Wall. Cr. CD18 21
Clifton Clo. Wey. AW55 83
Clifton Ct. NW8 BT38 1
Clifton Ct. NW8 BT38 56
Clifton Cres. SE15 CB43 67
Clifton Gdns. N15 CA32 48
Clifton Gdns. NW11 BR31 46
Clifton Gdns. W9 BT38 1
Clifton Gdns. W9 BT38 56
Clifton Gdns. Enf. BX24 29
Clifton Gdns. Uxb. AZ37 53
Clifton Hill NW8 BS37 1
Clifton Hill NW8 BS37 56
Clifton Marine Par. Grav. DF46 81
Clifton Pk. Av. SW20 BQ51 85
Approach Rd.
Clifton Pl. W2 BT40 56
Clifton Pl. Bans. BS61 104
Clifton Ri. Wind. AL44 61
Clifton Ri. SE14 CD43 67
Clifton Rd. E7 CJ36 58
Clifton Rd. E16 CG39 58
Clifton Rd. N3 BT30 38
Clifton Rd. N8 BW32 47
Clifton Rd. N22 BW30 38
Clifton Rd. NW10 BP37 55
Clifton Rd. SE25 BZ52 87
Clifton Rd. SW19 BQ50 75
Clifton Rd. W9 BT38 1
Clifton Rd. W9 BT38 56
Clifton Rd. Couls. BV61 104
Clifton Rd. Grav. DG48 81
Clifton Rd. Grnf. BG38 54
Clifton Rd. Har. BL32 46
Clifton Rd. Horn. CU32 50
Clifton Rd. Houns. AZ45 63
Conway Rd.
Clifton Rd. Ilf. CM32 49
Clifton Rd. Islw. BG44 64
Clifton Rd. Kings. On T. BL50 75
Clifton Rd. Loug. CK24 31
Clifton Rd. Sid. CN49 78
Clifton Rd. Slou. AQ41 62
Clifton Rd. Sthl. BE42 64
Clifton Rd. Tedd. BH49 74
Clifton Rd. Wall. BV56 95
Clifton Rd. Wat. BC25 26
Clifton Rd. Well. CO45 69
Cliftons La. Reig. BQ70 120
Clifton St. E8 CB36 57
Graham Rd.
Clifton St. EC2 CA39 2
Clifton St. EC2 CA39 57
Clifton St. St. Alb. BH13 9
Clifton Ter. N4 BY34 47
Cliftonville, Dor. BJ72 119
Clifton Vills. W9 BS39 1
Clifton Vills. W9 BS39 56
Clifton Way SE15 CB43 67
Clifton Way, Brwd. DE26 122
Clifton Way, Wem. BL37 55
Clift St. N1 BZ37 2
Clifton Way, Wok. AP62 100
Climb, The Rick. AW25 26
Clinch Ct. E16 CH39 58
Cline Rd. N11 BW29 38
Cline Rd. Guil. AS71 118
Clinger Ct. N1 CA37 2
Clinger St. N1 CA37 2
Clink St. SE1 BZ40 4
Clink St. SE1 BZ40 57
Clinton Av. E. Mol. BG52 84
Clinton Av. Well. CN45 68
Clinton Clo. Wok. AO62 100
Clinton Cres. Ilf. CN29 40
Clinton Rd. E3 CD38 57
Clinton Rd. E7 CH35 49
Clinton Rd. N15 BZ31 48
Clinton Rd. Lthd. BK65 102
Clipper Cres. Grav. DJ49 81
Clippesby Clo. Chess. BL57 94
Clipstone Ms. W1 BW38 1
Clipstone Mews BW39 56
Clipstone Rd. Houns. BF45 64
Clipstone St. W1 BV39 56
Clissold Clo. N2 BU31 47
Clissold Ct. N16 BZ34 48
Clissold Cres. N16 BZ35 48
Clissold Rd. N16 BZ34 48
Clitheroe Av. Har. BF33 45
Clitheroe Gdns. Wat. BD27 36
Clitheroe Rd. SW9 BX44 66
Clitheroe Rd. Rom. CS28 41
Clitherow Av. W7 BJ41 64
Clitherow Rd. Brent. BJ42 64
Clitterhouse Cres. NW2 BQ33 46
Clitterhouse Rd. NW2 BQ33 46
Clive Av. N18 CB29 39
Claremont St.
Clive Av. Dart. CT46 79
Clive Clo. Pot. B. BR19 19
Clive Ct. Slou. AO41 61
Clive Ct. Surb. BM55 85
Cliveden Clo. N12 BT28 38
Cliveden Clo. Brwd. DC26 122
Cliveden Pl. SW1 BV42 3
Cliveden Pl. Shep. AZ53 83
High St.
Cliveden Rd. SW19 BR51 85
Clivedon Pl. SW1 BV42 66
Clivedon Rd. E4 CG28 40
Clive Pass. SE21 BZ48 77
Chalford Rd.
Clive Pass. SE21 BZ48 77
Clive Rd.
Clive Rd. SE21 BZ48 77
Clive Rd. SW19 BU50 76
Clive Rd. Belv. CQ42 69
Clive Rd. Brwd. DB29 42
Clive Rd. Enf. CB24 30
Clive Rd. Esher BF56 93
Clive Rd. Felt. BC46 73
Clive Rd. Grav. DG46 81
Clive Rd. Rom. CU32 50
Clive Rd. Twick. BH49 74
Clivesdale Dr. Hayes BC40 53
Avondale Dr.
Clive Way, Couls. BX62 104
Clive Way, Enf. CB24 30
Clive Way, Stai. AV51 82
Clive Way, Wat. BD23 27
Cloak La. EC4 BZ40 4
Cloak La. EC4 BZ40 57
Clock House Clo. Wey. AY59 92
Clockhouse La.
Ashf. & Felt. AZ48 73
Clockhouse La. Grays DB40 60
Clockhouse La. Grays DC40 71
Clockhouse La. Rom. CR29 41
Clockhouse La. Sev. CU65 107
Clockhouse La. W. Egh. AT50 72
Clock House Mead. Lthd. BF60 93
Clock Ho. Rd. Beck. CC52 87
Clock Ho. Rd. Beck. CD51 87
Clock Pl. SE1 BY42 4
Clock Ter. Grav. DH46 81
Clock Tower Pl. N7 BX36 56
Clock Tower Rd. Islw. BH45 64
Clodhouse Hill, Wok. AO64 100
Cloister Gdns. SE25 CB53 87
Cloister Gdns. Edg. BO28 37
Cloister Garth. St. Alb. BH15 9
Cloister Rd. NW2 BR34 46
Cloister Rd. W3 BN39 55
Cloisters Av. Brom. CK53 88
Cloisters, The Rick. AY26 35
Clonard Way, Pnr. BF29 36
Clonbrock Rd. N16 CA35 48
Cloncurry St. SW6 BQ44 65
Clonmell Rd. N17 BZ31 48
Clonmel Rd. SW6 BR43 65
Clonmel Rd. Tedd. BG49 74
Clonmore St. SW18 BR47 75
Clonnel Clo. Har. BG34 45
Cloonmore Av. Orp. CN56 97
Clorane Gdns. NW3 BS34 47
Close, The E4 CF29 39
Close, The N10 BV30 38
Close, The N14 BW27 38
Close, The Barn. BU25 29
Close, The Beck. CD52 87
Close, The Bet. BM72 120
Close, The Bex. CR47 79
Close, The Brwd. DB27 42
Close, The Bush. BF25 27
Close, The Cars. BU58 95
Close, The Dart. CV48 80
Close, The Grays DD41 71
Close, The Har. BG30 36
Close, The Hat. BR16 19
Close, The Islw. BG44 64
Close, The Iver AU38 52
Close, The Mitch. BU52 86
Close, The N. Mal. BN51 85
Close, The N20 BR27 37
Close, The Orp. CN53 88
Close, The Pnr. BD33 45
Close, The Pnr. BE33 45
Close, The Pur. BX58 95
Close, The Pur. BY58 95
Close, The Rad. BH20 18
Close, The Reig. BS71 121
Close, The Rich. BM45 65
Close, The Rick. AW26 35
Close, The Rom. CQ32 50
Close, The Sev. CT65 107
Close, The Sid. CO49 79
Close, The Sutt. BR54 85
Close, The Uxb. AY36 53
Close, The Uxb. AZ37 53
Close, The Vir. W. AR53 82
Close, The Wem. BL36 55
Close, The Wem. BN34 46
Close, The Wey. AW60 92
Closemead Clo. Nthwd. BA29 35
Cloth Fair EC1 BY39 2
Cloth Fair EC1 BY39 56
Clothier St. E1 CA39 57
Cutler St.
Cloudberry Rd. Rom. CV29 42
Cloudesdale Rd. SW17 BV48 76
Cloudesley Pl. N1 BY37 2
Cloudesley Pl. N1 BY37 56
Cloudesley Rd. N1 BY37 2
Cloudesley Rd. N1 BY37 56
Cloudesley Rd. Bexh. CQ44 69
CLoudesley Rd. Erith CT44 69
Cloudesley Sq. N1 BY37 2
Cloudesley Sq. N1 BY37 56
Cloudesley St. N1 BY37 2
Cloudesley St. N1 BY37 56
Clova Rd. E7 CG36 58
Cloveley Av. Uxb. BA35 44
Cloveley Clo. Uxb. BA35 44
Clovelley Way, Orp. CN53 88
Clovelly Av. Warl. CB63 105
Clovelly Av. NW9 BO31 46
Clovelly Ct. Horn. CW34 51
Clovelly Ct. Horn. CX34 51
Clovelly Gdns. Enf. CA26 39
Clovelly Gdns. Rom. CR30 41
Clovelly Rd. N8 BW31 47
Clovelly Rd. W4 BN41 65
Clovelly Rd. W5 BK41 64
Clovelly Rd. Bexh. CQ43 69
Clovelly Way E1 CC39 57
Jamaica St.
Clovelly Way, Har. BE34 45
Clover Clo. E11 CF34 48
Norman Rd.
Cloverdale Gdns. Sid. CN46 78
Cloverfield, Welw. G. C. BR6 5
Clover Hill, Couls. BV64 104
Cloverland, Hat. BO14 10
Clover Leas, Epp. CN18 22
Cloverley Rd. Ong. CX18 24
Clover Ms. SW3 BU43 3
Clover Ms. SW3 BU43 66
Clover Rd. Guil. AP69 118
Clover Way, Hem. H. AW13 8
Clove St. E13 CH38 58
Clowders Rd. SE6 CD48 77
Cloyster Wood, Edg. BK29 36
Club Gdns. Rd. Brom. CH54 88
Club Row E1 CA38 57
Club Row E2 CA38 2
Club Row E2 CA38 57
Clump Av. Tad. BN69 120
Clump, The Rick. AW25 26
Clumps, The Felt. BA49 73
Clunas Gdns. Rom. CV31 51
Clunbury Av. Sthl. BE42 64
Clunbury St. N1 BZ37 2
Cluny Ms. SW5 BS42 66
Cluny Pl. SE1 CA41 4
Cluny Pl. SE1 CA41 67
Clutton St. E14 CE39 57
Clydach Rd. Enf. CA24 30
Clyde Av. Sth. Croy. CB61 105
Clyde Cir. N15 CA31 48
Clyde Clo. Red. BV70 121
Clyde Clo. Upmin. CZ32 51
Clyde Pl. E10 CE33 48
Clyde Pl. SE23 CC48 77
Clyde Rd. N15 BZ31 48
Clyde Rd. N22 BW30 38
Clyde Rd. Croy. CA55 87
Clyde Rd. Hodd. CF13 12
Clyde Rd. Stai. AX47 73
Clyde Rd. Sutt. BS56 95
Clyde Rd. Wall. BW56 95
Clydesdale Av. Stan. BK31 45
Clydesdale Clo. Borwd. BN25 28
Clydesdale Gdns. Rich. BM45 65
Clydesdale Path, Borwd. BN25 28
Clydesdale Clo.
Clydesdale Rd. W11 BR39 55
Clydesdale Rd. Enf. CC24 30
Clydesdale Rd. Horn. CT33 50
Clyde Sq. Hem. H. AY11 8
Clyde St. SE8 CD43 67
Clyde Ter. SE23 CC48 77
Clyde Val. SE23 CC48 77
Clyde Way, Rom. CT30 41
Clydon Clo. Erith CT43 69
Clyfford Rd. Ruis. BB35 44
Clyfton Clo. Brox. CD15 12
Clymping Dene, Felt. BC47 73
Clyston Rd. Wat. BB25 26
Clyston St. SW8 BW44 66
Coach & Horses Yd. W1 BW40 3
Coach & Horses Yd. W1 BW40 56
Old Burlington St.
Coach House. La. SW19 BQ48 75
Coach Rd. Cher. AU57 91
Coach Rd. Dor. & Bet. BL71 120
Coach Rd. Grav. DE46 81
Coach Rd. Grav. DF46 81
Coach Rd. Sev. DA65 108
Coach Rd. Sev. DA66 117
Coaldale Wk. SE24 BZ47 77
Rosendale Rd.
Coalecroft Rd. SW15 BQ45 65
Coaley Row, Dag. CQ37 59
Coal Rd. Til. DJ42 71
Coal Wharf Rd. W12 BQ42 65
Coalwith Rd. W6 BQ44 65
Coast Hill, Dor. BE73 119
Coast Hill La. Dor. BF72 119
Coates Hill Rd. Brom. CL51 88
Coates Rd. Borwd. BK26 36
Coates St. Harl. CM11 13
Coate St. E2 CB37 57
Coates Wk. Brent. BL42 65
Burford Rd.
Coates Way, Wat. BD20 18
Coat Wicks, Beac. AO29 34
Cob Clo. Borwd. BN25 28
Hunter Path
Cobb Ern. Wat. BC19 17
Cobbets Clo. Wok. AQ62 100
Cobbets Hill, Wey. AZ57 92
Cobbett, Guil. AP70 118
Cobbett Rd. SE9 CK45 68
Cobbett Rd. Twick. BF47 74
Cobbetts Av. Ilf. CJ32 49
Cobbinsend Rd. Wal. Abb. CJ18 22
Cobbins, The Wal. Abb. CG20 22
Cobbler's Wk. Tedd. BG50 74
Cobbles, The Brwd. DC27 122
Cobbles, The Upmin. CZ33 51
Cobbold Est. NW10 BO36 55
Cobbold Rd. E11 CG34 49
Cobbold Rd. NW10 BO36 55
Cobbold Rd. W12 BO41 65
Cobb Rd. Berk. AP13 7
Cobbs Rd. Houns. BE45 64
Cobb St. E1 CA39 2
Cobb St. E1 CA39 57
Leyden St.
Cobden Clo. Uxb. AX37 53
Wells Rd.
Cobden Hill, Rad. BJ21 27
Cobden Rd. E11 CG34 49
Cobden Rd. SE25 CB53 87
Cobden Rd. Orp. CM58 97
Cobden Rd. Sev. CV65 108
Cobham Av. N. Mal. BP53 85
Cobham Clo. SW11 BU46 76
Cobham Clo. Brom. CK54 88
Cobham Clo. Wall. BX57 95
Redford Av.
Cobham Pk. Rd. Cob. BC62 101
Cobham Pk. Rd. Cob. BD62 102
Cobham Rd. E17 CF30 39
Cobham Rd. N22 BY31 47
Cobham Rd. Bark. CM37 58
St. Margaret's Rd.
Cobham Rd. Cob. & Lthd. BF62 102
Cobham Rd. Houns. BC43 63
Cobham Rd. Ilf. CN34 49
Cobham Rd. Kings. on T. BM51 85
Cobham Rd. Lthd. BG64 102
Cobham St. Grav. DG47 81
Cobham Ter. Rd. Green. DA46 80
Cobham Ter. Rd. Green. DA47 80
Cobham Way, Leath. BB66 110
Cobill Clo. Horn. CV31 51
Cobland Rd. SE12 CJ49 78
Cobmead, Hat. BP11 10
Crop Common
Coborn Rd. E3 CD37 57
Coborn St. E3 CD38 57
Cobourg Rd. SE5 CA43 67
Cobourg Rd. SE5 CA45 4
Cobourg St. NW1 BW38 1
Cobourg St. NW1 BW38 56
Cobsdene, Grav. DH50 81
Cobs Way, Wey. AW58 92
Coburgh Cres. SW2 BX47 76
Coburg Rd. N22 BX31 47
Cochrane Clo. NW8 BT37 56
Cochrane Ms. NW8 BT37 56
Cochrane Rd. SW19 BR50 75
Cochrane St. NW8 BT37 1
Cochrane St. NW8 BT37 56
Cockcayne Wk. SE8 CD42 67
Cockerhurst Rd. Sev. CS57 98
Cocker Rd. Enf. CB21 30
Cockett Rd. Slou. AS41 62
Cockfosters Rd. Barn. BU22 29
Cock Gro. Berk. AO13 7
Cock Hill E1 CA39 57
New St.
Cock La. EC1 BY39 2
Cock La. EC1 BY39 56
Cock La. Hodd. CB13 12
Cock La. Lthd. BG64 102
Cockmannings La. Orp. CP54 89
Cockmannings Rd. Orp. CP54 89
Cockpit Yd. WC1 BX39 2
Cockpit Yd. WC1 BX39 56
Northington St.
Cock Robins La. Harl. CL7 6
Cock Robins La. Ware. CL6 6
Cocks Cres. N. Mal. BO52 85
Cocksett Av. Orp. CN57 97
Cockshot Hill, Reig. BS71 121
Cockshot Rd. Reig. BS71 121
Cockspur Ct. SW1 BW40 3
Cockspur Ct. SW1 BW40 56
Spring Gdns.
Cockspur St. SW1 BW40 3
Cockspur St. SW1 BW40 56
Cocksure La. Sid. CR48 79
Cock Yd. SE5 BZ44 67
Denmark Hill
Code St. E1 CA38 2
Code St. E1 CA38 57
Codham Hall La. Brwd. DB31 51
Codicote Dr. Wat. BD20 18
Codicote Rd. Welw. BN5 5
Codicote Row, Hem. H. AZ10 8
Codicote Ter. N4 BZ34 48
Colding Way, Wem. BK35 45
Codmore Cres. Chesh. AP18 16
Codmore Wood Rd. Chesh. AR20 16
Codrington Ct. Grav. DH49 81
Codrington Gdns. Grav. DH49 81
Codrington Hl. SE23 CD47 77
Codrington Ms. W11 BR39 55
Blenheim Cres.
Cody Clo. Har. BK31 45
Cody Clo. Wall. BW57 95
Alcock Clo.
Cody Rd. E16 CF38 57
Cofers Circ. Wem. BM34 46
Coftards, Slou. AR39 52
Cogan Av. E17 CO30 39
Coin St. SE1 BY40 56
Coisy St. NW5 BV36 56
Cokers La. SE21 BZ47 77
Perifield
Coke. S. La. Ch. St. G. AQ24 25
Coke St. E1 CB39 57
Colas Ms. NW6 BS37 56
Birchington Rd.
Colbeck Ms. SW7 BS42 3
Colbeck Ms. SW7 BS42 66
Colberg Pl. N16 CA33 48
Colborne Way, Wor. Pk. BQ55 85
Colbrook Av. Hayes BA41 63
Colbrook Clo. Hayes BA41 63
Colburn Av. Cat. CA65 105
Colburn Av. Pnr. BE29 36
Colburn Way, Sutt. BT55 86
Colby Rd. SE19 CA49 77
Colby Rd. Walt. BC54 83
Colchester Av. E12 CK34 49
Colchester Dr. Pnr. BD32 45
Colchester Rd. E10 CF33 48
Colchester Rd. E17 CE32 48
Colchester Rd. Edg. BN30 37
Colchester Rd. Nthwd. BC30 35
Colchester Rd. Rom. CV30 42
Colcokes Rd. Bans. BS61 104
Cold Arbor Rd. Sev. CS65 107
Coldbath Sq. EC1 BY38 56
Topham St.
Coldbath St. SE13 CE44 67
Cold Blow Cres. Bex. CS47 79
Cold Blow La. SE14 CC43 67
Cold Blows, Mitch. BU52 86
Coldershaw Rd. W13 BJ40 54
Coldfall Av. N10 BV30 38
Coldhabour Rd. Wey. AV60 91
Coldham Clo. Enf. CD22 30
Standard Rd.
Coldhara La. Pur. BY54 86
Coldharbour Clo. Egh. AV52 82
Coldharbour La.
Coldharbour La. SE5 BZ45 67
Coldharbour La. SW9 BY45 66
Coldharbour La. Bush. BF25 27
Coldharbour La. Dor. BH74 119
Coldharbour La. Egh. AU52 82
Coldharbour La. Hayes BC41 63
Coldharbour La. Pur. CH58 97
Coldharbour La. Red. CA70 114
Coldharbour La. Ton. CZ71 117
Coldharbour La. Wok. AV61 100
Coldharbour Rd. Croy. BY56 95
Coldharbour Rd. Grav. DF48 81
Coldharbour Rd. Harl. CK11 13
Coldharbour Rd. Wok. AV61 100
Coldharbour Way, Croy. BY56 95
Coldshott, Oxt. CH70 115
Coldstream Gdns. SW18 BR46 75
Cold St. EC1 BY38 2
Colebeck Mews N1 BY36 47
Colebert Av. E1 CC38 5
Colebrook, Cher. AU57 9
Colebrook Av. W13 BJ39 5
Colebrook Clo. SW15 BQ47 7
Colebrook Row N1 BY37
Colebrook Dr. E11 CH33 4
Colebrooke Rise, Brom. CG51 8
Colebrooke Row N1 BY37 5
Colebrook Gnds. Loug. CM23 3
Colebrook La. Loug. CL23 3
Colebrook Path. Loug. CL23 3
Colebrook Rd. E17 CD31 4
Colebrook Rd. SW16 BX51 8
Colebrook Rd. Red. BU69 12
Colebrook Way N11 BV28 3
High Rd.
Coleby Path SE5 BZ43 6
Elmington Estate
Cole Clo. SE28 CO40 5
Cole Ct. W6 BQ43 6
Coledale Dr. Stan. BK30 3
Coleford Clo. Loug. CL23 3
Colefod Rd. SW18 BT46 7
Colegrave Rd. E15 CF35 4
Cole Grn. Welw. G. C. BR9
Colegrove Rd. SE15 CA43 6
Coleherne Ct. SW5 BS42
Coleherne Ct. SW5 BS42 6
Coleherne Ms. SW10 BS42
Coleherne Ms. SW10 BS42 6
Coleherne Rd. SW10 BS42
Coleherne Rd. SW10 BS42 6
Colehill Gdns. SW6 BR44 6
Fulham Palace Rd.
Colehill La. SW6 BR44 6
Coleman Clo. E1 CC40 5
Garnet St.
Coleman Ct. E1 CC40 5
Garnet St.
Coleman Ct. SW18 BS47 7
Coleman Fields N1 BZ37
Coleman Fields N1 BZ37 5
Coleman Rd. SE5 CA43 6
Coleman Rd. Belv. CR42 6
Coleman Rd. Dag. CQ36 5
Colemans Hth. SE9 CL48 7
Coleman's La. Wal. Abb. CF16 2
Coleman's La. Wal. Abb. CG16 2
Coleman St. EC2 BZ39
Coleman St. EC2 BZ39 5
Colemorton Cres. Wind. AM42 61
Colenso Rd. E5 CC35 4
Colenso Rd. Ilf. CN33 4
Cole Pk. Gdns. Twick. BJ46 7
Cole Pk. Rd. Twick. BJ46 7
Colepits Wood Rd. SE9 CM46 7
Coleraine Rd. N8 BY31 4
Coleraine Rd. SE3 CG43 6
Coleridge Av. E12 CK36 5
Coleridge Clo. SW8 BV44 6
Coleridge Clo. Brwd. DE26 12
Byron Rd.
Coleridge Cr. Hem. H. AZ10 8
Coleridge Cres. Slou. AV44 62
Coleridge Gdns. NW6 BT36 56
Coleridge La. N8 BX32 47
Coleridge Rd.
Coleridge Rd. E17 CD31 48
Coleridge Rd. N4 BY34 47
Coleridge Rd. N8 BW32 47
Coleridge Rd. N12 BT28 38
Coleridge Rd. Ashf. AY49 73
Coleridge Rd. Croy. CC54 87
Coleridge Rd. Dart. CX45 70
Coleridge Rd. Rom. CU29 41
Coleridge Rd. Til. DH44 71
Coleridge Wk. NW11 BS31 47
Coleridge Way, Hayes BC39 53
Coleridge Way, Orp. CO53 89
Coleridge Way, West Dr. AY42 63
Cole Rd. Twick. BJ46 74
Cole Rd. Wat. BC23 26
Colesburg Rd. Beck. CD52 87
Coles Clo. Ong. CX16 24
Coles Cres. Har. BF34 45
Colescroft Hill, Pur. BY61 104
Colesdale, Pot. B. BX18 20
Coles Grn. Ct. NW2 BP34 46
Coles Grn. Rd. NW2 BP33 46
Coles Grn. Bush. BG26 36
Coles Grn. Loug. CL23 31
Coles Hill, Hem. H. AW12 8
Coleshill Rd. Tedd. BH50 74
Coles La. West. CP65 107
Colesmead Rd. Red. BU69 121
Colestown St. SW11 BU44 66
Cole St. SE1 BZ41 4
Cole St. SE1 BZ41 67
Cole St. SW11 BU44 66
Colet Ct. W6 BQ42 65
Colet Gdns. W14 BQ42 65
Colet Rd. Brwd. DE25 122
Colets Orch. Sev. CU61 107
Coley Av. Wok. AT62 100
Coley St. WC1 BX38 2
Coley St. WC1 BX38 56
Colfe Rd. SE23 CD47 77
Colgrove, Welw. G. C. BQ8 5
Colham Grn. Rd. Uxb. AZ39 53
Colham Rd. Uxb. AY38 53
Colham Rd. West Dr. AY40 53
Colina Ms. N8 BW31 47
Park Rd.
Colina Rd. N15 BY32 47
Colin Clo. NW9 BO31 46
Colin Clo. Croy. CD55 87
Colin Clo. Dart. CX46 80
Brent Clo.
Colin Clo. W. Wick. CG55 88
Colin Cres. NW9 BO31 46
Colindale Av. NW9 BN31 46
Colindale Av. Erith. CR43 69
Colindale Av. St. Alb. BH14 9
Colindale Rd. Slou. AV44 62
Colindeep Gdns. NW4 BP31 46
Colindeep La. NW9 BN31 46
Colin Dr. NW9 BO32 46
Colinette Rd. SW15 BQ45 65

Colin Gdns. NW9 BO32 46
Colin Pk. Rd. NW9 BO31 46
Colin Rd. NW10 BP36 55
Colin Rd. Cat. CB65 105
Colin St. SE1 BY40 4
Colinton Rd. Ilf. CO34 50
Colin Way, Slou. AN41 61
Coliston Rd. SW18 BS47 76
Collage Gate, Harl. CM11 13
Collamore Av. SW18 BU47 76
Collapit Clo. Har. BF32 45
Collard Av. Loug. CM23 31
Collard Grn. Loug. CM23 31
College App. SE10 CF43 67
College Av. Grays DD42 71
College Av. Slou. AP41 62
College Av. Egh. AT50 72
College Av. Epsom BO60 94
College Av. Har. BH30 36
College Clo. E9 CC35 48
Churchill Wk.
College Clo. N18 CA28 39
College Clo. Har. BH29 36
College Cres. NW3 BT36 56
College Cres. Wind. AN44 61
College Cross N1 BY36 56
College Dr. Ruis. BC33 44
College Gdns. E4 CE26 39
College Gdns. N18 CA28 39
College Gdns. SE21 CA47 77
College Gdns. Enf. BZ23 30
College Gdns. Ilf. CK32 49
College Gdns. N. Mal. BO53 85
College Grn. SE19 CA50 77
College Gro. NW1 BW37 1
College Hill EC4 BZ40 4
College Hill EC4 BZ40 57
College Hill Rd. Har. BH29 36
College Hill Rd. Har. BH30 36
College La. NW5 BV35 47
College La. Hat. BO13 10
College La. Wok. AR63 100
College Pk. Cl. SE13 CF46 77
College Pl. E17 CG31 49
College Pl NW1 BW37 1
College Pl. NW1 BW37 56
College Pl. St. Alb. BG13 9
College Rd. E17 CF32 48
College Rd. N17 CA29 39
College Rd. N21 BY27 38
College Rd. NW10 BQ37 55
College Rd. SE19 CA47 77
College Rd. SE21 CA47 77
College Rd. SW19 BT50 76
College Rd. W13 BJ39 54
College Rd. Brom. CH51 88
College Rd. Croy. BZ55 87
College Rd. Enf. BZ23 30
College Rd. Epsom BO60 94
College Rd. Grav. DD46 81
College Rd. Grays DE42 71
College Rd. Guil. AR71 118
College Rd. Har. BH30 36
College Rd. Har. BH32 45
College Rd. Hodd. CD11 12
College Rd. Islw. BH44 64
College Rd. St. Alb. BJ14 9
College Rd. Slou. AM40 61
College Rd. Swan. CT51 89
College Rd. Wal. Cr. CB18 21
College Rd. Wat. BB19 17
College Rd. Wem. BK33 45
College Rd. Wok. AT61 100
College Slip, Brom. CH51 88
College St. EC4 BZ40 4
College St. EC4 BZ40 57
College St. St. Alb. BG13 9
College Ter. E3 CD38 57
College Ter. N3 BR30 37
Hendon La.
College Vw. SE9 CJ47 78
College Way, Welw. G. C. BQ7 5
Collent St. E9 CC36 57
Collerston Rd. SE10 CG42 68
Colless Rd. N15 CA32 48
Collet Rd. Sev. CW62 108
Collett Clo. Wal. Cr. CC17 21
Collett Gdns. Wal Cr. CC17 21
Collett Clo.
Collett Rd. SE16 CB41 67
Collett Rd. Hem. H. AX13 8
Colley Hill La. Slou. AP34 43
Colley La. Reig. BR70 120
Colley La. Rick. AU24 25
Colley Manor Dr. Reig. BQ70 120
Colley Way, Reig. BR69 120
Collier Clo. Epsom BM57 94
Colliers Clo. Wok. AQ62 100
Collier Cres. Dart. CZ49 80
Collier Dr. Edg. BM30 37
Collier Row La. Rom. CR29 41
Collier Row Rd. Rom. CQ30 41
Colliers St. Cat. CB66 114
Collier St. N1 BX37 2
Collier St. N1 BX37 56
Colliers Water La. Th. Hth. BY53 86
Collindale Av. Sid. CO47 79
Collingbourne Rd. W12 BP40 55
Collingham Gdns. SW5 BS42 3
Collingham Gdns. SW5 BS42 66
Collingham Pl. SW5 BS42 3
Collingham Pl. SW5 BS42 66
Collingham Rd. SW5 BS42 3
Collingham Rd. SW5 BS42 66
Collington Clo. Grav. DF47 81
Beresford Rd.
Collingtree Rd. SE26 CC49 77
Collingtree Av. N10 BV31 47
Collingtree Av. Surb. BN54 85
Collingtree Clo. Twick. BF46 74
Collingwood Cres. Guil. AT70 118
Collingwood Est. E1 CB38 57
Collingwood Pl. SE18 CL41 68
Rodney St.
Collingwood Rd. E17 CE32 48
Collingwood Rd. N15 CA31 48
Collingwood Rd. Mitch. BU51 86
Collingwood Rd. Sutt. BR55 85
Collingwood Rd. Uxb. AZ38 53
Collingwood St. E1 CB38 57
Collins Av. Stan. BL30 37
Collins Dr. Ruis. BD34 45
Collins Meadow, Harl. CL11 13
Collinson St. SE1 BZ41 4
Collinson St. SE1 BZ41 67
Collinson Wk. SE1 BZ41 67
Scovell Rd.
Collins Rd. N5 BZ35 48
Collins St. SE3 CG44 68
Collins Yd. N1 BY37 2
Collinwood Av. Enf. CC24 30
Collinwood Gdns. Ilf. CK32 49
Collis Alley, Twick. BH47 74
Albion Rd.
Coll's Rd. SE15 CC44 67
Collum Grn. Slou. AO34 43
Collver Clo. N1 BX37 56
Eckford St.
Collyer Av. Croy. BX56 95
Collyer Pl. SE15 CA44 67
Peckham High St.
Collyer Rd. St. Alb. BK17 18
Collyer Rd. Croy. BX56 95
Colman Clo. Epsom BP62 103
Colman Rd. E16 CJ39 58
Colman St. E2 CB38 57
Colman Way, Red. BU69 121
Colmar Clo. E1 CC38 57
Alderney Rd.
Colmer Pl. Har. BG29 36
Colmer Rd. SW16 BX51 86
Colmore Rd. Enf. CC24 30
Colnbrook By-pass, Slou. AU43 62
Colnbrook By-pass, West Dr. AW43 63
Colnbrook St. SE1 BY41 4
Colnbrook St. SE1 BY41 66
Colndale Rd. Uxb. AX35 44
Colne Av. Rick. AW27 35
Colne Av. West. Dr. AX41 63
Colne Av. Wat. BC25 26
Colne Ct. Epsom BN56 94
Colne Dr. Rom. CW29 42
Colne Gdns. St. Alb. BL17 19
Colne Mead. Rick. AW27 35
Uxbridge Rd.
Colne Orchard, Iver AV39 52
Colne Rd. E5 CD35 48
Colne Rd. N21 BZ26 39
Colne Rd. Twick. BH47 74
Colne St. E13 CH38 58
Colne Valley, Upmin. CZ32 51
Colne Vw. Ter. St. Alb. BL15 10
Colne Way, Hem. H. AY11 8
Colne Way, Stai. AT48 72
Colney Hatch La. N10 BU29 38
Colney Hatch La. N11 BU29 38
Colney Heath La. St. Alb. BK13 9
Colney Heath La. St. Alb. BL13 10
Colney Rd. Dart. CW46 80
Cologne Rd. SW11 BT45 66
Colombo Rd. Ilf. CM33 49
Colombo St. SE1 BY40 4
Colombo St. SE1 BY40 56
Colomb St. SE10 CG42 68
Colonel's La. Cher. AW53 83
Colonial Av. Twick. BG46 74
Colonial Rd. Felt. BB47 73
Colonial Rd. Slou. AQ41 62
Colonial Way, Wat. BD23 27
Colonnade WC1 BX38 2
Colonnade WC1 BX38 56
Herbrand St.
Colridge Av. Sutt. BU56 95
Colson Gdns. Loug. CL24 31
Colson Path, Loug. CL24 31
Colson Rd. Croy. CA55 87
Colson Rd. Loug. CL24 31
Colson Way SW16 BW49 76
Colsterworth Rd. N15 CA31 48
Colston Av. Cars. BU56 95
Colston Ct. Cars. BU56 95
Colston Cres. Wal. Cr. BY17 20
Colston Rd. E7 CJ36 58
Colston Rd. SW14 BN45 65
Colt Hatch, Harl. CL10 6
Coltishall Rd. Horn. CV36 60
Coltness Cres. SE2 CO42 69
Colton Gdns. N17 BZ31 48
Coltsfoot Dr. Guil. AT69 118
Coltsfoot Path, Rom. CV29 42
Columbia Av. Edg. BM30 37
Columbia Av. Wor. Pk. BO54 85
Columbia Ct. N. Mal. BO54 85
Columbia Rd. E2 CA38 2
Columbia Rd. E2 CA38 57
Columbia Rd. E13 CG38 58
Columbia Sq. E2 CA38 2
Columbia Sq. SW14 BN45 65
Upr. Richmond Rd.
Columbine Av. Croy. BY57 95
Columbine Way SE13 CF44 67
Colvestone Cres. E8 CA35 48
Colville Est. N1 BZ37 57
Colville Gdns. W11 BR39 55
Colville Ho. W11 BR39 55
Colville Ms. W11 BR39 55
Colville Pl. W1 BW39 1
Colville Pl. W1 BW39 56
Colville Rd. E11 CF34 48
Colville Rd. E17 CD30 39
Colville Rd. N9 CB26 39
Colville Rd. W3 BM41 65
Colville Rd. W11 BR39 55
Colville Sq. W11 BR39 55
Colville Sq. Ms. W11 BR39 55
Portobello Rd.
Colville Ter. W11 BR39 55
Colvin Gdns. E4 CF27 39
Colvin Gdns. E11 CH31 49
Colvin Gdns. Ilf. CM30 40
Colvin Gdns. Wal. Cr. CC21 30
Colvin Rd. E6 CK36 58
Colvin Rd. Th. Hth. BY53 86
Colvin St. W6 BQ42 65
Glenthorne Rd.
Colwell Rd. SE22 CA46 77
Colwick Clo. N6 BW33 47
Colwith Rd. W6 BQ43 65
Colwood Gdns. SW19 BT50 76
Colworth Gro. SE17 BZ42 4
Colworth Gro. SE17 BZ42 67
Browning St.
Colworth Rd. E11 CG32 49
Colworth Rd. Croy. CB54 87
Colwyn Av. Grnf. BH37 54
Colwyn Cres. Houns. BG44 64
Colwyn Rd. NW2 BP34 46
Colyer Clo. SE9 CL48 78
Colyer Rd. Grav. DE48 81
Colyers Clo. Erith CS44 69
Colyers Clo. Welw. G. C. BR5 5
Colyers La. Erith CS44 69
Colyers Wk. Erith CT44 69
Colyton Clo. Well. CP44 69
Colyton Clo. Wem. BK36 54
Colyton Clo. Wok. AR62 100
Winnington Way
Colyton Rd. SE22 CB46 77
Colyton Way N18 CB28 39
Combe Av. SE3 CG43 68
Combedale Rd. SE10 CH42 68
Combe Lea, Brom. CK52 88
Combermartin Rd. SW18 BR47 75
Combe Ms. SE3 CG43 68
Comber Clo. NW2 BP34 46
Comber Gro. SE5 BZ43 67
Combermere Rd. SW9 BX45 66
Combermere Rd. Mord. BS53 86
Combe Rd. N16 CD35 48
Trumans Rd.
Combe Rd. Wat. BB25 26
Comberton Rd. E5 CB34 48
Combeside SE18 CN43 68
Combe St. Hem. H. AX13 8
Combfield Dr. Dart. CZ49 80
Combwell Cres. SE2 CO41 69
Comely Bank Rd. E17 CE32 48
Comeragh Clo. Wok. AQ63 100
Comeragh Ms. W14 BR42 65
Comeragh Rd.
Comeragh Rd. W14 BR42 65
Comerford Rd. SE4 CD45 67
Comet Clo. Grays CX42 70
Chieftan Dr.
Comet Clo. Wat. BB20 17
Comet Ho. Pl. SE8 CE43 67
Watson's St.
Comet Rd. Hat. BO12 10
Comet Rd. Stai. AX47 73
Comet St. SE8 CE43 67
Comforts Fm. Av. Oxt. CG70 115
Commerce Rd. N22 BX30 38
Commerce Rd. Brent. BK43 64
Commerce Way, Croy. BX55 86
Commercial Dock Pass. SE16 CD41 67
Commercial Rd. E1 CB39 2
Commercial Rd. E1 CB39 57
Commercial Rd. N18 CA29 39
Commercial Rd. Guil. AR71 118
Commercial Rd. Stai. AW50 73
Commercial St. E1 CA38 2
Commercial St. E1 CA38 57
Commercial Way SE15 CA43 67
Commercial Way, Wok. AS62 100
Commerell Pl. SE10 CG42 68
Blackwall La.
Commerell St. SE10 CG42 68
Commodore St. E1 CD38 57
Common Clo. Wok. AR60 91
Commondale SW15 BQ45 65
Commonfield La. SW17 BU49 76
Commonfield Rd. Bans. BS60 95
Commonfields, Harl. CN10 6
Common Grn. Berk. AT12 7
Common La. Dart. CU48 79
Common La. Esher BJ57 93
Common La. Kings. L. AY17 17
Common La. Red. BZ69 114
Common La. Wat. BH23 27
Common La. Wey. AX58 92
Common La. Wind. AO42 61
Common Meadow La. Wat. BG20 18
Common Rd. SW13 BP45 65
Common Rd. Brwd. DE28 122
Common Rd. Dor. BG70 119
Common Rd. Esher BJ57 93
Common Rd. Lthd. BE64 102
Common Rd. Red. BU71 121
Common Rd. Rick. AU24 25
Common Rd. Sev. DA65 108
Common Rd. Slou. AT42 62
Common Rd. Stan. BG28 36
Common Rd. Uxb. AX35 44
Common Rd. Wal. Abb. CJ14 13
Common Rd. Wind. AL42 61
Common Rd. Wind. AM42 61
Common Rd. Wind. AN42 61
Commonsgate Rd. Rick. AU25 25
Commonside, Harl. CN13 13
Commonside, Kes. CJ56 97
Commonside, Lthd. BF65 102
Commonside, Mitch. BW53 86
Commonside, E. Mitch. BV52 86
Commonside Rd. Harl. CN13 13
Commonside, W. Mitch. BU52 86
Commons La. Hem. H. AY13 8
Commons, The Welw. G. C. BS9 5
Common, The W5 BL40 55
Common, The Berk. AS12 7
Common, The Hat. BP12 10
Common, The Kings L. AW19 17
Common, The Rich. BK48 74
Common, The Stan. BH27 36
Common, The Sthl. BD42 64
Common Way, Esher BG58 93
Commonwealth Av. W12 BP40 55
Commonwealth Av. Hayes BA39 53
Commonwealth Rd. N17 CB29 39
Commonwealth Rd. Cat. CB65 105
Commonwealth Way SE2 CO42 69
Community Clo. Uxb. AZ34 44
Long La.
Community Rd. E15 CF35 48
Community Rd. Grnf. BG37 54
Como Rd. SE23 CD48 77
Como St. Rom. CS31 50
Compass Hill, Rich. BL46 75
Petersham Rd.
Compayne Gdns. NW6 BS36 56
Comport Gr. Croy. CG59 97
Compton Av. E6 CJ37 58
Compton Av. N1 BY36 56
Compton Av. N6 BU33 47
Compton Av. Brwd. DE26 122
Compton Av. Rom. CU31 50
Compton Clo. NW1 BV38 1
Compton Clo. NW1 BV38 56
Robert St.
Compton Clo. Esher BG56 93
Compton Ct. SE19 CA49 77
Compton Cres. N17 BZ29 39
Compton Cres. W4 BN43 65
Compton Cres. Chess. BL57 94
Compton Crs. Nthlt. BD37 54
Compton Gdns. St. Alb. BF16 18
Faringford Clo.
Compton Pass. EC1 BY38 2
Compton Pass. EC1 BY38 56
Compton St.
Compton Pl. Erith CT43 69
Compton Pl. Wat. BE28 36
Compton Rise, Pnr. BE32 45
Compton Rd. N1 BY36 56
Compton Rd. N21 BY26 38
Compton Rd. NW10 BQ38 55
Compton Rd. SW19 BR50 75
Compton Rd. Croy. CB54 87
Compton Rd. Hayes BB40 53
Compton Sq. N1 BY36 56
Canonbury Rd.
Compton St. E13 CH37 58
Compton St. EC1 BY38 2
Compton St. EC1 BY38 56
Compton Ter. N1 BY36 56
Comreddy Clo. Enf. BY22 29
Comus Pl. SE17 BZ42 4
Comus Pl. SE17 CA42 67
Comus Rd. N19 BW34 47
Comyne Rd. Wat. BB21 26
Comyn Rd. SW11 BU45 66
Comyns Clo. E16 CG39 58
Comyns Rd. Dag. CR36 59
Comyns, The Bush. BG26 36
Conaways Clo. Epsom BP58 94
Concanon Rd. SW2 BX45 66
Concert Hall App. SE1 BX40 4
Concert Hall App. SE1 BX40 56
Concorde Cl. Houns. BF44 64
Lampton Rd.
Concorde Clo. Uxb. AY37 53
Concorde Dr. Hem. H. AX13 8
Concorde Way, Slou. AO41 61
Concorde Rd. W3 BM38 55
Concorde Rd. Enf. CB25 30
Concourse, The N9 CB27 39
Condell Rd. SW8 BW44 66
Conder St. E14 CD39 57
Conderton Rd. SE5 BZ45 67
Condor Path, Nthlt. BF37 54
Leander Rd.
Condor Rd. Stai. AX52 83
Condor Wk. Rain. CU36 59
Condover Cres. SE18 CL43 68
Condray St. SW11 BT44 66
Conduct Rd. Barn. BR25 28
Conduit Ct. WC2 BX40 56
Long Acre
Conduit La. N18 BZ28 39
Hermitage La.
Conduit La. Enf. CC25 30
Conduit La. Hodd. CE12 12
Conduit La. Sth. Croy. CA56 96
Conduit Ms. W2 BT39 1
Conduit Ms. W2 BT39 56
Conduit Pl. W2 BT39 1
Conduit Pl. W2 BT39 56
London St.
Conduit Rd. SE18 CL42 68
Conduit St. W1 BV40 3
Conduit St. W1 BV40 56
Conduit Way NW10 BM36 55
Conegar Ct. Slou. AP40 52
Conewood Pl. N5 BY34 47
Conewood St.
Conewood St. N5 BY34 47
Coney Acre SE21 BZ47 77
Coney Berry, Reig. BT72 121
Coney Burrows E4 CG27 40
Normanton Pk.
Coneybury, Red. CA70 114
Coney Clo. Hat. BP13 10
Coney Dale, Welw. G. C. BQ7 7
Coney Grn. Saw. CP5 6
Coney Gro. Uxb. AZ38 53
Coneygrove Path, Nthlt. BE36 54
Arnold Rd.
Coney Hill Rd. W. Wick. CG55 88
Conference Rd. SE2 CP42 69
Congeton Gro. SE18 CM42 68
Congo Rd. SE18 CM42 68
Congress Rd. SE2 CP42 69
Congreve Rd. SE9 CK45 68
Congreve St. SE17 CA42 4
Congreve St. SE17 CA42 67
Conical Cnr. Enf. BZ23 30
Conifer Av. Hart. DC53 90
Conifer Av. Rom. CR28 41
Conifer Clo. Orp. CM56 97
Beechcroft Rd.
Conifer Clo. Reig. BS69 121
Reigate Hill
Conifer Gdns. SW16 BX48 76
Conifer Way, Hayes BC40 53
Longmead Rd.
Conifers, Wey. BB56 92
Conifers Clo. Tedd. BJ50 74
Coniger Rd. SW6 BS44 66
Coningham Ms. W12 BP40 55
Percy Rd.
Coningham Rd. W12 BP40 55
Coningsby Bnk. St. Alb. BG15 9
Coningsby Clo. Hat. BQ15 10
Coningsby Cott W5 BK41 64
Coningsby Rd.
Coningsby Dr. Pot. B. BT20 20
Coningsby Dr. Wat. BB23 26
Coningsby Gdns. E4 CE29 39
Coningsby La. Maid. AH44 61
Coningsby Rd. N4 BY33 47
Coningsby Rd. W5 BK41 64
Coningsby Rd. Sth. Croy. BZ58 96
Conington Rd. SE13 CE44 67
Conisbee Ct. N14 BW25 29
Conisborough Cres. SE6 CF48 77
Coniscliffe Rd. N13 BZ27 39
Conista Ct. Wok. AP61 100
Coniston Av. Bark. CN36 58
Coniston Av. Grnf. BJ38 54
Coniston Av. Upmin. CY35 51
Coniston Av. Well. CN45 68
Coniston Clo. N20 BT27 38
Coniston Clo. W4 BN43 65
Coniston Clo. Bark. CN36 58
Coniston Av.
Coniston Clo. Bexh. CS44 69
Coniston Clo. Dart. CU47 79
Coniston Clo. Erith. CT43 69
Coniston Clo. Hem. H. BA14 8
Coniston Clo. N. Mal. BQ53 85
Grand Dr.
Coniston Ct. Wall. BV56 95
Danbury Mews
Conistone Way N7 BX36 56
Sutterton St.
Coniston Gdns. N9 CC26 39
Coniston Gdns. NW9 BN32 46
Coniston Gdns. Ilf. CK31 49
Coniston Gdns. Pnr. BC31 44
Coniston Gdns. Sutt. BT57 95
Coniston Gdns. Wem. BK33 45
Coniston Rd. N10 BV30 38
Coniston Rd. N17 CB29 39
Coniston Rd. Bexh. CS44 69
Coniston Rd. Brom. CF50 77
Coniston Rd. Couls. BW61 104
Coniston Rd. Croy. CB54 87
Coniston Rd. Kings L. AY17 17
Coniston Rd. Twick. BF46 74
Coniston Rd. Wok. AT63 100
Coniston Wk. E9 CC35 48
Churchill Wk.
Coniston Way N7 BX36 56
Coniston Way, Chess. BL55 85
Coniston Way, Horn. CU35 50
Coniston Way, Red. BU70 121
Conlan St. W10 BR38 55
Conley Rd. NW10 BO36 55
Conley St. SE10 CG42 68
Connaught App. E16 CJ39 58
Baxter Rd.
Connaught Av. Grays DD41 71
Connaught Av. E4 CF26 39
Connaught Av. SW14 BN45 65
Connaught Av. Ashf. AX49 73
Connaught Av. Barn. BU26 38
Connaught Av. Enf. CA23 30
Connaught Av. Houns. BE45 64
Connaught Av. Loug. CJ24 31
Connaught Clo. E10 CD34 48
Connaught Clo. W2 BU39 1
Connaught Clo. W2 BU39 56
Connaught St.
Connaught Clo. Enf. CA23 30
Connaught Clo. Hem. H. AZ12 8
Connaught Clo. Sutt. BT55 86
Connaught Clo. Uxb. BA38 53
Connaught Dr. NW11 BS31 47
Connaught Gdns. N10 BW32 47
Connaught Gdns. N13 BY28 38
Connaught Hill, Loug. CJ24 31
Connaught La. Ilf. CM34 49
Connaught Ms. W2 BU39 1
Connaught Ms. W2 BU39 56
Connaught Pl.
Connaught Pl. W2 BU39 56
Connaught Pl. W2 BU40 3
Connaught Rd. E4 CG26 40
Springfield Rd.
Connaught Rd. E11 CF33 48
Connaught Rd. E16 CJ40 58
Connaught Rd. E17 CE32 48
Connaught Rd. N4 BY33 47
Connaught Rd. NW10 BO37 55
Connaught Rd. SE18 CL42 68
Connaught Rd. W13 BJ40 54
Connaught Rd. Barn. BQ25 28
Connaught Rd. Har. BH30 36
Connaught Rd. Horn. CV34 51
Connaught Rd. Ilf. CM34 49
Connaught Rd. N. Mal. BO52 85
Connaught Rd. Rich. BL46 75
Albert Rd.
Connaught Rd. St. Alb. BG12 9
Connaught Rd. Sutt. BT55 86
Connaught Rd. Tedd. BG49 74
Connaught Sq. W2 BU39 1
Connaught Sq. W2 BU39 56
Connaught St. W2 BU39 1
Connaught St. W2 BU39 56
Connaught Way N13 BY28 38
Connell Cres. W5 BL38 55
Connemara Clo. Borwd. BN25 28
Percheron Rd.
Connicut La. Lthd. BF67 111
Connington Cres. E4 CF27 39
Connop Rd. Enf. CC22 30
Connor Rd. Dag. CQ35 50
Connors All. W6 BR43 65
Bayonne Rd.
Connor St. E9 CC37 57
Lauriston Rd.
Conolly Rd. W7 BH40 54
Conquest Rd. Wey. AW56 92
Conquest St. SE1 BY41 66
Conrad Dr. Wor. Pk. BQ54 85
Conrad St. E9 CC36 57
Consfield Av. N. Mal. BP52 85
Consort Mews, Islw. BG46 74

Consort Rd. SE15 CB44 67
Cons St. SE1 BY41 4
Cons St. SE1 BY41 66
Windmill Wk.
Constable Clo. NW11 BS32 47
Constable Clo. Hayes BA37 53
Constable Clo. Islw. BG46 74
Constable Cres. N15 CB32 48
Constable Gdns. Edg. BM30 37
Constable Rd. Grav. DF48 81
Constable Wk. SE21 CA48 77
Constance Cres. Brom. CG54 88
Constance Rd. Croy. BY54 86
Constance Rd. Enf. CA25 30
Constance Rd. Sutt. BT56 95
Constance Rd. Twick. BF47 74
Constance St. E16 CK40 58
Constantine Rd. NW3 BU35 47
Constitution Hill SW1 BV41 3
Constitution Hill SW1 BV41 66
Constitution Hill, Grav. DH47 81
Constitution Hill, Wok. AS63 100
Constitution Rise SE18 CL44 68
Content St. SE17 BZ42 4
Content St. SE17 BZ42 67
Contessa Clo. Orp. CM56 97
Control Tower Rd. Houns. AZ45 63
Inner Ring West
Convair Wk. Nthlt. BD37 54
Convair Wk. Nthlt. BD38 54
Kittiwake Rd.
Convent Est. SE19 BZ50 77
Convent Gdns. W5 BK42 64
Convent Gdns. W11 BR39 55
Convent Hl. SE19 BZ50 77
Convent La. Cob. BB59 92
Convent Rd. Ashf. AZ49 73
Convent Rd. Wind. AM44 61
Convent Way, Sthl. BD42 64
Conway Clo. Rain. CU36 59
Conway Clo. Stan. BJ29 36
Conway Cres. Grnf. BH37 54
Conway Cres. Rom. CP33 50
Conway Dr. Ashf. BA50 73
Conway Dr. Hayes BA41 63
Conway Dr. Sutt. BS57 95
Conway Gdns. Enf. CA22 30
Conway Gdns. Mitch. BW52 86
Conway Gdns. Wem. BK33 45
Conway Gro. W3 BN39 55
Conway Rd. N14 BX27 38
Conway Rd. N15 BY32 47
Conway Rd. NW2 BQ34 46
Conway Rd. SE18 CM42 68
Conway Rd. SW20 BQ51 85
Conway Rd. Felt. BD49 74
Conway Rd. Houns. BE47 74
Conway St. E13 CH38 58
Philip St.
Conway St. W1 BW38 1
Conway St. W1 BW38 56
Conybeare NW3 BU36 56
Quickswood
Conybury Clo. Wal. Abb. CH19 22
Conyerd Rd. Sev. DC63 108
Conyers Clo. Walt. BD56 93
Conyers Clo. Wdf. Grn. CG29 40
Conyers Rd. E3 CD37 57
Conyers Rd. SW16 BW49 76
Conyers Way, Loug. CL24 31
Cooden Clo. Brom. CH50 78
Plaistow La.
Cookes La. Sutt. BR57 94
Church Rd.
Cookham Hill, Orp. CR55 89
Cookham Rd. Sid. CR50 79
Cookhill Rd. SE2 CO41 69
Cook's Hole Rd. Enf. BY22 29
Cook's Rd. E15 CE37 57
Cooks Rd. SE17 BY43 66
Cooks Spinney, Harl. CO10 6
Cooks Vennel, Hem. H. AW12 8
Coolfin Rd. E16 CH39 58
Coolgardie Av. E4 CF28 39
Coolgardie Av. Chig. CL27 40
Coolgardie Rd. Ashf. BA49 73
Coolhurst Rd. N8 BW32 47
Cool Oak La. NW9 BO33 46
Cool Oak Rd. NW4 BP33 46
Coomassie Rd. W9 BR38 55
Bravington Rd.
Coombe Av. Croy. CA56 96
Coombe Bank, Kings. on T. BO51 85
Coombe Clo. Edg. BL30 37
Coombe Clo. Houns. BF45 64
Coombe Cnr. N21 BY26 38
Coombe Cres. Hamptn. BE50 74
Coombe Cres. Kings. on T. BN50 75
Coombe Dr. Wey. AV57 91
Coombe Dr. Ruis. BC34 44
Coombe End, Kings. on T. BN50 75
Coombe La. W. Kingston BN51 83
Coombefield Clo. N. Mal. BO53 85
Coombe Gdns. SW20 BP51 85
Coombe Gdns. Berk. AP12 7
Coombe Gdns. N. Mal. BO52 85
Coombe Hill Clo.
Kings. on T. BO50 75
Coombe Hill Glade,
Kings. on T. BO50 75
Coombe Hill Rd.
Kings. on T. BO50 75
Coombe Hill Rd. Rick. AW26 35
Coombe Ho. Chase,
N. Mal. BN51 85
Coombehurst Clo. Barn. BU23 29
Coombelands La. Wey. AW57 92
Coombe La. Croy. CB56 96
Coombe La. Kings. on T. BM51 85
Coombe Moor,
Kings. on T. BO50 75
Coombe Nevile,
Kings. on T. BN50 75
Coombe Pk. Kings. on T. BN49 75
Coombe Ri. Kings. on T. BN51 85
Coombe Ridings,
Kings. on T. BN49 75
Coombermere Clo. Wind. AN44 61
Coombe Rd. NW10 BN34 46
Coombe Rd. SE26 CB49 77
Coombe Rd. W4 BO42 65
Coombe Rd. W13 BJ41 64
Northcroft Rd.
Coombe Rd. Bush. BG26 36
Coombe Rd. Croy. BZ56 96
Coombe Rd. Grav. DH48 81
Coombe Rd. Hamptn. BE50 74
Coombe Rd. Kings. on T. BM51 85
Coombe Rd. N. Mal. BO51 85
Coombe Rd. Rom. CW31 51
Coombe Rd. Sev. CV61 108
Coombe Springs,
Kings. on T. BN51 85
Coombes Rd. Dag. CQ37 59
Coombes Rd. St. Alb. BK16 18
Coombe, The Bet. BN69 120
Coombe Vale, Ger. Cr. AS33 43
Coombe Wk. Sutt. BS55 86
Coombe Wd. Hill, Pur. BZ59 96
Coombe W. La.
Kings. on T. BM51 85
Coombewood Dr. Rom. CR32 50
Coombe Wood Rd.
Kings. on T. BN49 75
Coomb La. Guil. AO67 109
Coombs St. N1 BY37 2
Coomb's St. N1 BY37 56
Remington St.
Coome Rise, Brwd. DC26 122
Coomer Rd. SW6 BR43 65
Cooms Wk. Edg. BM30 37
East Rd.
Cooper Av. E17 CD30 39
Cooper Clo. SE1 BY41 4
Morley St.
Cooper Ct. Wat. BC22 26
Cooper Cres. Cars. BU55 86
Coopers Grn. La. St. Alb. BL12 10
Cooper Rd. NW10 BP35 46
Cooper Rd. Croy. BY56 95
Cooper Rd. Guil. AS71 118
Coopersale Clo. Wdf. Grn. CJ29 40
Coopersale Common, Epp. CP17 23
Coopersale La. Epp. CO22 32
Coopersale La. Back La.
Rom. CO23 32
Coopersale Rd. E9 CC35 48
Coopersale Rd. Epp. CO18 23
Coopersale St. Epp. CP19 23
Coopers Cl. Stai. AV49 72
Coopers Clo. Chig. CO27 41
Coopers Clo. S. Dnth. CY51 90
Paddock Ct.
Coopers Green La.
Welw. G. C. BN10 5
Coopers Hill Ong. CX18 24
Coopers Hill La. Egh. AR49 72
Cooper's Hill Rd. Red. BX70 121
Coopers Hill Rd. Red. BY73 121
Coopers La. E10 CE33 48
Coopers La. SE12 CH48 78
Coopers La. Pot. B. BT19 20
Cooper's La. Til. DH43 71
Coopers Lane Rd. Pot. B. BU19 20
Coopers Rd. NW4 BQ32 46
Renters Av.
Cooper's Rd. SE1 CA42 4
Cooper's Rd. SE1 CA42 67
Coopers Rd. Grav. DF47 81
Coopers Rd. Pot. B. BT18 20
Cooper's Row, EC3 CA40 4
Cooper's Row, EC3 CA40 57
Coopers Row, Iver AU38 52
Cooper St. E16 CG39 58
Coote Gdns. Dag. CQ34 50
Coote Rd. Bexh. CQ44 69
Coote Rd. Dag. CQ34 50
Copeland Rd. E17 CE32 48
Copeland Rd. SE15 CB44 67
Copelia Rd. SE3 CG45 68
Copeman Rd. Brwd. DE26 122
Copenhagen Pl. E14 CD39 57
Copenhagen St. N1 BX37 2
Copenhagen St. N1 BX37 56
Copenhagen Way Walt. BC55 83
Copen Rd. Dag. CQ33 50
Cope Pl. W8 BS41 66
Copers Cope Rd. Beck. CD50 77
Cope St. SE16 CC42 67
Copeswood Rd. Wat. BC23 26
Copford Clo. Wdf. Grn. CK29 40
Green Wk.
Copford Wk. N1 BZ37 57
Popham St.
Copinger Wk. Edg. BM30 37
North Rd.
Copland Av. Wem. BK35 45
Copland Clo. Wem. BK35 45
Copland Rd. Wem. BL36 55
Copleigh Dr. Tad. BR63 103
Copleston Rd. SE15 CA45 67
Copley Clo. SE17 BY43 66
Hillingdon St.
Copley Clo. W7 BH39 54
Copley Clo. Red. BU69 121
Copley Clo. Wok. AP63 100
Copley Dene Brom. CJ51 88
Copley Pk. SW16 BX50 76
Copley Rd. Stan. BK28 36
Copley St. E1 CC39 57
Copley Way, Tad. BQ63 103
Copmans Wick, Rick. AU25 25
Copnor Way, SE15 CA43 67
Hordle Prom. W.
Copperas St. SE8 CE43 67
Copperbeech Clo. NW3 BT35 47
Akenside Rd.
Copper Beech Clo. Hem. H. AV15 7
Copper Beech Clo. Ilf. CL30 40
Copper Beech Gro. Wind. AL44 61
Copper Beech Rd. S. Ock. DB38 60
Copperdale Rd. Hayes BC41 63
Copperfield, Chig. CM28 40
Copperfield Approach,
Chig. CM29 40
Copperfield App. Ilf. CM29 40
Copperfield Av. Uxb. AZ39 53
Copperfield Clo. Grav. DK47 81
Copperfield Ct. Lthd. BJ64 102
Kingston Rd.
Copperfield Gdns. Brwd. DA26 42
Copperfield Mews, N18 CA28 39
Dickens La.
Copperfield Orchard, Sev. CW62 108
Copperfields
Copperfield Rise, Wey. AV56 91
Copperfield Rd. E3 CD38 57
Copperfields, Sev. CW62 108
Copperfield St. SE1 BY41 4
Copperfield St. SE1 BY41 66
Copperfield Way Chis. CM50 78
Coppermill La. E17 CC32 48
Copper Mill La. SW17 BT49 76
Coppermill La. Rick. AV29 34
Coppermill La. Uxb. AW29 35
Copper Mill Rd. Stai. AT46 72
Copper Ridge. Ger. Cr. AS28 34
Coppetts Clo. N12 BU29 38
Coppetts Rd. N10 BU29 38
Coppice Cl. Hat. BO14 10
Coppice Clo. SW20 BQ52 85
Coppice Clo. Guil. AO70 118
Coppice Clo. Ruis. BA32 44
Coppice Dr. SW15 BP46 75
Coppice Dr. Stai. AR47 72
Coppice Est. Brom. CL53 88
Coppice La. Reig. BR69 120
Coppice Path, Chig. CO28 41
Coppice Row, Epp. CM21 31
Coppice, The Ashf. AZ50 73
School Rd.
Coppice, The Brwd. CZ21 33
Coppice, The Enf. BY24 29
Coppice, The Wat. BD25 27
Coppice, The West Dr. AY39 53
Coppice Wk. N20 BS27 38
Coppice Way, E18 CG31 49
Coppifs Gro. N11 BV28 38
Copping Clo. Croy. CA56 96
Coppins Clo. Berk. AP13 7
Coppins La. Iver. AV39 52
Coppins, The Croy. CE57 96
Coppins, The Har. BH29 36
Coppley Way, Tad. BQ63 103
Coppock Clo. SW11 BU43 66
Copse Av. W. Wick. CE55 87
Copse Bnk. Sev. CW63 108
Copse Clo. Guil. AU73 118
Copse Clo. Nthwd. BA30 35
Copse Clo. West Dr. AX41 63
Copse Edge Av. Epsom. BO60 94
Copse Glade Surb. BK54 84
Copse Hill Pur. BX60 95
Copse Hill, Sutt. BS57 95
Copse Hl. SW20 BP51 85
Copse La. Beac. AP29 34
Copsem Dr. Esher BG57 93
Copsem La. Esher BG57 93
Copsem La. Lthd. BG59 93
Copse Rd. Cob. BC60 92
Copse Rd. Wok. AP62 100
Copse Side Hart. DC52 90
Copse, The E4 CG26 40
Copse, The Lthd. BF65 102
Copse Vw. Sth. Croy. CC58 96
Copse Wood, Iver AU37 52
Copse Wood Way, Nthwd. BA30 35
Copsleigh Av. Red. BV74 121
Copsleigh Clo. Red. BV73 121
Coptfold Rd. Brwd. DB27 42
Copthall Av. EC2 BZ39 2
Copthall Av. EC2 BZ39 57
Copthall Bldgs. EC2 BZ39 57
Telegraph St.
Copthall Cl. EC2 BZ39 2
Copthall Clo. EC2 BZ39 57
Copthall Clo. Ger. Cr. AS29 34
Copthall Corner. Ger. Cr. AS29 34
Copthall Ct. EC2 BZ39 57
Throgmorton St.
Copthall Dr. NW7 BP29 37
Copthall Gdns. NW7 BP29 37
Copthall Gdns. Twick. BH47 74
Copt Hall Rd. Sev. DA65 108
Copthall Rd. E. Uxb. AZ34 44
Copthall Rd. W. Uxb. AZ34 44
Copthall Way, Wey. AV58 91
Copthall Way, Wey. AW58 92
Copthorn Clo. Shep. BA53 83
Copthorne Av. SW12 BW47 76
Copthorne Av. Brom. CK55 88
Copthorne Av. Ilf. CL29 40
Copthorne Clo. Ashf. AY49 73
Ford Rd.
Copthorne Clo. Ilf. CL29 40
Copthorne Clo. Rick. AY25 26
Copthorne Gdns. Horn. CX32 51
Copthorne Rise Sth. Croy. BZ60 96
Copthorne Rd. Lthd. BJ63 102
Copthorne Rd. Rick. AY25 26
Copthorpe Ct. NW8 BT38 56
Maida Vale
Coptic St. WC1 BX39 2
Coptic St. WC1 BX39 56
Coral Clo. Rom. CP31 50
Coralline Wk. SE2 CP41 69
Coral Mead. Rick. AX26 35
Coral St. SE1 BY41 4
Coral St. SE1 BY41 66
Coram Clo. Berk. AR13 7
Coram Grn. Brwd. DE25 122
Coram St. WC1 BX38 2
Coram St. WC1 BX38 56
Coran Clo. N9 CC26 39
Corban Rd. Houns. BF45 64
Corbar Clo. Barn. BT23 29
Corbet Clo. Wall. BV55 86
Corbet Pl. E1 CA39 57
Jerome St.
Corbet Rd. Epsom BO58 94
Corbets Av. Upmin. CX35 51
Corbets Tey Rd. Upmin. CX35 51
Corbett Rd. E11 CJ32 49
Corbett Rd. E17 CF31 48
Corbett Rd. N22 BX29 38
Trinity Rd.
Corbetts La. SE16 CC42 67
Rotherhithe New Rd.
Corbetts Pass. SE16 CC42 67
Rotherhithe New Rd.
Corbett St. SW8 BX43 66
Corbicum E11 CG33 49
Corbiere Ct. SW19 BQ50 75
Thornton Rd.
Corbins La. Har. BF34 45
Corby Clo. St. Alb. BF16 18
Corby Cres. Enf. BX24 29
Corby Dr. Eng. AR50 72
Corbylands Rd. Sid. CN47 78
Corbyn St. N4 BX33 47
Corby Rd. NW10 BN37 55
Corby Way E3 CE38 57
Knapp Rd.
Corcorans Brwd. DA25 33
Elizabeth Rd.
Cordelia Gdns. Stai. AY47 73
Cordelia Rd. Stai. AY47 73
Cordelia St. E14 CE39 57
Cordelia St. N7 BX36 56
Cordell Clo. Wal. Cr. CD17 21
Corder Clo. St. Alb. BF15 9
Cordons Clo. Ger. Cr. AR30 34
Cordova Rd. E3 CD38 57
Cordrey Gdns. Couls. BX57 95
Cordrey Gdns. Couls. BX61 104
Cordwainers Wk. E13 CH37 58
Turpin Estate
Cord Way E14 CE41 67
Mellish St.
Cordwell Rd. SE13 CF46 77
Corelli Rd. SE3 CK44 68
Corfe Av. Har. BF35 45
Corfe Clo. Ash. BK62 102
Corfield St. E2 CB38 57
Corfton Rd. W5 BL39 55
Corinium Clo. Wem. BL35 46
Corinium Gte. St. Alb. BF14 9
Corinne Rd. N19 BW35 47
Corinthian Manorway, Erith CS42 69
Corinthian Rd. Erith CS42 69
Corinthian Way Stai. AX47 73
Clare Rd.
Corinth Par. Hayes BB39 53
Corinth Rd. N7 BX35 47
Corker Way N7 BX34 47
Andover Est.
Corkran Rd. Surb. BK54 84
Corkscrew Hill W. Wick. CF55 87
Cork St. W1 BW40 3
Cork St. W1 BW40 56
Corlett St. NW1 BU39 1
Corlett St. NW1 BU39 56
Bell St.
Cormongers La. Red. BV70 121
Cormont Rd. SE5 BY44 66
Cormorant Wk. Rain. CU36 59
Cornbury Rd. Edg. BK29 36
Corn Croft, Hat. BP11 10
Crop Common
Cornelia Pla. Erith CT43 69
Queen
Cornell Clo. Sid. CQ50 79
Cornell Way, Rom. CR28 41
Cornerfield Mo. Hat. BP11 10
Corner Hall, Hem. H. AX14 8
Cornerhall Av. Hem. H. AX14 8
Corner Mead NW9 BO30 37
Corner St. E16 CH39 58
Beckton Rd.
Corners Welw. G. C. BS7 5
Corney Rd. W4 BO43 65
Cornfield Clo. Uxb. AX37 53
Cornfield Rd. Bush. BF24 27
Cornfield Rd. Reig. BT71 121
Cornfields, Hem. H. AW13 8
Cornflower Ter. SE22 CB46 77
Cornford Clo. Brom. CH53 88
Cornford Gro. SW12 BV48 76
Cornhill EC3 BZ39 2
Cornhill EC3 BZ39 57
Cornish Gro. SE20 CB51 87
Corn Mead, Welw. G. C. BQ6 5
Cornmill, Wal. Abb. CE20 21
Cornmill Dr. Orp. CN54 88
Cornmill La. SE13 CF45 67
Cornshaw Rd. Dag. CP33 50
Cornsland, Brwd. DB27 42
Cornthwaite Rd. E5 CC34 48
Cornwall Av. E2 CC38 57
Cornwall Av. N3 BS29 38
Cornwall Av. N22 BX30 38
Cornwall Av. Esher BJ57 93
Cornwall Av. Sthl. BE39 54
Cornwall Av. Well. CN45 68
Cornwall Av. Wey. AY60 92
Cornwall Clo. Bark. CN36 58
Cornwall Clo. Wal. Cr. CD20 21
Cornwall Cres. W11 BR39 55
Cornwall Cres. W11 BR40 55
Cornwall Dr. Orp. CP50 79
Cornwall Gdns. NW10 BP36 55
Cornwall Gdns. SW7 BS41 3
Cornwall Gdns. SW7 BS41 66
Cornwall Gdns. Wk. SW7 BS41 3
Cornwall Gdns. Wk. SW7 BS41 66
Cornwall Gro. W4 BO42 65
Cornwallis Av. N9 CB27 39
Cornwallis Av. SE9 CM48 78
Cornwallis Gro. N9 CB27 39
Cornwallis Rd. E17 CC31 48
Cornwallis Rd. N9 CB27 39
Cornwallis Rd. N19 BX34 47
Cornwallis Rd. Dag. CP35 50
Cornwallis Wk. SE9 CK45 68
Cornwall Lo. Kings. on T. BM50 75
Cornwall Mews St. SW7 BT41 3
Cornwall Ms. St. SW7 BT41 66
Cornwall Rd. N4 BY33 47
Cornwall Rd. N15 BZ32 48
Cornwall Rd. N18 CB28 39
Fairfield Rd.
Cornwall Rd. SE1 BY40 4
Cornwall Rd. SE1 BY40 5
Cornwall Rd. Brwd. DA25 3
Cornwall Rd. Croy. BY55 8
Cornwall Rd. Har. BG32 4
Cornwall Rd. Pnr. BE29 3
Cornwall Rd. Ruis. BB34 4
Cornwall Rd. Ruis. BC34 4
Cornwall Rd. St. Alb. BH14
Cornwall Rd. Sutt. BS58 9
Cornwall Rd. Twick. BJ47 7
Cornwall Rd. Uxb. AX36 5
Cornwall St. Est. E1 CB40 5
Cornwall Ter. NW1 BU38
Cornwall Ter. NW1 BU38 5
Cornwall Way, Stai. AV50 7
Cornwell Av. Grav. DH48 8
Cornwell Rd. Wind. AQ46 7
Cornwood Clo. N2 BT32 4
Cornworthy Rd. Dag. CP35 5
Corona Rd. SE12 CH47 7
Coronation Av. Wind. AQ44 6
Coronation Av. N16 CA35 4
Coronation Av. Slou. AS39 5
Coronation Clo. Bex. CP46 7
Coronation Clo. Ilf. CM31 4
Coronation Cotts. W5 BL38 5
Coronation Cres. Grays DG41 7
Loewen Rd.
Coronation Dr. Horn. CU35 5
Coronation Hill, Epp. CN18 2
Coronation Rd. E13 CJ38 5
Coronation Rd. NW10 BL38 5
Coronation Rd. Hayes BB42 6
Coronation Wk. Twick. BF47 7
Coroner's Ct. W6 BQ42 6
Coronet St. N1 CA38
Coronet St. N1 CA38 5
Corporation Av. Houns. BE45 6
Corporation Row EC1 BY38
Corporation Row EC1 BY38 5
Corporation St. E15 CG37 5
Corporation St. N7 BX35 4
Corral Gdns. Hem. H. AY13
Corrall Rd. N7 BX36 5
Lough Rd.
Corrance Rd. SW2 BX45 6
Corran Way, S. Ock. DA40 6
Corri Av. N14 BW28 3
Corrie Gdns. Vir. W. AR54 8
Corrie Rd. Wey. AX56 9
Corrie Rd. Wok. AT63 10
Corrigan Av. Couls. BV61 10
Corringham Ct. NW11 BS33 4
Corringham Ct. St. Alb. BH13
Lemsford Rd.
Corringham Rd. NW11 BS33 4
Corringham Rd. Wem. BM34 4
Corrington Ms. W11 BR40 5
Blenheim Cres.
Corringway NW11 BS33 4
Corringway W5 BL39 5
Corsair Clo. Stai. AX47 7
Corsair Rd. Stai. AX47 7
Corscoombe Clo.
Kings. on T. BN49 7
Corsehill St. SW16 BW50 7
Corseley Way E9 CD36 5
Trowbridge Est.
Corsham St. N1 BZ38
Corsham St. N1 BZ38 5
Corsica St. N5 BY36 5
Cortayne Rd. SW6 BR44 6
Cortis Rd. SW15 BP46 7
Cortis Ter. SW15 BP46 7
Corunna Rd. SW8 BW44 6
Corunna Ter. SW8 BW44 6
Corve La. S. Ock. DA40 6
Corwall Ave. Wind. AM42 6
Corwall Ct. SW17 BU49 7
Broadwater Rd.
Corwell Gdns. Uxb. BA39 5
Corwell La. Uxb. BA39 5
Corwood Dr. E1 CC39 5
Cory Dr. Brwd. DD26 12
Cosbycote Av. SE24 BZ46 7
Cosdach Av. Wall. BW57 9
Cosedge Cres. Croy. BY56 9
Cosmo Pl. WC1 BX39
Cosmo Pl. WC1 BX39 5
Southampton Row
Cossall St. SE15 CB44 6
Cossall Wk. SE15 CC44 6
Cosser St. SE1 BY41
Cosser St. SE1 BY41 6
Costa St. SE15 CB44 6
Costan Clo. SE4 C45 6
Hainsford Clo.
Costead Manor Rd. Brwd. DA26 4
Coston's Av. Grnf. BG38 5
Coston's La. Grnf. BG38 5
Coston Wk. SE4 CD45 6
Frendsbury Rd.
Cosway St. NW1 BU39
Cosway St. NW1 BU39 5
Cotall St. E14 CE39 5
Coteford Clo. Pnr. BC32 4
Coteford St. SW17 BU49 7
Cotelands Croy. CA55 8
Cotesbach Rd. E5 CC34 4
Cotesmere Gdns. Dag. CP35 5
Coford Rd. Th. Hth. BZ52 8
Cotham St. SE17 BZ42
Cotham St. SE17 BZ42 6
Cotherstone, Epsom BN58 9
Cotherstone Rd. SW2 BX47 7
Cotlandswck, St. Alb. BK16 1
Cotleigh Av. Bex. CP48 7
Cotleigh Rd. NW6 BS36 5
Cotleigh Rd. Rom. CS32 5
Cotman Clo. NW11 BT32 4
Cotman Clo. SW15 BQ46 7
Cotmandene Cres. Orp. CO51 8
Cotman Gdns. Edg. BM30 3
Cotmans Ash La. Sev. CX60 9
Cotmans Ash La. Sev. CY62 10
Cotmans Clo. Hayes BC40 5
Coton Rd. Well. CO45 6
Cotsford Av. N. Mal. BN53 8

Cotswold Hem. H. AY12 8
Mendip Way
Cotswold Av. Bush. BG25 27
Cotswold Clo. Bexh. CT44 69
Cotswold Clo. Kings. on T. BM50 75
Cotswold Clo. St. Alb. BK11 9
Chiltern Rd.
Cotswold Clo. Slou. AN41 61
Cotswold Clo. Stai. AW49 73
Cotswold Clo. Uxb. AX37 53
Cotswold Gdns. E6 CJ38 58
Cotswold Gdns. NW2 BQ34 46
Cotswold Gdns. Brwd. DF26 122
Cotswold Gdns. Ilf. CM33 49
Cotswold Rd. Grav. DF48 81
Cotswold Rd. Hamptn. BF49 74
Cotswold Rd. Rom. CW30 42
Cotswold Rd. Sutt. BS58 95
Cotswold Rise, Orp. CN53 89
Perry Hall Rd.
Cotswolds, Hat. BP13 10
Cotswold St. SE27 BY49 76
Cotswold Way, Enf. BX24 29
Cottage Av. Brom. CK54 88
Cottage Clo. Cher. AU57 91
Cottage Clo. Ruis. BA33 44
Cottage Farm Way, Egh. AU52 82
Cottage Field Clo. Sid. CP47 79
Cottage Gro. SE5 BZ43 67
Cottage Gro. SW9 BX45 66
Cottage Gro. Surb. BK53 84
Cottage Park Rd. Slou. AO34 43
Cottage Pl. SW3 BU41 3
Cottage Pl. SW3 BU41 66
Cottage Rd. Epsom BN57 94
Cottage St. E14 CE40 57
Cottages, The St. Alb. BH14 9
Cottage, The Surb. BK54 84
Cottage Wk. N16 CA34 48
Smalley Rd.
Cottage Walk SE15 CA44 67
Sumner Estate
Cottage Wk. SW1 BU41 3
Cottage Wk. SW1 BU41 66
Cottenham Dr. SW20 BP50 75
Cottenham Pde. SW20 BP51 85
Durham Rd.
Cottenham Pk. Rd. SW20 BP51 85
Cottenham Pl. SW20 BP50 75
Cottenham Rd. E17 CD31 48
Cotterells, Hem. H. AX13 8
Cotterells Hill, Hem. H. AX13 8
Cotterill Rd. Surb. BL55 85
Cottesbrook Clo. Slou. AU44 62
Cottesbrook St. SE14 CD43 67
Nynehead St.
Cottesmore Av. Ilf. CL30 40
Cottesmore Gdns. W8 BS41 3
Cottesmore Gdns. W8 BS41 66
Cottimore Av. Walt. BC54 83
Cottimore Cres. Walt. BC54 83
Cottimore La. Walt. BC54 83
Cottimore Ter. Walt. BC54 83
Cottingham Chase Ruis. BC34 44
Cottingham Rd. SE20 CC50 77
Cottington St. SE11 BY42 4
Cottington St. SE11 BY42 66
Cotton Av. W3 BN39 55
Cotton Hl. Brom. CF49 77
Cotton La. Green. CY46 80
Cottonmill Cres. St. Alb. BG14 9
Cottonmill La. St. Alb. BG14 9
Cotton Rd. Pot. B. BT19 20
Cottons Approach, Rom. CS32 50
Pettley Gdns.
Cotton's Gdns. E2 CA38 2
Cotton's Gdns. E2 CA38 57
Hackney Rd.
Cotton St. E14 CF40 57
Cottrill Rd. E8 CB36 57
Couchmore Av. Esher BH55 84
Couchmore Av. Ilf. CK30 40
Coulgate St. SE4 CD45 67
Coulsdon Ct. Rd. Couls. BX61 104
Coulsdon La. Couls. BU63 104
Coulsdon Rise, Couls. BX62 104
Coulsdon Rd. Cat. BZ64 105
Coulsdon Rd. Couls. BX61 104
Coulsdon Rd. Couls. BX63 104
Coulser Clo. Hem. H. AW12 8
Coulson St. SW3 BU42 3
Coulson St. SW3 BU42 66
Coulter Clo. Pot. B. BW17 20
Coulter Rd. W6 BP41 65
Coulton Av. Grav. DF47 81
Council Av. Grav. DE46 81
Councillor St. SE5 BZ43 67
Counters Clo. Hem. H. AW13 8
Countess Clo. Uxb. AX30 35
Countess Rd. NW5 BW35 47
Countisbury Av. Enf. CA26 39
Country Way Felt. BC50 73
County Gdns. Bark. CN37 58
County Gate SE9 CM48 78
County Gate Barn. BS25 29
County Gro. SE5 BZ44 67
County Rd. Th. Hth. BY51 86
County St. SE1 BZ41 4
County St. SE1 BZ41 67
Coupland Pl. SE18 CM42 68
Courage Clo. Horn. CV32 51
Courage Wk. Brwd. DE25 122
Courcy Rd. N8 BY31 47
Courland Gro. SW8 BW44 66
Courlands Rd. Wey. AW55 83
Courland St. SW8 BW44 66
Coursers Rd. St. Alb. BN15 10
Course, The SE9 CL48 78
Courtaulds, Kings L. AW18 17
Courtauld Rd. N19 BW33 47
Court Av. Couls. BY63 104
Court Av. Belv. CQ42 69
Court Av. Rom. CX29 42
Court Bushes Rd. Whyt. CB63 105
Court Clo. Har. BL31 46
Court Clo. Maid. AH42 61
Court Clo. Twick. BF48 74
Court Clo. Wall. BW57 95
Court Clo. Av. Twick. BF48 74
Court Cres. Chess. BK57 93
Court Cres. Slou. AO39 52
Court Downs Rd. Beck. CE51 87
Court Dr. Croy. BX56 95
Court Dr. Stan. BL28 37
Court Dr. Sutt. BU56 95
Court Dr. Uxb. AY37 53
Courtenay Av. N6 BU33 47
Courtenay Av. Har. BG29 36
Courtenay Gdns. Har. BG30 36
Courtenay Gdns. Upmin. CY33 51
Coutenay Pl. E17 CD32 48
Courtenay Rd. E11 CG34 49
Coutenay Rd. E17 CC31 48
Courtenay Rd. Wok. AT61 100
Courtenay Rd. Wor. Pk. BQ55 85
Courtenay Sq. SE11 BY42 66
Courtenay St.
Courtenay St. SE11 BX42 4
Courtenay St. SE11 BY42 66
Court Farm La. Nthlt. BF36 54
Court Farm Rd. SE9 CK48 78
Court Farm Rd. Nthlt. BF36 54
Courtfield Av. Har. BH32 45
Courtfield Cres. Har. BH32 45
Courtfield Cres. Har. BJ32 45
Courtfield Av.
Courtfield Gdns. SW5 BS42 3
Courtfield Gdns. SW5 BS42 66
Courtfield Gdns. W13 BJ39 54
Courtfield Gdns. Ruis. BB34 44
Courtfield Gdns. Uxb. AW34 44
Courtfield Ms. SW7 BT42 3
Courtfield Ms. SW7 BT42 66
Courtfield Rise, W. Wick. CF55 87
Courtfield Rd. SW7 BS42 3
Courtfield Rd. SW7 BT42 66
Courtfield Rd. Ashf. AZ50 73
Court Fm. Av. Epsom BN56 94
Court Fm. Rd. Warl. CB62 105
Ct. Grn. Heights Wok. AR63 100
Fern Hill La.
Court Haw Bans. BU61 104
Court Hill Couls. BU62 104
Court Hill Sth. Croy. CA59 96
Courthill Rd. SE13 CF45 67
Courthope Rd. NW3 BU35 47
Mansfield Rd.
Courthope Rd. SW19 BR49 75
Courthope Rd. Grnf. BG37 54
Courthope Vill. SW19 BR50 75
Court House Gdns. N3 BS29 38
Court House Rd. N12 BS29 38
Courtland Av. E4 CG27 40
Courtland Av. Ilf. CK34 49
Courtland Cres. Bans. BS61 104
Courtland Dr. Chig. CL27 40
Courtlands Ave. Slou. AR42 62
Courtlands Av. NW7 BN27 37
Courtlands Av. SE12 CH46 78
Courtlands Av. SW16 BX50 76
Courtlands Av. Brom. CG54 88
Courtlands Av. Esher BE57 93
Courtlands Av. Hamptn. BE50 74
Courtlands Av. Rich. BM44 65
Courtlands Av. Est. SE12 CH46 78
Courtlands Clo. Sth. Croy. CA58 96
Courtlands Dr. Epsom BO57 94
Courtlands Dr. Wat. BB22 26
Courtlands Rd. Surb. BM54 85
Court La. SE21 CA46 77
Court La. Iver AV40 52
Court La. Wind. AK41 61
Court La. Gdns. SE21 CA47 77
Court Leas. Cob. BF60 93
Courtleet Dri. Erith CS44 69
Alberta Rd.
Courtleet Dr. Erith. CR44 69
Alberta Rd.
Courtleigh Av. Barn. BT22 29
Courtleigh Gdns. NW11 BR31 46
Courtman Rd. N17 BZ29 39
Court Mead Nthlt. BE38 54
Courtmead Clo. SE24 BZ46 77
Courtnell St. W2 BS39 56
Courtney Clo. SE19 CA50 77
Courtney Cres. Cars. BU57 95
Courtney Pl. Croy. BY55 86
Courtney Rd. N7 BY35 47
Courtney Rd. SE20 CC50 77
Courtney Rd. SW19 BU50 76
Courtney Rd. Croy. BY55 86
Courtney Rd. Grays DH41 71
Courtney Rd. Houns. AZ45 63
Courtney Way, Hounds. AZ45 63
Courtney Rd.
Court Pde. Wem. BJ34 45
Court Side N8 BW32 47
Courtrai Rd. SE23 CD46 77
Court Rd. SE9 CK48 78
Court Rd. SE25 CA51 87
Court Rd. Bans. BS61 104
Court Rd. Cat. BZ65 105
Court Rd. Dart. CZ49 80
Court Rd. Gdse. CC69 114
Court Rd. Orp. CO55 89
Court Rd. Sthl. BE42 64
Court Rd. Uxb. AZ35 44
Court Side SE26 CC48 77
Round Hill
Court St. E1 CB39 57
Durward St.
Court St. Brom. CH51 88
South St.
Court, The Ruis. BE35 45
Court, The Warl. CD62 105
Court Way NW9 BO31 46
Court Way W3 BN39 55
Court Way, Ilf. CM31 49
Court Way, Rom. CW30 42
Court Way, Twick. BH47 74
Courtway, Wdf. Grn. CJ28 40
Courtway, The Wat. BE27 36
Courtwood La. Croy. CD59 96
Court Wood Rd. Sev. CU65 107
Court Yard SE9 CK46 78
Cousin La. EC4 BZ40 4
Cousin La. EC4 BZ40 57
Couthurst Rd. SE3 CH43 68
Coutts Av. Chess. BL56 94
Coval Gdns. SW14 BM45 65
Coval La. SW14 BM45 65
Coval Passage SW14 BN45 65
Upper Richmond Rd.
Coval Rd. SW14 BN45 65
Coveham Cres. Cob. BC60 92
Covenbrook, Brwd. DD27 122
Covent Gdn. WC2 BX40 4
Covent Gdn. WC2 BX40 56
Coventry Clo. NW6 BS37 56
Coventry Cross Est. E3 CF38 57
Coventry Rd. E1 CB38 57
Coventry Rd. SE25 CB52 87
Coventry Rd. Ilf. CL34 49
Coventry St. W1 BW40 3
Coventry St. W1 BW40 56
Coverack Clo. N14 BV25 29
Coverdale Hem. H. AY12 8
Wharfedale
Coverdale Clo. Stan. BJ28 36
Coverdale Gdns. Croy. CB55 87
Park Hill Rise
Coverdale Rd. NW2 BQ36 55
Coverdale Rd. W12 BP41 65
Coverdales, The Bark. CM37 58
Covert Clo. Berk. AO12 7
Coverton Rd. SW17 BU49 76
Covert Rd. Berk. AO11 7
Covert Rd. Chig. CN28 40
Coverts Rd. Leath. BH58 93
Coverts, The Brwd. DD26 122
Covert, The Nthwd. BA30 35
Coverts, The Orp. CN53 88
Covert Way Barn. BT23 29
Covington Gdns. SW16 BY50 76
Covington Way SW16 BX50 76
Cowan St. SE5 CA43 4
Cowan St. SE5 CA43 67
Cowbridge La. Bark. CL36 58
Cowbridge Rd. Har. BL31 46
Cowcross St. EC1 BY39 2
Cowcross St. EC1 BY39 56
Cowdenbeath Path N1 BX37 56
Bemerton Est.
Cowden Rd. Orp. CN54 88
Cowden St. SE6 CE49 77
Cowdray Rd. Uxb. BA37 53
Cowdray Way, Horn. CU35 50
Cowdrey Clo. Enf. CA23 30
Cowdrey Ct. Dart. CU47 79
Cowdrey Rd. SW19 BS49 76
Cowdry Rd. E9 CD36 57
Cowen Av. Har. BG34 45
Cowgate Rd. Grnf. BG37 54
Cowick Rd. SW17 BU49 76
Cowings Mead Nthlt. BE36 54
Arnold Rd.
Cowland Av. Enf. CC24 30
Cow La. Grnf. BG37 54
Cow La. Wat. BD21 27
Cowleaze Rd. Kings. on T. BL51 85
Cowles, Wal. Cr. CA17 21
Cowley Av. Cher. AV54 82
Cowley Clo. Sth. Croy. CC58 96
Cowley Cres. Uxb. AX39 53
Cowley Cres. Walt. BD56 93
Cowley Hill Borwd. BM22 28
Cowley Hill Borwd. BM23 28
Cowley La. E11 CG34 49
Cathall Rd.
Cowley La. Cher. AV54 82
Cowley Mill Rd. Uxb. AW37 53
Cowley Peachey, Uxb. AX39 53
Cowley Rd. E11 CH32 49
Cowley Rd. SW9 BY44 66
Cowley Rd. SW14 BO45 65
Cowley Rd. W3 BO40 55
Cowley Rd. Ilf. CK33 49
Cowley Rd. Rom. CU29 41
Cowley Rd. Uxb. AX38 53
Cowley St. SW1 BX41 4
Cowley St. SW1 BX41 66
Little College St.
Cowling Clo. W11 BR40 55
Wilsham St.
Cowper Av. E6 CK36 58
Cowper Av. Sutt. BT56 95
Cowper Av. Til. DG44 71
Cowper Clo. Cher. AV53 82
Cowper Clo. Well. CO46 79
Cowper Gdns. N14 BV25 29
Cowper Gdns. Wall. BW57 95
Cowper Pl. EC2 BZ38 2
Cowper Rd. N14 BV26 38
Cowper Rd. N16 CA35 48
Cowper Rd. N18 CB28 39
Cowper Rd. SW19 BT50 76
Cowper Rd. W3 BN40 55
Cowper Rd. W7 BH40 54
Cowper Rd. Belv. CQ42 69
Cowper Rd. Berk. AQ13 7
Cowper Rd. Brom. CJ52 88
Cowper Rd. Hem. H. AW14 8
Cowper Rd. Kings. On T. BL49 75
Cowper Rd. Rain. CU38 59
Cowper Rd. Welw. G. C. BR9 5
Cowper St. EC2 BZ38 2
Cowper St. EC2 BZ38 57
Cowslip La. Dor. BJ67 111
Cowslip La. Wok. AQ60 91
Cowslip Rd. E18 CH31 49
Cowthorpe Rd. SW8 BW44 66
Coxdean, Epsom BQ62 103
Coxdean, Epsom BQ63 103
Coxfield Clo. Hem. H. AY13 8
Cox La. Chess. BL56 94
Cox La. Epsom BM56 94
Coxley Rise Pur. BZ56 96
Coxley Rise Pur. BZ60 96
Coxmount Rd. SE7 CJ42 68
Coxon Clo. Har. BF30 36
Cox's Ct. EC1 BZ39 2
Cox's Ct. EC1 BZ39 57
Cox's La. Wok. AS64 100
Coxson Pl. SE1 CA41 4
Coxson Pl. SE1 CA41 67
Cox's Wk. SE21 CB47 77
Coxtie Green Rd. Brwd. CW25 33
Coxwell Rd. SE18 CM42 68
Coxold Path. Chess. BL57 94
Crabbe Cres. Chesh. AO18 16
Crabbs Croft Clo. Orp. CL56 97
Crab Hill, Beck. CF50 77
Crab Hill La. Red. BX72 121
Crab La. Wat. BF21 27
Crabtree Av. Rom. CP31 50
Crabtree Av. Wem. BL37 55
Crabtree Clo. Bush. BF25 27
Crabtree Clo. Hem. H. AX14 8
Crabtree La. SW6 BQ43 65
Crabtree La. Dor. BJ68 111
Crabtree La. Hem. H. AX14 8
Crabtree La. Lthd. BF66 111
Crabtree Manorway Belv. CS41 69
Crabtree Rd. Egh. AU51 82
Crabtree Walk SE15 CA44 67
Sumner Estate
Crace St. NW1 BW38 56
Drummond Cres.
Craddock Rd. Enf. CA24 30
Craddock's Ave. Ash. BL62 103
Craddock St. NW3 BV36 56
Prince of Wales Rd.
Cradley Rd. SE9 CM47 78
Cragg Av. Rad. BH21 27
Craigavon Rd. Hem. H. AY11 8
Craigdale Rd. Horn. CT32 50
Craig Dr. Uxb. AZ39 53
Craigen Av. Croy. CB54 87
Craig Gdns. E18 CG30 40
Craigmore Tower Wok. AS63 100
Guildford Rd.
Craig Mount Rad. BJ21 27
Craigmuir Pk. Wem. BL37 55
Craignair Rd. SW2 BX47 76
Craignish Av. SW16 BX51 86
Craig Park Rd. N18 CB28 39
Criag Rd. Rich. BK49 74
Craig's Ct. SW1 BX40 4
Craig's Ct. SW1 BX40 56
Whitehall
Craigton Rd. SE9 CK45 68
Craig Wk. Wal. Cr. CC17 21
Davison Dr.
Craigweil Av. Rad. BJ21 27
Craigwell Av. Felt. BC48 73
Craigwell Clo. Stan. BK28 36
Craigwell Dr. Stan. BK28 36
Crail Row SE17 BZ42 4
Crail Row SE17 BZ42 67
Catesby St.
Crail Row SE17 BZ42 67
Darwin St.
Craithie Rd. SE12 CH46 78
Crakell Rd. BT71 121
Cramer St. W1 BV39 1
Cramer St. W1 BV39 56
Crammavill St. Grays DD40 71
Crammerville Wk. Rain. CV39 60
Crampshaw La. Ash. BL63 103
Crampton Rd. SE20 CC50 77
Crampton's Rd. Sev. CU63 107
Crampton St. SE17 BY42 4
Crampton St. SE17 BY42 66
Cranberry Clo. Nthlt. BE37 54
Cranberry St. E1 CB38 57
Cranborne Av. Sthl. BF42 64
Cranborne Cres. Pot. B. BR19 19
Cranborne Gdns. Upmin. CX34 51
Cranborne Rd. Hat. BP12 10
Cranborne Rd. Hodd. CE11 12
Cranborne Rd. Pot. B. BR18 19
Cranborne Rd. Pot. B. BR19 19
Cranborne Rd. Wal. Cr. CC19 21
Theobalds La.
Cranborne Way, Hayes BC39 53
Cranbourne Ave. Wind. AM44 61
Cranbourne Av. E11 CH31 49
Cranbourne Av. Surb. BM55 85
Cranbourne Clo. Slou. AO40 61
Cranbourne Clo. SW16 BX52 86
Pollards Cr.
Cranbourne Ct. E18 CH31 49
Cranbourne Dr. Pnr. BD32 45
Cranbourne Gdns. NW11 BR32 46
Cranbourne Gdns. Ilf. CM31 49
Cranbourne Gdns.
Welw. G. C. BR8 5
Cranbourne Rd. E12 CK35 49
High St. N.
Cranbourne Rd. E15 CF35 48
Cranbourne Rd. N10 BV30 38
Cranbourne Rd. Nthwd. BB31 44
Cranbourne Rd. Slou. AO40 61
Cranbourn Pass. SE16 CB41 67
Wilson Gro.
Cranbourn St. WC2 BW40 3
Cranbourn St. WC2 BW40 56
Long Acre
Cranbrook Clo. Brom. CH53 88
Cranbrook Dr. Esher BG55 84
Cranbrook Dr. Rom. CU31 50
Cranbrook Dr. Twick BF47 74
Cranbrook Est. E2 CC37 57
Cranbrook Pk. N22 BX30 38
Cranbrook Rise, Ilf. CK32 49
Cranbrook Rd. SE8 CE44 67
Cranbrook Rd. SW19 BR50 75
Cranbrook Rd. W4 BO42 65
Cranbrook Rd. Barn. BT25 29
Cranbrook Rd. Bexh. CQ44 69
Cranbrook Rd. Houns. BE45 64
Cranbrook Rd. Ilf. CL32 49
Cranbrook Rd. St. Alb. BL13 10
Cranbrook Rd. Th. Hth. BZ51 87
Cranbrook St. E2 CC37 57
Gathorne St.
Cranbrook Ter. E2 CC37 57
Roman Rd.
Cranbury Rd. SW6 BS44 66
Crane Av. W3 BO40 55
Cumberland Pk.
Crane Av. Islw. BJ46 74
Crane Clo. Dag. CR36 59
Crane Ct. Epsom BN56 94
Craneford Clo. Twick. BH47 74
Craneford Way Twick. BH47 74
Crane Gdns. Hayes. BB42 63
Crane Gro. N7 BY36 56
Furlong Rd.
Cranell Grn. S. Ock. DA40 60
Crane Lo. Houns. BC43 63
Crane Pk. Rd. Twick. BF48 74
Crane Rd. Twick. BH47 74
Cranes Dr. Surb. BL52 85
Cranes Pk. Surb. BL52 85
Cranes Pk. Av. Surb. BL52 85
Cranes Pk. Cres. Surb. BL52 85
Crane St. SE10 CF42 67
Cranes Water, Hayes. BB43 63
Craneswater Pk. Sthl. BE42 64
Cranes Way Borwd. BN25 28
Crane Way, Twick. BG47 74
Cranewood Clo. Wok. AS63 100
Guildford Rd.
Cranfield Cres. Pot. B. BX18 20
Cranfield Dr. Wat. BE19 18
Cranfield Rd. SE4 CD45 67
Cranfield Rd. E. Cars. BV58 95
Cranfield Rd. W. Cars. BV58 95
Cranfield Row SE1 BY41 4
Cranfield Villas, SE27 BZ49 77
Auckland Rd.
Cranleigh St. NW1 BW37 1
Cranfield Vills. SE27 BZ48 77
Norwood High St.
Cranford Av. N13 BX28 38
Cranford Av. Stai. AY47 73
Cranford Clo. SW20 BP50 75
Cranford Clo. Stai. AY47 73
Cranford Cotts. E1 CC40 57
Cranford St.
Cranford Dr. Hayes BB42 63
Cranford Dr. Hayes BC42 63
Cranford La. Hayes BA43 63
Cranford La. Houns. BB44 63
Cranford La. Houns. BC43 63
Cranford La. Est. Houns. BC43 63
Cranford Park Rd. Hayes BB42 63
Cranford Pk. Rd. Hayes BC42 63
Cranford Rd. Dart. CW47 80
Cranford Rd. Hayes BB42 63
Cranford St. E1 CC40 57
Cranham Gdns. Upmin. CZ33 51
Cranham Rd. Horn. CU32 50
Cranhurst Rd. NW2 BQ35 46
Cranleigh Clo. SE20 CB51 87
Cranleigh Clo. Bex. CR46 79
Cranleigh Clo. Orp. CN55 88
Cranleigh Clo. Sth. Croy. CB59 96
Cranleigh Dr. Swan. CT53 89
Cranleigh Gdns. N21 BY24 29
Cranleigh Gdns. SE25 CA52 87
Cranleigh Gdns. Berk. CM36 58
Cranleigh Gdns. Har. BL32 46
Cranleigh Gdns.
Kings. on T. BL50 75
Cranleigh Gdns. Loug. CK25 31
Cranleigh Gdns. Sth. Croy. CB59 96
Cranleigh Gdns. Sthl. BE39 54
Cranleigh Gdns. Sutt. BS55 86
Cranleigh Rd. N15 BZ32 48
Cranleigh Rd. SW19 BR52 85
Cranleigh Rd. Esher BG54 84
Cranleigh Rd. Felt. BB49 73
Cranleigh St. NW1 BW37 56
Cranley Clo. Guil. AT70 118
Cranley Dr. Ilf. CM33 49
Cranley Dr. Ruis. BC34 44
Cranley Gdns. N10 BV31 47
Cranley Gdns. N13 BX27 38
Cranley Gdns. SW7 BT42 3
Cranley Gdns. SW7 BT42 66
Cranley Gdns. Wall. BW57 95
Cranley Gro. Watt. BB57 92
Cranley Ms. SW7 BT42 3
Cranley Ms. SW7 BT42 66
Cranley Mews Ilf. CM32 49
Cranley Rd.
Cranley Pl. SW7 BT42 3
Cranley Pl. SW7 BT42 66
Cranley Rd. E13 CH39 58
Cranley Rd. Guil. AS70 118
Cranley Rd. Ilf. CM33 49
Cranley Rd. Watt. BB56 92
Cranmer Av. W13 BJ41 64
Cranmer Clo. Mord. BQ53 85
Cranmer Clo. Pot. B. BS18 20
Cranmer Clo. Ruis. BD33 45
Cranmer Clo. Stan. BK29 36
Cranmer Clo. Warl. CD62 105
Cranmer Gdns.
Cranmer Clo. Wey. AZ57 92
Cranmer Ct. SW3 BU42 3
Cranmer Ct. SW3 BU42 66
Cranmer Ct. Hamptn. BF49 74
Cranmer Gdns. Dag. CS35 50
Cranmer Rd. E7 CH35 49
Cranmer Rd. SW9 BY43 66
Cranmer Rd. Croy. BY55 86
Cranmer Rd. Edg. BM27 37
Cranmer Rd. Hayes. BA39 53
Cranmer Rd. Hamptn. BF49 74
Cranmer Rd. Kings. on T. BL49 75
Cranmer Rd. Mitch. BU52 86
Cranmer Rd. Sev. CT65 107
Cranmer Terr. SW17 BT49 76
Cranmer Ter. SW17 BU49 76
Tooting Gro.
Cranmern Farn Clo. Mitch. BU52 86
Cranmore Av. Chis. CK49 78
Cranmore Av. Islw. BG43 64
Cranmore Ct. St. Alb. BH13 9
Avenue Rd.
Cranmore Lane, Leath. AZ68 110
Cranmore Pk. Est. Chis. CK50 78
Cranmore Rd. Brom. CG48 78
Cranmore Way N10 BW31 47
Cranston Cl. Houns. BE44 64
Cranstoun Clo. Guil. AP68 109
Keens Park Rd.

Crosspath, The Rad. BJ21 27
Cross Rds. Loug. CH23 31
Cross Rd. E4 CF26 39
Cross Rd. N11 BV28 38
Cross Rd. N22 BY29 38
Cross Rd. SE5 CA44 67
Cross Rd. SW19 BS50 76
Cross Rd. Brom. CK55 88
Cross Rd. Croy. BZ54 87
Cross Rd. Dart. CV46 80
Cross Rd. Dart. CW49 80
Cross Rd. Enf. CA24 30
Cross Rd. Felt. BE49 74
Cross Rd. Har. BF34 45
Cross Rd. Har. BG31 45
Cross Rd. Har. BJ30 36
Cross Rd. Kings. on T. BL50 75
Cross Rd. Orp. CO53 89
Cross Rd. Pur. BY60 95
Cross Rd. Rom. CP33 50
Cross Rd. Rom. CR31 50
Cross Rd. Sid. CO49 79
Cross Rd. Sutt. BS58 95
Cross Rd. Sutt. BT56 95
Cross Rd. Tad. BQ64 103
Cross Rd. Wal. Cr. CD20 21
Cross Rd. Wat. BE25 27
Cross Rd. Wdf. Grn. CK29 40
Cross St. E1 CC39 57
Commercial Rd.
Cross St. E3 CE36 57
Monier Rd.
Cross St. N1 BY36 56
Cross St. N1 BY37 2
Cross St. N18 CB28 39
Wakefield St.
Cross St. SW13 BO44 65
Cross St. Erith CT43 69
Cross St. Harl. CM11 13
Cross St. Hmptn. BG49 74
Cross St. Uxb. AX37 53
Cross St. Wat. BD24 27
Cross Street N. St. Alb. BG13 9
Crosswall EC3 CA40 4
Crosswall EC3 CA40 57
Crossway N12 BT29 38
Crossway N16 CA35 48
Cross Way NW9 BO31 46
Cross Way SE2 CP40 59
Crossway SW20 BQ52 85
Crossway, Dag. CP34 50
Crossway, Enf. CA26 39
Crossway, Hayes BC40 53
Crossway, Orp. CM52 88
Crossway, Pnr. BC30 35
Crossway, Ruis. BD34 45
Crossway, Walt. BC55 83
Crossway, Wdf. Grn. CJ28 40
Crossway, Welw. G. C. BQ6 5
Cross Waye, The Uxb. AY37 53
Cross Ways N21 BZ25 30
Cross Ways, Berk. AP13 7
Crossways, Brwd. D25 122
Crossways, Egh. AU50 72
Crossways, Guil. AP71 118
Cross Ways, Hem. H. AZ13 8
Crossways, Rom. CU31 50
Crossways, Sth. Croy. CD57 96
Crossways, Sutt. BT57 95
Crossways La. Reig. BT67 113
Cross Ways Rd. Beck. CE52 87
Crossways Rd. Mitch. BV52 86
Crossways, The Couls. BX63 104
Crossways, The Houns. BE43 64
Crossways, The Red. BW68 113
Crossways, The Wem. BM34 46
Crossway, The N22 BY29 38
Cross Way, The SE9 CJ48 78
Cross Way, The Har. BH30 36
Crossway, The W13 BJ38 54
Crossways, West. CJ63 106
Crosswell Clo. Shep. BA51 83
Charlton Rd.
Crosthwaite Av. SE5 BZ45 67
Croston St. E8 CB37 57
Crouch Av. Bark. CO37 59
Crouch Clo. Beck. CE50 77
Abbey La.
Crouch Cft. SE9 CL48 78
Crouch End Hill N8 BW33 47
Crouchfield, Hem. H. AW14 8
Crouch Hall Rd. N8 BW32 47
Crouch Hill N4 BX32 47
Crouch Hill N8 BX32 47
Crouch La. Wal. Cr. BZ17 21
Crouchmans Clo. SE26 CB48 77
Crouchoak La. Wey. AW56 92
Crouch Rd. NW10 BN36 55
Crouch Rd. Grays DG42 71
Crouch Valley, Upmin. CZ33 51
Crowboro Dr. Warl. CD62 105
Crowborough Path. Wat. BD27 36
Crowborough Rd. SW17 BV50 76
Crow Clo. Warl. CD62 105
Crowder St. E1 CB40 57
Crowden Way SE2 CP40 59
Crow Grn. Brwd. DA25 33
Crow Green Rd. Brwd. CZ25 33
Crowhurst La. Sev. DA58 99
Crowhurst Rd. SW9 BY44 66
Crowhurst Rd. Sev. DB65 108
Crowhurst Way Orp. CP53 89
Crowland Ave. Hayes BB42 63
Crowland Gdns. N14 BX26 38
Crowland Rd. N15 CA32 48
Crowland Rd. Th. Hth. BZ52 87
Crowlands Av. Rom. CR32 50
Crowland Ter. N1 BZ36 57
Crowland Wk. Mord. BS53 86
Crow La. Rom. CQ33 50
Crowley Cres. Croy. BY56 95
Crowlin Wk. N1 BZ36 57
Marquess Est.
Crown Ash Hill, West. CH60 97
Crown Ash La. West. CH61 106
Crown Clo. E3 CE37 57
Wick La.
Crown Clo. NW6 BS36 56
Lymington Rd.
Crown Clo. NW7 BO27 37
Crown Clo. Bish. CS7 6
Crown Clo. Hayes BB41 63
Crown Clo. Orp. CO56 98
Crown Ct. EC2 BZ39 57
Cheapside
Crown Ct. N10 BV29 38
Crown Ct. SE12 CH46 78
Crown Ct. WC2 BX39 2
Crown Ct. WC2 BX39 56
Russell St.
Crown Ct. Brom. CK53 88
Crown Ct. Til. DG44 71
Newton Rd.
Crown Dale SE19 BY50 76
Crowndale Rd. NW1 BW37 1
Crowndale Rd. NW1 BW37 56
Crownfield Av. Ilf. CN32 49
Crown Field, Brox. CE14 12
Crownfield Rd. E15 CF35 48
Crownfields, Sev. CU66 116
Crown Gate, Harl. CM11 13
Crown Hill, Croy. BZ55 87
Crown Hill, Wal. Abb. CK20 22
Crown Hill Rd. NW10 BO37 55
Crownhill Rd. Wdf. Grn. CK29 40
Crown La. N14 BW26 38
Crown La. SW16 BY49 76
Crown La. Brom. CJ53 88
Crown La. Chis. CM51 88
Crown La. Mord. BS52 86
Crown La. Vir. W. AR53 82
Crown La. Spur. Brom. CJ53 88
Crownmead Way Rom. CR31 50
Crown Office Row EC4 BY40 4
Crown Office Row EC4 CM40 58
Crown Par. Hayes BB39 53
Crown Pass SW1 BW40 3
Crown Pass SW1 BW40 56
King St.
Crown Pass. Wat. BD24 27
Crown Pl. NW5 BV36 56
Raglan St.
Crown Point, Sev. CZ64 108
Crown Pt. SE19 BY50 76
Crown Rise, Wat. BD20 18
Crown Rd. N10 BV29 38
Crown Rd. Borwd. BM23 28
Crown Rd. Brwd. CY22 33
Crown Rd. Brwd. CY23 33
Crown Rd. Enf. CB24 30
Crown Rd. Grays DD43 71
Crown Rd. Ilf. CM31 49
Crown Rd. Mord. BS52 86
Crown Rd. N. Mal. BN51 85
Crown Rd. Orp. CO56 98
Crown Rd. Sev. CT58 98
Crown Rd. Sutt. BS56 95
Crown Rd. Twick. BJ46 74
Crown Rd. Vir. W. AR53 82
Crown Rd. West. CK63 106
Crownstone Rd. SW2 BY46 76
Crown St. SE5 BZ43 67
Crown St. W3 BM40 55
Crown St. Brwd. DB27 42
Crown St. Dag. CS36 59
Crown St. Egh. AT49 72
Crown St. Har. BG33 45
Crown Ter. Rich. BL45 65
Crown Wk. Uxb. AX36 53
High St.
Crown Wk. Wem. BL34 46
Crown Woods La. SE9 CL44 68
Crown Woods Way SE9 CM46 78
Crowood, Egh. AV51 82
Crowshott Av. Stan. BK30 36
Crows Rd. E15 CF38 57
Crows Rd. Epp. CN18 22
Crowstone Rd. Grays DE41 71
Crowther Av. Brent. BL42 65
Crowther Clo. Stan. BK30 36
Crowther Rd. SE25 CB52 87
Crowthorne St. W10 BQ39 55
Croxdale Rd. Borwd. BL23 28
Croxden Clo. Edg. BL31 46
Crosden Clo. Edg. BM31 46
Reynolds Dr.
Croxden Wk. Mord. BT53 86
Croxford Gdns. N22 BY29 38
Croxford Way Rom. CS33 50
Croxley Clo. Orp. CO51 89
Croxley Gn. Orp. CO51 89
Croxley Rd. W9 BR38 55
Croxted Clo. SE21 BZ47 77
Croxted Rd. SE21 BZ46 77
Croxted Rd. SE24 BZ46 77
Croyde Ave. Hayes BB42 63
Croyde Av. Grnf. BG38 54
Croyde Clo. Sid. CM47 78
Croydon Rd. Cat. CB65 105
Croydon Gro. Croy. BY54 86
Croydon La. Bans. BT60 95
Croydon Rd. E13 CG38 58
Croydon Rd. SE20 CB51 87
Croydon Rd. Beck. CC53 87
Croydon Rd. Brom. CJ55 88
Croydon Rd. Mitch. BV52 86
Croydon Rd. Reig. BS70 121
Croydon Rd. Wall. BV56 95
Croydon Rd. Warl. CE63 105
Croydon Rd. West. CK65 106
Croydon Rd. W. Wick. CG55 88
Croyland Rd. N9 CB26 39
Croylands Surb. BL54 85
Croysdale Av. Sun. BC52 83
Crozier Dri. Sth. Croy. CB58 96
Crozier Rd. Uxb. BA35 44
Crozier St. SE1 BX41 66
Crozier Ter. E9 CC35 48
Crucifix La. SE1 CA41 4
Crucifix La. SE1 CA41 67
Cruden Rd. Grav. DJ48 81
Cruden St. N1 BY37 2
Cruden St. N1 BY37 56
Cruik Ave. S. Ock. DB39 60
Cruikshank Rd. E15 CG35 49
Cruikshank St. WC1 BY38 2
Cruikshank St. WC1 BY38 56
Crummock Gdns. NW9 BO32 46
Crumpsall St. SE2 CP42 69
Crundale Av. NW9 BM32 46
Crunden Rd. Sth. Croy. BZ57 96
Crusader Clo. Grays CX42 70
Centurian Way
Crusader Gdns. Croy. CA55 87
Crushes Clo. Brwd. DF25 122
- Chelmer Dr.
Crusoe Rd. Erith CS42 69
Crusoe Rd. Mitch. BU50 76
Crutched Friars EC3 CA40 4
Crutched Friars EC3 CA40 57
Crutches La. Beac. AP29 34
Crutchfield La. Walt. BC55 83
Crutchley Rd. SE6 CG48 78
Crystal Av. Horn. CW35 51
Crystal Ct. SE19 CA49 77
Crystal Palace Pde. SE19 CA50 77
Crystal Palace Pk. Rd. SE26 CB49 77
Crystal Palace Rd. SE22 CB45 67
Crystal Palace Sta. Rd.
SE19 CB50 77
Crystal Ter. SE19 BZ50 77
Crystal Vw. Ct. Brom. CF49 77
Cuba Dr. Enf. CC23 30
Cuba St. E14 CE41 67
Cubitt Ter. SW4 BW45 66
Cubitts Clo. Welw. G. C. BR5 5
Cubitt's Cotts. SW18 BS47 76
Garratt La.
Cubitt St. WC1 BX38 2
Cubitt St. WC1 BX38 56
Cubitt St. Croy. BX56 95
Cuckmans Dr. St. Alb. BF16 18
Cuckoo Av. W7 BH38 54
Cuckoo Dene W7 BG39 54
Cuckoo Hall La. N9 CC26 39
Cuckoo Hill Pnr. BD31 45
Cuckoo Hill Dr. Pnr. BD31 45
Cuckoo Hill Rd. Pnr. BD31 45
Cuckoo La. W7 BH40 54
Cuckoo La. Grays DC40 71
Cucumber La. Hat. BU13 11
Cudas Clo. Epsom BO56 94
Cuddington Av. Wor. Pk. BO55 85
Cuddington Clo. Tad. BQ63 103
Cuddington Ct. Sutt. BQ58 94
Cuddington Way, Sutt. BQ59 94
Cudham La. N. Sev. CM58 97
Cudham La. S. Sev. CM61 106
Cudham Pk. Rd. Sev. CM58 97
Cudham Rd. Orp. CL59 97
Cudham Rd. West. CK63 106
Cudham St. SE6 CF47 77
Cudworth St. E1 CB38 57
Cuff Cres. SE9 CJ46 78
Cuffley Av. Wat. BD20 18
Cuffley Ct. Hem. H. BA11 8
Cuffley Hill, Wal. Cr. BY18 20
Cuff Pl. E2 CA38 57
Angela St.
Culfield Rd. Grays DE41 71
Culford Gdns. SW3 BU42 3
Culford Gdns. SW3 BU42 66
Culford Gro. N1 CA36 57
Culford Ms. N1 CA36 57
Southgate Rd.
Culford Rd. N1 CA36 57
Culgaith Gdns. Enf. BX24 29
Cullen Sq. S. Ock. DB40 60
Cullen Way NW10 BN38 55
Cullesden Rd. Ken. BY61 104
Culling Rd. SE16 CC41 67
Cullings Ct. Wal. Abb. CG20 22
Cullington Clo. BJ31 45
Cullingworth Rd. NW10 BP35 46
Culloden Rd. Enf. BY23 29
Cullum St. EC3 CA40 4
Cullum St. EC3 CA40 57
Culmington Rd. W13 BK40 54
Culmington Rd. Sth. Croy. BZ57 96
Culmore Cross SW12 BV47 76
Culmore Rd. SE15 CB43 67
Culmstock Rd. SW11 BV46 76
Culpeper Clo. Ilf. CL29 40
Culpeper St. N1 BY37 2
Culpeper St. N1 BY37 56
Culross Cl. N15 BZ31 48
Culross St. W1 BV40 3
Culross St. W1 BV40 56
Culsac Rd. Surb. BL55 85
Culverden Rd. SW12 BW48 76
Culverden Rd. Wat. BC27 35
Culver Dr. Oxt. CG68 115
Culver Gro. Stan. BK30 36
Culverhay, Ash. BL61 103
Culverhouse Gdns. SW16 BX48 76
Culverlands Clo. Stan. BJ28 36
Culverley Rd. SE6 CE47 77
Culver Pl. SW11 BV45 66
Culver Rd. St. Alb. BH12 9
Culvers Av. Cars. BU55 86
Culvers Retreat Cars. BU54 86
Culverstone Clo. Brom. CG53 88
Culver's Way Cars. BU55 86
Culvert La. Uxb. AW37 53
Culvert Pl. SW11 BV44 66
Culvert Rd. N15 CA32 48
Culvert Rd. SW11 BU44 66
Culvey Clo. Hart. DC53 90
Culworth St. NW8 BU37 1
Culworth St. NW8 BU37 56
Cumberland Av. NW10 BM38 55
Cumberland Av. Grav. DH47 81
Cumberland Av. Guil. AQ68 109
Cumberland Av. Horn. CW34 51
Cumberland Av. Well. CO45 69
Cumberland Clo. SW20 BQ50 75
Cumberland Clo. E8 CA36 57
Cumberland Clo. Amer. AQ23 25
Cumberland Clo. Epsom BO58 94
Longmead Rd.
Cumberland Clo. Hem. H. BB15 8
Cumberland Clo. Horn. CW34 51
Cumberland Dr.
Cumberland Clo. Twick. BJ46 74
Cumberland Ct. St. Alb. BH13 9
Carlisle Av.
Cumberland Cres. W14 BR42 65
Cumberland Dr. Bexh. CQ43 69
Cumberland Dr. Chess. BL55 85
Cumberland Dr. Dart. CW47 80
Cumberland Dr. Esher BJ55 84
Cumberland Gdns. NW4 BQ30 37
Cumberland Gdns. WC1 BX38 2
Cumberland Gdns. WC1 BX38 56
Cumberland Gte. W1 BU40 3
Cumberland Gte. W1 BU40 56
Cumberland Market NW1 BV38 1
Cumberland Mkt. NW1 BV38 56
Cumberland Mkt. Est. NW1 BV38 56
Cumberland Pk. W3 BN40 55
Cumberland Pl. NW1 BV38 1
Cumberland Pl. NW1 BV38 56
Outer Circle
Cumberland Pl. Sun. BC52 83
Cumberland Rd. E12 CJ35 49
Cumberland Rd. E13 CH39 58
Cumberland Rd. E17 CD30 39
Cumberland Rd. N9 CC26 39
Cumberland Rd. N22 BX30 38
Cumberland Rd. SE25 CB53 87
Cumberland Rd. SW13 BO44 65
Cumberland Rd. W3 BN40 55
Cumberland Rd. W7 BH41 64
Cumberland Rd. Ashf. AX48 73
Cumberland Rd. Brom. CG52 88
Cumberland Rd. Har. BF32 45
Cumberland Rd. Rich. BM43 65
Cumberland Rd. Stan. BL31 46
Cumberlands Ken. BZ57 96
Cumberlands Ken. BZ61 105
Cumberland St. SW1 BV42 3
Cumberland St. SW1 BV42 66
Cumberland St. Stai. AU49 72
Cumberland Ter. NW1 BV37 1
Cumberland Ter. NW1 BV37 56
Cumberland Ter. Ms. NW1 BV37 56
Albany St.
Cumberlow Av. SE25 CA52 87
Cumberlow Pl. Hem. H. BA14 8
Cumbernauld Gdns. Sun. BB49 73
Cumberton Rd. N17 BZ30 39
Cumbrae Gdns. Surb. BK54 84
Cumbrian Av. Bexh. CT44 69
Cumbrian Gdns. NW2 BQ34 46
Cum Cum Hill. Hat. BT14 11
Cumley Rd. Epp. CT18 23
Cumming Est. N1 BZ37 57
Cummings Hall La. Rom. CV27 42
Cumming St. N1 BX37 2
Cumming St. N1 BX37 56
Cumnor Gdns. Epsom BP57 94
Cumnor Rd. Sutt. BT57 95
Cumnor Ri. Ken. BZ62 105
Hayes La.
Cunard Pl. EC3 CA39 57
Bury St.
Cunard Rd. NW10 BN38 55
Cunard St. SE5 CA43 67
Cundy Rd. E16 CH39 58
Cundy St. Est. SW1 BV42 3
Cundy St. Est. SW1 BV42 66
Cundy St. SW1 BV42 3
Cundy St. SW1 BV42 66
Cunliffe Clo. Epsom. BM65 103
Cunliffe Rd. Wor. Pk. BO56 94
Cunliffe St. SW16 BW50 76
Cunningham Av. Enf. CD21 30
Cunningham Av. Guil. AT70 118
Cunningham Av. St. Alb. BH14 9
Cunningham Clo. W. Wick. CE55 87
Cunningham Hill Rd.
St. Alb. BH14 9
Cunningham Pk. Har. BG32 45
Cunningham Pl. NW8 BT38 1
Cunningham Pl. NW8 BT38 56
Cunningham Rd. N15 CB31 48
Cunningham Rd. Bans. BT61 104
Cunningham Rd. Wal. Cr. CD17 21
Cunnington St. W4 BN41 65
Cupar Rd. SW11 BV44 66
Cureton St. SW1 BW42 3
Cupid Grn. La. Hem. H. AZ11 8
Cupola Clo. Brom. CH49 78
Powster Rd.
Cureton St. SW1 BW42 66
Curfew Yard, Wind. AO43 61
Datchet Rd.
Curlew Clo. Berk. AR13 7
Curlew Clo. Croy. CC59 96
Curlew Clo. Sth. Croy. CC58 96
Curlew Gdns. Guil. AU69 118
Curlew St. SE1 CA41 4
Curlew St. SE1 CA41 67
Curling Vale, Guil. AQ71 118
Curnick's La. SE27 BZ49 77
Curnock Est. NW1 BW37 1
Curnock Est. NW1 BW37 56
Curran Av. Sid. CN46 78
Curran Av. Wall. BV55 86
Currch Path. Red. BV67 113
Currey Rd. Grnf. BG36 54
Curricle St. W3 BO40 55
Currie Hill Clo. SW19 BR49 75
Curry Ri. NW7 BQ29 37
Cursers Rd. St. Alb. BM17 19
Cursitor St. EC4 BY39 2
Cursitor St. EC4 BY39 56
Curtain Rd. EC2 CA38 2
Curtain Rd. EC2 CA38 57
Curthwaite Gdns. Enf. BW24 29
Curtis Clo. Rick. AW26 35
Curtis Gdns. Dor. BJ71 119
Spring Gdns.
Curtismill Clo. Orp. CO52 89
Curtis Mill La. Rom. CT24 32
Curtismill Way Orp. CO52 89
Curtis Rd. Dor. BJ71 119
Curtis Rd. Epsom BN56 94
Curti Rd. Hem. H. BA14 8
Curtis Rd. Horn. CW33 51
Curtis Rd. Houns. BE47 74
Curtis St. SE1 CA42 4
Curtis St. SE1 CA42 67
Curtis Way SE28 CO40 59
Curtis Way Berk. AR13 7
Curvan Clo. Epsom BO58 94
Curve, The W12 BP40 55
Curwen Av. E7 CH35 49
Woodford Rd.
Curwen Rd. W12 BP41 65
Curzon Av. Enf. CC25 30
Curzon Av. Stan. BJ30 36
Curzon Clo. Orp. CM56 97
Curzon Clo. Wey. AZ56 92
Curzon Cres. NW10 BO36 55
Curzon Cres. Berk. CN37 58
Curzon Dr. Grays DD43 71
Curzon Ho. W5 BJ38 54
Castlebar Pk. Rd.
Curzon La. E. Brox. CD14 12
Curzon La. W. Brox. CD14 12
Curzon Pl. W1 BV40 3
Curzon Pl. W1 BV40 56
Curzon St.
Curzon Pl. Pnr. BD32 45
Curzon Rd. N10 BV30 38
Curzon Rd. W5 BJ38 54
Curzon Rd. Th. Hth. BX53 86
Curzon Rd. Wey. AX56 92
Curzon St. W1 BV40 3
Curzon St. W1 BV40 56
Cusack Clo. Twick. BH49 74
Custom House Wf. EC3 CA40 4
Custom Ho. Wf. EC3 CA40 57
Cussons Clo. Wal. Cr. CB18 21
Cutcombe Rd. SE5 BZ44 67
Cutforth Rd. Saw. CQ5 6
Cuthbert Rd. E17 CF31 48
Cuthberth Rd. N18 CB28 39
Fairfield Rd.
Cuthbert Rd. Croy. BY55 86
Cuthbert St. W2 BT39 1
Cuthbert St. W2 BT39 56
Cuthbert St. W9 BT38 1
Cuthill Rd. SE5 BZ44 67
Cutler's Ter. N1 CA36 57
Balls Pond Rd.
Cutler St. E1 CA39 2
Cutler St. E1 CA39 57
Cutmere St. Grav. DG47 81
Cutmore Dr. St. Alb. BM14 10
Cut, The SE1 BY41 4
Cut, The SE1 BY41 66
Cutthroat La. Hodd. CD11 12
Cutting, The Red. BU71 121
Cuttsfield Ter. Hem. H. AV14 7
Cuxton Clo. Bexh. CQ46 79
Cyclamen Rd. Swan. CS52 89
Cyclamen Way, Epsom BN56 94
Cycle Track, Harl. CO11 14
Cygnet Av. Felt. BD47 74
Cygnet Clo. Nthwd. BA29 35
Cygnet Gdns. Grav. DF48 81
Cygnets, The Felt. BE49 74
Cygnet St. E1 CA38 2
Cygnet St. E1 CA38 57
Sclater St.
Cymbran Ct. Hem. H. AY11 8
Cynthia St. N1 BX37 2
Cynthis St. N1 BX37 56
Cyntra Pl. E8 CB36 57
Mare St.
Cypress Av. Enf. BY21 29
Cypress Av. Twick. BG47 74
Cypress Clo. Wal. Abb. CF20 21
Cypress Gro. Ilf. CN29 40
Cypress Pl. W1 BW38 1
Cypress Pl. W1 BW38 56
Maple St.
Cypress Rd. SE25 CA51 87
Cypress Rd. Guil. AR69 118
Cypress Rd. Har. BG30 36
Cypress Rd. Sun. BB51 83
Harris Way
Cypress Way, Bans. BQ60 94
Cyprus Av. N3 BR30 37
Cyprus Gdns. N3 BR30 37
Cyprus Pl. E2 CC37 57
Cyprus St.
Cyprus Pl. E6 CL40 58
Cyprus Rd. N3 BR30 37
Cyprus Rd. N9 CA27 39
Cyprus St. E2 CC37 57
Cyprus St. EC1 BY38 2
Cyprus St. EC1 BY38 56
Cyrena Rd. SE22 CA46 77
Cyril Mans. SW11 BU44 66
Cyril Rd. Bexh. CQ44 69
Cyril Rd. Orp. CO54 89
Czar St. SE8 CD43 67
Dabbshill La. Nthlt. BE35 45
D'abernon Clo. Esher BF56 93
D'abernon Dr. Cob. BD61 102
Dabin Cres. SE10 CF44 67
Lindsell St.
Dacca St. SE8 CD43 67
Dace Rd. E3 CE36 57
Dacorum Way, Hem. H. AX13 8
Dace Av. S. Ock. CW40 60
Dacre Av. Ilf. CL30 40
Dacre Clo. Chig. CM28 40
Dacre Cres. S. Ock. CW40 60
Dacre Gdns. SE13 CG45 68
Dacre Gdns. Borwd. BN25 28
Dacre Gdns. Chig. CM28 40
Dacre Pk. SE13 CG45 68
Dacre Pl. SE13 CG45 68
Dacre Rd. E11 CG33 49
Dacre Rd. E13 CH37 58
Dacre Rd. Croy. BX54 86
Dacres Clo. SE23 CC48 77
Dacres Rd. SE23 CC48 77
Dacre St. SW1 BW41 3
Dacre St. SW1 BW41 66
Daerwood Clo. Brom. CK54 88
Daffodil Av. Brwd. DA25 33
Daffodil St. W12 BO40 55
Dafforne Rd. SW17 BU48 76

Dagden Rd. Guil.	AS73	118
Dagenham Av. Dag.	CQ37	59
Dagenham Rd. E10	CD33	48
Dagenham Rd. Dag.	CR35	50
Dagenham Rd. Rain.	CS36	59
Dagenham Rd. Rom.	CS33	50
Dagger La. Borwd.	BJ25	27
Daggs Dell Rd. Hem. H.	AV12	7
Dagley La. Guil.	AR73	118
Dagmar Av. Wem.	BL35	46
Dagmar Gdns. NW10	BQ37	55
Dagmar Pass. N1	BY37	2
Dagmar Pass. N1	BY37	56
Cross St.		
Dagmar Rd. N4	BY33	47
Dagmar Rd. N15	BZ32	48
Cornwall Rd.		
Dagmar Rd. N22	BW30	38

[Index page — full transcription abbreviated]

Deans Ms. W1 BV39 1
Deans Ms. W1 BV39 56
Cavendish Sq.
Deans Rd. W7 BH40 54
Deans Rd. Red. BW68 113
Deans Rd. Sutt. BS55 86
Dean Stanley St. SW1 BX41 4
Dean Stanley St. SW1 BX41 66
Dean St. E7 CH35 49
Dean St. W1 BW39 1
Dean St. W1 BW39 56
Dean Trench St. SW1 BX41 4
Deans Wk. Couls. BY62 104
Deansway N2 BT31 47
Deansway N9 BZ27 39
Deans Way, Edg. BN28 37
Deansway, Hem. H. AY15 8
Deans Yd. SW1 BW41 66
Dean Trench St. SW1 BX41 66
Tufton St.
Dean Wk. Edg. BN29 37
Dean Wk. Lthd. BF66 111
Dean Way, Cat. BZ66 114
Dean Way, Ch. St. G. AQ27 34
Dean Wood Rd. Beac. AO30 34
Dearne Clo. Stan. BJ28 36
De'arn Gdns. Mitch. BU52 86
Deason St. E15 CF37 57
Debden Clo. Wdf. Grn. CJ29 40
Debden La. Loug. CM22 31
Debden Rd. Loug. CL22 31
Debden Wk. Horn. CU36 59
De Beauvoir Cres. N1 BZ37 2
De Beauvoir Cres. N1 CA37 57
De Beauvoir Rd. N1 CA37 57
De Beauvoir Rd. N1 CA37 2
De Beauvoir Sq. N1 CA36 57
Debenham Rd. Wal. Cr. CB17 21
Debnams Rd. SE16 CC42 67
Rotherhithe New Rd.
Debohun Av. N14 BV25 29
Deborah Cl. Islw. BH44 64
Osterley Road
De Burgh Pk. Bans. BS61 104
De Burgh Rd. SW19 BT50 76
Decies Way, Slou. AQ37 52
Decima St. SE1 CA41 4
Decima St. SE1 CA41 67
Decoy Av. NW11 BR32 46
De Crespigny Pk. SE5 BZ44 67
Dedswell Drive, Guil. AW68 110
Dedworth Dr. Wind. AM44 61
Dedworth Rd. Wind. AL44 61
Dee Clo. Upmin. CZ32 51
Dee Lees, Beac. AO29 34
Deeley Rd. SW8 BW44 66
Deena Clo. W3 BL39 55
Deepdale SW19 BQ49 75
Deepdale Av. Brom. CG52 88
Deepdene W5 BL38 55
Ridings, The
Deepdene, Pot. B. BQ19 19
Deepdene Av. Croy. CA55 87
Deepdene Av. Dor. BK71 119
Deepdene Av. Rd. Dor. BK70 119
Deepdene Clo. E18 CH31 49
Deepdene Ct. N21 BY25 29
Deepdene Dri. Dor. BK71 119
Deepdene Gdns. SW2 BX47 76
Deepdene Gdns. Dor. BJ71 119
Deepdene Pk. Rd. Dor. BK71 119
Deepdene Path. Loug. CL24 31
Deepdene Rd. SE5 BZ45 67
Deepdene Rd. Loug. CL24 31
Deepdene Rd. Well. CO45 69
Deepdene Vale, Dor. BK71 119
Deepdene Wood, Dor. BK71 119
Deepfield Way, Couls. BX57 95
Deepfield Way, Couls. BX61 104
Deep Pool La. Wok. AQ60 91
Deer Barn Rd. Guil. AQ70 118
Deerbrook Rd. SE24 BY47 76
Deerdale Rd. SE24 BZ45 67
Deere Av. Rain. CU36 59
Deerfield Cotts. NW9 BO32 46
Deerhurst Rd. NW2 BQ36 55
Deerhurst Rd. SW16 BX49 76
Deerings Rd. Reig. BS70 121
Deerleap Gro. E4 CE25 30
Deerleap Rd. Dor. BF72 119
Dee Rd. E13 CG38 58
Dee Rd. Rich. BL45 65
Deer Park, Harl. CL12 13
Deer Pk. Clo. Kings. On T. BM50 75
Crescent Rd.
Deer Pk. Gdns. Mitch. BT52 86
Deer Pk. Rd. SW19 BT51 86
Deerswood Av. Hat. BP13 10
Deeside Rd. SW17 BT48 76
Dee St. E14 CF39 57
Dee, The Hem. H. AY11 8
Deeves Hall La. Pot. B. BO20 19
Dee Way, Epsom BO58 94
Dee Way, Rom. CT29 41
Defiance Wk. SE18 CK41 68
Antelope Rd.
Defiant Way Wall. BX57 95
Defoe Av. Rich. BM43 65
Defoe Par. Grays. DG41 71
Defoe Rd. N16 CA34 48
Defoe Way Rom. CR29 41
De Frene Rd. SE26 CC49 77
Degema Rd. Chis. CL49 78
Dehar Cres. NW4 BP33 46
De Haviland Rd. Houns. BC43 63
De Haviland Way Stai. AX46 73
De Havilland Clo. Hat. BO12 10
De Havilland Rd. Edg. BM30 37
De Havilland Rd. Wall. BX57 95
Dekker Rd. SE21 CA46 77
Delabole Rd. Red. BX68 113
Delacourt Rd. SE3 CH43 68
Old Dover Rd.
Delafield Rd. SE7 CH42 68
Delafield Rd. Grays. DE42 71
Delaford Clo. Hayes AW39 53
Delaford Clo. Iver AV39 52
Delaford Rd. SE15 CB42 67
Delaford Rd. SE16 CB42 67
Delaford St. SW6 BR43 65
Delagarde Rd. West CM66 115
Delahay Rse. Berk. AQ12 7
Delamere Cres. SW9 BX45 66
Brighton Ter.
Delamere Cres. Croy. CC53 87
Delamere Gdns. NW7 BN29 37
Delamere Rd. SW20 BQ51 85
Delamere Rd. W5 BL40 55
Delamere Rd. Borwd. BM23 28
Delamere Rd. Hayes BD40 54
Delamere Rd. Reig. BS72 121
Delamere Ter. W2 BS39 1
Delamere Ter. W2 BS39 56
Delancey St. NW1 BV37 1
Delancey St. NW1 BV37 56
De La Mere Rd. Wal. Cr. CD18 21
De Lapre Clo. Orp. CP54 89
Delaporte, Epsom BO59 94
Delara Way, Wok. AR62 100
De Laune St. SE17 BY43 4
De Laune St. SE17 BY42 66
Delaware Rd. W9 BS38 56
Delawyk Cres. SE24 BZ46 77
Delbow Rd. Felt. BC46 73
Delcombe Av. Wor. Pk. BQ54 85
Delderfield, Ash. BK64 102
Hatherwood
Delft Way SE22 CA46 77
Dulwich Gro.
Delhi Rd. Enf. CA26 39
Delhi St. N1 BX37 2
Delhi St. N1 BX37 56
Delia St. SW18 BS47 76
Delius Clo. Borwd. BK25 27
Dell Clo. E15 CF37 57
Dell Clo. Dor. BK67 111
Dell Clo. Lthd. BH65 102
Dell Clo. Lthd. BJ66 111
Dell CLo. Wall. BW56 95
Dell Clo. Wdf. Grn. CH27 40
Dellcott Clo. Welw. G. C. BP7 5
Dellcut Rd. Hem. H. AZ12 8
Dell Farm Rd. Ruis. BA32 44
Dellfield, St. Alb. BH14 9
Dell Field Av. Berk. AQ12 7
Dell Field Clo. Berk. AQ12 7
Dellfield Clo. Brom. CS50 77
Foxgrove Rd.
Dellfield Clo. Rad. BH21 27
Dellfield Clo. Wat. BC23 26
Dellfield Cres. Uxb. AX38 53
Dellfield Rd. Hat. BP12 10
Dell La. Epsom BP56 94
Dellmeadow, Wat. BB19 17
Dellors Clo. Barn. BQ25 28
Dellow Clo. Ilf. CM33 49
Dellow St. E1 CB40 57
Dell Rise, St. Alb. BF17 18
Dell Rd. Berk. AO11 7
Dell Rd. Enf. CC22 30
Dell Rd. Epsom BP57 94
Dell Rd. Grays. DD42 71
Dell Rd. Wat. BC22 26
Dell Rd. West Dr. AY42 63
Dell Side, Amer. AO23 25
Dellside, Uxb. AX32 44
Dellsome La. St. Alb. BO15 10
Dellsome Pde. Hat. BQ15 10
Fourways
Dells, The Hem. H. AZ14 8
Dell, The Nthwd. BB27 35
Dell, The SE2 CO42 69
Dell, The SE19 CA51 87
Dell, The Beck. CE50 77
Dell, The Bex. CT47 79
Dell, The Brwd. DA29 42
Dell, The Felt. BC47 73
Dell, The Ger. Cr. AS29 34
Dell, The Pnr. BD30 36
Dell, The Reig. BS70 121
Dell, The St. Alb. BJ12 9
Dell, The Wall. BW56 95
Dell, The Wdf. Grn. CH27 40
Dell, The Wem. BJ35 45
Dell, The Wok. AR62 100
Dell Wk. N. Mal. BO51 85
Dell Way W13 BK39 54
Dellwood Cl. Rick. AW26 35
Dellwood Gdns. Ilf. CL31 49
Delmar Av. Hem. H. BA14 8
Delmare Clo. SW9 BX45 66
Brighton Ter.
Delme Cres. SE3 CH44 58
Delmey Clo. Croy. CA55 87
Delmos Dr. Hem. H. AZ12 8
Deloraine St. SE8 CE44 67
Delorme St. W6 BQ43 65
Delphian Ct. SW16 BY49 76
Delsa Ct. NW2 BP34 46
Delta Clo. Wok. AP58 91
Delta Gain. Wat. BD27 36
Delta Gro. Nthlt. BD37 54
Delta Gro. Nthlt. BD38 54
Kittiwake Rd.
Delta Rd. Brwd. DE25 122
Delta Rd. Wok. AP58 91
Delta Rd. Wok. AT61 100
Delta Rd. Wor. Pk. BO55 85
Delta St. E2 CB38 2
Delta St. E2 CB38 57
Wellington Row
Deluci Rd. Erith CS42 69
Delvers Mead. Dag. CS35 50
Felhurst Cr.
Delverton Rd. SE17 BY42 4
Delverton Rd. SE17 BZ42 67
Delvino Rd. SW6 BS44 66
Demense Rd. Wall. BW57 95
Demeta Clo. Wem. BN34 46
De Montfort Rd. SW16 BX48 76
De Morgan Rd. SW6 BS45 66
Dempster Rd. SW18 BT45 66
Denberry Dr. Sid. CO48 79
Denbigh Ch. W11 BR40 55
Denbigh Clo. NW10 BO36 55
Denbigh Clo. Chis. CK50 78
Denbigh Clo. Horn. CW31 51
Denbigh Clo. Ruis. BB34 44
Denbigh Clo. Sid. CQ48 79
Riverside Rd.
Denbigh Clo. Sthl. BE39 54
Denbigh Clo. Sutt. BR56 94
Denbigh Dr. Hayes. BA41 63
Denbigh Gdns. Rich. BL46 75
Denbigh Pl. SW1 BW42 3
Denbigh Pl. SW1 BW42 66
Denbigh Rd. E6 CJ38 58
Denbigh Rd. W11 BR40 55
Denbigh Rd. W13 BJ40 54
Denbigh Rd. Sthl. BE39 54
Denbigh Rd. Sthl. BF44 64
Denbigh St. SW1 BW42 3
Denbigh St. SW1 BW42 66
Denbigh Ter. W11 BR40 55
Denbridge Rd. Brom. CK51 88
Denby Rd. Cob. BD59 93
Den Clo. Beck. CF52 87
Dendy St. SW12 BV47 76
Dene Av. Houns. BE45 64
Dene Av. Sid. CO47 79
Dene Clo. SE4 CD45 67
Dene Clo. Brom. CG54 88
Dene Clo. Dart. CT49 79
Dene Clo. Wor. Pk. BO55 85
Dene Ct. Guil. AT69 118
Denecroft Cres. Uxb. AZ37 53
Denecroft Gdns. Grays. DE41 1
Dene Dr. Orp. CO55 89
Denefield Dr. Ken. BZ61 105
Dene Gdns. Stan. BK26 36
Dene Gdns. Surb. BJ54 84
Dene Holm Rd. Grav. DE48 81
Denehurst Gdns. NW4 BQ32 46
Denehurst Gdns. W3 BM40 55
Gunersbury La.
Denehurst Gdns. Rich. BM45 65
Denehurst Gdns. Twick. BG47 74
Denehurst Gdns. Wdf. Grn. CH28 40
Dene Path. S. Ock. DA39 60
Dene Pl. Wok. AQ62 100
Caradon Clo.
Dene Rd. NW11 BU26 38
Dene Rd. Ash. BL63 103
Dene Rd. Buck. H. CJ26 40
Dene Rd. Dart. CW47 80
Dene Rd. Guil. AS71 118
Dene Rd. Nthwd. BA29 35
Dene Rd. Nthwd. BB29 35
Dene St. Gdns. Dor. BJ71 119
Denes, The Hem. H. AY15 8
Dene St. Dor. BJ71 119
Dene, The W13 BJ39 54
Templewood
Dene, The Croy. CC55 87
Dene, The Dor. BC73 119
Dene The E. Mol. BE53 84
Dene, The Sev. CU66 116
Dene, The Sutt. BR59 94
Dene, The Wem. BL35 46
Dene Walk, Long. DC52 90
Denewood, Barn. BT25 29
Denewood Clo. Wat. BB22 26
Denewood Rd. N6 BU32 47
Denfield, Dor. BJ72 119
Denford Rd. SE10 CG42 68
Glenforth St.
Dengie Wk. N1 BZ37 57
Rasire St.
Denham Av. Uxb. AV34 43
Denham Clo. Hem. H. AZ11 8
Sarratt Av.
Denham Clo. Uxb. AW34 44
Denham Clo. Well. CP45 69
Park View Rd.
Denham Ct. SE26 CB48 77
Halifax St.
Denham Cres. Mitch. BU52 86
Denham Dr. Esher BJ57 93
Denham Dr. Ilf. CM32 49
Denham Green Clo. Uxb. AW33 44
Denham Green La. Uxb. AV31 43
Denham La. Ger. Cr. AS29 34
Denham Rd. N20 BU27 38
Denham Rd. SE10 CH42 68
Denham Rd. Egh. AT49 72
Denham Rd. Epsom BO59 94
Denham Rd. Felt. BD46 74
Denham Rd. Iver & Uxb. AU37 52
Denham Walk, Ger. Cr. AS29 34
Denham La.
Denham Way, Bark. CN37 58
Denham Way Rick. AV27 34
Denham Way, Uxb. AW34 44
Denholme Rd. W9 BR38 55
Denison Clo. N2 BT31 47
Denison Rd. SW19 BT50 76
Denison Rd. W5 BK38 54
Denison Rd. Felt. BB49 73
Deniston Av. Bex. CQ47 79
Denleigh Gdns. N21 BY26 38
Denleigh Gdns. E. Mol. BH53 84
Denman Dr. NW11 BS32 47
Denman Dr. Ashf. AZ50 73
Denman Dr. N. NW11 BS32 47
Denman Dr. S. NW11 BS32 47
Denman Rd. SE15 CA44 67
Denman St. W1 BW40 3
Denman St. W1 BW40 56
Denmark Av. SW19 BR50 75
Denmark Ct. Mord. BS53 86
Denmark Gdns. Cars. BU55 86
Denmark Gro. N1 BY37 2
Denmark Gro. N1 BY37 56
Denmark Hill SE5 BZ44 67
Denmark Pl. N8 BY31 47
Denmark Rd.
Denmark Pl. WC2 BW39 1
Denmark Rd. N8 BY31 47
Denmark Rd. NW6 BR37 55
Denmark Rd. SE5 BZ44 67
Denmark Rd. SE25 CB53 87
Denmark Rd. SW19 BQ50 75
Denmark Rd. W13 BJ40 54
Denmark Rd. Brom. CH51 88
Denmark Rd. Cars. BU55 86
Denmark Rd. Guil. AS71 118
Denmark Rd. Kings. On T. BL52 85
Denmark Rd. Twick. BG48 74
Denmark St. E11 CG34 49
High Rd.
Denmark St. N17 CB30 39
Denmark St. WC2 BW39 1
Denmark St. WC2 BW39 56
Denmark St. Wat. BC23 26
Denmark Wk. SE27 BZ49 77
Denmead Clo. Ger. Cr. AS33 43
Denmead Rd. Croy. BY54 86
Denmead Way SE15 CA43 67
Hordie Prom. S.
Dennan Rd. Surb. BL54 85
Denner Rd. E4 CE27 39
Dennets, Wok. AP62 100
Staveley Way
Dennett Rd. Croy. BY54 86
Dennetts Gro. SE14 CC44 67
Dennettsland Rd. Eden. CM70 115
Dennett's Rd. SE14 CC44 67
Denning Av. Croy. BY56 95
Denning Clo. NW8 BT38 1
Denning Clo. NW8 BT38 56
Denning Rd. NW3 BT35 47
Dennington Clo. E5 CB34 48
Southwold Rd.
Dennington Pk. Rd. NW6 BS35 56
Dennis Av. Wem. BL35 46
Dennis Clo. Ashf. BA50 73
Chertsey Rd.
Dennis Clo. Red. BU69 121
Dennis Reeve Cl. Mitch. BU51 86
Dennises La. Upmin. CZ37 60
Dennis Gdns. Stan. BK28 36
Dennis La. Stan. BJ27 36
Dennis La. Est. Stan. BJ28 36
Dennis Pk. Cres. SW20 BR51 85
Dennis Rd. E. Mol. BG52 84
Dennis Rd. Grnf. BJ37 54
Dennis Rd. Grav. DG48 81
Dennis Rd. S. Ock. DA37 60
Dennisville, Guil. AP71 118
Denny Av. Wal. Abb. CF20 21
Denny Cres. SE11 BY42 4
Denny Cres. SE11 BY42 66
Denny St.
Denny Gdns. Dag. CO36 59
Denny Rd. N9 CB26 39
Denny St. SE11 BY42 4
Denny St. SE11 BY42 66
Den Rd. Brom. CF52 87
Densham Rd. E15 CG37 58
Densley Clo. Welw. G. C. BQ7 5
Densole Clo. Beck. CD51 87
King's Hall Rd.
Densor Gdns. Est. W9 BS39 56
Densworthy Gro. N9 CC27 39
Denton Clo. Barn. BQ25 28
Denton Clo. Red. BV73 121
Denton Ct. Rd. Grav. DJ47 81
Denton Gro. Walt. BE55 84
Denton Rd. N8 BX32 47
Denton Rd. N18 CA28 39
Denton Rd. NW10 BN36 55
Denton Rd. Bex. CT48 79
Denton Rd. Twick. BK46 74
Denton Rd. Well. CP43 69
Denton St. SW18 BS46 76
Denton St. Grav. DJ47 81
Denton Ter. Bex. CT48 79
Denton Way E5 CC34 48
Millfields Rd.
Denton Way, Wok. AP62 100
Dent. S. Ock. DA39 60
Dunnine Clo.
Dents Rd. SW11 BU46 76
Denvale Wk. Wok. AQ62 100
Muirfield Rd.
Denver Clo. Orp. CN53 88
Denver Rd. N16 CA33 48
Denver Rd. Dart. CU47 79
Denyer St. SW3 BU42 3
Denyer St. SW3 BU42 66
Denzilde Av. Uxb. AZ38 53
Denzil Rd. NW10 BO35 46
Denil Rd. Guil. AQ71 118
Deodar Rd. SW15 BR45 65
Depot Rd. Epsom BO60 94
Depot Rd. Houns. BG45 64
Depot St. SE5 BZ43 67
Deptford Br. SE8 CE44 67
Deptford Broadway SE8 CE44 67
Deptford Church St. SE8 CE43 67
Deptford Church St. SE8 CE43 67
Deptford Ferry Rd. E14 CE42 67
Deptford Grn. SE8 CE43 67
Deptford High St. SE8 CE43 67
Deptford Strand SE8 CD42 67
De Quincey Rd. N17 BZ30 39
Derby Arms Rd. Epsom BO62 103
Derby Av. N12 BT28 38
Derby Av. Har. BG30 36
Derby Av. Rom. CS32 50
Derby Av. Upmin. CW35 51
Derby Gate SW1 BX41 4
Derby Gate SW1 BX41 66
Derby Gro. Croy. BY54 86
Derby Hl. SE23 CC48 77
Derby Hl. Cres. SE23 CC48 77
Derby Hl. Est. SE23 CC48 77
Derby Rd. E7 CJ36 58
Derby Rd. E9 CC37 57
Derby Rd. E18 CG30 40
Derby Rd. N15 BY31 47
Derby Rd. N18 CB28 39
Derby Rd. SW14 BM45 65
Derby Rd. SW19 BS50 76
Derby Rd. Croy. BY54 86
Derby Rd. Enf. CB25 30
Derby Rd. Grays. DD43 71
Derby Rd. Grnf. BF37 54
Derby Rd. Guil. AP70 118
Derby Rd. Hodd. CF13 12
Derby Rd. Houns. BF45 64
Derby Rd. Surb. BM54 85
Derby Rd. Sutt. BR57 94
Derby Rd. Uxb. AX37 53
Derby Rd. Wat. BD24 27
Derbyshire St. E2 CB38 57
Derby Stables Rd. Epsom BO62 103
Derby St. W1 BV40 3
Derby St. W1 BV40 56
Curzon St.
Dereham Pl. EC2 CA38 2
Dereham Pl. EC2 CA38 57
Dereham Rd. Bark. CN35 49
Derek Av. Epsom. BM57 94
Derek Av. Wall. BV56 95
Derek Av. Wem. BM36 55
Derham Gdns. Upmin. CY34 51
Deri. Av. Rain. CU38 59
Dericote Rd. E8 CB37 57
Croston St.
Deridene Clo. Stai. AY46 73
Dering Pl. Croy. BZ56 96
Dering Rd. Croy. BZ56 96
Dering St. W1 BV39 1
Dering St. W1 BV39 56
Derinton Rd. SW17 BU49 76
Derley Rd. Sthl. BD41 64
Dermody Gdns. SE13 CF46 77
Dermody Rd. SE13 CF46 77
Derns Wk. Couls. BY58 95
Deronda Est. SW2 BY47 76
Deronda Rd. SE24 BY47 76
Derrick Av. Sth. Croy. BZ58 96
Derrick Gdns. SE7 CJ41 68
Derrick Rd. Beck. CD52 87
Derry Ave. S. Ock. DA39 60
Derry Down, Wok. AR64 100
Derry Downs Orp. CP53 89
Derry Rd. Croy. BX55 86
Derry St. W8 BS41 66
Dersingham Av. E12 CK35 49
Dedsingham Rd. NW2 BR34 46
Derwent Av. N18 BZ28 39
Derwent Av. NW7 BN29 37
Derwent Av. NW9 BO32 46
Derwent Av. SW15 BO49 75
Derwent Av. Barn. BU26 38
Derwent Av. Pnr. BE29 36
Derwent Av. Uxb. AZ34 44
Derwent Clo. Dart. CU47 79
Derwent Clo. Esher BH57 93
Derwent Clo. Wey. AX56 92
Derwent Cres. N20 BT27 38
Derwent Cres. Bexh. CR44 69
Derwent Cres. Stan. BK30 36
Derwent Dr. Hayes BB39 53
Derwent Dr. Orp. CM54 88
Derwent Dr. Pur. BZ60 96
Derwent Gdns. Ilf. CK31 49
Derwent Gdns. Wem. BK33 45
Derwent Par. S. Ock. DA39 60
Derwent Ri. NW9 BO32 46
Derwent Rd. N13 BX28 38
Derwent Rd. N. Mal. BQ53 85
Grand Drive
Derwent Rd. SE20 CB51 87
Derwent Rd. SE22 CA45 67
Derwent Rd. W5 BK41 64
Derwent Rd. Sthl. BE39 54
Derwent Rd. Twick. BF46 74
Derwent St. SE10 CG42 68
Derwentwater Rd. W3 BN40 55
Derwentwater Rd. Hem. H. BA14 8
Derwent Way, Horn. CU35 50
Dessalis Rd. Uxb. BA38 53
Desborough Clo. Shep. AZ54 83
Ferry La.
Desborough St. W2 BS39 56
Cirencester St.
Desenfans Rd. SE21 CA46 77
Desford Ct. Ashf. AY48 73
Deford Rd. E16 CG38 58
Desford Way, Ashf. AY48 73
Desmond Rd. Wat. BB21 26
Desmond St. SE14 CD43 67
Despard Av. SW11 BV44 66
Despard Rd. N19 BW33 47
Detillens La. Oxt. CH68 115
Detling Clo. Horn. CV35 51
Detling Rd. Brom. CH49 78
Detling Rd. Erith CS43 69
Detling Rd. Grav. DE47 81
Deva Clo. St. Alb. BF14 9
Devana End Cars. BU55 86
Devas Rd. SW20 BQ51 85
Devas St. E3 CE38 57
Devenay Rd. E15 CG36 58
Devenish Rd. SE2 CO41 69
Deventer Cres. SE22 CA46 77
Dulwich Gro.
Devlan Clo. SE18 CL43 68
Llanover St.
De Vere Gdns. W8 BT41 3
De Vere Gdns. W8 BT41 66
De Vere Gdns. Ilf. CK34 49
Deverell St. SE1 BZ41 4
Deverell St. SE1 BZ41 67
Devereux Ct. EC4 BY40 56
Fountain Ct.
Devereux Dr. Wat. BB22 26
Devereux Rd. SW11 BU46 76
Devereux Rd. Wind. AO44 61
De Vere Wk. Wat. BB23 26
Deveron Gdns. S. Ock. DA39 60
Deveron Way Rom. CT30 41
Devils La. Egh. AU50 72
Devitt Clo. Ash. BM61 103
Devizes St. N1 BZ37 2
Devoke Way Walt. BD55 84
Devon Av. Slou. AO39 52
Devon Av. Twick. BG47 74
Devon Back, Guil. AR72 118
Devon Clo. N17 CA31 48
Devon Clo. Buck. H. CH27 40
Devon Clo. Grnf. BK37 54
Devon Clo. Ken. CA61 105
Devon Ct. W3 BM39 55
Links Rd.
Devon Ct. Hamptn. BF50 74

Devon Ct. St. Alb. BH14 9
Old London Rd.
Devon Cres. Grnf. BK37 54
Devon Cres. Red. BT70 121
Devoncroft Gdns. Twick. BJ47 74
Oak La.
Devon Gdns. N4 BY32 47
Devonia Gdns. N18 BZ29 39
Devonia Rd. N1 BY37 2
Devonia Rd. N1 BY37 56
Devonport Gdns. Ilf. CK32 49
Devonport Mews W12 BP41 65
Devonport Pass. E1 CC39 57
Devonport Rd. W12 BP40 55
Devonport St. E1 CC39 57
Devon Rise N2 BT31 47
Devon Rd. Bark. CN37 58
Devon Rd. Red. BW68 113
Devon Rd. S. At. H. CX51 90
Devon Rd. Sutt. BR58 94
Devon Rd. Walt. BD56 93
Devon Rd. Wat. BD23 27
Devons Est. E3 CE38 57
Devonshire Ave. Wok. AU60 91
Devonshire Av. Dart. CU46 79
Devonshire Av. Sutt. BT57 95
Devonshire Clo. E15 CG35 49
Devonshire Clo. N13 BY27 38
Devonshire Clo. W1 BV39 1
Devonshire Clo. W1 BV39 56
Devonshire Ct. Croy. CD54 87
Devonshire Ct. Rich. BL44 65
Holmersdale Rd.
Devonshire Cres. NW7 BQ29 37
Devonshire Dr. SE10 CE43 67
Devonshire Dr. Surb. BK54 84
Devonshire Gdns. N17 BZ29 39
Devonshire Rd.
Devonshire Gdns. N21 BZ26 39
Devonshire Gdns. W4 BN43 65
Devonshire Gdns. S. Le. H. DK41 71
Somerset Rd.
Devonshire Gro. SE15 CB43 67
Devonshire Hill La. N17 BY29 38
Devonshire Mews N. W1. BV38 56
Park Cres. Ms. West
Devonshire Mews S. W1 BV39 1
Devonshire Ms. S. W1 BV39 56
Devonshire Ms. W. W1 BV38 1
Devonshire Ms. W. W1 BV38 56
Devonshire Pl. W1 BV38 1
Devonshire Pl. W1 BV38 56
Devonshire Pl. W4 BO42 65
Devonshire Pl. Ms. W1 BV38 1
Devonshire Pl. Ms. W1 BV38 56
Devonshire Rd. E15 CG35 49
Devonshire Rd. E16 CH39 58
Devonshire Rd. E17 CE32 48
Devonshire Rd. N9 CC26 39
Devonshire Rd. N13 BX28 38
Devonshire Rd. N17 BZ29 39
Devonshire Rd. NW7 BQ29 37
Devonshire Rd. SE9 CK48 78
Devonshire Rd. SE23 CC47 77
Devonshire Rd. SW19 BU50 76
Devonshire Rd. W4 BO42 65
Devonshire Rd. W5 BK41 64
Devonshire Rd. AZ56 92
Devonshire Rd. Bexh. CQ45 69
Devonshire Rd. Croy. BZ54 87
Devonshire Rd. Felt. BE48 74
Devonshire Rd. Grav. DG48 81
Devonshire Rd. Har. BG32 45
Devonshire Rd. Horn. CV34 51
Devonshire Rd. Ilf. CM33 49
Devonshire Rd. Orp. CO54 89
Devonshire Rd. Pnr. BD32 45
Devonshire Rd. Pnr. BE30 36
Devonshire Rd. Sthl. BF39 54
Devonshire Rd. Sutt. BT57 95
Devonshire Rd. Wall. BV56 95
Devonshire Row EC2 CA39 2
Devonshire Row EC2 CA39 57
Devonshire Sq. EC2 CA39 2
Devonshire Sq. EC2 CA39 57
Devonshire Sq. Brom. CH52 88
Masons Hill
Devonshire St. W1 BV39 1
Devonshire St. W1 BV39 56
Devonshire St. W4 BO42 65
Devonshire Ter. W2 BT39 1
Devonshire Ter. W2 BT39 56
Devonshire Way, Croy. CD55 87
Devonshire Way, Hayes BC39 53
Devons Rd. E3 CE38 57
Devon St. SE15 CB44 67
Devon Way, Chess. BK56 93
Devon Way, Epsom. BM56 94
Devon Waye, Houns. BE43 64
De Walden St. W1 BV39 1
De Walden St. W1 BV39 56
Marylebone St.
Dewar St. SE15 CB45 67
Dewberry St. E14 CF39 57
Dewey Rd. N1 BY37 2
Dewey Rd. N1 BY37 56
Dewey Rd. Dag. CS36 59
Dewey St. SW17 BU49 76
Dew Grass Gdns. Enf. CC21 30
Holmesdale
Dewhurst Rd. W14 BQ41 65
Dewhurst Rd. Wal. Cr. CB18 21
Dewlands. Dart. CX47 80
Dewlands, Gdse. CC69 114
Dewport St. W6 BR43 65
Field Rd.
Dewsbury Clo. Pnr. BE32 45
Dewsbury Clo. Rom. CV29 42
Dewsbury Gdns. Rom. CV29 42
Dewsbury Gdns. Wor. Pk. BP55 85
Dewsbury Rd. NW10 BP35 46
Dewsbury Rd. Rom. CV29 42
Dewsbury Ter. NW1 BV36 56
Camden High St.
Dexter Clo. Grays. DD41 71
Dexter Rd. SE24 BY45 66
Dexter Rd. Barn. BQ25 28
Deyncourt Gdns. Upmin. CY34 51
Deyncourt Rd. N17 BZ30 39
Deynecourt Gdns. E11 CJ31 49
D'eynsford Rd. SE5 BZ44 67
Diadem Ct. W1 BW39 1
Gt. Chapel St.
Dial, The Wk. W8 BS41 66
Dial Walk, The SW7 BS41 3
Diamedes, Stai. AX47 73
Diameter Rd. Orp. CL54 88
Diamond Clo. E7 CH35 49
Stracey Rd.
Diamond Rd. Ruis. BE35 45
Diamond Rd. Slou. AQ41 62
Diamond Rd. Wat. BC22 26
Diamond St. SE15 CA43 67
Diamond Ter. SE10 CF43 67
Diana Clo. E18 CH30 40
Latchett Rd.
Diana Pl. NW1 BV38 1
Diana Pl. NW1 BV38 56
Diana Rd. E17 CD31 48
Dianthus Clo. SE CO42 69
Carnation St.
Dianthus Clo. Cher. AV54 82
Diban Av. Horn. CU35 50
Dibber Rd. SE23 CC48 77
Dibden La. Sev. CT66 116
Dibden's Cotts. SE27 BY49 76
Crown La.
Dibden St. N1 BY37 2
Dibden St. N1 BZ37 57
Dibdin Clo. Sutt. BS55 86
Dibdin Ho. NW6 BS38 56
Dibdin Ho. W9 BS37 1
Dibdin Rd. NW6 BS37 56
Dibdin Rd. SE1 BY41 66
Gerridge St.
Dibdin Rd. Sutt. BS55 86
Diceland Rd. Bans. BR61 103
Dicey Av. NW2 BQ35 46
Dickens Ave. Til. DG44 71
Dickens Av. N3 BT30 38
Dickens Av. Dart. CX45 70
Dickens Av. Uxb. AZ39 53
Dickens Clo. Hart. DC53 90
Dickens Clo. Rich. BL48 75
Dickens Clo. St. Alb. BG13 9
Dickens Ct. Hem. H. AZ10 8
Dickens Dr. Chis. CM50 78
Dickens Dr. Wey. AW56 92
Dickens Est. SE1 CB41 67
Dickens Est. SE16 CB41 4
Dickens La. N18 CA29 39
Dickenson Av. Rick. AZ25 26
Dickenson Rd. N8 BX33 47
Dickenson's La. SE25 CB53 87
Dickenson's Pl. SE25 CB53 87
Dickenson Rd. Felt. BD49 74
Dickenson Sq. Rick. AZ25 26
Dickens Rise, Chig. CL27 40
Dickens Rd. E6 CJ37 58
Dickens Rd. Grav. DJ47 81
Dickens Sq. SE1 BZ41 4
Dickens Sq. SE1 BZ41 67
Dickens St. SW8 BV44 66
Dickerage La. N. Mal. BN52 85
Dickerage Rd. Kings. On T. BN51 85
Dickins Clo. Wal. Cr. CB17 21
Spicersfield
Dickson Rd. SE9 CK45 68
Dickson's Fold. Pnr. BD31 45
Dickson, Wal. Cr. CA17 21
Dick Turpin Way, Felt. BB45 63
Didcot St. SW11 BT45 66
Didsbury Clo. E6 CK37 58
Barking Rd.
Digby Cres. N4 BZ34 48
Digby Est. E2 CC38 57
Digby Gdns. Dag. CR37 59
Digby Pl. Croy. CA55 87
Digby Rd. E9 CC35 48
Digby Rd. Bark. CN36 58
Digby St. E2 CC38 57
Digby Way, Wey. AY59 92
Digby Wk. Horn. CV35 51
Digdag Hill, Wal. Cr. CA17 21
Digdens Rise, Epsom BN61 103
Diggon St. E1 CC39 57
Dighton Rd. SW18 BT46 76
Dignum St. N1 BY37 2
Dignum St. N1 BY37 56
Digswellbury, Welw. G. C. BR6 5
Digswell Hill, Welw. G. C. BP6 5
Digswell La. Welw. G. C. BR6 5
Digswell Park Rd.
Welw. G. C. BQ5 5
Digswell Park Rd.
Welw. G. C. BR5 5
Digswell Rise, Welw G. C. BQ7 5
Digswell Rd. Welw. G. C. BQ7 5
Digswell St. N7 BY36 56
Holloway Rd.
Dilhorne Clo. SE12 CH48 78
Dilke St. SW3 BU43 66
Dillan Pl. N7 BX34 47
Dillwyn Clo. SE26 CD49 77
Dilston Clo. Nthlt. BD38 54
Dilston Gro. SE16 CC42 67
Abbeyfield Rd.
Dilston Rd. Lthd. BJ63 102
Dilton Gdns. SW15 BP47 75
Dimes Pl. W3 BP42 65
King St.
Dimmock Dr. Har. BG35 45
Dimmocks La. Rick. AW21 26
Dimond Clo. E7 CH35 49
Stracey Rd.
Dimsdale Dr. NW9 BN33 46
Dimsdale Dr. Enf. CB25 30
Dimsdale Wk. E13 CG37 58
Dinant Link Rd. Hodd. CE11 12
Dingle Gdns. E14 CE40 57
Dingle Rd. Ashf. AZ49 73
Dingle, The Uxb. AZ38 53
Dingley La. SW16 BW48 76
Dingley Pl. EC1 BZ38 2
Dingley Pl. EC1 BZ38 57
Dingley Rd.
Dingley Rd. EC1 BZ38 2
Dingley Rd. EC1 BZ38 57
Dingon Hill Clo. Hayes BC39 53
Dingwall Av. Croy. BZ55 87
Dingwall Gdns. NW11 BS32 47
Dingwall Pl. Croy. BZ55 87
Dingwall Rd. SW18 BT47 76
Dingwall Rd. Cars. BU58 95
Dingwall Rd. Croy. BZ54 87
Dinmont Est. E2 CB37 57
Dinmont St. E2 CB37 57
Dinmore, Hem. H. AS17 16
Dinsdale Clo. Wok. AT62 100
Dinsdale Gdns. SE25 CA52 87
Dinsdale Gdns. Barn. BS25 29
Dinsdale Rd. SE3 CG43 68
Dinsmore Rd. SW12 BV47 76
Dinton Rd. SW19 BT50 76
Dinton Rd. Kings. On T. BL50 75
Dione Rd. Hem. H. AY12 8
Dippers Clo. Sev. CW62 108
Dirdene Clo. Epsom BO59 94
Dirdene Gdns. Epsom BO59 94
Dirdene Gro. Epsom BO59 94
Dirleton Rd. E15 CG37 58
Dirtham La. Leath. BC67 110
Disbrowe Rd. W6 BR43 65
Dishforth La. NW9 BO30 37
Disney Pl. SE1 BZ41 1
Disney Pl. SE1 BZ41 67
Disney St.
Disney St. SE1 BZ41 4
Disney St. SE1 BZ41 67
Dison Clo. Enf. CC23 30
Disraeli Clo. SE28 CP40 59
Disraeli Clo. W4 BN41 65
Winston Wk.
Disraeli Gdns. SW15 BR45 65
Fawe Pk. Rd.
Disraeli Rd. E7 CH36 58
Disraeli Rd. NW10 BN37 55
Disraeli Rd. SW15 BQ45 65
Disraeli Rd. W5 BK40 54
Diss St. E2 CA38 2
Diss St. E2 CA38 57
Distaff La. EC4 BZ40 4
Distaff La. EC4 BZ39 57
Cannon St.
Distillery La. W6 BQ42 65
Distillery Wk. Brent. BL43 65
Pottery Rd.
Distin St. SE11 BY42 4
Distin St. SE11 BY42 66
District Rd. Wem. BJ35 45
Ditch Alley SE10 CE44 67
Ditchburn St. E14 CF40 57
Ditches La. Couls. BX63 104
Ditchfield Rd. Hodd. CE10 12
Dittisham Rd. SE9 CK49 78
Ditton Clo. Surb. BJ54 84
Ditton Gra. Clo. Surb. BK54 84
Ditton Grd. Dr. Surb. BK54 84
Ditton Hill Rd. Surb. BK54 84
Ditton Lawn Surb. BJ54 84
Ditton Park Rd. Slou. AS43 62
Ditton Pl. SE20 CB51 87
Ditton Rd. Bexh. CP46 79
Ditton Rd. Slou. AR44 62
Ditton Rd. Slou. AS43 62
Ditton Rd. Sthl. BE42 64
Ditton Rd. Surb. BK55 84
Divis Way SW15 BP46 75
Dover Pk. Dr.
Dixon Pl. W. Wick. CE54 87
Dixon Rd. SE14 CD44 67
Dixon Rd. SE25 CA52 87
Dixons Alley SE16 CB41 67
West La.
Dixon's Hill Clo. Hat. BP16 19
Dixon's Hill Rd. Hat. BP16 19
Dobb, S Weir Rd. Harl. CG13 13
Dobb, S Weir Rd. Hodd. CF12 12
Dobbin Clo. Har. BJ30 36
Dobell Rd. SE9 CK46 78
Dobree Rd. NW10 BP36 55
Dobson Clo. NW6 BT36 56
Belsize Rd.
Dobson Rd. Grav. DJ49 81
Dockett Eddy La. Shep. AY54 83
Dockhead SE1 CA41 67
Jamaica Rd.
Dockland St. E16 CL40 58
Dockley Rd. SE16 CB41 4
Dockley Rd. SE16 CB41 67
Dock Rd. E16 CG40 58
Dock Rd. Brent. BK43 64
Dock Rd. Grays. DE43 71
Dock Rd. Grays. DF43 71
Dock St. E1 CB40 4
Dock St. E1 CB40 57
Dockwell Clo. Felt. BC45 63
Doctor Johnsons Av. SW17 BV48 76
Doctors Common Rd.
Berk. AQ13 7
Doctors La. Cat. BY65 104
Docwras Bldgs. N1 BZ36 57
Docwra's Bldgs. N1 CA36 57
King Henry's Wk.
Dodbrooke Rd. SE27 BY48 76
Doddinghurst Rd. Brwd. DB23 33
Doddinghurst Rd. Brwd. DB26 42
Doddington Gro. SE17 BY43 4
Doddington Gro. SE17 BY43 66
Doddington Pl. SE17 BY43 4
Doddington Pl. SE17 BY43 66
Kennington Pk. Pl.
Dodds Cres. Wey. AW60 92
Dodds La. Ch. St. G. AQ27 34
Dodds La. Hem. H. AX10 8
Dodds La. Wey. AW60 92
Dodds Pk. Bet. BM71 120
Dodson St. SE1 BY41 4
Dodson St. SE1 BY41 6
Dod St. E14 CD39 57
Dodwood, Welw. G. C. BS8 5
Doel Cl. SW19 BT50 76
Doggets Clo. Barn. BU25 29
Doggets Farm Rd. Uxb. AU33 43
Doggets Rd. SE6 CE47 77
Doggetts Way, St. Alb. BG15 9
Doggetts Wood Clo.
Ch. St. G. AQ24 25
Doggetts Wood La.
Ch. St. G. AQ24 25
Doghurst Ave. Hayes. AZ43 63
Doghurst Dr. West Dr. AZ43 63
Doghurst La. Couls. BU63 104
Dog Kennel Hill, SE22 CA45 67
Dog Kennel La. Hat. BP12 10
Dog Kennel La. Rick. AV25 25
Dog La. NW10 BO35 46
Dognell Grn. Welw. G. C. BP7 5
Dog Wood Clo. Grav. DF49 81
Dogherty Rd. E13 CH38 58
Dolben St. SE1 BY40 4
Dolben St. SE1 BY40 56
Dolby Rd. SW6 BR44 65
Ewald Rd.
Dole St. NW7 BQ29 37
Dolland St. SE11 BX42 4
Dolland St. SE11 BX42 66
Dollis Av. N3 BR30 37
Dollis Brook Wk. Barn. BR25 28
Dollis Cres. Ruis. BD33 45
Dollis Hill Av. NW2 BP34 46
Dollis Hill La. NW2 BO35 46
Dollis Ms. N3 BS30 38
Dollis Pk.
Dollis Pk. N3 BR30 37
Dollis Rd. N3 BR29 37
Dollis Valley Way Barn. BR25 28
Dolman Rd. W4 BN42 65
Dolman St. SW4 BX45 66
Dolphin Clo. Surb. BK53 84
Dolphin Ct. Slou. AQ41 62
Dolphin Rd.
Dolphin Ct. Stai. AW48 73
Bremer Rd.
Dolphin La. E14 CE40 57
Dolphin, N. Rd. Sun. BB51 83
Dolphin Rd. Nthlt. BE37 54
Dolphin Rd. Slou. AQ41 62
Dolphin, S. Rd. Sun. BB51 83
Dolphin Sq. SW1 BW42 3
Dolphin Sq. SW1 BW42 66
Dolphin, W. Rd. Sun. BB51 83
Dombey St. WC1 BX39 2
Dombey St. WC1 BX39 56
Dome Hill, Cat. CA67 114
Dome Hill Pk. SE26 CA49 77
Dome Hill Peak. Cat. CA66 114
Domett Clo. SE5 BZ45 67
Dome Way, Red. BU70 121
Domingo St. EC1 BZ38 57
Baltic St.
Dominic Dr. SE9 CL49 78
Dominion Dr. Rom. CR29 41
Dominion Rd. Croy. CA54 87
Dominion St. EC2 BZ39 2
Dominion St. EC2 BZ39 57
Dominion Way, Rain. CU38 59
Domitian Pl. Enf. CA25 30
Domville Cl. N20 BT27 38
Sweets Way
Domville Gro. SE5 CA42 67
Domvill Gro. SE5 CA42 4
Donald Dr. Rom. CP32 50
Donald Rd. E13 CH37 58
Donald Rd. Croy. BX54 86
Donaldson Rd. NW6 BR37 55
Donaldson Rd. SE18 CL44 68
Doncaster Dr. Nthlt. BE35 45
Doncaster Gdns. N4 BY32 47
Stanhope Gdns.
Doncaster Gdns. Nthlt. BE35 45
Doncaster Rd. N9 CB26 39
Doncaster Way, Upmin. CW34 51
Donegal St. N1 BX37 2
Donegal St. N1 BX37 56
Doneraile St. SW6 BQ44 65
Dongola Rd. E13 CH38 58
Dongola Rd. N17 CA31 48
Donington Av. Ilf. CM32 49
Donkey La. Enf. CB23 30
Donkey La. Farn. CX55 90
Donkey La. West Dr. AX42 63
Donnefield Av. Edg. BL29 37
Donne Gdns. Wok. AV61 100
Donne Pl. SW3 BU42 3
Donne Pl. SW3 BU42 66
Donne Pl. Mitch. BV52 86
Donne Rd. Dag. CP34 50
Donnington Rd. NW10 BP36 55
Donnington Rd. Har. BK32 45
Donnington Rd. Sev. CS63 107
Donnington Rd. Wor. Pk. BP55 85
Donnybrook Rd. SW16 BW50 76
Donovan Av. N10 BV30 38
Donovan Clo. Epsom BN58 94
Don Phelan Clo. SE5 BZ44 67
Deynsford Rd.
Don Way Rom. CT29 41
Doods Pk. Rd. Reig. BT70 121
Doods Rd. Reig. BT70 121
Doods Way, Reig. BT70 121
Doone Clo. Tedd. BJ50 74
Doon St. SE1 BY40 4
Doon St. SE1 BY40 56
Dorado Gs. Orp. CP55 89
Doral Way Cars. BU56 95
Carshalton Pk. Rd.
Doran Dr. Reig. BT70 121
Doran Gdns. Reig. BT70 121
Doran Gro. SE18 CM43 68
Doran Mans. N2 BU32 47
Doran Wk. E15 CF36 57
Dora Rd. SW19 BS49 76
Dora St. E14 CD39 57
Dorcas Ct. St. Alb. BH14 9
Old London Rd.
Dorchester Av. N13 BZ28 39
Dorchester Av. Bex. CP47 79
Dorchester Av. Har. BF32 45
Dorchester Av. Hodd. CE11 12
Dorchester Clo. Dart. CW47 80
Dorchester Clo. Nthlt. BF35 45
Dorchester Ct. N14 BV26 38
Dorchester Court, Rick. BA25 26
Mayfare
Dorchester Ct. SE24 BZ46 77
Dorchester Dr. SE24 BZ46 77
Dorchester Gdns. E4 CE28 39
Dorchester Gdns. NW11 BS31 47
Gloucester Dr.
Dorchester Gdns. Mord. BS54 86
Dorchester Gro. W4 BO43 65
Dorchester Rd. Grav. DH48 81
Dorchester Rd. Mord. BS54 86
Dorchester Rd. Nthlt. BF35 45
Dorchester Rd. Wey. AZ55 83
Dorchester Rd. Wor. Pk. BQ54 85
Dorchester Way, Har. BL32 46
Dorchester Waye Hayes BC39 53
Dorcis Av. Bexh. CQ44 69
Dordrecht Rd. W3 BO40 55
Dore Av. E12 CL35 49
Dore Gdns. BT54 86
Doreen Av. NW9 BN33 46
Dorell Clo. Sthl. BE39 54
Doria Dri. Grav. DJ48 81
Dorian Rd. Horn. CU33 50
Doria Rd. SW6 BR44 65
Doric Way NW1 BW38 1
Doric Way NW1 BW38 56
Dorien Rd. SW20 BQ51 85
Dorincourt SW15 BN49 75
Dorin Ct. Wok. AV61 100
Dorinda St. N7 BY36 56
Dorinium Clo. Wem. BL35 46
Lea Gdns.
Doris Av. Erith. CR44 69
Doris Rd. E7 CH36 58
Dori Rd. Ashf. BA50 73
Doris St. SE11 BY42 66
Tracey St.
Dorking Clo. SE8 CD43 67
Dorking Clo. Wor. Pk. BQ55 85
Dorking Rise, Rom. CV28 42
Dorking Rd. Ash. BM61 103
Dorking Rd. Epsom BM61 103
Dorking Rd. Guil. AU73 118
Dorking Rd. Lthd. BF66 111
Dorking Rd. Lthd. BJ64 102
Dorking Rd. Rom. CV28 42
Dorking Rd. Tad. BO67 112
Dorking Wk. Rom. CV28 42
Dorkins Way, Upmin. CZ33 51
Dorlcote Rd. SW18 BT47 76
Dorling Dr. Epsom BO59 94
Dorly Clo. Shep. BB53 83
Dormans Clo. Nthwd. BA29 35
Dorman Way NW8 BT37 56
Dorman Wk. NW10 BN36 55
Garden Way
Dormay St. SW18 BS46 76
Dormer Clo. E15 CG36 58
Dormer Clo. Barn. BQ25 28
Dormer's Av. Sthl. BE39 54
Dormer's Rise Sthl. BF40 54
Dormer's Wells La. Sthl. BF39 54
Dormie Clo. St. Alb. BG12 9
Dormy Wood, Ruis. BB32 44
Dornbergh Clo. SE3 CH43 68
Dornbery Rd. SE3 CH43 68
Banchory Rd.
Dorncliffe Rd. SW6 BR44 65
Dornels, Slou. AR39 52
Dorney Gro. Wey. AZ55 83
Dorney Reach Rd. Maid. AJ41 61
Dorney Rise Orp. CN53 88
Dornfell St. NW6 BR35 46
Dornton Rd. SW12 BV48 76
Dornton Rd. Sth. Croy. BZ57 96
Dorothy Av. Wem. BL36 55
Dorothy Evans Clo.
Bexh. CR45 69
Dorothy Gdns. Dag. CO35 50
Dorothy Rd. SW11 BU45 66
Dorrington Gdns. Horn. CV33 51
Dorrington St. EC1 BY39 2
Dorrington St. EC1 BY39 56
Dorrit Mews N18 CA28 39
Dickens La.
Dorrit Way Chis. CM50 78
Dorrofield Clo. Rick. BA25 26
Dors Clo. NW9 BN33 46
Dorset Av. Hayes BB38 53
Dorset Av. Rom. CS31 50
Dorset Av. Sthl. BF42 64
Dorset Av. Well. CN45 68
Dorset Bldgs. EC4 BY39 56
Dorset Rise
Dorset Clo. NW1 BU39 1
Dorset Clo. NW1 BU39 56
Dorset Clo. Berk. AP12 7
Doret Clo. Hayes BB38 53
Dorset Cres. Grav. DJ49 81
Dorset Dr. Edg. BL29 37
Dorset Dr. Wok. AT62 100
Dorset Est. E2 CA38 57
Dorset Gdns. Mitch. BX52 86
Dorset Gdns. S. Le. H. DK41 71
Somerset Rd.
Dorset Ms. SW1 BV41 3
Dorset Ms. SW1 BV41 66
Wilton St.
Dorset Pl. E15 CF36 57
Dorset Pl. SW1 BW42 3
Dorset Pl. SW1 BW42 66
Rampayne St.
Dorset Rise EC4 BY39 2
Dorset Rise EC4 BY39 56
Dorset Rd. E7 CJ36 58
Dorset Rd. N15 BZ31 48
Dorset Rd. N22 BX30 38
Dorset Rd. SE9 CK48 78
Dorset Rd. SW8 BX43 66
Dorset Rd. SW19 BS51 86
Dorset Rd. W5 BK41 64
Dorset Rd. Ashf. AX48 73
Dorset Rd. Beck. CC52 87
Dorset Rd. Har. BG32 45
Dorset Rd. Mitch. BU51 86
Dorset Rd. Sutt. BS58 95

35

Street	Grid	Page
Duke Gdns. Ilf.	CM31	49
Duke Rd.		
Duke Humphrey Rd. SE3	CG44	68
Duke of Cambridge Clo. Twick.	BG46	74
Duke of Edinburgh Rd. Sutt.	BT55	86
Duke of Wellington Pl. SW1	**BV41**	**3**
Duke of Wellington Pl. SW1	BV41	66
Duke of York St. SW1	**BW40**	**3**
Duke of York St. SW1	BW40	56
Duke Rd. W4	BN42	65
Duke Rd. Ilf.	CM31	49
Duke St. Hill SE1	**BZ40**	**4**
Duke St. Hill SE1	BZ40	57
Duke St. Ms. NW8	BU38	56
Lisson Gro.		
Dukes Av. Grays.	DD41	71
Duke's Av. N3	BS30	38
Dukes Av. N10	BW31	47
Duke's Av. W4	BN42	65
Dukes Av. Edg.	BL29	37
Dukes Av. Epp.	CN21	31
Dukes Av. Har.	BE32	45
Duke's Av. Har.	BH31	45
Dukes Av. Houns.	BE45	64
Dukes Av. N. Mal.	BO52	85
Dukes Av. Nthlt.	BE36	54
Duke's Av. Twick.	BK49	74
Dukes Clo. Ashf.	BA49	73
Dukes Clo. Epp.	CR17	23
Dukes Clo. Ger. Cr.	AS33	43
Dukes Clo. Hamptn.	BE49	74
Duke's Clo. Kings. On T.	BK49	74
Dukes Ct. E6	CL37	58
Dukes Kiln Rd. Ger. Cr.	AR34	43
Dukes La. W8	BS41	66
Dukes La. Ger. Cr.	AS33	43
Dukes La. Ong.	DB12	15
Dukes Lodge, Nthwd.	BB28	35
Eastbury Av.		
Dukes Meadows W4	BN44	65
Dukes Mews N10	BV31	47
Dukes Av.		
Duke's Ms. W1	**BV39**	**1**
Duke's Ms. W1	BV39	56
Duke St.		
Dukes Pass. E17	CF31	48
Marlowe Rd.		
Duke's Pl. EC3	**CA39**	**2**
Duke's Pl. EC3	CA39	57
Dukes Ride, Ger. Cr.	AS33	43
Dukes Rd. E6	CL37	58
Dukes Rd. W3	BM38	55
Duke's Rd. WC1	**BW38**	**1**
Duke's Rd. WC1	BW38	56
Dukes Rd. Walt.	BD56	93
Dukesthorpe Rd. SE26	CC49	77
Duke St. SW1	**BW40**	**3**
Duke St. SW1	BW40	56
Duke St. St. James's SW1	**BW40**	**3**
Duke St. W1	**BV39**	**1**
Duke St. W1	BV39	56
Duke St. Hodd.	CE11	12
Duke St. Rich.	BK46	74
Duke St. Sutt.	BT56	95
Duke St. Wat.	BD24	27
Duke St. Wind.	AO44	61
Duke St. Wok.	AS62	100
Dukes Way, Berk.	AQ12	7
Dukes Way, W. Wick.	CG55	88
Dukes Wood Av. Ger. Cr.	AS33	43
Dukes Wood Dr. Ger. Cr.	AR33	43
Dulas St. N4	BX33	47
Everleigh St.		
Dulford St. W11	BR40	55
Dulka Rd. SW11	BU46	76
Dulton Clo. Hem. H.	AX14	8
Dulverton Rd. SE9	CM48	78
Dulverton Rd. Rom.	CV29	42
Dulverton Rd. Ruis.	BC33	44
Dulverton Rd. Sth. Croy.	CC58	96
Dulwich Common SE21	CA47	77
Dulwich Rd. SE24	BY46	76
Dulwich Vill. SE21	CA46	77
Dulwich Way, Rick.	AZ25	26
Dulwich Wood Av. SE19	CA49	77
Dulwich Wood Pk. SE19	CA49	77
Dumbarton Av. Wal. Cr.	CC20	21
Raglan Av.		
Dumbarton Rd. SW2	BX46	76
Dumbleton Clo. Kings. On T.	BM51	85
Gloucester Rd.		
Dumbreck Rd. SE9	CK45	68
Dumfries Clo. Wat.	BC27	35
Dumont Rd. N16	CA34	48
Dumpton Pl. NW1	BV36	56
Dunally Pk. Shep.	BA54	83
Dunbar Av. SW16	BY51	86
Dunbar Av. Beck.	CD52	87
Dunbar Av. Dag.	CR34	50
Dunbar Clo. Hayes	BC39	53
Dunbar Gdns. Dag.	CR35	50
Dunbar Pl. SE27	BZ48	77
Dunbar Rd. E7	CH36	58
Dunbar Rd. N22	BY30	38
Dunbar Rd. N. Mal.	BN52	85
Dunbar St. SE27	BY48	76
Norwood High St.		
Dunblane Rd. SE9	CK45	68
Dunboe Pl. Shep.	BA54	83
Russell Rd.		
Dunboyne Rd. NW3	BU35	47
Dunbridge St. E2	CB38	57
Duncan Clo. Barn.	BT24	29
Duncan Ct. St. Alb.	BH14	9
Duncan Dr. Guil.	AT70	118
Duncan Gro. W3	BO39	55
Duncannon Cres. Wind.	AL45	61
Duncannon St. WC2	**BX40**	**4**
Duncannon St. WC2	BX40	56
Adelaide St.		
Duncan Rd. E8	CB37	57
Duncan Rd. Rich.	BL45	65
Duncan Rd. Tad.	BR62	103
Duncan Rd. Tad.	BR63	103
Duncan St. N1	**BY37**	**2**
Duncan St. N1	BY37	56
Duncan Ter. N1	**BY37**	**2**
Duncan Ter. N1	BY37	56
Duncan Way, Bush.	BE23	27
Duncombe Clo. Amer.	AP22	25
Duncombe Hl. SE23	CD47	77
Duncombe Rd. N19	BW33	47
Duncombe Rd. Berk.	AP12	7
Duncrievie Rd. SE13	CF46	77
Duncroft SE18	CN43	68
Duncroft, Wind.	AM45	61
Duncroft Clo. Reig.	BR70	120
Dundalk Rd. SE4	CD45	67
Dundas Gdns. E. Mol.	BF52	84
Dundas Rd. SE15	CC44	67
Dundee Rd. E13	CH37	58
Dundee Rd. SE25	CB53	87
Dundee St. E1	CB40	57
Green Bank		
Dundela Gdns. Epsom	BP56	94
Dundonald Rd. NW10	BQ37	55
Dundonald Rd. SW19	BR51	85
Dundon Gdns. SE23	CC47	77
Dundrey Cres. Red.	BX68	113
Dunedin Dr. Cat.	CA66	114
Dunedin Rd. E10	CE34	48
Dunedin Rd. Ilf.	CM33	49
Dunedin Rd. Rain.	CT38	59
Dunedin Way, Hayes	BD38	54
Dunelm St. E1	CC39	57
Duneved Rd. S. Th. Hth.	BY53	86
Dunewood Clo. Wey.	AV59	91
Dunfield Gdns. SE6	CE49	77
Dunfield Rd. SE6	CE49	77
Dunford Rd. N7	BX35	47
Dungarvan Av. SW15	BP45	65
Dungates La. Bet.	BP70	120
Dunheved Clo. Th. Hth.	BY53	86
Dunheved Rd. N. Th. Hth.	BY53	86
Dunheved Rd. W. Th. Hth.	BY53	86
Dunholme Grn. N9	CA27	39
Dunholme La. N9	CA27	39
Dunholme Rd.		
Dunholme Rd. N9	CA27	39
Dunkeld Rd. SE25	BZ52	87
Dunkeld Rd. Dag.	CO34	50
Dunkellin Gro. S. Ock.	DA39	60
Dunkellin Way, S. Ock.	DA39	60
Dunkery Rd. SE9	CJ49	78
Dunkin Rd. Dart.	CX45	70
Dunkirk Clo. Grav.	DH49	81
Waring St.		
Dunlace Rd. E5	CC35	48
Dunleary Clo. Houns.	BE47	74
Dunley Dr. Croy	CE57	96
Dunlin, Hem. H.	AY11	8
Dunlin Rise, Guil.	AU69	118
Dunloe Av. N17	BZ31	48
Dunloe Pl. E2	**CA37**	**2**
Dunloe St. E2	**CA37**	**2**
Dunloe St. E2	CA37	57
Dunlop Pl. SE16	**CA41**	**4**
Dunlop Pl. SE16	CA41	67
Dunlop Rd. Til.	DF44	71
Dunmail Dr. Pur.	CA60	96
Dunmore, Guil.	AO70	118
Dunmore Rd. NW6	BR37	55
Dunmore Rd. SW20	BQ51	85
Dunmow Clo. Loug.	CK25	31
Dunmow Clo. Rom.	CP32	50
Dunmow Dr. Rain.	CT37	59
Dunmow Gdns. Brwd.	DE32	123
Dunmow Rd. E15	CF35	48
Dunmow Rd. Ong.	CZ13	15
Dunmow Wk. N1	BZ37	57
Popham St.		
Dunnine Clo. S. Ock.	DA39	60
Dunningford Clo. Horn.	CT35	50
Dunnings La. Brwd.	DC33	123
Dunnings La. Upmin.	DD34	123
Dunn St. E8	CA35	48
Dunny La. Kings L.	AV19	16
Dunollie Pl. NW5	BW35	47
Dunollie Rd.		
Dunollie Rd. NW5	BW35	47
Dunoon Rd. SE23	CC47	77
Dunraven Dr. Enf.	BY23	29
Dunraven Rd. W12	BP40	55
Dunraven St. W1	**BV40**	**3**
Dunraven St. W1	BU40	56
Green St.		
Dunsany Rd. W14	BQ41	65
Dunsbury Clo. Sutt.	BS58	95
Nettlecombe Clo.		
Dunsdon Av. Guil.	AQ71	118
Dunsfold Rise, Couls.	BW60	95
Dunsfold Way, Croy.	CE58	96
Dunsford Cres. SW18	BS47	76
Merton Rd.		
Dunsford Way SW15	BP46	75
Dover Pk. Dr.		
Dunsmore Rd. Walt.	BC53	83
Dunsmore Way, Bush.	BG25	27
Dunsmure Rd. N16	CA33	48
Dunspring La. Ilf.	CL30	40
Dunstable Clo. Rom.	CV29	42
Dunstable Ms. W1	**BV39**	**1**
Dunstable Ms. W1	BV39	56
Dunstable Rd. E. Mol.	BE52	84
Dunstable Rd. Rich.	BL45	65
Dunstable Rd. Rom.	CV29	42
Dunstall Rd. SW20	BP50	75
Dunstals, Harl.	CL13	13
Dunstall Way, E. Mol.	BF52	84
Dunstan Cl. N2	BT31	47
Benedict Way		
Dunstan Rd. NW11	BR33	46
Dunstan Rd. Couls.	BW62	104
Dunstan's Gro. SE22	CB46	77
Dunstans Rd. SE22	CB47	77
Dunstar Clo. Barn.	BQ24	28
Dunster Av. SW15	BP46	75
Dunster Av. Mord.	BQ54	85
Dunster Clo. Rom.	CS30	41
Dunster Clo. Uxb.	AW40	35
Dunster Ct. EC3	CA40	57
Mincing La.		
Dunster Cres. Horn.	CX34	51
Dunster Dr. NW9	BN33	46
Dunster Gdns. NW6	BR36	55
Dunster Way, Har.	BE34	45
Dunston Rd. E8	**CA37**	**2**
Dunston Rd. E8	CA37	57
Dunston Rd. SW8	BV44	66
Stanley Gro.		
Dunston Rd. SW11	BV45	66
Dunston St. E8	**CA37**	**2**
Dunston St. E8	CA37	57
Dunston Rd. Hem. H.	AZ10	8
Dunton Rd. E10	CE33	48
Dunton Rd. SE1	**CA42**	**4**
Dunton Rd. SE1	CA42	67
Dunton Rd. Rom.	CT31	50
Duntshill Rd. SW18	BS47	76
Dunvegan Clo. E. Mol.	BF52	84
Dunvegan Rd. SE9	CK45	68
Dunwich Rd. Bexh.	CQ44	69
Dupont Rd. SW20	BQ51	85
Dupont St. E14	CD39	57
Duppas Av. Croy.	BY56	95
Violet La.		
Duppas Clo. Shep.	BA53	83
Green La.		
Duppas Hill La. Croy.	BY56	95
Duppas Hill La. Croy.	BY55	86
Duppas Hill Rd. Croy.	BY56	95
Duppas Hill Ter. Croy.	BY55	86
Duppash La. Croy.	BY55	86
Duppash Rd. Croy.	BY55	86
Dupree Rd. SE7	CH42	68
Duraden Clo. Beck.	CE50	77
Durand Clo. Cars.	BU54	86
Durand Gdns. SW9	BX44	66
Durand Way NW10	BN36	55
Durant Dr. Swan.	CU50	79
Durants Pk. Av. Enf.	CC24	30
Durants Rd. Enf.	CC24	30
Durant St. E2	**CB37**	**2**
Durant St. E2	CB37	57
Durban Gdns. Dag.	CS36	59
Durban Ho. E7	CJ36	58
Durban Rd. E15	CG38	58
Durban Rd. E17	CD30	39
Durban Rd. N17	CA29	39
Durban Rd. SE27	BZ49	77
Durban Rd. Beck.	CD51	87
Durban Rd. Felt.	BC48	73
Durban Rd. Ilf.	CN33	49
Durban Rd. E. Wat.	BC24	26
Durban Rd. W. Wat.	BC24	26
Durbin Rd. Chess.	BL56	94
Durdans Rd. Sthl.	BE39	54
Durell Gdns. Dag.	CP35	50
Durell Rd. Dag.	CP35	50
Durfold Dr. Reig.	BT70	121
Durford Cres. SW15	BP47	75
Durham Av. Brom.	CG52	88
Durham Av. Houns.	BE42	64
Durham Av. Rom.	CV31	51
Durham Av. Wdf. Grn.	CJ28	40
Durham Bldgs. SW11	BT45	66
Durham Clo. SW20	BP51	85
Durham Clo. Guil.	AP69	118
Durham Hl. Brom.	CG49	78
Durham House St. WC2	**BX40**	**4**
Durham Pl. SW3	**BU42**	**3**
Durham Ho. St. WC2	BX40	56
Strand		
Durham Pl. SW3	BU42	66
Durham Rise SE18	CM42	68
Durham Rd. E12	CJ35	49
Durham Rd. E16	CG38	58
Durham Rd. N2	BU31	47
Durham Rd. N7	BX34	47
Durham Rd. N9	CB27	39
Durham Rd. SW20	BP51	85
Durham Rd. W5	BK41	64
Durham Rd. Borwd.	BN24	28
Durham Rd. Brom.	CG52	88
Durham Rd. Dag.	CS35	50
Durham Rd. Felt.	BD47	74
Durham Rd. Har.	BF32	45
Durham Rd. Sid.	CO49	79
Durham Row E1	CC39	57
Stepney High St.		
Durham St. SE11	**BX43**	**4**
Durham St. SE11	BX42	66
Durham Ter. W2	BS39	56
Durleston Pk. Dr. Lthd.	BG66	111
Durley Av. Pnr.	BE33	45
Durley Rd. N16	CA33	48
Durlston Rd. E5	CB34	48
Durlston Rd. Kings. On T.	BL50	75
Durndale La. Grav.	DF49	81
Durnell Way, Loug.	CL24	31
Durnford St. N15	CA32	48
Durnford St. SE10	CF43	67
Greenwich Church St.		
Durning Rd. SE19	BZ49	77
Durnsford Av. SW19	BS48	76
Durnsford Rd. N11	BW30	38
Durnsford Rd. SW19	BS48	76
Duro Pl. W8	BS42	66
Durrants Clo. Rain.	CV37	60
Durrants Dr. Rick.	BA24	26
Durrants Hill Rd. Hem. H.	AX15	8
Durrants La. Berk.	AP13	7
Durrant's La. Rick.	AY24	26
Durrants Rd. Berk.	AP12	7
Durrant Way, Orp.	CM56	97
Durrant Way, Swans.	DB46	80
Durrant Way, Swans.	DC47	81
Durrell Rd. SW6	BR44	65
Durrell Way, Shep.	BA53	83
Durrington Av. SW20	BQ50	75
Durrington Pk. Rd. SW20	BQ51	85
Durrington Rd. E5	CD35	48
Durrington Rd. Dev. E5	CD35	48
Dursley Clo. SE3	CJ44	68
Dursley Gdns. SE3	CJ44	68
Dursley Rd. SE3	CJ44	68
Durward St. E1	CB39	57
Durweston Mews W1	BV39	56
Crawford St.		
Durweston St. W1	BV39	56
York St.		
Dury Falls Clo. Horn.	CX33	51
Dury Rd. Barn.	BR23	28
Duseley Rd. Stai.	AR47	72
Duthie St. E14	CF40	57
Dutton St. SE10	CF44	67
Dutton Way, Iver	AV39	52
Duxford Clo. Horn.	CV36	60
Duxons Turn, Hem. H.	AZ13	8
Dyall Ho. Grays.	DD43	71
Hawkes Clo.		
Dyers Bldgs. EC1	BY39	56
Holborn		
Dyers Hall Rd. E11	CF34	48
Dyer's La. SW15	BP45	65
Dyers Way, Rom.	CU29	41
Dyke Dr. Orp.	CP54	89
Dykes Path, Wok.	AU61	100
Bentham Av.		
Dykewood Clo. Bex.	CT48	79
Dylan Rd. Belv.	CR41	69
Dylways SE5	BZ45	67
Dymchurch Clo. Ilf.	CL30	40
Dymchurch Clo. Orp.	CN56	97
Dymes Path SW19	BR48	75
Queensmere Rd.		
Dymock St. SW6	BS45	66
Dymoke Grn. St. Alb.	BJ11	9
Dymoke Rd. Horn.	CT33	50
Dymokes Way, Hodd.	CE10	12
Dyneley Rd. SE12	CJ49	78
Dyne Rd. NW6	BR36	55
Dynes Rd. Sev.	CW62	108
Dynemor Pl. Guil.	AO68	109
Dunevor Rd. N16	CA34	48
Dynevor Rd. Rich.	BL46	75
Dynham Rd. NW6	BS36	56
Dyott St. WC1	**BW39**	**1**
Dyott St. WC1	**BX39**	**2**
Dyott St. WC1	BW39	56
Dyrham La. Barn.	BP21	28
Dysart Av. Kings. On T.	BK49	74
Dysart St. EC2	**BZ38**	**2**
Dysart St. EC2	BZ38	57
Dyson Clo. Wind.	AN45	61
Dyson Rd. E11	CG32	49
Dyson Rd. E15	CG36	58
Dysons Clo. Wal. Cr.	CC19	21
Dyson's Rd. N18	CB29	39
Dytchleys La. Brwd.	CX24	33
Eade Rd. N4	BY33	47
Eagans Clo. N2	BT31	47
Eagle Av. Rom.	CO32	50
Eagle Clo. Enf.	CC24	30
Eagle Clo. Rain.	CU36	59
Eagle Ct. EC1	**BY39**	**2**
Eagle Ct. EC1	BY39	56
Albion Pl.		
Eagle Hill SE19	BZ50	77
Eagle La. E11	CH31	49
Eagle La. Brwd.	CZ22	33
Eagle Pl. E1	CC38	57
Mile End Rd.		
Eagle Pl. SW1	**BW40**	**3**
Eagle Pl. SW1	BW40	56
Jermyn St.		
Eagle Rd. Guil.	AR70	118
Eagle Rd. Wem.	BK36	54
Eagles Dri. West.	CJ62	106
Ricketts Hill		
Eaglesfield Rd. SE18	CL44	68
Eagles, The W6	BV34	47
Eagle St. WC1	**BX39**	**2**
Eagle St. WC1	BX39	56
High Holborn		
Eagle Ter. Wdf. Grn.	CH29	40
Eaglet Pl. E1	CC38	57
Mile End Rd.		
Eagle Way, Brwd.	DA29	42
Eagle Way, Hat.	BP13	10
Eagle Wharf Rd. N1	**BZ37**	**2**
Eagle Wharf Rd. N1	BZ37	57
Eakenwalk Clo. Cher.	AV53	82
Ealdham Sq. SE9	CJ45	68
Ealing Grn. W5	BK40	54
Ealing Pk. Gdns. W5	BK42	64
Ealing Pk. Ms. W5	BK41	64
Ealing Rd.		
Ealing Rd. Brent.	BK42	64
Ealing Rd. Nthlt.	BF37	54
Ealing Rd. Wem.	BL36	55
Ealing Vill. W5	BL39	55
Eamont St. NW8	**BU37**	**1**
Eamont St. NW8	BU37	56
Eardemont Clo. Dart.	CT45	69
Eardley Cres. SW5	BS42	66
Eardley Rd. SW16	BW49	76
Eardley Rd. Belv.	CR42	69
Eardley Rd. Sev.	CU65	107
Earl Cott. SE1	**CA42**	**4**
Earl Cotts. SE1	CA42	67
Earldom Rd. SW15	BQ45	65
Earle Gdn. Kings. On T.	BL50	75
Earlesmead Rd. NW10	BQ38	55
Earlham Gro. E7	CG35	49
Earlham Gro. N22	BX29	38
Earlham St. WC2	**BW39**	**1**
Earlham St. WC2	**BX39**	**2**
Earlham St. WC2	BW39	56
Earl Rise SE18	CM42	68
Earl Rd. SE1	**CA42**	**4**
Earl Rd. SE1	CA42	67
Earl Rd. SW14	BN45	65
Earl Rd. Grav.	DF48	81
Earlsbrook Rd. Red.	BU71	121
Earls Ct. Gdns. SW5	BS42	66
Earl's Ct. Rd. SW5	BS41	66
Earl's Ct. Rd. W8	BS41	66
Earl's Ct. Sq. SW5	BS42	66
Earl's Cres. Har.	BH31	45
Earlsferry Clo. N1	**BX37**	**2**
Earlsferry Clo. N1	BX36	56
Carnoustie Dr.		
Earlsferry Way N1	BX36	56
Earlsferry Clo.		
Earlsfield Rd. SW18	BT47	
Earlshall Rd. SE9	CK45	
Earls La. Pot. B.	BO19	
Earlsmead, Har.	BE35	
Earlsmead Rd. N15	CA32	
Earlsmead Rd. NW10	BQ39	
Earls Path, Loug.	CJ23	
Earls Ter. W8	BR41	
Earlsthorpe Rd. SE26	CC49	
Earlstroke St. EC1	BY38	
Earlstone Gro. E9	CB37	
Victoria Pk. Rd.		
Earl St. EC2	**BZ39**	
Earl St. EC2	BZ39	
Earl St. Wat.	BD24	
Earl's Wk. W8	BS41	
Earls Wk. Dag.	CO35	
Earlswood, Cob.	BD59	
Earlswood Av. Th. Hth.	BY53	
Earlswood Gdns. Ilf	CL31	
Earlswood Rd. Red.	BU71	
Earlswood St. SE10	CG42	
Early Ms. NW1	BV37	
Arlington Rd.		
Earnshaw St. WC2	**BW39**	
Earnshaw St. WC2	BW39	
Earsby St. W14	BR2	
Earsby Cres. Mord.	BS53	
Easebourne Rd. Dag.	CP35	
Easedale Dr. Horn.	CU35	
Easington Pl. Guil.	AS71	
Maori Rd.		
Easleys Ms. W1	**BV39**	
Easleys Ms. W1	BV39	
Wigmore St.		
East Acton La. W3	BO40	
Eastam Cres. Brwd.	DD28	
East Arbour Sq. E1	CC39	
East Av. E12	CK36	
East Av. E17	CE31	
East Av. Hayes	BB40	
East Av. Hayes	BC40	
East Av. Sthl.	BE40	
East Av. Wall.	BX56	
East Av. Watt.	BB58	
East Bank N16	CA33	
Eastbank Rd. Hamptn.	BG49	
East Barnet Rd. Barn.	BT24	
Eastbourne Av. W3	BN39	
Eastbourne Gdns. SW14	BN45	
Eastbourne Ms. W2	**BT39**	
Eastbourne Ms. W2	BT39	
Eastbourne Rd. E6	CL38	
Eastbourne Rd E15	CG37	
Eastbourne Rd. N15	CA32	
Eastbourne Rd. SW17	BV50	
Eastbourne Rd. W4	BN43	
Eastbourne Rd. Brent.	BK42	
Eastbourne Rd. Felt.	BD48	
Eastbourne Rd. Gdse.	CC69	
Eastbourne Ter. W2	**BT39**	
Eastbourne Ter. W2	BT39	
Eastbournia Av. N9	CB27	
Eastbrook Av. N9	CC26	
Eastbrook Av. Dag.	CS35	
East Brook Clo. Wok.	AT61	
Eastbrook Dr. Rom.	CT34	
Eastbrook Rd. SE3	CH43	
Eastbrook Rd. Wal. Abb.	CG20	
East Burrow Fld. Welw. G. C.	BQ9	
Eastbury Av. Nthwd.	BB28	
Eastbury Av. Bark.	CN37	
Eastbury Av. Enf.	CA23	
Eastbury Ct. St. Alb.	BH13	
Lemsford Rd.		
Eastbury Gro. W4	BO43	
Eastbury Rd.		
Eastbury Pl. Nthwd.	BB28	
Eastbury Av.		
Eastbury Rd. W4	BO42	
Eastbury Rd. Kings. on T.	BL50	
Eastbury Rd. Nthwd.	BB28	
Eastbury Rd. Nthwd.	BB29	
Eastbury Rd. Orp.	CM53	
Eastbury Rd. Rom.	CS32	
Eastbury Rd. Wat.	BC26	
Eastbury Sq. Bark.	CN37	
Eastbury Ter. E1	CC38	
Eastcastle St. W1	**BW39**	
Eastcastle St. W1	BW39	
Eastcheap EC3	**BZ40**	
Eastcheap EC3	CA40	
East Churchfield Rd. W3	BN40	
Eastchurch Rd. Houns.	BB44	
East Clo. W5	BM38	
East Clo. Barn.	BV24	
East Clo. Grnf.	BG37	
East Clo. Rain.	CU38	
Eastcombe Av. SE7	CH43	
East Common, Ger. Cr.	AS32	
Eastcote, Orp.	CN54	
Eastcote Av. E. Mol.	BE53	
Eastcote Av. Grnf.	BJ35	
Eastcote Av. Har.	BF34	
Eastcote Gdns. Well.	CM44	
Eastcote High Rd. Pnr.	BC32	
Eastcote La. Har.	BE35	
Eastcote La. Nthlt.	BE35	
Eastcote La. N. Nthlt.	BE36	
Eastcote Rd. Har.	BG34	
Eastcote Rd. Pnr.	BD32	
Eastcote Rd. Ruis.	BB33	
Eastcote Rd. Well.	CM44	
Eastcote St. SW9	BX44	
Eastcote Vw. Pnr.	BD31	
East Ct. Wem.	BK34	
East Cres. N11	BU28	
East Cres. Enf.	CA25	
East Cres. Wind.	AM44	
East Cres. Rd. Grav.	DH46	
Eastcroft Rd. Epsom	BO57	
Eastdean Av. Epsom	BM60	
Eastdene Dr. Rom.	CV28	
Eastdown Pk. SE13	CF45	
East Dr. SW11	BV43	
East Dr. Cars.	BU58	
East Dr. Nthwd.	BB27	

East Dr. Orp. CO53 89
East Dr. Saw. CQ6 6
East Dr. Slou. AP38 52
East Dr. St. Alb. BL13 10
East Dr. Vir. W. AQ53 82
East Dr. Wat. BC21 26
East Dulwich Est. SE22 CA45 67
East Dulwich Gro. SE22 CA46 77
East Dulwich Rd. SE22 CA45 67
East End Rd. N2 BS30 38
East End Rd. N3 BS30 38
East End Way, Pnr. BE31 45
East Entrance, Dag. CR37 59
Eastern Av. S. Ock. CW40 60
Eastern Av. Ilf. CH32 49
Eastern Av. Pnr. BD33 45
Eastern Av. Rom. CQ31 50
Eastern Av. S. Ock. CY41 70
Eastern Av. Wal. Cr. CD20 21
Eastern Av. E. Rom. CS30 41
Eastern Av. W. Ilf. CR31 50
Eastern Ind. Est. Belv. CR41 69
Eastern Perimeter Rd.
Houns. BB44 63
Eastern Rd. E13 CH37 58
Eastern Rd. E17 CF32 48
Eastern Rd. N2 BU31 47
Eastern Rd. N22 BX30 38
Eastern Rd. SE4 CE45 67
Eastern Rd. Grays. DE42 71
Eastern Rd. Rom. CT32 50
Eastern View, West. CJ61 106
Easternville Gdns. Ilf. CM32 49
Eastern Way, Grays. DD42 71
East Ferry Rd. E14 CE42 67
Eastfield Av. Wat. BD23 27
Eastfield Clo. Slou. AQ41 62
Eastfield Ct. St. Alb. BK12 9
Southfield Way
Eastfield Gdns. Dag. CR35 50
Eastfield Pde. Pot. B. BT19 20
Forbes Av.
Eastfield Rd. E17 CE31 48
Eastfield Rd. N8 BX31 47
Eastfield Rd. Brwd. DB27 42
Eastfield Rd. Dag. CQ35 50
Eastfield Rd. Enf. CC22 30
Eastfield Rd. Wal. Cr. CD19 21
Eastfields, Pnr. BD22 45
Eastfields Rd. W3 BN39 55
Eastfields Rd. Mitch. BV51 86
Eastfields St. E14 CD39 57
East Flint, Hem. H. AV13 7
East Gdns. SW17 BU50 76
Eastgate, Bans. BR60 94
East Gate, Harl. CM10 6
East Gate, Harl. CM11 13
Eastgate Gdns. Guil. AS71 118
East Gdn. Wok. AU62 100
Eastglade, Nthwd. BB28 35
East Glade, Pnr. BE31 45
East Grn. Hem. H. AY16 17
Easthall La. Rain. CV39 60
East Hall Rd. Orp. CQ54 89
East Ham Manor Way E6 CK38 58
East Ham Manor Way E16 CK38 58
East Harding St. EC4 BY39 2
East Harding St. EC4 BY39 56
East Heath Rd. NW3 BT34 47
East Hill SW18 BS46 76
East Hill, Dart. CW47 80
East Hill, Oxt. CG68 115
East Hill, Sev. CX59 99
East Hill, S. Dnth. CY51 90
East Hill, Sth. Croy. CA58 96
East Hill, Wem. BM34 46
East Hill, West. CH62 106
East Hill, Wok. AU61 100
East Hill Dr. Dart. CW47 80
East Hill Rd. Oxt. CG68 115
Eastholm NW11 BS31 47
East Holme, Erith CS44 69
East Holme, Hayes BC40 53
E. India Dock Rd. E14 CF39 57
E. India Dock Wall Rd. E14 CF40 57
Eastington Pl. Guil. AS71 118
Maori Rd.
E. Kent Av. Grav. DE46 81
Eastlake Rd. SE5 BZ44 67
Eastlands Clo. Oxt. CF67 114
Eastland Cres. SE21 CA46 77
Eastlands Way, Oxt. CF67 114
East La. SE16 CB41 4
East La. SE16 CB41 67
Chambers St.
East La. Kings. on T. BK52 84
High St.
East La. Leath. BA66 110
East La. Wat. BC18 17
East La. Wem. BJ34 45
Eastlea Av. Wat. BE22 27
Eastleigh Av. Har. BF34 45
Eastleigh Clo. NW2 BO34 46
E. Leigh Clo. Sutt. BS57 95
Eastleigh Rd. Bexh. CS44 69
Eastleigh Rd. Felt. BB45 63
Eastleigh Wk. SW15 BP47 75
East Lodge La. Enf. BW21 29
Eastman St. E1 CB38 57
Eastman Way, Hem. H. AZ12 8
Eastmead, Ruis. BD34 45
E. Mead. Welw. G. C. BS9 5
Eastmead Av. Grnf. BF38 54
East Mead Clo. Brom. CK51 88
East Meads, Guil. AQ71 118
Eastmearn Rd. SE21 BZ48 77
East Milton Rd. Grav. DH47 81
Eastminster E1 CA40 4
Eastminster E1 CA40 57
Royal Mint St.
Eastmont Rd. Esher BH55 84
Eastmoor Pl. SE7 CJ41 68
Eastmoor St.
Eastmoor St. SE7 CJ41 68
East Mount St. CB39 57
Eastney Rd. Croy. BY54 86
Eastney St. SE10 CF42 67
Eastnor, Hem. H. AT17 16
Eastnor Rd. SE9 CM47 78
Eastnor Rd. Reig. BS71 121
Easton Gdns. Browd. BN24 28
Easton St. WC1 BY38 2
Easton St. WC1 BY38 56
East Pk. Harl. CP9 6
East Pk. Saw. CQ6 6
E. Pk. Clo. Rom. CQ32 50
East Pl. SE27 BZ49 77
Dunkirk St.
East Pl. SE27 BZ49 77
Pilgrim Hill
East Ramp, Houns. AZ44 63
East Poultry Av. EC1 BY39 2
East Ridgeway, Pot. B. BX17 20
East Rd. E11 CH32 49
East Rd. E15 CH37 58
East Rd. N1 BZ38 2
East Rd. N1 BZ38 57
East Rd. SW19 BT50 76
East Rd. Barn. BV26 38
East Rd. Belv. CQ41 69
East Rd. Edg. BM30 37
East Rd. Enf. CC22 30
East Rd. Felt. BA47 73
East Rd. Grays. CX40 70
East Rd. Harl. CO9 6
East Rd. Kings. on T. BL51 85
East Rd. Reig. BR70 120
East Rd. Rom. CQ31 50
East Rd. Rom. CS33 50
East Rd. Well. CO44 69
East Rd. West Dr. AY42 63
East Rd. Wey. BA57 92
East Rochester Wa. CN46 7
East Row W10 BR38 55
Eastry Av. Brom. CG53 88
Eastry Rd. Erith. CR43 69
East Shalford La. Guil. AS73 118
East Sheen Av. SW14 BN46 75
Eastside Rd. NW11 BR31 46
East Smithfield E1 CA40 4
East Smithfield E1 CA40 57
East Sq. SE18 CL42 68
East St. EC2 BZ39 2
East St. EC2 BZ39 57
Blomfield St.
East St. SE17 BZ42 4
East St. SE17 BZ42 67
East St. Berk. CM36 58
East St. Bexh. CR45 69
East St. Brent. BK43 64
East St. Brom. CH51 88
East St. Epsom BO59 94
East St. Grays. DC43 71
East St. Grays. DE43 71
East St. Hem. H. AX13 8
East St. Lthd. BF66 111
East Tenter St. E1 CA39 2
East Tenter St. E1 CA39 57
East Ter. Grav. DH46 81
East Thurrock Rd. Grays. DD43 71
East Tilbury Rd. S. Le H. DJ40 71
East Towers, Pnr. BD32 45
East Vw. E4 CF28 39
East Vw. NW3 BT34 47
East Vw. Barn. BR23 28
East Vw. Hat. BU12 11
Eastview Av. SE18 CN43 68
Eastview Av. NW11 BR32 46
East Wk. Barn. BV26 38
East Wk. Hayes BC40 53
East Wk. Reig. BS70 121
Eastway E9 CD36 57
East Way E11 CH32 49
East Way, Brom. CH54 88
East Way, Croy. CD55 87
Eastway, Epsom BN59 94
East Way, Hayes BC40 53
Eastway, Mord. BQ53 85
Eastway, Ruis. BC33 44
East Way, Wal. Abb. CF21 30
Eastway, Wall. BW56 95
Eastwell Clo. Beck. CD51 87
King's Hall Rd.
Eastwick Cres. Rick. AV27 34
Eastwick Dr. Lthd. BF65 102
Eastwick Hall La. Harl. CL8 6
Eastwick Pk. Av. Lthd. BF66 111
Eastwick Pk. Av. Lthd. BF65 102
Eastwick Rd. Harl. CM9 6
Eastwick Rd. Lthd. BF66 111
Eastwick Rd. Walt. BC57 92
Eastwick Rd. Ware CK9 6
Eastwick Row, Hem. H. AZ14 8
Eastwood Clo. E18 CH30 40
Eastwood Dr. Rain. CU39 59
Eastwood Est. SW15 BP46 75
Eastwood Rd. E18 CH30 40
Eastwood Rd. N10 BV30 38
Eastwood Rd. Ilf. CO33 50
East Wood Side, Bex. CQ47 79
Eastwood St. SW16 BW50 76
Eastwood Rd. Cher. AW54 83
Eatington Rd. E10 CF32 48
Easton Cl. SW1 BV42 3
Eaton Clo. SW1 BV42 66
Eaton Clo. Stan. BJ28 36
Eaton Ct. Guil. AT69 118
Eaton Dr. SW9 BY44 66
Loughborough Pl. Dev.
Eaton Dr. Kings. on T. BM50 75
Eaton Dr. Rom. CR29 41
Eaton Gate SW1 BV42 3
Eaton Gate SW1 BV42 66
Eaton Gate, Nthwd. BA29 35
Eaton La. SW1 BV41 3
Eaton La. SW1 BV41 66
Eaton Ms. SW1 BV42 3
Eaton Ms. N. SW1 BV42 3
Eaton Ms. N. SW1 BV41 66
Eaton Ms. S. SW1 BV42 3
Eaton Ms. S. SW1 BV42 66
Eaton Ms. W. SW1 BV42 3
Eaton Ms. W. SW1 BV42 66
Eaton Pk. Cob. BE60 93
Eaton Pk. Rd. N13 BY27 38
Eaton Pk. Rd. Cob. BE60 93
Eaton Pl. SW1 BV41 3
Eaton Pl. SW1 BV41 66
Eaton Rise W5 BK39 54
Eaton Rd. E11 CJ32 49
Eaton Rd. NW4 BQ32 46
Eaton Rd. SW9 BY45 66
Eaton Rd. Enf. CA24 30
Eaton Rd. Hem. H. AZ12 8
Eaton Rd. Houns. BG45 64
Eaton Rd. St. Alb. BJ13 9
Eaton Rd. Sid. CP48 79
Eaton Rd. Sutt. BT57 95
Eaton Row SW1 BV41 3
Eaton Row SW1 BV41 66
Eatons Mead E4 CE27 39
Eaton Sq. SW1 BV42 3
Eaton Sq. SW1 BV42 66
Eaton Ter. SW1 BV42 3
Eaton Ter. SW1 BV42 66
Eaton Ter. Ms. SW1 BV42 66
Eaton Ter.
Eatonville Rd. SW17 BU48 76
Eatonville Vills SW17 BU48 76
Eatonville Rd.
Eaton Walk SE15 CA44 67
Sumner Estate
Eator, Welw. G. C. BS6 5
Ebbas Way, Epsom BM61 103
Ebberns Rd. Hem. H. AY15 8
Ebbisham Clo. Dor. BJ71 119
Ebbisham Dr. SW8 BX43 66
Ebbisham La. Tad. BP64 103
Ebbisham Rd. Epsom BM60 94
Ebbisham Rd. Epsom BM61 103
Ebbisham Rd. Epsom BN60 94
Ebbisham Rd. Wor. Pk. BQ55 85
Ebbsfleet Rd. NW2 BR35 46
Ebdon Way SE3 CH45 68
Ebenezer Rd. NW2 BS34 47
Ebenezer St. N1 BZ38 2
Ebenezer St. N1 BA38 57
Ebenezer Wk. SW16 BW51 86
Ebley Clo. SE15 CA43 67
St. George's Way
Ebner St. SW18 BS46 76
Ebor St. E1 CA38 2
Ebor St. E1 CA38 57
Ebrington Rd. Har. BK32 45
Ebsworth St. SE23 CC47 77
Eburne Rd. N7 BX34 47
Ebury App. Rick. AX26 35
Ebury Rd.
Ebury Br. SW1 BV42 3
Ebury Br. SW1 BV42 66
Ebury Br. Est. SW1 BV42 3
Ebury Br. Est. SW1 BV42 66
Ebury Br. Rd. SW1 BV42 3
Ebury Br. Rd. SW1 BV42 66
Ebury Clo. Kes. CK55 88
Ebury Clo. Nthwd. BA28 35
Ebury Ms. SW1 BV42 3
Ebury Ms. SW1 BV42 66
Ebury Ms. E. SW1 BV41 3
Ebury Rd. Rick. AX26 35
Ebury Rd. Wat. BD24 27
Ebury Sq. SW1 BV42 3
Ebury Sq. SW1 BV42 66
Ebury St. SW1 BV42 3
Ebury St. SW1 BV42 66
Ecclesbourne Clo. N13 BX28 38
Cranford Av.
Ecclesbourne Clo. N13 BY28 38
Ecclesbourne Gdns. N13 BY28 38
Ecclesbourne Rd. N1 BZ36 2
Ecclesbourne Rd. N1 BZ36 57
Ecclesbourne Rd. Th. Hth. BZ53 87
Eccles Hill, Dor. BK73 119
Eccles Rd. SW11 BU45 66
Eccleston Br. SW1 BV42 3
Eccleston Br. SW1 BV42 66
Eccleston Clo. Barn. BU24 29
Carson Rd.
Eccleston Clo. Orp. CM54 88
Eccleston Cres. Rom. CO33 50
Eccleston Ct. Wem. BL35 46
Eccleston Ms. Wem. BL35 46
Eccleston Ms. SW1 BV41 3
Eccleston Ms. SW1 BV42 3
Eccleston Ms. SW1 BV41 66
Eccleston Pl. SW1 BV42 3
Eccleston Pl. SW1 BV42 66
Eccleston Pl. Wem. BL35 46
Eccleston Rd. W13 BJ40 54
Eccleston Sq. SW1 BV42 3
Eccleston Sq. SW1 BV42 66
Eccleston Sq. Ms. SW1 BW42 66
Warwick Pl. N.
Eccleston St. SW1 BV41 3
Eccleston St. SW1 BV41 66
Echo Heights E4 CE26 39
Echo Pit Rd. Guil. AS72 118
Echo Sq. Grav. DH48 81
Eckersley St. E1 CA38 2
Eckersley St. E1 CA38 57
Eckford St. N1 BY37 2
Eckford St. N1 BY37 56
Wynford Rd.
Eckington Gdns. SE14 CC43 67
Eckerstein Rd. SW11 BU45 66
Eclipse Rd. E13 CH39 58
Ecob Clo. Guil. AP68 109
Ecton Rd. Wey. AW56 92
Ector Rd. SE6 CG48 78
Edale Rd. SE16 CC42 67
Edbrooke Rd. W9 BS38 56
Eddington St. N4 BY33 47
Everleigh St.
Eddiscombe Rd. SW6 BR44 65
Eddy Clo. Rom. CR32 50
Eddystone Rd. SE4 CD46 77
Eddystone Wk. Stai. AY47 73
Clare Rd.
Eddy St. Berk. AQ12 7
Edenbridge Clo. Orp. CP52 89
Edenbridge Rd. E9 CC36 57
Edenbridge Rd. Enf. CA25 30
Eden Clo. Bex. CS49 79
Eden Clo. Slou. AT42 62
Eden Clo. Wem. BK37 54
Eden Clo. Wey. AW58 92
Eden Ct. W5 BL39 55
Station Rd.
Edencourt Rd. SW16 BV50 76
Edendale W3 BM40 55
Julian Av.
Edendale Rd. Bexh. CS44 69
Edenfield Gdns. Wor. Pk. BO55 85
Eden Grn. E17 CE32 48
Eden Grn. S. Ock. DA39 60
Eden Gro. N7 BX35 47
Eden Grove Rd. Wey. AY60 92
Edenhall Rd. Rom. CV28 42
Edenham Way W10 BR39 55
Elkstone Rd.
Edenhurst Av. SW6 BR45 65
Eden Pk. Av. Beck. CD52 87
Eden Pk. Av. Beck CE53 87
Eden Rd. E17 CE32 48
Eden Rd. SE27 BY49 76
Eden Rd. Beck. CD52 87
Eden Rd. Bex. CS49 79
Eden Rd. Croy. BZ56 96
Edenside Rd. Lthd. BE65 102
Edensor Gdns. W4 BO43 65
Edensor Rd. W4 BO43 65
Eden St. Kings. On T. BL51 85
Edenvale Rd. Mitch. BV50 76
Edenvale St. SW6 BS44 66
Eden Way, Beck. CD53 87
Eden Way, Warl. CD62 105
Ederline Av. SW16 BX52 86
Edgar Clo. Swan. CT52 89
Edgarley Ter. SW6 BR44 65
Edgar Rd. E3 CE38 57
Edgar Rd. Houns. BE47 74
Edgar Rd. Rom. CP33 50
Edgar Rd. Sev. CW62 108
Edgar Rd. Sth. Croy. BZ58 96
Edgar Rd. West. CJ64 106
Edgar Rd. West Dr. AY40 53
Edgars Ct. Welw. G. C. BR8 5
Edgbaston Rd. Wat. BC27 35
Edgebury, Chis. CL49 78
Edgebury Est. Chis. CM49 78
Edgebury Wk. Chis. CM49 78
Edge Clo. Wey. AZ57 92
Edgecombe Clo.
Kings. On T. BN50 75
Edgecombe Rd. E11 CG33 49
Harvey Rd.
Edgecombe, Sth. Croy. CC57 96
Edgecot Gro. N15 CA32 48
Edgefield Av. Bark. CN36 58
Edgefield Clo. Dart. CX47 80
Edge Field Clo. Red. BV73 121
Edge Hill SE18 CL43 68
Edge Hill SW19 BQ50 75
Edge Hill Av. N3 BS31 47
Edge Hill Ct. SW19 BQ50 75
Edgehill Gdns. Dag. CR35 50
Edgehill Gdns. Grav. DF51 81
Edgehill Rd. W13 BJ39 54
Edgehill Rd. Chis. CM48 78
Edgehill Rd. Mitch. BV51 86
Edgehill Rd. Pur. BY58 95
Edgeley, Lthd. BE65 102
Edgeley La. SW4 BW45 66
Edgeley Rd. SW4 BW45 66
Edgell Clo. Vir. W. AS52 82
Edgell Rd. Stai. AV49 72
Edgel St. SW18 BS45 66
Ferrier St.
Edgepoint Clo. SE27 BY49 76
Knight's Hill
Edge St. W8 BS40 56
Edgewood Dr. Orp. CN58 97
Edgewood Grn. Croy. CC54 87
Edgeworth Av. NW4 BP32 46
Edgeworth Av. Barn. BU24 29
Edgeworth Clo. NW4 BP32 46
Edgeworth Cres. NW4 BP32 46
Edgeworth Rd. SE9 CJ45 68
Edgington Rd. SW16 BW50 76
Edgwarebury Gdns. Edg. BM28 37
Edgwarebury La. Borwd. BL26 37
Edgwarebury La. Edg. BM28 37
Edgware Ct. Edg. BM29 37
Edgware Rd. NW2 BP33 46
Edgware Rd. NW9 BN30 37
Edgware Rd. W2 BT38 1
Edgware Rd. W2 BT38 56
Edgware Way, Edg. BK26 36
Edinar Gdns. Wind. AO44 61
Edinburgh Av. Rick. AW25 26
Edinburgh Clo. Uxb. AZ35 44
Edinburgh Ct. SW20 BQ53 85
Edinburgh Cres. Wal. Cr. CD20 21
Edinburgh Dr. Stai. AX50 73
Edinburgh Dr. Uxb. AZ35 44
Edinburgh Dr. Uxb. AV32 43
Edinburgh Gate SW1 BU41 3
Edinburgh Gate SW1 BU41 66
Edinburgh Pl. Harl. CO9 6
Edinburgh Rd. E13 CH37 58
Edinburgh Rd. E17 CD32 48
Edinburgh Rd. N18 CB28 39
Edinburgh Rd. W7 BH41 64
Edinburgh Rd. Sutt. BT55 86
Edinburgh Way, Harl. CN9 6
Edington Rd. SE2 CO41 69
Edington Rd. Enf. CC23 30
Edison Av. Horn. CT33 50
Edison Clo. Horn. CT33 50
Edison Dr. Sthl. BF39 54
Edison Gro. SE18 CN43 68
Edison Rd. N8 BW32 47
Edison Rd. Brom. CH51 88
Church Rd.
Edison Rd. Well. CN44 68
Edis St. NW1 BV37 1
Edis St. NW1 BV37 56
Edith Dr. N11 BW29 38
Edith Gdns. Surb. BM54 85
Edith Gro. SW10 BT43 66
Edith Ms. SW6 BS44 66
Edith Row
Edithna St. SW9 BX45 66
Edith Rd. E6 CJ36 58
Edith Rd. E15 CF35 48
Edith Rd. SE25 BZ53 87
Edith Rd. SW19 BS50 76
Edith Rd. W14 BR42 65
Edith Rd. Orp. CO56 98
Edith Rd. Rom. CP33 50
Edith Row SW6 BS44 66
Edith's Rd. Sev. CX62 108
Edith Ter. SW10 BT43 66
Edith Yd. SW10 BT43 66
Worlds End
Edlyn Clo. Berk. AP12 7
Edmondscote W13 BJ39 54
Cleveland Rd.
Edmund Rd. Mitch. BU52 86
Edmund Rd. Orp. CP53 89
Edmund Rd. Rain. CT38 59
Edmund Rd. Well. CO45 69
Edmunds Av. Orp. CP52 89
Edmunds Clo. Hayes BD39 54
Edmunds Plover Clo. Berk. AR13 7
Edmund St. SE5 BZ43 67
Edmunds Wk. N2 BU31 47
Edmund Way, Slou. AQ39 52
Edna Rd. SW20 BQ51 85
Edna St. SW11 BU44 66
Edrick Rd. Edg. BN29 37
Edrick Wk. Edg. BN29 37
Edric Rd. SE14 CC43 67
Edridge Clo. Bush. BG25 27
Edridge Clo. Horn. CV35 51
Edridge Rd. Croy. BZ55 87
Edulf Rd. Borwd. BM23 28
Edward Av. E4 CE29 39
Edward Av. Mord. BT53 86
Edward Clo. N9 CA29 39
Edward Clo. Barn. BT25 29
Edward Clo. Hamptn. BG49 74
Edward Clo. Nthlt. BD37 54
Edward Clo. Rom. CV31 51
Edward Clo. St. Alb. BH14 9
Edward Ct. E16 CH39 58
Alexandra St.
Edward Ct. Wal. Abb. CG20 22
Ninefields
Edward Ms. W1 BV39 1
Edwardes Sq. W8 BR41 65
Edward ii Av. Wey. AY60 92
Edward Pl. SE8 CD43 67
Edward Rd. E17 CC31 48
Edward Rd. SE20 CC50 77
Edward Rd. Barn. BT24 29
Edward Rd. Belv. CR42 69
Edward Rd. Brom. CH50 78
Edward Rd. Chis. CL49 78
Edward Rd. Couls. BW61 104
Edward Rd. Croy. CA54 87
Edward Rd. Felt. BA46 73
Edward Rd. Har. BG31 45
Edward Rd. Hmptn. BG49 74
Edward Rd. Nthlt. BD37 54
Edward Rd. Rom. CQ32 50
Edward Rd. West. CK62 106
Edwards Av. Ruis. BC36 53
Edwards Clo. Brwd. DF25 122
Edwards Clo. Wor. Pk. BQ55 85
Edwards Gdns. Swan. CS52 89
Edward's La. N16 BZ34 48
Edwards Ter. Ong. CY19 24
Edward St. E16 CH38 58
Edward St. SE8 CD43 67
Edward St. SE14 CD43 67
Edwards Way, Brwd. DF25 122
Edward Way, Ashf. AY48 73
Edwins Gdns. Ilf. CK32 49
Edwin Av. E6 CL38 58
Edwin Clo. Bexh. CQ43 69
Edwin Clo. Rain. CT38 59
Edwin Rd. Dart. CU48 79
Edwin Rd. Edg. BN29 37
Edwin Rd. Leath. BA66 110
Edwin Rd. Twick. BH47 74
Edwin's Mead E9 CD35 48
Kings Mead Est.
Edwin St. E1 CC38 57
Edwin St. E16 CG39 58
Edwin St. Grav. DG47 81
Edw. Temme Av. E15 CG36 58
Edwyn Clo. Barn. BQ25 28
Effie Pl. SW6 BS43 66
Effie Rd. SW6 BS43 66
Effingham Clo. Sutt. BS57 95
Effingham Ct. Wok. AS62 100
Constitution Hill
Effingham Rd. N8 BY32 47
Effingham Rd. SE12 CG46 78
Effingham Rd. Croy. BX54 86
Effingham Rd. Reig. BS71 121
Effingham Rd. Surb. BJ54 84
Effort St. SW17 BU49 76
Effra Clo. SW19 BS50 76
Effra Pde. SW2 BY46 76
Effra Rd. SW2 BY45 66
Effra Rd. SW19 BS50 76
Egan Way SE16 CB42 67
Bonamy Est. East The
Egbert St. NW1 BV36 56
Egerton Av. Swan. CT50 79
Egerton Clo. Dart. CU47 79
Egerton Clo. Pnr. BC31 44
Egerton Ct. E11 CF33 48
Egerton Cres. SW3 BU42 3
Egerton Cres. SW3 BU42 66
Egerton Dr. SE10 CE44 67
Egerton Gdns. NW4 BP31 46
Egerton Gdns. NW10 BQ37 55
Egerton Gdns. SW3 BU41 3
Egerton Gdns. SW3 BU41 66
Egerton Gdns. W13 BJ39 54
Egerton Gdns. Ilf. CN34 49
Egerton Gdns. Ms. SW3 BU41 66
Egerton Ms. SW3 BU41 3
Egerton Ms. SW3 BU41 66
Egerton Pl. SW3 BU41 3
Egerton Pl. SW3 BU41 66
Egerton Pl. Wey. BA57 92

Egerton Rd. N16 CA33 48
Egerton Rd. SE25 CA52 87
Egerton Rd. Berk. AQ12 7
Egerton Rd. Guil. AP70 118
Egerton Rd. N. Mal. BO52 85
Egerton Rd. Twick. BH46 74
Egerton Rd. Wem. BL36 55
Egerton Rd. Wey. BA57 92
Egerton Ter. SW3 BU41 3
Egerton Ter. SW3 BU41 66
Egg Hall, Epp. CO18 23
Eggpie La. Sev. & Ton. CV70 117
Egham By-pass, Egh. AS49 72
Egham Clo. SW19 BR48 75
Frimley Clo.
Egham Clo. Sutt. BR55 85
Egham Cres. Sutt. BQ55 85
Egham Hill, Egh. AR50 72
Egham Rd. E13 CH39 58
Eglantine La. Hort. K. CX54 90
Eglantine Rd. SW18 BT46 76
Egleston Rd. Mord. BS53 86
Egley Dr. Wok. AR64 100
Egley Rd. Wok. AR64 100
Eglington Ct. SE17 BZ43 67
Carter St.
Eglington Rd. E4 CF26 39
Eglington Rd. Swans. DC48 81
Eglinton Hill SE18 CL43 68
Eglinton Rd. SE18 CL43 68
Eglise Rd. Warl. CD62 105
Egliston Ms. SW15 BQ45 65
Egliston Rd. SW15 BQ45 65
Egmont Av. Surb. BL54 85
Egmont Pk. Rd. Tad. BP66 112
Egmont Rd. N. Mal. BO52 85
Egmont Rd. Surb. BL54 85
Egmont Rd. Sutt. BT57 95
Egmont Rd. Walt. BC54 83
Egmont St. SE14 CC43 67
Egmont Way, Tad. BR63 103
Egremont Rd. SE27 BY48 76
Eider St. SE17 BZ42 67
Rodney Rd.
Eigth Av. E12 CK35 49
Eighth Av. Hayes BC40 53
Eileen Rd. SE25 BZ53 87
Eisenhower Dr. E6 CK39 58
Elaine Gro. NW5 BV35 47
Elam Clo. SE5 BY44 66
Eland Rd. SW11 BU45 66
Eland Rd. Croy. BY55 86
Elan Rd. S. Ock. DA39 60
Elba Pl. SE17 BA42 4
Elba Pl. SE17 BZ42 67
Rodney Rd.
Elberton Av. Croy. BW53 86
Elbe St. SW6 BT44 66
Elborough Rd. SE25 CB53 87
Elborough St. SW18 BS47 76
Elbury Dr. E16 CH39 58
Elcho St. SW11 BU43 66
Elcom St. W10 BR39 55
Kensal Rd.
Elcot Av. SE15 CB43 67
Elder Av. N8 BX32 47
Elderberry Rd. W5 BL41 65
Elder Ct. Bush. BH27 36
Elderfield Rd. E5 CC35 48
Elderfield Rd. Slou. AP36 52
Elderfield Wk. E11 CH32 49
Elder Oak Clo. SE20 CB51 87
Elder Rd. SE27 BZ49 77
Elders Ct. Bush. BH27 36
Eldersley Clo. Red. BU69 121
Elderslie Clo. Beck. CE53 87
Elderslie Rd. SE9 CL46 78
Elder St. E1 CA39 2
Elder St. E1 CA39 57
Elderton Rd. SE26 CD49 77
Eldertree Pl. Mitch. BV51 86
Eldertree Way, Mitch. BV51 86
Elder Wk. N1 BY37 56
Essex Rd.
Elder Way, Rain. CV38 60
Eldon Av. Borwd. BM23 28
Eldon Av. Croy. CC55 87
Eldon Av. Houns. BF43 64
Eldon Gro. NW3 BT35 47
Eldon Pk. SE25 CB52 87
Eldon Rd. E17 CD32 48
Eldon Rd. N9 CC27 39
Eldon Rd. N22 BY30 38
Eldon Rd. NW3 BT35 47
Eldon Rd. W8 BS41 3
Eldon Rd. W8 BS41 66
Eldon Rd. Cat. BZ64 105
Eldon Rd. Hodd. CF13 12
Eldon St. EC2 BZ39 2
Eldon St. EC2 BX39 57
Eldon Way NW10 BM37 55
Eldred Dr. Orp. CP54 89
Eldred Gdns. Upmin. CZ33 51
Eldred Rd. Bark. CM37 58
Eldridge Clo. Felt. BC47 73
Eldridge Clo. Horn. CV35 51
Eleanor Av. Epsom BN58 94
Eleanor Av. St. Alb. BG12 9
Eleanor Cres. NW7 BQ28 37
Eleanor Cross Rd. Wal. Cr. CD20 21
Eleanor Gdns. Dag. CQ34 50
Eleanor Gro. SW13 BO45 65
Eleanor Rd. E8 CB36 57
Eleanor Rd. E15 CG36 58
Eleanor Rd. N11 BX29 38
Eleanor Rd. Ger. Cr. AR30 34
Eleanor Rd. Wal. Cr. CD20 21
Eleanor St. E3 CE38 57
Eleanor Wk. SE18 CK42 68
Samuel St.
Eleanor Way, Brwd. DB28 42
Electric Av. SW9 BY45 66
Electric La. SW9 BY45 66
Electric Pde. Surb. BK53 84
Elephant & Castle SE1 BY42 4
Elephant & Castle SE1 BY42 66
Elephant La. SE16 CC41 67
Rotherhithe St.
Elephant Rd. SE17 BZ42 4
Elephant Rd. SE17 BZ42 67
Elers Rd. W13 BK41 64
Elers Rd. Hayes BA42 63
Eleven Acre Rise, Loug. CK24 31
Eley Rd. N18 CC28 39
Eleys Est. N18 CC28 39
Elfindale Rd. SE24 BZ46 77
Elfin Gro. Tedd. BH49 74
Elfin Rd. SE5 BY43 66
Warrior Rd.
Elford Clo. SE3 CJ45 68
Elfort Rd. N5 BY34 47
Elfrida Cres. SE6 CE49 77
Elfrida Rd. Wat. BD25 27
Elf Row E1 CC40 57
Elfwine Rd. W7 BH39 54
Elgal Clo. Orp. CL56 97
Elgar Av. SW16 BX52 86
Elgar Av. W5 BL41 65
Elgar Av. Surb. BM54 85
Elgar Clo. Borwd. BK26 36
Elgar Clo. Uxb. AZ34 44
Elgar Gdns. Til. DG44 71
Elgar St. SE16 CD41 67
Elgin Av. W9 BS38 1
Elgin Av. W9 BS38 56
Elgin Av. Ashf. BA50 73
Elgin Av. Har. BJ30 36
Elgin Av. Rom. CX29 42
Elgin Clo. Nthwd. BB29 35
Elgin Cres. W11 BR40 55
Elgin Cres. Cat. CB64 105
Elgin Cr. Felt. BB44 63
Eastern Perimeter Rd.
Elgin Gdns. Guil. AT70 118
Bladon Clo.
Elgin Ms. W11 BR39 55
Elgin Ms. N. W9 BS38 1
Elgin Ms. N. W9 BS38 56
Elgin Ms. S. W9 BS38 1
Elgin Ms. S. W9 BS38 56
Elgin Rd. N22 BW30 38
Elgin Rd. Brox. CD15 12
Elgin Rd. Croy. CA55 87
Elgin Rd. Ilf. CN33 49
Elgin Rd. Sutt. BT55 86
Elgin Rd. Wal. Cr. CC18 21
Elgin Rd. Wall. BW57 95
Elgin Rd. Wey. AZ56 92
Elgin Ter. W11 BR40 55
Elgood Av. Nthwd. BB29 35
Elham Clo. Brom. CJ50 78
Romney Dr.
Elia Mews EC1 BY37 56
Elia Mews N1 BY37 2
Elias Pl. SW8 BY43 66
Elia St. N1 BY37 2
Elia St. N1 BY37 56
Elibank Rd. SE9 CK45 68
Elim Est. SE1 BZ41 4
Elim Est. SE1 CA41 67
Elim Way E13 CG38 58
Eliot Bank SE23 CB48 77
Eliot Cotts. SE3 CG44 68
Eliot Dr. Har. BF34 45
Eliot Hill SE13 CF44 67
Eliot Pk. SE13 CF44 67
Eliot Pl. SE3 CG44 68
Eliot Rd. Dag. CP35 50
Eliot Rd. Dart. CX46 80
Eliot Vale SE3 CF44 67
Elizabethan Clo. Stai. AX47 73
Elizabethan Way, Stai. AX47 73
Elizabeth Av. Amer. AQ23 25
Elizabeth Av. N1 BZ37 2
Elizabeth Av. N1 BZ37 57
Elizabeth Av. Enf. BY24 29
Elizabeth Av. Ilf. CM34 49
Elizabeth Av. Stai. AX50 73
Elizabeth Br. SW1 BV42 3
Elizabeth Br. SW1 BV42 66
Elizabeth Clo. Barn. BQ24 28
Elizabeth Clo. E14 CE39 57
Grundy St.
Elizabeth Clo. W9 BT38 56
Randolph Av.
Elizabeth Clo. Rom. CR30 41
Elizabeth Clo. Wal. Abb. CF15 12
Nazeing Rd.
Elizabeth Clyde Clo. N15 CA31 48
Lawrence Rd.
Elizabeth Clyde Clo. N15 CA31 48
Lawrence Rd.
Elizabeth Cotts. Rich. BL44 65
Elizabeth Ct. Mord. BR54 85
Dudley Dr.
Elizabeth Ct. St. Alb. BK12 9
Villiers Cres.
Elizabeth Ct. Wat. BB22 26
Elizabeth Dr. Epp. CN21 31
Elizabeth Est. SE17 BZ43 4
Elizabeth Est. SE17 BZ43 67
Elizabeth Gdns. W3 BN40 55
Elizabeth Gdns. Stan. BK29 36
Elizabeth Gdns. Sun. BC52 83
Elizabeth Ms. NW3 BU36 56
Elizabeth Pl. N15 CA31 48
Elizabeth Pl. Til. DG45 71
Elizabeth Ride N9 CB26 39
Elizabeth Rd. E6 CJ37 58
Elizabeth Rd. N15 CA32 48
Elizabeth Rd. Brwd. DA23 33
Elizabeth St. SW1 BV42 3
Elizabeth St. SW1 BV42 66
Elizabeth St. Green. CZ46 80
Elizabeth Ter. SE9 CK46 78
Elizabeth Way, Felt. BD49 74
Elizabeth Way, Harl. CK11 13
Elizabeth Way, Harl. CM9 6
Elizabeth Way, Orp. CP53 89
Elizabeth Way, Slou. AP37 52
Elkington Rd. E13 CH38 58
Elkins, The Rom. CT30 41
Elkstone Rd. W10 BR39 55
Ellaline Rd. W6 BQ43 65
Ellanby Cres. N18 CB28 39
Elland Rd. SE15 CC45 67
Ellanor Gro. Uxb. AZ34 44
Ella Rd. N8 BX33 47
Ellement Clo. Pnr. BD32 45
Ellenborough Rd. N22 BY30 38
Ellenborough Rd. Sid. CP50 79
Ellenbridge Way, Sth. Croy. CA58 96
Ellenbrook La. Hat. BN12 10
Ellen Clo. Brom. CJ52 88
Ellen Ct. N9 CC27 39
Densworth Gro.
Ellen St. E1 CB39 2
Ellen St. E1 CB39 57
Elleray Rd. Tedd. BH50 74
Ellerby St. SW6 BQ44 65
Ellerdale Clo. NW3 BT35 47
Ellerdale Rd. NW3 BT35 47
Ellerdale St. SE13 CE45 67
Ellerdine Rd. Houns. BG45 64
Ellerker Gdns. Rich. BL46 75
Ellerman Av. Twick. BE47 74
Ellerman Rd. Til. DF44 71
Broadway
Ellerman Rd. Til. DF44 71
Church Rd.
Ellerslie Rd. W12 BP40 55
Ellers Rd. W13 BK41 64
Ellerton Gdns. Dag. CP36 59
Ellerton Rd. SW13 BP44 65
Ellerton Rd. SW18 BT47 76
Ellerton Rd. SW20 BP50 75
Ellerton Rd. Dag. CP36 59
Ellerton Rd. Surb. BL55 85
Ellery Rd. SE19 BZ50 77
Ellery St. SE15 CB44 67
Elles Av. Guil. AU70 118
Ellesborough Clo. Way. BD28 36
Ellesmere Av. NW7 BN27 37
Ellesmere Av. Beck. CE51 87
Ellesmere Clo. E11 CG32 49
Ellesmere Clo. Ruis. BA33 44
Ellesmere Ct. W4 BN42 65
Great W. Rd.
Ellesmere Dr. Sth. Croy. CB60 96
Ellesmere Gdns. Ilf. CK32 49
Ellesmere Gro. Barn. BR25 28
Ellesmere Rd. E3 CD37 57
Ellesmere Rd. NW10 BP35 46
Ellesmere Rd. W4 BN43 65
Ellesmere Rd. Berk. AR13 7
Ellesmere Rd. Grnf. BG38 54
Ellesmere Rd. Twick. BK46 74
Ellesmere Rd. Wey. BA57 92
Ellesmere St. E14 CE39 57
Ellias St. E1 CD39 57
Elliman Av. Slou. AP40 52
Ellingford Rd. E8 CB36 57
Ellingham Clo. Hem. H. AZ12 8
Ellingham Rd. E15 CF35 48
Ellingham Rd. W12 BP41 65
Ellingham Rd. Chess. BK57 93
Ellingham Rd. Hem. H. AY13 8
Ellington Rd. N10 BV31 47
Ellington Rd. Felt. BB49 73
Ellington Rd. Houns. BF44 64
Ellington St. N7 BY36 56
Elliot Clo. E15 CG36 58
Elliot Gdns. Rom. CU30 41
Elliot Gdns. Shep. AZ52 83
Elliot Rd. NW4 BP32 46
Elliot Rd. Stan. BJ29 36
Elliott Rd. SW9 BY43 66
Elliott Rd. W4 BO42 65
Elliott Rd. Brom. CJ52 88
Elliott Rd. Th. Hth. BY52 86
Elliotts Ct. EC4 BY39 56
Old Bailey
Elliotts Pl. N1 BY37 56
St. Peters St.
Elliott's Row SE11 BY42 4
Elliotts Row SE11 BT42 66
Elliott St. Grav. DH47 81
Ellis Av. Ger. Cr. AS30 34
Ellis Av. Slou. AR41 62
Ellis Av. Guil. AP71 118
Ellis Av. Rain. CU39 59
Ellis Clo. SE9 CM48 78
Elliscombe Rd. SE7 CJ42 68
Ellis David Rd. Croy. BY55 86
Ellis Fm. Clo. Wok. AR64 100
Ellisfield Dr. SW15 BP47 75
Ellis Ms. SE7 CJ43 68
Ellison Dr. Wind. AM45 61
Ellison Gdns. Sthl. BE42 64
Ellison Rd. SW13 BO44 65
Ellison Rd. SW16 BW50 76
Ellison Rd. Sid. CM47 78
Ellis Rd. Couls. BX63 104
Ellis Rd. Mitch. BU53 86
Ellis Rd. Oxt. CG68 115
Ellis St. SW1 BU42 3
Ellis St. SW1 BU42 66
Ellmore Clo. Rom. CU30 41
Ellora Rd. SW16 BW49 76
Ellsworth St. E2 CB38 57
Ellwood Gdns. Wat. BC20 17
Ellwood Gdns. Wat. BD21 27
Ellwood Ri. Ch. St. G. AR27 34
Elmar Rd. N15 BZ31 48
Elm Av. W5 BL40 55
Elm Av. Ruis. BC33 44
Elm Av. Upmin. CX35 51
Elm Av. Wat. BE26 36
Elm Bank N14 BX26 38
Elmbank Av. Barn. BQ24 28
Elmbank Av. Egh. AQ50 72
Elm Bank Av. Guil. AQ71 118
Elm Bank Gdns. SW13 BO44 65
Elmbank Way W7 BG39 54
Elmbourne Rd. SW17 BV48 76
Elmbridge Av. Surb. BM53 85
Elmbridge Clo. Ruis. BC32 44
Elmbridge Dr. Ruis. BB32 44
Elmbridge Dr. Ruis. BC32 44
Elmbridge Rd. Ilf. CO29 41
Elmbridge Wk. E8 CB36 57
Wilman Gro.
Elmbrook Gdns. SE9 CK45 68
Elmbrook Rd. Sutt. BR56 94
Elm Clo. E11 CH32 49
Elm Clo. NW4 BQ32 46
Elm Clo. SW20 BQ52 85
Elm Clo. Amer. AO22 25
Elm Clo. Buck. H. CJ27 40
Elm Clo. Cars. BU54 86
Elm Clo. Dart. CV47 80
Elm Clo. Epp. CL15 13
Elm Clo. Har. BF32 45
Elm Clo. Hayes BC39 53
Elm Clo. Lthd. BJ64 102
Elm Clo. Rom. CR30 41
Elm Clo. Sth. Croy. BZ57 96
Elm Clo. Surb. BN54 85
Elm Clo. Twick. BF48 74
Elm Clo. Wal. Abb. CF20 21
Elm Clo. Warl. CC62 105
Elm Clo. Wok. AR61 100
Elm Clo. Wok. AW65 101
Elmcote, Rick. AY25 26
Elm Ct. Mitch. BU51 86
Elmcourt Rd. SE27 BY48 76
Elm Ct. Wok. AO62 100
Beechwood Rd.
Elm Cres. W5 BL40 55
Elm Cres. Kings. on T. BL51 85
Elm Croft. Slou. AR44 62
Elmcroft Av. E11 CH32 49
Elmcroft Av. N9 CB25 30
Elmcroft Av. NW11 BR33 46
Elmcroft Av. Sid. CN46 78
Elmcroft Clo. E11 CH31 49
Elmcroft Clo. W5 BK39 54
Elmcroft Clo. Chess. BL55 85
Elmcroft Clo. Felt. BB46 73
Elmcroft Cres. NW11 BQ33 46
Elmcroft Cres. Har. BF31 45
Elm Croft Dr. Ashf. AZ49 73
Elmcroft Dr. Chess. BL55 85
Elmcroft Gdns. NW9 BM32 46
Elmcroft Rd. Orp. CO54 89
Elmcroft St. E5 CC35 48
Elmdale Rd. N13 BX28 38
Elmdene, Surb. BN54 85
Elmdene Av. Horn. CW32 51
Elmdene Clo. Beck. CD53 87
Elmdene Est. Beck. CD53 87
Elmdene Rd. SE18 CL42 68
Elmdon Rd. Houns. BB44 63
Elmdon Rd. Houns. BE44 64
Elm Dr. Wok. AP58 91
Elm Dr. Har. BF32 45
Elm Dr. Hat. BP13 10
Elm Dr. Lthd. BJ64 102
Elm Dr. St. Alb. BK13 9
Elm Dr. Sun. BD51 84
Elm Dr. Swan. CS51 89
Elm Dr. Wal. Cr. CD17 21
Elmer Av. Hav. CT27 41
Elmer Clo. Enf. BX24 29
Elmer Clo. Rain. CU36 59
Elmer Cotts. Lthd. BJ64 102
Elmer Gdns. Edg. BM29 37
Elmer Gdns. Islw. BG45 64
Elmer Gdns. Rain. CU36 59
Elmer Rd. SE6 CF47 77
Elmers Dr. Tedd. BJ50 74
Elmers End Rd. SE20 CC51 87
Elmers End Rd. Beck. CC51 87
Elmerside Rd. Beck. CD52 87
Elmers Rd. SE25 CB54 87
Elm Field, Lthd. BF65 102
Elmfield Av. N8 BX32 47
Elmfield Av. Mitch. BV51 86
Elmfield Av. Tedd. BH49 74
Elmfield Clo. Grav. DG47 81
Elmfield Clo. Pot. B. BR20 19
Elmfield Pk. Brom. CH52 88
Elmfield Rd. E4 CF27 39
Elmfield Rd. E17 CC32 48
Elmfield Rd. N2 BT31 47
Elmfield Rd. SW17 BV48 76
Elmfield Rd. Brom. CH51 88
Elmfield Rd. Pot. B. BR20 19
Elmfield Rd. Sthl. BE41 64
Elmfield Way, Sth. Croy. CA58 96
Elm Gdns. N2 BT31 47
Elm Gdns. Enf. BZ22 30
Elm Gdns. Epp. CR16 23
Elm Gdns. Epsom BQ63 103
Elm Gdns. Esher BH57 93
Elm Gdns. Mitch. BW52 86
Elm Gdns. Welw. G. C. BP8 5
Elmgate Av. Felt. BC48 73
Elmgate Gdns. Edg. BN28 37
Elm Grn. W3 BO39 55
Elm Grn. Hem. H. AV12 7
Elm Gro. N8 BX32 47
Elm Gro. NW2 BQ35 46
Elm Gro. SE15 CA44 67
Elm Gro. SW19 BR50 75
Elm Gro. Berk. AR13 7
Elm Gro. Cat. CA64 105
Elm Gro. Epsom BN60 94
Elm Gro. Erith CS43 69
Elm Gro. Har. BF33 45
Elm Gro. Horn. CW32 51
Elm Gro. Kings. on T. BL51 85
Elm Gro. Orp. CN54 88
Elm Gro. Sutt. BS56 95
High St.
Elm Gro. Wat. BC22 26
Elm Gro. Wdf. Grn. CG28 40
Elm Gro. West Dr. AY40 53
Elm Gro. Clo. Wok. AO63 100
Elmgrove Cres. Har. BH32 45
Elmgrove Gdns. Har. BJ32 45
Elmgrove Pde. Wall. BV55 86
Elm Grove Rd. SW13 BP44 65
Elmgrove Rd. W5 BL41 65
Elmgrove Rd. Cob. BD61 102
Elmgrove Rd. Croy. CB54 87
Elmgrove Rd. Har. BH32 45
Elmgrove Rd. Wey. AZ55 83
Elmhall Gdns. E11 CH32 49
Elmhurst, Belv. CQ43 69
Elmhurst Av. N2 BT31 47
Elmhurst Av. Mitch. BV50 76
Elmhurst Ct. Guil. AS71 118
Lwr. Edgeborough Rd.
Elmhurst Dr. E18 CH30 40
Elmhurst Dr. Dor. BJ72 119
Elmhurst Dr. Horn. CV33 51
Elmhurst Gdns. E18 CH30 40
Elmhurst Rd. N17 CA30 39
Elmhurst Rd. SE9 CK48 78
Elmhurst Rd. Enf. CC22 30
Elmhurst Rd. Slou. AT41 62
Elmhurst St. SW4 BW45 66
Elmhurst Way, Loug. CK26 40
Elmington Clo. Bex. CR46 79
Elmington Est. SE5 BZ43 67
Elmington Rd. SE5 BZ44 67
Elmira St. SE13 CE45 67
Elm La. SE6 CD48 77
Elm Lawn Clo. Uxb. AY36 53
Elmlea Dr. Hayes BB39 53
Grange Rd.
Elmlee Clo. Chis. CK50 78
Elmley St. SE18 CM42 68
Elm Ms. W2 BT41 66
Elm Nursery Est. Mitch. BV51 86
Elmore Rd. E11 CF34 4
Elmore Rd. Couls. BU64 10
Elmore Rd. Enf. CC22 3
Elmores, Loug. CL24 3
Elmore St. N1 BZ36 5
Elm Pk. SW2 BX46 7
Elm Pk. Stan. BJ28 3
Elm Pk. Av. N15 CA32 4
Elm Pk. Av. Horn. CU35 5
Elm Pk. Ct. Pnr. BD31 4
Elm Pk. Gdns. NW4 BQ32 4
Elm Pk. Gdns. SW10 BT42
Elm Pk. Gdns. SW10 BT42 6
Elm Pk. Gdns. W3 BN39 5
Noel Rd.
Elm Pk. Gdns. Sth. Croy. CC58 9
Elm Pk. La. SW3 BT42
Elm Pk. La. SW3 BT42 6
Elm Pk. Mans. SW10 BT43
Elm Pk. Mans. SW10 BT43 6
Elm Pk. Pde. W3 BN39 5
Noel Rd.
Elm Pk. Rd. E10 CD33 4
Elm Pk. Rd. N3 BR29 3
Elm Pk. Rd. N21 BZ26 3
Elm Pk. Rd. SE25 CA52 8
Elm Pk. Rd. SW3 BT43
Elm Pk. Rd. SW3 BT43 6
Elm Pk. Rd. Pnr. BD30 3
Elm Pl. SW7 BT42
Elm Pl. SW7 BT42 6
Elm Ridge La. Wok. AS63 10
Elm Rd. E7 CG36 5
Elm Rd. E11 CF34 4
Elm Rd. E17 CF32 4
Elm Rd. N22 BY30 3
Elm Rd. SW14 BO45 6
Elm Rd. Barn. BR24 2
Elm Rd. Beck. CD51 8
Elm Rd. Chess. BK56 9
Elm Rd. Dart. CV47 8
Elm Rd. Epsom BO57 9
Elm Rd. Erith. CU44 6
Elm Rd. Esher BH57 9
Elm Rd. Felt. BA47 7
Elm Rd. Grav. DH48 8
Elm Rd. Grays. DE43 7
Elm Rd. Green. CZ46 8
Elm Rd. Hodd. CE12 1
Elm Rd. Houns. BE44 6
Elm Rd. Kings. On T. BL51 8
Elm Rd. Lthd. BJ64 10
Elm Rd. N. Mal. BN52 8
Elm Rd. Orp. CO57 9
Elm Rd. Pur. BY60 9
Elm Rd. Red. BU70 12
Elm Rd. Rom. CR30 4
Elm Rd. Sid. CO49 7
Elm Rd. S. Ock. CW40 6
Elm Rd., Th. Hth. BZ52 8
Elm Rd. Wall. BV54 8
Elm Rd. Warl. CC62 1
Elm Rd. Wem. BL35 4
Elm Rd. West. CM66 1
Elm Rd. Wind. AN45 6
Elm Rd. Wok. AR62 1
Elm Rd. Wok. AS61 1
Elm Rd. W. Sutt. BR54 8
Elm Row NW3 BT34
Elmroyd Av. Pot. B. BR20
Elmroyd Av. Pot. B. CN20
Elmroyd Clo. Pot. B. BR20
Elmroyd Clo. Pot. B. CN20
Elms Av. N10 BV31
Elms Av. NW4 BQ32
Elmscott Gdns. N21 BZ25
Elmscott Rd. Brom. CG49
Elms Ct. Wem. BJ35
Elms Cres. SW4 BW46
Elmscroft Gdns. Pot. B. BR19
Elmsdale Rd. E17 CD31
Elms Fm. Rd. Horn. CV35
Elms Gdns. Dag. CQ35
Elms Gdns. Wem. BJ35
Elmshaw Rd. SW15 BP46
Elmshorn, Epsom BQ61 1
Elmshurst Cres. N2 BT31
Elmshurst Est. N2 BT31
Elmshurst Rd. E7 CH36
Elmside, Croy. CE57
Elmside, Guil. AQ71 1
Elmside Rd. Wem. BM34
Elms La. Wem. BJ34
Elmsleigh Av. Har. BJ31
Elmsleigh Ct. Sutt. BS55
Elmsleigh Rd. Stai. AV49
Thames St.
Elmsleigh Rd. Twick. BG48
Elmslie Clo. Epsom BN60
Elms Ms. W2 BT40
Elms Ms. W2 BT40
Elms Pk. Av. Wem. BJ35
Elms Rd. SW4 BW46
Elms Rd. Ger. Cr. AS29

lms Rd. Har. BH29 36
lmstead Av. Chis. CK49 78
lmstead Av. Wem. BL33 46
lmstead Clo. N20 BS27 38
lmstead Clo. Epsom BO56 94
lmstead Clo. Sev. CT64 107
lmstead Gdns. Wor. Pk. BP55 85
lmstead Glade, Chis. CK50 78
lmstead La. Chis. CK50 78
lmstead Rd. Erith CT44 69
lmstead Rd. Ilf. CN34 49
lmstead Rd. Wey. AW60 92
lmstead Cres. Well. CP43 69
lms, The SW13 BO45 65
lms, The Ong. CX18 24
Coopers Hill
lms, The Slou. BO53 85
lmstone Rd. SW6 BS44 66
lm St. WC1 BX38 2
lm St. WC1 BX38 56
lmsway, Ashf. AY49 73
lms Wood, Lthd. BE65 102
lmsworth Av. Houns. BF44 64
lm Ter. NW3 BS34 47
Finchley Rd.
lm Ter. SE9 CL46 78
lm Ter. Grays. DA43 70
lm Ter. Har. BG29 36
m Tree, Brwd. CZ22 33
mtree Av. Esher BG54 84
lm Tree Clo. NW8 BT38 1
stree Clo. Ashf. AZ49 73
m Tree Clo. Cher. AV55 82
m Tree Clo. Nthlt. BE37 54
m Tree Clo. Wey. AY60 92
m Tree Gdns. Nthlt. BE37 54
Elm Tree Clo.
lm Tree Rd. NW8 BT38 1
m Tree Rd. NW8 BT38 56
mtree Rd. Tedd. BH49 74
m Wk. NW3 BS34 47
West Heath Rd.
m Wk. SW20 BQ52 85
m Wk. Orp. CK55 88
m Wk. Rad. BH21 27
m Wk. Rom. CU31 50
m Way NW3 BS33 47
West Heath Rd.
m Way NW10 BO35 46
m Way, Brwd. DA28 42
m Way, Epsom BN56 94
mway, Grays DE40 71
m Way, Rick. AW26 35
m Way, Wor. Pk. BQ55 85
mwood Clo. Ash. BK62 102
Woodfield
mwood, Saw. CQ6 6
mwood, Welw. G. C. BP8 5
mwood Av. N13 BX28 38
mwood Av. Borwd. BM24 28
mwood Av. Felt. BC48 73
mwood Av. Har. BJ32 45
mwood Clo. Wall. BV55 86
mwood Ct. Wem. BJ34 45
mwood Cres. NW9 BN31 46
mwood Dr. Bex. CQ47 79
mwood Dr. Epsom BP57 94
mwood Gdns. W7 BH39 54
mwood Rd. SE24 BZ46 77
mwood Rd. W4 BN43 65
mwood Rd. Croy. BY54 86
mwood Rd. Mitch. BU52 86
mwood Rd. Red. BV69 121
mwood Rd. Slou. AQ40 52
mwood Rd. Wok. AO63 100
mworth Gro. SE21 BZ48 77
nathan Ms. W9 BS38 1
nathan Ms. W9 BS38 56
phinstone Rd. E17 CD30 39
phinstone St. N5 BY34 47
rick Clo. Erith CT43 69
Queen St.
rington Rd. E8 CB36 57
ruge Clo. West Dr. AX41 63
se Rd. Well. CO44 69
sa St. E14 CD39 57
sdale St. E9 CC36 57
sden Ms. E2 CC37 57
Old Ford Rd.
sden Rd. N17 CA30 39
sdon Rd. Wok. AQ62 100
senham Rd. E12 CK35 49
senham St. SW18 BR47 75
sham Rd. E11 CG34 49
sham Rd. W14 BR41 65
sham Ter. W14 BR41 65
siedene Rd. N21 BZ26 39
siemaud Rd. SE4 CD46 77
sie Rd. SE22 CA45 67
singe Rd. Enf. CB22 30
sinore Av. Stai. AY47 73
sinore Rd. SE23 CD47 77
sley Rd. SW11 BU45 66
speth Rd. SW11 BU45 66
speth Rd. Wem. BL35 46
srick Av. Mord. BS53 86
stan Way, Croy. CD54 87
sted St. SE17 BZ42 4
sted St. SE17 BZ42 67
sthorpe Rd. Rom. CR29 41
stow Clo. SE9 CL46 78
stow Clo. Ruis. BD33 45
stow Gdns. Dag. CQ37 59
stow Rd. Dag. CQ36 59
stree Gdns. N9 CB26 39
stree Gdns. Belv. CQ42 69
stree Gdns. Ilf. CM35 49
stree Hill N. Borwd. BK25 27
stree Hill S. Borwd. BK26 36
stree Hl. Brom. CG50 78
stree Rd. Borwd. BJ25 27
stree Rd. Bush. BG26 36
stree Rd. Hem. H. AZ10 8
stree Rd. Stan. BK27 36
stree Rd. Wat. BH23 27
stree Way, Borwd. BM23 28
swick Rd. SE13 CE44 67
swick St. SW6 BT44 66

Elsworth Rd. NW3 BU36 56
Elsworthy Rd. NW3 BU37 1
Elsworthy E. Mol. BH53 84
Elsworthy Ri. NW3 BU36 56
Elsynge Rd. SW18 BT46 76
Eltham Grn. SE9 CJ46 78
Eltham Grn. Rd. SE9 CJ45 68
Eltham High St. SE9 CK46 78
Eltham Hill SE9 CJ46 78
Eltham Palace Rd. SE9 CJ46 78
Eltham Pk. Gdns. SE9 CL45 68
Eltham Pl. Guil. AP69 118
Eltham Rd. SE9 CG46 78
Eltham Rd. SE12 CG46 78
Eltham St. SE17 BZ42 4
Eltham St. SE17 BZ42 67
Elthiron Rd. SW6 BS44 66
Elthorne Av. W7 BH41 64
Elthorne Ct. Felt. BD47 74
Elthorne Pk. Rd. W7 BH41 64
Elthorne Rd. NW9 BN33 46
Elthorne Rd. Uxb. AX37 52
Elthorne Way NW9 BN32 46
Elthruda Rd. SE13 CF46 77
Eltisley Rd. Ilf. CL35 49
Elton Av. Barn. BR25 28
Elton Av. Grnf. BH36 54
Elton Av. Wem. BJ35 45
Elton Clo. Kings. On T. BK50 74
Normansfield Av.
Elton Clo. Tedd. BK50 74
Elton Pl. N16 CA35 48
Elton Rd. Kings. On T. BL51 85
Elton Rd. Pur. BW59 95
Elton St. N16 CA35 48
Matthias Rd.
Elton Way, Wat. BF23 27
Elvaston Ms. SW7 BT41 3
Elvaston Ms. SW7 BT41 66
Elvaston Pl. SW7 BT41 3
Elvaston Pl. SW7 BT41 66
Elvaston Ter. SW7 BT42 66
Elveden Clo. Wok. AW62 101
Elveden Pl. NW10 BM37 55
Elveden Rd. NW10 BM37 55
Elvendon Rd. N13 BX29 38
Elver Gdns. E2 CB38 57
Avebury Est.
Elverson Rd. SE8 CE44 67
Elverton St. SW1 BW42 3
Elverton St. SW1 BW42 66
Elvet Av. Rom. CV31 51
Elvington Dr. NW9 BO30 37
Elvington Grn. Brom. CG53 88
Elvino Rd. SE26 CC49 77
Elwell Rd. SW4 BX44 66
Elwick Rd. S. Ock. DB39 60
Elwill Way, Beck. CF52 87
Elwill Way, Grav. DF51 81
Elwin St. E2 CB38 2
Elwin St. E2 CA38 57
Elwood St. N5 BY34 47
Elwyn Gdns. SE12 CH47 78
Ely Clo. Hat. BO12 10
Ely Clo. Amer. AP23 25
Ely Clo. Erith CT44 69
Ely Clo. N. Mal. BO51 85
Ely Gdns. Borwd. BN25 28
Ely Gdns. Dag. CS34 50
Elyne Rd. N4 BY32 47
Ely Pl. EC1 BY39 2
Ely Pl. EC1 BY39 56
Ely Pl. Wdf. Grn. CL29 40
Ely Pl. Welw. G. C. BR8 5
Ely Rd. E10 CF32 48
Ely Rd. Croy. BZ53 87
Ely Rd. Houns. BD45 64
Ely Rd. St. Alb. BJ14 9
Elysian Av. Orp. CN53 88
Elysium Pl. SW6 BR44 65
Elysium St.
Elysium St. SW6 BR44 65
Fulham Pk. Gdns.
Elystan Clo. Wall. BV57 95
Elystan Pl. SW3 BU42 3
Elystan Pl. SW3 BU42 66
Elystan St. SW3 BU42 3
Elystan St. SW3 BU42 66
Emanuel Av. W3 BN39 55
Embankment Gdns. SW3 BU43 66
Embankment Pl. WC2 BX40 4
Embankment Pl. WC2 BX40 56
Villiers St.
Embankment, The SW15 BQ44 65
Embankment, The Stai. AR47 72
Embankment, The Twick. BJ47 74
Emba St. SE16 CB41 67
Ember Clo. Orp. CM54 88
Ember Clo. Wey. AX56 92
Embercourt Rd. Surb. BG53 84
Ember Fm. Av. E. Mol. BG53 84
Ember Fm. Way, E. Mol. BG53 84
Ember Gdns. Surb. BH53 84
Ember La. Esher BG54 84
Ember Rd. Slou. AT41 62
Emberson Way, Epp. CR16 23
Embleton Rd. SE13 CE45 67
Embleton Rd. Wat. BC27 35
Embry Clo. Stan. BJ28 36
Embry Dr. Stan. BJ29 36
Embry Way, Stan. BJ28 36
Emden St. SW6 BS44 66
Emerald Gdns. Dag. CR33 50
Emerald St. WC1 BX39 2
Emerald St. WC1 BX39 56
Emerson Dr. Horn. CV33 51
Emerson Gdns. Har. BL33 46
Emerson Pl. SE1 BZ40 4
Emerson Rd. Ilf. CL33 49
Emerson St. SE1 BZ40 4
Emerson St. SE1 BZ40 57
Emery Hill St. SW1 BW41 3
Emery Hill St. SW1 BW41 66
Emery St. SE1 BY41 66
Morley St.
Emes Rd. Erith CS43 69
Emily Pl. N7 BY35 47
Queensland Rd.

Emily St. E16 CG39 58
Jude St.
Emlyn Gdns. W12 BO41 65
Emlyn La. Lthd. BJ64 102
Emlyn Rd. W12 BO41 65
Emlyn Rd. Red. BV71 121
Emmanuel Clo. Nthwd. BB29 35
Emmanuel Rd. SW12 BW47 76
Emmanuel Rd. Nthwd. BB29 35
Emma Rd. E13 CG37 58
Emma St. E2 CB37 57
Emma Ter. E11 CG34 49
Montague Rd.
Emmaus Way, Wdf. Grn. CL28 40
St. Marys Way
Emmett St. E14 CD40 57
Emmot Clo. NW11 BT32 47
Emmott Av. Ilf. CM32 49
Emmott St. E1 CD38 57
Emnetts Clo. Wok. AR62 100
Kirby Rd.
Emperor's Gate SW7 BS41 3
Emperors Gate SW7 BS41 66
Empire Av. N18 BZ28 39
Empire Ct. Wem. BM34 46
Empire Pde. N18 BZ29 39
Empire Rd. Grnf. BJ37 54
Empire Wharf Rd. E14 CF42 57
Empire Way, Wem. BL35 46
Empire Yd. N7 BX34 47
Empress Av. E4 CE29 39
Empress Av. E12 CJ34 49
Empress Av. Ilf. CK34 49
Empress Av. Wdf. Grn. CG29 40
Empress Dr. Chis. CL50 78
Empress Pl. SW6 BS42 66
Empress Rd. Grav. DJ47 81
Empress St. SE17 BZ43 4
Empress St. SE17 BZ43 67
Empson St. E3 CE38 57
Emsworth Clo. N9 CC26 39
Emsworth Rd. Ilf. CL30 40
Emsworth St. SW2 BX48 76
Emu Rd. SW8 BV44 66
Ena Rd. SW16 BX52 86
Enborne Grn. S. Ock. DA39 60
Enbrook St. W10 BR38 55
Endale Clo. Cars. BU55 86
Endeavour Rd. SW19 BS49 76
Endeavour Rd. Wal. Cr. CD17 21
Endeavour Way, Bark. CO37 59
Endell St. WC2 BX39 2
Endell St. WC2 BX39 56
Endensor Gdns. Est. W9 BS40 56
Enderley St. SE10 CG42 68
Enderley Clo. Har. BH30 36
Enderley Rd. Har. BH30 36
Endersby Rd. Barn. BQ25 28
Endersleigh Gdns. NW4 BP31 46
Endlebury Rd. E4 CE27 39
Endlesham Rd. SW12 BV47 76
Endsleigh Clo. Sth. Croy. CC58 96
Endsleigh Gdns. WC1 BW38 1
Endsleigh Gdns. WC1 BW38 56
Endsleigh Gdns. Ilf. CK34 49
Endsleigh Gdns. Surb. BK53 84
Endsleigh Gdns. Walt. BC56 92
Endsleigh Pl. WC1 BW38 1
Endsleigh Pl. WC1 BW38 56
Endsleigh Rd. Red. BW68 113
Endsleigh Rd. Sthl. BE42 64
Endsleigh Rd. W13 BJ40 54
Endsleigh St. WC1 BW38 1
Endsleigh St. WC1 BW38 56
End Way, Surb. BM54 85
Endwell Rd. SE4 CD44 67
Endymion Rd. N4 BY33 47
Endymion Rd. SW2 BX46 76
Endymion Rd. Hat. BQ12 10
Enfield Clo. Uxb. AX37 52
Enfield Rd. N1 CA36 2
Enfield Rd. N1 CA36 57
Enfield Rd. N8 BX32 47
Enfield Rd. W3 BM41 65
Enfield Rd. Brent. BK42 64
Enfield Rd. Enf. BW24 29
Enfield Rd. E. Brent. BK42 64
Enford St. W1 BU39 1
Enford St. W1 BU39 56
Engadine Clo. Croy. CA55 87
Engadine St. SW18 BR47 75
Engate St. SE13 CF45 67
Engayne Gdns. Upmin. CX33 51
Engel Pk. NW7 BQ29 37
Engineer Clo. SE18 CL43 68
Engineers Dr. Bush. BF24 27
Engineers Way, Wem. BM35 46
Englands La. NW3 BU36 56
Englands La. Loug. CL23 31
Englefield Clo. Croy. BZ53 87
Queen's Rd.
Englefield Clo. Enf. BY23 29
Englefield Clo. Orp. CN53 88
Englefield Cres. Orp. CN52 88
Englefield Path, Orp. CN52 88
Englefield Rd. N1 BZ36 57
Englefield Rd. Wok. AO62 100
Engleheart Dr. Felt. BB46 73
Engleheart Dr. Felt. BC46 73
Engleheart Rd. SE6 CE47 77
Englehurst, Egh. AR50 72
Englewood Rd. SW12 BV46 76
Engliff La. Wok. AV61 100
English Gdns. SE1 CA40 4
English Gdns. Stai. AR46 72
English Grounds SE1 CA40 57
English St. E3 CD38 57
Enid St. SE16 CA41 4
Enid St. SE16 CA41 67
Enkel St. N7 BX34 47
Enmore Av. SE25 CB53 87
Enmore Gdns. SW14 BN46 75
Enmore Rd. SE25 CB53 87
Enmore Rd. SW15 BQ45 65
Enmore Rd. Sthl. BF38 54
Ennerdale Av. Horn. CU35 50
Ennerdale Av. Stan. BK31 45
Ennerdale Clo. St. Alb. BJ14 9

Ennerdale Dr. NW9 BN32 46
Ennerdale Gdns. Wem. BK33 45
Ennerdale Rd. Bexh. CR44 69
Ennerdale Rd. Rich. BL44 65
Ennersdale Rd. SE13 CF46 77
Ennismore Av. W4 BO42 65
Ennismore Av. Grnf. BH36 54
Ennismore Av. Guil. AS70 118
Ennismore Gdns. SW7 BT41 3
Ennismore Gdns. SW7 BU41 66
Ennismore Gdns. E. Mol. BH53 84
Ennismore Gdns. Ms. SW7 BU41 3
Ennismore Gdns. Ms. SW7 BU41 66
Ennismore Ms. SW7 BT41 3
Ennismore Ms. SW7 BU41 3
Ennismore Ms. SW7 BU41 66
Ennismore St. SW7 BU41 66
Ennismore Gdns.
Ennis Rd. N4 BY33 47
Ennis Rd. SE18 CM43 68
Ensign Clo. Stai. AX47 73
Ensign Dr. N13 BZ27 39
Ensign St. E1 CB40 4
Ensign St. E1 CB40 57
Ensign Way, Stai. AX47 73
Ensleigh Rd. Red. BW68 113
Enslin Rd. SE9 CL46 78
Ensor Ms. SW7 BT42 3
Ensor Ms. SW7 BT42 66
Cranley Gdns.
Enstone Rd. Uxb. AY34 44
Enterdent, The Cdse. CC70 114
Entick St. E2 CC38 57
Epirus Ms. SW6 BR43 65
Epirus Rd. SW6 BR43 65
Epping Clo. Rom. CR31 50
Epping Glade E4 CF25 30
Epping Grn. Hem. H. AZ11 8
Epping La. Rom. BV14 32
Epping New Rd. Buck. H. CH27 40
Epping New Rd. Loug. CH25 31
Epping Pl. N7 BY36 56
Liverpool Rd.
Epping Rd. Epp. CL14 13
Epping Rd. Epp. CL21 31
Epping Rd. Epp. CM19 22
Epping Rd. Epp. CP17 23
Epping Rd. Epp. CS18 23
Epping Rd. Harl. CH11 13
Epping Rd. Ong. CT15 14
Epping Rd. Ong. CV16 24
Epping Way E4 CE25 30
Epple Rd. SW6 BR44 65
Epsom Clo. Bexh. CR45 69
Epsom Clo. Nthlt. BE35 45
Epsom Gap, Lthd. BJ61 102
Epsom La. Epsom BP63 103
Epsom La. S. Tad. BQ64 103
Epsom Rd. E10 CF32 48
Epsom Rd. Ash. BL62 103
Epsom Rd. Croy. BY56 95
Epsom Rd. Epsom BO59 94
Epsom Rd. Guil. AS71 118
Epsom Rd. Guil. AU70 118
Epsom Rd. Guil. AX69 110
Epsom Rd. Ilf. CN32 49
Epsom Rd. Lthd. BJ64 102
Epsom Rd. Mord. BR54 85
Epsom Way, Horn. CW35 51
Epstein Rd. SE28 CO40 59
Epworth Pl. EC2 BZ38 57
Epworth St.
Epworth Rd. Islw. BJ43 64
Epworth St. EC2 BZ38 2
Epworth St. EC2 BZ38 57
Erasmus St. SW1 BW42 3
Erasmus St. SW1 BW42 66
Erconwald St. W12 BO39 55
Eresby Pl. NW6 BS37 56
Kingsgate Pl.
Eresby Rd. NW6 BS36 56
Eresby Rd. Beck. CE54 87
Eresey Rd. Croy. CD54 87
Erica Ct. Swan. CT52 89
Erica Gdns. Croy. CE55 87
Erica St. W12 BP40 55
Eric Clo. E7 CH35 49
Ericcson Clo. SW18 BS46 76
Eric Rd. E7 CH35 49
Eric Rd. NW10 BO36 55
Eric Rd. Rom. CP33 50
Eric St. E3 CD38 57
Eridge Rd. W4 BN41 65
Erin Clo. Brom. CG50 78
Elstree Hill
Erindale SE18 CM43 68
Eriswell Cres. Watt. BB57 92
Eriswell Rd. Watt. BB56 92
Erith Cres. Rom. CS30 41
Erith Rd. Belv. CR42 69
Erith Rd. Bexh. CR45 69
Erith Rd. Erith CR44 69
Erlanger Rd. SE14 CC44 67
Erlesmere Gdns. W13 BJ41 64
Ermine Clo. Houns. BD45 64
Ermine Clo. St. Alb. BF14 9
Ermine Clo. Wal. Cr. CB19 21
Ermine Rd. SE13 CE45 67
Ermine Side, Enf. CB25 30
Ermington Rd. SE9 CM48 78
Ermyn Clo. Lthd. BK64 102
Ermyn Way, Lthd. BK64 102
Ernald Av. E6 CK37 58
Ernan Clo. S. Ock. DA39 60
Ernan Rd. S. Ock. DA39 60
Erncroft Way, Twick. BH46 74
Ernest Av. SE27 BY49 76
Ernest Gdns. W4 BM43 65
Ernest Gro. Beck. CD53 87
Ernest Gro. Clo. Beck. CE53 87
Ernest Rd. Horn. CW32 51
Ernest Rd. Kings. on T. BM51 85
Ernest Sq. Kings. on T. BM51 85
Ernest St. E1 CC38 57
Ernle Rd. SW20 BP50 75
Ernshaw Pl. SW15 BR46 75
Carlton Dr.

Erons Way, Grays DG42 71
Erpingham Rd. SW15 BQ45 65
Erridge Rd. SW19 BS51 86
Erriff Dr. S. Ock. DA39 60
Errington Clo. Grays. DG41 71
Cedar Rd.
Errington Rd. W9 BR38 55
Errol Gdns. Hayes BC38 53
Errol Gdns. N. Mal. BP52 85
Erroll Rd. Rom. CT31 50
Errol St. EC1 BZ38 2
Errol St. EC1 BZ38 57
Erskine Clo. Sutt. BU55 86
Erskine Cres. N15 CB31 48
Erskine Hl. NW11 BS32 47
Erskine Rd. E17 CD31 48
Erskine Rd. NW3 BU36 56
Erskine Rd. Sutt. BT56 95
Esam Way SW16 BY49 76
Escombe Dr. Guil. AQ68 109
Escott Gdns. SE9 CK49 78
Escot Way, Barn. BQ25 28
Escreet Gro. SE18 CL42 68
Esdaile La. Hodd. CE12 12
Esdaile Gdns. Upmin. CY33 51
Esher Av. Rom. CS32 50
Esher Av. Sutt. BQ55 85
Esher Av. Walt. BC54 83
Esher Clo. Bex. CQ47 79
Esher Clo. Esher BF56 93
Esher Cr. Felt. BB44 63
Eastern Perimeter Rd.
Esher Grn. Esher BF56 93
Esher Ms. Mitch. BU52 86
Esher Pk. Av. Esher BF56 93
Esher Pl. Av. Esher BF56 93
Esher Rd. E. Mol. BG53 84
Esher Rd. Ilf. CN34 49
Esher Rd. Walt. BE56 93
Eskdale, Hem. H. AY12 8
Lonsdale
Eskdale Av. Chesh. AO18 16
Eskdale Av. Nthlt. BE37 54
Eskdale Clo. Dart. CY47 80
Eskdale Gdns. Maid. AG42 61
Aysgarth Pk.
Eskdale Gdns. Pur. BZ60 96
Eskdale Rd. Bexh. CR44 69
Eskdale Rd. Uxb. AW37 53
Eskdale, St. Alb. BL17 19
Thamesdale
Eskdale Clo. Wem. BK34 45
Carlton Av. East
Eskley Gdns. S. Ock. DA39 60
Eskmont Ridge SE19 CA50 77
Esk Rd. E13 CH38 58
Esk Way, Rom. CS29 41
Esmar Cres. NW4 BP33 46
Esmeralda Rd. SE1 CB42 4
Esmeralde Rd. SE1 CB42 67
Esmond Clo. Rain. CU36 59
Esmond Gdns. W5 BK41 64
St. Marys Rd.
Esmond Rd. NW6 BR37 55
Esmond Rd. W4 BN42 65
Esmond St. SW15 BR45 65
Esparto St. SW18 BS47 76
Essen Clo. Belv. CR42 69
Essendene Rd. Cat. CA65 105
Essenden Rd. Belv. CR42 69
Essenden Rd. Sth. Croy. BZ57 96
Essendine Rd. W9 BS38 56
Essendon Clo. Hat. BU12 11
Essendon Gdns. Welw. G. C. BR8 5
Essendon Hill, Hat. BU12 11
Essendon Rd. Hert. BV11 11
Essex Av. Islw. BH45 64
Essex Av. Slou. AO39 52
Essex Clo. E17 CC31 48
Essex Clo. Mord. BQ54 85
Essex Clo. Rom. CR31 50
Essex Clo. Ruis. BD33 45
Essex Clo. Wey. AX56 92
Garfield Rd.
Essex Ct. EC4 BY39 2
Essex Ct. EC4 BY39 56
Essex Ct. EC4 BY39 56
Middle Temple La.
Essex Ct. SW13 BP44 65
Essex Gdns. N4 BY32 47
Rutland Gdns.
Essex Gdns. Horn. CX32 51
Essex Gdns. S. Le. H. DK41 71
Somerset Rd.
Essex Gro. SE19 BZ50 77
Essex la. Kings L. BA20 17
Essex Mead, Hem. H. AY10 8
Essex Pk. N3 BS29 38
Essex Pk. Ms. W3 BO40 55
Essex Pl. W4 BO42 65
Chiswick High Rd.
Essex Rd. E4 CG26 40
Essex Rd. E10 CF32 48
Essex Rd. E12 CK35 49
Essex Rd. E17 CD32 48
Essex Rd. E18 CH30 40
Essex Rd. N1 BY37 2
Essex Rd. N1 BY37 56
Essex Rd. NW10 BO36 55
Essex Rd. W3 BN40 55
Essex Rd. W4 BN42 65
Belmont Gro.
Essex Rd. Bark. CM36 58
Essex Rd. Borwd. BM24 28
Essex Rd. Dag. CS35 50
Essex Rd. Dart. CV46 80
Essex Rd. Enf. BZ24 30
Essex Rd. Grav. DG47 81
Essex Rd. Grays. DA43 70
Essex Rd. Hodd. CE11 12
Essex Rd. Long. DB51 90
Essex Rd. Rom. CP33 50
Essex Rd. Rom. CR31 50
Essex Rd. Wat. BC23 26
Essex St. E7 CH35 49
Essex St. EC4 BY39 2
Essex St. WC2 BY40 4
Essex St. WC2 BY39 56

Fairtrough La. Orp. CO60 98
Fair Vw. Cob. BD61 102
Fairview, Pot. B. BS18 20
Fairview Av. Brwd. DF26 122
Fairview Av. Rain. CV37 60
Fairview Av. Wem. BK36 54
Fairview Clo. E17 CD30 39
Fairview Clo. Chig. CN28 40
Fairview Clo. Epsom BQ59 94
Fairview Cres. Har. BF33 45
Fairview Dr. Chig. CN28 40
Fairview Dr. Orp. CM56 97
Fairview Dr. Shep. AY53 83
Fairview Dr. Wat. BB21 26
Fairview Gdns. Wdf. Grn. CH30 40
Fairview Pl. SW2 BX47 76
Holmewood Gdns.
Fairview Rd. N15 CA32 48
Fairview Rd. SW16 BX51 86
Fairview Rd. Chig. CN28 40
Fairview Rd. Enf. BX23 29
Fairview Rd. Epsom BO59 94
Fairview Rd. Erith. CT43 69
Fairview Rd. Grav. DE50 81
Fairview Rd. Sutt. BT56 95
Fairview Way, Edg. BM28 37
Fairwater Av. Well. CO45 69
Fairway SW20 BQ52 85
Fairway, Bexh. CQ46 79
Fairway, Cars. BT59 95
Fairway, Cher. AW54 83
Fairway, Grays. DD40 71
Fairway, Guil. AU70 118
Fairway, Hem. H. AY15 8
Fairway, Orp. CM53 88
Fairway, Saw. CQ6 6
Fairway, Wdf. Grn. CJ28 40
Fairway Av. NW9 BM31 46
Fairway Av. Borwd. BM23 28
Fairway Av. West Dr. AX40 53
Fairway Clo. NW11 BT33 47
Fairway Clo. Croy. CD53 87
Fairway Clo. Epsom BN55 85
Fairway Clo. St. Alb. BG17 18
Fairway Clo. West Dr. AX40 53
Fairway Dr. Dart. CX47 80
Fairway Gdns. Ilf. CM35 49
Fairways, Ashf. AZ50 73
Fairways, Ken. BZ62 105
Hayes La.
Fairways, Stan. BL30 37
Fairways, Tedd. BK50 74
Fairways, Wal. Abb. CG20 22
Fairways, The Harl. CO12 14
Fairway, The N13 BZ27 39
Fairway, The W3 BO39 55
Fairway, The Barn. BS25 29
Fairway, The Brom. CK53 88
Fairway, The E. Mol. BF52 84
Fairway, The Grav. DG48 81
Fairway, The Lthd. BJ62 102
Fairway, The N. Mal. BN51 85
Fairway, The Nthlt. BG36 54
Fairway, The Nthwd. BB28 35
Fairway, The NW7 BN27 37
Fairway, The N14 BV25 29
Fairway, The Ruis. BD35 45
Fairway, The Upmin. CY33 51
Fairway, The Uxb. AY37 53
Fairway, The Wat. BA19 17
Fairway, The Wem. BJ34 45
Fairway, The Wey. AZ59 92
Fairway, Vir. W. AR53 82
Fairweather Clo. N15 CA31 48
Lawrence Rd.
Fairweather Rd. N16 CB32 48
Fairwood Ct. E11 CF33 48
Fairwyn Rd. SE26 CD49 77
Fairy Lawns Clo. Horn. CW33 51
Falcon Av. Brom. CK52 88
Falconberg Ms. W1 BW39 1
Falconberg Ms. W1 BW39 56
Sutton Row
Falcon Cl. Hat. BP13 10
Falcon Clo. SE1 BZ40 4
Falcon Clo. SE1 BZ40 57
Falcon Clo. Saw. CP6 6
Falcon Cres. Enf. CC25 30
Falcon Dr. Stai. AX46 73
Falconer Rd. Bush. BE25 27
Falconer Rd. Ilf. CO28 41
Falconers Pk. Saw. CP6 6
Falconer Wk. N7 BX34 47
Andover Est.
Falconer Wk. N7 BX34 47
Corker Way
Falcon Ln. SW11 BU45 66
Lavender Hill
Falcon Pl. N16 CA34 48
Church St.
Falcon Ridge, Berk. AR13 7
Falcon Rd. SW11 BU44 66
Falcon Rd. SW11 BU45 66
Falcon Rd. Enf. CC25 30
Falcon Rd. Guil. AR71 118
Falcon Rd. Hamptn. BE50 74
Falcon St. E13 CG38 58
Falcon Ter. Est. SW11 BU45 66
Falcon Way, Har. BL32 46
Falcon Way, Rain. CU37 59
Falcon Way, Sun. BB51 83
Peregrine Rd.
Falcon Way, Wat. BE20 18
Falconwood Av. Well. CM44 68
Falconwood Pde. Well. CN45 68
Falconwood Rd. Croy. CD58 96
Falcourt Clo. Sutt. BS56 95
Robin Hood La.
Falkholt St. SW7 BU42 66
Rutland St.
Falkirk Clo. Horn. CX33 51
Falkirk Gdns. Wat. BD28 36
Falkirk St. N1 CA37 2
Falkirk St. N1 CA37 57
Falkland Av. N3 BS29 38
Falkland Av. N11 BV28 38
Falkland Gdns. Dor. BJ72 119
Falkland Clo.
Falkland Gro. Dor. BJ72 119
Vincents La.
Falklands Pk. Av. SE25 CA52 87
Falkland Pl. NW5 BW35 47
Falkland Rd.
Falkland Rd. N8 BY31 47
Falkland Rd. NW5 BW35 47
Falkland Rd. Barn. BR23 28
Falkland Rd. Dor. BJ72 119
Fallaise, Egh. AS49 72
Fallaize Av. Ilf. CL35 49
Riverdene Rd.
Falling La. West Dr. AY40 53
Falloden Way NW11 BS31 47
Fallon Trading Est. NW10 BO35 46
Fallow Clo. Chig. CN28 40
Fallow Ct. Av. N12 BT29 38
Fallowfield, Welw. G. C. BR6 5
Fallowfield, Stan. BJ27 36
Fallowfield Ct. Stan. BJ27 36
Fallowfield Wk. Hem. H. AW12 8
Fallow Hurst Path N3 BT29 38
Park Cres.
Fallsbrook Rd. SW16 BV50 76
Falmer Rd. E17 CE31 48
Falmer Rd. N15 BZ32 48
Falmer Rd. Enf. CA24 30
Falmouth Av. E4 CF28 39
Falmouth Clo. SE12 CG46 78
Taunton Rd.
Falmouth Clo. N22 BX29 38
Falmouth Gdns. Ilf. CJ31 49
Falmouth Rd. SE1 BZ41 4
Falmouth Rd. SE1 BZ41 67
Falmouth Rd. Walt. BD56 93
Falmouth St. E15 CF35 48
Falstaff Gdns. St. Alb. BG15 9
Falstone, Wok. AQ62 100
Fambridge Rd. SE26 CD49 77
Fambridge Rd. Dag. CR33 50
Famet Av. Pur. BZ60 96
Famet Clo. Pur. BZ60 96
Famet Wk. Pur. BZ60 96
Fane St. W14 BR43 65
Fann St. EC1 BZ38 2
Fann St. EC1 BZ38 57
Fanshawe Av. Bark. CM36 58
Fanshawe Cres. Dag. CQ35 50
Fanshawe Cres. Horn. CV32 51
Fanshawe Rd. Grays. DG41 71
Fanshawe Rd. Rich. BK49 74
Fanshaws La. Hert. BZ10 12
Fanshaw St. N1 CA38 2
Fanshaw St. N1 CA38 57
Fanthorpe St. SW15 BQ45 65
Fara Cl. N7 BX36 56
Faraday Av. Sid. CO48 79
Faraday Clo. Wat. BB25 26
Faraday Rd. E15 CG36 58
Faraday Rd. SE7 CJ41 68
Faraday Rd. SW19 BS50 76
Faraday Rd. W3 BN40 55
Faraday Rd. W10 BR39 55
Faraday Rd. E. Mol. BF52 84
Faraday Rd. Sthl. BF39 54
Faraday Rd. Well. CO45 69
Faraday Way, Orp. CO52 89
Fareham Rd. Felt. BD46 74
Far End, Hat. BP14 10
Farewell Pl. Mitch. BT51 86
Fairfield Clo. N12 BT28 38
Faringdon Av. Brom. CL54 88
Faringdon Av. Rom. CV30 42
Faringford Clo. St. Alb. BF16 18
Farisbarn Dr. Wey. AV59 91
Fari, S La. Wey. AV59 91
Farjeon Rd. SE3 CJ44 68
Farland Rd. Hem. H. AZ13 8
Farleigh Av. Brom. CG53 88
Farleigh Ct. Rd. Warl. CD60 96
Farleigh Dean Cres. Croy. CE58 96
Farleigh Dean Cres. Croy. CE59 96
Farleigh Pl. N16 CA35 48
Farleigh Rd. N16 CA35 48
Farleigh Rd. Warl. CC62 105
Farleigh Rd. Wey. AW59 92
Farleton Clo. Wey. BA57 92
Farley Cft. West. CM66 115
Farley Dr. Ilf. BT33 47
Farley Pl. SE25 CB52 87
Farley Rd. SE6 CE46 77
Farley Rd. Sth. Croy. CB58 96
Farleys Clo. Leath. BA66 110
Farlington Pl. SW15 BP47 75
Farlow Clo. Grav. DF48 81
Grieves Rd.
Farlow Rd. SW15 BQ45 65
Farlton Rd. SW18 BS47 76
Farman Gro. Nthlt. BD38 54
Wayfarer Rd.
Farm Av. NW2 BR34 46
Farm Av. SW16 BX49 76
Farm Av. Har. BE33 45
Farm Av. Orp. CM54 88
Farm Av. Swan. CS52 89
Farm Av. Wem. BK36 54
Farm Clo. Amer. AR23 25
Farm Clo. Barn. BP25 28
Farm Clo. Brwd. DE26 122
Farm Clo. Buck. H. CJ27 40
Farm Clo. Cher. AT53 82
Farm Clo. Dag. CS36 59
Farm Clo. Leath. BB67 110
Farm Clo. Lthd. BG65 102
Farm Clo. Maid. AG42 61
Farm Clo. Pot. B. BW17 20
Farm Clo. Shep. AZ54 83
Farm Clo. Stai. AV49 72
Farm Clo. Sthl. BF40 54
Farm Clo. Sutt. BT57 95
Farm Clo. Wall. BW58 95
Farm Clo. Welw. G. C. BQ8 5
Farm Clo. W. Wick. CG55 88
Farmcote Rd. SE12 CH47 78
Farm Ct. NW4 BP31 46
Farm Ct. Uxb. AZ34 44
Farmer Ct. Wal. Abb. CH20 22
Winters Way
Farm Cres. Slou. AR39 52
Farmcroft, Grav. DG48 81
Farmdale Rd. SE10 CH42 68
Farmdale Rd. Cars. BU57 95
Farm Dr. Croy. CD55 87
Farm Dr. Pur. BW59 95
Farm End E4 CG25 31
Farm End, Nthwd. AZ30 35
Farmer Rd. E10 CE33 48
Farmers Clo. Wat. BC20 17
Farmers Rd. Stai. AV49 72
Farmer St. W8 BS40 56
Farmers Way, Beac. AO29 34
Farm Field, Wat. BB22 26
Farmfield Clo. N12 BS28 38
Farmfield Rd. Brom. CF49 77
Farm Fields, Sth. Croy. CA59 96
Farm Hill Rd. Wal. Abb. CF20 21
Farm House Clo. Wok. AU61 100
Farmhouse Rd. SW16 BW50 76
Farmilo Rd. E17 CD33 48
Farmington Av. Sutt. BT55 86
Farmlands, Enf. CH23 31
Farmlands, Pnr. BC31 44
Farmlands, The Nthlt. BE36 54
Farmland Wk. Chis. CL49 78
Farm La. N14 BV25 29
Farm La. SW6 BS43 66
Farm La. Ash. BM61 103
Farm La. Croy. CD55 87
Farm La. Leath. BB67 110
Farm La. Pur. BW58 95
Farm La. Rick. AX24 26
Farm La. Slou. AO40 52
Farm La. Wok. AU65 100
Farmleigh Gro. Watt. BB56 92
Farmleigh Rd. N14 BW26 38
Farm Pl. W8 BS40 56
Farm Pl. Berk. AP12 7
Farm Pl. Dart. CU45 69
Farm Rd. N21 BY26 38
Farm Rd. Edg. BM29 37
Farm Rd. Epsom BN59 94
Farm Rd. Esher BF54 84
Farm Rd. Grays. DF41 71
Farm Rd. Mord. BS53 86
Farm Rd. Nthwd. BA28 35
Farm Rd. Rain. CV38 60
Farm Rd. Rick. AT24 25
Farm Rd. St. Alb. BJ13 9
Farm Rd. Sev. CV63 108
Farm Rd. Stai. AU46 72
Farm Rd. Stai. AW50 73
Farm Rd. Sutt. BT57 95
Farm Rd. Warl. CD63 105
Farm Rd. Wok. AT63 100
Farmstead Rd. SE6 CE49 77
Farmstead Rd. Har. BG30 36
Farm St. W1 BV40 3
Farm St. W1 BV40 56
Farm, The SW19 BQ47 75
Princes Way
Farm Vale, Bex. CR46 79
Farm Wk. NW11 BR32 46
Farm Wk. Guil. AP71 118
Farm Way, Buck. H. CJ28 40
Farm Way, Bush. BF24 27
Farmway, Dag. CP34 50
Farm Way, Horn. CU35 50
Farm Way, Nthwd. BB28 35
Farm Way, Stai. AV46 72
Farm Way, Wor. Pk. BQ55 85
Farmwell La. Leath. AZ67 110
Farnaby Dr. Sev. CU66 116
Farnaby Rd. SE9 CJ45 68
Farnaby Rd. Brom. CF50 77
Farnan Av. E17 CE30 39
Farnan Rd. SW16 BX49 76
Farnborough Av. E17 CD31 48
Farnborough Av. Sth. Croy. CC58 96
Farnborough Clo. Wem. BM34 46
Farnborough Com. Orp. CK55 88
Farnborough Cres.
Sth. Croy. CD58 96
Farnborough Hill, Orp. CM56 97
Farnborough Hill, Orp. CN56 97
Farnborough Way SE15 CA43 67
Farnborough Way, Orp. CL56 97
Farncombe St. SE16 CB41 67
Farndale Av. N13 BY27 38
Farndale Cres. Grnf. BG38 54
Farndon Mill La. Harl. CL9 6
Farnell Ms. SW5 BS42 66
Farnell Rd. Islw. BG45 64
Farnell Rd. Stai. AW48 73
Farnes Dr. Rom. CV30 42
Farnham Clo. N20 BT26 38
Farnham Clo. Hem. H. AT17 16
Farnham Gdns. SW20 BP51 85
Farnham Pk. La. Slou. AO37 52
Farnham Pl. SE1 BY40 4
Farnham Pl. SE1 BY40 56
Farnham Rd. Guil. AO72 118
Farnham Rd. Ilf. CN33 49
Farnham Rd. Rom. CV28 42
Farnham Rd. Well. CP44 69
Farnham Royal SE11 BX42 4
Farnham Royal SE11 BX43 66
Farningham Cres. Cat. CB65 105
Farningham Rd. N17 CB29 39
Farningham Rd. Cat. CB65 105
Farnley Rd. E4 CG26 40
Farnley Rd. SE25 BZ52 87
Farnley, Wok. AP62 100
Clifton Way
Farnol Rd. Dart. CX46 80
Farn Yd. Wind. AO43 61
Faroe Rd. W14 BQ41 65
Farorna Wk. Enf. BY23 29
Farquhar Rd. SE19 CA49 77
Farquhar Rd. SW19 BS48 76
Farquharson Rd. Croy. BZ54 87
Farraline Rd. Wat. BC24 26
Farrance Est. E14 CE39 57
Farrance Rd. Rom. CQ32 50
Farrance St. E14 CD39 57
Farrant Av. N22 BY30 38
Farrant Clo. Orp. CN57 97
Farrant Way, Borwd. BL23 28
Farr Av. Bark. CO37 59
Maybury Rd.
Farren Rd. SE23 CD48 77
Farrer Rd. N8 BW31 47
Farrer Rd. Har. BL32 46
Farrier Clo. Sun. BC52 83
Anvil Rd.
Farriers Clo. Grav. DJ47 81
Lwr. Higham Rd.
Farriers Rd. Nthlt. BF37 54
Farrier St. NW1 BW36 56
Farriers Way, Borwd. BN25 28
Farringdon Clo. Pot. B. BT19 20
Farringdon Rd. EC1 BY38 2
Farringdon Rd. EC1 BY38 56
Farringdon St. EC1 BY39 2
Farringdon St. EC4 BY39 2
Farringdon St. EC4 BY39 56
Farringford Rd. E15 CG36 58
Farrington Av. Orp. CO52 89
Faro Clo. Brom. CL51 88
Farrow Gdns. Grays. DD40 71
Farr Rd. Enf. BZ23 30
Farthing Alley SE1 CB41 67
Wolseley St.
Farthing Barn La. Orp. CK58 97
Farthings Clo. E4 CG27 40
Fathing Clo. Dart. CW45 70
Wellcome Av.
Farthing Fields E1 CB40 57
Raine St.
Farthing Grn. La. Slou. AQ37 52
Farthings, Wok. AP61 100
Green Acre
Farthings Clo. E4 CG27 40
Bernwell Rd.
Farthings Clo. Pnr. BC32 44
Farthing St. Orp. CK57 97
Farwell Rd. Sid. CO48 79
Farwig La. Brom. CG51 88
Fashion St. E1 CA39 2
Fashion St. E1 CA39 57
Fashoda Rd. Brom. CJ52 88
Fassett Rd. E8 CB36 57
Fassett Rd. Kings. On T. BL52 85
Fassett Sq. E8 CB36 57
Fauconberg Rd. W4 BN43 65
Faulkners Rd. Walt. BD56 93
Faulkner St. SE14 CC44 67
Fauna Clo. Rom. CP32 50
Faunce St. SE17 BY42 66
Faunce St. SE17 BY43 4
Favart Rd. SW6 BS44 66
Faversham Av. E4 CG26 40
Faversham Av. Enf. BZ25 30
Faversham Clo. Chig. CO27 41
Faversham Rd. SE6 CD47 77
Faversham Rd. Beck. CD51 87
Croydon Rd.
Faversham Rd. Mord. BS53 86
Fawcett Clo. SW11 BT44 66
Wye St.
Fawcett Est. E5 CB33 48
Fawcett Rd. NW10 BO37 55
Fawcett Rd. Croy. BZ55 87
Fawcett Rd. Wind. AN44 61
Fawcett St. SW10 BT43 66
Fawcus Clo. Esher BH57 93
Fawe Pk. Rd. SW15 BR45 65
Fawe St. E14 CE39 57
Fawke Comm. Rd. Sev. CX66 117
Fawkham Grn. Rd. Fawk. DA55 90
Fawkham Rd. Sev. CZ57 99
Fawkham Rd. S. Dnth. DB52 90
Fawley Rd. N17 CB31 48
Fawley Rd. NW6 BS35 47
Fawnbrake Av. SE24 BY46 76
Fawn Ct. Hat. BQ11 10
Fawn Rd. E13 CJ37 58
Fawn Rd. Chig. CN28 40
Fawns Manor Rd. Felt. BA47 73
Fawood Av. NW10 BN36 55
Fawsley Clo. Slou. AV44 62
Coleridge Cres.
Fawters Clo. Brwd. DE25 122
Fayerfield, Pot. B. BT19 20
Blunesfield
Faygate Cres. Bexh. CR46 79
Faygate Rd. SW2 BX48 76
Fay Grn. Wat. BA20 17
Fayland Av. SW16 BW49 76
Fayland Est. SW16 BW49 76
Faymore Gdns. S. Ock. DA39 60
Feacey Down, Hem. H. AW12 8
Fearn Clo. Leath. BB68 110
Fearney Mead, Rick. AW26 35
Hall Clo.
Fearnley Rd. SE5 CA44 67
Lettsom St.
Fearnley Rd. Welw. G. C. BQ8 5
Fearnley St. Wat. BC24 26
Fearon St. SE10 CH42 68
Featherbed La. Croy. CD57 96
Featherbed La. Hem. H. AW16 17
Featherbed La. Rom. CQ26 41
Featherbed La. Wat. BC16 17
Featherbed La. Wat. BD16 18
Feather Dell Cft. Hat. BO12 10
Feather Dell Wood, Hat. BO12 10
Feathers La. Stai. AT48 72
Feathers Pl. SE10 CF43 67
Featherstone Av. SE23 CB48 77
Featherstone Clo. Pot. B. BT19 20
Featherstone Ct. EC1 BZ38 57
Featherstone St.
Featherstone Gdns. Borwd. BN24 28
Featherstone Rd. NW7 BP29 37
Featherstone Rd. Sthl. BE41 64
Featherstone St. EC1 BZ38 2
Featherstone St. EC1 BZ38 57
Featherstone Ter. Sthl. BE41 64
Featley Rd. SW9 BY45 66
Angell Rd.
Federal Rd. Grnf. BK37 54
Federal Way, Wat. BD23 27
Federal Way, Wey. BD22 27
Federation Rd. SE2 CO42 69
Fee Farm Rd. Esher BH57 93
Feenan Highway, Til. DG43 71
Feilding Av. Til. DG44 71
Felbridge Av. Stan. BJ30 36
Felbridge Clo. SW16 BY49 76
Felbridge Clo. Sutt. BS58 95
Felbrigge Rd. Ilf. CN34 49
Felcott Clo. Walt. BD55 84
Felcott Rd. Walt. BD55 84
Felday Rd. SE13 CE46 77
Felden Clo. Pnr. BE29 36
Felden Clo. Wat. BD20 18
Felden Dr. Hem. H. AW15 8
Felden La. Hem. H. AW15 8
Felden Rd. Hem. H. AX15 8
Felden St. SW6 BR44 65
Feldman Clo. N16 CB33 48
Oldhill St.
Feldwick Pl. Red. BV70 121
Ladbroke Rd.
Felgate Ms. W6 BP42 65
Felhampton Rd. SE9 CL48 78
Felhurst Cres. Dag. CR35 50
Felicia Way, Grays. DG42 71
Felix Av. N8 BX32 47
Felix Dr. Guil. AW67 110
Felix La. Shep. BB53 83
Felix Rd. W13 BJ40 54
Felix Rd. Walt. BC53 83
Felixstowe Rd. N9 CB27 39
Felixstowe Rd. N17 CA31 48
Felixstowe Rd. NW10 BP38 55
Felixstowe Rd. SE2 CP41 69
Sedgemere Rd.
Felix St. E2 CB37 57
Cambridge Cres.
Felland Way, Reig. BT72 121
Fellbrigg Rd. SE22 CA46 77
Fellbrigg St. E1 CB38 57
Headlam St.
Fellbrook, Rich. BJ48 74
Fellowes La. St. Alb. BN15 10
Fellowes Rd. Cars. BU55 86
Fellows Rd. NW3 BT36 56
Fell Path, Borwd. BN25 28
Fell Rd. Croy. BZ55 87
Felltram Way SE7 CH42 68
Felmersham Clo. SW4 BW45 66
Hassel Rd.
Felmingham Rd. SE20 CC51 87
Felmongers, Harl. CO10 6
Felnex Est. NW10 BN38 55
Felsberg Rd. SW2 BX46 76
Fels Clo. Dag. CR34 50
Fels Fm. Av. Dag CS34 50
Felsham Rd. SW15 BQ45 65
Felspar Clo. SE18 CN42 68
Felstead Av. Ilf. CL30 40
Felstead Rd. E11 CH33 49
Felstead Rd. Epsom BN59 94
Felstead Rd. Loug. CK26 40
Felstead Rd. Orp. CO55 89
Felstead Rd. Rom. CS29 41
Felstead Rd. Wal. Cr. CD19 21
Felstead St. E9 CD36 57
Felsted Rd. E16 CJ39 58
Feltham Av. E. Mol. BH52 84
Feltham Hill Rd. Ashf. AZ49 73
Feltham Hill Rd. Felt. BC49 73
Feltham Rd. Ashf. AZ49 73
Feltham Rd. Mitch. BV51 86
Feltham Rd. Red. BU73 121
Feltham Wk. Red. BU73 121
Felton Clo. Borwd. BL22 28
Felton Clo. Brom. CL53 88
Felton Lea. Sid. CN49 78
Felton Rd. W13 BK41 64
Camborne Av.
Felton Rd. Bark. CN37 58
Felton St. N1 BZ37 2
Felton St. N1 BZ37 57
Fencepiece Rd. Chig. CM28 40
Fencepiece Rd. Ilf. CM30 40
Fenchurch Av. EC3 CA39 2
Fenchurch Av. EC3 CA39 57
Fenchurch Bldgs. EC3 CA39 2
Fenchurch Bldgs. EC3 CA39 57
Fenchurch Ct. EC3 CA39 2
Fenchurch St. EC3 CA40 4
Fenchurch St. EC3 BZ40 57
Fen Clo. Brwd. DD24 122
Fen Ct. EC3 CA39 57
Fendall Rd. Epsom BN56 94
Fendall St. SE1 CA41 4
Fendall St. SE1 CA41 67
Fendt Clo. E16 CG40 58
Bowman Av.
Fendyke Rd. Belv. CP42 69
Fenelon Pl. W14 BR42 65
Fengates Rd. Red. BU70 121
Fen Gro. Sid. CN46 78
Fenham Rd. SE15 CB43 67
Fenismead Av. Sutt. BQ58 94
Fen La. Upmin. DB35 51
Fen La. Upmin. DC35 123
Fenman Ct. N17 CB30 39
Shelbourne Rd.
Fenn Clo. Brom. CH50 78
Fennel Cl. Guil. AT69 118
Fennel St. SE18 CL43 68
Fennels, Harl. CM13 13
Fennels Mead, Epsom BO58 94
Fennings, The Amer. AO21 25
Fenning St. SE1 CA41 4
Fenning St. SE1 CA41 67
St. Thomas St.
Fenn St. E9 CC35 48
Fenns Way, Wok. AS61 100
Fenny Cft. Hem. H. AV12 7
Fen Pond Rd. Sev. DB62 108
Fensomes Alley, Hem. H. AY13 8
Fenstanton Av. N12 BT29 38
Fen St. E16 CG40 58
Huntingdon St.
Fens Way, Swan. CU50 79
Fentiman Av. Horn. CW33 51
Fentiman Rd. SW8 BX43 66
Fenton Av. Stai. AX50 73

Fenton Clo. SW9 BX44 66
Stockwell La.
Fenton Clo. Brom. CK49 78
Fenton Clo. Red. BV70 121
Fenton Ho. Est. NW3 BT34 47
Fenton Rd. N17 BZ29 39
Fenton Rd. Red. BV70 121
Fenton's Av. E13 CH37 58
Fentum Rd. Guil. AQ69 118
Fenwick Clo. SE18 CL43 68
Ritter St.
Fenwick Gro. SE15 CB45 67
Fenwick Pl. SW9 BX45 66
Fenwick Rd. SE15 CB45 67
Ferdinand Est. NW1 BV36 56
Ferdinand Pl. NW1 BV36 56
Ferdinand St.
Ferdinand Pl. NW5 BV36 56
Ferdinand St. NW1 BV36 56
Ferguson Av. Grav. DH49 81
Ferguson Av. Rom. CV30 42
Ferguson Av. Surb. BL53 85
Ferguson Cres. Rom. CV30 42
Fergus Rd. N5 BY35 47
Calabria Rd.
Ferme Pk. Rd. N4 BX32 47
Ferme Pk. Rd. N8 BX32 47
Fermor Rd. SE23 CD47 77
Fermoy Rd. W9 BR38 55
Fermoy Rd. Grnf. BF38 54
Fern Av. Mitch. BW52 86
Fernbank Av. Horn. CV35 51
Fernbank Av. Walt. BE54 84
Fernbank Av. Wem. BH35 45
Fernbank Rd. Wey. AW56 92
Fernbrook Av. Sid. CN46 78
Fernbrook Cres. SE13 CG46 78
Fernbrook Dr. Har. BF33 45
Fernbrook Rd. SE13 CG46 78
Ferncliffe Est. E8 CB35 48
Ferncliff Rd. E8 CB35 48
Fern Clo. Brox. CD15 12
Curzon La. E.
Fern Clo. Warl. CD62 105
Fern Cft. St. Alb. BG15 9
Fern Ct. Berk. AQ13 7
Charles St.
Ferncroft Av. N12 BU29 38
Ferncroft Av. NW3 BS34 47
Ferncroft Av. Ruis. BD34 45
Ferndale Brom. CJ51 88
Fern Dale, Guil. AP69 118
Ferndale Horn. CW32 51
Ferndale Av. E17 CF32 48
Ferndale Av. Cher. AV55 82
Ferndale Av. Houns. BE45 64
Ferndale Ct. SE3 CG43 68
Ferndale Ct. SW9 BX45 66
Ferndale Cres. Uxb. AX38 53
Ferndale Rd. E7 CH36 58
Ferndale Rd. E11 CG34 49
Ferndale Rd. N15 CA32 48
Ferndale Rd. SE25 CB53 87
Ferndale Rd. SW4 BX45 66
Ferndale Rd. SW9 BX45 66
Ferndale Rd. Ashf. AX49 73
Ferndale Rd. Bans. BR61 103
Ferndale Rd. Enf. CD22 30
Ferndale Rd. Grav. DG48 81
Ferndale Rd. Rom. CS30 41
Ferndale Rd. Wok. AS61 100
Ferndale St. E6 CL40 58
Ferndale Ter. Har. BH31 45
Ferndale Way Orp. CM56 97
Ferndell Av. Bex. CS48 79
Fern Dells, Hat. BO13 10
Fern Dene W13 BJ39 54
Dene, The
Ferndene Rd. SE24 BZ45 67
Ferndene Way, Rom. CR32 50
Ferndown Av. Orp. CM54 88
Ferndown Clo. Guil. AT71 118
Ferndown Clo. Pnr. BE29 36
Ferndown Clo. Sutt. BF57 95
Ferndown Gdns. Cob. BD60 93
Ferndown Rd. SE9 CJ47 78
Ferndown Rd. Nthwd. BC30 35
Ferndown Rd. Wat. BD27 36
Fern Dr. Felt. BC47 73
Fern Dr. Hem. H. AY14 8
Fernery, The Stai. AV49 72
Ferney Rd. Barn. BV26 38
Ferney Rd. Wey. AX59 92
Fern Gro. Welw. G. C. BQ6 5
Fernhall Dr. Ilf. CJ32 49
Fernhall La. Wal. Abb. CJ19 22
Fernham Rd. Th. Hth. BZ52 87
Fernhead Rd. W9 BR38 55
Fernhead Yd. W9 BR39 55
Fernhead Rd.
Fernheath Way, Dart. CS49 79
Fernhill, Harl. CN13 13
Fern Hill, Lthd. BG60 93
Fernhill Clo. Wok. AR63 100
Fernhill Ct. E17 CF30 39
Fernhill Ct. Kings. on T. BK49 74
Fernhill Gdns. Kings. on T. BK49 74
Fernhill La. Harl. CN13 13
Fern Hill La. Wok. AR63 100
Fernhill Pk. Wok. AR63 100
Fernhills, King L. BA20 17
Fernhill St. E16 CK40 58
Fernholme Rd. SE15 CC46 77
Fernhurst Gdns. Edg. BM29 37
Fernhurst Rd. SW6 BR44 65
Fernhurst Rd. Ashf. BA49 73
Fernhurst Rd. Croy. CB54 87
Fernie Clo. Chig. CO28 41
Fernlands Clo. Cher. AV55 82
Fern La. Houns. BE42 64
Fernlea, Lthd. BF65 102
Fernlea Rd. SW12 BV47 76
Fernlea Rd. Mitch. BV51 86
Fernleigh Ct. Har. BF30 36
Fernleigh Ct. Wem. BL34 46
Fernleigh Rd. N21 BY27 38
Fern Leys, St. Alb. BK12 9
Fernsbury St. WC1 BY38 2
Fernsbury St. WC1 BY38 57
Margery St.
Ferns Clo. Enf. CD21 30
Ferns Clo. Sth. Croy. CB58 96
Fernshaw Rd. SW10 BT43 66
Fernside NW3 BS34 47
Fernside NW4 BQ30 37
Fernside, Buck. H. CH26 40
Fernside Av. NW7 BN27 37
Fernside Av. Felt. BC49 73
Fernside La. Sev. CV68 117
Fernside Rd. SW12 BU47 76
Fernsleigh Clo. Ger. Cr. AS29 34
Ferns Rd. E15 CG36 58
Fern St. E3 CE38 57
Fernthorpe Rd. SW16 BW50 76
Ferntower Rd. N5 BZ35 48
Fernville La. Hem. H. AX13 8
Fern Way, Wat. BC21 26
Fernways, Ilf. CL35 49
Cecil Rd.
Fernwood Av. SW16 BW49 76
Fernwood Av. Wem. BK36 54
Fernwood Clo. Brom. CJ51 88
Fernwood Cres. N20 BU27 38
Ferranti Clo. SE7 CJ42 68
Ferrard Clo. Houns. BF43 64
Ferrers Ave. West Dr. AX41 63
Ferrers Av. Wall. BW56 95
Ferrers Rd. SW16 BW49 76
Ferrestone Rd. N8 BX31 47
Glebe Rd.
Ferrier St. SW18 BS45 66
Ferriers Way, Epsom. BQ63 103
Ferring Clo. Har. BG33 45
Ferrings, SE21 CA48 77
Ferris Av. Croy. CD55 87
Ferris Rd. SE22 CB45 67
Ferron Rd. E5 CB34 48
Ferro Rd. Rain. CU38 59
Ferry Approach SE18 CL41 68
Ferry Av. Stai. AV50 72
Ferryhills Clo. Wat. BD27 36
Ferry La. N17 CB31 48
Ferry La. SW13 BO43 65
Lonsdale Rd.
Ferry La. Brent. BL43 65
Ferry La. Guil. AR72 118
Ferry La. Rain. CT39 59
Ferry La. Rich. BL43 65
Ferry La. Shep. AZ54 83
Ferry La. Stai. AT48 72
Ferry La. Stai. AX52 83
Ferrymead Av. Grnf. BF38 54
Ferrymead Dr. Grnf. BF37 54
Ferrymead Gdns. Gfnf. BF37 54
Ferrymoor Rich. BJ48 74
Ferry Path, Cher. AW53 83
Ferry Pl. E14 CF42 67
Ferry Pl. SE18 CL41 68
Ferry Rd. SW13 BP43 65
Ferry Rd. E. Mol. BF52 84
Ferry Rd. Maid. AH41 61
Ferry Rd. Surb. BJ53 84
Ferry Rd. Tedd. BJ49 74
Ferry Rd. Til. DG45 71
Ferry Rd. Twick. BJ47 74
Ferry Sq. Shep. AZ54 83
Church Sq.
Ferry St. E14 CF42 67
Feryby Rd. Grays. DG41 71
Fesants Croft, Harl. CO9 6
Festing Rd. SW15 BQ45 65
Festival Clo. Bex. CP47 79
Festival Clo. Erith CT43 69
Festival Clo. Uxb. AZ37 53
Fetcham Comm. La. Lthd. BF64 102
Fetcham Pk. Dr. Lthd. BH65 102
Fetter La. EC4 BY39 2
Fetter La. EC4 BY39 56
Finch St. SE8 CE43 67
Fiddicroft Av. Bans. BS60 95
Fiddle Bri. Lane, Hat. BO12 10
Field Clo. E4 CE29 39
Field Clo. Brom. CJ51 88
Field Clo. Buck. H. CJ27 40
Field Clo. Chess. BK57 93
Field Clo. E. Mol. BF53 84
Field Cl. Guil. AU69 118
Field Clo. Houns. BC44 63
Field Clo. Rom. CO24 32
Field Clo. Ruis. BA33 44
Field Clo. Sth. Croy. CB60 96
Field Clo. Uxb. AZ34 44
Fieldcommon La. Walt. BE54 84
Field Ct. WC1 BX39 2
Field Ct. WC1 BX39 56
Field Ct. Oxt. CG67 115
Field End Barn. BP24 28
Field End Couls. BW56 95
Field End Couls. BW60 95
Field End Nthlt. BD36 54
Arnold Rd.
Field End Ruis. BD36 54
Field End Twick. BH49 74
Fieldend Rd. SW16 BW51 86
Field End Rd. Pnr. BC32 44
Field End Rd. Ruis. BD33 45
Field Gate La. Mitch. BU52 86
Fieldgate St E1 CB39 2
Fieldgate St. E1 CB39 57
Fieldhouse Rd. SW12 BW47 76
Fieldhurst Clo. Wey. AW56 92
Fielding Av. Twick. BG48 74
Fielding Rd. W4 BN41 65
Fielding Rd. W14 BQ41 65
Fielding St. SE17 BZ43 4
Fielding St. SE17 BZ43 67
Fieldings Rd. Wal. Cr. CD18 21
Fielding, The SE23 CC47 77
Fielding Ter. W5 BL40 55
Uxbridge Rd.
Fielding Way, Brwd. DE25 122
Field La. Brent. BK43 64
Field La. Tedd. BJ49 74
Fieldman Clo. N16 CC33 48
Oldhill St.
Field Mead NW9 BO29 37
Field Pk. Cres. Rom. CP32 50
Field Pl. EC1 BY37 2
Field Pl. EC1 BY37 56
St. John St.
Field Pl. N. Mal. BO53 85
Field Rd. E7 CG35 49
Field Rd. E17 CE31 48
Field Rd. N17 BZ31 48
Field Rd. NW10 BO38 55
Field Rd. W6 BR42 65
Field Rd. Felt. BC46 73
Field Rd. Slou. AT41 62
Field Rd. S. Ock. CW40 60
Field Rd. Uxb. AV35 43
Field Rd. Wat. BE25 27
Fields End La. Hem. H. AU12 7
Fieldsend Rd. Sutt. BR56 94
Fields Est. E8 CB36 57
Fieldside Rd. Brom. CF49 77
Field St. WC1 BX38 2
Field St. WC1 BX38 56
Fieldview SW18 BT47 76
Field View, Egh. AV49 72
Field Vw. Felt. BA49 73
Fieldview Rise, St. Alb. BE18 18
Field View Rd. Pot. B. BS20 20
Field Way NW10 BN36 55
Field Way, Berk. AS14 7
Fieldway, Croy. CE57 96
Field Way, Dag. CO35 50
Field Way, Ger. Cr. AR29 34
Fieldway, Grays. DD40 71
Field Way, Hem. H. AT17 16
Fieldway, Orp. CM53 88
Field Way, Rick. AW26 35
Field Way, Ruis. BA33 44
Fieldway Cres. N5 BY35 47
Field Waye, Uxb. AX38 53
Field Way, Wok. AV66 109
Burntcommon La.
Fife Ct. W3 BM39 55
Links Rd.
Fifehead Clo. Ashf. AY50 73
Fife Rd. E16 CH39 58
Fife Rd. N22 BY29 38
Fife Rd. SW14 BN46 75
Fife Rd. Kings. On T. BL51 85
Fife Ter. N1 BX37 56
Wynford Rd.
Fife Way Brom. CH51 88
White Hart Slip.
Fifeway, Lthd. BF66 111
Fifield La. Wind. AH45 61
Fifield Path SE23 CC48 77
Bampton Rd.
Fifield Rd. Hem. H. AZ14 8
Fifield Rd. Maid. AH43 61
Fifield Rd. Wind. AH44 61
Fifth Av. E12 CK35 49
Fifth Av. W10 BR38 55
Fifth Av. Enf. CA25 30
Fifth Av. Grays. DA43 70
First Av.
Fifth Av. Harl. CM10 6
Fifth Av. Harl. CM9 6
Fifth Av. Hayes. BB40 53
Fifth Av. Wat. BD21 27
Fifth Cross Rd. Twick. BG48 74
Figg's Rd. Mitch. BV50 76
Fig Tree Hill, Hem. H. AX13 8
Filby Rd. Chess. BL57 94
Filey Av. N16 CD33 48
Filey Clo. Sutt. BT57 95
Filey Clo. West. CH63 106
Filey Waye, Ruis. BC34 44
Fillebrook Av. Enf. CA23 30
Fillebrook Rd. E11 CF33 48
Filmer La. Sev. CW64 108
Filmer Rd. SW6 BR44 65
Filmer Rd. Wind. AL44 61
Filston La. Sev. CS61 107
Filston Rd. Belv. CR42 69
Riverdale Rd.
Filston Rd. Erith CR42 69
Riverdale Rd.
Filston Rd. Erith CS42 69
Holly Hill Rd.
Finborough Rd. SW10 BS42 66
Finborough Rd. SW17 BU50 76
Finchale Rd. SE2 CO41 69
Finch Av. SE27 BZ49 77
Finch Cl. Hat. BP13 10
Finch Clo. NW10 BN36 55
Finch Clo. Wok. AO62 100
Finchdale, Hem. H. AW14 8
Finchdean Way SE15 CA43 67
Finch Dr. Felt. BD47 74
Finches Dr. Guil. AU69 118
Finchingfield Av. Wdf. Grn. CJ29 40
Finch La. EC3 BZ39 2
Finch La. EC3 BZ39 57
Finch La. Amer. AP24 25
Finch La. Bush. BE24 27
Finchley Clo. Dart. CX46 80
Finchley Ct. N3 BS29 38
Finchley La. NW4 BQ31 46
Finchley Pk. N12 BT28 38
Finchley Pl. NW8 BT37 1
Finchley Pl. NW8 BT37 56
Finchley Rd. NW2 BR31 46
Finchley Rd. NW3 BR31 46
Finchley Rd. NW3 BT36 1
Finchley Rd. NW8 BR31 46
Finchley Rd. NW8 BT37 56
Finchley Rd. NW11 BR31 46
Finchley Rd. Grays. DD43 71
Finchley Way N3 BS29 38
Finchmoor Harl. CM12 13
Finch Rd. Berk. AQ12 7
Finch Rd. Guil. AR70 118
Finck St. SE1 BX41 4
Finck St. SE1 BX41 66
Finden Rd. E7 CH35 49
Findhorne Av. Hayes BC39 53
Findhorn St. E14 CF39 57
Aberfeldy St.
Findlay Dr. Guil. AP68 109
Findon Clo. SW18 BS46 76
Wimbledon Park Rd.
Findon Clo. Har. BF34 45
Findon Gdns. Rain. CU39 59
Findon Rd. N9 CB26 39
Findon Rd. W12 BP41 65
Fine Bush La. Uxb. AZ32 44
Fingal St. SE10 CG42 68
Fingrith Hall La. Ing. DC17 24
Finians Clo. Uxb. AY36 53
Finistock Rd. W10 BQ39 55
Finland Rd. SE4 CD45 67
Finlays Clo. Chess. BM56 94
Finlay St. SW6 BQ44 65
Finnis St. E2 CB38 57
Finnymore Rd. Dag. CQ36 59
Finsbury Av. EC2 BZ39 2
Finsbury Av. EC2 BZ39 57
Finsbury Cir. EC2 BZ39 2
Finsbury Cir. EC2 BZ39 57
Finsbury Cotts. N22 BX29 38
Finsbury Mkt. EC2 CA38 2
Finsbury Mkt. EC2 CA38 57
Finsbury Pk. Av. N4 BZ33 48
Finsbury Pk. Rd. N4 BY34 47
Finsbury Pavement EC2 BZ39 2
Finsbury Pavement EC2 BZ39 57
Finsbury Rd. N22 BX29 38
Finsbury Sq. EC2 BZ38 2
Finsbury Sq. EC2 BZ38 57
Finsbury St. EC2 BZ39 2
Finsbury St. EC2 BZ39 57
Finsen Rd. SE5 BZ45 67
Finstock Rd. W10 BQ40 55
Finucane Dr. Orp. CP54 89
Finucane Gdns. Rain. CU36 59
Finucane Rise, Bush. BG27 36
Fiona Clo. Lthd. BF65 102
Firbank Dr. Wat. BE26 36
Firbank Dr. Wok. AQ63 100
Firbank La. Wok. AQ63 100
Firbank La. Wok. AR62 100
Firbank Pl. Egh. AQ50 72
Firbank Rd. SE15 CB44 67
Firbank Rd. Rom. CR28 41
Firbank Rd. St. Alb. BH11 9
Fir Clo. Walt. BC54 83
Fircroft Av. Chess. BL56 94
Fircroft Clo. Slou. AQ36 52
Fircroft Clo. Wok. AS62 100
Ockenden Rd.
Fircroft Gdns. Har. BH34 45
Fircroft Rd. SW17 BU48 76
Firdene, Surb. BN54 85
Fire Bell Alley, Surb. BL53 85
Firefly Clo. Wall. BX57 95
Firfield Rd. Wey. AW56 92
Fir Grange Av. Wey. AZ56 92
Fir Gro. N. Mal. BO53 85
Fir Gro. Wok. AQ63 100
Firham Park Av. Rom. CX29 42
Firhill Rd. SE6 CE49 77
Firlands, Wey. BB57 92
Firmin Rd. Dart. CV46 80
Fir Park, Harl. CL12 13
Fir Rd. Felt. BD49 74
Fir Rd. Sutt. BR54 85
Firs Ave. Wind. AM45 61
Firs Av. N10 BV31 47
Firs Av. SW14 BN45 65
Firsby Av. Croy. CC54 87
Firsby Rd. N16 CA33 48
Firs Cl. Hat. BP13 10
Firs Clo. N10 BV31 47
Firs Av.
Firs Clo. Dor. BJ72 119
Firs Clo. Esher BH57 93
Firs Clo. SE23 CD47 77
Firscroft N13 BZ27 39
Firsdene Clo. Cher. AU57 91
Firs Dr. Loug. CK23 31
Firs Dr. Houns. BC44 63
Firs Dr. Loug. CK23 31
Firsgrove Cres. Brwd. DA28 42
Firsgrove Rd. Brwd. DA28 42
Firs La. N13 BZ27 39
Firs La. N21 BZ27 39
Firs La. Pot. B. BS20 20
Firs Pk. Av. N21 BZ26 39
Firs Pk. Gdns. N21 BZ26 39
Firs Rd. Ken. BY61 104
Firs, The Borwd. BL24 29
First Av. Amer. AO23 25
First Av. E12 CK35 49
First Av. E13 CH38 58
First Av. E17 CE32 48
First Av. N18 CC28 39
First Av. NW4 BQ31 46
First Av. SW14 BO45 65
First Av. W3 BO40 55
First Av. W10 BR38 55
First Av. Brwd. DB20 24
First Av. Dag. CR37 59
First Av. E. Mol. BE52 84
First Av. Enf. CA25 30
First Av. Epsom BO58 94
First Av. Grav. DF47 81
First Av. Grays DA43 70
First Av. Harl. CM10 6
First Av. Harl. CN10 6
First Av. Hayes BB40 53
First Av. Hayes BC40 53
Glebe Rd.
First Av. Rom. CP32 50
First Av. Walt. BC53 83
First Av. Wat. BD21 27
First Av. Well. CP43 69
First Av. Wem. BK34 45
First Clo. E. Mol. BG52 84
First Cross Rd. Twick. BH48 74
Firs, The N20 BT26 38
Athenaeum Rd.
Firs, The SW20 BP50 75
Firs, The W5 BK39 54
Firs, The Bex. CS47 79
Dartford Rd.
Firs, The Bex. CS48 79
Dartford Rd.
Firs, The St. Alb. BJ15
Firs, The Welw. G. C. BQ6
Firs, The Grays. DE40 7
First Slip, Lthd. BJ62 10
First St. SW3 BU42
First St. SW3 BU42 6
First Way SW20 BQ51 8
First Way, Guil. AQ70 11
First Way, Wem. BM35 4
Firs Wk. Nthwd. BA29 3
Firs Wk. Wdf. Grn. CH28 4
Firswood Av. Epsom BO56 9
Firth Gdns. SW6 BR44 6
Firtree Ave. West Dr. AZ41 6
Firtree Av. Mitch. BV51 8
Fir Tree Av. Slou. AP38 5
Fir Tree Clo. Epsom BO56 9
Fir Tree Clo. Epsom BQ61 10
Fir Tree Clo. Esher BG56 9
Fir Tree Clo. Hem. H. AZ14
Firtree Clo. Orp. CN56 9
Fir Tree Clo. Rom. CS31 5
Fir Tree Clo. Rom. CT31 5
Fir Tree Ct. Borwd. BL24 2
Fir Tree Gdns. Croy. CE56 9
Firtree Gro. Cars. BU57 9
Fir Tree Hill, Rick. AY22 2
Fir Tree Pl. Ashf. AZ49 7
Fir Tree Rd. Bans. BR60 9
Fir Tree Rd. Epsom BP61 10
Fir Tree Rd. Guil. AR69 11
Fir Tree Rd. Houns. BE45 6
Fir Tree Rd. Lthd. BK65 10
Fir Trees Epp. CO18 2
Tidy's La.
Firtree Wk. Dag. CS34 5
Fir Tree Wk. Enf. BZ24 3
Fir Tree Wk. Reig. BT70 12
Fir Wk. Sutt. BQ57 9
Firwood Av. St. Alb. BL13 1
Firwood Clo. Wok. AP63 10
Firwood Rd. Vir. W. AP53 8
Fisher Clo. Croy. CA54 8
Lwr. Addiscombe Rd.
Fisher Clo. Grnf. BF38 5
Fisher Clo. Kings L. AZ18 1
Fishermens Hill Grav. DD46 8
Warwick Pl.
Fisher Rd. Har. BH30 3
Fishers Ct. SE14 CC44 6
Fishers Hatch, Harl. CN10
Fishers Hill, Wok. AP64 10
Fisher's La. W4 BN42 6
Fishers La. Epp. CN19 2
Fisher St. E16 CG39 5
Fisher St. WC1 BX39
Fisher St. WC1 BX39 5
Fishers Way Belv. CS40 5
Fisher St. Est. NW8 BT38
Fisherton St. Est. NW8 BT38 5
Fisherton St. NW8 BT38
Fisherton St. NW8 BT38 5
Fishery Pl. Hem. H. AW14
Fishery Rd. Hem. H. AW14
Fishery Rd. Maid. AH40 6
Fishemongers Hall, St. EC4 BZ40 5
Swan Wf.
Fishponds Rd. SW17 BU49 7
Fishponds Rd. Kes. CJ56 9
Fishpool St. St. Alb. BF13
Fish St. Hill EC3 BZ40
Fish St. Hill EC3 BZ40 5
Lwr. Thames St.
Fitzalan Rd. N3 BR31 4
Fitzalan Rd. Esher BH57 9
Fitzalan St. SE11 BX42
Fitzalan St. SE11 BX42 6
Fitzgerald Rd. Surb. BJ53 8
Fitz George Av. W14 BR42 6
Fitzgeorge Av. N. Mal. BN51 8
Fitzgerald Av. SW14 BO45 6
Fitzgerald Rd. E11 CH32 4
Fitzgerald Rd. SW14 BN45 6
Fitzhardinge St. W1 BV39
Fitzhardinge St. W1 BV39 5
Fitzhugh Gro. SW18 BT46 7
Fitzilian Av. Rom. CW30 4
Fitz James Av. W14 BR42 6
Fitzjames Av. Croy. CB55 8
Fitzjohn Av. Barn. BR25 2
Fitzjohn's Av. NW3 BT35 4
Fitzmaurice Pl. W1 BV40
Fitzmaurice Pl. W1 BV40 5
Curzon St.
Fitz Neal St. W12 BO39 5
Fitzroy Clo. Har. BH30 3
Fitzroy Gdns. SE19 CA50 7
Fitzroy Ms. NW1 BW38 5
Cleveland St.
Fitzroy Ms. W1 BW38
Fitzroy Pk. N6 BU33 4
Fitzroy Rd.NW1 BU37
Fitzroy Sq. W1 BW38
Fitzroy Sq. W1 BW38 5
Fitzroy St. W1 BW38
Fitzroy St. W1 BW38 5
Fitzstephen Rd. Dag. CO35 5
Fitzwarren Gdns. N19 BW33 4
Fitzwilliam Av. Rich. BL44 6
Fitzwilliam Rd. SW4 BW45 6
Fitz Wygram Clo. Hamptn BG49 7
Five Acre NW9 BO30 3
Five Acre Wk. Welw. G. C. BR8
Salisbury Rd.
Five Acres. Chesh. AO20 1
Five Acres, Harl. CN12 1
Five Acres, St. Alb. BK16 1
Five Acres Av. St. Alb. BE18 1
Fiveash Rd. Grav. CF47 8
Five Elms Rd. Dag. CQ34 5
Five Oaks Clo. Wok. AP63 10
Five Oaks La. Chig. CQ29 4
Five Oaks, Wey. AV47 9
Fivewents Swan. CU51 8
Fladbury Rd. N15 BZ32 4
Fladgate Rd. E11 CG32 4
Flags, The Hem. H. AZ13
Flag Wk. Pnr. BC32 4

Fox Ct. EC1 BY39 56
Brooke St.
Foxcroft, St. Alb. BJ14 9
Foxcroft Rd. SE18 CL44 68
Fox Dell, Nthwd. BA29 35
Foxdell Way, Ger. Cr. AS28 34
Foxearth Clo. West. CK62 107
Foxearth Rd. Sth. Croy. CB58 96
Foxearth Spur, Sth. Croy. CC58 96
Foxenden Rd. Guil. AS71 118
Foxes Dale SE3 CG45 68
Foxes Vale Brom. CF52 87
Foxfield Clo. Nthwd. BB29 35
Foxfield Rd. Orp. CM55 88
Foxglove Clo. Hat. BP13 10
Foxglove Rd. S. Ock. DB39 60
Foxglove St. W12 BO40 55
Foxgrove N14 BX27 38
Foxgrove Av. Beck. CE50 77
Foxgrove Dr. Wok. AT61 100
Foxgrove Path, Wat. BD28 36
Foxgrove Rd. Beck. CE50 77
Foxhall Rd. Upmin. CY35 51
Foxham Rd. N19 BW34 47
Fox Hatch, Brwd. CZ22 33
Foxherne, Slou. AR41 62
Fox Hill SE19 CA50 77
Fox Hill Kes. CJ56 97
Fox Hills Clo. Cher. AU57 91
Foxhills Rd. Cher. AT56 91
Foxhills Rd. Grays DE40 71
Brookmans Av.
Fox Hl. Gdns. SE19 CA50 77
Foxhole Rd. SE9 CK46 78
Foxholes Wey. BA56 92
Foxholt Gdns. NW10 BN36 55
Foxhounds La. Grav. DD48 81
Fox Ho. Rd. Belv. CR42 69
Foxlake Rd. Wey. AY59 92
Foxlands Cres. Dag. CS35 50
Foxlands Rd. Dag. CS35 50
Fox La. N13 BX27 38
Fox La. W5 BL38 55
Fox La. Cat. BY64 104
Fox La. Kes. CH56 97
Fox La. Lthd. BE66 111
Fox La. North, Cher. AV54 82
Fox La. South, Cher. AV54 82
Foxley Clo. E8 CB35 48
Ferncliffe Est.
Foxley Clo. Loug. CL24 31
Foxley Clo. Red. BV73 121
Foxley Gdns. Pur. BY60 95
Foxley Hill Rd. Pur. BY59 95
Foxley La. Pur. BW59 95
Foxley Rd. SW9 BY43 66
Foxley Rd. Ken. BY60 95
Foxley Rd. Th. Hth. BY52 86
Foxleys Wat. BE27 36
Foxmanor Way Grays DA43 70
Foxmore St. SW11 BU44 66
Foxoak Hill, Watt. BB58 92
Foxon Clo. Cat. CA64 105
Foxon La. Cat. BZ64 105
Foxon La. Gdns. Cat. CA64 105
Fox Rd. E16 CG39 58
Fox Rd. Slou. AR42 62
Fox's La. Hat. BQ15 10
Fox's Path Mitch. BT51 86
Foxton Rd. Grays DB43 70
Foxton Rd. Hodd. CE12 12
Foxwarren Esher BH58 93
Fox Well Clo. Slou. AM40 61
Foxwell St. SE4 CD45 67
Foxwood Dr. Dart. DA48 80
Foxwood Rd. SE3 CG45 68
Foyle Dr. S. Ock. DA39 60
Foyle Rd. N17 CB30 39
Foyle Rd. SE3 CG43 68
Frailey Clo. Wok. AT61 100
Frailey Hill, Wok. AT61 100
Framewood Rd. Slou. AR36 52
Framfield Clo.N12 BS27 38
Framfield Rd. N5 BY35 47
Framfield Rd. W7 BH39 54
Framfield Rd. Mitch. BV50 76
Framlingham Clo. E5 CB34 48
Southwold Rd.
Framlingham Cres. SE9 CK49 78
Frampton Clo. Sutt. BS57 95
Frampton Pk. Est. E9 CC36 57
Frampton Pk. Rd. E9 CC36 57
Frampton Rd. Epp. CO17 23
Frampton Rd. Houns. BE45 64
Frampton Rd. Pot. B. BT18 20
Frampton St. NW8 BT38 1
Frampton St. NW8 BT38 56
Francemary Rd. SE4 CE46 77
Frances Gdns. S. Ock. CZ39 60
Frances Rd. E4 CE29 39
Frances Rd. Wind. AO44 61
Frances St. SE18 CK42 68
Frances St. Chesh. AO18 16
Franche Ct. Rd. SW17 BT48 76
Francis Av. Bexh. CR44 69
Francis Av. Felt. BC48 73
Francis Av. Grav. DJ49 81
Francis Av. Har. BJ32 45
Francis Av. Ilf. CM34 49
Francis Av. St. Alb. BG12 9
Franciscan Rd. SW17 BU49 76
Francis Chichester Way
SW11 BV44 66
Francis Clo. Epsom BN56 94
Francis Clo. Shep. AZ52 83
Francis Gro. SW19 BR50 75
Francis Rd. E10 CF33 48
Francis Rd. N2 BU31 47
Lynmouth Rd.
Francis Rd. Cat. BZ64 105
Francis Rd. Croy. BY53 86
Francis Rd. Dart. CV46 80
Francis Rd. Grnf. BJ37 54
Francis Rd. Har. BJ32 45
Francis Rd. Houns. BD44 64
Francis Rd. Ilf. CM34 49
Francis Rd. Orp. CP52 89
Francis Rd. Pnr. BD32 45
Francis Rd. Wall. BW57 95
Francis Rd. Wat. BC24 26
Francis St. E15 CG36 58
Francis St. SW1 BW42 3
Francis St. SW1 BW42 66
Francis St. Ilf. CM34 49
Francis Ter. N19 BW34 47
Francis Way, Grays. DH41 71
Francklyn Gdns. Edg. BM27 37
Franconia Rd. SW4 BW46 76
Francombe Gdns. Rom. CU32 50
Frank Bailey Wk. E12 CK35 49
Gainsborough Av.
Frank Dixon Clo. SE21 CA47 77
Frank Dixon Way SE21 CA47 77
Frankfurt Rd. SE24 BZ46 77
Frankham St. SE8 CE43 67
Frankland Clo. Rick. AZ26 35
Frankland Clo. Wdf. Grn. CJ28 40
Frankland Rd. E4 CE28 39
Frankland Rd. Rick. AZ25 26
Franklands Dr. Wey. AW57 92
Franklin Av. Wal. Cr. CB18 21
Franklin Clo. N20 BT26 38
Franklin Clo. BM52 85
Kings. on T.
Willingham Way
Franklin Clo. St. Alb. BO14 10
Franklin Cres. Mitch. BW52 86
Franklin Pass. SE9 CK45 68
Franklin Rd. NW10 BO36 55
Franklin Rd. SE20 CC50 77
Franklin Rd. Bexh. CQ44 69
Franklin Rd. Grav. DH49 81
Franklin Rd. Wat. BD23 26
Franklin Sq. SW5 BR42 65
Marchbank Rd.
Franklin's Row SW3 BU42 3
Franklin's Row SW3 BU42 66
Franklin St. E3 CE38 57
Bromley High St.
Franklin St. N15 CA32 48
Franklyn Clo. Dag. CS36 59
Franklyn Cres. Wind. AL45 61
Franklyn Gdns. Ilf. CM29 40
Franklyn Rd. NW10 BO36 55
Franklyn Rd. Walt. BC53 83
Franklyns Harl. CM11 13
Franks Av. N. Mal. BN52 85
Franks La. Hort. K. CX53 90
Franks Rd. Guil. AQ69 118
Frank St. E13 CH38 58
Franks Wd. Av. Orp. CL53 88
Franlaw Cres. N13 BZ28 39
Franmil Rd. Horn. CU33 50
Fransfield Gro. SE26 CB48 77
Frant Clo. SE20 CC50 77
Franthorne Way SE6 CE48 77
Randlesdown Rd.
Frant Rd. Th. Hth. BY53 86
Fraser Clo. Bex. CS47 79
Dartford Rd.
Fraser Clo. Bex. CS48 79
Dartford Rd.
Fraser Rd. E17 CE32 48
Fraser Rd. N9 CB27 39
Fraser Rd. Erith CS42 69
Fraser Rd. Grnf. BJ37 54
Fraser Rd. Wal. Cr. CD17 21
Fraser St. W4 BO42 65
Frating Cres. Wdf. Grn. CH29 40
Frays Ave. West Dr. AX41 63
Frays Pl. Uxb. AX37 53
Frays Waye, Uxb. AX37 53
Frazer Av. Ruis. BD35 45
Frazer Gdns. Dor. BJ71 119
Frazier St. SE1 BY41 4
Frazier St. SE1 BY41 66
Frean St. SE16 CB41 4
Frean St. SE16 CB41 67
Frederica Rd. E4 CF26 39
Frederica St. N7 BX36 56
Caledonian Rd.
Frederick Clo. W2 BU40 3
Frederick Clo. W2 BU39 56
Frederick Clo. Sutt. BR56 94
Frederick Cres. SW9 BY43 66
Frederick Cres. Enf. CC23 30
Frederick Pl. SE18 CL42 68
Frederick Rd. SE17 BY43 4
Frederick Rd. SE17 BY43 66
Frederick Rd. Rain. CS37 59
Frederick Rd. Sutt. BR56 94
Frederick's Pl. EC2 BZ39 57
Old Jewry
Frederick's Pl. N12 BT28 38
Frederick St. E17 CD32 48
Frederick St. WC1 BX38 2
Frederick Ter. E8 CA36 57
Haggerston Rd.
Fredora Av. Hayes BB38 53
Freeborne Gdns. Rain. CU36 59
Freedom St. SW11 BU44 66
Freedown La. Sutt. BT60 95
Freegrove Rd. N7 BX35 47
Freeland Pk. NW4 BR30 37
Freeland Rd. W5 BL40 55
Freelands Av. Sth. Croy. CC58 96
Freelands Gro. Brom. CH51 88
Freelands Rd. Brom. CH51 88
Freelands Rd. Cob. BC60 92
Freeling St. N1 BX36 56
Freeman Clo. Nthlt. BE36 54
Yeoman Rd.
Freeman Ct. Chesh. AO18 16
Barnes Av.
Freeman Rd. Grav. DJ48 81
Freeman Rd. Mord. BT53 86
Freemantle Av. Enf. CC25 30
Freemantle Rd. Belv. CR42 69
Freemans Clo. Slou. AQ36 52
Freemantle St. SE17 CA42 4
Freemason's Rd. Croy. CA54 87
Free Prae Rd. Cher. AW54 83
Freethorpe Clo. SE19 BZ20 77
Freke Rd. SW11 BV45 66
Fremantle Ho. Til. DG44 71
Leicester Rd.
Fremantle Rd. Ilf. CM30 40
Fremantle St. SE17 CA42 67
Fremont St. E9 CC37 57
Frencham Ct. Mitch. BT52 86
Belgrave Rd.
Frenchaye, Wey. AX56 92
Frenches Dr. Red. BV69 121
Franches, The
Frenches Rd. Red. BV69 121
Frenches, The Red. BV69 121
French Gdns. Cob. BD60 93
French Horn Lane, Hat. BP12 10
Frenchlands, Leath. BB67 110
French St. Sun. BD51 84
Frenchum Gdns. Slou. AM40 61
French Wells, Wok. AQ62 100
Frendsbury Rd. SE4 CC45 67
Frensham Dr. SW15 BO48 75
Frensham Dr. Croy. CF57 96
Frensham Rd. SE9 CM48 78
Frensham Rd. Ken. BY60 95
Frensham St. SE15 CB43 67
Frensham, Wal. Cr. CA17 21
Frensham Way, Epsom BQ61 103
Frere St. SW11 BU44 66
Freshborough Ct. Guil. AS71 118
Lwr. Edgeborough Rd.
Freshfield Dr. N14 BV25 38
Trent Gdns.
Freshfields Croy. CD54 87
Freshfields Av. Upmin. CX35 51
Freshford St. SW18 BT48 76
Fresh Water, Harl. CN10 6
Freshwater Clo. SW17 BV50 76
Freshwater Rd. SW17 BV50 76
Freshwater Rd. Dag. CP33 50
Freshwell Av. Rom. CP31 50
Freshwell Gdns. Brwd. DE32 123
Fresh Wharf Est. Bark. CL37 58
Fresh Wharf Rd. Bark. CL37 58
Freshwood Clo. Beck. CE51 87
Freshwood Way Wall. BV57 95
Fresley Clo. N15 BZ31 48
Clinton Rd.
Fresmount Gdns. Epsom. BM59 94
Freston Gdns. Barn. BU25 29
Freston Rd. W10 BQ40 55
Freta Rd. Bexh. CQ46 79
Fretherne Rd. Welw. G. C. BQ8 5
Frewin Rd. SW18 BT47 76
Friar Rd. Hayes BD38 54
Friar Rd. Orp. CO53 89
Friars Av. N20 BU27 38
Friars Clo. N2 BT31 47
Friars Clo. Nthlt. BD38 54
Broomcroft Av.
Friars Croft, Brox. CE13 12
Stafford Dr.
Friars Gdns. W3 BN40 55
St. Dunstan's Av.
Friar's Gate, Guil. AQ71 118
Friars La. Rich. BK46 74
Friars Orchard, Ltdh. BG64 102
Friar, S. Av. Brwd. DD26 122
Friar, S. Clo. Brwd. DD26 122
Friars Place La. W3 BN40 55
Friars Rise, Wok. AT62 100
Friars Rd. E6 CJ37 58
Friars Rd. Vir. W. AR52 82
Friars Stile Pl. Rich. BL46 75
Friars Stile Rd.
Friars Stile Rd. Rich. BL46 75
Friars, The Chig. CN28 40
Friars, The Harl. CL12 13
Friar St. EC4 BY39 2
Friar St. EC4 BY39 56
Carter La.
Friars Wk. N14 BV26 38
Friars Wk. SE2 CP42 69
Friars Wk. Har. BH29 36
Friars Way N14 BV26 38
Friars Way W3 BN39 55
Friars Way Bush. BE23 27
Friars Way, Kings L. AZ18 17
Friars Wd. Croy. CD58 96
Friary Clo. N12 BU28 38
Friary Est. SE15 CB43 67
Friary La. Wdf. Grn. CH28 40
Friary Rd. N12 BT28 38
Friary Rd. SE15 CB43 67
Friary Rd. W3 BN39 55
Friary Rd. Stai. AR47 72
Friary St. Guil. AR71 118
Friary, The Wind. AR46 72
Friary Way N12 BU28 38
Friday Hill E4 CG27 40
Friday Hill Belv. CR42 69
Friday Hill West E4 CG27 40
Friday Rd. Erith CS42 69
Friday Rd. Mitch. BU50 76
Friday St. EC4 BZ39 57
Cannon St.
Friday St. EC4 BZ40 4
Frideswide Pl. NW5 BW35 47
Islip St.
Friendly St. Ms. SE8 CE44 67
Friendly St. SE8 CE44 67
Friendship Wk. Nthlt. BD38 54
Wayfarer Rd.
Friends Rd. Croy. BZ55 87
Friends Rd. Pur. BY59 95
Friend St. EC1 BY38 2
Friend St. EC1 BY38 56
Friern Barnet La. N11 BT27 38
Friern Barnet La. N20 BT27 38
Friern Barnet Rd. N11 BU28 38
Friern Ct. N20 BT27 38
Friern Mt. Dr. N20 BT26 38
Friern Pk. N12 BT28 38
Friern Rd. SE22 CB47 77
Friern Watch Av. N12 BT28 38
Frieze Hill, Brwd. CX26 42
Frigo Ct. Epsom BN59 94
Frimley Av. Horn. CX33 51
Frimley Clo. SW19 BR48 75
Frimley Clo. Croy. CF57 96
Frimley Ct. Sid. CP49 79
Frimley Cres. Croy. CF57 96
Frimley Gdns. Mitch. BU52 86
Frimley Rd. Chess. BL56 94
Frimley Rd. Hem. H. AV13 7
Frimley Rd. Ilf. CN34 49
Frimley Vw. Wind. AL44 61
Fringewood Copse
Nthwd. AZ30 35
Frinstead Rd. Erith CS43 69
Frinsted Clo. Orp. CP52 89
Frinton Clo. Wat. BC27 35
Frinton Dr. Wdf. Grn. CF29 39
Frinton Mews, Ilf. CL32 49
Bramley Cres.
Frinton Rd. E6 CJ38 58
Frinton Rd. N15 CA32 48
Frinton Rd. SW17 BV50 76
Frinton Rd. Rom. CR29 41
Frinton Rd. Sid. CQ48 79
Friston Path Chig. CN28 40
Manford Way
Friston St. SW6 BS44 66
Fritham Clo. N. Mal. BO53 85
Frith Ct. NW7 BR29 37
Frithe, The Slou. AR40 52
Frith Gdns. SW6 BR45 65
Frith Knowle Walt. BC57 92
Frith La. NW7 BR29 37
Frith Rd. E11 CF35 48
Frith Rd. Croy. BZ55 87
Frith St. W1 BW39 1
Frith St. W1 BW39 56
Frithville Gdns. W12 BQ40 55
Frithwald Rd. Cher. AV54 82
Frithwood Av. Nthwd. BC29 35
Frizlands La. Dag. CR34 50
Frobish Ct. SE23 CB48 77
Sydenham Rise
Frobisher Clo. Pnr. BD33 45
Frobisher Clo. Ken. BZ62 105
Hayes La.
Frobisher Ct. W12 BP41 65
Frobisher Cres. Stai. AY47 73
Frobisher Gdns. Guil. AT70 118
Frobisher Gdns. Stai. AY47 73
Frobisher Rd. N8 BY31 47
Frobisher Rd. St. Alb. BK14 9
Frobisher St. SE10 CG43 68
Frobisher Way, Grav. DJ49 81
Froggy La. Uxb. AU34 43
Froghall La. Chig. CM28 40
Froghole La. Eden. CN70 115
Frog La. Guil. AS66 109
Frogley Rd. SE22 CA45 67
Frogmoor La. Rick. AX27 35
Frogmore SW18 BS46 76
Frogmore Av. Hayes BB38 53
Frogmore Clo. Sutt. BQ55 85
Frogmore Ct. Rick. AX27 35
Frogmore La.
Frogmore Dr. Wind. AP44 62
Frogmore Farm Est.
Hayes BA38 53
Frogmore Gdns. Hayes BB38 53
Frogmore Gdns. Sutt. BQ56 94
Fromore Rd. Hem. H. AX15 8
Frognal NW3 BT35 47
Frognal Gdns. NW3 BT35 47
Frognal Av. Sid. CO50 79
Frognal Clo. NW3 BT35 47
Frognall Gdns. NW3 BT35 47
Frognal La. NW3 BS35 47
Frognall Av. Har. BH31 45
Frognal Pa. NW3 BT36 56
Frognal Ct.
Frognal Pl. Sid. CO50 79
Frognal Rise NW3 BT34 47
Frognal Rd. NW3 BT36 56
Frognal Way NW3 BT35 47
Frog St. Brwd. CZ23 33
Froissart Rd. SE9 CJ46 78
Frome Sq. Hem. H. AY11 8
Frome St. N1 BZ37 2
Frome St. N1 BZ37 57
Fromondes Rd. Sutt. BR56 94
Front La. Upmin. CZ33 51
Front, The Berk. AT11 7
Frostic Pl. E1 CA39 57
Hopetown St.
Froude St. SW8 BV44 66
Dickens St.
Froude St. BW44 66
Robertson St.
Frowick Cl. Hat. BP15 10
Frowyke Cres. Pot. B. BP19 19
Fruen Rd. Felt. BB47 73
Fryatt Rd. N17 BZ29 39
Fryatt St. E14 CG39 58
Fry Clo. Rom. CR28 41
Fryent Clo. NW9 BM32 46
Fryent Cres. NW9 BO32 46
Fryent Fields NW9 BO32 46
Fryent Gro. NW9 BO32 46
Fryent Way NW9 BM32 46
Fryer Clo. Chesh. AO20 16
Frying Pan All. E1 CA39 2
Frying Pan Alley E1 CA39 57
Bell La.
Fry Rd. E6 CJ36 58
Fry Rd. NW10 BO37 55
Fry Rd. Ashf. AX49 73
Fryston Av. Couls. BV60 95
Fryston Av. Croy. CB55 87
Fryth Mead, St. Alb. BF13 9
Fuchsia St. SE2 CO42 69
Fulbeck Dr. NW9 BO30 37
Fulbeck Way Har. BG30 36
Fulbourne Est. E1 CB38 57
Fulbourne Rd. E17 CF30 39
Fulbrook La. S. Ock. CZ40 60
Fulbrook Ms. N19 BW35 47
Tufnell Pk. Rd.
Fulbrook Rd. N19 BW35 47
Fuley Rd. West CJ62 106
Fulford Gro. Wat. BC27 35
Fulford Rd. Cat. BZ64 105
Fulford Rd. Epsom BN57 94
Fulford St. SE16 CB41 6
Fulham Broadway SW6 BS43 6
Fulham Clo. Uxb. BA38 5
Fulham Ct. SW6 BS44 6
Fulham Est. SW6 BR43 6
Fulham High St. SW6 BR44 6
Fulham Palace Rd. SW6 BQ42 6
Fulham Palace Rd. W6 BQ42 6
Fulham Pk. Gdns. SW6 BR44 6
Fulham Pk. Rd. SW6 BR44 6
Fulham Rd. SW3 BR44 6
Fulham Rd. SW6 BR44 6
Fulham Rd. SW8 BR44 6
Fulham Rd. SW10 BT42
Fulham Rd. SW10 BR44 6
Fullarton Cres. S. Ock. DA40 6
Fullbrook Av. Wey. AW59 9
Fullbrooks Av. Wor. Pk. BO54 8
Fuller Clo. Orp. CN56 9
Fuller Gdns. Wat. BC22 2
Fuller Rd. Dag. CO34 5
Fuller Rd. Wat. BC22 2
Fullers Av. Surb. BL55 8
Fuller's Av. Wdf. Grn. CG29 4
Fullers Clo. Rom. CS29 4
Fullers Clo. Wal. Abb. CH20 2
Fullers Hill West. CM66 11
Fullers La. Rom. CS29 4
Fullers Mead, Harl. CP11 1
Fuller's Rd. E18 CG30 4
Fullers St. Sev. CX63 10
Fuller St. E2 CB38
Fuller St. E2 CB38 5
Cheshire St.
Fullers Way N. Surb. BL55 8
Fullers Way S. Chess. BL56 9
Fullers Wd. Croy. CE56 9
Fullers Wood La. Red. BW71 12
Fullerton Clo. Wey. AY60 9
Fullerton Dr. Wey. AY60 9
Fullerton Rd. SW18 BT46 7
Fullerton Rd. Cars. BU58 9
Fullerton Rd. Croy. CA54 8
Fullerton Rd. Wey. AY60 9
Fullerton Way, Wey. AY60 9
Fuller Way, Hayes BB42 6
Fuller Way, Rick. AZ25 2
Fullmer Way, Wey. AV58 9
Fullwell Av. Ilf. CK30 4
Fulmar Cres. Hem. H. AW14
Fulmar Rd. Rain. CU36 5
Fulmead St. SW6 BS44 6
Fulmer Common Rd.
Slou. & Iver AR36 5
Fulmer Dr. Ger. Cr. AR34 4
Fulmer La. Ger. Cr. AS34 4
Fulmer Rd. Ger. Cr. AS33 4
Fulmer Way W13 BJ41 6
Fulmer Way, Ger. Cr. AS32 4
Fulready Rd. E10 CF32 4
Fulstone Clo. Houns. BE45 6
Fulthorp Rd. SE3 CG44 6
Fulton Ms. W2 BT40
Fulton Ms. W2 BT40 5
Porchester Ter.
Fulton Rd. Wem. BM34 4
Fulton St. E16 CG39 5
George St.
Fulwell Pk. Av. Twick. BF48 7
Fulwell Rd. Tedd. BG49 7
Fulwich Rd. Dart. CW46 8
Fulwood Av. Wem. BL37 5
Fulwood Clo. Hayes BB39 5
Fulwood Gdns. Twick. BH46 7
Fulwood Pl. WC1 BX39
Fulwood Pl. WC1 BX39 5
Fulwood Wk. SW19 BR47 7
Furber St. W6 BP41 6
Furham Flds. Pnr. BF29 3
Furley Pl. N1 BY36 5
Islington Pk. St.
Furley Rd. SE15 CB44 6
Furlong Rd. N7 BY36 5
Furlong Rd. Dor. BG72 11
Furlongs, Hem. H. AW13
Furmage St. SW18 BS47 7
Furmigers Rd. Orp. CR56 9
Furnace Clo. Hem. H. AZ14
Furneaux Av. SE27 BY49 7
Furness Clo. Grays. DG42 7
St. Johns Rd.
Furness Pl. Wind. AL44 6
Furness
Furness Rd. NW10 BP37 5
Furness Rd. SW6 BS44 6
Furness Rd. Har. BF33 4
Furness Row, Wind. AL44 6
Furness
Furness Sq. Wind. AL44 6
Furness
Furness Walk, Wind. AL44 6
Furness
Furness Rd. Mord. BS54 8
Furness Way, Horn. CU35 5
Furness, Wind. AL44 6
Furness Way, Wind. AL44 6
Furness
Furnival Clo. Vir. W. AR53 8
Furnival St. EC4 BY39
Furnival St. EC4 BY39 5
Furrowfield, Hat. BP11 1
Crop Common
Furrow La. E9 CC35 4
Furrows Pl. Cat. CA65 10
Furrows, The Uxb. AX32 4
Furrows, The Walt. BD55 8
Fursby Av. N3 BS29 3
Furse Av. St. Alb. BJ11
Further Acre NW9 BO37 3
Further Grn. Rd. SE6 CG47 7
Furtherground, Hem. H. AY13
Furzebushes La. St. Alb. BE16 1
Furze Clo. Red. BU70 12
Furzedown Dr. La. SW17 BV49 7
Furzedown Rd. SW17 BV49 7
Furzedown Rd.. Sutt. BT59 9
Furze Farm Clo. Rom. CQ30 4
Furze Field Lthd. BH60 9

Furzefeld Wal. Cr. CB17 21
Maybury Av.
Furzefield Clo. Chis. CL50 78
Furzefield Cres. Reig. BT71 121
Furzefield Rd. SE3 CH43 68
Furzefield Rd. Reig. BT71 121
Furzefield Rd. Welw. G. C. BR8 5
Furze Gro. Tad. BR64 103
Furzeham Rd. West Dr. AY41 63
Furze Hill Pur. BX59 95
Furze Hill Red. BU70 121
Furze Hill, Tad. BR64 103
Furzehill Parade, Borwd. BM24 28
Furzehill Rd.
Furzehill Rd. Bowd. BM24 28
Furze La. Pur. BX59 95
Furzen Cr. Hat. BO14 10
Furze Rd. Hem. H. AV14 7
Furze Rd. Th. Hth. BZ52 87
Furze Rd. Wey. AV57 91
Furze St. E3 CE39 57
Furze View, Rick. AU25 25
Furze Wd. Sun. BC51 83
Fusedale Way, S. Ock. CZ40 60
Fyfe Ter. N1 BX37 2
Fyfield Clo. Brwd. DE32 123
Fyfield Rd. E17 CF31 48
Fyfield Rd. SW9 BY45 66
Fyfield Rd. Enf. CA24 30
Fyfield Rd. Ong. CW13 15
Tayfield Rd. Ong. DA13 15
Fyfield Rd. Rain. CT37 59
Fyfield Rd. Wdf. Grn. CJ29 40
Fynes St. SW1 BW42 3
Fynes St. SW1 BW42 66
Regency St.
Gable Clo. Dart. CU46 79
Gable Clo. Pnr. BF29 36
Gable Clo. Wat. BB19 17
Gable Ct. SE26 CB49 77
Gables Av. Ashf. AY49 73
Gables Av. Borwd. BL24 28
Gables Clo. Ger. Cr. AS28 34
Gables Clo. Slou. AQ43 62
Gables Clo. Wok. AS63 100
Gables, The Bans. BR62 103
Gabriel Clo. Rom. CS29 41
Gabriel St. SE23 CC47 77
Gadbrook Rd. Bet. BN73 120
Gaddesden Av. Wem. BL36 55
Gaddesden Cres. Wat. BD20 18
Gaddesden Gro.
Welw. G. C. BT8 5
Chilton Grn.
Gade Av. Wat. BB24 26
Gade Bk. Rick. BA24 26
Gadebridge La. Hem. H. AW12 8
Gadebridge Rd. Hem. H. AW12 8
Gade Clo. Hem. H. AW12 8
Gadesden Rd. Epsom BN57 94
Gadeside Wat. BA21 26
Gade Valley Clo. Kings L. AZ17 17
Gade View Gdns. Kings L. BA19 17
Gade View Rd. Hem. H. AX15 8
Gadsden Clo. Upmin. CZ32 51
Gadwell Clo. Wat. BE21 27
Gage Rd. E16 CG39 58
Gage St. WC1 BX39 56
Boswell St.
Gainford St. N1 BY37 2
Gainford St. N1 BY37 56
Gains Ave. E11 CF34 48
Gainsboro' Av. Dart. CV46 80
Gainsboro' Ct. Walt. BC55 83
Gainsboro' Rd. Rain. CU37 59
Gainsborough Ave. Til. DG44 71
Gainsborough Av. E12 CL35 49
Gainsborough Av. St. Alb. BH13 9
Gainsborough Dr. Grav. DE48 81
Gainsborough Gdns.
NW3 BT34 47
Gainsborough Gdns.
NW11 BR33 46
Gainsborough Gdns. Edg. BL30 37
Gainsborough Gdns. Grnf. BH35 45
Gainsborough Gdns. Islw. BG46 74
Gainsborough Rd. E11 CG33 49
Gainsborough Rd. E15 CG38 58
Gainsborough Rd. N12 BS28 38
Gainsborough Rd. W4 BO42 65
Gainsborough Rd. Dag. CO35 50
Gainsborough Rd. Epsom BN58 94
Gainsborough Rd. Hayes BA37 53
Gainsborough Rd. N. Mal. BN53 85
Gainsborough Rd. Rich. BL44 65
Gainsborough Rd.
Wdf. Grn. CK29 40
Gainsbough Sq. Erith CP45 69
Regency Way
Gainsford Rd. E17 CD31 48
Gainsford St. SE1 CA41 4
Gainsford St. SE1 CA41 67
Gains's Sq. Bexh. CP45 69
Gainsthorpe Rd. Ong. CV15 15
Gainswood, Welw. G. C. BR8 5
Gairloch Rd. SE5 CA44 67
Gaisford St. NW5 BW36 56
Gaitskell Rd. SE9 CM47 78
Galahad Rd. Brom. CH48 78
Gaeata Rd. SW13 BP43 65
Galatea Sq. SE15 CB45 67
Scylla Rd.
Galbraith St. E14 CF41 67
Galeborough Av.
Wdf. Grn. CF29 39
Gale Clo. Mitch. BT52 86
Gale Cres. Bans. BS62 104
Gale Grn. S. Ock. DA39 60
Galena Rd. W6 BP42 65
Galen Pl. WC1 BX39 2
Galen Pl. WC1 BX39 56
Bury Pl.
Galesbury Rd. SW18 BT46 76
Gales Clo. Guil. AU69 118
Gilliat Dri.
Gale's Gdns. E2 CB38 57
Bethnal Green Rd.
Gale St. E3 CE39 57
Gale St. Dag. CP37 59
Galesway Wdf. Grn. CK29 40
Gallants Farm Rd. Barn. BU26 38
Gallery Gdns. Nthlt. BD37 54
Gallery Rd. SE21 BZ47 77
Gallery Hill, Hem. H. AV12 7
Gallery Hill Rd. Grav. DC46 81
Galleyhill Rd. Wal. Abb. CG19 22
Galley La. Barn. BP22 28
Galley La. Barn. BP23 28
Galleymead Rd. Slou. AV44 62
Galleywall Rd. SE16 CB42 67
Galleywood Cres. Rom. CS29 41
Galliard Ct. N9 CB25 30
Galliard Rd. N9 CB26 39
Gallia Rd. N5 BY35 47
Calabria Rd.
Gallions Clo. Bark. CO38 59
Gallions La. Slou. AR38 52
Gallions Rd. E16 CL40 58
Gallions Rd. SE7 CH42 68
Gallon Clo. SE7 CJ42 68
Charlton Church Rd.
Gallop, The Sth. Croy. CB57 96
Gallop, The Sutt. BT58 95
Gallop, The Wind. AO47 72
Gallosson Rd. SE18 CN42 68
Galloway Rd. W12 BP40 55
Gallows Wood, Fawk. DA56 99
Gallows Hill, Kings L. BA19 17
Gallowshill La. Wat. BA19 17
Gallus Sq. SE3 CH45 68
Gallys Rd. Wind. AL44 61
Galpin's Rd. Th. Hth. BX53 86
Galsworthy Av. Rom. CO33 50
Galsworthy Clo. SE28 CO40 59
Epstein Rd.
Galsworthy Cres. SE3 CJ44 68
Merriman Rd.
Galsworthy Rd. NW2 BR35 46
Galsworthy Rd. Cher. AW54 83
Galsworthy Rd.
Kings. On T. BM50 75
Galsworthy Rd. Til. DH44 71
Galton St. W10 BR38 55
Galveston Rd. SW15 BR46 75
Galway St. EC1 BZ38 2
Gambetta St. SW8 BV44 66
Gambia St. SE1 BY40 4
Gambia St. SE1 BY40 56
Gambles La. Wok. AX65 101
Gambles La. Wok. AX66 110
Gambole Rd. SW17 BU49 76
Games Rd. Barn. BU24 29
Gamlen Rd. SW15 BQ45 65
Gammon's La. Brox. CA16 21
Gammon's La. Wat. BB21 26
Gamuel Rd. E17 CD32 48
Gandergreen La. Sutt. BR55 85
Ganders Ash. Wat. BC20 17
Gane Clo. Wall. BX57 95
Gangers Hill, Gdse. CD67 114
Ganghill, Guil. AT69 118
Gant Ct. Wal. Abb. CG20 22
Ganton St. W1 BW40 3
Ganton St. W1 BW40 56
Kingly St.
Gantshill Cres. Ilf. CL32 49
Gantshill Cross, Ilf. CL32 49
Ganymede Pl. Hem. H. AY12 8
Gap Rd. SW19 BS49 76
Garage Rd. NW4 BP32 46
Garage Rd. W3 BM39 55
Garbrand Walk, Epsom BO58 94
Garbutt Pl. W1 BV39 1
Garbutt Pl. W1 BV39 56
Gard St. EC1 BY38 56
Masons Pl.
Garden Av. Bexh. CR45 69
Garden Av. Hat. BP14 10
Garden Av. Mitch. BV50 76
Garden City Edg. BM29 37
Garden Clo. E4 CE28 39
Garden Clo. SW9 BX45 66
Garden Clo. SW15 BP47 75
Bristol Gdns.
Garden Clo. Ashf. BA50 73
Garden Clo. Bans. BS61 104
Garden Clo. Hamptn. BE49 74
Garden Clo. Lthd. BK66 111
Garden Clo. Nthlt. BE37 54
Garden Clo. Ruis. BB34 44
Garden Clo. Wall. BX56 95
Garden Clo. Wat. BB23 26
Garden Clo. Wey. AX56 92
Garden Cotts. Epsom BN59 94
Garden Cotts. Orp. CP51 89
Garden Court SE15 CA44 67
Sumner Estate
Garden Ct. Rich. BL44 65
Garden End, Amer. AP22 25
Gardener Gro. Felt. BE48 74
Gardeners Rd. E3 CC37 57
Gardeners Rd. Croy. BY54 86
Albion St.
Garden Fields, Ong. CW20 24
Gardenia Rd. Enf. CA25 30
Garden La. SW2 BX47 76
Garden La. Brom. CH50 78
Garden Pl. Dart. CV48 80
Garden Pl. Sid. CP50 79
Garden Reach, Ch. St. G. AR24 25
Garden Rd. NW8 BT38 1
Garden Rd. NW8 BT38 56
Garden Rd. SE20 CC51 87
Garden Rd. Brom. CH50 78
Garden Rd. Rich. BM45 65
Garden Rd. Sev. CV64 108
Garden Rd. Walt. BC53 83
Garden Rd. Wat. BB19 17
Garden Row SE1 BY41 4
Garden Row SE1 BY41 66
Gardens, The N8 BX31 47
Rectory Gdns.
Gardens, The N16 CA33 48
Gardens, The SE22 CB45 67
Gardens, The Beck. CF51 87
Gardens, The Esher BF56 93
Gardens, The Har. BG32 45
Gardens, The Hat. BR17 19
Gardens, The Pnr. BE32 45
Gardens, The Wat. BB23 26
Garden St. E1 CC39 57
Garden Terrace Rd. Harl. CP9 6
Garden Wk. EC2 CA38 2
Garden Wk. EC2 CA38 57
Rivington St.
Garden Wk. Couls. BV65 104
Garden Way NW10 BN36 55
Garden Way, Cat. BZ64 105
Garden Way, Loug. CL22 31
Gardiner Av. NW2 BQ35 46
Gardiner's Wk. Lthd. BF66 111
Gardner Clo. E11 CH32 49
Gardner Rd. E13 CH38 58
Gardner Rd. Guil. AR70 118
Gardners La. EC4 BZ40 4
Gardnor Rd. NW3 BT35 47
Flask Wk.
Gardon Clo. St. Alb. BJ13 9
Garendon Gdns. Mord. BS54 86
Garendon Rd. Mord. BS54 86
Gareth Clo. Wor. Pk. BQ55 85
Burnham Dr.
Gareth Gro. Brom. CH49 78
Garfield Pl. Wind. AO44 61
Albany Rd.
Garfield Rd. E4 CF26 39
Garfield Rd. E13 CG38 58
Garfield Rd. SW11 BV45 66
Garfield Rd. SW19 BT49 76
Garfield Rd. Enf. CC24 30
Garfield Rd. Twick. BJ47 74
York St.
Garfield Rd. Wey. AX56 92
Garfield St. Wat. BC22 26
Garford St. E14 CE40 57
Garibaldi Rd. Red. BU71 121
Garibaldi St. SE18 CN42 68
Garland Clo. Hem. H. AX13 8
Allandale
Garland Rd. SE18 CM43 68
Garland Rd. Stan. BL30 37
Garland Way, Horn. CW31 51
Garlands, Ton. CY71 117
Garlands Rd. Lthd. BJ64 102
Garlands Rd. Red. BU71 121
Garlichill Rd. Epsom BP62 103
Garlick Hill EC4 BZ40 4
Garlick Hill EC4 BZ40 57
Queen Victoria St.
Garlies Rd. SE23 CD48 77
Garlinge Rd. NW2 BR36 55
Garman Rd. N18 CB29 39
Garnault Ms. EC1 BY38 2
Garnault Ms. EC1 BY38 56
Hardwick St.
Garnault Rd. Enf. CA22 30
Garnault Pl. EC1 BY38 2
Garnault Pl. EC1 BY38 56
Myddelton St.
Garner Dri. Brox. CD16 21
Garner Rd. E17 CF30 39
Garners Clo. Ger. Cr. AS29 34
Garners End, Ger. Cr. AS29 34
Garners Rd. Ger. Cr. AS29 34
Garner St. E3 CB37 57
Coate St.
Garnet Rd. NW10 BO36 55
Garnet Rd. Th. Hth. BZ52 87
Garnet St. E1 CC40 57
Garnett Clo. SE9 CK45 68
Garnett Clo. Wat. BD22 27
Garnett Dr. St. Alb. BF18 18
Garnett Rd. NW3 BU35 47
Garnett Way E17 CD30 39
Mcentee Av.
Garnham Clo. N16 CA34 48
Smalley Rd.
Garnham St. N16 CA34 48
Garnies Clo. SE15 CA43 67
Garnles Clo. SE15 CA43 67
Thruxton Rd.
Garrad's Rd. SW16 BW48 76
Garrard Clo. Bexh. CR45 69
Garrard Clo. Chis. CL49 78
Garrard Rd. Bans. BS61 104
Garratt Clo. Croy. BX56 95
Croydon Rd.
Garratt La. SW17 BS46 76
Garratt La. SW18 BS46 76
Garratt Rd. Edg. BM29 37
Garratts La. Bans. BR61 103
Garratts Rd. Bush. BG26 36
Garratt Ter. SW17 BU49 76
Garrett St. EC1 BZ38 2
Garrett St. EC1 BZ38 57
Garrick Av. NW11 BR32 46
Garrick Clo. Croy. CB55 86
Garrick Cl. SW18 BT45 66
Garrick Clo. Rich. BK46 74
Green, The
Garrick Clo. Stai. AW50 73
Garrick Clo. Walt. BC56 92
Garrick Dr. NW4 BQ30 37
Garrick Gdns. N17 CA29 39
Garrick Gdns. E. Mol. BF52 84
Garrick Pk. NW4 BQ30 37
Garrick Rd. NW9 BO32 46
Garrick Rd. Grnf. BF38 54
Garrick Rd. Rich. BM44 65
Garrick St. WC2 BX40 4
Garrick St. WC2 BX40 56
Garrick Way NW4 BQ31 46
Garrison La. Chess. BK57 93
Garrod St. Grav. DG46 81
New Rd.
Garron La. S. Ock. CA40 60
Garrutt Rd. Upmin. CY34 51
Garry Clo. Rom. CT29 41
Garry Way Rom. CT29 41
Garside Clo. Hamptn. BF50 74
Garsmouth Way Wat. BD21 27
Garson La. Stai. AR47 72
Garston Cres. Wat. BD20 18
Garston Dr. Wat. BD20 18
Garston La. Ken. BZ60 96
Garston La. Wat. BD20 18
Garston La. Wat. BD21 27
Garston Park Pde. Wat. BD20 18
Garstons, The Lthd. BF66 111
Garth Clo. Kings. On T. BL49 75
Garth Clo. Mord. BQ54 85
Garth Clo. Ruis. BD33 45
Garth Ct. W4 BO42 65
Garth Rd.
Garthland Dr. Barn. BP25 28
Garthorne Rd. SE23 CC47 77
Garth Rd. W4 BN43 65
Garth Rd. Kings. On T. BL49 75
Garth Rd. Mord. BQ53 85
Garth Rd. Sev. CV67 117
Garth Rd. S. Ock. DB38 60
Garthside, Rich. BL49 75
Garth, The Cob. BE60 93
Garth, The Har. BL32 46
Garth, The Hamptn. BF50 74
Garth, The Wat. BA20 17
Garthay N12 BU29 38
Gartlett Rd. Wat. BC24 26
Gartmoor Gdns. SW19 BR47 75
Gartmore Rd. Ilf. CN34 49
Garton Pl. SW18 BT46 76
Garvary Rd. E16 CH39 58
Garvock Dr. Sev. CU66 116
Kippington Rd.
Garway Rd. W2 BS39 56
Gascoigne Gdns.
Wdf. Grn. CG29 40
Gascoigne Pl. E2 CA38 2
Gascoigne Pl. E2 CA38 57
Gascoigne Rd. Bark. CM37 58
Gascoigne Rd. Croy. CF58 96
Gascoigne Rd. Wey. AZ55 83
Gascony Av. NW6 BS36 56
Gascoyne Clo. Pot. B. BP19 19
Gascoyne Est. E9 CD36 57
Gascoyne Rd. E9 CC36 57
Gaselee St. E14 CF40 57
Gasholder Pl. SE11 BX42 4
Gasholder Pl. SE11 BX42 66
Gaskarth Rd. SW12 BV46 76
Gaskarth Rd. Edg. BN30 37
Gaskell Rd. N6 BU32 47
Gaskell St. SW4 BW44 66
Gaskin St. N1 BY37 2
Gaskin St. N1 BY37 56
Gaspar Ms. SW5 BS42 3
Gaspar Ms. SW5 BS42 66
Courtfield Gdns.
Gassiot Rd. SW17 BU49 76
Gassiot Way Sutt. BT55 86
Gasson Rd. Swans. DC46 81
Gastein Rd. W6 BQ43 65
Gaston Bell Clo. Rich. BL45 65
Stanmore Rd.
Gaston Bridge Rd. Shep. BA53 83
Gaston Rd. Mitch. BV52 86
Gaston Way, Shep. BA53 83
Gas Works Rd. Sthl. BE41 64
Gataker St. SE16 CB41 67
Gatcombe Rd. N19 BW34 47
Gate End, Nthwd. BC29 35
Gateford St. NW8 BU38 56
Gateforth St. NW8 BU38 1
Gateforth St. NW8 BU38 56
Gatehill, Nthwd. BB29 35
Gatehope Dr. S. Ock. CZ39 60
Gatehouse Clo.
Kings. On T. BN51 85
Gateley Rd. SW9 BX45 66
Gate Rd. Wey. AZ55 83
Gatesby St. SE17 BZ42 4
Gatesden Rd. Lthd. BG65 102
Gates Grn. Rd. W. Wick. CG55 88
Gateshead Rd. Borwd. BL23 28
Gateside Rd. SW17 BU48 76
Gatestone Rd. SE19 CA50 77
Gate St. WC2 BX39 2
Gate St. WC2 BX39 56
Kingsway
Gateway SE17 BZ43 4
Gateway SE17 BZ43 67
Walworth Rd.
Gateway Clo. Nthwd. BA29 35
Gateways, Guil. AT70 118
Gateways Surb. BL53 85
Surbiton Hill Rd.
Gateways, The SW3 BU42 3
Gateways, The SW3 BU42 66
Whiteheads Gro.
Gateway, The Wok. AU60 91
Gatewick Clo. Slou. AP40 52
Gathorne Rd. N22 BY30 38
Gathorne St. E2 CC37 57
Roman Rd.
Gatley Av. Epsom BM56 94
Gatliff Rd. SW1 BV42 3
Gatliff Rd. SW1 BV42 66
Gatling Rd. SE2 CO42 69
Gatton Bottom, Red. BU67 113
Gatton Clo. Reig. BT69 121
Gatton Clo. Sutt. BS58 95
Gatton Pk. Rd. Reig.
& Red. BT69 121
Gatton Rd. SW17 BU49 76
Gatton Rd. Reig. BT69 121
Gattons Way, Sid. CQ49 79
Gatward Clo. N21 BY25 29
Gatward Grn. N9 CA27 39
Gatwick Rd. SW18 BR47 75
Gatwick Rd. Grav. DG48 81
Gatwick Way, Horn. CW34 51
Gauden Clo. SW4 BW44 66
Gauden Rd. SW4 BW44 66
Gaunt Ct. Wem. BJ35 45
Harrow Rd.
Gauntlet Clo. BJ35 45
Gauntlet Clo. Nthlt. BE36 54
Yeoman Rd.
Gauntlett Rd. Sutt. BT56 95
Gaunt St. SE1 BY41 4
Gaunt St. SE1 BZ41 67
Newington Causeway
Gautrey Rd. SE15 CC44 67
Gavell Rd. Cob. BC60 92
Gavel St. SE17 BZ42 4
Gavel St. SE17 BZ42 67
Mason St.
Gaverick St. E14 CE42 67
Gaveston Dr. Berk. AQ12 7
Gavestone Clo. Wey. AY60 92
Gavestone Rd. SE12 CH47 78
Gaveston Rd. Lthd. BJ63 102
Gavina Clo. Mord. BT53 86
Gavin St. SE18 CN42 68
Gaviots Clo. Ger. Cr. AS33 43
Gaviots Grn. Ger. Cr. AS33 43
Gaviots Way, Ger. Cr. AS33 43
Gawber St. E2 CC38 57
Gawsworth Clo. E15 CG35 49
Gay Clo. NW2 BP35 46
Gayfere Rd. Epsom BP56 94
Gayfere Rd. Ilf. CK31 49
Gayfere St. SW1 BX41 4
Gayfere St. SW1 BX41 66
Gt. Peter St.
Gayford Rd. W12 BO41 65
Gay Gdns. Dag. CS35 50
Gayhurst Rd. E8 CB36 57
Gaylor Rd. Nthlt. BE35 45
Gaylor Rd. Til. DF44 71
Gaynes Ct. Upmin. CX35 51
Gaynesford Rd. SE23 CC48 77
Gaynesford Rd. Cars. BU57 95
Gaynes Hill Rd. Wdf. Grn. CK29 40
Gaynes Park Rd. Upmin. CX35 51
Gaynes Parkway, Upmin. CW34 51
Gaynes Rd. Upmin. CX34 51
Gay Rd. E15 CF37 57
Gaysham Av. Ilf. CL32 49
Gays La. Maid. AG43 61
Gayton Clo. Amer. AP21 25
Gayton Cres. NW3 BT35 47
Gayton Rd. NW3 BT35 47
Gayton Rd. SE2 CP42 69
Wilton Rd.
Gayton Rd. Har. BH32 45
Gayville Rd. SW11 BU46 76
Gaywood Av. Wal. Cr. CC18 21
Gaywood Clo. SW2 BY47 76
Gaywood Est. SE1 BY41 66
Gaywood Rd. E17 CE31 48
Gaywood Rd. Ash. BL62 103
Gaywood St. SE1 BY41 4
Gaywood St. SE1 BY41 66
Gaza St. SE17 BY42 4
Gaza St. SE17 BY42 66
Gazeley Ct. SE19 CA49 77
Gipsy Hill
Gazelle Glade, Grav. DJ49 81
Gean Wk. Hat. BP14 10
Geapins La. Upmin. CX36 60
Gear Ct. Brwd. DB26 42
Gear Dr.
Gear Dr. Brwd. DB26 42
Geariesville Gdns. Ilf. CL31 49
Geary Rd. NW10 BP35 46
Geary St. N7 BX35 47
Geddes Rd. Bush. BG24 27
Gedeney Rd. N17 BZ30 39
Gedling Pl. SE1 CA41 4
Gedling Pl. SE1 CA41 67
Abbey St.
Geere Rd. E15 CG37 58
Gees Ct. W1 BV39 1
Gees Ct. W1 BV39 56
Barrett St.
Gee St. EC1 BY38 2
Gee St. EC1 BY38 56
Geffrye Ct. N1 CA37 2
Geffrye Ct. N1 CA37 57
Geffrye St. E2 CA37 2
Geffrye St. E2 CA37 57
Geisthorp Ct. Wal. Abb. CH20 22
Winters Way
Geldart Rd. SE15 CB43 67
Geldeston Rd. E5 CB34 48
Gellatly Rd. SE14 CC44 67
Gell Clo. Uxb. AY35 44
Gemini Gro. Nthlt. BD38 54
Javeline Way
General Gordon Pl. SE18 CL42 68
General's Wk. The Enf. CD22 30
General Wolfe Rd. SE10 CF44 67
Genesta Glade, Grav. DJ49 81
Genesta Rd. SE18 CL43 68
Geneva Ct. N16 BZ33 48
Geneva Drive SW9 BY44 66
Loughborough Pk. Dev.
Geneva Gdns. Rom. CQ32 50
Geneva Rd. SW9 BY45 66
Geneva Rd. Kings. On T. BL52 85
Geneva Rd. Th. Hth. BZ53 87
Geneva Ter. SW9 BY45 66
Genever Clo. E4 CE28 39
Genista Rd. N18 CB28 39
Genoa Av. SW15 BQ46 75
Genoa Rd. SE20 CC51 87
Genotin Rd. Enf. BZ24 30
Gentian Row SE13 CF44 67
Sparta St.
Gentlemans Row, Enf. BZ24 30
Gentry Gdns. E13 CH38 58
Genyn Rd. Guil. AQ71 118
Geo. Crooks Ho. Grays DD43 71
New Rd.
Geoffrey Av. Rom. CX29 42
Geoffrey Gdns. E6 CK37 58
Geoffrey Rd. SE4 CD45 67
George Avey Cft. Epp. CR16 23
Church La.
George Comberton
Wk. E12 CK35 49
George Comberton
Wk. E12 CL35 49
Gainsborough Ave.
George Ct. WC2 BX40 56
Strand
George Cres. N10 BV29 38
George Downing Est.
N16 CA34 48

46

Street	Grid	Page
Glengall Rd. Edg.	BM27	37
Glengall Rd. Wdf. Grn.	CH29	40
Glengall Ter. SE15	**CA43**	**4**
Glengall Ter. SE15	CA43	67
Glen Gdns. Croy.	BY55	86
Glengarnock Av. E14	CF42	67
Glengarry Rd. SE22	CA46	77
Glenham Dr. Ilf.	CL32	49
Glenhaven Av. Borwd.	BM24	28
Glenhazel Chase Brwd.	DB21	33
Glenhead Clo. SE9	CL45	68
Glenhill Clo. N3	BS30	38
Glenhouse Rd. SE9	CL46	78
Glenhurst Av. NW5	BV35	47
Glenhurst Av. Bex.	CQ47	79
Glenhurst Av. Ruis.	BA33	44
Glenhurst Ri. SE19	BZ50	77
Glenhurst Rd. N12	BT28	38
Glenhurst Rd. Brent.	BK43	64
Glenilla Rd. NW3	BU36	56
Glenista Rd. N18	CB28	39
Glenister Pk. Rd. SW15	BW50	76
Glenister Pk. Rd. SW16	BW50	76
Glenister Rd. SE10	CG42	68
Glenister St. E16	CL40	58
Glenlea Rd. SE9	CK46	78
Glenloch Rd. NW3	BU36	56
Glenloch Rd. Enf.	CC23	30
Glenluce Rd. SE3	CH43	68
Glenlyn Av. St. Alb.	BJ14	9
Glenlyon Rd. SE9	CL46	78
Glenmere Av. NW7	BP29	37
Glenmore Clo. Wey.	AW55	83
Glenmore Rd. NW3	BU36	56
Glenmore Rd. Well.	CN43	68
Glenmore Way Bark.	CO37	59
Glenmount Path SE18	CM42	68
Raglan Rd.		
Glenn Av. Pur.	BY59	95
Glennie Rd. SE27	BY48	76
Glenny Rd. Bark.	CM36	58
Glenparke Rd. E7	CH36	58
Glen Rise Wdf. Grn.	CH29	40
Glen Rd. E13	CJ38	58
Glen Rd. E17	CD32	48
Glen Rd. Chess.	BL55	85
Glenrosa St. SW6	BT44	66
Glenroy St. W12	BQ39	55
Glensdale Rd. SE4	CD45	67
Glenshiel Rd. SE9	CL46	78
Glenside Chig.	CM29	40
Glenside Rd. SE18	CN42	68
Glentham Gdns. SW13	BP43	65
Glentham Rd.		
Glentham Rd. SW13	BP43	65
Glen, The Croy.	CC55	87
Glen, The Enf.	BY24	29
Glen, The Hem. H.	AY11	8
Glen, The Orp.	CK55	88
Glen, The Pnr.	BC32	44
Glen, The Pnr.	BE33	45
Glen, The Rain.	CV38	60
Glen, The Slou.	AR41	62
Glen, The Sthl.	BE42	64
Glen, The Wem.	BK35	45
Glen, The Wey.	AV56	91
Glenthorne Av. Croy.	CB54	87
Glenthorne Clo. Sutt.	BS54	86
Glenthorne Gdns. Sutt.	BS54	86
Glenthorne Rd. E17	CD32	48
Glenthorne Rd. N11	BU28	38
Glenthorne Rd. W6	BP42	65
Glenthorne Rd. Kings. on T.	BL52	85
Glenthorn Gdns. Ilf.	CL31	49
Glenthorpe Rd. Mord.	BQ53	85
Glenton Clo. Rom.	CT29	41
Glenton Rd. SE13	CG45	68
Glenton Way Rom.	CT29	41
Glentrammon Av. Orp.	CN57	97
Glentrammon Clo. Orp.	CN56	97
Glentrammon Gdns. Orp.	CN57	97
Glentrammon Rd. Orp.	CN57	97
Glentworth Pl. Slou.	AO40	61
Glentworth St. NW1	**BU38**	**1**
Glentworth St. NW1	BU38	56
Glenure Rd. SE9	CL46	78
Glenview SE2	CP43	69
Glen Vw. Grav.	DH47	81
Glenview Rd. Brom.	CJ51	88
Glenview Rd. Hem. H.	AW13	8
Glenville Av. Enf.	BZ22	30
Glenville Av. Enf.	BZ23	30
Glenville Clo. Surb.	BN54	85
Glenville Gro. SE8	CD43	67
Glenville Rd. Kings. On T.	BM51	85
Glen Way, Wat.	BB22	26
Glen Wood, Dor.	BK72	119
Glenwood Av. NW9	BN33	46
Glenwood Av. Rain.	CU38	59
Glenwood Clo. Har.	BH32	45
Glenwood Dr. Rom.	CU31	50
Glenwood Gdns. Ilf.	CL32	49
Glenwood Gro. NW9	BN33	46
Glenwood Rd. N15	BY32	47
Glenwood Rd. NW7	BO27	37
Glenwood Rd. SE6	CD47	77
Glenwood Rd. Epsom	BP57	94
Glenwood Rd. Houns.	BG45	64
Glenwood Way, Croy.	CC53	87
Glenworth Av. E14	CF42	67
Glevium Clo. St. Alb.	BE14	9
Gliddon Rd. W14	BR42	65
Glimpsing Grn. Belv.	CQ41	69
Glisson Rd. Uxb.	AZ37	53
Gload Cres. Orp.	CP55	89
Globe Cres. E15	CG35	49
Globe La. SE18	CL41	68
Globe Rd. E1	CC38	57
Globe Rd. E2	CC38	57
Globe Rd. E15	CG35	49
Globe Rd. Horn.	CU32	50
Gloe Rd. Wdf. Grn.	CJ29	40
Globe St. SE1	**BZ41**	**4**
Globe St. SE1	BZ41	67
Globe Ter. E2	CC38	57
Globe Rd.		
Glory Mead, Dor.	BJ73	119
Glossop Rd. Sth. Croy.	BZ58	96
Gloster Rd. N. Mal.	BO52	85
Gloster Rd. Wok.	AT63	100
Gloucester Ave. Grays.	DE41	71
Gloucester Av. NW1	**BV36**	**1**
Gloucester Av. NW1	BV6	56
Gloucester Av. Horn.	CW31	51
Gloucester Av. Sid.	CN48	78
Gloucester Av. Slou.	AO39	52
Gloucester Av. Wal. Cr.	CD20	21
Gloucester Av. Well.	CN45	68
Gloucester Cir. SE10	CF43	67
Gloucester Clo. NW10	BN36	55
Gloucester Clo. Surb.	BJ54	84
Gloucester Ct. EC3	**CA40**	**4**
Tower Hill		
Gloucester Ct. W3	BM39	55
Links Rd.		
Gloucester Ct. Rich.	BM43	65
Gloucester Cres. NW1	**BV37**	**1**
Gloucester Cres. NW1	BV37	56
Gloucester Cres. Stai.	AX50	73
Gloucester Dr. N4	BY34	47
Gloucester Dr. NW11	BS31	47
Gloucester Dr. Stai.	AU48	72
Gloucester Gdns. NW11	BR33	46
Gloucester Gdns. W2	**BT39**	**1**
Gloucester Gdns. W2	BT39	56
Gloucester Gdns. Barn.	BV24	29
Gloucester Gdns. Ilf.	CK33	49
Gloucester Gdns. Sutt.	BS55	86
Gloucester Gate NW1	**BV37**	**1**
Gloucester Gate NW1	BV37	56
Gloucester Gro. SE15	CA43	67
Gloucester Gro. Edg.	BN30	37
Gloucester Ms. NW1	BV37	56
Albany St.		
Gloucester Ms. W2	**BT39**	**1**
Gloucester Ms. W2	BT39	56
Gloucester Ms. W. W2	**BT39**	**1**
Gloucester Ms. W. W2	BT39	56
Gloucester Parade Sid.	CO46	79
Gloucester Pl. NW1	**BU38**	**1**
Gloucester Pl. NW1	BU38	56
Gloucester Pl. W1	BU39	56
Gloucester Pl. Wind.	AO44	61
Gloucester Pl. Ms. W1	**BU39**	**1**
Gloucester Pl. Ms W1	BU39	56
Gloucester Rd. E10	CE33	48
Gloucester Rd. E11	CH32	49
Gloucester Rd. E12	CK35	49
Gloucester Rd. E17	CC30	39
Gloucester Rd. N17	BZ30	39
Gloucester Rd. N18	CA28	39
Gloucester Rd. SW7	**BT41**	**3**
Gloucester Rd. SW7	BT41	66
Gloucester Rd. W3	BN41	65
Gloucester Rd. W5	BK41	64
Gloucester Rd. Barn.	BS25	29
Gloucester Rd. Belv.	CQ42	69
Gloucester Rd. Brwd.	DA25	33
Gloucester Rd. Croy.	BZ54	87
Gloucester Rd. Dart.	CU47	79
Gloucester Rd. Enf.	BZ22	30
Gloucester Rd. Felt.	BD47	74
Gloucester Rd. Grav.	DG49	81
Gloucester Rd. Guil.	AP69	118
Gloucester Rd. Har.	BF32	45
Gloucester Rd. Hmptn.	BF50	74
Gloucester Rd. Houns.	BE45	64
Gloucester Rd. Kings. On T.	BM51	85
Gloucester Rd. Red.	BU70	121
Gloucester Rd. Rich.	BM43	65
Gloucester Rd. Rom.	CT32	50
Gloucester Rd. Tedd.	BH49	74
Gloucester Rd. Twick.	BG47	74
Gloucester Sq. W2	**BT39**	**1**
Gloucester Sq. W2	BT39	56
Gloucester St. SW1	**BW42**	**3**
Gloucester St. SW1	BW42	66
Gloucester St. Red.	BU70	121
Gloucester Ter. NW1	BV37	56
Outer Circle		
Gloucester Ter. W2	**BS39**	**1**
Gloucester Ter. W2	BS39	56
Gloucester Wk. W8	BS41	66
Gloucester Way EC1	**BY38**	**2**
Gloucester Way EC1	BY38	56
Glover Rd. Pnr.	BD32	45
Glovers Field, Brwd.	CZ22	33
Glovers La. Harl.	CQ13	14
Glovers Rd. Reig.	BS71	121
Gloxinia Rd. Grav.	DD50	81
Glycena Rd. SW11	BU45	66
Glyn Av. Barn.	BT24	29
Glyn Clo. SE25	CA51	87
Grange Hill		
Glyn Clo. Epsom	BP58	94
Glyn Ct. SE27	BY48	76
Glynde Ms. SW3	**BU41**	**3**
Glynde Ms. SW3	BU41	66
Yeomans Row		
Glynde Rd. Bexh.	CP45	69
Glynde St. SE4	CD46	77
Glyndon Rd. SE18	CM42	68
Glyn Dr. Sid.	CO49	79
Glynfield Rd. NW10	BO36	55
Glynn Rd. Enf.	CC24	30
Glyn Rd. E5	CC34	48
Glyn Rd. Wor. Pk.	BQ55	85
Glyn St. SE11	**BX42**	**4**
Glyn St. SE11	BX42	66
Glynswood Ger. Cr.	AS29	34
Glynwood Ct. SE26	CC48	77
Glynwood Dr.		
Glynwood Dr. SE26	CC48	77
Goat Ho. Br. SE25	CB52	87
Goat La. Enf.	CA22	30
Goat La. Surb.	BJ55	84
Goat Rd. Mitch.	BU54	86
Goatsfield Rd. West.	CJ63	106
Goatswood La. Houns.	CU41	41
Gobions Rom.	CR30	41
Gobions Av. Rom.	CS29	41
Gobions Way, Pot. B.	BS17	20
Gobins Grn. Welw. G. C.	BQ8	5
Gobins Grn. Welw. G. C.	BR8	5
Godalming Av. Wall.	BX56	95
Godalming By Pass, Guil.	AR70	118
Godalming Rd. E14	CE39	57
Chrisp St.		
Godbold Rd. E15	CG38	58
Goddard Clo. Shep.	AY52	83
Magdalens Rd.		
Goddard Rd. Beck.	CC52	87
Goddard Rd. Grays.	DD40	71
Goddards Clo. Hert.	BW13	11
Goddington Chase Orp.	CO56	98
Goddington La. Orp.	CO55	89
Godfrey Av. Nthlt.	BE37	54
Godfrey Av. Twick.	BG47	74
Godfrey Hl. SE18	CK42	68
Godfrey Rd. SE18	CK42	68
Godfrey St. E15	CF37	57
Godfrey St. SW3	**BU42**	**3**
Godfrey St. SW3	BU42	66
Godfrey Way, Houns.	BE47	74
Godfrey Way, Houns.	BG45	64
Hanworth Rd.		
Godfries Clo. Welw.	BU5	5
Goding St. SE11	**BX42**	**4**
Goding St. SE11	BX42	66
Godley Rd. SW18	BT47	76
Godley Rd. Wey.	AY60	92
Godliman St. EC4	**BY39**	**2**
Godliman St. EC4	BY39	56
Godlophin Clo. Sutt.	BR58	94
Godman Rd. SE15	CB44	67
Godman Rd. Grays.	DG41	71
Godolphin Rd. W12	BP40	55
Godolphin Rd. Beac.	AO29	34
Godolphin Rd. Slou.	AO40	52
Godolphin Rd. Wey.	BA57	92
Godric Cres. Croy.	CF58	96
Godson Rd. Croy.	BY55	86
Godson St. N1	BY37	56
Godstone Hill, Gdse.	CB67	114
Godstone Rd. Cat.	CB65	105
Godstone Rd. Cat.	CB66	114
Godstone Rd. Oxt.	CE69	114
Godstone Rd. Pur.	BY59	95
Godstone Rd. Red.	CA70	114
Godstone Rd. Sutt.	BT56	95
Godstone Rd. Twick.	BJ46	74
Godstow Rd. SE2	CO41	69
Godwin Ct. NW1	**BW37**	**1**
Godwin Ct. NW1	BW37	56
Chalton St.		
Godwin Rd. E7	CH35	49
Godwin Rd. Brom.	CJ52	88
Goffers Rd. SE3	CG44	68
Goff's Cres. Wal. Cr.	BZ18	21
Goff's La. Wal. Cr.	BZ18	21
Goff's Oak Av. Wal. Cr.	BZ17	21
Goffs Rd. Ashf.	BA50	73
Gogmore Fm. Clo. Cher.	AV53	82
Gogmore La. Cher.	AW54	83
Goidel Clo. Wall.	BW56	95
Golborne Gdns. W10	BR38	55
Golborne Rd.		
Golborne Rd. W10	BR39	55
Golda Clo. Barn.	BQ25	28
Goldbeaters Gro. Edg.	BO29	37
Goldcliff Clo. Mord.	BS54	86
Goldcrest Way Bush.	BG26	36
Goldcrest Way Croy.	CF58	96
Goldcrest Way Pur.	BW58	95
Gt. Woodcote Dr.		
Gold Cft. Hem. H.	AZ14	8
Golden Ct. Rich.	BK46	74
George St.		
Golden Cres. Hayes	BB40	53
Golden Dell. Welw. G C.	BR10	5
Golden La. EC1	**BZ38**	**2**
Golden La. EC1	BZ38	57
Golden La. Est. EC1	BZ38	57
Golden Manor W7	BH40	54
Golden Sq. W1	**BW40**	**3**
Golden Sq. W1	BW40	56
Golders Clo. Edg.	BM28	37
Golders Gdns. NW11	BR33	46
Golders Gn. Cres. NW11	BR33	46
Golders Gn. Rd. NW11	BR32	46
Golders Grn. Rd. NW11	BR32	46
Golders Manor Dr. NW4	BQ32	46
Golders Pk. Clo.NW11	BS33	47
Golders Rise NW4	BQ32	46
Golders Way NW11	BR33	46
Goldfinch Gdn. Guil.	AU70	118
Goldfinch Rd. Sth. Croy.	CC58	96
Goldford Pl. NW1	**BU38**	**1**
Goldfort Wk. Wok.	AP61	100
Langmans Way		
Goldhawk Rd. W6	BO42	65
Goldhawk Rd. W12	BO42	65
Goldhawk Rd. W12	BP41	65
Titmuss St. W12		
Gold Hill Edg.	BN29	37
Gold Hill, E. Ger. Cr.	AR30	34
Gold Hill, N. Ger. Cr.	AR30	34
Gold Hill, West. Ger. Cr.	AR30	34
Goldhurst Ter. NW6	**BS36**	**1**
Goldhurst Ter. NW6	BS36	56
Goldingham Av. Loug.	CM23	31
Golding Rd. Sev.	CV64	108
Goldings Cross. Hat.	BP12	10
Goldings Hill, Loug.	CK22	31
Goldings Hill, Loug.	CK23	31
Goldings Rise, Loug.	CL23	31
Goldings Rd. Loug.	CL23	31
Golding St. E1	CB39	57
Goldington Clo. Hodd.	CD10	12
Goldington Cres. NW1	**BW37**	**1**
Goldington Cres. NW1	BW37	56
Goldington St. NW1	**BW37**	**1**
Goldington St. NW1	BW37	56
Gold La. Edg.	BN29	37
Goldman Clo. E2	**CA38**	**2**
Goldney Rd. W9	BS38	56
Goldrings Rd. Lthd.	BF60	93
Goldsboro' Rd. SW8	BW44	66
Goldsborough Cres. E4	CE27	39
Goldsdown Clo. Enf.	CD23	30
Goldsdown Rd. Enf.	CC23	30
Goldsell Rd. Swan.	CS53	89
Goldsmid St. SE18	CN42	68
Sladedale Rd.		
Goldsmith Av. E12	CK36	58
Goldsmith Av. NW9	BO32	46
Goldsmith Av. Rom.	CR33	50
Goldsmith Clo. W3	BN40	55
East Acton La.		
Goldsmith Clo. Har.	BF33	45
Goldsmith La. NW9	BM31	46
Goldsmith Rd. E10	CE33	48
Goldsmith Rd. E17	CC30	39
Goldsmith Rd. N11	BU28	38
Goldsmith Rd. SE15	CB44	67
Goldsmith Rd. W3	BN40	55
Goldsmiths Av. W3	BN40	55
Goldsmiths Clo. Wok.	AR62	100
Goldsmith's Row E2	**CB37**	**2**
Goldsmith's Row E2	CB37	57
Goldsmiths Sq. E2	CB37	57
Goldsmith St. EC2	BZ39	57
Gutter La.		
Goldsworth Orchard, Wok.	AQ62	100
Goldsworth Rd. Wok.	AR62	100
Goldsworthy Gdns. SE16	CC42	67
Goldwell Rd. Th. Hth.	BX52	86
Goldwin Clo. SE15	CC44	67
Pomeroy St.		
Golf Clo. Bush.	BD23	27
Golf Clo. Stan.	BK29	36
Golf Clo. Wok.	AV60	91
Golf Club Rd. Wey.	AZ58	92
Golf Club Rd. Wok.	AQ63	100
Gold Course Dr. Kings. On T.	BN50	75
Golfe Rd. Ilf.	CM34	49
Golf Links Av. Grav.	DG49	81
Golford Pl. NW1	BU38	56
Lisson Gro.		
Golf Ride Enf.	BY21	29
Golf Rd. W5	BL39	55
Boileau Rd.		
Golf Rd. Brom.	CL52	88
Golf Rd. Ken.	BZ62	105
Golf Side, Sutt.	BR59	94
Golf Side, Twick.	BG48	74
Golfside Clo. N. Mal.	BO51	85
Goliath Clo. Wall.	BX57	95
Gollogly Terr. SE7	CJ42	68
Nadine St.		
Gombards All. St. Alb.	BG13	9
Gomer Gdns. Tedd.	BJ50	74
Gomer Pl. Tedd.	BJ49	74
Gomm Rd. SE16	CC41	67
Gomshall Av. Wall.	BX56	95
Gomshall Gdns. Ken.	BZ61	105
Gomshall Rd. Sutt.	BQ58	94
Gonson Pl. SE8	CE43	67
Gonson St. SE8	CE43	67
Gonston Cl. SW19	BR48	75
Queensmere Rd.		
Gonston Cl. SW19	BQ48	75
Bodicott Cl.		
Gonville Av. Rick.	AZ25	26
Gonville Cres. Nthlt.	BF36	54
Gonville Rd. Th. Hth.	BX53	86
Gonville St. SW6	BR45	65
Putney Br. App.		
Goodall Rd. E11	CF35	48
Goodbury Rd. Sev.	CX60	99
Good Clo. Couls.	BY63	104
Gooden Ct. Har.	BH34	45
Goodenough Rd. SW19	BR50	75
Goodenough Wy. Couls.	BX63	104
Goodge Pl. W1	**BW39**	**1**
Goodge Pl. W1	BW39	56
Goodge St.		
Goodge St. W1	**BW39**	**1**
Goodge St. W1	BW39	56
Goodhall St. NW10	BO38	55
Goodhart Way W. Wick.	CG54	88
Goodhews Gdns. NW4	BP30	37
Goodinge Clo. N7	BX35	47
North Rd.		
Goodinge Rd. N7	BX36	56
Goodley Stock Rd. Eden.	CL69	115
Goodley Stock Rd. West.	CL67	115
Goodman Cres. SW2	BX48	76
Goodman Pk. Slou.	AR40	52
Goodman Pla. Stai.	AV49	72
High St.		
Goodman Rd. E10	CF33	48
Goodmans Stile Rd. E1	CA39	57
Alie St.		
Goodman St. E1	**CB39**	**2**
Goodman St. E1	CA39	57
Goodman's Yd. E1	CA40	57
Goodmayes Av. Ilf.	CO33	50
Goodmayes La. Ilf.	CO35	50
Goodmayes Rd. Ilf.	CO33	50
Goodmead Rd. Orp.	CO54	89
Goodrich Clo. Wat.	BC21	26
Goodrich Rd. SE22	CA46	77
Goodson Rd. NW10	BO36	55
Goodson St. N1	**BY37**	**2**
Goods Way NW1	**BW37**	**1**
Goods Way NW1	**BX37**	**2**
Goods Way NW1	BW37	56
Goodway Gdns. E14	CF39	57
Goodwin Dr. Sid.	CP48	79
Goodwin Gdns. Croy.	BY57	95
Goodwin Rd. N9	CC26	39
Goodwin Rd. W12	BP41	65
Goodwin Rd. Croy.	BY57	95
Goodwins Ct. WC2	**BX40**	**4**
Goodwin's Ct. WC2	BX40	56
St. Martins La.		
Goodwin St. N4	BY34	47
Fonthill Rd.		
Goodwood Av. Horn.	CW35	51
Goodwood Av. Wat.	BB21	26
Goodwood Clo. Hodd.	CE11	12
Goodwood Clo. Mord.	BS52	86
Goodwood Cres. Grav.	DH49	81
Goodwood Crs. Grav.	DH50	81
Goodwood Dr. Nthlt.	BF36	54
Goodwood Pde. Wat.	BB21	26
Goodwood Rd. SE14	CD43	67
Goodwood Rd. Red.	BU69	121
Goodwyn Av. NW7	BO28	37
Goodwyns Farm Est. Dor.	BJ73	119
Goodwyns Rd. Dor.	BJ73	119
Goodwyn's Vale N10	BV30	38
Goodyear Pl. SE5	BZ43	67
Addington Sq.		
Goodyear Ter. Grays.	DA43	70
Goodyers Av. Rad.	BH20	18
Goodyers Gdns. NW4	BQ32	46
Brent Green		
Goose Acre, Welw. G. C.	BR9	5
Gooseacre La. Har.	BK32	45
Goose Croft, Hem. H.	AV13	7
Goosefield, E. Mol.	BF52	84
Goose Grn. Cob.	BC63	101
Goose La. Wok.	AQ64	100
Gooseley La. E6	CL38	58
Goose Rye Rd. Guil.	AO66	109
Goose Yd. EC1	**BY37**	**2**
Goose Yd. EC1	BY37	56
St. John St.		
Gooshays Dr. Rom.	CW28	42
Gooshays Gdns. Rom.	CW29	42
Gophir La. EC4	BZ40	57
Bush La.		
Gopsall St. N1	**BZ37**	**2**
Gopsall St. N1	BZ37	57
Gorden Gdns. Edg.	BM30	37
Gordon Av. E4	CG29	40
Gordon Av. SW14	BO45	65
Gordon Av. Horn.	CT34	50
Gordon Av. Stan.	BH29	36
Gordon Av. Stan.	BJ29	36
Gordon Av. Sth. Croy.	BZ58	96
Gordon Av. Twick.	BJ46	74
Gordonbrock Rd. SE4	CE46	77
Gordon Clo. N19	BW33	47
Highgate Hill		
Gordon Clo. Cher.	AV55	82
Gordon Clo. Stai.	AW50	73
Gordon Clo. St. Alb.	BJ14	9
Gordon Ct. W12	BQ39	55
Gordon Cres. Croy.	CA54	87
Gordon Cres. Hayes	BC41	63
Gordondale Rd. SW19	BS48	76
Gordon Dr. Cher.	AV55	82
Gordon Gro. SE5	BY44	66
Gordon Hill Enf.	BZ23	30
Gordon House Rd. NW5	BV35	47
Gordon Pl. W8	BS41	66
Gordon Prom. Grav.	DH46	81
Gordon Rd. E4	CG26	40
Gordon Rd. E11	CH32	49
Gordon Rd. E12	CL34	49
Gordon Rd. E15	CF35	48
Gordon Rd. E17	CD32	48
Gordon Rd. E18	CH30	40
Gordon Rd. N3	BR29	37
Gordon Rd. N9	CB27	39
Gordon Rd. N11	BW29	38
Gordon Rd. NW6	BS38	56
Gordon Rd. SE15	CB44	67
Gordon Rd. W4	BM43	65
Gordon Rd. W5	BK40	54
Gordon Rd. W13	BJ40	54
Gordon Rd. Ashf.	AY48	73
Gordon Rd. Bark.	CN37	58
Gordon Rd. Beck.	CC51	87
Gordon Rd. Beck.	CD52	87
Gordon Rd. Belv.	CS42	69
Gordon Rd. Brwd.	DD26	122
Gordon Rd. Cars.	BU57	95
Gordon Rd. Cat.	BZ64	105
Gordon Rd. Chesh.	AO19	16
Gordon Rd. Dart.	CV47	80
Gordon Rd. Enf.	BZ23	30
Gordon Rd. Esher	BH57	93
Gordon Rd. Grav.	DF47	81
Gordon Rd. Grays.	DF41	71
Gordon Rd. Har.	BH31	45
Gordon Rd. Houns.	BG45	64
Gordon Rd. Ilf.	CM34	49
Gordon Rd. Kings. On T.	BL51	85
Gordon Rd. Red.	BV69	121
Gordon Rd. Rich.	BL44	65
Gordon Rd. Rom.	CQ32	50
Gordon Rd. Sev.	CU66	116
Gordon Rd. Shep.	BA53	83
Gordon Rd. Sid.	CN46	78
Gordon Rd. Stai.	AU49	72
Gordon Rd. Sthl.	BE42	64
Gordon Rd. Surb.	BL54	85
Gordon Rd. Wal. Abb.	CE20	21
Gordon Rd. West Dr.	AY40	53
Gordon Rd. Wind.	AM44	61
Gordon Sq. WC1	**BW38**	**1**
Gordon Sq. WC1	BW38	56
Gordon St. E13	CH38	58
Gordon St. WC1	**BW38**	**1**
Gordon St. WC1	BW38	56
Gordon St. Twick.	BJ46	74
Gordon Way, Barn.	BR24	28
Gordons Way, Oxt.	CF67	114
Gordon Way, Ch. St. G.	AQ27	34
Gore Clo. Wat.	BC21	26
Gore Ct. NW9	BM32	46
Gorefield Pl. NW6	BS37	56
Gorelands La. Ch. St. G.	AR26	34
Gore Rd. E9	CC37	57
Gore Rd. SW20	BQ51	85
Gore Rd. Dart.	CY47	80
Goresbrook Rd. Dag.	CO37	59
Gore St. SW7	**BT41**	**3**
Gore St. SW7	BT41	66
Gorhambury Dr. St. Alb.	BE12	9
Gorham Dr. St. Alb.	BH15	9
Gorham Pl. W11	BR40	55
Mary Pl.		
Goring Clo. Rom.	CS30	41
Goring Gdns. Dag.	CP35	50
Goring Rd. N11	BX29	38
Goring Rd. Dag.	CS36	59
Goring Rd. Stai.	AV49	72
Goring Rd. N. Dag.	CS36	59
Goring Sq. Stai.	AV49	72
Goring St. EC3	**CA39**	**2**

Street	Grid	Page
Goring St. EC3	CA39	57
Houndsditch		
Goring Way Grnf.	BG37	54
Gorle Station St. W14	BR43	65
Gorleston Rd. N15	BZ32	48
Gorleston St. W14	BR42	65
Gorman Rd. SE18	CK42	68
Gorringe Av. S. Dnth.	CY51	90
Gorringe Pk. Av. Mitch.	BU50	76
Gorse Cl. Hat.	BO14	10
Gorse Hill, Farn.	CX54	90
Gorse Hill La. Vir. W.	AR52	82
Gorse Hill Rd. Vir. W.	AR52	82
Gorse La. Wok.	AP57	91
Windsor Rd.		
Gorselands Clo. Wey.	AX59	92
Gorse Rise SW17	BV49	76
Gorse Rd. Croy.	CE56	96
Gorse Rd. Orp.	CQ54	89
Gorse Wk. West Dr.	AY39	53
Gorse Way Rom.	CT33	50
Gorsewood Rd. Wok.	AO63	100
Gorst Rd. NW10	BN38	55
Gorst Rd. SW11	BU46	76
Gorsuch Pl. E2	**CA38**	**2**
Gorsuch St. E2	**CA38**	**2**
Gorsuch St. E2	CA38	57
Gosberton Rd. SW12	BU47	76
Gosbury Hill Chess.	BL56	94
Gosden Hill Rd. Guil.	AU68	109
Gosfield Rd. Dag.	CR33	50
Gosfield Rd. Dag.	CR34	50
Gosfield Rd. Epsom	BN59	94
Gosfield St. W1	**BV39**	**1**
Gosfield St. W1	BW39	56
Gosford Gdns. Ilf.	CK32	49
Gosforth La. Wat.	BC27	35
Goshawk Gdns. Hayes	BB38	53
Goslett Yd. WC2	**BW39**	**1**
Goslett Yd. WC2	BW39	56
Charing Cross Rd.		
Gosling Clo. Grnf.	BF38	54
Gosling Green Rd. Slou.	AS41	62
Gosling Way SW9	BY44	66
Gospatrick Rd. N17	BZ29	39
Gospel Oak Est. NW5	BU35	47
Gosport Dr. Horn.	CV36	60
Gosport Rd. E17	CD32	48
Gosport Way SE15	CA43	67
Gossage Rd. SE18	CM42	68
Ancona Rd.		
Gossage Rd. Uxb.	AY36	53
Gossamers, The Wat.	BE21	27
Gosset St. E2	**CA38**	**2**
Gosset St. E2	CA38	57
Goss Hill Swan.	CV50	80
Gosshill Rd. Brom.	CL51	88
Gossoms End, Berk.	AQ12	7
Gosterwood St. SE8	CD43	67
Gostling Rd. Twick.	BF47	74
Goston Gdns. Th. Hth.	BY52	86
Goswell Pl. EC1	**BY38**	**2**
Goswell Pl. Wind.	AO44	61
Goswell Rd. EC1	**BY37**	**2**
Goswell Rd. EC1	BY37	56
Goswell Pl. EC1	BY38	56
Goswell Rd.		
Goswell Rd. Wind.	AO43	61
Gothic Clo. Dart.	CW48	80
Gothic Ct. Hayes	BA43	63
Gothic Rd. Twick.	BG48	74
Goudhurst Rd. Brom.	CG49	78
Gouge Av. Grav.	DF47	81
Gough Rd. E15	CG35	49
Gough Rd. Enf.	CB23	30
Gough Sq. EC4	**BY39**	**2**
Gough Sq. EC4	BY39	56
Gough St. WC1	**BX38**	**2**
Gough St. WC1	BX38	56
Gould Cl. Hat.	BP15	10
Gould Ct. SE19	CA49	77
Gould Ct. Guil.	AU69	118
Eustack Rd.		
Gould Rd. Felt.	BB47	73
Gould Rd. Twick.	BH47	74
Gould's Grn. Uxb.	AZ40	53
Goulston St. E1	**CA39**	**2**
Goulston St. E1	CA39	57
Goulton Rd. E5	CB35	48
Gourley St. N15	CA32	48
Gourock Rd. SE9	CL46	78
Govan St. E2	CB37	57
Whiston Rd.		
Government Row, Enf.	CE22	30
Governors Av. Uxb.	AV32	43
Govett Av. Shep.	BA53	83
Gowan Av SW6	BR44	65
Gowan Rd. NW10	BP36	55
Gower Clo. E15	CG36	58
Gower Ct. WC1	**BW38**	**1**
Gower Ms. WC1	**BW39**	**1**
Gower Ms. WC1	BW39	56
Gower Pl. WC1	**BW38**	**1**
Gower Pl. WC1	BW38	56
Gower Rd. E7	CH36	58
Gower Rd. Islw.	BH43	64
Gower Rd. Wey.	BA57	92
Gowers La. Grays.	DF41	71
Gowers, The Amer.	AP22	25
Gowers, The Harl.	CO10	6
Gower St. WC1	**BW38**	**1**
Gower St. WC1	BW38	56
Gowers Wk. E1	**CB39**	**2**
Gowers Wk. E1	CB39	57
Gower, The Egh.	AT52	82
Gowland Pl. Beck.	CD51	87
Gowlett Rd. SE15	CB45	67
Gowrie Rd. SW11	BV45	66
Graburn Way, E. Mol.	BG52	84
Grace Av. Bexh.	CQ44	69
Gracechurch St. EC3	**BZ40**	**4**
Gracechurch St. EC3	BZ40	57
Gracedale Rd. SW16	BV49	76
Gracefield Gdns. SW16	BX48	76
Grace Path SE26	CC49	77
Silverdale Rd.		
Grace Rd. Croy.	BZ53	87
Grace's Alley E1	CB40	57
Ensign St.		
Grace's Ms. SE5	BZ44	67
Grace's Rd. SE5	CA44	67
Grace St. E3	CE38	57
Gracious La. Sev.	CU68	116
Gracious Pond Rd. Wok.	AQ57	91
Gradient, The SE26	CB49	77
Graemar Turn, Hem. H.	AZ10	8
Graeme Rd. Enf.	BZ23	30
Graemesdyke Av. SW14	BM45	65
Graemes Dyke Rd. Berk.	AQ13	7
Grafton Clo. W13	BJ39	54
Grafton Clo. Slou.	AS39	52
Grafton Clo. Wey.	AV60	91
Grafton Clo. Wor. Pk.	BO55	85
Grafton Cres. NW1	BV36	56
Grafton Gdns. N4	CB32	48
Rutland Gdns.		
Grafton Gdns. Dag.	CQ34	50
Grafton Ms. W1	**BW38**	**1**
Grafton Ms. W1	BW38	56
Grafton Way		
Grafton Pk. Rd. N. Mal.	BO55	85
Grafton Pl. NW1	**BW38**	**1**
Grafton Pl. NW1	BW38	56
Grafton Rd. NW5	BV35	47
Grafton Rd. W3	BN40	55
Grafton Rd. Croy.	BY54	86
Grafton Rd. Dag.	CQ34	50
Grafton Rd. Enf.	BX24	29
Grafton Rd. Har.	BG32	45
Grafton Rd. N. Mal.	BO52	85
Grafton Rd. Wor. Pk.	BN55	85
Grafton Sq. SW4	BW45	66
Grafton St. NW3	BS34	47
Hermitage La.		
Grafton St. W1	**BV40**	**3**
Grafton St. W1	BV40	56
Grafton Ter. NW2	BS34	47
Hermitage La.		
Grafton Ter. NW5	BU35	47
Grafton Way NW1	BW38	56
Grafton Way W1	**BW38**	**1**
Grafton Way WC1	BW38	56
Grafton Yd. NW5	BV36	56
Prince of Wales Rd.		
Graham Av. W13	BJ41	64
Graham Av. Brox.	CD14	12
Graham Av. Mitch.	BV51	86
Graham Clo. Croy.	CE55	87
Grahame Park Est. NW9	BO30	37
Grahame Park Way NW9	BO30	37
Graham Gdns. Surb.	BL54	85
Graham Rd. E8	CB36	57
Graham Rd. E13	CH38	58
Graham Rd. N15	BY31	47
Graham Rd. NW4	BP32	46
Graham Rd. SW19	BR50	75
Graham Rd. W4	BN41	65
Graham Rd. Bexh.	CQ45	69
Graham Rd. Hamptn.	BF49	74
Graham Rd. Har.	BG31	45
Graham Rd. Mitch.	BV51	86
Graham Rd. Pur.	BY60	95
Graham St. N1	**BY37**	**2**
Graham St. N1	BY37	56
Graham Ter. SW1	**BV42**	**3**
Graham Ter. SW1	BV42	66
Grainger Clo. Nthlt.	BG35	45
Grainger Rd. N22	BZ30	39
Grainger Rd. Islw.	BH44	64
Grainges Yd. Uxb.	AX36	53
Windsor St.		
Gramer Clo. E11	CF34	48
Norman Rd.		
Grampian Clo. Orp.	CN53	89
Clovelly Way		
Grampian Gdns. NW2	BR33	46
Grampians, The W14	BQ41	65
Grampian Way, Hayes	BA43	63
Penine Way		
Grampian Way, Slou.	AT42	62
Granada St. SW17	BU49	76
Granard Av. SW15	BP46	75
Granard Rd. SW12	BU47	76
Granary Mead. Brwd.	DC21	33
Granby Pk. Rd. Wal. Cr.	CA17	21
Granby Rd. SE9	CK44	68
Granby Rd. Grav.	DE46	81
Granby's Bdgs. SE11	**BX42**	**4**
Granby's Bldgs. SE11	BX42	66
Salamanca St.		
Granby St. E2	**CA38**	**2**
Granby St. E2	CA38	57
Granby Ter. NW1	**BW37**	**1**
Granby Ter. NW1	BW37	56
Grand Av. EC1	**BY39**	**2**
Grand Av. EC1	BY39	56
Charterhouse St.		
Grand Av. N10	BV31	47
Grand Av. Surb.	BM53	85
Grand Av. Wem.	BM35	46
Grand Av. E. Wem.	BM35	46
Grand Central Wk. SE19	CB50	77
Grand Depot Rd. SE18	CL42	68
Grand Dr. SW20	BQ52	85
Granden Rd. SW16	BX51	86
Grandfield Av. Wat.	BC23	26
Grandison Rd. SW11	BU45	66
Grandison Rd. Wor. Pk.	BQ55	85
Grand Parade Mews SW15	BR46	75
Upper Richmond Rd.		
Grand Pde. Surb.	BM54	85
Grand Pde. Wem.	BM34	46
Grand Sq. SE10	CF42	67
Grand Stand Rd. Epsom	BO62	103
Grand, The Pde. NW3	BT35	47
Finchley Rd.		
Grand View Ave. West.	CJ62	106
Granfield St. SW11	BT44	66
Grange Av. N12	BT28	38
Grange Av. N20	BR26	37
Grange Av. SE25	CA51	87
Grange Av. Barn.	BU26	38
Grange Av. Stan.	BJ30	36
Grange Av. Twick.	BH48	74
Grange Av. Wdf. Grn.	CH29	40
Grangecliffe Gdns. SE25	CA51	87
Grange Clo. Brwd.	DE28	122
Grange Clo. Edg.	BN28	37
Grange Clo. Ger. Cr.	AS30	34
Grange Clo. Guil.	AQ68	109
Grange Clo. Hayes	BB39	53
Grange Clo. Hem. H.	AZ14	8
Grange Clo. Houns.	BE42	64
Grange Clo. Lthd.	BK63	102
Grange Clo. W. Mol.	BF52	84
Grange Rd.		
Grange Clo. N. Mal.	BP53	85
Grange Clo. Red.	BV67	113
Grange Clo. Sid.	CO48	79
Grange Clo. Stai.	AS46	72
Grange Clo. Wdf. Grn.	CH29	40
Grange Clo. West.	CM66	115
Grange Ct. WC2	**BX39**	**2**
Grange Ct. WC2	BX39	56
Grange Ct. Chig.	CM27	40
Grange Ct. Loug.	CJ25	31
Grange Ct. Nthlt.	BD37	54
Grange Ct. St. Alb.	BG13	9
Grange St.		
Grange Ct. Shep.	AZ52	83
Watersplash Rd.		
Grange Ct. Wal. Abb.	CE20	21
Grange Ct. Walt.	BC55	83
Grange Ct. Rd. N16	CA33	48
Grange Cres. Chig.	CM28	40
Grange Dr. Chis.	CK50	78
Grange Dr. Orp.	CP58	98
Grange Dr. Wok.	AS61	100
Grange Est. N2	BT30	38
Grange Farm Clo. Har.	BG34	45
Grangefields Ave. Guil.	AR67	109
Grange Flds. Ger. Cr.	AS30	34
Grange Gdns. N14	BW26	38
Grange Gdns. SE25	CA51	87
Grange Gdns. Bans.	BS60	95
Grange Gdns. Pnr.	BE31	45
Grange Gdns. Slou.	AO35	43
Grange Gro. N1	BY36	56
Grange Hill SE25	CA51	87
Grange Hill, Edg.	BN28	37
Grangehill Pl. SE9	CK45	68
Grangehill Rd. SE9	CK45	68
Grange La. SE21	CA48	77
Grange La. Harl.	CJ11	13
Grange Mead. Bans.	BS60	95
Grangemill Rd. SE6	CE48	77
Grangemill Way SE6	CE48	77
Grange Mt. Lthd.	BK63	102
Grange Par. Hayes.	BB39	53
Grange Pk. W5	BL40	55
Grange Pk. Wok.	AS60	91
Grange Pk. Wok.	AS61	100
Grange Pk. Av. N21	BY25	29
Grange Pk. Rd. E10	CE33	48
Grange Pk. Rd. Th. Hth	BZ52	87
Grange Pl. NW6	BS37	56
Kingsgate		
Grange Pl. Stai.	AW51	83
Grange Rd. E10	CE33	48
Grange Rd. E13	CG38	58
Grange Rd. E17	CD32	48
Grange Rd. N6	BU32	47
Grange Rd. N17	CB29	39
Grange Rd. NW10	BP36	55
Grange Rd. SE1	CA41	67
Grange Rd. SW13	BP44	65
Grange Rd. W4	BM42	65
Grange Rd. W5	BK40	54
Grange Rd. Borwd.	BL25	28
Grange Rd. Bush.	BE25	27
Grange Rd. Cat.	CA66	114
Grange Rd. Chess.	BL55	85
Grange Rd. E. Mol.	BF53	84
Grange Rd. Edg.	BN29	37
Grange Rd. Egh.	AS49	72
Grange Rd. Ger. Cr.	AS30	34
Grange Rd. Grav.	DG47	81
Grange Rd. Grays.	DD43	71
Grange Rd. Guil.	AQ68	109
Grange Rd. Guil.	AQ69	118
Grange Rd. Har.	BG34	45
Grange Rd. Har.	BJ47	74
Grange Rd. Hayes	BB39	53
Grange Rd. Ilf.	CL35	49
Grange Rd. Kings. On T.	BL52	85
Grange Rd. Lthd.	BK63	102
Grange Rd. Orp.	CM55	88
Grange Rd. Rom.	CU29	41
Grange Rd. Sev.	CU67	116
Grange Rd. S. Ock.	CW40	60
Grange Rd. Sth. Croy.	BZ58	96
Grange Rd. Sthl.	BE41	64
Grange Rd. Sutt.	BS57	95
Grange Rd. Th. Hth.	BZ52	87
Grange Rd. Walt.	BE56	93
Grange Rd. Wey.	AW58	92
Grange Rd. Wok.	AS60	91
Granger Way, Rom.	CU32	50
Grange St. N1	**BZ37**	**2**
Grange St. N1	BZ37	57
Grange St. St. Alb.	BG13	9
Grange, The N20	BT26	38
Grange, The NW3	BS34	47
Grange, The SE1	**CA41**	**4**
Grange, The SE1	CA41	67
Grange, The SW19	BQ49	75
Grange, The Croy.	CD55	87
Grange, The N. Mal.	BP53	85
Grange, The Sev.	CY57	99
Grange, The Wem.	BM36	55
Grange, The Wind.	AQ46	72
Grange, The Wor. Pk.	BN55	85
Grange, The Dr. N21	BY25	29
Grange Vale, Sutt.	BS57	95
Grange View Rd. N20	BT26	38
Grange Wk. SE1	**CA41**	**4**
Grange Wk. SE1	CA41	67
Grange Way N12	BS28	38
Grangeway NW6	BS36	56
Messina Av.		
Grange Way, Erith	CU43	69
Grange Way, Iver	AV39	52
Grangeway Wdf. Grn.	CJ28	40
Grangeway Gdns. Ilf.	CK32	49
Grangeway, The N21	BY25	29
Grangewood, Bex.	CQ47	79
Hurst Rd.		
Grangewood, Pot. B.	BS18	20
Grangewood Ave. Grays.	DF41	71
Grangewood Av. Rain.	CV38	60
Grangewood Clo. Brwd.	DD27	122
Grangewood Clo. Nthwd.	BB29	35
Grangewood Clo. Pnr.	BC32	44
Grangewood Dr. Sun.	BB50	73
Forest Dr.		
Grangewood La. Beck.	CD50	77
Grangewood, Slou.	AR39	52
Grangewood St. E6	CJ37	58
Grangewood Ter. SE25	BZ51	87
Grange Yd. SE1	**CA41**	**4**
Grange Yd. SE1	CA41	67
Granham Gdns. N9	CA27	39
Granite St. SE18	CN42	68
Granleigh Rd. E11	CG34	49
Gransden Av. E8	CB36	57
London La.		
Gransden Rd. W12	BO41	65
Wendell Rd.		
Grant Av. Slou.	AP39	52
Grantbridge St. N1	**BY37**	**2**
Grantbridge St. N1	BY37	56
Grant Clo. N14	BW26	38
Grant Clo. Shep.	AZ53	83
Grantham Clo. Edg.	BL27	37
Grantham Gdns. Rom.	CQ32	50
Grantham Grn. Borwd.	BN25	28
Grantham Pl. W1	**BV40**	**3**
Grantham Pl. W1	BV40	56
Old Park La.		
Grantham Rd. E12	CL34	49
Grantham Rd. SW9	BX44	66
Grantham Rd. W4	BO43	65
Grantham Way, Grays.	DD40	71
Grantley Clo. Guil.	AS74	118
Grantley Gdns. Guil.	AQ70	118
Grantley Rd. Guil.	AQ70	118
Grantley Rd. Houns.	BC44	63
Grantley St. E1	CC38	57
Grantock Rd. E17	CF30	39
Granton Av. Upmin.	CW34	51
Granton Rd. SW16	BW51	86
Granton Rd. Ilf.	CO33	50
Granton Rd. Sid.	CP50	79
Grant Pl. Croy.	CA54	87
Grant Rd. SW11	BT45	66
Grant Rd. Croy.	CA54	87
Grant Rd. Har.	BH31	45
Grants Clo. NW7	BQ29	37
Grants La. Oxt.	CJ70	115
Grant St. E13	CH38	58
Grant St. N1	**BY37**	**2**
Grantully Rd. W9	BS38	56
Grantwood Clo. Red.	BV73	121
Granville Av. Felt.	BC48	73
Granville Av. Houns.	BF46	74
Granville Av. Slou.	AO39	52
Granville Clo. Croy.	CB55	87
Granville Clo. Wey.	AY60	92
Church Rd.		
Granville Clo. Wey.	BA57	92
Granville Dene, Hem. H.	AT17	16
Granville Gdns. SW16	BX51	86
Granville Gdns. W5	BL40	55
Granville Gro. SE13	CF45	67
Granville Ms. NW2	BR34	46
Granville Pk. SE13	CF45	67
Granville Pl. N12	BT29	38
High Rd. Nth. Finchley		
Granville Pl. W1	**BV39**	**1**
Granville Pl. W1	BV39	56
Granville Rd. E17	CE32	48
Granville Rd. E18	CH30	40
Granville Rd. N4	BX32	47
Granville Rd. N9	CC27	39
Granville Rd. N12	BS29	38
Granville Rd. N13	BX29	38
Granville Rd. N22	BY30	38
Granville Rd. NW2	BR34	46
Granville Rd. NW6	BS37	56
Granville Rd. SW18	BR47	75
Granville Rd. SW19	BS50	76
Granville Rd. Barn.	BQ24	28
Granville Rd. Berk.	AP12	7
Granville Rd. Epp.	CO18	23
Granville Rd. Grav.	DF47	81
Granville Rd. Hayes.	BB42	63
Granville Rd. Ilf.	CL33	49
Granville Rd. Oxt.	CG68	115
Granville Rd. St. Alb.	BH13	9
Granville Rd. Sev.	CU65	107
Granville Rd. Sid.	CO49	79
Granville Rd. Uxb.	AZ36	53
Granville Rd. Wat.	BD24	27
Granville Rd. Well.	CP45	69
Granville Rd. West.	CM66	115
Granville Rd. Wey.	BA57	92
Granville Rd. Wok.	AS63	100
Granville Sq. WC1	**BX38**	**2**
Granville Sq. WC1	BX38	56
Granville St. WC1	**BX38**	**2**
Granville St. WC1	BXX38	56
Wharton St.		
Grape St. WC2	BX39	56
High Holborn		
Grasdene Rd. SE18	CO43	69
Grasmere Av. SW15	BN49	75
Grasmere Av. SW19	BS51	86
Grasmere Av. W3	BN40	55
Grasmere Av. Houns.	BF46	74
Grasmere Av. Orp.	CL55	88
Grasmere Av. Ruis.	BA33	44
Grasmere Av. Slou.	AQ40	52
Grasmere Av. Wem.	BK33	45
Grasmere Clo. Guil.	AT70	118
Grasmere Clo. Hem. H.	AZ14	8
Grasmere Clo. Loug.	CK23	31
Grasmere Ct. N22	BX29	38
Palmerston Rd.		
Grasmere Gdns. Har.	BJ30	36
Grasmere Gdns. Ilf.	CK32	49
Grasmere Gdns. Orp.	CL55	88
Grasmere Rd. E13	CH37	58
Grasmere Rd. N10	BV30	38
Grasmere Rd. N17	CB29	39
Grasmere Rd. SE25	CB53	87
Grasmere Rd. SW16	BX49	76
Grasmere Rd. Bexh.	CS44	69
Grasmere Rd. Brom.	CG51	88
Grasmere Rd. Horn.	CW31	51
Grasmere Rd. Orp.	CL55	88
Grasmere Rd. Pur.	BY59	95
Grasmere Rd. St. Alb.	BJ14	9
Grassmere Way, Wey.	AY59	92
Grassingham End, Ger. Cr.	AS29	34
Grassingham Rd. Ger. Cr.	AS29	34
Grassington Clo. St. Alb.	BF18	18
W. Riding		
Grassington Rd. Sid.	CO49	79
Grass Mt. SE23	CB48	77
Grassmount Pur.	BW58	95
Grass Pk. N3	BR30	37
Grass Warren, Welw.	BU6	5
Grassway Wall.	BW56	95
Grassy Clo. Hem. H	AW13	8
Grassy La. Sev.	CU66	116
Grasvenor Av. Barn.	BS25	29
Gratley Way SE15	CA43	67
Hordle Prom. N.		
Gratton Dr. Wind.	AM45	61
Gratton Rd. W14	BR41	65
Gratton Ter. NW2	BQ34	46
Gratton Way W1	BW38	56
Gravel Clo. Chig.	CO27	41
Graveley Av. Borwd.	BN24	28
Graveley Ct. Hem. H.	BA14	8
Graveley Dell, Welw. G. C.	BS8	5
Waterford Grn.		
Gravel Hill N3	BR30	37
Broadway, The		
Gravel Hill, Bexh.	CR46	79
Gravel Hill, Ger. Cr.	AS29	34
Gravel Hill, Hem. H.	AW13	8
Gravel Hill, Loug.	CH23	31
Gravel Hill, Lthd.	BJ64	102
Gravel Hill, Sth. Croy.	CC57	96
Gravel Hill, Uxb.	AX35	44
Gravel Hill Clo. Bexh.	CR46	7
Gravel Hill Ter. Hem. H.	AW14	
Gravel La. E1	**CA39**	
Gravel La. E1	CA39	57
Gravel La. Chig.	CO26	41
Gravel La. Chig.	CO27	41
Gravel La. Hem. H.	AW13	
Gravelly Ride SW19	BP49	75
Gravel Path, Berk.	AR13	
Gravel Path, Hem. H.	AW13	
Gravel Pit La. SE9	CM46	78
Gravel Rd. Brom.	CK55	88
Gravel Rd. Twick.	BH47	7
Gravel St. E1	CC40	5
Gravel Wood Clo. Chis.	CM48	7
Gravely Hill, Cat.	CA67	11
Graveney Gro. SE20	CC50	7
Graveney Rd. SW17	BU49	7
Gravesend Rd. W12	BP40	5
Gravetts La. Guil.	AO69	11
Gravetts La. Guil.	AP68	10
Gray Av. Dag.	CQ33	5
Grayburn Clo. Ch. St. G.	AQ27	3
Grayburne, Grav.	DB49	8
Graydon St. SE18	CL43	6
Grayfield Ter. N1	**BY37**	
Gray Gdns. Rain.	CU36	5
Grayham Cres. N. Mal.	BN52	8
Grayham Rd. N. Mal.	BN52	8
Graylands Clo. Wok.	AS61	10
Horsell Pk.		
Graylands, Epp.	CM22	3
Graylands, Wok.	AS61	10
Graylands La. Swans.	DB46	6
Graylands Sq. Swans.	DB46	6
Grayling Rd. N16	BZ34	4
Grayling Sq. E2	CB38	5
Avebury Est.		
Graylings, The Wat.	BA20	1
Grayscroft Rd. SW16	BW50	7
Graysend Clo. Gray.	DD41	7
Grays Farm Rd. Orp.	CO51	8
Graysfield, Welw. G. C.	BS9	
Grays Inn Rd. WC1	**BX38**	
Gray's Inn Rd. WC1	BX38	
Gray's Inn Sq. WC1	**BX39**	
Gray's Inn Sq. WC1	BY39	5
Gray's La. Ash.	BL63	10
Grays La. Ashf.	AZ49	7
Grays Pk. Rd. Slou.	AQ37	5
Grays Pl. Slou.	AP40	5
Grays Rd.	BQ51	8
Grays Rd. Slou.	AP40	5
Grays Rd. Uxb.	AY36	5
Grays Rd. West.	CL64	10
Gray St. SE1	**BY41**	
Gray St. SE1	BY41	6
Grays Wk. Brwd.	DE26	12
Grayswood Gdns. SW20	BP51	8
Graywood Ct. N12	BT29	3
Grazebrook Rd. N16	BZ34	4
Grazeley Clo. Bexh.	CS46	7
Gt. Acre Ct. SW4	BW45	6
Clapham Pk. Rd.		
Great Benty, West Dr.	AY42	6
Great Braitch La. Hat.	BO10	
Great Brays, Harl.	CO11	
Great Break, Welw. G. C.	BS8	
Gt. Brownings SE21	CA49	
Gt. Bushey Dr. N20	BS26	
Gt. Cambridge Rd. N9	BZ27	
Gt. Cambridge Rd. N17	BZ30	
Gt. Cambridge Rd. N18	BZ28	
Gt. Cambridge Rd. Brox.	CB20	
Gt. Cambridge Rd. Enf.	CB24	
Gt. Cambridge Rd. Wal. Cr.	CB20	
Gt. Cambridge Rd. Wal. Cr.	CB25	
Gt. Castle St. W1	**BV39**	
Gt. Castle St. W1	BV39	
Gt. Central Av. Ruis.	BD35	
Gt. Central St. NW1	**BU39**	

Street	Grid	Page
Gt. Central St. NW1	BU39	56
Melcombe Sq.		
Gt. Chapel St. W1	**BW39**	**1**
Gt. Chapel St. W1	BW39	56
Gt. Chertsey Rd. W4	BN44	65
Gt. Chertsey Rd. Felt.	BE48	74
Gt. Church La. W6	BQ42	65
Gt. College St. SW1	**BX41**	**4**
Gt. College St. SW1	BX41	66
Gt. Conduit, Welw. G. C.	BT7	5
Gt. Cross Av. SE10	CG43	68
Gt. Cullings, Rom.	CT34	50
Gt. Cumberland Ms. W1	**BU39**	**1**
Gt. Cumberland Ms. W1	BU39	56
Seymour Pl.		
Gt. Cumberland Pl. W1	**BU39**	**1**
Gt. Cumberland Pl. W1	BU39	56
Great Dell, Welw. G. C.	BQ7	7
Gt. Dover St. SE1	**BZ41**	**4**
Gt. Dover St. SE1	BZ41	67
Greatdown Rd. W7	BH38	54
Gt. Eastern Rd. E15	CF36	57
Gt. Eastern Rd. Brwd.	DB28	42
Great Eastern St. EC2	**CA38**	**2**
Gt. Eastern St. EC2	CA38	57
Gt. Ellshams, Bans.	BS61	104
Gt. Elms Rd. Brom.	CJ52	88
Gt. Elms Rd. Hem. H.	AY15	8
Great Field NW9	BO30	37
Greatfield Av. E6	CK38	58
Greatfield Clo. SE4	CE45	67
Greatfields Dr. Uxb.	AZ39	53
Greatfields Rd. Bark.	CM37	58
Great Field, Strand NW9	BO30	37
Greatford Dr. Guil.	AU70	118
Great Ganett, Welw. G. C.	BS9	5
Gt. Gardens Rd. Horn.	CU32	50
Gt. George St. SW1	**BW41**	**3**
Gt. George St. SW1	BW41	66
Gt. Goodwin Dr. Guil.	AT69	118
Gt. Grove, Bush.	BF24	27
Gt. Guildford St. SE1	**BZ40**	**4**
Gt. Guildford St. SE1	BZ40	57
Greatham Rd. Bush.	BD24	27
Greatham Wk. SW15	BP47	75
Foxcombe Rd.		
Gt. Harry Dr. SE9	CL48	78
Greatheart, Hem. H.	AY12	8
Gt. Heath, Hat.	BP11	10
Great Hobletts Rd. Hem. H.	AY13	8
Gt. Hurstend, Lthd.	BE65	102
Great James St. WC1	**BX39**	**2**
Gt. James St. WC1	BX39	56
Gt. Lawn, Ong.	CX17	24
Great Ley, Welw. G. C.	BR9	5
Great Leylands, Harl.	CO11	14
Gt. Marlborough St. W1	**BW39**	**1**
Gt. Marlborough St. W1	BW39	56
Great Mead, Brox.	CE14	12
Gt. Nelmes Chase, Horn.	CW32	51
Greatness La. Sev.	CV64	108
Greatness Rd. Sev.	CV64	108
Gt. Newport St. WC2	BW40	56
Upr. St. Martin's La.		
Great New St. EC4	**BY39**	**2**
Great North Rd. Hat.	BQ11	10
Gt. North Rd. N2	BU31	47
Great North Rd. N20	BT26	38
Gt. North Rd. Barn.	BR24	28
Great North Rd. Beac.	AP29	34
Great North Rd. Hat.	BT17	20
Great North Rd. Pot. B.	BT18	20
Gt. North Way NW4	BP30	37
Gt. Oaks, Brwd.	DD25	122
Great Oaks, Chig.	CM28	40
Gt. Oaks Pk. Guil.	AT68	109
Greatorex St. E1	**CB39**	**2**
Greatorex St. E1	CB39	57
Great Ormond St. WC1	**BX39**	**2**
Gt. Ormond St. WC1	BX39	56
Gt. Owl Rd. Chig.	CL27	40
Great Palmers, Hem. H.	AY11	8
Great Park, Kings L.	AY18	17
Great Parndon, Harl.	CL12	13
Great Percy St. WC1	**BX38**	**2**
Gt. Percy St. WC1	BX38	56
Gt. Peter St. SW1	**BW41**	**3**
Gt. Peter St. SW1	BX41	66
Great Plumtree, Harl.	CN10	6
Gt. Portland St. W1	**BV38**	**1**
Gt. Portland St. W1	BV38	56
Gt. Pulteney St. W1	**BW40**	**3**
Gt. Pulteney St. W1	BW40	56
Gt. Quarry, Guil.	AR72	118
Great Queen St. WC2	**BX39**	**2**
Gt. Queen St. WC2	BX39	56
Gt. Queen St. Dart.	CW47	80
Great Rd. Hem. H.	AY13	8
Great Ropers La. Brwd.	DA29	42
Gt. Russell St. WC1	**BW39**	**1**
Gt. Russell St. WC1	**BX39**	**2**
Gt. Russell St. WC1	BW39	56
Great St. Helen's EC3	**CA39**	**2**
Gt. St. Helen's EC3	CA39	57
St. Mary Axe		
Gt. St. Thomas Apostle EC4	**BZ40**	**4**
Gt. St. Thomas Apostle EC4	BZ40	57
Queen St.		
Great Saplings SE21	CA46	77
Gt. Scotland Yd SW1	**BX40**	**4**
Gt. Scotland Yd. SW1	BX40	56
Great Slades, Pot. B.	BR20	19
Gt. Smith St. SW1	**BW41**	**3**
Gt. Smith St. SW1	BW41	66
Great South West Rd. Felt.	BA47	73
Gt. Spilmans SE22	CA46	77
Gt. Suffolk St. SE1	**BY40**	**4**
Gt. Suffolk St. SE1	BY40	56
Gt. Sutton St. EC1	**BY38**	**2**
Gt. Sutton St. EC1	BY38	56
Gt. Swan All. EC2	**BZ39**	**2**
Gt. Swan All. EC2	BZ39	57
Gt. Tattenhams, Epsom	BP62	103
Gt. Thrift, Orp.	CM52	88
Gt. Titchfield St. W1	**BV38**	**1**
Gt. Titchfield St. W1	BV38	56
Gt. Tower St. EC3	CA40	57
Gt. Trinity La. EC4	**BZ40**	**4**
Gt. Trinity La. EC4	BZ40	57
Queen Victoria St.		
Gt. Turnstile WC1	BX39	56
High Holborn		
Great Turnstile WC2	**BX39**	**2**
Great Warley St. Borwd.	DA30	42
Great Warley St. Brwd.	DB31	51
Gt. Western Rd. W9	BR38	55
Gt. Western Rd. W11	BR38	55
Gt. West Rd. W4	BM42	65
Gt. West Rd. Brent.	BJ43	64
Gt. West Rd. Houns.	BE44	64
Great Whites Rd. Hem. H.	AY14	8
Great Winchester St. EC2	**BZ39**	**2**
Gt. Winchester St. EC2	BZ39	57
Gt. Windmill St. W1	**BW40**	**3**
Gt. Windmill St. W1	BW40	56
Greatwood, Chis.	CL50	78
Greatwood Clo. Cher.	AU58	91
Gt. Woodcote Dr. Pur.	BW58	95
Gt. Woodcote Pk. Pur.	BW58	95
Greaves Pl. SW17	BU49	76
Grecian Cres. SE19	BY50	76
Greek Ct. W1	BW39	56
Old Compton St.		
Greek St. W1	**BW39**	**1**
Greek St. W1	BW39	56
Greenacre, Dart.	CV48	80
Green Acre, Wind.	AM44	61
Green Acre, Wok.	AP61	100
Green Acre Clo. Barn.	BR22	28
Greenacres SE9	CL46	78
Green Acres, Croy.	CA55	87
Greenacres, Epp.	CN17	22
Lindsey St.		
Green Acres, Hem. H.	BA14	8
Green Acres, Lthd.	BF65	102
Greenacres, Oxt.	CG67	115
Green Acres, Welw. G. C.	BR9	5
Greenacres Av. Uxb.	AY34	44
Greenacres Clo. Rain.	CW38	60
Greenacres Dr. Stan.	BJ29	36
Greenacre Wk. N13	BX27	38
Cannon Hill		
Green Acre, Wok.	AP61	100
Lockfield Dr.		
Greenall Clo. Wal. Cr.	CD18	21
Roundmoor Dr.		
Green Arbour Ct. EC4	BY39	56
Old Bailey		
Green Av. NW7	BN28	37
Green Av. W13	BJ41	64
Greenaway Gdns. NW3	BS35	47
Green Bank E1	CB40	57
Green Bank N12	BS28	38
Greenbank, Wal. Cr.	CB17	21
Greenbank Av. Wem.	BJ35	45
Green Bank Clo. Rom.	CV27	42
Greenbank Cres. NW4	BR31	46
Greenbank Rd. Wat.	BA21	26
Green Banks, Upmin.	CZ34	51
Green Banks, Walt.	BE54	84
Greenbay Rd. SE7	CJ43	68
Greenbury St. NW8	**BU37**	**1**
Greenberry St. NW8	BU37	56
Greenbrook Av. Barn.	BT23	29
Greenbury Clo. Rick.	AU24	25
Green Clo. NW9	BN32	46
Green Clo. NW11	BT33	47
Green Clo. Brom.	CG52	88
Green Clo. Cars.	BU55	86
Green Clo. Epp.	CL15	13
Green Clo. Felt.	BE49	74
Green Clo. Hat.	BR16	19
Green Clo. Wal. Cr.	CD19	21
Greencoat Pl. SW1	**BW42**	**3**
Greencoat Pl. SW1	BW42	66
Greencoat Row SW1	**BW41**	**3**
Greencoat Row SW1	BW41	66
Francis St.		
Greencourt Av. Edg.	BM30	37
Green Ct. Edg.	BM29	37
Green Ct. Av. Croy.	CB55	87
Green Ct. Gdns. Croy.	CB54	87
Greencourt Rd. Orp.	CM53	88
Green Ct. Rd. Swan.	CS53	89
Greencroft, Guil.	AT70	118
Green Cft. Hat.	BP11	10
Greencroft Av. Ruis.	BD34	45
Greencroft Gdns. NW6	BS36	56
Greencroft Gdns. Enf.	CA24	30
Greencroft Rd. Houns.	BE44	64
Green Curve, Bans.	BR60	94
Green Dale NW7	BO28	37
Green Dale SE22	BZ45	67
Green Dale Clo. SE22	CA46	77
Green Dale		
Greendale Wk. Grav.	DF48	81
Green Dell Way, Hem. H.	AZ13	8
Green Dene, Leath	BA70	110
Green Dragon La. N21	BX25	29
Green Dragon La. Brent.	BL42	65
Green Dragon Yd. E1	**CB39**	**2**
Green Dragon Yd. E1	CB39	57
Old Montague St.		
Green Dr. Sthl.	BF40	54
Green East Rd. Beac.	AP29	34
Green End N21	BY27	38
Green End, Chess.	BK56	93
Green End, Hem. H.	AV13	7
Greenend Rd. W4	BO41	65
Green End Rd. Hem. H.	AW14	8
Greene Walk, Berk.	AR13	7
Greenfarm Clo. Orp.	CN57	97
Greenfield, Welw. G. C.	BQ6	5
Greenfield Av. Surb.	BM54	85
Greenfield Av. Wat.	BE27	36
Greenfielde End, Stai.	AX50	73
Greenfield End, Ger. Cr.	AS29	34
Greenfield Gdns. NW2	BR34	46
Greenfield Gdns. Dag.	CP37	59
Greenfield Gdns. Orp.	CM54	88
Greenfield, Hat.	BQ11	10
Greenfield, Link-couls.	BX57	95
Greenfield Rd. E1	CB39	57
Greenfield Rd. N15	CA32	48
Green Field Rd. Berk.	AR13	7
Greenfield Rd. Dag.	CP37	59
Greenfield Rd. Dart.	CS49	79
Greenfields NW7	BO27	37
Lawrence St.		
Greenfields, Loug.	CL24	31
Greenfields, Sthl.	BF40	54
Greenfields Clo. Loug.	CL24	31
Greenfield St. Wal. Abb.	CF20	21
Greenfield Way, Har.	BF31	45
Greenford Av. W7	BH38	54
Greenford Av. Sthl.	BE40	54
Greenford Gdns. Grnf.	BF38	54
Greenford Rd. Grnf.	BG37	54
Greenford Rd. Har.	BH35	45
Greenford Rd. Sthl.	BG40	54
Greenford Rd. Sutt.	BS56	95
Thorncroft Rd.		
Green Gdns. Orp.	CM56	97
Greengate, Grnf.	BJ36	54
Greengate St. E13	CH37	58
Green Glade, Epp.	CN22	31
Greenglades, Horn.	CW32	51
Greenhalgh Wk. N2	BT31	47
Greenham Rd. N10	BV30	38
Greenham Wk. Wok.	AR62	100
Winnington Way		
Greenhayes Av. Bans.	BS60	95
Greenhayes Gdns. Bans.	BS61	104
Greenheys Clo. Nthwd.	BB30	35
Greenheys Dr. E18	CG31	49
Greenheys Pl. Wok.	AS62	100
Green Hill SE18	CK42	68
Green Hill, Buck. H.	CJ26	40
Green Hill, Orp.	CK59	97
Greenhill, Sutt.	BT55	86
Greenhill, Wem.	BM34	46
Greenhill Av. Cat.	CB64	105
Greenhill Cres. Har.	BH32	45
Greenhill Cres. Wat.	BB25	26
Greenhill Gdns. Nthlt.	BE37	54
Greenhill Gro. E12	CK35	49
Green Hill La. Warl.	CD62	105
Greenhill Pk. NW10	BO37	55
Greenhill Pk. Barn.	BS25	29
Greenhill Rd. NW10	BO37	55
Greenhill Rd. Grav.	DF48	81
Greenhill Rd. Har.	BH32	45
Greenhill Rd. Sev.	CV61	108
Greenhills Clo. Rick.	AW25	26
Greenhill's Rents EC1	BY39	56
Cowcross St.		
Green Hill Ter. SE18	CK42	68
Greenhill Ter. Nthlt.	BE37	54
Greenhill Way, Wem.	BM34	46
Greenhithe Clo. Sid.	CN47	78
Greenholm Rd. SE9	CL46	78
Green Hundred Rd. SE15	CB43	67
Greenhurst La. Oxt.	CH69	115
Greenhurst Rd. SE27	BY49	76
Green Hythe Rd. Guil.	AR67	109
Greening St. SE2	CP42	69
Greenland Cres. Sthl.	BD41	64
Greenland Rd. NW1	**BV37**	**1**
Greenland Rd. NW1	BT37	56
Greenland Rd. Barn.	BQ25	28
Greenlands Rd. Sev.	CX63	108
Greenlands Rd. Stai.	AW49	73
Greenlands Rd. Wey.	AZ55	83
Greenland St. NW1	**BV37**	**1**
Green La. E4	CF24	30
Green La. NW4	BQ31	46
Green La. SE9	CL47	78
Green La. SE20	CC50	77
Green La. SW16	BX50	76
Green La. W7	BH41	64
Green La. Amer.	AO21	25
Green La. Amer.	AP22	25
Green La. Ash.	BK62	102
Green La. Berk.	AR13	7
Green La. Brox.	CE15	12
Green La. Brwd.	CY23	33
Green La. Brwd.	DA26	42
Green La. Brwd.	DA29	42
Green La. Brwd.	DB25	33
Green La. Cat.	BZ64	105
Green La. Cher.	AV55	82
Green La. Chesh.	AQ20	16
Green La. Chess.	BK58	93
Green La. Chig.	CM26	40
Green La. Chis.	CL49	78
Green La. Cob.	BE59	93
Green La. Dag.	CN34	49
Green La. Dag.	CP34	50
Green La. E. Mol.	BF53	84
Green La. Edg.	BL28	37
Green La. Egh.	AT49	72
Green La. Egh.	AT52	82
Green La. Egh.	AU51	82
Green La. Guil.	AT70	118
Green La. Guil.	AW67	110
Green La. Har.	BH34	45
Green La. Harl.	CR11	14
Green La. Hem. H.	BA14	8
Green La. Houns.	BC45	63
Green La. Ilf.	CM34	49
Green La. Ing.	DB19	24
Green La. Maid.	AG40	61
Green La. Maid.	AG44	61
Green La. Mord.	BQ52	85
Green La. Mord.	BS53	86
Green La. N. Mal.	BN53	85
Green La. Nthwd.	BA29	35
Green La. Pur.	BW59	95
Green La. Red.	BU69	121
Green La. Red.	CA68	114
Green La. Reig.	BR70	120
Green La. St. Alb.	BG12	9
Green La. Shep.	BA53	83
Green La. Slou.	AQ44	62
Green La. Slou.	AT44	62
Green La. Stan.	BJ28	36
Green La. Sun.	BB50	73
Green La. Th. Hth.	BX50	76
Green La. Upmin.	CY37	60
Green La. Uxb.	BA39	53
Green La. Wal. Abb.	CJ20	22
Green La. Walt.	BC57	92
Green La. Warl.	CD62	105
Green La. Wat.	BD26	36
Green La. Welw. G. C.	BO9	5
Green La. West.	CM65	106
Green La. Wey.	AY59	92
Green La. Wind.	AN44	61
Green La. Wok.	AP58	91
Green La. Wok.	AQ64	100
Green La. Wok.	AZ65	101
Green La. Wor. Pk.	BP54	85
Green La. Av. Walt.	BD56	93
Green La. Clo. Amer.	AO21	25
Green La. Clo. Cher.	AV55	82
Green La. Clo. Wey.	AY56	92
Green La. Gdns. Th. Hth.	BZ51	87
Green Lanes N4	BY32	47
Green Lanes N8	BY31	47
Green Lanes N13	BX29	38
Green Lanes N16	BZ34	48
Green Lanes N21	BY27	38
Green Lanes, Epsom	BO58	94
Green Lane West, Wok.	AZ66	110
Greenlaw Gdns. N. Mal.	BO54	85
Green Lawns, Ruis.	BD33	45
Greenlaw St. SE18	CK41	68
Greenleafe Dr. Ilf.	CL31	49
Greenleaf Rd. E6	CJ37	58
Greenleaf Rd. E17	CD31	48
Green Leas, Sun.	BB50	73
Green Leas, Wal. Abb.	CG20	22
Green Man Gdns. W13	BJ40	54
Green Man La. W13	BJ40	54
Green Man La. Felt.	BC45	63
Green Manor Way, Grav.	DC45	71
Green Man St. N1	**BZ36**	**2**
Green Man St. N1	BZ36	57
Green Mayes Clo. Reig.	BT70	121
Green Meadow, Pot. B.	BS18	20
Greenmeads, Wok.	AS64	100
Green Moor Link N21	BY26	38
Greenmoor Rd. Enf.	CC23	30
Greenoak Ri. West.	CJ62	106
Greenock Rd. SW16	BW51	86
Greenock Rd. W3	BM41	65
Corville Rd.		
Greenock Way, Rom.	CT29	41
Greeno Cres. Shep.	AZ53	83
Green Pk. Stai.	AV48	72
Vicarage Rd.		
Greenpark Ct. Wem.	BK36	54
Green Pl. Dart.	CT46	79
Green Pond Rd. E17	CD31	48
Green Ride, Epp.	CM20	22
Green Ride, Loug.	CH25	31
Green Rd. N14	BV25	29
Green Rd. N20	BT27	38
Green Rd. N22	BX29	38
Green Rd. Dart.	DA50	80
Green Rd. Grav.	DD49	81
Green's End SE18	CL42	68
Greenshaw, Brwd.	DA26	42
Greenside, Bex.	CQ47	79
Greenside, Dag.	CP33	50
Greenside, Rich.	BK46	74
Greenside, Swan.	CS51	89
Greenside Rd. W12	BP41	65
Greenside Rd. Croy.	BY54	86
Greenside Rd. Wey.	AZ55	83
Kings Rd.		
Greenside Wk. West.	CJ62	106
King's Rd.		
Green Slade Av. Ash.	BM63	103
Greenstead, Saw.	CQ6	6
Greenstead Av. Wdf. Grn.	CJ29	40
Greenstead Clo. Brwd.	DF26	122
Greenstead Clo. Wdf. Grn.	CJ29	40
Greenstead Gdns.		
Greenstead Gdns. SW15	BP46	75
Greenstead Gdns. Wdf. Grn.	CJ29	40
Greenstead Rd. Loug.	CK26	40
Greens, The Clo. Loug.	CL23	31
Green St. E7	CH35	49
Green St. E7	CH36	58
Green St. E13	CJ37	58
Green St. W1	**BV40**	**3**
Green St. W1	BV40	56
Green St. Dart.	CX47	80
Green St. Enf.	CC23	30
Green St. Hat.	BS13	11
Green St. Rad.	BM21	28
Green St. Rick.	AU23	25
Green St. Sun.	BC51	83
Green Ter. EC1	**BY38**	**2**
Green Ter. EC1	BY38	56
Green, The E4	CF26	39
Green, The E11	CH32	49
Green, The E15	CG36	58
Green, The N9	CB27	39
Green, The N14	BW27	38
Green, The N21	BY26	38
Green, The W3	BO39	55
Green, The W5	BK40	54
Green, The Amer.	AO22	25
Green, The Bexh.	CR44	69
Green, The Brom.	CH48	78
Green, The Brom.	CH54	88
Green, The Cat.	CE65	105
Green, The Epp.	CM21	31
Green, The Epsom	BP59	94
Green, The Gdse.	CB69	114
Green, The Hem. H.	AT18	16
Green, The Houns.	BF43	64
Heston Rd.		
Green, The Ing.	DC19	24
Green, The Mord.	BR52	85
Green, The N. Mal.	BN52	85
Green, The Orp.	CL56	97
Green, The Orp.	CO50	79
Green, The Rain.	CW40	60
Green, The Rich.	BK46	74
Green, The Rick.	AW21	26
Green, The Rick.	AY25	26
Green, The Sev.	CV64	108
Green, The Shep.	BB52	83
Holmbank Dr.		
Green, The Sid.	CO49	79
Green, The Slou.	AO41	61
Green, The Slou.	AQ43	62
Green, The Slou.	AL40	61
Green, The Stai.	AS46	72
Green, The Sthl.	BE41	64
Green, The Sutt.	BS55	86
Green, The Twick.	BH47	74
Green, The Wal. Cr.	CC17	21
Green, The Wat.	BC22	26
Green, The Watt.	BB58	92
Green, The Wdf. Grn.	CH28	40
Green, The Well.	CM45	68
Green, The Wem.	BJ34	45
Green, The West.	CM66	115
Green, The West Dr.	AX41	63
Greentiles La. Uxb.	AV33	43
Green Vale W5	BL39	55
Green Vale, Bexh.	CP46	79
Greenvale Rd. SE9	CK45	68
Green Vale Rd. Wok.	AO62	100
Southwood Av.		
Green Verges, Stan.	BK29	36
Green Vw. Chess.	BL57	94
Greenview Av. Croy.	CD53	87
Green View Clo. Hem. H.	AT18	16
Greenville Clo. Cob.	BD60	93
Green Wk. E4	CF26	39
Green Wk. NW4	BQ31	46
Green Wk. SE1	**CA41**	**4**
Green Wk. SE1	CA41	67
Green Wk. Dart.	CT46	79
Green Wk. Ong.	CW18	24
Green Wk. Ruis.	BB33	44
Green Wk. Ruis.	BC33	44
Green Wk. Sth. Croy.	CD57	96
Green Wk. Sthl.	BF42	64
Green Wk. Wdf. Grn.	CK29	40
Greenway N14	BX27	38
Greenway N20	BS27	38
Green Way SE9	CJ46	78
Greenway SW20	BQ52	85
Green Way, Berk.	AQ13	7
Green Way, Brom.	CK53	88
Greenway, Brwd.	DD26	122
Greenway, Chis.	CL49	78
Greenway, Dag.	CP34	50
Greenway, Har.	BL32	46
Green Way, Hart.	DC53	90
Greenway, Hayes	BC38	53
Greenway, Hem. H.	AZ13	8
Greenway, Lthd.	BF65	102
Greenway, Pnr.	BC30	35
Green Way, Red.	BU69	121
Greenway, Rom.	CX29	42
Green Way, Sun.	BC52	83
Greenway, Wall.	BW56	95
Greenway, Wdf. Grn.	CJ28	40
Greenway Av. E17	CF31	48
Greenway Clo. N16	BZ34	48
Greenway Clo. N20	BS27	38
Greenway Clo. NW9	BN30	37
Greenway Clo. Wey.	AW60	92
Greenway Ct. Har.	BH30	36
Greenway Dr. Stai.	AX51	83
Greenway Gdns. NW9	BN30	37
Greenway Gdns. Croy.	CD55	87
Greenway Gdns. Grnf.	BF38	54
Greenways, Beck.	CE52	87
Greenways, Esher	BH56	93
Greenways, Oxt.	CH70	115
Greenways, Tad.	BP66	112
Greenways, Wal. Cr.	BY18	20
Greenways, Wat.	BB19	17
Greenways Ct. Egh.	AS50	72
Greenways Est. E2	CC38	57
Greenway, The NW9	BN30	37
Greenway, The Enf.	CC21	30
Greenway, The Epsom	BM60	94
Greenway, The Ger. Cr.	AR31	43
Greenway, The Har.	BH30	36
Green Way, The Houns.	BE45	64
Greenway, The Orp.	CO53	89
Greenway, The Pnr.	BE32	45
Greenway, The Pot. B.	BS20	20
Greenway, The Rick.	AW26	35
Greenway, The Uxb.	AX37	53
Greenway, The Uxb.	AZ34	44
Greenway, The Epsom	BM61	103
Greenway, West.	CJ63	106
Greenwell St. W1	**BV38**	**1**
Greenwell St. W1	BV38	56
Green West Rd. Beac.	AP29	34
Greenwich Church St. SE10	CF43	67
Greenwich High Rd. SE10	CE44	67
Greenwich Mkt. SE10	CF43	67
Greenwich Pk. St. SE10	CF42	67
Greenwich S. St. SE10	CE44	67
Greenwood Av. Dag.	CR35	50
Greenwood Av. Enf.	CC23	30
Greenwood Av. Wal. Cr.	CB19	21
Greenwood Clo. Amer.	AP22	25
Greenwood Clo. Bush.	BH26	36
Langmead Dr.		
Greenwood Clo. Mord.	BR52	85
Greenwood Clo. Orp.	CN53	88
Greenwood Clo. Red.	BV73	121
Greenwood Clo. Sid.	CO48	79
Hurst Rd.		
Greenwood Clo. Surb.	BJ54	84
Greenwood Clo. Wey.	AV59	91
Greenwood Ct. Wal. Cr.	CB19	21
Greenwood Dr. E4	CF28	39
Avril Way		
Greenwood Dr. Red.	BV73	121
Greenwood Dr. Wat.	BC20	17
Greenwood Gdns. N13	BY27	38
Greenwood Gdns. Cat.	CB66	114
Greenwood Gdns. Ilf.	CM29	40
Greenwood Ho. Grays.	DD43	71
Hawkes Clo.		
Greenwood La. Hamptn.	BF49	74
Greenwood Pk. Kings. On T.	BO50	75
Greenwood Pl. NW5	BV35	47
Highgate Rd.		
Greenwood Rd. E8	CB36	57
Greenwood Rd. E13	CG37	58
Maud Rd.		
Greenwood Rd. Bex.	CS49	79

Greenwood Rd. Chig. CO28 41
Greenwood Rd. Croy. BY53 86
Greenwood Rd. Islw. BH45 64
Greenwood Rd. Mitch. BW52 86
Greenwood Rd. Surb. BJ54 84
Greenwood Rd. Wok. AP63 100
Greenwood Ter. NW10 BG37 54
Greenwood, The Guil. AT70 118
Greenwood Way, Sev. CT66 116
Greenwrythe Cres. Cars. BU54 86
Green Wrythe La. Cars. BT53 86
Green Yd. Wal. Abb. CF21 21
Greer Rd. Har. BG30 36
Greet St. SE1 BY40 4
Greet St. SE1 BY40 56
Gregor Mews SE3 CH43 68
Gregory Av. Pot. B. BT20 20
Gregory Cres. SE9 CJ47 78
Gregory Pl. W8 BS41 66
Gregory Rd. Rom. CP31 50
Gregory Rd. Slou. AO34 43
Gregory Rd. Sthl. BF41 64
Greig Clo. N8 BX32 47
Greig Ter. SE17 BY43 66
Lorrimore Sq.
Grenaby Av. Croy. BZ54 87
Grenaby Rd. Croy. BZ54 87
Grenada Rd. SE7 CJ43 68
Grenade St. E14 CD40 57
Grenadier St. E16 CK40 58
Grena Gdns. Rich. BL45 65
Grena Rd. Rich. BL45 65
Grendon Gdns. Wem. BM34 46
Grendon St. NW8 BU38 1
Grendon St. NW8 BU38 56
Grenfall St. SE10 CG41 68
Grenfell Av. Horn. CT33 50
Grenfell Clo. West. CJ59 97
Grenfell Gdns. Har. BL33 46
Grenfell Rd. W11 BQ40 55
Grenfell Rd. Mitch. BU50 76
Grenfell Wk. W11 BQ40 55
Lancaster Rd.
Grennell Clo. Sutt. BT55 86
Grennell Rd. Sutt. BT55 86
Grenoble Gdns. N13 BY29 38
Grenview Ct. Ashf. AY49 73
Grenville Av. Brox. CD14 12
Grenville Clo. Wal. Cr. CC19 21
Grenville Gdns. Wdf. Grn. CJ30 40
Grenville Ms. SW7 BT42 3
Grenville Ms. SW7 BT42 66
Grenville Ms. Hamptn. BF49 74
Grenville Pl. NW7 BN28 37
Grenville Pl. SW7 BT41 3
Grenville Pl. SW7 BT41 66
Grenville Rd. N19 BX33 47
Grenville Rd. Croy. CF58 96
Grenville St. WC1 BX38 2
Grenville St. WC1 BX38 56
Guilford St.
Gresham Av. Warl. CD62 105
Gresham Av. N20 BU28 38
Gresham Clo. Bex. CQ46 79
Gresham Clo. Enf. BZ24 30
Gresham Dr. Rom. CO32 50
Gresham Gdns. NW11 BR33 46
Gresham Rd. E6 CK37 58
Gresham Rd. E16 CH39 58
Gresham Rd. NW10 BN35 46
Gresham Rd. SE25 CB52 87
Gresham Rd. SW9 BY45 66
Gresham Rd. Beck. CD51 87
Gresham Rd. Brwd. DB27 42
Gresham Rd. Edg. BL29 37
Gresham Rd. Houns. BG44 64
Gresham Rd. Oxt. CG68 115
Gresham Rd. Stai. AV49 72
Gresham Rd. Uxb. AZ37 53
Gresham St. EC2 BZ39 2
Gresham St. EC2 BZ39 57
Gresley Rd. N19 BW33 47
Gressenhall Rd. SW18 BR46 75
Gresse St. W1 BW39 1
Gresse St. W1 BW39 56
Greswell Clo. Sid. CO48 79
Greswell Rd. SW6 BQ44 65
Greta Bank, Leath. BA66 110
Greton Rd. N17 CA29 39
Beaufoy Rd.
Greville Av. Sth. Croy. CC58 96
Greville Clo. Guil. AP70 118
Greville Clo. Hat. BQ15 10
Knolles Cres.
Greville Clo. Twick. BJ47 74
Greville Hall NW6 BS37 1
Greville Hall NW6 BS37 56
Greville Pk. Av. Ash. BL62 103
Greville Pk. Rd. Ash. BL62 103
Greville Pl. NW6 BS37 1
Greville Pl. NW6 BS38 56
Greville Rd. E17 CF31 48
Greville Rd. NW6 BS37 1
Greville Rd. NW6 BS37 56
Greville Rd. Rich. BL46 75
Greville St. EC1 BY39 2
Greville St. EC1 BY39 56
Greycaine Rd. Wat. BD22 27
Grey Clo. NW11 BT32 47
Greycoat Pl. SW1 BW41 3
Greycoat Pl. SW1 BW41 66
Greycoat St. SW1 BW41 3
Greycoat St. SW1 BW41 66
Greycott Rd. Beck. CE49 77
Grey Eagle St. E1 CA39 2
Grey Eagle St. E1 CA39 57
Greyfell Clo. Stan. BJ28 36
Coverdale Clo.
Greyfriars Pass. EC1 BY39 2
Greyfriars Pass. EC1 BY39 56
Newgate St.
Greyfriars Rd. Wok. AW65 101
Greygoose Pk. Harl. CL12 13
Greyhound Hl. NW4 BP31 46
Greyhound La. SW16 BW50 76
Greyhound La. Grays. DG41 71
Greyhound La. Pot. B. BP20 19
Greyhound Rd. N17 CA31 48
Greyhound Rd. NW10 BP38 55
Greyhound Rd. W6 BQ43 65
Greyhound Rd. W14 BR43 65
Greyhound Ter. SW16 BW51 86
Greyland Clo. Brom. CJ51 88
Greyshot Rd. SW11 BU44 66
Greys Pk. Clo. Kes. CJ56 97
Greys Rd. Uxb. AY37 53
Greystead Rd. SE23 CC47 77
Greystoke Av. Pnr. BF31 45
Greystoke Gdns. W5 BL38 55
Greystoke Gdns. Enf. BW24 29
Greystoke Lo. W5 BL38 55
Hanger La.
Greystoke Pk. Ter. W5 BK38 54
Greystoke Pl. EC4 BY39 56
Cursitor St.
Greystoke Clo. Berk. AQ13 7
Greystone Clo. Croy. CC59 96
Greystone Clo. Sth. Croy. CC58 96
Greystone Gdns. Har. BK32 45
Greystone Gdns. Ilf. CM30 40
Greystone Pk. Sev. CQ66 116
Greystones Clo. Red. BT71 121
Hardwicke Rd.
Greystones Dr. Reig. BT69 121
Grey St. E16 CJ40 58
Greyswood St. SW16 BV50 76
Greythorne Rd. Wok. AQ62 100
Grey Towers Av. Horn. CV33 51
Grey Towers Gdns. Horn. CV33 51
Grice Av. West. CH60 97
Grid Iron Pl. Upmin. CX34 51
Gridland St. E15 CG37 58
Church St.
Grierson Rd. SE23 CC47 77
Grieves Rd. Grav. CF48 81
Griffin Av. Upmin. CZ32 51
Griffin Clo. Slou. AN41 61
Griffin Manor Way SE28 CM41 68
Griffin Rd. N17 CA30 39
Griffin Rd. SE18 CM42 68
Griffins, The Grays. DD41 71
Griffin Way, Lthd. BF66 111
Griffin Way, Sun. BC51 83
Griffiths Clo. Wor. Pk. BP55 85
Griffiths Rd. SW19 BS50 76
Griggs Pl. SE1 CA41 4
Griggs Pl. SE1 CA41 67
Grange Rd.
Griggs Rd. E10 CF32 48
Grimsby St. E2 CA38 2
Grimsby St. E2 CA38 57
Grimsdell's La. Amer. AO22 25
Grimsdyke Cres. Barn. BQ24 28
Grimsdyke Rd. Pnr. BE29 36
Grimsel Path SE17 BY43 66
Brandon Est.
Grimshaw Clo. N6 BV33 47
Grimstone Clo. Rom. CR29 41
Grimston Rd. SW6 BR44 65
Grimston Rd. St. Alb. BH13 9
Grimthorpe Clo. St. Alb. BG12 9
Grimthorpe Ho. EC1 BY38 2
Grimwade Av. Croy. CB55 87
Grimwade Cres. SE15 CC45 67
Grimwood Rd. Twick. BH47 74
Grindal St. SE1 BY41 4
Grindal St. SE1 BY41 66
Lower Marsh
Grinling Pl. SE8 CE43 67
Grinstead Rd. SE8 CD42 67
Grisedale Clo. Pur. CA60 96
Grisedale Gdns. Pur. CA60 96
Grittledon Rd. W9 BS38 56
Grittleton Av. Wem. BM36 55
Grizedale Ter. SE23 CB48 77
Grocers Hall Ct. EC2 BZ39 57
Poultry
Groombridge Clo. Walt. BC56 92
Groombridge Clo. Well. CO46 79
Groombridge Rd. E9 CC36 57
Groom Cres. SW18 BT47 76
Groomfield Clo. SW17 BV49 76
Groom Pl. SW1 BV41 3
Groom Pl. SW1 BV41 66
Chapel St.
Grooms Cotts. Chesh. AQ18 16
Grosmont Rd. SE18 CN43 68
Grosse Way SW15 BP46 75
Dover Pk. Dr.
Grosvenor Av. N5 BZ35 48
Grosvenor Av. SW14 BO45 65
Grosvenor Av. Cars. BU57 95
Grosvenor Av. Har. BF33 45
Grosvenor Av. Hayes. BB37 53
Grosvenor Av. Kings L. BA17 17
Grosvenor Av. Rich. BL46 75
Grosvenor Rd.
Grosvenor Clo. Loug. CL23 31
Grosvenor Ct. N14 BW26 38
Grosvenor Ct. Guil. AT69 118
Grosvenor Ct. Mord. BS52 86
Grosvenor Ct. Rick. BA25 26
Mayfare
Grosvenor Cres. NW9 BM31 46
Grosvenor Cres. SW1 BV41 3
Grosvenor Cres. SW1 BV41 66
Grosvenor Cres. Dart. CV46 80
Grosvenor Cres. Uxb. AZ36 53
Grosvenor Cres. Uxb. BA37 53
Grosvenor Cres.
Ms. SW1 BV41 3
Grosvenor Cres.
Ms. SW1 BV41 66
Grosvenor Dr. Horn. CV33 51
Grosvenor Dr. Loug. CL23 31
Grosvenor Est. N5 BZ35 48
Grosvenor Est. SW1 BW42 3
Grosvenor Est. SW1 BW42 66
Grosvenor Gdns. E6 CJ38 58
Grosvenor Gdns. N10 BW31 47
Grosvenor Gdns. N14 BW24 29
Grosvenor Gdns. NW2 BQ36 55
Grosvenor Gdns. NW11 BR32 46
Grosvenor Gdns. SW1 BV41 3
Grosvenor Gdns. SW1 BV41 66
Grosvenor Gdns. SW14 BO45 65
Grosvenor Gdns.
Kings. On T. BK50 74
Grosvenor Gdns. Upmin. CY33 51
Grosvenor Gdns. Wall. BW57 95
Grosvenor Gdns. Wdf. Grn. CH29 40
Grosvenor Gdns.
Ms. N. SW1 BV41 3
Grosvenor Gdns.
Ms. N. SW1 BV41 66
Ebury St.
Grosvenor Hill SW19 BR50 75
Grosvenor Hill W1 BV40 3
Grosvenor Hill W1 BV40 56
Grosvenor Pk SE5 BZ43 67
Grosvenor Pk. Rd. E17 CE32 48
Grosvenor Path. Loug. CM23 31
Grosvenor Pl. SW1 BV41 3
Grosvenor Pl. SW1 BV41 66
Grosvenor Rise E. E17 CE32 48
Grosvenor Rd. E6 CJ37 58
Grosvenor Rd. E7 CH36 58
Grosvenor Rd. E10 CF33 48
Grosvenor Rd. E11 CH32 49
Grosvenor Rd. N3 BR29 37
Grosvenor Rd. N9 CB26 39
Grosvenor Rd. N10 BV30 38
Grosvenor Rd. SE25 CB52 87
Grosvenor Rd. SW1 BV43 3
Grosvenor Rd. SW1 BV43 66
Grosvenor Rd. W4 BM42 65
Grosvenor Rd. W7 BJ40 54
Grosvenor Rd. Belv. CQ43 69
Grosvenor Rd. Bexh. CP46 79
Grosvenor Rd. Borwd. BM24 28
Grosvenor Rd. Brent. BK43 64
Grosvenor Rd. Brox. CD13 12
Grosvenor Rd. Dag. CQ33 50
Grosvenor Rd. Epsom BN63 103
Grosvenor Rd. Houns. BE45 64
Grosvenor Rd. Ilf. CM34 49
Grosvenor Rd. Nthwd. BB28 35
Grosvenor Rd. Orp. CN53 88
Grosvenor Rd. Rich. BL46 75
Grosvenor Rd. Rom. CS33 50
Grosvenor Rd. St. Alb. BH14 9
Grosvenor Rd. Stai. AW50 73
Grosvenor Rd. Sthl. BE41 64
Grosvenor Rd. Twick. BJ47 74
Grosvenor Rd. Wall. BV57 95
Grosvenor Rd. Wat. BD24 27
Grosvenor Rd. W. Wick. CE55 87
Grosvenor Rd. Wok. AO60 91
Grosvenor Sq. W1 BV40 3
Grosvenor Sq. W1 BV40 56
Grosvenor St. W1 BV40 3
Grosvenor St. W1 BV40 56
Grosvenor Ter. SE17 BZ43 67
Grosvenor Ter. Hem. H. AW14 8
Grosvenor Vale, Ruis. BB34 44
Grosvenor, Wharf Rd. E14 CF42 67
Grotes Bldgs. SE3 CG44 68
Grotes Pl. SE3 CG44 68
Groton Rd. SW18 BS48 76
Grotto Rd. Twick. BH48 74
Grotto Rd. Wey. AZ55 83
Ground La. Hat. BP11 10
Grove Av. N3 BS29 38
Grove Av. N10 BW30 38
Grove Av. W7 BH39 54
Grove Av. Epsom BO60 94
Grove Av. Pnr. BE32 45
Grove Av. Sutt. BS57 95
Grove Av. Twick. BH47 74
Grove Bldgs. SW3 BU43 3
Grove Bldgs. SW3 BU43 66
Grovebury Clo. Erith CT43 69
Grovebury Rd. SE2 CO41 69
Grove Clo. SE23 CD47 77
Grove Clo. Brom. CH55 88
Grove Clo. Felt. BE49 74
Grove Clo. Ger. Cr. AR30 34
Grove Clo. Kings. On T. BL52 85
Grove Clo. Slou. AQ41 62
Grove Clo. Uxb. AZ35 44
Grove Clo. Wind. AQ47 72
Grove Ct. SE3 CH44 68
Grove Ct. E. Mol. BG53 84
Grove Ct. Tedd. BJ49 74
Cambridge Rd.
Grove Clo. Wal. Abb. CE20 21
Grove Cres. E18 CG30 40
Grove Cres. NW9 BN31 46
Grove Cres. SE5 CA44 67
Grove Cres. Felt. BE49 74
Grove Cres. Kings. On T. BL52 85
Grove Cres. Rick. AZ24 26
Grove Cres. Walt. BC54 83
Grove Cres. Rd. E15 CF36 57
Grovedale Rd. N19 BW34 47
Grove End. Ger. Cr. AR30 34
Grove End Gdns. NW8 BT37 1
Grove End Gdns. NW8 BT37 56
Grove End La. Esher BG54 84
Grove End Rd. NW8 BT38 1
Grove End Rd. NW8 BT38 56
Grove Est. SE5 CA44 67
Grove Est. Pnr. BE32 45
Grove F. P. Kings. On T. BL52 85
Grove Gdns. E15 CG36 58
Grove Gdns. NW4 BP31 46
Grove Gdns. NW8 BU38 1
Grove Gdns. NW8 BU38 56
Grove Gdns. Dag. CS34 50
Grove Gdns. Enf. CC23 30
Grove Gdns. Tedd. BJ49 74
Grove Grn. Nthwd. BA28 35
Grove Grn. Rd. E11 CF34 48
Grove Hall Ct. NW8 BT38 1
Grove Hall Ct. NW8 BT38 56
Grovehall Rd. Bush. BE24 27
Grove Heath La. Wok. AW65 101
Grove Heath North, Wok. AW64 101
Grove Hill E18 CG30 40
Grove Hill, Ger. Cr. AR29 34
Grove Hill, Har. BH33 45
Grove Hill Rd. SE5 CA45 67
Grove Hill Rd. Har. BH33 45
Grove Hill Rd. Red. BU70 121
Grove House Rd. N8 BX31 47
Groveland Av. SW16 BX50 76
Groveland Rd. Beck. CD52 87
Grovelands, W. Mol. BF52 84
Grovelands, St. Alb. BF17 18
Ringway Rd.
Grovelands Ct. N14 BW26 38
Grovelands Rd. N13 BX28 38
Grovelands Rd. N15 CB32 48
Grovelands Rd. Orp. CO50 79
Grovelands Rd. Pur. BX59 95
Grovelands Way, Grays. DC42 71
Grovelands Way, N. Mal. BN53 85
Grove La. SE5 BZ44 67
Grove La. Chesh. AQ17 16
Grove La. Chig. CN27 40
Grove La. Couls. BU59 95
Grove La. Ger. Cr. AQ30 34
Grove La. Kings. On T. BL52 85
Grove La. Uxb. AY38 53
Grove Lea, Hat. BP14 10
Groveley Rd. Sun. BB49 73
Grove Mkt. Pl. SE9 CK46 78
Grove Meadow, Welw. G. C. BS8 5
Grove Ms. W6 BQ41 65
Grove Mill La. Wat. BA22 26
Grove Mo. Hat. BO12 10
Grove Pk. E11 CH32 49
Grove Pk. NW9 BN31 46
Grove Pk. SE5 CA44 67
Grove Pk. Av. E4 CE29 39
Grove Pk. Gdns. W4 BM43 65
Grove Pk. Rd. N15 CA31 48
Grove Pk. Rd. SE9 CJ48 78
Grove Pk. Rd. W4 BM43 65
Grove Pk. Rd. Rain. CU37 59
Grove Pk. Ter. W4 BM43 65
Grove Pass. E2 CB37 57
Grove Pass. Tedd. BJ49 74
Grove Path, Wal. Cr. CB19 21
Grove Pl. NW3 BT34 47
Christchurch Hill
Grove Pl. W3 BN40 55
Grove Pl. W5 BK40 54
Grove Pl. Croy. BY54 86
Grove Pl. Wat. BF23 27
Grove Pl. Wey. BA56 92
Grover Clo. Hem. H. AX13 8
Grove Rd. Croy. BY52 86
Grove Rd. E3 CD37 57
Grove Rd. E4 CE28 39
Grove Rd. E9 CC37 57
Grove Rd. E11 CG33 49
Grove Rd. E17 CE32 48
Grove Rd. N11 BV28 38
Grove Rd. N12 BT28 38
Grove Rd. N15 CA32 48
Grove Rd. NW2 BQ36 55
Grove Rd. SW13 BO44 65
Grove Rd. SW19 BT50 76
Grove Rd. W3 BN40 55
Grove Rd. W5 BK40 54
Grove Rd. Amer. AP22 25
Grove Rd. Ash. BL62 103
Grove Rd. Barn. BU24 29
Grove Rd. Belv. CQ43 69
Grove Rd. Bexh. CS45 69
Grove Rd. Borwd. BL23 28
Grove Rd. Brent. BK42 64
Grove Rd. Cher. AV53 82
Grove Rd. E. Mol. BG52 84
Grove Rd. Edg. BM29 37
Grove Rd. Epsom BO60 94
Grove Rd. Grav. DD46 81
Grove Rd. Grays. DD43 71
Grove Rd. Guil. AU70 118
Grove Rd. Hem. H. AW14 8
Grove Rd. Houns. BF45 64
Grove Rd. Islw. BH44 64
Grove Rd. Mitch. BV51 86
Grove Rd. Nthwd. BA29 35
Grove Rd. Oxt. CF70 114
Grove Rd. Pnr. BE32 45
Grove Rd. Rich. BL46 75
Grove Rd. Rick. AW27 35
Grove Rd. Rom. CO33 50
Grove Rd. St. Alb. BG14 9
Grove Rd. Sev. CV64 108
Grove Rd. Sev. CX64 108
Grove Rd. Shep. BA53 83
Grove Rd. Surb. BK53 84
Grove Rd. Sutt. BS57 95
Grove Rd. Twick. BG48 74
Grove Rd. Uxb. AX36 53
Grove Rd. West. CJ63 106
Grove Rd. Wind. AO44 61
Grove Rd. Wok. AS61 100
Grove Rd. W. Enf. CC22 30
Grover Rd. Wat. BD26 36
Groveside Clo. Lthd. BF67 111
Grove Side
Grove Side, Lthd. BF66 111
Groveside Rd. E4 CG27 40
Grove Stile Waye, Felt. BA47 73
Grove St. N18 CA28 39
Grove St. SE8 CD42 67
Grove Ter. Tedd. BJ49 74
Grove, The E15 CG36 58
Grove, The N3 BS30 38
Ballard's La.
Grove, The N4 BX33 47
Grove, The N6 BV33 47
Grove, The N8 BW32 47
Grove, The N13 BY28 38
Grove, The NW5 BV35 47
Lissenden Gdns.
Grove, The NW9 BN32 46
Grove, The NW11 BR33 46
Grove, The SE21 CA47 77
Grove, The SW16 BW49 76
Grove, The W5 BK40 54
Grove, The Amer. AO21 25
Grove, The Bexh. CP45 69
Grove, The Brwd. CZ28 42
Grove, The Cat. BZ64 105
Grove, The Chesh. AR21 25
Grove, The Couls. BW61 104
Grove, The Edg. BM28 37
Grove, The Egh. AT49 72
Grove, The Enf. BY23 29
Grove, The Epsom BO58 94
Grove, The Epsom BO60 94
Grove, The Esher BF54 84
Grove, The Grav. DH47 81
Grove, The Grnf. BG39 54
Grove, The Hat. BS16 20
Grove, The Islw. BH44 64
Grove, The Pot. B. BT19 20
Grove, The Rad. BJ20 18
Grove, The Sev. CZ58 99
Grove, The Sid. CQ49 79
Grove, The Swans. DC46 81
Grove, The Tedd. BJ49 74
Grove, The Upmin. CX35 51
Grove, The Uxb. AZ35 44
Grove, The Walt. BC53 83
Grove, The West. CJ62 106
Grove, The W. Wick. CE55 87
Grove, The Wey. AW56 92
Grove, The Wok. AS61 100
Grove Val. SE22 CA45 67
Grove Val. Chis. CL50 78
Grove Vill. E14 CE40 57
Grove Wk. N1 CA38 2
Groveway SW9 BX44 66
Groveway, Dag. CP35 50
Grove Way, Esher BG54 84
Grove Way, Rick. AT25 25
Grove Way, Uxb. AX36 53
Groveway, Wem. BM35 46
Grove Wd. Hill, Couls. BW60 95
Grove Wood Clo. Rick. AT25 25
Grovewood Rd. Rich. BM44 65
Sandycombe Rd.
Greek Ct W1 BW39 1
Grt. Cambridge Rd.
Wal. Cr. CC19 21
Grt. Julians, Rick. AZ24 26
Grubb Rd. Oxt. CJ67 115
Grubs La. Hat. BS14 11
Grummant Rd. SE15 CA44 67
Grundy St. E14 CE39 57
Gruneisen Rd. N3 BS29 38
Grt. Fox Meadow, Brwd. CZ22 33
Guardsman Clo. Brwd. DB28 42
Woodman Rd.
Guards Rd. Wind. AL44 61
Guards Wk. Wind. AL44 61
Gubbins La. Rom. CW29 42
Gubyon Av. SE24 BY46 76
Guerin Sq. E3 CE37 58
Malmesbury Rd.
Guerin St. E3 CD38 57
Guernsey Clo. Houns. BF43 64
Guernsey Farm Dr. Wok. AR61 100
Guernsey Gro. SE24 BZ47 77
Guernsey Rd. E11 CF33 48
Guessens Ct. Welw. G. C. BQ8 5
Guessens Gro. Welw. G. C. BQ8 5
Guessens Wk. Welw. G. C. BQ7 5
Guibal Rd. SE12 CH47 78
Guildables La. Eden CK70 115
Guild Cft. Guil. AT70 118
Guildersfield Rd. SW16 BX50 76
Guildford Av. Felt. BB47 73
Guildford Av. Surb. BL53 85
Guildford & Goldalming
By Pass, Guil. AO72 118
Guildford Gro. SE10 CE44 67
Guildford La. Guil. AU71 118
Guildford Lodge Ri. Leath. BB68 110
Guildford Pk. Av. Guil. AQ71 118
Guildford Pk. Rd. Guil. AQ71 118
Guildford Pl. Wok. AS63 100
Guildford Rd. E17 CF30 39
Guildford Rd. N1 CA36 2
Guildford Rd. SW8 BX44 66
Guildford Rd. Cher. AU57 91
Guildford Rd. Cher. AV54 82
Guildford Rd. Croy. BZ53 87
Guildford Rd. Dor. BC73 119
Guildford Rd. Dor. BF72 119
Guildford Rd. Ilf. CN34 49
Guildford Rd. Leath. BB68 110
Guildford Rd. Lthd. BE67 111
Guildford Rd. Lthd. BH65 102
Guildford Rd. Rom. CV29 42
Guildford Rd. St. Alb. BJ14 9
Guildford Rd. Wok. AS63 100
Guilfords, Harl. CP9 6
Guildford St. Stai. AW50 73
Guildford Way, Wall. BX56 95
Guildhall Bldgs. EC2 BZ39 2
Guildhall Bldgs. EC2 BZ39 57
Basinghall St.
Guildhall Yd. EC2 BZ39 2
Guildhall Yd. EC2 BZ39 57
Gresham St.
Guildhouse St. SW1 BW42 3
Guildhouse St. SW1 BW42 66
Guildown Av. N12 BS28 38
Holden Rd.
Guildown Av. Guil. AQ72 118
Guildown Rd. Guil. AQ72 118
Guild Rd. SE7 CJ42 68
Guild Rd. Erith CT43 69
Guilds Way E17 CD30 39
Guileshill La. Wok. AY65 101
Guilford Pl. WC1 BX38 56
Guilford Rd. Guil. AR66 109
Guilford Pl. WC1 BX38 2
Guilford St. WC1 BX38 2
Guilford St. WC1 BX38 56
Guilsborough Clo. NW10 BO36 55
Guinne Clo. Hayes BA41 63
Guinness Bldgs. E2 CB37 2
Guinness Bldgs. SE1 CA42 67
Guinness Bldgs. SE11 BY42 4
Guinness Bldgs. SE17 BZ42 67
Guinness Bldgs. SW3 BU42 3
Guinness Bldgs. SW3 BU42 66
Guinness Bldgs. W6 BQ42 65
Fulham Palace Rd.
Guinness Clo. Hayes BA41 63
Bourne Av.

Guinness Ct. Wok. AP62 100
Ivergh Rd.
Guinness Sq. SE1 CA42 67
Page's Wk.
Guinness Trust SE24 BY45 66
Guinness Trust Bldgs. SW10 CN44 68
Guinness Trust Dws. N16 CA33 48
Guion Rd. SW6 BR44 65
Gulland Clo. Bush. BG24 27
Gulland Wk. N1 BZ36 57
Marquess Est.
Gullbrook, Hem. H. AW13 8
Gull Clo. Wall. BX57 95
Gullet Wood Rd. Wat. BC21 17
Ruston Av.
Gulliver Clo. Nthlt. BE37 54
Gulliver Rd. Sid. CN48 78
Gulliver St. SE16 CD41 67
Gull Wk. Rain. CU37 59
Gumleigh Rd. W5 BK42 64
Gumeley Rd. Islw. BJ45 64
Gumley Rd. Grays. DB43 70
Gumping Rd. Orp. CM55 88
Gunduff St. SE11 BY42 4
Gurnard Clo. West Dr. AX40 53
Trout Rd.
Gundulf St. SE11 BY42 66
Gundulph Rd. Brom. CJ52 88
Gunfleet Clo. Grav. DJ47 81
Roehampton Clo.
Gun Hill, Til. DH43 71
Gunmaker's La. E3 CD37 57
Gunner La. SE18 CL42 68
Gunnersbury Av. W3 BM41 65
Gunnersbury Av. W5 BL40 55
Gunnersbury Ct. W3 BM41 65
Bollo La.
Gunnersbury Cres. W3 BM41 65
Gunnersbury Dr. W5 BL41 65
Gunnersbury Gdns. W3 BM41 65
Gunnersbury La. W3 BM41 65
Gunnersbury Ms. Brent. BM42 65
Gunners Gro. E4 CF27 39
Gunners Rd. SW18 BT48 76
Gunning St. SE18 CN42 68
Gunn Rd. Swans. DC46 81
Gunstor Rd. N16 CA35 48
Gun St. E1 CA39 2
Gunter Gro. SW10 BT43 66
Gunter Gro. Edg. BN30 37
Gunterstone Rd. W14 BR42 65
Gunthorpe St. E1 CA39 2
Gunthorpe St. E1 CA39 57
Wentworth St.
Gunton Rd. E5 CB34 48
Gunton Rd. SW17 BV50 76
Gurdon Rd. SE7 CH42 68
Gurnell Gro. W13 BH38 54
Gurney Clo. E15 CG35 49
Gurney Rd.
Gurney Ct. Rd. St. Alb. BH12 9
Gurney Cres. Croy. BX54 86
Gurney Dr. N2 BT31 47
Gurney Rd. E15 CG35 49
Gurney Rd. Cars. BU56 95
Gurney Rd. Nthlt. BC38 53
Gurnsey Clo. Houns. BF44 64
Sutton Rd.
Guthrie St. SW3 BU42 3
Guthrie St. SW3 BU42 66
Cale St.
Gutter La. EC2 BZ39 2
Gutter La. EC2 BZ39 57
Guyatt Gdns. Mitch. BV51 86
Ormerod Gdns.
Guy Rd. Wall. BW55 86
Guyscliff Rd. SE13 CF46 77
Guysfield Clo. Rain. CU37 59
Guysfield Dr. Rain. CU37 59
Guy St. SE1 BZ41 4
Guy St. SE1 BZ41 67
Gwendolen Av. SW15 BQ45 65
Gwendolen Clo. SW15 BQ46 75
Gwendolen Av. E13 CH37 58
Gwendwr Rd. W14 BR42 65
Gwent Clo. Wat. BD20 18
Gwillim Clo. Sid. CO46 79
Gwydor Rd. Beck. CC52 87
Gwydyr Rd. Brom. CG52 88
Gwynne Av. Croy. CC54 87
Gwynne Clo. Wind. AM44 61
Cawcott Dr.
Gwynne Pl. WC1 BX38 56
King's Cross Rd.
Gwynne Rd. SW11 BT44 66
Gwynne Vaughan Av. Guil. AQ68 109
Gwynn Rd. Grav. DE48 81
Gyfford Wk. Wal. Cr. CB19 21
Gylcote Clo. SE5 BZ45 67
Gyles Pk. Stan. BK29 36
Gyllyngdune Gdns. Ilf. CN34 49
Gypsy La. Wey. AZ55 83
Haarlem Rd. W14 BQ41 65
Haberdasher St. N1 BZ38 2
Haberdasher St. W1 BZ38 57
Habet Rd. W1 BT39 1
Habgood Rd. Loug. CK24 31
Hackbridge Pk. Gdns. Cars. BU55 86
Hackbridge Rd. Wall. BV55 86
Hacketts La. Wok. AV60 91
Hackford Rd. SW9 BX44 66
Hackforth Clo. Barn. BP25 28
Hackington Cres. Beck. CE50 77
Hackney Clo. Borwd. BN25 28
Hackney Gro. E8 CB36 57
Hackney Rd. E2 CA38 2
Hackney Rd. E2 CA38 57
Hacombe Rd. SW19 BT50 76
Hacton Dr. Horn. CV35 51
Hacton La. Horn. CW34 51
Hacton Parkway, Upmin. CW35 51
Hadden Way SE28 CN41 68
Hadden Way, Grnf. BG36 54
Haddington Rd. Brom. CF48 77
Haddon Clo. Borwd. BM23 28
Haddon Clo. Enf. CB25 30
Haddon Clo. Hem. H. AZ14 8
Haddon Clo. N. Mal. BO53 85
Cromwell Av.
Haddon Gro. Sid. CN47 78
Haddon Rd. Orp. CP53 89
Haddon Rd. Rick. AU25 25
Haddon Rd. Sutt. BS56 95
Thorncroft Rd.
Haddo St. SE10 CE43 67
Haden Ct. N4 BY34 47
Hadfield Rd. Stai. AX47 73
Hadleigh Ct. Brox. CD14 12
Hadleigh Clo. E1 CC38 57
Martus Rd.
Hadleigh Rd. N9 CB26 39
Hadleigh St. E2 CC38 57
Hadley Clo. N21 BY25 29
Hadley Clo. Borwd. BL25 28
Hadley Comm. Barn. BS23 29
Hadley Gdns. W4 BN42 65
Hadley Gdns. Sthl. BE42 64
Hadley Grn. Rd. Barn. BR23 28
Hadley Grn. W. Barn. BR23 28
Hadley Gro. Barn. BR23 28
Hadley Highstone, Barn. BR23 28
Hadley Ridge, Barn. BR24 28
Hadley Rd. Barn. BS24 29
Hadley Rd. Barn. BU22 29
Hadley Rd. Barn. BX23 29
Hadley Rd. Belv. CQ42 69
Hadley Rd. Mitch. BW52 86
Hadley St. NW1 BV36 56
Hadley Way N21 BY25 29
Hadley Wood Ri. Sth. Croy. BY61 104
Hadlow Pl. SE19 CB50 77
Hadlow Rd. Sid. CO49 79
Hadlow Rd. Well. CP43 69
Hadlow Way, Grav. DF50 81
Hadrian Clo. Stai. AY47 73
Hadrian Clo. Wall. BX57 95
Hadrian Est. E2 CB37 57
Hadrians Clo. St. Alb. BE15 9
Hadrians Ride, Enf. CA25 30
Hadrian St. SE10 CG42 68
Hadrian Way, Stai. AX47 73
Hadyn Pk. Rd. W12 BP41 65
Hafer Rd. SW11 BU45 66
Hafton Rd. SE6 CG47 78
Hagden La. Wat. BB25 26
Haggard Rd. Twick. BJ47 74
Haggerston Est. E8 CA37 2
Haggerston Est. E8 CA37 57
Haggerston Rd. E8 CA36 2
Haggerston Rd. E8 CA36 57
Haggerston Rd. Borwd. BL22 28
Hague St. E2 CB38 57
Derbyshire St.
Ha-ha Rd. SE18 CK43 68
Haig Clo. St. Alb. BJ14 9
Haig Cres. Red. BV71 121
Haig Rd. Stan. BK28 36
Haig Rd. Uxb. AZ39 53
Haig Rd. West. CK62 106
Haig Rd. E. E13 CJ38 58
Haig Rd. W. E13 CJ38 58
Haigville Gdns. Ilf. CL31 49
Haileybury Av. Enf. CA25 30
Haileybury Rd. Orp. CO56 98
Hailey Rd. Belv. CR41 69
Hailsham Av. SW2 BX48 76
Hailsham Clo. Rom. CV28 42
Hailsham Clo. Surb. BK54 84
Hailsham Gdns. Rom. CV28 42
Hailsham Rd. SW17 BV50 76
Hailsham Rd. Rom. CV28 42
Hailsham Ter. N18 BZ28 39
Haimo Rd. SE9 CJ46 78
Hainault Ct. E17 CF31 48
Hainault Gore, Rom. CQ32 50
Hainault Gro. Chig. CM28 40
Hainault Rd. E11 CF33 48
Hainault Rd. Chig. CL27 40
Hainault Rd. Rom. CO29 41
Hainault Rd. Rom. CQ32 50
Hainault Rd. Rom. CS30 41
Hainault St. SE9 CL47 78
Hainault St. Ilf. CM34 49
Haines Ct. Wey. BA56 93
Haines St. SW8 BW43 66
Haines Way, Wat. BC20 17
Hainford Clo. SE4 CD45 67
Frendsbury Rd.
Hainsford Clo. SE4 CC45 67
Hainthorpe Rd. SE27 BY48 76
Hainton Path E1 CB39 57
Watney Market
Halbert Ms. E5 CB34 48
Knightland Rd.
Halbutt Gdns. Dag. CQ34 50
Halbutt Gdns. Dag. CQ34 50
Halbutt St. Dag. CQ34 50
Halcomb St. N1 CA37 2
Halcomb St. N1 CA37 57
Orsman Rd.
Halcot Av. Bexh. CR46 79
Halcrow St. E1 CB39 57
Halcyon Way, Horn. CW33 51
Haldane Clo. N10 BV29 38
Haldane Clo. N11 BV29 38
Hampden Rd.
Haldane Pl. SW18 BS47 76
Haldane Rd. E6 CJ38 58
Haldane Rd. SW6 BR43 65
Haldane Rd. Sthl. BG40 54
Haldan Rd. E4 CF29 39
Haldens, Welw. G. C. BR6 5
Haldon Clo. Chig. CN28 40
Arrowsmith Rd.
Haldon Rd. SW18 BR46 75
Hale Clo. E4 CF27 39
Hale Clo. Edg. BN28 37
Hale Clo. Orp. CM56 97
Broadwater Gdns.
Hale Ct. Edg. BN28 37
Hale Dr. NW7 BN29 37
Hale End, Rom. CU29 41
Hale End Rd. E4 CF29 39
Hale End Rd. E17 CF29 39
Hale End Rd. Wdf. Grn. CF29 39
Halefield Rd. N17 CB30 39
Hale Gdns. N17 CB31 48
High Cross Rd.
Hale Gdns. W3 BM40 55
Hale Grove Gdns. NW7 BN28 37
Hale La. NW7 BN28 37
Hale La. Edg. BM28 37
Hale La. Sev. CT62 107
Hale Oak Rd. Sev. CU70 116
Hale Pit Rd. Lthd. BG66 111
Hale Rd. E6 CK38 58
Hale Rd. N17 CB31 48
Halesowen Rd. Mord. BS54 86
Hales St. SE8 CE43 67
Hale St. E14 CE40 57
Haleswood, Cob. BC60 83
Haleswood Rd. Hem. H. AZ13 8
Halesworth Clo. E5 CB34 48
Southwold Rd.
Halesworth Clo. Rom. CW29 42
Halesworth Rd. SE13 CE45 67
Halesworth Rd. Rom. CW29 42
Hale, The E4 CF29 39
Hale, The N17 CB31 48
Hale, The Wem. BJ35 45
Hale, Wk. W7 BH39 54
Haley Rd. NW4 BQ32 46
Renters Av.
Half Acre, Brent. BK43 64
Half Acre Hill, Ger. Cr. AS30 34
Half Acre Rd. W7 BH40 54
Half End Clo. Ruis. BC32 44
Halfhide La. Wal. Cr. CC16 21
Halfhides, Wal. Abb. CF20 21
Halfield Est. W2 BT40 56
Half Moon Cres. N1 BX37 2
Half Moon Cres. N1 BX37 56
Half Moon La. SE24 BZ46 77
Half Moon Pass. E1 CA39 2
Half Moon Pass. E1 CA39 57
Braham St.
Half Moon St. W1 BV40 3
Half Moon St. W1 BV40 56
Halford Rd. E10 CF32 48
Halford Rd. SW6 BS43 66
Halford Rd. Rich. BL46 75
Halford Rd. Uxb. AZ35 44
Halfpenny Clo. Guil. AU73 118
Halfpenny La. Guil. AU71 118
Halfway Grn. Walt. BC55 83
Halfway St. Sid. CM47 78
Haliburton Rd. Twick. BJ46 74
Halidon Clo. E9 CC35 48
Churchill Wk.
Halidon Rise, Rom. CX29 42
Halifax Rd. Enf. BZ23 30
Halifax Rd. Grnf. BF37 54
Halifax St. SE26 CB49 77
Haling Gro. Sth. Croy. BZ57 96
Haling Pk. Gdns. Sth. Croy. BY57 95
Haling Rd. Sth. Croy. BZ57 96
Halings La. Uxb. AU31 43
Halings La. Uxb. AV31 43
Halkin Arc. SW1 BV41 3
Halkin Arc. SW1 BV41 66
Motcomb St.
Halkingcroft Slou. AR41 62
Halkin Ms. SW1 BV41 66
Motcomb St.
Halkin Pl. SW1 BV41 3
Halkin Pl. SW1 BV41 66
Halkin St. SW1 BV41 3
Halkin St. SW1 BV41 66
Hallam Clo. Brwd. DA22 33
Hallam Clo. Chis. CK49 78
Hallam Gdns. Pnr. BE29 36
Hallam Ms. W1 BV39 56
Hallam St.
Hallam Rd. N2 BY31 47
Stanley Rd.
Hallam St. W1 BV38 1
Hallam St. W1 BV38 56
Halland Way, Nthwd. BA29 35
Hall Av. S. Ock. CW40 60
Hall Clo. Rick. AW26 35
Hall Ct. Slou. AQ43 62
Hall Cres. S. Ock. CY41 70
Hall Dene Clo. Guil. AU70 118
Hall Dr. SE26 CB49 77
Hall Dr. W7 BH39 54
Hall Dr. Uxb. AX29 35
Halley Pl. E14 CD39 57
Halley Rd. E7 CJ36 58
Halley Rd. E12 CJ36 58
Halley St. E14 CD39 57
Hall Farm Clo. Stan. BJ27 36
Hall Farm Dr. Twick. BG47 74
Hallfield Est. W2 BS39 1
Hallfield Est. W2 BT39 56
Hallford Way, Dart. CV46 80
Hall Gdns. E4 CD28 39
Hall Gdns. St. Alb. BN15 10
Hall Gate NW8 BT38 1
Hall Gate NW8 BT38 56
Hall Rd.
Hall Grn. La. Brwd. DE26 122
Hall Gro. Welw. G. C. BS9 5
Hall Heath Clo. St. Alb. BJ12 9
Hall Hill, Oxt. CF69 114
Hall Hill, Sev. CX65 108
Halliford Clo. Shep. BB52 83
Halliford Rd. Shep. BB53 83
Halliford Rd. Sun. BB52 83
Halliford St. N1 BX36 2
Halliford St. N1 BZ36 57
Halling, Harl. CN10 6
Hallingbury Rd. Saw. CR5 6
Halling Hill, Harl. CN10 6
Halliwell Rd. SW2 BX46 76
Halliwick Rd. N10 BV30 38
Hall La. E4 CD28 39
Hall La. NW4 BP30 37
Hall La. Brwd. DC24 122
Hall La. Brwd. DC25 122
Hall La. Hayes BA43 63
Hall La. Upmin. CY30 42
Hall La. Upmin. CY33 51
Hallmead, Sutt. BS55 86
Hall Mores, Brox. CE13 12
Hall Oak Wk. NW6 BR36 55
Maygrove Rd.
Hallowell Av. Croy. BX56 95
Hallowell Clo. Mitch. BV52 86
Hallowell Rd. Nthwd. BB29 35
Hallowell Cres. Wat. BC27 35
Hayling Rd.
Hall Pk. Berk. AS13 7
Hall Pk. Gate, Berk. AS14 7
Hall Pk. Hill, Berk. AS14 7
Hall Pk. Rd. Upmin. CY35 51
Hall Pl. W2 BT38 1
Hall Pl. W2 BT38 56
Hall Pl. Wok. AT61 100
Hall Pl. Dr. Wey. BB56 92
Hall Pl. Gdns. St. Alb. BH13 9
Hall Pl. Cres. Bex. CS46 79
Hall Rd. E6 CK37 58
Hall Rd. E15 CF35 48
Hall Rd. NW8 BT38 1
Hall Rd. NW8 BT38 56
Hall Rd. Dart. CW45 70
Hall Rd. Grav. DE48 81
Hall Rd. Islw. BG46 74
Hall Rd. Rom. CP32 50
Hall Rd. Rom. CV31 51
Hall Rd. S. Ock. CY41 70
Hall Rd. Wall. BV58 95
Halls Farm Clo. Wok. AO62 100
Hallside Rd. Enf. CA22 30
Hall St. EC1 BY38 2
Hall St. EC1 BY38 56
Hall St. N12 BT28 38
Hallsville Rd. E16 CG39 58
Hallswelle Rd. NW11 BR32 46
Hall Ter. S. Ock. CY41 70
Hall, The SE3 CH45 68
Hall View SE9 CJ48 78
Hall Way, Pur. BY60 95
Hallwood Ct. Welw. G. C. BR8 5
Hallwood Cres. Brwd. DC26 122
Halons Rd. SE9 CL47 78
Halpin Pl. SE17 BZ42 67
Halsbrook Rd. SE3 CJ45 68
Halsbury Clo. Stan. BJ28 36
Halsbury Rd. E. Nthlt. BG35 45
Halsbury Rd. W. Nthlt. BF35 45
Halsbury St. W12 BP40 55
Halsend, Hayes BC41 63
Halsey Pl. Wat. BC22 26
Halsey St. SW3 BU42 3
Halsey St. SW3 BU42 66
Halsham Cres. Bark. CN35 49
Halsmere Rd. SE5 BY44 66
Halstead Gdns. N21 BZ26 39
Halstead Hill, Wal. Cr. CA18 21
Halstead Rd. E11 CH32 49
Halstead Rd. N21 BZ26 39
Halstead Rd. Enf. CA24 30
Halstead Rd. Erith. CT44 69
Halston Cl. SW11 BU46 76
Northcote Rd.
Halstow Rd. NW10 BQ38 55
Halstow Rd. SE10 CH42 68
Halsway, Hayes BC40 53
Halt Dr. S. Le H. DK42 71
Halt Hill, Egh. AS49 72
Halton Rd. N1 BY36 2
Halton Rd. N1 BY36 56
Halt Robin La. Belv. CR42 69
Halt Robin Rd.
Halt Robin Rd. Belv. CR42 69
Hambalt Rd. SW4 BW46 76
Hamberlins La. Berk. AO11 7
Hamble Clo. Ruis. BB34 44
Hambledon Gdns. SE25 CA52 87
Hambledon Hill, Epsom BN61 103
Hambledon Rd. SW18 BR47 75
Hambledon Rd. Sid. CM47 78
Hambledon Vale, Epsom BN61 103
Hamble La. S. Ock. CZ39 60
Hamble St. SW6 BS45 66
Hamble Wk. Nthlt. BF37 54
Leander Rd.
Hambro Av. Brom. CH54 88
Hambrook Rd. SE25 CB52 87
Hambro Rd. SW16 BW50 76
Hambro Rd. Brwd. DB27 42
Ingrave Rd.
Hambrough Rd. Sthl. BE40 54
Ham Clo. Rich. BK48 74
Hamden Cres. Brwd. DB28 42
Hamden Cres. Dag. CR34 50
Hamelin St. E14 CF39 57
Hamerton Rd. Grav. DD46 81
Hameway E6 CL38 58
Ham Farm Rd. Rich. BK49 74
Hamfield Clo. Oxt. CF67 114
Hamfrith Rd. E15 CG36 58
Ham Gate Av. Rich. BK48 74
Hamilton Av. N9 CB26 39
Hamilton Av. Cob. BC60 92
Hamilton Av. Hodd. CE11 12
Hamilton Av. Ilf. CL31 49
Hamilton Av. Rom. CS30 41
Hamilton Av. Surb. BM55 85
Hamilton Av. Sutt. BR54 85
Hamilton Av. Wok. AV61 100
Hamilton Clo. N17 CA31 48
Hamilton Clo. NW8 BT38 1
Hamilton Clo. NW8 BT38 56
Hamilton Clo. Barn. BU24 29
Hamilton Clo. Cher. AV54 82
Hamilton Clo. Epsom BN59 94
Hamilton Clo. Felt. BB49 73
Hamilton Clo. Pot. B. BP20 19
Hamilton Clo. St. Alb. BF19 18
Hamilton Clo. Stan. BH27 36
Hamilton Ct. W5 BL40 55
Hamilton Rd.
Hamilton Ct. W9 BT38 1
Hamilton Ct. W9 BT38 56
Hamilton Cres. N13 BY28 38
Hamilton Cres. Brwd. DB28 42
Hamilton Cres. Har. BE34 45
Hamilton Cres. Houns. BF46 74
Hamilton Dr. Guil. AQ68 109
Hamilton Dr. Rom. CW30 42
Hamilton Gdns. NW8 BT38 1
Hamilton Gdns. NW8 BT38 56
Hamilton La. N5 BY35 47
Hamilton Mead, Hem. H. AT17 16
Hamilton Pk. N5 BY35 47
Hamilton Pk. Way N5 BY35 47
Hamilton Pl. SE20 CB51 87
Hamilton Pl. W1 BV40 3
Hamilton Pl. W1 BV40 56
Hamilton Pl. Sun. BC50 73
Hamilton Rd. E15 CG38 58
Hamilton Rd. E17 CD30 39
Hamilton Rd. N2 BT31 47
Hamilton Rd. N9 CB26 39
Hamilton Rd. NW10 BP35 46
Hamilton Rd. NW11 BQ33 46
Hamilton Rd. SE27 BZ49 77
Hamilton Rd. SW19 BS50 76
Hamilton Rd. W4 BO41 65
Hamilton Rd. W5 BL40 55
Hamilton Rd. Barn. BU24 29
Hamilton Rd. Berk. AQ13 7
Hamilton Rd. Bexh. CQ44 69
Hamilton Rd. Brent. BK43 64
Hamilton Rd. Felt. BB49 73
Hamilton Rd. Har. BH32 45
Hamilton Rd. Hayes BC40 53
Hamilton Rd. Ilf. CL35 49
Hamilton Rd. Kings L. BA20 17
Hamilton Rd. Rom. CU32 50
Hamilton Rd. St. Alb. BJ13 9
Hamilton Rd. Sid. CO49 79
Hamilton Rd. Sthl. BE40 54
Hamilton Rd. Th. Hth. BZ52 87
Hamilton Rd. Twick. BH47 74
Hamilton Rd. Uxb. AX38 53
Hamilton Rd. Wat. BC27 35
Hamilton Sq. SE1 BZ41 4
Hamilton Sq. SE1 BZ41 67
Kipling St.
Hamilton St. SE8 CD43 67
Deptford High St.
Hamilton St. Wat. BD25 27
Hamilton Ter. NW8 BS37 1
Hamilton Ter. NW8 BT38 56
Hamilton Way N3 BS29 38
Hamilton Way, Wall. BW58 95
Hamish St. SE11 BX42 4
Hamish St. SE11 BX42 66
Lambeth Wk.
Ham La. Egh. AQ49 72
Ham La. Wind. AQ46 72
Ham La. Wind. AR45 62
Hamlea Clo. SE12 CH46 78
Hamlet Clo. Rom. CR29 41
Hamlet Clo. Wdf. Grn. CH29 40
Hamlet Gdns. W6 BP62 65
Hamlet Hill, Harl. CH13 13
Hamlet Rd. SE19 CA50 77
Hamlet Rd. Rom. CQ29 41
Hamlets Way E3 CD38 57
Hamlet, The Berk. AT11 7
Hamlin Cres. Pnr. BD32 45
Hamlin Rd. Sev. CT64 107
Hamlyn Gdns. SE19 CA50 77
Hammarskjold Rd. Harl. CM10 6
Hammelton Rd. Brom. CG51 88
Hammer La. Hem. H. AY13 8
Hammers Gate, St. Alb. BF16 18
Hammers La. NW7 BP28 37
Hammersley Av. E16 CG39 58
Hammersmith Br. Rd. W6 BQ42 65
Hammersmith Gro. W6 BQ41 65
Hammersmith Rd. W6 BQ42 65
Hammersmith Rd. W14 BR42 65
Hammersmith Ter. W6 BP42 65
Hammett St. EC3 CA40 57
Minories
Hamm Moor La. Wey. AY56 92
Hammond Av. Mitch. BV51 86
Hammond Clo. Barn. BR25 28
Hammond Clo. Hamptn. BF51 84
Hammond Clo. Har. BG35 45
Lilian Board Way
Hammond Clo. Wal. Cr. CA16 21
Hammond Clo. Wok. AR61 100
Hammond Rd. Enf. CB23 30
Hammond Rd. Sthl. BE41 64
Hammond Rd. Wok. AR61 100
Hammond St. Rd. Wal. Cr. BZ16 21
Hammonds La. Brwd. DA29 42
Hammond St. NW5 BW36 56
Hammond Way SE28 CO40 59
Hamonde Clo. Edg. BM27 37
Hamond Sq. N1 CA37 2
Hamond Sq. N1 CA37 57
Hoxton St.
Ham Pk. Rd. E7 CH36 58
Ham Pk. Rd. E15 CG36 58
Hampden Av. Beck. CD51 87
Hampden Clo. Slou. AQ37 52
Hampden Ct. N10 BV29 38
Hampden Cres. Wal. Cr. CB19 21
Hampden Gurney St. W1 BU39 56
Seymour Pl.
Hampden La. N17 CA30 39
Hampden Rd. N8 BY31 47
Hampden Rd. N10 BV29 38
Hampden Rd. N17 CB30 39
Hampden Rd. Beck. CD51 87
Hampden Rd. Ger. Cr. AR30 34
Hampden Rd. Grays DD42 71
Hampden Rd. Har. BG30 36
Hampden Rd. Kings. On T. BM51 85
Hampden Rd. Rom. CR29 41
Hampden Rd. Slou. AS41 62
Hampden Sq. N14 BV26 38
Hampden Way N14 BV26 38
Hampden Way, Wat. BB21 26
Hampdon Pl. St. Alb. BH18 18
Hamper Mill La. Wat. BC26 35
Hampshire Av. Slou. AO39 52
Hampshire Clo. N18 CB28 39
Berkshire Gdns.
Hampshire Gdns. S. Le H. DK41 71
Somerset Rd.
Hampshire Rd. N22 BX29 38

Hampshire Rd. Horn. CX31 51
Hampshire St. NW5 BW36 56
Torriano Av.
Hampson Way SW8 BX44 66
Hampstead Gdns. NW3 BU35 47
Rosslyn Hill
Hampstead Gdns. NW11 BS32 47
Hampstead Gro. NW3 BT34 47
Hampstead High St. NW3 BT35 47
Hampstead Hill Gdns. NW3 BT35 47
Hampstead La. N6 BU33 47
Hampstead La. NW3 BT33 47
Hampstead La. Dor. BH72 119
Hampstead Rd. NW1 BW37 1
Hampstead Rd. NW1 BW37 56
Hampstead Rd. Dor. BJ72 119
Hampstead Sq. NW3 BT34 47
Hampstead Way NW11 BS32 47
Hampton Clo. NW6 BS38 56
Hampton Clo. SW20 BQ50 75
Hampton Ct. Av. E. Mol. BG53 84
Hampton Ct. Rd. Hamp. BG51 84
Hampton Ct. Rd. E. Mol. BH52 84
Hampton Ct. Rd.
Kings. on T. BH52 84
Hampton Ct. Way, E. Mol. BH53 84
Hampton Ct. Way, Surb. BH55 84
Hampton Cres. Grav. DJ48 81
Hampton Gro. NW3 BU35 47
Pond St.
Hampton Gro. Epsom BO59 94
Hampton La. Felt. BE49 74
Hampton Mead. Loug. CL24 31
Hampton Pl. NW6 BS39 56
Hampton Rise, Har. BL32 46
Hampton Rd. E4 CD28 39
Hampton Rd. E7 CH35 49
Hampton Rd. E11 CF33 48
Hampton Rd. NW6 BS38 56
Hampton Rd. Croy. BZ53 87
Hampton Rd. Ilf. CL35 49
Hampton Rd. Red. BU73 121
Hampton Rd. Tedd. BG49 74
Hampton Rd. Twick. BG48 74
Hampton Rd. Wor. Pk. BP55 85
Hampton Rd. E. Felt. BE48 74
Hampton Rd. W. Felt. BE48 74
Hampton St. SE17 BY42 4
Hampton St. SE17 BY42 66
Ham Ridings, Rich. BL49 75
Hamsey Grn. Gdns. Warl. CB61 105
Hamsey Way, Sth. Croy. CB61 105
Ham Shades Clo. Sid. CO48 79
Hamstel Rd. Harl. CM10 6
Ham St. Rich. BK47 74
Ham, The Brent. BK43 64
Ham Vw. Croy. CD53 87
Hanameel St. E16 CH40 58
Hanbury Clo. Wal. Cr. CC18 21
Hanbury Dr. West. CH60 97
Hanbury Path, Wok. AU60 91
Hanbury Rd. N17 CB30 39
Hanbury Rd. W3 BM41 65
Hanbury St. E1 CA39 2
Hanbury St. E1 CB39 2
Hanbury St. E1 CB39 57
Hanbury Wk. Bex. CS48 79
Hancock Rd. E3 CF38 57
Hancock Rd. SE19 BZ50 77
Handa Clo. Hem. H. AZ15 8
Handa Wk. N1 BZ36 57
Marquess Est.
Hand Ct. WC1 BX39 2
Hand Ct. WC1 BX39 56
Sandland St.
Handcroft Rd. Croy. BY54 86
Handel Clo. Edg. BL29 37
Handel Cres. Til. DG43 71
Handel St. WC1 BX38 2
Handel St. WC1 BX38 56
Handel Way, Edg. BM29 37
Handen Rd. SE12 CG46 78
Handford Rd. S. Ock. CW40 60
Handforth Rd. SW9 BY43 66
Hand La. Saw. CP6 6
Handley Rd. E9 CC37 57
Victoria Pk. Rd.
Handover Rd. N15 CA31 48
Handpost Hill, Pot. B. BV17 20
Handside Clo. Welw. G. C. BQ8 5
Handside Clo. Wor. Pk. BQ54 85
Handside Grn. Welw. G. C. BQ7 5
Handside La. Welw. G. C. BP9 5
Hands Wk. E16 CH39 58
Butcher's Rd.
Handsworth Av. E4 CF29 39
Handsworth Clo. Wat. BC27 35
Handsworth Rd. N17 BZ31 48
Handtrough Way, Bark. CL37 58
Fresh Wharf Rd.
Hanford Clo. SW18 BS47 76
Hanford Row SW19 BQ50 75
Hanger Ct. W5 BL38 55
Heathcroft
Hanger Grn. W5 BM38 55
Western Av.
Hanger Hill, Wey. AZ57 92
Hanger La. W5 BL37 55
Hanger Ruding, Wat. BE27 36
Hanger Vale La. W5 BL39 55
Hang Grove Hill, Orp. CL60 97
Hanging Hill La. Brwd. DD27 122
Hankey Pl. SE1 BZ41 4
Hankey Pl. SE1 BZ41 67
Hankins La. NW7 BO27 37
Hanks Vw. Cob. BE60 93
Hanley Clo. Wind. AL44 61
Hanley Rd. N4 BX33 47
Hanmer Wk. N7 BX34 47
Andover Est.
Hanmer Wk. N7 BX34 47
Newington Way
Hannell Rd. SW6 BR43 65
Hannen Rd. SE27 BY48 76
Hannibal Rd. E1 CC39 57
Hannibal Rd. Stai. AX47 73
Hannington Rd. SW4 BV45 66
Hanover Av. Felt. BC47 73
Hanover Cir. Hayes BA39 53
Hanover Clo. Red. BW67 113
Hanover Clo. Rich. BM43 65
Cambridge Rd.
Hanover Clo. Sutt. BR56 94
Hanover Ct. W12 BP40 55
Hanover Gdns. SE11 BY43 66
Hanover Gdns. Ilf. CM29 40
Hanover Gate NW1 BU38 1
Hanover Gate NW1 BU38 56
Hanover Gate
Mans. NW1 BU38 1
Hanover Grn. Hem. H. AW14 8
Hanover Pk. SE15 CB44 67
Hanover Pl. WC2 BX40 56
Long Acre
Hanover Pl. Egh. AR50 72
Blay's La.
Hanover Rd. NW10 BQ36 55
Hanover Rd. SW19 BT50 76
Hanover Sq. W1 BV39 1
Hanover Sq. W1 BV39 56
Hanover St. W1 BV39 1
Hanover St. W1 BV39 56
Hanover St. Croy. BY55 86
Latimer Rd.
Hanover Ter. NW1 BU38 1
Hanover Ter. NW1 BU38 56
Hanover Ter. Ms. NW1 BU38 1
Hanover Ter. Ms. NW1 BU38 56
Hanover Wk. Wey. BB55 83
Hanover Way, Bexh. CP45 69
Hanover Way, Wind. AM44 61
Hanover Yd. N1 BY37 56
Noel Rd.
Hansard Ms. W14 BQ41 65
Hansart Way, Enf. BY23 29
Hans Cres. SW1 BU41 3
Hans Cres. SW1 BU41 66
Hanselin Clo. Stan. BH28 36
Chenduit Way
Hansells Mead, Harl. CH11 13
Hanshades Clo. Sid. CO48 79
Hanshaw Dr. Edg. BN30 37
Hansler Gro. E. Mol. BG53 84
Hansler Rd. SE22 CA46 77
Hansol Rd. Bexh. CQ46 79
Hanson Clo. SW12 BV47 76
Hanson Clo. Loug. CM23 31
Hanson Dr. Loug. CM23 31
Hanson Gdns. Sthl. BE41 64
Hanson Grn. Loug. CM23 31
Hanson St. W1 BW39 1
Hanson St. W1 BW39 56
Hans Pl. SW1 BU41 3
Hans Pl. SW1 BU41 66
Hans Rd. SW3 BU41 3
Hans Rd. SW3 BU41 66
Hans St. SW1 BU41 3
Hans St. SW1 BU41 66
Pavilion Rd.
Hanway Pl. W1 BW39 1
Hanway Pl. W1 BW39 56
Hanway St.
Hanway Rd. W7 BG39 54
Hanway St. W1 BW39 1
Hanway St. W1 BW39 56
Hanworth Clo. Felt. BE49 74
Hanworth La. Cher. AV54 82
Hanworth Rd. Felt. BC47 73
Hanworth Rd. Hamptn. BE49 74
Hanworth Rd. Houns. BE47 74
Hanworth Rd. Red. BU73 121
Hanworth Rd. Sun. BC50 73
Hanworth Trd. Est. Felt. BE48 74
Hanyards End, Pot. B. BW17 20
Hill Rise
Hanyards La. Pot. B. BW17 20
Hapgood Clo. Har. BG35 45
Harad's Pl. E1 CB40 57
Ensign St.
Harb Clo. Slou. AL40 61
Harben Rd. NW6 BT36 56
Harberson Rd. E15 CG37 58
Harberson Rd. SW12 BV47 76
Harberton Rd. N19 BW33 47
Harberts Rd. Harl. CL11 13
Harbert Rd. E4 CC28 39
Harbet Rd. W2 BT39 1
Harbet Rd. W2 BT39 56
Harbex Clo. Bex. CR47 79
Harbinger Rd. E14 CE42 67
Harbledown Pl. Orp. CP52 89
Okemore Gdns.
Harbledown Rd. SW6 BS44 66
Harbledown Rd. Sth. Croy. CB59 96
Harbord St. SW6 BQ44 65
Harborough Av. Sid. CN47 78
Harborough Rd. SW16 BX49 76
Harbourer Clo. Ilf. CO28 41
Harbourer Rd. Ilf. CO29 41
Harbourfield Rd. Bans. BS61 104
Harbour Rd. SE5 BZ45 67
Harbridge Av. SW15 BO47 75
Harbury Rd. Cars. BU58 95
Harbut Rd. SW11 BT45 66
Harcombe Rd. N16 CA34 48
Harcourt Av. E12 CK35 49
Harcourt Av. Edg. BN27 37
Harcourt Av. Sid. CP46 79
Harcourt Av. Wall. BV56 95
Harcourt Clo. Egh. AV50 72
Harcourt Fld. Wall. BV56 95
Harcourt La. Maid. AJ41 61
Harcourt Rd. E15 CG37 58
Harcourt Rd. N22 BW30 38
Harcourt Rd. SE4 CD45 67
Harcourt Rd. SW19 BS50 76
Harcourt Rd. Bexh. CQ45 69
Harcourt Rd. Bush. BF25 27
Harcourt Rd. Maid. AJ41 61
Harcourt Rd. Th. Hth. BX53 86
Harcourt Rd. Wall. BV56 95
Harcourt Rd. Wind. AM44 61
Harcourt St. W1 BU39 1
Harcourt St. W1 BU39 56
Harcourt Ter. SW10 BS42 3
Harcourt Ter. SW10 BS42 66
Harcroft, Dor. BK73 119
Hardcourts Clo. W. Wick. CE55 87
Hardel Rise SW2 BY47 76
Harden Rd. Grav. DF48 81
Harden's Manor Way SE7 CJ41 68
Harden St. SE18 CK42 68
Harder's Rd. Ms. SE15 CB44 67
Hardess St. SE24 BY45 66
Hardie Clo. NW10 BN35 46
Hardie Rd. Dag. CS34 50
Hardinge Clo. Uxb. AZ39 53
Hardinge Rd. N18 CA29 39
Hardinge Rd. NW10 BP37 55
Hardinge St. E1 CC39 57
Harding Rd. Bexh. CQ44 69
Harding Rd. Chesh. AO18 16
Harding Rd. Epsom. BO63 103
Harding Rd. Grays. DG41 71
Hardings La. SE20 CC50 77
Hardings Row, Iver AU38 52
Hardings, Welw. G. C. BT7 5
Hardley Cres. Horn. CV31 51
Hardman Rd. SE7 CH42 68
Hardman Rd. Kings. On T. BL51 85
Hardwick Clo. Stan. BK28 36
Marsh La.
Hardwicke Av. Houns. BF44 64
Hardwicke Clo. Cob. BG61 102
Hardwicke Clo. St. Alb. BK17 18
Hardwicke Rd. N13 BX29 38
Hardwicke Rd. W4 BN42 65
Hardwicke Rd. Reig. BS70 121
Hardwicke Rd. Rich. BK49 74
Hardwicke St. Bark. CM37 58
Hardwick Gn. W13 BJ39 54
Templewood
Hardwicke Rd. Red. BT71 121
Hardwick La. Cher. AU54 82
Hardwick St. EC1 BY38 2
Hardwick St. EC1 BY38 56
Hardwicks Way SW18 BS46 76
Hardwidge St. SE1 CA41 4
Hardwidge St. SE1 CA41 67
Snows Fields
Hardy Av. Grav. DF48 81
Hardy Av. Ruis. BC35 44
Hardy Clo. Dor. BJ74 119
Spook Hill
Hardy Clo. Pnr. BD33 45
Hardy Gro. Dart. CX45 70
Hardy Pass N22 BY30 38
Cranbrook Pk.
Hardy Rd. SE3 CG43 68
Hardy Rd. SW19 BS50 76
Hardy Rd. Hem. H. AY13 8
Hardy Way, Enf. BY23 29
Harebell Hill, Cob. BD60 93
Harebell Way, Rom. CV29 42
Hare & Billet Rd. SE3 CF44 67
Hare Bl. Welw. G. C. BR9 5
Harebreaks, The Wat. BC21 26
Harecourt Rd. N1 BZ36 57
Hare Cres. Wat. BC19 17
Harecroft, Lthd. BF65 102
Haredale Rd. SE24 BZ45 67
Haredon Clo. SE23 CC47 77
Harefield, Esher BH55 84
Harefield, Harl. CO10 6
Harefield Av. Sutt. BQ58 94
Harefield Grn. NW7 BQ29 37
Harefield Ms. SE4 CD45 67
Harefield Pl. Est. Uxb. AY35 44
Harefield Pl. St. Alb. BK12 9
Villiers Cres.
Harefield Rd. N8 BW32 47
Harefield Rd. SE4 CD45 67
Harefield Rd. SW16 BX50 76
Harefield Rd. Rick. AX27 35
Harefield Rd. Sid. CP48 79
Harefield Rd. Uxb. AX36 53
Hare Hall La. Rom. CU31 50
Hare Hill, Wey. AV57 91
Hare Hill Clo. Wok. AW61 101
Harelands Clo. Wok. AR62 100
Harelands La. Wok. AQ62 100
Hare La. Esher BG57 93
Hare La. Esher BH57 93
Hare La. Hat. BP13 10
Hare Pk. Clo. Hem. H. AV13 7
Hare Pl. EC4 BY39 2
Hares Bank, Croy. CF58 96
Haresfield Rd. Dag. CR36 59
Harestone Dr. Cat. CA66 114
Harestone Dr. Cat. CA65 105
Harestone Valley Rd. Cat. CA66 114
Hare St. SE18 CL41 68
Hare St. Springs, Harl. CL11 13
Harewood SW15 BN49 75
Harewood, Rick. AX25 26
Harewood Av. NW1 BU38 1
Harewood Av. NW1 BU38 56
Harewood Av. Nthlt. BE36 54
Harewood Clo. Nthlt. BE36 54
Harewood Clo. Reig. BT69 121
Harewood Dr. Ilf. CK30 40
Harewood Gdns. Sth. Croy. CB61 105
Harewood Hill, Epp. CN21 31
Harewood Pl. W1 BV39 1
Harewood Pl. Slou. AQ41 62
Harewood Rd. SW19 BU50 76
Harewood Rd. Brwd. DA25 33
Harewood Rd. Ch. St. G. AR24 25
Harewood Rd. Islw. BH43 64
Harewood Rd. Sth. Croy. CA57 96
Harewood Rd. Wat. BC27 35
Harewood Row NW1 BU39 1
Harewood Ter. Sthl. BE42 64
Harew Pl. W1 BV39 56
Hanover Sq.
Harfield Dr. Sun. BD51 84
Harfield Gdns. SE5 CA45 67
Harfield Rd. Sun. BD51 84
Harford Clo. E4 CE26 39
Harford Dr. Wat. BB22 26
Harford Rd. E4 CE26 39
Harford St. E1 CD38 57
Harford Wk. N2 BT31 47
Hargood Rd. SE3 CJ44 68
Hargrave Pk. N19 BW34 47
Hargrave Pl. N7 BW35 47
Brecknock Rd.
Hargrave Rd. N19 BW34 47
Hargreaves Av. Wal. Cr. CB18 21
Hargreaves Clo. Wal. Cr. CB19 21
Hargwyne St. SW9 BX45 66
Haringey Pk. N8 BX32 47
Haringey Pass. N4 BY31 47
Haringey Rd. N8 BX31 47
Harkness Clo. Epsom BQ61 103
Harland Av. Croy. CA55 87
Harland Av. Sid. CM48 78
Harland Rd. SE12 CH47 78
Harlech Gdns. Houns. BD43 64
Harlech Rd. N14 BX27 38
Harlequin Av. Brent. BJ43 64
Harlequin Rd. Tedd. BJ50 74
Fairfax Rd.
Harlescott Rd. SE15 CC45 67
Harlesden Clo. Rom. CW29 42
Harlesden Gdns. NW10 BO37 55
Harlesden La. NW10 BP37 55
Harlesden Rd. NW10 BP36 55
Harlesden Rd. Rom. CW29 42
Harlesden Rd. St. Alb. BJ13 9
Harlesden Wk. Rom. CW29 42
Harleston Clo. E5 CB34 48
Southwold Rd.
Harley Clo. Wem. BK36 54
Harley Ct. Har. BG31 45
Harley Ct. St. Alb. BK11 9
Villiers Cres.
Harley Cres. Har. BG31 45
Harleyfood, Brom. CJ51 88
Harleyford Rd. SE11 BX43 4
Harleyford Rd. SE11 BX43 66
Harleyford St. SE11 BY43 66
Harley Gdns. SW10 BT42 3
Harley Gdns. SW10 BT42 66
Harley Gdns. Orp. CN56 97
Harley Gro. E3 CD38 57
Harley Pl. W1 BV39 1
Harley Pl. W1 BV39 56
Harley Rd. NW3 BT36 1
Harley Rd. NW3 BT36 56
Harley Rd. NW10 BO37 55
Harley Rd. Har. BG31 45
Harley St. SE11 BY43 66
Harley St. W1 BV38 1
Harley St. W1 BV38 56
Harling St. SE5 BZ43 67
Harlington Clo. Hayes BA43 63
Harlington High St. Hayes BA43 63
Harlington Rd. Bexh. CQ45 69
Harlington Rd.
Uxb. & Hayes AZ38 53
Harlington Rd. E. Felt. BC47 73
Harlington Rd. W. Felt. BC46 73
Harlow Common Rd. Harl. CP12 14
Harlow Gdns. Rom. CS29 41
Harlow Rd. N13 BZ27 39
Harlow Rd. Bish. CR7 6
Harlow Rd. Harl. CJ11 13
Harlow Rd. Harl. CP8 6
Harlow Rd. Harl. CR8 6
Harlow Rd. Ong. CV13 15
Harlow Rd. Rain. CT37 59
Harlow Rd. Saw. CP7 6
Harlow St. Hem. H. AZ11 8
Harlton Ct. Wal. Abb. CG20 22
Harlyn Dr. Pnr. BC31 44
Harman Av. Grav. DG49 81
Harman Av. Wdf. Grn. CG29 40
Harman Clo. E4 CF28 39
Harman Clo. NW2 BR35 46
Harman Dr. NW2 BR35 46
Harman Dr. Sid. CN46 78
Harman Rd. Enf. CA25 30
Harmer Grn. La. Welw. G. C. BR5 5
Harmer Rd. Swans. DC46 81
Harmer St. Grav. DH46 81
Harmondsworth La.
West Dr. AY43 63
Harmondsworth Rd.
W. Dray. AY42 63
Harmony Clo. NW11 BR32 46
Harmood St. NW1 BV36 56
Harmsworth St. SE17 BY42 4
Harmsworth St. SE17 BY42 66
Harmsworth Way N20 BR26 37
Harnage Rd. Brent. BL42 65
Harness Rd. SE28 CO41 69
Harold Av. Hayes BB41 63
Harold Av. Belv. CQ42 69
Harold Av. Hayes BC41 63
Harold Ct. Rd. Rom. CX29 42
Harold Cres. Wal. Abb. CF19 21
Harold Est. Wal. Abb. CF19 21
Harold Gibbons Ct. SE7 CJ43 68
Harold Hill Ind. Est. Rom. CV29 42
Harold Rd. E4 CF27 39
Harold Rd. E11 CG33 49
Harold Rd. E13 CH37 58
Harold Rd. N8 BX32 47
Harold Rd. N15 CA32 48
Harold Rd. NW10 BN38 55
Harold Rd. SE19 BZ50 77
Harold Rd. Dart. CW49 80
Harold Rd. Sutt. BT56 95
Harold Rd. Wal. Cr. CE20 21
Harold Rd. Wdf. Grn. CH30 40
Harolds Rd. Harl. CK11 13
Haroldstone Rd. E17 CC32 48
Harold Vw. Rom. CW30 42
Heath Rd.
Harp All. EC4 BY39 2
Harp All. EC4 BY39 56
St. Bride St.
Harpenden Rd. E12 CJ34 49
Harpenden Rd. SE27 BY48 76
Harpenden Rd. St. Alb. BH12 9
Harper La. Rad. BJ19 18
Harper Rd. SE1 BZ41 4
Harper Rd. SE1 BZ41 67
Harper La. Brwd. DB22 33
Harper's Yd. N17 CA30 39
Ruskin Rd.
Harpesford Av. Vir. W. AQ53 82
Harp La. EC3 CA40 4
Harp La. EC3 CA40 57
Lwr. Thames St.
Harpley Sq. E1 CC38 57
Harpour Rd. Bark. CM36 58
Harp Rd. W7 BH38 54
Harpsden St. SW11 BV44 66
Battersea Pk. Rd.
Harpsfield, Hat. BO12 10
Harps Oak La. Red. BU66 113
Harptree Way, St. Alb. BJ12 9
Harpur St. WC1 BX39 2
Harpur St. WC1 BX39 56
Dombey St.
Harraden Rd. SE3 CJ44 68
Harrier Clo. Rain. CU36 59
Harriers Clo. W5 BL40 55
Harries Rd. Hayes BD38 54
Harriet Clo. E8 CA37 57
Broadway Mkt. Est.
Harriet Gdns. Croy. CB55 87
Harriet St. SW1 BU41 3
Harriet St. SW1 BU41 66
Sloane St.
Harriet Wk. SW1 BU41 3
Harriet Wk. SW1 BU41 66
Harriet Way, Bush. BG26 36
Harriets Cres. Wal. Abb. CH19 22
Harringay Gdns. N15 BY31 47
Harringay Rd. N15 BY32 47
Harring Sq. NW1 BW37 56
Harrington Clo. Croy. BX55 86
Beddington La.
Harrington Clo. Wind. AM45 61
Harrington Gdns. SW7 BS42 3
Harrington Gdns. SW7 BS42 66
Harrington Hill E5 CB33 48
Harrington Pl. Reig. BS69 121
Reigate Hill
Harrington Rd. E11 CG33 49
Harrington Rd. SE25 CB52 87
Harrington Rd. SW7 BT42 3
Harrington Rd. SW7 BT42 66
Harrington Sq. NW1 BW37 1
Harrington St. NW1 BW38 1
Harrington St. NW1 BW38 56
Harrington Ter. N18 BZ27 39
Harrington Way SE18 CJ41 68
Harriot's La. Ash. BK63 102
Harriott Clo. SE10 CG42 68
Tunnel Av.
Harris Clo. Enf. BY23 29
Harris Clo. Grav. DF48 81
Harris Clo. Houns. BF44 64
Sutton La.
Harris La. Rad. BM20 19
Harrison Clo. Brwd. DE25 122
Harrison Clo. Nthwd. BA29 35
Harrison Clo. Reig. BS71 121
Lymden Gdns.
Harrison Dr. Epp. CR16 23
High Rd.
Harrison Rd. Dag. CR36 59
Harrisons Rise, Croy. BY55 86
Harrison St. WC1 BX38 2
Harrison St. WC1 BX38 56
Harrison Way, Slou. AL40 61
Harris Rd. Bexh. CQ44 69
Harris Rd. Dag. CQ35 50
Harris Rd. Wat. BC21 26
Harris St. E17 CD33 48
Harris St. SE5 BZ43 67
Harris Way, Sun. BB51 83
Harrogate Clo. Slou. AT42 62
Harrogate Rd. Wat. BD27 36
Harrold Rd. Dag. CO35 50
Harrow Av. Enf. CA25 30
Harrow Bottom Rd. Vir. W. AS53 82
Harrowby St. W1 BU39 1
Harrowby St. W1 BU39 56
Harrow Clo. Chess. BK57 93
Harrow Clo. Dor. BJ72 119
Harrow Clo. Wey. AW55 83
Harrow Cotts. Felt. AZ48 73
Harrow Cres. Rom. CU29 41
Harrowdene Clo. Wem. BK35 45
Harrowdene Gdns. Tedd. BJ50 74
Harrowdene Rd. Wem. BK34 45
Harrow Dr. N9 CA26 39
Harrow Dr. Horn. CU32 50
Harrowes Meade, Edg. BM27 37
Harrow Gdns. Warl. CD61 105
Harrowgate Rd. E9 CD36 57
Harrow La. E14 CF40 57
Harrow La. West CM63 106
Harrow Manorway SE2 CP40 59
Harrow Pk. Har. BH34 45
Harrow Pl. E1 CA39 2
Harrow Pl. E1 CA39 57
Harrow Rd. E6 CK37 58
Harrow Rd. E11 CG34 49
Harrow Rd. NW10 BP38 55
Harrow Rd. W2 BS39 56
Harrow Rd. W2 BT39 1
Harrow Rd. W9 BR38 55
Harrow Rd. W10 BR38 55
Harrow Rd. Bark. CN37 58
Harrow Rd. Cars. BU57 95
Harrow Rd. Felt. AZ48 73
Harrow Rd. Ilf. CM35 49
Harrow Rd. Sev. CQ61 107
Harrow Rd. Slou. AS41 62
Harrow Rd. Warl. CD61 105
Harrow Rd. Wem. BH34 45
Harrow Rd. E. Dor. BJ72 119
Harrow Rd. W. Dor. BJ72 119
Harrow View, Har. BG31 45
Harrow Vw. Hayes BC39 53
Harrow Vw. Uxb. BA38 53
Harrow Vw. Rd. W5 BJ38 54
Harrow Way, Shep. BA51 83
Harrow Way, Wat. BE27 36
Harrow Weald, Har. BG29 36
Harrow Weald Pk. Har. BG29 36
Hart Cres. Chig. CN28 40
Hart Dyke Cres. Swan. CS52 89
Hartdyke Rd. Orp. CP55 89

Hart Dyke Rd. Swan. CS52 89
Harte Rd. Houns. BE44 64
Hartfield Av. Borwd. BM25 28
Hartfield Av. Nthlt. BC37 53
Hartfield Clo. Borwd. BM25 28
Hartfield Cres. SW19 BR50 75
Hartfield Cres. Kes. CH55 88
Hartfield Gro. SE20 CB51 87
Hartfield Rd. SW19 BR50 75
Hartfield Rd. Chess. BK56 93
Hartfield Rd. Kes. CH56 97
Hartfield Ter. E3 CE37 57
Hartford Av. Har. BJ31 45
Hartforde Rd. Borwd. BM23 28
Hartford Pl. Grav. DE47 81
Hartford Rd. Bex. CR46 79
Hart Gro. W5 BM40 55
Hart Gro. Sthl. BF39 54
Hart Gro. Clo. W5 BM40 55
Hart Gro.
Harthall La. Hem. H. AZ17 17
Hartham Clo. N7 BX35 47
Hartham Clo. Islw. BJ44 64
Hartham Rd. N7 BX35 47
Hartham Rd. N17 CA30 39
Hartham Rd. Islw. BH44 64
Hartin Clo. Uxb. AY37 53
Harting Rd. SE9 CK49 78
Hartington Clo. Har. BH35 45
Hartington Ct. W4 BM43 65
Hartington Rd. E16 CH39 58
Hartington Rd. E17 CD32 48
Hartington Rd. SW8 BX44 66
Hartington Rd. W4 BM43 65
Hartington Rd. W13 BJ40 54
Hartington Rd. Sthl. BE41 64
Hartington Rd. Twick. BJ46 74
Hartismere Rd. SW6 BR43 65
Hartlake Rd. E9 CC36 57
Hartland Clo. Edg. BM27 37
Hartland Clo. Wey. AX58 92
Hartland Dr. Edg. BM27 37
Hartland Dr. Ruis. BC34 44
Hartland Gro. NW1 BV36 56
Hartland Rd.
Hartland Rd. E15 CG36 58
Hartland Rd. N11 BU28 38
Hartland Rd. NW1 BV36 56
Hartland Rd. NW6 BR37 55
Hartland Rd. Epp. CO19 23
Hartland Rd. Hamptn. BF49 74
Hartland Rd. Horn. CU34 50
Hartland Rd. Mord. BS54 86
Hartland Rd. Wal. Cr. CC18 21
Hartland Rd. Wey. AW57 92
Hartland St. NW1 BV36 56
Hartland Way, Croy. CD55 87
Hartland Way, Mord. BR54 85
Hartley Av. E6 CK37 58
Hartley Av. NW7 BO28 37
Hartley Clo. NW7 BO28 37
Hartley Clo. W3 BM40 55
Uxbridge Rd.
Hartley Clo. Brom. CK51 88
Hartley Clo. Slou. AR37 52
Hartley Down Rd. Pur. BX61 104
Hartley Farm Est. Pur. BX61 104
Hartley Hill, Pur. BX61 104
Hartley Old Rd. Pur. BX61 104
Hartley Rd. E11 CG33 49
Hartley Rd. Croy. BY54 86
Hartley Rd. Long. DC51 90
Hartley Rd. Well. CP43 69
Hartley Rd. West. CM66 115
Hartley St. E2 CC38 57
Hartley Way, Pur. BX61 104
Hartmann Rd. E16 CJ40 58
Harton Rd. N9 CB27 39
Harton St. SE8 CE44 67
Hart Rd. Dor. BJ71 119
Hart Rd. Harl. CP8 6
Hart Rd. St. Alb. BG14 9
Hart Rd. Wey. AY60 92
Hartsbourne Av. Bush. BG27 36
Hartsbourne Rd. Bush. BG27 36
Hartsbourne Way, Hem. H. BA14 8
Harts Clo. Bush. BF23 27
Hartscroft, Croy. CD58 96
Harts Gdns. Guil. AQ69 118
Hartshill, Guil. AO70 118
Harts Hill Clo. Uxb. AZ36 53
Hartshill Rd. Grav. DF48 81
Hartshill Wk. Wok. AQ61 100
Hartshorn Gdns. E6 CL38 58
Hameway
Hartslands Rd. Sev. CV65 108
Hart's La. SE14 CC43 67
Harts La. Bark. CL36 58
Hartslock Dr. SE2 CP41 69
Hartsmead Rd. SE9 CK48 78
Hartspring La. Bush. BF23 27
Hart St. EC3 CA40 4
Hart St. EC3 CA40 57
Mark La.
Hart St. WC2 BX39 2
Hart St. Brwd. DB27 42
Hartsway, Enf. CC24 30
Hartswood Av. Reig. BS72 121
Hartswood Clo. Brwd. DB28 42
Hartswood Clo. Brwd. DC28 122
Hartswood Rd. W12 BO41 65
Hartswood Rd. Brwd. DC28 122
Hartville Rd. SE18 CO42 69
Hartwell Dr. E4 CF29 39
Hartwell St. E8 CA36 57
Dalston La.
Harty Clo. Grays DD40 71
Harvard Ct. NW6 BS35 47
West End La.
Harvard Hill W4 BM43 65
Wolseley Gdns.
Harvard La. W4 BN42 65
Harvard Rd.
Harvard Rd. SE13 CF46 77
Harvard Rd. W4 BM42 65
Harvard Rd. Islw. BH44 64
Harvard Wk. Horn. CU35 50
Harvel Cres. SE2 CP42 69
Harvest Bank Rd. W. Wick. CG55 88
Harvest End, Wat. BD21 27
Harvester Rd. Epsom BN58 94
Harvest Mead, Hat. BP12 10
Harvest Rd. Bush. BF24 27
Harvest Rd. Egh. AR49 72
Harvest Rd. Felt. BC48 73
Harvest Way, Swan. CS54 89
Harvey Centre, Harl. CM11 13
Harvey Fields, Wal. Abb. CF20 21
Harvey Gdns. SE7 CJ42 68
Harvey Gdns. Loug. CL24 31
Harvey Rd. E11 CG33 49
Harvey Rd. N8 BX32 47
Harvey Rd. SE5 BZ44 67
Harvey Rd. Guil. AS71 118
Harvey Rd. Houns. BE47 74
Harvey Rd. Ilf. CL35 49
Harvey Rd. Nthlt. BD36 54
Harvey Rd. Rick. AZ25 26
Harvey Rd. St. Alb. BK16 18
Harvey Rd. Slou. AT41 62
Harvey Rd. Uxb. AZ37 53
Harvey Rd. Walt. BC54 83
Harvey's La. Rom. CS34 50
Harvey St. N1 BZ37 2
Harvey St. N1 BZ37 57
Harvil Rd. Sid. CP49 79
Harvil Rd. Uxb. AX31 44
Harvington Wk. E8 CB36 57
Wilman Gro.
Harvist Rd. NW6 BQ37 55
Harwater Dr. Loug. CK23 31
Harwell Clo. Ruis. BA33 44
Harwell Pass N2 BU31 47
Harwood Av. Brom. CH51 88
Harwood Av. Horn. CW31 51
Harwood Av. Mitch. BU52 86
Harwood Clo. Welw. G. C. BU6 5
Harwood Ct. SW15 BQ45 65
Upr. Richmond Rd.
Harwood Gdns. Wind. AQ47 72
Harwood Hall La. Upmin. CX36 60
Harwood Hill, Welw. G. C. BS6 5
Harwood Rd. SW6 BS43 66
Harwood Sewells, Welw. G. C. BR6 5
Harwoods Rd. Wat. BC24 26
Harwoods Yd. N21 BY26 38
Wades Hill
Harwood Ter. SW6 BS44 66
Hasedines Rd. Hem. H. AW13 8
Haselbury Rd. N9 CA27 39
Haselbury Rd. N18 CA28 39
Haseldene Rd. St. Alb. BK16 18
Haseldine Meads. Hat. BO13 10
Haselmere Av. Houns. BD44 64
Haselrigge Rd. SW4 BW45 66
Haskard Rd. Dag. CP35 50
Hasker St. SW3 BU42 3
Hasker St. SW3 BU42 66
Haslam Av. Sutt. BR54 85
Haslemere Av. SW18 BS48 76
Haslemere Av. W7 BJ41 64
Haslemere Av. W13 BJ41 64
Haslemere Av. Barn. BU26 38
Haslemere Av. Mitch. BT51 86
Haslemere Clo. Hamptn. BE49 74
Haslemere Clo. Wall. BX56 95
Haslemere Gdns. N3 BR31 46
Haslemere Gdns. NW4 BQ32 46
Haslemere Rd. N8 BW33 47
Haslemere Rd. N21 BY27 38
Haslemere Rd. Bexh. CQ44 69
Haslemere Rd. Th. Hth. BY53 86
Haslemere Rd. Wind. AN44 61
Haslet Rd. Wat. BC24 26
Haslett Rd. Shep. BB51 83
Haslewood Av. Hodd. CE12 12
Haslewood Dr. Enf. BY24 29
Haslock Gdns. Barn. BS25 29
Hassard St. E2 CA38 2
Hassendean Rd. SE3 CH43 68
Hassett Rd. E9 CC36 57
Hassocks Clo. SE26 CB48 77
Hassocks Rd. SW16 BW51 86
Hassop Rd. NW2 BQ35 46
Hassop Wk. SE9 CK49 78
Hasted Rd. SE7 CJ42 68
Hastings Av. Ilf. CL31 49
Hastings Clo. Maid. AH42 61
Hastings Clo. SE15 CB43 67
Bells Gdns.
Hastings Rd. N11 BW28 38
Hastings Rd. W13 BJ40 54
Hastings Rd. Brom. CK54 88
Hastings Rd. Croy. CA54 87
Hastings Rd. Rom. CU32 50
Hastings St. WC1 BX38 2
Hastings St. WC1 BX38 56
Hastings Way, Bush. BE24 27
Hastings Way, Rick. BA24 26
Hastingwood Rd. Harl. CP13 14
Hatcham Pk. Rd. SE14 CC44 67
Hatcham Rd. SE15 CC43 67
Hatchard Rd. N19 BW34 47
Hatch Clo. Wey. AW55 83
Hatchcroft NW4 BP31 46
Hatch End, Pnr. BE29 36
Hatchett Rd. Felt. BA47 73
Hatch Gdns. Tad. BQ63 103
Hatch Gro. Rom. CQ31 50
Hatchlands Rd. Red. BU70 121
Hatch La. E4 CF28 39
Hatch La. Bans. BU61 104
Hatch La. West Dr. AX43 63
Hatch La. Wok. AZ63 101
Hatch Rd. SW16 BX51 86
Hatch Rd. Brwd. DA25 33
Hatch Side, Chig. CL28 40
Hatch, The Enf. CC23 30
Hatch, The Wind. AL43 61
Hatcliffe Clo. SE3 CG45 68
Hatcliffe St. SE10 CG42 68
Hatfield Clo. SE14 CC43 67
Reaston St.
Hatfield Clo. Brwd. DE26 122
Hutton Dr.
Hatfield Clo. Horn. CV35 51
Hatfield Clo. Ilf. CL31 49
Hatfield Clo. Mitch. BT52 86
Hatfield Cres. Hem. H. AY11 8
Hatfield Mead. Mord. BS53 86
Hatfield Rd. E15 CG35 49
Hatfield Rd. W4 BN41 65
Hatfield Rd. W13 BJ40 54
Hatfield Rd. Ash. BL62 103
Hatfield Rd. Dag. CQ36 59
Hatfield Rd. Hat. BU10 5
Hatfield Rd. Pot. B. BT19 20
Hatfield Rd. Slou. AQ41 62
Hatfield Rd. St. Alb. BH13 9
Hatfield Rd. St. Alb. BL13 10
Hatfield Rd. Wat. BC23 26
Hatfields SE1 BY40 4
Hatfields SE1 BY40 56
Hatfields Rd. Loug. CL24 31
Hathaway Clo. Stan. BJ28 36
Uxbridge Rd.
Hathaway Ct. St. Alb. BL13 10
Hatfield Rd.
Hathaway Cres. E12 CK36 58
Hathaway Gdns. W13 BJ39 54
Hathaway Gdns. Rom. CP32 50
Hathaway Rd. Croy. BY54 86
Hathaway Rd. Grays DD41 71
Hatherleigh Clo. Chess. BK56 93
Hatherleigh Clo. Mord. BS52 86
Hatherleigh Gdns. Pot. B. BT19 20
Hatherleigh Rd. Ruis. BC34 44
Hatherleigh Way, Rom. CV30 42
Hatherley Cres. Sid. CO48 79
Hatherley Gdns. E6 CJ37 58
Hatherley Gdns. N8 BX32 47
Hatherley Gro W2 BS39 1
Hatherley Gro. W2 BS39 56
Hatherley Ms. E17 CE31 48
Hatherley Rd.
Hatherley Rd. E17 CD31 48
Hatherley Rd. Rich. BL44 65
Hatherley Rd. Sid. CO49 79
Hatherley St. SW1 BW42 3
Hatherley St. SW1 BW42 66
Vincent Sq.
Hathern Gdns. SE9 CL49 78
Hatherop Rd. Hamptn. BE50 74
Hatherside Gdns. Slou. AO34 43
Hatherwood, Ash. BK64 102
Hathorne Clo. SE15 CC44 67
Hathway Rd. Grays DD42 71
Hathway St. SE15 CC44 67
Gibbon Rd.
Hatley Av. Ilf. CM31 49
Hatley Clo. N11 BU28 38
Hatley Rd. N4 BX34 47
Hatrel Dr. Horn. CV35 51
Hatton Av. Slou. AO38 52
Hatton Gdns. Mitch. BU53 86
Hatton Gdn. EC1 BY39 2
Hatton Gdn. EC1 BY38 56
Hatton Grn. Felt. BC45 63
Hatton Pl. EC1 BY39 2
Hatton Pl. EC1 BY39 56
Hatton Wall.
Hatton Rd. Croy. BY54 86
Hatton Rd. Felt. BA47 73
Hatton Rd. Felt. BB45 63
Hatton Rd. N. Houns. BA44 63
Hatton Rd. Wal. Cr. CC18 21
Hatton Row NW8 BT38 1
Hatton St. NW8 BT38 1
Hatton St. NW8 BT38 56
Hatton Wall EC1 BY39 2
Hatton Wall EC1 BY39 56
Hattor Rd. N. West Dr. AX40 53
Haunch of Venison Yd. W1 BV39 1
Haunch of Venison Yd. W1 BV39 56
Brook St.
Havana Clo. Rom. CT32 50
Havana Rd. SW19 BS48 76
Havannah St. E14 CE41 67
Havant Rd. E17 CF31 48
Havant Way SE15 CA43 67
Landport Way
Havelius Clo. SE10 CG42 68
Flamstead Est.
Havelock Ct. Sthl. BE41 64
Havelock Pl. SE18 CL42 68
Anglesea Rd.
Havelock Pl. Har. BH32 45
Havelock Rd. N17 CB30 39
Havelock Rd. SW19 BT49 76
Havelock Rd. Belv. CQ42 69
Havelock Rd. Brom. CJ52 88
Havelock Rd. Croy. CA55 87
Havelock Rd. Dart. CU46 79
Havelock Rd. Grav. DF47 81
Havelock Rd. Har. BH31 45
Havelock Rd. Kings L. AY17 17
Havelock Rd. Sthl. BE41 64
Havelock St. N1 BX37 56
Havelock St. Ilf. CL34 49
Havelock Ter. SW8 BV43 66
Havelock Wk. SE23 CC47 77
Haven Clo. Hat. BP12 10
Haven Clo. SW19 BQ48 75
Haven Clo. Grav. DF50 81
Haven Clo. Hayes BB39 53
Haven Clo. Swan. CT51 89
Haven Ct.
Haven Grn. W5 BK39 54
W. Side Rd.
Haven Grn. Ct. W5 BK39 54
Haven Grn.
Havenhurst Rise, Enf. BY23 29
Haven La. W5 BK39 54
Haven Pl. W5 BK40 54
Broadway, The
Haven Pl. Grays DE41 71
Haven Rd. NW1 BV36 56
Castle Rd.
Haven Rd. Ashf. AZ49 73
Reedsfield Rd.
Haven Ter. W5 BK40 54
Haven Pl.
Haven, The Grays DG42 71
Haven, The Rich. BM45 65
Havenwood, Wem. BM34 46
Haverfield Gdns. Rich. BN43 65
Haverfield Rd. E3 CD38 57
Haverford Way, Edg. BL30 37
Haverhill Rd. E4 CF26 39
Pretoria Rd.
Haverhill Rd. SW12 BW47 76
Havering Dr. Rom. CT31 50
Havering Gdns. Rom. CP32 50
Havering Pl. Hav. CS27 41
Havering Rd. Rom. CS30 41
Havering St. E1 CC39 57
Havering Way, Bark. CO38 59
Havers Av. Walt. BD56 93
Haversham Clo. Twick. BK46 74
Haversham Gra. Twick. BK46 74
Haverstock Hl. NW3 BU35 47
Haverstock Rd. NW5 BU35 47
Haverstock St. N1 BY37 2
Haverstock St. N1 BY37 56
Haverthwaite Rd. Orp. CM55 88
Havil St. SE5 CA43 67
Havisham Rd. Grav. DK48 81
Hawarden Av. Wal. Cr. CC20 21
Hawarden Gro. SE24 BZ47 77
Hawarden Rd. E17 CC31 48
Hawarden Rd. Cat. BZ64 105
Haward Rd. Hodd. CF11 12
Hawbridge Rd. E11 CF33 48
Hawes Clo. Nthwd. BB29 35
Hawes La. E4 CF22 30
Hawes La. W. Wick. CF54 87
Hawes Rd. N18 CB29 39
Hawes Rd. Brom. CH51 88
Hawes Rd. Tad. BQ63 103
Hawes St. N1 BY36 2
Hawes St. N1 BY36 56
Hawfield Gdns. St. Alb. BG16 18
Hawgood St. E3 CE39 57
Hawkdene E4 CE25 30
Hawkenbury, Harl. CL12 13
Hawker Clo. Wall. BX57 95
Hawke Rd. SE19 BZ50 77
Hawkesbury Rd. SW15 BP46 75
Hawkes Clo. Grays DD43 71
Hawkesfield Rd. SE23 CD48 77
Hawkesley Clo. Twick. BJ49 74
Hawkes Rd. Mitch. BU51 86
Hawkesworth Rd. Brom. CH52 88
Hawkewood Rd. Sun. BC52 83
Hawkfield Ct. Islw. BH44 64
Hawkfield Wk. Orp. CP55 89
Hawkhirst Rd. Ken. BZ61 105
Hawkhurst Gdns. Chess. BL56 94
Orchard Rd.
Hawkhurst Gdns. Rom. CS29 41
Hawkhurst Rd. SW16 BW51 86
Hawkhurst Someroile Rd. Cob. BF60 93
Hawkhurst Way, N. Mal. BN53 85
Hawkhurst Way, W. Wick. CE55 87
Hawkinge Wk. Orp. CO52 89
Robin Way
Hawkinge Way, Horn. CV36 60
Hawkins Av. Grav. DH49 81
Hawkins Clo. Har. BG33 45
Hawkins Rd. Tedd. BJ50 74
Hawk Pk. Rd. N22 BY31 47
Hawkridge Clo. Rom. CP32 50
Hawks Brook La. Beck. CF53 87
Hawkshaw Clo. SW2 BX47 76
Hawkshead Clo. Brom. CG50 78
Coniston Rd.
Hawkshead Clo. Enf. CC21 30
Hawkshead La. Hat. BQ17 19
Hawkshead Rd. NW10 BO36 55
Hawkshead Rd. W4 BO41 65
Hawkshead Rd. Pot. B. BS18 20
Hawks Hill, Lthd. BH65 102
Hawkshill Clo. Esher BF57 93
Hawks Hill Clo. Lthd. BH64 102
Hawkshill Way, Esher BF57 93
Hawkslade Rd. SE15 CC46 77
Hawksley Rd. N16 BZ34 48
Hawks Mews SE10 CF43 67
Luton Pl.
Hawksmoor Grn. Brwd. DE25 122
Hawks Moor, Rad. BM20 19
Hawksmoor St. W6 BQ43 65
Hawksmouth E4 CF26 39
Hawks Rd. Kings. On T. BL51 85
Hawkstone Rd. SE16 CC42 67
Hawks Way, Stai. AV48 72
Hawkswood Est. Chis. CM52 88
Hawkswood Gro. Slou. AS36 52
Hawkswood La. Ger. Cr. AS35 43
Hawksworth Clo. Nthwd. BA29 35
Hawkwell Wk. N1 BZ37 57
Rasire St.
Hawkwood Cres. E4 CE25 30
Hawkwood Dell, Lthd. BF66 111
Hawkwood La. Chis. CM51 88
Hawkwood Mt. E5 CB33 48
Hawkwood Ri. Lthd. BF66 111
Hawlands Dr. Pnr. BE33 45
Hawley Cres. NW1 BV36 1
Hawley Cres. NW1 BV36 56
Hawley Gdns. SE27 BY48 76
Hawley Rd. NW1 BV36 56
Hawley Rd. Dart. CW48 80
Hawley St. NW1 BV36 56
Hawley Way, Ashf. AZ49 73
Haws La. Stai. AW46 73
Hawstead La. Orp. CQ56 98
Hawstead Ranch, Buck. H. CH26 40
Hawstead Rd. SE6 CE46 77
Hawthorn Av. N13 BX28 38
Hawthorn Av. Brwd. DC27 122
Hawthorn Av. Cars. BV57 95
Hawthorn Av. Rain. CU38 59
Hawthorn Clo. Hmptn. BF49 74
Hawthorn Clo. Orp. CM53 88
Hawthorn Clo. Oxt. CH70 115
Holland La.
Hawthorn Clo. Red. BV73 121
Hawthorn Clo. Wat. BB22 26
Hawthorn Clo. Wok. AS63 100
Hawthorn Cres. Croy. CC59 96
Hawthorndene Clo. Brom. CG55 88
Hawthorndene Rd. Brom. CG55 88
Hawthorn Dr. Har. BE32 45
Hawthorn Dr. Uxb. AX36 53
Hawthorn Dr. W. Wick. CG56 97
Hawthorne Av. West. CJ61 106
Hawthorne Av. Har. BJ32 45
Hawthorne Av. Mitch. BT51 86
Hawthorne Av. Ruis. BC32 44
Hawthorne Av. Th. Hth. BY51 86
Hawthorne Av. Wal. Cr. CB19 21
Hawthorne Clo. N1 CA34 57
Hathorne Clo. Brom. CK52 88
Hawthorne Clo. Sutt. BT55 86
Hawthorne Clo. Wal. Cr. CB19 21
Hawthorne Cres. Slou. AP39 52
Hawthorne Cres. Sth. Croy. CC58 96
Hawthorne Gro. NW9 BN33 46
Hawthorne La. Sev. CT64 107
Hawthorne Pl. Epsom BO59 94
Hawthorne Rd. Brom. CK52 88
Hawthornes, Hat. BO13 10
Hawthorne Way, Guil. AT68 109
Hawthorne Farm Av. Nthlt. BE37 54
Hawthorn Gdns. W5 BK41 64
Hawthorn Gro. Enf. BZ22 30
Hawthorn Hatch, Brent. BJ43 64
Hawthorn La. Hem. H. AV13 7
Hawthorn Pl. Hayes BB40 53
Hawthorn Pl. Hayes BC40 53
Hawthorn Rd. E17 CE31 48
Hawthorn Rd. N8 BW31 47
Hawthorn Rd. N18 CA29 39
Hawthorn Rd. NW10 BP36 55
Hawthorn Rd. Bexh. CQ46 79
Hawthorn Rd. Brent. BJ43 64
Hawthorn Rd. Buck. H. CJ28 40
Hawthorn Rd. Dart. CV47 80
Hawthorn Rd. Hodd. CE11 12
Hawthorn Rd. Stai. AU49 72
Hawthorn Rd. Sutt. BT56 95
Hawthorn Rd. Wall. BV57 95
Hawthorn Rd. Wok. AR63 100
Hawthorn Rd. Wok. AV65 100
Hawthorns, Rick. AU28 34
Hawthorns, The Hem. H. AV15 7
Beechwood Pk.
Hawthorns, Wdf. Grn. CG27 40
Hawthorns, Welw. G. C. BQ7 5
Hawthorns' The Loug. CL24 31
Hawthorn, The Berk. AQ12 7
Hawthorn Way N9 CA27 39
Hawthorn Way, Chesh. AO18 16
Hawthorn Way, St. Alb. BF15 9
Hawthorn Way, St. Alb. BF16 18
Hawthorn Way, Shep. BA52 83
Hawthorn Way, Wey. AW58 92
Hawthorn Wk. W10 BR38 55
Droop St.
Hawtrees, Rad. BH21 27
Hawtrey Clo. Slou. AQ41 62
Hawtrey Dr. Ruis. BC33 44
Hawtrey Rd. NW3 BU36 56
Hawtrey Rd. Wind. AO44 61
Hawtrey Av. Nthlt. BD37 54
Haxtead Rd. Brom. CH51 88
Haybourn Mead. Hem. H. AW14 8
Hayburn Way, Horn. CT33 50
Hay Clo. E15 CG36 58
Haycroft Clo. Ken. BY62 104
Haycroft Gdns. NW10 BP37 55
Haycroft Rd. SW2 BX46 76
Haycroft Rd. Surb. BK55 84
Hay Currie St. E14 CE39 57
Hayday Rd. E16 CH39 58
Hayden Ct. Wey. AW59 92
Hayden Pl. Guil. AR71 118
Haydens Clo. Orp. CP54 89
Haydens Rd. Harl. CM11 13
Hayden Way, Rom. CS30 41
Haydn Av. Pur. BY60 95
Haydock Av. Nthlt. BE36 54
Haydock Clo. Horn. CW35 51
Haydock Grn. Nthlt. BF36 54
Haydon Clo. NW9 BN31 46
Haydon Dr. Pnr. BC31 44
Haydon Rd. Dag. CP34 50
Haydon Rd. Wat. BE25 27
Haydons Pk. Rd. SW19 BS49 76
Haydon Sq. E1 CA39 57
Haydons Rd. SW19 BS49 76
Haydon St. EC3 CA40 4
Haydon St. EC3 CA40 57
Hayes Barton, Wok. AV61 100
Hayes Chase, W. Wick. CF53 87
Hayes Clo. Brom. CH55 88
Hayes Ct. SW2 BX47 76
Hayes Cres. NW11 BR32 46
Hayes Cres. Sutt. BQ56 94
Hayes Dr. Rain. CU36 59
Hayes End Clo. Hayes BA38 53
Hayes End Dr. Hayes BA38 53
Hayes End Rd. Hayes BA38 53
Hayesford Pk. Dr. Brom. CG53 88
Hayesford Pk. Est. Brom. CH53 88
Hayes Gdns. Brom. CH55 88
Hayes Hill Rd. Brom. CG54 88
Hayes La. Beck. CF52 87
Hayes La. Brom. CH54 88
Hayes La. Ken. BY61 104
Hayes La. Ken. BZ63 105
Hayes Mead. Brom. CG54 88
Hayes Pl. NW1 BU40 56
Hayes Rd. Brom. CH52 88
Hayes Rd. Green. CZ47 80
Hayes Rd. Sthl. BC42 63
Hayes St. Brom. CH54 88
Hayes, The Epsom BN63 103
Hayes Wk. Pot. B. BS20 20
Willow Way
Hayes Way, Beck. CF52 87
Hayes Wd. Av. Brom. CH54 88
Hayfield Clo. Bush. BF24 27
Hayfield Pass. E1 CC38 57

Hayfield Rd. Orp. CO53 89
Hay Grn. La. Brwd. DB21 33
Hay Grn. La. Ing. DC20 24
Hay Hill W1 BV40 3
Hay Hill W1 BV40 56
Hayland Clo. NW9 BN31 46
Hay La. NW9 BN31 46
Hay La. Slou. AR35 43
Hayles St. SE11 BY42 4
Hayles St. SE11 BY42 66
Hayling Av. Felt. BC48 73
Hayling Rd. Wat. BC27 35
Hayman Cres. Hayes BA37 53
Haymarket SW1 BW40 3
Hayman St. N1 BY37 2
Haymarket SW1 BW40 56
Haymeads Dr. Esher BG57 93
Haymeads Hill, Welw. G. C. BR6 5
Haymer Gdns. Wor. Pk. BP55 85
Haymerle Rd. SE15 CB43 67
Hayne Rd. Beck. CD51 87
Haynes Clo. N17 CB29 39
Haynes Clo. SE3 CG45 68
Haynes Clo. Slou. AS42 62
Haynes Clo. Welw. G. C. BS8 5
Haynes La. SE19 CA50 77
Haynes Mead. Berk. AQ12 7
Haynes Rd. Grav. DF48 81
Haynes Rd. Horn. CV32 51
Haynes Rd. Wem. BL36 55
Hayne St. EC1 BY39 2
Hayne St. EC1 BY39 56
Haynt Wk. SW20 BR52 85
Hayse Hill, Wind. AL44 61
Hays La. SE1 BZ40 4
Hays La. SE1 CA40 57
Haysleigh Gdns. SE20 CB51 87
Hay's Ms. W1 BV40 3
Hays Ms. W1 BV40 56
Haysoms Clo. Rom. CT31 50
Ingrave Rd.
Haystall Clo. Hayes BB37 53
Hays Wk. Sutt. BQ58 94
Hayter Rd. SW2 BX46 76
Hayton Clo. E8 CA36 57
Rhodes Dev.
Hay Wk. E1 CA40 57
Hayward Clo. SW19 BS51 86
Hayward Clo. Bex. CS46 79
Bourne Rd.
Hayward Gdns. SW15 BQ46 75
Hayward Rd. N20 BT27 38
Haywards Clo. Brwd. DF25 122
Haywards Pl. EC1 BY38 56
Sekforde St.
Haywood Ct. Wal. Abb. CG20 22
Haywood Rise, Orp. CN56 97
Haywood Rd. Brom. CJ52 88
Haywoods Clo. Pnr. BD30 36
Haywoods Pl. EC1 BY38 2
Hazel Av. Guil. AR68 109
Hazel Av. West Dr. AZ41 63
Hazel Bnk. Surb. BN54 85
Hazelbank Rd. SE6 CF48 77
Hazelbank Rd. Cher. AX54 83
Hazelbourne Rd. SW12 BV46 76
Hazelbrouck Gdns. Ilf. CM29 40
Hazelbury Av. Wat. BA19 17
Hazelbury Grn. N9 CA27 39
Hazelbury La. N9 CA27 39
Hazel Clo. N13 BZ27 39
Hazel Clo. Brent. BJ43 64
Hazel Clo. Horn. CU34 50
Hazel Clo. Mitch. BW52 86
Hazel Clo. Reig. BT71 121
Hazel Clo. Twick. BG47 74
Hazel Clo. Welw. G. C. BR5 5
Hazelcote, Wok. AW64 101
Hazel Cft. Pnr. BF29 36
Hazeldean Rd. NW10 BN36 55
Hazeldean Rd. Croy. BZ55 87
Hazeldell Rd. Hem. H. AV14 7
Hazelden Clo. Sev. DA58 99
Hazeldene Clo. Wey. AX56 92
Crockford Pk. Rd.
Hazeldene Ct. Ken. BZ61 105
Hazeldene Dr. Pnr. BD31 45
Hazeldene Gdns. Uxb. BA37 53
Hazeldene Rd. Ilf. CO34 50
Hazeldene Rd. Well. CP44 69
Hazeldon Rd. SE4 CD46 77
Hazel Dr. Erith. CU44 69
Hazel Dr. Wok. AV65 100
Hazeleigh, Brwd. DD27 122
Hazeleigh Gdns. Wdf. Grn. CK28 40
Hazel End, Swan. CT53 89
Hazel Gdns. Edg. BM28 37
Hazel Gdns. Grays DF41 71
Hazel Gr. Hat. BO14 10
Hazel Gro. SE26 CC49 77
Hazel Gro. Enf. CB25 30
Dimsdale Dr.
Hazel Gro. Orp. CL55 88
Hazel Gro. Rom. CQ31 50
Hazel Gro. Stai. AW50 73
Hazel Gro. Welw. G. C. BS7 5
Hazel Gro. Wem. BL37 55
Carlyon Rd.
Hazelhurst, Beck. CF51 87
Hazelhurst Rd. SW17 BT49 76
Hazel La. Rich. BL48 75
Hazell Clo. Egh. AQ50 72
Hazell Cres. Rom. CR29 41
Hazell Gr. Hat. BO14 10
Hazells Rd. Grav. DD49 81
Hazellville Rd. N19 BW33 47
Hazel Mead. Barn. BP25 28
Hazel Mead. Epsom BP58 94
Hazelmere Clo. Felt. BA46 73
Hazelmere Clo. Lthd. BJ63 102
Hazelmere Clo. Nthlt. BE37 54
Hazelmere Rd.
Hazelmere Dr. Nthlt. BE37 54
Hazelmere Rd.
Hazelmere Gdns. Horn. CU32 50
Hazelmere Rd. NW6 BS37 56
Hazelmere Rd. Nthlt. BE37 54
Hazelmere Rd. Orp. CM52 88
Hazelmere Rd. St. Alb. BK12 9
Hazelmere Wk. Nthlt. BE37 54
Hazelmere Rd.
Hazelmere Way, Brom. CH53 88
Hazel Rise, Horn. CV32 51
Hazel Rd. NW10 BQ38 55
Hazel Rd. Berk. AR13 7
Hazel Rd. Dart. CV47 80
Hazel Rd. Erith CU44 69
Hazel Rd. Reig. BT71 121
Hazel Rd. St. Alb. BF17 18
Hazel Rd. Wey. AV60 91
Hazel Rd. Wey. AW60 92
Hazeltree La. Nthlt. BE38 54
Hazel Tree Rd. Wat. BC22 26
Hazel Wk. Brom. CL53 88
Hazel Way E4 CD29 39
Hazel Way, Lthd. BG64 102
Hazel Way, Slou. AP36 52
Hazelwood, S. Le H. DK42 71
Hazelwood Clo. W5 BL41 65
Hazelwood Clo. Chesh. AO18 16
Hazelwood Ct. Surb. BL53 85
Hazelwood Cres. N13 BY28 38
Hazelwood Cres. W10 BR38 55
Hazelwood Dr. Pnr. BC30 35
Hazelwood Dr. St. Alb. BK12 9
Hazelwood Gdns. Brwd. DA25 33
Hazelwood Ho. SE8 CD42 67
Hazelwood La. N13 BY28 38
Hazelwood La. Couls. BU62 104
Hazelwood La. Couls. BU63 104
Hazelwood La. Wat. BA19 17
Hazelwood Rd. E17 CD32 48
Hazelwood Rd. Enf. CA25 30
Hazelwood Rd. Mord. BS52 86
Hazelwood Rd. Oxt. CH69 115
Hazelwood Rd. Rick. BA25 26
Hazelwood Rd. Sev. CM59 97
Hazlebury Rd. SW6 BS44 66
Hazledene Rd. W4 BN43 65
Hazlemere Clo. Lthd. BJ63 102
Hazlemere Gdns. Wor. Pk. BP54 85
Hazlemere Rd. Ilf. CN34 49
Hazlemere Rd. Slou. AQ40 52
Hazlewell Rd. SW15 BP46 75
Hazlewood, Loug. CJ25 31
Hazlewood Cres. W10 BR39 55
Hazlewood Gro. Sth. Croy. CB60 96
Hazlitt Rd. W14 BR41 65
Hazon Way, Epsom BN59 94
Headcorn Pl. Th. Hth. BX52 86
Headcorn Rd. N17 CA29 39
Tenterden Rd.
Headcorn Rd. Brom. CG49 78
Headcorn Rd. Th. Hth. BX52 86
Headfort Pl. SW1 BV41 3
Headfort Pl. SW1 BV41 66
Headingley Clo. Wal. Cr. CA16 21
Holbeck La.
Heading St. NW4 BQ31 46
Headington Rd. SW18 BT47 76
Headlam Rd. SW4 BW46 76
Headlam St. E1 CB38 57
Headley App. Ilf. CL32 49
Headley Av. Wall. BX56 95
Headley Chase, Brwd. DB28 42
Headley Clo. Epsom BM57 94
Headley Common Rd.
Epsom BN67 112
Headley Dr. Croy. CE57 96
Headley Dr. Ilf. CL32 49
Headley Heath App. Tad. BM69 120
Headley Rd. Dor. BK68 111
Headley Rd. Epsom BM62 103
Headley Rd. Epsom BN64 103
Headley Rd. Lthd. BK64 102
Headley St. SE15 CB44 67
Gordon Rd.
Headley Vw. Tad. BP63 103
Headly Dr. Epsom BP63 103
Head Mews W10 BS39 56
Needham Rd.
Head Mews W10 BS39 56
Headstone Dr. Har. BG31 45
Headstone Gdns. Har. BG31 45
Headstone La. Har. BF31 45
Headstone Rd. Har. BG32 45
Head St. E1 CC39 57
Headway, The Epsom BO58 94
Headworth Rd. SW17 BT48 76
Heald St. SE8 CE44 67
Heston St.
Healey Dr. Orp. CN56 97
Healey Rd. Wat. BB25 26
Healey St. NW1 BV36 56
Health Dr. Epp. CN21 31
Heards La. Brwd. DC23 122
Hearne Rd. W4 BM42 65
Hearnes Clo. Beac. AO28 34
Hearn Rise, Nthlt. BD37 54
Hearn Rd. Rom. CT32 50
Hearn's Bldgs. SE17 BZ42 4
Hearn's Bldgs. SE17 BZ42 67
Elsted St.
Hearns Clo. Orp. CP52 89
Hearn's Mead. Beac. AO28 34
Hearns Rise, Orp. CP52 89
Hearns Rd. Orp. CP52 89
Hearn St. EC2 CA38 2
Hearn St. EC2 CA38 57
Curtain Rd.
Hearnville Rd. SW12 BV47 76
Heatham Pk. Twick. BH47 74
Heath Av. Bexh. CP43 69
Heath Av. St. Alb. BG12 9
Heathbourne Rd. Bush. BH26 36
Heathbrow NW3 BT34 47
North End Way
Heath Clo. NW11 BS33 47
Heath Clo. W5 BL38 55
Heath Clo. Bans. BS60 95
Heath Clo. Hayes BA43 63
Heath Clo. Hem. H. AX14 8
Heath Clo. Orp. CP54 89
Heath Clo. Pot. B. BS18 20
Heath Clo. Rom. CU31 50
Heath Clo. Stai. AX46 73
Heath Clo. Vir. W. AR52 82
Heathclose Av. Dart. CU47 79
Heathclose Rd. Dart. CU47 79
Heathcote Av. Hat. BP11 10
Heathcote Av. Ilf. CK30 40
Heathcote Gro. E4 CF27 39
Heathcote Rd. Epsom BN60 94
Heathcote Rd. Twick. BJ46 74
Heathcote St. WC1 BX38 2
Heathcote St. WC1 BX38 56
Heath Ct. W5 BL38 55
Heath Cft. NW11 BS33 47
Heathcroft W5 BL38 55
Heathcroft Av. Sun. BB50 73
Heathcroft Grn. BB50 73
Heathdale Rd. Houns. BE45 64
Heathdene Rd. SW16 BX50 76
Heathdene Rd. Wall. BV57 95
Heathdown Rd. Wok. AU61 100
Heath Dr. NW3 BS35 47
Heath Dr. SW20 BQ52 85
Heath Dr. Pot. B. BS18 20
Heath Dr. Rom. CU30 41
Heath Dr. Sutt. BT58 95
Heath Dr. Tad. BP66 112
Heath Edge SE26 CB48 77
Heathend Rd. Bex. CT47 79
Heather Av. Rom. CS30 41
Heatherbank SE9 CK44 68
Heatherbank, Chis. CL51 88
Heather Clo. Brwd. DA25 33
Mounolid Way
Heather Clo. Brwd. DB25 42
Heather Clo. Hamptn. BE51 84
Heather Clo. Rom. CS30 41
Heather Clo. Tad. BR64 103
Heather Clo. Uxb. AY39 53
Heather Clo. Wey. AW58 92
Heather Clo. Wok. AR61 100
Heatherdale Clo.
Kings. on T. BM50 75
Heatherdean Clo. Mitch. BT52 86
Heatherdene, Leath. BA66 110
Heatherden Grn. Iver AU37 52
Heather Dr. Rom. CS30 41
Heather Dr. Dart. CU47 79
Heather Gdns. NW11 BR32 46
Heather Gdns. Rom. CS30 41
Heather Gdns. Sutt. BS57 95
Heather Glen, Rom. CS30 41
Heatherlands, Sun. BC50 73
Heather La. West Dr. AY39 53
Heatherley Pl. E5 CB34 48
Heatherley St.
Heatherley St. E5 CB34 48
Heatherley Dr. Ilf. CK31 49
Heather Pk. Dr. Wem. BM36 55
Heather Pl. Esher BF56 93
Heather Rise, Bush. BE23 27
Heather Rd. NW2 BO34 46
Heather Rd. SE12 CH48 78
Heather Rd. Welw. G. C. BQ8 5
Heatherset Gdns. SW16 BX50 76
Heatherside Dr. Vir. W. AQ53 82
Heatherside Rd. Epsom BN57 94
Heatherside Rd. Sid. CP48 79
Bexley La.
Heathers Land. Dor. BK73 119
Heatherton Ter. N3 BS30 38
Squires La.
Heathervale Rd. Wey. AW58 92
Heather Wk. W10 BR38 55
Droop St.
Heather Wk. Edg. BM28 37
Heather Wk. Watt. BB58 92
Heather Way, Hem. H. AX13 8
Heather Way, Pot. B. BR19 19
Heather Way, Rom. CS30 41
Heather Way, Stan. BH29 36
Heather Way, Sth. Croy. CC58 96
Heather Way, Wok. AP57 91
Heatherwood Clo. E12 CJ34 49
Heath Farm La. St. Alb. BH12 9
Heath Farm Ct. Wat. BA22 26
Grove Mill La.
Heathfield E4 CF27 39
Heathfield SW17 BU47 76
Burntwood Gra. Rd.
Heathfield, Chis. CM50 78
Heathfield, Cob. BF60 93
Heathfield Av. SW18 BT47 76
Heathfield Clo. Kes. CJ56 97
Heathfield Clo. Pot. B. BS18 20
Church Rd.
Heathfield Clo. Wok. AT62 100
Heathfield Ct. W4 BN42 65
Heathfield Ter.
Heathfield Ct. St. Alb. BH13 9
Avenue Rd.
Heathfield Dr. Red. BU73 121
Heathfield Gdns. NW11 BQ32 46
Heathfield Gdns. SW18 BT46 76
Heathfield Gdns. W4 BN42 65
Heathfield Gdns. Croy. BZ56 96
Heathfield La. Chis. CL50 78
Heathfield North, Twick. BH47 74
Heathfield Pk. NW2 BQ36 55
Heathfield Rise, Ruis. BA33 44
Heathfield Rd. SW18 BT46 76
Heathfield Rd. W3 BM41 65
Heathfield Rd. Bexh. CQ45 69
Heathfield Rd. Brom. CG50 78
Heathfield Rd. Bush. BE24 27
Heathfield Rd. Croy. BZ56 96
Heathfield Rd. Kes. CJ56 97
Heathfield Rd. Sev. CT64 107
Heathfield Rd. Walt. BE56 93
Heathfield Rd. Wok. AT62 100
Heathfield South, Twick. BH47 74
Heathfield Sq. SW18 BT47 76
Heathfield St. W11 BR40 55
Portland Rd.
Heathfield Ter. SE18 CN43 68
Heathfield Ter. W4 BN42 65
Heathfield Vale, Sth. Croy. CC58 96
Heathfield Way, Ger. Cr. AR32 43
Heath Gdns. Twick. BH47 74
Heathgate NW11 BS32 47
Heath Gro. SE20 CC50 77
Heath Hill, Dor. BJ71 119
Heath House La. Wok. AO64 100
Heath Hurst Rd. NW3 BT35 47
Keats Gro.
Heathland Rd. N16 CA33 48
Heathlands NW3 BT34 47
Heathlands Clo. Sun. BC51 83
Heathlands Dr. St. Alb. BH12 9
Heathlands Rise, Dart. CU46 79
Heath Rise, Dor. BG72 119
Heath La. SE3 CF44 67
Heath La. Dart. CU47 79
Heath La. Dart. CV47 80
Heath La. Hem. H. AX14 8
Heathlee Rd. SE3 CG45 68
Heathley End, Chis. CM50 78
Heathmans Yd. SW6 BR44 65
Heathmead SW19 BQ48 75
Heath Pk. Ct. Rom. CU32 50
Heath Pk. Rd. Rom. CU32 50
Heath Ri. Wok. AW65 101
Heath Ridge Grn. Cob. BF60 93
Heath Rise SW15 BQ46 75
Heath Rise, Brom. CG53 88
Heath Rise, Vir. W. AR52 82
Heath Rd. SW8 BV45 66
Heath Rd. Bex. CS47 79
Heath Rd. Cat. BZ65 105
Heath Rd. Dart. CT46 79
Heath Rd. Grays DF40 71
Heath Rd. Har. BG33 45
Heath Rd. Houns. BF45 64
Heath Rd. Lthd. BG59 93
Heath Rd. Pot. B. BS18 20
Heath Rd. Red. CB70 114
Heath Rd. Rom. CP33 50
Heath Rd. St. Alb. BH12 9
Heath Rd. Th. Hth. BZ52 87
Heath Rd. Twick. BH47 74
Heath Rd. Uxb. BA38 53
Heath Rd. Wat. BD26 36
Heath Rd. Wey. AZ56 92
Heath Rd. Wok. AS61 100
Heathrow Clo. West. Dr. AW44 63
Heaths Clo. Enf. CA23 30
Heath Side NW3 BT35 47
Heathside, Esher BH55 84
Heath Side, Houns. BE47 74
Heath Side, Orp. CM54 88
Heathside, Wey. AZ56 92
Heathside Av. Bexh. CQ44 69
Heathside Clo. Esher BH55 84
Heathside Clo. Nthwd. BA28 35
Heathside Cres. Wok. AS62 100
Heathside Gdns. Wok. AT62 100
Heathside Pk. Rd. Wok. AS62 100
Heathside Rd. Nthwd. BA28 35
Heathside Rd. Wok. AS62 100
Heathstan Rd. W12 BP40 55
Heath St. NW3 BT34 47
Heath St. Bark. CM37 58
Heath St. Dart. CV47 80
Heath, The W7 BH40 54
Lwr. Boston Rd.
Heath, The Cat. BZ65 105
Heath, The Rad. BJ20 18
Heathurst Rd. Sth. Croy. BZ58 96
Heath Vw. N2 BT31 47
Heath View, Leath. BB66 110
Heathview Av. Dart. CT47 79
Heath Vw. Clo. N2 BT31 47
Heathview Cres. Dart. CU47 79
Heathview Gdns. SW15 BQ47 75
Heath View Gdns. Grays DE41 71
Heath View Rd. Grays DE41 71
Heathview Rd. Th. Hth. BT52 86
Heath Vill. SE18 CN42 68
Heathville Rd. N19 BX33 47
Heathwall St. SW11 BU45 66
Heath Way SE3 CH43 68
Heath Way, Croy. CD55 87
Heathway, Dag. CQ34 50
Heath Way, Erith. CS44 69
Heathway, Iver. AU37 52
Heathway, Lthd. BB65 101
Heathway, Wdf. Grn. CJ28 40
Heath Way, West. Dr. AX40 53
Heathway, Cat. BZ66 114
Heathwood Gdns. SE7 CK42 68
Heathwood Gdns. Swan. CS51 89
Heaton Av. Rom. CU29 41
Heaton Clo. Rom. CV29 42
Heaton Gra. Rd. Rom. CT30 41
Heaton Pl. E15 CF35 48
Heaton Rd. SE15 CB45 67
Heaton Rd. Mitch. BV50 76
Heaton Way, Rom. CV29 42
Heaver Clo. SW11 BT45 66
Heaverham Rd. Sev. CX62 108
Heaver Rd. SW11 BT45 66
Heavitree Rd. SE18 CM42 68
Heayfield, Welw. G. C. BT7 5
Hebden Ct. E2 CA37 2
Hebdon Rd. SW17 BU48 76
Heber Rd. NW2 BQ35 46
Heber Rd. SE22 CA46 77
Hebron Rd. W6 BP41 65
Hecham Clo. E17 CD30 39
Heckfield Pl. SW6 BS43 66
Fulham Rd.
Heckford St. E1 CC40 57
Hector St. SE18 CN42 68
Heddon Ct. Av. Barn. BU25 29
Heddon Rd. Barn. BU25 29
Heddon St. W1 BW40 3
Heddon St. W1 BW40 56
Hedge Brooms, Welw. G. C. BT7 5
New Wood
Hedge Hill, Enf. BY23 29
Hedge La. N13 BY27 38
Hedgeley, Ilf. CK31 49
Hedgeman's Rd. Dag. CP36 59
Hedgemans Way, Dag. CQ36 59
Hedge Pl. Rd. Green. CZ46 80
Hedgerley Gdns. Grnf. BG37 54
Hedgerley Hill, Slou. AO34 43
Hedgerley La. Slou. AP32 43
Hedge Row, Ger. Cr. AS29 34
Hedgerows, Saw. CQ6 6
Hedgers Rd. E9 CD36 57
Hedges Clo. Hat. BP12 10
Stonecross Rd.
Hedgeside, Berk. AT11 7
Hedgeside Rd. Nthwd. BA28 35
Hedge Wk. SE6 CE49 77
Lushington Rd.
Hedgeway, Guil. AQ71 118
Hedgewood Gdns. Ilf. CL31 49
Hedgley St. SE12 CG46 78
Hedingham Clo. N1 BZ36 57
Poplar Rd.
Hedingham Clo. N1 BZ37 2
Popham Rd.
Hedingham Rd. Dag. CO35 50
Hedingham Rd. Horn. CX33 51
Hedley Av. Grays DB43 70
Hedley Rd. St. Alb. BJ13 9
Hedworth Av. Wal. Cr. CC20 21
Heene Rd. Enf. BZ23 30
Heigham Rd. E6 CJ36 58
Heighams, Harl. CK12 13
Heighton Gdns. Croy. BY56 95
Heights Clo. Bans. BR61 103
Heights, The SE7 CJ42 68
Heights, The Beck. CF50 77
Heights, The Nthlt. BE35 45
Heights, The Hem. H. AY12 8
Saturn Way
Heiron St. SE17 BY43 66
Helby Rd. SW4 BW46 76
Helder Gro. SE12 CG47 78
Helder St. Sth. Croy. BZ57 96
Heldman Clo. Islw. BG45 64
Helen Clo. N2 BT31 47
Benedict Way
Helena Clo. Barn. BT22 29
Helena Clo. Wall. BX57 95
Helena Ct. W5 BK39 54
Eaton Rise
Helena Rd. E13 CG37 58
Helena Rd. E17 CE32 48
Helena Rd. NW10 BP35 46
Helena Rd. W5 BK39 54
Helena Rd. Wind. AO44 61
Helena St. WC1 BY38 56
Fernsbury St.
Helen Av. Felt. BC47 73
Helen Clo. E. Mol. BF52 84
Helen Rd. Horn. CV31 51
Helenslea Av. NW11 BR33 46
Helen's Pl. E2 CC38 57
Roman Rd.
Helen St. SE18 CL42 68
Helford Clo. Ruis. BB34 44
Chichester Av.
Helford Way, Upmin. CY33 51
Helgiford Gdns. Sun. BB50 73
Helions Rd. Harl. CL11 13
Helix Gdns. SW2 BX46 76
Helix Rd. SW2 BX46 76
Helling St. E1 CB40 4
Helling St. E1 CB40 57
Hermitage Wall
Helmet Row EC1 BZ38 2
Helmet Row EC1 BZ38 57
Helmsdale Clo. Rom. CT29 41
Helmsdale Rd. SW16 BW51 86
Helmsdale Rd. Rom. CT29 41
Helmsley St. E8 CB36 57
Helston Dene, Hem. H. AX11 8
Washington Av.
Helstone Clo. Pnr. BE29 36
Helston Pl. Wat. BB19 17
Helvetia St. SE6 CD48 77
Hemans St. SW8 BX43 66
Wandsworth Rd.
Hemberton Rd. SW9 BX45 66
Hemel Hempstead Rd.
Hem. H. BB14 8
Hemel Hempstead Rd.
Wat. BA21 26
Hemingford Rd. N1 BX37 2
Hemingford Rd. N1 BX37 56
Hemingford Rd. Sutt. BQ56 94
Hemingford Rd. Wat. BB21 26
Heming Rd. Edg. BM29 37
Hemington Av. N11 BU28 38
Hemlock Rd. W12 BO40 55
Hemmen La. Hayes BB39 53
Hemming Clo. Hamptn. BF51 84
Hemming St. E1 CB38 57
Hemming Way, Wat. BC21 26
Hemnall St. Epp. CN19 22
Hempshaw Av. Bans. BU61 104
Hempson Av. Slou. AR41 62
Hempstead Clo. Buck. H. CH27 40
Hempstead Rd. E17 CF31 48
Hempstead Rd. Berk. AT12 7
Hempstead Rd. Hem. H. AT16 16
Hempstead Rd. Kings L. AY16 17
Hempstead Rd. Kings L. AZ19 17
Hemp Wk. SE17 BZ42 4
Hemp Wk. SE17 BZ42 67
Chatham St.
Hemsby Rd. Chess. BL57 94
Hemstal Rd. NW6 BS36 56
Hemstead Rd. St. Alb. BE14 9
Hemstead Rd. Erith. CT43 69
Hemswell Dr. NW9 BO30 37
Hemsworth Ct. N1 CA37 2
Hemsworth St. N1 CA37 2
Hemsworth St. N1 CA37 57
Hemus Pl. SW3 BU42 3
Hemus Pl. SW3 BU42 66
Chelsea Manor St.
Hemwood Rd. Wind. AL45 61
Henbane Path, Rom. CV29 42
Clematis Clo.
Henbain Pth. Rom. CV29 42
Henbury Way, Wat. BD27 36
Hen & Chickens Ct. EC4 BY39 56
Fleet St.
Henchley Dene, Guil. AU69 118
Henchman St. W12 BO39 55
Hencroft St. Slou. AP41 62

Street	Grid	Page
Hendale Av. NW4	BP31	46
Henderson Av. Guil.	AQ68	109
Henderson Clo. NW10	BN36	55
Henderson Clo. St. Alb.	BG11	9
Henderson Dr. NW8	BT38	56
St. Johns Wood La.		
Henderson Dr. Dart.	CW45	70
Henderson Pl. Wat.	BB17	17
Henderson Rd. E7	CJ36	58
Henderson Rd. N9	CB26	39
Henderson Rd. SW18	BU47	76
Henderson Rd. Croy.	BZ53	87
Henderson Rd. West.	CJ59	97
Hendham Rd. SW17	BU48	76
Hendon Av. N3	BR30	37
Hendon Clo. Islw.	BJ45	64
Hendon Clo. Rom.	CS29	41
Hendon La. N3	BR31	46
Hendon Pk. Mans. NW4	BQ32	46
Hendon Pk. Row NW11	BR32	46
Hendon Rd. N9	CB27	39
Hendon Way, Maid.	AG42	61
Hendon Way NW2	BQ33	46
Hendon Way NW4	BP32	46
Hendon Way, Stai.	AX46	73
Hendon Wood La. NW7	BO26	37
Hendre Rd. SE1	**CA42**	**4**
Hendre Rd. SE1	CA42	67
Hendren Clo. Har.	BG35	45
Dimmock Dr.		
Hendrick Av. SW12	BU47	76
Hendricks Ter. N17	CB31	48
Heneage Cres. Croy.	CF58	96
Heneage La. EC3	**CA39**	**2**
Heneage La. EC3	CA39	57
Bevis Marks		
Heneage St. E1	**CA39**	**2**
Heneage St. E1	CA39	57
Henfield Clo. N19	BW33	47
Henfield Clo. Bex.	CR46	79
Henfield Rd. SW19	BR51	85
Hengeld Gdns. Mitch.	BT52	86
Hengist Rd. SE12	CH47	78
Hengist Rd. Erith	CF43	69
Hengist Way, Brom.	CF52	87
Hengrave Rd. SE23	CC46	77
Hengrove Ct. Bex.	CQ47	79
Hurst Rd.		
Hen Grove Cres. Ashf.	AX48	73
Henhurst Rd. Grav.	DJ50	81
Henley Av. Sutt.	BR55	85
Henley Clo. SW11	CA44	67
Henley Clo. Grn.	BG37	54
Henley Clo. Islw.	BH44	64
Henley Ct. N14	BW26	38
Henley Dr. Kings. on T.	BO50	75
Henley Gdns. Pnr.	BC31	44
Henley Gdns. Rom.	CQ32	50
Henley Gate, Guil.	AQ71	118
Henley Rd. E16	CK41	68
Henley Rd. N18	CA28	39
Henley Rd. NW10	BQ37	55
Henley Rd. Ilf.	CM35	49
Henley St. SW11	BV44	66
Henley Way, Felt.	BD49	74
Hennel Clo. SE23	CC48	77
Henniker Gdns. E6	CJ38	58
Henniker Ms. SW3	**BT42**	**3**
Henniker Ms. SW3	BT44	66
Callow St.		
Henniker Rd. E15	CF35	48
Henningham Rd. N17	BZ30	39
Henning St. SW11	BU44	66
Shuttleworth Rd.		
Henrietta Ms. WC1	**BX38**	**2**
Henrietta Ms. WC1	BX38	56
Brunswick Sq.		
Henrietta Pl. W1	**BV39**	**1**
Henrietta Pl. W1	BV40	56
Henrietta St. WC2	**BX40**	**4**
Henrietta St. WC2	BX40	56
Henriques St. E1	CB39	57
Henry Darlot Dr. NW7	BQ28	37
Henry Dickens Ct. W11	BQ40	55
Henry Jackson Rd. SW15	BQ45	65
Henry Rd. E6	CK37	58
Henry Rd. N4	BY33	47
Henry Rd. Barn.	BT25	29
Henry Rd. Slou.	AO41	61
Henry's Av. Wdf. Grn.	CG28	40
Henryson Rd. SE4	CD46	77
Henry's Ter. Brwd.	DA20	24
Henry St. Brom.	CH51	88
Henry St. Hem. H.	AX15	8
Henrys Wk. Ilf.	CM29	40
Henry Wells Sq. Hem. H.	AY11	8
Hensford Gdns. SE26	CB48	77
Wells Pk. Rd.		
Henshall St. N1	BZ36	57
Balls Pond Rd.		
Henshawe Rd. Dag.	CP34	50
Henshaw St. SE17	**BZ42**	**4**
Henshaw St. SE17	BZ42	67
Henslowe Rd. SE22	CB46	77
Henslow Way, Wok.	AU60	91
Henson Av. NW2	BQ35	46
Henson Clo. Orp.	CL55	88
Henson Path, Har.	BK31	45
Henson Pl. Nthlt.	BD37	54
Henstridge Pl. NW8	**BU37**	**1**
Henstridge Pl. NW8	BU37	56
Hensworth Rd. Ashf.	AX49	73
Henty Clo. SW11	BU43	66
Henty Wk. SW15	BP46	75
Sunnymead Rd.		
Henville Rd. Brom.	CH51	88
Henwick Rd. SE9	CJ45	68
Henwood Rd. SE16	CC41	67
Henwood Side, Chig.	CK29	40
Henwood Side, Wdf. Grn.	CK29	40
Hepburn Gdns. W. Wick.	CG54	88
Hepple Clo. Islw.	BJ44	64
Hepplestone Clo. SW15	BP46	75
Dover Pk. Dr.		
Hepscott Rd. E9	CE36	57
Hepwell Rd. Grav.	DG46	81
Hepworth Gdns. Bark.	CO35	50
Hepworth Rd. SW16	BX50	76
Hepworth Way, Walt.	BB54	83
Heracles Clo. Wall.	BX57	95
Herald St. E2	CB38	57
Birkbeck St.		
Herbal Hill EC1	**BY38**	**2**
Herbal Hill EC1	BY38	56
Ray St.		
Herbal Pl. EC1	BY38	56
Ray St.		
Herbert Cres. SW1	**BU41**	**3**
Herbert Cres. SW1	BU41	66
Pavilion Rd.		
Herbert Cres. Wok.	AP62	100
Herbert Gdns. NW10	BP37	55
Herbert Gdns. W4	BM43	65
Magnolia Rd.		
Herbert Gdns. Rom.	CP33	50
Herbert Rd. E12	CK35	49
Herbert Rd. E17	CD33	48
Herbert Rd. N11	BX29	38
Herbert Rd. N15	CA32	48
Herbert Rd. NW9	BP32	46
Herbert Rd. SE18	CL43	68
Herbert Rd. SW19	BR50	75
Herbert Rd. Bexh.	CQ44	69
Herbert Rd. Brom.	CJ53	88
Herbert Rd. Horn.	CW33	51
Herbert Rd. Ilf.	CN34	49
Herbert Rd. Kings. On T.	BL52	85
Herbert Rd. Sthl.	BE40	54
Herbert Rd. Swan.	CU50	79
Herbert Rd. Swans.	DC46	81
Herbert St. E13	CH37	58
Herbert St. NW5	BV35	47
Herbert St. Hem. H.	AX13	8
Herbert St. Wat.	BD24	27
Herbrand St. WC1	**BX38**	**2**
Herbrand St. WC1	BX38	56
Hercies Rd. Uxb.	AY36	53
Hercules Pl. N7	BX34	47
Hercules Rd. SE1	**BX41**	**4**
Hercules Rd. SE1	BX41	66
Hercules St. N7	BX34	47
Hereford Av. Barn.	BU26	38
Hereford Clo. Epsom	BN60	94
Hereford Clo. Guil.	AP69	118
Hereford Clo. Stai.	AW51	83
Hereford Gdns. Ilf.	CK33	49
Hereford Gdns. Pnr.	BE32	45
Hereford Gdns. Twick.	BG47	74
Hereford Ms. W2	BS39	56
Hereford Rd.		
Hereford Pl. SE14	CD43	67
Hereford Retreat SE15	CB43	67
Bird-in-bush Rd.		
Hereford Rd. E11	CH32	49
Hereford Rd. W2	BS39	56
Hereford Rd. W3	BM40	55
Hereford Rd. W5	BK41	64
Hereford Rd. Felt.	BD47	74
Hereford Sq. SW7	**BT42**	**3**
Hereford Sq. SW7	BT42	66
Hereford St. E2	**CB38**	**2**
Hereford St. E2	CB38	57
Hereford Way, Chess.	BK56	93
Herent Dr. Ilf.	CK31	49
Hereward Av. Pur.	BY59	95
Hereward Clo. Wal. Abb.	CF19	21
Hereward Gdns. N13	BY28	38
Hereward Rd. SW17	BU49	76
Herga Ct. Har.	BH34	45
Herga Ct. Wat.	BC23	26
Herga Rd. Har.	BH31	45
Herington Gro. Brwd.	DD26	122
Heriot Av. E4	CD27	39
Heriot Pl. NW5	BV35	47
Mansfield Rd.		
Heriot Rd. NW4	BQ32	46
Heriot Rd. Cher.	AW54	83
Heriots Clo. Stan.	BJ28	36
Heritage Clo. St. Alb.	BG13	9
High St.		
Heritage Clo. Uxb.	AX38	53
Herkomer Clo. Bush.	BF25	27
Herkomer Rd. Bush.	BF25	27
Herlwyn Av. Ruis.	BB34	44
Herlwyn Gdns. SW17	BU49	76
Hermes St. N1	BY37	56
Hermes Wk. Nthlt.	BF37	54
Leander Rd.		
Hermes Way, Wall.	BW57	95
Hermiston Av. N8	BX32	47
Hermitage Clo. E18	CG31	49
Hermitage Clo. Enf.	BY23	29
Hermitage Clo. Esher	BJ57	93
Hermitage Clo. Pot. B.	BT20	20
Hermitage Clo. Shep.	AZ52	83
Hermitage Clo. Slou.	AR41	62
Hermitage Ct. E18	CH31	49
Hermitage Gdns. NW3	BS34	47
Hermitage Gdns. SE19	BZ50	77
Hermitage La. NW3	BS34	47
Hermitage La. SE25	CB53	87
Hermitage La. SW16	BX50	76
Hermitage Rd. N4	BZ33	48
Hermitage Rd. N15	BZ32	48
Hermitage Rd. SE19	BZ50	77
Hermitage Rd. Ken.	BZ61	105
Hermitage Rd. Wok.	AO63	100
Hermitage, The SE23	CC47	77
Hermitage, The SW13	BO44	65
Hermitage, The Rich.	BL46	75
Hermitage, The Uxb.	AX36	53
Hermitage Wk. E18	CG31	49
Hermitage Wall E1	**CB40**	**4**
Hermitage Wall E1	CB40	57
Hermitage Way, Stan.	BJ30	36
Hermitage Woods Cres. Wok.	AO63	100
Hermit La. N18	BZ28	39
Hermit Rd. E16	CG39	58
Hermit St. EC1	**BY38**	**2**
Hermit St. EC1	BY38	56
Rawstorne St.		
Hermon Gro. Hayes	BC40	53
Hermon Hill E11	CH32	49
Hermon Hill E18	CH31	49
Herndon Rd. SW18	BT46	76
Herne Clo. NW10	BN35	46
Herne Hill SE24	BZ46	77
Herne Hill Rd. SE24	BZ45	67
Herne Ms. N18	CB28	39
Lyndhurst Rd.		
Herne Pl. SE24	BY46	76
Herne Rd. Bush.	BF25	27
Herne Rd. Surb.	BK55	84
Herne-Shaw, Hat.	BO13	10
Herns La. Welw. G. C.	BS7	5
Herns Way, Welw. G. C.	BS7	5
Heron Clo. E17	CD30	39
Heron Clo. NW10	BO36	55
Heron Clo. Buck. H.	CH26	40
Heron Clo. Guil.	AQ69	118
Heron Clo. Rick.	AX27	35
Heron Clo. Uxb.	AX36	53
Heron Ct. Brom.	CJ52	88
Heron Ct. Rich.	BK46	74
Bridge St.		
Heron Cres. Sid.	CN48	78
Herondale, Sth. Croy.	CC58	96
Heron Dale, Wey.	AX56	92
Herondale Av. SW18	BT47	76
Heronfield, Pot. B.	BT18	20
Heron Flight Av. Rain.	CU36	59
Herongate Rd. E12	CJ34	49
Herongate Rd. Swan.	CT50	79
Herongate Rd. Wal. Cr.	CD17	21
Heron Hill, Belv.	CQ42	69
Heron Mews, Ilf.	CL34	49
Heron Rd. SE24	BZ45	67
Heron Rd. Croy.	CA54	87
Heron Rd. Twick.	BJ45	64
Heronry, The Walt.	BC57	92
Herons Cft. Wey.	BA57	92
Heronsford W13	BK39	54
Heronsgate, Edg.	BM28	37
Heronsgate, Rick.	AT25	25
Herons La. Ong.	CY14	15
Heronslea Dr. Stan.	BL28	37
Heronslea, Wat.	BD21	27
Herons Rise, Barn.	BU24	29
Herons, The E11	CG32	49
Herons Way, St. Alb.	BJ15	9
Herons Wood, Harl.	CL10	6
Heronswood, Wal. Abb.	CG20	22
Roundhills		
Herons Wood Rd. Welw. G. C.	BS8	5
Heronway, Brwd.	DD26	122
Heron Way, Hat.	BP13	10
Heron Way, Upmin.	CZ33	51
Heronway, Wdf. Grn.	CJ28	40
Herrick Rd. N5	BZ34	48
Herrick St. SW1	**BW42**	**3**
Herrick St. SW1	BW42	66
Herries St. W10	BR37	55
Herringham Rd. SE7	CJ41	68
Herrings La. Cher.	AW53	83
Herring St. SE5	CA43	67
Herrongate Clo. Enf.	CA23	30
Hersant Clo. NW10	BP37	55
Herschel St. Slou.	AP41	62
Herschell Rd. SE23	CC47	77
Hersham Clo. SW15	BP47	75
Hersham Rd. Walt.	BC55	83
Hersham Trd. Est. Walt.	BE55	84
Hers St. Slou.	AP41	62
Hertford Av. SW14	BN46	75
Hertford Clo. Barn.	BT24	29
Hertford Pl. W1	**BW38**	**1**
Hertford Pl. W1	BW38	56
Whitfield St.		
Hertford Rd. N1	**CA37**	**2**
Hertford Rd. N1	CA37	57
Hertford Rd. N2	BU31	47
Hertford Rd. N9	CB27	39
Hertford Rd. Bark.	CL36	58
Hertford Rd. Barn.	BT24	29
Hertford Rd. Enf.	CC24	30
Hertford Rd. Epsom	BM57	94
Hertford Rd. Hat.	BQ11	10
Hertford Rd. Hodd.	CC10	12
Hertford Rd. Ilf.	CN32	49
Hertford Rd. Welw. G. C.	BU6	5
Hertford Rd. Welw. G. C.	BR5	5
Hertford Sq. Mitch.	BX52	86
Hertford St. W1	**BV40**	**3**
Hertford St. W1	BV40	56
Hertford Way, Mitch.	BX52	86
Hertslet Rd. N7	BX34	47
Hervey Clo. N3	BS30	38
Hervey Pk. Rd. E17	CD31	48
Hervey Rd. SE3	CH44	68
Hervey Way N3	BS30	38
Hervey Clo.		
Hesa Rd. Hayes	BC39	53
Heseltine Rd. SE26	CD49	77
Green La.		
Hesham Rd. Berk.	AP15	7
Hesiers Hill, Warl.	CG62	106
Hesiers Rd. Warl.	CG61	106
Hesketh Av. Dart.	CX47	80
Hesketh Pl. W11	BR40	55
Hesketh Rd. E7	CH34	49
Heslop Rd. SW12	BU47	76
Hesper Ms. SW5	**BS42**	**3**
Hesper Ms. SW5	BS42	66
Hesperus Cres. E14	CE42	67
Hessell St. E1	CB39	57
Hessel Rd. W13	BJ41	64
Hesselyn Dr. Rain.	CU36	59
Hessle Gro. Epsom	BO59	94
Hestercombe Av. SW6	BR44	65
Hester Rd. N18	CB28	39
Hester Rd. SW11	BU43	66
Heston Av. Houns.	BE43	64
Heston Grange La. Houns.	BE43	64
Heston Grn. Houns.	BE43	64
Walnut Tree Rd.		
Heston Ho. SE8	CD44	67
Heston Rd. Houns.	BF43	64
Heston Rd. Red.	BU72	121
Heston St. SE8	CD44	67
Heston Wk. Red.	BU72	121
Hetchleys, Hem. H.	AW12	8
Hetherington Rd. SW4	BX45	66
Hetherington Rd. Shep.	BA51	83
Hetherington Way, Uxb.	AY35	44
Hetley Gdns. SE19	CA50	77
Fox Hill		
Hetley Rd. W12	BP40	55
Hetton St. W6	BQ42	65
Glenthorne Rd.		
Hevelius Clo. SE10	CG42	68
Hever Av. Sev.	CZ57	99
Hever Ct. Rd. Grav.	DH50	81
Hever Croft SE9	CL49	78
Hever Gdns. Brom.	CL51	88
Heverham Rd. SE18	CN42	68
Hever Rd. Sev.	CZ57	99
Heversham Rd. Bexh.	CR44	69
Hever Wood Rd. Sev.	CZ57	99
Hewens Rd. Uxb.	BA38	53
Hewer St. W10	BQ39	55
Hewers Way, Tad.	BQ63	103
Hewett Clo. Stan.	BJ28	36
Stanmore Hill		
Hewett Pl. Swan.	CS52	89
Hewett Rd. Dag.	CP35	50
Hewish Rd. N18	CA28	39
Hewitt Av. N22	BY30	38
Hewitt Rd. N8	BY32	47
Hewitts Rd. Orp.	CQ57	98
Hewlett Rd. E3	CD37	57
Hexagon, The N6	BU33	47
Hexal Rd. SE6	CG48	78
Hexham Gdns. Islw.	BJ43	64
Hexham Rd. SE27	BZ48	77
Hexham Rd. Barn.	BS24	29
Hexham Rd. Mord.	BS54	86
Hextalls La. Red.	BZ67	114
Heybourne Rd. N17	CB29	39
Heybridge Av. SW16	BX50	76
Heybridge Dr. Ilf.	CM31	49
Heydons Clo. St. Alb.	BG12	9
Heyford Av. SW8	BX43	66
Heyford Av. SW20	BR52	85
Heyford Rd. Mitch.	BU51	86
Heyford Rd. Rad.	BJ21	27
Heygate St. SE17	**BZ42**	**4**
Heygate St. SE17	BZ42	67
Heylyn Sq. E3	CE37	58
Malmesbury Rd.		
Heymede, Lthd.	BK65	102
Heynes Rd. Dag.	CP35	50
Heysham Dr. Wat.	BD28	36
Heysham Rd. N15	BZ32	48
Heythorpe Clo. Wok.	AP62	100
Kenton Way		
Heythorpe St. SW18	BR47	75
Heyworth Rd. E5	CB35	48
Heyworth Rd. E15	CG35	49
Hibbert Av. Wat.	BD22	27
Hibbert Rd. E17	CD33	48
Hibbert Rd. Har.	BH30	36
Hibbert Rd. Maid.	AG41	61
Hibberts Alley, Wind.	AO44	61
Peascod St.		
Hibbert St. SW11	BT45	66
Hibernia Dr. Grav.	DJ48	81
Hibernia Gdns. Houns.	BF45	64
Hibernia Rd. Houns.	BF45	64
Hichisson Rd. SE15	CC46	77
Hickin Clo. SE7	CJ42	68
Charlton Church Rd.		
Hickling Rd. Ilf.	CL35	49
Hickman Av. E4	CF28	39
Hickman Rd. Rom.	CP33	50
Hickmans Clo. Gdse.	CC69	114
Hickmore Walk SW4	BW45	66
Cubitt Terr.		
Hicks Av. Grnf.	BG37	54
Hicks Cl. SW11	BU44	66
Hicks St. SE8	CD42	67
Hidalgo Ct. Hem. H.	AY12	8
Hide Pl. SW1	**BW42**	**3**
Hide Pl. SW1	BW42	66
Hide Rd. Har.	BG31	45
Hides, The Harl.	CM10	6
Higgs Row SW15	BQ45	65
Felsham Rd.		
High Acres, Wat.	BA19	17
Higham Av. Hem. H.	AX14	8
Higham Hill Rd. E17	CD30	39
Higham La. Ton.	DC70	117
Higham Pl. E17	CD31	48
Higham Rd. E17	CD30	39
Higham Rd. N17	BZ31	48
Higham Rd. Wdf. Grn.	CH29	40
Highams Hill, War.	CH59	97
Higham Station Av. E4	CE29	39
Highams, The Park, Wdf. Grn.	CG28	40
Higham View Epp.	CR16	23
Highash Clo. S. Le. H.	DK42	71
Highbanks Clo. Well.	CO43	69
Highbanks Rd. Hem. H.	AZ16	17
High Banks Rd. Pnr.	BF29	36
Highbarn Rd. Lthd.	BD68	111
Highbarrow Rd. Croy.	CA54	87
High Beech Sth. Croy.	CA57	96
High Beeches, Bans.	BQ60	94
High Beeches, Ger. Cr.	AR33	43
High Beeches Orp.	CO57	98
High Beeches, Sid.	CQ49	79
High Beech Rd. Loug.	CK24	31
High Bois La. Amer.	AO21	25
High Bridge SE10	CF42	67
Highbridge Rd. Bark.	CL37	58
High Bri. St. Wal. Abb.	CE20	21
Highbrook Rd. SE3	CJ45	68
Highbroom Cres. W. Wick.	CE54	87
Highbury Av. Hodd.	CE11	12
Highbury Av. Th. Hth.	BY51	86
Highbury Clo. W. Wick.	CE55	87
Highbury Cres. N5	BY35	47
Highbury Gdns. Ilf.	CN34	49
Highbury Gra. N5	BY35	47
Highbury Gro. N5	BY36	56
Highbury Gro. N. Mal.	BN52	85
Highbury Hill N5	BY35	47
Highbury Mews N5	BY35	47
Ronalds Rd.		
Highbury New Pk. N5	BZ34	48
Highbury Pk. N5	BY35	47
Highbury Park Ms. N5	BZ35	48
Highbury Gra.		
Highbury Pl. N5	BY36	56
Highbury Quadrant N5	BY34	47
Highbury Quadrant Est. N5	BZ34	48
Highbury Rd. SW19	BR49	75
Highbury Station Rd. N1	BY36	56
Highbury Ter. N5	BY35	47
Highbury Ter. Ms. N5	BY35	47
Ronalds Rd.		
High Canons, Borwd.	BN22	28
High Clere Clo. Ken.	BZ57	96
Highclere Clo. Ken.	BZ61	105
Highclere Ct. St. Alb.	BH13	9
Avenue Rd.		
Highclere Dr. Hem. H.	AZ15	8
Highclere Gdns. Wok.	AO62	100
Highclere Rd. N. Mal.	BN52	85
Highclere Rd. Wok.	AO62	100
Highclere St. SE26	CD49	77
Highcliffe Dr. SW15	BO46	75
Highcliffe Gdns. Ilf.	CK32	49
High Clo. Rick.	AX25	26
Highcombe, SE7	CH43	68
Highcombe Clo. SE9	CJ47	78
Highcotts La. Wok.	AV66	109
High Ct. Wdf. Grn.	CH29	40
Higham Rd.		
Highcroft, NW9	BO32	46
Highcroft Av. Wem.	BL36	55
Highcroft Gdns. NW11	BR32	46
Highcroft Rd. N19	BX33	47
Highcroft Rd. Hem. H.	AW16	17
High Cross Rd. N17	CA31	48
Highcross Rd. Grav.	DB49	80
High Cross Rd. Sev.	DA66	117
Highcross Walk, SW15	BP47	75
Bessborough Rd.		
Highdaun Dr. SW16	BX52	86
High Dells, Hat.	BO13	10
Highdown Wor. Pk.	BO55	85
Highdown Rd. SW15	BP46	75
High Dr. Lthd.	BG60	93
High Dr. Cat.	CE64	105
High Dr. Lthd.	BG60	93
High Dr. N. Mal.	BN51	85
High Elms, Chig.	CN28	40
High Elms, Upmin.	CZ33	51
High Elms, Wdf. Grn.	CH28	40
High Elms Clo. Nthwd.	BA29	35
Highelms La. Wat.	BC18	17
Highelms La. Wat.	BD19	18
High Elms Rd. Orp.	CL59	97
Higher Dr. Bans.	BQ59	94
Higher Dr. Pur.	BY60	95
Higher Grn. Epsom	BP60	94
Higher Tubs, Bush.	BG26	36
High Field, Bans.	BU62	104
Highfield, Harl.	CO11	14
Highfield Rom.	CS29	41
High Fld. Wind.	AM45	
Highfield Av. NW9	BN32	46
Highfield Av. NW11	BQ33	46
Highfield Av. Erith.	CR43	69
Highfield Av. Grnf.	BH35	45
Highfield Av. Orp.	CN56	97
Highfield Av. Pnr.	BE32	45
Highfield Av. Wem.	BL34	46
Highfield, Ch. St. G.	AR26	34
Highfield Clo. NW9	BN32	46
Highfield Clo. Amer.	AO22	25
Highfield Clo. Egh.	AR50	72
Highfield Clo. Nthwd.	BB30	35
Highfield Clo. Rom.	CS29	41
Highfield Clo. Surb.	BK54	84
Highfield Clo. Wey.	AW60	92
Highfield Ct. N14	BW25	29
Highfield Cres. Horn.	CW34	51
Highfield Cres. Nthwd.	BB30	35
Highfield Dr. Brom.	CG52	88
Highfield Dr. Brox.	CD14	12
Highfield Dr. Epsom	BO57	94
Highfield Dr. Uxb.	AY34	44
Highfield Dr. Uxb.	AY35	44
Highfield Dr. W. Wick.	CE55	87
Highfield Gdns. NW11	BR32	46
Highfield Gdns. Grays	DE41	71
Highfield Grn. Epp.	CN19	22
Highfield Hill SE19	BZ50	77
Highfield La. Hem. H.	AY12	8
Highfield La. Red.	BK14	9
Highfield Pl. Epp.	CN19	22
Highfield Rd. N21	BY26	38
Highfield Rd. NW11	BR32	46
Highfield Rd. W3	BM39	55
Highfield Rd. Berk.	AR13	7
Highfield Rd. Bexh.	CQ46	79
Highfield Rd. Brom.	CK52	88
Highfield Rd. Bush.	BE25	27
Highfield Rd. Cat.	CB64	105
Highfield Rd. Cher.	AW54	83
Highfield Rd. Chis.	CN52	88
Highfield Rd. Dart.	CV47	80
Highfield Rd. Felt.	BC47	73
Highfield Rd. Horn.	CW34	51
Highfield Rd. Islw.	BH44	64
Highfield Rd. Nthwd.	BB30	35
Highfield Rd. Pur.	BX58	95
Highfield Rd. Rom.	CS29	41
Highfield Rd. St. Alb.	BJ10	9
Highfield Rd. St. Alb.	BK14	9
Highfield Rd. Sun.	BB53	83
Highfield Rd. Surb.	BN54	85
Highfield Rd. Sutt.	BU56	95
Highfield Rd. Wal. Cr.	CA16	21
Highfield Rd. Walt.	BC54	83
Highfield Rd. Wdf. Grn.	CK29	40
Highfield Rd. West.	CJ62	106
Highfield Rd. Wey.	AW60	92
Highfield Rd. S. Dart.	CV47	80
Highfields, Ash.	BK63	102
Highfields, Leath.	BB67	110
Highfields, Pot. B.	BX17	20
Highfield Way, Horn.	CW34	51
Highfield Way, Pot. B.	BS19	20
Highfield Way, Rick.	AW25	26

High Firs Swan. CT52 89
High Foleys Esher BJ57 93
High Gables Loug. CJ25 31
Highgate Av. N6 BV32 47
Highgate Clo. N6 BV33 47
Highgate High St. N6 BV33 47
Highgate Hill N19 BV33 47
Highgate Rd. NW5 BV34 47
Highgate West Hill, N6 BV33 47
High Gro. SE18 CM43 68
High Gro. Welw. G. C. BQ7 5
Highgrove Rd. Dag. CP35 50
Highgrove Way, Ruis. BC33 44
High Hill Est. E5 CB33 48
High Hill Rd. Warl. CF60 96
High Holborn WC1 BX39 2
High Holborn WC1 BX39 56
High House La. Til. DH41 71
Highland Av. W7 BH39 54
Highland Av. Brwd. DB26 42
Highland Av. Dag. CS34 50
Highland Av. Loug. CK25 31
Highland Cotts. Wall. BV56 95
Highland Croft, Beck. CE50 77
Highland Dr. Bush. BG26 36
Highland Dr. Hem. H. AZ13 8
Highland Pk. Felt. BB49 73
Highland Rd. SE19 CA50 77
Highland Rd. Amer. AO23 25
Highland Rd. Bexh. CR46 79
Highland Rd. Brom. CG51 88
Highland Rd. Nthwd. BB31 44
Highland Rd. Nthwd. BC31 44
Highland Rd. Pur. BY60 95
Highland Rd. Sev. CR59 98
Highland Rd. Wal. Abb. CG14 13
Highlands, Wat. BD27 36
Highlands, Wat. BD26 36
Highlands, Wok. AS64 100
Highland Av. W3 BN40 55
Highlands Av. Lthd. BK64 102
Highlands Clo. Ger. Cr. AS29 34
Highlands Clo. Houns. BF44 64
Highlands Clo. Lthd. BJ64 102
Highlands End, Ger. Cr. AS29 34
Highlands Gdns. Ilf. CK33 49
Highlands Hat. BQ11 10
Highlands Heath SW15 BQ47 75
Bristol Gdns.
Highlands Hill, Swan. CU51 89
Highlands La. Ger. Cr. AS29 34
Highlands Pk. Lthd. BK65 102
Highlands Rd. Barn. BS25 29
Highlands Rd. Beac. AO28 34
Highlands Rd. Lthd. BJ64 102
Highlands Rd. Orp. CO54 89
Highlands Rd. Reig. BT70 121
Highlands, The Edg. BM30 37
Highlands, The Leath. BB66 110
Highlands, The Pot. B. BT18 20
Highlands, The Rick. AW26 35
High La. W7 BG39 54
High La. Warl. CD62 105
High Laver La. Ong. CU12 14
Highlea Clo. NW9 BO30 37
High Level Dr. SE25 CB49 77
High Lever Rd. W10 BQ39 55
Highmead SE18 CN43 68
Highmead Chig. CL27 40
High Mead Har. BH32 45
High Mead W. Wick. CF55 87
Highmead Cres. Wem. BL36 55
Highmeadows Clo. Pnr. BC31 44
High Meadow Cres. NW9 BN32 46
High Meadows Chig. CM28 40
High Moor, Amer. AO23 25
Highmore Rd. SE3 CG43 68
High Oaks, Enf. BX22 29
High Oaks, St. Alb. BG11 9
High Oaks Rd. Welw. G. C. BP7 5
High Ongar Rd. Ong. CX17 24
Highover Park, Amer. AO23 25
High Park Av. Leath. BB66 110
High Pk. Av. Rich. BM44 65
High Pk. Rd. Rich. BM44 65
High Pastures, Bish. CS7 6
High Path SW19 BS51 86
High Path Rd. Guil. AU70 118
High Pine Clo. Wey. BA56 92
High Point SE9 CL48 78
High Point, Wey. AZ56 92
High Ridge N10 BV30 38
High Ridge, Pot. B. BX17 20
High Ridge Clo. Epsom BO60 94
Highridge La. Bet. BM73 120
Highridge Pla. Enf. BY23 29
The Ridgeway
High Ridge Rd. Hem. H. AX16 17
High Rd. E11 CG34 49
High Rd. E18 CG29 40
High Rd. N11 BV28 38
High Rd. N15 CA32 48
High Rd. N17 CA30 39
High Rd. N22 BX29 38
High Rd. NW10 BO36 55
High Rd. NW10 BP36 55
High Rd. Brox. CD15 12
High Rd. Buck. H. CH27 40
High Rd. Bush. BG26 36
High Rd. Couls. BU65 104
High Rd. E. Finchley N2 BT30 38
High Rd. Epp. CO15 14
High Rd. Epp. CO17 23
High Rd. Epp. CR16 23
High Rd. Epp. CS15 14
High Rd. Grays DC40 71
High Rd. Har. Weald BH29 36
High Rd. Hat. BU12 11
High Rd. Ilf. CL34 49
High Rd. Leytonstone E11 CG35 49
High Rd. Leytonstone E15 CG35 49
High Rd. Loug. CJ25 31
High Rd. N. Finchley N12 BT28 38
High Rd. Reig. BT67 113
High Rd. Rom. CO33 50
High Rd. Uxb. AX39 53
High Rd. Uxb. AZ34 44
High Rd. Wat. BB20 17
High Rd. Wat. BB21 26
High Rd. Wdf. Grn. CG29 40
High Rd. Wem. BK35 45
High Rd. Wey. AY59 92
High Rd. Whet. BT26 38
High Road Willesden Grn. NW10 BO36 55
High Rd. Wilmington CV48 80
High St. Ms. SW19 BR49 75
Courthope Rd.
High St. Southgate N14 BW26 38
Highshore Rd. SE15 CA44 67
High Silver Loug. CJ24 31
Highstead Cres. Erith CT43 69
Highstone E11 CG32 49
Highstone Av. E11 CH32 49
High St. E11 CH32 49
High St. E13 CH37 58
High St. E15 CF37 57
High St. E17 CD32 48
High St. N8 BX31 47
High St. NW7 BP28 37
High St. NW10 BO37 55
High St. SE20 CB50 77
High St. SW6 BR45 65
High St. SW19 BO49 75
High St. W3 BM40 55
High St. W5 BK40 54
High St. Bans. BS61 104
High St. Barkingside CM31 49
High St. Barn. BR24 28
High St. Beck. CE51 87
High St. Bedmond. Wat. BB17 17
High St. Berk. AP11 7
High St. Bex. CR47 79
High St. Brent. BK43 64
High St. Brom. CG51 88
High St. Brwd. DB27 42
High St. Bush. BE25 27
High St. Cars. BU56 95
High St. Cheam BR57 94
High St. Chis. CL50 78
High St. Ch. St. G. AR27 34
High St. Claygate BH57 93
High St. Cob. BC60 92
High St. Cob. BC61 101
High St. Col. Heath. BN14 10
High St. Colliers Wood SW19 BT50 76
High St. Cranford BC43 63
High St. Croy. BZ55 87
High St. Dart. CW46 80
High St. Dart. DA48 80
High St. Dor. BJ71 119
High Silver Edg. BM29 37
High St. Egh. AS49 72
High St. Elstree BK25 27
High St. E. Mol. BF52 84
High St. Epp. CN19 22
High St. Epsom BN60 94
High St. Erith CT42 69
High St. Esher BF56 93
High St. Ewell BO58 94
High St. Farn. CW53 90
High St. Farn. CL56 97
High St. Felt. BC48 73
High St. Ger. Cr. AS30 34
High St. Grav. DD46 81
High St. Grav. DG46 81
High St. Grays DD43 71
High St. Green. DA45 70
High St. Green St. Green. CN57 97
High St. Guil. AR71 118
High St. Har. BH33 45
High St. Harl. CH10 13
High St. Harl. CP9 6
High St. Hem. H. AT17 16
High St. Hem. H. AX12 8
High St. Hmptn. BF51 84
High St. Hmptn. BG51 84
High St. Hodd. CE13 12
High St. Horn. CV33 51
High St. Houns. BF45 64
High St. Iver. AV39 52
High St. Kings L. AZ18 17
High St. Kings. on T. BK51 84
High St. Kings. on T. BK52 84
High St. Lthd. BF66 111
High St. Lthd. BJ64 102
High St. Maid. AH41 61
High St. Merton SW19 BS50 76
High St. Nthwd. BB30 35
High St. Ong. CX17 24
High St. Orp. CL59 97
High St. Orp. CO55 89
High St. Oxt. CF68 114
High St. Oxt. CH67 115
High St. Pnr. BE31 45
High St. Ponders End CC25 30
High St. Pot. B. BT19 20
High St. Pur. BY59 95
High St. Red. BU70 121
High St. Red. BV67 113
High St. Red. BX70 121
High St. Red. BZ70 114
High St. Reig. BS70 121
High St. Rick. AX26 35
High St. Rom. CT32 50
High St. Ruis. BB33 44
High St. St. Alb. BG13 9
High St. St. Alb. BK16 18
High St. St. Mary Cray CP53 89
High St. S. Norwood SE25 CA52 87
High St. S. Ock. CW40 60
High St. S. Ock. DB38 60
High St. Sev. CS64 107
High St. Sev. CT58 98
High St. Sev. CU61 107
High St. Sev. CV66 117
High St. Sev. CW64 108
High St. Sev. CX62 108
High St. Sev. DC67 117
High St. Shep. AZ54 83
High St. Sid. CP50 79
High St. Slou. AO41 61
High St. Slou. AP41 62
High St. Slou. AQ44 62
High St. Slou. AU43 62
High St. Stai. AS46 72
High St. Stai. AV49 72
High St. Stai. AX46 73
High St. Sthl. BE40 54
High St. Sutt. BS56 95
High St. Swan. CT52 89
High St. Swans. DC46 81
High St. Tad. BQ65 103
High St. Tedd. BJ49 74
High St. Thames Ditton BJ54 84
High St. Th. Hth. BZ52 87
High St. Uxb. AX30 35
High St. Uxb. AX36 53
High St. Uxb. AX39 53
High St. Wal. Cr. CC18 21
High St. Wal. Cr. CD20 21
High St. Walt. BC54 83
High St. Wat. BD24 27
High St. Wealdstone BH30 36
High St. Well. CO45 69
High St. Wem. BL35 46
High St. West. CM67 115
High St. West Dr. AX40 53
High St. Wey. AW56 92
High St. Wey. AZ56 92
High St. Whitton. BG47 74
High St. Wind. AO43 61
High St. Wind. AO44 61
High St. Wok. AP59 91
High St. Wok. AR61 100
High St. Wok. AS62 100
High St. Wok. AT64 100
High St. Wok. AW64 101
High St. W. Wick. CE54 87
High Street Green Hem. H. AZ12 8
High St. N. E6 CK36 58
High St. N. E12 CK35 49
High Timber St. EC4 BZ40 4
High Timber St. EC4 BZ40 57
Broken Wharf
Hightor Clo. Brom. CH50 78
High Tor Clo. Brom. CH50 77
Babbacombe Rd.
High Tree Clo. Wey. AW56 92
High Trees SW2 BY47 76
High Trees, Barn. BU25 29
High Trees, Croy. CD54 87
High Trees Clo. Cat. CA64 105
High Trees Rd. Reig. BT71 121
High View, Hat. BO13 10
Highview, Pnr. BD31 45
High Vw. Rick. AW24 26
High Vw. Sutt. BR59 94
High Vw. Wat. BB25 26
High View Ave. Grays DE42 71
Highview Av. Edg. BN28 37
Highview Av. Wall. BX56 95
High Vw. Clo. SE19 CA51 87
High Vw. Clo. Loug. CJ25 31
Highview Cres. Brwd. DE25 122
Highview Gdns. N3 BR31 46
High View Gdns. N11 BW28 38
Highview Gdns. Edg. BN28 37
High View Gdns. Pot. B. BT20 20
Highview Gdns. Upmin. CX34 51
Highview Pk. Bans. BS61 104
High View Rd. E18 CG31 49
High View Rd. SE19 BZ50 77
Highview Rd. W13 BJ39 54
High View Rd. Guil. AO72 118
High Vw. Rd. Orp. CL58 97
High View Rd. Sid. CO49 79
Highway, The E1 CB40 4
Highway, The E1 CB40 57
Highway, The Orp. CO56 98
Highway, The Stan. BH30 36
Highway, The Sutt. BT58 95
High Wickfield, Welw. G. C. BT8 5
Highwold Couls. BV62 104
Highwood Av. N12 BT28 38
Highwood Av. Bush. BE23 27
Highwood Clo. Brwd. DA26 42
Highwood Clo. Ken. BZ58 96
Highwood Clo. Ken. BZ62 105
Highwood Clo. Orp. CM55 88
Highwood Dr. Orp. CM55 88
Highwood Gdns. Ilf. CK32 49
Highwood Gro. NW7 BN28 37
Highwoodhall La. Hem. H. AZ16 17
Highwood Hill NW7 BO27 37
Highwood La. Loug. CL25 31
Highwood Rd. N19 BX34 47
Highwood Rd. Hodd. CD10 12
Highwoods, Lthd. BK64 102
High Worple Har. BE33 45
Highworth Rd. N11 BW29 38
High Wych La. Saw. CO6 6
High Wych Rd. Harl. CN7 6
High Wych Rd. Harl. CN8 6
Highwych Way, Hem. H. AZ10 8
Elstree Rd.
Hilary Av. Mitch. BV52 86
Hilary Clo. SW6 BS43 66
Hilary Clo. Bexh. CR44 69
Hilary Clo. Horn. CV35 51
Hilary Rd. W12 BO39 55
Hilary Rd. Hem. H. AZ13 8
Hilbert Rd. Sutt. BQ55 85
Hilborough Rd. Orp. CM56 97
Hilda May Av. Swan. CT52 89
Hilda Rd. E6 CJ36 58
Hilda Rd. E16 CG38 58
Hilda Terr. SW9 BY44 66
Myatts Fields Dev.
Hilda Vale Clo. Orp. CL56 97
Hilda Vale Rd. Orp. CL56 97
Hildenborough Gdns. Brom. CG50 78
Hilden Dr. Erith. CU43 69
Hildenley Clo. Red. BW67 113
Malmstone Av.
Hildens, The Dor. BG72 119
Hilders, The Ash. BM62 103
Hildreth St. SW12 BV47 76
Hildyard Rd. SW6 BS43 66
Hiley Rd. NW10 BQ38 55
Hilfield La. Wat. BF23 27
Hilfield La. S. Bush. BH25 27
Hilfield La. Sth. Bush. BH25 27
Hilgrove Est. NW6 BT36 56
Hiliard Rd. Nthwd. BC30 35
Hiliary Gdns. Stan. BK30 36
Hillards Rd. Uxb. AX39 53
Hillars Hth. Rd. Couls. BX61 104
Hillary Av. Grav. DF48 81
Hillary Cres. Walt. BD54 84
Hilary Rd. Slou. AS41 62
Hillary Rd. Sthl. BF41 64
Hillary Rise, Barn. BS24 29
Hillbeck Clo. SE15 CB43 67
Hillbeck Way Grnf. BG37 54
Hillborne Clo. Hayes BC42 63
Hillborough Ave. Sev. CV64 108
Hillborough Clo. SW19 BT50 76
Hillbrook Rd. SW17 BU48 76
Hill Brow, Brom. CJ51 88
Hill Brow, Dart. CT46 79
Hillbrow, N. Mal. BO52 85
Hillbrow Clo. Bex. CS49 79
Hillbrow Ct. Gdse. CC69 114
Hickmans Clo.
Hillbrow Rd. Brom. CG50 78
Hillbrow Rd. Esher BG56 93
Hillbury, Hat. BO13 10
Hillbury Av. Har. BJ32 45
Hillbury Clo. Warl. CC62 105
Hillbury Rd. SW17 BV48 76
Hillbury Rd. Warl. CB62 105
Hill Clo. NW2 BP34 46
Hill Clo. NW11 BS32 47
Hill Clo. Barn. BQ25 28
Hill Clo. Chesh. AP20 16
Hill Clo. Chis. CL49 78
Hill Clo. Grav. DF50 81
Hill Clo. Har. BH34 45
Hill Clo. Pur. BZ60 96
Hill Clo. Rom. CV28 42
Hill Clo. Stan. BJ28 36
Hill Clo. Wok. AR61 100
Hill Common, Hem. H. AZ15 8
Hillcote Av. SW16 BY50 76
Hill Ct. SW15 BQ46 75
Putney Hill
Hill Ct. W5 BL38 55
Ridings, The
Hillcourt Av. N12 BS29 38
Hillcourt Est. N16 BZ33 48
Hillcourt Rd. SE22 CB46 77
Hill Cres. N20 BS27 38
Hill Cres. Bex. CS47 79
Hill Cres. Har. BJ32 45
Hill Cres. Horn. CV32 51
Hill Cres. Surb. BL53 85
Hill Cres. Wor. Pk. BQ55 85
Hillcrest N6 BV33 47
Hillcrest N21 BY26 38
Hillcrest, Hat. BO12 10
Hillcrest, Pot. B. BT20 20
Hillcrest, Sev. CU64 107
Hill Crest, Sid. CO47 79
Hillcrest Av. NW11 BR32 46
Hillcrest Av. Cher. AV55 82
Hillcrest Av. Edg. BM28 37
Hillcrest Av. Grays DA43 70
Hillcrest Av. Pnr. BD31 45
Hillcrest Clo. Beck. CD53 87
Hillcrest Clo. Epsom BO61 103
Treadwell Rd.
Hillcrest Dr. Green. DA46 80
Hill Crest Gdns. N3 BR31 46
Hillcrest Gdns. NW2 BP34 46
Hillcrest Gdns. Esher BH55 84
Hillcrest Gdns. Ruis. BD34 45
Hillcrest Rd. E17 CF30 39
Hillcrest Rd. E18 CG30 40
Hillcrest Rd. SE26 CB49 77
Hillcrest Rd. W3 BM40 55
Hillcrest Rd. W5 BL39 55
Hillcrest Rd. Brom. CH49 78
Hillcrest Rd. Dart. CT47 79
Hillcrest Rd. Epp. CT18 23
Hillcrest Rd. Guil. AP70 118
Hillcrest Rd. Horn. CU33 50
Hillcrest Rd. Loug. CJ25 31
Hillcrest Rd. Orp. CO55 89
Hillcrest Rd. Pur. BX58 95
Hillcrest Rd. Rad. BM20 19
Hill Crest Rd. West. CJ61 106
Hillcrest Rd. Whyt. CA62 105
Hillcrest Vw. Beck. CD53 87
Hillcrest Way Epp. CO19 23
Bower Hill
Hillcrest Waye, Ger. Cr. AS32 43
Hillcrest, Wey. AZ56 92
Hillcroft Loug. CL23 31
Hill Croft Av. Pnr. BE32 45
Hillcroft Av. Pur. BW60 95
Hillcroft Cres. W5 BK39 54
Hillcroft Cres. Ruis. BD34 45
Hillcroft Cres. Wat. BC26 35
Hillcroft Cres. Wem. BL35 46
Hillcroft Rd. Chesh. AO18 16
Hillcroome Rd. Sutt. BT57 95
Hillcross Av. Mord. BQ53 85
Hilldale Rd. Sutt. BR56 94
Hilldene Av. Rom. CV29 42
Hilldown Rd. SW16 BX50 76
Hilldown Rd. Brom. CG54 88
Hilldown Rd. Hem. H. AW12 8
Hill Dr. NW9 BN33 46
Hill Dr. SW16 BX52 86
Hilldrop Cres. N7 BW35 47
Hilldrop Est. N7 BW35 47
Hilldrop La. N7 BW35 47
Hilldrop Rd. N7 BW35 47
Hilldrop Rd. Brom. CH50 78
Hillend SE18 CL44 68
Hill End, Orp. CN55 88
Hill End La. St. Alb. BK14 9
Hill End Rd. Uxb. AX29 35
Hillerdon Av. Edg. BL28 37
Hillers Av. Uxb. AZ38 53
Hillersdon Av. SW13 BP44 65
Hillersdon Moat, Slou. AQ39 52
Hillery Clo. SE17 BZ42 67
Catesby St.
Hillery Rd. SE17 BZ42 4
Hill Farm Av. Wat. BC20 17
Hill Farm Clo. Wat. BC20 17
Hill Farm La. Ch. St. G. AQ26 34
Hill Farm Rd. W10 BQ39 55
Hill Farm Rd. Chesh. AO20 16
Hillfarm Rd. Ger. Cr. AS29 34
Hill Farm Rd. Uxb. BA35 44
Hillfield Av. N8 BX32 47
Hillfield Av. NW9 BO32 46
Hillfield Av. Mitch. BU53 86
Hillfield Av. Wem. BL36 55
Hillfield Clo. Guil. AU69 118
Hillfield Clo. Har. BG31 45
Hillfield Clo. Red. BV70 121
Hillfield Ct. NW3 BU35 47
Belsize Av.
Hillfield Ct. Esher BF56 93
Hillfield Pk. N10 BV31 47
Hillfield Pk. N21 BY27 38
Hillfield Pk. Ms. N10 BV31 47
Hillfield Pk.
Hillfield Rd. NW6 BR35 46
Hillfield Rd. Ger. Cr. AS29 34
Hillfield Rd. Hamptn. BE50 74
Hillfield Rd. Hem. H. AX13 8
Hillfield Rd. Red. BV70 121
Hillfield Rd. Sev. CT63 107
Hillfield Rd. Sev. CW61 108
Hillfield Sq. Ger. Cr. AS29 34
Hillfoot Av. Rom. CS30 41
Hillfoot Rd. Rom. CS30 41
Hillford Pl. Red. BV73 121
Hill Gdns. Wey. AV56 91
Hillgate Pl. W8 BS40 56
Hillgate St. W8 BS40 56
Hillgay Clo. Guil. AS70 118
Hillgay Ct. Guil. AS70 118
Hill Gro. Rom. CT31 50
Hillgrove Rd. NW6 BT36 1
Hillgrove Rd. NW6 BT36 56
Hillhouse, Wal. Abb. CG20 22
Hill Ho. Av. Stan. BH29 36
Hill Ho. Clo. N21 BY26 38
Hill House Clo. Ger. Cr. AS29 34
Rickmansworth La.
Hill House Dr. Reig. BS71 121
Hillhouse La. Wey. AZ58 92
Hill House Rd. SW16 BX49 76
Hillhouse Rd. Dart. CY47 80
Hillhurst Gdns. Cat. CA63 105
Hilliards Ct. E1 CC40 57
Hilliards Rd. Nthwd. BB30 35
Hillier Clo. Barn. BS25 29
Hillier Rd. SW11 BU46 76
Hillier Rd. Guil. AT70 118
Hilliers La. Croy. BX55 86
Hillingdon Ave. Sev. CV64 108
Hillingdon Av. Stai. AY47 73
Hillingdon Cir. Uxb. AZ36 53
Hillingdon Hill, Uxb. AY37 53
Hillingdon Ri. Sev. CV64 108
Hillingdon Rd. Bexh. CS44 69
Hillingdon Rd. Grav. DG48 81
Hillingdon Rd. Uxb. AX37 53
Hillingdon Rd. Wat. BC20 17
Hillingdon St. SE17 BY43 66
Hillingdon St. SW9 BY43 66
Hillingsdale, West. CH62 106
Hillington Gdns. Wdf. Grn. CJ30 40
Hill La. Ruis. BA33 44
Hill La. Tad. BR64 103
Hill La. Wind. AO44 61
Hill Leys Pot. B. BX17 20
Homewood Av.
Hillman Clo. Uxb. AY35 44
Hillman St. E8 CB36 57
Hillmarton Rd. N7 BX35 47
Hillmay Dr. Hem. H. AW14 8
Hillmont Rd. Esher BH55 84
Hillmore Gro. SE26 CC49 77
Hill Path SW16 BX49 76
Hill Place St. E14 CE39 57
Hillreach SE18 CK42 68
Hill Ri. Dart. CY49 80
Hill Ri. Dor. BJ70 119
Hill Ri. Ger. Cr. AR30 34
Hill Ri. Rick. AW26 35
Hill Ri. Slou. AT43 62
Hill Rise N9 CB25 30
Hill Rise NW11 BS31 47
Hill Rise SE23 CB47 77
Hill Rise, Esher BJ55 84
Hill Rise, Grnf. BG36 54
Hill Rise, Pot. B. BT20 20
Hill Rise, Pot. B. BW17 20
Hill Rise, Rich. BK46 74
Hill Rise, Ruis. BA33 44
Hill Rise, Upmin. CX34 51
Hill Rise, Walt. BB54 83
Hillrise Av. Wat. BD22 27
Hill Rise Cres. Ger. Cr. AS30 34
Hillrise Rd. N19 BX33 47
Hillrise Rd. Rom. CS29 41
Hill Rd. N10 BU30 38
Hill Rd. NW8 BT38 1
Hill Rd. NW8 BT38 56
Hill Rd. Amer. AO22 25
Hill Rd. Brwd. DA27 42
Hill Rd. Cars. BU57 95
Hill Rd. Dart. CW48 80
Hill Rd. Epp. CN22 31
Hill Rd. Har. BJ32 45
Hill Rd. Hem. H. AV14 7
Hill Rd. Lthd. BF64 102
Hill Rd. Mitch. BV51 86
Hill Rd. Nthwd. BA29 35
Hill Rd. Pnr. BE32 45
Hill Rd. Pur. BX59 95
Hill Rd. Sutt. BS56 95
Hill Rd. Wem. BJ34 45

Holmdale Gdns. NW4 BQ32 46
Holmdale Lo. Ct. W3 BM40 55
Whitehall Gdns.
Holmdale Rd. NW6 BS35 47
Holmdale Rd. Chis. CM49 78
Holmdale Ter. N15 CA32 48
Holmdene Av. NW7 BP29 37
Holmdene Av. SE24 BZ46 77
Holmdene Av. Har. BF31 45
Holmdene Clo. Beck. CF51 87
Holmdene Rd. N15 CA33 48
Holmead Rd. SW6 BS43 66
Holmebury Clo. Bush. BH27 36
Holme Chase Mord. BR53 85
Holme Chase, Wey. BA57 92
Holme Cl. Hat. BO11 10
Holme Clo. Wal. Cr. CD19 21
Holmecote Gdns. N5 BZ35 48
Holmedale, Slou. AR40 52
Holme Lacey Rd. SE12 CG46 78
Holme Lea, Wat. BD20 18
Holme Park Borwd. BL23 28
Holme Rd. E6 CK37 58
Holme Rd. Hat. BO11 10
Holme Rd. Horn. CW33 51
Holme Rd. Horn. CX33 51
Holmes Av. E17 CD31 48
Holmes Av. NW7 BR28 37
Holmes Dale, Guil. AT70 118
Holmesdale, Wal. Cr. CC21 30
Holmesdale Av. SW14 BM45 65
Holmesdale Clo. SE25 CA52 87
Holmesdale Hill St. Dnth. CY51 90
Holmesdale Rd. N6 BV32 47
Holmesdale Rd. Bexh. CP44 69
Holmesdale Rd. Croy. BZ53 87
Holmesdale Rd. Dor. BJ73 119
Holmesdale Rd. Red. BX71 121
Holmesdale Rd. Reig. BS70 121
Holmesdale Rd. Rich. BL44 65
Holmesdale Rd. S. Dnth. CY51 90
Holmesdale Rd. Tedd. BK50 74
Holmesley Rd. SE23 CD46 77
Holmes Rd. NW5 BV36 56
Holmes Rd. SW19 BT50 76
Holme Rd. Twick. BH48 74
Homes Way, Stan BH29 36
Holmethorpe Av. Red. BV69 121
Holmewood Gdns. SW2 BX47 76
Holmewood Rd. SE25 CA52 87
Holmewood Rd. SW2 BX47 76
Holmfield Av. NW4 BQ32 46
Holmfield Ct. NW3 BU35 47
Holmhurst Rd. Belv. CR42 69
Holmlea Wlk. Slou. AR44 62
Holmleigh Av. Dart. CV45 70
Holmleigh Rd. N16 CA33 48
Holmsdale Clo. Iver. AV39 52
Holmsdale Gro. Bexh. CT44 69
Holmsdale Rd. N11 BW28 38
Homsdale Rd. Sev. CV65 108
Holmshaw Rd. SE26 CD49 77
Holmshill La. Borwd. BN21 28
Holmside Rise Wat. BC27 35
Holmside Rd. SW12 BV46 76
Holmsley Clo. N. Mal. BO53 85
Holms St. E2 CA37 57
Holms St. E2 **CB37** **2**
Holmstall Av. Edg. BN30 37
Holmsworth Ct. Har. BG32 45
Holm Wk. SE3 CH44 68
Blackheath Pk.
Holmwood Croy. BW53 86
Holmwood Kings. On T. BN49 75
Holmwood Av. Brwd. DD25 122
Holmwood Av. Sth. Croy. CA60 96
Holmwood Clo. Har. BG31 45
Holmwood Clo. Leath. BB67 110
Holmwood Clo. Nthlt. BF36 54
Holmwood Clo. Sutt. BQ58 94
Holmwood Clo. Wey. AW56 92
Holmwood Gdns. N3 BS30 38
Holmwood Gdns. Wall. BV57 95
Holmwood Gro. NW7 BN28 37
Holmwood Rd. Chess. BL56 94
Holmwood Rd. Enf. CC21 30
Holmwood Rd. Ilf. CN34 49
Holmwood Rd. Sutt. BQ58 94
Holne Chase N2 BT32 47
Holness Rd. E15 CG36 58
Holroyd Clo. Esher BJ58 93
Holroyd Rd. SW15 BQ45 65
Holroyd Rd. Leath. BH58 93
Holstein Av. Wey. AZ56 92
Holstein Way Belv. CP41 69
Holsworthy Way, Chess. BK56 93
Holt Cl. N10 BV31 47
Holt Clo. Chig. CN28 40
Holton St. E1 CC38 57
Holt Rd. E16 CK40 58
Holt Rd. Wem. BJ34 45
Holtsmere Clo. Wat. BD21 27
Holt, The Hem. H. AY14 8
Holt, The Ilf. CM29 40
Holt, The Wall. BW56 95
Holt Way Chig. CN28 40
Holtwhites Av. Enf. BZ23 30
Holtwhite's Hill Enf. BY23 29
Holtwood Rd. Lthd. BG60 93
Holwell Ct. Hat. BU10 11
Holwell Hyde La.
Welw. G. C. BT9 5
Holwell Hyde Welw. G. C. BT8 5
Holwell Manor Rd. Hat. BU10 11
Holwell Pl. Pnr. BE31 45
Holwell Rd. Welw. G. C. BR8 5
Holwood Clo. Walt. BD55 84
Holwood Pk. Av. Orp. CK56 97
Holwood Pl. SW4 BW45 66
Holwood Rd. Brom. CH51 88
Holybourne Av. SW15 BP47 75
Holy Cross Hill, Brox. CB15 12
Holyfield Rd. Wal. Abb. CF18 21
Holy Hedge Rd. Cob. BC60 92
Holyoake Av. Wok. AR62 100
Holyoake Cres. Wok. AR62 100
Holyoake Rd. SE11 **BY41** **4**
Holyoak Rd. SE11 BY42 66
Holyoake Ter. Sev. CU65 107
Holyoake Wk. N2 BT31 47
Holyoake Wk. W5 BK38 54
Holyoak Rd. SE11 **BY42** **4**
Holyport Rd. SW6 BQ43 65
Holyrood Av Har. BE35 45
Holyrood Cres. St. Alb. BG15 9
Holyrood Gdns. Edg. BM31 46
Holyrood Gdns. Grays DH42 71
Holyrood Rd. Barn. BT25 29
Holywell Clo. Stai. AY47 73
Holyrood St. SE1 **CA41** **4**
Holywell Hill, St. Alb. BG14 9
Holywell La. EC2 **CA38** **2**
Holywell La. EC2 CA38 57
Holywell Rd. Wat. BC25 26
Holywell Row EC2 **CA38** **2**
Holywell Row EC2 CA38 57
Scrutton St.
Holywell Way, Stai. AY47 73
Home Clo. Brox. CD15 12
Macer's La.
Home Clo. Cars. BU55 86
Home Clo. Harl. CN11 13
Home Clo. Lthd. BG64 102
Home Clo. Nthlt. BE38 54
Homecroft Gdns. Loug. CL24 31
Homecroft Rd. N22 BY30 38
Homecroft Rd. SE26 CC49 77
Homedean Rd. Sev. CS64 107
Home Farm Clo. Esher BF57 93
Home Farm Clo. Shep. BB52 83
Upper Halliford Rd.
Homefarm Rd. W7 BH39 54
Home Farm Rd. Brwd. DC30 42
Home Farm Rd. Rick. AZ28 35
Home Farm Way, Slou. AR37 52
Home Field, Berk. AT11 7
Homefield Gdns. N2 BT31 47
Stanley Rd.
Homefield Hem. H. AT17 16
Homefield Wal. Abb. CH19 22
Homefield Walt. BD56 93
Homefield Av. Ilf. CN32 49
Homefield Clo. NW10 BN36 55
Homefield Clo. Epp. CO18 23
Homefield Clo. Hem. H. AZ13 8
Homefield Clo. Lthd. BK64 102
Homefield Clo. Swan. CT52 89
Homefield Clo. Wey. AV59 91
Homefield Gdns. Mitch. BT51 86
Homefield Gdns. Tad. BQ63 103
Homefield Pk. Sutt. BS57 95
Sutton Pk. Rd.
Homefield Rise Orp. CO54 89
Homefield Rd. SW19 BQ50 75
Homefield Rd. W4 BO42 65
Homefield Rd. Brom. CJ51 88
Homefield Rd. Bush. BF25 27
Homefield Rd. Couls. BY63 104
Homefield Rd. Edg. BN29 37
Homefield Rd. Rad. BH22 27
Homefield Rd. Rick. AU24 25
Homefield Rd. Sev. CT64 107
Homefield Rd. Walt. BE54 84
Homefield Rd. Warl. CC63 105
Homefield Rd. Wem. BJ35 45
Homefield Sq. N1 **CA37** **2**
Homefield St. N1 CA37 57
Regan Way
Home Fm. Clo. Epsom BQ62 103
Home Fm. Clo. Surb. BH54 84
Home Fm. Gdns. Walt. BD55 84
Home Fm. Rd. Berk. AO11 7
Home Gdns. Dag. CS34 50
Home Gdns. Dart. CW46 80
Home Hill Swan. CT50 79
Home Lea, Orp. CN56 97
Osgood Av.
Homelands, Lthd. BK64 102
Homelands Dr. SE19 CA50 77
Homeleigh Rd. SE15 CC46 77
Home Mead Stan. BK30 36
Home Mead Clo. Grav. DG47 81
Homemead Rd. Brom. CK53 88
Homemead Rd. Croy. BW53 86
Home Orchard Dart. CW46 80
Home Pk. Oxt. CH69 115
Home Pk. Rd. SW19 BR49 75
Home Pk. Wk.
Kings. on T. BK52 84
Homer Ct. Bexh. CS44 69
Homerfield, Welw. G. C. BQ7 5
Home Rd. SW11 BU44 66
Homer Rd. E9 CD36 57
Homer Rd. Croy. CC53 87
Homer Row W1 **BU39** **1**
Homer Row W1 BU39 56
Homersham Rd.
Kings. on T. BM51 85
Homers Rd. Wind. AL44 61
Homer St. W1 **BU39** **1**
Homer St. W1 BU39 56
Homerswood La. Welw. BP6 5
Homerton Gro. E9 CC35 48
Homerton High St. E9 CC35 48
Homerton Rd. E9 CD35 48
Homerton Row E9 CC35 48
Churchill Walk
Homerton Ter. E9 CC36 57
Homesdale Rd. Brom. CJ52 88
Homesdale Rd. Cat. BZ65 105
Homesdale Rd. Orp. CN54 88
Homesfield Rd. NW11 BS32 47
Homestall, Guil. AO70 118
Homestall Rd. SE22 CC46 77
Homestead Gdns. Esher BH56 93
Homestead La. Welw. G. C. BR9 5
Homestead Paddock N14 BV25 29
Homestead Pk. NW2 BO34 46
Homestead Rd. SW6 BR43 65
Homestead Rd. Cat. BZ65 105
Homestead Rd. Dag. CQ34 50
Homestead Rd. Hat. BP11 10
Homestead Rd. Orp. CO57 98
Homestead Rd. Rick. AX26 35
Homestead Rd. Stai. AW50 73
Homestead, The Dart. CV46 80
Homestead Way, Croy. CF59 96
Homewater Av. Sun. BB51 83
Home Way, Rick. AV26 34
Homeway, Rom. CX29 42
Homewood, Slou. AR39 52
Homewood Av. Pot. B. BX17 20
Homewood Cres. Chis. CN50 78
Home Wood La. Pot. B. BW17 20
Homewood Rd. Mitch. BT52 86
Homewood Rd. St. Alb. BJ12 9
Homland Dr. Sutt. BS58 95
Hulverston Clo.
Honduras St. EC1 **BZ38** **2**
Honduras St. EC1 BZ38 57
Baltic St.
Hone Par. SE11 BX42 66
Lambeth Wk.
Honeybourne Rd. NW6 BS35 47
Honeybourne Way Orp. CM54 88
Honeybrook Rd. SW12 BW47 76
Honeybrook, Wal. Abb. CG20 22
Honey Clo. Brwd. DB21 33
Honeycrock La. Red. BV74 121
Honeycroft Loug. CL24 31
Honey Croft, Welw. G C. BQ8 5
Honeycroft Hill, Uxb. AY36 53
Honeycross Rd. Hem. H. AV14 7
Honeyden Rd. Sid. CQ50 79
Honeyhill, Harl. CN13 13
Honey Hill, Uxb. AY36 53
Honey La. EC2 **BZ39** **2**
Honey La. EC2 BZ39 57
Cheapside
Honey La. Wal. Abb. CG20 22
Honey La. Wal. Abb. CH21 31
Honey Meade, Saw. CP7 6
Honeypot Clo. Har. BL31 46
Honeypot La. Brwd. DA27 42
Honeypot La. Sev. CX63 108
Honeypot La. Stan. BK36 29
Honeypots Rd. Wok. AR64 100
Honeysett Rd. N17 CA30 39
Reform Row
Honeysuckle Bottom
Leath. BB70 110
Honeysuckle Clo. Brwd. DA25 33
Honeysuckle Clo. Rom. CV29 42
Cloudberry Rd.
Honeysuckle Gdns. Hat. BP13 10
Honeysuckle La. N22 BZ30 39
Crawley Rd.
Honeywell Rd. SW11 BU46 76
Honeywood Clo. Pot. B. BT20 20
Honeywood Rd. NW10 BO37 55
Honeywood Rd. Islw. BJ45 64
Honister Clo. Stan. BJ29 36
Honister Clo. Stan. BK30 36
Honister Gdns. Stan. BJ29 36
Honister Gdns. Stan. BJ30 36
Honister Heights Pur. BZ60 96
Honister Pl. Stan. BJ30 36
Honiton Rd. NW6 BR37 55
Honiton Rd. Rom. CS32 50
Honiton Rd. Well. CN44 68
Honley Rd. SE6 CE47 77
Honnor Rd. Stai. AX50 73
Bingham Dr.
Honor Oak Est. SE4 CD45 67
Honor Oak Ri. SE23 CC46 77
Honor Oak Rd. SE23 CC47 77
Hood Av. N14 BV25 29
Hood Av. N14 BW26 38
Hood Av. SW14 BN46 75
Hood Av. Orp. CO53 89
Hood Clo. Croy. BY54 86
Hoodcote Gdns. N21 BY26 38
Hood Rd. SW20 BO50 75
Hood Rd. Rain. CT37 59
Hood Wk. Rom. CR30 41
Hook End La. Brwd. DB20 24
Hook End La. Brwd. DB21 33
Hook End Rd. Brwd. DA21 33
Hooke Rd. Leath. BB66 110
Hookers Rd. E17 CC31 48
Hookfarm Rd. Brom. CJ53 88
Hookfield Epsom BN60 94
Hookfield, Harl. CN12 13
Hookfield, Harl. CM13 13
Hook Field, Harl. CN12 13
Hook Fields, Grav. DF48 81
Hookgate, Enf. CB21 30
Hook Grn. La. Dart. CT48 79
Hook Grn. Rd. Grav. DC50 81
Hook Heath Av. Wok. AQ63 100
Hook Heath Gdns. Wok. AQ64 100
Hook Heath Rd. Wok. AP64 100
Hook Hill Sth. Croy. CA58 96
Hook Hill La. Wok. AQ64 100
Hook Hill Pk. Wok. AQ64 100
Hooking Grn. Har. BF32 45
Hook La. Pot. B. BU19 20
Hook La. Rom. CQ25 32
Hook La. Rom. CQ26 41
Hook La. Well. CN46 78
Hook Rise N. Surb. BL55 85
Hook Rise S. Surb. BL55 85
Hook Rd. Chess. BK56 93
Hook Rd. Epsom BN57 94
Hooks Hall Dr. Dag. CS34 50
Hook, The Barn. BT25 29
Hook Wk. Edg. BN29 37
Hookwood Rd. Orp. CP59 98
Hooley La. Red. BU71 121
Hooper Rd. E16 CH39 58
Hoopers Ct. SW3 **BU41** **3**
Hoopers Ct. SW3 BU41 66
Basil St.
Hooper's Ms. W3 BM40 55
Churchfield Rd.
Hooper St. E1 CB39 57
Hoopers Yd. Sev. CV66 117
Hoop La. NW11 BR33 46
Hoo, The Harl. CP8 6
Hopedale Rd. SE7 CH43 68
Hopefield Av. NW6 BR37 55
Hope Green, Wat. BC20 17
Hope Pk. Brom. CG50 78
Hope St. SW11 BT45 66
Hopetown St. E1 **CA39** **2**
Hopetown St. E1 CA39 57
Hopewell Dr. Grav. DJ49 81
Hopewell St. SE5 BZ43 67
Hopfield Av. Wey. AY59 92
Hop Fields, Wok. AS61 100
Hopgarden La. Sev. CU67 116
Hop Gdns. WC2 BX40 56
Bedfordbury
Hopgood St. W12 BQ40 55
Macfarlane Rd.
Hopground Clo. St. Alb. BJ14 9
Hopkins Cres. St. Alb. BJ10 9
Hopkins St. W1 **BW39** **1**
Hopkins St. W1 BW39 56
Hopland Rd. W14 BR42 65
Hopper's Rd. N13 BY27 38
Hopper's Rd. N21 BY27 38
Hoppett Rd. E4 CG27 40
Hoppety, The Tad. BQ64 103
Hopping La. N1 BY36 56
St. Mary's Gro.
Hoppingwood Av. N. Mal. BO52 85
Hoppit Rd. Wal. Abb. CE19 21
Hoppner Rd. Hayes BA37 53
Hopton Gdns. N. Mal. BP53 85
Hopton Rd. SW16 BX49 76
Hopton St. SE1 **BY40** **4**
Hopton St. SE1 BY40 56
Hopwood Rd. SE17 BZ43 67
Hopwood Wk. E8 CB36 57
Wilman Gro.
Horace Av. Rom. CS33 50
Horace Rd. E7 CH35 49
Horace Rd. Ilf. CM31 49
Horace Rd. Kings. On T. BL52 85
Horatio St. E2 **CA37** **2**
Horatio St. E2 CA37 57
Horbury Cres. W11 BS40 56
Horbury Ms. W11 BR40 55
Horder Rd. SW6 BR44 65
Hordle Gdns. St. Alb. BH14 9
Hordle Promenade E. SE15 CA43 67
Hordle Promenade N. SE15 CA43 67
Hordle Promenade S. SE15 CA43 67
Hordle Promenade W. SE15 CA43 67
Horley Clo. Bexh. CR46 79
Horley Rd. SE9 CK49 78
Horley Rd. Red. BU71 121
Hormead Rd. W9 BR38 55
Hornbeam Clo. Borwd. BM23 28
Hornbeam Av. Upmn. CX35 51
Hornbeam Clo. Brwd. DD27 122
Hornbeam Cres. Brent. BJ43 64
Hornbeam Gro. E4 CG27 40
Hornbeam La. E4 CG25 31
Hornbeam La. Hat. BU14 11
Hornbeam Rd. Buck. H. CJ27 40
Hornbeam Rd. Epp. CM22 31
Hornbeam Rd. Guil. AR69 118
Hornbeam Rd. Hayes BD39 54
Hornbeam Rd. Reig. BS71 121
Hornbeam Rd. Reig. BS72 121
Hornbeams, St. Alb. BE18 18
Hornbeams Av. Enf. CC21 30
Hornbeams, The Harl. CM10 6
Hornbeam Walk, Watt. BB58 92
Hornbeam Way, Brom. CL53 88
Hornbill Clo. Uxb. AX39 53
Hornby Clo. NW3 BT36 56
Chakots Est.
Horncastle Clo. SE12 CH47 78
Horncastle Rd. SE12 CH47 78
Hornchurch Hill Whyt CA62 105
Hornchurch Rd. Horn. CT33 50
Horndean Clo. SW15 BP47 75
Bessborough Rd.
Horndon Clo. Rom. CS30 41
Horndon Grn. Rom. CS30 41
Horndon Rd. Rom. CS30 41
Horne Rd. Shep. AZ52 83
Hornets, The Wat. BC24 26
Horne Way SW15 BQ44 65
Hornfair Rd. SE7 CJ43 68
Hornford Way, Rom. CT33 50
Hornhatch, Guil. AT73 118
Hornhatch Clo. Guil. AT73 118
Horn Hill Rd. Rick. AU28 34
Horniman Dr. SE23 CB47 77
Horning Clo. SE9 CK49 78
Horn La. SE10 CH42 68
Horn La. W3 BN40 55
Horn La. Wdf. Grn. CH29 40
Hornminster Glen. Horn. CX34 51
Horn Pk. Clo. SE12 CH46 78
Horn Pk. La. SE12 CH46 78
Hornsby La. Grays DG41 71
Hornsey La. N6 BX33 47
Hornsey La. Est. N19 BW33 47
Hornsey La. Gdns. N6 BW33 47
Hornsey Pk. Rd. N8 BX31 47
Hornsey Rise N19 BW33 47
Hornsey Rise Gdns. N19 BW33 47
Hornsey Rise Mews N19 BW33 47
Hornsey Rise
Hornsey Rd. N7 BX34 47
Hornsey Rd. N19 BX33 47
Hornsey St. N7 BX35 47
Horns Field, Welw. G. C. BT7 5
Hornshay Pl. SE15 CC43 67
Hornshay St. SE15 CC43 67
Horns Meadow, West. CP65 107
Horns Rd. Ilf. CM32 49
Hornton Pl. W8 BS41 66
Hornton St.
Hornton St. W8 BS41 66
Horsa Rd. SE12 CJ47 78
Horsa Rd. Erith CR43 69
Horsbury Cres. W11 BS40 56
Horscroft Bans. BS62 104
Horsecroft Clo. Harl. CK11 13
Horsecroft Clo. Orp. CO54 89
Horsecroft Rd. Edg. BN29 37
Horsecroft Rd. Harl. CK11 13
Horsecroft Rd. Hem. H. AW14 8
Horse Fair Kings. On T. BL51 85
Wood St.
Horseferry Pl. SE10 CF43 67
Horseferry Rd. SW1 **BW41**
Horseferry Rd. SW1 BW41 6
Horse Guards Av. SW1 **BX40**
Horse Guards Av. SW1 BX40 5
Horse Guards Rd. SW1 **BW40**
Horse Guards Rd. SW1 BW40 5
Horse Hill, Chesh. AR19 1
Horselers, Hem. H. AY15
Horsell Birch, Wok. AQ61 10
Horsell Common Rd. Wok. AR60 9
Horsell Ct. Cher. AW54 8
Horsell Moor, Wok. AR62 10
Horsell Pk. Wok. AS61 10
Horsell Pk. Clo. Wok. AR61 10
Horsell Rise, Wok. AR61 10
Horsell Rise, Clo. Wok. AR61 10
Horsell Rd. N5 BY35 4
Horsell Rd. Orp. CO51 8
Horsell Vale, Wok. AS61 10
Horsell Way, Wok. AR61 10
Horselydown La. SE1 CA41 6
Horsemonden Clo. Orp. CN54 8
Horsemoor Clo. Slou. AT42 6
Parlaunt Rd.
Horsenden Av. Grnf. BH35 4
Horsenden Cres. Grnf. BH35 4
Horsenden La. N. Grnf. BH36 5
Horsenden La. S. Grnf. BJ37 5
Horseshoe Alley SE1 BZ40 5
Bankside
Horseshoe Co. NW2 BP34 4
Horse Shoe Cres. Nthlt. BF37 5
Horseshoe Grn. Sutt. BS55 8
Horseshoe Hill, Wal. Abb. CJ19 2
Horseshoe Lane N20 BQ26 3
Horseshoe La. Enf. BZ24 3
Chase Side
Horseshoe La. Guil. AT70 11
Horseshoe La. Wat. BC19 1
Horseshoe La. Wat. BD20 1
Horseshoe, The Bans. BR61 10
Horseshoe, The Couls. BW60 9
Horseshoe, The Hem. H. BA14
Horse Yd. N1 BY37 5
Essex Rd.
Horsfield Gdns. SE9 CK46 7
Horsfield Rd. SE9 CJ46 7
Horsford Rd. SW2 BX46 7
Horsham Av. N12 BU28 3
Horsham Rd. Bexh. CR46 7
Horsham Rd. Dor. BJ72 11
Horsham Rd. Felt. BA46 7
Horsham Rd. Guil. AS74 11
Horsley Clo. Epsom BN60 9
Horsleydown La. SE1 **CA41**
Horsley Dr. Croy. CF57 9
Horsley Rd. E4 CF27 3
Horsley Rd. Brom. CH51 8
Horsley Rd. Cob. BC64 10
Horsleys Rick. AU28 3
Long Croft Rd.
Horsley St. SE17 **BZ43**
Horsley St. SE17 BZ43 6
Horsman Side, Brwd. CV25 3
Horsmonden Rd. SE4 CD46 7
Hortensia Ho. SW10 BT43 6
Hortensia Rd. SW10 BT43 6
Horticultural Pl. W4 BN42 6
Heathfield Ter.
Horton Av. NW2 BR35 4
Horton Bri. Rd. West Dr. AY40 5
Horton Cres. West Dr. AY40 5
Horton Gdns. Hem. H. AZ10
Elstree Rd.
Horton Hill Epsom BN59 94
Horton La. Epsom BM59 94
Horton La. West Dr. AY40 53
Horton Rd. E8 CB36 57
Horton Rd. Hort. K. CY52 90
Horton Rd. Slou. AQ43 62
Horton Rd. Slou. AT44 62
Horton Rd. Slou. AU45 62
Horton Rd. Stai. AW46 73
Horton Rd. West Dr. AY40 53
Horton St. SE13 CE45 67
Horton St. Hort. K. CX52 90
Horton Way, Farn. CW54 90
Hortons Way, West CM66 115
Hortus Rd. E4 CF26 39
Hortus Rd. Sthl. BE41 64
Hosack Rd. SW17 BU47 76
Hoser Av. SE12 CH48 78
Hosey Common La. Eden. CM70 115
Hosey Common Rd. West. CM67 115
Hosier La. EC1 **BY39** **2**
Hosier La. EC1 BY39 56
Hoskins Clo. E16 CJ39 58
Hoskins Clo. Hayes BB42 63
Hoskins Rd. Oxt. CG68 115
Hoskins St. SE10 CF42 67
Hospital Bridge Rd. Twick. BF47 74
Hospital Hill, Chesh. AO19 16
Hospital Rd. Houns. BF45 64
Hospital Rd. Sev. CV64 108
Hospital Rd. Sutt. BS59 95
Hotham Clo. E. Mol. BF52 84
Hotham Rd. SW15 BQ45 65
Hotham Rd. SW19 BT50 76
Hotham St. E15 CG37 58
Hothfield Pl. SE16 CC41 67
Hotspur Rd. Nthlt. BF37 54
Hotspur St. SE11 **BY42** **4**
Hotspur St. SE11 BY42 66
Hottsfield Hart. DC52 90
Houblon Rd. Rich. BL46 75
Houblons Hill Epp. CP19 23
Houghin Dri. Ong. CY14 15
Hough St. SE18 CL41 68
Houghton Clo. E8 CA36 57
Rhodes Dev.
Houghton Rd. N15 CA31 48
Houghton St. WC2 **BX39** **2**
Houghton St. WC2 BX39 56
Houlder Cres. Croy. BY57 95
Houndsditch EC3 **CA39** **2**
Houndsditch EC3 CA39 57
Houndsfield Rd. N9 CB26 39
Houndsden Rd. N21 BX26 38

Hounslow Av. Houns. BF46 74
Hounslow Gdns. Houns. BF46 74
Hounslow Rd. Felt. BC47 73
Hounslow Rd. Felt. BD49 74
Hounslow Rd. Twick. BF46 74
House La. St. Alb. BK10 9
Housewood End. Hem. H. AW12 8
Houston Rd. SE23 CD48 77
Hove Av. E17 CD32 48
Hoveden Rd. NW2 BQ35 46
Hove St. SE15 CC43 67
Culmore Rd.
Howard Av. Bex. CP47 79
Howard Av. Epsom BP58 94
Howard Av. Slou. AO39 52
Howard Clo. N11 BV27 38
Howard Clo. NW2 BR35 46
Marnham Av.
Howard Clo. W3 BM39 55
Howard Clo. Ash. BL62 103
Howard Clo. Bush. BH26 36
Howard Clo. Hamptn. BG50 74
Howard Close, Leath. BA66 110
Howard Clo. Lthd. BK65 102
Howard Clo. St. Alb. BK14 9
Howard Clo. Tad. BO66 112
Howard Clo. Wat. BC22 26
Howard Cres. Beac. AO28 34
Howard Dr. Borwd. BN24 28
Howard Gdns. SE25 CB53 87
Howard Gdns. Guil. AT70 118
Howard Lodge Rd. Brwd. CY22 33
Howard Pl. SW1 BW41 66
Vauxhall Bridge Rd.
Howard Ridge, Guil. AT68 109
Howard Rd. E6 CK37 58
Howard Rd. E11 CG34 49
Howard Rd. E17 CE31 48
Howard Rd. N15 CA32 48
Howard Rd. N16 BZ35 48
Howard Rd. NW2 BQ35 46
Howard Rd. SE20 CC51 87
Howard Rd. SE25 CB53 87
Howard Rd. Ashf. AX49 73
Howard Rd. Bark. CM37 58
Howard Rd. Beac. AO28 34
Howard Rd. Brom. CG50 78
Howard Rd. Couls. BW61 104
Howard Rd. Dart. CX46 80
Howard Rd. Dor. BJ71 119
Howard Rd. Ilf. CL35 49
Howard Rd. Islw. BH45 64
Howard Rd. Lthd. BC64 101
Howard Rd. Lthd. BF67 111
Howard Rd. N. Mal. BO52 85
Howard Rd. Reig. BS71 121
Howard Rd. Sthl. BF39 54
Howard Rd. Surb. BL53 85
Howard Rd. Upmin. CY34 51
Howards Clo. Pnr. BC30 35
Howards Dr. Hem. H. AW12 8
Howardsgate, Welw. G. C. BQ8 5
Howards La. SW15 BP45 65
Howards La. Wey. AV57 91
Howards Rd. E13 CH38 58
Howards Rd. Wok. AS63 100
Howards Thicket. Ger. Cr. AR33 43
Howard St. WC2 BX40 56
Arundel St.
Howard St. Surb. BJ54 84
Howards Wood Dr. Ger. Cr. AR34 43
Howards Yd. SE18 CL41 68
Powis St.
Howard Wk. N2 BT31 47
Howard Way, Harl. CN10 6
Howard Way, Harl. CN9 6
Howarth Rd. SE2 CO42 69
Howberry Clo. Edg. BK29 36
Howberry Rd. Edg. BK29 36
Howberry Rd. Th. Hth. BZ51 87
Howbury La. Erith CT44 69
Howbury Rd. SE15 CC45 67
Howcroft Cres. N3 BS29 38
Howden Clo. SE2 CP40 59
Howden Rd. SE25 CA51 87
Howden St. SE15 CB45 67
Howe Clo. Rom. CR30 41
Howe Dell, Hat. BP12 10
Howell Clo. Rom. CP32 50
Howell Hill Clo. Epsom BQ59 94
Howell Hill Gro. Epsom BQ58 94
Howe Rd. Hem. H. AZ15 8
Howfield Grn. Hodd. CD10 12
Howgate Rd. SW14 BO45 65
Howick Pl. SW1 BW41 3
Howick Pl. SW1 BW41 66
Howicks Grn. Welw. G. C. BS9 5
Howie St. SW11 BU43 66
Howitt Rd. NW3 BU36 56
Howland Garth, St. Alb. BG15 9
Howland Ms. E. W1 BW39 1
Howland Ms. E. W1. BW39 56
Howland St.
Howland Ms. W. W1 BW39 1
Howland Ms. W. W1 BW39 56
Howland St.
Howlands, Welw. G. C. BQ9 5
Howland St. W1 BW39 1
Howland St. W1 BW39 56
How La. Couls. BU63 104
Howlett, S. La. Ruis. BA32 44
Howletts Rd. SE24 BZ46 77
Howley Pl. W2 BT39 1
Howley Pl. W2 BT39 56
Howley Rd. Croy. BY55 86
Hows Clo. Uxb. AX37 53
Howsman Rd. SW13 BP43 65
Hows Mead. Epp. CS15 14
Howson Rd. SE4 CD45 67
Howson Ter. Rich. BL46 75
Hows Rd. Uxb. AX37 53
Hows St. E2 CA37 2
Hows St. E2 CA37 57
Howton Pl. Bush. BG26 36
How Wood St. Alb. BF17 18
Hoxton Mkt. N1 CA38 57
Boot St.
Hoxton Sq. N1 CA38 2
Hoxton Sq. N1 CA38 57
Hoxton St. N1 CA37 2
Hoxton St. N1 CA37 57
Hoylake Cres. Uxb. AZ34 44
Hoylake Gdns. Mitch. BW52 86
Hoylake Gdns. Rom. CW30 42
Hoylake Gdns. Ruis. BC33 44
Hoylake Gdns. Wat. BD28 36
Hoylake Rd. W3 BO39 55
Hoyle Rd. SW17 BU49 76
Hoyle St. W1 BW40 3
Hoy St. E16 CG40 58
Hubbard Rd. SE27 BZ49 77
Hubbards Chase, Horn. CX32 51
Hubbards Clo. Horn. CX32 51
Hubbards Hill, Sev. CU68 116
Hubbards Rd. Rick. AU25 25
Hubbard St. E15 CG37 58
Hubert Gro. SW9 BX45 66
Hubert Rd. E6 CJ38 58
Hubert Rd. Brwd. DA27 42
Hubert Rd. Rain. CT38 59
Hubert Rd. Slou. AR42 62
Hucknall Clo. Rom. CW29 42
Petersfield Avenue
Huddlestone Cres. Red. BW67 113
Huddlestone Rd. E7 CG35 49
Huddlestone Rd. NW2 BP36 55
Huddleston Rd. N7 BW34 47
Hudson Clo. NW3 BU36 56
Hudson Clo. Wat. BB21 26
Hudson Pl. SW1 BV42 3
Hudson Pl. SE18 CM42 68
Hudson Pl. SW1 BW42 66
Hudson Rd. Bexh. CQ44 69
Hudson Rd. Hayes BA43 63
Hudson Rd. Kings. On T. BL51 85
Hugenot Sq. SE15 CB45 67
Scylla Rd.
Huggin HIll EC4 BZ40 57
Queen Victoria St.
Huggin La. EC4 BZ40 4
Huggin's La. Hat. BQ15 10
Hughan Rd. E15 CF35 48
Hughenden Av. Har. BJ32 45
Hughenden Gdns. Nthlt. BD38 54
Hughenden Rd. St. Alb. BJ12 9
Hughenden Rd. Slou. AO39 52
Hughenden Rd. Wor. Pk. BP54 85
Hughendon Ter. E15 CF35 48
Hughes Rd. Ashf. BA50 73
Hughes Rd. Grays DG41 71
Hughes Rd. Hayes BC40 53
Hugh Ms. SW1 BV42 3
Hughes Wk. Croy. BZ54 87
St. Saviour's Rd.
Hugh Ms. SW1 BV42 66
Hugh St.
Hugh St. SW1 BV42 3
Hugh St. SW1 BV42 66
Hugo Gdns. Rain. CU36 59
Hugon Rd. SW6 BS45 66
Hugo Rd. N19 BW35 47
Hug Sq. SE15 CB45 67
Huguenot Pl. SW18 BT46 76
Huitt Sq. SW11 BT45 66
Winstanley Rd.
Hulletts La. Brwd. CZ24 33
Hull Gro. Harl. CL13 13
Hull Pl. SE18 CN42 68
Hull Rd. Rom. CQ32 50
Hull St. EC1 BZ38 2
Hull St. EC1 BZ38 57
Hulmlea Rd. Slou. AR44 62
Hulse Av. Bark. CM36 58
Hulse Av. Rom. CR30 41
Hulsewood Clo. Dart. CU48 79
Hulton Clo. Lthd. BK65 102
Hulverston Clo. Sutt. BS58 95
Humber Ave. S. Ock. CZ39 60
Humber Dr. Upmin. CY32 51
Humber Rd. NW2 BP34 46
Humber Rd. SE3 CG43 68
Humberstone Rd. E13 CJ38 58
Humberton Clo. E9 CD35 48
Swinnerton St.
Humber Way, Slou. AT42 62
Humbolt Clo. Guil. AP70 118
Humbolt Rd. W6 BR43 65
Hume Ave. Til. DG44 71
Humes Av. W7 BH41 64
Hume Way, Ruis. BC32 44
Hummer Rd. Egh. AT49 72
Humphrey Clo. Ilf. CK30 40
Humphrey Clo. Lthd. BG64 102
Humphrey St. SE1 CA42 4
Humphrey St. SE1 CA42 67
Humphries Clo. Dag. CQ35 50
Hundred Acre NW9 BO30 37
Hundred Acre La. Amer. AO23 25
Hungerdown E4 CF26 39
Hungerford Av. Slou. AP39 52
Hungerford Bridge WC2 BX40 4
Hungerford La. WC2 BX40 56
Craven St.
Hungerford Rd. N7 BW36 56
Hungerford St. E1 CB39 57
Commercial Rd.
Hungry Hill, Wok. AX66 110
Hunsdon Clo. Dag. CQ36 59
Hunsdon Est. E5 CB34 48
Hunsdon Rd. SE14 CC43 67
Hunslett St. E2 CC37 57
Royston St.
Hunsoon Dr. Sev. CU65 107
Hunston Rd. Mord. BS54 86
Hunt Clo. St. Alb. BK12 9
Hunter Av. Brwd DD25 122
Hunter Clo. SE1 BZ41 4
Hunter Clo. SW12 BV47 76
Balham Pk. Rd.
Hunter Clo. Borwd. BN25 28
Clydesdale Clo.
Hunter Clo. Pot. B. BS20 20
Huntercombe Gdns. Wat. BD28 36
Huntercombe La. Maid. AK40 61
Hunter Clo. SE1 BZ41 67
Hunter Dr. Horn. CV35 51
Hunter Path, Borwd. BN25 28
Hunter Rd. SW20 BQ51 85
Hunter Rd. Guil. AS71 118
Hunter Rd. Ilf. CL35 49
Hunter Rd. Th. Hth. BZ52 87
Hunters Clo. SW12 BV47 76
Balham Park Rd.
Hunters Clo. Epsom BN60 94
Hunters Clo. Hem. H. AT18 16
Huntersfield Clo. Reig. BS69 121
Hunters Gro. Har. BK31 45
Hunters Gro. Hayes BC40 53
Hunter's Gro. Rom. CR28 41
Hunters Hall Rd. Dag. CR35 50
Hunter's Hill, Ruis. BD34 45
Hunter, S La. Wat. BB20 17
Hunters Ride, St. Alb. BF19 18
Hunters Rd. Chess. BL55 85
Hunters Sq. Dag. CR35 50
Hunter St. WC1 BX38 2
Hunter St. WC1 BX38 56
Hunters Way Enf. BY23 29
Hunter's Way, Welw. G. C. BR9 5
Hunter Wk. E13 CG37 58
Hunter Wk. E13 CH37 58
Hunting Clo. Esher BF56 93
Hunting Gate, Hem. H. AY11 8
Huntingdon Clo. Brox. CD15 12
Huntingdon Clo. Mitch. BX52 86
Huntingdon Gdns. Wor. Pk. BQ55 85
Huntingdon Rd. N2 BU31 47
Huntingdon Rd. N9 CC26 39
Huntingdon Rd. Red. BU70 121
Cromwell Rd.
Huntingdon St. E16 CG39 58
Huntingdon St. N1 BX36 56
Huntingdon Way, Croy. CA56 96
Huntingfield Croy. CD57 96
Huntingfield Rd. SW15 BP45 65
Huntingfield Way, Egh. AU50 72
Huntings Rd. Dag. CR36 59
Huntley Av. Grav. DD46 81
Huntley Dr. N3 BS29 38
Nether St.
Huntley St. WC1 BW38 1
Huntley St. WC1 BW38 56
Huntley Way SW10 BP51 85
Huntly Rd. SE25 CA52 87
Huntonbridge Hill, Kings L. BA20 17
Hunton St. E1 CB38 57
Hunton St. E1 CB39 2
Hunt Rd. Grav. DF48 81
Hunt Rd. Sthl. BF41 64
Hunts Clo. SE3 CH44 68
Hunts Clo. Guil. AO70 118
Hunt's La. E15 CF37 57
Huntsman Rd. Ilf. CO29 41
Huntsman Dr. Upmin. CY35 51
Huntsman St. SE17 BZ42 4
Huntsman St. SE17 BZ42 67
Barlow St.
Huntsmead Enf. CC24 30
Hunts Mead Clo. Brom. CK50 78
Bullerswood Dr.
Huntsmead Clo. Chis. CK50 78
Bullerswood Dr.
Hunts Mill Rd. Hem. H. AV14 7
Huntsmoor Rd. Epsom BN56 94
Huntspill St. SW17 BT48 76
Hunts Slip Rd. SE21 CA48 77
Hunt St. W11 BQ40 55
Huntsworth Ms. NW1 BU38 1
Huntsworth Ms. NW1 BU38 56
Hurley Clo. Walt. BC55 83
Hurley Rd. Grnf. BF39 54
Hurlingham Ct. SW6 BR45 65
Hurlingham Gdns. SW6 BR45 65
Hurlingham Rd. SW6 BR44 65
Hurlingham Rd. Bexh. CQ43 69
Hurlock St. N5 BY34 47
Hurlstone Rd. SE25 BZ53 87
Hurnford Clo. Sth. Croy. CA58 96
Huron Rd. SW17 BV48 76
Hurry Clo. E15 CG36 58
Hursley Rd. Chig. CN28 40
Hart Cres.
Hurst Av. E4 CE28 39
Hurst Av. N6 CW32 47
Hurstbourne Gdns. Bark. CM36 58
Hurstbourne Rd. SE23 CD47 77
Hurst Clo. E4 CE27 39
Hurst Clo. NW11 BS32 47
Hurst Clo. Brom. CG54 88
Hurst Clo. Chess. BM56 94
Hurst Clo. Nthlt. BE35 45
Hurst Clo. Wok. AR63 100
Hurstcourt Rd. Sutt. BS55 86
Hurst Cft. Guil. AS72 118
Hurstdene Av. Brom. CG54 88
Hurstdene Av. Stai. AW50 73
Hurstdene Gdns. N15 CA32 48
Hurst Dr. Tad. BP66 112
Hurst Dr. Wal. Cr. CC20 21
Hurst Farm Rd. Sev. CU69 116
Hurstfield Brom. CH53 88
Hurstfield Cres. Hayes BB39 53
Hurstfield Rd. E. Mol. BF52 84
Hurst Grn. Oxt. CG69 115
Hurst Green Rd. Oxt. CG69 115
Hurst Gro. Walt. BB54 83
Hursthead Ct. Edg. BM28 37
Hurstlands, Oxt. CH69 115
Hurstlands Clo. Horn. CV32 51
Hurst La. SE2 CP42 69
Hurst La. E. Mol. BG52 84
Hurst La. Egh. AT51 82
Hurst La. Epsom BN65 103
Hurstleigh Clo. Red. BU69 121
Hurstleigh Dr. Red. BU69 121
Hurstleigh Gdns. Ilf. CK30 40
Hurst Pk. Av. Horn. CW35 51
Hurst Place Est. SE2 CP42 69
Hurst Rise Barn. BS24 29
Hurst Rd. E17 CE31 48
Hurst Rd. N21 BY26 38
Hurst Rd. Buck. H. CJ26 40
Hurst La. SE2 CP42 69
Hurst Rd. E. Mol. BF52 84
Hurst Rd. Epsom BN59 94
Hurst Rd. Erith CS44 69
Hurst Rd. Sid. CO48 79
Hurst Rd. Tad. BP65 103
Hurst Rd. Walt. BD53 84
Hurst Springs Bex. CQ47 79
Hurst St. SE24 BY46 76
Hurst St. W11 BQ40 55
Hurst Vw. Rd. Sth. Croy. CA57 96
Hurst Way, Sev. CV57 117
Hurst Way Sth. Croy. CA57 96
Hurst Way, Wok. AV60 91
Hurstway Walk W11 BQ40 55
Lancaster Road
Hurstwood Av. E18 CH31 49
Hurstwood Av. Bex. CQ47 79
Hurstwood Av. Brwd. DA26 42
Hurstwood Av. Erith CT44 69
Hurstwood Ct. N12 BU29 38
Woodleigh Av.
Hurstwood Ct. NW11 BR31 46
Hurstwood Dr. Brom. CK52 88
Hurstwood Rd. NW11 BR31 46
Hurtwood Rd. Walt. BE54 84
Hurworth Rd. Slou. AR41 62
Husseywell Cres. Brom CH54 88
Hutchings St. E14 CE41 67
Hutchings Wk. NW11 BS31 47
Hutchins Clo. E15 CF36 57
Hutchinson Ter. Wem. BK34 45
Hutton Clo. Har. BG35 45
Mary Peters Dr.
Hutton Clo. Wdf. Grn. CH28 40
Hutton Dr. Brwd. DE26 122
Hutton Gdns. Har. BG29 36
Hutton Gro. N12 BS28 38
Hutton La. Har. BG29 36
Hutton Rd. Brwd. DC26 122
Hutton St. EC4 BY39 56
Dorset Rise
Hutton Vill. Brwd. DF26 122
Hutton Wk. Har. BG29 36
Huxbear St. SE4 CD46 77
Huxley Clo. Uxb. AX38 53
Huxley Dr. Rom. CO33 50
Huxley Gdns. NW10 BL38 55
Huxley Pde. N18 BZ28 39
Huxley Pl. N13 BY27 38
Huxley Rd. E10 CF34 48
Huxley Rd. N18 BZ28 39
Huxley Rd. Well. CN45 68
Huxley Sayze N18 BZ28 39
Gt. Cambridge Rd.
Huxley St. W10 BR38 55
Hyacinth Ct. Pnr. BD31 45
Nursery Rd.
Hyacinth Rd. SW15 BP47 75
Hyburn Clo. St. Alb. BE18 18
Hycliffe Gdns. Chig. CM28 40
Hyde Av. Pot. B. BS20 20
Hyde Clo. E13 CH37 58
Turpin Estate
Hyde Clo. Barn. BR24 28
Hyde Cres. NW9 BO32 46
Hydefield Clo. N21 BZ26 39
Hydefield Ct. N9 CA27 39
Hyde La. SW11 BU44 66
Westbridge Rd.
Hyde Lane SW11 BU44 66
Battersea Bridge Rd.
Hyde La. Hem. H. AT17 16
Hyde La. Hem. H. AZ17 17
Hyde La. St. Alb. BH17 18
Hyde La. Wok. AZ63 101
Hyde Mead. Wal. Abb. CG15 13
Hyde Mead. Hem. H. AT17 16
Hyde Pk. Av. N21 BZ26 39
Hyde Park Corner W1 BV41 3
Hyde Pk. Corner W1 BV41 66
Hyde Park Cres. W2 BU39 1
Hyde Pk. Cres. W2 BU39 56
Hyde Pk. Gdns. N21 BZ26 39
Hyde Park Gdns. W2 BT40 3
Hyde Park Gdns. W2 BT40 56
Hyde Park Gdns. Ms. W2 BT40 3
Hyde Park Gdns. Ms. W2 BU39 56
Hyde Park Gate SW7 BT41 1
Hyde Pk. Gte. SW7 BT41 66
Hyde Pk. Gte. Ms. SW7 BT41 66
Hyde Pk. Mans. NW1 BU39 1
Hyde Pk. Mans. NW1 BU39 56
Edgeware Rd.
Hyde Park Ms. SW7 BT41 3
Hyde Park Pl. W2 BU40 3
Hyde Pk. Pl. W2 BU40 56
Bayswater Rd.
Hyde Park Sq. W2 BU39 1
Hyde Park Sq. W2 BU39 56
Hyde Park St. W2 BU39 1
Hyde Park St. W2 BU39 56
Hyde Pl. N1 BY36 56
Compton Av.
Hyde Rd. N1 BZ37 2
Hyde Rd. N1 BZ37 57
Hyde Rd. Bexh. CQ44 69
Hyde Rd. Rich. BL46 75
Albert Rd.
Hyde Rd. Sth. Croy. BZ60 96
Hyde Rd. Wat. BC23 26
Hyder Rd. Grays. DH41 71
Hydeside Gdns. N9 CA27 39
Hyde St. SE8 CD43 67
Deptford High St.
Hyde Ter. Ashf. BB50 73
Hydethorpe Av. N9 CA27 39
Hydethorpe Rd. SW12 BW47 76
Hyde Val. SE10 CF43 67
Hyde Valley, Welw. G. C. BR9 5
Hyde Wk. Mord. BS54 86
Hyde Way N9 CA27 39
Hyde Way, Hayes BB42 63
Hyde Way, Welw. G. C. BR8 5
Hyland Clo. Horn. CU33 50
Hylands Mews, Epsom BM61 103
Hylands Mews, Epsom BN61 103
Hylands Rd. E17 CF31 48
Hylands Rd. Epsom BN61 103
Hyland Way, Horn. CU33 50
Hylle Clo. Wind. AM44 61
Cawcott Dr.
Hylton St. SE18 CN42 68
Hyndman Gro. SE15 CB43 67
Hyndman St. SE15 CB43 67
Hynton Rd. Dag. CP34 50
Hyperion Ct. Hem. H. AY12 8
Hyperion Pl. Epsom BN58 94
Hyrons La. Amer. AO22 25
Hyrst Dene Sth. Croy. BY56 95
Hyson Rd. SE16 CB42 67
Hythe Av. Bexh. CQ43 69
Hythe Cl. N18 CB28 39
Hythe End Rd. Stai. AT48 72
Hythe Field Av. Egh. AU50 72
Hythe Park Rd. Egh. AV49 72
Hythe Rd. Stai. AU49 72
Hythe Rd. Th. Hth. BZ51 87
Hythe St. Dart. CW46 80
Hythe, The Stai. AV49 72
Hyver Hill NW7 BN26 37
Ian Sq. Enf. CC23 30
Ibbetson Pa. Loug. CL24 31
Ibbotson Av. E16 CG39 58
Iberian Av. Wall. BW56 95
Ibis La. W4 BN44 65
Ibscott Clo. Dag. CS36 59
Ibsley Gdns. SW15 BP47 75
Ibsley Way, Barn. BU24 29
Icehouse Wood, Oxt. CG69 115
Iceland Rd. E3 CE37 57
Ickburgh Est. E5 CB34 48
Ickburgh Rd. E5 CB34 48
Ickenham Clo. Ruis. BA34 44
Ickenham Rd. Ruis. BA33 44
Ickenham Rd. Uxb. BA34 44
Ickleton Rd. SE9 CK49 78
Icklingham Rd. Cob. BD59 93
Icknield Clo. St. Alb. BE15 9
Icknield Dr. Ilf. CL32 49
Ickworth Pk. Rd. E17 CD31 48
Ida Rd. N15 BZ32 48
Ida St. E14 CF39 57
Ide Hill, Sev. CS65 107
Ide Hill Rd. Sev. CQ69 116
Iden Clo. Brom. CG52 88
Idenden Cotts. SE10 CG41 68
Idlecombe Rd. SW17 BV50 76
Idmiston Rd. E15 CG35 49
Idmiston Rd. SE27 BZ48 77
Idmiston Rd. Wor. Pk. BO54 85
Idmiston Sq. Wor. Pk. BO54 85
Idol La. EC3 CA40 4
Idol La. EC3 CA40 57
Idonia St. SE8 CD43 67
Iffley Clo. Uxb. AX36 53
Iffley Rd. W6 BP41 65
Ifield Rd. SW10 BS43 66
Ifield Ter. Green. DA46 80
Ifield Way, Grav. DH50 81
Ightham By-Pass, Sev. DB64 108
Ightham Mote, Sev. DA67 117
Ightham Rd. Erith CR43 69
Ikona Ct. Way. BA56 92
Ilbert St. W10 BQ38 55
Ilchester Gdns. W2 BS40 56
Ilchester Pl. W14 BR41 65
Ilchester Rd. Dag. CO35 50
Ildersley Gro. SE21 BZ48 77
Ilderton Rd. SE15 CC43 67
Ilderton Rd. SE16 CB42 67
Ilex Clo. Egh. AQ50 72
Ilex Ct. Berk. AQ13 7
Angle Pl.
Ilex Rd. NW10 BO36 55
Ilex Way SW16 BY49 76
Ilford Hill, Ilf. CL34 49
Ilford La. Ilf. CL34 49
Ilfracombe Gdns. Rom. CO33 50
Ilfracombe Rd. Brom. CG48 78
Iliffe St. SE17 BY42 4
Iliffe St. SE17 BY42 66
Iliffe Yd. SE17 BY42 4
Iliffe Yd. SE17 BY42 66
Amelia St.
Ilkley Rd. E16 CJ39 58
Ilkley Rd. Wat. BD28 36
Illingworth Clo. Mitch. BT52 86
Belgrave Wk.
Illingworth, Wind. AM45 61
Illingworth Way, Enf. CA25 30
Ilmington Rd. Har. BK32 45
Ilminster Gdns. SW11 BU45 66
Imber Clo. N14 BW26 38
Imber Ct. E. Mol. BG54 84
Imber Gro. Esher BG54 84
Imber Pk. Rd. Esher BG54 84
Imber St. N1 BZ37 2
Imilking La. Orp. CK59 97
Imperial Av. N16 CA35 48
Imperial Clo. Har. BF32 45
Imperial Dr. Grav. DJ49 81
Imperial Dr. Har. BF33 45
Imperial Institute Rd. SW7 BT41 3
Imperial Institute Rd. SW7 BT41 66
Imperial Mews E6 CJ37 58
Imperial Rd. N22 BX30 38
Imperial Rd. SW6 BS44 66
Imperial Rd. Felt. BB47 73
Imperial Rd. Wind. AN45 61
Imperial Sq. SW6 BS44 66
Imperial St. E3 CF38 57
Imperial Way SE18 CK43 68
Imperial Way, Chis. CM48 78
Imperial Way, Croy. BY57 95
Imperial Way, Har. BL32 46
Imperial Way, Wat. BD23 27
Inca Dr. SE9 CL47 78
Ince Rd. Watt. BB57 92
Inchmery Rd. SE6 CE48 77
Indells, Hat. BO13 10
Independents Rd. SE3 CG45 68
Inderwick Rd. N8 BX32 47
India Rd. Slou. AQ41 62
India St. EC3 CA39 2

India St. EC3 CA39 57
Jewry St.
India Way W12 BP40 55
Indus Rd. SE7 CJ43 68
Industrial Est. Grnf. BF37 54
Industrial Est. Iver. AV40 52
Industrial Est. Mitch. BU53 86
Ingate Pl. SW8 BV44 66
Ingatestone Rd. E12 CJ33 49
Ingatestone Rd. SE25 CB52 87
Ingatestone Rd. Ing. DC19 24
Ingatestone Rd. Wdf. Grn. CH29 40
Ingelow Rd. SW8 BV44 66
Ingels Mead. Epp. CN18 22
Ingersoll Rd. W12 BP40 55
Ingersoll Rd. Enf. CC22 30
Ingestre Pl. W1 BW39 1
Ingestre Pl. W1 BW39 56
Ingestre Rd. E7 CH35 49
Ingestre Rd. NW5 BV35 47
Ingford St. N1 BY37 2
Ingham Clo. Sth. Croy. CC58 96
Ingham Rd. NW6 BS35 47
Ingham Rd. Sth. Croy. CC58 96
Inglebert St. EC1 BY38 2
Inglebert St. EC1 BY38 56
Ingleboro. Dr. Pur. BZ60 96
Ingleby Clo. Dag. CR36 59
Ingleby Dr. Har. BG34 45
Ingleby Gdns. Chig. CO27 41
Lambourne Rd.
Ingleby Rd. N7 BX34 47
Ingleby Rd. N7 BX34 47
Tollington Way
Ingleby Rd. Dag. CR36 59
Ingleby Rd. Grays DG41 71
Ingleby Rd. Ilf. CL33 49
Ingleby Way, Chis. CL49 78
Ingleby Way, Wall. BW57 95
Ingle Clo. Pnr. BE31 45
Ingledew Rd. SE18 CM42 68
Ingleglen, Horn. CX33 51
Inglehurst, Wey. AW58 92
Inglehurst Gdns. Ilf. CK32 49
Inglemere Rd. SE23 CC48 77
Inglemere Rd. Mitch. BU50 76
Ingles, Welw. G. C. BQ6 5
Inglesham Wk. E9 CD36 57
Trowbridge Est.
Ingleside Clo. Beck. CE50 77
Ingleside Gro. SE3 CG43 68
Inglethorpe St. SW6 BQ44 65
Ingleton Av. Well. CO46 79
Ingleton Rd. N18 CB29 39
Ingleton Rd. Cars. BU58 95
Ingleway N12 BT29 38
Inglewood Clo. Chig. CN29 40
Inglewood Copse Brom. CK51 88
Inglewood Rd. NW6 BS35 47
Inglewood Rd. Bexh. CS45 69
Inglewood Wok. AQ62 100
Inglis Rd. W5 BL40 55
Inglis Rd. Croy. CA54 87
Inglis St. SE5 BY44 66
Ingoldsby Rd. Grav. DJ47 81
Ingram Av. NW11 BT33 47
Ingram Clo. Stan. BK28 36
Ingram Ho. Kings. On T. BK51 84
Ingram Rd. N2 BU31 47
Ingram Rd. Dart. CW47 80
Ingram Rd. Grays DE42 71
Ingram Rd. Th. Hth. BZ51 87
Ingrams Clo. Walt. BD56 93
Ingram Way, Grnf. BG37 54
Ingrave Rd. Brwd. DB27 42
Ingrave Rd. Brwd. DC27 122
Ingrave Rd. Rom. CS31 50
Ingrave St. SW11 BT45 66
Ingrebourne Gdns. CY33 51
Ingrebourne Rd. Rain. CU38 59
Ingress Gdns. Green. DB46 80
Ingreway, Rom. CX29 42
Inholms La. Dor. BJ73 119
Inigo Jones Rd. SE7 CJ43 68
Inkerman Rd. NW5 BV36 56
Inkerman Rd. St. Alb. BH14 9
Inkerman Rd. Wind. AM42 61
Inkerman Rd. Wok. AP62 100
Inkerman Ter. Chesh. AO20 16
Inkerman Way, Wok. AP62 100
Inks Grn. E4 CE28 39
Inman Rd. NW10 BO37 55
Inman Rd. SW18 BT47 76
Inman's Row, Wdf. Grn. CH28 40
Inner Circ. NW1 BV38 1
Inner Circ. NW1 BV38 56
Inner Pk. Rd. SW19 BQ47 75
Inner Ring East Houns. AZ45 63
Conway Rd.
Inner Ring West Houns. AZ45 63
Chester Rd.
Inner Staithe W4 BN43 65
Upper Staithe
Innes Clo. SW20 BR51 85
Innes Gdns. SW15 BP46 75
Innes Lo. SE23 CC48 77
Innes Yd. Croy. BZ55 87
Whitgift St.
Inniskilling Rd. E13 CJ37 58
Inskip Dr. Horn. CW33 51
Inskip Rd. Dag. CP33 50
Institute Pl. E8 CB35 48
Amhurst Rd.
Institute Rd. Epp. CP18 23
Institution Rd. Dor. BG72 119
Instone Clo. Wall. BX57 95
Instone Rd. Dart. CV47 80
Instow Pl. N7 BY35 47
Queensland Rd.
Insurance St. WC1 BY38 2
Insurance St. WC1 BY38 56
Margery St.
International Av. Houns. BD42 64
Inverarey Pl. SE18 CM43 68
Inver Clo. E5 CB34 48
Southwold Rd.
Inverclyde Gdns. Rom. CP31 50
Inveresk Gdns. Wor. Pk. BO55 85
Inverforth Rd. N11 BV28 38
High Rd.
Inverine Rd. SE7 CH42 68
Invermore Pl. SE18 CM42 68
Inverna Gdns. W8 BS42 66
Inverness Av. Enf. CA23 30
Inverness Ct. W3 BM39 55
Links Rd.
Inverness Dr. Ilf. CN29 40
Inverness Gdns. W8 BS40 56
Inverness Ms. W2 BS40 3
Inverness Ms. W2 BS40 56
Inverness Ter.
Inverness Pl. W2 BS40 3
Inverness Pl. W2 BS40 56
Inverness Ter.
Inverness Rd. N18 CB28 39
Inverness Rd. Houns. BE45 64
Inverness Rd. Sthl. BE42 64
Inverness Rd. Wor. Pk. BQ54 85
Inverness St. NW1 BV37 1
Inverness St. NW1 BV37 56
Inverness Ter. W2 BS39 1
Inverness Ter. W2 BS40 56
Inverton Rd. SE15 CC45 67
Invicta Clo. Chis. CL49 78
Invicta Gro. Nthlt. BE38 54
Invicta Rd. SE3 CH43 68
Invicta Rd. Dart. CX46 80
Inwood Av. Couls. BY63 104
Inwood Av. Houns. BG45 64
Inwood Clo. Croy. CD55 87
Inwood Ct. Walt. BD55 84
Inwood Rd. Houns. BF45 64
Inworth St. SW11 BU44 66
Inworth Wk. N1 BZ37 57
Popham St.
Iona Clo. SE6 CD47 77
Iona Clo. SE6 CE47 77
Ravensbourne Pk.
Ionian Way, Hem. H. AY12 8
Ipswich Rd. SW17 BV50 76
Ireland Yd. EC4 BY39 2
Ireland Yd. EC4 BY39 56
St. Andrew's Hill
Irene Rd. SW6 BS44 66
Irene Rd. Cob. BF61 102
Irene Rd. Orp. CN54 88
Ireston Rd. Grays DD42 71
Ireton Av. Walt. BB55 83
Ireton St. E3 CE38 57
Iris Av. Bex. CQ46 79
Iris Clo. Brwd. DA25 33
Iris Clo. Surb. BL54 95
Iris Ct. Pnr. BD31 45
Nursery Rd.
Iris Cres. Bexh. CQ43 69
Iris Path, Rom. CV29 42
Iris Rd. Epsom BM56 94
Iris Way E4 CD29 39
Irkdale Av. Enf. CA23 30
Iron Br. Rd. West Dr. AZ40 53
Irongate Wf. Rd. W2 BT39 56
Iron Mill La. Dart. CT45 69
Iron Mill Pl. Dart. CT45 69
Iron Mill Rd. SW18 BS46 76
Ironmonger La. EC2 BZ39 2
Ironmonger La. EC2 BZ39 57
Ironmonger Row EC1 BZ38 2
Ironmonger Row EC1 BZ38 57
Irons Bottom Rd. Reig. BS74 121
Irons Way Rom. CS29 41
Irvine Av. Har. BJ31 45
Irvine Clo. N20 BU27 38
Irvine Gdns. S. Ock. CZ39 60
Irvine Way Orp. CN54 88
Irving Av. Nthlt. BD37 54
Irving Gro. SW9 BX44 66
Irving Rd. W14 BQ41 65
Irving St. WC2 BW40 3
Irving St. WC2 BW40 56
Leicester Sq.
Irving Wk. Swans. DC47 81
Irving Way Swan. CS51 89
Irwin Av. SE18 CN43 68
Irwin Gdns. NW10 BP37 55
Irwin Rd. Guil. AQ71 118
Isabella Dri. Orp. CM56 97
Isabella Rd. E9 CC35 48
Isabel St. SW9 BX44 66
Isambard Clo. Uxb. AX38 53
Isbell Gdns. Rom. CT29 41
Isbells Dr. Reig. BS71 121
Isel Way SE22 CA46 77
Dulwich Gro.
Isham Rd. SW16 BX51 86
Isis Dr. Upmin. CZ32 51
Isis St. SW18 BT48 76
Island Clo. Stai. AV49 72
Island Fm. Av. E. Mol. BF53 84
Island Fm. Rd. E. Mol. BE53 84
Island Rd. Mitch. BU50 76
Island Row E14 CD39 57
Island, The Stai. AT48 72
Isla Rd. SE18 CM43 68
Islay Gdns. Houns. BD46 74
Islay Wk. N1 BZ36 57
Marquess Est.
Isledon Rd. N7 BX34 47
Islehurst Clo. Chis. CL51 88
Summer Hill
Islehurst Cr. Chis. CL51 88
Islington Grn. N1 BY37 2
Islington High St. N1 BY37 2
Islington High St. N1 BY37 56
Islington Pk. St. N1 BY36 56
Islip Gdns. Edg. BN29 37
Islip Gdns. Nthlt. BE36 54
Islip Manor Rd. Nthlt. BE36 54
Islip St. NW5 BW35 47
Ismailia Rd. E7 CH36 58
Ismays Rd. Sev. DA66 117
Istead Rise, Grav. DF50 81
Itchingwood Common Rd. Oxt. CJ70 115
Ivanhoe Clo. Uxb. AX39 53
Ivanhoe Dr. Har. BJ31 45
Ivanhoe Rd. SE5 CA45 67
Ivanhoe Rd. Houns. BD45 64
Ivatt Way N17 BZ31 48
Iveagh Av. NW10 BM37 55
Iveagh Clo. NW10 BM37 55
Iveagh Clo. Nthwd. AZ30 35
Iveagh Rd. Guil. AQ71 118
Iveagh Rd. Wok. AP62 100
Ivedon Rd. Well. CP44 69
Ive Farm Clo. E10 CE34 48
Iveley Rd. SW4 BW44 66
Iverdale Clo. Iver. AU40 52
Ivere Dr. Barn. BS25 29
Iver La. Iver & Uxb. AW39 53
Iverna Gdns. W8 BS41 66
Iverna Gdns. Felt. BA46 73
Iverson Rd. NW6 BR36 55
Ivers Way Croy. CE57 96
Ives Rd. E16 CG39 58
Ives Rd. Slou. AS41 62
Ives St. SW3 BU42 3
Ives St. SW3 BU42 66
Ivestor Ter. SE23 CC47 77
Ivimey St. E2 CB38 57
Pollard Row
Ivinghoe Clo. Enf. BZ23 30
Ivinghoe Clo. Wat. BD21 27
Ivinghoe Rd. Bush. BG26 36
Ivinghoe Rd. Dag. CO35 50
Ivinghoe Rd. Rick. AV26 34
Ivinghoe Rd. Rick. AW26 35
Ivor Clo. Guil. AT71 118
Ivor Gro. SE9 CL47 78
Ivor Pl. NW1 BU38 1
Ivor Pl. NW1 BU38 56
Ivor St. NW1 BW36 56
Ivorydown, Brom. CH49 78
Ivybridge, Brox. CE13 12
Ivybridge La. W12 BX40 56
Savoy Pl.
Ivychimneys Rd. Epp. CN20 22
Ivy Clo. Dart. CX47 80
Ivy Clo. Grav. DH49 81
Ivy Clo. Har. BE35 45
Ivy Clo. Pnr. BD33 45
Ivy Clo. Sun. BD51 84
Ivy Cres. W4 BN42 65
Ivydale Rd. SE15 CC46 77
Ivydale Rd. Cars. BU55 86
Ivyday Gro. SW16 BX48 76
Ivydene E. Mol. BE53 84
Ivy Dene Clo. Red. BV73 121
Ivydene Clo. Sutt. BT56 95
Ivydene Rd. E8 CB36 57
Ivy Gdns. N8 BX32 47
Ivy Gdns. Mitch. BW52 86
Ivy House La. Berk. AR13 7
Ivy House La. Sev. CS62 107
Ivyhouse Rd. Dag. CP36 59
Ivyhouse Rd. Uxb. AZ34 44
Ivy La. Houns. BE45 64
Ivy La. Wok. AT62 100
Ivy Lodge La. Rom. CX30 42
Ivy Mill Clo. Gdse. CB69 114
Ivy Mill La. Gdse. CB69 114
Ivymount Rd. SE27 BY48 76
Ivy Pl. Surb. BL53 85
Ivy Rd. E16 CH39 58
Ivy Rd. E17 CE32 48
Ivy Rd. N14 BW26 38
Ivy Rd. NW2 BQ35 46
Ivy Rd. SE4 CD45 67
Ivy Rd. Houns. BF45 85
Ivy Rd. Surb. BM54 85
Ivy St. N1 CA37 2
Ivy St. N1 CA37 57
Ivy Ter. Hodd. CF11 12
Ivy Wk. Dag. CQ36 59
Ixworth Pl. SW3 BU42 3
Ixworth Pl. SW3 BU42 66
Izane Rd. Bexh. CQ45 69
Jackass La. Kes. CH57 97
Jackass La. Oxt. CD69 114
Jack Barnett Way N22 BX30 38
Mayes Rd.
Jack Cornwell St. E12 CL35 49
Jackdaws, Welw. G. C. BT8 5
Grove Meadow
Jackets La. Nthwd. AZ29 35
Jacketts Fld. Wat. BB18 17
Jacklin Grn. Wdf. Grn. CH28 40
Jackman Ms. NW10 BO34 46
North Circular Rd.
Jackman's La. Wok. AQ63 100
Jackman St. E8 CB37 57
Jackson Clo. Epsom BN60 94
Jackson Rd. N7 BX35 47
Jackson Rd. Bark. CM37 58
Jackson Rd. Barn. BT25 29
Jackson Rd. Brom. CK55 88
Jackson Rd. Grnf. BJ37 54
Sindall Rd.
Jackson Rd. Uxb. AY36 53
Jackson St. SE18 CL43 68
Jackson's La. N6 BV33 47
Jackson's Ms. NW10 BO34 46
Jackson's Pl. Croy. BZ54 87
Jacobs Clo. Wind. AM44 61
Jacobs Ladder, Warl. CB63 105
Jacob St. SE1 CA41 4
Jacob St. SE1 CB41 67
Jacobs Wells Ms. W1 BV39 56
George St.
Jaffray Pl. SE27 BY49 76
Jaffray Rd. Brom. CJ52 88
Jago Clo. SE18 CM43 68
Jago Wk. SE5 BZ43 67
Lomond Gro.
Jail La. Biggin Hl.
Jamaica Rd. SE1 CA41 4
Jamaica Rd. SE16 CA41 67
Jamaica Rd. Th. Hth. BY53 86
Jamaica St. E1 CC39 57
James Av. NW2 BQ35 46
James Av. Dag. CQ33 50
James Bedford Clo. Pnr. BD30 36
James Clo. E13 CH37 58
Turpin Est.
James Clo. Bush. BE25 27
James Clo. Rom. CU32 50
James Gdns. N22 BY29 38
James Gdns. Wem. BK36 54
James La. E10 CF33 48
James La. E11 CF33 48
James Newman Ct. SE9 CL49 78
Jameson Ct. St. Alb. BH13 9
Avenue Rd.
Jameson St. W8 BS40 56
James Pass. N17 CA29 39
Church Rd.
James Rd. Dart. CT47 79
James's Cotts. Rich. BM43 65
Kew Rd.
James St. W1 BV39 1
James St. W1 BV39 56
James St. W1 BW40 3
James St. WC2 BX39 2
James St. WC2 BX40 56
Long Acre
James St. Bark. CM36 58
James St. Enf. CA25 30
James St. Epp. CO17 23
James St. Houns. BG45 64
James St. Wem. BK36 54
James St. Wind. AO44 61
Peascod St.
Jamestown Rd. NW1 BV37 1
Jamestown Rd. NW1 BV37 56
Jamnagar Clo. Stai. AV50 72
Jane Clo. Hem. H. AZ11 8
Jane Pl. Uxb. AX36 53
Vine St.
Janet St. E14 CE41 67
Janeway Pl. SE16 CB41 67
Janeway St.
Janeway St. SE16 CB41 67
Janice Ms. Ilf. CL34 49
Oakfield Rd.
Jan Mead. Brwd. DD26 122
Janoway Hill La. Wok. AR63 100
Jansen Wk. SW11 BT45 66
Wayland Rd.
Janson Clo. E15 CG35 49
Janson Rd.
Janson Rd. E15 CG35 49
Jansons Rd. N15 CA31 48
Japan Cres. N4 BX33 47
Japan Rd. Rom. CP32 50
Japonica Clo. Wok. AR62 100
Silversmiths Way
Jaqueline Clo. Nthlt. BE37 54
Jarman Clo. Hem. H. AY14 8
Jarrow Rd. N15 CB31 48
Jarrow Rd. SE16 CC42 67
Jarrow Rd. Rom. CP32 50
Jarrow Way E9 CD35 48
King's Mead Est.
Jarvis Rd. SE22 CA45 67
Jarvis Rd. Sth. Croy. BZ57 96
Jasmine Clo. Orp. CL55 88
Jasmine Clo. Red. BV73 121
Jasmine Clo. Wok. AP61 100
Jasmine Gdns. Croy. CE55 87
Jasmine Gdns. Har. BF34 45
Sandringham Cres.
Jasmine Gro. SE20 CB51 87
Jasmine Ter. West Dr. AZ41 63
Jasmine Way, E. Mol. BH52 84
Jasmin Rd. Epsom BM57 94
Jason Clo. E15 CG35 49
Jason Rd.
Jason Clo. Brwd. CZ28 42
Jason Clo. Red. BU73 121
Jason Clo. Wey. BA56 92
Jasons Hill, Chesh. AQ17 16
Jason Wk. SE9 CL49 78
Jasper Clo. Enf. CC22 30
Jasper Pass. SE19 CA50 77
Jasper Rd. SE19 CA50 77
Javelin Way, Nthlt. BD38 54
Jay Ms. SW7 BT41 3
Jay Ms. SW7 BT41 66
Jays Bldgs. W1 BX37 56
Rodney St.
Jebb Av. SW2 BX46 76
Jebb St. E3 CE37 57
Jedburgh Rd. E13 CJ38 58
Jedburgh St. SW11 BV45 66
Jeddo Rd. W12 BO41 65
Jefferson Clo. Ilf. CL32 49
Jefferson Wk. SE18 CL43 68
Kempt St.
Jeffrey Clo. Slou. AT42 62
Jeffreys Pl. NW1 BW36 56
Jeffreys St.
Jeffrey's Rd. SW4 BX44 66
Jeffreys Rd. Enf. CD24 30
Jeffrey's St. NW1 BW36 56
Jeffrey's Walk SW9 BX44 66
Jeffreys Walk
Jeffreys Way, Enf. CD24 50
Jeffs Rd. Sutt. BR56 94
Jeken Rd. SE9 CJ45 68
Jelf Rd. SW2 BY46 76
Jellicoe Av. Grav. DH48 81
Jellicoe Gdns. Stan. BJ29 36
Jellicoe Rd. N17 BZ29 39
Jenkins Av. St. Alb. BE18 18
Jenkins La. Bark. CL37 58
Jenkins Rd. E13 CH38 58
Jenner Pl. SW13 BP43 65
Jenner Rd. N16 CA34 48
Jenner Rd. Guil. AS71 118
Jennett Rd. Croy. BY55 86
Jennifer Rd. Brom. CG48 78
Jenningham Dr. Grays. DD40 71
Jennings Rd. SE22 CA46 77
Jennings Rd. St. Alb. BH13 9
Jennings Way, Barn. BQ24 28
Jenningtree Rd. Erith CU43 69
Jenningtree Way, Belv. CS41 69
Jenny Path, Rom. CV29 42
Jenson Way SE19 CA50 77
Fox Hill
Jenton Av. Bexh. CQ44 69
Jephson Rd. E7 CJ36 58
Jephson St. SE5 BZ44 6
Grove La.
Jephtha Rd. SW18 BS46 7
Jeppo's La. Mitch. BU52 8
Jerdan Pl. SW6 BS43 6
Fulham Broadway
Jeremiah St. E14 CE39 5
Jeremys Grn. N18 CB28 3
Jericho Pl. Ing. DC19 2
Jermyn St. SW1 BW40
Jermyn St. SW1 BW40 5
Jerningham Av. Ilf. CL30 4
Jerningham Rd. SE14 CD44 6
Jerome Cres. NW8 BU38
Jerome Cres. NW8 BU38 5
Jerome Dr. St. Alb. BF15
Jerome Pl. SE17 BZ43
Jerome Pl. SE17 BZ43 6
Hillingdon St.
Jerome St. E1 CA38
Jerome St. E1 CA38 5
Calvin St.
Jerounds Harl. CL12 1
Jerrard St. N1 CA37
Jerrard St. SE13 CE45 6
Jersey Av. Stan. BJ30 3
Jersey Clo. Hodd. CE11 1
Jersey Dr. Orp. CM53 8
Jersey La. St. Alb. BJ12
Jersey Rd. E11 CF33 4
Jersey Rd. E16 CH39 5
Jersey Rd. SW17 BV50 7
Jersey Rd. W7 BJ41 6
Jersey Rd. Houns. BF44 6
Jersey Rd. Ilf. CL35 4
Jersey Rd. Rain. CU36 5
Jersey St. E2 CB38 5
Bethnal Green Rd.
Jerusalem Pass. EC1 BY38
Jerusalem Pass. EC1 BY38 5
Jerusalem Pl. EC1 BY38 5
Aylesbury St.
Jervis Av. Enf. CD21 3
Jerviston Gdns. SW16 BY50 7
Jesmond Av. Wem. BL36 5
Jesmond Rd. Croy. CA54 8
Jesmond Rd. Grays. DE40 7
Jesmond St. SE17 BZ42
Jesmond Way, Stan. BL28 3
Jessam Av. E5 CB33 48
Jessamine Rd. W7 BH40 5
Jessamin Pl. Dart. CY47 8
Jessamy St. Wey. AZ55 8
Jessel Dr. Loug. CM23 3
Jesse Rd. E10 CF33 48
Jessica Rd. SW18 BT46 7
Jessiman Ter. Shep. AZ53 8
Jessop Rd. SE24 BZ45 6
Jetstar Way, Nthlt. BE38 5
Jevington Way SE12 CH47 78
Jewel Rd. E17 CE31 48
Jewels Hill, War. CH59 9
Jewry St. EC3 CA39
Jewry St. EC3 CA39 5
Jews Row SW18 BS45 6
Jews Wk. SE26 CB49 7
Jeymer Av. NW2 BP35 4
Jeymer Dr. Grnf. BG37 5
Jeypore Rd. SW18 BT46 7
Jillian Clo. Hmptn. BF50 74
Jinnings, The Welw. G. C. BS9 5
Joan Cres. SE9 CJ47 78
Joan Gdns. Dag. CQ34 5
Joan Rd. Dag. CQ34 5
Joan St. SE1 BY40 4
Joan St. SE1 BY40 56
Jocelyn Rd. Rich. BL45 65
Jocelyns, Harl. CP9 6
Jocketts Hill, Hem. H. AV14 7
Jocketts Rd. Hem. H. AV14 7
Jockey's Fields WC1 BX39 2
Jockey's Fields WC1 BX39 56
Jodrell Rd. E3 CD37 57
Joel St. Nthwd. BC31 44
Johanna St. SE1 BY41 4
Johanna St. SE1 BY41 66
John Adam St. WC2 BX40 4
John Adam St. WC2 BX40 56
Villiers St.
John Aird Ct. W2 BT39 56
Howley Pl.
John Barnes Wk. E15 CG36 58
John Bradshaw Rd. N14 BW26 38
John Burns Dr. Bark. CN36 58
Johnby Cl. Enf. CD22 30
Manly Dixon Dr.
John Campbell Rd. N16 CA35 48
John Carpenter St. EC4 BY40 4
John Carpenter St. EC4 BY40 56
John Clay Gdns. Grays. DD40 71
Whitmore Av.
John Clynge Ct. SW15 BP45 65
Woodborough Rd.
John Cobb Rd. Wey. AZ57 92
John Dwight Ho. SW6 BS45 66
John Elict Clo. Wal. Abb. CG14 13
John Felton Rd. SE16 CB41 4
John Felton Rd. SE16 CB41 67
John Fisher St. E1 CB40 4
John Fisher St. E1 CB40 57
John Islip St. SW1 BW42 3
John Islip St. SW1 BW42 66
John Newton Ct. Well. CO45 69
John Parker Clo. Dag. CR36 59
John Penn St. SE13 CD44 67
John Perrin Pl. Harrow BL33 46
Preston Hill
John Prince's St. W1 BV39 1
John Prince's St. W1 BV39 56
John Rennie Walk E1 CB40 57
Agatha Clo.
John Ruskin St. SE5 BY43 66
John's Av. NW4 BQ31 46
John's Clo. Ashf. BA49 73
Johnsdale, Oxt. CG68 115
John's Gro. Rich. BL45 65
Kew Foot Rd.
John's La. Mord. BT53 86

John's Ms. WC1 BX38 2
John's Ms. WC1 BX38 56
Johnson Clo. Grav. DE48 81
Johnson Clo. Mitch. BV52 86
Johnson Rd. Brom. CJ53 88
Johnson Rd. Houns. BD43 64
Johnsons Av. Sev. CR58 98
Johnson's Clo. Cars. BU55 86
Johnsons Dr. Hamptn. BG51 84
Johnsons Pl. SW1 BW42 3
Johnson St. E1 CC40 57
Johnson St. Sthl. BD41 64
Johnson Way NW10 BM38 55
John Spencer Sq. N1 BY36 47
John's Pla. E1 CB39 57
Nelson St.
Johns Rd. West. CJ63 106
John's Ter. Croy. CA54 87
Johns, The Ong. CX17 24
Johnstone Rd. E6 CK38 58
Johnstone Ter. NW2 BQ34 46
Johnston Grn. Guil. AQ68 109
Johnston Rd. Wdf. Grn. CH29 40
Johnston Walk, Guil. AQ68 109
John St. E15 CG37 58
John St. SE25 CB52 87
John St. WC1 BX38 2
John St. WC1 BX38 56
John St. Enf. CA25 30
John St. Grays. DE43 71
John St. Houns. BE44 64
Johns Wk. Whyt. CB63 105
John Taylor Ct. Slou. AO40 61
Tuns La.
John Wilson St. SE18 CL41 68
Joiners Clo. Chesh. AQ18 16
Joiners Clo. Ger. Cr. AS29 34
Joiner's La. Ger. Cr. AS29 34
Joiner St. SE1 BZ40 4
Joiner St. SE1 BZ40 57
Joiners Way, Ger. Cr. AS29 34
Jolleys La. Har. BG33 45
Jolliffe Rd. Red. BW66 113
Jonathan St. SE11 BX42 4
Jonathan St. SE11 BX42 66
Jones Rd. E13 CH38 58
Holborn Rd.
Jones Rd. Wal. Cr. BY18 20
Jones St. W1 BV40 3
Jones St. W1 BV40 56
Bourdon St.
Jones Way, Slou. AO34 43
Jonson Clo. Hayes BC39 53
Joram Way, SE16 CB42 67
Egan Way
Jordan Clo. Red. BV73 121
Jordan Rd. Grnf. BJ37 54
Jordans Clo. Guil. AT70 118
Beatty Av.
Jordans Clo. Islw. BH44 64
Jordans Clo. Stai. AX47 73
Jordans Clo. Sth. Croy. CA59 96
Jordans Clo. Wat. BB21 26
Jordans Way, Beac. AP29 34
Jordans Way, Rain. CV37 60
Jordans Way, St. Alb. BE18 18
Jordon Dr. Red. BV73 121
Josephine Av. Tad. BR67 112
Josephine Av. SW2 BX46 76
Joseph Powell Clo. SW12 BW46 76
Hazelbourne Rd.
Joseph's Rd. Guil. AR70 118
Joseph St. E3 CD38 57
Joshua St. E14 CF39 57
Joslin Rd. Grays. CY42 70
Joubert St. SW11 BU44 66
Journeys End, Slou. AP38 52
Jowett St. SE15 CA43 67
Joyce Av. N18 CA28 39
Joyce Ct. Wal. Abb. CF20 21
Joyce Grn. La. Dart. CW45 70
Joyce Grn. Wk. Dart. CW46 80
Joycroft, Enf. BY23 29
Hansart Way
Joydens Wd. Rd. Bex. CS48 79
Joydon Dr. Rom. CO32 50
Joyners Field, Harl. CM13 13
Joy Rd. Grav. DH47 81
Jubilee Av. E4 CF28 39
Jubilee Av. Rom. CR32 50
Jubilee Av. Twick. BG47 74
Jubilee Clo. NW9 BN32 46
Jubilee Clo. Green. DB46 80
Jubilee Clo. Pnr. BD30 36
Jubilee Clo. Rom. CR32 50
Jubilee Clo. Stai. AX47 73
Jubilee Cotts. SE9 CK46 78
Jubilee Ct. Hat. BP11 10
Northfield
Jubilee Ct. Th. Hth. BY52 86
Jubilee Cres. E14 CF41 67
Jubilee Cres. N9 CB26 39
Jubilee Cres. Grav. DJ48 81
Jubilee Cres. Wey. AX56 92
Jubilee Dr. Ruis. BD35 45
Jubilee Gdns. Sthl. BF39 54
Jubilee Pl. SW3 BU42 3
Jubilee Pl. SW3 BU42 66
Jubilee Ri. Sev. CW64 108
Jubilee Rd. Grays. DA43 70
Jubilee Rd. Grnf. BJ37 54
Jubilee Rd. Orp. CQ57 98
Jubilee Rd. St. Alb. BK16 18
Jubilee Rd. Sutt. BQ57 94
Jubilee Rd. Wat. BC22 26
Jubilee St. E1 CC39 57
Jubilee Ter. Bet. BN72 120
Jubilee Ter. Dor. BJ71 119
Jubilee Way Chess. BM56 94
Jubilee Way, Sid. CO48 79
Jubilee Way SW19 BS51 86
Judd St. WC1 BX38 2
Judd St. WC1 BX38 56
Jude St. E16 CG39 58
Judeth Gdns. Grav. DJ49 81
Judge Heath La. Hayes BA39 53
Judges Hill, Pot. B. BU18 20
Judge St. Wat. BC22 26
Judges Wk. NW3 BT34 47
Judith Ann Ct. Upmin. CZ34 51
Judith Av. Rom. CR29 41
Juer St. SW11 BU43 66
Jug Hill, West. CG61 106
Julia Gdns. Bark. CP37 59
Julian Av. W3 BM40 55
Julian Clo. Barn. BS24 29
Julian Clo. Wok. AR62 100
Silversmiths Way
Julian Hill Har. BH34 45
Julian Hill, Wey. AZ57 92
Julian Rd. Orp. CO57 98
Julians Clo. Sev. CU67 116
Julians Way, Sev. CU67 116
Julia St. NW5 BV35 47
Oak Village
Julien Rd. W5 BK42 64
Julien Rd. Couls. BW61 104
Junction App. SE13 CF45 67
Junction Ms. W2 BU39 1
Junction Ms. W2 BU39 56
Sale Pl.
Junction Rd. E13 CH37 58
Junction Rd. N9 CB26 39
Junction Rd. N17 CB31 48
Junction Rd. N19 BW35 47
Junction Rd. W5 BK42 64
Junction Rd. Ashf. BA49 73
Junction Rd. Brwd. DB28 42
Junction Rd. Dart. CV46 80
Junction Rd. Dor. BJ71 119
Junction Rd. Har. BG32 45
Junction Rd. Rom. CT31 50
Junction Rd. Sth. Croy. BZ57 96
Junction Rd. E. Rom. CQ33 50
Kenneth Rd.
Junction Rd. W. Rom. CQ33 50
June Clo. Couls. BV60 95
June La. Red. BV74 121
Juniper Av. St. Alb. BF19 18
Juniper Clo. Brox. CD16 21
Juniper Clo. Guil. AR68 109
Juniper Clo. Reig. BT71 121
Juniper Clo. Rick. AX27 35
Juniper Gate Rick. AX27 35
Stockers Fm. Rd.
Juniper Grn. Hem. H. AV13 7
Juniper Gro. Wat. BC22 26
Juniper Rd. Ilf. CL35 49
Riverdene Rd.
Juniper Rd. Reig. BT71 121
Juniper Wk. Bet. BN71 120
Juniper Way, Hayes BA40 53
Juno Rd. Hem. H. AY12 8
Juno Way SE14 CC43 67
Jupiter Dr. Hem. H. AY12 8
Jupiter Way, N7 BX36 47
Jupp Rd. W. E15 CF37 57
Jupps Rd. E3 CD38 57
Jurgen's Rd. Grays. CY43 70
Justice Wk. SW3 BU43 66
Lawrence St.
Justin Clo. Brent. BK43 64
Jute La. Enf. CD23 30
Jutland Rd. E13 CH38 58
Jutland Rd. SE6 CF47 77
Jutsums Av Rom. CR32 50
Jutsums La. Rom. CR32 50
Juxton St. SE11 BX42 4
Juxon St. SE11 BX42 66
Kadona Clo. Pnr. BC32 44
Kale Rd. Belv. CQ41 69
Kambala Clo. SW11 BT45 66
Wye St.
Kambala Rd. SW11 BT44 66
Kandle Wood, Brwd. DD26 122
Kangley Bri. Rd. SE26 CD49 77
Karen Clo. Rain. CT37 59
Karen Ct. Brom. CG51 88
Karen Ter. E11 CG34 49
Montague Rd.
Karoline Gdns. Grnf. BG37 54
Kashgar Rd. SE18 CN42 68
Kashmir, Wey. AX58 92
Kashmir Rd. SE7 CJ43 68
Kassala Rd. SW11 BU44 66
Kates Croft, Welw. G C. BR10 5
Kate St. SW12 BV47 76
Katharine St. Croy. BZ55 87
Katherine Clo. Wey. AW57 92
Katherine Gdns. SE9 CJ45 68
Katherine Gdns. Ilf. CM29 40
Katherine Rd. E6 CJ36 58
Katherine Rd. E7 CJ35 49
Katherine Sq. W11 BQ40 55
Wilsham St.
Kathleen Av. W3 BN39 55
Kathleen Av. Wem. BL36 55
Kathleen Rd. SW11 BU45 66
Katrine Sq. Hem. H. AX11 8
Kavanagh, S Rd. Brwd. DA27 42
Kavanagh, S Ter. Brwd. DA27 42
Kayemoor Rd. Sutt. BT57 95
Kay Rd. SW9 BX44 66
Kay St. E2 CB37 2
Kay St. E2 CB37 57
Kay St. E15 CF36 57
New Mk. St.
Kay St. Well. CO44 69
Kaywood Clo. Slou. AR41 62
Kean St. WC2 BX39 2
Kean St. WC2 BX39 56
Kearn Clo. Brwd. DB26 42
Kearton Clo. Ken. BZ62 105
Keary Rd. Swans. DC47 81
Keats Av. Rom. CU30 41
Keats Clo. NW3 BU35 47
Keats Gro.
Keats Clo. Chig. CM29 40
Keats Clo. Hem. H. AZ10 8
Bronte Cres.
Keats Clo. Hayes BC39 53
Keats Gdns. Til. DG44 71
Keats Gro. NW3 BT35 47
Keats La. Wind. AO43 61
Keats Rd. Belv. CS41 69
Keats Rd. Well. CN44 68
Keats Wk. Brwd. DE26 122
Keats Way Croy. CC53 87
Keats Way Grnf. BF39 54
Keats Way, West Dr. AY42 63
Keble Clo. Nthlt. BG35 45
Keble Clo. Wor. Pk. BO54 85
Keble St. SW17 BT49 76
Keble Ter. Wat. BB19 17
Kechill Gdns. Brom. CH54 88
Kedeston Ct. Sutt. BS55 86
Kedleston Dr. Orp. CN53 88
Kedleston Wk. E2 CB38 57
Keedonwood Rd. Brom. CG49 78
Keel Dr. Slou. AN40 61
Keeler Clo. Wind. AM45 61
Keeley Rd. Croy. BZ55 87
Keeley St. WC2 BX39 2
Keeley St. WC2 BX39 56
Keeling Rd. SE9 CJ46 78
Keemor Clo. SE18 CL43 68
Llanover St.
Keensacre, Iver AU37 52
Keens La. Guil. AP68 109
Keens Park Rd. Guil. AP68 109
Keen's Rd. Croy. BZ56 96
Keen's Yd. N1 BY36 56
St. Paul's Rd.
Keepers Clo. Guil. AU69 118
Keepers Walk, Vir. W. AR53 82
Keep, The SE3 CH44 68
Keeton's Rd. SE16 CB41 67
Keevil Dr. SW19 BQ47 75
Keighley Cl. N7 BX35 47
Penn Rd.
Keighley Rd. Rom. CW29 42
Keightley Dr. SE9 CK47 78
Keilder Clo. Chig. CN29 40
Keilder Clo. Uxb. AZ37 53
Charnwood Rd.
Keildon Rd. SW11 BU45 66
Keir Hardie Ho. W6 BQ43 65
Keir Hardie Way, Bark. CO36 59
Keir, The SW19 BQ49 75
Keith Ave. S. Dnth. CX50 80
Keith Gro. W12 BP41 65
Keith Park Cres. West. CH59 97
Keith Pk. Rd. Uxb. AY36 53
Keith Rd. E17 CD30 39
Keith Rd. Bark. CM37 58
Keith Rd. Hayes BB41 63
Keiths Rd. Hem. H. AZ14 8
Keithway Horn. CW33 51
Kelbrook Rd. SE3 CK44 68
Kelburn Way Rain. CT38 59
Kelbys, Welw. G. C. BT7 5
Kelby Path SE9 CL48 78
Kelceda Clo. NW2 BP34 46
Kelfield Gdns. W10 BQ39 55
Kelland Clo. N8 BW32 47
Kelland Rd. E13 CH38 58
Kellaway Rd. SE3 CJ44 68
Kellerton Rd. SE13 CG46 78
Kellett Rd. SW2 BY45 66
Kelling Gdns. Croy. BY54 86
Kellino St. SW17 BU49 76
Kelliwell Ct. SE22 CB46 77
Kellner Rd. SE28 CN41 68
Kellway Pl. W14 BR42 65
Kelly Rd. NW7 BR29 37
Kelly St. NW1 BV36 56
Kelly Way, Rom. CQ32 50
Kelman Clo. SW4 BW44 66
Kelmore Gro. SE22 CB45 67
Kelmscott Clo. E17 CD30 39
Kelmscott Clo. Wat. BC25 26
Kelmscott Cres. Wat. BC25 26
Kelmscott Gdns. W12 BP41 65
Kelmscott Rd. SW11 BU46 76
Kelross Rd. N5 BY35 47
Kelsall Clo. SE3 CH44 68
Kelsey La. Beck. CE52 87
Kelsey Pk. Av. Beck. CE51 87
Kelsey Pk. Rd. Beck. CE51 87
Kelsey Rd. Orp. CO51 89
Kelsey St. E2 CB38 57
Kelsey Way Beck. CE52 87
Kelshall Wat. BE21 27
Kelsie Way, Ilf. CN29 40
Kelso Dr. Grav. DJ49 81
Kelso Pl. W8 BS41 3
Kelso Pl. W8 BS41 66
Kelso Rd. Cars. BT54 86
Kelston Rd. Ilf. CL30 40
Kelvedon Av. Watt. BB57 92
Kelvedon Clo. Kings. On T. BM50 75
Kelvedon Grn. Brwd. CZ22 33
Kelvedon Hall Brwd. CX21 33
Kelvedon Rd. SW6 BR43 65
Kelvedon Wk. Rain. CT37 59
Kelvedon Way, Wdf. Grn. CK29 40
Kelvin Av. N13 BX29 38
Kelvin Av. Tedd. BH50 74
Kelvinbrook E. Mol. BF52 84
Kelvin Clo. Epsom BM57 94
Kelvin Cres. Har. BH29 36
Kelvin Dr. Twick. BJ46 74
Kelvin Gdns. Sthl. BF39 54
Kelvin Gro. SE26 CB48 77
Kelvin Gro. Chess. BK55 84
Kelvington Clo. Croy. CD53 87
Kelvington Clo. Orp. CO52 89
Kelvington Rd. SE15 CC46 77
Kelvin Pde. Orp. CN54 88
Kelvin Rd. N5 BZ35 48
Kelvin Rd. Til. DG44 71
Kelvin Rd. Well. CO45 69
Kelway Pl. W14 BR43 65
Kemble Clo. Pot. B. BT20 20
Kemble Clo. Wey. BA56 92
Kemble Dr. Brom. CK55 88
Kemble Rd. N17 CB30 39
Kemble Rd. SE23 CC47 77
Kemble Rd. Croy. BY55 86
Kembleside Rd. West. BP53 106
Kings Rd.
Kembleside Rd. West. CJ62
King's Rd.
Kemble St. WC2 BX39 2
Kemble St. WC2 BX39 56
Kemerton Rd. SE5 BZ45 67
Kemerton Rd. Beck. CE51 87
Kemerton Rd. Croy. CA54 87
Kemeys St. E9 CD35 48
Kemnal Rd. Chis. CM50 78
Kempe Clo. St. Alb. BG15 9
Kempe Rd. NW6 BQ37 55
Kempe Rd. Enf. CB21 30
Kemp Gdns. Croy. BZ53 87
St. Saviour's Rd.
Kempis Way SE22 CA46 77
Dulwich Gro.
Kemp Pl. Bush. BT25 27
Kemplay Rd. NW3 BT35 47
Kemple Rd. NW6 BQ37 55
Kemp Rd. Dag. CP33 50
Kemps Dri. E1 CE40 57
Oriental St.
Kemps Dr. Nthwd. BB29 35
Kempsford Gdns. SW5 BS42 66
Kempsford Rd. SE11 BY42 4
Kempshead Rd. SE5 CA42 4
Kempshead Rd. SE5 CA42 67
Kempshott Rd. SW16 BW50 76
Kempson Rd. SW6 BS43 66
Kempton Av. Horn. CW35 51
Kempton Av. Nthlt. BF36 54
Kempton Av. Sun. BC51 83
Kempton Clo. Erith CS43 69
Kempton Clo. Uxb. BA35 44
Lawrence Dr.
Kempton Rd. E6 CK37 58
Kempton Rd. Hamptn. BE51 84
Kempton Wk. Croy. CD53 87
Kempt St. SE18 CL43 68
Kemsing Clo. Bex. CQ47 79
Kemsing Clo. Brom. CG55 88
Bourne Way
Kemsing Clo. Th. Hth. BZ52 87
Kemsing Rd. SE10 CH42 68
Kemsing Rd. Sev. DA62 108
Kemsley Clo. Grav. DF49 81
Kemsley Cl. Green. DA46 80
Kemsley Rd. West CJ63 106
Kenbury Clo. Uxb. AZ34 44
Kenbury St. SE5 BZ44 67
Kendal Av. N18 BZ28 39
Kendal Av. W3 BM39 55
Kendal Av. Bark. CN37 58
Kendal Av. Epp. CO18 23
Kendal Av. Epp. CO19 23
Kendal Clo. Reig. BT70 121
Kendal Clo. Slou. AQ40 52
Kendal Clo. Wdf. Grn. CG27 40
Kendal Croft Horn. CU35 50
Kendal Dr. Slou. AQ40 52
Kendale Grays DG41 71
Godman Rd.
Kendale, Hem. H. AZ14 8
Kendale Clo. Hayes BB37 53
Kendale Rd. Brom. CG49 78
Kendal Gdns. N18 BZ28 39
Kendall Av. Beck. CD51 87
Kendall Av. Sth. Croy. BZ58 96
Kendall Av. S. Sth. Croy. BZ58 96
Kendall Gdns. Sutt. BT55 86
Kendall Pl. W1 BV39 1
Kendall Pl. W1 BV39 56
George St.
Kendall Rd. Beck. CD51 87
Kendall Rd. Islw. BJ44 64
Kendal Rd. NW10 BP35 46
Kendals Clo. Rad. BH21 27
Kendal St. W2 BU39 1
Kendal St. W2 BU39 56
Kender Est. SE14 CC44 67
Kender St. SE14 CC44 67
Kendoa Rd. SW4 BW45 66
kendon Clo. E11 CH32 49
Avenue, The
Kendor Av. Epsom BN59 94
Kendra Hall Rd. Sth. Croy. BY57 95
Kendrey Gdns. Twick. BH46 74
Kendrick Ms. SW7 BT42 3
Kendrick Ms. SW7 BT42 66
Brompton Rd.
Kendrick Rd. Slou. AQ41 62
Kenelm Clo. Har. BJ34 45
Kenerne Dr. Barn. BR25 28
Kenford Clo. Wat. BC19 17
Kenia Walk, Grav. DJ48 81
Cervia Way
Kenilford Rd. SW12 BV47 76
Kenilworth Ave. Cob. BF60 93
Kenilworth Av. E17 CE30 39
Kenilworth Av. SW19 BS49 76
Kenilworth Av. Har. BE35 45
Kenilworth Av. Rom. CX29 42
Kenilworth Clo. Bans. BS61 104
Kenilworth Clo. Borwd. BN24 28
Kenilworth Clo. Slou. AP41 62
Mere Rd.
Kenilworth Ct. SW15 BQ45 65
Kenilworth Ct. Twick. BG48 74
Kenilworth Ct. Wat. BC23 26
Kenilworth Cres. Enf. CA23 30
Kenilworth Dr. Borwd. BN24 28
Kenilworth Dr. Rick. AZ24 26
Kenilworth Gdns. SE18 CL44 68
Kenilworth Gdns. Hayes BB39 53
Kenilworth Gdns. Horn. CV34 51
Kenilworth Gdns. Ilf. CN34 49
Kenilworth Gdns. Loug. CK25 31
Kenilworth Gdns. Stai. AX49 73
Kenilworth Gdns. Sthl. BE38 54
Kenilworth Gdns. Wat. BD28 36
Kenilworth Rd. E3 CD37 57
Kenilworth Rd. NW6 BR37 55
Kenilworth Rd. SE20 CC51 87
Kenilworth Rd. W5 BL40 55
Kenilworth Rd. Ashf. AX48 73
Kenilworth Rd. Edg. BN27 37
Kenilworth Rd. Epsom BP56 94
Kenilworth Rd. Orp. CM53 88
Kenilworth Way, Slou. AP41 62
Mere Rd.
Kenley Av. NW9 BO30 37
Kenley Clo. Bex. CR47 79
Kenley Clo. Cat. BZ63 105
Kenley Clo. Chis. CN52 88
Kenley Gdns. Horn. CW34 51
Kenley Gdns. Th. Hth. BY52 86
Kenley La. Ken. BZ61 105
Kenley Rd. SW19 BR51 85
Kenley Rd. Kings. On T. BM51 85
Kenley Rd. Twick. BJ46 74
Kenley St. W11 BR40 55
Kenley Wk. W11 BR40 55
Kenley Wk. Sutt. BQ56 94
Kenlor Rd. SW17 BT49 76
Kenmare Dr. Mitch. BU50 76
Kenmare Gdns. N13 BZ28 39
Kenmare Rd. Th. Hth. BX53 86
Kenmere Rd. Well. CP44 69
Kenmont Gdns. NW10 BP38 55
Kenmore N2 BT33 47
Kenmore Av. Har. BJ32 45
Kenmore Cres. Hayes BB38 53
Kenmore Gdns. NW10 BM37 55
Kenmore Gdns. Edg. BM30 37
Kenmore Rd. Har. BK31 45
Kenmore Rd. Ken. BY60 95
Kenmure Rd. E8 CB35 48
Kennard Rd. E15 CF36 57
Kennard Rd. N11 BU28 38
Kennard St. E16 CK40 58
Kenneally, Wind. AL44 61
Kenneally Clo. Wind. AL44 61
Kenneally
Kenneally Pl. Wind. AL44 61
Kenneally
Kenneally Walk, Wind. AL44 61
Kenneally
Kennedy Av. Enf. CC25 30
Kennedy Av. Hodd. CD12 12
Kennedy Clo. E13 CH37 58
Kennedy Clo. Orp. CM54 88
Kennedy Clo. Pnr. BE29 36
Kennedy Clo. Wal. Cr. CD17 21
High St. Cheshunt
Kennedy Gardens, Sev. CV65 108
Kennedy Rd. W7 BH39 54
Kennedy Rd. Bark. CN37 58
Kennel Clo. Lthd. BG65 102
Kennel La. Brwd. CY23 33
Kennal La. Lthd. BF64 102
Kennelwood Cres. Croy. CF59 96
Kennel Wood Lane, Hat. BP12 10
Kenners La. Wal. Abb. CK13 13
Kennet Cl. SW11 BT45 66
Maysoule Rd.
Kennet Clo. Upmin. CZ32 51
Kenneth Av. Ilf. CL35 49
Kenneth Cres. NW2 BP35 46
Kenneth Gdns. Stan. BJ29 36
Kenneth Rd. Bans. BT61 104
Kenneth Rd. Rom. CP33 50
Kennet Rd. W9 BR38 55
Kennet Rd. Dart. CU45 69
Kennet Rd. Islw. BH45 64
Kennet Rd. Slou. AT41 62
Kenninghall Rd. E5 CB34 48
Kenninghall Rd. N18 CC28 39
Kenning Rd. Hodd. CE11 12
Kennings Est. SE11 BY42 66
Kenning St. SE16 CC41 67
Kennings Way SE11 BY42 4
Kennings Way SE11 BY42 66
Kenning Ter. N1 CA37 2
Kenning Ter. N1 CA37 57
Branch Pl.
Kennington Gro. SE11 BX43 4
Kennington Gro. SE11 BX43 66
Kennington La. SE11 BX42 4
Kennington La. SE11 BX42 66
Kennington Oval SE11 BX43 66
Kennington Park Est. SE11 BY43 66
Kennington Pk. Gdns. SE11 BY43 66
Kennington Pk. Pl. SE11 BY43 4
Kennngton Pk. Pl. SE11 BY43 66
Kennington Pk. Rd. SE11 BY43 4
Kennington Pk. Rd. SE11 BY43 66
Kennington Rd. SE1 BY41 4
Kennington Rd. SE1 BY41 66
Kennington Rd. SE11 BY42 66
Kennyland Ct. NW4 BP32 46
Kenny Rd. NW7 BR29 37
Kenrick Pl. W1 BV39 1
Kenrick Pl. W1 BV39 56
Dorset St.
Kenrick Sq. Red. CA70 114
Kensal Rd. W10 BR38 55
Kensington Av. E12 CK36 58
Kensington Av. Th. Hth. BY51 86
Kensington Av. Wat. BB24 26
Kensington Church St. W8 BS40 56
Kensington Church Wk. W8 BS41 66
Holland St.
Kensington Ct. W8 BS41 3
Kensington Ct. W8 BS41 66
Kensington Ct. Ms. W8 BS41 66
Kensington Ct. Pl.
Kensington Ct. Pl. W8 BS41 3
Kensington Ct. Pl. W8 BS41 66
Kensington Dr. Wdf. Grn. CJ30 40
Kensington Gdns. Ilf. CK33 49
Kensington Gdns. Sq. W2 BS39 56
Kensington Gte. W8 BT41 3
Kensington Gte. W8 BT41 66
Kensington Gore SW7 BT41 3
Kensington Gore SW7 BT41 66
Kensington High St. W8 BR41 65
Kensington High St. W14 BR41 65
Kensington Mall W8 BS40 56
Kensington Palace Gdns. W8 BS40 56
Kensington Pk. Gdns. W11 BR40 55
Kensington Pk. Ms. W11 BR39 55
Kensington Pk. Rd. W11 BR39 55
Kensington Pl. W8 BS40 56
Kensington Rd. SW7 BT41 66
Kensington Rd. W8 BS41 3
Kensington Rd. W8 BT41 66
Kensington Rd. Brwd. DA25 33

Kensington Rd. Nthlt. BF38 54
Kensington Rd. Rom. CS32 50
Kensington Sq. W8 BS41 3
Kensington Sq. W8 BS41 66
Kensington Ter. Sth. Croy. BZ57 96
Kent Av. W13 BJ39 54
Kent Av. Dag. CR39 59
Kent Av. Hem. H. AX15 8
Kent Av. Slou. AO39 52
Kent Av. Well. CN46 78
Kent Clo. Mitch. BX52 86
Kent Clo. Orp. CN57 97
Kent Clo. Stai. AX50 73
Kent Dr. Barn. BV24 29
Kent Dr. Horn. CV35 51
Kent Dr. Tedd. BH49 74
Kentford Way, Nthlt. BE37 54
Kent Gdns. W13 BJ39 54
Kent Gdns. Ruis. BC32 44
Kent Gate Way, Croy. CD57 96
Kent Hatch Rd. Oxt. CJ68 115
Kent House La. Beck. CD50 77
Kent House. Rd. Beck. CD50 77
Kentish La. Hat. BT16 20
Kentish Rd. Belv. CR42 69
Kentish Town Rd. NW1 BV37 1
Kentish Town Rd. NW1 BV36 56
Kentish Town Rd. NW5 BV36 56
Kentmere Rd. SE18 CN42 68
Kenton Av. Har. BH33 45
Kenton Av. Sthl. BF40 54
Kenton Av. Sun. BD51 84
Kenton Ct. Har. BJ32 45
Kenton Gdns. Har. BK32 45
Kenton Gdns. St. Alb. BH14 9
Kenton La. Har. BH29 36
Kenton Park Av. Har. BK31 45
Kenton Park Clo. Har. BK32 45
Kenton Park Cres. Har. BK31 45
Kenton Park Rd. Har. BK31 45
Kenton Rd. E9 CC36 57
Kenton Rd. Har. BH33 45
Kenton's La. Wind. AM44 61
Kenton St. WC1 BX38 2
Kenton St. WC1 BX38 56
Kenton Way, Hayes BB38 53
Kenton Way, Wok. AP61 100
Kent Pass. NW1 BU38 1
Kent Pass. NW1 BU38 56
Kent Rd. N15 CA32 48
Kent Rd. N21 BZ26 39
Kent Rd. SE1 CA42 4
Kent Rd. W4 BN41 65
Kent Rd. Dag. CR35 50
Kent Rd. Dart. CV46 80
Kent Rd. E. Mol. BG52 84
Kent Rd. Grav. DG47 81
Kent Rd. Grays. DE43 71
Kent Rd. Kings. on T. BK52 84
Kent Rd. Long. DB51 90
Kent Rd. Orp. CO53 89
Kent Rd. Rich. BM43 65
Kent Rd. W. Wick. CE54 87
Kent Rd. Wok. AT61 100
Kents La. Epp. CS14 14
Kents Pass. Hmptn. BE51 84
Kent St. E2 CA37 2
Kent St. E2 CA37 57
Kent St. E13 CH38 58
Kent Ter. NW1 BU38 1
Kent Ter. NW1 BU38 56
Kent View S. Ock. CY41 70
Kent Vw. Gdns. Ilf. CN34 49
Kent Walk SW9 BY45 66
Somerleyton Rd. Dev.
Kent Way SE15 CA44 67
Sumner Estate
Kent Way Surb. BL55 85
Kentwode Grn. SW13 BP43 65
Kentwyns Ri. Red. BX71 121
Kenver Av. N12 BT29 38
Kenward Rd. SE9 CJ46 78
Kenway Rain. CV38 60
Kenway Rom. CS30 41
Ken Way Wem. BN34 46
Kenway Clo. Rain. CV38 60
Kenway Dr. Amer. AQ23 25
Kenway Rd. SW5 BS42 66
Kenway Wk. Rain. CV38 60
Kenwood Av. N14 BW25 29
Kenwood Clo. West Dr. AZ43 63
Kenwood Dr. Beck. CF52 87
Kenwood Dr. Rick. AV27 34
Kenwood Dr. Walt. BC57 92
Kenwood Gdns. E18 CH31 49
Kenwood Gdns. Ilf. CL31 49
Kenwood Rd. N6 BU32 47
Kenwood Rd. N9 CB26 39
Kenworth Clo. Wal. Cr. CC20 21
Kenworthy Rd. E9 CD35 48
Kenwyn Dr. NW2 BO34 46
Kenwyn Rd. SW4 BW45 66
Kenwyn Rd. SW20 BQ51 85
Kenya Rd. SE7 CJ43 68
Kenyington Dr. Sun. BC49 73
Kenyington Pl. Har. BK32 45
Kenyons, Leath. AZ67 110
Kenyon St. SW6 BQ44 65
Keogh Rd. E15 CG36 58
Kepler Rd. SW4 BX45 66
Keppell Rd. Dor. BJ70 119
Keppel Rd. E6 CK36 58
Keppel Rd. Dag. CQ35 50
Keppel Row SE1 BZ40 4
Keppel Row SE1 BZ40 57
Great Guildford St.
Keppel Spur, Wind. AQ47 72
Keppel St. WC1 BW39 1
Keppel St. WC1 BW39 56
Malet St.
Keppel St. Wind. AO44 61
Helena Rd.
Kerbela St. E2 CB38 2
Kerbela St. E2 CA38 57
Kerbey St. E14 CE39 57
Kerdistone Clo. Pot. B. BS18 20
Kerfield Cres. SE5 BZ44 67
Kerfield Pl. SE5 BZ44 67
Kernick Clo. N7 BX36 56
Sutterton St.
Kernow Clo. Horn. CW34 51
Kerrill Ave. Couls. BY63 104
Kerrison Rd. E15 CF37 57
Kerrison Pl. W5 BK40 54
Kerrison Rd. SW11 BU45 66
Kerrison Rd. W5 BK40 54
Kerry Av. Stan. BK28 36
Kerry Clo. E16 CH39 58
Kerry Clo. Barn. BQ24 28
Kerry Clo. Upmin. CZ33 51
Kerry Dr. Upmin. CZ33 51
Kerry Rd. SE14 CD43 67
Kerry Rd. Grays. DE40 71
Kerry Ter. Wok. AT61 100
Kersey Dr. Sth. Croy. CC59 96
Kersey Gdns. SE9 CK49 78
Kersey Gdns. Rom. CW29 42
Kersfield Rd. SW15 BQ46 75
Kershaw Rd. Dag. CR34 50
Kersley Ms. SW11 BU44 66
Kersley Rd. N16 CA34 48
Kersley St. SW11 BU44 66
Kerstin Clo. Hayes BB40 53
Kerswell Cr. N15 CA32 48
Kerwick Clo. N7 BX36 56
Blundell St.
Keslake Rd. NW6 BQ37 55
Kessock Clo. N15 CB32 48
Kesters Rd. Chesh. AO19 16
Kesteven Clo. Chig. CN29 40
Kesteven Clo. Ilf. CN29 40
New North Rd.
Keston Ave. Couls. BY63 104
Keston Av. Kes. CJ56 97
Keston Av. Wey. AW59 92
Keston Clo. N18 BZ27 39
Keston Clo. Well. CP43 69
Keston Gdns. Kes. CJ56 97
Keston Rd. N17 BZ31 48
Keston Rd. SE15 CB45 67
Keston Rd. Th. Hth. BX53 86
Kestrel Av. Stai. AV48 72
Kestrel Clo. Berk. AR13 7
Kestrel Clo. Guil. AV69 118
Kestrel Clo. Ilf. CP28 41
Kestrel Clo. Rain. CU36 59
Kestrel Grn. Hat. BP13 10
Kestrel Rd. SE24 BY46 76
Kestrel Way Croy. CF58 96
Keswick Av. SW15 BO49 75
Keswick Av. SW19 BS51 85
Keswick Av. Horn. CV33 51
Keswick Clo. Sutt. BT56 95
Keswick Dr. Enf. CC22 30
Keswick Gdns. Ilf. CK31 49
Keswick Gdns. Ruis. BA32 44
Keswick Gdns. Wem. BL35 46
Keswick Mews W5 BK40 54
Keswick Rd. SW15 BR46 75
Keswick Rd. Bexh. CR44 69
Keswick Rd. Lthd. BF66 111
Keswick Rd. Orp. CN54 88
Keswick Rd. Twick. BF46 74
Keswick Rd. W. Wick. CG55 88
Kettering Rd. Enf. CC22 30
Kettering Rd. Rom. CW29 42
Kettering St. SW16 BV50 76
Kett Gdn. SW2 BX46 76
Kettlebaston Rd. E10 CD33 48
Kettlebury Way Ong. CW18 24
Kettlewell Clo. Swan. CT51 89
Kettlewell Clo. Wok. AR61 100
Kettlewell Dri. Wok. AS60 91
Kettlewell Hill, Wok. AS60 91
Ketton Grn. Red. BW67 113
Malmstone Av.
Kevan Dr. Wok. AV65 100
Kevelioc Rd. N17 BZ30 39
Kevin Clo. Houns. BD44 64
Kevington Dr. Brom. CN52 88
Kevington Dr. Chis. CN52 88
Kevington Dr. Orp. CN52 88
Keway Ct. Berk. AQ13 7
Cross Oak Rd.
Kew Bridge Rd. Brent. BL43 65
Kew Ct. W4 BM42 65
Kew Cres. Sutt. BR55 85
Kewferry Dr. Nthwd. AZ28 35
Kewferry Rd. Nthwd. BA29 35
Kew Foot Rd. Rich. BL45 65
Kew Gdns. Rd. Rich. BL43 65
Kew Grn. Rich. BL43 65
Kew Meadow Path Rich. BM44 65
Kew Palace, Rich. BL43 65
Kew Rd. Rich. BL43 65
Kew Rd. Rich. BL45 65
Kew Clo. E1 CC38 57
Cambridge Heath Rd.
Keyes Rd. NW2 BQ35 46
Keyes Rd. Dart. CW45 70
Keyfield Ter. St. Alb. BG14 9
Keymer Clo. West. CJ61 106
Keymer Rd. SW2 BX48 76
Keynes Clo. N2 BU31 47
Keynsham Av. Wdf. Grn. CG28 40
Keynsham Gdns. SE9 CK46 78
Keynsham Rd. SE9 CJ46 78
Keynsham Rd. Mord. BS54 86
Keynsham Wk. Mord. BS54 86
Keyse Rd. SE1 CA41 4
Keyse Rd. SE1 CA41 67
Keysers Rd. Brox. CE14 12
Keysham Av. Houns. BC43 63
Keystone Cres. N1 BX37 2
Keystone Cres. N1 BX37 56
Caledonian Rd.
Keywood Dr. Sun. BC50 73
Keyworth St. SE1 BY41 4
Keyworth St. SE1 BY41 66
Khama Rd. SW17 BU49 76
Khartoum Rd. E13 CH38 58
Khartoum Rd. SW17 BT49 76
Khartoum Rd. Ilf. CL35 49
Khyber Rd. SW11 BU44 66
Kibworth St. SW8 BX43 66
Dorset Rd.
Kidborough Down Lthd. BF67 111
Grove Side
Kidbrooke Gdns. SE3 CH44 68
Kidbrooke Gro. SE3 CH44 68
Kidbrooke La. SE9 CK45 68
Kidbrooke Pk. Clo. SE3 CH44 68
Kidbrooke Pk. Rd. SE3 CH44 68
Kidbrooke Way SE3 CH44 68
Kidderminster Pl. Croy. BY54 86
Kidderminster Rd. Croy. BY54 86
Kidderpore Av. NW3 BS35 47
Kidderpore Gdns. NW3 BS35 47
Kidd Pl. SE7 CK42 68
Maryon Rd.
Kidlington Way BO30 37
Kidrow Way E9 CC37 57
Clermont Rd.
Kielder Clo. Ilf. CN29 40
New North Rd.
Kier Hardie Way, Hayes BC38 53
Kiffen St. EC2 BZ38 2
Kilbride Ct. Hem. AY11 8
Kilburn Bldgs. NW6 BS37 56
Kilburn High St.
Kilburn Gate NW6 BS37 1
Kilburn Gate NW6 BS37 56
Kilburn High Rd. NW6 BR36 55
Kilburn La. W10 BQ38 55
Kilburn Pk. Rd. NW6 BS38 56
Kilburn Pl. NW6 BS37 56
Kilburn Priory NW6 BS37 56
Kilburn Sq. NW6 BS37 56
Kilburn Vale Est. NW6 BS37 56
Kilby Clo. Wat. BD20 18
Kilcorral Clo. Epsom BP60 94
Kildare Clo. Ruis. BD33 45
Kildare Gdns. W2 BS39 56
Kildare Rd. E16 CH39 58
Kildare Ter. W2 BS39 56
Kildare Wk. E14 CE39 58
Farrance St.
Kildonan Clo. Wat. BB23 26
Kildonan Clo. Wat. BC23 26
Kildoran Rd. SW2 BX46 76
Kildowan Rd. Ilf. CO33 50
Kilfillan Gdns. Berk. AQ13 7
Kilgour Rd. SE23 CD46 77
Kilgowan Rd. Ilf. CO33 50
Kilkie St. SW6 BT44 66
Killasser Ct. Tad. BQ65 103
Killearn Rd. SE6 CF47 77
Killearney Rd. SW18 BT46 76
Killester Gdns. Wor. Pk. BP56 94
Killewarren Way, Orp. CP54 89
Chelsfield Rd.
Killick St. N1 BX37 2
Killick St. N1 BX37 56
Killieser Av. SW2 BX48 76
Killip Clo. E16 CG39 58
Killowen Av. Nthlt. BG35 45
Killowen Rd. E9 CC36 57
Killy Hill, Wok. AP57 91
Killyon Rd. SW8 BW44 66
Kilmaine Rd. SW6 BR43 65
Kilmarnock Rd. Wat. BD28 36
Woodhall La.
Kilmarsh St. W6 BQ42 65
Kilmartin Av. SW16 BX52 86
Kilmartin Rd. Ilf. CO34 50
Kilmartin Way Horn. CU35 50
Kilmeston Way SE15 CA43 67
Kilmington Clo. Brwd. DD27 122
Kilmington Rd. SW13 BP43 65
Kilmiston Av. Shep. BA53 83
Kilmorey Gdns. Twick. BJ46 74
Kilmorey Rd. Twick. BJ45 64
Kilmorie Rd. SE23 CD47 77
Kiln Ave. Amer. AR23 25
Kiln Clo. Hayes BA43 63
Kilncroft, Hem. H. AZ14 8
Kiln Field Brwd. DB21 33
Kiln Field, Welw. G. C. BR6 5
Kiln Ground, Hem. H. AZ14 8
Kiln La. Bet. BN70 120
Kiln La. Chesh. AQ19 16
Kiln La. Epsom BO59 94
Kiln La. Slou. AO33 43
Kiln La. Wok. AW65 101
Kiln Mead. Guil. AO68 109
Kiln Pl. NW5 BV35 47
Kiln Rd. Epp. CR17 23
Kilnside, Esher BJ57 93
Kilravock St. W10 BR38 55
Kilrue La. Walt. BB56 92
Kilrush Ter. Wok. AT61 100
Kilsby Wk. Dag. CO36 59
Rugby Rd.
Kilsha Rd. Walt. BD53 84
Kilsmore La. Wal. Cr. CC18 21
Kilvinton Dr. Enf. BZ22 30
Kilworth Av. Brwd. DD25 122
Kimbell Gdns. SW6 BR44 65
Kimber Clo. Wind. AN45 61
Kimber Ct. Guil. AU69 118
Gilliat Dr.
Kimberley Av. E6 CK37 58
Kimberley Av. SE15 CB44 67
Kimberley Av. Ilf. CM33 49
Kimberley Av. Rom. CS32 50
Kimberley Dr. Sid. CP48 79
Kimberley Gdns. Enf. CA24 30
Kimberley Pl. Pur. BY59 95
Brighton Rd.
Kimberley Rd. E4 CG26 40
Kimberley Rd. E11 CF34 48
Kimberley Rd. E16 CG38 58
Kimberley Rd. E17 CD30 39
Kimberley Rd. N4 BY32 47
Kimberley Rd. N17 CB30 39
Kimberley Rd. N18 CB29 39
Kimberley Rd. NW6 BR37 55
Kimberley Rd. SW9 BX44 66
Kimberley Rd. Beck. CC51 87
Kimberley Rd. Croy. BY53 86
Kimberley Rd. St. Alb. BG13 9
Kimberley Way E4 CG26 40
Kimber Rd. SW18 BS47 76
Kimble Cres. Bush. BG26 36
Kimble Rd. SW19 BT50 76
Kimbolton Clo. SE12 CG46 78
Kimbolton Grn. Borwd. BN24 28
Kimbolton Row SW3 BU42 66
Fulham Rd.
Kimbur Rd. SW18 BS47 76
Kimmeridge Gdns. SE9 CK49 78
Kimmeridge Rd. SE9 CK49 78
Kimps Way, Hem. H. AZ15 8
Kimpton Av. Brwd. DA26 42
Kimpton Clo. Hem. H. AZ11 8
Cleves Rd.
Kimpton Clo. Wat. BD20 18
Kimpton Rd. SE5 BZ44 67
Kimpton Rd. Sutt. BR55 85
Kimptons Clo. Ong. CW16 24
Kimptons Mead. Pot. B. BQ19 19
Kimptons Mead. Clo. Pot. B. BQ19 19
Kinburn Dr. Egh. AS49 72
Kinburn St. SE16 CC41 67
Kincaid Rd. SE15 CB43 67
Kinch Gro. Har. BL33 46
Kinder Clo. SE2 CP40 59
Kinder Scout, Hem. H. AZ14 8
Kindersley Way, Wat. BA19 17
Kinder St. E1 CB39 57
Kinfauns Av. Horn. CV32 51
Kinfauns Rd. SW2 BY48 76
Kinfauns Rd. Ilf. CO33 50
Kingaby Gdns. Rain. CU36 59
King Alfred Av. SE6 CE49 77
King Alfred Rd. Rom. CW30 42
King Arthur St. SE15 CC43 67
Kg. Charles Cres. Surb. BL54 85
King Charles's Rd. Surb. BL53 85
King Charles St. SW1 BW41 3
King Charles St. SW1 BW41 66
King Charles Wk. SW13 BR47 75
Princes Way
Kingcraig Dr. Sev. CU65 107
King David La. E1 CC40 57
Kingdon Rd. NW6 BS36 56
King Edward Av. Dart. CV46 80
King Edward Av. Rain. CV37 60
King Edward Ct. Wind. AO44 61
King Edward Dr. Chess. BK55 84
King Edward Dr. Grays. DF42 71
King Edward Rd. E10 CF33 48
King Edward Rd. E17 CD31 48
King Edward Rd. Barn. BS24 29
King Edward Rd. Brwd. DB27 42
King Edward Rd. Green. DA46 80
King Edward Rd. Rad. BL20 19
King Edward Rd. Rom. CT32 50
King Edward Rd. Wal. Cr. CD20 21
King Edward Rd. Wat. BE25 27
King Edwards Gdns. W3 BM40 55
King Edward's Gro. Tedd. BJ50 74
King Edward's Rd. Ruis. BA33 44
King Edward's Rd. E9 CB37 57
King Edward's Rd. N9 CB26 39
King Edward's Rd. Bark. CM37 58
King Edward's Rd. Enf. CC24 30
King Edward St. EC1 BZ39 2
King Edward St. EC1 BZ39 57
King Edward St. Hem. H. AX15 8
King Edward St. Slou. AO41 61
King Edward VII, Av. Wind. AO43 61
King Edward Wk. SE1 BY41 4
King Edward Wk. SE1 BY41 66
Kingfield Clo. Wok. AS63 100
Kingfield Dr. Wok. AS63 100
Kingfield Gdns. Wok. AS63 100
Kingfield Rd. W5 BK38 54
Kingfield Rd. Wok. AS63 100
Kingfield St. E14 CF42 67
Kingfisher Clo. Brwd. DD26 122
Kingfisher Clo. Walt. BE56 93
Kingfisher Dr. Guil. AU69 118
Kingfisher Dr. Red. BV69 121
Kingfisher Dr. Rich. BK49 74
Kingfisher Dr. Stai. AV49 72
Kingfisher Gdns. Sth. Croy. CC59 96
Kingfisher Lure, Rick. AW24 26
Kingfisher Rd. Upmin. CZ33 51
Kingfisher Sq. SE8 CD43 67
Dorking Clo.
Kingfisher Sq. SE8 CD43 67
Staunton St.
King George Ave. West. CJ61 106
King George Av. E16 CJ39 58
King George Av. Bush. BF25 27
King George Av. Walt. BD54 84
King George Clo. Rom. CS31 50
King George Rd. Wal. Abb. CF20 21
King George's Av. Wat. BB24 26
King Georges Dr. Sthl. BE39 54
Lady Maragaret Rd.
King Georges Dr. Wey. AW58 92
King George's Rd. Brwd. CZ25 33
King George St. SE10 CF43 67
King George VI Av. Mitch. BU52 86
Kingham Clo. SW18 BT47 76
King Harold's Way, Bexh. CP43 69
King Harry La. St. Alb. BF14 9
King Harry St. Hem. H. AX13 8
King Henry's Dr. Croy. CF58 96
King Henry's Rd. NW3 BT36 1
King Henry's Rd. NW3 BT36 56
Kg. Henry's Rd. Kings. Kings. On T. BM52 85
King Henry St. N16 CA35 48
King Henry's Wk. N1 CA36 57
King James Av. Pot. B. BX18 20
King James St. SE1 BY41 4
King James St. SE1 BY41 66
King Jame & Tinker Rd. CA21 30
King John Ct. EC2 CA38 2
King John Ct. EC2 CA38 57
New Inn Yd.
King Johns Clo. Stai. AR46 72
King John's Ct. EC2 CA38 57
New Inn Yd.
King John St. E1 CC39 57
King John's Wk. SE9 CJ47 78
Kinglake Est. SE17 CA42 4
Kinglake Est. SE17 CA42 67
Kinglake St. SE17 CA42 4
Kinglake St. SE17 CA42 67
Kingly Ct. W1 BW40 3
Kingly St. W1 BW39 1
Kingly St. W1 BW38 56
King & Queen St. SE17 BZ42 4
King & Queen St. SE17 BZ42 67
Kingsand Rd. SE12 CH48 78
Kings Arms Ct. E1 CB39 2
Kings Arms Ct. E1 CB39 57
Old Montague St.
King's Arms Yd. EC2 BZ39 2
King's Arms Yd. EC2 BZ39 57
Kings Arms Yd. SW18 BS46 76
Wandsworth High St.
Kings Av. N10 BV31 47
King's Av. N21 BY26 38
King's Av. SW4 BW47 76
King's Av. SW12 BW47 76
Kings Av. W5 BK39 54
King's Av. Brom. CG50 78
King's Av. Buck. H. CJ27 40
King's Av. Cars. BU57 95
King's Av. Grnf. BF39 54
King's Av. Hem. H. AY15 8
Kings Av. Houns. BF44 64
Kings Av. N. Mal. BO52 85
Kings Av. Red. BU71 121
Kings Av. Rom. CQ32 50
Kings Av. Sun. BB49 73
King's Av. Wat. BB25 26
King's Av. Wdf. Grn. CH29 40
Kings Av. Wey. AX59 92
King's Av. Gdns. SW4 BX46 76
King's Bench St. SE1 BY41 4
King's Bench St. SE1 BY41 66
King's Bench Wk. EC4 BY40 4
Kingsbridge Av. W3 BL41 65
Kingsbridge Cir. Rom. CW29 42
Kingsbridge Clo. Rom. CW29 42
Kingsbridge Cres. Sthl. BE39 54
Kingsbridge Rd. W10 BQ39 55
Kingsbridge Rd. Bark. CM37 58
Kingsbridge Rd. Mord. BQ53 85
Kingsbridge Rd. Rom. CW29 42
Kingsbridge Rd. Sthl. BE42 64
Kingsbridge Rd. Walt. BC54 83
Kingsbridge Way, Hayes BB38 53
Weymouth Dr.
Kings Brook Lthd. BJ62 102
Kingston Rd.
Kingsbury Av. St. Alb. BG13 9
Kingsbury Cir. NW9 BM32 46
Kingsbury Dr. Wind. AQ47 72
Kingsbury Rd. N1 CA36 57
Kingsbury Rd. NW9 BM32 46
Kingsbury Ter. N1 CA36 57
Kings Cft. Welw. G. C. BS7 5
Hazel Gro.
Kingsclere Clo. SW15 BP47 75
Kingscliffe Gdns. SW19 BR47 75
Kings Clo. E10 CE33 48
Kings Clo. NW4 BQ31 46
Kings Clo. Ch. St. G. AR27 34
King's Clo. Dart. CT45 69
Kings Clo. Stai. AX50 73
King's Clo. Walt. BC54 83
Kings College Rd. NW3 BT36 56
Eton Av.
Kings College Rd. Ruis. BB32 44
Kingscote Rd. W4 BN41 65
Kingscote Rd. Croy. CB54 87
Kingscote Rd. N. Mal. BN52 85
Kingscote St. EC4 BY40 4
Kingscote St. EC4 BY40 56
Tudor St.
King's Ct. E13 CH37 58
King's Ct. SW19 BS50 76
Kings Ct. W5 BK39 54
Castlebar Pk.
King's Ct. W6 BP42 65
Kings Ct. Har. BF34 45
King's Ct. Wem. BM34 46
Kingscourt Rd. SW16 BW48 76
King's Cres. N4 BZ34 48
Kingscroft Rd. NW2 BR36 55
Kingscroft Rd. Bans. BT61 10
Kingscroft Rd. Lthd. BJ63 10
Kingscross La. Red. BW71 12
Kings Crss Rd. WC1 BX38
King's Cross Rd. WC1 BX38 5
Kingsdale Est. SE18 CN43 6
Kingsdale Rd. SE18 CN43 6
Kingsdale Rd. SE20 CC50 7
Kingsdale Rd. Berks. AQ13
Kingsdene, Tad. BP64 10
Kingsdon La. Harl. CP11 1
Kingsdown Av. W3 BO40 5
Kingsdown Av. W13 BJ41 6
Kingsdown Av. Sth. Croy. BY58 9
Kingsdown Cl. W11 BQ39 5
Kingsdowne Rd. Surb. BL54 8
Kingsdown Rd. E11 CG34 4
Kingsdown Rd. N19 BX34 4
Kingsdown Rd. Epsom BP60 9
Kingsdown Rd. Sutt. BR56 9
Kingsdown Way Brom. CH53 8
Kings Dr. Edg. BL28 3
Kings Dr. Edg. BL28 3
Kings Dr. Grav. DG48 8
King's Dr. Surb. BJ53 8
King's Dr. Surb. BM54 8
Kings Dr. Tedd. BG49 7
Kings Dr. Walt. BB58 9
King's Dr. Wem. BM34 4
Kingsend, Ruis. BA33 4
King's Farm Av. Rich. BM45 6
Kingsfield, Wind. AL44 6
Kingsfield Av. Har. BF31 4
Kingsfield Dr. Enf. CC21 3
Kingsfield Rd. Har. BG33 4
Kingsfield Rd. Sev. CZ58 9
Kingsfield Rd. Wat. BD26 3
Kingsfield Ter. Dart. CV46 8
Kingsfield Ter. Har. BG33 4
Kingsfield Way, Enf. CC21 3
Kingsford Av. Wall. BX57 9

Kings Gdns. Croy. BY56 95
Kings Gdns. Ilf. CM33 49
Kings Gdns. Upmin. CZ33 51
Kingsgate, Wem. BM34 46
Kingsgate Av. N3 BS31 47
Kingsgate Clo. Bexh. CQ44 69
Kingsgate Clo. Orp. CP52 89
Main Rd.
Kingsgate Pl. NW6 BS36 56
Kingsgate Rd. NW6 BS36 56
Kings Grn. Loug. CK24 31
Kingsground SE9 CK47 78
King's Gro. SE15 CB44 67
Kings Gro. Rom. CU32 50
King's Hall Rd. Beck. CD50 77
Kings Head Ct. EC3 BZ40 57
Fish St. Hill
Kings Head Ct. Saw. CQ6 6
London Rd.
King's Head Hill E4 CE26 39
Kingshead La. Wey. AX59 92
Kings Head Pass. SW4 BW45 66
Clapham Pk. Rd.
King's Head Yd. SE1 BZ40 4
King's Head Yd. SE1 BZ40 57
Borough High St.
Kings Highway SE18 CN43 68
Kings Hill Loug. CK23 31
Kingshill Av. Har. BJ31 45
Kingshill Av. Hayes BB38 53
Kingshill Av. Nthlt. BD38 54
Kinshill Av. Rom. CS29 41
Kingshill Av. St. Alb. BJ11 9
Kingshill Av. Wor. Pk. BP54 85
Kinshill Dr. Har. BJ30 36
Kingshill Rd. E2 CA38 57
Kingshill Way, Berk. AQ14 7
Kingshold Est. E9 CC37 57
Kingshold Rd. E9 CC36 57
Kingsholm Gdns. SE9 CJ45 68
Kingshurst Rd. SE12 CH47 78
Kingsland Harl. CM12 13
Kingsland Est. E2 CA37 2
Kingsland Est. E2 CA37 57
Kingsland Grn. N16 CA36 57
Kingsland High St. E8 CA36 57
Kingsland Pk. Hem. H. AW14 8
Kingsland River, Hem. H. AW14 8
Kingsland Rd. E2 CA37 57
Kingsland Rd. E8 CA37 57
Kingsland Rd. E13 CJ38 58
Kingsland Rd. Hem. H. AW14 8
King's La. Egh. AQ49 72
King's La. Sutt. BT56 95
Kingslawn Clo. SW15 BQ45 65
Howards La.
Kingslea, Lthd. BJ63 102
Kingsley Ave. Dart. CX46 80
Kingsley Av. W13 BJ39 54
Kingsley Av. Bans. BS61 104
Kingsley Av. Borwd. BL23 28
Kingsley Av. Houns. BG44 64
Kingsley Av. Sthl. BF40 54
Kingsley Av. Sutt. BT56 95
Kingsley Av. Wal. Cr. CB18 21
Kingsley Clo. N2 BT32 47
Kingsley Clo. Dag. CR35 50
Kingsley Cres. SE19 CA51 87
Kingsley Dr. Egh. AQ50 72
Kingsley Dr. Wor. Pk. BO55 85
Kingsley Gdns. E4 CE28 39
Kingsley Gdns. Horn. CV31 51
Kingsley Gro. Reig. BS72 121
Kingsley Ms. W8 BS41 3
Kingsley Ms. W8 BS41 66
Stanford Rd.
Kingsley Pl. N6 BV33 47
Kingsley Rd. E7 CH36 58
Kingsley Rd. E17 CF30 39
Kingsley Rd. N13 BY28 38
Kingsley Rd. NW6 BR37 55
Kingsley Rd. SW19 BS49 76
Kingsley Rd. Brwd. DE26 122
Kingsley Rd. Croy. BY54 86
Kingsley Rd. Har. BG35 45
Kingsley Rd. Houns. BF44 64
Kingsley Rd. Ilf. CM30 40
Kingsley Rd. Loug. CM24 31
Kingsley Rd. Orp. CN57 97
Kingsley Rd. Pnr. BE31 45
Kingsley St. SW11 BU45 66
Kingsley Wk. Grays DG42 71
Kingsley Way N2 BT32 47
Kingsley Wood Dr. SE9 CK48 78
Kings Lynn Clo. Rom. CV29 42
Kings Lynn Dr. Rom. CV29 42
Kings Lynn Path, Rom. CV29 42
Kings Lynn Dr.
Kingsman St. SE18 CK41 68
Kingsmead Barn. BS24 29
Kings Mead. Pot. B. BX17 20
Kingsmead, Saw. CQ6 6
Kingsmead, St. Alb. BK12 9
Villiers Cres.
Kingsmead, West. CJ61 106
Kingsmead Av. N9 CB26 39
Kingsmead Av. NW9 BN33 46
Kingsmead Av. Mitch. BW52 86
Kingsmead Av. Rom. CT32 50
Kingsmead Av. Sun. BD51 84
Kingsmead Av. Surb. BM55 85
Kingsmead Av. Wor. Pk. BP55 85
Kingsmead Clo. Epsom BN57 94
Kingsmead Clo. Harl. CH11 13
Kingsmead Clo. Sid. CO48 79
Kingsmead Dr. Nthlt. BE36 54
King's Mead. Est. E9 CD35 48
Kingsmead Rd. SW2 BY48 76
King's Mead. Way E9 CD35 48
Kingsmere Pk. NW9 BM33 46
Kingsmere Rd. SW19 BQ48 75
King's Ms. WC1 BX38 2
King's Ms. WC1 BX38 56
Kingsmill Gdns. Dag. CQ35 50
Kings Mill La. Red. BW73 121
Kingsmill Rd. Dag. CQ35 50
Kingsmill Ter. NW8 BT37 1
Kingsmill Ter. NW8 BT37 56
Kingsmoor, Harl. CL13 13
Kingsmoor Rd. Harl. CL12 13
Kingsnympton Pk.
Kings. on T. BM50 75
Kings Orchard, SE9 CK46 78
King's Chase, Brwd. DB27 42
King's Farm Rd. Rick. AU25 25
King's La. Kings L. AW19 17
King's Rd. Brwd. DB27 42
Kingspark Ct. E18 CH31 49
Kingspark Ct. Ilf. CK33 49
Drive, The
Kings Pass. Kings. on T. BK51 84
Kings Pl. SE1 BZ41 4
Kings Pl. SE1 BZ41 67
Kings Pl. W4 BN42 65
Kings Pl. Buck. H. CJ27 40
King Sq. EC1 BZ38 2
King Sq. Est. EC1 BY38 56
Kings Ride Gate, Rich. BM45 65
Kingsridge Gdns. Dart. CV46 80
King's Rd. E4 CF26 39
King's Rd. E6 CJ37 58
King's Rd. E11 CG33 49
King's Rd. N17 CA30 39
King's Rd. N18 CB28 39
King's Rd. N22 BX30 38
King's Rd. NW10 BP36 55
King's Rd. SE25 CB52 87
King's Rd. SW1 BV42 3
Kings Rd. SW1 BV42 66
King's Rd. SW3 BS43 66
King's Rd. SW3 BT43 3
King's Rd. SW6 BS44 66
King's Rd. SW10 BT43 66
King's Rd. SW14 BN45 65
King's Rd. SW19 BS50 76
Kings Rd. W5 BK39 54
Kings Rd. Bark. CM36 58
North St.
Kings Rd. Barn. BQ24 28
Kings Rd. Berk. AQ13 7
Kings Rd. Ch. St. G. AR27 34
King's Rd. Egh. AT49 72
King's Rd. Felt. BD47 74
Kings Rd. Guil. AR70 118
Kings Rd. Har. BE34 45
King's Rd. Kings. on T. BL51 85
King's Rd. Mitch. BV52 86
King's Rd. Orp. CN56 97
Kings Rd. Rich. BL46 75
Kings Rd. Rom. CU31 50
Kings Rd. St. Alb. BF13 9
Kings Rd. St. Alb. BK16 18
Kings Rd. Slou. AP41 62
King's Rd. Surb. BK54 84
Kings Rd. Sutt. BS58 95
King's Rd. Tedd. BG49 74
Kings Rd. Twick. BJ46 74
Kings Rd. Uxb. AX37 52
Kings Rd. Wal. Cr. CD20 21
Kings Rd. Walt. BC55 83
Kings Rd. West. CJ62 106
Kings Rd. West Dr. AY41 63
Kings Rd. Wey. AW58 92
King's Rd. Wind. AO45 61
Kings Rd. Wok. AT61 100
King's Scholar's Pass. SW1 BW42 3
Kings Scholars Pass. SW1 BW41 66
Carlisle Pl.
King Stable St. Wind. AO43 61
King's Ter. NW1 BW37 1
Kings Ter. NW1 BW37 56
Plender St.
King's Ter. Islw. BJ45 64
Kingsthorpe Rd. SE26 CC49 77
Kingston Av. Felt. BB46 73
Kingston Av. Leath. BB66 110
Kingston Av. Lthd. BJ64 102
Kingston Av. Sutt. BR55 85
Kingston Av. West Dr. AY40 53
Kingston Br. Kings. on T. BK51 84
Kingston By-pass, Esher BH55 84
Kingston By-pass,
New Malden BO53 85
Kingston By-pass, Surb. BL55 85
Kingston By-pass, SW15 BO49 75
Kingston By-pass, SW20 BP51 85
Kingston Clo. Nthlt. BE36 54
Kingston Clo. Tedd. BJ50 74
Kingston Ct. Grav. DD46 81
Warwick Pl.
Kingston Cres. Ashf. AX49 73
Kingston Cres. Beck. CD51 87
Kingston Hall Rd.
Kings. on T. BK52 84
Kingston Hill Av. Rom. CQ30 41
Kingston Hl. Kings. on T. BM51 85
Kingston Ho Gdns. Lthd. BJ64 102
Upr. Fairfield Rd.
Kingston Lane, Leath. AZ67 110
Kingston La. Tedd. BJ49 74
Kingston La. Uxb. AY38 53
Kingston La. West Dr. AY41 63
Kingston Pk. Est.
Kings. on T. BM50 75
Kingston Pl. Sthl. BE41 64
Kingston Rise, Wey. AW58 92
Kingston Rd. N9 CB27 39
Kingston Rd. SW15 BP48 75
Kingston Rd. SW19 BR51 85
Kingston Rd. SW20 BQ51 85
Kingston Rd. Ashf. AY50 73
Kingston Rd. Barn. BT25 29
Kingston Rd. Epsom BO57 94
Kingston Rd. Ilf. CL35 49
Kingston Rd. Lthd. BJ62 102
Kingston Rd. N. Mal. BM52 85
Kingston Rd. Rom. CT31 50
Kingston Rd. Stai. & Ashf. AW49 73
Kingston Rd. Sun. BE51 84
Kingston Rd. Surb. BM55 85
Kingston Rd. Tedd. BJ49 74
Kingston Vale SW15 BN49 75
Kingstown St. NW1 BV37 56
King St. E13 CH38 58
King St. EC2 BZ39 2
King St. EC2 BZ39 57
King St. N2 BT31 47
King St. SW1 BW40 3
King St. SW1 BW40 56
King St. W3 BM40 55
King St. W6 BO42 65
King St. WC2 BX40 4
King St. WC2 BX40 56
King St. Cher. AV54 82
King St. Grav. DG46 81
King St. Ong. CZ17 24
King St. Rich. BK46 74
King St. Sthl. BE41 64
King St. Twick. BJ47 74
King St. Wat. BC24 26
Kings Wk. Grays DD43 71
Argent St.
King's Wk. Kings. On T. BK51 84
Kings Wk. Sth. Croy. CR60 96
Kingsway N12 BT29 38
Kingsway NW8 BU37 56
Kingsway SW14 BM45 65
Kingsway WC2 BX39 2
Kingsway WC2 BX39 56
Kingsway, Croy. BX56 95
Kingsway, Enf. CB25 30
Kingsway, Ger. Cr. AS30 34
Kingsway, Ger. Cr. AS31 43
King's Way Har. BH31 45
Kingsway, Hayes BA39 53
Kingsway, Iver AV39 52
Kingsway, N. Mal. BQ52 85
Kingsway Orp. CM53 88
Kingsway, Pot. B. BX18 20
Kingsway, Stai. AX47 73
Kingsway, Wat. BB21 26
Kingsway, Wat. BD20 18
Kingsway, Wdf. Grn. CJ28 40
Kingsway, Wem. BL35 46
Kingsway W. Wick. CG55 88
Kingsway, Wok. AR62 100
Kingsway Av. Sth. Croy. CC58 96
Kingsway Av. Wok. AR62 100
Kingsway Cres. Har. BG31 45
Kingsway Industrial Est.
N18 CC29 39
Kingsway Rd. Sutt. BR57 94
Kingsway, The, Epsom BO59 94
Kingswear Rd. NW5 BV34 47
Kingswear Rd. Ruis. BC34 44
Kingswell Ride, Pot. B. BX18 20
Kingswood Av. NW6 BR37 55
Kingswood Av. Belv. CQ42 69
Kingswood Av. Houns. BE44 64
Kingswood Av. Sth. Croy. CB61 105
Kingswood Av. Swan. CT52 89
Kingswood Av. Th. Hth. BY53 86
Kingswood Clo. Egh. AR49 72
Kingswood Clo. N20 BT26 38
Kingswood Clo. Dart. CV46 80
Kingswood Clo. Guil. AU70 118
Kingswood Clo. N. Mal. BO53 85
Kingswood Clo. Orp. CM54 88
Woodcote Rd.
Kingswood Clo. Surb. BL54 85
Kingswood Clo. Wey. AZ57 92
Kingswood Ct. Rich. BL46 75
Marchmont Rd.
Kingswood Creek, Stai. AR46 72
Kingswood Dr. SE19 CA49 77
Kingswood Dr. Cars. BU54 86
Kingswood Est. SE21 CA49 77
Kingswood La. Warl. CC61 105
Kingswood Pk. N3 BR30 37
Kingswood Pl. SE13 CG45 68
Kingswood Rise, Egh. AR49 72
Kingswood Rd. SE20 CC50 77
Kingswood Rd. SW2 BX46 76
Kingswood Rd. SW19 BR50 75
Kingswood Rd. W4 BN41 65
Kingswood Rd. Brom. CF52 87
Kingswood Rd. Ilf. CO33 50
Kingswood Rd. Sev. CT64 107
Kingswood Rd. Tad. BP64 103
Kingswood Rd. Wat. BC20 17
Kingswood Way, Croy. CC60 96
Kingswood Way Wall. BX56 95
Kingthorpe Rd. NW10 BN36 55
Kingthorpe Ter. NW10 BN36 55
Kingwell Rd. Barn. BT22 29
King William St. EC4 BZ39 2
King William St. EC4 BZ39 57
King William Wk. SE10 CF43 67
Kingwood Av. Brom. CG52 88
Kingwood Av. Hamptn. BF50 74
Kingwood Rd. SW6 BR44 65
Kinlet Clo. SE18 CM44 68
Kinlet Rd.
Kinlet Rd. SE18 CL44 68
Kinloch Dr. NW9 BN33 46
Kinloch St. N7 BX34 47
Kinloss Ct. N3 BR31 46
Kinloss Gdns.
Kinloss Gdns. N3 BR31 46
Kinloss Rd. Cars. BT54 86
Kinnaird Av. W4 BN43 65
Kinnaird Av. Brom. CG50 78
Kinnaird Clo. Brom. CG50 78
Kinnear Rd. W12 BO41 65
Kinnersley Wk. Reig. BS72 121
Castle Dr.
Kinnerton Pl. N. SW1 BU41 3
Kinnerton Pl. N. SW1 BU41 66
Kinnerton St.
Kinnerton Pl. S. SW1 BU41 3
Kinnerton Pl. S. SW1 BU41 66
Kinnerton St.
Kinnerton St. SW1 BU41 3
Kinnerton St. SW1 BV41 66
Kinnoul Rd. W6 BR43 65
Kinross Av. Wor. Pk. BP55 85
Kinross Clo. Har. BL32 46
Kinross Clo. Sun. BB49 73
Kinross Dr. Sun. BB49 73
Kinsale Rd. SE15 CB45 67
Kinsfield, Hodd. CE11 12
Kintore St. SE1 CA42 4
Kintore St. SE1 CA42 67
Kintore Way SE1 CA42 4
Kintore Way SE1 CA42 67
Grange Rd.
Kints Clo. Wind. AL44 61
Kintyre Clo. SW16 BX56 86
Kinveachy Gdns. SE7 CK42 68
Kinver Rd. North SE26 CC49 77
Kinver Rd. South SE26 CC49 77
Kipling Ave. Til. DG44 71
Kipling Est. SE1 BZ41 4
Kipling Estate SE1 BZ41 67
Kipling Pl. Stan. BH29 36
Kipling Rd. Bexh. CQ44 69
Kipling Rd. Dart. CX46 80
Kipling St. SE1 BZ41 4
Kipling St. SE1 BZ41 67
Kipling Ter. N9 BZ27 39
Kirby Clo. Epsom BO56 94
Kirby Clo. Ilf. CN29 40
Kirby Clo. Loug. CK26 40
Kirby Est. SE16 CB41 67
Kirby Gro. SE1 CA41 4
Kirby Gro. SE1 CA41 67
Kirby Rd. Dart. CY47 80
Kirby Rd. Wok. AR61 100
Kirby St. EC1 BY39 2
Kirby St. EC1 BY39 56
Kirby Way Walt. BD53 84
Kircaldy Grn. Wat. BD27 36
Trevose Way
Kirchen Rd. W13 BJ40 54
Kirkdale SE26 CB48 77
Kirkdale Rd. E11 CG33 49
Kirkham St. SE18 CN43 68
Kirkland Av. Ilf. CL30 40
Kirkland Av. Wok. AP61 100
Kirkland Pl. SE10 CG41 68
Kirkland Wk. E8 CA36 57
Rhodes Dev.
Kirklands, Welw. G. C. BQ6 5
Kirk La. SE18 CM43 68
Kirklees Rd. Th. Hth. BX52 86
Kirkley Rd. SW19 BS50 76
Kirkly Clo. Sth. Croy. CA58 96
Kirkside Rd. SE3 CH43 68
Kirkstall Av. N17 BZ31 48
Kirkstall Gdns. SW2 BW47 76
Kirkstall Rd. SW2 BW47 76
Kirksted Rd. Mord. BS54 86
Kirkstone Way Brom. CG50 78
Kirkton Clo. W4 BN42 65
Dolman Rd.
Kirkton Gdns. E2 CA38 57
Chambo Rd.
Kirkton Rd. N15 CA32 48
Kirkwall Pl. E2 CC38 57
Kirkwood Rd. SE15 CB44 67
Kirn Rd. W13 BJ40 54
Kirchen Rd.
Kirtling St. SW8 BW43 66
Gringle St.
Kirton Rd. E13 CJ37 58
Kirton Wk. Edg. BN29 37
Kirwyn Way SE5 BY43 66
Kitchener Clo. St. Alb. BJ14 9
Kitchener Rd. E7 CH36 58
Kitchener Rd. E17 CE30 39
Kitchener Rd. N2 BU31 47
Kitchener Rd. N17 BZ31 48
Kitchener Rd. Dag. CR36 59
Kitchener Rd. Th. Hth. BZ52 87
Kitchener's La. Red. CA70 114
Kitchenor Av. Grav. DH48 81
Kitkat Ter. E3 CE38 57
Kitley Gdns. SE19 CA51 87
Kitsbury Rd. Berk. AQ13 7
Kitsbury Ter. Berk. AQ13 7
Kitsmead La. Cher. AS55 82
Kitson Rd. SE5 BZ43 67
Kitson Rd. SW13 BP44 65
Kitswell Way, Rad. BH20 18
Kittiwake Clo. Sth. Croy. CD58 96
Kittiwake Rd. Nthlt. BD38 54
Kitto Rd. SE14 CC44 67
Kitt's End Rd. Barn. BQ21 28
Kiver Rd. N19 BW34 47
Klea Ave. SW4 BW46 76
Knapdale Clo. SE23 CB48 77
Knapmill Rd. SE6 CE48 77
Knapmill Way SE6 CE48 77
Knapp Clo. NW10 BO36 55
Knappe Rd. Ashf. AY49 73
Knapp Rd. E3 CE38 57
Knaresboro' Pl. SW5 BS42 3
Knaresborough Pl. SW5 BS42 66
Knaresborough Rd. SW5 BS43 66
Knatchbull Rd. NW10 BN37 55
Knatchbull Rd. SE5 BY44 66
Knatts La. Sev. CY59 99
Knatts Valley Rd. Sev. CY59 99
Knebworth Av. E17 CE30 39
Knebworth Path, Borwd. BN24 28
Knebworth Rd. N16 CA35 48
Knee Hill SE2 CP42 69
Knee Hill Cres. SE2 CP42 69
Knella Grn. Welw. G. C. BS8 5
Knella Rd. Welw. G. C. BR8 5
Kneller Gdns. Islw. BG46 74
Kneller Rd. SE4 CD45 67
Kneller Rd. N. Mal. BN54 85
Kneller Rd. Twick. BG46 74
Knightland Rd. E5 CB34 48
Knighton Clo. Rom. CS32 50
Knighton Clo. Sth. Croy. BY57 95
Knighton Clo. Wdf. Grn. CH28 40
Knighton Dr. Wdf. Grn. CH28 40
Knighton La. Buck. H. CH27 40
Knighton Park Rd. SE26 CC49 77
Knighton Rd. E7 CH34 49
Knighton Rd. Red. BV71 121
Knighton Rd. Rom. CS32 50
Knighton Rd. Sev. CT61 107
Knighton Way La. Uxb. AW36 53
Knightrider St. EC4 BZ39 57
Godliman St.
Knightrider St. EC4 BZ40 4
Knightrider St. EC4 BZ40 57
Queen Victoria St.
Knights Av. W5 BL41 65
Knightsbridge SW1 BU41 66
Knightsbridge SW7 BU41 3
Knightsbridge SW7 BU41 66
Knightsbridge Clo. SW1 BU41 3
Knightsbridge Clo. SW1 BU41 66
Knightsbridge
Knightsbridge Cres. AW50 73
Knightsbridge Gdns. Rom. CS32 50
Knightsbridge Grn. SW1 BU41 3
Knightsbridge Grn. SW1 BU41 66
Knightsbridge
Knightsbridge Way,
Hem. H. AY13 8
Knights Clo. E9 CC35 48
Churchill Wk.
Knights Clo. Egh. AU50 72
Knights Ct. Kings. on T. BL52 85
Knightsfield, Welw. G. C. BQ5 5
Knight's Hill, SE27 BY49 76
Knight's Hill Sq. SE27 BY49 76
Knight's Hill
Knights La. N9 CB27 39
Knight, S Way, Brwd. DD27 122
Knights Pk. Kings. on T. BL52 85
Knight's Rd. E16 CH41 68
Knights Rd. Stan. BK28 36
Knight St. Saw. CQ6 6
Knights Walk Rom. CO24 32
Knights Way, Ilf. CM29 40
Knightswood, Wok. AP62 100
Knightswood Clo. Edg. BN27 37
Knightwood Clo. Reig. BS71 121
Knightwood Cres. N. Mal. BO53 85
Knipp Hl. Cob. BE60 93
Knivett Rd. SW6 BS43 66
Knob's Hill Rd. E15 CE37 57
Knockhall Chase, Green. DB46 80
Knockholt Main Rd. Sev. CN63 106
Knockholt Rd. SE9 CJ46 78
Knockholt Rd. Sev. CO61 107
Knockholt Rd. Sev. CQ60 98
Knole Clo. Croy. CC53 87
Knole La. Sev. CV66 117
Knole Rd. Dart. CU47 79
Knole Rd. Sev. CV65 108
Knole, The SE9 CL49 78
Knole, The Grav. DF50 81
Knole Way, Sev. CV66 117
Knoll Cres. Nthwd. BB30 35
Knoll Dr. N14 BV26 38
Knolles Cr. Hat. BP15 10
Knollmead Surb. BN54 85
Knoll Rise Orp. CN54 88
Knoll Rd. SW18 BT46 76
Knoll Rd. Bex. CR47 79
Knoll Rd. Dor. BJ72 119
Knoll Rd. Sid. CO49 79
Knolls Clo. Wor. Pk. BP55 85
Knolls, The Epsom BQ61 103
Knoll, The W13 BK39 54
Knoll, The Beck. CE51 87
Knoll, The Brom. CH55 88
Knoll, The Cob. BF60 93
Knoll, The Orp. CN54 88
Knollys Clo. SW16 BY48 76
Knollys Rd. SW16 BX48 76
Knolton Way, Slou. AQ39 52
Knottisford St. E2 CC38 57
Knott's Grn. Rd. E10 CE32 48
Knotts Pl. Sev. CU65 107
Knowle Av. Bexh. CQ43 69
Knowle Clo. SW9 BY45 66
Knowle Grn. Stai. AW49 73
Knowle Gdns. Wey. AV60 91
Madeira Rd.
Knowle Gro. Vir. W. AR54 82
Knowle Grove Clo. Vir. W. AR54 82
Knowle Hill, Vir. W. AR54 82
Knowle Pk. Cob. BE61 102
Knowle Park Av. Stai. AW50 73
Knowle Rd. Brom. CK55 88
Knowle Rd. Twick. BH47 74
Knowles Hl. Cres. SE13 CF46 77
Knowl Hill, Wok. AT63 100
Knowlton Grn. Brom. CG53 88
Knowl Way Borwd. BL24 28
Knowsley Av. Sthl. BF40 54
Knowsley Rd. SW11 BU44 66
Knox Rd. E7 CG36 58
Knox Rd. Guil. AQ68 109
Knox St. W1 BU39 1
Knox St. W1 BU39 56
Knoyle St. SE14 CD43 67
Chubworthy St.
Knutsford Av. Wat. BD22 27
Kohat Rd. SW19 BS49 76
Koh-i-noor Av. Bush. BF25 27
Koonowla Clo. West. BQ52 106
Dowding Rd.
Kossuth St. SE10 CG42 68
Kramer Ms. SW5 BS42 66
Kuala Gdns. SW16 BX51 86
Kuhn Way, E7 CH35 49
Kydbrook Clo. Orp. CM54 88
Kylemore Rd. NW6 BS36 56
Kymberley Rd. Har. BH32 45
Kyme Rd. Rom. CT32 50
Kynance Gdns. Stan. BK30 36
Kynance Ms. SW7 BS41 3
Kynance Ms. SW7 BS41 66
Kynance Pl. SW7 BT41 3
Kynance Pl. SW7 BT41 66
Kynaston Av. N16 CA34 48
Dynevor Rd.
Kynaston Av. Th. Hth. BZ53 87
Kynaston Clo. Har. BG29 36
Kynaston Cres. Th. Hth. BZ53 87
Kynaston Rd. N16 CA34 48
Kynaston Rd. Brom. CH49 78
Kynaston Rd. Enf. BZ23 30
Kynaston Rd. Orp. CO54 89
Kynaston Rd. Th. Hth. BZ53 87
Kynaston Wood, Har. BG29 36
Kynnersley Clo. Cars. BU55 86
Kynock Rd. N18 CC28 39
Kyrle Rd. SW11 BU46 76
Kytes Dr. Wat. BD20 18

Kyverdale Rd. N16 CA33 48
Labour-in-Vain Rd. Sev. DB60 99
Laburnam Ct. E2 CA37 2
Laburnam St. E2 CA37 2
Laburnham Av. West. Dr. AY40 53
Laburnham Ct. Stan. BK28 36
Laburnham Gdns. Upmin. CZ33 51
Laburnham Rd. Epp. CP18 23
Laburnham Way Brom. CL54 88
Laburnum Av. N9 CA27 39
Laburnum Av. N17 BZ29 39
Laburnum Av. Dart. CV47 80
Laburnum Av. Horn. CT34 50
Laburnum Av. Sutt. BU55 86
Laburnum Av. Swan. CS52 89
Laburnum Clo. E4 CD29 39
Maple Av.
Laburnum Clo. Guil. AR69 118
Laburnum Clo. Upmin. DA33 51
Laburnum Clo. Wal. Cr. CC19 21
Laburnum Cres. Sun. BC51 83
Laburnum Gdns. N21 BZ27 39
Laburnum Gro. N21 BZ27 39
Laburnum Gro. NW9 BN33 46
Laburnum Gro. Grav. DE47 81
Laburnum Gro. Houns. BE45 64
Laburnum Gro. N. Mal. BN51 85
Laburnum Gro. St. Alb. BF16 18
Laburnum Gro. Slou. AT43 62
Laburnum Gro. Sthl. BE38 54
Laburnum Pl. SE9 CL46 78
Laburnum Pl. Egh. AQ50 72
Laburnum Rd. SW19 BT50 76
Laburnum Rd. Cher. AW54 83
Laburnum Rd. Epsom. BO60 94
Laburnum Rd. Hayes BB42 63
Laburnum Rd. Hayes BC42 63
Laburnum Rd. Hodd. CE11 12
Laburnum Rd. Mitch. BV51 86
Laburnum Rd. Wok. AR63 100
Laburnum St. E2 CA37 57
Laburnum Wk. Horn. CV35 51
Laburnum Way, Stai. AY47 73
Laburnum Way, Wal. Cr. BY17 20
Lacey Ave. Couls. BY63 104
Lacey Clo. Egh. AU50 72
Lacey Dri. Edg. BL28 37
Lacey Dr. Hamptn. BE51 84
Lacey Grn. Couls. BY63 104
Lacey Wk. E3 CE37 57
Morville St.
Lackford Rd. Couls. BU62 104
Lackington St. EC2 BZ39 2
Lackington St. EC2 BZ39 57
Lackmore Rd. Enf. CC21 30
Lacon Rd. SE2 CB45 67
Lacy Dr. Couls. BY63 104
Lacy Rd. SW15 BQ45 65
Ladas Rd. SE27 BZ49 77
Ladbrook Cl. W11 BR39 55
Ladbroke Grove
Ladbroke Cres. W11 BR39 55
Ladbroke Gro.
Ladbroke Gdns. W11 BR40 55
Ladbroke Gro. W10 BQ38 55
Ladbroke Gro. W11 BR39 55
Ladbroke Gro. Red. BV70 121
Ladbroke Rd. W11 BR40 55
Ladbroke Rd. Enf. CA25 30
Ladbroke Rd. Epsom. BN60 94
Ladbroke Rd. Red. BV70 121
Ladbroke Sq. W11 BR40 55
Ladbroke Sq. Gdns. W11 BR40 55
Ladbroke Ter. W11 BR40 55
Ladbroke Wk. W11 BR40 55
Ladbrook Clo. Pnr. BE32 45
Ladbrook Cres. Sid. CP48 79
Ladbrooke Dr. Pot. B. BS19 20
Ladbrook Rd. SE25 BZ52 87
Ladbrook Rd. Slou. AO41 61
Ladderstile Ride,
Kings. on T. BN49 75
Ladderswood Rd. N11 BW28 38
Ladds Way Swan. CS52 89
Ladenhatch La. Swan. CS51 89
Ladies Gro. St. Alb. BF13 9
Ladworth Lo. Est. Mitch. BV52 86
Lady Amherst's Dri. Sev. CR69 116
Ladycroft Gdns. Orp. CM56 97
Ladycroft Rd. SE13 CE45 67
Ladycroft Wk. Stan. BK30 36
Ladycroft Way, Orp. CM56 97
Ladyfields, Grav. DF49 81
Ladyfields Loug. CL24 31
Ladyfields Clo. Loug. CL24 31
Ladygate La. Ruis. AZ32 44
Ladygate Rd. Dor. BK71 119
Ladygrove, Croy. CD58 96
Lady Gro. Welw. G. C. BR9 5
Lady Hay Wor. Pk. BO55 85
Lady Margaret Rd. N19 BW35 47
Lady Margaret Rd. NW5 BW35 47
Lady Margaret Rd. Sthl. BE40 54
Ladymeadow, Kings L. AX17 17
Ladymead Parkway, Guil. AR70 118
Lady's Clo. Wat. BC24 26
Vicarage Rd.
Ladyshot, Harl. CO10 6
Ladysmith Av. E6 CK37 58
Ladysmith Av. Ilf. CM33 49
Ladysmith Rd. E16 CG38 58
Ladysmith Rd. N17 CB30 39
Ladysmith Rd. N18 CB28 39
Ladysmith Rd. SE9 CL46 78
Ladysmith Rd. Enf. CA24 30
Ladysmith Rd. Har. BH30 36
Ladysmith Rd. Kes. CG57 97
Ladysmith Rd. St. Alb. BG13 9
Lady Somerset Rd. NW5 BV35 47
Lady Spencer Gro. St. Alb. BG14 9
Lady Vane Clo. Ton. DB68 117
Stumble Hill
Ladywell Rd. SE13 CE46 77
Ladywell St. E15 CG37 58
Ladywood Av. Orp. CN53 88
Ladywood Clo. Rick. AX24 26
Ladywood Rd. Dart. CZ49 80
Ladywood Rd. Surb. BM55 85
Lafone Av. Felt. BD48 74
Lafone St. SE1 CA41 67
Lagger Clo. Ch. St. G. AQ27 34
Lagger, The Ch. St. G. AQ27 34
Laglands Clo. Reig. BT69 121
Lagonda Av. Ilf. CN29 40
Lagoon Rd. Orp. CO53 89
Lahore Rd. Croy. BZ53 87
Sydenham Rd.
Laidon Sq. Hem. H. AX11 8
Laindon Av. E15 CG35 49
Leytonstone Rd.
Laing Dene Nthlt. BD37 54
Laings Av. Mitch. BU51 86
Lainson St. SW18 BS47 76
Laird Ave. Grays. DE41 71
Lairdale Clo. SE24 BZ47 77
Rosendale Rd.
Laitwood Rd. SW12 BV47 76
Lake Av. Brom. CH50 78
Lake Av. Rain. CV37 60
Lake Av. Slou. AO40 52
Lake Clo. SW19 BR49 75
Lake Rd.
Lake Clo. Wey. AX59 92
Lakedale Rd. SE18 CG43 68
Lake End Rd. Maid. AK40 61
Lakefield Rd. N22 BY30 38
Lakefields Clo. Rain. CV37 60
Lake Gdns. Dag. CR35 50
Lake Gdns. Rich. BJ48 74
Lake Gdns. Wall. BV55 86
Lakehall Gdns. Th. Hth. BY53 86
Lakehall Rd. Th. Hth. BY53 86
Lake House Rd. E11 CH34 49
Lakehurst Rd. Epsom BO56 94
Lakeland Clo. Chig. CO28 41
Lakeland Clo. Har. BG29 36
Lakenheath N14 BW25 29
Lake Rise Rom. CT30 41
Lake Rd. SW19 BR49 75
Lake Rd. Croy. CD55 87
Lake Rd. Rom. CP31 50
Lake Rd. Vir. W. AQ52 82
Lake Rd. Wal. Abb. CG14 13
Lakers Rise Bans. BU61 104
Lakeside W13 BK39 54
Edge Hill Rd.
Lakeside Enf. BW24 29
Lakeside Rain. CV37 60
Lakeside Red. BV69 121
Kingfisher Dr.
Lakeside Wall. BV56 95
Lakeside, Wey. BB55 83
Lakeside, Wok. AP63 100
Lakeside Av. Ilf. CJ31 49
Lakeside Clo. SE25 CA51 87
Lakeside Clo. Ruis. BA32 44
Lakeside Clo. Sid. CP46 79
Lakeside Clo. Wok. AP63 100
Lakeside Ct. Borwd. BM25 28
Lakeside Cres. Barn. BU25 29
Lake Side Cres. Brwd. DB27 42
Lakeside Dr. Brom. CK55 88
Lakeside Dr. Esher BG57 93
Lakeside Dr. Slou. AP37 52
Lakeside Rd. N13 BX28 38
Lakeside Rd. W14 BQ41 65
Lakeside Rd. Slou. AW43 63
Lakeside Rd. Wal. Cr. CC17 21
Lakeside Way, Wem. BM35 46
Lakes Rd. Kes. CJ56 97
Lakeswood Rd. Orp. CL53 88
Lake, The Bush. BG26 36
Lake Vw. Edg. BL28 37
Lake View, Pot. B. BT20 20
Lakeview Rd. SE27 BY49 76
Lakeview Rd. Sev. CU65 107
Lake View Rd. Well. CO45 69
Lakis Clo. NW3 BT35 47
Flask Walk
Laleham Av. NW7 BN27 37
Laleham Ct. Wok. AS61 100
Chobham Rd.
Laleham Rd. SE6 CF47 77
Laleham Rd. Shep. AY52 83
Laleham Rd. Stai. AV49 72
Lalor St. SW6 BR44 65
Lambarde Av. SE9 CL49 78
Lambarde Rd. Sev. CU64 107
Lamb Cl. Hat. BP13 10
Lamb Clo. Til. DH44 71
Coleridge Rd.
Lamberhurst Clo. Orp. CP54 89
Lamberhurst Rd. SE27 BY49 76
Lamberhurst Rd. Dag. CQ33 50
Lambert Av. Rich. BM45 65
Lambert Av. Slou. AS41 62
Lambert Clo. West. CJ61 106
Sunningvale Av.
Lambert Rd. E16 CH39 58
Lambert Rd. N12 BT28 38
Lambert Rd. SW2 BX46 76
Lambert Rd. Bans. BS60 95
Lamberts Pl. Croy. BZ54 87
Lamberts Rd. Surb. BL53 85
Lambert St. N1 BY36 56
Lambert Way N12 BT28 38
Lambeth Bridge SW1 BX42 4
Lambeth High St. SE1 BX42 4
Lambeth High St. SE1 BX42 66
Lambeth Hill EC4 BZ40 57
Upper Thames St.
Lambeth Mews SE11 BX42 2
Lambeth Mews SE11 BX42 66
Lambeth Palace Rd. SE1 BX41 4
Lambeth Palace Rd. SE1 BX41 66
Lambeth Rd. SE1 BX41 4
Lambeth Rd. SE1 BX41 66
Lambeth Rd. Croy. BY54 86
Lambeth St. E1 CB39 2
Lambeth St. E1 CB39 57
Lambeth St. N1 BY37 2
Lambeth Wk. SE11 BX42 4
Lambeth Wk. SE11 BX42 66
Lambert Wk. Wem. BK34 45
Hutchinson Ter.
Lamb La. E8 CB36 57
Lamble St. NW5 BV35 47
Lambley Rd. Dag. CO36 59
Lambolle Pl. NW3 BU36 56
Lambolle Rd. NW3 BU36 56
Lambourn Clo. W7 BH41 64
Lambourne Av. SW19 BR49 75
Lambourne Cres. Chig. CO27 41
Lambourne Cres. Wok. AU60 91
Lambourne Dr. Brwd. DF26 122
Lambourne Gdns. E4 CE27 39
Lambourne Gdns. Bark. CN36 58
Lambourne Rd.
Lambourne Gdns. Enf. CA23 30
Lambourne Gdns. Horn. CV34 51
Lambourne Gro.
Kings. On T. BM51 85
Gloucester Rd.
Lambourne Pl. SE3 CH44 68
Shooter's Hill Rd.
Lambourne Rd. E11 CF33 48
Lambourne Rd. Bark. CN36 58
Lambourne Rd. Chig. CN28 40
Lambourne Rd. Ilf. CN34 49
Lambourn Rd. SE17 BZ42 4
Lambourn Rd. SE17 BZ43 67
Lambourn Rd. SW4 BV45 66
Lambridge Dr. Sev. CU65 107
Lambrook Ter. SW6 BR44 65
Lambs Bldgs. EC1 BZ38 2
Lambs Bldgs. EC1 BZ38 57
Errol St.
Lambs Clo. Pot. B. BX18 20
Lambs Conduit Pass. WC1 BX39 2
Lamb's Conduit Pass. WC1 BX39 56
Red Lion Sq.
Lambs Conduit St. WC1 BX38 2
Lambs Conduit St. WC1 BX38 56
Lambscroft Av. SE9 CJ48 78
Lambs Croft Way, Ger. Cr. AS30 34
Lambs La. Rain. CU39 59
Lambs Meadow Wdf. Grn. CJ30 40
Lambs Pass. EC1 BZ39 2
Lambs Pass. EC1 BZ39 57
Lambs Pass. Brent. BL42 65
Lambs Ter. N9 BZ27 39
Lamb St. E1 CA39 2
Lamb St. E1 CA39 57
Lambs Wk. Enf. BZ23 30
Lambton Av. Wal. Cr. CC19 21
Lambton Pl. W11 BS40 56
Lambton Rd. N19 BX33 47
Lambton Rd. SW20 BQ51 85
Lamb Wk. SE1 CA41 4
Lamb Wk. SE1 CA41 67
Lamb Yd. Wat. BD24 27
Lamerock Rd. Brom. CG49 78
Lamerton Rd. Ilf. CL30 40
Lamerton St. SE8 CE43 67
Lamford Clo. N17 BZ29 39
Lamington St. W6 BP42 65
Lamlash St. SE11 BY42 4
Lamlash St. SE11 BY42 66
Hayles St.
Lammas Av. Mitch. BV51 86
Lammas Ct. Stai. AU48 72
Lammas Ct. Wind. AO44 61
Lammas Dr. Stai. AU49 72
Lammas Gn. SE26 CB48 77
Lammas Hill, Esher BF56 93
Lammas La. Esher BF56 93
Lammas Mead. Brox. CD15 12
Lammas Pk. Gdns. W5 BK40 54
Lammas Pk. Rd. W5 BK40 54
Lammas Rd. E9 CC36 57
Lammas Rd. E10 CD33 48
Lammas Rd. Rich. BK49 74
Lammas Rd. Wat. BD25 27
Lammermoor Rd. SW12 BV47 76
Lamont Rd. SW10 BT43 66
Lamorbey Clo. Sid. CN47 78
Lamorna Av. Grav. DH48 81
Lamorna Clo. Orp. CO54 89
Lamorna Clo. Rad. BJ20 18
The Avenue
Lamorna Gro. Stan. BK30 36
Lampard Gro. N16 CA33 48
Lampern Sq. E2 CB38 57
Nelson Gdns.
Lampeter Clo. Wok. AS62 100
Lampeter St. N1 BZ37 2
Lampeter St. N1 BZ37 57
Lampits, Hodd. CE12 12
Lampmead Rd. SE12 CG46 78
Lamport Clo. SE18 CK42 68
Lampton Av. Houns. BF44 64
Lampton Ho. Clo. SW19 BQ49 75
Lampton Pk. Rd. Houns. BF44 64
Lampton Rd. Houns. BF44 64
Lamsey Rd. Hem. H. AX14 8
Lanacre Av. NW9 BO30 37
Lanark Clo. W5 BK39 54
Lanark Pl. W9 BT38 1
Lanark Pl. W9 BT38 56
Lanark Rd. W9 BS37 1
Lanark Rd. W9 BS38 56
Lanbury Rd. SE15 CC45 67
Lancashire Gate W1 BV40 56
Avery Row
Lancashire Rd. E17 CD30 39
Lancaster Av. E18 CH31 49
Lancaster Av. SE27 BY48 76
Lancaster Av. SW19 BQ49 75
Lancaster Av. Bark. CN36 58
Lancaster Av. Barn. BT22 29
Lancaster Av. Mitch. BX53 86
Lancaster Clo. Brom. CG52 88
Lancaster Clo. Brwd. DA25 33
Lancaster Clo.
Kings. On T. BK49 74
Lancaster Clo. Wall. BX55 86
Beddington La.
Lancaster Cotts. Rich. BL46 75
Lancaster Pk.
Lancaster Ct. SW6 BR43 65
Lancaster Ct. W2 BT40 3
Lancaster Ct. W2 BT40 56
Lancaster Ct. Bans. BR60 94
Lancaster Dr. NW3 BU36 56
Lancaster Dr. Horn. CU35 50
Lancaster Gdns. SW19 BR49 75
Lancaster Gdns. W2 BT40 56
Lancaster Gdns. W13 BJ40 54
Lancaster Gdns.
Kings. On T. BK49 74
Lancaster Gate W2 BT40 3
Lancaster Gate W2 BT40 56
Lancaster Gds. NW3 BU36 56
Lambolle Pla.
Lancaster Gro. NW3 BT36 56
Lancaster Ms. W2 BT40 3
Lancaster Ms. W2 BT40 56
Lancaster Ms. Rich. BL46 75
Richmond Hill
Lancaster Pk. Rich. BL46 75
Lancaster Pl. SW19 BQ49 75
Lancaster Pl. WC2 BX40 4
Lancaster Pl. WC2 BX40 56
Lancaster Pl. Houns. BD44 64
Lancaster Rd. E7 CH36 58
Lancaster Rd. E11 CG34 49
Lancaster Rd. E17 CC30 39
Lancaster Rd. N4 BY33 47
Lancaster Rd. N11 BW29 38
Lancaster Rd. N18 CA28 39
Lancaster Rd. NW10 BP35 46
Lancaster Rd. SE25 CA51 87
Lancaster Rd. SW19 BQ49 75
Lancaster Rd. W5 BK40 54
Lancaster Rd. W10 BQ41 65
Lancaster Rd. W11 BQ40 55
Lancaster Rd. Barn. BT24 29
Lancaster Rd. Enf. BZ23 30
Lancaster Rd. Epp. CR16 23
Lancaster Rd. Har. BF32 45
Lancaster Rd. Nthlt. BG36 54
Lancaster Rd. St. Alb. BH12 9
Lancaster Rd. Sthl. BE40 54
Lancaster Rd. Uxb. AX36 53
Lancaster St. SE1 BY41 4
Lancaster St. SE1 BY41 66
Lancaster Ter. W2 BT40 3
Lancaster Way, Welw. BQ5 5
Lancaste Wk. Hayes BA39 53
Lancefield St. W10 BR38 55
Lancell St. N16 CA34 48
Lancelot Av. Wem. BK35 45
Lancelot Cres. Wem. BK35 45
Lancelot Gdns. Barn. BV26 38
Lancelot Pl. SW7 BU41 3
Lancelot Pl. SW7 BU41 66
Lancelot Rd. Ilf. CN29 40
Lancelot Rd. Well. CO45 69
Lancelot Rd. Wem. BK35 45
Lance Rd. Har. BG33 45
Lanchester Rd. N6 BU32 47
Lancing Av. Felt. BB48 73
Lancing Gdns. N9 CA26 39
Lancing Rd. W13 BJ40 54
Drayton Gn. Rd.
Lancing Rd. Croy. BX54 86
Lancing Rd. Ilf. CM32 49
Lancing Rd. Orp. CO55 89
Lancing Rd. Rom. CW29 42
Lancing St. NW1 BW38 1
Lancing St. NW1 BW38 56
Lancing Way, Rick. AZ25 26
Landcroft Rd. SE22 CA46 77
Landells Rd. SE22 CA46 77
Land End, Hat. BO14 10
Lander Rd. Grays. DE42 71
Landfield St. E5 CB34 48
Landfold Clo. Rick. AY27 35
Landford Rd. SW15 BQ45 65
Landgrove Rd. SW19 BS49 76
Landguard, Saw. CQ6 6
Landmead Rd. Wal. Cr. CD18 21
Landon Pl. SW1 BU41 3
Landon Pl. SW1 BU41 66
Landon Way, Ashf. BA50 73
Landon Wk. E1 CE40 57
Shirbutt St.
Landor Rd. SW9 BX45 66
Landor Wk. W12 BP41 65
Landport Way SE15 CA43 67
Landra Gdns. N21 BY25 29
Landridge Rd. SW6 BR44 65
Landrock Rd. N8 BX32 47
Landsbury Dr. Hayes BC38 53
Landscape Rd. Warl. CB63 105
Landscape Rd. Wdf. Grn. CH29 40
Lands End, Bush. BK25 27
Landseer Av. E12 CL35 49
Landseer Av. Grav. DE48 81
Landseer Clo. Edg. BM30 37
Landseer Rd. N19 BX34 47
Landseer Rd. Enf. CB25 30
Landseer Rd. N. Mal. BN54 85
Landseer Rd. Sutt. BS57 95
Lanstead Rd. SE18 CM43 68
Land St. N1 BZ38 2
Landview Gdns. Ong. CX18 24
Landway, The Orp. CP52 89
Landway, The Sev. CW63 108
Landway, The Sev. CX62 108
Lane App. NW7 BR28 37
Lane Ave. Green. DB46 80
Lanebridge Rd. Welw. G C. BQ7 5
Lane Clo. NW2 BP34 46
Lane Clo. Wey. AW56 92
Lane Ct. SW11 BU46 76
Thurleigh Rd.
Lane End, Bexh. CR45 69
Lane End, Epsom BN60 94
Lanefield Wk.
Welw. G. C. BQ8 5
Lane Gdns. Bush. BH26 36
La Plata Gro. Brwd. DA27 42
Lanercost Gdns. N14 BX26 38
Lanercost Rd. SW2 BY48 76
Lanes Av. Grav. DF48 81
Laneside, Chis. CL49 78
Laneside, Edg. BN28 37
Laneside Av. Dag. CQ33 50
Lane, The NW8 BT37 1
Lane, The NW8 BT37 56
Lane, The SE3 CH45 68
Casterbridge Rd.
Lane, The Vir. W. AS52 82
La Tourne Gdns. Orp. CM55 88
Lane Way SW15 BP46 75
Sunnymead Rd.
Lanfranc Rd. E3 CD37 57
Lanfranc St. SE1 BY41 4
Lanfrey Pl. W14 BR42 65
North End Rd.
Langafel Clo. Long. DC51 90
Langaller La. Lthd. BF64 102
Langbourne Av. N6 BV34 47
Langbourne Way, Esher BJ56 93
Langbrook Rd. SE3 CJ45 68
Lang Clo. Lthd. BF65 102
Langcroft Clo. Cars. BU55 86
Langdale Av. Mitch. BU52 86
Langdale Clo. SE17 BY44 66
Olney St.
Langdale Clo. Wok. AR61 100
Langdale Ct. Hem. H. AY12 8
Wharfedale
Langdale Ct. Hem. H. AY12 8
Langdale Cr. Bexh. CR43 69
Langdale Dr. Hayes BB37 53
Langdale Gdns. Grnf. BJ38 54
Langdale Gdns. Horn. CU35 50
Langdale Gdns. Wal. Cr. CC21 30
Langdale Rd. SE10 CE43 67
Langdale Rd. Th. Hth. BY52 86
Langdale St. E1 CB39 57
Langdale Wk. Grav. DF48 81
Langdon Ct. NW10 BO37 55
Craven Park
Langdon Cres. E6 CL37 58
Langdon Dr. NW9 BN33 46
Langdon Pk. Rd. N6 BW33 47
Langdon Pl. SW14 BN45 65
Rosemary La.
Langdon Rd. E6 CL37 58
Langdon Rd. Brom. CH52 88
Langdon Rd. Mord. BT53 86
Langdon Shaw, Sid. CN49 78
Langford Clo. NW8 BT37 1
Langford Clo. E8 CB35 48
Ferncliffe Est.
Langford Clo.NW8 BT37 56
Langford Ct. NW8 BT37 56
Langford Cres. Barn. BU24 29
Langford Green Gdns. SE5 CA45 67
Langford Pl.NW8 BT37 1
Langford Pl. NW8 BT37 56
Langford Pl. Sid. CO48 79
Langford Rd. SW6 BS44 66
Langford Rd. Barn. BU24 29
Langford Rd. Wdf. Grn. CJ29 40
Langfords, Buck. H. CJ27 40
Langham Clo. N15 BY31 47
Langham Rd.
Langham Ct. Horn. CV33 51
Langham Dene Ken. BY57 95
Langham Dene Ken. BY61 104
Langham Dr. Rom. CO32 50
Langham Gdns. N21 BY25 29
Langham Gdns. W13 BJ40 54
Garden Rd.
Langham Gdns. Edg. BN29 37
Langham Gdns. Rich. BK49 74
Langham Gdns. Wem. BK34 45
Langham Ho. Rich. BK49 74
Langham Pl. N15 BY31 47
Langham Pl. W1 BV39 1
Langham Pl. W1 BV39 56
Langham Pl. Egh. AS49 72
Langham Rd. N15 BY31 47
Langham Rd. SW20 BQ51 85
Langham Rd. Edg. BN29 37
Langham Rd. Tedd. BJ49 74
Langham St. W1 BV39 1
Langham St. W1 BV39 56
Langhedge Clo. N18 CA29 39
Langhorne Rd. Dag. CR36 59
Langland Ct. Nthwd. BA29 35
Langland Cres. E. Stan. BK30 36
Langland Cres. N. Stan. BL30 36
Langland Cres. S. Stan. BL31 46
Langland Cres. W. Stan. BK30 36
Langland Dr. Pnr. BE29 36
Langland Gdns. NW3 BS35 47
Langland Gdns. Croy. CD55 87
Langlands Dr. Dart. CZ49 80
Langlands Rise, Epsom BN60 94
Langler Rd. NW10 BQ37 55
Langler Rd. NW10 BQ38 55
Langley Av. Hem. H. AY15 8
Langley Av. Ruis. BC34 44
Langley Av. Surb. BK54 84
Langley Av. Wor. Pk. BQ54 85
Langley Broom Ave. Slou. AS42 62
Langleybury La. Kings L. AZ22 26
Langley Clo. Epsom BN63 103
Langley Clo. Guil. AR70 118
Langley Cl. Rom. CV29 42
Clematis Cl.
Langley Ct. SE9 CL46 78
Langley Ct. WC2 BX40 4
Langley Ct. WC2 BX40 56
Long Acre
Langley Ct. W. Wick. CF54 87
Langley Cres. E11 CH33 49
Langley Cres. Dag. CP36 59
Langley Cres. Edg. BN27 37
Langley Cres. Hayes BB43 63
Langley Cres. St. Alb. BG12 9
Langley Dr. E11 CH33 49
Langley Dr. W3 BM41 65
Langley Dr. Brwd. DA27 42
Langley Gdns. Dag. CP36 59
Langley Gdns. Orp. CL53 88
Langley Gro. N. Mal. BO51 85
Langley High St. Slou. AT42 62
Langley Hill, Kings L. AY18 17
Langley Hill Clo. Kings L. AZ18 17
Langley La. SW8 BX43 66
Langley La. Epsom BM66 112
Langley La. Wat. BB19 17

65

Leadenhall Pl. EC3 CA39 2
Leadenhall Pl. EC3 CA39 57
Lime St.
Leadenhall St. EC3 CA39 2
Leadenhall St. EC3 CA39 57
Leadenham Ct. E3 CE38 57
Campbell Rd.
Leader Av. E12 CL35 49
Leadings, The Wem. BN34 46
Leaf Clo. Nthwd. BA29 35
Leaf Gro. SE27 BY49 76
Leafield Clo. SW16 BY50 76
Leafield Clo. Wok. AQ62 100
Winnington Way
Leafield La. Sid. CQ49 79
Leafield Rd. SW20 BR52 85
Leafield Rd. Sutt. BS55 86
Leaford Cres. Wat. BB22 26
Leafy Gro. Kes. CJ56 97
Leafy Oak Rd. SE12 CJ49 78
Leafy Way, Brwd. DE26 122
Leafy Way, Croy. CB55 87
Leagrave St. E5 CC34 48
Lea Hall Rd. E10 CE33 48
Leaholme Waye, Ruis. BA32 44
Leahurst Rd. SE13 CF46 77
Leake Ct. SE1 BX41 4
Leake Ct. SE1 BX41 66
Addington St.
Leake St. SE1 BX41 4
Leake St. SE1 BX41 66
Lealand Rd. N15 CA32 48
Leamead Av. Nthlt. BE36 54
Leamington Av. E17 CE32 48
Leamington Av. Brom. CJ49 78
Leamington Av. Mord. BR52 85
Leamington Av. Orp. CN56 97
Leamington Clo. E12 CK35 49
Leamington Clo. Brom. CJ49 78
Leamington Clo. Houns. BG46 74
Leamington Clo. Rom. CW29 42
Leamington Cres. Har. BE34 45
Leamington Gdns. Ilf. CN34 49
Leamington Pk. W3 BN39 55
Leamington Pl. Hayes BB38 53
Leamington Pl. Hayes BC38 53
Leamington Rd. Rom. CX29 42
Leamington Rd. Sthl. BD42 64
Leamington Rd. Vill. W11 BR39 55
Leamore St. W6 BQ42 65
Leamouth Rd. E14 CF39 57
Leander Dr. Grav. DJ49 81
Leander Gdns. Wat. BE22 27
Eastlea Av.
Leander Rd. SW2 BX46 76
Leander Rd. Nthlt. BF37 54
Leander Rd. Th. Hth. BX52 86
Leapale La. Guil. AR71 118
Lea Pl. Sutt. BS56 95
Lea Rd. Beck. CD51 87
Lea Rd. Enf. BZ23 30
Lea Rd. Grays. DG42 71
Lea Rd. Hodd. CF11 12
Lea Rd. Sev. CV67 117
Lea Rd. Sthl. BE42 64
Lea Rd. Wal. Abb. CE20 21
Learoyd Gdns. E6 CL40 58
Leas Clo. Chess. BL57 94
Leas Dale SE9 CL48 78
Leas Dr. Iver. AV39 52
Leas Green, Chis. CN50 78
Lea Side, Lthd. BF65 102
Leaside Av. N10 BV31 47
Leaside Rd. E5 CB33 48
Leas La. Warl. CC62 105
Leasowes Rd. E10 CE33 48
Leas Rd. Guil. AR71 118
Leas Rd. Warl. CC62 105
Leas, The Bush. BE23 27
Leas, The Hem. H. AZ16 17
Leas, The Upmin. CY33 51
Leasway, Brwd. DB27 42
Leasway, Grays. DE40 71
Leasway, Upmin. CY35 51
Leat Clo. E. Mol. BH53 84
Leat Clo. Saw. CQ5 6
Station Rd.
Lea, The Egh. AV51 82
Leather Bottle Grn. Belv. CQ41 69
Leather Bottle La. Belv. CQ42 69
Leather Clo. Mitch. BV51 86
Leatherdale St. E1 CC38 57
Portelet Rd.
Leather Gdns. E15 CG37 58
Leatherhead By-pass, Lthd. BH65 102
Leatherhead Clo. N16 CA33 48
Leatherhead Rd. Chess. BK59 93
Leatherhead Rd. Cob. BG61 102
Leatherhead Road, Leath. AZ68 110
Leatherhead Rd. Lthd. BF66 111
Leatherhead Rd. Lthd. BG60 93
Leatherhead Rd. Lthd. & Ash. BK64 102
Leather La. EC1 BY39 2
Leather La. EC1 BY38 56
Leathermarket St. SE1 CA41 4
Leathermarket St. SE1 CA41 67
Leathsail Rd. Har. BF34 45
Leathwaite Rd. SW11 BU45 66
Leathwell Rd. SE8 CE44 67
Lea Vale Dart. CS45 69
Lea Valley Rd. E4 CC25 30
Lea Valley Rd. Enf. CC24 30
Lea Valley Trading Est. E4 CC28 39
Leaveland Clo. Beck. CE52 87
Leaver Gdns. Grnf. BH37 54
Leavesden Rd. Stan. BJ29 36
Leavesden Rd. Wat. BC22 26
Leavesden Rd. Wey. AZ56 92
Leaves Green Cres. Kes. CJ59 97
Leaves Grn. Rd. Kes. CJ58 97
Lea Vw. Wal. Abb. CE20 21
Lea View Ho. E5 CB33 48
Leavsden Rd. Stan. BJ29 36
Leaway E10 CC33 48
Leazes Ave. Cat. BY65 104
Lebanon Av. Felt. BD49 74
Lebanon Clo. Wat. BA21 26
Lebanon Ct. Twick. BJ47 74
Lebanon Dr. Cob. BF60 93
Lebanon Gdns. SW18 BS46 76
Lebanon Gdns. West. CJ62 106
Lebanon Pk. Twick. BJ47 74
Lebanon Rd. SW18 BS46 76
Lebanon Rd. Croy. CA54 87
Lebrun Sq. SE3 CH45 68
Lechmere Av. Chig. CM28 40
Lechmere Av. Wdf. Grn. CJ30 40
Lechmere Rd. NW2 BP36 55
Leckford Rd. SW18 BT47 76
Leckwith Av. Bexh. CQ43 69
Lecky St. SW7 BT42 3
Lecky St. SW7 BT42 66
Leconfield Av. SW13 BO45 65
Leconfield Rd. N5 BZ35 48
Leconfield Wk. Horn. CV36 60
Airfield Way
Lectern Ct. St. Alb. BH15 9
Creighton Av.
Leda Av. Enf. CC22 30
Leda Rd. SE18 CK41 68
Ledbury Ms. N. W11 BS40 56
Ledbury Ms. W. W11 BS40 56
Ledbury Pl. Croy. BZ56 96
Ledbury Rd. W11 BR39 55
Ledbury Rd. Croy. BZ56 96
Ledbury Rd. Reig. BS70 121
Ledbury St. SE15 CB43 67
Ledger Clo. Guil. AT69 118
Ledger Dri. Wey. AV56 91
Ledger La. Maid. AH44 61
Ledger's Rd. Slou. AO41 61
Ledgers Rd. Warl. CE62 105
Ledrington Rd. SE19 CA50 77
Ledway Dr. Wem. BL33 46
Lee Av. Rom. CQ32 50
Lee Bri. SE13 CF45 67
Leechcroft Av. Sid. CN46 78
Leechcroft Av. Swan. CT52 89
Leech La. Lthd. BM66 112
Lee Church St. SE13 CG45 68
Lee Clo. E17 CC30 39
Lee Conservancy Rd. E9 CD35 48
Leecroft Rd. Barn. BR24 28
Leecroft Rd. Wall. BV55 86
Leeds Pl. N4 BX33 47
Leeds Rd. Ilf. CM33 49
Leeds Rd. Slou. AP40 52
Leeds St. N18 CB28 39
Lee Farm Clo. Chesh. AQ18 16
Lee Gdns. Av. Horn. CX33 51
Leegate Ho. SE12 CG46 78
Lee Grn. SE12 CG45 68
Lee Grn. Orp. CO53 89
Lee Green La. Epsom. BM65 103
Lee Gro. Chig. CL27 40
Lee High Rd. SE12 CG45 68
Lee High Rd. SE13 CF45 67
Leeke St. WC1 BX38 2
Leeke St. WC1 BX38 56
Leeland Rd. W13 BJ40 54
Broadway
Leeland Ter. W13 BJ40 54
Leeland Way, NW10 BO35 46
Lee La. St. Alb. BH15 9
Leeming Rd. Borwd. BL22 28
Lee Pk. SE3 CG45 68
Lee Park Way, N18 CC28 39
Lee Rd. NW7 BQ29 37
Lee Rd. SE3 CG45 68
Lee Rd. SW19 BS51 86
Lee Rd. Enf. CB25 30
Lee Rd. Grnf. BK37 54
Lees Av. Nthwd. BB30 35
Leeside Barn. BR25 28
Leeside Cres. NW11 BR32 46
Leeside Rd. N18 CC29 39
Leeson Rd. SE24 BY45 66
Mayall Rd.
Leesons Hill Brom. CO52 89
Leesons Hill Chis. CN52 88
Leesons Way Orp. CN51 88
Lees Pl. W1 BV40 3
Lees Pl. W1 BV40 56
Lees Rd. Uxb. AZ38 53
Lees, The Croy. CD55 87
Lee St. E8 CA37 2
Lee St. E8 CA37 57
Lee Ter. SE3 CG45 68
Lee Vw. Enf. BY23 29
Leeward Gdns. SW19 BR49 75
Leeway SE8 CD42 67
Leewood Pl. Swan. CS52 89
Leewood Way, Lthd. BD67 111
Lefevre Wk. E3 CD37 57
Lefroy Rd. W12 BO41 65
Legard Rd. N5 BY34 47
Legatt Rd. SE9 CJ46 78
Leggatt Rd. E15 CF37 57
Leggatts Clo. Wat. BB21 26
Leggatts Rise, Wat. BC21 26
Leggatts Way, Wat. BB21 26
Leggatts Wood Av. Wat. BC21 26
Legge St. SE13 CF46 77
Leggfield Ter. Hem. H. AV13 7
Leghorn Rd. NW10 BO37 55
Leghorn Rd. SE18 CM42 68
Legion Clo. N1 BY36 56
Legion Ct. Mord. BS53 86
Legion Rd. Grnf. BG37 54
Legon Av. Rom. CS33 50
Legrace Av. Houns. BD44 64
Leicester Av. Mitch. BX52 86
Leicester Clo. Wor. Pk. BQ56 94
Leicester Ct. WC2 BW40 3
Leicester Ct. WC2 BW40 56
Cranbourn St.
Leicester Gdns. Ilf. CN33 49
Leicester Pl. WC2 BW40 3
Leicester Pl. WC2 BW40 56
Lisle St.
Leicester Rd. E11 CH32 49
Leicester Rd. N2 BU31 47
Leicester Rd. NW10 BN36 55
Leicester Rd. Barn. BS25 29
Leicester Rd. Croy. CA54 87
Leicester Rd. Til. DF44 71
Leicester Sq. WC2 BW40 3
Leicester Sq. WC2 BW40 56
Leicester St. WC2 BW40 3
Leicester St. WC2 BW40 56
Lisle St.
Leigham Av. SW16 BX48 76
Leigham Ct. Rd. SW16 BX48 76
Leigham Dr. Islw. BH43 64
Leigham Vale SW16 BX48 76
Leigh Av. Ilf. CJ31 49
Leigh Clo. N. Mal. BN52 85
Leigh Clo. Wey. AV57 91
Leigh Common. Welw. G. C. BR9 5
Leigh Court Clo. Cob. BD60 93
Leigh Ct. Har. BH33 45
Leigh Cres. Croy. CE57 96
Leigh Dr. Rom. CV28 42
Leigh Gdns. NW10 BQ37 55
Leigh Hill Rd. Cob. BD60 93
Leigh Hunt St. SE1 BZ41 4
Leigh Hunt St. SE1 BZ41 67
Leigh Orchard Clo. SW16 BX48 76
Ivyday Gro.
Leigh Pk. Slou. AQ43 62
Leigh Pl. Cob. BD61 102
Leigh Pl. Well. CO44 69
Leigh Place La. Gdse. CC69 114
Leigh Place Rd. Reig. BP73 120
Leigh Rd. E6 CL36 58
Leigh Rd. E10 CF33 48
Leigh Rd. N5 BY35 47
Leigh Rd. Cob. BC60 92
Leigh Rd. Grav. DG48 81
Leigh Rd. Houns. BG45 64
Leigh Rood Wat. BE27 36
Leigh St. WC1 BX38 2
Leigh St. WC1 BX38 56
Leigh Ter. Orp. CO52 89
Leighton Av. E12 CL35 49
Leighton Av. Pnr. BE31 45
Leighton Buzzard Rd. Hem. H. AW10 8
Leighton Clo. Edg. BM30 37
Leighton Cres. NW5 BW35 47
Leighton Gro.
Leighton Gdns. NW10 BP37 55
Leighton Gdns. Sth. Croy. CB60 96
Leighton Gdns. Til. DG43 71
Leighton Gro. NW5 BW35 47
Leighton Ho. W14 BR41 65
Leighton Pl. NW5 BW35 47
Leighton Rd.
Leighton Rd. NW5 BW35 47
Leighton Rd. W13 BJ41 64
Leighton Rd. Enf. CA25 30
Leighton Rd. Har. BG30 36
Leighton St. E. Croy. BY54 86
Leighton St. W. Croy. BY54 86
Leighton Way, Epsom BN60 94
Leinster Av. SW14 BN45 65
Leinster Gdns. W2 BT39 1
Leinster Gdns. W2 BT39 56
Leinster Ms. W2 BT40 3
Leinster Ms. W2 BT40 56
Leinster Pl. W2 BT39 1
Leinster Pl. W2 BT39 56
Leinster Rd. N10 BV31 47
Leinster Rd. NW6 BS38 56
Leinster Sq. W2 BS40 56
Leinster Ter. W2 BT40 3
Leinster Ter. W2 BT40 56
Leith Clo. NW9 BN33 46
Leithcote Gdns. SW16 BX49 76
Leithcote Path SW16 BX48 76
Ivyday Gro.
Leith Hill Orp. CN51 88
Leith Hill Gn. Orp. CO51 89
Leigh Hill
Leith Park Rd. Grav. DG47 81
Leith Rd. N22 BY30 38
Leith Rd. Epsom BO59 94
Lela Av. Houns. BD44 64
Lelitia Clo. E8 CA37 57
Broadway Mkt. Est.
Leman Pl. E1 CB39 2
Leman St. E1 CA39 2
Leman St. E1 CA39 57
Leman St. E1 CB39 57
Good St.
Lemark Clo. Stan. BK28 36
Haig Rd.
Le May Av. SE12 CH48 78
Lemmon Rd. SE10 CG43 68
Lemna Rd. E11 CG33 49
Lemonfield Dr. Wat. BE19 18
Lemonwell Ct. SE9 CM46 78
Lemsford Clo. N15 CB32 48
Lemsford Ct. Borwd. BN24 28
Lemsford Rd. Hat. BP11 10
Lemsford Rd. St. Alb. BH13 9
Lemsfor La. Welw. G. C. BP8 5
Lena Gdns. W6 BQ41 65
Lendal Ter. SW4 BX45 66
Lenelby Rd. Surb. BM54 85
Lenham Rd. SE12 CG45 68
Lenham Rd. Bexh. CQ43 69
Lenham Rd. Sutt. BS56 95
Lenham Rd. Th. Hth. BZ51 87
Lenmore Ave. Grays. DE41 71
Lennard Av. W. Wick. CG55 88
Lennard Clo. W. Wick. CG55 88
Lennard Rd. SE20 CC50 77
Lennard Rd. Beck. CD50 77
Lennard Rd. Brom. CK54 88
Lennard Rd. Croy. BZ54 87
Lennard Rd. Sev. CT63 107
Lennard Row, S. Ock. CW40 60
Lennox Av. E17 CE32 48
Lennox Av. Grav. DF47 81
Lennox Clo. Rom. CT32 50
Lennox Gdns. NW10 BO35 46
Lennox Gdns. SW1 BU41 3
Lennox Gdns. SW1 BU41 66
Lennox Gdns. Croy. BY56 95
Lennox Gdns. Ilf. CK33 49
Lennox Gdns. Ms. SW1 BU41 3
Lennox Gdns. Ms. SW1 BU41 66
Lennox Rd. E17 CD32 48
Lennox Rd. N4 BX34 47
Lennox Rd. Grav. DF46 81
Lennox Rd. E. Grav. DG47 81
Lensbury Clo. Wal. Cr. CD17 21
Lensbury Way SE2 CP41 69
Lens Rd. E7 CJ36 58
Lenthall Ave. Grays. DD41 71
Lenthall Pl. SW7 BT42 66
Gloucester Rd.
Lenthall Rd. E8 CA36 57
Lenthall Rd. Loug. CM24 31
Lenthorpe Rd. SE10 CG42 68
Lentmead Rd. Brom. CG48 78
Lenton Ri. Rich. BL45 65
Lenton St. SE18 CM42 68
Leof Cres. SE6 CE49 77
Leominster Rd. Mord. BT53 86
Leominster Wk. Mord. BT53 86
Leonard Ave. Sev. CU61 107
Leonard Av. Mord. BT53 86
Leonard Av. Rom. CS33 50
Leonard Av. Swans. DC47 81
Leonard Rd. E4 CE29 39
Leonard Rd. E7 CH35 49
Leonard Rd. N9 CA27 39
Leonard Rd. SW16 BW51 86
Leonard Rd. Sthl. BD41 64
Leonard Robbins Path SE28 CO40 59
Tawney Rd.
Leonard St. E16 CK40 58
Leonard St. EC2 BZ38 2
Leonard St. EC2 BZ38 57
Leonard Way, Brwd. CZ28 42
Leontine Clo. SE15 CB43 67
Bells Gdns.
Leopold Av. SW19 BR49 75
Leopold Rd. E17 CE32 48
Leopold Rd. N2 BT31 47
Leopold Rd. N18 CB28 39
Albany Rd.
Leopold Rd. NW10 BO36 55
Leopold Rd. SW19 BR49 75
Leopold Rd. W5 BL40 55
Leopold St. E3 CD39 57
Leo St. SE15 CB43 67
Leo Yd. EC1 BY38 2
Leo Yard EC1 BY38 56
Gt. Sutton St.
Lepale Rd. Guil. AR71 118
Lepe Clo. Brom. CG49 78
Le Personne Rd. Cat. BZ64 105
Leppoc Rd. SW4 BW46 76
Leroy St. SE1 CA41 4
Leroy St. SE1 CA42 4
Leroy St. SE1 CA42 67
Lesbourne Rd. Reig. BS71 121
Lescombe Clo. SE23 CD48 77
Lescombe Rd. SE23 CD48 77
Lesley Clo. Bex. CR47 79
Lesley Clo. Grav. DF50 81
Lesley Clo. Swan. CS52 89
Leslie Gdns. Sutt. BS57 95
Leslie Gro. Croy. BZ54 87
Leslie Pk. Rd. Croy. CA54 87
Leslie Pl. Croy. CA54 87
Leslie Rd. E11 CF35 48
Leslie Rd. E16 CH39 58
Leslie Rd. N2 BT31 47
Leslie Rd. Dor. BK70 119
Leslie Rd. Wok. AP58 91
Leslie Smith Sq. SE18 CL43 68
Nightingale Vale
Lesness Rd. Belv. CR43 69
Lesney Fm. Est. Erith CT43 69
Lesney Pk. Erith CS43 69
Lesney Pk. Rd. Erith CS43 69
Lessada St. E3 CC37 57
Lessar Av. SW4 BV46 76
Lessingham Av. Ilf. CL31 49
Lessingham Rd. SW17 BU49 76
Lessing St. SE23 CD47 77
Lessington Av. Rom. CS32 50
Lessness Av. Bexh. CP43 69
Lessness Pk. Belv. CQ42 69
Lessness Rd. Belv. CR43 69
Stapley Rd.
Lessness Rd. Mord. BT53 86
Lester Av. E15 CG38 58
Leston Spur. Slou. AP39 52
Leswin Pl. N16 CA34 48
Leswin Rd.
Leswin Rd. N16 CA34 48
Letchfield Chesh. AQ19 16
Letchford Cotts. Har. BF30 36
Letchford Gdns. NW10 BP38 55
Letchford Mews NW10 BP38 55
Letchford Gdns.
Letchmore Heath Rd. Wat. BG22 27
Letchmore Hth. Rd. Wat. BG23 27
Letchmore Rd. Rad. BJ21 27
Letchworth Av. Felt. BB47 73
Letchworth Clo. Brom. CH53 88
Letchworth Clo. Wat. BD28 36
Letchworth Dr. Brom. CH53 88
Letchworth St. SW17 BU49 76
Lethbridge Clo. SE13 CF44 67
Letter Box La. Sev. CV68 117
Letterstone Rd. SW6 BR43 65
Varna Rd.
Lettice St. SW6 BR44 65
Lettsom St. SE5 CA44 67
Leucha Rd. E17 CD32 48
Levana Ct. SW19 BR47 75
Victoria Dr.
Levehurst Way SW4 BX44 66
Leven Clo. Wal. Cr. CC20 21
Leven Clo. Wat. BD28 36
Levendale Rd. SE23 CD48 77
Leven Dr. Wal. Cr. CC20 21
Leven Rd. E14 CF39 57
Leven Way, Hayes BB39 53
Leven Way, Hem. H. AX11 8
Lomond Rd.
Leveret Clo. Croy. CF58 96
Leveret Clo. Croy. CF59 9
Leveret Clo. Wat. BC20 1
Leveret Pla. SW3 BU42 6
Denyer St.
Leverett St. SW1 BU42 6
Denyer St.
Leverholme Gdns. SE9 CL49 7
Leverington Pl. N1 BZ38
Leverson St. SW16 BW50 7
Lever Sq. Grays. DF42 7
Leverstock Grn. Hem. H. AZ13
Leverstock Grn. Rd. Hem. H. AZ13
Leverstock Grn. Way, Hem. H. BA13
Lever St. EC1 BY38
Lever St. EC1 BY38 5
Leverton St. NW5 BW35 4
Leveson Rd. Grays. DG41 7
Levett Gdns. Ilf. CN35 4
Levett Rd. Bark. CN36 5
Levett Rd. Lthd. BJ63 10
Levine Gdns. Bark. CP37 5
Levison Way N19 BW33 4
Ashbrook Rd.
Levyisdene, Guil. AU70 11
Lewes Clo. Nthlt. BF36 5
Lewesdon Clo. SW19 BQ47 7
Lewes Rd. N12 BU28 3
Lewes Rd. Brom. CJ51 8
Lewes Rd. Rom. CV28 4
Leweston Pl. N16 CA33 4
Lewes Way, Rick. BA24 2
Lewgars Av. NW9 BN32 4
Lewin Rd. SW14 BN45 6
Lewin Rd. SW16 BW50 7
Lewin Rd. Bexh. CQ46 7
Lewins Rd. Epsom BM60 9
Lewins Rd. Ger. Cr. AR31 4
Lewis Av. E17 CE30 3
Lewis Clo. Brwd. DC26 12
Lewis Cres. NW10 BN35 4
Lewis Field, Guil. AO68 10
Lewis Gdns. N2 BT30 3
Lewis Gro. SE13 CF45 6
Lewisham High St. SE13 CE46 7
Lewisham Hill SE13 CF44 6
Lewisham Pk. SE13 CE46 7
Lewisham Rd. SE13 CE44 6
Lewisham St. SW1 BW41
Lewisham St. SW1 BW41 6
Lewisham Way SE4 CD44 6
Lewisham Way SE14 CD44 6
Lewis La. Ger. Cr. AS30 3
Lewis Rd. Grav. DF51 8
Lewis Rd. Mitch. BT51 8
Lewis Rd. Rich. BK46 7
Red Lion St.
Lewis Rd. Sid. CP48 7
Lewis Rd. Sthl. BE41 6
Lewis Rd. Sutt. BS55 8
Lewis Rd. Swans. DC46 8
Lewis Rd. Well. CP45 6
Lewis St. NW1 BV36 5
Lewis Trust Blds. SW3 BU42
Lewis Trust Bldgs. SW3 BU42 6
Lewville Way SE16 CB42 6
Bonamy Estate West, The
Lexden Dr. Rom. CO32 5
Lexden Rd. W3 BM40 5
Lexden Rd. Mitch. BW52 8
Lexham Clo. Nthlt. BE36 5
Lexham Gdns. W8 BS41
Lexham Gdns. W8 BS42 6
Leham Gdns. Amer. AO22 2
Lexham Gdns. Ms. W8 BS41
Lexham Gdns. Ms. W8 BS41 6
Lexham Ms. W8 BS42 6
Lexham Wk. W8 BS41
Lexham Wk. W8 BS41 6
Lexington Clo. Borwd. BM24 2
Lexington Clo. Pur. BZ58 9
Lexington St. W1 BW39
Lexington St. W1 BW40
Lexington St. W1 BW39 5
Lexington Way, Barn. BQ24 2
Lexington Way, Upmin. CZ32 5
Lexton Gdns. SW12 BW47 7
Ley Wk. Welw. G. C. BT8
Leyborne Av. W13 BJ41 6
Leyborne Pk. Rich. BM44 6
Leybourne Av. Wey. AY60 9
Leybourne Clo. Brom. CH53 8
Leybourne Clo. Wey. AY60 9
Leybourne Rd. E11 CG33 4
Leybourne Rd. NW1 BV36 5
Leybourne Rd. NW9 BM32 4
Leybourne Rd. Uxb. BA37 5
Leybridge Ct. SE12 CH46 7
Leyburn Clo. E17 CE31 4
Leyburn Cres. Rom. CW29 4
Leyburn Gdns. Croy. CA55 8
Leyburn Gro. N18 CB29 3
Leyburn Rd. N18 CB29 3
Leyburn Rd. Rom. CV29 4
Leycroft Clo. Loug. CL25 3
Leycroft Gdns. Erith CU44 6
Leyden St. E1 CA39
Leyden St. E1 CA39 5
Leyes Rd. E16 CJ39 5
Leyfield Wor. Pk. BO54 8
Leyhill Clo. Swan. CT53 8
Ley Hill Rd. Hem. H. AR18 1
Leyland Av. St. Alb. BG14
Leyland Clo. Wal. Cr. CC17 2
Leyland Gdns. Wdf. Grn. CJ28 4
Leyland Rd. SE12 CG46 7
Leyland Rd. Enf. CD23 3
Leylands La. Slou. AV45 6
Leylang Rd. SE14 CC43 6
Leys Av. Dag. CS37 5
Leys Clo. Dag. CS36 5
Leys Clo. Har. BG32 4
Leys Clo. Uxb. AX30 3
Leysdown Av. Bexh. CS45 6
Leysdown Rd. SE9 CK48 7
Leysfield Rd. W12 BP41 6
Leys Gdns. Barn. BV25 2

Lister Rd. E11 CG33 49
Lister Rd. Til. DG45 71
Liston Rd. N17 CB30 39
Liston Rd. SW4 BW45 66
Liston Way Wdf. Grn. CJ29 40
Listowel Rd. Dag. CR34 50
Listria Pk. N16 CA34 48
Litcham Spur, Slou. AO39 52
Litchfield Av. E15 CG36 58
Litchfield Av. Mord. BR54 85
Litchfield Gdns. NW10 BP36 55
Litchfield Rd. Sutt. BT56 95
Litchfield St. WC2 BW40 56
Litchfield Way NW11 BS32 47
Litchfield Way, Brox. CD14 12
Litchfield Way, Guil. AP71 118
Litford Rd. SE5 BY44 66
Lithgows Rd. Felt. BB45 63
Lithos Rd. NW3 BS36 56
Litlington St. SE16 CB42 67
Little Acre Beck. CE52 87
Lit. Albany St. NW1 BV38 1
Lit. Albany St. NW1 BV38 56
Lit. Argyle St. W1 BW39 1
Lit. Argyll St. W1 BW39 56
Argyll St.
Lit. Aston Rd. Rom. CW30 42
Lit. Belhus Clo. S. Ock. DA38 60
Little Benty, West Dr. AX42 63
Lit. Birches Sid. CN48 78
Lit. Boltons, The SW10 BS42 3
Little Boltons, The, SW10 BS42 66
Little Bookham St. Lthd. BE66 111
Lit. Borough, Bet. BM71 120
Lit. Bournes SE21 CA49 77
Little Brays, Harl. CO11 14
Little Britain EC1 BY39 2
Little Britain EC1 BY39 56
Littlebrook Gdns. Wal. Cr. CC18 21
Littlebrook Manor Way, Dart. CX46 80
Little Brownings SE23 CB48 77
Little Buntings, Wind. AM45 61
Little Burrow, Welw. G. C. BQ9 5
Littlebury Ct. Brwd. CZ22 33
Kelvedon Grn.
Littlebury Rd. SW4 BW45 66
Little Bury St. N9 BZ26 39
Lit. Bushey La. Bush. BF23 27
Little Catkins, Harl. CK13 13
Little Cedars N12 BT28 38
Woodside Av.
Lit. Chester St. SW1 BV41 3
Little Chester St. SW1 BV41 66
Wilton Ms.
Little College La. EC4 BZ40 57
College St.
Lit. College St. SW1 BX41 4
Little College St. SW1 BX41 66
Littlecombe SE7 CH43 68
Littlecombe Cl. SW15 BQ46 75
Lytton Grove
Lit. Comm. La. Red. BY69 121
Littlecote Clo. SW19 BR47 75
Beaumont Rd.
Littlecote Pl. Pnr. BE30 36
Little Ct. W. Wick. CG55 88
Little Court Rd. Sev. CU65 107
Little Cranmore Lane, Leath. AZ67 110
Little Croft SE9 CL45 68
Littlecroft, Grav. DF50 81
Littlecroft Rd. Egh. AS49 72
Littledale SE2 CO43 69
Little Dell, Welw. G. C. BQ7 7
Little Dimocks SW12 BV48 76
Lit. Dorrit Ct. SE1 BZ41 4
Little Dorrit Ct. SE1 BZ41 67
Lit. Ealing La. W5 BK42 64
Lit. Edward St. NW1 BV37 1
Lit. Edward St. NW1 BV37 56
Little Elms, Hayes BA43 63
Little Ferry Rd. Twick. BJ47 74
Ferry Rd.
Littlefield Ct. West Dr. AX43 63
Littlefield Rd. Edg. BN29 37
Little Friday Hill E4 CG27 40
Lit. Friday Rd. E4 CG27 40
Little Ganett, Welw. G. C. BS9 5
Little Gaynes Gdns. Upmin. CX35 51
Little Gaynes La. Upmin. CX35 51
Little Gearies Ilf. CL31 49
Lit. George St. SW1 BX41 4
Little George St. SW1 BX41 66
Gt. George St.
Lit. Gerpins La. Upmin. CW37 60
Little Graylings, Wat. BB20 17
Little Grn. Rick. AZ24 26
Little Green La. Cher. AV55 82
Lit. Green La. Rick. AZ24 26
Lit. Green St. NW5 BV35 47
College La.
Lit. Gregories La. Epp. CM21 31
Little Gro. Barn. BU25 29
Lit. Grove Bush. BF24 27
Littlegrove Field, Harl. CM11 13
Little Hardings, Welw. G. C. BT7 5
Little Heath SE7 CK43 68
Little Heath Rom. CO31 50
Littleheath La. Cob. BF60 93
Little Heath Rd. Berk. AT13 7
Little Heath Rd. Bexh. CQ44 69
Littleheath Rd. Sth. Croy. CB58 96
Little Heath Rd. Wok. AP58 91
Lit. Hide, Guil. AT69 118
Little Hill, Rick. AU25 25
Little Holt E11 CH32 49
Lit. How. Croft Wat. BA19 17
Abbots Rd.
Little Ilford La. E12 CK35 49
Little John Rd. W7 BH39 54
Littlejohn Rd. Orp. CO53 89
Little Julian Hill, Sev. CU67 116
Lit. Lake, Welw. G. C. BS9 5
Little Laver Road, Ong. CW11 15
Little Ley, Welw. G. C. BR9 5
Lit. Marlborough St. W1 BW39 1
Little Marlborough St. W1 BW39 56
Gt. Marlborough St.
Lit. Martins Bush. BF25 27
Littlemead Esher BG56 93
Littlemede SE9 CK48 78
Littlemore Rd. SE2 CO41 69
Littlemore Rd. Ilf. CM34 49
Lit. Moss La. Pnr. BE30 36
Little Mount, Hat. BP11 10
Little Newport St. WC2 BW40 56
Charing Cross Rd.
Little New St. EC4 BY39 2
Little New St. EC4 BY39 56
Little Orchard, Wey. AV59 91
Lit. Orchard Clo. Pnr. BE30 36
Little Orchard Rd. Wok. AT60 91
Lit. Oxhey La. Wat. BE28 36
Little Pk. Dr. Felt. BD48 74
Little Pk. Gdns. Enf. BZ24 30
Lit. Pastures Brwd. CZ28 42
River Rd.
Lit. Pipers Clo. Wal. Cr. BZ18 21
Lit. Platt. Guil. AO70 118
Lit. Plucketts Way, Buck. H. CJ26 40
Roebuck La.
Lit. Portland St. W1 BV39 1
Lit. Portland St. W1 BW39 56
Lit. Port Spur, Slou. AP39 52
Little Potters Bush. BG26 36
Little Pynchons, Harl. CN12 13
Little Queen's Rd. Tedd. BH50 74
Lit. Queen St. Dart. CW47 80
Lit. Queen St. Tedd. BH50 74
Little Redlands Brom. CK51 88
Little Reeves Ave. Amer. AP23 25
Little Ridge, Welw. G. C. BS8 5
Little Rivers, Welw. G. C. BS7 5
Little Rd. Hayes. BB41 63
Little Rd. Hem. H. AY13 8
Lit. Roke Av. Ken. BY60 95
Lit. Roke Rd. Ken. BZ60 96
Littler's Clo. SW19 BT51 86
Little Russell St. WC1 BX39 2
Lit. Russell St. WC1 BX39 56
Lit. St. James's St. SW1 BW40 3
Little St. James's St. SW1 BW40 56
Little St. Leonard's SW14 BO45 65
Lit. Sanctuary SW1 BW41 3
Little Sanctuary SW1 BX41 66
Broad Sanctuary
Lit. Smith St. SW1 BW41 3
Little Somerset St. E1 CA39 2
Little Somerset St. E1 CA39 57
Littlestone Clo. Beck. CE50 77
Abbey La.
Little Strand NW9 BO30 37
Little St. Guil. AQ68 109
Little Sutton La. Slou. AU42 62
Little Thistle, Welw. G. C. BT9 5
Lit. Thrift, Orp. CM52 88
Lit. Tichfield St. W1 BW39 1
Lit. Tichfield St. W1 BW39 56
Gt. Tichfield St.
Littleton Av. E4 CG26 40
Valance Av.
Littleton Cres. Har. BH34 45
Littleton Gdns. Ashf. BA50 73
Littleton La. Guil. AQ73 118
Littleton La. Reig. BQ71 120
Littleton La. Shep. AX54 83
Littleton Rd. Har. BH34 45
Littleton St. SW18 BT48 76
Lit. Trinity La. EC4 BZ40 2
Lit. Trinity La. EC4 BZ40 57
Queen Victoria St.
Lit. Turnstile WC1 BX39 56
High Holborn
Little Turnstile, WC2 BX39 2
Little Wade, Welw. G. C. BR9 5
Little Walk, Harl. CM11 13
Little Warley Hall La. Brwd. DC30 123
Lit. Warren Clo. Guil. AT71 118
Littlewick Rd. Wok. AP61 100
Littlewick Rd. Wok. AR60 91
Lit. Woodcote La. Cars. BV59 95
Littlewood Rd. SE13 CF46 77
Littlewood Rd. Sev. CV64 108
Littleworth Av. Esher BG56 93
Littleworth Common Rd. Esher BG55 84
Littleworth La. Esher BG56 93
Littleworth Rd. Esher BG56 93
Lit. Youngs. Welw. G. C. BQ8 5
Livermere Rd. E8 CA37 2
Liverpool Gro. SE17 BZ42 4
Liverpool Gro. SE17 BZ42 67
Liverpool Rd. E10 CF32 48
Liverpool Rd. E16 CG38 58
Liverpool Rd. N1 BY36 2
Liverpool Rd. N1 BY36 56
Liverpool Rd. N7 BY35 47
Liverpool Rd. W5 BK41 64
Liverpool Rd. Kings. on T. BM50 75
Liverpool Rd. St. Alb. BH13 9
Liverpool Rd. Th. Hth. BZ52 87
Liverpool Rd. Wat. BC25 26
Liverpool St. EC2 CA39 2
Liverpool St. EC2 CA39 57
Livesey Pl. SE15 CB43 67
Peckham Park Rd.
Livingstone Ct. E10 CF32 48
Livingstone Gdns. Grav. DH49 81
Livingstone Rd. E15 CF37 57
Livingstone Rd. E17 CE32 48
Livingstone Rd. N13 BX29 38
Livingstone Rd. SW11 BT45 66
Winstanley Rd.
Livingstone Rd. Cat. BZ64 105
Livingstone Rd. Grav. DH49 81
Livingstone Rd. Houns. BG45 64
Livingstone Rd. Sthl. BD40 54
Livingstone Rd. Th. Hth. BZ51 87
Livingstone St. E6 CL40 58
Livingstone Ter. Rain. CT37 59
Livingstone Wk. SW11 BT45 66
Plough Rd.
Livingstone Walk, Hem. H. AY11 8
Livonia St. W1 BW39 1
Livonia St. W1 BW39 56
Berwick St.
Lizard St. EC1 BZ38 2
Lizard St. EC1 BZ38 57
Lixban St. SE3 CH43 68
Llanvanor Rd. NW2 BR34 46
Llanbury Clo. Ger. Cr. AS29 34
Llanelly La.NW2 BR34 46
Llanelly Rd. NW2 BR34 46
Crewys Rd.
Llanover Rd. Wem. BK34 45
Llanover St. SE18 CL43 68
Llanthony Rd. Mord. BT53 86
Llewellyn St. SE16 CB41 67
Chambers St.
Lloyd Av. SW16 BX51 86
Lloyd Av. Couls. BV60 95
Lloyd Baker St. WC1 BX38 2
Lloyd Baker St. WC1 BX38 56
Lloyd Ct. Pnr. BD32 45
Lloyd Pk. Av. Croy. CA56 96
Lloyd Rd. E6 CK37 58
Lloyd Rd. E17 CC31 48
Lloyd Rd. Dag. CQ36 59
Lloyd Rd. Wor. Pk. BQ55 85
Lloyd's Av. EC3 CA39 2
Lloyd's Av. EC3 CA39 57
Lloyds Pl. SE3 CG44 68
Lloyd Sq. WC1 BY38 2
Lloyd Sq. WC1 BY38 56
Lloyd's Row, EC1 BY38 2
Lloyds Row EC1 BY38 56
Lloyd St. WC1 BY38 2
Lloyd St. WC1 BY38 56
Lloyds Way Beck. CD53 87
Loampit Hill SE13 CE44 67
Loampit Vale SE13 CE45 67
Loates La. Wat. BD24 27
Lobbell La. St. Alb. BL17 19
Local Board Rd. Wat. BD25 27
Locarno Rd. W3 BO41 65
High St.
Locarno Rd. Grnf. BG38 54
Lochaline St. W6 BQ43 65
Lochinvar St. SW12 BV47 76
Lochmere Clo. Erith CR43 69
Lochnagar St. E14 CF39 57
Lochnell Rd. Berk. AP12 7
Lockaber Rd. SE13 CG45 68
Lock Chase SE3 CG45 68
Locke Clo. Rain. CT36 59
Locke Gdns. Slou. AR41 62
Locke King Clo. Wey. AZ57 92
Locke King Rd. Wey. AZ57 92
Lockers Park La. Hem. H. AW13 8
Lockesley Dr. Orp. CN53 88
Lockesley Sq. Surb. BK53 84
Locket Rd. Har. BH30 36
Lockets Clo. Wind. AL44 61
Lockfield Av. Enf. CD23 30
Lockfield Dr. Wok. AP61 100
Lockhart Clo. N7 BX36 56
Mackenzie Rd.
Lockhart Rd. Cob. BD60 93
Lockhart St. E3 CD38 57
Lockhurst Rd. E5 CC35 48
Lockier Wk. Wem. BK34 45
Hutchinson Ter.
Lock La. Wok. AW61 101
Lockley Cres. Hat. BP11 10
Lockmead Rd. N15 CB32 48
Lockmead Rd. SE13 CF45 67
Lock Pth. Wind. AL43 61
Lock Rd. Guil. AR69 118
Lock Rd. Rich. BK49 74
Lock's La. Mitch. BU51 86
Locksley Est. E14 CD39 57
Locksley St. E14 CD39 57
Lock St. W10 BQ40 55
Lockwood Cl. SE26 CC49 77
Mayow Rd.
Lockwood Path, Wok. AV60 91
Lockwood Rd. Ilf. CM34 49
Lockwood Sq. SE16 CB41 67
Southwark Pk. Rd.
Lockwood Wk. Rom. CT32 50
Lockwood Way, Chess. BM56 94
Lockyer Rd. Grays CY43 70
Lockyer St. SE1 BZ41 4
Locton Est. E3 CD37 57
Loddiges Rd. E9 CC36 57
Loder Clo. Wok. AU60 91
Loder St. SE15 CC43 67
Lodge Av. SW14 BN45 65
South Worple Way
Lodge Av. Borwd. BL25 28
Lodge Av. Croy. BX55 86
Lodge Av. Dag. CO37 59
Lodge Av. Dart. CV46 80
Lodge Av. Har. BL31 46
Lodge Av. Rom. CT32 50
Lodgebottom Rd. Lthd. BL67 112
Lodge Clo. N18 BZ28 39
Lodge Clo. Chig. CO28 41
Lodge Clo. Cob. BE61 102
Lodge Clo. Dor. BK73 119
Lodge Clo. Edg. BL29 37
Lodge Clo. Egh. AR49 72
Lodge Cl. Islw. BJ44 65
London Rd.
Lodge Clo. Lthd. BG64 102
Lodge Clo. Orp. CO54 89
Lodge Clo. Slou. AO41 61
Lodge Clo. Sutt. BS56 95
Lodge Clo. Uxb. AX38 53
Lodge Clo. Wall. BV54 86
Lodge Ct. Horn. CW34 51
Lodge Cres. Orp. CO54 89
Lodge Cres. Wal. Cr. CC20 21
Lodge Dr. N13 BY28 38
Lodge Dr. Hat. BQ11 10
Lodge End, Rad. BJ20 18
Lodge Field, Welw. G. C. BR6 5
Lodge Gnds. Beck. CD53 87
Lodge Hall, Harl. CN13 13
Lodge Hill, Ilf. CK31 49
Lodge Hill, Pur. BY61 104
Lodge Hill, Well. CO43 69
Lodge La. N12 BT28 38
Lodge La. Bex. CP46 79
Lodge La. Ch. St. G. AS23 25
Lodge La. Croy. CE57 96
Lodge La. Grays. DD41 71
Lodge La. Wal. Abb. CF21 30
Lodge La. West. CM67 115
Lodge La. Est. Rom. CR29 41
Lodge Rd. NW4 BQ31 46
Lodge Rd. NW8 BT38 1
Lodge Rd. NW8 BT38 56
Lodge Rd. Brom. CH50 78
Lodge Rd. Croy. BY53 86
Lodge Rd. Epp. CL20 22
Lodge Rd. Lthd. BG64 102
Lodge Rd. Sutt. BS56 95
Lodge Rd. Wall. BV56 95
Lodge Vill. Wdf. Grn. CG29 40
Lodge Way, Ashf. AY48 73
Lodge Way, Shep. BA51 83
Lodge Way, Wind. AM45 61
Lodore Gdns. NW9 BN32 46
Lodore Grn. Uxb. AY34 44
Lodore St. E14 CF39 57
Loewen Rd. Grays. DG41 71
Loftie St. SE16 CB41 67
Chambers St.
Lofting Rd. N1 BX36 2
Lofting Rd. N1 BX36 56
Loftus Rd. W12 BP40 55
Logan Clo. Enf. CC23 30
Logan Ms. W8 BS42 66
Logan Pl. W8 BS42 66
Logan Rd. N9 CB27 39
Logan Rd. Houns. BE45 64
Logan Rd. Wem. BK34 45
Logmore La. Dor. BF72 119
Logs Hill, Chis. CK51 88
Logs Hill Clo. Chis. CK51 88
Lois Dr. Shep. BA53 83
Lolesworth St. E1 CA39 2
Lolesworth St. E1 CA39 57
Wentworth St.
Lollard Pl. SE11 BY42 4
Lollard Pl. SE11 BY42 66
Lollard St. SE11 BX42 4
Lollard St. SE11 BX42 66
Lollesworth La. Leath. BA66 110
Loman Path, S. Ock. CZ39 60
Loman St. SE1 BY41 4
Loman St. SE1 BY41 66
Lomas St. E1 CB39 57
Vallence Rd.
Lombard Av. N11 BW28 38
Lombard Av. Enf. CC23 30
Lombard Av. Ilf. CN33 49
Lombard La. EC4 BY39 2
Lombard La. EC4 BY39 56
Lombard Rd. SW11 BT44 66
Lombard Rd. SW19 BS51 86
Lombard St. EC3 BZ39 2
Lombard St. EC3 BZ39 57
Lombard Wall SE7 CH41 68
Lombardy Dr. Berk. AR13 7
Lomond Clo. N15 CA31 48
Kirton Rd.
Lomond Clo. Wem. BL36 55
Lomond Gro. SE5 BZ43 67
Lomond Rd. Hem. H. AZ11 8
Loncin Mead. Av. Wey. AX58 92
Loncroft Rd. SE5 CA43 4
Londale Clo. Pnr. BE29 36
Londesborough Rd. N16 CA35 48
London Av. Gro. SE26 CB49 77
London Bridge, SE1 BZ40 4
London Bridge St. SE1 BZ40 4
London Br. St. SE1 BZ40 57
London Br. Wk. SE1 BZ40 57
Tooley St.
London Colney By-pass, St. Alb. BL16 19
London Fields E8 CB37 57
London Fields, E. Side E8 CB37 57
London Fields, W. Side E8 CB36 57
London La. E8 CB36 57
London La. Brom. CG50 78
London Lane, Leath. BC68 110
London La. Uxb. AZ38 53
London Ms. W2 BT39 1
London Ms. W2 CJ39 58
London St.
London Rd. E13 CH37 58
London Rd. SE1 BY41 4
London Rd. SE1 BY41 66
London Rd. SE23 CB47 77
London Rd. SW16 BX51 86
London Rd. SW17 BU53 86
London Rd. Bark. CL37 58
London Rd. Berk. AS13 7
London Rd. Brom. CG50 78
London Rd. Brwd. CZ28 42
London Rd. Bush. BE25 27
London Rd. Cat. BZ65 105
London Rd. Ch. St. G. AR27 34
London Rd. Croy. BY52 86
London Rd. Dart. CS46 79
London Rd. Dart. CX47 80
London Rd. Dor. BJ71 119
London Rd. Enf. BZ25 30
London Rd. Epsom BP58 94
London Rd. Grav. DE46 81
London Rd. Grays CX42 70
London Rd. Guil. AS71 118
London Rd. Har. BH34 45
London Rd. Harl. CP11 14
London Rd. Harl. CP13 14
London Rd. Harl. CP14 14
London Rd. Harl. CP9 6
London Rd. Hat. BQ12 10
London Rd. Hem. H. AX15 8
London Rd. Hem. H. AY16 17
London Rd. Houns. BG45 64
London Rd. Islw. BH44 64
London Rd. Kings. on T. BL51 85
London Rd. Mitch. BU53 86
London Rd. Mitch. BV53 86
London Rd. Mord. BS53 86
London Rd. Ong. CV20 24
London Rd. Purfleet CW42 70
London Rd. Rad. BL20 19
London Rd. Red. BU70 12
London Rd. Reig. BS70 12
London Rd. Rick. AY27 35
London Rd. Rom. CO24 32
London Rd. Rom. CR32 50
London Rd. Rom. CS23 32
London Rd. St. Alb. BG13 9
London Rd. Saw. CP6 6
London Rd. Sev. CQ58 98
London Rd. Sev. CR59 98
London Rd. Sev. CS62 107
London Rd. Sev. CT65 107
London Rd. Sev. CU66 116
London Rd. Sev. CY56 99
London Rd. Sev. & Ton. CW70 117
London Rd. Slou. AQ43 62
London Rd. Stai. Ashf. & Felt. AW49 7
London Rd. Stan. BK28 3
London Rd. Sutt. BQ55 8
London Rd. Swan. CS51 8
London Rd. Swan. CU52 8
London Rd Th. Hth. & Croy. BX51 8
London Rd. Til. DG44 7
London Rd. Twick. BJ47 7
London Rd. Vir. W. AQ51 8
London Rd. Wall. BV55 8
London Rd. Welw. BQ5 5
London Rd. Wem. BL35 4
London Rd. West. CM66 11
London Rd. Wok. AU67 10
London Rd. East. Amer. AP24 2
London Rd. N. Red. BW67 11
London Rd. S. Red. BV68 11
London Rd. West. Amer. AO23 2
Londons Clo. Upmin. CY35 5
London Stile W4 BM42 6
Wellesley Rd.
London St. EC3 CA40 5
Fenchurch St.
London St. W2 BT39
London St. W2 BT39 5
London St. Cher. AW54 8
London Ter. EC3 CA40
London Tilbury Rd. Rain. CV38 6
London Wall, EC2 BZ39
London Wall, EC2 BZ39 5
Londrina Ter. Berk. AR13
Lonesome La. Reig. BS71 12
Long Acre, WC2 BX40
Long Acre, WC2 BX40 5
Long Acre Orp. CP55 8
Longacre Pl. Cars. BV57 9
Longacre Rd. E17 CF30 3
Longacres St. Alb. BK13
Longaford Way, Brwd. DE26 12
Long Arrotts, Hem. H. AW12
Long Banks, Harl. CM12 1
Long Barn Cl. Wat. BC19 1
Long Barn Rd. Sev. CU70 11
Longbeach Rd. SW11 BU45 6
Longberrys Rd. NW2 BR34 4
Longbottom La. Beac. AO29 3
Longbourne Way, Cher. AV53 8
Longbridge Rd. Bark. CM36 5
Longbridge Way SE13 CF46 7
Longbridge Way, Uxb. AW37 5
Longbury Dr. Orp. CO52 8
Long Chaulden, Hem. H. AV13
Longcliffe Path Wat. BC27 3
Gosforth La.
Long Copse Clo. Lthd. BF65 10
Longcroft SE9 CK48 7
Long Cft. Wat. BC26 3
Longcroft Av. Bans. BT60 9
Longcroft Dr. Wal. Cr. CD20 2
Longcroft Grn. Welw. G. C. BQ8
Longcroft La. Hem. H. AU17 1
Longcroft La. Welw. G. C. BQ8
Longcroft Rise Loug. CL25 3
Longcroft Rd. SE5 CA43 6
Longcroft Rd. Edg. BK29 3
Long Croft Rd. Rick. AU28 3
Longcrofts Wal. Abb. CG20 2
Roundhills
Longcross Rd. Cher. AP55 8
Long Deacon Rd. E4 CG26 4
Longdean Pk. Hem. H. AZ16 1
Longden Wood Av. Kes. CK56 9
Longdown La. N. Epsom BP60 9
Longdown La. S. Epsom BP61 10
Longdown Rd. SE6 CE49 7
Longdown Rd. Epsom BP60 9
Longdown Rd. Guil. AT72 11
Long Dr. W3 BO39 5
Long Dr. Grnf. BF37 5
Long Dr. Ruis. BD35 4
Long Dyke, Guil. AT69 11
Long Elmes, Har. BF30 3
Long Elms, Wat. BA20 1
Long Fallow, St. Alb. BF17 1
Longfellow Dr. Brwd. DE26 12
Longfellow Rd. E3 CD38 5
Longfellow Rd. E17 CE32 4
Longfellow Rd. Wor. Pk. BP54 8
Longfield NW9 BO29 3
Longfield, Brom. CG51 8
Longfield, Hem. H. AZ14
Longfield, Loug. CJ25 3
Long Field, Slou. AO34 4
Longfield Av. E17 CD31 4
Longfield Av. NW7 BP29 3
Longfield Av. W5 BK40 5
Longfield Av. Enf. CC22 3
Longfield Av. Horn. CT33 5
Longfield Av. Wall. BV54 8
Longfield Av. Wem. BL33 4
Longfield Cres. SE26 CC48 7
Longfield Cres. Tad. BQ63 10
Longfield Dr. SW14 BM46 7
Longfield Est. SE1 CA42
Longfield Est. SE1 CA42 6

Longfield, Harl. CO12 14
Longfield La. Wal. Cr. CB17 21
Longfield Rd. W5 BK40 54
Longfield Rd. Dor. BH72 119
Longfields, Ong. CX18 24
Longfield St. SW18 BS47 76
Longfield Wk. W5 BK39 54
Longford Av. Felt. BB46 73
Longford Av. Stai. AY47 73
Longford Av. Sthl. BF40 54
Longford Clo. N15 CA32 48
Albert Rd.
Longford Clo. Hamptn. BF49 74
Longford Ct. Epsom BN56 94
Longford Gdns. Hayes BD40 54
Longford Gdns. Sutt. BT55 86
Longford Rd. Twick. BF47 74
Longford St. NW1 BV38 1
Longford St. NW1 BV38 56
Longford Way, Stai. AY47 73
Longford Av.
Long Grn. Chig. CN28 40
Long Gro. Beac. AO29 34
Long Gro. Rd. Epsom BM58 94
Longhayes Av. Rom. CP31 50
Longheath Gdns. Croy. CC53 87
Longhedge St. SW11 BV44 66
Rowditch Lane
Long Hill, Cat. CC64 105
Longhill Rd. SE6 CF48 77
Longhook Cres. Nthlt. BC37 53
Longhouse Rd. Grays. DG41 71
Longhurst Rd. SE13 CF46 77
Longhurst Rd. Croy. CB53 87
Longhurst Rd. Leath. BB68 110
Long John, Hem. H. AY14 8
Longland Dr. N20 BS27 38
Longlande Clo. Wal. Cr. CC19 21
Longlands Av. Couls. BV60 95
Longlands Ct. W11 BR40 55
Westbourne Gro.
Longlands, Hem. H. AY13 8
Longlands Pk. Cres. Sid. CN48 78
Longlands Rd. Sid. CN48 78
Longlands Rd. Welw. G. C. BR8 5
Long La. EC1 BY39 2
Long La. EC1 BY39 56
Long La. N2 BT30 38
Long La. N3 BS30 38
Long La. SE1 BZ41 4
Long La. SE1 BZ41 67
Long La. Bexh. CP43 69
Long La. Croy. CB53 87
Long La. Hem. H. AS19 16
Long La. Rick. AU25 25
Long La. Rick. AV27 34
Long La. Stai. AY48 73
Long La. Uxb. AZ35 44
Longleat Rd. Enf. CA25 30
Longleat Way, Felt. BA47 73
Longlees Rick. AU28 34
Long Croft Rd.
Longleigh La. SE2 CO43 69
Long Ley, Harl. CN11 13
Long Ley, Harl. CO11 14
Long Ley, Welw. G. C. BT8 5
Longley Av. Wem. BL37 55
Longley Rd. SW17 BU50 76
Longley Rd. Croy. BY54 86
Longley Rd. Har. BG32 45
Long Leys E4 CE29 39
Longley St. SE1 CB42 4
Longley St. SE1 CB42 67
Long Lodge Dr. Walt. BD55 84
Longmans Way, Wok. AP61 100
Longmarsh View, S. At. H. CX51 90
Long Mead. NW9 BO30 37
Longmead, Chis. CL51 88
Longmead, Guil. AU70 118
Long Mead, Hat. BP11 10
Longmead, Wind. AM44 61
Longmead Clo. Brwd. DC26 122
Longmead Clo. Cat. CA64 105
Longmead Dr. Sid. CP48 79
Long Meadow NW5 BW35 47
Long Meadow, Brwd. DE27 122
Long Meadow, Lthd. BE66 111
Longmeadow Rd. Sid. CN47 78
Longmead Rd. SW17 BU49 76
Longmead Rd. Epsom BN59 94
Longmead Rd. Hayes BB40 53
Longmead Rd. Surb. BH54 84
Longmere Gdns. Tad. BQ63 103
Longmoor St. SW1 BW42 3
Longmoor St. SW1 BW42 66
Longmoor, Wal. Cr. CD18 21
Longmore Av. Barn. BT25 29
Longmore Clo. AV28 34
Longmore Gdns.
Welw. G. C. BR8 5
Longmore Rd. Walt. BE56 93
Longnor Rd. E1 CC38 57
Long Park, Amer. AO21 25
Long Pond Rd. SE3 CG44 68
Longport Clo. Ilf. CO29 41
Long Reach, Wok. AZ65 101
Long Reach Rd. Bark. CN38 58
Longreach Rd. Erith. CU43 69
Long Wk. SE1 CA41 6
Longridge Gro. Wok. AV60 91
Woking Rd.
Longridge La. Sthl. BF40 54
Longridge Rd. SW5 BS42 66
Long Ridings Av. Brwd. DD25 122
Longs Clo. Wok. AW61 101
Long Shaw, Lthd. BJ63 102
Longshaw Rd. E4 CF27 39
Longshore SE8 CD42 67
Longside Clo. Egh. AU51 82
Longspring, Wat. BC22 26
Longstaff Cres. SW18 BS46 76
Longstaff Rd. SW18 BS46 76
Longstone Av. NW10 BO37 55
Longstone Rd. SW17 BV49 76
Longstone Rd. Iver AU37 52
Long St. E2 CA38 2
Long St. E2 CA38 57
Long St. Wal. Abb. CK19 22
Long String, St. Alb. BH11 9
Longthornton Rd. SW16 BW51 86
Longton Gro. SE26 CB49 77
Longtown Clo. Rom. CV28 42
Longtown Rd. Rom. CV28 42
Long View, Berk. AQ12 7
Longview Way, Rom. CS30 41
Longville Rd. SE11 BY42 4
Longville Rd. SE11 BY42 66
Long Wk. SE1 CA41 4
Long Wk. SE18 CL43 68
Dale Rd.
Long Wk. SW13 BO44 65
Terrace, The
Long Walk, Ch. St. G. AR24 25
Long Wk. Epsom. BQ63 103
Long Wk. Grav. DF51 81
Long Walk, Guil. AY68 110
Long Wk. N. Mal. BN52 85
Long Wk. Wal. Abb. CE18 21
Long Walk, The Wind. AO47 72
Longways, Stai. AV51 82
Longwood Clo. Upmin. CY35 51
Longwood Dr. SW15 BP46 75
Long Wood Dr. Beac. AP29 34
Longwood Gdns. Ilf. CK31 49
Longwood La. Amer. AO23 25
Longwood Rd. Ken. BZ61 105
Long Yd. WC1 BX38 2
Long Yd. WC1 BX38 56
Loning, The NW9 BO31 46
Loning, The Enf. CC22 30
Lonsdale, Hem. H. AY12 8
Lonsdale Av. E6 CJ38 58
Lonsdale Av. Brwd. DE25 122
Lonsdale Av. Rom. CS32 50
Lonsdale Av. Wem. BL35 46
Lonsdale Clo. E6 CK38 58
Lonsdale Clo. Edg. BL29 37
Lonsdale Clo. Uxb. BA39 53
Lonsdale Cres. Dart. CY47 80
Lonsdale Cres. Ilf. CL32 49
Lonsdale Dr. Enf. BW24 29
Lonsdale Dr. N. Enf. BX25 29
Lonsdale Gdns. Th. Hth. BX52 86
Lonsdale Mews, Rich. BL44 65
Lonsdale Ms. Rich. BM44 65
Elizabeth Cott.
Lonsdale Pl. N1 BY36 56
Lonsdale Pla. N1 BY37 2
Lonsdale Rd. E11 CG33 49
Lonsdale Rd. NW6 BR37 55
Lonsdale Rd. SE25 CB52 87
Lonsdale Rd. SW13 BO44 65
Lonsdale Rd. W4 BO42 65
Lonsdale Rd. W11 BR39 55
Lonsdale Rd. Bexh. CQ44 69
Lonsdale Rd. Dor. BJ71 119
Lonsdale Rd. Sthl. BD41 64
Lonsdale Rd. Wey. AZ57 92
Lonsdale Sq. N1 BY36 2
Lonsdale Sq. N1 BY36 56
Lonsdale Way, Maid. AH42 61
Springfield Pk.
Loobert Rd. N15 CA31 48
Looe Gdns. Ilf. CL31 49
Loom La. Rad. BH22 27
Loom Pl. Rad. BJ21 27
Loop Rd. Chis. CL50 78
Loop Rd. Epsom BN61 103
Loop Rd. Wal. Abb. CE19 21
Loop Rd. Wok. AS64 100
Lopen Rd. N18 CA28 39
Loraine Clo. Enf. CC25 30
Loraine Gdns. Ash. BL62 103
Loraine Rd. N7 BX35 47
Loraine Rd. W4 BM43 65
Lorbet Pl. E1 CA39 2
Lord Av. Ilf. CK31 49
Lord Chancellor Wk.
Kings. on T. BN51 85
Lorden Wk. E2 CB38 2
Lorden Wk. E2 CB38 57
Lord Gdns. Ilf. CK31 49
Lord Hills Br. W2 BS39 56
Lord Hills Rd. W2 BS39 1
Lord Hills Rd. W2 BS39 56
Lord Holland La. SW9 BY44 66
Myatts Fields Dev.
Lord Knyvetts Clo. AX46 73
Lord Napier Pl. W6 BP42 65
Upper Mall
Lord North St. SW1 BX41 4
Lord North St. SW1 BX41 66
Lordsbury Fld. Wall. BW58 95
Lords Clo. Felt. BE48 74
Lordship Clo. Brwd. DE26 122
Lordship Gro. N16 BZ34 48
Lordship Rd.
Lordship La. N17 BZ30 39
Lordship La. N22 BY30 38
Lordship La. SE22 CA46 77
Lordship Pk. N16 BZ34 48
Lordship Pl. SW3 BU43 66
Cheyne Row
Lordship Rd. N16 BZ33 48
Lordship Rd. Nthlt. BE36 54
Lordship Rd. Wal. Cr. CB18 21
Lordship Ter. N16 BZ34 48
Lordsmead Rd. N17 CA30 39
Lord St. E16 CK40 58
Lord St. Hodd. CB11 12
Lords Wood, Welw. G. C. BT8 5
Lord Warwick St. SE18 CK41 68
Lorenzo St. WC1 BX38 2
Lorenzo St. WC1 BX38 56
Loretto Gdns. Har. BL31 46
Lorian Av. N12 BS28 38
Holden Rd.
Lorian Clo. N12 BS28 38
Guildown Av.
Lorian Dr. Reig. BT70 121
Loring Rd. N20 BU27 38
Loring Rd. Berk. AR13 7
Loring Rd. Islw. BH44 64
Loring Rd. Wind. AM44 61
Loris Rd. W6 BQ41 65
Lorne Av. Croy. CC54 87
Lorne Clo. Slou. AN41 61
Lorne Gdns. E11 CJ31 49
Lorne Gdns. W11 BQ41 65
Lorne Gdns. W14 BQ32 46
Lorne Gdns. Croy. CC54 87
Lorne Rd. E7 CH35 49
Lorne Rd. E17 CE32 48
Lorne Rd. N4 BX33 47
Lorne Rd. Brwd. DB28 42
Lorne Rd. Har. BH30 36
Lorne Rd. Rich. BL46 75
Albert Rd.
Lorne, The Lthd. BF66 111
Lorn Rd. SW9 BX44 66
Lorraine Pk. Har. BH29 36
Lorrimore Rd. SE17 BY43 66
Lorrimore Sq. SE17 BY43 4
Lorrimore Sq. SE17 BY43 66
Lorton Clo. Grav. DJ48 81
Losberne Way SE16 CB42 67
Bonamy Est. West, The
Loseberry Rd. Esher BG56 93
Losfield Rd. Wind. AM44 61
Lothair Rd. W5 BK41 64
Lothair Rd. N. N4 BY32 47
Lothair Rd. S. N4 BY33 47
Lothbury EC2 BZ39 2
Lothbury EC2 BZ39 57
Lothian Av. Hayes BC39 53
Lothian Rd. SW9 BY44 66
Lothian Wd. Tad. BP64 103
Lothrop St. W10 BR38 55
Lots Rd. SW6 BT44 66
Lots Rd. SW10 BT43 66
Lotus Rd. West. CK62 106
Loubet St. SW17 BU50 76
Loudhams Rd. Amer. AR23 25
Loudhams Wood La.
Ch. St. G. AR23 25
Loudon Rd. NW8 BT36 1
Loudon Av. Ilf. CL32 49
Loudon Rd. NW8 BT36 56
Loudwater Clo. Sun. BC52 83
Loudwater Dr. Rick. AX24 26
Loudwater Heights, Rick. AW24 26
Loudwater Hill, Rick. AX25 26
Loudwater La. Rick. AX 4 26
Loudwater Rd. Sun. BC52 83
Loughborough Est. SW9 BY44 66
Loughborough Pk. SW9 BY45 66
Loughborough Pk.
Dev. SW9 BY44 66
Loughborough Rd. SW9 BY44 66
Loughborough St. SE11 BX42 4
Loughborough St. SE11 BX42 66
Loughton Ct. Wal. Abb. CH20 22
Stanway Rd.
Loughton La. Epp. CM22 31
Loughton Way, Buck. H. CJ26 40
Louisa St. E1 CC38 57
Louise Gdns. Rain. CT38 59
Louise Rd. E15 CG36 58
Louisville Rd. SW17 BV48 76
Lourdon Rd. Mews NW8 BT37 56
Lourdon Rd.
Lousehall La. Wal. Abb. CF16 21
Louvaine Rd. SW11 BT45 66
Louvain Rd. Green. CZ47 80
Louvain Way, Wat. BC19 17
Lovat Clo. NW2 BO34 46
Lovat La. EC3 CA40 4
Lovat La. EC3 CA40 57
Lovatt Clo. Edg. BM29 37
Lovatt Dr. Ruis. BB32 44
Lovatt Dr. Ruis. BC32 44
Lovatts, Rick. AZ24 26
Lovat Wk. Houns. BE43 64
Cranford La.
Loveday Rd. W13 BJ40 54
Love Grn. La. Iver. AV39 52
Lovegrove St. SE1 CB43 67
Love Hill La. Slou. AT40 52
Lovejoy La. Wind. AL44 61
Lovekyn Clo. Kings. on T. BL51 85
Lovelace Av. Brom. CL53 88
Lovelace Clo. Lthd. BC65 101
Lovelace Clo. Sev. CZ57 99
Lovelace Dr. Wok. AV61 100
Lovelace Gdns. Bark. CO35 50
Lovelace Gdns. Surb. BK54 84
Lovelace Gdns. Walt. BD56 93
Lovelace Grn. SE9 CK45 68
Lovelace Rd. SE21 BZ48 77
Lovelace Rd. Barn. BU26 38
Lovelace Rd. Surb. BK54 84
Loveland La. Tad. BS67 113
Lovelands La. Wok. AO60 91
Love La. EC2 BZ39 2
Love La. EC2 BZ39 57
Love La. N17 CA29 39
Love La. SE18 CL42 68
Thomas St.
Love La. SE25 CB52 87
Love La. Bex. CQ46 79
Love La. Brom. CH51 88
Love La. Gdse. CC69 114
Love La. Grav. CH47 81
Love La. Hat. BP17 19
Love La. Iver AU39 52
Love La. Kings L. AY18 17
Love La. Mitch. BU52 86
Love La. Mord. BS54 86
Love La. Ong. CX17 24
Love La. Pnr. BE31 45
Love La. S. Ock. CW40 60
Love La. Surb. BK55 84
Love La. Sutt. BR57 94
Love La. Tad. BO67 112
Love La. Wat. BB18 17
Love La. Wdf. Grn. CK29 40
Lovel Av. Well. CO44 69
Lovel Clo. Hem. H. AW13 8
Lovel End, Ger. Cr. AR29 34
Lovelinch Clo. SE14 CC43 67
Rollins St.
Lovell Rd. Enf. CB21 30
Lovell Rd. Rich. BK48 74
Lovell Rd. Sthl. BF39 54
Lovell Wk. Rain. CT36 59
Lovel Mead. Ger. Cr. AR29 34
Lovel Rd. Ger. Cr. AR29 34
Loveridge Rd. NW6 BR36 55
Lovers La. Green. DB45 70
Lovers Wk. N3 BS29 38
Lover's Wk. SE10 CF43 67
Lover's Wk. Rom. CS28 41
Lovett Clo. Uxb. AX31 44
Lovett Dr. Cars. BT54 86
Lovett Rd. Egh. AV49 72
Lovetts Pl. SW18 BS45 66
York Rd.
Lovett Way NW10 BN35 46
Love Wk. SE5 BZ44 67
Lovibonds Av. Orp. CL56 97
Lowbrook Rd. Ilf. CL35 49
Lowburys, Dor. BJ73 119
Low Cross Wood La. SE21 CA48 77
Lowdell Clo. West Dr. AY39 53
Lowden Rd. N9 CB26 39
Lowden Rd. SE24 BY45 66
Lowden Rd. Sthl. BE40 54
Lowe Av. E16 CH39 58
Watford Rd.
Lowe Clo. Chig. CO28 41
Lowell St. E14 CD39 57
Lwr. Addiscombe Rd. Croy. CA54 87
Lower Barn. Hem. H. AY15 8
Lwr. Barn Rd. Pur. BZ59 96
Lwr. Bedfords Rd. Rom. CT29 41
Lwr. Belgrave St. SW1 BV41 3
Lwr. Belgrave St. SW1 BV41 66
Lwr. Boston Rd. W7 BH40 54
Lwr. Bridge Rd. Red. BU70 121
Lwr. Broad St. Dag. CR37 59
Lwr. Bury La. Epp. CN19 22
Lwr. Camden, Chis. CK50 78
Lwr. Church Hill, Green. CZ46 80
Lwr. Church St. Croy. BY55 86
Wadden New Rd.
Lwr. Cippenham La. Slou. AM40 61
Lwr. Clapton Rd. E5 CB34 48
Lwr. Clarendon Wk. W11 BQ40 55
Lancaster Rd.
Lwr. Common S. SW15 BP45 65
Lwr. Coombe St. Croy. BZ56 96
Lwr. Ct. Rd. Epsom BN59 94
Lwr. Cres. S. Le H. DK41 71
Lwr. Cft. Swan. CT52 89
Lwr. Dagnal St. St. Alb. BG13 9
Lwr. Derby Rd. Wat. BD24 27
Lwr. Downs Rd. SW20 BQ51 85
Lwr. Drayton Pl. Croy. BY55 86
Lwr. Edgeborough Rd. Guil. AS71 118
Lwr. Farm Rd. Lthd. BC65 101
Lowerfield, Welw. G. C. BS8 5
Lwr. Form, Wor. Pk. BQ55 85
Lwr. George St. Rich. BK46 74
George St.
Lwr. Gravel Rd. Brom. CK54 88
Lwr. Green Rd. Esher BF55 84
Lwr. Green W. Mitch. BU52 86
Lwr. Grosvenor Pl. SW1 BV41 3
Lwr. Grosvenor Pl. SW1 BV41 66
Lwr. Guildford Rd. Wok. AO62 100
Lwr. Hall La. E4 CD28 39
Lwr. Hampton Rd. Sun. BD52 84
Lwr. Ham Rd. Kings. on T. BK50 74
Lwr. Hatfield Rd. Hert. BW11 11
Lwr. Higham Rd. Grav. DJ47 81
Lwr. Hill Rd. Epsom BM59 94
Lwr. Hythe St. Dart. CW46 80
Lwr. James St. W1Z BW40 56
Brewer St.
Lwr. John St. W1 BW40 3
Lwr. John St. W1 BW40 56
Brewer St.
Lwr. Kenwood Av. Enf. BW25 29
Lwr. Kings Rd. Berk. AR13 7
Lwr. Maidstone Rd. N11 BW29 38
Lwr. Mall W6 BP42 65
Lwr. Mardyke Av. Rain. CS37 59
Lwr. Marsh SE1 BY41 4
Lwr. Marsh SE1 BY41 66
Lwr. Marsh La. Kings. on T. BL52 85
Lwr. Mead, Iver AU38 52
Lwr. Meadow, Harl. CN13 13
Lwr. Merton Rise NW3 BU36 1
Lwr. Merton Rd. NW3 BU36 56
Lwr. Morden La. Mord. BQ53 85
Lwr. Mortlake Rd. Rich. BL45 65
Lwr. Newport St. WC2 BW40 3
Lwr. Paddock Rd. Wat. BE25 27
Lwr. Pk. Rd. N11 BW29 38
Lwr. Pk. Rd. Bans. BU62 104
Lwr. Pk. Rd. Belv. CR41 69
Lwr. Pk. Rd. Loug. CJ25 31
Lwr. Paxton Rd. St. Alb. BH14 9
Paxton Rd.
Lwr. Peryers, Leath. BB67 110
Lwr. Pillory Downs. Cars. BV60 95
Lwr. Plantation, Rick. AX24 26
Lwr. Pyrford Rd. Wok. AW61 101
Lwr. Queen's Rd. Buck. H. CJ27 40
Lwr. Range Rd. Grav. DJ47 81
Lwr. Richmond Rd. SW14 BM45 65
Lwr. Richmond Rd. SW15 BP45 65
Lwr. Richmond Rd. Rich. BM45 65
Lwr. Rd. E13 CH38 58
Lwr. Rd. SE8 CC42 67
Lwr. Rd. SE16 CC41 67
Lwr. Rd. Belv. CR41 69
Lwr. Rd. Brwd. DE23 122
Lwr. Rd. Erith CS42 69
Lwr. Rd. Ger. Cr. AS31 43
Lwr. Rd. Grav. DC45 71
Lwr. Rd. Grav. DK47 81
Lwr. Rd. Har. BG34 45
Lwr. Rd. Hem. H. AZ16 17
Lwr. Rd. Ken. BY60 95
Lwr. Rd. Loug. CL23 31
Lwr. Rd. Lthd. BD67 111
Lwr. Rd. Lthd. BG65 102
Lwr. Rd. Orp. CO54 89
Lwr. Rd. Rain. CS37 59
Lwr. Rd. Red. BT71 121
Lwr. Rd. Rick. AU24 25
Lwr. Rd. Sutt. BT56 95
Lwr. Rd. Swan. CT50 79
Lwr. Rd. Uxb. AU33 43
Lwr. Sales, Hem. H. AV14 7
Lwr. Shot, Lthd. BF66 111
Lwr. Shot Clo. Lthd. BF66 111
Lwr. Sloane St. SW1 BU42 3
Lwr. Sloane St. SW1 BV42 66
Lwr. Sq. Islw. BJ45 64
Lwr. Staithe W4 BN44 65
Lwr. Station Rd. Crayford CT46 79
Lwr. Strand NW9 BO30 37
Lwr. Sunbury Rd. Hamptn. BE51 84
Lwr. Swaines, Epp. CN18 22
Lwr. Tail. Wat. BE27 36
Lwr. Teddington Rd.
Kings. on T. BK50 74
Lwr. Ter. NW3 BT34 47
Lwr. Thames St. EC3 BZ40 4
Lwr. Thames St. EC3 BZ40 57
Lwr. Trinity La. EC4 BZ40 4
Lwr. Tubs, Bush. BG26 36
Lwr. Vernon Rd. Sutt. BT56 95
Lwr. Wood, Harl. CK12 13
Lwr. Wood Rd. Esher BJ57 93
Lwr. Yott. Hem. H. AY13 8
Lowestoft Clo. E5 CB34 48
Southwold Rd.
Lowestoft Rd. Wat. BC23 26
Loweswater Clo. Wem. BK34 45
Carlton Av. East
Lowe, The Chig. CO28 41
Lowfield, Saw. CQ6 6
Brook Rd.
Lowfield La. Hodd. CE12 12
Lowfield Rd. NW6 BS36 56
Lowfield Rd. W3 BM39 55
Lowfield St. Dart. CW48 80
Low Hall Clo. E4 CE26 39
Lowhall La. E17 CD32 48
Low Hill, Harl. CG12 13
Low Hill Rd. Harl. CG12 13
Lowick Rd. Har. BH31 45
Lowlands Gdns. Rom. CR32 50
Lowlands Rd. Har. BH33 45
Lowlands Rd. Pnr. BD33 45
Lowlands Rd. S. Ock. CX40 60
Lowman Rd. N7 BX35 47
Lowndes Clo. SW1 BV41 3
Lowndes Clo. SW1 BV41 66
Lowndes Pl. SW1 BV41 3
Lowndes Pl. SW1 BV41 66
Lowndes Sq. SW1 BU41 3
Lowndes Sq. SW1 BU41 66
Lowndes St. SW1 BU41 3
Lowndes St. SW1 BU41 66
Lownds Av. Brom. CH51 88
Lowood St. E1 CB40 57
Low Rd. Hat. BU11 11
Lowshoe La. Rom. CR30 41
Lowson Gro. Wat. BE26 36
Low St. La. Til. DJ43 71
Lowswood Clo. Nthwd. BA30 35
Lowther Dr. Enf. BW24 29
Lowther Hl. SE23 CD47 77
Lowther Rd. E17 CD30 39
Lowther Rd. N7 BY35 47
Mackenzie Rd.
Lowther Rd. SW13 BO44 65
Lowther Rd. Kings. on T. BL51 85
Lowther Rd. Stan. BL31 46
Lowth Rd. SE5 BZ44 67
Loxford Av. E6 CJ37 58
Loxford La. Ilf. CM35 49
Loxford Rd. Bark. CL36 58
Loxham Rd. E4 CE29 39
Loxham St. WC1 BX38 2
Loxham St. WC1 BX38 56
Argyle Wk.
Loxley Rd. SW18 BT47 76
Loxley Rd. Berk. AP12 7
Loxley Rd. Hamptn. BE49 74
Loxton Rd. SE23 CC47 77
Loxwood Clo. Orp. CP55 89
Chelsfield La.
Loxwood Rd. N17 CA31 48
Lubbock Rd. Chis. CK50 78
Lubbock St. SE14 CC43 67
Lucan Dr. Stai. AX50 73
Bingham Dr.
Lucan Pl. SW3 BU42 3
Lucan Pl. SW3 BU42 66
Lucan Rd. Barn. BR24 28
Lucas Av. E13 CH37 58
Lucas Av. Har. BF34 45
Lucas Ct. Har. BF33 45
Lucas Ct. Wal. Abb. CG20 22
Mason Way
Lucas Rd. SE20 CC50 77
Lucas Rd. Grays. DD41 71
Lucas St. SE8 CD44 67
Lucerne Clo. N13 BX27 38
Lucerne Clo. Wok. AS63 100
Claremont Av.
Lucerne Gro. E17 CF31 48
Lucerne Ms. W8 BS40 56
Kensington Mall
Lucerne Rd. N5 BY35 47
Lucerne Rd. Orp. CN54 88
Lucerne Rd. Th. Hth. BY52 86
Lucerne Way, Rom. CV29 42
Lucie Av. Ashf. AZ50 73
Lucien Rd. SW17 BV49 76
Lucien Rd. SW19 BS48 76
Lucknow St. SE18 CN43 68
Lucks Hill, Hem. H. AV13 7
Lucorn Clo. SE12 CG46 78
Luctons Av. Buck. H. CJ26 40
Lucy Cres. W3 BN39 55
Lucy Gdns. Dag. CQ34 50
Luddesdon Rd. Erith CR43 69
Luddington Av. Vir. W. AS51 82
Ludford Clo. NW9 BO30 37
Ludgate Cir. EC4 BY39 2
Ludgate Cir. EC4 BY39 56
Ludgate Hill EC4 BY39 2
Ludgate Hill EC4 BY39 56
Ludgate Sq. EC4 BY39 2

70

71

Mansion House St. EC2 BZ39 57
Cornhill
Mansion La. Iver AU40 52
Mans St. SW10 BT44 66
Manson Ms. SW7 BT42 3
Manson Ms. SW7 BT42 66
Manson Pl. SW7 BT42 3
Manson Pl. SW7 BT42 66
Manstead Clo. Rain. CU39 59
Mansted Gdns. Rom. CP33 50
Manston Av. Sthl. BF42 64
Manston Clo. Wal. Cr. CC18 21
Manstone Rd. NW2 BR35 46
Manston Rd. Harl. CN11 13
Manston Way, Horn. CU36 59
Mantell St. N1 BY37 2
Mantell St. N1 BY37 56
Manthorp Rd. SE18 CM42 68
Mantilla Rd. SW17 BV49 76
Mantle Rd. SE4 CD45 67
Manton Av. W7 BH41 64
Manton Clo. SE15 CB45 67
Manton Clo. Hayes BB40 53
Manton Rd. SE2 CO42 69
Mantua Clo. SW11 BT45 66
Wye St.
Mantua Rd. SW11 BT45 66
Mantus Clo. E1 CC38 57
Mantus Rd.
Mantus Rd. E1 CC38 57
Manus Way N20 BT27 38
Manville Gdns. SW17 BV48 76
Manville Rd. SW17 BX48 76
Manwood Rd. SE4 CD46 77
Manwood St. E16 CK40 58
Manygate La. Shep. BA54 83
Many Gates SW12 BV48 76
Mapel Rd. Wok. AV65 100
Mapesbury Rd. NW2 BR36 55
Mape St. E2 CB38 57
Maple Av. E4 CD28 39
Maple Av. W3 BO40 55
Maple Av. Har. BF34 45
Maple Av. St. Alb. BG11 9
Maple Av. Upmin. CX35 51
Maple Av. West. Dr. AY40 53
Maple Clo. Hat. BP13 10
Maple Clo. N16 CB32 48
Timberwharf Rd.
Maple Clo. SW4 BW46 76
Clarence Av.
Maple Clo. Brwd. DC27 122
Maple Clo. Buck. H. CJ27 40
Maple Clo. Bush. BE23 27
Maple Clo. Horn. CU34 50
Maple Clo. Mitch. BV51 86
Maple Clo. Orp. CM53 88
Maple Clo. Ruis. BC32 44
Maple Ct. Egh. AQ50 72
Maple Ct. N. Mal. BO52 85
Maple Cres. Sid. CO46 79
Maple Cres. Slou. AQ40 52
Maplecroft La. Wal. Abb. CG14 13
Mapledale Av. Croy. CB55 87
Mapledene, Chis. CM50 78
Mapledene Rd. E8 CA36 57
Maplefield, St. Alb. BF18 18
Maplefield La. Ch. St. G. AQ24 25
Maple Gdns. Edg. BO29 37
Maple Grn. Hem. H. AV12 7
Maple Gro. NW9 BN33 46
Maple Gro. W5 BK41 64
Maple Gro. Brent. BJ43 64
Maple Gro. Guil. AR69 118
Maple Gro. Sthl. BE39 54
Maple Gro. Welw. G. C. BR6 5
Maple Gro. Wok. AS64 100
Maple Hill, Hem. H. AR18 16
Maple Ho. SE8 CD43 67
Idonia St.
Mapleleafe Gdns. Ilf. CL31 49
Maple Pl. E1 CB39 57
Maple Pl. W1 BW38 1
Maple Pl. W1 BW38 56
Maple St.
Maple Pl. Bans. BQ60 94
Maple Pl. West. Dr. AY40 53
Maple Rd. E11 CG32 49
Maple Rd. SE20 CB51 87
Maple Rd. Ash. BK63 102
Maple Rd. Dart. CV47 80
Maple Rd. Grav. DH49 81
Maple Rd. Grays. DE43 71
Maple Rd. Hayes BD38 54
Maple Rd. Red. BU72 121
Maple Rd. Surb. BK53 84
Maple Rd. Whyt. CA62 105
Maple Wk. Sutt. BS58 95
Cotswold Rd.
Maple Wk. W10 BR38 55
Droop St.
Maplescombe La. Farn. CX55 90
Maplescombe La. Farn. CX56 99
Maples Pl. E1 CB39 57
Raven Row
Maple Springs, Wal. Abb. CH20 22
Maplestead Rd. SW2 BX47 76
Maplestead Rd. Dag. CO37 59
Maples, The Bans. BS60 95
Maples, The Cher. AU57 91
Maples, The Harl. CL13 13
Maple St. W1 BW39 1
Maple St. W1 BW39 56
Maple St. Rom. CS31 50
Maple Ter. Rick. AV28 34
Maplethorpe Rd. Th. Hth. BY52 86
Mapleton Clo. Brom. CH53 88
Mapleton Cres. SW18 BS46 76
Mapleton Rd.
Mapleton Cres. Enf. CC22 30
Mapleton Rd. SW18 BS46 76
Mapleton Rd. Enf. CB23 30
Mapleton Rd. West. CN68 115
Maple Wy. Couls. BV64 104
Maplin Clo. N21 BX25 29
Maplin Rd. E16 CH39 58
Mapperley Dr. Wdf. Grn. CG29 40
Forest Dr.
Maquire St. SE1 CA41 4
Maran Way, Belv. CP41 69
Marbeck Clo. Wind. AL44 61
Marble Arch W1 BU40 3
Marble Arch W1 BU40 56
Marble Clo. W3 BM40 55
Gunnersbury La.
Marble Hill River Path, Twick. BK47 74
Orleans Rd.
Marble Hl. Clo. Twick. BJ47 74
Marble Hl. Gdns. Twick. BJ47 74
Marbles Way, Tad. BQ63 103
Marbrook Ct. SE12 CJ48 78
Marcet Rd. Dart. CV46 80
Marchbank Rd. SW5 BR43 65
Marchmont Rd. Rich. BL46 75
Marchmont Rd. Wall. BW57 95
Marchmont St. WC1 BX38 2
Marchmont St. WC1 BX38 56
March Rd. Twick. BJ47 74
March Rd. Wey. AZ56 92
Marchwood Clo. SE5 CA43 67
Southampton Way
Marchwood Cres. W5 BK39 54
Marcia Rd. SE1 CA42 4
Marcia Rd. SE1 CA42 67
Marcilly Rd. SW18 BT46 76
Marconi Rd. Grav. DE48 81
Marconi Way, Sthl. BF39 54
Marcon Pl. E8 CB35 48
Marco Rd. W6 BP41 65
Marcus Ct. E15 CG37 58
Marcus Rd. Dart. CU47 79
Marcus St. E15 CG37 58
Marcus St. SW18 BS46 76
Marcus Ter. SW18 BS46 76
Denton St.
Mardale Dr. NW9 BN32 46
Mardell Rd. Croy. CC53 87
Marden Av. Brom. CG53 88
Marden Clo. Chig. CO27 41
Marden Cres. Bex. CS46 79
Marden Cres. Croy. BX53 86
Marden Rd. N17 CA30 39
Avenue, The
Marden Rd. Croy. BX53 86
Marden Rd. Rom. CT32 50
Marden Sq. SE16 CB41 67
Drummond Rd.
Marder Rd. W13 BJ41 64
Mardyke Rd. Harl. CO10 6
Mardyke St. SE17 BZ42 4
Mardyke St. SE17 BZ42 67
Townsend St.
Marechal Niel Av. Sid. CM48 78
Mareschal Rd. Guil. AR71 118
Mares Field, Croy. CA55 87
Maresfield Gdns. NW3 BT35 47
Mare St. E8 CB37 57
Marfield Ct. N. Mal. BO54 85
Margaret Av. E4 CE25 30
Margaret Av. Brwd. DC26 122
Margaret Av. St. Alb. BG12 9
Margaret Bondfield Av. Bark. CO36 59
Margaret Bldgs. N16 CA33 48
Margaret Rd.
Margaret Clo. Epp. CN18 22
Margaret Rd.
Margaret Clo. Pot. B. BT20 20
Margaret Clo. Rom. CU32 50
Margaret Clo. Stai. AX50 73
Margaret Clo. Wal. Abb. CF20 21
Moremead
Margaret Ct. W1 BW39 56
Margaret St.
Margaret Dr. Horn. CW33 51
Margaret Rd.N16 CA33 48
Margaret Rd. Barn. BT24 29
Margaret Rd. Bex. CP46 79
Margaret Rd. Epp. CO18 23
Margaret Rd. Guil. AR71 118
Margaret Rd. Rom. CU32 50
Margaret St. W1 BV39 1
Margaret St. W1 BV39 56
Margaret St. Uxb. AX36 53
Cross St.
Margaretta Ter. SW3 BU43 3
Margaretta Ter. SW3 BU43 66
Margaretting Rd. E12 CJ34 49
Margaret Way, Couls. BY58 95
Margaret Way, Ilf. CJ32 49
Margate Rd. SW2 BX46 76
Margeholes, Wat. BE27 36
Margery Gro. Tad. BR68 112
Margery La. Tad. BR68 112
Margery Pk. Rd. E7 CH36 58
Margery Rd. Dag. CP34 50
Margery St. WC1 BY38 2
Margery St. WC1 BY38 56
Margin Dr. SW19 BQ49 75
Margravine Gdns. W6 BQ42 65
Margravine Rd. W6 BQ42 65
Marham Gdns. SW18 BU47 76
Marham Gdns. Mord. BT53 86
Maria Clo. SE1 CB42 67
Beatrice Rd.
Marian Clo. Grays DC40 60
Marian Clo. Hayes BD38 54
Marian Ct. Sutt. BS56 95
Marian Gdns. Horn. CW34 51
Marian Pl. E2 CB37 57
Marian Rd. SW16 BW51 86
Marian Way NW10 BO36 55
Maria Ter. E1 CC38 57
Maricas Av. Har. BG29 36
Marie Therese Clo. N. Mal. BN53 85
Marigold St. SE16 CB41 67
Marina Av. N. Mal. BP53 85
Marina Clo. Brom. CG52 88
Marina Clo. Rom. CS32 50
Marina Dr. Dart. CX47 80
Marina Dr. Dart. CW47 80
Marina Dr. Grav. DF47 81
Marina Dr. Well. CN44 68
Marina Gdns. Wal. Cr. CC18 21
Marina Pl. SW8 BX44 66
Priory Gro.
Marina Way, Hayes AW40 53
Marina Way, Iver AV40 52
Marine Way, Tedd. BK50 74
Fairways
Marine Av. Well. CO45 69
Marinefield Rd. SW6 BS44 66
Mariner Gdns. Rich. BJ48 74
Ashburnham Rd.
Mariner Rd. E12 CL35 49
Mariner Way, Hem. H. AZ14 8
Dersingham Av.
Marine St. SE16 CB41 4
Marine St. SE16 CB41 67
Enid St.
Marion Av. Shep. AZ53 83
Marion Clo. Bush. BE23 27
Marion Clo. Grays. DC40 71
Marion Clo. Ilf. CM29 40
Marion Cres. Orp. CO53 89
Marion Gro. Wdf. Grn. CG28 40
Marion Rd. NW7 BP28 37
Marion Rd. Th. Hth. BZ53 87
Mariott Rd. Dart. CW47 80
Marischal Rd. SE13 CF45 67
Marish La. Uxb. AU31 43
Mariso Clo. Grays. DG42 71
Maritime St. E3 CD38 57
Marius Rd. SW17 BV48 76
Marjorams Av. Loug. CL23 31
Marjorie Gro. SW11 BU45 66
Murkab Nthwd. BB28 35
Markab Rd. Nthwd. BC28 35
Mark Av. E4 CE25 30
Mark Clo. Bexh. CQ44 69
Mark Clo. Sthl. BF40 54
Mark Dr. Ger. Cr. AR28 34
Marke Clo. Kes. CK56 97
Markedge La. Couls. BU65 104
Markedge La. Red. BU66 113
Markenfield Rd. Guil. AR70 118
Market Ct. W1 BW39 56
Market Pl.
Market Field Rd. Red. BU70 121
Market Hill SE18 CL41 68
Market Link, Rom. CT31 50
Mkt. Meadow Pl. Orp. CP52 89
Market Ms. W1 BV40 3
Market Ms. W1 BV40 56
Market Oak La. Hem. H. AZ15 8
Market Pde. SE15 CB44 67
Market Pl. N2 BU31 47
Market Pl. NW11 BS31 47
Market Pl. W1 BW39 1
Market Pl. W1 BW39 56
Market Pl. W3 BN40 55
Market Pl. Brent. BK43 64
Market Pl. Dart. CW47 80
Market Pl. Dor. BJ71 119
Market Pl. Enf. BZ24 30
Market Pl. Ger. Cr. AR30 34
Market Pl. Grav. DH47 81
Market Pl. Grays. DD43 71
Market Pl. Hat. BP12 10
Market Pl. Kings. on T. BK51 84
Market Pl. Rom. CO24 32
Market Pl. Rom. CT32 50
Market Pl. St. Alb. BG13 9
Market Pl. Wat. BD24 27
Market Rd. N7 BX36 56
Market Rd. Rich. BM45 65
Market Row SW9 BY45 66
Atlantic Rd.
Market Sq. N9 CB27 39
Market Sq. Brom. CH51 88
Market Sq. Hem. H. AX13 8
Market Sq. Uxb. AX36 53
High St.
Market Sq. Wal. Abb. CF20 21
Market Sq. Wok. AS62 100
Market St. E6 CK37 58
Market St. SE18 CL42 68
Market St. Dart. CW47 80
Market St. Guil. AR71 118
Market St. Harl. CP9 6
Market St. Wat. BC24 26
Market, The Cars. BT54 86
Market Way, Slou. AU42 62
Market Way, West. CM66 115
Castells Meadows
Markfield, Croy. CB58 96
Markfield Gdns. CE26 39
Markfield Rd. W15 CB31 48
Markfield Rd. Cat. CB66 114
Mark Grn. Wat. BD28 36
Mark Hall Moors, Harl. CO9 6
Markham Sq. SW3 BU42 3
Markham Sq. SW3 BU42 66
Markham St. SW3 BU42 3
Markham St. SW3 BU42 66
Markhole Clo. Hampton. BE50 74
Markhouse Av. E17 CD32 48
Mark House Rd. E17 CD32 48
Mark La. EC3 CA40 4
Mark La. EC3 CA40 57
Mark La. Grav. DJ47 81
Markmanor Av. E17 CD33 48
Mark Oak La. Lthd. BF64 102
Mark Pl. Sthl. BF40 54
Mark Rd. N22 BY30 38
Mark Rd. Hem. H. AZ12 8
Mark St. E15 CG36 58
Marks Av. Grav. DF47 81
Marks Av. Ong. CW17 24
Marksbury Av. Rich. BM45 65
Marks Rd. Rom. CS32 50
Marks Rd. Warl. CD62 105
Marks St. E1 CA39 57
Mark St. EC2 CA38 2
Mark St. EC2 CA38 57
Mark St. Reig. BS70 121
Markville Gdns. Cat. CB66 114
Markway, Sun. BD51 84
Mark Way, Swan. CU53 89
Markwell Clo. SE26 CB49 77
Taylors La.
Markyate Rd. Dag. CO35 50
Marland Ms. N1 BY36 56
Lofting Rd.
Marlands Rd. Ilf. CK31 49
Marlboro' Rd. Dart. CV46 80
Marlboro' Rd. Sth. Croy. BZ57 96
Marlboro' Rd. Sthl. BD41 64
Marlboro' Rd. Wat. BC24 26
Marlboro' St. SW3 BU42 3
Marlborough Av. E8 CB37 2
Marlborough Av. E8 CB37 57
Marlborough Av. N14 BW27 38
Marlborough Av. Edg. BM27 37
Marlborough Av. Ruis. BA32 44
Marlborough Bldgs. SW3 BU42 3
Marlborough Bldgs. SW3 BU42 66
Marlborough Clo. N20 BU27 38
Marlborough Clo. SW19 BU50 76
Marlborough Clo. Grays. DE41 71
Marlborough Clo. Orp. CN54 88
Marlborough Clo. Upmin. CZ33 51
Marlborough Clo. Walt. BD55 84
Marlborough Ct. W1 BW39 1
Marlborough Ct. W8 BS42 66
Marlborough Cres. W4 BN41 65
Marlborough Cres. Sev. CT65 107
Marlborough Dr. Ilf. CK31 49
Marlborough Dr. Wey. BA55 83
Marlborough Gdns. N20 BU27 38
Marlborough Gdns. Surb. BK54 84
Marlborough Gdns. Upmin. CY33 51
Marlborough Gate, St. Alb. BH13 9
Marlborough Gro. SE1 CB42 4
Marlborough Gro. SE1 CB42 67
Marlborough Hill NW8 BT37 1
Marlborough Hill NW8 BT37 56
Marlborough Hill, Har. BG32 45
Marlborough Pk. Av. Sid. CO47 79
Marlborough Pl. NW8 BT37 1
Marlborough Pl. NW8 BT37 56
Marlborough Rise, Hem. H. AY12 8
Marlborough Rd. E4 CE29 39
Marlborough Rd. E7 CJ36 58
Marlborough Rd. E15 CG35 49
Borthwick Rd.
Marlborough Rd. E18 CH31 49
Marlborough Rd. N9 CA26 39
Marlborough Rd. N19 BW34 47
Marlborough Rd. N22 BX29 38
Marlborough Rd. SE7 CJ43 68
Marlborough Rd. SW1 BW40 3
Marlborough Rd. SW1 BW40 56
Marlborough Rd. SW19 BT50 76
Marlborough Rd. W4 BN42 65
Marlborough Rd. W5 BK41 64
Marlborough Rd. Ashf. AX49 73
Marlborough Rd. Bexh. CP45 69
Marlborough Rd. Brom. CJ52 88
Marlborough Rd. Brwd. DA25 33
Marlborough Rd. Dag. CO35 50
Marlborough Rd. Dor. BJ71 119
Marlborough Rd. Felt. BD48 74
Marlborough Rd. Har. BH31 45
Marlborough Rd. Hmptn. BF50 74
Marlborough Rd. Islw. BJ44 64
Marlborough Rd. Rich. BL46 75
Marlborough Rd. Rom. CR31 50
Marlborough Rd. St. Alb. BH13 9
Marlborough Rd. Slou. AR42 62
Marlborough Rd. Sutt. BS55 86
Marlborough Rd. Uxb. AZ38 53
Marlborough Rd. Wok. AT61 100
Marlborough St. SW3 BU42 66
Marle Gdns. Wal. Abb. CF19 21
Marler Rd. SE23 CD47 77
Marlescroft, Loug. CL25 31
Marley Av. Bexh. CP43 69
Marley Clo. Grnf. BF37 54
Marley Clo. Wey. AV57 91
Marley Rd. Welw. G. C. BS9 5
Marlin Clo. Berk. AP12 7
Marlingdene Clo. Hmptn. BF50 74
Marlings Clo. Chis. CN52 88
Marlings Clo. Whyt. CA62 105
Marlings Pk. Av. Chis. CN52 88
Marling Way, Grav. DJ49 81
Marlin Sq. Wat. BB19 17
Marlins Clo. Rick. AV23 25
Marlins Turn, Hem. H. AW12 8
Marloes Clo. Wem. BK35 45
Marloes Rd. W8 BS41 66
Marloes, The NW8 BT37 1
Marloes, The NW8 BT37 56
Marlo, The Ash. BL62 103
Marlow Clo. SE20 CB52 87
Marlow Ct. NW6 BQ36 55
Marlow Cres. Twick. BH46 74
Marlow Dr. Sutt. BQ55 85
Marlowe Clo. Chis. CM50 78
Marlowe Clo. Ilf. CM30 40
Marlowe Gdns. SE9 CL46 78
Foot's Cray Rd.
Marlowe Gdns. Rom. CV30 42
Shenstone Gdns.
Marlowe Rd. E17 CF31 48
Marlowes, Hem. H. AX14 8
Marlowe Sq. Mitch. BW52 86
Marlowes, The Dart. CS45 69
Marlow Gdns. Hayes BA41 63
Marlow Gdns. Rom. CV30 42
Marlow Rd. E6 CK38 58
Marlow Rd. SE20 CB52 87
Marlow Rd. Sthl. BE41 64
Marlpit Av. Couls. BX62 104
Marlpit La. Couls. BW61 104
Listria Pk.
Marl St. SW18 BT45 66
Marlton St. SE10 CG42 68
Marlyns Clo. Guil. AT68 109
Marlyns Dr. Guil. AT68 109
Marlyns Dr. Guil. AT69 118
Marlyon Rd. Ilf. CO28 41
Marmadon Rd. SE18 CN42 68
Marmion App. E4 CE28 39
Marmion Clo.
Marmion Av. E4 CD28 39
Marmion Clo. E4 CE28 39
Marmion Rd. SW11 BV45 66
Marmount Rd. SE15 CB44 67
Marmora Rd. SE22 CC46
Marmot Rd. Houns. BD45
Marne Av. N11 BV28
Marne Av. Well. CO45
Marnell Way, Houns. BD45
Marne St. W10 BR38
Marney Rd. SW11 BV45
Marneys Clo. Epsom BM61 1
Woodlands Rd.
Marnham Av. NW2 BR35
Marnham Cres. Grnf. BF37
Marnham Rise, Hem. H. AW12
Marnock Rd. SE4 CD46
Maroon St. E14 CD39
Marquess Gro. N1 BZ36
Marquess Rd. N1 BZ36
Marquis Clo. Wem. BL36
Marquis Rd. N4 BX33
Marquis Rd. N22 BX29
Marquis Rd. NW1 BW36
Marrick Clo. SW15 BP45
Marrilyne Av. Enf. CD22
Marriot Clo. Felt. BA46
Marriot Rd. Barn. BQ24
Marriots Clo. BO32
Marriots, The Harl. CP8
Old Rd.
Marriott Rd. E15 CG37
Marriott Rd. N4 BX33
Marriott Rd. N10 BU30
Marrowells, Wey. BB55
Mar Rd. S. Ock. DB38
Marryat Rd. SW19 BQ49
Marryat Rd. Enf. CB21
Marryatt Pl. SW19 BR49
Marsala Rd. SE13 CE45
Marsden Clo. Welw. G. C. BP9
Marsden Grn. Welw. G. C. BP8
Marsden Rd. N9 CB27
Marsden Rd. SE15 CA45
Marsden Rd. Welw. G. C. BP8
Marsden St. NW5 BV36
Marshall Av. St. Alb. BH12
Marshall Clo. Houns. BE46
Marshall Dr. Hayes BB39
Marshall Gdns. SE1 BY41
London Rd.
Marshall Path SE28 CO40
Titmuss Av.
Marshall Rd. N17 BZ30
Marshalls Clo. Epsom BN60
Marshall Dr. Rom. CT31
Marshall's Gro. SE18 CK42
Marshalls Rd. Rom. CS31
Marshall's Rd. Sutt. BS56
Lewis Rd.
Marshall St. W1 BW39
Marshall St. W1 BW39
Marshals Dr. St. Alb. BJ12
Marshalsea Rd. SE1 BZ41
Marshalsea Rd. SE1 BZ41
Marshalswick La. St. Alb. BJ12
Marsham Clo. Chis. CL49
Marsham La. Ger. Cr. AS32
Marsham St. SW1 BW41
Marsham St. SW1 BW41
Marsham Way, Ger. Cr. AS32
Marsh Av. Epsom BO58
Marsh Av. Loug. CM23
Marsh Av. Mitch. BU51
Marshbrooke Clo SE3 CJ45
Marsh Clo. NW7 BO27
Marsh Clo. Wal. Cr. CD20
Marshcroft Dr. Wal. Cr. CD18
Southmead Cr.
Marsh Dr. NW9 BO32
Marshe Clo. Pot. B. BT19
Marsh Farm Rd. Twick. BH47
Marshfield St. E14 CF41
Marshfoot Rd. Grays. DF42
Marshgate La. E15 CE37
Marsh Grn. Rd. Dag. CR37
Marsh Hill E9 CD35
Marsh Hill, Wal. Abb. CG17
Marsh La. E10 CE34
Marsh La. NW7 BN28
Marsh La. W17 CB30
Marsh La. Harl. CQ8
Marsh La. Maid. AJ40
Marsh La. Stan. BK28
Marsh La. Wey. AW56
Marsh Rd. Pnr. BE31
Marsh Rd. Wem. BK37
Marsh St. E14 CE42
Marsh St. Dart. CW45
Marsh St. Dart. CX45
Marsh St. Dart. CX46
Marshmoor Cres. Hat. BQ15
Marshmoor La. Hat. BQ14
Marsland Rd. SE17 BY42
Marston, Epsom BN58
Marston Av. Chess. BL57
Marston Av. Dag. CR34
Marston Clo. NW6 BT36
Marston Clo. Dag. CR34
Marston Clo. Hem. H. AZ14
Marston Rd. Hodd. CE11
Marston Rd. Ilf. CK30
Marston Rd. Tedd. BJ49
Marston Rd. Wok. AQ62 1
Marston Way SE19 BY50
Marston Way SE19 BY50
Marsworth Av. Pnr. BD30
Martaban Rd. N16 CA34
Listria Pk.
Martello St. E8 CB36
Martell Rd. SE21 BZ48
Marten Gate, St. Alb. BJ11
Marten Rd. E17 CE30
Martens Av. Bexh. CR45
Martens Clo. Bexh. CS45
Martha Rd. E15 CG36
Martha St. E1 CB39
Marthorne Cres. Har. BG30
Martian Av. Hem. H. AZ12
Martin Bowes Rd. SE9 CK45
Martin Cl. Hat. BP13
Martin Clo. Croy. CC59

artin Clo. Sth. Croy.	CC58	96
artin Clo. Warl.	CB61	105
artin Clo. Sth. Croy.	CC58	96
artin Cres. Croy.	BY54	86
artindale SW14	BN46	75
artindale Av. Orp.	CN56	97
artindale Clo. Guil.	AU69	118
Gilliat Dr.		
artindale Rd. SW12	BV47	76
artindale Rd. Hem. H.	AV13	7
artindale Rd. Houns.	BE45	64
artindale Rd. Wok.	AQ62	100
artin Dene, Bexh.	CQ46	79
artin Dr. Nthlt.	BE35	45
artin Dr. Rain.	CU38	59
artineau Dr. Dor.	BJ72	119
artineau Rd. N5	BY35	47
artineau St. Est. E1	CC40	57
artingale Clo. Rich.	BK48	74
artingale Clo. Sun.	BC52	83
artin Gdns. Dag.	CP35	50
artin Gro. Mord.	BS52	86
lartin La. EC4	**BZ40**	**4**
artin La. EC4	BZ40	57
artin Rise, Bexh.	CQ46	79
artin Rd. Dag.	CP35	50
artin Rd. Dart.	CV48	80
artin Rd. Guil.	AQ69	118
artin Rd. Slou.	AP41	62
artin Rd. S. Ock.	CW40	60
artins Bldgs. SW18	BS46	76
Frogmore		
artins Clo. Guil.	AU70	118
artins Clo. Orp.	CP52	89
artins Dr. Wal. Cr.	CD17	21
artins Mt. Barn.	BS24	29
artin's Rd. Brom.	CG51	88
artins Shaw, Sev.	CT64	107
High St.		
artins, The SE26	CB49	77
Lawrie Pk. Gdns.		
artins Wk. N10	BV29	38
artin Way SW20	BQ51	85
artin Way, Wok.	AQ62	100
artlesham Clo. Horn.	CV35	51
artlet Gro. Nthlt.	BD38	54
Javelin Way		
lartlett Ct. WC2	**BX39**	**2**
artlett Ct. WC2	BX39	56
Drury La.		
artley Dr. Ilf.	CL32	49
lart St. WC2	**BX40**	**4**
art St. WC2	BX40	56
Floral St.		
artyr Clo. St. Alb.	BG15	9
Creighton Av.		
artyr S. La. Wok.	AT59	91
arvell Av. Hayes	BC39	53
arvels Clo. SE12	CH48	78
arvels La. SE12	CH48	78
arville Rd. SW6	BR43	65
arwell, West.	CM66	115
Farley Croft		
arwood Clo. Kings L.	AY18	17
arwood Clo. Well.	CO45	69
arwood Way SE16	CB42	67
Catlin St.		
ary Ann's Bldgs SE8	CE43	67
ary Clo. Har.	BL31	46
aryatt Av. Har.	BF34	45
arybank SE18	CK42	68
Frances St.		
ary Datchelor Clo. SE5	BZ44	57
Deynsford Rd.		
aryfield Clo. Bex.	CT48	79
ary Hill Clo. Ken.	BZ62	105
lary Kingsley Pl. N6	BV33	47
laryland, Hat.	BO13	10
laryland Pk. E15	CG35	49
laryland Rd. E15	CF35	48
laryland Rd. N22	BX29	38
laryland Rd. Th. Hth.	BY51	86
laryland Sq. E15	CG35	49
larylands Rd. W9	BS38	56
laryland St. E15	CF35	48
laryland Way, Sun.	BC51	83
larylebone Cir. NW1	**BU39**	**1**
larylebone High St. W1	**BV39**	**1**
laryland Wk. N1	BZ37	57
Popham St.		
larylebone High St. W1	BV39	56
larylebone La. W1	**BV39**	**1**
larylebone La. W1	BV39	56
larylebone Ms. W1	BV39	1
larylebone Ms. W1	BV39	56
larylebone Pass. W1	**BW39**	**1**
larylebone Rd. NW1	**BU39**	**1**
larylebone Rd. NW1	BU39	56
larylebone St. W1	**BV39**	**1**
larylebone St. W1	BV39	56
larylee Way SE11	**BX42**	**4**
larylee Way SE11	BX42	66
lary Macarthur Ho. W14	BR43	65
larylee Way SE11	**BX42**	**4**
larylee Way SE11	BX42	66
lary Macarthur Ho W14	BR43	65
lary Peters Dr. Har.	BG35	45
laryon Gro. SE7	CK42	68
laryon Ms. NW3	BU35	47
South End Rd.		
laryon Rd. SE7	CK42	68
lary Pl. W11	BR40	55
lary Rd. Guil.	AR71	118
lary's Av. Berk.	AO12	7
laryside, Slou.	AS41	62
lary's Ter. Twick.	BJ47	74
lary St. N1	**BZ37**	**2**
lary St. N1	BZ37	57
lary Ter. NW1	**BV37**	**1**
lary Ter. NW1	BV37	56
lasbro' Rd. W14	BQ41	65
lascalls Ct. SE7	CJ43	68
Victoria Way		
lascalls Gdns. Brwd.	CZ28	42
lascalls La. Brwd.	CZ28	42
lascalls Rd. SE7	CJ43	68
lascotts Clo. NW2	BP34	46
lasefield Av. Borwd.	BM25	28
Masefield Av. Stan.	BH28	36
Masefield Av. Sthl.	BF40	54
Masefield Clo. Erith	CT44	69
Masefield Clo. Rom.	CU30	41
Masefield Cres. N14	BV25	29
Masefield Cres. Rom.	CV30	42
Masefield Dr. Upmin.	CY33	51
Masefield Gdns. E6	CL38	58
Masefield La. Hayes	BC38	53
Masefield Rd. Dart.	CX46	80
Masefield Rd. Grav.	DE48	81
Masefield Rd. Grays.	DF41	71
Masefield Rd. Hamptn.	BE49	74
Mashie Rd. W3	BO39	55
Mashiters Hill, Rom.	CS30	41
Mashiters Wk. Rom.	CT30	41
Maskell Rd. SW17	BT48	76
Maskelyn Clo. SW11	BU44	66
Mason Clo. E16	CH40	58
Mason Clo. Bexh.	CR45	69
Mason Clo. Hamptn.	BE51	84
Masonic Hall Rd. Cher.	AV53	82
Mason Pl. Mitch.	BU51	86
Mason Rd. Wdf. Grn.	CG28	40
Mason's Arms Ms. W1	**BV40**	**3**
Mason's Arms Yd. W1	BV40	56
Maddox St.		
Masons Av. EC2	**BZ39**	**2**
Mason's Av. EC2	BZ39	57
Mason Av. Croy.	BZ55	87
Masons Av. Har.	BH31	45
Mason's Br. Rd. Red.	BV73	121
Masons Ct. Wem.	BM34	46
Mason's Grn. La. W3	BM38	55
Masons Hill SE18	CL42	68
Masons Hill, Brom.	CH52	88
Masons Paddock, Dor.	BJ70	119
Masons Pl. EC1	**BY38**	**2**
Masons Pl. EC1	BY38	56
Masons Rd. Enf.	CB21	30
Mason's Rd. Hem. H.	AZ13	8
Mason St. SE17	**BZ42**	**4**
Mason St. SE17	BZ42	67
Mason's Yd. SW1	**BW40**	**3**
Mason's Yd. SW1	BW40	56
Duke St.		
Mason Way, Wal. Abb.	CG20	22
Massey Clo. N11	BV28	38
Grove Rd.		
Massie Rd. E8	CB36	57
Graham Rd.		
Massinger St. SE17	**CA42**	**4**
Massinger St. SE17	CA42	67
Massingham St. E1	CC38	57
Masson Av. Ruis.	BD36	54
Master Gunner Pl. SE18	CK43	68
Masterman Rd. E6	CK38	58
Masters St. E1	CC39	57
Mast House Ter. E14	CE42	67
Maswell Pk. Cres. Houns.	BG46	74
Maswell Pk. Rd. Houns.	BF46	74
Matcham Rd. E11	CG34	49
Matching Rd. Harl.	CR9	6
Matfield Clo. Brom.	CH53	88
Matfield Rd. Belv.	CR43	69
Matham Gro. SE22	CA45	67
Matham Rd. E. Mol.	BG53	84
Matheson Pl. W14	BR42	65
Matheson Rd. W14	BR43	65
Mathews Av. E6	CL37	58
Mathews La. Stai.	AV49	72
Mathews Yd. WC2	BX39	56
Shorts Gdns.		
Matilda House E1	**CB40**	**4**
Matilda St. N1	**BX37**	**2**
Matilda St. N1	BX37	56
Matlock Ct. SE5	BZ45	67
Matlock Cres. Sut.	BR55	85
Matlock Cres. Wat.	BD27	36
Matlock Gdns. Horn.	CW34	51
Matlock Gdns. Sutt.	BR56	94
Matlock Pl. Sutt.	BR56	94
Matlock Rd. E10	CF32	48
Matlock Rd. Cat.	CA64	105
Matlock St. E14	CD39	57
Matlock Way, N. Mal.	BN51	85
Matrimony Pl. SW8	BW44	66
Wandsworth Rd.		
Matt Arnold Clo. Cob.	BC60	92
Matthew Parker St. SW1	**BW41**	**3**
Matthew Parker St. SW1	BW41	66
Matthews Av. E6	CL37	58
Folkestone Rd.		
Matthews Pk. Av. E15	CG36	58
Matthews Rd. Har.	BG35	45
Matthew St. SW11	BU44	66
Matthew St. Reig.	BS72	121
Matthias Rd. N16	BZ35	48
Mattingley Way SE15	CA43	67
Mattison Rd. N4	BY32	47
Mattock La. W5	BK40	54
Mattock La. W13	BJ40	54
Mattock Rd. W5	BK40	54
Mattock La.		
Matyr Rd. Guil.	AR71	118
Maude Cres. Wat.	BC22	26
Maude Rd. E17	CD32	48
Maude Rd. SE5	CA44	67
Maude Rd. Swan.	CU50	79
Maudesville Cotts. W7	BH40	54
Maude Ter. E17	CD31	48
Maud Gdns. E13	CG37	58
Maud Rd.		
Maud Gdns. Bark.	CN37	58
Maud Rd. E10	CF34	48
Maud Rd. E13	CG37	58
Maudslay Rd. SE9	CK45	68
Maud St. E16	CG39	58
Mauleverer Rd. SW2	BX46	76
Maunder Rd. W7	BH40	54
Maunolid Way, Brwd.	DA25	33
Maunsel St. SW1	**BW42**	**3**
Maunsel St. SW1	BW42	66
Maurice Av. Cat.	BZ64	105
Maurice Av. N22	BY30	38
Maurice Brown Clo. NW7	BQ28	37
Maurice Wk. NW11	BT31	47
Maurier Clo. Nthlt.	BD38	54
Mauritius Rd. SE10	CG42	68
Maurne St. W12	BP39	55
Maury Rd. N16	CB34	48
Mauve St. E14	CF39	57
St. Leonard's Av.		
Mavelstone Clo. Brom.	CK51	88
Mavelstone Rd. Brom.	CJ51	88
Mavis Av. Epsom	BO56	94
Mavis Clo. Epsom	BO56	94
Mavis Gro. Horn.	CW34	51
Mawbey Est. SE1	**CA42**	**4**
Mawbey Est. SE1	CB42	67
Mawbey Pl. SE1	**CA42**	**4**
Mawbey Pl. SE1	CA42	67
Mawbey Rd.		
Mawbey Rd. SE1	**CA42**	**4**
Mawbey Rd. SE1	CA42	67
Mawbey St. SW8	BX43	66
Mawney Rd. Rom.	CR30	41
Mawneys Clo. Rom.	CR30	41
Mawson Clo. SW20	BR51	85
Mawson Ho. EC1	BY39	56
Baldwin's Gdns.		
Mawson La. W4	BO43	65
Chiswick La. S.		
Maxey Gdns. Dag.	CQ35	50
Maxey Rd. SE18	CM42	68
Maxey Rd. Dag.	CQ35	50
Maxilla Gdns. W10	BQ39	55
Maxilla Wk. W10	BQ39	55
Maxilla Gdns.		
Maximfeldt Rd. Erith	CT42	69
Maxim Rd. N21	BY25	29
Maxim Rd. Dart.	CT46	79
Maxim Rd. Dart.	CT46	79
Wosley Clo.		
Maxim Rd. Erith	CS42	69
Maxted Clo. Hem. H.	AZ12	8
Maxted Pk. Har.	BH33	45
Maxted Rd. SE15	CA45	67
Maxted Rd. Hem. H.	AZ12	8
Maxwell Clo. Rick.	AW27	35
Maxwell Dr. Wey.	AX59	92
Maxwell Gdns. Orp.	CN55	88
Maxwell Rise, Wat.	BE26	36
Maxwell Rd. SW6	BS43	66
Maxwell Rd. Ashf.	BA50	73
Maxwell Rd. Borwd.	BN23	28
Maxwell Rd. Nthwd.	BA29	35
Maxwell Rd. St. Alb.	BJ14	9
Maxwell Rd. Well.	CO45	69
Maxwell Rd. West Dr.	AY42	63
Maxwelton Av. NW7	BN28	37
Maxwelton Clo. NW7	BN28	37
Mayall Rd. SE24	BY45	66
May Av. Grav.	DF47	81
May Av. Orp.	CO53	89
Maybank Av. E18	CH30	40
Maybank Av. Horn.	CU35	50
Maybank Av. Wem.	BH35	45
Maybank Gdns. Pnr.	BC32	44
Maybank Rd. E18	CH30	40
Maybank Vil. Ilf.	CO33	50
Mayberry Pl. Surb.	BL54	85
Maybourne Clo. SE26	CB49	77
Maybourne Rise, Wok.	AR65	100
Maybrick Rd. Horn.	CV32	51
Maybrook Meadow Est.		
Bark.	CO36	59
Maybury Av. Dart.	CY47	80
Maybury Av. Wal. Cr.	CB17	21
Maybury Clo. Orp.	CL53	88
Maybury Clo. Tad.	BR63	103
Maybury Gdns. NW10	BP36	55
Maybury Hill, Wok.	AT61	100
Maybury Rd. E13	CJ38	58
Maybury Rd. Bark.	CN37	58
Maybury Rd. Wok.	AS62	100
Maybury St. SW17	BU49	76
Maybush Rd. Horn.	CW33	51
Maychurch Clo. Stan.	BK29	36
May Clo. Chess.	BL57	94
May Clo. St. Alb.	BG12	9
May Ct. Hem. H.	AX13	8
Maycock Gro. Nthwd.	BB29	35
Carew Rd.		
Maycroft Gdns. Grays.	DE42	71
Maycroft, Pnr.	BC30	35
Maycroft Av. Grays.	DE42	71
Maycroft Rd. Wal. Cr.	CA16	21
Maycross Av. Mord.	BR52	85
Mayday Gdns. SE3	CK44	68
Mayday Rd. Th. Hth.	BY53	86
Maye Clo. Lthd.	BK65	102
Mayerne Rd. SE9	CJ46	78
Mayesbrook Rd. Bark.	CN37	58
Mayesbrook Rd. Ilf.	CO34	50
Mayes Clo. Swan.	CU52	89
Mayes Clo. Warl.	CC62	105
Mayesford Rd. Rom.	CP33	50
Mayes Rd. N22	BX30	38
Mayeswood Rd. SE12	CJ48	78
Mayfair Av. Bexh.	CP44	69
Mayfair Av. Ilf.	CK34	49
Mayfair Av. Rom.	CP32	50
Mayfair Av. Twick.	BG47	74
Mayfair Av. Wor. Pk.	BP54	85
Mayfair Clo. Surb.	BL54	85
Mayfair Ct. Beck.	CE51	87
Mayfair Gdns. N17	BZ29	39
Mayfair Gdns. Wdf. Grn.	CH29	40
Mayfair Pl. W1	**BV40**	**3**
Mayfair Pl. W1	BV40	56
Mayfair Rd. Dart.	CV46	80
Mayfair Ter. N14	BW26	38
Mayfare, Rick.	BA25	26
Mayfield, Bexh.	CQ45	69
Church Rd.		
Mayfield Clo. Walt.	BC56	92
Mayfield Gdns. Walt.	BC56	92
Mayfield, Wal. Abb.	CF20	21
Roundhills		
Mayfield, Welw. G. C.	BQ6	5
Mayfield Av. Ger. Cr.	AR31	43
Mayfield Av. N12	BT28	38
Mayfield Av. N14	BW27	38
Mayfield Av. W4	BO42	65
Mayfield Av. W13	BJ41	64
Mayfield Av. Har.	BJ32	45
Mayfield Av. Orp.	CN54	88
Mayfield Av. Wdf. Grn.	CH29	40
Mayfield Av. Wey.	AW58	92
Mayfield Clo. E8	CA36	57
Forest Rd.		
Mayfield Clo. Ashf.	AZ50	73
Mayfield Clo. Harl.	CQ9	6
Mayfield Clo. Surb.	BJ54	84
Mayfield Clo. Wey.	AW58	92
Mayfield Cres. N9	CB25	30
Mayfield Cres. Th. Hth.	BX52	86
Mayfield Dr. Pnr.	BE31	45
Mayfield Gdns. NW4	BQ32	46
Mayfield Gdns. W7	BG39	54
Mayfield Gdns. Brwd.	DA26	42
Mayfield Gdns. Stai.	AV50	72
Mayfield Rd. E4	CF27	39
Mayfield Rd. E8	CA36	57
Mayfield Rd. E13	CG38	58
Mayfield Rd. E17	CD30	39
Mayfield Rd. N8	BX32	47
Mayfield Rd. SW19	BR51	85
Mayfield Rd. W3	BM40	55
Mayfield Rd. Belv.	CS42	69
Mayfield Rd. Brom.	CK53	88
Mayfield Rd. Dag.	CP33	50
Mayfield Rd. Enf.	CC23	30
Mayfield Rd. Grav.	DF47	81
Mayfield Rd. Sth. Croy.	BZ58	96
Mayfield Rd. Sutt.	BT57	95
Mayfield Rd. Th. Hth.	BX52	86
Mayfield Rd. Walt.	BC56	92
Mayfield Rd. Wey.	AZ56	92
Mayfields, Grays.	DE41	71
Mayfields, Wem.	BM34	46
Mayfields Clo. Wem.	BM34	46
Mayflower Av. Hem. H.	AX13	8
Mayflower Clo. Ruis.	BA32	44
Mayflower Clo. S. Ock.	DB38	60
Mayflower Clo. Wal. Abb.	CG15	13
Crooked Way		
Mayflower Path, Brwd.	DB29	42
Mayflower Rd. SW9	BX44	66
Mayflower Rd. St. Alb.	BF17	18
Mayflower St. SE16	CC41	67
St. Mary Ch. St.		
Mayflower Way, Ong.	CX17	24
Mayflower Way, Slou.	AO35	43
Mayfly Gdns. Nthlt.	BD38	54
Valliant Clo.		
Mayford, Wok.	AR64	100
Mayford Clo. SW12	BU47	76
Mayford Clo. Wok.	AR64	100
Mayford Rd. SW12	BU47	76
May Gdns. Wem.	BK37	54
Maygold Wk. Amer.	AR23	25
Maygoods Clo. Uxb.	AX39	53
Maygoods Grn. Uxb.	AX39	53
Maygood St. N1	**BX37**	**2**
Maygood St. N1	BX37	56
Maygoods Vw. Uxb.	AX39	53
Maygreen Cres. Horn.	CU33	50
Maygrove Rd. NW6	BR36	55
Mayh Av. Wok.	AU61	100
Mayh Clo. Wok.	AU61	100
Mayh Cres. Wok.	AU61	100
Mayhew Clo. E4	CE27	39
Mayhill Av. SE7	CH43	68
Mayhill Rd. Barn.	BR25	28
Mayh St. Wok.	AU61	100
Mayland Av. Hem. H.	AZ12	8
Maylands Av. Horn.	CU35	50
Maylands Clo. Wat.	BD28	36
Maylands Dr. Sid.	CP48	79
Maylands Dr. Uxb.	AX36	53
Maylands Way, Rom.	CY29	42
Maylins Dr. Saw.	CP6	6
Maynard Clo. Erith	CT43	69
Maynard Ct. Wal. Abb.	CG20	22
Shernbroke Rd.		
Maynard Dr. St. Alb.	BG15	9
Maynard Pl. Pot. B.	BX18	20
Station Rd.		
Maynard Rd. E17	CE32	48
Maynards, Horn.	CW33	51
Clairvale		
Mayne Av. St. Alb.	BE14	9
Mayne Av. St. Alb.	BF15	9
Mayo Clo. Wal. Cr.	CC17	21
Mayola Rd. E5	CC35	48
Mayo Rd. NW10	BO36	55
Mayo Rd. Croy.	BZ53	87
Mayo Rd. Walt.	BB54	83
Mayo Rd. Walt.	BC54	83
Mayow Rd. SE23	CC48	77
Mayow Rd. SE26	CC49	77
May Pl. Av. Dart.	CU45	69
Mayplace Clo. Bexh.	CR45	69
May Pl. La. SE18	CL43	68
Mayplace Rd. E. Bexh.	CR45	69
Mayplace Rd. W. Bexh.	CR45	69
Maypole Cres. Ilf.	CM29	40
Maypole Dr. Chig.	CO27	41
Maypole Rd. Orp.	CO56	98
May Rd. E4	CE29	39
May Rd. E13	CH37	58
May Rd. Dart.	CW49	80
May Rd. Twick.	BH47	74
Maryroyd Av. Surb.	BM55	85
May's Bldgs. Ms. SE10	CF43	67
Croom's Hill		
Mays Ct. WC2	**BX40**	**4**
Mays Ct. WC2	BX40	56
St. Martin's La.		
Mays Hill Rd. Brom.	CG51	88
Mays La. E4	CF27	39
May's La. Barn.	BP26	37
May's Pl. SE15	CB45	67
Scylla Rd.		
Mays Rd. Tedd.	BG49	74
Mayswood Gdns. Dag.	CS36	59
Maythorn Clo. Wat.	BB24	26
Mayton St. N7	BX34	47
Maytree Clo. Edg.	BN27	37
Maytree Clo. Guil.	AR68	109
Maytree Clo. Guil.	AR69	118
Maytree Clo. Rain.	CT37	59
Maytree Cres. Wat.	BB21	26
Maytree Wk. SW2	BY48	76
Mayville Est. N16	CA35	48
Mayville Rd. E11	CG34	49
Mayville Rd. Ilf.	CL35	49
Mayville St. N16	CD35	48
Woodville Rd.		
May Wk. E13	CH37	58
Mayward Rd. Hem. H.	AX14	8
Maywater Clo. Sth. Croy.	BZ59	96
Maywin Dr. Horn.	CW33	51
Maywood Clo. Beck.	CE50	77
Maze Hill SE3	CG43	68
Maze Hill SE10	CG43	68
Mazenod Av. NW6	BS36	56
Maze Rd. Rich.	BM43	65
McAdam Clo. Hodd.	CE11	12
Mcadam Dr. Enf.	BY23	29
Mccall Cres. SE7	CK42	68
Maccarthy Rd. Felt.	BD49	74
McCoid Wk. SE1	BZ41	67
Scovell Rd.		
Mcdermott Clo. SW11	BU44	66
Mcdermott Rd. SE15	CB45	67
McDonough Clo. Chess.	BL56	94
Hook Rd.		
Mcdowall Rd. SE5	BZ44	67
Mcddwell Clo. E16	CH39	58
Mcentree Av. E17	CD30	39
Mcewan Clo. E15	CF37	57
Mcgarth Rd. E15	CG35	49
Mcgregor Rd. W11	BR39	55
Mcintosh Clo. Rom.	CT31	50
McIntosh Clo. Wall.	BX57	95
Redford Av.		
Mcintosh Rd. Rom.	CT31	50
Mckay Rd. SW20	BP50	75
Mckellar Clo. Bush.	BG27	36
McKenzie Rd. Brox.	CD13	12
Mckerrell Rd. SE15	CB44	67
Mcleod Rd. SE2	CO42	69
Mcleod's Ms. SW7	**BS41**	**3**
Mcleod's Ms. SW7	BS41	66
Mcmillan St. SE8	CE43	67
McNeil Rd. SE5	CA44	67
Mead Av. Slou.	AT41	62
Mead Clo. Egh.	AT50	72
Mead Clo. Grays.	DD41	71
Mead Clo. Har.	BG30	36
Mead Clo. Red.	BU69	121
Mead Clo. Rom.	CU30	41
Mead Clo. Slou.	AT41	62
Mead Clo. Swan.	CU53	89
Mead Clo. Uxb.	AW34	44
Mead Ct. NW9	BN32	46
Mead Ct. Wal. Abb.	CE20	21
Mead Ct. Wok.	AP61	100
Mead Cres. E4	CF28	39
Mead Cres. Dart.	CV47	80
Mead Cres. Lthd.	BF66	111
Mead Cres. Sutt.	BU56	95
Mead End, Ash.	BL62	103
Meadfield, Edg.	BM27	37
Meadfield Av. Slou.	AT41	62
Meadfield Grn. Edg.	BM27	37
Meadfoot Rd. SW16	BW50	76
Meadgate Av. Wdf. Grn.	CK28	40
Meadgate Rd. Harl.	CG13	13
Mead Gro. Croy.	BY54	86
Mead Gro. Rom.	CP31	50
Meadhurst Rd. Cher.	AW54	83
Meadlands Dr. Rich.	BK48	74
Meadow Av. Croy.	CC53	87
Meadow Bk. Oxt.	CF68	114
Meadow Bank N21	BX25	29
Meadowbank NW3	**BU36**	**1**
Meadowbank SE3	CG45	68
Meadowbank, Surb.	BL53	85
Meadow Bank, Wat.	BD26	36
Meadowbank Gdns. Houns.	BC44	63
Meadowbank Rd. NW9	BN33	46
Meadow Brook Clo. Slou.	AV44	62
Meadowbrook Rd. Dor.	BJ71	119
Meadow Clo. Hat.	BQ15	10
Meadow Clo. SW20	BQ52	85
Meadow Clo. Barn.	BR25	28
Meadow Clo. Chis.	CL49	78
Meadow Clo. Enf.	CC22	30
Meadow Clo. Esher	BH55	84
Meadow Clo. Houns.	BF46	74
Meadow Clo. Nthlt.	BF37	54
Meadow Clo. Pur.	BW60	95
Meadow Clo. Rich.	BL47	75
Petersham Rd.		
Meadow Clo. Ruis.	BB32	44
Meadow Clo. St. Alb.	BF18	18
Meadow Clo. St. Alb.	BK11	9
Meadow Clo. St. Alb.	BK17	18
Meadow Clo. Sutt.	BT55	86
Meadow Clo. Walt.	BE56	93
Meadow Clo. Wind.	AQ46	72
Meadow Ct. Stai.	AV48	72
Moor La.		
Meadowcourt Rd. SE3	CG45	68
Meadowcourt, Brom.	CK52	88
Meadowcourt, Ger. Cr.	AR30	34
Meadow Cft. Hat.	BO12	10
Meadowcroft, St. Alb.	BJ15	9
Meadowcroft Rd. N13	BY27	38
Meadow Cross, Wal. Abb.	CG20	22
Meadow Dell, Hat.	BO12	10
Meadow Dr. Amer.	AP22	25
Meadow Dr. N10	BV31	47
Meadow Dr. NW4	BQ30	37
Meadow Dr. Sev.	CU65	107
Lambarde Rd.		
Meadow Dr. Wok.	AV65	100
Meadow Gdns. Edg.	BM29	37
Meadow Gdns. Stai.	AV49	72
Meadow Garth NW10	BN36	55
Meadow Grn. Welw. G. C.	BQ8	5
Meadow Hill, N. Mal.	BO53	85
Meadow Hill, Pur.	BW60	95
Meadowlands, Cob.	BC60	92
Meadowlands, Guil.	AW68	110
Meadowlands, Horn.	CW33	51
Meadowlands, Oxt.	CH70	115
Meadowlands, Sev.	CW63	108

Meadow La. Lthd. BG64 102
Meadow La. Wind. AO43 61
Meadow Mead, Rad. BH20 18
Meadow Ms. SW8 BX43 66
Meadow Pk. Ger. Cr. AR33 43
Meadow Pl. SW8 BX43 66
Meadow Rise, Couls. BW60 95
Meadow Rise, Ing. DC19 24
Meadow Rd. SW8 BX43 66
Meadow Rd. SW19 BT50 76
Meadow Rd. Ash. BL62 103
Meadow Rd. Ashf. BA49 73
Meadow Rd. Bark. CN36 58
Meadow Rd. Berk. AQ12 7
Meadow Rd. Borwd. BM23 28
Meadow Rd. Brom. CG51 88
Meadow Rd. Bush. BF24 27
Meadow Rd. Dag. CQ36 59
Meadow Rd. Epp. CN18 22
Meadow Rd. Esher BH57 93
Meadow Rd. Felt. BE48 74
Meadow Rd. Grav. DE47 81
Meadow Rd. Grav. DG48 81
Meadow Rd. Grays. DD40 71
Meadow Rd. Guil. AT68 109
Meadow Rd. Hem. H. AZ16 17
Meadow Rd. Loug. CK25 31
Meadow Rd. Pnr. BE31 45
Meadow Rd. Rom. CS33 50
Meadow Rd. Slou. AS42 62
Meadow Rd. Sthl. BE40 54
Meadow Rd. Sutt. BU56 95
Meadow Rd. Vir. W. AP53 82
Meadow Rd. Wat. BC20 17
Meadow Row SE1 BZ41 4
Meadow Row SE1 BZ41 67
Meadows Clo. Brwd. DE29 122
The Meadows
Meadows End, Sun. BC51 83
Meadowside SE9 CJ45 68
Meadowside, Beac. AP29 34
Meadowside, Dart. CV47 80
Beech Rd.
Meadowside, Lthd. BF65 102
Meadowside, Walt. BD55 84
Meadowside Rd. Sutt. BR58 94
Meadowside Rd. Upmin. CY35 51
Meadows, The Amer. AP23 25
Meadows, The Brwd. DE29 122
Meadows, The Guil. AR72 118
Meadows, The Orp. CP57 98
Meadows, The Sev. CQ60 98
Meadows, The Welw. G. C. BT8 5
Meadow Stile, Croy. BZ55 87
Meadow, The Chis. CM50 78
Meadow Vw. Orp. CP52 89
Meadow Vw. Sid. CO47 79
Meadowview Clo. SE6 CE49 77
Meadowview Rd. SE6 CD49 77
Meadowview Rd. Bex. CQ46 79
Meadowview Rd. Epsom BO58 94
Meadow Vw. Rd. Hayes BA38 53
Meadow Vw. Rd. Th. Hth. BY53 86
Meadow Wk. E18 CH31 49
Meadow Wk. Dag. CQ36 59
Meadow Wk. Dart. CV49 80
Meadow Wk. Epsom BO57 94
Meadow Wk. Tad. BP65 103
Meadow Wk. Wall. BV55 86
Meadow Way NW9 BN32 46
Meadow Way, Chess. BL56 94
Meadow Way, Chig. CM27 40
Meadow Way, Dart. CY47 80
Meadow Way, Hem. H. AW15 8
Meadow Way, Kings L. AZ18 17
Meadow Way, Leath. BA66 110
Meadow Way, Lthd. BF65 102
Meadow Way, Maid. AH44 61
Meadow Way, Maid. AJ41 61
Meadow Way, Orp. CL55 88
Meadow Way, Pot. B. BS20 20
Meadow Way, Reig. BS72 121
Meadow Way, Rick. AX26 35
Meadow Way, Ruis. BC32 44
Meadow Way, St. Alb. BN15 10
Meadow Way, Saw. CR6 6
Meadow Way, Tad. BR62 103
Meadow Way, Upmin. CY35 51
Meadow Way, Wat. BB17 17
Meadow Way, Wem. BK35 45
Meadow Way, Wey. AW56 92
Meadow Way, Wind. AQ46 72
Meadow Waye, Houns. BE43 64
Meadow Way, The Har. BH30 36
Mead La. Cher. AW54 83
Mead Path SW19 BT49 76
Mead Pl. E9 CC36 57
Mead Pl. Croy. BY54 86
Mead Plat. NW10 BN36 55
Mead Rd. Cat. CA65 105
Mead Rd. Chis. CM50 78
Mead Rd. Dart. CV47 80
Mead Rd. Grav. DG48 81
Mead Rd. Hayes BA38 53
Mead Rd. Rich. BK48 74
Mead Rd. Uxb. AX36 53
Mead Rd. Walt. BE56 93
Mead Row SE1 BY41 4
Mead Row SE1 BY41 66
Westminster Br. Rd.
Mead's La. Ilf. CN33 49
Meads Rd. N22 BY30 38
Meads Rd. Edg. BM29 37
Meads Rd. Enf. CD23 30
Meads Rd. Guil. AT70 118
Meads, The Berk. AP12 7
Meads, The Edg. BN29 37
Meads, The St. Alb. BF18 18
Meads, The Sutt. BQ55 85
Meads, The Upmin. CZ34 51
Meads, The Uxb. AY38 53
Mead, The N2 BT30 38
Mead, The W13 BJ39 54
Templewood
Mead, The Ash. BL63 103
Mead, The Beck. CF51 87
Mead, The Rom. CO24 32
Mead, The Uxb. AZ34 44
Mead, The Wal. Cr. CC18 21
Mead, The Wall. BW57 95
Mead, The Wat. BE27 36
Mead, The W. Wick. CF54 87
Meadvale Rd. W5 BJ38 54
Meadvale Rd. Croy. CA54 87
Mead Wk. Ong. CW18 24
Mead Wk. Slou. AT41 62
Meadway N14 BW27 38
Meadway N14 BX27 38
Mead Way NW10 BN36 55
Meadway NW11 BS32 47
Meadway SW20 BQ52 85
Meadway, Ashf. AZ49 73
Meadway, Barn. BR24 28
Mead Way, Beck. CF51 87
Meadway, Berk. AS12 7
Mead Way, Brom. CG53 88
Mead Way, Bush. BE23 27
Meadway, Couls. BX62 104
Mead Way, Croy. CD55 87
Meadway, Enf. CC21 30
Meadway, Epsom M59 94
Meadway, Esher BF58 93
Meadway, Grays. DE42 71
Meadway, Guil. AU68 109
Meadway, Hodd. CE13 12
Meadway, Ilf. CN35 49
Meadway, Lthd. BE67 111
Meadway, Lthd. BH60 93
Meadway, Rom. CT30 41
Meadway, Sev. CQ60 98
Meadway, Stai. AV50 72
Meadway, Stai. AW50 73
Meadway, Surb. BN54 85
Meadway, Twick. BG47 74
Mead Way, Warl. CC61 105
Meadway, Wdf. Grn. CJ28 40
Meadway, Welw. G. C. BR9 5
Meadway Clo. NW11 BS32 47
Meadway Clo. Barn. BS24 29
Meadway Clo. Pnr. BF29 36
High Banks Rd.
Meadway Clo. Stai. AV50 72
Meadway Clo. Stai. AW50 73
Meadway Ct. NW11 BS32 47
Meadway Dr. Wey. AX57 92
Meadway Dr. Wok. AR61 100
Meadway Gdns. Ruis. BA32 44
Meadway Gate NW11 BS32 47
Meadway, The SE3 CF44 67
Meadway, The Buck. H. CJ26 40
Meadway, The Loug. CK25 31
Meadway, The Orp. CO56 98
Meadway, The Pot. B. BX18 20
Mead Way, The Sev. CT64 107
Meaford Way SE20 CB50 77
Meakin Est. SE1 CA41 4
Meakin Est. SE1 CA41 67
Meald St. SE14 CD44 67
Meanley Rd. E12 CK35 49
Meard St. W1 BW39 1
Meard St. W1 BW39 56
Meath Clo. Orp. CO53 89
Meath Rd. E15 CG37 58
Meath Rd. Ilf. CM34 49
Meath St. SW11 BV44 66
Meautys, St. Alb. BF15 9
Mechanic's Pass. SE8 CE43 67
Mecklenburgh Pl. WC1 BX38 2
Mecklenburgh Pl. WC1 BX38 56
Guilford St.
Mecklenburgh Sq. WC1 BX38 2
Mecklenburgh Sq. WC1 BX38 56
Medburn St. NW1 BW37 1
Medburn St. NW1 BW37 56
Medcalf Pl. N1 BY37 2
Medcalf Rd. Enf. CD22 30
Medcroft Gdns. SW14 BM45 65
Medebourne Clo. SE3 CH45 68
Mede Clo. Stai. AR47 72
Mede Ct. Stai. AV48 72
Medfield St. SW15 BP47 75
Medhurst Cres. Grav. DJ48 81
Medhurst Gdns. Grav. DJ48 81
Median Rd. E5 CC35 48
Medina Av. Esher BH55 84
Medina Gro. N7 BY34 47
Medina Rd. N7 BY34 47
Medina Rd. Grays. DE42 71
Medlake Rd. Egh. AU50 72
Medland Clo. Wall. BV54 86
Medlar Clo. Guil. AR69 118
Medlar Clo. Nthlt. BD37 54
Medlar St. SE5 BZ44 67
Medley Rd. NW6 BS36 56
Medomsley Clo. Sid. CO48 79
Medora Rd. SW2 BX47 76
Medora Rd. Rom. CS31 50
Medusa Rd. SE6 CE46 77
Medway, Wat. BD20 18
Medway Clo. Croy. CC53 87
Medway Clo. Ilf. CM35 49
Loxford La.
Medway Dr. Grnf. BH37 54
Medway Gdns. Wem. BJ35 45
Medway Ms. E3 CD37 57
Medway Pde. Grnf. BH37 54
Medway Rd. E3 CD37 57
Medway Rd. Dart. CU45 69
Medway Rd. Hem. H. AY11 8
Medway St. SW1 BW41 3
Medway St. SW1 BW41 66
Medwin St. SW4 BX45 66
Meek St. SW10 BT43 66
Ulverdale Rd.
Meerbrook Rd. SE3 CJ45 68
Meeson Rd. E15 CG37 58
Meeson St. E5 CD35 48
Meeting Flds. Path E9 CC36 57
Homerton Ter.
Meeting Ho. All. E1 CB40 57
Watts St.
Meeting House La. SE15 CB44 67
Meggs La. Kings L. AW18 17
Meggs Pl. E1 CB39 57
Kingward St.
Mehetabel Rd. E9 CC35 48
Melanda Clo. Chis. CK49 78
Melanie Clo. Bexh. CQ44 69
Melba Gdns. Til. DG43 71
Melba Way SE13 CE44 67
Morden St.
Melbourne Av. N13 BX29 38
Melbourne Av. W13 BJ40 54
Melbourne Av. Pnr. BF31 45
Melbourne Clo. Orp. CN54 88
Melbourne Clo. St. Alb. BH11 9
Melbourne Clo. Wall. BW56 95
Melbourne Clo. Wey. AW60 92
Melbourne Ct. SE20 CB50 77
Melbourne Ct. Welw. G. C. BP8 5
Melbourne Flds. SW9 BY44 66
Melbourne Gdns. Rom. CQ31 50
Melbourne Gro. SE22 CA45 67
Melbourne Pl. WC2 BX40 56
Melbourne Rd. E6 CK37 58
Melbourne Rd. E10 CE33 48
Melbourne Rd. E17 CD31 48
Melbourne Rd. SW19 BS51 86
Melbourne Rd. Bush. BF25 27
Melbourne Rd. Ilf. CL33 49
Melbourne Rd. Tedd. BK50 74
Melbourne Rd. Til. DF44 71
Melbourne Rd. Wal. Cr. CE20 21
Melbourne Rd. Wall. BV56 95
Melbourne Sq. SW9 BY44 66
Melbourne Way, Enf. CA25 30
Melbury Av. Sthl. BF41 64
Melbury Clo. Cher. AW54 83
London St.
Melbury Clo. Chis. CK50 78
Melbury Clo. Esher BJ57 93
Melbury Ct. W8 BR41 65
Melbury Gdns. SW20 BP51 85
Melbury Rd. W14 BR41 65
Melbury Rd. Har. BL32 46
Melbury Ter. NW1 BU38 56
Harewood Av.
Melcombe Gdns. Har. BL32 46
Melcombe Pl. NW1 BU39 1
Melcombe Pl. NW1 BU39 56
Melcombe St. NW1 BU38 1
Melcombe St. NW1 BU38 56
Meldrum Clo. Orp. CP54 89
Killewarren Way
Meldrum Clo. Oxt. CG69 115
Meldrum Rd. Ilf. CO34 50
Melfield Clo. SE6 CF49 77
Melford Av. Bark. CN36 58
Melford Rd. E6 CK38 58
Melford Rd. E11 CG34 49
Melford Rd. E13 CH38 58
Melford Rd. E17 CD32 48
Melford Rd. SE22 CB47 77
Melford Rd. Ilf. CM34 49
Melfort Av. Th. Hth. BY52 86
Melfort Rd. Th. Hth. BY52 86
Melgund Rd. N5 BY35 47
Melina Clo. Hayes BA39 53
Middleton Rd.
Melina Pl. NW8 BT38 1
Melina Pl. NW8 BT38 56
Melina Rd. W12 BP41 65
Melior St. SE1 BZ41 4
Melior St. SE1 CA41 67
Weston St.
Meliot Rd. SE6 CF48 77
Melksham Clo. Rom. CW29 42
Melksham Dr. Rom. CW29 42
Melksham Gdns. Rom. CW29 42
Melksham Grn. Rom. CW29 42
Meller Clo. Croy. BX55 86
Melling St. SE18 CN43 68
Mellison Rd. SW17 BU49 76
Mellitus St. W12 BO39 55
Mellow Clo. Bans. BS60 95
Mellow La. Uxb. BA38 53
Mellow La. E. Hayes BA38 53
Mellows Rd. Ilf. CK31 49
Mellows Rd. Wall. BW56 95
Mells Cres. SE9 CK49 78
Mell St. SE10 CG42 68
Melody Rd. SW18 BT46 76
Melody Rd. West. CH62 106
Melon Pl. W8 BS41 56
Kensington Church St.
Melon Rd. SE15 CA44 67
Melrose Av. N22 BY30 38
Melrose Av. NW2 BP35 46
Melrose Av. SW16 BX52 86
Melrose Av. SW19 BR48 75
Melrose Av. Borwd. BM25 28
Melrose Av. Grnf. BF37 54
Melrose Av. Mitch. BV50 76
Melrose Av. Pot. B. BS19 20
Melrose Av. Twick. BF47 74
Melrose Clo. Grnf. BF37 54
Melrose Clo. Hayes BC39 53
Melrose Cres. Orp. CM56 97
Melrose Dr. Sthl. BF40 54
Melrose Gdns. W6 BQ41 65
Melrose Gdns. Edg. BM30 37
Melrose Gdns. N. Mal. BN52 85
Melrose Gdns. Walt. BD56 93
Melrose Pl. Wat. BB22 26
Melrose Rd. SW13 BO44 65
Melrose Rd. SW18 BR46 75
Melrose Rd. SW19 BS51 86
Melrose Rd. W3 BM41 65
Melrose Rd. Couls. BV61 104
Melrose Rd. Pnr. BE31 45
Melrose Rd. West. CJ61 106
Melrose Rd. Wey. AZ56 92
Melrose Ter. W6 BQ41 65
Melsa Rd. Mord. BT53 86
Melsted Rd. Hem. H. AW13 8
Melstock Av. Upmin. CY35 51
Meltham Way SE16 CB42 67
Egan Way
Melthorpe Dr. Ruis. BD34 45
Melthorpe Gdns. SE3 CJ44 68
Melton Clo. Ruis. BD33 45
Melton Ct. SW7 BT42 3
Melton Ct. SW7 BT42 66
Melton Gdns. Rom. CT33 50
Melton Pl. Epsom BN58 94
Melton Rd. Red. BW68 113
Melton St. NW1 BW38 1
Melton St. NW1 BW38 56
Melville Av. SW20 BP50 75
Melville Av. Grnf. BH35 45
Melville Av. Sth. Croy. CA56 96
Melville Ct. W12 BP41 65
Melville Gdns. N13 BY28 38
Melville Rd. E17 CD31 48
Melville Rd. N1 BZ37 2
Essex Rd.
Melville Rd. NW10 BN37 55
Melville Rd. SW13 BP44 65
Melville Rd. Rain. CU38 59
Melville Rd. Rom. CR29 41
Melville Rd. Sid. CP48 79
Melville St. N1 BZ36 2
Melville St. N1 BZ36 57
Essex Rd.
Melville Vill. Rd. W3 BO40 55
Melvin Rd. SE20 CC51 87
Melvin Shaw, Lthd. BK64 102
Melvyn Clo. Wal. Cr. BY17 20
Melyn Clo. N19 BW35 47
Anson Rd.
Memel St. EC1 BZ38 57
Baltic St.
Memess Path SE18 CL43 68
Engineer Clo.
Memorial Av. E15 CG38 58
Memorial Clo. Houns. BF43 64
Heston Rd.
Mendip Clo. SW19 BR48 75
Queensmere Rd.
Mendip Clo. Hayes BA43 63
Penine Way
Mendip Clo. St. Alb. BK11 9
Chiltern Rd.
Mendip Clo. Slou. AT42 62
Mendip Cres. SW11 BT45 66
Mendip Dr. NW2 BQ34 46
Mendip Rd. SW11 BT45 66
Mendip Rd. Bexh. CT44 69
Mendip Rd. Bush. BG25 27
Mendip Rd. Horn. CU33 50
Mendip Rd. Ilf. CN32 49
Mendip Way, Hem. H. AY12 8
Mendora Rd. SW6 BR43 65
Mendoza Clo. Horn. CW32 51
Menelik Rd. NW2 BR35 46
Menlo Gdns. SE19 BZ50 77
Menor Clo. Walt. BE54 84
Menotti St. E2 CB38 57
Dunbridge St.
Mense Way, Sev. CT59 98
Menthone Pl. Horn. CV33 51
North St.
Mentmore Clo. Har. BK32 45
Mentmore Rd. St. Alb. BG14 9
Mentmore Ter. E8 CB36 57
Meon Clo. Tad. BP64 103
Meon Rd. W3 BN41 65
Meopham Rd. Mitch. BW51 86
Mepham Cres. Har. BG29 36
Mepham Gdns. Har. BG29 36
Mepham St. SE1 BX40 4
Mepham St. SE1 BX40 56
Mera Dr. Bexh. CR45 69
Mercator Rd. SE13 CF45 67
Mercer Clo. Surb. BJ54 84
Giggs Hill Rd.
Merceron St. E1 CB38 57
Mercer Pl. Pnr. BD30 36
Mercers, Harl. CL12 13
Mercers, Hem. H. AY12 8
Mercers Clo. SE10 CG42 68
Tunnel Av.
Mercer's Rd. N19 BW34 47
Mercer St. WC2 BW39 1
Mercer St. WC2 BX39 2
Mercer St. WC2 BX39 56
Mercer Wk. Uxb. AX36 53
High St.
Merchant St. E3 CD38 57
Merchiston Rd. SE6 CF48 77
Merchland Rd. SE9 CM47 78
Mercia Gro. SE13 CF45 67
Mercian Way, Slou. AL40 61
Mercia Way, Wok. AS62 100
Ch. St. W.
Mercier Rd. SW15 BR46 75
Mercury Gdns. Rom. CT31 50
Mercury Rd. Brent. BK42 64
Mercury Wk. Hem. H. AY12 8
Mercy Ter. SE13 CE45 67
Merebank La. Wall. BX56 95
Mere Clo. SW19 BQ47 75
Mere Clo. Orp. CL55 88
Mere Clo. Tad. BP65 103
Meredith Av. NW2 BQ35 46
Meredith Clo. Pnr. BD29 36
Meredith Rd. Grays. DG42 71
Meredith St. E13 CH38 58
Meredith St. EC1 BY38 2
Meredith St. EC1 BY38 56
Meredyth Rd. SW13 BP44 65
Mere End, Croy. CC54 87
Merefield Gdns. Tad. BQ63 103
Mere Rd. Shep. AZ53 83
Mere Rd. Slou. AP41 62
Mere Rd. Tad. BP65 103
Mere Rd. Wey. BA55 83
Mere Side, Orp. CL55 88
Mereside Pl. Vir. W. AQ54 82
Mere, The Slou. AP41 62
Mere Rd.
Meretone Clo. SE4 CD45 67
Meretune Ct. Mord. BR52 85
Merevale Cres. Mord. BT53 86
Mereway Rd. Twick. BG47 74
Merewood Clo. Brom. CL51 88
Merewood Rd. Bexh. CS44 69
Mereworth Clo. Brom. CG53 88
Mereworth Dr. SE18 CL43 68
Meriden Clo. Ilf. CM30 40
Meriden Way, Wat. BE21 27
Meridian Rd. SE7 CJ43 68
Meridian Wk. N18 CA29 3
Commercial Rd.
Merifield Rd. SE9 CJ45 6
Merino Pl. Sid. CO46 7
Merivale Rd. SW15 BR45 6
Merivale Rd. Har. BG33 4
Merland Grn. Tad. BQ63 10
Merland Ri. Epsom BQ63 10
Merle Av. Uxb. AW30 3
Merlewood, Sev. CU65 10
Merlewood Clo. Cat. BZ63 10
Ninehams Rd.
Merlewood Rd. Chis. CK51 8
Merley Ct. NW9 BN33 4
Merlin Clo. Croy. CA55 8
Merlin Clo. Ilf. CP28 4
Merlin Clo. Nthlt. BD38 5
Merlin Clo. Rom. CS29 4
Merlin Cres. Edg. BL29 3
Merlin Gdns. Brom. CH48 7
Merlin Gdns. Rom. CS29 4
Merlin Gro. Beck. CD52 8
Merlin Gro. Ilf. CL29 4
Merlin Rd. E12 CJ34 4
Merlin Rd. Rom. CS29 4
Merlin Rd. Well. CO45 6
Merlins Av. Har. BE34 4
Merlin St. WC1 BY38
Merlin St. WC1 BY38 5
Wilmington St.
Mermagen Dr. Rain. CU36 5
Mermaid Ct. SE1 BZ41
Mermaid Ct. SE1 BZ41 6
Merona Clo. Uxb. AX39 5
Merredene St. SW2 BX46 7
Merrick Sq. SE1 BZ41
Merrick Sq. SE1 BZ41 6
Merridene N21 BY25 2
Merrielands Cres. Bark. CQ37 5
Merrilands Rd. Wor. Pk. BQ54 8
Merrilees Rd. Sid. CN47 7
Merrilyn Clo. Esher BJ57 9
Merriman Rd. SE3 CJ44 6
Merrington Rd. SW6 BS43 6
Merrion Av. Stan. BK28 3
Merritt Rd. SE4 CD46 7
Merritts Bldgs. EC2 CA38
Merritts Bldgs. EC2 CA38 5
Worship St.
Merrivale N14 BW25 2
Merrivale Av. Ilf. CJ31 4
Merrow Chase, Guil. AU70 11
Merrows Clo. Nthwd. BA29 3
Rickmansworth Rd.
Merrow Common Rd. Guil. AU69 11
Merrow Copse, Guil. AT70 11
Merrow Croft, Guil. AU70 11
Merrow Dr. Hem. H. AV13
Merrow La. Guil. AU68 10
Merrow Rd. Sutt. BA58 9
Merrow St. SE17 BZ43
Merrow St. SE17 BZ43 6
Merrow St. Guil. AU69 11
Merrow Way, Croy. CF57 9
Merrow Woods, Guil. AT69 11
Merryfield SE3 CG44 6
Merryfield Gdns. Stan. BK28 3
Merryfields, Uxb. AX37 5
Merryfields Wall Clo. Uxb. AY37 5
Merryhill Clo. E4 CE26 3
Merry Hill, Mt. Bush. BF26 3
Merry Hill Rd. Bush. BE25 2
Merryhills Clo. West. CJ61 10
Merryhills Dr. Enf. BW24 2
Merrylands, Cher. AV55 8
Merrylands Rd. Lthd. BE65 10
Merrymeet, Bans. BU60 9
Merrywood Pk. Reig. BS69 12
Mersey Av. Upmin. CY32 5
Mersey Pl. Hem. H. AY11
Mersey Rd. E17 CD31 4
Mersey Wk. Nthlt. BF37 5
Leander Rd.
Mersham Dr. NW9 BM32 4
Mersham Pl. SE20 CB51 8
Mersham Rd. Th. Hth. BZ52 8
Merstham Rd. Red. BY68 11
Merten Rd. Rom. CQ33 5
Merthyr Ter. SW13 BP43 6
Merton Abbey Sta.
Rd. SW19 BT51 8
Merton Av. W4 BO42 6
Merton Av. Hart. DC52 9
Merton Av. Nthlt. BG35 4
Merton Av. Uxb. AZ36 5
Merton Gdns. Orp. CL53 8
Merton Gdns. Tad. BQ63 10
Merton Hall Gdns. SW20 BR51 8
Merton Hall Rd. SW19 BR50 7
Merton La. N6 BU34 4
Merton Mansions SW20 BQ51 8
Merton Pl. SE10 CF44 6
Merton Pl. Grays. DG42 7
Merton Ri. NW3 BU36 5
Merton Rd. E17 CF32 4
Merton Rd. SE25 CB53 8
Merton Rd. SW18 BS46 7
Merton Rd. SW19 BS50 7
Merton Rd. Bark. CN36 5
Merton Rd. Enf. BZ22 3
Merton Rd. Har. BG33 4
Merton Rd. Ilf. CN33 4
Merton Rd. Slou. AQ41 6
Merton Rd. Wat. BC24 2
Merton Spur SW20 BP52 8
Bushey Rd.
Merton Wk. Lthd. BJ62 10
Merton Way
Merton Way, E. Mol. BF52 8
Merton Way, Lthd. BJ63 10
Merton Way, Uxb. AZ36 5
Merttins Rd. SE15 CC46 7
Ivydale Rd.
Mervan Rd. SW2 BY45 6
Mervyn Av. SE9 CM48 7
Mervyn Rd. W13 BJ41 6
Mervyn Rd. Shep. AZ54 8
Russell Rd.

Merwin Way, Wind. AL45 61
Messaline Av. W3 BN39 55
Messent Rd. SE9 CJ46 78
Messeter Pl. SE9 CL46 78
Messina Av. NW6 BS36 56
Messon's La. Grays. DC42 71
Metcalf Rd. Ashf. AZ49 73
Meteor St. SW1 BV45 66
Meteor Way, Wall. BX57 95
Methley St. SE11 BY42 4
Methley St. SE11 BY42 66
Methuen Clo. Edg. BM29 37
Methuen Rd. Edg. BM29 37
Methuen Pk. N10 BV30 38
Methuen Rd. Belv. CR42 69
Methuen Rd. Bexh. CQ45 69
Methwold Rd. W10 BQ39 55
Mews End, West. CJ62 106
Mews, The N1 BZ37 2
Mews, The N1 BZ37 2
Linton St.
Mews, The N1 BZ37 57
Linton St.
Mews, The Ilf. CJ32 49
Mews, The Rom. CT31 50
Mews, The Saw. CQ5 6
Mews, The Slou. AP41 62
Mews, The Twick. BJ46 74
Bridge Rd.
Mexfield Rd. SW15 BR46 75
Meyer Grn. Enf. CB22 30
Meyer Rd. Erith. CS43 69
Meymott St. SE1 BY40 4
Meymott St. SE1 BY40 56
Meynell Cres. E9 CC36 57
Meynell Rd. E9 CC36 57
Meynell Rd. Rom. CU29 41
Meyrick Clo. Wok. AP61 100
Creston Av.
Meyrick Rd. NW10 BP36 55
Meyrick Rd. SW11 BT45 66
Mezen Clo. Nthwd. BA29 35
Miall Wk. SE26 CD49 77
Dillwyn Clo.
Micawber Av. Uxb. AZ39 53
Micawber St. N1 BZ38 2
Micawber St. N1 BZ38 57
Michael Faraday Ho. SE17 BZ42 4
Michael Faraday Ho. SE17 BZ42 67
Michael Gdns. Grav. DJ49 81
Michael Gdns. Horn. CV31 51
Michael Rd. E11 CG33 49
Michael Rd. SE25 CA52 87
Michael Rd. SW6 BS44 66
Michaels Clo. SE13 CG45 68
Michael's Rd. NW2 BQ35 46
Michehan Gdns. Tad. BQ63 103
Micheldever Rd. SE12 CG46 78
Michelham Gdns. Twick. BJ48 74
Michel's Row, Rich. BL45 65
Kew Foot Rd.
Michigan Av. E12 CK35 49
Michelham Down N12 BR28 37
Micklefield Rd. Hem. H. BA13 8
Mickleford Way, Borwd. BL22 28
Mickleham By-pass, Dor. BJ67 111
Mickleham Clo. Orp. CN51 88
Mickelham Rd.
Mickleham Dr. Lthd. BK66 111
Mickleham Gdns. Sutt. BR57 94
Mickleham Rd. Orp. CN51 88
Mickleham Way, Croy. CF57 96
Micklem Dr. Hem. H. AV13 7
Micklethwaite Rd. SW6 BS43 66
Midcot Way, Berk. AP12 7
Mid Croft, Ruis. BB33 44
Mid Cross La. Ger. Cr. AS28 34
Middfield, Hat. BP12 10
Lemsford Rd.
Middle Boy, Rom. CP24 32
Middle Clo. Amer. AP22 25
Middle Clo. Couls. BY63 104
Middle Clo. Epsom BO59 94
Middle Cres. Uxb. AU33 43
Middlecroft, Croy. CD58 96
Middle Dene NW7 BN27 37
Middlefield NW8 BT37 56
Boundary Rd.
Middlefield, Hat. BP11 10
Lemsford Rd.
Middle Field Av. Hodd. CE11 12
Middlefield Clo. St. Alb. BK12 9
Middlefield Cres. Ilf. CL32 49
Middle Fielde W13 BJ39 54
Templewood
Middle Field Rd. Hodd. CE11 12
Middle Furlong, Bush. BF24 27
Middle Grn. Brwd. DB22 33
Middlegreen, Slou. AR41 62
Middle Grn. Slou. AS40 52
Middle Grn. Stai. AX50 73
Middleham Gdns. N18 CB29 39
Middleham Rd. N18 CB29 39
Middle Hill, Egh. AR49 72
Middle Hill, Hem. H. AV13 7
Middleknights Hill, Hem. H. AW12 8
Middle La. N8 BX32 47
Middle La. Epsom BO59 94
Middle La. Hem. H. AT18 16
Middle La. Tedd. BH50 74
Middle La. Mews N8 BX32 47
Middle La.
Middle Meadow, Ch. St. G. AQ27 34
Middlemead Rd. Lthd. BE66 111
Middle Ope, Wat. BC22 26
Middle Pk. Av. SE9 CJ46 78
Middle Path, Har. BG33 45
Middle Rd. SW16 BW51 86
Middle Rd. Barn. BU25 29
Middle Rd. Berk. AQ13 7
Middle Rd. Brwd. DE28 122
Middle Rd. Har. BG34 45
Middle Rd. Lthd. BJ64 102
Up. Fairfield Rd.
Middle Rd. Uxb. AU33 43
Middle Rd. Wal. Abb. CE19 21
Middle Row N10 BR38 55
Middle Row Pl. WC1 BY39 56
High Holborn
Middlesborough Rd. N18 CB29 39
Middlesex Rd. Mitch. BX53 86
Middlesex St. E1 CA39 2
Middlesex St. E1 CA39 57
Middlesex Wharf E5 CC34 48
Southwold Rd.
Middle St. EC1 BZ39 2
Middle St. EC1 BZ39 57
Bartholomew Clo.
Middle St. Bet. BM71 120
Middle St. Croy. BZ55 87
Middle St. Wal. Abb. CG14 13
Middle Temple La. EC4 BY39 2
Middle Temple La. EC4 BY39 56
Middleton Av. E4 CD28 39
Middleton Av. Grnf. BG37 54
Middleton Av. Sid. CO50 79
Middleton Bldgs. W1 BW39 56
Langham St.
Middleton Clo. E4 CD27 39
Middleton Dr. Pnr. BC31 44
Middleton Gdns. Ilf. CL32 49
Middleton Gro. N7 BX35 47
Middleton Hall La. Brwd. DC27 122
Middleton Ind. Est. Rd. Guil. AQ70 118
Middleton Mews N7 BX35 47
Middleton Gro.
Middleton Pas. EC1 BY38 2
Middleton Rd. E8 CA36 57
Middleton Rd. NW11 BS33 47
Middleton Rd. Brwd. DC26 122
Middleton Rd. Cob. BD63 102
Middleton Rd. Guil. AP71 118
Middleton Rd. Hayes BA39 53
Middleton Rd. Mord. BS53 86
Middleton Rd. N. Mal. BN51 85
Middleton Rd. Rick. AW26 35
Middleton St. E2 CB38 57
Canrobert St.
Middleton Way SE13 CF45 67
Middle Wk. Wok. AS62 100
Ch. St. W.
Middleway NW11 BS32 47
Middle Way SW16 BW51 86
Middle Way, Hayes BD38 54
Middle Way, Wat. BC22 26
Middle Way, The Har. BH30 36
Middlings Ri. Sev. CT66 116
Middlings, The Sev. CT66 116
Middlings Wood, Sev. CT66 116
Midfield Av. Bexh. CS45 69
Midfield Pl. W1 BW38 1
Midfield Way, Orp. CO51 89
Midford Pl. W1 BW38 56
Tottenham Court Rd.
Midholm NW11 BS31 47
Midholm, Wem. BM33 46
Midholm Clo. NW11 BS31 47
Midholm Rd. Croy. CD55 87
Midhope Clo. Wok. AS63 100
Midhope Rd.
Midhope Gdns. Wok. AS63 100
Midhope Rd.
Midhope Rd. Wok. AS63 100
Midhope St. WC1 BX38 2
Midhope St. WC1 BX38 56
Argyle Wk.
Midhurst Av. N10 BV31 47
Midhurst Av. Croy. BY54 86
Midhurst Clo. Horn. CU35 50
Cowdray Way
Midhurst Hill, Bexh. CR46 79
Midhurst Rd. W13 BJ41 64
Midland Mead SE16 CC42 67
Midland Rd. E10 CF33 48
Midland Rd. NW1 BW37 1
Midland Rd. NW1 BW37 56
Midland Rd. Hem. H. AX13 8
Midland Ter. NW2 BQ34 46
Midland Ter. NW10 BO38 55
Midmoor Rd. SW12 BW47 76
Midmoor Rd. SW19 BQ50 75
Mid Sto. Red. BX72 121
Midstrath Rd. NW10 BO35 46
Balnacraig Av.
Midway, St. Alb. BF15 9
Midway, Sutt. BR54 85
Midway, Walt. BC55 83
Midway Av. Egh. AT52 82
Midwood Clo. NW2 BP34 46
Miers Clo. E6 CL37 58
Mighell Av. Ilf. CJ32 49
Milborne Gro. SW10 BT42 3
Milborne Gro. SW10 BT42 66
Gilston Rd.
Milborne St. E9 CC36 57
Well St.
Milborough Cres. SE12 CG46 78
Milbourne La. Esher BG57 93
Milbourne Rd. Felt. BE49 74
Milbrook, Esher BG57 93
Milburn Wk. Epsom BO61 103
Milcombe Clo. Wok. AQ62 100
Inglewood
Milcote St. SE1 BY41 4
Milcote St. SE1 BY41 66
Mildenhall Rd. E5 CB35 48
Mildenhall Rd. Slou. AP39 52
Mildmay Av. N1 BZ36 57
Mildmay Gro. N1 BZ35 48
Mildmay Pk. N1 BZ35 48
Mildmay Pl. Sev. CT59 98
Mildmay Rd. N1 BZ35 48
Mildmay Rd. Rom. CS32 50
Mildmay St. N1 BZ36 57
Mildred Av. Hayes BA42 63
Mildred Av. Borwd. BM24 28
Mildred Av. Nthlt. BF35 45
Mildred Av. Wat. BB24 26
Mildred Clo. Dart. CX46 80
Mildred Rd. Erith CS42 69
Mildreds Rd. Guil. AS70 118
Midsummer Av. Houns. BE45 64
Midwood Clo. NW2 BP34 46
Mile Clo. Wal. Abb. CF19 21
Mile End Pl. E1 CC38 57
Mile End Rd. E1 CC38 57
Mile End Rd. E3 CD38 57
Mile House Clo. St. Alb. BJ15 9
Mile House La. St. Alb. BJ15 9
Mile Path, Wok. AQ63 100
Mile Rd. Wall. BV54 86
Miles Clo. Harl. CL11 13
Miles La. EC4 BZ40 4
Miles La. EC4 BZ40 57
Arthur St.
Milespit Hl. NW7 BP28 37
Miles Pl. NW1 BT39 56
Miles Pl. Surb. BL52 85
Miles Rd. N8 BX31 47
Miles Rd. Epsom BN59 94
Miles Rd. Mitch. BT52 86
Miles's La. Cob. BE60 93
Miles St. SW8 BX43 66
Milestone Clo. Sutt. BT57 95
Milestone Clo. Wok. AW64 101
Milestone Rd. SE19 CA50 77
Milestone Rd. Dart. CX47 80
Miles Way N20 BU27 38
Mile, The End E17 CC30 39
Milfoil St. W12 BP40 55
Milford Clo. SE2 CQ43 69
Milford Gdns. Edg. BM29 37
Milford Gdns. Wem. BK35 45
Milford Gro. Sutt. BT56 95
Milford La. WC2 BX39 56
Milford La. WC2 BX40 4
Milford Rd. W13 BJ40 54
Milford Rd. Grays. DE40 71
Milford Rd. Sthl. BF40 54
Milford St. SW8 BV45 66
Milford Way SE15 CA44 67
Sumner Estate
Milhill La. Bet. BM70 120
Milhog Ct. Wal. Abb. CG20 22
Haywood Ct.
Milhoo Ct. Wal. Abb. CG20 22
Haywood Ct.
Milking La. Kes. CJ59 97
Milk St. E16 CL40 58
Milk St. EC2 BZ39 2
Milk St. EC2 BZ39 57
Milk St. Brom. CH50 78
Milkwell Gdns. Wdf. Grn. CH29 40
Milkwell Yd. SE5 BZ44 67
Denmark Hill
Milkwood Rd. SE24 BY46 76
Milk Yd. E1 CC40 57
Millais Av. E12 CL35 49
Millais Pl. Til. DG43 71
Millais Rd. E11 CF35 48
Millais Rd. Enf. CA25 30
Millais Rd. N. Mal. BO53 85
Millais Way, Epsom BN56 94
Millard Ter. Dag. CR36 59
Mill Av. Uxb. AX37 53
Millbank SW1 BW42 3
Millbank SW1 BW42 66
Millbank SW1 BX41 4
Millbank Av. Ong. CW18 24
Mill Bank Way SE12 CH46 78
Osberton Rd.
Millbro, Swan. CV51 89
Millbrook, Wey. BB56 92
Millbrook Av. Well. CM45 68
Millbrook Ct. SW15 BR46 75
Keswick Rd.
Millbrook Gdns. Rom. CQ32 50
Millbrook Gdns. Rom. CT30 41
Millbrook Gdns. Wey. AZ57 92
Millbrook Rd. N9 CB26 39
Millbrook Rd. SW9 BY45 66
Millbrooks Rd. Bush. BE23 27
Millbourne Rd. Felt. BE49 74
Mill Brook St. Guil. AR71 118
Mill Clo. Cars. BV55 86
Mill Clo. Chesh. AP20 16
Mill Clo. Hem. H. AW11 8
Mill Clo. Hem. H. AZ16 17
Mill Clo. Lthd. BF65 102
Mill Clo. Wal. Cr. CD17 21
Mill Clo. Welw. G. C. BP8 5
Mill Clo. West Dr. AX41 63
Mill Corner, Barn. BR23 28
Millcrest Rd. Wal. Cr. BY17 20
Millen Clo. Wey. AW58 92
Miller Clo. Pnr. BD30 36
Miller Grn. Rd. Ong. DA13 15
Miller Rd. SW19 BT50 76
Miller Rd. Croy. BX54 86
Miller Rd. Grav. DK48 81
Miller Rd. Guil. AU69 118
Millers Av. E8 CA35 48
Miller's Clo. Chig. CO27 41
Millers Copse, Epsom BN63 103
Millers Ct. W6 BO42 65
Millersdale, Harl. CL13 13
Millers Grn. Enf. BY24 29
Miller's La. Chig. CO26 41
Miller's La. Chig. CO27 41
Millers La. Wind. AP46 72
Millers Ter. E8 CA35 48
Miller St. NW1 BW37 1
Miller St. NW1 BW37 56
Millett Rd. Grnf. BF38 54
Millfarm Av. Sun. BB50 73
Mill Farm Clo. Pnr. BD30 36
Mill Farm Cres. Houns. BE47 74
Mill Field, Berk. AR12 7
Mill Field, Harl. CP9 6
Mill Field, Welw. G. C. BT7 5
Millfield, Sun. BA51 83
Millfield Av. E17 CD30 39
Millfield La. N6 BU34 47
Millfield La. New. A. G. DC55 90
Millfield La. Tad. BR66 112
Millfield Pl. N6 BV34 47
Millfield Rd. Edg. BN30 37
Millfield Rd. Houns. BE47 74
Millfield Rd. Sev. CY57 99
Mill Fields, Saw. CQ5 6
Millfields Clo. Orp. CO52 89
Millfields, Ong. CY17 24
Millfields Rd. E5 CC35 48
Millfield Wk. Hem. H. AZ15 8
Mill Gdns. SE26 CB49 77
Mill Grn. La. Hat. BR11 10
Millgreen Rd. Mitch. BU54 86
Mill Grn. Rd. Welw. G. C. BR8 5
Milgrove St. SW11 BV44 66
Dagnall St.
Mill Hedge Clo. Cob. BE61 102
Mill Hill, Brwd. DC26 122
Mill Hill Gr. NW7 BO28 37
Mill Hill Gro. W3 BN40 55
Mill Hill Rd. SW13 BP44 65
Mill Hill Rd. W3 BM41 65
Mill Hill Ter. W3 BM40 55
Mill Hill NW3 BT34 47
Mill House La. Cher. AT52 82
Millhouse La. Wat. BB17 17
Millias Gdns. Edg. BM30 37
Millicent Rd. E10 CD33 48
Milling Rd. Edg. BN29 37
Mill La. E4 CE24 30
Mill La. NW6 BR35 46
Mill La. SE18 CL42 68
Mill La. Brox. CD14 12
Mill La. Brwd. CZ22 33
Mill La. Brwd. DB21 33
Mill La. Cars. BU56 95
Mill La. Ch. St. G. AQ27 34
Mill La. Croy. BX55 86
Mill La. Dor. BJ71 119
Mill La. Egh. AU52 82
Mill La. Epsom BO58 94
Mill La. Ger. Cr. AS32 43
Mill La. Grays. DB41 70
Mill La. Harl. CQ9 6
Mill La. Kings L. AZ18 17
Mill La. Kings. on T. BL52 85
Mill La. Lthd. BJ64 102
Mill La. Ong. CT18 23
Mill La. Ong. CV12 15
Mill La. Ong. CY18 24
Mill La. Orp. CL58 97
Mill La. Orp. CO52 89
Mill La. Oxt. CG69 115
Mill La. Oxt. CK69 115
Mill La. Red. BW69 121
Mill La. Rom. CQ32 50
Mill La. Rom. CU23 32
Mill La. Rom. CV22 33
Mill La. Saw. CQ6 6
Mill La. Sev. CT58 98
Mill La. Sev. CY69 117
Mill La. Sev. CT64 107
Mill La. Sev. CV64 108
Mill La. Sev. DB64 108
Mill La. Slou. AT45 62
Mill La. Ton. CX71 117
Mill La. Wal. Cr. CD17 21
Mill La. Wdf. Grn. CG28 40
Mill La. Wey. AY60 92
Mill La. Wind. AN43 61
Mill La. Wok. AX63 101
Mill La. Clo. Brox. CD14 12
Millman Ms. WC1 BX38 56
Millman St. WC1 BX38 2
Millman St. WC1 BX38 56
Millmark Gro. SE14 CD44 67
Millmarsh La. Enf. CD23 30
Millmead, Guil. AR71 118
Mill Mead, Stai. AV49 72
Mill Mead, Wey. AY59 92
Mill Mead Rd. N17 CB31 48
Millmead Ter. Guil. AR71 118
Millmead Way, Loug. CK23 31
Mill Pk. Av. Horn. CW34 51
Mill Pl. E14 CD39 57
Mill Pl. Chis. CL51 88
Mill Pl. Dart. CU45 69
Mill Pl. Kings. on T. BL52 85
Mill Pl. Slou. AR44 62
Mill Plat, Islw. BJ44 64
Mill Plat Av. Islw. BJ44 64
Millpond Est. SE16 CB41 67
Mill Pond Rd. Dart. CW46 80
Mill Ridge, Edg. BL28 37
Mill Rd. E16 CH40 58
Mill Rd. SW19 BT50 76
Mill Rd. Dart. CW49 80
Mill Rd. Epsom BO59 94
Mill Rd. Erith CS43 69
Mill Rd. Esher BF55 84
Mill Rd. Eyns. CW54 90
Mill Rd. Grav. DF47 81
Mill Rd. Grays. CX43 70
Mill Rd. Ilf. CL34 49
Mill Rd. S. Ock. CW40 60
Mill Rd. Twick. BG48 74
Mill Rd. West Dr. AX41 63
Mill Row N1 CA37 2
Mill Row N1 CA37 57
Mill Row W4 BN42 65
Belmont Rd.
Mills Clo. Uxb. AZ37 53
Mills Ct. E11 CG34 49
Harrow Rd.
Mills Ct. EC2 CA38 2
Mills Cres. Sev. CW62 108
Mills Gro. E14 CF39 57
Mills Gro. NW4 BQ31 46
Mill Shaw, Oxt. CG69 115
Mill Shot Dr. Amer. AO23 25
Millside, Cars. BU55 86
Millson Clo. N20 BT27 38
Sweets Way
Mill's Pl. NW8 BT39 1
Mills Rd. Walt. BD56 93
Mills Spur, Wind. AQ47 72
Millstead Clo. Tad. BP65 103
Spindlewoods
Millstream La. Slou. AM40 61
Millstream Rd. SE1 CA41 4
Milstream Rd. SE1 CA41 67
Mill St. SE1 CA41 4
Mill St. SE1 CA41 67
Mill St. W1 BV40 3
Mill St. W1 BV40 56
Mill St. Berk. AR13 7
Mill St. Hem. H. AX15 8
Mill St. Kings. on T. BL52 85
Mill St. Red. BU71 121
Mill St. Slou. AP40 52
Mill St. Slou. AU43 62
Mill St. West. CM67 115
Mills Way, Brwd. DE26 122
Milthorn Clo. Rick. AY25 26
Mill Vale, Brom. CG51 88
Millview Clo. Reig. BT69 121
Mill View Gdns. Croy. CC55 87
Millwall Dock Rd. E14 CE41 67
Tiller St.
Millwall Est. E14 CE41 67
Millwards, Hat. BP14 10
Millward St. W10 BQ40 55
Charles Sq.
Millway NW7 BO28 37
Mill Way, Bush. BE23 27
Mill Way, Felt. BC46 73
Mill Way, Reig. AV26 34
Millway Gdns. Nthlt. BE36 54
Millway, Reig. BT70 121
Millwell Cres. Chig. CM28 40
Millwood Rd. Houns. BG46 74
Millwood Rd. Orp. CP52 89
Millwood St. W10 BQ39 55
Chesterton Rd.
Milman Clo. Pnr. BD30 36
Milman Rd. NW6 BQ37 55
Milmans St. SW10 BT43 66
Milne Est. SE18 CK42 68
Milne Fld. Pnr. BF29 36
Milne Gdns. SE9 CK46 78
Milne Pk. E. Croy. CF59 96
Milne Pk. W. Croy. CF59 96
Milner App. Cat. CB64 105
Milner Clo. Cat. CA64 105
Milner Clo. Wat. BC20 17
Milner Dr. Cob. BE59 93
Milner Dr. Twick. BR47 74
Milner Pl. N1 BY37 2
Milner Pl. N1 BY37 56
Milner Rd. E15 CG38 58
Milner Rd. SW19 BS51 86
Milner Rd. Cat. CA64 105
Milner Rd. Dag. CP34 50
Milner Rd. Kings. on T. BK52 84
Milner Rd. Mord. BT53 86
Milner Rd. Th. Hth. BZ52 87
Milner Sq. N1 BY36 2
Milner Sq. N1 BY36 56
Milner St. SW1 BU42 66
Milner St. SW3 BU42 3
Milner St. SW3 BU42 66
Milner St. EC1 BY38 2
Milne Way, Uxb. AW30 35
Milnthorpe Rd. W4 BN43 65
Milo Rd. SE22 CA46 77
Milroy Av. Grav. DF48 81
Milroy Wk. SE1 BY40 4
Milroy Wk. WC2 BY40 56
Rennie St.
Milson Rd. W14 BQ41 65
Milton Av. Ger. Cr. AR31 43
Milton Av. E6 CJ36 58
Milton Av. N6 BW33 47
Milton Av. NW9 BM31 46
Milton Av. NW10 BO37 55
Milton Av. Barn. BR25 28
Milton Av. Croy. BZ54 87
Milton Av. Dor. BG72 119
Milton Av. Grav. DH47 81
Milton Av. Horn. CT34 50
Milton Av. Sev. CR58 98
Milton Av. Sutt. BT55 86
Milton Clo. N2 BT32 47
Milton Clo. Hayes BC39 53
Milton Clo. Pnr. BE29 36
Milton Clo. Slou. AT45 62
Milton Clo. Sutt. BT55 86
Milton Ct. EC2 BZ39 2
Milton Ct. EC2 BZ39 57
Milton St.
Milton Ct. Kings. on T. BL49 75
Milton Ct. Uxb. AZ34 44
Miltoncourt La. Dor. BH71 119
Milton Ct. Rd. SE14 CD43 67
Milton Cres. Ilf. CM33 49
Milton Dene, Hem. H. AZ10 8
Coleridge Cr.
Milton Dr. Borwd. BM25 28
Milton Dr. Shep. AY52 83
Milton Flds. Ch. St. G. AQ27 34
Milton Gdns. Epsom BO60 94
Milton Gdns. Til. DG44 71
Milton Gro. N11 BW28 38
Milton Gro. N16 BZ35 48
Milton Hall Rd. Grav. DH47 81
Milton Hill, Ch. St. G. AQ27 34
Milton Lawns, Amer. AO21 25
Milton Pk. N6 BW33 47
Milton Pl. N7 BY35 47
George's Rd.
Milton Pl. Grav. DH46 81
Milton Rd. E17 CE31 48
Milton Rd. N6 BW33 47
Milton Rd. N15 BY31 47
Milton Rd. NW7 BP28 37
Milton Rd. NW9 BO33 46
Broadway, The
Milton Rd. NW9 BP33 46
Milton Rd. SE24 BY46 76
Milton Rd. SW14 BN45 65
Milton Rd. SW19 BT50 76
Milton Rd. W3 BN40 55
Milton Rd. W7 BH40 54
Milton Rd. Belv. CR42 69
Milton Rd. Brwd. DA28 42
Milton Rd. Cat. BZ64 105
Milton Rd. Croy. BZ54 87
Milton Rd. Egh. AS49 72
Milton Rd. Grav. DG46 81
Milton Rd. Grays. DD42 71
Milton Rd. Hamptn. BF50 74
Milton Rd. Har. BH31 45

76

78

New Burlington Pl. W1 BW40 56
Savile Row
New Burlington St. W1 BW40 3
New Burlington St. W1 BW40 56
Newburn St. SE11 BX42 4
Newburn St. SE11 BX42 66
Newbury Av. Enf. CD22 30
Newbury Clo. Nthlt. BE36 54
Newbury Clo. Rom. CV29 42
Newbury Ct. E11 CH31 49
Newbury Gdns. Epsom BO56 94
Newbury Gdns. Rom. CV29 42
Newbury Gdns. Upmin. CW34 51
Newbury Rd. E4 CF29 39
Newbury Rd. Brom. CH52 88
Newbury Rd. Houns. AY44 63
Newbury Rd. Ilf. CN32 49
Newbury Rd. Rom. CV28 42
Newbury St. EC1 BZ39 2
Newbury St. EC1 BZ39 57
Newbury Wk. Rom. CV28 42
Newbury Way, Nthlt. BE36 54
New Butts Gdns. Slou. AT44 62
Newby Clo. Enf. CA23 30
Newby Pl. E14 CF39 57
Newby St. SW8 BV44 66
Newcastle Av. Ilf. CO29 41
Newcastle Ct. EC4 BY39 2
Newcastle Ct. EC4 BY39 56
Farringdon St.
Newcastle Pl. W2 BT39 1
Newcastle Pl. W2 BT39 56
Newcastle St. W8 BS41 66
New Causeway, Reig. BS72 121
New Cavendish St. W1 BV39 1
New Cavendish St. W1 BV39 56
New Change, EC4 BZ39 2
New Change EC4 BZ39 57
New Chapel Rd. Felt. BC47 73
New Church Rd. SE5 BZ43 67
New City Rd. E13 CJ38 58
New College Mews N1 BY36 56
College Cross
New Clo. SW19 BT51 86
New Clo. Felt. BE49 74
New Clo. Est. Mitch. BT51 86
Newcombe Pk. NW7 BO28 37
Newcombe Pk. Wem. BL37 55
Newcombe Rd. Rad. BM20 19
Newcombe St. W8 BS40 56
Newcomen Rd. E11 CG34 49
Newcomen Rd. SW11 BT45 66
Newcomen St. SE1 BZ41 4
Newcomen St. SE1 BZ41 67
Newcome Path, Rad. BM20 19
New Compton St. WC2 BW39 1
New Compton St. WC2 BW39 56
New Ct. WC2 BX39 2
New Ct. Dart. CW46 80
New Ct. Uxb. AX39 53
New Ct. Wey. AX55 83
Newcourt St. NW8 BU37 1
Newcourt St. NW8 BU37 56
New Coventry St. W1 BW40 3
New Coventry St. W1 BW40 56
Coventry St.
Newcroft Clo. Uxb. AY39 53
New Cross Gate SE14 CC44 67
New Cross Rd. SE14 CC43 67
New Cross Rd. Guil. AQ69 118
Newdale Clo. N9 CB27 39
Balham Rd.
Newdene Av. Nthlt. BD37 54
Newdigate Gdn. Uxb. AX30 35
Newdigate Rd. Uxb. AX30 35
Newdigate Rd. East. Uxb. AX30 35
Newell Rd. Hem. H AY15 8
Newell St. E14 CD39 57
New End NW3 BT35 47
New End Sq. NW3 BT35 47
New England St. St. Alb. BG13 9
Newenham Rd. Lthd. BF66 111
Newent Clo. SE15 CA43 67
Coleman Rd.
Newent Clo. Cars. BU54 86
New Euston Col. NW1 BW38 1
New Farm Dr. CP24 32
New Farm La. Nthwd. BB30 35
New Fetter La. EC4 BY39 2
New Fetter La. EC4 BY39 56
Newfield Clo. Hamptn. BF51 84
Newfield La. Hem. H. AY13 8
Newfield Rise NW2 BP34 46
Newfields, Welw. G. C. BP8 5
New Fm. Av. Brom. CH52 88
Newford Clo. Hem. H. AZ13 8
New Ford Rd. Wal. Cr. CD20 21
New Forest La. Chig. CL29 40
Newgale Gdns. Edg. BL30 37
Newgate, Croy. BZ54 87
Newgate Clo. Felt. BE48 74
Newgate Clo. St. Alb. BK12 9
Newgate St. E4 CG27 40
Newgate St. EC1 BY39 2
Newgate St. EC1 BY39 56
Newgate St. Hert. BX15 11
Newgatestreet Rd.
Wal. Cr. BY16 20
New Goulston St. E1 CA39 2
New Goulston St. E1 CA39 57
Middlesex St.
New Greens Av. St. Alb. BG11 9
Newhall Ct. Wal. Abb. CG20 22
Mason Way
New Hall Dr. Rom. CW20 42
Newham Rd. Houns. BA44 63
Newall Rd.
Newhams Clo. Brom. CK52 88
Newhams Row, SE1 CA41 4
Newhams Row SE1 CA41 67
Newham Way E16 CJ39 58
Newham Way, Har. BL31 46
Newhaven Clo. Hayes BB42 63
Newhaven Cres. Ashf. BA49 73
Newhaven Gdns. SE9 CJ45 68
Newhaven Rd. SE25 BZ53 87
New Haw Rd. Wey. AX56 92
New Heston Rd. Houns. BE43 64
New Hill Rd. Orp. CK58 97
Newhouse Av. Rom. CP31 50
Newhouse Clo. N. Mal. BO54 85
Newhouse Cres. Wat. BC19 17
New House La. Epp. CS16 23
New House La. Grav. DF48 81
Newhouse La. Ong. CV14 15
Newhouse La. Sev. DC61 108
Newhouse Pk. St. Alb. BJ15 9
Newhouse Rd. Hem. H. AT16 16
Newhouse Way, Mord. BT54 86
Newick Clo. Bex. CR46 79
Newick Rd. E5 CB34 48
Newing Grn. Brom. CJ50 78
Newington Barrow Way
N7 BX34 47
Andover Est.
Newington Butts, SE1 BY42 4
Newington Butts, SE1 BY42 66
Newington Causeway,
SE1 BY41 4
Newington Causeway,
SE1 BY41 66
Newington Gn. N16 BZ35 48
Newington Gn. Rd. N1 BZ35 48
Newington Way, N7 BX34 47
New Inn, Broadway EC2 CA38 57
New Inn Yd.
New Inn La. Guil. AT68 109
New Inn St. EC2 CA38 2
New Inn Yd. EC2 CA38 2
New Inn Yd. EC2 CA38 57
New James St. SE15 CB45 67
New James St. SE15 CB45 67
Scylla Rd.
New Kent Rd. SE1 BZ41 4
New Kent Rd. SE1 BZ41 67
New King's Rd. SW6 BR44 65
New King St. SE8 CE43 67
Newland Clo. St. Alb. BJ15 9
Mile Ho. Clo.
Newland Gdns. W13 BJ41 64
Newland Rd. N8 BX31 47
Newlands Av. Rad. BH20 18
Newlands Av. Surb. BH54 84
Newlands Av. Wok. AS64 100
Newlands Clo. Brwd. DE26 122
Newlands Clo. Edg. BL27 37
Newlands Clo. Sthl. BE42 64
Newlands Clo. Walt. BE56 93
Newlands Clo. Wem. BK36 54
Newlands Ct. Wem. BM34 46
Newlands Dr. Enf. CB23 30
Newlands Est. SW17 BV49 76
Newlands Pk. SE26 CC50 77
Newlands Pl. Barn. BQ25 28
Newlands Rd. SW16 BX51 86
Newlands Rd. Hem. H. AV13 7
Newlands Rd. Wdf. Grn. CG27 40
Newlands, The Wall. BW57 95
Newland St. E16 CK40 58
Newlands Wk. Wat. BD20 18
Newlands Way, Chess. BK56 93
Newlands Wd. Croy. CD58 96
New La. Guil. AS66 109
New La. Wok. & Guil. AS64 100
Newling Est. E2 CA38 57
New London St. EC3 CA40 57
Hart St.
Newlyn Clo. St. Alb. BE18 18
Newlyn Clo. Uxb. AZ39 53
Newlyn Gdns. Har. BE33 45
Newlyn Rd. N17 CA30 39
Newlyn Rd. Barn. BR24 28
Newlyn Rd. NW2 BQ33 46
Newlyn Rd. Well. CN44 68
Newman Cl. Horn. CW31 51
Newman Pass. W1 BW39 1
Newman Pass. W1 BW39 56
Newman St.
Newman Rd. E13 CH38 58
Newman Rd. E17 CC32 48
Newman Rd. Brom. CH51 88
Newman Rd. Croy. BX54 86
Newman Rd. Hayes BC40 53
Newman Rd. Houns. AZ44 63
Nimrod Rd.
Newmans Clo. Loug. CL24 31
Newmans Dr. Brwd. DE26 122
Newmans La. Loug. CL24 31
Newmans Rd. Grav. DF48 81
Newmans Row, WC2 BX39 2
Newman's Row WC2 BV39 56
Gt. Turnstile
Newman St. W1 BW39 1
Newman St. W1 BW39 56
Newmans Way, Barn. BT23 29
Newman Yd. W1 BW39 1
Newmarket Av. Nthlt. BF35 45
Newmarket Grn. SE9 CJ47 78
Newmarket Way, Horn. CW35 51
New Martan St. E1 CA40 57
New Martan St. E1 CB40 4
New Meadows Path, Rich. BM44 65
Townmead Rd.
Newminster Rd. Mord. BT53 86
New Mount St. E15 CF36 57
Newnham Av. Ruis. BD33 45
Newnham Clo. Loug. CJ25 31
Newnham Clo. Nthlt. BG35 45
Newnham Clo. Slou. AQ40 52
Newnham Gdns. Nthlt. BG36 54
Newnham Pk. Wal. Cr. CC18 21
Newnham Pl. Grays. DG42 71
Newnham Rd. N22 BX30 38
Newnham St. E1 CA39 2
Newnham Ter. SE1 BY41 4
Newnham Ter. SE1 BY41 66
New North Pl. EC2 CA38 2
New North Pl. EC2 CA38 57
Luke St.
New North Rd. N1 BZ36 2
New North Rd. N1 BZ36 57
New North Rd. Ilf. CM29 40
New North Rd. Reig. BR72 120
New North St. WC1 BX39 2
New North St. WC1 BX39 56
Newnton Clo. N4 BZ33 48
New Oak Rd. N2 BT30 38
New Orleans Walk N19 BW33 47
New Oxford St. WC1 BW39 1
New Oxford St. WC1 BX39 2
New Oxford St. WC1 BW39 56
New Pa. Hayes BA39 53
New Palace Yd. SW1 BX41 4
New Pde. Ashf. AY49 73
Church Rd.
New Pk. Av. N13 BY27 38
New Park Clo. Nthlt. BE36 54
Arnold Rd.
New Pk. Ct. SW2 BX47 76
New Park Dr. Hem. H. AZ13 8
New Park Rd. SW2 BW47 76
New Park Rd. Ashf. BA49 73
New Park Rd. Hert. BV15 11
New Park Rd. Uxb. AX30 35
New Peachey La. Uxb. AX39 53
New Peachey La. Clo.
Uxb. AX39 53
Newpiece, Loug. CL24 31
New Place Gdns. Upmin. CY34 51
New Pl. Sq. SE16 CB41 67
Southwark Pk. Rd.
New Plaistow Rd. E15 CG37 58
New Pond Rd. Guil. AO74 118
Newport Av. E13 CH38 58
Palmer Rd.
Newport Ct. WC2 BW40 3
Newport Ct. WC2 BW40 56
Charing Cross Rd.
Newport Est. E3 CD38 57
Newport Mead. Wat. BD28 36
Newport Pl. WC2 BW40 3
Newport Pl. WC2 BW40 56
Shaftesbury Av.
Newport Rd. E10 CF34 48
Newport Rd. E17 CD31 48
Newport Rd. SW13 BP44 65
Newport Rd. Hayes BA39 53
Newport Rd. Houns. AY44 63
Newbury Rd.
Newports, Saw. CP6 6
Newports, Swan. CS54 89
Newport St. SE11 BX42 4
Newport St. SE11 BX42 66
Newport St. WC2 BW40 3
Newport St. WC2 BW41 66
Charing Cross Rd.
Newquay Cres. Har. BE34 45
Newquay Gdns. Wat. BC27 35
Newquay Rd. SE6 CE48 77
New Quebec St. W1 BU39 1
New Quebec St. W1 BU39 56
New River Clo. Hodd. CE11 12
New River Ct. N5 BZ35 48
New River Cres. N13 BY28 38
New River Gdns. N22 BY29 38
New River Wk. N1 BZ36 57
New Rd. E1 CA39 57
New. Rd. E4 CE28 39
New Rd. E16 CG39 58
New Rd. N8 BX32 47
New Rd. N9 CB27 39
New Rd. N17 CA30 39
New Rd. N22 BZ30 39
New Rd. NW7 BO26 37
New Rd. NW7 BR29 37
New Rd. SE2 CP42 69
New Rd. Amer. AP22 25
New Rd. Berk. AS11 7
New Rd. Berks. AP12 7
New Rd. Borwd. BK25 27
High St.
New Rd. Brent. BK43 64
New Rd. Brox. CD13 12
New Rd. Brwd. DB27 42
Coptfold Rd.
New Rd. Ch. St. G. AS24 25
New Rd. Dag. CR37 59
New Rd. Dor. BK72 119
New Rd. E. Mol. BF52 84
New Rd. Epp. CR19 23
New Rd. Esher BG55 84
New Rd. Felt. BA46 73
New Rd. Felt. BC47 73
New Rd. Felt. BE49 74
New Rd. Grav. DG46 81
New Road. Guil. AY69 110
New Rd. Har. BH35 45
New Rd. Harl. CP9 6
New Rd. Hayes BA43 63
New Rd. Ilf. CN34 49
New Rd. Kings L. AV18 16
New Rd. Kings. on T. BM50 75
New Rd. Leath. BH58 93
New Rd. Lthd. BH59 93
New Rd. Maid. AG43 61
New Rd. Mord. BU54 86
New Rd. Orp. CO54 89
New Rd. Oxt. CH68 115
New Rd. Pot. B. BP20 19
New Rd. Rad. BH21 27
New Rd. Rad. BM20 19
New Rd. Rain. CS37 59
New Rd. Rich. BK49 74
New Rd. Rick. AV23 25
New Rd. Rick. AZ25 26
New Rd. Rom. CP25 32
New Rd. Shep. AZ52 83
New Rd. Slou. AR44 62
New Rd. Slou. AT41 62
New Rd. S. Dnth. CY51 90
New Rd. Stai. AU49 72
New Rd. Swan. CT50 79
New Rd. Swan. CT52 89
New Rd. Tad. BQ65 103
New Rd. Uxb. BA38 53
New Rd. Wat. BD24 27
New Rd. Wat. BH23 27
New Rd. Well. CO44 69
New Rd. Welw. G. C. BP9 5
New Rd. Welw. G. C. BR5 5
New Rd. Wey. BA56 92
New Row, WC2 BX40 4
New Row WC2 BX40 56
Newry Rd. Twick. BJ46 74
New St. Hill EC4 BY39 56
Lit. New St.
New St. Hill Brom. CH49 78
New St. Sq. EC4 BY39 56
Newsam Av. N15 BZ32 48
New Scotland Yd. SW1 BX41 66
Derby Gate
New Spring Gdns. Brent. BK43 64
Albany Road
New Spring Gdns. Wk.
SE11 BX42 66
Albert Embankment
New Sq. WC2 BX39 2
New Sq. WC2 BX39 56
Newstead, Hat. BO14 10
Newstead Av. Orp. CM65 88
Newstead Ri. Cat. CB66 114
Newstead Rd. SE12 CG47 78
Newstead Rd. Cat. CB66 114
Newstead Wk. Cars. BT54 86
Newstead Way SW19 BQ49 75
New St. EC2 CA39 2
New St. EC2 CA39 57
New St. Berk. AR13 7
New St. Saw. CQ5 6
New Street Sq. EC4 BY39 2
New St. Stai. AW49 73
New St. Wat. BD24 27
Church St.
New St. West. CM67 115
Newteswell Dri. Wal. Abb. CF19 21
Newton Abbot Rd. Grav. DF48 81
Newton Av. N10 BV30 38
Newton Av. W3 BN41 65
Newton Clo. Slou. AS41 62
Newton Dr. Saw. CP6 6
Newton Gro. N1 BZ37 2
Newton Gro. N1 BZ37 57
Northport St.
Newton Gro. W4 BO41 65
Newton La. Wind. AO46 72
Newton Rd. E15 CF35 48
Newton Rd. N15 CA32 48
Newton Rd. NW2 BQ35 46
Newton Rd. SW19 BR50 75
Newton Rd. W2 BS39 56
Newton Rd. Chig. CO28 41
Newton Rd. Har. BH30 36
Newton Rd. Houns. AY44 63
Newton Rd. Islw. BH44 64
Newton Rd. Pur. BW59 95
Newton Rd. Til. DG44 71
Newton Rd. Well. CO45 69
Newton Rd. Wem. BL36 55
Newtons Clo. Rain. CT36 59
Newton St. WC2 BX39 2
Newton St. WC2 BX39 56
Newton's Yd. SW18 BS46 76
Wandsworth High St.
Newton Walk, Edg. BM30 37
North Rd.
Newton Way N18 BZ28 39
Newton Wood Rd. Ash. BL61 103
Newtown Rd. Uxb. AW36 53
Newtown St. SW11 BV44 66
New Trinity Rd. N2 BT31 47
New Turnstile WC1 BX39 56
High Holborn
New Turnstile, WC2 BX39 2
New Union Clo. E14 CF41 68
Stewart Clo.
New Walk, Sev. DC61 108
Battlefields Rd.
New Wanstead E11 CG32 49
New Way La. Harl. CR11 14
New Way Rd. NW9 BO31 46
New Wharf. N1 BX37 2
New Wharf Rd. N1 BX37 56
New Wickham La. Egh. AT50 72
New Windsor St. Uxb. AX37 53
New Wood, Welw. G C. BT7 5
Newyears Green La. Uxb. AY32 44
New Years La. Sev. CN61 106
New Zealand Av. Walt. BB54 83
New Zealand Way W12 BP40 55
New Zealand Way, Rain. CT38 59
Niagra Av. W5 BK42 64
Nibthwaite Rd. Har. BH32 45
Nicholas Clo. St. Alb. BG11 9
Nicholas Clo. S. Ock. DB38 60
Nicholas Clo. Wat. BC22 26
Nicholas Dr. Sev. CV66 117
Nicholas Gdns. W5 BK40 54
Nicholas Gdns. Wok. AV61 100
Nicholas La. EC4 BZ40 4
Nicholas La. EC4 BZ40 57
Nicholas Rd. E1 CC38 57
Nicholas Rd. Borwd. BM25 28
Nicholas Rd. Croy. BX56 95
Nicholas Rd. Dag. CQ34 50
Nicholas Rd. Houns. BF45 64
Nicholas Way, Hem. H. AY12 8
Nicholas Way, Nthwd. BA30 35
Nicholas Way, Sev. CV64 108
Nicholay Rd. N19 BW33 47
Calverland Gr.
Nichol Clo. N14 BW26 38
Nichol La. Brom. CH50 78
Nicholl Rd. Epp. CN19 22
Nicholls Av. Uxb. AZ38 53
Nicholls Field, Harl. CO11 14
Nichols Grn. W5 BK39 54
Montpelier Rd.
Nicholson Dr. Bush. BG26 36
Nicholson Rd. Croy. CA54 87
Nicholson St. SE1 BY40 4
Nicholson St. SE1 BY40 56
Nickelby Clo. Uxb. AZ39 53
Thackeray Clo.
Nickelby Rd. Grav. DK47 81
Nicola Clo. Har. BG30 36
Nicola Clo. Sth. Croy. BZ57 96
Nicolas Wk. Grays. DG41 71
Nicol Clo. Twick. BJ46 74
Cassilis Rd.
Nicol End, Ger. Cr. AR30 34
Nicoll Rd. NW10 BO37 55
Nicoll Way Borwd. BN24 28
Nicol Pl. NW4 BP32 46
Nicol Rd. Ger. Cr. AR30 34
Nicolson Rd. Orp. CP54 89
Nicosia Rd. SW18 BU47 76
Niddersdale, Hem. H. AY12 8
Niederwald Rd. SE26 CD49 77
Nield Rd. Hayes BB41 63
Nigel Clo. Nthlt. BE37 54
Nigel Ms. Ilf. CL35 49
Nigel Playfair Av. W6 BP42 65
Nigel Rd. E7 CJ35 49
Nigel Rd. SE15 CB45 67
Nigeria Rd. SE7 CJ43 68
Nightingales La. Ch. St. G. AR26 34
Nightingale Ave. Lthd. BA65 101
Nightingale Av. E4 CG28 40
Nightingale Av. Leath. BA66 110
Nightingale Av. Upmin. CZ33 51
Nightingale Clo. E4 CF28 39
Nightingale Clo. W4 BN43 65
Nightingale Clo. Cars. BV55 86
Nightingale Clo. Cob. BD59 93
Nightingale Cl. Grav. DF49 81
Mulberry Rd.
Nightingale Cres. SW11 BU46 76
Blenkarne Rd.
Nightingale Cres.
Leath. BA66 110
Nightingale Cres. Lthd. BA65 101
Nightingale Dr. Epsom BM57 94
Nightingale Gro. SE13 CF46 77
Nightingale Gro. Dart. CX45 70
Nightingale La. E11 CH32 49
Nightingale La. N6 BU33 47
Nightingale La. N8 BX31 47
Nightingale La. SW4 BV46 76
Nightingale La. SW12 BV47 76
Nightingale La. Brom. CJ51 88
Nightingale La. Rich. BL47 75
Nightingale La. St. Alb. BK15 9
Nightingale La. Sev. CR68 116
Nightingale Pl. SE18 CL43 68
Nightingale Rd. E5 CB34 48
Nightingale Rd. N9 CC26 39
Nightingale Rd. N22 BX30 38
Nightingale Rd. NW10 BO37 55
Nightingale Rd. W7 BH40 54
Nightingale Rd. Bush. BF25 27
Nightingale Rd. Cars. BU55 86
Nightingale Rd. Croy. CC59 96
Nightingale Rd. E. Mol. BF53 84
Nightingale Rd. Esher BE56 93
Nightingale Rd. Guil. AR70 118
Nightingale Rd. Hamptn. BF49 74
Nightingale Rd. Leath. BB66 110
Nightingale Rd. Orp. CM53 88
Nightingale Rd. Rick. AX26 35
Nightingale Rd. Sev. CW62 108
Nightingale Rd. Sth. Croy. CC58 96
Nightingales, Wal. Abb. CG20 22
Roundhills
Nightingales La. Ch. St. G. AR24 25
Nightingale Sq. SW12 BV47 76
Nightingale Vale SE18 CL43 68
Nightingale Wk. SW4 BV46 76
Nightingale Way, Uxb. AV33 43
Nijmegen Way SE22 CA46 77
Dulwich Gro.
Nile Path, SE18 CL43 68
Jackson St.
Nile Rd. E13 CJ37 58
Nile St. N1 BZ38 2
Nile St. N1 BZ38 57
Nile Ter. SE15 CA42 4
Nile Ter. SE15 CA42 67
Nimbus Rd. Epsom BN58 94
Nimmo Dr. Bush. BG26 36
Nimrod Rd. SW17 BV50 76
Nimrod Rd. Houns. AZ44 63
Nimrod Way, Houns. AZ44 63
Nimrod Rd.
Nine Acres Clo. E12 CK35 49
Nine Ashes Rd. Brwd. DA20 24
Nine Ashes Rd. Ing. DC18 24
Nine Elms Av. Uxb. AX39 53
Nine Elms Clo. Uxb. AX39 53
Nine Elms Gro. Grav. DG47 81
Nine Elms La. SW8 BW43 66
Ninefields, Wal. Abb. CG20 22
Ninehams Clo. Cat. BZ63 105
Ninehams Gdns. Cat. BZ63 105
Ninehams Rd.
Ninehams Rd. Cat. BZ64 105
Ninehams Rd. West. CH64 106
Nine Stiles Clo. Uxb. AW36 53
Nineteenth Rd. Mitch. BX52 86
Carisbrooke Rd.
Ninhams Wd. Orp. CK56 97
Ninian Rd. Hem. H. AY11 8
Ninnings Rd. Ger. Cr. AS29 34
Ninnings Way, Ger. Cr. AS29 34
Ninth Av. Hayes BC40 53
Nisbet Ho. E9 CC35 48
Nita Rd. Brwd. DB28 42
Nithdale Rd. SE18 CL43 68
Niton Clo. Barn. BQ25 28
Niton Rd. Rich. BM45 65
Niton St. SW6 BQ43 65
Nizels La. Ton. CW71 117
Nizels Rd. Ton. CW70 117
Noak Hill Rd. Rom. CV28 42
Noble Rd. N18 CC28 39
Noble St. EC2 BZ39 2
Noble St. EC2 BZ39 57
Nobles Way, Egh. AS50 72
Nockhall Rd. Green. DB46 80
Noel Park Rd. N22 BY30 38
Noel Rd. E6 CK38 58
Noel Rd. N1 BY37 2
Noel Rd. N1 BY37 56
Noel Rd. W3 BM40 55
Noel Sq. Dag. CP35 50
Noel St. W1 BW39 1
Noel St. W1 BW39 56
Noke Dr. Red. BV70 121
Noke La. St. Alb. BE16 18
Nokes, The Hem. H. AW12 8
Nolan Way E5 CB35 48

Nolton Pl. Edg. BL30 37
Nonsuch Clo. Ilf. CL29 40
Nonsuch Court Av. Epsom BP58 94
Nonsuch Wk. Sutt. BQ58 94
Nora Gdns. NW4 BQ31 46
Norah St. E2 CB38 57
Nora Ter. Har. BH33 45
Norbiton Av. Kings. on T. BM51 85
Norbiton Common Rd. N. Mal. BM52 85
Norbiton Hall Kings. on T. BL51 85
Norbiton Rd. E14 CD39 57
Norbreck Gdns. NW10 BL38 55
Norbreck Pde. W5 BL38 55
Norbroke St. W12 BO40 55
Norburn St. W10 BR39 55
Chesterton Rd.
Norbury Av. SW16 BX51 86
Norbury Av. Houns. BG45 64
Norbury Av. Th. Hth. BY51 86
Norbury Clo. SW16 BY51 86
Norbury Ct. Rd. SW16 BX52 86
Norbury Cres. SW16 BX51 86
Norbury Cross SW16 BX52 86
Norbury Gdns. Rom. CP32 50
Norbury Gro. NW7 BO27 37
Norbury Hl. SW16 BY50 76
Norbury Ms. SW16 BX51 86
Norbury Cres.
Norbury Rise SW16 BX52 86
Norbury Rd. E4 CE28 39
Norbury Rd. Reig. BR70 120
Norbury Rd. Th. Hth. BZ51 87
Norbury Way, Lthd. BG66 111
Norcombe Gdns. Har. BK32 45
Norcott Clo. Hayes BD38 54
Norcott Rd. N16 CB34 48
Norcroft Gdns. SE22 CB47 77
Norcutt Rd. Twick. BH47 74
Nordenfeldt Rd. Erith CS42 69
Norfield Rd. Bex. CS49 79
Norfolk Av. N13 BY29 38
Norfolk Av. N15 CA32 48
Norfolk Av. Slou. AO39 52
Norfolk Av. Sth. Croy. CA58 96
Norfolk Av. Wat. BD22 27
Norfolk Clo. N2 BU31 47
Park Rd.
Norfolk Clo. N13 BY29 38
Norfolk Clo. Barn. BV24 29
Norfolk Clo. Twick. BJ46 74
Norfolk Cres. W2 BU39 1
Norfolk Cres. W2 BU39 56
Norfolk Cres. Sid. CN47 78
Norfolk Est. E1 CC38 57
Norfolk Farm Clo. Wok. AU61 100
Norfok Farm Rd. Wok. AU61 100
Norfolk Gdns. Bexh. CQ44 69
Norfolk Gdns. Borwd. BN24 28
Norfolk Ho. Rd. SW16 BW48 76
Norfolk Pl. W2 BT39 1
Norfolk Pl. W2 BT39 56
Norfolk Pl. Well. CO44 69
Norfolk Rd. E6 CK37 58
Norfolk Rd. E17 CC30 39
Norfolk Rd.NW8 BT37 1
Norfolk Rd. NW8 BT37 56
Norfolk Rd. NW10 BO36 55
Norfolk Rd. SW19 BU50 76
Norfolk Rd. Bark. CN36 58
Norfolk Rd. Barn. BS24 29
Norfolk Rd. Dag. CR35 50
Norfolk Rd. Dor. BJ71 119
Norfolk Rd. Enf. CB25 30
Norfolk Rd. Felt. BD47 74
Norfolk Rd. Grav. DH46 81
Norfolk Rd. Grav. DH47 81
Norfolk Rd. Har. BF32 45
Norfolk Rd. Ilf. CN33 49
Norfolk Rd. Rick. AY26 35
Norfolk Rd. Rom. CS32 50
Norfolk Rd. Th. Hth. BZ52 87
Norfolk Rd. Upmin. CX34 51
Norfolk Rd. Uxb. AX36 53
Norfolk Row, SE11 BX42 4
Norfolk Row, SE11 BX42 66
Old Paradise St.
Norfolk Sq. W2 BT39 1
Norfolk Sq. W2 BT39 56
Norfolk St. E7 CH35 49
Norfolk Ter. W6 BR42 65
Norgrove St. SW12 BV47 76
Norheads, West. CH62 106
Norheads La. West. CJ61 106
Norhyrst Av. SE25 CA52 87
Nork Gdns. Bans. BR60 94
Nork Rise, Bans. BQ61 103
Nork Way, Bans. BQ61 103
Norland Pl. W11 BR40 55
Norland Rd. W11 BQ40 55
Norlands Cres. Chis. CL51 88
Norland Sq. W11 BR40 55
Norley Rd. SE13 CF45 67
Norley Vale SW15 BP47 75
Norlington Rd. E10 CF33 48
Norlington Rd. E11 CF33 48
Norman Av. N22 BY30 38
Norman Av. Epsom BO59 94
Norman Av. Felt. BE48 74
Norman Av. Sth. Croy. BZ58 96
Norman Av. Sthl. BE40 54
Norman Av. Twick. BJ47 74
Normanby Rd. NW10 BO35 46
Normanby Cl. SW15 BR46 75
Manfred Rd.
Norman Clo. N22 BZ30 39
Norman Av.
Norman Clo. Dart. CW47 80
Norman Clo. Orp. CM55 88
Norman Clo. Rom. CR30 41
Norman Clo. Wal. Abb. CF20 21
Norman Ct. N4 BY33 47
Norman Ct. Pot. B. BT19 20
Norman Cres. Brwd. DD27 122
Norman Cres. Houns. BD43 64
Norman Cres. Pnr. BD30 36
Normand Ms. W14 BR43 65
Normand Rd. W14 BR43 65
Normandy Av. Barn. BR25 28
Normandy Dr. Berk. AQ12 7
Normandy Dr. Hayes BA39 53
Normandy Rd. SW9 BY44 66
Normandy Rd. St. Alb. BG12 9
Normandy Ter. E16 CH39 58
Coolfin Rd.
Normandy Way, Erith CT44 69
Norman Gro. E3 CD37 57
Norman Ho. Felt. BE48 74
Norman Hurst, Ashf. AZ49 73
Normanhurst Av. Bexh. CP44 69
Normanhurst, Brwd. DE25 122
Rayleigh Rd.
Normanhurst Dr. Twick. BJ46 74
St. Margaret's Rd.
Normanhurst Rd. SW2 BX48 76
Normanhurst Rd. Orp. CO51 89
Normanhurst Rd. Walt. BD55 84
Norman Rd. E6 CK38 58
Norman Rd. N15 CA32 48
Norman Rd. SE10 CE43 67
Norman Rd. SW19 BT50 76
Norman Rd. Ashf. BA50 73
Norman Rd. Belv. CR41 69
Norman Rd. Dart. CW47 80
Norman Rd. Horn. CU33 50
Norman Rd. Ilf. CL35 49
Norman Rd. Sutt. BS56 95
Norman Rd. Th. Hth. BY53 86
Norman Rd. Welw. G. C. BP5 5
Norman's Bldgs. EC1 BZ38 2
Norman's Bldgs. EC1 BZ38 57
Norman's Clo. NW10 BN36 55
Normans Clo. Grav. DG47 81
Normans Clo. Uxb. AY39 53
Normansfield, Tedd. BK50 74
Normansfield Av. Tedd. BK50 74
Normansfield Clo. Bush. BF26 36
Normanshire Av. E4 CF28 39
Normanshire Dr. E4 CE28 39
Normansmead NW10 BN36 55
Normans, The Slou. AQ39 52
Norman St. EC1 BZ38 2
Norman St. EC1 BZ38 57
Normanton Av. SW19 BS48 76
Normanton Pk. E4 CG27 40
Normanton Rd. Sth. Croy. CA57 96
Normanton St. SE23 CC48 77
Norman Way N14 BX27 38
Norman Way W3 BM39 55
Normington Clo. SW16 BY49 76
Norrell's Dri. Leath. BB66 110
Norrells Ride, Leath. BB66 110
Norrice Lea N2 BT32 47
Norris Gro. Brox. CD13 12
Norris La. Hodd. CE11 12
Norris Rise, Hodd. CD11 12
Norris Rd. Hodd. CD11 12
Norris Rd. Stai. AV49 72
Norris St. SW1 BW40 3
Norris St. SW1 BW40 56
Haymarket
Norroy Rd. SW15 BQ45 65
Norrys Clo. Barn. BU24 29
Norrys Rd. Barn. BU24 29
Norseman Ct. Brwd. CZ22 33
Kelvedon Grn.
Norseman Way, Grnf. BF37 54
Olympic Way
Norstead Pl. SW15 BP48 75
Norsted La. Orp. CO59 98
North Acess Rd. E17 CC32 48
North Acre NW9 BO30 37
North Acre, Bans. BR61 103
North Acton Rd. NW10 BN37 55
North Albert Rd. Reig. BR70 120
Northallerton Way, Rom. CV28 42
Northall Rd. Bexh. CS44 69
Northampton Bldgs. EC1 BY38 2
Northampton Bldgs. EC1 BY38 56
Skinner St.
Northampton Gro. N1 BZ35 48
St. Pauls Pl.
Northampton Pk. N1 BZ36 57
Northampton Rd. EC1 BY38 2
Northampton Rd. EC1 BY38 56
Northampton Rd. Croy. CB55 87
Northampton Rd. Enf. CD25 30
Northampton Sq. EC1 BY38 2
Northampton Sq. EC1 BY38 56
Northampton St. N1 BZ36 57
Northanger Rd. SW16 BX50 76
North App. Nthwd. BA27 35
North App. Wat. BB21 26
North App. Wat. BC20 17
North Ash Rd. New. A. G. DC55 90
North Audley St. W1 BV39 56
North Av. N18 CB28 39
North Av. W13 BJ39 54
North Av. Cars. BU57 95
North Av. Har. BF32 45
North Av. Hayes BC40 53
North Av. Rich. BM44 65
Sandycombe Rd.
North Av. Sthl. BE40 54
North Av. Watt. BB58 92
Northaw Clo. Hem. H. AZ11 8
Northaw Rd. East, Pot. B. BW19 20
Northaw Rd. West, Pot. B. BV18 20
North Bank NW8 BU38 1
Northbank NW8 BU38 56
Northbank Rd. E17 CF30 39
North Barns, Brox. CE14 12
Northborough Rd. SW16 BW52 86
Northbourne Brom. CH54 88
Northbourne Rd. SW4 BW45 66
North Bridge Rd. Berk. AP12 7
Northbrook Dr. Nthwd. BB30 35
Northbrook Rd. N22 BX29 38
Northbrook Rd. SE13 CF46 77
Northbrook Rd. Barn. BR25 28
Northbrook Rd. Croy. BZ53 87
Northbrook Rd. Ilf. CL34 49
Northbrooks Harl. CM11 13
Northburgh St. EC1 BY38 2
Northburgh St. EC1 BY38 56
Northchurch Rd. N1 BZ36 57
North Church Rd. Wem. BM36 55
North Circular Rd. E4 CD28 39
North Circular Rd. N3 BS31 47
North Circular Rd. N12 BU29 38
North Circular Rd. N13 BY28 38
North Circular Rd. NW2 BQ34 46
North Circular Rd. NW10 BL38 55
North Circular Rd. NW11 BQ32 46
Northcliffe Dr. N20 BR26 37
Northcliffe Rd. Grav. DF47 81
North Clo. Barn. BQ25 28
North Clo. Bexh. CP45 69
North Clo. Chig. CO28 41
North Clo. Dag. CR37 59
North Clo. Dor. BK73 119
North Clo. Mord. BR52 85
North Clo. St. Alb. BF16 18
North Common, Wey. BA56 92
N. Common Rd. W5 BL40 55
Northcote, Wey. AX56 92
Northcote Av. W5 BL40 55
Northcote Av. Islw. BJ46 74
Northcote Av. Sthl. BE40 54
Northcote Av. Surb. BM54 85
Northcote Close, Leath. BA66 110
Northcote Cres. Leath. BA66 110
Northcote Rd. E17 CD31 48
Northcote Rd. NW10 BO36 55
Northcote Rd. SW11 BU46 76
Northcote Rd. Croy. BZ53 87
Northcote Rd. Leath. BA66 110
Northcote Rd. N. Mal. BN52 85
Northcote Rd. Sid. CN49 78
Northcote Rd. Twick. BJ46 74
Northcott Av.N22 BX30 38
N. Countess Rd. E17 BX30 38
North Ct. W1 BW39 1
North Ct. W1 BW39 56
Chitty St.
North Cray Rd. Bex. CQ50 79
North Cray Rd. Sid. CQ50 79
North Cres. N3 BR30 37
North Cres. WC1 BW39 1
North Cres. WC1 BW39 56
Store St.
Northcroft Clo. Egh. AQ49 72
Northcroft Gdns. Egh. AQ49 72
Northcroft Rd. W13 BJ41 64
Northcroft Rd. Egh. AQ49 72
Northcroft Rd. Epsom BN57 94
Northcroft Vill. Egh. AQ49 72
N. Cross Rd. SE22 CA46 77
North Cross Rd. Ilf. CM31 49
North Dene NW7 BN27 37
Northdene, Chig. CM28 40
North Dene, Houns. BF44 64
Northdene Gdns. N15 CA32 48
Northdon Clo. Ruis. BB34 44
North Down Sth. Croy. CA59 96
Northdown Gdns. Ilf. CN32 49
North Down La. Guil. AS72 118
Northdown Rd. Cat. CE65 105
North Down Rd. Ger. Cr. AS29 34
Northdown Rd. Hat. BP14 10
Northdown Rd. Horn. CU33 50
Northdown Rd. Long. DB51 90
Northdown Rd. Sev. CW62 108
North Down Rd. Sutt. BS58 95
Northdown Rd. Well. CO44 69
Northdowns Cres. Croy. CE58 96
North Downs Rd. Croy. CE58 96
Northdown St. N1 BX37 2
North Downs Way, Bet. BP68 112
North Downs Way, Dor. BD72 119
North Downs Way, Red. BW67 113
North Downs Way, Sev. DB61 108
North Downs Way, Tad. BS68 113
North Downs Way, West. CL65 106
Northdown St. N1 BX37 56
North Dr. SW11 BU43 66
North Dr. SW16 BW49 76
North Dr. Houns. BG44 64
North Dr. Orp. CN56 97
North Dr. Rom. CV31 51
North Dr. Ruis. BB33 44
North Dr. Vir. W. AO53 82
North Dr. Vir. W. AP53 82
Northeast Pl. N1 BY37 56
Chapel Mkt.
North End NW3 BT34 47
North End W14 BR43 65
Northend, Brwd. DB28 42
North End, Buck. H. CJ26 40
North End, Croy. BZ54 87
Northend, Hem. H. AZ14 8
North End Av. NW3 BT34 47
North End Cres. W14 BR42 65
North End Ho. W14 BR42 65
North End La. Orp. CL58 97
North End Pde. W14 BR42 65
North End Rd.
North End Rd. NW11 BS33 47
North End Rd. SW6 BR43 65
North End. Rd. W14 BR42 65
Northend Rd. Erith CT44 69
North End Rd. Wem BM34 46
North End Way NW3 BT34 47
Northern Av. N9 CA27 39
Northernhay Wk. Mord. BR52 85
Northern Perimeter Rd. Houns. AX44 63
Nohtern Rd. E13 CH37 58
Northern Rd. Slou. AO38 52
Northey Av. Sutt. BQ58 94
North Eyot Gdns. W6 BO42 65
Berestead Rd.
North Eyot St. W6 BP42 65
St. Peter's Sq.
Northey St. E14 CD40 57
North Feltham Trd. Est. Felt. BC46 73
Northfield Av. W5 BK41 64
Northfield Av. W13 BJ40 54
Northfield Av. Orp. CP53 89
Northfield Av. Pnr. BD31 45
Northfield Cres. Sutt. BR56 94
Abbotts Rd.
Northfield Gdns. Dag. CQ35 50
Northfield Gdns. Wat. BD22 27
Northfield, Hat. BP11 10
Northfield Industrial Est. Wem. BM37 55
Northfield Park Clo. Hayes BB41 63
Northfield Path, Dag. CQ34 50
Northfield Pl. Wey. AZ57 92
Northfield Rd. E6 CK36 58
Northfield Rd. N16 CA33 48
Northfield Rd. W13 BJ41 64
Northfield Rd. Barn. BU24 29
Northfield Rd. Borwd. BM23 28
Northfield Rd. Cob. BC60 92
Northfield Rd. Dag. CQ35 50
Northfield Rd. Enf. CB25 30
Northfield Rd. Houns. BD43 64
Northfield Rd. Stai. AW51 83
Northfield Rd. Wal. Cr. CD19 21
Northfield Rd. Wind. AM42 61
Northfields SW18 BS45 66
Northfields, Ash. BL63 103
Northfields Rd. W3 BM39 55
North Gdns. SW19 BT50 76
North Gate, Harl. CM10 6
North Gate Path, Borwd. BL22 28
Northgate Path, Borwd. BL23 28
North Gower St. NW1 BW38 1
North Gower St.NW1 BW38 56
North Gro. N6 BV33 47
North Gro. N15 BZ32 48
North Gro. Cher. AV53 82
North Gro. Harl. CO11 14
N. Harrow Est. Har. BF31 45
North Hill, Rick. AV23 25
North Hill Av. N6 BU32 47
North Hill Dr. Rom. CV27 42
North Hill Grn. Rom. CV28 42
Nort Hl. N6 BU32 47
North Hyde Gdns. Hayes BC42 63
North Hyde La. Houns. BE42 64
North Hyde La. Sthl. BD42 64
North Hyde Rd. Hayes BB41 63
Northiam N12 BS28 38
Northiam St. E8 CB37 57
Northington St. WC1 BX38 2
Northington St. WC1 BX38 56
North Kent Rd. St. Alb. BG13 9
Northlands, Pot. B. BT19 20
Northlands Av. Orp. CM56 97
Northlands St. SE5 BZ44 67
North La. Tedd. BH50 74
North Lodge W5 BK40 54
North Lodge Clo. SW15 BQ46 75
North Looe Rd. Epsom BP60 94
North Mall N9 CB27 39
North Mead Rd. Red. BU69 121
North Moors, Guil. AS68 109
North Ms. WC1 BX38 2
North Ms. WC1 BX38 56
Northolm, Edg. BN28 37
Northolme Gdns. Edg. BM30 37
Northolme Rise, Orp. CN55 88
Northolme Rd. N5 BY35 47
Northolt Av. Ruis. BC35 44
Northolt Gdns. Grnf. BH35 45
Northolt Rd. Har. BF35 45
Northolt Rd. Houns. AX44 63
Northold Way, Horn. CV36 60
North Orbital, Rick. AV25 25
North Orbital Rd. St. Alb. BE18 18
North Orbital Rd. Uxb. AV33 43
North Orbital Rd. Uxb. AW32 44
North Orbital Rd. Wat. BC20 17
North Orbital Rd. Wat. BD19 18
Northover, Brom. CG48 78
North Pde. Chess. BL56 94
North Parade, Hat. BO12 10
North Pk. SE9 CK46 78
North Park, Ger. Cr. AS31 43
North Pk. Iver. AU41 62
North Park La. Gdse. CB68 114
North Pass. SW18 BS46 76
North Pl. Mitch. BU50 76
North Pl. Wal. Abb. CE20 21
North Pole W10 BQ40 55
North Pole La. Kes. CG57 97
Northpole Rd. W10 BQ39 55
Northport St. N1 BZ37 2
Northport St. N1 BZ37 57
North Quay E1 CB40 57
North Ride, W2 BU40 3
North Ride W2 BU40 56
Northridge Rd. Grav. DH48 81
Northridge Way, Hem. H. AV14 7
North Riding, St. Alb. BF18 18
North Rd. N2 BT30 38
North Rd. N6 BV33 47
North Rd. N7 BX36 56
North Rd. N9 CB26 39
North Rd. SE18 CN42 68
North Rd. SW19 BR48 75
North Rd. SW19 BT50 76
North Rd. Amer. AO21 25
North Rd. Belv. CR41 69
North Rd. Berk. AQ13 7
North Rd. Brent. BL43 65
North Rd. Brom. CH51 88
North Rd. Brwd. DB26 42
North Rd. Dart. CT46 79
North Rd. Edg. BM30 37
North Rd. Felt. BA46 73
North Rd. Grays CY42 70
North Rd. Guil. AQ69 118
North Rd. Hav. CT27 41
North Rd. Hayes BA39 53
North Rd. Hodd. CE11 12
North Rd. Ilf. CN34 49
North Rd. Reig. BR72 120
North Rd. Rich. BM45 65
North Rd. Rick. AU25 25
North Rd. Rom. CQ32 50
North Rd. S. Ock. DA37 60
North Rd. Sthl. BF40 54
North Rd. Surb. BK53 84
North Rd. Wal. Cr. CD20 21
North Rd. Walt. BD56 93
North Rd. West Dr. AY41 63
North Rd. W. Wick. CE54 87
North Rd. Wok. AT61 100
North Road Av. Brwd. DB26 42
Northrop Rd. Houns. BB44 63
North Row, W1 BU40 3
North Row W1 BU40 56
North St. Pass. E13 CH37 58
North Several SE3 CF44 67
North Side SW18 BT46 76
Northspur Rd. Sutt. BS55 86
North Sq. N9 CB27 39
Town Rd.
North Sq. NW11 BS32 47
Northstead Rd. SW2 BY48 76
North St. E13 CH37 58
North St. NW4 BQ32 46
Heriot Rd.
North St. SW4 BW45 66
North St. BJ71 119
North St. Bark. CL36 58
North St. Bexh. CR45 69
North St. Brom. CH51 88
North St. Cars. BU55 86
North St. Dart. CV47 80
North St. Dor. BG72 119
North St. Egh. AS49 72
North St. Guil. AR71 118
North St. Horn. CV33 51
North St. Islw. BJ45 64
North St. Lthd. BJ64 102
North St. Red. BU70 121
North St. Rom. CS31 50
North St. Rom. CT32 50
North St. Wal. Abb. CG14 13
North Tenter St. E1 CA39 2
North Tenter St. E1 CA39 57
North Ter. SW3 BU41 3
North Ter. SW3 BU41 66
North, The Glade, Bex. CQ47 79
Northumberlnd All. EC3 CA39 2
Northumberland All. EC3 CA39 57
Northumberland Av. E12 CJ33 49
Northumberland Av. WC2 BX40 4
Northumberland Av. WC2 BX40 56
Northumberland Av. Enf. CB22 30
Northumberland Av. Horn. CV32 51
Northumberland Av. Islw. BH44 64
Northumberland Av. Well. CM45 68
Northumberland Clo. Erith CS43 69
Northumberland Clo. Stai. AY46 73
Northumberland Cres. Felt. BB46 73
Northumberland Gdns. N9 CA27 39
Northumberland Gdns. Mitch. BW53 86
Northumberland Gro. N17 CB29 39
Northumberland Pk. N17 CA29 39
Northumberland Pk. Erith CR43 69
Northumberland Pk. Clo. N17 CB29 39
Northumberland Pk.
Northumberland Pl. W2 BS39 56
Northumberland Rd. E17 CE33 48
Northumberland Rd. Barn. BT26 38
Northumberland Rd. Grav. DF50 81
Northumberland Rd. Har. BE32 45
Northumberland Rd. S. Le H. DJ41 71
Northumberland Row Twick. BH47 74
Colne Rd.
Northumberland St. WC2 BX40 4
Northumberland St. WC2 BX40 56
Northumberland Way, Erith CS44 69
Northumbria St. E14 CE39 57
North Verbena Gdns. W6 BP42 65
St. Peter's Sq.
North Vw. SW19 BP49 75
North Vw. W5 BK38 54
North Vw. Ilf. CO29 41
North Vw. Pnr. BD33 45
Northview, Swan. CT51 89
North View Av. Til. DG44 71
North View Cres. NW10 BO35 46
North View Cres. Epsom BP62 103
North View Dr. Wdf. Grn. CJ30 40
North View Rd. N8 BW31 47
Northview Rd. Sev. CV64 108
North Vill. NW1 BW36 56
North Wk. Croy. CF57 96
North Wk. Sutt. BQ59 94
North Way N9 CC27 39
Northway N11 BW29 38
North Way NW9 BM31 46
Northway NW11 BS32 47
Northway, Guil. AQ69 118
North Way, Mord. BR52 85
North Way, Pnr. BD31 45
Northway, Rick. AX26 35
North Way, Uxb. AY36 53
Northway, Wall. BW56 95
North Way, Welw. G. C. BR6 5
Northway Cir. NW7 BN28 37
Northway Cres. NW7 BN28 37
Northway Rd. SE5 BZ45 67
Northway Rd. Croy. CA53 87
Northways NW3 BT36 56
College Cres.
Northwestern Av. Wat. BB21 17
North Western Av. Wat. BB21 26
North Western Av. Wat. BD21 27
North Western Av. Wat. BG24 27
Northwest Pl. N1 BY37 2
Northwest Pl. N1 BY37 56
Chapel Mkt.
North Wharf Rd. W2 BT39 56
Northwick Av. Har. BJ32 45
Northwick Circle Har. BK32 45
Northwick Clo. NW8 BT38 1
Northwick Clo. NW8 BT38 56
Norwood Cres.

Northwick Rd. Wat. BD28 36
Northwick Sq. Houns. BA44 63
Northwick Ter. NW8 BT38 1
Northwick Ter. NW8 BT38 56
Northwick Wk. Har. BH33 45
Northwold Dr. Pnr. BD30 36
Northwold Est. E5 CB34 48
Northwold Rd. E5 CB34 48
Northwold Rd. N16 CA34 48
North Wolf W13 BJ40 54
North Wood, Grays DG41 71
Northwood Av. Horn. CU35 50
Northwood Av. Pur. BY59 95
Northwood Av. Wok. AO62 100
Northwood Gdns. N12 BT28 38
Northwood Gdns. Grnf. BH35 45
Northwood Gdns. Ilf. CL31 49
Northwood Hills, Nthwd. BC30 35
Northwood Hills Cir. Nthwd. BC30 35
Northwood Pla. Belv. CQ41 69
Yarnton Way
Northwood Rd. N6 BV33 47
Northwood Rd. SE23 CD47 77
Northwood Rd. Cars. BV57 95
Northwood Rd. Houns. AX44 63
Northwood Rd. Th. Hth. BY51 86
Northwood Rd. Uxb. AX30 35
Northwood Way, SE19 CA50 77
Central Hill Est.
Northwood Way, Nthwd. BB29 35
Northwood Way, Uxb. AX30 35
N. Woolwich Rd. E16 CH40 58
North Worple Way SW14 BN45 65
Nortoft Rd. Ger. Cr. AS29 34
Norton Av. Surb. BM54 85
Norton Clo. E4 CE28 39
Norton Clo. Enf. CB23 30
Norton Folgate E1 CA39 2
Norton Folgate E1 CA39 57
Norton Gdns. SW16 BX51 86
Norton Heath Rd. Ong. DB15 15
Norton La. Cob. BB63 101
Norton La. Ong. DA16 24
Norton Rd. E10 BX33 47
Dagenham Rd.
Norton Rd. Dag. CS36 59
Norton Rd. Uxb. AX38 53
Norton Rd. Wem. BK36 54
Norval Grn. SW9 BY44 66
Myatts Fields Dev.
Norval Rd. Wem. BJ34 45
Norway Dr. Slou. AQ39 52
Norway Pl. E14 CD39 57
Norway St. SE10 CE43 67
Norway Wk. Rain. CV39 60
Norwich Mews, Ilf. CO33 50
Ashgrove Rd.
Norwich Rd. E7 CH35 49
Norwich Rd. E8 CB37 57
Norwich Rd. Dag. CR37 59
Norwich Rd. Grnf. BF37 54
Norwich Rd. Nthwd. BB31 44
Norwich Rd. Th. Hth. BZ52 87
Norwich St. EC4 BY39 2
Norwich St. EC4 BY39 56
Norwich Wk. Edg. BN29 37
Norwich Way, Rick. AZ24 26
Norwood Av. Rom. CS33 50
Norwood Av. Wem. BL37 55
Norwood Clo. Lthd. BE67 111
Norwood Clo. Sthl. BF42 64
Norwood Cres. Houns. BA44 63
Norwood Dr. Har. BE32 45
Norwood End. Ong. CX11 15
Norwood Gdns. Hayes BD38 54
Norwood Gdns. Sthl. BE42 64
Norwood Grn. Rd. Sthl. BF42 64
Norwood High St. SE27 BY48 76
Norwood La. Iver AU38 52
Norwood Pk. Rd. SE27 BZ49 77
Norwood Rd. SE17 BZ43 4
Norwood Rd. SE24 BY47 76
Norwood Rd. SE27 BY47 76
Norwood Rd. SE27 BY48 76
Norwood Rd. Lthd. BE67 111
Norwood Rd. Sthl. BE41 64
Norwood Ter. Sthl. BF42 64
Notley St. SE5 BZ43 67
Notre Dame Est. SW4 BW46 76
Notson Rd. SE25 CB52 87
Nott Ct. WC2 BX39 56
Shorts Gdns.
Nottingham Av. E16 CJ39 58
Nottingham Clo. Wat. BC20 17
Nottingham Clo. Wok. AP62 100
Nottingham Ct. WC2 BX39 2
Nottingham Pl. W1 BV38 1
Nottingham Pl. W1 BV38 56
Nottingham Rd. E10 CF32 48
Nottingham Rd. SW17 BU47 76
Nottingham Rd. Islw. BH44 64
Nottingham Rd. Sth. Croy. BZ56 96
Nottingham St. W1 BV39 1
Nottingham St., W1 BV39 56
Nottingham Ter. NW1 BV38 1
Nottingham Ter. NW1 BV38 56
Allsop Pl.
Notting Hill Gte. W11 BS40 56
Nottingdale Sq. W11 BR40 55
Wilsham St.
Nova Mews, Sutt. BR54 85
Nova Rd. Croy. BY54 86
Novar Rd. SE9 CM47 78
Novello St. SW6 BS44 66
Nowell Rd. SW13 BP43 65
Nower Hill Pnr. BE31 45
Nower Rd. Dor. BJ71 119
Nower, The Sev. CN63 106
Noyna Rd. SW17 BU48 76
Nth. Audley St. W1 BV40 3
Nth. Birbeck Rd. E11 CF34 48
Nth. Kent Av. Grav. DE46 81
Nth. Ockham Rd. Sth. Leath. BA66 110
Nth. Orbital Rd. Hat. BP10 5
Nth. Orbital Rd. Wat. AW25 26
Nth. Station App. Red. BX71 121
Nth. Wharf Rd. W2 BT39 1
Nth. Western Av. Wat. BA21 26
Nuding Clo. SE13 CE45 67
Nuding Rd. SE13 CE45 67
Nufield Rd. Swan. CU50 79
Nugent Rd. N19 BX33 47
Nugent Rd. SE25 CA52 87
Nugents Ct. Pnr. BE30 36
Nugents Pk. Pnr. BE30 36
Nugent Ter. NW8 BT37 1
Nugent Ter. NW8 BT38 56
Nunappleton Way, Oxt. CH69 115
Nuneaton Rd. Dag. CP36 59
Nunfield, Kings L. AW19 17
Nunhead Cres. SE15 CB45 67
Nunhead Grn. SE15 CB45 67
Nunhead Gro. SE15 CB45 67
Nunhead La. SE15 CB45 67
Nunnery Clo. St. Alb. BH14 9
Nunnington Clo. SE9 CK48 78
Nunns Rd. Enf. BZ23 30
Nunns Way, Grays DE42 71
Nunsbury Dr. Brox. CD16 21
Nuns La. St. Alb. BH15 9
Nuns Walk, Vir. W. AR53 82
Nupton Dr. Barn. BQ25 28
Nursery Av. N3 BT30 38
Nursery Av. Bexh. CQ45 69
Nursery Av. Croy. CC55 87
Nursery Clo. SW15 BQ45 65
Nursery Clo. Amer. AP23 25
Nursery Clo. Croy. CC55 87
Nursery Clo. Dart. CY47 80
Nursery Clo. Enf. CC23 30
Nursery Clo. Epsom BO58 94
Nursery Clo. Felt. BC47 73
Nursery Clo. Hamptn. BE49 74
Nursery Clo. Orp. CO54 89
Nursery Clo. Rom. CP32 50
Nursery Clo. Sev. CV64 108
Nursery Clo. S. Ock. DB38 60
Nursery Clo. Swan. CS51 89
Nursery Clo. Tad. BP66 112
Nursery Clo. Wdf. Grn. CH28 40
Nursery Clo. Wey. AV58 91
Nursery Clo. Wok. AR61 100
Nursery Gdns. Enf. CC23 30
Nursery Gdns. Stai. AW50 73
Nursery Gdns. Sun. BB51 83
Nursery Gdns. Sun. BC51 83
Nursery Gdns. Welw. G. C. BR6 5
Nursery Hill, Welw. G. C. BR6 5
Nursery La. E7 CH36 58
Nursery La. W10 BQ39 55
Highlever Road
Nursery La. Uxb. AX38 53
Nursery La. Rd. Slou. AR40 52
Nursery Pl. Sev. CS65 107
Nursery Rd. N14 BW26 38
Nursery Rd. SW9 BX45 66
Nursery Rd. SW19 BR50 75
Nursery Rd. Brox. CD16 21
Nursery Rd. Brwd. DB20 24
Nursery Rd. Hodd. CE10 12
Nursery Rd. Loug. CH23 31
Nursery Rd. Loug. CJ25 31
Nursery Rd. Pnr. BD31 45
Nursery Rd. Sun. BB51 83
Nursery Rd. Tad. BP66 112
Nursery Rd. Th. Hth. BZ52 87
Nursery Rd. Wal. Abb. CF14 12
Nursery Rd. Wok. AO62 100
Nursery Row SE17 BZ42 4
Nursery Row SE17 BZ42 67
Nursery, The West. CM67 115
Nursery St. N17 CA29 39
Nursery St. SW4 BV45 66
Heath Rd.
Nursery Ter. Berk. AT11 7
Nursery, The, Erith CT43 69
Nursery Wk. NW4 BP31 46
Nursery Wk. Rom. CS32 50
Nursery Way, Stai. AR46 72
Nursery Waye, Uxb. AX37 53
Nurstead Rd. Erith. CR43 69
Nutberry Av. Grays DD41 71
Nutbourne St. W10 BR38 55
Nutbrook St. SE15 CA45 67
Nut Browne Rd. Dag. CQ37 59
Nutcombe La. Dor. BH71 119
Nutcroft Gro. Lthd. BH64 102
Nutcroft Rd. SE15 CB43 67
Nutfield Clo. N18 CB29 39
Fore St.
Nutfield Gdns. Ilf. CO34 50
Nutfield Gdns. Nthlt. BD37 54
Nutfield Marsh Rd. Red. BW69 121
Nutfield Pl. Th. Hth. BY52 86
Nutfield Rd. E15 CF35 48
Nutfield Rd. NW2 BP34 46
Nutfield Rd. SE22 CA45 67
Nutfield Rd. Couls. BV61 104
Nutfield Rd. Red. BW70 121
Nutfield Rd. Red. BW68 113
Nutfield Rd. Red. BW69 121
Nutfield Rd. Th. Hth. BY52 86
Nutfield Way, Orp. CL55 88
Nutford Pl. W1 BU39 1
Nutford Pl. W1 BU39 56
Nut Gro. Welw. G. C. BQ6 5
Nuthurst Av. SW2 BX48 76
Nutley Clo. Swan. CT51 89
Nutley Gro. Reig. BR70 120
Nutley La. Reig. BR70 120
Nutley Ter. NW3 BT36 56
Nutmead Clo. Bex. CS47 79
Nuttall St. N1 CA37 2
Nuttall St. N1 CA37 57
Nutter La. E11 CH32 49
Nuttfield Clo. Rick. AZ25 26
Nutt Gro. Stan. BK27 36
Nut Tree Clo. Orp. CP55 89
Nut St. SE15 CA43 67
Sumner Rd.
Nutty La. Shep. BA52 83
Nutwell St. SW17 BU49 76
Nutwood Av. Bet. BN71 120
Nutwood Clo. Bet. BN71 120
Nuxley Rd. Belv. CQ43 69
Nyanza St. SE18 CM43 68
Nye Bevan Est. E5 CC34 48
Nye Way, Hem. H. AT17 16
Nylands Av. Rich. BM44 65
Nymans Gdns. SW20 BP51 85
Nynehead St. SE14 CD43 67
Nyon Gro. SE6 CD48 77
Nyth Clo. Upmin. CY32 51
Oakapple Clo. Sth. Croy. CB60 96
Cherry Tree Grn.
Oak Av. Sev. CU67 116
Oak Av. West Dr. AZ41 63
Oak Av. N8 BX31 47
Oak Av. N10 BV29 38
Oak Av. N17 BZ29 39
Oak Av. Croy. CE54 87
Oak Av. Egh. AU50 72
Oak Av. Enf. BX22 29
Oak Av. Hamptn. BE49 74
Oak Av. Houns. BE43 64
Oak Av. St. Alb. BF18 18
Oak Av. Upmin. CX35 51
Oak Av. Uxb. AZ34 44
Oakbank, Brwd. DF25 122
Oakbank, Croy. CF57 96
Oak Bank, Wok. AS63 100
Oakbank Av. Walt. BE54 84
Oakbank Gro. SE24 BZ45 67
Oakbury Rd. SW6 BS44 66
Oak Clo. N14 BV26 38
Oak Clo. Hem. H. AY15 8
Oak Clo. Sutt. BT55 86
Oak Clo. Wal. Abb. CF20 21
Oak Clo. West Dr. AZ41 63
Oakcombe Clo. N. Mal. BO51 85
Traps La. Coombe Rd.
Oak Com. W3 BO39 55
Common La.
Oak Corner, Berk. AO13 7
Oak Cottage Clo. SE6 CG47 78
Oak Ct. N1 CA38 2
Oak Ct. Barn. BU25 29
Oak Cres. E16 CG39 58
Oakcroft Clo. Wey. AV60 91
Oakcroft Rd. SE13 CF44 67
Oakcroft Rd. Chess. BL56 94
Oakcroft Rd. Wey. AV60 91
Oakcroft Vill. Chess. BL56 94
Oakdale N14 BV26 38
Oakdale, Welw. G. C. BQ6 5
Oakdale Av. Har. BL32 46
Oakdale Av. Nthwd. BC30 35
Oakdale Clo. Wat. BD28 36
Oakdale Ct. E4 CF28 39
Oakdale La. Eden. CM70 115
Oakdale Rd. E7 CH36 58
Oakdale Rd. E11 CF34 48
Oakdale Rd. E18 CH30 40
Oakdale Rd. N4 BZ32 48
Oakdale Rd. SE15 CC45 67
Ivydale Rd.
Oakdale Rd. SW16 BX49 76
Oakdale Rd. Epsom BN57 94
Oakdale Rd. Wat. BD27 36
Oakdale Rd. Wey. AZ55 83
Oak Dene W13 BJ39 54
Dene, The
Oak Dene, Tad. BR63 103
Oakdene, Wal. Cr. CD18 21
Oakdene, Wok. AP58 91
Oakdene Av. Chis. CL49 78
Oakdene Av. Erith. CS43 69
Oakdene Av. Surb. BJ54 84
Oakdene Clo. Bet. BN71 120
Oakdene Clo. Horn. CU32 50
Oakdene Clo. Lthd. BF67 111
Oakdene Dr. Surb. BN54 85
Oakdene Pk. N3 BR29 37
Oakdene Rd. Bet. BM72 120
Oakdene Rd. Cob. BC60 92
Oakdene Rd. Hem. H. AY15 8
Oakdene Rd. Lthd. BE65 102
Oakdene Rd. Orp. CN53 88
Oakdene Rd. Red. BU70 121
Oakdene Rd. Sev. CU64 107
Oakdene Rd. Uxb. AZ37 53
Oakdene Rd. Wat. BC21 26
Oakdene Way, St. Alb. BK13 9
Oakden St. SE11 BY42 4
Oakden St. SE11 BY42 66
Oak Dr. Berk. AR13 7
Oak Dr. Saw. CP7 6
Oaken Coppice La. Ash. BM63 103
Oak End, Harl. CN12 13
Oaken Dr. Esher BH57 93
Oakend Way, Ger. Cr. AS32 43
Oak End Way, Wey. AV59 91
Oaken Gro. Welw. G. C. BR9 5
Oaken La. Esher BH56 93
Oakenshaw Clo. Surb. BL54 85
Oakes Gro. E4 CG27 40
Oakeshott Av. N6 BV34 47
Oak Farm Clo. Borwd. BM25 28
Oakfield, Rick. AV26 34
Oakfield Av. Slou. AN40 61
Oakfield Av. Har. BJ31 45
Oak Field Clo. N. Mal. BO53 85
Oakfield Ct. N8 BX33 47
Oakfield Ct. NW11 BQ33 46
Oakfield Dr. Reig. BS69 121
Reigate Hill Rd.
Oakfield Gdns. N18 CA28 39
Oakfield Gdns. SE19 CA49 77
Oakfield Gdns. Beck. CE53 87
Oakfield Gdns. Cars. BU54 86
Oakfield Gdns. Grnf. BG38 54
Oakfield Glade, Wey. BA56 92
Oakfield La. Dart. CV48 80
Oakfield La. Kes. CJ56 97
Oakfield Pk. Rd. Dart. CV48 80
Oakfield Pl. Dart. CV48 80
Oakfield Rd. E6 CK37 58
Oakfield Rd. E17 CD30 39
Oakfield Rd. N3 BS30 38
Oakfield Rd. N4 BY32 47
Oakfield Rd. N14 BX27 38
Oakfield Rd. SE20 CB51 87
Oakfield Rd. SW19 BQ48 75
Oakfield Rd. Ash. BL62 103
Oakfield Rd. Ashf. AZ49 73
Oakfield Rd. Croy. BZ54 87
Oakfield Rd. Ilf. CL34 49
Oakfield Rd. Orp. CO54 89
Oakfields, Guil. AP69 118
Oakfields, Sev. CU66 116
Oakfields, Walt. BC54 83
Oak Fields, Wey. AW60 92
Oakfields Rd. NW11 BR32 46
Oakfield St. SW10 BT43 3
Oakfield St. SW10 BT43 66
Oakfield, Wok. AP61 100
Oakford Rd. NW5 BW35 47
Oak Gdns. Croy. CE54 87
Oak Gdns. Edg. BN30 37
Oak Glade, Nthwd. BA30 35
Oak Glen, Horn. CW31 51
Oak Grange Rd. Guil. AW68 110
Oak Gro. NW2 BQ35 46
Oak Gro. Ruis. BC33 44
Oak Gro. Sun. BC50 73
Oak Gro. W. Wick. CF55 87
Oakgrove Rd. SE20 CC51 87
Oakhall Ct. E11 CH32 49
Cambridge Pk.
Oakhall Rd. E11 CH32 49
Oakham Dr. Brom. CG52 88
Oakhampton Clo. N12 BT28 38
Oakhampton Rd. NW7 BQ29 37
Oakhampton Rd. Rom. CV29 42
Oakhampton Sq. Rom. CV29 42
Oak Hill, Epsom BN61 103
Oakhill, Esher BJ57 93
Oak Hill, Guil. AU68 109
Oak Hill, Surb. BL54 85
Oak Hill, Wdf. Grn. CF29 39
Oakhill Av. Pnr. BE30 36
Oakhill Clo. Ash. BK62 102
Oak Hill Clo. Wdf. Grn. CF29 39
Oak Hill Ct. SE23 CC46 77
Oak Hill Ct. Wdf. Grn. CF29 39
Oakhill Cres. Surb. BL54 85
Oak Hill Cres. Wdf. Grn. CF29 39
Oakhill Dr. Sun. BB49 73
Oak Hill Dr. Surb. BL54 85
Oakhill Gdns. Wdf. Grn. CG30 40
Oakhill Gdns. Wey. BB55 83
Oakhill Gro. Surb. BL53 85
Oak Hill Ms. NW3 BT35 47
Oak Hill Pk. NW3 BS35 47
Oakhill Path, Surb. BL53 85
Oakhill Pl. SW15 BS46 76
Oakhill Rd.
Oakhill Rd. SW15 BR46 75
Oakhill Rd. SW16 BX51 86
Oakhill Rd. Ash. BK62 102
Oak Hill Rd. Beck. CF51 87
Oak Hill Rd. Orp. CN54 88
Oakhill Rd. Reig. BS71 121
Oakhill Rd. Rick. AU28 34
Oak Hill Rd. Rom. CS26 41
Oak Hill Rd. Sev. CV65 107
Oakhill Rd. Surb. BL53 85
Oakhill Rd. Sutt. BS55 86
Oakhill Rd. Wey. AV57 91
Oak Hill Way NW3 BS35 47
Oakhouse Rd. Bexh. CR46 79
Oakhurst, Wok. AP58 91
Oakhurst Av. Barn. BU26 38
Oakhurst Av. Bexh. CQ44 69
Oakhurst Clo. E17 CG31 49
Oakhurst Gdns. E4 CG26 40
Oakhurst Gdns. E17 CG31 49
Oakhurst Gdns. Bexh. CQ43 69
Oakhurst Gro. SE22 CB45 67
Oakhurst Rise, Cars. BU58 95
Oakhurst Rd. Enf. CC21 30
Oakhurst Rd. Epsom BN57 94
Oakhurst Rd. Kings. on T. BL50 75
Oakington Av. Amer. AS23 25
Oakington Av. Hayes BA42 63
Oakington Av. Har. BF33 45
Oakington Av. Wem. BL34 46
Oakington Dr. Sun. BD51 84
Oakington Manor Dr. Wem. BM35 46
Oakington Rd. W9 BS38 56
Oakington Way N8 BX32 47
Oakland Dr. S. Ock. DB39 60
Oakland Gdns. Brwd. DE25 122
Oaklands N21 BX27 38
Oaklands, Chess. BK56 93
Oaklands, Ken. BZ61 105
Oaklands, Twick. BG47 74
Oaklands Av. N9 CB25 30
Oaklands Av. Esher BG54 84
Oaklands Av. Hat. BR17 19
Oaklands Av. Islw. BH43 64
Oaklands Av. Rom. CT31 50
Oaklands Av. Sid. CN47 78
Oaklands Av. Th. Hth. BY52 86
Oaklands Av. Wat. BC26 35
Oaklands Av. W. Wick. CE55 87
Oaklands Clo. Bexh. CQ46 79
Oaklands Clo. Grav. DF49 81
Oaklands Clo. Orp. CN53 88
Oaklands Clo. Sev. CZ57 99
Oaklands Clo. Wem. BK35 45
Oaklands Ct. SE26 CB49 77
Oaklands Ct. Wat. BC23 26
Oaklands Est. SW4 BW46 76
Oaklands Gdns. Ken. BZ60 96
Oaklands Gro. W12 BP40 55
Oaklands La. Barn. BP24 28
Oaklands La. St. Alb. BM13 10
Oaklands La. West. CH60 97
Oaklands Pk. Av. Ilf. CM34 49
Oaklands Rd. N20 BR26 37
Oaklands Rd. NW2 BQ35 46
Oaklands Rd. SW14 BN45 65
Oaklands Rd. W7 BH41 64
Oaklands Rd. Bexh. CQ45 69
Oaklands Rd. Brom. CG50 78
Oaklands Rd. Dart. CX47 80
Oaklands Rd. Wal. Cr. CA16 21
Oakland Way, Epsom BN57 94
Oak La. E14 CD40 57
Oak La. N2 BT30 38
Oak La. N11 BW29 38
Oak La. Egh. AR48 72
Oak La. Islw. BH45 64
Oak La. Pot. B. BX17 20
Oak La. Sev. CT68 116
Oak La. Twick. BJ47 74
Oak La. Wdf. Grn. CG28 40
Oak La. Wind. AN44 61
Oak La. Wok. AT61 100
Oaklawn Rd. Lthd. BH62 102
Oakleafe Gdns. Ilf. CL31 49
Oaklea Pass. Kings. on T. BK52 84
Oakleigh Av. N20 BT27 38
Oakleigh Av. Edg. BM30 37
Oakleigh Av. Surb. BM54 85
Oakleigh Clo. N20 BU27 38
Oakleigh Ct. Edg. BN30 37
Oakleigh Cres. N20 BU27 38
Oakleigh Dr. Rick. BA25 26
Oakleigh Gdns. N20 BT26 38
Oakleigh Gdns. Edg. BL28 37
Oakleigh Gdns. Orp. CN56 97
Oakleigh Pk. Av. Chis. CL51 88
Oakleigh Pk. N. N20 BT27 38
Oakleigh Pk. S. N20 BU26 38
Oakleigh Rd. Pnr. BE29 36
Oakleigh Rd. Uxb. BA36 53
Oakleigh Rd. N. N20 BT27 38
Oakleigh Rd. S. N11 BV27 38
Oakleigh Way, Mitch. BV51 86
Oakleigh Way, Surb. BM54 85
Oakley Av. W5 BM40 55
Oakley Av. Bark. CN36 58
Oakley Av. Croy. BX56 95
Oakley Clo. W7 BH40 54
Oakley Clo. Islw. BG44 64
Oakley Clo. Wey. AX56 92
Oakley Cres. N1 BY37 56
City Rd.
Oakley Cres. Slou. AP40 52
Oakley Dr. Brom. CK55 88
Oakley Dr. Rom. CX28 42
Oakley Dr. Sid. CM47 78
Oakley Gdns. N8 BX32 47
Oakley Gdns. SW3 BU43 3
Oakley Gdns. SW3 BU43 66
Oakley Gdns. Bans. BS61 104
Oakley Grn. Rd. Wind. AK44 61
Oakley Ho. W5 BM40 55
Oakley Pk. Sid. CP47 79
Oakley Pl. SE1 CA42 4
Oakley Pl. SE1 CA42 67
Oakley Rd. N1 BZ36 57
Oakley Rd. SE25 CB53 87
Oakley Rd. Brom. CK55 88
Oakley Rd. Har. BH32 45
Oakley Rd. Warl. CB62 105
Oakley Sq. NW1 BW37 1
Oakley Sq. NW1 BW37 56
Oakley St. SW3 BU42 3
Oakley St. SW3 BU42 66
Oak Lodge Av. Chig. CM28 40
Oak Lodge Clo. Stan. BJ28 36
Oak Lodge Clo. Walt. BD56 93
Oak Lodge Dr. W. Wick. CE54 87
Oak Lodge La. West. CM66 115
Oakmead Av. Brom. CH53 88
Oakmeade, Pnr. BF29 36
Oakmead Gdns. Edg. BN28 37
Oakmead Rd. SW12 BV47 76
Oakmead Rd. Croy. BW53 86
Oakmere Av. Pot. B. BT20 20
Oakmere Clo. Pot. B. BT19 20
Oakmere La. Pot. B. BT19 20
Oakmere Rd. SE2 CO43 69
Oakmoor Way, Chig. CN28 40
Parkes Rd.
Oakmount Pl. Orp. CM54 88
Oak Pk. Wey. AV60 91
Oak Piece, Epp. CS16 23
Oak Ridge, Dor. BJ73 119
Oakridge Av. Rad. BH20 18
Oakridge La. Rad. BH20 18
Oakridge La. Wat. BG21 27
Oakridge La. Wat. BH20 18
Oakridge Rd. Brom. CF49 77
Oak Rise, Buck. H. CJ27 40
Oak Rd. Cat. CA64 105
Oak Rd. Cob. BE61 102
Oak Rd. Epp. CN18 22
Oak Rd. Erith CS43 69
Oak Rd. Erith CU44 69
Oak Rd. Grav. DH48 81
Oak Rd. Grays DE43 71
Oak Rd. Green. CZ46 80
Oak Rd. Lthd. BJ63 102
Oak Rd. N. Mal. BN51 85
Oak Rd. Orp. CO57 98
Oak Rd. Reig. BS70 121
Oak Rd. Rom. CW30 42
Oak Rd. West. CM66 115
Oak Row, Mitch. BW51 86
Rowan Rd.
Oakroyd Av. Pot. B. BR20 19
Oakroyd Clo. Pot. B. BR20 19
Oak St. Bakers La. W5 BK40 54
Grove, The
Oaks Av. SE19 BZ49 77
Oaks Av. Felt. BE48 74
Oaks Av. Rom. CS30 41
Oaks Av. Wor. Pk. BP55 85
Oaks Clo. Lthd. BJ64 102
Oaksford Av. SE26 CB49 77
Oakshade Rd. Brom. CF49 77
Oakshade Rd. Lthd. BG60 93
Oakshaw Rd. SW18 BS47 76
Oakside, Uxb. AW35 44
Oak Side, Uxb. AW36 53
Oaks La. Croy. CB56 96
Oaks La. Croy. CC55 87
Oaks La. Ilf. CN31 49
Oaks Rd. Croy. CB56 96
Oaks Rd. Ken. BY60 95
Oaks Rd. Pur. BY60 95
Oaks Rd. Reig. BT70 121

Opal Mews, Ilf. CL34 49
Ley St.
Opal St. SE11 BY42 4
Opal St. SE11 BY42 66
Openshaw Rd. SE2 CO42 69
Openview SW18 BT47 76
Ophir Ter. SE15 CB44 67
Oppossum Way, Houns. BD45 64
Oppidans Ms. NW3 BU36 56
Oppidans Rd. NW3 BU36 1
Oppidans Rd. NW3 BU36 56
Orange Ct. E1 CB40 57
Hermitage Wall
Orange Hill Rd. Edg. BN29 37
Orange Pl. SE16 CC41 67
Orangery La. SE9 CK46 78
Orange St. WC2 BW40 3
Orange St. WC2 BW40 56
Orange Tree Hill, Hav. CS28 41
Orantham Clo. Edg. BL27 37
Orbain Rd. SW6 BR43 65
Orbel St. SW11 BU44 66
Orbital Cres. Wat. BB21 26
Orb St. SE17 BZ42 4
Orb St. SE17 BZ42 67
Orchard Av. Berk. AQ13 7
Orchard Av. Wey. AV59 91
Orchard Av. Wind. AN44 61
Orchard Av. N3 BS31 47
Orchard Av. N14 BW26 38
Orchard Av. N20 BT27 38
Orchard Av. Ashf. BA50 73
Orchard Av. Belv. CQ43 69
Orchard Av. Berk. AQ13 7
Orchard Av. Brwd. DC27 122
Orchard Av. Croy. CD54 87
Orchard Av. Dart. CU47 79
Orchard Av. Felt. BA46 73
Orchard Av. Grav. DG49 81
Orchard Av. Houns. BE43 64
Orchard Av. Mitch. BV54 86
Orchard Av. N. Mal. BO51 85
Orchard Av. Rain. CV38 60
Orchard Av. Sthl. BE40 54
Orchard Av. Surb. BJ54 84
Orchard Av. Wat. BC19 17
Orchard Clo. SE23 CC46 67
Honor Oak Ri.
Orchard Clo. SW20 BQ52 85
Orchard Clo. Ashf. BA50 73
Orchard Clo. Bans. BS60 95
Orchard Clo. Bexh. CQ44 69
Orchard Clo. Bish. CS7 6
Orchard Clo. Borwd. BL24 28
Orchard Clo. Bush. BG26 36
Orchard Clo. Edg. BL29 37
Orchard Clo. Egh. AT49 72
Orchard Clo. Hem. H. AZ12 8
Orchard Clo. Hert. BW13 11
Orchard Clo. Lthd. BB65 101
Orchard Clo. Lthd. BB64 102
Orchard Clo. Pot. B. BX17 20
Orchard Clo. Rad. BH22 27
Orchard Clo. Rick. AU24 25
Orchard Clo. Ruis. BA33 44
Orchard Clo. St. Alb. BH14 9
Orchard Clo. Sev. CV63 108
Orchard Clo. S. Ock. DB38 60
Orchard Clo. Surb. BJ54 84
Orchard Clo. Uxb. AW36 53
Orchard Clo. Wat. BB23 26
Orchard Clo. Wem. BL36 55
Orchard Clo. Wok. AT61 100
Orchard Cotts. Brwd. DC32 123
Orchard Ct. Edg. BL28 37
Orchard Ct. Islw. BG44 64
Thornbury Av.
Orchard Ct. Wor. Pk. BP54 85
Orchard Cres. Edg. BN28 37
Orchard Cres. Enf. CA23 30
Orchard Croft. Harl. CO10 6
Orchard Dr. Rick. AU24 25
Orchard Dr. SE3 CF44 67
Orchard Dr. Ash. BK63 102
Orchard Dr. Edg. BL28 37
Orchard Dr. Epp. CN21 31
Orchard Dr. Grays DD41 71
Orchard Dr. St. Alb. BF17 18
Orchard Dr. Uxb. AX38 53
Orchard Dr. Wat. BB23 26
Orchard Dr. Wok. AS61 100
Orchard End, Wey. BB55 83
Orchard End Av. Amer. AP23 25
Orchard Est. SE13 CE44 67
Orchard Gdns. Chess. BL56 94
Orchard Gdns. Epsom BN60 94
Orchard Gdns. Lthd. BE67 111
Orchard Gdns. Sutt. BS56 95
Orchard Gdns. Wal. Abb. CF20 21
Orchard Gate NW9 BO31 46
Orchard Gate, Esher BG54 84
Orchard Gate, Grnf. BJ36 54
Orchard Grn. Orp. CN55 88
Orchard Gro. Croy. CD54 87
Orchard Gro. Edg. BM30 37
Orchard Gro. Ger. Cr. AR30 34
Orchard Gro. Har. BL32 46
Orchard Gro. Orp. CN55 88
Orchard Hill SE13 CE44 67
Coldbath St.
Orchard Hill, Cars. BU56 95
Orchard Hill, Dart. CT46 79
Orchard La. SW20 BP51 85
Orchard La. Amer. AO22 25
Orchard La. Brwd. CZ25 33
Orchard La. E. Mol. BG53 84
Orchard La. Wdf. Grn. CJ28 40
Orchard Leas, Wok. AV61 100
Orchardleigh, Lthd. BJ64 102
St. Nicholas Hill
Orchardleigh Av. Enf. CC23 30
Orchard Mains, Wok. AR63 100
Orchardmede N21 BZ25 30
Orchard North, The Epp. CO19 23
Orchard Piece, Ing. DC18 24
Orchard Pl. E14 CG40 58
Orchard Pl. N17 CA29 39
Orchard Pl. Brom. CH51 88
Orchard Rise, Croy. CD54 87
Orchard Rise, Kings. on T. BN51 85
Orchard Rise, Rich. BM46 75
Orchard Rise, E. Sid. CN46 78
Orchard Rise, W. Sid. CN45 67
Orchard Rd. N6 BV33 47
Orchard Rd. SE3 CG44 68
Orchard Rd. SE18 CM42 68
Orchard Rd. Barn. BR24 28
Orchard Rd. Beac. AO28 34
Orchard Rd. Belv. CR42 69
Orchard Rd. Brent. BK43 64
Orchard Rd. Brom. CJ51 88
Orchard Rd. Chess. BL56 94
Orchard Rd. Ch. St. G. AR27 34
Orchard Rd. Dag. CR37 59
Orchard Rd. Dor. BJ72 119
Horsham Rd.
Orchard Rd. Enf. CC25 30
Orchard Rd. Grav. DE48 81
Orchard Rd. Guil. AP71 118
Orchard Rd. Guil. AS73 118
Orchard Rd. Guil. AT68 109
Orchard Rd. Hamptn. BE50 74
Orchard Rd. Hayes BC40 53
Orchard Rd. Houns. BE46 74
Orchard Rd. Kings. on T. BL52 85
Orchard Rd. Mitch. BV54 86
Orchard Rd. Orp. CL56 97
Orchard Rd. Orp. CP58 98
Orchard Rd. Reig. BS70 121
Orchard Rd. Rich. BM45 65
Orchard Rd. Rom. CR30 41
Orchard Rd. Sev. CT61 107
Orchard Rd. Sev. CT64 107
Orchard Rd. Sid. CN49 78
Orchard Rd. S. Ock. DB38 60
Orchard Rd. Sth. Croy. CB60 96
Orchard Rd. Sun. BC50 73
Orchard Rd. Sutt. BS56 95
Orchard Rd. Swans. DC46 81
Orchard Rd. Twick. BJ46 74
Orchard Rd. Well. CO45 69
Orchard Rd. Wind. AQ46 72
Orchardson St. NW8 BT38 1
Orchardson St. NW8 BT38 56
Orchard Sq. W14 BR42 65
Sun Rd.
Orchard Sq. Brox. CD15 12
Orchards S. The Epp. CO19 23
Orchards, The Saw. CQ6 6
Orchard St. E17 CD31 48
Orchard St. W1 BV39 1
Orchard St. W1 BV39 56
Orchard St. Dart. CW46 80
Orchard St. Hem. H. AX15 8
Orchard St. St. Alb. BG14 9
Orchard, The N21 BZ25 30
Orchard, The NW11 BS32 47
Orchard, The SE3 CF44 67
Orchard, The W4 BN42 65
Orchard, The W5 BK39 54
Orchard, The Dor. BK73 119
Orchard, The Houns. BG44 64
Orchard, The Kings L. AZ18 17
Orchard, The Welw. G. C. BQ7 5
Orchard, The Wok. AS64 100
Orchard Vw. Uxb. AX38 53
Orchard Way, Ashf. AY48 73
Orchard Way, Chig. CO27 41
Orchard Way, Croy. CD54 87
Orchard Way, Dart. CV48 80
Orchard Way, Enf. CA24 30
Orchard Way, Esher BG57 93
Orchard Way, Hem. H. AT17 16
Orchard Way, Oxt. CH70 115
Orchard Way, Pot. B. BS18 20
Orchard Way, Reig. BS72 121
Orchard Way, Rick. AW26 35
Orchard Way, Sev. CX62 108
Orchard Way, Sutt. BT56 95
Orchard Way, Tad. BR66 112
Orchard Way, Wal. Cr. BY17 20
Orchard Way, Wey. AW56 92
Orchard Way, Wok. AU66 109
Orchard Waye, Uxb. AX37 53
Orchard Mead. Hat. BO12 10
Orchehill Av. Ger. Cr. AR31 43
Orchehill Rise, Ger. Cr. AS32 43
Orchid Rd. N14 BW26 38
Orchid St. W12 BP40 55
Orchid Way, Rom. CW29 42
Orde Hall St. WC1 BX39 2
Orde Hall St. WC1 BX39 56
Ordell Rd. E3 CD37 57
Ordnance Clo. Felt. BC48 73
Ordnance Cres. SE10 CG41 68
Ordnance Hill NW8 BT37 1
Ordnance Hill NW8 BT37 56
Ordnance Rd. E16 CG39 58
Ordnance Rd. SE18 CL43 68
Ordnance Rd. Enf. CC22 30
Ordnance Rd. Grav. DH46 81
Oregon Av. E12 CK35 49
Oregon Sq. Orp. CM54 88
Oreston La. Leath. BC67 110
Oreston Rd. Rain. CV38 60
Orford Ct. SE27 BY48 76
Orford Gdns. Twick. BH48 74
Orford Rd. E17 CE32 48
Orford Rd. E18 CH31 49
Organ Hall Rd. Borwd. BK22 27
Organ La. E4 CF27 39
Oriel Clo. Mitch. BW52 86
Holly Way
Oriel Ct. Mitch. BW52 86
Oriel Gdns. Ilf. CK31 49
Oriel Pl. NW3 BT35 47
Oriel Rd. E9 CC36 57
Oriel Way, Nthlt. BF36 54
Oriental Clo. Wok. AS62 100
Oriental Rd. Wok. AS62 100
Oriental St. E14 CE40 57
Orient Rd. Til. DG45 71
Orient St. SE11 BY42 4
Orient St. SE11 BY42 66
West Sq.
Orient Way E5 CC34 48
Millfields Rd.
Orion Way, Nthwd. BB28 35
Orissa Rd. SE18 CN42 68
Orkney St. SW11 BV44 66
Dagnall St.
Orlando Gdns. Epsom BN58 94
Orlando Rd. SW4 BW45 66
Orleans Rd. SE19 BZ50 77
Orleans Rd. Twick. BJ47 74
Orleston Gdns. Orp. CQ56 98
Orleston Ms. N7 BY36 56
Orleston Rd. N7 BY36 56
Orley Farm Rd. Har. BH34 45
Orlick Rd. Grav. DK48 81
Orlop St. SE10 CG42 68
Ormanton Rd. SE26 CB49 77
Orme Ct. W2 BS40 3
Orme Ct. W2 BS40 56
Orme Ct. Ms. W2 BS40 56
Orme La.
Orme La. W2 BS40 3
Orme La. W2 BS40 56
Ormeley Rd. SW12 BV47 76
Orme Ms. W2 BS40 56
Orme Ct.
Orme Rd. Kings. on T. BM51 85
Ormerod Gdns. Mitch. BV51 86
Ormesby Dr. Pot. B. BQ19 19
Ormesby Gdns. Grnf. BG37 54
Ormesby Way, Har. BL32 46
Orme Sq. W2 BS40 3
Orme Sq. S2 BS40 56
Ormiston Gro. W12 BP40 55
Ormiston Rd. SE10 CH42 68
Ormond Av. Hamptn. BF51 84
Ormond Av. Rich. BK46 74
Ormond Rd.
Ormond Clo. WC1 BX39 56
Boswell St.
Ormond Cres. Hamptn. BF51 84
Ormond Dr. Hamptn. BF50 74
Ormonde Av. Epsom BN58 94
Ormonde Av. Orp. CM55 88
Ormonde Ct. SW15 BQ45 65
Upr. Richmond Rd.
Ormonde Gate, SW3 BU42 3
Ormonde Gte, SW3 BU42 66
Ormonde Pl. SW1 BV42 66
Bourne St.
Ormonde Rise Buck. H. CJ26 40
Ormonde Rd. SW14 BM45 65
Ormonde Rd. Nthwd. BA28 35
Ormonde Rd. Wok. AR61 100
Ormonde Ter. NW8 BU37 1
Ormonde Ter. NW8 BU37 56
Ormond Ms. WC1 BX38 2
Ormond Ms. WC1 BX38 56
Guilford St.
Ormond Rd. N19 BX33 47
Ormond Rd. Rich. BK46 74
Ormond Yd. SW1 BW40 3
Ormond Yd. SW1 BW40 56
Duke of York St.
Ormsby Pl. N16 CD34 48
Victorian Gro.
Ormsby St. E2 CA37 2
Ormsby St. E2 CA37 57
Ormskirk Rd. Wat. BD28 36
Ornan Rd. NW3 BU35 47
Oronsay, Hem. H. AZ14 8
Oronsay Wk. N1 BZ36 57
Marquess Est.
Orphanage Rd. Wat. BD23 27
Orpheus St. SE5 BZ44 67
Orpington By-pass, Orp. CP56 98
Orpington Gdns. N18 CA27 39
Orpington Rd. N21 BY26 38
Orpington Rd. Chis. CN51 88
Orpin Rd. Red. BV68 113
Orris Ms. W6 BQ42 65
Beadon Rd.
Orsett Heath Cres. Grays DG41 71
Orsett St. SE11 BX42 4
Orsett Rd. Grays DD42 71
Orsett St. SE11 BX42 66
Orsett Ter. W2 BS39 1
Orsett Ter. W2 BT39 56
Orsett Ter. Wdf. Grn. CJ29 40
Orsman Rd. N1 CA37 2
Orsman Rd. N1 CA37 57
Orton St. E1 CB40 4
Orton St. E1 CB40 57
Hermitage Wall
Orville Rd. SW11 BT44 66
Orwell Clo. Wind. AO45 61
Orwell Ct. N5 BZ35 48
Orwell Gdns. Reig. BS71 121
Orwell Rd. E13 CJ37 58
Osbaldeston Rd. N16 CA34 48
Osberton Rd. SE12 CH46 78
Osbert St. SW1 BW42 3
Osbert St. SW1 BW42 66
Vincent Sq.
Osborn Clo. E14 CE40 57
Osborne Av. Stai. AY47 73
Osborne Clo. Beck. CD52 87
Osborne Clo. Horn. CU32 50
Osborne Clo. Sutt. BT56 95
Albert Rd.
Osborne Gdns. Th. Hth. BZ51 87
Osborne Gro. E17 CD32 48
Osborne Mews, Wind. AO44 61
Osborne Rd. E7 CH35 49
Osborne Rd. E9 CD36 57
Osborne Rd. E10 CE34 48
Osborne Rd. N4 BX33 47
Osborne Rd. N13 BY27 38
Osborne Rd. NW2 BP36 55
Osborne Rd. W3 BM41 65
Osborne Rd. Belv. CQ42 69
Osborne Rd. Brox. CE13 12
Osborne Rd. Brwd. DA25 33
Osborne Rd. Buck. H. CH26 40
Osborne Rd. Dag. CQ35 50
Osborne Rd. Egh. AS50 72
Osborne Rd. Enf. CC23 30
Osborne Rd. Horn. CU32 50
Osborne Rd. Houns. BE45 64
Osborne Rd. Kings. on T. BL50 75
Osborne Rd. Pot. B. BS18 20
Osborne Rd. Red. BV69 121
Osborne Rd. Sthl. BF39 54
Osborne Rd. Th. Hth. BZ51 87
Osborne Rd. Wal. Cr. CD17 21
Osborne Rd. Walt. BC54 83
Osborne Rd. Wat. BD22 27
Osborne Rd. Wind. AO44 61
Osborne Sq. Dag. CQ35 50
Osborne St. SE17 BZ42 4
Osborne St. SE17 BZ42 67
Osborne St. Slou. AP41 62
Osborn Gdns. NW7 BQ29 37
Osborn Rd. Uxb. AX36 53
High St.
Osborn St. E1 CA39 2
Osborn St. E1 CA39 57
Osborn Ter. SE3 CG45 68
Osbourne Av. Kings L. AY17 17
Osbourne Clo. Felt. BD49 74
Oscar St. SE8 CE44 67
Oseney Cres. NW5 BW35 47
Osgood Av. Orp. CN56 97
Osgood Gdns. Orp. CN56 97
O'shea Gro. E3 CD37 57
Osidge La. N14 BV26 38
Osiers Rd. SW18 BS45 66
Osier St. E1 CC38 57
Cephas Av.
Osier Way, Bans. BR60 94
Osier Way E10 CE34 48
Osier Way, Mitch. BU53 86
Oslac Rd. SE6 CE49 77
Oslo Ct. NW8 BU37 1
Oslo Ct. NW8 BU37 56
Osman Clo. N15 BZ32 48
Tewkesbury Rd.
Osman Rd. N9 CB27 39
Osmond Clo. Har. BG34 45
Osmond Gdns. Wall. BW56 95
Osmund St. W12 BO39 55
Braybrook St.
Osnaburgh St. NW1 BV38 1
Osnaburgh St. NW1 BV38 56
Osnaburgh Ter. NW1 BV38 1
Osnaburgh Ter. NW1 BV38 56
Osnaburgh St.
Osney Wk. Cars. BT53 86
Osney Way, Grav. DJ48 81
Osprey Gdns. Sth. Croy. CC58 96
Ospringe Ct. SE9 CM46 78
Ospringe Rd. NW5 BW35 47
Osric Pth. N1 CA37 57
Ossian Rd. N4 BX33 47
Ossie Dr. Iver. AU40 52
Ossington Bldgs. W1 BV39 56
Moxon St.
Ossington Clo. W2 BS40 56
Ossington St.
Ossington St. W2 BS40 56
Ossory Rd. SE1 CB43 4
Ossory Rd. SE1 CB42 67
Ossulston Est. NW1 BW38 1
Ossulston Est. NW1 BW38 56
Ossulston St. NW1 BW37 1
Ossulston St. NW1 BW37 56
Ossulton Pla. N2 BT31 47
Ossulton Way
Ossulton Way N2 BT31 47
Ostade Rd. SW2 BX47 76
Osten Ms. SW7 BS41 3
Osten Ms. SW7 BS41 66
Osterberg Rd. Dart. CW45 70
Osterley Av. Islw. BG43 64
Osterley Clo. Orp. CO51 88
Leith Hill
Osterley Ct. Islw. BG44 64
Osterley Cres. Islw. BH44 64
Osterley Gdns. Th. Hth. BZ51 87
Osterley La. Sthl. BF42 64
Osterley Pk. Rd. Sthl. BE41 64
Osterley Pk. Vw. Rd. W7 BH41 64
Osterley Rd. N16 CA35 48
Osterley Rd. Islw. BH43 64
Oster St. St. Alb. BG13 9
Oswald Clo. Lthd. BG64 102
Oswald Rd. Lthd. BG64 102
Oswald Rd. St. Alb. BH14 9
Oswald Rd. Sthl. BE40 54
Oswald's Mead. E9 CD35 48
King's Mead. Est.
Osward Croy. CD58 96
Osward Pl. N9 CB27 39
Osward Rd. SW17 BU48 76
Oswin St. SE11 BY42 4
Oswin St. SE11 BY42 66
Oswyth Rd. SE5 CA44 67
Otford Clo. Bex. CR46 79
Otford Clo. Brom. CL52 88
Otford Cres. SE4 CD46 77
Otford La. Sev. CQ59 98
Otford Rd. Sev. CU63 107
Otis St. E3 CF38 57
Otley App. Ilf. CL32 49
Otley Dr. Ilf. CL32 49
Otley Rd. E16 CJ39 58
Otley Rd. Chesh. AP18 16
Otley Ter. E5 CC34 48
Otley Way, Wat. BD27 36
Otlinge Clo. Orp. CP52 89
Ottawa Gdns. Dag. CS36 59
Ottawa Rd. Til. DG44 71
Ottaway St. E5 CB34 48
Otterbourne Rd. E4 CF27 39
Otterbourne Rd. Croy. BY55 86
Ruskin Rd.
Otterburn Gdns. Islw. BJ63 64
Otterburn St. SW17 BU50 76
Otterden Clo. Orp. CN56 97
Otterden St. SE6 CE49 77
Otterfield Rd. West Dr. AY40 53
Otter Gds. Hat. BP13 10
Ottermead La. Cher. AU57 91
Otter Rd. Grnf. BG38 54
Otterspool La. Wat. BE22 27
Otterspool Way, Wat. BE23 27
Ottesbrook St. SE14 CD43 67
Otto Clo. SE26 CB48 77
Sydenham Hill
Ottoman Ter. Wat. BD24 27
Ebury Rd.
Otto St. SE17 BY43 66
Ottway's Av. Ash. BK63 102
Ottway's La. Ash. BK63 102
Otways Clo. Pot. B. BS19 20
Oulton Clo. E5 CB34 48
Southwold Rd.
Oulton Cres. Bark. CN35 49
Oulton Cres. Pot. B. BQ19 19
Oulton Rd. N15 BZ32 48
Oulton Rd. Pot. B. BQ19 19
Oulton Way Wat. BE28 36
Oundle Av. Bush. BG25 27
Ousden Clo. Wal. Cr. CD18 21
Ousden Dr. Wal. Cr. CD18 21
Ouseley Rd. SW12 BU47 76
Ouseley Rd. Wind. AR47 72
Outer Circle NW1 BV38 1
Outer Circle NW1 BV38 56
Outfield Rd. Ger. Cr. AR29 34
Outgate Rd. NW10 BO36 55
Outing's La. Brwd. DA21 33
Outram Pl. N1 BX37 56
Havelock St.
Outram Pl. Wey. BA56 92
St. Georges Av.
Outram Rd. E6 CK37 58
Outram Rd. N22 BW30 38
Outram Rd. Croy. CA55 87
Outward La. Red. BZ71 114
Outwich St. EC3 CA39 57
Houndsditch
Outwood La. Couls. BU62 104
Outwood La. Couls. BU63 104
Outwood La. Tad. BS64 104
Oval Gdns. Grays DE41 71
Oval Pl. SW8 BX43 66
Oval Rd. NW1 BV36 56
Oval Rd. NW1 BV37 1
Oval Rd. Croy. BZ55 87
Oval Rd. N. Dag. CR37 59
Oval Rd. S. Dag. CR37 59
Oval, The E2 CB37 57
Oval, The Bans. BS60 95
Oval, The Brox. CD16 21
Oval, The Guil. AQ71 118
Oval, The Sid. CO47 79
Oval Way SE11 BX42 4
Oval Way SE11 BX42 66
Oval Way, Ger. Cr. AS31 43
Ovenden Rd. Sev. CP63 107
Over Brae, Beck. CE50 77
Overbrook, Leath. AZ68 110
Overbrook Wk. Edg. BM29 37
Methven Clo.
Overbury Av. Beck. CE52 87
Overbury Cres. Croy. CF58 96
Overbury Rd. N15 BZ32 48
Overbury St. E5 CC35 48
Overcliffe, Grav. DF46 81
Overcliffe Rd. Grays DE42 71
Overcliff Rd. SE13 CD45 67
Overcourt Clo. Sid. CO46 79
Blackfen Rd.
Overdale, Ash. BL61 103
Overdale, Dor. BK71 119
Overdale, Red. BZ70 114
Overdale Av. N. Mal. BN51 85
Overdale Rd. W5 BK41 64
Overdown Rd. SE6 CE49 77
Overhill Gdns. SE22 CB47 77
Overhill Rd. SE22 CB47 77
Overhill Rd. Pur. BY58 95
Overhill Way, Beck. CF53 87
Overlea Rd. E5 CB33 48
Overmead, Sid. CM47 78
Overmead, Swan. CT53 89
Overstand Clo. Beck. CE53 87
Overstone Rd. W6 BQ41 65
Overstream, Rick. AW24 26
Over, The Misbourne, Ger. Cr. AT32 43
Overton Clo. NW10 BN36 55
Overton Clo. Islw. BH44 64
Overton Dr. E11 CH33 49
Overton Dr. Rom. CP33 50
Overton Gdns. Croy. CD54 87
Overton Rd. E10 CD33 48
Overton Rd. N14 BX25 29
Overton Rd. SE2 CP41 69
Overton Rd. East SE2 CP41 69
Overton Rd.
Overton Rd. SW9 BY44 66
Overton Rd. Sutt. BS57 95
Overton's Yd. Croy. BZ55 87
Ovex Clo. E14 CF41 68
Stewart Clo.
Overy Liberty Dart. CW47 80
Overy St. Dart. CW46 80
Ovesdon Av. Har. BE33 45
Oveton Way, Lthd. BF66 111
Ovington Ct. Wok. AP61 100
Roundthorne Way
Ovington Gdns. SW3 BU41 3
Ovington Gdns. SW3 BU41 66
Ovington Ms. SW3 BU41 3
Ovington Ms. SW3 BU41 66
Ovington Sq. SW3 BU41 3
Ovington Sq. SW3 BU41 66
Ovington St. SW3 BU42 3
Ovington St. SW3 BU42 66
Owen Clo. SE28 CP40 59
Owen Clo. Hayes BC38 53
Owen Rd. N13 BZ28 39
Owen Rd. Hayes BC38 53
Owen St. EC1 BY37 2
Owen Way NW10 BN35 46
Owens Ct. EC1 BY38 2
Owens Ct. EC1 BY38 56
Goswell Rd.
Owens Rd. EC1 BY38 56
St. John St.

Owens Row EC1	**BY38**	**2**
Owens Way, Rick.	AZ24	26
Owenite St. SE2	CO42	69
Owgan Close SE5	BZ43	67
Elmington Estate		
Owl Clo. Sth. Croy.	CC58	96
Kingfisher Gdns.		
Owlets Hall Clo. Rom.	CW31	51
Ownstead Gdns. Sth. Croy.	CA59	96
Ownstead Hill Croy.	CF58	96
Oxberry Av. SW6	BR44	65
Oxdowne Clo. Cob.	BF60	93
Oxenden Wd. Rd. Orp.	CO57	98
Oxendon Dr. Hodd.	CE12	12
Oxendon St. SW1	**BW40**	**3**
Oxendon St. SW1	BW40	56
Oxenford St. SE15	CA45	67
Oxenhill Rd. Sev.	CW62	108
Oxenpark Av. Wem.	BL33	46
Oxestalls Rd. SE8	CD42	67
Oxfield Clo. Ber.	AQ13	7
Oxford Av. Grays	DG42	71
Oxford Av. Hayes	BB43	63
Oxford Av. SW20	BR51	85
Oxford Av. Horn.	CX31	51
Oxford Av. Houns.	BF43	64
Oxford Av. St. Alb.	BK14	9
Oxford Circus W1	**BV39**	**1**
Oxford Clo. N9	CB27	39
Oxford Clo. Ashf.	BA50	73
Oxford Clo. Grav.	DJ48	81
Oxford Clo. Mitch.	BW52	86
Oxford Ct. Felt.	BD49	74
Oxford Cres. N. Mal.	BN53	85
Oxford Dr. Ruis.	BD34	45
Oxford Gdns. N20	BT26	38
Oxford Gdns. N21	BZ26	39
Oxford Gdns. W4	BM42	65
Oxford Gdns. W10	BQ39	55
Oxford Gdns. Uxb.	AW34	44
Oxford La. Guil.	AR71	118
Oxford Rd. E15	CF36	57
Oxford Rd. N4	BY33	47
Oxford Rd. N9	CB27	39
Oxford Rd. NW6	BS37	56
Oxford Rd. SE19	BZ50	77
Oxford Rd. SW15	BR45	65
Oxford Rd. W5	BK40	54
Oxford Rd. Cars.	BU57	95
Oxford Rd. Cat.	CA66	114
Oxford Rd. Enf.	CB25	30
Oxford Rd. Ger. Cr.	AO31	43
Oxford Rd. Guil.	AR71	118
Oxford Rd. Har.	BG32	45
Oxford Rd. Ilf.	CM35	49
Oxford Rd. Red.	BU70	121
Oxford Rd. Rom.	CW29	42
Oxford Rd. Sid.	CO49	79
Oxford Rd. Tedd.	BG49	74
Oxford Rd. Uxb.	AW34	44
Oxford Rd. Uxb.	AX36	53
Oxford Rd. Wall.	BW56	95
Oxford Rd. Wdf. Grn.	CJ28	40
Oxford Rd. N. W4	BM42	65
Oxford Rd. S. W4	BM42	65
Oxford Sq. W2	**BU39**	**1**
Oxford Sq. W2	BU39	56
Oxford St. W1	**BV39**	**1**
Oxford St. W1	BV39	56
Oxford St. Bark.	CL36	58
Oxford St. Wat.	BC25	26
Oxford Way, Cat.	CA66	114
Oxford Way Felt.	BD49	74
Oxfort Ct. Brwd.	DB28	42
Oxgate Gdns. NW2	BP34	46
Oxgate La. NW2	BP34	46
Oxhawth Cres. Brom.	CL53	88
Oxhey Av. Wat.	BD26	36
Oxhey Dr. Nthwd.	BC28	35
Oxhey La. Wat.	BE26	36
Oxhey Rd. Wat.	BD25	27
Ox La. Epsom	BP58	94
Oxleas Clo. Well.	CM44	68
Oxlease Dr. Hat.	BP13	10
Oxleay Av. Har.	BF33	45
Oxleay Ct. Har.	BF33	45
Oxleigh Clo. N. Mal.	BO53	85
Oxley Clo. Rom.	CV30	42
Oxleys Rd. NW2	BP34	46
Oxleys Rd. Wal. Abb.	CH20	22
Oxleys, The Harl.	CQ9	6
Oxlow La. Dag.	CQ35	50
Oxonian St. SE22	CA45	67
Oxshott Av. Cob.	BF61	102
Oxshott Rise, Cob.	BE60	93
Oxshott Way, Cob.	AM52	102
Oxted Clo. Mitch.	BT52	86
Oxted Rd. Gdse.	CC68	114
Oxtoby Way SW16	BW51	86
Oyster Hill, Epsom	BN65	103
Oyster La. Wey.	AY59	92
Pachesham Dr. Lthd.	BH61	102
Pachesham Park. Lthd.	BJ61	102
Pacific Rd. E16	CH39	58
Packet Boat La. Uxb.	AX39	53
Packham Rd. Grav.	DF48	81
Packhorse Clo. St. Alb.	BK11	9
Packhorse La. Borwd.	BN20	19
Packhorse La. Borwd.	BO22	28
Packhorse La. Pot. B.	BN18	19
Packhorse Path, Stai.	AV49	72
South St.		
Packhorse Rd. Ger. Cr.	AS31	43
Packhorse Rd. Sev.	CS65	107
Packington Sq. N1	BZ37	57
Packington St. N1	**BY37**	**2**
Packington St. N1	BY37	56
Packington St. N1	**BZ37**	**2**
Packmores Rd. SE9	CM46	78
Padbury Ct. E2	**CA38**	**2**
Padbury Ct. E2	CA38	57
Padcroft Rd. West Dr.	AX40	53
Paddenswick Ct. W6	BP41	65
Paddenswick Rd.		
Paddenswick Rd. W6	BP41	65
Paddington Basin W2	**BT39**	**1**
Paddington Grn. W2	**BT39**	**1**
Paddington Grn. W2	BT39	56
Paddington St. W1	**BV39**	**1**
Paddington St. W1	BV39	56
Paddock Clo. SE26	CC49	77
Paddock Clo. Har.	BF35	45
Paddock Clo. Nthlt.	BF37	54
Paddock Clo. Oxt.	CG69	115
Paddock Clo. S. Dnth.	CY51	90
Paddock Gdns. SE19	CA50	77
Paddock Mead. Harl.	CM13	13
Paddock Rd. NW2	BP34	46
Paddock Rd. Bexh.	CQ45	69
Paddock Rd. Ruis.	BD34	45
Paddocks Clo. Ash.	BL62	103
Paddocks Clo. Orp.	CP55	89
Paddocks Mead. Wok.	AP61	100
Paddocks Rd. Guil.	AT68	109
Paddocks, The Barn.	BU24	29
Chalk La.		
Paddocks, The Guil.	AU70	118
Paddocks, The Lthd.	BF66	111
Leatherhead Rd.		
Paddocks, The Wem.	BM34	46
Paddocks, The Welw. G. C.	BS7	5
Brooksfield		
Paddocks, The Wey.	BB55	83
Paddocks, The Barn.	BU24	29
Paddocks Way, Ash.	BL62	103
Paddocks Way, Ash.	BL63	103
Paddocks Way, Cher.	AW54	83
Paddock, The Brox.	CE13	12
Paddock, The Dor.	BG72	119
Paddock, The Ger. Cr.	AR28	34
Paddock, The Hat.	BP11	10
Lemsford Rd.		
Paddock, The Slou.	AQ44	62
Paddock, The Uxb.	AZ35	44
Paddock, The West.	CM66	115
Paddock Way, Hem. H.	AV13	7
Paddock Way, Oxt.	CG69	115
Paddock Way, Wok.	AT60	91
Padfield Rd. SE5	BZ45	67
Padgets, The Wal. Abb.	CG20	22
Honey La.		
Padnall Rd. Rom.	CP31	50
Padstow Rd. Enf.	BY23	29
Padua Rd. SE20	CC51	87
Pagden St. SW8	BV44	66
Pageant Clo. Til.	DG44	71
Pageant Rd. St. Alb.	BG14	9
Pageant Wk. Croy.	CA55	87
Page Clo. Harrow	BL32	46
Page Cres. Croy.	BY57	95
Page Cres. Erith	CT43	69
Page Gdns. Chis.	CL51	88
Page Green Rd. N15	CB32	48
Page Green Ter. N15	CA32	48
Page Hth. La. Brom.	CJ52	88
Page Hth. Villas Brom.	CJ52	88
Pagehurst Rd. Croy.	CB54	87
Page Rd. Felt.	BA46	73
Pages Croft, Berk.	AQ12	7
Page's Hill N10	BV30	38
Page's La. N10	BV30	38
Page's Sq. SE1	**CA42**	**4**
Page St. NW7	P29	37
Page St. SW1	**BW42**	**3**
Page St. SW1	BW42	66
Page's Wk. SE1	**CA42**	**4**
Page's Wk. SE1	CA42	67
Paget Av. Sutt.	BT55	86
Paget Clo. Hamptn.	BG49	74
Paget Rise SE18	CL43	68
Paget Rd. N16	BZ33	48
Paget Rd. Ilf.	CL35	49
Paget Rd. Slou.	AS42	62
Paget Rd. Uxb.	BA38	53
Paget St. EC1	**BY38**	**2**
Paget St. EC1	BY38	56
Paget Ter. SE18	CL43	68
Pagles Field Brwd.	DE25	122
Rayleigh Rd.		
Pagnell St. SE14	CD43	67
Pagoda Av. Rich.	BL45	65
Pagoda Av. Rich.	BL45	65
Pagoda Gdns. SE3	CF44	67
Paignton Rd. N15	CA32	48
Paignton Rd. Ruis.	BC34	44
Paine's Brook Rd. Rom.	CW29	42
Paine's Brook Way, Rom.	CW29	42
Paines Clo. Pnr.	BE31	45
Paines Hill, Oxt.	CJ69	115
Paines La. Pnr.	BE30	36
Pains Clo. Mitch.	BV51	86
Painters Ash La. Grav.	DE48	81
Painters La. Enf.	CD21	30
Painters Rd. Ilf.	CN31	49
Paisley Rd. N22	BY30	38
Paisley Rd. Cars.	BT54	86
Pakeman St. N7	BX34	47
Pakenham Cl. SW12	BV47	76
Balham Pk. Rd.		
Pakenham St. WC1	**BX38**	**2**
Pakenham St. WC1	BX38	56
Pakes Way, Epp.	CN22	31
Palace Av. W8	BS40	56
Palace Av. W8	**BS41**	**3**
Palace Clo. Kings L.	AY18	17
Palace Ct. W2	BS40	56
Palace Ct. Brom.	CH51	88
Palace Ct. Har.	BL32	46
Palace Court Gdns. N10	BW30	38
Palace Gdns. Buck. H.	CJ26	40
Palace Gdns. Enf.	BZ24	30
Palace Gdns. Surb.	BH54	84
Palace Gdns. Ms. W8	BS40	56
Palace Gdns. Ter. W8	BS40	56
Palace Gdns. Ter. W8	BS41	66
Palace Gate W8	**BT41**	**3**
Palace Gte. W8	BT41	66
Palace Gates Rd. N22	BW30	38
Palace Grn. Croy.	CD57	96
Palace Gro. SE19	CA50	77
Palace Gro. Brom.	CH51	88
Palace Mews, Enf.	BZ24	30
Palace Gdns.		
Palace Pl. SW1	**BV41**	**3**
Palace Pl. SW1	BW41	66
Palace St.		
Palace Rd. N8	BW32	47
Palace Rd. N11	BW29	38
Palace Rd. SE19	CA50	77
Palace Rd. SW2	BX47	76
Palace Rd. Brom.	CH51	88
Palace Rd. E. Mol.	BG52	84
Palace Rd. Kings. on T.	BK52	84
Palace Rd. Ruis.	BE35	45
Palace Rd. West.	CL64	106
Palace Sq. SE19	CA50	77
Palace St. SW1	**BW41**	**3**
Palace St. SW1	BW41	66
Palace Vw. SE12	CH48	78
Palace Vw. Brom.	CH52	88
Palace Vw. Croy.	CD55	87
Palace Vw. Rd. E4	CE28	39
Palamos Rd. E10	CE33	48
Palatine Rd. N16	CA35	48
Palermo Rd. NW10	BP37	55
Palestine Gro. SW19	BT51	86
Palewell Clo. Orp.	CO51	89
Palewell Common Dr.		
SW14	BN46	75
Palewell Pk. SW14	BN46	75
Paley Gdns. Loug.	CL24	31
Palfrey Clo. St. Alb.	BG12	9
Palfrey Pl. SW8	BX43	66
Palgrave Av. Sthl.	BF40	54
Palgrave Rd. W12	BO41	65
Palins Way, Grays	DD40	71
Palissy St. E2	**CA38**	**2**
Palissy St. E2	CA38	57
Pallas Rd. Hem. H.	AY12	8
Pallet Way SE18	CJ44	68
Tellson Av.		
Palliser Rd. W14	BR42	65
Palliser Rd. Ch. St. G.	AQ27	34
Pall Mall SW1	**BW40**	**3**
Pall Mall SW1	BW40	56
Pall Mall E. SW1	**BW40**	**3**
Pall Mall E. SW1	BW40	56
Pall Mall Pl. SW1	**BW40**	**3**
Pall Mall Pl. SW1	BW40	56
Palmar Cres. Bexh.	CR45	69
Palmar Rd. Bexh.	CR44	69
Palmarsh Clo. Orp.	CP52	89
Palm Av. Sid.	CP50	79
Palmeira Rd. Bexh.	CP45	69
Palmer Av. Bush.	BF25	27
Palmer Av. Grav.	DH49	81
Palmer Av. Sutt.	BQ56	94
Palmer Clo. Houns.	BF44	64
Palmer Cres.		
Kings. on T.	BL52	85
Palmer Pl. N7	BY35	47
Palmer Rd. E13	CH38	58
Palmer's Ave. Grays	DE42	71
Palmers Clo. Red.	BV71	121
Palmersfield Rd. Bans.	BS60	95
Palmers Gro. Mol.	BF52	84
Palmers Gro. Wal. Abb.	CG14	13
Palmers La. Enf.	CB23	30
Palmers Moor La. Iver	AW38	53
Palmers Pass, SW14	BN45	65
Palmers Rd.		
Palmer's Rd. E2	CC37	57
Palmers Rd. N11	BW28	38
Palmers Rd. SW14	BN45	65
Palmers Rd. SW16	BX51	86
Palmers Rd. Borwd.	BM23	28
Palmerston Clo.		
Welw. G. C.	BQ8	5
Palmerston Clo. Wok.	AS60	91
Palmerston Ct. E17	CD31	48
Palmerston Rd.		
Palmerston Cres. N13	BX28	38
Palmerston Cres. SE18	CM43	68
Palmerston Gdns. Grays	DB42	70
Palmerston Gro. SW19	BS50	76
Palmerston Rd. E7	CH35	49
Palmerston Rd. E17	CD31	48
Palmerston Rd. N22	BX29	38
Palmerston Rd. SE18	CM43	68
Palmerston Rd. SW14	BN45	65
Palmerston Rd. SW19	BS50	76
Palmerston Rd. W3	BN41	65
Palmerston Rd. Buck. H.	CH27	40
Palmerston Rd. Cars.	BU56	95
Palmerston Rd. Grays	DB43	70
Palmerston Rd. Har.	BH31	45
Palmerston Rd. Orp.	CM56	97
Palmerston Rd. Rain.	CV37	60
Palmerston Rd. Sutt.	BT56	95
Palmerston Rd. Th. Hth.	BZ53	87
Palmerston Rd. Twick.	BH46	74
Palmerston Way SW8	BV43	66
Bradmead		
Palmer St. SW1	**BW41**	**3**
Palmer St. SW1	BW41	66
Palmer St. W10	BQ40	55
Palmers Way, Wall. Cr.	CD18	21
Palm Gro. W5	BL41	65
Palm Gro. Guil.	AR68	109
Palm Rd. Rom.	CS32	50
Palm St. E3	CD38	57
Pamber St. W10	BQ39	55
Pamela Av. Hem. H.	AY15	8
Pamela Gdns. Pnr.	BC32	44
Pampisford Rd. Pur.	BY59	95
Pams Way, Epsom	BN56	94
Pamcake La. Hem. H.	BA14	8
Pancras La. EC4	**BZ39**	**2**
Pancras La. EC4	BZ39	57
Qn. Victoria St.		
Pancras Rd. NW1	**BW37**	**1**
Pancras Rd. NW1	BW37	56
Pancroft, Rom.	CO24	32
Pandora Rd. NW6	BS36	56
Panfield Mews, Ilf.	CL32	49
Panfield Rd. SE2	CO41	69
Pangbourne Av. W10	BQ39	55
Pangbourne Dr. Stan.	BK28	36
Panmuir Rd. SW20	BP51	85
Panmure Rd. SE26	CB48	77
Pannard Pl. Sthl.	BF40	54
Panshanger Dr.		
Welw. G. C.	BS8	5
Pansy Gdns. W12	BP40	55
Panters, Swan.	CT50	79
Pantile Rd. Wey.	BA56	92
Pantile Row, Slou.	AT42	62
Pantiles Clo. Wok.	AQ62	100
Pantiles, The NW11	BR31	46
Pantiles, The Bexh.	CQ43	69
Pantiles, The Brom.	CJ52	88
Pantiles, The Bush.	BG26	36
Butts, The		
Pantile Wk. Uxb.	AX36	53
High St.		
Panton St. SW1	**BW40**	**3**
Panton St. SW1	BW40	56
Haymarket		
Panyer Alley EC4	BY39	56
Newgate St.		
Panyer Al. EC4	**BZ39**	**2**
Papercourt La. Wok.	AU64	100
Paper Mews, Dor.	BJ71	119
High St.		
Papworth Gdns. N7	BX35	47
Chill Rd.		
Parade Mans. NW4	BP32	46
Parade Ms. SW2	BY48	76
Norwood Rd.		
Parade, The Brwd.	DB27	42
Kg. Edward Rd.		
Parade, The Dart.	CT46	79
Crayford Way		
Parade, The Epsom	BN60	94
Parade, The Esher	BH57	93
Parade, The S. Ock.	CY41	70
Parade, The Sun.	BB50	73
Parade, The Sun.	BC50	73
Parade, The Wind.	AL44	61
Paradise Clo. Wal. Cr.	CB17	21
Paradise Cotts. Rich.	BL46	75
Paradise Rd.		
Paradise Hill, Brox.	CB16	21
Paradise Pass. N7	BY35	47
Ingham Rd.		
Paradise Pl. SE18	CK42	68
Samuel St.		
Paradise Rd. SW4	BX44	66
Paradise Rd. Rich.	BK46	74
Paradise Row E2	CB38	57
Bethnal Green Rd.		
Paradise Row, Wal. Abb.	CF20	21
Paradise St. SE16	CB41	67
Paradise Wk. SW3	**BU43**	**3**
Paradise Wk. SW3	BU43	66
Paradise Wood La.		
Hem. H.	AX14	8
Paragon Gro. Surb.	BL53	85
Paragon Mews SE1	BZ42	67
Searles Rd.		
Paragon Pl. SE3	CG44	68
Paragon Pl. Surb.	BL53	85
Paragon Rd. E9	CB36	57
Paragon Row SE17	BZ42	67
Paragon, The SE3	CG44	68
Parbury Rise, Ches.	BL57	94
Parbury Rd. SE23	CD46	77
Parchment Clo. Amer.	AP22	25
Chestnut La.		
Parchmore Rd. Th. Hth.	BY51	86
Parchmore Way Th. Hth.	BY51	86
Pardoner St. SE1	BZ41	67
Pardon St. EC1	**BY38**	**2**
Pardon St. EC1	BY38	56
Dallington St.		
Pares Clo. Wok.	AR61	100
Parfett St. E1	CB39	57
Parfour Dri. Ken.	BZ61	105
Abbots La.		
Parfrey St. W6	BQ43	65
Parham Dr. Ilf.	CL32	49
Parham Way N10	BW30	38
Paringdon Rd. Harl.	CL13	13
Paris Gdn. SE1	**BY40**	**4**
Paris Gdn. SE1	BY40	56
Parish La. SE20	CC50	77
Parish La. Slou.	AO34	43
Park App. Well.	CO45	69
Park Ave. Harl.	CP12	14
Park Av. E6	CL37	58
Park Av. E15	CG36	58
Park Av. N3	BS30	38
Park Av. N13	BY27	38
Park Av. N18	CB28	39
Park Av. N22	BX30	38
Park Av. NW2	BP36	55
Park Av. NW10	BL37	55
Park Av. NW11	BS33	47
Park Av. SW14	BO45	65
Park Av. Bark.	CM36	58
Park Av. Barn.	BT25	29
Park Av. Brom.	CG50	78
Park Av. Brwd.	DE26	122
Park Av. Bush.	BD24	27
Park Av. Bush.	BE23	27
Park Av. Cars.	BV57	95
Park Av. Cat.	CA65	105
Park Av. Egh.	AU50	72
Park Av. Enf.	BZ25	30
Park Av. Grav.	DF47	81
Park Av. Grav.	DH47	81
Park Av. Grays	DA43	70
Park Av. Houns.	BF46	74
Park Av. Ilf.	CL33	49
Park Av. Mitch.	BV50	76
Park Av. Orp.	CK55	88
Park Av. Orp.	CO55	89
Park Av. Pot. B.	BT20	20
Park Av. Rad.	BJ20	18
Park Av. Ruis.	BA32	44
Park Av. St. Alb.	BJ13	9
Park Av. Stai.	AR46	72
Park Av. Stai.	AV50	72
Park Av Sthl.	BE41	64
Park Av. Upmin.	CZ33	51
Park Av. Wat.	BC24	26
Park Av. Wdf. Grn.	CH28	40
Park Av. W. Wick.	CF55	87
Park Av. E. Epsom	BP57	94
Park Avenue Mews,		
Mitch	BV50	76
Park Av.		
Park Av. N. N8	BW31	
Park Av. N. NW10	BP35	
Park Av. Rd. N17	CB29	
Park Av. S. N8	BW31	
Park Av. W. Epsom	BP57	
Park Barn Dr. Guil.	AP69	
Park Barn Est. Guil.	AP70	
Park Boul. Rom.	CT30	
Park Chase, Guil.	AS70	
Park Chase, Wem.	BL35	
Park Clo. Hat.	BQ12	
Park Clo. NW2	BP34	
Park Clo. NW10	BL38	
Park Clo. SW1	**BU41**	
Park Clo. SW1	BU41	
Park Clo. W8	BR42	
Park Clo. W14	BR41	
Park Clo. Bet.	BM73	
Park Clo. Bush.	BD24	
Park Clo. Cars.	BU57	
Park Clo. Epp.	CR17	
Park Clo. Esher	BF57	
Park Clo. Har.	BH30	
Park Clo. Hamptn.	BG51	
Park Clo. Houns.	BG46	
Park Clo. Lthd.	BG65	
Park Clo. Rick.	AZ28	
Park Clo. Walt.	BB55	
Park Clo. Wey.	AW58	
Park Clo. Wind.	AO44	
Park Copner Dr. Leath.	BB67	
Park Copse, Dor.	BK71	
Park Corner, Wind.	AM45	
Park Cor. Ms. W. W1	BV38	
Park Corner Rd. Grav.	DC49	
Park Ct. N12	BT28	
Park Ct. Harl.	CN10	
Park Ct. Kings. on T.	BK51	
Park Ct. Lthd.	BF66	
Church Rd.		
Park Ct. N. Mal.	BN52	
Park Ct. Wall.	BX56	
Park Ct. Wem.	BL35	
Park Ct. Wok.	AS62	
Park Cres. N3	BS29	
Park Cres. W1	**BV38**	
Park Cres. W1	BV38	
Park Cres. Borwd.	BL24	
Park Cres. Enf.	BZ24	
Park Cres. Erith	CS43	
Park Cres. Har.	BH30	
Park Cres. Hem. H.	AZ11	
Park Cres. Horn.	CU3?	
Park Cres. Ms. E. W1	**BV38**	
Park Cres. Ms. E. W1	BV38	
Gt. Portland St.		
Park Cres. Ms. W. W9	**BV38**	
Park Cres. Ms. W. W1	BV39	
Park Cres. Rd. Erith	CS43	
Park Croft, Edg.	BN30	
Parkcroft Rd. SE12	CG47	
Parkdale N11	BW29	
Bounds Green Rd.		
Parkdale Cres. Wor. Pk.	BN55	
Parkdale Rd. SE18	CN42	
Park Dr. N21	BZ25	
Park Dr. NW11	BS33	
Park Dr. SW14	BN45	
Park Dr. W3	BM41	
Park Dr. Dag.	CS34	
Park Dr. Har.	BF33	
Park Dr. Har.	BG29	
Park Dr. Pot. B.	BS19	
Park Dr. Rom.	CS31	
Park Dr. Upmin.	CX35	
Park Dr. Wok.	AS62	
Park Drive Clo. SE7	CK42	
Park End Brom.	CG51	
Park End Rd. Rom.	CT31	
Parker Av. Til.	DH44	
Parker Clo. E16	CK40	
Parker St.		
Parke Rd. SW13	BP44	
Parke Rd. Sun.	BC52	
Parker Rd. Croy.	BZ56	
Parker Rd. Grays	DC42	
Parkers La. Ash.	BL63	
Parker's Row SE1	CA41	
Parker St. E16	CK40	
Parker St. WC2	**BX39**	
Parker St. WC2	BX39	
Parker St. Wat.	BC23	
Parkes Rd. Chig.	CN28	
Park Farm Dr. Guil.	AP70	
Park Farm E. Guil.	AP70	
Park Farm Rd. Brom.	CJ51	
Park Farm Rd. Kings. on T.	BL50	
Parkfield, Sev.	CW65	
Parkfield Av. Amer.	AO22	
Parkfield Av SW14	BO45	
Parkfield Av. Felt.	BC48	
Parkfield Av. Har.	BG30	
Parkfield Av. Nthlt.	BD37	
Parkfield Av. Uxb.	AZ38	
Parkfield Clo. Edg.	BM29	
Parkfield Clo. Nthlt.	BE37	
Parkfield Cres. Felt.	BC48	
Parkfield Cres. Har.	BG30	
Parkfield Cres. Ruis.	BE34	
Parkfield Dr. Nthlt.	BD37	
Parkfield Gdns. Har.	BF31	
Parkfield Rd. NW10	BP36	
Parkfield Rd. SE14	CD44	
Parkfield Rd. Felt.	BC48	
Parkfield Rd. Har.	BG34	
Parkfield Rd. Nthlt.	BE37	
Parkfield Rd. Uxb.	AZ34	
Parkfields SW15	BQ45	
Park Fields, Harl.	CH11	
Parkfields, Welw. G. C.	BQ8	
Parkfields Av. NW9	BN33	
Parkfields Av. SW20	BP51	
Parkfields Rd. Kings. on T.	BL49	
Parkfield St. N1	**BY37**	
Parkfield St. N1	BY37	
Parkfield Way Brom.	CK53	
Park Flds. Croy.	CD54	
Park Fm. Clo. N2	BT31	

85

Paulet Rd. SE5 BY44 66
Paul Gdns. Croy. CA55 87
Paulham Rd. Har. BK31 45
Paulin Dr. N21 BY26 38
Paulin Cres. Twick. BG47 74
Paulins Clo. Orp. CP51 89
Pauls La. Hodd. CE12 12
Pauls Pl. Ash. BM62 103
Paul St. E15 CF37 57
Paul St. EC2 BZ38 2
Paul St. EC2 BZ38 57
Paultons Sq. SW3 BT43 66
Paulton's St. SW3 BT43 66
Old Church St.
Pauntley St. N19 BW33 47
Paved Ct. Rich. BK46 74
King St.
Paveley St. NW8 BU38 1
Paveley St. W1 BU38 56
Pavement Mews, Rom. CP33 50
Pavement Sq. Croy. CA54 87
Teevan Rd.
Pavement, The SW4 BW45 66
Pavet Clo. Dag. CR36 59
Pavilion Gdns. Stai. AW50 73
Pavilion Rd. E15 CG38 58
Springfield Rd.
Pavilion Rd. SW1 BU41 3
Pavilion Rd. SW1 BU41 66
Pavilion Rd. Ilf. CK33 49
Pavilion St. SW1 BU41 3
Pavilion Way, Ruis. BD34 45
Pawleyne Clo. SE20 CC50 77
Pawsey Clo. E13 CH37 58
Plashet Rd.
Pawson's Rd. Croy. BZ53 87
Paxford Rd. Wem. BJ34 45
Paxton Av. Slou. AO41 61
Paxton Ct. Rich. BL44 65
Paxton Gdns. Wok. AU59 91
Paxton Pl. SE27 CA49 77
Paxton Rd. N17 CA29 39
Paxton Rd. W4 BO43 65
Paxton Rd. Berk. AR13 7
Paxton Rd. Brom. CH50 78
College Rd.
Paxton Rd. St. Alb. BH14 9
Paxton Ter. SW1 BV42 66
Churchill Gdns. Rd.
Paxton Ter. SW1 BV43 3
Paycock Rd. Harl. CL12 13
Payne Rd. E3 CE37 57
Old Ford Rd.
Paynesfield Av. SW14 BN45 65
Paynesfield Rd. Bush. BH26 36
Paynesfield Rd. West. CJ63 106
Paynes La. Wal. Abb. CF15 12
Payne St. SE8 CD43 67
Peabody Av. SW1 BV42 3
Peabody Av. SW1 BV42 66
Peabody Bldgs. SE1 BY40 4
Peabody Bldgs. WC1 BX38 2
Peabody Bldgs. SE17 BZ42 4
Peabody Bldgs. WC1 BX38 56
Peabody Clo. SE10 CE44 67
Devonshire Dr.
Peabody Est. EC1 BZ38 57
Peabody Est. N17 CA30 39
Peabody Est. SE1 BY40 56
Peabody Est. SE24 BY47 76
Peabody Est. SW11 BU45 66
Peabody Est. W6 BQ42 65
Peabody Sq. N1 BZ37 2
Peabody Sq. SE1 BY41 4
Peabody Trust SW3 BU43 3
Peabody Hill Est. SE21 BZ47 77
Peabody Trust SW3 BU43 66
Chealsea Manor St.
Peabody Yd. N1 BZ37 2
Peabody Yd. N1 BZ36 57
Green Man St.
Peace St. E1 CB38 2
Peace St. E1 CB38 57
Peaches Clo. Sutt. BR57 94
Peachy La. Uxb. AX39 53
Peach Tree Av. West Dr. AY39 53
Peachum Rd. SE3 CG43 68
Peacock Gdns. Sth. Croy. CD58 96
Peacocks, Harl. CK12 13
Peacock St. SE17 BY42 4
Peacock St. SE17 BY42 66
Peacock St. Grav. DH47 81
Peacock Wk. N6 BV33 47
Chomeley Cres.
Peacock Wk. Dor. BJ72 119
Rose Hill
Peacock Yd. SE17 BY42 66
Iliffe St.
Peahen Ct. EC2 CA39 57
Bishopsgate
Peakes La. Wal. Cr. CA17 21
Peakes Way, Wal. Cr. CA17 21
Peaketon Av. Ilf. CJ31 49
Peak Hill SE26 CC49 77
Peak Hill Av. SE26 CC49 77
Peak Hill Gdns. SE26 CC49 77
Peaks Hill, Pur. BW58 95
Peaks Hill Rise, Pur. BX58 95
Peak, The SE26 CC49 77
Pea La. Berk. AO12 7
Pea La. Upmin. DA36 60
Peal Gdns. W13 BJ38 54
Peall Rd. Croy. BX53 86
Pearcefield Av. SE23 CC47 77
Pear Clo. NW9 BN31 46
Pearcroft Rd. E11 CF34 48
Peardon St. SW8 BV44 66
Silverthorne Rd.
Peareswood Gdns. Stan. BK30 36
Pearfield Rd. SE23 CD48 77
Pearl Ct. Wok. AP61 100
Langmans Way
Pearle Rd. E. Mol. BF51 84
Pearl Rd. E17 CE31 48
Pearl St. E1 CB40 57
Penang St.
Pearman St. SE1 BY41 4
Pearman St. SE1 BY41 66
Pearscroft Ct. SW6 BS44 66
Pearscroft Rd. SW6 BS44 66
Pearson's Av. SE14 CD44 67
Tanner's Hill
Pearson St. E2 CA37 2
Pearson St. E2 CA37 57
Pears Rd. Houns. BG45 64
Pearswood Rd. Erith. CT43 69
Peartree Av. Ashf. BA49 73
Pear Tree Av. West Dr. AY39 53
Peartree Chase, S. Ock. CA37 60
Pear Tree Clo. Brwd. DB22 33
Peartree Clo. Erith. CS44 69
Peartree Clo. Mitch. BU51 86
Peartree Clo. Sth. Croy. CB60 96
Orchard Rd.
Peartree Clo. Welw. G. C. BR8 5
Pear Tree Ct. EC1 BY38 2
Peartree Ct. EC1 BY38 56
Peartree Ct. Welw. G. C. BR8 5
Peartree Gdns. Dag. CO35 50
Peartree Gdns. Rom. CR30 41
Peartree La. Brwd. DB22 33
Peartree La. Welw. G. C. BR8 5
Peartree Mead. Harl. CO12 14
Peartree Rd. Enf. CA24 30
Peartree Rd. Hem. H. AW13 8
Pear Tree Rd. Wey. AW56 92
Pear Trees, Brwd. DE29 122
Pear Tree St. EC1 BY38 2
Pear Tree St. EC1 BY38 56
Pear Tree Wk. Wal. Cr. BZ16 21
Peary Pl. E2 CC38 57
Kirkwall Pl.
Peascond Pl. Wind. AO44 61
Peascod St.
Peascod St. Wind. AO44 61
Peascroft Rd. Hem. H. AZ15 8
Pease Hill, Sev. DC57 99
Peatmore Av. Wok. AW61 101
Pebble Clo. Tad. BO67 112
Pebble Hill, Leath. BA70 110
Pebblehill Rd. Bet. BO69 120
Pebblehill Rd. Tad. BO68 112
Pebble La. Epsom BL64 103
Pebble la. Lthd. BL65 103
Pebworth Rd. Har. BJ34 45
Peckarmans Wood SE26 CB48 77
Peckford Yd. SW9 BY44 66
Peckford Pl.
Peckham Gro. SE5 CA43 67
Peckham Gro. SE15 CA43 67
Peckham High St. SE15 CA44 67
Peckham Hill St. SE15 CB43 67
Peckham Pk. Rd. SE15 CB43 67
Peckham Rd. SE5 CA44 67
Peckham Rd. SE15 CA44 67
Peckham Rye SE15 CB45 67
Peckham Rye SE22 CB45 67
Peckham Wk. Av.
Sev. & Ton. DC67 117
Pecks Hill, Wal. Abb. CG14 13
Peckwater St. Est. NW5 BW35 47
Peckwater St. NW5 BW35 47
Islip St.
Pedlars End, Ong. CU14 14
Pedlars Way N7 BX36 56
Pedley St. E1 CA38 2
Pedley St. E1 CA38 57
Pedro St. E5 CC34 48
Pedworth Gdns. SE16 CC42 67
Rotherhithe New Rd.
Peek Cres. SW19 BQ49 75
Peel Clo. Wind. AN45 61
Peel Dr. Ilf. CK31 49
Peel Gro. E2 CC37 57
Peel Prec. NW6 BS37 56
Peel Rd. E18 CG30 40
Peel Rd. NW6 BR37 55
Peel Rd. NW9 BP31 46
Peel Rd. Har. BH31 45
Peel Rd. Orp. CM56 97
Peel Rd. Wem. BK34 45
Peel St. W8 BS40 56
Peel Way, Rom. CW30 42
Peel Way, Uxb. AY39 53
Peerless St. EC1 BZ38 2
Pearless St. EC1 BZ38 57
Peer Way, Horn. CW33 51
Pegamoid Rd. N9 CC27 39
Pegasus Pl. SE11 BY43 66
Clayton St.
Pegasus Rd. Croy. BY57 95
Pegelm Gdns. Horn. CW33 51
Peggotty Waye, Uxb. AZ39 53
Pegg Rd. Houns. BC43 63
Pegley Gdns. SE12 CH48 78
Pegmire La. Wat. BF23 27
Pegrams Rd. Harl. CM12 13
Pegwell St. SE18 CN43 68
Peket Clo. Stai. AV51 82
Pekin Clo. E14 CE39 57
Pekin St. E14 CE39 57
Peldon Ct. Rich. BL45 65
Peldon Pass. Rich. BL45 65
Sheen Rd.
Peldon Rd. Harl. CL12 13
Peldon Wk. N1 BZ37 57
Popham St.
Pelham Av. Bark. CN37 58
Pelham Clo. SE5 CA44 67
Pelham Ct. SW3 BU42 3
Pelham Ct. SW3 BU42 66
Fulham Rd.
Pelham Ct. Hem. H. BA13 8
Pelham Ct. Stai. AW49 73
Pelham Ct. Welw. G. C. BT8 5
Pelham Cres. SW7 BU42 3
Pelham Cres. SW7 BU42 66
Pelham Pl. SW7 BT42 3
Pelham Pl. SW7 BU42 66
Pelham Rd. E18 CH31 49
Pelham Rd. N15 CA31 48
Pelham Rd. N22 BY30 38
Pelham Rd. SW19 BS50 76
Pelham Rd. Beck. CC51 87
Pelham Rd. Bexh. CR45 69
Pelham Rd. Grav. DF47 81
Pelham Rd. Ilf. CM34 49
Pelham St. SW7 BT42 3
Pelham St. SW7 BT42 66
Pelham Way, Lthd. BF66 111
Dawnay Rd.
Pelhams Clo. Esher BF56 93
Pelham's Wk. Esher BF55 84
Pelhams, Wat. BD21 27
Pelican Wk. SW9 BY45 66
Somerleyton Rd. Dev.
Pelier St. SE17 BZ43 4
Pelier St. SE17 BZ43 67
Pelinore Rd. SE6 CG48 78
Pellant Rd. SW6 BR43 65
Pellatt Gro. N22 BY30 38
Pellatt Rd. SE22 CA46 77
Pellerin Rd. N16 CA35 48
Pelling Hill, Wind. AQ47 72
Pelling St. E14 CE39 57
Pellipar Clo. SE18 CK42 68
Hillreach
Pellipar Clo. N13 BY27 38
Pellipar Gdns. SE18 CK42 68
Ogilby St.
Pellipar Rd. SE18 CK42 68
Pells La. Sev. DA59 99
Pell St. E1 CB40 57
Pelly Rd. E13 CH37 58
Pelter St. E2 CA38 2
Pelter St. E2 CA38 57
Diss St.
Pelton Av. Sutt. BS58 95
Pelton Rd. SE10 CG42 68
Pembar Av. E17 CD31 48
Pember Rd. NW10 BQ38 55
Pemberton Av. Rom. CV31 51
Pemberton Clo. St. Alb. BG15 9
Pemberton Gdns. N19 BW34 47
Pemberton Gdns. Rom. CQ32 50
Pemberton Rd. N4 BY32 47
Pemberton Rd. E. Mol. BG52 84
Pemberton Row EC4 BY39 56
E. Harding St.
Pemberton Ter. N19 BW34 47
Pembrey Way, Horn. CV36 60
Pembridge Av. Twick. BE47 74
Pembridge Clo. Hem. H. AS17 16
Pembridge Cres. W11 BS40 56
Pembridge Gdns. W2 BS40 56
Pembridge La. Brox. BZ14 12
Pembridge La. Hert. BZ13 12
Pembridge Ms. W8 BS43 66
Earls Ct. Rd.
Pembridge Ms. W11 BS40 56
Pembridge Pl. W2 BS40 56
Pembridge Pl. W8 BS42 66
Pembridge Rd. W11 BS40 56
Pembridge Rd. Hem. H. AT17 16
Pembridge Sq. W2 BS40 56
Pembridge Studios W8 BS42 66
Pembridge Vill. W11 BS40 56
Pembroke Av. Enf. CB23 30
Pembroke Av. Har. BJ31 45
Pembroke Av. Surb. BM53 85
Pembroke Av. Walt. BD56 93
Pembroke Clo. SW1 BV41 3
Pembroke Clo. SW1 BV41 66
Pembroke Clo. Bans. BS62 104
Pembroke Clo. Brox. CD15 12
Church La.
Pembroke Clo. Horn. CW31 51
Pembroke Dr. Wal. Cr. BY18 20
Pembroke Gdns. W8 BR42 65
Pembroke Gdns. Dag. CR34 50
Pembroke Gdns. Wok. AT62 100
Pembroke Rd.
Pembroke Gdns. Clo. W8 BS41 66
Pembroke Ms. W8 BS41 66
Earl's Ct. Rd.
Pembroke Pl. W8 BS41 66
Pembroke Pl. Edg. BM29 37
Pembroke Pl. Islw. BH44 64
Clifton Rd.
Pembroke Pl. S. At. H. CX51 90
Main Rd.
Pembroke Rd. E17 CE32 48
Pembroke Rd. N8 BX31 47
Pembroke Rd. N10 BV29 38
Pembroke Rd. N13 BZ27 39
Pembroke Rd. N15 CA32 48
Pembroke Rd. SE25 CA52 87
Pembroke Rd. W8 BR42 65
Pembroke Rd. Brom. CJ51 88
Pembroke Rd. Erith CS42 69
Pembroke Rd. Grnf. BF38 54
Pembroke Rd. Ilf. CN33 49
Pembroke Rd. Mitch. BV51 86
Pembroke Rd. Nthwd. BA27 35
Pembroke Rd. Ruis. BB33 44
Pembroke Rd. Sev. CU66 116
Pembroke Rd. Wem. BK34 45
Pembroke Rd. Wok. AT62 100
Pembroke Sq. W8 BS41 66
Pembroke St. N1 BX36 2
Pembroke St. N1 BX36 56
Gifford St.
Pembroke Studios W8 BR41 65
Pembroke Vill. W8 BS41 66
Pembroke Vill, Rich. BK45 64
Pembroke Way, Hayes BA41 63
Pembury Av. Wor. Pk. BP54 85
Pembury Clo. E5 CB35 48
Pembury Clo. Brom. CG54 88
Pembury Clo. Couls. BV60 95
Pembury Ct. Hayes BA43 63
Pembury Cres. Sid. CQ48 79
Pembury Est. E5 CB35 48
Pembury Gro. E5 CB35 48
Pembury Pl. E5 CB35 48
Pembury Rd.
Pembury Rd. E5 CB35 48
Pembury Rd. N17 CA30 39
Pembury Rd. SE25 CB52 87
Pembury Rd. Bexh. CQ43 69
Pemdevon Rd. Croy. BY54 86
Pemell Clo. E1 CC38 57
Colebert Av.
Pemerich Clo. Hayes BB42 63
Penally Pl. N1 BZ37 2
Penang St. E1 CB40 57
Farthing Flds.
Penarth St. SE15 CC43 67
Penberth Rd. SE6 CF47 77
Penbury Rd. Sthl. BE42 64
Pencraig Way SE15 CB43 67
Pendall Rd. Red. BY69 121
Penda Rd. Erith. CR43 69
Hengist Rd.
Penda Rd. Erith. CS43 69
Pendarves Rd. SW20 BQ51 85
Penda's Mead. E9 CD35 48
King's Mead. Est.
Pendell Av. Hayes BB43 63
Pendennis Clo. Wey. AW60 92
Pendennis Rd. N17 BZ31 48
Pendennis Rd. SW16 BX49 76
Pendennis Rd. Orp. CP55 89
Pendennis Rd. Sev. CV65 108
Penderel Rd. Houns. BF46 74
Penderry Ri. SE6 CF48 77
Penderyn Way N7 BW35 47
Carlton Rd.
Pendle Rd. SW16 BV50 76
Pendlestone Rd. E17 CE32 48
Pendleton Rd. Red. BU71 121
Sandpit Rd.
Pendleton Rd. Reig. & Red. BT72 121
Pendragon Rd. Brom. CG48 78
Pendrell Rd. SE4 CD44 67
Pendrell St. SE18 CM43 68
Pendridge Clo. Enf. CB22 30
Pen Dr. Uxb. AV32 43
Penerley Rd. SE6 CE47 77
Penerly Rd. Rain. CU39 59
Penfold La. Bex. CP48 79
Penfold Pl. NW1 BU39 1
Penfold Pl. NW1 BU39 56
Penfold Rd. N9 CC26 39
Penfold St. NW1 BT38 56
Penfold St. NW8 BT38 1
Penfold St. NW8 BT38 56
Penfold Gdns. SE9 CJ45 68
Penfold St. SE5 BY44 66
Pengarth Rd. Bex. CP46 79
Penge La. SE20 CC50 77
Pengelly Clo. Wal. Cr. CB18 21
Burygreen Rd.
Penge Rd. E13 CJ37 58
Penge Rd. SE20 CB51 87
Penge Rd. SE25 CB52 87
Penhall Rd. SE7 CJ42 68
Penhill Rd. Bex. CP47 79
Penhurst Rd. Ilf. CL29 40
Penhurst Rd. Pot. B. BT19 20
Penhurst Rd. Th. Hth. BY53 86
Penine Way, Hayes BA43 63
Peninsular Clo. Felt. BA46 73
Peninsular Rd. Til. DG45 71
Penistone Rd. SW16 BX50 76
Penistone Wk. Rom. CV29 42
Okehampton Rd.
Penketh Dr. Har. BG34 45
Penlow Rd. Harl. CM12 13
Penman Clo. St. Alb. BF17 18
Pen Meadow, Slou. AQ37 52
Penmon Rd. SE2 CO41 69
Pennack Rd. SE15 CA43 67
Sumner Rd.
Pennack St. SE15 CA43 67
Willowbrook Est.
Pennant Ms. W8 BS42 66
Pennant Ter. E17 CD30 39
Pennard Rd. W12 BQ41 65
Pennards, The Sun. BD52 84
Penn Clo. Grnfd. BF37 54
Penn Clo. Har. BK31 45
Penn Clo. Rick. AU25 25
Penn Ct. Chis. CL51 88
Penner Clo. SW19 BR48 75
Queensmere Rd.
Penner Clo. SW19 BR48 75
Victoria Dr.
Pennethorne Clo. E9 CC37 57
Victoria Pk. Rd.
Pennethorne Rd. SE15 CB43 67
Penney Clo. Dart. CV47 80
Penn Gdns. Rom. CR29 41
Penn Gaskell La. Ger. Cr. AS28 34
Pennine Dr. NW2 BQ34 46
Pennine La. NW2 BQ34 46
Pennine Dr.
Pennine Way, Bexh. CT44 69
Pennine Way, Grav. DF48 81
Pennine Way, Hem. H. AY12 8
Pennington Clo. Rom. CR28 41
Pennington Dr. Wey. BB55 83
Pennington Rd. AR29 34
Penningtons, The Amer. AP22 25
Pennington St. E1 CB40 57
Pennins Av. Guil. AP69 118
Penn La. Bex. CP46 79
Penn Pl. Rick. AX26 35
Northway
Penn Rd. N7 BX35 47
Penn Rd. Rick. AV26 34
Penn Rd. St. Alb. BG17 18
Penn Rd. Slou. AO38 52
Penn Rd. Slou. AR44 62
Penn Rd. Wat. BC23 26
Penn St. N1 BZ37 2
Penn St. N1 BZ37 57
Penn Way, Rick. AU25 25
Pennycroft, Croy. CC58 96
Pennyfield, Cob. BC60 92
Pennyfields E14 CE40 57
Penny Flds, Brwd. DB28 42
Junction Rd.
Penny La. Shep. BB54 83
Pennylets Grn. Slou. AP36 52
Pennymead Dr. Leath. BB67 110
Pennymead, Harl. CO11 14
Pennypot La. Wok. AO59 91
Penny Rd. NW10 BM38 55
Penpoll Rd. E8 CB36 57
Penpool La. Well. CO45 69
Penrhyn Av. E17 CD30 39
Penrhyn Cres. E17 CE30 39
Penrhyn Cres. SW14 BO45 65
Penrhyn Gdns. Kings. on T. BK52 84
Penrhyn Gro. E17 CE30 39
Penrhyn Rd. Kings. on T. BL52 85
Penrith Clo. Brom. CE51 87
Albemarle Rd.
Penrith Clo. SW15 BR46 75
Penrith Clo. Red. BU70 121
Penrith Cres. Horn. CU35 50
Penrith Rd. N15 BZ32 48
Penrith Rd. Ilf. CN29 40
Penrith Rd. N. Mal. BN52 85
Penrith Rd. Rom. CX29 42
Penrith Rd. Th. Hth. BZ51 87
Penrith St. SW16 BW50 76
Pen Rd. Ger. Cr. AR30 34
Penrose Av. Wat. BE27 36
Penrose Ct. Hem. H. AY11 8
Penrose Gro. SE17 BZ42 4
Penrose Gro. SE17 BZ42 67
Penrose Ho. SE17 BZ42 4
Penrose Ho. SE17 BZ42 67
Penrose Rd. Lthd. BG64 102
Penrose St. SE17 BZ42 4
Penrose St. SE17 BZ42 67
Penryn St. NW1 BW37 1
Penryn St. NW1 BW37 56
Penry St. SE1 CA42 4
Penry St. SE1 CA42 67
Marcia Rd.
Pensbury Pl. SW8 BW44 66
Pensbury St. SW8 BW44 66
Penscroft Gdns. Borwd. BN24 28
Pensford Av. Rich. BM44 65
Penshurst Av. Sid. CO46 79
Penshurst Clo. Ger. Cr. AR30 34
Penshurst Gdns. Edg. BM28 37
Penshurst Grn. Brom. CG53 88
Penshurst Rd. E9 CC36 57
Penshurst Rd. N17 CA29 39
Penshurst Rd. Bexh. CQ44 69
Penshurst Way, Sutt. BS57 95
Pensmead Ter. E4 CF28 39
Mead Cres.
Pentelowe Gdns. Felt. BC46 73
Pentire Clo. Upmin. CZ32 51
Pentire Rd. E17 CF30 39
Pentland, Hem. H. AY12 8
Mendip Way
Pentland Av. Shep. AZ53 83
Pentland Rd. Bush. BG25 27
Pentlands Clo. Mitch. BV52 86
Pentland St. SW18 BT46 76
Pentley Clo. Welw. G. C. BQ6 5
Pentley Pk. Welw. G. C. BQ6 5
Pentlow St. SW15 BQ45 65
Pentlow Way, Buck. H. CK26 40
Pentney Rd. E4 CF26 39
Pretoria Rd.
Pentney Rd. SW12 BW47 76
Pentney Rd. SW19 BR51 85
Midmoor Rd.
Penton Av. Stai. AV50 72
Penton Dr. Wal. Cr. CC18 21
Penton Hall Dr. Stai. AW51 83
Penton Pl. SE17 BY42 4
Penton Pl. SE17 BY42 66
Penton Pl. WC1 BX38 56
Penton Rise WC1 BX38 2
Penton Rd. Stai. AV50 72
Penton St. N1 BY37 2
Penton St. N1 BY37 56
Pentonville Rd. N1 BY37 2
Pentonville Rd. N1 BX37 56
Pentreath Av. Guil. AP71 118
Pentrich Av. Enf. CB22 30
Pentridge St. SE15 CA43 67
Pentyre Av. N18 BZ28 39
Penwerris Av. Islw. BG43 64
Penwith Rd. SW18 BS48 76
Penwood End, Wok. AQ64 100
Penwortham Rd. SW16 BV50 76
Penwortham Rd. Sth. Croy. BA58 96
Penylan Pl. Edg. BM29 37
Penywern Rd. SW5 BS42 66
Penzance Clo. Uxb. AX30 35
Penzance Gdns. Rom. CX29 42
Penzance Pl. W11 BR40 55
Penzance Rd. Rom. CX29 42
Penzance St. W11 BR40 55
Peony Clo. Brwd. DA25 33
Lavender Av.
Peony Gdns. W12 BP40 55
Curve, The
Pepler Rd. SE15 CA43 4
Pepler Rd. SE15 CA43 67
Peplins Clo. Hat. BR16 19
Peplins Way, Hat. BR16 19
Peploe Rd. NW6 BQ37 55
Pepper Alley, Loug. CG23 31
Peppercroft St. Grav. DG47 81
Pepper Hill, Grav. DE48 81
Pepper St. SE1 BZ41 4
Pepper St. SE1 BZ41 67
Pepys Clo. Ash. BL62 103
Pepys Clo. Dart. CX45 70
Pepys Clo. Grav. DE48 81
Pepys Clo. Slou. AT43 62
Pepys Clo. Til. DH44 71
Pepys Clo. Uxb. AZ35 44
Pepys Cres. Barn. BQ25 28
Pepys Rd. SE14 CC44 67
Pepys Rd. SW20 BO50 75
Pepys St. EC3 CA40 4
Pepys St. EC3 CA40 57
Perceval Av. NW3 BU35 47
Percheron Rd. Borwd. BN25 28
Perch St. E8 CA35 48
Percival Ct. N17 CA29 39
High Rd.
Percival Gdns. Rom. CP32 50
Percival Rd. SW14 BN46 75
Percival Rd. Enf. CA24 30
Percival Rd. Felt. BB48 73
Percival Rd. Horn. CV32 51
Percival Rd. Orp. CL55 88

Pitt Rd. Epsom BO60 94
Pitt Rd. Orp. CM56 97
Pitt Rd. Th. Hth. BZ53 87
Pittsfield, Welw. G. C. BQ6 5
Pitts Head Ms. W1 BV40 56
Pitts Rd. Slou. AO40 61
Pitt Street SE15 CA44 67
Sumner Est.
Pitt St. W8 BS41 66
Pittville Gdns. SE25 CB52 87
Pit Wood Grn. Tad. BQ63 103
Pix Farm La. Berk. AT14 7
Pixfield Ct. Brom. CG51 88
Pixham La. Dor. BK70 119
Pixholme Gro. Dor. BK70 119
Pixie Cres. Hem. H. AV1L 7
Pixley St. E14 CD39 57
Pixton Way, Croy. CD58 96
Place Farm Rd. Brwd. DA21 33
Place Farm Rd. Red. BZ68 114
Place House La. Couls. BX63 104
Placket Way, Slou. AL40 61
Plain, The Epp. CO18 23
Plaistow Grn. Brom. CH50 78
Plaistow Gro. E15 CG37 58
Plaistow Gro. Brom. CH50 78
Plaistow La. Brom. CH50 78
Plaistow Pk. Rd. E13 CH37 58
Plaistow Rd. E15 CG37 58
Plaitford Clo. Rick. AY27 35
Plane Av. Grav. DE47 81
Plane St. SE26 CB48 77
Planes, The Cher. AX54 83
Bridge Rd.
Plane Tree Walk SE19 CA50 77
Central Hill Est.
Plantagenet Clo. Wor. Pk. BN56 94
Plantagenet Gdns. Rom. CP33 50
Plantagenet Pl. Rom. CP33 50
Broomfield Rd.
Plantagenet Rd. Barn. BT24 29
Plantation Dr. Orp. CP54 89
Plantation La. Warl. CD63 105
Plantation Rd. Amer. AP22 25
Plantation Rd. Erith. CU43 69
Plantation Rd. Swan. CU50 79
Plantation, The SE3 CH44 68
Plantation Wk. Hem. H. AW12 8
Plantation Way, Amer. AP22 25
Plashet Gdns. Brwd. DD28 122
Plasher Gro. E6 CJ36 58
Plashet Rd. E13 CH37 58
Plashetts, Bish. CS7 6
Plassy Rd. SE6 CE47 77
Platina St. EC2 BZ38 2
Platina St. EC1 BZ38 57
Tabernacle St.
Platford Grn. Horn. CW31 51
Plato Rd. SW2 BX45 66
Platt Mead. Guil. AU69 118
Eustack Rd.
Platts Av. Wat. BC24 26
Platt's La. NW3 BS35 47
Platts Rd. Enf. CC23 30
Platt St. NW1 BW37 1
Platt St. NW1 BW37 56
Platt, The SW15 BQ45 65
Plawsfield Rd. SE20 CC51 87
Plaxtol Clo. Brom. CJ51 88
Plaxtol Pl. SE10 CH42 68
Westcombe Hill
Plaxtol Rd. Erith. CR43 69
Playfield Av. Rom. CS30 41
Playfield Cres. SE22 CA46 77
Playfield Rd. Edg. BN30 37
Playford Rd. N4 BX34 47
Playgreen Way SE6 CE48 77
Playhouse Yd. EC4 BY39 2
Playhouse Rd. EC4 BY39 56
Pleasance Rd. SW15 BP45 65
Pleasance Rd. Orp. CO51 89
Pleasance, The SW15 BP45 65
Pleasance Rd.
Pleasant Gro. Croy. CD55 87
Pleasant Pl. N1 BY36 2
Pleasant Pl. N1 BY36 56
Pleasant Pl. Har. BG33 45
Pleasant Pl. Walt. BD57 93
Pleasant Rise, Hat. BQ11 10
Pleasant Rd. Kings. on T. BN52 85
Pleasant Row NW1 BV37 1
Pleasant Row NW1 BV37 56
Camden High St.
Pleasant Vw. Erith. CT42 69
Pleasant Vw. Orp. CL56 97
Pleasant Vw. Pl. Orp. CM56 97
Pleasant Way, Wem. BK37 54
Pleasure Pit Rd. Ash. BM62 103
Plender Pl. NW1 BW37 1
Plender Pl. NW1 BW37 56
Plender St.
Plender St. Est. NW1 BW37 56
Plender St. NW1 BW37 1
Plender St. NW1 BW37 56
Pleshey Rd. N7 BW35 47
Plevna Cres. N15 CA32 48
Plevna Rd. N9 CB27 39
Plevna Rd. Hamptn. BF51 84
Plevna St. E6 CL40 58
Plevna St. E14 CF41 67
Plevny Clo. N15 BY31 47
Shepstone St.
Pleydell Av. SE19 CA50 77
Pleydell Av. W6 BO42 65
Pleydell Ct. EC4 BZ39 57
Fleet St.
Plimsoll Rd. N4 BY34 47
Plough All. E1 CB40 57
Hermitage Wall
Plough Est. SE8 CC42 67
Plough Hill, Pot. B. BX18 20
Plough La. SE22 CA46 77
Plough La. SW17 BS49 76
Plough La. SW19 BS49 76
Plough La. Berk. AT11 7
Plough La. Cob. BC62 101
Plough La. Pur. BX58 95
Plough La. Rick. AV20 16
Plough La. Slou. AQ37 52
Plough La. Wall. BX56 95
Plough La. Clo. Wall. BX56 95
Plough Lees La. Slou. AP40 52
Plough Pl. EC4 BY39 2
Plough Pl. EC4 BY39 56
New Fetter La.
Plough Rise, Upmin. CZ33 51
Plough Rd. SW11 BT45 66
Plough Rd. Brent. BK43 64
Brent Way
Plough Rd. Epsom BN58 94
Plough St. SW11 BT45 66
Plough Way SE16 CC42 67
Plough Yd. EC2 CA38 2
Plough Yd. EC2 CA38 57
Hearn St.
Plover Clo. Stai. AV48 72
Plover Gdns. Upmin. CZ33 51
Plovers Baron, Brwd. DB21 33
Plovers Mead. Brwd. DB21 33
Ployters Rd. Harl. CM13 13
Pluckington Pl. Sthl. BE41 64
Plumbers Row E1 CB39 2
Plumbers Row E1 CB39 57
Plumbridge St. SE10 CE44 67
Plum Garth, Brent. BK42 64
Plum La. SE18 CL43 68
Plummer La. Mitch. BU51 86
Plummer Rd. SW4 BW46 76
Plumpton Av. Horn. CW35 51
Plumpton Clo. Nthlt. BF36 54
Plumpton Rd. Hodd. CF11 12
Plumpton Way, Cars. BU55 86
Wrythe La.
Plumstead Com. Rd. SE18 CL43 68
Plumstead High St. SE18 CN42 68
Plumstead Rd. SE18 CL42 68
Plumtree Ct. EC4 BY39 2
Plumtree Ct. EC4 BY39 56
Shoe La.
Plumtree Mead. Loug. CL24 31
Pluto Rise, Hem. H. AY12 8
Plymouth Dr. Sev. CV65 108
Plymouth Pk. Sev. CV65 108
Plymouth Rd. E16 CH39 58
Plymouth Rd. Brom. CH51 88
Plympton Pl. NW8 BU38 1
Plympton Rd. NW6 BR36 55
Plympton St. NW8 BU38 1
Plympton St. NW8 BU38 56
Plymstock Rd. Well. CP43 69
Pocketsdell La. Hem. H. AR17 16
Pocklington Clo. NW9 BO30 37
Pocock St. SE1 BY41 4
Pocock St. SE1 BY41 66
Podmore Rd. SW18 BT45 66
Poets Corner SW1 BX41 4
Poet's Rd. N5 BZ35 48
Pointalls Clo. N3 BT30 38
Point Clo. SE10 CF44 67
Point Hill
Pointers Hill, Dor. BG72 119
Pointers Rd. Cob. BA61 101
Point Hill SE10 CF43 67
Point Pleasant SW18 BS45 66
Point, The Ruis. BB35 44
Poland St. W1 BW39 1
Poland St. W1 BW39 56
Polaym Garth, Welw. G. C. BQ7 5
Polebrook Rd. SE3 CJ45 68
Pole Cat Alley, Brom. CG55 88
Polecroft La. SE6 CD48 77
Pole Hanger La. Hem. H. AV12 7
Pole Hill Rd. E4 CF26 39
Pole Hill Rd. Uxb. AZ38 53
Pole La. Ong. CT12 14
Polesden Gdns. SW20 BP51 85
Polesden La. Wok. AV65 100
Polesden Rd. Dor. BF68 111
Poles Hill, Rick. AV20 16
Polesteeple Hill, West. CJ62 106
Polesworth Rd. Dag. CP36 59
Pol Hill, Sev. CS61 107
Police Sta. Rd. Walt. BD57 93
Police Stn La. Bush. BF26 36
School La.
Pollard Av. Ger. Cr. AV32 43
Pollard Clo. E16 CH40 58
Munday Rd.
Pollard Clo. N7 BX35 47
Pollard Clo. Chig. CO28 41
Pollard Clo. Wind. AQ46 72
Pollard Hatch, Harl. CL12 13
Pollard Rd. N20 BU27 38
Pollard Rd. NW9 BO33 46
Broadway, The
Pollard Rd. Mord. BT53 86
Pollard Rd. Wok. AT61 100
Pollard Row E2 CB38 57
Pollards, Loug. CJ25 31
Pollards, Rick. AU28 34
Pollards Clo. Wal. Cr. BZ18 21
Pollards Cres. SW16 BX52 86
Pollards Hill E. SW16 BX52 86
Pollards Hill N. SW16 BX52 86
Pollards Hill S. SW16 BX52 86
Pollards Hill W. SW16 BX52 86
Pollards Oak Cres. Oxt. CH69 115
Pollards Oak Rd. Oxt. CH69 115
Pollard St. E2 CB38 57
Pollards Wd. Rd. SW16 BX52 86
Pollards Wood Rd. Oxt. CH69 115
Pollard Wk. Sid. CP50 79
Evry Rd.
Pollard Wood Hill, Oxt. CH68 115
Pollen St. W1 BV39 1
Pollen St. W1 BW39 56
Hanover St.
Pollitt Dr. NW8 BT38 56
Henderson Dr.
Polls La. Sev. DA60 99
Polperro Clo. Orp. CN53 89
Cotswold Rise
Polsted La. Guil. AO73 118
Polsted Rd. SE6 CD47 77
Polthorne Gro. SE18 CM42 68
Poltimore Ms. W3 BN41 65
Mill Hill Gro.
Poltimore Rd. Guil. AQ71 118
Polworth Rd. SW16 BX49 76
Polygon Ms. W2 BU39 1
Polygon Rd. NW1 BW37 1
Polygon Rd. NW1 BW37 56
Polytechnic St. SE18 CL42 68
Pomeroy Clo. Amer. AO23 25
Pomeroy Cres. Wat. BC21 26
Pomeroy Sq. SE14 CC43 67
Pomeroy St.
Pomeroy St. SE14 CC44 67
Pomfret Rd. SE5 BZ45 67
Flaxman Rd.
Pompadour Clo. Brwd. DB28 42
Queen St.
Pond Clo. SE3 CG44 68
Pond Clo. Uxb. AX30 35
Pond Cotts. SE21 CA47 77
Pond Ct. Ash. BL62 103
Marlo, The
Pond Croft, Hat. BO12 10
Pondcroft, Welw. G. C. BR8 5
Ponder St. N7 BX36 56
Pondfield, Welw. G. C. BS6 5
Lumbards
Pondfield Cres. St. Alb. BJ11 9
Pondfield La. Brwd. DD27 122
Pondfield Rd. Brom. CG54 88
Pondfield Rd. Dag. CR35 50
Pondfield Rd. Ken. BY61 104
Pondfield Rd. Orp. CL55 88
Pond Grn. Ruis. BB34 44
Pond Hill, Sutt. BR57 94
Pond Hill Gdns. Sutt. BR57 94
Pond Ho. SW3 BU42 3
Pond Ho. SW3 BU42 66
Pond La. Ger. Cr. AQ30 34
Pond La. Sev. CZ66 117
Pond Mead. Guil. AP70 118
Pond Piece, Lthd. BF60 93
Pond Pl. SW3 BU42 3
Pond Pl. SW3 BU42 66
Pond Pl. Ash. BL62 103
Pond Rd. E15 CG37 58
Pond Rd. Egh. AU50 72
Pond Rd. Hem. H. AZ16 17
Pond Rd. SE3 CG45 68
Pond Rd. Wok. AQ63 100
Pondside Clo. Hayes BA43 63
Pondside Clo. Hayes BB42 63
Harlington High St.
Pond Sq. N6 BV33 47
Pond St. NW3 BU35 47
Pond Wk. Upmin. CZ34 51
Pond Way, Tedd. BK50 74
Pondwicks Clo. St. Alb. BG14 9
Pondwood Rise, Orp. CN54 88
Ponler St. E1 CB39 57
Ponsard Rd. NW10 BP38 55
Ponsford St. E9 CC36 57
Ponsonby Pl. SW1 BW42 3
Ponsonby Pl. SW1 BW42 66
Ponsonby Rd. SW15 BP47 75
Ponsonby Ter. SW1 BW42 3
Ponsonby Ter. SW1 BW42 66
Pontefract Rd. Brom. CG49 78
Ponton Rd. SW8 BW43 66
Pontosie Clo. Sev. CT64 107
Pont St. Ms. SW1 BU41 3
Pont St. Ms. SW1 BU41 66
Pont St. SW1 BU41 3
Pont St. SW1 BU41 66
Pontypool Wk. Rom. CV29 42
Saddleworth Rd.
Pony Chase, Cob. BE60 93
Pool Clo. E. Mol. BF53 84
Poole Clo. Ruis. BB34 44
Poole Ct. Rd. Houns. BE44 64
Poole Rd. E9 CC36 57
Poole Rd. Epsom BN57 94
Poole Rd. Horn. CX33 51
Poole Rd. Wok. AS62 100
Pooles Cotts. Rich. BK48 74
Clifford Rd.
Pooles La. Dag. CQ37 59
Pooles Pk. N4 BY34 47
Poole St. N1 BZ37 2
Poole St. N1 BZ37 57
Poole Way, Hayes BB38 53
Pooley Av. Egh. AT49 72
Pooley Grn. Clo. Egh. AV49 72
Pooley Grn. Rd. Egh. AT49 72
Pooley's La. Hat. BP15 10
Poolmans Rd. Wind. AL45 61
Pool Rd. E. Mol. BE53 84
Poolsford Rd. NW9 BO31 46
Pootings Rd. Eden. CM70 115
Pope Rd. Brom. CJ53 88
Pope's Av. Twick. BH48 74
Popes Clo. Amer. AP22 25
Popes Clo. Slou. AT43 62
Popes Dr. N3 BS30 38
Popes Gro. Croy. CD55 87
Pope's Gro. Twick. BH48 74
Popes La. W5 BK41 64
Popes La. Oxt. CG70 115
Popes La. Wat. BC22 26
Popes Rd. SW9 BY45 66
Popes Rd. Wat. BB19 17
Pope St. SE1 CA41 4
Pope St. SE1 CA41 67
Popham Clo. Felt. BE48 74
Popham Gdns. Rich. BM45 65
Marksbury Av.
Popham Rd. N1 BZ37 2
Popham Rd. N1 BZ37 57
Popham St. N1 BZ37 2
Popham St. N1 BY37 56
Essex Rd.
Poplar Av. Amer. AP23 25
Poplar Av. Grav. DH49 81
Poplar Av. Lthd. BJ64 102
Poplar Av. Mitch. BU51 86
Poplar Av. Orp. CL55 88
Poplar Av. Sthl. BF41 64
Poplar Av. West Dr. AY40 53
Poplar Bath St. E14 CE40 57
Lawless St.
Poplar Clo. Ing. DC19 24
Poplar Clo. Pnr. BD30 36
Poplar Clo. Slou. AV44 62
Poplar Clo. Wat. BC19 17
Poplar Ct. SW19 BS49 76
Poplar Cres. Epsom BN57 94
Poplar Dr. Bans. BQ60 94
High Beeches
Poplar Fm. Clo. Epsom BN57 94
Poplar Gdns. N. Mal. BN51 85
Poplar Gro. W6 BQ41 65
Poplar Gro. N. Mal. BN52 85
Poplar Gro. Wem. BN34 46
Poplar Gro. Wok. AS63 100
Poplar High St. E14 CE40 57
Poplar, Mt. Belv. CR42 69
Poplar Pl. SE2 CP40 59
Poplar Pl. W2 BS40 3
Poplar Pl. W2 BS40 56
Poplar Rd. SE24 BZ45 67
Poplar Rd. SW19 BS51 86
Poplar Rd. Ashf. BA49 73
Poplar Rd. Guil. AS74 118
Poplar Rd. Lthd. BJ64 102
Poplar Rd. Sutt. BR54 85
Poplar Rd. Uxb. AX35 44
Poplar Rd. Uxb. AX36 53
Poplar Rd. S. SW19 BS52 86
Poplar Row, Epp. CN22 31
Poplars, Welw. G. C. BS7 5
Poplars Av. NW2 BQ36 55
High Rd.
Poplars Av. Hat. BN12 10
Poplars Clo. Hat. BN12 10
Poplars Clo. Ruis. BB33 44
Poplar Shaw, Wal. Abb. CG20 22
Poplars Rd. E17 CE32 48
Poplars, The N14 BV25 29
Poplars, The Hem. H. AW14 8
Poplars, The Rom. CO24 32
Poplars, The St. Alb. BJ15 9
Poplar St. Rom. CS31 50
Poplar Wk. SE24 BZ45 67
Poplar Wk. Croy. BZ54 87
Poplar Way, Ilf. CM31 49
Ashurst Dr.
Poppins Ct. EC4 BY39 2
Poppin's Ct. EC4 BY39 56
St. Bride St.
Poppleton Rd. E11 CG32 49
Poppy Clo. Brwd. DA25 33
Porchester Clo. Horn. CW32 51
Porchester Gdns. W2 BS40 3
Porchester Gdns. W2 BS40 56
Porchester Gdns. Ms. W1 BT39 1
Porchester Pl. NW1 BW36 56
Agar Gro.
Porchester Pl. W2 BU39 1
Porchester Pl. W2 BU39 56
Porchester Rd. W2 BS39 1
Porchester Rd. W2 BS39 56
Porchester Rd.
Kings. on T. BM51 85
Porchester Sq. W2 BS39 1
Porchester Sq. W2 BS39 56
Porchester Sq. Ms. W2 BS39 1
Porchester Ter. W2 BT40 3
Porchester Ter. W2 BT39 1
Porchester Ter. W2 BT39 56
Porchester Ter. N. W2 BS39 1
Porchester Ter. N. W2 BS40 56
Porchfield Clo. Grav. DH48 81
Porchfield Clo. Sutt. BS58 95
Hulverston Clo.
Porch Way N20 BU27 38
Porcupine Clo. SE9 CK48 78
Porden Rd. SW2 BX45 66
Porlock Av. Har. BG33 45
Porlock Rd. Enf. CA26 39
Porlock St. SE1 BZ41 4
Porlock St. SE1 BZ41 67
Porrington Clo. Brom. CL51 88
Lubbock Rd.
Portal Clo. SE27 BY48 76
Portal Clo. Ruis. BC35 44
Portal Clo. Uxb. AY36 53
Port Av. Green. DA46 80
Port Cres. E13 CH38 58
Portcullis Lo. Rd. Enf. BZ24 30
Baker St.
Portelet Rd. E1 CC38 57
Porten Rd. W14 BR41 65
Porter's Av. Dag. CO36 59
Porters Clo. Brwd. DA26 42
Greenshaw
Porter, S. Wood St. Alb. BH11 9
Porter's Rd. W2 BT39 56
Porter St. W1 BU39 1
Porter St. W1 BU39 56
Baker St.
Porters Way, West Dr. AY41 63
Porteus Rd. W2 BT39 1
Porteus Rd. W2 BT39 56
Portgate Clo. W9 BR38 55
Ashmore Rd.
Porthcawe Rd. SE26 CD49 77
Porthester Mead. Beck. CE50 77
Port Hill, Orp. CO59 98
Porthkerry Av. Well. CO45 69
Portinscale Rd. SW15 BR46 75
Portland Av. N16 CA33 48
Portland Av. Grav. DG48 81
Portland Av. N. Mal. BO54 85
Portland Av. Sid. CO46 79
Portland Cres. SE9 CK48 78
Portland Cres. Felt. BA49 73
Portland Cres. Grnf. BF38 54
Portland Dr. Red. BW68 113
Portland Gdns. N4 BY32 47
Portland Gdns. Rom. CP32 50
Portland Gro. SW8 BX44 66
Lansdowne Way
Portland Mews W1 BW39 1
Darblay St.
Portland Pl. W1 BV38 1
Portland Pl. W1 BV38 56
Portland Pl. Epsom BO59 94
Portland Rise N4 BY33 47
Portland Rise, Est. N4 BY33 47
Portland Rd. N15 CA31 48
Portland Rd. SE9 CK48 78
Portland Rd. SE25 CB52 87
Portland Rd. W11 BR40 55
Portland Rd. Ashf. AY49 73
Portland Rd. Brom. CJ49 78
Portland Rd. Dor. BJ71 119
Portland Rd. Grav. DE46 81
Portland Rd. Grav. DG47 81
Portland Rd. Hayes BB38 53
Portland Rd. Kings. on T. BL52 85
Portland Rd. Mitch. BU51 86
Portland Rd. Sthl. BE41 64
Portland St. SE17 BZ42 4
Portland St. SE17 BZ42 67
Portland St. St. Alb. BG13 9
Portland Ter. Rich. BK45 64
Portley La. Cat. CA64 105
Portman Av. SW14 BN45 65
Portman Bldgs. NW1 BU38 1
Portman Bldgs. NW1 BU38 56
Portman Clo. W1 BU39 1
Portman Clo. W1 BV39 56
Portman Clo. Bex. CS47 79
Portman Clo. Erith CP45 69
Glynde Rd.
Portman Dr. Wdf. Grn. CJ30 40
Portman Gdns. NW9 BN30 37
Portman Ms. S. W1 BV39 1
Portman Ms. S. W1 BV39 56
Portman Pl. E2 CC38 57
Portman Rd. Kings. on T. BL51 85
Portman Sq. W1 BV39 1
Portman Sq. W1 BV39 56
Portman St. W1 BV39 1
Portman St. W1 BV39 56
Portmeadow Wk. SE2 CP41 69
Portmore Gdns. Rom. CR28 41
Portmore Pk. Rd. Wey. AY56 92
Portnall Dr. Vir. W. AP53 82
Portnall Rise, Vir. W. AP53 82
Portnall Rd. W9 BR38 55
Portnall Rd. Vir. W. AP53 82
Portnall's Clo. Couls. BV61 104
Portnall's Rise, Couls. BV61 104
Portnalls Rd. Couls. BV62 104
Portnoi Clo. Rom. CS30 41
Portobello Ct. W11 BR40 55
Portobello Ms. W11 BS40 56
Portobello Rd.
Portobello Rd. W10 BR39 55
Portobello Rd. W11 BR39 55
Portpool La. EC1 BY39 2
Portpool La. EC1 BY39 56
Portree Clo. N22 BX29 38
Nightingate Rd.
Portree St. E14 CF39 57
Portsdown Av. NW11 BR32 46
Portsdown La. Edg. BM28 37
Portsea Ms. W2 BU39 1
Portsea Ms. W2 BU39 56
Kendal St.
Portsea Pl. W2 BU39 1
Portsea Pl. W2 BU39 56
Kendal St.
Portsea Rd. Til. DH44 71
Portslade Rd. SW8 BW44 66
Portsmouth Av. Surb. BJ54 84
Portsmouth Bldgs. NW1 BU39 56
Portsmouth Rd. Cob. BB60 92
Portsmouth Rd. Cob. BD59 93
Portsmouth Rd. Esher BE58 93
Portsmouth Rd. Esher BG56 93
Portsmouth Rd. Wok. AW65 101
Portsmouth Rd. Wok. AZ62 101
Portsmouth St. WC2 BX39 56
Portugal St.
Portsoken St. E1 CA40 4
Portsoken St. E1 CA40 57
Portswood Pl. SW15 BO46 75
Danebury Av.
Portugal Gdns. Twick. BG48 74
Portugal Rd. Wok. AS61 100
Portugal St. WC2 BX39 2
Portugal St. WC2 BX39 56
Portway, E15 CG37 58
Portway, Epsom BP58 94
Portway Cres. Epsom BP58 94
Portway Gdns. SE18 CJ43 68
Postern Grn. Enf. BY24 29
Post House La. Lthd. BF66 111
Post Mead. Iver AU38 52
Post Office Alley
Hamptn. BF51 84
Thames St.
Post Office App. E7 CH35 49
Post Office La. Slou. AR39 52
Postway Ms. Ilf. CL34 49
Clements Rd.
Potier St. SE1 BZ41 4
Potier St. SE1 BZ41 67
Potkin La. Beac. AO30 34
Potten End, Berk. AT12 7
Potter Clo. Mitch. BV51 86
Potter Heights Clo. Pnr. BC29 35
Potterne Clo. SW19 BQ47 75
Castlecombe Dr.
Potter St. Hill. Pnr. BC29 35
Potter St. Nthwd. BC30 33
Potters Clo. Loug. CK23 31
York Hill
Potter's Flds. SE1 CA40 4
Potter's Fields, SE1 CA40 57
Potters Field, St. Alb. BH11 9
Potters Gro. N. Mal. BN52 85
Potter's La. SW16 BW50 76
Potter's La. Bans. BR61 103
Potter's La. Barn. BS24 29
Potter's La. Borwd. BN23 28
Potters La. Guil. AT66 109
Potters La. Wok. AT65 100
Potters Lane, Wok. AU67 109
Potter's Rd. Barn. BS24 29
Potter St. Pnr. BC30 35
Potters Way, Reig. BT72 121

Street	Grid	Page
Potters La. W11	BR40	55
Portland Rd.		
Pottery Rd. Bex.	CS48	79
Whenman Av.		
Pottery Rd. Brent.	BL43	65
Pottery St. SE16	CB41	67
Wilson Gro.		
Pott St. Est. E2	CB36	57
Pott St. E2	CB38	57
Bethnal Green Rd.		
Pouchen End La. Hem. H.	AU14	7
Pouchen Hill La. Hem. H.	AU13	7
Poulcott, Stai.	AS46	72
Poulett Gdns. Twick.	BJ47	74
Poulett Rd. E6	CK37	58
Poulner Way, SE15	CA43	67
Poulton Av. Sutt.	BT55	86
Poulton Clo. E8	CB35	48
Marcon Pl.		
Poulton Clo. E8	CB35	48
Spurstowe Ter.		
Poultry EC2	**BZ39**	**2**
Poultry EC2	BZ39	57
Cheapside		
Poultry Av. EC1	**BY39**	**2**
Pound Clo. Surb.	BK54	84
Pount Clo. Wal. Abb.	CG15	13
Pound Ct. Dr. Orp.	CM55	88
Pound Crescent, Lthd.	BG64	102
Pound Field, Wat.	BB21	17
Ashfields		
Poundfield Gdns. Wok.	AU63	100
Poundfield Rd. Loug.	CL25	31
Pound La. NW10	BP36	55
Pound La. Epsom	BN59	94
Pound La. Sev.	CP61	107
Pound La. Sev.	CV65	108
Pound Park Rd. SE7	CJ42	68
Pound Pl. SE9	CL46	78
Pound Pla. Guil.	AS73	118
Pound Rd. Bans.	BR62	103
Pound Rd. Cher.	AW54	83
Pound St. Cars.	BU56	95
Poundwell, Welw. G. C.	BS8	5
Pounsley Rd. Sev.	CT64	107
Pountney Rd. SW11	BV45	66
Poverest Rd. Orp.	CN53	88
Powderham Ct. Wok.	AO62	100
Powder Mill La. Dart.	CW48	80
Powder Mill La. Twick.	BE47	74
Powell Clo. Edg.	BL29	37
Powell Clo. Guil.	AP71	118
Powell Gdns. Dag.	CR35	50
Powell Rd. E5	CB34	48
Powell Rd. Buck. H.	CJ26	40
Powells Clo. Dor.	BJ73	119
Powell's Wk. W4	BO43	65
Power Rd. W4	BM42	65
Powers Ct. Twick.	BK47	74
Cambridge Pk.		
Powerscroft Rd. E5	CC35	48
Powerscroft Rd. Sid.	CP50	79
Powis Gdns. NW11	BR33	46
Powis Gdns. W11	BR39	55
Powis Ms. W11	BR39	55
Powis Pl. WC1	**BX38**	**2**
Powis Pl. WC1	BX38	56
Powis Rd. E3	CE38	57
Powis Sq. W11	BR39	55
Powis St. SE18	CL41	68
Powis Ter. W11	BR39	55
Powlett Pla. NW1	BV36	56
Harmood St.		
Pownall Gdns. Houns.	BF45	64
Pownall Rd. E8	**CA37**	**2**
Pownall Rd. E8	CA37	57
Pownall Rd. Houns.	BF45	64
Powster Rd. Brom.	CH49	78
Powy's Clo. Bexh.	CP43	69
Powys La. N13	BX28	38
Powys La. N14	BX28	38
Poyle Rd. Guil.	AS71	118
Poyle Rd. Slou.	AV45	62
Poynder Rd. Til.	DG44	71
Poynders Ct. SW4	BW46	76
Poynders Gdns. SW4	BW47	76
Poynders Hill, Hem. H.	BA14	8
Poynder's Rd. SW4	BW46	76
Plummer Rd.		
Poynings Clo. Orp.	CO55	89
Poynings Rd. N19	BW34	47
Poynings, The Iver	AV42	62
Poynings Way N12	BS28	38
Poynings Way, Rom.	CW30	42
Poyntell Cres. Chis.	CM50	78
Poynter Rd. Enf.	CA25	30
Poynton Rd. N17	CB30	39
Poyntz Rd. SW11	BU44	66
Poyser St. E2	CB37	57
Old Bethnal Grn. Rd.		
Prae Clo. St. Alb.	BF13	9
Praed Ms. W2	**BT39**	**1**
Praed Ms. W2	BT39	56
Norfolk Pl.		
Praed St. W2	**BT39**	**1**
Praed St. W2	BT39	56
Pragel St. E13	CJ37	58
Pragnell Rd. SE12	CH48	78
Prague Pl. SW2	BX46	76
Prah Rd. N4	BY34	47
Prairie Clo. Wey.	AW55	83
Prairie Rd. Wey.	AW55	83
Prairie St. SW8	BV44	66
Pratt Ms. NW1	**BW37**	**1**
Pratt Ms. NW1	BW37	56
Pratt St.		
Pratts La. Walt.	BD56	93
Pratt St. NW1	**BW37**	**1**
Pratt St. NW1	BW37	56
Pratt Wk. SE11	**BX42**	**4**
Pratt Wk. SE11	BX42	66
Prayle Gro. NW2	BQ33	46
Prebend Gdns. W4	BO42	65
Prebend Gdns. W6	BO42	65
Prebend St. N1	**BZ37**	**2**
Prebend St. N1	BZ37	57
Precinct Rd. Hayes	BC40	53
Premier Ave. Grays	DE41	71
Premier Pl. SW15	BQ45	65
Putney High St.		
Prendergast Rd. SE3	CG45	68
Prentice Pl. Harl.	CP12	14
Prentis Rd. SW16	BW49	76
Prentiss Ct. SE7	CJ42	68
Prescelly Pl. Edg.	BL30	37
Prescot Rd. Slou.	AV44	62
Prescot St. E1	**CA40**	**4**
Prescot St. E1	CA40	57
Prescott Av. Orp.	CL53	88
Prescott Grn. Loug.	CM24	31
Prescott Pl. SW4	BW45	66
Prescott Rd. Wal. Cr.	CD17	21
Pressland St. W10	BR39	55
Kensal Rd.		
Press Rd. NW10	BN34	46
Press Rd. Uxb.	AX36	53
Prestage St. E14	CF40	57
Quixley St.		
Prestburg Rd. N. Mal.	BO53	85
Prestbury Cres. Bans.	BU61	104
Prestbury Rd. E7	CJ36	58
Prestbury Sq. SE9	CK49	78
Prestead Rd. SW11	BU45	66
St. John's Hill		
Prested Rd. SW11	BU45	66
Preston Cl. SE1	**CA42**	**4**
Preston Clo. SE1	CA42	67
Preston Clo. Twick.	BH48	74
Preston Ct. Shep.	AZ53	83
Preston Rd.		
Preston Dr. E11	CJ32	49
Preston Dr. Bexh.	CP44	69
Preston Dr. Epsom	BO57	94
Preston Gdns. NW10	BO36	55
Preston Gdns. Enf.	CD22	30
Preston Gdns. Ilf.	CK32	49
Preston Gro. Ash.	BK62	102
Preston Hill, Chesh.	AO18	16
Preston Hill, Har.	BL32	46
Preston La. Tad.	BQ63	103
Preston Pk. N3	BR30	37
Preston Pl. NW2	BP36	55
Belton Rd.		
Preston Pl. NW6	BP36	55
Preston Pl. Rich.	BL46	75
Preston Rd. E4	CF29	39
Preston Rd. E11	CG32	49
Preston Rd. SE19	BY50	76
Preston Rd. SW20	BO50	75
Preston Rd. Grav.	DF47	81
Preston Rd. Har.	BL33	46
Preston Rd. Rom.	CV28	42
Preston Rd. Shep.	AZ53	83
Preston Rd. Slou.	AR40	52
Preston Rd. Wem.	BL33	46
Preston's Rd. E14	CF40	57
Preston Waye, Har.	BL33	46
Prestwick Clo. Sthl.	BE42	64
Prestwick Rd. Wat.	BC28	35
Prestwood Gdns. Croy.	BZ54	87
Queen's Rd.		
Prestwood, Slou.	AQ39	52
Prestwood Av. Har.	BJ31	45
Prestwood Clo. Har.	BJ31	45
Prestwood Dr. Rom.	CS28	41
Prestwood St. N1	**BZ37**	**2**
Prestwood St. N1	BZ37	57
Wenlock Rd.		
Pretoria Av. E17	CD31	48
Pretoria Clo. N17	CA29	39
Pretoria Cres. E4	CF26	39
Pretoria Rd. E4	CF26	39
Pretoria Rd. E11	CF33	48
Pretoria Rd. E16	CG38	58
Pretoria Rd. N17	CA29	39
Pretoria Rd. N18	CA29	39
Pretoria Rd. SW16	BV50	76
Pretoria Rd. Cher.	AV54	82
Pretoria Rd. Ilf.	CL35	49
Pretoria Rd. Rom.	CS31	50
Pretoria Rd. Wat.	BC24	26
Pretoria Rd. N. N18	CA29	39
Prey Heath Clo. Wok.	AR65	100
Prey Heath Rd. Wok.	AQ65	100
Preyost Rd. N11	BV27	38
Price Clo. NW7	BR29	37
Price Clo. SW17	BU48	76
Price Rd. Croy.	BY56	95
Price's La. Reig.	BS72	121
Prices St. SE1	**BY40**	**4**
Prices St. SE1	BY40	56
Prices Yd. N1	**BX37**	**2**
Prices Yard, N1	BX37	56
Caledonian Rd.		
Pricklers Hill, Barn.	BS25	29
Prickley Wk. Brom.	CG54	88
Prideaux Pl. WC1	**BX38**	**2**
Prideaux Pl. WC1	BX38	56
Prideux Rd. SW9	BX45	66
Pridham Rd. E. Th. Hth.	BZ52	87
Priestfield Rd. SE23	CD48	77
Priest Hill, Egh. & Wind.	AR48	72
Priestlands Pk. Rd. Sid.	CN48	78
Priestley Gdns. Rom.	CO32	50
Priestley Rd. Mitch.	BV51	86
Priestley Way E17	CC31	48
Priestley Way NW2	BP33	46
Priests Av. Rom.	CS30	41
Priests Br. SW14	BO45	65
Priests Ct. EC2	BZ39	57
Foster La.		
Priest, S Fld. Brwd.	DE28	122
Priest, S La. Brwd.	DC26	122
Priest Wk. Grav.	DK48	81
Prima Rd. SW9	BY43	66
Primley Lane, Bish.	CS6	6
Primrose Av. Enf.	BZ23	30
Primrose Av. Rom.	CO33	50
Primrose Cl. Hat.	BP13	10
Primrose Clo. Har.	BE34	45
Primrose Ct. E15	CF36	57
Angel La.		
Primrose Field, Harl.	CN12	13
Primrose Gdns. NW3	BU36	56
Primrose Gdns. Bush.	BF26	36
Primrose Gdns. Ruis.	BD35	45
Primrose Glen. Horn	CW31	51
Primrose Hill EC4	**BY39**	**2**
Primrose Hill EC4	BY39	56
Primrose Hill, Brwd.	DB27	42
Primrose Hill, Bri. NW8	**BU37**	**1**
Primrose Hill, Kings L.	AZ17	17
Primrose Hill, Orp.	CN58	97
Primrose Hill, Cat. NW3	BU36	56
Primrose Hill Rd. NW3	**BU36**	**1**
Primrose Hill Rd. NW3	BU36	56
Primrose La. Maid.	AG43	61
Primrose Path, Wal. Cr.	CB19	21
Primrose Rd. E10	CE33	48
Primrose Rd. E18	CH30	40
Primrose Rd. Walt.	BD56	93
Primrose St. EC2	**CA39**	**2**
Primrose St. EC2	CA39	57
Primrose Way, Wem.	BK37	54
Primula St. W12	BP39	55
Prince Albert Rd. NW1	BU37	56
Prince Albert Rd. NW8	**BU38**	**1**
Prince Albert Rd. NW8	BU38	56
Prince Albert Sq. Red.	BU73	121
Prince Alberts Rd. Wind.	AP43	62
Prince Alberts Wk. Wind.	AP43	62
Prince Arthur Ms. NW3	BT35	47
Perrins La.		
Prince Arthur Rd. NW3	BT35	47
Prince Charles Av. S. Dnth.	CY51	90
Prince Charles Rd. SE3	CG44	68
Prince Charles Way, Wall.	BV55	86
Prince Consort Dr. Chis.	CM51	88
Prince Consort Rd. SW7	**BT41**	**3**
Prince Consort Rd. SW7	BT41	66
Princedale Rd. W11	BR40	55
Prince Edward Rd. E9	CD36	57
Prince Edward St. Berk.	AR13	7
Prince George Av. N14	BW24	29
Prince George Rd. N16	CA35	48
Prince George Rd. SW19	BT51	86
Prince Georges Av. SW20	BQ51	85
Prince Henry Rd. SE7	CJ43	68
Prince Imperial Rd. Chis.	CL50	78
Prince Imperial Way SE18	CL43	68
Prince John Rd. SE9	CK46	78
Princelet St. E1	**CA39**	**2**
Princelet St. E1	CA39	57
Prince of Wales Cl. NW4	BP31	46
Church Terr.		
Prince of Wales Dr. SW11	BU44	66
Prince of Wales Rd. E16	CJ39	58
Prince of Wales Rd. NW5	BV36	56
Prince of Wales Rd. SE3	CG44	68
Prince of Wales Rd. Red.	BY74	121
Prince of Wales Rd. Sutt.	BT55	86
Prince of Wales Ter. W4	BO42	65
Devonshire Rd.		
Prince of Wales Ter. W8	BS41	66
Prince Pk. Hem. H.	AW14	8
Prince Philip Ave. Grays	DD40	71
Prince Regent Rd. Houns.	BG45	64
Prince Regent's La. E13	CH38	58
Prince Regent's La. E16	CJ39	58
Prince Rd. SE25	CA53	87
Prince Rupert Rd. SE9	CK45	68
Princes Ave. Dart.	CX47	80
Prince's Av. N10	BV31	47
Princes Av. N13	BY28	38
Prince's Av. N22	BW30	38
Princes Av. NW9	BM31	46
Princes Av. W3	BM41	65
Princes Av. Cars.	BU57	95
Princes Av. Enf.	CD21	30
Princes Av. Grnf.	BF39	54
Princes Av. Orp.	CN53	88
Princes Av. Sth. Croy.	CB61	105
Princes Av. Surb.	BM54	85
Prince's Av. Wat.	BB25	26
Princes Av. Wdf. Grn.	CH28	40
Princes Clo. NW9	BM31	46
Princes Clo. Berk.	AQ12	7
Princes Clo. Edg.	BM28	37
Princes Clo. Epp.	CS16	23
Princes Clo. Sid.	CP48	79
Princes Clo. Sth. Croy.	CB61	105
Princes Clo. Tedd.	BG49	74
Princes Ct. Wem.	BL35	46
Prince's Dr. Har.	BH31	45
Princes Dr. Lthd.	BH59	93
Princesfield Rd. Wal. Abb.	CH20	22
Princes Gdns. SW7	**BT41**	**3**
Princes Gdns. SW7	BM41	66
Princes Gdns. Ms. SW7	**BT41**	**3**
Princes Gdns. W3	BM39	55
Princes Gdns. W5	BK38	54
Princes Gte. SW7	**BT41**	**3**
Princes Gte. SW7	BU41	66
Princes Gte. Ct. SW7	**BT41**	**3**
Princes Gte. Ct. SW7	BT41	66
Exhibition Rd.		
Princes Gte. Ms. SW7	BT41	66
Princes La. N10	BV31	47
Princes Ms. SW7	**BT41**	**3**
Prince's Ms. SW7	BT42	66
Princes Ms. W2	BS40	56
Prince, S Rd. Rom.	CW23	33
Princes Pde. Pot. B.	BS20	20
High St.		
Princes Pk. Rain.	CU36	59
Princes Pk. Av. NW11	BR32	46
Princes Park Av. Hayes	BA40	53
Princes Park Cir. Hayes	BA40	53
Princes Park Clo. Hayes	BA40	53
Princes Pk. La. Hayes	BA50	53
Princes Park Par. Hayes	BA40	53
Princes Pl. W11	BR40	55
Prince's Plain, Brom.	CK54	88
Princes Rise, SE13	CF44	67
Princes Rd. N18	CC28	39
Princes Rd. SE20	CC50	77
Princes Rd. SW14	BN45	65
Prince's Rd. SW19	BS50	76
Princes Rd. W13	BJ40	54
Mattock La.		
Princes Rd. Ashf.	AY49	73
Princes Rd. Buck. H.	CJ27	40
Princes Rd. Dart.	CU46	79
Princes Rd. Dart.	CY47	80
Princes Rd. Felt.	BB48	73
Princes Rd. Grav.	DG49	81
Prince's Rd. Ilf.	CM31	49
Princes Rd. Kew.	BL44	65
Prince's Rd. Kings. on T.	BM51	85
Prince's Rd. Red.	BU71	121
Princes Rd. Rich.	BL46	75
Princes Rd. Rom.	CU32	50
Princes Rd. Tedd.	BG49	74
Prince's Rd. Wey.	AZ56	92
Princess Ave. Wind.	AN45	61
Princess Av. N3	BS30	38
Princess Av. Wem.	BL34	46
Carlton Av. E.		
Princess Cres. N4	BY34	47
Princess Gdns. Wok.	AT61	100
Princess Margaret Rd. S. Le H.	DK41	71
Princess May Rd. N16	CA35	48
Princess Mews NW3	BT35	47
Princess Pde. Dag.	CR37	59
Whitebarn La.		
Princess Pde. Orp.	CL55	88
Princes Sq. W2	BS40	56
Princess Rd. NW1	**BV37**	**1**
Princess Rd. NW1	BV37	56
Princess Rd. NW6	BS37	56
Princess Rd. Croy.	BZ53	87
Princess Rd. Egh.	AS50	72
Princess Rd. Swan.	CU50	79
Princess Rd. Wok.	AT61	100
Princes St. SE1	**BY41**	**4**
Princess St. SE1	BY41	66
Princes St. EC2	**BZ39**	**2**
Princes St. EC2	BZ39	57
Princes St. N17	CA29	39
Queen St.		
Prince's St. W1	**BV39**	**1**
Prince's St. W1	BV39	56
Princes St. Bexh.	CQ45	69
Princes St. Rich.	BL46	75
Princes St. Sutt.	BT56	95
Princes Ter. E13	CH37	58
Princes Ter. W3	BN41	65
Church Rd.		
Prince St. SE8	CD43	67
Prince St. Wat.	BD24	27
Prnces Vw. Dart.	CX47	80
Princes Way, SW19	BQ47	75
Princes Way, Brwd.	DD27	122
Prince's Way, Buck. H.	CJ27	40
Princes Way, Croy.	BX57	95
Princes Way, Ruis.	BE35	45
Princes Way, W. Wick.	CG56	97
Princethorpe Rd. SE26	CC49	77
Princeton St. WC1	**BX39**	**2**
Princeton St. WC1	BX39	56
Pringle Gdns. SW16	BW49	76
Pring St. W10	BQ40	55
Freston Road		
Printer St. EC4	BY39	56
Gough Sq.		
Printing House La. Hayes	BB41	63
Printing House Yd. E2	CA38	57
Hackney Rd.		
Priolo Rd. SE7	CJ42	68
Prior Av. Sutt.	BT57	95
Prior Boulton St. N1	BY36	56
Compton Rd.		
Prioress St. SE1	BZ41	67
Prior Gro. Chesh.	AO18	16
Priors Croft E17	CD30	39
Priors Cft. Wok.	AT64	100
Priors Field, Nthlt.	BE36	54
Arnold Rd.		
Priorsford Av. Orp.	CO52	89
Priors Gdns. Ruis.	BD35	45
Priors Mead. Enf.	CA23	30
Priors Mead. Lthd.	BF66	111
Priors Pk. Horn.	CV34	51
Priors, The Ash.	BK63	102
Prior St. SE10	CF43	67
Priors Way, Maid.	AG42	61
Priory Av. E4	CD27	39
Priory Av. E17	CE32	48
Priory Av. N8	BW31	47
Priory Av. W4	BO42	65
Priory Av. Harl.	CP8	6
Priory Av. Orp.	CM53	88
Priory Av. Sutt.	BQ56	94
Priory Av. Uxb.	AX31	44
Priory Av. Wem.	BH35	45
Priory Br. SW14	BO45	65
Priory Clo. E4	CD27	39
Priory Clo. E18	CH30	40
Priory Clo. N14	BW25	29
Priory Clo. N20	BR26	37
Priory Clo. Beck.	CD52	87
Priory Clo. Brox.	CD15	12
Priory Clo. Brwd.	DA25	33
Priory Clo. Chis.	CK51	88
Priory Clo. Dart.	CV46	80
Priory Clo. Dor.	BJ72	119
Harrow Rd. W.		
Priory Clo. Hamptn.	BE51	84
Priory Clo. Hodd.	CE12	12
Priory Clo. Ruis.	BB33	44
Priory Clo. Stan.	BH27	36
Priory Clo. Sun.	BC50	73
Priory Clo. Uxb.	AW34	44
Priory Clo. Uxb.	AX31	44
Priory Clo. Wem.	BH35	45
Priory Clo. Wok.	AU60	91
Priory Cotts. Uxb.	AX31	44
Priort Ct. E17	CD30	39
Priory Ct. SW8	BW44	66
Priory Ct. St. Alb.	BH14	9
Old London Rd.		
Priory Ct. Est. E17	CD30	39
Priory Cres. SE19	BZ50	77
Priory Cres. Sutt.	BQ56	94
Priory Cres. Wem.	BJ34	45
Priory Dr. SE2	CP42	69
Priory Dr. Reig.	BS71	121
Priory Dr. Stan.	BH27	36
Priory Gdns. N6	BV32	47
Priory Gdns. N8	BW31	47
Priory Gdns. SW13	BO45	65
Priory Gdns. W5	BL38	55
Priory Gdns. Berk.	AR13	7
Priory Gdns. Dart.	CV46	80
Priory Gdns. Hamptn.	BE50	74
Priory Gdns. Uxb.	AX31	44
Priory Gdns. Walt.	BC55	83
Priory Gdns. Wem.	BJ35	45
Priory Grn. Stai.	AW49	73
Priory Green Est. N1	**BX37**	**2**
Priory Green Est. N1	BX37	56
Priory Gro. SW8	BX44	66
Priory Gro. Rom.	CW27	42
Priory Hill, Dart.	CV46	80
Priory Hill, Wem.	BJ35	45
Priory La. SW15	BO46	75
Priory La. E. Mol.	BF52	84
Priory La. Farn.	CW54	90
Priory Mead. Brwd.	DB21	33
Priory Ms. SW8	BW44	66
Priory Pde. Wem.	BH35	45
Priory Pk. SE3	CG45	68
Priory Pk. Rd. NW6	BR37	55
Priory Pk. Rd. Wem.	BJ35	45
Priory Path, Rom.	CW27	42
Priory Pl. SW15	BO45	65
Upr. Richmond Rd.		
Priory Pl. Dart.	CV46	80
Priory Rd. E6	CJ37	58
Priory Rd. N8	BW31	47
Priory Rd. NW6	BS37	56
Priory Rd. SW19	BT50	76
Priory Rd. W4	BN41	65
Priory Rd. Bark.	CM36	58
Priory Rd. Chess.	BL55	85
Priory Rd. Croy.	BY54	86
Priory Rd. Dart.	CV45	70
Priory Rd. Dart.	CV46	80
Priory Rd. Ger. Cr.	AR31	43
Priory Rd. Hamptn.	BE50	74
Priory Rd. Houns.	BG46	74
Priory Rd. Loug.	CK24	31
Priory Rd. Reig.	BS71	121
Priory Rd. Rich.	BM43	65
Priory Rd. Rom.	CW27	42
Priory Rd. Sutt.	BQ56	94
Priory St. E3	CE38	57
Bromley High St.		
Priory Ter. NW6	**BS37**	**1**
Priory Ter. NW6	BS37	56
Priory Ter. Sun.	BC50	73
Priory, The SE3	CG45	68
Priory, The Gdse.	CB69	114
Priory Vw. Bush.	BH26	36
Priory Wk. SW10	**BT42**	**3**
Priory Wk. SW10	BT42	66
Priory Wk. St. Alb.	BH15	9
Priory Way, Har.	BF31	45
Priory Way, Slou.	AQ43	62
Priory Way, Sthl.	BD41	64
Western Rd.		
Pritchards Rd. E2	CB37	57
Priter Rd. SE16	**CB41**	**4**
Priter Rd. SE16	CB41	67
St. James's Rd.		
Priter Way SE16	**CB41**	**4**
Priter Way SE16	CB41	67
Private Rd. Enf.	BZ25	30
Private Rd. Grav.	DD47	81
Private Rd. S. Ock.	CX41	70
Private Rd. Wal. Cr.	BZ19	21
Priyor Clo. Wat.	BB19	17
Probert Rd. SW2	BY45	66
Probyn Rd. SW2	BY48	76
Procter Gdns. Lthd.	BF66	111
Procter St. WC1	**BX39**	**2**
Procter St. WC1	BX39	56
High Holborn		
Proctors Cl. Felt.	BC47	73
Profumo Rd. Walt.	BD56	93
Profwales Ter. W8	**BS41**	**3**
Progress Way N22	BY30	38
Progress Way, Croy.	BX55	86
Progress Way, Enf.	CB25	30
Promenade Approach Rd. W4	BO43	65
Promenade De Verdun Pur.	BW59	95
Promenade, The W4	BO44	65
Prospect Clo. SE10	CF44	67
Point Hill		
Prospect Clo. SE26	CB49	77
Wells Park Rd.		
Prospect Clo. Belv.	CR42	69
Prospect Clo. Houns.	BE43	64
Prospect Clo. Ruis.	BD33	45
Prospect Cotts. SW18	BS45	66
Point Pleasant		
Prospect Cres. Twick.	BG46	74
Prospect Gro. Grav.	DH47	81
Prospect Hill, E17	CE31	48
Prospect La. Egh.	AQ49	72
Prospect Pla. Brom.	CH52	88
Prospect Pl. N2	BT31	47
Prospect Pl. N17	CA29	39
Prospect Pl. NW2	BR34	46
Prospect Rd.		
Prospect Pl. Epsom	BO60	94
Prospect Pl. Grav.	DH47	81
Prospect Pl. Grays	DD43	71
Prospect Pl. Rom.	CS30	41
Prospect Pl. Stai.	AV49	72
Prospect Ring N2	BT31	47
Prospect Rd. E17	CD32	48
Prospect Rd. NW2	BR34	46
Prospect Rd. SE26	CB49	77
Prospect Rd. Barn.	BS24	29
Prospect Rd. Horn.	CW31	51
Prospect Rd. St. Alb.	BG14	9
Prospect Rd. Sev.	CV65	108
Prospect Rd. Surb.	BK53	84
Prospect Rd. Wdf. Grn.	CJ29	40
Prospect Val. SE18	CK42	68
Prospect Wk. E2	CC38	57
Prospero Rd. N19	BW33	47
Protheroe Rd. SW6	BR43	65
Prothero Gdns. NW4	BP32	46
Prout Gro. NW10	BO35	46

Prout Rd. E5 CB34 48
Provence St. N1 BZ37 2
Providence Ct. W1 BV40 3
Providence Ct. W1 BV40 56
Providence La. Hayes BA43 63
Providence Pl. N1 BY37 2
Providence Pl. N1 BY37 56
Upper St.
Providence Pl. Epsom BO59 94
Providence Row N1 BX37 56
Northdown St.
Providence Rd. West Dr. AY40 53
Providence Ter. Reig. BS70 121
Provost Dwellings N1 BZ37 57
Provost Rd. NW3 BU36 56
Provost St. N1 BZ37 2
Provost St. N1 BZ37 57
Prowse Av. Bush. BG27 36
Prowse Pl. NW1 BW36 56
Bonny St.
Pruden Clo. N14 BW27 38
Prune Hill, Egh. AR50 72
Prusom St. E1 CB40 57
Pryors, The NW3 BT34 47
Puckshill, Wok. AO62 100
Beechwood Rd.
Puck La. Wal. Abb. CF18 21
Pudding La. EC3 BZ40 57
Pudding La. Chig. CN26 40
Pudding La. Hem. H. AW12 8
Pudding La. Sev. CX64 108
Church Rd.
Pudding Mill La. E15 CE37 57
Puddle Dock EC4 BY40 4
Puddle Dock EC4 BY40 56
Upper Thames St.
Puddledock La. Dart. CT49 79
Puddledock La. West CN70 115
Puers La. Beac. AP29 34
Pulborough Rd. SW18 BR47 75
Pulborough Way Houns. BD45 64
Pulford Rd. N15 BZ32 48
Pulham Av. N2 BT31 47
Puller Rd. Barn. BR23 28
Puller Rd. Hem. H. AW14 8
Pulleyns Av. E6 CK38 58
Pulleys Clo. Hem. H. AV13 7
Pulleys La. Hem. H. AV12 7
Pullman Ct. SW2 BX47 76
Pullman Gdns. SW15 BQ46 75
Pulross Rd. SW9 BX45 66
Pulteney Clo. E3 CD37 57
Pulteney Rd. E18 CH31 49
Pulteney Ter. N1 BX37 2
Pulteney Ter. N1 BX37 56
Pulton Rd. SW6 BS43 66
Puma Ct. E1 CA39 2
Puma Ct. E1 C39 57
Commercial St.
Pump All. Brent. BK53 64
High St.
Pump Hill, Loug. CK23 31
Pumping Station Rd. W4 BO43 65
Pump La. Chesh. AP20 16
Pump La. Epp. CL15 13
Pump La. Hayes BB41 63
Pump La. Orp. CR56 98
Pump Pail N. Croy. BZ55 87
Pump Pail S. Croy. BZ55 87
Punchbowl La. Dor. BK71 119
Punch Bowl La. Hem. H.
& St. Alb. BA12 8
Pundersons Gdns. E2 CB38 57
Purbeck Av. N. Mal. BO53 85
Purbeck Dr. Wok. AS60 91
Purbeck Dr. NW2 BQ34 46
Purbeck Rd. Horn. CU33 50
Purberry Gro. Epsom BO58 94
Purbrock Av. Wat. BD21 27
Purbrook Clo. Red. B67 113
Purbrook Est. SE1 CA41 4
Purbrook Est. SE1 CA41 67
Purbrook St. SE1 CA41 4
Purbrook St. SE1 CA41 67
Purcell Clo. Borwd. BK23 27
Stainer Rd.
Purcell Cres. SW6 BR43 65
Purcell Rd. Grnf. BF39 54
Purcells Av. Edg. BM28 37
Purcells Clo. Ash. BL62 103
Purcell St. N1 CA37 2
Purcell St. N1 CA37 57
Purcer's Cross Rd. SW6 BR44 65
Purcers Rd. SW6 BR45 65
Purchese St. NW1 BW37 1
Purchese St. NW1 BW37 56
Purdy St. E3 CE38 57
Purex Rd. Grnf. BG37 54
Purfleet Art Rd. S. Ock. CX41 70
Purfleet By-pass CX42 70
Purfleet Rd. S. Ock. CX41 70
Purford Grn. Harl. CO11 14
Purland Clo. Dag. CQ33 50
Purland Rd. SE28 CN41 68
Purleigh Av. Wdf. Grn. CK29 40
Purley Av. NW2 BR34 46
Purley Bury Av. Pur. BZ59 96
Purley Bury Clo. Pur. BZ59 96
Purley Clo. Ilf. CL30 40
Purley Ct. Pur. BY58 95
Purley Downs Rd. Pur. BZ58 96
Purley Hill, Pur. BY59 95
Purley Knoll, Pur. BX59 95
Purley Oaks Rd.
Sth. Croy. BZ58 96
Purley Pk. Rd. Pur. BY58 95
Purley Pl. N1 BY36 56
Islington Pk. St.
Purley Rise, Pur. BX59 95
Purley Rd. N9 BZ27 39
Purley Rd. Pur. BY59 95
Purley Rd. Sth. Croy. BZ57 96
Purley Vale Pur. BY60 95
Purley Way Croy. BX54 86
Purlieu Way, Epp. CN21 31
Purlings Rd. Bush. BF25 27
Purney's Rd. SE9 CJ45 68
Purrett Rd. SE18 CN42 68
Pursley Rd. NW7 BP29 37
Purves Rd. NW10 BQ37 55
Putney Br. App. SW6 BR45 65
Putney Br. Rd. SW15 BR45 65
Putney Br. Rd. SW18 BS46 76
Putney Hth. SW15 BP47 75
Putney Hth. La. SW15 BQ46 75
Putney High St. SW15 BQ45 65
Putney Hl. SW15 BQ46 75
Putney Pk. Av. SW15 BP45 65
Putney Pk. La. SW15 BP45 65
Putney Rd. Enf. CC21 30
Puttenham Clo. Wat. BD27 36
Putters Cft. Hem. H. AY11 8
Puttocks Cl. Hat. BQ15 10
Puttocks Dr. Hat. BQ15 10
Pyecombe Cor. N12 BR28 37
Pyenest Rd. Harl. CL12 13
Pyghtle, The Uxb. AW33 44
Pykhill, Grays DG41 71
Pylbrook Rd. Sutt. BS55 86
Pyle Hill, Guil. AS66 109
Pyle Hill, Wok. AR65 100
Pym Clo. Barn. BT25 29
Pymers Mead. SE21 BZ47 77
Pymme's Clo. N13 BX28 38
Pymmes Gdns. N. N9 CA27 39
Pymmes Gdns. S. N9 CA27 39
Pymmes Grn. Rd. N11 BV27 38
Pymmes Rd. N13 BX29 38
Pymms Gdns. Barn. BU24 29
Pym Pl. Grays DD42 71
Pynchester Clo. Uxb. AZ34 44
Pyne Rd. Surb. BM54 85
Pynestgreen Grn.
Wal. Abb. CH22 31
Pynham Clo. SE2 CO41 69
Pynnacles Clo. Stan. BJ28 36
Pypers Hatch, Harl. CN11 13
Pyrcroft La. Wey. AZ56 92
Pycroft Rd. Cher. AV54 82
Pyrford Common Rd.
Wok. AU61 100
Pyrford Heath, Wok. AV61 100
Pyrford Rd. Wey. AW60 92
Pyrford Rd. Wok. AW61 101
Pyford Woods, Wok. AV61 100
Pyrford Woods Clo.
Wok. AV61 100
Pyrford Woods Rd. Wok. AV61 100
Pyrland Rd. N5 BZ35 48
Pyrland Rd. Rich. BL46 75
Pyrles Grn. Loug. CL23 31
Pyrles La. Loug. CL23 31
Pyrmont Gro. SE27 BY48 76
Pyrmont Rd. W4 BM43 65
Pyrmont Rd. Ilf. CM34 49
Pytchley Cres. SE19 BZ50 77
Pytchley Rd. SE22 CA45 67
Pytt Field, Harl. CO11 14
Quadrangle, The Guil. AQ71 118
Quadrangle, The
Welw. G. C. BQ7 5
Quadrant Arc. Rom. CT32 50
Quadrant Clo. NW4 BP32 46
Quadrant Gro. NW5 BU35 47
Quadrant Rd. N1 BZ36 57
Essex Rd.
Quadrant Rd. Rich. BK45 64
Quadrant Rd. Th. Hth. BY52 86
Quadrant, The SE24 BZ46 77
Quadrant, The SW20 BR51 85
Quadrant, The Bexh. CP43 69
Quadrant, The Grays CY42 70
Quadrant, The Rich. BK46 74
Quadrant, The St. Alb. BJ12 9
Quadrant, The Wey. AZ56 92
Quaggy Wk. SE3 CH45 68
Quail Gdns. Sth. Croy. CD58 96
Quainton St. NW10 BN34 46
Quaker Clo. Sev. CV65 108
Quaker La. Islw. BJ44 64
Quaker La. Sthl. BF41 64
Quakers Clo. Hart. DC52 90
Quakers Course NW9 BO30 37
Quaker's Hall La. Sev. CV64 108
Quakers La. Pot. B. BS18 20
Quaker St. E1 CA38 2
Quaker St. E1 CA38 57
Quaker St. Wal. Abb. CF20 21
Quaker's Wk. N21 BZ25 30
Quality Ct. WC2 BY39 2
Quality Ct. WC2 BT39 56
Chancery La.
Quality St. Red. BV67 113
Quantock Clo. Hayes BA43 63
Quantock Clo. Slou. AT42 62
Quantock Clo. St. Alb. BK11 9
Chiltern Rd.
Quantock Gdns. NW2 BQ34 46
Quantock Rd. Bexh. CT44 69
Quantocks, Hem. H. AY12 8
Malvern Way
Quarles Clo. Rom. CR29 41
Quarley Way SE15 CA43 67
Quarrendon Rd. Amer. AO23 25
Quarrendon St. SW6 BS44 66
Quarr Rd. Cars. BT53 86
Quarry, Guil. AR71 118
Quarry Clo. Couls. BX57 95
Quarry Clo. Couls. BX61 104
Quarry Clo. Oxt. CG68 115
Quarry Hill, Grays DD42 71
Quarry Hill, Sev. CV65 108
Quarry Hill Rd. Sev. DC64 108
Quarry Pk. Rd. Sutt. BR57 94
Quarry Rise, Sutt. BR57 94
Quarry Rd. SW18 BT46 76
Quarry Rd. Oxt. CG68 115
Quarry Spring, Harl. CO11 14
Quartermaine Av. Wok. AS64 100
Quartermass Clo. Hem. H. AW13 8
Quartermass Rd. Hem. H. AW13 8
Quarter Mile La. E10 CE35 48
Quarter Mile La. E15 CE35 48
Quaves Rd. Slou. AQ41 62
Quebec Ave. West. CM66 115
Quebec Ms. W1 BU39 1
Quebec Ms. W1 BU39 56
Quebec Rd. Hayes BD39 54
Quebec Rd. Ilf. CL33 49
Quebec Rd. Til. DG44 71
Quebec Sq. West. CM66 115
Queen Adelaide Rd.
SE20 CC50 77
Queen Alexandra's Ct.
SW19 BR49 75
Queen Ann Clo. Esher BH58 93
Queen Anne Av. Brom. CG52 88
Queen Anne Gate, Erith CP45 69
Glynde Rd.
Queen Anne Gdns. Mitch. BU52 86
Qn. Anne Ms. W1 BV39 1
Qn. Anne Rd. E9 CD36 57
Queen Anne's Clo. Twick. BG48 74
Queen Anne's Dr. Wind. AO41 61
Queen Annes Gdns. W5 BL41 65
Queen Anne's Gdns. Enf. CA25 30
Queen Anne's Gate SW1 BW41 3
Queen Anne's Gate SW1 BW41 66
Queen Annes Gro. W4 BO41 65
Bedford Rd.
Queen Annes Gro. W5 BL41 65
Queen Anne's Gro. Enf. BZ26 39
Queen Anne's Pl. Enf. CA25 30
Queen Anne's Rd. Wind. AO45 61
Queen Anne St. W1 BV39 1
Queen Anne St. W1 BV39 56
Queen Anne's Wk. WC1 BX39 56
Guilford St.
Queen Ann Gate, Bexh. CP45 69
Regency Way
Queen Ann Ms. W1 BV39 56
Chandos St.
Queen Anns Gdns. Lthd. BJ64 102
Up. Fairfield Rd.
Queen Anns Ter. Lthd. BJ64 102
Up. Fairfield Rd.
Queenborough Gdns. Ilf. CL31 49
Queen Caroline Est. W6 BQ42 65
Queen Caroline St. W6 BQ42 65
Queen Clo. Wey. BB57 92
Queen Court Ride, Cob. BC60 92
Queen Dale Ct. Wok. AP61 100
Queen Eleanor Clo. Ash. BL63 103
Queen Eleanor's Rd. Guil. AP71 118
Queen Elizabeth Clo. N16 BZ34 48
Queen Elizabeth Rd. E17 CD31 48
Qn. Elizabeth Rd.
Kings. on T. BL51 85
Queen Elizabeth's Dr. N14 BW26 38
Queen Elizabeth's Dr.
Croy. CF58 96
Qn. Elizabeths Gdns. Croy. CF58 96
Qn. Elizabeths Dr.
Queen Elizabeth Gdns.
Mord. BS52 86
Hatherleigh Clo.
Queen Elizabeth St. SE1 CA41 4
Queen Elizabeth St. SE1 CA41 67
Queen Elizabeth Wk. N16 BZ33 48
Queen Elizabeth Wk. Wall. BW56 95
Queen Elizabeth Way,
Wok. AS63 100
Queenhill Rd. Sth. Croy. CB58 96
Queenhithe, EC4 BZ40 4
Queenhithe EC4 BZ40 57
Queen Margaret's Gro. N1 CA35 48
Queen Mary Av. Mord. BQ53 85
Queen Mary Av. Wat. BB24 26
Queen Mary Clo. Wok. AU61 100
Queen Mary Rd. SE19 BY50 76
Queen Mary Rd. Shep. BA51 83
Queen Mary's Av. Cars. BU57 95
Queen Marys Dri. Wey. AV58 91
Queen Mothers Dri. Uxb. AV32 43
Queens Acre Sutt. BQ57 94
Queen St. Pl. EC4 BZ40 4
Queen St. Pl. EC4 BZ40 57
Queens Alley, Epp. CN19 22
Hemnall St.
Queen's Av. N3 BT29 38
Queen's Av. N10 BV31 47
Queen's Av. N20 BT27 38
Queen's Av. N21 BY26 38
Queen's Av. Felt. BD49 74
Queens Av. Grnf. BF39 54
Queens Av. Stan. BK31 45
Queen's Av. Wat. BB24 26
Queen's Av. Wdf. Grn. CH28 40
Queens Av. Wey. AX59 92
Queensberry Ms. W. SW7 BT42 66
Queen's Gte.
Queensberry Pl. SW7 BT42 66
Queensberry Way SW7 BT42 66
Harrington Rd.
Queensborough Ct. N3 BR31 46
N. Circular Rd.
Queensborough Pass. W2 BT40 56
Queensborough Ter.
Queensborough Ter. W2 BS40 3
Queensborough Ter. W2 BT40 56
Queensbridge Ct. E2 CA37 2
Queensbridge Ms. Islw. BH46 74
Queensbridge Pk. Islw. BH46 74
Queensbridge Rd. E2 CA36 57
Queensbridge Rd. E2 CA37 2
Queensbridge Rd. E8 CA36 57
Queensbridge Rd. E8 CA37 2
Queensbury Ms. W. SW7 BT42 3
Queensbury Pl. SW7 BT42 3
Queensbury Pl. Rich. BK46 74
Retreat Rd.
Queensbury Rd. NW9 BN33 46
Queensbury Rd. Wem. BL37 55
Queensbury Sta. Par. Edg. BL31 46
Queensbury St. N1 BZ36 57
Morton Rd.
Queensbury Way SW7 BT42 3
Queen's Cir. SW11 BV43 66
Queens Clo. Dg. BM28 37
Queens Clo. Tad. BP66 112
Queens Clo. Wind. AQ46 72
Queen's Club Gdns. W14 BR43 65
Queens Ct. NW11 BR32 46
Queens Ct. SE23 CC48 77
Queens Ct. W5 BK39 54
Queen's Wk.
Queens Ct. Rich. BL46 75
Queens Ct. St. Alb. BJ13 9
Queens Ct. Wem. BL35 46
Queen's Cres. NW5 BV36 56
Queen's Cres. Rich. BL46 75
Queens Cres. St. Alb. BJ12 9
Queenscroft Rd. SE9 CJ46 78
Queensdale Cres. W11 BQ40 55
Queensdale Pl. W11 BR40 55
Queensdale Rd. W11 BQ40 55
Queensdale Wk. W11 BR40 55
Queensdown Rd. E5 CB35 48
Queens Dr. Rick. AV25 25
Queens Dr. E10 CE33 48
Queen's Dr. N4 BY34 47
Queens Dr. W3 BL39 55
Queens Dr. Guil. AQ69 118
Queens Dr. Lthd. BG59 93
Queen's Dr. Slou. AS37 52
Queen's Dr. Surb. BJ54 84
Queen's Dr. Surb. BM54 85
Queens Dr. Wal. Cr. CE20 21
Queens Dr. Wat. BB19 17
Queens Elm Sq. SW3 BT42 3
Queen's Elm Sq. SW3 BT42 66
Queen's Gdns. NW4 BQ32 46
Queen's Gdns. W2 BT40 3
Queen's Gdns. W2 BT40 56
Queens Gdns. W5 BK38 54
Queens Gdns. Dart. CX47 80
Queens Gdns. Houns. BE43 64
Queens Gdns. Rain. CS37 59
Queens Gdns. Upmin. CZ32 51
Queen's Gte. SW7 BT41 3
Queen's Gte. SW7 BT41 66
Queen's Gte. Gdns.
SW7 BT41 3
Queen's Gte. Gdns. SW7 BT41 66
Queensgate Gdns. Chis. CM51 88
Prince Consort Dr.
Queen's Gte. Ms. SW7 BT41 3
Queen's Gte. Ms. SW7 BT41 66
Queen's Gte. Pl. SW7 BT41 3
Queensgate Pl. NW6 BS37 56
Kingsgate Pl.
Queen's Gte. Pl. SW7 BT41 66
Queen's Gate Pl. Ms.
SW7 BT41 3
Queen's Gte. Pl. Ms. SW7 BT41 66
Queen's Gate Ter. SW7 BT41 3
Queen's Gte. Ter. SW7 BT41 66
Queen's Gro. NW8 BT37 1
Queen's Gro. NW8 BT37 56
Queens Gro. Rd. E4 CF26 39
Queen, S. Head St. N1 BY37 2
Queen's Gro. Studios,
NW8 BT37 1
Queens Hd. Wk. Brox. CD15 12
High Rd.
Queens Head St. N1 BY37 56
Raleigh St.
Queen's Ho. Tedd. BH50 74
Queensland Av. N18 BZ29 39
Queensland Av. SW19 BS51 86
Queensland Pl. N7 BY35 47
Queensland Rd.
Queensland Rd. N7 BY35 47
Queens La. Ashf. AY49 73
Clarendon Rd.
Queens Mns. NW4 BP32 46
Queen's Mkt. E13 CJ37 58
Queensmead NW8 BT37 56
Queensmead, Slou. AQ44 62
Queens Rd.
Queensmead Av. Epsom BP58 94
Queens Mead Rd. Brom. CG51 88
Queensmere Clo. SW19 BQ48 75
Queensmere Rd. SW19 BQ48 75
Queen's Ms. W2 BS40 3
Queen's Ms. W2 BS40 56
Salem Rd.
Queensmill Rd. SW6 BQ43 65
Queen, S. Rd. Brwd. DB27 42
Queens Pde. Clo. N12 BU28 38
Hollyfield Av.
Queens Pk. Ct. W10 BQ38 55
Queen's Pk. Gdns. Felt. BC48 73
Queens Park Rd. Cat. CA65 105
Queens Pk. Rd. Rom. CW30 42
Queen's Pl. Mord. BS52 86
Queen's Pl. Wat. BD24 27
Queen's Place, Watt. BB56 92
Queens Prom.
Kings. on T. BK52 84
Queen Sq. WC1 BX38 2
Queen Sq. WC1 BX38 56
Queen's Ride SW13 BP45 65
Queen's Rise, Rich. BL46 75
Queen's Rd. E11 CF33 48
Queen's Rd. E13 CH37 58
Queen's Rd. E17 CD32 48
Queen's Rd. N3 BT30 38
Queens Rd. N9 CB27 39
Queen's Rd. N11 BX29 38
Queen's Rd. NW4 BQ32 46
Queens Rd. SE15 CB44 67
Queen's Rd. SW14 BN45 65
Queen's Rd. SW19 BR50 75
Queens Rd. W5 BL39 55
Queen's Rd. Bark. CM36 58
Queens Rd. Barn. BQ24 28
Queens Rd. Beck. CD51 87
Queens Rd. Berk. AQ12 7
Queen's Rd. Brom. CH51 88
Queen's Rd. Buck. H. CH27 40
Queens Rd. Chis. CL50 78
Queen's Rd. Croy. BY53 86
Queens Rd. Egh. AS49 72
Queen's Rd. Enf. CA24 30
Queens Rd. Epp. CR16 23
Queen's Rd. Erith CT43 69
Queens Rd. Felt. BC47 73
Queens Rd. Grav. DH48 81
Queens Rd. Guil. AR70 118
Queens Rd. Hayes BB39 53
Queen's Rd. Hamptn. BF49 74
Queen's Rd. Houns. BF45 64
Queens Rd. Ilf. CM34 49
Queen's Rd. Kings. on T. BM50 75
Queen's Rd. Loug. CK24 31
Queens Rd. Mitch. BT52 86
Phipps Bridge Rd.
Queen's Rd. Mord. BS52 86
Queens Rd. N. Mal. BO52 85
Queen's Rd. Rich. BL47 75
Queens Rd. Slou. AP40 52
Queens Rd. Slou. AQ44 62
Queen's Rd. Sthl. BE41 64
Queens Rd. Surb. BH53 84
Queen's Rd. Sutt. BS59 95
Queen's Rd. Tedd. BH50 74
Queen's Rd. Twick. BJ47 74
Queens Rd. Uxb. AX38 53
Queens Rd. Wal. Cr. CD20 21
Queen's Rd. Wall. BV56 95
Queens Rd. Wat. BD23 27
Queens Rd. Watt. BB56 92
Queen's Rd. Well. CO44 69
Queens Rd. West Dr. AY41 63
Queens Rd. Wey. AZ56 92
Queens Rd. Wind. AM42 61
Queens Rd. Wind. AO44 61
Queens Rd. Wok. AO62 100
Queen's Rd. W. E13 CH37 58
Queen's Row SE17 BZ43 4
Queen's Row SE17 BZ43 67
Queen's Sq. The
Hem. H. AY13 8
Queen's Ter. E13 CH37 58
Queen's Ter. NW8 BT37 1
Queen's Ter. NW8 BT37 56
Queen's Ter. Islw. BJ45 64
Queen's Ter. Wind. AO45 61
Queens, The Dr. Rick. AV26 34
Queensthorpe Rd. SE26 CC49 77
Queenstown Gdns. Rain. CT38 59
Queenstown Rd. SW8 BV45 66
Queen St. EC4 BZ40 4
Queen St. EC4 BZ40 57
Queen St. N17 CA29 39
Queen St. Bexh. CQ45 69
Queen St. Brwd. DB28 42
Queen St. Cher. AW54 83
Queen St. Croy. BZ55 87
Queen St. Erith CT43 69
Queen St. Grav. DG46 81
Queen St. Kings L. AW19 17
Queen St. Mayfair W1 BV40 3
Queen St. Mayfair W1 BV40 56
Queen St. Ong. LZ14 15
Queen St. Rom. CS32 50
Queen St. St. Alb. BG13 9
Queensville Rd. SW12 BW47 76
Queens Wk. E4 CF26 39
Green Wk.
Queen's Wk. NW9 BN34 46
Queen's Walk SW1 BW40 3
Queen's Wk. SW1 BW40 56
Queens Wk. W5 BK38 54
Queens Wk. Ashf. AX49 73
Queen's Wk. Har. BH31 45
Queen's Wk. Ruis. BD34 45
Queensway NW4 BQ32 46
Queensway W2 BS39 1
Queensway W2 BS40 56
Queensway, Croy. BX57 95
Queensway, Enf. CB24 30
Queen's Way, Felt. BD49 74
Queensway, Hat. BP12 10
Queensway, Hem. H. AX13 8
Queensway North, Cob. BD56 93
Beech Clo.
Queensway, Orp. CM53 88
Queens Way, Rad. BL19 19
Queensway, Red. BU70 121
Queensway, Sun. BC51 83
Queensway, Wal. Cr. CD20 21
Longcroft Dr.
Queensway, Walt. BD56 93
Queensway W. Wick. CG55 88
Queensway, Ong. CW16 24
Queensway, The Ger. Cr. AR31 43
Queenswell Av. N20 BU28 38
Queenswood Av. E17 CF30 39
Queenswood Av. Brwd. DE25 122
Queenswood Av. Hmptn. BF50 74
Queenswood Av. Houns. BE44 64
Queenswood Av. Th. Hth. BY53 86
Queenswood Av. Wall. BW56 95
Queenswood Ct. SW4 BX46 76
Queenswood Cres. Wat. BC20 17
Queenswood Gdns. E11 CH33 49
Queenswood Pk. N3 BR30 37
Queen's Wood Rd. N10 BV32 47
Queenswood Rd. SE23 CC48 77
Queenswood Rd. Sid. CN46 78
Queenswood Rd. Wok. AO63 100
Queen Victoria Av. Wem. BK36 54
Queen Victoria St. EC4 BY40 4
Queen Victoria St. EC4 BY40 56
Quemerford Rd. N7 BX35 47
Quendon Dr. Wal. Abb. CF20 21
Quentin Pl. SE13 CG45 68
Quentin Rd. SE13 CG45 68
Quentin Way, Vir. W. AQ52 82
Quenton Pl. SE13 CG45 68
Quen Way, Brwd. DE26 122
Quernmore Clo. Brom. CH50 78
Quernmore Rd. N4 BY32 47
Quernmore Rd. Brom. CH50 78
Querrin St. SW6 BT44 66
Quex Ms. NW6 BS37 56
Quex Rd. NW6 BS37 56
Quickbeams, Welw. G. C. BS6 5
Rowans
Quickberry Pl. Amer. AO23 25
Quickett St. E3 CE38 57
Quickley La. Rick. AU25 25
Quickley Rise, Rick. AU25 25
Quickmoor La. Kings L. AW20 17
Quick Pl. N1 BY37 2
Quick Pl. N1 BY36 56
Essex Rd.
Quick Rd. W4 BO42 65

Quicks Rd. SW19 BS50 76
Quick St. N1 BY37 2
Quick St. N1 BY37 56
Quickswood NW3 BU36 56
Quickwood Clo. Rick. AV25 25
Quiet Clo. Wey. AW56 92
Quiet Nook, Kes. CJ55 88
Quill Hall La. Amer. AP22 25
Quill Lane, SW15 BQ45 65
Cardinal Place
Quilot, The Watt. BB56 92
Quilp St. SE1 BZ41 4
Quilp St. SE1 BZ41 67
Redcross Way
Quilter Gdns. Orp. CP54 89
Quilter Rd. Orp. CP54 89
Quilter St. E2 CA38 2
Quilter St. E2 CA38 57
Quinbrookes, Slou. AR39 52
Quinces Cft. Hem. H. AW12 8
Quinta Dr. Barn. BP25 28
Quinton Av. SW20 BR51 85
Quinton Clo. Beck. CF52 87
Quinton Clo. Wall. BV56 95
Quinton Rd. Surb. BJ54 84
Quinton St. SW18 BT48 76
Quintrol Clo. Wok. AQ62 100
Quixley St. SW18 CF40 57
Quorn Rd. SE22 CA45 67
Rabbit Row W8 BS40 56
Kensington Mall
Rabbits Rd. E12 CK35 49
Rabbits Rd. S. Dnth. CZ51 90
Rabbs Mill, Uxb. AX37 53
Rabies Heath Rd. Red. CA70 114
Raby Rd. N. Mal. BN52 85
Raby St. E14 CD39 57
Raccoon Way, Houns. BD44 64
Rachels Way, Chesh. AO20 16
Cresswell Rd.
Rack Rd. W3 BM41 65
Racquet Ct. EC4 BY39 56
Fleet St.
Racton Rd. SW6 BS43 66
Radbourne Av. W5 BK42 64
Radbourne Clo. E5 CC35 48
Glyn Rd.
Radbourne Cres. E17 CF31 48
Radbourne Rd. SW12 BW47 76
Radburn Clo. Harl. CO13 14
Radcliffe Av. NW10 BP37 55
Radcliffe Av. Enf. BZ23 30
Radcliffe Gdns. Cars. BU57 95
Radcliffe Path SW8 BW44 66
St. Rule St.
Radcliffe Rd. N21 BY26 38
Radcliffe Rd. Croy. CA55 87
Radcliffe Rd. Har. BJ30 36
Radcliffe Sq. SW15 BQ46 75
Radcliffe Way, Nthlt. BD38 54
Radcot Ave. Slou. AU41 62
Radcot St. SE11 BY42 4
Radcot St. SE11 BY42 66
Raddington Rd. W10 BR39 55
Radfield Way, Sid. CM47 78
Radford Rd. SE13 CF46 77
Radipole Rd. SW6 BR44 65
Radland Rd. E16 CG39 58
Radlett Av. SE26 CB48 77
Radlett Park Rd. Rad. BJ20 18
Radlett Pl. NW8 BU37 1
Radlett Pl. NW8 BU37 56
Radlett Rd. Rad. BK20 18
Radlett Rd. Rad. BK21 27
Radlett Rd. Rad. BL20 19
Radlett Rd. St. Alb. BH18 18
Radlett Rd. Wat. BD24 27
Radley Av. Ilf. CO35 50
Radley Gdns. Har. BL31 46
Radley La. E18 CH30 40
Radley Ms. W8 BS41 66
Radley Rd. N17 CA30 39
Radleys Mead. Dag. CR36 59
Radix Rd. E10 CE33 48
Radnor Av. Har. BH32 45
Radnor Av. Well. CO46 79
Radnor Clo. Chis. CN50 88
Homewood Cres.
Radnor Clo. Mitch. BX52 86
Radnor Ct. Red. BU70 121
Linkfield St.
Radnor Cres. Ilf. CK32 49
Radnor Gdns. Enf. CA23 30
Radnor Gdns. Twick. BH48 74
Radnor Gro. Uxb. AZ37 53
Charnwood Rd.
Radnor Ho. Twick. BJ48 74
Radnor Ms. W2 BT39 1
Radnor Ms. W2 BT39 56
Radnor Pl. W2 BT39 1
Radnor Pl. W2 BU39 56
Radnor Rd. NW6 BR37 55
Radnor Rd. SE15 CB43 67
Radnor Rd. Har. BG32 45
Radnor Rd. Twick. BH47 74
Radnor Rd. Wey. AZ55 83
Radnor St. EC1 BZ38 2
Radnor St. EC1 BZ38 57
Radnor Ter. SW8 BX43 66
South Lambeth Rd.
Radnor Ter. W14 BR42 65
Radnor Wk. SW3 BU42 3
Radnor Wk. SW3 BU42 66
Radnor Wk. Croy. CD53 87
Radnor Way NW10 BM38 55
Radnor Way, Slou. AS42 62
Radstock Av. Har. BJ31 45
Radstock St. SW11 BU43 66
Parkgate Rd.
Radstock Way, Red. BW67 113
Radstock Way, Red. BX68 113
Radstone Ct. Wok. AS62 100
Hill Vw. Rd.
Raebarn Gdns. Barn. BP25 28
Raeburn Av. Dart. CU46 79
Raeburn Av. Surb. BM54 85
Raeburn Clo. NW11 BS32 47
Raeburn Clo. Kings. on T. BK50 74
Lower Teddington Rd.
Raeburn Ho. Kings. on T. BK50 74
Raeburn Rd. Edg. BM30 37
Raeburn Rd. Hayes BA37 53
Raeburn Rd. Sid. CN46 78
Raeburn St. SW2 BX45 66
Rafford Way, Brom. CH51 88
Raft Rd. SW18 BS46 76
Ragged Hall La. St. Alb. BE15 9
Ragge Way, Sev. CW63 108
Landway, The
Raggleswood, Chis. CL51 88
Rag Hill Rd. W. J64 106
Raglan Av. Wal. Cr. CC20 21
Raglan Clo. Reig. BT69 121
Raglan Ct. Sth. Croy. BY56 95
Raglan Ct. Wem. BL35 46
Raglan Gdns. Wat. BC26 35
Raglan Rd. E17 CF32 48
Raglan Rd. SE18 CL42 68
Raglan Rd. Belv. CQ42 69
Raglan Rd. Brom. CJ52 88
Raglan Rd. Enf. CA26 39
Raglan Rd. Reig. BS69 121
Raglan Rd. Wok. AP62 100
Raglan St. NW5 BV36 56
Raglan Ter. Har. BF35 45
Stroud Gate
Raglan Way. Nthlt. BG36 54
Ragley Clo. W3 BM41 65
Avenue Rd.
Rags La. Wal. Cr. CA17 21
Ragstone Rd. Slou. AO41 61
Rahn Rd. Epp. CN19 22
Rahn Rd. Epp. CO19 23
Raider Clo. Rom. CR30 41
Raikes La. Dor. BC74 119
Railey Ms. NW5 BW35 47
Leverton St.
Railpit La. Warl. CG61 106
Railshed Rd. Twick. BJ45 64
St. Margaret's Rd.
Railston Way, Wat. BD27 36
Railton Rd. SE24 BY45 66
Railway App. SE1 BZ40 4
Railway App. SE1 BZ40 57
Railway App. Cheam BR57 94
Railway App. Cher. AV54 82
Railway App. Har. BH31 45
Railway App. Pur. BW61 104
Railway App. Twick. BJ47 74
Railway App. Wall. BV56 95
Railway Arches SE8 CE43 67
Deptford High St.
Railway Av. SE16 CC41 67
Railway Cotts. Ilf. CN29 40
Railway Cotts. St. Alb. BH10 9
Railway Ms. W10 BR39 55
Ladbroke Gro.
Railway Pass. Tedd. BJ50 74
Clarence Rd.
Railway Pl. EC3 CA40 4
Railway Pl. EC3 CA40 57
Fenchurch St.
Railway Pl. SW19 BR50 75
Hartfield Rd.
Railway Pl. Belv. CR41 69
Railway Rd. Tedd. BH49 74
Railway Side SW13 BO45 65
White Hart La.
Railway Sq. Brwd. DB27 42
Railway St. N1 BX37 2
Railway St. N1 BX37 56
Railway St. Grav. DD46 81
Railway St. Rom. CP33 50
Railway Ter. SE13 CE46 77
Railway Ter. Felt. BC47 73
Railway Ter. Slou. AP40 52
Railway Ter. Stai. AV49 72
Rainborough Clo. NW10 BN36 55
Rainbow Ct. Wok. AP61 100
Langmans Way
Rainbow St. SE5 CA43 67
Raine St. E1 CB40 57
Rainham Clo. SE9 CN46 78
Rainham Clo. SW11 BU46 76
Rainham Rd. NW10 BQ38 55
Rainham Rd. Rain. CT36 59
Rainham Rd. N. Dag. CR34 50
Rainham Rd. S. Dag. CR35 50
Rainhill Way E3 CE38 57
Rainsborough Av. SE8 CD42 67
Rainsford Rd. NW10 BM38 55
Rainsford St. W2 BU39 1
Rainsford St. W2 BU39 56
Sale Pl.
Rainsford Way, Horn. CU33 50
Rainton Rd. SE7 CH42 68
Rainville Rd. W6 BQ43 65
Raisins Hill, Pnr. BC31 44
Raith Av. N14 BW27 38
Raleana Rd. E14 CF40 57
Raleigh Av. Hayes BC39 53
Raleigh Av. Wall. BW56 95
Raleigh Clo. N13 BZ27 39
Raleigh Clo. NW4 BQ32 46
Raleigh Clo. Pnr. BD33 45
Raleigh Clo. Ruis. BB34 44
Ralegh Ct. Beck. CE51 87
Raleigh Ct. Stai. AW49 73
Leacroft
Raleigh Ct. Wall. BV57 95
Raleigh Dr. N20 BU27 38
Raleigh Dr. Esher BG56 93
Raleigh Dr. Surb. BN54 85
Raleigh Gdns. Mitch. BU51 86
Raleigh Rd. N8 BY31 47
Raleigh Rd. SE20 CC50 77
Raleigh Rd. Enf. BZ24 30
Raleigh Rd. Felt. BB48 73
Raleigh Rd. Rich. BL45 65
Raleigh Rd. Sthl. BE42 64
Raleigh St. N1 BY37 2
Raleigh St. N1 BY37 56
Raleigh Way N14 BW26 38
Raleigh Way, Felt BD49 74
Ralliwood Rd. Ash. BM63 103
Ralph St. SE1 BZ41 4
Ralph St. SE1 BZ41 67
Ralston St. SW3 BU42 3
Ralston St. SW3 BU42 66
Tedworth Sq.
Rama Ct. Har. BH34 45
Ramaney Dr. Enf. CD22 30
Rambler Clo. SW16 BW49 76
Rambler La. Slou. AR41 62
Ramblings, The E4 CF28 39
Ram Gorse, Harl. CL10 6
Ramilles Clo. SW2 BX46 76
Ramillies Pl. W1 BW39 1
Ramillies St. W1 BW39 1
Ramilles St. W1 BW39 56
Gt. Marlborough St.
Ramillies Pl. W1 BW39 56
Ramillies Rd. NW7 BO27 37
Ramillies Rd. W4 BN42 65
Ramillies Rd. Sid. CO46 79
Ramorne Clo. Walt. BE56 93
Rampart St. E1 CB39 57
Commercial Rd.
Rampayne St. SW1 BW42 3
Rampayne St. SW1 BW42 66
Ram Pl. E9 CC36 57
Chatham Pl.
Rampton Clo. E4 CE27 39
Ramsay Gdns. Rom. CV30 42
Ramsay Rd. E7 CG35 49
Ramsay Rd. W3 BN41 65
Ramsbury Rd. St. Alb. BH14 9
Ramscroft Clo. N9 CA26 39
Ramsdale Rd. SW17 BV49 76
Ramsden Clo. Orp. CP54 89
Ramsden Rd.
Ramsden Dr. Rom. CR29 41
Ramsden Rd. N11 BU28 38
Ramsden Rd. SW12 BV46 76
Ramsden Rd. Erith CS43 69
Ramsden Rd. Orp. CO54 89
Ramsey Clo. Brox. CD14 12
Ramsey Clo. Har. BG35 45
Ramsey Clo. Hat. BT17 20
Ramsey Clo. St. Alb. BJ14 9
Ramsey Ct. N8 BW32 47
Ramsey Rd. NW9 BO32 46
Broadway, The
Ramsey Rd. Th. Hth. BX53 86
Ramsey St. E2 CB38 2
Ramsey St. E2 CB38 57
Ramsey Wk. N1 BZ36 57
Marquess Est.
Ramsey Way N14 BW26 38
Windsor Ct.
Ramsgate St. E8 CA36 57
Ramsgill App. Ilf. CN31 49
Ramsgill Dr. Ilf. CN32 49
Rams Gro. Rom. CQ31 50
Ramus Wd. Av. Orp. CN56 97
Rancliffe Gdns. SE9 CK45 68
Rancliffe Rd. E6 CK38 58
Randal Cres. Reig. BS71 121
Randall Av. NW2 BO34 46
Randall Clo. SW11 BU44 66
Randall Clo. Erith CS43 69
Randall Clo. Slou. AS42 62
Randall Dr. Horn. CU35 51
Randall Pl. SE10 CF43 67
Randall Rd. SE11 BX42 4
Randall Rd. SE11 BX42 66
Randall Rd. Rom. CT32 50
Randall Row SE11 BX42 4
Randall Row. SE11 BX42 66
Randall Cres. Lthd. BJ63 102
Randalls Dr. Brwd. DF25 122
Randalls Farm La. Lthd. BJ63 102
Randall's Mkt. E14 CE39 57
Ricardo St.
Randalls Pk. Av. Lthd. BJ63 102
Randalls Ride, Hem. H. AX12 8
Randalls Rd. Lthd. BH63 102
Randalls Rode, Hem. H. AX12 8
Randalls Way, Lthd. BJ64 102
Randell Hill Rd. Sev. DC61 108
Battlefields Rd.
Randell's Rd. N1 BX37 2
Randell's Rd. N1 BX37 56
Randle Rd. Rich. BK49 74
Randlesdown Gdns. SE6 CE48 77
Randlesdown Rd. SE6 CE49 77
Randles La. Sev. CP60 98
Randolph App. E16 CJ39 58
Baxter Rd.
Randolph Av. W9 BS37 1
Randolph Av. W9 BT38 56
Randolph Clo. Bexh. CS45 69
Randolph Clo. Cob. BF61 102
Randolph Clo. Kings. on T. BN49 75
Randolph Clo. Slou. AS42 62
Randolph Clo. Wok. AP62 100
Randolph Cres. W9 BT38 1
Randolph Cres. W9 BT38 56
Randolph Gdns. NW6 BS37 56
Randolph Ms. W9 BT38 1
Randolph Ms. W9 BT38 56
Randolph Rd. E17 CE32 48
Randolph Rd. W9 BT38 1
Randolph Rd. W9 BT38 56
Randolph Rd. Epsom BO60 94
Randolph Rd. Sthl. BE41 64
Randolph St. NW1 BW36 56
Randon Clo. Har. BF30 36
Ranelagh Av. SW6 BR45 65
Ranelagh Av. SW13 BP44 65
Ranelagh Br. W2 BS39 1
Ranelagh Br. W2 BS40 56
Ranelagh Clo. Edg. BM28 37
Ranelagh Dr. Edg. BM28 37
Ranelagh Dr. Twick. BJ45 64
Ranelagh Est. SW15 BQ44 65
Ranelagh Gdns. E11 CJ32 49
Ranelagh Gdns. SW6 BR45 65
Ranelagh Gdns. W4 BN43 65
Grove Pk. Gdns.
Ranelagh Gdns. Grav. DF47 81
Ranelagh Gdns. Ilf. CK33 49
Ranelagh Gro. SW1 BV42 3
Ranelagh Gro. SW1 BV42 66
Ranelagh Mews W5 BK41 64
Ranelagh Rd.
Ranelagh Pl. N. Mal. BO53 85
Ranelagh Rd. E6 CL37 58
Ranelagh Rd. E11 CG35 49
Ranelagh Rd. E15 CG37 58
Ranelagh Rd. N17 CA31 48
Ranelagh Rd. N22 BX30 38
Ranelagh Rd. NW10 BO37 55
Ranelagh Rd. SW1 BW42 66
Lupus St.
Ranelagh Rd. W5 BK41 64
Ranelagh Rd. Hem. H. AZ13 8
Ranelagh Rd. Red. BU70 121
Ranelagh Rd. Sthl. BD40 54
Ranelagh Rd. Wem. BK35 45
Ranelagh St. SW1 BW42 3
Ranfurly Rd. Sutt. BS55 86
Rangefield Rd. Brom. CG49 78
Rangemoor Rd. N15 CA32 48
Range Rd. Grav. DJ47 81
Rangers Rd. E4 CG26 40
Rangers Sq. SE10 CF44 67
Range Way, Shep. AZ54 83
Rangoon St. EC3 CA39 2
Rangoon St. EC3 CA39 57
Northumberland Alley
Rankin Clo. NW9 BO31 46
Ranleigh Gdns. Bexh. CQ43 69
Ranmere Clo. Red. BV69 121
Ranmere St. SW12 BV47 76
Ranmoor Clo. Har. BG31 45
Ranmoor Gdns. Har. BG31 45
Ranmore Av. Croy. CA55 87
Ranmore Comm. Rd. Dor. BD70 119
Ranmore Path, Orp. CO52 89
Ranmore Rd. Couls. BX62 104
Ranmore Rd. Dor. BG70 119
Ranmore Rd. Dor. BJ71 119
Ranmore Rd. Sutt. BQ58 94
Rannoch Rd. W6 BQ43 65
Rannoch Wk. Hem. H. AX11 8
Rannock Dr. NW9 BN33 46
Ranskill Rd. Borwd. BM23 28
Ransom Rd. SE7 CJ42 68
Ranston St. NW1 BU39 1
Ranston St. NW1 BU39 56
Rant Meadow, Hem. H. AZ14 8
Ranulf Rd. NW2 BR35 46
Ranworth Clo. Erith CT44 69
Ranworth Clo. Hem. H. AX14 8
Ranworth Rd. N9 CC27 39
Ranworth Rd. Hem. H. AX14 8
Raans Rd. Amer. AP22 25
Raphael Av. Til. DG44 71
Raphael Av. Rom. CT30 41
Raphael Rd. Grav. DH47 81
Raphael St. SW7 BU41 3
Raphael St. SW7 BU41 66
Rapier Clo. Grays. CW42 70
Rasher Mead. Dor. BK73 119
Rashleigh St. SW8 BV44 66
Rashleigh Way, Hort. K. CY52 90
Rasper Rd. N20 BT27 38
Rastell Av. SW2 BW48 76
Ratcliffe Cross St. E1 CC39 57
Ratcliffe Gro. EC1 BZ38 2
Ratcliffe La. E14 CD39 57
Ratcliffe Rd. Uxb. AX38 53
Ratcliff Orchard E1 CC40 57
Ratcliff Rd. E7 CJ35 49
Rathbone Mkt. E16 CG39 58
Rathbone Pl. W1 BW39 1
Rathbone Pl. W1 BW39 56
Rathbone St. E16 CG39 58
Rathbone St. W1 BW39 1
Rathbone St. W1 BW39 56
Rathcoole Av. N8 BX31 47
Rathcoole Gdns. N8 BX32 47
Rathfen Rd. SE6 CD47 77
Rathgar Av. W13 BJ40 54
Rathgar Clo. N3 BR30 37
Rathgar Clo. Red. BV73 121
Rathlin, Hem. H. AZ14 8
Rathlin Wk. N1 BZ36 57
Marquess Est.
Rathmell Dr. SW4 BW46 76
Rathmore Rd. SE7 CH42 68
Ratmore Rd. Wal. Abb. CG20 22
Rat's La. Loug. CH22 31
Rattray Rd. SW2 BY45 66
Ratty's La. Hodd. CF12 12
Raul Rd. SE15 CB44 67
Raveley St. NW5 BW35 47
Ravel Gdns. S. Ock. CW39 60
Ravel Rd. S. Ock. CW39 60
Raven Clo. Rick. AX26 35
Raven Ct. Hat. BP13 10
Ravendale Rd. Sun. BB51 83
Ravenet St. SW11 BV44 66
Ravenfield Rd. SW17 BU48 76
Ravenfield Rd. Welw. G. C. BR8 5
Ravenhill Rd. E13 CJ37 58
Ravenna Rd. SW15 BQ45 65
Ravenor Pk. Rd. Grnf. BF38 54
Raven Rd. E18 CJ30 40
Raven Row E1 CB39 57
Ravensbourne Av. Brom. CF50 77
Ravensbourne Av. Ilf. CL30 40
Ravensbourne Av. Stai. AY47 73
Ravensbourne Cres. SE6 CD47 77
Ravensbourne Est. Brom. CF49 77
Ravensbourne Gdns. W13 BJ39 54
Ravensbourne Gdns. Ilf. CL30 40
Ravensbourne Pk. SE6 CD47 77
Ravensbourne Pk.
Cres. SE6 CD47 77
Ravensbourne Rd. SE6 CD47 77
Ravensbourne Rd. Brom. CH52 88
Ravensbourne Rd. Dart. CU45 69
Ravensbourne Rd. Twick. BK46 74
Ravensbury Av. Mord. BT53 86
Ravensbury Gro. Mitch. BT52 86
Ravensbury La. Mitch. BT52 86
Ravensbury Path, Mitch. BT52 86
Ravensbury Rd. SW18 BS48 76
Ravensbury Rd. Orp. CN52 88
Ravenscar Rd. Brom. CG49 78
Ravenscar Rd. Surb. BL55 85
Ravens Clo. Brom. CG51 88
Ravens Clo. Enf. CA23 30
Ravens Clo. Red. BU70 121
Ravens Clo. Wok. AO61 100
Ravens Ct. Sun. BB51 83
Ravenscourt Av. W6 BP42 65
Ravenscourt Clo. Horn. CW34 51
Ravenscourt Dr.
Ravens Ct. Clo. Ruis. BA33 44
Ravenscourt Dr. Horn. CW34 51
Ravenscourt Gdns. W6 BP42 65
Ravenscourt Gro. Horn. CW34 51
Ravenscourt Pk. W6 BP42 65
Ravenscourt Pl. W6 BP42 65
King St.
Ravenscourt Rd. W6 BP41 65
Ravenscourt Rd. Orp. CO51 89
Ravenscourt Sq. W6 BP41 65
Ravenscraig Rd. N11 BW28 38
Ravenscroft Av. NW11 BR33 46
Ravenscroft Av. Wem. BL33 46
Ravenscroft Clo. E16 CH39 58
Ravenscroft Pk. Barn. BQ24 28
Ravenscroft Pk. Rd. Barn. BQ24 28
Ravenscroft Rd. E16 CG39 58
Ravenscroft Rd. W4 BN42 65
Ravenscroft Rd. Beck. CC51 87
Ravenscroft Rd. Wey. BA59 92
Ravenscroft St. E2 CA37 2
Ravenscroft St. E2 CA37 57
Ravensdale Av. N12 BT28 38
Ravensdale Gdns. SE19 BZ50 77
Ravensdale Rd. N16 CA33 48
Ravensdale Rd. Houns. BE45 64
Ravens Dell, Hem. H. AV13 7
Ravensdon St. SE11 BY42 4
Ravensdon St. SE11 BY42 66
Ravensfield, Slou. AR41 62
Ravensfield St. SE11 BY42 66
Ravensfield Clo. Dag. CP35 50
Ravensfield Gdns. Epsom BO56 94
Ravenshaw St. NW6 BR35 46
Ravensfield St. NW6 BR35 46
Ravenshead Clo. Sth. Croy. CC59 96
Ravenshill, Chis. CL51 88
Ravenshurst Av. NW4 BQ31 46
Ravens La. Berk. AR13 7
Ravenslea Rd. SW12 BU47 76
Ravens Mead. Ger. Cr. AS28 34
Ravensmead Rd. Brom. CF50 77
Ravensmede Way W4 BO42 65
Chiswick High Rd.
Ravensmere, Epp. CO19 23
Ravenstone Rd. N8 BY31 47
Ravenstone Rd. NW9 BO32 46
Broadway, The
Ravenstone St. SW12 BV47 76
Ravens Way SE12 CH46 78
Ravenswold, Ken. BZ61 105
Ravenswood, Bex. CQ47 79
Ravenswood, Ken. BZ57 96
Ravenswood Av. Surb. BL55 85
Ravenswood Av. W. Wick. CF54 87
Ravenswood Clo. Croy. BY55 86
Ravenswood Rd.
Ravenswood Clo. Rom. CR28 41
Ravenswood Ct.
Kings. on T. BN50 75
Ranvenswood Ct. Wok. AS62 100
Hill Vw. Rd.
Ravenswood Cres. Har. BE34 45
Ravenswood Cres.
W. Wick. CF54 87
Ravenswood Gdns. Islw. BH44 64
Ravenswood Pk. Nthwd. BC29 35
Ravenswood Rd. E17 CE31 48
Ravenswood Rd. SW12 BV47 76
Ravenswood Rd. Croy. BY55 86
Ravenswood Rd. NW10 BP38 55
Ravenswood Rd. SE9 CK48 78
Ravent Rd. SE11 BX42 4
Ravent Rd. SE11 BX42 66
Ravey St. EC2 CA38 2
Ravey St. EC2 CA38 57
Ravine Gro. SE18 CN43 68
Rawcester Clo. SW18 BR47 75
Rawdon Dr. Hodd. CE12 12
Rawlings Clo. Orp. CN56 97
Rawlings La. Beac. AO27 34
Rawlings St. SW3 BU42 3
Rawlings St. SW3 BU42 66
Rawlins Clo. Sth. Croy. CD57 96
Rawnsley Av. Mitch. BU53 86
Rawreth Wk. N1 BZ37 57
Rasire St.
Rawson St. SW11 BV44 66
Despard Av.
Rawstone Wk. E13 CH37 58
Rawstorne Pl. EC1 BY38 2
Rawstorne St.
Rawstorne Pl. EC1 BY38 56
Rawstorne St.
Rawstorne St. EC1 BY38 2
Rawstorne St. EC1 BY38 56
Raybarn Rd. Hem. H. AW12 8
Rayburn Rd. Horn. CX33 51
Raydean Rd. Barn. BS25 29
Raydon Rd. Wal. Cr. CC19 21
Theobalds La.
Raydons Gdns. Dag. CQ35 50
Raydons Rd. Dag. CQ35 50
Raydon St. N19 BV34 47
Rayfield, Epp. CN18 22
Ray Field, Welw. G. C. BQ6 5
Rayfield Clo. Brom. CK53 88
Rayford Av. SE12 CG47 78
Rayford Clo. Dart. CV46 80
Ray Gdns. Bark. CO37 59
Ray Gdns. Stan. BJ28 36
Rayleas Clo. SE18 CL44 68
Rayleigh Av. Tedd. BH50 74
Rayleigh Clo. Brwd. DE25 122
Rayleigh Ct. N22 BZ30 39
Rayleigh Ct. Kings. on T. BM51 85
Cambridge Rd.
Rayleigh Rise, Sth. Croy. CA57 96

Rayleigh Rd. N13 BZ27 39
Rayleigh Rd. SW19 BR51 85
Rayleigh Rd. Brwd. DD25 122
Rayleigh Rd. Wdf. Grn. CJ29 40
Rayley La. Epp. CQ14 14
Ray Lodge Rd. Wdf. Grn. CJ29 40
Raymead NW4 BQ31 46
Raymead Av. Th. Hth. BY53 86
Raymead Clo. Loug. CM25 31
Raymead Clo. Lthd. BH64 102
Raymead Way, Lthd. BH64 102
Raymer Ct. St. Alb. BH13 9
Raymer Clo.
Raymere Gdns. SE18 CM43 68
Raymond Av. E18 CG31 49
Raymond Av. W13 BJ41 64
Raymond Bldgs. WC1 BX39 2
Raymond Bldgs. WC1 BX39 56
Raymond Clo. SE26 CC49 77
Raymond Clo. Slou. AV44 62
Raymond Cres. Guil. AP71 118
Raymond Gdns. Chig. CO27 41
Raymond Rd. E13 CJ36 58
Raymond Rd. SW19 BR50 75
Raymond Rd. Beck. CD52 87
Raymond Rd. Ilf. CM33 49
Raymond Rd. Slou. AT42 62
Raymonds Clo. Welw. G. C. BR9 5
Raymonds Plain, Welw. G. C. BR9 5
Raymond Way, Esher BJ57 93
Raymouth Rd. SE16 CB42 67
Rayne Ct. E18 CG31 49
Rayner's Ct. Har. BF33 45
Rayners Cres. Nthlt. BC38 53
Rayners Gdns. Nthlt. BC38 53
Rayner's La. Har. BF33 45
Rayners La. Pnr. BE32 45
Rayners Rd. SW15 BQ46 75
Rayner St. E9 CC36 57
Raynes Av. E11 CJ33 49
Raynham Av. N18 CB29 39
Raynham Rd. N18 CB28 39
Raynham Rd. W6 BP42 65
Raynham Ter. N18 CB28 39
Raynor Clo. Sthl. BE40 54
Raynors Clo. Wem. BK35 45
Raynton Clo. Har. BE33 45
Raynton Clo. Hayes BB38 53
Raynton Dr. Hayes BB38 53
Raynton Dr. Hayes BC38 53
Raynton Rd. Enf. CC22 30
Ray Rd. E. Mol. BF53 84
Rays Av. Wind. AM43 61
Rays Av. N18 CC28 39
Rays Rd. N18 CB28 39
Ray St. EC1 BY38 2
Ray St. EC1 BY38 56
Ray Wk. N7 BX34 47
Andover Est.
Ray Wk. N7 BX34 47
Briset Way
Raywood St. SW8 BV44 66
Read Ct. Wal. Abb. CH20 22
Winters Way
Readens, The Bans. BU61 104
Readgold St. W11 BQ40 55
Reading Arch Rd. Red. BU70 121
Reading La. E8 CB36 57
Reading Rd. Nthlt. BF35 45
Reading Rd. Sutt. BT56 95
Readings, The Harl. CN12 13
Readings, The Rick. AV24 25
Reading Way NW7 BR28 37
Read Rd. Ash. BK62 102
Reads Rest La. Tad. BS63 104
Read Way, Grav. DH49 81
Reardon Path E1 CB40 57
Reardon St. E1 CB40 57
Reaston St. SE14 CC43 67
Rebble Rd. Swans. DC46 81
Reckinham Rd. Guil. AQ69 118
Reckitt Rd. W4 BO42 65
Record St. SE15 CC43 67
Recovery St. SW17 BU49 76
Recreation Av. Rom. CS32 50
Recreation Av. Rom. CW30 42
Recreation Rd. SE26 CC49 77
Recreation Rd. Brom. CG51 88
Recreation Rd. Guil. AR70 118
Recreation Rd. Sthl. BE42 64
Recreation Way, Mitch. BW52 86
Rector St. N1 BZ37 2
Rector St. N1 BZ37 57
Rectory Chase, Brwd. DB22 33
Rectory Chase, Brwd. DB31 51
Rectory Chase, Brwd. DC31 123
Rectory Clo. E4 CE27 39
Brindwood Rd.
Rectory Clo. N3 BR30 37
Rectory Clo. Ash. BL63 103
Rectory Clo. Dart. CT45 69
Rectory Clo. Guil. AU69 118
Rectory Clo. Hat. BU12 11
Rectory Clo. Shep. AZ52 83
Rectory Clo. Sid. CO49 79
Rectory Clo. Stan. BJ28 36
Rectory Clo. Surb. BK54 84
Rectory Clo. Wey. AY60 92
Rectory Clo. Wind. AN44 61
Rectory Cres. E11 CJ32 49
Rectory Field, Harl. CL12 13
Rectory Field Cres. SE7 CJ43 68
Rectory Gdns. N8 BX31 47
Rectory Gdns. SW4 BW45 66
Rectory Gro.
Rectory Gdns. Hayes BA42 63
Rectory Gdns. Nthlt. BE37 54
Rectory Gdns. Upmin. CZ34 51
Rectory Grn. Beck. CD51 87
Rectory Grn. La. Bet. BO69 120
Rectory Gro. SW4 BW45 66
Rectory Gro. Croy. BY55 86
Rectory Gro. Hamptn. BE49 74
Rectory La. SW17 BV50 76
Rectory La. Ash. BL62 103
Rectory La. Bans. BU60 95
Rectory La. Berk. AR13 7
Rectory La. Edg. BM29 37
Rectory La. Grays. DE41 71
Rectory La. Kings L. AZ17 17
Rectory La. Loug. CL23 31
Rectory La. Lthd. BE66 111
Rectory La. Pot. B. BN19 19
Rectory La. Rad. BM19 19
Rectory La. Rick. AX26 35
Rectory La. Sev. CV66 117
Rectory La. Sev. BD64 108
Rectory La. Sid. CO49 79
Rectory La. Stan. BJ28 36
Rectory La. Surb. BJ54 84
Rectory La. Wall. BW55 86
Rectory La. West. CP65 107
Rectory La. Wey. AY60 92
Rectory Mead. Grav. DD50 81
Rectory Pk. Sth. Croy. CA60 96
Rectory Pk. Av. Nthlt. BE38 54
Rectory Pl. SE18 CL42 68
Rectory Rd. E12 CK35 49
Rectory Rd. E17 CE31 48
Rectory Rd. N16 CA34 48
Rectory Rd. SW13 BP44 65
Rectory Rd. W3 BM40 55
Rectory Rd. Beck. CE51 87
Rectory Rd. Couls. BS66 113
Rectory Rd. Dag. CR36 59
Rectory Rd. Green. CZ46 80
Church Rd.
Rectory Rd. Hayes BC39 53
Rectory Rd. Houns. BC44 63
Rectory Rd. Kes. CJ57 97
Rectory Rd. Rick. AX26 35
Rectory Rd. Sthl. BE41 64
Rectory Rd. Sutt. BS55 86
Rectory Rd. Swans. DC47 81
Rectory Rd. Til. DH43 71
Rectory Rd. Welw. G. C. BP6 5
Rectory Rd. West. CK65 106
Rectory Sq. E1 CC39 57
Rectory Way, Uxb. AZ34 44
Rectory Wood, Harl. CM10 6
Reculver Ms. N18 CB28 39
Lyndhurst Rd.
Reculver Rd. SE16 CC42 67
Redan Pl. W2 BS39 1
Redan Pl. W2 BS40 56
Redan St. W14 BQ41 65
Redan Ter. SE5 BZ44 67
Flaxman Rd.
Redberry Gro. SE26 CC48 77
Redbourne Av. N3 BS30 38
Redbourne Rd. Hem. H. AZ11 8
Redbourne Rd. St. Alb. BE12 9
Redbridge Gdns. SE5 CA44 67
Dalwood St.
Redbridge La. E. Ilf. CJ32 49
Redbridge La. W. E11 CH32 49
Red Bull Yd. EC4 BZ40 57
Upr. Thames St.
Redburn St. SW3 BU43 3
Redburn St. SW3 BU43 66
Redburn Ter. Enf. CC25 30
South St.
Redbury Clo. Rain. CV39 60
Redcar Clo. Nthlt. BF36 54
Redcar Rd. Rom. CW28 42
Redcar St. SE5 BZ43 67
Redcastle Clo. E1 CC40 57
Juniper St.
Red Cedars Rd. Orp. CN54 88
Redchurch St. E2 CA38 2
Redchurch St. E2 CA38 57
Redcliffe Clo. SW5 BS42 66
Redcliffe Gdns. SW10 BS42 3
Redcliffe Gdns. SW10 BS42 66
Redcliffe Gdns. Ilf. CL33 49
Redcliffe Ms. SW10 BS42 3
Redcliffe Ms. SW10 BS42 66
Redcliffe Pl. SW10 BT43 66
Redcliffe Rd. SW10 BT42 3
Redcliffe Rd. SW10 BT42 66
Redcliffe Sq. SW10 BS42 3
Redcliffe Sq. SW10 BS42 66
Redcliffe St. SW10 BS43 3
Redcliffe St. SW10 BS43 66
Redclose Av. Mord. BS53 86
Redclyffe Rd. E6 CJ37 58
Red Ct. Slou. AP40 52
Redcourt, Wok. AU61 100
Redcroft Rd. Sthl. BG40 54
Red Cross, Reig. BS70 121
Redcross Pl. SE1 BZ41 4
Redcross Pl. SE1 BZ41 67
Redcross Way
Redcross Way SE1 BZ41 4
Redcross Way SE1 BZ41 67
Reddea Ct. Rd. Rom. CW31 51
Redden Ct. Rd. Horn. CW31 51
Reddings, Hem. H. AY14 8
Reddings, Welw. G. C. BQ7 5
Reddings Av. Bush. BF25 27
Reddings Clo. NW7 BO28 37
Reddings, The Borwd. BL24 28
Red Rd.
Reddings, The NW7 BO27 37
Reddington Clo. Sth. Croy. CA58 96
Reddington Dr. Slou. AS42 62
Reddings Rd. SE15 CB43 67
Redditch Ct. Hem. H. AY11 8
Reddons Rd. Beck. CD50 77
Reddown Rd. Couls. BW62 104
Reddy Rd. Erith CT43 69
Rede Pl. W2 BS39 56
Redesdale Gdns. Islw. BJ43 64
Redesdale St. SW3 BU42 3
Redesdale St. SW3 BU42 66
Redfern Av. Twick. BF47 74
Redfern Clo. Uxb. AX37 53
Rockingham Clo.
Redfern Gdns. Rom. CV30 42
Redfern Rd. NW10 BO36 55
Redfern Rd. SE6 CF47 77
Brownhill Rd.
Redfield La. SW5 BS42 66
Redford Av. Couls. BV60 95
Redford Av. Th. Hth. BX52 86
Redford Av. Wall. BX57 95
Redford Rd. Wind. AL44 61
Redford Wk. N1 BZ37 57
Popham St.
Redford Way, Uxb. AX36 53
Redgate Dr. Brom. CH55 88
Redgate Ter. SW15 BQ46 75
Lytton Gro.
Redgrave Rd. SW15 BQ45 65
Redhall Clo. Hat. BO14 10
Redhall Dr. Hat. BO14 10
Red Hall La. Rick. AY23 26
Redheath Clo. Wat. BC20 17
Red Hill, Chis. CL49 78
Red Hill, Cob. BA61 101
Redhill, Uxb. AU33 43
Redhill Dr. Edg. BN30 37
Redhill Rd. Cob. AZ59 92
Redhill St. NW1 BV37 1
Redhill St. NW1 BV37 56
Redholm Vill. N16 BZ35 48
Winston Rd.
Red House La. Bexh. CP45 69
Red Ho. La. Walt. BC55 83
Red Ho. Rd. Croy. BW53 86
Redhouse Rd. West. CJ64 106
Redington Gdns. NW3 BS35 47
Redington Rd. NW3 BS35 47
Redlands, Couls. BX57 95
Redlands, Couls. BX61 104
Redlands Gdns. E. Mol. BE52 84
Redlands Rd. Enf. CD23 30
Redlands Rd. Sev. CT65 107
Redlands Way SW2 BX47 76
Red La. Dor. BL74 120
Red La. Esher BJ57 93
Red La. Oxt. CH69 115
Redlaw Way SE16 CB42 67
Bonamy Est. West, The
Redleaf Clo. Belv. CR43 69
Redleaves Av. Ashf. AZ50 73
Redlees Clo. Islw. BJ45 64
Red Lion Clo. Orp. CP53 89
Red Lion Ct. EC4 BY39 2
Red Lion Ct. EC4 BY39 56
Fleet St.
Red Lion Cres. Harl. CP12 14
Red Lion Hl. N2 BT30 38
Red Lion La. SE18 CL44 68
Red Lion La. Harl. CP12 14
Red Lion La. Rick. AW21 26
Red Lion La. Wok. AP58 91
Red Lion Rd. Surb. BL55 85
Red Lion Rd. Wok. AP58 91
Red Lion Row SE17 BZ43 67
Boundary La.
Red Lion Sq. WC1 BX39 2
Red Lion Sq. WC1 BX39 56
Red Lion Sq. Hmptn. BF51 84
Red Lion St. WC1 BX39 2
Red Lion St. WC1 BX39 56
Theobalds Rd.
Red Lion St. Rich. BK46 74
Red Lion Yd. Wat. BD24 27
Red Lo. Cres. Bex. CS48 79
Red Lo. Rd. Bex. CS48 79
Red Lodge Rd. W. Wick. CF54 87
Redmans La. Sev. CT57 98
Redman's Pl. Sev. CV66 117
Redman's Rd. E1 CC39 57
Redmead La. E1 CB40 4
Redmead La. E1 CB40 57
Redmead Rd. Hayes BB42 63
Redmore Rd. W6 BP42 65
Red Oak Clo. Orp. CL55 88
Red Oaks Mead. Epp. CM22 31
Red Pl. W1 BV40 3
Red Pl. W1 BV40 56
Park St.
Redpoll Way SE2 CP41 69
Maren Way
Redpoll Way, Belv. CP41 69
Maran Way
Red Post Hl. SE21 BZ45 67
Red Post Hl. SE24 BZ45 67
Redrick La. Harl. CN8 6
Redriffe Rd. E13 CG37 58
Redriff Est. SE16 CD41 67
Redriff Rd. SE16 CC41 67
Redriff Rd. Rom. CR30 41
Red Rd. Bet. BN69 120
Red Rd. Borwd. BL24 28
Red Rd. Brwd. DA28 42
Red Rose La. Ing. DC18 24
Redruth Clo. N22 BX29 38
Redruth Clo. Rom. CW28 42
Redruth Rd. Rom. CW28 42
Redruth Wk. Rom. CW28 42
Redstart Clo. Croy. CF58 96
Redstone Hill, Red. BV70 121
Redstone Hollow, Red. BV71 121
Redstone Mans. Red. BV70 121
Redstone Pk. Red. BV70 121
Redstone Rd. Red. BV71 121
Redston Rd. N8 BW31 47
Red St. Grav. DD50 81
Redvers Rd. N22 BY30 38
Redvers Rd. Warl. CC62 105
Redwald Rd. E5 CC35 48
Redway Dr. Twick. BG46 74
Redwell La. Sev. DA65 108
Red Willow, Harl. CK12 13
Redwing Clo. Croy. CC59 96
Redwing Clo. Sth. Croy. CC58 96
Redwing Ri. Guil. AU69 118
Redwood Ri. Guil. AU69 118
Redwood Clo. Guil. AU73 118
Redwood Clo. N14 BW26 38
The Vale
Redwood Clo. Ken. BZ60 96
Redwood Clo. Uxb. AZ37 53
Redwood Dr. Hem. H. AY14 8
Redwood Gdns. Chig. CO28 41
Red Wood Mt. Reig. BS69 121
Redwoods SW15 BP47 75
Alton Rd.
Reece Ms. SW7 BT42 3
Reece Ms. SW7 BT42 66
Reechfield Rd. Welw. G. C. BR9 5
Reedan Clo. St. Alb. BF18 18
Reed Av. Orp. CM55 88
Reed Clo. E16 CH39 58
Plymouth Rd.
Reed Clo. SE12 CH46 78
Reede Gdns. Dag. CR35 50
Reede Rd. Dag. CR36 59
Reede Way, Dag. CR36 59
Reedham Pk. Av. Pur. BY61 104
Reedham St. SE15 CB44 67
Reed Pl. NW1 BW36 56
Rochester Pl.
Reed Pond Wk. Rom. CT30 41
Reed Rd. N17 CA30 39
Reedsfield Rd. Ashf. AZ49 73
Reeds La. Ton. DC68 117
Reedworth St. SE11 BY42 4
Reedworth St. SE11 BY42 66
Reeham Clo. N15 CB31 48
Reenglass Rd. Stan. BK28 36
Rees Gdns. Croy. CA53 87
Reesland Clo. E12 CL35 49
Reesland Clo. E12 CL49 78
Rees Rd. Red. BU70 121
High St.
Rees St. N1 BZ37 2
Rees St. N1 BZ37 57
Reets Farm Clo. NW9 BO32 46
Reeve Rd. Maid. AG43 61
Reeve Rd. Reig. BT72 121
Reeves Av. NW9 BN33 46
Reeves Clo. Brwd. DA20 24
Reeves Corner, Brwd. BY55 86
Church St.
Reeves Cres. Swan. CS52 89
Reeves La. Harl. CJ13 13
Reeves Ms. W1 BV40 3
Reeves Ms. W1 BV40 56
Reeves Rd. E3 CE38 57
Reform Row N17 CA30 39
Reform St. SW11 BU44 66
Regal Clo. W5 BK39 54
Regal Cres. Wall. BV55 86
Prince Charles Way
Regal Ct. N18 CA28 39
Regal Field Clo. Guil. AP68 109
Regal La. NW1 BV37 1
Regent La. NW1 BV37 56
Regents Pk. Rd.
Regal Way, Harl. BK32 45
Regan Clo. Guil. AQ68 109
Regan Way N1 CA37 2
Regan Way N1 CA37 57
Regarder Rd. Chig. CO28 41
Regarth Av. Rom. CT32 50
Regency Clo. W5 BL39 55
Regency Clo. Chig. CM28 40
Regency Clo. Hamptn. BE49 74
Regency Ct. Brwd. DB27 42
High St.
Regency Dr. Wey. AV60 91
Regency Ms. NW10 BO36 55
High Rd.
Regency Mews, Islw. BH46 74
Regency St. SW1 BW42 3
Regency St. SW1 BW42 66
Regency Wk. Croy. CD53 87
Regency Way, Bexh. CP45 69
Regency Waye, Wok. AU61 100
Regent Av. N13 BY28 38
Regent Av. Uxb. AZ36 53
Regent Clo. Har. BL32 46
Regent Clo. Houns. BC44 63
Regent Clo. Wey. AX58 92
Regent Cres. Red. BU69 121
Linkfield La.
Regent Ho. Surb. BL53 85
Regency Pl. SW1 BW42 3
Regent Pl. W1 BW40 3
Regent Pl. W1 BW40 56
Warwick St.
Regent Pl. Croy. CA54 87
Regent Rd. SE24 BY46 76
Regent Rd. Epp. CN18 22
Regent Rd. Surb. BL53 85
Regents Av. N13 BY28 38
Regents Clo. Grays. DE41 71
Regents Clo. Rad. BJ20 18
Regents Clo. Sth. Croy. CA57 96
Regents Clo. Whyt. CA62 105
Regents Dr. Kes. CJ56 97
Regents Pk. Est. NW1 BV38 1
Regents Pk. Est. NW1 BV38 56
Regents Pk. Rd. N3 BR31 46
Regent's Pk. Rd. NW1 BU37 1
Regents Pk. Rd. NW1 BU37 56
Regent's Pk. Ter. NW1 BU37 1
Regents Pk. Ter. NW1 BV37 56
Oval Rd.
Regent Sq. E3 CE38 57
Regent Sq. WC1 BX38 2
Regent Sq. WC1 BX38 56
Regent Sq. Belv. CR42 69
Regents Row E8 CB37 57
Regents Row E8 CB37 57
Regent St. NW10 BQ38 55
Kilburn La.
Regent St. SW1 BW40 3
Regent St. SW1 BW40 56
Regent St. W1 BV39 1
Regent St. W1 BV39 56
Regent St. W4 BM42 65
Regent St. Wat. BC22 26
Regina Clo. Barn. BQ24 28
Reginald Rd. E7 CG36 58
Reginald Rd. SE8 CE43 67
Reginald Rd. Nthwd. BB30 35
Reginald Rd. Rom. CX30 42
Reginald Sq. SE8 CE43 67
Regina Rd. N4 BX33 47
Regina Rd. SE25 CB52 87
Regina Rd. W13 BJ40 54
Regina Rd. Sthl. BE42 64
Regis Way SE17 BY43 66
Regnart Bldgs. NW1 BW38 56
Euston St.
Reid Av. Cat. BZ64 105
Reid Clo. Pnr. BC31 44
Reidhaven Rd. SE18 CN42 68
Reid St. N1 BY37 56
Reigate Av. Sutt. BS55 86
Reigate Hill, Reig. BS68 113
Reigate Hill Clo. Reig. BS69 121
Reigate Hill Rd. Reig. BS70 121
Reigate Rd. Bet. BN70 120
Reigate Rd. Brom. CG48 78
Reigate Rd. Dor. BK71 119
Reigate Rd. Epsom BP58 94
Reigate Rd. Ilf. CN34 49
Reigate Rd. Lthd. BK65 102
Reigate Rd. Reig. BS70 121
Reigate Rd. Reig. BS74 121
Reigate Way, Wall. BX56 95
Reighton Rd. E5 CB34 48
Reinters Cotts. Rich. BK48 74
Relf Rd. SE15 CB45 67
Relinque Rd. SE26 CD49 77
Porthcawe Rd.
Relko Ct. Epsom BN59 94
Relko Gdns. Sutt. BT56 95
Sutton Gro.
Rembrandt Dr. Grav. DE48 81
Rembrandt Rd. SE13 CG45 68
Rembrandt Rd. Edg. BM30 37
Rembrant Way, Walt. BC55 83
Remington Rd. N15 BZ32 48
Remington St. N1 BY37 2
Remington St. N1 BY37 56
Remnant St. WC2 BX39 2
Remnant St. WC2 BX39 56
Kingsway
Remus Rd. E3 CD36 57
Remus Rd. E3 CE36 57
Monter Rd.
Rendlesham Av. Rad. BH22 27
Rendlesham Rd. E5 CB35 48
Rendlesham Rd. Enf. BY22 29
Rendlesham Way, Rick. AU25 25
Renforth St. SE16 CC41 67
Renfrew Rd. SE11 BY42 4
Renfrew Rd. SE11 BY42 66
Renfrew Rd. Houns. BD44 64
Renfrew Rd. Kings. on T. BN50 75
Renmans, The Ash. BL61 103
Renmuir St. SW17 BU50 76
Rennell St. SE13 CF45 67
Renness Rd. E17 BX31 47
Rennetts Clo. SE9 CM46 78
Rennetts Wood Rd. SE9 CM46 78
Rennie Clo. Ashf. AX48 73
Rennie St. SE1 BY40 4
Rennie St. SE1 BY40 56
Rennie Ter. Red. BV71 121
Renown Clo. Croy. BY54 86
Renown Clo. Rom. CR30 41
Rensburg Rd. E17 CC32 48
Renters Av. NW4 BQ32 46
Renton Dr. Orp. CP54 89
Renwick Rd. Bark. CO38 59
Replingham Rd. SW18 BR47 75
Reporton Rd. SW6 BR43 65
Repository Rd. SE18 CK43 68
Repton Av. Hayes BA42 63
Repton Av. Rom. CU31 50
Repton Av. Wem. BK35 45
Repton Clo. Cars. BU56 95
Repton Ct. Beck. CE51 87
Repton Dr. Rom. CU31 50
Repton Gdns. Rom. CU31 50
Repton Gro. Ilf. CK30 40
Repton Rd. Har. BL31 46
Repton Rd. Orp. CN55 88
Repton St. E14 CD39 57
Repton Way, Rick. AZ25 26
Repulse Clo. Rom. CR30 41
Reservoir Rd. N14 BW25 29
Reservoir Rd. SE4 CD44 67
Reservoir Rd. Loug. CH23 31
Reservoir Rd. Ruis. BA32 44
Resolution Wk. SE18 CK41 68
Venus Rd.
Reson Way, Hem. H. AW14 8
Restell Clo. SE3 CG43 68
Reston Clo. Borwd. BM22 28
Reston Path, Borwd. BM22 28
Reston Path, Borwd. BM23 28
Reston Pl. SW7 BT41 3
Reston Pl. SW7 BT41 66
Palace Gte.
Restons Cres. SE9 CM46 78
Retcar Clo. N19 BV34 47
Raydon St.
Retcar St. N6 BV34 47
Retford Clo. Rom. CW29 42
Retford Path, Rom. CX29 42
Retford Rd. Rom. CW29 42
Retingham Way E4 CE27 39
Retreat Clo. Har. BK32 45
Retreat Pl. E9 CC36 57
Retreat Rd. Rich. BK46 74
Retreat Ter. Brent. BK43 64
Brickfield Clo.
Retreat, The NW4 BQ31 46
Heading St.
Retreat, The NW9 BN32 46
Highfield Av.
Retreat, The SE15 CC44 67
Retreat, The SW14 BO45 65
South Worple Way
Retreat, The Amer. AS23 25
Retreat, The Brwd. DA26 42
Costead Manor Rd.
Retreat, The Brwd. DD25 122
Retreat, The Egh. AR49 72
Retreat, The Grays. DG43 71
Retreat, The Har. BF33 45
Retreat, The NW9 BN32 46
Retreat, The Orp. CO57 98
Retreat, The Surb. BL53 85
Retreat, The Th. Hth. BZ52 87
Retreat, The Wor. Pk. BP55 85
Retreat Way, Chig. CO27 41
Rettiward Clo. SW15 BQ45 65
Colinette Rd.
Reubens Rd. Brwd. DD25 122

Revell Clo. Lthd. BF64 102
Revell Dr. Lthd. BF64 102
Revell Rise SE18 CN43 68
Revell Rd. Kings. on T. BM51 85
Revell Rd. Sutt. BR57 94
Revelon Rd. SE4 CD45 67
Revelstoke Rd. SW18 BR48 75
Reventlow Rd. SE9 CM47 78
Reverdy Rd. SE1 CB42 4
Reverdy Rd. SE1 CB42 67
Revesby Rd. Cars. BT53 86
Review Rd. NW2 BO34 46
Review Rd. Dag. CR37 59
Rewell St. SW6 BT43 66
Rewley Rd. Cars. BT53 86
Rex Av. Ashf. AZ50 73
Rex Clo. Rom. CR29 41
Rex Pl. W1 BV40 3
Rex Pl. W1 BV40 56
Reydon Av. E11 CJ32 49
Reynard Clo. Brom. CL52 88
Blackbrook La.
Reynard Dr. SE19 CA50 77
Reynardson Rd. N17 BZ29 39
Reynards Way, St. Alb. BE18 18
Reynolds Av. E12 CL35 49
Reynolds Av. Ches. BL57 94
Reynolds Av. Rom. CP33 50
Reynolds Clo. NW11 BS33 47
Reynolds Clo. Cars. BU54 86
Reynolds Clo. Hem. H. AW13 8
Reynolds Cres. St. Alb. BJ11 9
Reynolds Dr. Edg. BL31 46
Reynolds Pl. SE3 CH43 68
Reynolds Rd. SE15 CC45 67
Reynolds Rd. W4 BN41 65
Reynolds Rd. Hayes BD38 54
Reynolds Rd. N. Mal. BN54 85
Reynolds Way, Croy. CA56 96
Rheidol Mews N1 BZ37 2
Rheidol Ter. N1 BY37 2
Rheidol Ter. N1 BY37 56
Rheola Clo. N17 CA30 39
Rhoda St. E2 CA38 2
Rhoda St. E2 CA38 57
Rhodes Av. N22 BW30 38
Rhodes Dev. E8 CA36 57
Rhodesia Rd. E11 CF34 48
Rhodesia Rd. SW9 BX44 66
Rhodes Moorhouse Ct. Mord. BS53 86
Rhodes St. N7 BX35 47
Mackenzie Rd.
Rhodes Way, Wat. BD23 27
Rhodeswell Rd. E14 CD39 57
Rhodedendron Ride, Egh. AP49 72
Rhodrons Av. Chess. BL56 94
Rhondda Gro. E3 CD38 57
Rhyl Rd. Grnf. BH37 54
Rhyl St. NW5 BV36 56
Rhys Av. N11 BW29 38
Rialto Rd. Mitch. BV51 86
Ribbledade, St. Alb. BL17 19
Thamesdale
Ribblesdale, Dor. BJ72 119
Roman Rd.
Ribblesdale, Hem. H. AY12 8
Wharfedale
Ribblesdale Av. Nthlt. BF36 54
Ribblesdale Rd. N8 BX31 47
Ribblesdale Rd. SW16 BV50 76
Ribbleside Rd. Dart. CY47 80
Ribchester Av. Grnf. BH38 54
Ribston Clo. Brom. CK54 88
Ricardo Path SE28 CP40 59
Byron Clo.
Ricardo Rd. Wind. AQ46 72
Ricardo St. E14 CE39 57
Ricards Clo. Surb. BL54 85
Ricards Rd. SW19 BR49 75
Ricebridge La. Reig. BP72 120
Richard Clo. SE18 CK42 68
Samuel St.
Richards Av. Rom. CS32 50
Richards Clo. Har. BJ32 45
Richards Clo. Uxb. AZ37 53
Richard's Cotts. W3 BN40 55
Churchfield Rd.
Richardson Clo. Hayes BA43 63
Richardson Clo. St. Alb. BL17 19
Richardson Ms. NW1 BW39 56
Warren St.
Richardson Pl. St. Alb. BM14 10
Richardson Rd. E15 CG37 58
Richards Pl. E17 CE31 48
Richard's Pl. SW3 BU42 3
Richards Pl. SW3 BU42 66
Richards Rd. Cob. BF60 93
Richard St. E1 CB39 57
Richard St. E16 CH39 58
Richbell Clo. Ash. BK62 102
Richbell Pl. WC1 BX39 56
Emerald St.
Richborne Ter. SW8 BX43 66
Richborough Rd. NW2 BQ35 46
Rich Clo. West. CH62 106
Richfield Rd. Bush. BG26 36
Richford Rd. E15 CG37 58
Richford St. W6 BQ41 65
Richings Way, Iver. AV41 62
Rich La. SW5 BS42 66
Earl's Ct. Sq.
Richland Av. Couls. BV60 95
Richlands Av. Epsom BP56 94
Richmer Rd. Erith. CT43 69
Richmond Av. E4 CF28 39
Richmond Av. N1 BX37 2
Richmond Av. N1 BX37 56
Richmond Av. NW10 BQ36 55
Richmond Av. SW20 BR51 85
Richmond Av. Felt. BB46 73
Richmond Av. Uxb. AZ36 53
Richmond Br. Rich. & Twick. BK46 74
Richmond Bldgs. W1 BW39 1
Richmond Bldgs. W1 BW39 56
Dean St.
Richmond Clo. Epsom BO60 94
Richmond Clo. Lthd. BF65 102
Richmond Clo. Wal. CR. CC18 21
Dewhurst Rd.
Richmond Ct. SW20 BP51 85
Richmond Rd.
Richmond Cres. E4 CF28 39
Richmond Cres. N1 BX37 2
Richmond Cres. N1 BY37 56
Richmond Cres. N9 CB26 39
Richmond Cres. Slou. AQ40 52
Richmond Cres. Stai. AV49 72
Richmond Dr. Shep. BA53 83
Richmond Dr. Wat. BB23 26
Richmond Gdns. NW4 BP31 46
Richmond Gdns. Har. BH29 36
Richmond Grn. Croy. BX55 86
Richmond Gro. N1 BY36 56
Halton Rd.
Richmond Gro. Surb. BL53 85
Richmond Hl. Rich. BL46 75
Richmond Hl. Ct. Rich. BL46 75
Richmond Ms. W1 BW39 56
Dean St.
Richmond Pl. SE18 CM42 68
Richmond Pk. Rd. SW14 BN46 75
Richmond Pk. Rd. Kings. on T. BL51 85
Richmond Rd E4 CF26 39
Richmond Rd. E7 CH35 49
Richmond Rd. E8 CA36 57
Richmond Rd. E11 CF34 48
Richmond Rd. E17 CD32 48
Richmond Rd. N2 BT30 38
Brighton Rd.
Richmond Rd. N3 BT30 38
Chamberlain Rd.
Richmond Rd. N11 BX29 38
Richmond Rd. N15 CA32 48
Richmond Rd. SW20 BP51 85
Richmond Rd. W5 BL41 65
Richmond Rd. Barn. BS25 29
Richmond Rd. Couls. BV61 104
Richmond Rd. Croy. BX55 86
Richmond Rd. Grays. DE43 71
Richmond Rd. Ilf. CM34 49
Richmond Rd. Islw. BJ45 64
Richmond Rd. Kings. on T. BK49 74
Richmond Rd. Pot. B. BT19 20
Richmond Rd. Rom. CT32 50
Richmond Rd. Stai. AV49 72
Richmond Rd. Th. Hth. BY52 86
Richmond Rd. Twick. BJ47 74
Richmond St. E13 CH37 58
Richmond Ter. SW1 BX41 4
Richmond Ter. SW1 BX41 66
Parliament St.
Richmond Ter. Ms. SW1 BX41 4
Richmond Ter. Ms. SW1 BX41 66
Parliament St.
Richmond Way E11 CH34 49
Richmond Way W12 CH34 49
Richmond Way W14 BQ41 65
Richmond Way, Lthd. BF65 102
Richmond Way, Rick. BA24 26
Richmount Gdns. SE3 CH45 68
Rich St. E14 CD40 57
Richard Clo. SW2 BX47 76
Rickard Clo. West. Dr. AX41 63
Ricketts Hill Rd. West. CJ62 106
Ricketts St. SW6 BS43 66
Rickfield Clo. Hat. BP13 10
Woods Av.
Rickman Cres. Wey. AW55 83
Rickman Hill, Couls. BV62 104
Rickman Hill Rd. Couls. BV62 104
Rickmans La. Slou. AP35 43
Rickmans La. Slou. AP36 52
Rickman St. E1 CC38 57
Mantos Rd.
Rickmansworth By-pass, Rick. AX26 35
Rickmansworth La. Ger. Cr. AS29 34
Rickmansworth Rd. Amer. AO22 25
Rickmansworth Rd. Nthwd. AZ28 35
Rickmansworth Rd. Pnr. BC30 35
Rickmansworth Rd. Rick. AV24 25
Rickmansworth Rd. Rick. AX26 35
Rickmansworth Rd. Uxb. AX30 35
Rickmansworth Rd. Wat. BB24 26
Ricksons La. Leath. AZ67 110
Rickyard, Guil. AO70 118
Rickyard Path SE9 CK45 68
Elmbrook Gdns.
Ridding La. Grnf. BH35 45
Riddings La. Harl. CO13 14
Riddlesdown Av. Pur. BZ59 96
Riddlesdown Rd. Pur. BZ59 96
Riddons Rd. SE12 CJ48 78
Riders Way, Gdse. CC69 114
Ride, The Brent. BJ42 64
Ride, The Enf. CC24 30
Ride, The Leath. BB66 110
Ridgdale Rd. E3 CE37 57
Ridge Av. N21 BZ26 39
Ridge Av. Dart. CT46 79
Ridgebrook Rd. SE3 CJ45 68
Ridgebrook Ter. SE3 CJ45 68
Ridge Clo. NW4 BQ30 37
Ridge Clo. NW9 BN31 46
Ridge Clo. Bet. BM72 120
Ridge Clo. Houns. BF45 64
Ridge Crest. Enf. BX23 29
Ridgecroft Clo. Bex. CS47 79
St. Mary's Rd.
Ridgegate Clo. Reig. BT69 121
Ridge Grn. Red. BX72 121
Ridge Grn. Clo. Red. BX72 121
Ridge Hl. Pot. B. BN18 19
Ridge Hl. NW11 BR33 46
Ridgehurst Av. Wat. BB20 17
Ridgelands, Lthd. BG65 102
Ridge La. Pot. B. BO20 19
Ridge La. Wat. BB21 26
Ridge Langley, Sth. Croy. CB58 96
Ridgemead Rd. Egh. AQ48 72
Ridgemount, Guil. AQ71 118
Ridgemount Av. Couls. BV62 104
Ridgemount Av. Croy. CC55 87
Ridgemount Clo. SE20 CB50 77
Ridgemount End, Ger. Cr. AS28 34
Misbourne Av.
Ridgemount Gdns. Enf. BY23 29
Ridgemount, Wey. BB55 83
Ridge Pk. Pur. BW58 95
Ridge Rd. N8 BX32 47
Ridge Rd. N21 BZ26 39
Ridge Rd. NW2 BR34 46
Ridge Rd. Mitch. BV50 76
Ridge Rd. Sutt. BR54 85
Ridge Rd. W. Red. BW66 113
Ridge St. Wat. BC22 26
Ridge, The Bex. CQ47 79
Ridge, The Cat. CE66 114
Ridge, The Couls. BX60 95
Ridge, The Epsom BN62 103
Ridge, The Guil. AR73 118
Ridge, The Orp. CM55 88
Ridge, The Pur. BW58 95
Ridge, The Surb. BM53 85
Ridge, The Twick. BG47 74
Ridge, The Wok. AT62 100
Ridge, The Way, Sth. Croy. CA58 96
Ridge Vw. Clo. Barn. BQ25 28
Ridgeview Rd. N20 BS27 38
Ridgeway N14 BX27 38
Ridge Way SE19 CA50 77
Central Hill Est.
Ridgeway SW19 BQ50 75
Ridgeway, Berk. AP13 7
Ridgeway, Brom. CH55 88
Ridgeway, Brwd. DD26 122
Ridge Way, Dart. CT46 79
Ridgeway, Dart. CZ49 80
Ridgeway, Epsom BN59 94
Ridgeway Way, Felt. BE48 74
Ridgeway, Grays. DF42 71
Ridge Way, Iver. AV40 52
Ridgeway, Rick. AW26 35
Ridgeway, Rom. CW30 42
Ridgeway, Walt. BB54 83
Ridgeway, Wdf. Grn. CJ28 40
Ridgeway, Welw. G. C. BS8 5
Ridgeway, Wok. AR61 100
Ridgeway Av. Barn. BU25 29
Ridgeway Av. Grav. DG48 81
Ridgeway Clo. Dor. BJ72 119
Ridgeway Rd.
Ridgeway Clo. Lthd. BG60 93
Ridgeway Clo. Red. BU71 121
Ridgeway Clo. Wok. AR61 100
Ridgeway Cres. Orp. CN55 88
Ridgeway Cres. Gdns. Orp. CN55 88
Ridgeway Dr. Brom. CH49 78
Ridgeway Dr. Dor. BJ73 119
Ridgeway East, Sid. CN46 78
Ridgeway Gdns. Ilf. CK32 49
Ridgeway Gdns. Wok. AR61 100
Ridgeway Rd. E4 CF26 39
Ridgeway Rd. Dor. BJ72 119
Ridgeway Rd. Islw. BH43 64
Ridgeway Rd. Red. BU70 121
Ridgeway Rd. The Pot. B. BU21 29
Ridgeway, The E4 CE27 39
Ridgeway, The N3 BS29 38
Ridgeway, The N11 BU28 38
Ridgeway, The NW7 BP27 37
Ridgeway, The NW9 BN31 46
Ridgeway, The NW11 BR33 46
Ridgeway, The W3 BM41 65
Ridgeway, The Amer. AO23 25
Ridgeway, The Croy. BX55 86
Ridgeway, The Enf. BV21 29
Ridgeway, The Enf. BY23 29
Ridgeway, The Ger. Cr. AR31 43
Ridgeway, The Guil. AT71 118
Ridgeway, The Har. BF32 45
Ridgeway, The Har. BK32 45
Ridgeway, The Lthd. BG60 93
Ridgeway, The Lthd. BG65 102
Ridgeway, The Pot. B. BV17 20
Ridgeway, The Rad. BJ21 27
Ridgeway, The Rom. CU31 50
Ridgeway, The Ruis. BC33 44
Ridgeway, The St. Alb. BJ11 9
Ridgeway, The Stan. BK29 36
Ridgeway, The Wat. BB22 26
Ridgeway Wk. Nthlt. BE36 54
Ridgeway West, Sid. CN46 78
Ridgewell Clo. N1 BZ37 57
Rasire St.
Ridgewell Clo. Dag. CR37 59
Ridgewell Rd. E16 CJ39 58
Ridgmont Gdns. Edg. BN28 37
Ridgmont Rd. St. Alb. BH14 9
Ridgmount Gdns. WC1 BW38 56
Ridgmount Gdns. WC1 BW39 1
Ridgmount Pl. WC1 BW39 1
Ridgmount Rd. SW18 BS46 76
Ridgmount St. WC1 BW39 56
Store St.
Ridgway SW19 BQ50 75
Ridgway Clo. Wok. AR61 100
Ridgway Gdns. SW19 BQ50 75
Ridgway Ms. SW19 BR50 75
Ridgway Pl. SW19 BR50 75
Ridgway Rd. SW9 BY45 66
Ridgway, The Sutt. BT57 95
Riding Ct. Rd. Slou. AR43 62
Ridinge, The Amer. AO21 25
Riding Hill, Sth. Croy. CB60 96
Riding Ho. St. W1 BV39 56
Riding House St. W1 BV39 1
Riding La. Ton. & Sev. CY71 117
Ridings Av. Enf. BY24 29
Rigings La. Wok. AZ65 101
Ridings Rd. Kings. on T. BN49 75
Ridings, The W5 BL39 55
Ridings, The Ash. BK62 102
Ridings, The Ches. AR21 25
Ridings, The Cob. BF59 93
Ridings, The Epsom BO61 103
Ridings, The Iver. AV42 62
Ridings, The Leath. BB66 110
Ridings, The Loug. CJ24 31
Ridings, The Reig. BT69 121
Ridings, The Sun. BC51 83
Ridings, The Surb. BM53 85
Ridings, The Tad. BR63 103
Ridings, The West. CK62 106
Ridings, The Wey. AV57 91
Riding, The NW1 BR33 46
Golders Grn. Rd.
Riding, The Wok. AT60 91
Ridlands Clo. Oxt. CK68 115
Ridlands La. Oxt. CJ68 115
Ridlands Ri. Oxt. CK68 115
Ridler Rd. Enf. CA22 30
Ridley Av. W13 BJ41 64
Ridley Clo. Brom. CG52 88
Ridley Clo. Rom. CU30 41
Ridley Rd. E7 CJ35 49
Ridley Rd. E8 CA35 48
Ridley Rd. NW10 BP37 55
Ridley Rd. SW19 BS50 76
Ridley Rd. Brom. CG52 88
Ridley Rd. Warl. CC62 105
Ridley Rd. Well. CO44 69
Ridley Several SE3 CH44 68
Blackheath Pk.
Ridout St. SE18 CK42 68
Ridsdale Rd. SE20 CB51 87
Ridsdale Rd. Wok. AQ62 100
Riefield Rd. SE9 CM46 78
Riesco Dr. Croy. CC57 96
Riffel Rd. NW2 BQ35 46
Riffhams, Brwd. DD27 122
Rifle Butts Alley, Epsom BO60 94
Rifle Ct. SE11 BY43 4
Rifle Ct. SE11 BY43 66
Kennington Pk. Rd.
Rifle Pl. W11 BQ40 55
Rifle St. E14 CE39 57
Rigault Rd. SW6 BR44 65
Rigby Clo. Croy. BY55 86
Rigby Gdns. Grays. DG42 71
Rigby La. Hayes BA40 53
Rigby La. Hayes BA41 63
Rigby Mews, Ilf. CL34 49
Rigden St. E14 CE39 57
Rigeley Rd. NW10 BP38 55
Rigg App. E10 CC33 48
Rigge Clo. Wok. AQ64 100
Riggindale Rd. SW16 BW49 76
Riley Rd. SE1 CA41 4
Riley Rd. SE1 CA41 67
Riley Rd. Enf. CC22 30
Riley St. SW10 BT43 66
Ring Clo. Brom. CH50 77
Ringcroft Rd. N7 BY35 47
Madras Pl.
Ringers Rd. Brom. CH52 88
Ringford Rd. SW18 BR46 75
Ringlestone Clo. West Dr. AY43 63
Ringley Pk. Av. Reig. BT71 121
Ringley Pk. Rd. Reig. BT70 121
Ringmer Av. SW6 BR44 65
Ringmer Gdns. N19 BX34 47
Ringmer Pk. N7 BX35 47
Ringmer Pl. N21 BZ25 30
Ringmore Dr. Guil. AU69 118
Ringmore Ri. SE23 CB47 77
Ringmore Rd. Walt. BD55 84
Ring Rd. D. Hayes BC40 53
Ringshall Rd. Orp. CO52 89
Ringslade Rd. N22 BX30 38
Ringstead Rd. SE6 CE47 77
Ringstead Rd. Sutt. BT56 95
Ring, The W2 BT40 3
Ring, The W2 BT40 56
Ringway N11 BW29 38
Ringway, Sthl. BE42 64
Ring Way Rd. St. Alb. BG17 18
Ringwold Clo. Beck. CD50 77
Aldersmead Rd.
Ringswood Av. N2 BU30 38
Ringwood Av. Croy. BX54 86
Ringwood Av. Horn. CV34 51
Ringwood Av. Orp. CP58 98
Ringwood Av. Red. BU69 121
Ringwood Clo. Pnr. BD31 45
Ringwood Gdns. SW15 BP47 75
Alton Rd.
Ringwood Rd. E17 CD32 48
Ringwood Way N21 BY26 38
Ringwood Way, Hamptn. BF49 74
Ripley Av. Egh. AS50 72
Ripley-by-Pass, Wok. AX65 101
Ripley By Pass, Wok. AV66 109
Ripley Clo. Croy. CF57 96
Ripley Clo. Slou. AS42 62
Ripley Gdns. SW14 BN45 65
Ripley Gdns. Sutt. BT56 95
Ripley La. Leath. HZ66 110
Ripley La. Wok. AY65 101
Ripley Rd. E16 CJ39 58
Ripley Rd. Belv. CR42 69
Ripley Rd. Guil. AW67 110
Ripley Rd. Hmptn. BF50 74
Ripley Rd. Ilf. CN34 49
Ripley Vw. Loug. CL22 31
Ripley Way, Hem. H. AV13 7
Ripley Way, Wal. Cr. CB18 21
Ripling Gro. Hem. H. AZ10 8
Riplington Ct. SW15 BP47 75
Ripon Clo. Guil. AP69 118
Ripon Clo. Nthlt. BF36 54
Ripon Gdns. Chess. BK56 93
Ripon Gdns. Ilf. CK32 49
Ripon Rd. N9 CB26 39
Ripon Rd. N17 BZ31 48
Ripon Rd. SE18 CL43 68
Ripon Way, Borwd. BN24 28
Rippersley Rd. Well. CO44 69
Ripple Rd. Bark. CM36 58
Ripplevale Gro. N1 BX36 2
Ripplevale Gro. N1 BX36 56
Rippolson Rd. SE18 CN42 68
Ripston Rd. Ashf. BA49 73
Risborough Dr. Wor. Pk. BP54 85
Risborough St. SE1 BY41 4
Risborough St. SE1 BY41 66
Risdon St. SE16 CC41 67
Risebridge Chase, Rom. CT29 41
Risebridge Rd. Rom. CT30 41
Risedale Clo. Hem. H. AY15 8
Risedale Hill, Hem. H. AY15 8
Risedale Rd. Bexh. CR45 69
Risedale Rd. Hem. H. AY15 8
Riseldine Rd. SE23 CD46 77
Rise Pk. Boul. Rom. CT30 41
Rise Pk. Pde. Rom. CT30 41
Rise, The E11 CH32 49
Rise, The N13 BY28 38
Rise, The NW7 BO29 37
Rise, The NW10 BN34 46
Rise, The Amer. AO22 25
Rise, The Bex. CP47 79
Rise, The Borwd. BL25 28
Rise, The Buck. H. CJ26 40
Rise, The Couls. BW60 95
Rise, The Dart. CT45 69
Rise, The Edg. BM28 37
Rise, The Epsom BO58 94
Rise, The Grav. DJ49 81
Rise, The Grnf. BJ35 45
Rise, The St. Alb. BG16 18
Rise, The Sev. CV67 117
Rise, The Sid. CP47 79
Rise, The Sth. Croy. CC58 96
Rise, The Uxb. AY37 53
Riseway, Brwd. DC27 122
Rising Hill Clo. Nthwd. BA29 35
Risinghill St. N1 BX37 2
Risinghill St. N1 BX37 56
Risingholme Clo. Bush. BF26 36
Risingholme Clo. Har. BH30 36
Risingholme Rd. Har. BH30 36
Risings, The E17 CF31 48
Risley Av. N17 BZ30 39
Rita Rd. SW8 BX43 66
Ritches Rd. N15 BZ32 48
Ritchie Rd. Croy. CB53 87
Ritchie St. N1 BY37 2
Ritchie St. N1 BY37 56
Ritchings Av. E17 CD31 48
Ritcroft Clo. Hem. H. AZ14 8
Ritcroft St. Hem. H. AZ14 8
Ritherdon Rd. SW17 BV48 76
Ritson Rd. E8 CB36 57
Ritter St. SE18 CL43 68
Ritz Ct. Pot. B. BS19 20
Rivaz Pl. E9 CC36 57
Rivenhall Gdns. E18 CG31 49
River Av. N13 BY27 38
River Av. Hodd. CE11 12
River Av. Surb. BJ54 84
River Bnk. N21 BZ26 39
River Bnk. SE10 CF41 67
Riverbk. E. Mol. BH52 84
River Bnk. Surb. BH53 84
River Clo. E11 CJ32 49
River Clo. Rain. CU39 59
River Clo. Ruis. BB32 44
River Clo. Surb. BK53 84
Rivercourt Rd. W6 BP42 65
Riverdale Dr. Wok. AS64 100
Riverdale Gdns. Twick. BK46 74
Riverdale Rd. SE18 CN42 68
Riverdale Rd. Bex. CQ47 79
Riverdale Rd. Erith CR42 69
Riverdale Rd. Felt. BE49 74
Riverdale Rd. Twick. BK46 74
Riverdene, Edg. BN27 37
Riverdene Rd. Ilf. CL34 49
River Dr. Upmin. CY32 51
Riverfield Rd. Stai. AV50 72
River Front, Enf. BZ24 30
River Gdns. Cars. BV55 86
River Gdns. Felt. BD46 74
River Grove Pk. Beck. CD51 87
River Hill, Sev. CW68 117
Riverholme Dr. Epsom BN58 94
River La. Lthd. BG64 102
River La. Rich. BK47 74
Rivermead Clo. Tedd. BJ49 74
Rivermead Clo. Wey. AX57 92
Rivermead, Wey. AY60 92
River Mead Ct. SW6 BR45 65
Ranelagh Gdns.
River Meads. Av. Twick. BF48 74
River Meads. Est. Twick. BF48 74
Rivermount Gdns. Guil. AR72 118
Rivermill, Harl. CM10 6
Rivermount, Walt. BB54 83
River Nook Clo. Walt. BD53 84
River Pk. Gdns. Brom. CF50 77
River Park Rd. N22 BX30 38
River Pl. N1 BZ36 2
River Pl. N1 BZ36 57
River Reach, Tedd. BK49 74
Broom Water
River Reach, Tedd. BK50 74
River Rd. Bark. CN37 58
River Rd. Brwd. CZ28 42
River Rd. Buck. H. CK26 40
River Rd. Stai. AV51 82
Riversdale Rd. N5 BY34 47
Riversdale Rd. Rom. CR29 41
Riversdale Rd. Surb. BJ53 84
Riversdell Rd. Cher. AV54 82
Rivers End Rd. Hem. H. AX15 8
Riversfield Rd. Enf. CA24 30
Riverside NW4 BP33 46
Riverside SE7 CH41 68
Riverside, Dor. BK70 119
Riverside, Guil. AR69 118
Riverside, Stai. AR47 72
Riverside, Stai. AT48 72
Riverside, Stai. AV51 82
Riverside, Twick. BJ47 74
Riverside Av. Brox. CE14 12
Riverside Av. E. Mol. BG53 84
Riverside Clo. W7 BH38 54
Riverside Clo. Kings. on T. BK52 84
Riverside Clo. St. Alb. BH14 9
Riverside Clo. Stai. AV50 72
Riverside Clo. Stai. AV51 82
Riverside Clo. Wall. BV55 86
Riverside Dr. W4 BN43 65
Riverside Dr. Esher BF56 93

Riverside Dr. Mitch. BU53 86
Riverside Dr. Rich. BJ48 74
Riverside Dr. Rick. AX26 35
Riverside Dr. Stai. AV49 72
Riverside Dr. Stai. AV51 82
Riverside Gdns. W6 BP42 65
Riverside Gdns. Berk. AQ12 7
Riverside Gdns. Enf. BZ23 30
Riveride Gdns. Wem. BL37 55
Riverside Gdns. Wok. AT64 100
High St.
Riverside Path, Wal. Cr. CC18 21
Riverside Pl. Stai. AX46 73
Riverside Rd. E15 CF37 57
Riverside Rd. N15 CB32 48
Riverside Rd. SW17 BS49 76
Riverside Rd. St. Alb. BH14 9
Riverside Rd. Sid. CQ48 79
Riverside Rd. Stai. AV50 72
Riverside Rd. Stai. AX46 73
Riverside Rd. Walt. BE56 93
Riverside Rd. Wat. BC25 26
Riverside, Shep. BB54 83
Riverside Wk. SE1 BX41 4
Riverside Wk. SE1 BX41 66
Riverside Wk. Bex. CP47 79
Riverside Wk. Islw. BH45 64
Riverside Way, Dart. CW46 80
Riverside Way, Uxb. AW37 53
Riversmead, Hodd. CE12 12
Rivers Rd. Slou. AS41 62
River St. EC1 BY38 2
River St. EC1 BY38 56
River St. Wind. AO43 61
River Ter. W6 BQ42 65
Crisp Rd.
River Ter. Berk. AQ12 7
Riverton Clo. W9 BR38 55
Ashmore Rd.
River Vw. Enf. BZ24 30
River Vw. Grays. DF42 71
River Vw. Welw. G. C. BR6 5
River View Gdns. SW13 BP43 65
River Vw. Gdns. Twick. BH48 74
Riverview Gro. W4 BM43 65
Riverview Pk. SE6 CE48 77
Riverview Rd. W4 BM43 65
Riverview Rd. Epsom BN55 85
Riverview Rd. Epsom BN56 94
River View Rd. Green. DA46 80
River Wk. Uxb. AX35 44
River Wk. Walt. BC53 83
Riverway N13 BY28 38
River Way SE10 CG41 68
River Way Epsom BN56 94
Riverway, Harl. CO9 6
River Way Loug. CK25 31
Riverway, Stai. AW51 83
River Way Twick. BF48 74
Riverwood La. Chis. CM51 88
Rivett Drake Rd. Guil. AQ58 109
Rivey Clo. Wey. AV60 91
Rivfield La. Saw. CQ5 6
Rivington Av. Wdf. Grn. CJ30 40
Rivington Cres. NW9 BO29 37
Rivington Ct. NW10 BO36 55
Rivington Ct. NW10 BP37 55
Longstone Av.
Rivington Pl. EC2 CA38 2
Rivington St. EC2 CA38 2
Rivington St. EC2 CA38 57
Rivulet Rd. N17 BZ29 39
Rixon Ho. SE18 CL43 68
Rixsen Rd. E12 CK35 49
Roach Rd. E3 CE36 57
Road Pl. N4 BW34 47
Hornsey Rd.
Roads Pl. N4 BX34 47
Roakes Av. Wey. AW55 83
Roan St. SE10 CE43 67
Roasthill La. Wind. AL43 61
Robart House E11 CG33 49
Robb Rd. Stan. BJ29 36
Robbs Clo. Hem. H. AW12 8
Robe End, Hem. H. AV12 7
Robert Adam St. W1 BV39 56
Roberta St. E2 CB38 2
Roberta St. E2 CB38 57
Robert Av. St. Alb. BF15 9
Robert Clo. W9 BT38 1
Robert Clo. W9 BT38 56
Robert Clo. Chig. CN28 40
Robert Clo. Pot. B. BR20 19
Robert Clo. Walt. BC56 92
Robert Gentry Ho. W14 BR42 65
Robert Keen Clo. SE15 CB44 67
Moncrieff Est.
Robert Keen Clo. SE15 CB44 67
Cicely Rd.
Robert Ms. NW1 BW38 56
Hampstead Rd.
Roberton Dr. Brom. CJ51 88
Robert Owen Ho. SW6 BQ44 65
Robert Rd. Slou. AO34 43
Roberts Alley W5 BK41 64
Church Gdns.
Robertsbridge Rd. Cars. BT54 86
Roberts Clo. Rom. CU30 41
Roberts Clo. Stai. AX46 73
Park Rd.
Roberts La. Ger. Cr. AT28 34
Robertson Rd. E15 CF37 57
Robertson St. SW8 BV45 66
Roberts Rd. E17 CE30 39
Roberts Rd. NW7 BR29 37
Roberts Rd. Belv. CR42 69
Roberts St. Wat. BD25 27
Robert St. E2 CB37 57
Old Bethnal Green Rd.
Robert St. E16 CL40 56
Robert St. NW1 BV38 1
Robert St. NW1 BV38 56
Robert St. SE18 CM42 68
Robert St. WC2 BX40 4
Robert St. WC2 BX40 56
Savoy Pl.
Robert St. Croy. BZ55 87
High St.
Roberts Way, Egh. AR50 72
Robina Clo. Bexh. CP45 69
Brunswick Rd.
Robin Clo. Rom. CS29 41
Robin Gdns. Red. BV69 121
Kingfisher Dr.
Robin Gro. N6 BV34 47
Robin Gro. Brent. BK43 64
Robin Gro. Harrow BL32 46
Robin Hill, Berk. AR13 7
Robin Hill Dr. Chis. CK50 78
Wood Dr.
Robin Hood Clo. Mitch. BW52 86
Robinhood Clo. Slou. AM40 61
Robin Hood Clo. Wok. AP62 100
Robin Hood Cres. Wok. AP62 100
Robin Hood Dr. Bush. BE23 27
Robin Hood Dr. Har. BH29 36
Robin Hood Grn. Orp. CO53 89
Robin Hood La. E14 CF39 57
Robin Hood La. SW15 BO48 75
Robin Hood La. Bexh. CQ46 79
Robin Hood La. Guil. AS65 100
Robin Hood La. Guil. AS66 109
Robin Hood La. Hat. BP12 10
Common, The
Robin Hood La. Mitch. BW52 86
Robin Hood Mead.
Hem. H. AY11 8
Robin Hood Rd. SW19 BO49 75
Robin Hood Rd. Brwd. DB26 42
Robin Hood Rd. Sutt. BS56 95
Robin Hood Rd. Wok. AP62 100
Robin Hood Way SW15 BO49 75
Robin Hood Way SW20 BO49 75
Robin Hood Way, Grnf. BH36 54
Robin Hood Yd. EC1 BY39 56
Leather Lane
Robinia Av. Grav. DE47 81
Robinia Clo. Chig. CN29 40
Robin Md. Welw. G C. BS6 5
Robin Rd. Hem. H. AZ14 8
Robins Clo. Uxb. AX39 53
Robin's Ct. SE12 CJ48 78
Robins Ct. Beck. CF51 87
Robins Dale, Wok. AO62 100
Robinsfield, Hem. H. AW13 8
Robins Gro. Kes. CH55 88
Robins Ness Hill, Hert. BW11 11
Robinson Av. Wal. Cr. BY17 20
Robinson Cres. Bush. BG27 36
Robinson Rd. E2 CC37 57
Robinson Rd. SW17 BU50 76
Robinson Rd. Dag. CR35 50
Robinsons Clo. W13 BJ39 54
Robins Orchard, Ger. Cr. AS29 34
Robins, The Brwd. DB21 33
Robin St. SW3 BU42 66
Flood St.
Robin St. SW3 BU43 3
Robinsway, Wal. Abb. CG20 22
Roundhills
Robinsway, Walt. BD56 93
Robins Way, Hat. BO14 10
Robin Way, Guil. AQ68 109
Robin Way Orp. CO52 89
Robin Way, Pot. B. BX17 20
Robin Way, Stai. AV48 72
Roborough Wk. Horn. CV36 60
Robsart St. SW9 BX44 66
Robson Clo. Enf. BY23 29
Robson Clo. Ger. Cr. AR28 34
Robson Rd. SE27 BY48 76
Robyn's Way, Sev. CT64 107
Roch Av. Edg. BL30 37
Rochdale Rd. E17 CE33 48
Rochdale Rd. SE2 CO42 69
Rochdale Way SE8 CD43 67
Idonia St.
Rochelle Cl. SW11 BT45 66
Nantes Cl.
Rochelle St. E2 CA38 2
Rochelle St. E2 CA38 57
Swanfield St.
Rochemont Walk E8 CA37 57
Broadway Mkt. Est.
Roche Rd. SW16 BX51 86
Rochester Av. E13 CJ37 58
Rochester Av. Brom. CH51 88
Rochester Av. Felt. BB48 73
Rochester Clo. SE3 CJ45 68
Rochester Clo. Enf. CA23 30
Rochester Clo. Sid. CO46 79
Rochester Dr. Bexh. CR46 79
Rochester Dr. Pnr. BD32 45
Rochester Gdns. Croy. CA55 87
Rochester Gdns. Ilf. CK33 49
Rochester Mews NW1 BW36 56
Rochester Rd.
Rochester Pl. NW1 BW36 56
Rochester Rd. NW1 BW36 56
Rochester Rd. Cars. BU56 95
Rochester Rd. Dart. CX47 80
Rochester Rd. Grav. DJ47 81
Rochester Rd. Nthwd. BB31 41
Rochester Row SW1 BW42 3
Rochester Row SW1 BW42 66
Rochester Sq. NW1 BW36 56
Rochester St. SW1 BW41 3
Rochester St. SW1 BW42 66
Rochester Row
Rochester Ter. NW1 BW36 56
Rochester Wk. Reig. BS73 121
Castle Dr.
Rochester Way SE3 CH44 68
Rochester Way SE9 CH44 68
Rochester Way, Dart. CT47 79
Rochester Way, Rick. AZ24 26
Rochester Way, Sid. CN46 78
Roche Wk. Cars. BT53 86
Rochford Av. Brwd. DD25 122
Rochford Av. Loug. CM24 31
Rochford Av. Rom. CP32 50
Rochford Av. Wal. Abb. CF20 21
Rochford Clo. E6 CJ37 58
Boleyn Rd.
Rochford Clo. E13 CJ37 58
Boleyn Rd.
Rochford Clo. Brx. CD16 21
Rochford Clo. Horn. CU36 59
Rochford Grn. Loug. CM24 31
Rochford St. NW5 BU35 47
Rochford Wk. E8 CB36 57
Wilman Gro.
Rochford Way, Croy. BX53 86
Rock Av. SW14 BN45 65
South Worple Way
Rockbourne Rd. SE23 CC47 77
Rockchase Gdns. Horn. CW32 51
Rockcliffe Av. Kings L. AZ18 17
Rockdale Rd. Sev. CU66 116
Rockells Pl. SE22 CB46 77
Rockfield Rd. Oxt. CG68 115
Rockford Av. Grnf. BJ37 54
Rock Gro. SE16 CB42 67
Blue Anchor La.
Rockhall Rd. NW2 BQ35 46
Rockhampton Rd. SE27 BY49 76
Rockhampton Rd.
Sth. Croy. BZ57 96
Rock Hill SE26 CA49 77
Rock Hill, Orp. CR57 98
Rockingham Av. Horn. CU32 50
Rockingham Cl. SW15 BO45 65
Priory Lane
Rockingham Clo. Uxb. AX37 53
Rockingham Est. SE1 BA41 4
Rockingham Est. SE1 BZ41 67
Rockingham Par. Uxb. AX37 53
Rockingham Rd. Uxb. AW37 53
Rockingham St. SE1 BZ41 4
Rockingham St. SE1 BZ41 67
Rocklands Dr. Stan. BJ30 36
Rocklands Rd. SW15 BR45 65
Rock La. Dag. CR35 50
Rockley Rd. W14 BQ41 65
Rockmead Rd. E9 CC37 57
Rockmount Rd. SE18 CN42 68
Rockmount Rd. SE19 BZ50 77
Rockshaw Rd. Red. BW67 113
Rocks La. SW13 BP44 65
Rock St. N4 BY34 47
Rockware Av. Grnf. BH37 54
Rockways, Barn. BO25 28
Rockwell Gdns. Dag. CR35 50
Rockwell Rd. Dag. CR35 50
Rockwells Ct. SE19 CA49 77
Rockwells Gdns. SE19 CA49 77
Rockwood Gdns.
Wdf. Grn. CH27 40
Whitehall La.
Rockwood Pl. W12 BQ41 65
Shepherds Bush Grn.
Rocky La. Reig. BU67 113
Rocliffe St. N1 BY37 2
Rocliffe St. N1 BY37 56
Rocombe Cres. SE23 CC47 77
Rocque La. SE3 CG45 68
Rodborough Rd. NW11 BS33 47
Rodd La. EC3 CA40 57
Roden Clo. Harl. CQ9 6
Roden Gdns. Croy. CA53 87
Rodenhurst Rd. SW4 BW46 76
Roden St. N7 BX34 47
Roden St. Ilf. CK34 49
Roden Way, Ilf. CL34 49
Roden St.
Roderick Rd. NW3 BU35 47
Roding Av. Bark. CL36 58
Roding Av. Wdf. Grn. CK29 40
Roding Clo. Ong. BY14 15
Roding Ho. Wdf. Grn. CK29 40
Roding La. Buck. H. CJ27 40
Roding La. N. Wdf. Grn. CJ30 40
Roding La. S. Ilf. CJ31 49
Roding Rd. E5 CC35 48
Roding Rd. Loug. CK25 31
Rodings Clo. Ong. CY14 15
Ongar Rd.
Rodings, The Upmin. CY32 51
Rodings, The Wdf. Grn. CJ29 40
Snakes La.
Roding St. E7 CH35 49
Oakhurst Rd.
Roding Trading Est. Bark. CL36 58
Roding Vw. Buck. H. CJ26 40
Roding Vw. Ong. CX17 24
Roding Way, Rain. CV37 60
Briscoe Rd.
Rodmarton St. W1 BU39 1
Rodmarton St. W1 BU39 56
Rodmell Slope N12 BR28 37
Rodmere St. SE10 CG42 68
Rodmill La. SW2 BX47 76
Rodney Av. St. Alb. BJ14 9
Rodney Clo. Croy. BY54 86
Rodney Clo. N. Mal. BO52 85
Rodney Clo. Pnr. BE33 45
Rodney Clo. Walt. BD55 84
Rodney Rd.
Rodney Cres. Hodd. CE11 12
Rodney Gdns. Kes. CH56 97
Rodney Gdns. Pnr. BC32 44
Rodney Grn. Walt. BD55 84
Rodney Rd.
Rodney Pl. E17 CD30 39
Rodney Pl. SE17 BZ42 4
Rodney Pl. SE17 BZ42 67
Rodney Pl. SW19 BT51 86
Rodney Rd. E11 CH31 49
Rodney Rd. SE17 BZ42 4
Rodney Rd. SE17 BZ42 67
Rodney Rd. Mitch. BU51 86
Rodney Rd. N. Mal. BO53 85
Rodney Rd. Ong. CW18 24
Rodney Rd. Twick. BF46 74
Rodney Rd. Walt. BC55 83
Rodney St. N1 BX37 2
Rodney St. N1 BX37 56
Rodney St. SE18 CL41 68
Rodney Way, Guil. AT70 118
Rodney Way, Rom. CR30 41
Rodney Way, Slou. AV44 62
Rodona La. Wey. AB59 92
Rodsley Pl. SE15 CB44 67
Commercial Way
Rodsley St. SE1 CB43 67
Old Kent Rd.
Rodway Rd. SW15 BP47 75
Rodwell Clo. Ruis. BD33 45
Rodwell Ct. Wey. AV57 91
Rodwell Rd. SE22 CA46 77
Roebourne Way E16 CL40 58
Pier Rd.
Roebuck Clo. N17 CA29 39
High Rd.
Roebuck Gdns. Slou. AM40 61
Roebuck La. Buck. H. CJ26 40
Roebuck Rd. Chess. BM56 94
Roebuck Rd. Ilf. CO28 41
Roedean Av. Enf. CC23 30
Roedean Clo. Enf. CC23 30
Roedean Cres. SW15 BO46 75
Roe End, NW9 BN31 46
Roe Fields Clo. Hem. H. AW15 8
Roe Grn. NW9 BN32 46
Roe Green Clo. Hat. BO13 10
Roe Green La. Hat. BO12 10
Roehampton Clo. SW15 BP45 65
Roehampton Clo. Grav. DJ47 81
Roehampton Dr. Chis. CM50 78
Roehampton Gate SW15 BO46 75
Roehampton High St.
SW15 BP47 75
Roehampton La. SW15 BP45 65
Roehampton Vale SW15 BO48 75
Roe Hill Cl. Hat. BO13 10
Roe La. NW9 BM31 46
Roestock Gdns. St. Alb. BO14 10
Roestock La. St. Alb. BN15 10
Roestock La. St. Alb. BO14 10
Roe Way, Wall. BX57 95
Rofant Rd. Nthwd. BB29 35
Roffes La. Cat. BZ66 114
Roffey Clo. Pur. BY61 104
Roffey St. E14 CF41 67
Roffords, Wok. AQ62 100
Marston Rd.
Roger's Cl. Cat. CB64 105
Rogers Clo. Couls. BY62 104
Rogers Gdns. Dag. CR35 50
Rogers La. Slou. AP36 52
Rogers Mead. Gdse. CB69 114
Rogers Rd. E16 CG39 58
Rogers Rd. SW17 BT49 76
Rogers Rd. Dag. CR35 50
Rogers Rd. Grays DE42 71
Rogers Ruff. Nthwd. BA30 35
Roger St. WC1 BX38 2
Roger St. WC1 BX38 56
Rogers Walk, N12 BS27 38
Brook Meadow
Rogers Wood La. Fawk. DA56 99
Rojack Rd. SE23 CC47 77
Rokeby Gdns. Wdf. Grn. CH30 40
Rokeby Rd. SE4 CD44 67
Rokeby St. E15 CF37 57
Roke Clo. Ken. BZ60 96
Roke Lodge Rd. Ken. BY60 95
Roke Rd. Ken. BY61 104
Roker Park Av. Uxb. AY35 44
Rokesby Clo. Well. CM44 68
Rokesby Clo. Wem. BK35 45
Rokesly Av. N8 BX32 47
Roland Gdns. SW7 BT42 66
Roland Gdns. SW10 BT42 3
Roland Gdns. SW10 BT42 66
Roland Gdns. Felt. BE48 74
Roland Rd. E17 CF32 48
Roland St. St. Alb. BJ13 9
Roland Way SE17 BZ42 4
Roland Way SE17 BZ42 67
Roland Way SW7 BT42 66
Roland Way SW10 BT42 3
Roland Way, Wor. Pk. BO55 85
Roles Gro. Rom. CP31 50
Rolfe Clo. Barn. BU24 29
Rolfe Rd. SE7 CK42 68
Rollesby Rd. Chess. BM57 94
Rolleston Av. Orp. CL53 88
Rolleston Clo. Orp. CL54 88
Rolleston Rd. Sth. Croy. BZ57 96
Roll Gdns. Ilf. CL32 49
Rollins St. SE15 CC43 67
Rollit Cres. Houns. BF46 74
Rollit St. N7 BY35 47
Hornsey Rd.
Rollitt St. N7 BY35 47
Rollo Rd. Swan. CT50 79
Rolls Bldgs. EC4 BY39 2
Rolls Bldgs. EC4 BY39 56
Fetter La.
Rollscourt Av. SE24 BZ46 77
Rolls Park Av. E4 CE28 39
Rolls Park Rd. E4 CE28 39
Rolls Pass. EC4 BY39 2
Rolls Pass. EC4 BY39 56
Chancery La.
Rolls Rd. SE1 CA42 4
Rolls Rd. SE1 CA42 67
Rollswood, Welw. G. C. BR9 5
Rolt St. SE8 CD43 67
Rolvenden Gdns. Brom. CJ50 78
Roman Clo. Felt. BC46 73
Roman Clo. Rain. CS37 59
Romanhurst Av. Brom. CG52 88
Romanhurst Gdns. Brom. CG52 88
Roman Rise SE19 BZ50 77
Roman Rd. E2 CC38 57
Roman Rd. E3 CC38 57
Roman Rd. E6 CK38 58
Roman Rd. N10 BV29 38
Roman Rd. W4 BO42 65
Roman Rd. Dor. BJ72 119
Roman Rd. Epsom BL65 103
Roman Rd. Grav. DE48 81
Roman Rd. Ilf. CL36 58
Roman St. Hodd. CE11 12
Romans Way, Wok. AW61 101
Roman Villa Hill.
S. Dnth. CY50 80
Roman Way N7 BX36 56
Roman Way, Croy. BY55 86
Roman Way, Enf. CA25 30
Romany Gdns. E17 CD30 39
Mcentee Ave.
Romany Gdns. Sutt. BS54 86
Romany Rise, Orp. CM54 88
Romany Rd. Grav. DF48 81
Romany Rd. Wok. AO60 91
Roma Rd. E17 CD31 48
Romberg Rd. SW17 BV48 76
Romborough Gdns. SE13 CF46 77
Romborough Way SE13 CE46 77
Romeland, St. Alb. CF20 21
Romeland Hill, St. Alb. BG13 9
Romero Sq. SE9 CJ45 68
Romeyn Rd. SW16 BX48 76
Romford Cres. Rom. CT33 50
Romford Rd. E7 CG36 58
Romford Rd. E12 CG36 58
Romford Rd. E15 CG36 58
Romford Rd. Chig. CO27 41
Romford Rd. Ong. CW19 24
Romford Rd. Rom. CP28 41
Romford Rd. S. Ock. CW39 60
Romford St. E1 CB39 57
Romilly Dr. Wat. BE28 36
Romilly Rd. N4 BY34 47
Romilly St. W1 BW40 3
Romilly St. W1 BW40 56
Rommany Rd. SE27 BZ48 77
Romney Chase, Horn. CW32 51
Romney Chase, Horn. CX32 51
Romney Clo. N17 CB30 39
Romney Clo. NW11 BT33 47
Romney Clo. Ashf. BA49 73
Romney Clo. Chess. BL56 94
Romney Clo. Har. BF33 45
Romney Dr. Brom. CJ50 78
Romney Dr. Har. BF33 45
Romney Gdns. Bexh. CQ44 69
Romney Lock Rd. Wind. AP43 61
Romney Rd. SE10 CF43 67
Romney Rd. Hayes BA37 53
Romney Rd. N. Mal. BN53 85
Romney St. SW1 BW41 3
Romney St. SW1 BW41 66
Romola Rd. SE24 BY47 76
Romsey Clo. Slou. AS41 62
Romsey Dr. Slou. AO34 43
Romsey Gdns. Dag. CP37 59
Romsey Rd. W13 BJ40 54
Romsey Rd. Dag. CP37 59
Ronald Av. E15 CG38 58
Ronald Clo. Beck. CD52 87
Ronald Rd. Rom. CX30 42
Ronald St. E1 CC39 57
Devonport St.
Ronalds Rd. N5 BY35 47
Ronald's Rd. Brom. CH51 88
Ronaldstone Rd. Sid. CN46 78
Rona Rd. NW3 BV35 47
Rona Wk. N1 BZ36 57
Marquess Est.
Rondu Rd. NW2 BR35 46
Ronelean Rd. Surb. BL55 85
Ronfearn Av. Orp. CP53 89
Ronneby Clo. Wey. BB55 83
Ronson Way, Lthd. BJ64 102
Ronver Rd. SE12 CG47 78
Rood La. EC3 CA40 4
Rook Clo. Rain. CU37 59
Rook Dean, Sev. CS64 107
Rookeries Clo. Felt. BC48 73
Rookery Clo. NW9 BO32 46
Rookery Clo. Grays. DA43 70
Rookery, The
Rookery Clo. Lthd. BG65 102
Rookery Cres. Dag. CR36 59
Rookery Dr. Dor. BF72 119
Rookery Dr. Chis. CL51 88
Rookery Gdns. Orp. CP53 89
Rookery Grays. DA43 70
Rookery La. Brom. CJ53 88
Rookery La. Wal. Abb. CF18 21
Rookery Rd. SW4 BW45 66
Rookery Rd. Ing. DB17 24
Rookery Rd. Orp. CK58 97
Rookery Rd. Stai. AW49 73
Rookery, The Dor. BF72 119
Rookery, The Wat. BC26 35
Rookery Vw. Grays. DE42 71
Rookery Way NW9 BO32 46
Rookery Way, Tad. BR67 112
Rookesley Rd. Orp. CP54 89
Rooke Way SE10 CG42 68
Glenister Rd.
Rookfield Av. N10 BW31 47
Rookfield Clo. N10 BW31 47
Cranmore Way
Rook Hill Cat. BY65 104
Rook La. Cat. BX65 104
Rookley Clo. Sutt. BS58 95
Hulverston Clo.
Rooks Hill, Rick. AX24 26
Rooks Hill, Sev. CY68 117
Rooks Hill, Welw. G. C. BQ8 5
Rooksmead Rd. Sun. BB51 83
Rookstone Rd. SW17 BU49 76
Rookwood Av. Loug. CM24 31
Rookwood Av. N. Mal. BP52 85
Rookwood Av. Wall. BW56 95
Rookwood Clo. Grays. DD42 71
Rookwood Clo. Red. BV68 113
Rookwood Gdns. E4 CG27 40
Whitehall Rd.
Rookwood Gdns. Ilf. CO29 41
Rookwood Gdns. Loug. CM24 31
Rookwood Rd. N16 CA32 48
Roosevelt Way, Dag. CS36 59
Roothill La. Bet. BM73 120
Ropemakers Flds. E14 CD40 57
Ropemaker St. EC2 BZ39 57
Ropers Av. E4 CE28 39
Roper St. SE9 CK46 78
Roper Way, Mitch. BV51 86
Ropery St. E3 CD38 57
Rope Wk. Sun. BD52 84
Rope Wk. Gdns. E1 CB39 57
Commercial Rd.
Rope Yard Rails, SE18 CL41 68

Ropley St. E2 CB37 2
Ropley St. E2 CB37 57
Shipton St.
Rosa Alba Ms. N5 B35 48
Kelross Rd.
Rosa Av. Ashf. AZ49 73
Rosaline Rd. SW6 BR43 65
Rosamond St. SE26 CB48 77
Rosary Clo. Houns. BE44 64
Rosary Clo. Pot. B. BS18 20
Rosary Gdns. SW7 BT42 3
Rosary Gdns. SW7 BT42 66
Rosary Gdns. Ashf. AZ49 73
Rosary, The Egh. AV51 82
Rosavale Rd. SW6 BR43 65
Rosco St. EC1 BZ38 2
Rosco St. EC1 BZ38 57
Roscoff Cl. Edg. BM30 37
East Rd.
Roseacre, Oxt. CH70 115
Rose Acre, Saw. CP5 6
Roseacre Clo. W13 BJ39 54
Roseacre Clo. Horn. CW33 51
Curtis Rd.
Roseacre Gdns. Guil. AV73 118
Roseacre Rd. Well. CO45 69
Rose Alley SE1 BZ40 4
Rose Alley SE1 BZ40 57
Roseary Clo. West Dr. AX42 63
Rose Av. E18 CH30 40
Rose Av. Grav. DJ47 81
Rose Av. Mitch. BU51 86
Rose Av. Mord. BT53 86
Rose Bank SE20 CB50 77
Rose Bank SW6 BQ43 65
Rose Bank, Brwd. DB27 42
Rosebank, Epsom BN60 94
Rosebank, Wal. Abb. CG20 22
Rosebank Av. Horn. CV35 51
Rosebank Av. Wem. BH35 45
Rosebank Cotts. Wok. AS64 100
Rosebank Gdns. E3 CD37 57
St. Stephens Rd.
Rosebank Gdns. W3 BN39 55
York Rd.
Rosebank Gro. E17 CD31 48
Rosebank Rd. E3 CD37 57
Norman Gro.
Rosebank Rd. E17 CE32 48
Rosebank Rd. W7 BH41 64
Rosebank Vill. E17 CE31 48
High St.
Rosebank Wk. SE18 CK42 68
Samuel St.
Rosebank Way W3 BN39 55
Roseberry Av. EC1 BY38 56
Roseberry Clo. Mord. BQ53 85
Roseberry Clo. Upmin. CZ32 51
Roseberry Gdns. Dart. CV47 80
Roseberry Gdns. Orp. CN55 88
Roseberry Gdns. Upmin. CZ32 51
Roseberry Gdns. Upmin. CZ33 51
Roseberry Pl. E8 CA36 57
Roseberry Rd. Epsom BN63 103
Roseberry St. SE16 CB42 67
Rosebery Av. E12 CK36 58
Rosebery Av. EC1 BY38 2
Rosebery Av. EC1 BY38 56
Rosebery Av. N17 CB30 39
Rosebery Av. Epsom BO60 94
Rosebery Av. Har. BE35 45
Rosebery Av. N. Mal. BO51 85
Rosebery Av. Sid. CN47 78
Rosebery Av. Th. Hth. BZ51 87
Rosebery Cres. Wok. AS64 100
Rosebery Gdns. N4 BY32 47
Rosebery Gdns. N8 BX32 47
Rosebery Gdns. W13 BJ39 54
Rosebery Gdns. Sutt. BS56 95
Lewis Rd.
Rosebery Mews, N10 BW30 38
Rosebery Rd.
Rosebery Rd. N9 CB27 39
Rosebery Rd. N10 BW30 38
Rosebery Rd. SW2 BX46 76
Rosebery Rd. Bush. BF26 36
Rosebery Rd. Grays. DC43 71
Rosebery Rd. Houns. BG46 74
Rosebery Rd. Kings. on T. BM51 85
Rosebery Rd. Sutt. BR57 94
Rosebery Sq. Kings. on T. BM51 85
Rosebine Av. Twick. BG47 74
Rose Briar Clo. Wok. AW61 101
Pyrford Rd.
Rosebriar Wk. Wat. BB21 26
Rosebrook Villas E17 CD31 48
High St.
Rosebury Rd. SW6 BS44 66
Rosebury Vale, Ruis. BB33 44
Rosebushes, Epsom BP61 103
Rose Cott. W5 BK40 54
Western Rd.
Rose Ct. SE26 CB48 77
Rose Ct. Pnr. BD31 45
Nursery Rd.
Rosecourt Rd. Croy. BX53 86
Rosecroft Av. NW3 BS34 47
Rosecroft Clo. Orp. CP53 89
Rosecroft Dr. Wat. BB22 26
Rosecroft Gdns. NW2 BP34 46
Rosecroft Gdns. Twick. BG47 74
Rosecroft Rd. Sthl. BF38 54
Rosecroft Wk. Pnr. BD32 45
Rosecorft Wk. Wem. BK35 45
Rose & Crown Ct. EC2 BZ39 57
Foster La.
Rose & Crown La. W6 BQ40 65
Talgarth Rd.
Rose & Crown Yd. SW1 BW40 3
Rose & Crown Yd. SW1 BW40 56
King St.
Rosedale, Ash. BK62 102
Rosedale, Orp. CL55 88
Rosedale, Wal. Cr. CA17 21
Rosedale, Welw. G. C. BR6 5
Rosedale Av. Hayes BA39 53
Rosedale Av. Wal. Cr. CB18 21
Rosedale Clo. SE2 CO41 69
Finchdale Rd.
Rosedale Clo. Dart. CX47 80
Rosedale Clo. St. Alb. BE18 18
Rosedale Clo. Stan. BJ29 36
Rosedale Cotts. W7 BH41 64
Rosedale Gdns. Dag. CO36 59
Rosedale Rd. E7 CJ35 49
Rosedale Rd. Dag. CO36 59
Rosedale Rd. Epsom BP56 94
Rosedale Rd. Grays. DE42 71
Rosedale Rd. Rich. BL45 65
Rosedale Rd. Rom. CS30 41
Rosedale Way, Wal. Cr. CB17 21
Rosedene Av. SW16 BX48 76
Rosedene Av. Croy. BX54 86
Rosedne Av. Grnf. BF38 54
Rosedene Av. Mord. BS53 86
Rosedene Ct. Dart. CV47 80
Shepherds Lane
Rosedene Ct. Ruis. BB33 44
Rosedene Gdns. Ilf. CL31 49
Rosedene Ter. E10 CE34 48
Rosedew Rd. W6 BQ43 65
Rose Dr. Chesh. AO19 16
Rose End Wor. Pk. BQ54 85
Rosefield, Sev. CU65 107
Rosefield Gdns. E14 CE40 57
Morant St.
Rosefield Gdns. Cher. AU57 91
Rosefield Rd. Stai. AW49 73
Rose Garden Clo. Edg. BL29 37
Rose Gdns. W5 BK41 64
Rose Gdns. Felt. BC48 73
Rose Gdns. Sthl. BF38 54
Rose Gdns. Wat. BC25 26
Rose Glen NW9 BN31 46
Rose Glen, Rom. CT33 50
Rosehart Mews W11 BS39 56
Westbourne Grove
Rosehatch Av. Rom. CP31 50
Rose Heath, Hem. AV13 7
Roseheath Rd. Houns. BE46 74
Rose Hill, Dor. BJ71 119
Rosehill, Esher BJ57 93
Rose Hill, Hamptn. BF51 84
Rose Hill, Sutt. BS55 86
Rosehill Av. Sutt. BT54 86
Rose Hill Av. Wok. AR61 100
Rosehill Clo. Hodd. CD12 12
Rosehill Gdns. Grnf. BH35 45
Rosehill Gdns. Sutt. BS55 86
Rosehill Gdns. Wat. BA19 17
Rosehill Pk. W. Sutt. BS54 86
Rosehill Rd. SW18 BT46 76
Rosehill Rd. West. CJ62 106
Roseland Cl. N17 BZ29 39
Roselands Av. Hodd. CD11 12
Rose La. Rom. CP31 50
Rose La. Wok. AX64 101
Rose Lawn, Bush. BG26 36
Roseleigh Av. N5 BY35 47
Roseleigh Clo. Twick. BK46 74
Rosemaker St. EC2 BZ39 2
Rosemary Av. N3 BS30 38
Rosemary Av. N9 CB26 39
Rosemary Av. E. Mol. BF52 84
Rosemary Av. Enf. BZ23 30
Rosemary Av. Houns. BD44 64
Rosemary Av. Rom. CT31 50
Rosemary Clo. Harl. CP9 6
Garden Ter. Rd.
Rosemary Clo. S. Ock. DB38 60
Rosemary Clo. Oxt. CH70 115
Holland La.
Rosemary Clo. Uxb. AZ39 53
Rose Mary Cres. Guil. AP68 109
Rosemary Dr. Ilf. CJ32 49
Rosemary Gdns. SW14 BN45 65
Rosemary La.
Rosemary Gdns. Chess. BL56 94
Rosemary Gdns. Dag. CQ33 50
Rosemary La. SW14 BN45 65
Rosemary La. Egh. AT52 82
Rosemary Rd. SE15 CA43 67
Sumner Rd.
Rosemary Rd. Well. CN44 68
Rosemary St. N1 BZ37 2
Rosemary St. N1 BZ37 57
Rose Mead. BO33 46
Rose Mead. Pot. B. BT18 20
Rosemead Av. Felt. BB48 73
Rosemead Av. Mitch. BW52 86
Rosemead Av. Wem. BL35 46
Rosemead Clo. Red. BT71 121
Rosemead Gdns. Brwd. DF24 122
Rosemont Av. N12 BT29 38
Rosemont Cotts. Wem. BL37 55
Rosemont Ct. W3 BM40 55
Rosemont Rd.
Rosemont Rd. NW3 BT36 56
Rosemont Rd. W3 BM40 55
Rosemont Rd. N. Mal. BN52 85
Rosemont Rd. Rich. BL46 75
Rosemoor St. SW3 BU42 3
Rosemoor St. SW3 BU42 66
Rosemount Harl. CL12 13
Rosemount Av. Wey. AW60 92
Rosemount Dr. Brom. CK52 88
Rosemount Rd. W13 BJ39 54
Rosenau Cres. SW11 BU44 66
Rosenau Rd. SW11 BU44 66
Rosendale Rd. SE21 BZ47 77
Rosendale Rd. SE24 BZ47 77
Rosendale St. E5 CB34 48
Roseneath Av. N21 BY26 38
Roseneath Clo. Orp. CP57 98
Roseneath Rd. SW11 BV46 76
Roseneath Wk. Enf. BZ24 30
Rosens Wk. Edg. BM27 37
Rosenthal Rd. SE6 CE46 77
Rosenthorpe Rd. SE15 CC46 77
Roserton St. E14 CF41 67
Rosert St. E14 CF41 67
Manchester Rd.
Rosery, The Croy. CC53 87
Roses La. Wind. AL44 61
Roses, The Wdf. Grn. CG29 40
Bunches La.
Rose St. WC2 BX40 4
Rose St. WC2 BX40 56
Floral St.
Rose St. Grav. DD46 81
Rosetrees, Guil. AT71 118
Rose Vale, Hodd. CE12 12
Rosevale Rd. SW6 BR44 65
Rose Vall. Brwd. DB27 42
Roseveare Rd. SE12 CJ49 78
Roseville Av. Houns. BF46 74
Roseville Rd. Hayes BC42 63
Rosevine Rd. SW20 BQ51 85
Rose Wk. Pur. BW59 95
Rose Wk. St. Alb. BK12 9
Rose Wk. Surb. BM53 85
Rose Wk. W. Wick. CF55 87
Roseway SE21 BZ46 77
Rosewood Bex. CT49 79
Rosewood Av. Grnf. BJ35 45
Rosewood Av. Horn. CU35 50
Rosewood Clo. Sid. CP48 79
Birchwood Av.
Rosewood Dr. Enf. BY21 29
Rosewood Dr. Shep. AY53 83
Rose Wood Gdns. Wall. BV57 95
Rosewood Gro. Sutt. BT55 86
Rosher Clo. E15 CF36 57
Rosina St. E9 CC35 48
Roskell Rd. SW15 BQ45 65
Roslin Rd. W3 BM41 65
Roslin Way, Brom. CH49 78
Roslyn Clo. Brox. CD14 12
Roslyn Clo. Mitch. BT51 86
Rosly Gdns. Rom. CT30 41
Roslyn Rd. N15 BZ32 48
Rosmead Rd. W11 BR40 55
Rosoman St. EC1 BY38 2
Rosoman St. EC1 BY38 56
Rossall Clo. Horn. CU32 50
Rossall Cres. NW10 BL38 55
Ross Av. NW7 BR28 37
Ross Av. Dag. CQ34 50
Ross Clo. Hat. BP11 10
Ross Clo. E4 CF27 39
Ross Clo. Hayes BA42 63
Ross Ct. NW1 BU38 1
Ross Cres. Wat. BC21 26
Rossdale, Sutt. BU56 95
Rossdale Dr. N9 CC25 30
Rossdale Dr. NW9 BN33 46
Rossdale Rd. SW15 BQ45 65
Rosse Ms. SE3 CH44 68
Rossendale St. E5 CB34 48
Rossgate, Hem. H. AW12 8
Galley Hill
Rossindale Rd. Houns. BF46 74
Rossington Av. Borwd. BL22 28
Rossington St. E5 CB34 48
Rossiter Clo. Slou. AS42 62
Rossiter Rd. SW12 BV47 76
Rossland Clo. Bexh. CR46 79
Rosslyn Av. E4 CG27 40
Rosslyn Av. SW13 BO45 65
Rosslyn Av. Barn. BU25 29
Rosslyn Av. Dag. CQ33 50
Rosslyn Av. Felt. BC46 73
Rosslyn Av. Rom. CW30 42
Rosslyn Clo. Hayes BA39 53
Rosslyn Clo. W. Wick. CG55 88
Rosslyn Ct. Wok. AQ62 100
St. John's Rd.
Rosslyn Cres. Har. BH31 45
Rosslyn Cres. Wem. BL35 46
Rosslyn Cres. N. Har. BH31 45
Rosslyn Cres. S. Har. BH32 45
Rosslyn Hl. NW3 BT35 47
Rosslyn Pk. Ms. NW3 BT35 47
Rosslyn Rd. E17 CF31 48
Rosslyn Rd. Bark. CM36 58
Rosslyn Rd. Twick. BK46 74
Rosslyn Rd. Wat. BC24 26
Rossmore Rd. NW1 BU38 1
Rossmore Rd. NW1 BU38 56
Ross Oak Rd. Ber. AQ13 7
Ross Pde. Wall. BV57 95
Ross Rd. SE25 BZ52 87
Ross Rd. Cob. BD60 93
Ross Rd. Dart. CU46 79
Ross Rd. Twick. BG47 74
Ross Rd. Wall. BW56 95
Ross Way SE9 CK45 68
Rossway Dr. Bush. BG25 27
Ross Way, Nthwd. BB28 35
Rossway La. Berk. AO13 7
Rostella Rd. SW17 BT49 76
Rostrevor Av. N15 CA32 48
Rostrevor Gdns. Hayes BB40 53
Rostrevor Gdns. Iver. AU37 52
Rostrevor Gdns. Sthl. BE42 64
Rostrevor Mews SW6 BR45 65
Rostrevor Rd. SW6 BR44 65
Rostrevor Rd. SW19 BS49 76
Rotary St. SE1 BY41 4
Rotary St. SE1 BY41 66
Rothbury Av. Rain. CU39 59
Rothbury Gdns. Islw. BJ43 64
Rothbury Rd. E9 CD36 57
Rothbury Wk. N17 CB29 39
Park La.
Rother Clo. Wat. BD20 18
Rotherfield Rd. Cars. BV56 95
Rotherfield Rd. Enf. CC22 30
Rotherfield St. N1 BZ36 2
Rotherfield St. N1 BZ36 57
Rotherhill Av. SW16 BW50 76
Rotherhithe New Rd. SE16 CB42 67
Rotherhithe Old Rd. SE16 CC42 67
Rotherhithe St. SE16 CB41 67
Rotherhithe Tunnel App. E14 CD40 57
Rothermere Rd. Croy. BX56 95
Rotherwick Hill W5 BL38 55
Rotherwick Rd. NW11 BS33 47
Rotherwood Rd. SW15 BQ45 65
Rothery St. N1 BY37 56
Gaskin St.
Rothesay Av. SW20 BR51 85
Rothesay Av. Grnf. BG36 54
Rothesay Av. Rich. BM45 65
Rothesay Rd. SE25 BZ52 87
Rothes Rd. Dor. BJ71 119
Rothfild Rd. Cars. BV56 95
Rothsay Rd. E7 CJ36 58
Rothsay St. SE1 BZ41 4
Rothsay St. SE1 CA41 67
Rothschild Rd. W4 BN41 65
Rothschild St. SE27 BY49 76
Roth Wk. N7 BX34 47
Andover Est.
Roth Wk. N7 BX34 47
Durham Rd.
Rothwell Gdns. Dag. CP37 59
Rothwell Rd. Dag. CP37 59
Rothwell St. NW1 BU36 56
Rotten Row SE3 CG44 68
Rotten Row SW7 BT41 3
Rotten Row SW7 BU41 66
Rotten Row SW11 BU43 66
Rouel Rd. SE16 CB41 4
Rouel Rd. SE16 CB41 67
Rougemont Av. Mord. BS53 86
Roughdown Av. Hem. H. AW15 8
Roughdown, Hem. H. AW15 8
Rough Down Rd. Hem. H. AW15 8
Roughetts La. Red. CA68 114
Roughlands, Wok. AV60 100
Rough Rew, Dor. BJ73 119
Rough Rd. Wok. AO64 100
Roughs, The Nthwd. BB27 35
Rough Wood Clo. Wat. BB22 26
Roughwood La. Ch. St. G. AS25 25
Roughwood La. Ch. St. G. AS26 34
Roundabout's, The Dor. BE71 119
Roundacre Est. SW19 BQ48 75
Round Ash Way, Hart. DC53 90
Roundaway Rd. Ilf. CK30 40
Round Gro. Croy. CC54 87
Roundhay Clo. SE23 CC48 77
Round Hedge Mews, Enf. BX22 29
Roundhill Clo. Wok. AT62 100
Roundhill Dr. Enf. BX24 29
Roundhill Dr. Wok. AT63 100
Roundhills, Wal. Abb. CF20 21
Roundhills, Wal. Abb. CG20 22
Roundhill Way, Cob. BF59 93
Roundhill Way, Guil. AP70 118
Round Hl. SE26 CB48 77
Roundmead Av. Loug. CL24 31
Roundmead Clo. Loug. CL24 31
Roundmoor Dr. Wal. Cr. CD18 21
Round Oak Rd. Wey. AY55 83
Roundtable Rd. Brom. CG48 78
Roundthorne Way. Wok. AP61 100
Roundtree Rd. Wem. BJ36 54
Round Way, Egh. AV49 72
Roundway, West. CJ61 106
Sunningvale Av.
Roundways, The Ruis. BB34 44
Roundway, The N17 BZ29 39
Roundway, The Esher BH57 93
Roundway, The Wat. BB25 26
Roundwood, Chis. CL51 88
Roundwood, Kings L. AY17 17
Roundwood Av. Brwd. DD26 122
Roundwood Clo. Ruis. BA33 44
Roundwood Dr. Welw. G. C. BQ7 5
Roundwood Gro. Brwd. DD26 122
Roundwood Pk. Av. NW10 BP37 55
Roundwood Rd. NW10 BO36 55
Round Wood Rd. Amer. AP22 25
Round Wood Vw. Bans. BQ61 103
Roundwood Way, Bans. BQ61 103
Rounton Dr. Wat. BB22 26
Rounton Rd. E3 CE38 57
Rounton Rd. Wal. Abb. CG20 22
Roupell Rd. SW2 BX47 76
Roupell St. SE1 BY40 4
Roupell St. SE1 BY40 56
Rousebarn La. Rick. AY22 26
Rousebarn La. Wat. BB24 26
Rouse Gdns. SE21 CA49 77
Rous Rd. Buck. H. CK26 40
Routh Rd. SW18 BU47 76
Rover Av. Ilf. CN29 40
Rovington Clo. W2 BS39 1
Rowallan Rd. SW6 BR43 65
Rowan Av. E4 CD29 39
Rowan Av. Egh. AV49 72
Rowan Clo. SW16 BW51 86
Rowan Clo. Guil. AR69 118
Rowan Clo. Reig. BT71 121
Rowan Clo. N. Mal. BO51 85
Rowan Clo. St. Alb. BF19 18
Rowan Clo. Uxb. AW30 35
Rowan Ct. SE12 CG47 78
Rowan Cres. SW16 BW51 86
Rowan Cres. Dart. CV47 80
Rowan Dr. Brox. CD16 21
Rowan Gdns. W6 BQ42 65
Bute Gdns.
Rowan Gdns. Croy. CA55 87
Rowan Grn. Couls. BV64 104
Rowanhurst Dr. Slou. AO35 43
Rowan Pl. Hayes BB40 53
Rowan Rd. SW16 BW51 86
Rowan Rd. W6 BQ42 65
Rowan Rd. Bexh. CQ45 69
Rowan Rd. Brent. BJ43 64
Rowan Rd. Swan. CS52 89
Rowan Rd. West Dr. AX42 63
Rowan Wk. W10 BR38 55
Droop St.
Rowans, Welw. G. C. BS6 5
Rowans, The N13 BY27 38
Rowans The Ger. Cr. AR31 43
Rowans, The Hem. H. AW13 8
Rowans, The Sun. BB49 73
Rowantree Clo. N21 BZ26 39
Rowantree Rd. N21 BZ26 39
Rowantree Rd. Enf. BY23 29
Rowan Wk. N2 BT32 47
Rowan Wk. Brom. CK55 88
Rowan Wk. Hat. BP14 10
Rowan Wk. Horn. CV31 51
Rowan Way, Rom. CP31 50
Rowbarns Way, Leath. BB68 110
Rowben Clo. N20 BS26 38
Row Croft, Hem. H. AV14 7
Rowcross St. SE1 CA42 4
Rowcross St. SE1 CA42 67
Rowdell Rd. Nthlt. BF37 54
Rowden Pk. Gdns. E4 CE29 39
Rowden Rd.
Rowden Rd. E4 CE29 39
Rowden Rd. Beck. CD51 87
Rowden Rd. Epsom BM56 94
Rowditch La. SW11 BV44 66
Rowdon Av. NW10 BP36 55
Rowdon La. Sev. CV60 99
Rowdon La. Sev. CV61 108
Rowdown Cres. Croy. CF58 96
Rowdowns Rd. Dag. CQ37 59
Rowe Gdns. Bark. CN37 58
Rowe La. E9 CC35 48
Urswick Rd.
Rowena Cres. SW11 BU44 66
Rowen Grn. Brwd. DC27 122
Rowe Wk. Har. BF34 45
Rowfant Rd. SW17 BV47 76
Rowhedge, Brwd. DD27 122
Rowhill, Wey. AV57 91
Rowhill Rd. E5 CB35 48
Rowhill Rd. Dart. CT50 79
Row Hill St. NW3 BU35 47
Rowhurst Av. Lthd. BH62 102
Rowington Clo. W2 BS39 56
Rowland Av. Har. BK31 45
Rowland Clo. Wind. AL45 61
Rowland Ct. E13 CG38 58
Rowland Ct. E16 CG38 58
Beaconsfield Rd.
Rowland Cres. Chig. CN28 40
Fairview Dr.
Rowland Gro. SE26 CB49 77
Rowland Gro. SE26 CB48 77
Dallas Rd.
Rowland Hill Av. N17 BZ29 39
Rowland Hill St. NW3 BU35 47
Rowland Rd. SW4 BW45 66
Rowlands Av. Pnr. BF28 36
Rowlands Rd. Dag. CQ34 50
Rowland Way SW19 BS51 86
Hayward Cl.
Rowland Wk. Hav. CT27 41
Rowland Way, Ashf. BA50 73
Rowlatt Clo. Dart. CV49 80
Rowlatt Rd. Dart. CV49 80
Rowlett Dr. St. Alb. BF14 9
Rowley Av. Sid. CO47 79
Rowley Clo. Wat. BE25 27
Rowley Clo. Wem. BL36 55
Rowley Gdns. N4 BZ33 48
Rowley Grn. Rd. Barn. BO25 28
Rowley La. Borwd. BN23 28
Rowley La. Slou. AR37 52
Rowley Mead. Epp. CP16 23
Rowley Rd. N15 BZ32 48
Rowley Ter. NW5 BV36 56
Rowley Way NW8 BS37 56
Abbey Rd.
Rowlls Rd. Kings. on T. BL52 85
Rowney Gdns. Dag. CO36 59
Rowney Gdns. Saw. CP7 6
Rowney Rd. Dag. CO36 59
Rowney Wood, Saw. CP6 6
Rowns Way, Loug. CK24 31
Rowntree Path SE28 CO40 59
Macauley Way
Rowntree Rd. Twick. BH47 74
Rowse Clo. E15 CF37 57
Rowsley Av. NW4 BQ31 46
Rowstock Gdns. N7 BW35 47
Rowton Rd. SE18 CM43 68
Roxborough Av. Har. BG33 45
Roxborough Av. Islw. BH43 64
Roxborough Pk. Har. BH33 45
Roxborough Rd. Har. BG32 45
Roxbourne Clo. Nthlt. BE36 54
Arnold Rd.
Roxburgh Av. Upmin. CY35 51
Roxburgh Rd. SE27 BY49 76
Roxburn Way, Ruis. BB34 44
Roxby Pl. SW6 BS43 66
Roxeth Ct. Ashf. AZ49 73
Roxeth Grn. Av. Har. BF34 45
Roxeth Gro. Har. BF35 45
Roxeth Hill, Har. BG34 45
Roxford Clo. Shep. BB53 83
Roxford Clo. Sth. Croy. CC59 96
Roxley Rd. SE13 CE46 77
Roxton Gdns. Croy. CE56 96
Roxwell Rd. W12 BP41 65
Roxwell Rd. Bark. CO37 59
Roswell Way, Wdf. Grn. CJ29 40
Roxy Av. Rom. CP33 50
Royal Arc. SW1 BW40 3
Royal Arc. SW1 BW40 56
Pall Mall
Royal Av. SW3 BU42 3
Royal Av. SW3 BU42 66
Royal Av. Wal. Cr. CD20 21
Royal Av. Wor. Pk. BO55 85
Royal Cir. SE27 BY48 76
Royal Clo. Uxb. AY39 53
Royal Clo. Wor. Pk. BO55 85
Royal College St. NW1 BW36 1
Royal College St. NW1 BW36 56
Royal Cres. W11 BQ40 55
Royal Cres. Ruis. BE35 45
Royal Cres. Ms. W11 BQ40 55
Royal Ct. Hem. H. AV15 8
Royal Dr. Epsom BP62 103
Royal Exchange Bldgs. EC3 BZ39 2
Royal Exchange Bldgs. EC3 BZ39 57
Cornhill
Royal Hl. SE10 CF43 67
Royal Hospital Rd. SW3 BU43 3
Royal Hospital Rd. SW3 BU43 66
Royal La. Uxb. & West Dr. AY38 53

Royal Mint Pla. E1 CA40 57
Royal Mint St.
Royal Mint St. E1 CA40 4
Royal Mint St. E1 CA40 57
Royal Naval Pl. SE14 CD43 67
Hereford Pl.
Royal Oak Ct. N1 CA38 57
Royal Oak Rd. E8 CB36 57
Wilton Way
Royal Oak Rd. Bexh. CQ46 79
Royal Oak Rd. Wok. AR62 100
Royal Oak Shopping Cen. Pur. BY54 86
Royal Pde. SE3 CG44 68
Royal Pde. W5 BL38 55
Western Av.
Royal Pde. Chis. CM50 78
Royal Pier Rd. Grav. DG46 81
Royal Pl. SE10 CF43 67
Royal Rd. E16 CJ39 58
Royal Rd. SE17 BY43 66
Royal Rd. Dart. CX49 80
Royal Rd. St. Alb. BJ13 9
Royal Rd. Sid. CP48 79
Royal Rd. Tedd. BG49 74
Royal St. SE1 BX41 4
Royal St. SE1 BX41 66
Royalty Mews W1 BW39 56
Dean St.
Royal Victor Pl. E3 CC37 57
Old Ford Rd.
Royal Wk. Wall. BV55 86
Prince Charles Way
Royce Clo. Brox. CD14 12
Roycraft Av. Bark. CN37 58
Roycraft Clo. Bark. CN37 58
Roycroft Clo. E18 CH30 40
Roydene Rd. SE18 CN43 68
Roydon Clo. SW11 BU44 66
Reform St.
Roydon Clo. Loug. CK26 40
Roydon Ct. Hem. H. AZ10 8
Elstree Rd.
Roydon Rd. Harl. CK10 13
Roydon St. SW11 BV44 66
Royd Way, Cob. BF60 93
Roy Gdns. Ilf. CN31 49
Roy Gro. Hamptn. BF50 74
Royle Gro. Ger. Cr. AS29 34
Royle Clo. Rom. CU32 50
Royle Cres. W13 BJ38 54
Roymount Ct. Twick. BH48 74
Roy Rd. Nthwd. BB29 35
Roysdon Rd. Rom. CW29 42
Ryston Av. E4 CE28 39
Royston Av. Sutt. BT55 86
Royston Av. Wall. BW56 95
Royston Av. Wey. AY60 92
Royston Chase, Wey. AY59 92
Royston Clo. Houns. BC44 63
Royston Clo. Walt. BC54 83
Royston Ct. Rich. BL44 65
Royston Ct. Surb. BM55 85
Royston Gdns. Ilf. CJ32 49
Royston Gro. Pnr. BE29 36
Royston Pk. Rd. Pnr. BE29 36
Royston Rd. SE20 CC51 87
Royston Rd. Dart. CT46 79
Royston Rd. Rich. BL46 75
Royston Rd. St. Alb. BJ14 9
Royston Rd. Wey. AY59 92
Roystons, The Surb. BM53 85
Royston St. E2 CC38 57
Rozel Rd. SW4 BW44 66
Rubastic Rd. Sthl. BC41 63
Rubens Rd. Nthlt. BD37 54
Rubens St. SE6 CD48 77
Ruberoid Rd. Enf. CD24 30
Ruby Rd. E17 CE31 48
Ruby St. SE15 CB43 67
Ruccles Brice Rd. Ashf. AX49 73
Ruckholt Clo. E10 CE34 48
Ruckholt Rd. E10 CE35 48
Rucklers La. Kings L. AW17 17
Ruckles Way, Amer. AO23 25
Station Rd.
Rucklidge Av. NW10 BO37 55
Rudall Cres. NW3 BT35 47
Willoughby Rd.
Ruddigore Rd. SE14 CD43 67
Ruddles Way, Wind. AL44 61
Rudd St. SE18 CL42 68
Ruden Way, Epsom BP61 103
Rudford Rd. SE16 CC42 67
Rudge Rd. Wey. AV56 91
Rudgewick Ct. Guil. AS71 118
Chesham Rd.
Rudland Rd. Bexh. CR45 69
Rudloe Rd. SW12 BW47 76
Rudolph Rd. E13 CG37 58
Rudolph Rd. NW6 BS37 56
Rudolph Rd. Bush. BF25 27
Rudwick Clo. Wal. Cr. CD17 21
Ashdown Cres.
Rudyard Gro. NW7 BN29 37
Ruffetts Clo. Sth. Croy. CB57 96
Ruffetts, The Sth. Croy. CB57 96
Ruffetts Way, Tad. BR62 103
Rufford St. N1 BX37 2
Rufford St. N1 BX37 56
Rufus Clo. Ruis. BE34 45
Rufus St. EC1 CA38 57
Old St.
Rufus St. N1 CA38 2
Rugby Av. N9 CA26 39
Rugby Av. Grnf. BG36 54
Rugby Av. Wem. BJ35 45
Rugby Clo. Har. BH31 45
Rugby Gdns. Dag. CP36 59
Rugby La. Sutt. BQ58 94
Rugby Rd. NW9 BM31 46
Rugby Rd. W4 BO41 65
Rugby Rd. Dag. CO36 59
Rugby Rd. Twick. BH46 74
Rugby St. WC1 BX38 2
Rugby St. WC1 BX38 56
Rugby Way, Rick. AZ25 26
Rugged La. Wal. Abb. CJ20 22
Rugg St. E14 CE40 57
Ruislip Clo. Grnf. BF38 54
Ruislip Rd. Grnf. BE38 54
Ruislip Rd. Nthlt. BD37 54
Ruislip Rd. E. W7 BG38 54
Ruislip Rd. E. W13 BG38 54
Ruislip Rd. E. Grnf. BG38 54
Ruislip St. SW17 BU49 76
Rumania Wk. Grav. DJ48 81
Cervia Way
Rumballs Clo. Hem. H. AZ15 8
Rumballs Rd. Hem. H. AZ15 8
Rumbold Rd. SW6 BS43 66
Rumbold Rd. Hodd. CF11 12
Rum Clo. E1 CB40 57
Agatha Clo.
Rumsley Rd. SW9 BX45 66
Runbury Circle NW9 BN34 46
Runciman Clo. Orp. CP58 98
Runcorn Cres. Hem. H. AY11 8
Runcorn Pl. W11 BR40 55
Rundell Cres. NW4 BP32 46
Rundells, Harl. CO13 14
Runham Rd. Hem. H. AY14 8
Runham St. SE17 BZ42 67
Runnelfield, Har. BH34 45
Runnemede, Egh. AS49 72
Runnemede Ct. Egh. AT49 72
Running Horse Yd. Brent. BL43 65
Pottery Rd.
Running Waters, Brwd. DD28 122
Runn Way E7 CH35 49
Runnymede SW19 BT51 86
Runnymede Clo. Twick. BF46 74
Runnymede Cres. SW16 BW51 86
Runnymede Gdns. Grnf. BG37 54
Runnymede Gdns. Twick. BF46 74
Runnymede Rd. Twick. BF46 74
Runrig Hill, Amer. AP21 25
Runsley, Welw. G. C. BR6 5
Runtley Wood La. Guil. AS66 109
Runton St. N19 BW33 47
Runway, The Ruis. BD35 45
Rupack St. SE16 CC41 67
St. Mary Church St.
Rupert Av. Wem. BL35 46
London Rd.
Rupert Gdns. SW9 BY44 66
Rupert Rd. N19 BW34 47
Rupert Rd. NW6 BR37 55
Rupert Rd. W4 BO41 65
Rupert Rd. Guil. AQ71 118
Rupert St. W1 BW40 3
Rupert St. W1 BW40 56
Rural Vale, Grav. DF47 81
Rural Way SW16 BV50 76
Rural Way, Red. BV70 121
Ruscoe Dr. Wok. AT62 100
Pembroke Rd.
Ruscoe Rd. E16 CG39 58
Ruscombe Dr. St. Alb. BG16 18
Ruscombe Way, Felt. BB47 73
Bedfont La.
Rusham Pk. Av. Egh. AS50 72
Rusham Rd. SW12 BU46 76
Rusham Rd. Egh. AS50 72
Rushbrook Cres. E17 CD30 39
Rushbrook Rd. SE9 CM48 78
Rushcroft Rd. E4 CE29 39
Rushcroft Rd. SW2 BY45 66
Rushden Clo. SE19 BZ50 77
Rushdene SE2 CP41 69
Rushdene Av. Barn. BU26 38
Rushdene Clo. Nthlt. BD37 54
Rushdene Cres. Nthlt. BD37 54
Rushdene Rd. Brwd. DB26 42
Rushdene Rd. Pnr. BD32 45
Rushdene Wk. West. BQ53
Polesteeple Hill
Rushdene Gdn. NW7 BQ29 37
Rushdene Gdns. Ilf. CL30 40
Rushdon Clo. Grays. DD41 71
Rushen Wk. Cars. BT54 86
Rushes Mead. Harl. CN12 13
Rushet Rd. Orp. CO51 89
Rushett Clo. Surb. BJ54 84
Rushett Dr. Dor. BJ73 119
Rushett Gdns. Surb. BJ54 84
Rushett La. Chess. BK59 93
Rushett Rd. Surb. BJ54 84
Rushetts Rd. Reig. BT72 121
Rushett's Rd. Sev. CZ57 99
Rushey Clo. N. Mal. BN52 85
Rushey Grn. SE6 CE47 77
Rushfield, Pot. B. BQ20 19
Rushfield, Saw. CQ6 6
Rushford Rd. SE4 CD46 77
Rush Grn. Gdns. Rom. CS33 50
Rush Grn. Rd. Rom. CR33 50
Rushgrove Av. NW9 BO32 46
Rushgrove St. SE18 CK42 68
Rush Hill Rd. SW11 BV45 66
Rushleigh Av. Wal. Cr. CC18 21
Rushley Clo. Grays. DE40 71
Rushley Clo. Kes. CJ56 97
Rushmead E2 CB38 57
Florida St.
Rushmead, Rich. BJ48 74
Rushmead, Sev. CX62 108
Rushmead Clo. Croy. CA56 96
Rushmead Clo. Edg. BM27 37
Rushmere Av. Upmin. CY35 51
Rushmere La. Ches. AQ17 16
Rushmoor Clo. Guil. AP69 118
Rushmoor Clo. Pnr. BC31 44
Rushmoor Clo. Rick. AX27 35
Rushmoor Clo. Brom. CK52 88
Rushmoor Ct. Wor. Pk. BP55 85
Rushmore Cres. E5 CC35 48
Rushmore Hill, Orp. CP58 98
Rushmore Rd. E5 CC35 48
Rusholme Rd. SW15 BQ46 75
Rusholme Rd. Dag. CR34 50
Rushout Av. Har. BJ32 45
Rushton Av. Wat. BC21 26
Rushton St. N1 BZ37 2
Rushton St. N1 BZ37 57
Rushworth Gdns. NW4 BP31 46
Rushworth Rd. Reig. BS70 121
Rushworth St. SE1 BY41 4
Rushworth St. SE1 BY41 66
Ruskin Av. E12 CK36 58
Ruskin Av. Felt. BB46 73
Ruskin Av. Rich. BM43 65
Ruskin Av. Upmin. CY33 51
Ruskin Av. Wal. Abb. CG20 22
Ruskin Av. Well. CO45 69
Ruskin Clo. NW11 BS32 47
Ruskin Clo. Wal. Cr. CA16 21
Hammond St. Rd.
Ruskin Ct. N21 BX26 38
Ruskin Dr. Orp. CN55 88
Ruskin Dr. Well. CO45 69
Ruskin Dr. Wor. Pk. BP55 85
Ruskin Dr. Wor. Pk. BQ54 85
Ruskin Gdns. W5 BK38 54
Ruskin Gdns. Har. BL32 46
Ruskin Gdns. Rom. CU30 41
Ruskin Gro. Dart. CX46 80
Ruskin Gro. Well. CO44 69
Ruskin Pk. Ho. SE5 BZ45 67
Ruskin Rd. N17 CA30 39
Ruskin Rd. Belv. CR42 69
Ruskin Rd. Cars. BU56 95
Ruskin Rd. Croy. BY55 86
Ruskin Rd. Grays. DG42 71
Ruskin Rd. Islw. BH45 64
Ruskin Rd. Stai. AV50 72
Ruskin Rd. Sthl. BE40 54
Ruskin Wk. N9 CB27 39
Ruskin Wk. SE24 BZ46 77
Ruskin Wk. Brom. CK53 88
Rusland Av. Orp. CM55 88
Rusland Rd. Har. BH31 45
Rusper Clo. Stan. BK28 36
Rusper Clo. SW9 BX44 66
Clapham Rd.
Rusper Rd. N22 BY30 38
Rusper Rd. Dag. CP36 59
Russ Clo. E4 CF28 39
Larkshall Rd.
Russel Av. St. Alb. BG13 9
Russelcroft Rd. Welw. G. C. BQ7 5
Russell Av. N22 BY30 38
Russell Clo. NW10 BN36 55
Russell Clo. Amer. AR23 25
Russell Clo. Beck. CE52 87
Russell Clo. Bexh. CR45 69
Russell Clo. Brwd. DA26 42
Russell Clo. Dart. CU45 69
Russell Clo. Ruis. BD34 45
Russell Clo. Tad. BP66 112
Russell Clo. Wok. AR61 100
Russell Ct. SW1 BW40 3
Russell Ct. SW1 BW40 56
Cleveland Row
Russell Ct. Chesh. AO18 16
Russell Ct. Lthd. BJ64 102
Russell Ct. St. Alb. BF18 18
Black Boy Wd.
Russell Cres. Wat. BB21 26
Russell Dr. Stai. AX46 73
Russell Gdns. N20 BU27 38
Russell Gdns. NW11 BR32 46
Russell Gdns. W14 BR41 65
Russell Gdns. Rich. BK48 74
Russell Gdns. Ms. W14 BR41 65
Russell Grn. Clo. Pur. BY58 95
Russell Gro. NW7 BO28 37
Russell Gro. SW9 BY43 66
Russell Hill, Pur. BX58 95
Russell Hill Pl. Pur. BY55 86
Russell Hill Pl. Pur. BY59 95
Russell Hill Rd. Pur. BY58 95
Russell La. N20 BU27 38
Russell La. Wat. BA21 26
Russell Mead, Har. BH29 36
Russell Pl. SW1 BW42 3
Russell Pl. SW1 BW42 66
Vauxhall Br. Rd.
Russell Pl. Hem. H. AW15 8
Russell Pl. S. at. H. CX51 90
Russell Rd. E4 CD28 39
Russell Rd. E10 CE32 48
Russell Rd. E16 CH39 58
Russell Rd. E17 CD31 48
Russell Rd. N8 BW32 47
Russell Rd. N13 BX29 38
Russell Rd. N15 CA32 48
Russell Rd. N20 BU27 38
Russell Rd. NW9 BO32 46
Russell Rd. SW19 BS50 76
Russell Rd. W14 BR41 65
Russell Rd. Buck. H. CH26 40
Russell Rd. Enf. CA22 30
Russell Rd. Grav. DH46 81
Russell Rd. Grays. DD42 71
Russell Rd. Nthlt. BG35 45
Russell Rd. Nthwd. BA27 35
Russell Rd. Shep. AZ54 83
Russell Rd. Til. DF44 71
Russell Rd. Twick. BH46 74
Russell Rd. Walt. BC53 83
Russell Rd. Wok. AR61 100
Russell's Footpath SW16 BX49 76
Russell Sq. WC1 BX38 2
Russell Sq. WC1 BW38 56
Russells Ride, Wal. Cr. CD19 21
Russell St. E13 CH37 58
Russell St. WC1 BX40 4
Russell St. WC2 BX40 56
Russell Rd. Mitch. BU52 86
Russell Rd. Wind. AO44 61
Russet Clo. Stai. AV46 72
Russet Clo. Uxb. BA38 53
Russet Cres. N7 BX35 47
Stockorchard Cres.
Russett Clo. Orp. CO56 98
Russett Way, Swan. CS51 89
Russet Way SE13 CE44 67
Conington Rd.
Russia La. E2 CC37 57
Russia Row EC2 BZ39 2
Russia Row EC2 BZ39 57
Milk St.
Russington Rd. Shep. BA53 83
Rusthall Av. W4 BN42 65
Rusthall Clo. Croy. CC53 87
Rustic Av. SW16 BV50 76
Rustic Clo. Upmin. CZ33 51
Rustic Pl. Wem. BK35 45
Rustington Wk. Mord. BR54 85
Ruson Av. Surb. BM54 85
Ruston Ms. W11 BR39 55
Ruston St. E3 CD37 57
Rust Sq. SE5 BZ43 67
Rutford Rd. SW16 BX49 76
Ruth Clo. Epsom BM60 94
Ruth Clo. Har. BL31 46
Ruthen Clo. Epsom BN60 94
Rutherford Clo. Sutt. BT57 95
Rutherford St. SW1 BW42 3
Rutherford Way, Bush. BG26 36
Rutherglen Rd. SE2 CO43 69
Rutherland St. SW1 BW42 66
Rutherwick Rise BX62 104
Rutherwick Rise, Couls. BX57 95
Rutherwyke Clo. Epsom BP57 94
Rutherwyk Rd. Cher. AV54 82
Ruthin Rd. SE3 CH43 68
Ruthven Av. Wal. Cr. CC20 21
Ruthven St. E9 CC37 57
Lauriston Rd.
Rutland App. Horn. CW32 51
Rutland App. Horn. CX32 51
Rutland Av. Sid. CO47 79
Rutland Av. Slou. AO39 52
Rutland Clo. SW14 BN45 65
Rutland Clo. SW19 BU50 76
Rutland Rd.
Rutland Clo. Bex. CP47 79
Rutland Clo. Chess. BL57 94
Rutland Clo. Dart. CV46 80
Rutland Clo. Epsom BN58 94
Sefton Rd.
Rutland Clo. Red. BU70 121
Rutland Ct. SE5 BZ45 67
Rutland Dr. Horn. CW32 51
Rutland Dr. Horn. CX32 51
Rutland Dr. Mord. BR53 85
Rutland Gdns. N4 BY32 47
Rutland Gdns. SW7 BU41 3
Rutland Gdns. SW7 BU41 66
Rutland Gdns. W13 BJ39 54
Rutland Gdns. Croy. CA56 96
Rutland Gdns. Dag. CP35 50
Rutland Gnds. Rich. BK47 74
Rutland Gate SW7 BU41 3
Rutland Gate SW7 BU41 66
Rutalnd Gate, Belv. CR41 69
Rutland Gate, Brom. CG52 88
Rutland Gate Ms. SW7 BU71 3
Rutland Gate Ms. SW7 BU41 66
Rutland Gro. W6 BP42 65
Rutland Ms. NW8 BT37 1
Rutland Ms. NW8 BS37 56
Rutland Ms. S. SW7 BU42 66
Rutland St.
Rutland Ms. St. SW7 BU41 3
Rutland Ms. St. SW7 BU42 66
Ennismore Ms. Gdns.
Rutland Pl. Bush. BG26 36
The Butts
Rutland Pk. NW2 BQ36 55
Rutland Pk. SE6 CD48 77
Rutland Rd. E7 CJ36 58
Rutland Rd. E9 CC37 57
Rutland Rd. E11 CH32 49
Rutland Rd. E17 CE32 48
Rutland Rd. SW19 BU50 76
Rutland Rd. Har. BG32 45
Rutland Rd. Hayes BA42 63
Rutland Rd. Ilf. CL35 49
Rutland Rd. Sthl. BF38 54
Rutland Rd. Twick. BH48 74
Rutland St. SW7 BU41 3
Rutland St. SW7 BU41 66
Rutland Wk. SE6 CD48 77
Rutland Way, Orp. CP53 89
Rutlish Rd. SW19 BS51 86
Rutson Rd. Wey. AY60 92
Rutter Gdns. Mitch. BT52 86
Rutters Clo. West Dr. AZ41 63
Ruttesland St. N1 CA37 57
Hoxton St.
Rutts Ter. SE14 CC44 67
Ruvigny Gdns. SW15 BQ45 65
Ruxbury Rd. Cher. AU53 82
Ruxley Clo. Epsom BM56 94
Ruxley Clo. Sid. CP50 79
Ruxley Cres. Esher BJ57 93
Ruxley La. Epsom BM57 94
Ruxley Ridge, Esher BJ57 93
Ryan Clo. SE3 CJ45 68
Ryarsh Cres. Orp. CN56 97
Rycott Path SE22 CB47 77
Lordship La.
Rycroft Cres. Barn. BP25 28
Rycroft La. Sev. CT68 116
Ryculff Sq. SE3 CG44 68
Rydal Clo. SW16 BW49 76
Rydal Clo. Pur. BZ60 96
Rydal Ct. NW4 BR30 37
Rydal Cres. Grnf. BJ37 54
Rydal Dr. Bexh. CQ44 69
Rydal Gdns. NW9 BO32 46
Rydal Gdns. SW15 BO49 75
Rydal Gdns. Houns. BF46 74
Rydal Gdns. Wem. BK33 45
Rydal Rd. SW16 BW49 76
Rydal Way, Enf. CC25 30
Rydal Way, Ruis. BD35 45
Ryde Clo. Wok. AX64 101
Ryde Heron, Wok. AP62 100
Rydens Av. Walt. BC55 83
Rydens Av. Walt. BD55 84
Rydens Clo. Walt. BD55 84
Rydens Gro. Walt. BD56 93
Rydens Rd. Walt. BC55 83
Rydens Rd. Walt. BD54 84
Rydens Way, Wok. AT63 100
Ryder Clo. Brom. CH49 78
Ryder Clo. Bush. BF25 27
Ryder Clo. Hem. H. AT17 16
Ryder Gdns. E6 CL39 58
Ryder Gdns. Rain. CT36 59
Ryders Av. Hat. BO13 10
Ryders Ter. NW8 BT37 1
Ryder's Ter. NW8 BT37 56
Ryder St. SW1 BW40 3
Ryder St. SW1 BW40 56
Ryde's Av. Guil. AP69 118
Rydes Clo. Wok. AY63 100
Ryde's Hill Cres. Guil. AP68 109
Rydes Hill Est. Guil. AP69 118
Ryde's Hill Rd. Guil. AP69 118
Ryde, The Hat. BQ11 10
Ryde, The Stai. AW51 83
Ryde Vale Rd. SW12 BV48 76
Rydings, Wind. AM45 61
Rydons Clo. SE9 CK45 68
Rydons La. Couls. BZ63 105
Rydons Pk. Walt. BD55 84
Rydon St. N1 BZ37 2
Rydon St. N1 BZ37 57
St. Paul St.
Rydons Wood Clo. Couls. BZ63 105
Rydston Clo. N7 BX36 56
Sutterton St.
Rydston Clo. N7 BX36 56
S. Jtt. St.
Ryebrook Clo. Lthd. BJ62 102
Ryebrook Rd. Lthd. BJ62 102
Rye Clo. Bex. CR46 79
Rye Clo. Guil. AP69 118
Ryecotes Mead. SE21 CA47 77
Rye Cres. Orp. CP54 89
Ryecroft, Harl. CL11 13
Ryecroft, Hat. BO13 10
Ryecroft, Wind. AM45 61
Ryecroft Av. Ilf. CL30 40
Ryecroft Av. Twick. BF47 74
Ryecroft Clo. Hem. H. BA14 8
Ryecroft Ct. St. Alb. BL13 10
Fourways
Ryecroft N17 CA31 48
Ryecroft Rd. SE13 CF46 77
Ryecroft Rd. SW16 BY50 76
Ryecroft Rd. Orp. CM53 88
Ryecroft Rd. Sev. CU61 107
Ryecroft St. SW6 BS44 66
Ryecroft Way N17 CA31 48
Chesnut Rd.
Ryedale SE22 CB46 77
Ryefield, Orp. CP55 89
Ryefield Av. Uxb. AZ36 53
Ryefield Cres. Pnr. BC30 35
Ryefield Rd. SE19 BZ50 77
Ryefield Rd. Croy. CC60 96
Ryehill Ct. N. Mal. BO54 85
Rye Hill Est. SE15 CC45 67
Rye Hill Pk. SE15 CC45 67
Rye Hill Rd. Epp. CO15 14
Rye Hill Rd. Harl. CM13 13
Ryeland Clo. West Dr. AY39 53
Ryelands Clo. Cat. CA64 105
Ryelands. Welw. G. C. BR9 5
Ryelands Cres. SE12 CJ46 78
Ryelands Ct. Lthd. BJ62 102
Kingston Rd.
Rye La. SE15 CB44 67
Rye La. Sev. CT63 107
Rye La. Sev. CU61 107
Rye Rd. SE15 CC45 67
Rye Rd. Harl. CG10 13
Rye Rd. Hodd. CE11 12
Rye, The N14 BW26 38
Rye Wk. SW15 BQ46 75
Chartfield Av.
Rye Way, Edg. BL29 37
Ryfold Rd. SW19 BS48 76
Ryhope Rd. N11 BV28 38
Rylandes Rd. NW2 BP34 46
Ryland Rd. NW5 BV36 56
Rylands Rd. Sth. Croy. CD58 96
Rylett Cres. W12 BO41 65
Rylett Rd. W12 BO41 65
Rylston Rd. N13 BZ27 39
Rylston Rd. SW6 BR43 65
Ryman Ct. Rick. AU25 25
Stag La.
Rymer Rd. SW18 BT45 66
Alma Rd.
Rymer Rd. Croy. CA54 87
Rymer St. SE24 BY46 76
Rymill Clo. Hem. H. AT17 16
Rymill St. E16 CL40 58
Rysbrack St. SW3 BU41 66
Rysbrook St. SW3 BU41 3
Rysted La. West. CM66 115
Rythe Ct. Surb. BJ54 84
Rythe Rd. Esher BH56 93
Sabbarton St. E16 CG39 58
Victoria Dock Rd.
Sabella Ct. E3 CE37 57
Mostyn Gro.
Sabella St. SE1 BY40 4
Sabella St. SE1 BY40 56
Sabina Rd. Grays. DH42 71
Sabine Rd. SW11 BU45 66
Sabines Rd. Rom. CV23 33
Sable Clo. Houns. BD45 64
Sable St. N1 BY36 56
Sach Rd. E5 CB34 48
Sackville Av. Brom. CH54 88
Sackville Clo. Har. BG34 45
Sackville Clo. Sev. CU64 107
Sackville Cres. Rom. CW30 42
Sackville Est. SW16 BX48 76
Sackville Gdns. Ilf. CK33 49
Sackville Rd. Dart. CV48 80
Sackville Rd. Sutt. BS57 95
Sackville St. W1 BW40 3
Sackville St. W1 BW40 56
Sacombe Rd. Hem. H. AV12 7
Saddington St. Grav. DH47 81
Saddlers Mead. Harl. CO11 14
Saddlescombe Way N12 BS28 38
Saddleworth Rd. Rom. CV29 42
Saddleworth Sq. Rom. CV29 42
Sadie St. SE5 BZ44 67
Orpheus St.

Sadler Clo. Mitch. BU51 86
Sadler Clo. Guil. AU70 118
Sadlers Ride, E. Mol. BG51 84
Sadlers Way, Epsom BN63 103
Sadlier Rd. St. Alb. BH14 9
Saffron Clo. NW11 BR32 46
Saffron Clo. Hodd. CD11 12
Saffron Hill EC1 BY38 56
Saffron Hill EC1 BY39 2
Saffron La. Hem. H. AW13 8
Saffron Platt. Guil. AQ68 109
Saffron Rd. Rom. CS30 41
Saffron St. EC1 BY39 56
Saffron Hill
Safron Clo. Brwd. DE32 123
Saftesbury Rd. Cars. BT54 86
Sail St. SE11 BX42 4
Sail St. SE11 BX42 66
Sainsbury Rd. SE19 BZ49 77
St. Agatha's Dr. Kings. on T. BL50 75
Latchmere Rd.
St. Agathas Gro. Cars. BU54 86
St. Agatha's Wk. Kings. on T. BM50 75
Alexandra Rd.
St. Agnell's La. Hem. H. AY11 8
St. Agnes Clo. E9 CC37 57
Gore Rd.
St. Agnes Pl. SE11 BY43 66
St. Aidan's Rd. SE22 CB46 77
St. Aidan's Rd. W13 BJ41 64
St. Aidan's Way, Grav. DJ48 81
St. Albans Av. E6 CK38 58
St. Albans Av. W4 BN42 65
St. Albans Av. Felt. BD49 74
St. Albans Av. Upmin. CZ34 51
St. Albans Av. Wey. AZ55 83
St. Albans Clo. NW11 BS33 47
North End Rd.
St. Alban's Clo. Grav. DH48 81
St. Alban's Cres. N22 BY30 38
St. Alban's Cres. Wdf. Grn. CH29 40
St. Alban's Gdns. Grav. DH48 81
St. Alban's Gdns. Tedd. BJ49 74
St. Alban's Gro. W8 BS41 3
St. Alban's Gro. W8 BS41 66
St. Alban's Gro. Cars. BU54 86
St. Albans Hill, Hem. H. AY15 8
St. Albans La. NW11 BS33 47
West Heath Br.
St. Albans Ms. W2 BT39 1
St. Albans La. St. Alb. BC16 18
St. Alban's Ms. W2 BT39 56
Edgware Rd.
St. Albans Pl. N1 BY37 2
St. Albans Pl. W1 BY37 56
St. Alban's Rd. NW5 BV34 47
St. Alban's Rd. NW10 BO37 55
St. Albans Rd. Barn. BQ22 28
St. Albans Rd. Dart. CW47 80
St. Albans Rd. Epp. CP18 23
St. Albans Rd. Hat. BO12 10
St. Albans Rd. Hat. BP12 10
St. Albans Rd. Hem. H. AX14 8
St. Albans Rd. Ilf. CN33 49
St. Alban's Rd. Kings. on T. BL50 75
St. Albans Rd. Pot. B. BO19 19
St. Albans Rd. Reig. BS70 121
St. Albans Rd. St. Alb. BJ11 9
St. Alban's Rd. Sutt. BR56 94
St. Albans Rd. Wat. BC23 26
St. Albans Rd. Wat. BD20 18
St. Albans Rd. Wat. BD21 27
St. Alban's Rd. Wdf. Grn. CH29 40
St. Albans Rd. East, Hat. BP12 10
St. Albans Rd. West, Hat. BN12 10
St. Albans St. SW1 BW40 3
St. Alban's St. SW1 BW40 56
Jermyn St.
St. Albans St. Wind. AO44 61
St. Alban's Ter. W6 BR43 65
St. Alfege Pass SE10 CF43 67
Roan St.
St. Alfege Rd. SE7 CJ43 68
St. Alphage Ct. NW9 BN31 46
St. Alphages Gdns. EC2 BZ39 2
St. Alphages Gdns. EC2 BZ39 57
St. Alphege Rd. N9 CC26 39
St. Alphonsus Rd. SW4 BW45 66
St. Andrew's Av, Wind. AM44 61
St. Andrews Av. Horn. CU35 50
St. Andrews Av. Wem. BJ35 45
St. Anne's Clo. Wal. Cr. CA17 21
St. Andrews Clo. N12 BT28 38
Woodside Av.
St. Andrews Clo. NW2 BP34 46
St. Andrews Clo. Epp. CS15 14
St. Andrew's Clo. Islw. BH44 64
St. Andrews Clo. Reig. BS71 121
St. Mary's Rd.
St. Andrew's Clo. Ruis. BD34 45
St. Andrews Clo. Shep. BA52 83
St. Andrews Clo. Stan. BK30 36
St. Andrews Clo. Wind. AQ46 72
St. Andrews Ct. SW18 BT48 76
Waynflete St.
St. Andrew's Cres. Wind. AM44 61
St. Andrew's Dr. Orp. CO53 89
St. Andrew's Dr. Stan. BK30 36
St. Andrews Grn. Welw. G. C. BR8 5
St. Andrew's Gro. N16 BZ33 48
St. Andrews Hill EC4 BY39 2
St. Andrew's Hill EC4 BY39 5
St. Andrew's Hill EC4 BY40 4
St. Andrew's Ms. N16 CA33 48
Dunsmure Rd.
St. Andrew's Pl. NW1 BV38 1
St. Andrews Pl. NW1 BV38 56
St. Andrews Pl. Brwd. DC27 122
St. Andrew's Rd. E11 CG32 49
St. Andrew's Rd. E13 CH38 58
St. Andrew's Rd. N9 CC26 39
St. Andrews Rd. NW9 BN33 46
St. Andrews Rd. NW10 BP36 55
St. Andrews Rd. NW11 BR32 46
St. Andrew's Rd. W3 BO40 55
St. Andrew's Rd. W7 BH41 64
St. Andrews Rd. W14 BR43 65
St. Andrews Rd. Cars. BU55 86
St. Andrew's Rd. Couls. BV61 104
St. Andrew's Rd. Croy. BZ56 96
St. Andrews Rd. Enf. BZ24 30
St. Andrews Rd. Hem. H. AX15 8
St. Andrew's Rd. Ilf. CK33 49
St. Andrews Rd. Rom. CS32 50
St. Andrews Rd. Sid. CP48 79
St. Andrews Rd. Surb. BK53 84
St. Andrews Rd. Til. DF44 71
St. Andrews Rd. Uxb. AY37 53
St. Andrews Sq. W11 BR39 55
St. Mark's Rd.
St. Andrews Sq. Surb. BK53 84
St. Andrew St. EC4 BY39 2
St. Andrew St. EC4 BY39 56
St. Andrew St. W14 BR43 65
St. Andrews Wk. Cob. BC61 101
St. Andrews Way, Oxt. CK69 115
St. Anne's Av. Stai. AX47 73
St. Anne's Clo. N6 BV34 47
St. Anne's Clo. Wal. Cr. CA17 21
St. Anne's Ct. W1 BW39 1
St. Anne's Ct. W1 BW39 56
Wardour St.
St. Anne's Gdns. NW10 BL38 55
St. Annes La. SW1 BW41 66
Old Pye St.
St. Anne's Rd. E11 CF34 48
St. Annes Rd. Brwd. DE23 122
St. Anne's Rd. Cher. AV53 82
St. Anne's Rd. Har. BH32 45
St. Anne's Rd. St. Alb. BK17 18
St. Annes Rd. Uxb. AX31 44
St. Anne's Rd. Wem. BK35 45
St. Ann's, Bark. CM37 58
St. Ann's Clo. Cher. AV53 82
St. Ann's Cres. SW18 BT46 76
St. Ann's Gdns. NW5 BV36 56
Queen's Cres.
St. Anns Hill Rd. Cher. AU53 82
St. Ann's Hill SW18 BS46 76
St. Ann's La. SW1 BW41 3
St. Anns La. SW1 BW41 66
Old Pye St.
St. Ann's Pk. Rd. SW18 BT46 76
St. Ann's Pass. SW13 BO45 65
Cross St.
St. Ann's Rd. N9 CA27 39
St. Ann's Rd. N15 BY32 47
St. Anns Rd. SW13 BO44 65
St. Anns Rd. W11 BQ40 55
St. Ann's St. SW1 BW41 3
St. Ann's St. SW1 BW41 66
St. Anns St. Bark. CM37 58
Morley Rd.
St. Ann's Ter. NW8 BT37 1
St. Ann's Ter. NW8 BT37 56
St. Ann's Vill. W11 BQ40 55
St. Ann's Way, Sth. Croy. BY57 95
St. Anselms Ct. SW16 BX49 76
St. Anselm's Pl. W1 BV40 3
St. Anselms Pl. W1 BV40 56
Davies St.
St. Anselms Rd. Hayes BB41 63
St. Anthony's Av. Wdf. Grn. CJ29 40
St. Anthonys Clo. Hem. H. AZ14 8
St. Anthony's La. Swan. CU51 89
St. Anthony's Rd. E7 CH36 58
St. Anthony's Way, Felt. BB45 63
St. Arvans Clo. Croy. CA55 87
St. Asaph Rd. SE4 CC45 67
St. Aubyns Av. SW19 BR49 75
St. Aubyn's Av. Houns. BF46 74
St. Aubyn's Clo. Orp. CN55 88
St. Aubyn's Gdns. Orp. CN55 88
St. Aubyn's Rd. SE19 CA50 77
St. Audrey Av. Bexh. CR44 69
St. Audreys Clo. Hat. BP13 10
St. Augustine Rd. Grays. DG42 71
St. Augustine's Av. W5 BL37 55
St. Augustines Av. Brom. CK53 88
St. Augustine's Av. Sth. Croy. BZ57 96
St. Augustine's Av. Wem. BL34 46
St. Augustine, S. Clo. Brox. CD13 12
St. Augustine, S. Dr. Brox. CD13 12
St. Augustine's Rd. NW1 BW36 56
St. Augustines Rd. Belv. CQ42 69
St. Austell Clo. Edg. BL30 37
St. Austell Rd. SE13 CF44 67
St. Awdry's Rd. Bark. CM36 58
St. Awdry's Wk. Bark. CM36 58
St. Barnabas Clo. Beck. CF51 87
St. Barnabas Rd. E17 CE32 48
St. Barnabas Rd. Mitch. BV50 76
St. Barnabas Rd. Sutt. BT56 95
St. Barnabas Rd. Wood Grn. CH30 40
St. Barnabas St. SW1 BV42 3
St. Barnabas St. SW1 BV42 66
St. Barnabas Vil. SW8 BX44 66
Guildford Rd.
St. Bartholomew's Rd. E6 CK37 58
St. Benedict's Av. Gray. DJ48 81
St. Benedicts Clo. SW17 BV49 76
Rectory La.
St. Benet Pl. EC3 BZ40 57
Gravechurch St.
St. Benets Gro. Cars. BT54 86
St. Bernard's, Croy. CA55 87
St. Bernard's Rd. E6 CJ37 58
St. Bernards Rd. St. Alb. BH13 9
St. Bernards Rd. Slou. AR41 62
St. Blaise Av. Brom. CH51 88
St. Botolph Rd. Grav. DE48 81
Pepper Hill
St. Botolph Row EC3 CA39 57
Houndsditch
St. Botolph's Av. Sev. CU65 107
St. Botolph's Rd. Sev. CU65 107
St. Botolph St. EC3 CA39 2
St. Botolph St. EC3 CA39 57
St. Brelades Clo. Dor. BJ72 119
Knoll Rd.
St. Bride's Av. Edg. BL30 37
St. Brides Clo. Belv. CP41 69
St. Katherines Rd.
St. Bride's Pass. EC4 BY39 56
Dorset Rise
St. Bride St. EC4 BY39 2
St. Bride St. EC4 BY39 56
St. Catharine, S. Rd. Brox. CE13 12
St. Catherines Clo. Wok. AR63 100
St. Catherines Ct. W4 BO42 65
Newton Gro.
St. Catherine's Dr. SE14 CC44 67
Kitto Rd.
St. Catherines Dr. Guil. AQ72 118
St. Catherines Est. AR63 100
St. Catherine's Rd. E4 CE27 39
St. Catherines Rd. Ruis. BA32 44
St. Cecilia Rd. Grays. DG42 71
St. Chads Gdns. Rom. CQ33 50
St. Chads Pl. WC1 BX38 2
St. Chads Pl. WC1 BX38 56
St. Chads Rd. Rom. CQ32 50
St. Chads St. WC1 BX38 56
St. Chads Dr. Grav. DJ48 81
St. Charles' Pl. W10 BR39 55
Chesterton Rd.
St. Charles Rd. Brwd. DA26 42
St. Charles Sq. W10 BQ39 55
St. Christopher Rd. Uxb. AX39 53
St. Christophers Clo. Islw. BG44 64
Thornbury Rd.
St. Christopher's Pl. W1 BV39 1
St. Christopher's Pl. W1 BV39 56
Barrett St.
St. Clair Clo. Oxt. CF68 114
St. Clair Clo. Ilf. CK30 40
St. Clair Clo. Reig. BT70 121
St. Clair Dr. Wor. Pk. BP55 85
St. Clair Rd. E13 CH37 58
St. Clair's Rd. Croy. CA55 87
St. Clare Hill Rd. Sev. CY60 99
St. Clare St. EC3 CA39 2
St. Clare St. EC3 CA39 57
Minories
St. Clements Av. Grays. DA43 70
St. Clement's La. WC2 BX39 2
St. Clement's La. WC2 BX39 56
Portugal St.
St. Clement's Rd. Grays. DB43 70
St. Clement St. N7 BY36 56
Offord Rd.
St. Clement Way, Uxb. AX39 53
St. Clere Hill Rd. Sev. CY60 99
St. Cloud Rd. SE27 BZ49 77
St. Columba's Clo. Grav. DJ48 81
St. Crispin's Clo. Sthl. BE39 54
St. Crispins Way, Cher. AU58 91
St. Cross St. EC1 BY39 2
St. Cross St. EC1 BY39 56
St. Cuthbert's NW3 BS34 47
St. Cuthberts Gdns. Prn. BE29 36
Westfield Pk.
St. Cuthbert's Rd. NW2 BR36 55
St. Cuthberts Rd. Hodd. CF10 12
St. Cyprian's St. SW17 BU49 76
St. David Clo. Uxb. AX39 53
St. David's Clo. Hem. H. BA14 8
St. Davids Clo. Iver. AU37 52
St. Davids Clo. Reig. BT70 121
St. David's Clo. Wem. BN34 46
St. Davids Clo. W. Wick. CE54 87
St. David's Cres. Grav. DH49 81
St. David's Dr. Edg. BL30 37
St. David S. Dr. Brox. CD13 12
St. Davids Pl. NW4 BP33 46
St. Davids, Pur. BX62 104
St. David's Rd. Swan. CT50 79
St. Denis Rd. SE27 BZ49 77
St. Denys Clo. Wok. AO62 100
St. Dionis Rd. SW6 BR44 65
St. Donatt's Rd. SE14 CD44 67
St. Dunstan's Alley EC3 CA40 57
Idol La.
St. Dunstan's Av. W3 BN40 55
St. Dunstans Clo. Hayes BB42 63
St. Dunstan's Clo. Hayes BC42 63
St. Dunstan's Dr. Grav. DJ49 81
St. Dunstans Gdns. W3 BN40 55
St. Dunstan's Av.
St. Dunstans Hill EC3 CA40 4
St. Dunstan's Hill EC3 CA40 57
St. Dunstan's Hill, Sutt. BR57 94
St. Dunstan's La. EC3 CA40 4
St. Dunstan's La. EC3 CA40 57
Idol La.
St. Dunstans La. Beck. CF53 87
St. Dunstans Rd. E7 CJ36 58
St. Dunstan's Rd. SE25 CA52 87
St. Dunstan's Rd. W6 BQ42 65
St. Dunstans Rd. W7 BH41 64
St. Dunstans Rd. Felt. BB48 73
St. Dunstan's Rd. Houns. BC44 63
St. Edmunds Av. Ruis. BA32 44
St. Edmund's Clo. NW8 BU37 1
St. Edmunds Clo. NW8 BU37 56
St. Edmunds Ter.
St. Edmund's Clo. Belv. CP41 69
St. Katherine's Rd.
St. Edmunds Dr. Stan. BJ30 36
St. Edmunds La. Twick. BF47 74
St. Edmund's Rd. N9 CB26 39
St. Edmunds Rd. Dart. CX45 70
St. Edmunds Rd. Dart CX46 80
St. Edmunds Rd. Ilf. CK32 49
St. Edwards Ter. NW8 BU37 1
St. Edmunds Ter. NW8 BU37 56
St. Edmunds Way, Harl. CP9 6
St. Edwards Clo. NW11 BS32 47
Finchley Rd.
St. Edwards Clo. Croy. CF58 96
St. Edwards Clo. Croy. CF59 96
St. Edwards Way, Rom. CS31 50
St. Egberts Way E4 CF26 39
St. Elmo Rd. W12 BO40 55
St. Erkenwald Rd. Bark. CM37 58
St. Ermins Hill SW1 BW41 66
Broadway
St. Ervan's Rd. W10 BR39 55
St. Ethelredas Dr. Hat. BQ12 10
St. Faiths Clo. Enf. BZ23 30
St. Faith's Rd. SE21 BY47 76
St. Fidelis Rd. Erith CS42 69
St. Fillans Rd. SE6 CF47 77
St. Francis Clo. Orp. CN53 88
St. Francis Clo. Pot. B. BT20 20
St. Vincents Way
St. Francis Clo. Wat. BC26 35
Oaklands Av.
St. Francis Rd. SE22 CA45 67
St. Francis Rd. Erith. CS42 69
West St.
St. Francis Rd. Uxb. AV32 43
St. Francis Way, Brwd. DA27 42
St. Francis Way, Grays. DH42 71
St. Gabriel's Rd. NW2 BQ35 46
St. Gabriel St. SE11 BY42 4
St. George's Av. Grays. DE42 71
St. George's Av. E7 CH36 58
St. George's Av. N7 BW35 47
St. George's Av. NW9 BN31 46
St. George's Av. W5 BK41 64
St. George's Av. Horn. CW33 51
St. Georges Av. Sthl. BE40 54
St. Georges Av. Wey. AZ57 92
St. George's Cir. SE1 BY41 4
St. George's Cir. SE1 BY41 66
St. George's Clo. NW11 BR32 46
St. George's Clo. Wem. BJ34 45
St. Georges Clo. Wey. BA56 92
St. Georges Clo. Wind. AM44 61
St. Georges Ct. E6 CK38 58
St. George's Ct. SW7 BT41 3
St. Georges Ct. W8 BT41 66
St. George's Cres. Grav. DH49 81
St. George's Dr. SW1 BV42 3
St. George's Dr. SW1 BV42 66
St. George's Dr. Wat. BE27 36
St. Georges Est. Amer. AQ23 25
St. Georges Fields W2 BU39 1
St. Georges Fields W2 BU39 56
Albion St.
St. Georges Gdns. Epsom BO60 94
St. Georges Grove SW17 BT48 76
St. George's La. EC3 BZ40 57
Pudding La.
St. Georges Ms. NW1 BU36 56
Regents Pk. Rd.
St. George, S. Dr. Uxb. AY34 44
St. George's Pl. Twick. BJ47 74
Church St.
St. George's Rd. E7 CH36 58
St. George's Rd. E10 CF34 48
St. George's Rd. N9 CB27 39
St. George's Rd. N15 CA32 48
St. George's Rd. N21 BX27 38
St. George's Rd. NW11 BR32 46
St. George's Rd. SE1 BY41 4
St. George's Rd. SE1 BY41 66
St. George's Rd. SW19 BR50 75
St. George's Rd. W4 BN41 65
St. George's Rd. W7 BH40 54
St. George's Rd. Beck. CE51 87
St. George's Rd. Brom. CK51 88
St. George's Rd. Dag. CQ35 50
St. George's Rd. Enf. CA22 30
St. George's Rd. Felt. BD49 74
St. George's Rd. Hem. H. AX15 8
St. George's Rd. Ilf. CK33 49
St. George's Rd. Kings. on T. BM50 75
St. Georges Rd. Mitch. BV52 86
St. Georges Rd. Orp. CM53 88
St. George's Rd. Rich. BL45 65
St. George's Rd. Sev. CU64 107
St. George's Rd. Sid. CP50 79
St. George's Rd. Swan. CT52 89
St. George's Rd. Twick. BJ46 74
St. George's Rd. Wall. BV56 95
St. George's Rd. Wat. BC22 26
St. George's Rd. Wey. AX56 92
St. George's Rd. Wey. BA57 92
St. George's Rd. W. Brom. CK51 88
St. George's Sq. E7 CH36 58
St. George's Sq. SW1 BW42 3
St. George's Sq. SW1 BW42 66
St. George's Sq. Ms. SW1 BW42 3
St. George's St. Cat. BZ64 105
St. Georges Ter. NW1 BU36 56
Regents Pk. Rd.
St. George St. W1 BV39 56
St. George St. W1 BV40 3
St. George's Way SE15 CA43 67
St. Georges Way, Croy. BZ55 87
St. German's Bungs. SE3 CG44 68
St. German's Pl. SE3 CH44 68
St. German's Rd. SE23 CD47 77
St. Giles Av. Dag. CR36 59
St. Giles Av. Pot. B. BP20 19
St. Giles Cir. W1 BW39 56
St. Giles Cir. WC1 BW39 1
St. Giles Clo. Dag. CH36 59
St. Giles Clo. Orp. CM56 97
St. Giles Ct. WC2 BW39 1
St. Giles Ct. WC2 BX39 2
St. Giles High St. WC2 BW39 1
St. Giles High St. WC2 BW39 56
St. Giles Rd. SE5 CA43 67
St. Giles S. Av. Uxb. BA35 44
St. Gothard Rd. SE27 BZ49 77
St. Gregory's Cres. Grav. DJ48 81
St. Helena Rd. SE16 CC42 67
St. Helena St. WC1 BY38 2
St. Helena Ter. Rich. BK46 74
Friars La.
St. Helens Clo. Uxb. AX39 53
St. Helens Ct. Epp. CO18 23
St. Helens Ct. Rain. CU38 59
St. Helen's Cres. SW16 BX51 86
St. Helen's Gdns. W10 BQ39 55
St. Helen's Pl. EC3 CA39 2
St. Helen's Pl. EC3 CA39 57
Bishopgate
St. Helen's Rd. SE2 CP41 69
St. Helen's Rd. SW16 BX51 86
St. Helen's Rd. W13 BJ40 54
Dane Rd.
St. Helens Rd. Belv. CP41 69
St. Helen's Rd. Ilf. CK32 49
St. Helier Av. Mord. BT54 86
St. Helier's Av. Houns. BF46 74
St. Helier's Rd. E10 CF32 48
St. Helier's Rd. St. Alb. BJ11 9
St. Hilda's Av. Ashf. AY49 73
St. Hilda's Clo. NW6 BQ36 55
St. Hilda's Clo. Wok. AO62 100
St. Hilda's Rd. SW13 BP43 65
St. Hilda's Way, Grav. DJ49 81
St. Hilds's Clo. Ashf. AY49 73
St. Huberts Clo. AS34 43
St. Huberts La. Ger. Cr. AS34 43
St. Hugh's Rd. SE20 CB51 87
Ridsdale Rd.
St. Ives Clo. Welw. G. C. BR5 5
St. Ivians Dr. Rom. CU31 50
St. Jame's Av. Beck. CD52 87
St. James Av. Epsom CO59 94
St. James Av. Ong. CW18 24
St. James' Av. Sutt. BS56 95
St. Jame's Clo. SE18 CM42 68
Congeton Gro.
St. James Clo. Epsom BO60 94
St. James Clo. Ruis. BD34 45
St. James Clo. Wok. AQ62 100
St. James' Ct. N22 BX29 38
St. James Hatcham SE14 CD44 67
St. James' La. Green. CZ47 80
St. James Pl. Dart. CV46 80
St. James Pl. Enf. CC25 30
South St.
St. James' Rd. E15 CG35 49
St. James Rd. N9 CB27 39
Queens Rd.
St. James Rd. SE16 CB41 4
St. James Rd. Mitch. BV50 76
St. James Rd. Pur. BY60 95
St. James Rd. Surb. BK53 84
St. James' Rd. Sutt. BS56 95
St. James' SE14 CD44 67
St. James' Av. E2 CC37 57
St. James' Av. N20 BU27 38
St. James's Av. W13 BJ40 54
St. James's Av. Grav. DG47 81
St. James's Av. Hmptn. BG49 74
St. James's Clo. N20 BU27 38
St. James's Clo. SW12 BU48 76
St. James's Dr.
St. James's Clo. N. Mal. BO53 85
St. James's Cott. Rich. BL46 75
Paradise Rd.
St. James's Cres. SW9 BY45 66
St. James's Dr. SW17 BU47 76
St. James's Gdns. W11 BR40 55
St. James's Gro. SW11 BU44 66
Battersea Pk. Rd.
St. James's La. N10 BV31 47
St. James's Mkt. SW1 BW40 3
St. James S. Rd. Brwd. DB27 42
St. James's Pk. Croy. BZ54 87
St. James's Pass. EC3 CA39 57
Duke's Pl.
St. James's Path E17 CD32 48
St. James's Pl. SW1 BW40 3
St. James's Pl. SW1 BW40 56
St. James's Rd. SE1 CB41 67
St. James's Rd. SE16 CB41 67
St. James's Rd. Cars. BU55 86
St. James's Rd. Croy. BY54 86
St. James's Rd. Grav. DG47 81
St. James's Rd. Hmptn. BF49 74
St. James's Rd. Kings. on T. BK51 84
St. James's Rd. Sev. CU64 107
St. James's Rd. Wal. Cr. BZ17 21
St. James's Rd. Wat. BC25 26
St. James's Row EC1 BY38 2
St. James's Row EC1 BY38 56
Clerkenwell Clo.
St. James's Sq. SW1 BW40 3
St. James's Sq. SW1 BW40 56
St. James's St. E17 CD32 48
St. James's St. SW1 BW40 3
St. James's St. SW1 BW40 56
St. James's St. W6 BQ42 65
St. James's St. Grav. DG46 81
St. James's Ter. Ms. NW8 BU37 1
St. James's Ter. Ms. NW8 BU37 56
St. James's Wk. EC1 BY38 2
St. James's Wk. EC1 BY38 56
Sekforde St.
St. James Wk. SE15 CA44 67
Sumner Est.
St. James Wk. Iver. AV41 62
St. James Way, Sid. CQ49 79
St. Jeromes Gro. Hayes BA39 53
St. Joan's Rd. N9 CA27 39
St. John's, Dor. BK73 119
St. Johns Av. N11 BU28 38
St. John's Av. NW10 BO37 55
St. John's Av. SW15 BQ46 75
St. John's Av. Epsom BO59 94
St. John's Av. Harl. CP9 6
St. John's Av. Lthd. BJ64 102
St. John's Church Rd. E9 CC35 48
Urswick Rd.
St. Johns Church Rd. Dor. BE73 119
St. John's Clo. Guil. AQ71 118
St. Johns Clo. Lthd. BK64 102
St. John's Clo. Pot. B. BT20 20
St. John's Clo. Rain. CU36 59
St. John's Clo. Wem. BL35 46
St. John's Cotts. SE20 CC50 77
Maple Rd.
St. John's Cotts. Rich. BL45 65
Kew Foot Rd.
St. John's Ct. N4 BY34 47
St. Johns Ct. Buck. H. CJ26 40
St. Johns Ct. Nthwd. BB29 35
Murray Rd.
St. Johns Ct. Islw. BH44 64

St. Johns Ct. St. Alb. BJ12 9
Beaumont Av.
St. John's Cres. SW9 BY45 66
St. Johns Dr. Walt. BD54 84
St. Johns Dr. Wind. AM44 61
St. Johns Est. N1 BZ37 57
St. Johns Est. SE1 CA41 4
St. Johns Est. SE1 CA41 67
St. Johns Est. SW11 BT44 66
St. John's Gdns. W11 BR40 55
St. John's Gro. N19 BW34 47
St. John's Gro. SW13 BQ44 65
Terrace Gdns.
St. John's Gro. Rich. BL45 65
Kew Foot Rd.
St. John's Hill, Couls. BY62 104
St. Johns Hill, Pur. BY57 95
St. John's Hill, Pur. BY61 104
St. John's Hill, Sev. CV64 108
St. John's Hill Rd. Wok. AQ63 100
St. John's Hill SW11 BT46 76
St. John's Hill Gro. SW11 BT45 66
St. John's La. EC1 BY38 56
St. John's La. EC1 BY39 2
St. Johns Av. Brwd. DB28 42
St. John's Pde. Sid. CO49 79
St. John's Pk. SE3 CG43 68
St. John's Pass. SW19 BR50 75
St. John's Ri. Wok. AQ62 100
St. John's Rd. E4 CE28 39
St. John's Rd. E6 CK37 58
St. John's Rd. E16 CH39 58
St. John's Rd. E17 CE30 39
St. John's Rd. N15 CA32 48
St. John's Rd. NW11 BR32 46
St. John's Rd. SE20 CC50 77
St. John's Rd. SW11 BU45 66
St. John's Rd. SW19 BR50 75
St. John's Rd. Bark. CG37 58
St. John's Rd. Cars. BU55 86
ST. John's Rd. Croy. BY55 86
Sylverdale Rd.
St. Johns Rd. Croy. BY55 86
Silverdale Rd.
St. John's Rd. Dart. CY47 80
St. John's Rd. Dor. BG72 119
St. John's Rd. E. Mol. BG52 84
St. John's Rd. Epp. CN18 22
St. John's Rd. Erith. CS42 69
St. John's Rd. Felt. BE49 74
St. John's Rd. Grav. DH47 81
St. John's Rd. Grays. DG42 71
St. John's Rd. Guil. AQ71 118
St. John's Rd. Har. BH32 45
St. John's Rd. Hem. H. AW14 8
St. John's Rd. Ilf. CM33 49
St. John's Rd. Islw. BH44 64
St. John's Rd. Islw. BJ45 64
St. John's Rd. Kings. on T. BK51 84
St. John's Rd. Loug. CK23 31
St. John's Rd. Lthd. BK64 102
St. John's Rd. N. Mal. BN52 85
St. John's Rd. Orp. CM53 88
St. John's Rd. Red. BU71 121
St. John's Rd. Rich. BL45 65
St. John's Rd. Rom. CS28 41
St. John's Rd. Sev. CU64 107
St. John's Rd. Sid. CO49 79
St. John's Rd. Slou. AQ40 52
St. Johns Rd. Sthl. BE41 64
St. John's Rd. Sutt. BS55 86
St. Johns Rd. Uxb. AW37 53
St. John's Rd. Wat. BC23 26
St. John's Rd. Well. CO45 69
St. John's Rd. Wem. BK35 45
St. John's Rd. Wind. AN44 61
St. John's Rd. Wok. AQ62 100
St. John's Sq. EC1 BY38 2
St. John's Sq. EC1 BY38 56
Clerkenwell Rd.
St. Johns St. EC1 BY37 2
St. John's St. W10 BQ39 55
Harrow Rd.
St. John's Ter. E7 CH36 58
St. John's Ter. SE18 CM43 68
St. John's Ter. W10 BQ38 55
Harrow Rd.
St. Johns Ter. Enf. BZ22 30
St. Johns Ter. Rd. Red. BU71 121
St. John St. EC1 BY37 56
St. John's Vale SE8 CE44 67
St. John's Vill. N19 BW34 47
St. John's Way N19 BW34 47
St. Johns Well. La. Berk. AQ12 7
St. John's Wood Ct. NW8 BT38 1
St. John's Wood Ct. NW8 BT38 56
St. John's Wood Rd.
St. John's Wood High St. NW8 BT37 1
St. John's Wood High St. NW8 BT37 56
St. John's Wood Pk. NW8 BT37 1
St. John's Wood Pk. NW8 BT37 56
St. John's Wood Rd. NW8 BT38 1
St. John's Wood Rd. NW8 BT38 56
St. John's Wood Ter. NW8 BT37 1
St. John's Wood Ter. NW8 BT37 56
St. Joseph's Dr. Sthl. BE40 54
St. Joseph's Rd. N9 CB26 39
St. Judes Clo. Egh. AR49 72
St. Jude's Rd. E2 CB37 57
St. Jude's Rd. Egh. AR49 72
St. Jude St. N16 CA35 48
St. Julian's Clo. SW16 BY49 76
St. Julian's Farm. Rd. SE27 BY49 76
St. Julians Hill, St. Alb. BG15 9
St. Julians Rd. NW6 BR37 55
St. Julians Rd. St. Alb. BG14 9
St. Julians Rd. Sev. CW68 117
St. Justin Rd. Sev. CW68 117
St. Justin Clo. Orp. CP52 89
St. Katharine's Precinct. NW1 BV37 56
Outer Circle
St. Katherine's Way E1 CA40 4
St. Katherine's Way E1 CA40 57
St. Katherine's Cross, Red. CA70 114
St. Katherine's Rd. Belv. CP41 69
St. Katherine's Rd. Cat. CB66 114
St. Kevverne Rd. SE9 CK49 78
St. Kilda Rd. W13 BJ40 54
St. Kilda Rd. Orp. CN54 88
St. Kilda's Rd. N16 BZ33 48
St. Kilda's Rd. Brwd. DA26 42
St. Kilda's Rd. Har. BH32 45
St. Laurence Dr. Brox. CD15 12
High Rd.
St. Lawrence Clo. Hem. H. AT17 16
St. Lawrence Clo. Edg. BL29 37
Whitchurch La.
St. Laurence Way, Slou. AQ41 62
St. Lawrence Clo. Orp. CP52 89
St. Lawrence Clo. St. Alb. BE19 18
St. Lawrence Clo. Wat. BB18 17
St. Lawrence Dr. Pnr. BC32 44
St. Lawrence Gdns. Ing. DC19 24
St. Lawrence Rd. SW9 BY4 66
St. Lawrence Rd. Upmin. CY34 51
St. Lawrence, Rue De Wal. Abb. CF20 21
John Foxe Pl.
St. Lawrence St. E14 CF40 57
St. Lawrence Ter. W10 BR39 55
St. Lawrence Way SW9 BY44 66
Myatts Fields Dev.
St. Lawrence Way, St. Alb. BE19 18
St. Leonards Av. E4 CF29 39
St. Leonards Av. Har. BK32 45
St. Leonard's Clo. Well. CO45 69
Hook La.
St. Leonard's Ct. SW14 BN45 65
St. Leonard's Rd.
St. Leonards Cres. St. Alb. BK10 9
St. Leonards Gdns. Houns. BE43 64
St. Leonards Gdns. Ilf. CM35 49
St. Leonard's Hill, Wind. AM45 61
St. Leonard, S. Rd. Wal. Abb. CF15 12
St. Leonard, S. Rd. Wal. Abb. CG15 13
St. Leonard's Rise, Orp. CM56 97
St. Leonard's Rd. E14 CE39 57
St. Leonards Rd NW10 BN38 55
St. Leonard's Rd. SW14 BM45 65
St. Leonard's Rd. W13 BK40 54
St. Leonards Rd. Amer. AP21 25
St. Leonards Rd. Croy. BY55 86
St. Leonards Rd. Epsom BQ63 103
St. Leonard's Rd. Esher BH57 93
St. Leonards Rd. Surb. BJ53 84
St. Leonards Rd. Surb. BK53 84
St. Leonard's Rd. Wal. Abb. CF16 21
St. Leonard's Rd. Wal. Abb. CG16 22
St. Leonards Rd. Wind. AN45 61
St. Leonard's Sq. NW5 BV36 56
St. Leonards Sq. Surb. BK53 84
St. Leonard's St. E3 CE38 57
St. Leonard's Ter. SW3 BU42 3
St. Leonards Ter. SW3 BU42 66
St. Leonards Wk. Iver. AV41 62
St. Leon Av. Wind. AO44 61
St. Loo Av. SW3 BU43 3
St. Loo Av. SW3 BU43 66
St. Louis Rd. SE27 BZ49 77
St. Loy's Rd. N17 CA30 39
St. Luke Clo. Uxb. AX39 53
St. Luke's Clo. SE25 CB53 87
St. Luke's Av. SW4 BW45 66
St. Luke's Av. Enf. BZ22 30
St. Lukes Av. Ilf. CL35 49
St. Lukes Ms. W11 BR39 55
St. Lukes Pass. Kings. on T. BL51 85
St. Lukes Pl. St. Alb. BJ14 9
St. Luke's Rd. W11 BR39 55
St. Luke's Rd. Whyt. CA62 105
St. Luke's Rd. Wind. AQ46 72
St. Luke's Sq. E16 CG39 58
St. Luke's St. SW3 BU42 3
St. Luke's St. SW3 BU42 66
St. Luke's Yd. W9 BR38 55
St. Malo Av. N9 CC27 39
St. Margaret's NW3 BS34 47
St. Margarets, Bark. CM37 58
St. Margarets, Guil. AS70 118
St. Margaret's Av. N15 BY31 47
St. Margaret's Av. N20 BT27 38
St. Margarets Av. Ashf. AZ49 73
St. Margaret's Av. Har. BG34 45
St. Margarets Av. Sid. CM48 78
St. Margaret's Av. Sutt. BR55 85
St. Margarets Av. Uxb. AZ38 53
St. Margarets Clo. EC2 BZ39 2
Lothbury
St. Margarets Clo. Berk. AR13 7
St. Margarets Clo. Iver AU37 52
St. Margaret's Clo. Orp. CO55 89
St. Margaret's Cres. SW15 BP46 75
St. Margaret's Cres. Grav. DJ48 81
St. Margaret's Dr. Twick. BJ46 74
St. Margarets Gate, Iver. AU37 52
St. Margaret's Gro. SE18 CM43 68
St. Margaret's Gro. Twick. BJ46 74
St. Margarets Ms. WC2 BX40 4
St. Margaret's Pass. SE13 CG45 68
St. Margaret's Path SE18 CM42 68
St. Margarets Pl. SW1 BW41 3
St. Margarets Pl. SW1 BX41 66
Spencer Pl.
St. Margarets Rd. E12 CJ34 49
St. Margarets Rd. N17 CA31 48
St. Margarets Rd. NW10 BQ38 55
St. Margaret's Rd. SE4 CO45 67
St. Margaret's Rd. W7 BH41 64
St. Margaret's Rd. Beck. CC52 87
St. Margaret's Rd. Edg. BM28 37
St. Margaret's Rd. Grav. DF47 81
Perry St
St. Margaret's Rd. Ruis. BA32 44
St. Margarets Rd. S. Dnth. CZ50 80
St. Margarets Rd. Twick. BJ45 64
St. Margarets St. SW1 BX41 4
St. Margarets St. SW1 BX41 66
St. Margaret's Ter. SE18 CM42 68
St. Margaret's Way, Hem. H. BA13 8
St. Marg. Rd. Couls. BV64 104
St. Mark's Clo. W11 BQ40 55
Lancaster Rd.
St. Mark's Clo. Barn. BS24 29
St. Marks Cres. NW1 BV37 1
St. Mark's Cres. NW1 BV37 56
St. Marks Gro. SW10 BS43 66
St. Mark's Hill, Surb. BL53 85
St. Marks Pl. SW19 BR50 75
Wimbledon Hill Rd.
St. Marks Pl. W11 BR39 55
St. Mark's Pl. Wind. AO44 61
St. Mark's Rise E8 CA35 48
St. Mark's Rd. SE25 CB52 87
St. Marks Rd. W5 BL40 55
Common, The
St. Marks Rd. W7 BH41 64
St. Marks Rd. W10 BQ39 55
St. Marks Rd. Brom. CH52 88
St. Mark's Rd. Enf. CA25 30
St. Mark's Rd. Epsom BQ62 103
St. Marks Rd. Mitch. BU51 86
St. Mark's Rd. Tedd. BJ50 74
St. Mark's Rd. Wind. AO44 61
St. Mark's Sq. NW1 BV37 1
St. Mark's Sq. NW1 BV37 56
Regents Pk. Rd.
St. Marks Sq. Grav. DF49 81
St. Mark St. E1 CA39 2
St. Martha's Av. Wok. AS64 100
St. Martin Clo. Uxb. AX39 53
St. Martins App. Ruis. BB33 44
St. Martin's Av. E6 CJ37 58
St. Martins Av. Epsom BO60 94
St. Martins Clo. Belv. CP41 69
St. Helens Rd.
St. Martins Clo. Brwd. DE26 122
St. Martin's Clo. Enf. CB23 30
St. Martins Clo. Epsom BO60 94
St. Martins Clo. Leath. BB68 110
St. Martins Clo. West Dr. AX41 63
St. Martin's Ct. WC2 BX40 56
St. Martin's La.
St. Martins Ct. Ashf. AX49 73
St. Martins Dr. Eyns. CV56 99
St. Martins Dr. Walt. BD55 84
St. Martin's La. WC2 BX40 4
St. Martin's La. WC2 BX40 56
St. Martins Le Grand EC1 BZ39 2
St. Martins Le Grand EC1 BZ39 57
St. Martins Mead. West. CP65 107
St. Martin's Ms. WC2 BX40 56
Adelaide St.
St. Martin's Pl. WC2 BX40 4
St. Martin's Rd. N9 CB27 39
St. Martin's Rd. SW9 BX44 66
St. Martin's Rd. Dart. CW46 80
St. Martins Rd. W. Dr. AX41 63
St. Martins St. WC2 BW40 3
St. Martins St. WC2 BX40 56
Whitcomb St.
St. Mary Abbot's Pl. W8 BR41 65
St. Mary Abbots Ter. W14 BR41 65
St. Mary at Hill EC3 CA40 4
St. Mary at Hill EC3 CA40 57
Lwr. Thames St.
St. Mary Av. Wall. BV55 86
St. Mary Axe EC3 CA39 2
St. Mary Axe EC3 CA39 57
St. Mary Church St. SE16 CC41 67
St. Mary Clo. N17 CB30 39
Kemble Rd.
St. Mary Rd. E17 CE32 48
St. Marys, Bark. CM37 58
St. Mary's App. E12 CK35 49
Church Rd.
St. Mary's Av. Nthwd. BB28 35
St. Mary's Av. E11 CH32 49
St. Mary's Av. N3 BR30 37
St. Mary's Av. Brom. CG52 88
St. Mary's Av. Stai. AX47 73
St. Mary's Av. Sthl. BF42 64
St. Mary's Av. Tedd. BH50 74
St. Mary's Av. Wal. Cr. CC18 21
St. Mary's Clo. E12 CK35 49
Church Rd.
St. Mary's Clo. Chess. BL57 94
St. Mary's Clo. Epsom BO57 94
St. Mary's Clo. Grav. DH48 81
St. Mary's Clo. Lthd. BG65 102
St. Mary's Clo. Orp. CO51 89
St. Marys Clo. Stai. AX47 73
St. Marys Cres.
St. Mary's Clo. Sun. BC52 83
St. Mary's Clo. Uxb. AW31 44
St. Mary's Clo. Wat. BC24 26
St. Mary's Cotts. SW19 BS51 86
St. Mary's Rd.
St. Mary's Ct. E6 CK38 58
St. Mary's Ct. W5 BK41 64
St. Mary's Rd.
St. Mary's Cres. NW4 BP31 46
St. Mary's Cres. Hayes BB40 53
St. Mary's Cres. Hayes BC40 53
St. Mary's Rd.
St. Mary's Cres. Islw. BG43 64
St. Mary's Cres. Stai. AX47 73
St. Mary's Dr. Felt. BA47 73
St. Mary's Dr. Sev. CT65 107
St. Mary's Gdns. SE11 BY42 4
St. Mary's Gdns. SE11 BY42 66
St. Mary's Gdns. W2 BT39 1
St. Marys Grn. BT31 47
Benedict Way
St. Marys Gr. West. CJ62 106
St. Marys Grn. West. BQ53 106
St. Marys Gro.
St. Mary's Gro. N1 BY36 56
St. Mary's Gro. SW13 BP45 65
St. Mary's Gro. W4 BM43 65
St. Mary's Gro. Rich. BL45 65
St. Marys La. Upmin. CX34 51
St. Mary's La. Upmin. DB33 51
St. Mary's Mans. W2 BT39 1
St. Mary's Mews NW6 BB36 56
Priory Rd.
St. Mary's Ms. W2 BT39 56
St. Marys Path N1 BY37 56
Gaskin St.
St. Mary, S. Av. Brwd. DD25 122
St. Mary, S. La. Upmin. DC33 123
St. Mary, S'rd Wok. AR62 100
St. Marys Path N1 BY37 2
St. Mary's Rd. E10 CF34 48
St. Mary's Rd. E13 CH37 58
St. Mary's Rd. N8 BX31 47
High St.
St. Mary's Rd. N9 CB26 39
St. Mary's Rd. NW10 BO37 55
St. Mary's Rd. NW11 BR33 46
St. Mary's Rd. SE15 CC44 67
St. Mary's Rd. SE25 CA52 87
St. Mary's Rd. SW19 BR49 75
St. Mary's Rd. W5 BK40 54
St. Mary's Rd. Barn. BU26 38
St. Mary's Rd. Bex. CS47 79
St. Marys Rd. E. Mol. BG53 84
St. Mary's Rd. Grays. DG42 71
St. Mary's Rd. Green. CZ45 70
St. Mary's Rd. Hayes BB40 53
St. Mary's Rd. Hem. H. AX13 8
St. Mary's Rd. Ilf. CM34 49
St. Mary's Rd. Lthd. BJ64 102
St. Mary's Rd. Merton SW19 BS51 86
St. Mary's Rd. Reig. BS71 121
St. Marys Rd. Slou. AS40 52
St. Mary's Rd. Sth. Croy. BZ58 96
St. Marys Rd. Surb. BK53 84
St. Mary's Rd. Surb. BK54 84
St. Mary's Rd. Swan. CS52 89
St. Mary's Rd. Uxb. AV32 43
St. Marys Rd. Uxb. AW31 44
St. Marys Rd. Wal. Cr. CC18 21
St. Mary's Rd. Wat. BC24 26
St. Mary's Rd. Wey. BA56 92
St. Mary's Rd. Wimb. SW19 BR49 75
St. Mary's Rd. Wok. AR62 100
St. Mary's Rd. Wor. Pk. BO55 85
St. Mary's Sq. W2 BT39 1
St. Mary's Sq. W2 BT39 56
St. Mary's Ter. Gdns.
St. Mary's Ter. W2 BT31 1
St. Mary's Ter. W2 BT39 1
St. Mary's Ter. W2 BT39 56
St. Mary St. SE18 CK42 68
St. Marys Way, Wdf. Grn. CL28 40
St. Mary's Wk. SE11 BY42 4
St. Mary's Wk. SE11 BY42 66
St. Mary's Wk. Hayes BB40 53
St. Marys Wk. St. Alb. BJ11 9
St. Mary's Way, Ger. Cr. AR30 34
St. Marys Way, Long. DC52 90
St. Mathew's Rd. SW2 BX45 66
St. Mathew St. SW1 BW41 3
St. Matthew Clo. Uxb. AX39 53
St. Matthew Rd. Red. BU70 121
St. Matthew's Av. Surb. BL54 85
St. Matthew's Clo. Rain. CU36 59
St. Matthews Dr. Brom. CK52 88
St. Matthews Rd. W5 BL40 55
Common, The
St. Matthews Row E2 CB38 2
St. Matthews Row E2 CB38 57
St. Matthews St. SW1 BW41 66
Old Pye St.
St. Matthias Clo. BO32 46
St. Maur Rd. SW6 BR44 65
St. Merryn Clo. SE18 CM43 68
St. Meryl Est. Wat. BE27 36
St. Michael's Alley EC3 BZ39 57
Cornhill
St. Michael's Av. N9 CC26 39
St. Michael's Av. NW2 BQ35 46
St. Michaels Av. Hem. H. AZ14 8
St. Michael's Av. Wem. BM36 55
St. Michaels Clo. N3 BR30 37
Hendon La.
St. Michaels Clo. N12 BU28 38
St. Michaels Clo. Belv. BP41 69
St. Helens Rd.
St. Michaels Clo. Brom. CK52 88
St. Michaels Clo. Pot. B. BS18 20
Church Rd.
St. Michael's Clo. Walt. BD55 84
St. Michael's Cres. Pnr. BE32 45
St. Michael's Dr. Sev. CV61 108
St. Michael's Gdns. W10 BR39 55
Ladbroke Gro.
St. Michael, S. Rd. Brox. CD13 12
St. Michael's Rise, Well. CO44 69
St. Michael's Rd. SW9 BX44 66
St. Michael's Rd. Ashf. AZ49 73
St. Michael's Rd. Cat. BZ64 105
St. Michael's Rd. Croy. BZ54 87
St. Michaels Rd. Grays. DG42 71
St. Michael's Rd. Wall. BW56 95
St. Michaels Rd. Well. CO45 69
St. Michaels Rd. Wok. AU60 91
St. Michaels St. SE8 CD44 67
Tanner's Hill
St. Michael's St. W2 BT39 1
St. Michael's St. W2 BT39 56
St. Michaels St. St. Alb. BF13 9
St. Michael's Ter. N22 BX30 38
St. Michaels Vw. Hat. BP11 10
Drovers Way
St. Michaels Way, Pot. B. BS18 20
Church Rd.
St. Mildred's Ct. EC2 BZ39 57
Poultry
St. Mildred's Rd. SE12 CG47 78
St. Monica's Rd. Tad. BR64 103
St. Neots Rd. Rom. CW29 42
St. Nicholas Av. Lthd. BF66 111
St. Nicholas Av. Horn. CU34 50
St. Nicholas Clo. Amer. AQ23 25
St. Nicholas Clo. Borwd. BK25 27
Elstree Hill, N.
St. Nicholas Clo. Uxb. AX39 53
St. Nicholas Dr. Shep. AZ54 83
St. Nicholas Glebe SW17 BV49 76
St. Nicholas Gro. Borwd. DE28 122
St. Nicholas Hill, Lthd. BJ64 102
St. Nicholas La. Chis. CK51 88
St. Nicholas Mnt. Hem. H. AV13 7
St. Nicholas Rd. SE18 CN42 68
St. Nicholas Rd. Surb. BH53 84
St. Nicholas Rd. Sutt. BS56 95
St. Nicholas St. SE8 CE44 67
Lucas St.
St. Nicholas Way, Sutt. BS56 95
St. Norbert Gn. SE4 CD45 67
St. Norbert Rd. SE4 CC46 77
St. Norman's Way, Epsom BP58 94
St. Olaf's Rd. SW6 BR43 65
St. Olaves Clo. AV50 72
St. Olaves Ct. EC2 BZ39 2
St. Olave's Est. SE1 CA41 4
St. Olave's Est. SE1 CA41 67
St. Olave's Rd. E6 CL37 58
St. Olaves Wk. SW16 BW51 86
St. Omer Rd. Guil. AT71 118
St. Omer's Ridge, Guil. AT71 118
St. Oswald's Pl. SE11 BX42 4
St. Oswalds Pl. SE11 BX42 66
St. Oswald's Rd. SW16 BY51 86
St. Oswolf St. SW1 BW42 66
Erasmus St.
St. Oswulf St. SW1 BW42 3
St. Oswulf St. SW1 BW42 66
Erasmus St.
St. Pancras Ct. N2 BT30 38
St. Pancras Way NW1 BW36 56
St. Pancras Way NW1 BW37 1
St. Pancras Way Est. NW1 BW36 56
St. Pancras Way
St. Patrick's Gdns. Grav. DH48 81
St. Patricks Pl. Grays. DG42 71
St. Paul Clo. Uxb. AX39 53
St. Paul's Alley EC4 BY39 56
St. Paul's Churchyard
St. Paul's Av. NW2 BP36 55
St. Paul's Av. SE16 CC40 57
St. Pauls Av. Har. BL32 46
St. Pauls Av. Slou. AP40 52
St. Paul's Churchyard EC4 BY39 2
St. Pauls Churchyard EC4 BY39 56
St. Pauls Clo. W5 BL41 65
St. Paul's Clo. Ashf. BA49 73
St. Paul's Clo. Chess. BK56 93
St. Pauls Clo. Hayes BA42 63
St. Pauls Clo. Houns. BE44 64
St. Pauls Clo. S. Ock. CW40 60
St. Paul's Cray Est. Chis. CN52 88
St. Paul's Cray Rd. Chis. CM50 78
St. Paul's Cres. NW1 BW36 56
St. Paul's Dr. E15 CF35 48
St. Paul's Pl. N1 BZ36 57
St. Pauls Pl. St. Alb. BJ13 9
St. Paul's Rd. N1 BY36 56
St. Pauls Rd. N17 CB29 39
St. Paul's Rd. Bark. CM37 58
St. Paul's Rd. Brent. BK43 64
St. Paul's Rd. Erith CS43 69
St. Pauls Rd. Hem. H. AX13 8
St. Pauls Rd. Rich. BL45 65
St. Paul's Rd. Stai. AU50 72
St. Paul's Rd. Th. Hth. BZ52 87
St. Pauls Rd. Wok. AT62 100
St. Paul's Rd. E. Dor. BJ71 119
St. Paul's Rd. W. Dor. BJ72 119
St. Paul's Shrubbery N1 BZ36 57
St. Paul's Rd.
St. Pauls Sq. Brom. CG51 88
Church Rd.
St. Paul's St. E3 CD39 57
St. Paul's Ter. SE17 BY43 4
St. Pauls Ter. SE17 BY43 66
St. Paul St. N1 BZ37 2
St. Paul St. N1 BZ37 57
St. Paul's Way E3 CD39 57
St. Paul's Way N3 BS29 38
St. Pauls Way, Wal. Abb. CF20 21
Rochford Av.
St. Paul's Way Est. E14 CD39 57
St. Pauls Wood Hill, Orp. CN51 88
St. Peter's Av. E17 CG31 49
St. Peter's Av. N18 CB28 39
St. Peters Av. Ong. CW16 24
St. Petersburgh Ms. W2 BS40 3
St. Petersburgh Ms. W2 BS40 56
St. Petersburgh Pl. W2 BS40 56
St. Peters Clo. E2 CB38 57
St. Peters Clo. Barn. BP25 28
St. Peters Clo. Bush. BG26 36
St. Peters Clo. Chis. CM50 78
St. Peters Clo. Ger. Cr. AS30 34
St. Peters Clo. Ger. Cr. AS30 34
St. Peters Clo. Ilf. CN31 49
St. Peters Clo. Rick. AW26 35
Church La.
St. Peter's Clo. Ruis. BD34 45
St. Peters Clo. Wind. AQ46 72
St. Peters Clo. Wok. AU63 100
St. Peters Ct. SE3 CG45 68
St. Peters Ct. Ger. Cr. AS30 34
St. Peter's Gro. W6 BP42 65
St. Peter, S. Clo. St. Alb. BG13 9
St. Peter, S. Rd. Brwd. DA28 42
St. Peters St. Mews N1 BY37 56
St. Peters St.
St. Peter, S. St. St. Alb. BG13 9
St. Peter's Rd. N9 CB26 39
St. Peter's Rd. SW6 BR44 65
Filmer Rd.
St. Peter's Rd. W6 BP42 65
St. Peter's Rd. Croy. BZ56 96
St. Peters Rd. E. Mol. BF52 84
St. Peters Rd. Grays. DG42 71
St. Peters Rd. Kings. on T. BM51 85
Cambridge Rd.
St. Peters Rd. St. Alb. BH13 9
St. Peter's Rd. Stai. AV50 72

Sarsfield Rd. SW12 BU47 76
Sarsfield Rd. Grnf. BJ37 54
Sartor Rd. SE15 CC45 67
Sarum Grn. Wey. BB55 83
Sarum Pl. Hem. H. AY11 8
Satchwell Rd. E2 CA38 57
Bethnal Green Rd.
Saturn Way, Hem. H. AY12 8
Saunders Copse, Wok. AQ64 100
Saunders La. Wok. AP64 100
Saunders Ness Rd. E14 CF42 67
Saunders Rd. SE18 CN42 68
Saunders Rd. Uxb. AY36 53
Saunders St. SE11 BX42 4
Saunders St. SE11 BY42 66
Saunder's Way SE28 CO40 59
Saunderton Rd. Wem. BJ35 45
Saunton Ave. Hayes BB43 63
Saunton Rd. Horn. CU34 50
Savage Gdns. E6 CK39 58
Savage Gdns. EC3 CA40 4
Savage Gdns. EC3 CA40 57
Savay Clo. Uxb. AW33 44
Savay La. Uxb. AW32 44
Savernake Rd. N9 CB25 30
Savernake Rd. NW3 BU35 47
Savile Gdns. Croy. CA55 87
Savile Row W1 BW40 56
Saville Clo. N. Mal. BO53 85
Saville Cres. Ashf. BA50 73
Saville Gdns. Croy. CA55 87
Saville Rd. E16 CK40 58
Saville Rd. W4 BN41 65
Saville Rd. Rom. CQ32 50
Saville Rd. Twick. BH47 74
Saville Row W1 BW40 3
Saville Row, Wdf. Grn. CH29 40
Savill Gdns. SW20 BP52 85
Saviours Est. SE1 CA41 4
Savona Clo. SW19 BQ50 75
Savona Est. SW8 BW43 66
Savona St. SW8 BW43 66
Savoy Av. Hayes BB42 63
Savoy Clo. Edg. BM28 37
Savoy Clo. Uxb. AX30 35
Savoy Ct. WC2 BX40 4
Savoy Ct. WC2 BX40 56
Strand
Savoy Hill WC2 BX40 4
Savoy Pl. WC2 BX40 4
Savoy Pl. WC2 BX40 56
Savoy Pl. W12 BX40 56
Savoy St.
Savoy Rd. Dart. CV46 80
Savoy St. WC2 BX40 4
Savoy St. WC2 BX40 56
Savoy Way WC2 BX40 56
Carting La.
Sawells, Brox. CD14 12
Sawkin Clo. SW19 BQ48 75
Thursley Gdns.
Sawkins Clo. SW19 BR48 75
Queensmere Rd.
Sawley Rd. W12 BP40 55
Sawpit Lane, Guil. AY69 110
Sawtry Clo. Cars. BT54 86
Sawyers Clo. Dag. CS36 59
Sawyers Clo. Wind. AM43 61
Sawyers La. Borwd. BJ23 27
Sawyers La. Pot. B. BQ20 19
Sawyer, S. Hall La. Brwd. DB26 42
Sawyer St. SE1 BZ41 4
Sawyer St. SE1 BZ41 67
Sawyers Way, Hem. H. AY13 8
Saxbys Rd. Sev. CY64 108
Saxby St. SW2 BX47 76
Saxham Rd. Bark. CN37 58
Saxlingham Rd. E4 CF27 39
Saxon Av. Felt. BE48 74
Saxon Rd. E3 CD37 57
Saxonbury Av. Sun. BC51 83
Saxonbury Clo. Mitch. BT52 86
Saxonbury Gdns. Surb. BK54 84
Saxon Clo. Brwd. DD27 122
Saxon Clo. Grav. DE48 81
Saxon Clo. Rom. CW30 42
Saxon Clo. Slou. AS41 62
Saxon Clo. Uxb. AY39 53
Saxon Dr. W3 BM39 55
Saxon Gdns. Sthl. BE40 54
Saxon Ho. Felt. BE48 74
Saxon Pl. Hort. K. CY53 90
Saxon Rd. E6 CK38 58
Saxon Rd. N22 BY30 38
Saxon Rd. SE25 BZ53 87
Saxon Rd. Ashf. BA50 73
Saxon Rd. Brom. CG50 78
Saxon Rd. Dart. CW49 80
Saxon Rd. Ilf. CL36 58
Saxon Rd. Sthl. BE40 54
Saxon Rd. Walt. BD55 84
Saxon Rd. Welw. BP5 5
Saxon Rd. Wem. BM34 46
Saxon Wk. Sid. CP50 79
Cray Rd.
Saxon Way N14 BW25 29
Saxon Way, Reig. BR70 120
Saxon Way, Wal. Abb. CF20 21
Saxony Par. Hayes BA39 53
Saxton Clo. SE13 CF45 67
Saxville Rd. Orp. CO52 89
Sayers Clo. Lthd. BG65 102
Sayesbury Av. Saw. CP5 6
Sayesbury Rd. Saw. CQ6 6
Sayes Ct. Est. SE8 CD42 67
Sayes Ct. Gdns. SE8 CD42 67
Sayes Ct. Rd. Orp. CO52 89
Sayes Ct. St. SE8 CD43 67
Sayes Ct. Wey. AW56 92
Sayers Gdns. Berk AQ11 7
Sayward Clo. Chesh. AO18 16
Scabharbour Rd. Sev. CV70 117
Scad's Hill Clo. Orp. CN53 88
Scala St. W1 BW39 1
Scales Rd. N17 CA31 48
Scampston Ms. W10 BQ39 55
Scampton Rd. Houns. AY46 73
Southampton Rd.
Scandrett St. E1 CB40 57
Wapping High St.
Scarba Wk. N1 BZ36 57
Marquess Est.
Scarborough Clo. Sutt. BR59 94
Scarborough Clo. West. CJ62 106
Scarborough Rd. E11 CF33 48
Scarborough Rd. N4 BY33 47
Scarborough Rd. N9 CC26 39
Scarborough St. E1 CA39 2
Scarbrook Rd. Croy. BZ55 87
Scarle Rd. Wem. BK36 54
Scarlet Rd. SE6 CG48 78
Scarlett Clo. Wok. AP62 100
Scarsbrook Rd. SE3 CJ45 68
Scarsdale Gro. SE5 CA43 67
Neate St.
Scarsdale Pl. W8 BS41 66
Wrights La.
Scarsdale Rd. SE5 CA43 4
Scarsdale Rd. Har. BG34 45
Scarsdale Vill. W8 BS41 66
Scarth Rd. SW13 BO45 65
Scatterdells La. Kings L. AV18 16
Scatterdells La. Kings L. AW18 17
Scawen Rd. SE8 CD42 67
Scawfell St. E2 CA37 2
Scawfell St. E2 CA37 57
Scaynes Link N12 BS28 38
Sceaux Est. SE5 CA44 67
Sceptre Rd. E2 CC38 57
Sceyness Link N12 BS28 38
Chanctonbury Way
Schofield Rd. SE3 CH43 68
Schofield Wk. SE3 CH43 68
Dornbergh Clo.
Scholars Rd. E4 CF26 39
Scholars Rd. SW12 BW47 76
Scholars Wk. Hat. BP14 10
Scholefield Rd. N19 BW33 47
School Alley, Twick. BJ47 74
School La. Welw. BU6 5
School Clo. Guil. AR69 118
Bellfields Rd.
Schoolfield Rd. Grays DA43 70
School Gdns. Berk. AT12 7
School Green La. Epp. CS16 23
School Hill, Red. BW67 113
Schoolhouse La. E1 CC40 57
School Ho. La. Tedd. BJ50 74
School La. Beac. AO29 34
School La. Brwd. DE29 122
School La. Bush. BF26 36
School La. Ch. St. G. AQ27 34
School La. Dor. BG72 119
School La. Egh. AT49 72
School La. Ger. Cr. AR30 34
School La. Guil. AY69 110
School La. Harl. CN10 6
School La. Hat. BQ12 10
School La. Hat. BU12 11
School La. Hort. K. CY52 90
School La. Kings. on T. BK51 84
Park Rd.
School La. Leath. AZ68 110
School La. Lthd. BF66 111
School La. Lthd. BG65 102
School La. Ong. CS12 14
School La. Ong. CZ10 15
School La. Ong. DA11 15
School La. Pnr. BE31 45
School La. Sev. CW64 108
School La. Sev. CZ59 99
School La. Sev. & Ton. DC67 117
School La. Shep. AZ53 83
School La. Slou. AQ36 52
School La. St. Alb. BF20 18
School La. Surb. BM54 85
School La. Swan. CU51 89
School La. Tad. BP66 112
School La. Wat. BE20 18
School La. Well. CO45 69
School La. Welw. BO5 5
School La. Wey. AW56 92
School La. Wok. AZ64 101
School Mead. Wat. BA19 17
School Pass. Kings. on T. BL51 85
School Pass. Sthl. BE40 54
School Pl. E1 CB38 57
Buckhurst St.
School Rd. E12 CK35 49
School Rd. NW10 BN38 55
School Rd. W4 BN42 65
Belmont Rd.
School Rd. Ashf. AZ49 73
School Rd. Brwd. CZ22 33
School Rd. Chis. CM51 88
School Rd. Dag. CR37 59
School Rd. E. Mol. BG52 84
School Rd. Grav. DH48 81
School Rd. Hamptn. BG50 74
School Rd. Houns. BG45 64
School Rd. Kings. on T. BK51 84
Park Rd.
School Rd. Ong. CT18 23
School Rd. Pot. B. BT18 20
School Rd. Sev. DA64 108
School Rd. West Dr. AX43 63
School Rd. Av. Hamptn. BG50 74
School Row, Hem. H. AV14 7
School Wk. Slou. AQ40 52
School Wk. Sun. BC52 83
School Way N12 BT28 38
School Way N12 BT29 38
School Way, Dag. CP34 50
Schroder Ct. Egh. AQ49 72
Schubert Clo. Borwd. BK25 27
Schurbert Rd. SW15 BR46 75
Scillonian Rd. Guil. AQ71 118
Sclater St. E1 CA38 2
Sclater St. E1 CA38 57
Scobie Pl. N16 CA35 48
Amhurst Rd.
Scoresby St. SE1 BY40 4
Scoresby St. SE1 BY40 56
Scorton Av. Grnf. BJ37 54
Scotch Common W13 BJ39 54
Scoter Clo. Wdf. Grn. CH29 40
Mallards Rd.
Scot Gro. Pnr. BE29 36
Scothey Wk. Horn. CV36 60
Pembrey Way
Scotland Bridge Rd. Wey. AW59 92
Scotland Grn. N17 CA30 39
Scotland Grn. Rd. Enf. CC25 30
Scotland Grn. Rd. N. Enf. CC24 30
Scotland Rd. Buck. H. CJ26 40
Scots Clo. Stai. AX47 73
Scotscraig, Rad. BH21 27
Scotsdale Clo. Orp. CN52 88
Scotsdale Clo. Sutt. BR57 94
Scotsdale Rd. SE12 CH46 78
Scotshall La. Warl. CF61 105
Scots Hill, Rick. AY25 26
Scots Hill Clo. Rick. AY25 26
Scotswold Wk. N17 CB29 39
Waverley Rd.
Scotswood Wk. N17 CB29 39
Northumberland Pk.
Scott Clo. SW16 BX51 86
Fairview Rd.
Scott Clo. Epsom BN56 94
Scott Clo. West Dr. AY42 63
Scott Cres. Erith CT44 69
Scott Cres. Har. BF33 45
Scott Ellis Gdns. NW8 BT38 1
Scott Ellis Gdns. NW8 BT38 56
Scottes La. Dag. CP33 50
Valence Av.
Scott Lidgett Cres. SE16 CB41 4
Scott Lidgett Cres. SE16 CB41 67
Scott Rd. Grav. DH49 81
Scott Rd. Grays DG42 71
Scotts Av. Brom. CF51 87
Scotts Av. Sun. BB50 73
Scotts Dr. Hamptn. BF50 74
Scotts Fm. Rd. Epsom BN57 94
Scotts Gro. Clo. Wok. AO60 91
Scotts Gro. Rd. Wok. AO60 91
Scott's La. Brom. CF52 87
Scotts Mill Rd. Rick. AY25 26
Scott's Rd. E10 CF33 48
Scott's Rd. W12 BP41 65
Scott's Rd. Brom. CH50 78
Scott's Rd. Sthl. BD41 64
Scott St. E1 CB38 57
Scotts Way, Sev. CT64 107
Scotts Way, Sun. BB50 73
Scotts Wol. Clo. Bush. BE23 27
Scotts Wol. Rd. Bush. BE23 27
Scoulding Rd. E16 CG39 58
Roger's Rd.
Scouler St. E14 CF40 57
Harrap St.
Scout App. NW10 BN35 46
Scout La. SW4 BW45 66
Scout Way NW7 BN28 37
Scovell Rd. SE1 BZ41 4
Scovell Rd. SE1 BZ41 67
Scovell Wk. SE1 BZ41 67
Scovell Rd.
Scrafton Rd. Ilf. CL34 49
Scratchers La. Farn. CY55 90
Scrattons Ter. Bark. CP37 59
Scriven St. E8 CA37 57
Scrive St. E8 CA37 2
Scrooby St. SE6 CE46 77
Scrubbits Pk. Rd. Rad. BJ21 27
Scrubs La. NW10 BP38 55
Scrubs La. W10 BP38 55
Scrutton Clo. SW12 BW47 76
Scrutton Pl. EC2 CA38 2
Scrutton St. EC2 CA38 2
Scrutton St. EC2 CA38 57
Scudamore La. NW9 BN31 46
Scudders Hill, Fawk. DA53 90
Scutari Rd. SE22 CB46 77
Scylla Rd. SE15 CB45 67
Scylla Rd. Houns. AZ46 73
Seaborough Rd. Grays. DH41 71
Seabrook Dr. W. Wick. CF55 87
Seabrooke Ri. Grays. DD43 71
Seabrook Gdns. Rom. CR33 50
Seabrook Rd. Dag. CP34 50
Seabrook Rd. Kings L. BA17 17
Seaburn Clo. Rain. CT38 59
Seacoal La. EC4 BY39 2
Seacoal La. EC4 BY39 56
Seacourt Rd. SE2 CP41 69
Seacourt Rd. Slou. AT42 62
Seacroft Gdns. Wat. BD27 36
Seafield Rd. N11 BW28 38
Seaford Rd. E17 CE31 48
Seaford Rd. N15 BZ31 48
Seaford Rd. W13 BJ40 54
Seaford Rd. Enf. CA24 30
Seaford Rd. Houns. AX46 73
Sandringham Rd.
Seaford St. WC1 BX38 2
Seaford St. WC1 BX38 56
Seaforth Av. N. Mal. BP53 85
Seaforth Clo. Rom. CT29 41
Seaforth Cr. N5 BZ35 48
Seaforth Dr. Wal. Cr. CC20 21
Seaforth Gdns. N21 BX26 38
Seaforth Gdns. Epsom BO56 94
Seaforth Gdns. Wdf. Grn. CJ28 40
Seaforth Pl. SW1 BW41 3
Seaforth Pl. SW1 BW41 66
Buckingham Gate
Seager Pl. E3 CD39 57
Burdett Rd.
Seagrave Clo. E1 CC39 57
Seagrave Clo. Wey. AZ57 92
Seagrave Rd. SW6 BS43 66
Seagry Rd. E11 CH32 49
Sealand Rd. Houns. AZ46 73
Sealand Wk. Nthlt. BD38 54
Wayfarer Rd.
Seal Chart, Sev. CY64 108
Seal Dr. Sev. CW64 108
Seale Hill, Reig. BS71 121
Seal Hill, Sev. CX64 108
Seal Hollow Rd. Sev. CV65 108
Sealord Clo. Ruis. BA34 44
Seal Rd. Sev. CV64 108
Seal St. E8 CA35 48
Seaman Clo. St. Alb. BG16 18
Searches La. Wat. BC17 17
Searches La. Wat. BD17 18
Searchwood Rd. Warl. CB62 105
Searle Clo. SW11 BU43 66
Searles Rd. SE1 BZ42 4
Searles Rd. SE1 BZ42 67
Sears St. SE5 BZ43 67
Seasprite Clo. Nthlt. BD38 54
Seaton Av. Ilf. CN35 49
Seaton Clo. E13 CH38 58
New Barn St.
Seaton Clo. Twick. BG46 74
Seaton Dr. Ashf. AY48 73
Seaton Gdns. Ruis. BC34 44
Seaton Pl. NW1 BW38 1
Seaton Pl. NW1 BW38 56
Seaton Rd. Dart. CU47 79
Seaton Rd. Hayes BA42 63
Seaton Rd. Hem. H. AX15 8
Seaton Rd. Mitch. BU51 86
Seaton Rd. St. Alb. BK17 18
Seaton Rd. Twick. BG46 74
Seaton Rd. Well. CP43 69
Seaton Rd. Wem. BL37 55
Seaton St. N18 CB28 39
Sebastian Av. Brwd. DD25 122
Sebastian St. EC1 BY38 2
Sebastian St. EC1 BY38 56
Sebastopool Rd. N9 CB28 39
Sebbon St. N1 BY36 2
Sebbon St. N1 BY36 56
Sebert Rd. E7 CH35 49
Sebright Pass. E CB37 57
Sebright Rd. Barn. BQ23 28
Sebright Rd. Hem. H. AW14 8
Secker Cres. Har. BG30 36
Secker St. SE1 BY40 4
Secker St. SE1 BY40 56
Second Av. Harl. CN11 13
Second Av. E12 CK35 49
Second Av. E13 CH38 58
Second Av. E17 CE32 48
Second Av. N18 CC28 39
Second Av. NW4 BQ31 46
Second Av. SW14 BO45 65
Second Av. W3 BO40 55
Second Av. W10 BR38 55
Second Av. Brwd. DB20 24
Second Av. Dag. CR37 59
Second Av. Enf. CA25 30
Second Av. Grays DA43 70
Second Av. Hayes BB40 53
Second Av. Hayes BC40 53
Glebe Rd.
Second Av. Rom. CP32 50
Second Av. Walt. BC53 83
Second Av. Wat. BD21 27
Second Av. Wem. BK34 45
Second Clo. E. Mol. BG52 84
Second Cross Rd. Twick. BG48 74
Second Way, Wem. BM35 46
Secretan Rd. SE5 CA42 4
Secretan Rd. SE5 CA42 67
Sedan Way SE17 CA42 4
Sedcote Rd. Enf. CC25 30
Sedding St. SW1 BV42 3
Sedding St. SW1 BV42 66
Sloane Sq.
Seddon Rd. Mord. BT53 86
Sedgebrook Rd. SE3 CJ44 68
Sedgecombe Av. Har. BK32 45
Sedgefield Clo. Rom. CV28 42
Sedgefield Cres. Rom. CW28 42
Sedgeford Rd. W12 BP40 55
Sedgehill Rd. SE6 CE49 77
Sedgemere Av. N2 BT31 47
Sedgemere Rd. SE2 CP41 69
Sedgemoor Dr. Dag. CR35 50
Sedge Way SE6 CG47 78
Sedgewick Av. Uxb. AZ36 53
Sedgewood Clo. CG54 88
Sedgmoor Pl. SE5 CA43 67
Sedgwick Rd. E10 CF34 48
Sedgwick St. E9 CC35 48
Sedleigh Rd. SW18 BR46 75
Sedlescombe Rd. SW6 BS43 66
Sedley, Grav. DD49 81
Sedley Pl. W1 BV39 1
Sedley Pl. W1 BV39 56
Oxford St.
Sedley Ri. Loug. CK23 31
Seeley Dr. SE21 CA49 77
Seelig Av. NW9 BP33 46
Seely Rd. SW17 BV50 76
Seer Green La. Beac. AP29 34
Seer Mead. Beac. AO29 34
Seething La. EC3 CA40 4
Seething La. EC3 CA40 57
Seething Wells La. Surb. BK53 84
Sefton Av. NW7 BN28 37
Sefton Av. Har. BG30 36
Sefton Clo. Orp. CN52 88
Sefton Clo. Slou. AP37 52
Sefton Pad. Slou. AQ36 52
Sefton Rd. Croy. CB54 87
Sefton Rd. Epsom BN58 94
Sefton Rd. Orp. CN52 88
Sefton St. SW15 BQ45 65
Sefton Way, Uxb. AY39 53
Sekforde St. EC1 BY38 2
Sekforde St. EC1 BY38 56
Selan Gdns. Hayes BC39 53
Selbie Av. NW10 BO35 46
Selborne Av. E12 CL35 49
Selborne Av. Bex. CQ47 79
Selborne Gdns. NW4 BP31 46
Selborne Gdns. Grnf. BJ37 54
Selborne Rd. E17 CD32 48
Selborne Rd. N14 BX27 38
Selborne Rd. N22 BX30 38
Selborne Rd. SE5 BZ44 67
Selborne Rd. Croy. CA55 87
Selborne Rd. Ilf. CL34 49
Selborne Rd. N. Mal. BO51 85
Selborne Rd. Sid. CO49 79
Selbourne Av. Surb. BL55 85
Selbourne Av. Wey. AW58 92
Selbourne Clo. Wey. AW58 92
Selbourne Rd. E17 CD32 48
Selbourne Sq. Gdse. CC68 114
Selby Av. St. Alb. BG13 9
Selby Chase, Ruis. BC34 44
Selby Clo. Chess. BL57 94
Selby Clo. Chis. CL50 78
Selby Gdns. Sth. BF38 54
Selby Grn. Cars. BU54 86
Selby Rd. E11 CG34 49
Selby Rd. E13 CH39 58
Selby Rd. N17 CA29 39
Selby Rd. SE20 CB51 87
Selby Rd. W5 BJ38 54
Selby Rd. Ashf. BA50 73
Selby Rd. Cars. BU54 86
Selby St. E1 CB38 57
Selcroft Rd. SE10 CG42 68
Selcroft Rd. Pur. BY59 95
Selden Rd. SE15 CC44 67
Selden Wk. N7 BX34 47
Andover Est.
Seldon Hill, Hem. H. AX14 8
Seldon Wk. N7 BX34 47
Durham Rd.
Selhurst Clo. Wok. AS61 100
Selhurst New Rd. SE25 CA53 87
Selhurst Pl. SE25 CA53 87
Selhurst Rd. N9 BZ27 39
Selhurst Rd. SE25 CA53 87
Selinas La. Dag. CQ33 50
Selkirk Rd. SW17 BU49 76
Selkirk Rd. Twick. BG48 74
Sellers Hall Clo. N3 BS29 38
Sellincourt Rd. SW17 BU49 76
Sellindge Clo. Beck. CD50 77
Sellon Ms. SE11 BX42 4
Sellon Ms. SE11 BX42 66
Sellons Av. NW10 BO37 55
Selma Ho. W12 BP39 55
Due Cane Rd.
Selous St. NW1 BW37 1
Selous St. NW1 BW37 56
Selsdon Av. Sth. Croy. BZ57 96
Selsdon Clo. Rom. CS30 41
Selsdon Clo. Surb. BL53 85
Selsdon Cres. Sth. Croy. CC58 96
Selsdon Pk. Rd. Sth. Croy. CC58 96
Selsdon Rd. E11 CH33 49
Selsdon Rd. E13 CJ37 58
Selsdon Rd. NW2 BO34 46
Selsdon Rd. SE27 BY48 76
Selsdon Rd. Sth. Croy. BZ56 96
Selsdon Rd. Wey. AW59 92
Selsey Cres. Well. CP44 69
Selsey Pl. N6 CA35 48
Crossway
Selsey St. E14 CE39 57
Selvage La. NW7 BN28 37
Selway Clo. Pnr. BC31 44
Selwins Clo. Horn. CV32 51
Selworth Clo. E11 CH32 49
Selwood Clo. Stai. AX46 73
Selwood Gdns. Stai. AX46 73
Selwood Pl. SW7 BT42 3
Selwood Pl. SW7 BT42 66
Selwood Rd. Brwd. CZ27 42
Selwood Rd. Chess. BK56 93
Selwood Rd. Croy. CB55 87
Selwood Rd. Sutt. BR54 85
Selwood Rd. Wok. AT63 100
Selwood Ter. SW7 BT42 3
Selwood Ter. SW7 BT42 66
Selworthy Rd. SE6 CD48 77
Selwyn Av. E4 CF29 39
Selwyn Av. NW10 BN36 55
Selwyn Av. Hat. BN13 10
Selwyn Av. Ilf. CN32 49
Selwyn Av. Rich. BL45 65
Selwyn Ct. SE3 CG45 68
Selwyn Ct. Edg. BM29 37
Selwyn Cres. Hat. BO12 10
Selwyn Cres. Well. CO45 69
Selwyn Dr. Hat. BN12 10
Selwyn Grn. Walt. BD54 84
Cromwell Rd.
Selwyn Rd. E3 CD37 57
Selwyn Rd. E13 CH37 58
Selwyn Rd. N17 CA31 48
Selwyn Rd. N. Mal. BN53 85
Selwyn Rd. Orp. CO52 89
Selwyn Rd. Til. DF44 71
Selwyn Rd. Walt. BD54 84
St. John's Dr.
Semaphore Rd. Guil. AS71 118
Semley Pl. SW1 BV42 3
Semley Pl. SW1 BV42 66
Semley Rd. SW16 BX51 86
Semper Clo. Wok. AP62 100
Sempter Rd. Grays DH41 71
Semphill Rd. Hem. H. AY15 8
Send Clo. Wok. AU65 100
Send Hill Rd. Wok. AU65 100
Send Hill Rd. Wok. AU66 109
Sendmarsh Rd. Wok. AU65 100
Send Rd. Wok. AT65 100
Seneca Rd. SW4 BX45 66
Seneca Rd. Th. Hth. BZ52 87
Senga Rd. Wall. BV54 86
Senhouse Rd. Sutt. BQ55 85
Senior St. W2 BS39 56
Senlac Rd. SE12 CH47 78
Sennen Walk SE9 CK48 78
Nunnington Clo.
Sennon Rd. Enf. CA26 39
Senrab St. E1 CC39 57
Sentinal Sq. NW4 BQ31 46
September Way, Stan. BJ29 36
Septimus Pl. Enf. CB25 30
Ermine Side
Sequoia Clo. Bush. BG26 36
Sequoia Gdns. Orp. CN54 88
Sequoia Pk. Pnr. BF29 36
Serbin Clo. E10 CG33 49
Sergeants Green La.
Wal. Abb. CJ20 22

101

Sherrards Pk. Rd.
Welw. G. C. BQ7 5
Sherrards Way, Barn. BS25 29
Sherrick Grn. Rd. NW10 BP35 46
Sherriff Rd. NW6 BS36 56
Sherringham Av. N17 CB30 39
Sherrock Gdns. NW4 BP31 46
Sherwin Rd. SE14 CC44 67
Sherwood, Grays. DC40 71
Sherwood Av. E18 CH31 49
Sherwood Av. SW16 BW50 76
Sherwood Av. Grnf. BH36 54
Sherwood Av. Hayes BC38 53
Sherwood Av. Pot. B. BR19 19
Sherwood Av. Ruis. BB32 44
Sherwood Av. St. Alb. BJ12 9
Sherwood Clo. SW15 BP45 65
Sherwood Clo. W13 BJ40 54
Sherwood Clo. Slou. AS42 62
Sherwood Clo. Wok. AP62 100
Sherwood Cres. Reig. BS72 121
Sherwood Gdns. Bark. CM36 58
Sherwood Pk. Av. Sid. CO47 79
Sherwood Pk. Rd. Mitch. BW52 86
Sherwood Pk. Rd. Sutt. BS56 95
Sherwood Rd. NW4 BQ31 46
Sherwood Rd. SW19 BR50 75
Sherwood Rd. Couls. BW61 104
Sherwood Rd. Croy. CB54 87
Sherwood Rd. Har. BG34 45
Sherwood Rd. Hmptn. BG49 74
Sherwood Rd. Ilf. CM31 49
Sherwood Rd. Well. CO44 69
Sherwoods Rd. Wat. BE26 36
Sherwood St. N20 BT27 38
Sherwood St. W1 BW40 3
Sherwood St. W1 BW40 56
Brewer St.
Sherwood Ter. N20 BT27 38
Sherwood Way, W. Wick. CE55 87
Shetland Clo. Borwd. BN25 28
Percheron Rd.
Shetland Rd. E3 CD37 57
Shevon Way, Brwd. CZ28 42
Shey Copse, Wok. AU62 100
Shieldhall St. SE2 CP42 69
Shield Rd. Ashf. BA49 73
Shiliber Wk. Chig. CN27 40
Shilburn Way, Wok. AQ62 100
Thursby Rd.
Shilling St. N1 BY36 56
Cross St.
Shillington St. SW11 BU44 66
Shillitoe Av. Pot. B. BQ19 19
Shillitoe Rd. N13 BY28 38
Shimmings, The Guil. AT70 118
Shinfield St. W12 BQ39 55
Shingle Ct. Wal. Abb. CH20 22
Winters Way
Shinglewell Rd. Erith. CR43 69
Ship All. E1 CB40 57
Wellclose Sq.
Shipbourne Rd.
Sev. & Ton. CY69 117
Shipfield Clo. West. CJ64 106
Shipford Path SE23 CC48 77
Ship & Half Moon
Pass. SE18 CL41 68
Ship Hill, West. CJ64 106
Shipka Rd. SW12 BV47 76
Ship La. SW14 BN45 65
Ship La. S. At H. CV51 90
Ship La. S. Ock. CW40 60
Shipman Rd. E16 CH39 58
Shipman Rd. SE23 CC48 77
Ship & Mermaid Row SE1 BZ41 67
Weston St.
Ship St. SE8 CE44 67
Ship Tavern Pass EC3 CA39 57
Lime St.
Shipton Clo. Dag. CP34 50
Shipton Rd. Uxb. AY35 44
Shipton St. E2 CA38 2
Shipton St. E2 CA38 57
Shipwa Ter. N16 CA34 48
Victorian Rd.
Shirburn Clo. SE23 CC47 77
Shirbutt St. E14 CE40 57
Shirebrook Rd. SE3 CJ45 68
Shirehall Clo. NW4 BQ32 46
Shirehall Gdns. NW4 BQ32 46
Shirehall La. NW4 BQ32 46
Shirehall Pk. NW4 BQ32 46
Shirehall Rd. Dart. CV49 80
Shire La. Ger. Cr. AT27 34
Shire La. Orp. CK57 97
Shire La. Orp. CN56 97
Shire La. Rick. AT25 25
Shire Meade, Borwd. BL25 28
Shires Houses, Wey. AY60 92
Shires, The Rich. BL49 75
Shirland Ms. W9 BR38 55
Shirland Rd. W9 BR38 55
Shirley Av. Couls. BY63 104
Shirley Av. Wind. AM44 61
Shirley Av. Bex. CP47 79
Shirley Av. Croy. CC54 87
Shirley Av. Red. BU73 121
Shirley Av. Sutt. BR58 94
Shirley Av. Sutt. BT56 95
Shirley Ch. Rd. Croy. CC55 87
Shirley Clo. Brox. CD15 12
Westlea Rd.
Shirley Clo. Dart. CV45 70
Shirley Clo. Houns. BG46 74
Shirley Clo. Wal. Cr. CB18 21
Shirley Cres. Beck. CC52 87
Shirley Dr. Houns. BG46 74
Shirley Gdns. W7 BH40 54
Shirley Gdns. Bark. CN36 58
Shirley Gdns. Horn. CV34 51
Shirley Gro. N9 CC26 39
Shirley Gro. SW11 BV45 66
Shirley Heights, Erith. CQ45 69
Avenue Rd.
Shirley Hills Rd. Croy. CC56 96
Shirley Ho. Dr. SE7 CJ43 68
Shirley Oak Rd. Croy. CC54 87
Shirley Pk. Rd. Croy. CB54 87
Shirley Pl. Wok. AO62 100
Shirley Rd. E15 CG36 58
Shirley Rd. W4 BN41 65
Shirley Rd. Croy. CB54 87
Shirley Rd. Enf. BZ24 30
Shirley Rd. St. Alb. BH14 9
Shirley Rd. Sid. CN48 78
Shirley Rd. Wall. BW58 95
Shirley Rd. Wat. BB19 17
Shirley Rd. E16 CG39 58
Shirley St. N1 BX37 2
Shirley St. N1 BX37 56
Shirley Way, Croy. CD55 87
Shirlock Rd. NW3 BU35 47
Mansfield Rd.
Shobden Rd. N17 BZ30 39
Shoebury Rd. E6 CK36 58
Shoe La. EC4 BY39 2
Shoe La. EC4 BY39 56
Shoe La. Harl. CQ11 14
Sholdon Gdns. Orp. CP53 89
Shonk's Mill, Rom. CU22 32
Shooters Av. Har. BK31 45
Shooters Dr. Wal. Abb. CG14 13
Shooters Hill SE18 CK44 68
Shooters Hill, Well. CK44 68
Shooter's Hill Rd. SE3 CF44 67
Shooter's Hill Rd. SE18 CF44 67
Shooters Rd. Enf. BY22 29
Shooters Way, Berk. BY22 29
Shooters Way Pk. Berk. AP13 7
Shooters Way, Berk. AO12 7
Shootersway La. Berk. AP13 7
Shoot Up Hill NW2 BR35 46
Shootery Clo. SE9 CK48 78
Shoplands, Welw. G. C. BQ6 5
Shord Hill, Ken. BZ57 96
Shord Hill, Ken. BZ61 105
Shore Clo. Felt. BB47 73
Bedfont La.
Shoreditch Clo. Uxb. AY34 44
Shoreditch High St. E1 CA38 2
Shoreditch High St. E1 CA38 57
Shore Est. E9 CC36 57
Shore Gro. Felt. BF48 74
Shoreham Clo. SW18 BS46 76
York Rd.
Shoreham Clo. Bex. CP47 79
Stansted Cres.
Shoreham Clo. Croy. CC53 87
Shoreham La. Orp. CR57 98
Shoreham La. Sev. CQ59 98
Shoreham La. Sev. CT64 107
Shoreham Rd. Orp. CO51 89
Shoreham Rd. Sev. CU59 98
Shoreham Rd. E. Houns. AY46 73
Shoreham Rd. W. Houns. AY46 73
Shoreham St. SW18 BS46 76
Barchard St.
Shoreham Way, Brom. CH53 88
Shore Pl. E9 CC36 57
Shore Rd. E9 CC36 57
Shores Rd. Wok. AS60 91
Shore St. SW19 BT51 86
Shore, The Grav. DE46 81
Shorncliffe Rd. SE1 CA42 4
Shorncliffe Rd. SE1 CA42 67
Shorndeen St. SE6 CF47 77
Shorne Clo. Sid. CO46 79
Park Mead
Shornefield Clo. Brom. CL52 88
Shorrolds Rd. SW6 BR43 65
Shortcroft Rd. Epsom BO57 94
Shortcrofts Rd. Dag. CQ36 59
Shorter Av. Brwd. DC26 122
Short Gate N12 BR28 37
Shortland Rd. E10 CE33 48
Shortlands W6 BQ42 65
Shortlands, Hayes BA43 63
Shortlands Av. Ong. CW16 24
Shortlands Clo. N18 BZ27 39
Shortlands Gdns. Brom. CG51 88
Shortlands Grn. Welw. G. C. BR8 5
Shortlands Gro. Brom. CF51 87
Shortlands Ms. W6 BQ42 65
Shortlands Rd. Brom. CF52 87
Shortlands Rd. Kings. on T. BL50 75
Short La. Oxt. CH69 115
Short La. St. Alb. BE18 18
Short La. Stai. AY47 73
Short La. Dr. Wal. Cr. CD19 21
Short Path SE18 CL43 68
Herbert Rd.
Short Path SE18 CL43 68
Dale Rd.
Short Rd. E11 CG34 49
Short Rd. E15 CF37 57
Short Rd. W4 BO43 65
Short Rd. Houns. AY46 73
Shorts Croft NW9 BM31 46
Shorts Gdns. WC2 BX39 2
Shorts Gdns. WC2 BX39 56
Shorts Rd. Cars. BU56 95
Short St. NW4 BQ31 46
Short St. SE1 BY41 4
Short St. SE1 BY41 66
Short Way N12 BU29 38
Short Way SE9 CK45 68
Short Way, Amer. AO22 25
Short Way, Twick. BG47 74
Shortwood Av. Stai. AW48 73
Shotfield, Wall. BV57 95
Shothamger Way, Hem. H. AU16 16
Shottendane Rd. SW6 BS44 66
Shottfield Av. SW14 BO45 65
Shoulder Of Mutton All.
E14 CD40 57
Narrow St.
Shouldham St. W1 BU39 1
Shouldham St. W1 BU39 56
Showers Way, Hayes BC40 53
Shrapnel Clo. SE18 CK43 68
Stadium Rd.
Shrapnel Rd. SE9 CK45 68
Shrewsbury Av. SW14 BN45 65
Shrewsbury Av. Har. BL31 46
Shrewsbury Clo. Surb. BK55 84
Shrewsbury Cres. NW10 BN37 55
Shrewsbury Ho. SW3 BU43 66
Shrewsbury Ho. Surb. BL55 85
Shrewsbury La. SE18 CL44 68
Shrewsbury Ms. W2 BS39 56
Chepstow Rd.
Shrewsbury Rd. E7 CJ35 49
Shrewsbury Rd. N11 BW29 38
Shrewsbury Rd. NW10 BO37 55
Shrewsbury Rd. W2 BS39 56
Shrewsbury Rd. Beck. CD52 87
Shrewsbury Rd. Cars. BU53 86
Shrewsbury Rd. Red. BU70 121
Shrewsbury Wk. Islw. BJ45 64
South St.
Shrewton Rd. SW17 BU50 76
Shroffold Rd. Brom. CG49 78
Shropshire Clo. Mitch. BX52 86
Shropshire Rd. N22 BX29 38
Shroton St. NW1 BU39 1
Shroton St. NW1 BU39 56
Shrubberies, The Chig. CM28 40
Shrubberies, The E18 CH30 40
Shrubbery Gdns. N21 BY26 38
Shrubbery Rd. N9 CB27 39
Shrubbery Rd. SW16 BX49 76
Shrubbery Rd. Grav. DH47 81
Shrubbery Rd. S. Dnth. CY51 90
Shrubbery Rd. Sthl. BF40 54
Shrubbery, The Upmin. CY34 51
Shrubbs Hill, Wok. AO58 91
Shrubhill Rd. Hem. H. AV14 7
Shrubland Est. E8 CA36 57
Shrubland Gro. Wor. Pk. BQ55 85
Shrubland Rd. E8 CA37 2
Shrubland Rd. E8 CA37 57
Shrubland Rd. E10 CE33 48
Shrubland Rd. E17 CE32 48
Shrubland Rd. Bans. BR61 103
Shrublands, Hat. BS16 20
Shrublands Av. Berk. AQ13 7
Shrublands Av. Croy. CE55 87
Shrublands Clo. N20 BT26 38
Shrublands Clo. Chig. CM29 40
Shrublands Rd. Berk. AQ12 7
Shrublands, The Pot. B. BR20 19
Shrubs Rd. Rick. AY28 35
Shuna Wk. N1 BZ36 57
Marquess Est.
Shurland Gdns. SE15 CA43 67
Rosemary Rd.
Shurlock Av. Swan. CS51 89
Shurlock Dr. Orp. CM56 97
Broadwater Gdns.
Shuter Sq. W14 BR42 65
Sun Rd.
Shuttle Clo. Sid. CN47 78
Shuttle Mead. Bex. CQ47 79
Shuttle Rd. Dart. CU45 69
Shuttle St. E1 CB38 2
Shuttle St. E1 CA38 57
Buxton St.
Shuttleworth Rd. SW11 BT44 66
Sibella Rd. SW4 BW44 66
Sibley Clo. Bexh. CQ46 79
Mount Rd.
Sibley Gro. E12 CK36 58
Sibthorpe Rd. SE12 CH47 78
Sibthorpe Rd. Hat. BQ15 10
Sibthorp Rd. Mitch. BU51 86
Sibton Rd. Cars. BU54 86
Sicilian Av. WC1 BX39 2
Sicilian Av. WC1 BX39 56
Bloomsbury Way
Sickert Ct. N1 BZ36 57
Sickle Cnr. Dag. CR38 59
Sicklefield Clo. Wal. Cr. CA16 21
Sidbury Av. SW6 BR45 65
Sidbury St. SW6 BR44 65
Sidcup By-pass, Sid. CM48 78
Sidcup Hill Gdns. Sid. CP49 79
Sidcup High St. Sid. CO49 79
Sidcup Hill, Sid. CO49 79
Sidcup Hill Gdns. Sid. CP49 79
Sidcup Rd. SE9 CJ47 78
Sidcup Rd. SE12 CJ47 78
Siddons La. NW1 BU38 1
Siddons La. NW1 BU38 56
Siddons Rd. N17 CB30 39
Siddons La. NW1 BU38 56
Siddons Rd. N17 CB30 39
Siddons Rd. SE23 CC48 77
Siddons Rd. Croy. BY55 86
Side Rd. E17 CD32 48
South Gro.
Side Rd. Uxb. AU33 43
Sidewood Rd. SE9 CM47 78
Sidford Pl. SE1 BX41 4
Sidford Pl. SE1 BX41 66
Sidmouth Av. Islw. BH44 64
Sidmouth Clo. Wat. BC27 35
Sidmouth Dr. Ruis. BC34 44
Sidmouth Rd. E10 CF34 48
Sidmouth Rd. NW2 BQ36 55
Sidmouth Rd. SE15 CA44 67
Sumner Est.
Sidmouth Rd. Orp. CO53 89
Sidmouth Rd. Well. CP43 69
Sidmouth St. WC1 BX38 2
Sidmouth St. WC1 BX38 56
Sidney Av. N13 BX28 38
Sidney Gdns. Brent. BK43 64
Boston Manor Rd.
Sidney Gdns. Sev. CV62 108
Sidney Gro. N1 BY38 56
Wakley St.
Sidney Rd. E7 CH34 49
Sidney Rd. N22 BX29 38
Sidney Rd. SE25 CB53 87
Sidney Rd. SW9 BX44 66
Sidney Rd. Beck. CD51 87
Sidney Rd. Epp. CM21 31
Sidney Rd. Har. BG31 45
Sidney Rd. Sutt. BS56 95
Sidney Rd. Twick. BJ46 74
Sidney Rd. Wal. Cr. CE20 21
Sidney Rd. Walt. BC54 83
Sidney St. Est. E1 CC39 57
Sidney Sq. E1 CC39 57
Sidney St. E1 CB39 57
Sidney St. Stai. AW49 73
Sidworth St. E8 CB36 57
Siebert Rd. SE3 CH43 68
Siemens Rd. SE18 CJ41 68
Sigdon Rd. E8 CB35 48
Sigers, The Pnr. BC32 44
Sigismund St. SE10 CG41 68
Silas St. Est. NW5 BV36 56
Silbury St. N1 BZ38 2
Silbury St. N1 BZ38 57
East Rd.
Silcester Ct. Th. Hth. BY52 86
Silchester Ms. W10 BQ40 55
Walmer Rd.
Silchester Rd. W10 BQ39 55
Silcote Rd. SE5 CA42 4
Silcote Rd. SE5 CA42 67
Albany Rd.
Silecroft Rd. Bexh. CR44 69
Silesia Bldgs. E8 CB36 57
London La.
Silex St. SE1 BY41 4
Silex St. SE1 BY41 66
Silkfield Rd. NW9 BO32 46
Silkham Rd. Oxt. CF67 114
Silkins, The Rom. CT30 41
Silk Mill Rd. Wat. BS26 35
Silk Mills Path SE13 CF44 67
Silkmore La. Leath. HZ66 110
Silkstream Rd. Edg. BN30 37
Silk St. EC2 BZ39 2
Silk St. EC2 BZ39 57
Silsden Cres. Ch. St. G. AR27 34
Silsoe Rd. N22 BX30 38
Silver Birch Av. E4 CD29 39
Silver Birch Av. Epp. CQ17 23
Silver Birch Clo. Dart. CT49 79
Silver Birch Clo. Uxb. AY35 44
Silver Birch Clo. Wey. AV59 91
Silver Birches, Brwd. DD26 122
Silverbirch Wk. NW3 BU36 56
Maitland Pk. Vw.
Silvercliffe Gdns. Barn. BU24 29
Silver Clo. Har. BG29 36
Silver Clo. Sutt. BR56 94
Silver Cres. W4 BM42 65
Silverdale SE26 CC49 77
Silverdale, Enf. BX24 29
Silverdale, Stai. AW49 73
Leacroft
Silverdale Av. Lthd. BG60 93
Silverdale Av. Ilf. CN32 49
Silverdale Av. Walt. BB55 83
Silverdale Av. Watt. BB56 92
Silverdale Clo. W7 BH40 54
Cherington Rd.
Silverdale Clo. W13 BH40 54
Silverdale Clo. Har. BE35 45
Silverdale Ct. Stai. AW49 73
Silverdale Dr. Horn. CU35 50
Silverdale Dr. Sun. BC51 83
Silverdale Gdns. Hayes BC41 63
Silverdale Rd. E4 CF29 39
Silverdale Rd. Bexh. CR44 69
Silverdale Rd. Bush. BE25 27
Silverdale Rd. Hayes BB41 63
Silverdale Rd. Orp. CM52 88
Silverdale Rd. Orp. CO52 89
Silver Dell, Wat. BB21 26
Silverfield, Brox. CD14 12
Silverhall St. Islw. BJ45 64
Silver Hill, Ch. St. G. AQ27 34
Silverholme, Har. BK33 45
Silver Jubilee Way, Houns. BC44 63
Silverland St. E16 CK40 58
Silver La. Pur. BW59 95
Silver La. W. Wick. CF55 87
Silverleigh Rd. Th. Hth. BX52 86
Silverlocke Rd. Grays. DE43 71
Silvermere Av. Rom. CR28 41
Silvermere Rd. SE6 CE47 77
Silver Pl. W1 BW40 3
Silver Pl. W1 BW40 56
Lexington St.
Silver Rd. Grav. DJ48 81
Silversmiths Way, Wok. AR62 100
Silver Spring Clo. Erith. CR43 69
Silversted La. West. CM64 106
Silverstone Clo. Red. BU69 121
Goodwood Rd.
Silverstone Way, Stan. BK29 36
Silver St. EC2 BZ39 57
Wood St.
Silver St. N18 BZ28 39
Silver St. Enf. BZ24 30
Silver St. Rom. CO24 32
Silver St. Wal. Abb. CF20 21
Silver St. Wal. Cr. BZ18 21
Silverthorn Dr. Hem. H. AZ15 8
Silverthorne Gdns. E4 CE27 39
Silverthorne Rd. SW8 BV44 66
Silverton Rd. W6 BQ43 65
Silvertown By-pass E16 CJ40 58
Silvertown Way E16 CG39 58
Silvertree Clo. Walt. BC55 83
Silver Wk. SE16 CD40 57
Silver Way, Rom. CR31 50
Silverwood Clo. Beck. CE50 77
Brackley Rd.
Silverwood Clo. Nthwd. BA29 35
Silvester Rd. SE22 CA46 77
Silvester St. SE1 BZ41 4
Silvesters, Harl. CK12 13
Silvester St. SE1 BZ41 67
Silwood Est. SE16 CC42 67
Silwood St. SE16 CC42 67
Simla Clo. SE14 CD43 67
Chubworthy St.
Simmil Rd. Esher BH56 93
Simmons Clo. N20 BU27 38
Simmons Clo. Slou. AT42 62
Common Rd.
Simmons La. E4 CF27 39
Simmons Pl. Grays. DD40 71
Simmons Rd. SE18 CL42 68
Brookhill Rd.
Simmons Wk. E15 CF35 48
Waddington Rd.
Simmons Way N20 BU27 38
Simm's Clo. Cars. BU55 86
Simms Rd. SE1 CB42 4
Simms Rd. SE1 CB42 67
Simnel Rd. SE12 CH47 78
Simon Clo. W11 BS40 56
Portobello Rd.
Simon Dean, Hem. H. AT17 16
Simonds Rd. E10 CE34 48
Simone Clo. Brom. CJ51 88
Simone Dr. Ken. BZ62 105
Simons Clo. Cher. AU57 91
Simons Wk. E15 CF35 48
Simons Wk. E15 CF36 57
Simons Wk. Egh. AR50 72
Simplemarsh Rd. Wey. AW56 92
Simpson Rd. Houns. BE46 74
Simpson Rd. Rain. CT36 59
Simpson Rd. Rich. BK49 74
Simpsons Rd. E14 CE40 57
Simpsons Rd. Brom. CH52 88
Simpson St. SW11 BU44 66
Simrose Ct. SW18 BS46 76
Sims Clo. Rom. CT31 50
Junction Rd.
Sims Wk. SE3 CG45 68
Lee Rd.
Sinclaire Clo. Enf. CA23 30
Sinclair Gdns. W14 BQ41 65
Sinclair Gro. NW4 BQ32 46
Sinclair Rd. E4 CD28 39
Sinclair Rd. W14 BQ41 65
Sinclair Clo. Enf. CA23 30
Carterhatch La.
Sincots Rd. Red. BU70 121
Lwr. Bridge Rd.
Sindall Rd. Grnf. BJ37 54
Sinderby Clo. Borwd. BL23 28
Sinderby Clo. Borwd. BL23 28
Singapore Rd. W13 BJ40 54
Singer St. EC2 BZ38 2
Singer St. EC2 BZ38 57
Cowper St.
Singles Cross La. Sev. CP60 98
Single St. Orp. CL60 97
Singleton Clo. Croy. BZ54 87
St. Saviour's Rd.
Singleton Clo. Horn. CT35 50
Cowdray Way
Singleton Clo. Horn. CU35 50
Cowdray Way
Singleton Clo. Mitch. BU50 76
Singleton Rd. Dag. CQ35 50
Singleton Scarp N12 BS28 38
Singlewell Rd. Grav. DG48 81
Singret Pl. Uxb. AX38 53
Sinnott Rd. E17 CC30 39
Sion Rd. Twick. BJ47 74
Sipsom La. West Dr. AZ43 63
Sipson Clo. West Dr. AY41 63
Sipson Rd. West Dr. AZ43 63
Sipson Way, West Dr. AZ44 63
Sir Alexander Clo. W3 BO40 55
Sir Alexander Rd.
Sir Alexander Rd. W3 BO40 55
Sirdar Rd. N22 BY31 47
Sirdar Rd. W11 BQ40 55
Sirdar Rd. Mitch. BU50 76
Sirdar Strand, Grav. DJ49 81
Sir Thom More Est. SW3 BT43 66
Sirus Rd. Nthwd. BC28 35
Sisley Rd. Bark. CN37 58
Sispare Gdns. SW18 BR46 75
Sissinghurst Rd. Croy. CB54 87
Sisters Av. SW11 BU45 66
Sistova Rd. SW12 BV47 76
Sittingburne Av. Enf. BZ25 30
Sitwell Gro. Stan. BH28 36
Siverst Clo. Nthlt. BF36 54
Siviter Way, Dag. CR36 59
Siward Rd. N17 BZ30 39
Siward Rd. SW17 BT48 76
Siward Rd. Brom. CH52 88
Six Acres, Hem. H. AZ15 8
Six Bells La. Sev. CV66 117
Sixth Av. W10 BR38 55
Sixth Av. E12 CK35 49
Sixth Av. Enf. CA25 30
Sixth Av. Hayes BB40 53
Sixth Av. Wat. BD21 27
Sixth Cross Rd. Twick. BG48 74
Skardu Rd. NW2 BR35 46
Skarnings Ct. Wal. Abb. CH20 22
Winters Way
Skeena Hill SW18 BR47 75
Skeet Hill La. Orp. CQ54 89
Skeffington Rd. E6 CK37 58
Skelbrook St. SW18 BS48 76
Skelgill Rd. SW15 BR45 65
Skelton Clo. E8 CA36 57
Rhodes Dev.
Skelton Rd. E7 CH36 58
Skeltons La. E10 CE33 48
Skelwith Rd. W6 BQ43 65
Sketty Rd. Enf. CA24 30
Skibbs La. Orp. CQ56 98
Skid Hill La. War. CG60 97
Skidmore Way, Rick. AY26 35
Skiers St. E15 CF37 57
Skiffington Clo. SW2 BY47 76
Skillet Hill, Wal Abb. CH21 31
Skimpans Clo. Hat. BQ15 10
Skin Market Pl. SE1 BZ40 4
Skin Market Pl. SE1 BZ40 57
Skinner Ct. E2 CB37 57
Parmiter St.
Skinner Pl. SW1 BV42 66
Bourne St.
Skinners La. EC4 BZ40 4
Skinners La. Ash. BK62 102
Skinners La. Garlick Hill EC4 BZ40 57
Queen Victoria St.
Skinner St. EC1 BY38 2
Skips Cor. Epp. CS16 23
Skipsey Av. E6 CK38 58
Skipton Dr. Hayes BA42 63

105

Station App. (Cray.) Dart.	CT46	79
Station Rd.		
Station App. E. Red.	BU71	121
Station App. Elm Pk. Horn.	CU35	50
Station App. N. Sid.	CO48	79
Station Rd.		
Station App. Nth. Sid.	CO48	79
Station Rd.		
Station App. Rd. W4	BM43	65
Grove Park Rd.		
Station App. Rd. Tad.	BQ64	103
Station App. Rd. Til.	DG45	71
Station App. Southgate N14	BW26	38
Station App. Sth. Sid.	CO48	79
Station Rd.		
Station App. W. Red.	BU71	121
Station Ave. Cat.	CB65	105
Station Av. Ewell W.	BO58	94
Station Av. N. Mal.	BO52	85
Station Av Rich.	BM44	65
Station Pde.		
Station Av. Watt.	BB56	92
Station Av. Wey.	AW59	92
Station Bldgs. Hayes	CG54	88
Station Clo. N3	BS30	38
Station Clo. Hat.	BR16	19
Station Clo. Hamptn.	BF51	84
Station Clo. Pot. B.	BR19	19
Station Clo. Pot. B.	BS19	20
Station Cres. N15	BZ31	48
Station Cres. SE3	CH42	68
Station Cres. Ashf.	AX49	73
Station Cres. Wem.	BJ36	54
Station Dr. NW1	BW38	56
Station Est. Elmers End	CC52	87
Station Est. Rd. Felt.	BC47	73
Station Fore Ct. NW1	**BW38**	**1**
Station Garage Mews SW16	BW50	76
Estreham Rd.		
Station Gdns. W4	BN43	65
Station Gate SE16	CC41	67
Station Gro. Wem.	BL36	55
Station Hill, Hayes	CH55	88
Station La. Brwd.	DE32	123
Station La. Edg.	BM29	37
Station La. Horn.	CV34	51
Station Pde. E11	CH32	49
High St.		
Station Pde. NW2	BQ36	55
Station Pde. W3	BM39	55
Station Pde. Chipstead	BU62	104
Station Parade, Vir. W.	AR52	82
Station Pk. Sev.	CU65	107
Station Pass E18	CH30	40
Maybank Rd.		
Station Path, Stai.	AV49	72
Station Pl.N4	BY34	47
Station Rise SE27	BY48	76
Norwood Rd.		
Station Rd. E4	CF26	39
Station Rd. E7	CH35	49
Station Rd. E10	CF34	48
Station Rd. E12	CJ35	49
Station Rd. E15	CF36	57
Station Rd. E17	CD32	48
Station Rd. N3	BS30	38
Station Rd. N11	BV28	38
Station Rd. N17	CB31	48
Station Rd. N18	CA28	39
Silver St.		
Station Rd. N19	BW34	47
Junction Rd.		
Station Rd. N22	BX30	38
Station Rd. NW4	BP32	46
Station Rd. NW7	BO28	37
Station Rd. NW10	BO37	55
Station Rd. SE20	CC50	77
Station Rd. SW13	BQ44	65
Station Rd. W5	BL39	55
Station Rd.	BJ71	119
Station Rd. Amer.	AO23	25
Station Rd. Ash.	BL61	103
Station Rd. Ashf.	AY49	73
Station Rd. Barkingside	CM31	49
Station Rd. Barn.	BS25	29
Station Rd. Belmont	BS58	95
Station Rd. Belv.	CR41	69
Station Rd. Berk.	AR12	7
Station Rd. Bet.	BO69	120
Station Rd. Bexh.	CQ45	69
Station Rd. Borwd.	BM24	28
Station Rd. Brom.	CH51	88
Station Rd. Brox.	CD13	12
Station Rd. Cars.	BU56	95
Station Rd. Cat.	CD64	105
Station Rd. Cher.	AV54	82
Station Rd. Chess.	BL56	94
Station Rd. Chig.	CL27	40
Station Rd. Chingford E4	CF26	39
Station Rd. Claygate	BH56	93
Station Rd. Cob.	BE62	102
Station Rd. Crayford	CT47	79
Station Rd. Dag.	CP33	50
Station Rd. Edg.	BM29	37
Station Rd. Egh.	AS49	72
Station Rd. Epp.	CO19	23
Station Rd. Epp.	CR17	23
Station Rd. Esher	BG55	84
Station Rd. Ger. Cr.	AS32	43
Station Rd. Grav.	DD46	81
Station Rd. Grav.	DD49	81
Station Rd. Green	DA46	80
Station Rd. Guil.	AS73	118
Station Rd. Hmptn.	BK51	84
Station Rd. Hanwell W7	BH40	54
Station Rd. Har.	BH31	45
Station Rd. Har.	CM9	6
Station Rd. Harl.	CP8	6
Station Rd. Harold Wd.	CW30	42
Station Rd. Hat.	BQ15	10
Station Rd. Hayes	BB41	63
Station Rd. Hayes	BB42	63
Station Rd. Hem. H.	AW14	8
Station Rd. Hmptn.	BF51	84
Station Rd. Houns.	BF45	64
Station Rd. Ilf.	CL34	49
Station Rd. Ken.	BZ60	96
Station Rd. Kings L.	AZ18	17
Station Rd. Kings. on T.	BM51	85
Station Rd. Knockholt	CQ58	98
Station Rd. Long.	DC52	90
Station Rd. Loug.	CK24	31
Station Rd. Lthd.	BJ64	102
Station Rd. Motspur Pk.	BP53	85
Station Rd. Norwood Junc. SE25	CA52	87
Station Rd. Orp.	CN55	88
Station Rd. Pnr.	BE31	45
Station Rd. Pot. B.	BX18	20
Station Rd. Rad.	BJ21	27
Station Rd. Red.	BU70	121
Station Rd. Red.	BW67	113
Station Rd. Rick.	AX26	35
Station Rd. St. Alb.	BF19	18
Station Rd. St. Alb.	BM13	10
Station Rd. St. Mary Cray	CP52	89
Station Rd. Saw	CQ5	6
Station Rd. Sev.	CQ59	98
Station Rd. Sev.	CT63	107
Station Rd. Sev.	CU59	98
Station Rd. Sev.	CU61	107
Station Rd. Shep.	BA53	83
Station Rd. Shortlands	CG51	88
Station Rd. Sid.	CO49	79
Station Rd. Slou.	AT41	62
Station Rd. Slou.	BO53	85
Station Rd. S. Dnth.	CX51	90
Station Rd. S. Ock.	DB38	60
Station Rd. Stai.	AS46	72
Station Rd. Sun.	BC50	73
Station Rd. Swan.	CT52	89
Station Rd. Tedd.	BH49	74
Station Rd. Thames Ditton	BH54	84
Station Rd. Til.	DJ43	71
Station Rd. Twick.	BH47	74
Station Rd. Upmin.	CY34	51
Station Rd. Upr. Warl.	CA62	105
Station Rd. Uxb.	AX38	53
Station Rd. Wal. Cr.	CE20	21
Station Rd. Wat.	BC23	26
Station Rd. West.	CO65	107
Station Rd. Welw. G. C.	BR5	5
Station Rd. W. Croy.	BZ54	87
Station Rd. W. Wick.	CF54	87
Station Rd. Wey.	AW59	92
Station Rd. Wey.	AX56	92
Station Rd. Winchmore Hill N21	BY26	38
Station Rd. Wok.	AP59	91
Station Rd. Wok.	AS62	100
Station Rd. E. Oxt.	CG67	115
Station Rd. Gidea Pk. Rom.	CU31	50
Station Rd. N. Belv.	CR41	69
Station Rd. N. Harl.	BF32	45
Station Rd. N. Red.	BW67	113
Station Rd. S. Red.	BW67	113
Station Rd. W. Oxt.	CG68	115
Station Row, Guil.	AS73	118
Station Sq. Pett's Wd.	CM53	88
Station Sq. St. Mary Cray	CO52	89
Station St. E15	CF36	57
Station St. E16	CL40	58
Station Ter. NW10	BQ37	55
Station Ter. SE5	BZ44	67
Station Rd.		
Station Vw. Grnf.	BG37	54
Station Vill. NW7	BQ29	37
Bittacy Hill		
Station Way, Cheam	BR57	94
Station Way, Claygate	BH57	93
Station Way, Roding Vall.	CJ28	40
Station Way, St. Alb.	BH13	9
Station Way, Welw. G. C.	BQ7	5
Station Yd. Twick.	BJ47	74
Staunton Rd. Kings. on T.	BL50	75
Staunton Rd. Slou.	AO39	52
Staunton St. SE8	CD43	67
Staveley Cl. N7	BX35	47
Penn Rd.		
Staveley Clo. E9	CC35	48
Churchill Wk.		
Staveley Gdns. W4	BN44	65
Staveley Rd. W4	BN43	65
Staveley Rd. Ashf.	BA50	73
Staveley Way, Wok.	AP62	100
Staverton Rd. NW2	BQ36	55
Staverton Rd. Horn.	CV32	51
Stavordale Rd. N5	BY35	47
Stavordale Rd. Cars.	BT54	86
Stayne End, Vir. W.	AQ52	82
Stayners Rd. E1	CC38	57
Stayton Rd. Sutt.	BS55	86
Steadman Clo. Bex.	CT48	79
Stead St. SE17	**BZ42**	**4**
Stead St. SE17	BZ42	67
Steam Farm La. Felt.	BB45	63
Stean St. E8	**CA37**	**2**
Stean St. E8	CA37	57
Stebbing Way, Bark.	CO37	59
Stebondale St. E14	CF42	67
Stedman Clo. Uxb.	AZ34	44
Steedman St. SE17	BY42	66
Steedman St. SE17	**BZ42**	**4**
Steeds Rd. N10	BU30	38
Steeds Way, Loug.	CK24	31
Steele Rd. E11	CG35	49
Steele Rd. N17	CA31	48
Steele Rd. NW10	BN37	55
Steele Rd. W4	BN41	65
Steele Rd. Islw.	BJ45	64
Steele's Ms. NW3	BU36	56
Steele's Rd. NW3	BU36	56
Steel's La. E1	CC39	57
Devonport St.		
Steel's La. Lthd.	BF60	93
Steen Way SE22	CA46	77
Dulwich Gro.		
Steep Clo. Orp.	CN57	97
Steep Hill, SW16	BW48	76
Steep Hill, Wok.	AO57	91
Steeple Clo. SW6	BR45	65
Steeple Clo. SW19	BR49	75
Steeplestone Clo. N18	BZ28	39
Steeple Wk. N1	BZ37	57
Rasire St.		
Steerforth St. SW18	BS48	76
Steerlands, Bush.	BF26	36
Steer's Mead. Mitch.	BU51	86
Stella Rd. SW17	BU50	76
Stelling Rd. Erith	CS43	69
Stembridge Rd. SE10	CB51	87
Stents La. Cob.	BE63	102
Stepgates Mead. La. Cher.	AW54	83
Stephen Av. Rain.	CU36	59
Stephen Clo. Egh.	AU50	72
Stephendale Rd. SW6	BS45	66
Stephen Rd. Bexh.	CS45	69
Stephens Clo. Pnr.	BD32	45
Stephens Gro. SE13	CF45	67
Stephen's Ms. W1	BW39	56
Gresse St.		
Stephenson Av. Til.	DG44	71
Stephenson Dr.	????	61
Clewer Ct. Rd.		
Stephenson Rd. W7	BH39	54
Stephenson St. E16	CG38	58
Stephenson St. NW10	BO38	55
Stephenson Way NW1	**BW38**	**1**
Stephenson Way NW1	BW38	56
Stephens Rd. E15	CG37	58
Stephen St. W1	**BW39**	**1**
Stephen St. W1	BW39	56
Stepney Causeway E1	CC39	57
Stepney Green E1	CC39	57
Stepney Grn. Dws. E1	CC39	57
Hayfield Pass		
Stepney High St. E1	CC39	57
Stepney Way E1	CB39	57
Sterling Av. Edg.	BL28	37
Sterling Av. Wal. Cr.	CC20	21
Sterling Rd. Enf.	BZ22	30
Sterling Rd. Enf.	BZ23	30
Sterling St. SW7	**BU41**	**3**
Sterling St. SW7	BU41	66
Montpelier Pl.		
Sterndale Rd. W14	BQ41	65
Sterndale Rd. Dart.	CW47	80
Sterne St. W12	BQ41	65
Sternhall La. SE15	CB44	67
Sternhold Av. SW2	BW48	76
Sterry Cres. Dag.	CR35	50
Sterry Dr. E. Mol.	BH53	84
Sterry Dr. Epsom	BO56	94
Sterry Gdns. Dag.	CR36	59
Sterry Rd. Bark.	CN37	58
Sterry Rd. Dag.	CR35	50
Sterry St. SE1	**BZ41**	**4**
Sterry St. SE1	BZ41	67
Stevedale Rd. Well.	CP44	69
Stevenage Cres. Borwd.	BL23	28
Stevenage Rise, Hem. H.	AY11	8
Stevenage Rd. E12	CL36	58
Stevenage Rd. SW6	BQ43	65
Stevens Av. E9	CC36	57
Stevens Clo. Beck.	CE50	77
Stumps Hill La.		
Stevens Clo. Bex.	CS49	79
Stevens Clo. Epsom	BO60	94
High St.		
Stevens Cott. NW2	BP36	55
High Rd.		
Stevens Grn. Bush.	BG26	36
Stevenson Clo. Erith.	CU43	69
Stevenson Rd. Slou.	AO34	43
Stevens Rd. Dag.	CO34	50
Steven's La. Esher	BJ57	93
Stevens Way, Chig.	CN28	40
Steventon Rd. W12	BO40	55
Steward Clo. Wal. Cr.	CD18	21
Stewards Clo. Epp.	CO20	23
Steward's Green Rd. Epp.	CO19	23
Steward's Green Rd. Epp.	CO20	23
Steward St. E1	**CA39**	**2**
Steward St. E1	CA39	57
Steward Wk. Rom.	CT32	50
Stewart Av. Shep.	AZ52	83
Stewart Av. Slou.	AP39	52
Stewart Clo. NW9	BN32	46
Stewart Clo. Maid.	AH44	61
Stewart Clo. Wat.	BB19	17
Stewart Rd. E15	CF35	48
Stewarts Av. Upmin.	CX34	51
Stewartsby Clo. N18	BZ28	39
Stewart's Gro. SW3	**BT42**	**3**
Stewart's La. SW8	BV43	66
Stewarts Rd. SW8	BW44	66
Stewart St. E14	CF41	67
Stewart's Wk. SW3	BU42	66
Stewart Way, Stai.	AW50	73
Stew La. EC4	**BZ40**	**4**
High Timber St.		
Stew La. EC4	BZ40	57
Broken Wharf		
Steyne Rd. W3	BM40	55
Steyning Clo. Ken.	BY61	104
Steyning Gro. SE9	CK49	78
Steynings Way N12	BS28	38
Steyning Way, Houns.	BD45	64
Steynton Av. Bex.	CP48	79
Sth. Audley St. W1	**BV40**	**3**
Sth. Birbeck Rd. E11	CF34	48
Sth. Black Lion La. W6	BP42	65
Sth. Common Rd. Uxb.	AY36	53
Sth. Countess Rd. E17	CD31	48
Sth. Croxted Rd. SE21	BZ48	77
Sth. Eaton Pl. SW1	**BV42**	**3**
Sth. Eldon Pl. EC2	BZ39	57
Sth. Esk Rd. E7	CJ36	58
Sth. Hill Rd. Grav.	DH47	81
Sth. Kent Av. Grav.	DE46	81
Sth. Lodge W5	BK40	54
Webster Gdns.		
Sth. Molton La. W1	**BV39**	**1**
Sth. Molton Rd. E16	CH39	58
Sth. Molton St. W1	**BV39**	**1**
Sth. Norwood Hl. SE25	CA51	87
Sth. Tenter St. E1	**CA40**	**4**
Sth. Tenter St. E1	CA40	57
Sth. Vw. Ct. Wok.	AS62	100
Constitution Hill		
Sth. View Rd. Ash.	BK63	102
Sth. Western Rd. Twick.	BJ46	74
Sth. Wharf Rd. W2	**BT39**	**1**
Stickland Rd. Belv.	CR42	69
Stickleton Clo. Grnf.	BF38	54
Stifford Clays Rd. Grays	DC40	71
Stifford Est. E1	CC39	57
Stifford Hill, S. Ock.	DB40	60
Stifford Ho. E1	CC39	57
Stifford Rd. S. Ock.	CZ40	60
Stilecroft, Harl.	CO12	14
Stilecroft Gdns. Wem.	BJ34	45
Stile Hall Gdns. W4	BM42	65
Stile Path, Sun.	BC52	83
Stiles Clo. Brom.	CK53	88
Stillingfleet Rd. SW13	BP43	65
Stillington St. SW1	**BW42**	**3**
Stillington St. SW1	BW42	66
Stillness Rd. SE23	CD46	77
Stilton Cres. NW10	BN36	55
Stirling Clo. Bans.	BR62	103
Stirling Clo. Rain.	CU38	59
Stirling Clo. Uxb.	AX38	53
Stirling Clo. Wind.	AL44	61
Stirling Dr. Orp.	CO56	98
Stirling Rd. E13	CH37	58
Stirling Rd. E17	CD31	48
Stirling Rd. N17	CB30	39
Stirling Rd. N22	BY30	38
Stirling Rd. SW9	BX44	66
Stirling Rd. W3	BM41	65
Stirling Rd. Har.	BH31	45
Stirling Rd. Hayes	BC40	53
Stirling Rd. Houns.	AY46	73
Southampton Rd.		
Stirling Rd. Twick.	BF47	74
Stirling Rd. Pth. E17	CD31	48
Stirling St. SW7	BU41	66
Stirling Wk. Surb.	BM53	85
Stirling Way N18	BZ28	39
Stirling Way, Borwd.	BN25	28
Stites Hill Rd. Cat.	BY64	104
Stiven Cres. Har.	BE34	45
Stk. Station App. Red.	BX71	121
Stoats Nest Rd. Couls.	BX60	95
Stoats Nest Village, Couls.	BX61	104
Stockbreach Cl. Hat.	BP12	10
Stockbreach Rd. Hat.	BP12	10
Stockbury Rd. Croy.	CC53	87
Stockdale Rd. Dag.	CQ34	50
Stockdales Rd. Wind.	AM42	61
Stockdove Way, Grnf.	BH38	54
Stockers Farm Rd. Rick.	AX27	35
Stockers La. Wok.	AT63	100
Stockfield, Brwd.	CZ22	33
Stockfield Av. Hodd.	CE11	12
Stockfield Rd. SW16	BX48	76
Stockfield Rd. Esher	BH56	93
Stock Hill, West.	CJ61	106
Stockhurst Cl. SW15	BQ45	65
Ashlone Rd.		
Stocking La. Hert.	BW11	11
Stocking La. Hert.	BY12	11
Stockingswater La. Enf.	CD23	30
Stockland Rd. Rom.	CS32	50
Stock La. Dart.	CV49	80
Stockleigh Hall, NW8	**BU37**	**1**
Stockley Clo. West Dr.	AZ41	63
Stockley Rd. West Dr.	AZ40	53
Stockley Rd. West Dr.	AZ42	63
Stock Orchard Cres. N7	BX35	47
Stock Orchard St. N7	BX35	47
Stockport Rd. SW16	BW51	86
Stocksfield Rd. E17	CF31	48
Stocks La. Brwd.	CZ22	33
Stock St. E13	CH37	58
Stock St. WC2	**BX39**	**2**
Stockton Gdns. N17	BZ29	39
Stockton Gdns. NW7	BN27	37
Stockton Rd. N17	BZ29	39
Stockton Rd. N18	CB29	39
Stockton Rd. Reig.	BS72	121
Stockwell Av. SW9	BX45	66
Stockwell Clo. Wal. Cr.	CB17	21
Stockwell Gdns. SW9	BX44	66
Stockwell Grn. SW9	BX44	66
Stockwell La. SW9	BX44	66
Stockwell La. Wal. Cr.	CB17	21
Stockwell Pk. SW9	BX45	66
Stockwell Park Cres. SW9	BX44	66
Stockwell Pk. Est. SW9	BX44	66
Stockwell Pk. Rd. SW9	BX44	66
Stockwell Rd. SW9	BX44	66
Stockwell St. SE10	CF43	67
Stockwood St. SW11	BT45	66
Plough Rd.		
Stocton Clo. Guil.	AR70	118
Stocton Rd. Guil.	AR70	118
Stodart Rd. SE20	CC51	87
Sto Elmo Cres. Slou.	AO38	52
Stofield Gdns. SE9	CJ48	78
Stoford Clo. SW19	BR47	75
Southmead Rd.		
Sto Johns Rd. Dart.	CY47	80
Stoke Av. Ilf.	CO29	41
Stoke Clo. Cob.	BE61	102
Stoke Common Rd. Slou.	AQ35	43
Stoke Ct. Dr. Slou.	AP37	52
Stokefields, Guil.	AR71	118
Stoke Gdns. Slou.	AP40	52
Stoke Grn. Slou.	AQ38	52
Stokenchurch St. SW6	BS44	66
Stoke Newington Church St. N16	BZ34	48
Stoke Newington Common N16	CA34	48
Stoke Newington High St. N16	CA34	48
Stoke Newington Rd. N16	CA35	48
Stoke Pl. NW10	BO38	55
Stoke Poges La. Slou.	AP40	52
Stoke Rd. Cob.	BD61	102
Stoke Rd. Guil.	AR70	118
Stoke Rd. Kings. on T.	BN50	75
Stoke Rd. Rain.	CV37	60
Stoke Rd. Slou.	AP40	52
Stoke Rd. Walt.	BD55	84
Stokesby Rd. Chess.	BL57	94
Stokesheath Rd. Lthd.	BG59	93
Stokesley St. W12	BO39	55
Stokes Rd. E6	CK38	58
Stokes Rd. Croy.	CC53	87
Stoke St. Cob.	BD61	102
Stoke Wood La. Slou.	AP35	43
Stompits Rd. Maid.	AG43	61
Stompond La. Walt.	BC55	83
Stonard Rd. N13	BY27	38
Stonard Rd. Dag.	CO35	50
Stonards Hill, Epp.	CO18	23
Stonards Hill, Loug.	CK25	31
Sondon Pk. SE23	CD47	77
Stondon Rd. Ong.	CX18	24
Stondon Wk. E6	CJ37	58
Abbot's Rd.		
Stonebridge Est. E8	**CA37**	**2**
Stonebridge Est. E8	CA37	57
Stonebridge Pk. NW10	BN36	55
Stonebridge Rd. N15	CA32	48
Stonebridge Rd. Grav.	DD46	81
Stonebridge Way, Wem.	BM36	55
Stone Bldgs. WC2	**BX39**	**2**
Stone Bldgs. WC2	BX39	56
Stone Clo. Dag.	CQ34	50
Stone Clo. West Dr.	AY40	53
Stonecot Clo. Sutt.	BR54	85
Stonecot Hill, Sutt.	BR54	85
Stonecroft Av. Iver.	AV39	52
Stonecroft Rd. Erith	CS43	69
Stonecroft Way, Croy.	BX54	86
Stone Cross, Harl.	CM10	6
Stonecross, St. Alb.	BH13	9
Stonecross Rd. Hat.	BP11	10
Stone Cross Rd. Swan.	CS53	89
Stonecutter St. EC4	**BY39**	**2**
Stonecutter St. EC4	BY39	56
Shoe La.		
Stonefield Clo. Bexh.	CR45	69
Stonefield Clo. Ruis.	BE35	45
Stonefield St. N1	**BY37**	**2**
Stonefield Way SE7	CJ43	68
Green Bay Rd.		
Stonefield Way, Ruis.	BE35	45
Stonegate Clo. Orp.	CP52	89
Main Rd.		
Stonegrove, Edg.	BL28	37
Stone Gro. Ct. Edg.	BL28	37
Stone Gro. Gdns. Edg.	BL28	37
Stonehall Av. Ilf.	CK32	49
Stone Hall Rd. N21	BX26	38
Stoneham Rd. E5	CB34	48
Stoneham's Hill, Dart.	CT45	69
Stonehill Clo. SW14	BN46	75
Stonehill Cres. Wok.	AS57	91
Stonehill Grn. Rd. Dart.	CS50	79
Stonehill Rd. SW14	BN46	75
Stonehill Rd. W4	BM42	65
Wellesley Rd.		
Stonehill Rd. Wok.	AR58	91
Stonehills, Welw. G. C.	BQ7	5
Stonehills Ct. SE21	CA48	77
Stone Ho. Ct. EC3	CA39	57
Hounsditch		
Stonehouse Gdns. Cat.	CA66	114
Stonehouse La. Grays	CZ43	70
Stonehouse La. Sev.	CP58	98
Stonehouse Rd. N11	BW28	38
Stonehouse Rd. Sev.	CP58	98
Stonehurst Rd. Enf.	CC25	30
High Street		
Stoneings La. Sev.	CN62	106
Stonelea Rd. Hem. H.	AY14	8
Stoneleigh Av. Enf.	CB22	30
Stoneleigh Av. Wor. Pk.	BP55	85
Stoneleigh Clo. Wal. Cr.	CC20	21
Stoneleigh Ct. Ilf.	CK31	49
Stoneleigh Cres. Epsom	BO56	94
Stoneleigh Dr. Hodd.	CE10	12
Stoneleigh Pk. Av. Croy.	CC53	87
Stoneleigh Pk. Rd. Epsom	BO57	94
Stoneleigh Pl. W11	BQ40	55
Stoneleigh Rd. N17	CA31	48
Stoneleigh Rd. Cars.	BU54	86
Stoneleigh Rd. Ilf.	CK31	49
Stoneleigh Rd. Oxt.	CK68	115
Stoneleigh, Saw.	CQ5	6
Stoneleigh St. W11	BQ40	55
Stoneleigh Ter. N19	BV34	47
Chester Rd.		
Stonell's Rd. SW11	BU46	76
Chatham Rd.		
Stonemead. Welw. G. C.	BQ5	5
Stone Ness Rd. Grays	DA43	70
Stonenest St. N4	BX33	47
Evershot Rd.		
Stone Pk. Av. Beck.	CE52	87
Stone Pl. Wor. Pk.	BP55	85
Stone Place Rd. Green.	CZ46	80
Stone Rd. Brom.	CG53	88
Stones Alley, Wat.	BC24	26
Stones End St. SE1	**BZ41**	**4**
Stones End St. SE1	BZ41	67
Stones La. Dor.	BG72	119
Stone's Rd. Epsom	BO59	94
Stone St. Croy.	BY56	95
Stone St. Grav.	DG47	81
Stone St. Sev.	CY65	108
Stone St. Sev.	CZ66	117
Stoneswood Rd. Oxt.	CH68	115
Stonewood, Dart.	DB48	80
Stonewood Rd. Erith	CT42	69
Stone Yard La. E14	CF40	57

Stoney Brook, Guil. AP70 118
Stoney Ct. Welw. G. C. BS7 5
Stoneycroft, Hem. H. AW13 8
Long Chaulden
Stoneycroft Clo. SE12 CG47 78
Stoneycroft Rd. Wdf. Grn. CK29 40
Stoneydown Av. E17 CD31 48
Stoneyfield Rd. Couls. BX62 104
Stoneyfields Gdns. Edg. BN28 37
Stoneyfields La. Edg. BN28 37
Stoneylands Ct. Egh. AS49 72
Stoneylands Rd. Egh. AS49 72
Stoney La. E1 CA39 57
Stoney La. EC3 CA39 2
Stoney La. SE19 CA50 77
Stoney La. Hem. H. AT17 16
Stoney La. Kings L. AV19 16
Stoney Meade, Slou. AN40 61
Stoney St. SE1 BZ40 4
Stoney St. SE1 BZ40 57
Stonhouse St. SW4 BW45 66
Stonny Coft, Ash. BL62 103
Stonor Rd. W14 BR42 65
Stony Hill, Esher BE57 93
Stony La. Amer. AS22 25
Stony La. Ong. CU15 14
Stony La. Ong. CV16 24
Stony Path, Loug. CK23 31
Stonyshotts, Wal. Abb. CG20 22
Stopford Rd. E13 CH37 58
Stopford Rd. SE17 BY42 4
Store Gdns. Brwd. DE25 122
Store Rd. E16 CL41 68
Store St. E15 CF35 48
Store St. WC1 BW39 1
Store St. WC1 BW39 56
Storey Rd. E17 CD32 48
Storey Rd. N6 BU32 47
Storeys Gate SW1 BW41 3
Storey's Gate SW1 BW41 66
Storey St. E16 CL40 58
Storey St. Hem. H. AX15 8
Stories Ms. SE5 CA44 67
Stories Rd. SE5 CA45 67
Stork Rd. E7 CG36 58
Storksmead Rd. Edg. BO29 37
Storks Rd. SE16 CB41 67
Stormont Rd. N6 BU33 47
Stormong Rd. SW11 BV45 66
Stormont Way, Chess. BK56 93
Stormount Dr. Hayes BA41 63
Stornaway Strand, Grav. DJ49 81
Stornoway, Hem. H. AZ14 8
Northend
Storrington Rd. Croy. CA54 87
Stortford Rd. Hodd. CE11 12
Story St. N1 BX36 2
Stothard St. E1 CC38 57
Colebert Av.
Stoughton Av. Sutt. BQ56 94
Stoughton Cl. SW15 BP47 75
Bessborough Rd.
Stoughton Rd. Guil. AQ69 118
Stour Av. Sthl. BF41 64
Stourcliffe St. W1 BU39 1
Stourcliffe St. W1 BU39 56
Stour Clo. Kes. CJ56 97
Stour Clo. Slou. AN41 61
Stourhead Clo. SW19 BQ47 75
Castlecombe Dr.
Stourhead Gdns. SW20 BP51 85
Stour Rd. E3 CE36 57
Stour Rd. Dag. CR34 50
Stour Rd. Dart. CU45 69
Stour Rd. Grays DG42 71
Stourton Av. Felt. BE49 74
Stour Way, Upmin. CZ32 51
Stovell Rd. Wind. AN43 61
Stowage, The SE8 CE43 67
Stow Cres. E17 CD29 39
Stowe Cres. Ruis. BA32 44
Stowe Gdns. N9 CA26 39
Stowell Av. Croy. CF58 96
Stowe Pl. N15 CA31 48
Stowe Rd. W12 BP41 65
Stowe Rd. Orp. CO56 98
Stow, The Harl. CN10 6
Stowting Rd. Orp. CN56 97
Stox Mead. Har. BG30 36
Stracey Rd. E7 CH35 49
Stracey Rd. NW10 BN37 55
Strachen Pl. SW19 BQ50 75
Stradbroke Dr. Chig. CL29 40
Stradbroke Gro. Ilf. CK31 49
Stradbroke Rd. N5 BZ35 48
Balfour Rd.
Stradbrooke Gro.
Buck. H. CJ26 40
Stradella Rd. SE24 BZ46 77
Strafford Av. Ilf. CL30 40
Strafford Clo. Pot. B. BS19 20
Strafford Gate, Pot. B. BS19 20
Strafford Rd. W3 BN41 65
Bollo Bridge Rd.
Strafford Rd. Barn. BR24 28
Strafford Rd. Houns. BE45 64
Strafford Rd. Twick. BJ47 74
Strahan Rd. E3 CD38 57
Straight Rd. Rom. CU28 41
Straight Rd. Wind. AQ46 72
Straight, The Sthl. BE41 64
Straitsmouth SE10 CF43 67
Straits, The Wal. Abb. CE19 21
Strakers Rd. SE22 CB45 67
Strand, WC2 BX40 4
Strand, WC2 BY39 2
Strand, WC2 BX40 56
Strand Clo. Epsom BN63 103
Strandfield Clo. SE18 CN42 68
Strand La. WC2 BX40 4
Strand La. WC2 BX40 56
Temple Pl.
Strand On The Green
W4 BM43 65
Strand Pl. N18 CA28 39
Strangeways, Wat. BB21 26
Strangways Terr. W14 BR41 65
Melbury Rd.
Stranraer Rd. Houns. AY46 73
Southampton Rd.
Stranraer Way N1 BX36 56
Gifford St.
Stratfield Dr. Brox. CD13 12
Stratfield Rd. Borwd. BL24 28
Stratford Av. W8 BS41 66
Stratford Av. Uxb. AY37 53
Stratford Clo. Bark. CO36 59
Stratford Clo. Dag. CS36 59
Stratford Gro. SW15 BQ45 65
Stratford Pl. W1 BV39 1
Stratford Pl. W1 BV39 56
Stratford Rd. E13 CG37 58
Stratford Rd. NW4 BQ31 46
Stratford Rd. W3 BN41 65
Stratford Rd. W8 BS41 66
Stratford Rd. Hayes BC38 53
Stratford Rd. Sthl. BE42 64
Stratford Rd. Th. Hth. BY52 86
Stratford Rd. Wat. BC23 26
Stratford St. E14 CE41 67
Stratford Vill. NW1 BW36 56
Stratford Way, Hem. H. AW15 8
Stratford Way, Wat. BB23 26
Strathairn St. SE1 CB42 4
Strathan Clo. SW18 BR46 75
Strathaven Rd. SE12 CH46 78
Strathblaine Rd. SW11 BT45 66
Strathbrook Rd. SW16 BX50 76
Strathcona Av. Lthd. BE67 111
Strathcona Rd. Wem. BK34 45
Strathdale SW16 BX49 76
Strathdon Dr. SW17 BT48 76
Strathearn Av. Hayes BB43 63
Strathearn Av. Twick. BF47 74
Strathearn Pl. W2 BU40 56
Strathearn Rd. SW19 BS49 76
Strathearn Rd. Sutt. BS56 95
Stratheden Rd. SE3 CH44 68
Strathern Pl. W2 BT40 3
Strathfield Gdns. Bark. CM36 58
Strathleven Rd. SW2 BX45 66
Strathmore Clo. Cat. CA64 105
Strathmore Gdns. N3 BS30 38
Hervey Clo.
Strathmore Gdns. W8 BS40 56
Strathmore Gdns. Edg. BM30 37
Strathmore Gdns. Horn. CT33 50
Strathmore Rd. SW19 BS48 76
Strathmore Rd. Croy. BZ54 87
Strathnairn St. SE1 CB42 67
Strathray Gdns. NW3 BU36 56
Strath Ter. SW11 BU45 66
Strathville Rd. SW18 BS48 76
Strathyre Av. SW16 BX52 86
Stratmore Rd. Tedd. BH49 74
Stratton Av. Enf. BZ22 30
Stratton Av. Wall. BW58 95
Stratton Chase Dr. Ch.
St. G. AQ26 34
Stratton Clo. SW19 BS51 86
Stratton Clo. Bexh. CQ45 69
Stratton Clo. Edg. BL29 37
Stratton Clo. Houns. BF44 64
Stratton Ct. Guil. AQ69 118
Shepherds Hill
Strattondale St. E14 CF41 67
Stratton Dr. Bark. CN35 49
Stratton Gdns. Sthl. BE39 54
Stratton Rd. SW19 BS51 86
Stratton Rd. Bexh. CQ45 69
Stratton Rd. Rom. CX28 42
Stratton Rd. Sun. BB51 83
Stratton St. W1 BV40 3
Stratton St. W1 BV40 56
Stratton Wk. Rom. CX28 42
Strauss Rd. W4 BN41 65
Strawberry Field, Hat. BP14 10
Old Leys
Strawberry Hill Clo.
Twick. BH48 74
Strawberry Hill Rd.
Twick. BH48 74
Strawberry La. Cars. BU55 86
Strawberry Vale N2 BT30 38
Strawberry Vale, Twick. BJ48 74
Strawfields, Welw. G. C. BS7 5
Strawmead, Hat. BP11 10
Crop Common
Strayfield Rd. Enf. BY21 29
Stream Ct. SW16 BX48 76
Streamdale SE2 CO43 69
Stream La. Edg. BM28 37
Streamside Clo. CH52 88
Sandford Rd.
Streamway, Belv. CQ43 69
Streatfield Av. E6 CK37 58
Streatfield Rd. Har. BK31 45
Streatfield St. E14 CD39 57
Streatham Clo. SW16 BX48 76
Leigham Ct. Rd.
Streatham Common N.
SW16 BX49 76
Streatham Common S.
SW16 BX50 76
Streatham High Rd.
SW16 BX49 76
Streatham Hill SW2 BX48 76
Streatham Hl. Est. SW16 BX48 76
Streatham Pl. SW2 BX47 76
Streatham Rd. SW16 BU51 86
Streatham Rd. Mitch. BU51 86
Streatham St. WC1 BX39 2
Streatham St. WC1 BX39 56
Streatham Vale SW16 BW51 86
Streathbourne Rd. SW17 BV48 76
Streatley Pl. NW3 BT35 47
Streatley Rd. NW6 BR36 55
Street Cobham, Cob. BC60 83
Street, The Ash. BL62 103
Street, The Bet. BP70 120
Street, The Guil. AR73 118
Street, The Guil. AW69 110
Street, The Kings. L. AW19 17
Street, The Leath. AZ67 110
Street, The Lthd. BD67 111
Street, The Lthd. BG64 102
Street, The Ong. CY17 24
Street, The Sev. DB56 99
Street, The Sev. DB64 108
Streimer Rd. E15 CF37 57
Strelley Way W3 BO40 55
Stretton Rd. Croy. CA54 87
Stretton Rd. Rich. BK48 74
Stretton Way, Borwd. BL22 28
Strickland Av. Dart. CW45 70
Strickland Row SW18 BT47 76
Strickland St. SE8 CE44 67
Stride Rd. E13 CG37 58
Stringer Ave. Guil. AR67 109
Stringhams Copse, Wok. AV65 100
Linden Way
Strode Cl. N10 BV29 38
Strode Rd. E7 CH35 49
Strode Rd. N17 CA30 39
Strode Rd. NW10 BP36 55
Strode Rd. SW6 BR43 65
Strode's Cres. Stai. AX49 73
Strode St. Egh. AT49 72
Stroma Clo. Hem. H. BA14 8
Strone Rd. E7 CJ36 58
Strone Rd. E12 CJ36 58
Strongbow Cres. SE9 CK46 78
Strongbow Rd. SE9 CK46 78
Strongbridge Clo. Har. BF33 45
Stronsa Rd. W12 BO41 65
Stronsay Clo. Hem. H. AZ14 8
Strood Av. Rom. CS33 50
Stroud Clo. Wind. AL45 61
Stroud Cres. SW15 BP48 75
Stroude Rd. Egh. AT50 72
Stroude Rd. Egh. AT51 82
Stroude Rd. Vir. W. AS53 82
Stroudes Clo. Wor. Pk. BO54 85
Stroud Farm Rd. Maid. AG43 61
Stroud Field, Nthlt. BE36 54
Arnold Rd.
Stroud Gate, Har. BF35 45
Stroud Grn. Gdns. Croy. CC53 87
Stroud Green Gdns. Croy. CC54 87
Stroud Green Rd. N4 BX33 47
Stroud Grn. Way, Croy. CB54 87
Stroudley Wk. E1 CE38 57
Devons Rd.
Stroud Rd. SE25 CB53 87
Stroud Rd. SW19 BS48 76
Stroud Way, Ashf. AZ50 73
Strutton Av. Grav. DF48 81
Strutton Ground SW1 BW41 3
Strutton Ground SW1 BW41 66
Strype St. E1 CA39 2
Strype St. E1 CA39 57
Leyden St.
Stuart Av. NW4 BP33 46
Stuart Av. W5 BL40 55
Stuart Av. Brom. CH54 88
Stuart Av. Har. BE34 45
Stuart Av. Walt. BC54 83
Stuart Clo. Brwd. DA25 33
Stuart Clo. Swan. CU51 89
Victoria Hill Rd.
Stuart Clo. Uxb. AZ36 53
Stuart Clo. Wal. Cr. CB19 21
Stuart Clo. Wind. AM44 61
Stuart Cres. N22 BX30 38
Stuart Cres. Croy. CD55 87
Stuart Cres. Hayes BA39 53
Stuart Cres. Reig. BS72 121
Stuart Evans Clo. Well. CP45 69
Stuart Gdns. Tedd. BH49 74
Stuart Mantle Way, Erith CS43 69
Stuart Pl. Mitch. BU51 86
Stuart Rd. NW6 BS38 56
Stuart Rd. SE15 CC45 67
Stuart Rd. SW19 BS48 76
Stuart Rd. W3 BN40 55
Stuart Rd. Bark. CN36 58
Dawson Av.
Stuart Rd. Barn. BU26 38
Stuart Rd. Grav. DG46 81
Stuart Rd. Grays DD42 71
Stuart Rd. Har. BH31 45
Stuart Rd. Reig. BS72 121
Stuart Rd. Rich. BJ48 74
Stuart Rd. Th. Hth. BZ52 87
Stuart Rd. Warl. CB63 105
Stuart Rd. Well. CO44 69
Stuart Rd. Welw. BP5 5
Stuart Way, Vir. W. AQ52 82
Stuart Way, Wind. AM44 61
Stubbers La. Upmin. CZ36 60
Stubbings Hall La.
Wal. Abb. CF17 21
Stubbs Clo. Dor. BK72 119
Stubbs End Clo. Amer. AP21 25
Stubbs Hill, Dor. BK72 119
Stubbs Hill, Orp. CP60 98
Stubbs La. Tad. BR67 112
Stubbs Wood, Amer. AP21 25
Stucley Pl. NW1 BV37 56
Camden High St.
Stucley Rd. Houns. BG43 64
Studd St. N1 BY37 2
Studdridge St. SW6 BS44 66
Stud Grn. Wat. BC19 17
Studholme Ct. NW6 BS35 47
Studholm St. SE15 CB43 67
Studio Dr. Wem. BM34 46
Empire Way
Studios Rd. Shep. AZ52 83
Studland Clo. Sid. CN48 78
Studland Rd. SE26 CC49 77
Studland Rd. W7 BG39 54
Studland Rd. Kings. on T. BL50 75
Studland Rd. Wey. AY60 92
Studland St. W6 BP42 65
Studley Av. E4 CF29 39
Studley Clo. E5 CD35 48
Durrington Rd.
Studley Ct. Sid. CO49 79
Studley Dr. Ilf. CJ32 49
Studley Gra. Rd. W7 BH41 64
Studley Rd. E7 CH36 58
Studley Rd. SW4 BX44 66
Studley Rd. Dag. CP36 59
Stukeley Rd. E7 CH36 58
Stukeley St. WC2 BX39 2
Stukeley St. WC2 BX39 56
Stumble Hill, Ton. DB68 117
Stump Rd. Epp. CP17 23
Stumps Hl. La. Beck. CE50 77
Stumps La. Whyt. CA62 105
Sturdy Rd. SE15 CB44 67
Sturge Av. E17 CE30 39
Sturges Field, Chis. CM50 78
Sturgess Av. NW4 BP33 46
Sturge St. SE1 BZ41 4
Sturge St. SE1 BZ41 67
Sturmer Way N7 BX35 47
Stockorchard Cres.
Sturrock Clo. N15 BZ31 48
Ida Rd.
Sturry St. E14 CE39 57
Sturt St. N1 BZ37 2
Sturt St. N1 BZ37 57
Stutfield St. E1 CB39 57
Styants Bottom La. Sev. CZ64 108
Stychens Clo. Red. BZ70 114
Stychens La. Red. BZ69 114
Stylecroft Rd. Ch. St. G. AR27 34
Style Rd. Slou. AR41 62
Styles End, Lthd. BF67 111
Styles Gdns. SW9 BY45 66
Styles Way, Beck. CF52 87
Styventon Pl. Cher. AV54 82
Cowley Av.
Succombs Hill, Warl. CB63 105
Sudbourne Rd. SW2 BX46 76
Sudbrooke Rd. SW12 BU46 76
Sudbrook Gdns. Rich. BK48 74
Sudbrook La. Rich. BL47 75
Sudbury Av. Wem. BK34 45
Sudbury Ct. Dr. Har. BH34 45
Sudbury Ct. Rd. Har. BH34 45
Sudbury Cres. Brom. CH50 78
Sudbury Cres. Wem. BJ35 45
Sudbury Cft. Wem. BH35 45
Sudbury Gdns. Croy. CA55 87
Sudbury Heights Av. Grnf. BH35 45
Sudbury Hill, Har. BH34 45
Sudbury Hill Clo. Wem. BH35 45
Sudbury Pde. Wem. BJ35 45
Sudbury Rd. Bark. CN35 49
Sudeley St. N1 BY37 2
Sudeley St. N1 BY37 56
Sudicamps Ct. Wal. Abb. CH20 22
Winters Wy.
Sudlow Rd. SW18 BS46 76
Sudrey St. SE1 BZ41 4
Sudrey St. SE1 BZ41 67
Sudridge Hill, Sev. CP62 107
Suez Av. Grnf. BH37 54
Suez Rd. Enf. CD24 30
Suffield Clo. Sth. Croy. CC59 96
Suffield Rd. E4 CE28 39
Suffield Rd. N15 CA32 48
Suffield Rd. SE17 BY42 4
Suffield Rd. SE20 CC51 87
Suffolk Clo. Borwd. BN25 28
Suffolk Clo. St. Alb. BK16 18
Suffolk Ct. Ilf. CN32 49
Suffolk Gro. SE16 CC42 67
Hawkstone Rd.
Suffolk La. EC4 BZ40 4
Suffolk La. EC4 BZ40 57
Suffolk Pl. E17 CD31 48
Suffolk Pl. SW1 BW40 3
Suffolk Pl. SW1 BW40 56
Suffolk St.
Suffolk Rd. E13 CG38 58
Suffolk Rd. N15 BZ32 48
Suffolk Rd. NW10 BO36 55
Suffolk Rd. SE25 CA52 87
Suffolk Rd. SW13 BO43 65
Suffolk Rd. Bark. CM36 58
Suffolk Rd. Dag. CS35 50
Suffolk Rd. Dart. CW46 80
Suffolk Rd. Enf. CB25 30
Suffolk Rd. Grav. DH46 81
Suffolk Rd. Har. BE32 45
Suffolk Rd. Ilf. CN32 49
Suffolk Rd. Pot. B. BR19 19
Suffolk Rd. Sid. CP50 79
Suffolk Rd. Wor. Pk. BO55 85
Suffolk St. E7 CH35 49
Suffolk St. SW1 BW40 3
Suffolk St. SW1 BW40 56
Suffolk Way, Sev. CV66 117
Buckhurst La.
Suffolk Way, Horn. CX31 51
Sugar House La. E15 CF37 57
Sugar Lane, Berk. AT14 7
Sugar Loaf Wk. E2 CC38 57
Sugden Rd. SW11 BV45 66
Sugden Rd. Surb. BJ54 84
Sugden St. SE5 BZ43 67
Sugden Way, Bark. CN37 58
Sulgrave Rd. W6 BQ41 65
Sulina Rd. SW2 BX47 76
Sulivan Ct. SW6 BS44 66
Sulivan Rd. SW6 BS45 66
Sullivan Av. E16 CJ39 58
Sullivan Clo. SW11 BU45 66
Ingrave St.
Sullivan Ct. SW6 BS45 66
Sullivan Cres. Uxb. AX30 35
Sullivan Rd. SE11 BY42 66
Brook Drive
Sullivan Rd. E. Mol. BF52 84
Sullivan Rd. Til. DG44 71
Sullivan Way, Borwd. BK25 27
Sultan Rd. E11 CH31 49
Sultan St. SE5 BZ43 67
Sultan St. Beck. CC51 87
Sumatra Rd. NW6 BS35 47
Sumburgh Rd. SW12 BV46 76
Summer Av. E. Mol. BH53 84
Summer Ct. Rd. E1 CC39 57
W. Arbour St.
Summer Dale,
Welw. G. C. BQ6 5
Summerfield, Hat. BP14 10
Hollyfield
Summerfield Av. NW6 BR37 55
Summerfield Clo.
St. Alb. BK16 18
Summerfield Clo. Wey. AW56 92
Summerfield La. Surb. BK55 84
Summerfield Rd. W5 BJ38 54
Summerfield Rd. Loug. CJ25 31
Summerfield Rd. Wat. BC21 26
Summerfield St. SE12 CG47 78
Summer Gdns. E. Mol. BH53 84
Summer Hayes Clo. Wok. AS60 91
Summer Hayes Clo. Wok. AS61 100
Summerhays, Cob. BD60 93
Summer Hill, Chis. CL51 88
Summerhill Clo. Orp. CN56 97
Summerhill Ct. St. Alb. BH13 9
Avenue Rd.
Summerhill Gro. Enf. CA25 30
Summerhill Rd. N15 BZ31 48
Summerhill Rd. Dart. CV47 80
Summer Hill Vill. Chis. CL51 88
Summerhouse Av. Houns. BE44 64
Summerhouse Dr. Bex. CS49 79
Summerhouse Dr. Dart. CS48 79
Summerhouse La. Uxb. AW29 35
Summerhouse La. Wat. BG23 27
Summerhouse La.
West Dr. AX43 63
Summer House Rd. N16 CA34 48
Summerhouse Way, Wat. BB18 17
Summerland Gdns. N10 BV31 47
Muswell Hill, Broadway
Summerlands Av. W3 BN40 55
Summerlands Rd. St. Alb. BK11 9
Ridgeway, The
Summerlea, Slou. AN41 61
Summerlee Av. N2 BU31 47
Summerlee Gdns. N2 BU31 47
Summerley St. SW18 BS48 76
Summer Rd. E. Mol. BG53 84
Summersby Rd. N6 BV32 47
Summers Clo. Sutt. BS57 95
Overton Rd.
Summers Clo. Wey. AZ59 92
Summers La. N12 BT29 38
Summers Row N12 BU29 38
Summers St. EC1 BY38 2
Summers St. EC1 BY38 56
Back Hill
Summerstown SW17 BT48 76
Summerswood La. Borwd. BO21 28
Summertrees Sun. BC51 83
Summerville Gdns. Sutt. BR57 94
Summerville Rd. Dart. CW46 80
Summerwood Rd. Islw. BH46 74
Summit Av. NW9 BN32 46
Summit Clo. N14 BW27 38
Summit Clo. NW2 BR35 46
Summit Clo. NW9 BN31 46
Summit Clo. Edg. BM29 37
Summit Clo. Wey. AV56 91
Summit Dr. Wdf. Grn. CJ30 40
Summit Est. N16 CB33 48
Summit Rd. E17 CE31 48
Summit Rd. Nthlt. BF36 54
Summit, The Loug. CK23 31
Summit Way N14 BV27 38
Summit Way SE19 CA50 77
Sumner Av. SE15 CA44 67
Sumner Rd.
Sumner Blds. SE1 BZ40 4
Sumner Bldgs. SE1 BZ40 57
Sumner St.
Sumner Clo. Orp. CM56 97
Isabella Dr.
Sumner Gdns. Croy. CY54 86
Sumner Pl. SW7 BT42 3
Sumner Pl. SW7 BR42 66
Sumner Pl. Ms. SW7 BT42 3
Sumner Pl. Ms. SW7 BT42 66
Sumner Pl.
Sumner Rd. SE15 CA43 67
Sumner Rd. Croy. BY54 86
Sumner Rd. Har. BG33 45
Sumner Rd. S. Croy. BY54 86
Sumner St. SE1 BY40 4
Sumner St. SE1 BY40 56
Sumpter Clo. NW3 BT36 56
Sumpter Yd. St. Alb. BG13 9
Sun All. Rich. BL45 65
Sunbeam Rd. NW10 BN38 55
Sunbridge Rd. Croy. CA54 87
Sunbury Av. NW7 BN28 37
Sunbury Av. SW14 BN45 65
Sunbury Ct. Rd. Sun. BD51 84
Sunbury Cres. Felt. BB48 73
Sunbury Gdns. NW7 BN28 37
Sunbury La. SW11 BT44 66
Sunbury La. Walt. BC53 83
Sunbury Rd. Felt. BB48 73
Sunbury Rd. Sutt. BQ55 85
Sunbury Rd. Wind. AO43 61
Sunbury St. SE18 CK41 68
Suncourt, Erith CT44 69
Suncroft Pl. SE26 CC48 77
Sundale Av. Sth. Croy. CC58 96
Sunderland Av. St. Alb. BJ13 9
Sunderland Ct. SE22 CB47 77
Sunderland Mt. SE23 CC48 77
Sunderland Rd. SE23 CC48 77
Sunderland Rd. W5 BK41 64
Sunderland Rd. Houns. AY46 73
Southampton Rd.
Sunderland Ter. W2 BS39 56
Sunderland Way E12 CJ34 49
Sundew Av. W12 BP40 55
Sundial Av. SE25 CA52 87
Sundon Cres. Vir. W. AQ53 82
Sundorne Rd. SE7 CH42 68
Sundown Av. Sth. Croy. CA59 96
Sundown Pl. Ilf. CL34 49
Ilford Hill
Sundown Rd. Ashf. BA49 73
Sundra Wk. E1 CC38 57
Beaumont Gr.
Sundridge Av. Brom. CJ51 88
Sundridge Av. Well. CM44 68
Sundridge Clo. Dart. CX46 80

Street	Grid	Page
Sundridge Ho. Brom.	CH49	78
Sundridge La. Sev.	CO62	107
Sundridge Rd. Wok.	AT63	100
Sunfields Pl. SE3	CH43	68
Sun Hill, Fawk.	CZ55	90
Sunland Av. Bexh.	CQ45	69
Sun La. SE3	CH43	68
Sun La. Grav.	DH48	81
Sunleigh Rd. Wem.	BL37	55
Sunley Gdns. Grnf.	BJ37	54
Sunmead Clo. Lthd.	BH64	102
Sunmead Rd. Hem. H.	AX13	8
Sunmead Rd. Sun.	BC52	83
Sunna Gdns. Sun.	BC51	83
Sunningdale Av. W3	BO39	55
Sunningdale Av. Bark.	CM37	58
Sunningdale Av. Felt.	BE48	74
Sunningdale Av. Rain.	CU38	59
Sunningdale Av. Ruis.	BD33	45
Sunningdale Clo. Stan.	BJ29	36
Sunningdale Gdns. NW9	BN32	46
Sunningdale Rd. Brom.	CK52	88
Sunningdale Rd. Rain.	CU36	59
Sunningdale Rd. Sutt.	BR55	85
Sunningfields Cres. NW4	BP30	37
Sunningfields Rd. NW4	BP30	37
Sunning Hill, Grav.	DF48	81
Sunninghill Rd. SE13	CE44	67
Sunnings La. Upmin.	CW36	60
Sunningvale Av. West.	CJ61	106
Sunningvale Av. West.	CJ62	106
Sunningvale Clo. West.	CJ61	106
Sunny Bank SE25	CB52	87
Sunny Bank, Epsom	BN61	103
Sunny Bank, Warl.	CD62	105
Sunny Bank Rd. Pot. B.	BS20	20
Sunny Cres. NW10	BN36	55
Sunnycroft Gdns. Upmin.	CZ33	51
Sunnycroft Rd. SE25	CB52	87
Sunnycroft Rd. Houns.	BF44	64
Sunnycroft Rd. Sthl.	BF39	54
Sunnydale Rd. SE12	CH46	78
Sunnydale, Orp.	CL55	88
Sunnydale Gro. NW7	BN29	37
Sunnydell, St. Alb.	BF16	18
Sunnydene Av. E4	CF28	39
Sunnydene Av. Ruis.	BC33	44
Sunnydene Clo. Rom.	CW29	42
Sunnydene Rd. Pur.	BY60	95
Sunnydene St. SE26	CD49	77
Sunnyfield NW7	BO27	37
Sunnyfield, Hat.	BQ11	10
Sunnyfield Rd. Chis.	CO52	89
Sunny Gdns. Rd. NW4	BP30	37
Sunnyhill Rd. SW16	BX49	76
Sunny Hill Rd. Ger. Cr.	AU29	34
Sunnyhill Rd. Hem. H.	AW13	8
Sunny Hl. NW4	BP31	46
Sunnyhurst Clo. Sutt.	BS55	86
Sunnymead Av. Chesh.	AP17	16
Sunnymead Av. Mitch.	BW52	86
Sunnymead Rd. NW9	BN33	46
Sunnymead Rd. SW15	BP46	75
Sunnymede, Chig.	CO27	41
Sunnymede Av. Cars.	BT59	95
Sunnymede Av. Epsom	BO58	94
Sunnymede Dr. Ilf.	CL32	49
Sunnymede Gdns. Wem.	BK36	54
Sunny Nook Gdns. Sth. Croy.	BZ57	96
Selsdon Rd.		
Sunny Ri. Cat.	BZ65	105
Sunnyside SW19	BR50	75
Sunny Side Walt.	BD53	84
Sunny Side, Wal. Abb.	CG14	13
Hoe La.		
Sunnyside Dr. E4	CF26	39
Sunnyside Gdns. Upmin.	CY34	51
Sunnyside Pass SW19	BR50	75
Sunnyside Rd. E10	CE33	48
Sunnyside Rd. N19	BW33	47
Sunnyside Rd. NW2	BR34	46
Sunnyside Rd. W5	BK40	54
Sunnyside Rd. Epp.	CN19	22
Sunnyside Rd. Ilf.	CM34	49
Sunnyside Rd. Tedd.	BG49	74
Sunnyside Rd. E. N9	CB27	39
Sunnyside Rd. N. N9	CB27	39
Sunnyside Rd. S. N9	CA27	39
Sunny, The Rd. Enf.	CC23	30
Sunny Vw. NW9	BN32	46
Sunny Way N12	BU29	38
Sun Pass. Wind.	AO44	61
Peascod St.		
Sunray Av. West Dr.	AX41	63
Sunray Av. SE24	BZ45	67
Sunray Av. Brom.	CK53	88
Sun Ray Av. Brwd.	DF25	122
Sunray Av. Surb.	BM55	85
Sunrise Av. Horn.	CV34	51
Sunrise Clo. Felt.	BE48	74
Sunrise Cres. Hem. H.	AY15	8
Sun Rd. W14	BR42	65
Sun Rd. Swans.	DC46	81
Sun St. EC2	**BZ39**	**2**
Sun St. Pass. EC2	**CA39**	**2**
Sun St. Pass EC2	CA39	57
Sunset Av. E4	CE26	39
Sunset Av. Wdf. Grn.	CG28	40
Sunset Dr. Hav.	CU28	41
Sunset Gdns. SE25	CA51	87
Sunset Rd. SE5	BZ45	67
Sunset Vw. Barn.	BR23	28
Sunshine Way, Mitch.	BU51	86
Sun Sq. Hem. H.	AX13	8
High St.		
Sunstone Grn. Red.	BX68	113
Sun St. EC2	BZ39	57
Sun St. Wal. Abb.	CF20	21
Sunwell Clo. SE15	CB44	67
Gordon Rd.		
Sunwell St. SE15	CB44	67
Surbiton Ct. Surb.	BK53	84
Surbiton Cres. Surb.	BL53	85
Surbiton Hall Clo. Kings. on T.	BL52	85
Surbiton Hill Pk. Surb.	BL53	85
Surbiton Hill Rd. Surb.	BL52	85
Surbiton Pk. Ter. Kings. on T.	BL52	85
Surbiton Rd. Kings. on T.	BK52	84
Surgeon St. SE18	CL41	68
Surly Hall Wk. Wind.	AM44	61
Surman Cres. Brwd.	DE26	122
Surrendale Pl. W9	BS38	56
Surrey Av. Slou.	AO39	52
Surrey Cres. W4	BM42	65
Chiswick High Rd.		
Surrey Dr. Horn.	CW31	51
Surrey Gdns. W4	BM42	65
Chiswick High Rd.		
Surrey Gdns. Lthd.	BB64	101
Surrey Gro. SE17	**CA42**	**4**
Surrey Gro. SE17	CA42	67
Surrey La. SW11	BU44	66
Surrey Ms. SE27	CA49	77
Hamilton Rd.		
Surrey Mt. SE23	CB47	77
Surrey Rd. SE15	CC46	77
Surrey Rd. Bark.	CN36	58
Surrey Rd. Dag.	CR35	50
Surrey Rd. Har.	BG32	45
Surrey Rd. W. Wick.	CE54	87
Surrey Row, SE1	**BY41**	**4**
Surrey Row, SE1	BY41	66
Surrey Sq. SE17	**CA42**	**4**
Surrey Sq. SE17	CA42	67
Surrey St. E13	CH38	58
Surrey St. WC2	**BX40**	**4**
Surrey St. WC2	BX40	56
Temple Pl.		
Surrey St. Croy.	BZ55	87
Surrey Ter. SE17	**CA42**	**4**
Surrey Ter. SE17	CA42	67
Surrey Sq.		
Surridge Clo. Rain.	CV38	60
Surridge Gdns. SE19	BZ50	77
Surr St. N7	BX35	47
Surry Gro. Sutt.	BT55	86
Susan Clo. Rom.	CR31	50
Susannah St. E14	CE39	57
Susan Rd. SE3	CH44	68
Susan Wood, Chis.	CL51	88
Sussex Av. Islw.	BH45	64
Sussex Av. Rom.	CW29	42
Sussex Clo. N19	BX34	47
Sussex Clo. Ch. St. G.	AQ27	34
Sussex Clo. Ilf.	CK32	49
Radnor Cres.		
Sussex Clo. N. Mal.	BO52	85
Sussex Clo. Reig.	BT71	121
Sussex Clo. Slou.	AQ41	62
Sussex Clo. Twick.	BJ46	74
Westmorland Clo.		
Sussex Cres. Nthlt.	BF36	54
Sussex Gdns. N4	BZ32	48
Rosebery Gdns.		
Sussex Gdns. W2	**BT39**	**1**
Sussex Gdns. W2	BT39	56
Sussex Gdns. Chess.	BK57	93
Sussex Ms. NW1	**BU38**	**1**
Sussex Ms. NW1	BU38	56
Sussex Place		
Sussex Ms. E. W2	**BT40**	**3**
Sussex Ms. E. W2	BT40	56
Clifton Pl.		
Sussex Ms. W. W2	**BT40**	**3**
Sussex Pl. Erith.	CR43	69
Sussex Pl. W2	**BT39**	**1**
Sussex Pl. W2	BT39	56
Sussex Pl. W6	BQ42	65
Sussex Pl. N. Mal.	BO52	85
Sussex Rd.		
Sussex Pl. Slou.	AQ41	62
Sussex Rd. E6	CL37	58
Sussex Rd. SW9	BY45	66
Sussex Rd. Brwd.	DA28	42
Sussex Rd. Cars.	BU57	95
Sussex Rd. Dart.	CX47	80
Sussex Rd. Erith	CR43	69
Sussex Rd. Har.	BF32	45
Sussex Rd. N. Mal.	BO52	85
Sussex Rd. Orp.	CP53	89
Sussex Rd. Sid.	CO49	79
Sussex Rd. Sth. Croy.	BZ57	96
Sussex Rd. Sthl.	BD41	64
Sussex Rd. Uxb.	BA35	44
Sussex Rd. Wat.	BC22	26
Sussex Rd. W. Wick.	CE54	87
Sussex Sq. W2	**BT40**	**3**
Sussex Sq. W2	BT40	56
Sussex St. E13	CH38	58
Sussex St. SW1	**BV42**	**3**
Sussex St. SW1	BV42	66
Sussex Wk. SW9	BY45	66
Somerleyton Rd. Dev.		
Sussex Way N7	BX34	47
Sussex Way N19	BX34	47
Sussex Way, Barn.	BV25	29
Sussex Way, Uxb.	AV32	43
Sutcliffe Clo. NW11	BS32	47
Sutcliffe Clo. Bush.	BG24	27
Sutcliffe Rd. SE18	CN43	68
Sutcliffe Rd. Well.	CP44	69
Sutherland Av. West.	CJ62	106
Sutherland Av. W9	**BS38**	**1**
Sutherland Av. W9	BS38	56
Sutherland Av. W13	BJ39	54
Sutherland Av. Guil.	AS67	109
Sutherland Av. Hayes	BC42	63
Sutherland Av. Orp.	CN53	88
Sutherland Av. Pot. B.	BW17	20
Hillary Av.		
Sutherland Av. Sun.	BB51	83
Sutherland Av. Well.	CN45	68
Sutherland Clo. Barn.	BR24	28
Sutherland Ct. NW9	BM32	46
Sutherland Gdns. SW14	BO45	65
Sutherland Gdns. Sun.	BB51	83
Sutherland Gdns. Wor. Pk.	BP54	85
Sutherland Gro. SW18	BR46	75
Sutherland Gro. Tedd.	BH49	74
Sutherland Pl. W2	BS39	56
Sutherland Rd. E3	CD37	57
Sutherland Rd. E17	CC30	39
Sutherland Rd. N9	CB26	39
Sutherland Rd. N17	CB29	39
Sutherland Rd. W4	BO43	65
Sutherland Rd. W13	BJ39	54
Sutherland Rd. Belv.	CR41	69
Sutherland Rd. Croy.	BY54	86
Sutherland Rd. Enf.	CC25	30
Sutherland Rd. Sthl.	BE39	54
Sutherland Rd. Path E17	CC31	48
Sutherland Row SW1	**BV42**	**3**
Sutherland Row SW1	BV42	66
Sutherland St.		
Sutherlands Av. Sun.	BC51	83
Sutherland Sq. SE17	**BZ42**	**4**
Sutherland Sq. SE17	BZ42	67
Sutherland St. E3	CD37	57
Sutherland St. SW1	**BV42**	**3**
Sutherland St. SW1	BV42	66
Sutherland Wk. SE17	**BZ42**	**4**
Sutherland Wk. SE17	BZ42	67
Sutherland Way, Pot. B.	BW17	20
Sutlej Rd. SE7	CJ43	68
Sutterton St. N7	BX36	56
Blundell St.		
Sutton Av. Slou.	AR41	62
Sutton Av. Wok.	AP63	100
Sutton Clo. Brom.	CE51	87
Albermarle Rd.		
Sutton Clo. Brox.	CD13	12
Sutton Clo. Loug.	CK26	40
Sutton Clo. Pnr.	BC32	44
Sutton Com. Rd. Sutt.	BR54	85
Sutton Ct. W4	BN43	65
Sutton Ct. Rd. E13	CJ38	58
Sutton Ct. Rd. W4	BN43	65
Sutton Ct. Rd. Sutt.	BT57	95
Sutton Ct. Rd. Uxb.	AZ37	53
Sutton Cres. Barn.	BQ25	28
Sutton Dene, Houns.	BF44	64
Sutton Dws. N1	BY36	56
Sutton Dws. SE8	CC42	67
Sutton Dwellings SW3	**BU42**	**3**
Sutton Dws. SW3	BU42	66
Sutton Dws. W10	BQ39	55
Sutton Gdns. Croy.	CA53	87
Sutton Gdns. Red.	BW68	113
Sutton Grn. Bark.	CN37	58
Saxham Rd.		
Sutton Grn. Rd. Guil.	AS66	109
Sutton Gro. Sutt.	BT56	95
Sutton Hall Rd. Houns.	BF43	64
Sutton La. W4	BN42	65
Sutton La. Houns.	BE45	64
Sutton La. Slou.	AT43	62
Sutton La. Sutt.	BS59	95
Sutton La. S. W4	BN43	65
Sutton Model Dws. EC1	**BZ38**	**2**
Sutton Pk. Rd. Sutt.	BS57	95
Sutton Path, Borwd.	BM23	28
Sutton Pl. E9	CC35	48
Sutton Pl. Slou.	AT43	62
Sutton Rd. E13	CG38	58
Sutton Rd. E17	CC30	39
Sutton Rd. N10	BV30	38
Sutton Rd. Bark.	CN37	58
Sutton Rd. Houns.	BF44	64
Sutton Rd. St. Alb.	BJ14	9
Sutton Rd. Wat.	BD24	27
Sutton Row W1	**BW39**	**1**
Sutton Row W1	BW39	56
Suttons Av. Horn.	CV34	51
Suttons Gdns. Horn.	CV34	51
Suttons La. Horn.	CV35	51
Suttons Parkway, Upmin.	CW35	51
Sutton Sq. Houns.	BE44	64
Sutton St. E1	CC40	57
Sutton Way W10	BQ38	55
Sutton Way, Houns.	BE44	64
Swabey Rd. Slou.	AT42	62
Swaby Rd. SW18	BT47	76
Swaffham Way N22	BY29	38
Swaffield Rd. SW18	BS47	76
Swaffield Rd. Sev.	CV64	108
Swain Rd. Th. Hth.	BZ53	87
Swain Clo. West Dr.	AY41	63
Swain's La. N6	BV34	47
Swainson Rd. W3	BO41	65
Swain's Rd. SW17	BU50	76
Swaisland Rd. Dart.	CU46	79
Swaislands Dr. Dart.	CT45	69
Crayford Rd.		
Swaislands Dr. Dart.	CT46	79
Crayford Way		
Swaislands Dr. Dart.	CT46	79
Crayford Way		
Swakeleys Dr. Uxb.	AZ35	44
Swakeleys Rd. Uxb.	AY35	44
Swale Clo. S. Ock.	CW39	60
Swaledale Rd. Dart.	CY47	80
Swale Rd. Dart.	CU45	69
Swallands Rd. SE6	CE48	77
Swallow Clo. SE14	CC44	67
Swallow Clo. Bush.	BF26	36
Swallow Clo. Stai.	AV49	72
Swallow Clo. Rick.	AX26	35
Nightingale Rd.		
Swallowdale, Iver	AU38	52
Swallowdale, Sth. Croy.	CC58	96
Swallowdale Est. Iver.	AU38	52
Swallowdale La. Hem. H.	AZ12	8
Swallow Dr. Nthlt.	BE37	54
Hazelmere Rd.		
Swallow End, Welw. G. C.	BR8	5
Swallowfield Rd. SE7	CH42	68
Swallowfields, Grav.	DF48	81
Swallow Fields, Welw. G. C.	BR8	5
Swallowfield Way, Hayes	BA41	63
Swallow Gdns. Hat.	BP13	10
Swallows, Harl.	CP9	6
Swallow Pl. W1	**BV39**	**1**
Swallow St. W1	**BW40**	**3**
Swallow St. W1	BW40	56
Piccadilly		
Swallow St. Iver	AU38	52
Swallow Wk. Rain.	CU36	59
Swanage Rd. E4	CF29	39
Swanage Rd. SW18	BT46	76
Swanage Waye, Hayes	BD39	54
Swan Av. Upmin.	CZ33	51
Swanbourne Dr. Horn.	CV35	51
Swanbridge Rd. Bexh.	CR44	69
Swan Clo. Felt.	BE49	74
Swan Clo. Orp.	CO52	89
Swan Ct. N20	BT27	38
Swan Ct. SW3	**BU42**	**3**
Swan Ct. SW3	BU42	66
Swanfield Rd. Wal. Cr.	CD20	21
Swanfield St. E2	**CA38**	**2**
Swanfield St. E2	CA38	57
Swanhill, Welw. G. C.	BS6	5
Swan La. EC4	**BZ40**	**4**
Swan La. EC4	BZ40	57
Wharfside		
Swan La. N20	BT27	38
Swan La. Brwd.	CZ22	33
Swan La. Dart.	CT47	79
Swan La. Guil.	AR71	118
Swanley Bar. La. Pot. B.	BS17	20
Swanley By-pass, Swan.	CS52	89
Swanley Cres. Pot. B.	BS18	20
Swanley La. Swan.	CT52	89
Swanley Rd. Well.	CN44	68
Swanley Vill. Rd. Swan.	CU51	89
Swan Mead SE1	**CA41**	**4**
Swan Mead SE1	CA41	67
Swan Mews SW9	BX44	66
Stockwell Pk. Rd.		
Swan Ms. SW9	BX44	66
Stockwell Rd.		
Swan Mill Gdns. Dor.	BK70	119
Swann's Meadow, Lthd.	BF66	111
Swan Paddock, Brwd.	DB27	42
Chestnut Gr.		
Swan Passage E1	CA40	57
Royal Mint St.		
Swan Pl. SW13	BO44	65
Swan & Pike Rd. Enf.	CE22	30
Swan Rd. SE7	CJ41	68
Swan Rd. SE16	CC41	67
Swan Rd. Felt.	BE49	74
Swan Rd. Iver	AV39	52
Swan Rd. Sthl.	BF39	54
Swan Rd. West. Dr.	AX41	63
Swans Clo. St. Alb.	BL14	10
Swanscombe Rd. W4	BO42	65
Swanscombe Rd. W11	BQ40	55
Swanscombe Rd. Swans.	DC46	81
Swansea Rd. Enf.	CC24	30
Swansfield La. Green.	DA47	80
Swansland Gdns. E17	CD30	39
Mcentee Av.		
Swanston Path, Wat.	BD27	36
Swan St. SE1	**BZ41**	**4**
Swan St. SE1	BZ41	67
Swan St. Islw.	BJ45	64
Swan Ter. Wind.	AN43	61
Swanton Gdns. SW19	BQ47	75
Swanton Rd. Erith.	CR43	69
Swan Wk. SW3	BU43	66
Swan Wk. Rom.	CT32	50
Swan Way, Enf.	CC23	30
Swan Wf. EC4	BZ40	57
Wharfside		
Swanwick Clo. SW15	BO47	75
Swanworth La. Dor.	BJ67	111
Swan Yd. N1	BY36	56
Highbury Stn. Rd.		
Swanzy Rd. Sev.	CV63	108
Sward Rd. Orp.	CO53	89
Swaton Rd. E3	CE38	57
Swaylands Rd. Belv.	CR43	69
Swaynesland Rd. Eden.	CK70	115
Swayne's La. Guil.	AV70	118
Swedenborg St. E1	CB40	57
Swedewborg Gdns. E1	CB40	57
Sweeney Cres. SE1	**CA41**	**4**
Sweeney Cres. SE1	CA41	67
Sweeps La. Egh.	AS49	72
Sweeps La. Orp.	CP53	89
Sweet Briar, Welw. G. C.	BS8	5
Sweetbriar Clo. Hem. H.	AW12	8
Sweet Briar Grn. N9	CA27	39
Briary La.		
Sweet Briar Gro. N9	CA27	39
Sweetbriar La. Epsom	BN60	94
Sweet Briar Wk. N18	CA28	39
Sweetcroft La. Uxb.	AY36	53
Sweetenham Wk. SE18	CM42	68
Sandbach Pl.		
Sweetmans Av. Pnr.	BD31	45
Sweets Way N20	BT27	38
Swete St. E13	CH37	58
Sweyne Rd. Swans.	DC46	81
Sweyn Pl. SE3	CH44	68
Sweyn Rd. Green.	DB46	80
Swievelands Hill Rd. West.	CH63	106
Swift Clo. Har.	BF34	45
Swift Clo. Hayes	BB39	53
Swift Clo. Upmin.	CZ33	51
Swift Rd. Felt.	BD49	74
Swift Rd. Sthl.	BF41	64
Swiftsden Way, Brom.	CG50	78
Swift St. SW6	BR44	65
Swinborn Ct. SE5	BZ45	67
Basingdon Way		
Swinbourne Gdns. Til.	DG44	71
Swinbrook Rd. W10	BR39	55
Swinburne Cres. Croy.	CC53	87
Swinburne Rd. SW15	BP45	65
Swinderby Rd. Wem.	BL36	55
Swindon Clo. Ilf.	CN34	49
Salisbury Rd.		
Swindon Clo. Rom.	CW28	42
Swindon Gdns. Rom.	CW28	42
Swindon La. Rom.	CW28	42
Swindon St. W12	BP40	55
Swinford Gdns. SW9	BY45	66
Swingate La. SE18	CN43	68
Swing Gate La. Berk.	AR14	7
Swinnerton St. E9	CD35	48
Swinton Clo. Wem.	BM33	46
Swinton Pl. WC1	**BX38**	**2**
Swinton Pl. WC1	BX38	56
Swinton St.		
Swinton St. WC1	**BX38**	**2**
Swinton St. WC1	BX38	56
Swiss Av. Wat.	BB24	2
Swiss Clo. Wat.	BB24	2
Swithland Gdns. SE9	CK49	7
Swyncombe Av. W5	BJ42	6
Sybourn St. E17	CD33	4
Sycamore App. Rick.	BA25	2
Sycamore Av. W5	BK41	6
Sycamore Av. Hat.	BP13	1
Sycamore Av. Hayes	BB40	5
Sycamore Av. Sid.	CN46	7
Sycamore Av. Upmin.	CX35	5
Sycamore Clo. Bush.	BE23	2
Sycamore Clo. Ch. St. G.	AQ27	3
Sycamore Clo. Nthlt.	BE37	5
Sycamore Clo. Wat.	BC21	2
Sycamore Clo. West Dr.	AY40	5
Sycamore Dean, Chesh.	AO17	1
Sycamore Dr. St. Alb.	BG17	1
Radlett Rd.		
Sycamore Dr. Swan.	CT52	8
Sycamore Field, Harl.	CL12	1
Sycamore Gdns. W6	BP41	6
Sycamore Gro. NW9	BN33	4
Sycamore Gro. N. Mal.	BN52	8
Sycamore Ri. Bans.	BQ60	9
High Beeches		
Sycamore Ri. Ch. St. G.	AQ27	3
Sycamore Rd. SW19	BQ50	7
Sycamore Rd. Amer.	AO22	2
Sycamore Rd. Ch. St. G.	AQ27	3
Sycamore Rd. Dart.	CV47	8
Sycamore Rd. Guil.	AR70	11
Sycamore Rd. Rick.	BA25	2
Sycamore St. EC1	BZ38	5
Baltic St.		
Sycamore Wk. W10	BR38	5
Droop St.		
Sycamore Wk. Ilf.	CM31	4
Civic Way		
Sycamore Wk. Slou.	AS39	5
Sycamore Way, Th. Hth.	BY53	8
Sydenham Av. SE26	CB49	7
Sydenham Hill SE23	CB47	7
Sydenham Hill SE26	CB47	7
Sydenham Pk. SE26	CC49	7
Sydenham Pk. Rd. SE26	CC48	7
Sydenham Rise SE23	CC48	7
Sydenham Rd. SE26	CC49	7
Sydenham Rd. Croy.	BZ54	8
Sydenham Rd. Guil.	AR71	11
Sydmons St. SE23	CC47	7
Sydner Rd. N16	CA35	4
Sydney Av. Pur.	BX59	9
Sydney Clo. SW3	BT42	6
Sydney Clo. SW7	**BT42**	
Sydney Cres. Ashf.	AZ50	7
Sydney Gro. NW4	BQ32	4
Sydney Gro. Slou.	AO39	5
Sydney Ms. SW3	BT42	6
Sydney Ms. SW7	**BT42**	
Sydney Ms. Clo. SW7	BT42	6
Sydney Pl. SW7	**BT42**	
Sydney Pl. SW7	BU42	6
Sydney Rd. E11	CH32	4
Sydney Rd. N8	BY31	4
Sydney Rd. N10	BV30	3
Sydney Rd. SE2	CP41	6
Sydney Rd. SW20	BQ51	8
Sydney Rd. W13	BJ40	5
Sydney Rd. Bexh.	CP45	6
Sydney Rd. Enf.	BZ24	3
Sydney Rd. Felt.	BC47	7
Sydney Rd. Guil.	AS71	11
Sydney Rd. Ilf.	CM30	4
Sydney Rd. Rich.	BL45	6
Sydney Rd. Sid.	CN49	7
Sydney Rd. Tedd.	BH49	7
Sydney Rd. Til.	DG44	7
Sydney Rd. Wat.	BB25	2
Sydney Rd. Wdf. Grn.	CH28	4
Sydney Sq. SE15	CB43	6
Latona Rd.		
Sydney St. SW3	**BT42**	
Sydney St. SW3	BU42	6
Sykecluan, Iver	AV41	6
Sykeings, Iver	AV41	6
Sylvana Clo. Uxb.	AY37	5
Sylvan Av. N3	BS30	3
Sylvan Av. N22	BX29	3
Sylvan Av. NW7	BO29	3
Sylvan Av. Horn.	CW32	5
Sylvan Av. Rom.	CQ32	5
Sylvan Clo. Grays	DC42	7
Sylvan Clo. Hem. H.	AZ14	
Sylvan Clo. Sth. Croy.	CB58	9
Sylvan Clo. Wok.	AT62	10
Sylvan Gdns. Surb.	BK54	8
Sylvan Gro. SE15	CB43	6
Sylvan Hl. SE19	CA51	8
Sylvan Rd. E7	CH36	5
Sylvan Rd. E11	CH32	4
Sylvan Rd. E17	CE32	4
Sylvan Rd. SE19	CA51	8
Sylvan Rd. Ilf.	CM34	4
Sylvan Way, Dag.	CO34	5
Sylvan Way, Red.	BV71	12
Sylvan Way, W. Wick.	CG56	9
Sylverdale Rd. Croy.	BY55	8
Sylverdale Rd. Ken.	BY60	9
Sylvester Av. Chis.	CK50	7
Sylvester Gdns. Ilf.	CO28	4
Sylvester Rd. E8	CB36	5
Sylvester Rd. E17	CD33	4
Sylvester Rd. N2	BT30	3
Sylvester Rd. Wem.	BK35	4
Sylvia Av. Brwd.	DE27	12
Sylvia Av. Pnr.	BE29	3
Sylvia Ct. N1	**BZ37**	
Sylvia Ct. Wem.	BM36	5
Sylvia Gdns. Wem.	BM36	5
Symes Ms. NW1	**BW37**	
Symes Ms. NW1	BW37	5
Symonds Clo. Sev.	CZ56	9
Symondshyde La. Hat.	BM9	
Symons St. SW3	**BU42**	
Symons St. SW3	BU42	6
Syon La. Islw.	BH43	64
Syon Pk. Gdns. Islw.	BH43	64

111

Trederwen Rd. E8 CB37 57
Tredown Rd. SE26 CC49 77
Tree Bourne Rd. West CJ62 106
Treebys Av. Guil. AR67 109
Tree Clo. Rich. BK47 74
Tree Mt. Ct. Epsom BO60 94
Treen Av. SW13 BO45 65
Tree Rd. E16 CJ39 58
Treeside Clo. West Dr. AX42 63
Tree Tops, Brwd. DB26 42
Tree Tops, Grav. DG49 81
Tree Tops Clo. Belv. CQ42 69
Tree Tops Clo. Nthwd. BA28 35
Treewall Gdns. Brom. CH49 78
Trefgarne Rd. Dag. CR34 50
Trefil Walk N7 BX35 47
Warlters Rd.
Trefil Wk. N7 BX35 47
Parkhurst Rd.
Trefoil Rd. SW18 BT46 76
Trefusis Wk. Wat. BB23 26
Tregaron Av. N8 BX32 47
Tregarvon Rd. SW11 BV45 66
Tregelles Rd. Hodd. CE11 12
Tregenna Av. Har. BE35 45
Tregenna Clo. N14 BW25 29
Trego Rd. E3 CD36 57
Tregothnan Rd. SW9 BX45 66
Tregunter Rd. SW10 BS43 3
Tregunter Rd. SW10 BS43 66
Trehaven Pde. Reig. BS72 121
Hornbeam Rd.
Trehearn Rd. Ilf. CM29 40
Treherne Ct. SW17 BV49 76
Treherne Rd. SW9 BY44 66
Trehern Rd. SW14 BN45 65
Trehurst St. E5 CD35 48
Trelawney Est. E9 CC36 57
Trelawney Rd. Ilf. CM29 40
Trelawn Clo. Cher. AU57 91
Trelawn Rd. E10 CF34 48
Trelawn Rd. SW2 BY46 76
Trelawney Gro. Wey. AZ57 92
Elgin Rd.
Trellis Sq. E3 CE37 58
Malmesbury Sq.
Treloar Gdns. SE19 BZ50 77
Tremadoc Rd. SW4 BW45 66
Tremaine Clo. SE4 CE44 67
Tremaine Gro. Hem. H. AY11 8
Tremaine Rd. SE20 CB51 87
Trematon, Tedd. BK50 74
Tremlett Gro. N19 BW34 47
Tremlett Ms. N19 BW34 47
Junction Rd.
Trenance Gdns. Ilf. CO34 50
Trenchard Av. Ruis. BC35 44
Trenchard Clo. Stan. BJ29 36
Trenchard Clo. Walt. BD56 93
Trenchard Ct. Mord. BS53 86
Trenchard Rd. Maid. AG43 61
Trenchard St. SE10 CF42 67
Trenches La. Slou. AT40 52
Trenham Dr. Warl. CC61 105
Trenholme Clo. SE20 CB50 77
Trenholme Rd. SE20 CB50 77
Trenmar Gdns. NW10 BP38 55
Trent Av. W5 BK41 64
Trent Av. Upmin. CY32 51
Trent Gdns. N14 BV25 29
Trentham Cres. Wok. AT64 100
Trentham Dr. Orp. CO53 89
Trentham Rd. Red. BV71 121
Trentham St. SW18 BS47 76
Trentham Way, Red. BU71 121
Trent Rd. SW2 BX46 76
Trent Rd. Buck. H. CH26 40
Trent Way, Hayes BB37 53
Trent Way, Wor. Pk. BQ55 85
Trentwood Side Enf. BX24 29
Treport St. SW18 BS47 76
Tresco Clo. Brom. CG50 78
Hillbrow Rd.
Trescoe Gdns. Har. BE33 45
Trescoe Gdns. Rom. CS28 41
Tresco Gdns. Ilf. CO34 50
Tresco Rd. SE15 CB45 67
Tresco Rd. Berk. AP12 7
Tresham Cres. NW8 BU38 1
Tresham Cres. W1 BU38 56
Tresham Rd. Bark. CN36 58
Tresham Wk. E9 CC35 48
Churchill Wk.
Tresilian Sq. Hem. H. AY11 8
Tressillian Cres. SE4 CE45 67
Tressillian Rd. SE4 CD45 67
Tresta Wk. Wok. AQ61 100
Treswell Rd. Dag. CQ37 59
Tretawn Gdns. NW7 BO28 37
Tretawn Pk. NW7 BO28 37
Trevanion Rd. W14 BR42 65
Treve Av. Har. BG33 45
Trevelance Way, Wat. BD20 18
Trevelga Way, Hem. H. AY11 8
Tremaine Gro.
Trevelyan Av. E12 CK35 49
Trevelyan Clo. Dart. CW45 70
Trevelyan Cres. Har. BL33 46
Trevelyan Gdns. NW10 BQ37 55
Trevelyan Rd. E15 CG35 49
Trevelyan Rd. SW17 BU49 76
Trevelyan Way, Berk. AQ12 7
Trevelyn Ct. N. Mal. BO54 85
Trevereux Hill, Oxt. CK69 115
Treveris St. SE1 BY40 4
Treveris St. SE1 BY40 56
Bear Lane
Treverton Est. W10 BQ39 55
Treverton St. W10 BQ38 55
Treville St. SW15 BP47 75
Trevisco Rd. SE23 CC47 77
Farren Rd.
Trevithick Dr. Dart. CW45 70
Trevithick Rd. Dart. CW46 80
Trevithick St. SE8 CE42 67
Watergate St.
Trevone Gdns. Pnr. BE32 45
Trevor Clo. Barn. BT25 29
Trevor Clo. Brom. CG54 88
Trevor Clo. Islw. BH46 74
Trevor Clo. Nthlt. BD37 54
Trevor Clo. Stan. BH29 36
Trevor Ct. Stai. AW46 73
Horton Rd.
Trevor Cres. Ruis. BB35 44
Trevor Gdns. Edg. BN30 37
Trevor Gdns. Nthlt. BD37 54
Trevor Pl. SW7 BU41 3
Trevor Pl. SW7 BU41 66
Trevor Rd. SW19 BR50 75
Trevor Rd. Edg. BN30 37
Trevor Rd. Hayes BB41 63
Trevor Rd. Wdf. Grn. CH29 40
Trevor Sq. SW7 BU41 3
Trevor Sq. SW7 BU41 66
Trevor St. SW7 BU41 3
Trevor St. SW7 BU41 66
Trevose Av. Wey. AV60 91
Trevose Rd. E17 CF30 39
Trevose Way Wat. BD27 36
Trewenna Dri. Chess. BK56 93
Hook Road
Trewenna Dr. Pot. B. BT19 20
Trewince Rd. SW20 BQ51 85
Trewint St. SW18 BT48 76
Trewsbury Rd. SE26 CC49 77
Triangle, Wok. AR62 100
Triangle Ct. E16 CJ39 58
Tollgate Rd.
Triangle Pl. SW4 BW45 66
Triangle Rd. E8 CB37 57
Triangle, The Bark. CM36 58
Park Av.
Triangle, The Hamptn BG51 84
Triangle, The Kings. on T. BN51 85
Trident Gdns. Nthlt. BD38 54
Jetstar Way
Trident Rd. Wat. BB20 17
Trident Way, Sthl. BC41 63
Triggs Clo. Wok. AR63 100
Triggs La. Wok. AR63 100
Trigon Rd. SW8 BX43 66
Trilby Rd. SE23 CC48 77
Trimmer Wk. Brent. BL43 65
Netley Rd.
Trim St. SE14 CD43 67
Trinder Gdns. N19 BX33 47
Trinder Rd. N19 BX33 47
Trinder Rd. Barn. BQ25 28
Trindles Rd. Red. BX71 121
Tring Av. W5 BL40 55
Tring Av. Sthl. BE39 54
Tring Av. Wem. BM36 55
Tring Clo. Ilf. CM32 49
Tring Clo. Rom. CW28 42
Tring Gdns. Rom. CW28 42
Tring Grn. Rom. CW28 42
Tringham Clo. Cher. AU56 91
Tring Rd. Berk. AO11 7
Tring Wk. Rom. CW28 42
Trinidad Gdns. Dag. CS36 59
Trinidad St. E14 CD40 57
Trinity Av. N2 BT31 47
Trinity Av. Enf. CA25 30
Trinity Ch. Rd. SW13 BP43 65
Trinity Church Sq. SE1 BZ41 4
Trinity Church Sq. SE1 BZ41 67
Trinity Cl. SE13 CF45 67
Wisteria Rd.
Trinity Clo. NW3 BT35 47
Hampstead High St.
Trinity Clo. Brom. CK54 88
Trinity Clo. Houns. BE45 64
Trinity Clo. Nthwd. BB29 35
Trinity Clo. Stai. AX46 73
Trinity Clo. Sth. Croy. CA58 96
Trinity Cotts. Rich. BL45 65
Trinity Rd.
Trinity Ct. N1 CA37 2
Trinity Ct. N1 CA37 57
Trinity Cres. SW17 BU48 76
Trinity Est. SE8 CD42 67
Trinity Gdns. E16 CG39 58
Trinity Gdns. SW9 BX45 66
Trinity Grn. E1 CC38 57
Trinity Gro. SE10 CF44 67
Trinity La. Wal. Cr. CD19 21
Trinity Pl. Bexh. CQ45 69
Trinity Pl. Wind. AO44 61
Trinity Ri. SW2 BY47 76
Trinity Rd. N2 BT31 47
Trinity Rd. N22 BX29 38
Trinity Rd. SW17 BT46 76
Trinity Rd. SW18 BT46 76
Trinity Rd. SW19 BS50 76
Trinity Rd. Ilf. CM31 49
Trinity Rd. Rich. BL45 65
Trinity Rd. Sthl. BE40 54
Trinity Sq. EC3 CA40 4
Trinity Sq. EC3 CA40 57
Trinity St. E16 CG39 58
Trinity St. SE1 BZ41 4
Trinity St. SE1 BZ41 67
Trinity St. Enf. BZ23 30
Trinity Wk. NW3 BT36 56
College Cres.
Trinity Way W3 BO40 55
Trio Pl. SE1 BZ41 4
Trio Pl. SE1 BZ41 67
Tripps Hill Clo. Ch. St. G. AQ27 34
Tripton Rd. Harl. CN11 13
Trisian Sq. SE3 CG45 68
Tristram Clo. E17 CF31 48
Tristram Rd. Brom. CG49 78
Triton Sq. NW1 BW38 1
Triton Sq. NW1 BW38 56
Triton Way, Hem. H. AY12 8
Tritton Av. Croy. BX56 95
Tritton Rd. SE21 BZ48 77
Triumph Clo. Hayes BA43 63
Trodd's La. Guil. AU70 118
Trojan Way Croy. BX55 86
Trolling Down Hill, Dart. CY48 80
Tronsay Wk. N1 BZ36 57
Marquess Est.
Troon St. E1 CD39 57
Trosley Av. Grav. DG48 81
Trosley Rd. Belv. CR43 69
Trossachs Rd. SE22 CA46 77
Trothy Rd. SE1 CB42 4
Trothy Rd. SE1 CB42 67
Trots La. West. CM67 115
Trotsworth Av. Vir. W. AS52 82
Trotters Bottom Barn. BP22 28
Trotters La. Wok. AQ59 91
Trotters Rd. Harl. CO12 14
Trott Rd. N10 BU29 38
Trott St. SW11 BT44 66
Troughton Rd. SE7 CH42 68
Troutbeck Rd. E14 CD44 67
Trout La. West Dr. AX40 53
Trout Rise, Rick. AW24 26
Trout Rd. West Dr. AX40 53
Troutstream Way, Rick. AW24 26
Trouville Rd. SW4 BW46 76
Trowbridge Est. E9 CD35 48
Trowbridge Rd. E9 CD36 57
Trowbridge Rd. Rom. CV29 42
Trowers Way, Red. BV69 121
Trowley Rise, Wat. BB19 17
Trowlock Av. Tedd. BK50 74
Trowlock Way, Tedd. BK50 74
Broom Rd.
Troy Ct. SE18 CL42 68
Troy Ct. W8 BS41 66
Troy Rd. SE19 BZ50 77
Troy Town SE15 CB45 67
Nutbrook St.
Trucks Alley Swan. CR51 89
Truesdale Dr. Uxb. AX31 44
Trulock Ct. N17 CB29 39
Trulock Rd. N17 CB29 39
Truman's Rd. N16 CA35 48
Truman St. SE16 CB41 67
Trumper's Way W7 BH41 64
Trumper Way, Uxb. AX37 53
Trumpetshill Rd. Reig. BP71 120
Trumpington Dr. St. Alb. BG15 9
Trumpington Rd. E7 CG35 49
Trumpsgreen Av. Vir. W. AR53 82
Trumps Green Clo. Vir. W. AS53 82
Trumpsgreen Rd.
Trumpsgreen Rd. Vir. W. AR53 82
Trumpsgreen Rd. Vir. W. AR54 82
Trumps Mill La. Vir. W. AS53 82
Trump St. EC2 BZ39 2
Trump St. EC2 BZ39 57
King St.
Trundlers Way Bush. BH26 36
Trundle St. SE1 BZ41 4
Trundle St. SE1 BZ41 67
Weller St.
Trundley's Rd. SE8 CC42 67
Trundley's Ter. SE8 CC42 67
Truro Gdns. Ilf. CK33 49
Truro Rd. E17 CD32 48
Truro Rd. N22 BX29 38
Truro Rd. Grav. DH48 81
Truro St. NW3 BV36 56
Truro Wk. Rom. CV29 42
Truro Way, Hayes BB38 53
Truslove Rd. SE27 BY49 76
Trussley Rd. W6 BQ41 65
Trustees Wy. Uxb. AV32 34
Trustings Clo. Esher BJ57 93
Trustons Gdns. Horn. CU33 50
Trycewell La. Sev. DB64 108
Tryfan Clo. Ilf. CJ32 49
Tryon St. SW3 BU42 3
Tryon St. SW3 BU42 66
Trys Hill, Cher. AT55 82
Tuam Rd. SE18 CM43 68
Tubbenden Clo. Orp. CN55 88
Tubbenden Dr. Orp. CM56 97
Tubbenden La. Orp. CM56 97
Tubbenden La. South Orp. CM56 97
Tubbs Rd. NW10 BO37 55
Tubs Hill, Sev. CU65 107
Tubwell Rd. Slou. AQ37 52
Tucker St. Wat. BD25 27
Tuckley Gro. Wok. AV65 100
Tuck Rd. Rain. CU36 59
Tudor Av. Hamptn. BF50 74
Tudor Av. Rom. CU31 50
Tudor Av. Wal. Cr. CB19 21
Tudor Av. Wat. BD22 27
Tudor Av. Wor. Pk. BP55 85
Tudor Clo. NW3 BU35 47
Tudor Clo. NW7 BP29 37
Tudor Clo. NW9 BN34 46
Tudor Clo. SW2 BX46 76
Tudor Clo. Ashf. AY49 73
Tudor Clo. Bans. BR61 103
Tudor Clo. Brwd. DD25 122
Tudor Clo. Chess. BL56 94
Tudor Clo. Chig. CL27 40
Tudor Clo. Chis. CK51 88
Tudor Clo. Cob. BE60 93
Tudor Clo. Couls. BY62 104
Tudor Clo. Dart. CU46 79
Tudor Clo. Lthd. BE65 102
Tudor Clo. Pnr. BC32 44
Tudor Clo. Sth. Croy. CB61 105
Tudor Clo. Sutt. BQ57 94
Tudor Clo. Wal. Cr. CB19 21
Tudor Clo. Wall. BW57 95
Tudor Clo. Wdf. Grn. CH28 40
Tudor Clo. Welw. BP5 5
Tudor Ct. E17 CD32 48
Tudor Ct. SE9 CK45 68
Tudor Ct. N. Wem. BM35 46
Tudor Ct. S. Wem. BM35 46
Tudor Cres. Ilf. CL29 40
Tudor Cres. Sev. CV61 108
Tudor Dr. Kings. on T. BK49 74
Tudor Dr. Mord. BQ53 85
Tudor Dr. Rom. CU31 50
Tudor Dr. Sev. CV61 108
Tudor Dr. Walt. BD54 84
Tudor Dr. Wat. BD22 27
Tudor Est. NW10 BM38 55
Tudor Gdns. NW9 BN34 46
Tudor Gdns. SW13 BO45 65
Treen Av.
Tudor Gdns. W3 BM39 55
Tudor Gdns. Rom. CU31 50
Tudor Gdns. Twick. BH47 74
Tudor Gdns. Upmin. CY34 51
Tudor Gdns. W. Wick. CF55 87
Tudor Gro. E9 CC36 57
Tudor Hill, Hem. H. AX14 8
Tudor Parade, Rick. AW26 35
Berry La.
Tudor Pl. W1 BW39 1
Tudor Pl. W1 BW39 56
Gresse St.
Tudor Pl. Mitch. BU50 76
Tudor Rd. E4 CE29 39
Tudor Rd. E6 CJ37 58
Tudor Rd. E9 CB37 57
Tudor Rd. N9 CB26 39
Tudor Rd. SE19 CA50 77
Tudor Rd. SE25 CB53 87
Tudor Rd. Ashf. BA50 73
Tudor Rd. Bark. CN37 58
Tudor Rd. Barn. BS24 29
Tudor Rd. Beck. CE52 87
Tudor Rd. Brox. CD14 12
Tudor Rd. Hamptn. BF50 74
Tudor Rd. Har. BG30 36
Tudor Rd. Hayes BA39 53
Tudor Rd. Houns. BG45 64
Tudor Rd. Kings. on T. BM50 75
Tudor Rd. Pnr. BD30 36
Tudor Rd. St. Alb. BH11 9
Tudor Rd. Sthl. BE40 54
Tudor Sq. Hayes BA39 53
Tudor St. EC4 BY39 56
Tudor St. EC4 BY40 4
Tudor Wk. Bex. CQ46 79
Tudor Walk, Lthd. BH63 102
Tudor Wk. Wat. BD22 27
Tudor Way N14 BW26 38
Tudor Way W3 BL41 65
Tudor Way Orp. CM53 88
Tudor Way, Rick. AW26 35
Tudor Way, Uxb. AZ36 53
Tudor Way, Wal. Abb. CF20 21
Tudor Way, West Dr. AY42 63
Tudor Way, Wind. AM44 61
Tudor Well Clo. Stan. BJ28 36
Old Church La.
Tudway Rd. SE3 CJ45 68
Tudway Rd. SE9 CJ45 68
Tufnail Rd. Dart. CW46 80
Tufnell Park Rd. N7 BW35 47
Tufter Rd. Chig. CN28 40
Tufton Gdns. E. Mol. BF51 84
Tufton Rd. E4 CE28 39
Tufton St. SW1 BW41 3
Tufton St. SW1 BW41 66
Tugela Rd. Croy. BZ53 87
Tugela St. SE6 CD48 77
Tuilerie St. E2 CB37 2
Tulip Clo. Brwd. DA25 33
Poppy Clo.
Tulip Clo. Rom. CV29 42
Tulip Ct. Pnr. BD31 45
Nursery Rd.
Tullerie St. E2 CB37 57
Tulse Clo. Beck. CF52 87
Tulse Hill SW2 BY46 76
Tulse Hl. Est. SW2 BY46 76
Tulsemere Rd. SE27 BZ48 77
Tumber St. Epsom BN66 112
Tumblefield Rd. Sev. DC60 99
Tumbler Rd. Harl. CO11 14
Tumblewood Rd. Bans. BR61 103
Tumbling Way, Walt. BC53 83
Tuncombe Rd. N18 CA28 39
Tunfield Rd. Hodd. CE10 12
Tunis Rd. W12 BP40 55
Tunley Rd. NW10 BO37 55
Tunley Rd. SW17 BV47 76
Tunmarsh La. E13 CH38 58
Tunmers End, Ger. Cr. AR30 34
Tunnel Av. SE10 CF40 57
Tunnel Gdns. N11 BW29 38
Tunnel Wood Clo. Wat. BB22 26
Tunnel Wood Rd. Wat. BB22 66
Tunnmead, Harl. CO10 6
Tunsgate, Guil. AR71 118
Tuns La. Slou. AO40 61
Tunstall Av. Ilf. CO29 41
Tunstall Clo. Orp. CN56 97
Tunstall Rd. SW9 BX45 66
Tunstall Rd. Croy. CA54 87
Tunstall Wk. Brent. BK42 64
Ealing Rd.
Tunworth Clo. NW9 BN32 46
Tunworth Cres. SW15 BO46 75
Tupwood La. Cat. CB66 114
Tupwood Scrubs La. Cat. CB67 114
Tures Clo. Uxb. AZ38 53
Turenne Cl. SW18 BT45 66
Garrick Cl.
Turfhouse La. Wok. AP58 91
Turin Ct. Egh. AR49 72
Turin Rd. N9 CC26 39
Turin St. E2 CB38 2
Turin St. E2 CB38 57
Turkey St. Enf. CB21 30
Turks Head Yd. EC1 BY39 2
Turks Head Yd. EC1 BY38 56
Turnhill St.
Turk's Row SW3 BU42 3
Turk's Row SW3 BU42 66
Turle Rd. N4 BX33 47
Turle Rd. SW16 BW51 86
Turlewray Clo. N19 BX33 47
Turley Clo. E15 CG37 58
Turmore Dale Welw. G. C. BQ8 5
Turnagain La. EC4 CM39 58
Farringdon St.
Turnagain La. Dart. CU48 79
Turnage Rd. Dag. CQ33 50
Turnant Rd. N17 BZ30 39
Lordship La.
Turnberry Way Orp. CM54 88
Turnbull Clo. Green. CZ47 80
Turner Av. N15 CA31 48
Turner Av. Mitch. BU51 86
Turner Av. Twick. BG48 74
Turner Clo. NW11 BS32 47
Turner Clo. Hayes BA37 53
Turner Dr. NW11 BS32 47
Turner Rd. E17 CF31 48
Turner Rd. Bush. BG24 27
Turner Rd. Dart. DA48 80
Turner Rd. Edg. BL30 37
Turner Rd. N. Mal. BN54 85
Turner Rd. West. CJ59 97
Turners Clo. Ong. CW18 24
Turner's Hill, Hem. H. AY14 8
Turners Hill, Wal. Cr. CC18 21
Turners La. Walt. BC57 92
Turner Sq. N1 CA37 2
Turners Rd. E3 CD39 57
Turner St. E1 CB39 57
Turner St. E16 CG39 58
Turners Way NW11 BT33 47
Wildwood Rd.
Turner's Wood NW11 BT33 47
Wildwood Rd.
Turners Wood Dr. Ch. St. G. AR27 34
Turneville Rd. W14 BR43 65
Turney Rd. SE21 BZ47 77
Turney Rd.. W14 BR43 65
Turnham Grn. Ter. W4 BO42 65
Turnham Rd. SE4 CD46 77
Turnmill St. EC1 BY38 56
Turnmill St. EC1 BY39 2
Turnoak Av. Wok. AS63 100
Turnoak La. Wok. AS63 100
Turnpike Cl. SE14 CD43 67
Amersham Vale
Turnpike Ct. Bexh. CP45 69
Crook Log
Turnpike Dr. Orp. CP58 98
Turnpike La. N8 BX31 47
Turn Pike La. Uxb. AY37 53
Turnpike Link Croy. CA55 87
Turnpin La. SE10 CF43 67
King William Wk.
Turnstone Clo. Sth. Croy. CC58 96
Turnstones, The Wat. BE21 27
Turnville Rd. W14 BR44 65
Turp Av. Grays DE41 71
Turpentine La. SW1 BV42 3
Turpentine La. SW1 BV42 66
Sutherland St.
Turpin Av. Rom. CR29 41
Turpin Estate E13 CH37 58
Turpington Clo. Brom. CK54 88
Turpington La. Brom. CK54 88
Turpin's La. Wdf. Grn. CK28 40
Turpin Road, Felt. BB46 73
Staines Rd.
Turpin Way N19 BW33 47
Ashbrook Rd.
Turpin Way Wall. BV57 95
Turquand St. SE17 BZ42 4
Turquand St. SE17 BZ42 67
Turret Gro. SW4 BW45 66
Turtle Rd. SW17 BT48 76
Turton Mkt. Wem. BL35 46
Turton Rd.
Turton Rd. Wem. BL35 46
Turton Way, Slou. AO41 61
Turve St. E2 CA38 2
Turville St. E2 CA38 57
Old Nichol St.
Tuscan Rd. SE18 CM42 68
Tuskar St. SE10 CG42 68
Tuttlebee La. Buck. H. CH27 40
Tuxford Clo. Borwd. BL22 28
Twedwell Clo. Brom. CK52 88
Tweedale Rd. Cars. BT54 86
Tweed Glen Rom. CS29 41
Tweed Grn. Rom. CS29 41
Tweed La. Bet. BM72 120
Tweedmouth Rd. E13 CH37 58
Tweed Way Rom. CS29 41
Tweedy Rd. Brom. CH51 88
Twelve Acre Clo. Lthd. BE65 102
Twelve Acres, Welw G. C. BR9 5
Twelve Trees Cr. E3 CF38 57
Devas St.
Twentyman Clo. Wdf. Grn. CH28 40
Twickenham Br. Rich. BK46 74
Twickenham Br. Twick. BK46 74
Twickenham Clo. Croy. BX55 86
Twickenham Gdns. Grnf. BJ35 45
Twickenahm Gdns. Har. BH29 36
Twickenham Rd. E11 CF34 48
Twickenham Rd. Felt. BE49 74
Twickenham Rd. Islw. BJ46 74
Twickenham Rd. Rich. BK45 64
Twickenham Rd. Tedd. BJ49 74
Twigs Clo. Erith CT43 69
Twilley St. SW18 BS47 76
Twinches La. Slou. AN40 61
Twineham Grn. N12 BS28 38
Twining Av. Twick. BG48 74
Twinn Rd. NW7 BR29 37
Twinoaks, Cob. BF60 93
Twisden Rd. NW5 BV35 47
Twitchells La. Beac. AP29 34
Twitton Bungalows Sev. CA52 107
Twitton La. Sev. CS61 107
Two Acres, Welw G. C. BR9 5
Two Dells Lane, Chesh. AP16 16
Two Waters Rd. Hem. H. AX15 8
Twybridge Way NW10 BN36 55
Twyford Abbey Rd. NW10 BL38 55
Twyford Av. N2 BU31 47
Twyford Av. W3 BM40 55
Twyford Cres. W3 BM40 55
Twyford Pl. WC2 BX39 2
Twyford Pl. WC2 BX39 56
Kingsway

Twyford Rd. Cars. BT54 86
Twyford Rd. Har. BF33 45
Twyford Rd. Ilf. CM35 49
Twyford St. N1 BX37 2
Twyford St. N1 BX37 56
Twysdens Ter. Hat. BQ15 10
Station Rd.
Tyas Rd. E16 CG38 58
Tybalds Est. WC1 BX39 2
Tybenham Rd. SW19 BR52 85
Tyberry Rd. Enf. CB24 30
Tyburn La. Har. BH33 45
Tyburns, The Brwd. DE27 122
Tyburn Way W1 BU40 3
Tycehurst Gdns. Ilf. CM35 49
Tycehurst Hill Loug. CK24 31
Tychbourne Dri. Guil. AU69 118
Tydcombe Rd. Warl. CC63 105
Tye Green Village Harl. CN12 13
Tye La. Epsom BN67 112
Tye La. Orp. CM56 97
Tyer's Est. SE1 CA41 4
Tyer's Gate SE1 CA41 4
Tyers St. SE11 BX42 4
Tyers St. SE11 BX42 66
Tyers Ter. SE11 BX42 4
Tyers Ter. SE11 BX42 66
Tyeshurst Clo. SE2 CQ42 69
Tykeswater La. Borwd. BK23 27
Tylecroft Rd. SW16 BX51 86
Tyle Green Horn. CW31 51
Tylehost, Guil. AQ68 109
Tyler Gro. Dart. CW45 70
Spielman Rd.
Tylers Causeway, Hert. BW14 11
Tylers Clo. Gdse. CB68 114
Tylers Clo. Kings L. AY18 17
Tylers Clo. Loug. CK26 40
Tylers Est. SE1 CA41 67
Tylers Gate SE1 CA41 67
Tylers Gate, Har. BL32 46
Tylers Grn. Rd. Swan. CS53 89
Tylers Hill Rd. Ches. AP18 16
Tylers La. Harl. CJ13 13
Tylers Rd. Harl. CJ13 13
Tyler St. SE10 CG42 68
Tylers Way Wat. BG24 27
Tylney Av. SE19 CA49 77
Tylney Croft, Harl. CM12 13
Tylney Rd. E7 CJ35 49
Tylney Rd. Brom. CJ51 88
Tyndale La. N1 BY36 56
Upper St.
Tyndall Rd. E10 CF34 48
Tyndall Rd. Well. CN45 68
Tyne Gdns. S. Ock. CW40 60
Tyne Clo. Upmin. CY32 51
Tynedale, St. Alb. BL17 19
Thamesdale
Tynedale Rd. Bet. BM72 120
Tyneham Rd. SW11 BV44 66
Tynemouth Dr. Enf. CB22 30
Tynemouth Rd. N15 CA31 48
Tynemouth Rd. Mitch. BV50 76
Tynemouth St. SW6 BT44 66
Tyne Rd. Ilf. CM34 49
Tynley Gro. Guil. AR67 109
Type St. E2 CC37 57
Tyrawley Rd. SW6 BS44 66
Tyrell Clo. Har. BH35 45
Tyrell Gdns. Wind. AM45 61
Tyrell Rise Brwd. DB28 42
Chindits La.
Tyrells Clo. Upmin. CX34 51
Tyrone Rd. E6 CK37 58
Tyron Way, Sid. CN49 78
Tyrrell Av. Well. CO46 79
Tyrrell Rd. SE22 CB45 67
Tyrrells Hall Clo. Grays DE42 71
Tyrrells Wood Dr. Lthd. BL65 103
Tyrrel Way NW9 BO33 46
Tyrwhitt Av. Guil. AQ68 109
Tyrwhitt Rd. SE4 CE45 67
Tysea Clo. Harl. CN12 13
Tysea Hill, Rom. CT26 41
Tysea Rd. Harl. CN12 13
Tysoe Av. Enf. CD22 30
Tysoe St. EC1 BY38 2
Tysoe St. EC1 BY38 56
Tyson Rd. SE23 CC47 77
Tyssen Pl. E8 BT36 56
Ramsgate St.
Tyssen Rd. N16 CA34 48
Stoke Newington High St.
Tyssen St. E8 CA36 57
Tytherton Rd. N19 BW34 47
Tyttenhanger La. St. Alb. BK14 9
Tyttenhanger La. St. Alb. BL15 10
Uamvar St. E14 CE39 57
Uckfield Gro. Mitch. BV51 86
Uckfield Rd. Enf. CC22 30
Udall Gdns. Rom. CR29 41
Udall St. SW1 BW42 3
Udall St. SW1 BW42 66
Vincent Sq.
Udney Pk. Rd. Tedd. BJ50 74
Uffington Rd. NW10 BP37 55
Uffington Rd. SE27 BY49 76
Ufford Clo. Har. BF29 36
Ufford Rd. Har. BF29 36
Ufford St. SE1 BY41 4
Ufford St. SE1 BY41 66
Ufton Gro. N1 BZ36 57
Ufton Rd. N1 BZ36 2
Ufton Rd. N1 BZ36 57
Ullathorne Rd. SW16 BW49 76
Ulleswater Rd. N14 BX28 38
Ullswater Clo. SW15 BN49 75
Ullswater Clo. Brom. CG50 78
Ullswater Clo. Hayes BB37 53
Ullswater Cres. Couls. BW61 104
Ullswater Rd. SE27 BY48 76
Ullswater Rd. SW13 BP43 65
Ullswater Rd. Hem. H. AZ14 8
Ullswater Way, Horn. CU35 50
Ulstan Clo. Cat. CE65 105
Ulster Gdns. N13 BZ28 39
Ulster Pl. NW1 BV38 56
Ulundi Rd. SE3 CG43 68
Ulva Rd. SW15 BQ45 65
Ravenna Rd.
Ulverdale Rd. SW10 BT43 66
Ulverscroft Rd. SE22 CA46 77
Ulverstone Rd. SE27 BY48 76
Ulverston Rd. E17 CF30 39
Ulwyn Av. Wey. AY60 92
Ulysses Rd. NW6 BR35 46
Umberston St. E1 CB39 57
Umbria St. SW15 BP46 75
Umfreville Rd. N4 BY32 47
Ummer Gro. Borwd. BK25 27
Underacres Clo. Hem. H. AZ13 8
Underbridge Way Enf. CD24 30
Undercliff Rd. SE13 CE45 67
Underhill Barn. BS25 29
Underhill Pk. Rd. Reig. BS69 121
Underhill Rd. SE22 CB46 77
Underne Av. N14 BV27 38
Underriver House Rd. Sev. CX68 117
Undershaft EC3 CA39 57
St. Mary Axe
Undershaw Rd. Brom. CG48 78
Underwood Croy. CF57 96
Underwood Rd. E1 CB38 2
Underwood Rd. E1 CB38 57
Underwood Rd. E4 CE28 39
Underwood Rd. Cat. CA66 114
Underwood Row N1 BZ38 2
Underwood Row N1 BZ38 57
Underwood St. E1 CB38 2
Underwood St. N1 BZ38 2
Underwood St. N1 BZ38 57
Underwood, The SE9 CK48 78
Undine St. SW17 BU49 76
Uneeda Dr. Grnf. BG37 54
Union Cotts. E15 CG36 58
Union Ct. E15 CF37 57
Union Ct. EC2 CA39 2
Broad St.
Union Ct. EC2 CA39 57
Wormwood St.
Union Ct. Ilf. CL34 49
Ilford Hill
Union Gro. SW8 BW44 66
Union La. Islw. BJ44 64
Park Rd.
Union Rd. E17 CD32 48
Union Rd. N11 BW29 38
Union Rd. SW4 BW44 66
Union Rd. SW8 BW44 66
Union Rd. Brom. CJ53 88
Union Rd. Croy. BZ54 87
Union Rd. Nthlt. BF37 54
Union Rd. Wem. BL36 55
Union Row N18 CB29 39
Union Sq. N1 BZ37 2
Union Sq. N1 BZ37 57
Union St. E15 CF37 57
Union St. SE1 BY41 4
Union St. SE1 BY41 66
Union St. Barn. BR24 28
Union St. Hem. H. AX12 8
Union St. Kings. on T. BK51 84
Union Wk. E2 CA38 2
Union Wk. E2 CA38 57
Unity Rd. Enf. CC22 30
Unity Way SE18 CJ41 68
University Cl. NW9 BO29 37
Rivington Cres.
University Pl. Erith CR43 69
Belmont Rd.
University Pl. Erith CR44 69
Becton Pl.
University Rd. SW19 BT50 76
University St. WC1 BW38 1
University St. WC1 BW38 56
Unwin Av. Felt. BA46 73
Unwin Clo. SE15 CB43 67
Unwin Rd. Islw. BH45 64
Upbrook Ms. W2 BT39 1
Upbrook Ms. W2 BT39 56
Upcerne Rd. SW10 BT43 66
Kings Rd.
Upchurch Clo. SE20 CB50 77
Woodbin Gro.
Upcroft, Wind. AN45 61
Upcroft Av. Edg. BN28 37
Updale Clo. Pot. B. BQ20 19
Updale Rd. Sid. CN49 78
Upfield, Croy. CB55 87
Upfield Rd. W7 BH38 54
Uphall Rd. Ilf. CL34 49
Upham Pk. Rd. W4 BO42 65
Uphill Dr. NW7 BO28 37
Uphill Dr. NW9 BN32 46
Uphill Gro. NW7 BO28 37
Uphill Rd. NW7 BO28 37
Upland Ct. Rd. Rom. CW30 42
Upland Rd. E13 CG38 58
Upland Rd. SE22 CB46 77
Upland Rd. Bexh. CQ45 69
Upland Rd. Cat. CE63 105
Upland Rd. Epp. CM16 22
Upland Rd. Sth. Croy. BZ56 96
Upland Rd. Sutt. BT57 95
Uplands SW16 BY49 76
Uplands, Ash. BK63 102
Uplands, Beck. CE51 87
Uplands, Rick. AY25 26
Uplands, Welw. G. C. BQ6 5
Uplands Av. E17 CC30 39
Uplands Clo. SW14 BM46 75
Uplands Clo. Ger. Cr. AS33 43
Uplands Clo. Sev. CT65 107
Uplands Ct. N21 BY26 38
Uplands Dr. Hat. BS16 20
Uplands End, Wdf. Grn. CK29 40
Uplands Pk. Rd. Enf. BY24 29
Uplands Rd. N8 BX32 47
Uplands Rd. Barn. BV26 38
Uplands Rd. Brwd. DC28 122
Uplands Rd. Ken. BZ61 105
Uplands Rd. Orp. CO54 89
Uplands Rd. Rom. CP31 50
Uplands Rd. Wdf. Grn. CK29 40
Uplands, The Ger. Cr. AS33 43
Uplands, The Loug. CK24 31
Uplands, The Ruis. BC33 44
Uplands, The St. Alb. BE18 18
Uplands Way N21 BY25 29
Uplands Way, Sev. CT65 107
Upland Way, Epsom BQ62 103
Upminster Rd. Horn. CW34 51
Upminster Rd. N. Rain. CV38 60
Upminster Rd. S. Rain. CU38 59
Upney La. Bark. CN35 49
Upnor Way SE17 CA42 4
Upnor Way SE17 CA42 67
Uppark Dr. Ilf. CM32 49
Upr. Abbey Rd. Belv. CQ42 69
Upr. Addison Gdns. W14 BR41 65
Upr. Ashlyns Rd. Berk. AQ13 7
Upr. Austin Lodge Rd. Eyns. CV56 99
Upr. Av. Grav. DF51 81
Upr. Bardsey Wk. N1 BZ36 57
Marquess Est.
Upr. Barn, Hem. H. AY15 8
Upr. Belgrave St. SW1 BV41 3
Upr. Belgrave St. SW1 BV41 66
Upr. Berkeley St. W1 BU39 1
Upr. Berkeley St. W1 BU39 56
Upr. Beulah Hl. SE19 CA51 87
Upr. Bray Rd. Maid. AH42 61
Upr. Brentwood Rd. Rom. CV31 51
Upr. Bridge Rd. Red. BU70 121
Upr. Brighton Rd. Surb. BK53 84
Upr. Brockley Rd. SE4 CD45 67
Upr. Brook St. W1 BV40 3
Upr. Brook St. W1 BV40 56
Upr. Butts, Brent. BK43 64
Upr. Caldy Wk. N1 BZ36 57
Marquess Est.
Upr. Camelford Walk W11 BQ40 55
Lancaster Road
Upr. Cavendish Av. N3 BS31 47
Upr. Cheyne Row SW3 BU43 66
Upr. Church Hill Grn. CZ46 80
Upr. Clapton Rd. E5 CB33 48
Upr. Clarendon Walk W11 BQ40 55
Lancaster Road
Upr. Corner Pl. Ch. St. G. AQ27 34
Upr. Cornsland, Brwd. DB27 42
Upr. Court Rd. Cat. CE65 105
Upr. Court Rd. Epsom BN59 94
Upr. Culver Rd. St. Alb. BH12 9
Upr. Dagnal St. St. Alb. BG13 9
Upr. Drayton Pl. Croy. BY55 86
Upr. Dr. West. CJ62 106
Upr. Edgeborough Rd. Guil. AS71 118
Upr. Elmers End Rd. Beck. CD52 87
Upr. Fairfield Rd. Lthd. BJ64 102
Upr. Farm Rd. BE52 84
Upr. Field Rd. Welw. G. C. BR9 5
Upr. Fosters NW4 BQ32 46
Upr. George St. Chesh. OP18 16
Upr. Green E. Mitch. BU51 86
Upr. Green La. Ton. DB68 117
Upr. Green Rd.
Upr. Green Rd. Ton. DB68 117
Upr. Green, W. Mitch. BU51 86
Upr. Grosvenor St. W1 BV40 3
Upr. Grenfell Wk. W11 BQ40 55
Lancaster Rd.
Upr. Grosvenor St. W1 BV40 56
Upr. Grotto Rd. Twick. BH48 74
Upr. Ground SE1 BY40 4
Upr. Ground SE1 BY40 56
Upr. Gro. SE25 CA52 87
Upr. Grove Rd. Belv. CQ43 69
Upr. Guildown Rd. Guil. AQ72 118
Upr. Gulland Wk. N1 BZ36 57
Marquess Est.
Upr. Haliford Rd. Shep. BB52 83
Upr. Hall Pk. Berk. AR13 7
Upr Ham Rd. Rich. BK49 74
Upr. Handa Wk. N1 BZ36 57
Marquess Est.
Upr. Harley St. NW1 BV38 1
Upr. Harley St. NW1 BV38 56
Upr. Heath Rd. St. Alb. BH12 9
Upr. High St. Epsom BO60 94
Upr. Highway, Kings L. BA19 17
Upr. Highway, Wat. BA20 17
Upr. Hill Rise, Rick. AW25 26
Upr. Hill Vw. Rd. Pnr. BE29 36
Upr. Hitch, Wat. BE27 36
Upr. Holly Hill Rd. Belv. CR42 69
Upr. James St. W1 BW40 3
Upr. James St. W1 BW40 56
Beak St.
Upr. John St. W1 BW40 56
Beak St.
Upr. Lattimore Rd. St. Alb. BH13 9
Upr. Lismore Wk. N1 BZ36 57
Marquess Est.
Upr. Mall W6 BP42 65
Upr. March La. Hodd. CE12 12
Upr. Marlborough Rd. St. Alb. BH13 9
Upr. Marsh SE1 BX41 4
Upr. Marsh SE1 BX41 66
Upr. Mealines, Harl. CO12 14
Upr. Montagu St. W1 BU39 1
Upr. Montagu St. W1 BU39 56
Upr. Mulgrave Rd. Sutt. BR57 94
Upr. North St. E14 CE39 57
Upr. Paddock Rd. Wat. BE25 27
Upr. Palace Rd. E. Mol. BG52 84
Upr. Pk. Harl. CL10 6
Upr. Pk. Loug. CJ24 31
Upr. Pk. Rd. N11 BV28 38
Upr. Pk. Rd. NW3 BU35 47
Upr. Pk. Rd. Belv. CR42 69
Upr. Pk. Rd. Brom. CH51 88
Upr. Park Rd. Kings. on T. BM50 75
Upr. Phillimore Gdns. W8 BS41 66
Upr. Pillory Downs, Cars. BV60 95
Upr. Pines, Bans. BU62 104
Upr. Rainham Rd. Horn. CT33 50
Upr. Ramsey Wk. N1 BZ36 57
Marquess Est.
Upr. Richmond Rd. SW14 BM45 65
Upr. Richmond Rd. SW15 BM45 65
Upr. Richmond Rd. Rich. BM45 65
Upr. Rd. E13 CH38 58
Upr. Rd. Uxb. AU33 43
Upr. Rd. Wall. BW56 95
Upr. Rose Hill, Dor. BJ72 119
Upr. Ryle, Brwd. DA26 42
Upr. St. Martin's La. WC2 BX40 4
Upr. St. Martin's La. WC2 BX40 56
Long Acre
Upr. Sales, Hem. H. AV14 7
Upr. Selsdon Rd. Sth. Croy. CA57 96
Upr. Sheppey Wk. N1 BZ36 57
Marquess Est.
Upr. Sheridan Rd. Belv. CR42 69
Coleman Rd.
Upr. Shirley Rd. Croy. CC55 87
Upr. Shot. Welw. G. C. BS7 5
Upr. Spring La. Sev. DA64 108
Upr. Sq. Islw. BJ45 64
Upr. Staithe W4 BN44 65
Upr. Station Rd. Rad. BJ21 27
Upr. Stoneyfield, Harl. CL11 13
Upr. St. N1 BY37 2
Upr. St. N1 BY37 56
Upr. Sunbury Rd. Hamptn. BE51 84
Upr. Sutton La. Houns. BF44 64
Upr. Swaines, Epp. CN18 22
Upr. Tail, Wat. BE27 36
Upr. Talbot Wk. W11 BQ40 55
Lancaster Rd.
Upr. Teddington Rd. Kings. on T. BK50 74
Upr. Teddington Rd. Tedd. BK50 74
Upr. Ter. NW3 BT34 47
Windmill Hill
Upr. Thames St. EC4 BY40 4
Upr. Thames St. EC4 BY40 56
Upr. Tollington Pk. N4 BY33 47
Upperton Rd.Rd. E13 CJ38 58
Upperton Rd. Guil. AR71 118
Upperton Rd. Sid. CN49 78
Upr. Tooting Pk. SW17 BU48 76
Upr. Tooting Rd. SW17 BU49 76
Upr. Town Rd. Grnf. BF38 54
Upr. Tulse Hill SW2 BX47 76
Upr. Walthamstow Rd. E17 CF31 48
Upr. West St. Reig. BR70 120
Upr. Wickham La. Well. CO45 69
Upr. Wimpole St. W1 BV39 1
Upr. Wimpole St. W1 BV39 56
Upr. Woburn Pl. WC1 BW38 1
Upr. Woburn Pl. WC1 BW38 56
Upr. Wood, Harl. CK12 13
Uppingham Av. Stan. BJ30 36
Upsdell Av. N13 BY29 38
Upshire Rd. Wal. Abb. CG19 22
Upshire Rd. Wal. Abb. CH20 22
Upshot La. Wok. AV62 100
Upstall St. SE5 BY44 66
Upton Av. E7 CH36 58
Upton Av. St. Alb. BG13 9
Upton Clo. Bex. CQ46 79
Upton Clo. St. Alb. AP41 62
Upton Pk.
Upton Clo. St. Alb. BG16 18
Upton Clo. Slou. AP41 62
Upton Pk.
Upton Ct. Rd. Slou. AQ41 62
Upton Dene, Sutt. BS57 95
Upton Gdns. Har. BJ32 45
Upton Gro. Slou. AP41 62
Upton La. E7 CH37 58
Upton Lo. Clo. Bush. BG26 36
Upton Pk. Slou. AP41 62
Upton Pk. Rd. E7 CH36 58
Upton Rd. N18 CB28 39
Upton Rd. SE18 CM43 68
Upton Rd. Bexh. CQ45 69
Upton Rd. Houns. BF45 64
Upton Rd. Slou. AQ41 62
Upton Rd. Th. Hth. BZ51 87
Upton Rd. Wat. BC24 26
Upton Rd. S. Bex. CQ45 69
Upway N12 BU29 38
Upway, Ger. Cr. AS30 34
Upwood Rd. SE12 CG46 78
Upwood Rd. SW16 BX51 86
Uranus Rd. Hem. H. AY12 8
Urban Av. Horn. CV34 51
Urlwin St. SE5 BZ43 67
Urlwin Wk. SW9 BY44 66
Myatts Fields Dev.
Urmston Dr. SW19 BR47 75
Ursula St. SW11 BU44 66
Urswick Gdns. Dag. CQ36 59
Urswick Rd. E9 CC35 48
Urswick Rd. Dag. CQ36 59
Usk Rd. SW11 BT45 66
Usk Rd. S. Ock. CW39 60
Usk St. E2 CC38 57
Usk St. E16 CG40 58
Utterton Way, Red. BT72 121
Uvedale Cres. Cro. CF59 96
Uverdale Rd. SW10 BT43 66
Kings Rd.
Uvedale Rd. Dag. CR34 50
Uvedale Rd. Enf. BZ25 30
Uvedale Rd. Oxt. CG68 115
Uverdale Rd. SW10 BT43 66
Uxbridge Cir, Uxb. AY35 44
Uxbridge Gdns. Felt. BD48 74
Uxbridge Rd. W3 BJ40 54
Uxbridge Rd. W5 BJ40 54
Uxbridge Rd. W12 BP40 55
Uxbridge Rd. W13 BJ40 54
Uxbridge Rd. Felt. BD48 74
Uxbridge Rd. Hmptn. BF49 74
Uxbridge Rd. Kings. on T. BK52 84
Uxbridge Rd. Pnr. BC30 35
Uxbridge Rd. Rick. AV27 34
Uxbridge Rd. Rick. AW27 35
Uxbridge Rd. Slou. AQ41 62
Uxbridge Rd. Slou. & Iver AS39 52
Uxbridge Rd. Sthl. BF40 54
Uxbridge Rd. Uxb. & Hayes AZ38 53
Uxbridge St. W8 BS40 56
Uxendon Cres. Wem. BL33 46
Uxendon Hill, Wem. BL33 46
Vache La. Ch. St. G. AR27 34
Valan Leas, Brom. CG52 88
Valance Av. E4 CG26 40
Vale Av. Borwd. BM25 28
Vale Clo. NW8 BT38 1
Vale Clo. W9 BT38 56
Vale Clo. Brwd. CZ25 33
Vale Clo. Couls. BX60 95
Vale Clo. Twick. BJ48 74
Vale Cotts. Brom. CH52 88
Vale Ct. Wey. BA55 83
Vale Cres. SW15 BO49 75
Valecroft, Pnr. BE32 45
Vale Dr. Barn. BR24 28
Vale End SE22 CA45 67
Grove Vale
Vale Farm Rd. Wok. AS62 100
Vale Gro. N4 BZ33 48
Vale Gro. W3 BN40 55
Vale Gro. Slou. AP41 62
Vale La. W3 BM39 55
Valence Av. Dag. CP33 50
Valence Cir. Dag. CP34 50
Valence Ho. Dag. CQ34 50
Valence Rd. Erith CS43 69
Valence Wood Rd. Dag. CP34 50
Valencia Rd. Stan. BK28 36
Valency Clo. Nthwd. BB28 35
Valentine Av. Bex. CQ48 79
Valentine Ct. SE23 CC48 77
Valentine Pl. SE1 BY41 4
Valentine Pl. SE1 BY41 66
Valentine Rd. Har. CC36 57
Valentine Rd. Har. BG34 45
Valentine Row SE1 BY41 4
Valentine Row SE1 BY41 66
Valentines Rd. Ilf. CL33 49
Valentine Way, Ch. St. G. AR27 34
Valentines Way, Rom. CS34 50
Vale of Heath NW3 BT34 47
East Heath Rd.
Vale Pl. W14 BQ41 65
Spring Vale Ter.
Valerian Way E15 CG38 58
Valerie Clo. St. Alb. BJ13 9
Valerie Ct. Bush. BG26 36
Vale Rise NW11 BR33 46
Vale Rd. E7 CH36 58
Vale Rd. N4 BZ33 48
Vale Rd. Brom. CL51 88
Vale Rd. Bush. BE25 27
Vale Rd. Chesh. AO16 16
Vale Rd. Dart. CU47 79
Vale Rd. Esher BH58 93
Vale Rd. Grav. DE47 81
Vale Rd. Mitch. BW52 86
Vale Rd. Sutt. BS56 95
Vale Rd. Wey. BA55 83
Vale Rd. Wind. AM44 61
Vale Rd. Wor. Pk. BO55 85
Vale Rd. N. Surb. BL55 85
Vale Rd. S. Surb. BL55 85
Vale Row N5 BY34 47
Gillespie Rd.
Vale Royal N7 BX36 56
Valeswood Rd. Brom. CG49 78
Vale Ter. N4 BZ32 48
Vale, The N10 BV30 38
Vale, The N14 BW26 38
Vale, The NW11 BQ34 46
Vale, The SW3 BT43 3
Vale, The SW3 BT43 66
Vale, The W3 BO40 55
Vale, The Brwd. DB26 42
Vale, The Couls. BW60 95
Vale, The Croy. CC55 87
Vale, The Felt. BC46 73
Vale, The Houns. BE43 64
Vale, The Ruis. BD34 45
Vale, The Sun. BC50 73
Vale, The Wdf. Grn. CH29 40
Vale, The Ger. Cr. AR30 34
Valetta Gro. E13 CG37 58
Valetta Rd. W3 BO41 65
Valette St. E9 CB36 57
Vale Way, Horn. CU35 50
Valiant Clo. Nthlt. BD38 54
Ruislip Rd.
Valiant Clo. Rom. CR30 41
Vallance Rd. E1 CB38 57
Vallance Rd. E2 CB38 57
Vallance Rd. N22 BW30 38
Vallentin Ct. E17 CF31 48
Vallentin Rd.
Vallentin Rd. E17 CF31 48
Valley Av. N12 BT28 38
Valley Clo. Dart. CT46 79
Valley Clo. Loug. CK25 31
Valley Clo. Pnr. BC30 35
Valley Clo. Wal. Abb. CF19 21
Valley Clo. Wdf. Grn. CH29 40
Valley Dr. NW9 BM32 46
Valley Dr. Grav. DH49 81
Valley Dr. Sev. CU66 116
Valleyfield Rd. SW16 BX49 76
Valley Flds. Cres. Enf. BY23 29
Valley Gdns. SW19 BT50 76
Valley Gdns. Wem. BL36 55
Valley Grn. The Welw. G. C. BQ7 5
Valley Gro. SE7 CJ42 68
Valley Hill, Loug. CK26 40
Valley Ms. Twick. BJ48 74
Cross Deep
Valley Rise, Wat. BC20 17
Valley Rd. N12 BT28 38
Valley Rd. SW16 BX49 76
Valley Rd. Belv. CR42 69
Valley Rd. Berk. AP12 7

Valley Rd. Brom. CG51 88
Valley Rd. Dart. CT46 79
Valley Rd. Erith CS42 69
Valley Rd. Fawk. DB53 90
Valley Rd. Ken. BZ60 96
Valley Rd. Orp. CO51 89
Valley Rd. Rick. AV25 25
Valley Rd. Rick. AW25 26
Valley Rd. St. Alb. BH11 9
Valley Rd. Uxb. AY37 53
Valley Rd. Welw. G. C. BP8 5
Valley Side E4 CE27 39
Valley Side, Hem. H. AV13 7
Valley, The Guil. AR72 118
Valley Vw. Barn. BR25 28
Valley Vw. Green. DA46 80
Valley Vw. Wal. Cr. BZ17 21
Valley Vw. West. CJ62 106
Valley Vw. Gdns. Ken. CA57 96
Valley Vw. Gdns. Ken. CA61 105
Valley Wk. Croy. CC55 87
Valley Wk. Rick. BA25 26
Valley Way, Ger. Cr. AR32 43
Valliant Clo. Nthlt. BD38 54
Valliere Rd. NW10 BP38 55
Valliers Wood Rd. Sid. CM47 78
Vallis Way W13 BJ39 54
Vallis Way, Chess. BK56 93
Valmar Rd. SE5 BZ44 67
Valnay St. SW17 BU49 76
Valognes Av. E17 BX30 38
Valonia Gdns. SW18 BR46 75
Vambery Rd. SE18 CM43 68
Vanbrough Cres. Nthlt. BD37 54
Vanbrugh Clo. Orp. CN54 88
Vanbrugh Fields SE3 CG43 68
Vanbrugh Hill SE3 CG42 68
Vanbrugh Hill SE10 CG42 68
Vanbrugh Pk. SE3 CG43 68
Vanbrugh Pk. Rd. SE3 CG43 68
Vanbrugh Pk. Rd. W. SE3 CG43 68
Vanbrugh Rd. W4 BN41 65
Vanbrugh Ter. SE3 CG44 68
Vancouver Clo. Epsom BN59 94
Vancouver Cotts. Epsom BN59 94
Vancouver Rd. SE23 CD48 77
Vancouver Rd. Edg. BM29 37
Vancouver Rd. Hayes BC38 53
Vancouver Rd. Rich. BK49 74
Vanda Cres. St. Alb. BH14 9
Vanderbilt Rd. SW18 BS47 76
Vandome Clo. E16 CH39 58
Vandon Pass. SW1 BW41 3
Vandon Pass. SW1 BW41 66
Petty France
Vandon St. SW1 BW41 3
Vandon St. SW1 BW41 66
Van Dyck Av. N. Mal. BN54 85
Vandyke Clo. SW15 BQ46 75
Vandyke Clo. Red. BU69 121
Vandyke Cross SE9 CK46 78
Vandy St. EC2 CA38 2
Vandy St. EC2 CA38 57
Vane Clo. Har. BL32 46
Vanessa Clo. Belv. CR42 69
Vanessa Wk. Grav. DJ49 81
Vanessa Way, Bex. CS48 79
Vane St. SW1 BW42 3
Vane St. SW1 BW42 66
Vincent Sq.
Vanguard Clo. Croy. BY54 86
Vanguard Clo. Rom. CR30 41
Vanguard St. SE8 CE44 67
Vanguard Way, Wall. BX57 95
Vanoc Gdns. Brom. CG48 78
Vanquisher Wk. Grav. DJ48 81
Cervia Way
Vansittart Dr. Wind. AN44 61
Vansittart Rd. E7 CG35 49
Vansittart Rd. Wind. AN44 61
Vansittart St. SE14 CD43 67
Vanston Pl. SW6 BS43 66
Vantage Rd. Slou. AN41 61
Vantorts Clo. Saw. CQ6 6
Vantorts Rd. Saw. CQ6 6
Vant Rd. SW17 BU49 76
Varcoe Rd. SE16 CB42 67
Vardens Rd. SW11 BT45 66
Varden St. E1 CB39 57
Varley Rd. E16 CH39 58
Varna Rd. SW6 BR43 65
Varna Rd. Hmptn. BF51 84
Varndell St. NW1 BV38 1
Varndell St. NW1 BW38 56
Varney Clo. Hem. H. AV13 7
Varney Clo. Wal. Cr. CB17 21
Varney Rd. Hem. H. AV13 7
Vartry Rd. N15 BZ32 48
Vassall Rd. SW9 BY43 66
Vauban Est. SE16 CA41 4
Vauban Est. SE16 CA41 67
Vauban St. SE16 CA41 4
Vauban St. SE16 CA41 67
Vaudrey Clo. E1 CC38 57
Vaughan Av. NW4 BP32 46
Vaughan Av. W6 BO42 65
Vaughan Av. Horn. CV35 51
Vaughan Gdns. Ilf. CK33 49
Vaughan Pl. SE15 CB43 67
Vaughan Rd. E15 CG36 58
Vaughan Rd. SE5 BZ44 67
Vaughan Rd. Har. BG32 45
Vaughan Rd. Surb. BJ54 84
Vaughan Rd. Well. CN44 68
Vaughan Way, Dor. BJ71 119
Westcott Rd.
Vaughan Williams Clo. SE8 CE43 67
Watson's St.
Vaux Cres. Walt. BC57 92
Vauxhall Br. BX42 66
Vauxhall Br. SW1 BX42 4
Vauxhall Br. Rd. SW1 BW41 3
Vauxhall Br. Rd. SW1 BW41 66
Vauxhall Clo. Grav. DF47 81
Vauxhall Cross SW8 BX42 4
Vauxhall Cross SW8 BX43 66
Vauxhall Gdns. Sth. Croy. BZ57 96
Vauxhall Gdns. Est. SE11 BX42 4
Vauxhall Gdns. Est. SE11 BX42 66
Vauxhall Gro. SW8 BX43 4
Vauxhall Gro. SW8 BX43 66
Vauxhall Pl. Dart. CW47 80
Vauxhall Rd. Hem. H. AZ13 8
Vauxhall St. SE11 BX42 4
Vauxhall St. SE11 BX42 66
Vauxhall Wk. SE11 BX42 4
Vauxhall Wk. SE11 BX42 66
Vectis Gdns. SW17 BV50 76
Vectis Rd.
Vectis Rd. SW17 BV50 76
Veda Rd. SE13 CE45 67
Veevers Rd. Reig. BT72 121
Vega Cres. Nthwd. BB28 35
Vegal Cres. Egh. AQ49 72
Vega Rd. Bush. BG26 36
Velde Way SE22 CA46 77
Dulwich Gro.
Velizy Av. Harl. CM10 6
Venables St. NW8 BT38 56
Venables St. W9 BT38 1
Vencourt Pl. W6 BP42 65
King St.
Venetian Rd. SE5 BZ44 67
Venetia Rd. N4 BY32 47
Venetia Rd. W5 BK41 64
Ventte Clo. Rain. CU39 59
Venner Rd. SE26 CC49 77
Venners Clo. Bexh. CT44 69
Venn St. SW4 BW45 66
Venour Rd. E3 CD38 57
Maidman St.
Ventnor Av. Stan. BJ30 36
Ventnor Dr. N20 BS27 38
Ventnor Gdns. Bark. CN36 58
Ventnor Rd. SE14 CC43 67
Ventnor Rd. Sutt. BS57 95
Venture Clo. Bex. CQ47 79
Elmwood Dr.
Venue St. E14 CF39 57
Venus Hill, Her. H. AT19 16
Venus Rd. SE18 CK41 68
Veny Cres. Horn. CV36 60
Vera Av. N21 BY25 29
Vera Rd. SW6 BR44 65
Verbena Clo. S. Ock. DB39 60
Verbena Gdns. W6 BP42 65
Verdan Rd. Bexh. CQ44 69
Verdant Ct. SE6 CG47 78
Verdant La. SE6 CG47 78
Verdayne Av. Croy. CC55 87
Verdayne Gdns. Warl. CC61 105
Verderers Rd. Chig. CO28 41
Verdun Rd. SE18 CO43 69
Verdun Rd. SW13 BP43 65
Vereker Dr. Sun. BC52 83
Vereker Rd. W14 BR42 65
Vere Rd. Loug. CM24 31
Vere St. W1 BV39 1
Vere St. W1 BV39 56
Vermont Rd. SE19 BZ50 77
Vermont Rd. SW18 BS46 76
Vermont Rd. Sutt. BS55 86
Verney Clo. Berk. AP12 7
Verney Gdns. Dag. CQ35 50
Verney Rd. SE16 CB42 67
Verney Rd. Dag. CQ35 50
Verney Rd. Slou. AT42 62
Verney St. NW10 BN34 46
Verney Way SE16 CB42 67
Vernham Rd. SE18 CM43 68
Vernon Av. E12 CK35 49
Vernon Av. SW20 BQ51 85
Vernon Av. Enf. CD21 30
Vernon Av. Wdf. Grn. CH29 40
Vernon Clo. Cher. AU57 91
Vernon Clo. Epsom BN57 94
Vernon Clo. Orp. CO52 89
Vernon Clo. St. Alb. BG14 9
Vernon Clo. Sev. CZ58 99
Vernon Cres. Barn. BV25 29
Vernon Cres. Brwd. DD27 122
Vernon Dr. Stan. BJ30 36
Vernon Dr. Uxb. AX30 35
Vernon Pl. WC1 BX39 2
Vernon Pl. WC1 BX39 56
Bloomsbury Way
Vernon Rise WC1 BX38 2
Vernon Rise WC1 BX38 56
Percy Circus
Vernon Rise, Grnf. BG35 45
Vernon Rd. E3 CD37 57
Vernon Rd. E11 CG33 49
Vernon Rd. E15 CG36 58
Vernon Rd. E17 BX32 47
Vernon Rd. N8 BY31 47
Vernon Rd. SW14 BO45 65
Vernon Rd. Bush. BE25 27
Vernon Rd. Felt. BB48 73
Vernon Rd. Ilf. CN33 49
Vernon Rd. Rom. CS28 41
Vernon Rd. Sutt. BT56 95
Vernon Rd. Swans. DC46 81
Vernon Sq. WC1 BX38 2
Vernon Sq. WC1 BX38 56
Penton Rise
Vernon St. W14 BR42 65
Vernon Wk. Tad. BQ63 103
Vernon Way, Guil. AP70 118
Vernon Yd. W11 BR40 55
Portobello Rd.
Verona Dr. Surb. BL55 85
Verona Gdns. Grav. DJ49 81
Verona Rd. E7 CH36 58
Upton La.
Veronica Clo. Rom. CV29 42
Veronica Rd. SW17 BV48 76
Veronique Gdns. Ilf. CM32 49
Verran Rd. SW12 BV47 76
Balham Gro.
Ver Rd. St. Alb. BG13 9
Versailles Rd. SE20 CB50 77
Verulam Av. E17 CD32 48
Verulam Av. Pur. BW59 95
Verulam Bldgs. WC1 BX39 2
Verulam Clo. Welw. G. C. BR8 5
Verulam Rd. Grnf. BF38 54
Verulam Rd. St. Alb. BG13 9
Verulam St. EC1 BY39 56
Verulam St. WC1 BY39 2
Verwood Rd. Har. BG30 36
Vespan Rd. W12 BP41 65
Vesta Av. St. Alb. BG15 9
Vesta Rd. SE4 CD44 67
Vesta Rd. Hem. H. AY12 8
Vestris Rd. SE23 CC48 77
Vestry Ms. SE5 CA44 67
Vestry Rd. E17 CE32 48
Vestry Rd. SE5 CA44 67
Vestry Rd. Sev. CV63 108
Vestry St. N1 BZ38 2
Vestry St. N1 BZ38 57
Vevey St. SE6 CD48 77
Veysey Gdns. Dag. CR34 50
Viaduct Bldgs. EC1 BY39 56
Saffron Hill
Viaduct Pl. E2 CB38 57
Viaduct St. E2 CB38 57
Viaduct, The E18 CH30 40
Viaduct Way, Welw. G. C. BR6 5
Vian Av. Enf. CD21 30
Vian St. SE13 CE45 67
Vibart Gdns. SW2 BX47 76
Vicarage Av. SE3 CH44 68
Vicarage Av. Egh. AT49 72
Vicarage Clo. Brwd. CZ28 42
Vicarage Clo. Erith CS43 69
Vicarage Clo. Lthd. BF66 111
Vicarage Clo. Pot. B. BU18 20
Vicarage Clo. Ruis. BA33 44
Vicarage Clo. St. Alb. BG15 9
Vicarage Clo. Tad. BR65 103
Vicarage Ct. W8 BS41 66
Vicarage Gate
Vicarage Ct. Egh. AT49 72
Vicarage Rd.
Vicarage Ct. Felt. BA47 73
Vicarage Cres. Egh. AT49 72
Vicarage Cres. SW11 BT44 66
Vicarage Dr. SW14 BN46 75
Vicarage Dr. Bark. CM36 58
Vicarage Dr. Grav. DE46 81
Vicarage Dr. Maid. AH41 61
Vicarage Farm Rd. Houns. BE44 64
Vicarage Flds. Walt. BD53 84
Vicarage Gdns. SW14 BN46 75
Vicarage Gdns. W8 BS41 66
Vicarage Gdns. Mitch. BU52 86
Vicarage Gate W8 BS41 66
Vicarage Gate, Guil. AQ71 118
Vicarage Gro. SE5 BZ44 67
Vicarage La. E6 CK38 58
Vicarage La. E15 CG36 58
Vicarage La. Chig. CM27 40
Vicarage La. Epp. CR15 14
Vicarage La. Epsom BP58 94
Vicarage La. Grav. DK48 81
Vicarage La. Hem. H. AT17 16
Vicarage La. Ilf. CM33 49
Vicarage La. Kings L. AY18 17
Vicarage La. Lthd. BJ64 102
Vicarage La. Stai. AS47 72
Vicarage La. Stai. AX52 83
Vicarage La. Wok. AU66 109
Vicarage Pk. SE18 CM42 68
Vicarage Path N8 BW33 47
Vicarage Pl. Slou. AQ41 62
Vicarage Rd. E10 CE33 48
Vicarage Rd. E15 CG36 58
Vicarage Rd. N17 CG30 39
Vicarage Rd. SE18 CM42 68
Vicarage Rd. SW14 BN46 75
Vicarage Rd. Berk. AT11 7
Vicarage Rd. Bex. CR47 79
Vicarage Rd. Croy. BY55 86
Vicarage Rd. Dag. CR36 59
Vicarage Rd. Egh. AT49 72
Vicarage Rd. Egh. AT50 72
Vicarage Rd. Epp. CP18 23
Vicarage Rd. Horn. CU33 50
Vicarage Rd. Kings. on T. BK51 84
Vicarage Rd. Stai. AV48 72
Vicarage Rd. Sun. BB49 73
Vicarage Rd. Sutt. BS56 95
Vicarage Rd. Tedd. BJ49 74
Vicarage Rd. Twick. BG46 74
Vicarage Rd. Twick. BH48 74
Vicarage Rd. Wat. BC26 35
Vicarage Rd. Wdf. Grn. CK29 40
Vicarage Rd. Wok. AO59 91
Vicarage Rd. Wok. AS64 100
Vicarage Wk. SW11 BT44 66
Battersea Church Rd.
Vicarage Wk. Walt. BC54 83
Vicarage Way NW10 BN34 46
Vicarage Way, Ger. Cr. AS32 43
Vicarage Way, Har. BF33 45
Vicarage Way, Slou. AU43 62
Vicarage Wood, Harl. CO10 6
Vicars Clo. E15 CH37 58
Vicars Clo. Enf. CA23 30
Vicars Hill SE13 CE45 67
Vicar's Moor La. N21 BY26 38
Vicars Rd. NW5 BV35 47
Vicars Wk. Dag. CO34 50
Vicerage Way, Hem. H. AT16 16
Viceroy Ct. NW8 BU37 1
Viceroy Ct. NW8 BU37 56
Viceroy Rd. SW8 BX44 66
Hartington Rd.
Vickers Rd. Erith CS42 69
Victor App. Horn. CV33 51
Victor Gdns. Horn. CV33 51
Victor Gro. Wem. BL36 55
Victoria Arc, Sthl. BE40 54
Victoria Av. Grays DE41 71
Victoria Av. E6 CJ37 58
Victoria Av. EC2 CA39 57
New St.
Victoria Av. N3 BR30 37
Victoria Av. Barn. BT24 29
Victoria Av. E. Mol. BF52 84
Victoria Av. Grav. DG47 81
Victoria Av. Houns. BE46 74
Victoria Av. Rom. CR29 41
Victoria Av. Sth. Croy. BZ58 96
Victoria Av. Surb. BK54 84
Victoria Av. Uxb. AZ36 53
Victoria Av. Wall. BV55 86
Victoria Av. Wem. BM36 55
Victoria Clo. Barn. BT24 29
Victoria Clo. Grays. DE41 71
Victoria Av.
Victoria Clo. Hayes BA39 53
Victoria Clo. Rick. AX26 35
Nightingale Rd.
Victoria Clo. Wey. BA55 83
Victoria Clo. Wey. BB55 83
Victoria Cotts. N10 BV30 38
Victoria Ct. W3 BM41 65
Victoria Ct. Wem. BM36 55
Victoria Cres. N15 CA32 48
Victoria Cres. SE19 CA50 77
Victoria Cres. SW19 BR50 75
Victoria Cres. Hayes AW40 53
Victoria Cres. Iver AV40 52
Victoria Dock Rd. E16 CG39 58
Victoria Dr. SW19 BQ47 75
Victoria Dr. S. Dnth. CY51 90
Victoria Emb. SW1 BX41 4
Victoria Emb. SW1 BX41 66
Victoria Gdns. W11 BS41 66
Church St.
Victoria Gdns. Houns. BE44 64
Victoria Gdns. West. CJ61 106
Victoria Gro. N12 BT28 38
Victoria Gro. W2 BS40 56
Victoria Gro. W8 BT41 3
Victoria Gro. W8 BT41 66
Victoria Hill Rd. Swan. CT51 89
Victoria La. Barn. BR24 28
Victoria La. Hayes BA42 63
Victoria Ms. NW6 BS37 56
Victoria Ms. SW4 BV45 66
Victoria Rise
Victorian Gro. N16 CA34 48
Victorian Rd. N16 CA34 48
Victorian Pk. Rd. E9 CB37 57
Victoria Pk. Sq. E2 CC38 57
Victoria Pl. Epsom BO59 94
Victoria Pl. Rich. BK46 74
Victoria Rise SW4 BV45 66
Victoria Rd. BJ50 74
Victoria Rd. E4 CG26 40
Victoria Rd. E13 CH37 58
Victoria Rd. E17 CF30 39
Victoria Rd. E18 CH30 40
Victoria Rd. N4 BX33 47
Victoria Rd. N9 CA27 39
Victoria Rd. N15 CB31 48
Victoria Rd. N18 CA28 39
Victoria Rd. N22 BW30 38
Victoria Rd. NW4 BQ31 46
Victoria Rd. NW6 BR37 55
Victoria Rd. NW7 BO28 37
Victoria Rd. NW10 BN39 55
Victoria Rd. SW14 BN45 65
Victoria Rd. W3 BN39 55
Victoria Rd. W5 BJ39 54
Victoria Rd. W8 BS41 3
Victoria Rd. W8 BT41 66
Victoria Rd. Bark. CL36 58
Victoria Rd. Barn. BT24 29
Victoria Rd. Berk. AR13 7
Victoria Rd. Bexh. CR46 79
Victoria Rd. Brom. CJ53 88
Victoria Rd. Brwd. DB28 42
Victoria Rd. Buck. H. CJ27 40
Victoria Rd. Bush. BF26 36
Victoria Rd. Chis. CL49 78
Victoria Rd. Couls. BW61 104
Victoria Rd. Dag. CR35 50
Victoria Rd. Dart. CV46 80
Victoria Rd. Erith CT43 69
Victoria Rd. Felt. BC47 73
Victoria Rd. Grav. DF47 81
Victoria Rd. Guil. AS71 118
Victoria Rd. Guil. AS71 118
Victoria Rd. Kings. on T. BL51 85
Victoria Rd. Mitch. BU50 76
Victoria Rd. Red. BV71 121
Victoria Rd. Rich. BL44 65
Victoria Rd. Rom. CT32 50
Victoria Rd. Ruis. BC33 44
Victoria Rd. Sev. CU66 116
Victoria Rd. Sid. CN48 78
Victoria Rd. Slou. AQ40 52
Victoria Rd. Stai. AV48 72
Victoria Rd. Sthl. BE41 64
Victoria Rd. Surb. BK53 84
Victoria Rd. Sutt. BT56 95
Victoria Rd. Twick. BJ47 74
Victoria Rd. Uxb. AX36 53
Victoria Rd. Wal. Abb. CF20 21
Victoria Rd. Wat. BC22 26
Victoria Rd. Wey. AX56 92
Victoria Rd. Wey. BA55 83
Victoria Rd. Wind. AM42 61
Victoria Rd. Wok. AO62 100
Victoria Rd. Wok. AS62 100
Victoria Sq. SW1 BU41 3
Victoria Sq. SW1 BV41 66
Beeston Pl.
Victoria St. E15 CG36 58
Victoria St. SW1 BV41 3
Victoria St. SW1 BV41 66
Victoria St. Belv. CQ42 69
Victoria St. Egh. AR50 72
Victoria St. St. Alb. BG13 9
Victoria St. Slou. AP41 62
Victoria St. Wind. AO44 61
Victoria Ter. N4 BY33 47
Victoria Ter. Dor. BJ71 119
Victoria Ter. Har. BG33 45
Victoria Vills. Rich. BL45 65
Victoria Way SE7 CH42 68
Victoria Way, Wok. AS62 100
Victor Rd. NW10 BP38 55
Victor Rd. SE20 CC50 77
Victor Rd. Har. BG31 45
Victor Rd. Tedd. BH49 74
Victor Rd. Wind. AO45 61
Victor, S. Cres. Brwd. DD27 122
Victor Vill. N9 BZ27 39
Victor Wk. Horn. CV33 51
Victory Av. Mord. BT53 86
Victory Pk. Rd. Wey. AX56 92
Victory Pl. SE17 BZ42 4
Victory Pl. SE17 BZ42 67
Victory Pl. SE19 CA50 77
Victory Rd. SW19 BT50 76
Victory Rd. Berk. AQ12 7
Victory Rd. Cher. AW54 83
Victory Rd. Rain. CU37 59
Victory Sq. SE5 BZ43 67
Victory Wk. SE8 CE44 67
Ship St.
Victory Way, Rom. CR30 41
View Clo. N6 BU33 47
View Clo. Chig. CM28 40
View Clo. Har. BG31 45
View Clo. West. CJ61 106
Viewfield Rd. SW18 BR46 75
Viewfield Rd. Sid. CP47 79
Viewland Rd. SE18 CN42 68
Viewlands Av. Sev. CN63 106
View Rd. N6 BU33 47
View Rd. Grays. DD43 71
View Rd. Pot. B. BT19 20
View, The SE2 CQ42 69
View, The Gray. DH47 81
Viga Rd. N21 BY25 29
Viggory La. Wok. AR61 100
Vigilant Clo. SE26 CB49 77
Vigilant, The SE26 CB49 77
Vigilant Way, Grav. DJ49 81
Vigors Cft. Hat. BO13 10
Vigo St. W1 BW40 3
Vigo St. W1 BW40 56
Viking Rd. Grav. DE48 81
Viking Rd. Sthl. BE40 54
Viking Way, Brwd. DA25 33
Viking Way, Sev. CZ57 99
Villa Clo. Grav. DK48 81
Villacourt Rd. SE18 CO43 69
Village Clo. E4 CF28 39
Village Grn. Av. West. CK62 106
Village Grn. Rd. Dart. CU45 69
Village Grn. Way West. CK62 106
Village La. Slou. AO33 43
Village Rd. N3 BR29 37
Village Rd. Egh. AU52 82
Village Rd. Enf. BZ26 39
Village Rd. Enf. CA25 30
Village Rd. Uxb. AV34 43
Village Rd. Uxb. AW33 44
Village Rd. Wind. AK41 61
Village Row, Sutt. BS57 95
Village, The SE7 CJ43 68
Village, The Ong. DB13 15
Village Way NW10 BN35 46
Village Way SE21 BZ46 77
Village Way, Amer. AR23 25
Village Way, Ashf. AY49 73
Village Way, Beck. CE52 87
Village Way, Pnr. BE33 45
Village Way, Sth. Croy. CB60 96
Village Way, E. Har. BE33 45
Villa Rd. SW9 BY45 66
Villas Rd. SE18 CM42 68
Villa St. SE17 BZ42 4
Villa St. SE17 BZ42 67
Villiers Av. Surb. BL53 85
Villiers Av. Twick. BE47 74
Villiers Clo. E10 CE34 48
Villiers Clo. Kings. on T. BL52 85
Villiers Cres. St. Alb. BK12 9
Villiers Ct. N20 BT26 38
Villiers Path, Surb. BL53 85
Villiers Rd. NW2 BP36 55
Villiers Rd. Beck. CC51 87
Villiers Rd. Islw. BH44 64
Villiers Rd. Kings. on T. BL52 85
Villiers Rd. Slou. AO39 52
Villiers Rd. Sthl. BE40 54
Villiers Rd. Wat. BE25 27
Villiers St. WC2 BX40 4
Villiers St. WC2 BX40 56
Villiers St. Uxb. AX37 53
Vincam Clo. Twick. BF47 74
Vincent Av. Cars. BT59 95
Vincent Av. Surb. BM54 85
Vincent Clo. Barn. BS24 29
Vincent Clo. Brom. CH52 88
Vincent Clo. Cher. AV54 82
Vincent Clo. Couls. BU63 104
Vincent Clo. Esher BF55 84
Vincent Clo. Ilf. CM29 40
Vincent Clo. Lthd. BF65 102
Vincent Clo. Sid. CN47 79
Valliers Wood Rd.
Vincent Clo. West Dr. AZ43 63
Vincent Ct. NW4 BQ31 46
Vincent Dr. Shep. BB52 83
Vincent Gdns. NW2 BO34 46
Vincent Rd. E4 CF29 39
Vincent Rd. N15 BZ31 48
Vincent Rd. N22 BY30 38
Vincent Rd. SE18 CL42 68
Vincent Rd. W3 BN41 65
Palmerston Rd.
Vincent Rd. Cher. AV54 82
Vincent Rd. Cob. AM52 102
Vincent Rd. Couls. BW61 104
Vincent Rd. Croy. CA54 87
Vincent Rd. Dag. CQ36 59
Vincent Rd. Houns. BD44 64
Vincent Rd. Islw. BG44 64
Vincent Rd. Kings. on T. BM52 85
Vincent Rd. Rain. CV38 60
Vincent Rd. Wal. Cr. CD17 21
Vincent Rd. Wem. BL36 55
Vincent Row, Hamptn. BG50 74
Vincent's Dr. Dor. BJ72 119
Vincents La. Dor. BJ71 119
Vincents Path, Nthlt. BE36 54
Arnold Rd.
Vincent Sq. SW1 BW42 3
Vincent Sq. SW1 BW42 66
Vincent Sq. West. CJ60 97
Vincent's Rd. Dor. BJ71 119

Wardell Clo. NW9 BO29 37
Wardell Field NW9 BO30 37
Warden Av. Har. BE33 45
Warden Av. Rom. CS28 41
Warden Ct. Har. BE33 45
Warden Rd. NW5 BV36 56
Wardens Gro. SE1 BZ40 4
Wardens Gro. SE1 BZ40 57
Ward Gdns. Slou. AM40 61
Ward Hatch, Harl. CO9 6
Ward La. Warl. CC61 105
Wardle St. E9 CC35 48
Wardley St. SW18 BS47 76
Wardo Av. SW6 BR44 65
Wardour Ms. W1 BW39 1
Wardour St. W1 BW39 1
Wardour St. W1 BW39 56
Wardour St. W1 BW40 3
Ward Rd. E15 CF37 57
Ward Rd. N19 BW34 47
Wardrobe, The Rich. BK46 74
Old Palace Yd.
Wards La. Borwd. BH23 27
Wards Rd. Ilf. CM33 49
Ward St. Guil. AR71 118
Wareham Clo. Houns. BF45 64
Wareham St. N1 BZ37 2
Wareham St. N1 BZ37 57
Rushton St.
Waremead Rd. Ilf. CL32 49
Warenford Way Borwd. BM23 28
Warenne Rd. Lthd. BG64 102
Ware Rd. Hodd. CE10 12
Warescot Clo. Brwd. DA26 42
Warescot Rd. Brwd. DA26 42
Wareside Clo. Welw. G. C. BS8 5
Waterford Grn.
Wareside, Hem. H. AZ10 8
Elstree Rd.
Warfield Rd. NW10 BQ39 55
Warfield Rd. Felt. BB47 73
Warfield Rd. Hamptn. BF51 84
Wargrave Av. N15 CA32 48
Wargrave Rd. Har. BG34 45
Warham Rd. N4 BY32 47
Warham Rd. Har. BH30 36
Warham Rd. Sev. CU61 107
Warham Rd. Sth. Croy. BY56 95
Waring Clo. Orp. CN57 97
Waring Dr. Orp. CN57 97
Waring Rd. Sid. CP50 79
Waring St. SE27 BZ49 77
Warkworth Gdns. Islw. BJ43 64
Warkworth Rd. N17 BZ29 39
Warland Rd. SE18 CM43 68
Warland Rd. Sev. CZ58 99
Warley Av. Dag. CQ33 50
Warley Av. Hayes BC39 53
Warley Gap, Brwd. DA29 42
Warley Hall La. Upmin. DC33 123
Warley Hill, Brwd. DA29 42
Warley Par. NW9 BO31 46
Warley Rd. N9 CC27 39
Warley Rd. Brwd. DA29 42
Warley Rd. Hayes BC39 53
Warley Rd. Ilf. CL30 40
Warley Rd. Upmin. CY30 42
Warley Rd. Wdf. Grn. CH29 40
Warley St. E2 CC38 57
Warley St. Brwd. DB32 51
Warley St. Upmin. DB33 51
Warlingham Rd. Th. Hth. BY52 86
Warlock Rd. W9 BR38 55
Warlters Clo. N7 BX35 47
Warlters Mews N7 BX35 47
Warlters Rd. N7 BX35 47
Warltersville Rd. N19 BX33 47
Warmark Rd. Hem. H. AV12 7
Warmington Clo. E5 CC34 48
Millfields Rd.
Warmington Rd. SE24 BZ46 77
Warmington St. E13 CH38 58
Warminster Gdns. SE25 CB51 87
Warminster Rd. SE25 CA51 87
Warminster Sq. SE25 CB51 87
Warminster Way, Mitch. BV51 86
Warndon St. SE16 CC42 67
Warneford Pl. Wat. BE25 27
Warneford Rd. Har. BK31 45
Warneford St. E9 CB37 57
Warner Av. Sutt. BR55 85
Warner Clo. E15 CG35 49
Warner Clo. NW9 BO33 46
Warner Clo. Hayes BA43 63
Warner Clo. Slou. AM40 61
Warner Par. Hayes BA43 63
Warner Pl. E2 CB37 2
Warner Pl. E2 CB37 57
Warner Rd. E17 CD31 48
Warner Rd. N8 BW31 47
Warner Rd. SE5 BZ44 67
Warner Rd. Brom. CG50 78
Warners Av. Hodd. CD13 12
Warners Clo. Wdf. Grn. CH28 40
Warners End Rd.
Hem. H. AW13 8
Warner's La. Kings. on T. BK49 74
Warner St. EC1 BY38 2
Warner St. EC1 BY38 56
Warnford Rd. Orp. CN56 97
Warnham Court Rd. Cars. BU57 95
Warnham Rd. N12 BU28 38
Warple Way W3 BO40 55
Warren Av. E10 CF34 48
Warren Av. Brom. CG50 78
Warren Av. Orp. CN56 97
Warren Av. Rich. BM45 65
Warren Av. Sth. Croy. CC57 96
Warren Av. Sutt. BR58 94
Warren Clo. Hat. BP11 10
Warren Clo. N9 CC26 39
Warren Clo. SE24 BZ47 77
Rosendale Rd.
Warren Clo. Bexh. CR46 79
Warren Clo. Esher BF56 93
Warren Clo. Slou. AS41 62
Warren Clo. Tad. BR65 103
Warren Ct. Beck. CD50 77
Warren Ct. Chig. CM28 40
Warren Ct. Sev. CV66 117
Warren Ct. Wey. AZ56 92
Elgin Rd.
Warren Cres. N9 CA26 39
Warren Cutting,
Kings. on T. BN50 75
Warren Dale
Welw. G. C. BQ6 5
Warrender Rd. N19 BW34 47
Warrender Rd. Chesh. AP18 16
Warrender Way Ruis. BC33 44
Warren Dr. Grnf. BF38 54
Warren Dr. Horn. CU35 50
Warren Dr. Orp. CO56 98
Warren Dr. Ruis. BD33 45
Warren Dr. S. Surb. BN54 85
Warren Dr. Tad. BR64 103
Warren Dr. Tad. BS65 104
Warren Dr. N. Surb. BM54 85
Warreners La. Wey. BA57 92
Warren Farm Clo. E11 CJ32 49
Warren Rd.
Warren Fld. Epp. CO19 23
Charles St.
Warren Field, Iver. AU37 52
Warren Flds. Stan. BK28 36
Warren Gdns. E15 CF35 48
Warren Gdns. Orp. CO56 98
Warrengate La. Pot. B. BQ19 19
Warrengate Rd. Hat. BQ17 19
Warren Green, Hat. BP11 10
Warren Gro. Borwd. BN24 28
Warren Hill Epsom BN61 103
Warren Hill Lough. CJ25 31
Warren Hill Ho. Loug. CH25 31
Warren Ho. Kings. on T. BN50 75
Warren La. SE18 CL41 68
Warren La. Brwd. CZ23 33
Warren La. Grays. DB42 70
Warren La. Lthd. BG59 93
Warren La. Oxt. CG70 115
Warren La. Stan. BH27 36
Warren La. Wok. AW62 101
Warren Mead Bans. BQ61 103
Warren Ms. W1 BV38 1
Warrenne Rd. Bet. BN71 120
Warren Pk. Kings. on T. BN50 75
Warren Pk. Warl. CC62 105
Warren Pk. Rd. Sutt. BT57 95
Warren Pond Rd. E4 CG26 40
Warren Rise N. Mal. BN51 85
Warren Rd. E4 CF27 39
Warren Rd. E10 CF34 48
Warren Rd. E11 CJ32 49
Warren Rd. NW2 BO34 46
Warren Rd. SW19 BU50 76
Warren Rd. Ashf. BB50 73
Warren Rd. Bans. BQ60 94
Warren Rd. Bexh. CR46 79
Warren Rd. Brom. CH55 88
Warren Rd. Bush. BG26 36
Warren Rd. Croy. CA54 87
Warren Rd. Dart. CW48 80
Warren Rd. Grav. DD49 81
Warren Rd. Guil. AS71 118
Warren Rd. Ilf. CM32 49
Warren Rd. Kings. on T. BN50 75
Warren Rd. Orp. CN56 97
Warren Rd. Pur. BY59 95
Warren Rd. Reig. BS70 121
Warren Rd. St. Alb. BG15 9
Warren Rd. Sid. CP48 79
Warren Rd. Twick. BG46 74
Warren Rd. Uxb. AY35 44
Warren Rd. Wey. AW58 92
Warrens Shawe Lane,
Edg. BM27 37
Springwood Cres.
Warren St. Ms. W1 BW38 56
Warren St.
Warren, S The Hart. DC53 90
Warren St. W1 BV38 1
Warren St. W1 BW38 56
Warren Ter. Rom. CP31 50
Warren, The E12 CK35 49
Warren, The Ash. BL63 103
Warren, The Cars. BT58 95
Warren, The Grav. DH49 81
Warren, The Ger. Cr. AS30 34
Warren, The Hayes BC39 53
Warren, The Houns. BE43 64
Warren, The Leath BB68 110
Warren, The Rad. BJ20 18
Warren, The Tad. BR65 103
Warren, The Wor. Pk. BN56 94
Warren, The Dr. E11 CJ33 49
Warren Wk. SE7 CJ43 68
Warren Way NW7 BR29 37
Warren Way, Welw. G. C. BR5 5
Warren Way, Wey. BA56 92
Warren Wd. Rd. Brom. CG55 88
Warren Wood Clo. Brom. CG55 88
Warrick Gro. Croy. CA55 87
Warriner Av. Horn. CV34 51
Warriner Gdns. SW11 BU44 66
Warrington Av. Slou. AO39 52
Warrington Cres. W9 BT38 1
Warrington Cres. W9 BT38 56
Warrington Gdns. W9 BS38 56
Warwick Av.
Warrington Gdns. Horn. CV32 51
Warrington Rd. Croy. BY55 86
Warrington Rd. Dag. DP34 50
Warrington Rd. Har. BH32 45
Warrington Rd. Rich. BL46 75
Hermitage, The
Warrington Spur, Wind. AQ47 72
Warrington Sq. Dag. CP34 50
Warrington St. E13 CH38 58
Warrior Av. Grav. DH49 81
Warrior Rd. SE5 BY43 66
Warrior Sq. E12 CL35 49
Warsaw Clo. Ruis. BC36 53
Warspite Rd. SE18 CK41 68
Warton Rd. E15 CF37 57
Warwick Av. W2 BS38 56
Warwick Av. W9 BS38 1
Warwick Av. W9 BS38 56
Warwick Av. Edg. BM27 37
Warwick Av. Egh. AU51 82
Warwick Av. Har. BE35 45
Warwick Av. Pot. B. BW17 20
Warwick Av. Slou. AO38 52
Warwick Av. Stai. AX50 73
Warwick Clo. Bush. BH26 36
Warwick Clo. Hamptn. BG50 74
Warwick Clo. Orp. CO55 89
Warwick Cotts. Barn. BT25 29
Warwick Ct. WC1 BX39 2
Warwick Ct. WC1 BX39 56
Warwick Ct. Surb. BL55 85
Warwick Cres. W2 BT39 1
Warwick Cres. W2 BT39 56
Warwick Cres. Hayes BB38 53
Warwick Dene W5 BL40 55
Warwick Dr. SW15 BP45 65
Warwick Dr. Wal. Cr. CC17 21
Warwick Est. W2 BS39 1
Warwick Est. W2 BS39 56
Warwick Gdns. N4 BZ32 48
Warwick Gdns. W14 BR41 65
Warwick Gdns. Ash. BK62 102
Warwick Gdns. Ilf. CL33 49
Warwick Gdns. Rom. CV31 51
Warwick Gdns. Surb. BH53 84
Warwick Gro. E5 CB33 48
Warwick Gro. Surb. BL54 85
Warwick House St. SW1 BW40 3
Warwick Ho. St. SW1 BW40 56
Warwick La. EC4 BY39 2
Warwick La. EC4 BY39 56
Warwick La. Upmin. CW38 60
Warwick La. Wok. AQ63 100
Warwick Ms. W9 BT39 1
Warwick Ms. W2 BS39 1
Warwick Pl. SW1 BW42 3
Warwick Pl. W5 BK41 64
Warwick Rd.
Warwick Pl. W9 BT39 1
Warwick Pl. W9 BT39 56
Warwick Pl. Grav. DD46 81
Warwick Pl. Uxb. AX36 53
Warwick Pl. West Dr. AX40 53
Warwick Pl. Ms. W9 BT39 56
Warwick Pl. N. SW1 BW42 66
Warwick Rd. E4 CE28 39
Warwick Rd. E11 CH32 49
Warwick Rd. E12 CK35 49
Warwick Rd. E15 CG36 58
Warwick Rd. E17 CD30 39
Warwick Rd. N11 BW29 38
Warwick Rd. N18 CA28 39
Warwick Rd. SE20 CB52 87
Warwick Rd. SW5 BR42 65
Warwick Rd. W5 BK41 64
Warwick Rd. W14 BR42 65
Warwick Rd. Ashf. AY49 73
Warwick Rd. Barn. BS24 29
Warwick Rd. Borwd. BN24 28
Warwick Rd. Couls. BW60 95
Warwick Rd. Enf. CD22 30
Warwick Rd. Houns. BC45 63
Warwick Rd. Kings. on T. BK51 84
Warwick Rd. N. Mal. BN52 85
Warwick Rd. Rain. CV38 60
Warwick Rd. Red. BU70 121
Warwick Rd. St. Alb. BH12 9
Warwick Rd. Sid. CO49 79
Warwick Rd. Sthl. BE41 64
Warwick Rd. Surb. BH53 84
Warwick Rd. Sutt. BT56 95
Warwick Rd. Th. Hth. BY52 86
Warwick Rd. Twick. BH47 74
Warwick Rd. Well. CP45 69
Warwick Rd. West Dr. AY40 53
Warwick Row SW1 BV41 3
Warwick Row SW1 BV41 66
Warwick's Bench, Guil. AS72 118
Warwick's Bench Rd.
Guil. AS72 118
Warwickshire Path SE8 CD43 67
Payne St.
Warwick Sq. EC4 BY39 2
Warwick Sq. EC4 BY39 56
Warwick Sq. SW1 BW42 3
Warwick Sq. SW1 BW42 66
Warwick Sq. Ms. SW1 BW42 3
Warwick St. W1 BW40 3
Warwick St. W1 BW40 56
Warwick Ter. SE18 CM43 68
Warwick Way SW1 BV42 3
Warwick Way SW1 BV42 66
Warwick Way, Rick. BA24 26
Warwick Wold Rd. Red. BY68 113
Warwick Yd. EC1 BZ38 2
Washington Av. Hem. H. AY11 8
Washington Av. E12 CK35 49
Washington Clo. Reig. BS69 121
Washington Rd. E6 CJ36 58
St. Stephen's Rd.
Washington Rd. E18 CG30 40
Washington Rd. SW13 BP43 65
Washington Rd.
Kings. on T. BM51 85
Washington Rd. Wor. Pk. BP55 85
Wash La. Barn. BQ21 28
Washneys La. Orp. CO60 98
Washpond La. Warl. CF62 105
Wash Rd. Brwd. DE25 122
Wash Rd. Pot. B. BP20 19
Wastdale Rd. SE23 CC47 77
Watchfield Ct. W4 BN42 65
Watchgate, Dart. CY49 80
Watchlytes, Welw. G. C. BT8 5
Watch Mead, Welw. G. C. BS7 5
Watcombe Cotts. Rich. BM43 65
Bushwood Rd.
Watcombe Pl. SE25 CB52 87
Waterbank Rd. SE6 CE48 77
Waterbeach Rd. Dag. CP35 50
Watercroft Rd. Sev. CQ58 98
Waterdale Rd. SE2 CO43 69
Waterdale St. Grav. DE48 81
Waterden Clo. Guil. AS71 118
Waterden Rd. E15 CE35 48
Waterden Rd. Guil. AS71 118
Waterend La. St. Alb. BN7 5
Water End Rd. Berk. AT12 7
Waterer Gdns. Tad. BR62 103
Waterer Rise Wall. BW57 95
Waterer Rd. N20 BT27 38
Waterers Rise, Wok. AO62 100
Waterfall Clo. N14 BW27 38
Waterfall Rd.
Waterfall Clo. Vir. W. AQ52 82
Waterfall Cotts. SW19 BT50 76
Waterfall Rd. N11 BV28 38
Waterfall Rd. N14 BV28 38
Waterfall Rd. SW19 BT50 76
Waterfield, Tad. BP63 103
Water Field, Welw. G. C. BS7 5
Waterfield Clo. SE28 CO40 59
Waterfield Dr. Warl. CB62 105
Waterfield Dr. Warl. CC63 105
Waterfield Grn. Tad. BP63 103
Waterfields, Lthd. BJ63 102
Waterford Grn. Welw. G. C. BS8 5
Waterford Rd. SW6 BS43 66
Watergate EC4 BY40 4
Watergate EC4 BY40 56
Tudor St.
Watergate Wat. BD27 36
Watergate St. SE8 CE43 67
Watergate Wk. WC2 BX40 4
Watergate Wk. WC2 BX40 56
Waterhall Av. E4 CG27 40
Waterhead Clo. Erith CT43 69
Waterhouse La. Ken. BZ63 105
Waterhouse La. Red. CA69 114
Waterhouse La. Tad. BR64 103
Waterhouse Moor, Harl. CN11 13
Waterhouse St. Hem. H. AX13 8
Water La. E15 CG36 58
Water La. Berk. AR13 7
Water La. Brwd. CY23 33
Water La. Cob. BE61 102
Water La. Harl. CK12 13
Water La. Hem. H. AT18 16
Water La. Ilf. CN34 49
Water La. Kings L. AZ18 17
Water La. Kings. on T. BK51 84
Water La. Lthd. BD66 111
Water La. Oxt. CH66 115
Water La. Rich. BK46 74
Water La. Sid. CQ48 79
Water La. Twick. BJ47 74
Water La. Wat. BD24 27
Waterloo Br. SE1 BX40 56
Waterloo Bridge WC2 BX40 4
Waterloo Br. WC2 BX40 56
Waterloo Gdns. Rom. CT32 50
St. Andrews Rd.
Waterloo Est. E2 CB37 57
Waterloo Gdns. E2 CC37 57
Waterloo Ms. SE5 BZ43 67
Elmington Rd.
Waterloo Pl. NW6 BR36 55
Willesdon La.
Waterloo Pl. SW1 BW40 3
Waterloo Pl. SW1 BW40 56
Waterloo Pl. Rich. BL45 65
Quadrant, The
Waterloo Pl. Rich. BM43 65
Waterloo Rd. E6 CJ36 58
Waterloo Rd. E7 CG35 49
Wellington Rd.
Waterloo Rd. E10 CE33 48
Waterloo Rd. NW2 BP33 46
Waterloo Rd. SE1 BX40 4
Waterloo Rd. SE1 BX40 56
Waterloo Rd. Brwd. DB26 42
Waterloo Rd. Epsom BN59 94
Waterloo Rd. Ilf. CM30 40
Waterloo Rd. Rom. CT32 50
Waterloo Rd. Sutt. BT56 95
Waterloo Rd. Uxb. AX37 53
Waterloo St. EC1 BZ38 2
Waterloo St. EC1 BZ38 57
Lever St.
Waterloo Ter. N1 BY36 56
Waterloo Ter. N1 BY37 2
Waterloo Wk. E9 CC35 48
Churchill Wk.
Waterlow Ct. NW11 BS33 47
Waterlow Rd. N19 BW33 47
Waterlow Rd. Reig. BT71 121
Waterman Clo. Wat. BC25 26
Waterman St. SW15 BQ45 65
Waterman Way Epp. CR17 23
Watermead La. Cars. BU53 86
Watermead Rd. SE6 CE49 77
Watermede, Felt. BB47 73
Water Mill Clo. Rich. BK48 74
Water Mill La. N18 CA28 39
Water Mill Way, Felt. BE48 74
Water Mill Way, S. Dnth. CX51 90
Waterpetty La. Wok. AP58 91
Water Rd. Wem. BL37 55
Waters Dr. Stai. AV48 72
Watersedge, Epsom BN56 94
Watersfield Way, Edg. BK29 36
Waters Gdns. Dag. CR35 50
Waterside, Beck. CD51 87
Waterside Chesh. AO20 16
Waterside Dart. CT46 79
Waterside, Kings L. AZ18 17
Waterside, St. Alb. BL17 19
Waterside, Uxb. AX39 53
Waterside, Welw. G. C. BS7 5
Waterside Clo. SE16 CB41 67
Bevington St.
Waterside Pla. NW1 BV37 56
Princess Rd.
Waterside Rd. Guil. AR69 118
Waterside Rd. Sthl. BF41 64
Waters Mead, Harl. CL13 13
Waterson Rd. Grays. DG42 71
Waterson St. E2 CA38 2
Waterson St. E2 CA38 57
Watersplash La. hayes BC42 63
Watersplash Rd. Shep. AZ52 83
Waters Rd. SE6 CG48 78
Waters Rd. Kings. on T. BM51 85
Waters Side Way Wok. AQ62 100
Winnington Way
Waters Sq. Kings. on T. BM52 85
Water St. WC2 BX40 4
Water St. WC2 BY40 56
Maltravers St.
Water St. Kings. on T. BL51 85
Canbury Pass
Waterton Av. Grav. DJ47 81
Water Tower Hill Croy. BZ56 96
Waterville Rd. N17 BZ30 39
Waterway Rd. Lthd. BJ64 102
Waterworks La. E5 CC34 48
Lea Bridge Rd.
Waterworks Rd. SW2 BX46 76
Watery La. SW20 BR51 85
Watery La. Brox. CD16 21
Watery La. Cher. AV54 82
Watery La. Hat. BO13 10
Watery La. Hayes BB42 63
Watery La. Nthlt. BD37 54
Watery Lane, Ong. CV11 15
Watery Lane, Ong. DA13 15
Watery La. Sev. CY64 108
Watery La. Sid. CO50 79
Watery La. St. Alb. BK17 18
Watery La. Wok. AO58 91
Wates Way, Mitch. BU53 86
Watford By-pass Borwd. BJ26 36
Watford Clo. SW11 BU44 66
Petworth St.
Watford Clo. Guil. AS70 118
Watford Flds. Rd. Wat. BD25 27
Watford Rd. E16 CH39 58
Watford Rd. Borwd. BK25 27
Watford Rd. Har. BJ33 45
Watford Rd. Kings. L. AZ18 17
Watford Rd. Nthwd. BB29 35
Watford Rd. Rick. AZ25 26
Watford Rd. St. Alb. BF17 18
Watford Rd. Wat. BF22 27
Watford Rd. Wat. BF23 27
Watford Way NW4 BN28 37
Watford Way NW7 BN28 37
Wathen Rd. Dor. BJ71 119
Watkin Rd.. Wem. BM34 46
Watkinson Rd. N7 BX36 56
Watling Av. Edg. BN30 37
Watling Clo. Hem. H. AY11 8
Watling Ct. EC4 BZ39 57
Watling St.
Watling Ct. Bush. BK25 27
Watling Farm Clo. Stan. BJ26 36
Watling Gdns. NW2 BR36 55
Watling Knoll, Rad. BH20 18
Watling St. EC4 BZ39 2
Watling St. EC4 BZ39 57
Watling St. Bexh. CR45 69
Watling St. Borwd. BK23 27
Watling St. Grav. DE48 81
Watling St. Rad. BH19 18
Watling St. St. Alb. BD10 9
Watlington Gro. SE26 CD49 77
Watlington Rd. Harl. CP9 6
Watling Vw. St. Alb. BG15 9
Watney Rd. SW14 BN45 65
Watney's Rd. Mitch. BW53 86
Watson Av. E6 CL36 58
Watson Av. Sutt. BR55 85
Watson Clo. N16 BZ35 48
Matthias Rd.
Watson Clo. SW19 BU50 76
Watson Rd. Dor. BG72 119
Watson Rd. Wok. AS61 100
Watsons Av. St. Alb. BH12 9
Watsons Ms. W1 BU39 56
Crawford Pl.
Watson, S Wk. St. Alb. BH14 9
Watson's Rd. N22 BX30 38
Watson's St. SE8 CD43 67
Watson St. E13 CH37 58
Watsons Yd. NW2 BO34 46
Watson Way, Grnf. BJ37 54
Sindall Dr.
Wattendon Rd. Ken. BY61 104
Wattisfield Rd. E5 CC34 48
Watt's Bri. Rd. Erith CT43 69
Watts Cres. Grays CY42 70
Watts Farm Par. Wok. AP58 91
Watts Gro. E3 CE39 57
Watt's La. Chis. CL51 88
Watts La. Tad. BQ64 103
Watts La. Tedd. BJ49 74
Watts Mead, Tad. BQ64 103
Watts Rd. Surb. BJ54 84
Watts St. E1 CB40 57
Wat Tyler Rd. SE10 CF44 67
Wauthier Clo. N13 BY28 38
Wavell Clo. Wal. Cr. CD17 21
Wavell Dr. Sid. CN46 78
Wavel Ms. NW6 BS36 56
Wavendene Av. Egh. AT50 72
Wavendon Av. W4 BN42 65
Waveney Av. SE15 CB45 67
Waveney, Hem. H. AY11 8
Waverley Av. E4 CD28 39
Waverley Av. Ken. CA61 105
Waverley Av. Surb. BM53 85
Waverley Av. Sutt. BS55 86
Waverley Av. Twick. BE47 74
Waverley Av. Wem. BL36 55
Waverley Clo. E18 CJ30 40
Waverley Clo. Brom. CJ53 88
Waverley Clo. Hayes BA42 63
Waverley Cres. SE18 CM42 68
Waverley Cres. Rom. CV29 42
Waverley Dr. Cher. AU56 91
Waverley Dr. Cher. AU55 82
Waverley Dr. Vir. W. AQ52 82
Waverley Gdns. NW10 BL37 55
Waverley Gdns. Bark. CN37 58
Waverley Gdns. Grays. DD41 71
Waverley Gdns. Ilf. CM30 40
Waverley Gdns. Nthwd. BC30 35
Waverley Gro. N3 BQ31 46
Waverley Pl. NW8 BT37 1
Waverley Pl. NW8 BT37 56

Waverley Pl. Lthd. BJ64 102
Church Rd.
Waverley Rd. E17 CF31 48
Waverley Rd. E18 CJ30 40
Waverley Rd. N8 BW32 47
Waverley Rd. N17 CA30 39
Waverley Rd. N17 CB29 39
Waverley Rd. SE18 CM42 68
Waverley Rd. SE25 CB52 87
Waverley Rd. Cob. BF60 93
Waverley Rd. Enf. BY24 29
Waverley Rd. Epsom BP57 94
Waverley Rd. Har. BE33 45
Waverley Rd. Rain. CU38 59
Waverley Rd. St. Alb. BG12 9
Waverley Rd. Sthl. BF40 54
Waverley Rd. Wey. AZ56 92
Waverley Wk. W2 BS39 56
Waverley Way Cars. BU57 95
Waverton Rd. SW18 BT47 76
Waverton St. W1 BV40 3
Waverton St. W1 BV41 66
Wavertree Ct. SW2 BX47 76
Wavertree Rd. E18 CH30 40
Wavertree Rd. SW2 BX47 76
Wave Tock Side, Brwd. CY23 33
Waxlow Cres. Sthl. BF39 54
Waxlow Rd. NW10 BN37 55
Waxwell Clo. Pnr. BD30 36
Waxwell La. Pnr. BD30 36
Waxwell Ter. SE1 BX41 4
Waxwell Ter. SE1 BX41 66
Waycross Rd. Upmin. CZ33 51
Waye Av. Houns. BC44 63
Wayfarer Rd. Nthlt. BD38 54
Wayford St. SW11 BU44 66
Wayland Av. E8 CB35 48
Waylands Swan. CT52 89
Waylett Pl. Wem. BK34 45
Wayne Clo. Orp. CN55 88
Waynefleet Tower Av.
Esher BF55 84
Wayneflete Sq. W10 BQ40 55
Wayneflete St. SW18 BT48 76
Waynfleet Av. Croy. BY55 86
Wayre Rd. Harl. CP9 6
Wayside NW11 BR33 46
Wayside SW14 BN46 75
Way Side, Kings L. AW18 17
Wayside, Pot. B. BT20 20
Wayside Av. Bush. BG25 27
Wayside Av. Horn. CV34 51
Wayside Clo. N14 BW25 29
Wayside Clo. Rom. CT31 50
Wayside Ct. Twick. BK46 74
Arlington Rd.
Wayside Gdns. SE9 CK49 78
Wayside Gro.
Wayside Gdns. Dag. CR35 50
Wayside Gro. SE9 CK49 78
Wayside Mews, Ilf. CL32 49
Gaysham Av.
Wayside, The Hem. H. AZ14 8
Way, The Reig. BT70 121
Wayville Rd. Dart. CX47 80
Way Volante, Grav. DJ49 81
Weald Bridge Rd. Epp. CS15 14
Weald Clo. Brom. CK55 88
Weald Clo. Brwd. DA27 42
Weald Clo. Sev. CU70 116
Weald Clo. Sev. CV70 117
Weald Hall La. Epp. CP16 23
Weald La. Har. BG30 36
Weald Park Way, Brwd. CZ27 42
Weald Rise, Har. BH29 36
Weald Rd. Brwd. CX26 42
Weald Rd. Sev. CU67 116
Weald Rd. Uxb. AZ37 53
Weald Sq. E5 CB34 48
Rossington St.
Wealdstone Rd. Sutt. BR55 85
Weald, The Chis. CK50 78
Weald, The Grav. DF50 81
Weald Way, Cat. CA67 114
Weald Way, Hayes BB38 53
Weald Way, Reig. BT72 121
Weald Way, Rom. CR32 50
Wealdwood Gdns. Pnr. BF29 36
High Banks Rd.
Weale Rd. E4 CF27 39
Weall Grn. Wat. BC19 17
Weardale Av. Dart. CY47 80
Weardale Gdns. Enf. BZ23 30
Weardale Rd. SE13 CF45 67
Wear Pl. E2 CB38 57
Bethnal Green Rd.
Wearside Rd. SE13 CE45 67
Wear St. E2 CB38 57
Teesdale St.
Weasdale Ct. Wok. AP61 100
Weatherall Clo. Wey. AW56 92
Weatherley Clo. E3 CD39 57
Weavers Clo. Grav. DG47 81
Weaver's La. SE1 CA40 4
Weavers La. SE1 CA40 57
Weavers La. Sev. CV64 108
Weaver St. E1 CB38 2
Weaver St. E1 CB38 57
Weaver Wk. SE27 BY49 76
Webb Clo. Slou. AR42 62
Webber Clo. Erith CU43 69
Webber Row SE1 BY41 4
Webber Row SE1 BY41 66
Webber St. SE1 BY41 4
Webber St. SE1 BY41 66
Webb Est. E5 CB33 48
Webb Gdns. E13 CH38 58
Kelland Rd.
Webb Rd. SE3 CG43 68
Webb's Alley, Sev. CV66 117
Webbs Rd. SW11 BU45 66
Webbs Rd. Hayes BC38 53
Webb St. SE1 CA41 4
Webb St. SE1 CA41 67
Webster Clo. Cob. BF60 93
Webster Clo. Uxb. AX38 53
Webster Clo. Wal. Abb. CG20 22
Webster Gdns. W5 BK40 54
Webster Rd. E11 CF34 48
Webster Rd. SE16 CB41 67
Webster Vill. W5 BK40 54
Webster Gdns.
Wedderburn Rd. NW3 BT35 47
Wedderburn Rd. Bark. CM37 58
Wedgewood Clo. Epp. CO18 23
Theydon Clo.
Wedgewood Clo. Nthwd. BA29 35
Wedgewood Way SE19 BZ50 77
Beulah Hill
Wedgewood Wk. NW6 BS36 56
Lymington Rd.
Wedhey Harl. CM11 13
Wedlake Clo. Horn. CW33 51
Wedlake St. W10 BR38 55
Kensal Rd.
Wedmore Av. Ilf. CL30 40
Wedmore Gdns. N19 BW34 47
Holloway Rd.
Wedmore Ms. N19 BW34 47
Wedmore St.
Wedmore Rd. Grnf. BG38 54
Wedmore St. N19 BW34 47
Wednesbury Gdns. Rom. CW29 42
Wednesbury Grn. Rom. CW29 42
Wednesbury Rd. Rom. CW29 42
Weech Rd. NW6 BS35 47
Weedington Rd. NW5 BV35 47
Weekes Dr. Slou. AN40 61
Weekley Sq. SW11 BT45 66
Th. Baines Rd.
Weetfield Av. Sth. Croy. BZ60 96
Weetman St. SE10 CG41 68
Weigall Rd. SE12 CH46 78
Weighouse St. W1 BV40 3
Weighouse St. W1 BV40 56
Weighton Ms. SE20 CB51 87
Weighton Rd.
Weighton Rd. SE20 CB51 87
Weighton Rd. Har. BG30 36
Weimar St. SW15 BR45 65
Weind, The Epp. CN21 31
Weint, The Slou. AU43 62
Weinurst Gdns. Sutt. BT56 95
Weir Clo. Bex. CR47 79
Weirdale Av. N20 BU27 38
Weir Hall Av. N18 BZ29 39
Weir Hall Clo. N17 BZ29 39
Weir Hall Gdns. N18 BZ28 39
Weir Hall Rd. N17 BZ29 39
Weir Hall Rd. N18 BZ29 39
Weir Pl. Stai. AV51 82
Weir Rd. SW12 BW47 76
Weir Rd. SW19 BS49 76
Weir Rd. Cher. AW54 83
Weir Rd. Walt. BC53 83
Weirs Pass NW1 BW38 1
Weirs Pass NW1 BW38 56
Chalton St.
Weiss Rd. SW15 BQ45 65
Welbeck Av. Brom. CH49 78
Welbeck Av. Hayes BC38 53
Welbeck Av. Sid. CO47 79
Welbeck Clo. N12 BT28 38
Welbeck Clo. Borwd. BM24 28
Welbeck Clo. Epsom BP57 94
Welbeck Clo. N. Mal. BO53 85
Welbeck Rd. E6 CJ38 58
Welbeck Rd. Barn. BT25 29
Welbeck Rd. Cars. BU54 86
Welbeck Rd. Har. BF33 45
Welbeck Rd. Sutt. BT55 86
Welbeck St. W1 BV39 1
Welbeck St. W1 BV39 56
Welbeck Wk. Cars. BT54 86
Welbeck Rd.
Welbeck Way W1 BV39 1
Welbeck Way W1 BV39 56
Welbourne Rd. N17 CA31 48
Hale The
Welby St. SE5 BY44 66
Welch Pl. Pnr. BC30 35
Welcomes Rd. Ken. BZ61 105
Weld Pl. N11 BW28 38
Welders La. Beac. AP29 34
Weldon Clo. Ruis. BC36 53
Weldon Way, Red. BW68 113
Welfare Rd. E15 CG36 58
Welford Clo. E5 CC34 48
Millfields Rd.
Welford Pl. SW19 BR49 75
Welham Cl. Hat. BQ15 10
Welham Rd. SW17 BV49 76
Welhouse Rd. Cars. BU54 86
Wellacre Rd. Har. BJ32 45
Wellan Clo. Well. CO46 79
Welland Gdns. Grnf. BH37 54
Wellands Clo. Brom. CK51 88
Welland St. SE10 CF43 67
Creek Rd.
Well App. Barn. BQ25 28
Wellbrook Rd. Orp. CL56 97
Wellbury Ter. Hem. H. BA13 8
Well Cl. E1 CB40 57
Well Clo. Ruis. BE34 45
Well Clo. Wok. AR62 100
Wellclose Sq. E1 CB40 4
Wellclose Sq. E1 CB40 57
Wellclose St. E1 CB40 57
Wellclose Sq.
Wellclose St. St. Alb. BG13 9
Wellcome Av. Dart. CW45 70
Well Cottage Clo. E11 CJ32 49
Well Ct. EC4 BZ39 57
Queen St.
Well Ct.NW8 BT37 1
Well Ct. SE18 BT37 56
Well Ct. NW8 BT38 56
Well Croft, Hem. H. AW13 8
Wellcroft Clo.
Welw. G. C. BS9 5
Wellcroft Rd. Slou. AN40 61
Welldale Rd. SE16 CC42 67
Welldon Cres. Har. BH32 45
Well End La. Borwd. BN22 28
Wellen Rise, Hem. H. AY15 8
Weller Clo. Amer. AP22 25
Weller Rd. Amer. AP22 25
Wellers Ct. NW1 BX37 2
Wellers Ct. NW1 BX37 56
Weller St. SE1 BZ41 67
Wellesford Clo. Bans. BR62 103
Wellesley Av. Iver. AV41 62
Wellesley Av. Nthwd. BB28 35
Wellesley Av. W6 BP41 65
Wellesley Av. Nthwd. BC28 35
Wellesley Ct. W9 BT38 56
Wellesley Ct. Rd. Croy. BZ55 87
Wellesley Gro.
Wellesley Cres. Pot. B. BR20 19
Wellesley Cres. Twick. BH48 74
Wellesley Gro. Croy. BZ55 87
Wellesley Path, Slou. AQ41 62
Wellesley Rd.
Wellesley Pl. NW5 BV35 47
Wellesley Rd. E11 CH32 49
Wellesley Rd. E17 CE32 48
Wellesley Rd. N22 BY30 38
Redvers Rd.
Wellesley Rd. NW5 BV35 47
Wellesley Rd. W4 BM42 65
Wellesley Rd. Brwd. DB26 42
Wellesley Rd. Croy. BZ55 87
Wellesley Rd. Har. BH32 45
Wellesley Rd. Ilf. CL34 49
Wellesley Rd. Slou. AQ41 62
Wellesley Rd. Sutt. BT57 95
Wellesley Rd. Twick. BG48 74
Wellesley St. E1 CC39 57
Welley Av. Stai. AS45 62
Welley Dr. Slou. AS45 62
Welley Rd. Stai. AS45 62
Welley Rd. Stai. AS46 72
Wellfarm Rd. Whyt. CB63 105
Well Field Hart. DC52 90
Wellfield Av. N10 BV31 47
Wellfield Clo. Hat. BP12 10
Wellfield Rd. SW16 BX49 76
Wellfield Rd. Hat. BP11 10
Wellfields Rd. Loug. CL24 31
Wellfield Wk. SW16 BX49 76
Wellgarth Gdns. Grnf. BJ36 54
Wellgarth Rd. NW11 BS33 47
Well Hall Rd. SE9 CK45 68
Wellham Rd. Uxb. AX37 53
Well Hill Orp. CR57 98
Wel Hill La. Orp. CR57 98
Well Hill Rd. Sev. CS57 98
Wellhouse La. Barn. BQ24 28
Wellhouse La. Bet. BN72 120
Wellhouse Rd. Beck. CD52 87
Wellington Arch W1 BV41 3
Wellington Arch SW1 BV42 66
Wellington Av. E4 CE27 39
Wellington Av. N9 CB27 39
Wellington Av. N15 CA32 48
Wellington Av. Houns. BF46 74
Wellington Av. Pnr. BE30 36
Wellington Av. Sid. CO46 79
Wellington Av. Vir. W. AQ52 82
Wellington Av. Wor. Pk. BQ56 94
Wellington Clo. E4 CE27 39
Wellington Av.
Wellington Cl. SE14 CC44 67
Wild Goose Dri.
Wellington Clo. W11 BS39 56
Ledbury Rd.
Wellington Clo. Dag. CS36 59
Wellington Cotts. Leath. BB68 110
Wellington Cres. N. Mal. BN52 85
Wellington Dr. Dag. CS36 59
Wellington Gdns. SE7 CJ42 68
Wellington Gdns. Hamptn. BG49 74
Wellington Hill, Loug. CH2 31
Wellingtonia Av. Hav. CS27 41
Wellington Pass E11 CH32 49
Wellington Rd.
Wellington Pl. N2 BU32 47
Wellington Pl. NW8 BT38 1
Wellington Pl. NW8 BT38 56
Wellington Rd. E6 CK37 58
Wellington Rd. E7 CG35 49
Wellington Rd. E10 CD33 48
Wellington Rd. E11 CH32 49
Wellington Rd. E17 CD31 48
Wellington Rd. NW8 BT37 1
Wellington Rd. NW8 BT37 56
Wellington Rd. NW10 BQ39 55
Wellington Rd. SW19 BS48 76
Wellington Rd. W5 BK41 64
Wellington Rd. Ashf. AY49 73
Wellington Rd. Belv. CQ42 69
Wellington Rd. Bex. CP46 79
Wellington Rd. Brom. CJ52 88
Wellington Rd. Cat. BZ64 105
Wellington Rd. Croy. BY54 86
Wellington Rd. Dart. CV46 80
Wellington Rd. Enf. CA26 39
Wellington Rd. Felt. BB46 73
Wellington Rd. Har. BH31 45
Wellington Rd. Hmptn. BG49 74
Wellington Rd. Orp. CO53 89
Wellington Rd. Pnr. BE29 36
Wellington Rd. St. Alb. BJ14 9
Wellington Rd. St. Alb. BK16 18
Wellington Rd. Til. DG45 71
Wellington Rd. Wat. BC23 26
Wellington Rd. N. Houns. BE45 64
Wellington Rd. S. Houns. BE45 64
Wellington Row E2 CA38 2
Wellington Row E2 CA38 57
Wellington Sq. SW3 BU42 3
Wellington Sq. SW3 BU42 66
Wellington St. E5 CB34 48
Wellington St. SE18 CL42 68
Wellington St. WC2 BX40 4
Wellington St. WC2 BX40 56
Wellington St. Grav. DH47 81
Wellington St. Slo. AQ41 62
Wellington Ter. Har. BG33 45
Wellington Way E3 CE38 57
Wellington Yd. Rich. BK46 74
George St.
Welling Way SE9 CM45 68
Welling Way Well. CM45 68
Well La. SW14 BN46 75
Well La. Brwd. CZ24 33
Well La. Grays. DC40 61
Well La. Harl. CL10 6
Well La. Wok. AR62 100
Wellmeade Dr. Sev. CU67 116
Wellmeadow Rd. SE6 CG46 78
Wellmeadow Rd. SE13 CG46 78
Wellmeadow Rd. W7 BJ42 64
Wellow Wk. Cars. BT54 86
Well Pass NW3 BT34 47
Well Path, Wok. AR62 100
Well Rd. NW10 BO38 55
Well Rd. Barn. BQ25 28
Well Rd. Pot. B. BU17 20
Well Rd. Sev. CV62 108
Well Row, Hert. BX12 11
Wells Clo. Nthlt. BD38 54
Wells Cres. SE5 CA43 67
Wells Dr. NW9 BN33 46
Wells Gdns. Dag. CR35 50
Wells Gdns. Ilf. CK33 49
Wells Gdns. Rain. CT36 59
Wellshouse Rd. NW10 BO39 55
Wellside Clo. Barn. BQ24 28
Wellside Gdns. SW14 BN46 75
Wells Ms. W1 BW39 1
Wells Ms. W1 BW39 56
Wellsmoor Gdns. Brom. CL5 88
Wells Pk. Rd. SE26 CB48 77
Wells Pl. W5 BK40 54
Wellsprings Cres. Wem. BM34 46
Wells Rise NW8 BU37 1
Wells Rise NW8 BU37 56
Wells Rd. W12 BQ41 65
Wells Rd. Brom. CK51 88
Wells Rd. Epsom BM60 94
Wells St. W1 BW39 1
Wells St. W1 BW39 56
Wellstead Av. N9 CC26 39
Wellstead Rd. E6 CL37 58
Wells Ter. N4 BY34 47
Wells, The N14 BW26 38
Wellstones, Wat. BC24 26
Market St.
Well St. E9 CB36 57
Well St. E15 CG36 58
Wells Way SE5 BZ43 67
Wellswood Clo. Hem. H. AZ13 8
Well Way, Epsom BM61 103
Wellwood Clo. Couls. BX56 95
Wellwood Clo. Couls. BX60 95
Wellwood Rd. Ilf. CO33 50
Welsford St. SE1 CB42 4
Welsford St. SE1 CB42 67
Welsh Clo. E13 CH38 58
Welshpool St. E8 CB37 57
Weltje Rd. W6 BP42 65
Welton Rd. SE18 CN43 68
Welwyn Av. Felt. BB46 73
Welwyn Ct. Hem. H. AY11 8
Welwyn St. E2 CC38 57
Globe Rd.
Welwyn Way, Hayes BB38 53
Wembley Hill Rd. Wem. BL34 46
Wembley Park Dr. Wem. BL35 46
Wembley Rd. Hamptn. BF51 84
Wembley Way, Wem. BM36 55
Wemborough Rd. Stan. BK30 36
Wembury Rd. N6 BV33 47
Wemyss Rd. SE3 CG44 68
Wendela Clo. Wok. AS62 100
Wendela Ct. Har. BH34 45
Wendell Rd. W12 BO41 65
Wend End Ct. Slou. AP37 2
Wendley Dri. Wey. AV58 91
Wendling Rd. Sutt. BT55 86
Wendon St. E3 CD37 57
Wendover Dr. N. Mal. BO53 85
Wendover Pl. Stai. AV49 72
Wendover Rd. NW10 BO37 55
Wendover Rd. SE9 CJ45 68
Wendover Rd. Brom. CH52 88
Wendover Rd. Stai. AV49 72
Wendover Way Bush. BG25 27
Wendover Way Orp. CO53 89
Wendover Way, Well. CO46 79
Wendron Clo. Wok. AQ62 100
Shilburn Way
Wend. The Couls. BW60 95
Wendy Clo. Enf. CA25 30
First Av.
Wendy Cres. Guil. AQ69 118
Wendy Way, Wem. BL37 55
Weneth Hall Rd. Ilf. CK31 49
Wenloch Edge, Dor. BK72 119
Wenlock Ct. N1 BZ37 2
Wenlock Rd. N1 BZ37 2
Wenlock Rd. N1 BZ37 57
Wenlock Rd. Edg. BM29 37
Wenlocks La. Ing. BZ37 24
Wenlock St. N1 BZ37 2
Wenlock St. N1 BZ37 57
Wennington Rd. E3 CC37 57
Grove Rd.
Wennington Rd. Rain. CU38 59
Wensley Av. Wdf. Grn. CG29 40
Wensley Clo. Rom. CR28 41
Wensleydale, Hem. H. AY12 8
Wensleydale Av. Ilf. CK30 40
Wensleydale Gdns.
Hamptn. BF50 74
Wensleydale Pass
Hamptn. BF51 84
Wensleydale Rd. Hamptn. BF50 74
Wensley Rd. N18 CB29 39
Wensum Way, Rick. AX26 35
Wentbridge Path Borwd. BL22 28
Wentland Rd. SE6 CF48 77
Wentworth Av. N3 BS29 38
Wentworth Clo. N3 BS29 38
Wentworth Clo. Ashf. AZ49 73
Reedsfield Rd.
Wentworth Clo. Mord. BS54 86
Wentworth Clo. Orp. CN56 97
Wentworth Clo. Surb. BK55 84
Wentworth Clo. Wat. BB22 26
Wentworth Clo. Wok. AW64 101
Wentworth Cres. SE15 CB43 67
Bells Gdns.
Wentworth Cres. Hayes BA41 63
Wentworth Dr. Dart. CU46 79
Wentworth Dr. Pnr. BC32 44
Wentworth Dr. Vir. W. AP52 82
Wentworth Gdns. N13 BY28 38
Wentworth Hill, Wem. BL33 46
Wentworth Ms. E3 CD38 57
Eric St.
Wentworth Pk. N3 BS29 38
Wentworth Rd. E12 CJ35 49
Wentworth Rd. NW11 BR32 46
Wentworth Rd. Barn. BQ24 28
Wentworth Rd. Croy. BY54 86
Wentworth Rd. Sthl. BD42 64
Wentworth St. E1 CA39 2
Wentworth St. E1 CA39 57
Wentworth Way, Pnr. BD31 45
Wentworth Way, Rain. CU38 59
Wentworth Way,
Sth. Croy. CB60 96
Wenvoe Av. Bexh. CR44 69
Wernbrook St. SE18 CM43 68
Werndee Rd. SE25 CB52 87
Werrington St. NW1 BW37 1
Warrington St. NW1 BW37 56
Werter Rd. SW15 BR45 65
Wesley Av. NW10 BN38 55
Wesley Av. Houns. BE44 64
Wesley Clo. N7 BX34 47
Durham Rd.
Wesley Clo. Har. BG34 45
Wesley Clo. Orp. CP52 89
Main Rd.
Wesley Clo. Wal. Cr. BZ17 21
Wesley Rd. E10 CF33 48
Wesley Rd. NW10 BN37 55
Wesley Rd. Hayes BC39 53
Wesley Square W11 BQ40 55
Lancaster Road
Wesley St. W1 BV39 56
Weymouth St.
Wessex Av. SW19 BS52 86
Wessex Bldgs. N19 BW34 47
Wedmore St.
Wessex Clo. Ilf. CN32 49
Suffolk Rd.
Wessex Clo. Kings. on T. BM51 85
Gloucester Rd.
Wessex Dr. Erith CT44 69
Wessex Dr. Pnr. BE29 36
Wessex Gdns. NW11 BR33 46
Wessex Rd. Houns. AW45 63
Wessex St. E2 CC38 57
Wessex Way NW11 BR33 46
Westacott, Hayes BB39 53
Westacott Clo. N19 BW33 47
Hazelville Rd.
Westacres Esher BE57 93
Westall Rd. Loug. CL24 31
Westanley Av. Amer. AO23 25
West App. Orp. CM53 88
West Arbour St. E1 CC39 57
West Av. E17 CE31 48
West Av. N3 BS29 38
West Av. NW4 BQ32 46
West Av. Hayes BB40 53
West Av. Hayes BC40 53
West Av. Pnr. BE32 45
West Av. Red. BV73 121
West Av. St. Alb. BF16 18
West Av. Sthl. BE40 54
West Av. Wall. BX56 95
West Av. Watt. BB58 92
West Av. Rd. E17 CE31 48
West Bank N16 CA33 48
West Bank, Bark. CL37 58
West Bank, Dor. BH72 119
West Bank, Enf. BZ23 30
Westbank Rd. Hamptn. BG50 74
West Barnes La. SW20 BP51 80
West Barnes La. N. Mal. BP52 85
West Barnes La. N. Mal. BP53 85
West Beech Rd. N22 BY31 47
Westbere Dr. Stan. BK28 36
Westbere Rd. NW2 BR35 46
Westbourne Av. N9 CB27 39
Eastbournia Av.
Westbourne Av. W3 BN39 55
Westbourne Av. Sutt. BR55 85
Westbourne Br. W2 BT39 1
Westbourne Br. W2 BT39 56
Westbourne Clo. Hayes BD38 54
Westbourne Cres. W2 BT40 3
Westbourne Cres. W2 BT40 56
Westbourne Dr. SE23 CC48 77
Westbourne Dr. Brwd. CZ28 42
Westbourne Gdns. W2 BS39 1
Westbourne Gdns. W2 BS39 56
Westbourne Gte. W2 BS39 56
Westbourne Gr. W11 BR40 55
Westbourne Gro. Ms.
W11 BS39 56
Westbourne Gro.
Westbourne Gro. W2 BS39 56
Westbourne Gro. Ter. W2 BS39 1
Westbourne Gro. Ter. W2 BS39 56
Westbourne Pk. Ms. W2 BS39 1
Westbourne Pk. Ms. W2 BS39 56
Westbourne Gdns.
Westbourne Pk. Pass W2 BS39 56
Westbourne Pk. Rd. W2 BR39 55
Westbourne Pk. Rd. W11 BR39 55
Westbourne Pk. Vill. W2 BS39 56
Westbourne Pl. N9 CB27 39
Eastbournia Av.
Westbourne Rd. N7 BY36 56
Arundel Sq.
Westbourne Rd. SE26 CC50 77
Westbourne Rd. Bexh. CP43 69
Westbourne Rd. Croy. CA53 87
Westbourne Rd. Felt. BB48 73
Westbourne Rd. Stai. AW50 73
Westbourne Rd. Uxb. AZ38 53
Westbourne St. W2 BT40 3
Westbourne St. W2 BT40 56

Westbourne Ter. W2 BT39 1
Westbourne Ter. W2 BT39 56
Westbourne Ter. Ms. W2 BT39 1
Westbourne Ter. Ms. W2 BT39 56
Westbourne Ter. Rd. W2 BT39 1
Westbourne Ter. Rd. W2 BT39 56
Westbridge Rd. SW11 BT44 66
West Brook, Harl. CK12 13
Westbrook, Maid. AJ42 61
Westbrook Av. Hamptn. BE50 74
Westbrook Clo. Barn. BT24 29
Westbrook Cres. Barn. BT24 29
Westbrook Dr. Orp. CP54 89
Westbrooke Cres. Well. CP45 69
Westbrooke Rd. Sid. CM48 78
Westbrooke Rd. Well. CP45 69
Westbrook Rd. SE3 CH44 68
Westbrook Rd. Houns. BE43 64
Westbrook Rd. Th. Hth. BZ51 87
Westbrook Sq. Barn. BT24 29
West Burrow Fld. Welw. G. C. BQ9 5
Westbury Av. N22 BY31 47
Westbury Av. Esher BH57 93
Westbury Av. Sthl. BF38 54
Westbury Av. Wem. BL36 55
Westbury Clo. Ruis. BC33 44
Westbury Clo. Shep. AZ53 83
Burchetts Way
Westbury Dr. Brwd. DA27 42
Westbury Gro. N3 BS29 38
Westbury La. Buck. H. CH27 40
Westbury Lodge Clo. Pnr. BD31 45
Chapel La.
Westbury Pl. Brent. BK43 64
Hamilton Rd.
Westbury Rd. E7 CH35 49
Westbury Rd. E17 CD31 48
Westbury Rd. N11 BX29 38
Westbury Rd. N12 BS29 38
Westbury Rd. SE20 CC51 87
Westbury Rd. W5 BL39 55
Westbury Rd. Bark. CM37 58
Westbury Rd. Beck. CD52 87
Westbury Rd. Brom. CJ51 88
Westbury Rd. Brwd. DB27 42
Westbury Rd. Buck. H. CH27 40
Westbury Rd. Buck. H. CJ27 40
Westbury Rd. Croy. BZ53 87
Westbury Rd. Felt. BD47 74
Westbury Rd. Ilf. CK34 49
Westbury Rd. N. Mal. BN52 85
Westbury Rd. Nthwd. BA28 35
Westbury Rd. Wat. BC25 26
Westbury Rd. Wem. BL36 55
Westbury St. SW8 BW44 66
Westbury Ter. E7 CH36 58
Westbury Ter. Upmin. CZ34 51
Westbury Ter. West. CM66 115
Westbush Clo. Hodd. CD10 12
Westcar La. Walt. BC57 92
West Central Pl. WC1 BX39 2
West Central St. WC1 BX39 56
New Oxford St.
Westchester Dr. NW4 BQ31 46
West Clo. N9 CA27 39
West Clo. Ashf. AY49 73
West Clo. Barn. BP25 28
West Clo. Barn. BV24 29
West Clo. Grnf. BG37 54
West Clo. Hodd. CE11 12
West Clo. Rain. CU38 59
West Clo. Wem. BL33 46
Westcombe Av. Croy. BX53 86
Westcombe Ct. SE3 CG43 68
Westcombe Dr. Barn. BS25 29
Westcombe Hill SE3 CH42 68
Westcombe Pk. Rd. SE3 CG43 68
West Common, Ger. Cr. AR32 43
West Common Clo. Ger. Cr. AS32 43
West Common Rd. Brom. CH55 88
West Common Rd. Uxb. AX35 44
W. Common Rd. Uxb. AX36 53
Westcoombe Av. SW20 BO51 85
Westcote Rise, Ruis. BA33 44
Westcote Rd. SW16 BW49 76
West Cotts. NW6 BS35 47
Westcott Clo. N15 CA32 48
Ermine Rd.
Westcott Clo. Croy. CE58 96
Westcott Cres. W7 BH39 54
Westcott Rd. SE17 BY43 4
Westcott Rd. SE17 BY43 66
Westcott Rd. Dor. BH72 119
Westcott St. Dor. BF72 119
Westcott Way Sutt. BQ58 94
Westcott Waye, Uxb. AX37 52
West Ct. SE18 CL43 68
Prince Imperial Way
West Ct. Wem. BK34 45
Westcourt Av. Grav. DG48 81
West Cres. Wind. AM44 61
West Cres. Rd. Grav. DG46 81
Westcroft Clo. NW2 BR35 46
Westcroft Est. NW2 BR35 46
Westcroft Gdns. Mord. BR52 85
Westcroft Rd. Cars. BV56 95
Westcroft Sq. W6 BO42 65
Westcroft Way. NW2 BR35 46
West Cromwell Rd. SW5 BR42 65
West Cromwell Rd. W14 BR42 65
Westdale Rd. SE18 CL43 68
W. Drayton Rd. Uxb. AY39 53
Westdean Av. SE12 CH47 78
Westdean Cl. SW18 BS46 76
Denton St.
West Dene Sutt. BR57 94
Park La.
Westdene Dr. Rom. CV28 42
West Dene Way, Wem. BB55 83
Westdown, Lthd. BF67 111
Westdown Rd. E15 CF35 48
Westdown Rd. SE6 CE47 77
West Drayton Park Ave. West Dr. AY41 63
West Dr. N8 BW31 47
Redston Rd.
West Dr. SW11 BU43 66
Wet Dr. SW16 BW49 76
West Dr. Ascot. AO53 82
West Dr. Cars. BT58 95
West Dr. Har. BG29 36
West Dr. Sutt. BQ58 94
West Dr. Tad. BQ62 103
West Dr. Vir. W. AO53 82
West Dr. Wat. BC21 26
West Dr. Gdns. Har. BG29 36
West Eaton Pl. SW1 BV42 3
West Eaton Pl. SW1 BV42 66
Wested La. Swan. CU54 89
West Ella Rd. NW10 BO36 55
West End, Sev. CW62 108
West End Av. E10 CF32 48
West End Av. Pnr. BD31 45
West End Ct. Pnr. BD31 45
West End Gdns. Esher BE56 93
West End Gdns. Nthlt. BD37 54
West End La. NW6 BS35 47
West End La. Barn. BQ24 28
West End La. Esher BE57 93
West End La. Esher BF56 93
West End La. Hat. BT12 11
West End La. Hayes BA43 63
West End La. Pnr. BD31 45
West End La. Slou. AP37 52
West End Rd. Brox. CA14 12
West End Rd. Nthlt. BD36 54
West End Rd. Ruis. BB33 44
West End Rd. Sthl. BE40 54
Westerdale, Hem. H. AY12 8
Westerdale Rd. SE10 CH42 68
Westerfield Rd. N15 CA32 48
Wester Folds Clo. Wok. AU62 100
Westergate Rd. SE2 CQ43 69
Westerham Av. N9 BZ27 39
Westerham Clo. Wey. AX57 92
Westerham Dr. Sid. CO46 79
Westerham Rd. E10 CE32 48
Westerham Rd. Kes. CJ58 97
Westerham Rd. Oxt. CG68 115
Westerham Rd. Sev. CR65 107
Westerham Rd. West. CJ60 97
Westerley Cres. SE26 CD49 77
Western Av. NW9 BQ32 46
Western Av. W3 BJ38 54
Western Av. W5 BJ38 54
Western Av. Brwd. DB26 42
Western Av. Dag. CS36 59
Western Av. Egh. AT52 82
Western Av. Epp. CN19 22
Western Av. Grnf. BJ38 54
Western Av. Rom. CV30 42
Western Av. Ruis. BC36 53
Western Av. Uxb. AX35 44
Western Av. Uxb. BA36 53
Western Circus W3 BO40 55
Western Ct. N3 BS29 38
Western Ct. W3 BN39 55
York Rd.
Western Dr. Shep. BA53 83
Western Gdns. W5 BM40 55
Western Gdns. Brwd. DB27 42
Western La. SW12 BV47 76
Western Pde. Barn. BS25 29
Western Perimeter Rd. Houns. AW45 63
Western Perimeter Rd. Houns. AX46 73
Western Rd. E13 CJ37 58
Western Rd. E17 CF32 48
Western Rd. N2 BU31 47
Western Rd. N22 BX30 38
Western Rd. NW10 BN38 55
Western Rd. SW9 BY45 66
Western Rd. SW19 BT51 86
Western Rd. W5 BK40 54
Western Rd. Brwd. DB27 42
Western Rd. Epp. CN19 22
Western Rd. Mitch. BT51 86
Western Rd. Rom. CT32 50
Western Rd. Sthl. BD42 64
Western Rd. Sutt. BS56 95
Western Rd. Wal. Abb. CG14 13
Western St. E15 CF36 57
Western Trading Est. NW10 BN38 55
Westernville Gdns. Ilf. CM33 49
Western Vn. Hayes BB41 63
Western Way Barn. BS25 29
West Farm Av. Ash. BK62 102
West Farm Clo. Ash. BK63 102
West Farm Dr. Ash. BK63 102
West Ferry Est. E14 CE42 67
Westferry Rd. E14 CE40 57
Westfield Rd. Guil. AS68 109
Westfield N6 BV34 47
West Field SW13 BO45 65
Cross St.
Westfield, Harl. CN11 13
Westfield, Reig. BS69 121
Westfield, Sev. CV64 108
Westfield, Welw. G. C. BS7 5
Daniells
Westfield, Ash. BL62 103
Westfield Av. SW13 BO45 65
Westfield Av. Wat. BD22 27
Westfield Av. Wok. AS64 100
Westfield Clo. Enf. CD24 30
Westfield Clo. Grav. DH49 81
Westfield Clo. Sutt. BR56 94
Westfield Clo. Wal. Cr. CD19 21
Westfield Ct. St. Alb. BK12 9
Southfield Way
Westfield Dr. Har. BK32 45
Westfield Dr. Lthd. BF64 102
Westfield Gdns. Har. BK31 45
Westfield Gro. Wok. AS63 100
Westfield La. Harrow BK31 45
Westfield La. Slou. AR40 52
Westfield Pde. Wey. AX58 92
Westfield Pk. Pnr. BE29 36
Westfield Rd. N8 BX31 47
Westfield Rd. NW7 BN27 37
Westfield Rd. SE18 CJ41 68
Westfield Rd. W13 BJ40 54
Westfield Rd. Beck. CD51 87
Westfield Rd. Berk. AP12 7
Westfield Rd. Bexh. CS44 69
Westfield Rd. Croy. BY55 86
Westfield Rd. Dag. CQ35 50
Westfield Rd. Hodd. CD11 12
Westfield Rd. Mitch. BU51 86
Westfield Rd. Surb. BK53 84
Westfield Rd. Sutt. BR56 94
Westfield Rd. Walt. BE54 84
Westfield Rd. Wok. AR64 100
Westfields SW13 BO45 65
Railway Side
Westfields, Loug. CJ25 31
Longfield
Westfields, St. Alb. BF14 9
Westfields, St. Alb. BF15 9
Westfields Rd. W3 BM39 55
Westfield Wk. Wal. Cr. CD19 21
Westfield Way, Ruis. BB34 44
Westfield Way, Wok. AS64 100
West Gdns. E1 CB40 57
West Gardens E1 CB40 57
Agatha Clo.
West Gdns. SW17 BU50 76
West Gdns. Epsom BO58 94
West Gate SE16 CC41 67
West Gate, Harl. CM11 13
West Gate Ms. W10 BQ38 55
West Row
Westgate Rd. SE25 CB52 87
Westgate Rd. Beck. CE51 87
Westgate Rd. Dart. CV46 80
Westgate St. E8 CB37 57
Westgate Ter. SW10 BS42 3
Westgate Ter. SW10 BS42 66
Westglade Ct. Har. BK32 45
West Green Rd. N15 BY31 47
West Gro. SE10 CF44 67
West Gro. Walt. BC56 92
West Gro. Wdf. Grn. CJ29 40
Westgrove La. SE10 CF44 67
West Halkin St. SW1 BV41 3
West Halkin St. SW1 BV41 66
West Hall Ct. N6 BV34 47
West Hallows SE9 CJ47 78
Westhall Park Rd. Warl. CC63 105
Westhall Rd. SE5 BY43 66
West Hall Rd. Rich. BM44 65
Westhall Rd. Warl. CB62 105
Westhall Rd. Warl. CB63 105
West Ham La. E15 CG36 58
West Hampstead Ms. NW6 BS36 56
West Harding St. EC4 BY39 2
West Harding St. EC4 BY39 56
Fetter La.
Westharold Swan. CS52 89
West Hatch Manor, Ruis. BB33 44
Westhay Gdns. SW14 BM46 75
West Hth. Av. NW11 BS33 47
West Hth. Clo. NW3 BS34 47
West Hth. Clo. Dart. CT46 79
West Hth. Ct. NW11 BS33 47
West Hth. Dr. NW11 BS33 47
West Hth. Gdns. NW3 BS34 47
West Hth. La. Sev. CU67 116
West Hth. Rd. NW3 BS34 47
West Hth. Rd. SE2 CP43 69
West Hth. Rd. Dart. CT46 79
West Hill SW15 BQ47 75
West Hill SW18 BQ47 75
West Hill, Ash. BL63 103
West Hill, Dart. CV46 80
West Hill Epsom BN60 94
West Hill Har. BH34 45
West Hill, Orp. CK59 97
West Hill Sth. Croy. CA58 96
West Hill, Wem. BL33 46
West Hill Av. Epsom BM60 94
West Hill Bk. Oxt. CF68 114
Westhill Clo. Grav. DG47 81
Leith Pk. Rd.
West Hill Ct. SW18 BR46 75
West Hill Rd.
West Hill Dr. Dart. CV46 80
West Hill Rise, Dart. CV46 80
West Hill Rd. SW18 BR46 75
Westhill Rd. Hodd. CD11 12
West Hill Rd. Wok. AR63 100
West Hill Way N20 BS26 38
Westholm NW11 BS31 47
West Holme Erith CS44 69
Westholme Orp. CN54 88
Westholme Gdns. Ruis. BC33 44
Westhorne Av. SE9 CH47 78
Westhorne Av. SE12 CH47 78
Westhorpe Gdns. NW4 BQ31 46
Westhorpe Rd. SW15 BQ45 65
Westhouse Clo. SW19 BR47 75
Westhumble St. Dor. BJ69 119
Westhurst Dr. Chis. CL49 78
West Hyde La. Ger. Cr. AS29 34
West India Dock Rd. E14 CD39 57
West Kent Av. Grav. DE46 81
West Kentish Town Est. NW5 BV35 47
Westlake Clo. N13 BY27 38
Westlake Rd. Bex. CP46 79
Blendon Rd.
Westland Av. Horn. CW33 51
Westland Ct. Epsom BN60 94
Westland Dr. Brom. CG55 88
Westland Dr. Hat. BR17 19
Westland Pl. N1 BZ38 2
Westland Pl. N1 BZ38 57
Westland Rd. Wat. BC23 26
Westlands Ct. Epsom BN61 103
Westlands Ter. SW12 BW46 76
Gaskarth Rd.
Westlands Way, Oxt. CF67 114
Westland Way. Grays DD40 71
West La. SE16 CB41 67
West La. Dor. BD73 119
Westlea Av. Wat. BE21 27
Westlea Rd. W7 BJ41 64
Westlea Rd. Brox. CD15 12
Westleigh Av. SW15 BP46 75
Westleigh Av. Couls. BV61 104
Westleigh Dr. Brom. CK51 88
Westleigh Gdns. Edg. BM30 37
Westley St. W1 BV39 1
Westley Wood, Welw. G. C. BS7 5
West Lodge Av. W3 BM40 55
Westlyn Clo. Rain. CV38 60
West Mall W8 BS40 56
West Malling Way, Horn. CV35 51
Westmead SW15 BP46 75
Westmead Epsom BO57 94
Westmead Ruis. BD35 45
West Mead. Welw. G. C. BS9 5
Westmead, Wind. AN45 61
Westmead Rd. Sutt. BT56 95
West Mead, Wok. AQ62 100
West Meads, Guil. AP71 118
West Mede Chig. CM29 40
Westmere Dr. NW7 BN27 37
West Mews N18 CB29 39
Westminster Av. Th. Hth. BY51 86
Westminster Br. SE1 BX41 66
Westminster Bridge SW1 BX41 4
Westminster Br. SW1 BX41 66
Westminster Bridge Rd. SE1 BX41 4
Westminster Bridge Rd. SE1 BX41 66
Westminster Clo. Ilf. CM30 40
Westminster Clo. Tedd. BJ49 74
Cambridge Rd.
Westminster Ct. St. Alb. BG14 9
Westminster Dr. N13 BX28 38
Westminster Gdns. Bark. CN37 58
Westminster Gdns. Ilf. CM30 40
Westminster Ms. W2 BS40 56
Shrewsbury Rd.
Westminster Rd. N9 CB26 39
Westminster Rd. W7 BH40 54
Westminster Rd. Sutt. BT55 86
Westmoat Clo. Beck. CF50 77
Westmont Rd. Esher BH55 84
Westmoor Gdns. Enf. CC23 30
Westmoor Rd. Enf. CC23 30
Westmoor St. SE7 CJ41 68
Westmoreland Bldgs. EC1 BZ39 2
Westmoreland Bldgs. EC1 BZ39 57
Aldersgate St.
Westmoreland Dr. Sutt. BS57 95
Westmoreland Pl. SW1 BV42 3
Westmoreland Pl. SW1 BV42 66
Westmoreland Pl. W5 BK39 54
Mount Av.
Westmoreland Rd. NW9 BL31 46
Westmoreland Rd. Brom. CG53 88
Westmoreland Rd. Har. BF32 45
Westmoreland St. W1 BV39 56
Westmoreland Ter. SW1 BV42 3
Westmoreland Ter. SW1 BV42 66
Westmoreland Way Mitch. BW52 86
Westmore Rd. West. CJ64 106
Westmorland Av Horn. CV32 51
Westmorland Av. Well. CN45 68
Westmorland Clo. E12 CJ33 49
Westmorland Clo. Epsom BO58 94
Longmead Rd.
Westmorland Clo. Twick. BJ46 74
St. Margaret's Rd.
Westmorland Rd. E17 CE32 48
Westmorland Rd. SE17 BZ43 4
Westmorland Rd. SW13 BO44 65
Westmorland St. W1 BV39 1
West Mount, Guil. AR71 118
The Mount
West Mount Av. Amer. AO23 25
Westmount Rd. SE9 CK44 68
West Oak, Beck. CF51 87
Westoe Rd. N9 CB27 39
Weston Av. E. Mol. BE52 84
Weston Av. Surb. BH54 84
Weston Av. Wey. AW56 92
Weston Clo. Brwd. DE26 122
Weston Clo. Couls. BX63 104
Weston Dr. Stan. BJ30 36
Weston Grn. Dag. CQ35 50
Weston Grn. Surb. BH54 84
Weston Grn. Rd. Esher BG54 84
Weston Grn. Rd. Surb. BH54 84
Weston Gro. Brom. CG50 78
Weston Gro. Wok. AV61 100
Weston Park N8 BX32 47
Weston Pk. Kings. on T. BL51 85
Fairfield West
Weston Pk. Surb. BH54 84
Weston Pk. Clo. Surb. BH54 84
Weston Rise WC1 BX38 2
Weston Rise WC1 BX38 56
Weston Rd. W4 BN41 65
Weston Rd. Brom. CG50 78
Weston Rd. Dag. CQ35 50
Weston Rd. Enf. BZ23 30
Weston Rd. Guil. AQ70 118
Weston Rd. Surb. BH54 84
Weston St. SE1 BZ41 67
Weston Way, Wok. AV61 100
Weston Yd. SE1 BZ41 67
Weston St.
Westover Clo. Sutt. BS58 95
Hulverston Clo.
Westover Hill NW3 BS34 47
Westover Rd. SW18 BT47 76
Westow Hill SE19 CA50 77
Westow St. SE19 CA50 77
West Palace Gdns. Wey. AZ55 83
West Park SE9 CK48 78
West Pk. Av. Rich. BM44 65
West Park Clo. Rom. CQ32 50
West Park Hill, Brwd. DA27 42
West Park Rd. Epsom BL59 94
West Pk. Rd. Rich. BM44 65
West Pl. SW19 BQ49 75
West Point, Slou. AL40 61
Westpole Av. Barn. BV24 29
Westport Rd. E13 CH38 58
Westport St. E1 CC39 57
West Poultry Av. EC1 BY39 2
West Poultry Av. EC1 BY39 56
Charterhouse St.
West Quarters W12 BP39 55
Du Cane Rd.
Westray, Hem. H. AZ14 8
West Ramp, Houns. AZ44 63
West Ridge Clo. Hem. H. AV13 7
West Ridge Gdns. Grnf. BG37 54
West Riding, St. Alb. BE18 18
West Riding, St. Alb. BF18 18
West Rd. E15 CG37 58
West Rd. N17 CB29 39
West Rd. SW4 BW46 76
West Rd. SW14 BN45 65
West Rd. W5 BL39 55
West Rd. Barn. BV26 38
West Rd. Berk. AQ12 7
West Rd. Chess. BK59 93
West Rd. Felt. BA46 73
West Rd. Guil. AS71 118
West Rd. Harl. CO9 6
West Rd. Kings. on T. BN51 85
West Rd. Reig. BS71 121
West Rd. Rom. CQ32 50
West Rd. Rom. CS33 50
West Rd. Saw. CO5 6
West Rd. S. Ock. DA38 60
West Rd. West Dr. AY41 63
West Rd. Wey. AZ58 92
West Row W10 BQ38 55
West St. E11 CG34 49
High Rd. Leytonstone
Westrow Dr. Bark. CO35 50
Westrow Gdns. Ilf. CN34 49
West St. La. Cars. BU56 95
West Sheen Vale, Rich. BL45 65
Westside NW4 BP30 37
West Side SW18 BT46 76
West Side, Common SW19 BQ49 75
West Smithfield EC1 BY39 2
West Smithfield EC1 BY39 56
West Sq. SE1 BY41 66
West Sq. SE11 BY41 4
West Sq. SE18 CK42 68
West Sq. Iver AV39 52
West St. E11 CG34 49
West St. E17 CE32 48
West St. EC2 BZ39 2
West St. EC2 BZ39 57
Moorgate
West St. WC2 BW39 1
West St. WC2 BW39 56
Litchfield St.
West St. Bexh. CQ45 69
West St. Brom. CH51 88
West St. Cars. BU55 86
West St. Croy. BZ56 96
West Dr. Dor. BJ71 119
West St. Epsom BN60 94
West St. Epsom BO58 94
West St. Erith CS42 69
West St. Grav. DG46 81
West St. Grays DB43 70
West St. Grays DD43 71
West St. Har. BG33 45
West St. Reig. BR70 120
West St. Sutt. BS56 95
West St. Wat. BC23 26
West Temple Sheen SW14 BM45 65
West Tenter St. E1 CA39 2
West Tenter St. E1 CA39 57
West Thurrock Art Rd. Grays CZ41 70
West Towers Pnr. BD32 45
West Valley Rd. Hem. H. AX16 17
West View NW4 BQ31 46
West View, Ches. AO18 16
West View, Felt. BA47 73
Westview, Hat. BP11 10
West View Lough. CK24 31
West View Av. Whyt. CA62 105
West View Clo. NW10 BO35 46
West View Cres. N9 CA26 39
West View Dr. Wdf. Grn. CJ30 40
West View Rise, Hem. H. AX13 8
West View Rd. Dart. CW46 80
West View Rd. St. Alb. BG13 9
West View Rd. Swan. CS53 89
West View Rd. Swan. CU52 89
West View Rd. Warl. CB63 105
Westville Rd. W12 BP41 65
Westville Rd. Surb. BJ54 84
West Way N18 BZ28 39
West Wk. W5 BL39 55
West Wk. Barm. BV26 38
West Walk, Harl. CM11 13
West Wk. Hayes BC40 53
Westward Dri. Amer. AR23 25
Westward Rd. E4 CD28 39
Westward Way, Har. BL32 46
West Warwick Pl. SW1 BV42 3
West Warwick Pl. SW1 BW42 66
West Way NW10 BN35 46
Westway SW20 BP52 85
Westway W12 BO40 55
West Way, Brwd. DA27 42
West Way Cars. BT58 95
Westway, Cat. BZ64 105
West Way Croy. CD55 87
West Way, Edg. BM29 37
Westway, Guil. AP69 118
West Way Houns. BE44 64
Westway Orp. CM53 88
West Way Pnr. BD31 45
West Way, Rick. AW26 35
West Way, Ruis. BB33 44
West Way, Sev. CT64 107
West Way, Shep. BA53 83
West Way, Wal. Abb. CE21 30
West Way, West. CM66 115
West Way, W. Wick. CG53 88
West Way Clo. SW20 BP52 85
West Way Gdns. Croy. CC55 87
Westway Gdns. Red. BV69 121
Westways Epsom BO56 94

Street	Grid	Page
Westwell App. SW16	BX50	76
Westwell Rd.		
Westwell Clo. Orp.	CP54	89
Westwell Rd. SW16	BX50	76
Westwick Gdns. W14	BQ41	65
Westwick Gdns. Houns.	BC44	63
Westwick Row, Hem. H.	BA13	8
Westwood Av. Wey.	AV59	91
Westwood Av. SE19	BZ51	87
Westwood Av. Brwd.	DA28	42
Westwood Av. Har.	BF35	45
Westwood Clo. Amer.	AR23	25
Westwood Clo. Esher	BG55	84
Westwood Clo. Pot. B.	BS18	20
Westwood Clo. Ruis.	AZ32	44
Westwood Gdns. SW13	BO45	65
Westwood Hill SE26	CB49	77
West Wood Ho. Guil.	AS69	118
Westwood La. Sid.	CO46	79
Westwood La. Well.	CN45	68
Westwood Pk. SE23	CB47	77
Westwood Rd. E16	CH40	58
Westwood Rd. SE26	CB49	77
Westwood Rd. SW13	BO45	65
Westwood Rd. Couls.	BW62	104
Westwood Rd. Grav.	DC50	81
Westwood Rd. Ilf.	CN33	49
West Wood Side, Bex.	CO47	79
Westyoke Rd. Fawk.	DA55	90
Wetheral Dr. Stan.	BJ30	36
Wetherby Clo. Nthlt.	BF36	54
Wetherby Gdns. SW5	**BS42**	**3**
Wetherby Gdns. SW5	BS42	66
Wetherby Ms. SW5	**BS42**	**3**
Wetherby Ms. SW5	BS42	66
Bolton Gdns.		
Wetherby Pk. Wey.	BB56	92
Wetherby Pl. SW7	**BT42**	**3**
Wetherby Pl. SW7	BT42	66
Gloucester Rd.		
Wetherby Rd. Borwd.	BL23	28
Wethrby Rd. Enf.	BZ22	30
Wetherby Way Chess.	BL57	94
Wetherden St. E17	CD33	48
Wetherell Rd. E9	CC37	57
Wetherill Rd. N10	BV30	38
Wexford Rd. SW12	BU47	76
Wexham Pk. La. Slou.	AQ38	52
Wexham Rd. Slou.	AQ40	52
Wexham St. Slou.	AQ38	52
Weybanks, Wok.	AY61	101
Wey Barton, Wey.	AY60	92
Weybourne St. SW18	BT48	76
Weybridge Park, Wey.	AZ56	92
Weybridge Rd. Th. Hth.	BY52	86
Weybridge Rd. Wey.	AX55	83
Weybridge St. SW11	BV44	66
Culvert Rd.		
Wey Clo. Wey.	AW60	92
Wey Ct. Epsom	BN56	94
Wey Ct. Wey.	AX58	92
Weydon Cl. SW19	BR47	75
Weydown Clo. SW19	BR47	75
Princes Way		
Weydown Clo. Guil.	AQ68	109
Cumberland Av.		
Weyhill Rd. E1	CB39	57
Holly St.		
Weylond Rd. Dag.	CQ34	50
Wey Manor Rd. Wey.	AX58	92
Weyman Rd. SE3	CJ44	68
Weymarks, The N17	BZ29	39
Weymead Clo. Cher.	AX54	83
Weymouth Av. NW7	BO28	37
Weymouth Av. W5	BK41	64
Weymouth Ct. Sutt.	BS57	95
Weymouth Dr. Hayes	BB38	53
Weymouth Ms. W1	**BV39**	**1**
Weymouth Ms. W1	BV39	56
Weymouth Pl. E2	**CA37**	**2**
Weymouth Pl. E2	CA37	57
Weymouth Ter.		
Weymouth St. W1	**BV39**	**1**
Weymouth St. W1	BV39	56
Weymouth St. Hem. H.	AX15	8
Weymouth Ter. E2	**CA37**	**2**
Weymouth Ter. E2	CA37	57
Weymouth Wk. Stan.	BJ29	36
Wey Rd. Wey.	AY55	83
Wey Side Clo. Wey.	AY59	92
Weyside Gdns. Guil.	AR69	118
Weyside Rd. Guil.	AQ70	118
Weystone Rd. Wey.	AY56	92
Whadcoat St. N4	BY34	47
Whalebone Av. Rom.	CQ32	50
Whalebone Gro. Rom.	CQ32	50
Whalebone La. E15	CG36	58
Whalebone Lane North Rom.	CQ29	41
Whalebone La. S. Dag.	CQ32	50
Whalebone La. S. Rom.	CQ32	50
Whaley Rd. Pot. B.	BT20	20
Whally St. E1	CC39	57
Wharfdale Rd. N1	**BX37**	**2**
Wharfdale Rd. N1	BX37	56
Wharfedale, Hem. H.	AY12	8
Wharfedale Gdns. Th. Hth.	BX52	86
Wharfedale St. SW10	BS42	66
Wharf La. Berk.	AO11	7
Wharf La. Rick.	AY26	35
Wharf La. Twick.	BJ47	74
Wharf La. Wok.	AU65	100
Wharf La. Wok.	AX62	101
Wharf Pl. E2	CB37	57
Wharf Rd. E15	CF37	57
Wharf Rd. N1	**BZ37**	**2**
Wharf Rd. N1	BZ37	57
Wharf Rd. Brox.	CD15	12
Wharf Rd. Brwd.	DB27	42
Wharf Rd. Enf.	CD25	30
Wharf Rd. Grav.	DJ46	81
Wharf Rd. Grays.	DC43	71
Wharf Rd. Hem. H.	AW14	8
Wharf Rd. Stai.	AR47	72
Wharfside EC4	**BZ40**	**4**
Wharfside EC4	BZ40	57
Wharfside Rd. E16	CG39	58
Barking Rd.		
Wharf St. E16	CG39	58
Wharley Hook, Harl.	CN12	13
Wharncliffe Dr. Sthl.	BG40	54
Wharncliffe Gdns. NW8	**BT38**	**1**
Wharncliffe Gdns. NW8	BT38	56
St. John's Wood Rd.		
Wharncliffe Gdns. SE25	CA51	87
Wharncliffe Rd. SE25	BZ51	87
Wharncliffe St. E2	CC37	57
Royston St.		
Wharton Clo. NW10	BO36	55
Wharton Rd. Brom.	CH51	88
Wharton St. WC1	**BX38**	**2**
Wharton St. WC1	BX38	56
Whateley Rd. SE20	CC50	77
Whateley Rd. SE22	CA46	77
Whateley Rd. Guil.	AQ68	109
Whatley Av. SW20	BQ52	85
Whatman Rd. SE23	CC47	77
Whatmore Clo. Stai.	AW46	73
Wheatash Rd. Wey.	AW55	83
Wheat Barn, Welw. G. C.	BS7	5
Wheatfield, Hat.	BP12	10
Crop Common		
Wheatfields, Enf.	CC23	30
Wheathill Rd. SE20	CB51	87
Wheat Knoll Ken.	BZ61	105
Wheatland Rd. Slou.	AQ41	62
Wheatlands Rd. SW17	BV48	76
Wheatlands, The Houns.	BF43	64
Wheatley Clo. Saw.	CP6	6
Wheatley Clo. Welw. G. C.	BS9	5
Wheatley Cres. Hayes	BC40	53
Wheatley Gdns. N9	CA27	39
Wheatley Rd. Islw.	BH45	64
Wheatley Rd. Welw. G. C.	BR8	5
Wheat Leys, St. Alb.	BK12	9
Wheatley St. W1	BV39	56
Marylebone St.		
Wheatley Ter. Rd. Erith	CT43	69
Wheatley Way, Ger. Cr.	AS29	34
Wheatsheaf Clo. Cher.	AU57	91
Wheatsheaf Clo. Wok.	AS61	100
Wheatsheaf Hill Orp.	CQ58	98
Wheatsheaf Hill, Sev.	CQ69	116
Wheasheaf La. SW8	BX43	66
Wheatsheaf La. Stai.	AV50	72
Wheatsheaf Rd. Rom.	CT32	50
Wheatstone Rd. W10	BR39	55
Wheat St. W1	**BV39**	**1**
Wheat St. W1	BV39	56
Marylebone St.		
Wheeler Av. Oxt.	CF68	114
Wheelers, Epp.	CN18	22
Wheelers Clo. Wal. Abb.	CG14	13
Wheelers Cross, Bark.	CM37	58
Wheelers Farm Gdns. Epp.	CR16	23
Wheelers La. Bet.	BM71	120
Wheelers La. Brwd.	CX24	33
Wheelers La. Epsom	BM60	94
Wheelers La. Hem. H.	AY14	8
Wheelers Orchard, Ger. Cr.	AS29	34
Wheel Fm. Dr. Dag.	CS34	50
Wheelwright St. N7	BX36	56
Wheler St. E1	**CA38**	**2**
Wheler St. E1	CA38	57
Whellock Rd. W4	BO41	65
Whenman Av. Bex.	CS48	79
Wherwell Rd. Guil.	AR71	118
Whetstone Clo. N20	BT27	38
Whetstone Park WC2	**BX39**	**2**
Whetstone Pk. WC2	BX39	56
Gate St.		
Whetstone Rd. SE3	CJ44	68
Whewell Rd. N19	BX34	47
Whichcote Gdns. Chesh.	AO20	16
Whickcliffe Gdns. Wem.	BM34	46
Whidborne St. WC1	**BX38**	**2**
Whidborne St. WC1	BX38	56
Whinfell Clo. SW16	BW49	76
Whinfell Way, Grav.	DJ49	81
Whinyates Rd. SE9	CK45	68
Whippendale Way, Orp.	CO51	89
Whippend Clo. Orp.	CO51	89
Whippendell Rd. Wat.	BB25	26
Whippendell Rd. Wat.	BC25	26
Whipps Cross Rd. E11	CF32	48
Whiskin St. EC1	**BY38**	**2**
Whiskin St. EC1	BY38	56
Gloucester Way		
Whisper Wood, Rick.	AW24	26
Whister Wk. SW10	BT43	66
Worlds End		
Whistler Gdns. Edg.	BL30	37
Whistler St. N5	BY35	47
Whiston Rd. E2	**CA37**	**2**
Whiston Rd. E2	CA37	57
Whittakers Way, Loug.	CK23	31
Whitbread Rd. SE4	CD45	67
Whitburn Rd. SE13	CE45	67
Whitby Av. NW10	BM38	55
Whitby Av. Brwd.	DE29	122
Whitby Clo. West.	CH62	106
Whitby Gdns. NW9	BM31	46
Whitby Gdns. Sutt.	BT55	86
Whitby Rd. Har.	BG34	45
Whitby Rd. Ruis.	BC34	44
Whitby Rd. Slou.	AO40	52
Whitby Rd. Sutt.	BT55	86
Whitby St. E1	**CA38**	**2**
Whitby St. E1	CA38	57
Whitcher Clo. SE14	CD43	67
Chubworthy St.		
Whitcher Pl. NW1	BW36	56
Rochester Rd.		
Whitchurch Av. Edg.	BL29	37
Whitchurch Clo. Edg.	BL29	37
Whitchurch Gdns. Edg.	BL29	37
Whitchurch La. Edg.	BK29	36
Whitchurch Rd. Rom.	CV28	42
Whitcomb St. WC2	**BW40**	**3**
Whitcomb St. WC2	BW40	56
White Acre NW9	BO30	37
Whitear Wk. E15	CF36	57
White Av. Grav.	DF48	81
Whitebarn La. Dag.	CR37	59
Whitebeam Av. Brom.	CL54	88
Whitebeam Clo. SW9	BX43	66
Whitebeams, Hat.	BP14	10
White Beam Way, Tad.	BP64	103
White Beans, St. Alb.	BG17	18
Whitebeam Tower E17	CD31	48
Oatland Rise		
Whitebridge Clo. Felt.	BB46	73
White Broom Rd. Hem. H.	AV12	7
Whitebutts Rd. Ruis.	BD34	45
Whitechapel High St. E1	**CA39**	**2**
Whitechapel High St. E1	CA39	57
Whitechapel Rd.		
Whitechapel Rd. E1	**CB39**	**2**
Whitechapel Rd. E1	CB39	57
Whitechurch La. E1	**CB39**	**2**
White Church La. E1	CB39	57
White City Clo. W12	BQ40	55
South Africa Rd.		
White City Est. W12	BP40	55
White City Rd. W12	BP40	55
White Clo. Slou.	AO40	61
White Conduit St. N1	**BY37**	**2**
White Conduit St. N1	BY37	56
Whitecote Rd. Sthl.	BF39	54
White Craig Clo. Pnr.	BF28	36
White Craig Clo. Stan.	BL31	46
Everton Dr.		
Whitecroft, St. Alb.	BJ15	9
Whitecroft Clo. Beck.	CF52	87
Whitecroft Way, Beck.	CF53	87
Whitecross Pl. EC2	**BZ39**	**2**
Whitecross Pl. EC2	BZ39	57
White Cross Row, Rich.	BK46	74
Water La.		
Whitecross St. EC1	**BZ38**	**2**
Whitecross St. EC1	BZ38	57
Whitecross St. Sth. EC2	**BZ39**	**2**
Whitecross St. Sth. EC2	BZ39	57
White Downs, Dor.	BC73	119
Whitefield Av. NW2	BQ33	46
Whitefield Av. Pur.	BY61	104
Whitefield Clo. Orp.	CP52	89
Whitefields Rd. Wal. Cr.	CC17	21
Whitefoot La. Brom.	CF49	77
Whitefoot Ter. Brom.	CG48	78
Whiteford Rd. Slou.	AP39	52
Whitefriars Av. Har.	BG30	36
Whitefriars St. EC4	**BY39**	**2**
Whitefriars St. EC4	BY39	56
Whitefrost Hill, Red.	BU70	121
White Gdns. Dag.	CR36	59
White Gate Gdns. Har.	BH29	36
Whitegates, Wok.	AS63	100
Loop Rd.		
White Gates Clo. Rick.	AZ24	26
Whitehall E7	CH35	49
Forest St.		
Whitehall SW1	**BX40**	**4**
Whitehall SW1	BX40	56
Whitehall Clo. Chig.	CO27	41
Whitehall Clo. Uxb.	AX37	53
Whitehall Clo. Wal. Abb.	CG14	13
Whitehall Ct. SW1	**BX40**	**4**
Whitehall Ct. SW1	BX40	56
Whitehall Cres. Chess.	BK56	93
Whitehall Farm La. Vir. W.	AS52	82
Whitehall Gdns. E4	CG26	40
Whitehall Gdns. W3	BM40	55
Whitehall Gdns. W4	BM43	65
Whitehall Gdns. SW1	**BX40**	**4**
Whitehall La. Buck. H.	CH27	40
Whitehall La. Egh.	AS50	72
Whitehall La. Erith	CT44	69
Whitehall La. Grays.	DE43	71
Whitehall La. Reig.	BR72	120
Whitehall La. Stai.	AT46	72
Whitehall Pk. N19	BW33	47
Whitehall Pk. Rd. W4	BM43	65
Whitehall Pl. E7	CH35	49
Kuhn Way		
Whitehall Pl. SW1	**BX40**	**4**
Whitehall Pl. SW1	BX40	56
Whitehall Rd. E4	CG27	40
Whitehall Rd. W7	BJ41	64
Whitehall Rd. Brom.	CJ53	88
Whitehall Rd. Grays.	DE42	71
Whitehall Rd. Har.	BH33	45
Whitehall Rd. Th. Hth.	BY53	86
Whitehall Rd. Uxb.	AX37	53
Whitehall Rd. Wdf. Grn.	CG27	40
Whitehall St. N17	CA29	39
White Hands Clo. Hodd.	CD12	12
Whitehart Av. Uxb.	BA39	53
White Hart Clo. Hayes	BA43	63
White Hart Clo. Sev.	CV68	117
White Hart Dr. Hem. H.	AY14	8
White Hart La. N17	BX30	38
White Hart La. N22	BX30	38
White Hart La. SW13	BO44	65
White Hart La. Brwd.	DB27	42
White Hart La. Hem. H.	AS17	16
White Hart La. Rom.	CR30	41
White Hart Meadows, Wok.	AX64	101
White Hart Rd. SE18	CN42	68
White Hart Rd. Hem. H.	AZ14	8
Whitehart Rd. Orp.	CO54	89
White Hart Rd. Slou.	AO41	61
Whitehart Slip, Brom.	CH51	88
White Hart St. SE11	**BY42**	**4**
White Hart St. SE11	BY42	66
White Hart Wood, Sev.	CV68	117
White Hart Yd. SE1	**BZ40**	**4**
White Hart Yd. SE1	BZ40	57
Borough High St.		
Whitehart Yd. Cher.	AW54	83
Whitehaven St. NW8	**BU38**	**1**
Whitehaven St. NW8	BU38	56
Whitehead Clo. SW18	BT47	76
Whitehead Clo. Dart.	CV48	80
Whiteheads Gro. SW3	**BU42**	**3**
Whiteheads Gro. SW3	BU42	66
Whiteheath Av. Ruis.	BA33	44
White Hedge Dr. St. Alb.	BG12	9
White Hill, Berk.	AR15	7
White Hill, Chesh.	AO18	16
White Hill, Couls.	BU65	104
White Hill, Hem. H.	AV14	7
White Hill, Rick.	AZ29	35
White Hill, Welw.	BP5	5
White Hill Clo. Chesh.	AO18	16
Whitehill Ct. Berk.	AR12	7
White Hill		
Whitehall La. Grav.	DH48	81
White Hill La. Red.	BZ67	114
Whitehill La. Wok.	BA65	101
White Hill Rd. Berk.	AQ14	7
Whitehill Rd. Dart.	CU46	79
Whitehill Rd. Grav.	DH48	81
Whitehill Rd. Loug.	DB51	90
Whitehills Rd. Loug.	CL24	31
White Horse Alley EC1	BY39	56
Cowcross St.		
White Horse Dr. Epsom	BN60	94
White Horse Hill, Chis.	CK49	78
White Horse La. E1	CC38	57
Whitehorse La. SE25	BZ52	87
Whitehorse La. St. Alb.	BK16	18
Whitehorse La. St. Alb.	BL16	19
White Horse Rd. E1	CD39	57
White Horse Rd. E6	CK38	58
Whitehorse Rd. Croy.	BZ54	87
White Horse Rd. Wind.	AL45	61
White Horse St. W1	**BV40**	**3**
White Horse St. W1	BV40	56
White Horse Yd. EC2	BZ39	57
Coleman St.		
White Ho. SW11	BT44	66
Whitehorse Av. Borwd.	BM24	28
Whitehorse Clo. Ger. Cr.	AS29	34
Whitehouse Ct. N14	BW27	38
Whitehouse Dr. Stan.	BJ28	36
Whitehouse Est. E10	CF32	48
White House La. Guil.	AR68	109
Whitehouse La. Wat.	BC16	17
Whitehouse Rd. Enf.	BZ23	30
White House Rd. Sev.	CT68	116
Whitehouse Way N14	BV27	38
Whitehouse Way, Iver	AU38	52
White Kennett St. E1	**CA39**	**2**
White Kennett St. E1	CA39	57
White Knobs Way, Cat.	CB66	114
Whiteland Av. Rick.	AT24	25
Whiteland Way, Rom.	CV30	42
Whitehouse Dr. Stan.	BK28	36
White La. Guil.	AU71	118
White La. Oxt.	CH65	106
Whiteleaf Rd. Hem. H.	AX15	8
Whiteledges W13	BK39	54
Whitelegg Rd. E13	CG37	58
Whiteley, Wind.	AM43	61
Whiteley Rd. SE19	BZ49	77
Whiteley's Cotts. W14	BR42	65
Whiteley Way, Felt.	BF48	74
White Lion Hill EC4	**BY40**	**4**
White Lion Hill EC4	BY40	56
White Lion Rd. Amer.	AP23	25
White Lion St. EC1	**BZ38**	**2**
Fann St.		
White Lion St. N1	**BY37**	**2**
White Lion Sq. Hat.	BP12	10
Common, The		
White Lion St. N1	BY37	56
White Lion St. Hem. H.	AX15	8
White Lodge Clo. NW3	BT33	47
White Lodge Clo. Sutt.	BT57	95
White Lodge Est. SE19	BZ50	77
White Lyons Rd. Brwd.	DB27	42
Kings Rd.		
Whitemore Rd. Guil.	AR68	109
Whiteoak Dr. Beck.	CF51	87
White Orchard N20	BR26	37
White Orchards, Stan.	BJ28	36
White Post, Farn.	CX54	90
White Post Field, Saw.	CP6	6
Gilder St.		
White Post La. E9	CD36	57
White Post St. SE15	CC43	67
White Rd. E15	CG36	58
White Rd. Bet. & Tad.	BM70	120
White Rose La. Wok.	AS62	100
Whites Av. Ilf.	CN32	49
Whites Grounds SE1	**CA41**	**4**
Whites Grounds SE1	CA41	67
Whites Grounds Est. SE1	**CA41**	**4**
Whites Grounds Est. SE1	CA41	67
White Shack La. Wat.	AY22	26
Whites La. Slou.	AQ43	62
White's Row E1	**CA39**	**2**
White's Row E1	CA39	57
Whites Sq. SW4	BW45	66
Nelson's Row		
Whitestile Rd. Brent.	BK42	64
Whitestone La. NW3	BT34	47
Heath St.		
Whitestone Wk. NW3	BT34	47
North End Way		
Whitestone Wk. Hem. H.	AW12	8
White St. Sthl.	BD41	64
White Stubb La. Hert.	BX13	11
White Stubbs La. Brox.	BZ14	12
Whitethorn, Welw. G. C.	BS8	5
Whitethorn Av. Couls.	BV61	104
Whitethorn Av. West.	AY40	53
Whitehorn Gdns. Croy.	CB55	87
Whitehorn Gdns. Enf.	BZ25	30
Whitehorn Gdns. Horn.	CV32	51
Whitehorn St. E3	CE38	57
Whitewaits, Harl.	CN10	6
White Way, Lthd.	BF66	111
Whitewebbs, Enf.	BY21	29
Whitewebbs La. Enf.	CA21	30
Whitewebbs Way, Orp.	CN51	88
Whitewood Cotts. West.	CJ63	106
White Wood Rd. Berk.	AQ13	7
Whitfield Pl. W1	**BW38**	**1**
Whitfield Pl. W1	BW38	56
Whitfield St.		
Whitfield Rd. E6	CJ36	58
Whitfield Rd. SE3	CF44	67
Whitfield Rd. Bexh.	CQ43	69
Whitfield St. W1	**BW38**	**1**
Whitfield St. W1	BW38	56
Whitfield Way, Rick.	AV26	34
Whitford Gdns. Mitch.	BU52	86
Whitgift Av. Sth. Croy.	BY56	95
Whitgift St. SE11	**BX42**	**4**
Whitgift St. SE11	BX42	66
Whitgift St. Croy.	BZ55	87
Whiting Av. Bark.	CL36	58
Whiting Hill Est. Barn.	BP25	28
Whitings Rd. Barn.	BQ25	28
Whitland Rd. Cars.	BT54	86
Whitlars Dr. Kings L.	AV17	17
Whitley Clo. Stai.	AY46	73
Whitley Rd. N17	CA30	39
Whitley Rd. Hodd.	CE11	12
Whitlock Dr. SW18	BR47	75
Whitman Rd. E3	CD38	57
Whitmoor La. Guil.	AR66	109
Whitmore Av. Grays.	DD40	71
Whitmore Clo. N11	**BV28**	**39**
High Rd.		
Whitmore Est. N1	**CA37**	**2**
Whitmore Gdns. NW10	BQ37	55
Whitmore Rd. N1	**CA37**	**2**
Whitmore Rd. N1	CA37	57
Whitmore Rd. Beck.	CD52	87
Whitmore Rd. Har.	BF33	45
Whitmores Clo. Epsom	BN61	103
Whitnell Way SW15	BQ46	75
Chartfield Av.		
Whitnell Way SW15	BQ46	75
Whitney Av. Ilf.	CJ31	49
Whitney Rd. E10	CE33	48
Whitney Wk. Sid.	CQ50	79
Maidstone Rd.		
Whitstable Clo. Beck.	CD51	87
Whitstable Clo. Ruis.	BB34	44
Chichester Av.		
Whittaker Av. Rich.	BK46	74
Whittaker Rd. E6	CJ36	58
Whittaker Rd. Sutt.	BR55	85
Whittaker St. SW1	**BV42**	**3**
Whittaker St. SW1	BV42	66
Bourne St.		
Whitta Rd. E12	CJ35	49
Whittel Gdns. SE26	CC48	77
Whitting Av. Bark.	CL36	58
Whittingstall Rd. SW6	BR44	65
Whittingstall Rd. Hodd.	CE11	12
Whittington Av. EC3	CA39	57
Leadenhall St.		
Whittington Av. Hayes	BB39	53
Whittington Ct. N2	BU32	47
Whittington Rd. N22	BX29	38
Whittington Rd. Brwd.	DE25	122
Whittington Way, Pnr.	BE32	45
Whittlebury Clo. Cars.	BU57	95
Whittle Clo. Sthl.	BF39	54
Whittle Rd. Houns.	BD43	64
Whittlesea Path, Har.	BG30	36
Whittlesea Rd. Har.	BG29	36
Whittlesey St. SE1	**BY40**	**4**
Whittlesey St. SE1	BY40	56
Whitton Av. E. Grnf.	BH35	45
Whitton Av. W. Grnf.	BF35	45
Whitton Av. W. Nthlt.	BF35	45
Whitton Clo. Grnf.	BJ36	54
Whitton Dene, Houns.	BF46	74
Whitton Dr. Grnf.	BJ36	54
Whitton Manor Rd. Islw.	BG46	74
Whitton Rd. Houns.	BF45	64
Whitton Rd. Twick.	BH46	74
Whitton Wk. E3	CE37	58
Malmesbury Rd.		
Whitton Waye, Houns.	BF46	74
Whitwell Rd. E13	CH38	58
Whitwell Rd. Wat.	BD21	27
Whitworth Rd. SE18	CL43	68
Whitworth Rd. SE25	CA52	87
Whitworth St. SE10	CG42	68
Whopshot Av. Wok.	AR61	100
Whopshot Clo. Wok.	AR61	100
Whopshot Dr. Wok.	AR61	100
Whorlton Rd. SE15	CB45	67
Whybridge Clo. Rain.	CT37	59
Whymark Av. N22	BY31	47
Whytecliffe Rd. Pur.	BY59	95
Whytecroft, Houns.	BD43	64
Whyteleafe Rd. Cat.	CA63	105
Whyteleaf Hill, Whyt.	CA63	105
Whyteville Rd. E7	CH36	58
Wickenden Rd. Sev.	CV64	108
Wickersley Rd. SW11	BV44	66
St. John's Hill		
Wicker St. E1	CB39	57
Wicket, The Croy.	CE56	96
Wickford Clo. Rom.	CW28	42
Wickford Dr. Rom.	CW28	42
Wickford St. E1	CC38	57
Wickham Av. Croy.	CD55	87
Wickham Av. Sutt.	BQ56	94
Wickham Chase, W. Wick.	CF54	87
Wickham Clo. Enf.	CB24	30
Wickham Clo. N. Mal.	BO53	85
Wickham Clo. Uxb.	AX30	35
Wickham Ct. Rd. W. Wick.	CF55	87
Wickham Cres. W. Wick.	CF55	87
Wickham Fld. Sev.	CT61	107
Wickham Gdns. SE4	CD45	67
Wickham La. SE2	CO42	69
Wickham La. Egh.	AT50	72
Wickham Rd. E4	CF29	39
Wickham Rd. SE4	CD45	67
Wickham Rd. Beck.	CE51	87
Wickham Rd. Croy.	CC55	87
Wickham Rd. Grays.	DH41	71
Wickham Rd. Har.	BG30	36
Wickham St. SE11	**BX42**	**4**
Wickham St. SE11	BX42	66
Wickham St. Well.	CN44	68
Wickham Way, Beck.	CF52	87
Wickhurst Rd. Sev.	CT69	116
Wick La. E3	CD36	57
Wick La. Egh.	AP50	72
Wickliffe Av. N3	BR30	37
Wicklow St. WC1	**BX38**	**2**
Wicklow St. WC1	BX38	56
Wick Rd. E9	CC36	57
Wick Rd. Egh.	AQ51	82
Wick Rd. Tedd.	BJ50	74

Wicks Rd. Rick. AU28 34
Wick Way, St. Alb. BJ12 9
Wickwood St. SE5 BY44 66
Wid Clo. Brwd. DE25 122
Widenham Clo. Pnr. BD32 45
Widdenham Rd. N7 BX35 47
Widdin St. E15 CF36 57
Widecombe Clo. Rom. CV30 42
Widecombe Ct. N2 BT32 47
Widecombe Gdns. Ilf. CK31 49
Widecombe Rd. SE9 CK48 78
Widecombe Way N2 BT32 47
Widecroft Rd. Iver AV39 52
Wide Gates E1 CA39 2
Widegate St. E1 CA39 57
Sandy's Row
Wide Way, Mitch. BW52 86
Widdicombe Av. Har. BE34 45
Widford Rd. Welw. G. C. BS8 5
Widford Ter. Hem. H. AZ10 8
Elstree Rd.
Widley Rd. W9 BS38 56
Widmore Dr. Hem. H. AZ12 8
Widmore Lo. Rd. Brom. CJ51 88
Widmore Rd. Brom. CH51 88
Widmore Rd. Uxb. AZ38 53
Widworthy Hayes, Brwd. DD26 122
Wieland Rd. Nthwd. BC29 35
Wigan Ho. E5 CB33 48
Wiggenhall Rd. Wat. BC24 26
Wiggie La. Red. BV69 121
Wiggington Av. Wem. BM36 55
Wiggins La. Rich. BK48 74
Wiggins Mead NW9 BO30 37
Wiggins & Pointers Cotts. Rich. BK48 74
Ham St.
Wightman Rd. N4 BY31 47
Whightman Rd. N8 BY31 47
Wigley Bush La. Brwd. CZ27 42
Wigley Rd. Felt. BD48 74
Wigmore Pl. W1 BV39 1
Wigmore Pl. W1 BV39 56
Wigmore Rd. Cars. BT55 86
Wigmores North, Welw. G. C. BQ7 5
Wigmores Sth. Welw. G. C. BQ8 5
Wigmore St. W1 BV39 1
Wigmore St. W1 BV39 56
Wigmore Wk. Cars. BT55 86
Wigram Rd. E11 CJ32 49
Wigram Sq. E17 CF31 48
Wigston Rd. E13 CH38 58
Wigton Gdns. Stan. BL30 37
Wigton Pl. SE11 BY42 66
Milver St.
Wigton Rd. E17 CD30 39
Wigton Rd. Rom. CW28 42
Wigton Way, Rom. CW28 42
Wilberforce Rd. N4 BY34 47
Wilberforce Rd. NW9 BP32 46
Wilberforce Way SW19 BQ50 75
Wilberforce Way, Grav. DH49 81
Wilbraham Pl. SW1 BU42 3
Wilbraham Pl. SW1 BU42 66
Wilbury Av. Sutt. BR58 94
Wilbury Rd. Wok. AR62 100
Wilbury Way N18 BZ28 39
Wilby Ms. W11 BR40 55
Wilby Rd. SE5 BZ44 67
Grove La.
Wilcot Av. Wat. BE26 36
Wilcox Pl. SW1 BW41 66
Victoria St.
Wilcox Rd. SW8 BX43 66
Wilcox Rd. Sutt. BS56 95
Brandon Rd.
Wilcox Rd. Tedd. BG49 74
Wild Acres, Wey. AX59 92
Wild Ct. WC2 BX39 2
Wild Ct. WC2 BX39 56
Wildcroft Gdns. Edg. BK29 36
Wildcroft Manor SW15 BQ47 75
Bristol Gdns.
Wildcroft Rd. SW15 BQ47 75
Wilde Clo. Til. DH44 71
Coleridge Rd.
Wildernesse Av. Sev. CW64 108
Wildernesse Mt. Sev. CV64 108
Wilderness Rd. Chis. CL50 78
Wilderness Rd. Guil. AP71 118
Wilderness Rd. Oxt. CF68 114
Wilderness Rd. Oxt. CG68 115
Wilderness, The Hamptn. BF49 74
Park Rd.
Wilders Clo. Wok. AR62 100
Wilderton Rd. N16 CA33 48
Wildfell Rd. SE6 CE47 77
Wild Goose Dr. SE14 CC44 67
Wild Grn. Slou. AT42 62
Wild Hatch NW11 BS32 47
Wild Hill Rd. Hat. BS14 11
Wild Oaks Clo. Nthwd. BB29 35
Wild's Rents SE1 BZ41 4
Wild's Rents SE1 CA41 67
Wild St. WC2 BX39 2
Wild St. WC2 BX39 56
Wildwood, Nthwd. BA29 35
Wildwood Av. St. Alb. BE18 18
Wildwood Clo. SE12 CG47 78
Wildwood Clo. Leath. BB66 110
Wildwood Clo. Wok. AV60 91
Wildwood Clo. Wok. AV61 100
Wildwood Rise NW11 BT33 47
Wildwood Rd. NW11 BT33 47
Wilford Clo. Enf. BZ24 30
Lit Pk. Gdns.
Wilford Clo. Nthwd. BA29 35
Wilford Rd. Slou. AS42 62
Wilfred Av. Rain. CU39 59
Wilfred St. SW1 BW41 3
Wilfred St. SW1 BW41 66
Wilfred St. Wok. AR62 100
Wilfred Turney Est. W6 BQ41 65
Wilfrid Gdns. W3 BN39 55
Wilhelmena Av. Couls. BW63 104
Wilkes Rd. Brwd. DE25 122
Wilkins Clo. Hayes BB42 63
Wilkin's Grn. La. Hat. BN13 10
Wilkins Grn. La. St. Alb. BM13 10
Wilkinson Clo. Dart. CW45 70
Wilkinson RD. E16 CJ39 58
Wilkinson St. SW8 BX43 66
Wilkinson Way W4 BN41 65
Willan Rd. N17 BZ30 39
Willard Est. SW8 BV45 66
Willcocks Clo. Chess. BL55 85
Willcott Rd. W3 BM40 55
Will Crook's Gdns. SE9 CJ45 68
Willenhall Av. Barn. BS25 29
Willenhall Rd. SE18 CL42 68
Willersley Av. Orp. CM55 88
Willersley Av. Sid. CN47 78
Willersley Clo. Sid. CN47 78
Willesden Grn. NW2 BQ36 55
Willesden La. NW2 BQ36 55
Willesden La. NW6 BQ36 55
Willes Rd. NW5 BV36 56
Willets La. Uxb. AV35 43
Willets La. Uxb. AV36 52
Willett Clo. Nthlt. BD38 54
Broomcroft Av.
Willett Clo. Orp. CN53 88
Willett Clo. Th. Hth. BY53 86
Willett Rd. Th. Hth. BY53 86
Willett Way, Orp. CM53 88
Willett Way SE16 CB42 67
Egan Way
Willey Broom La. Cat. BY66 113
Willey Farm. La. Cat. BZ66 114
Willey La. Cat. BZ66 114
William Barefoot Dr. SE9 CK49 78
William Bonney Est. SW4 BW45 66
William Clo. Rom. CS30 41
William Covell Clo. Enf. BX22 29
William Ellis Clo. Wind. AQ46 72
William IV St. WC2 BX40 4
William IV St. WC2 BX40 56
William Guy Gdns. E3 CF38 57
Talwin St.
William Hayne Gdns. Wor. Pk. BQ55 85
William Margrei Clo. SE15 CB44 67
Moncrieff Est.
William Margrie Clo. SE15 CB44 67
Moncrieff St.
William Mews SW1 BV41 3
William Mews SW1 BV41 66
William Morris Clo. E17 CD31 48
William Morris Ho. W6 BQ43 65
William Parnell Ho. SW6 BS44 66
William Rd. NW1 BV38 1
William Rd. NW1 BV38 56
William Rd. SW19 BR50 75
William Rd. Cat. BZ64 105
William Rd. Guil. AR70 118
William Rd. Sutt. BT56 95
Williams Av. E17 CD30 39
Williams Gro. N22 BY30 38
William's La. SW14 BN45 65
Williams La. Mord. BT53 86
Williamson Clo. SE10 CG42 68
Lenthorpe Rd.
Williamson St. N7 BX35 47
Williamson Way NW7 BR29 37
Williams Rd. W13 BJ40 54
Alfred Rd.
Williams Rd. Sthl. BE42 64
Williams St. Slou. AP40 52
Williams Ter. Well. CN44 68
William St. E10 CE32 48
William St. E15 CF36 57
William St. N12 BT28 38
Lodge La.
William St. N17 CA29 39
William St. SW1 BU41 3
William St. SW1 BU41 66
William St. Bark. CM36 58
William St. Berk. AR13 7
William St. Bush. BD24 27
William St. Cars. BU55 86
William St. Grav. DG47 81
William St. Grays. DB43 70
William St. Grays. DD43 71
William St. Wind. AO44 61
Williams Way, Rad. BJ21 27
William Ter. Croy. BY57 95
William Willisom Est. SW19 BR47 75
Willifield Way NW11 BS31 47
Willingale Clo. Brwd. DF25 122
Fairview Av.
Willingale Clo. Loug. CM23 31
Willingale Clo. Wdf. Grn. CJ29 40
Willingale Rd. Ing. DC16 24
Willingale Rd. Loug. CM24 31
Willingale Rd. Ong. CZ14 15
Willingale Rd. Ong. DB15 15
Willingdon Rd. N22 BY30 38
Willingham Clo. NW5 BW35 47
Leighton Rd.
Willingham Ter. NW5 BW35 47
Willingham Way, Kings. on T. BM52 85
Willington Rd. SW9 BX45 66
Willis Av. Sutt. BU57 95
Willis Rd. E15 CG37 58
Willis Rd. Croy. BZ54 87
Willis Rd. Erith CS42 69
Willis St. E14 CE39 57
Willmore End SW19 BS51 86
Willoughby Av. Croy. BX56 95
Willoughby Clo. Brox. CD14 12
Willoughby Dr. Rain. CT36 59
Willoughby Gro. N17 CB29 39
Willoughby La. N17 CB29 39
Willoughby Pk. Rd. N17 CB29 39
Willoughby Rd. N8 BY31 47
Willoughby Rd. NW3 BT35 47
Willoughby Rd. Kings. on T. BL51 85
Willoughby Rd. Slou. AT41 62
Willoughby Rd. Twick. BK46 74
Willow Av. SW13 BO44 65
Willow Av. Sid. CO46 79
Willow Av. Swan. CT52 89
Willow Av. Uxb. AX35 44
Willow Av. Uxb. AX36 53
Willow Av. West. Dr. AY40 53
Willow Bank SW6 BR45 65
Willowbank, Rich. BJ48 74
Willow Br. Rd. N1 BZ36 57
Willowbrook Clo. Sthl. BF41 64
Willowbrook Gro. SE15 CA43 67
Willowbrook Rd. SE15 CA43 67
Willow Brook Rd. Stai. AY48 73
Willow Clo. W5 BK39 54
Willow Clo. Bex. CQ46 79
Willow Clo. Brent. BK43 64
Willow Clo. Brom. CK53 88
Willow Clo. Brwd. DB22 33
Willow Clo. Brwd. DD25 122
Willow Clo. Buck. H. CJ27 40
Willow Clo. Erith. CU44 69
Willow Clo. Horn. CU34 50
Willow Clo. Orp. CO54 89
Willow Clo. Slou. AU43 62
Willow Clo. Th. Hth. BY53 86
Willow Clo. Wal. Cr. CA16 21
Willow Clo. Wey. AV59 91
Willow Cotts. Rich. BM43 65
Waterloo Pl.
Willow Cott. Rd. Cars. BU53 86
Willow Ct. Edg. BL28 37
Willowcourt Av. Har. BJ32 45
Willow Cres. St. Alb. BK13 9
Willow Cres. E. Uxb. AX35 44
Willow Cres. W. Uxb. AX35 44
Willowdene N6 BU33 47
Denewood Rd.
Willowdene, Brwd. CZ25 42
Willowdene, Brwd. CZ25 33
Ongar Rd.
Willowdene, Bush. BH26 36
Willow Dene, Pnr. BD30 36
Willowdene Clo. Twick. BG47 74
Willowdene Ct. Brwd. DB28 42
Warley Mt.
Willow Dr. Barn. BR24 28
Willow End N20 BS27 38
Willow End, Surb. BL54 85
Willowfield, Harl. CM12 13
Willowfield, Saw. CQ6 6
Springham Rd.
Willow Gdns. N16 CA34 48
Cazenove Rd.
Willow Gdns. Houns. BF44 64
Willow Gdns. Ruis. BB34 44
Willow Grn. Dor. BJ73 119
Willow Gro. E13 CH37 58
Willow Gro. SE1 CA42 4
Willow Gro. SE1 CA42 67
Curtis St.
Willow Gro. Chis. CL50 78
Willow Gro. Ruis. BB34 44
Willow Gro. Welw. G. C. BQ5 5
Willow Hayne Dr. Walt. BC54 83
Willow Herb Wk. Rom. CV29 42
Clematis Clo.
Willow La. Amer. AP24 25
Willow La. Mitch. BU53 86
Willow La. Wat. BC25 26
Willow Mead, Chig. CO27 41
Willowmead Clo. W5 BK38 54
Brenthan Way
Willowmere, Esher BG56 93
Willow Pk. Sev. CA53 107
Willow Pk. Slou. AQ37 52
Willow Path, Wal. Abb. CG20 22
Willow Pl. SW1 BW42 3
Willow Pl. SW1 BW42 66
Francis St.
Willow Pth. Epsom BM60 94
Willow Rd. NW3 BT35 47
Willow Rd. W5 BL41 65
Willow Rd. Dart. CV47 80
Willow Rd. Enf. CA24 30
Willow Rd. Erith. CU44 69
Willow Rd. N. Mal. BN52 85
Willow Rd. Red. BT71 121
Willow Rd. Rom. CQ32 50
Willow Rd. Slou. AV44 62
Willow Rd. Wall. BV57 95
Willows Av. Mord. BS53 86
Willows Clo. Pnr. BD30 36
Willow Side, St. Alb. BL17 19
Willows Path, Wind. AL44 61
Willows, The Grays. DE43 71
Willows, The St. Alb. BJ15 9
Willows, The Wey. AY60 92
Willow St. E4 CF26 39
Willow St. EC2 CA38 2
Willow St. EC2 CA38 57
Willow St. Rom. CS31 50
Willow Tree Clo. SW18 BS47 76
Cargill Rd.
Willow Tree Clo. Hayes BD38 54
Willowtree Clo. Uxb. BA34 44
Willow Tree La. Hayes BD38 54
Willowtree La. Nthlt. BE38 54
Willow Val. Chis. CL50 78
Willow Vale W12 BP40 55
Willow Vale, Lthd. BF65 102
Willow View SW19 BT51 86
Palestine Gro.
Willow Wk. E17 CD32 48
Willow Wk. N2 BT30 38
Willow Wk. N15 BY31 47
Willow Wk. N21 BX25 29
Willow Wk. SE1 CA42 4
Willow Wk. SE1 CA42 67
Willow Wk. Cher. AW54 83
Willow Wk. Croy. CE55 87
Willow Wk. Dart. CV45 70
Willow Wk. Egh. AR49 72
Willow Wk. Ilf. CL34 49
Station Rd.
Willow Wk. Orp. CL55 88
Willow Wk. Sutt. BR55 85
Willow Wk. Upmin. CZ33 51
Willow Way N3 BS29 38
Willow Way SE26 CB48 77
Willow Way, Epsom BN57 94
Willow Way, Gdse. CB69 114
Willow Way, Guil. AR68 109
Willow Way, Hat. BO14 10
Willow Way, Hem. H. AW12 8
Willow Way, Pot. B. BS20 20
Willow Way, Rad. BH21 27
Willow Way, Rom. CX29 42
Willow Way, St. Alb. BF17 18
Willow Way, Sun. BC52 83
Willow Way, Twick. BF48 74
Willow Way, Wem. BJ34 45
Willow Way, Wey. AX59 92
Willow Way, Wok. AR64 100
Willow Wd. Cres. SE25 CA53 87
Wills Cres. Houns. BF46 74
Wills Gro. NW7 BP28 37
Willshaw St. SE14 CE44 67
Willson Rd. Egh. AQ49 72
Willwood Way NW3 BT33 47
North End Rd.
Willy St. WC1 BX39 2
Willy St. WC1 BX39 56
Gt. Russell St.
Wilman Gro. E8 CB36 57
Wilmar Clo. Hayes BA38 53
Wilmar Clo. Uxb. AX36 53
Wilmar Gdns. W. Wick. CE54 87
Wilmar Way, Sev. CW63 108
Landway, The
Wilmer Clo. Kings. on T. BL49 75
Wilmer Cres. Kings. on T. BL49 75
Wilmer Gdns. N1 CA37 2
Wilmer Gdns. N1 CA37 57
Wilmerhatch La. Epsom BM62 103
Wilmer Ho. Kings. on T. BL49 75
Wilmerlee Clo. E15 CF36 57
Wilmer Way N14 BW28 38
Wilmington Av. W4 BN43 65
Wilmington Av. Orp. CP55 89
Wilmington Ct. Rd. Dart. CU48 79
Wilmington Gdns. Bark. CM36 58
Wilmington Sq. WC1 BY38 2
Wilmington Sq. WC1 BY38 56
Wilmington St. WC1 BY38 2
Wilmot Clo. N3 BT30 38
Sylvester Rd.
Wilmot Clo. SE15 CB43 67
Bells Gdns.
Wilmot Pl. NW1 BW36 56
Wilmot Pl. W7 BH40 54
Wilmot Rd. E10 CE34 48
Wilmot Rd. N17 BZ31 48
Wilmot Rd. Dart. CU46 79
Wilmot Rd. Pur. BY59 95
Wilmots Clo. Reig. BT70 121
Wilmot St. E2 CB38 57
Wilmot Way, Bans. BS60 95
Wilmount St. SE18 CL42 68
Wilna Rd. SW18 BS47 76
Wilna Yd SW18 BS47 76
Wilna Rd.
Wilrose Cres. SE2 CO42 69
Wilsham St. W11 BQ40 55
Wilshere Av. St. Alb. BG15 9
Wilsman Rd. S. Ock. CA37 60
Wilsmere Dr. Har. BH29 36
Wilsmere Dr. Nthlt. BE35 45
Wilsmere Dr. Nthlt. BE36 54
Wilson Av. Mitch. BU50 76
Wilson Clo. Dag. CS36 59
Wilson Gdns. Har. BG33 45
Wilson Gro. SE16 CB41 67
Wilson Rd. E6 CJ38 58
Wilson Rd. SE5 BZ44 67
Wilson Rd. Chess. BL57 94
Wilson Rd. Har. BG33 45
Wilson Rd. Ilf. CK33 49
Wilson's Pl. E14 CD39 57
Salmon La.
Wilsons Rd. W6 BQ42 65
Wilson St. E13 CH37 58
Wilson St. E17 CF32 48
Wilson St. EC2 BZ39 2
Wilson St. EC2 BZ39 57
Wilson St. N21 BY26 38
Wilson Way, Wok. AR61 100
Wilton Av. W4 BO42 65
Wilton Clo. West. Dr. AX43 63
Hatch La.
Wilton Ct. N10 BV30 38
Wilton Cres. SW1 BV41 3
Wilton Cres. SW1 BV41 66
Wilton Cres. SW19 BR51 85
Wilton Cres. Wind. AL45 61
Wilton Dr. Rom. CS29 41
Wilton Gdns. Walt. BD54 84
Wilton Gro. SW19 BR50 75
Wilton Gro. N. Mal. BO53 85
Wilton La. Beac. AO29 34
Wilton Ms. SW1 BV41 3
Wilton Ms. SW1 BV41 66
Wilton Pde. Felt. BC48 73
Wilton Pk. Ct. SE18 CL43 68
Prince Imperial Rd.
Wilton Pl. SW1 BV41 3
Wilton Pl. SW1 BV41 66
Wilton Pl. Wey. AX58 92
Wilton Rd. N10 BV30 38
Wilton Rd. SW1 BV41 3
Wilton Rd. SW1 BV41 66
Wilton Rd. SW19 BU50 76
Wilton Rd. Barn. BU24 29
Wilton Rd. Houns. BD45 64
Wilton Rd. Ilf. CL35 49
Cecil Rd.
Wilton Rd. Red. BU71 121
Wilton Rd. SE2 CP42 69
Wilton Row SW1 BV41 3
Wilton Row SW1 BV41 66
Wilton Sq. N1 BZ37 2
Wilton Sq. N1 BZ37 57
Wilton St. SW1 BV41 3
Wilton St. SW1 BV41 66
Wilton Ter. SW1 BV41 3
Wilton Ter. SW1 BV41 66
Wilton Vil. N1 BZ37 2
Wilton Way E8 CB36 57
Wilton Yd. W10 BQ40 55
Bard Rd.
Wiltshire Av. Horn. CW31 51
Wiltshire Clo. SW3 BU42 3
Wiltshire Clo. SW3 BU42 66
Wiltshire Gdns. Twick. BG47 74
Wiltshire La. Pnr. BB31 44
Wiltshire Rd. N1 BZ37 2
Wiltshire Rd. N1 BZ37 57
Wiltshire Rd. SW9 BY44 66
Loughborough Rd.
Wiltshire Rd. Orp. CO54 89
Wiltshire Rd. Th. Hth. BY52 86
Wilverley Cres. N. Mal. BO53 85
Wimbart Rd. SW2 BX47 76
Wimbledon Clo. SW20 BQ50 75
Wimbledon Hl. Rd. SW19 BR50 75
Wimbledon Pk. Est. SW19 BR47 75
Wimbledon Pk. Rd. SW18 BR48 75
Wimbledon Pk. Rd. SW19 BP48 75
Wimbledon Rd. SW17 BT49 76
Wimbolt St. E2 CB38 2
Wimbolt St. E2 CB38 57
Wimborne Av. Hayes BC39 53
Wimborne Av. Orp. CN52 88
Wimborne Av. Red. BU73 121
Wimborne Av. Sthl. BF42 64
Wimborne Clo. SE12 CG46 78
Wimborne Clo. Epsom BO60 94
Wimborne Clo. Saw. CP6 6
Wimborne Clo. Wor. Pk. BQ54 85
Dorchester Rd.
Wimborne Ct. N1 BZ37 2
Wimborne Dr. NW9 BM31 46
Wimborne Dr. Pnr. BD33 45
Wimborne Gdns. W13 BJ39 54
Wimborne Gro. Wat. BB22 26
Wimborne Rd. N9 CB27 39
Wimborne St. N1 BZ37 2
Wimborne Way, Beck. CC52 87
Wimbourne Clo. Buck. H. CH27 40
Wimbourne Ct. N1 BZ37 57
Wimbourne Rd. N17 CA30 39
Wimbourne St. N1 BZ37 57
Wimpole Clo. Kings. on T. BL51 85
Wimpole Ms. W1 BV39 1
Wimpole Ms. W1 BV39 56
Wimpole Rd. West. Dr. AX40 53
Wimpole St. W1 BV39 1
Wimpole St. W1 BV39 56
Winans Wk. SW9 BY44 66
Wincanton Cres. Nthlt. BF35 45
Wincanton Gdns. Ilf. CL30 40
Wincanton Rd. SW18 BR47 75
Wincanton Rd. Rom. CV27 42
Winchcombe Rd. Cars. BT54 86
Winchcomb Gdns. SE9 CJ45 68
Winch Dells, Hem. H. AZ15 8
Winchelsea Av. Bexh. CQ43 69
Winchelsea Clo. SW15 BQ46 75
Chartfield Av.
Winchelsea Cres. E. Mol. BG51 84
Winchelsea Rd. E7 CH34 49
Winchelsea Rd. N17 CA31 48
Winchelsea Rd. NW10 BN37 55
Winchelsey Rd. Sth. Croy. CA57 96
Winchendon Rd. SW6 BR44 65
Winchendon Rd. Tedd. BG49 74
Winchester Av. NW6 BR37 55
Winchester Av. NW9 BM31 46
Winchester Av. Houns. BE43 64
Winchester Av. Upmin. CZ33 51
Winchester Clo. Brom. CG52 88
Winchester Clo. Enf. CA25 30
Winchester Clo. Esher BF56 93
Winchester Clo. Kings. on T. BM50 75
Winchester Clo. Slou. AV44 62
Rodney Way
Winchester Cres. Grav. DH48 81
Winchester Dr. Pnr. BD32 45
Winchester Ms. NW3 BT36 56
Winchester Rd.
Winchester Pk. Brom. CG52 88
Winchester Pl. E8 CA35 48
Kingsland High St.
Winchester Pl. N6 BV33 47
Winchester Pl. W3 BN41 65
Park Rd. E.
Winchester Rd. E4 CF29 39
Winchester Rd. N6 BV33 47
Winchester Rd. N9 CA26 39
Winchester Rd. NW3 BT36 56
Winchester Rd. Bexh. CP44 69
Winchester Rd. Brom. CG52 88
Winchester Rd. Felt. BE48 74
Winchester Rd. Har. BL31 46
Winchester Rd. Hayes BB43 63
Winchester Rd. Ilf. CM34 49
Winchester Rd. Nthwd. BB31 44
Winchester Rd. Nthwd. BC30 35
Winchester Rd. Orp. CO56 98
Winchester Rd. Twick. BJ46 74
Winchester Rd. Walt. BC54 83
Winchester Sq. SE1 BZ40 4
Winchester Sq. SE1 BZ40 57
Winchester Wk.
Winchester St. SW1 BV42 3
Winchester St. SW1 BV42 66
Winchester St. W3 BN41 65
Winchester Wk. SE1 BZ40 4
Winchester Wk. SE1 BZ40 57
Winchester Way, Rick. AZ25 26
Winchfield Clo. Har. BK32 45
Winchfield Rd. SE26 CD49 77
Winchfield Way, Rick. AX26 35
Winchmore Hill Rd. N14 BW26 38
Winchmore Hill Rd. N21 BW26 38
Winchstone Clo. Shep. AY52 83
Winckley Clo. Har. BL32 46
Wincott St. SE11 BY42 4
Wincott St. SE11 BY42 66
Wincrofts Dr. SE9 CM45 68
Windborough Rd. Cars. BV57 95
Windermere Av. N3 BS31 47
Windermere Av. NW6 BR37 55
Windermere Av. SW19 BS52 86
Windermere Av. Horn. CU35 50
Windermere Av. Ruis. BD33 45
Windermere Av. St. Alb. BJ14 9
Windermere Av. Wem. BK33 45

Windermere Clo. Dart. CU47 79
Windermere Clo. Hem. H. BA14 8
Windermere Clo. Orp. CL55 88
Windermere Ct. SW13 BO43 65
Windermere Gdns. Ilf. CK32 49
Windermere Gro. Wem. BK33 45
Windermere Av.
Windermere Rd. N10 BV30 38
Windermere Rd. N19 BW34 47
Holloway Rd.
Windermere Rd. SW15 BO49 75
Windermere Rd. SW16 BW51 86
Windermere Rd. W5 BK41 64
Windermere Rd. Bexh. CR44 69
Windermere Rd. Bexh. CS44 69
Windermere Rd. Couls. BX61 104
Windermere Rd. Croy. CA54 87
Windermere Rd. Sthl. BE39 54
Windermere Rd. W. Wick. CG55 88
Windermere Way, Red. BU70 121
Winders Rd. SW11 BU44 66
Windfield, Lthd. BJ64 102
Windfield Clo. SE26 CC49 77
Windgates, Guil. AU69 118
Windham Av. Croy. CF58 96
Windham Rd. Rich. BL45 65
Wind Hill, Ong. CU13 14
Wind Hill, Welw G. C. BS7 5
Windhover Way, Gray. DJ49 81
Winding Shot, Hem. H. AW13 8
Windings, The Sth. Croy. CA59 96
Winding Way, Dag. CP34 50
Winding Way, Har. BH35 45
Windlass Pl. SE8 CD42 67
Windlesham Gro. SW19 BQ47 75
Windlesham Rd. SW19 BQ47 75
Windlesham Rd. Wok. AO58 91
Windley Clo. SE23 CC48 77
Windmill Av. Epsom BO59 94
Windmill Av. St. Alb. BK11 9
Windmill Clo. SE1 CB42 67
Beatrice Rd.
Windmill Clo. Cat. BZ64 105
Coulsdon Rd.
Windmill Clo. Epsom BO59 94
Windmill Clo. Sun. BB50 73
Windmill Clo. Surb. BK54 84
Windmill Clo. Upmin. CX34 51
Windmill Clo. Wal. Abb. CG20 22
Windmill Clo. Wind. AN44 61
Windmill Dr. SW4 BV46 76
Windmill Dr. Lthd. BK65 102
Windmill Dr. Reig. BT69 121
Windmill Dr. Rick. AY25 26
Windmill End, Epsom BO59 94
Windmill Gdns. Enf. BY23 29
Windmill Hill, Enf. BY24 29
Windmill Hill, Kings L. AV19 16
Windmill Hill, Ruis. BB33 44
Windmill La. E15 CF36 57
Windmill La. Barn. BO25 28
Windmill La. Bush. BG26 36
Windmill La. Epsom BO59 94
Windmill La. Grnf. BG38 54
Windmill La. Sthl. BG40 54
Windmill La. Surb. BJ53 84
Windmill La. Wal. Cr. CD18 21
Windmill Rd. N18 BZ28 39
Windmill Rd. SW18 BT46 76
Windmill Rd. SW19 BP47 75
Windmill Rd. W4 BO42 65
Windmill Rd. W5 BK42 64
Windmill Rd. Brent. BK42 64
Windmill Rd. Croy. BZ54 87
Windmill Rd. Dag. CQ34 50
Windmill Rd. Ger. Cr. AR29 34
Windmill Rd. Hem. H. AY13 8
Windmill Rd. Hmptn. BF49 74
Windmill Rd. Mitch. BW53 86
Windmill Rd. Sev. CU68 116
Windmill Rd. Sev. CU70 116
Windmill Rd. Slou. AO40 61
Windmill Rd. Slou. AR35 43
Windmill Rd. Sun. BB51 83
Windmill Rd. West. Sun. BB51 83
Windmill Row SE11 BY42 4
Windmill Row SE11 BY42 66
Windmill St. W1 BW39 1
Windmill St. W1 BW39 56
Windmill St. Bush. BH26 36
Windmill St. Grav. DG47 81
Windmill Wk. SE1 BY40 4
Windmill Wk. SE1 BY40 56
Windmill Way, Reig. BT69 121
Windmill Way, Ruis. BB33 44
Windmore Av. Pot. B. BQ19 19
Windover Av. NW9 BN31 46
Windridge Clo. St. Alb. BF15 9
Windridge Rd. St. Alb. BD15 9
Windrush Av. Slou. AT42 62
Windrush Clo. SW11 BT45 66
Maysoule Rd.
Windrush Clo. W4 BN43 65
Bolton Rd.
Windrush Clo. Uxb. AY35 44
Windrush La. SE23 CC48 77
Winds End Clo. Hem. H. AZ12 8
Windsland Ms. W2 BT39 56
London St.
Windsor Av. Grays. DD41 71
Windsor Av. Rick. AW26 35
Windsor Av. E17 CD30 39
Windsor Av. SW19 BT51 86
Windsor Av. E. Mol. BF52 84
Windsor Av. Edg. BM28 37
Windsor Av. N. Mal. BN53 85
Windsor Av. Sutt. BR55 85
Windsor Av. Uxb. AZ37 53
Windsor Clo. N3 BR30 37
Windsor Rd.
Windsor Clo. Borwd. BM23 28
Windsor Clo. Guil. AP71 118
Powell Clo.
Windsor Clo. Har. BF34 45
Windsor Clo. Nthwd. BC30 35
Windsor Clo. Wal. Cr. CB18 21
Windsor Clo. Welw. G. C. BP5 5
Windsor Ct. N14 BW26 38
Windsor Ct. Rd. Wok. AP58 91
Windsor Cres. Har. BF35 45
Windsor Cres. Wem. BM34 46
Windsor Dr. Ashf. AX49 73
Windsor Dr. Barn. BU25 29
Windsor Dr. Dart. CU46 79
Windsor Dr. Orp. CO57 98
Windsor Gdns. Hayes BA41 63
Windsor Gro. SE27 BZ49 77
Windsor Pk. Rd. Hayes BB43 63
Windsor Pl. SW1 BW42 3
Windsor Pl. SW1 BW42 66
Francis St.
Windsor Rd. E4 CE28 39
Chivers Rd.
Windsor Rd. E7 CH35 49
Windsor Rd. E10 CE34 48
Windsor Rd. E11 CH33 49
Windsor Rd. N3 BR30 37
Windsor Rd. N7 BX34 47
Windsor Rd. N13 BY27 38
Windsor Rd. N17 CB30 39
Windsor Rd. NW2 BP36 55
Windsor Rd. W5 BK40 54
Windsor Rd. Barn. BQ25 28
Windsor Rd. Bexh. CQ45 69
Windsor Rd. Brwd. DA25 33
Windsor Rd. Dag. CQ34 50
Windsor Rd. Egh. AR47 72
Windsor Rd. Enf. CC21 30
Windsor Rd. Grav. DG48 81
Windsor Rd. Har. BG30 36
Windsor Rd. Horn. CV33 51
Windsor Rd. Houns. BC44 63
Windsor Rd. Ilf. CL35 49
Windsor Rd. Kings. on T. BL50 75
Windsor Rd. Maid. AG41 61
Windsor Rd. Rich. BL44 65
Windsor Rd. Sid. CO50 79
Windsor Rd. Slou. AQ35 43
Windsor Rd. Slou. AQ43 62
Windsor Rd. Stai. AS46 72
Windsor Rd. Sthl. BE41 64
Windsor Rd. Sun. BC50 73
Windsor Rd. Tedd. BG49 74
Windsor Rd. Th. Hth. BY51 86
Windsor Rd. Wat. BD22 27
Windsor Rd. Welw. BP5 5
Windsor Rd. Wind. AO42 61
Windsor Rd. Wok. AO56 91
Windsor Rd. Wor. Pk. BP55 85
Windsor St. N1 BY37 2
Windsor St. N1 BY37 56
Windsor St. Cher. AW53 83
Windsor St. Uxb. AX36 53
Windsor Ter. N1 BZ38 2
Windsor Ter. N1 BZ38 57
Windsor Wk. SE5 BZ44 67
Windsor Wk. Wey. AZ56 92
Windsor Way, Wok. AU61 100
Winds Ridge, Wok. AU66 109
Windus Rd. N16 CA33 48
Windus Wk. N16 CA33 48
Alkham Rd.
Windward Clo. Enf. CC21 30
Windy Hill, Brwd. DE26 122
Windy Ridge, Brom. CK51 88
Windyridge Clo. SW19 BQ49 75
Wine Clo. E1 CB40 57
Agatha Clo.
Wine Office Ct. EC4 BY39 2
Wine Office Ct. EC4 BY39 56
Winern Glebe, Wey. AY60 92
Winford Dr. Brox. CD14 12
Winforton St. SE10 CF44 67
Winfrith Rd. SW18 BT47 76
Wingate Cres. Croy. BW53 86
Wingate Rd. W6 BP41 65
Wingate Rd. Ilf. CL35 49
Wingate Rd. Sid. CP49 79
Sidcup-hill
Wingate Rd. Sid. CP50 79
Sidcup Hill
Wingate Way, St. Alb. BJ14 9
Wingfield Clo. Brwd. DD27 122
Wingfield Clo. Wey. AW58 92
Wingfield Gdns. Upmin. CZ32 51
Wingfield Ms. SE15 CB45 67
Wingfield St.
Wingfield Pl. Sid. CN48 78
Wingfield Rd. E15 CF35 48
Wingfield Rd. E17 CE32 48
Wingfield Rd. Grav. DG47 81
Wingfield Rd. Kings. on T. BL50 75
Wingfield St. SE15 CB45 67
Wingfield Way, Ruis. BC35 44
Wingford Rd. SW2 BX46 76
Wingletye La. Horn. CW31 51
Wingletye La. Horn. CX32 51
Wingmore Rd. SE24 BZ45 67
Wingrave Cres. Brwd. CZ28 42
Wingrave Rd. W6 BQ43 65
Wingrove Rd. SE6 CG48 78
Wing Way, Brwd. DB26 42
Winifred Av. Horn. CV35 51
Winifred Gro. SW11 BU45 66
Marjorie Gro.
Winifred Rd. SW19 BS51 86
Winifred Rd. Couls. BV61 104
Winifred Rd. Dag. CQ34 50
Winifred Rd. Dart. CU46 79
Winifred Rd. Erith CT42 69
Winifred Rd. Hamptn. BF49 74
Winifred Rd. Hem. H. AX15 8
Winifred St. E16 CK40 58
Winifred Ter. Enf. CA26 39
Winkers Clo. Ger. Cr. AS30 34
Winkers La. Ger. Cr. AS30 34
Winkfield Rd. E13 CH37 58
Winkfield Rd. N22 BY30 38
Winkfield Rd. Wind. AM46 61
Winkley St. E2 CB38 57
Canrobert St.
Winkworth Pl. Bans. BR60 94
Winkworth Pl. Bans. BS60 95
Winkworth Rd. Bans. BS60 95
Winlaton Rd. Brom. CF49 77
Winn Common Rd. SE18 CN43 68
Winnings Wk. Nthlt. BE36 54
Arnold Rd.
Winnington Clo. N2 BT32 47
Winnington Rd. N2 BT32 47
Winnington Rd. Enf. CC22 30
Winnington Way, Wok. AQ62 100
Winnock Rd. West Dr. AX40 53
Winn Rd. SE12 CH47 78
Winns Av. E17 CD31 48
Winns Ms. N15 CD31 48
Grove Pk. Rd.
Winns Ter. E17 CE30 39
Winsbeach E17 CF31 48
Winscombe Cres. W5 BK38 54
Winscombe St. N19 BV34 47
Winscombe Way, Stan. BJ28 36
Winsford Rd. SE6 CD48 77
Winsford Ter. N18 BZ28 39
Winsham Gro. SW11 BV46 76
Winslade Rd. SW2 BX46 76
Winslade Way SE6 CE47 77
Winsland Ms. W2 BT39 1
Winsland Ms. W2 BT39 56
Winsland St.
Winsland St. W2 BT39 1
Winsland St. W2 BT39 56
Winsley St. W1 BW39 1
Winsley St. W1 BW39 56
Winslow Clo. Pnr. BC32 44
Winslow Gro. E4 CG27 40
Hoppett Rd.
Winslow Rd. W6 BQ43 65
Winslow Way, Felt. BE48 74
Winslow Way, Walt. BD55 84
Winsor Est. W9 BS39 56
Winsor Ter. E6 CL39 58
Winstanley Rd. SW11 BT45 66
Winstead Gdns. Dag. CS35 50
Winston Av. NW9 BO33 46
Winston Clo. Har. BH29 36
Winston Clo. Rom. CR31 50
Winston Ct. Har. BF29 36
Winston Dr. Cob. BE62 102
Winstone Clo. Rom. CR31 50
Marlborough Rd.
Winstone Wk. W4 BN41 65
Winston Rd. N16 BZ35 48
Winston Way, Pot. B. BS20 20
Winston Way, Wok. AT63 100
Winstre Rd. Borwd. BM23 28
Winter Av. E6 CK37 58
Winterbourne Av. Orp. CM55 88
Winterbourne Gro. Wey. BA57 92
Winterbourne Rd. SE6 CD47 77
Winterbourne Rd. Dag. CP34 50
Winterbourne Rd. Th. Hth. BY52 86
Winter Box Wk. Rich. BL46 75
Kings Rd.
Winterbrook Rd. SE24 BZ46 77
Winterdown Gdns. Esher BE57 93
Winterdown Rd. Esher BE57 93
Winterdown Rd. Esher BE59 93
Winterfold Clo. SW19 BR48 75
Winterhill Way, Guil. AT68 109
Winterscroft Rd. Hodd. CD11 12
Winters Rd. Surb. BJ54 84
Winterstoke Gdns. NW7 BP28 37
Winterstoke Rd. SE6 CD47 77
Winters Way, Wal. Abb. CH20 22
Winterton Pl. SW10 BT43 3
Winterton Pl. SW10 BT43 66
Winterwell Rd. SW2 BX46 76
Winthorpe Rd. SW15 BR45 65
Winthrop Pl. E1 CB39 57
Winthrop St.
Winthrop St. E1 CB39 57
Winthrop Wk. Wem. BK34 45
Hutchinson Ter.
Winton App. Rick. BA25 26
Winton Av. N11 BW29 38
Winton Clo. N9 CC26 39
Winton Cres. Rick. AZ25 26
Winton Dr. Rick. AZ25 26
Winton Dr. Wal. Cr. CD18 21
Winton Gdns. Edg. BL29 37
Whitchurch La.
Winton Rd. Orp. CL56 97
Winton Way SW16 BY49 76
Winvale, Slou. AP41 62
Winwood, Slou. AR39 52
Wippendell Hill, Kings L. AX18 17
Wisbeach Rd. Croy. BZ53 87
Wisborough Rd. Sth. Croy. CA58 96
Wisdons Clo. Dag. CR34 50
Wise La. NW7 BP28 37
Wise La. West Dr. AX41 63
Wiseman Rd. E10 CE34 48
Wisemans Gdns. Saw. CP6 6
Wise Rd. E15 CF37 57
Wise's La. Hat. BQ17 19
Wise's La. Sev. DC57 99
Wiseton Rd. SW17 BU47 76
Wishart Rd. SE3 CJ44 68
Wistlea Cres. St. Alb. BM14 10
Wisley La. Wok. AX61 101
Wisley La. Wok. AY62 101
Wisley Rd. SW11 BU46 76
Wisley Rd. Orp. CO50 79
Wisteria Clo. Brwd. DB25 33
Lavender Av.
Wisteria Clo. Orp. CL55 88
Wisteria Gdns. Swan. CS51 89
Wisteria Rd. SE13 CF45 67
Witan St. E2 CB38 57
Coventry Rd.
Witches La. Sev. CT65 107
Witham Clo. Loug. CK25 31
Witham Rd. SE20 CC52 87
Witham Rd. Dag. CR35 50
Witham Rd. Horn. CU32 50
Witham Rd. Islw. BG44 64
Withens Clo. Orp. CP52 89
Witherby Clo. Croy. CA56 96
Witherfield Way SE16 CB42 67
Egan Way
Witherings, The Horn. CW32 51
Witherington Rd. N5 BY35 47
Withers Mead NW9 BO30 37
Withers Pl. EC1 BZ38 2
Withers Pl. EC1 BZ38 57
Old St.
Witherston Way SE9 CL48 78
Witney Clo. Pnr. BE29 36
Withey Clo. Wind. AM44 61
Witheygate Av. Stai. AW50 73
Withies, The Lthd. BJ63 102
Withycombe Rd. SW19 BQ47 75
Victoria Dr.
Withycroft, Slou. AS39 52
Withy Mead E4 CF27 39
Witley Ct. Sthl. BE32 45
Witley Cres. Croy. CF57 96
Witley Gdns. Sthl. BE42 64
Witley Rd. N19 BW34 47
Holloway Rd.
Witney Clo. Uxb. AY35 44
Witney Path SE23 CC48 77
Wittenham Clo. Slou. AQ40 52
Wittenham Way E4 CF27 39
Wittersham Rd. Brom. CG49 78
Wittering Wk. Horn. CV36 60
Witton Gdns. E. Mol. BF52 84
Wivenhoe Clo. SE15 CB45 67
Wivenhoe Rd. Bark. CO37 59
Wiverton Rd. SE26 CC50 77
Wix Hill, Leath. AZ68 110
Wix Rd. Dag. CP37 59
Wix's La. SW4 BV45 66
Woburn Av. Epp. CN22 31
Woburn Av. Horn. CU35 50
Woburn Av. Pur. BY59 95
Woburn Clo. Bush. BG25 27
Woburn Pl. WC1 BX38 2
Woburn Pl. WC1 BW38 56
Woburn Rd. Cars. BU54 86
Woburn Rd. Croy. BZ54 87
Woburn Sq. WC1 BW38 1
Woburn Sq. WC1 BW38 56
Woburn Wk. WC1 BW38 1
Woburn Wk. WC1 BW38 56
Wodeham St. E1 CB39 57
Woffingham Clo.
Kings. on T. BK51 84
Woffington Clo. Tedd. BK50 74
Upr. Teddington Rd.
Woking Clo. SW15 BO45 65
Wokingdon Rd. Grays. DG41 71
Woking Rd. Guil. AR67 109
Woking Rd. Wey. AV60 91
Woldham Rd. Brom. CJ52 88
Woldingham Rd. Cat. CF66 114
Woldingham Slines New
Rd. Cat. CB63 105
Wolds Dri. Orp. CL56 97
Wolfe Clo. Brom. CH53 88
Wolfe Clo. Hayes BC38 53
Ayels Rd.
Wolfe Cres. SE7 CJ42 68
Wolftencroft Cl. SW11 BU44 66
Wolferton Rd. E12 CK35 49
Wolffe Gdns. E15 CG36 58
Wolfington Rd. SE27 BY49 76
Wolf La. Wind. AL45 61
Wolf La. Wind. AM45 61
Wolfram Clo. SE13 CG46 78
Wolfs Hill, Oxt. CH69 115
Wolfs Rd. Oxt. CH68 115
Wolfs Row, Oxt. CH68 115
Wolfstan St. W12 BO40 55
Wolfs Wood, Oxt. CH69 115
Wolmer Clo. Edg. BM28 37
Wolmer Gdns. Edg. BM27 37
Wolseley Av. SW19 BS48 76
Wolseley Gdns. W4 BM43 65
Wolseley Rd. E7 CH36 58
Wolseley Rd. N8 BW32 47
Wolseley Rd. N22 BX30 38
Wolseley Rd. W4 BN42 65
Wolseley Rd. Har. BH31 45
Wolseley Rd. Mitch. BV54 86
Wolseley Rd. Rom. CS33 50
Wolseley St. SE1 CA41 4
Wolseley St. SE1 CA41 67
Wolsen St. E1 CC39 57
Sidney St.
Wolsey Av. E6 CL38 58
Wolsey Av. E17 CD31 48
Wolsey Av. Surb. BH53 84
Wolsey Clo. Houns. BG46 74
Wolsey Clo. Kings. on T. BM51 85
Wolsey Clo. Sthl. BG41 64
Wolsey Clo. Wor. Pk. BO56 94
Wolsey Cres. Croy. CF58 96
Wolsey Cres. Mord. BR54 85
Wolsey Dr. Kings. on T. BL49 75
Wolsey Dr. Walt. BD54 84
Wolsey Gdns. Ilf. CL29 40
Wolsey Gro. Edg. BN29 37
Wolsey Gro. Esher BF56 93
Wolsey Ms. NW5 BW36 56
Caversham Rd.
Wolsey Rd. N1 BZ35 48
Wolsey Rd. Ashf. AY49 73
Wolsey Rd. E. Mol. BG52 84
Wolsey Rd. Enf. CB23 30
Wolsey Rd. Esher BF56 93
Wolsey Rd. Hmptn. BF50 74
Wolsey Rd. Nthwd. BA27 35
Wolsey Rd. Sun. BB50 73
Wolsey Rd. Sun. BC50 73
Wolsey St. E1 CC39 57
Sidney St.
Wolsey Wk. Wok. AS62 100
Ch. St. W.
Wolsey Way, Chess. BM56 94
Wolsley Clo. Dart. CT46 79
Wolstonbury N12 BR28 37
Wolvens La. Dor. BF73 119
Wolvercote Rd. SE2 CP41 69
Wolverley St. E2 CB38 57
Bethnal Green Rd.
Wolverton Av.
Kings. on T. BM51 85
Wolverton Gdns. W5 BL40 55
Wolverton Gdns. W6 BQ42 65
Wolverton Rd. Stan. BK29 36
Wolverton Way N14 BW25 29
Wolves La. N13 BY29 38
Wolves La. N22 BY29 38
Womersley Rd. N8 BX32 47
Wonersh Way, Sutt. BQ58 94
Wonford Clo. Tad. BP66 112
Wonham La. Bet. BO71 120
Wonford Clo. Kings. on T. BO51 85
Wontford Rd. Pur. BY61 104
Wontner Rd. SW17 BU48 76
Woodall Cres. Horn. CW33 51
Woodall Road, Enf. CC25 30
Wood Av. Grays. CY42 70
Woodbank N12 BS28 38
Woodbank Rd. Brom. CG48 78
Woodbarn Way, Wal. Cr. CD19 21
Woodbastwick Rd. SE26 CC50 77
Woodberry Av. N12 BT29 38
Woodberry Av. N21 BY27 38
Woodberry Av. Har. BF31 45
Woodberry Clo. Sun. BC50 73
Woodberry Cres. N10 BV31 47
Woodberry Down N4 BZ33 48
Woodberry Down Est. N4 BZ33 48
Woodberry Gdns. N12 BT29 38
Woodberry Gro. N4 BZ33 48
Woodberry Gro. N12 BT29 38
Woodberry Grove, Bex. CS48 79
Briar Rd.
Woodberry Way E4 CF26 39
Woodberry Way N12 BT29 38
Woodbery Down Epp. CO17 23
Woodbine Clo. Twick. BG48 74
Woodbine Clo. Wal. Abb. CJ21 31
Woodbine Gro. SE20 CB50 77
Woodbine Gro. Enf. BZ22 30
Woodbine La. Wor. Pk. BP55 85
Woodbine Pl. E11 CH32 49
Woodbine Rd. Sid. CN47 78
Woodbines Av.
Kings. on T. BK52 84
Woodbine Ter. E9 CC36 57
Homerton Ter.
Woodborough Rd. SW15 BP45 65
Woodbourne Av. SW16 BW48 76
Woodbourne Clo. SW16 BW48 76
Woodbourne Dr. Esher BH57 93
Woodbridge Av. Lthd. BJ62 102
Woodbridge Clo. NW2 BP34 46
Newfield Rise
Woodbridge Clo. N7 BX34 47
Durham Rd.
Woodbridge Clo. Rom. CV28 42
Woodbridge Ct. Wdf. Grn. CK29 40
Vicarage Rd.
Woodbridge Gdns. Lthd. BJ62 102
Woodbridge Hill, Guil. AQ70 118
Woodbridge Hill Gdns.
Guil. AQ70 118
Woodbridge La. Rom. CV27 42
Woodbridge Meadows
Guil. AQ70 118
Woodbridge Rd. Bark. CN35 49
Woodbridge Rd. Guil. AR70 118
Woodbridge Rd. Guil. AR71 118
North St.
Woodbridge St. EC1 BY38 2
Woodbridge St. EC1 BY38 56
Woodbrook Clo.
Wal. Abb. CG20 22
Woodbrook Rd. SE2 CO43 69
Woodburn Cl. NW4 BQ32 46
Woodbury Clo. E11 CH31 49
Woodbury Clo. Croy. CA55 87
Woodbury Clo. West. CK62 106
Belvedere Rd.
Woodbury Dr. Sutt. BT58 95
Woodbury Hill Loug. CK23 31
Woodbury Pk. Rd. W13 BJ38 54
Woodbury Rd. E17 CE31 48
Woodbury Rd. West. CK62 106
Woodbury St. SW17 BU49 76
Woodchester Sq. W2 BS39 56
Woodchurch Clo. Sid. CM48 78
Wood Church Dri. Brom. CJ50 78
Woodchurch Rd. NW6 BS36 56
Wood Cl. Hat. BP12 10
Wood Clo. E2 CB38 57
Wood Clo. NW9 BN33 46
Wood Clo. Amer. AQ23 25
Wood Clo. Bex. CT48 79
Wood Clo. Har. BG33 45
Wood Clo. Wind. AO45 61
Woodclyffe Dr. Chis. CL51 88
Woodcock Dell Av. Har. BK33 45
Woodcock Hill Borwd. BM25 28
Woodcock Hill Har. BK32 45
Woodcock Hill, St. Alb. BK10 9
Woodcock Hill Trd. Est.
Rick. AX23 35
Woodcombe Cres. SE23 CC47 77
Wood Common, Hat. BP11 10
Woodcote Av. NW7 BQ29 37
Woodcote Av. Horn. CU35 50
Woodcote Av. Th. Hth. BY52 86
Woodcote Av. Wall. BV58 95
Woodcote Clo. Enf. CC25 30
Woodcote Clo. Epsom BN60 94
Woodcote Clo.
Kings. on T. BL50 75
Woodcote Dr. Pur. BW58 95
Woodcote End Epsom BN61 103
Woodcote Grn. Rd.
Epsom BN61 103
Woodcote Grn. Rd. Wall. BW58 95
Woodcote Gro. Cars. BV59 95
Woodcote Gro. Rd. Couls. BW61 104
Woodcote Hurst Epsom BN61 103
Woodcote La. Pur. BW59 95
Woodcote Pk. Av. Pur. BW59 95
Woodcote Pk. Rd. Epsom BN61 103
Woodcote Pl. SE27 BY49 76
Dassett Rd.
Woodcote Rd. E11 CH33 49
Woodcote Rd. Epsom BN60 94
Woodcote Rd. Orp. CN54 88
Woodcote Rd. Wall. BV57 95
Woodcote Side, Epsom BM61 103

Woodcote Valley Rd. Pur. BW60 95
Woodcote Village Pur. BW59 95
Woodcourt Clo. Wal. Cr. CC18 21
Wood Cres. Hem. H. AX14 8
Woodcrest Rd. Pur. BX60 95
Woodcrest Wk. Reig. BU69 121
Woodcroft N21 BX26 38
Woodcroft SE9 CK48 78
Woodcroft Av. NW7 BO29 37
Woodcroft Av. Stan. BJ30 36
Woodcroft Cres. Grnf. BJ36 54
Woodcroft Cres. Uxb. AZ37 53
Woodcroft Rd. Chesh. AO17 16
Woodcroft Rd. Th. Hth. BY53 86
Woodcutters Av. Grays. DE41 71
Wood Dene Leath BG58 93
Wood Dene, Lthd. BG59 93
Wood Dr. Chis. CK50 78
Wood Dr. Sev. CT66 116
Woodedge Clo. E4 CG26 40
Forest Side
Woodend SE19 BZ50 77
Wood End Esher BG55 84
Wood End, Hayes BB39 53
Wood End, Lthd. BK66 111
Wood End, St. Alb. BG17 18
Woodend, Sutt. BT55 86
Wood End Av. Har. BF35 45
Wood End Clo. Nthlt. BG35 45
Wood End Clo. Slou. AO34 43
Woodend Clo. Wok. AQ63 100
Woodend Gdns. Enf. BX24 29
Wood End Gdns. Nthlt. BG35 45
Wood End Grn. Rd.
Hayes BA39 53
Wood End La. Nthlt. BF36 54
Woodend Park, Cob. BD61 102
Woodend Rd. E17 CF30 39
Woodend, The Wall. BV58 95
Wood End Way Nthlt. BG35 45
Wooder Gdns. E7 CG35 49
Woodfall Av. Barn. BR25 28
Woodfall Rd. N4 BY33 47
Woodfall St. SW3 BU42 3
Woodfall St. SW3 BU42 66
Wood Farm Rd. Hem. H. AY14 8
Woodfarrs SE5 BZ45 67
Woodfield Av. Nthwd. BB28 35
Woodfield Av. NW9 BO31 46
Woodfield Av. SW16 BW48 76
Woodfield Av. W5 BK38 54
Woodfield Av. Cars. BV57 95
Woodfield Av. Grav. DG48 81
Woodfield Av. Wem. BK34 45
Woodfield Clo. SE19 BZ50 77
Woodfield Clo. Ash. BK62 102
Woodfield Clo. Couls. BW63 104
Woodfield Clo. Red. BU70 121
Woodfield Cres. W5 BK38 54
Woodfield Dr. Barn. BV26 38
Woodfield Dr. Rom. CU31 50
Woodfield Gdns. W9 BR39 55
Woodfield Rd.
Woodfield Gdns. N. Mal. BO53 85
Woodfield Gro. SW16 BW48 76
Woodfield Hill, Couls. BV63 104
Woodfield La. SW16 BW48 76
Woodfield La. Ash. BL62 103
Woodfield La. Hat. BT15 11
Woodfield Pl. W9 BR39 55
Woodfield Rise Bush. BG26 36
Woodfield Rd. W5 BK38 54
Woodfield Rd. W9 BR39 55
Woodfield Rd. Ash. BK62 102
Woodfield Rd. Houns. BC44 63
Woodfield Rd. Rad. BJ21 27
Woodfield Rd. Surb. BH55 84
Woodfield Rd. Welw. G. C. BR8 5
Woodfields, Sev. CS65 107
Woodfields, The Sth. Croy. CA59 96
Woodfield Way N11 BW29 38
Woodfield Way, Horn. CV33 51
Woodfield Way, Red. BU70 121
Woodfield Way, St. Alb. BK12 9
Woodford Av. Ilf. CJ31 49
Woodford Bridge Rd. Ilf. CJ31 49
Woodford Cres. Pnr. BC30 35
Woodford Ct. Wal. Abb. CH20 22
Abbots Dr.
Woodford New Rd. E17 CG31 49
Woodford New Rd. E18 CG31 49
Woodford New Rd.
Wdf. Grn. CG31 49
Woodford Pl. Wem. BL33 46
Woodford Rd. E7 CH35 49
Woodford Rd. E18 CG33 49
Woodford Rd. Wat. BC23 26
Wood Gate, Wat. BC20 17
Woodgate Av. Chess. BK56 93
Woodgate Cres. Nthwd. BC29 35
Woodgavil Bans. BR61 103
Woodgers Gro. Swan. CT51 89
Swanley La.
Woodger Rd. W12 BQ41 65
Goldhawk Rd.
Woodgrange Av. N12 BT29 38
Woodgrange Av. W5 BL40 55
Woodgrange Av. Enf. CB25 30
Woodgrange Av. Har. BK32 45
Woodgrange Clo. Har. BK32 45
Woodgrange Gdns. Enf. CB25 30
Woodgrange Rd. E7 CH35 49
Woodgreen La. Wal. Abb. CH20 22
Woodgreen Rd. Wal. Abb. CJ20 22
Woodhall Av. SE21 CA48 77
Woodhall Av. Pnr. BE30 36
Woodhall Clo. Uxb. AX35 44
Woodhall Cres. Horn. CW33 51
Woodhall Ct. Welw. G. C. BR8 5
Woodhall Dr. SE21 CA48 77
Woodhall Dr. Pnr. BD30 36
Woodhall Gate Pnr. BD29 36
Woodhall La. Hem. H. AY13 8
Woodhall La. Rad. BL21 28
Woodhall La. Wat. BD27 36
Woodhall La. Welw. G. C. BR8 5
Woodhall Rd. Pnr. BD29 36
Woodham Ct. E18 CG31 49
Woodham La. Wey. AV59 91
Woodham La. Wey. AX58 92
Woodham La. Wok. AT60 91
Woodham Park Rd. Wey. AV58 91
Woodham Park Way, Wey. AV59 91
Woodham Rise, Wok. AT61 100
Woodham Rd. SE6 CF48 77
Woodham Rd. Wok. AS61 100
Woodham Rd. Wok. AT60 91
Woodham Waye, Wok. AT60 91
Woodhatch Rd. Reig. &
Red. BT72 121
Woodhatch Spinney Couls. BX57 95
Woodhatch Spinney Couls. BX61 104
Woodhaven Gdns. Ilf. CL31 49
Brandville Gdns.
Woodhaven Gdns. Ilf. CM31 49
Brandville Gdns.
Woodhaw, Egh. AT49 72
Woodhayes Rd. SW19 BQ50 75
Woodhead Dr. Orp. CN55 88
Woodheyes Rd. NW10 BN35 46
Woodhill SE18 CK41 68
Woodhill Harl. CN13 13
Woodhill Av. Ger. Cr. AS32 43
Woodhill Cres. Har. BK32 45
Woodhill, Wok. AU66 109
Woodhouse Av. Grnf. BH37 54
Woodhouse Clo. Grnf. BH37 54
Woodhouse Clo. Hayes BB41 63
Woodhouse Gro. E12 CK36 58
Woodhouse Rd. E11 CG34 49
Woodhouse Rd. N12 BT29 38
Woodhurst Av. Orp. CL53 88
Woodhurst Av. Wat. BD21 27
Woodhurst Dr. Uxb. AV32 43
Woodhurst Pk. Oxt. CG68 115
Woodhurst Rd. SE2 CO42 69
Woodhurst Rd. W3 BN40 55
Woodhurst Rd. Oxt. CG68 115
Woodhyrst Gdns. Ken. BY57 95
Woodhyrst Gdns. Ken. BY61 104
Wooding Grove, Harl. CL11 13
Woodington Clo. SE9 CL46 78
Woodison St. E3 CD38 57
Woodknoll Dr. Brom. CK51 88
Woodland App. Grnf. BJ36 54
Whitton Dr.
Woodland Av. Wind. AM45 61
Woodland Av. Brwd. DD25 122
Woodland Av. Guil. AQ71 118
Woodland Av. Hem. H. AW14 8
Woodland Av. Slou. AO40 52
Woodland Clo. NW9 BN32 46
Woodland Clo. Brwd. DE25 122
Woodland Clo. Epsom BO57 94
Woodland Clo. Uxb. AZ34 44
Woodland Clo. Wdf. Grn. CH27 40
Woodland Ct. Oxt. CF67 114
Woodland Ct. Oxt. CG67 115
Woodland Cres. SE10 CG43 68
Woodland Dri. Leath. BB67 110
Woodland Dr. St. Alb. BK12 9
Woodland Dr. Wat. BB23 26
Woodland Gdns. N10 BV32 47
Woodland Gdns. Croy. CC59 96
Woodland Gdns. Islw. BH45 64
Woodland Gdns. Sth. Croy. CC58 96
Woodland Gro. SE10 CG42 68
Woodland Gro. Wey. BA56 92
Woodland Hl. SE19 CA50 77
Woodland La. Rick. AU24 25
Woodland Pl. Hem. H. AW14 8
Woodland Rise, Oxt. CG68 115
Woodland Rise, Sev. CW65 108
Woodland Rise N10 BV31 47
Woodland Rise, Grnf. BJ36 54
Woodland Rise
Welw. G. C. BQ7 7
Woodland Rd. E4 CF26 39
Woodland Rd. N11 BW28 38
Woodland Rd. SE19 CA49 77
Woodland Rd. Loug. CK24 31
Woodland Rd. Rick. AU28 34
Woodland Rd. Th. Hth. BY52 86
Woodlands NW11 BR32 46
Woodlands SW20 BQ52 85
Woodlands, Har. BF31 45
Woodlands, Hat. BS17 20
Woodlands, Rad. BJ20 18
Woodlands Av. Wey. AV60 91
Woodlands Av. E11 CH33 49
Woodlands Av. N12 BT29 38
Woodlands Av. W3 BM40 55
High St.
Woodlands Av. Berk. AR13 7
Woodlands Av. Berk. AU11 7
Woodlands Av. Horn. CV32 51
Woodlands Av. N. Mal. BN51 85
Woodlands Av. Red. BU71 121
Woodlands Av. Rom. CQ32 50
Woodlands Av. Ruis. BD33 45
Woodlands Av. Sid. CN47 78
Woodlands Av. Wor. Pk. BO55 85
Woodlands Clo. NW11 BR32 46
Woodlands Clo. Borwd. BM24 28
Woodlands Clo. Brom. CK51 88
Woodlands Clo. Cher. AT58 91
Woodlands Clo. Esher BH57 93
Woodlands Clo. Ger. Cr. AT32 43
Woodlands Clo. Grays. DF41 71
Woodlands Clo. Hem. H. AW14 8
Woodlands Clo. Swan. CT52 89
Woodlands Clo. Wey. BA56 92
Woodlands Ct. Wok. AS63 100
Constitution Hill
Woodlands Dr. Har. BH29 36
Woodlands Dr. Hodd. CE13 12
Woodlands Dr. Kings L. BA17 17
Woodlands Dr. Sun. BD51 84
Woodlands Dr. Wat. BC23 26
Woodlands Gdns. E17 CG31 49
Woodford New Rd.
Woodlands Gro. Couls. BV62 104
Woodlands Gro. Islw. BH44 64
Woodlands La. Cob. BF62 104
Woodlands Pde. Ashf. BA50 73
Hogarth Av.
Woodlands Pk. Bex. CS49 79
Woodlands Pk. Guil. AT70 118
Woodlands Pk. Tad. BM69 120
Woodlands Pk. Wey. AV56 91
Woodlands Pk. Rd. N15 BY32 47
Woodlands Pk. Rd. SE10 CG43 68
Woodlands Rise Swan. CT51 89
Woodlands Rd. E11 CG34 49
Woodlands Rd. E17 CF31 48
Woodlands Rd. N9 CC26 39
Woodlands Rd. SW13 BO45 65
Woodlands Rd. Bexh. CQ45 69
Woodlands Rd. Brom. CK51 88
Woodlands Rd. Bush. BE24 27
Woodlands Rd. Enf. BZ23 30
Woodlands Rd. Epsom BM61 103
Woodlands Rd. Guil. AR68 109
Woodlands Rd. Har. BH32 45
Woodlands Rd. Hem. H. AZ17 17
Woodlands Rd. Ilf. CM34 49
Woodlands Rd. Islw. BG45 64
Woodlands Rd. Islw. BH44 64
Woodlands Rd. Lthd. BE67 111
Woodlands Rd. Lthd. BG62 102
Woodlands Rd. Orp. CO57 98
Woodlands Rd. Red. BU71 121
Woodlands Rd. Rom. CT31 50
Woodlands Rd. Rom. CX30 42
Woodlands Rd. Sev. CX60 99
Woodlands Rd. Sthl. BD40 54
Woodlands Rd. Surb. BK54 84
Woodlands Rd. Vir. W. AR52 82
Woodlands Rd. Wey. AV60 91
Woodlands Rd. East
Vir. W. AR52 82
Woodlands Rd. West
Vir. W. AR52 82
Woodlands St. SE13 CF47 77
Woodlands, The N14 BV26 38
Woodlands, The SE13 CF47 77
Woodlands, The SE19 BZ50 77
Woodlands, The Amer AO21 25
Woodlands, The Esher BG55 84
Woodlands, The Ger. Cr. AS32 43
Woodlands, The Islw. BH44 64
Woodlands, The Orp. CO57 98
Woodlands, The Wall. BV58 95
Woodlands, The Wind. AM45 61
Nelson Rd.
Woodlands Way SW15 BR46 75
Woodlands Way Ash. BL62 103
Woodfield La.
Woodlands Way, Ash. BM61 103
Woodland Ter. SE7 CK42 68
Woodland Ter. SE18 CK42 68
Woodland View, Chesh. AO20 16
Woodland Wk. SE10 CG42 68
Woodland Way N21 BY27 38
Woodland Way NW7 BO29 37
Woodland Way NW11 BS32 47
Woodland Way SE2 CP42 69
Woodland Way, Cat. CA67 114
Woodland Way, Croy. CD54 87
Woodland Way, Epp. CM21 31
Woodland Way, Mitch. BV50 76
Woodland Way, Mord. BR52 85
Woodland Way, Ong. CW18 24
Woodland Way, Orp. CM52 88
Woodland Way, Pur. BY60 95
Woodland Way, Surb. BM55 85
Woodland Way, Tad. BR64 103
Woodland Way, Wal. Cr. BY17 20
Woodland Way, Wdf. Grn. CH27 40
Woodland Way, W. Wick. CE56 96
Woodland Way, Wey. BA56 92
Wood La. N6 BV32 47
Wood La. NW9 BN33 46
Wood La. W12 BQ39 55
Wood La. Cat. BZ65 105
Wood La. Dag. CP35 50
Wood La. Dart. CY49 80
Wood La. Horn. CU35 50
Wood La. Islw. BH43 64
Wood La. Iver AU38 52
Wood Lane, Ong. DC13 15
Wood La. Ruis. BA33 44
Wood La. Slou. AN41 61
Wood La. Slou. AO35 43
Wood La. Stan. BJ27 36
Wood La. Tad. BR62 103
Wood La. Wdf. Grn. CG28 40
Wood La. Wey. BA58 92
Wood La. Wok. AO62 100
Wood La. Clo. Iver AU38 52
Wood Lane End, Hem. H. AZ13 8
Woodlawn Cres. Twick. BF48 74
Woodlawn Dr. Felt. BD48 74
Woodlawn Gro. Wok. AS61 100
Woodlawn Rd. SW6 BQ43 65
Woodlea Dr. Brom. CG53 88
Woodlea Est. Brom. CG53 88
Woodlea Gro. Nthwd. BA29 35
Woodlea Rd. N16 CA34 48
Woodleigh Av. N12 BU29 38
Woodleigh Gdns. SW16 BX48 76
Woodley Clo. SW17 BU50 76
Woodley Hill, Chesh. AO20 16
Woodley Rd. Orp. CP55 89
Wood Lodge La.
W. Wick. CF55 87
Woodmancote Gdns.
Wey. AW60 92
Elmstead Rd.
Woodman La. E4 CG25 31
Woodman Path Chig. CN29 40
Woodman Pl. SE7 CK42 68
Maryon Rd.
Woodman Rd. Brwd. DB28 42
Woodman Rd. Couls. BW61 104
Woodman Rd. Hem. H. AY14 8
Woodmans Ct. Stan. BL30 37
Woodmans Mews W12 BP39 55
Woodmansterne La. Bans. BS61 104
Woodmansterne La. Cars. BU59 95
Woodmansterne Rd.
SW16 BW50 76
Woodmansterne Rd. Cars. BU58 76
Woodmansterne Rd.
Couls. BW61 104
Woodmansterne St. Bans. BU61 104
Wood Meads Epp. CO18 23
Woodmere SE9 CK47 78
Woodmere Av. Croy. CC54 87
Woodmere Av. Wat. BD22 27
Woodmere Clo. Croy. CC54 87
Woodmere Gdns. Croy. CC54 87
Woodmere Way Beck. CF53 87
Wood Mt. Hat. BP12 10
Woodmount Swan. CS54 89
Woodnook Rd. SW16 BV49 76
Woodpecker Clo. N9 CB25 30
Woodpecker Clo. Bush. BG26 36
Woodpecker Mt. Croy. CD58 96
Woodpecker Rd. SE14 CD43 67
Woodpecker Way, Wok. AR65 100
Woodplace Clo. Couls. BW63 104
Woodplace La. Couls. BW62 104
Woodplace La. Couls. BW64 104
Woodquest Av. SE24 BZ46 77
Woodridden Hill,
Wal. Abb. CJ21 31
Woodride Barn. BT23 29
Wood Ride Orp. CM52 88
Woodridge Way, Nthwd. BB29 35
Woodridings Av. Pnr. BE30 36
Woodridings Clo. Pnr. BE29 36
Woodriffe Rd. E11 CF33 48
Wood Rise, Guil. AP69 118
Wood Rise Pnr. BC32 44
Wood Rd. Sev. CZ57 99
Wood Rd. Shep. AZ52 83
Wood Rd. West. CJ62 106
Woodrow SE18 CK42 68
Woodrow Av. Hayes BB39 53
Woodrow Clo. Grnf. BJ36 54
Woodruff Av. Guil. AT69 118
Woodrush Way, Rom. CP31 50
Woods Av. Hat. BP12 10
Woods Av. Hat. BP13 10
Woods Bldgs. E1 CB39 57
Durward St.
Woodseer St. E1 CA39 2
Woodseer St. E1 CA39 57
Woodsford Sq. W14 BR41 65
Woodshire Rd. Dag. CR34 50
Woodside NW11 BS32 47
Woodside SW19 BR50 75
Woodside, Borwd. BL24 28
Woodside, Buck. H. CJ27 40
Woodside, Lthd. BF64 102
Woodside, Orp. CO56 98
Woodside, Tad. BR67 112
Woodside, Wat. BC22 26
Woodside Av. Amer. AO21 25
Woodside Av. N6 BU32 47
Woodside Av. N10 BU32 47
Woodside Av. N12 BS28 38
Woodside Av. SE25 CB53 87
Woodside Av. Chis. CL49 78
Woodside Av. Esher BH54 84
Woodside Av. Walt. BC56 92
Woodside Av. Wem. BL37 55
Woodside Clo. Amer. AO22 25
Woodside Clo. Bexh. CS45 69
Woodside Clo. Brwd. DE25 122
Woodside Clo. Ger. Cr. AS30 34
Woodside Clo. Rain. CV38 60
Woodside Clo. Stan. BJ28 36
Woodside Clo. Surb. BN54 85
Woodside Clo. Vir. W. AQ53 82
Woodside Clo. Wem. BL37 55
Woodside Clo. Wok. AO62 100
Woodside Ct. Croy. CB54 87
Woodside Ct. Rd. Croy. CB54 87
Woodside Cres. Sid. CN48 78
Woodside Dr. Dart. CT49 79
Woodside End, Wem. BL37 55
Woodside Epp. CP16 23
Woodside Gdns. E4 CE28 39
Woodside Gdns. N17 CA30 39
Woodside Grange Rd. N12 BS28 38
Woodside Grn. SE25 CB53 87
Woodside Gro. N12 BT27 38
Woodside Hill, Ger. Cr. AS30 34
Woodside La. N12 BS27 38
Woodside La. Bex. CP46 79
Woodside La. Hat. BR15 10
Woodside La. Hat. BS15 11
Woodside, Leath. BA66 110
Woodside Pk. SE25 CB53 87
Woodside Pk. Av. E17 CF32 48
Woodside Pk. Rd. N12 BS28 38
Woodside Pl. Wem. BL37 55
Woodside Rd. E13 CJ38 58
Woodside Rd. N22 BX29 38
Woodside Rd. SE25 CB53 87
Woodside Rd. Amer. AO22 25
Woodside Rd. Bexh. CS45 69
Woodside Rd. Brom. CK53 88
Woodside Rd. Cob. BF60 93
Woodside Rd. Guil. AP70 118
Woodside Rd.
Kings. on T. BL50 75
Woodside Rd. N. Mal. BN51 85
Woodside Rd. Nthwd. BB29 35
Woodside Rd. Nthwd. BC29 35
Woodside Rd. Pur. BW60 95
Woodside Rd. St. Alb. BE18 18
Woodside Rd. Sev. CP65 107
Woodside Rd. Sev. CU65 107
Woodside Rd. Sid. CN48 78
Woodside Rd. Sutt. BT55 86
Woodside Rd. Wat. BC19 17
Woodside Rd. Wdf. Grn. CH28 40
Woodside Rd. Welw. G. C. BR5 5
Woodside Vw. SE25 CB53 87
Woodside Vw. Sev. CR58 98
Woodside Way, Croy. CC53 87
Woodside Way, Mitch. BV51 86
Woodside Way, Rad. BV71 121
Woodside Way, Red. BV73 121
Woods Ms. W1 BV40 3
Woods Ms. W1 BV40 56
Woodsome Clo. Wey. BA57 92
Woodsome Rd. NW5 BV34 47
Woods Pl. SE1 CA41 4
Woods Pl. SE1 CA41 67
Woodspring Rd. SW19 BR48 75
Woods Rd. SE15 CB44 67
Wood St. E16 CH39 58
Ethel Rd.
Woodstead Gro. Edg. BL29 37
Woods, The Nthwd. BC28 35
Woods, The Uxb. AZ35 44
Woodstock Surb. BK55 84
Woodstock Av. Slou. AR42 62
Woodstock Av. NW11 BR33 46
Woodstock Av. W13 BJ41 64
Woodstock Av. Islw. BJ46 74
Woodstock Av. Rom. CX28 42
Woodstock Av. Sthl. BE38 54
Woodstock Av. Sutt. BR54 85
Woodstock Clo. Bex. CQ47 79
Woodstock Clo. Stan. BL30 37
Woodstock Ct. SE12 CH46 78
Woodstock Cres. N9 CA25 30
Woodstock Dr. Uxb. AY35 44
Woodstock Gdns. Beck. CE50 77
Woodstock Gdns. Hayes BB39 53
Woodstock Gdns. Ilf. CO34 50
Woodstock Gro. W12 BQ41 65
Woodstock, Guil. AW67 110
Woodstock La. Esher BJ57 93
Woodstock Ms. W1 BV39 1
Woodstock Rise, Sutt. BR54 85
Woodstock Rd. E7 CJ36 58
Woodstock Rd. E17 CF30 39
Woodstock Rd. N4 BY33 47
Woodstock Rd. NW11 BR33 46
Woodstock Rd. W4 BO42 65
Woodstock Rd. Brox. CD13 12
Woodstock Rd. Bush. BH26 36
Woodstock Rd. Cars. BV56 95
Woodstock Rd. Couls. BV61 104
Woodstock Rd. Croy. BZ55 87
Woodstock Rd. Wem. BL37 55
Woodstock Rd. N.
St. Alb. BJ12 9
Woodstock Road S.
St. Alb. BJ13 9
Woodstock St. E16 CG39 58
Woodstock St. W1 BV39 1
Woodstock St. W1 BV39 56
Oxford St.
Woodstock Ter. E14 CE40 57
Woodstock Way, Mitch. BV51 86
Woodstone Av. Epsom BP56 94
Wood St. E17 CF31 48
Wood St. EC2 BZ39 2
Wood St. EC2 BZ39 57
Wood St. W4 BO42 65
Wood St. Barn. BQ24 28
Wood St. Grays. DE43 71
Wood St. Kings. on T. BK51 84
Wood St. Mitch. BU54 86
Wood St. Red. BW68 113
Wood St. Swan. CV51 90
Woods Wy. Lthd. BH60 93
Woodsyre Est. SE26 CA49 77
Wood, The Surb. BL53 85
Woodthorpe Rd. SW15 BP45 65
Woodthorpe Rd. Ashf. AX50 73
Wood Vale N10 BW32 47
Wood Vale SE23 CB47 77
Woodvale Av. SE25 CA52 87
Wood Vale Est. SE23 CB47 77
Wood View, Chess. BK59 93
Wood Vw. Grays. DE41 71
Wood View, Hem. H. AW12 8
Wood View, Pot. B. BW17 20
Woodview Av. E4 CF28 39
Woodview Clo. Sev. CZ57 99
Woodview Clo.
Sth. Croy. CB60 96
Woodview Rd. Swan. CS51 89
Woodville SE3 CH44 68
Woodville Clo. Tedd. BJ49 74
Woodville Ct. Wat. BC23 26
Woodville Gdns. NW11 BQ33 46
Hendon Way
Woodville Gdns. W5 BL39 55
Woodville Gdns. Ilf. CL31 49
Woodville Gdns. Ruis. BA33 44
Woodville Gro. N16 CA35 48
Woodville Rd.
Woodville Pl. Cat. BZ64 105
Woodville Rd. E11 CG33 49
Woodville Rd. E17 CD32 48
Woodville Rd. E18 CH30 40
Woodville Rd. N16 CA35 48
Woodville Rd. NW6 BR37 55
Woodville Rd. NW11 BQ33 46
Woodville Rd. W5 BK39 54
Woodville Rd. Barn. BS24 29
Woodville Rd. Mord. BS52 86
Woodville Rd. Rich. BJ48 74
Woodville Rd. Th. Hth. BZ52 87
Woodville St. SE18 CK42 68
Woodvill Rd. Lthd. BJ63 102
Woodward Av. NW4 BP32 46
Woodward Clo. Grays. DD42 71
Woodwarde Rd. SE22 CA46 77
Woodward Gdns. Dag. CO36 59
Woodward Rd.
Woodward Rd. Dag. CO36 59
Woodwards, Harl. CM12 13
Woodward Ter. Green. CZ46 80
Woodway, Brwd. DD26 122
Woodway, Guil. AT70 118
Wood Way, Orp. CL55 88
Wood Way, Sev. CT64 107
Woodway Cres. Harl. BJ32 45
Woodwaye Wat. BD26 36
Woodwell St. SW18 BT46 76
North Side
Wood Wharf SE10 CF43 67
Wood Yard Clo. NW5 BV35 47
Gillies St.
Woodyard La. SE21 CA47 77
Woodyates Rd. SE12 CG46 78
Woolacombe Rd. SE3 CH44 68
Woolacombe Way, Hayes BB42 63

Woolaston Rd. N4 BY32 47
Umfreville Rd.
Wooler St. SE17 BZ42 4
Wooler St. SE17 BZ42 67
Woolf Clo. SE28 CO40 59
Woolf Wk. Til. DH44 71
Coleridge Rd.
Woolhampton Way Chig. CO27 41
Woollam Cres. St. Alb. BG11 9
Woollard St. Wal. Abb. CF20 21
Woollard Way Ing. DC19 24
Woolmans Clo. Brox. CD14 12
Woolmead Av. NW4 BP33 46
Woolmer Dr. Hem. H. BA13 8
Woolmer Gdns. N18 CB29 39
Woolmer Rd. N18 CB28 39
Woolmongers La. Ing. DA19 24
Woolmore St. E14 CF40 57
Woolneigh St. SW6 BS45 66
Wool Rd. SW20 BP50 75
Woolsey Rd. Hem. H. AX14 8
Woolstone Rd. SE23 CD48 77
Woolwich Church St. SE18 CK41 68
Woolwich Common SE18 CL43 68
Woolwich High St. SE18 CK41 68
Woolwich Industrial Est. SE28 CN41 68
Woolwich Manor Way E16 CL40 58
Woolwich New Rd. SE18 CL42 68
Woolwich Rd. SE2 CP43 69
Woolwich Rd. SE7 CG42 68
Woolwich Rd. SE10 CG42 68
Woolwich Rd. Belv. CP43 69
Woolwich Rd. Bexh. CR45 69
Wooster Gdns. E14 CF39 57
Woosters Mews, Har. BG31 45
Fairfield Dr.
Wooton Dr. Hem. H. AY11 8
Wootton Clo. Horn. CV32 51
Wootton Gro. N3 BS30 38
Station Rd.
Wootton St. SE1 BY41 4
Wootton St. SE1 BY41 66
Worbeck Rd. SE20 CB51 87
Worcester Av. N17 CB29 39
Worcester Av. Enf. CB22 30
Worcester Av. Upmin. CZ34 51
Worcester Clo. Croy. CD55 87
Worcester Cl. Green DA45 70
Worcester Clo. Mitch. BV51 86
Worcester Cres. NW7 BO27 37
Worcester Cres. Wdf. Grn. CH28 40
Worcester Gdns. Grnf. BG36 54
Worcester Gdns. Ilf. CK33 49
Worcester Gdns. Sutt. BS57 95
Worchester Gdns. Wor. Pk. BO55 85
Worcester Mews NW6 BS36 56
Lymington Rd.
Worcester Pk. Rd. Wor. Pk. BN55 85
Worcester Rd. E12 CK35 49
Worcester Rd. SW19 BR49 75
Worcester Rd. Guil. AP69 118
Worcester Rd. Hat. BO12 10
Worcester Rd. Reig. BS70 121
Worcester Rd. Sutt. BS57 95
Worcester Rd. Uxb. AX39 53
Wordsworth Av. E12 CK36 58
Wordsworth Av. E18 CG31 49
Wordsworth Av. Grnf. BG38 54
Wordsworth Av. Pur. BZ61 105
Valley Rd.
Wordsworth Clo. Rom. CV30 42
Wordsworth Clo. Til. DH44 71
Coleridge Rd.
Wordsworth Dr. Sutt. BQ56 94
Wordsworth Pde. N8 BY31 47
Alfoxton Av.
Wordsworth Rd. N16 CA35 48
Wordsworth Rd. SE20 CC50 77
Wordsworth Rd. Hamptn. BE49 74
Wordsworth Rd. Har. BH31 45
Wordsworth Rd. Wall. BW57 95
Wordsworth Rd. Well. CN44 68
Wordsworth Rd. Wey. AX56 92
Wordsworth Wk. NW11 BS31 47
Wordsworth Way, Dart. CX45 70
Wordsworth Way, West Dr. AY42 63
Worfield St. SW11 BU43 66
Worgan St. SE11 BX42 4
Worgan St. SE11 BX42 66
Worgate St. N1 BZ37 2
Worgate St. N1 BZ37 57
Rushton St.
Worland Rd. E15 CG36 58
Worlds End SW10 BT43 66
World's End La. N21 BX25 29
Worlds End, Cob. BC60 92
Worlds End, Epsom BN61 103
Worlds End La. Orp. CN57 97
Worlds End Pass SW10 BT43 66
Worlds End Pl. SW10 BT43 66
Worlds End
Worley Rd. St. Alb. BG13 9
Worlidge St. W6 BQ42 65
Worlingham Rd. SE22 CA45 67
Wormholt Est. W12 BO40 55
Wormholt Rd. W12 BP40 55
Wormley Ct. Wal. Abb. CH20 22
Winters Wy.
Wormley Lo. Clo. Brox. CD15 12
High Rd.
Wormwood St. EC2 CA39 2
Wormwood St. EC2 CA39 57
Wormingford Ct. Wal. Abb. CH20 22
Ninefields
Wornington Rd. W10 BR38 55
Wornington Yd. W10 BR38 55
Wornington Rd.
Woronzow Rd. NW8 BT37 1
Woronzow Rd. NW8 BT37 56
Worple Av. SW19 BQ50 75
Worple Av. Islw. BJ46 74
Worple Av. Stai. AW50 73
Worple Clo. Har. BE33 45
Worple Rd. SW19 BQ51 85
Worple Rd. SW20 BQ51 85
Worple Rd. Epsom BN61 103
Worple Rd. Islw. BJ45 64
Worple Rd. Lthd. BJ64 102
Worple Rd. Lthd. BJ65 102
Worple Rd. Stai. AW50 73
Worple Rd. Stai. AW51 83
Worple Rd. Ms. SW19 BR50 75
Worplesdon Rd. Guil. AP67 109
Worple St. SW14 BN45 65
Worple, The Stai. AS46 72
Worple Way Har. BE33 45
Worple Way, Rich. BL46 75
Worrin Clo. Brwd. DC26 122
Worrin Rd. Brwd. DC26 122
Worship's Hill, Sev. CT65 107
Worship St. EC2 BZ38 2
Worship St. EC2 BZ38 57
Worslade Rd. SW17 BT49 76
Worsley Bri. Rd. SE26 CD49 77
Worsley Bri. Rd. Beck. CD49 77
Worsley Rd. E11 CG35 49
Worsopp Dr. SW4 BW45 66
Worsted Grn. Red. BW68 113
Worth Clo. Orp. CN56 97
Worthfield Clo. Epsom BN57 94
Worthing Clo. E15 CG37 58
Worthing Rd. Houns. BE43 64
Worthington Rd. Surb. BL54 85
Worthydown Ct. SE18 CL43 68
Prince Imperial Rd.
Wortley Rd. E6 CJ36 58
Wortley Rd. Croy. BY54 86
Worton Gdns. Islw. BG44 64
Worton Rd. Islw. BG45 64
Worton Way Islw. BG44 64
Wotton Dri. Dor. BD73 119
Wotton Grn. Orp. CP52 89
Wotton Rd. NW2 BQ35 46
Wotton Way, Sutt. BQ58 94
Wouldham Rd. E16 CG39 58
Wrabness Way, Stai. AW51 83
Wragby Rd. E11 CG34 49
Wrangley Ct. Wal. Abb. CH20 22
Winters Way.
Wray Av. Ilf. CL31 49
Wray Cl. Horn. CV33 51
Wray Comm. Rd. Reig. BT70 121
Wray Cres. N4 BX34 47
Wrayfield Av. Reig. BT70 121
Wrayfield Rd. Sutt. BQ55 85
Wraylands Dr. Reig. BT69 121
Wray La. Reig. BT68 113
Wray Park Rd. Reig. BS70 121
Wray Rd. Sutt. BR58 94
Wraysbury Rd. Stai. AT48 72
Wrays Way, Hayes BB38 53
Wrekin Rd. SE18 CM43 68
Wren Av. NW2 BQ35 46
Wren Av. Sthl. BE42 64
Wren Clo. Sth. Croy. CC58 96
Wren Cres. Bush. BG26 36
Wren Cres. Wey. AX56 92
Wren Gdns. Dag. CP35 50
Wren Gdns. Horn. CT33 50
Wren Pl. Brwd. DB27 42
Wren Rd. SE5 BZ44 67
Wren Rd. Dag. CP35 50
Wren Rd. Sid. CP49 79
Wrens Av. Ashf. BA49 73
Wrensfield, Hem. H. AW13 8
Wrens Hill, Lthd. BG61 102
Wren St. WC1 BX38 2
Wren St. WC1 BX38 56
Gray's Inn Rd.
Wrentham Av. NW10 BQ37 55
Wrenthorpe Rd. Brom. CG49 78
Wren Wk. Til. DG44 71
Poynder Rd.
Wren Wood, Welw. G. C. BS7 5
Wrenwood Way Pnr. BC31 44
Wrestlers Clo. Hat. BQ11 10
Lockley Cres.
Wrestlers Ct. EC3 CA39 2
Camomile St.
Wrexham Rd. E3 CE37 57
Wrexham Rd. Rom. CV27 42
Wrexham Rd. Slou. AQ41 62
Wricklemarsh Rd. SE3 CH44 68
Wrigglesworth St. SE14 CC43 67
Wright Wind. AL45 61
Wright Rd. NW4 BQ33 46
Wright Rd. N1 CA36 57
Pond Rd.
Wright Rd. Houns. BC43 63
Wright's Alley SW19 BQ50 75
Wrightsbridge Rd. Rom. CW27 42
Wrights Bldgs. SE1 CA41 67
Grange Rd.
Wrights Clo. SE13 CF45 67
Wisteria Rd.
Wright's La. W8 BS41 66
Wrights La. Brwd. DB21 33
Wright's Rd. E3 CD37 57
Wright's Rd. SE25 CA52 87
Wrights Row Wall. BV56 95
Wright Sq. Wind. AL45 61
Wright
Wrights Wk. SW14 BN45 65
North Worple Way
Wright Way, Wind. AL45 61
Wright
Wrigley Clo. E4 CF28 39
Avenue, The
Writtle Wk. Rain. CT37 59
Wrotham Rd. NW1 BW36 56
St. Pancras Way
Wrotham Rd. W13 BJ40 54
Mattock La.
Wrotham Rd. Barn. BR23 28
Wrotham Rd. Grav. DF51 81
Wrotham Rd. Well. CP44 69
Wroths Path Loug. CK23 31
Wrottesley Rd. NW10 BP37 55
Wrottesley Rd. SE18 CL43 68
Wroughton Rd. SW11 BU46 76
Wroughton Ter. NW4 BP31 46
Babington Rd.
Wroxall Rd. Dag. CP36 59
Wroxham Av. Hem. H. AX14 8
Wroxham Gdns. N11 BW29 38
Wroxham Gdns. Enf. BY21 29
Wroxham Gdns. Pot. B. BQ19 19
Wroxton Rd. SE15 CB44 67
Wrythe Grn. Rd. Cars. BU55 86
Wrythe La. Cars. BT54 86
Wulfred Way, Sev. CX62 108
Wulfstan St. W12 BO39 55
Wyatt Clo. Hayes BC39 53
Wyatt Clo. Nthlt. BE36 54
Wyatt Clo. Sev. DC63 108
Wyatt La. Wind. AL45 61
Wyatt Pk. Rd. SW2 BX48 76
Wyatt Rd. E7 CH36 58
Wyatt Rd. N5 BZ34 48
Wyatt Rd. Stai. AW49 73
Wyatts Clo. Rick. AW24 26
Wyatt's Green La. Brwd. DB21 33
Wyatt's Green Rd. Brwd. DB21 33
Wyatts La. E17 CF31 48
Wyatts Rd. Rick. AV24 25
Wybert St. NW1 BV38 56
Munster Sq.
Wyborne Way NW10 BN36 55
Wyburn Av. Barn. BR24 28
Wyche Gro. Sth. Croy. BZ57 96
Wych Elm, Harl. CM10 6
Wych Elm Clo. Horn. CX32 51
Wych Elm Pass Kings. on T. BL50 75
Wych Elm Rise, Guil. AS72 118
Wych Elm Rd. Horn. CX32 51
Wychelms, St. Alb. BF17 18
Wycherley Cres. Barn. BS25 29
Wychford Dr. Saw. CP6 6
Wych Hill, Wok. AR63 100
Wych Hill La. Wok. AS63 100
Wych Hill Waye, Wok. AR63 100
Wychill Rise, Wok. AR63 100
Wychling Clo. Orp. CP54 89
Wychwood Av. Edg. BK29 36
Wychwood Av. Th. Hth. BZ52 87
Wychwood Clo. Edg. BK29 36
Wychwood End N6 BW33 47
Wychwood Gdns. Ilf. CK31 49
Wychwood Wk. Edg. BK29 36
Wychwood Way SE19 CA50 77
Central Hill Est.
Wychwood Way, Nthwd. BB29 35
Wycliffe Clo. Wel. CN44 68
Wycliffe Rd. SW19 BS50 76
Wyclif St. EC1 BY38 2
Wyclif St. EC1 BY38 56
Wycliffe Way, Grav. DF47 81
Dover Road East
Wycombe Gdns. NW11 BS34 47
Wycombe Rd. N17 CB30 39
Wycombe Rd. Ilf. CK32 49
Wycombe Rd. Wem. BM37 55
Wyddial Grn. Welw. G. C. BS8 5
Widford Rd.
Wydehurst Rd. Croy. CB54 87
Wydell Clo. Mord. BQ53 85
Wydeville Manor Rd. SE12 CH49 78
Wyecliffe Gdns. Red. BW68 113
Wye Clo. Ashf. AZ49 73
Wye Clo. Orp. CN54 88
Wyedale, St. Alb. BL17 19
Thamesdale
Wyemead Cres. E4 CG27 40
Normanton Pk.
Wye Rd. Grav. DH48 81
Wye St. SW11 BT44 66
Wye, The Hem. H. AZ11 8
Wyeth's Rd. Epsom BO60 94
Wyevale Clo. Pnr. BC31 44
Wyfields Ilf. CL30 40
Wyfold Rd. SW6 BR44 65
Wyhill Wk. Dag. CS36 59
Wyke Gdns. W7 BJ41 64
Wykeham Av. Dag. CP36 59
Wykeham Av. Horn. CV32 51
Wykeham Grn. Dag. CP36 59
Wykeham Hill, Wem. BL33 46
Wykeham Rd. NW4 BQ31 46
Wykeham Rd. Guil. AU70 118
Wykeham Rd. Har. BJ31 45
Wyke Rd. E3 CE36 57
Wyke Rd. SW20 BQ51 85
Wylands Rd. Slou. AT42 62
Wylchin Clo. Pnr. BB31 44
Fore St.
Wyldfield Gdns. N9 CA27 39
Latymer Rd.
Wyld Way, Wem. BM36 55
Wyleu St. SE23 CD47 77
Wylie Rd. Sthl. BF41 64
Wyllen Clo. E1 CC38 57
Wyllyotts Clo. Pot. B. BR19 19
Wylo Dr. Barn. BO25 28
Wymering Rd. W9 BS38 56
Wymond St. SW15 BQ45 65
Wynaud Ct. N22 BX29 38
Palmerston Rd.
Wyncham Av. Sid. CN47 78
Wynchgate N14 BW26 38
Wynchgate, Har. BH29 36
Wynchlands Cres. St. Alb. BK13 9
Wyncote Way, Sth. Croy. CC58 96
Wyncroft Clo. Brom. CK52 88
Wyndale Av. NW9 BM32 46
Wyndcliff Rd. SE7 CH42 68
Wyndcroft Clo. Enf. BY24 29
Wyndham Av. Barn. BU26 38
Wyndham Av. Cob. BC60 92
Wyndham Clo. Orp. CM54 88
Wyndham Cres. N19 BW34 47
Wyndham Cres. Houns. BF46 74
Wyndham Est. SE5 BZ43 67
Wyndham Ms. W1 BU39 1
Wyndham Ms. W1 BU39 56
Upr. Montagu St.
Wyndham Pl. W1 BU39 1
Wyndham Pl. W1 BU39 56
Wyndham Rd. E6 CJ36 58
Wyndham Rd. SE5 BY43 66
Wyndham Rd. W13 BJ41 64
Wyndham Rd. Kings. on T. BL50 75
Wyndham Rd. Wok. AQ62 100
Wyndham St. W1 BU39 1
Wyndham St. W1 BU39 56
Wyneham Rd. SE24 BZ46 77
Wynell Rd. SE23 CC48 77
Wynford Gro. Orp. CO52 89
Wynford Rd. N1 BX37 2
Wynford Rd. N1 BX37 56
Wynford Way SE9 CK48 78
Wynlie Gdns. Pnr. BC30 35
Wynndale Rd. E18 CH30 40
Wynne Rd. SW9 BY44 66
Wynn's Av. Sid. CN46 78
Lyndon Av.
Wynn's Av. Sid. CO46 79
Lyndon Av.
Wynnstay Gdns. W8 BS41 66
Wynnstow Pk. Oxt. CG69 115
Wynter St. SW11 BT45 66
Wynton Gdns. SE25 CA52 87
Wynton Gro. Walt. BC55 83
Wynton Pl. W3 BM39 55
Wynyard Clo. Rick. AW21 26
Wynyard Ter. SE11 BX42 4
Wynyard Ter. SE11 BX42 66
Aveline St.
Wynyatt St. EC1 BY38 2
Wyre Gro. Edg. BM27 37
Wyre Gro. Hayes BC42 63
Wyresdale Cres. Grnf. BH38 54
Wyte Leaf Clo. Ruis. BA32 44
Wythburn Pl. W1 BU39 1
Wythburn Pl. W1 BU39 56
Seymour Pl.
Wythenshawe Rd. Dag. CR34 50
Wythens Wk. SE9 CL46 78
Southend Cres.
Wythes Clo. Brom. CK51 88
Wythes Rd. E16 CK40 58
Wythfield Rd. SE9 CK46 78
Wyvenhoe Rd. Har. BG34 45
Wyver Ct. St. Alb. BH13 9
Avenue Rd.
Wyvern Clo. Dart. CV47 80
Wyvern Clo. Orp. CO55 89
Wyvern Rd. Pur. BY58 95
Wyvil Est. SW8 BX43 66
Wyvil Rd. SW8 BX43 66
Wyvis St. E14 CE39 57
Yabsley St. E14 CF40 57
Yalding Clo. Orp. CP52 89
Yalding Rd. SE16 CB41 4
Yalding Rd. SE16 CB41 67
Yarborough Rd. SW19 BT51 86
Runnymede
Yardbridge, Sutt. BS58 95
Hulverston Clo.
Yardley Clo. E4 CE25 30
Yardley Clo. Reig. BS69 121
Yardley La. E4 CE25 30
Yardley St. WC1 BY38 2
Yardley St. WC1 BY38 56
Yard Mead, Stai. AT48 72
Yarm Ct. Rd. Lthd. BK65 102
Yarmouth Cres. N15 CB32 48
Yarmouth Pl. W1 BV40 3
Yarmouth Pl. W1 BV40 56
Brick St.
Yarmouth Rd. Wat. BD22 27
Yarm Way, Lthd. BK65 102
Yarnton Way SE2 CP41 69
Yarnton Way Belv. CP41 69
Yarrow Fld. Wok. AR65 100
Yarrow Side, Amer. AQ23 25
Yateley St. SE7 CJ41 68
Yates Ct. NW2 BQ36 55
Yeading Av. Har. BE34 45
Yeading Gdns. Hayes BC39 53
Yeading La. Hayes BC39 53
Yeading La. Nhtlt. BD38 54
Yeading La. Fork Hayes BD38 54
Yeading Wk. Har. BE32 45
Yeate St. N1 BZ36 2
Yeate St. N1 BZ36 57
Yeatman Rd. N6 BU32 47
Yeats Clo. SE13 CF44 67
Eliot Pk.
Yeats Clo. Red. BT72 121
Yeldham Rd. W6 BQ42 65
Yellowpine Way, Ilf. CO28 41
Yelverton Cl. Rom. CV30 42
Neave Cres.
Yelverton Rd. SW11 BT44 66
Yens, The Ashf. AZ49 73
Reedsfield Rd.
Yenston Clo. Mord. BS53 86
Yeoman Rd. Nthlt. BE36 54
Yeoman Way, Red. BV73 121
Spencer Way
Yeomans Acre Ruis. BC32 44
Yeomans Meadow, Sev. CU66 116
Yeomans Mews, Islw. BG46 74
Yeomans Mews, Islw. BH46 74
Yeomans Rd. Hem. H. AZ10 8
Yeomans Row SW3 BU41 3
Yeomans Row SW3 BU41 66
Yeoman St. SE8 CD42 67
Yeomans Way, Enf. CB23 30
Yeomen Way, Ilf. CM29 40
Yeo St. E3 CE39 57
Yeoveney Clo. Stai. AU48 72
Yeovil Clo. Orp. CN55 88
Yerbury Rd. N19 BW34 47
Yester Dr. Chis. CK50 78
Yester Pk. Chis. CK50 78
Yester Rd. Chis. CL50 78
Yevale Way, Horn. CW33 51
Yew Av. West Dr. AY40 53
Yew Clo. Buck. H. CJ27 40
Albert Rd.
Yewdale Clo. Brom. CG50 78
Yewfield Rd. NW10 BO36 55
Yew Gro. NW2 BQ35 46
Yewlands, Hodd. CE12 12
Yewlands, Saw. CQ6 6
Yewlands Clo. Bans. BT61 104
Yews Av. Enf. CB21 30
Yew Tree Bottom Rd. Epsom BP61 103
Yew Tree Clo. NW1 BY26 38
Yew Tree Clo. Brwd. DD25 122
Yew Tree Clo. Chesh. AQ18 16
Yew Tree Clo. Couls. BU63 104
Yew Tree Clo. Hem. H. AW14 8
Yew Tree Clo. Well. CO44 69
Yew Tree Clo. Wor. Pk. BO54 85
Yew Tree Dri. Guil. AR68 109
Yew Tree Dr. Cat. CA66 114
Yewtree End, St. Alb. BF17 18
Yewtree Gdns. Epsom BM61 103
Yew Tree Gdns. Rom. CS32 50
Pettley Gdns.
Yew Tree Gdns. Rom. CS32 50
Yewtree La. Dor. BF69 119
Yew Tree La. Reig. BS69 121
Yew Tree Rd. W12 BO40 55
Yewtree Rd. Beck. CD52 87
Yew Tree Rd. Dor. BJ70 119
Yew Tree Rd. Slou. AQ41 62
Yew Tree Rd. Uxb. AY37 53
Yew Trees, Egh. AU52 82
Yew Trees, Shep. AY52 83
Laleham Rd.
Yew Tree Wk. Houns. BE46 74
Yewtree Wlk. Pur. BZ58 96
Yew Wk. Har. BH33 45
Yiewsley By-pass, Uxb. & West Dr. AZ39 53
Yiewsley Sta. Rd. West. Dr. AY40 53
Yoakley Rd. N16 CA34 48
Yolande Gdns. SE9 CK46 78
Yonge Pk. N4 BY34 47
York Av. Wind. AN44 61
York Av. SW14 BN46 75
York Av. W7 BH40 54
York Av. Hayes BA39 53
York Av. Sid. CN48 78
York Av. Slou. AO39 52
York Av. Stan. BJ30 36
York Blds. WC2 BX40 4
York Bldgs. WC2 BX40 56
Watergate Wk.
York Clo. SE5 BZ44 67
York Clo. W7 BH40 54
York Clo. Brwd. DC26 122
York Clo. Kings L. AZ18 17
York Clo. Wey. AY59 92
York Ct. Borwd. BN23 28
York Ct. Mord. BS52 86
York Cres. Loug. CK24 31
Yorke Gdns. Reig. BS70 121
Yorke Rd. Reig. BS70 121
Yorke Rd. Rick. AZ25 26
York Gdns. N18 CB29 39
York Gdns. Walt. BD55 84
York Gate N14 BX26 38
York Gate NW1 BV38 1
York Gate NW1 BV38 56
York Gro. SE15 CC44 67
York Hill SE27 BY48 76
York Hill Loug. CK23 31
York Hill Loug. CK24 31
York Ho. Pl. W8 BS41 66
Yorkland Av. Well. CN45 68
York Ms. NW5 BV35 47
York Mews, Ilf. CL34 49
York Rd.
York Pl. SW11 BT45 66
York Pl. W7 BH40 54
York Pl. WC2 BX40 4
York Pl. WC2 BX40 56
Villiers St.
York Pl. Grays. DD43 71
York Pl. Ilf. CL34 49
York Rd.
York Pl. Wind. AO44 61
York Rise NW5 BV34 47
York Rd. E4 CD28 39
York Rd. E7 CH36 58
York Rd. E10 CF34 48
York Rd. E17 CC32 48
York Rd. N11 BW29 38
York Rd. N18 CB29 39
York Rd. N21 BZ26 39
York Rd. NW9 BO32 46
Broadway, The
York Rd. SE1 BX41 4
York Rd. SE1 BX41 66
York Rd. SW11 BS46 76
York Rd. SW18 BS46 76
York Rd. SW19 BS50 76
York Rd. W3 BN39 55
York Rd. W5 BK41 64
York Rd. Barn. BT24 29
York Rd. Brent. BK42 64
York Rd. Brwd. DC26 122
York Rd. Croy. BY54 86
York Rd. Dart. CW47 80
York Rd. Grav. DE47 81
York Rd. Grav. DH48 81
York Rd. Guil. AR71 118
York Rd. Houns. BF45 64
York Rd. Ilf. CL34 49
York Rd. Kings. on T. BL50 75
York Rd. Nthwd. BC30 35
York Rd. Rain. CT36 59
York Rd. Rich. BL46 75
Albert Rd.
York Rd. St. Alb. BH13 9
York Rd. Sth. Croy. CC58 96
York Rd. Sutt. BS57 95

York Rd. Tedd.	BH49	74
York Rd. Uxb.	AX36	53
York Rd. Wal. Cr.	CD20	21
York Rd. Wat.	BD25	27
York Rd. West.	CH63	106
York Rd. Wey.	AX59	92
York Rd. Wey.	BA56	92
York Rd. Wind.	AN44	61
York Rd. Wok.	AR63	100
Yorks Hl. Sev.	CR69	116
Yorkshire Gdns. N18	CB28	39
Yorkshire Grey Pla. NW3	BT35	47
Heath St.		
Yorkshire Rd. E14	CD39	57
Yorkshire Rd. Mitch.	BX53	86
York Sq. E14	CD39	57
York St. W1	**BU39**	**1**
York St. W1	BU39	56
York St. Bark.	CL37	58
Abbey Rd.		
York St. Mitch.	BV54	86
York St. Twick.	BJ47	74
York Ter. E. NW1	BV38	56
York Ter. E. NW1	**BV38**	**1**
York Ter. Enf.	BZ22	30
York Ter. Erith	CR44	69
York Ter. W. NW1	BV38	56
Yorkton St. E2	**CB37**	**2**
Yorkton St. E2	CB37	57
York Way N1	**BX36**	**2**
York Way N1	BW36	56
York Way N7	BW36	56
York Way N20	BU27	38
York Way, Chess.	BL57	94
York Way, Felt.	BE48	74
York Way, Wat.	BD21	27
York Way, Welw.	BP5	5
York Way Ct. N1	**BX37**	**2**
York Way Ct. N1	BX37	56
Young Field, Hem. H.	AV13	7
Youngmans Clo. Enf.	BZ23	30
Young Rd. E16	CJ39	58
Youngs Rise,		
Welw. G. C.	BP8	5
Youngs Rd. Ilf.	CM32	49
Young St. W8	**BS41**	**3**
Young St. W8	BS41	66
Young St. Lthd.	BH65	102
Youngstroat La. Wok.	AS59	91
Yoxley App. Ilf.	CM32	49
Yoxley Dr. Ilf.	CM32	49
Yukon Rd. SW12	BV47	76
Zambra Way, Sev.	CW63	108
Zampa Rd. SE16	CC42	67
Zander Ct. E2	CB38	57
St. Peters Clo.		
Zangwill Rd. SE3	CJ 4	68
Zealand Av. West. Dr.	AX43	63
Zealand Clo. NW2	BQ33	46
Zealand Rd. E3	CD37	57
Zelah Rd. Orp.	CO54	89
Zennor Rd. SW12	BV47	76
Zenoria St. SE22	CA45	67
Zermatt Rd. Th. Hth.	BZ52	87
Zetland St. E14	CE39	57
Zig-zag Rd. Ken.	BZ61	105
Zig-zag Rd. Tad.	BL69	120
Zion Pl. Th. Hth.	BZ52	87
Zion Rd. Th. Hth.	BZ52	87
Zion St. Grav.	DG47	81
Zoffany St. N19	BW34	47
Ashbrook Rd.		

ADMINISTRATIVE AREAS

BEDFORDSHIRE
DAGNALL
MARKYATE
WELWYN
STAPLEFORD
EAS
AYLESBURY
FLAMSTEAD
HARPENDEN
WHEATHAMPSTEAD
ASTON CLINTON
ALDBURY
LITTLE GADDESDEN
WELWYN GARDEN CITY
5
HER
TRING
Gade
REDBOURN
LEMSFORD
AYLESBURY VALE
STOKE MANDEVILLE
WESTON TURVILLE
SANDRIDGE
WELWYN
LETTY GREEN
WIGGINTON
DACORUM
ST. ALBANS
ESSENDON
ROE GREEN
HATFIELD
NORTHCHURCH
BERKHAMSTED
HEMEL HEMPSTEAD
ST. ALBANS
HATFIELD
BERKH
WENDOVER
7
BOURNE END
8
9
10
COLNEY HEATH
WILDHILL
N
ST. LEONARDS
LEVERSTOCK GREEN
EPPING GREEN
GREAT KIMBLE
ASHLEY GREEN
HERTFORDSHIRE
NEWG STR
MONKS RISBOROUGH
CHARTRIDGE
LYE GREEN
BOVINGDON
KINGS LANGLEY
CHISWELL GREEN
PARK STREET
LONDON COLNEY
WELHAM GREEN
BROOKMANS PARK
PRINCES RISBOROUGH
SOUTH HEATH
16
CHIPPERFIELD
17
BRICKET WOOD
18
COLNEY STREET
19
20
ABBOTS LANGLEY
LACEY GREEN
PRESTWOOD
CHESHAM
SOUTH MIMMS
POTTERS BAR
GREAT MISSENDEN
HYDE HEATH
FLAUNDEN
GARSTON
Colne
SHENLEY
Chess
SARRATT
RADLETT
RIDGE
BOT
BUCKINGHAMSHIRE
CHESHAM BOIS
THREE RIVERS
HADLEY WOOD
CHENIES
26
HERTSMERE
NAPHILL
GREAT KINGSHILL
CHILTERN
25
27
28
29
AMERSHAM
LITTLE CHALFONT
WATFORD
WATFORD
BOREHAMWOOD
NEW BARNET
COCKFOST
WYCOMBE
PENN STREET
CROXLEY GREEN
BARNET
ARKLEY
WINCHM
WEST WYCOMBE
HAZLEMERE
COLESHILL
CHORLEYWOOD
OXHEY
ELSTREE
EAST BARNET
Misbourne
BUSHEY
TOTTERIDGE
HIGH WYCOMBE
TYLERS GREEN
CHALFONT ST. GILES
RICKMANSWORTH
BATCHWORTH
WHETSTONE
SEER GREEN
34
CHALFONT COMMON
35
36
STANMORE
37
MILL HILL
FRIERN BARNET
38
PALME GREE
LOUDWATER
BATCHWORTH HEATH
SOUTH OXHEY
EDGWARE
BARNET
WOOD GREEN
BEACONSFIELD
HAREFIELD
HARROW
FINCHLEY
FLACKWELL HEATH
NORTHWOOD
PINNER
WEALDSTONE
MUSWELL HILL
CHALFONT ST. PETER
Colne
EASTCOTE
HENDON
HA
LITTLE MARLOW
HARROW
KINGSBURY
GOLDERS GREEN
CROUCH END
GERRARDS CROSS
WOOBURN
43
44
RUISLIP
RAYNERS LANE
45
Kenton
46
47
HIGHG
DENHAM
NEASDEN
GREATER LONDON
MARLOW
BOURNE END
ICKENHAM
SUDBURY
BRENT
SOUTH BUCKS
CRICKLEWOOD
HAMPSTEAD
FARNHAM COMMON
HILLINGDON
WEMBLEY
COOKHAM
CAMDEN
KENTISH TOWN
UXBRIDGE
NORTHOLT
WILLESDEN
KILBURN
STOKE POGES
IVER HEATH
HURLEY
HILLINGDON
ALPERTON
CAMDEN TOWN
HARLESDEN
TAPLOW
52
53
YEADING
Greenford
54
55
PARK ROYAL
MAIDENHEAD
IVER
COWLEY
EALING
HOLBORN
BURNHAM
NOTTING HILL
PADDINGTON
SLOUGH
YIEWSLEY
SOUTHALL
HANWELL
EALING
ACTON
KENSINGTON & CHELSEA
WESTMINSTER
WOODLANDS PARK
SLOUGH
WEST DRAYTON
HAYES
SHEPHERDS BUSH
KENSINGTON
HAMMERSMITH
LANGLEY
Colne Brook
HARLINGTON
Chiswick
WESTMINSTER
DORNEY
HOLYPORT
Thames
BRENTFORD
CHELSEA
WALTHAM ST. LAWRENCE
61
ETON
62
COLNBROOK
63
HESTON
64
HAMMERSMITH & FULHAM
65
66
DATCHET
OSTERLEY
KEW
BARNES
FULHAM
BATTERSEA
WINDSOR & MAIDENHEAD
HEATHROW AIRPORT LONDON
CRANFORD
HOUNSLOW
PALEY STREET
FIFIELD
WINDSOR
HORTON
HOUNSLOW
BERKSHIRE
RICHMOND
PUTNEY
LONDON
SHURLOCK ROW
OLD WINDSOR
WRAYSBURY
STANWELL
ISLEWORTH
ROEHAMPTON
WANDSWORTH
CLAPHAM
WINKFIELD
FELTHAM
TWICKENHAM
RICHMOND UPON THAMES
PETERSHAM
WANDSWORTH
STREAT
72
EAST BEDFONT
73
74
75
76
BINFIELD
EARLSFIELD
WOKINGHAM
ENGLEFIELD GREEN
EGHAM
STAINES
ASHFORD
HANWORTH
TEDDINGTON
WIMBLEDON
TOOTING GRAVENEY
BRACKNELL
SPELTHORNE
HAMPTON
NORBITON
MERTON
ASCOT
VIRGINIA WATER
THORPE
LALEHAM
SUNBURY
MERTON
MITCHAM
WOKINGHAM
BRACKNELL
KINGSTON UPON THAMES
NORB
SUNNINGHILL
SUNNINGDALE
82
83
SHEPPERTON
WEST MOLESEY
84
THAMES DITTON
85
MORDEN
86
RUNNYMEDE
CHERTSEY
WALTON-ON-THAMES
SURBITON
MALDEN
ST. HELIER
BROOMHALL
TOLWORTH
CROWTHORNE
WINDLESHAM
ADDLESTONE
WORCESTER PARK
CARSHALTON
BEDDING
OTTERSHAW
WEYBRIDGE
ESHER
HOOK
SUTTON
SUTTON
WALLING
BAGSHOT
ELMBRIDGE
CHESSINGTON
EWELL
CHEAM
LIGHTWATER
NEW HAW
KINGSTON UPON THAMES
SANDHURST
91
92
93
94
95
WOODHAM
EPSOM
SURREY HEATH
CHOBHAM
WEST END
Mole
EPSOM
BELMONT
PURLEY
OXSHOTT
EPSOM & EWELL
YATELEY
CAMBERLEY
WEST BYFLEET
BYFLEET
COBHAM
WOODMANSTER
YORK TOWN
WOKING
BANSTEAD
KNAPHILL
STOKE D'ABERNON
FRIMLEY
BISLEY
Wey
HAWLEY
WOKING
ASHTEAD
BURGH HEATH
COULSDO
CHIPSTEAD
100
OLD WOKING
101
102
103
104
FRIMLEY GREEN
RIPLEY
OCKHAM
PIRBRIGHT
SEND
FETCHAM
LEATHERHEAD
TADWORTH
HOOLEY
HARTLEY WINTNEY
FLEET
MAYFORD
MYTCHETT
LITTLE BOOKHAM
FARNBOROUGH
WALTON-ON-THE-HILL
WORPLESDON
JACOBSWELL
WEST HORSLEY
GREAT BOOKHAM
REIGATE & BANSTEAD
MERST
RUSHMOOR
109
WEST CLANDON
110
111
MICKLEHAM
112
113
CHURCH CROOKHAM
NORMANDY
EAST HORSLEY
HANTS
ALDERSHOT
STOUGHTON
Wey
SURREY
BUCKLAND
REDHILL
EAST CLANDON
FLEXFORD
GUILDFORD
MOLE VALLEY
HEATH END
ASH
BROCKHAM
118
119
120
REIGATE
121
WANBOROUGH
HALE
TONGHAM
GUILDFORD
WESTCOTT
DORKING
EARLSWOOD
GOMSHALL
SEALE
STROOD GREEN
FARNHAM
RUNFOLD
COMPTON
SHALFORD
ALBURY
SHERE
Mole
ABINGER HAMMER
NORTH HOLMWOOD
LEIGH
SALFORDS
SHACKLEFORD
HURTMORE
BROOK
WONERSH
NALDERSWOOD
BRAMLEY
HOLMBURY ST. MARY
SHAMLEY GREEN
BEARE GREEN
ELSTEAD
GODALMING
HORLEY

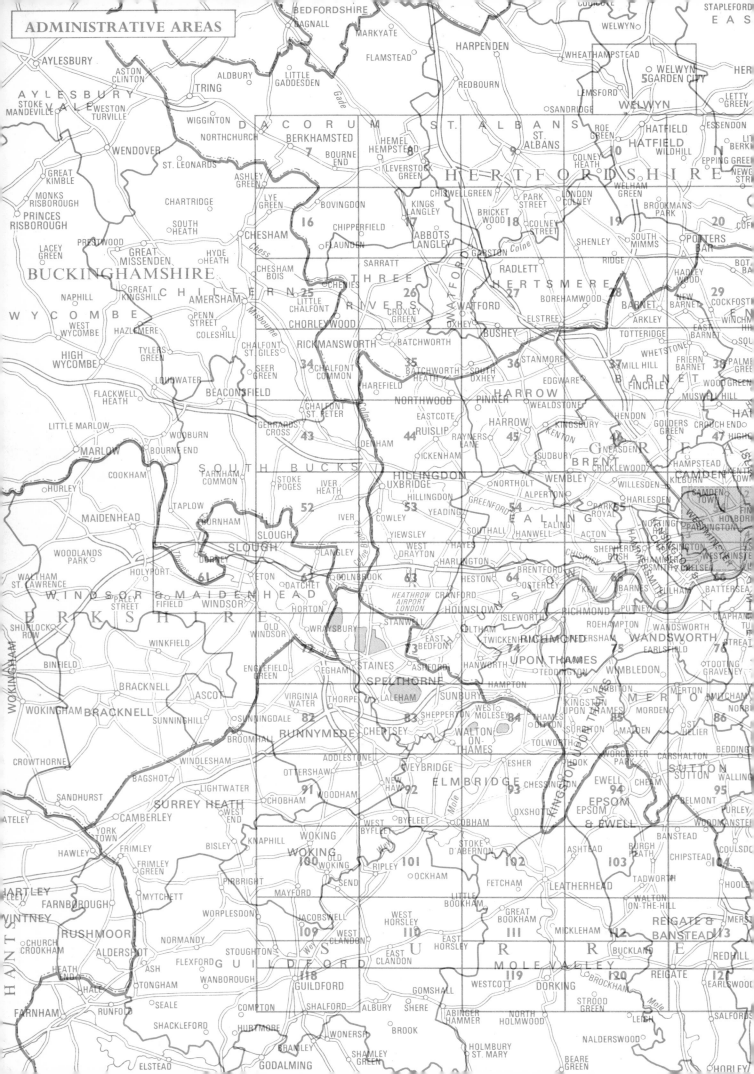